AMERICAN CONSTITUTIONAL LAW

Otis H. Stephens, Jr.
John M. Scheb, II

Department of Political Science
University of Tennessee, Knoxville

WEST PUBLISHING COMPANY

Minneapolis/St. Paul • New York • Los Angeles • San Francisco

Copyeditor: Marilyn Taylor
Cover and Text Design: Lois Stanfield/LightSource Images
Indexer: Schroeder Indexing Services
Composition: Carlisle Communications
Cover Image: Supreme Court by John Haymson. Courtesy of Aaron Ashley Inc., Yonkers, N.Y.

Production, Prepress, Printing and Binding by West Publishing Company

PHOTO CREDITS

1, 4 Library of Congress; **6** Historical Pictures/Stock Montage; **13** H. Armstrong Roberts, Inc.; **20** Collection of the Supreme Court of the United States; **24** Supreme Court Historical Society; **45** Historical Pictures/Stock Montage; **85** Library of Congress; **94, 95** Historical Pictures/Stock Montage; **117, 124** Library of Congress; **166** Bohdan Hrynewych/Stock Boston; **256, 263,** Library of Congress; **270** Joseph Kovac/Stock Boston; **281** Library of Congress; **325** Tony Stone Worldwide/Chicago Ltd.; **327, 334** Historical Pictures/Stock Montage; **385** Supreme Court Archives; **395** UPI/Bettmann Newsphotos; **399, 471** Library of Congress; **472** UPI/Bettmann; **475** James H. Pickerell/Stock Boston; **522, 529** Historical Pictures/Stock Montage; **530** Collection of the Supreme Court of the United States; **533** The Bettmann Archive; **536** National Archives; **543** Supreme Court Historical Society; **603** Library of Congress; **614, 617** AP/Wide World Photos; **620, 622** Stock Boston; **673** Collection of the Supreme Court of the United States; **676** UPI/Bettmann Newsphotos; **678** Collection of the Supreme Court of the United States; **755** UPI/Bettmann Newsphotos; **758** Collection of the Supreme Court of the United States; **823** Historical Pictures/Stock Montage; **826, 832, 833** AP/Wide World Photos; **843, 961, 964** UPI/Bettmann; **969** Reuters/Bettmann; **971** Stock Boston; **975** AP/Wide World Photos; **1043** Historical Pictures/Stock Montage; **1050** The Bettmann Archive; **1052** Historical Pictures/Stock Montage; **1054** AP/Wide World Photos; **1055, 1062** UPI/Bettmann; **1073** AP/Wide World Photos; **1153** Collection of the Supreme Court of the United States

WEST'S COMMITMENT TO THE ENVIRONMENT

In 1906, West Publishing Company began recycling materials left over from the production of books. This began a tradition of efficient and responsible use of resources. Today, up to 95 percent of our legal books and 70 percent of our college and school texts are printed on recycled, acid-free stock. West also recycles nearly 22 million pounds of scrap paper annually—the equivalent of 181,717 trees. Since the 1960s, West has devised ways to capture and recycle waste inks, solvents, oils, and vapors created in the printing process. We also recycle plastics of all kinds, wood, glass, corrugated cardboard, and batteries, and have eliminated the use of styrofoam book packaging. We at West are proud of the longevity and the scope of our commitment to the environment.

Copyright © 1993   BY WEST PUBLISHING COMPANY
610 Opperman Drive
P.O. Box 64526
St. Paul, MN 55164-0526

Printed in the United States of America
00 99 98 97 96   8 7 6 5 4 3 2
Library of Congress Cataloging-in-Publication Data
Stephens, Otis H., 1936–
    American constitutional law : essays and cases / Otis H. Stephens,
John M. Scheb, II.
        p.   cm.
    Includes index.
    ISBN 0-314-01223-0 (hard)
        1. United States—Constitutional law—Cases.   I. Scheb, John M.
II. Title.
KF4549.S745   1993
342.73 —dc20   92-30208
[347.302]   CIP

ABOUT THE AUTHORS

Otis H. Stephens, Jr. is Alumni Distinguished Service Professor of Political Science at the University of Tennessee, Knoxville. He holds a Ph.D. in political science from Johns Hopkins University and a J.D. from the University of Tennessee. Professor Stephens is the author of *The Supreme Court and Confessions of Guilt* (1973) and co-author, with Gregory J. Rathjen, of *The Supreme Court and the Allocation of Constitutional Power* (1980) and, with John M. Scheb, II, of *American Constitutional Law: Essays and Cases* (1988). He has contributed chapters to *Comparative Human Rights* (1976) and *The Reagan Administration and Human Rights* (1985). He has also authored or coauthored a number of articles in professional journals, including the *Georgetown Law Journal*, the *Journal of Public Law*, the *Tennessee Law Review*, and the *Criminal Law Bulletin*. Dr. Stephens is also a member of the Tennessee Bar.

John M. Scheb, II is Associate Professor of Political Science and is currently a Fellow in the Social Science Research Institute at the University of Tennessee, Knoxville. He received his Ph.D. from the University of Florida. He has authored or co-authored numerous articles in professional journals, including *The Journal of Politics, American Politics Quarterly, Western Political Quarterly, Law and Policy, Judicature, State and Local Government Review, Southeastern Political Review*, and the *Tennessee Law Review*. He has also co-authored two textbooks, *American Constitutional Law: Essays and Cases* (1988), with Otis H. Stephens, Jr., and *Criminal Law and Procedure* (1989), with Judge John M. Scheb.

Professors Stephens and Scheb regularly teach graduate and undergraduate courses in American government, constitutional law, administrative law, the judicial process, and law in society.

Dedicated with love, to Mary Stephens and Sherilyn Scheb

CONTENTS

Preface		xv
About the Authors		iii
Introduction		**1**
What is Constitutional Law?		2
The Adoption and Ratification of the Constitution		2
The "Living Constitution"		7
PART I	**THE SUPREME COURT IN THE CONSTITUTIONAL SYSTEM**	**11**
Chapter 1	**The Supreme Court in the American Judicial Process**	**13**
	Introduction	14
	An Overview of American Courts	14
	Appointment and Removal of Federal Judges	22
	The Genesis of Constitutional Law Cases	25
	The Supreme Court's Decision-Making Process	28
	Factors that Influence the Court's Decisions	35
	Conclusion	38
Chapter 2	**The Establishment and Exercise of Judicial Review**	**43**
	Introduction	43
	The Establishment of Judicial Review	44
	The Development of Judicial Review	47
	Theories of Constitutional Interpretation	56
	Conclusion	58
	Cases and Readings:	
	Marbury v. Madison	60
	Eakin v. Raub	63
	President Jackson's Message to the Senate in Support of his Veto of a Bill to Renew the Bank of the United States	66
	Dred Scott v. Sandford	69
	United States v. Nixon	72
	Texas v. Johnson	77

Chapter 3   **External Constraints on Judicial Power**   **85**

Introduction   86
Judicial Dependency on Congress   86
Appointment and Removal of Federal Judges   92
Enforcement of Court Decisions   95
Conclusion   97
Cases and Readings:
    Alexander Hamilton, The Federalist No. 78   *99*
    Ex parte McCardle   *103*
    President Franklin D. Roosevelt's "Fireside Chat,"
    March 9, 1937   *104*
    Chief Justice Charles Evans Hughes's Letter to
    Senator Burton K. Wheeler, March 21, 1937   *107*
    Senate Judiciary Committee Report on
    Roosevelt's Court-Packing Plan   *109*
    Cooper v. Aaron   *112*

Chapter 4   **Internal Limitations on Judicial Power**   **117**

Introduction   118
Threshold Requirements   118
Decisions on the Merits   128
Conclusion   135
Cases and Readings:
    Poe v. Ullman   *137*
    Valley Forge Christian College v. Americans United
    for Separation of Church and State   *140*
    DeFunis v. Odegaard   *143*
    Younger v. Harris   *146*
    Luther v. Borden   *149*
    Baker v. Carr   *151*
    Massachusetts v. Laird   *155*
    Crockett v. Reagan   *158*
    Ashwander v. Tennessee Valley Authority   *161*

PART II   **SHARED POWERS: THE INSTITUTIONAL**
ARRANGEMENTS OF GOVERNMENT   **163**

Chapter 5   **Congress and the Development of National Power**   **165**

Introduction   165
Structural Aspects of Congress   166
Constitutional Sources of Congressional Power   168
The Power to Investigate   172
Regulation of Interstate Commerce   176
Taxing and Spending Powers   188
Congressional Enforcement of Civil Rights Amendments   194
Conclusion   197

Cases and Readings:
  M'Culloch v. Maryland — *199*
  McGrain v. Daugherty — *203*
  Watkins v. United States — *206*
  Barenblatt v. United States — *212*
  Gibbons v. Ogden — *216*
  United States v. E.C. Knight Company — *221*
  Carter v. Carter Coal Company — *226*
  National Labor Relations Board v. Jones & Laughlin
  Steel Corporation — *228*
  Wickard v. Filburn — *233*
  Heart of Atlanta Motel v. United States — *237*
  Katzenbach v. McClung — *240*
  United States v. Butler — *241*
  Chas. C. Steward Machine Company v. Davis — *246*
  South Dakota v. Dole — *249*

Chapter 6   The Powers of the Presidency   255
Introduction — 255
Structural Aspects of the American Presidency — 256
Theories of Presidential Power — 259
Specific Powers of the Presidency — 263
The Power to Make Foreign Policy — 272
Presidential War Powers — 277
Conclusion — 282
Cases and Readings:
  Articles of Impeachment against President
  Richard M. Nixon Recommended by the House
  Judiciary Committee — *284*
  Youngstown Sheet and Tube Company v. Sawyer — *286*
  Schick v. Reed — *293*
  Wiener v. United States — *296*
  United States v. Curtiss-Wright Export Corporation — *298*
  The Prize Cases — *301*
  The War Powers Resolution of 1973 — *304*
  The Persian Gulf War Resolution — *307*
  Ex Parte Milligan — *308*
  Korematsu v. United States — *311*
  United States v. United States District Court — *315*

Chapter 7   The Constitution and the Modern Administrative State   323
Introduction — 323
The Delegation of Legislative Power — 324
Congressional Control of Administrative Action — 333
Judicial Oversight of the Bureaucracy — 336
Agency Actions and Other Individual Rights — 338
Conclusion — 340

Cases and Readings:

J.W. Hampton & Company v. United States   *342*

A.L.A. Schechter Poultry Corporation v. United States   *343*

Bowsher v. Synar   *348*

Mistretta v. United States   *353*

Immigration and Naturalization Service v. Chadha   *357*

Metropolitan Washington Airports, Authority v. Citizens
for the Abatement of Aircraft Noise   *364*

Vermont Yankee Nuclear Power Corporation v. Natural
Resources Defense Council, Inc.   *368*

Mathews v. Eldridge   *370*

Marshall v. Barlow's, Inc.   *374*

Dow Chemical Company v. United States   *378*

Chapter 8   The Dynamics of "Our Federalism"   **385**

Introduction   386

Development of the Federal System   386

Characteristics of the Contemporary Federal System   393

State Power to Regulate Commerce   397

State Taxing Power   406

Interstate Relations   411

Conclusion   416

Cases and Readings:

Chisholm v. Georgia   *418*

M'Culloch v. Maryland   *421*

Gibbons v. Ogden   *421*

Hammer v. Dagenhart   *421*

United States v. Darby Lumber Company   *424*

National League of Cities v. Usery   *428*

Garcia v. San Antonio Metropolitan Transit Authority   *432*

Silkwood v. Kerr-McGee Corporation   *438*

Cooley v. Board of Wardens   *441*

South Carolina Highway Department v. Barnwell   *444*

Southern Pacific Railroad Company v. Arizona   *446*

Philadelphia v. New Jersey   *450*

Kassel v. Consolidated Freightways Corporation   *453*

Maine v. Taylor   *458*

PART III   CIVIL RIGHTS AND LIBERTIES   **463**

Chapter 9   Constitutional Sources of Civil Rights and Liberties   **465**

Introduction   465

Rights Recognized in the Original Constitution   467

The Bill of Rights   471

The Fourteenth Amendment   478

Amendments Protecting Voting Rights   485

Standards of Judicial Review   487
The Importance of State Constitutions   488
Conclusion   489
Cases and Readings:
   United States v. Brown   490
   DeShaney v. Winnebago Social Services   493
   Barron v. Baltimore   496
   Hurtado v. California   498
   Chicago, Burlington and Quincy Railroad
   Company v. Chicago   501
   Palko v. Connecticut   503
   Adamson v. California   505
   Rochin v. California   510
   Duncan v. Louisiana   513

Chapter 10   Property Rights and Economic Freedom   521
Introduction   521
Evolving Judicial Perspectives   522
The Contract Clause   524
The Rise and Fall of Economic Due Process   527
Equal Protection and Economic Regulation   539
Property Rights and the "Takings" Issue   540
Property Rights and Free Expression   543
Conclusion   544
Cases and Readings:
   Dartmouth College v. Woodward   546
   Charles River Bridge Company v. Warren
   Bridge Company   550
   Home Building and Loan Association v. Blaisdell 554
   The Slaughter-House Cases   558
   Munn v. Illinois   564
   Chicago, Milwaukee & St. Paul Railway
   Company v. Minnesota   567
   Lochner v. New York   569
   Adkins v. Children's Hospital   573
   Nebbia v. New York   579
   West Coast Hotel Company v. Parrish   581
   Ferguson v. Skrupa   585
   Hawaii Housing Authority v. Midkiff   587
   Nollan v. California Coastal Commission   590
   PruneYard Shopping Center v. Robins   593

Chapter 11   Freedom of Expression, Assembly and Association   599
Introduction   599
"Subversive" Speech and Internal Security Concerns   602
"Fighting Words"   609
Symbolic Speech   612

Obscenity, Indecency, and Profanity 616
Restricting Speech by Public Employees and Beneficiaries 618
Freedom of Assembly 619
Time, Place, and Manner Regulations 623
Freedom of Association 626
The Overbreadth Doctrine 628
Conclusion 629
Cases and Readings:
   Schenck v. United States 631
   Dennis v. United States 632
   Brandenburg v. Ohio 637
   Feiner v. New York 638
   Cohen v. California 641
   *Tinker v. Des Moines Independent Community
   School District* 645
   Texas v. Johnson [note] 649
   Barnes v. Glen Theatre, Inc. 650
   Rankin v. McPherson 653
   Rust v. Sullivan 657
   Edwards v. South Carolina 660
   Adderley v. Florida 662
   *National Association for the Advancement of
   Colored People v. Alabama* 665
   Roberts v. United States Jaycees 667

Chapter 12   **Freedom of the Press: Mass Media and
the Constitution** **673**
Introduction 674
Freedom of the Press—A Basic National Commitment 674
Libel 677
A Free Press and the "Peoples Right to Know" 680
Obscenity 682
Commerical Advertising 685
The Special Case of Broadcast Media 687
Conclusion 689
Cases and Readings:
   Near v. Minnesota 691
   *New York Times Company v. United States
   (The Pentagon Papers Case)* 695
   Nebraska Press Association v. Stuart 700
   New York Times Company v. Sullivan 705
   Hustler Magazine v. Falwell 709
   Branzburg v. Hayes 712
   Cohen v. Cowles Media Company 716
   Miller v. California 720
   Jenkins v. Georgia 723
   New York v. Ferber 725

American Booksellers Ass'n., Inc. v. Hudnut   *728*
Federal Communications Commission v. Pacifica
Foundation   *732*

Chapter 13   Religious Liberty and Church-State Relations   739
Introduction   739
What is Religion?   740
Free Exercise of Religion   742
Separation of Church and State   750
Conclusion   761
Cases and Readings:
  West Virginia State Board of Education v. Barnette   *763*
  Goldman v. Weinberger   *766*
  Wisconsin v. Yoder   *770*
  Employment Division v. Smith   *778*
  Everson v. Board of Education   *784*
  Abington School District v. Schempp   *788*
  Wallace v. Jeffree   *790*
  Edwards v. Aguillard   *794*
  Marsh v. Chambers   *799*
  Lynch v. Donnelly   *803*
  Walz v. Tax Commission   *808*

Chapter 14   The Constitution and Criminal Justice   815
Introduction   815
Search and Seizure   816
Arrest   823
The Fourth Amendment Exclusionary Rule   825
Police Interrogation and Confessions of Guilt   828
The Right to Counsel   832
Bail and Pretrial Detention   835
Plea Bargaining   836
Trial by Jury   837
The Protection Against Double Jeopardy   841
Cruel and Unusual Punishments   842
Appeal and Postconviction Relief   847
Juvenile Justice   851
Conclusion   852
Cases and Readings:
  Olmstead v. United States   *855*
  Katz v. United States   *858*
  Illinois v. Gates   *862*
  Chimel v. California   *868*
  United States v. Ross   *870*
  Terry v. Ohio   *874*
  United States v. Sokolow   *878*
  Weeks v. United States   *882*

Mapp v. Ohio   *885*
United States v. Leon   *889*
Miranda v. Arizona   *894*
Nix v. Williams   *899*
New York v. Quarles   *903*
Powell v. Alabama (The Scottsboro Case)   *907*
Gideon v. Wainwright   *911*
Bordenkircher v. Hayes   *913*
Batson v. Kentucky   *916*
Johnson v. Louisiana   *922*
Furman v. Georgia   *925*
Gregg v. Georgia   *933*
McCleskey v. Kemp   *938*
Hutto v. Finney   *942*
In Re Gault   *945*

**Chapter 15   Personal Autonomy and the Constitutional
Right of Privacy**   **953**
Introduction   953
Constitutional Foundations of the Right of Privacy   955
Procreation and Birth Control   957
The Abortion Controversy   960
The Right of Privacy and Living Arrangements   970
Privacy and Gay Rights   971
Other "Victimless Crimes"   972
Refusal of Medical Treatment and the "Right to Die"   973
The Protection of Private Information   976
Conclusion   976
Cases and Readings:
Jacobson v. Massachusetts   *978*
Meyer v. Nebraska   *980*
Buck v. Bell   *981*
Poe v. Ullman   *982*
Griswold v. Connecticut   *987*
Roe v. Wade   *993*
Maher v. Roe   *1000*
Bellotti v. Baird   *1005*
Akron v. Akron Center for Reproductive Health   *1010*
Webster v. Reproductive Health Services   *1017*
Moore v. City of East Cleveland   *1023*
Dronenburg v. Zech   *1028*
Bowers v. Hardwick   *1030*
Cruzan v. Director, Missouri Health Department   *1035*

**Chapter 16   Equal Protection and the Antidiscrimination
Principle**   **1043**
Introduction   1044
Levels of Judicial Scrutiny in Equal Protection Cases   1045

The Struggle for Racial Equality 1047

Sex Discrimination 1061

Other Forms of Discrimination 1067

The Ongoing Problem of Private Discrimination 1072

Conclusion 1075

Cases and Readings:

The Civil Rights Cases 1077

Plessy v. Ferguson 1081

Shelley v. Kraemer 1084

Sweatt v. Painter 1087

Brown v. Board of Education of Topeka I 1089

Brown v. Board of Education of Topeka II 1092

Loving v. Virginia 1093

Swann v. Charlotte-Meeklenburg Board of Education 1096

Milliken v. Bradley 1099

Fullilove v. Klutznick 1103

City of Richmond v. J.A. Croson Company 1108

Frontiero v. Richardson 1117

Rostker v. Goldberg 1121

Mississippi University for Women v. Hogan 1124

Plyler v. Doe 1128

City of Cleburne, Texas v. Cleburne Living Center 1134

San Antonio Independent School District v. Rodriguez 1138

Chapter 17   Representation and Voting Rights **1147**

Introduction 1147

Racial Discrimination in Voting Rights 1149

The Reapportionment Decisions 1157

Political Parties and Electoral Fairness 1161

Conclusion 1162

Cases and Readings:

Smith v. Allwright 1164

Gomillion v. Lightfoot 1167

South Carolina v. Katzenbach 1169

Mobile v. Bolden 1172

Rogers v. Lodge 1176

Reynolds v. Sims 1181

Karcher v. Daggett 1184

Brown v. Thomson 1189

Davis v. Bandemer 1194

Appendix A: The Constitution of the United States of America **A-1**

Appendix B: Chronology of Justices of the United States Supreme Court **B-1**

Appendix C: Supreme Court Justices: By Appointing President, State Appointed from, and Political Party **C-1**

Appendix D: Glossary of Legal Terms   **D-1**

Appendix E: Summary of the Supreme Court's 1991 Term   **E-1**
    Chemical Waste Management, Inc. v. Hunt   *E-3*
    R.A.V. v. City of St. Paul   *E-6*
    Lee v. Weisman   *E-10*
    Planned Parenthood v. Casey   *E-14*
    Freeman v. Pitts   *E-25*
    U.S. Department of Commerce v. Montana   *E-29*

Table of Cases   **T-1**

Index   **I-1**

PREFACE

This book is designed for political science courses in American constitutional law. The study of constitutional law should include far more than an examination of authoritative legal rules and principles, important though such examination is. Constitutional law is a dynamic process, continuously woven into the fabric of American history, politics, and culture. Therefore, each of the essays introducing the chapters in this book—in addition to the entire Introduction—is intended to provide historical, political, and cultural context for the judicial decisions that follow. In selecting and editing United States Supreme Court cases and other materials, we have emphasized recent trends in major areas of constitutional interpretation. At the same time, we have included many landmark decisions, some of which retain importance as precedents while others illustrate the transient nature of constitutional interpretation.

The bicentennial of the Constitution in 1987 underscored the themes of continuity and change emphasized in this book. The Philadelphia Convention of 1787 is typically recognized as the starting point in a dynamic governing process that endures to the present day. Yet it is clear that this starting point by no means represented a complete departure from political events immediately preceding it. The Constitution also reflects the influence of seventeenth- and eighteenth-century political theory, especially the writings of Locke and Montesquieu. The drafting and ratification of the Constitution, followed by adoption of the Bill of Rights four years later, represents the culmination of the American Revolution, as well as the birth of the Republic. Appropriate as it is to commemorate the work of those who drafted the Constitution and Bill of Rights, it is the living Constitution, further amended and interpreted over the years, that underscores the meaning of the bicentennial.

The original Constitution, amended only twenty-seven times (seventeen excluding the Bill of Rights), continues as the ultimate basis of legal authority in a country vastly larger, more diverse, and more complex—socially, politically, commercially, industrially, and technologically—than the United States of the late eighteenth century. We can appreciate the durable quality of the Constitution, however, without indulging in the excessive, uncritical praise expressed by many of those who took part in the centennial celebration of 1887. As Benjamin F. Wright pointed out, sometimes these people "seemed to confuse the work of the Convention of 1787 with the Tables handed down from Sinai, or at least with the writings which had their origin on Olympus." According to this view, "the authors of the Constitution were divinely inspired patriots of unsurpassed wisdom in whose work there is to be found no human flaw." The opposite view is hardly less objectionable. Most influential during the early part of this century, and still endorsed by some critics, this latter interpretation brands the Constitution as "the product of a reactionary movement engineered by the selfish rich" and "an antidemocratic document skillfully designed to secure the blessings of liberty only to the prosperous and the predatory."

The Constitution of 1787 was in fact addressed to immediate, practical problems. The primary objective was to establish a system of government with enough centralized power to ensure the survival and enhance the stability of the United States politically and economically, while preserving the states as basic units of the political system and protecting fundamental individual rights and liberties.

The Constitution did grant extensive powers to the national government, but it distributed them among legislative, executive, and judicial branches and provided a number of internal checks designed to prevent concentration of power at any single point. James Madison described this "security" against the concentration of power as "giving to those who administer each department the necessary constitutional means and personal motives to resist encroachments of the others." Beyond this limitation, the Tenth Amendment made explicit what had been implied in the structure of the constitutional system: that the powers not granted to the national government were reserved to the states or to the people. Taken together, the Constitution and Bill of Rights provided for a distribution of powers among branches of the national government, for a division of power between the national government and the states, and for the establishment of outer limits beyond which government could not legitimately exert power in relation to individuals.

Although the original Constitution contained many innovations, it did not represent a neat, unified theory of government. It emerged as a practical political document, a "bundle of compromises" reflecting a diversity of national, regional, and local interests. Of course, the Constitution endorsed a number of eighteenth-century practices and institutions long since discredited and abandoned. For example, it recognized and accommodated slavery, although the Framers fastidiously avoided use of that term. Similarly, the Framers deferred to state voting qualifications that limited the franchise to white males and in most instances included some requirement of property ownership.

In addition, the Constitution reflected to a large extent the economic interests of creditors. It removed the control of currency from the states, centralizing that power in the national government. It gave Congress full power to regulate commerce among the states—a vast, open-ended source of authority, as the past half-century of constitutional development has made clear. While granting major fiscal and regulatory powers to the national government, the Constitution also prohibited the states from impairing contractual obligations.

Although the Framers represented diverse, often conflicting, interests, they shared the prevailing view of that period (not much different from that of today) that those in public office are not to be trusted. The Framers' recognition of human limitations (including their own) is reflected not only in the system of checks and balances written into the Constitution but in the provisions for amending the basic law. Although the Framers held a skeptical view of human nature, they nevertheless presumed the possibility of human progress, a concept implicit in their stated intention to "form a more perfect union."

It seems clear that the members of the Philadelphia Convention in the summer of 1787 were more preoccupied with granting and allocating power than with guaranteeing specific rights and liberties. A few individual safeguards were recognized in the original Constitution, including *habeas corpus,* trial by jury in criminal cases, and bans on *ex post facto* laws and bills of attainder. Several of these provisions reflected the Framers' knowledge of and strong opposition to certain arbitrary practices of English government during the colonial period. For similar reasons, the original Constitution also prohibited the granting of titles of nobility and provided that "no religious test shall ever be required as a qualification to any office or public trust under the United States." A more detailed Bill of Rights was suggested during the closing days of the Convention, but the idea was dropped prior to the signing of the

Constitution on September 17. A short time later, however, during debates on ratification, a number of supporters agreed to exert their influence to bring about the addition of a Bill of Rights as soon as possible once the new Constitution went into effect. This promise paved the way for ratification and led to adoption of the first ten amendments in 1791. Subsequent amendments, notably the Thirteenth, Fourteenth, Fifteenth, and Nineteenth, added constitutional impetus to the drive for legal equality and democracy beginning in the nineteenth century and continuing to the present day.

Some of the language of the Constitution is explicit, leaving little if any doubt about its precise meaning: Age qualifications and terms of office for the president and members of Congress are straightforward and unambiguous. But terms such as "commerce," "necessary and proper," "executive power," and "judicial power" invite varying interpretations. In the amendments the difficulty of interpretation is compounded by such phrases as "establishment of religion," "freedom of speech," "unreasonable searches and seizures," "cruel and unusual punishments," "due process of law," and "equal protection of the laws."

All public officials who by oath or affirmation promise to support the Constitution share, in theory if not always in fact, some responsibility for constitutional interpretation. As a practical matter, however, the courts have taken the lead in this area almost from the beginning. And since the time that John Marshall was chief justice (1801–1835), the United States Supreme Court has assumed preeminence as the authoritative interpreter of the Constitution. The dynamic quality of judicial interpretation has contributed enormously to the ongoing relevance of the original Constitution and its historic amendments. The work of state and lower federal courts in the field of constitutional law is of course important. Accordingly, we have included a few excerpts from decisions at these levels; however, this book is written from a widely shared perspective that accords primary emphasis to the work of the Supreme Court.

Although the Court plays a very important role in American politics, its role is limited to deciding cases that pose legal questions. Accordingly, its political decisions are rendered in legal terms. Because it is both a legal and a political institution, a complete understanding of the Court requires some knowledge of both law and politics. Although political discourse is familiar to most college students, the legal world can seem rather bewildering. Terms such as *habeas corpus, ex parte, subpoena duces tecum,* and *certiorari* leave the impression that one must master an entirely new language just to know what is going on, much less achieve a sophisticated understanding. Although we do not believe that a complete mastery of legal terminology is necessary to glean the political from the legal, we recognize that understanding the work of the Supreme Court is a complex task. We have tried to minimize this complexity by deleting as much technical terminology as possible from the decisions excerpted in this book wihout damaging the integrity of those decisions. Where citations to cases, statutes, or other legal materials have been deleted from opinions, we have so indicated using three asterisks (***). Deletions of text are indicated by ellipses (...). Nevertheless, despite our attempts at editing out distracting citations, technical terms, and mere verbiage, the task of understanding Supreme Court decisions remains formidable. It is one that requires concentration, patience, and above all the determination to grasp what may at times seem hopelessly abstruse. We firmly believe that all students of American politics, indeed all citizens, should make the effort.

As noted above, this book emphasizes the historical, political and cultural contexts of constitutional law. This emphasis is reflected both in the introductory essays and in the selection of cases and related materials. While we have grouped the cases in a manner consistent with our own pedagogical preferences, we recognize that no single organizational arrangement will suit the needs of all teachers of constitutional law. Accordingly, we have endeavored to indicate the relevance of important cases to several areas of constitutional law by frequent cross-references. We hope that this device will enable instructors to choose the sequence of issues and cases most suitable to their approach.

This book includes Supreme Court decisions handed down through June 1992. To maintain the currency of the book, we plan to publish annual supplements summarizing major developments in constitutional law, beginning in the summer of 1993.

In completing this project, our efforts have been aided by numerous individuals. First and foremost, we wish to thank the secretaries in the political science department at the University of Tennessee, Knoxville, who spent innumerable hours doing the word processing: Naina Bowen, Carolyn Gose, Deborah McCauley, and Phyllis Moyers. Next, we would like to thank the following students (and former students) at the University of Tennessee, Knoxville, who provided invaluable research assistance and/or read parts of the manuscript and made suggestions for its improvement: Gordon S. Church, Stephen Clark, Jason Epstein, Carol S. Frazier, Steve Garrett, Richard A. Glenn, Sarah Hall, Nancy Hay, Ann S. Henderson, Judy Jessie, Sylvia Myers, Nathan Nelson and Jason R. Ward. A special word of thanks is due to John Shanks, our graduate assistant, for his thorough and conscientious research efforts.

The following colleagues at the University of Tennessee, Knoxville, read parts of the manuscript and offered useful comments and suggestions: Joseph Anderson, Terry Bowen, William Lyons, and Glenn H. Reynolds. We sincerely appreciate their help.

We would also like to express our appreciation to Hon. John M. Scheb, Florida Court of Appeal, 2nd District (ret.); Professor Anthony Simones, Southwest Missouri State University; and attorneys Charles S.P. Hodge and Durward K. McDaniel of Washington, D.C., and Austin, Texas, respectively, for their valuable suggestions and comments.

We wish to express our gratitude to Joan Gill, our editor at West, for her enthusiastic support and steadfast encouragement throughout the project. Thanks are due as well to Holly Henjum, Poh Lin Khoo, and Ann Swift. We deeply appreciate the efforts of all these individuals.

Finally, we wish to acknowledge the support and assistance in manuscript preparation provided by our wives, Mary Stephens and Sherilyn Scheb. This book is dedicated to them.

While many people contributed to the development and production of this book, we, of course, assume full responsibility for any errors that may appear herein.

Otis H. Stephens, Jr.
John M. Scheb, II
Knoxville, Tennessee
December 18, 1992

REVIEWERS AND AFFILIATIONS

The authors and publisher wish to thank the following individuals who reviewed the manuscript:

Henry Abraham
University of Virginia

Ralph Baker
Ball State University

Paul R. Benson
The Citadel

Robert Bradley
Illinois State University

Saul Brenner
University of North Carolina–Charlotte

Robert V. Burns
South Dakota State University

Larry Elowitz
Georgia College

William Haltom
University of Puget Sound

William E. Kelly
Auburn University

Kent A. Kirwan
University of Nebraska–Omaha

Mark Landis
Hofstra University

Timothy O. Lenz
Florida Atlantic University

William P. McLauchlan
Purdue University

R. Christopher Perry
Indiana State University

E.C. Price
California State University–Northridge

Donald I. Ranish
Antelope Valley College

Wilfred E. Rumble
Vassar College

Elliot E. Slotnick
Ohio State University

Diane E. Wall
Mississippi State University

John Winkle
University of Mississippi

INTRODUCTION

If men were angels, no government would be necessary. If angels were to govern men, neither external nor internal controls would be necessary. In framing a government which is to be administered by men over men, the great difficulty lies in this: you must first enable the government to control the governed; and in the next place oblige it to control itself.

James Madison
The Federalist No. 51

The signing of the
Constitution

WHAT IS CONSTITUTIONAL LAW?

Constitutional law deals with the organization, powers, and limits of government and with the relationship between a nation's government and its citizenry. *American constitutional law,* as used in the title of this book, refers to the Constitution of the United States and its application to the social, economic, and political issues that have confronted the country over the past two centuries.

It is largely through judicial interpretation that the Constitution takes on continuing meaning, force, and relevance. Of chief importance are the interpretations rendered by the United States Supreme Court. While other governmental actors, such as Congress and the president, also participate in deciding what the Constitution means, the Supreme Court's interpretations of the nation's charter are usually accorded finality. Thus, the study of American constitutional law is to a great extent the analysis of the constitutional decisions of the Supreme Court.

Constitutional law is generally divided into two basic components. The first deals with the powers of and relationships among the various institutions and levels of government in this country. In this area of constitutional law, one encounters questions of presidential, Congressional, and judicial power, as well as questions of state versus national authority. The second great area of constitutional law, usually referred to as **civil rights and liberties,** concerns the relationship between the individual and government. Here, one encounters issues involving claims of personal freedom and legal and political equality.

Why Study Constitutional Law?

Questions of constitutional law may seem abstract, remote, or even hopelessly esoteric to the average citizen. But in reality, the Constitution touches the lives of ordinary Americans in countless ways, many of which will be revealed in this book. In constitutional law, one sees all of the theoretical and philosophical questions underlying our political system, as well as the great public issues of the day, acted out in a series of real-life dramas. Questions of constitutional law are therefore too important to be reserved exclusively to judges, lawyers, and scholars. Every citizen, and certainly every student of American government, ought to have at least a rudimentary understanding of constitutional law.

THE ADOPTION AND RATIFICATION OF THE CONSTITUTION

The study of constitutional law begins logically with the adoption and ratification of the Constitution itself. The Constitution was adopted in 1787 by a convention of delegates representing twelve of the thirteen states in the Union at that time. Fifty-five delegates convened at Independence Hall in Philadelphia during the hot summer of 1787 to try to devise a plan for a successful national government.

The Articles of Confederation

The country had been governed since late in the American Revolution by a weak national government consisting only of the Congress and a few administrators. This arrangement had been formalized under the **Articles of Confederation,** proposed in 1777 but not ratified until 1781. Under the Articles, there was no real system of national government—no presidency to provide leadership, no courts to settle disputes between the states. Congress, the sole organ of the government, was lacking in both power and prestige. Congress had no power to tax and was reduced to pleading with the state legislatures for revenue.

Under the Articles of Confederation, Congress lacked the power to regulate interstate commerce. It was therefore powerless to prevent the states from engaging in trade protectionism that frustrated the emergence of an integrated national economy and exacerbated the depressed and unstable economy that existed in the wake of the Revolutionary War. At this stage in its history, the United States was hardly a nation at all, but rather a mere collection of independent states, each jealous and suspicious of the others. Most ominous of all was the ever-present threat of the European colonial powers, which still had designs on the New World and were ready to intervene should the United States government collapse.

Shays' Rebellion

By 1786, it was widely recognized that the Articles of Confederation were in serious need of repair, if not replacement. This recognition was reinforced by a seminal event that occurred in Massachusetts in the summer of 1786. Daniel Shays, a veteran of the Battle of Bunker Hill, led a ragtag army composed primarily of disgruntled farmers in a rebellion against state tax-collectors and courts. The object of Shays' Rebellion was to prevent foreclosure on numerous farms whose owners were bankrupt. Unable to put down the rebellion by itself, the Massachusetts government requested assistance from the national confederation. Congress adopted a plan to raise an army, but most states were unwilling to provide the necessary funds. Shays' army succeeded in taking over a considerable area of western Massachusetts until it was defeated by a band of mercenaries hired by wealthy citizens who feared a popular uprising. The inability of the national government to respond effectively to Shays' Rebellion was the single most important event in generating broad support for a constitutional convention.

The Constitutional Convention

In September 1786, shortly after Shays' Rebellion, delegates from five states met in Annapolis, Maryland, to consider ways to resolve the growing problems of interstate commerce. While the Annapolis Convention resolved nothing, two of the delegates, James Madison of Virginia and Alexander Hamilton of New York, took this opportunity to call for a national convention to consider a general revision of the Articles of Confederation. Responding to this initiative, Congress, on February 21, 1787, issued the call for a federal convention to meet in Philadelphia "for the sole and express purpose of revising the Articles of Confederation." The states were invited to send delegations, each of which would have an equal vote at the convention. The delegates were chosen by their respective state legislatures. Only Rhode Island refused to participate.

The fifty-five representatives of twelve states who gathered in Philadelphia were drawn, for the most part, from the nation's elite: landowners, lawyers,

James Madison: the principal
architect of the Constitution

bankers, manufacturers, physicians, and businessmen. The delegates were, on
the whole, highly educated men of wealth and influence. Some commentators,
most notably Charles A. Beard, have suggested that the delegates to the Constitutional Convention were motivated primarily by their own upper-class economic interests, interests that would be threatened by political instability. In
Beard's view, the overriding motivation of the delegates was the protection of
private property rights against actions of the state legislatures. Yet others, such as
John P. Roche, have argued that the delegates were first and foremost practical
politicians who were concerned both about the economic interests of their
respective states and about their common nationality. Certainly those who gathered in Philadelphia were aware that whatever document they produced would
have to be approved by their respective states. Their goal was to design an
effective system of national government that could win popular approval in a
nation that had just fought a revolution against a monarch and was still highly
suspicious of centralized power.

The men who participated in the drafting of the Constitution were quite
familiar with the writings of John Locke and other **social contract** theorists.
They were also well aware of the principles of **separation of powers** and
checks and balances advocated by the French philosopher Montesquieu.
More important than abstract concepts of individual rights and limited government, however, was the actual experience of the Framers in the shaky aftermath
of the Revolution. In particular, the Framers could draw on the recent experience of the states in adopting their own new constitutions shortly after independence from England was declared.

Like most of their fellow citizens, the delegates to the Constitutional Convention were sensitive to the dangers of concentrated power and recognized the
necessity for broad popular representation. But they were equally mindful of the

danger that unchecked representative government might degenerate into the "tyranny of the majority." They certainly accorded great importance to the need to protect the liberty and property of the individual.

The Framers accepted the existence of the states as sovereign political entities, but they also recognized that without a strong national government, economic growth and political stability would be seriously undermined by interstate rivalries. Thus, the underlying theme of the Framers' thinking was the need for balance, moderation, and prudence. This level-headed, pragmatic approach to the daunting task of designing a new system of government was largely responsible for the success of the Constitutional Convention.

After electing George Washington as the presiding officer and deciding to conduct their business in secret, the delegates chose to abandon the Articles of Confederation altogether and fashion a wholly new constitution. The decision to "start from scratch" was risky because, although there was broad consensus on the need for a new and improved governmental system, many issues sharply divided the delegates. There was no guarantee that they would ever be able to agree on a substitute for the Articles of Confederation. The questions of how states would be represented in the new Congress, the nature of the executive power, and the need for a national judiciary were all potential stumbling blocks. Perhaps most difficult was the question of slavery, which had already divided Northern and Southern sentiment. After many long weeks of intense debate, many conflicts and many compromises, and the departure of sixteen delegates, the Constitution was finally approved on September 17, 1787.

A Conservative Document?

The document the Framers produced has been characterized as "conservative," and when the Constitution is compared to the Declaration of Independence, the label is not altogether inappropriate. Whereas the Declaration of Independence sought to justify a revolution, the Framers of the Constitution were concerned with the inherently more conservative task of nation-building. But in 1787, the political philosophy underlying the Constitution was fairly revolutionary. It fused classical republican ideas of the rule of law and limited government with eighteenth-century liberal principles of individual liberty and popular sovereignty.

Equally radical in the late eighteenth century was the notion of a written constitution to which government would be forever subordinated. The English constitution, with which the Framers were well-acquainted, consists of unwritten traditions and parliamentary enactments that are seen as fundamental but that may be altered through ordinary legislation. The Framers rejected the concept of legislative supremacy, opting instead for a government subordinated to a supreme written charter that could not be easily changed. As James Wilson, one of the delegates to the Constitutional Convention, commented,

> The idea of a Constitution, limiting and superintending the operations of legislative authority, seems not to have been accurately understood in Britain. . . . To control the power and conduct of the legislature by an overruling Constitution was an improvement in the science of government reserved to the American states.

Patrick Henry: A critic of the
Constitution

The framework of government delineated in the new Constitution was built
on four fundamental principles: (1) **separation of powers** among the legislative, executive, and judicial branches of government; (2) a system of **checks
and balances** among these branches; (3) a system of **federalism,** or division
of power between the national government and the states; and (4) the **rule of
law.** As James Madison, the principal architect of the Constitution, observed, "the
accumulation of all powers . . . in the same hands . . . may be pronounced the
very definition of tyranny." Therefore, in the Madisonian view, power must be
divided, checked, balanced, and limited. Perhaps most important, it must be
subordinated to the rule of law. Thus, the Constitution, in Article VI, Section 2,
is proclaimed to be "the supreme law of the land."

The Battle over Ratification

The Philadelphia Convention was only the first step in winning approval of the
new Constitution. The document still had to be ratified, as provided in Article VII,
by at least nine states before it could become "the supreme law of the land."
Ratification was by no means a foregone conclusion. Critics of the Constitution
pointed to a number of antidemocratic features. The U.S. Senate was not to be
chosen by the people directly; rather, its members were to be selected by the
state legislatures. Nor was the chief executive subject to direct popular election;
the president was to be chosen by an elite body called the **Electoral College.**
Finally, federal judges, including the justices of the Supreme Court, were to be
appointed for life by the president with the consent of the Senate. For men such
as Patrick Henry and Richard Henry Lee of Virginia, these elitist features were too
much to bear, and they led the movement to defeat the Constitution.

The Federalist Papers

The strongest arguments in favor of the Constitution were made by James Madison, Alexander Hamilton, and John Jay in a series of newspaper essays published under the pseudonym Publius and now known collectively as *The Federalist Papers*. In this classic work of American political theory, Madison, Hamilton, and Jay expounded on the design of the Constitution. For example, in *The Federalist* No. 78, Alexander Hamilton made a persuasive argument that the judiciary would be the "least dangerous branch" of the newly proposed national government. The publication of *The Federalist Papers* is generally recognized to have been a useful exercise in consensus-building. It probably helped allay fears about the dramatic changes in the American political system that would be ushered in by the ratification of the Constitution. More important, however, *The Federalist Papers* represented a clear statement of the theoretical underpinnings of the Constitution. They continue to be relied upon, not only by scholars but also by judges and legislators, in addressing questions of constitutional interpretation.

The Bill of Rights

Thomas Jefferson, who has been described as the "missing giant" of the Constitutional Convention, was disappointed that the Framers failed to include a bill of rights in the document they adopted. This omission was the greatest deficiency of the Constitution and in fact threatened to derail its ratification. Finally, a "gentlemen's agreement" was worked out whereby ratification was obtained in Virginia and other key states on the condition that Congress would immediately take up the matter of creating a bill of rights. The first ten amendments to the Constitution, known collectively as the Bill of Rights, were adopted by the First Congress in 1789 and ratified by the requisite nine states in 1791. Today, issues arising under various provisions of the Bill of Rights (for example, abortion, pornography, and the rights of criminal suspects) are among the most salient questions of American constitutional law.

THE "LIVING CONSTITUTION"

The Constitution has been amended seventeen times since the ratification of the Bill of Rights. Undoubtedly the most important of these amendments are the Thirteenth, Fourteenth, and Fifteenth, ratified in 1865, 1868, and 1870, respectively. The Thirteenth Amendment abolished slavery, or "involuntary servitude." The Fourteenth Amendment was designed primarily to prohibit states from denying equal protection and due process of law to the former slaves. The Fifteenth Amendment forbade the denial of voting rights on the basis of race. These so-called Civil War Amendments attempted to eradicate the institution of slavery and the inferior legal status of black Americans. Although the abstract promises of the Civil War Amendments went unfulfilled for many years (some would say they remain unfulfilled even today), they represented the beginning of a process of democratization that has fundamentally altered the character of the American political system. It is important to recognize that the Fourteenth Amendment in particular, with its broad requirements of equal protection and due process, has become a major source of legal protection for civil rights and liberties, extending far beyond issues of racial discrimination.

Constitutional Democracy

When the Framers met in Philadelphia in 1787, the right to vote was, for the most part, limited to white men of property. In fact, all fifty-five of the delegates to the Constitutional Convention were drawn from this segment of the population. Women were regarded as second-class citizens, and most blacks, being slaves, held no legal rights. The Civil War, industrial and commercial expansion, and waves of immigration in the late nineteenth century, together with two world wars and the Great Depression in the twentieth century, produced fundamental changes in the nature of American society. Inevitably, social forces have brought about dramatic changes in the legal and political systems. The basic thrust of these changes has been to render the polity more democratic, that is, more open to participation by those who were once excluded. Through constitutional amendment and changing interpretations of existing constitutional language, the "constitutional republic" designed by the Framers has become a "constitutional democracy." This fundamental change in the character of the political system testifies to the remarkable adaptability of the Constitution itself.

Built-in Flexibility

Although the Constitution was intended to limit the power of government, it was not designed as a straitjacket. Through a number of general, open-ended provisions, the Constitution enables government to respond to changing social, political, and economic conditions. When the first Congress convened in 1789, the United States consisted of thirteen states stretching along the Atlantic coast. The economy was primarily agricultural, and most of the nation's four million people lived in rural areas. The pace of life was slow. Little was expected from the national government. Its total expenditures up to 1792 were $4,269,000, and the national debt stood at just over $77 million. The federal government was staffed by approximately eight hundred employees. There was no standing army.

Today, the United States stretches across the continent and beyond into the islands of the Pacific. The nation's population has exceeded 250 million. The United States is the only nation in the world that is both a military and an industrial superpower. The U.S. people now live mostly in gigantic metropolitan areas, restless hubs of transportation, communications, and business. The pace of life has become extremely quick. While we enjoy a standard of living undreamed of by the Founders, we also experience collective problems that did not greatly trouble the eighteenth century: environmental degradation, crime, racial conflict, social disorganization and others. Americans now look to government, especially to Washington, to address these problems. Consequently, the annual federal budget is well over a trillion dollars. The national debt exceeds $4 trillion and is growing rapidly. Federal employees number about three million, not counting the armed forces.

Obviously, the United States in the 1990s is a radically different place from the nation the Founders knew. Yet the United States is governed essentially by the same set of institutions the Framers designed and by the same Constitution (with twenty-seven amendments) adopted in 1787. In fact, the U.S. Constitution is the oldest written constitution still in effect in the world.

The adaptability of the Constitution is fundamentally due to the open-ended nature of numerous key provisions of the document. This is particularly evident in the broad language outlining the legislative, executive, and judicial powers. Article I permits Congress to tax and spend to further the "general welfare," a term that has taken on new meaning in modern times. Article II gives the "executive power" to the president but does not define the precise limits thereof. Article III likewise invests the Supreme Court with "judicial power" without elaborating on the limits of that power. Such open-ended provisions endow the Constitution with a built-in flexibility that has enabled it to withstand the test of time.

Judicial Interpretation of the Constitution

The Constitution's remarkable adaptability is also a function of the power of the courts, and especially the U.S. Supreme Court, to authoritatively interpret the provisions of the document. In *Marbury v. Madison* (1803), the most important case in American constitutional law, the Supreme Court asserted that "[i]t is, emphatically, the province and duty of the judicial department, to say what the law is." In *Marbury,* Chief Justice John Marshall was referring not only to the interpretation of ordinary legislation but also to the interpretation of the Constitution itself. While the courts do not have a monopoly on constitutional interpretation, ever since *Marbury v. Madison,* it has been widely recognized and generally accepted that the interpretations rendered by the courts are authoritative.

Judges, lawyers, politicians, and scholars have long debated theories of how the eighteenth-century Constitution should be understood and applied to the issues of the day. As the federal courts have assumed a more central role in the public policy-making process, the debate over constitutional interpretation has become more heated and more public. On one side of the debate are those who subscribe to the **doctrine of original intent,** which holds that in applying a provision of the Constitution to a contemporary question, judges should attempt to determine what the Framers intended the provision to mean. On the other side are those who champion the idea of a "living Constitution," the meaning of which must change to reflect the spirit of the age. This debate is often lurking behind disagreements over particular constitutional questions ranging from abortion to school prayer. It is being constantly reargued and rekindled by the decisions of the Supreme Court.

In some instances, the language of the Constitution leaves little room for varying judicial interpretation. For example, the Article I, Section 3 provides unequivocally that "[t]he Senate of the United States shall be composed of two Senators from each State. . . ." But not all of the Constitution's provisions are so obvious in their meaning. Perhaps the best example is the Necessary and Proper Clause of Article I, Section 8. It is through this clause that the Supreme Court, in what can certainly be considered the second most important case in American constitution law, *M'Culloch v. Maryland* (1819), endowed Congress with a deep reservoir of **implied powers.** Another example of broad language is that clause of Article I, Section 8 that gives Congress the authority to "regulate commerce . . . among the several states." Under this clause, the Supreme Court has upheld sweeping congressional action in the fields of labor relations, antitrust policy, highway construction, airline safety, environmental protection, and civil rights, just to name a few of the more prominent examples.

The Constitution and Modern Government

The central tendency of modern constitutional interpretation has been to increase the power and scope of the national government. Some would say that this expansion has occurred at the expense of **states' rights** and individual freedom. There is no doubt that the modern Constitution, largely by necessity, allows for a far more extensive and powerful federal government than the Framers would have desired or could have imagined. Yet the Supreme Court has not lost sight of the Framers' ideal of limited government, and in recent years, it has showed its willingness and ability to curtail the exercise of governmental power. In *United States v. Nixon* (1974), the Watergate tapes case, the Court refused to condone an assertion of presidential power that flatly contradicted the Framers' principle of the rule of law. And in *Immigration and Naturalization Service v. Chadha* (1983), the Court stood up to Congress, telling it that many of its laws governing congressional control over executive agencies were invalid. However one feels about the correctness of the decisions rendered in *Nixon* and *Chadha*, these cases demonstrate that the Court takes the Constitution seriously and that the Constitution still embodies the Framers' idea that the government may not always do what it pleases.

FOR FURTHER READING

Beard, Charles A. *An Economic Interpretation of the Constitution of the United States.* New York: Macmillan, 1935.

Farrand, Max, ed. *The Records of the Federal Convention of 1787.* New Haven: Yale University Press, 1937.

Hamilton, Alexander, John Jay, and James Madison. *The Federalist Papers.* Originally published in serial form, 1787–88, by J. and A. M'Lean, New York. Now available in numerous editions.

Jensen, Merrill. *The Articles of Confederation.* Madison: University of Wisconsin Press, 1940.

Kelly, Alfred H., Winfred A. Harbison, and Herman Belz. *The American Constitution: Its Origins and Development,* 7th ed., 2 vols. New York: Norton, 1991.

Kenyon, Cecilia, ed. *The Antifederalists.* Indianapolis: Bobbs-Merrill, 1966.

McDonald, Forrest. *We the People: The Economic Origins of the Constitution.* Chicago: University of Chicago Press, 1958.

McDonald, Forrest. *Novus Ordo Seclorum: The Intellectual Origins of the Constitution.* Lawrence: University of Kansas Press, 1985.

Roche, John P. "The Founding Fathers: A Reform Caucus in Action." *American Political Science Review* 55 (1961).

Swisher, Carl Brent. *American Constitutional Development.* 2d ed. New York: Houghton-Mifflin, 1954.

Warren, Charles. *The Making of the Constitution.* Boston: Little, Brown, 1928.

PART ONE

THE SUPREME COURT IN THE CONSTITUTIONAL SYSTEM

CHAPTER ONE

THE SUPREME COURT IN THE AMERICAN JUDICIAL PROCESS

The answers that the Supreme Court is required to give are based on questions and on data that preclude automatic or even undoubting answers. If the materials on which judicial judgments must be based could be fed into a machine so as to produce ineluctable answers, if such were the nature of the problems that come before the Supreme Court and such were the answers expected, we could have IBM machines doing the work instead of judges.

—Justice Felix Frankfurter, from "Some Observations on the Nature of the Judicial Process and Supreme Court Litigation," 98 Proceedings of the American Philosophical Society 233 (1954).

The U.S. Supreme Court Building. *The Court has occupied this building since 1935*

INTRODUCTION

The U.S. Supreme Court is the leading actor on the stage of American constitutional law. While other courts (federal and state) have occasion to interpret the Constitution, the Supreme Court is the preeminent court of law in the country. Its decisions interpreting the Constitution are most significant and authoritative. Thus, *constitutional law is comprised chiefly, but not exclusively, of the Supreme Court's decisions applying the Constitution to a broad range of social, economic, and political issues.*

The Supreme Court operates within an elaborate framework of legal principles, precedents, and procedures. However, by virtue of its institutional status as an independent branch of government and the fact that the legal issues it addresses often involve important questions of public policy, the Court is a profoundly political entity. The Court's political role is most obvious when it decides controversial cases requiring a determination of the meaning of the nation's fundamental law. Because the Supreme Court is at once a legal and a political institution, an understanding of the Court and its most significant product, constitutional law, requires knowledge of both law and politics.

Part I of this book examines the Supreme Court as an institution—its practices, powers, and procedures. It also looks at limitations on the Court's power, some of which are self-imposed. This chapter focuses on the Court's decision-making process and its role in the American judicial system. It also examines the genesis of constitutional law cases and explains how such cases reach the Court. As a preliminary matter, it is necessary to review some basic information about courts of law generally.

AN OVERVIEW OF AMERICAN COURTS

Courts of law exist primarily to decide cases, which are legal disputes arising between parties. The parties to such disputes may be individuals, groups of individuals, corporations, or even agencies of government, depending on the nature of the dispute. The issues presented in such cases may be factual or legal. **Trial courts** make factual determinations based on the presentation of evidence and apply established legal principles to resolve disputes. **Appellate courts,** on the other hand, exist to correct legal errors made by trial courts and to settle controversies about disputed legal principles.

Jurisdiction is the power of a court to hear and decide certain categories of cases. **Original jurisdiction** is the authority to hear a case for the first time, usually for the purpose of conducting a trial or hearing. **Appellate jurisdiction** is the authority to review the decisions of lower courts.

A **court system** thus consists of a set of trial and appellate courts arranged in a hierarchy, with one supreme appellate court assigned the responsibility of making final decisions within that system. In the United States, there are at least fifty-one separate and distinct court systems, one for the federal government and one for each of the fifty states. Indeed, one might argue that the federal courts comprise more than one system, in that Congress has created separate sets of courts for the District of Columbia, Puerto Rico, and Guam. These subsystems are roughly comparable in structure and function to individual state court systems.

State Court Systems

Each of the fifty state court systems is designed to settle cases arising under the laws of that state, which include the state **constitution,** the **statutes** enacted by the state legislature, the **orders** issued by the governor, the **regulations** promulgated by various state agencies, and the **ordinances** (local laws) adopted by cities and counties.

No two state court systems are identical. Substantial variation exists in how state courts are organized and administered, the exact procedures they follow in adjudicating cases, and the means whereby judges are selected, retained, and removed from office. Yet there are many common features. Fundamentally, every state court system is equipped to adjudicate civil and criminal cases. **Civil cases** occur when one party, referred to as the **plaintiff,** sues another party, known as the **defendant,** to vindicate a legal right, quite often to recover monetary damages for a personal injury or breach of contract. Civil suits are usually brought by individuals but may be initiated by corporations or government agencies in some instances. Persons representing large groups of "similarly situated" individuals sometimes institute **class actions** to redress widespread injuries. **Criminal cases,** on the other hand, occur when the government (state or federal) prosecutes a party (usually an individual) for the alleged commission of a crime. In addition to handling both civil and criminal matters, every state court system is equipped to conduct trials and to consider appeals from the outcomes of trials. Thus, every state court system has at least one tier of trial courts and at least one appellate tribunal.

Figure 1.1 illustrates a model state court system. It is composed of four tiers. At the bottom are the **courts of limited jurisdiction,** trial courts that handle minor civil cases (often called **small claims**) and lesser crimes (refer- red to as **misdemeanors**). At the next level of the hierarchy are the **courts of general jurisdiction,** trial courts that handle major civil matters and more serious crimes (called **felonies**). Above these are the **intermediate appellate courts,** which consider routine appeals brought by losing parties in the trial courts below. At the apex of the hierarchy is the state supreme court, which decides the most important issues of state law and, ideally, provides legal clarity and consistency for lower appellate and trial courts. (In New York, the "supreme court" is a trial court of general jurisdiction; the highest appellate court is called the "court of appeals.") It is important to recognize that, although federal constitutional questions often arise in state courts, the decisions of the state supreme court are final with respect to questions of state law.

The national government operates its own court system, which has authority throughout the United States and its territories. This system is commonly referred to as the **federal courts.** The federal courts decide cases arising under the statutes enacted by Congress, **executive orders** issued by the president, regulations established by various federal agencies, and treaties and other agreements between the United States and foreign countries. The federal courts also decide cases involving provisions of the U.S. Constitution. Such disputes, called **constitutional cases,** comprise the subject matter of this text.

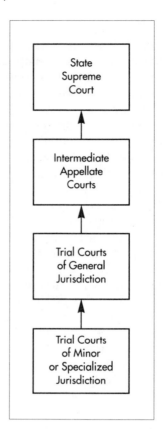

FIGURE 1.1
A Model State
Court System

The Federal Courts

Under the **Articles of Confederation,** in effect from 1781 to 1789, there was no court of law capable of fairly and effectively resolving disputes between states or between citizens of different states. Very early during the Constitutional Convention of 1787, delegates unanimously approved a resolution proposed by Edmund Randolph of Virginia calling for the establishment of a national judiciary. Yet the Constitution provided little guidance for the structure, powers, and functions of the national courts.

Article III of the Constitution provides that "[t]he judicial Power of the United States, shall be vested in one supreme Court, and in such inferior Courts as the Congress may from time to time ordain and establish." This language gives Congress the authority to create, and to some extent control, the federal court system. When Congress convened in 1789, the first order of business was the creation of a federal judiciary. Not all members of Congress, however, saw the need for lower federal courts. Rather, they preferred that state courts (in existence since the American Revolution) be given the power to decide federal cases. The advocates of an independent federal court system eventually prevailed, and the **Judiciary Act of 1789** became law.

In addition to the Supreme Court, which had been provided for by Article III of the Constitution, the Judiciary Act of 1789 created a two-tiered system of federal trial courts. At the base of the hierarchy were the district courts, which were afforded fairly limited jurisdiction. Above them were the circuit courts, which were given broad original and appellate jurisdiction, including the authority to hear **diversity of citizenship cases** (suits between citizens of different states). The circuit courts were not provided their own judges but were staffed by judges of the district courts sitting alongside Supreme Court justices, who were required to "ride circuit." Supreme Court justices regarded their circuit-riding duties as onerous and routinely complained to Congress. The justices' circuit-riding responsibilities were progressively diminished during the nineteenth century as Congress provided for circuit court judges. The circuit courts were finally abolished in 1911, making the district courts the major trial courts in the federal judiciary.

The U.S. District Courts

Section 2 of the Judiciary Act of 1789 created thirteen district courts, one for each of the eleven states then in the Union and one each for the parts of Massachusetts and Virginia that were later to become the states of Maine and Kentucky, respectively. From the outset, then, the district courts have been state-contained, with Congress adding new districts as the nation has grown. Today, there are ninety-four federal judicial districts, each state being allocated at least one. Tennessee, for example, has three federal judicial districts following the traditional "grand division" among the western, middle, and eastern regions of the state. California, New York, and Texas are the only states with four federal judicial districts.

FIGURE 1.2 The Federal Judicial System

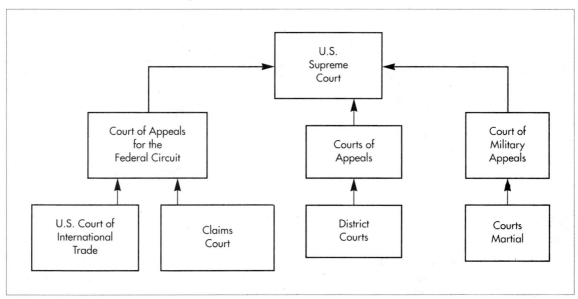

Since 1911, the district courts have been the major trial courts in the federal system. They are empowered to conduct trials and hearings in civil and criminal cases arising under federal law. Normally, one federal judge presides at such hearings and trials, although federal law permits certain exceptional cases to be decided by panels of three judges. In 1990, the federal district courts disposed of nearly 258,000 cases, of which roughly sixteen percent were criminal prosecutions.

The U.S. Courts of Appeals

Federal law provides opportunities for losing parties in the district courts to appeal to the U.S. courts of appeal. These intermediate appellate courts did not exist until the enactment of the **Judiciary Act of 1891.** Prior to that time, appeals from the decisions of the district courts were heard by the old circuit courts or by the Supreme Court.

Like the district courts, the courts of appeals are organized geographically. The nation is divided into twelve circuits, with each circuit comprising a number of federal judicial districts (there is also a "federal circuit," discussed below in

FIGURE 1.3 The Federal Judicial Circuits

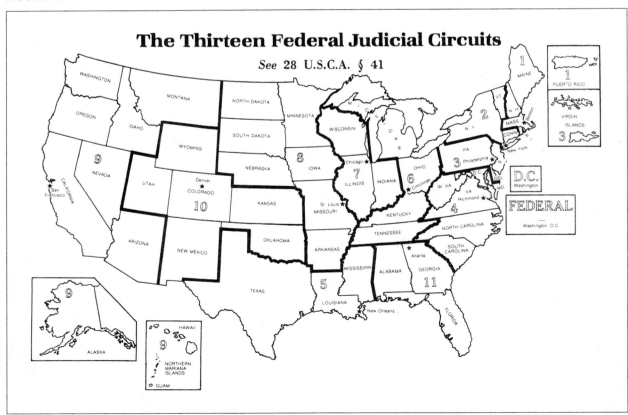

Source: *Federal Reporter,* 2d series (West Publishing Co.).

relation to specialized federal courts). Each of the so-called "circuit courts" hears appeals from the federal districts within its circuit. For example, the U.S. Court of Appeals for the Eleventh Circuit, based in Atlanta, hears appeals from the district courts located in Alabama, Georgia, and Florida. The Court of Appeals for the District of Columbia Circuit, based in Washington, has the very important function of hearing appeals from numerous "quasi-judicial" bodies in the federal bureaucracy.

Appeals in the circuit courts are normally decided by rotating panels of three judges, although under exceptional circumstances, these courts will decide cases **en banc,** meaning that all of the judges assigned to the court will participate in the decision. On average, there are twelve judges assigned to each circuit, but the number varies according to caseload. In 1990, the courts of appeals collectively disposed of more than thirty-eight thousand appeals, of which roughly fifteen percent were criminal cases.

Specialized Federal Tribunals

Over the years, Congress has provided for a number of specialized courts. The U.S. Claims Court (first established in 1855 as the Court of Claims) is responsible for adjudicating **tort claims** (civil suits for damages) against the federal government. The U.S. Court of International Trade (first established in 1926 as the Customs Court) adjudicates controversies between the federal government and importers of foreign goods. Finally, the Tax Court (once an appendage of the Internal Revenue Service [IRS], now an independent tribunal) performs the very important function of interpreting the labyrinthine federal tax code and deciding who prevails in disputes between citizens or corporations and the IRS. Appeals from the Claims Court, the Court of International Trade, and the Tax Court are directed to the Court of Appeals for the Federal Circuit, which is the thirteenth federal circuit court (not to be confused with the D.C. Circuit).

Under the **Uniform Code of Military Justice,** crimes committed by persons in military service are prosecuted before **courts-martial.** In 1950, a civilian court, the U.S. Court of Military Appeals, was created by Congress to review criminal convictions rendered by courts-martial. Appeals are decided in the Court of Military Appeals by a panel of five judges.

The U.S. Supreme Court

Although the Supreme Court is explicitly recognized in Article III of the Constitution, it was not formally established until passage of the Judiciary Act of 1789. The act provided for a Court comprised of a chief justice and five associate justices. The Supreme Court was given the authority to hear certain appeals brought from the lower federal courts and the state courts. The Court was also given the power to issue various kinds of orders, or **writs,** to enforce its decisions. Yet the powers of the Court, both under Article III of the Constitution and the Judiciary Act of 1789, remained somewhat vague, and its role in the governmental system was unclear.

John Jay: Chief Justice of the
United States, 1789–1795

Article III of the Constitution declares that the Supreme Court shall have
original jurisdiction "[i]n all Cases affecting Ambassadors, other public Ministers
and Consuls, and those in which a state shall be a party . . ." (modified by the
Eleventh Amendment). Congress has enacted legislation giving the district
courts **concurrent jurisdiction** in cases dealing with "Ambassadors, other
public Ministers and Consuls," as well as in cases between the U.S. government
and one or more state governments. Essentially, the Supreme Court retains
exclusive original jurisdiction only in suits between state governments, which
often involve boundary disputes. These cases, while important in themselves,
represent a minute proportion of the Court's caseload.

The Supreme Court's appellate jurisdiction extends to all federal cases "with
such Exceptions, and under such Regulations as the Congress shall make" (U.S.
Constitution, Article III, Section 2). Appellate cases coming to the Supreme
Court from the lower federal courts usually come from the thirteen courts of
appeals, although they may come from the Court of Military Appeals or, under
special circumstances, directly from the district courts. Appellate cases may also
come from the state courts of last resort.

Prior to 1891, losing parties in the lower federal courts and state courts of
last resort had the right to automatically appeal their cases to the Supreme Court,
using the old common law **writ of error.** The Court's docket was crowded with
appeals, many of which raised routine or even frivolous claims. In 1891, Congress created nine courts of appeals to perform the function of **error correction** in routine appeals from the lower federal courts. This reduced the High
Court's caseload and permitted it to concentrate its efforts on important issues.
Nevertheless, losing parties in the courts of appeals and the state courts of last
resort retained in many cases a statutory right to have their cases reviewed by the
Supreme Court.

ARTICLE III, Sections 1 and 2, United States Constitution

Section 1. The judicial power of the United States, shall be vested in one Supreme Court, and in such inferior courts as the Congress may from time to time ordain and establish. The judges, both of the Supreme and inferior courts, shall hold their offices during good behavior, and shall, at stated times, receive for their services, a compensation, which shall not be diminished during their continuance in office.

Section 2. (1) The judicial power shall extend to all cases, in law and equity, arising under this Constitution, the laws of the United States, and treaties made, or which shall be made, under their authority; — to all cases affecting ambassadors, other public ministers and consuls; — to all cases of admiralty and maritime jurisdiction; — to controversies to which the United States shall be a party; — to controversies between two or more States; — between a State and citizens of another State;*—between citizens of different States; — between citizens of the same State claiming lands under grants of different States, and between a State, or the citizens thereof, and foreign States, citizens or subjects.

(2) In all cases affecting ambassadors, other public ministers and consuls, and those in which a State shall be party, the Supreme Court shall have original jurisdiction. In all the other cases before mentioned, the Supreme Court shall have appellate jurisdiction, both as to law and fact, with such exceptions, and under such regulations as the Congress shall make.

(3) The trial of all crimes, except in cases of impeachment, shall be by jury; and such trial shall be held in the State where the said crimes shall have been committed; but when not committed within any State, the trial shall be at such place or places as the Congress may by law have directed.

---

*Restricted by the Eleventh Amendment.

In 1925, Congress reformed the Supreme Court's appellate jurisdiction by restricting the categories of cases in which litigants were afforded an **appeal by right** to the Supreme Court. In addition, the **Judiciary Act of 1925,** commonly known as the Judges' Bill, gave the Court the power to issue **writs of certiorari** to review all cases, federal or state, posing "federal questions of substance." The writ of certiorari is issued at the discretion of the Court, thus giving the Court the power to address some issues and deflect others.

In 1988, the statute governing the Supreme Court's jurisdiction was further amended to eliminate most appeals by right. Under the Act to Improve the Administration of Justice (1988), the Court is required to hear appeals only in cases involving federal civil rights laws, legislative reapportionment, federal antitrust actions, and a few other matters. Yet even in these areas, the Court may invoke jurisdictional and procedural grounds to dismiss "mandatory" appeals. Consequently, the Court's appellate jurisdiction is almost entirely discretionary. It is difficult to overstate the importance of this discretion. Since a wide range of policy questions appear in the continuous stream of petitions for certiorari, the Court is able to set its own agenda. Students of public policy will recognize the importance of agenda setting as the necessary first phase in any autonomous institutional policy-making process.

The power to set its own agenda is only one aspect of the Court's institutional authority. Another aspect, already alluded to, is the fact that the Supreme Court has the power to interpret the Constitution with finality, barring a constitutional amendment. But the real bulwark of the Court's authority is its power of **judicial review,** the power to invalidate government policies that are found to be contrary to the Constitution. The Court's power of judicial review was first articulated in 1803 in the seminal case of *Marbury v. Madison,* which will be treated extensively in Chapter 2. Suffice it to say that in *Marbury,* the Court assumed the power to strike down laws passed by Congress. The power of judicial review has since been extended to cover legislative and executive actions at every level of government—local, state, and federal. The power of judicial review renders the American judiciary unique among the world's court systems. It has also helped the U.S. Supreme Court become the most prestigious and powerful judicial body in the world.

APPOINTMENT AND REMOVAL OF FEDERAL JUDGES

As provided by the Constitution, federal judges (with the exception of those serving on the specialized tribunals) are appointed for life terms by the president, subject to the consent of the Senate. Normally, the Senate consents to presidential judicial appointments with a minimum of controversy. However, as was demonstrated in 1987, senatorial approval is by no means *pro forma,* especially when it involves appointments to the Supreme Court. In fact, historically, the Senate has rejected about 25 percent of the presidential nominations to the Supreme Court.

In the summer of 1987, President Ronald Reagan nominated Judge Robert Bork of the Court of Appeals for the District of Columbia Circuit to fill a vacancy on the Supreme Court created by the retirement of Justice Lewis Powell. Reagan, a conservative Republican, wanted to place a conservative jurist on the High Court, and Bork seemed ideally suited to this purpose. After a long and bitter hearing and debate, the Democrat-controlled Senate rejected Bork by a vote of 58 to 42.

President Reagan was forced to withdraw the name of his next nominee, Judge Douglas Ginsberg, but less for ideological or partisan reasons than because of revelations that Ginsberg had used marijuana. After two embarrassing defeats for the Reagan administration, the vacancy on the Supreme Court was ultimately filled when the Senate confirmed Judge Anthony Kennedy in 1988.

In sharp contrast to the rancorous Bork affair, the 1990 appointment of David Souter to fill the vacancy left by the retirement of Justice William Brennan was both dignified and harmonious. Many were surprised that President George Bush would nominate a relatively obscure, recently appointed federal judge who had spent most of his judicial career on the New Hampshire Supreme Court. Although regarded by his colleagues as a serious and thoughtful jurist, Souter's judicial philosophy was virtually unknown. Yet this may have been precisely the president's strategy. Whereas Bork, a former law professor and solicitor general, had written widely on a number of controversial legal issues and thus provided ammunition to his critics, Souter had generally avoided public controversy and had written little to signal his judicial philosophy. Although there was some concern from both sides of the political spectrum over Souter's judicial proclivities, he was ultimately approved by the Senate by the overwhelming majority of 90 to 9.

The Clarence Thomas Episode

Without question, the most bizarre episode involving a nomination to the Supreme Court took place in the fall of 1991, when the Senate Judiciary Committee held hearings on the nomination of Clarence Thomas. Thomas, a federal appeals court judge, had been nominated by President Bush to fill the vacancy left by the retirement of Justice Thurgood Marshall, the first African-American to serve on the High Court. In nominating Judge Thomas, a conservative black, Bush attempted to satisfy two constituencies. During the initial hearings in the judiciary committee, Thomas was evasive as to his views on abortion and other controversial questions of public law. The committee, being evenly divided, forwarded the matter to the Senate floor without recommendation. During floor debate, charges of sexual harassment against Judge Thomas that had not been made public by the committee were brought to light. The charges had been made by Anita Hill, a law professor who formerly worked for Thomas when he chaired the Equal Employment Opportunity Commission. After learning of the charges, the full Senate sent the nomination back to the judiciary committee for an additional hearing. During the hearing of several days, much of which was carried on live television, the nation watched as Hill detailed her charges and Thomas responded with vehement denials. Ultimately, after an embarrassing public spectacle, the committee and the full Senate narrowly approved the Thomas nomination. Political commentators speculated about the effect of the hearings on Justice Thomas's future decisions and on the appointment process itself.

Presidential Influence on the Judiciary

The shared presidential-senatorial power of appointing federal judges is an important means of influencing the judiciary (see Chapter 3). By appointing all the judges in the newly created federal courts, George Washington left a lasting impression on the judiciary. More recently, President Jimmy Carter also left a deep imprint on the federal courts, even though he was unable to appoint a single Supreme Court justice. Largely due to a dramatic expansion in the number of federal judgeships in 1978, Carter was able to select 40 percent of the federal bench during his one-term presidency. Carter's judicial appointments were shaped not only by the traditional considerations of merit, partisanship, and ideology but also by a desire to diversify the federal bench, traditionally the domain of white males.

Ronald Reagan likewise made a significant impression on the federal courts. In his eight years as president, Reagan appointed three new Supreme Court justices (including the first woman on the Court, Sandra Day O'Connor), elevated Associate Justice William Rehnquist to be Chief Justice, and appointed

William H. Rehnquist: Associate Justice, 1972–1986; Chief Justice, 1986–

roughly half of the lower federal judges in service at the end of his second term. The Reagan judicial appointments reflected less emphasis on "affirmative action" than the Carter appointments but equal emphasis on partisanship and ideology. Again, this is in line with long-standing tradition. Federal judgeships are used both to reward political party allies and to ensure that the president's political agenda will be carried forward in the courts.

Tenure of Federal Judges

Article III, Section 1 of the Constitution states that "judges, both of the supreme and inferior Courts, shall hold their Offices during good Behaviour. . . ." This grant of life tenure to federal judges was intended to make the federal courts independent of partisan forces and transitory public passions so that they could dispense justice impartially, according to the law. In *The Federalist* No. 78, Alexander Hamilton argued that

> The standard of good behavior for the continuance in office of the judicial magistracy is certainly one of the most valuable of the modern improvements in the practice of government. In a monarchy it is an excellent barrier to the despotism of the prince; in a republic it is a no less excellent barrier to the encroachments and oppressions of the representative body. And it is the best expedient which can be devised in any government to secure a steady, upright and impartial administration of the laws.

Hamilton's views on the need for a life-tenured, appointed federal judiciary were not universally accepted in 1788, nor are they today. In a democratic nation that extols the "will of the people," such sentiments are apt to be viewed as elitist, even aristocratic. While states vary widely in their mechanisms for judicial selection, only in Rhode Island are judges given life tenure. From time to time, proposals have surfaced to impose limitations on the terms of federal judges, but no such effort has ever gained serious political momentum. Life tenure for federal judges, like most of the elements of our eighteenth-century Constitution, remains a firmly established principle of the political order.

Impeachment

The only means of removing a federal judge is through the **impeachment** process provided in the Constitution. First, the House of Representatives must approve one or more articles of impeachment by at least a majority vote. Then, a trial is held in the Senate. To be removed from office, a judge must be convicted by a vote of at least two-thirds of the Senate.

Since 1789, the House of Representatives has initiated impeachment proceedings against thirteen federal judges, and only seven of these have been convicted in the Senate. Only once has a Supreme Court justice been impeached by the House. In 1804, Justice Samuel Chase fell victim to President Thomas Jefferson's attempt to control a federal judiciary largely comprised of Washington and Adams appointees. Justice Chase had irritated the Jeffersonians with his haughty and arrogant personality and his extreme partisanship. Nevertheless, there was no evidence that he was guilty of any crime. Consequently, Chase narrowly escaped conviction in the Senate.

The Chase affair set an important precedent—a federal judge may not be removed simply for reasons of partisanship, ideology, or personality. Thus, despite some support in conservative quarters for the impeachment of Chief Justice Earl Warren during the 1960s, there was never any real prospect of Warren's removal. Barring criminal conduct or serious breaches of judicial ethics, federal judges do not have to worry that their decisions might cost them their jobs.

THE GENESIS OF CONSTITUTIONAL LAW CASES

Before examining Supreme Court decision making, it is important to understand how constitutional law cases get started. Essentially, all cases, including constitutional cases, begin in one of two ways—as civil suits or criminal prosecutions.

Civil Suits

A civil suit begins when one party, the **plaintiff,** files suit against another party, the **defendant.** In a constitutional case, the plaintiff alleges that the defendant has violated his or her constitutional rights or has taken some action in violation of constitutional limitations. Since constitutional rights are essentially limitations on the actions of government, the respondent in such a civil suit is generally a governmental official. Suits against government agencies *per se* are often, but not always, barred by the doctrine of **sovereign immunity.** Congress and the state legislatures have passed laws waiving sovereign immunity with regard to certain types of claims.

Every civil suit seeks a **remedy** for an alleged wrong. The remedy may be monetary compensation for actual or punitive **damages,** it may be a court order requiring specified action by the defendant, or it may be a simple **declaratory judgment**—a statement from the court as to which party is in the right. Often, a plaintiff will seek an **injunction** against a defendant to cause an ongoing injury to cease or to prevent an injury from occurring.

In a civil suit alleging the violation of a constitutional right, all of the afore-mentioned remedies are available to the plaintiff. However, because many government officials (judges, legislators, governors, and so on) are immune from suits for monetary damages stemming from their official decisions or actions, suits against government officials tend to seek declaratory judgments and/or injunctions.

An example of a civil suit being employed to vindicate a constitutional right is *Tinker v. Des Moines Community School District,* decided by the Supreme Court in 1969. In this case, public school officials suspended students for wearing black armbands to school to protest the Vietnam War. The students' parents filed a suit in U.S. district court seeking an injunction to prevent school officials from disciplining the students. The parents eventually won their injunction, but only after pursuing the case through three levels of the federal judiciary (for further discussion of the *Tinker* case, see Chapter 11).

In some instances, individuals whose constitutional rights have been violated may recover monetary damages. The Civil Rights Act of 1866 (Title 42, U.S. Code, Section 1983) permits courts to award monetary damages to plaintiffs whose constitutional rights are violated by private persons acting under "color of law." An example of this type of action is *Monroe v. Pape* (1961). A citizen filed suit against thirteen Chicago police officers, alleging that they had invaded and searched his home in violation of the Fourth Amendment ban on unreasonable searches. Although the district court initially dismissed the suit, the Supreme Court reinstated the complaint, and the plaintiff ultimately prevailed.

Criminal Prosecutions

Constitutional issues are often implicated by criminal prosecutions. One who is threatened with prosecution under an unconstitutional statute may seek an injunction against enforcement of the law by filing a civil suit against the prosecutor. *Roe v. Wade,* the landmark abortion decision, began when Jane Roe, an unmarried pregnant woman, brought suit against Henry Wade, the district attorney in Dallas, Texas, seeking to restrain Wade from enforcing the state's abortion law against her and other women "similarly situated" (see Chapter 15).

Once a prosecution is underway, the usual remedy is to challenge the statute in the trial court through a **demurrer** to an **indictment** or through the appropriate **pretrial motion.** If one is convicted under an arguably unconstitutional statute, the appropriate remedy is, of course, an appeal to a higher court. Most criminal convictions are challenged in this way. As an illustration, consider the case of *Texas v. Johnson* (1989), the landmark flag burning case. Gregory Johnson was convicted of violating the Texas law making it a crime to desecrate the American flag. He appealed his conviction to the Texas Court of Criminal Appeals, the state court of last resort in criminal cases, arguing that the conviction violated his constitutional rights. The appellate court agreed, saying the state flag desecration law was unconstitutional. The state of Texas obtained review in the U.S. Supreme Court on a writ of certiorari, but to no avail. The Supreme Court, in a highly publicized and controversial decision, agreed with the Texas Court of Criminal Appeals—it was held unconstitutional to punish someone for the act of burning the American flag (see Chapter 11).

Very often, constitutional issues arise in criminal cases owing to the actions of the police or the prosecutor or decisions made by the trial judge on the admission of evidence or various trial procedures. The federal Constitution provides a host of protections to persons accused of crimes; these protections are often invoked by persons challenging their convictions on appeal.

As one of many possible examples, consider the case of *Katz v. United States* (1967). Katz, a suspected bookie, was convicted in federal district court for violating the federal act making it a crime to use interstate communications devices to transmit wagering information. Katz appealed his conviction on the grounds that the Federal Bureau of Investigation had illegally obtained the evidence against him. The court of appeals upheld Katz's conviction, but the Supreme Court reversed, saying that Katz's rights had been violated (see Chapter 14).

Habeas Corpus

The Constitution explicitly recognizes the **writ of habeas corpus,** an ancient common law device that citizens may use to challenge the legality of arrest or imprisonment. One who believes that he or she is being illegally detained, even if that person is in prison after being duly convicted and exhausting the ordinary appeals process, may seek a writ of habeas corpus in a federal district court.

An example of federal habeas corpus can be seen in *Brewer v. Williams* (1977). Williams was convicted of murder and sentenced to life imprisonment by an Iowa court. He exhausted his appeals in the Iowa state courts, but his conviction and sentence were upheld. Williams then initiated a federal habeas corpus action against Brewer, the warden of the prison where Williams was being held. The district court granted relief, holding that evidence had been wrongly admitted against Williams at trial. The court ordered that Williams be released from custody pending a new trial. Brewer appealed without success to the court of appeals. Brewer then petitioned the Supreme Court for certiorari. The High Court agreed to review the case but upheld the lower-court decisions. Williams thus won a new trial, but only after his case had progressed through all levels of the state and federal court systems (see *Nix v. Williams* [1984], reprinted in Chapter 14).

The federal habeas corpus statute affords opportunities to convicted criminals to obtain review of their convictions in federal courts, even if they received extensive appellate review in the state courts. Critics of federal habeas corpus have long called for its curtailment or outright abolition. The Supreme Court has restricted access to federal habeas corpus somewhat, and Congress has considered legislation that would impose further restrictions (see Chapter 14). At this time, however, it remains a fairly common means by which constitutional questions are raised in the federal courts.

Taking a Case to the Supreme Court

The exclamation "I'll fight it all the way to the Supreme Court if I have to!" is a stock phrase in American legal rhetoric. Yet it is extremely difficult to get one's case before the High Court. The Supreme Court uses its limited resources to address the most important questions in American law. The rectification of injustices in individual cases is usually accorded much lower priority.

Mechanisms of Supreme Court Review

The Supreme Court reviews lower-court decisions by three mechanisms. By far the rarest is **certification,** where a federal appeals court formally asks the Supreme Court to certify or "make certain" a point of law. The second is on **appeal by right,** where, at least theoretically, the Court must rule on the merits of the appeal. As noted earlier, however, Congress has restricted such appeals to a few narrow categories of cases. The most common means by which the Court grants review is the **writ of certiorari.**

One who loses an appeal in a state court of last resort or a federal court of appeals may file a petition for certiorari in the Supreme Court. The filing fee is currently two hundred dollars, which may be waived for indigent litigants on the filing of a motion to proceed *in forma pauperis.*

The chances of the Supreme Court granting review in a given case are very slim. The chances are somewhat improved if the case originated in a federal court. The odds are much better still if the **petitioner** is the federal government, the most frequent litigator in the federal courts. Of the more than five thousand petitions for certiorari coming to it each year, the Court will normally grant review in only a few hundred, and even some of these cases will be dismissed later without a **decision on the merits.** Others will be disposed of through brief **memorandum decisions,** where the Court does not provide its reasoning through the issuance of opinions. In most Supreme Court terms, fewer than 150 cases are treated as **full opinion decisions.**

THE SUPREME COURT'S DECISION-MAKING PROCESS

Although the Constitution provided the broad parameters of the federal judicial power, it permitted Congress to largely determine the Court's decision-making process. Congress decides, for example, how many justices will serve on the Court. Initially, Congress set the number at six, but in 1807, the Court was expanded to include seven justices. In 1837, Congress increased the number of justices to nine. During the Civil War, the number of justices was increased to ten. Since 1869, the membership of the Court has remained constant at nine.

While Congress is authorized to regulate the appellate jurisdiction of the Supreme Court, it has rarely used this power to curtail the Court (but see *Ex Parte McCardle* [1869], discussed in Chapter 3). Rather, Congress has facilitated the institutional development of the Court by minimizing its mandatory appellate jurisdiction and thus giving it control over its own agenda. Likewise, Congress has delegated to the Court the authority to promulgate **rules of**

Three Examples of Memorandum Decisions from the 1989 Term

In the first case, *Barrow v. Illinois,* the Supreme Court denies certiorari to a man challenging the constitutionality of his death sentence, thus leaving the death sentence intact.

No. 89-7380.

Ronald Barrow, Petitioner v Illinois

June 25, 1990. Petition for writ of certiorari to the Supreme Court of Illinois denied.

Same case below, 133 Ill 2d 226, 549 NE2d 240.

Justice Brennan and Justice Marshall, dissenting. . . .

In the second case, *Georgia v. Stewart,* the Court grants certiorari and renders a judgment remanding the case to a state court for reconsideration in light of a recent Supreme Court decision.

No. 89-944.

Georgia, Petitioner v Thomas D. Stewart, et ux.

June 25, 1990. On petition for writ of certiorari to the Court of Appeals of Georgia. The petition for writ of certiorari is granted. The judgment is vacated and the case is remanded to the Court of Appeals of Georgia for further consideration in light of Illinois v Rodriguez, 497 US – – –, 111 L Ed 2d 148, 110 S Ct – – – (1990). Justice Stevens dissents.

Same case below, 191 Ga App 750, 382 SE2d 677.

In the final example, *Parker v. Dugger,* the Court grants certiorari indicating that it will hear arguments in the case.

No. 89-5961.

Robert Lacy Parker, Petitioner v Richard L. Dugger, Secretary, Florida Department of Corrections, et al.

June 28, 1990. Motion of petitioner for leave to proceed in forma pauperis and petition for writ of certiorari to the United States Court of Appeals for the Eleventh Circuit granted.

Same case below, 876 F2d 1470.

---

procedure for itself and the lower federal courts. Consequently, the Supreme Court is nearly autonomous with respect to the determination of its decision-making process.

The Supreme Court Term

The Supreme Court's first session was held in February 1790. It had no cases on the docket and adjourned after ten days. During its first decade, 1790 to 1801, the Court met twice a year for brief terms beginning in February and August. Over the years, the Court's annual sessions have expanded, along with its workload and its role in the political and legal system. Since 1917, the Court's annual term has begun on the "first Monday of October."

Until 1979, the Court adjourned its sessions for the summer, necessitating special sessions to handle urgent cases arising in July, August, or September. Such was the case in July 1972, when the Court held a special session to consider *O'Brien v. Brown,* a case involving the seating of delegates at the Democratic National Convention, slated to open in a matter of days. In 1974, the Court was forced to postpone adjournment to render an immediate decision in the famous

Watergate tapes case, *United States v. Nixon.* Since 1979, however, the Court has stayed in continuous session throughout the year, merely declaring a recess for its summer vacation.

The Court's Caseload

In 1800, the Supreme Court had a mere handful of cases on its docket. As litigation in the federal courts steadily increased, so did the Court's caseload. The creation of the U.S. courts of appeals in 1891 reduced the High Court's caseload substantially, but only for the short term. In the twentieth century, as society grew more complex and the American people became more numerous (and more litigation-prone), the Supreme Court's docket began to swell. In 1990, the Court disposed of more than five thousand petitions for certiorari, and there is no indication that this aspect of the Court's caseload is declining. Fortunately, Congress has seen fit to eliminate nearly all of the Supreme Court's mandatory appellate jurisdiction. This allows the Court to regulate its workload somewhat, in that the Court may reject petitions for certiorari.

Case Selection

The process of case selection begins as the justices' **law clerks** (staff attorneys) read the many petitions for certiorari and prepare summary memoranda. With the assistance of his clerks, the chief justice, who bears primary responsibility for Court administration, prepares a "discuss list" of cases to be considered for certiorari. The associate justices may add cases to the list. Unless at least one justice indicates that a petition should be discussed, review is automatically denied, which disposes of more than 70 percent of the petitions for certiorari.

The Court considers petitions on the "discuss list" in private conferences. A conference usually lasting the better part of a week is held immediately before the commencement of the Court's term in October. This preterm conference is devoted entirely to consideration of "cert" petitions. Regular conferences are

TABLE 1.1 Disposition of Cases, 1990 Supreme Court Term

Jurisdiction	Dispositions
Original	3
Appellate	
on the merits	238
review denied	5168
TOTAL	5409

Source: Administrative Office of the United States Courts

held throughout the term, both for the purpose of reviewing cert petitions and for discussing and deciding the cases in which the Court has granted review.

At least four justices must vote to grant certiorari in order for the Court to accept a case from the discuss list. The **Rule of Four** permits a minority of justices to set the Court's agenda. In such situations, it would be possible for the five justices who voted against "cert" to later vote to dismiss the case without reaching the merits. Yet institutional norms militate against this strategy, suggesting the collegiality of the Court's decision making.

More than 95 percent of the petitions for certiorari coming to the Supreme Court are denied. A denial of certiorari, just like the dismissal of an appeal, has the effect of sustaining the lower-court decision under challenge. An important distinction is made, however, between denials of certiorari and dismissals of appeals. According to the Supreme Court's decision in *Hopfmann v. Connolly* (1985), a denial of certiorari carries no weight as precedent, while dismissal of an appeal "for want of a substantial federal question" has binding precedential effect on lower courts. The fact that the Court has decided not to review a lower-court decision does not mean that the Court necessarily approves of the way it was decided. There is nothing to prevent the Court from reviewing the same issue in a future case and deciding it differently. Denial of certiorari thus may be as much a function of scarce judicial resources as it is an expression of approval of the lower-court decision. Yet as a manifestation of the authoritative allocation of values by government, the Court's case selection process must be viewed as inescapably political.

Summary Decisions

As noted previously, not all cases accepted by the Supreme Court are afforded plenary review, or "full-dress treatment." Some cases are decided summarily, that is, quickly, without the benefit of full argumentation before the Court. These decisions are rendered in the form of a memorandum or *per curiam* (unsigned) opinion, usually with little discussion or justification. Although memorandum decisions are fully binding on the parties to the case, they are accorded little significance as precedents. The major function of summary decisions is error correction; thus, they have very little impact on constitutional lawmaking. Accordingly, it is debatable whether the High Court should consume any of its precious resources dealing with such matters. Dissenting in *Florida v. Meyers* (1984), Justice John Paul Stevens complained that summary dispositions might well encourage petitions for certiorari in routine cases and thus have the effect of further taxing the Court's capacity to decide important issues:

> . . . [I]f we take it upon ourselves to review and correct every incorrect disposition of a federal question, . . . we will soon become so busy that we will either be unable to discharge our primary responsibilities effectively, or be forced to make still another adjustment in the size of our staff in order to process cases effectively. We should focus our attention on methods of using our scarce resources wisely rather than laying another course of bricks in the building of a federal judicial bureaucracy.

Submission of Briefs

In cases slated for plenary review, lawyers for both parties (the petitioner and the respondent, or the appellant and the appellee) are requested to submit **briefs.** Briefs are written documents containing legal arguments in support of a party's position. By Court rule, the parties' briefs are limited to fifty pages. In addition to the briefs submitted by the parties to the litigation, the Court may permit outside parties to file *amicus curiae* briefs. *Amicus* briefs are often filed on behalf of organized groups that have an interest in the outcome of a case. Examples of interest groups that routinely file *amicus* briefs in the Supreme Court are the American Civil Liberties Union, the National Association for the Advancement of Colored People, the National Rifle Association, and the American Medical Association.

Oral Argument

After the briefs of parties and *amici* have been submitted, the case is scheduled for **oral argument,** a public hearing where lawyers for both sides appear before the Court to make verbal presentations and, more important, answer questions from the bench. The oral argument is the only occasion on which lawyers in a case have any direct contact with the justices.

Oral arguments are normally held on Mondays, Tuesdays, and Wednesdays beginning on the first Monday in October and ending in late April. Oral argument on a given case is usually limited to one hour. Four cases will be argued before the Court on any given oral argument day. "Court watchers" (including representatives of interest groups, the media, and academia) often attend oral argument hoping to learn something about the Court's predisposition with respect to the case under consideration or something about the general proclivities of the justices, especially the most recent appointees.

Conference and Decision

Within days after a case is orally argued, it is discussed in private conference among the justices. Conferences are usually held on Wednesdays, Thursdays, and Fridays. At conference, the chief justice opens the discussion by reviewing the essential facts of the case at hand, summarizing the history of the case in the lower courts, and stating his view as to the correct decision. This provides the chief with a chance to influence his colleagues, an opportunity that only a few occupants of the office have been able to exploit. It is well known, however, that Chief Justice Charles Evans Hughes was on occasion able to overwhelm other members of the Court with a photographic memory that gave him command of legal and factual details.

After the chief justice has presented the case, associate justices, speaking in descending order of seniority, present their views of the case and indicate their "votes" as to the proper judgment. This original vote on the merits is not binding, however, and justices have been known to change their votes prior to the announcement of the decision. The final vote is not recorded until the decision is formally announced.

In deciding a case that has been fully argued, the Court has several options. First, the Court may decide that it should not have granted review in the first place, whereupon the case is dismissed. Of course, this occurs rarely. Alternatively, the Court may instruct the parties to reargue the case, focusing on somewhat different issues, in which case the matter is likely to be carried over to the next term and final decision delayed for at least a year. This is precisely what happened in the two most significant cases of the twentieth century, *Brown v. Board of Education* (1954), the school desegregation case, and *Roe v. Wade* (1973), the abortion case. It is interesting to note that in the *Brown* case, the Court not only called for reargument of the issues but, under the leadership of the newly appointed Chief Justice Earl Warren, delayed its decision until unanimity could be achieved.

If the Court decides to render judgment, it will either **affirm,** that is, uphold, or **reverse,** that is, overturn, the decision of the lower court. Alternatively, it may modify the lower court's decision in some respect. Reversal or modification of a lower-court decision requires a majority vote, a quorum being six justices. A tie vote (in cases where one or more justices is unable to participate) always results in the affirmance of the decision under review.

Supreme Court Opinions

Once a judgment has been reached, it remains for the decision to be explained and justified in one or more written **opinions.** In the early days of the Court, opinions were issued *seriatim,* that is, each justice would produce an opinion reflecting his views of the case. John Marshall, who became chief justice in 1801, instituted the practice of issuing an **opinion of the Court,** which reflects the views of at least a majority of justices. The opinion of the Court, referred to as the **majority opinion** when the Court is not unanimous, has the great advantage of providing a coherent statement of the Court's position to the parties, the lower courts, and the larger legal and political communities.

It must be understood, however, that even a unanimous vote in support of a particular judgment does not guarantee that there will be an opinion of the Court. Justices can and do differ on the rationales they adopt for voting a particular way. Every justice retains the right to produce an opinion in every case, either for or against the judgment of the Court. A **concurring opinion** is one written in support of the Court's decision; a **dissenting opinion** is one that disagrees with the decision. An opinion **concurring in the judgment** is one that supports the Court's decision but disagrees with the rationale expressed in the majority opinion.

Dissenting opinions, while indicative of intellectual conflict on the Court, are very important in the development of American constitutional law. It is often said that "yesterday's dissent is tomorrow's majority opinion." Usually, the time lag is much longer, but a number of examples exist of dissents being vindicated by later Court decisions. Of course, it is more frequently the case that a dissenting vote is merely a defense of a dying position.

The modern Supreme Court has seen a dramatic rise in the frequency of dissenting opinions, reflecting both the increased complexity of the law and the demise of consensual norms in the Court itself. The modern Court has become less of a collegial decision-making body and more like "nine separate law firms."

When the Court fails to produce a majority opinion, at least one opinion will announce the judgment of the Court and state the views of those justices who endorse that opinion. This is referred to as the **plurality opinion** if it garners the most signatures among those justices who support the Court's decision. It should be noted that, because it does not express the views of a majority of justices, the plurality opinion has no official weight as precedent.

Alternatively, the judgment of the Court may be expressed in a ***per curiam opinion,*** which is not attributed to any particular justice. Thus, the maximum number of opinions that may be produced in one decision is ten: one *per curiam* opinion announcing the decision of the Court followed by nine individual concurring or dissenting opinions. This occurred in the famous Pentagon papers case of 1971. The Court voted 6 to 3 to permit the *New York Times* and the *Washington Post* to publish the Pentagon papers, despite an attempt by the Nixon Administration to prevent the newspapers from doing so. The decision was announced in a three-paragraph *per curiam* opinion. Six justices (Hugo Black, William O. Douglas, William Brennan, Potter Stewart, Thurgood Marshall, and Byron White) authored concurring opinions. Three justices (Warren Burger, Harry Blackmun, and John Harlan) wrote dissenting opinions (see *New York Times Co. v. United States* [1971] reprinted in Chapter 12).

In recent years, the Court's frequent inability to produce majority opinions in important cases has generated considerable criticism. Legal and political communities definitely prefer decisions that contain an opinion of the Court. This requires both a high degree of collegiality on the part of the justices and leadership from the chief justice. It is also facilitated by relatively clear-cut legal issues that the Court has some experience in addressing. Today, many of the issues coming before the Court are highly complex, allowing for a wide range of responses from the individual justices. This reduces the probability that a majority will agree on one opinion.

Assignment and Preparation of Opinions

In an effort to obtain a majority opinion, the chief justice, assuming he is in the majority, will either prepare a draft opinion himself or assign the task to one of his colleagues in the majority. If the chief is in dissent, the responsibility of opinion assignment falls on the senior associate justice in the majority. Sometimes, in a 5-to-4 decision, a majority opinion may be "rescued" by assigning it to the swing voter, that is, that justice who was most likely to dissent. On the modern Court, the task of writing majority opinions is more or less evenly distributed among the nine justices. However, majority opinions in important decisions are more apt to be authored by the chief justice or a senior member of the Court.

After the opinion has been assigned to one of the justices, work begins on a rough draft. At this stage, the law clerks play an important role by performing legal research and assisting the justice in the writing of the opinion. When a draft is ready, it is circulated among those justices in the majority for their suggestions and, ultimately, their signatures. A draft opinion that fails to receive the approval of a majority of justices participating in a given decision cannot be characterized as the opinion of the Court. Accordingly, a draft may be subject to considerable revision before it attains the status of majority opinion.

Opinion Day

The Supreme Court announces most of its plenary decisions in open court, a large number coming late in the term. A decision is announced by the author of the majority or plurality opinion, who may even read excerpts from that opinion. In important and controversial cases, concurring and dissenting justices will read excerpts from their opinions as well. When several decisions are to be announced, the justices making the announcements will speak in reverse order of their seniority on the Court. After the decisions are announced, summaries are released to the media by the Court's public information office. Today, it is not uncommon for the nation to be informed of an important Supreme Court decision within minutes of its being handed down.

Publication of Supreme Court Decisions

The decisions of the Supreme Court, indeed of all appellate courts in this country, are published in books known as **case reporters.** The official reporter, published by the United States Government Printing Office, is entitled the *United States Reports* (abbreviated **U.S.**). West Publishing Company (the publisher of this textbook) publishes a commercial edition entitled *Supreme Court Reporter* (abbreviated **S.Ct.**). Finally, the Lawyers' Cooperative Publishing Company publishes the *United States Supreme Court Reports, Lawyers' Edition* (abbreviated **L.Ed.**). Lawyers, judges, academics, and students wishing to read the decisions of the Supreme Court may utilize any of these reporters, and references to the Court's decisions usually cite all three reporters. For example, the Pentagon papers case, *New York Times v. United States,* is cited 403 U.S. 713, 91 S. Ct. 2140, 29 L. Ed. 2d 822 (1971). This citation indicates that the Supreme Court's decision in the Pentagon papers case can be located beginning on page 713 of volume 403 of the *United States Reports;* in volume 91 of the *Supreme Court Reporter,* beginning on page 2140; or starting on page 820 of volume 29 of the second series of the *Lawyers' Edition*.

FACTORS THAT INFLUENCE THE COURT'S DECISIONS

Since *Marbury v. Madison* (1803), commentators have sought to explain and predict, as well as evaluate, Supreme Court decision making. Traditional legal commentary relied almost exclusively on legal factors—principles, provisions, procedures, and precedents. Modern analysis tends to look beyond the law to explain judicial decision making. Political scientists in particular are interested in the political factors that influence judicial behavior.

How to Brief a Case

Many instructors of constitutional law, including the authors of this textbook, require students to prepare "briefs" of a number of assigned cases. Even in the absence of such a requirement, students may find that briefing a case helps them "digest" its contents. Preparing briefs is also an excellent means of studying for an examination that covers court cases. Below is an example of a case brief prepared in the style that we recommend to students. Students will note that the "brief" below is exactly that: a very brief summary of the case. It highlights the basic issue, the essential facts, the decision of the Court, and the arguments set forth in the majority and dissenting opinions. We also encourage students to include a brief comment on the significance of the case. Of course, other instructors may prefer a somewhat different approach.

PLESSY V. FERGUSON (1896)

Issue: Is a state law requiring "separate but equal" facilities for whites and blacks a violation of the Thirteenth or Fourteenth Amendment?

Facts: Homer Plessy, who was ⅞ white and ⅛ black, was arrested after refusing to vacate a seat in a railroad car reserved for whites. He was convicted under a Louisiana statute mandating "equal but separate" accommodations on railroads. After unsuccessfully attacking the statute in the Louisiana state courts, Plessy appealed to the U.S. Supreme Court.

Supreme Court Decision: Judgment of lower court affirmed; conviction and statute upheld. Vote: 7-1 (Brewer not participating).

Opinions: *Majority* (Brown): Segregation is a reasonable exercise of the state's police power in that it is conducive to the maintenance of public order and peace. Segregation is not *per se* a "badge of slavery" and is therefore not a violation of the Thirteenth Amendment. The compulsory segregation of the races is permissible under the Equal Protection Clause of the Fourteenth Amendment as long as equal accommodations are provided. The Fourteenth Amendment was not intended to abolish all distinctions based on color, or to enforce social, as distinct from political, equality.

Dissenting (Harlan): Compulsory segregation is an infringement on the personal liberties of blacks. The Constitution is color-blind; therefore, government is prohibited from treating people differently merely on account of their race. Forcible segregation is a badge of inferiority, a vestige of slavery, and therefore a violation of the Thirteenth Amendment.

Comment: The "separate but equal doctrine" propounded in *Plessy* provided a justification for the entire regime of "Jim Crow" laws enacted in the late nineteenth century. The Supreme Court eventually repudiated this doctrine, beginning in *Brown v. Board of Education* (1954).

The law is complex, rich, and subtle. And judicial decision making, especially at the level of the Supreme Court, is hardly a mechanical process. Legal reasoning is certainly important, but it is inevitably colored by extralegal factors. It is not only possible, but likely, that two judges, equally well-trained and capable in legal research, will reach different conclusions about what "the law" requires in a given case. The fluidity of judicial decision making is most apparent when the Supreme Court is called upon to interpret the many open-ended clauses of the Constitution. Although the Court's constitutional decisions are rendered in a legal context, they cannot be fully explained by legalistic analysis.

Ideologies of the Justices

Political scientists who have studied Supreme Court decision making have amassed considerable evidence that the Court's decisions are influenced by the ideologies of the justices. This is inferred from regularities in the voting behavior of the justices, mainly the tendency of certain groups of justices to vote as **blocs.** In the 1989–90 term, for example, the Court was divided into two opposing ideological camps: a liberal bloc comprising Justices Brennan, Marshall, Blackmun, and Stevens; and a conservative bloc comprised of Justices Rehnquist, White, O'Connor, Scalia, and Kennedy. In the 1990s, the Court is becoming increasingly dominated by justices with conservative ideologies. Perhaps the most significant recent ideological shift on the Court occurred when Justices Brennan and Marshall, both staunch liberals, retired in 1990 and 1991, respectively. Their replacements, David Souter and Clarence Thomas, are considerably more conservative.

Although observers tend to characterize Supreme Court decisions and voting patterns in simplistic liberal-conservative terms, judicial ideology may well include more than general political attitudes or views on specific issues of public policy (for example, school prayer or abortion). It may also embrace philosophies regarding the proper role of courts in a democratic society. There is reason to believe that, at least for some justices, considerations of **judicial activism** versus **judicial restraint** weigh as heavily as policy preferences in determining how the vote will be cast in a given case. Justices inclined toward activism are more likely to support expansion of the Court's jurisdiction and powers and to embrace innovative constitutional doctrines. Activists are less likely than restraintists to follow precedent or defer to the judgment of elected officials. Judicial activists are more prone to see cases in terms of their public policy significance than as abstract questions of law.

The Political Environment

In addition to the ideologies of the justices, research has pointed to a number of political factors that appear to influence Supreme Court decision making. While the Supreme Court is ostensibly a countermajoritarian institution, there is reason to believe that public opinion will on occasion influence the Court. Certainly, ample evidence exists that the actions, or threatened actions, of Congress and the president will have an impact on Court decisions. And in a constitutional system that emphasizes checks and balances, one should not expect that it would be otherwise! Unquestionably, the political environment provides stimuli to, support for, and constraints upon Supreme Court decision making.

The Internal Politics of the Court

Finally, the Court's decision making is intensely political in the sense that the internal dynamics of the Court are characterized by conflict, bargaining, and compromise, the very essence of politics. Such activities are difficult to observe since they occur behind the "purple curtain" that separates the Court from its attentive public. Conferences are held in private, votes on certiorari are not routinely made public, and the justices tend to be tight-lipped about what goes on behind the scenes in the "marble temple." Yet from time to time, evidence of the Court's internal politics appears in the form of memoirs, autobiographies, and other writings of the justices and in the occasional interviews the justices and/or their clerks give to journalists and academicians.

Some may be offended at the attempts of journalists and scholars to penetrate the purple curtain, to examine the political realities lurking behind the veil of law and mythology in which the Supreme Court is shrouded. However, in a democratic society, it is the right, and arguably the duty, of citizens to have a realistic understanding of the institutions of their government. Armed with such an understanding of the Supreme Court, one can begin to make reasonable judgments about its decisions. Realism does not lead inexorably to cynicism.

It would be unfortunate and incorrect to assume that because the Supreme Court engages in politics, it is nothing more than a miniature legislature and the justices are nothing more than "politicians in black robes." The Supreme Court is at once a legal *and* a political institution, which makes it unique in the scheme of American government. This may also account for the reverence with which the American people (even the most jaded political scientists) tend to regard the Court.

CONCLUSION

The Supreme Court has evolved considerably over two hundred years. It began as a vaguely conceived tribunal, with no cases to decide and no permanent home. Over the years, the Court's caseload increased, as did its prominence in national affairs. The Court assumed increasing power and managed to hold its own against the legislative and executive branches of government. Eventually, the Court found a home in the Capitol, although its chambers were less than spectacular. In 1935, the Court moved into its own building, the majestic marble structure across the street from the Capitol. After many years of sharing space with Congress, the Court had finally arrived! Today, the Court is not only a co-equal branch of the national government but the most powerful and prestigious judicial body in the world.

The tremendous growth in the power and prestige of the Supreme Court was the inevitable consequence of the constitutional design that created the judiciary as a separate branch of the federal government. It is also a function of the Court's institutional development, which was accomplished through numerous assertions of power and equally numerous instances of prudent self-restraint. Through U.S. history, moreover, the elected branches of government have found it useful to permit the life-tenured Court to decide difficult and controversial issues. Perhaps most fundamentally, the growth in the Court's power and prestige can be attributed to the degree to which the American people and their elected representatives have accepted the political role that the Court has established for itself.

FOR FURTHER READING

Abraham, Henry J. *Justices and Presidents: A Political History of Appointments to the Supreme Court,* 2d ed. New York: Oxford University Press, 1985.

Abraham, Henry J. *The Judicial Process,* 5th ed. New York: Oxford University Press, 1986.

Ball, Howard. *Courts and Politics: The Federal Judicial System,* 2d ed. Englewood Cliffs, N.J.: Prentice-Hall, 1987.

Barrow, Deborah, and Thomas Walker. *A Court Divided: The Fifth Circuit Court of Appeals and the Politics of Judicial Reform.* New Haven: Yale University Press, 1988.

Bartee, Alice Fleetwood. *Cases Lost, Causes Won: The Supreme Court and the Judicial Process.* New York: St. Martin's Press, 1984.

Baum, Lawrence. *The Supreme Court,* 3d ed. Washington, D.C.: Congressional Quarterly Press, 1989.

Baum, Lawrence. *American Courts: Process and Policy.* Boston: Houghton-Mifflin, 1986.

Becker, Theodore, and Malcolm M. Feeley, eds. *The Impact of Supreme Court Decisions,* 2d ed. New York: Oxford University Press, 1973.

Brigham, John. *The Cult of the Court.* Philadelphia: Temple University Press, 1987.

Calvi, James V., and Susan Coleman. *American Law and Legal Systems.* Englewood Cliffs, N.J.: Prentice-Hall, 1989.

Cannon, Mark W. and David M. O'Brien, eds. *Views from the Bench: The Judiciary and Constitutional Politics.* Chatham, N.J.: Chatham House, 1985.

Cardozo, Benjamin Nathan. *The Nature of the Judicial Process.* New Haven: Yale University Press, 1921.

Carp, Robert A., and Ronald Stidham. *The Federal Courts,* 2d ed. Washington, D.C.: Congressional Quarterly Press, 1991.

Carp, Robert A., and Ronald Stidham. *Judicial Process in America.* Washington, D.C.: Congressional Quarterly Press, 1990.

Congressional Quarterly, Inc. *The Supreme Court at Work.* Washington, D.C.: Congressional Quarterly Press, 1990.

Cooper, Phillip J. *Hard Judicial Choices.* New York: Oxford University Press, 1988.

Douglas, William O. *The Court Years.* New York: Random House, 1980.

Epstein, Lee. *Conservatives in Court.* Knoxville: University of Tennessee Press, 1985.

Fish, Peter. *The Politics of Federal Judicial Administration.* Princeton, N.J.: Princeton University Press, 1973.

Frankfurter, Felix, and James Landis. *The Business of the Supreme Court.* New York: Macmillan, 1928.

Freund, Paul A., ed. *History of the Supreme Court of the United States,* 11 vols. New York: Macmillan, 1971-.

Gates, John B., and Charles A. Johnson, eds., *The American Courts: A Critical Assessment.* Washington, D.C.: Congressional Quarterly Press, 1991.

Goldman, Sheldon, and Thomas P. Jahnige. *The Federal Judicial System: Readings in Process and Behavior.* New York: Holt, Rinehart and Winston, 1968.

Goldman, Sheldon, and Austin Sarat. *American Court Systems: Readings in Judicial Process and Behavior.* San Francisco: W. H. Freeman, 1978.

Howard, J. Woodford. *Courts of Appeals in the Federal Judicial System: A Study of the Second, Fifth and District of Columbia Circuits.* Princeton, N.J.: Princeton University Press, 1981.

Hughes, Charles Evans. *The Supreme Court of the United States.* New York: Columbia University Press, 1928.

Johnson, Charles A., and Bradley C. Canon. *Judicial Policies: Implementation and Impact.* Washington, D.C.: Congressional Quarterly Press, 1984.

Krislov, Samuel. *The Supreme Court in the Political Process.* New York: Macmillan, 1965.

Lamb, Charles M., and Stephen C. Halpern, eds. *The Burger Court: Political and Judicial Profiles.* Urbana: University of Illinois Press, 1991.

Lewis, Anthony. *Gideon's Trumpet.* New York: Random House, 1964.

Melone, Albert P. *Researching Constitutional Law.* Glenview, Ill.: Scott, Foresman, 1990.

Murphy, Walter. *Elements of Judicial Strategy.* Chicago: University of Chicago Press, 1964.

Neubauer, David W. *Judicial Process: Law, Courts and Politics in the United States.* Pacific Grove, Calif.: Brooks/Cole, 1991.

O'Brien, David. *Storm Center: The Supreme Court in American Politics,* 2d ed. New York: Norton, 1990.

Perry, H. W. *Deciding to Decide: Agenda Setting in the U.S. Supreme Court.* Cambridge: Harvard University Press, 1991.

Pritchett, C. Herman. *The Roosevelt Court*. New York: Macmillan, 1948.

Provine, Doris Marie. *Case Selection in the United States Supreme Court*. Chicago: University of Chicago Press, 1980.

Rehnquist, William H., *Grand Inquests: The Historic Impeachments of Justice Samuel Chase and President Andrew Johnson*. New York: Morrow, 1992.

Rehnquist, William. *The Supreme Court: How It Was, How It Is*. New York: Morrow, 1987.

Schubert, Glendon. *Quantitative Analysis of Judicial Behavior*. Glencoe, Ill.: Free Press, 1959.

Schubert, Glendon. *The Judicial Mind*. Evanston, Ill.: Northwestern University Press, 1965.

Schwartz, Bernard, with Stephen Lesher. *Inside the Warren Court*. Garden City, N.Y.: Doubleday, 1983.

Shapiro, Martin. *Law and Politics in the Supreme Court: New Approaches to Political Jurisprudence*. New York: Free Press of Glencoe, 1964.

Sheldon, Charles. *The Judicial Process: Models and Approaches*. New York: Dodd, Mead, 1974.

Stumpf, Harry P. *American Judicial Politics*. San Diego: Harcourt Brace Jovanovich, 1988.

Van Geel, T. R. *Understanding Supreme Court Opinions*. New York: Longman, 1991.

Warren, Charles. *The Supreme Court in United States History,* rev. ed., 2 vols. Boston: Little, Brown, 1926.

Wasby, Stephen. *The Supreme Court in the Federal Judicial System*, 3d ed. Chicago: Nelson-Hall, 1988.

Westin, Alan F. *The Anatomy of a Constitutional Law Case*. New York: Macmillan, 1958.

Westin, Alan F., ed. *The Supreme Court: Views from Inside*. New York: W. W. Norton, 1961.

Wheeler, Russell, and Cynthia Harrison. *Creating the Federal Judicial System*. Washington, D.C.: Federal Judicial Center, 1989.

Woodward, Bob, and Scott Armstrong. *The Brethren: Inside the Supreme Court*. New York: Simon and Schuster, 1979.

CHAPTER TWO

THE ESTABLISHMENT AND EXERCISE OF JUDICIAL REVIEW

Hardly any question arises in the United States that is not resolved sooner or later into a judicial question.

Alexis de Tocqueville

INTRODUCTION

The study of American constitutional law begins logically with an examination of the power of **judicial review.** In its most general sense, the term "judicial review" simply refers to a court's authority to review a particular case or issue. In American constitutional law, judicial review denotes the power of a court of law to review a policy of government (usually a legislative act) and to invalidate that policy if it is found to be contrary to constitutional principles. In effect, a court of law has the power to nullify an action of the people's elected representatives, if what they have done is determined to be unconstitutional.

Judicial review is a uniquely American invention. Although English **common law** courts exercised the power to make law in some instances, no English court claimed the authority to nullify an act of Parliament. However, in *Dr. Bonham's Case* (1610), the great English jurist Sir Edward Coke recognized that parliamentary enactments were subordinate to the fundamental principles of the common law. While this was not an outright endorsement of judicial review as we know it today, Coke's holding was important in recognizing that legislative acts must conform to some higher law.

While judicial review is normally associated with the U.S. Supreme Court, it is a power possessed by most courts of law in this country. In fact, a nascent form of judicial review had already been exercised by a few state courts prior to the adoption of the U.S. Constitution (see, for example, *Trevett v. Weeden* [1786], Rhode Island). The Framers, however, did not resolve the question of whether the newly created federal courts should have this power. Article III is silent on the subject. It remained for the Supreme Court, in a bold stroke of legal and political genius, to assume this power for itself and the rest of the federal courts.

THE ESTABLISHMENT OF JUDICIAL REVIEW

The Supreme Court assumed the power to review legislation as early as 1796, when it upheld a federal tax on carriages as a valid exercise of the congressional taxing power (see *Hylton v. United States*). While this decision approving congressional action implied the power of judicial review, it did not establish it; to do that, the Court would have to *strike down* an act of Congress. The opportunity to do so came in 1803.

Marbury v. Madison

The *Marbury* case arose out of what may be fairly described as a bizarre set of circumstances. After the national election of 1800, in which the Federalists lost the presidency and both houses of Congress to the Jeffersonian Republicans, the Federalists sought to preserve their influence within the national government by enlarging their control over the federal courts. The "lame duck" Congress, in which the Federalists held a majority, quickly passed the **Judiciary Act of 1801,** which was signed into law by the lame duck president, John Adams. The Judiciary Act created a number of additional federal judgeships, which under the Constitution President Adams would be able to fill with good Federalists, of course. Congress also adopted legislation creating a number of minor judgeships for the newly established District of Columbia. Here again, the power to fill these posts lay primarily with the president.

William Marbury was one of the many Federalist politicians appointed to judicial office in the waning days of the Adams administration. Marbury's commission as justice of the peace for the District of Columbia had been signed by the president following Senate confirmation on March 3, 1801, President Adam's last day in office. Everything was in order, and after Secretary of State John Marshall placed the seal of the United States on the letter of commission, it was ready to be delivered to Marbury. But for some reason, yet to be fully explained, the delivery, which was entrusted to John Marshall's brother James, never took place. Marbury's commission was returned to John Marshall's office on the evening of March 3 or the morning of March 4, along with sixteen other justice of the peace commissions that James Marshall also failed to deliver. The commissions simply disappeared in the last-minute confusion of moving records and other papers from the office of the outgoing secretary of state, who was moving from the Cabinet to his new post as chief justice of the United States.

Thomas Jefferson was sworn in as the nation's third president on March 4, 1801. The new secretary of state, James Madison, failed to deliver copies of the commissions to Marbury and the sixteen other Federalists who were to get judgeships. After Marbury and the other Federalists began to press the issue, Jefferson mounted an effort to repeal the Judiciary Act of 1801. A willing Congress, now dominated by Republicans, was happy to oblige. Not only did Congress repeal the Judiciary Act, but it abolished the Supreme Court term of 1802! (Whether Congress could take such a bold step today is highly unlikely, since the annual Supreme Court term has become an institution in itself.)

John Marshall: Chief Justice,
1801–1835

Although he had to wait until 1803 for a decision, Marbury filed suit against James Madison in the Supreme Court, invoking the Court's **original jurisdiction.** In his suit, Marbury asked the Court to issue a **writ of mandamus,** an order directing Madison to deliver the disputed judicial commission to Marbury. The stage was now set for a head-on collision between the Court, staffed entirely by Federalists, and the Jefferson administration.

It seems not to have occurred to the new chief justice, John Marshall, that he should have **recused** himself (abstained) in the *Marbury* case. By today's standards of professional responsibility, Marshall's impartiality would have been doubted, to say the least. At the time of Marbury's appointment, John Marshall was a leader in the Federalist Party. He was central to the planning of the Judiciary Act of 1801 that had so enraged the Jeffersonians. Moreover, it was Marshall's failure as secretary of state to deliver Marbury's commission that necessitated the lawsuit!

John Marshall and his Federalist brethren on the Supreme Court found themselves in a dilemma. On the one hand, they could issue the writ of mandamus and risk the very real possibility that the Jefferson administration would refuse to obey the Court, in which case the Court would suffer a serious blow to its prestige. To make matters worse, President Jefferson had made it clear that if the Court were to issue the mandamus, he would seek to have several members of the Court, including his distant cousin John Marshall, brought before Congress on articles of impeachment! On the other hand, if the Court were to deny Marbury his commission, it would have been widely perceived as an admission of weakness and would have damaged the prestige of the Court, not to mention that of the Federalist Party. While Chief Justice Marshall, a long-time opponent of Thomas Jefferson, welcomed an opportunity to confront the new administration, neither of the aforementioned alternatives seemed palatable.

John Marshall was an imposing figure—a man of great intellect and forceful personality who dominated the Court during his thirty-four year tenure as chief justice. There is no doubt that Marshall arrived at the solution to the *Marbury* puzzle and persuaded his colleagues on the Court to embrace it. John Marshall's solution was as follows. William Marbury was held to have a legal right to his commission; by implication, the Jefferson administration was legally and morally wrong to deny it to him. However, the Court would not issue the writ of mandamus. The reason it would not do so, said John Marshall, was that the Court had no authority to issue the writ.

The Supreme Court's presumed authority to issue the writ of mandamus was based on Section 13 of the Judiciary Act of 1789. Section 13 granted the Court the authority to "issue . . . writs of mandamus, in cases warranted by the principles and usages of law. . . ." According to John Marshall's opinion in *Marbury,* the Court could not issue the writ because the relevant provision of Section 13 was unconstitutional. It was invalid, in his view, because it expanded the Court's original jurisdiction.

In Chapter 1, we pointed out that Article III, Section 2 of the Constitution expressly provides that Congress has authority to regulate the appellate jurisdiction of the Supreme Court. The implication is that Congress has no such authority with respect to the Court's original jurisdiction. In Marshall's view, Section 13 was invalid insofar as it permitted the Court to issue a writ of mandamus in a case under the Court's original jurisdiction. The Court had held for the first time that an act of Congress was null and void.

Not all legal scholars are persuaded by John Marshall's reasoning. One can argue that all that Congress had done in crafting Section 13 of the Judiciary Act was to recognize the Court's power to issue certain kinds of writs in cases appropriately before it. In other words, Congress had not expanded the Court's jurisdiction at all but merely recognized a legal remedy that the Court might have possessed even in the absence of the statute! At the time, however, no one appeared to be very interested in challenging John Marshall's reasoning on this issue.

A much larger question is posed in *Marbury v. Madison* than the validity of Section 13 of the Judiciary Act of 1789. Even assuming the invalidity of the act, where does the Supreme Court get the power to strike down the law? After all, the Constitution does not explicitly recognize judicial review. In support of this assumption of power, John Marshall reasoned that, since the Constitution is the "supreme law of the land" and given the judiciary's duty to interpret the law, judicial review is both necessary and inevitable. Perhaps because the Supremacy Clause of Article VI focuses on the subordinate relationship of state to federal law, Marshall relied more heavily on Article III, which established and broadly defined federal judicial power. It was in this context that Marshall made his frequently quoted assertion that "[i]t is emphatically the province and duty of the judicial department, to say what the law is." In reaching this conclusion, Marshall stressed the fact that judges take an oath to support and defend the Constitution. Marshall posed the question: "Why does a judge swear to discharge his duties agreeable to the Constitution of the United States, if that constitution forms no rule for his government?"

Rejoinder to John Marshall

One of the most effective refutations of Marshall's position was offered by Justice John B. Gibson of the Pennsylvania Supreme Court. In a dissenting opinion in an otherwise unremarkable decision, *Eakin v. Raub* (1825), Gibson contended that the courts had no more authority to strike down legislative acts than the legislatures had to strike down judicial decisions. In Gibson's view, each branch of the government is ultimately responsible to the people for the constitutionality of its own acts. In support of this argument, Gibson noted that "[t]he oath to support the Constitution is not peculiar to the judges, but is taken indiscriminately by every officer of the government. . . ."

While Justice Gibson's position might still have some appeal in the realm of academic theory, judicial review has long been accepted as a legitimate power of American courts and an important feature of the system of checks and balances. Indeed, one can argue that without judicial review, the system of checks and balances is incomplete, for judicial review is really the only check that the courts have on the actions of the legislative and executive branches.

THE DEVELOPMENT OF JUDICIAL REVIEW

The Supreme Court's assertion of judicial review in *Marbury v. Madison* went largely unchallenged for two reasons. First, although claiming the right to review legislation, the Court ostensibly backed away from a confrontation with the president and Congress. Second, the provision invalidated by the Court was not a major element of public policy. Rather, it was a minor provision of a law dealing with the judicial process itself, an area in which the Supreme Court might be presumed to have greater expertise and hence a greater claim to exercise judicial review.

Marbury v. Madison was the only instance in which the Supreme Court under John Marshall struck down an act of Congress. The Marshall Court did, however, use its power of judicial review to invalidate a number of state laws in some very important cases. The Court first exercised this power in 1810, in the highly politicized case of *Fletcher v. Peck* (see Chapter 10). Perhaps the most important of these cases was *M'Culloch v. Maryland* (1819), where the Court invalidated an attempt by a state to tax a branch of the Bank of the United States (see Chapter 5). Nearly as important was *Gibbons v. Ogden* (1824), in which the Court struck down a New York law granting a monopoly to a steamboat company in contravention of a federal law granting a license to another company (see Chapter 5). Not only were the decisions in *M'Culloch v. Maryland* and *Gibbons v. Ogden* important as assertions of power by the Supreme Court, they were instrumental in enlarging the powers of Congress vis-à-vis the states.

In addition to asserting the power to invalidate state laws, the Marshall Court established its authority to overrule decisions of the highest state appellate courts on questions of federal law, constitutional and statutory. Article VI provides that the Constitution, laws, and treaties of the United States "shall be the Supreme law of the land; and the judges in every state shall be bound thereby, anything in the constitution or laws of any state to the contrary notwithstanding."

Section 25 of the Judiciary Act of 1789 provided that appeals could be brought to the Supreme Court from certain decisions of the highest state courts. Against the strenuous objections of **states' rights** advocates, led by Judge Spencer Roane of Virginia, the Marshall Court successfully asserted federal judicial authority over the states with respect to the interpretation of federal law. Judge Roane conceded that state judges were bound by federal law but asserted that state court decisions ought to be final in regard to the interpretation of federal law, including the U.S. Constitution.

When the Supreme Court invalidated Virginia's alien-inheritance and confiscation laws in 1813, the Virginia Supreme Court responded with an opinion by Chief Judge Roane declaring Section 25 of the Judiciary Act of 1789 unconstitutional. This action brought the case back to the U.S. Supreme Court. In a detailed opinion by Justice Joseph Story (John Marshall having recused himself due to earlier participation in this litigation, which had begun in the 1780s), the Supreme Court reversed the Virginia Supreme Court and affirmed its power to review state court decisions on matters of federal law (*Martin v. Hunter's Lessee* [1816]).

States' rights advocates continued to assail Supreme Court authority to review the decisions of state courts on matters of federal law. The issue reached the Supreme Court once again in *Cohens v. Virginia* (1821). P. J. and M. J. Cohen had been convicted in a Virginia court of violating that state's law prohibiting the sale of lottery tickets. The Cohens had been selling tickets in Norfolk for the Washington, D.C., lottery, which had been authorized by Congress to finance civic improvements in the Nation's capital. The Cohens challenged their convictions in the Supreme Court, arguing that the federal law authorizing the lottery took precedence over the Virginia law criminalizing the sale of lottery tickets. On this point, the Cohens ultimately lost, the Supreme Court concluding that Congress had not authorized the sale of lottery tickets outside the District of Columbia. From a technical standpoint, this was a minor criminal case involving a fine of only $100. However, the competing forces of states' rights and national supremacy converted it into a major constitutional battle. Responding to Virginia's denial of the Supreme Court's authority to hear the Cohens' appeal, Chief Justice Marshall forcefully asserted the Supreme Court's jurisdiction over state court decisions "which may contravene the Constitution or the laws of the United States. . . ."

Although the Supreme Court under John Marshall succeeded in establishing and expanding the scope of judicial review, under Marshall's successor, the Court damaged its credibility and prestige by an impolitic use of this power. The case was *Dred Scott v. Sandford* (1857), the first instance after *Marbury v. Madison* where the Supreme Court struck down an act of Congress.

The *Dred Scott* Case

Slavery had been a divisive political issue as early as the Constitutional Convention of 1787. By the early nineteenth century, it was clear that slavery threatened to disunite the United States. Congress responded by adopting a series of compromises on the issue. Perhaps the most important of these was the Missouri

Compromise of 1820. Under this act of Congress, Missouri was admitted to the Union as a "slave state," that is, one in which slavery would be legal, but slavery would be prohibited in the western territories north of thirty-six degrees, thirty minutes latitude.

The *Dred Scott* case began when Scott, a slave backed by abolitionist forces, brought suit seeking emancipation from his owner, John Sandford. Scott was formerly owned by a U.S. Army surgeon named Emerson. In 1834, Emerson had taken Scott from Missouri, where he had long resided, into the free state of Illinois and from there to Fort Snelling in the Wisconsin territory, which was also "free" under the Missouri Compromise. After several years, Emerson and Scott returned to Missouri. Within a short time, Emerson died, and title to Scott ultimately passed to John Sandford, a New Yorker. In 1846, Scott brought suit against Sandford in the Missouri courts to obtain his freedom, arguing that his several-year residency on free soil had nullified his status as a slave. After a favorable decision at the lower-court level, the Missouri Supreme Court rejected Scott's claim. Scott then initiated a federal lawsuit on the jurisdictional ground that he and Sandford were citizens of different states. In response to Scott's claim, Sandford contended that since Scott was black, he was not a citizen of Missouri and that, accordingly, the federal courts had no jurisdiction in his case. Scott filed a **demurrer** in answer to this plea, arguing that Sandford's contention had no legal effect. Although the federal trial court sustained Scott's demurrer, thus possibly conceding his citizenship, it ruled against Scott's claim that his residency in a free territory entitled him to freedom. Scott appealed.

By the time the *Dred Scott* case reached the Supreme Court, it had become highly politicized. Both sides in the slavery controversy looked to the Court for a constitutional ruling vindicating their divergent views on the legal status of blacks and the power of Congress to regulate slavery in the territories. In 1857, five members of the Court, Chief Justice Roger B. Taney and four southern colleagues (Justices John Campbell, John Catron, Peter Daniel, and James Wayne) supported the institution of slavery without reservation. Two of the four northerners on the Court, Justices Samuel Nelson and Robert Grier, if not supporters of slavery, were at least antiabolitionist in their sentiments. These seven justices comprised the majority in the *Dred Scott* decision. Justices Benjamin Curtis and John McLean wrote strong dissenting opinions.

The *Dred Scott* decision was rendered in an atmosphere of intense emotion and political partisanship. Chief Justice Taney's impassioned majority opinion went far beyond the jurisdictional question presented in the case. The opinion held that blacks, not just slaves but free blacks as well, were not citizens of the United States and could "therefore claim none of the rights and privileges which [the Constitution] provides . . ." Indeed, in Taney's view, blacks ". . . had no rights or privileges except such as those who held the power and the Government might choose to grant them." The Court further ruled that the Missouri Compromise was an arbitrary deprivation of the property rights of slaveholders and, as such, offended the provision of the Fifth Amendment that prohibits government from depriving persons of property without "due process of law."

The *Dred Scott* decision is the source of the doctrine of **substantive due process,** which holds that the Due Process Clause forbids government policies that are unreasonable, unfair, or unjust. The more conventional interpretation of the Due Process Clause is that government must follow certain procedures before taking a person's life, liberty, or property. In *Dred Scott*, the Court used the Due Process Clause not to scrutinize government procedures but to condemn the very substance of a government policy. This controversial doctrine would later be used by the Supreme Court in very different contexts from slavery.

Extreme Judicial Activism

Dred Scott was also an extreme form of **judicial activism.** The decision was activist in the sense that the Court invalidated an act of Congress by invoking a novel, some would say dubious, constitutional doctrine. More fundamentally, it was activist in that the Court inserted itself into the slavery controversy, a deeply divisive issue that it could well have avoided. Far from resolving the slavery issue, the Court's decision greatly intensified the sectional conflict. A large and growing segment of the public simply rejected the legitimacy of the Court's constitutional theorizing on the slavery question. The *Dred Scott* decision and Chief Justice Taney soon became objects of ridicule in abolitionist circles. The Court's intemperate decision thus not only hastened the arrival of the Civil War but also severely damaged the Court's prestige and credibility.

The *Dred Scott* decision itself was eventually nullified by the ratification of the Thirteenth Amendment, which outlawed slavery, and the Fourteenth Amendment, which provides that "*all persons* [emphasis added] born or naturalized in the United States . . . are citizens of the United States and of the State wherein they reside. . . ."

The Post-Civil War Era

In light of the furor produced by the *Dred Scott* decision, it is significant that the institution of judicial review survived the Civil War intact. While the Court conspicuously avoided conflict with Congress and the president during the Civil War, soon after the war ended, the Court began to invalidate acts of Congress. In the decades to follow, the Court would exercise the power of judicial review much more frequently than it did in the early nineteenth century (see Table 2.1). Yet the Court managed to avoid the great issues of public debate and, accordingly, avoided the conflict that had characterized the *Dred Scott* decision. The period from 1865 to 1890 was thus one in which the Court quietly went about the task of rebuilding its prestige and credibility.

The Age of Conservative Activism, 1890–1937

Judicial review again became a subject of political controversy in the late nineteenth century as the Supreme Court exercised its power to limit government activity in the economic realm (see Chapter 10). In *Chicago, Milwaukee and St. Paul Railway Co. v. Minnesota* (1890), the Court invoked the doctrine of substantive due process to strike down a state law establishing a commission to set railroad rates. This case ushered in the Age of Conservative Activism, a period in which the Court often interpreted the Constitution as prohibiting governmental regulation of business. This tendency to insulate laissez-faire capitalism from government intervention brought the Court, and its power of judicial review, under an increasing barrage of criticism from Populists and Progressives.

The Income Tax Case

In *Pollock v. Farmers' Loan and Trust Company* (1895), the Court invalidated a federal law that imposed a 2 percent tax on incomes of more than four thousand dollars a year. Fourteen years earlier, the Court had upheld an income tax measure adopted by Congress during the Civil War (see *Springer v. United States,* 1881). Article I of the Constitution requires that ". . . direct taxes shall be apportioned among the several States . . . according to their respective numbers. . . ." In *Springer,* the Court had concluded that the income tax was an indirect tax not subject to the apportionment requirement. But in *Pollock,* the Court, by 5 to 4, changed direction. The Court held that the new income tax was a direct tax insofar as it was based on incomes derived from land and, as such, had to be apportioned among the states. Since the law did not provide for apportionment, it was unconstitutional.

TABLE 2.1 Supreme Court Decisions Invalidating Acts of Congress, 1867–1888

Case	Year	Act(s) of Congress Invalidated
Ex Parte Garland	1867	January 24, 1865, 13 Stat. 424
In re: The Alicia	1869	June 30, 1864, 13 Stat. 311, Sec. 13
Hepburn v. Griswold	1870	February 25, 1862, 12 Stat. 345, Sec. 2 July 11, 1862, 12 Stat. 532, Sec. 1 March 3, 1863, 12 Stat. 711, Sec. 3
Justices v. Murray	1870	March 3, 1863, 12 Stat. 756, Sec. 5
United States v. Dewitt	1870	March 2, 1867, 14 Stat. 484, Sec. 29
United States v. Klein	1872	July 12, 1870, 16 Stat. 235
United States v. Reese	1876	May 31, 1870, 16 Stat. 140, Secs. 3, 4
United States v. Fox	1878	March 2, 1867, 14 Stat. 539
Trade-Mark Cases	1879	July 8, 1870, 16 Stat. 210 August 14, 1876, 19 Stat. 141
United States v. Harris	1883	April 20, 1871, 17 Stat. 13, Sec. 2
Civil Rights Cases	1883	March 1, 1875, 18 Stat. 336, Secs. 1, 2
Boyd v. United States	1886	June 22, 1874, 18 Stat. 1878, Sec. 4
Callan v. Wilson	1888	June 17, 1870, 16 Stat. 154, Sec. 3

Note: *Stat.* refers to *United States Statutes-at-Large*

The Supreme Court was influenced in *Pollock* by the imposing briefs and oral arguments of prominent attorneys, including Joseph H. Choate, who, representing corporate interests, branded the income tax as a populistic assault on the institutions of capitalism. Choate condemned the tax as part of the "Communist march," which if not blocked would lead to further incursions on private property, "the very keystone of the arch upon which all civilized government rests." The Court was heavily influenced by this point of view, as evidenced by the following passage from a concurring opinion by Justice Stephen J. Field:

> The present assault upon capital is but the beginning. It will be a stepping stone to others larger and more sweeping till our political contests will become a war of the poor against the rich, a war constantly growing in intensity and bitterness.

The *Pollock* decision was assailed by numerous critics as proof that the Court was aligning itself with business interests and in opposition to a moderate revenue measure broadly supported by the American people. The Court itself had exhibited deep internal division in reaching final disposition of the case. With Justice Howell Jackson not participating due to illness, the Court was evenly split when the case was first argued. Prior to reargument before a full Court later in the year, one of the justices changed his position, underscoring the shakiness of the majority. Consequently, *Pollock* was regarded as a dubious precedent.

Some observers believed that if Congress enacted another income tax measure, the Court would return to the *Springer* rationale and uphold the tax. This view was furthered by the replacement of several members of the *Pollock* majority in the late 1890s, Justice Field among them. In 1900, the Court upheld a graduated inheritance tax in *Knowlton v. Moore*. Then, in *Flint v. Stone Tracy Co.* (1911), the Court sustained a tax levied on corporations as an excise tax on the privilege of doing business, even though the tax was measured by income. Before this ruling, however, Congress had proposed the Sixteenth Amendment, specifically authorizing taxation of income from any source without the requirement of apportionment among the states. By early 1913, the requisite three-fourths of the states had ratified the amendment, thus formally overruling the *Pollock* decision. As in the case of *Dred Scott v. Sandford,* a controversial Supreme Court decision had been nullified through constitutional amendment.

The Sugar Trust Case

Another great case decided in 1895 was *United States v. E. C. Knight Co.* The case arose when the federal government, relying on the Sherman Antitrust Act of 1890, blocked a corporate merger in an attempt to prevent one company from monopolizing the sugar refining industry. In *E. C. Knight,* the Supreme Court held that Congress's power to regulate interstate commerce (see Article I, Section 8, clause 3) did not extend to the regulation of manufacturing *per se.* Although the Court did not actually strike down the Sherman Act altogether, it greatly limited its scope.

Early Twentieth-Century Developments

Perhaps the best known decision of the early twentieth century is *Lochner v. New York* (1905), where the Supreme Court struck down a state law regulating working hours in bakeries. In the Court's view, the law was an unjustified interference with "the right to labor, and with the right of free contract on the part of the individual, either as employer or employee." In an oft-quoted dissent, Justice Oliver Wendell Holmes, Jr. argued for **judicial restraint:**

> This case is decided upon an economic theory which a large part of the country does not entertain. If it were a question of whether I agreed with that theory, I should desire to study it further and long before making up my mind. But I do not conceive that to be my duty, because I strongly believe that my agreement or disagreement has nothing to do with the right of a majority to embody their opinions in law. . . .

In Justice Holmes's view, the Court in *Lochner* had transcended the proper judicial role and usurped the function of the legislature. Today, *Lochner,* like *Dred Scott,* tends to be equated with extreme judicial activism.

Throughout the early twentieth century, the Supreme Court continued to use its power of judicial review to frustrate state and federal attempts at economic regulation. In *Hammer v. Dagenhart* (1918), for example, the Court struck down an act of Congress that sought to discourage the industrial exploitation of child labor. Relying on its earlier decision in *United States v. E. C. Knight* (1895), the Court found that the federal law went beyond the regulation of interstate commerce and invaded the legislative realm reserved to the states under the Tenth Amendment. In another notable case, *Adkins v. Children's Hospital* (1923), the Court invoked the "freedom of contract" doctrine it had developed in *Lochner v. New York* and like cases to invalidate a law authorizing a minimum wage for women and children working in the District of Columbia.

The Constitutional Battle over the New Deal

The Age of Conservative Activism entered its final phase in a constitutional showdown between the Supreme Court on one side and Congress and the president on the other. In 1932, in the depths of the Great Depression, Franklin D. Roosevelt was elected president in a landslide over the Republican incumbent, Herbert Hoover. Roosevelt promised the American people a "New Deal" from the federal government. A bold departure from the traditional theory of laissez-faire capitalism, the New Deal greatly expanded the role of the federal government in the economic life of the nation. Inevitably, the New Deal would face a serious challenge in the Supreme Court, which in the 1930s was still dominated by justices with conservative views on economic matters.

The first New Deal program to be struck down was the National Recovery Administration. In *A.L.A. Schechter Poultry Corporation v. United States* (1935), the Supreme Court held that Congress had gone too far in delegating legislative power to the executive branch (see Chapter 7). In the period 1935 to 1937, a host of New Deal programs were declared unconstitutional by the Supreme Court (see Table 2.2 on p. 54).

President Roosevelt responded to the adverse judicial decisions by trying to "pack" the Court with new appointees (see Chapter 3). Although the infamous Court-packing plan ultimately failed to win approval in Congress, the Supreme Court may have gotten the message. In an abrupt turnabout, the Court approved a key New Deal measure. In *National Labor Relations Board v. Jones and Laughlin Steel Corp.* (1937), the Court upheld the controversial Wagner Act, which guaranteed to industrial workers the right to unionize and bargain collectively with management.

The Constitutional Revolution of 1937

The Court's sudden turnabout in *Jones and Laughlin* presaged a veritable constitutional revolution. For decades to come, the Court would cease to interpret the Constitution as a barrier to social and economic legislation. In the late 1930s and 1940s, the Court would permit Congress to enact sweeping legislation affecting labor relations, agricultural production, and social welfare. The Court exercised similar restraint with respect to state laws regulating economic activity. Indeed, in *Ferguson v. Skrupa* (1963), the Court appeared to give states carte blanche in the area of economic regulation. Justice Hugo Black's opinion for the unanimous Court echoed Justice Holmes's dissent in *Lochner v. New York* fifty-eight years earlier:

> We have returned to the original constitutional proposition that courts do not substitute their social and economic beliefs for the judgment of legislative bodies, who are elected to pass laws. . . . Whether a legislature takes for its textbook Adam Smith, Herbert Spencer, Lord Keynes, or some other is no concern of ours.

TABLE 2.2 New Deal Legislation Invalidated by the Supreme Court

Case	Year	Law Invalidated
Schechter Corp. v. United States	1935	National Industrial Recovery Act of 1933 (48 Stat. 195)
Hopkins Savings Assoc. v. Cleary	1935	Provision, Home Owners' Loan Act of 1933 (48 Stat. 646, Sec. 6)
Railroad Retirement Board v. Alton	1935	Railroad Retirement Act of 1934 (48 Stat. 1283)
Louisville Bank v. Radford	1935	Frazier-Lemke Act of 1934, Amending the Bankruptcy Act (48 Stat. 1289, Ch. 869)
United States v. Butler	1936	Agricultural Adjustment Act of 1933 (48 Stat. 31)
Rickert Rice Mills v. Fontenot	1936	1935 Amendments to the Agricultural Adjustment Act of 1933 (49 Stat. 750)
Carter v. Carter Coal Company	1936	Bituminous Coal Act of 1935 (49 Stat. 991)
Ashton v. Cameron County District	1936	Act of May 24, 1934, Amending Bankruptcy Act (48 Stat. 798)

Notes: 1. Other federal statutes were invalidated by the Court during the period 1935 to 1937, but these laws were enacted prior to the New Deal. 2. *Stat.* refers to *United States Statutes-at-Large*

The Priorities of the Modern Supreme Court

The modern Supreme Court's restraint in the area of economic regulation was counterbalanced by a heightened concern for civil rights and liberties. This concern was foreshadowed in a footnote in Justice Harlan Fiske Stone's majority opinion in *United States v. Carolene Products* (1938). In an otherwise unremarkable case, Justice Stone maintained that "[t]here may be a narrower scope for the . . . presumption of constitutionality when legislation appears on its face to be within a specific prohibition of the Constitution, such as those of the first ten amendments. . . ." In essence, Justice Stone was suggesting that the traditional presumption of validity accorded to legislation ought to be reversed when that legislation touches on freedoms protected by the Bill of Rights. Stone's footnote also expressed the Court's willingness to be especially solicitous of the claims of minorities, saying that ". . . prejudice against discrete and insular minorities may be a special condition, which tends seriously to curtail the operation of those political processes ordinarily to be relied upon to protect minorities and . . . may call for a more searching judicial scrutiny."

Supreme Court activity in the modern era, at least up until the 1980s, tended to follow the philosophy stated in *Carolene Products*. This was especially true under the leadership of Chief Justice Earl Warren, from 1953 to 1969. The Warren Court had an enormous impact on civil rights and liberties. Its most notable decision was *Brown v. Board of Education* (1954), where the Court declared racially segregated public schools unconstitutional. In *Brown* and numerous other decisions, the Warren Court expressed its commitment to ending discrimination against African-Americans and other minority groups.

The Warren Court used its power of judicial review liberally to expand the rights not only of racial minorities but also of persons accused of crimes, members of extremist political groups, and the poor. Moreover, the Court revolutionized American politics by entering the "political thicket" of legislative reapportionment in *Baker v. Carr* (1962) and subsequent cases. Without question, the Warren era represents the most significant period in the Supreme Court's history since the clash over the New Deal in the 1930s. The Warren Court has been praised as heroic and idealistic; it has also been denounced as lawless and accused of "moral imperialism."

President Richard Nixon's appointment of Chief Justice Warren E. Burger and three associate justices (Harry Blackmun, Lewis Powell, and William Rehnquist) had the effect of tempering somewhat the liberal activism of the Warren Court. Yet it was the Burger Court that handed down the blockbuster decision in *Roe v. Wade* (1973), effectively legalizing abortion throughout the United States.

In the 1980s, the Supreme Court became increasingly conservative as older members retired and were replaced by appointments made by Presidents Reagan and Bush. In 1986, Associate Justice Rehnquist was elevated to Chief Justice when Burger resigned to work on the national celebration of the bicentennial of the Constitution. The Rehnquist Court has continued the Burger Court's movement to the right, although it has not dismantled most of what was accomplished by the Warren Court in the realm of civil rights and liberties.

Indeed, the Court's 5 to 4 decision in *Texas v. Johnson* (1989), in which the Court struck down a state law making it a crime to burn the American flag, was surprisingly reminiscent of the Warren Era. With the recent retirements of Justices William Brennan and Thurgood Marshall, both of whom were members of the majority in *Texas v. Johnson,* it is likely, however, that the Rehnquist Court will move further away from the civil liberties commitments of the Warren Court.

THEORIES OF CONSTITUTIONAL INTERPRETATION

As the foregoing historical sketch indicates, the Supreme Court's power of judicial review may be used boldly or with caution. To some extent, the approach the Court adopts in a given case depends on the nature of the issue and the complexion of political forces surrounding the case. It also depends, however, on the philosophies of the justices who happen to be on the Court at a given time. The justices tend to have varying views about the role of the Court in the political system and the conditions under which judicial review ought to be exercised. They also vary in their understandings of the Constitution and their theories as to how the Constitution should be interpreted.

Interpretivism

The most orthodox judicial philosophy is known as "interpretivism," so-called because of its insistence that the proper judicial function is interpretation, as opposed to lawmaking. Interpretivism holds that judicial review is legitimate only insofar as judges base their decisions squarely on the Constitution. In interpreting the Constitution, judges must be guided by the plain meaning of the text when it is clear. In the absence of plain textual meaning, judges should attempt to determine the original intentions of the Framers.

The so-called "jurisprudence of original intent" took on a distinctly political aspect during the 1980s. It was very much a part of the Reagan administration's judicial philosophy. U.S. Attorney General Edwin Meese made a series of public speeches in 1985 in which he castigated the modern Court for allegedly ignoring original intent. In a highly publicized speech at Georgetown University, Justice Brennan rebutted Meese, saying, "It is arrogant to pretend that from our vantage point we can gauge accurately the intent of the Framers on application of principle to specific, contemporary questions." Brennan argued that judges must "read the Constitution the only way we can: as twentieth century Americans . . ." (*Newsweek,* October 28, 1985).

The doctrine of original intent also played an important role in the Reagan administration's attempt to reshape the federal judiciary. It was in large measure due to his adherence to this doctrine that Robert Bork was nominated to the Supreme Court when Justice Powell retired in 1987. Bork's defense of strict originalism was also somewhat responsible for his rejection by the Senate following a heated confirmation battle.

In addition to its emphasis on original intent, interpretivism stresses the need for judges to respect history and tradition and, in particular, legal precedent. Essentially, interpretivism calls for judges to maintain as best they can the original Constitution, with a minimum of judicial modification.

Noninterpretivism

Many judges and scholars of the Constitution do not share the interpretivist view. Serious questions have been raised about the practicability and/or desirability of interpretivism, especially on the issue of original intent. It is often argued that the "intent of the Framers" is impossible to discern on many issues. Many would argue that original intent, even if knowable, should not control contemporary constitutional decision making. These commentators are apt to view the Constitution as a living document, the meaning of which evolves according to what Justice Oliver Wendell Holmes called the "felt necessities" of the times.

Numerous noninterpretive theories have been developed, drawing on a number of schools of legal thought. Some have suggested that the Court should strive to reflect societal consensus. Others have urged that the Court adopt an explicit position of moral leadership, striving to elevate and enlighten society, rather than merely reflect prevailing norms. Noninterpretivists, whatever their particular philosophies, are united in their rejection of the idea that the meaning of the Constitution is rigid and static.

Natural Law

Another perspective, not easily identified with either interpretivism or noninterpretivism, is one which argues for judicial reliance on **natural law.** Natural law is a complex term with many connotations, but it generally refers to a set of principles transcending human authority that may be discovered through reason. Natural law is often associated with religion and, in particular, the moral and ethical values of the Judeo-Christian tradition. Although occasionally invoked by individual justices, the natural law perspective has, for the most part, been eschewed by the modern Supreme Court. Students should recall, however, that natural law and the related concept of **natural rights,** with its emphasis on inalienable freedoms, contributed significantly to the intellectual foundations of the American republic.

An Ongoing Dialogue

The Supreme Court has never committed itself to any one judicial philosophy or theory of constitutional interpretation. Rather, the Court's numerous constitutional decisions reflect an ongoing philosophical and theoretical dialogue, both from within and without the Court. The Court's opinions are rife with arguments about "narrow" versus "broad construction" of the Constitution, about judicial activism and restraint, about the "intent of the Framers" versus the need to keep the Constitution "in tune with the times," and so on. These debates are fundamentally about the proper role of a powerful, life-tenured, black-robed elite within a democratic polity and about the duty of that elite to ensure that our eighteenth-century Constitution is both meaningful and relevant as the United States enters the twenty-first century.

CONCLUSION

Students of American government must consider whether the power of judicial review is compatible not only with the intentions of the Framers of the Constitution but also with our modern notions of democracy. Is judicial review an arrogation of power by the courts? Is it a vestige of aristocracy? Or is it a necessary and desirable element of constitutional democracy? Before reaching conclusions on these questions, one should examine the way in which judicial review has been applied over the years since *Marbury v. Madison*. It is also important to take into account the constraints, both external and self-imposed, under which judicial review is exercised. The topic of external constraints on judicial power is examined in Chapter 3.

FOR FURTHER READING

Abraham, Henry J. *The Judiciary: The Supreme Court in the Governmental Process,* 7th ed. Boston: Allyn and Bacon, 1987.

Agresto, John. *The Supreme Court and Constitutional Democracy.* Ithaca: Cornell University Press, 1980.

Beveridge, Albert J. *The Life of John Marshall,* 4 vols. Boston: Houghton-Mifflin, 1916–1919.

Bickel, Alexander M. *The Least Dangerous Branch: The Supreme Court at the Bar of Politics.* Indianapolis: Bobbs-Merrill, 1962.

Bickel, Alexander M. *The Supreme Court and the Idea of Progress,* rev. ed. New Haven: Yale University Press, 1978.

Black, Charles L. *Perspectives in Constitutional Law,* rev. ed. Englewood Cliffs, N.J.: Prentice-Hall, 1970.

Black, Charles L. *The People and the Court: Judicial Review in a Democracy.* New York: Macmillan, 1960.

Black, Hugo L. *A Constitutional Faith.* New York: Knopf, 1969.

Bobbitt, Philip. *Constitutional Fate: Theory of the Constitution.* New York: Oxford University Press, 1982.

Bork, Robert H. *The Tempting of America: The Political Seduction of the Law.* New York: Free Press, 1990.

Bork, Robert H. *Tradition and Morality in Constitutional Law.* Washington, D.C.: American Enterprise Institute, 1984.

Carter, Lief H. *Contemporary Constitutional Lawmaking: The Supreme Court and the Art of Politics.* New York: Pergamon, 1985.

Choper, Jesse H. *Judicial Review and the National Political Process.* Chicago: University of Chicago Press, 1980.

Ely, John Hart. *Democracy and Distrust: A Theory of Judicial Review.* Cambridge: Harvard University Press, 1980.

Ervin, Sam J., and Ramsey Clark. *Role of the Supreme Court: Policymaker or Adjudicator?* Washington, D.C.: American Enterprise Institute, 1970.

Fehrenbacher, Don E. *The Dred Scott Case: Its Significance in American Law and Politics.* New York: Oxford University Press, 1978.

Fisher, Louis. *Judicial Power and the Constitution.* New York: Macmillan, 1990.

Funston, Richard. *A Vital National Seminar: The Supreme Court in American Political Life.* Palo Alto, Calif.: Mayfield, 1978.

Garraty, John A., ed. *Quarrels that have Shaped the Constitution,* rev. ed. New York: Harper and Row, 1987.

Garvey, John, and T. A. Aleinikoff, *Modern Constitutional Theory,* 2d ed. St. Paul: West, 1991.

Halpern, Stephen C., and Charles M. Lamb, eds., *Supreme Court Activism and Restraint.* Lexington, Mass.: Lexington Books, 1982.

Konefsky, Samuel J. *The Legacy of Holmes and Brandeis: A Study in the Influence of Ideas.* New York: Macmillan, 1956.

Lasser, William. *The Limits of Judicial Power: The Supreme Court in American Politics.* Chapel Hill: University of North Carolina Press, 1988.

Levinson, Sanford. *Constitutional Faith.* Princeton, N.J.: Princeton University Press, 1988.

Levy, Leonard, ed., *Judicial Review and the Supreme Court.* New York: Harper, 1967.

Lusky, Louis. *By What Right? A Commentary on the Supreme Court's Power to Revise the Constitution.* Charlottesville, Va.: Michie, 1975.

Mason, Alpheus T. *The Supreme Court from Taft to Burger.* Baton Rouge: Louisiana State University Press, 1979.

McCloskey, Robert G. *The American Supreme Court.* Chicago: University of Chicago Press, 1960.

McPherson, James M. *Battle Cry of Freedom: The Civil War Era.* New York: Oxford University Press, 1988.

Miller, Arthur Selwyn. *Toward Increased Judicial Activism: The Political Role of the Supreme Court.* Westport, Conn.: Greenwood Press, 1982.

Rodell, Fred. *Nine Men: A Political History of the Supreme Court from 1790 to 1955.* New York: Random House, 1955.

Swisher, Carl B. *Roger B. Taney.* New York: Macmillan, 1935.

Swisher, Carl B. *The Supreme Court in Modern Role,* 2d ed. New York: New York University Press, 1965.

Warren, Earl. *A Republic, If You Can Keep It.* New York: Quadrangle, 1972.

Wolfe, Christopher. *Judicial Activism: Bulwark of Freedom or Precarious Security?* Pacific Grove, Calif.: Brooks/Cole, 1991.

CASES AND READINGS

Marbury v. Madison
1 Cranch (5 U.S.) 137; 2 L. Ed. 60 (1803)
Vote: 4-0

In the election of 1800, the Federalists lost control of the presidency as well as both houses of Congress. In an obvious attempt to preserve Federalist influence in the government, the "lame duck" Congress passed the Judiciary Act of 1801. This act created sixteen federal circuit judgeships. Under the Constitution, outgoing President John Adams was able to appoint a number of "midnight judges." In addition to the Judiciary Act, the Congress also adopted organic legislation for the District of Columbia providing for forty-two justices of the peace. William Marbury was appointed by President Adams to one of these positions. However, in the confusion surrounding the change of presidential administrations, Mr. Marbury did not actually receive his commission. It seems that John Marshall, secretary of state in the Adams administration, and newly appointed Chief Justice, had neglected to deliver the commission to Marbury. Upon assuming the presidency, Thomas Jefferson ordered his secretary of state, James Madison, not to deliver Marbury's commission. Hence Marbury filed suit in the Supreme Court, seeking a writ of mandamus to force Madison to deliver his commission.

[**Mr. Chief Justice Marshall** delivered the opinion of the Court.]

. . . It is, then, the opinion of the Court,

1st. That by signing the commission of Mr. Marbury, the President of the United States appointed him a justice of peace for the county of Washington, in the District of Columbia; and that the seal of the United States, affixed thereto by the Secretary of State, is conclusive testimony of the verity of the signature, and of the completion of the appointment; and that the appointment conferred on him a legal right to the office for the space of five years.

2d. That, having this legal title to the office, he has a consequent right to the commission; a refusal to deliver which is a plain violation of the right, for which the laws of his country afford him a remedy.

. . . It remains to be inquired whether,

3d. He is entitled to the remedy for which he applies. This depends on 1st. The nature of the writ applied for; and,

2d. The power of this court.

After a lengthy discussion of the nature of the writ of mandamus *and its historical basis, Marshall continues:*

. . . The act [the Judiciary Act of 1789] to establish the judicial courts of the United States authorizes the Supreme Court, "to issue writs of *mandamus*, in cases warranted by the principles and usages of law, to any courts appointed or persons holding office, under the authority of the United States" [Section 13].

The Secretary of State, being a person holding an office under the authority of the United States, is precisely within the letter of this description; and if this court is not authorized to issue a writ of *mandamus* to such an officer, it must be because the law is unconstitutional, and therefore, absolutely incapable of conferring the authority, and assigning the duties which its words purport to confer and assign.

The Constitution vests the whole judicial power of the United States in one Supreme Court, and such inferior courts as congress shall, from time to time, ordain and establish. This power is expressly extended to all cases arising under the laws of the United States; and consequently, in some form, may be exercised over the present case; because the right claimed is given by a law of the United States.

In the distribution of this power, it is declared, that "the Supreme Court shall have original jurisdiction, in all cases affecting ambassadors, other public ministers and consuls, and those in which a state shall be a party. In all other cases, the Supreme Court shall have appellate jurisdiction."

It has been insisted, at the bar, that as the original grant of jurisdiction to the Supreme and inferior courts, is general, and the clause, assigning original jurisdiction to the Supreme Court, contains no negative or restrictive words, the power remains to the legislature, to assign original jurisdiction to that court, in other cases than those specified in the article which has been recited; provided those cases belong to the judicial power of the United States.

If it had been intended to leave it in the discretion of the legislature, to apportion the judicial power between the Supreme and inferior courts, according to the will of that body, it would certainly have been useless to have proceeded further than to have defined the judicial power, and the tribunals in which it should be vested. The subsequent part of the section is mere surplusage—is entirely without meaning, if such is to be the construction. If Congress remains at liberty to give this court appellate jurisdiction, where the Constitution has declared their jurisdiction shall be original; and original jurisdiction where the Constitution has declared it shall be appellate; the distribution of jurisdiction, made in the constitution, is form without substance.

Affirmative words are often, in their operation, negative of other objects than those affirmed; and in this case, a negative or exclusive sense must be given to them, or they have no operation at all.

It cannot be presumed, that any clause in the Constitution is intended to be without effect; and therefore, such a construction is inadmissible, unless the words require it.

If the solicitude of the convention, respecting our peace with foreign powers, induced a provision that the Supreme Court should take original jurisdiction in cases which might be supposed to affect them; yet the clause would have proceeded no further than to provide for such cases, if no further restriction on the powers of Congress had been intended. That they should have appellate jurisdiction in all other cases, with such exceptions as Congress might make, is no restriction; unless the words be deemed exclusive of original jurisdiction.

When an instrument organizing, fundamentally, a judicial system, divides it into one supreme, and so many inferior courts as the legislature may ordain and establish; then enumerates its powers, and proceeds so far to distribute them, as to define the jurisdiction of the Supreme Court, by declaring the cases in which it shall take original jurisdiction, and that in others it shall take appellate jurisdiction, the plain import of the words seems to be, that in one class of cases, its jurisdiction is original, and not appellate; in the other, it is appellate, and not original. If any other construction would render the clause inoperative, that is an additional reason for rejecting such other construction, and for adhering to their obvious meaning.

To enable this Court, then, to issue a *mandamus,* it must be shown to be an exercise of appellate jurisdiction; or to be necessary to enable them to exercise appellate jurisdiction.

It has been stated at the bar, that the appellate jurisdiction may be exercised in a variety of forms, and that if it be the will of the legislature that a *mandamus* should be used for that purpose, that will must be obeyed. This is true, yet the jurisdiction must be appellate, not original.

It is the essential criterion of appellate jurisdiction, that it revises and corrects the proceedings in a cause already instituted, and does not create that cause. Although, therefore, a *mandamus* may be directed to courts, yet to issue such a writ to an officer, for the delivery of a paper, is, in effect, the same as to sustain an original action for that paper, and therefore, seems not to belong to appellate, but to original jurisdiction. Neither is it necessary in such a case as this, to enable the court to exercise its appellate jurisdiction.

The authority, therefore, given to the Supreme Court by the act establishing the judicial courts of the United States, to issue writs of *mandamus* to public officers, appears not to be warranted by the Constitution; and it becomes necessary to inquire, whether a jurisdiction so conferred can be exercised.

The question, whether an act, repugnant to the Constitution, can become the law of the land, is a question deeply interesting to the United States; but, happily, not of an intricacy proportioned to its interest. It seems only necessary to recognize certain principles, supposed to have been long and well established, to decide it.

That the people have an original right to establish, for their future government, such principles as, in their opinion, shall most conduce to their own happiness, is the basis on which the whole American fabric has been erected. The exercise of this original right is a very great exertion; nor can it, nor ought it, to be frequently repeated. The principles, therefore, so established, are deemed fundamental: and as the authority from which they proceed is supreme, and can seldom act, they are designed to be permanent.

This original and supreme will organizes the government, and assigns to different departments their respective powers. It may either stop here, or establish certain limits not to be transcended by those departments.

The government of the United States is of the latter description. The powers of the legislature are defined and limited; and that those limits may not be mistaken or forgotten, the Constitution is written. To what purpose are powers limited, and to what purpose is that limitation committed to writing, if these limits may, at any time, be passed by those intended to be restrained? The distinction between a government with limited and unlimited powers is abolished, if those limits do not confine the persons on whom they are imposed, and if acts prohibited and acts allowed, are of equal obligation. It is a proposition too plain to be contested, that the constitution controls any legislative act repugnant to it; or that the legislature may alter the Constitution by an ordinary act.

Between these alternatives, there is no middle ground. The Constitution is either a superior paramount law, unchangeable by ordinary means, or it is on a level with ordinary legislative acts, and, like other acts, is alterable when the legislature shall please to alter it.

If the former part of the alternative be true, then a legislative act, contrary to the Constitution, is not law; if the latter part be true, then written constitutions are absurd attempts, on the part of the people, to limit a power, in its own nature, illimitable.

Certainly, all those who have framed written constitutions contemplate them as forming the fundamental and paramount law of the nation, and consequently, the theory of every such government must be, that an act of the legislature, repugnant to the Constitution, is void.

This theory is essentially attached to a written constitution, and is, consequently, to be considered, by this Court, as one of the fundamental principles of our society. It is not, therefore, to be lost sight of, in the further consideration of this subject.

If an act of the legislature, repugnant to the Constitution, is void, does it notwithstanding its invalidity, bind the courts, and oblige them to give it effect? Or, in other words, though it be not law, does it constitute a rule as operative as if it was a law? This would be to overthrow, in fact, what was established in theory; and would seem, at first view, an absurdity too gross to be insisted on. It shall, however, receive a more attentive consideration.

It is, emphatically, the province and duty of the judicial department, to say what the law is. Those who apply the rule to particular cases, must of necessity expound and interpret that rule. If two laws conflict with each other, the courts must decide on the operation of each.

So, if a law be in opposition to the Constitution; if both the law and the Constitution apply to a particular case, so that the court must either decide that case, conformable to the law, disregarding the Constitution; or conformable to the Constitution, disregarding the law; the court must determine which of these conflicting rules governs the case: this is of the very essence of judicial duty.

If then, the courts are to regard the Constitution, and the constitution is superior to any ordinary act of the legislature, the Constitution, and not such ordinary act, must govern the case to which they both apply.

Those, then, who controvert the principle, that the Constitution is to be considered, in court, as a paramount law, are reduced to the necessity of maintaining that courts must close their eyes on the Constitution, and see only the law.

This doctrine would subvert the very foundation of all written constitutions. It would declare that an act which, according to the principles and theory of our government, is entirely void, is yet, in practice, completely obligatory. It would declare, that if the legislature shall do what is expressly forbidden, such act, notwithstanding the express prohibition, is in reality effectual. It would be given to the legislature a practical and real omnipotence, with the same breath which professes to restrict their powers within narrow limits. It is prescribing limits, and declaring that those limits may be passed at pleasure....

The judicial power of the United States is extended to all cases arising under the Constitution. Could it be the intention of those who gave this power, to say, that in using it, the constitution should not be looked into? That a case arising under the Constitution should be decided, without examining the instrument under which it arises?

This is too extravagant to be maintained.

In some cases, then, the constitution must be looked into by the judges. And if they can open it at all, what part of it are they forbidden to read or to obey? . . .

. . . [I]t is apparent, that the framers of the Constitution contemplated that instrument as a rule for the government of courts, as well as the legislature.

Why otherwise does it direct the judges to take an oath to support it? This oath certainly applies in an especial manner, to their conduct in their official character. How immoral to impose it on them, if they were to be used as the instruments, and the knowing instruments, for violating what they swear to support!

. . . Why does a judge swear to discharge his duties agreeable to the Constitution of the United States, if that constitution forms no rule for his government? If it is closed upon him, and cannot be inspected by him?

If such be the real state of things, this is worse than solemn mockery. To prescribe, or to take this oath, becomes equally a crime.

It is also not entirely unworthy of observation, that in declaring what shall be the supreme law of the land, the Constitution itself is first mentioned; and not the laws of the United States, generally, but those only which shall be made in pursuance of the Constitution, have that rank.

Thus, the particular phraseology of the Constitution of the United States confirms and strengthens the principle, supposed to be essential to all written constitutions, that a law repugnant to the Constitution is void; and that courts, as well as other departments, are bound by that instrument.

The rule must be discharged.

[**Justices Cushing** and **Moore** did not participate in the decision.]

Eakin v. Raub

12 Sergeant & Rawle (Pennsylvania Supreme Court) 330 (1825)

Although the specific issue before the Pennsylvania Supreme Court is of little interest today, Justice Gibson's dissenting opinion is still considered to be the most effective rejoinder to Chief Justice Marshall's argument in support of judicial review.

Gibson, J. [dissenting].

. . . I will avail myself of it to express an opinion which I have deliberately formed, on the abstract right of the judiciary to declare an unconstitutional act of the legislature void.

. . . I am aware, that a right to declare all unconstitutional acts void . . . is generally held as a professional dogma; but, I apprehend rather as a matter of faith than of reason. I admit that I once embraced the same doctrine, but without examination, and I shall therefore state the arguments that impelled me to abandon it, with great respect for those by whom it is still maintained. . . .

. . . The Constitution and the *right* of the legislature to pass the act, may be in collision; but is that a legitimate subject for judicial determination? If it be, the judiciary must be a peculiar organ, to revise the proceedings of the legislature, and to correct its mistakes; and in what part of the Constitution are we to look for this proud pre-eminence? Viewing the matter in the opposite direction, what would be thought of an act of assembly in which it should be declared that the Supreme Court had, in a particular case, put a wrong construction on the Constitution of the United States, and that the judgment should therefore be reversed? It would doubtless be thought a usurpation of judicial power. But it is by no means clear, that to declare a law void which has been enacted according to the forms prescribed in the Constitution, is not a usurpation of legislative power. . . .

. . . But it has been said to be emphatically the business of the judiciary, to ascertain and pronounce what the law is; and that this necessarily involves a consideration of the Constitution. It does so: but how far? If the judiciary will inquire into any thing beside the form of enactment, where shall it stop? There must be some point of limitation to such an inquiry; for no one will pretend that a judge would be justifiable in calling for the election returns, or scrutinizing the qualifications of those who composed the legislature. . . .

Every one knows how seldom men think exactly alike on ordinary subjects; and a government constructed on the principle of assent by all its parts, would be inadequate to the most simple operations. The notion of a complication of counter checks has been carried to an extent in theory, of which the framers of the Constitution never dreamt. When the entire sovereignty was separated into its elementary parts, and distributed to the appropriate branches, all things incident to the exercise of its powers were committed to each branch exclusively. The negative which each part of the legislature may exercise, in regard to the acts of the other, was thought sufficient to prevent material infractions of the restraints which were put on the power of the whole; for, had it been intended to interpose the judiciary as an additional barrier, the matter would surely not have been left in doubt. Thus judges would not have been left to stand on the insecure and ever-shifting ground of public opinion as to constructive powers; they would have been placed on the impregnable ground of an express grant; they would not have been compelled to resort to the debates in the convention, or the opinion that was generally entertained at the time. A constitution, or a statute, is supposed to contain the whole will of the body from which it emanated; and I would just as soon resort to the debates in the legislature for the construction of an act of assembly, as to the debates in the convention for the construction of the Constitution.

The power is said to be restricted to cases that are free from doubt or difficulty. But the abstract existence of a power cannot depend on the clearness or obscurity of the case in which it is to be exercised; for that is a consideration that cannot present itself, before the question of the existence of the power shall have been determined; and, if its existence be conceded, no considerations of policy arising from

the obscurity of the particular case ought to influence the exercise of it. . . . The grant of a power so extraordinary ought to appear so plain, that he who should run might read. Now, put the Constitution into the hands of any man of plain sense, whose mind is free from an impression on the subject, and it will be impossible to persuade him, that the exercise of such a power was ever contemplated by the Convention.

But the judges are sworn to support the Constitution, and are they not bound by it as the law of the land? In some respects they are. In the very few cases in which the judiciary, and not the legislature, is the immediate organ to execute its provisions, they are bound by it in preference to any act of assembly to the contrary. In such cases, the Constitution is a rule to the courts. But what I have in view in this inquiry, is the supposed right of the judiciary, to interfere, in cases where the constitution is to be carried into effect through the instrumentality of the legislature, and where that organ must necessarily first decide on the constitutionality of its own act. The oath to support the Constitution is not peculiar to the judges, but is taken indiscriminately by every officer of the government, and is designed rather as a test of the political principles of the man, than to bind the officer in the discharge of his duty; otherwise it were difficult to determine what operation it is to have in the case of a recorder of deeds, for instance, who, in the execution of his office, has nothing to do with the Constitution. But granting it to relate to the official conduct of the judge, as well as every other officer, and not to his political principles, still it must be understood in reference to supporting the Constitution, *only as far as that may be involved in his official duty;* and consequently, if his official duty does not comprehend an inquiry into the authority of the legislature, neither does his oath.

It is worthy of remark here that the foundation of every argument in favor of the right of the judiciary, is found at last to be an assumption of the whole ground in dispute. Granting that the object of the oath is to secure a support of the Constitution in the discharge of official duty, its terms may be satisfied by restraining it to official duty in the exercise of the *ordinary* judicial powers. Thus, the Constitution may furnish a rule of construction, where a particular interpretation of a law would conflict with some constitutional principle; and such interpretation, where it may, is always to be avoided. But the oath was more probably designed to secure the powers of each of the different branches from being usurped by any of the rest; for instance, to prevent the house of representatives from erecting itself into a court of judicature, or the Supreme Court from attempting to control the legislature; and in this view, the oath furnishes an argument equally plausible *against* the right of the judiciary. But if it require a support of the Constitution in any thing beside official duty, it is in fact an oath of allegiance to a particular form of government; and, considered as such, it is not easy to see why it should not be taken by the citizens at large, as well as by the officers of the government. It has never been thought that an officer is under greater restraint as to measures which have for their avowed end a total change of the Constitution, than a citizen who has taken no oath at all. The official oath, then, relates only to the official conduct of the officer, and does not prove that he ought to stray from the path of his ordinary business to search for violations of duty in the business of others; nor does it, as supposed, define the powers of the officer.

But do not the judges do a *positive* act in violation of the Constitution, when they give effect to an unconstitutional law? Not if the law has been passed according to the forms established in the Constitution. The fallacy of the question is in supposing that the judiciary adopts the acts of the legislature as its own; whereas the enactment of a law and the interpretation of it are not concurrent acts, and as the judiciary is not required to concur in the enactment, neither is it in the breach of the Constitution which may be the consequence of the enactment; the fault is imputable to the legislature, and on it the responsibility exclusively rests. In this respect, the judges are in the predicament of jurors who are bound to serve in capital cases, although unable, under any circumstance, to reconcile it to their duty to deprive a human being of life. To one of these, who applied to be discharged from the panel, I once heard it remarked, by an eminent and humane judge, "You do not deprive a prisoner of life by finding him guilty of a capital crime; you but pronounce his case

to be within the law, and it is, therefore, those who declare the law, and not you, who deprive him of life."

... But it has been said that this construction would deprive the citizen of the advantages which are peculiar to written constitution, by at once declaring the power of the legislature, in practice, to be illimitable. I ask, what are those advantages? The principles of a written constitution are more fixed and certain, and more apparent to the apprehension of the people than principles which depend on tradition and the vague comprehension of the individuals who compose the nation, and who cannot all be expected to receive the same impressions or entertain the same notions on any given subject. But there is no magic or inherent power in parchment and ink, to command respect and protect principles from violation. In the business of government, a recurrence to first principles answers the end of an observation at sea with a view to correct the dead reckoning; and, for this purpose, a written constitution is an instrument of inestimable value. It is of inestimable value, also, in rendering its principles familiar to the mass of the people; for, after all, there is no effectual guard against legislative usurpation but public opinion, the force of which, in this country, is inconceivably great. Happily this is proved, by experience, to be a sufficient guard against palpable infractions. The Constitution of this state has withstood the shocks of strong party excitement for thirty years, during which no act of the legislature has been declared unconstitutional, although the judiciary has constantly asserted a right to do so in clear cases. But it would be absurd to say, that this remarkable observance of the Constitution has been produced, not by the responsibility of the legislature to the people, but by an apprehension of control by the judiciary. Once let public opinion be so corrupt as to sanction every misconstruction of the constitution and abuse of power which the temptation of the moment may dictate, and the party which may happen to be predominant, will laugh at the puny effort of a dependent power to arrest it in its course.

For these reasons, I am of opinion that it rests with the people, in whom full and absolute sovereign power resides to correct abuses in legislation, by instructing their representatives to repeal the obnoxious act. What is wanting to plenary power in the government, is reserved by the people for their own immediate use; and to redress an infringement of their rights in this respect, would seem to be an accessory of the power thus reserved. It might, perhaps, have been better to vest the power in the judiciary; as it might be expected that its habits of deliberation, and the aid derived from the arguments of counsel, would more frequently lead to accurate conclusions. On the other hand, the judiciary is not infallible; and an error by it would admit of no remedy but a more distinct expression of the public will, through the extraordinary medium of a convention; whereas, an error by the legislature admits of a remedy by an exertion of the same will, in the ordinary exercise of the right of suffrage—a mode better calculated to attain

the end, without popular excitement. It may be said, the people would probably not notice an error of their representatives. But they would as probably do so, as notice an error of the judiciary; and, beside, it is a *postulate* in the theory of our government, and the very basis of the superstructure, that the people are wise, virtuous, and competent to manage their own affairs; and if they are not so, in fact, still every question of this sort must be determined according to the principles of the Constitution, as it came from the hands of its framers, and the existence of a defect which was not foreseen, would not justify those who administer the government, in applying a corrective in practice, which can be provided only by a convention. . . .

President Jackson's Message to the Senate in Support of His Veto of a Bill to Renew the Bank of the United States (July 10, 1832)
3 *Messages and Papers of the Presidents* 1139–1143
(Richardson, ed.)

The Second Bank of the United States, the constitutionality of which had been sustained by the Supreme Court in M'Culloch v. Maryland *(1819), came under renewed political attack during the 1820s. Critics of the bank alleged that it was a corrupt institution that favored the aristocracy. In 1832, the bank's supporters persuaded Congress to renew the bank's charter. An opponent of the bank, President Andrew Jackson vetoed the legislation extending the charter. His accompanying message suggests that the executive branch has an important role in the process of constitutional interpretation.*

To the Senate:

The bill "to modify and continue" the act entitled "An Act to incorporate the subscribers to the Bank of the United States" was presented to me on the 4th July instant. Having considered it with that solemn regard to the principles of the Constitution which the day was calculated to inspire, and come to the conclusion that it ought not to become a law, I here-

with return it to the Senate, in which it originated, with my objections.

A bank of the United States is in many respects convenient for the Government and useful to the people. Entertaining this opinion, and deeply impressed with the belief that some of the powers and privileges possessed by the existing bank are unauthorized by the Constitution, subversive of the rights of the States, and dangerous to the liberties of the people, I felt it my duty at an early period of my Administration to call the attention of Congress to the practicability of organizing an institution combining all its advantages and obviating these objections. I sincerely regret that in the act before me I can perceive none of those modifications of the bank charter which are necessary, in my opinion, to make it compatible with justice, with sound policy, or with the Constitution of our country. . . .

It is maintained by the advocates of the bank that its constitutionality in all its features ought to be considered as settled by precedent and by the decision of the Supreme Court. To this conclusion I can not assent. Mere precedent is a dangerous source of authority, and should not be regarded as deciding questions of constitutional power except where the acquiescence of the people and the States can be considered as well settled. So far from this being the case on this subject, an argument against the bank might be based on precedent. One Congress, in 1791, decided in favor of a bank; another, in 1811, decided against it. One Congress, in 1815, decided against a bank; another, in 1816, decided in its favor. Prior to the present Congress, therefore, the precedents drawn from that source were equal. If we resort to the States, the expressions of legislative, judicial, and executive opinions against the bank have been probably to those in its favor as 4 to 1. There is nothing in precedent, therefore, which, if its authority were admitted, ought to weigh in favor of the act before me.

If the opinion of the Supreme Court covered the whole ground of this act, it ought not to control the coordinate authorities of this Government. The Congress, the Executive, and the Court, must each for itself be guided by its own opinion of the Constitution. Each public officer who takes an oath to support the Constitution swears that he will support it as he understands it, and not as it is understood by others. It is as much the duty of the House of Representatives, of the Senate, and of the President to decide upon the constitutionality of any bill or resolution which may be presented to them for passage or approval as it is of the supreme judges when it may be brought before them for judicial decision. The opinion of the judges has no more authority over Congress than the opinion of Congress has over the judges, and on that point the President is independent of both. The authority of the Supreme Court must not, therefore, be permitted to control the Congress or the Executive when acting in their legislative capacities, but to have only such influence as the force of their reasoning may deserve.

But in the case relied upon the Supreme Court have not decided that all the features of this corporation are compatible with the Constitution. It is true that the courts have said that the law incorporating the bank is a constitutional exercise of power by Congress; but taking into view the whole opinion of the court and the reasoning by which they have come to that conclusion, I understand them to have decided that inasmuch as a bank is an appropriate means for carrying into effect the enumerated powers of the General Government, therefore the law incorporating it is in accordance with that provision of the Constitution which declares that Congress shall have power "to make all laws which shall be necessary and proper for carrying those powers into execution." Having satisfied themselves that the word *"necessary"* in the Constitution means *"needful," "requisite," "essential," "conducive to,"* and that "a bank" is a convenient, a useful, and essential instrument in the prosecution of the Government's "fiscal operations," they conclude that to "use one must be within the discretion of Congress" and that "the act to incorporate the Bank of the United States is a law made in pursuance of the Constitution"; "but," say they, *"where the law is not prohibited and is really calculated to effect any of the objects intrusted to the Government, to undertake here to inquire into the degree of its necessity would be to pass the line which circumscribes the judicial department and to tread on legislative ground."*

The Principle here affirmed is that the "degree of its necessity," involving all the details of a banking institution, is a question exclusively for legislative consideration. A bank is constitutional, but it is the province of the Legislature to determine whether this or that particular power, privilege, or exemption is "necessary and proper" to enable the bank to discharge its duties to the Government, and from their decision there is no appeal to the courts of justice. Under the decision of the Supreme Court, therefore, it is the exclusive province of Congress and the President to decide whether the particular features of this act are *necessary* and *proper* in order to enable the bank to perform conveniently and efficiently the public duties assigned to it as a fiscal agent, and therefore constitutional, or *unnecessary* and *improper,* and therefore unconstitutional.

Without commenting on the general principle affirmed by the Supreme Court, let us examine the details of this act in accordance with the rule of legislative action which they have laid down. It will be found that many of the powers and privileges conferred on it can not be supposed necessary for the purpose for which it is proposed to be created, and are not, therefore, means necessary to attain the end in view, and consequently not justified by the Constitution. . . .

It is maintained by some that the bank is a means of executing the constitutional power "to coin money and regulate the value thereof." Congress have established a mint to coin money and passed laws to regulate the value thereof. The money so coined, with its value so regulated, and such foreign coins as Congress may adopt are the only currency known to the Constitution. But if they have other power to regulate the currency, it was conferred to be exercised by themselves, and not to be transferred to a corporation. If the bank be established for that purpose, with a charter unalterable without its consent, Congress have parted with their power for a term of years, during which the Constitution is a dead letter. It is neither necessary nor proper to transfer its legislative power to such a bank, and therefore unconstitutional.

By its silence, considered in connection with the decision of the Supreme Court in the case of M'Culloch against the State of Maryland, this act takes from the States the power to tax a portion of the banking business carried on within their limits, in subversion of one of the strongest barriers which secured them against Federal encroachments.

Upon the formation of the Constitution the States guarded their taxing power with peculiar jealousy. They surrendered it only as it regards imports and exports. In relation to every other object within their jurisdiction, whether persons, property, business, or professions, it was secured in as ample a manner as it was before possessed. All persons, though United States officers, are liable to a poll tax by the States within which they reside. The lands of the United States are liable to the usual land tax, except in the new States, from whom agreements that they will not tax unsold lands are exacted when they are admitted into the Union. Horses, wagons, any beasts or vehicles, tools, or property belonging to private citizens, though employed in the service of the United States, are subject to State taxation. Every private business, whether carried on by an officer of the General Government or not, whether it be mixed with public concerns or not, even if it be carried on by the Government of the United States itself, separately or in partnership, falls within the scope of the taxing power of the State. Nothing comes more fully within it than banks and the business of banking, by whomsoever instituted and carried on. Over this whole subject-matter it is just as absolute, unlimited, and uncontrollable as if the Constitution had never been adopted, because in the formation of that instrument it was reserved without qualification.

The principle is conceded that the States can not rightfully tax the operations of the General Government. They can not tax the money of the Government deposited in the State banks, nor the agency of those banks in remitting it; but will any maintain that their mere selection to perform this public service for the General Government would exempt the State banks and their ordinary business from State taxation? Had the United States, instead of establishing a bank at Philadelphia, employed a private banker to keep and transmit their funds, would it have deprived Pennsylvania of the right to tax his bank and his usual banking operations? It will not be pretended. Upon what principle, then, are the banking establishments of the Bank of the United States and their usual banking operations to be exempted from taxation? It is not their public agency or the deposits of the Government which the States claim a right to tax, but their banks and their banking powers, instituted and exercised within State jurisdiction for their private emolument—those powers and privileges for which they pay a bonus, and which the States tax in their own banks. . . .

Dred Scott v. Sandford

19 Howard (60 U.S.) 393; 15 L. Ed. 691 (1857)
Vote: 7-2

Dred Scott was a slave belonging to a surgeon in the U.S. Army. He was taken by his master into territories in which slavery was forbidden by the Missouri Compromise of 1820. Several years after his return to Missouri, Dred Scott brought suit in federal court to obtain his freedom, arguing that his temporary residence in a "free" territory had abolished his servitude. After an adverse ruling in the lower court, Scott took the case to the Supreme Court on a writ of error.

Mr. Chief Justice Taney delivered the opinion of the Court.

. . . The question is simply this: Can a negro, whose ancestors were imported into this country, and sold as slaves, become a member of the political community formed and brought into existence by the Constitution of the United States, and as such become entitled to all the rights, and privileges, and immunities, guaranteed by that instrument to the citizen? One of which rights is the privilege of suing in a court of the United States in the cases specified in the Constitution. . . .

We think . . . [that Negroes] . . . are not included, and were not intended to be included, under the word "citizens" in the Constitution, and can therefore claim none of the rights and privileges which that instrument provides for and secures to citizens of the United States. On the contrary, they were at that time considered as a subordinate and inferior class of beings, who had been subjugated by the dominant race, and, whether emancipated or not, yet remained subject to their authority, and had no rights or privileges but such as those who held the power and the Government might choose to grant them.

It is not the province of the court to decide upon the justice or injustice, the policy or impolicy, of these laws. The decision of that question belonged to the political or law-making power; to those who formed the sovereignty and framed the Constitution. The duty of the court is, to interpret the instrument they have framed, with the best lights we can obtain on the subject, and to administer it as we find it, according to its true intent and meaning when it was adopted. . . .

The question then arises, whether the provisions of the Constitution, in relation to the personal rights and privileges to which the citizen of a State should be entitled, embraced the negro African race, at that time in this country, or who might afterwards be imported, who had then or should afterwards be made free in any State; and to put it in the power of a single State to make him a citizen of the United States, and endow him with the full rights of citizenship in every other State without their consent? Does the Constitution of the United States act upon him whenever he shall be made free under the laws of a State, and raised there to the rank of a citizen, and immediately clothe him with all the privileges of a citizen in every other State, and in its own courts?

The court thinks the affirmative of these propositions cannot be maintained. And if it cannot, the plaintiff in error could not be a citizen of the State of Missouri, within the meaning of the Constitution of the United States, and, consequently, was not entitled to sue in its courts. . . .

In the opinion of the court, the legislation and histories of the times, and the language used in the Declaration of Independence, show, that neither the class of persons who had been imported as slaves, nor their descendants, whether they had become free or not, were then acknowledged as a part of the people, nor intended to be included in the general words used in that memorable instrument. . . .

They had for more than a century before been regarded as beings of an inferior order, and altogether unfit to associate with the white race, either in social or political relations; and so far inferior, that they had no rights which the white man was bound to respect; and that the negro might justly and lawfully be reduced to slavery for his benefit. He was bought and sold, and treated as an ordinary article of merchandise and traffic, whenever a profit could be made by it. This opinion was at that time fixed and universal in the civilized portion of the white race. It was regarded as an axiom in morals as well as in politics, which no one thought of disputing, or supposed to be open to dispute; and men in every grade and position in society daily and habitually acted upon it in their private pursuits, as well as in matters of public concern, without doubting for a moment the correctness of this opinion. . . .

The only two provisions [of the Constitution] which point to them [slaves] and include them [Article I, Section 9, and Article IV, Section 2], treat them as property, and make it the duty of the Government to protect it; no other power, in relation to this race, is to be found in the Constitution; and as it is a Government of special, delegated, powers, no authority beyond these two provisions can be constitutionally exercised. The Government of the United States had no right to interfere for any other purpose but that of protecting the rights of the owner, leaving it altogether with the several States to deal with this race, whether emancipated or not, as each State may think justice, humanity, and the interests and safety of society, require. The States evidently intended to reserve this power exclusively to themselves.

No one, we presume, supposes that any change in public opinion or feeling, in relation to this unfortunate race, in the civilized nations of Europe or in this country, should induce the court to give to the words of the Constitution a more liberal construction in their favor than they were intended to bear when the instrument was framed and adopted. Such an argument would be altogether inadmissible in any tribunal called on to interpret it. If any of its provisions are deemed unjust, there is a mode prescribed in the instrument itself by which it may be amended; but while it remains unaltered, it must be construed now as it was understood at the time of its adoption. It is not only the same in words, but the same in meaning, and delegates the same powers to the Government, and reserves and secures the same rights and privileges to the citizen; and as long as it continues to exist in its present form, it speaks not only in the same words, but with the same meaning and intent with which it spoke when it came from the hands of its framers, and was voted on and adopted by the people of the United States. Any other rule of construction would abrogate the judi-

cial character of this court, and make it the mere reflex of the popular opinion of the day. . . .

What the construction was at that time, we think can hardly admit of doubt. We have the language of the Declaration of Independence and of the Articles of Confederation, in addition to the plain words of the Constitution itself; we have the legislation of the different States, before, about the time, and since, the Constitution was adopted; we have the legislation of Congress, from the time of its adoption to a recent period; and we have the constant and uniform action of the Executive Department, all concurring together, and leading to the same result. And if anything in relation to the construction of the Constitution can be regarded as settled, it is that which we now give to the word "citizen" and the word "People." . . .

The act of Congress, upon which the plaintiff relies, declares that slavery and involuntary servitude, except as a punishment for crime, shall be forever prohibited in all that part of the territory ceded by France, under the name of Louisiana, which lies north of thirty-six degrees thirty minutes north latitude, and not included within the limits of Missouri. And the . . . inquiry is whether Congress was authorized to pass this law under any of the powers granted to it by the Constitution; for if the authority is not given by that instrument, it is the duty of this court to declare it void and inoperative, and incapable of conferring freedom upon any one who is held as a slave under the laws of any one of the States.

The counsel for the plaintiff has laid much stress upon that article in the Constitution which confers on Congress the power "to dispose of and make all needful rules and regulations respecting the territory or other property belonging to the United States," but, in the judgment of the court, that provision has no bearing on the present controversy, and the power there given, whatever it may be, is confined, and was intended to be confined, to the territory which at that time belonged to, or was claimed by the United States, and was within their boundaries as settled by the treaty with Great Britain, and can have no influence upon a territory afterwards acquired from a foreign Government. It was a special provision for a known and particular territory, and to meet a present emergency, and nothing more.

. . . The powers of the Government and the rights and privileges of the citizen are regulated and plainly defined by the Constitution itself. And when the Territory becomes a part of the United States, the Federal Government enters into possession in the character impressed upon it by those who created it. It enters upon it with its powers over the citizen strictly defined, and limited by the Constitution, from which it derives its own existence, and by virtue of which alone it continues to exist and act as a Government and sovereignty. It has no power of any kind beyond it; and it cannot, when it enters a Territory of the United States, put off its character and assume discretionary or despotic powers which the Constitution has denied to it. It cannot create for itself a new character separated from the citizens of the United States, and the duties it owes them under the provisions of the Constitution. The Territory being a part of the United States, the Government and the citizen both enter it under the authority of the Constitution, with their respective rights defined and marked out; and the Federal Government can exercise no power over his person or property, beyond what that instrument confers, nor lawfully deny any right which it has reserved. . . .

. . . An Act of Congress which deprives a citizen of the United States of his liberty or property, merely because he came himself or brought his property into a particular Territory of the United States, and who had committed no offense against the laws, could hardly be dignified with the name of due process of law.

The powers over person and property of which we speak are not only not granted to Congress, but are in express terms denied, and they are forbidden to exercise them. And this prohibition is not confined to the States, but the words are general, and extend to the whole territory over which the Constitution gives it power to legislate, including those portions of it remaining under Territorial Government, as well as that covered by States. It is a total absence of power everywhere within the dominion of the United States, and places the citizens of a Territory, so far as these rights are concerned, on the same footing with citizens of the States and guards them as firmly and plainly against any inroads which the General Government might attempt, under the

plea of implied or incidental powers. And if Congress itself cannot do this—if it is beyond the powers conferred on the Federal Government—it will be admitted, we presume, that it could not authorize a Territorial Government to exercise them. It would confer no power on any local Government, established by its authority, to violate provisions of the Constitution. . . .

Upon these considerations, it is the opinion of the court that the act of Congress which prohibited a citizen from holding and owning property of this kind in the territory of the United States north of the line therein mentioned, is not warranted by the Constitution, and is therefore void; and that neither Dred Scott himself, nor any of his family, were made free by being carried into this territory; even if they had been carried there by the owner, with the intention of becoming a permanent resident. . . .

Mr. Justice Curtis, joined by ***Mr. Justice McLean,*** dissenting.

I dissent from the opinion pronounced by the Chief Justice, and from the judgment which the majority of the court think it proper to render in this case. . . .

To determine whether any free persons, descended from Africans held in slavery, were citizens of the United States under the Confederation, and consequently at the time of the adoption of the Constitution of the United States, it is only necessary to know whether any such persons were citizens of either of the States under the Confederation, at the time of the adoption of the Constitution.

Of this there can be no doubt. At the time of the ratification of the Articles of Confederation, all free native-born inhabitants of the States of New Hampshire, Massachusetts, New York, New Jersey, and North Carolina, though descended from African slaves, were not only citizens of those States, but such of them as had the other necessary qualifications possessed the franchise of electors, on equal terms with other citizens. . . .

I dissent, therefore, from that part of the opinion of the majority of the court, in which it is held that a person of African descent cannot be a citizen of the United States; and I regret I must go further, and dissent both from what I deem their assumption of authority to examine the constitutionality of the act of Congress commonly called the Missouri Compromise act, and the grounds and conclusions announced in their opinion.

Having first decided that they were bound to consider the sufficiency of the plea to the jurisdiction of the Circuit Court, and having decided that this plea showed that the Circuit Court had no jurisdiction, and consequently that this is a case to which the judicial power of the United States does not extend, they have gone on to examine the merits of the case as they appear on the trial before the court and jury, on the issues joined on the pleas in bar, and so have reached the question of the power of Congress to pass the act of 1820. On so grave a subject as this, I feel obliged to say that, in my opinion, such an exertion of judicial power transcends the limits of the authority of the court. . . .

United States v. Nixon

418 U.S. 683; 94 S. Ct. 3090, 41 L. Ed. 2d 1039 (1974)

Vote: 8-0

Mr. Chief Justice Burger delivered the opinion of the Court.

. . . [This case presents] for review the denial of a motion, filed on behalf of the President of the United States, . . . to quash a third-party *subpoena duces tecum* issued by the United States District Court for the District of Columbia. *** The subpoena directed the President to produce certain tape recordings and documents relating to his conversations with aides and advisers. The court rejected the President's claims of absolute executive privilege, of lack of jurisdiction. . . . The President appealed to the Court of Appeals. We granted the United States' petition for *certiorari* before judgment . . . because of the public importance of the issues presented and the need for their prompt resolution. ***

On March 1, 1974, a grand jury of the United States District Court for the District of Columbia returned an indictment charging seven named individuals with various offenses, including conspiracy to defraud the United States and to obstruct justice. Although he was not designated as such in the indictment, the grand jury named the President, among others, as an unindicted co-conspirator. On April 18, 1974, upon motion of the Special Prosecutor, . . . a *subpoena duces tecum* was issued *** to the President by the United States District Court and made returnable on May 2, 1974. This subpoena required the production, in advance of the September 9 trial date, of certain tapes, memoranda, papers, transcripts, or other writings relating to certain precisely identified meetings between the President and others. The Special Prosecutor was able to fix the time, place and persons present at these discussions because the White House daily logs and appointment records had been delivered to him. On April 30, the President publicly released edited transcripts of 43 conversations; portions of 20 conversations subject to subpoena in the present case were included. On May 1, 1974, the President's counsel, filed a "special appearance" and a motion to quash the subpoena. *** This motion was accompanied by a formal claim of privilege. . . .

On May 20, 1974, the District Court denied the motion to quash. . . . It further ordered "the President or any subordinate officer, official or employee with custody or control of the documents or objects subpoenaed," *** to deliver to the District Court, on or before May 31, 1974, the originals of all subpoenaed items, as well as an index and analysis of those items, together with tape copies of those portions of the subpoenaed recordings for which transcripts had been released to the public by the President on April 30. The District Court rejected jurisdictional challenges based on a contention that the dispute was nonjusticiable because it was between the Special Prosecutor and the Chief Executive and hence "intra-executive" in character; it also rejected the connection that the judiciary was without authority to review an assertion of executive privilege by the President. The court's rejection of the first challenge was based on the authority and powers vested in the Special Prosecutor by the regulation promulgated by the Attorney General; the court concluded that a justiciable controversy was presented. . . .

The District Court held that the judiciary, not the President, was the final arbiter of a claim of executive privilege. The court concluded that, under the circumstances of this case, the presumptive privilege was overcome by the Special Prosecutor's *prima facie* "demonstration of need sufficiently compelling to warrant judicial examination in chambers. . . ." ***

JUSTICIABILITY

In the District Court, the President's counsel argued that the court lacked jurisdiction to issue the subpoena because the matter was an intrabranch dispute between a subordinate and superior officer of the Executive Branch and hence not subject to judicial resolution. That argument has been renewed in this Court with emphasis on the contention that the dispute does not present a "case" or "controversy" which can be adjudicated in the federal courts. The President's counsel argues that the federal courts should not intrude into areas committed to the other branches of Government. He views the present dispute as essentially a "jurisdictional" dispute within the Executive Branch which he analogizes to a dispute between two congressional committees. Since the Executive Branch has exclusive authority and absolute discretion to decide whether to prosecute a case, *** it is contended that a President's decision is final in determining what evidence is to be used in a given criminal case. Although his counsel concedes the President has delegated certain specific powers to the Special Prosecutor, he has not "waived nor delegated to the Special Prosecutor the President's duty to claim privilege as to all materials . . . which fall within the President's inherent authority to refuse to disclose to any executive officer." *** The Special Prosecutor's demand for the items therefore presents, in the view of the President's counsel, a political question under *Baker v. Carr* [1962], ***

since it involves a "textually demonstrable" grant of power under Art. II.

The mere assertion of a claim of an "intrabranch dispute," without more, has never operated to defeat federal jurisdiction; justiciability does not depend on such a surface inquiry. . . .

Our starting point is the nature of the proceeding for which the evidence is sought—here a pending criminal prosecution. It is a judicial proceeding in a federal court alleging violation of federal laws and is brought in the name of the United States as sovereign. *** Under the authority of Art. II, Sec. 2, Congress has vested in the Attorney General the power to conduct the criminal litigation of the United States Government. *** It has also vested in him the power to appoint subordinate officers to assist him in the discharge of his duties. *** Acting pursuant to those statutes, the Attorney General had delegated the authority to represent the United States in these particular matters to a Special Prosecutor with unique authority and tenure. The regulation gives the Special Prosecutor explicit power to contest the invocation of executive privilege in the process of seeking evidence deemed relevant to the performance of these specially delegated duties. ***

. . . So long as this regulation remains in force the Executive Branch is bound by it, and indeed the United States as the sovereign composed of the three branches is bound to respect and to enforce it. Moreover, the delegation of authority to the Special Prosecutor in this case is not an ordinary delegation by the Attorney General to a subordinate officer: with the authorization of the President, the Acting Attorney General provided in the regulation that the Special Prosecutor was not to be removed without the "consensus" of eight designated leaders of Congress. ***

The demands of and the resistance to the subpoena present an obvious controversy in the ordinary sense, but that alone is not sufficient to meet constitutional standards. In the constitutional sense, controversy means more than disagreement and conflict; rather it means the kind of controversy courts traditionally resolve. Here at issue is the production or nonproduction of specified evidence deemed by the Special Prosecutor to be relevant and admissible in a pending criminal case. It is sought by one official of the Government within the scope of his express authority; it is resisted by the Chief Executive on the ground of his duty to preserve the confidentiality of the communications of the President. Whatever the correct answer on the merits, these issues are "of a type which are traditionally justiciable." . . .

In light of the uniqueness of the setting in which the conflict arises, the fact that both parties are officers of the Executive Branch cannot be viewed as a barrier to justiciability. It would be inconsistent with the applicable law and regulation and the unique facts of this case to conclude other than that the Special Prosecutor has standing to bring this action and that a justiciable controversy is presented for decision. . . .

THE CLAIM OF PRIVILEGE

A

. . . [W]e turn to the claim that the subpoena should be quashed because it demands "confidential conversations between a President and his close advisors that it would be inconsistent with the public interest to produce." *** The first contention is a broad claim that the separation of powers doctrine precludes judicial review of a President's claim of privilege. The second contention is that if he does not prevail on the claim of absolute privilege, the court should hold as a matter of constitutional law that the privilege prevails over the *subpoena duces tecum*.

In the performance of assigned constitutional duties each branch of the Government must initially interpret the Constitution, and the interpretation of its power by any branch is due great respect from the others. The President's counsel, as we have noted, reads the Constitution as providing an absolute privilege of confidentiality for all presidential communications. Many decisions of this Court, however, have unequivocally reaffirmed the holding of *Marbury v. Madison* *** that "[i]t is emphatically the province and duty of the judicial department to say what the law is." ***

No holding of the Court has defined the scope of judicial power specifically relating to the enforce-

ment of a subpoena for confidential presidential communications for use in a criminal prosecution, but other exercises of powers by the Executive Branch and the Legislative Branch have been found invalid as in conflict with the Constitution. . . . Since this Court has consistently exercised the power to construe and delineate claims arising under express powers, it must follow that the Court has authority to interpret claims with respect to powers alleged to derive from enumerated powers.

Our system of government "requires that federal courts on occasion interpret the Constitution in a manner at variance with the construction given the document by another branch." *** And in *Baker v. Carr* *** the Court stated:

[d]eciding whether a matter has in any measure been committed by the Constitution to another branch of government, or whether the action of that branch exceeds whatever authority has been committed, is itself a delicate exercise in constitutional interpretation, and is a responsibility of this Court as ultimate interpreter of the Constitution.

Notwithstanding the deference each branch must accord the others, the "judicial power of the United States" vested in the federal courts by Art. III, Sec. 1 of the Constitution can no more be shared with the Executive Branch than the Chief Executive, for example, can share with the Judiciary the veto power, or the Congress share with the Judiciary the power to override a Presidential veto. Any other conclusion would be contrary to the basic concept of separation of powers and the checks and balances that flow from the scheme of a tripartite government. *** We therefore reaffirm that it is the province and the duty of this Court "to say what the law is" with respect to the claim of privilege presented in this case. ***

B

In support of his claim of absolute privilege, the President's counsel urges two grounds, one of which is common to all governments and one of which is peculiar to our system of separation of powers. The first ground is the valid need for protection of communications between high government officials and those who advise and assist them in the performance of their manifold duties; the importance of this confidentiality is too plain to require further discussion.

Human experience teaches that those who expect public dissemination of their remarks may well temper candor with a concern for appearances and for their own interests to the detriment of the decision-making process. Whatever the nature of the privilege of confidentiality of presidential communications in the exercise of Art. II powers, the privilege can be said to derive from the supremacy of each branch within its own assigned area of constitutional duties. Certain powers and privileges flow from the nature of enumerated powers; the protection of confidentiality of Presidential communications has similar constitutional underpinnings.

The second ground asserted by the President's counsel in support of the claim of absolute privilege rests on the doctrine of separation of powers. Here it is argued that the independence of the Executive Branch within its own sphere *** insulates a president from a judicial subpoena in an ongoing criminal prosecution, and thereby protects confidential presidential communications.

However, neither the doctrine of separation of powers, nor the need for confidentiality of high level communications, without more, can sustain an absolute, unqualified presidential privilege of immunity from judicial process under all circumstances. The President's need for complete candor and objectivity from advisers calls for great deference from the courts. However, when the privilege depends solely on the broad, undifferentiated claim of public interest in the confidentiality of such conversations, a confrontation with other values arises. Absent a claim of need to protect military, diplomatic or sensitive national security secrets, we find it difficult to accept the argument that even the very important interest in confidentiality of presidential communications is significantly diminished by production of such material for *in camera* inspection with all the protection that a district court will be obliged to provide.

The impediment that an absolute, unqualified privilege would place in the way of the primary constitutional duty of the Judicial Branch to do justice in criminal prosecutions would plainly conflict with the function of the courts under Art. III. In designing the structure of our Government and dividing and allocating the sovereign power among three co-equal branches, the Framers of the Constitution sought to provide a comprehensive system, but the separate powers were not intended to operate with absolute independence. . . . To read the Art. II powers of the President as providing an absolute privilege as against a subpoena essential to enforcement of criminal statutes on no more than a generalized claim of the public interest in confidentiality of nonmilitary and nondiplomatic discussions would upset the constitutional balance of "a workable government" and gravely impair the role of the courts under Art. III.

C

Since we conclude that the legitimate needs of the judicial process may outweigh presidential privilege, it is necessary to resolve those competing interests in a manner that preserves the essential functions of each branch. The right and indeed the duty to resolve that question does not free the judiciary from according high respect to the representations made on behalf of the President. ***

The expectation of a President to the confidentiality of his conversations and correspondence, like the claim of confidentiality of judicial deliberations, for example, has all the values to which we accord deference for the privacy of all citizens and added to those values the necessity for protection of the public interest in candid, objective, and even blunt or harsh opinions in presidential decision making. A President and those who assist him must be free to explore alternatives in the process of shaping policies and making decisions and to do so in a way many would be unwilling to express except privately. These are the considerations justifying a presumptive privilege for presidential communications. The privilege is fundamental to the operation of government and inextricably rooted in the separation of powers under the Constitution. . . .

But this presumptive privilege must be considered in light of our historic commitment to the rule of law. . . . We have elected to employ an adversary system of criminal justice in which the parties contest all issues before a court of law. The need to develop all relevant facts in the adversary system is both fundamental and comprehensive. The ends of criminal justice would be defeated if judgments were to be founded on a partial or speculative presentation of the facts. The very integrity of the judicial system and public confidence in the system depend on full disclosure of all the facts, within the framework of the rules of evidence. To ensure that justice is done, it is imperative to the function of courts that compulsory process be available for the production of evidence needed either by the prosecution or by the defense. . . .

In this case the President challenges a subpoena served on him as a third party requiring the production of materials for use in a criminal prosecution on the claim that he has a privilege against disclosure of confidential communications. He does not place his claim of privilege on the ground they are military or diplomatic secrets. As to these areas of Art. II duties the courts have traditionally shown the utmost deference to presidential responsibilities. . . . No case of the Court, however, has extended this high degree of deference to a President's generalized interest in confidentiality. Nowhere in the Constitution, as we have noted earlier, is there any explicit reference to a privilege of confidentiality, yet to the extent this interest relates to the effective discharge of a President's powers, it is constitutionally based.

The right to the production of all evidence at a criminal trial similarly has constitutional dimensions. The Sixth Amendment explicitly confers upon every defendant in a criminal trial the right "to be confronted with the witnesses against him" and "to have compulsory process for obtaining witnesses in his favor." Moreover, the Fifth Amendment also guarantees that no person shall be deprived of liberty without due process of law. It is the manifest duty of the courts to vindicate those guarantees and to accomplish that it is essential that all relevant and admissible evidence be produced.

In this case we must weigh the importance of the general privilege of confidentiality of presidential communications in performance of his responsibilities against the inroads of such a privilege on the fair administration of criminal justice. The interest in preserving confidentiality is weighty indeed and entitled to great respect. However, we cannot conclude that advisers will be moved to temper the candor of their remarks by the infrequent occasions of disclosure because of the possibility that such conversations will be called for in the context of a criminal prosecution.

On the other hand, the allowance of the privilege to withhold evidence that is demonstrably relevant in a criminal trial would cut deeply into the guarantee of due process of law and gravely impair the basic function of the courts. A President's acknowledged need for confidentiality in the communications of his office is general in nature, whereas the constitutional need for production of relevant evidence in a criminal proceeding is specific and central to the fair adjudication of a particular criminal case in the administration of justice. Without access to specific facts a criminal prosecution may be totally frustrated. The President's broad interest in confidentiality of communications will not be vitiated by disclosure of a limited number of conversations preliminarily shown to have some bearing on the pending criminal cases.

We conclude that when the ground for asserting privilege as to subpoenaed materials sought for use in a criminal trial is based only on the generalized interest in confidentiality, it cannot prevail over the fundamental demands of due process of law in the fair administration of criminal justice. The generalized assertion of privilege must yield to the demonstrated, specific need for evidence in a pending criminal trial. . . .

*[**Justice Rehnquist** did not participate in this decision.]*

Texas v. Johnson

491 U.S. 397; 109 S. Ct. 2533; 105 L. Ed. 2d 342 (1989)
Vote: 5-4

After burning an American flag as part of a public protest, Gregory Lee Johnson was convicted of desecrating a flag in violation of Texas law. The Texas Court of Criminal Appeals reversed the conviction, holding that the statute under which Johnson was convicted was unconstitutional as applied to his particular conduct. The State of Texas petitioned the U.S. Supreme Court for certiorari.

Justice Brennan delivered the opinion of the Court.

I

While the Republican National Convention was taking place in Dallas in 1984, respondent Johnson participated in a political demonstration dubbed the "Republican War Chest Tour." As explained in literature distributed by the demonstrators and in speeches made by them, the purpose of this event was to protest the policies of the Reagan administration and of certain Dallas-based corporations. The demonstrators marched through the Dallas streets, chanting political slogans and stopping at several corporate locations to stage "die-ins" intended to dramatize the consequences of nuclear war. On several occasions they spray-painted the walls of buildings and overturned potted plants, but Johnson himself took no part in such activities. He did, however, accept an American flag handed to him by a fellow protestor who had taken it from a flag pole outside one of the targeted buildings.

The demonstration ended in front of Dallas City Hall, where Johnson unfurled the American flag, doused it with kerosene, and set it on fire. While the flag burned, the protestors chanted, "America, the red, white, and blue, we spit on you." After the demonstrators dispersed, a witness to the flag-burning collected the flag's remains and buried them in his backyard. No one was physically injured or threatened with injury, though several witnesses testified that they had been seriously offended by the flag-burning.

Of the approximately 100 demonstrators, Johnson alone was charged with a crime. The only criminal offense with which he was charged was the desecration of a venerated object in violation of Tex. Penal Code Ann. Sec. 42.09 (a)(3) (1989). After a trial, he was convicted, sentenced to one year in prison, and fined $2,000. The Court of Appeals for the Fifth District of Texas at Dallas affirmed Johnson's conviction, *** but the Texas Court of Criminal Appeals reversed, *** holding that the State could not, consistent with the First Amendment, punish Johnson for burning the flag in these circumstances.

Because it reversed Johnson's conviction on the ground that Sec. 42.09 was unconstitutional as applied to him, the state court did not address Johnson's argument that the statute was, on its face, unconstitutionally vague and overbroad. We granted certiorari, *** and now affirm.

II

Johnson was convicted of flag desecration for burning the flag rather than for uttering insulting words. This fact somewhat complicates our consideration of his conviction under the First Amendment. We must first determine whether Johnson's burning of the flag constituted expressive conduct, permitting him to invoke the First Amendment in challenging his conviction. *** If his conduct was expressive, we next decide whether the State's regulation is related to the suppression of free expression. *** If the State's regulation is not related to expression, then the less stringent standard we announced in *United States v. O'Brien* [1968] for regulations of noncommunicative conduct controls. *** If it is, then we are outside of *O'Brien*'s test, and we must ask whether this interest justifies Johnson's conviction under a more demanding standard. *** A third possibility is that the State's asserted interest is simply not implicated on these facts, and in that event the interest drops out of the picture. ***

The First Amendment literally forbids the abridgement only of "speech," but we have long recognized that its protection does not end at the spoken or written word. While we have rejected "the view that an apparently limitless variety of conduct can be labeled 'speech' whenever the person engaging in the conduct intends thereby to express an idea," *** we have acknowledged that conduct may be "sufficiently imbued with elements of communication to fall within the scope of the First and Fourteenth Amendments." ***

In deciding whether particular conduct possesses sufficient communicative elements to bring the First Amendment into play, we have asked whether "[a]n intent to convey a particularized message was present, and [whether] the likelihood was great that the message was present, and [whether] the likelihood was great that the message would be understood by those who viewed it." Hence, we have recognized the expressive nature of students' wearing of black armbands to protest American military involvement in Vietnam, *** of the wearing of American military uniforms in a dramatic presentation criticizing American involvement in Vietnam, *** and of picketing about a wide variety of causes. ***

Especially pertinent to this case are our decisions recognizing the communicative nature of conduct relating to flags. Attaching a peace sign to the flag, *** saluting the flag, *** and displaying a red flag, *** we have held, all may find shelter under the First Amendment. *** That we have had little difficulty identifying an expressive element in conduct relating to flags should not be surprising. The very purpose of a national flag is to serve as a symbol of our country; it is, one might say, "the one visible manifestation of two hundred years of nationhood." *** Pregnant with expressive content, the flag as readily signifies this Nation as does the combination of letters found in "America."

We have not automatically concluded, however, that any action taken with respect to our flag is expressive. Instead, in characterizing such action for First Amendment purposes, we have considered the context in which it occurred.

The State of Texas conceded for purposes of its oral argument in this case that Johnson's conduct was expressive conduct. *** Johnson burned an American flag as part—indeed, as the culmination—of a political demonstration that coincided with the convening of the Republican Party and its renomination of Ronald Reagan for President. The expressive, overtly political nature of this conduct was both intentional and overwhelmingly apparent. . . .

III

The government generally has a freer hand in restricting expressive conduct than it has in restricting the written or spoken word. *** It may not, however, proscribe particular conduct *because* it has expressive elements. . . . It is, in short, not simply the verbal or nonverbal nature of the expression, but the governmental interest at stake, that helps to determine whether a restriction on that expression is valid. . . .

In order to decide whether *O'Brien*'s test applies here, therefore we must decide whether Texas has asserted an interest in support of Johnson's conviction that is unrelated to the suppression of expression. If we find that an interest asserted by the State is simply not implicated on the facts before us, we need not ask whether *O'Brien*'s test applies. *** The State offers two separate interests to justify this conviction: preventing breaches of the peace, and preserving the flag as a symbol of nationhood and national unity. We hold that the first interest is not implicated on this record and that the second is related to the suppression of expression.

A

Texas claims that its interest in preventing breaches of the peace justifies Johnson's conviction for flag desecration. However, no disturbance of the peace actually occurred or threatened to occur because of Johnson's burning of the flag. Although the State stresses the disruptive behavior of the protestors during their march toward City Hall, *** it admits that no actual breach of the peace "occurred at the time of the flagburning or in response to the flagburning." The State's emphasis on the protestors' disorderly actions prior to arriving at City Hall is not only somewhat surprising given that no charges were brought on the basis of this conduct, but it also fails to show that a disturbance of the peace was a likely reaction to Johnson's conduct. The only evidence offered by the State at trial to show the reaction to Johnson's actions was the testimony of several persons who had been seriously offended by the flag-burning.

The State's position, therefore, amounts to a claim that an audience that takes serious offense at particular expression is necessarily likely to disturb the peace and that the expression may be prohibited on this basis. Our precedents do not countenance such a presumption. On the contrary, they recognize that a principal "function of free speech under our system of government is to invite dispute. It may indeed best serve its high purpose when it induces a condition of unrest, creates dissatisfaction with conditions as they are, or even stirs people to anger." ***

... Johnson's expressive conduct [does not] fall within that small class of "fighting words" that are "likely to provoke the average person to retaliation, and thereby cause a breach of the peace." *** No reasonable onlooker would have regarded Johnson's generalized expression of dissatisfaction with the policies of the Federal Government as a direct personal insult or an invitation to exchange fisticuffs.

We thus conclude that the State's interest in maintaining order is not implicated on these facts. The State need not worry that our holding will disable it from preserving the peace. We do not suggest that the First Amendment forbids a State to prevent "imminent lawless action." *** ...

B

The State also asserts an interest in preserving the flag as a symbol of nationhood and national unity.... The State, apparently, is concerned that ... [flag burning] will lead people to believe either that the flag does not stand for nationhood and national unity, but instead reflects other, less positive concepts, or that the concepts reflected in the flag do not in fact exist, that is, we do not enjoy unity as a Nation. These concerns blossom only when a person's treatment of the flag communicates some message, and thus are related "to the suppression of free expression" within the meaning of *O'Brien*. We are thus outside of *O'Brien*'s test altogether.

IV

It remains to consider whether the State's interest in preserving the flag as a symbol of nationhood and national unity justifies Johnson's conviction.

... Johnson was not ... prosecuted for the expression of just any idea; he was prosecuted for his ex-

pression of dissatisfaction with the policies of this country, expression situated at the core of our First Amendment values. ***

Moreover, Johnson was prosecuted because he knew that his politically charged expression would cause "serious offense." If he had burned the flag as a means of disposing of it because it was dirty or torn, he would not have been convicted of flag desecration under this Texas law: federal law designates burning as the preferred means of disposing of a flag "when it is in such condition that it is no longer a fitting emblem for display," *** and Texas has no quarrel with this means of disposal. The Texas law is thus not aimed at protecting the physical integrity of the flag in all circumstances, but is designed instead to protect it only against impairments that would cause serious offense to others....

Whether Johnson's treatment of the flag violated Texas law thus depended on the likely communicative impact of his expressive conduct. ... [T]his restriction on Johnson's expression is content-based.

... Johnson's political expression was restricted because of the content of the message he conveyed. We must therefore subject the State's asserted interest in preserving the special symbolic character of the flag to "the most exacting scrutiny." ***

If there is a bedrock principle underlying the First Amendment, it is that Government may not prohibit the expression of an idea simply because society finds the idea itself offensive or disagreeable. ***

... [N]othing in our precedents suggests that a State may foster its own view of the flag by prohibiting expressive conduct relating to it....

There is, moreover, no indication—either in the text of the Constitution or in our cases interpreting it—that a separate judicial category exists for the American flag alone. Indeed, we would not be surprised to learn that the persons who framed our Constitution and wrote the Amendment that we now construe were not known for their reverence for the Union Jack. The First Amendment does not guarantee that other concepts virtually sacred to our Nation as a whole—such as the principle that discrimination on the basis of race is odious and destructive—will go unquestioned in the marketplace of ideas. *** We decline, therefore to create for the flag an exception to the joust of principles protected by the First Amendment.

It is not the State's ends, but its means, to which we object. It cannot be gainsaid that there is a special place reserved for the flag in this Nation, and thus we do not doubt that the Government has a legitimate interest in making efforts to "preserv[e] the national flag as an unalloyed symbol of our country." . . . Congress has, for example, enacted precatory regulations describing the proper treatment of the flag *** and we cast no doubt on the legitimacy of its interest in making such recommendations. To say that the Government has an interest in encouraging proper treatment of the flag, however, is not to say that it may criminally punish a person for burning a flag as a means of political protest. . . .

We are tempted to say . . . that the flag's deservedly cherished place in our community will be strengthened, not weakened, by our holding today. Our decision is a reaffirmation of the principles of freedom and inclusiveness that the flag best reflects, and of the conviction that our toleration of criticism such as Johnson's is a sign and source of our strength.

The way to preserve the flag's special role is not to punish those who feel differently about these matters. It is to persuade them that they are wrong.

. . . [P]recisely because it is our flag that is involved, one's response to the flag-burners may exploit the uniquely persuasive power of the flag itself. We can imagine no more appropriate response to burning a flag than waving one's own, no better way to counter a flag-burner's message than by saluting the flag that burns, no surer means of preserving the dignity even of the flag that burned than by—as one witness here did—according its remains a respectful burial. We do not consecrate the flag by punishing its desecration, for in doing so we dilute the freedom that this cherished emblem represents.

V

. . . The judgment of the Texas Court of Criminal Appeals is . . . affirmed.

Justice Kennedy, concurring.

I write not to qualify the words Justice Brennan chooses so well, for he says with power all that is necessary to explain our ruling. I join his opinion without reservation, but with a keen sense that this case, like others before us from time to time, exacts its personal toll. This prompts me to add to our pages these few remarks.

The case before us illustrates better than most that the judicial power is often difficult in its exercise. We cannot here ask another branch to share responsibility, as when the argument is made that a statute is flawed or incomplete. For we are presented with a clear and simple statute to be judged against a pure command of the Constitution. The outcome can be laid at no door but ours.

The hard fact is that sometimes we must make decisions we do not like. We make them because they are right, right in the sense that the law and the Constitution, as we see them, compel the result. And so great is our commitment to the process that, except in the rare case, we do not pause to express distaste for the result, perhaps for fear of undermining a valued principle that dictates the decision. This is one of those rare cases.

Our colleagues in dissent advance powerful arguments why respondent may be convicted for his expression, reminding us that among those who will be dismayed by our holding will be some who have had the singular honor of carrying the flag in battle. And I agree that the flag holds a lonely place of honor in an age when absolutes are distrusted and simple truths are burdened by unneeded apologetics.

With all respect to those views, I do not believe the Constitution gives us the right to rule as the dissenting members of the Court urge, however painful this judgment is to announce. Though symbols often are what we ourselves make of them, the flag is constant in expressing beliefs in law and peace and that freedom which sustains the human spirit. The case here today forces recognition of the costs to which those beliefs commit us. It is poignant but fundamental that the flag protects those who hold it in contempt.

For all the record shows, this respondent was not a philosopher and perhaps did not even possess the ability to comprehend how repellent his statements must be to the Republic itself. But whether or not he could appreciate the enormity of the offense he gave, the fact remains that his acts were speech, in both the technical and the fundamental meaning of the Constitution. So I agree with the Court that he must go free.

Chief Justice Rehnquist, with whom ***Justice White*** and ***Justice O'Connor*** join, dissenting.

In holding this Texas statute unconstitutional, the Court ignores Justice Holmes' familiar aphorism that "a page of history is worth a volume of logic." *** For more than 200 years, the American flag has occupied a unique position as the symbol of our Nation, a uniqueness that justifies a governmental prohibition against flag burning in the way respondent Johnson did here. . . .

Here it may equally well be said that the public burning of the American flag by Johnson was no essential part of any exposition of ideas, and at the same time it had a tendency to incite a breach of the peace. Johnson was free to make any verbal denunciation of the flag that he wished; indeed, he was free to burn the flag in private. He could publicly burn other symbols of the Government or effigies of political leaders. He did lead a march through the streets of Dallas, and conducted a rally in front of the Dallas City Hall. He engaged in a "die-in" to protest nuclear weapons. He shouted out various slogans during the march, including: "Reagan, Mondale which will it be? Either one means World War III"; "Ronald Reagan, killer of the hour, perfect example of US power"; and "red, white and blue, we spit on you, you stand for plunder, you will go under." *** For none of these acts was he arrested or prosecuted; it was only when he proceeded to burn publicly an American flag stolen from its rightful owner that he violated the Texas statute. . . .

The Court concludes its opinion with a regrettably patronizing civics lecture, presumably addressed to the Members of both Houses of Congress, the members of the 48 state legislatures that enacted prohibitions against flag burning, and the troops fighting under that flag in Vietnam who objected to its being burned: "The way to preserve the flag's special role is not to punish those who feel differently about these matters. It is to persuade them that they are wrong." *** The Court's role as the final expositor of the Constitution is well established, but its role as a platonic guardian admonishing those responsible to public opinion as if they were truant school children has no similar place in our system of government. The cry of "no taxation without representation" animated those who revolted against the English Crown to found our Nation—the idea that those who submitted to government should have some say as to what kind of laws would be passed. Surely one of the high purposes of a democratic society is to legislate against conduct that is regarded as evil and profoundly offensive to the majority of people—whether it be murder, embezzlement, pollution, or flag burning.

Our Constitution wisely places limits on powers of legislative majorities to act, but the declaration of such limits by this Court "is, at all times, a question of much delicacy which ought seldom, if ever, to be decided in the affirmative, in a doubtful case." *** Uncritical extension of constitutional protection to the burning of the flag risks the frustration of the very purpose for which organized governments are instituted. The Court decides that the American flag is just another symbol, about which not only must opinions pro and con be tolerated, but for which the most minimal public respect may not be enjoined. The government may conscript men into the Armed Forces where they must fight and perhaps die for the flag, but the government may not prohibit the public burning of the banner under which they fight. I would uphold the Texas statute as applied in this case.

Justice Stevens, dissenting.

As the Court analyzes this case, it presents the question whether the State of Texas, or indeed the Federal Government, has the power to prohibit the public desecration of the American flag. The question is unique. In my judgment rules that apply to a host of other symbols, such as state flags, armbands, or various privately promoted emblems of political or commercial identity, are not necessarily controlling. Even if flag burning could be considered just another species of symbolic speech under the logical application of the rules that the Court has developed in its interpretation of the First Amendment in other contexts, this case has an intangible dimension that makes those rules inapplicable.

A country's flag is a symbol of more than "nationhood and national unity." *** It also signifies the ideas that characterize the society that has chosen that emblem as well as the special history that has animated the growth and power of those ideas. The fleur-de-lis and the tricolor both symbolized "nationhood and national unity," but they had vastly different meanings. The message conveyed by some flags—the swastika, for example—may survive long after it has outlived its usefulness as a symbol of regimented unity in a particular nation.

So it is with the American flag. It is more than a proud symbol of the courage, the determination, and the gifts of nature that transformed 13 fledgling Colonies into a world power. It is a symbol of freedom, of equal opportunity, of religious tolerance, and of goodwill for other peoples who share our aspirations. The symbol carries its message to dissidents both at home and abroad who may have no interest at all in our national unity or survival.

The value of the flag as a symbol cannot be measured. Even so, I have no doubt that the interest in preserving that value for the future is both significant and legitimate. Conceivably that value will be enhanced by the Court's conclusion that our national commitment to free expression is so strong that even the United States as ultimate guarantor of that freedom is without power to prohibit the desecration of its unique symbol. But I am unpersuaded. The creation of a federal right to post bulletin boards and graffiti on the Washington Monument might enlarge the market for free expression, but at a cost I would not pay. . . .

The Court is . . . quite wrong in blandly asserting that respondent "was prosecuted for his expression of dissatisfaction with the policies of this country, expression situated at the core of our First Amendment values." *** Respondent was prosecuted because of the method he chose to express his dissatisfaction with those policies. Had he chosen to spray paint—or perhaps convey with a motion picture projector—his message of dissatisfaction on the facade of the Lincoln Memorial, there would be no question about the power of the Government to prohibit his means of expression. The prohibition would be supported by the legitimate interest in preserving the quality of an important national asset. Though the asset at stake in this case is intangible, given its unique value, the same interest supports a prohibition on the desecration of the American flag.

The ideas of liberty and equality have been an irresistible force in motivating leaders like Patrick Henry, Susan B. Anthony, and Abraham Lincoln, schoolteachers like Nathan Hale and Booker T. Washington, the Philippine Scouts who fought at Bataan, and the soldiers who scaled the bluff at Omaha Beach. If those ideas are worth fighting for—and our history demonstrates that they are—it cannot be true that the flag that uniquely symbolizes their power is not itself worthy of protection from unnecessary desecration.

I respectfully dissent.

CHAPTER THREE

EXTERNAL CONSTRAINTS ON JUDICIAL POWER

The Supreme Court is a tribunal of limited jurisdiction, narrow processes, and small capacity for handling mass litigation; it has no force to coerce obedience, and is subject to being stripped of jurisdiction or smothered with additional Justices any time such a disposition exists and is supported strongly enough by public opinion. I think the Court can never quite escape consciousness of its own infirmities. . . .

Justice Robert H. Jackson,
The Supreme Court in the American System of Government (1955)

Robert Jackson, Associate
Justice, 1941–1954

INTRODUCTION

The concept of checks and balances is one of the fundamental principles of the American Constitution. Each branch of the national government is provided specific means of limiting the exercise of power by the other branches. For example, the president may veto acts of Congress, which will not become law unless the veto is overridden by a two-thirds vote in both houses.

Although the federal courts, and the Supreme Court in particular, are often characterized as guardians of the Constitution, the judicial branch is by no means immune to the abuse of power. Accordingly, the federal judiciary is subject to checks and balances imposed by Congress and the president. In a constitutional system that seeks to prevent any agency of government from exercising unchecked power, even the Supreme Court is subject to external limitations. These limitations may not be as great as suggested in the passage by former Supreme Court Justice Robert Jackson, but they are significant nevertheless.

JUDICIAL DEPENDENCY ON CONGRESS

Article III of the Constitution recognizes the judiciary as a separate branch of government, but it also requires the courts to depend on Congress in a number of ways. The federal courts, including the Supreme Court, depend on Congress for their budgets, although Congress is prohibited from reducing the salaries of federal judges. The organization and jurisdiction, indeed the very existence, of the lower federal courts is left entirely to Congress by Article III. It is quite conceivable that Congress might have chosen not to create a system of lower federal courts at all. It could have granted existing state tribunals original jurisdiction in federal cases, although it certainly would have been required to provide some degree of appellate review by the U.S. Supreme Court, the one federal tribunal recognized by the Constitution. Rather quickly, however, Congress passed the Judiciary Act of 1789, which provided the basis for the contemporary system of lower federal courts (see Chapter 1).

Lower Federal Court Jurisdiction

Under Article III, Congress also controls the jurisdiction, both original and appellate, of the lower federal courts. The tendency over the years has been to expand federal jurisdiction, but recently proposals have surfaced that would limit the authority of federal courts to hear certain types of cases. In particular, some have suggested that the statute permitting federal courts to issue writs of habeas corpus to review state criminal cases be restricted or repealed. The federal courts acquired this authority from Congress shortly after the Civil War. In passing the Habeas Corpus Act of 1867, Congress was concerned about the possibility that southern state courts would mistreat blacks and other persons sympathetic to the Union during the Civil War. The purpose of the act was to extend a measure of federal judicial supervision over state court systems to ensure that federal constitutional rights would be observed. Today, federal habeas corpus is frequently used by state prisoners who have exhausted their appeals in the state courts and wish to carry on their fight in federal court. Critics argue that this causes the federal courts to be inundated with frivolous claims and permits federal judges to second-guess the decisions of the state courts. Defenders of the status quo argue that federal habeas corpus is necessary to prevent miscarriages of justice and ensure that federal constitutional rights are uniformly respected throughout the states. The essential point is that this jurisdiction was created by Congress and can be removed by Congress through ordinary legislation. It remains to be seen what, if anything, Congress will do in this area.

It is unclear how far Congress may go in reducing federal jurisdiction. At some point, restriction of jurisdiction would undermine the system of checks and balances and endanger individual rights. In *Battaglia v. General Motors Corp.* (1948), the Supreme Court said that "...while Congress has the undoubted power to give, withhold and restrict the jurisdiction of courts other than the Supreme Court, it must not exercise that power so as to deprive any person of life, liberty or property without due process of law or to take private property without just compensation." It is unlikely that the Supreme Court would uphold a statute seriously eroding lower-court jurisdiction, but such a law is not likely to be enacted. Clearly, Congress has the authority to restrict federal jurisdiction on a limited basis.

Just as Congress may expand or delimit federal jurisdiction, it may also increase or reduce the powers of the lower federal courts to render certain kinds of judgments and issue certain types of orders. The Judiciary Act of 1789 gave the federal courts authority to issue a variety of writs in support of their judgments. Since 1789, the authority of federal judges to issue judgments, orders, and decrees has expanded. For example, Congress has authorized the federal courts to render **declaratory judgments** and issue **injunctions** in order to prevent injuries to plaintiffs' legal rights. On the other hand, Congress has on occasion restricted the power of the federal courts to issue certain types of orders. Under the Norris-LaGuardia Act of 1932, Congress restricted the power of federal district courts to issue injunctions in labor disputes. In *Lauf v. E.G. Skinner & Co.* (1938), the Supreme Court upheld the Norris-LaGuardia Act, saying that "there can be no question of the power of Congress thus to define and limit the jurisdiction of the inferior courts of the United States."

Congress has even been permitted to frustrate judicial review in the lower federal courts by granting those courts the authority to enforce laws but denying them the right to rule on the constitutionality thereof. The Emergency Price Control Act adopted during World War II provided for criminal prosecution of parties who violated emergency price controls imposed by a federal agency. Yet the act prohibited all lower federal courts except the Emergency Court of Appeals from entertaining challenges to the constitutionality of the controls. In *Yakus v. United States* (1944), the Supreme Court upheld this arrangement, saying that "there is no constitutional requirement that [determinations of constitutionality] ... be made in one tribunal rather than another, so long as there is the opportunity to be heard...." Dissenting, Justice Wiley Rutledge complained that "[i]t is one thing for Congress to withhold jurisdiction. It is entirely another to confer it and direct that it be exercised in a manner inconsistent with constitutional requirements. . . ." It should be pointed out, however, that *Yakus* was decided amidst the crisis atmosphere of World War II; it is unlikely that the Supreme Court would allow Congress to restrict the lower courts' power of judicial review under more conventional circumstances.

Restriction of the Supreme Court's Jurisdiction

The Supreme Court's original jurisdiction is fixed by Article III of the Constitution. *Marbury v. Madison* made clear that Congress may alter neither the Court's original jurisdiction nor its power to issue orders in such cases. Congress may, however, authorize lower federal courts to share the Court's original jurisdiction. The Supreme Court's appellate jurisdiction is another matter. Article III indicates that the Court ". . . shall have appellate Jurisdiction, both as to Law and Fact, with such Exceptions, and under such Regulations as the Congress shall make."

The McCardle Case

On only one occasion since 1789 has Congress significantly limited the appellate jurisdiction of the Supreme Court. It happened in 1869, during the turbulent Reconstruction period. After the Civil War, Congress passed the Reconstruction Acts, which, among other things, imposed military rule on most of the southern states formerly comprising the Confederacy. As part of this program, military tribunals were authorized to try civilians who interfered with Reconstruction. William H. McCardle, editor of the *Vicksburg Times,* published a series of editorials highly critical of Reconstruction. Consequently, he was arrested by the military and held for trial by a military tribunal. McCardle sought release from custody through a petition for habeas corpus in federal court. As noted earlier, Congress in 1867 had extended federal habeas corpus jurisdiction to cover state prisoners. This applied to McCardle, since he was in the custody of the military government of Mississippi. The 1867 Reconstruction Act also provided a right of appeal to the Supreme Court. Having lost his bid for relief in the lower court, McCardle exercised his right to appeal.

After *Ex Parte McCardle* was argued in the Supreme Court, Congress enacted legislation, over President Andrew Johnson's veto, withdrawing the Supreme Court's appellate jurisdiction in habeas corpus cases. The obvious motive was to prevent the Court from ruling on the constitutionality of the Reconstruction Acts, which McCardle had challenged in his appeal. The Court could have declared unconstitutional this blatant attempt to prevent the Court from exercising its power of judicial review. But the Court chose to capitulate. By acquiescing in the withdrawal of its jurisdiction in *McCardle,* the Court avoided a direct confrontation with Congress at a time when that institution was dominant in the national government. Shortly before *McCardle* was decided, the House of Representatives had impeached President Andrew Johnson, and he escaped conviction in the Senate by only one vote. It is likely that the Court's decision to back down was somewhat influenced by the Johnson impeachment.

Does *Ex Parte McCardle* imply that Congress could completely abolish the Court's appellate jurisdiction? Whatever the answer might have been in 1869, the answer today would certainly be no. It is highly unlikely that Congress would ever undertake such a radical measure, but if it did, the Supreme Court would almost certainly declare the act invalid. Since the Court's major decision-making role is a function of its appellate jurisdiction, any serious curtailment of that jurisdiction would in effect deny the Court the ability to perform its essential function in the constitutional system.

There is even doubt that the *McCardle* decision would be reaffirmed if the contemporary Supreme Court were faced with a similar question. In *Glidden v. Zdanok* (1962), Justice William O. Douglas mused that "there is a serious question whether the *McCardle* case could command a majority today." One can argue that the Court would not, and should not, permit Congress to restrict its appellate jurisdiction if by so doing Congress would curtail the Court's ability to enforce constitutional principles or protect citizens' fundamental rights.

More Recent Developments

Congress has, on several occasions, debated limitations on the Supreme Court's appellate jurisdiction. In the late 1950s, there was a movement in Congress to deny the Supreme Court appellate jurisdiction in cases involving national security, a reaction to Warren Court decisions protecting the rights of suspected Communists. Although the major legislative proposals were narrowly defeated, the Court retreated from the most controversial decisions of 1956 and 1957. In this regard, it is instructive to compare *Pennsylvania v. Nelson* (1956) and *Watkins v. United States* (1957) with *Uphaus v. Wyman* (1959) and *Barenblatt v. United States* (1959).

In the early 1980s, a flurry of activity in Congress was aimed at restricting Supreme Court jurisdiction to hear appeals in cases dealing with abortion. A number of proposals surfaced, but none was adopted. The constitutionality of such proposals is open to question, in that they might be construed as undermining the Court's ability to protect fundamental constitutional rights. The question remains academic, however, as Congress has not enacted such a restriction on the Court. Denial of jurisdiction as a limiting strategy depends greatly on the substantive-issue area involved, what the Court has done in the area thus far, and what it is likely to do in the future. As a retaliation against the Court for one controversial decision, the curtailment of appellate jurisdiction is not likely to be an effective strategy.

Constitutional Amendment

By far the most effective means of overruling a Supreme Court or any federal court decision is for Congress to use its power of amendment. If Congress disapproves of a particular judicial decision, it may be able to override that decision through a simple statute, but only if the decision was based on statutory interpretation. In *Grove City College v. Bell* (1984), for example, the Court was called upon to interpret Title IX of the Education Amendments of 1972, which prohibited sex discrimination by educational institutions receiving federal funds. In *Grove City,* the Court interpreted Title IX narrowly, so as to limit a potential plaintiff's ability to sue a college or university for sex discrimination. Congress disapproved of the Court's interpretation of Title IX and effectively nullified the Court's decision by adopting the Civil Rights Restoration Act of 1988 over President Reagan's veto. Since *Grove City College v. Bell* was based on the interpretation of a statute, rather than the Constitution, Congress could overrule the Court simply by amending the statute.

It is much more difficult for Congress to override a federal court decision that is based on the Constitution. Indeed, Congress alone cannot do so. Ever since *Marbury v. Madison,* our system of government has conceded to the courts the power to authoritatively interpret the nation's charter. A Supreme Court decision interpreting the Constitution is therefore final unless and until one of two things occurs. First, the Court may overrule itself in a later case. This has happened numerous times, the most notable example being the repudiation of official racial segregation in *Brown v. Board of Education* (1954). The only other way to overturn a constitutional decision of the Supreme Court is through constitutional amendment. This is not easily done, since Article V of the Constitution prescribes a two-thirds majority in both houses of Congress, followed by ratification by three-fourths of the states. Yet four times in our history, specific Supreme Court decisions have been overturned in this manner.

The Eleventh Amendment

The first ten amendments to the Constitution were adopted simultaneously in 1789 (ratified in 1791) and are known collectively as the **Bill of Rights.** These amendments were not responses to judicial decisions but rather to a perception that the original Constitution was incomplete. The Eleventh Amendment, however, was added to the Constitution in the aftermath of the Supreme Court's first major decision—*Chisholm v. Georgia* (1793).

Alexander Chisholm brought suit against the state of Georgia in the Supreme Court to recover a sum of money he owed to an estate of which he was executor. Because Chisholm was a citizen of South Carolina, the federal courts had jurisdiction, and since a state government was a party to the case, the case came under the original jurisdiction of the High Court. The state of Georgia denied that the Supreme Court had jurisdiction, claiming **sovereign immunity.** The state relied on statements made by James Madison, John Marshall, and Alexander Hamilton during the debates over ratification of the Constitution that states could not be made parties to federal cases against their consent. Indeed, Georgia failed to send a legal representative to defend its position when *Chisholm v. Georgia* came up for oral argument in the Supreme Court.

Dividing 4 to 1, the Supreme Court decided that the state of Georgia was subject to the lawsuit, sovereign immunity notwithstanding. This decision precipitated considerable outrage in the state legislatures, which feared an explosion of federal litigation at their expense. One newspaper, *The Independent Chronicle,* predicted that "... refugees, Tories, etc. ... will introduce such a series of litigations as will throw every State in the Union into the greatest confusion." Five years later, in 1798, the Eleventh Amendment was ratified. It reads:

> The Judicial power of the United States shall not be construed to extend to any suit in law or equity, commenced or prosecuted against one of the United States by Citizens of another State, or by Citizens or Subjects of any Foreign States.

The adoption of the Eleventh Amendment assuaged widespread fears of the new national government, and of the federal courts in particular. The Amendment also demonstrated that an unpopular Supreme Court decision was reversible, given sufficient political consensus. Despite its unequivocal language, the Eleventh Amendment has not proved to be a great barrier to federal judicial power vis-à-vis the states (see Chapter 8).

The Civil War Amendments

In *Dred Scott v. Sandford* (1857) (discussed in Chapter 2), the Supreme Court invalidated the Missouri Compromise of 1820, by which Congress had forbidden slavery in the northern federal territories. The Court's decision generated an outpouring of hostility, not only from abolitionists but also from moderate elements who supported congressional efforts to achieve a national compromise on the slavery question. After the Union victory in the Civil War, Congress adopted and the states ratified three constitutional amendments designed to protect the civil rights of the newly freed slaves. The Thirteenth Amendment outlawed slavery. The Fourteenth Amendment recognized "all persons born or naturalized in the United States" as citizens and forbade states from denying persons within their jurisdictions due process and equal protection of the law. The Fifteenth Amendment prohibited the state and federal governments from denying persons the right to vote "on account of race, color or previous condition of servitude." These three amendments, known collectively as the Civil War Amendments, not only nullified the *Dred Scott* decision but greatly expanded the rights of black Americans. Ironically, in light of *Dred Scott,* blacks would later look to the Supreme Court to enforce the provisions of the Civil War Amendments.

The Sixteenth Amendment

The Supreme Court's decision in *Pollock v. Farmer's Loan and Trust Co.* (1895) (also discussed in Chapter 2) invalidated an attempt by Congress to levy a national income tax. While the Court evidently considered the tax "a populistic assault on the institutions of private property and capitalism," Congress and the public perceived the Court's decision as reactionary and elitist. Ultimately, public opinion prevailed when the Sixteenth Amendment was ratified in 1913. It provides that:

> The Congress shall have power to lay and collect taxes on incomes, from whatever source derived, without apportionment among the several States, and without regard to any census or enumeration.

Interestingly, from time to time, one hears news reports of tax protesters who refuse to pay their federal income taxes on the ground that Congress lacks constitutional authority to tax incomes. The language of the Sixteenth Amendment to the contrary is quite clear and makes such a defense untenable in a prosecution for income tax evasion.

The Twenty-Sixth Amendment

In 1970, Congress enacted a statute lowering the voting age to eighteen in both state and federal elections. The states of Oregon and Texas filed suit under the original jurisdiction of the Supreme Court seeking an injunction preventing the attorney general from enforcing the statute with respect to the states. In *Oregon v. Mitchell* (1970), the Supreme Court ruled that Congress had no power to regulate the voting age in state elections. The Twenty-Sixth Amendment, ratified in 1971, accomplished what Congress was not permitted to do through statute. The Amendment provides:

> The right of citizens of the United States, who are eighteen years of age or older, to vote shall not be denied or abridged by the United States or by any State on account of age.

Other Proposed Constitutional Amendments

Over the years, numerous unsuccessful attempts have been made to overrule Supreme Court decisions through constitutional amendments. In 1983, an amendment providing that "[t]he right to an abortion is not secured by this Constitution," obviously aimed at *Roe v. Wade*, failed to pass the Senate by only one vote. In November 1971, a proposal designed to overrule the Supreme Court's school prayer decisions (see, for example, *Abington Township v. Schempp*, 1963) fell twenty-eight votes short of the necessary two-thirds majority in the House of Representatives. In his 1980 presidential campaign, Ronald Reagan called on Congress to resurrect the proposed school prayer amendment, but Congress proved unwilling to give the measure serious consideration. In the mid-1960s, a widely publicized effort to overrule the Supreme Court's reapportionment decisions (for example, *Reynolds v. Sims*, 1964) was spearheaded by Senate minority leader Everett Dirksen (R-Ill.). Despite auspicious beginnings, the Dirksen amendment ultimately proved to be a flash in the pan.

The most recent example of a proposed constitutional amendment aimed at a Supreme Court decision dealt with the emotional issue of flag-burning. In *Texas v. Johnson* (1989) [reprinted in Chapter 2], the Court held that burning the American flag as part of a public protest was a form of symbolic speech protected by the First Amendment. Many, including President Bush, called on Congress to overrule the Court. Congress considered an amendment that read, "The Congress and the States shall have power to prohibit the physical desecration of the flag of the United States." Votes were taken in both houses, but neither achieved the necessary two-thirds majority. In the wake of the failed constitutional amendment, Congress adopted a statute making flag desecration a federal offense. Like the state law struck down in *Texas v. Johnson*, this measure was declared unconstitutional by the Supreme Court (see *United States v. Eichman*, 1990).

APPOINTMENT AND REMOVAL OF FEDERAL JUDGES

As provided by the Constitution, federal judges, including Supreme Court justices, are appointed for life terms by the president, subject to the consent of the Senate. The grant of life tenure was intended to make the federal courts independent of partisan forces and public passions so that they could dispense justice impartially, according to the law. There is no question that life tenure has the effect of insulating the federal judiciary from political pressures. The only way to remove a sitting federal judge who refuses to resign is to initiate the cumbersome impeachment process. While a number of lower federal judges have been removed from office through impeachment, no justice of the Supreme Court has ever been removed from his position involuntarily (for more detailed discussion of impeachment, see Chapter 1).

Life tenure and the difficulty of impeachment make a president's appointments to the federal bench extremely critical. Recognizing that their judicial appointments will almost certainly outlast their time in office, presidents are apt to choose judicial nominees carefully. Lower federal court appointments are heavily influenced by considerations of patronage, however, with senators from the president's party exercising significant influence in the selection of federal judges within their states. The president exercises far more independence in nominating individuals to the Supreme Court.

Presidents cannot predict with certainty what their judicial nominees will do once on the bench. Consequently, presidents are not always happy with their judicial appointments. Dwight D. Eisenhower once remarked that his nomination of Earl Warren to be chief justice in 1953 was "the biggest damn fool mistake I ever made."

The Appointment Power as a Check on the Judiciary

As noted in Chapter 1, the shared presidential-senatorial power of appointing federal judges is an important means of influencing the judiciary. For example, President Richard Nixon made a significant impact on the Supreme Court and on American constitutional law through his appointment of four justices. During the 1968 presidential campaign, Nixon criticized the Warren Court's liberal decisions, especially in the criminal law area, and promised to appoint "strict constructionists" (widely interpreted to mean "conservatives") to the bench. President Nixon's first appointment came in 1969, when Warren E. Burger was selected to succeed Earl Warren as chief justice. In 1970, after the abortive nominations of Clement Haynsworth and G. Harold Carswell, Harry Blackmun was appointed to succeed Justice Abe Fortas, who had resigned from the Court in a scandal in 1969. Then, in 1972, President Nixon appointed Lewis Powell to fill the vacancy left by Hugo Black's retirement and William Rehnquist to succeed John M. Harlan, who had also retired. The four Nixon appointments had a definite impact on the Supreme Court, although the resulting swing to the right was less dramatic than many observers had predicted.

FDR's Court-Packing Plan

Unquestionably, the most dramatic attempt by a president to control the Supreme Court through the appointment power was launched by Franklin D. Roosevelt (FDR) in 1937. As discussed in Chapter 2, the Court had invalidated a number of key elements of FDR's New Deal program, beginning in 1935 with the National Industrial Recovery Act (*A.L.A. Schechter Poultry Corp. v. United States*).

President Franklin D. Roosevelt

Roosevelt criticized the Court for being out of touch with the realities of an industrialized economy and holding to a "horse-and-buggy definition of interstate commerce." Privately, FDR, who referred to the Court as the "nine old men," began to plan a strategy to curb the Court. His resolve was strengthened by his landslide reelection in 1936 and by the Court's continuing willingness to invalidate New Deal legislation. Finally, in early 1937, Roosevelt proposed his "court packing plan" to Congress. The plan called for Congress to increase the number of justices on the Court, allowing the president to nominate a new justice for each incumbent beyond the age of 70 who refused to retire. This would have given the president the opportunity to appoint as many as six additional justices, raising the membership of the Court to fifteen.

Roosevelt attempted initially to sell his plan to Congress and the American people by portraying it merely as a measure to enhance the efficiency of the Supreme Court. He suggested that some of the incumbent justices were too old or infirm to stay abreast of their caseloads. Roosevelt soon admitted in one of his famous "fireside chats" that his motivation in trying to pack the Court was to produce a Supreme Court that would "not undertake to override the judgment of Congress on legislative policy."

Responding to the president's assault on the Court, Chief Justice Charles Evans Hughes sent a carefully timed letter to Senator Burton K. Wheeler, chairman of the Senate Judiciary Committee, stating that the Court was fully abreast of its docket and implying the Court-packing plan might be unconstitutional. Senator Wheeler read this letter aloud at a session of the Judiciary Committee, which was being broadcast by radio into millions of homes around the country.

FDR's court-packing plan was denounced by the Senate Judiciary Committee as "needless, futile and utterly dangerous." The plan failed to win the approval

Charles Evans Hughes:
Associate Justice 1910–1916;
Chief Justice, 1930–1941

of Congress. Nevertheless, the Supreme Court manifested a dramatic about-face in the spring of 1937, when it upheld the Wagner Act, another important element of New Deal policy (see *National Labor Relations Board v. Jones and Laughlin Steel Corporation*). The Court's famous "switch in time that saved nine" obviated the need for FDR to pack the Court. Within five years, eight of the "nine old men" had retired or died in office, and Roosevelt was able to "pack" the Court through normal procedures. The Roosevelt Court, as it came to be known, brought about a revolution in American constitutional law.

Without question, the shared presidential-senatorial power to appoint judges and justices is the most effective means of controlling the federal judiciary. Congress and the president may not be able to achieve immediate results using the appointment power, but they can bring about long-term changes in the Court's direction. The appointment power ensures that the Supreme Court and the other federal courts may not continue for very long to defy a clear national consensus.

ENFORCEMENT OF COURT DECISIONS

Courts generally have adequate means of enforcing their decisions on the parties directly involved in litigation. Any party that fails to comply with a court order, such as a **subpoena** or an injunction, may be held in **contempt.** The Supreme Court's decisions interpreting the federal Constitution are typically nationwide in scope. As such, they automatically elicit the compliance of state and federal judges. Occasionally, one hears of a recalcitrant judge who, for one reason or another, defies a Supreme Court decision, but this phenomenon, while not uncommon in the early days of the Republic, is an eccentric curiosity today.

Courts have greater difficulty enlisting the compliance of the general public, especially when they render unpopular decisions. Despite the Supreme Court's repeated rulings against officially sponsored prayer in the public schools, such activities continue in some parts of the country. The school prayer decisions, even after three decades, have failed to generate broad public acceptance. Without the assistance of local school officials, there is little the Court can do to effect compliance with its mandates regarding school prayer unless and until an unhappy parent files a lawsuit.

An interesting case that arose in 1982 nicely illustrates the difficulties of implementing the Supreme Court's school prayer rulings. Ishmael Jaffree, a parent with three children in public schools in Mobile, Alabama, filed suit in U.S. district court against various school officials. Jaffree claimed that his children were routinely being subjected to "religious indoctrination" and that their teachers were routinely leading their classes in "saying certain prayers in unison," despite Jaffree's repeated complaints to school officials. The federal judge who heard the case dismissed Jaffree's complaint, blatantly rejecting the Supreme Court's earlier rulings on prayer in the public schools (*Jaffree v. Board of School Commissioners of Mobile County* [1983]). Not surprisingly, Jaffree appealed to the court of appeals, which reversed the district court and ordered that the prayer activities be terminated.

Sometimes the Supreme Court must depend on congressional and/or presidential cooperation to secure compliance with its decisions. This is particularly true when Supreme Court decisions are actively resisted by state and local officials. For example, the efforts of Arkansas Governor Orval Faubus to block the court-ordered desegregation of Central High School in Little Rock in 1957 resulted in President Eisenhower's commitment of federal troops to enforce the court order. A year later, in *Cooper v. Aaron* (1958), the Supreme Court issued a stern rebuke to Faubus, reminding him of his duty to uphold the Constitution of the United States. Would the Court have been able to take the "high constitutional ground" if Eisenhower, who had reservations about court-ordered desegregation, had decided not to send the troops to Little Rock? In using military force to implement a Supreme Court decision about which he had doubts, Eisenhower was recognizing the authority of the Court to speak with finality on matters of constitutional interpretation. However, the ultimate decision to enforce the Court's authority belonged to the president. Accordingly, *Cooper v. Aaron* is more a testament to judicial dependency on the executive than an assertion of judicial power.

Unlike the president, Congress is seldom in a position to enforce a decision of the Supreme Court. On the other hand, Congress has often enacted legislation without which the broad objectives of the Court's decisions could not have been fully realized. This was certainly the case during the 1960s in the field of civil rights. The Supreme Court in a series of decisions had stated the general policy objective of eradicating racial discrimination. It remained for Congress to adopt sweeping legislation in pursuit of this goal, namely, the Civil Rights Act of 1964, the Voting Rights Act of 1965, and the Fair Housing Act of 1968.

The Supreme Court often depends on the president to enforce and the Congress to flesh out its decisions. But the Court cannot force either of the coordinate branches of the national government to do anything. This limitation is perhaps best encapsulated in a famous comment attributed to President Andrew Jackson: "Well, John Marshall has made his decision. Now let him enforce it." In *Worcester v. Georgia* (1832), the Court had held that the state of Georgia's attempt to regulate the Cherokee Indian nation violated the Constitution and certain treaties. The decision required Georgia to release missionaries whom it had prosecuted for ministering to the Cherokees in violation of state law. Georgia's refusal to comply with the decision of the Supreme Court led to President Jackson's oft-quoted remark.

The Supreme Court's lack of enforcement power is an inherent limitation on the power of the Court, but one that makes sense in terms of the principle of separation of powers. Law enforcement, after all, is an aspect of executive power. To permit a court of law to mobilize law enforcement authorities *without the consent of the chief executive* would be to concentrate governmental powers in a manner flatly inconsistent with the Framers' plan. As James Madison observed in *The Federalist* No. 47,

> [t]he accumulation of all powers, legislative, executive, and judiciary, in the same hands . . . may justly be pronounced the very definition of tyranny.

CONCLUSION

In *The Federalist* No. 78, Alexander Hamilton sought to persuade his countrymen that the Supreme Court would be the "least dangerous" branch of the national government under the new Constitution, which had yet to be ratified.

> [T]he judiciary . . . has no influence over either the sword or the purse; no direction of the strength or of the wealth of a society; and can take no active resolution whatever. It may be truly said to have neither force nor will, but merely judgment.

It is true that the Supreme Court's power of enforcement is limited; it is also true that the Court does not determine taxing and spending policies. Yet the almost hallowed character of the Court's "mere judgment" makes the Court as likely to secure compliance with its policy pronouncements as institutions having direct control over appropriations or law enforcement agencies. Clearly, the power of the federal courts, and of the Supreme Court in particular, to secure compliance goes far beyond the issuance of orders and decrees and the availability of a few federal marshals to enforce them.

The power and prestige of the Supreme Court, indeed of the entire federal judiciary, have grown tremendously over the past two centuries. It is no exaggeration to say that the Supreme Court now stands as the most influential tribunal in the world. Nevertheless, the Court works within a constitutional and political system that imposes significant constraints on its power. The Supreme Court can, and occasionally does, speak with finality on important questions of constitutional law and public policy. But it must consider the probable responses of Congress, the president and, ultimately, the American people.

It should be recognized that American government, especially at the national level, is vastly more powerful and pervasive than the Framers of the

Constitution could have imagined. The increased authority of the federal judiciary has kept pace with the growth of governmental activity generally but has not placed it in a dominant position in the American system of government. Two hundred years after the ratification of the Constitution, Alexander Hamilton's characterization of the federal judiciary as the "least dangerous" branch of the national government remains credible.

FOR FURTHER READING

Abraham, Henry J. *Justices and Presidents: A Political History of Appointments to the Supreme Court,* 2d ed. New York: Oxford University Press, 1985.

Becker, Theodore L., and Malcolm M. Feeley, eds. *The Impact of Supreme Court Decisions.* New York: Oxford University Press, 1973.

Berger, Raoul. *Congress versus the Supreme Court.* Cambridge: Harvard University Press, 1969.

Berger, Raoul. *Impeachment: The Constitutional Problem.* Cambridge: Harvard University Press, 1973.

Bickel, Alexander M. *Politics and the Warren Court.* New York: Harper and Row, 1966.

Breckenridge, Adam C. *Congress Against the Court.* Lincoln: University of Nebraska Press, 1971.

Dolbeare, Kenneth M., and Phillip E. Hammond. *The School Prayer Decisions: From Court Policy to Local Practice.* Chicago: University of Chicago Press, 1971.

Jackson, Robert H. *The Struggle for Judicial Supremacy.* New York: Knoph, 1941.

Johnson, Charles A., and Bradley C. Canon. *Judicial Policies: Implementation and Impact.* Washington, D.C.: Congressional Quarterly Press, 1984.

Kutler, Stanley L. *Judicial Power and Reconstruction Politics.* Chicago: University of Chicago Press, 1968.

Lytle, Clifford M. *The Warren Court and Its Critics.* Tucson: University of Arizona Press, 1968.

Murphy, Walter F. *Congress and the Court.* Chicago: University of Chicago Press, 1962.

Peltason, Jack W. *Federal Courts in the Political Process.* New York: Random House, 1955.

Peltason, Jack W. *Fifty-Eight Lonely Men: Southern Federal Judges and School Desegregation.* Urbana: University of Illinois Press, 1961.

Pritchett, C. Herman. *Congress versus the Supreme Court, 1957–1960.* Minneapolis: University of Minnesota Press, 1961.

Scigliano, Robert. *The Supreme Court and the Presidency.* New York: Free Press, 1971.

Schmidhauser, John R., and Larry L. Berg. *The Supreme Court and Congress: Conflict and Interaction, 1945–1968.* New York: Free Press, 1972.

Steamer, Robert J. *The Supreme Court in Crisis.* Amherst: University of Massachusetts Press, 1971.

Vile, John R. *The Constitutional Amending Process in American Political Thought.* New York: Praeger, 1992.

Vose, Clement E. *Constitutional Change: Amendment Politics and Supreme Court Litigation Since 1900.* Lexington, Mass.: D.C. Heath, 1972.

Warren, Charles. *Congress, the Constitution and the Supreme Court.* Boston: Little, Brown, 1935.

Alexander Hamilton, *The Federalist* No. 78

We proceed now to an examination of the judiciary department of the proposed government.

In unfolding the defects of the existing confederation, the utility and necessity of a federal judicature have been clearly pointed out. It is the less necessary to recapitulate the considerations there urged; as the propriety of the institution in the abstract is not disputed: The only questions which have been raised being relative to the manner of constituting it, and to its extent. To these points, therefore, our observations shall be confined.

The manner of constituting it seems to embrace these several objects: 1st. The mode of appointing the judges: 2nd. The tenure by which they are to hold their places: 3rd. The partition of the judiciary authority between different courts, and their relations to each other.

First. As to the mode of appointing the judges: This is the same with that of appointing the officers of the union in general, and has been so fully discussed . . . that nothing can be said here which would not be useless repetition.

Second. As to the tenure by which the judges are to hold their places: This chiefly concerns their duration in office; the provisions for their support; the precautions for their responsibility.

According to the plan of the convention, all the judges who may be appointed by the United States are to hold their offices during good behavior; which is conformable to the most approved of the state constitutions—among the rest, to that of this state. Its propriety having been drawn into question by the adversaries of that plan, is no light symptom of the rage for objection, which disorders their imaginations and judgments. The standard of good behavior for the continuance in office of the judicial magistracy is certainly one of the most valuable of the modern improvements in the practice of government. In a monarchy, it is an excellent barrier to the despotism of the prince; in a republic, it is a no less excellent barrier to the encroachments and oppression of the representative body. And it is the best expedient which can be devised in any government, to secure a steady, upright, and impartial administration of the laws.

Whoever attentively considers the different departments of power must perceive, that, in a government in which they are separated from each other, the judiciary, from the nature of its functions, will always be the least dangerous to the political rights of the constitution; because it will be least in a capacity to annoy or injure them. The executive not only dispenses the honors, but holds the sword of the community: The legislature not only commands the purse, but prescribes the rules by which the duties and rights of every citizen are to be regulated: The judiciary, on the contrary, has no influence over either the sword or the purse; no direction either of the strength or of the wealth of the society; and can take no active resolution whatever. It may truly be said to have neither FORCE nor WILL, but merely judgment; and must ultimately depend upon the aid of the executive arm for the efficacious exercise even of this faculty.

This simple view of the matter suggests several important consequences: it proves incontestably, that the judiciary is beyond comparison, the weakest of the three departments of power, that it can never attack with success either of the other two; and that all possible care is requisite to enable it to defend itself against their attacks. It equally proves, that, though individual oppression may now and then proceed from the courts of justice, the general liberty of the people can never be endangered from that quarter: I mean so long as the judiciary remains truly distinct from both the legislature and executive. For I agree, that "there is no liberty, if the power of judging be not separated from the legislative and executive powers." It proves, in the last place, that as liberty can have nothing to fear from the judiciary alone, but would have everything to fear from its union with either of the other departments; that, as all the effects of such a union must ensue from a dependence of the former on the latter, notwithstanding a nominal and apparent separation; that as, from the natural feebleness of the judiciary, it is in continual jeopardy of being overpowered, awed or influenced by its co-ordinate branches; that, as nothing can contribute so much to its firmness and independence as PERMANENCY IN OFFICE, this quality may therefore be justly regarded as an indispensable ingredient in its constitution; and, in a great measure, as the CITADEL of the public justice and the public security.

The complete independence of the courts of justice is peculiarly essential in a limited constitution. By a limited constitution, I understand one which contains certain specified exceptions to the legislative authority; such, for instance, as that it shall pass no bills of attainder, no ex post facto laws, and the like. Limitations of this kind can be preserved in practice no other way than through the medium of the courts of justice; whose duty it must be to declare all acts contrary to the manifest tenor of the constitution void. Without this, all the reservations of particular rights or privileges would amount to nothing.

Some perplexity respecting the right of the courts to pronounce legislative acts void, because contrary to the constitution, has arisen from an imagination that the doctrine would imply a superiority of the judiciary to the legislative power. It is urged that the authority which can declare the acts of another void, must necessarily be superior to the one whose acts may be declared void. As this doctrine is of great importance in all the American constitutions, a brief discussion of the grounds on which it rests cannot be unacceptable.

There is no position which depends on clearer principles than that every act of a delegated authority, contrary to the tenor of the commission under which it is exercised, is void. No legislative act, therefore, contrary to the constitution, can be valid. To deny this would be to affirm, that the deputy is greater than his principal; that the servant is above his master; that the representatives of the people are superior to the people themselves; that men, acting by virtue of powers, may do not only what their powers do not authorize, but what they forbid.

If it be said that the legislative body are themselves the constitutional judges of their own powers, and that the construction they put upon them is conclusive upon the other departments, it may be answered, that this cannot be the natural presumption, where it is not to be collected from any particular provisions in the constitution. It is not otherwise to be supposed that the constitution could intend to enable the representatives of the people to substitute their will to that of their constituents. It is far more rational to suppose that the courts were designed to be an intermediate body between the people and the legislature, in order, among other things, to keep the latter within the limits assigned to their authority. The interpretation of the laws is the proper and peculiar province of the courts. A constitution is, in fact, and must be, regarded by the judges as a fundamental law. It must therefore belong to them to ascertain its meaning, as well as the meaning of any particular act proceeding from the legislative body. If there should happen to be an irreconcilable variance between the two, that which has the superior obligation and validity ought, of course, to be preferred; in other words, the constitution ought to be preferred to the statute, the intention of the people to the intention of their agents.

Nor does the conclusion by any means suppose a superiority of the judicial to the legislative power. It only supposes that the power of the people is superior to both; and that where the will of the legislature declared in its statutes, stands in opposition to that of the people declared in the constitution, the judges ought to be governed by the latter, rather than the former. They ought to regulate their decisions by the fundamental laws, rather than by those which are not fundamental.

This exercise of judicial discretion, in determining between two contradictory laws, is exemplified in a familiar instance. It not uncommonly happens, that there are two statutes existing at one time, clashing in whole or in part with each other, and neither of them containing any repealing clause or expression. In such a case, it is the province of the courts to liquidate and fix their meaning and operation: So far as they can, by any fair construction be reconciled to each other, reason and law conspire to dictate that this should be done: Where this is impracticable, it becomes a matter of necessity to give effect to one, in exclusion of the other. The rule which has obtained in the courts for determining their relative validity is, that the last in order of time shall be preferred to the first. But this is a mere rule of construction, not derived from any positive law, but from the nature and reason of the thing. It is a rule not enjoined upon the courts by legislative provision, but adopted by themselves, as consonant to truth and propriety, for the direction of their conduct as interpreters of the law. They thought it reasonable, that between the interfering acts of an equal authority, that which was the last indication of its will should have the preference.

But in regard to the interfering acts of a superior and subordinate authority, of an original and derivative power, the nature and reason of the thing indicate the converse of that rule as proper to be followed. They teach us, that the prior act of a superior ought to be preferred to the subsequent act of an inferior and subordinate authority; and that, accordingly, whenever a particular statute contravenes the constitution, it will be the duty of the judicial tribunals to adhere to the latter, and disregard the former.

It can be of no weight to say, that the courts, on the pretense of a repugnancy, may substitute their own pleasure to the constitutional intentions of the legislature. This might as well happen in the case of two contradictory statutes; or it might as well happen in every adjudication upon any single statute. The courts must declare the sense of the law; and if they should be disposed to exercise WILL instead of JUDGMENT, the consequence would equally be the substitution of their pleasure to that of the legislative body. The observation, if it proved anything, would prove that there ought to be no judges distinct from that body.

If then the courts of justice are to be considered as the bulwarks of a limited constitution, against legislative encroachments, this consideration will afford a strong argument for the permanent tenure of judicial offices, since nothing will contribute so much as this to that independent spirit in the judges, which must be essential to the faithful performance of so arduous a duty.

This independence of the judges is equally requisite to guard the constitution and the rights of individuals, from the effects of those ill-humors which

the arts of designing men, or the influence of particular conjunctures, sometimes disseminate among the people themselves, and which, though they speedily give place to better information, and more deliberate reflection, have a tendency, in the meantime, to occasion dangerous innovations in the government, and serious oppression of the minor party in the community. Though I trust the friends of the proposed constitution will never concur with its enemies, in questioning that fundamental principle of republican government, which admits the right of the people to alter or abolish the established constitution whenever they find it inconsistent with their happiness; yet it is not to be inferred from this principle that the representatives of the people, whenever a momentary inclination happens to lay hold of a majority of their constituents incompatible with the provisions in the existing constitution, would, on that account, be justifiable in a violation of those provisions; or that the courts would be under a greater obligation to connive at infractions in this shape, than when they had proceeded wholly from the cabals of the representative body. Until the people have, by some solemn and authoritative act, annulled or changed the established form, it is binding upon themselves collectively, as well as individually; and no presumption, or even knowledge of their sentiments, can warrant their representatives in a departure from it, prior to such an act. But it is easy to see, that it would require an uncommon portion of fortitude in the judges to do their duty as faithful guardians of the constitution, where legislative invasions of it had been instigated by the major voice of the community.

But it is not with a view to infractions of the constitution only, that the independence of the judges may be an essential safeguard against the effects of occasional ill-humors in the society. These sometimes extend no farther than to the injury of the private rights of particular classes of citizens, by unjust and partial laws. Here also the firmness of the judicial magistracy is of vast importance in mitigating the severity, and confining the operation of such laws. It not only serves to moderate the immediate mischiefs of those which may have been passed, but it operates as a check upon the legislative body in passing them; who, perceiving that obstacles to the success of an iniquitous intention are to be expected from the scruples of the courts, are in a manner compelled by the very motives of the injustice they mediate, to qualify their attempts. This is a circumstance calculated to have more influence upon the character of our governments than but few may imagine. The benefits of the integrity and moderation of the judiciary have already been felt in more states than one; and though they may have displeased those whose sinister expectations they may have disappointed, they must have commanded the esteem and applause of all the virtuous and disinterested. Considerate men, of every description, ought to prize whatever will tend to beget or fortify that temper in the courts; as no man can be sure that he may not be tomorrow the victim of a spirit of injustice, by which he may be a gainer today. And every man must now feel that the inevitable tendency of such a spirit is to sap the foundations of public and private confidence, and to introduce in its stead universal distrust and distress.

That inflexible and uniform adherence to the rights of the constitution, and of individuals, which we perceive to be indispensable in the courts of justice, can certainly not be expected from judges who hold their offices by a temporary commission. Periodical appointments, however regulated, or by whomsoever made, would, in some way or other, be fatal to their necessary independence. If the power of making them was committed either to the executive or legislature, there would be danger of an improper complaisance to the branch which possessed it: if to both, there would be an unwillingness to hazard the displeasure of either; if to the people, or to persons chosen by them for the special purpose, there would be too great a disposition to consult popularity, to justify a reliance that nothing would be consulted but the constitution and the laws.

There is yet a further and a weighty reason for the permanency of judicial offices; which is deducible from the nature of the qualifications they require. It has been frequently remarked, with great propriety, that a voluminous code of laws is one of the inconveniences necessarily connected with the advantages of a free government. To avoid an arbitrary discretion in the courts, it is indispensable that they should be bound down by strict rules and precedents, which serve to define and point out their duty in every particular case that comes before them; and it will readily be conceived, from the variety of controversies which grow out of the folly and wickedness of mankind, that the records of those precedents must unavoidably swell to a very considerable bulk, and must demand long and laborious study to acquire a competent knowledge of them. Hence it is, that there can be but few men in the society, who will have sufficient skill in the laws to qualify them for the stations of judges. And making the proper deductions for the ordinary depravity of human nature, the number must be still smaller, of those who unite the requisite integrity with the requisite knowledge. These considerations apprise us, that the government can have no great option between fit characters; and that a temporary duration in office, which would naturally discourage such characters from quitting a lucrative line of practice to accept a seat on the bench, would have a tendency to throw the administration of justice into hands less able, and less well qualified, to conduct it with utility and dignity. In the present circumstances of this country, and in those in which it is likely to be for a long time to come, the disadvantages on this score would be greater than they may at first sight appear; but it must be confessed, that they are far inferior to those which present themselves under the other aspects of the subject.

Upon the whole, there can be no room to doubt, that the convention acted wisely in copying from the models of those constitutions which have established good behavior as the tenure of judicial offices, in point of duration; and that, so far from being blameable on this account, their plan would have been inexcusably defective, if it had wanted this important feature of good government. The experience of Great Britain affords an illustrious comment on the excellence of the institution.

Ex parte McCardle
7 Wall. (74 U.S.) 506; 19 L. Ed. 264 (1869)
Vote: 8-0

In the wake of the Civil War, Congress chose to rely on military rule as the most effective means to "reconstruct" the South. As part of this regime, the Reconstruction Acts authorized military commissions to try civilians who interfered with the program. William H. McCardle, editor of the Vicksburg Times, *published a series of editorials that were highly critical of Reconstruction and of the military government which ruled Mississippi. He was subsequently arrested and held for trial by a military commission on the charge of sedition. McCardle sought release by filing a* habeas corpus *petition in federal circuit court. Shortly before McCardle's case arose, the Congress had authorized the circuit courts to hear* habeas corpus *cases involving anyone held by state authorities in violation of the U.S. Constitution or federal statutes. The act included the right to appeal a circuit court denial of* habeas corpus *to the Supreme Court. McCardle lost his bid for release in the circuit court and exercised his option to appeal. After the case was argued in the Supreme Court, but before a decision on the constitutionality of the Reconstruction Acts was reached, the Congress amended the law to remove the Supreme Court's appellate jurisdiction in* habeas corpus *cases. Quite obviously, Congress was attempting to prevent the Supreme Court from ruling on the constitutionality of the Reconstruction Acts.*

Mr. Chief Justice Chase delivered the opinion of the Court.

This cause came here by appeal from the Circuit Court for the Southern District of Mississippi.

A Petition for the writ of *habeas corpus* was preferred in that court by [McCardle], alleging unlawful restraint by military force.

The writ was issued and a return was made by the military commander, admitting the restraint, but denying that it was unlawful.

It appeared that the petitioner was not in the military service of the United States, but was held in custody by military authority, for trial before a Military Commission, upon charge founded upon the

publication of articles alleged to be incendiary and libelous, in a newspaper of which he was editor.

Upon the hearing, [McCardle] was remanded to military custody; but upon his prayer, an appeal was allowed him to this court, and upon filing the usual appeal bond for costs, he was admitted to bail. . . .

Subsequently, the case was argued very thoroughly and ably upon the merits, and was taken under advisement. While it was held, and before conference in regard to the decision proper to be made, an Act was passed by Congress, *** returned, with objections by the President, and repassed by the constitutional majority, which, it is insisted, takes from this court jurisdiction of the appeal. The 2d section of this act was as follows:

And be it further enacted, that so much of the Act approved February 5, 1867, . . . as authorized an appeal from the judgment of the circuit court to the Supreme Court of the United States, . . . is hereby repealed.

The attention of the court was directed to this statute at the last term, but counsel having expressed a desire to be heard in argument upon its effect, and the Chief Justice being detained from his place here by his duties in the Court of Impeachment, the cause was continued under advisement.

At this term we have heard arguments upon the effect of the repealing Act, and will now dispose of the case.

The first question necessarily is that of jurisdiction; for, if the Act . . . takes away the jurisdiction defined by the Act of February, 1867, it is useless, if not improper, to enter into any discussion of other questions.

It is quite true, as was argued by the counsel for [McCardle], that the appellate jurisdiction of this court is not derived from acts of Congress. It is, strictly speaking, conferred by the Constitution. But it is conferred "with such exceptions and under such regulations as Congress shall make." . . .

The exception to appellate jurisdiction in the case before us . . . is not an inference from the affirmation of other appellate jurisdiction. It is made in terms.

The provision of the act of 1867, affirming the appellate jurisdiction of this court in cases of *habeas corpus* is expressly repealed. It is hardly possible to imagine a plainer instance of positive exception.

We are not at liberty to inquire into the motives of the legislature. We can only examine into its power under the Constitution; and the power to make exceptions to the appellate jurisdiction of this court is given by express words.

What, then, is the effect of the repealing act upon the case before us? We cannot doubt as to this. Without jurisdiction the court cannot proceed at all in any cause. Jurisdiction is power to declare the law, and when it ceases to exist, the only function remaining to the court is that of announcing the fact and dismissing the cause. And this is not less clear upon authority than upon principle.

Several cases were cited by the counsel for [McCardle] in support of the position that jurisdiction of this case is not affected by the repealing act. But none of them, in our judgment, afford any support to it. They are all cases of the exercise of judicial power by the legislature, or of legislative interference with courts in the exercising of continuing jurisdiction. ***

On the other hand, the general rule, supported by the best elementary writers *** is, that "when an act of the legislature is repealed, it must be considered, except as to transactions past and closed, as if it never existed." And the effect of repealing acts upon suits under acts repealed, has been determined by the adjudications of this court. . . .

It is quite clear, therefore, that this court cannot proceed to pronounce judgment in this case, for it has no longer jurisdiction of the appeal; and judicial duty is not less fitly performed by declining ungranted jurisdiction than in exercising firmly that which the Constitution and the laws confer.

Counsel seem to have supposed, if effect be given to the repealing act in question, that the whole appellate power of the court, in cases of *habeas corpus*, is denied. But this is an error. The act of 1868 does not except from that jurisdiction any cases but appeals from Circuit Courts under the act of 1867. It does not affect the jurisdiction which was previously exercised. ***

The appeal of [*McCardle*] must be dismissed for want of jurisdiction.

President Franklin D. Roosevelt's "Fireside Chat," March 9, 1937

. . . Tonight, sitting at my desk in the White House, I make my first radio report to the people in my second term of office.

I am reminded of that evening in March 4 years ago, when I made my first radio report to you. We were then in the midst of the great banking crisis. . . .

In 1933 you and I knew that we must never let our economic system get completely out of joint again — that we could not afford to take the risk of another great depression.

We also became convinced that the only way to avoid a repetition of those dark days was to have a government with power to prevent and to cure the abuses and the inequalities which had thrown that system out of joint.

We then began a program of remedying those abuses and inequalities. . . .

Today we are only part way through that program — and recovery is speeding up to a point where the dangers of 1929 are again becoming possible, not this week or month perhaps, but within a year or two.

National laws are needed to complete that program. Individual or local or State effort alone cannot protect us in 1937 any better than 10 years ago. . . .

The courts have cast doubts on the ability of the elected Congress to protect us against catastrophe by meeting squarely our modern social and economic conditions.

We are at a crisis in our ability to proceed with that protection. It is a quiet crisis. There are no lines of depositors outside closed banks. But to the far-sighted it is far-reaching in its possibilities of injury to America.

I want to talk with you very simply about the need for present action in this crisis—the need to meet the unanswered challenge of one-third of a nation ill-nourished, ill-clad, ill-housed.

Last Thursday I described the American form of government as a three-horse team provided by the Constitution to the American people so that their field might be plowed. The three horses are, of course, the three branches of government—the Congress, the executive, and the courts. Two of the horses are pulling in unison today; the third is not. Those who have intimated that the President of the United States is trying to drive that team overlook the simple fact that the President, as Chief Executive, is himself one of the three horses.

It is the American people themselves who are in the driver's seat.

It is the American people themselves who want the furrow plowed.

It is the American people themselves who expect the third horse to pull in unison with the other two.

I hope that you have reread the Constitution of the United States. Like the Bible, it ought to be read again and again.

. . . In its preamble the Constitution states that it was intended to form a more perfect Union and promote the general welfare; and the powers given to the Congress to carry out those purposes can be best described by saying that they were all the powers needed to meet each and every problem which then had a national character and which could not be met by merely local action.

But the framers went further. Having in mind that in succeeding generations many other problems then undreamed of would become national problems, they gave to the Congress the ample broad powers "to levy taxes *** and provide for the common defense and general welfare of the United States."

That, my friends, is what I honestly believe to have been the clear and underlying purpose of the patriots who wrote a Federal Constitution to create a National Government with national power, intended as they said, "to form a more perfect union . . . for ourselves and our posterity." . . . .

. . . [S]ince the rise of the modern movement for social and economic progress through legislation, the Court has more and more often and more and more boldly asserted a power to veto laws passed by the Congress and State legislatures. . . .

In the last 4 years the sound rule of giving statutes the benefit of all reasonable doubt has been cast aside. The Court has been acting not as a judicial body, but as a policy-making body.

When the Congress has sought to stabilize national agriculture, to improve the conditions of labor, to safeguard business against unfair competition, to protect our national resources, and in many other ways to serve our clearly national needs, the majority of the Court has been assuming the power to pass on the wisdom of these acts of the Congress—and to approve or disapprove the public policy written into these laws.

That is not only my accusation. It is the accusation of most distinguished Justices of the present Supreme Court. I have not the time to quote to you all the language used by dissenting Justices in many of these cases. But in the case holding the Railroad Retirement Act unconstitutional, for instance, Chief Justice Hughes said in a dissenting opinion that the majority opinion was "a departure from sound principles," and placed "an unwarranted limitation upon the commerce clause." And three other justices agreed with him.

In the face of these dissenting opinions, there is no basis for the claim made by some members of the Court that something in the Constitution has compelled them regretfully to thwart the will of the people.

The Court in addition to the proper use of its judicial functions has improperly set itself up as a third House of the Congress—a superlegislature, as one of the Justices has called it, "reading into the Constitution words and implications which are not there, and which were never intended to be there."

We have, therefore, reached the point as a Nation where we must take action to save the Constitution from the Court and the Court from itself. We must find a way to take an appeal from the Supreme Court to the Constitution itself. We want a Supreme Court which will do justice under the Constitution—not over it. In our courts we want a government of laws and not of men.

I want—as all Americans want—an independent judiciary as proposed by the framers of the Constitution. That means a Supreme Court that will enforce the Constitution as written—that will refuse to amend the Constitution by the arbitrary exercise of judicial power—amendment by judicial say-so. It does not mean a judiciary so independent that it can deny the existence of facts universally recognized.

How, then, could we proceed to perform the mandate given us? . . .

. . . I came by a process of elimination to the conclusion that short of amendments the only method which was clearly constitutional, and would at the same time carry out other much needed reforms, was to infuse new blood into all our courts. . . . [W]e must have judges who will bring to the courts a present-day sense of the Constitution—judges who will retain in the courts the judicial functions of a court and reject the legislative powers which the courts have today assumed. . . .

What is my proposal? It is simply this: Whenever a judge or justice of any Federal court has reached the age of 70 and does not avail himself of the opportunity to retire on a pension, a new member shall be appointed by the President then in office, with the approval, as required by the Constitution of the Senate of the United States.

That plan has two chief purposes: By bringing into the judicial system a steady and continuing stream of new and younger blood, I hope, first, to make the administration of all Federal justice speedier and therefore less costly; secondly, to bring to the decision of social and economic problems younger men who have had personal experience and contact with modern facts and circumstances under which average men have to live and work. This plan will save our National Constitution from hardening of the judicial arteries.

The number of judges to be appointed would depend wholly on the decision of present judges now over 70 or those who would subsequently reach the age of 70.

If, for instance, any one of the six Justices of the Supreme Court now over the age of 70 should retire as provided under the plan, no additional place would be created. Consequently, although there never can be more than 15, there may be only 14, or 13, or 12, and there may be only 9.

There is nothing novel or radical about this idea. It seeks to maintain the Federal bench in full vigor. . . .

The statute would apply to all the courts in the Federal system. There is general approval so far as the lower Federal courts are concerned. The plan has met opposition only so far as the Supreme Court of the United States itself is concerned. If such a plan is good for the lower courts, it certainly ought to be equally good for the highest court, from which there is no appeal.

Those opposing this plan have sought to arouse prejudice and fear by crying that I am seeking to "pack" the Supreme Court and that a baneful precedent will be established.

What do they mean by the words "packing the Court?"

Let me answer this question with a bluntness that will end all honest misunderstanding of my purposes.

If by that phrase "packing the Court" it is charged that I wish to place on the bench spineless puppets who would disregard the law and would decide specific cases as I wished them to be decided, I make this answer: That no President fit for his office would appoint, and no Senate of honorable men fit for their office would confirm, that kind of appointees to the Supreme Court.

But if by that phrase the charge is made that I would appoint and the Senate would confirm Justices worthy to sit beside present members of the Court who understand those modern conditions; that I will appoint Justices who will not undertake to override the judgment of the Congress on legislative policy; that I will appoint Justices who will act as Justices and not as legislators—if the appointment of such Justices can be called "packing the Courts"—then I say that I, and with me the vast majority of the American people, favor doing just that thing—now. . . .

I now propose that we establish by law an assurance against any such ill-balanced Court in the future. I propose that hereafter, when a judge reaches the age of 70, a new and younger judge shall be added to the Court automatically. In this way I propose to enforce a sound public policy by law instead of leaving the composition of our Federal courts, including the highest, to be determined by change or the personal decision of individuals. . . .

Like all lawyers, like all Americans, I regret the necessity of this controversy. But the welfare of the

United States, and indeed of the Constitution itself, is what we all must think about first. Our difficulty with the Court today rises not from the Court as an institution but from human beings within it. But we cannot yield our constitutional destiny to the personal judgment of a few men who, being fearful of the future, would deny us the necessary means of dealing with the present.

This plan of mine is no attack on the Court; it seeks to restore the Court to its rightful and historic place in our system of constitutional government and to have it resume its high task of building anew on the Constitution "a system of living law." . . .

During the past half century the balance of power between the three great branches of the Federal Government has been tipped out of balance by the courts in direct contradiction of the high purpose of the framers of the Constitution.

It is my purpose to restore that balance. You who know me will accept my solemn assurance that in a world in which democracy is under attack I seek to make American democracy succeed.

Chief Justice Charles Evans Hughes's Letter to Senator Burton K. Wheeler, March 21, 1937

My Dear Senator Wheeler:

In response to your inquiries, I have the honor to present the following statement with respect to the work of the Supreme Court:

1. The Supreme Court is fully abreast of its work. When we rose on March 15 (for the present recess) we have heard argument in cases in which *certiorari* had been granted only 4 weeks before—February 15.

During the current term, which began last October and which we call "October term, 1936," we have heard argument on merits in 150 cases (180 numbers) and we have 28 cases (30 numbers)' awaiting argument. We shall be able to hear all these cases, and such others as may come up for argument, before our adjournment for the term. There is no congestion of cases upon our calendar.

This gratifying condition has obtained for several years. We have been able for several terms to adjourn after disposing of all cases which are ready to be heard.

2. The cases on our docket are classified as original and appellate. Our original jurisdiction is defined by the Constitution and embraces cases to which States are parties. There are not many of these. At the present time they number 13 and are in various stages of progress to submission for determination.

Our appellate jurisdiction covers those cases in which appeal is allowed by statute as a matter of right and cases which come to us on writs of *certiorari*. . . .

3. The statute relating to our appellate jurisdiction is the act of February 13, 1925. *** That act limits to certain cases the appeals which come to the Supreme Court as a matter of right. Review in other cases is made to depend upon the allowance by the Supreme Court of a writ of *certiorari*.

Where the appeal purports to lie as a matter of right, the rules of the Supreme Court (rule 12) require the appellant to submit a jurisdictional statement showing that the case falls within that class of appeals and that a substantial question is involved. We examine that statement, and the supporting and opposing briefs, and decide whether the Court had jurisdiction. As a result, many frivolous appeals are forthwith dismissed and the way is open for appeals which disclose substantial questions.

4. The act of 1925, limiting appeals as a matter of right and enlarging the provisions for review only through *certiorari* was most carefully considered by Congress. I call attention to the reports of the Judiciary Committees of the Senate and House of Representatives. *** That legislation was deemed to be essential to enable the Supreme Court to perform its proper function. No single court of last resort, whatever the number of judges, could dispose of all the cases which arise in this vast country and which litigants would seek to bring up if the right of appeal were unrestricted. Hosts of litigants will take appeals so long as there is a tribunal accessible. In protracted

litigation, the advantage is with those who command a long purse. Unmeritorious appeals cause intolerable delays. Such appeals clog the calendar and get in the way of those that have merit.

Under our Federal system, when litigants have had their cases heard in the courts of first instance, and the trier of the facts, jury or judge, as the case may require, has spoken and the case on the facts and law has been decided, and when the dissatisfied party has been accorded an appeal to the circuit court of appeals, the litigants, so far as mere private interests are concerned, have had their day in court. If further review is to be had by the Supreme Court it must be because of the public interest in the questions involved. That review, for example, should be for the purpose of resolving conflicts in judicial decisions between different circuit courts of appeals or between circuit courts of appeals and State courts where the question is one of State law; or for the purpose of determining constitutional questions or settling the interpretation of statutes; or because of the importance of the questions of law that are involved. Review by the Supreme Court is thus in the interest of the law, its appropriate exposition and enforcement, not in the mere interest of the litigants.

It is obvious that if appeal as a matter of right is restricted to certain described cases, the question whether review should be allowed in other cases must necessarily be confided to some tribunal for determination, and, of course, with respect to review by the Supreme Court, that Court should decide.

5. Granting *certiorari* is not a matter of favor but of sound judicial discretion. It is not the importance of the parties or the amount of money involved that is in any sense controlling. The action of the Court is governed by its rules. . . .

I should add that petitions of *certiorari* are not apportioned among the Justices. In all matters before the Court, except in the more routine of administration, all the Justices—unless for some reason a Justice is disqualified or unable to act in a particular case—participate in the decision. This applies to the grant or refusal of petitions for *certiorari*. Furthermore, petitions for *certiorari* are granted if four Justices think they should be. A vote by a majority is not required in such cases. Even if two or three of the Justices are strongly of the opinion that *certiorari*

should be allowed, frequently the other Justices will acquiesce in their view, but the petition is always granted if four so vote.

6. The work of passing upon these applications for *certiorari* is laborious but the Court is able to perform it adequately. Observations have been made as to the vast number of pages of records and briefs that are submitted in the course of a term. The total is imposing but the suggested conclusion is hasty and rests on an illusory basis. Records are replete with testimony and evidence of facts. But the questions on *certiorari* are questions of law. So many cases turn on the facts, principles of law not being in controversy. It is only when the facts are interwoven with the questions of law which we should review that the evidence must be examined and then only to the extent that it is necessary to decide the questions of law.

This at once disposes of a vast number of factual controversies where the parties have been fully heard in the courts below and have no right to burden the Supreme Court with the dispute which interests no one but themselves.

This is also true of controversies over contracts and documents of all sorts which involve only questions of concern to the immediate parties. The applicant for *certiorari* is required to state in his petition the grounds for his application and in a host of cases that disclosure itself disposes of his request. So that the number of pages of records and briefs afford no satisfactory criterion of the actual work involved. It must also be remembered that Justices who have been dealing with such matters for years have the aid of a long and varied experience in separating the chaff from the wheat.

I think that it is safe to say that about 60 percent of the applications for *certiorari* are wholly without merit and ought never to have been made. There are probably about 20 percent or so in addition which have a fair degree of plausibility but which fail to survive critical examination. The remainder, falling short, I believe, of 20 percent, show substantial grounds and are granted. I think that it is the view of the members of the Court that if any error is made in dealing with these applications it is on the side of liberality.

7. An increase in the number of Justices of the Supreme Court, apart from any question of policy,

which I do not discuss, would not promote the efficiency of the Court. It is believed that it would impair that efficiency so long as the Court acts as a unit. There would be more judges to hear, more judges to confer, more judges to discuss, more judges to be convinced and to decide. The present number of Justices is thought to be large enough so far as the prompt, adequate, and efficient conduct of the work of the Court is concerned. As I have said, I do not speak of any considerations in view of the appropriate attitude of the Court in relation to questions of policy.

I understand that it has been suggested that with more Justices the Court could hear cases in divisions. It is believed that such a plan would be impracticable. A large proportion of the cases we hear are important and a decision by a part of the Court would be unsatisfactory.

I may also call attention to the provisions of Article III, Section 1, of the Constitution that the judicial power of the United States shall be vested "in one Supreme Court" and in such inferior courts as the Congress may from time to time ordain and establish. The Constitution does not appear to authorize two or more Supreme Courts or two or more parts of a supreme court functioning in effect as separate courts.

On account of the shortness of time I have not been able to consult with the members of the Court generally with respect to the foregoing statement, but I am confident that it is in accord with the views of the Justices. I should say, however, that I have been able to consult with Mr. Justice Van Devanter and Mr. Justice Brandeis, and I am at liberty to say that the statement is approved by them.

Senate Judiciary Committee Report on President Roosevelt's Court-Packing Plan

(S. Rept. No. 711, 75th Cong., 1st Sess., June 7, 1937)

The Committee on the Judiciary, to whom was referred the bill (S. 1392) to reorganize the judicial branch of the Government, after full consideration, having unanimously amended the measure, hereby reports the bill adversely with the recommendation that it does not pass. . . .

THE ARGUMENT

The committee recommends that the measure be rejected for the following primary reasons:

   I. The bill does not accomplish any one of the objectives for which it was originally offered.
   II. It applies force to the judiciary and in its initial and ultimate effect would undermine the independence of the courts.
   III. It violates all precedents in the history of our Government and would in itself be a dangerous precedent for the future.
   IV. The theory of the bill is in direct violation of the spirit of the American Constitution and its

employment would permit alteration of the Constitution without the people's consent or approval; it undermines the protection our constitutional system gives to minorities and is subversive of the rights of individuals.
   V. It tends to centralize the Federal district judiciary by the power of assigning judges from one district to another at will.
   VI. It tends to expand political control over the judicial department by adding to the powers of the legislative and executive departments respecting the judiciary.

BILL DOES NOT DEAL WITH INJUNCTIONS

The measure was sent to the Congress by the President on February 5, 1937, with a message setting forth the objectives sought to be attained.

It should be pointed out here that a substantial portion of the message was devoted to a discussion of the evils of conflicting decisions by inferior courts on constitutional questions and to the alleged abuse of the power of injunction by some of the Federal courts. These matters, however, have no bearing on the bill before us, for it contains neither a line nor a sentence dealing with either of those problems.

Nothing in this measure attempts to control, regulate, or prohibit the power of any Federal court to pass upon the constitutionality of any law—State or National.

Nothing in this measure attempts to control, regulate, or prohibit the issuance of injunctions by any court, in any case, whether or not the Government is a party to it.

If it were to be conceded that there is need of reform in these respects, it must be understood that this bill does not deal with these problems.

OBJECTIVES AS ORIGINALLY STATED

As offered to the Congress, this bill was designed to effectuate only three objectives, described as follows in the President's message:

1. To increase the personnel of the Federal courts "so that cases may be promptly decided in the first instance, and may be given adequate and prompt hearing on all appeals";
2. To "invigorate all the courts by the permanent infusion of new blood";
3. To "grant to the Supreme Court further power and responsibility in maintaining the efficiency of the entire Federal judiciary."

The third of these purposes was to be accomplished by the provisions creating the office of the Proctor and dealing with the assignment of judges to courts other than those to which commissioned.

The first two objectives were to be attained by the provisions authorizing the appointment of not to exceed 50 additional judges when sitting judges of retirement age, as defined in the bill, failed to retire or resign. How totally inadequate the measure is to achieve either of the named objectives, the most cursory examination of the facts reveals.

BILL FAILS OF ITS PURPOSE

In the first place, as already pointed out, the bill does not provide for any increase of personnel unless

judges of retirement age fail to resign or retire. Whether or not there is to be an increase of the number of judges, and the extent of the increase if there is to be one, is dependent wholly upon the judges themselves and not at all upon the accumulation of litigation in any court. To state it another way the increase of the number of judges is to be provided, not in relation to the increase of work in any district or circuit, but in relation to the age of the judges and their unwillingness to retire.

In the second place, as pointed out in the President's message, only 25 of the 237 judges serving in the Federal courts on February 5, 1937, were over 70 years of age. Six of these were members of the Supreme Court at the time the bill was introduced. At the present time there are 24 judges 70 years of age or over distributed among the 10 circuit courts, the 84 district courts, and the 4 courts in the District of Columbia and of that 24, only 10 are serving in the 84 district courts, so that the remaining 14 are to be found in 4 special courts and in the 10 circuit courts. Moreover, the facts indicate that the courts with the oldest judges have the best records in the disposition of business. It follows, therefore, that since there are comparatively few aged justices in service and these are among the most efficient on the bench, the age of sitting judges does not make necessary an increase of personnel to handle the business of the courts.

There was submitted with the President's message a report from the Attorney General to the effect that in recent years the number of cases has greatly increased and that delay in the administration of justice is interminable. It is manifest, however, that this condition cannot be remedied by the contingent appointment of new judges to sit beside the judges over 70 years of age, most of whom are either altogether equal to their duties or are commissioned in courts in which congestion of business does not exist. It must be obvious that the way to attack congestion and delay in the courts is directly by legislation which will increase the number of judges in those districts where the accumulation exists, not indirectly by the contingent appointment of new judges to courts where the need does not exist, but where it may happen that the sitting judge is over 70 years of age. . . .

QUESTION OF AGE NOT SOLVED

The next question is to determine to what extent "the persistent infusion of new blood" may be expected from this bill.

It will be observed that the bill before us does not and cannot compel the retirement of any judge, whether on the Supreme Court or any other court, when he becomes 70 years of age. It will be remembered that the mere attainment of three score and ten by a particular judge does not, under this bill, require the appointment of another. The man on the bench may be 80 years of age, but this bill will not authorize the President to appoint a new judge to sit beside him unless he has served as a judge for 10 years. In other words, age itself is not penalized; the penalty falls only when age is attended with experience.

No one should over look the fact that under this bill the President, whoever he may be and whether or not he believes in the constant infusion of young blood in the courts, may nominate a man 69 years and 11 months of age to the Supreme Court, or to any court, and, if confirmed, such nominee, if he never had served as a judge, would continue to sit upon the bench unmolested by this law until he had attained the ripe age of 79 years and 11 months.

We are told that "modern complexities call also for a constant infusion of new blood in the courts, just as it is needed in executive functions of the Government and in private business." Does this bill provide for such? The answer is obviously no. As has been just demonstrated, the introduction of old and inexperienced blood into the courts is not prevented by this bill.

More than that, the measure, by its own terms, makes impossible the "constant" or "persistent" infusion of new blood. It is to be observed that the word is "new," not "young." . . .

It thus appears that the bill before us does not with certainty provide for increasing the personnel of the Federal judiciary, does not remedy the law's delay, does not serve the interest of the "poorer litigant" and does not provide for the "constant" or "persistent infusion of new blood" into the judiciary. What, then, does it do?

THE BILL APPLIES FORCE TO THE JUDICIARY

The answer is clear. It applies force to the judiciary. It is an attempt to impose upon the courts a course of action, a line of decision which, without that force, without that imposition, the judiciary might not adopt.

Can there be any doubt that this is the purpose of the bill? Increasing the personnel is not the object of this measure; infusing young blood is not the object; for if either one of these purposes had been in the minds of the proponents, the drafters would not have written the following clause to be found on page 2, lines 1 to 4, inclusive:

"Provided, That no additional judge shall be appointed hereunder if the judge who is of retirement age dies, resigns, or retires prior to the nomination of such additional judge."

Let it also be borne in mind that the President's message submitting this measure contains the following sentence:

"If, on the other hand, any judge eligible for retirement should feel that his Court would suffer because of an increase of its membership, he may retire or resign under already existing provisions of law if he wishes to do so."

Moreover, the Attorney General in testifying before the committee *** said:

"If the Supreme Court feels that the addition of six judges would be harmful to that Court, it can avoid that result by resigning."

Three invitations to the members of the Supreme Court over 70 years of age to get out despite all the talk about increasing personnel to expedite the disposition of cases and remedy the law's delay. One by the bill. One by the President's message. One by the Attorney General.

Can reasonable men by any possibility differ about the constitutional impropriety of such a course?

Those of us who hold office in this Government, however humble or exalted it may be, are creatures of the Constitution. To it we owe all the power and authority we possess. Outside of it we have none. We are bound by it in every official act.

We know that this instrument, without which we would not be able to call ourselves presidents, judges, or legislators, was carefully planned and deliberately framed to establish three coordinate branches of government, every one of them to be independent of the others. For the protection of the people, for the preservation of the rights of the individual, for the maintenance of the liberties of minorities, for maintaining the checks and balances of our dual system, the three branches of the Government were so constituted that the independent expression of honest difference of opinion could never be restrained in the people's servants and no one branch could overawe or subjugate the others. That is the American system. It is immeasurably more important, immeasurably more sacred to the people of America, indeed, to the people of all the world than the immediate adoption of any legislation however beneficial. . . .

A PRECEDENT OF LOYALTY TO THE CONSTITUTION

Shall we now, after 150 years of loyalty to the constitutional ideal of an untrammeled judiciary, duty bound to protect the constitutional rights of the humblest citizen even against the Government itself, create the vicious precedent which must necessarily undermine our system? The only argument for the increase which survives analysis is that Congress should enlarge the Court so as to make the policies of this administration effective.

We are told that a reactionary oligarchy defies the will of the majority, that this is a bill to "unpack" the Court and give effect to the desires of the majority; that is to say, a bill to increase the number of Justices for the express purpose of neutralizing the views of some of the present members. In justification we are told, but without authority, by those who would rationalize this program, that Congress was given the power to determine the size of the Court so that the legislative branch would be able to impose its will upon the judiciary. This amounts to nothing more than the declaration that when the Court stands in the way of a legislative enactment, the Congress may reverse the ruling by enlarging the Court. When such a principle is adopted, our constitutional system is overthrown!

This, then is the dangerous precedent we are asked to establish. When proponents of the bill assert, as they have done, that Congress in the past has altered the number of Justices upon the Supreme Court and that this is reason enough for our doing it now, they show how important precedents are and prove that we should now refrain from any action that would seem to establish one which could be followed hereafter whenever a Congress and an executive should become dissatisfied with the decisions of the Supreme Court.

This is the first time in the history of our country that a proposal to alter the decisions of the court by enlarging its personnel has been so boldly made. Let us meet it. Let us now set a salutary precedent that will never be violated. Let us, of the Seventy-fifth Congress, in words that will never be disregarded by any succeeding Congress, declare that we would rather have an independent Court, a fearless Court, a Court that will dare to announce its honest opinions in what it believes to be the defense of the liberties of the people, than a Court that, out of fear or sense of obligation to the appointing power, or factional passion, approves any measure we may enact. We are not the judges of the judges. We are not above the Constitution.

Even if every charge brought against the so-called "reactionary" members of this Court be true, it is far better that we await orderly but inevitable change of personnel than that we impatiently overwhelm them with new members. Exhibiting this restraint, thus demonstrating our faith in the American system, we shall set an example that will protect the independent American judiciary from attack as long as this Government stands. . . .

Cooper v. Aaron
358 U.S. 1; 78 S. Ct. 1401; 3 L. Ed. 2d 5 (1958)
Vote: 9-0

Opinion of the Court by *The Chief Justice, Mr. Justice Black, Mr. Justice Frankfurter, Mr. Justice Douglas, Mr. Justice Burton, Mr. Justice Clark, Mr. Justice Harlan, Mr. Justice Brennan,* and *Mr. Justice Whittaker.*

As this case reaches us it raises questions of the highest importance to the maintenance of our federal system of government. It necessarily involves a claim by the Governor and Legislature of a State that there is no duty on state officials to obey federal court orders resting on this Court's considered interpretation of the United States Constitution. Specifically it involves actions by the Governor and Legislature of Arkansas upon the premise that they are not bound by our holding in *Brown v. Board of Education.* *** That holding was that the Fourteenth Amendment forbids States to use their governmental powers to bar children on racial grounds from attending schools where there is state participation through any arrangement, management funds or property. We are urged to uphold a suspension of the Little Rock School Board's plan to do away with segregated public schools in Little Rock until state laws and efforts to upset and nullify our holding in *Brown v. Board of Education* have been further challenged and tested in the courts. We reject these contentions. . . .

On May 17, 1954, this Court decided that enforced racial segregation in the public schools of a State is a denial of the equal protection of the laws enjoined by the Fourteenth Amendment. *** The Court postponed, pending further argument, formulation of a decree to effectuate this decision. That decree was rendered May 31, 1955. *** In the formulation of that decree the Court recognized that good faith compliance with the principles declared in *Brown* might in some situations "call for elimination of a variety of obstacles in making the transition to school systems operated in accordance with the constitutional principles set forth in our May 17, 1954, decision." ***

. . . [T]he District Courts were directed to require "a prompt and reasonable start toward full compliance," and to take such action as was necessary to bring about the end of racial segregation in the public schools "with all deliberate speed." *** . . . It was made plain that delay in any guise in order to deny the constitutional rights of Negro children could not be countenanced, and that only a prompt start, diligently and earnestly pursued, to eliminate racial segregation from the public schools could constitute good faith compliance. State authorities were thus duty bound to devote every effort toward initiating desegregation and bringing about the elimination of racial discrimination in the public school system. . . .

While the School Board was . . . going forward with its preparation for desegregating the Little Rock school system, other state authorities, in contrast, were actively pursuing a program designed to perpetuate in Arkansas the system of racial segregation which this Court had held violated the Fourteenth Amendment. . . .

The School Board and the Superintendent of Schools nevertheless continued with preparations to carry out the first stage of the desegregation program. Nine Negro children were scheduled for admission in September 1957 to Central High School. . . .

On September 2, 1957, the day before these Negro students were to enter Central High, the school authorities were met with drastic opposing action on the part of the Governor of Arkansas who dispatched units of the Arkansas National Guard to the Central High school grounds and placed the school "off limits" to colored students. As found by the District Court in subsequent proceedings, the Governor's action had not been requested by the school authorities, and was entirely unheralded. . . .

The Governor's action caused the School Board to request the Negro students on September 2 not to attend the high school "until the legal dilemma was solved." The next day, September 3, 1957, the Board petitioned the District Court for instructions, and the court, after a hearing, found that the Board's request of the Negro students to stay away from the high school had been made because of the stationing of the military guards by the state authorities. The court determined that this was not a reason for departing from the approved plan, and ordered the School Board and Superintendent to proceed with it.

On the morning of the next day, September 4, 1957, the Negro children attempted to enter the high school but . . . [the] National Guard "acting pursuant to the Governor's order, stood shoulder to shoulder at the school grounds and thereby forcibly prevented the 9 Negro students . . . from entering," as they continued to do every school day during the following three weeks. ***

. . . After hearings, . . . the District Court found that the School Board's plan had been obstructed by the

Governor through the use of National Guard troops, and granted a preliminary injunction ... enjoining the Governor and the officers of the Guard from preventing the attendance of Negro children at Central High School, and from otherwise obstructing or interfering with the orders of the court in connection with the plan. *** The National Guard was then withdrawn from the school.

The next school day was Monday, September 23, 1957. The Negro children entered the high school that morning under the protection of the Little Rock Police Department and members of the Arkansas State Police. But the officers caused the children to be removed from the school during the morning because they had difficulty controlling a large and demonstrating crowd which had gathered at the high school. *** On September 25, however, the President of the United States dispatched federal troops to Central High School and admission of the Negro students to the school was thereby effected. ...

We come now to the aspect of the proceedings presently before us. ... [T]he School Board and the Superintendent of Schools filed a petition in the District Court seeking a postponement of their program for desegregation. Their position in essence was that because of extreme public hostility, which they stated had been engendered largely by the official attitudes and actions of the Governor and the Legislature, the maintenance of a sound educational program at Central High School, with the Negro students in attendance, would be impossible. The Board therefore proposed that the Negro students already admitted to the school be withdrawn and sent to segregated schools, and that all further steps to carry out the Board's desegregation program be postponed for a period later suggested by the Board to be two and one-half years. ...

One may well sympathize with the position of the Board in the face of the frustrating conditions which have confronted it, but, regardless of the Board's good faith, the actions of the other state agencies responsible for those conditions compel us to reject the Board's legal position. Had Central High School been under the direct management of the State itself, it could hardly be suggested that those immediately in charge of the school should be heard to assert their own good faith as a legal excuse for delay in implementing the constitutional rights of these respondents, when vindication of those rights were rendered difficult or impossible by the actions of other state officials. The situation here is in no different posture because the members of the School Board and the Superintendent of Schools are local officials; from the point of view of the Fourteenth Amendment, they stand in this litigation as the agents of the State.

The constitutional rights of respondents are not to be sacrificed or yielded to the violence and disorder which have followed upon the actions of the Governor and Legislature. ... Thus law and order are not here to be preserved by depriving the Negro children of their constitutional rights. The record before us clearly established that the growth of the Board's difficulties to a magnitude beyond its unaided power to control is the product of state action. ...

The controlling legal principles are plain. The command of the Fourteenth Amendment is that no "State" shall deny to any person within its jurisdiction the equal protection of the laws. ... [T]he prohibitions of the Fourteenth Amendment extend to all action of the State denying equal protection of the laws; whatever the agency of the State taking the action. *** In short, the constitutional rights of children not to be discriminated against in school admission on grounds of race or color declared by this Court in the *Brown* case can neither be nullified openly and directly by state legislators or state executive or judicial officers, nor nullified indirectly by them through evasive schemes for segregation whether attempted "ingeniously or ingenuously." ***

What has been said, in the light of the facts developed, is enough to dispose of the case. However, we should answer the premise of the actions of the Governor and Legislature that they are not bound by our holding in the *Brown* case. It is necessary only to recall some basic constitutional propositions which are settled doctrine.

Article 6 of the Constitution makes the Constitution the "supreme Law of the Land." ... Chief Justice Marshall ... declared in *Marbury v. Madison:* *** "It is emphatically the province and duty of the judicial department to say what the law is." This decision declared the basic principle that the federal judiciary is supreme in the exposition of the law of the Constitution, and that principle has ever since been respected by this Court and the Country as a permanent and indispensable feature of our constitutional system. It follows that the interpretation of the Fourteenth Amendment enunciated by this Court in the Brown Case is the supreme law of the land, and Art 6 of the Constitution makes it of binding effect on the States "any Thing in the Constitution or Laws of any State to the Contrary notwithstanding." Every state legislator and executive and judicial officer is solemnly committed by oath taken pursuant to Art 6, cl 3, "to support this Constitution." . . .

No state legislator or executive or judicial officer can war against the Constitution without violating his undertaking to support it. Chief Justice Marshall spoke for a unanimous Court in saying that: "If the legislatures of the several states may, at will, annul the judgments of the courts of the United States, and destroy the rights acquired under those judgments, the Constitution itself becomes a solemn mockery. . . ." *** A Governor who asserts a power to nullify a federal court order is similarly restrained. . . .

It is, of course, quite true that the responsibility for public education is primarily the concern of the States, but it is equally true that such responsibilities, like all other state activity, must be exercised consistently with federal constitutional requirements as they apply to state action. . . . State support of segregated schools through any arrangement, management, funds, or property cannot be squared with the Amendment's command that no State shall deny to any person within its jurisdiction the equal protection of the laws. . . . The basic decision in *Brown* was unanimously reached by this Court. . . . Since the first *Brown* opinion three new Justices have come to the Court. They are at one with the Justices still on the Court who participated in that basic decision as to its correctness, and that decision is now unanimously reaffirmed. The principles announced in that decision and the obedience of the States to them, according to the command of the Constitution, are indispensable for the protection of the freedoms guaranteed by our fundamental charter for all of us. Our constitutional ideal of equal justice under law is thus made a living truth.

Mr. Justice Frankfurter, concurring. . . .

CHAPTER FOUR

INTERNAL LIMITATIONS ON JUDICIAL POWER

Lewis Powell: Associate Justice, 1972–1987

I . . . believe that repeated and essentially head-on confrontations between the life-tenured branch and the elected branches of government will not, in the long run, be beneficial to either. The public confidence essential to the former and the vitality crucial to the latter may well erode if we do not exercise self-restraint in the utilization of our power. . . .

Justice Lewis F. Powell, Concurring in *United States v. Richardson* (1974)

INTRODUCTION

The exercise of judicial review by the federal courts is limited by the constitutional system of checks and balances. It is further constrained by judicial doctrines that limit the exercise of judicial power. These doctrines reflect an underlying philosophy of **judicial restraint,** a philosophy that counsels courts to exercise their powers cautiously. Advocates of judicial restraint point to the inherent tensions surrounding the existence of judicial review in a democracy and the consequences that may result when the judiciary contravenes the wishes of the elected branches of government. American constitutional history demonstrates that the imprudent exercise of judicial review can be costly to the institutional prestige and credibility of the courts. In addition, courts, like all government agencies, have limited resources. Doctrines of judicial restraint assist courts in allocating these scarce resources more efficiently.

The **limiting doctrines** discussed in this chapter are both complex and imprecise and their employment by the federal courts is anything but mechanical. Indeed, the self-imposed limitations are often "honored in the breach." Yet they reflect a fairly long-standing and pervasive commitment within the federal judiciary to the principle that, as the Supreme Court said in *Broadrick v. Oklahoma* (1974), "courts are not roving commissions assigned to pass judgment on the nation's laws."

THRESHOLD REQUIREMENTS

Before reaching the merits of a case, a federal court must first resolve a number of **threshold issues.** Far from being mere legal technicalities, threshold considerations are an important aspect of the judicial policy-making process. These considerations determine which policy questions will be addressed by the courts, as well as how and when such questions will be examined. From an institutional perspective, these self-imposed constraints may ultimately help to insulate the courts from external retaliation.

Jurisdiction

The fundamental threshold question that must be addressed in any lawsuit is that of jurisdiction, the legal authority to hear and decide a case. A court must have jurisdiction, both over the subject matter of a case and the parties to a case, before it may proceed to adjudicate that controversy. The jurisdiction of the federal courts is determined both by the language of Article III of the Constitution and by statutes enacted by Congress.

The jurisdiction of the federal courts, while broad, is not unlimited. There are two basic categories of federal jurisdiction. First, and most important for students of constitutional law, is **federal question jurisdiction.** The essential requirement here is that a case must present a "federal question," that is, a question arising under the U.S. Constitution or a federal statute, regulation, executive order, or treaty. Of course, given its expansive modern role, the federal government has produced a myriad of statutes, regulations, and executive orders. Consequently, most important questions of public policy can be framed as issues of federal law, thus permitting the federal courts to play a tremendous role in the policy-making process.

The second broad category, **diversity jurisdiction,** applies only to civil suits and is unrelated to the presence of a question of federal law. To qualify under federal diversity jurisdiction, a case must involve parties from different states and an amount in controversy that exceeds fifty thousand dollars.

Jurisdiction: An Internal as Well as an External Constraint

While the issue of jurisdiction can be viewed as an external constraint on the courts, in that Congress actually writes the statutes that define jurisdiction, it functions as an internal constraint as well. This is especially true at the Supreme Court level, where the exercise of jurisdiction is subject to the discretion of the justices. As noted in Chapter 1, Congress in 1988 made the appellate jurisdiction of the Supreme Court almost entirely discretionary by greatly limiting the so-called appeals by right. Rather, the Court's appellate jurisdiction is exercised almost exclusively through the writ of certiorari, which is, of course, issued at the Court's discretion. Federal law authorizes the Court to grant certiorari to review all cases, state or federal, which raise substantial federal questions. This extremely wide discretion permits the Court to set its own agenda, which enhances its role as a policymaker. But it also permits the Court to avoid certain issues that may carry undesirable institutional consequences. The Court may deflect, or at least postpone dealing with, issues that it considers too hot to handle. The Court's flexible jurisdiction, then, can be used as a means to expand or limit the Court's policy-making role, depending on the issue. Thus, jurisdiction, at least at the level of the Supreme Court, can function as a self-imposed constraint on the exercise of judicial power.

The "Case or Controversy" Requirement

Unlike some state courts, the federal courts are not in the business of rendering **advisory opinions.** Rather, their decisions are limited to real controversies between adverse parties. This limitation may be inferred from the language of Article III, which extends the federal judicial power to "cases" arising under federal law and "controversies" involving certain types of parties. Yet it remained for the Supreme Court to recognize and enforce this limitation on judicial power. In 1793, Chief Justice John Jay first asserted the ban on advisory opinions by rebuffing an attempt by President George Washington to obtain the Court's advice on matters of international law.

The Supreme Court has said that the exercise of the federal judicial power is limited to "flesh and blood" cases and does not extend to contrived lawsuits. Thus in *Muskrat v. United States* (1911), the Court refused to take jurisdiction in a case where Congress had authorized members of the Cherokee tribe to sue the federal government to challenge a law redistributing tribal properties. Referring to the power of judicial review, the Court's opinion in *Muskrat* said:

> The exercise of this, the most important and delicate duty of this court, is not given to it as a body with revisory power over the actions of Congress, but because the

rights of the litigants in justiciable controversies require the court to choose between the fundamental law and a law purporting to be enacted within constitutional authority, but in fact beyond the power delegated to the legislative branch of government.

The case-or-controversy limitation is perhaps the most basic application of the philosophy of judicial restraint. Nevertheless, federal judges and justices from time to time render miniature advisory opinions on hypothetical issues—in the form of **obiter dicta** contained in their written opinions. Dicta are statements that are not essential to the resolution of the case at hand. Although dicta are not legally binding, they are important in that they signal how the courts might respond to a given issue in the future.

Arranged Test Cases

Sometimes, the parties to litigation may stretch the truth a bit to meet the case-or-controversy requirement. The historic case of *Plessy v. Ferguson* (1896) provides a ready example. In 1890, Louisiana enacted a law requiring railroads to carry black passengers in separate cars. A civil rights organization based in New Orleans sought to challenge this statute. Railroads, which incurred the expense of providing additional railroad cars to comply with the law, proved sympathetic to the challenge. On the basis of mutual interest, civil rights lawyers and railroad officials arranged a test case. According to plan, Homer Plessy, not readily identifiable as a black person, was arrested by a railroad detective immediately after taking his seat in the "whites only" car. Plessy's attorneys argued that the Louisiana law violated the Equal Protection Clause of the Fourteenth Amendment and ultimately carried the case all the way to the Supreme Court. Ironically, this challenge led to the Court's upholding the law on the basis of the infamous "separate but equal" doctrine (see Chapter 16).

Standing to Sue

After determining that a real case or controversy exists, a federal court must ascertain whether the parties to the litigation have standing. This is simply a determination of whether the litigants are the appropriate parties to raise the legal questions in the case. The Supreme Court has developed an elaborate body of principles defining the nature and contours of standing. Essentially, to have standing, a party must have a personal stake in the case. A plaintiff must have suffered some direct and substantial injury or be likely to suffer such an injury if a particular legal wrong is not redressed. A defendant must be the party responsible for perpetrating the alleged legal wrong.

One may challenge a law or policy on constitutional grounds if he or she can show that the enforcement of the law or implementation of the policy infringes on an individual constitutional right, such as freedom of speech. Thus, in *Tinker v. Des Moines Community School District* (1969), there was no question that parents had standing to challenge public school authorities' restrictions on their children's wearing black armbands to protest the Vietnam War. On the other hand, mere ideological opposition to a particular government policy is not sufficient grounds to challenge that policy in a federal court.

Certainly a significant economic injury or burden is sufficient to provide standing to sue. For example, in *Singleton v. Wulff* (1976), the Supreme Court held that a doctor had standing to challenge an abortion law that would have an adverse impact on his practice and his relationship with patients. Writing for the Court, Justice Blackmun noted that

> ... the constitutionally protected abortion decision is one in which the physician is intimately involved. Aside from the woman herself, therefore, the physician is uniquely qualified to litigate the constitutionality of the State's interference with, or discrimination against, that decision.

Taxpayer Suits

Not every economic burden is sufficient to confer standing. In most situations, a taxpayer does not have standing to challenge policies or programs that he or she is forced to support. In *Frothingham v. Mellon* (1923), the Supreme Court denied a federal taxpayer the right to challenge a federal program that she claimed violated the Tenth Amendment, which reserves certain powers to the states. The Court said:

> The party who invokes the [federal judicial] power must be able to show that he has sustained or is immediately in danger of sustaining some direct injury as the result of the statute's enforcement, and not merely that he suffers in some indefinite way common with people generally.

The Supreme Court's long-held prohibition against taxpayer standing was qualified somewhat in *Flast v. Cohen* (1968). There the Court granted standing to a taxpayer to challenge federal spending that would benefit parochial schools in possible violation of the Establishment of Religion Clause of the First Amendment. The *Flast* decision created a narrow exception to the bar against taxpayer lawsuits, an exception that has not been expanded, despite numerous opportunities to do so. Indeed, there is question as to the continued vitality of the *Flast* decision, especially in light of such decisions as *United States v. Richardson* (1974).

In *Richardson,* the Court denied standing to a taxpayer who sought to challenge a provision of the Central Intelligence Act exempting the Central Intelligence Agency from the constitutional requirement that government expenditures be publicly reported (see Article I, Section 9, clause 7). Writing for a majority of five justices, Chief Justice Burger argued that although Richardson, as a federal taxpayer, had "a genuine interest in the use of funds," he had not alleged that he was "in danger of suffering any particular concrete injury...." Burger recognized that if a taxpayer "is not permitted to litigate this issue, no one can do so." Nevertheless, he concluded:

> In a very real sense, the absence of any particular individual or class to litigate these claims gives support to the argument that the subject matter is committed to the surveillance of Congress, and ultimately to the political process. Any other conclusion would mean that the Founding Fathers intended to set up something in the nature of an Athenian democracy or New England town meeting to oversee the conduct of the National Government by means of lawsuits in the federal courts.

In a stinging dissent, Justice William O. Douglas wrote:

> The sovereign in this Nation are the people, not the bureaucracy. The statement of accounts of public expenditures goes to the heart of the problem of sovereignty. If taxpayers may not ask that rudimentary question, their sovereignty becomes an empty symbol and a secret bureaucracy is allowed to run our affairs.

Another decision casting doubt on the continued vitality of *Flast v. Cohen* is *Valley Forge Christian College v. Americans United for Separation of Church and State, Inc.* (1982). In this case, the Supreme Court denied standing to a group of taxpayers who sought to challenge the transfer of federal property to a private Christian college. Writing for a sharply divided Court, Justice Rehnquist said:

> We simply cannot see that respondents have alleged an *injury of any kind,* economic or otherwise, sufficient to confer standing. Respondents complain of a transfer of property located in Chester County, Pa. The named plaintiffs reside in Maryland and Virginia; their organizational headquarters are located in Washington, D.C. They learned of the transfer from a news release. Their claim that the Government has violated the Establishment Clause does not provide a special license to roam the country in search of wrongdoing and to reveal their discoveries in federal court. The federal courts were simply not constituted as ombudsmen of the general welfare.

Decisions such as *United States v. Richardson* and *Valley Forge Christian College v. Americans United* indicate that the traditional barrier against taxpayer lawsuits remains very much intact.

Standing to Assert Environmental Interests

An issue of considerable contemporary significance is standing to sue to prevent damage to the natural environment. In *Sierra Club v. Morton* (1972), the Supreme Court denied an environmental group standing to challenge a decision by the secretary of the interior to permit the construction of a resort complex in a national forest. The Court acknowledged that conservational interests might be protected through litigation but held that the Sierra Club had not demonstrated that its members would be substantially adversely affected by the secretary's decision.

In *United States v. Students Challenging Regulatory Agency Procedures (SCRAP)* (1973), the Supreme Court granted standing to a group of law students to challenge a regulation of the Interstate Commerce Commission (ICC). This regulation permitted an increase in railroad freight surcharges for recyclable materials, which made recycling more expensive. Perhaps picking up on the cue provided by the Court in *Sierra Club,* SCRAP argued that its members "suffered economic, recreational and aesthetic harm directly as a result of the railroad freight rate structure . . ." because the increased cost of recycling would mean an increase in litter in the natural environment. Moreover, SCRAP argued that the decision to permit a rate increase for the transportation of recyclable materials was illegal because the ICC had failed to perform an environmental impact study as required by the National Environmental Policy Act of 1969. The Supreme Court distinguished the *SCRAP* case from *Sierra Club v. Morton,* saying,

In *Sierra Club* ... we went on to stress the importance of demonstrating that the party seeking review be himself among the injured, for it is this requirement that gives a litigant a direct stake in the controversy and prevents the judicial process from becoming no more than a vehicle for the vindication of the value interests of concerned bystanders. No such specific injury was alleged in *Sierra Club*. ... [T]he Sierra Club failed to allege that it or its members would be affected in any of their activities or pastimes. ... Here, by contrast, the appellees [SCRAP] claimed that the specific and allegedly illegal action of the Commission [ICC] would directly harm them in their use of the natural resources of the Washington Metropolitan Area.

In *Duke Power v. Carolina Environmental Study Group* (1978), the Court permitted residents of a community near the site of a proposed nuclear power plant to challenge the constitutionality of the federal Price-Anderson Act, which facilitates construction of nuclear plants by limiting liability for accidents. The Court said that:

> ... [T]he emission of non-natural radiation into appellees' environment would ... seem a direct and present injury, given our generalized concern about exposure to radiation and the apprehension flowing from the uncertainty about the health and genetic consequences of even small emissions like those concededly emitted by nuclear power plants.

Reaching the merits of the case, the Court upheld the Price-Anderson Act, saying that "limiting liability is an acceptable method for Congress to utilize in encouraging the private development of electric energy by atomic power. ..." The *Duke Power* case thus demonstrates that the grant of standing to sue is no guarantee that plaintiffs will ultimately prevail in their challenge to government action.

Opposing Philosophies of Standing

The issue of standing is far more than a mere technical aspect of the judicial process. A grant or denial of standing determines who may challenge government policies and, to some extent, what types of policies may be challenged. Arguments over standing reflect different conceptions of the role of the federal courts in the political system. In a concurring opinion in *United States v. Richardson* (1974), Justice Lewis Powell wrote:

> Relaxation of standing requirements is directly related to the expansion of judicial power. It seems to me that allowing unrestricted ... standing would significantly alter the allocation of power at the national level, with a shift away from a democratic form of government.

A contrasting perspective is offered by Justice William O. Douglas, dissenting in *Warth v. Seldin* (1975):

> Standing has become a barrier to access to the federal courts. ... The mounting caseload of the federal courts is well known. But cases such as this one reflect festering sores in our society; and the American dream teaches that if one reaches high enough and persists there is a forum where justice is dispensed. I would lower the technical barriers and let the courts serve that ancient need.

William O. Douglas: Associate
Justice, 1939–1975

Mootness

A case is moot if the issues that gave rise to it have been resolved or have otherwise disappeared. Such a case is apt to be dismissed, because a court decision would have no practical effect. An excellent example of a constitutional case being dismissed for **mootness** is *DeFunis v. Odegaard* (1974). Marco De-Funis was denied admission to the University of Washington Law School. When he discovered that minority students with lower grade point averages and test scores had obtained admission under an affirmative action program, he filed suit in the state courts. The state trial court held that DeFunis had been denied the "equal protection of the laws" required by the Fourteenth Amendment and ordered that he be admitted to the law school. On appeal, the Washington Supreme Court reversed the trial court, holding that the affirmative action plan did not violate the Constitution. By then, DeFunis was in his second year of law school. The U.S. Supreme Court granted DeFunis's petition for certiorari, and Justice Douglas issued an order staying the decision of the state supreme court. By the time the case was orally argued in the U.S. Supreme Court, DeFunis was in his third and final year of law school. When the Court finally dismissed the case on mootness grounds, DeFunis was within weeks of graduation.

In the *DeFunis* case, the Supreme Court was able to delay dealing with the difficult and controversial political issue of affirmative action. The delay was rather short, however, as the Court reached the merits of the affirmative action issue in *University of California Board of Regents v. Bakke* (1978) (see Chapter 16).

If the federal courts strictly adhered to the mootness rule, certain inherently time-bound questions would never be addressed. Such issues are, in the Supreme Court's words, "capable of repetition yet evading review." *Roe v. Wade* (1973), the landmark abortion case, provides an excellent example. The gestation period of the human fetus is nine months; the gestation period for constitutional litigation tends to be much longer! Thus, by the time the *Roe* case reached the Supreme Court, Jane Roe had given birth to her child. Explaining the Court's refusal to dismiss the case as moot, Justice Blackmun's majority opinion stated:

> The usual rule . . . is that an actual controversy must exist at stages of appellate or certiorari review, and not simply at the date the action is initiated. *** But when, as here, pregnancy is a significant fact in the litigation, the normal 266-day human gestation period is so short that the pregnancy will come to term before the usual appellate process is complete. If that termination makes a case moot, pregnancy litigation will seldom survive much beyond the trial stage, and appellate review will be effectively denied. Our law should not be that rigid. Pregnancy often comes more than once to the same woman, and in the general population, if man is to survive, it will always be with us. Pregnancy provides a classic justification for a conclusion of nonmootness.

In *Roe,* the Court chose to relax the mootness rule to address an important issue. However, had the Court been disinclined to deal with the divisive abortion question, the mootness doctrine would have provided the Court a convenient out.

Ripeness

A case that comes to an appellate court too late, such as *DeFunis v. Odegaard,* may be dismissed as moot; one that comes to court too soon may be dismissed as "not ripe for review." The purpose of this doctrine is to prevent the courts from getting prematurely involved in issues that may ultimately be resolved through other means. Like the doctrines of standing and mootness, the **ripeness** doctrine is not merely a means of conserving judicial power but also can be used flexibly as part of the judicial agenda-setting process.

A classic example of the Supreme Court using the ripeness doctrine to avoid an important constitutional issue occurred in *United Public Workers v. Mitchell* (1947). The Political Activities Act of 1939, better known as the Hatch Act, prohibits federal employees from active involvement in political campaigns. The purpose of the law is to maintain the appearance of political neutrality in the federal civil service. A number of federal employees, fearful of losing their jobs, brought suit, arguing that the act violated their First Amendment rights. The Supreme Court dismissed the case, saying:

> The power of courts, and ultimately of this Court, to pass upon the constitutionality of acts of Congress arises only when the interests of litigants require the use of this judicial authority for their protection against actual interference. A hypothetical threat is not enough. We can only speculate as to the kinds of political activity the appellants desire to engage in or as to the contents of their proposed public statements or the circumstances of their publication.

Justices Black and Douglas dissented from the dismissal of the suit, arguing that "to require these employees first to suffer the hardship of an actual discharge is not only to make them incur a penalty; it makes inadequate . . . any legal remedy they might have."

Another classic example of the application of the ripeness doctrine is *Poe v. Ullman* (1961). In this case, the Supreme Court dismissed a challenge to a nineteenth-century Connecticut law that prohibited practicing birth control through artificial means (see Chapter 15). The Court said that since the law had not yet been enforced against the plaintiffs, the case was not ripe for judicial review. Eventually, the Court reviewed and struck down the Connecticut statute, but only after an individual was convicted and fined for violating the law (see *Griswold v. Connecticut* [1965]).

Exhaustion of Remedies

A close cousin of the ripeness doctrine is the **exhaustion of remedies** requirement. For a case to be ripe for judicial consideration, the parties must have first exhausted all their nonjudicial remedies. The primary application of this doctrine is to cases that involve decisions by administrative or regulatory agencies. Thus, for example, a corporation that has been denied a broadcasting license by the Federal Communications Commission (FCC) must first exhaust all means of appeal within the FCC before taking the case to federal court. The exhaustion doctrine avoids unnecessary litigation and allows the courts to defer to agency "experts" in the resolution of what can be complex and technical issues.

In *Natural Gas Pipeline Co. v. Slattery* (1937), the Supreme Court said that the exhaustion requirement had "especial force" when the case involved a state, as distinct from a federal, agency. In such cases, the Court's customary deference to the executive branch is compounded with its traditional deference to state governments. Judicial intervention into state or federal agency decision making may be justified, however, in order to prevent "irreparable injury" from being inflicted on a citizen or company (see *Oklahoma Natural Gas Co. v. Russell* [1923]).

The Doctrine of Abstention

Closely akin to exhaustion of remedies is the doctrine of **abstention.** Whereas the principal application of the exhaustion doctrine is to bureaucratic decision making, the primary application of abstention is to the state court systems. Essentially, the abstention doctrine prohibits the federal courts from intervening in state court proceedings until they have been finalized. Thus, a person convicted of a crime in a state court normally must exhaust all means of appeal in the state judiciary before petitioning the U.S. Supreme Court for a writ of certiorari or a federal district court for a writ of habeas corpus.

Under the doctrine of abstention, federal judges normally abstain from issuing injunctions to prevent persons from being prosecuted under unconstitutional state statutes. For example, in *Younger v. Harris* (1971), the Supreme Court said it was improper for a federal court to enjoin a state prosecutor from trying a man under a state law virtually identical to one that had recently been declared unconstitutional (see *Brandenburg v. Ohio* [1969]). Writing for the Court, Justice Black stressed the notion of "comity," which entails mutual respect between the state and federal governments.

The Political Questions Doctrine

Even though a case may meet the formal prerequisites of jurisdiction, standing, ripeness, and so forth, the federal courts may still refuse to consider the merits of the dispute. Under the doctrine of political questions, cases may be dismissed as nonjusticiable if the issues they present are regarded as extremely "political" in nature. Of course, in a broad sense, all of the cases that make their way into the federal courts are political in nature. The political questions doctrine really refers to those issues that are likely to draw the courts into a political battle with the executive or legislative branch or are simply more amenable to executive or legislative decision making.

The doctrine of political questions originated in *Luther v. Borden* (1849). There, the Supreme Court refused to take sides in a dispute between two rival governments in Rhode Island, one based on a popular referendum, the other based on an old royal charter. Writing for the Court, Chief Justice Roger B. Taney observed that the argument in the case "turned on political rights and political questions." Not insignificantly, President John Tyler had agreed to send in troops to support the charter government before the case ever went to the Supreme Court.

Foreign Policy and Military Affairs

Perhaps the best established application of the political questions doctrine is the federal courts' unwillingness to enter the fields of international relations, military affairs, and foreign policy-making. This was demonstrated in *Massachusetts v. Laird* (1970), where the Supreme Court dismissed a suit challenging the constitutionality of the Vietnam War. This position was reaffirmed in *Goldwater v. Carter* (1979), where the Court refused to entertain a lawsuit brought by a U.S. senator challenging President Jimmy Carter's unilateral termination of a defense treaty with Taiwan. It was invoked more recently in 1982, when a federal district judge in Washington, D.C., dismissed a lawsuit brought by members of Congress challenging President Reagan's decision to supply military aid to the government of El Salvador (see *Crockett v. Reagan* [1982]).

Legislative Reapportionment

For a number of years, the federal courts stayed out of controversies involving the apportionment of legislative districts. In *Colegrove v. Green* (1946), Justice Felix Frankfurter warned of the dangers of entering the "political thicket" of reapportionment. But in *Baker v. Carr* (1962), the Supreme Court held that legislative malapportionment (that is, gross disparities in population among districts) was a justiciable question in federal court. This decision signaled a veritable revolution, in which federal courts directed the reapportionment of legislative districts at all levels of government, from the U.S. House of Representatives to local school boards, on the basis of "one person, one vote."

In an interview given after his retirement from the Court, former Chief Justice Earl Warren said, "[I]n my mind, the most important case we have had in all those years was *Baker v. Carr,* which is what we might call the parent of the one man, one vote doctrine." (Television interview, WGBH-TV, Boston, 1972.) Arguably, the reapportionment decisions were the most important contributions of the Warren Court to American constitutional law. (For an extensive discussion of the reapportionment issue, see Chapter 17.)

Justice Brennan's Summary of the Political Questions Doctrine

Justice Brennan's majority opinion in *Baker v. Carr* contains a useful summary of the matters to which the political questions doctrine would apply: (1) those demonstrably committed by the Constitution to some other branch of government; (2) those lacking judicially discoverable standards; (3) those requiring initial policy determinations clearly reserved for nonjudicial discretion; (4) those in which a court decision would express disrespect for a coordinate branch of government; (5) those in which there is a need for firm adherence to "political decisions" already made; and (6) those in which there is a danger of embarrassment by multiple pronouncements by various branches of government.

Although Brennan's summary is helpful, it by no means eliminates all of the ambiguities inherent in the political questions doctrine. One can say, however, that political questions are now confined to matters involving separation of powers and thus function primarily as a means of maintaining good relations between the federal courts and the other branches of the national government.

DECISIONS ON THE MERITS

The philosophy of judicial restraint counsels judges to avoid broad or dramatic constitutional pronouncements. Accordingly, various doctrines limit the exercise of judicial review, even after a federal court has reached the merits of a case. Some of these rules are codified in Justice Louis Brandeis's oft-cited concurring opinion in *Ashwander v. Tennessee Valley Authority* (1936). In *Ashwander,* the Supreme Court upheld the federal government's program of building dams to generate electrical power in the Tennessee Valley region. Justice Brandeis's concurring opinion has become a classic statement of the principles of judicial restraint. The **Ashwander Rules,** as they have come to be known, seek to protect judicial power not only by deflecting constitutional questions but by making narrow rulings when constitutional pronouncements cannot be avoided.

The Doctrine of Strict Necessity

Under the **doctrine of strict necessity,** federal courts will attempt to avoid a constitutional question if a case can be decided on nonconstitutional grounds. As formulated in *Ashwander v. Tennessee Valley Authority,* "It is not the habit of the court to decide questions of a constitutional nature unless absolutely necessary to the decision of a case." For example, in *Communist Party of the United States v. Subversive Activities Control Board* (1956), the Supreme Court remanded a case to a government agency for further proceedings, rather than reach the sensitive political issue of whether the Communist Party enjoyed constitutional protection. Similarly, in *Hurd v. Hodge* (1948), the Court addressed the issue of "restrictive covenants," private agreements prohibiting the sale and rental of housing to African-Americans and other minorities. The Court held that enforcement of restrictive covenants by federal courts in the District of Columbia would violate national public policy but did not reach the question of whether such enforcement would violate the Constitution. The Court said: "It is a well settled principle that this court will not decide constitutional questions where other grounds are available and dispositive of the issues of the case." The Court chose not to avoid this constitutional issue in a similar case arising in a state court, ruling that state judicial enforcement violates the Equal Protection Clause of the Fourteenth Amendment (see *Shelley v. Kraemer* [1948], discussed and reprinted in Chapter 16).

The Doctrine of Saving Construction

Before a court can determine the constitutionality of a statute, it must first determine its exact meaning. This is known as **statutory construction.** In construing statutes, courts often must look beyond the language of the law to the intent of the legislature. Sometimes, the intent is clearly revealed in the legislative debate surrounding the adoption of the law. At other times, legislative intent is not clear, allowing the courts to exercise discretion in deciding what the law means.

Sometimes, the judicial interpretation of the statute may determine its constitutionality. Where a challenged law is subject to different interpretations, judicial restraint demands that a court choose an interpretation that results in saving the constitutionality of the law. This is known as the **doctrine of saving construction.** The doctrine is articulated by Justice Brandeis in *Ashwander v. Tennessee Valley Authority:*

> When the validity of an act of the Congress is drawn in question, and even if a serious doubt of constitutionality is raised, it is a cardinal principle that this Court will first ascertain whether a construction of the statute is fairly possible by which the question may be avoided.

In *National Labor Relations Board v. Jones & Laughlin Steel Corporation* (1937), the Supreme Court upheld the Wagner Act of 1935, a controversial federal statute regulating labor-management relations in major industries (see Chapter 5). The Jones-Laughlin Steel Corporation argued that the act was a thinly disguised attempt to regulate all industries, rather than merely those that affected interstate commerce. This point was crucial, as Congress's power in this field is limited to the regulation of interstate commerce. Given the choice between two interpretations of the act, the Court chose the narrower one, leading to a conclusion that the act was valid. Writing for the majority, Chief Justice Charles Evans Hughes observed,

> The cardinal principle of statutory construction is to save and not to destroy. We have repeatedly held that as between two possible interpretations of a statute, by one of which it would be unconstitutional and by the other valid, our plain duty is to adopt that which will save the act.

The Narrowness Doctrine

When a federal court does invalidate a statute, it usually does so on narrow grounds, so as to avoid a broad pronouncement that might carry unforeseen implications for future cases. As expressed in the *Ashwander* Rules, courts should not "formulate a rule of constitutional law broader than is required by the precise facts to which it is to be applied." A narrowly grounded decision accomplishes the desired result, striking down an unconstitutional statute, but preserving both judicial and legislative options in the future.

In *Bowsher v. Synar* (1986), the Supreme Court struck down a provision of the Gramm-Rudman-Hollings Act, a law designed to reduce the federal deficit through automatic spending cuts. The plaintiff, Representative Mike Synar (D.-Oklahoma), asked the Court to invalidate the statute on the grounds that it delegated Congress's lawmaking power to the comptroller general, an appointed official. Rather, the Court ruled that the law impermissibly assigned executive powers to an official under the control of Congress. Thus, the Court avoided the issue of congressional delegation of legislative power altogether. The delegation issue is potentially explosive because so many of the regulations promulgated by the federal bureaucracy are based on authority delegated by Congress to the executive branch (see Chapter 7).

Similarly, in *Watkins v. United States* (1957), the Supreme Court refused to rule on the question of whether witnesses testifying before congressional committees had a First Amendment right to refuse to answer certain questions about the "subversive" activities of other persons. Yet the Court did reverse Watkins' conviction for contempt of Congress on due process grounds, signaling its displeasure with the unbridled investigations of the House Un-American Activities Committee (see Chapter 5).

Avoiding the Creation of New Principles

A variation on the narrowness doctrine is that courts should not create a new principle if a case may be decided on the basis of an existing one. Thus, in *Stanley v. Georgia* (1969), the Supreme Court struck down a state law making it a crime to possess obscene material in the home. Stretching the boundaries of the First Amendment, the Court held that this law was a violation of the freedom of expression. The Court could have created a right of privacy to engage in certain activities in the home that might be subject to criminal prosecution outside the home. This, however, would have required the Court to consider the constitutionality of numerous criminal prohibitions, including laws governing possession and use of "recreational" drugs.

The federal appellate courts are not bound to address constitutional issues precisely as they have been framed by the litigants. In its grant of certiorari, the

Supreme Court may direct the parties to address certain issues and then refuse to decide these issues. For example, in *Illinois v. Gates* (1983), the Supreme Court directed the parties to argue the so-called "good faith exception" to the Fourth Amendment exclusionary rule (see Chapter 14). In its final decision in *Gates,* the Court did not address the highly controversial good faith exception but decided the case on other grounds. Thus, the Court refrained, at least temporarily, from creating a new principle of constitutional law.

Stare Decisis

The term *stare decisis* ("stand by decided matters") refers to the doctrine of **precedent.** It is axiomatic that American courts of law should follow precedent whenever possible, thus maintaining stability and continuity in the law. Justice Louis Brandeis once remarked, "*Stare decisis* is usually the wise policy, because in most matters it is more important that the applicable rule of law be settled than that it be settled right" (*Burnet v. Coronado Oil Co.* [1932], dissenting opinion).

Devotion to precedent is considered a hallmark of judicial restraint. Obviously, following precedent limits a judge's ability to determine the outcome of a case in a way that he or she might choose if it were a matter of first impression. The decision in *Roe v. Wade* poses an interesting problem for new Supreme Court justices who believe the decision legalizing abortion was incorrect. Should a new justice who believes *Roe* was wrongly decided vote to overrule it, or should *stare decisis* be observed? This question was put to Judge Robert Bork by the Senate Judiciary Committee during the 1987 confirmation hearings on Bork's ill-fated nomination to the Supreme Court. The committee was anxious to find out Bork's predisposition toward *Roe v. Wade* since, if confirmed, his vote might well be decisive. Like many nominees faced with a difficult and sensitive question of judicial policy, Bork equivocated. Still, anxiety among Senate Democrats about Bork's propensities on the abortion issue was one of the major reasons for his failure to win confirmation.

The doctrine of *stare decisis* certainly applies to American constitutional law, although there are numerous examples of the Supreme Court departing from precedent in constitutional matters. Perhaps the most famous reversal is *Brown v. Board of Education* (1954), where the Supreme Court repudiated the "separate but equal" doctrine of *Plessy v. Ferguson* (1896). The separate but equal doctrine had legitimated racial segregation in this country for nearly six decades. Beginning with the *Brown* decision, official segregation was abolished as a denial of the "equal protection of the laws" (for further discussion, see Chapter 16).

Presumption of Constitutionality

Perhaps the most fundamental self-imposed limitation on the exercise of judicial review is the **presumption of constitutionality.** Under this doctrine, courts will presume a challenged statute is valid until it is demonstrated otherwise. In other words, the party attacking the validity of the law carries the burden of proof. This doctrine is based on an appreciation for the countermajoritarian character of judicial review and a fundamental respect for the legislative bodies in a democratic system.

The modern Supreme Court has modified the doctrine of presumptive constitutionality with respect to laws impinging on civil rights and liberties. In a famous footnote in *United States v. Carolene Products* (1938), Justice Harlan Fiske Stone suggested that there may be a "narrower scope" for the usual presumption of constitutionality where a law arguably infringes on a provision of the Bill of Rights or discriminates against a "discrete and insular minority." Since *Korematsu v. United States* (1944), government policies that discriminate on the basis of race have been viewed as "inherently suspect" and thus presumptively unconstitutional by the federal courts. (For further discussion, see Chapter 16.)

The Severability Doctrine

Under the doctrine of **severability,** federal courts will generally attempt to excise the unconstitutional elements of a statute while leaving the rest of the law intact. In *Champlin Refining Co. v. Corporation Commission of Oklahoma* (1932), the Supreme Court said that invalid provisions of a law are to be severed "unless it is evident that the Legislature would not have enacted those provisions which are within its power, independently of that which is not." The severability doctrine is consistent with the philosophy of judicial restraint, in that judicial review is employed with a minimum of "damage" to the work of the legislature.

In *Immigration and Naturalization Service v. Chadha* (1983), for example, the Supreme Court invalidated Section 244(c)(2) of the Immigration and Nationality Act. This specific provision permitted one house of Congress to veto decisions of the executive branch regarding deportation of aliens. The Supreme Court found this "legislative veto" to be an unconstitutional exercise of power by Congress (see Chapter 7). The remainder of the Immigration and Nationality Act, a very important statute from the standpoint of immigration policy, was left intact.

Frequently, Congress will attach a severability clause to a piece of legislation, indicating its desire that any unconstitutional provisions be severed from the rest of the statute. The Immigration and Nationality Act at issue in the *Chadha* case contained such a clause:

> If any particular provision of this Act, or the application thereof to any person or circumstance, is held invalid, the remainder of the Act and the application of such provision to other persons or circumstances shall not be affected.

Absent a severability clause, federal courts may presume an enactment was intended to be judged as a whole.

Related to the concept of severability is the inclusion of a "saving" clause in many statutes. In attempting to keep pace with social change and current demands on government, Congress routinely enacts legislation repealing earlier statutes. Logically, an absolute repeal would set aside or bring to an end all pending matters governed by the repealed statute. To avoid the disruption and confusion that would result, Congress typically includes a "saving" clause in the act of repeal. The saving clause simply indicates that repeal of the earlier statute is subject to certain exceptions. For example, in repealing criminal statutes, Congress often provides that prosecutions initiated prior to repeal may be pursued under repealed provisions. Although serious constitutional questions may be raised with respect to such clauses, the Supreme Court generally recognizes their validity.

The point is well illustrated by the decision in *Bradley v. United States* (1973). Bradley was convicted in 1971 of conspiring to sell cocaine in violation of a federal statute that imposed a mandatory five-year prison term on offenders. The statute under which he was prosecuted was repealed five days before his conviction and sentencing. The new law contained less punitive sentencing requirements. Nevertheless, Bradley was sentenced to the mandatory five-year term under the original statute. The Supreme Court affirmed his conviction and sentence, upholding the validity of the saving clause contained in the act of repeal.

"Unconstitutional as Applied . . ."

The severability clause from the Immigration and Nationality Act quoted above distinguishes between judicial invalidation of a law as *inherently* unconstitutional and invalidation of a law *as applied* to particular persons or circumstances. The philosophy of judicial restraint suggests that, if possible, courts refrain from making declarations that a challenged statute is invalid "on its face." Whether a federal court will invalidate a statute on its face or as applied depends on the language of the law and the facts of the case in which the law is challenged.

By way of illustration, consider the Supreme Court's decision in *Cohen v. California* (1971). There, the Supreme Court held that a state "offensive conduct" law was unconstitutional as applied to a case where a man was prosecuted for wearing a jacket bearing the slogan "Fuck the Draft." The Court held that to punish Cohen's "immature antic" as offensive conduct would be to deny his right of free speech guaranteed by the First Amendment. On the other hand, in *Brandenburg v. Ohio* (1969), the Court struck down a state **criminal syndicalism** law as inherently unconstitutional under the First Amendment, because the law prohibited the "mere advocacy" of violence. (Both *Cohen* and *Brandenburg* are discussed and reprinted in Chapter 11.)

Distinguishing the Unconstitutional from the Merely Objectionable

The federal courts are constantly besieged with cases seeking to have state or federal laws declared unconstitutional. The courts deflect many of these cases by invoking the threshold doctrines discussed previously in this chapter. When the federal courts do reach the merits of such cases, they are nevertheless apt to uphold challenged laws if a reasonable case can be made for their validity. One who challenges the constitutionality of a law must make a specific attack on the statute, showing why the law offends some particular provision of the Constitution. It is not enough to assert that a challenged statute offends "natural law" or "human dignity" or other sources of authority beyond the Constitution. Nor is it sufficient to argue that a particular enactment be regarded by some as poor or unfortunate public policy. Federal judges tend to draw a sharp distinction between questions of constitutional propriety and questions of desirable public policy.

Justice Hugo Black, writing for the Supreme Court in *Ferguson v. Skrupa* (1963), commented: "We refuse to sit as a super-legislature to weigh the wisdom of legislation. . . ." Similarly, Justice Potter Stewart, dissenting in *Griswold v. Connecticut* (1965), said, ". . . we are not asked in this case to say whether we think [the state law under review] is unwise, or even asinine." In his classic dissent in *Lochner v. New York* (1905), Justice Oliver Wendell Holmes, Jr., put it this way: "I strongly believe that my agreement or disagreement [with a policy] has nothing to do with the right of a majority to embody their opinions in law." Holmes went on to observe that the Constitution "is made for people of fundamentally differing views."

Chief Justice Warren E. Burger, dissenting in the landmark death penalty case *Furman v. Georgia* (1972), commented on the need for judges to distinguish between their policy preferences and their judgments regarding the constitutionality of statutes:

> If [the Supreme Court] were possessed of legislative power, I would . . . restrict the use of capital punishment to a small category of the most heinous crimes. Our constitutional inquiry, however, must be divorced from personal feelings as to the morality and efficacy of the death penalty, and be confined to the meaning and applicability of the uncertain language of the Eighth Amendment. There is no novelty in being called upon to interpret a constitutional provision that is less than self-defining, but, of all our fundamental guarantees, the ban on 'cruel and unusual punishments' is one of the most difficult to translate into judicially manageable terms. . . . Yet it is essential to our role as a court that we not seize on the enigmatic character of the guarantee as an invitation to enact our personal predilections into law.

In *Furman,* the Supreme Court struck down Georgia's death penalty law, despite Chief Justice Burger's plea for judicial restraint. While most judges agree on the abstract distinction between matters of constitutional law and questions of public policy, the vague language of the Constitution often blurs this distinction when actual cases must be decided. Grand terms like "liberty," "due process," and "equal protection of the laws" are not given to precise formulations.

It must be noted that all of the self-imposed limitations on judicial power are subject to a degree of manipulation to achieve desired outcomes. The doctrines are sufficiently complex and imprecise to permit two judges to reach opposite conclusions about their application to a given case. Nevertheless, the creation and continuance of these doctrines suggest a certain sensitivity on the part of the federal judiciary to the inherent tensions surrounding the exercise of judicial review in a democratic polity.

CONCLUSION

Under the philosophy of **judicial restraint,** federal courts are viewed as performing a circumscribed role in the political system. They are not seen as "platonic guardians" or "philosopher kings." They are not the primary custodians of the general welfare, as that role belongs to Congress and the state legislatures. Such doctrines as standing, mootness, ripeness, and the like are reflections of judicial restraint since they serve to limit the scope of judicial inquiry. Similarly, such doctrines as presumptive constitutionality and narrowness reflect the respect for the legislature that is the hallmark of judicial restraint.

The countervailing philosophy to judicial restraint is **judicial activism.** Activist judges tend to see the courts as coequal participants, along with the legislative and executive branches, in the process of public policy-making. Activists are thus impatient with self-imposed limitations on judicial review and tend to brush aside doctrinal restraints. A jurist of activist views, Justice Douglas once remarked, "It is far more important to be respectful to the Constitution than to a coordinate branch of government" (*Massachusetts v. Laird* [1970], dissenting opinion). Dissenting in *Paul v. Davis* (1976), Justice Brennan expressed similar sentiments regarding the role of the Supreme Court:

> I had always thought that one of this court's most important roles was to provide a bulwark against governmental violation of the constitutional safeguards securing in our free society the legitimate expectations of every person to innate human dignity and a sense of worth.

In the modern era, judicial restraint tends to be equated with political conservatism, judicial activism with liberalism. Yet one must remember that judicial power can be used for liberal or conservative policy goals. The debate over judicial activism is a long-standing one and can be traced to such decisions as *Dred Scott v. Sandford* (1857), where a conservative Supreme Court actively defended the institution of slavery on highly dubious constitutional grounds. Along the same lines, in *Lochner v. New York* (1905), a conservative Court used its power without restraint to frustrate the implementation of progressive economic legislation.

Much of American constitutional law can be seen as an ongoing dialectic between judicial activism and judicial restraint. In a system committed both to representative democracy and the preservation of individual rights, it is inevitable that the courts will wrestle with the problem of defining the proper judicial role. This dynamic tension is most visible in the Supreme Court's exercise of the power of judicial review.

FOR FURTHER READING

Abraham, Henry J. *The Judiciary: The Supreme Court in the Governmental Process,* 7th ed. Boston: Allyn and Bacon, 1987.

Agresto, John. *The Supreme Court and Constitutional Democracy.* Ithaca, N.Y.: Cornell University Press, 1984.

Antieau, Chester J. *Modern Constitutional Law,* 2 vols. Rochester, N.Y.: Lawyers Co-operative, 1969. See, in particular, Chapter 15, "The Courts and Judicial Review of Constitutional Issues."

Bickel, Alexander M. *The Least Dangerous Branch: The Supreme Court at the Bar of Politics.* Indianapolis: Bobbs-Merrill, 1962.

Cannon, Mark W., and David M. O'Brien. *Views from the Bench.* Chatham, N.J.: Chatham House, 1985.

Carp, Robert A., and Ronald Stidham. *The Federal Courts,* 2d ed. Washington, D.C.: Congressional Quarterly Press, 1991. See, in particular, Chapter 2, "Jurisdiction, Workload, and Policy-Making Boundaries of Federal Courts."

Forte, David F. *The Supreme Court in American Politics: Judicial Activism vs. Judicial Restraint.* Lexington, Mass.: D.C. Heath, 1972.

Halpern, Stephen C., and Charles M. Lamb, eds. *Supreme Court Activism and Restraint.* Lexington, Mass.: D.C. Heath, 1982.

Jackson, Robert H. *The Supreme Court in the American System of Government.* Cambridge: Harvard University Press, 1955.

Moore, Blaine F. *The Supreme Court and Unconstitutional Legislation.* New York: Columbia University Press, 1913.

Post, C. Gordon. *The Supreme Court and Political Questions.* Baltimore: Johns Hopkins University Press, 1936.

Radcliffe, James E. *The Case-or-Controversy Provision.* University Park, Pennsylvania: University of Pennsylvania Press, 1978.

Strum, Philippa. *The Supreme Court and "Political Questions."* Tuscaloosa: University of Alabama Press, 1974.

Poe v. Ullman

367 U.S. 497; 81 S. Ct. 1752; 6 L. Ed.2d 989 (1961)
Vote: 5-4

Paul and Pauline Poe, a married couple, and Jane Doe, a housewife, filed suits in federal court against the Connecticut state's attorney seeking a declaratory judgment as to the constitutionality of a Connecticut law forbidding the use of contraceptives.

Mr. Justice Frankfurter announced the judgment of the Court and an opinion in which **The Chief Justice [Warren], Mr. Justice Clark** and **Mr. Justice Whittaker** join.

These appeals challenge the constitutionality, under the Fourteenth Amendment, of Connecticut statutes which, as authoritatively construed by the Connecticut Supreme Court of Errors, prohibit the use of contraceptive devices and the giving of medical advice in the use of such devices. In proceedings seeking declarations of law, not on review of convictions for violation of the statutes, that court has ruled that these statutes would be applicable in the case of married couples and even under claim that conception would constitute a serious threat to the health or life of the female spouse.

. . . The [first] complaint . . . alleges that the plaintiffs, Paul and Pauline Poe, are a husband and wife, thirty and twenty-six years old respectively, who live together and have no children. Mrs. Poe has had three consecutive pregnancies terminating in infants with multiple congenital abnormalities from which each died shortly after birth. Plaintiffs have consulted Dr. Buxton, an obstetrician and gynecologist of eminence, and it is Dr. Buxton's opinion that the cause of the infants' abnormalities is genetic, although the underlying "mechanism" is unclear. In view of the great emotional stress already suffered by plaintiffs, the probable consequence of another pregnancy is psychological strain extremely disturbing to the physical and mental health of both husband and wife. . . . [I]t is Dr. Buxton's opinion that the best and safest medical treatment which could be prescribed

for their situation is advice in methods of preventing conception. Dr. Buxton knows of drugs, medicinal articles and instruments which can be safely used to effect contraception. Medically, the use of these devices is indicated as the best and safest preventive measure necessary for the protection of plaintiffs' health. Plaintiffs, however, have been unable to obtain this information for the sole reason that its delivery and use may or will be claimed by the defendant State's Attorney (appellee in this Court) to constitute offenses against Connecticut law. The State's Attorney . . . claims that the giving of contraceptive advice and the use of contraceptive devices would be offenses forbidden by Conn. Gen. Stat. Rev. 1958, Sections 53–32 and 54–196.

. . . [Paul and Pauline Poe] ask a declaratory judgment that sections 53–32 and 54–196 are unconstitutional, in that they deprive the plaintiffs of life and liberty without due process of law.

The second action . . . is brought by Jane Doe, a twenty-five-year-old housewife. Mrs. Doe, it is alleged, lives with her husband, they have no children; Mrs. Doe recently underwent a pregnancy which induced in her a critical physical illness—two weeks' unconsciousness and a total of nine weeks' acute sickness which left her with partial paralysis, marked impairment of speech, and emotional instability. Another pregnancy would be exceedingly perilous to her life. She, too, has consulted Dr. Buxton, who believes that the best and safest treatment for her is contraceptive advice. The remaining allegations of Mrs. Doe's complaint, and the relief sought, are similar to those in the case of Mr. and Mrs. Poe.

Appellants' complaints in these declaratory judgment proceedings do not clearly, and certainly do not in terms, allege that appellee Ullman threatens to prosecute them for use of, or for giving advice concerning, contraceptive devices. The allegations are merely that, in the course of his public duty, he intends to prosecute any offenses against Connecticut law, and that he claims that use of and advice concerning contraceptives would constitute offenses. The lack of immediacy of the threat described by these allegations might alone raise serious questions of non-justiciability of appellants' claims. *** But even were we to read the allegations to convey a clear threat of imminent prosecutions, we are not bound to accept as true all that is alleged on the face of the complaint and admitted, technically, by demurrer, any more than the Court is bound by stipulation of the parties. *** Formal agreement between parties that collides with plausibility is too fragile a foundation for indulging in constitutional adjudication.

The Connecticut law prohibiting the use of contraceptives has been on the State's books since 1879. *** During the more than three-quarters of a century since its enactment, a prosecution for its violation seems never to have been initiated, save in *State v. Nelson.* *** The circumstances of that case, decided in 1940, only prove the abstract character of what is before us. There, a test case was brought to determine the constitutionality of the Act as applied against two doctors and a nurse who had allegedly disseminated contraceptive information. After the Supreme Court of Errors sustained the legislation on appeal from a demurrer to the information, the State moved to dismiss the information. Neither counsel nor our own researchers have discovered any other attempt to enforce the prohibition of distribution or use of contraceptive devices by criminal process. The unreality of these law suits is illumined by another circumstance. We were advised by counsel for appellants that contraceptives are commonly and notoriously sold in Connecticut drug stores. Yet no prosecutions are recorded; and certainly such ubiquitous, open, public sales would more quickly invite the attention of enforcement officials than the conduct in which the present appellants wish to engage—the giving of private medical advice by a doctor to his individual patients, and their private use of the devices prescribed. The undeviating policy of nullification by Connecticut of its anti-contraceptive laws throughout all the long years that they have been on the statute books bespeaks more than prosecutorial paralysis. What was said in an-

other context is relevant here. "Deeply embedded traditional ways of carrying out state policy" *** —or not carrying it out—"are often tougher and truer law than the dead words of the written text." ***

The restriction of our jurisdiction to cases and controversies within the meaning of Article III of the Constitution, see *Muskrat v. United States,* *** is not the sole limitation on the exercise of our appellate powers, especially in cases raising constitutional powers. The policy reflected in numerous cases and over a long period was thus summarized in the oft-quoted statement of Mr. Justice Brandeis: "The Court [has] developed, for its own governance in the cases confessedly within its jurisdiction, a series of rules under which it has avoided passing upon a large part of all the constitutional questions pressed upon it for decision." *** In part the rules summarized in the *Ashwander* opinion had derived from the historically defined, limited nature and function of courts and from the recognition that, within the framework of our adversary system, the adjudicatory process is most securely founded when it is exercised under the impact of a lively conflict between antagonistic demands, actively pressed, which make resolution of the controverted issue a practical necessity. *** In part they derive from the fundamental federal and tripartite character of our National Government and from the role—restricted by its very responsibility—of the federal courts, and particularly this Court, within that structure. ***

These considerations press with special urgency in cases challenging legislative action or state judicial action as repugnant to the Constitution. "The best teaching of this Court's experience admonishes us not to entertain constitutional questions in advance of the strictest necessity." *** ... "This court can have no right to pronounce an abstract opinion upon the constitutionality of a State law. Such law must be brought into actual or threatened operation upon rights properly falling under judicial cognizance, or a remedy is not to be had here." *** "The party who invokes the power [to annul legislation on grounds of its unconstitutionality] must be able to show not only that the statute is invalid, but that he has sustained or is immediately in danger of sustaining some direct injury as the result of its enforcement." ***

Insofar as appellants seek to justify the exercise of our declaratory power by the threat of prosecution, facts which they can no more negative by complaint and demurrer than they could by stipulation preclude our determining their appeals on the merits. *** It is clear that the mere existence of a state penal statute would constitute insufficient grounds to support a federal court's adjudication of its constitutionality in proceedings brought against the State's prosecuting officials if real threat of enforcement is wanting. *** If the prosecutor expressly agrees not to prosecute, a suit against him for declaratory and injunctive relief is not such an adversary case as will be reviewed here. *** Eighty years of Connecticut history demonstrate a similar, albeit tacit agreement. The fact that Connecticut has not chosen to press to enforcement of this statute deprives these controversies of the immediacy which is an indispensable condition of constitutional adjudication. This Court cannot be umpire to debates concerning harmless, empty shadows. To find it necessary to pass on these statutes now, in order to protect appellants from the hazards of prosecution, would be to close our eyes to reality.

Nor does the allegation by the Poes and Doe that they are unable to obtain information concerning contraceptive devices from Dr. Buxton, "for the sole reason that the delivery and use of such information and advice may or will be claimed by the defendant State's Attorney to constitute offenses," disclose a necessity for present constitutional decision. It is true that this Court has several times passed upon criminal statutes challenged by persons who claimed that the effects of the statutes were to deter others from maintaining profitable or advantageous relations with the complainants. *** But in these cases the deterrent effect complained of was one which was grounded in a realistic fear of prosecution. We cannot agree that if Dr. Buxton's compliance with these statutes is uncoerced by the risk of their enforcement, his patients are entitled to a declaratory judgment concerning the statutes' validity. And, with due regard to Dr. Buxton's standing as a physician and to his personal sensitiveness, we cannot accept, as the basis of constitutional adjudication, other than as chimerical the fear of enforcement of provisions that have during so many years gone uniformly and without exception unenforced.

Justiciability is of course not a legal concept with a fixed content or susceptible of scientific verification. Its utilization is the result of many subtle pressures, including the appropriateness of the issues for decision by this Court and the actual hardship to the litigants of denying them the relief sought. Both these factors justify withholding adjudication of the constitutional issue raised under the circumstances and in the manner in which they are now before the Court.

Dismissed.

Mr. Justice Black dissents because he believes that the constitutional questions should be reached and decided.

Mr. Justice Brennan, concurring in the judgment.

I agree that this appeal must be dismissed for failure to present a real and substantial controversy which unequivocally calls for adjudication of the rights claimed in advance of any attempt by the State to curtail them by criminal prosecution. I am not convinced, on this skimpy record, that these appellants as individuals are truly caught in an inescapable dilemma. The true controversy in this case is over the opening of birth-control clinics on a large scale; it is that which the State has prevented in the past, not the use of contraceptives by isolated and individual married couples. It will be time enough to decide the constitutional questions urged upon us when, if ever, that real controversy flares up again. Until it does, or until the State makes a definite and concrete threat to enforce these laws against individual married couples—a threat which it has never made in the past except under the provocation of the litigation—this Court may not be compelled to exercise its most delicate power of constitutional adjudication.

Mr. Justice Stewart, dissenting . . . .

Mr. Justice Douglas, dissenting.

These cases are dismissed because a majority of the members of this Court conclude, for varying reasons, that this controversy does not present a justiciable question. That question is too transparent to require an extended reply. . . .

Mr. Justice Harlan, dissenting.

I am compelled, with all respect, to dissent from the dismissal of these appeals. In my view the course which the Court has taken does violence to established concepts of "justiciability," and unjustifiably leaves these appellants under the threat of unconstitutional prosecution. . . . Between them these suits seek declaratory relief against the threatened enforcement of Connecticut's antibirth-control laws making criminal the use of contraceptives, insofar as such laws relate to the use of contraceptives by married persons and the giving of advice to married persons in their use. The appellants, a married couple, a married woman, and a doctor, ask that it be adjudged, contrary to what the Connecticut courts have held, that such laws, as threatened to be applied to them in circumstances described in the opinion announcing the judgment of the Court violate the Fourteenth Amendment, in that they deprive appellants of life, liberty, or property without due process.

The plurality opinion of the Court gives, as the basis for dismissing the appeals, the reason that, as to the two married appellants, the lack of demonstrated enforcement of the Connecticut statute bespeaks an absence of exigent adversity which is posited as the condition for evoking adjudication from us, and, as to the doctor, that his compliance with the state statute is uncoerced by any "realistic fear of prosecution," giving due recognition to his "standing as a physician and to his personal sensitiveness." With these reasons it appears that the concurring opinion agrees.

. . . In my view of these cases a present determination of the Constitutional issues is the only course which will advance justice, and I can find no sound reason born of considerations as to the possible inadequacy or ineffectiveness of the judgment that might be rendered which justifies the Court's contrary disposition. . . .

The remainder of Justice Harlan's dissent is reprinted in Chapter 15.

Valley Forge Christian College v. Americans United for Separation of Church and State

454 U.S. 464; 102 S. Ct. 752; 70 L. Ed.2d 700 (1982)
Vote: 5-4

This case raises the issue of standing to sue in the context of a dispute over the First Amendment principle of separation of church and state. The essential facts are contained in Justice Rehnquist's majority opinion.

Justice Rehnquist delivered the opinion of the Court.

. . . Article IV, Sec. 3, cl. 2, of the Constitution vests Congress with the "Power to dispose of and make all needful Rules and Regulations respecting the . . . Property belonging to the United States." Shortly after the termination of hostilities in the Second World War, Congress enacted the Federal Property and Administrative Services Act of 1949. *** The Act was designed, in part, to provide "an economical and efficient system for . . . the disposal of surplus

property." *** In furtherance of this policy, federal agencies are directed to maintain adequate inventories of the property under their control and to identify excess property for transfer to other agencies able to use it. *** Property that has outlived its usefulness to the Federal Government is declared "surplus" and may be transferred to private or other public entities. ***

The Act authorizes the Secretary of Health, Education, and Welfare (now the Secretary of Education) to assume responsibility for disposing of surplus real property "for school, classroom, or other educational use." *** Subject to the disapproval of the Administrator of General Services, the Secretary may sell or lease the property to non-profit, tax exempt educational institutions for consideration that takes into account "any benefit which has accrued or may accrue to the United States" from the transferee's use of the property. *** By regulation, the Secretary has provided for the computation of a "public benefit allowance," which discounts the transfer price of the property "on the basis of benefits to the United States from the use of such property for educational purposes." ***

The property which spawned this litigation was acquired by the Department of the Army in 1942, as part of a larger tract of approximately 181 acres of land northwest of Philadelphia. The Army built on that land the Valley Forge General Hospital, and for 30 years thereafter, that hospital provided medical care for members of the Armed Forces. In April 1973, as part of a plan to reduce the number of military installations in the United States, the Secretary of Defense proposed to close the hospital, and the General Services Administration declared it to be "surplus property."

The Department of Health, Education, and Welfare (HEW) eventually assumed responsibility for disposing of portions of the property, and in August 1976, it conveyed a 77-acre tract to petitioner, the Valley Forge Christian College. The appraised value of the property at the time of conveyance was $577,500. This appraised value was discounted, however, by the Secretary's computation of a 100% public benefit allowance, which permitted petitioner to acquire the property without making any financial payment for it. . . .

In September 1976, respondents Americans United for Separation of Church and State, Inc. (Americans United), and four of its employees, learned of the conveyance through a news release. Two months later, they brought suit in the United States District Court for the District of Columbia, later transferred to the Eastern District of Pennsylvania, to challenge the conveyance on the ground that it violated the Establishment Clause of the First Amendment. *** In its amended complaint, Americans United described itself as a nonprofit organization composed of 90,000 "tax-payer members." The complaint asserted that each member "would be deprived of the fair and constitutional use of his (her) tax dollar for constitutional purposes in violation of his (her) rights under the First Amendment of the United States Constitution." Respondents sought a declaration that the convey-

ance was null and void, and an order compelling petitioner to transfer the property back to the United States. ***

On petitioner's motion, the District Court granted summary judgment and dismissed the complaint. *** The court found that respondents lacked standing to sue as taxpayers under *Flast v. Cohen* *** (1968), and had "failed to allege that they have suffered any actual or concrete injury beyond a generalized grievance common to all taxpayers." ***

Respondents appealed to the Court of Appeals for the Third Circuit, which reversed the judgment of the District Court by a divided Court. *** All members of the court agreed that respondents lacked standing as taxpayers to challenge the conveyance under *Flast v. Cohen* *** since that case extended standing to taxpayers qua taxpayers only to challenge congressional exercises of the power to tax and spend conferred by Art I., Sec. 8, of the Constitution, and this conveyance was authorized by legislation enacted under the authority of the Property Clause, Art. IV, Sec. 3, cl. 2. Notwithstanding this significant factual difference from *Flast,* the majority of the Court of Appeals found that respondents also had standing merely as "citizens," claiming "injury in fact to their shared individuated right to a government that 'shall make no law respecting the establishment of religion.' " *** In the majority's view, this "citizen standing" was sufficient to satisfy the "case or controversy" requirement of Art. III. . . .

Because of the unusually broad and novel view of standing to litigate a substantive question in the federal courts adopted by the Court of Appeals, we granted certiorari, *** and we now reverse. . . .

Article III of the Constitution limits the "judicial power" of the United States to the resolution of "cases" and "controversies." The constitutional power of federal courts cannot be defined, and indeed has no substance, without reference to the necessity "to adjudge the legal rights of litigants in actual controversies." *** The requirements of Art. III are not satisfied merely because a party requests a court of the United States to declare its legal rights, and has couched that request for forms of relief historically associated with courts of law in terms that have a familiar ring to those trained in the legal process. The judicial power of the United States defined by Art. III is not an unconditioned authority to determine the constitutionality of legislative or executive acts. The power to declare the rights of individuals and to measure the authority of governments, this Court said 90 years ago, "is legitimate only in the last resort, and as a necessity in the determination of real, earnest and vital controversy." *** Otherwise, the power "is not judicial . . . in the sense in which judicial power is granted by the Constitution to the courts of the United States." ***

As an incident to the elaboration of this bedrock requirement, this Court has always required that a litigant have "standing" to challenge the action sought to be adjudicated in the lawsuit. . . .

. . .[A]t an irreducible minimum, Art. III requires the party who invokes the court's authority to "show that he personally has suffered some actual or threatened injury as a result of the putatively illegal conduct of the defendant," *** and that the injury "fairly can be traced to the challenged action" and "is likely to be redressed by a favorable decision." *** In this manner does Art. III limit the federal judicial power "to those disputes which confine federal courts to a role consistent with a system of separated powers and which are traditionally thought to be capable of resolution through the judicial process." ***

We need not mince words when we say that the concept of "Art. III standing" has not been defined with complete consistency in all of the various cases decided by this Court which have discussed it, nor when we say that this very fact is probably proof that the concept cannot be reduced to a one-sentence or one-paragraph definition. But of one thing we may be sure: Those who do not possess Art. III standing may not litigate as suitors in the courts of the United States. Article III, which is every bit as important in its circumscription of the judicial power of the United States as in its granting of that power, is not merely a troublesome hurdle to be overcome if possible so as to reach the "merits" of a lawsuit which a party desires to have adjudicated; it is a part of the basic charter promulgated by the Framers of the Constitution at Philadelphia in 1787, a charter which created a general government, provided for the interaction between the government and the governments of the several States, and was later amended

so as to either enhance or limits its authority with respect to both States and individuals. . . .

Unlike the plaintiffs in *Flast*, respondents fail the first prong of the test for taxpayer standing. Their claim is deficient in two respects. First, the source of their complaint is not a congressional action, but a decision by HEW to transfer a parcel of federal property. *Flast* limited taxpayer standing to challenges directed "only [at] exercises of congressional power." ***

Second, and perhaps redundantly, the property transfer about which respondents complain was not an exercise of authority conferred by the Taxing and Spending Clause of Art. I, Sec. 8. The authorizing legislation, the Federal Property and Administrative Services Act of 1949, was an evident exercise of Congress' power under the Property Clause, Art. IV, Sec. 3, cl. 2. Respondents do not dispute this conclusion, *** and it is decisive of any claim of taxpayer standing under the *Flast* precedent. . . .

Respondents, therefore, are plainly without standing to sue as taxpayers. . . . It remains to be seen whether respondents have alleged any other basis for standing to bring this suit. . . .

. . . It is evident that respondents are firmly committed to the constitutional principle of separation of church and State, but standing is not measured by the intensity of the litigant's interest or the fervor of his advocacy.

. . . Their claim that the Government has violated the Establishment Clause does not provide a special license to roam the country in search of governmental wrongdoing and to reveal their discoveries in federal court. The federal courts were simply not constituted as ombudsmen of the general welfare.

Were we to accept respondents' claim of standing in this case, there would be no principled basis for confining our exception to litigants relying on the Establishment Clause. Ultimately, that exception derives from the idea that the judicial power requires nothing more for its invocation than important issues and able litigants. The existence of injured parties who might not wish to bring suit becomes irrelevant. Because we are unwilling to countenance such a departure from the limits on judicial power contained in Art. III, the judgment of the Court of Appeals is reversed. . . .

Justice Brennan with whom *Justice Marshall* and *Justice Blackmun* join, dissenting.

. . . The opinion of the Court is a stark example of this unfortunate trend of resolving cases at the "threshold" while obscuring the nature of the underlying rights and interests at stake. The Court waxes eloquent on the blend of prudential and constitutional considerations that combine to create our misguided "standing" jurisprudence. But not one word is said about the Establishment Clause right that the plaintiff seeks to enforce. And despite its pat recitation of our standing decisions, the opinion utterly fails . . . to explain why this case is unlike *Flast v. Cohen,* *** and is controlled instead by *Frothingham v. Mellon* *** (1923).

It may of course happen that a person believing himself injured in some obscure manner by government action will be held to have no legal right under the constitutional or statutory provision upon which he relies, and will not be permitted to complain of the invasion of another person's "rights." It is quite another matter to employ the rhetoric of "standing" to deprive a person, whose interest is clearly protected by the law, of the opportunity to prove that his own rights have been violated. It is in precisely that dissembling enterprise that the Court indulges today. . . .

In 1947, nine Justices of this Court recognized that the Establishment Clause does impose a very definite restriction on the power to tax. The Court held in *Everson v. Board of Education* *** that the " 'establishment of religion' clause of the First Amendment means at least this:"

"No tax in any amount, large or small, can be levied to support any religious activities or institutions, whatever they may be called, or whatever form they may adopt, to teach or practice religion." ***

It is at once apparent that the test of standing formulated by the Court in *Flast* sought to reconcile the developing doctrine of taxpayer "standing" with the Court's historical understanding that the Establishment Clause was intended to prohibit the Federal Government from using tax funds for the advancement of religion, and thus the constitutional imperative of taxpayer standing in certain cases brought pursuant to the Establishment Clause. . . .

It may be that Congress can tax for almost any reason, or for no reason at all. There is, so far as I have been able to discern, but one constitutionally imposed limit on that authority. Congress cannot use tax money to support a church, or to encourage religion. That is "the forbidden exaction." In absolute terms the history of the Establishment Clause of the First Amendment makes this clear. . . .

Blind to history, the Court attempts to distinguish this case from *Flast* by wrenching snippets of language from our opinions, and by perfunctorily applying that language under color of the first prong of *Flast*'s two-part nexus test. The tortuous distinctions thus produced are specious, at best: at worst, they are pernicious to our constitutional heritage. . . .

Plainly hostile to the Framer's understanding of the Establishment Clause, and *Flast*'s enforcement of that understanding, the Court vents that hostility under the guise of standing, "to slam the courthouse door against plaintiffs who [as the Framers intended] are entitled to full consideration of their [Establishment Clause] claims on the merits." *** Therefore I dissent.

Justice Stevens, dissenting. . . .

DeFunis v. Odegaard
416 U.S. 312; 94 S. Ct. 1704; 40 L.Ed.2d 164 (1974)
Vote: 5-4

This is the first case in which the Supreme Court is asked to rule on the constitutionality of a state affirmative action program. The pertinent facts are supplied in the Court's opinion.

Per Curiam.

In 1971 the petitioner Marco DeFunis, Jr., applied for admission as a first year student at the University of Washington Law School, a state-operated institution. The size of the incoming first-year class was to be limited to 150 persons, and the Law School received some 1,600 applications for these 150 places. DeFunis was eventually notified that he had been denied admission. He thereupon commenced this suit in a Washington trial court, contending that the procedures and criteria employed by the Law School Admissions Committee invidiously discriminated against him on account of his race in violation of the Equal Protection Clause of the Fourteenth Amendment to the United States Constitution.

DeFunis brought the suit on behalf of himself alone, and not as the representative of any class, against the various respondents, who are officers, faculty members, and members of the Board of Regents of the University of Washington. He asked the trial court to issue a mandatory injunction commanding the respondents to admit him as a member of the first-year class entering in September 1971, on the ground that the Law School admissions policy had resulted in the unconstitutional denial of his application for admission. The trial court agreed with his claim and granted the requested relief.

DeFunis was, accordingly, admitted to the Law School and began his legal studies there in the fall of 1971. On appeal, the Washington Supreme Court reversed the judgment of the trial court and held that the Law School admissions policy did not violate the Constitution. By this time DeFunis was in his second year at the Law School. He then petitioned this Court for a writ of certiorari, and Mr. Justice Douglas, as Circuit Justice, stayed the judgment of the Washington Supreme Court pending the "final disposition of the case by this Court." By virtue of this stay, DeFunis has remained in law school, and was in the first term of his third and final year when this Court first considered his certiorari petition in the fall of 1973. Because of our concern that DeFunis' third-year standing in the Law School might have rendered this case moot, we requested the parties to brief the question of mootness before we acted on the petition. In response, both sides contended that the case was not moot. The respondents indicated that, if the decision of the Washington Supreme Court were permitted to stand, the petitioner could complete the term for which he was then enrolled but would have to apply to the faculty for permission to con-

tinue in the school before he could register for another term.

We granted the petition for certiorari on November 19, 1973. *** The case was in due course orally argued on Feb. 26, 1974.

In response to questions raised from the bench during the oral argument, counsel for the petitioner has informed the Court that DeFunis has now registered "for his final quarter in law school." Counsel for the respondents have made clear that the Law School will not in any way seek to abrogate this registration. In light of DeFunis' recent registration for the last quarter of his final law school year, and the Law School's assurance that his registration is fully effective, the insistent question again arises whether this case is not moot, and to that question we now turn.

The starting point for analysis is the familiar proposition that "federal courts are without power to decide questions that cannot affect the rights of litigants in this case before them." *** The inability of the federal judiciary "to review most cases derives from the requirement of Article III of the Constitution under which the exercise of judicial power depends upon the existence of a case or controversy." *** Although as a matter of Washington state law it appears that this case would be saved from mootness by "the great public interest in the continuing issues raised by this appeal," *** the fact remains that under Art III "[e]ven in cases arising in the state courts, the question of mootness is a federal one which a federal court must resolve before it assumes jurisdiction." ***

The respondents have represented that, without regard to the ultimate resolution of the issues in this case, DeFunis will remain a student in the Law School for the duration of any term in which he has already enrolled. Since he has now registered for his final term, it is evident that he will be given an opportunity to complete all academic and other requirements for graduation, and, if he does so, will receive his diploma regardless of any decision this Court might reach on the merits of this case. In short, all parties agree that DeFunis is now entitled to complete his legal studies at the University of Washington and to receive his degree from that institution. A determination by this Court of the legal issues tendered by the parties is no longer necessary to compel that result, and could not serve to prevent it. DeFunis did not cast his suit as a class action, and the only remedy he requested was an injunction commanding his admission to the Law School. He was not only accorded that remedy, but he now has also been irrevocably admitted to the final term of the final year of the Law School course. The controversy between the parties has thus clearly ceased to be "definite and concrete" and no longer "touch[es] the legal relations of parties having adverse legal interests." ***

It matters not that these circumstances partially stem from a policy decision on the part of the respondent Law School authorities. The respondents, through their counsel, the Attorney General of the State, have professionally represented that in no event will the status of DeFunis now be affected by any view this Court might express on the merits of this controversy. And it has been the settled practice of the Court, in contexts no less significant, fully to accept representations such as these as parameters for decision. ***

There is a line of decisions in this Court standing for the proposition that the "voluntary cessation of allegedly illegal conduct does not deprive the tribunal of power to hear and determine the case, i.e., does not make the case moot. *** These decisions and the doctrine they reflect would be quite relevant if the question of mootness here had arisen by reason of a unilateral change in the admissions procedures of the Law School. For it was the admissions procedures that were the target of this litigation, and a voluntary cessation of the admissions practices complained of could make this case moot only if it could be said with assurance "that 'there is no reasonable expectation that the wrong will be repeated.' " *** Otherwise, "[t]he defendant is free to return to his old ways," *** and this fact would be enough to prevent mootness because of the "public interest in having the legality of the practices settled." *** But mootness in the present case depends not at all upon a "voluntary cessation" of the admissions practices that were the subject of this litigation. It depends, instead, upon the simple fact that DeFunis is now in the final quarter of the final year of his course of study, and the settled and unchallenged policy of the Law School to permit him to complete the term for which he is now enrolled.

It might also be suggested that this case presents a question that is "capable of repetition, yet evading review," *** and is thus amenable to federal adjudication even though it might otherwise be considered moot. But DeFunis will never again be required to run the gauntlet of the Law School's admission process, and so the question is certainly not "capable of repetition" so far as he is concerned. Moreover, just because this particular case did not reach the Court until the eve of the petitioner's graduation from Law School, it hardly follows that the issue he raises will in the future evade review. If the admissions procedures of the Law School remain unchanged, there is no reason to suppose that a subsequent case attacking those procedures will not come with relative speed to this Court, now that the Supreme Court of Washington has spoken. This case, therefore, in no way presents the exceptional situation ...[that] might permit a departure from "[t]he usual rule in federal cases ... that an actual controversy must exist at stages of appellate or certiorari review, and not simply at the date the action is initiated." ***

Because the petitioner will complete his law school studies at the end of the term for which he has now registered regardless of any decision this Court might reach on the merits of this litigation, we conclude that the Court cannot, consistently with the limitations of Art III of the Constitution, considerthe substantive constitutional issues tendered by the parties. Accordingly, the judgment of the Supreme Court of Washington is vacated, and the cause is remanded for such proceedings as by that Court may be deemed appropriate.

It is so ordered.

Mr. Justice Brennan, dissenting. . . .

Mr. Justice Douglas, dissenting.

I agree with Mr. Justice Brennan that this case is not moot, and because of the issues raised I think it is important to reach the merits. . . .

Younger v. Harris

401 U.S. 37; 91 S. Ct. 746; 27 L. Ed. 2d 669 (1971)

Vote: 8-1

Mr. Justice Black delivered the opinion of the Court.

Appellee, John Harris, Jr., was indicted in a California state court, charged with violation of the . . . California Criminal Syndicalism Act. . . . He then filed a complaint in the Federal District Court, asking that court to enjoin the appellant, Younger, the District Attorney of Los Angeles County, from prosecuting him, and alleging that the prosecution and even the presence of the Act inhibited him in the exercise of his rights of free speech and press, rights guaranteed him by the First and Fourteenth Amendments. . . . A three-judge Federal District court . . . held that it had jurisdiction and power to restrain the District Attorney from prosecuting, held that the State's Criminal Syndicalism Act was void for vagueness and overbreadth in violation of the First and Fourteenth Amendments, and accordingly restrained the District Attorney from "further prosecution of the currently pending action against the plaintiff Harris for alleged violation of the Act." ***

The case is before us on appeal by the State's District Attorney Younger. . . . [W]e have concluded that the judgment of the District Court, enjoining appellant Younger from prosecuting under these California statutes, must be reversed as a violation of the national policy forbidding federal courts to stay or enjoin pending state court proceedings except under special circumstances. We express no view about the circumstances under which federal courts may act when there is no prosecution pending in state courts at the time the federal proceeding is begun.

Appellee Harris has been indicted, and was actually being prosecuted by California for a violation of its Criminal Syndicalism Act at the time this suit was filed. He thus has an acute, live controversy with the State and its prosecutor. . . . A federal lawsuit to stop a prosecution in a state court is a serious matter. And persons having no fears of state prosecution, except those that are imaginary or speculative, are not to be accepted as appropriate plaintiffs in such cases. ***

Since Harris is actually being prosecuted under the challenged laws, however, we proceed with him as a proper party.

Since the beginning of this Country's history Congress has, subject to few exceptions, manifested a desire to permit state courts to try state cases free from interference by federal courts. In 1793 an Act unconditionally provided: ". . . nor shall a writ of injunction be granted to stay proceedings in any court of any state. . . ." *** A comparison of the 1793 Act with *** its present-day successor, graphically illustrates how few and minor have been the exceptions granted from the flat, prohibitory language of the old Act. During all this lapse of years from 1793 to 1970 the statutory exceptions to the 1793 congressional enactment have been only three: (1) "except as expressly authorized by Act of Congress"; (2) "where necessary in aid of its jurisdiction"; and (3) "to protect or effectuate its judgments." In addition, a judicial exception to the longstanding policy evidenced by the statute has been made where a person about to be prosecuted in a state court can show that he will, if the proceeding in the state court is not enjoined, suffer irreparable damages. ***

The precise reasons for this longstanding public policy against federal court interference with state court proceedings have never been specifically identified but the primary sources of the policy are plain. One is the basic doctrine of equity jurisprudence that courts of equity should not act, and particularly should not act to restrain a criminal prosecution, when the moving party has an adequate remedy at law and will not suffer irreparable injury if denied equitable relief. The doctrine may originally have grown out of circumstances peculiar to the English judicial system and not applicable in this country, but its fundamental purpose of restraining equity jurisdiction within narrow limits is equally important under our Constitution, in order to prevent erosion of the role of the jury and avoid a duplication of legal proceedings and legal sanctions where a single suit would be adequate to protect the rights asserted. This underlying reason for restraining courts of equity from interfering with criminal prosecutions is reinforced by an even more vital consideration, the notion of "comity," that is, a proper respect for state functions, a recognition of the fact that the entire country is made up of a Union of separate state governments, and continuance of the belief that the National Government will fare best if the States and their institutions are left free to perform their separate functions in their separate ways. This, perhaps for lack of a better and clearer way to describe it, is referred to by many as "Our Federalism," and one familiar with the profound debates that ushered our Federal Constitution into existence is bound to respect those who remain loyal to the ideals and dreams of "Our Federalism." The concept does not mean blind deference to "States' Rights" any more than it means centralization of control over every important issue in our National Government and its courts. The Framers rejected both these courses. What the concept does represent is a system in which there is sensitivity to the legitimate interests of both State and National Governments, and in which the National Government, anxious though it may be to vindicate and protect federal rights and federal interests, always endeavors to do so in ways that will not unduly interfere with the legitimate activities of the States. It should never be forgotten that this slogan, "Our Federalism," born in the early struggling days of our Union of States, occupies a highly important place in our Nation's history and its future.

This brief discussion should be enough to suggest some of the reasons why it has been perfectly natural for our cases to repeat time and time again that the normal thing to do when federal courts are asked to enjoin pending proceedings in state courts is not to issue such injunctions. . . .

In all of these cases the Court stressed the importance of showing irreparable injury, the traditional prerequisite to obtaining an injunction. In addition, however, the Court also made clear that in view of the fundamental policy against federal interference with state criminal prosecutions, even irreparable injury is insufficient unless it is "both great and immediate." *** Certain types of injury, in particular, the cost, anxiety, and inconvenience of having to defend against a single criminal prosecution could not by themselves be considered "irreparable" in the special legal sense of that term. Instead, the threat to the plaintiff's federally protected rights must be one that cannot be eliminated by his defense against a single criminal prosecution. . . .

This is where the law stood when the Court decided *Dombrowski v. Pfister* [1965] *** and held that an injunction against the enforcement of certain state criminal statues could properly issue under the circumstances presented in the case. . . . The appellants in *Dombrowski* had offered to prove that their offices had been raided and all their files and records seized pursuant to search and arrest warrants that were later summarily vacated by a state judge for lack of probable cause. They also offered to prove that despite the state court order quashing the warrants and suppressing the evidence seized, the prosecutor was continuing to threaten to initiate new prosecutions of appellants under the same statutes, was holding public hearings at which photostatic copies of the illegally seized documents were being used, and was threatening to use other copies of the illegally seized documents to obtain grand jury indictments against the appellants on charges of violating the same statutes. These circumstances, as viewed by the Court, sufficiently establish the kind of irreparable injury, above and beyond that associated with the defense of a single prosecution brought in good faith, that had always been considered sufficient to justify federal intervention. . . . [T]he Court in *Dombrowski* went on to say:

> But the allegations in this complaint depict a situation in which defense of the State's criminal prosecution will not assure adequate vindication of constitutional rights. They suggest that a substantial loss of or impairment of freedoms of expression will occur if appellants must await the state court's disposition and ultimate review in this Court of any adverse determination. These allegations, if true, clearly show irreparable injury. ***

. . . The District Court . . . thought that the *Dombrowski* decision substantially broadened the availability of injunctions against state criminal prosecutions and that under that decision the federal courts may give equitable relief, without regard to any showing of bad faith or harassment, whenever a state statute is found "on its face" to be vague or overly broad, in violation of the First Amendment. We recognize that there are some statements in the *Dombrowski* opinion that would seem to support this argument. But as we have already seen, such statements were unnecessary to the decision of that case, because the Court found that the plaintiffs had alleged a basis for equitable relief under the long-established standards. In addition, we do not regard the reasons adduced to support this position as sufficient to justify such a substantial departure from the established doctrines regarding the availability of injunctive relief. It is undoubtedly true, as the Court stated in *Dombrowski,* that "a criminal prosecution under a statute regulating expression usually involves imponderables and contingencies that themselves may inhibit the full exercise of First Amendment freedoms." *** But this sort of "chilling effect," as the court called it, should not by itself justify federal intervention. . . .

Moreover, the existence of a "chilling effect," even in the area of First Amendment rights, has never been considered a sufficient basis, in and of itself, for prohibiting state action. Where a statute does not directly abridge free speech, but—while regulating a subject within the State's power—tends to have the incidental effect of inhibiting First Amendment rights, it is well settled that the statute can be upheld if the effect on speech is minor in relation to the need for control of the conduct and the lack of alternative means for doing so. *** Just as the incidental "chilling effect" of such statutes does not automatically render them unconstitutional, so the chilling effect that admittedly can result from the very existence of certain laws on the statute books does not in itself justify prohibiting the State from carrying out the important and necessary task of enforcing these laws against socially harmful conduct that the State believes in good faith to be punishable under its laws and the Constitution.

Beyond all this is another, more basic consideration. Procedures for testing the constitutionality of a statute "on its face" in the manner apparently contemplated by *Dombrowski,* and for then enjoining all action to enforce the statute until the State can obtain court approval for a modified version, are fundamentally at odds with the function of the federal courts in our constitutional plan. The power and duty of the judiciary to declare laws unconstitutional is in the final analysis derived from its responsibility for resolving concrete disputes brought before the courts for decision; a statute apparently governing a dispute cannot be applied by judges, consistently with their obligations under the Supremacy Clause, when such an application of the statute would conflict with the Constitution. *** But this vital responsibility, broad as it is, does not amount to an unlimited power to survey the statute books and pass judgment on laws before the courts are called upon to enforce them. Ever since the Constitutional Convention rejected a proposal for having members of the Supreme Court render advice concerning pending legislation it has been clear that, even when suits of this kind involve a "case or controversy" sufficient to satisfy the requirements of Article III of the Constitution, the task of analyzing a proposed statute, pinpointing its deficiencies, and requiring correction of these deficiencies before the statute is put into effect, is rarely if ever an appropriate task for the judiciary. The combination of the relative remoteness of the controversy, the impact on the legislative process of the relief sought, and above all the speculative and amorphous nature of the required line-by-line analysis of detailed statutes *** ordinarily results in a kind of case that is wholly unsatisfactory for deciding constitutional questions, whichever way they might be decided. In light of this fundamental conception of the Framers as to the proper place of the federal courts in the governmental processes of passing and enforcing laws, it can seldom be appropriate for these courts to exercise any such power of prior approval or veto over the legislative process.

For these reasons, fundamental not only to our federal system but also to the basic functions of the Judicial Branch of the National Government under our Constitution, we hold that the *Dombrowski* decision should not be regarded as having upset the settled doctrines that have always confined very narrowly the availability of injunctive relief against state criminal prosecutions. We do not think that opinion stands for the proposition that a federal court can properly enjoin enforcement of a statute solely on the basis of showing that the statute "on its face" abridges First Amendment rights. There may, of course, be extraordinary circumstances in which the necessary irreparable injury can be shown even in the absence of the usual prerequisites of bad faith and harassment. . . . Other unusual situations calling for federal intervention might also arise, but there is no point in our attempting now to specify what they might be. It is sufficient for purposes of the present case to hold, as we do, that the possible unconstitutionality of a statute "on its face" does not in itself justify an injunction against good faith attempts to enforce it, and that . . . Harris has failed to make any showing of bad faith, harassment, or any other unusual circumstances that would call for equitable relief. . . .

The judgment of the District Court is reversed, and the case is remanded for further proceedings not inconsistent with this opinion.

Reversed.

Mr. Justice Stewart, with whom *Mr. Justice Harlan* joins, concurring. . . .

Mr. Justice Brennan, with whom *Mr. Justice White* and *Mr. Justice Marshall* join, concurring in the result. . . .

Mr. Justice Douglas, dissenting.

The fact that we are in a period of history when enormous extrajudicial sanctions are imposed on those who assert their First Amendment rights in unpopular causes emphasizes the wisdom of *Dombrowski v. Pfister.* *** There we recognized that in times of repression, when interests with powerful spokesmen generate symbolic pogroms against nonconformists, the federal judiciary, charged by Congress with special vigilance for protection of civil rights, has special responsibilities to prevent an erosion of the individual's constitutional rights. . . .

The special circumstances when federal intervention in a state criminal proceeding is permissible are not restricted to bad faith on the part of state officials or the threat of multiple prosections. They also exist where for any reason the state statute being enforced is unconstitutional on its face. . . .

In *Younger,* "criminal syndicalism" is defined so broadly as to jeopardize "teaching" that socialism is preferable to free enterprise.

Harris' "crime" was distributing leaflets advocating change in industrial ownership through political action. The statute under which he was indicted was the one involved in *Whitney v. California,* [1927], *** a decision we overruled in *Brandenburg v. Ohio.* [1969]. ***

If the "advocacy" which Harris used was an attempt at persuasion through the use of bullets, bombs, and arson, we would have a different case. But Harris is charged only with distributing leaflets advocating political action toward his objective. He tried unsuccessfully to have the state court dismiss the indictment on constitutional grounds. He resorted to the state appellate court for writs of prohibition to prevent the trial, but to no avail. He went to the federal court as a matter of last resort in an effort to keep this unconstitutional trial from being saddled on him. . . .

The eternal temptation, of course, has been to arrest the speaker rather than to correct the conditions about which he complains. I see no reason why [petitioners like Harris] should be made to walk the treacherous ground of these statutes. They, like other citizens, need the umbrella of the First Amendment as they study, analyze, discuss, and debate the troubles of these days. When criminal prosecutions can be leveled against them because they express unpopular views, the society of the dialogue is in danger.

Luther v. Borden

7 Howard (48 U.S.) 1; 12 L. Ed. 581 (1849)
Vote: 8-1

This case arose out of the Dorr Rebellion in Rhode Island in 1842. Essentially, the conflict involved rival governments competing for sovereignty—an established government founded on a charter issued by the

English king prior to the American Revolution and a rival government based on a new constitution that had been approved by popular referendum. The charter government declared martial law, called out the state militia, and appealed to President John Tyler for aid in putting down the rebellion. The president agreed to provide assistance, thus in effect recognizing the charter government, but the insurrection collapsed before federal troops were mobilized. Thomas Dorr, the leader of the rebellion, was captured, convicted of treason, and sentenced to life imprisonment. Dorr unsuccessfully sought relief on a writ of habeas corpus (see Ex Parte Dorr, 1845), although he was later pardoned and released. During the fracas, Borden, a member of the state militia under the charter government, broke into the home of Luther, a supporter of the Dorr movement. Luther brought suit for trespass against Borden in the U.S. Circuit Court for the District of Rhode Island. Borden defended on the ground that he was acting pursuant to martial law. Luther countered that the act of the state legislature declaring martial law was invalid, since the charter government was no longer the legitimate government of the state. After a jury trial, the circuit court returned a verdict in favor of Borden, the defendant. Luther appealed to the Supreme Court on a writ of error. Daniel Webster, the most famous lawyer of his time, argued the case on behalf of Luther in the Supreme Court. Nevertheless, the Supreme Court affirmed the Circuit Court's decision for Borden.

Mr. Chief Justice Taney delivered the opinion of the court.

... The Constitution of the United States, as far as it has provided for an emergency of this kind, and authorized the general government to interfere in the domestic concerns of a State, has treated the subject as political in its nature, and placed the power in the hands of that department.

The fourth section of the fourth article of the Constitution of the United States provides that the United States shall guarantee to every state in the Union a republican form of government, and shall protect each of them against invasion; and on the application of the legislature or of the executive (when the legislature cannot be convened) against domestic violence.

Under this article of the Constitution it rests with Congress to decide what government is the established one in a State. For as the United States guarantees to each State a republican government, Con-

gress must necessarily decide what government is established in the State before it can determine whether it is republican or not. And when the senators and representatives of a State are admitted into councils of the Union, the authority of the government under which they are appointed, as well as its republican character, is recognized by the proper constitutional authority. And its decision is binding on every other department of the government, and could not be questioned in a judicial tribunal. It is true that the contest in this case did not last long enough to bring the matter to this issue; and as no senators or representatives were elected under the authority of the government of which Mr. Dorr was the head, Congress was not called upon to decide the controversy. Yet the right to decide is placed there, and not in the courts.

So, too, as relates to the clause in the above-mentioned article of the Constitution, providing for cases of domestic violence. It rested with Congress, too, to determine upon the means proper to be adopted to fulfill this guarantee. They might, if they had deemed it most advisable to do so, have placed it in the power of a court to decide when the contingency had happened which required the federal government to interfere. But Congress thought otherwise, and no doubt wisely; and by the act of February 28, 1795, provided, that, "in case of an insurrection in any State against the government thereof, it shall be lawful for the President of the United States, on application of the legislature of such State or of the executive, when the legislature cannot be convened, to call forth such number of the militia of any other State or States, as may be applied for, as he may judge sufficient to suppress such insurrection."

By this act, the power of deciding whether the exigency had risen upon which the government of the United States is bound to interfere, is given to the President. He is to act upon the application of the legislature, or of the executive, and consequently he must determine what body of men constitute the legislature, and who is the governor, before he can act. The fact that both parties claim the right to the government, cannot alter the case, for both cannot be entitled to it. If there is an armed conflict, like the one of which we are speaking, it is a case of domestic violence, and one of the parties must be in insurrection against the lawful government. And the President must, of necessity, decide which is the government, and which party is unlawfully arrayed against it, before he can perform the duty imposed upon him by the act of Congress. . . .

It is said that this power in the President is dangerous to liberty, and may be abused. All power may be abused if placed in unworthy hands. But it would be difficult, we think, to point out any other hands in which this power would be more safe, and at the same time equally effectual. When citizens of the same State are in arms against each other and the constituted authorities unable to execute the laws, the interposition of the United States must be prompt, or it is of little value. The ordinary course of proceedings in courts of justice would be utterly unfit for the crisis. And the elevated office of the President, chosen as he is by the people of the United States, and the high responsibility he could not fail to feel when acting in a case of so much moment, appear to furnish as strong safeguards against a wilful abuse of power as human prudence and foresight could well provide. . . .

Much of the argument on the part of the plaintiff turned upon political rights and political questions, upon which the court has been urged to express an opinion. We decline doing so. The high power has been conferred on this court of passing judgment upon the acts of the State sovereignties, and of the legislative and executive branches of the federal government, and of determining whether they are beyond the limits of power marked out for them respectively by the Constitution of the United States. This tribunal, therefore, should be the last to overstep the boundaries which limit its own jurisdiction. And while it should always be ready to meet any question confided to it by the Constitution, it is equally its duty not to pass beyond its appropriate sphere of action, and to take care not to involve itself in discussions which properly belong to other forums. No one, we believe, has ever doubted the proposition, that, according to the institutions of this country, the sovereignty in every State resides in the people of the State, and that they may alter and change their form of government at their own pleasure. But whether they have changed it or not, by abolishing an old government, and establishing a new one in its place, is a question to be settled by the political power. And when that power has decided, the courts are bound to take notice of its decision, and to follow it. . . .

Mr. Justice Woodbury, dissenting. . . .

Baker v. Carr

369 U.S. 186; 82 S. Ct. 691; 7 L. Ed. 2d 663 (1962)
Vote: 6-2

The term "apportionment" refers to the way in which legislative districts are drawn. "Malapportionment" exists to the extent that numbers of voters are unequal across legislative districts. In a malapportioned system, voters in the more populous districts are underrepresented, while voters in the less populous districts are overrepresented in the legislature (see Chapter 17 for a discussion of the apportionment issue). In the middle of the twentieth century, critics of malapportionment turned to the courts for relief. In Colegrove v. Green *(1946) the Supreme Court dismissed a lawsuit directed against the mal-*

apportionment of Congressional districts in Illinois. In his plurality opinion, Justice Felix Frankfurter argued that "due regard for the Constitution as a viable system precludes judicial correction" of the problem. In Frankfurter's view, "[t]he remedy for unfairness in districting is to secure State legislatures that will apportion properly, or to invoke the ample powers of Congress." In what became the most frequently quoted language from the opinion, Frankfurter admonished courts not to enter the "political thicket" of reapportionment. Sixteen years after Colegrove v. Green, *the Supreme Court reconsidered Jus-*

*tice Frankfurter's admonition in the landmark case
of* Baker v. Carr. *The case began when voters residing
in Chattanooga, Knoxville, Memphis, and Nashville
brought a federal class action challenging the apportionment of the Tennessee General Assembly. The
General Assembly had not been reapportioned since
1901 and, as a result of population growth in the
cities, had become badly malapportioned. Plaintiffs
argued that they were being "denied the equal protection of the laws accorded them by the Fourteenth
Amendment . . . by virtue of the debasement of their
votes." As expected, the federal district court dismissed the case on the authority of* Colegrove v.
Green. *The plaintiffs appealed.*

Mr. Justice Brennan delivered the opinion of the
Court.

. . .[Baker et al.] seek relief in order to protect or
vindicate an interest of their own, and of those similarly situated. Their constitutional claim is, in substance, that the 1901 [Tennessee apportionment] statute constitutes arbitrary and capricious state action,
offensive to the Fourteenth Amendment in its irrational disregard of the standard of apportionment
prescribed by the State's Constitution or of any standard, effecting a gross disproportion of representation to voting population. The injury which appellants
assert is that this classification disfavors the voters in
the counties in which they reside, placing them in a
position of constitutionally unjustifiable inequality
vis-à-vis voters in irrationally favored counties. . . .

In holding that the subject matter of this suit was not
justiciable, the District Court relied on *Colegrove v. Green.* *** . . . We understand the District Court
to have read the . . . case as compelling the conclusion
that since [Baker] sought to have a legislative apportionment held unconstitutional, [his] suit presented a
"political question" and was therefore nonjusticiable.
We hold that this challenge to an apportionment presents no nonjusticiable "political question." . . .

We have said that "In determining whether a question falls within [the political question] category, the
appropriateness under our system of government of
attributing finality to the action of the political departments and also the lack of satisfactory criteria for
a judicial determination are dominant consider-

ations." *** The nonjusticiability of a political question is primarily a function of the separation of powers. Much confusion results from the capacity of the
"political question" label to obscure the need for
case-by-case inquiry. Deciding whether a matter has
in any measure been committed by the Constitution
to another branch of government, or whether the
action of that branch exceeds whatever authority has
been committed, is itself a delicate exercise in constitutional interpretation, and is a responsibility of
this Court as ultimate interpreter of the Constitution.
To demonstrate this requires no less than to analyze
representative cases and to infer from them the analytical threads that make up the political question
doctrine. We shall then show that none of those
threads catches this case.

*Brennan discusses several categories of cases in
which the Court has labeled particular controversies
as "political." He concludes:*

It is apparent that several formulations which vary
slightly according to the settings in which the questions arise may describe a political question, although each has one or more elements which identify it as essentially a function of the separation of
powers. Prominent on the surface of any case held to
involve a political question is found a textually demonstrable constitutional commitment of the issue
to a coordinate political department; or a lack of
judicially discoverable and manageable standards for
resolving it; or the impossibility of deciding without
an initial policy determination of a kind clearly for
nonjudicial discretion; or the impossibility of a
court's undertaking independent resolution without
expressing lack of the respect due coordinate
branches of government; or an unusual need for
unquestioning adherence to a political decision already made; or the potentiality of embarrassment
from multifarious pronouncements by various departments on one question.

Unless one of these formulations is inextricable
from the case at bar there should be no dismissal for
nonjusticiability on the ground of a political question's presence. The doctrine of which we treat is
one of "political questions," not one of "political

cases." The courts cannot reject as "no law suit" a bona fide controversy as to whether some action denominated "political" exceeds constitutional authority. The cases we have reviewed show the necessity for discriminating inquiry into the precise facts and posture of the particular case, and the impossibility of resolution by any semantic cataloguing. . . .

We come, finally, to the ultimate inquiry whether our precedents as to what constitutes a nonjusticiable "political question" bring the case before us under the umbrella of that doctrine. A natural beginning is to note whether any of the common characteristics which we have been able to identify and label descriptively are present. We find none: The question here is the consistency of state action with the Federal Constitution. We have no question decided, or to be decided, by a political branch of government coequal with this Court. Nor do we risk embarrassment of our government abroad, or grave disturbance at home if we take issue with Tennessee as to the constitutionality of her action here challenged. Nor need [Baker], in order to succeed in this action, ask the Court to enter upon policy determinations for which judicially manageable standards are lacking. Judicial standards under the Equal Protection Clause are well developed and familiar, and it has been open to courts since the enactment of the Fourteenth Amendment to determine, if on the particular facts they must, that a discrimination reflects no policy, but simply arbitrary and capricious action.

This case does, in one sense, involve the allocation of political power within a State, and [Baker] might conceivably have added a claim under Guaranty Clause. Of course, as we have seen, any reliance on that clause would be futile. But because my reliance on the Guaranty Clause could not have succeeded it does not follow that [Baker] may not be heard on the equal protection claim which in fact [he tenders]. True, it must be clear that the Fourteenth Amendment claim is not so enmeshed with those political question elements which render Guaranty Clause claims nonjusticiable as actually to present a political question itself. But we have found that not to be the case here. . . .

. . . [I]n *Gomillion v. Lightfoot* [1960] *** we applied the Fifteenth Amendment to strike down a redrafting

of municipal boundaries which effected a discriminatory impairment of voting rights, in face of what a majority of the Court of Appeals thought to be a sweeping commitment to state legislatures of the power to draw and redraw such boundaries. . . .

. . . [To the argument] that *Colegrove v. Green* *** was a barrier to hearing the merits of the case, the Court responded that *Gomillion* was lifted "out of the so-called 'political' arena and into the conventional sphere of constitutional litigation" because here was discriminatory treatment of a racial minority violating the Fifteenth Amendment. . . .

We conclude that the complaint's allegations of a denial of equal protection present a justiciable constitutional cause of action upon which [Baker is] entitled to a trial and a decision. The right asserted is within the reach of judicial protection under the Fourteenth Amendment.

The judgment of the District Court is reversed and the Cause is remanded for further proceedings consistent with this opinion.

Reversed and remanded.

Mr. Justice Whittaker did not participate in the decision of this case.

Mr. Justice Douglas, concurring. . . .

Mr. Justice Clark, concurring.

One emerging from the rash of opinions with their accompanying clashing of views may well find himself suffering a mental blindness. The Court holds that [Baker has] alleged a cause of action. However, it refuses to award relief here—although the facts are undisputed—and fails to give the District Court any guidance whatever. One dissenting opinion, bursting with words that go through so much and conclude with so little, condemns the majority action as "a massive repudiation of the experience of our whole past." Another describes the complaint as merely asserting conclusory allegations that Tennessee's apportionment is "incorrect," "arbitrary," "obsolete," and "unconstitutional." I believe it can be shown that this case is distinguishable from earlier cases dealing with the distribution of political power by a State, that a patent violation of the Equal Protection Clause of the United

States Constitution has been shown, and that an appropriate remedy may be formulated. . . .

. . . The widely heralded case of *Colegrove v. Green* *** was one not only in which the Court was bobtailed [composed of less than all nine Justices] but in which there was no majority opinion. Indeed, even the "political question" point in Mr. Justice Frankfurter's opinion was no more than an alternative ground. Moreover, [*Colegrove*] did not present an equal protection argument. While it has served as a Mother Hubbard to most of the subsequent cases, I feel it was in that respect ill-cast and for all of these reasons put it to one side. Likewise, I do not consider the Guaranty Clause cases based on Art. IV, Sec. 4, of the Constitution, because it is not invoked here and it involves different criteria, as the Court's opinion indicates. . . .

Although I find the Tennessee apportionment statute offends the Equal Protection Clause, I would not consider intervention by this Court into so delicate a field if there were any other relief available to the people of Tennessee. But the majority of the people of Tennessee have no "practical opportunities for exerting their political weight at the polls" to correct the existing "invidious discrimination." Tennessee has no initiative and referendum. I have searched diligently for other "practical opportunities" present under the law. I find none other than through the federal courts. The majority of the voters have been caught up in a legislative strait jacket. Tennessee has an "informed, civically militant electorate" and "an aroused popular conscience," but it does not sear "the conscience of the people's representatives." This is because the legislative policy has riveted the present seats in the Assembly to their respective constituencies, and by the votes of their incumbents a reapportionment of any kind is prevented. The people have been rebuffed at the hands of the Assembly; they have tried the constitutional convention route, but since the call must originate in the Assembly it, too, has been fruitless. They have tried Tennessee courts with the same result, and Governors have fought the tide only to flounder. It is said that there is recourse in Congress and perhaps that may be, but from a practical standpoint this is without substance. To date Congress has never undertaken such a task in any State. We therefore must conclude that the people of Tennessee are stymied and without judicial intervention will be saddled with the present discrimination in the affairs of their state government. . . .

In view of the detailed study that the Court has given this problem, it is unfortunate that a decision is not reached on the merits. The majority appears to hold, at least *sub silentio,* that an invidious discrimination is present, but it remands to the three-judge court for it to make what is certain to be that formal determination. It is true that Tennessee has not filed a formal answer. However, it has filed voluminous papers and made extended arguments supporting its position. At no time has it been able to contradict [Bakers's] factual claims; it has offered no rational explanation for the present apportionment; indeed, it has indicated that there are none known to it. As I have emphasized, the case proceeded to the point before the three-judge court that it was able to find an invidious discrimination factually present, and the State has not contested that holding here. In view of all this background I doubt if anything more can be offered or will be gained by the State on remand, other than time. Nevertheless, not being able to muster a court to dispose of the case on the merits, I concur in the opinion of the majority and acquiesce in the decision to remand. . . .

Mr. Justice Stewart, concurring. . . .

Mr. Justice Frankfurter, whom ***Mr. Justice Harlan*** joins, dissenting.

The Court today reverses a uniform course of decision established by a dozen cases. . . . The impressive body of rulings thus cast aside reflected the equally uniform course of our political history regarding the relationship between population and legislative representation—a wholly different matter from denial of the franchise to individuals because of race, color, religion or sex. Such a massive repudiation of the experience of our whole past in asserting destructively novel judicial power demands a detailed analysis of the role of this Court in our constitutional scheme. Disregard of inherent limits in the effective exercise of the Court's "judicial Power" not only presages the futility of judicial intervention in the essentially political conflict of forces by which the relation between population and representation has time out of mind been and now is determined. It may well impair the Court's position as the ultimate organ of "the supreme Law of the Land" in that vast range of legal problems, often strongly entangled in popular feeling, on which this Court must pronounce. The Court's authority—possessed of neither the purse nor the sword—ultimately rests on sustained public confidence in its moral sanction. Such feeling must be nourished by the Court's complete detachment, in fact and in appearance, from political entanglements and by abstention from injecting itself into the clash of political forces in political settlements. . . .

[In *Colegrove v. Green,* now overturned,] [t]wo opinions were written by the four Justices who composed the majority of the seven sitting members of the Court. Both opinions joining in the result in *Colegrove v. Green* agreed that considerations were controlling which dictated denial or jurisdiction though not in the strict sense of want of power. While the two opinions show a divergence of view regarding some of these considerations, there are important points of concurrence. Both opinions demonstrate a predominant concern, first, with avoiding federal judicial involvement in matters traditionally left to legislative policy making; second, with respect to the difficulty—in view of the nature

of the problems of apportionment and its history in this country—of drawing on or devising judicial standards for judgment, as opposed to legislative determinations, of the part which mere numerical equality among voters should play as a criterion for the allocation of political power; and, third, with problems of finding appropriate modes of relief—particularly, the problem of resolving the essentially political issue of the relative merits of at-large elections held in districts of unequal population.

The broad applicability of these considerations—summarized in the loose shorthand phrase, "political question"—in cases involving a State's apportionment of voting power among its numerous localities has led the Court, since 1946, to recognize their controlling effect in a variety of situations. . . .

The *Colegrove* doctrine, in the form in which repeated decisions have settled it, was not an innovation. It represents long judicial thought and experience. From its earliest opinions this Court has consistently recognized a class of controversies which do not lend themselves to judicial standards and judicial remedies. To classify the various instances as "political questions" is rather a form of stating this conclusion than revealing of analysis. . . .

Dissenting opinion of **Mr. Justice Harlan,** whom **Mr. Justice Frankfurter** joins. . . .

Massachusetts v. Laird

400 U.S. 886; 91 S. Ct. 128; 27 L. Ed.2d 130 (1970)
Vote: 6-3

The plaintiff, the Commonwealth of Massachusetts, attempted to bring suit against Melvin Laird, the secretary of defense during the Nixon administration, seeking to challenge the constitutionality of the Vietnam War. At issue before the Court is whether to grant the Commonwealth's motion to file a complaint. Students should note that this case comes under the original, as opposed to the appellate, jurisdiction of the Supreme Court. Although the Court denies the motion to file a complaint, Justice

Douglas's dissenting opinion is noteworthy for its activist approach to constitutional adjudication.

Memorandum.

The motion for leave to file a bill of complaint is denied.

Mr. Justice Douglas, dissenting.

This motion was filed by the Commonwealth of Massachusetts against the Secretary of Defense, a citizen of another State. It is brought pursuant to a mandate contained in an act of the Massachusetts Legislature. *** Massachusetts seeks to obtain an adjudication of the constitutionality of the United States' participation in the Indochina war. It requests that the United States' participation be declared "unconstitutional in that it was not initially authorized or subsequently ratified by Congressional declaration"; it asks that the Secretary of Defense be enjoined "from carrying out, issuing, or causing to be issued any further orders which would increase the present level of United States troops in Indochina" and it asks that, if appropriate congressional action is not forthcoming within 90 days of this Court's decree, that the Secretary of Defense be enjoined "from carrying out, issuing, or causing to be issued any further order directing any inhabitant of the Commonwealth of Massachusetts to Indochina for the purpose of participating in combat or supporting combat troops in the Vietnam war." Today this Court denies leave to file the complaint. I dissent.

The threshold issues for granting leave to file a complaint in this case are standing and justiciability. At the very least, however, it is apparent that the issues are not so clearly foreclosed as to justify a summary denial of leave to file.

STANDING

In *Massachusetts v. Mellon* [1923], *** the Court held a State lacked standing to challenge, as *parens patriae* [guardian of its citizens], a federal grant-in-aid program under which the Federal Government was allegedly usurping powers reserved to the States . . .

. . . [T]he ruling of the Court in that case is not dispositive of this one. The opinion states "we need not go so far as to say that a state may never intervene by suit to protect its citizens against any form of enforcement of unconstitutional acts of Congress; but we are clear that the right to do so does not arise here." *** Thus the case did not announce a per se rule to bar all suits against the Federal Government as *parens patriae.* . . .

Mellon relates to an Act of Congress signed by the Executive, a distinction noted in other original actions. ***

Massachusetts attacks no federal statute. In fact, the basis of Massachusetts' complaint is the absence of congressional action.

It is said that the Federal Government "represents" the citizens. Here the complaint is that only one representative of the people, the Executive, has acted and the other representatives of the citizens have not acted, although, it is argued, the Constitution provides that they must act before an overseas "war" can be conducted. . . .

In *South Carolina v Katzenbach,* [1965] *** we denied standing to South Carolina to assert claims under the Bill of Attainder Clause of Article I and the principle of separation of powers which were regarded "only as protections for individual persons and private groups who are particularly vulnerable to nonjudicial determinations of guilt." *** Yet we went on to allow South Carolina to challenge the Voting Rights Act of 1965 as beyond congressional power under the Fifteenth Amendment.

The main interest of South Carolina was in the continuing operation of her election laws. Massachusetts' claim to standing in this case is certainly as strong as South Carolina's was in the *Katzenbach* case.

Massachusetts complains, as *parens patriae,* that her citizens are drafted and sent to fight in an unconstitutional overseas war. Their lives are in jeopardy. Their liberty is impaired. . . . The allegation in . . . *Mellon* . . . was that Congress had exceeded the general powers delegated to it by Art I, § 8, and invaded the reserved powers of the States under the Tenth Amendment. The claim was not specific. . . . Here Massachusetts points to a specific provision of the Constitution. Congress by Art I, § 8, has the power "To declare War." . . .

. . . [It] has been settled at least since 1901 that "if the health and comfort of the inhabitants of a State are threatened, the State is the proper party to represent and defend them." *** Those cases involved injury to inhabitants of one State by water or air pollution of another State, by interference with navigation, by economic losses caused by an out-of-state agency, and the like. The harm of citizens of Massachusetts suffered by being drafted for a war are certainly of no less a magnitude. Massachusetts would clearly seem to have standing as *parens patriae* to represent, as alleged in its complaint, its male citizens being drafted for overseas combat in Indochina.

JUSTICIABILITY

A question that is "political" is opposed to one that is "justiciable." In reviewing the dimensions of the "political" question we said in *Baker v Carr,* ***

"... Prominent on the surface of any case held to involve a political question is found a textually demonstrable constitutional commitment of the issue to a coordinate political department; or a lack of judicially discoverable and manageable standards for resolving it; or the impossibility of deciding without an initial policy determination of a kind clearly for nonjudicial discretion; or the impossibility of a court's undertaking independent resolution without expressing lack of the respect due coordinate branches of government; or an unusual need for unquestioning adherence to a political decision already made; or the potentiality of embarrassment from multifarious pronouncements by various departments on one question."

1. *A textually demonstrable constitutional commitment of the issue to a coordinate political department.* At issue here is the phrase in Art I, § 8, cl 11: "To declare War." Congress definitely has that power. The Solicitor General argues that only Congress can determine whether it has that power. The Solicitor General argues that only Congress can determine whether it has declared war. He states, " 'To declare War' includes a power to determine, free of judicial interference, the form which its authorization of hostilities will take." This may be correct. But as we stated in *Powell v. McCormack* [1969], *** the question of a textually demonstrable commitment and "what is the scope of such commitment are question [this Court] ... must resolve." *** It may well be that it is for Congress, and Congress alone, to determine the form of its authorization, but if that is the case we should only make that determination after full briefs on the merits and oral argument.

2. *A lack of judicially discoverable and manageable standards for resolving the issue. The standards that are applicable are not elusive.* The case is not one where the Executive is repelling a sudden attack. The present Indochina "war" has gone on for six years. The question is whether the Gulf of Tonkin Resolution was a declaration of war or whether other acts of Congress were its equivalent.

3. *The impossibility of deciding without an initial policy determination of a kind clearly for nonjudicial discretion.* In *Ex parte Milligan* [1866] *** (concurring opinion), it was stated that "neither can the President, in war more than in peace, intrude upon the proper authority of Congress. . . ." That issue in this case is not whether we ought to fight a war in Indochina, but whether the Executive can authorize it without congressional authorization. This is not a case where we would have to determine the wisdom of any policy.

4. *The impossibility of a court's undertaking independent resolution without expressing lack of respect due coordinate branches of government.* The Solicitor General argues it would show disrespect of the Executive to go behind his statements and determine his authority to act in these circumstances. Both *Powell* and the Steel Seizure Case [1952], *** however, demonstrate that the duty of this Court is to interpret the Constitution, and in the latter case we did go behind an executive order to determine his authority. ***

   It is far more important to be respectful to the Constitution than to a coordinate branch of government.

5. *An unusual need for unquestioning adherence to a political decision already made.* This test is essentially a reference to a commitment of a problem and its solution to a' coordinate branch of government.

6. *The potentiality of embarrassment from multifarious pronouncements by various departments of government on one question.* Once again this relates back to whether the problem and its solution are committed to a given branch of government.

We have never ruled, I believe, that when the Federal Government takes a person by the neck and submits him to punishment, imprisonment, taxation, or submission to some ordeal, the complaining person may not be heard in court. The rationale in cases such as the present is that government cannot take life, liberty, or property of the individual and escape adjudication by the courts of the legality of its action.

That is the heart of this case. It does not concern the wisdom of fighting in Southeast Asia. Likewise no question of whether the conflict is either just or necessary is present. We are asked instead whether the Executive has power, absent a congressional declaration of war, to commit Massachusetts citizens in armed hostilities on foreign soil. Another way of putting the question is whether under our Constitution presidential wars are permissible. Should that question be answered in the negative we would then have to determine whether Congress has declared war. That question which Massachusetts presents is in my view justiciable. . . .

"The war power of the United States like its other powers . . . is subject to constitutional limitations." *** No less than the war power—the greatest leveler of them all—is the power of the Commander-in-Chief subject to constitutional limitations. . . .

This Court has previously faced issues of presidential war making. The legality of Lincoln's blockade was considered in the Prize Cases [1863] *** and although the Court narrowly split in supporting the President's position, the split was on the merits, not on whether the claim was justiciable. And even though that war was the Civil War and not one involving an overseas expedition, the decision was 5 to 4.

In the Steel Seizure Case, members of this Court wrote seven opinions and each reached the merits of the Executive's seizure. In that case, as here, the issue related to the President's powers as Commander-in-Chief and the fact that all nine Justices decided the case on the merits and construed the powers of a coordinate branch at a time of extreme emergency should be instructive. . . .

If we determine that the Indochina conflict is unconstitutional because it lacks a congressional declaration of war, the Chief Executive is free to seek one, as was President Truman free to seek congressional approval after our Steel Seizure decision.

There is, of course, a difference between this case and the Prize Cases and the Steel Seizure Case. In those cases a private party was asserting a wrong to him: his property was being taken and he demanded a determination of the legality of the taking. Here the lives and liberties of Massachusetts citizens are in jeopardy. Certainly the Constitution gives no greater protection to property than to life and liberty. It might be argued that the authority in the Steel Seizure Case was not textually apparent in the Constitution, while the power of the Commander-in-Chief to commit troops is obvious and therefore a different determination on justiciability is needed. The Prize Cases, however, involved Lincoln's exercise of power in ordering a blockade by virtue of his powers as the Commander-in-Chief.

Since private parties—represented by Massachusetts as *parens patriae*—are involved in this case, the teaching of the Prize Cases and the Steel Seizure Case is that their claims are justiciable. . . .

Today we deny a hearing to a State which attempts to determine whether it is constitutional to require its citizens to fight in a foreign war absent a congressional declaration of war. . . . The question of an unconstitutional war is neither academic nor "political." . . . It should be settled here and now.

I would set the motion for leave to file down for argument and decide the merits only after full argument.

Mr. Justice Harlan and **Mr. Justice Stewart** dissent. They would set this motion for argument on the questions of standing and justiciability.

Crockett v. Reagan
558 F.Supp. 893 (D.D.C. 1982)

Members of Congress brought suit against President Reagan, claiming that the president had provided military aid to El Salvador in violation of the War Powers Resolution of 1973. Plaintiffs sought an injunction that would force the president to discontinue military aid.

Joyce Hens Green, District Judge.

This case was brought by 29 Members of Congress against Ronald Reagan, individually and in his capacity as President of the United States, Caspar W. Weinberger, individually and in his capacity as Secretary of Defense, and Alexander M. Haig, Jr., individually and in his capacity as Secretary of State. Plaintiffs have alleged that defendants have supplied military equipment and aid to the government of El Salvador in violation of the War Powers Clause of the Constitution, the War Powers Resolution, *** and section 502B of the Foreign Assistance Act of 1961. *** More specifically, plaintiffs aver that a civil war is now in progress throughout El Salvador, with the Salvadoran Revolutionary Government Junta and its armed forces on one side, and the Democratic Revolutionary Front and its armed forces known as the Faribundo Marti National Liberation Front (FMLN) on the other. According to the complaint, in addition to the provision of monetary aid and military equipment, the defendants have dispatched at least 56 members of the United States Armed Forces to El Salvador in aid of the Junta. These forces allegedly are in situations where imminent involvement in hostilities is clearly indicated by the circumstances, and are allegedly taking part in the war effort and assisting in planning operations against the FMLN. Plaintiffs claim that this involvement violates Article 1, Section 8, clause 11 of the Constitution, granting to Congress the exclusive power to declare war, as implemented by the War Powers Resolution (WPR). The WPR requires that absent a declaration of war, a report be made to the Congress within 48 hours of any time when United States Armed Forces have been introduced into hostilities or into situations where imminent involvement in hostilities is clearly indicated by the circumstances, and that 60 days after a report is submitted or is required to be submitted, the President shall terminate any use of United States Armed Forces unless Congress declares war, enacts a specific authorization for such use of United States Armed Forces, or extends the 60-day period for 30 additional days. *** No report pursuant to the WPR has been made, and American forces have remained more than 60 days since they allegedly were introduced into a situation of hostilities or imminent hostilities without a declaration of war.

A cause of action is also stated under Section 502B of the Foreign Assistance Act of 1961, which prohibits the provision of security assistance to "any country the government of which engages in a consistent pattern of gross violations of internationally recognized human rights," which, plaintiffs contend, is the situation in El Salvador. A separate cause of action was originally stated under various provisions of international law, *** but plaintiffs have since stated that they recognize that there is no cause of action under international law, except as specifically implemented by Section 502B of the Foreign Assistance Act. ***

Plaintiffs seek declaratory judgements that the actions of defendants have violated the above described provisions of law, and a writ of mandamus and/or an injunction directing that defendants immediately withdraw all United States Armed Forces, weapons, and military equipment and aid from El Salvador and prohibiting any further aid of any nature. ***

THE WAR POWERS RESOLUTION

If the merits were reached, the Court would have to decide whether the Resolution is applicable to the American military presence in El Salvador, and if so, what remedial action is appropriate. The Court decides that the cause of action under the WPR in its present posture is non-justiciable because of the nature of the factfinding that would be required, and that the 60-day automatic termination provision is not operative unless a report has been submitted or required to be submitted by Congress or a court.

Although defendants have not emphasized the factual issues, which need not be reached if their motion to dismiss is granted, their pleadings and exhibits do make clear that the position of the government is that the factual circumstances in El Salvador do not trigger the WPR, that is, U.S. Armed Forces have not been "introduced into hostilities or into situations where imminent involvement in hostilities is clearly indicated by the circumstances." Plaintiffs present a significantly different picture of what is actually occurring in El Salvador, and the relationship of U.S. military personnel to it. Although consideration of the merits might reveal disagreements about the meaning of WPR terms such as "imminent involvement in hostilities," the most striking feature of the pleadings at this stage of the case is the discrepancy as to the facts.

In support of their position, defendants have submitted the declaration of Lieutenant General Ernest Graves, Director of the Defense Security Assistance Agency, whose responsibilities include the administration and oversight of all security assistance programs conducted by the Department of Defense, *** and a statement by the Department of State provided to Congressman William Broomfield in response to questions about the applicability of the WPR to the dispatch of military personnel to El Salvador and reprinted in the Congressional Record. *** According to General Graves, the Military Mobile Training Teams which have been dispatched to El Salvador since November, 1979 have the sole function of training Salvadoran military personnel so as to create a self-training capability in particular skills, and have never served as advisors, accompanied military units on combat operations, or given those units advice on or worked with them to plan or coordinate the actual performance of offensive or defensive combat operations. Although not exactly claiming that American military personnel have never been exposed to hostile fire, Graves asserts that at no time has insurgent activity directly or immediately threatened the security of training personnel sufficiently to warrant withdrawal of those individuals. The State Department statement echoes General Graves' assessment of the situation. It states that U.S. forces in El Salvador have not and will not act as combat advisors, accompany Salvadoran forces in combat, on operational patrols, or in any situation where combat is likely, and that they have not been subject to attack.

In contrast, plaintiffs contend that American military personnel in El Salvador are taking part in co-ordinating the war effort and are assisting in planning specific operations against the FMLN. Also, many of the 56 military personnel are alleged to work in and around areas where there is heavy combat. *** Two armed attacks on locations where U.S. military personnel were stationed are described in the Complaint, and another is described in Plaintiff's Opposition to Defendants' Motion to Dismiss. . . .

More recently, plaintiffs have supplemented their pleadings to bolster their contention that American forces in El Salvador have been introduced into hostilities or imminent hostilities. They rely upon two news articles. The first is to the effect that U.S. Armed Forces are "fighting side by side" with government troops battling against the FMLN. The second concerns a General Accounting Office (GAO) report which reportedly disclosed that U.S. military personnel in El Salvador are drawing "hostile fire pay," and that a tentative Pentagon ruling that all of El Salvador qualified as a "hostile fire area" was reversed for "policy reasons" possibly to avoid the necessity of reporting to Congress under the WPR. (The actual GAO report has not been submitted).

In sum, if plaintiff's allegations are correct, the executive branch does not merely have a different view of the application of the WPR to the facts, but also is distorting the reality of our involvement in El Salvador. This discrepancy as to factual matters is also evident in the contrast between plaintiffs' allegations regarding the human rights situation in El Salvador, and the President's certifications under the Foreign Assistance Act, discussed *infra*. Plaintiffs' allegations, which are to be accepted as true for the purpose of a motion to dismiss, are, at a minimum, disturbing. This nonetheless does not mean that judicial resolution is appropriate to vindicate, allay or obviate plaintiff's concerns.

The Court concludes that the factfinding that would be necessary to determine whether U.S. forces have been introduced into hostilities or imminent hostilities in El Salvador renders this case in its current posture non-justiciable. The questions as to the nature and extent of the United States' presence in El Salvador and whether a report under the WPR is mandated because our forces have been subject to hostile fire or are taking part in the war effort are appropriate for congressional, not judicial, investigation and determination. Further, in order to determine the application of the 60-day provision, the Court would be required to decide at exactly what point in time U.S. forces had been introduced into hostilities or imminent hostilities, and whether that situation continues to exist. This inquiry would be even more inappropriate for the judiciary.

... Even if the plaintiffs could introduce admissible evidence concerning the state of hostilities in various geographical areas in El Salvador where U.S. forces are stationed and the exact nature of U.S. participation in the conflict (and this information may well be unavailable except through inadmissible newspaper articles), the Court no doubt would be presented conflicting evidence on those issues by defendants. The Court lacks the resources and expertise (which are accessible to the Congress) to resolve disputed questions of fact concerning the military situation in El Salvador. ***

... Here the Court faces a dispute as to whether a small number of American military personnel who apparently have suffered no casualities have been introduced into hostilities or imminent hostilities. The subtleties of factfinding in this situation should be left to the political branches. If Congress doubts or disagrees with the Executive's determination that U.S. forces in El Salvador have not been introduced into hostilities or imminent hostilities, it has the resources to investigate the matter and assert its wishes. The Court need not decide here what type of congressional statement or action would constitute an official congressional stance that our involvement in El Salvador is subject to the WPR, because Congress has taken absolutely no action that could be interpreted to have that effect. Certainly, were Congress to pass a resolution to the effect that a report was required under the WPR, or to the effect that the forces should be withdrawn, and the President disregarded it, a constitutional impasse appropriate for judicial resolution would be presented. ***

... When a member of Congress is a plaintiff in a lawsuit, concern about separation of powers counsels judicial restraint even where a private plaintiff may be entitled to relief. Where the plaintiff's dispute appears to be primarily with his fellow legislators, "[j]udges are presented not with a chance to mediate between two political branches but rather with the possibility of thwarting Congress' will by allowing a plaintiff to circumvent the process of democratic decisionmaking." ***

While a court upon scrutiny of detailed discovery might not agree with the President's assessment of the human rights situation in El Salvador, and could possibly conclude that the provision of security assistance under these circumstances violates section 502B of the Foreign Assistance Act, the equitable discretion doctrine prevents consideration of these issues on behalf of congressional plaintiffs. Their dispute is primarily with their fellow legislators. Action by this Court would not serve to mediate between branches of government, but merely aid plaintiffs in circumventing the democratic processes available to them.

Ashwander v. Tennessee Valley Authority

297 U.S. 288; 56 S. Ct. 466; 80 L. Ed. 688 (1936)

Stockholders in the Alabama Power Company brought suit to block the sale of electric power by the Tennessee Valley Authority (TVA) to the Alabama Power Company. As part of their effort the stockholders challenged the constitutionality of the federal government's building the dam generating the electric power and the constitutionality of contracting to dispose of that power. The Court sustained the government on both counts. The excerpt reproduced below, referred to as the Ashwander *Rules, is part of Justice Brandeis's concurring opinion pointing out the importance of judicial restraint.*

Mr. Justice Brandeis, concurring.

The Court has frequently called attention to the "great gravity and delicacy" of its function in passing upon the validity of an act of Congress; and has restricted exercise of this function by rigid insistence that the jurisdiction of federal courts is limited to actual cases and controversies; and that they have no power to give advisory opinions. . . .

The Court developed, for its own governance in the cases confessedly within its jurisdiction, a series of rules under which it has avoided passing upon a large part of all the constitutional questions pressed upon it for decision. They are:

1. The court will not pass upon the constitutionality of legislation in a friendly, non-adversary proceeding, declining because to decide such questions "is legitimate only in the last resort, and as a necessity in the determination of a real, earnest and vital controversy between individuals. It never was the thought that, by means of a friendly suit, a party beaten in the legislature could transfer to the courts an inquiry as to the constitutionality of the legislative act." ***

2. The Court will not "anticipate a question of constitutional law in advance of the necessity of deciding it." *** "It is not the habit of the court to decide questions of a constitutional nature unless absolutely necessary to a decision of the case." ***

3. The Court will not "formulate a rule of constitutional law broader than is required by the precise facts to which it is to be applied." ***

4. The Court will not pass upon a constitutional question although properly presented by the record, if there is also present some other ground upon which the case may be disposed of. This rule has found most varied application. Thus, if a case can be decided on either of two grounds, one involving a constitutional question, the other a question of statutory construction or general law, the Court will decide only the latter. *** Appeals from the highest court of a state challenging its decision of a question under the Federal Constitution are frequently dismissed because the judgment can be sustained on an independent state ground. ***

5. The Court will not pass upon the validity of a statute upon complaint of one who fails to show that he is injured by its operation. *** Among the many applications of this rule, none is more striking than the denial of the right of challenge to one who lacks a personal or property right. Thus, the challenge by a public official interested only in the performance of his official duty will not be entertained. ***

6. The Court will not pass upon the constitutionality of a statute at the instance of one who has availed himself of its benefits. ***

7. "When the validity of an act of the Congress is drawn in question, and even if a serious doubt of constitutionality is raised, it is a cardinal principle that this Court will first ascertain whether a construction of the statute is fairly possible by which the question may be avoided." *** . . .

PART TWO

SHARED POWERS: THE INSTITUTIONAL ARRANGEMENTS OF GOVERNMENT

CONGRESS AND THE DEVELOPMENT OF NATIONAL POWER

. . .[I]t is not possible to give each department [of the government] an equal power of self-defense. In republican government, the legislative authority necessarily predominates. The remedy for this inconvenience is to divide the legislature into different branches; and to render them by different modes of election, and different principles of action, as little connected with each other, as the nature of their common functions, and their common dependence on the society will admit. It may even be necessary to guard against dangerous encroachments, by still further precautions.

James Madison, *The Federalist* No. 51.

INTRODUCTION

The first three articles of the Constitution are known as the **distributive articles,** because they deal with the three branches of the national government and distribute powers among them. It is no accident that the first article deals with Congress, because the legislature is the most basic institution of republican government. One will recall that under the Articles of Confederation, the national government consisted exclusively of the Congress and a few administrators. There was no executive branch and no system of federal courts. Thus, it is not surprising that the Framers of the Constitution placed the legislative article before the articles dealing with the executive and judicial branches.

Over the years, as government at all levels has expanded in size and responsibility, the power of the executive and judicial branches has grown more dramatically than that of Congress. Moreover, in attempting to address ever more complicated social and economic problems, Congress has created and delegated extensive authority to numerous administrative and regulatory agencies. As a result of this transformation of American government in the twentieth century, Congress, once recognized as preeminent, now shares essentially co-equal status with the presidency and the judiciary. Indeed, many observers would contend that today all three constitutional branches of the national government are overmatched by a mammoth bureaucracy that has emerged as a virtual fourth branch of government. (Constitutional issues relative to the bureaucracy are addressed in Chapter 7.) Nevertheless, Congress, through its vast

The Capitol

legislative powers, has been dominant in establishing and defining the authority of executive departments, federal courts, and regulatory agencies. It also continues to play a key role in the formulation of public policy. Accordingly, the legislative branch merits careful attention.

STRUCTURAL ASPECTS OF CONGRESS

Article I, Section 1 of the Constitution provides that "[a]ll legislative powers herein granted shall be vested in a Congress of the United States, which shall consist of a Senate and a House of Representatives." Article I delineates the composition of both houses of Congress, indicates minimal requirements for members, specifies how members are to be chosen, grants broad authority to each house to determine its own procedures, and extends certain privileges to members of Congress. Article I also defines the legislative powers of Congress, although grants of congressional authority are also found elsewhere in the Constitution.

Bicameralism

The most fundamental change in the institution of Congress brought about by the Constitution was to make it a bicameral, or two-house, body. Under the Articles of Confederation, the Congress was unicameral and each state delegation had only one vote. During the Constitutional Convention of 1787, there was near unanimity on the need for a bicameral Congress, although delegates were divided over the mechanisms of representation in the two houses. Eventually, they compromised on a plan calling for popular election of the members of the House and election of Senators by the state legislatures. This plan remained in effect until 1913, when the Seventeenth Amendment was ratified, instituting direct popular election of Senators.

Under the Constitution, each state is represented in the Senate by two senators. Thus, the size of the Senate has grown from twenty-six members (two from each of the thirteen original states) to one hundred members today. Each state, regardless of its population, is entitled to at least one representative in the House. Beyond this threshold level of representation, House seats are allocated among the states on the basis of population. Members of the House are elected from districts within their respective states. Originally, the House consisted of sixty-five members; today, that number is 435. Although the drawing of House district lines is left to the state legislatures, the Supreme Court has held that House districts must be equal in population so that, in the words of Justice Hugo Black, "one man's vote in a congressional election is to be worth as much as another's" (*Wesberry v. Sanders* [1964]). This ruling necessitates the redrawing of House district lines after each decennial census.

Bicameralism is an important part of the system of checks and balances established by the Constitution. Bicameralism makes it more difficult for Congress to act precipitously, since majorities in both houses must agree for any bill to become law. This is precisely what the Framers had in mind: they wanted to make the process of governance more deliberate in order to prevent transitory public passions from prompting the legislature to adopt ill-considered and unwise legislation. Writing for the Supreme Court in *Immigration and Naturalization Service v. Chadha* (1983), Chief Justice Warren E. Burger observed that:

> By providing that no law could take effect without the concurrence of the prescribed majority of the Members of both Houses, the Framers reemphasized their belief . . . that legislation should not be enacted unless it has been carefully and fully considered by the Nation's elected officials.

Congressional Terms

The original constitutional provisions regarding congressional terms remain unchanged. Members of the House serve two-year terms; senators hold their offices for six-year terms. Unlike the president, who is limited to two consecutive terms in office by the Twenty-second Amendment, members of Congress may be reelected to an unlimited number of terms. Today, support is growing for a constitutional amendment that would limit the number of terms for members of Congress. As an alternative to a national constitutional amendment, several states have considered measures that would limit the terms of members of their congressional delegations. There is also some support for making the terms for the House of Representatives four years, instead of two years. As it now stands, members of the House are no sooner elected than they must begin campaigning for reelection. Like most proposals for constitutional reform, these ideas are not likely to be adopted.

Qualifications of Members of Congress

Article I specifies qualifications for members of the House and the Senate. All members of Congress must reside (at least officially) within the state they represent. Members of the House must be at least twenty-five years of age; members of the Senate must be thirty. Representatives must have been citizens of the United States for at least seven years; for senators, the citizenship requirement is nine years. No member of Congress may simultaneously hold a position in the executive branch, save for temporary diplomatic duties. According to Article I, Section 6, "Each house shall be the Judge of the . . . Qualifications of its own Members. . . ," but the Supreme Court has held that members may be denied seats only if they fail to meet the qualifications specified in Article I (see *Powell v. McCormack* [1969]).

Immunities of Members of Congress

Article I, Section 6 provides that members of Congress "shall in all cases, except treason, felony and breach of the peace, be privileged from arrest during their attendance at the session of their respective houses, and in going to and returning from the same; and for any speech or debate in either house, they shall not be questioned in any other place." These protections reflect the Framers' concern over possible harassment of legislators by executive officials, a concern inherited from the English political experience.

The Speech or Debate Clause of Section 6 provides members of Congress a degree of immunity against criminal prosecution. In *United States v. Johnson* (1966), for example, the Court held that the Speech or Debate Clause insulated members from having their speeches in Congress used as evidence against them in criminal prosecutions. However, in *United States v. Brewster* (1972), the Court said that newsletters mailed to constituents were outside the sphere of legislative activity and could therefore be used as evidence in a criminal case. The Speech or Debate Clause also provides a degree of immunity from civil suits. In *Hutchinson v. Proxmire* (1979), the Supreme Court held that a senator could not be sued for libel for statements he made on the Senate floor. He could, however, be sued for allegedly libelous statements contained in press releases and newsletters to his constituents.

CONSTITUTIONAL SOURCES OF CONGRESSIONAL POWER

The **enumerated powers** of Congress are found in Article I and in provisions scattered throughout the Constitution. For example, Article I, Section 2 provides the House of Representatives the power to return articles of **impeachment,** although Section 3 gives the Senate the power to try impeachments and remove individuals from public office. No president or Supreme Court justice has ever been removed from office by the Senate. In 1868, President Andrew Johnson was impeached by the House but escaped conviction in the Senate by one vote. Richard Nixon resigned the presidency on August 9, 1974, to avoid certain impeachment by the House and likely conviction in the Senate. In 1804,

Justice Samuel Chase narrowly escaped conviction after being impeached by the House. Not since 1801 has any justice of the High Court been subjected to impeachment proceedings. During the 1950s and 1960s, however, a number of House members, including Republican minority leader Gerald Ford, attempted unsuccessfully to bring impeachment charges against Justice William O. Douglas. Moreover, in 1969, Justice Abe Fortas resigned from the Court rather than face charges of financial impropriety that might have led to impeachment.

Article I, Section 8

Most of the enumerated powers of Congress are located in Article I, Section 8, which consists of seventeen brief paragraphs enumerating specific powers followed by a general clause permitting Congress to "make all laws which shall be necessary and proper for carrying into Execution the foregoing powers, and all other powers vested by this Constitution in the Government of the United States. . . ." The powers enumerated in Article I, Section 8 authorize Congress to: lay and collect taxes; borrow money; regulate commerce among the states; control immigration and naturalization; regulate bankruptcy; coin money; fix standards of weights and measures; establish post offices and post roads; grant patents and copyrights; establish tribunals "inferior to the Supreme Court"; declare and wage war; raise and support an army and a navy; regulate the militia when called into service; and perform other more restricted functions.

In reading Article I, Section 8, one will note that, although Congress is empowered to "provide for the common defense and general welfare of the United States," there is no general grant of **police power** to Congress. The power to make any and all laws deemed necessary for the protection of the public health, safety, welfare, and morals is thus reserved to the states under the Tenth Amendment. Yet Congress exercises substantial police power indirectly, by linking laws to the specific powers contained in Section 8. For example, Congress is not empowered to prohibit prostitution *per se,* but it may make it a crime to transport persons across state lines for "immoral purposes" by drawing on its broad power to regulate "commerce among the states" (see *Hoke v. United States* [1913]).

Other Enumerated Powers

Article I, Section 9 authorized Congress to abolish the importation of slaves into the United States, but only after 1808, in deference to the slave-trading states of the Deep South. Congress did act to ban the slave trade in 1808, although the institution of slavery remained legal until the Thirteenth Amendment was ratified in 1865. Section 9 also permits Congress to suspend the writ of habeas corpus in cases of rebellion or national emergency. It is unclear whether this power is vested in Congress alone. At the outset of the Civil War, President Abraham Lincoln suspended habeas corpus in parts of the Union where secessionist sentiment was strong. Congress, which was not in session at the time, ratified Lincoln's action a few months later.

Article II confers on the Senate the power to participate in the treaty-making process and to approve or reject presidential appointments of ambassadors, federal judges, and "all other officers of the United States whose appointments are not herein otherwise provided for..." (Article II, Section 2, clause 2). Article III authorizes Congress to define the jurisdiction of the lower federal courts and to regulate the appellate jurisdiction of the Supreme Court. Article IV empowers Congress to implement uniform procedures under the clause providing that "full faith and credit shall be given in each State to the public acts, records and judicial proceedings of every other State" (Article IV, Section 1). Section 3 of this article authorizes Congress to admit new states to the Union, provided that it respects the territorial integrity of existing states. The same section confers on Congress the power to regulate and dispose of "the territory or other property belonging to the United States." Article V grants Congress authority to propose constitutional amendments and specifies their mode of ratification; that is, by state legislatures or conventions.

Several constitutional amendments confer additional powers on Congress. Of particular importance, the Sixteenth Amendment permits Congress to "lay and collect taxes on incomes from whatever source derived, without apportionment among the states." This amendment nullified an earlier Supreme Court decision striking down an income tax levied by Congress (see *Pollock v. Farmers' Loan and Trust Co.* [1895]).

A number of constitutional amendments endow Congress with the power to legislate in support of civil rights and liberties. For example, the Civil War Amendments—Thirteen, Fourteen, and Fifteen—authorize Congress to enforce civil rights through "appropriate legislation." These rights include freedom from slavery and involuntary servitude (Amendment XIII); the enjoyment of the privileges and immunities of national citizenship (Amendment XIV); guarantees against state deprivation or denial of due process or equal protection of law (Amendment XIV); and prohibition of governmental interference with the right to vote "on account of race, color, or previous condition of servitude" (Amendment XV, Section 1). The Nineteenth Amendment removes sex as an impediment to voting and the Twenty-sixth Amendment lowers the voting age in state and federal elections to eighteen. Both amendments contain clauses permitting Congress to enforce their terms by "appropriate legislation." The Twenty-third and Twenty-fourth Amendments, which give, respectively, the District of Columbia representation in the **Electoral College** and abolish **poll taxes** in federal elections, are likewise subject to Congressional enforcement.

The Doctrine of Implied Powers

When the Constitution was being debated in state ratifying conventions, its supporters argued that the enumeration of specific powers effectively limited the scope of national authority. The argument went as follows: The national government may exercise only those powers specifically delegated to it by the Constitution. The Constitution enumerates certain powers of Congress. Therefore, Congress may exercise only those powers that are specifically enumerated.

It is obvious that Congress today exercises far more powers than are specifically enumerated in the Constitution. Over the years, the American people have come to expect, even demand, as much. Yet one may argue that Congress has remained within the scope of powers delegated to it by the Constitution. The linchpin of this argument is the Necessary and Proper Clause (Article I, Section 8, clause 18) and the related doctrine of **implied powers.** In fact, the Necessary and Proper Clause is today, along with the Commerce, Taxing, and Spending Clauses, one of the key sources of congressional power.

The theory of implied powers originated with Alexander Hamilton, an advocate of strong centralized government. In Hamilton's view, the term "necessary" in the Necessary and Proper Clause referred to powers that could be appropriately exercised by Congress. In constitutional law, Hamilton's interpretation first appeared in an opinion by Chief Justice John Marshall in the obscure case of *United States v. Fisher* (1805). But the doctrine was firmly established in the landmark case of *M'Culloch v. Maryland* (1819), which ranks second only to *Marbury v. Madison* (1803) in importance in American constitutional law. It is important not only in relation to the powers of Congress but also in terms of federalism, the division of power between the national and state governments (see Chapter 8).

The M'Culloch Case

The *M'Culloch* case grew out of a conflict between national and state authority in the area of monetary policy. In 1791, Congress had granted a twenty-year charter to the Bank of the United States. In 1816, five years after the charter expired, Congress established a second Bank of the United States, once again with a twenty-year charter. For a variety of reasons, including its heavy speculation and alleged fraudulent practices, the bank soon became the center of political controversy. Eight states passed legislation designed to prevent or discourage the bank from doing business within their jurisdictions. Maryland chose the latter course by levying a tax on the bank's Baltimore branch. A penalty of five hundred dollars was imposed for each violation of the tax measure. James W. M'Culloch, cashier of the Baltimore branch, violated the Maryland statute by refusing the pay the tax, and a judgment was rendered against him by the Baltimore County Court. Agreeing on a statement of facts, the Maryland attorney general and federal officials converted this legal action into a test case on the constitutionality of the state law and, ultimately, of the bank itself. Critics of the bank argued that Congress had no constitutional warrant to charter a national bank and that, in any event, the states were well within their authority to impose a tax on the bank's operations.

The Maryland Court of Appeals upheld the state's tax on the National Bank, and the U.S. Supreme Court took the case at M'Culloch's behest. The greatest lawyers of their day argued the case for nine days before the Supreme Court. Daniel Webster, William Wirt, and William Pinckney represented M'Culloch; the state of Maryland was represented by Luther Martin, Joseph Hopkinson, and Walter Jones. In a strong show of support for the national government, the Supreme Court unanimously reversed the Maryland Court of Appeals. "Strict constructionists" and proponents of "states rights" were outraged by the High Court's decision. In an action uncharacteristic of a distinguished jurist, Judge Spencer Roane of Virginia went so far as to publish a series of newspaper columns attacking the *M'Culloch* decision. In state legislatures around the country, there were calls for constitutional amendments to restrict the Supreme Court's power of judicial review and reverse the Court's decision in *M'Culloch v. Maryland*. None of these proposals was taken seriously in Congress, which was preoccupied at that time with the slavery issue and the debate over the Missouri Compromise of 1820. Thus, the *M'Culloch* decision remained intact.

Chief Justice Marshall's opinion of the Court in *M'Culloch* is widely regarded as a judicial *tour de force* not unlike *Marbury v. Madison*. In *M'Culloch,* Marshall asserted that although none of the enumerated powers of Congress explicitly authorized the incorporation of a bank, the Necessary and Proper Clause provided the textual basis for Congress's action. In keeping with his general view of the Constitution as an adaptable instrument of government, Marshall construed the Necessary and Proper Clause broadly, concluding that it was not confined merely to authority that was *indispensable* to the exercise of the enumerated powers. Rather, it was sufficient for Congress to adopt "appropriate" means to carry out its legitimate objectives. Among these were the powers to tax, to coin and borrow money, and to regulate commerce. In Marshall's view, the establishment of a national bank was an appropriate means of achieving these broad objectives and was, accordingly, permissible under the Necessary and Proper Clause. Marshall provided a detailed exposition of the doctrine of implied powers, concluding with the following statement:

> Let the end be legitimate, let it be within the scope of the Constitution, and all means which are plainly adapted to that end, which are not prohibited, but consist with the letter and spirit of the Constitution, are constitutional.

Implied Powers: Congress Unbound?

Under the doctrine of implied powers, scarcely any area exists in which Congress is absolutely barred from acting, since most problems have a conceivable relationship to the broad powers and objectives contained in the Constitution. Thomas Jefferson, an opponent of the doctrine of implied powers, perceived as much in 1790 when, as secretary of state, he opposed the establishment of the First Bank of the United States. In a memorandum to President Washington, Jefferson wrote, "To take a single step beyond the boundaries thus specially drawn around the powers of Congress is to take possession of a boundless field of power, no longer susceptible of any definition." Today, the powers of Congress, while not exactly "boundless," are certainly far greater than most of the Founders could have imagined.

THE POWER TO INVESTIGATE

Nowhere in Article I is there any mention of Congress having the power to conduct investigations. Yet one readily recalls the highly publicized congressional investigation into the Iran-Contra affair when Lt. Col. Oliver North was summoned to testify before a committee of Congress. Over the years, Congress has conducted hundreds of investigations and called thousands of witnesses to testify. Sometimes these investigations have been great public events, such as the Watergate hearings of 1973 and 1974, which led to the demise of the Nixon presidency. More often, they have involved more mundane questions of public policy, such as consumer product safety or the regulation of the trucking industry.

One of the important functions of legislative investigations is **oversight**— Congress serving as a watchdog over the actions of executive and regulatory agencies. This function has become increasingly important in the modern era as Congress has created so many agencies and delegated to them broad powers within their areas of expertise. In a democracy, it is vital that the people's elected representatives keep tabs on the activities of a powerful, unelected government bureaucracy (for elaboration on this theme, see Chapter 7).

From where does Congress derive its power to investigate? There are several theories. The first is that Congress inherited this power from the English Parliament at the time of the Declaration of Independence in 1776. This theory views the power to investigate as inherent in any duly constituted legislature. Under this theory, Congress's power to investigate does not depend on any grant of authority in the Constitution (for a treatment of the general theme of inherited powers, see *United States v. Curtiss-Wright Export Corporation* [1936], reprinted in Chapter 6).

A second theory is that Congressional investigations may be justified under the doctrine of implied powers. In this argument, the power to investigate is seen as both necessary and proper to the exercise of Congress's most basic function—crafting legislation. Investigation is a necessary means of obtaining information about the issues and subjects around which Congress is considering legislation. Finally, Congress's power to conduct investigations may be justified under a theory of an evolving system of checks and balances. Under this theory, the system of checks and balances enumerated by the Framers was incomplete in that it failed to grant Congress the power to investigate, since investigation is an obvious means whereby Congress can check the other branches. In this argument, Congress was justified in asserting the power to investigate for the same reason that the Supreme Court was justified in assuming the power to rule on the constitutionality of legislation.

The Supreme Court Recognizes Congress's Power to Investigate

Congress conducted a number of important investigations during the early and mid-1800s. These included an inquiry into the Lewis and Clark exploration of the Louisiana Territory acquired during the Jefferson administration and an investigation of John Brown's abortive raid on the federal arsenal at Harper's Ferry in 1859. The Supreme Court did not, however, address the constitutionality of the investigative power until its decision in *Kilbourn v. Thompson* (1881). The case involved a House of Representatives investigation into the collapse of the Jay Cooke banking firm, with which the United States had deposited funds. In the course of the investigation, Hallet Kilbourn was called to testify and bring with him documents pertaining to his "real estate pool" and its dealings with the Jay Cooke company. Kilbourn refused both to testify and to produce the records.

He was cited for contempt of Congress and was jailed for forty-five days. Upon his release from custody, Kilbourn sued John G. Thompson, the House sergeant-at-arms, for false imprisonment. Reviewing a lower court decision in Thompson's favor, the Supreme Court held that, although Congress possessed the power to investigate, the power must be exercised in furtherance of the legislative function. Writing for a unanimous bench, Justice Samuel F. Miller stated that Congress could not employ its power of investigation to accomplish functions that were reserved to the other branches of government. In this case, the House had no intent to legislate; its inquiry into the Jay Cooke company was entirely investigatory in nature. Thus, Kilbourn's contempt citation and imprisonment were invalid.

The *Kilbourn* decision established the basic policy of the Supreme Court toward legislative investigations. The power to investigate is a necessary auxiliary of the legislative function. Yet the implied power to investigate is not unlimited. It must be exercised only in relation to potential legislation. Of course, today, there are few areas in which Congress may not potentially legislate; thus, there are few areas off limits to congressional investigation. Still, an investigation purely for its own sake is subject to judicial challenge.

Compulsory Process

When a congressional committee wishes to obtain testimony, it issues a **subpoena** to an individual. If it wishes to obtain documents for its inspection, it issues a **subpoena duces tecum.** A subpoena is often referred to as **compulsory process,** because the individual is compelled to comply or risk being held in contempt. The Supreme Court upheld Congress's power to enforce a subpoena in *McGrain v. Daugherty* (1927), a case stemming from a Senate investigation into the Teapot Dome scandal during the administration of President Warren G. Harding. There, the Court stated that "the power of inquiry—with the process to enforce it—is an essential and appropriate auxiliary to the legislative function."

The Rights of Individuals Called before Congressional Committees

Congress's power to conduct investigations and compel witnesses to disclose information is generally regarded as both necessary and proper, but the power is certainly subject to abuse. Individuals who are called to testify before congressional committees may under certain circumstances legitimately refuse to answer questions. The Fifth Amendment protection against compulsory self-incrimination applies to legislative investigations, as well as to police interrogations and questioning in a court of law. An individual may legitimately refuse to answer questions if the answers to such questions might reveal criminal wrong-doing on his or her part. Yet, like a court of law, Congress may grant **immunity** to a witness to circumvent the Fifth Amendment. A witness who is granted immunity from prosecution has no grounds to invoke the Fifth Amendment, since the danger of self-incrimination has been removed. This was the case during the Iran-Contra investigation, when Oliver North was granted **use immunity** in exchange for his testimony before Congress. Under the grant of immunity, federal prosecutors were barred from using North's testimony before Congress as evidence against him in a subsequent criminal prosecution. Under the grant of immunity, North ultimately avoided criminal liability.

In addition to the protection against compulsory self-incrimination, a person called to testify before Congress enjoys certain protections under the Due Process Clause of the Fifth Amendment. In particular, one is entitled to know the subject matter of the investigation. Moreover, questions must be pertinent to that subject (see *Watkins v. United States* [1957]).

Perhaps the best example of the abuse of the investigatory power occurred during the early days of the Cold War, when suspicions of Communist subversion verged on hysteria. In the 1950s, the House Un-American Activities Committee (HUAC) sought to expose Communist infiltration and corruption by subjecting suspected Communists to far-ranging and probing questions about their beliefs, affiliations, activities, and relationships. Justifying the committee's commitment to expose Communists, its first chairman, Congressman Martin Dies, said, "I am not in a position to say whether we can legislate effectively as to this matter, but I do know that exposure in a democracy of subversive activities is the most effective weapon that we have in our possession." In the climate of near-hysteria over Communist subversion, the admonitions in *Kilbourn v. Thompson* about the proper scope and function of the investigatory power were all but forgotten. Individuals who refused to answer the committee's questions on grounds of compulsory self-incrimination were apt to be branded "Fifth Amendment Communists."

In *Watkins v. United States* (1957), the Supreme Court reversed a conviction for contempt of Congress in a case where a witness had refused to answer questions put to him by HUAC. John Watkins answered questions about his own beliefs and activities but refused to "name names" of other suspected Communists, saying:

> I am not going to plead the Fifth Amendment, but I refuse to answer certain questions that I believe are outside the scope of your committee's activities.... I do not believe ... that this committee has the right to undertake public exposure of persons because of their past activities.

The Supreme Court reversed Watkins's conviction primarily on procedural grounds, holding that he had been denied due process of law. The Court also expressed concern that First Amendment values were being threatened by HUAC's public hearings. Critics of HUAC hoped the Court's decision in *Watkins* presaged a desire on the part of the Court to limit congressional investigations on First Amendment grounds. In Congress, however, critics of *Watkins* and similar Warren Court decisions introduced legislation to remove the Court's appellate jurisdiction in cases where persons are held in contempt of Congress. The Court evidently took note of these efforts and soon backed away from its First Amendment concerns regarding congressional investigations. In *Barenblatt v. United States* (1959), the Court upheld a conviction for contempt of Congress, holding that the public interest in exposing Communist infiltration outweighed a witness's First Amendment rights in refusing to answer questions. The *Barenblatt* decision went a long way toward deflating Court-curbing efforts and rehabilitating the Court's standing in Congress. Over the last three decades, the Court has continued to show deference to congressional investigations and has generally refused to allow uncooperative witnesses to invoke the protections of the First Amendment (see, for example, *Wilkinson v. United States* [1961] and *Eastland v. United States Servicemen's Fund* [1975]).

REGULATION OF INTERSTATE COMMERCE

The Articles of Confederation contained no provision authorizing Congress to regulate commerce among the states. This serious deficiency, along with the absence of a national taxing power and the inability to enforce decisions either against states or individuals, undermined the effectiveness of the national government during the Confederation period. The experience of that government was brief and frustrating. Growing commercial rivalries among the thirteen largely independent states could not be resolved by a weak Congress in which each state, regardless of its population, had an equal vote.

By 1787, it had become clear to most political observers (including the Framers of the Constitution), that the issue of commercial rivalry among the states was simply part of a larger set of problems stemming from the weakness of the national government under the Articles of Confederation. At the Philadelphia Convention and for many years thereafter, attention was directed to easing the economic friction among the states. It was the control of interstate rivalry, and not the exercise of national power on a broad scale, that chiefly concerned those who drafted the original Constitution. Concessions were necessary to persuade all the states to give up their autonomy in interstate commerce. One of these was the so-called commerce and slave trade compromise, through which several southern states were persuaded to drop their opposition to the national regulation of commerce in exchange for the assurance that their participation in the slave trade would not be restricted for twenty years (Article I, Section 9, clause 1).

Clause 3 of Article I, Section 8 provides that ". . . Congress shall have power . . . to regulate commerce with foreign nations, and among the several states, and with the Indian Tribes." This clause is important both as a source of national power and as an implicit restriction on state power. But the two dimensions of the Commerce Clause—source of national power and basis of state restraint—are closely interrelated, and this dual character should be kept in mind.

Early Interpretation of the Commerce Clause

During the first century following adoption of the Constitution, Congress made little use of the Commerce Clause as a source of positive power. It is true that this clause served as partial authority for the creation of the second Bank of the United States, as upheld in *M'Culloch v. Maryland* (1819). The range of potential congressional power was thus recognized at an early date. Nevertheless, during the nineteenth century, the primary function of the Commerce Clause was as a barrier against state legislation. Neither the states nor the national government engaged in extensive regulation of commerce during this early period, but most of the governmental activity that did occur emanated from the states. It was in this setting that the first major Commerce Clause case, *Gibbons v. Ogden* (1824), reached the Supreme Court.

Gibbons v. Ogden

As in most other areas of constitutional interpretation, the starting point in the interpretation of the Commerce Clause is found in one of Chief Justice John Marshall's opinions. As in *Marbury v. Madison* (1803) and *M'Culloch v. Maryland* (1819), Marshall's opinion in the *Gibbons* case is one of those fundamental statements of constitutional jurisprudence that has grown in influence with the passage of time. Marshall and his colleagues on the Supreme Court of the early 1800s had the advantage of addressing major questions of constitutional law for the first time, unguided—but also unencumbered—by the weight of precedent. Marshall, far more than any other jurist of his era, displayed the ability to use this advantage effectively.

At issue in *Gibbons v. Ogden* was the constitutionality of New York's grant of a steamboat monopoly to Robert Fulton and Robert Livingston. Aaron Ogden succeeded to the ownership of the Fulton-Livingston interest, which extended to commercial steamboat traffic between New York and New Jersey. Thomas Gibbons challenged this exclusive grant on the ground that it interfered with the power of Congress to regulate commerce among the states. Gibbons was licensed under federal law to engage in the "coasting" trade—commerce and navigation in coastal waters—and he contended that this authorization gave him the right to transact business of an interstate nature within the boundaries of New York, irrespective of that state's monopoly grant to others. Marshall and his colleagues agreed with Gibbons.

In the course of declaring the New York steamboat monopoly unconstitutional, Marshall wrote expansively about the scope of congressional power embodied in the Commerce Clause. In this instance, an obvious conflict existed between the federal licensing provision and the state grant of monopoly. Invoking the Supremacy Clause of Article VI of the Constitution, Marshall resolved this conflict in favor of the national government. He went on to assert that the power of Congress over commerce among the states was plenary—that is, full and complete—and subject to no competing exercise of state power in the same area. The federal law under which Gibbons operated was a modest exercise of that plenary power, but it was enough to warrant invalidation of the state law because the monopoly granted by the state interfered with the commercial privileges provided by the federal government.

It was clear from Marshall's perspective that Congress had acted well within its constitutional authority. In fact, Marshall defined the phrase "commerce among the several states" so broadly, and spoke in such sweeping terms about the power of Congress to regulate it, that his opinion came to be read as an endorsement of regulatory authority on a grand scale—far beyond anything dreamed of in the 1820s. Marshall acknowledged that commerce among the states was "restricted to that commerce which concerns more states than one." Nevertheless, it encompassed a vast range of relationships and transactions summed up in the phrase "commercial intercourse." When Marshall spoke of commerce as intercourse, he included more than the isolated movement of an article of trade from a point in one state to a point in another state. He had in mind commercial activity within and between states and maintained that realistic distinctions could not be automatically equated with state lines. Marshall recognized that some commerce might be altogether internal, or intrastate, in nature; but because that type of commerce was not at issue in this case, he did not elaborate on its precise meaning.

In asserting that the power of Congress under the Commerce Clause was plenary and superior to any competing state power, Marshall skirted one vitally important question: Would state legislation affecting commerce among the states be constitutional in the absence of any conflicting federal law? In a concurring opinion, Justice William Johnson answered this question in the negative. In his view, the power of Congress was not only plenary but also exclusive; he maintained that the states were absolutely barred from legislating in this broad area. Johnson was not supported in this view by other members of the Court, and his interpretation has never been adopted by a court majority. However, the Court has generally recognized the exclusive power of Congress to regulate commerce "with foreign nations . . . and with the Indian Tribes."

Justice Johnson's statement endorsing exclusive congressional control of commerce among the states served to sharpen the underlying issue in *Gibbons v. Ogden* and in a long line of cases decided since that decision. The basic issue is this: If the power of Congress is plenary, as Marshall and his colleagues in *Gibbons* maintained, does the failure of Congress to regulate a particular aspect of commerce mean that this aspect is not to be regulated at all? And if the answer to this question is no (as the Court has subsequently indicated), then does it follow that the states are free to regulate commerce in any area not already covered by federal legislation? Broadly speaking, and with varying degrees of imprecision, the Supreme Court has also answered this question in the negative. As Chapter 8 will explain, the states may, in the absence of conflicting federal law, regulate certain local aspects of interstate commerce. But even when no conflict with federal law exists, those aspects of interstate commerce that require uniform nationwide regulation cannot be touched by the states. The problem that remains unresolved to the present day is where to draw the line between permissible and impermissible state regulation of commerce in specific cases. It was not necessary in *Gibbons v. Ogden* to explore that problem; but as demands for greater governmental regulation at state and national levels increased, the issue became more and more perplexing.

Gibbons v. Ogden furnished John Marshall with an opportunity to lay down an all-encompassing definition of national power under the Commerce Clause. The decision was widely acclaimed by business leaders because it placed restrictions on state grants of commercial monopoly, thus encouraging competitive commercial and industrial activity at a time when the national government played no significant role in regulating business. To the advocate of private enterprise in the 1820s, it no doubt seemed safe enough to talk in the abstract about broad national power to regulate commerce, especially if such discussion provided a justification for curbing state regulation. Until late in the nineteenth century, that is precisely what the national commerce power symbolized.

During this period, the states, under an expanding definition of their police power, adopted an increasing number and variety of economic regulations, many of which were aimed at large corporations with growing political clout, especially in the post-Civil War era. The concept of police power refers to the state's basic function in protecting the health, safety, morals, and general welfare of the people. It is embraced within the broader concept of reserved power, formally recognized by the Tenth Amendment to the Constitution. Police power is inherent in the governing process. In the twentieth century, it has been advanced as a broad justification for national as well as state authority. It was first used, however, as a rationale for the expansion of state power. As this process of expansion continued, especially in the 1870s and 1880s, it came into conflict with the power of Congress to regulate commerce—not so much the actual exercise of that power but the potential power that, according to the Supreme Court, Congress alone could exert (see *Wabash, St. Louis & Pacific Railway Company v. Illinois* [1886]).

Congress Exercises the Commerce Power

As the popular demand for economic regulation increased and restrictions on state power multiplied, the national government came under greater pressure to limit the concentration of corporate influence and reduce what many Americans regarded as economic injustice and exploitation. Strong commercial interests countered this pressure to some extent, but ultimately, Congress responded by passing the Interstate Commerce Act of 1887 and the Sherman Antitrust Act of 1890. The first of these measures established the Interstate Commerce Commission (ICC), granting this independent agency limited authority to regulate railroads engaged in commerce among the states. The Sherman Act was aimed at controlling on a national scale the concentration of economic power in the form of monopolies or "combinations in restraint of trade," as the statute phrased it.

Both the ICC and the Sherman Act represented the beginning of a national counterpart to state police power. Both rested squarely on the Commerce Clause and both encountered rough sledding in the Supreme Court for a number of years. By 1890, the Court had come under the influence of an economic philosophy that stressed the values of individual and corporate freedom and minimized the legitimate sphere of governmental regulation. Although the Court never fully subscribed to the doctrine of laissez-faire, most of its members, including several former corporation lawyers, were sympathetic to this perspective. This view was reflected in changing interpretations of the Commerce Clause, the Tenth Amendment, and the Due Process Clauses of the Fifth and Fourteenth Amendments. Until the judicial revolution of 1937, the Court accorded great importance to the protection of property and other business-related rights against growing regulatory efforts at all levels of government. This subject is discussed more fully in Chapter 10, but it is important to recognize at this point that the restrictive view of the Commerce Clause, characteristic of Supreme Court decisions of the late nineteenth and early twentieth centuries, was part of a larger pattern of constitutional interpretation.

The Supreme Court Restricts the Commerce Power

The first major change in Commerce Clause interpretation as applied to the exercise of national power came in the 1895 case of *United States v. E. C. Knight Company*. The decision resulted from the federal government's effort to break up a powerful sugar monopoly by invoking the Sherman Antitrust Act. In this initial interpretation of the act, a Supreme Court majority held that its regulatory provisions, as applied to the manufacture of sugar, went beyond the proper scope of the commerce power.

Commerce Distinguished from Production

By contrast with John Marshall's broad perspective in *Gibbons v. Ogden,* Chief Justice Melville Fuller, writing for the majority in *E. C. Knight,* emphasized the boundaries of the commerce power. He acknowledged the "evils" of monopoly and conceded that the E. C. Knight Company was indeed engaged in monopolistic practices in the manufacture of refined sugar. He also recognized a connection between the control of the manufacture of "a given thing" and "control of its disposition." But he brushed aside the obvious relationship between commerce and manufacturing, maintaining that it was secondary, not primary, in nature. The connection, in his view, was incidental and indirect. Fuller did not clearly indicate why such a distinction should be made or precisely where the line should be drawn. He simply asserted that "commerce succeeds to manufacture and is not a part of it." Under their police power, states were free to regulate monopolies, but the national government had no general police power under the Commerce Clause. He thus accorded a narrow interpretation to the enumerated powers of Congress. Only if the business activity in question was itself a "monopoly of commerce" could the national government suppress it. This neat distinction between commerce and manufacturing, adopted over the strong dissent of Justice John M. Harlan (the elder), temporarily gutted the Sherman Act without formally declaring it unconstitutional. If the government could move only against the postmanufacturing phases of monopolistic activity, and not against the entire enterprise, its hands were effectively tied.

The Court followed similar reasoning in *Hammer v. Dagenhart,* (1918), invalidating by a 5-to-4 margin federal restrictions on child labor. The manufacture of goods by children, even when those goods were clearly destined for shipment in interstate commerce, was not a part of commerce and could not be regulated by Congress. Here the Court, over the scathing dissent of Justice Oliver Wendell Holmes, added the observation that there was nothing harmful in the manufactured goods themselves, implying that such a showing would have been necessary to justify their prohibition in interstate commerce.

Interestingly, the Court had upheld several equally far-reaching exercises of congressional power under the Commerce Clause between the *E. C. Knight* and *Dagenhart* decisions. In fact, some of these statutes imposed severe criminal penalties in addition to the civil remedies exclusively applied in the latter case. For example, Congress enacted laws imposing fines and imprisonment for participation in lotteries and prostitution. Activities of this sort, unlike child labor and business monopoly, were widely regarded as immoral. And when it came to punishing what most people believed to be sinful behavior, the Commerce Clause was seen as an appropriate weapon (see, for example, *Champion v. Ames* [1903], upholding the federal antilottery statute, and *Hoke v. United States* [1913], sustaining a federal law penalizing the transportation of women across state lines for "immoral purposes"). Throughout this period, the Court was also willing to uphold national legislation designed to protect consumers against adulterated food and the improper processing, packaging, and branding of meat shipped across state lines (see *Hipolite Egg Company v. United States* [1911], in which the Court upheld the Pure Food and Drug Act).

In the field of transportation, particularly the regulation of railroad freight rates, the scope of national power under the Commerce Clause developed in accordance with the broad language of *Gibbons v. Ogden*. Even intrastate rates might be regulated by the ICC if states created rate structures that discriminated against interstate carriers in favor of their local competitors. This was the situation in the Shreveport rate case (*Houston, East & West Texas Railway Company v. United States* [1914]). The Texas Railroad Commission permitted three railroads to charge lower rates for intrastate shipments in east Texas than for interstate shipments of comparable distances in the same geographical area. The impact of this arrangement was to generate business among East Texas cities at the expense of Shreveport, Louisiana, a commercial center naturally linked to such cities as Dallas. The Louisiana Railroad Commission began administrative proceedings before the Interstate Commerce Commission (ICC), challenging the differential rate structures. The ICC established uniform maximum rates for interstate and intrastate movement of freight and ordered the three railroads to cease their discriminatory practices. In a 7-to-2 decision, the Supreme Court affirmed the decree of a specialized tribunal, the Commerce Court, upholding the ICC decision. In his opinion for the majority, Associate Justice (later Chief Justice) Charles Evans Hughes declared that Congress is authorized

> to supply the needed correction where the relation between intrastate and interstate rates presents the evil to be corrected, and this it may do completely, by reason of its control over the interstate carrier in all matters having such a close and substantial relation to interstate commerce that it is necessary or appropriate to exercise the control for the government of that commerce. . . . Congress is entitled to maintain its own standard as to these rates, and to forbid any discriminatory action . . . which will obstruct the freedom of movement of interstate traffic over their lines in accordance with the terms it establishes.

Congress could provide for the execution of this power "through the aid of a subordinate body." Thus, the decision and the order of the ICC were lawful.

The "Stream of Commerce" Doctrine

In spite of broad interpretation of the commerce power in the field of transportation, prior to the late 1930s, the Court resisted congressional efforts to expand the Commerce Clause as a nonselective basis of national police power. Instead, the Court developed several concepts designed to assist it in defining the outer limits of the commerce power. We identify only two of the most prominent of these to illustrate the elusiveness and complexity of constitutional development in this field of congressional regulation. The "stream of commerce" doctrine was first articulated by Justice Holmes in the 1905 decision of *Swift and Co. v. United States*. There, the Court held that the power of the national government under the Sherman Act extended to "conspiracies in restraint of trade" among a combination of Chicago meatpackers. Even though the challenged activities, the buying and selling of cattle in Chicago, were local in nature, Holmes found that they were in the "current of commerce" among the states. The same rationale was applied by Chief Justice William Howard Taft seventeen years later in a decision upholding federal regulation under the Packers and Stockyards Act of 1921 (*Stafford v. Wallace* [1922]).

"Direct" Versus "Indirect" Effects on Interstate Commerce

The second concept is a presumed distinction between the direct and indirect effect of a particular regulation on commerce. In a number of cases during this period, the Court indicated that even though the activity in question might not be defined as commerce *per se,* it could still be regulated if it had a direct effect on interstate commerce. It followed that a mere indirect effect would not alone be sufficient to justify the exercise of congressional power. Although the "direct-indirect" test was usually applied in such a way that it sustained the regulation under review, the Court used this distinction as a means of indicating that congressional authority was subject to limitation. For example, when the National Industrial Recovery Act, a major piece of New Deal legislation, was declared unconstitutional in *A.L.A. Schechter Poultry Corporation v. United States* (1935), one of the principal conclusions reached by the Court was that what the government sought to regulate had only an indirect effect on interstate commerce. (The other principal constitutional basis of the decision, a violation of the rule against congressional delegation of authority, is discussed in Chapter 7.)

The distinction between manufacturing and commerce was reaffirmed in principle and extended to the differentiation between mining and commerce in the 1936 case of *Carter v. Carter Coal Company*. Thus, a Supreme Court majority from the mid-1890s through the mid-1930s treated the commerce power of Congress as inherently limited in nature. Then came the confrontation between President Franklin D. Roosevelt and the "nine old men." In the aftermath of Roosevelt's effort to pack the Supreme Court in 1937, the Court moved away from a defense of economic freedom and toward an affirmation of broad regulatory power, both national and state. One very important aspect of this transition was a return to John Marshall's expansive definition of congressional power under the Commerce Clause. As a result, the Commerce Clause came to be recognized as a source of far-reaching national police power.

Modern Interpretation of the Commerce Clause

Under President Roosevelt's leadership, the Democratic Congress of the middle and late 1930s enacted sweeping legislation to replace, and in some instances amplify, measures that the Supreme Court had invalidated prior to 1937. Such areas as labor-management relations, agriculture, social insurance, and national resource development became focal points of national policy, and the Commerce Clause figured prominently as a constitutional source for most of the new legislation. Beginning with its decision upholding the National Labor Relations Act (*National Labor Relations Board v. Jones & Laughlin Steel Corporation* [1937]), the reoriented Supreme Court swept away distinctions between commerce and manufacturing, between direct and indirect burdens on commerce, and between activities that directly or indirectly affected commerce.

The post-New Deal perspective on the Commerce Clause is well-illustrated by the case of *Wickard v. Filburn* (1942). At issue was the constitutionality of a federal acreage allotment for wheat. On their face, the questions might have seemed easy to resolve in light of the expanded power of Congress in the post-New Deal era. But the specific violation consisted of a farmer's raising a wheat crop in excess of the prescribed allotment not for sale or distribution in interstate commerce but for his own consumption. Writing for a unanimous Court, Justice Robert H. Jackson concluded:

> Even if appellant's activity be local and though it may not be regarded as commerce, it may still, whatever its nature, be reached by Congress if it exerts a substantial economic effect on interstate commerce, and this irrespective of whether such effect is what might at some earlier time have been defined as "direct" or "indirect."

A comparison between the sweeping language of *Wickard v. Filburn* and the restrictive view of Chief Justice Fuller in *E. C. Knight* illustrates the extent to which a single clause of the Constitution is subject to contrasting interpretations. Under the currently prevailing interpretation of the Commerce Clause, the federal government is permitted to play a very active role in the regulation of economic activity. This is seen in the enforcement of antitrust laws, the control over farm commodities, the supervision of financial markets, the oversight of labor-management relations, and the regulation of various transportation industries. It is also seen in areas of "commerce" that fall outside conventional regulation of business, such as civil rights legislation applicable to places of public accommodation.

Decline of the Tenth Amendment

With the decision in *United States v. Darby* (1941), another major post-New Deal ruling, the Tenth Amendment for all intents and purposes vanished as a significant restraint on the commerce power. It was not to reappear in this context for some thirty-five years (*National League of Cities v. Usery,* 1976). In *Darby,* the Court unanimously upheld the Fair Labor Standards Act of 1938. Writing for a unanimous Court, Justice (later Chief Justice) Harlan F. Stone found nothing in the Tenth Amendment that barred expansion of the national police power under the Commerce Clause. In upholding the Fair Labor Standards Act with its minimum wage and anti-child-labor provisions, Stone's opinion relegated the Tenth Amendment to the status of a historical monument.

Ignoring the emphasis accorded this amendment only a few years earlier, Stone observed that it stated "a mere truism that all is retained which has not been surrendered." The *Darby* decision explicitly overruled *Hammer v. Dagenhart*, rejecting the former ruling's narrow interpretation of the Commerce Clause, as well as its reliance on the Tenth Amendment. (*Hammer v. Dagenhart*, *United States v. Darby*, and *National League of Cities v. Usery*, along with the related case *Garcia v. San Antonio Metropolitan Transit Authority*, are reprinted in Chapter 8).

In contrast with his expansive interpretation of the commerce power in *Darby*, Stone virtually read the Tenth Amendment out of the Constitution. He emphasized the supposed intent of those who drafted the Amendment, "to allay fears that the new national government might seek to exercise powers not granted, and that the states might not be able to exercise fully their reserved powers." Stone conveniently omitted consideration of intervening judicial interpretation, especially that of the preceding generation, through which the scope of the Tenth Amendment had been enlarged.

Stone's approach in the *Darby* case reveals much about the nature of constitutional interpretation. His emphasis on "original intent" as a yardstick for determining the narrow scope of the Tenth Amendment contrasted sharply with his analysis of the Commerce Clause and the great national power exercised in its name 150 years after the Philadelphia Convention. Stone's selective emphasis on such concepts as original intent, on the one hand, and the changing conditions of society, on the other, is by no means unique in Supreme Court annals. It suggests in a single opinion the divergent approaches to constitutional interpretation (see Chapter 2). It is just this type of intellectual ambivalence that has led many observers to conclude that the Supreme Court has never conformed to any particular theory of constitutional interpretation.

In the 1976 case of *National League of Cities v. Usery*, the Court appeared to resurrect the Tenth Amendment as it struck down provisions of the 1974 amendments to the Fair Labor Standards Act extending minimum-wage coverage to most state and local government employees. In doing so, the Court overruled *Maryland v. Wirtz* (1968). Writing for a 5-to-4 majority in *Usery*, Justice (later Chief Justice) William Rehnquist concluded that the national commerce power must yield to the Tenth Amendment when the former infringes upon "traditional aspects of state sovereignty." Nevertheless, he made it clear that, at least for a majority of the Court, the Tenth Amendment would not be regarded as a "mere truism." Acknowledging the broad power of Congress to regulate commerce among the states, Rehnquist drew a sharp distinction between that authority as applied to business activity on the one hand and to the function of "states as states" on the other.

It is difficult to discern the specific Tenth Amendment interest that, for the *Usery* majority, justified restricting the commerce power. Justice Rehnquist expressed some concern about the adverse economic impact the 1974 amendments would have on already overburdened state and local governments. In his view, blanket minimum-wage requirements would not only be costly, but the national law that imposed them would also displace state policies structuring delivery of those governmental services that their citizens require.

In a sharp dissent, Justice Brennan assailed the *Usery* ruling as an irresponsible departure from modern views regarding the national commerce power and federal-state relations. A number of legal scholars endorsed this view, but others praised the decision as a welcome reassertion of the principle of federalism.

Controversy over *Usery* continued into the 1980s, until the decision was overruled in *Garcia v. San Antonio Metropolitan Transit Authority* (1985). Again the court was divided 5 to 4. Justice Harry A. Blackmun, who had concurred in the *Usery* ruling, switched sides and delivered the majority opinion in *Garcia*. Supported by Justices Brennan, White, Marshall, and Stevens, he concluded that

> the attempt to draw the boundaries of state regulatory immunity in terms of "traditional governmental function" is not only unworkable but is inconsistent with established principles of federalism and, indeed, with those very . . . principles on which *National League of Cities* purported to rest.

In a lengthy dissent, Justice Lewis Powell, joined by Chief Justice Burger and Justices Rehnquist and O'Connor, deplored what he characterized as the Court's abrupt departure from precedent and its reduction of the Tenth Amendment to "meaningless rhetoric when Congress acts pursuant to the Commerce Clause." He maintained that this decision "reflects a serious misunderstanding, if not an outright rejection, of the history of our country and the intention of the Framers of the Constitution."

In overruling *National League of Cities v. Usery,* the Court in *Garcia* specifically reaffirmed the ruling in *Maryland v. Wirtz,* which, in turn, had relied heavily on the reasoning of Justice Stone in the *Darby* case. Given the razor-thin majority in *Garcia* and the possibility that recent Supreme Court appointees might be philosophically receptive to the dissenting view in that case, we could witness still another change of direction in this important area of constitutional interpretation.

The Commerce Clause and Civil Rights

In the 1960s, Congress relied on the Commerce Clause as a basis for vast legislative undertakings, some of them well beyond the field of economic regulation. The most important illustration of the commerce power as a source of noncommercial legislation is within the area of race relations. In *Heart of Atlanta Motel v. United States* (1964), the Supreme Court unanimously upheld the public accommodations section of the 1964 Civil Rights Act as a proper exercise of the commerce power. The motel in question did a substantial volume of business with persons from outside Georgia. The Court ruled that its racially restrictive practices could impede commerce among the states and could therefore be appropriately regulated by Congress.

In the companion case of *Katzenbach v. McClung* (1964), the Court went even further by recognizing the power of Congress under the Commerce Clause to bar racial discrimination in a restaurant (Ollie's Barbecue in Birmingham, Alabama) patronized almost entirely by local customers. The Court found a connection with interstate commerce in the purchase of food and equipment from sources outside Alabama.

Five years later in *Daniel v. Paul* (1969), the Court followed the same approach in barring racial discrimination as practiced by the owners of an amusement park near Little Rock, Arkansas. After passage of the 1964 Civil Rights Act, the Pauls, who had been operating their establishment as a public, racially segregated recreational area, began to refer to it as a "private club." They resorted to the additional subterfuge of charging a twenty-five cent "membership fee" and issuing "membership cards" as a means of excluding black patrons from the snack bar and other park facilities. The federal district court before which this case was tried took **judicial notice** of the fact that the "principal ingredients going into the bread were produced and processed in other states" and that "certain ingredients (of the soft drinks) were probably obtained . . . from out-of-state sources." Writing for the Supreme Court, Justice Brennan concluded: "There can be no serious doubt that a 'substantial portion of the food' served at the snack bar [had] moved in interstate commerce."

Under such a broad definition, it is questionable whether any local enterprise that opens its doors to the public could remain outside the scope of the Commerce Clause. Today, few businesses attempt to challenge the applicability of the Civil Rights Act, as racial segregation in places of business has become socially, as well as legally, unacceptable.

Environmental Protection

Since the 1960s, government at all levels has been under pressure to do more to protect natural resources and combat pollution. Relying to a great extent on its powers under the Commerce Clause, Congress has enacted sweeping laws designed to promote conservation and protect the natural environment and workers from the adverse effects of an industrialized economy. Some of the more important federal laws in this regard are the Clean Air, Environmental Protection, and Occupational Safety and Health acts. These acts involve broad delegations of power from Congress to regulatory agencies, which raises a constitutional question in and of itself (see Chapter 7).

Federal environmental legislation has generally been favorably received in the Supreme Court. For example, in *Hodel v. Virginia Surface Mining and Reclamation Association, Inc.* (1981), the Supreme Court upheld a federal statute aimed at reducing the environmental impact of surface coal mining by establishing uniform national standards on the industry. The Court said that Congress could reasonably conclude that unregulated surface mining could "adversely affect the public welfare by destroying or diminishing the utility of land." Similarly, in *Federal Energy Regulatory Commission v. Mississippi* (1982), the Court upheld an act of Congress regulating local electric power transmissions, taking note of the impact of local electric power generation and transmission on the national supply of electrical power. Finally, in *Preseault v. Interstate Commerce Commission* (1990), the Court upheld a federal statute permitting local governments to convert abandoned railroad rights-of-way for purposes of recreation and conservation. The Court said that the law furthered a legitimate objective under the Commerce Clause—preservation of railroad rights-of-way for possible future reactivation.

The Supreme Court has gone so far as to hold that certain federal laws passed under the aegis of the Commerce Clause are so comprehensive and are of such overriding national importance as to preempt state and local governments from legislating in a given area. By way of illustration, the Court has held that the federal Noise Control Act of 1972 preempts a city from adopting its own aircraft noise abatement ordinance (see *Burbank v. Lockheed Air Terminal* [1973]). Clearly, the Supreme Court has given Congress broad latitude to use the Commerce Clause as a basis for environmental legislation.

The Commerce Clause and Federal Criminal Law

The expansive scope of the modern interpretation of the Commerce Clause has also facilitated increased federal activity in the enactment and enforcement of criminal law, an area traditionally left to the states. For example, in 1970, Congress enacted the Organized Crime Control Act, Title IX of which is entitled "Racketeer Influenced and Corrupt Organizations" (RICO). The federal RICO act, as it is widely known, essentially prohibits infiltration of organized crime into organizations or enterprises engaged in interstate commerce. The act permits the Federal Bureau of Investigation and other federal law enforcement agencies to become more involved in the investigation of organized crime, even into activities that are ostensibly confined to local areas. For instance, in *United States v. Gambino* (1978), a federal appeals court upheld the RICO convictions of two organized crime figures who had engaged in "a conspiracy to acquire and maintain control of the private sanitation industry in the Coop City area of the Bronx [New York] through a pattern of racketeering activity."

In *Perez v. United States* (1971), the Supreme Court upheld Title II of the Consumer Credit Protection Act, a federal statute aimed at loan-sharking. Even though loan-sharking is primarily a local activity, the Court held that Congress could reasonably have concluded that it is a major revenue source for organized crime, which is a national problem with a detrimental impact on interstate commerce. In a dissenting opinion, Justice Potter Stewart observed that

> the Framers of the Constitution never intended that the National Government might define as a crime and prosecute such wholly local activity through the enactment of federal criminal laws. . . . [I]t is not enough to say that some loan sharking is a national problem, for all crime is a national problem. It is not enough to say that some loan sharking has interstate characteristics, for any crime may have an interstate setting.

The interpretation of the Commerce Clause, like that of other constitutional provisions, is undertaken, in large part, to facilitate the achievement of practical political goals, as well as to preserve the continuity of legal doctrine. As substantial segments of the American public have demanded that the national government become increasingly active in such areas as economic regulation, civil rights, and environmental and crime control, the Commerce Clause has been stretched far beyond the intentions or expectations of the Framers of the Constitution.

TAXING AND SPENDING POWERS

If the absence of power to regulate commerce stifled economic growth under the Articles of Confederation, the inability to tax and resulting limits on the ability to spend threatened the continued existence of the national government itself. The Framers of the Constitution proposed to remedy these weaknesses by providing in the very first clause of Article I, Section 8 the following enumerated powers: "to lay and collect taxes, duties, imports and excises to pay the debts and provide for the common defense and general welfare of the United States." The vast taxing and spending powers exercised by the national government today are based on this broad-gauged constitutional provision.

Taxation as a Source of Congressional Power

We must distinguish between two important functions relating to taxation, raising revenue and regulation. It is in the second of these areas that the more enduring and important questions of constitutional interpretation have been debated. Although the modern Supreme Court accords wide latitude to both the revenue-raising and regulatory aspects of national taxation, it is at least theoretically more likely to entertain constitutional objections to the latter.

The taxing power is independent of any of the specific regulatory powers listed in other provisions of the Constitution. However, through linkage with the Necessary and Proper Clause, this power can be used far beyond the supposed limits of its own enumeration to implement various regulatory programs. In other words, the taxing power is not confined to the objectives set forth in Article I, Section 8, clause 1; that is, those of paying the debt and providing "for the common defense and general Welfare of the United States." Congress, as Justice Felix Frankfurter pointed out, may also "make an oblique use of the taxing power in relation to activities with which it may deal directly, as, for instance, commerce between the states" (*United States v. Kahriger* [1953], dissenting opinion).

The national taxing power, like the taxing power of the states, is exercised on the people directly. But within strict limits, the national government and the states may also tax each other, provided that fundamental considerations of sovereignty are observed. Sovereignty is an exceedingly elusive concept, and its meaning in this context is determined by the Supreme Court on a case-by-case basis. The doctrine of reciprocal immunity has historically imposed some limits on intergovernmental taxation. Although those limits still exist in theory, as a practical matter they are seldom recognized (see Chapter 8).

The Constitution distinguishes between direct and indirect taxes but leaves those vague categories largely undefined. Two separate provisions in Article I specify that direct taxes shall be apportioned among the states on the basis of population (Section 2, clause 3, and Section 9, clause 4). The second of these provisions refers to "capitation or other direct tax," suggesting that the Framers had in mind a distinction between direct taxes, such as those imposed on persons without regard to particular activities, and indirect taxes, such as those levied on businesses, goods, services, and various privileges. Nevertheless, the distinction between direct and indirect taxes was and is a muddy one. Fortunately, it is of little constitutional significance today. It figured prominently in the income tax controversy of the 1890s, but the relevance of the distinction in this field was rendered moot by passage of the Sixteenth Amendment in 1913.

Most constitutional issues in the field of taxation have involved levies on various aspects of business. The indirect nature of such taxes can be seen in the capacity of the individuals and corporations taxed to pass the burden on to consumers of the product or service in question. The only limitation the Constitution imposes on indirect taxes is that of geographic uniformity: They must be "uniform throughout the United States," that is, uniform in their application among the states, not identical as applied to each person taxed.

Federal Taxation as a Means of Regulation

The Supreme Court has always given wide latitude to the taxing power as a source of regulatory authority when used in combination with other enumerated powers. The case of *Veazie Bank v. Fenno* (1869) provides a classic example. There, the court upheld a tax of 10 percent on notes issued by state banks, a measure designed by the federal government to drive this unstable form of currency out of existence. Because the tax was linked with the congressional power to regulate currency, a power that emanates from several provisions in Article I, Section 8, Chief Justice Salmon P. Chase, Lincoln's former secretary of the treasury, expressed no doubts regarding its constitutionality:

> Having thus, in the exercise of undisputed congressional power, undertaken to provide a currency for the whole country, it cannot be questioned that Congress may, constitutionally, secure the benefit of it to the people by appropriate legislation.

Historically, the Court has expressed less certainty about the use of the taxing power as an independent regulatory device. By the mid-1930s, two conflicting lines of constitutional precedent bearing on this question had emerged, one endorsing and the other denying broad constitutional authority. In *McCray v. United States* (1904), a divided Court upheld an act under which Congress, responding to pressure from the dairy industry, levied a tax of ten cents a pound on oleomargarine colored to look like butter. In contrast, there was a tax of only one-fourth of a cent per pound on uncolored oleomargarine. The majority conceded that both the Fifth Amendment's Due Process Clause and the Tenth Amendment's recognition of the states' reserved powers imposed limits on the taxing power of Congress. But, according to Justice (later Chief Justice) Edward D. White, who wrote the majority opinion, those limits had not been breached by this tax. If it were "plain to the judicial mind" that the taxing power was not being used to raise revenue "but solely for the purpose of destroying rights" implicit in constitutional principles of freedom and justice, courts would be duty-bound to declare that Congress had acted beyond the authority conferred by the Constitution. The difference between the abuse of legislative power and the exercise of reasonable discretion was simply a matter of judgment, to be made in each case. Applying this elusive standard, White concluded that "the manufacture of artificially colored oleomargarine may be prohibited by a free government without a violation of fundamental rights."

It should be noted that unlike other exercises of the national police power early in the twentieth century, this law was not clearly identified with the promotion of public health, safety, or morality. At best, it discouraged the deceptive marketing of a food product with which the dairy industry did not want to compete.

The *McCray* decision served as a precedent for using the taxing power to regulate the sale of narcotics and firearms (*United States v. Doremus* [1919]; *Sonzinsky v. United States* [1937]). But the *McCray* rationale was not applied to the regulation of child labor (*Bailey v. Drexel Furniture Company* [1922]) or to the regulation of agricultural production (*United States v. Butler* [1936]). In the *Doremus* and *Sonzinsky* cases, the Court chose to recognize the validity of the revenue-raising features of the taxation in question and to view their regulatory aspects as consistent with the constitutional exercise of legislative power. In *Bailey v. Drexel* and *United States v. Butler,* the Court did just the opposite, choosing to view the taxes not as revenue measures (although they obviously produced revenue) but as penalties or coercive regulations infringing on either individual liberty or the reserved powers of the states.

In *Bailey* (better known as the child labor tax case), Chief Justice William Howard Taft maintained that Congress through the taxing power was attempting to regulate an activity properly within the scope of state authority. He noted the Court's previous recognition of state autonomy regarding the control of child labor (*Hammer v. Dagenhart*), concluding that Congress could not accomplish through the taxing power an objective previously denied it as an unconstitutional exercise of the commerce power. The tax amounted to 10 percent of the annual net income of mills, factories, mines, and quarries employing children under certain ages. This act singled out certain employment practices for tax purposes, just as the oleomargarine law singled out a particular marketing practice. Both were designed to discourage specific activities through the application of differential tax burdens. Yet the Court viewed one as an appropriate revenue measure and the other as an impermissible use of the taxing power.

The Court also invalidated the Agricultural Adjustment Act of 1933, as, among other things, an unconstitutional exercise of the taxing power. *United States v. Butler* thus nullified a major component of Franklin D. Roosevelt's New Deal program. The decision rejected congressional use of the taxing power as a basis for regulating agricultural production. In fact, the Court's condemnation of the processing tax at issue in this case is, to this day, the last repudiation of national legislative authority based on the distinction between the regulatory and revenue-raising features of a federal tax. In this respect, the *Butler* decision simply reiterated the rationale applied in the child labor tax case, but its constitutional importance is greater because it provided the Court with its first clear opportunity to consider the scope of the spending power as well.

The Spending Power of Congress

The source of the spending power is, of course, found in the same clause of the Constitution that grants Congress the power to tax. The provision simply states: "Congress shall have the power to . . . pay the debts and provide for the common defense and general welfare of the United States." The latter phrase—known as the General Welfare Clause (not to be confused with the "general welfare" provision in the Preamble to the Constitution)—has been used in combination with other enumerated powers since *United States v. Butler* as a basis for the establishment of vast governmental programs.

Under the Agricultural Adjustment Act of 1933, proceeds from the processing tax were used to pay farmers in exchange for their promises to reduce crop acreage. Thus, the scheme of regulation at issue embodied both taxing and spending features and rested squarely on Article I, Section 8, clause 1 as its constitutional source. Justice Owen J. Roberts, writing one of his most influential majority opinions, recognized that Congress could use appropriations for regulatory purposes by making them conditional—that is, by withholding them until the potential recipients either performed or failed to perform specified actions. In this way, the spending power could serve the same indirect regulatory function as the taxing power. He found the act objectionable primarily because both its taxing and spending aspects sought to regulate agricultural production, an area then regarded as reserved to the states by the Tenth Amendment. His detailed analysis of the spending power, however, did not necessarily point to this result.

Justice Roberts adopted the view widely held by constitutional scholars that the General Welfare Clause was not an unrestricted grant of power but was linked to the taxing power granted in the same constitutional provision. According to this view, the General Welfare Clause conferred no independent regulatory power as such but only a power to spend. However, he rejected the narrow interpretation advanced by James Madison that the taxing and spending power would amount to a "mere tautology." He accepted the broader alternative view first articulated by Alexander Hamilton and later endorsed by Justice Joseph Story in his influential *Commentaries on the Constitution*. Under this interpretation, the taxing and spending power, although not unrestricted, is subject to limitations found within the General Welfare Clause itself, rather than in other enumerated powers. Thus, Roberts, in effect, recognized an independent source of congressional power to tax and spend but at the same time attempted to place internal limits on that power. He was drawing what he regarded as a crucial distinction between special, enumerated powers and a broad unrestricted grant of national authority. Considerations of classical federalism—the division of power between the national government and the states—were of key importance in his analysis. This is evident from the structure of his detailed and elaborate opinion. After commenting on the internal limits of the taxing and spending power, he shifted abruptly to a consideration of the regulatory scheme contemplated by the Agricultural Adjustment Act, concluding that it violated the reserved powers of the states.

Justice Roberts's opinion has a quality of ambivalence, reflecting his apparent uncertainty about the emergence of sweeping regulatory power at the national level—an uncertainty shared by several other justices during this chaotic period in the Court's history. In any event, his interpretation of the General Welfare Clause proved untenable as a workable standard for assessing the constitutionality of other federal programs based on the taxing and spending power.

Dissenting in *Butler,* Justice Harlan Fiske Stone accused the majority of second-guessing Congress on the "wisdom" of the Agricultural Adjustment Act, remarking caustically: "Courts are not the only agency of government that must be assumed to have the capacity to govern." Stone was unimpressed by Justice Roberts's disingenuous claim that in reviewing the constitutionality of an act of Congress

> the judicial branch of the government has only one duty: to lay the article of the Constitution which is invoked beside the statute which is challenged and to decide whether the latter squares with the former.

In Stone's view, the *Butler* majority was exercising far more judicial discretion than Roberts's mechanical depiction of judicial review implied. Stone's call for the imposition of greater judicial self-restraint became a central theme of majority opinions in the fields of commerce and fiscal policy from 1937 forward.

The Modern Approach

Beginning with two 1937 decisions upholding the newly enacted social security and unemployment compensation programs, the Court abandoned the *Butler* rationale (*Chas. C. Steward Machine Company v. Davis* and *Helvering v. Davis*). In the *Steward Machine* case, the Court upheld the unemployment compensation features of the Social Security Act of 1935. Justice Benjamin N. Cardozo's majority opinion recognized extensive congressional power to tax and spend based on an interpretation of the General Welfare Clause as a source of plenary power. Cardozo asserted: "The subject matter of taxation open to the power of the Congress is as comprehensive as that open to the power of the states. . . ." After citing statistics on the high rate of unemployment between 1929 and 1936, he observed:

> It is too late today for the argument to be heard with tolerance that in a crisis so extreme [as the Great Depression] the use of the money of the nation to relieve the unemployed and their dependents is a use for any purpose narrower than the promotion of the general welfare.

In *Mulford v. Smith* (1939), the Court underscored this liberal view of national economic policy by upholding a second Agricultural Adjustment Act that, for all practical purposes, was as far-reaching as the 1933 statute that had been struck down by the "nine old men" in *United States v. Butler* (1936). Writing for the Court in *Mulford,* Justice Roberts adopted a rather different posture from that which he had taken in *Butler* three years earlier:

> Any rule, such as that embodied in the [Agricultural Adjustment] Act, which is intended to foster, protect and conserve [interstate] commerce, or to prevent the flow of commerce from working harm to the people of the nation, is within the competence of Congress. Within these limits the exercise of the power, the grant being unlimited in its terms, may lawfully extend to the prohibition of such

commerce, and ... to limitation of the amount of a given commodity which may be transported in such commerce. The motive of Congress in exerting the power is irrelevant to the validity of the legislation.

Another illustration of the broad scope accorded the national spending power in the modern era is *Buckley v. Valeo* (1976). One of the many issues raised in this case was the constitutionality of certain provisions of the Internal Revenue Code calling for public financing of presidential campaigns. The Court rejected the contention that the General Welfare Clause placed limits on the spending power in this regard. Rather, it viewed the clause as a "grant of power the scope of which is quite expansive, particularly in view of the enlargement of power by the Necessary and Proper Clause." According to well-established precedent, Congress could regulate presidential elections and primaries; thus, it followed that "public financing of presidential elections as a means to reform the electoral process was clearly a choice within the granted power." It was up to Congress "to decide which expenditures [would] promote the general welfare."

A more recent illustration of the broad spending powers of the modern Congress involves the effort to persuade the states to raise their drinking ages. In 1984, Congress adopted an act directing the secretary of transportation to withhold federal highway funds from states whose drinking age was lower than twenty-one years. South Dakota brought suit, attacking the right of the federal government to impose this condition on the receipt of federal funds. In *South Dakota v. Dole* (1987), the Supreme Court rejected the state's challenge, saying that "the condition imposed by Congress is directly related to one of the main purposes for which highway funds are expended—safe interstate travel." In a dissenting opinion harkening back to *United States v. Butler,* Justice Sandra Day O'Connor said:

> If the Spending Power is to be limited only by Congress' notion of the general welfare, the reality, given the vast financial resources of the Federal Government, is that the Spending Clause gives 'power to the Congress to tear down the barriers, to invade the states' jurisdiction, and to become a parliament of the whole people, subject to no restrictions save such as are self-imposed.' This, of course, ... was not the Framers' plan. ...

Another use of the spending power to affect social policy can be seen in the case of *Fullilove v. Klutznick* (1980). Under the Public Works Employment Act of 1977, Congress provided federal monies to state and local governments for public works projects. One section of the act required that at least 10 percent of the money in each grant be expended for contracts with "minority business enterprises." Not surprisingly, this provision was challenged in federal court at a time when the constitutionality of affirmative action programs was very much in question. The Supreme Court upheld the set-aside provision by a 6-to-3 margin. In his opinion announcing the judgment of the Court, Chief Justice Burger stressed the broad spending power of Congress, as well as its power to regulate interstate commerce. The set-aside provision was not found to be violative of the government's duty to provide equal protection of the laws (see Chapter 16).

Individual Rights as Restraints on the Taxing and Spending Powers

The potential limits imposed by various provisions of the Bill of Rights remain important in determining the extent of the taxing and spending powers. Due process standards place significant procedural requirements on all legislation, including taxing and spending measures. As a practical matter, however, the Fifth Amendment protection against compulsory self-incrimination has served as the primary constitutional basis in recent years for invalidating the exercise of such power. Justice Black first articulated this source of constitutional restraint in a dissenting opinion in a case sustaining the "wagering tax" provisions of the Revenue Act of 1951 (*United States v. Kahriger* [1953]). He read the registration provisions of the act as requiring persons to confess that they were engaged in the illegal "business of gambling." In his view, such compulsion, however, indirect, was condemned by the Fifth Amendment.

In the years following the *Kahriger* decision, the Supreme Court, under the leadership of Chief Justice Earl Warren, greatly expanded the constitutional rights of persons accused of crimes. Consistent with this trend, Justice Black's dissenting view was adopted by a Court majority in 1968, and *Kahriger* was expressly overruled (*Marchetti v. United States; Grosso v. United States*). Writing for the Court in *Marchetti,* Justice Harlan was careful to distinguish between the scope of the taxing power, which he did not wish to diminish, and the specific individual safeguards of the Fifth Amendment, which he sought to recognize. The issue was "whether the methods employed by Congress in the Federal Wagering Tax statutes [were] in this situation consistent with the limitations created by the privilege against self-incrimination." Because the registration requirements forced gamblers to expose their own illegal activities, he concluded that the Fifth Amendment was violated.

The Court made it clear in a 1976 decision, however, that the protection against compulsory self-incrimination does not come into play automatically—one must positively assert the right (*Garber v. United States*). Thus, it rejected a defendant's contention that the introduction into evidence of his income tax return, which listed his occupation as that of "professional gambler," violated his immunity against compulsory self-incrimination. In another attempt to strike a balance between procedural safeguards and substantive powers, the Court recognized that the taxing power cannot be used in such a way as to undermine Fourth Amendment restrictions against unreasonable searches and seizures. Thus, in *General Motors Leasing Corporation v. United States* (1977), it held that a warrantless entry into a business office under the purported authority of the Internal Revenue Code was, under the circumstances, a violation of the Fourth Amendment.

CONGRESSIONAL ENFORCEMENT OF CIVIL RIGHTS AMENDMENTS

A number of constitutional Amendments provide for congressional enforcement of various rights through "appropriate legislation." All three Civil War Amendments (Thirteen, Fourteen, and Fifteen) contain such provisions, and Congress frequently relied on this enforcement authority in developing civil rights legislation during the Reconstruction Era. For example, the Civil Rights Act of 1866, based on the Thirteenth Amendment's enforcement provision, sought to remove vestiges of slavery perpetuated in the "Black Codes," which had been enacted in Southern states to lessen the full force of the Amendment. The 1866 legislation provided, among other things, that all citizens were to be accorded the same right "as enjoyed by white citizens" to have access to the courts, to enter into enforceable contracts, and to buy and sell real estate.

In 1968, the Supreme Court held that the Civil Rights Act of 1866 prohibited racial discrimination in the sale of private housing (see *Jones v. Alfred H. Mayer Company*). Shortly thereafter, Congress adopted the Fair Housing Act, which prohibits racial discrimination in the rental and sale of private residences where such transactions are handled by agents or brokers (transactions by private individuals are not covered). The Fair Housing Act strengthens the prohibition of racial discrimination in housing transactions by authorizing the Department of Housing and Urban Development to refer cases of racial discrimination to the Justice Department for possible prosecution.

The Voting Rights Act of 1965

Aside from the Civil Rights Act of 1964 (discussed previously in connection with the Commerce Clause), the most significant modern legislation in the field of civil rights is the Voting Rights Act of 1965. This far-reaching statute (reenacted in 1982 in spite of initial reservations by the Reagan administration) authorizes the attorney general to suspend voting tests and assign federal voting registrars and poll watchers to any state or political subdivision in which fewer than fifty percent of the voting age population was registered as of a certain specified date (November 1, 1964, under the original act).

In a civil action originating in the U.S. Supreme Court, South Carolina challenged the constitutionality of the Voting Rights Act (*South Carolina v. Katzenbach* [1966]). The Court, in an opinion by Chief Justice Warren, rejected this challenge, concluding that Congress had established an ample factual basis for the legislation and that the provisions in question "are a valid means for carrying out the commands of the Fifteenth Amendment." Warren stated that "the basic test to be applied in a case involving Section 2 of the Fifteenth Amendment [the enforcement section] is the same as in all cases concerning the express powers of Congress with relation to the reserved powers of the states." Warren was relying specifically on Chief Justice Marshall's formulation in *M'Culloch v. Maryland*:

> Let the end be legitimate, let it be within the scope of the Constitution, and all means which are appropriate, which are plainly adapted to that end, which are not prohibited, but consist with the letter and spirit of the Constitution, are constitutional.

The Voting Rights Act met this basic standard of rationality and was thus deemed an "appropriate" mode for enforcing the Fifteenth Amendment command that "the right of citizens of the United States to vote shall not be denied or abridged by the United States or by any state on account of race, color, or previous condition of servitude."

In *Katzenbach v. Morgan* (1966), the Supreme Court upheld another provision of the Voting Rights Act of 1965 as an "appropriate" exercise of constitutional power to enforce the equal protection guarantee of the Fourteenth Amendment. The section in question provided that no person completing the sixth grade in an accredited non-English-language Puerto Rican school can be denied the right to vote through inability to read or write English. John P. and Christine Morgan, registered voters in New York City, challenged this section on the ground that it prohibited enforcement of the requirement that New York's English literacy test be passed in order to register to vote. In an earlier decision, the Supreme Court had held that a similar North Carolina literacy requirement did not violate the Equal Protection Clause of the Fourteenth Amendment (*Lassiter v. Northampton County Board of Elections* [1959]). The New York attorney general argued that Congress could not prohibit the implementation of a state law by invoking the enforcement provision of the Fourteenth Amendment unless the judicial branch determined that the state law violated the Constitution. Justice Brennan, writing for a 7-to-2 majority, disagreed, observing that such an interpretation would "depreciate both constitutional resourcefulness and congressional responsibility for implementing the Amendment." The central question, as he viewed it, was not whether the Supreme Court itself regarded English literacy tests as unconstitutional but whether Congress could "prohibit the enforcement of the state law by legislating under Section 5 of the Fourteenth Amendment." Thus, the Court's task was "limited to determining whether such legislation is, as required by Section 5, appropriate legislation to enforce the Equal Protection Clause."

Justice Brennan maintained that the authors of the Fourteenth Amendment intended through Section 5 to give Congress enforcement power under the Fourteenth Amendment comparable to the "broad powers expressed in the Necessary and Proper Clause. . . ." Again the Court relied on *M'Culloch v. Maryland*, finding that the challenged section of the Voting Rights Act was "appropriate" legislation because it met the rationality standard articulated by Chief Justice Marshall in that landmark decision.

The remedy that Congress chose to provide in protecting the voting rights of non-English-speaking Puerto Ricans could be justified on the basis of two alternative theories: (a) it might provide these persons with a "political weapon" that could be used to fight discriminatory practices by government (a rationale similar to that employed in *South Carolina v. Katzenbach*), or (b) Congress might have concluded that New York's English literacy test requirement violated the Equal Protection Clause of the Fourteenth Amendment, regardless of the Supreme Court's previous position on this issue. The importance of this justification is that it in effect recognizes Congress as a "constitutional interpreter." The implications of this rationale have fascinated legal scholars, some of whom regard *Morgan* as potentially undercutting the authority of the Supreme Court as a final interpreter of the Constitution. Moreover, if Congress has the power to define the scope of constitutional protections, as Brennan's opinion suggests, it logically follows that Congress might at some time narrow, rather than broaden, such protections. In his dissenting opinion, Justice Harlan expressed concern about this possibility. He maintained that Congress could define constitutional rights "so as, in effect, to dilute the equal protection and due process decisions of this Court." However, the *Morgan* decision is confined to the enforcement of rights explicitly recognized in provisions of the Constitution—in this instance, the Equal Protection Clause of the Fourteenth Amendment. Nevertheless, it serves to remind us that other branches of the national government have important roles to play in defining and implementing constitutional rights.

It is difficult to overstate the importance of the Voting Rights Act on American politics. In the first year after passage of the Act, the percentage of blacks registered to vote in Mississippi increased from roughly 7 percent to nearly 60 percent. Whereas less than 4 million blacks voted in 1964, by 1984, that number had exceeded 10 million. While very few blacks held elected office in the United States between the end of the Reconstruction Era and adoption of the Voting Rights Act, by the end of 1985, there were more than six thousand. In 1988, Jesse Jackson, a black, ran a serious race for the presidential nomination of the Democratic Party. By 1990, four of the nation's five largest cities had black mayors. And in 1990, Douglas Wilder of Virginia was elected the nation's first black governor. Moreover, the increased levels of black participation in the electoral process has forced white politicians to consider the interests of their black constituencies, people whose interests were all too often ignored in the past. The result has been that Congress and state legislatures have become more receptive to policies promoting civil rights for blacks and other minorities.

CONCLUSION

From the foregoing discussion it is clear that Congress has many sources of constitutional authority. Some of these are quite explicit, as the list of enumerated powers in Article I, Section 8 makes clear. Others are implicit, open-ended, and subject to no complete or conclusive definition. These implied powers are fully recognized, however, in the Necessary and Proper Clause and in the enforcement provisions of several constitutional amendments, most notably the Thirteenth, Fourteenth, and Fifteenth. Within this broad range of explicit and implicit powers, Congress has been accorded ample latitude to address the major problems, needs, and goals of the nation, as perceived by succeeding generations of Americans during two centuries of constitutional history. Today, many question the effectiveness of Congress, but there is no question of the adequacy of Congress's constitutional authority. Indeed, some conservatives question the expansive scope accorded to Congress's enumerated and implied powers. On the other hand, liberals tend to question the power of the modern presidency. That issue is the central theme of the next chapter.

FOR FURTHER READING

Alexander, Herbert E. *Financing Politics: Money, Elections and Political Reform*. Washington, D.C.: Congressional Quarterly Press, 1984.

Baker, Leonard. *Back to Back: The Duel Between FDR and the Supreme Court*. New York: Macmillan, 1967.

Beck, Carl. *Contempt of Congress*. New Orleans: Hauser Press, 1959.

Berger, Raoul. *Impeachment: The Constitutional Problems*. Cambridge: Harvard University Press, 1973.

Corwin, Edward S. *Liberty Against Government*. Baton Rouge: Louisiana State University Press, 1948.

Fisher, Louis. *The Politics of Shared Power: Congress and the Executive*. Washington, D.C.: Congressional Quarterly Press, 1987.

Fisher, Louis. *Constitutional Conflicts Between Congress and the President*. Princeton, N.J.: Princeton University Press, 1985.

Frankfurter, Felix. *The Commerce Clause Under Marshall, Taney and Waite*. Chapel Hill: University of North Carolina Press, 1971.

Goodman, Walter. *The Committee: The Extraordinary Career of the House Committee on Un-American Activities*. New York: Farrar, Straus and Giroux, 1968.

Gunther, Gerald, ed. *John Marshall's Defense of M'Culloch v. Maryland*. Stanford, Calif.: Stanford University Press, 1969.

Hamilton, James. *The Power to Probe: A Study of Congressional Investigations*. New York: Random House, 1976.

Harris, Joseph P. *The Advice and Consent of the Senate: A Study of the Confirmation of Appointments by the United States Senate*. Berkeley: University of California Press, 1953.

Kelly, Alfred H., Winifred A. Harbison, and Herman Belz. *The American Constitution: Its Origins and Development,* 7th ed. New York: Norton, 1991.

McCloskey, Robert. *American Conservatism: In the Age of Enterprise, 1865 – 1910*. Cambridge: Harvard University Press, 1951.

McGeary, M. Nelson. *The Development of Congressional Investigative Power*. New York: Octagon Books, 1966.

Morgan, Donald. *Congress and the Constitution*. Cambridge: Harvard University Press, 1966.

Murphy, Walter F. *Congress and the Court*. Chicago: University of Chicago Press, 1962.

Pritchett, C. Herman. *Congress versus the Supreme Court, 1957 – 1960*. Minneapolis: University of Minnesota Press, 1961.

Pritchett, C. Herman. *The Roosevelt Court: A Study in Judicial Politics and Values*. New York: Octagon Books, 1963.

Schmidhauser, John, and Larry Berg. *The Supreme Court and Congress: Conflict and Interaction, 1945 – 1968*. New York: Free Press, 1972.

Taylor, Telford. *The Grand Inquest: The Story of Congressional Investigations*. New York: Simon and Schuster, 1955.

Wilson, Woodrow. *Congressional Government*. Boston: Houghton-Mifflin, 1885.

CASES AND READINGS

M'Culloch v. Maryland
4 Wheat. (17 U.S.) 316; 4 L. Ed. 579 (1819)
Vote: 7-0

The first Bank of the United States was created by Congress in 1791 and given a twenty-year charter. Congress failed to extend the expiration date, and in 1811, the bank went out of business. Five years later, and after intensive controversy, Congress established the second Bank of the United States, again granting it a charter for twenty years. This bank, like its predecessor, was bitterly opposed by many local economic interests identified first with the Jeffersonian Republican Party and later with its successor, the Democratic Party under the leadership of Andrew Jackson. The bitter struggle over the issue of rechartering the second Bank of the United States was of central importance during Jackson's administration. It is against this background of partisan politics that the decision in M'Culloch v. Maryland *should be read.*

One of the branches of the second Bank of the United States was located in Baltimore, and in 1818, the Maryland legislature imposed a tax on all banks not chartered by the state. The act imposed an annual fee of fifteen thousand dollars payable in advance or a 2-percent tax on the value of notes issued by such banks. A penalty of five hundred dollars was imposed for each violation of this tax measure, which, as everyone recognized, was aimed squarely at the Bank of the United States. M'Culloch, the cashier of the Baltimore branch, refused to comply with the state law. A lower court judgment against M'Culloch was upheld by the Maryland Court of Appeals.

Mr. Chief Justice Marshall delivered the opinion of the Court.

... The first question made in the cause is, has Congress power to incorporate a bank? ...

The power now contested was exercised by the first Congress elected under the present Constitution.... Its principle was completely understood, and was opposed with equal zeal and ability. After being resisted, first in the fair and open field of debate, and afterwards in the executive cabinet, ... it became a law. The original act was permitted to expire; but a short experience of the embarrassments to which the refusal to revive it exposed the government, convinced those who were most prejudiced against the measure of its necessity and induced the passage of the present law....

This government is acknowledged by all to be one of enumerated powers. The principle, that it can exercise only the powers granted to it, would seem too apparent to have required to be enforced by all those arguments which its enlightened friends, while it was depending before the people, found it necessary to urge. That principle is now universally admitted. But the question respecting the extent of the powers actually granted, is perpetually arising, and will probably continue to arise, as long as our system shall exist.

In discussing these questions, the conflicting powers of the general and state governments must be brought into view, and the supremacy of their respective laws, when they are in opposition, must be settled.

If any one proposition could command the universal assent of mankind, we might expect it would be this—that the government of the Union, though limited in its powers, is supreme within its sphere of action. This would seem to result necessarily from its nature. It is the government of all; its powers are delegated by all; it represents all, and acts for all. Though any one state may be willing to control its operations, no state is willing to allow others to control them. The nation, on those subjects on which it can act, must necessarily bind its component parts. But this question is not left to mere reason; the people have, in express terms, decided it by saying, "this Constitution, and the laws of the United States, which shall be made in pursuance thereof," "shall be the supreme law of the land," and by requiring that the members of the state legislatures, and the officers of the executive and judicial departments of the states shall take the oath of fidelity to it.

The government of the United States, then, though limited in its powers, is supreme; and its laws, when made in pursuance of the Constitution, form the supreme law of the land, "anything in the Constitution or laws of any state to the contrary notwithstanding."

Among the enumerated powers, we do not find that of establishing a bank or creating a corporation. But there is no phrase in the instrument which, like the Articles of Confederation, excludes incidental or implied powers; and which requires that everything granted shall be expressly and minutely described. Even the 10th Amendment, which was framed for the purpose of quieting the excessive jealousies which had been excited, omits the word "expressly," and declares only that the powers "not delegated to the United States, nor prohibited to the states, are reserved to the states or to the people:" thus leaving the question, whether the particular power which may become the subject of contest has been delegated to the one government, or prohibited to the other, to depend on a fair construction of the whole instrument.... A constitution, to contain an accurate detail of all the subdivisions of which its great powers will admit, and of all the means by which they may be carried into execution, would partake of a prolixity of a legal code, and could scarcely be embraced by the human mind. It would probably never be understood by the public. Its nature, therefore, requires, that only its great outlines should be marked, its important objects designated, and the minor ingredients which compose those objects be deduced from the nature of the objects themselves.... In considering this question, then, we must never forget that it is a constitution we are expounding.

Although, among the enumerated powers of government, we do not find the word "bank" or "incorporation," we find the great powers to lay and collect taxes; to borrow money; to regulate commerce; to declare and conduct a war; and to raise and support armies and navies. The sword and the purse, all the external relations, and no inconsiderable portion of the industry of the nation, are entrusted to its gov-

ernment.... [I]t may with great reason be contended, that a government, entrusted with such ample powers, on the due execution of which the happiness and prosperity of the nation so vitally depends, must also be entrusted with ample means for their execution. The power being given, it is the interest of the nation to facilitate its execution. It can never be their interest, and cannot be presumed to have been their intention, to clog and embarrass its execution by withholding the most appropriate means....

The government which has a right to do an act, and has imposed on it the duty of performing that act, must, according to the dictates of reason, be allowed to select the means; and those who contend that it may not select any appropriate means, that one particular mode of effecting the object is excepted, take upon themselves the burden of establishing that exception.

But the Constitution of the United States has not left the right of Congress to employ the necessary means for the execution of the powers conferred on the government to general reasoning. To its enumeration of powers is added that of making "all laws which shall be necessary and proper, for carrying into execution the foregoing powers, and all other powers vested by this Constitution, in the government of the United States, or in any department thereof."

The counsel for the State of Maryland have urged various arguments, to prove that this clause, though in terms a grant of power, is not so in effect.... In support of this proposition, they have found it necessary to contend, that this clause was inserted for the purpose of conferring on Congress the power of making laws. That, without it, doubts might be entertained whether Congress could exercise its powers in the form of legislation.

But could this be the object for which it was inserted? A government is created by the people, having legislative, executive, and judicial powers. Its legislative powers are vested in a Congress.... That a legislature, endowed with legislative powers, can legislate, is a proposition too self-evident to have been questioned.

But the argument on which most reliance is placed, is drawn from the peculiar language of this clause. Congress is not empowered by it to make all laws, which may have relation to the powers conferred on the government, but such only as may be "necessary and proper" for carrying them into execution. The word "necessary" is considered as controlling the whole sentence, and as limiting the right to pass laws for the execution of the granted powers, to such as are indispensable, and without which the power would be nugatory. That it excludes the choice of means, and leaves to Congress, in each case, that only which is most direct and simple.

Is it true that this is the sense in which the word "necessary" is always used? Does it always import an absolute physical necessity, so strong that one thing, to which another may be termed necessary, cannot exist without the other? We think it does not. . . . To employ the means necessary to an end, is generally understood as employing any means calculated to produce the end, and not as being confined to those single means, without which the end would be entirely unattainable. Such is the character of human language, that no word conveys to the mind, in all situations, one single definite idea. . . .

It is, we think, impossible to compare the sentence which prohibits a state from laying "imposts or duties on imports or exports, except what may be absolutely necessary for executing its inspection laws," with that which authorizes Congress "to make all laws which shall be necessary and proper for carrying into execution" the powers of the general government, without feeling a conviction that the convention understood itself to change materially the meaning of the word "necessary," by prefixing the word "absolutely." This word, then, like others, is used in various senses; and, in its construction, the subject, the context, the intention of the person using them, are all to be taken into view.

Let this be done in the case under consideration. The subject is the execution of those great powers on which the welfare of a nation essentially depends. It must have been the intention of those who gave these powers, to insure, as far a human prudence could insure, their beneficial execution. This could not be done by confiding the choice of means to such narrow limits as not to leave it in the power of Congress to adopt any which might be appropriate, and which were conducive to the end. This provision

is made in a Constitution intended to endure for ages to come, and, consequently, to be adapted to the various crises of human affairs. . . .

The result of the most careful and attentive consideration bestowed upon this clause is, that if it does not enlarge, it cannot be construed to restrain the powers of Congress, or to impair the right of the legislature to exercise its best judgment in the selection of measures to carry into execution the constitutional powers of the government. If no other motive for its insertion can be suggested, a sufficient one is found in the desire to remove all doubts respecting the right to legislate on the vast mass of incidental powers which must be involved in the Constitution, if that instrument be not a splendid bauble.

We admit, as all must admit, that the powers of the government are limited, and that its limits are not to be transcended. But we think the sound construction of the Constitution must allow to the national legislature that discretion, with respect to the means by which the powers it confers are to be carried into execution, which will enable the body to perform the high duties assigned to it, in the manner most beneficial to the people. Let the end be legitimate, let it be within the scope of the Constitution, and all means which are appropriate, which are plainly adapted to that end, which are not prohibited, but consist with the letter and spirit of the Constitution, are constitutional.

That a corporation must be considered as a means not less usual, not of higher dignity, not more requiring a particular specification than other means, has been sufficiently proved. . . . [W]e find no reason to suppose that a constitution, omitting, and wisely omitting, to enumerate all the means for carrying into execution the great powers vested in government, ought to have specified this. . . .

If a corporation may be employed indiscriminately with other means to carry into execution the powers of the government, no particular reason can be assigned for excluding the use of a bank, if required for its fiscal operations. To use one, must be within the discretion of Congress, if it be an appropriate mode of executing the powers of government. That it is a convenient, a useful, and essential instrument in the prosecution of its fiscal operations, is not now a subject of controversy.

... [W]ere its necessity less apparent, none can deny its being an appropriate measure; and if it is, the degree of its necessity, as has been very justly observed, is to be discussed in another place. Should Congress, in the execution of its powers, adopt measures which are prohibited by the Constitution; or should Congress, under the pretext of executing its powers pass laws for the accomplishment of objects not entrusted to the government, it would become the painful duty of this tribunal, should a case requiring such a decision come before it, to say that such an act was not the law of the land. But where the law is not prohibited, and is really calculated to effect any of the objects entrusted to the government, to undertake here to inquire into the degree of its necessity, would be to pass the line which circumscribes the judicial department, and to tread on legislative ground. This court disclaims all pretensions to such a power....

After the most deliberate consideration, it is the unanimous and decided opinion of this court that the act to incorporate the bank of the United States is a law made in pursuance of the Constitution, and is a part of the supreme law of the land....

It being the opinion of the court that the act incorporating the bank is constitutional, ... we proceed to inquire:

Whether the state of Maryland may, without violating the Constitution, tax that branch?

That the power of taxation is one of vital importance; that it is retained by the states; that it is not abridged by the grant of a similar power to the government of the Union: that it is to be concurrently exercised by the two governments: are truths which have never been denied. But, such is the paramount character of the Constitution that its capacity to withdraw any subject from the action of even this power, is admitted. The states are expressly forbidden to lay any duties on imports or exports, except what may be absolutely necessary for executing their inspection laws. If the obligation of this prohibition must be conceded—if it may restrain a state from the exercise of its taxing power on imports and exports—the same paramount character would seem to restrain, as it certainly may restrain, a state from such other exercise of this power, as is in its nature incompatible with, and repugnant to, the constitutional laws of the Union....

This great principle is, that the Constitution and the laws made in pursuance thereof are supreme; that they control the constitution and laws of the respective states, and cannot be controlled by them. From this, which may be almost termed an axiom, other propositions are deduced as corollaries, on the truth or error of which, and on their application to this case the cause has been supposed to depend. These are, 1st. that a power to create implies a power to preserve. 2d. That a power to destroy, if wielded by a different hand, is hostile to, and incompatible with these powers to create and to preserve. 3d. That where this repugnancy exists, that authority which is supreme must control, not yield to that over which it is supreme....

That the power to tax involves the power to destroy; that the power to destroy may defeat and render useless the power to create; that there is a plain repugnance, in conferring on one government a power to control the constitutional measures of another, which other, with respect to those very measures, is declared to be supreme over that which exerts the control, are propositions not to be denied....

If the states may tax one instrument, employed by the government in the execution of its powers, they may tax any and every other instrument. They may tax the mail; they may tax the mint; they may tax patent-rights; they may tax all the means employed by the government, to an excess which would defeat all the ends of government. This was not intended by the American people....

The question is, in truth, a question of supremacy; and if the right of the states to tax the means employed by the general government be conceded, the declaration that the constitution, and the laws made in pursuance thereof, shall be the supreme law of the land, is empty and unmeaning declaration....

It has also been insisted, that, as the power of taxation in the general and state governments is acknowledged to be concurrent, every argument which would sustain the right of the general government to tax banks chartered by the states, will equally sustain the right of the states to tax banks chartered by the general government.

But the two cases are not on the same reason. The people of all the states have created the general government, and have conferred upon it the general power of taxation. The people of all the states, and the states themselves, are represented in Congress, and, by their representatives, exercise this power. When they tax the chartered institutions of the states, they tax their constituents; and these taxes must be uniform. But, when a state taxes the operations of the government of the United States, it acts upon institutions created, not by their own constituents, but by people over whom they claim no control. It acts upon the measures of a government created by others as well as themselves, for the benefit of others in common with themselves. The difference is that which always exists, and always must exist, between the action of the whole on a part, and the action of a part on the whole—between the laws of a government declared to be supreme, and those of a government which, when in opposition to those laws, is not supreme.

But if the full application of this argument could be admitted, it might bring into question the right of Congress to tax the state banks, and could not prove the right of the states to tax the Bank of the United States.

The court has bestowed on this subject its most deliberate consideration. The result is a conviction that the states have no power, by taxation or otherwise, to retard, impede, burden, or in any manner control the operations of the constitutional laws enacted by Congress to carry into execution the powers vested in the general government. This is, we think, the unavoidable consequence of that supremacy which the Constitution has declared.

We are unanimously of opinion that the law passed by the legislature of Maryland, imposing a tax on the Bank of the United States, is unconstitutional and void.

This opinion does not deprive the states of any resources which they originally possessed. It does not extend to a tax paid by the real property of the bank, in common with the other real property within the state, nor to a tax imposed on the interest which the citizens of Maryland may hold in this institution, in common with other property of the same description throughout the state. But this is a tax on the operations of the bank, and is, consequently, a tax on the operation of an instrument of the Union to carry its powers into execution. Such a tax must be unconstitutional. . . .

McGrain v. Daugherty

273 U.S. 135; 47 S. Ct. 319; 71 L. Ed. 580 (1927)
Vote: 8-0

This case stems from a Senate investigation into allegations of misconduct in the Department of Justice. As part of the investigation, a Senate special committee subpoenaed Mally S. Daugherty, a bank president and brother of Attorney General Harry M. Daugherty, who had resigned as the investigation was beginning. The witness failed to appear and was held in contempt of Congress. Daugherty sought relief on a writ of habeas corpus, challenging the authority of the Senate to compel his testimony.

Mr. Justice Van Devanter delivered the opinion of the Court.

. . . The first of the principal questions, the one which the witness particularly presses on our atten-

tion, is . . . whether the Senate—or the House of Representatives, both being on the same plane in this regard—has power, through its own process, to compel a private individual to appear before it or one of its committees and give testimony needed to enable it efficiently to exercise a legislative function belonging to it under the Constitution.

The Constitution provides for a Congress, consisting of a Senate and House of Representatives, and invests it with "all legislative powers" granted to the United States, and with power "to make all laws which shall be necessary and proper" for carrying into execution these powers and "all other powers" vested by the Constitution in the United States or in any department or officer thereof. . . . Other provisions show that, while bills can become laws only after being considered and passed by both houses of Congress, each house is to be distinct from the other, to have its own officers and rules, and to exercise its legislative function independently. . . . But there is no provision expressly investing either house with power to make investigations and exact testimony, to the end that it may exercise its legislative function advisedly and effectively. So the question arises whether this power is so far incidental to the legislative function as to be implied.

In actual legislative practice, power to secure needed information by such means has long been treated as an attribute of the power to legislate. It was so regarded in the British Parliament and in the colonial Legislatures before the American Revolution, and a like view has prevailed and been carried into effect in both houses of Congress and in most of the state Legislatures.

This power was both asserted and exerted by the House of Representatives in 1792, when it appointed a select committee to inquire into the [Gen. Arthur] St. Clair expedition and authorized the committee to send for necessary persons, papers and records. Mr. Madison, who had taken an important part in framing the Constitution only five years before, and four of his associates in that work, were members of the House of Representatives at the time, and all voted for the inquiry. . . . [T]he Senate . . . inquiry ordered in 1859 respecting the raid by John Brown and his adherents on the armory and arsenal of the United States at Harper's Ferry is of special significance. The resolution directing the inquiry authorized the committee to send for persons and papers, to inquire into the facts pertaining to the raid and the means by which it was organized and supported, and to report what legislation, if any, was necessary to preserve the peace of the country and protect the public property. The resolution was briefly discussed and adopted without opposition. . . .

The state courts quite generally have held that the power to legislate carries with it by necessary implication ample authority to obtain information needed in the rightful exercise of that power, and to employ compulsory process for the purpose. . . .

We have referred to the practice of the two houses of Congress, and we now shall notice some significant congressional enactments. . . . They show very plainly that Congress intended thereby (a) to recognize the power of either house to institute inquiries and exact evidence touching subjects within its jurisdiction and on which it was disposed to act; (b) to recognize that such inquiries may be conducted through committees; (c) to subject defaulting and contumacious witnesses to indictment and punishment in the courts, and thereby to enable either house to exert the power of inquiry "more effectually"; and (d) to open the way for obtaining evidence in such an inquiry, which otherwise could not be obtained, by exempting witnesses required to give evidence therein from criminal and penal prosecutions in respect of matters disclosed by their evidence. . . .

. . . [I]n *Kilbourn v. Thompson* *** (1880) . . . [t]he question there was whether the House of Representatives had exceeded its power in directing one of its committees to make a particular investigation. The decision was that it had. The principles announced and applied in the case are—that neither house of Congress possesses a "general power of making inquiry into the private affairs of the citizen"; that the power actually possessed is limited to inquiries relating to matters of which the particular house "has jurisdiction" and in respect of which it rightfully may take other action; that if the inquiry relates to "a matter wherein relief or redress could be had only by a judicial proceeding" it is not within the range of this power, but must be left to the courts, conformably to the constitutional separation of governmental powers; and that for the purpose of determining the essential character of the inquiry recourse may be had to the resolution or order under which it is made. . . .

. . . [In] *In re Chapman* *** (1896) . . . [t]he inquiry there in question was conducted under a resolution of the Senate and related to charges, published in the press, that Senators were yielding to corrupt influences in considering a tariff bill then before the Senate and were speculating in stocks the value of which would be affected by pending amendments to the bill. Chapman appeared before the committee in response to a subpoena, but refused to answer questions pertinent to the inquiry, and was indicted and convicted under the act of 1857 for his refusal. The court sustained the constitutional validity of the act of 1857, and, after referring to the constitutional provision empowering either house to punish its members for disorderly behavior and by a vote of two-thirds to expel a member, held that the inquiry related to the integrity and fidelity of Senators in the discharge of their duties, and therefore to a matter "within the range of the constitutional powers of the Senate" and in respect of which it could compel witnesses to appear and testify. . . .

The latest case is *Marshall v. Gordon* *** (1916). The question there was whether the House of Representatives exceeded its power in punishing, as for a contempt of its authority, a person—not a member—who had written, published, and sent to the chairman of one of its committees an ill-tempered and irritating letter respecting the action and purposes of the committee. Power to make inquiries and obtain evidence by compulsory process was not involved. The court recognized distinctly that the House of Representatives has implied power to punish a person not a member for contempt, as was ruled in *Anderson v. Dunn,* supra, but held that its action in this instance was without constitutional justification.

While these cases are not decisive of the question we are considering, they definitely settle two propositions which we recognize as entirely sound and having a bearing on its solution: One, that the two houses of Congress, in their separate relations, possess, not only such powers as are expressly granted to them by the Constitution, but such auxiliary powers as are necessary and appropriate to make the express powers effective; and the other, that neither house is invested with "general" power to inquire into private affairs and compel disclosures, but only with such limited power of inquiry as is shown to exist when the rule of constitutional interpretation just stated is rightly applied. . . .

We are of opinion that the power of inquiry—with process to enforce it—is an essential and appropriate auxiliary to the legislative function. It was so regarded and employed in American legislatures before the Constitution was framed and ratified. Both houses of Congress took this view of it early in their history. . . .

We come now to the question whether it sufficiently appears that the purpose for which the witness's testimony was sought was to obtain information in aid of the legislative function. The court below answered the question in the negative and put its decision largely on this ground. . . .

We are of opinion that the court's ruling on this question was wrong, and that it sufficiently appears, when the proceedings are rightly interpreted, that the object of the investigation and of the effort to secure the witness's testimony was to obtain information for legislative purposes.

It is quite true that the resolution directing the investigation does not in terms avow that it is intended to be in aid of legislation; but it does show that the subject to be investigated was the administration of the Department of Justice—whether its functions were being properly discharged or were being neglected or misdirected, and particularly whether the Attorney General and his assistants were performing or neglecting their duties in respect of the institution and prosecution of proceedings to punish crimes and enforce appropriate remedies against the wrongdoers; specific instances of alleged neglect being recited. Plainly the subject was one on which legislation could be had and would be materially aided by the information which the investigation was calculated to elicit. This becomes manifest when it is reflected that the functions of the Department of Justice, the powers and duties of the Attorney General, and the duties of his assistants are all subject to regulation by congressional legislation, and that the department is maintained and its activities are carried on under such appropriations as in the judgment of Congress are needed from year to year.

The only legitimate object the Senate could have in ordering the investigation was to aid it in legislating, and we think the subject-matter was such that the presumption should be indulged that this was the real object. An express avowal of the object would have been better, but in view of the particular subject-matter was not indispensable. . . .

We conclude that the investigation was ordered for a legitimate object; that the witness wrongfully refused to appear and testify before the committee and was lawfully attached; that the Senate is entitled to have him give testimony pertinent to the inquiry, either at its bar or before the committee; and that the district court erred in discharging him from custody under the attachment. . . .

What has been said requires that the final order in the district court discharging the witness from custody be reversed.

Mr. Justice Stone did not participate in the consideration or decision of the case.

Watkins v. United States

354 U.S. 178; 77 S. Ct. 1173; 1 L. Ed. 2d 1273 (1957)
Vote: 6-1

Mr. Chief Justice Warren delivered the opinion of the Court.

. . . [Watkins] was prosecuted for refusing to make certain disclosures which he asserted to be beyond the authority of the [House Un-American Activities] committee to demand. The controversy thus rests upon fundamental principles of the power of the Congress and the limitations upon that power. We approach the questions presented with conscious awareness of the far-reaching ramifications that can follow from a decision of this nature.

On April 29, 1954, [Watkins] appeared as a witness in compliance with a subpoena issued by a Subcommittee of the Committee on Un-American Activities of the House of Representatives. The Subcommittee elicited from [him] a description of his background in labor union activities. . . .

[Watkins's] name had been mentioned by two witnesses who testified before the Committee at prior hearings. . . .

[Watkins] answered . . . freely and without reservation . . . when the questioning turned to the subject of his past conduct, associations and predilections:

I am not now nor have I ever been a card-carrying member of the Communist Party. . . .

I would like to make it clear that for a period of time from approximately 1942 to 1947 I cooperated with the Communist Party and participated in Communist activities to such a degree that some persons may honestly believe that I was a member of the party.

I have made contributions upon occasions to Communist causes. I have signed petitions for Communist causes. . . .

. . . I never carried a Communist Party card. I never accepted discipline and indeed on several occasions I opposed their position.

The Subcommittee . . . was apparently satisfied with [Watkins's] disclosures. After some further discussion elaborating on the statement, counsel for the Committee read [a] list of names to petitioner. [Watkins] stated that he did not know several of the persons. Of those whom he did know, he refused to tell whether he knew them to have been members of the Communist Party. He explained to the Subcommittee why he took such a position:

I am not going to plead the Fifth Amendment, but I refuse to answer certain questions that I believe are outside the proper scope of your committee's activities. I will answer any questions which this committee puts to me about myself. I will also answer questions about those persons whom I knew to be members of the Communist Party and whom I believe still are. I will not, however, answer any questions with respect to others with whom I associated in the past. I do not believe that any law in this country requires me to testify about persons who may in the past have been Communist Party members or otherwise engaged in Communist Party activity but who to my best knowledge and belief have long since removed themselves from the Communist movement.

I do not believe that such questions are relevant to the work of this committee nor do I believe that this committee has the right to undertake the public exposure of persons because of their past activities. I may be wrong, and the committee may have this power, but until and unless a court of law so holds and directs me to answer, I most firmly refuse to discuss the political activities of my past associates.

The Chairman of the Committee submitted a report of petitioner's refusal to answer questions to the House of Representatives. *** The House directed the Speaker to certify the Committee's report to the United States Attorney for initiation of criminal prosecution. *** A seven-count indictment was returned. [Watkins] waived his right to jury trial and was found guilty on all counts by the court. The sentence, a fine of $100 and one year in prison, was suspended, and petitioner was placed on probation.

An appeal was taken to the Court of Appeals [and the conviction was affirmed.] . . . We granted certiorari because of the very important questions of constitutional law presented. ***

We start with several basic premises on which there is general agreement. The power of the Congress to conduct investigations is inherent in the legislative process. That power is broad. It encompasses inquiries concerning the administration of existing laws as well as proposed or possible needed statutes.

It includes surveys of defects in our social, economic or political system for the purpose of enabling the Congress to remedy them. It comprehends probes into departments of the Federal Government to expose corruption, inefficiency or waste. But broad as is this power of inquiry, it is not unlimited. There is no general authority to expose the private affairs of individuals without justification in terms of the functions of the Congress. . . . Nor is the Congress a law enforcement or trial agency. These are functions of the executive and judicial departments of government. No inquiry is an end in itself; it must be related to and in furtherance of a legitimate task of the Congress. Investigations conducted solely for the personal aggrandizement of the investigators or to "punish" those investigated are indefensible.

It is unquestionably the duty of all citizens to cooperate with the Congress in its efforts to obtain the facts needed for intelligent legislative action. It is their unremitting obligation to respond to subpoenas, to respect the dignity of the Congress and its committees and to testify fully with respect to matters within the province of proper investigation. This, of course, assumes that the constitutional rights of witnesses will be respected by the Congress as they are in a court of justice. The Bill of Rights is applicable to investigations as to all forms of governmental action. Witnesses cannot be compelled to give evidence against themselves. They cannot be subjected to unreasonable search and seizure. Nor can the First Amendment freedoms of speech, press, religion, or political belief and association be abridged. . . .

In the decade following World War II, there appeared a new kind of congressional inquiry unknown in prior periods of American history. Principally this was the result of the various investigations into the threat of subversion of the United States Government, but other subjects of congressional interest also contributed to the changed scene. This new phase of legislative inquiry involved a broadscale intrusion into the lives and affairs of private citizens. It brought before the courts novel questions of the appropriate limits of congressional inquiry. Prior cases . . . had defined the scope of investigative power in terms of the inherent limitations of the sources of that power. In the recent cases, the emphasis shifted to problems of accommodating the interests of the Government with the rights and privileges of individuals. The central theme was the application of the Bill of Rights as a restraint upon the assertion of governmental power in this form.

It was during this period that the Fifth Amendment privilege against self-incrimination was frequently invoked and recognized as a legal limit upon the authority of a committee to require that a witness answer its questions. Some early doubts as to the applicability of that privilege before a legislative committee never matured. When the matter reached this Court, the Government did not challenge in any way that the Fifth Amendment protection was available to the witness, and such a challenge could not have prevailed. . . .

A far more difficult task evolved from the claim by witnesses that the committee's interrogations were infringements upon the freedoms of the First Amendment. Clearly, an investigation is subject to the command that the Congress shall make no law abridging freedom of speech or press or assembly. While it is true that there is no statute to be reviewed, and that an investigation is not a law, nevertheless an investigation is part of law-making. It is justified solely as an adjunct to the legislative process. The First Amendment may be invoked against infringement of the protected freedoms by law or by law-making.

Abuses of the investigative process may imperceptibly lead to abridgment of protected freedoms. The mere summoning of a witness and compelling him to testify, against his will, about his beliefs, expressions or associations is a measure of governmental interference. And when those forced revelations concern matters that are unorthodox, unpopular, or even hateful to the general public, the reaction in the life of the witness may be disastrous. This effect is even more harsh when it is past beliefs, expressions or associations that are disclosed and judged by current standards rather than those contemporary with the matters exposed. Nor does the witness alone suffer the consequences. Those who are identified by witnesses and thereby placed in the same glare of publicity are equally subject to public stigma, scorn and obloquy. Beyond that, there is the more subtle and immeasurable effect upon those who tend to adhere to the most orthodox and uncontroversial views and associations in order to avoid a similar fate at some future time. That this impact is partly the result of non-governmental activity by private persons cannot relieve the investigators of their responsibility for initiating the reaction.

The Court recognized the restraints of the Bill of Rights upon congressional investigations in *United States v. Rumely.* *** The magnitude and complexity of the problem of applying the First Amendment to that case led the Court to construe narrowly the resolution describing the committee's authority. It was concluded that, when First Amendment rights are threatened, the delegation of power to the committee must be clearly revealed in its charter.

Accommodation of the congressional need for particular information with the individual and personal interest in privacy is an arduous and delicate task for any court. We do not underestimate the difficulties that would attend such an undertaking. It is manifest that despite the adverse effects which follow upon compelled disclosure of private matters, not all such inquiries are barred.... The critical element is the existence of, and the weight to be ascribed to, the interest of the Congress in demanding disclosures from an unwilling witness. We cannot simply assume, however, that every congressional investigation is justified by a public need that overbalances any private rights affected. To do so would be to abdicate the responsibility placed by the Constitution upon the judiciary to insure that the Congress does not unjustifiably encroach upon an individual's right to privacy nor abridge his liberty of speech, press, religion or assembly.

[Watkins] has earnestly suggested that the difficult questions of protecting these rights from infringement by legislative inquiries can be surmounted in this case because there was no public purpose served in his interrogation. His conclusion is based upon the thesis that the Subcommittee was engaged in a program of exposure for the sake of exposure. The sole purpose of the inquiry, he contends, was to bring down upon himself and others the violence of public reaction because of their past beliefs, expressions and associations....

We have no doubt that there is no congressional power to expose for the sake of exposure. The public is, of course, entitled to be informed concerning the workings of its government. That cannot be inflated into a general power to expose where the predominant result can only be an invasion of the private rights of individuals. But a solution to our problem is not to be found in testing the motives of committee members for this purpose. Such is not our function. Their motives alone would not vitiate an investigation which had been instituted by a House of Congress if that assembly's legislative purpose is being served.

... The theory of a committee inquiry is that the committee members are serving as the representatives of the parent assembly in collecting information for a legislative purpose. Their function is to act as the eyes and ears of the Congress in obtaining facts upon which the full legislature can act. To carry out this mission, committees and subcommittees, sometimes one Congressman, are endowed with the full power of the Congress to compel testimony. In this case, only two men exercised that authority in demanding information over petitioner's protest.

An essential premise in this situation is that House or Senate shall have instructed the committee members on what they are to do with the power delegated to them. It is the responsibility of the Congress, in the first instance, to insure that compulsory process is used only in furtherance of a legislative purpose. That requires that the instructions to an investigating committee spell out that group's jurisdiction and purpose with sufficient particularity. Those instructions are embodied in the authorizing resolution. That document is the committee's charter. Broadly drafted and loosely worded, however, such resolutions can leave tremendous latitude to the discretion of the investigators. The more vague the committee's charter is, the greater becomes the possibility that the committee's specific actions are not in conformity with the will of the parent House of Congress.

The authorizing resolution of the Un-American Activities Committee was adopted in 1938.... Several years later, the Committee was made a standing organ of the House with the same mandate. It defines the Committee's authority as follows:

The Committee on Un-American Activities, as a whole or by subcommittee, is authorized to make from time to time investigations of (i) the extent, character, and objects of un-American propaganda activities in the United States, (ii) the diffusion within the United States of subversive and un-American propaganda that is instigated from foreign countries or of a domestic origin and attacks the principle of the form of government as guaranteed by our Constitution, and (iii) all other questions in relation thereto that would aid Congress in any necessary remedial legislation.

It would be difficult to imagine a less explicit authorizing resolution. Who can define the meaning of "un-American"? What is that single, solitary "principle of the form of government as guaranteed by our Constitution"? . . .

Combining the language of the resolution with the construction it has been given, it is evident that the preliminary control of the Committee exercised by the House of Representatives is slight or non-existent. No one could reasonably deduce from the charter the kind of investigation that the Committee was directed to make. As a result, we are asked to engage in a process of retroactive rationalization. Looking backward from the events that transpired, we are asked to uphold the Committee's actions unless it appears that they were clearly not authorized by the charter. As a corollary to this inverse approach, the Government urges that we must view the matter hospitably to the power of the Congress—that if there is any legislative purpose which might have been furthered by the kind of disclosure sought, the witness must be punished for withholding it. No doubt every reasonable indulgence of legality must be accorded to the actions of a coordinate branch of our Government. But such deference cannot yield to an unnecessary and unreasonable dissipation of precious constitutional freedoms.

The Government contends that the public interest at the core of the investigations of the Un-American Activities Committee is the need by the Congress to be informed of efforts to overthrow the Government by force and violence so that adequate legislative safeguards can be erected. From this core, however, the Committee can radiate outward infinitely to any topic thought to be related in some way to armed insurrection. The outer reaches of this domain are known only by the content of "un-American activities." . . . A third dimension is added when the investigators turn their attention to the past to collect minutiae on remote topics, on the hypothesis that the past may reflect upon the present. . . .

It is, of course, not the function of this Court to prescribe rigid rules for the Congress to follow in drafting resolutions establishing investigating committees. That is a matter peculiarly within the realm of the legislature, and its decisions will be accepted by the courts up to the point where their own duty to enforce the constitutionally protected rights of individuals is affected. An excessively broad charter, like that of the House Un-American Activities Committee, places the courts in an untenable position if they are to strike a balance between the public need for a particular interrogation and the right of citizens to carry on their affairs free from unnecessary governmental interference. . . .

Since World War II, the Congress has practically abandoned its original practice of utilizing the coercive sanction of contempt proceedings at the bar of the House. The sanction there imposed is imprisonment by the House until the recalcitrant witness agrees to testify or disclose the matters sought, provided that the incarceration does not extend beyond adjournment. The Congress has instead invoked the aid of the federal judicial system in protecting itself against contumacious conduct. It has become customary to refer these matters to the United States Attorneys for prosecution under criminal law.

The appropriate statute . . . provides:

Every person who having been summoned as a witness by the authority of either House of Congress to give testimony . . . willfully makes default, or who, having appeared, refuses to answer any question pertinent to the question under inquiry, shall be deemed guilty of a misdemeanor, punishable by a fine of not more than $1,000 nor less than $100 and imprisonment in a common jail for not less than one month nor more than twelve months.

In fulfillment of their obligation under this statute, the courts must accord to the defendants every right which is guaranteed to defendants in all other criminal cases. Among these is the right to have available, through a sufficiently precise statute, information revealing the standard of criminality before the commission of the alleged offense. Applied to persons prosecuted under [the statute] *** this raises a special problem in that the statute defines the crime as refusal to answer "any question pertinent to the question under inquiry." Part of the standard of criminality, therefore, is the pertinency of the questions propounded to the witness.

The problem attains proportion when viewed from the standpoint of the witness who appears before a congressional committee. He must decide at the time the questions are propounded whether or not to answer.... An erroneous determination on his part, even if made in the utmost good faith, does not exculpate him if the court should later rule that the questions were pertinent to the question under inquiry.

It is obvious that a person compelled to make this choice is entitled to have knowledge of the subject to which the interrogation is deemed pertinent. That knowledge must be available with the same degree of explicitness and clarity that the Due Process Clause requires in the expression of any element of a criminal offense. The "vice of vagueness" must be avoided here as in all other crimes. There are several sources that can outline the "question under inquiry" in such a way that the rules against vagueness are satisfied. The authorizing resolution, the remarks of the chairman or members of the committee, or even the nature of the proceedings themselves might sometimes make the topic clear. This case demonstrates, however, that these sources often leave the matter in grave doubt.

... [Watkins] was not accorded a fair opportunity to determine whether he was within his rights in refusing to answer, and his conviction is necessarily invalid under the Due Process Clause of the Fifth Amendment.

We are mindful of the complexities of modern government and the ample scope that must be left to the Congress as the sole constitutional depository of legislative power. Equally mindful are we of the indispensable function, in the exercise of that power, of congressional investigations. The conclusions we have reached in this case will not prevent the Congress, through its committees, from obtaining any information it needs for the proper fulfillment of its role in our scheme of government. The legislature is free to determine the kinds of data that should be collected. It is only those investigations that are conducted by use of compulsory process that give rise to a need to protect the rights of individuals against

illegal encroachment. That protection can be readily achieved through procedures which prevent the separation of power from responsibility and which provide the constitutional requisites of fairness for witnesses. A measure of added care on the part of the House and the Senate in authorizing the use of compulsory process and by their committees in exercising that power would suffice. That is a small price to pay if it serves to uphold the principles of limited, constitutional government without constricting the power of the Congress to inform itself.

The judgment of the Court of Appeals is reversed, and the case is remanded to the District Court with instructions to dismiss the indictment.

It is so ordered.

Mr. Justice Burton and **Mr. Justice Whittaker** took no part in the consideration or decision of this case.

Mr. Justice Frankfurter, concurring....

Mr. Justice Clark, dissenting.

As I see it the chief fault in the majority opinion is its mischievous curbing of the informing function of the Congress. While I am not versed in its procedures, my experience in the executive branch of the government leads me to believe that the requirements laid down in the opinion for the operation of the committee system of inquiry are both unnecessary and unworkable....

It may be that at times the House Committee on Un-American Activities has, as the Court says, "conceived of its task in the grand view of its name." And, perhaps, as the Court indicates, the rules of conduct placed upon the Committee by the House admit of individual abuse and unfairness. But that is none of our affair. So long as the object of a legislative inquiry is legitimate and the questions propounded are pertinent thereto, it is not for the courts to interfere with the committee system of inquiry. To hold otherwise would be an infringement on the power given the Congress to inform itself, and thus a trespass upon the fundamental American principle of separation of powers. The majority has substituted the judiciary as the grand inquisitor and supervisor of congressional investigations. It has never been so....

I think the Committee here was acting entirely within its scope and that the purpose of its inquiry was set out with "undisputable clarity." In the first place, the authorizing language of the Reorganization Act must be read as a whole, not dissected. It authorized investigation into subversive activity, its extent, character, objects, and diffusion. While the language might have been more explicit than using such words as "un-American," or phrases like "principle of the form of government," still these are fairly well understood terms. We must construe them to give them meaning if we can. Our cases indicate that rather than finding fault with the use of words or phrases, we are bound to presume that the action of the legislative body in granting authority to the Committee was with a legitimate object "if [the action] is *capable* of being so construed." (Emphasis added.) *** Before we can deny the authority "it must be obvious that" the Committee has "exceeded the bounds of legislative power." *** The fact that the Committee has often been attacked has caused close scrutiny of its acts by the House as a whole and the House has repeatedly given the Committee its approval. "Power" and "responsibility" have not been separated. But the record in this case does not stop here. It shows that at the hearings involving Watkins, the Chairman made statements explaining the functions of the committee. And, furthermore, Watkins' action at the hearing clearly reveals that he was well acquainted with the purpose of the hearing. It was to investigate Communist infiltration into his union. This certainly falls within the grant of authority from the Reorganization Act and the House has had ample opportunity to limit the investigative scope of the Committee if it feels that the Committee has exceeded its legitimate bounds.

The Court makes much of petitioner's claim of "exposure for exposure's sake" and strikes at the purposes of the Committee through this catch phrase. But we are bound to accept as the purpose of the Committee that stated in the Reorganization Act together with the statements of the Chairman at the hearings involved here. Nothing was said of exposure. The statements of a single Congressman cannot transform the real purpose of the Committee into something not authorized by the parent resolution. *** The Court indicates that the questions propounded were asked for exposure's sake and had no pertinency to the inquiry. It appears to me that they were entirely pertinent to the announced purpose of the Committee's inquiry. Undoubtedly Congress has the power to inquire into the subjects of communism and the Communist Party. *** As a corollary of the congressional power to inquire into such subject matter, the Congress, through its committees, can legitimately seek to identify individual members of the Party. ***

The pertinency of the questions is highlighted by the need for the Congress to know the extent of infiltration of communism in labor unions. This technique of infiltration was that used in bringing the downfall of countries formerly free but now still remaining behind the Iron Curtain. . . . [T]he Party is not an ordinary political party and has not been at least since 1945. Association with its officials is not an ordinary association. Nor does it matter that the questions related to the past. Influences of past associations often linger. . . . The techniques used in the infiltration which admittedly existed here, might well be used again in the future. If the parties about whom Watkins was interrogated were Communists and collaborated with him, as a prior witness indicated, an entirely new area of investigation might have been opened up. Watkins' silence prevented the Committee from learning this information which could have been vital to its future investigation. The Committee was likewise entitled to elicit testimony showing the truth or falsity of the prior testimony of the witnesses who had involved Watkins and the union with collaboration with the Party. If the testimony was untrue a false picture of the relationship between the union and the Party leaders would have resulted. For these reasons there were ample indications of the pertinency of the questions.

. . . [T]he Court honors Watkins' claim of a "right to silence" which brings all inquiries, as we know, to a "dead end." I do not see how any First Amendment rights were endangered here. There is nothing in the First Amendment that provided the guarantees Watkins claims. That Amendment was designed to prevent attempts by law to curtail freedom of speech. *** It forbids Congress from making any law "abridging the freedom of speech, or of the press." It guarantees Watkins' right to join any organization and make any speech that does not have an intent to incite to crime. *** But Watkins was asked whether he knew named individuals and whether they were Communists. He refused to answer on the ground that his rights were being abridged. What he was actually seeking to do was to protect his former associates, not himself, from embarrassment. He had already admitted his own involvement. He sought to vindicate the rights, if any, of his associates. It is settled that one cannot invoke the constitutional rights of another. ***

. . . We should afford to Congress the presumption that it takes every precaution possible to avoid unnecessary damage to reputations. Some committees have codes of procedure, and others use the executive hearing technique to this end. The record in this case shows no conduct on the part of the Un-American Activities Committee that justifies condemnation. That there may have been such occasions is not for us to consider here. Nor should we permit its past transgressions, if any, to lead to the rigid restraint of all congressional committees. To carry on its heavy responsibility the compulsion of truth that does not incriminate is not only necessary to the Congress but is permitted within the limits of the Constitution.

Barenblatt v. United States

360 U.S. 109; 79 S. Ct. 1081; 3 L. Ed. 2d 1115 (1959)
Vote: 5-4

As part of its investigation into Communist infiltration into the education system, the House Un-American Activities Committee subpoenaed Lloyd Barenblatt, a former college professor. Barenblatt appeared before the committee but refused to answer its questions, which dealt primarily with his political beliefs and associations. Barenblatt based his refusal not on the selfincrimination clause of the Fifth Amendment, but on the First Amendment protections of political speech and association. Barenblatt was convicted of contempt of Congress.

Mr. Justice Harlan delivered the opinion of the Court.

. . . Once more the Court is required to resolve the conflicting constitutional claims of congressional power and of an individual's right to resist its exercise. The congressional power in question concerns the internal process of Congress in moving within its legislative domain; it involves the utilization of its committees to secure "testimony needed to enable it efficiently to exercise a legislative function belonging to it under the Constitution." *** The power of inquiry has been employed by Congress throughout our history, over the whole range of the national interests concerning which Congress might legislate or decide upon due investigation not to legislate; it has similarly been utilized in determining what to appropriate from the national purse, or whether to appropriate. The scope of the power of inquiry, in short, is as penetrating and far-reaching as the potential power to enact and appropriate under the Constitution.

Broad as it is, the power is not, however, without limitations. Since Congress may only investigate into those areas in which it may potentially legislate or appropriate, it cannot inquire into matters which are within the exclusive province of one of the other branches of the Government. Lacking the judicial power given to the Judiciary, it cannot inquire into matters that are exclusively the concern of the Judiciary. Neither can it supplant the Executive in what exclusively belongs to the Executive. And the Congress, in common with all branches of the Government, must exercise its powers subject to the limitations placed by the Constitution on governmental action, more particularly in the context of this case the relevant limitations of the Bill of Rights.

The congressional power of inquiry, its range and scope, and an individual's duty in relation to it, must be viewed in proper perspective. . . . The power and the right of resistance to it are to be judged in the concrete, not on the basis of abstractions. In the present case congressional efforts to learn the extent of a nationwide, indeed worldwide, problem have brought one of its investigating committees into the field of education. Of course, broadly viewed, inquiries cannot be made into the teaching that is pursued in any of our educational institutions. When academic teaching-freedom and its corollary learning-freedom, so essential to the well-being of the Nation, are claimed, this Court will always be on the alert against intrusion by Congress into this constitutionally protected domain. But this does not mean that the Congress is precluded from interrogating a witness merely because he is a teacher. An educational institution is not a constitutional sanctuary from inquiry into matters that may otherwise be within the constitutional legislative domain merely for the reason that inquiry is made of someone within its walls.

In the setting of this framework of constitutional history, practice and legal precedents, we turn to the particularities of this case.

We here review petitioner's conviction for contempt of Congress, arising from his refusal to answer certain questions put to him by a Subcommittee of the House Committee on Un-American Activities during the course of an inquiry concerning alleged Communist infiltration into the field of education. . . .

Petitioner's various contentions resolve themselves into three propositions: First, the compelling of testimony by the Subcommittee was neither legislatively authorized nor constitutionally permissible because of the vagueness of Rule XI of the House of Representatives, Eighty-third Congress, the charter of authority of the parent Committee. Second, petitioner was not adequately apprised of the pertinency of the Subcommittee's questions to the subject matter of the inquiry. Third, the questions petitioner refused to answer infringed rights protected by the First Amendment. . . .

. . . At the outset it should be noted that Rule XI authorized this Subcommittee to compel testimony within the framework of the investigative authority conferred on the Un-American Activities Committee. Petitioner contends that *Watkins v. United States* *** nevertheless held the grant of this power in all cir-

cumstances ineffective because of the vagueness of Rule XI in delineating the Committee jurisdiction to which its exercise was to be appurtenant. This view of *Watkins* was accepted by two of the dissenting judges below.

The Watkins Case cannot properly be read as standing for such a proposition. A principal contention in *Watkins* was that the refusals to answer were justified because the requirement . . . that the questions asked be "pertinent to the question under inquiry" had not been satisfied. This Court reversed the conviction solely on that ground, holding that Watkins had not been adequately apprised of the subject matter of the Subcommittee's investigation or the pertinency thereto of the questions he refused to answer. In so deciding the Court drew upon Rule XI only as one of the facets in the total *mise en scène* in its search for the "question under inquiry" in that particular investigation. The Court, in other words, was not dealing with Rule XI at large, and indeed in effect stated that no such issue was before it. That the vagueness of Rule XI was not alone determinative is also shown by the Court's further statement that aside from the Rule "the remarks of the chairman of members of the committee, or even the nature of the proceedings themselves, might sometimes make the topic [under inquiry] clear." In short, while *Watkins* was critical of Rule XI, it did not involve the broad and inflexible holding petitioner now attributes to it.

Petitioner also contends, independently of *Watkins,* that the vagueness of Rule XI deprived the Subcommittee of the right to compel testimony in this investigation into Communist activity. We cannot agree with this contention, which in its furthest reach would mean that the House Un-American Activities Committee under its existing authority has no right to compel testimony in any circumstances. Granting the vagueness of the Rule, we may not read it in isolation from its long history in the House of Representatives. Just as legislation is often given meaning by the gloss of legislative reports, administrative interpretation, and long usage, so the proper meaning of an authorization to a congressional committee is not to be derived alone from its abstract terms unrelated to the definite content furnished them by the course of congressional actions. The Rule comes to us with a "persuasive gloss of legislative history," which shows beyond doubt that in pursuance of its legislative concerns in the domain of "national security" the House has clothed the Un-American Activities Committee with pervasive authority to investigate Communist activities in this country. . . .

. . . In light of this long and illuminating history it can hardly be seriously argued that the investigation of Communist activities generally, and the attendant use of compulsory process, was beyond the purview of the Committee's intended authority under Rule XI. . . .

. . . In this framework of the Committee's history we must conclude that its legislative authority to conduct the inquiry presently under consideration is unassailable, and that independently of whatever bearing the broad scope of Rule XI may have on the issue of "pertinency" in a given investigation into Communist activities, as in *Watkins*, the Rule cannot be said to be constitutionally infirm on the score of vagueness. The constitutional permissibility of that authority otherwise is a matter to be discussed later. . . .

. . . Undeniably a conviction for contempt . . . cannot stand unless the questions asked are pertinent to the subject matter of the investigation. *** But the factors which led us to rest decision on this ground in *Watkins* were very different from those involved here.

In *Watkins* the petitioner had made specific objection to the Subcommittee's questions on the ground of pertinency; the question under inquiry had not been disclosed in any illuminating manner; and the questions asked the petitioner were not only amorphous on their face, but in some instances clearly foreign to the alleged subject matter of the investigation—"Communism in labor."

In contrast, petitioner in the case before us raised no objections on the ground of pertinency at the time any of the questions were put to him. . . .

We need not, however, rest decision on petitioner's failure to object on this score, for here "pertinency" was made to appear "with undisputable clarity." First of all, it goes without saying that the scope of the Committee's authority was for the House, not a witness, to determine, subject to the ultimate reviewing responsibility of this Court. What we deal with here is whether petitioner was sufficiently ap-

prised of "the topic under inquiry" thus authorized "and the connective reasoning whereby the precise questions asked relate[d] to it." In light of his prepared memorandum of constitutional objections there can be no doubt that this petitioner was well aware of the Subcommittee's authority and purpose to question him as it did. In addition the other sources of this information which we recognized in *Watkins* leave no room for a "pertinency" objection on this record. The subject matter of the inquiry had been identified at the commencement of the investigation as Communist infiltration into the field of education. Just prior to petitioner's appearance before the Subcommittee, the scope of the day's hearings had been announced as "in the main communism in education and the experiences and background in the party by Francis X. T. Crowley. It will deal with activities in Michigan, Boston, and in some small degree, New York." *** Petitioner had heard the Subcommittee interrogate the witness Crowley along the same lines as he, petitioner, was evidently to be questioned, and had listened to Crowley's testimony identifying him as a former member of an alleged Communist student organization at the University of Michigan while they both were in attendance there. Further, petitioner had stood mute in the face of the Chairman's statement as to why he had been called as a witness by the Subcommittee. And, lastly, unlike Watkins, petitioner refused to answer questions as to his own Communist Party affiliations, whose pertinency of course was clear beyond doubt. . . .

. . . The precise constitutional issue confronting us is whether the Subcommittee's inquiry into petitioner's past or present membership in the Communist Party transgressed the provisions of the First Amendment, which of course reach and limit congressional investigations. ***

The Court's past cases establish sure guides to decision. Undeniably, the First Amendment in some circumstances protects an individual from being compelled to disclose his associational relationships. However, the protections of the First Amendment, unlike a proper claim of the privilege against self-incrimination under the Fifth Amendment, do not afford a witness the right to resist inquiry in all circumstances. Where First Amendment rights are asserted to bar governmental interrogation, resolution of the issue always involves a balancing by the courts of the competing private and public interests at stake in the particular circumstances shown. These principles were recognized in the Watkins Case.... ***

The first question is whether this investigation was related to a valid legislative purpose, for Congress may not constitutionally require an individual to disclose his political relationships or other private affairs except in relation to such a purpose. ***

That Congress has wide power to legislate in the field of Communist activity in this Country, and to conduct appropriate investigations in aid thereof, is hardly debatable. The existence of such power has never been questioned by this Court, and it is sufficient to say, without particularization, that Congress has enacted or considered in this field a wide range of legislative measures, not a few of which have stemmed from recommendations of the very Committee whose actions have been drawn in question here. In the last analysis this power rests on the right of self-preservation, "the ultimate value of any society" ... *** Justification for its exercise in turn rests on the long and widely accepted view that the tenets of the Communist Party include the ultimate overthrow of the Government of the United States by force and violence, a view which has been given formal expression by the Congress....

... To suggest that because the Communist Party may also sponsor peaceable political reforms the constitutional issues before us should not be judged as if that Party were just an ordinary political party from the standpoint of national security, is to ask this Court to blind itself to world affairs which have determined the whole course of our national policy since the close of World War II, ... and to the vast burdens which these conditions have entailed for the entire Nation.

We think that investigatory power in this domain is not to be denied Congress solely because the field of education is involved.... Indeed we do not understand the petitioner here to suggest that Congress in no circumstances may inquire into Communist activity in the field of education. Rather, his position is in effect that this particular investigation was aimed not at the revolutionary aspects but at the theoretical classroom discussion of communism.

In our opinion this position rests on a too constricted view of the nature of the investigatory process, and is not supported by a fair assessment of the record before us. An investigation of advocacy of or preparation for overthrow certainly embraces the right to identify a witness as a member of the Communist Party ... and to inquire into the various manifestations of the Party's tenets. The strict requirements of a prosecution under the Smith Act, *** are not the measure of the permissible scope of a congressional investigation into "overthrow," for of necessity the investigatory process must proceed step by step. Nor can it fairly be concluded that this investigation was directed at controlling what is being taught at our universities rather than at overthrow. The statement of the Subcommittee Chairman at the opening of the investigation evinces no such intention, and so far as this record reveals nothing thereafter transpired which would justify our holding that the thrust of the investigation later changed. The record discloses considerable testimony concerning the foreign domination and revolutionary purposes and efforts of the Communist Party. That there was also testimony on the abstract philosophical level does not detract from the dominant theme of this investigation—Communist infiltration furthering the alleged ultimate purpose of overthrow. And certainly the conclusion would not be justified that the questioning of petitioner would have exceeded permissible bounds had he not shut off the Subcommittee at the threshold.

Nor can we accept the further contention that this investigation should not be deemed to have been in furtherance of a legislative purpose because the true objective of the Committee and of the Congress was purely "exposure." So long as Congress acts in pursuance of its constitutional power, the Judiciary lacks authority to intervene on the basis of the motives which spurred the exercise of that power. "It is of course, true," *** "that if there be no authority in the judiciary to restrain a lawful exercise of power by another department of the government, where a wrong motive or purpose has impelled to the exertion of the power, that abuses of a power conferred may be temporarily effectual. The remedy for this, however, lies, not in the abuse by the judicial authority of its functions, but in the people, upon whom, after all, under our institutions, reliance must be placed for the correction of abuses committed in the exercise of a lawful power." These principles of course apply as well to committee investigations into the need for legislation as to the enactments which such investigations may produce. . . . Thus, in stating in the Watkins Case . . . that "there is no congressional power to expose for the sake of exposure, we at the same time declined to inquire into the "motives of committee members," and recognized that their "motives alone would not vitiate an investigation which had been instituted by a House of Congress if that assembly's legislative purpose is being served." Having scrutinized this record we cannot say that the unanimous panel of the Court of Appeals which first considered this case was wrong in concluding that "the primary purposes of the inquiry were in aid of legislative processes." Certainly this is not a case like *Kilbourn v. Thompson* ***, where "the House of Representatives not only exceeded the limit of its own authority, but assumed a power which could only be properly exercised by another branch of government, because it was in its nature clearly judicial." The constitutional legislative power of Congress in this instance is beyond question.

Finally, the record is barren of other factors which in themselves might sometimes lead to the conclusion that the individual interests at stake were not subordinate to those of the state. There is no indication in this record that the Subcommittee was attempting to pillory witnesses. Nor did petitioner's

appearance as a witness follow from indiscriminate dragnet procedures, lacking in probable cause for belief that he possessed information which might be helpful to the Subcommittee. And the relevancy of the questions put to him by the Subcommittee is not open to doubt.

We conclude that the balance between the individual and the governmental interests here at stake must be struck in favor of the latter, and that therefore the provisions of the First Amendment have not been offended.

We hold that petitioner's conviction for contempt of Congress discloses no infirmity and that the judgment of the Court of Appeals must be Affirmed.

Mr. Justice Black, with whom **Chief Justice Warren** and **Mr. Justice Douglas** concur, dissenting. . . .

Mr. Justice Brennan, dissenting.

. . . I would reverse this conviction. It is sufficient that I state my complete agreement with my Brother Black that no purpose for the investigation of Barenblatt is revealed by the record except exposure purely for the sake of exposure. This is not a purpose to which Barenblatt's rights under the First Amendment can validly be subordinated. An investigation in which the processes of law-making and law-evaluating are submerged entirely in exposure of individual behavior—in adjudication, of a sort, through the exposure process—is outside the constitutional pale of congressional inquiry. ***

Gibbons v. Ogden
9 Wheat. (22 U.S.) 1; 6 L. Ed. 23 (1824)
Vote: 7-0

Aaron Ogden held an exclusive right to navigate steamboats in New York waters, a monopoly granted by the New York state legislature. Gibbons held a "coasting license" from the federal government. When Gibbons began operating a steamboat ferry service between New York and New Jersey, Ogden obtained an injunction in the New York courts.

Mr. Chief Justice Marshall delivered the opinion of the Court.

[Gibbons] contends that [New York's injunction] is erroneous, because the laws [of New York] which purport to give the exclusive privilege (to Ogden to navigate steamboats on New York waters) are repugnant to the Constitution and laws of the United States.

They are said to be repugnant . . . to that clause in the Constitution which authorizes Congress to regulate commerce. . . .

The words are: "Congress shall have power to regulate commerce with foreign nations, and among the several states, and with the Indian tribes."

The subject to be regulated is commerce; and our Constitution being, as was aptly said at the bar, one of enumeration, and not of definition, to ascertain the extent of the power it becomes necessary to settle the meaning of the word. The counsel for [Ogden] would limit it to traffic, to buying and selling, or the interchange of commodities, and do not admit that it comprehends navigation. This would restrict a general term, applicable to many objects, to one of its significations. Commerce, undoubtedly, is traffic, but it is something more; it is intercourse. It describes the commercial intercourse between nations, and parts of nations, in all its branches, and is regulated by prescribing rules for carrying on that intercourse. The mind can scarcely conceive a system for regulating commerce between nations, which shall exclude all laws concerning navigation, which shall be silent on the admission of the vessels of the one nation into the ports of the other, and be confined to prescribing rules for the conduct of individuals, in the actual employment of buying and selling or of barter.

If commerce does not include navigation, the government of the Union has no direct power over that subject, and can make no law prescribing what shall constitute American vessels, or requiring that they shall be navigated by American seamen. Yet this power has been exercised from the commencement of the government, has been exercised with the consent of all, and has been understood by all to be a commercial regulation. All America understands, and has uniformly understood, the word "commerce" to comprehend navigation. It was so understood, and must have been so understood, when the constitution was framed. The power over commerce, including navigation, was one of the primary objects for which the people of America adopted their government, and must have been contemplated in forming it. The convention must have used the word in that sense; because all have understood it in that sense, and the attempt to restrict it comes too late. . . .

The word used in the Constitution, then, comprehends, and has been always understood to comprehend, navigation within its meaning; and a power to regulate navigation is as expressly granted as if that term had been added to the word "commerce."

To what commerce does this power extend? The Constitution informs us, to commerce "with foreign nations, and among the several states, and with the Indian tribes."

It has, we believe, been universally admitted that these words comprehend every species of commercial intercourse between the United States and foreign nations. No sort of trade can be carried on between this country and any other, to which this power does not extend. It has been truly said, that commerce, as the word is used in the Constitution, is a unit, every part of which is indicated by the term.

If this be the admitted meaning of the word, in its application to foreign nations, it must carry the same meaning throughout the sentence, and remain a unit, unless there be some plain intelligible cause which alters it.

The subject to which the power is next applied, is to commerce "among the several states." The word "among" means intermingled with. A thing which is among others, is intermingled with them. Commerce among the states cannot stop at the external boundary line of each state, but may be introduced into the interior.

It is not intended to say that these words comprehend that commerce which is completely internal, which is carried on between man and man in a state, or between different parts of the same state, and which does not extend to or affect other states. Such a power would be inconvenient, and is certainly unnecessary.

Comprehensive as the word "among" is, it may very properly be restricted to that commerce which concerns more states than one. The phrase is not one which would probably have been selected to indicate the completely interior traffic of a state, because it is not an apt phrase for that purpose; and the enumeration of the particular classes of commerce to which the power was to be extended, would not have been made had the intention been to extend the power to every description. The enumeration presupposes something not enumerated; and that something, if we regard the language or the subject of the sentence, must be the exclusively internal commerce of a state. The genius and character of the whole government seem to be, that its action is to be applied to all the external concerns of the nation, and to those internal concerns which affect the states generally; but not to those which are completely within a particular state, which do not affect other states, and with which it is not necessary to interfere, for the purpose of executing some of the general powers of the government. The completely internal commerce of a state, then, may be considered as reserved for the state itself.

But, in regulating commerce with foreign nations the power of Congress does not stop at the jurisdictional lines of the several states. It would be a very useless power if it could not pass those lines. The commerce of the United States with foreign nations, is that of the whole United States. Every district has a right to participate in it. The deep streams which penetrate our country in every direction, pass through the interior of almost every state in the Union, and furnish the means of exercising this right. If Congress has the power to regulate it, that power must be exercised whenever the subject exists. If it exists within the states, if a foreign voyage may commence or terminate at a port within a state, then the power of Congress may be exercised within a state. . . .

We are now arrived at the inquiry, What is this power?

It is the power to regulate; that is, to prescribe the rule by which commerce is to be governed. This power, like all others vested in Congress, is complete in itself, may be exercised to its utmost extent, and acknowledges no limitations, other than are prescribed in the Constitution. These are expressed in plain terms, and do not affect the questions which arise in this case, or which have been discussed at the bar. If, as has always been understood, the sovereignty of Congress, though limited to specified objects, is plenary as to those objects, the power over commerce with foreign nations, and among the several States, is vested in Congress as absolutely as it would be in a single government, having in its constitution the same restrictions on the exercise of the power as are found in the Constitution of the United

States. The wisdom and the discretion of Congress, their identity with the people, and the influence which their constituents possess at election, are, in this, as in many other instances, as that, for example, of declaring war, the sole restraints on which they have relied, to secure them from its abuse. They are the restraints on which the people must often rely solely, in all representative governments.

The power of Congress, then, comprehends navigation within the limits of every state in the Union; so far as that navigation may be, in any manner, connected with "commerce with foreign nations, or among the several states, or with the Indian tribes." It may, of consequence, pass the jurisdictional line of New York, and act upon the very waters to which the prohibition now under consideration applies.

But it has been urged with great earnestness, that although the power of Congress to regulate commerce with foreign nations, and among the several states, be co-extensive with the subject itself, and have no other limits than are prescribed in the Constitution, yet the states may severally exercise the same power within their respective jurisdictions. In support of this argument, it is said that they possessed it as an inseparable attribute of sovereignty, before the formation of the Constitution, and still retain it, except so far as they have surrendered it by that instrument; that this principle results from the nature of the government, and is secured by the Tenth Amendment; that an affirmative grant of power is not exclusive, unless in its own nature it be such that the continued exercise of it by the former possessor is inconsistent with the grant, and that this is not of that description.

[Gibbons] conceding these postulates, except the last, contends that full power to regulate a particular subject, implies the whole power, and leaves no residuum; that a grant of the whole is incompatible with the existence of a right in another to any part of it.

Both parties have appealed to the Constitution, to legislative acts, and judicial decisions; and have drawn arguments from all these sources to support and illustrate the propositions they respectively maintain.

The grant of the power to lay and collect taxes is, like the power to regulate commerce, made in general terms, and has never been understood to interfere with the exercise of the same power by the states; and hence has been drawn an argument which has been applied to the question under consideration. But the two grants are not, it is conceived, similar in their terms or their nature. Although many of the powers formerly exercised by the states, are transferred to the government of the Union, yet the state governments remain, and constitute a most important part of our system. The power of taxation is indispensable to their existence, and is a power which, in its own nature, is capable of residing in, and being exercised by, different authorities at the same time. . . . Congress is authorized to lay and collect taxes, etc., to pay the debts, and to provide for the common defense and general welfare of the United States. This does not interfere with the power of the states to tax for the support of their own governments; nor is the exercise of that power by the states an exercise of any portion of the power that is granted to the United States. In imposing taxes for state purposes, they are not doing what Congress is empowered to do. Congress is not empowered to tax for those purposes which are within the exclusive province of the states. When, then, each government exercises the power of taxation, neither is exercising the power of the other. But, when a state proceeds to regulate commerce with foreign nations, or among the several states, it is exercising the very power that is granted to Congress, and is doing the very thing which Congress is authorized to do. There is no analogy, then, between the power of taxation and the power of regulating commerce.

In discussing the question, whether this [commerce] power is still in the states, in the case under consideration, we may dismiss from it the inquiry, whether it is surrendered by the mere grant to Congress, or is retained until Congress shall exercise the power. We may dismiss that inquiry, because it has been exercised, and the regulations which Congress deemed it proper to make, are now in full operation. The sole question is, can a state regulate commerce with foreign nations and among the states, while Congress is regulating it? . . .

In our complex system, presenting the rare and difficult scheme of one general government, whose action extends over the whole, but which possesses only certain enumerated powers, and of numerous state governments, which retain and exercise all powers not delegated to the Union, contests respecting power must arise. Were it even otherwise, the measures taken by the respective governments to execute their acknowledged powers, would often be of the same description, and might, sometimes, interfere. This, however, does not prove that the one is exercising, or has a right to exercise, the powers of the other. . . .

Since, . . . in exercising the power of regulating their own purely internal affairs, whether of trading or police, the states may sometimes enact laws, the validity of which depends on their interfering with, and being contrary to, an act of Congress passed in pursuance of the Constitution, the court will enter upon the inquiry, whether the laws of New York, as expounded by the highest tribunal of that state, have, in their application to this case, come into collision with an act of Congress, and deprived a citizen of a right to which that act entitles him. Should this collision exist, it will be immaterial whether those laws were passed in virtue of a concurrent power "to regulate commerce with foreign nations and among the several states," or in virtue of a power to regulate their domestic trade and police. In one case and the other, the acts of New York must yield to the law of Congress; and the decision sustaining the privilege they confer, against a right given by a law of the Union, must be erroneous.

. . . [It] has been contended that if a law, passed by a state in the exercise of its acknowledged sovereignty, comes into conflict with a law passed by Congress in pursuance of the Constitution, they affect the subject, and each other, like equal opposing powers.

But the framers of our constitution foresaw this state of things, and provided for it, by declaring the supremacy not only of itself, but of the laws made in pursuance of it. The nullity of any act, inconsistent with the Constitution, is produced by the declaration that the Constitution is the supreme law. The appropriate application of that part of the clause which confers the same supremacy on laws and treaties, is to such acts of the state legislatures as do not transcend their powers, but, though enacted in the execution of acknowledged state powers, interfere with, or are contrary to the laws of Congress, made in pursuance of the Constitution, or some treaty made under the authority of the United States. In every such case, the act of Congress, or the treaty, is supreme; and the law of the state, though enacted in the exercise of powers not controverted, must yield to it. . . .

. . . To the court it seems very clear, that the whole act on the subject of the coasting trade, according to those principles which govern the construction of statutes, implies, unequivocally, an authority to licensed vessels to carry on the coasting trade. . . .

If the power reside in Congress, as a portion of the general grant to regulate commerce, then acts applying that power to vessels generally, must be construed as comprehending all vessels. If none appear to be excluded by the language of the act, none can be excluded by construction. Vessels have always been employed to a greater or less extent in the transportation of passengers, and have never been supposed to be, on that account, withdrawn from the control or protection of Congress. . . .

. . . The real and sole question seems to be, whether a steam machine, in actual use, deprives a vessel of the privileges conferred by a license.

In considering this question, the first idea which presents itself, is that the laws of Congress, for the regulation of commerce, do not look to the principle by which vessels are moved. That subject is left entirely to individual discretion; and, in that vast and complex system of legislative enactment concerning it, which embraces everything that the legislature thought it necessary to notice, there is not, we believe, one word respecting the peculiar principle by which vessels are propelled through the water, except what may be found in a single act, granting a particular privilege to steamboats. With this exception, every act, either prescribing duties, or granting privileges, applies to every vessel, whether navigated by the instrumentality of wind or fire, of sails or machinery. . . .

This act demonstrates the opinion of Congress, that steamboats may be enrolled and licensed, in common with vessels using sails. They are, of course, entitled to the same privileges, and can no more be restrained from navigating waters, and entering ports which are free to such vessels, than if they were wafted on their voyage by the winds, instead of being propelled by the agency of fire. The one element may be as _legitimately_ used as the other, for every

commercial purpose authorized by the laws of the Union; and the act of a state inhibiting the use of either to any vessel having a license under the act of Congress, comes, we think, in direct collision with the act. . . .

Mr. Justice Johnson [concurring]. The judgment entered by the court in this cause has my entire approbation; but having adopted my conclusions on views of the subject materially different from those of my brethren, I feel it incumbent on me to exhibit those views. . . .

In attempts to construe the Constitution, I have never found much benefit resulting from the inquiry, whether the whole, or any part of it, is to be construed strictly, or literally. The simple, classical, precise, yet comprehensive language in which it is couched, leaves, at most, but very little latitude for construction; and when its intent and meaning is discovered nothing remains but to execute the will of those who made it, in the best manner to effect the purposes intended. The great and paramount purpose, was to unite this mass of wealth and power, for the protection of the humblest individual; his rights, civil and political, his interests and prosperity, are the sole end; the rest are nothing but the means. But the principal of those means, one so essential as to approach nearer the characteristics of an end, was the independence and harmony of the states, that they may the better subserve the purposes of cherishing and protecting the respective families of this great republic. . . .

The "power to regulate commerce," here meant to be granted, was that power to regulate commerce which previously existed in the states. But what was that power? The states were, unquestionably, supreme, and each possessed that power over commerce which is acknowledged to reside in every sovereign state. . . . The power of a sovereign state over commerce, therefore, amounts to nothing more than a power to limit and restrain it at pleasure. And since the power to prescribe the limits to its freedom necessarily implies the power to determine what shall remain unrestrained, it follows that the power must be exclusive; it can reside but in one potentate; and hence, the grant of this power carries with it the whole subject, leaving nothing for the state to act upon. . . .

It is impossible, with the views which I entertained of the principle on which the commercial privileges of the people of the United States, among themselves, rests, to concur in the view which this Court takes of the effect of the coasting license in this cause. I do not regard it as the foundation of the right set up in behalf of [Gibbons]. If there was any one object riding over every other in the adoption of the Constitution, it was to keep the commercial intercourse among the states free from all invidious and partial restraints. And I cannot overcome the conviction, that if the licensing act was repealed tomorrow, the rights of [Gibbons] to a reversal of the decision complained of, would be as strong as it is under this license. . . .

United States v. E. C. Knight Company

156 U.S. 1; 15 S. Ct. 249; 39 L. Ed. 325 (1895)

Vote: 8-1

Mr. Chief Justice Fuller delivered the opinion of the Court.

. . . By the purchase of the stock of the four Philadelphia refineries, with shares of its own stock, the American Sugar Refining Company acquired nearly complete control of the manufacture of refined sugar within the United States. The bill charged that the contracts under which these purchases were made constituted combinations in restraint of trade, and that in entering into them the defendants combined and conspired to restrain the trade and commerce in refined sugar among the several states and with foreign nations, contrary to . . . [the Sherman Antitrust Act].

The relief sought was the cancellation of the agreements under which the stock was transferred; the redelivery of the stock to the parties respectively; and an injunction against the further performance of the agreements and further violations of the Act. . . .

The fundamental question is whether conceding that the existence of a monopoly in manufacture is established by the evidence, that monopoly can be directly suppressed under the Act of Congress in the mode attempted by this bill.

It cannot be denied that the power of a state to protect the lives, health, and property of its citizens, and to preserve good order and the public morals, "the power to govern men and things within the limits of its dominion," is a power originally and always belonging to the states, not surrendered by them to the general government, nor directly restrained by the Constitution of the United States, and essentially exclusive. The relief of the citizens of each state from the burden of monopoly and the evils resulting from the restraint of trade among such citizens was left with the states to deal with, and this court has recognized their possession of that power. . . . On the other hand, the power of Congress to regulate commerce among the several states is also exclusive. The Constitution does not provide that interstate commerce shall be free, but, by the grant of this exclusive power to regulate it, it was left free except as Congress might impose restraints. . . . That which belongs to commerce is within the jurisdiction of the United States, but that which does not belong to commerce is within the jurisdiction of the police power of the state. ***

The argument is that the power to control the manufacture of refined sugar is a monopoly over a necessary of life, to the enjoyment of which by a large population of the United States interstate commerce is indispensable, and that, therefore, the general government in the exercise of the power to regulate commerce may repress such monopoly directly and set aside the instruments which have created it. But this argument cannot be confined to necessaries of life merely, and must include all articles of general consumption. Doubtless the power to control the manufacture of a given thing involves in a certain sense the control of its disposition, but this is a secondary and not the primary sense; and although the exercise of that power may result in bringing the operation of commerce into play, it does not control it, and affects it only incidentally and indirectly. Commerce succeeds to manufacture, and is not a part of it. The power to regulate commerce is the power to prescribe the rule by which commerce shall be governed, and is a power independent of the power to suppress monopoly. But it may operate in repression of monopoly whenever that comes within the rules by which commerce is governed or whenever the transaction is itself a monopoly of commerce.

It is vital that the independence of the commercial power and of the police power, and the delimitation between them, however sometimes perplexing, should always be recognized and observed, for while the one furnishes the strongest bond of union, the other is essential to the preservation of the autonomy of the states as required by our dual form of government; and acknowledged evils, however grave and urgent they may appear to be, had better be borne, than the risk be run, in the effort to suppress them, of more serious consequences by resort to expedients of even doubtful constitutionality.

It will be perceived how far reaching the proposition is that the power of dealing with a monopoly directly may be exercised by the general government whenever interstate or international commerce may be ultimately affected. The regulation of commerce applies to the subjects of commerce and not to matters of internal police. Contracts to buy, sell, or exchange goods to be transported among the several states ... may be regulated, but this is because they form part of interstate trade or commerce. The fact that an article is manufactured for export to another state does not of itself make it an article of interstate commerce, and the intent of the manufacture does not determine the time when the article or product passes from the control of the state and belongs to commerce....

Contracts, combinations, or conspiracies to control domestic enterprise in manufacture, agriculture, mining, production in all its forms, or to raise or lower prices or wages might unquestionably tend to restrain external as well as domestic trade, but the restraint would be an indirect result, however inevitable and whatever its extent, and such result would not necessarily determine the object of the contract, combination, or conspiracy.

Again, all the authorities agree that in order to vitiate a contract or combination it is not essential that its result should be a complete monopoly; it is sufficient if it really tends to that end and to deprive the public of the advantages which flow from free competition. Slight reflection will show that if the national power extends to all contracts and combinations in manufacture, agriculture, mining, and other productive industries, whose ultimate result may affect external commerce, comparatively little of business operations and affairs would be left for state control.

It was in the light of well settled principles that the Act of July 2, 1890, was framed. Congress did not attempt thereby to assert the power to deal with monopoly directly as such; or to limit and restrict the rights of corporations created by the states or the citizens of the states in the acquisition, control, or disposition of property; or to regulate or prescribe the price or prices at which such property or the products thereof should be sold; or to make criminal the acts of persons in the acquisition and control of property which the states of their residence or creation sanctioned or permitted.... [W]hat the law struck at was combinations, contracts, and conspiracies to monopolize trade and commerce among the several states or with foreign nations; but the contracts and acts of the defendants related exclusively to the acquisition of the Philadelphia refineries and the business of sugar refining in Pennsylvania, and bore no direct relation to commerce between the states or with foreign nations. The object was manifestly private gain in the manufacture of the commodity, but not through the control of interstate or foreign commerce. It is true that the bill alleged that the products of these refineries were sold and distributed among the several states, and that all the companies were engaged in trade or commerce with the several states and with foreign nations; but this was no more than to say that trade and commerce served manufacture to fulfill its function. Sugar was refined for sale, and sales were probably made at Philadelphia for consumption, and undoubtedly for resale by the first purchasers throughout Pennsylvania and other states, and refined sugar was also forwarded by the companies to other states for sale. Nevertheless it does not follow that an attempt to monopolize, or the actual monopoly of, the manufacture was an attempt, whether executory or consummated to monopolize commerce, even though, in order to dispose of the product, the instrumentality of commerce was necessarily invoked. There was nothing in the proofs to indicate any intention to put a restraint upon trade or commerce, and the fact, as we have seen, that trade or commerce might be indirectly affected was not enough to entitle [the government] to a decree. The subject matter of the sale was shares of manufacturing stock, and the relief sought was the surrender of property which had already passed and the suppression of the alleged monopoly in manufacture by the restoration of the status quo before the transfers, yet the Act of Congress only authorized the circuit courts to proceed by way of preventing and restraining violations of the Act in respect of contracts, combinations, or conspiracies in restraint of interstate or international trade or commerce. . . .

Decree affirmed.

Mr. Justice Harlan dissenting.

Prior to the 4th day of March, 1892, the American Sugar Refining Company, a corporation organized under a general statute of New Jersey for the purpose of buying, manufacturing, refining, and selling sugar in different parts of the country, had obtained the control of all the sugar refineries in the United States except five, of which four were owned and operated by Pennsylvania corporations—the E. C. Knight Company, the Franklin Sugar Refining Company, Spreckels' Sugar Refining Company, and the Delaware Sugar House—and the other, by the Revere Sugar Refinery of Boston. These five corporations were all in active competition with the American Sugar Refining Company and with each other. The product of the Pennsylvania companies was about thirty-three per cent, and that of the Boston company about two percent, of the entire quantity of sugar refined in the United States.

In March, 1892, by means of contacts or arrangements with stockholders of the four Pennsylvania companies, the New Jersey corporation—using for that purpose its own stock—purchased the stock of these companies, and thus obtained absolute control of the entire business of sugar refining in the United States except that done by the Boston company, which is too small in amount to be regarded in this discussion.

. . . In its consideration of the important constitutional question presented, this court assumes on the record before us that the result of the transactions disclosed by the pleadings and proof was the creation of a monopoly in the manufacture of a necessary of life. If this combination, so far as its operations necessarily or directly affect interstate commerce, cannot be restrained or suppressed under some power granted to Congress, it will be cause for regret that the patriotic statesmen who framed the Constitution did not foresee the necessity of investing the national government with power to deal with gigantic monopolies holding in their grasp, and injuriously controlling in their own interest, the entire trade among the states in food products that are essential to the comfort of every household in the land.

The Court holds it to be vital in our system of government to recognize and give effect to both the commercial power of the nation and the police powers of the states, to the end that the Union be strengthened and the autonomy of the states preserved. In this view I entirely concur. Undoubtedly, the preservation of the just authority of the states is an object of deep concern to every lover of his country. No greater calamity could befall our free institutions than the destruction of that authority, by whatever means such a result might be accomplished. . . . But it is equally true that the preservation of the just authority of the general government is essential as well to the safety of the states as to the attainment of the important ends for which that government was ordained by the people of the United States; and the destruction of that authority would be fatal to the peace and well-being of the American people. The Constitution which enumerates the powers committed to the nation for objects of interest to the people of all the states should not, therefore, be subjected to an interpretation so rigid, technical and narrow, that those objects cannot be accomplished. . . .

Congress is invested with power to regulate commerce with foreign nations and among the several states. . . .

. . . It is the settled doctrine of this court that interstate commerce embraces something more than the mere physical transportation of articles of property, and the vehicles or vessels by which such transportation is effected. . . . Interstate commerce does not consist in transportation simply. It includes the purchase and sale of articles that are intended to be transported from one state to another—every species of commercial intercourse among the states and with foreign nations. . . .

The fundamental inquiry in this case is, What, in a legal sense, is an unlawful restraint of trade? . . .

. . . [A] general restraint of trade has often resulted from combinations formed for the purpose of controlling prices by destroying the opportunity of buyers and sellers to deal with each other upon the basis of fair, open, free competition. Combinations of this character have frequently been the subject of judicial scrutiny, and have always been condemned as illegal because of their necessary tendency to restrain trade. Such combinations are against common right and are crimes against the public. . . .

The power of Congress covers and protects the absolute freedom of such intercourse and trade among the states as may or must succeed manufacture and precede transportation from the place of purchase. This would seem to be conceded; for, the Court in the present case expressly declare that "contracts to buy, sell, or exchange goods to be transported among the several states, the transportation and its instrumentalities, and articles, bought, sold, or exchanged for the purpose of such transit among the states, or put in the way of transit, may be regulated, but this is because they form part of interstate trade or commerce." Here is a direct admission— one which the settled doctrines of this court justify— that contracts to buy and the purchasing of goods to be transported from one state to another, and transportation, with its instrumentalities, are all parts of interstate trade or commerce. Each part of such trade is then under the protection of Congress. And yet, by the opinion and judgment in this case, if I do not misapprehend them, Congress is without power to protect the commercial intercourse that such purchasing necessarily involves against the restraints and burdens arising from the existence of combinations that meet purchasers from whatever state they come, with the threat—for it is nothing more nor less than a threat—that they shall not purchase what they desire to purchase, except at the prices fixed by such combinations. A citizen of Missouri has the right to go in person, or send orders, to Pennsylvania and New Jersey for the purpose of purchasing refined sugar. But of what value is that right if he is confronted in those states by a vast combination which absolutely controls the price of that article by reason of its having acquired all the sugar refineries in the United States in order that they may fix prices in their own interest exclusively?

In my judgment, the citizens of the several states composing the Union are entitled, of right, to buy goods in the state where they are manufactured, or in any other state, without being confronted by an illegal combination whose business extends throughout the whole country, which by the law everywhere is an enemy to the public interests, and which prevents such buying, except at prices arbitrarily fixed by it. I insist that the free course of trade among the states cannot coexist with such combinations. When I speak of trade I mean the buying and selling of articles of every kind that are recognized articles of interstate commerce. Whatever improperly obstructs the free course of interstate intercourse and trade, as involved in the buying and selling of articles to be carried from one state to another, may be reached by Congress, under its authority to regulate commerce among the states, the exercise of that authority so as to make trade among the states, in all recognized articles of commerce, absolutely free from unreasonable or illegal restrictions imposed by combinations, is justified by an express grant of power to Congress and would redound to the welfare of the whole country. I am unable to perceive that any such result would imperil the autonomy of the states, especially as that result cannot be attained through the action of any one state. . . .

While the opinion of the Court in this case does not declare the Act of 1890 to be unconstitutional, it defeats the main object for which it was passed. For, it is, in effect, held that the statute would be unconstitutional if interpreted as embracing such unlawful restraints upon the purchasing of goods in one state to be carried to another state as necessarily arise from the existence of combinations formed for the purpose and with the effect, not only [of] monopolizing the ownership of all such goods in every part of the country, but of controlling the prices for them in all the states. This view of the scope of the Act leaves the public, so far as national power is concerned, entirely at the mercy of combinations which arbitrarily control the prices of articles purchased to be transported from one state to another state. I cannot assent to that view. In my judgment, the general government is not placed by the Constitution in such a condition of helplessness that it must fold its arms and remain inactive while capital combines, under the name of a corporation, to destroy competition, not in one state only, but throughout the entire country, in the buying and selling of articles—especially the necessaries of life—that go into commerce among the states. The doctrine of the autonomy of the states cannot properly be invoked to justify a denial of power in the national government to meet such an emergency, involving as it does that freedom of commercial intercourse among the states which the Constitution sought to attain.

It is said that there are no proofs in the record which indicate an intention upon the part of the American Sugar Refining Company and its associates to put a restraint upon trade or commerce. Was it necessary that formal proof be made that the persons engaged in this combination admitted, in words, that they intended to restrain trade or commerce? Did anyone expect to find in the written agreements which resulted in the formation of this combination a distinct expression of a purpose to restrain interstate trade or commerce? Men who form and control these combinations are too cautious and wary to make such admissions orally or in writing. Why, it is conceded that the object of this combination was to obtain control of the business of making and selling refined sugar throughout the entire country. Those interested in its operations will be satisfied with nothing less than to have the whole population of America pay tribute to them. That object is disclosed upon the very face of the transactions described in the bill. And it is proved—indeed, is conceded—that that object has been accomplished to the extent that the American Sugar Refining Company now controls ninety-eight per cent of all the sugar refining business in the country, and therefore controls the price

of that article everywhere. Now, the mere existence of a combination having such an object and possessing such extraordinary power is itself, under settled principles of law—there being no adjudged case to the contrary in this country—a direct restraint of trade in the article for the control of the sales of which in this country that combination was organized. And that restraint is felt in all the states, for the reason, known to all, that the article in question goes, was intended to go, and must always go, into commerce among the several states, and into the homes of people in every condition of life....

We have before us the case of a combination which absolutely controls, or may, at its discretion, control the price of all refined sugar in this country. Suppose another combination, organized for private gain and to control prices, should obtain possession of all the large flour mills in the United States; another, of all the grain elevators; another, of all the oil territory; another, of all the salt-producing regions; another, of all the cotton mills; and another, of all the great establishments for slaughtering animals, and the preparation of meats. What power is competent to protect the people of the United States against such dangers except a national power—one that is capable of exerting its sovereign authority throughout every part of the territory and over all the people of the nation?

To the general government has been committed the control of commercial intercourse among the states, to the end that it may be free at all times from any restraints except such as Congress may impose or permit for the benefit of the whole country. The common government of all the people is the only one that can adequately deal with a matter which directly and injuriously affects the entire commerce of the country, which concerns equally all the people of the Union, and which, it must be confessed, cannot be adequately controlled by any one state. Its authority should not be so weakened by construction that it cannot reach and eradicate evils that, beyond all question, tend to defeat an object which that government is entitled, by the Constitution, to accomplish....

For the reasons stated I dissent from the opinion and judgment of the Court.

Carter v. Carter Coal Company

298 U.S. 238; 56 S. Ct. 855; 80 L. Ed. 1160 (1936)
Vote: 5-4

The Bituminous Coal Act of 1935 created a national commission with authority to regulate wages and prices for the coal industry. A 15 percent tax was levied on all coal sold at the mine, and producers who accepted the federal regulations were entitled to a 90 percent rebate of assessed taxes. Carter, a stockholder in the Carter Coal Company, brought suit seeking to enjoin the company from paying the tax or complying with the code.

Mr. Justice Sutherland delivered the opinion of the Court.

... The proposition, often advanced and as often discredited, that the power of the federal government inherently extends to purposes affecting the nation as a whole with which the states severally cannot deal or cannot adequately deal, and the related notion that Congress, entirely apart from the powers delegated by the Constitution, may enact laws to promote the general welfare, have never been accepted but always definitely rejected by this court. ...

... [T]he general purposes which the act recites ... are beyond the power of Congress except so far, and only so far, as they may be realized by an exercise of some specific power granted by the Constitution. ... [W]e shall find no grant of power which authorized Congress to legislate in respect of these general purposes unless it be found in the commerce clause— and this we now consider. ...

... [T]he word "commerce" is the equivalent of the phrase "intercourse for the purposes of trade." Plainly, the incidents leading up to and culminating in the mining of coal do not constitute such intercourse. The employment of men, the fixing of their wages, hours of labor and working conditions, the bargaining in respect of these things—whether carried on separately or collectively—each and all constitute intercourse for the purposes of production, not of trade. The latter is a thing apart from the relation of employer and employee, which in all producing occupations is purely local in character. Extraction of coal from the mine is the aim and the completed result of local activities. Commerce in the coal mined is not brought into being by force of these activities, but by negotiations, agreements, and circumstances entirely apart from production. Mining brings the subject matter of commerce into existence. Commerce disposes of it.

... [T]he effect of the labor provisions of the act, including those in respect of minimum wages, wage agreements, collective bargaining, and the Labor Board and its powers, primarily falls upon production and not upon commerce; and confirms the further resulting conclusion that production is a purely local activity. It follows that none of these essential antecedents of production constitutes a transaction in or forms any part of interstate commerce. *** ... Everything which moves in interstate commerce has had a local origin. Without local production somewhere, interstate commerce, as now carried on, would practically disappear. Nevertheless, the local character of mining, or manufacturing and of crop growing is a fact, and remains a fact, whatever may be done with the products. ...

That the production of every commodity intended for interstate sale and transportation has some effect upon interstate commerce may be, if it has not already been, freely granted; and we are brought to the final and decisive inquiry, whether here that effect is direct, as the "preamble" recites, or indirect. The distinction is not formal, but substantial in the highest degree, as we pointed out in the *Schechter* case. *** ...

Whether the effect of a given activity or condition is direct or indirect is not always easy to determine. The word "direct" implies that the activity or condition invoked or blamed shall operate proximately— not mediately, remotely, or collaterally—to produce the effect. It connotes the absence of an efficient intervening agency or condition. And the extent of the effect bears no logical relation to its character. The distinction between a direct and an indirect effect turns, not upon the magnitude of either the cause or the effect, but entirely upon the manner in which the effect has been brought about. If the production by one man of a single ton of coal intended for interstate sale and shipment, and actually so sold and shipped, affects interstate commerce indirectly, the effect does not become direct by multiplying the tonnage, or increasing the number of men employed, or adding to the expense or complexities of the business, or by all combined. It is quite true that rules of law are sometimes qualified by considerations of degree, as the government argues. But the matter of degree has no bearing upon the question here, since the question is not—What is the *extent* of the local activity or condition, or the *extent* of the effect produced upon interstate commerce? but—What is the *relation* between the activity or condition and the effect?

Much stress is put upon the evils which come from the struggle between employers and employees over the matter of wages, working conditions, the right of collective bargaining, etc., and the resulting strikes, curtailment and irregularity of production and effect on prices; and it is insisted that interstate commerce is *greatly* affected thereby. But, in addition to what has just been said, the conclusive answer is that the evils are all local evils over which the federal government has no legislative control. The relation of employer and employee is a local relation. . . . And the controversies and evils, which it is the object of the act to regulate and minimize, are local controversies and evils affecting local work undertaken to accomplish that local result. Such effect as they may have upon commerce, however extensive it may be, is secondary and indirect. An increase in the greatness of the effect adds to its importance. It does not alter its character. . . .

. . . [We] now declare, that the want of power on the part of the federal government is the same whether the wages, hours or service, and working conditions, and the bargaining about them, are related to production before interstate commerce has begun, or to sale and distribution after it has ended. . . .

Separate opinion of **Mr. Chief Justice Hughes** [dissenting]. . . .

The power to regulate interstate commerce embraces the power to protect that commerce from injury, whatever may be the source of the dangers which threaten it, and to adopt any appropriate means to that end. *** Congress thus has adequate authority to maintain the orderly conduct of interstate commerce and to provide for the peaceful settlement of disputes which threaten it. . . . But Congress may not use this protective authority as a pretext for the exertion of power to regulate activities and relations within the States which affect interstate commerce only indirectly. . . .

But . . . [t]he Act also provides for the regulation of the prices of bituminous coal sold in interstate commerce and prohibits unfair methods of competition in interstate commerce. Undoubtedly transactions in carrying on interstate commerce are subject to the federal power to regulate that commerce and the control of charges and the protection of fair competition in that commerce are familiar illustrations of the exercise of the power, as the Interstate Commerce Act, the Packers and Stockyards Act, and the Anti-Trust Acts abundantly show. . . .

. . . The marketing provisions in relation to interstate commerce can be carried out as provided in Part II without regard to the labor provisions contained in Part III. That fact, in the light of the congressional declaration of separability, should be considered of controlling importance.

In this view, the Act, and the Code for which it provides, may be sustained in relation to the provisions for marketing in interstate commerce, and the decisions of the courts below, so far as they accomplish that result, should be affirmed.

Mr. Justice Cardozo . . . [dissenting].

. . . I am satisfied that the Act is within the power of the central government in so far as it provides for minimum and maximum prices upon sales of bituminous coal in the transactions of interstate commerce and in those of intrastate commerce where interstate commerce is directly or intimately affected. Whether it is valid also in other provisions that have been considered and condemned in the opinion of the Court, I do not find it necessary to determine at this time. Silence must not be taken as importing acquiescence. . . .

Regulation of prices being an exercise of the commerce power in respect of interstate transactions, the question remains whether it comes within that power as applied to intrastate sales where interstate prices are directly or intimately affected. Mining and agriculture and manufacture are not interstate commerce considered by themselves, yet their relation to that commerce may be such that for the protection of the one there is need to regulate the other. *** Sometimes it is said that the relation must be "direct" to bring that power into play. In many circumstances such a description will be sufficiently precise to meet the needs of the occasion. But a great principle of constitutional law is not susceptible of comprehensive statement in an adjective. The underlying thought is merely this, that "the law is not indifferent to considerations of degree." *** It cannot be indifferent to them without an expansion of the commerce clause that would absorb or imperil the reserved powers of the states. At times, as in the case cited, the waves of causation will have radiated so far that their undulatory motion, if discernible at all, will be too faint or obscure, too broken by crosscurrents, to be heeded by the law. In such circumstances the holding is not directed at prices or wages considered in the abstract, but at prices or wages in particular conditions. The relation may be tenuous or the opposite according to the facts. Always the setting of the facts is to be viewed if one would know the closeness of the tie. Perhaps, if one group of adjectives is to be chosen in preference to another, "intimate" and "remote" will be found to be as good as any. At all events, "direct" and "indirect," even if accepted as sufficient, must not be read narrowly. *** A survey of the cases shows that the words have been interpreted with suppleness of adaptation and flexibility of meaning. The power is as broad as the need that evokes it.

One of the most common and typical instances of relating characterized as direct has been that between interstate and intrastate rates for carriers by rail where the local rates are so low as to divert business unreasonably from interstate competitors. In such circumstances Congress has the power to protect the business of its carriers against disintegrating encroachments. *** To be sure, the relation even then may be characterized as indirect if one is nice or over-liberal in the choice of words. Strictly speaking, the intrastate rates have a primary effect upon the intrastate traffic and not upon any other, though the repercussions of the competitive system may lead to secondary consequences affecting interstate traffic also. *** What the cases really mean is that the causal relation in such circumstances is so close and intimate and obvious as to permit it to be called direct without subjecting the word to an unfair or excessive strain. There is a like immediacy here. Within rulings the most orthodox, the prices for intrastate sales of coal have so inescapable a relation to those for interstate sales that a system of regulation for transactions of the one class is necessary to give adequate protection to the system of regulation adopted for the other. The argument is strongly pressed by intervening counsel that this may not be true in all communities or in exceptional conditions. If so, the operators unlawfully affected may show that the Act to that extent is invalid as to them. . . .

I am authorized to state that *Mr. Justice Brandeis* and *Mr. Justice Stone* join in this opinion.

National Labor Relations Board v. Jones & Laughlin Steel Corporation
301 U.S. 1; 57 S. Ct. 615; 81 L. Ed. 893 (1937)
Vote: 5-4

Mr. Chief Justice Hughes delivered the opinion of the Court.

In a proceeding under the National Labor Relations Act of 1935, the National Labor Relations Board found that the respondent, Jones & Laughlin Steel Corporation, had violated the Act by engaging in unfair labor practices affecting commerce. . . . The unfair labor practices charged were that the corporation was discriminating against members of the union with regard to hire and tenure of employment, and was coercing and intimidating its employees in order to interfere with their self-organization. The discriminatory and coercive action alleged was the discharge of certain employees.

The National Labor Relations Board, sustaining the charge, ordered the corporation to cease and desist from such discrimination and coercion, to offer reinstatement to ten of the employees named, to make good their losses in pay, and to post for thirty days notices that the corporation would not discharge or discriminate against members, or those desiring to become members, of the labor union. As the corporation failed to comply, the Board petitioned the Circuit Court of Appeals to enforce the order. The court denied the petition, holding that the order lay beyond the range of federal power. *** We granted *certiorari*.

The scheme of the National Labor Relations Act . . . may be briefly stated. The first section sets forth findings with respect to the injury to commerce resulting from the denial by employers of the right of employees to organize and from the refusal of employers to accept the procedure of collective bargaining. There follows a declaration that it is the policy of the United States to eliminate these causes of obstruction to the free flow of commerce. The Act then defines the terms it uses, including the terms "commerce" and "affecting commerce." *** It creates the National Labor Relations Board and prescribes its organization. *** It sets forth the right of employees to self-organization and to bargain collectively through representatives of their own choosing. *** It defines "unfair labor practices." *** It lays down rules as to the representation of employees for the purpose of collective bargaining. *** The board is empowered to prevent the described unfair labor practices affecting commerce and the Act prescribes the procedure to that end. The board is authorized to petition designated courts to secure the enforcement of its orders. The findings of the Board as to the facts, if supported by evidence, are to be conclusive. If either party on application to the court shows that additional evidence is material and that there were reasonable grounds for the failure to adduce such evidence in the hearings before the Board, the court may order the additional evidence to be taken. Any person aggrieved by a final order of the Board may obtain a review in the designated courts with the same procedure as in the case of an application by the Board for the enforcement of its order. *** The Board has broad powers of investigation. *** Interference with members of the Board or its agents in the performance of their duties is punishable by fine and imprisonment. *** Nothing in the Act is to be construed to interfere with the right to strike. . . .

The procedure in the instant case followed the statute. . . .

Contesting the ruling of the Board, [Jones & Laughlin] argues (1) that the Act is in reality a regulation of labor relations and not of interstate commerce; [and] (2) that the act can have no application to the respondent's relations with its production employees because they are not subject to regulation by the federal government. . . .

First. The scope of the Act. — The Act is challenged in its entirety as an attempt to regulate all industry, thus invading the reserved powers of the States over their local concerns. It is asserted that the references in the Act to interstate and foreign commerce are colorable at best; that the Act is not a true regulation of such commerce or of matters which directly affect it but on the contrary has the fundamental object of placing under the compulsory supervision of the federal government all industrial labor relations within the nation. . . .

If this conception of terms, intent and consequent inseparability were sound, the Act would necessarily fall by reason of the limitation upon the federal power which inheres in the constitutional grant, as well as because of the explicit reservation of the Tenth Amendment. *** The authority of the federal government may not be pushed to such an extreme as to destroy the distinction, which the commerce clause itself establishes, between commerce "among the several States" and the internal concerns of a State. That distinction between what is national and what is local in the activities of commerce is vital to the maintenance of our federal system. ***

But we are not at liberty to deny effect to specific provisions, which Congress has constitutional power to enact, by superimposing upon them inferences from general legislative declarations of an ambiguous character, even if found in the same statute. The cardinal principle of statutory construction is to save and not to destroy. We have repeatedly held that as between two possible interpretations of a statute, by one of which it would be unconstitutional and by the other valid, our plain duty is to adopt that which will save the act. . . .

We think it clear that the National Labor Relations Act may be construed so as to operate within the sphere of constitutional authority. . . .

There can be no question that the commerce . . . contemplated by the Act . . . is interstate and foreign commerce in the constitutional sense. The Act also defines the term "affecting commerce." *** . . .

This definition is one of exclusion as well as inclusion. The grant of authority to the Board does not purport to extend to the relationship between all industrial employees and employers. Its terms do not impose collective bargaining upon all industry regardless of effects upon interstate or foreign commerce. It purports to reach only what may be deemed to burden or obstruct that commerce and, thus qualified, it must be construed as contemplating the exercise or control within constitutional bounds. It is a familiar principle that acts which directly burden or obstruct interstate or foreign commerce, or its free flow, are within the reach of the congressional power. Acts having that effect are not rendered immune because they grow out of labor disputes. *** It is the effect upon commerce, not the source of the injury, which is the criterion. *** Whether or not particular action does affect commerce in such a close and intimate fashion as to be subject to federal control, and hence to lie within the authority conferred upon the Board, is left by the statute to be determined as individual cases arise. We are thus to inquire whether in the instant case the constitutional boundary has been passed.

Second. The unfair labor practices in question. . . .

. . . [I]n its present application, the statute goes no further than to safeguard the right of employees to self-organization and to select representatives of their own choosing for collective bargaining or other mutual protection without restraint or coercion by their employer.

That is a fundamental right. Employees have as clear a right to organize and select their representatives for lawful purposes as the respondent has to organize its business and select its own officers and agents. Discrimination and coercion to prevent the free exercise of the right of employees to self-organization and representation is a proper subject for condemnation by competent legislative authority. Long ago we stated the reason for labor organizations. We said that they were organized out of the necessities of the situation; that a single employee was helpless in dealing with an employer; that he was dependent ordinarily on his daily wage for the maintenance of himself and family; that if the employer refused to pay him the wages that he thought fair, he was nevertheless unable to leave the employ and resist arbitrary and unfair treatment; that union was essential to give laborers opportunity to deal on an equality with their employer. *** . . . Fully recognizing the legality of collective action on the part of employees in order to safeguard their proper interests, we said that Congress was not required to ignore this right but could safeguard it. Congress could seek to make appropriate collective action of employees an instrument of peace rather than of strife. We said that such collective action would be a mockery if representation were made futile by interference with freedom of choice. Hence the prohibition by Congress of interference with the selection of representatives for the purpose of negotiation and conference between employers and employees, "instead of being an invasion of the constitutional right of either, was based on the recognition of the rights of both." ***

Third. The application of the Act to employees engaged in production.—The principle involved.—Respondent [Jones & Laughlin Steel Corporation] says that whatever may be said of employees engaged in interstate commerce, the industrial relations and activities in the manufacturing department . . . are not subject to federal regulation. The argument rests upon the proposition that manufacturing in itself is not commerce. ***

. . . The various parts of respondent's enterprise are described as interdependent and as thus involving "a great movement of iron ore, coal and limestone along well-defined paths to the steel mills, thence through them, and thence in the form of steel products into the consuming centers of the country—a definite and well-understood course of business." It is urged that these activities constitute a "stream" or "flow" of commerce . . . and that industrial strife at [the central manufacturing plant of Jones & Laughlin] would cripple the entire movement. *** . . .

We do not find it necessary to determine whether these features of [Jones & Laughlin's] business dispose of the asserted analogy to the "stream of commerce" cases. The instances in which that metaphor has been used are but particular, and not exclusive, illustrations of the protection power which the Government invokes in support of the present Act. The congressional authority to protect interstate commerce from burdens and obstructions is not limited to transactions which can be deemed to be an essential part of a "flow" of interstate or foreign commerce. Burdens and obstructions may be due to injurious action springing from other sources. The fundamental principle is that the power to regulate commerce is the power to enact "all appropriate legislation" for "its protection and advancement"; *** to adopt measures "to promote its growth and insure its safety"; *** "to foster, protect, control and restrain." *** That power is plenary and may be exerted to protect interstate commerce "no matter what the source of the dangers which threaten it." *** Although activities may be intrastate in character when separately considered, if they have such a close and substantial relation to interstate commerce that their control is essential or appropriate to protect that commerce from burdens and obstructions, Congress cannot be denied the power to exercise that control. *** Undoubtedly the scope of this power must be considered in the light of our dual system of government and may not be extended so as to embrace effects upon interstate commerce so indirect and remote that to embrace them, in view of our complex society, would effectually obliterate the distinction between what is national and what is local and create a completely centralized government. *** The question is necessarily one of degree. . . .

That intrastate activities, by reason of close and intimate relation to interstate commerce, may fall within federal control is demonstrated in the case of carriers who are engaged in both interstate and intrastate transportation. There federal control has been found essential to secure the freedom of interstate traffic from interference or unjust discrimina-

tion and to promote the efficiency of the interstate service. *** It is manifest that intrastate rates deal primarily with a local activity. But in rate-making they bear such a close relation to interstate rates that effective control of the one must embrace some control over the other. . . .

The close and intimate effect which brings the subject within the reach of federal power may be due to activities in relation to productive industry although the industry when separately viewed is local. . . .

It is . . . apparent that the fact that the employees here concerned were engaged in production is not determinative. The question remains as to the effect upon interstate commerce of the labor practice involved. In the *Schechter* case, *** we found that the effect there was so remote as to be beyond the federal power. To find "immediacy or directness" there was to find it "almost everywhere," a result inconsistent with the maintenance of our federal system. In the *Carter* case, *** the Court was of the opinion that the provisions of the statute relating to production were invalid upon several grounds,—that there was improper delegation of legislative power, and that the requirements not only went beyond any sustainable measure of protection of interstate commerce but were also inconsistent with due process. These cases are not controlling here.

Fourth. Effects of the unfair labor practice in respondent's enterprise.—. . . [T]he stoppage of [Jones & Laughlin's] operations by industrial strife would have a most serious effect upon interstate commerce. In view of respondent's far-flung activities, it is idle to say that the effect would be indirect or remote. It is obvious that it would be immediate and might be catastrophic. We are asked to shut our eyes to the plainest facts of our national life and to deal with the question of direct and indirect effects in an intellectual vacuum. Because there may be but indirect and remote effects upon interstate commerce in connection with a host of local enterprises throughout the country, it does not follow that other industrial activities do not have such a close and intimate relation to interstate commerce as to make the presence of industrial strife a matter of the most urgent national concern. When industries organize themselves on a national scale, making their relation to interstate commerce the dominant factor in their activities, how can it be maintained that their industrial labor relations constitute a forbidden field into which Congress may not enter when it is necessary to protect interstate commerce from the paralyzing consequences of industrial war? We have often said that interstate commerce itself is a practical conception. It is equally true that interferences with that commerce must be appraised by a judgment that does not ignore actual experience.

Experience has abundantly demonstrated that the recognition of the right of employees to self-organization and to have representatives of their own choosing for the purpose of collective bargaining is often an essential condition of industrial peace. Refusal to confer and negotiate has been one of the most prolific causes of strife. This is such an outstanding fact in the history of labor disturbances that it is a proper subject of judicial notice and requires no citation of instances. . . .

These questions have frequently engaged the attention of Congress and have been the subject of many inquiries. The steel industry is one of the great basic industries of the United States, with ramifying activities affecting interstate commerce at every point. . . . It is not necessary again to detail the facts as to respondent's enterprise. Instead of being beyond the pale, we think that it presents in a most striking way the close and intimate relation which a manufacturing industry may have to interstate commerce and we have no doubt that Congress had constitutional authority to safeguard the right of [Jones & Laughlin's] employees to self-organization and freedom in the choice of representatives for collective bargaining. . . .

Our conclusion is that the order of the Board was within its competency and that the act is valid as here applied. The judgment of the Circuit Court of Appeals is reversed and the cause is remanded for further proceedings in conformity with this opinion.

Reversed.

Mr. Justice McReynolds delivered the following dissenting opinion.

Mr. Justice Van Devanter, Mr. Justice Sutherland, Mr. Justice Butler and I are unable to agree with the [decision] just announced. . . .

Considering [its] far-reaching import . . . , the departure from what we understand has been consistently ruled here, and the extraordinary power confirmed to a Board of three, the obligation to present our views becomes plain. . . .

Any effect on interstate commerce by the discharge of employees shown here, would be indirect and remote in the highest degree, as consideration of the facts will show. In [this case] ten men out of ten thousand were discharged. . . . The immediate effect in the factory may be to create discontent among all those employed and a strike may follow, which, in turn, may result in reducing production, which ultimately may reduce the volume of goods moving in interstate commerce. By this chain of indirect and progressively remote events we finally reach the evil with which it is said the legislation under consideration undertakes to deal. A more remote and indirect interference with interstate commerce or a more definite invasion of the powers reserved to the states is difficult, if not impossible, to imagine.

The Constitution still recognizes the existence of states with indestructible powers; the Tenth Amendment was supposed to put them beyond controversy.

We are told that Congress may protect the "stream of commerce" and that one who buys raw material without the state, manufactures it therein, and ships the output to another state is in that stream. Therefore it is said he may be prevented from doing anything which may interfere with its flow.

This, too, goes beyond the constitutional limitations heretofore enforced. If a man raises cattle and regularly delivers them to a carrier for interstate shipment, may Congress prescribe the conditions under which he may employ or discharge helpers on the ranch? The products of a mine pass daily into interstate commerce; many things are brought to it from other states. Are the owners and the miners within the power of Congress in respect of the miners' tenure and discharge? May a mill owner be prohibited from closing his factory or discontinuing his business because to do so would stop the flow of products to and from his plant in interstate commerce? May employees in a factory be restrained from quitting work in a body because this will close the factory and thereby stop the flow of commerce? May arson of a factory be made a Federal offense whenever this would interfere with such flow? If the business cannot continue with the existing wage scale, may Congress command a reduction? If the ruling of the Court just announced is adhered to, these questions suggest some of the problems certain to arise.

And if this theory of a continuous "stream of commerce" as now defined is correct, will it become the duty of the Federal Government hereafter to suppress every strike which by possibility may cause a blockage in that stream? *** Moreover, since Congress has intervened, are labor relations between most manufacturers and their employees removed from all control by the State? *** . . .

There is no ground on which reasonably to hold that refusal by a manufacturer, whose raw materials come from states other than that of his factory and whose products are regularly carried to other states, to bargain collectively with employees in his manufacturing plant, directly affects interstate commerce. In such business, there is not one but two distinct movements or streams in interstate transportation. The first brings in raw material and there ends. Then follows manufacture, a separate and local activity. Upon completion of this, and not before, the second distinct movement or stream in interstate commerce begins and the products go to their states. Such is the common course for small as well as large industries. It is unreasonable and unprecedented to say the commerce clause confers upon Congress power to govern relations between employers and employees in these local activities. *** In Schechter's case we condemned as unauthorized by the commerce clause the assertion of federal power in respect of commodities which had come to rest after interstate transportation. And, in Carter's case, we held Congress lacked power to regulate labor relations in respect of commodities before interstate commerce has begun.

It is gravely stated that experience teaches that if any employer discourages membership in "any organization of any kind" "in which employees participate, and which exists for the purpose in whole or in part of dealing with employers concerning grievances, labor disputes, wages, rates of pay, hours of employment or conditions of work," discontent may follow and this in turn may lead to a strike, and as the outcome of the strike there may be a block in the stream of interstate commerce. Therefore Congress may inhibit the discharge! Whatever effect any cause of discontent may ultimately have upon commerce is far too indirect to justify Congressional regulations. Almost anything—marriage, birth, death—may in some fashion affect commerce.

That Congress has power by appropriate means, not prohibited by the Constitution, to prevent direct and material interference with the conduct of interstate commerce is settled doctrine. But the interference struck at must be direct and material, not some mere possibility contingent on wholly uncertain events; and there must be no impairment of rights guaranteed. . . .

The right to contract is fundamental and includes the privilege of selecting those with whom one is willing to assume contractual relations. This right is unduly abridged by the act now upheld. A private owner is deprived of power to manage his own property by freely selecting those to whom his manufacturing operations are to be entrusted. We think this cannot lawfully be done in circumstances like those here disclosed.

It seems clear to us that Congress has transcended the powers granted.

Wickard v. Filburn

317 U.S. 111; 63 S. Ct. 82; 87 L. Ed. 122 (1942)
Vote: 9-0

Mr. Justice Jackson delivered the opinion of the Court.

. . . [Roscoe C. Filburn] for many years past has owned and operated a small farm in Montgomery Country, Ohio, maintaining a herd of dairy cattle, selling milk, raising poultry, and selling poultry and eggs. It has been his practice to raise a small acreage of winter wheat, sown in the Fall and harvested in the following July; to sell a portion of the crop; to feed part to poultry and livestock on the farm, some of which is sold; to use some in making flour for home consumption; and to keep the rest for the following seeding. The intended disposition of the crop here involved has not been expressly stated.

In July of 1940, pursuant to the Agricultural Adjustment Act of 1938, as then amended, there were established for [Filburn's] 1941 crop a wheat acreage allotment of 11.1 acres and a normal yield of 20.1 bushels of wheat an acre. He was given notice of such allotment in July of 1940 before the Fall planting of his 1941 crop of wheat, and again in July of 1941, before it was harvested. He sowed, however, 23 acres, and harvested from his 11.9 acres of excess acreage 239 bushels, which under the terms of the Act . . . constituted farm marketing excess, subject to a penalty of 49 cents a bushel, or $117.11 in all. [Filburn] has not paid the penalty and he has not postponed or avoided it by storing the excess under regulations of the Secretary of Agriculture. . . .

The general scheme of the Agricultural Adjustment Act of 1938 as related to wheat is to control the volume moving in interstate and foreign commerce in order to avoid surpluses and shortages and the consequent abnormally low or high wheat prices and obstructions to commerce. Within prescribed limits and by prescribed standards the Secretary of Agriculture is directed to ascertain and proclaim each year a national acreage allotment for the next crop of wheat, which is then apportioned to the states and their counties, and is eventually broken up into allotments for individual farms. Loans and payments to wheat farmers are authorized in stated circumstances.

The Act provides further that whenever it appears that the total supply of wheat as of the beginning of any marketing year . . . will exceed a normal year's domestic consumption and export . . . a compulsory national marketing quota shall be in effect with respect to the marketing of wheat. . . . [T]he Secretary must . . . conduct a referendum of farmers who will be subject to the quota to determine whether they favor or oppose it; and if more than one third of the farmers voting in the referendum do oppose, the Secretary must prior to the effective date of the quota by proclamation suspend its operation. . . .

Pursuant to the Act, the referendum of wheat growers was held on May 31, 1941. According to the required published statement of the Secretary of Agriculture, 81 per cent of those voting favored the marketing quota, with 19 per cent opposed. . . .

It is urged that under the Commerce Clause of the Constitution, Article I, Sec. 8, clause 3, Congress does not possess the power it has in this instance sought to exercise. The question would merit little consideration since our decision in *United States v. Darby* *** sustaining the federal power to regulate production of goods for commerce except for the fact that this Act extends federal regulation to production not intended in any part for commerce but wholly for consumption on the farm. The Act includes a definition of "market" and its derivatives so that as related to wheat in addition to its conventional meaning it also means to dispose of "by feeding (in any form) to poultry or livestock which, or the products of which, are sold, bartered, or exchanged, or to be so disposed of." Hence, marketing quotas not only embrace all that may be sold without penalty but also what may be consumed on the premises. Wheat produced on excess acreage is designated as "available for marketing" as so defined and the penalty is imposed thereon. Penalties do not depend upon whether any part of the wheat either within or without the quota is sold or intended to be sold. The sum of this is that the Federal Government fixes a quota including all that the farmer may harvest for sale or for his own farm needs, and declares that wheat produced on excess acreage may neither be disposed of nor used except upon payment of the penalty or except it is stored as required by the Act or delivered to the Secretary of Agriculture.

[Filburn] says that this is a regulation of production and consumption of wheat. Such activities are, he urges, beyond the reach of congressional power under the Commerce Clause, since they are local in character, and their effects upon interstate commerce are at most "indirect." In answer the Government argues that the statute regulates neither production nor consumption, but only marketing; and, in the alternative, that if the Act does go beyond the regulation of marketing it is sustainable as a "necessary and proper" implementation of the power of Congress over interstate commerce.

The Government's concern lest the Act be held to be a regulation of production or consumption rather than of marketing is attributable to a few *dicta* and decisions of this Court which might be understood to lay it down that activities such as "production," "manufacturing," and "mining" are strictly "local" and, except in special circumstances which are not present here, cannot be regulated under the commerce power because their effects upon interstate commerce are, as matter of law, only "indirect." Even today, when this power has been held to have great latitude, there is no decision of this Court that such activities may be regulated where no part of the product is intended for interstate commerce or intermingled with the subjects thereof. We believe that a review of the course of decision under the Commerce Clause will make plain, however, that questions of the power of Congress are not to be decided by reference to any formula which would give controlling force to nomenclature such as "production" and "indirect" and foreclose consideration of the actual effects of the activity in question upon interstate commerce.

At the beginning Chief Justice Marshall described the federal commerce power with a breadth never yet exceeded. *** He made emphatic the embracing and penetrating nature of this power by warning that effective restraints on its exercise must proceed from political rather than from judicial processes. ***

For nearly a century, however, decisions of this Court under the Commerce Clause dealt rarely with questions of what Congress might do in the exercise of its granted power under the Clause and almost entirely with the permissibility of state activity which it was claimed discriminated against or burdened interstate commerce. During this period there was perhaps little occasion for the affirmative exercise of the commerce power, and the influence of the Clause on American life and law was a negative one, resulting almost wholly from its operation as a restraint upon the powers of the states. In discussion and decision the point of reference, instead of being what was "necessary and proper" to the exercise by Congress of its granted power, was often some concept of sovereignty thought to be implicit in the status of statehood. Certain activities such as "production," "manufacturing," and "mining" were occasionally said to be within the province of state governments and beyond the power of Congress under the Commerce Clause.

It was not until 1887 with the enactment of the Interstate Commerce Act that the interstate commerce power began to exert positive influence in American law and life. This first important federal resort to the commerce power was followed in 1890 by the Sherman Anti-Trust Act and, thereafter, mainly after 1903, by many others. These statutes ushered in new phases of adjudication, which required the Court to approach the interpretation of the Commerce Clause in the light of an actual exercise by Congress of its power thereunder.

When it first dealt with this new legislation, the Court adhered to its earlier pronouncements, and allowed but little scope to the power of Congress. *** ...

Even while important opinions in this line of restrictive authority were being written, however, other cases called forth broader interpretations of the Commerce Clause destined to supersede the earlier ones,—and to bring about a return to the principles first enunciated by Chief Justice Marshall in *Gibbons v. Ogden.* *** ...

The Court's recognition of the relevance of the economic effects in the application of the Commerce Clause ... has made the mechanical application of legal formulas no longer feasible. Once an economic measure of the reach of the power granted to Congress in the Commerce Clause is accepted, questions of federal power cannot be decided simply by finding the activity in question to be "production" nor can consideration of its economic effects be foreclosed by calling them "indirect." ...

Whether the subject of the regulation in question was "production," "consumption," or "marketing" is, therefore, not material for purposes of deciding the question of federal power before us. That an activity is of local character may help in a doubtful case to determine whether Congress intended to reach it. The same consideration might help in determining whether in the absence of congressional action it would be permissible for the state to exert its power on the subject matter, even though in so doing it to some degree affected interstate commerce. But even if [Filburn's] activity be local and though it may not be regarded as commerce, it may still, whatever its nature, be reached by Congress if it exerts a substantial economic effect on interstate commerce, and this irrespective of whether such effect is what might at some earlier time have been defined as "direct" or "indirect." . . .

The wheat industry has been a problem industry for some years. . . . The decline in the export trade has left a large surplus in production which in connection with an abnormally large supply of wheat and other grains in recent years caused congestion in a number of markets; tied up railroad cars; and caused elevators in some instances to turn away grains, and railroads to institute embargoes to prevent further congestion. . . .

In the absence of regulation the price of wheat in the United States would be much affected by world conditions. . . .

The effect of consumption of home-grown wheat on interstate commerce is due to the fact that it constitutes the most variable factor in the disappearance of the wheat crop. Consumption on the farm where grown appears to vary in an amount greater than 20 per cent of average production. The total amount of wheat consumed as food varies but relatively little, and use as seed is relatively constant.

The maintenance by government regulation of a price for wheat undoubtedly can be accomplished as effectively by sustaining or increasing the demand as by limiting the supply. The effect of the statute before us is to restrict the amount which may be produced for market and the extent as well to which one may forestall resort to the market by producing to meet his own needs. That [Filburn's] own contribution to the demand for wheat may be trivial by itself is not enough to remove him from the scope of federal regulation where, as here, his contribution, taken together with that of many others similarly situated, is far from trivial. ***

It is well established by decisions of this Court that the power to regulate commerce includes the power to regulate the prices at which commodities in that commerce are dealt in and practices affecting such prices. One of the primary purposes of the Act in question was to increase the market price of wheat and to that end to limit the volume thereof that could affect the market. It can hardly be denied that a factor of such volume and variability as home-consumed wheat would have a substantial influence on price and market conditions. This may arise because being in marketable condition such wheat overhangs the market and if induced by rising prices tends to flow into the market and check price increases. But if we assume that it is never marketed, it supplies a need of the man who grew it which would otherwise be reflected by purchases in the open market. Home-grown wheat in this sense competes with wheat in commerce. The stimulation of commerce is a use of the regulatory function quite as definitely as prohibitions or restrictions thereon. This record leaves us in no doubt that Congress may properly have considered that wheat consumed on the farm where grown if wholly outside the scheme of regulation would have a substantial effect in defeating and obstructing its purpose to stimulate trade therein at increased prices.

It is said, however, that this Act, forcing some farmers into the market to buy what they could provide for themselves, is an unfair promotion of the markets and prices of specializing wheat growers. It is of the essence of regulation that it lays a restraining hand on the self-interest of the regulated and that advantages from the regulation commonly fall to others. The conflicts of economic interest between the regulated and those who advantage by it are wisely left under our system to resolution by the Congress under its more flexible and responsible legislative process. Such conflicts rarely lend themselves to judicial determination. And with the wisdom, workability, or fairness, of the plan of regulation we have nothing to do. . . .

Heart of Atlanta Motel v. United States

379 U.S. 241; 85 S. Ct. 348; 13 L. Ed. 2d 258 (1964)
Vote: 9-0

As the Supreme Court held in The Civil Rights Cases, *109 U.S. 3 (1883), Congress cannot use its power to enforce the Fourteenth Amendment to outlaw racial discrimination by privately owned places of public accommodation unless there is some significant degree of official state action supporting the discriminatory practices. Thus, in the 1964 Civil Rights Act, Congress sought to prohibit racial discrimination by hotels, restaurants, and other public facilities by invoking its broad authority to regulate interstate commerce. The constitutionality of this approach is before the Supreme Court in this case.*

Mr. Justice Clark delivered the opinion of the Court.

. . . Appellant owns and operates the Heart of Atlanta Motel which has 216 rooms available to transient guests. The motel is located on Courtland Street, two blocks from downtown Peachtree Street. It is readily accessible to interstate highways 75 and 85 and state highways 23 and 41. Appellant solicits patronage from outside the State of Georgia through various national advertising media, including magazines of national circulation; it maintains over 50 billboards and highway signs within the State, soliciting patronage for the motel; it accepts convention trade from outside Georgia and approximately 75% of its registered guests are from out of State. Prior to passage of the [Civil Rights Act of 1964] the motel had followed a practice of refusing to rent rooms to Negroes, and it alleged that it intended to continue to do so. In an effort to perpetuate that policy this suit was filed.

The appellant contends that Congress in passing [the Civil Rights Act] exceeded its power to regulate commerce under Art. I, Sec. 8, cl. 3, of the Constitution of the United States; that the Act violates the Fifth Amendment because appellant is deprived of the right to choose its customers and operate its business as it wishes, resulting in a taking of its liberty and property without due process of law and a taking of its property without just compensation; and, finally, that by requiring appellant to rent available rooms to Negroes against its will. Congress is subjecting it to involuntary servitude in contravention of the Thirteenth Amendment.

The appellees counter that the unavailability to Negroes of adequate accommodations interferes significantly with interstate travel, and that Congress, under the Commerce Clause, has power to remove such obstructions and restraints; that the Fifth Amendment does not forbid reasonable regulation and that consequential damage does not constitute a "taking" within the meaning of that amendment; that the Thirteenth Amendment claim fails because it is entirely frivolous to say that an amendment directed to the abolition of human bondage and the removal of widespread disabilities associated with slavery places discrimination in public accommodations beyond the reach of both federal and state law. . . .

. . . Title [II of the Civil Rights Act] is divided into seven sections beginning with Sec. 201 (a) which provides that:

All persons shall be entitled to the full and equal enjoyment of the goods, services, facilities, privileges, advantages, and accommodations of any place of public accommodation, as defined in this section without discrimination or segregation on the ground of race, color, religion, or national origin.

There are listed in 201 (b) four classes of business establishments, each of which "serves the public" and "is a place of public accommodation" within the meaning of 201 (a) "if its operation affects commerce, or if discrimination or segregation by it is supported by State action." The covered establishments are:

(1) any inn, hotel, motel, or other establishment which provides lodging to transient guests. . . .
(2) any restaurant, cafeteria . . . [not here involved];
(3) any motion picture house . . . [not here involved]
(4) any establishment . . . which is physically located within the premises of any establishment otherwise covered by this subsection, or . . . within the premises of which is physically located any such covered establishment . . . [not here involved].

Section 201 (c) defines the phrase "affect commerce" as applied to the above establishments. It first declares that "any inn, hotel, motel, or other establishment which provides lodging to transient guests" affects commerce per se. . . .

It is admitted that the operation of the motel brings it within the provisions of 201 (a) of the Act and that appellant refused to provide lodging for transient Negroes because of their race or color and that it intends to continue that policy unless restrained.

The sole question posed is, therefore, the constitutionality of the Civil Rights Act of 1964 as applied to these facts. The legislative history of the Act indicates that Congress based on the Act on Sec. 5 and the Equal Protection Clause of the Fourteenth Amendment as well as its power to regulate interstate commerce under Art. I, Sec. 8, cl. 3, of the Constitution.

The Senate Commerce Committee made it quite clear that the fundamental object of Title II was to vindicate "the deprivation of personal dignity that surely accompanies denials of equal access to public establishments." At the same time, however, it noted that such an objective has been and could be readily achieved "by congressional action based on the commerce power of the Constitution." *** Our study of the legislative record, made in the light of prior cases, has brought us to the conclusion that Congress possessed ample power in this regard, and we have therefore not considered the other grounds relied upon. This is not to say that the remaining authority upon which is acted was not adequate, a question upon which we do not pass, but merely that since the commerce power is sufficient for our decision here we have considered it alone. . . .

While the Act as adopted carried no congressional findings, the record of its passage through each house is replete with evidence of the burdens that discrimination by race or color places upon interstate commerce. *** This testimony included the fact that our people have become increasingly mobile with millions of people of all races traveling from State to State; that Negroes in particular have been the subject of discrimination in transient accommodations, having to travel great distances to secure the same; that often they have been unable to obtain accommodations and have had to call upon friends to put them up overnight, *** and that these conditions had become so acute as to require the listing of available lodging for Negroes in a special guidebook which was itself "dramatic testimony to the difficulties" Negroes encounter in travel. *** These exclusionary practices were found to be nationwide, the Under Secretary of Commerce testifying that there is "no question that this discrimination in the North still exists to a large degree" and in the West and Midwest as well. *** This testimony indicated a qualitative as well as quantitative effect on interstate travel by Negroes. The former was the obvious impairment of the Negro traveler's pleasure and convenience that resulted when he continually was uncertain of finding lodging. As for the latter, there was evidence that this uncertainty stemming from racial discrimination had the effect of discouraging travel on the part of a substantial portion of the Negro community. *** This was the conclusion not only of the Under Secretary of Commerce but also of the Administrator of the Federal Aviation Agency who wrote the Chairman of the Senate Commerce Committee that it was his "belief that air commerce is adversely affected by the denial to a substantial segment of the traveling public of adequate and desegregated public accommodations." *** [T]he voluminous testimony presents overwhelming evidence that discrimination by hotels and motels impedes interstate travel.

The power of Congress to deal with these obstructions depends on the meaning of the Commerce Clause. . . . [T]he determinative test of the exercise of power by the Congress under the Commerce Clause is simply whether the activity sought to be regulated is "commerce which concerns more States than one" and has a real and substantial relation to the national interest. Let us now turn to this facet of the problem.

That the "intercourse" of which the Chief Justice spoke included the movement of persons through more States than one was settled as early as 1849, in the Passenger Cases, *** where Mr. Justice McLean stated: "That the transportation of passengers is a part of commerce is not now an open question." ***

The same interest in protecting interstate commerce which led Congress to deal with segregation in interstate carriers and the white-slave traffic has prompted it to extend the exercise of its power to gambling, *** to deceptive practices in the sale of products, *** to fraudulent security transactions, *** to misbranding of drugs, *** to wages and hours, *** to members of labor unions, *** to crop control, *** to discrimination against shippers, *** to the protection of small business from injurious price cutting, *** to resale price maintenance, *** to professional football, *** and to racial discrimination by owners and managers of terminal restaurants. ***

That Congress was legislating against moral wrongs in many of these areas rendered its enactments no less valid. In framing Title II of this Act Congress was also dealing with what it considered a moral problem. But that fact does not detract from the overwhelming evidence of the disruptive effect that racial discrimination has had on commercial intercourse. It was this burden which empowered Congress to enact appropriate legislation, and, given this basis for the exercise of its power, Congress was not restricted by the fact that the particular obstruction to interstate commerce with which it was dealing was also deemed a moral and social wrong.

It is said that the operation of the motel here is of a purely local character. But, assuming this to be true, "[i]f it is interstate commerce that feels the pinch, it does not matter how local the operation which applies the squeeze." *** Thus the power of Congress to promote interstate commerce also included the power to regulate the local incidents thereof, including local activities in both the States of origin and destination, which might have a substantial and harmful effect upon that commerce. One need only examine the evidence which we have discussed above to see that Congress may—as it has—prohibit racial discrimination by motels serving travelers, however "local" their operations may appear. . . .

We, therefore, conclude that the action of the Congress in the adoption of the Act as applied here to a motel which concededly serves interstate travelers is within the power granted it by the Commerce Clause of the Constitution, as interpreted by this Court for 140 years. It may be argued that Congress could have pursued other methods to eliminate the obstructions it found in interstate commerce caused by racial discrimination. But this is a matter of policy that rests entirely with the Congress, not with the courts. How obstructions in commerce may be removed—what means are to be employed—is within the sound and exclusive discretion of the Congress. It is subject only to one caveat—that the means chosen by it must be reasonably adapted to the end permitted by the Constitution. We cannot say that its choice here was not so adapted. The Constitution requires no more.

Mr. Justice Black, concurring. . . .

Mr. Justice Douglas, concurring.

Though I join the Court's opinion, I am somewhat reluctant here . . . to rest solely on the Commerce Clause. My reluctance is not due to any conviction that Congress lacks power to regulate commerce in the interests of human rights. It is rather my belief that the right of people to be free of state action that discriminates against them because of race, like the "right of persons to move freely from State to State" *** "occupies a more protected position in our constitutional system than does the movement of cattle, fruit, steel, and coal across state lines." *** . . .

Hence I would prefer to test on the assertion of legislative power contained in Sec. 5 of the Fourteenth Amendment which states: "The Congress shall have power to enforce, by appropriate legislation, the provisions of this article"—a power which the Court concedes was exercised at least in part in this Act.

A decision based on the Fourteenth Amendment would have a more settling effect, making unnecessary litigation over whether a particular customer is an interstate traveler. Under my construction, the Act would apply to all customers in all the enumerated places of public accommodation. And that construction would put an end to all obstructionist strategies and finally close one door on a bitter chapter in American history. . . .

Katzenbach v. McClung

379 U.S. 294; 85 S. Ct. 377; 13 L. Ed. 2d 290 (1964)

Vote: 9-0

Mr. Justice Clark delivered the opinion of the Court.

This case was argued with ... *Heart of Atlanta Motel v. United States,* *** in which we upheld the constitutional validity of Title II of the Civil Rights Act of 1964 against an attack by hotels, motels, and like establishments. ...

Ollie's Barbecue is a family-owned restaurant in Birmingham, Alabama, specializing in barbecued meats and homemade pies, with a seating capacity of 220 customers. It is located on a state highway 11 blocks from an interstate ... and a somewhat greater distance from railroad and bus stations. The restaurant caters to a family and white-collar trade with a take-out service for Negroes. It employs 36 persons, two-thirds of whom are Negroes.

In the 12 months preceding the passage of the Act, the restaurant purchased locally approximately $150,000 worth of food, $69,683 or 46% of which was meat that it bought from a local supplier who had procured it from outside the State. The district Court expressly found that a substantial portion of the food served in the restaurant had moved in interstate commerce. The restaurant has refused to serve Negroes in its dining accommodations since its original opening in 1927, and since July 2, 1964, it has been operating in violation of the Act. The court below concluded that if it were required to serve Negroes it would lose a substantial amount of business.

... The activities that are beyond the reach of Congress are "those which are completely within a particular State, which do not affect other states, and with which it is not necessary to interfere, for the purpose of executing some of the general powers of the government." *Gibbons v. Ogden* *** (1824). This rule is as good today as it was when Chief Justice Marshall laid it down almost a century and a half ago.

This Court has held time and again that this power extends to activities of retail establishments, including restaurants, which directly or indirectly burden or obstruct interstate commerce. ...

Nor are the cases holding that interstate commerce ends when goods come to rest in the State of destination apposite here. That line of cases has been applied with reference to state taxation or regulation but not in the field of federal regulation. ...

Here, as there, Congress has determined for itself that refusals of service to Negroes have imposed burdens both upon the interstate flow of food and upon the movement of products generally. Of course, the mere fact that Congress has said when particular activity shall be deemed to affect commerce does not preclude further examination by this Court. But where we find that the legislators, in light of the facts and testimony before them, have a rational basis for finding a chosen regulatory scheme necessary to the protection of commerce, our investigation is at an end. The only remaining question—one answered in the affirmative by the court below—is whether the particular restaurant either serves or offers to serve interstate travelers or serves food a substantial portion of which has moved in interstate commerce. ...

Confronted as we are with the facts laid before Congress, we must conclude that it had a rational basis for finding that racial discrimination in restaurants had a direct and adverse effect on the free flow of interstate commerce. ...

The power of Congress in this field is broad and sweeping; where it keeps within its sphere and violates no express constitutional limitation it has been the rule of this Court, going back almost to the founding days of the Republic, not to interfere. The Civil Rights Act of 1964, as here applied, we find to be plainly appropriate in the resolution of what the Congress found to be a national commercial problem of the first magnitude. We find it in no violation of any express limitations of the Constitution and we therefore declare it valid. ...

United States v. Butler

297 U.S. 1; 56 S. Ct. 312; 80 L. Ed. 477 (1936)
Vote: 6-3

Mr. Justice Roberts delivered the opinion of the Court.

In this case we must determine whether certain provisions of the Agricultural Act of 1933 conflict with the federal Constitution. . . .

On July 14, 1933, the Secretary of Agriculture, with the approval of the President, proclaimed that he had determined rental and benefit payments should be made with respect to cotton; that the marketing year for that commodity was to begin August 1, 1933; and calculated and fixed the rates of processing and floor taxes on cotton in accordance with the terms of the [Agricultural Adjustment Act].

The United States presented a claim to [Butler *et al.*] as receivers of the Hoosac Mills Corporation for processing and floor taxes on cotton levied under [provisions] of the act. The receivers recommended that the claim be disallowed. The District Court found the taxes valid and ordered them paid. Upon appeal the Circuit Court of Appeals reversed the order. . . .

First. At the outset the United States contends that [Butler has] no standing to question the validity of the tax. The position is that the act is merely a revenue measure levying an excise upon the activity of processing cotton—a proper subject for the imposition of such a tax—the proceeds of which go into the federal treasury and thus become available for appropriation for any purpose. It is said that what [Butler is] endeavoring to do is challenge the intended use of the money pursuant to Congressional appropriation when, by confession, that money will have become the property of the Government and the taxpayer will no longer have any interest in it. [*Frothingham v. Mellon*] is claimed to foreclose litigation by [Butler] or other taxpayers, as such, looking to restraint of the expenditure of Government funds. That case might be an authority in the [government's] favor if we were here concerned merely with a suit by a taxpayer to restrain the expenditure of the public moneys. . . . Obviously the asserted interest of a taxpayer in the federal government's funds and the supposed increase of the future burden of taxation are minute and indeterminable. But here [Butler, who is] called upon to pay moneys as taxes, resist[s] the exaction as a step in an unauthorized plan. This circumstance clearly distinguishes the case. . . .

The tax can only be sustained by ignoring the avowed purpose and operation of the act, and holding it a measure merely laying an excise upon processors to raise revenue for the support of government. Beyond cavil the sole object of the legislation is to restore the purchasing power of agricultural products to a parity with that prevailing in an earlier day; to take money from the processor and bestow it upon farmers who will reduce their acreage for the accomplishment of the proposed end, and, meanwhile, to aid these farmers during the period required to bring the prices of their crops to the desired level.

The tax plays an indispensable part in the plan of regulation. . . . A tax automatically goes into effect for a commodity when the Secretary of Agriculture determines that rental or benefit payments are to be made for reduction of production of that commodity. The tax is to cease when rental or benefit payments cease. The rate is fixed with the purpose of bringing about crop-reduction and price-raising. . . . If the Secretary finds the policy of the act will not be promoted by the levy of the tax for a given commodity, he may exempt it. *** The whole revenue from the levy is appropriated in aid of crop control; none of it is made available for general governmental use. The entire agricultural adjustment program *** is to become inoperative when, in the judgment of the President, the national economic emergency ends. . . .

The statute not only avows an aim foreign to the procurement of revenue for the support of government, but by its operation shows the exaction laid upon processors to be the necessary means for the intended control of agricultural production. . . .

We conclude that the act is one regulating agricultural production; that the tax is a mere incident of such regulation and that [Butler has] standing to challenge the legality of the exaction.

It does not follow that as the act is not an exertion of the taxing power and the exaction not a true tax, the statute is void or the exaction uncollectible.... [I]f this is an expedient regulation by Congress, of a subject within one of its granted powers, "and the end to be attained is one falling within that power, the act is not void, because, within a loose and more extended sense than was used in the Constitution," the exaction is called a tax.

Second. The Government asserts that even if [Butler] may question the propriety of the appropriation embodied in the statute their attack must fail because Article 1, Sec. 8 of the Constitution authorizes the contemplated expenditure of the funds raised by the tax. This contention presents the great and the controlling question in the case. We approach its decision with a sense of our grave responsibility to render judgment in accordance with the principles established for the governance of all three branches of the Government.

There should be no misunderstanding as to the function of this court in such a case. It is sometimes said that the court assumes a power to overrule or control the action of the people's representatives. This is a misconception. The Constitution is the supreme law of the land ordained and established by the people. All legislation must conform to the principles it lays down. When an act of Congress is appropriately challenged in the courts as not conforming to the constitutional mandate the judicial branch of the Government has only one duty,—to lay the article of the Constitution which is invoked beside the statute which is challenged and to decide whether the latter squares with the former. All the court does, or can do, is to announce its considered judgment upon the question. The only power it has, if such it may be called, is the power of judgment. This court neither approves nor condemns any legislative policy. Its delicate and difficult office is to ascertain and declare whether the legislation is in accordance with, or in contravention of, the provisions of the Constitution; and, having done that, its duty ends.

The question is not what power the federal Government ought to have but what powers in fact have been given by the people.... Each State has all governmental powers save such as the people, by their Constitution, have conferred upon the United States, denied to the States, or reserved to themselves. The federal union is a government of delegated powers. It has only such as are expressly conferred upon it and such as are reasonably to be implied from those granted. In this respect we differ radically from nations where all legislative power, without restriction or limitation, is vested in a parliament or other legislative body subject to no restrictions except the discretion of its members.

Article I, Section 8, of the Constitution vests sundry powers in the Congress....

The clause thought to authorize the legislation,—the first,— confers upon the Congress power "to lay and collect Taxes, Duties, Imposts and Excises, to pay the Debts and provide for the common Defence and general Welfare of the United States...." It is not contended that this provision grants power to regulate agricultural production upon the theory that such legislation would promote the general welfare. The Government concedes that the phrase "to provide for the general welfare" qualifies the power "to lay and collect taxes." The view that the clause grants power to provide for the general welfare, independently of the taxing power, has never been authoritatively accepted. Mr. Justice Story points out that if it were adopted "it is obvious that under color of the generality of the words, to 'provide for the common defence and general welfare,' the government of the United States is, in reality, a government of general and unlimited powers, notwithstanding the subsequent enumeration of specific powers." The true construction undoubtedly is that the only thing granted is the power to tax for the purpose of providing funds for payment of the nation's debts and making provision for the general welfare.

Nevertheless the Government asserts that warrant is found in this clause for the adoption of the Agricultural Adjustment Act. The argument is that Congress may appropriate and authorize the spending of moneys for the "general welfare"; that the phrase should be liberally construed to cover anything conducive to national welfare; that decision as to what will promote such welfare rests with Congress alone, and the courts may not review its determination; and finally that the appropriation under attack was in fact for the general welfare of the United States.

The Congress is expressly empowered to lay taxes to provide for the general welfare. Funds in the Treasury as a result of taxation may be expected only through appropriation. *** They can never accomplish the objects for which they were collected unless the power to appropriate is as broad as the power to tax. The necessary implication from the terms of the grant is that the public funds may be appropriated "to provide for the general welfare of the United States." These words cannot be meaningless, else they would not have been used. The conclusion must be that they were intended to limit and define the granted power to raise and to expend money. . . .

We are now required to ascertain the scope of the phrase "general welfare of the United States" or to determine whether an appropriation in aid of agriculture falls within it. Wholly apart from that question, another principle embedded in our Constitution prohibits the enforcement of the Agricultural Adjustment Act. The act invades the reserved rights of the states. It is a statutory plan to regulate and control agricultural production, a matter beyond the powers delegated to the federal government. The tax, the appropriation of the funds raised, and the direction for their disbursement, are but parts of the plan. They are but means to an unconstitutional end.

From the accepted doctrine that the United States is a government of delegated powers, it follows that those not expressly granted, or reasonably to be implied from such as are conferred, are reserved to the states or to the people. To forestall any suggestion to the contrary, the Tenth Amendment was adopted. The same proposition, otherwise stated, is that powers not granted are prohibited. None to regulate agricultural production is given, and therefore legislation by Congress for that purpose is forbidden.

It is an established principle that the attainment of a prohibited end may not be accomplished under the pretext of the exertion of powers which are granted. . . .

The power of taxation, which is expressly granted, may, of course, be adopted as a means to carry into operation another power also expressly granted. But resort to the taxing power to effectuate an end which is not legitimate, not within the scope of the Constitution, is obviously inadmissible. . . .

Third. If the taxing power may not be used as the instrument to enforce a regulation of matters of state concern with respect to which the Congress has no authority to interfere, may it, as in the present case, be employed to raise the money necessary to purchase a compliance which the Congress is powerless to command? The Government asserts that whatever might be said against the validity of the plan, if compulsory, it is constitutionally sound because the end is accomplished by voluntary cooperation. There are two sufficient answers to the contention. The regulation is not in fact voluntary. The farmer, of course, may refuse to comply, but the price of such refusal is the loss of benefits. The amount offered is intended to be sufficient to exert pressure on him to agree to the proposed regulation. The power to confer or withhold unlimited benefits is the power to coerce or destroy. If the cotton grower elects not to accept the benefits, he will receive less for his crops; those who receive payment will be able to undersell him. The result may well be financial ruin. . . . This is coercion by economic pressure. The asserted power of choice is illusory.

But if the plan were one for purely voluntary cooperation it would stand no better so far as federal power is concerned. At best it is a scheme for purchasing with federal funds submission to federal regulation of a subject reserved to the states. . . .

Congress has no power to enforce its commands on the farmer to the ends sought by the Agricultural Adjustment Act. It must follow that it may not indirectly accomplish those ends by taxing and spending to purchase compliance. The Constitution and the entire plan of our government negate any such use of the power to tax and to spend as the act undertakes to authorize. It does not help to declare that local conditions throughout the nation have created a situation of national concern; for this is but to say that whenever there is a widespread similarity of local conditions, Congress may ignore constitutional limitations upon its own powers and usurp those reserved to the states. If, in lieu of compulsory regulation of subjects within the states' reserved jurisdiction, which is prohibited, the Congress could invoke the taxing and spending power as a means to accomplish the same end, clause 1 of Sec. 8 of Article I would become the instrument for total subversion of the governmental powers reserved to the individual states. . . .

Hamilton himself, the leading advocate of broad interpretation of the power to tax and to appropriate for the general welfare, never suggested that any power granted by the Constitution could be used for the destruction of local self-government in the states. Story countenances no such doctrine. It seems never to have occurred to them, or to those who have agreed with them, that the general welfare of the United States, . . . might be served by obliterating the constituent members of the Union. But to this fatal conclusion the doctrine contended for would inevitably lead. And its sole premise is that, though the makers of the Constitution, in erecting the federal government, intended sedulously to limit and define its powers, so as to reserve to the states and the people sovereign power, to be wielded by the states and their citizens and not be invaded by the United States, they nevertheless by a single clause gave power to the Congress to tear down the barriers, to invade the states' jurisdiction, and to become a parliament of the whole people, subject to no restrictions save such as are self-imposed. The argument when seen in its true character and in the light of the inevitable results must be rejected. . . .

The judgment is affirmed.

Mr. Justice Stone, dissenting.

I think the judgment should be reversed. The present stress of widely held and strongly expressed differences of opinion of the wisdom of the Agricultural Adjustment Act makes it important, in the interest of clear thinking and sound result, to emphasize at the outset certain propositions which should have controlling influence in determining the validity of the Act. They are:

1. The power of courts to declare a statute unconstitutional is subject to two guiding principles of decision which ought never to be absent from judicial consciousness. One is that courts are concerned only with the power to enact statutes, not with their wisdom. The other is that while unconstitutional exercise of power by the executive and legislative branches of the government is subject to judicial restraint, the only check upon our own exercise of power is our own sense of self-restraint. For the re-

moval of unwise laws from the statute books appeal lies not to the courts but to the ballot and to the processes of democratic government.

2. The constitutional power of Congress to levy an excise tax upon the processing of agricultural products is not questioned. The present levy is held invalid, not for any want of power in Congress to lay such a tax to defray public expenditures, including those for the general welfare, but because the use to which its proceeds are put is disapproved.

3. As the present depressed state of agriculture is nationwide in its extent and effects, there is no basis for saying that the expenditure of public money in aid of farmers is not within the specifically granted power of Congress to levy taxes to "provide for the . . . general welfare." The opinion of the Court does not declare otherwise. . . .

It is with these preliminary and hardly controverted matters in mind that we should direct our attention to the pivot on which the decision of the Court is made to turn. It is that a levy unquestionably within the taxing power of Congress may be treated as invalid because it is a step in a plan to regulate agricultural production and is thus a forbidden infringement of state power. The levy is not any the less an excise of taxing power because it is intended to defray an expenditure for the general welfare rather than for some other support of government. Nor is the levy and collection of the tax pointed to as effecting the regulation. While all federal taxes inevitably have some influence on the internal economy of the states, it is not contended that the levy of a processing tax upon manufacturers using agricultural products as raw material has any perceptible regulatory effects upon either their production or manufacture. The tax is unlike the penalties which were held invalid in the Child Labor Tax Case *** because they were themselves the instruments of regulation by virtue of their coercive effect on matters left to the control of the states. Here regulation, if any there be, is accomplished not by the tax but by the method by which its proceeds are expended, and would equally be accomplished by any like use of public funds, regardless of their source. . . .

It is upon the contention that state power is infringed by purchased regulation of agricultural production that chief reliance is placed. It is insisted that, while the Constitution gives to Congress, in specific and unambiguous terms, the power to tax and spend, the power is subject to limitations which do not find their origin in any express provision of the Constitution and to which other expressly delegated powers are not subject.

The Constitution requires that public funds shall be spent for a defined purpose, the promotion of the general welfare. . . . The power of Congress to spend is inseparable from persuasion to action over which Congress has no legislative control. Congress may not command that the science of agriculture be taught in state universities. But if it would aid the teaching of that science by grants to state institutions, it is appropriate, if not necessary, that the grant be on the condition *** that it be used for the intended purpose. Similarly it would seem to be compliance with the Constitution, not violation of it, for the government to take and the university to give a contract that the grant would be so used. It makes no difference that there is a promise to do an act which the condition is calculated to induce. Condition and promise are alike valid since both are in furtherance of the national purpose for which the money is appropriated.

These effects upon individual action, which are but incidents of the authorized expenditure of government money, are pronounced to be themselves a limitation upon the granted power, and so the time-honored principle of constitutional interpretation that the granted power includes all those which are incident to it is reversed. . . .

. . . The spending power of Congress is in addition to the legislative power and not subordinate to it. This independent grant of the power of the purse, and its very nature, involving in its exercise the duty to insure expenditure within the granted power, presuppose freedom of selection among diverse ends and aims, and the capacity to impose such conditions as will render the choice effective. It is a contradiction in terms to say that there is power to spend for the national welfare, while rejecting any power to impose conditions reasonably adapted to the attainment of the end which alone would justify the expenditure.

The limitation now sanctioned must lead to absurd consequences. The government may give seeds to farmers, but may not condition the gift upon their being planted in places where they are most needed or even planted at all. The government may give money to the unemployed, but may not ask that those who get shall give labor in return, or even use it to support their families. It may give money to sufferers from earthquake, fire, tornado, pestilence or flood, but may not impose conditions—health precautions designed to prevent the spread of disease, or induce the movement of population to safer or more sanitary areas. All that, because it is purchased regulation infringing state powers, must be left for the states, who are unable or unwilling to supply the necessary relief. . . . Do all its activities collapse because, in order to effect the permissible purpose, in myriad ways the money is paid out upon terms and conditions which influence action of the recipients within the states, which Congress cannot command? The answer would seem plain. If the expenditure is for a national public purpose, that purpose will not be thwarted because payment is on condition which will advance that purpose. The action which Congress induces by payments of money to promote the general welfare, but which it does not command or coerce, is but an incident to a specifically granted power, but a permissible means to a legitimate end. If appropriation in aid of a program of curtailment of agricultural production is constitutional, and it is not denied that it is, payment to farmers on condition that they reduce their crop acreage is constitutional. It is not any the less so because the farmer at his own option promises to fulfill the condition.

That the governmental power of the purse is a great one is not now for the first time announced. Every student of the history of government and economics is aware of its magnitude and of its existence in every civilized government. Both were well understood by the framers of the Constitution when they sanctioned the grant of the spending power to the federal government, and both were recognized by Hamilton and Story, whose views of the spending power as standing on a parity with the other powers specifically granted, have hitherto been generally accepted.

The suggestion that it must now be curtailed by judicial fiat because it may be abused by unwise use hardly rises to the dignity of argument. So may judicial power be abused. "The power to tax is the power to destroy," but we do not, for that reason, doubt its existence, or hold that its efficacy is to be restricted by its incidental or collateral effects upon the states. *** The power to tax and spend is not without constitutional restraints. One restriction is that the purpose must be truly national. Another is that it may not be used to coerce action left to state control. Another is the conscience and patriotism of Congress and the Executive. . . .

A tortured construction of the Constitution is not to be justified by recourse to extreme examples of reckless congressional spending which might occur if courts could not prevent—expenditures which, even if they could be thought to effect any national purpose, would be possible only by action of a legislature lost to all sense of public responsibility. Such suppositions are addressed to the mind accustomed to believe that it is the business of courts to sit in judgment on the wisdom of legislative action. Courts are not the only agency of government that must be assumed to have the capacity to govern. Congress and the courts both unhappily may falter or be mistaken in the performance of their constitutional duty. But interpretation of our great charter of government which proceeds on any assumption that the responsibility for the preservation of our institution is the exclusive concern of any one of the three branches of government, or that it alone can save them from destruction, is far more likely, in the long run, "to obliterate the constituent members" of "an indestructible union of indestructible states" than the frank recognition of that language, even of a constitution, may mean what it says: that the power to tax and spend includes the power to relieve a nation-wide economic maladjustment by conditional gifts of money.

Mr. Justice Brandeis and *Mr. Justice Cardozo* join in this opinion.

Chas. C. Steward Machine Company v. Davis

301 U.S. 548; 57 S. Ct. 883; 81 L. Ed. 1279 (1937)
Vote: 5-4

Mr. Justice Cardozo delivered the opinion of the Court.

The validity of the tax imposed by the Social Security Act on employers of eight or more is here to be determined.

[Steward Machine Company] paid a tax in accordance with the statute, filed a claim for refund with the Commissioner of Internal Revenue, and sued to recover the payment ($46.14), asserting a conflict between the statute and the Constitution of the United States. . . . An important question of constitutional law being involved, we granted certiorari. ***

The Social Security Act *** is divided into eleven separate titles, of which only titles IX and III are so related to this case as to stand in need of summary . . . [Under Title IX] every employer (with stated exceptions) is to pay for each calendar year "an excise tax, with respect to having individuals in his hisemploy," the tax to be measured by prescribed percentages of the total wages payable by the employer during the calendar year with respect to such employment. ***

Under [Title III] certain sums of money are "authorized to be appropriated for the purpose of assisting the states in the administration of their unemployment compensation laws. . . . The appropriations when made were not specifically out of the proceeds of the employment tax, but out of any moneys in the Treasury. Other sections of the title prescribe the method by which the payments are to be made to the state *** and also certain conditions to be established. . . . They are designed to give assurance to the Federal Government that the moneys granted by it will not be expended for purposes alien to the grant, and will be used in the administration of genuine unemployment compensation laws.

The assault on the statute proceeds on an extended front. Its assailants take the ground that the tax is not an excise; that it is not uniform throughout the United States as excises are required to be; that its exceptions are so many and arbitrary as to violate the Fifth Amendment; that its purpose was not revenue, but an unlawful invasion of the reserved powers of the states; and that the states in submitting to it have yielded to coercion and have abandoned governmental functions which they are not permitted to surrender. . . .

First: The tax, which is described in the statute as an excise, is laid with uniformity throughout the United States as a duty, an impost or an excise upon the relation of employment.

1. We are told that the relation of employment is one so essential to the pursuit of happiness that it may not be burdened with a tax. Appeal is made to history. From the precedents of colonial days we are supplied with illustrations of excises common in the colonies. They are said to have been bound up with the enjoyment of particular commodities. . . .

. . . Doubtless there were many excises in colonial days and later that were associated, more or less intimately, with the enjoyment or the use of property. This would not prove, even if no others were then known, that the forms then accepted were not subject to enlargement. *** But in truth other excises *were* known, and known since early times. . . . Our colonial forebears knew more about ways of taxing than some of their descendants seem to be willing to concede.

The historical prop failing, the prop or fancied prop of principle remains. We learn that employment for lawful gain is a "natural" or "inherent" or "inalienable" right, and not a "privilege" at all. But natural rights, so called, are as much subject to taxation as rights of less importance. An excise is not limited to vocations or activities that may be prohibited altogether. It is not limited to those that are the outcome of a franchise. It extends to vocations or activities pursued as of common right. What the individual does in the operation of a business is amenable to taxation just as much as what he owns, at all events if the classification is not tyrannical or arbitrary. . . .

The subject matter of taxation open to the power of Congress is as comprehensive as that open to the power of the states, though the method of apportionment may at times be different. . . . The statute

books of the states are strewn with illustrations of taxes laid on occupations pursued of common right. We find no basis for a holding that the power in that regard which belongs by accepted practice to the legislatures of the states, has been denied by the Constitution to the Congress of the nation.

2. The tax being an excise, its imposition must conform to the canon of uniformity. There has been no departure from this requirement. According to the settled doctrine the uniformity exacted is geographical, not intrinsic. ***

Second: The excise is not invalid under the provisions of the Fifth Amendment by force of its exemptions.

The statute does not apply . . . to employers of less than eight. It does not apply to agricultural labor, or domestic service in a private home or to some other classes of less importance. [Steward Machine Company] contends that the effect of these restrictions is an arbitrary discrimination vitiating the tax.

The Fifth Amendment unlike the Fourteenth has no equal protection clause. *** But even the states, though subject to such a clause, are not confined to a formula of rigid uniformity in framing measures of taxation. *** They may tax some kinds of property at one rate, and others at another, and exempt others altogether. *** They may lay an excise on the operations of a particular kind of business, and exempt some other kind of business closely akin thereto. *** If this latitude of judgment is lawful for the states, it is lawful . . . in legislation by the Congress, which is subject to restraints less narrow and confining. ***

The classifications and exemptions directed by the statute now in controversy have support in considerations of policy and practical convenience that cannot be condemned as arbitrary. The classifications and exemptions would therefore be upheld if they had been adopted by a state and the provisions of the Fourteenth Amendment were invoked to annul them. . . . The act of Congress is therefore valid, so far at least as its system of exemptions is concerned, and this though we assume that discrimination, if gross enough, is equivalent to confiscation and subject under the Fifth Amendment to challenge and annulment.

Third: The excise is not void as involving the coercion of the States in contravention of the Tenth

Amendment or of restrictions implicit in our federal form of government.

The proceeds of the excise when collected are paid into the Treasury at Washington, and thereafter are subject to appropriation like public moneys generally. *** No presumption can be indulged that they will be misapplied or wasted. Even if they were collected in the hope or expectation that some other and collateral good would be furthered as an incident, that without more would not make the act invalid. *** . . .

To draw the line intelligently between duress and inducement there is need to remind ourselves of facts as to the problem of unemployment that are now matters of common knowledge. *** Of the many available figures a few only will be mentioned. During the years 1929 to 1936, when the country was passing through a cyclical depression, the number of the unemployed mounted to unprecedented heights. Often the average was more than 10 million; at times a peak was attained of 16 million or more. Disaster to the breadwinner means disaster to dependents. Accordingly the roll of the unemployed, itself formidable enough, was only a partial roll of the destitute or needy. The fact developed quickly that the states were unable to give the requisite relief. The problem had become national in areas and dimensions. There was need of help from the nation if the people were not to starve. It is too late today for the argument to be heard with tolerance that in a crisis so extreme the use of the moneys of the nation to relieve the unemployed and their dependents is a use for any purpose narrower than the promotion of the general welfare. *** . . .

In the presence of this urgent need for some remedial expedient, the question is to be answered whether the expedient adopted has overleapt the bounds of power. The assailants of the statute say that its dominant end and aim is to drive the state legislatures under the whip of economic pressure into the enactment of unemployment compensation laws at the bidding of the central government. Supporters of the statute say that its operation is not constraint, but the creation of a larger freedom, the states and the nation joining in a cooperative endeavor to avert a common evil. . . .

The Social Security Act is an attempt to find a method by which all these public agencies may work together to a common end. Every dollar of the new taxes will continue in all likelihood to be used and needed by the nation as long as states are unwilling, whether through timidity or for other motives, to do what can be done at home. At least the inference is permissible that Congress so believed, though retaining undiminished freedom to spend the money as it pleased. On the other hand fulfillment of the home duty will be lightened and encouraged by crediting the taxpayer upon his account with the Treasury of the nation to the extent that his contributions under the laws of the locality have simplified or diminished the problem of relief and the probable demand upon the resources of the fisc. . . .

Who then is coerced through the operation of this statute? Not the taxpayer. He pays in fulfillment of the mandate of the local legislature. Not the state. Even now she does not offer a suggestion that in passing the unemployment law she was affected by duress. *** For all that appears she is satisfied with her choice, and would be sorely disappointed if it were now to be annulled. The difficulty with the petitioner's contention is that it confuses motive with coercion. "Every tax is in some measure regulatory. To some extent it interposes an economic impediment to the activity taxed as compared with others not taxed." *** In like manner, every rebate from a tax when conditioned upon conduct is in some measure a temptation. But to hold that motive or temptation is equivalent to coercion is to plunge the law in endless difficulties. The outcome of such a doctrine is the acceptance of a philosophical determinism by which choice becomes impossible. Till now the law has been guided by a robust common sense which assumes the freedom of the will as a working hypothesis in the solution of its problems. The wisdom of the hypothesis has illustration in this case. Nothing in the case suggests the exertion of a power akin to undue influence, if we assume that such a concept can ever be applied with fitness to the relations between state and nation. Even on that assumption the location of the point at which pressure turns into compulsion, and ceases to be inducement, would be a question of degree,—at times, perhaps, of fact. . . .

In ruling as we do, we leave many questions open. We do not say that a tax is valid, when imposed by act of Congress, if it is laid upon the condition that a state may escape its operation through the adoption of a statute unrelated in subject matter to activities fairly within the scope of national policy and power. No such question is before us. . . .

Fourth: The statute does not call for a surrender by the states of powers essential to their quasi-sovereign existence. . . .

The judgment is affirmed.

Separate opinion of **Mr. Justice McReynolds** [dissenting].

That portion of the Social Security legislation here under consideration, I think, exceeds the power granted to Congress. It unduly interferes with the orderly government of the State by her own people and otherwise offends the Federal Constitution. . . .

The doctrine thus announced and often repeated, I had supposed was firmly established. Apparently the States remained really free to exercise governmental powers, not delegated or prohibited, without interference by the Federal Government through threats of punitive measures or offers of seductive favors. Unfortunately, the decision just announced opens the way for practical annihilation of this theory. . . .

No defense is offered for the legislation under review upon the basis of emergency. The hypothesis is that hereafter it will continuously benefit unemployed members of a class. Forever, so far as we can see, the States are expected to function under federal direction concerning an internal matter. By the sanction of this adventure, the door is open for progres-sive inauguration of others of like kind under which it can hardly be expected that the States will retain genuine independence of action. And without independent States a Federal Union as contemplated by the Constitution becomes impossible. . . .

Ordinarily, I must think, a denial that the challenged action of Congress and what has been done under it amount to coercion and impair freedom of government by the people of the State would be regarded as contrary to practical experience. Unquestionably our federate plan of government confronts an enlarged peril.

Separate opinion of **Mr. Justice Sutherland** [dissenting in part].

. . . If we are to survive as the United States, the balance between the powers of the nation and those of the states must be maintained. There is grave danger in permitting it to dip in either direction, danger—if there were no other—in the precedent thereby set for further departures from the equipoise. The threat implicit in the present encroachment upon the administrative functions of the states is that of greater encroachments, and encroachments upon other functions, will follow.

For the foregoing reasons, I think the judgment below should be reversed.

Mr. Justice Van DeVanter joins in this opinion.

Mr. Justice Butler [dissenting]. . . .

South Dakota v. Dole
483 U.S. 203; 107 S. Ct. 2793; 97 L. Ed. 2d 171 (1987)
Vote: 7-2

Chief Justice Rehnquist delivered the opinion of the Court.

Petitioner South Dakota permits persons 19 years of age or older to purchase beer containing up to 3.2% alcohol. *** In 1984 Congress enacted 23 U.S.C. Sec. 158 (1982 ed., Supp. III) ("Sec. 158"), which directs the Secretary of Transportation to withhold a percentage of federal highway funds otherwise allo-cable from States "in which the purchase or public possession of any alcoholic beverage by a person who is less than twenty-one years of age is lawful." The State sued in United States District Court seeking a declaratory judgment that Sec. 158 violates the constitutional limitations on congressional exercise of the spending power and violates the Twenty-first Amendment to the United States Constitution. The

District Court rejected the State's claims, and the Court of Appeals for the Eighth Circuit affirmed. ***

In this Court, the parties direct most of their efforts to defining the proper scope of the Twenty-first Amendment. Relying on our statement in *California Retail Liquor Dealers Assn. v. Midcal Aluminum, Inc.* *** (1980), that the "Twenty-First Amendment grants the States virtually complete control over whether to permit importation or sale of liquor and how to structure the liquor distribution system," South Dakota asserts that the setting of minimum drinking ages is clearly within the "core powers" reserved to the States under Sec. 2 of the Amendment. *** Section 158, petitioner claims, usurps that core power. The Secretary in response asserts that the Twenty-first Amendment is simply not implicated by Sec. 158; the plain language of Sec. 2 confirms the States' broad power to impose restrictions on the sale and distribution of alcoholic beverages but does not confer on them any power to *permit* sales that Congress seeks to *prohibit*. *** That Amendment, under this reasoning, would not prevent Congress from affirmatively enacting a national minimum drinking age more restrictive than that provided by the various state laws; and it would follow *a fortiori* that the indirect inducement involved here is compatible with the Twenty-first Amendment.

These arguments present questions of the meaning of the Twenty-first Amendment, the bounds of which have escaped precise definition. *** Despite the extended treatment of the question by the parties, however, we need not decide in this case whether that Amendment would prohibit an attempt by Congress to legislate directly a national minimum drinking age. Here, Congress has acted indirectly under its spending power to encourage uniformity in the States' drinking ages. As we explain below, we find this legislative effort within constitutional bounds even if Congress may not regulate drinking ages directly.

The Constitution empowers Congress to "lay and collect Taxes, Duties, Imposts, and Excises, to pay the Debts and provide for the common Defense and general Welfare of the United States." Art. I, Sec. 8, c. 1. Incident to this power, Congress may attach conditions on the receipt of federal moneys upon compliance by the recipient with federal statutory and ad-

ministrative directives. *** The breadth of this power was made clear in *United States v. Butler* *** (1936), where the court, resolving a longstanding debate over the scope of the Spending Clause, determined that "the power of Congress to authorize expenditure of public moneys for public purposes is not limited by the direct grants of legislative power found in the Constitution." Thus, objectives not thought to be within Article I's enumerated legislative fields *** may nevertheless be attained through the use of the spending power and the condition grant of federal funds.

The spending power is of course not unlimited, *** but is instead subject to several general restrictions articulated in our cases. The first of these limitations is derived from the language of the Constitution itself; the exercise of the spending power must be in pursuit of "the general welfare." *** In considering whether a particular expenditure is intended to serve general public purposes, courts should defer substantially to the judgment of Congress. *** Second, we have required that if Congress desires to condition the States' receipt of federal funds, it "must do so unambiguously. . . , enabl[ing] the States to exercise their choice knowingly, cognizant of the consequences of their participation." *** Third, our cases have suggested (without significant elaboration) that conditions on federal grants might be illegitimate if they are unrelated "to the federal interest in particular national projects or programs." ***

South Dakota does not seriously claim that Sec. 158 is inconsistent with any of the first three restrictions mentioned above. We can readily conclude that the provision is designed to serve the general welfare, especially in light of the fact that "the concept of welfare or the opposite is shaped by Congress. . . ." *** Congress found that the differing drinking ages in the States created particular incentives for young persons to combine their desire to drink with their ability to drive, and that this interstate problem required a national solution. The means it chose to address this dangerous situation were reasonably calculated to advance the general welfare. The conditions upon which States receive the funds, moreover, could not be more clearly stated by Congress. *** And the State itself, rather than challenging the germaneness of the condition to federal purposes, admits that it "has never contended that the congressional action was . . . unrelated to a national concern in the absence of the Twenty-first Amendment." *** Indeed, the condition imposed by Congress is directly related to one of the main purposes for which highway funds are expended—safe interstate travel. *** This goal of the interstate highway system had been frustrated by varying drinking ages among the States. A presidential commission appointed to study alcohol-related accidents and fatalities on the Nation's highways concluded that the lack of uniformity in the states' drinking ages created "an incentive to drink" because "young persons commut[e] to border States where the drinking age is lower." *** By enacting Sec. 158, Congress conditioned the receipt of federal funds in a way reasonably calculated to address this particular impediment to a purpose for which the funds are expended.

The remaining question about the validity of Sec. 158—and the basic point of disagreement between the parties—is whether the Twenty-first Amendment constitutes an "independent constitutional bar" to the conditional grant of federal funds. *** Petitioner, relying on its view that the Twenty-first Amendment prohibits *direct* regulation of drinking ages by Congress, asserts that "Congress may not use the spending power to regulate that which it is prohibited from regulating directly under the Twenty-first Amendment." *** But our cases show that this "independent constitutional bar" limitation on the spending power is not of the kind petitioner suggests. *United States v. Butler,* *** for example, established that the constitutional limitations on Congress when exercising its spending power are less exacting than those on its authority to regulate directly.

We have also held that a perceived Tenth Amendment limitation on congressional regulation of state affairs did not concomitantly limit the range of conditions legitimately placed on federal grants. In *Oklahoma v. Civil Service Comm'n.* *** (1947), the Court considered the validity of the Hatch Act insofar as it was applied to political activities of state officials whose employment was financed in whole or in part with federal funds. The State contended that an order under this provision to withhold certain federal funds unless a state official was removed invaded its sovereignty in violation of the Tenth Amendment.

Though finding that "the United States is not concerned with, and has no power to regulate, local political activities as such of state officials," the Court nevertheless held that the Federal Government "does have power to fix the terms upon which its money allotments to states shall be disbursed." *** The Court found no violation of the State's sovereignty because the State could, and did, adopt "the 'simple expedient' of not yielding to what she urges is federal coercion. The offer of benefits to a state by the United States dependent upon cooperation by the state with federal plans, assumedly for the general welfare, is not unusual." ***

These cases establish that the "independent constitutional bar" limitation on the spending power is not, as petitioner suggests, a prohibition on the indirect achievement of objectives which Congress is not empowered to achieve directly. Instead, we think that the language in our earlier opinions stands for the unexceptionable proposition that the power may not be used to induce the States to engage in activities that would themselves be unconstitutional. Thus, for example, a grant of federal funds conditioned on invidiously discriminatory state action or the infliction of cruel and unusual punishment would be an illegitimate exercise of the Congress' broad spending power. But no such claim can be or is made here. Were South Dakota to succumb to the blandishments offered by Congress and raise its drinking age to 21, the State's action in so doing would not violate the constitutional rights of anyone.

Our decisions have recognized that in some circumstances the financial inducement offered by Congress might be so coercive as to pass the point at which "pressure turns into compulsion." *Steward Machine Co. v. Davis.* *** Here, however, Congress has directed only that a State desiring to establish a minimum drinking age lower than 21 lose a relatively small percentage of certain federal highway funds. Petitioner contends that the coercive nature of this program is evident from the degree of success it has achieved. We cannot conclude, however, that a conditional grant of federal money of this sort is unconstitutional simply by reason of its success in achieving the congressional objective.

When we consider, for a moment, that all South Dakota would lose if she adheres to her chosen course as to a suitable minimum drinking age is 5% of the funds otherwise obtainable under specified highway grant programs, the argument as to coercion is shown to be more rhetoric than fact. . . .

Here Congress has offered relatively mild encouragement to the States to enact higher minimum drinking ages than they would otherwise choose. But the enactment of such laws remains the prerogative of the States not merely in theory but in fact. Even if Congress might lack the power to impose a national minimum drinking age directly, we conclude that encouragement to state action found in Sec. 158 is a valid use of the spending power. Accordingly, the judgment of the Court of Appeals is affirmed.

Justice Brennan, dissenting. . . .

Justice O'Connor, dissenting.

The Court today upholds the National Minimum Drinking Age Amendment *** as a valid exercise of the Spending Power conferred by Article I, Sec. 8. But Sec. 158 is not a condition on spending reasonably related to the expenditure of federal funds and cannot be justified on that ground. Rather, it is an attempt to regulate the sale of liquor, an attempt that lies outside Congress' power to regulate commerce because it falls within the ambit of Sec. 2 of the Twenty-first Amendment.

My disagreement with the Court is relatively narrow on the Spending Power issue; it is a disagreement about the application of a principle rather than a disagreement on the principle itself. I agree with the Court that Congress may attach conditions on the receipt of federal funds to further "the federal interest in particular national projects or programs." *** I also subscribe to the established proposition that the reach of the Spending Power "is not limited by the direct grants of legislative power found in the Constitution." *** Finally, I agree that there are four separate types of limitations on the Spending Power: the expenditure must be for the general welfare, *** the conditions imposed must be unambiguous, *** they must be reasonably related to the purpose of the expenditure, *** and the legislation may not violate any independent constitutional prohibition. *** Insofar as two of these limitations are concerned, the Court is clearly correct that Sec. 158 is wholly unob-

jectionable. Establishment of a national minimum drinking age certainly fits within the broad concept of the general welfare and the statute is entirely unambiguous. I am also willing to assume *arguendo* that the Twenty-first Amendment does not constitute an "independent constitutional bar" to a spending condition. ***

But the Court's application of the requirement that the condition imposed be reasonably related to the purpose for which the funds are expended, is cursory and unconvincing. We have repeatedly said that Congress may condition grants under the Spending Power only in ways reasonably related to the purpose of the federal program. *** In my view, establishment of a minimum drinking age of 21 is not sufficiently related to interstate highway construction to justify so conditioning funds appropriated for that purpose.

In support of its contrary conclusion, the Court relies on a supposed concession by counsel for South Dakota that the State "has never contended that the congressional action was . . . unrelated to a national concern in the absence of the Twenty-first Amendment." *** In the absence of the Twenty-first Amendment, however, there is a strong argument that the Congress might regulate the conditions under which liquor is sold under the Commerce Power, just as it regulates the sale of many other commodities that are in or affect interstate commerce. The fact that the Twenty-first Amendment is crucial to the State's argument does not, therefore, amount to a concession that the condition imposed by Sec. 158 is reasonably related to highway construction. The Court also relies on a portion of the argument transcript in support of its claim that South Dakota conceded the reasonable relationship point. *** But counsel's statements there are at best ambiguous. Counsel essentially said no more than that he was not prepared to argue the reasonable relationship question discussed at length in the Brief for the National Conference of State Legislatures *et al.* as *Amici Curiae.*

Aside from these "concessions" by counsel, the Court asserts the reasonableness of the relationship between the supposed purpose of the expenditure—"safe interstate travel"—and the drinking age condition. *** The Court reasons that Congress wishes that the roads it builds may be used safely, that drunk drivers threaten highway safety, and that young people are more likely to drive while under the influence of alcohol under existing law than would be the case if there were a uniform national drinking age of 21. It hardly needs saying, however, that if the purpose of Sec. 158 is to deter drunken driving, it is far too over- and under-inclusive. It is over-inclusive because it stops teenagers from drinking even when they are not about to drive on interstate highways. It is under-inclusive because teenagers pose only a small part of the drunken driving problem in this Nation.

When Congress appropriates money to build a highway, it is entitled to insist that the highway be a safe one. But it is not entitled to insist as a condition of the use of highway funds that the State impose or change regulations in other areas of the State's social and economic life because of an attenuated or tangential relationship to highway use or safety. Indeed, if the rule were otherwise, the Congress could effectively regulate almost any area of a State's social, political, or economic life on the theory that use of the interstate transportation system is somehow enhanced. If, for example, the United States were to condition highway moneys upon moving the state capital, I suppose it might argue that interstate transportation is facilitated by locating local governments in places easily accessible to interstate highways—or, conversely, that highways might become overburdened if they had to carry traffic to and from the state capital. In my mind, such a relationship is hardly more attenuated than the one which the Court finds to support Sec. 158. ***

There is a clear place at which the Court can draw the line between permissible and impermissible conditions on federal grants. It is the line identified in the Brief for the National Conference of State Legislatures *et al.* as *Amici Curiae:*

Congress has the power to *spend* for the general welfare, it has the power to *legislate* only for delegated purposes. . . .

The appropriate inquiry, then, is whether the spending requirement or prohibition is a condition on a grant or whether it is regulation. The difference turns on whether the requirement specifies in some way how the money should be spent, so that Congress' intent in making the grant will be effectuated. Congress has no power under the

Spending Clause to impose requirements on a grant that go beyond specifying how the money should be spent. A requirement that is not such a specification is not a condition, but a regulation, which is valid only if it falls within one of Congress' delegated regulatory powers. ***

This approach harks back to *United States v. Butler,* *** the last case in which this Court struck down an Act of Congress as beyond the authority granted by the Spending Clause. The *Butler* Court saw the Agricultural Adjustment Act for what it was—an exercise of regulatory, not spending, power. The error in *Butler* was not the Court's conclusion that the Act was essentially regulatory, but rather its crabbed view of the extent of Congress' regulatory power under the Commerce Clause. The Agricultural Adjustment Act was regulatory but it was regulation that today would likely be considered within Congress' Commerce Power. ***

While *Butler's* authority is questionable insofar as it assumes that Congress has no regulatory power over farm production, its discussion of the Spending Power and its description of both the power's breadth and its limitations remains sound. The Court's decision in *Butler* also properly recognizes the gravity of the task of appropriately limiting the Spending Power. If the Spending Power is to be limited only by Congress' notion of the general welfare, the reality, given the vast financial resources of the Federal Government, is that the Spending Clause gives "power to the Congress to tear down the barriers, to invade the state's jurisdiction, and to become a parliament of the whole people, subject to no restrictions save such as are self-imposed." *** This, of course, as *Butler* held, was not the Framers' plan and it is not the meaning of the Spending Clause. . . .

The immense size and power of the Government of the United States ought not obscure its fundamental character. It remains a Government of enumerated powers. *** Because [Sec. 158] cannot be justified as an exercise of any power delegated to the Congress, it is not authorized by the Constitution. The Court errs in holding it to be the law of the land, and I respectfully dissent.

CHAPTER SIX

THE POWERS OF THE PRESIDENCY

> There is an idea, which is not without its advocates, that a vigorous executive is inconsistent with the genius of republican government. . . . Energy in the executive is the leading character in the definition of good government. It is essential to the protection of the community against foreign attacks; it is not less essential to the steady administration of the laws, to the protection of property. . .; [and] to the security of liberty against the enterprises and assaults of ambition, of faction and anarchy.
>
> Alexander Hamilton, *The Federalist* No. 70

INTRODUCTION

The Constitution devotes considerably more attention to Congress than to the other branches of government. Reflecting this emphasis, James Madison, in *The Federalist* No. 51, asserted that "in republican government, the legislative authority necessarily predominates." Perhaps Madison's observation was true of a small republic in the late eighteenth century. It does not, however, apply to the experience of the United States after more than two centuries of constitutional development. Without question, the dominant tendency of American constitutional history has been to concentrate power in the executive branch.

The expansion of presidential power has occurred despite a Constitution that provides little to the president by way of specific, **enumerated powers.** Throughout history, presidents have taken advantage of opportunities to enhance the power of the executive branch, opportunities afforded by crises such as the Civil War, two world wars, the Great Depression, and, more recently, the Cold War. The tendency of presidents to seize power to cope with the exigencies of their times is what led noted constitutional scholar Edward S. Corwin to remark that "the history of the Presidency has been a history of aggrandizement."

The American presidency has experienced setbacks, to be sure. In recent decades, such events as the ill-fated Vietnam War, the Watergate scandal, the Iran hostage crisis, and the Iran-Contra affair have exacted a toll on the presidency in terms of diminished public confidence and trust. Botched wars, inept covert activities, and political scandals have led to increased congressional oversight

Alexander Hamilton: Apostle of presidential power

and control of the executive branch. Nevertheless, the American presidency remains a powerful institution, without question the most powerful executive position in the world. This fact was made abundantly clear during the recent war with Iraq, when President George Bush demonstrated the awesome power of the American presidency to the entire world.

In the 1970s, in the wake of the Vietnam and Watergate debacles, some observers perceived a significant decline in presidential power and prestige. If a decline occurred, it was short-lived. In the 1980s, the Reagan and Bush administrations regained for the presidency a position comparable to the pre-eminence that it held prior to the late 1960s. Whatever the Framers might have intended regarding the scope of presidential power, it is obvious that the office has expanded far beyond their expectations.

STRUCTURAL ASPECTS OF THE AMERICAN PRESIDENCY

Some delegates to the Constitutional Convention of 1787 favored a multiple executive, in which power would be exercised simultaneously by three or more individuals. Others insisted on limiting the president to a single term of seven years or to two three-year terms. Still others maintained that the president, in concert with the Supreme Court, should function as a "council of revision," which would in effect pass on the constitutionality of acts of Congress. The Framers, who had recently participated in a successful revolution against the English crown, were understandably wary of creating an executive institution that could "degenerate" into a monarchy. Widespread recognition that George Washington would assume a central role of leadership greatly reduced these fears. In fact, Washington's daily presence as the presiding officer at the Convention probably contributed to the decision to create a single executive.

Presidential Terms

Ultimately, the Framers not only vested power in a single executive, elected for a term of four years, but also refused to limit the number of terms the president might serve. Washington, as the first president, displayed both the leadership and self-restraint that the American people expected. He established an important precedent by refusing to seek a third term, a tradition that survived until Franklin D. Roosevelt was elected to a third term in 1940, followed by a fourth term in 1944. Roosevelt died in office in 1945, and the Republican Party gained control of both Houses of Congress after the 1946 elections. Reacting to Roosevelt's break with tradition, Congress then proposed the Twenty-second Amendment, ratified in 1951, prohibiting future presidents from being elected to more than two consecutive terms. In the aftermath of Ronald Reagan's popular first term and landslide reelection in 1984, some political activists began to urge repeal of the Twenty-second Amendment. Attention to this issue was effectively diverted by the Iran-Contra affair and other problems during Reagan's second term.

The Electoral College

Contemporary Americans look to the quadrennial presidential elections as symbols of a deep national commitment to democracy. Yet the Framers of the Constitution, far less sanguine about democracy, provided for an indirect method of presidential selection. Under this arrangement, each state was authorized to appoint as many electors as it had senators and representatives in Congress (Article II, Section 1). This **Electoral College,** as it came to be called, was empowered to choose the president, and the person receiving the second highest number of votes would serve as vice-president. The Framers assumed that the electors would act independently of the people in making their selections. But with the advent of the **two-party system** in the late 1790s and the gradual extension of the suffrage, the electors soon lost this independent role. Reflecting the importance of party identity, the Twelfth Amendment was adopted in 1804, placing the offices of president and vice-president on separate ballots. The effect of this change was that each party developed its own presidential and vice-presidential "tickets," to which designated slates of electors were pledged. With rare exception, the presidential candidate receiving a plurality of the popular vote in a given state automatically received that state's entire electoral vote. Thus, the Electoral College, within less than twenty years after its creation, became a vestigial organ of American government. Although many have called for its abolition, it remains intact in the 1990s.

Succession and Disability

The constitutional problem of presidential succession has troubled generations of Americans. The problem first arose in 1841, when President William Henry Harrison died after only a month in office. The immediate question was whether Vice-President John Tyler would assume the full duties and powers of the office for the remaining forty-seven months of Harrison's term or serve merely as an acting president. Unwilling to settle for less than the full measure of presidential authority, Tyler set an important precedent, which has been followed by the eight other individuals who have succeeded to the office because of the death or resignation of an incumbent president.

The related problem of presidential disability has proved more perplexing. Several presidents have been temporarily disabled during their terms of office, with resulting uncertainty and confusion as to the locus of actual decision-making authority. For example, President Woodrow Wilson was seriously disabled by a stroke in 1919 and for a number of weeks was totally incapable of performing his official duties. No constitutional provision existed at that time for the temporary replacement of a disabled president. The result was that Wilson's wife, Edith, took on much of the responsibility of the office, an arrangement that evoked sharp criticism.

The problem of presidential disability is addressed by the Twenty-fifth Amendment, ratified in 1967. This amendment, which was proposed in the aftermath of the assassination of President John F. Kennedy, establishes, among other things, a procedure under which the vice-president may assume the role of acting president during periods of presidential disability. The amendment provides alternative means for determining presidential disability. Section 3 allows the president to transmit to Congress a written declaration that he is unable to discharge the duties of the office, upon which the vice-president assumes the role of acting president. The vice-president continues in this role unless and until the president is able to transmit a declaration to the contrary. If, however, the president is unable or unwilling to acknowledge the inability to perform the duties of the office, the vice-president and a majority of the Cabinet members are authorized to make this determination.

Removal of the Chief Executive

The ultimate constitutional sanction against the abuse of presidential power is **impeachment** and removal from office. Only twice in our history has the serious possibility of impeachment been raised. President Andrew Johnson was impeached by the House of Representatives in 1868 but narrowly escaped conviction by the Senate. President Richard Nixon almost certainly would have been impeached and convicted had he not resigned following the Supreme Court's 1974 decision in *United States v. Nixon* (discussed below).

Considering the power of impeachment in the context of both the Johnson and Nixon episodes, an interesting constitutional question comes to mind. The Constitution, in Article II, Section 4 states:

> The President, Vice-President and all civil officers of the United States shall be removed from office on impeachment for, and conviction of, treason, bribery or other **high crimes and misdemeanors.** [Emphasis added.]

Andrew Johnson was impeached for overtly political reasons, stemming from his clash with Congress over Reconstruction policy. His ultimate acquittal can be attributed to the fact that he had not committed indictable offenses, although many in Congress were willing to interpret the "high crimes and misdemeanors" language in the Constitution quite broadly!

Although they were made moot by the president's voluntary departure, similar questions surrounded the possible impeachment of Richard Nixon. Members of the House Judiciary Committee vigorously debated the meaning of "high crimes and misdemeanors." A majority of the committee's members seemed to believe Nixon could be impeached for "undermining the integrity of office, disregard of constitutional duties and oath of office, arrogation of power, abuse of the governmental process, and adverse impact on the system of government." On the other hand, Nixon's defenders held that the president could be impeached only for offenses against the criminal law, offenses for which he could be indicted by a grand jury. In light of information currently available regarding the president's role in the Watergate scandal, it seems that he could have been impeached, and convicted, under either interpretation of the Constitution.

The Supreme Court has not been called upon to render an authoritative construction of the "high crimes and misdemeanors" language of Article II. Should it be asked to do so in the future, the Court might well refuse by labeling the issue a "political question" (see Chapter 4). It has been suggested, however, that in light of *Powell v. McCormack* (1969), the Court could define "high crimes and misdemeanors." In *Powell,* the Court refused to view as "political" the question of whether Congress could exclude one of its members for reasons other than residency, age, or citizenship. From a formal legal standpoint, this argument is compelling, but the Court's decisions reflect more than legal arguments. Realistically, the Court could severely jeopardize the delicate balance of its coequal status were it to intervene between president and Congress in an impeachment controversy. Judicial self-restraint would counsel doing otherwise.

THEORIES OF PRESIDENTIAL POWER

Article II, Section 1 of the Constitution provides that the "executive power shall be vested in a President of the United States." Sections 2 and 3 enumerate specific powers granted to the president. These include authority to appoint judges and ambassadors, veto legislation, call Congress into special session, grant pardons and serve as **commander in chief** of the armed forces. Each of these designated powers is obviously a part of "executive power," but that general term is not defined in Article II. Thus, it is debatable whether the opening statement of Article II is merely a summary of powers later enumerated in the Article or, as many have argued, an independent grant of power to the president.

Enumerated and Inherent Powers

In the early days of the republic, James Madison and Alexander Hamilton engaged in the first of what was to be a long series of sharp disagreements among constitutional theorists about the proper scope of presidential power. Madison argued that presidential power is restricted to those powers specifically enumerated in Article II. By contrast, Hamilton argued for a transcendent conception of presidential power. Believing the opening statement in Article II to be a grant of power in its own right, he stated that "the difficulty of a complete enumeration of all cases of executive authority would naturally dictate the use of general terms and would render it improbable that a specification of certain particulars was designed as a substitute for the term [executive power]. . . ." Thus, Hamilton held that "the general doctrine of our Constitution . . . is that the executive power of the nation is vested in the President; subject only to the exceptions and qualifications which are expressed in that instrument." For Madison, if new exercises of power could be continually justified by invoking inherent executive power, "no citizen could any longer guess at the character of the government under which he lives; the most penetrating jurist would be unable to scan the extent of constructive prerogative." These competing theories correspond to very different notions of the proper role of the president in the newly created national government. While Madison envisaged a passive role for the president, who would faithfully execute the laws adopted by Congress, Hamilton viewed the presidency in more activist terms.

The "Stewardship" Theory of Presidential Power

The debate over the scope of presidential power was by no means confined to the early years of the republic. A vigorous argument occurred early in this century between those who espoused the "stewardship" theory and those who embraced the "constitutional" theory of presidential power. The constitutional theory, derived from Madison's ideas, finds its best and most succinct expression in the words of President William Howard Taft. In his view, the president can "exercise no power which cannot be fairly and reasonably traced to some specific grant of power or justly implied and included within such express grant as proper and necessary to its exercise." The stewardship theory, the modern counterpart to Hamilton's perspective, was best encapsulated by President Theodore Roosevelt. In his view, the Constitution permits the president "to do anything that the needs of the nation [demand] unless such action [is] forbidden by the Constitution or the laws." According to this perspective, the president is a steward of the people empowered to do anything deemed necessary, short of what is expressly prohibited by the Constitution, in the pursuit of the general welfare for which he is primarily responsible.

American constitutional history has, for the most part, vindicated the views of Alexander Hamilton and Theodore Roosevelt. Although some observers advocate scaling down the modern presidency, few really expect such diminution to occur. The exigencies of modernization, the complexities of living in a technological age, and the need for the United States as a superpower to speak to other nations with a unified voice and to respond quickly to threats to the national security have forced us to recognize the stewardship presidency as both necessary and legitimate. The inherent vagueness of Article II has facilitated this recognition.

The Supreme Court Legitimates Stewardship

For the most part, the Supreme Court has been willing to allow expansion of executive power over constitutional objections. It would be somewhat naive to expect the Court to stem the flow of power into the executive branch, given the fundamental economic, social, technological, and military needs that have promoted the stewardship presidency. There are cases in which the Court has invalidated particular exercises of executive power—for example, the steel seizure case (*Youngstown Sheet & Tube Company v. Sawyer* [1952]) and the Nixon tapes case (*United States v. Nixon* [1974]), but the overall trend has been to legitimize the "history of aggrandizement."

Because the Supreme Court generally reacts to issues arising elsewhere, it is odd that the first instance in which the Court grappled with abstract notions of executive power was a case that involved the not-so-abstract issue of the justices' personal safety (*In re Neagle,* 1890). In 1890, a federal marshal named David Neagle was charged with first-degree murder by the state of California for having killed a man while attempting to protect the life of a Supreme Court justice. At that time, justices were required to "ride circuit;" that is, while the Supreme Court was not in session, they had to travel extensively over particular geographic areas to conduct trials and hear appeals. During one such excursion to California, the life of Justice Stephen J. Field was threatened by a disgruntled litigant (and prominent member of the California bar) named David Terry. Learning of this threat, the U.S. attorney general assigned Neagle to accompany Justice Field when he next rode circuit in California. Upon Field's return to that state, he encountered David Terry in a restaurant. Terry struck Justice Field, whereupon Neagle shot Terry dead. Interestingly, no weapon was found on Terry's corpse, raising the question of whether Neagle's response to the attack had been excessive. In any event, Neagle was promptly arrested by California authorities acting on a complaint from the wife of the deceased. Neagle then brought a federal habeas corpus action in order to challenge his arrest and prosecution. Under federal law, Neagle could secure release if he could show that he had acted "in pursuance of a law of the United States."

Unfortunately for Neagle, his assignment to protect Justice Field was not based on any statutory authority. However, the Supreme Court held that the Attorney General's order assigning Neagle to protect Justice Field was tantamount to federal law. Opting essentially for the stewardship view of presidential power, the Court reasoned that the president was not "limited to enforcement of acts of Congress . . . according to their express terms." Rather, because the Constitution vests the government and particularly the executive with the obligation to protect "the peace of the United States," the executive is authorized to do whatever is necessary to fulfill that obligation (and this authorization is equivalent to a law). The president can and must take action to secure the peace, and he appropriately did so in the *Neagle* case. Thus, Neagle was held to be immune to prosecution by the state of California. In reaching this decision, the Court opted for Alexander Hamilton's broad view of executive power: this power stems not only from specific statutory authorizations or enumerations in Article II of the Constitution—it also derives from the power to protect the public safety implicit in the very nature of executive power.

The Outer Limits of Stewardship

Although the Supreme Court had several opportunities to elaborate on the scope of inherent executive power after *In re Neagle* (see, for example *In re Debs* [1895]; *United States v. Midwest Oil Company* [1915]; and *Korematsu v. United States* [1944]), it did not deal with the issue in any real depth until the steel seizure case of 1952 *(Youngstown Sheet & Tube Company v. Sawyer)*. In December 1951, President Harry S. Truman was informed that negotiations between labor and management in the steel industry had broken down. Concerned about the possible consequences of a stoppage in steel production, both for the domestic economy and for the Korean War effort, Truman acted to delay a strike by referring the issue to the Wage Stabilization Board for further negotiation. By April 1952, it became clear that negotiations were fruitless, and the workers announced their plans to strike. To prevent this, Truman ordered Secretary of Commerce Charles Sawyer to seize the steel mills and maintain full production. Not surprisingly, this action was challenged in the courts, and very soon the issue was before the Supreme Court.

Much to President Truman's chagrin, the Supreme Court (splitting 6 to 3) refused to allow the government to seize and operate the steel plants. Writing for the Court, Justice Hugo Black rejected inherent executive power as a justification for Truman's order. This reflected Justice Black's strong inclination to adhere closely to the language of the Constitution, an inclination characteristic of the interpretivist approach to constitutional adjudication. In a separate concurrence, Justice Robert Jackson took a position more characteristic of the historic mainstream of the Court. Jackson recognized an inherent executive power transcending particular enumerations in Article II but nevertheless found Truman's action to be impermissible. Noting that Congress had already considered and rejected legislation permitting such an executive order, Jackson wrote, "when the President takes measures incompatible with the expressed or implied will of Congress, his power is at its lowest ebb."

From the various opinions rendered in the steel seizure case, it is clear that several justices were swayed by the fact that Truman acted not only without congressional approval but irrespective of implied disapproval. In considering the Taft-Hartley bill, Congress had rejected an amendment that would have given the president a power similar to that exercised by Truman in seizing the steel mills. Thus, the steel seizure case was by no means a wholesale repudiation of the stewardship theory of presidential power—rather, it was a reminder that the steward's authority is neither entirely self-derived nor without limitation. Moreover, the decision served notice to the chief executive that his actions, at least those in the domestic sphere, are subject to judicial scrutiny.

Another important instance in which the Court imposed limits on the stewardship presidency was in the Pentagon papers case of 1971 *(New York Times Co. v. United States)*. In the most celebrated case arising from the Vietnam controversy, the Court refused to issue an injunction against newspapers that had come into possession of the "Pentagon papers," a set of classified documents detailing the history of American strategy in Vietnam. Basing his position on inherent executive power and not on any act of Congress, President Richard M. Nixon sought to restrain the press from disclosing classified information that, he argued,

President Harry S. Truman

would be injurious to the national security. The Court, obviously skeptical of the alleged threat to national security and sensitive to the values protected by the First Amendment, refused to defer to the president.

It is interesting to speculate whether the results reached in the steel seizure and Pentagon papers cases would have been different in other sociopolitical contexts. If the nation had been engaged in a world war, rather than in limited and divisive conflicts in Korea and Vietnam, it is hard to believe that the Court would have been willing to challenge such assertions of inherent executive power. One must realize that Supreme Court decisions on executive power, as on other constitutional issues, are influenced not simply by legal principles but by complex political forces as well.

SPECIFIC POWERS OF THE PRESIDENCY

Having considered general perspectives on presidential power, it is now appropriate to examine specific powers of the presidency. We begin our discussion with key enumerated powers: the power of appointment, the power to grant pardons, and the veto power. The discussion then moves to specific unenumerated powers: executive privilege, immunity from liability, and impoundment.

The Power to Veto Legislation

Under Article I, Section 7, "every bill" and "every order, resolution or vote to which the concurrence of the Senate and the House of Representatives may be necessary" must be presented to the president for approval. There are but three exceptions to this "presentment" requirement: it is not applicable to actions involving a single house, such as the adoption of procedural rules; it does not apply to concurrent resolutions, such as those establishing joint committees or setting a date for adjournment; finally, it does not apply to constitutional amendments proposed by the Congress. Until 1983, there was another category of congressional decisions not subject to presidential approval. The so-called legislative veto was a device whereby one or both houses of Congress passed resolutions to veto certain decisions made in the executive branch. In the case of *Immigration and Naturalization Service v. Chadha* (1983), the Supreme Court invalidated the legislative veto partly on the ground that it violated the presentment requirement of Article I.

The "Pocket Veto"

The president has ten days (not counting Sundays) in which to consider legislation presented for approval. The president has several options: (1) signing the bill into law, which is what usually occurs; (2) vetoing the bill, which can be overridden by a two-thirds majority of both houses of Congress; or (3) neither signing nor vetoing the bill, thus allowing it to become law automatically after ten days. A major exception applies, however, to the third option: if Congress adjourns before the ten days have expired and the president has still not signed the bill, it is said to have been subjected to a **"pocket veto."** The beauty of the pocket veto (at least from the president's standpoint) is that it deprives Congress of the chance to override a formal veto. This device was first used by President James Madison in 1812.

The pocket veto has been controversial since its inception. The crucial question is: What constitutes an adjournment of Congress? In the pocket veto case (*Okanogan Indians v. United States* [1929]), the Supreme Court upheld President Calvin Coolidge's authority to pocket-veto a bill between sessions of the same Congress. The Court held that "adjournment" means any congressional break that prevents the return of a bill within the requisite ten-day period.

Questions have persisted about whether adjournments between sessions of the same Congress do in fact prevent the president from returning a bill within the ten-day period. The issue was dramatized during Congress's holiday recess in November 1983, when President Reagan pocket-vetoed a bill linking U.S. aid to El Salvador to that country's progress in the area of human rights. Representative Michael Barnes, the sponsor of the bill, and thirty-two other House Democrats filed suit challenging the president's action. According to these plaintiffs, Congress's break between sessions had not really prevented the president from returning the bill because both the House and Senate had appointed officers to receive presidential messages, and it was possible to reconvene the Congress in short order at the call of the leadership.

Although the administration won the lawsuit at the district court level, a panel of the Court of Appeals for the District of Columbia Circuit reversed, splitting 2 to 1. According to the court of appeals, the holiday recess had not really prevented the president from returning the bill, either signed or vetoed, during the required ten-day period (see *Barnes v. Kline* [1985]). Until the Supreme Court addresses the issue, uncertainty will remain as to whether a pocket veto is limited to the final adjournment of a given Congress or is permissible between sessions of the same Congress and, if the latter, under what circumstances.

An "Item Veto"?

Although the Supreme Court has not faced the question, tradition dictates that the president must accept or veto a bill as a whole. Recent presidents, most notably Ronald Reagan and George Bush, have called for a constitutional amendment providing the president with a line-item veto, a power exercised by many state governors. Supporters of this measure argue that such a veto would allow the president to control the swelling federal budget more effectively. Arguably a line-item veto would also allow the President to defeat the congressional tactic of attaching disagreeable "riders" to bills the president basically supports. At present, it is unlikely that such an amendment will be adopted. It is unrealistic to expect Congress to approve a measure depriving itself of powers in order to further enhance the presidency.

The Powers of Appointment and Removal

Long before the advent of the modern stewardship presidency, it was obvious that presidents could not be expected to fulfill their duties alone. As presidential power has expanded, so too has the size and complexity of the executive branch. Originally, Congress provided for three cabinet departments—state, war, and treasury—to assist the president in the execution of policy. Today, there are fourteen cabinet departments, as well as a plethora of agencies, boards, and commissions in the executive establishment. While in 1790 less than a thousand employees worked for the executive branch, today that number has grown to approximately 3 million. Although almost all of these are **civil service** employees, the president directly appoints more than two thousand upper-level officials. The power to appoint these officials, as well as federal judges and ambassadors, emanates from Article II, Section 2, which provides that the president

> shall nominate, and by and with the advice and consent of the Senate, shall appoint ambassadors, other public ministers and consuls, judges of the Supreme Court, and all other officers of the United States, whose appointments are not herein otherwise provided for, which shall be established by law; but the Congress may by law vest the appointment of such inferior officers, as they think proper, in the President alone, in the courts of law, or in the heads of departments.

Thus, the Constitution permits some upper-level officials in the executive branch to be selected solely at the discretion of the president and some to be appointed solely by the heads of departments, while the ostensibly more important federal officials are to be appointed by the president with the advice and consent of the Senate. In the case of appointments requiring senatorial consent, the president nominates a candidate, awaits Senate approval by majority vote, and then commissions the confirmed nominee as an "officer of the United States."

The Supreme Court has made it clear that this process of nomination, approval, and commission is mandatory and that the nomination aspect of the process belongs solely to the president. Thus, in *Buckley v. Valeo* (1976), the Court struck down a section of the Federal Election Campaign Act of 1972 that provided Congress with a role in the nomination of members of the newly created Federal Election Commission.

In *Morrison v. Olson* (1988), the Court upheld a provision of the Ethics in Government Act of 1978 under which a "Special Division" of the U.S. Court of Appeals for the District of Columbia is empowered to appoint **special prosecutors** to investigate allegations of misconduct involving high government officials. The Court held that the special prosecutor is an "inferior officer" whose appointment may be assigned to the courts under Article II, Section 2.

The Removal Problem

Although the Constitution is reasonably clear on the subject of the presidential appointment power, the issue of removal of an appointed official has been rather problematic. Obviously, the president has a strong interest in being able to remove those appointees whose performance displeases him. However, the Constitution addresses the question of removal only in the context of the cumbersome impeachment process. It is unlikely that the Framers intended that administrative officials whose performance is unacceptable to the president be subject to removal only by impeachment. Given the difficulty of this method of removal, such a limitation could paralyze government.

Most observers agree that officers of the United States can be removed by means other than impeachment—except for judges, whose life tenure (assuming good behavior) is guaranteed by the Constitution. The problem is the role of Congress in the removal of executive officers. Given that the Constitution requires senatorial consent for certain presidential appointments, is it not reasonable to expect Congress to play a role in the removal of such officials? The Supreme Court first dealt with the question of the president's removal powers in *Myers v. United States* (1926).

The *Myers* case arose when President Woodrow Wilson removed Frank Myers, a Portland, Oregon, postmaster, before his term had expired. In removing Myers, Wilson ignored provisions of an 1876 act of Congress requiring Senate approval for the removal of postmasters. Consequently, Myers brought suit to recover wages lost between the time he was fired and the time his term was to expire. In a lengthy opinion for the Court, Chief Justice William Howard Taft (himself a former president) held that the removal of Myers was valid and that the senatorial consent provisions were unconstitutional. Taft's opinion stated that, given the president's constitutional duty to faithfully execute the laws, it would be unreasonable to expect an administration to retain an official on whom it could no longer count to follow orders. The upshot of the *Myers* decision is that purely executive officials performing purely executive functions may be removed at will by the president, unchecked by the Congress.

Dicta in Taft's opinion in *Myers* suggested that the president might also remove at will officials appointed to serve in the independent regulatory agencies, such as the Interstate Commerce Commission. This assertion contradicted the statutes establishing such commissions, which provided that the executive show cause (that is, malfeasance or neglect of duty) before removing commissioners. After all, the motivation behind the creation of such commissions was to allow for government by experts free of partisan political concerns. Inevitably, the Supreme Court was to decide whether Congress could limit presidential removal power as applied to independent regulatory agencies.

In *Humphrey's Executor v. United States* (1935), the Supreme Court considered whether President Franklin D. Roosevelt could fire a member of the Federal Trade Commission (FTC) solely on policy grounds. In 1931, President Herbert Hoover reappointed William Humphrey to serve on the FTC. According to an act of Congress, Humphrey's seven-year term was subject to presidential curtailment only for malfeasance, inefficiency, or neglect of duty. When Roosevelt took office, he fired Humphrey, believing that the goals of his administration would be better served by people of his own choosing. Although Humphrey died shortly after his removal, the executor of his estate brought suit to recover wages lost between the time of removal and the time of his death.

In *Humphrey's Executor,* the Supreme Court narrowed Chief Justice Taft's broad view of executive removal powers expressed in the *Myers* case. The Court maintained the view that purely executive officials performing purely executive functions could be removed at will by the president. However, in the case of regulatory commissions like the FTC, Congress had created a "quasi-legislative" body designed to perform tasks independent of executive control. Thus, said the Court, Congress could regulate the removal of such officials. At the time, some observers viewed the *Humphrey's Executor* decision as a politically motivated departure from the *Myers* precedent. They saw *Humphrey's Executor* as part of the larger struggle between the Court and Roosevelt. Although in 1935 this interpretation was quite plausible, a subsequent decision by the Court indicates that the *Humphrey* case was by no means an anomaly created by transitory political forces.

The Supreme Court expanded on the *Humphrey* rationale in *Wiener v. United States* (1958) by holding that the unique nature of independent agencies requires that removal must be for cause, whether or not Congress has so stipulated. The case involved a member of the War Claims Commission who had been appointed by President Harry S. Truman and who was removed for partisan reasons by President Dwight D. Eisenhower. Noting the adjudicatory character of the commission, the Court stated that "it must be inferred that Congress did not wish to have hang over the Commission the Damocles' sword of removal by the President for no other reason than that he preferred to have on the Commission men of his own choosing."

Thus, the Court's decisions hold that the legality of presidential removal of an official in the executive branch depends on the nature of the duties performed by the official in question. Officials performing purely executive functions may be removed by the president at will; those performing quasi-legislative or quasi-judicial functions can be removed only for cause.

The Power to Grant Pardons

President Gerald Ford's full and unconditional pardon of former President Richard Nixon following the Watergate affair may have been politically unwise, but it was unquestionably constitutional. Article II, Section 2 states that the president shall have the power to "grant reprieves and pardons for offenses against the United States, except in cases of impeachment." Although impeachment proceedings were initiated against Nixon, his sudden resignation foreclosed any possibility of impeachment, let alone conviction by the Senate. Thus, Ford acted constitutionally in issuing the pardon to Nixon. (Lest there be doubt about Nixon's culpability in the Watergate scandal, note that the acceptance of a presidential pardon is tantamount to an admission of guilt, for one cannot be pardoned unless one has committed an offense.)

Although President Ford issued a full pardon in the Nixon case, the president may also issue "conditional" pardons. In *Schick v. Reed* (1974), the Supreme Court said:

> The plain purpose of the broad [pardoning] power conferred . . . was to allow . . . the President to "forgive" the convicted person in part or entirely, to reduce a penalty a specified number of years, or to alter it with conditions which are themselves constitutionally unobjectionable.

Maurice Schick had been convicted of murder and sentenced to death by a military tribunal. Subsequently, President Eisenhower commuted Schick's sentence to life imprisonment on the condition he be ineligible for parole. However, in *Furman v. Georgia* (1972), the Supreme Court ruled that the death penalty was in certain instances unconstitutional (see Chapter 14). Consequently, Schick went back to court arguing in light of the Court's capital punishment decision, which had been applied retroactively, that his own original death sentence was unconstitutional and that, accordingly, the no-parole provision should likewise be set aside. The Court disagreed, holding that the conditional pardon was lawful when issued and that the later decision in *Furman* did not alter its validity.

An unqualified presidential pardon fully restores any civil rights forfeited upon conviction of the crime. In *Ex parte Garland* (1867), the Court held that a pardon restores an individual's innocence as though a crime had never been committed. In the *Garland* case, this meant that one who had fought for the Confederacy could practice law before the Supreme Court without the need to take an oath that he had not voluntarily borne arms against the United States. The Court held that a full pardon by President Andrew Johnson absolved Garland of the need to take such an oath.

Amnesties

Although the presidential pardon was traditionally thought to be a private transaction between the president and the recipient, this did not prevent President Jimmy Carter from granting an **amnesty** that was, in effect, a blanket pardon to those who were either deserters or draft evaders during the Vietnam War.

President Carter's amnesty was not challenged in the courts; neither was it criticized on constitutional grounds, although many considered it to be an insult to those who had fought and died in Vietnam. It should be noted that amnesties have traditionally been granted by Congress to those who deserted or evaded service in America's wars.

Executive Privilege

Beginning with George Washington, presidents have asserted a right to withhold information from Congress and the courts. Known as **executive privilege,** this "right" has been defended as inherent in executive power. Indeed, it must be defended as such because it is nowhere mentioned in the Constitution. Scholars are divided over whether the Framers envisaged such a power in the presidency; but the point is moot in light of two centuries of history, as well as explicit Supreme Court recognition, supporting executive privilege.

Although the term "executive privilege" was coined during the Eisenhower administration of the 1950s, the practice dates from 1792. In that year, President Washington refused to provide the House of Representatives certain documents it had requested relative to the bewildering defeat of military forces under Gen. Arthur St. Clair by the Ohio Indians. Washington again asserted the privilege in 1795 when the House requested information dealing with the negotiation of the Jay Treaty with England. A few years later, President Thomas Jefferson, once a sharp critic of George Washington's imperious approach to the presidency, would rely on inherent executive in defying a subpoena duces tecum issued during the trial of Aaron Burr for treason in 1807.

Later presidents invoked executive privilege primarily to maintain the secrecy of information related to national security. Presidents Truman, Eisenhower, Kennedy, and Johnson all found occasion to invoke the doctrine to protect the confidentiality of their deliberations. However, the power of executive privilege did not become a major point of contention until the Nixon presidency.

The Watergate Tapes Controversy

During his first term (1969–1973), President Nixon invoked executive privilege on four separate occasions; others in the Nixon administration did so in more than twenty instances. But after his landslide reelection in 1972, Nixon and his lieutenants routinely employed executive privilege to evade queries from Congress regarding the Watergate break-in and subsequent cover-up.

Although Nixon was able to use executive privilege to withhold information requested by Congress, he was unable to avoid a subpoena duces tecum issued by the federal courts at the request of Watergate special prosecutor Leon Jaworski. Earlier, Nixon had fired Archibald Cox, Jaworski's predecessor, when Cox refused to back down in his efforts to subpoena the infamous tapes on which Nixon had recorded conversations with principals in the Watergate scandal. In an episode that became known as the "Saturday Night Massacre," Nixon fired Attorney General Elliot Richardson and Assistant Attorney General William

President Richard M. Nixon

Rockelshaus, both of whom refused to follow the president's order to dismiss Cox. Ultimately, Cox was dismissed on the order of Robert H. Bork, who was solicitor general at the time. Although there was no question of Nixon's constitutional authority to dismiss Cox—who was, after all, an employee of the Justice Department—the dismissal was politically disastrous: the Saturday Night Massacre led Congress to consider the possibility of impeachment of the president. Succeeding Cox, Leon Jaworski pursued the Watergate investigation with alacrity. When the federal district court denied Nixon's motion to quash a new subpoena duces tecum obtained by Jaworski, the question of executive privilege went before the Supreme Court.

When *United States v. Nixon* reached the Supreme Court, Justice William Rehnquist, who had served in the Justice Department during Nixon's first term, recused himself. In deciding the Nixon tapes case, the other eight justices unanimously ordered that the subpoenaed tapes be surrendered. Recognizing the general legitimacy of executive privilege, the Court nevertheless held that the needs of criminal justice outweighed the presidential interest in confidentiality in this case. The Court refused to view executive privilege as an absolute presidential immunity from the judicial process. Thus, the Court asserted the primacy of the rule of law over the power of the presidency. Although Nixon was reportedly tempted to defy the Court's ruling, wiser counsel prevailed, and the tapes were produced. Shortly thereafter, recognizing the inevitable, Richard Nixon resigned the presidency in disgrace.

Presidential Immunity from Civil Suits

In addition to a limited power of executive privilege, the Supreme Court has held that presidents enjoy nearly absolute immunity against private civil suits.

Not surprisingly, the recent cases in which the Court was asked to decide the scope of executive immunity stemmed from controversies that began during the Nixon administration. Morton Halperin, a political scientist, was a staff member of the National Security Council during the Nixon administration. After learning that his home telephone had been illegally wiretapped, Halperin brought suit seeking monetary damages against Nixon, his secretary of state, Henry Kissinger, and his attorney general, John Mitchell. In *Kissinger v. Halperin* (1981), the Court divided 4 to 4 (Justice Rehnquist not participating), thus letting stand a lower federal court decision upholding President Nixon's susceptibility to lawsuit.

In *Nixon v. Fitzgerald* (1982), the Court was able to reach majority agreement on the question of presidential immunity. The case involved A. Ernest Fitzgerald, a former management analyst with the Air Force. Fitzgerald had attracted much attention in 1968 when he embarrassed the Department of Defense by revealing huge cost overruns on the C-5A transport plane. In 1970, Fitzgerald was dismissed, ostensibly as part of a departmental reorganization. Later, the Civil Service Commission found that Fitzgerald had been illegally removed for his whistle-blowing on the Pentagon. Following the commission's decision, Fitzgerald filed suit in federal court. On appeal, the Supreme Court held that the president was entitled to absolute immunity against private civil suits. Writing for the Court, Justice Lewis Powell opined that "[b]ecause of the singular importance of the President's duties, diversion of his energies by concern with private lawsuits would raise unique risks to the effective functioning of government." Justice Byron White dissented:

> Attaching absolute immunity to the office of the President, rather than to particular activities the President might perform, places the President above the law. It is a reversion to the old notion that the King can do no wrong.

The Power of Impoundment

Another controversial presidential power is that of **impoundment,** or the refusal to allow expenditure of funds appropriated by Congress. The first instance occurred in 1803, when President Jefferson withheld fifty thousand dollars that Congress had allocated to build gunboats to defend the Mississippi River. Jefferson's purpose was merely to delay the expenditure, primarily because the Louisiana Purchase, which was transacted shortly after Congress appropriated the money for gunboats, minimized the need for defenses along the Mississippi. During the remainder of the nineteenth century, presidents rarely invoked Jefferson's precedent. In 1905, Congress gave the president statutory authority to engage in limited impoundments to avoid departmental deficits. And in 1921, Congress extended this authority to allow the president to withhold funds to save money should Congress authorize more than was needed to secure its goals. Although Congress provided for a limited power of impoundment, these concessions to the president did not significantly undermine Congress's basic "power of the purse."

President Franklin D. Roosevelt consistently spent less than Congress appropriated. After Roosevelt, presidents increasingly used impoundment to pursue policy goals. Presidents Truman, Eisenhower, and Johnson used impoundment in the area of defense spending, justifying their actions on the basis of the president's role as commander in chief. Although these actions produced some criticism in Congress, they were not of sufficient magnitude to produce legislation or constitutional litigation.

Richard Nixon, however, extended the power of impoundment beyond limits acceptable to either Court or Congress. Nixon not only used impoundment to suit his fiscal preferences, but he also attempted to dismantle certain programs of which he disapproved. The most notorious example was his attempt to shut down the Office of Economic Opportunity (OEO) by refusing to spend any of the funds Congress had designated for it. (Congressional and public pressures forced Nixon to capitulate on the OEO issue.) In one of his far-reaching uses of the impoundment power, Nixon ordered the head of the Environmental Protection Agency, Russell Train, to withhold a substantial amount of money allocated for sewage treatment plants under the Water Pollution Control Act of 1972. Particularly disturbing to some members of Congress was the fact that Nixon had originally vetoed the act and Congress had overridden the veto. Thus, Nixon was seeking to have his way, a two-thirds majority of Congress to the contrary notwithstanding, by using the power to impound funds. In *Train v. City of New York* (1975), the Supreme Court invalidated Nixon's impoundment effort, concluding that the president did not possess a "seemingly limitless power to withhold funds from allotment and obligation."

The Budget and Impoundment Act of 1974

Prior to the Court's decision in the *Train* case, Congress adopted the Congressional Budget and Impoundment Control Act of 1974. Although the act recognizes a limited presidential power to impound funds, it requires the president to inform Congress of the reasons for an intended impoundment and provides for a bicameral legislative veto to prevent the president from proceeding. However, the Supreme Court's decision in *Immigration and Naturalization Service v. Chadha* rendered the legislative veto provision of the impoundment act presumptively unconstitutional (see Chapter 7).

THE POWER TO MAKE FOREIGN POLICY

Scholars have written of the "two presidencies." One presidency, concerned with domestic affairs, is severely limited by the Constitution, the Supreme Court, and Congress. The other presidency, that involving foreign affairs and international relations, is less susceptible to constitutional and political constraints. Although the thesis may have been overstated, the basic point is valid. Throughout American history, Congress, the courts, and the American public have been highly deferential to the president in the conduct of foreign policy. A serious reading of the Constitution indicates to some commentators that the Framers intended for Congress to play a greater role in the foreign policy process; however, the exigencies of history, more than the intentions of the Framers, determine the roles played by the institutions of government.

Another factor contributing to presidential dominance of foreign policy is the distinctive structures of Congress and the executive branch. Congress is comprised of 535 members, each representing either a state or localized constituency. On the other hand, the president represents a national constituency. Is it not reasonable that the president alone should speak for the nation in the international arena?

The "Sole Organ" in the Field of International Relations?

In *United States v. Curtiss-Wright Export Corporation* (1936), the Supreme Court placed its stamp of approval on presidential primacy in the realm of foreign affairs. In May 1934, Congress adopted a joint resolution authorizing the president to forbid U.S. companies from selling munitions (under such limitations and exceptions as the president might determine) to the warring nations of Paraguay and Bolivia. Additionally, Congress provided for criminal penalties for those violating presidential prohibitions. Shortly after this resolution was adopted, President Roosevelt issued an executive order imposing an embargo on arms sales to the belligerent countries. In 1936, the Curtiss-Wright Export Corporation was indicted for conspiring to sell arms to Bolivia in violation of the embargo. Curtiss-Wright sought to avoid prosecution by arguing that Congress had unconstitutionally delegated its lawmaking power to the president, because the resolution allowed the president to make the specific rules controlling arms shipments.

Despite the fact that just one year earlier it had taken a tough stand on the issue of delegation of legislative power (*see A.L.A. Schechter Poultry Corporation v. United States* [1935] discussed and reprinted in Chapter 7), the Court refused to find anything unconstitutional in the *Curtiss-Wright* case. The Court distinguished between two classes of power, domestic and foreign, and held that the rule against legislative delegation applied only to the former. Furthermore, the Court suggested that the president would have inherent power to impose such an embargo, even without an authorizing resolution from the Congress. Expounding on presidential primacy in foreign affairs, the Court referred to the president as the "sole organ of the federal government in the field of international relations." Justice George Sutherland's opinion in *Curtiss-Wright* went so far as to assert that this class of presidential power transcended the Constitution itself.

Even assuming that it is possible to draw a neat distinction between domestic powers and those pertaining to foreign affairs, many scholars would challenge the Court's sweeping endorsement of presidential power to make foreign policy. Few would argue that, in making and executing the foreign policy of this nation, the president is subject to no constitutional limitations. Clearly, though, the degree of freedom afforded the president in the field of foreign policy has been substantial indeed. For example, in *Haig v. Agee* (1981), the Court upheld the Reagan administration's decision to revoke the passport of a former agent of the Central Intelligence Agency (CIA) whose activities in foreign countries were deemed a threat to national security. And in *Regan v. Wald* (1984), the Court sustained the Reagan administration's unilateral restrictions on travel to Cuba.

Writing for the Court in *Haig v. Agee,* Chief Justice Burger invoked the expansive view of presidential authority in the field of foreign affairs taken by the Court in *Curtiss-Wright.* And, according to Justice Rehnquist's majority opinion in *Regan v. Wald,* matters involving "the conduct of foreign relations . . . are so entirely entrusted to the political branches of government as to be largely immune from judicial inquiry or interference."

The Iran-Contra Scandal

In the wake of Vietnam and Watergate, and fueled by revelations about covert CIA activities during the 1960s, Congress in the 1970s adopted a series of laws limiting presidential power to employ covert means of pursuing foreign policy objectives. In the 1980s, when Congress learned of CIA efforts to support the Contras battling to overthrow the Marxist government of Nicaragua, it adopted the Boland Amendments, a series of measures restricting the use of U.S. funds to aid the Contras. The Reagan administration attempted an end run around the Boland Amendments by secretly selling weapons to Iran and using the profits to aid the Contras. When the operation was uncovered, an outraged Congress conducted an investigation that included the testimony of Lt. Col. Oliver North, a staff member of the National Security Council who was heavily involved in the covert operation. In a later criminal trial, North was convicted of perjury and obstruction of justice. (His conviction was overturned on appeal in 1991. The appeals court held that prosecutors had illegally introduced evidence covered by the grant of immunity under which North had testified before Congress.)

Although the Iran-Contra affair was a blow to the credibility and prestige of the Reagan administration, it remains shrouded in legal uncertainty. It is not clear whether the administration actually violated the Boland Amendments, although there is little doubt that it sought to undermine the policy objective behind them. Second, given the Supreme Court's pronouncements in *United States v. Curtiss-Wright,* there is a serious question about the extent to which Congress may exercise control over presidential actions in the foreign policy sphere. Clearly, Congress may impose restrictions on the expenditure of government funds, since Congress possesses the "power of the purse." But may Congress prevent the president from carrying out a foreign policy objective through "creative enterprises," such as the deal to sell weapons to Iran?

Troubling constitutional questions involving the allocation of powers in the field of foreign policy are unlikely to be resolved in the courts of law. Rather, as "political questions," they are apt to be resolved in the court of public opinion. As the underwhelming public response to the Iran-Contra scandal demonstrates, the American people are not particularly squeamish about broad presidential latitude in the foreign policy arena.

Specifics of Conducting Foreign Affairs

Although presidential authority in international relations rests in large part on inherent executive power, the Constitution also enumerates specific powers important in the everyday management of foreign affairs. Article II, Section 3 authorizes the president to receive ambassadors and emissaries from foreign nations. In effect, this provides the president the power to recognize the legitimate governments of foreign nations. This power is of obvious importance in international relations, as attested by Roosevelt's recognition of the Soviet government in the 1930s, Truman's recognition of Israel, Kennedy's severance of ties with Cuba, and Carter's recognition of the People's Republic of China.

Treaties

In addition to the authority to recognize foreign governments, the president is empowered by Article II to make treaties with foreign nations, subject to the consent of the Senate. A treaty is an agreement between two or more nations containing promises to behave in specified ways. The atmospheric nuclear test-ban treaty negotiated under President Kennedy's leadership, the SALT I treaty reached with the Soviets during the Nixon presidency, and the Panama Canal Treaty negotiated during the Carter administration illustrate the foreign-policy importance of the treaty-making power.

A constitutional problem has arisen from the fact that the terms of a treaty can affect the domestic policy of the nation. This issue was addressed by the Supreme Court in *Missouri v. Holland* (1920). The case stemmed from a treaty between the United States and Canada designed to protect migratory birds. The treaty required both nations to pass laws restricting the hunting of certain species of fowl during their migrations between the United States and Canada. In 1918, Congress adopted a statute to effectuate the treaty. The state of Missouri brought suit, claiming ownership of the protected birds while they were within its borders and that, accordingly, Congress had usurped the powers reserved to the states by the Tenth Amendment. The Supreme Court, rejecting Missouri's claim of ownership, held the statute valid under the "elastic clause" of Article I, Section 8: "If the treaty is valid there can be no dispute about the validity of the statute . . . as a necessary and proper means to execute the powers of the Government." Addressing the ultimate validity of the treaty, the Court held that "acts of Congress are the supreme law of the land only when made in pursuance of the Constitution, while treaties are declared to be so when made under the authority of the United States." Thus, the Court at once upheld both a treaty and a related statute that probably would not have been upheld in the absence of the treaty.

Missouri v. Holland dramatized the close connection between the foreign and domestic spheres of power and pointed up potential problems inherent in a government whose domestic authority supposedly emanates from a constitution but whose power to deal with foreign nations is preconstitutional or meta-constitutional in nature. Indeed, the holding in *Missouri v. Holland* raised the possibility of using treaties as means of expanding the legislative powers of the national government. In response to the argument that reliance on treaties might override the limitations of the Constitution, Senator John Bricker in the early 1950s proposed a constitutional amendment that would have nullified any treaty provision conflicting with the Constitution. The Bricker Amendment was never submitted to the states for ratification, falling one vote short of the necessary two-thirds majority in the Senate. Nevertheless, interest in the amendment remained strong throughout the decade. Despite the failure of the Bricker Amendment, the fears that motivated its supporters have not been borne out by subsequent experience.

Executive Agreements

Support for the Bricker proposal was not based wholly on fears that the treaty power would be used to strengthen the national government at the expense of the states. The amendment also sought to curtail the increasing presidential tendency to bypass Congress altogether through the use of executive agreements. Like treaties, executive agreements require certain national commitments. However, such agreements are negotiated solely between heads of state acting independently of their legislative bodies. Most of these agreements involve minor matters of international concern, such as specification of the details of postal relations or the use of radio airwaves. In recent years, however, the executive agreement has emerged as an important tool of foreign policy-making. This development was legitimated by the Supreme Court in *United States v. Belmont* (1937) and *United States v. Pink* (1942). Both cases challenged the domestic aspects of the Litvinov Agreements that Franklin Roosevelt had struck with Joseph Stalin without any authorization or approval from the Senate. In addition to providing the Soviet Union with formal recognition, the agreements granted Soviet claims involving Russian companies that had been nationalized but whose assets were in the hands of U.S. banks. A legal controversy arose, however, when the state of New York refused to allow the transfer of assets to the Soviet government. The Supreme Court ultimately overruled the state *(United States v. Belmont),* holding that the executive agreement was legally equivalent to a treaty and thus the supreme law of the land, New York's policy notwithstanding.

The *Belmont* and *Pink* decisions, combined with the inherent uncertainty of treaty ratification, had the effect of making executive agreements all the more enticing to presidents. As the Senate's role in foreign policy-making declined, support increased in Congress for the provision of the Bricker Amendment that required congressional authorization of executive agreements before they could have any domestic effect. However, during the late 1950s and early 1960s, many of the forces motivating this proposal had diminished with shifts in international concern, changes in domestic public opinion, and the electoral defeat of Senator Bricker. Although there was some talk during and after the Vietnam War of reviving the Bricker Amendment, no formal proposals were forthcoming.

Perhaps the most dramatic recent use of the executive agreement was President Carter's agreement with Iran that secured the release of fifty-two American hostages in early 1981. The agreement negated all attachments against Iranian assets in the United States and transferred claims against Iran from American to international tribunals. In *Dames and Moore v. Regan* (1981), the Supreme Court upheld the validity of Carter's executive agreement. The Court found in the Emergency Powers Act of 1977 sufficient presidential authority to cancel attachments against Iranian assets. Finding no statutory authority for the transfer of claims to international tribunal, the Court held that Congress had tacitly approved the president's actions by its traditional pattern of acquiescence to executive agreements. Thus, merely by use may a power arguably in conflict with the Constitution gain legitimacy.

PRESIDENTIAL WAR POWERS

Presidential dominance in international affairs is not limited to or based on the formalities of recognizing and striking agreements with other governments. Integral to the president's foreign policy role is the tremendous power of the U.S. military, over which the Constitution makes the president commander in chief. Force is often threatened, and sometimes used, to protect U.S. allies and interests, maintain national security against possible attack, or defend the nation against actual attack. The success of American foreign policy would be severely limited if the Constitution curbed the nation's ability to respond effectively to threats against its interests or security. On the other hand, the Constitution was designed as a limitation on the power of our government. Should not such limitations apply (as Justice Black said in the Pentagon papers case) "to prevent the government from deceiving the people and sending them off to distant lands to die of foreign fevers and foreign shot and shell"?

The Framers of the Constitution did attempt to provide some limitation on the war-making power, as they did with respect to government power generally, by dividing power between the president and Congress. Although Article II recognizes the president as commander in chief, Article I provides Congress with the authority to declare war. Certainly the military conflicts in Vietnam and Korea qualify as wars; yet in neither case was there a formal declaration by Congress.

Presidential power to commit military forces to combat situations has a long heritage. It was first exercised in 1801, when Thomas Jefferson sent the U.S. Marines to "the shores of Tripoli" to root out the Barbary pirates. In 1846, James K. Polk sent American troops to instigate a war with Mexico that Congress formally approved by declaring war. In 1854, Franklin Pierce authorized a show of American force that led to the total destruction of an entire city in Central America. In none of these instances, however, did the Supreme Court have the opportunity to decide the scope of the president's power as commander-in-chief.

The Court's opportunity came in 1863 in *The Prize Cases*. These cases involved the disposition of vessels captured by the Union navy during the block-ade of Southern ports ordered by President Abraham Lincoln in the absence of a congressional declaration of war. Under existing laws of war, the captured vessels would become the property of the Union navy only if the conflict were a declared war. Given the extremely sensitive politics of the day, the Court could do nothing but find the seizures to be legal, even though Congress had not formally declared war against the Confederacy. The Court held that "the President is not only authorized, but bound to resist force. He does not initiate the war, but is bound to accept the challenge without waiting for any special legislative authority." Additionally, Justice Robert C. Grier noted that the "President was bound to meet [the Civil War] in the shape it presented itself, without waiting for the Congress to baptize it with a name; and no name given to it by him or them could change the fact." In *The Prize Cases,* the Court acknowledged the necessity of deferring to the president's decisions in times of crisis.

The Vietnam War

President Lincoln's unprecedented exercise of war powers presaged President Lyndon Johnson's actions in Vietnam a century later. Absent a formal declaration of war by Congress, the Johnson administration maintained that inherent presidential power essentially included the power to make war. In a 1966 *Department of State Bulletin,* Leonard Meeker asserted the president's power to

> deploy American forces abroad and commit them to military operations when the President deems such action necessary to maintain the security and defense of the United States. . . . If he considers that deployment of U.S. forces to South Vietnam is required, and that military measures against the source of communist aggression in North Vietnam are necessary, he is constitutionally empowered to take these measures.

In the Gulf of Tonkin Resolution of 1964, Congress did give limited authority to the president to take whatever actions were necessary to defend the government of South Vietnam and American interests and personnel in the region. The resolution was adopted in response to an alleged attack on American ships operating near North Vietnam. Later evidence indicated that the attack was exaggerated at the very least and was perhaps contrived to force Congress to sanction the growing American involvement in Southeast Asia. It was not long before the war was expanded far beyond anything envisioned by Congress in 1964. In a later development in the Vietnam War, President Nixon's covert war in Cambodia certainly fell beyond any authority granted the president by the Gulf of Tonkin Resolution. Amidst the harsh strains of sometimes violent antiwar protest, calmer voices began to be heard questioning the legality of the war effort.

During the Vietnam era, the Supreme Court had ample opportunity to rule on the constitutionality of the war and the concomitant use of presidential power, but it declined to do so, viewing the issue a "political question" (see *Massachusetts v. Laird* [1970]). The Court drew some criticism for this deferential posture. However, it is likely that the Court would have been more criticized if it had chosen to review the constitutionality of the Vietnam War—and it certainly would have been, had its ruling been adverse to the president. It is beyond question that the influence of the Court over the conduct of wars, foreign or domestic, is minimal at best. The philosophy of judicial self-restraint dictates that the Court maintain a low profile on such issues.

The War Powers Resolution

As the Supreme Court's unwillingness to address the issue became clear, Congress began to question the unbridled conception of presidential war powers. In

1973, Congress adopted the War Powers Resolution over the veto of President Nixon. The act was designed to limit the president's unilateral power to send troops into foreign combat. It requires the president to make a full report to Congress when sending troops into foreign areas, limits the duration of troop commitment without congressional authorization, and provides a veto mechanism whereby Congress can force the recall of troops at any time.

Given the Supreme Court's decision in *Immigration and Naturalization Service v. Chadha* (1983), the legislative veto provision of the War Powers Resolution is presumptively unconstitutional (see Chapter 7). Yet the provision remains on the books. Since Congress has not yet invoked the War Powers Resolution, the courts have had no occasion to address the specific question of its constitutionality. It is unlikely that the War Powers Resolution will ever be subjected to judicial review, as it is unlikely that it will ever be invoked against the president. Even if it were invoked and litigation resulted, it is probable that the courts would view the matter as a "political question" (see Chapter 4). In 1982, a federal judge did dismiss as "political" a lawsuit brought by members of Congress against President Reagan. Members were attempting to get the courts to invoke the War Powers Resolution to prevent the Reagan administration from providing military aid to the government of El Salvador (see *Crockett v. Reagan* [1982]).

Aside from the question of its constitutionality, the War Powers Resolution is probably not an effective constraint on the presidential war power. It can be viewed as little more than a symbolic gesture of defiance from a Congress displeased with the conduct of the Vietnam War. The existence of the War Powers Act did not prevent President Reagan from employing military force in pursuit of his foreign policy objectives. Reagan sent the U.S. Marines into Beirut and even used naval gunfire against the rebels in the Lebanese civil war. Reagan employed U.S. troops to topple the Marxist government of Grenada. And he ordered an air strike on Libya to punish the Khadaffi regime for its support of international terrorism. Although President Reagan chose to comply with the War Powers Act in all three cases by notifying Congress of his actions, he still made the decisions to send troops into hostile situations. Congressional disapproval would have made no difference in the cases of Grenada and Libya; the hostilities had practically ceased by the time Congress was notified.

The Persian Gulf War of 1991

Soon after Saddam Hussein's Iraq invaded and annexed tiny Kuwait in August 1990, President Bush ordered military forces into Saudi Arabia in a defensive posture. When it became clear that Iraq had no intention of leaving Kuwait, Bush ordered a massive build-up of forces in the region and began to threaten the use of force to remove Iraqi troops from Kuwait. Bush's critics soon suggested that the War Powers Act had been triggered because American troops were in a situation of imminent hostility. Yet Congress did not attempt to "start the clock" under the War Powers Act. When the president did finally decide to move against Iraq in January 1991, he first obtained a resolution from Congress supporting the use of force. Had Bush refused to obtain congressional approval, it would have been interesting to see whether and how Congress would have asserted itself. There is little question, however, that Bush's decision to seek congressional approval ultimately enhanced political support for the war. The war was executed with overwhelming force, resulting in minimal losses to allied forces. Iraq, which suffered enormous losses in both life and property, capitulated quickly. In the wake of the war, President Bush's approval ratings soared to levels not seen since the end of World War II. Presidential popularity is a volatile phenomenon, however, and Bush's approval ratings dropped steadily during the remainder of 1991.

Domestic Affairs during Wartime

Although there is a serious constitutional question over who has the power to *make* war, an equally difficult question arises over the extent of presidential power in the domestic sphere *during* wartime. Does the president's inherent power and duty to protect national security override express constitutional limitations and the rights of citizens? The Supreme Court's answer to the question has been mixed.

Civil War Cases

One of the early cases raising the question of individual rights versus presidential power during wartime was *Ex parte Merryman* (1861). Although it was not a Supreme Court decision, it did involve Chief Justice Roger B. Taney, acting in his capacity as circuit judge. John Merryman, a resident of Maryland, was a well-known advocate of secession. Fearing that Merryman's statements and potential actions would adversely affect the Union cause, military officials arrested him under the authority of a presidential directive. As a civilian, Merryman asserted that his arrest and detention by the military were illegal. He sought a writ of habeas corpus from Chief Justice Taney, who was "riding circuit" in Baltimore at the time. Earlier, President Lincoln had issued an order authorizing military commanders to suspend habeas corpus, thus facilitating military arrest and detention of civilians. However, Chief Justice Taney believed that only Congress could suspend the habeas corpus privilege (see Article I, Section 9). Taney issued the writ ordering Merryman's release, but it was ignored at Fort McHenry, where Merryman was in custody. Infuriated, Taney wrote an indignant letter to the president. The letter was widely publicized in the press. Although Lincoln never replied directly to Taney, he did ask Congress for legislation suspending habeas corpus, and in 1863, Congress complied with this request. Eventually, Merryman was turned over to civilian authorities.

Although the *Merryman* case never reached the Supreme Court, the justices eventually had an opportunity to rule on the constitutional limits of executive power during wartime. Lambdin P. Milligan, a civilian residing in Indiana, was an active collaborator with the Confederacy. In 1864, he was arrested and tried for treason by a military commission established by order of President Lincoln. Milligan was convicted and sentenced to death, but the sentence was not carried out. In 1866, some time after hostilities had ceased, the Supreme Court reviewed the conviction. Its landmark decision in *Ex parte Milligan* was a ringing endorsement of civil liberties. The Supreme Court took note of the fact that the

President Abraham Lincoln

civilian courts were open and operating in Indiana when Milligan was arrested and tried by the military. In ordering Milligan's release, the Court condemned Lincoln's directive establishing military jurisdiction over civilians outside of the immediate war area. It strongly affirmed the fundamental right of a civilian to be tried in a regular court of law, with all the procedural safeguards that characterize the criminal process. It must be remembered that this strong assertion of constitutional principles occurred a year after the close of the Civil War and the assassination of Abraham Lincoln. Viewed in this light, *Ex parte Milligan* may be more aptly described as an admission of judicial weakness during time of war than as a bold pronouncement of constitutional limits on presidential power.

The "Relocation" of Japanese-Americans

Early in the Second World War, President Roosevelt issued orders authorizing the establishment of "military areas" from which ostensibly dangerous persons could be expelled or excluded. Congressional legislation supported Roosevelt's orders by establishing criminal penalties for violators. Under these executive and congressional mandates, Gen. J. L. DeWitt, who headed the Western Defense Command, proclaimed a curfew and issued an order excluding all Japanese-Americans from a designated West Coast military area. The exclusion order led first to the imprisonment of some 120,000 persons in barbed wire-enclosed "assembly centers." Later, these persons were removed to "relocation centers" in rural areas as far inland as Arkansas. Although these actions were justified at the time on grounds of military necessity, overwhelming evidence indicates that they were in fact based on the view that all Japanese-Americans were "subversive" members of an "enemy race." In spite of the blatant racism reflected in these policies, the Supreme Court upheld both the curfew and the exclusion order (*Hirabayashi v. United States* [1943]; *Korematsu v. United States* [1944]). While recognizing that racial classifications are **inherently suspect** (a term discussed in detail in Chapter 16), a majority of the justices concluded that, under the pressure of war, the government had a **compelling interest** justifying such extreme measures. The *Korematsu* case stands for the sobering proposition that in time of war, the Supreme Court will defer to presidential assessments of threats to national security, whether real or imaginary.

It has now been well established that the forced relocation of thousands of Japanese-Americans was not justified on grounds of military necessity and was motivated chiefly by racial animus. In 1988, Congress belatedly acknowledged the government's responsibility for this gross miscarriage of justice by awarding reparations to survivors of the internment camps.

Peacetime Threats to National Security

During peacetime, presidential responses to perceived domestic threats to the national security are not as likely to win judicial approval. A good example is the Supreme Court's decision in *United States v. United States District Court* (1972). Reflecting Richard Nixon's deep-seated suspicions of the motives and affiliations of political opponents, the government had engaged in extensive wiretapping and other forms of electronic surveillance directed at U.S. citizens. The Supreme Court held that these activities, which were conducted without **probable cause** or judicial approval, offended the Fourth Amendment prohibition against unreasonable searches. The Court rejected the Nixon administration's argument that inherent executive power permitted the government to take these actions to obtain intelligence regarding foreign agents acting in the domestic sphere. In 1978, Congress buttressed the Court's decision by adopting the Foreign Intelligence Surveillance Act, which requires government agents to obtain a **search warrant** before subjecting U.S. citizens to electronic surveillance for the purpose of gathering foreign intelligence.

CONCLUSION

American constitutional development has witnessed the transformation of the presidency into the most powerful executive position in the world. The American president possesses awesome powers, most notably the authority to command the world's most formidable military. Yet the presidency is not without constitutional and statutory constraints, as dictated by the principle of checks and balances. Ultimately, the power of the presidency is less determined by congressional or judicial action than by public opinion.

Although the presidency occasionally experiences setbacks—as in the aftermath of the Iran-Contra scandal of 1986 and 1987—such reverses tend to be short-lived. The American people simply demand too much from the presidency to allow it to sink to a position of institutional inferiority. The Hamiltonian conception of the presidency has become institutionalized to the extent that neither the personality of the occupant nor the occasional crisis of credibility can produce any significant dismantling of the office.

FOR FURTHER READING

Barber, James David. *The Presidential Character,* 3d ed. Englewood Cliffs, N.J.: Prentice-Hall, 1985.

Berger, Raoul. *Impeachment: The Constitutional Problems.* Cambridge: Harvard University Press, 1973.

Burns, James MacGregor. *Presidential Government: The Crucible of Leadership.* Boston: Houghton Mifflin, 1973.

Corwin, Edward S. *The President: Office and Powers,* 4th ed. New York: New York University Press, 1957.

Cronin, Thomas E. *The State of the Presidency,* 2d ed. Boston: Little, Brown, 1980.

Hamilton, John C., ed. *Works of Alexander Hamilton.* New York: Macmillan, 1851.

Longley, Lawrence D., and Alan G. Braun. *The Politics of Electoral College Reform,* 2d ed. New Haven: Yale University Press, 1975.

Madison, James. *Letters and Other Writings of James Madison.* Edited by Philip R. Fendall. Philadelphia: Lippincott, 1865.

McConnell, Grant. *The Modern Presidency,* 2d ed. New York: St. Martin's, 1976.

Meeker, Leonard C. "The Legality of United States Participation in the Defense of Vietnam." *Department of State Bulletin* 54 (1966): 474–83.

McPherson, James M. *Abraham Lincoln and the Second American Revolution.* New York: Oxford University Press, 1991.

Mullen, William F. *Presidential Power and Politics.* New York: St. Martin's Press, 1976.

Reedy, George E. "The Presidency in 1976: Focal Point of Political Unity?" In *200 Years of the Republic in Retrospect,* edited by William C. Harvard and Joseph L. Bernd. Charlottesville: University Press of Virginia, 1976, pp. 228–38.

Roosevelt, Theodore. *Autobiography.* New York: Macmillan, 1913.

Rossiter, Clinton. *The American Presidency,* 2d ed. New York: Harcourt, Brace, 1960.

Schlesinger, Arthur. *The Imperial Presidency.* Boston: Houghton Mifflin, 1973.

Swisher, Carol Brent. *Stephen J. Field: Craftsman of the Law.* Washington, D.C.: Brookings Institution, 1930.

Taft, William Howard. *Our Chief Magistrate and His Powers.* New York: Columbia University Press, 1916.

Watson, Richard, and Norman Thomas. *The Politics of the Presidency.* New York: Wiley, 1983.

Westin, Alan. *The Anatomy of a Constitutional Law Case.* New York: Macmillan, 1958.

Wildavsky, Aaron. "The Two Presidencies." In *The Presidency,* edited by Aaron Wildavsky. Boston: Little, Brown, 1975.

CASES AND READINGS

Articles of Impeachment against President Richard M. Nixon Recommended by the House Judiciary Committee

On July 27, 1974, the House Judiciary Committee approved one article of impeachment against President Richard M. Nixon based on information the committee had obtained about Nixon's role in the cover-up of the infamous Watergate break-in that had occurred two years earlier. Two more articles of impeachment were later approved by the committee. All three articles are reprinted here. The House of Representatives never acted on the articles as Nixon resigned the presidency on August 9. On September 8, President Gerald Ford pardoned Nixon for any crimes he may have committed as president.

Resolved, That Richard M. Nixon, President of the United States, is impeached for high crimes and misdemeanors, and that the following articles of impeachment be exhibited to the Senate:

Articles of impeachment exhibited by the House of Representatives of the United States of America in the name of itself and of all of the people of the United States of America, against Richard M. Nixon, President of the United States of America, in maintenance and support of its impeachment against him for high crimes and misdemeanors.

ARTICLE I

In his conduct of the office of President of the United States, Richard M. Nixon, in violation of his constitutional oath faithfully to execute the office of President of the United States and, to the best of his ability, preserve, protect, and defend the Constitution of the United States, and in violation of his constitutional duty to take care that the laws be faithfully executed, has prevented, obstructed, and impeded the administration of justice, in that:

On June 17, 1972, and prior thereto, agents of the Committee for the Re-election of the President com-

mitted unlawful entry of the headquarters of the Democratic National Committee in Washington, District of Columbia, for the purpose of securing political intelligence. Subsequent thereto, Richard M. Nixon, using the powers of his high office, engaged, personally and through his subordinates and agents, in a course of conduct or plan designed to delay, impede, and obstruct the investigation of such unlawful entry; to cover up, conceal and protect those responsible; and to conceal the existence and scope of other unlawful covert activities.

The means used to implement this course of conduct or plan included one or more of the following:

1. Making or causing to be made false or misleading statements to lawfully authorized investigative officers and employees of the United States;
2. Withholding relevant and material evidence or information from lawfully authorized investigative officers and employees of the United States;
3. Approving, condoning, acquiescing in, and counseling witnesses with respect to the giving of false or misleading statements to lawfully authorized investigative officers and employees of the United States and false or misleading testimony in duly instituted judicial and congressional proceedings;
4. Interfering or endeavoring to interfere with the conduct of investigations by the Department of Justice of the United States, the Federal Bureau of Investigation, the Office of Watergate Special Prosecution Force, and Congressional committees;
5. Approving, condoning, and acquiescing in, the surreptitious payment of substantial sums of money for the purpose of obtaining the silence or influencing the testimony of witnesses, potential witnesses or individuals who participated in such illegal entry and other illegal activities;
6. Endeavoring to misuse the Central Intelligence Agency, an agency of the United States;

7. Disseminating information received from officers of the Department of Justice of the United States to subjects of investigations conducted by lawfully authorized investigative officers and employees of the United States, for the purpose of aiding and assisting such subjects in their attempts to avoid criminal liability;

8. Making false or misleading public statements for the purpose of deceiving the people of the United States into believing that a thorough and complete investigation had been conducted with respect to allegations of misconduct on the part of personnel of the executive branch of the United States and personnel of the Committee for the Re-election of the President, and that there was no involvement of such personnel in such misconduct; or

9. Endeavoring to cause prospective defendants, and individuals duly tried and convicted, to expect favored treatment and consideration in return for their silence or false testimony, or rewarding individuals for their silence or false testimony.

In all of this, Richard M. Nixon has acted in a manner contrary to his trust as President and subversive of constitutional government, to the great prejudice of the cause of law and justice and to the manifest injury of the people of the United States.

Wherefore Richard M. Nixon, by such conduct, warrants impeachment and trial, and removal from office.

ARTICLE II

Using the powers of the office of president of the United States, Richard M. Nixon, in violation of his constitutional oath faithfully to execute the office of president of the United States and, to the best of his ability, preserve, protect and defend the Constitution of the United States, and in disregard of his constitutional duty to take care that the laws be faithfully executed, has repeatedly engaged in conduct violating the constitutional rights of citizens, impairing the due and proper administration of justice and the conduct of lawful inquiries, or contravening the laws governing agencies of the executive branch and the purposes of these agencies.

This conduct has included one or more of the following:

1. He has, acting personally and through his subordinates and agents, endeavored to obtain from the Internal Revenue Service, in violation of the constitutional rights of citizens, confidential information contained in income tax returns for purposes not authorized by law and to cause, in violation of the constitutional rights of citizens, income tax audits or other income tax investigations to be initiated or conducted in a discriminatory manner.

2. He misused the Federal Bureau of Investigation, the Secret Service and other executive personnel in violation or disregard of the constitutional rights of citizens by directing or authorizing such agencies or personnel to conduct or continue electronic surveillance or other investigations for purposes unrelated to national security, the enforcement of laws or any other lawful function of his office; and he did direct the concealment of certain records made by the Federal Bureau of Investigation of electronic surveillance.

3. He has, acting personally and through his subordinates and agents, in violation or disregard of the constitutional rights of citizens, authorized and permitted to be maintained a secret investigative unit within the office of the president, financed in part with money derived from campaign contributions to him, which unlawfully utilized the resources of the Central Intelligence Agency, engaged in covert and unlawful activities and attempted to prejudice the constitutional right of an accused to a fair trial.

4. He has failed to take care that the laws were faithfully executed by failing to act when he knew or had reason to know that his close subordinates endeavored to impede and frustrate lawful inquiries by duly constituted executive, judicial and legislative entities concerning the unlawful entry into the headquarters of the Democratic National Committee and the coverup thereof, and concerning other unlawful activities including those relating to the confirmation of Richard Kleindienst as attorney general of the United States, the electronic surveillance

of private citizens, the break-in into the office of Dr. Lewis Fielding and the campaign financing practices of the Committee to Re-elect the President.

5. In disregard to the rule of law, he knowingly misused the executive power by interfering with agencies of the executive branch, including the Federal Bureau of Investigation, the Criminal Division and the Office of Watergate Special Prosecution Force, of the Department of Justice and the Central Intelligence Agency, in violation of his duty to take care that the laws be faithfully executed.

In all of this, Richard M. Nixon has acted in a manner contrary to his trust as president and subversive of constitutional government, to the great prejudice of the cause of law and justice and to the manifest injury of the people of the United States.

Wherefore Richard M. Nixon, by such conduct, warrants impeachment and trial and removal from office.

ARTICLE III

In his conduct of the office of president of the United States, Richard M. Nixon, contrary to his oath faithfully to execute the office of president of the United States and, to the best of his ability, preserve, protect and defend the Constitution of the United States, and in violation of his constitutional duty to take care that the laws be faithfully executed, has failed without lawful cause or excuse to produce papers and things as directed by duly authorized subpoenas issued by the Committee on the Judiciary of the House of Representatives on April 11, 1974; May 15, 1974; May 30, 1974, and June 24, 1974, and willfully disobeyed such subpoenas.

The subpoenaed papers and things were deemed necessary by the committee in order to resolve by direct evidence fundamental, factual questions relating to presidential direction, knowledge or approval of actions demonstrated by other evidence to be substantial grounds for impeachment of the president.

In refusing to produce these papers and things Richard M. Nixon, substituting his judgment as to what materials were necessary for the inquiry, interposed the powers of the presidency against the lawful subpoenas of the House of Representatives, thereby assuming to himself functions and judgments necessary to the exercise of the sole power of impeachment vested by the Constitution in the House of Representatives.

In all of this, Richard M. Nixon has acted in a manner contrary to his trust as president and subversive of constitutional government, to the great prejudice of the cause of law and justice and to the manifest injury of the people of the United States.

Wherefore, Richard M. Nixon by such conduct, warrants impeachment and trial and removal from office.

Youngstown Sheet and Tube Company v. Sawyer
343 U.S. 579; 72 S. Ct. 863; 96 L. Ed. 1153; (1952)
Vote: 6-3

Mr. Justice Black delivered the opinion of the Court.

We are asked to decide whether the President was acting within his constitutional power when he issued an order directing the Secretary of Commerce to take possession of and operate most of the Nation's steel mills. The mill owners argue that the President's order amounts to lawmaking, a legislative function which the Constitution has expressly con-fided to the Congress and not to the President. The Government's position is that the order was made on findings of the President that his action was necessary to avert a national catastrophe which would inevitably result from a stoppage of steel production, and that in meeting this grave emergency the President was acting within the aggregate of his constitutional powers as the Nation's Chief Executive and the Commander in Chief of the Armed Forces of the

United States. The issue emerges here from the following series of events:

In the latter part of 1951, a dispute arose between
the steel companies and their employees over terms
and conditions that should be included in new collective bargaining agreements. Long-continued conferences failed to resolve the dispute. On December 18, 1951, the employees' representative, United
Steelworkers of America, C.I.O., gave notice of an
intention to strike when the existing bargaining
agreements expired on December 31. The Federal
Mediation and Conciliation Service then intervened
in an effort to get labor and management to agree.
This failing, the President on December 22, 1951,
referred the dispute to the Federal Wage Stabilization Board to investigate and make recommendations for fair and equitable terms of settlement. This
Board's report resulted in no settlement. On April 4,
1952, the Union gave notice of a nation-wide strike
called to begin at 12:01 A.M. April 9. The indispens-
ability of steel as a component of substantially all
weapons and other war materials led the President
to believe that the proposed work stoppage would
immediately jeopardize our national defense and
that governmental seizure of the steel mills was necessary in order to assure the continued availability of
steel. Reciting these considerations for his action, the
President, a few hours before the strike was to begin,
issued Executive Order 10340.... The order directed the Secretary of Commerce to take possession
of most of the steel mills and keep them running.
The Secretary immediately issued his own posses-
sory orders, calling upon the presidents of the various seized companies to serve as operating managers for the United States. They were directed to carry
on their activities in accordance with regulations and
directions of the Secretary. The next morning the
President sent a message to Congress reporting his
action. *** Twelve days later he sent a second message. *** Congress has taken no action.

Obeying the Secretary's orders under protest, the
companies brought proceedings against him in the
District Court. Their complaints charged that the seizure was not authorized by an Act of Congress or by
any constitutional provisions. The District Court was
asked to declare the orders of the President and the
Secretary invalid and to issue preliminary and permanent injunctions restraining their enforcement.
Opposing the motion for preliminary injunctions,
the United States asserted that a strike disrupting
steel production for even a brief period would so
endanger the well-being and safety of the Nation that
the President had "inherent power" to do what he
had done—power "supported by the Constitution,
by historical precedent, and by court decisions." The
Government also contended that in any event no
preliminary injunction should be issued because the
companies had made no showing that their available
legal remedies were inadequate or that their injuries
from seizure would be irreparable. Holding against
the Government on all points, the District Court on
April 30 issued a preliminary injunction restraining
the Secretary from "continuing the seizure and possession of the plants . . . and from acting under the
purported authority of Executive Order No. 10340."
*** On the same day the Court of Appeals stayed the
District Court's injunction. *** Deeming it best that
the issues raised be promptly decided by this Court,
we granted *certiorari* on May 3 and set the cause for
argument on May 12. *** . . .

The President's power, if any, to issue the order
must stem either from an act of Congress or from the
Constitution itself. There is no statute that expressly
authorizes the President to take possession of property as he did here. Nor is there any act of Congress
to which our attention has been directed from which
such a power can fairly be implied. Indeed, we do
not understand the Government to rely on statutory
authorization for this seizure. There are two statutes
which do authorize the President to take both personal and real property under certain conditions.
However, the Government admits that these conditions were not met and that the President's order was
not rooted in either of the statutes. The Government
refers to the seizure provisions of one of these statutes *** (the Defense Production Act) as "much too
cumbersome, involved, and time-consuming for the
crisis which was at hand."

Moreover, the use of the seizure technique to
solve labor disputes in order to prevent work stop-
pages was not only unauthorized by any congressional enactment; prior to this controversy, Congress

had refused to adopt that method of settling labor disputes. When the Taft-Hartley Act was under consideration in 1947, Congress rejected an amendment which would have authorized such governmental seizures in cases of emergency. Apparently it was thought that the technique of seizure, like that of compulsory arbitration, would interfere with the process of collective bargaining. Consequently, the plan Congress adopted in that Act did not provide for seizure under any circumstances. Instead, the plan sought to bring about settlements by use of the customary devices of mediation, conciliation, investigation by boards of inquiry, and public reports. In some instances temporary injunctions were authorized to provide cooling-off periods. All this failing, unions were left free to strike after a secret vote by employees as to whether they wished to accept their employers' final settlement offer.

It is clear that if the President had authority to issue the order he did, it must be found in some provision of the Constitution. And it is not claimed that express constitutional language grants this power to the President. The contention is that presidential power should be implied from the aggregate of his powers under the Constitution. Particular reliance is placed on provisions in Article II which say that "The executive Power shall be vested in a President . . ."; that "he shall take Care that the Laws be faithfully executed"; and that he "shall be Commander in Chief of the Army and Navy of the United States."

The order cannot properly be sustained as an exercise of the President's military power as Commander in Chief of the Armed Forces. The Government attempts to do so by citing a number of cases upholding broad powers in military commanders engaged in day-to-day fighting in a theater of war. Such cases need not concern us here. Even though "theater of war" be an expanding concept, we cannot with faithfulness to our constitutional system hold that the Commander in Chief of the Armed Forces has the ultimate power as such to take possession of private property in order to keep labor disputes from stopping production. This is a job for the Nation's lawmakers, not for its military authorities.

Nor can the seizure order be sustained because of the several constitutional provisions that grant executive power to the President. In the framework of our Constitution, the President's power to see that the laws are faithfully executed refutes the idea that he is to be a lawmaker. The Constitution limits his functions in the lawmaking process to the recommending of laws he thinks wise and the vetoing of laws he thinks bad. And the Constitution is neither silent nor equivocal about who shall make laws which the President is to execute. The first section of the first article says that "All legislative Powers herein granted shall be vested in a Congress of the United States. . . ." After granting many powers to the Congress, Article I goes on to provide that Congress may "make all Laws which shall be necessary and proper for carrying into Execution the foregoing Powers, and all other Powers vested by this Constitution in the Government of the United States, or in any Department or Officer thereof."

The President's order does not direct that a congressional policy be executed in a manner prescribed by Congress—it directs that a presidential policy be executed in a manner prescribed by the President. The preamble of the order itself, like that of many statutes, sets out reasons why the President believes certain policies should be adopted, proclaims these policies as rules of conduct to be followed, and again, like a statute, authorizes a government official to promulgate additional rules and regulations consistent with the policy proclaimed and needed to carry that policy into execution. The power of Congress to adopt such public policies as those proclaimed by the order is beyond question. It can make laws regulating the relationships between employers and employees, prescribing rules designed to settle labor disputes, and fixing wages and working conditions in certain fields of our economy. The Constitution does not subject this lawmaking power of Congress to presidential or military supervision or control.

It is said that other Presidents without congressional authority have taken possession of private business enterprises in order to settle labor disputes. But even if this be true, Congress has not thereby lost its exclusive constitutional authority to make laws necessary and proper to carry out the powers vested by the Constitution "in the Government of the United States, or any Department or Officer thereof."

The Founders of this Nation entrusted the lawmaking power to the Congress alone in both good and bad times. It would do no good to recall the historical events, the fears of power and the hopes for freedom that lay behind their choice. Such a review would but confirm our holding that this seizure order cannot stand.

The judgment of the District Court is affirmed.

Mr. Justice Frankfurter, [concurring] . . .

Mr. Justice Douglas, concurring . . .

Mr. Justice Jackson, concurring in the judgment and opinion of the Court.

That comprehensive and undefined presidential powers hold both practical advantages and grave dangers for the country will impress anyone who has served as legal adviser to a President in time of transition and public anxiety. While an interval of detached reflection may temper teachings of that experience, they probably are a more realistic influence on my views than the conventional materials of judicial decision which seem unduly to accentuate doctrine and legal fiction. . . . The tendency is strong to emphasize transient results upon policies—such as wages or stabilization—and lose sight of enduring consequences upon the balanced power structure of our Republic.

A judge, like an executive advisor, may be surprised at the poverty of really useful and unambiguous authority applicable to concrete problems of executive power as they actually present themselves. Just what our forefathers did envision, or would have envisioned had they foreseen modern conditions, must be divined from materials almost as enigmatic as the dreams Joseph was called upon to interpret for Pharaoh. A century and a half of partisan debate and scholarly speculation yields no net result but only supplies more or less apt quotations from respected sources on each side of any question. They largely cancel each other. And other decisions are indecisive because of the judicial practice of dealing with the largest questions in the most narrow way.

The actual art of governing under our Constitution does not and cannot conform to judicial definitions of the power of any of its branches based on isolated clauses or even single Articles torn from context. While the Constitution diffuses power the better to secure liberty, it also contemplates that practice will integrate the dispersed powers into a workable government. It enjoins upon its branches separateness but interdependence, autonomy but reciprocity. Presidential powers are not fixed but fluctuate, depending upon their disjunction or conjunction with those of Congress. We may well begin by a somewhat over-simplified grouping of practical situations in which a President may doubt, or others may challenge, his powers, and by distinguishing roughly the legal consequences of this factor of relativity.

1. When the President acts pursuant to an express or implied authorization of Congress, his authority is at its maximum, for it includes all that he possesses in his own right plus all that Congress can delegate. In these circumstances, and in these only, may he be said (for what it may be worth) to personify the federal sovereignty. . . .

2. When the President acts in absence of either a congressional grant or denial of authority, he can only rely upon his own independent power, but there is a zone of twilight in which he and Congress may have concurrent authority, or in which its distribution is uncertain. . . . In this area, any actual test of power is likely to depend on the imperatives of events and contemporary imponderables rather than on abstract theories of law.

3. When the President takes measures incompatible with the expressed or implied will of Congress, his power is at its lowest ebb, for then he can rely only upon his own constitutional powers minus any constitutional powers of Congress over the matter. . . . Presidential claim to a power at once so conclusive and preclusive must be scrutinized with caution, for what is at stake is the equilibrium established by our constitutional system.

Into which of these classifications does this executive seizure of the steel industry fit? It is eliminated from the first by admission, for it is conceded that no congressional authorization exists for this seizure. . . .

Can it then be defended under flexible tests available to the second category? It seems clearly eliminated from that class because Congress has not left seizure of private property an open field but has covered it by three statutory policies inconsistent with this seizure. . . .

This leaves the current seizure to be justified only by the severe tests under the third grouping. . . . In short, we can sustain the President only by holding that seizure of such strike-bound industries is within his domain and beyond control by Congress. Thus, this Court's first review of such seizures occurs under circumstances which leave presidential power most vulnerable to attack and in the least favorable of possible constitutional postures.

I did not suppose, and I am not persuaded, that history leaves it open to question, at least in the courts, that the executive branch, like the Federal Government as a whole, possesses only delegated powers. . . . Some clauses could be made almost unworkable, as well as immutable, by refusal to indulge some latitude of interpretation of changing times. I have heretofore, and do now, give to the enumerated powers the scope and elasticity afforded by what seem to be reasonable, practical implications instead of the rigidity dictated by a doctrinaire textualism. . . .

[One] clause on which the Government . . . relies is that "The President shall be Commander in Chief of the Army and Navy of the United States. . . ." These cryptic words have given rise to some of the most persistent controversies in our constitutional history. Of course, they imply something more than an empty title. . . .

That military powers of the Commander in Chief were not to supersede representative government of internal affairs seems obvious from the Constitution and from elementary American history. . . .

We should not use this occasion to circumscribe, much less to contract, the lawful role of the President as Commander in Chief. I should indulge the widest latitude of interpretation to sustain his exclusive function to command the instruments of national force, at least when turned against the outside world for the security of our society. But, when it is turned inward, not because of rebellion but because of a lawful economic struggle between industry and labor, it should have no such indulgence. His command power is not such an absolute as might be implied from that office in a militaristic system but is subject to limitations consistent with a constitutional

Republic whose law and policy-making branch is a representative Congress. The purpose of lodging dual titles in one man was to insure that the civilian would control the military, not to enable the military to subordinate the presidential office. No penance would ever expiate the sin against free government of holding that a President can escape control of executive powers by law through assuming his military role. What the power of command may include I do not try to envision, but I think it is not a military prerogative, without support of law, to seize persons or property because they are important or even essential for the military and naval establishment. . . .

The Solicitor General lastly grounds support of the seizure upon nebulous, inherent powers never expressly granted but said to have accrued to the office from the customs and claims of preceding administrations. The plea is for a resulting power to deal with a crisis or an emergency according to the necessities of the case, the unarticulated assumption being that necessity knows no law.

Loose and irresponsible use of adjectives colors all nonlegal and much legal discussion of presidential powers. "Inherent" powers, "implied" powers, "incidental" powers, "war" powers and "emergency" powers are used, often interchangeably and without fixed or ascertainable meanings.

The vagueness and generality of the clauses that set forth presidential powers afford a plausible basis for pressures within and without an administration for presidential action beyond that supported by those whose responsibility it is to defend his actions in court. . . .

In view of the ease, expedition and safety with which Congress can grant and has granted large emergency powers, certainly ample to embrace this crisis, I am quite unimpressed with the argument that we should affirm possession of them without statute. Such power either has no beginning or it has no end. If it exists, it need submit to no legal restraint. I am not alarmed that it would plunge us straightway into dictatorship, but it is at least a step in that wrong direction.

As to whether there is imperative necessity for such powers, it is relevant to note the gap that exists between the President's paper powers and his real powers. The Constitution does not disclose the measure of the actual controls wielded by the modern presidential office. That instrument must be understood as an eighteenth-century sketch of a government hoped for, not as a blueprint of the Government that is. Vast accretions of federal power, eroded from that reserved by the States, have magnified the scope of presidential activity. Subtle shifts take place in the centers of real power that do not show on the face of the Constitution. . . .

But I have no illusion that any decision by this Court can keep power in the hands of Congress if it is not wise and timely in meeting its problems. . . . We may say that power to legislate for emergencies belongs in the hands of Congress, but only Congress itself can prevent power from slipping through its fingers. . . .

Mr. Justice Burton, concurring. . . .

Mr. Justice Clark, concurring in the judgment of the Court. . . .

Mr. Chief Justice Vinson, with whom **Mr. Justice Reed** and **Mr. Justice Minton** join, dissenting.

. . . In passing upon the question of Presidential powers in this case, we must first consider the context in which those powers were exercised.

Those who suggest that this is a case involving extraordinary powers should be mindful that these are extraordinary times. A world not yet recovered from devastation of World War II has been forced to face the threat of another and more terrifying global conflict.

Accepting in full measure its responsibility in the world community, the United States was instrumental in securing adoption of the United Nations Charter. . . . In 1950, when the United Nations called upon member nations "to render every assistance" to repel aggression in Korea, the United States furnished its vigorous support. . . .

Further efforts to protect the free world from aggression are found in the congressional enactments of the Truman Plan for assistance to Greece and Turkey and the Marshall Plan for economic aid needed to build up the strength of our friends in Western Europe. In 1949, the Senate approved the North Atlantic Treaty under which each member nation agrees that an armed attack against one is an armed attack against all. . . . The concept of mutual security recently has been extended by treaty to friends in the Pacific. . . .

Even this brief review of our responsibilities in the world community discloses the enormity of our undertaking. Success of these measures may, as has often been observed, dramatically influence the lives of many generations of the world's peoples yet unborn. Alert to our responsibilities, which coincide with our own self-preservation through mutual security, Congress has enacted a large body of implementing legislation. . . .

Chief Justice Vinson here discusses these legislative acts as well as the seizure authorizations included in the statutes. In addition, he chronicles instances of seizures, both based on these statutes and deriving their legitimacy from other sources.

Focusing now on the situation confronting the President on the night of April 8, 1952, we cannot but conclude that the President was performing his duty under the Constitution to "take Care that the Laws be faithfully executed." . . .

The President reported to Congress the morning after the seizure that he acted because a work stoppage in steel production would immediately imperil the safety of the Nation by preventing execution of the legislative programs for procurement of military equipment. And, while a shutdown could be averted by granting the price concessions requested by [Youngstown Sheet & Tube Company], granting such concessions would disrupt the price stabilization program also enacted by Congress. Rather than fail to execute either legislative program, the President acted to execute both.

Much of the argument in this case has been directed at straw men. We do not now have before us the case of a President acting solely on the basis of his own notions of the public welfare. Nor is there any question of unlimited executive power in this case. The President himself closed the door to any such claim when he sent his Message to Congress stating his purpose to abide by any action of Congress, whether approving or disapproving his seizure action. Here, the President immediately made sure that Congress was fully informed of the temporary action he had taken only to preserve the legislative programs from destruction until Congress could act.

The absence of a specific statute authorizing seizure of the steel mills as a mode of executing the laws—both the military procurement program and the anti-inflation program—has not until today been thought to prevent the President from executing the laws. . . . Flexibility as to mode of execution to meet critical situations is a matter of practical necessity. . . .

[A]s of December 22, 1951, the President had a choice between alternate procedures for settling the threatened strike in the steel mills: one route [the Taft-Hartley Act] created to deal with peacetime disputes; the other route [the Defense Production Act] specially created to deal with disputes growing out of the defense and stabilization program. There is no question of bypassing a statutory procedure because both of the routes available to the President in December were based upon statutory authorization. Both routes were available in the steel dispute. The Union, by refusing to abide by the defense and stabilization program, could have forced the President to invoke Taft-Hartley at that time to delay the strike a maximum of 80 days. Instead, the Union agreed to cooperate with the defense program and submit the dispute to the Wage Stabilization Board [WSB]. . . .

When the President acted on April 8, he had exhausted the procedures for settlement available to him. Taft-Hartley was a route parallel to, not connected with, the WSB procedure. The strike had been delayed 99 days as contrasted with the maximum delay of 80 days under Taft-Hartley. There had been a hearing on the issue in dispute and bargaining which promised settlement up to the very hour before seizure had broken down. Faced with immediate national peril through stoppage in steel production on the one hand and faced with destruction of the wage and price legislative programs on the other, the President took temporary possession of the steel mills as the only course open to him consistent with his duty to take care that the laws be faithfully executed.

. . . The President's action has thus far been effective, not in settling the dispute, but in saving the various legislative programs at stake from destruction until Congress could act in the matter.

The diversity of views expressed in the six opinions of the majority, the lack of reference to authoritative precedent, the repeated reliance upon prior dissenting opinions, the complete disregard of the uncontroverted facts showing the gravity of the emergency and the temporary nature of the taking all serve to demonstrate how far afield one must go to affirm the order of the District Court.

The broad executive power granted by Article II to an officer on duty 365 days a year cannot, it is said, be invoked to avert disaster. Instead, the President must confine himself to sending a message to Congress recommending action. Under this messenger-boy concept of the Office, the President cannot even act to preserve legislative programs from destruction so that Congress will have something left to act upon. There is no judicial finding that the executive action was unwarranted because there was in fact no basis for the President's finding of the existence of an emergency for, under this view, the gravity of the emergency and the immediacy of the threatened disaster are considered irrelevant as a matter of law.

Seizure of [the steel companies'] property is not a pleasant undertaking. Similarly unpleasant to a free country are the draft which disrupts the home and military procurement which causes economic dislocation and compels adoption of price controls, wage stabilization and allocation of materials. The President informed Congress that even a temporary Government operation of [the steel mills] was "thoroughly distasteful" to him, but was necessary to prevent immediate paralysis of the mobilization program. Presidents have been in the past, and any man worthy of the Office should be in the future, free to take at least interim action necessary to execute legislative programs essential to survival of the Nation. A sturdy judiciary should not be swayed by the unpleasantness or unpopularity of necessary executive action, but must independently determine for itself whether the President was acting, as required by the Constitution, to "take Care that the Laws be faithfully executed."

As the District Judge stated, this is no time for "timorous" judicial action. But neither is this a time for timorous executive action. Faced with the duty of executing the defense programs which Congress had enacted and the disastrous effects that any stoppage in steel production would have on these programs, the President acted to preserve those programs by seizing the steel mills. There is no question that the possession was other than temporary in character and subject to congressional direction—either approving, disapproving or regulating the manner in which the mills were to be administered and returned to the owners. The President immediately informed Congress of his action and clearly stated his intention to abide by the legislative will. No basis for claims of arbitrary action, unlimited powers or dictatorial usurpation of congressional power appears from the facts of this case. On the contrary, judicial, legislative and executive precedents throughout our history demonstrate that in this case the President acted in full conformity with his duties under the Constitution. Accordingly, we would reverse the order of the District Court.

Schick v. Reed

419 U.S. 256; 95 S. Ct. 379; 42 L. Ed. 2d 430 (1974)
Vote: 6-3

Mr. Chief Justice Burger delivered the opinion of the Court.

... The pertinent facts are undisputed. In 1954 [Schick], then a master sergeant in the United States Army stationed in Japan, was tried before a court-martial for the brutal murder of an eight-year-old girl. He admitted the killing, but contended that he was insane at the time that he committed it. Medical opinion differed on this point.... The court-martial rejected [Schick's] defense and he was sentenced to death on March 27, 1954, pursuant to *** the Uniform Code of Military Justice ***....

The case was then forwarded to President Eisenhower for final review.... The President acted on March 25, 1960:

[P]ursuant to the authority vested in me as President of the United States by Article II, Section 2, Clause 1, of the Constitution, the sentence to be put to death is hereby commuted to dishonorable discharge, forfeiture of all pay and allowances becoming due on and after the date of this action, and confinement at hard labor for the term of his ... natural life. This commutation of sentence is expressly made on the condition that the said Maurice L. Schick shall never have any rights, privileges, claims, or benefits arising under the parole and suspension or remission of sentence laws of the United States and the regulations promulgated thereunder governing Federal prisoners confined in any civilian or military penal institution ***....

... [Schick] was accordingly discharged from the Army and transferred to the Federal Penitentiary at Lewisburg, Pa. He has now served 20 years of his sentence. Had he originally received a sentence of life imprisonment he would have been eligible for parole consideration in March 1969; the condition in the President's order of commutation barred parole at any time....

When the death sentence was imposed in 1954 it was, as [Schick] concedes, valid under the Constitution of the United States and subject only to final action by the President. Absent the commutation of March 25, 1960, the sentence could, and in all probability would, have been carried out prior to 1972. Only the President's action in commuting the sentence under his Art. II powers, on the conditions stipulated, prevented execution of the sentence imposed by the court-martial.

The essence of [Schick's] case is that, in light of this Court's holding in *Furman v. Georgia* [1972], *** which he could not anticipate, he made a "bad bargain" by accepting a no-parole condition in place of a death sentence. He does not cast his claim in those terms, of course. Rather, he argues that the conditions attached to the commutation put him in a worse position than he would have been in had he contested his death sentence—and remained alive—until the Furman case was decided 18 years after that sentence was originally imposed.

It is correct that pending death sentences not carried out prior to *Furman* were thereby set aside without conditions such as were attached to [Schick's] commutation. However, [Schick's] death sentence was not pending in 1972 because it had long since been commuted. The question here is whether *Furman* must now be read as nullifying the condition attached to that commutation when it was granted in 1960. Alternatively, [Schick] argues that even in 1960 President Eisenhower exceeded his powers under Art. II by imposing a condition not expressly authorized by the Uniform Code of Military Justice.

In sum [Schick's] claim gives rise to [these] questions:... was the conditional commutation of his death sentence lawful in 1960;... if so, did *Furman* retroactively void such conditions....

The express power of Art. II, Sec. 2, cl. 1, from which the Presidential power to commute criminal sentences derives, is to "grant Reprieves and Pardons ... except in Cases of Impeachment." Although the authors of this clause surely did not act thoughtlessly, neither did they devote extended debate to its meaning. This can be explained in large part by the fact that the draftsmen were well acquainted with the English Crown authority to alter and reduce punishments as it existed in 1787. The history of that power, which was centuries old, reveals a gradual contract to avoid its abuse and misuse. Changes were made as potential or actual abuses were perceived....

At the time of the drafting and adoption of our Constitution it was considered elementary that the prerogative of the English Crown could be exercised upon conditions....

Various types of conditions, both penal and non-penal in nature, were employed. For example, it was common for a pardon or commutation to be granted on condition that the felon be transported to another place, and indeed our own Colonies were the recipients of numerous subjects of "banishment." This practice was never questioned despite the fact that British subjects generally could not be forced to leave the realm without an Act of Parliament and banishment was rarely authorized as a punishment for crime.... In short, by 1787 the English prerogative to pardon was unfettered except for a few specifically enumerated limitations.

The history of our executive pardoning power reveals a consistent pattern of adherence to the English common-law practice....

... [T]he draftsmen of Art. II, Sec. 2, spoke in terms of a "prerogative" of the President, which ought not be "fettered or embarrassed." In light of the English common law from which such language was drawn, the conclusion is inescapable that the pardoning power was intended to include the power to commute sentences on conditions which do not in themselves offend the Constitution, but which are not specifically provided for by statute.

The few cases decided in this area are consistent with the view of the power described above....

... [T]his Court has long read the Constitution as authorizing the President to deal with individual cases by granting conditional pardons. The very essence of the pardoning power is to treat each case individually....

Presidents throughout our history as a Nation have exercised the power to pardon or commute sentences upon conditions that are not specifically authorized by statute. Such conditions have generally gone unchallenged and, ... attacks have been firmly rejected by the courts. *** These facts are not insignificant for our interpretation of Art. II, Sec. 2, cl. 1, because, as observed by Mr. Justice Holmes: "If a thing has been practiced for two hundred years by common consent, it will need a strong case" to overturn it. ***

A fair reading of the history of the English pardoning power, from which our Art. II, Sec. 2, cl. 1, derives, of the language of that clause itself, and of the unbroken practice since 1790 compels the conclusion that the power flows from the Constitution alone, not from any legislative enactments, and that it cannot be modified, abridged, or diminished by the Congress. Additionally, considerations of public policy and humanitarian impulses support an interpretation of that power so as to permit the attachment of any condition which does not otherwise offend the Constitution. The plain purpose of the broad power conferred by Sec. 2, cl. 1, was to allow plenary authority in the President to "forgive" the convicted person in part or entirely, to reduce a penalty in terms of a specified number of years, or to alter it with conditions which are in themselves constitutionally unobjectionable. If we were to accept [Schick's] contentions, a commutation of his death sentence of 25 to 30 years would be subject to the same challenge as is now made, i.e., that parole must be available to [Schick] because it is to others. That such an interpretation of Sec. 2, cl. 1, would in all probability tend to inhibit the exercise of the pardoning power and reduce the frequency of commutations is hardly open to doubt. We therefore hold that the pardoning power is an enumerated power of the Constitution and its limitations, if any, must be found in the Constitution itself. It would be a curious logic to allow a convicted person who petitions for mercy to retain the full benefit of a lesser punishment with conditions, yet escape burdens readily assumed in accepting the commutation which he sought.

[Schick's] claim must therefore fail. The no-parole condition attached to the commutation of his death sentence is similar to sanctions imposed by legislatures such as mandatory minimum sentences or statutes otherwise precluding parole; it does not offend the Constitution. Similarly, the President's action derived solely from his Art. II powers; it did not depend upon *** any ... statute fixing a death penalty for murder....

We are not moved by [Schick's] argument that it is somehow "unfair" that he be treated differently from persons whose death sentences were pending at the time that *Furman* was decided. Individual acts of clemency inherently call for discriminating choices because no two cases are the same. Indeed, as noted earlier, [Schick's] life was undoubtedly spared by President Eisenhower's commutation order of March 25, 1960. Nor is [Schick] without further remedies since he may, of course, apply to the present or future Presidents for a complete pardon, commutation to time served, or relief from the no-parole condition. We hold only that the conditional commutation of his death sentence was lawful when made and that intervening events have not altered its validity.

Affirmed.

Mr. Justice Marshall, with whom ***Mr. Justice Douglas*** and ***Mr. Justice Brennan*** join, dissenting.

... The Court misconstrues [Schick's] retroactivity argument. Schick does not dispute the constitutional validity of the death penalty in 1954 under then-existing case law. Nor does he contend that he was under sentence of death in 1972 when the decision issued in *Furman,* invalidating "the imposition and carrying out" of discretionary death sentences. *** Rather he argues that the retroactive application of *Furman* to his no-parole commutation is required because the imposition of the death sentence was the indispensable vehicle through which he became subject to his present sentence. In other words, the no-parole condition could not now exist had the court-martial before which Schick was tried not imposed the death penalty....

Since *Furman* is fully retroactive [Schick's] case should be simple to resolve.... A death sentence was imposed by the court-martial and affirmed by the Board of Review and the United States Court of Military Appeals. *** The death sentence so imposed was declared unconstitutional by *Furman* and is therefore null and void as a matter of law. The only legal alternative—simple life imprisonment—must be substituted. Concomitantly, the adverse consequence of the death sentence—the no-parole condition of [Schick's] 1960 commutation—must also be voided, as it exceeds the lawful alternative punishment that should have been imposed. [He] should now be subject to treatment as a person sentenced to life imprisonment on the date of his original sentence and eligible for parole....

Since the majority devotes its opinion to a discussion of the scope of Presidential power, I am compelled to comment. I have no quarrel with the proposition that the source of the President's commutation power is found in Art. II, Sec. 2, cl. 1, of the Constitution....

... I take issue with the Court's conclusion that annexation of the "no-parole condition ... does not offend the Constitution." *** In my view the President's action exceeded the limits of the Art. II pardon power. In commuting a sentence under Art. II the Chief Executive is not imbued with the constitutional power to create unauthorized punishments.

The congressionally prescribed limits of punishment mark the boundaries within which the Executive must exercise his authority. By virtue of the pardon power the Executive may abstain from enforcing a judgment by judicial authorities; he may not, under the aegis of that power, engage in lawmaking or adjudication....

While the clemency function of the Executive in the federal criminal justice system is consistent with the separation of powers, the attachment of punitive conditions to grants of clemency is not. Prescribing punishment is a prerogative reserved for the law-making branch of government, the legislature. As a consequence, President Eisenhower's addition to Schick's commutation of a condition that did not coincide with punishment prescribed by the legislature for *any* military crime, much less this specific offense, was a usurpation of a legislative function. While the exercise of the pardon power was proper, the imposition of this penal condition was not embraced by that power. . . .

In conclusion I note that where a President chooses to exercise his clemency power he should be mindful that

The punishment appropriate for the diverse federal offenses is a matter for the discretion of Congress, subject only to constitutional limitations, more particularly the Eighth Amendment. ***

*** The Congress has not delegated such authority to the President. I do not challenge the right of the President to issue pardons on nonpenal conditions, but where the Executive elects to exercise the Presidential power for commutation, the clear import of the Constitution mandates that the lesser punishment imposed be sanctioned by the legislature.

In sum, the no-parole condition is constitutionally defective in the face of the retrospective application of *Furman* and the extra-legal nature of the Executive action. I would nullify the condition, and direct the lower court to remand the case for resentencing to the only alternative available—life with the opportunity for parole—and its attendant benefits.

Wiener v. United States
357 U.S. 349; 78 S. Ct. 1275; 2 L. Ed. 2d 1377 (1958)
Vote: 9-0

Mr. Justice Frankfurter delivered the opinion of the Court.

This is a suit for back pay, based on [Wiener's] alleged illegal removal as a member of the War Claims Commission. The facts are not in dispute. By the War Claims Act of 1948, *** Congress established that Commission with "jurisdiction to receive and adjudicate according to law" *** claims for compensating internees, prisoners of war, and religious organizations *** who suffered personal injury or property damage at the hands of the enemy in connection with World War II. The Commission was to be composed of three persons, at least two of whom were to be members of the bar, to be appointed by the President, by and with the advice and consent of the Senate. The Commission was to wind up its affairs not later than three years after the expiration of the time for filing claims, originally limited to two years but extended by successive legislation. . . . This limit on the Commission's life was the mode by which the tenure of the Commissioners was defined,

and Congress made no provision for removal of a Commissioner.

Having been duly nominated by President Truman, [Wiener] was confirmed on June 2, 1950, and took office on June 8. . . . On his refusal to heed a request for his resignation, he was, on December 10, 1953, removed by President Eisenhower in the following terms: "I regard it as in the national interest to complete the administration of the War Claims Act of 1948, as amended, with personnel of my own selection." The following day, the President made recess appointments to the Commission, including petitioner's post. After Congress assembled, the President, on February 15, 1954, sent the names of the new appointees to the Senate. The Senate had not confirmed these nominations when the Commission was abolished, July 1, 1954. *** Thereupon, [Wiener] brought this proceeding in the Court of Claims for recovery of his salary as a War Claims Commissioner from December 10, 1953, the day of his removal by the President, to June 30, 1954, the last day of the

Commission's existence.... We brought the case here ***....

Controversy pertaining to the scope and limits of the President's power of removal fills a thick chapter of our political and judicial history. The long stretches of its history, beginning with the very first Congress, with early echoes in the Reports of this Court, were laboriously traversed in *Myers v. United States* *** and need not be retraced. President Roosevelt's reliance upon the pronouncements of the Court in that case in removing a member of the Federal Trade Commission on the ground that "the aims and purposes of the Administration with respect to the work of the Commission can be carried out most effectively with personnel of my own selection" reflected contemporaneous professional opinion regarding the significance of the *Myers* decision. Speaking through a Chief Justice who himself had been President, the Court did not restrict itself to the immediate issue before it, the President's inherent power to remove a postmaster, obviously an executive official. As of set purpose and not by way of parenthetic casualness, the Court announced that the President had inherent constitutional power of removal also of officials who have "duties of a quasi-judicial character ... whose decisions after hearing affect interests of individuals, the discharge of which the President can not in a particular case properly influence or control." *** This view of presidential power was deemed to flow from his "constitutional duty of seeing that the laws be faithfully executed." ***

The assumption was short-lived that the *Myers* case recognized the President's inherent constitutional power to remove officials, no matter what the relation of the executive to the discharge of their duties and no matter what restrictions Congress may have imposed regarding the nature of their tenure.... Within less than ten years a unanimous Court, in *Humphrey's Executor v. United States* *** narrowly confined the scope of the *Myers* decision to include only "all purely executive officers," *** The Court explicitly "disapproved" the expressions in *Myers* supporting the President's inherent constitutional power to remove members of quasi-judicial bodies. *** Congress had given members of the Federal Trade Commission a seven-year term and also provided for the removal of a Commissioner by the President for inefficiency, neglect of duty or malfeasance in office....

Humphrey's case was a *cause célèbre*—and not least in the halls of Congress. And what is the essence of the decision in *Humphrey's* case? It drew a sharp line of cleavage between officials who were part of the Executive establishment and were thus removable by virtue of the President's constitutional powers and ... those whose tasks require absolute freedom from Executive interference. "For it is quite evident," again to quote *Humphrey's Executor,* "that one who holds his office only during the pleasure of another, cannot be depended upon to maintain an attitude of independence against the latter's will." ***

Thus, the most reliable factor for drawing an inference regarding the President's power of removal in our case is the nature of the function that Congress vested in the War Claims Commission. What were the duties that Congress confided to this Commission? And can the inference fairly be drawn from the failure of Congress to provide for removal that these Commissioners were to remain in office at the will of the President? For such is the assertion of power on which [Wiener's] removal must rest. The ground of President Eisenhower's removal ... was precisely the same as President Roosevelt's removal of Humphrey. Both Presidents desired to have Commissioners to be their men. The terms of removal in the two cases are identical and express the assumption that the agencies of which the two Commissioners were members were subject in the discharge of their duties to the control of the Executive. An analysis of the Federal Trade Commission Act left this Court in no doubt that such was not the conception of Congress in creating the Federal Trade Commission. The terms of the War Claims Act of 1948 leave no doubt that such was not the conception of Congress regarding the War Claims Commission.

The history of this legislation emphatically underlines this fact. The short of it is that the origin of the Act was a bill *** passed by the House that placed the administration of a very limited class of claims in the hands of the Federal Security Administrator ... The Federal Security Administrator was indubitably an arm of the President. When the House bill reached the Senate, it struck out all but the enacting clause, rewrote the bill, and established a Commission with "jurisdiction to receive and adjudicate according to law." ... The Commission was established as an adjudicating body with all the paraphernalia by which legal claims are put to the test of proof, with finality of determination "not subject to review by any other official of the United States or by any court, by *mandamus* or otherwise." *** Awards were to be paid out of a War Claims fund in the hands of the Secretary of the Treasury, whereby such claims were given even more assured collectability than adheres to judgments rendered in the Court of Claims. *** With minor amendment *** this Senate bill became a law.

... For Congress itself to have made appropriations for the claims with which it dealt under the War Claims Act was not practical in view of the large number of claimants and the diversity in the specific circumstances giving rise to the claims. The House bill in effect put the distribution of the narrow class of claims that it acknowledged into Executive hands, by vesting the procedure in the Federal Security Administrator. The final form of the legislation, as we have seen, left the widened range of claims to be determined by adjudication. Congress could, of course, have given jurisdiction over these claims to the District Courts or to the Court of Claims. The fact that it chose to establish a Commission to "adjudicate according to law' the classes of claims defined in the statute did not alter the intrinsic judicial

character of the task with which the Commission was charged. The claims were to be "adjudicated according to law," that is, on the merits of each claim, supported by evidence and governing legal considerations, by a body that was "entirely free from the control or coercive influence, direct or indirect," *** of either the Executive or the Congress. If, as one must take for granted, the War Claims Act precluded the President from influencing the Commission in passing on a particular claim, *a fortiori* must it be inferred that Congress did not wish to have hang over the Commission the Damocles' sword of removal by the President for no reason other than that he preferred to have on that Commission men of his own choosing.

For such is this case. We have not a removal for cause involving the rectitude of a member of an adjudicatory body, nor even a suspensory removal until the Senate could act upon it by confirming the appointment of a new Commissioner or otherwise dealing with the matter. Judging the matter in all the nakedness in which it is presented, ... we are compelled to conclude that no such power is given to the President directly by the Constitution, and none is impliedly conferred upon him by statute simply because Congress said nothing about it. The philosophy of *Humphrey's Executor,* in its explicit language as well as its implications, precludes such a claim....

United States v. Curtiss-Wright Export Corporation
299 U.S. 304; 57 S. Ct. 216; 81 L. Ed. 255 (1936)
Vote: 7-1

Mr. Justice Sutherland delivered the opinion of the Court.

On January 27, 1936, an indictment was returned in the court below, the first count of which charges that [Curtiss-Wright], beginning with the 29th of May, 1934, conspired to sell in the United States certain arms of war, namely fifteen machine guns, to Bolivia, a country then engaged in armed conflict in the Chaco, in violation of the Joint Resolution of Congress approved May 28, 1934, and the provisions of a

proclamation issued on the same day by the President of the United States pursuant to authority conferred by *** the resolution. ... [The United States District Court for the Southern District of New York sustained Curtiss-Wright's demurrer to the indictment, and the federal government appealed directly to the Supreme Court.] The Joint Resolution *** follows:

Resolved by the Senate and House of Representatives of the United States of America in Congress assembled, that if the

President finds that the prohibition of the sale of arms and munitions of war in the United States to those countries now engaged in armed conflict in the Chaco may contribute to the reestablishment of peace between those countries, and if after consultation with the governments of other American Republics and with their cooperation, as well as that of such other governments as he may deem necessary, he makes proclamation to that effect, it shall be unlawful to sell, except under such limitations and exceptions as the President prescribes, any arms or munitions of war in any place in the United States to the countries now engaged in that armed conflict, or to any person, company, or association acting in the interest of either country, until otherwise ordered by the President or by Congress.

... Whoever sells any arms or munitions of war in violation of section 1 shall, on conviction, be punished by a fine not exceeding $10,000 or by imprisonment not exceeding two years, or both.

The President's proclamation [May 28, 1934] *** after reciting the terms of the Joint Resolution [barred the sale of arms to Bolivia and Paraguay]. ...

On November 14, 1935, this proclamation was revoked. ***

... It is contended that by the Joint Resolution, the going into effect and continued operation of the resolution was conditioned (a) upon the President's judgment as to its beneficial effect upon the reestablishment of peace between the countries engaged in armed conflict in the Chaco; (b) upon the making of a proclamation, which was left to his unfettered discretion, thus constituting an attempted substitution of the President's will for that of Congress; (c) upon the making of a proclamation putting an end to the operation of the resolution, which again was left to the President's unfettered discretion; and (d) further, that the extent of its operation in particular cases was subject to limitation and exception by the President, controlled by no standard. In each of these particulars, [Curtiss-Wright urges] that Congress abdicated its essential functions and delegated them to the Executive.

Whether, if the Joint Resolution had related solely to internal affairs it would be open to the challenge that it constituted an unlawful delegation of legislative power to the Executive, we find it unnecessary to determine. The whole aim of the resolution is to affect a situation entirely external to the United States, and falling within the category of foreign affairs. The determination which we are called to make, therefore, is whether the Joint Resolution, as applied to that situation, is vulnerable to attack under the rule that forbids a delegation of the law-making power. In other works, assuming (but not deciding) that the challenged delegation, if it were confined to internal affairs, would be invalid, may it nevertheless be sustained on the ground that its exclusive aim is to afford a remedy for a hurtful condition within foreign territory?

It will contribute to the elucidation of the question if we first consider the differences between the powers of the Federal government in respect of foreign or external affairs and those in respect of domestic or internal affairs. That there are differences between them, and that these differences are fundamental, may not be doubted.

The two classes of powers are different, both in respect of their origin and their nature. The broad statement that the Federal government can exercise no powers except those specifically enumerated in the Constitution, and such implied powers as are necessary and proper to carry into effect the enumerated powers, is categorically true only in respect of our internal affairs. In that field, the primary purpose of the Constitution was to carve from the general mass of legislative powers *then possessed by the states* such portions as it was thought desirable to vest in the Federal government, leaving those not included in the enumerations still in the states. *** That this doctrine applies only to powers which the states had, is self-evident. And since the states severally never possessed international powers, such powers could not have been carved from the mass of state powers but obviously were transmitted to the United States from some other source. During the colonial period, those powers were possessed exclusively by and were entirely under the control of the Crown. By the Declaration of Independence, "the Representatives of the United States of America" declared the United [not the several] Colonies to be free and independent states, and as such to have "full Power to levy War, conclude Peace, contract Alliances, establish Commerce and to do all other Acts and Things which Independent States may of right do."

As a result of the separation from Great Britain by the colonies, acting as a unit, the powers of external sovereignty passed from the Crown not to the colonies severally, but to the colonies in their collective and corporate capacity as the United States of America. Even before the Declaration, the colonies were a unit in foreign affairs, acting through a common agency— namely the Continental Congress, composed of delegates from the thirteen colonies. That agency exercised the powers of war and peace, raised an army, created a navy, and finally adopted the Declaration of Independence. Rulers come and go; governments end and forms of government change; but sovereignty survives. A political society cannot endure without a supreme will somewhere. Sovereignty is never held in suspense. When, therefore, the external sovereignty of Great Britain in respect of the colonies ceased, it immediately passed to the Union. *** ...

The union existed before the Constitution, which was ordained and established among other things to form "a more perfect Union." Prior to that event, it is clear that the Union, declared by the Articles of Confederation to be "perpetual," was the sole possessor of external sovereignty, and in the Union it remained without change save in so far as the Constitution in express terms qualified its exercise. ...

It results that the investment of the Federal government with the powers of external sovereignty did not depend upon the affirmative grants of the Constitution. The powers to declare and wage war, to conclude peace, to make treaties, to maintain diplomatic relations with other sovereignties, if they had never been mentioned in the Constitution, would have vested in the Federal government as necessary concomitants of nationality. ...

Not only ... is the federal power over external affairs in origin and in essential character different from that over internal affairs, but participation in the exercise of power is significantly limited. In this vast external realm, with its important, complicated, delicate and manifold problems, the President alone has the power to speak or listen as a representative of the nation. He *makes* treaties with the advice and consent of the Senate; but he alone negotiates. Into the field of negotiation the Senate cannot intrude; and Congress itself is powerless to invade it. ...

It is important to bear in mind that we are here dealing not alone with an authority vested in the President by an exertion of legislative power, but with such an authority plus the very delicate, plenary and exclusive power of the President as the sole organ of the federal government in the field of international relations—a power which does not require as a basis for its exercise an act of Congress, but which, of course, like every other governmental power, must be exercised in subordination to the applicable provisions of the Constitution. It is quite apparent that if, in the maintenance of our international relations, embarrassment—perhaps serious embarrassment— is to be avoided and success for our aims achieved, congressional legislation which is to be made effective through negotiation and inquiry within the international field must often accord to the President a degree of discretion and freedom from statutory restriction which would not be admissible were domestic affairs alone involved. Moreover, he, not Congress, has the better opportunity of knowing the conditions which prevail in foreign countries, and especially is this true in time of war. He has his confidential sources of information. He has his agents in the form of diplomatic, consular and other officials. Secrecy in respect of information gathered by them may be highly necessary, and the premature disclosure of it productive of harmful results. ...

The marked difference between foreign affairs and domestic affairs in this respect is recognized by both houses of Congress in the very form of their requisitions for information from the executive departments. In the case of every department except the Department of State, the resolution *directs* the official to furnish the information. In the case of the State Department, dealing with foreign affairs, the President is *requested* to furnish the information "if not incompatible with public interest." A statement that to furnish the information is not compatible with the public interest rarely, if ever, is questioned.

When the President is to be authorized by legislation to act in respect of a matter intended to affect a situation in foreign territory, the legislator properly bears in mind the important consideration that the form of the President's action—or, indeed, whether he shall act at all—may well depend, among other things, upon the nature of the confidential information which he has or may thereafter receive, or upon the effect which his action may have upon our foreign relations. This consideration, in connection with what we have already said on the subject, disclosed the unwisdom of requiring Congress in this field of governmental power to lay down narrowly definite standards by which the President is to be governed. . . .

In the light of the foregoing observations, it is evident that this court should not be in haste to apply a general rule which will have the effect of condemning legislation like that under review as constituting an unlawful delegation of legislative power. The principles which justify such legislation find overwhelming support in the unbroken legislative practice which has prevailed almost from the inception of the national government to the present day. . . .

Practically every volume of the United States Statutes contains one or more acts or joint resolutions of Congress authorizing action by the President in respect of subjects affecting foreign relations, which either leave the exercise of the power to his unrestricted judgment, or provide a standard far more general than that which has always been considered requisite with regard to domestic affairs. . . .

The result of holding that the joint resolution here under attack is void and unenforceable as constituting an unlawful delegation of legislative power would be to stamp this multitude of comparable acts and resolutions as likewise invalid. And while this court may not and should not, hesitate to declare acts of Congress, however many times repeated, to be unconstitutional if beyond all rational doubt it finds them to be so, an impressive array of legislation such as we have just set forth, enacted by nearly every Congress from the beginning of our national existence to the present day, must be given unusual weight, in the process of reaching a correct determination of the problem. A legislative practice such

as we have here, evidenced not by only occasional instances, but marked by the movement of a steady stream for a century and half of time, goes a long way in the direction of proving the presence of unassailable ground for the constitutionality of the practice, to be found in the origin and history of the power involved, or in its nature, or on both combined. . . .

The uniform, long-continued and undisputed legislative practice just disclosed rests upon an admissible view of the Constitution which, even if the practice found far less support in principle than we think it does, we should not feel at liberty at this late day to disturb.

. . . It is enough to summarize by saying that, both upon principle and in accordance with precedent, we conclude there is sufficient warrant for the broad discretion vested in the President to determine whether the enforcement of the statute will have a beneficial effect upon the reestablishment of peace in the affected countries; whether he shall make proclamation to bring the resolution into operation; whether and when the resolution shall cease to operate and to make proclamation accordingly; and to prescribe limitations and exceptions to which the enforcement of the resolution shall be subject. . . .

The judgment of the court below must be reversed and the cause remanded for further proceedings in accordance with the foregoing opinion.

Reversed.

Mr. Justice McReynolds does not agree. He is of opinion that the court below reached the right conclusion and its judgment ought to be affirmed.

Mr. Justice Stone took no part in the consideration or decision of this case.

The Prize Cases

2 Black (67 U.S.) 635; 17 L. Ed. 459 (1863)
Vote: 5-4

A few days after the Confederate attack on Fort Sumter but before Congress had formally recognized the existence of civil war, President Abraham Lincoln ordered a blockade of Southern ports. Owners of

ships seized by the blockade brought suit in federal court challenging the legality of the president's order. From adverse judgments in the lower courts, the owners took an appeal to the Supreme Court.

Mr. Justice Grier. . . . By the Constitution, Congress alone has the power to declare a national or foreign war. It cannot declare war against a State, or any number of States, by virtue of any clause in the Constitution. . . .

If a war be made by invasion of a foreign nation, the President is not only authorized but bound to resist force by force. He does not initiate the war, but is bound to accept the challenge without waiting for any special legislative authority. . . .

This greatest of civil wars was not gradually developed by popular commotion, tumultuous assemblies, or local unorganized insurrections. However long may have been its previous conception, it nevertheless sprung forth suddenly from the parent brain, a Minerva in the full panoply of *war.* The President was bound to meet it in the shape it presented itself, without waiting for Congress to baptize it with a name; and no name given to it by him or them could change the fact.

It is not the less a civil war, with belligerent parties in hostile array, because it may be called an "insurrection" by one side, and the insurgents be considered as rebels or traitors. It is not necessary that the independence of the revolted province or State be acknowledged in order to constitute it a party belligerent in a war according to the law of nations. Foreign nations acknowledge it as war by a declaration of neutrality. The condition of neutrality cannot exist unless there be two belligerent parties. . . .

As soon as the news of the attack on Fort Sumter, and the organization of a government by the seceding States, assuming to act as belligerents, could become known in Europe, to wit, on the 13th of May, 1861, the Queen of England issued her proclamation of neutrality, "recognizing hostilities as existing between the Government of the United States of America and certain States styling themselves the Confederate States of America." This was immediately followed by similar declarations or silent acquiescence by other nations.

After such an official recognition by the sovereign, a citizen of a foreign State is stopped to deny the existence of a war with all its consequences as regards neutrals. They cannot ask a Court to affect a technical ignorance of the existence of a war, which all the world acknowledges to be the greatest civil war known in the history of the human race, and thus cripple the arm of the Government and paralyze its power by subtle definitions and ingenious sophisms. . . .

Whether the President in fulfilling his duties, as Commander-in-chief, in suppressing an insurrection, has met with such armed hostile resistance, and a civil war of such alarming proportions as will compel him to accord to them the character of belligerents, is a question to be decided *by him,* and this Court must be governed by the decisions and acts of the political department of the Government to which this power was entrusted. "He must determine what degree of force the crisis demands." The proclamation of blockade is itself official and exclusive evidence to the Court that a state of war existed which demanded and authorized a recourse to such a measure, under the circumstances peculiar to the case. . . .

If it were necessary to the technical existence of a war, that it should have a legislative sanction, we find it in almost every act passed at the extraordinary session of the Legislature of 1861, which was wholly employed in enacting laws to enable the Government to prosecute the war with vigor and efficiency. And finally, in 1861, we find Congress . . . in anticipation of such astute objections, passing an act "approving legalizing, and making valid all the acts, proclamations, and orders of the President, &c., as if they had been *issued and done under the precious express authority* and direction of the Congress of the United States."

Without admitting that such an act was necessary under the circumstances, it is plain that if the President had in any manner assumed powers which it was necessary should have the authority or sanction of Congress . . . this ratification has operated to perfectly cure the defect. . . .

The objection made to this act of ratification, that it is *ex post facto,* and therefore unconstitutional and void, might possibly have some weight on the trial of an indictment in a criminal Court. But precedents from that source cannot be received as authoritative in a tribunal administering public and international law.

On this first question, therefore, we are of the opinion that the President had a right . . . to institute a blockade of ports in possession of the States in rebellion, which neutrals are bound to regard.

We come now to the consideration of the second question. What is included in the term *"enemies' property"*?

The appellants contend that the term "enemy" is properly applicable to those only who are subjects or citizens of a foreign State at war with our own. . . .

They contend, also, that insurrection is the act of individuals and not of a government or sovereignty; that the individuals engaged are subjects of law. That confiscation of their property can be effected only under a municipal law. That by the law of the land such confiscation cannot take place without the conviction of the owner of some offense, and finally that the secession ordinances are nullities and ineffectual to release any citizen from his allegiance to the national Government, and consequently that the Constitution and Laws of the United States are still operative over persons in all the States for punishment as well as protection.

This argument rests on the assumption of two propositions, each of which is without foundation on the established law of nations. It assumes that where a civil war exists, the party belligerent claiming to be sovereign, cannot, for some unknown reason, exercise the rights of belligerents, although the revolutionary party may. Being sovereign, he can exercise only sovereign rights over the other party. The insurgent may be killed on the battle-field or by the executioner; his property on land may be confiscated under the municipal law; but the commerce on the ocean, which supplies the rebels with means to support the war, cannot be made the subject of capture under the laws of war, because it is *"unconstitutional*!!!" Now, it is a proposition never doubted, that the belligerent party who claims to be sovereign, may exercise both belligerent and sovereign rights ***. Treating the other party as a belligerent and using only the milder modes of coercion which the law of nations has introduced to mitigate the rigors of war, cannot be a subject of complaint by the party to whom it is accorded as a grace or granted as a necessity. We have shown that a civil war such as that now waged between the Northern and Southern States is properly conducted according to the humane regulations of public law as regards capture on the ocean.

Under the very peculiar Constitution of this Government, although the citizens owe supreme allegiance to the Federal government, they owe also a qualified allegiance to the State in which they are domiciled. Their persons and property are subject to its laws.

Hence, in organizing this rebellion, they have *acted as States* claiming to be sovereign over all persons and property within their respective limits, and asserting a right to absolve their citizens from their allegiance to the Federal Government. Several of these States have combined to form a new confederacy, claiming to be acknowledged by the world as a sovereign State. Their right to do so is now being decided by wager of battle. . . .

Mr. Justice Nelson, dissenting. . . . The truth is, this idea of the existence of any necessity for clothing the President with the war power, under the Act of 1795, is simply a monstrous exaggeration; for, besides having the command of the whole of the army and navy, Congress can be assembled within any thirty days, if the safety of the country requires that the war power shall be brought into operation.

The Acts of 1795 and 1807 did not, and could not under the Constitution, confer on the President the power of declaring war against a State of this Union, or of deciding that war existed, and upon the ground authorize the capture and confiscation of the property of every citizen of the State whenever it was found on the waters. The laws of war . . . convert every citizen of the hostile State into a public enemy, and treat him accordingly, whatever may have been his previous conduct. This great power over the business and property of the citizen is reserved to the legislative department by the express words of the Constitution. It cannot be delegated or surrendered to the Executive. Congress alone can determine whether war exists or would be declared; and until they have acted, no citizen of the State can be punished in his person or property, unless he has committed some offence against a law of Congress passed before the act was committed, which made it a crime, and defined the punishment. The penalty of confiscation for the acts of others with which he had no concern cannot lawfully be inflicted.

Mr. Justice Taney, Mr. Justice Catron and **Mr. Justice Clifford,** concurred in the dissenting opinion of **Mr. Justice Nelson.**

The War Powers Resolution of 1973

JOINT RESOLUTION

Concerning the war powers of Congress and the President.

Resolved by the Senate and House of Representatives of the United States of America in Congress assembled,

Short Title

Section 1. This joint resolution may be cited as the "War Powers Resolution."

Purpose and Policy

Sec. 2. (a) It is the purpose of this joint resolution to fulfill the intent of the framers of the Constitution of the United States and insure that the collective judgment of both the Congress and the President will apply to the introduction of United States Armed Forces into hostilities, or into situations where imminent involvement in hostilities is clearly indicated by the circumstances, and to the continued use of such forces in hostilities or in such situations.

(b) Under Article I, section 8, of the Constitution, it is specifically provided that the Congress shall have the power to make all laws necessary and proper for carrying into execution, not only its own powers but also all other powers vested by the Constitution in the Government of the United States, or in any department or officers thereof.

(c) The constitutional powers of the President as Commander-in-Chief to introduce United States Armed Forces into hostilities, or into situations where imminent involvement in hostilities is clearly indicated by the circumstances, are exercised only pursuant to (1) a declaration of war, (2) specific statutory authorization, or (3) a national emergency created by attack upon the United States, its territories or possessions, or its armed forces.

Consultation

Sec. 3. The President in every possible instance shall consult with Congress before introducing United States Armed Forces into hostilities or into situations where imminent involvement in hostilities is clearly indicated by the circumstances, and after every such introduction shall consult regularly with the Congress until United States Armed Forces are no longer engaged in hostilities or have been removed from such situations.

Reporting

Sec. 4. (a) In the absence of a declaration of war, in any case in which United States Armed Forces are introduced—

(1) into hostilities or into situations where imminent involvement in hostilities is clearly indicated by the circumstances;

(2) into the territory, airspace or waters of a foreign nation, while equipped for combat, except for deployments which relate solely to supply, replacement, repair, or training of such forces; or

(3) in numbers which substantially enlarge United States Armed Forces equipped for combat already located in a foreign nation;

the President shall submit within 48 hours to the Speaker of the House of Representatives and to the President pro tempore of the Senate a report, in writing, setting forth—

(A) the circumstances necessitating the introduction of United States Armed Forces;

(B) the constitutional and legislative authority under which such introduction took place; and

(C) the estimated scope and duration of the hostilities or involvement.

(b) The President shall provide such other information as the Congress may request in the fulfillment of its constitutional responsibilities with respect to committing the Nation to war and to the use of United States Armed Forces abroad.

(c) Whenever United States Armed Forces are introduced into hostilities or into any situation described in subsection (a) of this section, the President shall, so long as such armed forces continue to be engaged in such hostilities or situation, report to the Congress periodically on the status of such hostilities or situation as well as on the scope and duration of such hostilities or situation, but in no event shall he report to the Congress less often than once every six months.

Congressional Action

Sec. 5. (a) Each report submitted pursuant to section 4(a) (1) shall be transmitted to the Speaker of the House of Representatives and to the President pro tempore of the Senate on the same calendar day. Each report so transmitted shall be referred to the Committee on Foreign Affairs of the House of Representatives and to the Committee on Foreign Relations of the Senate for appropriate action. If, when the report is transmitted, the Congress has adjourned sine die or has adjourned for any period in excess of three calendar days, the Speaker of the House of Representatives and the President pro tempore of the Senate, if they deem it advisable (or if petitioned by at least 30 percent of the membership of their respective Houses) shall jointly request the President to convene Congress in order that it may consider the report and take appropriate action pursuant to this section.

(b) Within sixty calendar days after a report is submitted or is required to be submitted pursuant to section 4(a) (1), whichever is earlier, the President shall terminate any use of United States Armed Forces with respect to which such report was submitted (or required to be submitted), unless the Congress (1) has declared war or has enacted a specific authorization for such use of United States Armed Forces, (2) has extended by law such sixty-day period, or (3) is physically unable to meet as a result of an armed attack upon the United States. Such sixty-day period shall be extended for not more than an additional thirty days if the President determines and certifies to the Congress in writing that unavoidable military necessity respecting the safety of United States Armed Forces requires the continued use of such armed forces in the course of bringing about a prompt removal of such forces.

(c) Notwithstanding subsection (b), at any time that United States Armed Forces are engaged in hostilities outside the territory of the United States, its possessions and territories without a declaration of war or specific statutory authorization, such forces shall be removed by the President if the Congress so directs by concurrent resolution.

Congressional Priority Procedures for Joint Resolution or Bill

Sec. 6. (a) Any joint resolution or bill introduced pursuant to section 5(b) at least thirty calendar days before the expiration of the sixty-day period specified in such section shall be referred to the Committee on Foreign Affairs of the House of Representatives or the Committee on Foreign Relations of the Senate, as the case may be, and such committee shall report one such joint resolution or bill, together with its recommendations, not later than twenty-four calendar days before the expiration of the sixty-day period specified in such section, unless such House shall otherwise determine by the yeas and nays.

(b) Any joint resolution or bill so reported shall become the pending business of the House in question (in the case of the Senate the time for debate shall be equally divided between the proponents and the opponents), and shall be voted on within three calendar days thereafter, unless such House shall otherwise determine by yeas and nays.

(c) Such a joint resolution or bill passed by one House shall be referred to the committee of the other House named in subsection (a) and shall be reported out not later than fourteen calendar days before the expiration of the sixty-day period specified in section 5(b). The joint resolution or bill so reported shall become the pending business of the House in question and shall be voted on within three calendar days after it has been reported, unless such House shall otherwise determine by yeas and nays.

(d) In the case of any disagreement between the two Houses of Congress with respect to a joint resolution or bill passed by both Houses, conferees shall be promptly appointed and the committee of conference shall make and file a report with respect to such resolution or bill not later than four calendar days before the expiration of the sixty-day period specified in section 5(b). In the event the conferees are unable to agree within 48 hours, they shall report back to their respective Houses in disagreement. Notwithstanding any rule in either House concerning the printing of conference reports in the Record or concerning any delay in the consideration of such reports, such report shall be acted on by both Houses not later than the expiration of such sixty-day period.

Congressional Priority Procedures for Concurrent Resolution

Sec. 7. (a) Any concurrent resolution introduced pursuant to section 5(c) shall be referred to the Committee on Foreign Affairs of the House of Representatives or the Committee on Foreign Relations of the Senate, as the case may be, and one such concurrent resolution shall be reported out by such committee together with its recommendations within fifteen calendar days, unless such House shall otherwise determine by the yeas and nays.

(b) Any concurrent resolution so reported shall become the pending business of the House in question (in the case of the Senate the time for debate shall be equally divided between the proponents and the opponents) and shall be voted on within three calendar days thereafter, unless such House shall otherwise determine by yeas and nays.

(c) Such a concurrent resolution passed by one House shall be referred to the committee of the other House named in subsection (a) and shall be reported out by such committee together with its recommendations within fifteen calendar days and shall thereupon become the pending business of such House and shall be voted upon within three calendar days, unless such House shall otherwise determine by yeas and nays.

(d) In the case of any disagreement between the two Houses of Congress with respect to a concurrent resolution passed by both Houses, conferees shall be promptly appointed and the committee of conference shall make and file a report with respect to such concurrent resolution within six calendar days after the legislation is referred to the committee of conference. Notwithstanding any rule in either House concerning the printing of conference reports in the Record or concerning any delay in the consideration of such reports, such report shall be acted on by both Houses not later than six calendar days after the conference report is filed. In the event the conferees are unable to agree within 48 hours, they shall report back to their respective Houses in disagreement.

Interpretation of Joint Resolution

Sec. 8. (a) Authority to introduce United States Armed Forces into hostilities or into situations wherein involvement in hostilities is clearly indicated by the circumstances shall not be inferred—

(1) from any provision of law (whether or not in effect before the date of the enactment of this joint resolution), including any provision contained in any appropriation Act, unless such provision specifically authorizes the introduction of United States Armed Forces into hostilities or into such situations and states that it is intended to constitute specific statutory authorization within the meaning of this joint resolution; or

(2) from any treaty heretofore or hereafter ratified unless such treaty is implemented by legislation specifically authorizing the introduction of United States Armed Forces into hostilities or into such situations and stating that it is intended to constitute specific statutory authorization within the meaning of this joint resolution.

(b) Nothing in this joint resolution shall be construed to require any further specific statutory authorization to permit members of United States Armed Forces to participate jointly with members of the armed forces of one or more foreign countries in the headquarters operations of high-level military commands which were established prior to the date of enactment of this joint resolution and pursuant to the United Nations Charter or any treaty ratified by the United States prior to such date.

(c) For purposes of this joint resolution, the term "introduction of United States Armed Forces" includes the assignment of members of such armed forces to command, coordinate, participate in the movement of, or accompany the regular or irregular military forces of any foreign country or government when such military forces are engaged, or there exists an imminent threat that such forces will become engaged, in hostilities.

(d) Nothing in this joint resolution—

(1) is intended to alter the constitutional authority of the Congress or of the President, or the provisions of existing treaties; or

(2) shall be construed as granting any authority to the President with respect to the introduction of United States Armed Forces into hostilities or into situations wherein involvement in hos-

tilities is clearly indicated by the circumstances which authority he would not have had in the absence of this joint resolution.

Separability Clause
Sec. 9. If any provision of this joint resolution or the application thereof to any person or circumstance is held invalid, the remainder of the joint resolution and the application of such provision to any other person or circumstance shall not be affected thereby.

Effective Date
Sec. 10. This joint resolution shall take effect on the date of its enactment.

The Persian Gulf War Resolution
January 12, 1991

The following resolution, House Joint Resolution 77, was adopted by the House of Representatives by a vote of 250 to 183. The Senate approved the measure (originally introduced as Senate Joint Resolution 2) by a vote of 52 to 47.

To authorize the use of United States Armed Forces pursuant to United Nations Security Council Resolution 678.

Whereas the Government of Iraq without provocation invaded and occupied the territory of Kuwait on August 2, 1990; and

Whereas both the House of Representatives *** and the Senate *** have condemned Iraq's invasion of Kuwait and declared their support for international action to reverse Iraq's aggression; and

Whereas, Iraq's conventional, chemical, biological, and nuclear weapons and ballistic missile programs and its demonstrated willingness to use weapons of mass destruction pose a grave threat to world peace; and

Whereas the international community has demanded that Iraq withdraw unconditionally and immediately from Kuwait and that Kuwait's independence and legitimate government be restored; and

Whereas the U.N. Security Council repeatedly affirmed the inherent right of individual or collective self-defense in response to the armed attack by Iraq against Kuwait in accordance with Article 51 of the U.N. Charter; and

Whereas, in the absence of full compliance by Iraq with its resolutions, the U.N. Security Council in Resolution 678 has authorized member states of the United Nations to use all necessary means, after January 15, 1991, to uphold and implement all relevant Security Council resolutions and to restore international peace and security in the area; and

Whereas Iraq has persisted in its illegal occupation of, and brutal aggression against, Kuwait: Now, therefore be it

Resolved by the Senate and House of Representatives of the United States of America in Congress assembled,

Section 1. Title. This joint resolution may be cited as the "Authorization for Use of Military Force Against Iraq Resolution."

Section 2. Authorization for Use of United States Armed Forces

(a) AUTHORIZATION. The President is authorized, subject to subsection (b), to use United States Armed Forces pursuant to United Nations Security Council Resolution 678 (1990) in order to achieve implementation of Security Council Resolutions 660, 661, 662, 664, 665, 666, 667, 669, 670, 674, and 677.

(b) REQUIREMENT FOR DETERMINATION THAT USE OF MILITARY FORCE IS NECESSARY. Before exercising the authority granted in subsection (a), the President shall make available to the Speaker of the House of Representatives and the President pro tempore of the Senate his determination that—

(1) the United States has used all appropriate diplomatic and other peaceful means to obtain compliance by Iraq with the United Nations Security Council resolutions cited in subsection (a); and

(2) that those efforts have not been successful in obtaining such compliance.

(c) WAR POWERS RESOLUTION REQUIREMENTS.

(1) SPECIFIC STATUTORY AUTHORIZATION. Consistent with section 8(a)(1) of the War Powers Resolution, the Congress declares that this section is intended to constitute specific statutory authorization within the meaning of section 5(b) of the War Powers Resolution.

(2) APPLICABILITY OF OTHER REQUIREMENTS. Nothing in this resolution supersedes any requirement of the War Powers Resolution.

Section 4. REPORTS TO CONGRESS.

At least once every 60 days, the President shall submit to the Congress a summary on the status of efforts to obtain compliance by Iraq with the resolutions adopted by the United Nations Security Council in response to Iraq's aggression.

Ex Parte Milligan

4 Wall. (71 U.S.) 2; 18 L. Ed. 281 (1866)
Vote: 9-0

Lambdin Milligan, a citizen of Indiana and a civilian, was a Confederate sympathizer during the Civil War. In 1864, he was arrested by the military on charges of inciting insurrection and giving aid and comfort to the Confederacy. After being tried and convicted by a military court, Milligan was sentenced to death by hanging. In 1865, he petitioned the federal circuit court for a writ of habeas corpus, arguing that the military did not have jurisdiction over him since, at the time of his arrest, he was a civilian living in a state where the civilian courts were still open and that, even if the military court had jurisdiction, it had violated his right to trial by jury guaranteed by the Sixth Amendment. The circuit court was unable to reach a decision on these issues and thus certified the case to the Supreme Court. After the Supreme Court's decision, Milligan was released from custody. He later prevailed in a civil action against the military commander who had ordered his arrest.

Mr. Justice Davis delivered the opinion of the Court:

. . . The controlling question in the case is this: Upon the *facts* stated in Milligan's petition, and the exhibits filed, had the military commission mentioned in it *jurisdiction,* legally, to try and sentence him? Milligan, not a resident of one of the rebellious states, or a prisoner of war, but a citizen of Indiana for twenty years past, and never in the military or naval service, is, while at his home, arrested by the military power of the United States, imprisoned, and, on certain criminal charges preferred against him, tried, convicted, and sentenced to be hanged by a military commission, organized under the direction of the military commander of the military district of Indiana. Had this tribunal the legal power and authority to try and punish this man?

. . . The Constitution of the United States is a law for rulers and people, equally in war and in peace, and covers with the shield of its protection all classes of men, at all times, and under all circumstances. No doctrine involving more pernicious consequences was ever invented by the wit of man than that any of its provisions can be suspended during any of the great exigencies of government. Such a doctrine leads directly to anarchy or despotism, but the theory of necessity on which it is based is false; for the government, within the Constitution, has all the powers granted to it which are necessary to preserve its existence; as has been happily proved by the result of the great effort to throw off its just authority.

Have any of the rights guaranteed by the Constitution been violated in the case of Milligan? And if so, what are they?

Every trial involves the exercise of judicial power; and from what source did the military commission that tried him derive their authority? Certainly no part of the judicial power of the country was conferred on them; because the Constitution expressly vests it "in one supreme court and such inferior courts as the Congress may from time to time ordain and establish," and it is not pretended that the commission was a court ordained and established by Congress. They cannot justify on the mandate of the President; because he is controlled by law, and has his appropriate sphere of duty, which is to execute, not to make, the laws; and there is "no unwritten criminal code to which resort can be had as a source of jurisdiction."

But it is said that the jurisdiction is complete under the "laws and usages of war."

It can serve no useful purpose to inquire what those laws and usages are, whence they originated, where found and on whom they operate; they can never be applied to citizens in states which have upheld the authority of the government, and where the courts are open and their process unobstructed. This court has judicial knowledge that in Indiana the Federal authority was always unopposed, and its courts always open to hear criminal accusations and redress grievances; and no usage of war could sanction a military trial there for any offence whatever or a citizen in civil life, in nowise connected with the military service. Congress could grant no such power; and to the honor of our national legislature be it said, it has never been provoked by the state of the country even to attempt its exercise. One of the plainest constitutional provisions was, therefore, infringed when Milligan was tried by a court not ordained and established by Congress, and not composed of judges appointed during good behavior.

Why was he not delivered to the Circuit Court of Indiana to be proceeded against according to law? No reason of necessity could be urged against it; because Congress had declared penalties against the offences charged, provided for their punishment, and directed that court to hear and determine them. And soon after this military tribunal was ended, the Circuit Court met, peacefully transacted its business, and adjourned. It needed no bayonets to protect it, and required no military aid to execute its judgments. It was held in a state, eminently distinguished for patriotism, by judges commissioned during the Rebellion, who were provided with juries, upright,

intelligent, and selected by a marshal appointed by the President. The government had no right to conclude that Milligan, if guilty, would not receive in that court merited punishment; for its records disclose that it was constantly engaged in the trial of similar offences, and was never interrupted in its administration of criminal justice. If it was dangerous, in the distracted condition of affairs, to leave Milligan unrestrained of his liberty, because he "conspired against the government, afforded aid and comfort to rebels, and incited the people to insurrection," the law said arrest him, confine him closely, render him powerless to do further mischief; and then present his case to the grand jury of the district, with proofs of his guilt, and, if indicted, try him according to the course of the common law. If this had been done, the Constitution would have been vindicated, the law of 1863 enforced, and the securities for personal liberty preserved and defended.

Another guarantee of freedom was broken when Milligan was denied a trial by jury.... The Sixth Amendment affirms that "in all criminal prosecutions the accused shall enjoy the right to a speedy and public trial by an impartial jury," language broad enough to embrace all persons and cases; but the Fifth, recognizing the necessity of an indictment, or presentment, before any one can be held to answer for high crimes, "excepts cases arising in the land or naval forces, or in the militia, when in actual service in time of war or public danger"; and the framers of the Constitution, doubtless, meant to limit the right of trial by jury, in the Sixth Amendment, to those persons who were subject to indictment or presentment in the Fifth.

The discipline necessary to the efficiency of the army and navy required other and swifter modes of trial than are furnished by the common law courts; and, in pursuance of the power conferred by the Constitution, Congress has declared the kinds of trial, and the manner in which they shall be conducted, for offences committed while the party is in the military or naval service. Everyone connected with these branches of the public service is amenable to the jurisdiction which Congress has created for their government, and, while thus serving, surrenders his right to be tried by the civil courts. *All other persons,* citizens of states where the courts are open, if charged with crime, are guaranteed the inestimable privilege of trial by jury. This privilege is a vital principle, underlying the whole administration of criminal justice. . . .

It is claimed that martial law covers with its broad mantle the proceedings of this military commission. The proposition is this: that in a time of war the commander of an armed force (if in his opinion the exigencies of the country demand it, and of which he is to judge), has the power, within the lines of his military district, to suspend all civil rights and their remedies, and subject citizens as well as soldiers to the role of his will; and in the exercise of his lawful authority cannot be restrained, except by his superior officer or the President of the United States.

If this position is sound to the extent claimed, then when war exists, foreign or domestic, and the country is subdivided into military departments for mere convenience, the commander of one of them can, if he chooses, within his limits, on the plea of necessity, with the approval of the Executive, substitute military force for and to the exclusion of the laws, and punish all persons, as he thinks right and proper, without fixed or certain rules.

The statement of this proposition shows its importance; for, if true, republican government is a failure, and there is an end of liberty regulated by law. Martial law, established on such a basis, destroys every guaranty of the Constitution, and effectually renders the "military independent of and superior to the civil power"—the attempt to do which by the King of Great Britain was deemed by our fathers such an offence, that they assigned it to the world as one of the causes which impelled them to declare their independence. Civil liberty and this kind of martial law cannot endure together; the antagonism is irreconcilable; and in the conflict, one or the other must perish.

. . . But, it is insisted that the safety of the country in time of war demands that this broad claim for martial law shall be sustained. If this were true, it could be well said that a country preserved at the sacrifice of all the cardinal principles of liberty, is not worth the cost of preservation. Happily, it is not so.

It will be borne in mind that this is not a question of the power to proclaim martial law, when war

exists in a community and the courts and civil authorities are overthrown. Nor is it a question what rule a military commander, at the head of his army, can impose on states in rebellion to cripple their resources and quell the insurrection. The jurisdiction claimed is much more extensive. The necessities of the service, during the late Rebellion, required that the loyal states should be placed within the limits of certain military districts and commanders appointed in them; and, it is urged, that this, in a military sense, constituted them the theater of military operations; and, as in this case, Indiana had been and was again threatened with invasion by the enemy, the occasion was furnished to establish martial law. The conclusion does not follow from the premises. If armies were collected in Indiana, they were to be employed in another locality, where the laws were obstructed and the national authority disputed. On her soil there was no hostile foot; if one invaded, that invasion was at an end, and with it all pretext for martial law. Martial law cannot arise from a threatened invasion. The necessity must be actual and present; the invasion real, such as effectually closes the courts and deposes the civil administration.

It is difficult to see how the safety of the country required martial law in Indiana. If any of her citizens were plotting treason, the power of arrest could secure them, until the government was prepared for their trial, when the courts were open and ready to try them. It was as easy to protect witnesses before a civil as a military tribunal; and as there could be no wish to convict, except on sufficient legal evidence, surely an ordained and established court was better able to judge of this than a military tribunal composed of gentlemen not trained to the profession of the law.

It follows, from what has been said on this subject, that there are occasions when martial rule can be properly applied. If, in foreign invasions or civil war, the courts are actually closed, and it is impossible to administer criminal justice according to law, then, in the theater of active military operations, where war really prevails, there is a necessity to furnish a substitute for the civil authority, thus overthrown, to preserve the safety of the army and society; and as no power is left but the military, it is allowed to govern by martial rule until the laws can have their free course. As necessity creates the rule, so it limits its duration; for, if this government is continued after the courts are reinstated, it is a gross usurpation of power. Martial rule can never exist where the courts are open, and in the proper and unobstructed exercise of their jurisdiction. It is also confined to the locality of actual war. Because, during the late Rebellion it could have been enforced in Virginia, where the national authority was overturned and the courts driven out, it does not follow that it should obtain in Indiana, where that authority was never disputed, and justice was always administered. And so in the case of a foreign invasion martial rule may become a necessity in one state, when, in another, it would be "mere lawless violence." . . .

The two remaining questions in this case must be answered in the affirmative. The suspension of the privilege of the writ of *habeas corpus* does not suspend the writ itself. The writ issues as a matter of course; and on the return made to it the court decides whether the party applying is denied the right of proceeding any further with it.

If the military trial of Milligan was contrary to law, then he was entitled, on the facts stated in his petition, to be discharged from custody by the terms of the act of Congress of March 3d, 1863. . . .

But it is insisted that Milligan was a prisoner of war, and, therefore, excluded from the privileges of the statute. It is not easy to see how he can be treated as a prisoner of war, when he lived in Indiana for the past twenty years, was arrested there, and had not been, during the late troubles, a resident of any of the states in rebellion. If in Indiana he conspired with bad men to assist the enemy, he is punishable for it in the courts of Indiana; but, when tried for the offence, he cannot plead the rights of war; for he was not engaged in legal acts of hostility against the government, and only such persons, when captured, are prisoners of war. If he cannot enjoy the immunities attached to the character of a prisoner of war, how can he be subject to their pains and penalties? . . .

The Chief Justice delivered the following [concurring] opinion:

Four members of the Court . . . unable to concur in some important particulars with the opinion which has just been read, think it their duty to make a separate statement of their views of the whole case. . . .

The opinion . . . as we understand it, asserts not only that the military commission held in Indiana was not authorized by Congress, but that it was not in the power of Congress to authorize it; from which it may be thought to follow that Congress has no power to indemnify the officers who composed the commission against liability in civil courts for acting as members of it. We cannot agree to this. . . .

We think that Congress had power, though not exercised, to authorize the military commission which was held in Indiana. . . .

Mr. Justice Wayne, Mr. Justice Swayne, and *Mr. Justice Miller* concur with me in these views.

Korematsu v. United States
323 U.S. 214; 65 S. Ct. 193; 89 L. Ed. 194 (1944)
Vote: 6-3

Mr. Justice Black delivered the opinion of the Court.

The petitioner [Korematsu], an American citizen of Japanese descent, was convicted in a federal district court for remaining in San Leandro, California, a "Military Area," contrary to Civilian Exclusion Order No. 34 . . . which directed that after May 9, 1942, all persons of Japanese ancestry should be excluded from that area. No question was raised as to [Korematsu's] loyalty to the United States. The Circuit Court of Appeals affirmed, and the importance of the constitutional question involved caused us to grant *certiorari*.

It should be noted, to begin with, that all legal restrictions which curtail the civil rights of a single racial group are immediately suspect. That is not to say that all such restrictions are unconstitutional. It is to say that courts must subject them to the most rigid scrutiny. Pressing public necessity may sometime justify the existence of such restrictions; racial antagonism never can.

In the instant case prosecution of [Korematsu] was begun by information charging violation of an Act of Congress, of March 21, 1942, *** which provides that" ... whoever shall enter, remain in, leave, or commit any act in any military area or military zone prescribed, under the authority of an Executive order of the President, ... contrary to the restrictions applicable to any such area or zone ... shall, if it appears that he knew or should have known of the existence and extent of the restrictions or order and that his act was in violation thereof, be guilty of a misdemeanor and upon conviction shall be liable to a fine of not to exceed $5,000 or to imprisonment for not more than one year, or both, for each offense."

Exclusion Order No. 34, which [Korematsu] knowingly and admittedly violated, was one of a number of military orders and proclamations, all of which were substantially based upon Executive Order No. 9066. *** That order, issued after we were at war with Japan, declared the "the successful prosecution of the war requires every possible protection against espionage and against sabotage to national-defense material, national-defense premises, and national-defense utilities. . . ."

One of the series of orders and proclamations, a curfew order, ... subjected all persons of Japanese ancestry in prescribed West Coast military areas to remain in their residences from 8 P.M. to 6 A.M. As is the case with the exclusion order here, that prior curfew order was designed as a "protection against espionage and against sabotage." In *Hirabayashi v. United States* *** we sustained a conviction obtained for violation of the curfew order. . . .

The 1942 Act was attacked in the *Hirabayashi* case as an unconstitutional delegation of power; it was contended that the curfew order and other orders on which it rested were beyond the war powers of the Congress, the military authorities and of the President, as Commander in Chief of the Army; and finally that to apply the curfew order against none but citizens of Japanese ancestry amounted to a constitutionally prohibited discrimination solely on account of race. . . .

In the light of the principles we announced in the *Hirabayashi* case, we are unable to conclude that it was beyond the war power of Congress and the Executive to exclude those of Japanese ancestry from the West Coast war area at the time they did. True, exclusion from the area in which one's home is located is a far greater deprivation than constant confinement to the home from 8 P.M. to 6 A.M. Nothing short of apprehension by the proper military authorities of the gravest imminent danger to the public safety can constitutionally justify either. But exclusion from a threatened area, no less than curfew, has a definite and close relationship to the prevention of espionage and sabotage. The military authorities, charged with the primary responsibility of defending our shores, concluded that curfew provided inadequate protection and ordered exclusion. They did so, as pointed out in our *Hirabayashi* opinion, in accordance with Congressional authority to the military to say who should, and who should not, remain in the threatened areas.

In this case [Korematsu] challenges the assumptions upon which we rested our conclusions in the *Hirabayashi,* case. He also urges that by May 1942, when Order No. 34 was promulgated, all danger of Japanese invasion of the West Coast had disappeared. After careful consideration of these contentions we are compelled to reject them.

Here, as in the *Hirabayashi* case, *** " ... we cannot reject as unfounded the judgment of the military authorities and of Congress that there were disloyal members of that population, whose number and strength could not be precisely and quickly ascertained. We cannot say that the war-making branches of the Government did not have grounds for believing that in a critical hour such persons could not readily be isolated and separately dealt with, and constituted a menace to the national defense and safety, which demanded that prompt and adequate measures be taken to guard against it."

Like curfew, exclusion of those of Japanese origin was deemed necessary because of the presence of an unascertained number of disloyal members of the group, most of whom we have no doubt were loyal to this country. It was because we could not reject the finding of the military authorities that it was impossible to bring about an immediate segregation of the disloyal from the loyal that we sustained the validity of the curfew order as applying to the whole group. In the instant case, temporary exclusion of the entire group was rested by the military on the same ground. The judgment that exclusion of the entire group was for the same reason a military imperative answers the contention that the exclusion was in the nature of group punishment based on antagonism to those of Japanese origin. That there were members of the group who retained loyalties to Japan has been confirmed by investigations made subsequent to the exclusion. Approximately five thousand American citizens of Japanese ancestry refused to swear unqualified allegiance to the United States and to renounce allegiance to the Japanese Emperor, and several thousand evacuees requested repatriation to Japan.

We uphold the exclusion order as of the time it was made and when [Korematsu] violated it. *** In doing so, we are not unmindful of the hardships imposed by it upon a large group of American citizens. *** But hardships are part of war, and war is an aggregation of hardships. All citizens alike, both in and out of uniform, feel the impact of war in greater or lesser measure. Citizenship has its responsibilities as well as its privileges, and in time of war the burden is always heavier. Compulsory exclusion of large groups of citizens from their homes, except under circumstances of direst emergency and peril, is inconsistent with our basic governmental institutions. But when under conditions of modern warfare our shores are threatened by hostile forces, the power to protect must be commensurate with the threatened danger. . . .

It is said that we are dealing here with the case of imprisonment of a citizen in a concentration camp solely because of his ancestry, without evidence or inquiry concerning his loyalty and good disposition towards the United States. Our task would be simple, our duty clear, were this a case involving the imprisonment of a loyal citizen in a concentration camp because of racial prejudice. Regardless of the true nature of the assembly and relocation centers—and we deem it unjustifiable to call them concentration camps with all the ugly connotations that term

implies—we are dealing specifically with nothing but an exclusion order. To cast this case into outlines of racial prejudice, without reference to the real military dangers which were presented, merely confused the issue. Korematsu was not excluded from the Military Area because of hostility to him or his race. He was excluded because we are at war with the Japanese Empire, because the properly constituted military authorities feared an invasion of our West Coast and felt constrained to take proper security measures, because they decided that the military urgency of the situation demanded that all citizens of Japanese ancestry be segregated from the West Coast temporarily, and finally, because Congress, reposing its confidence in this time of war in our military leaders—as inevitably it must—determined that they should have the power to do just this. There was evidence of disloyalty on the part of some, the military authorities considered that the need for action was great, and time was short. We cannot—by availing ourselves of the calm perspective of hindsight—now say that at that time these actions were unjustified.

Affirmed.

Mr. Justice Frankfurter, concurring. . . .

Mr. Justice Roberts [dissenting]. . . .

Mr. Justice Murphy, dissenting. . . . The judicial test of whether the Government, on a plea of military necessity, can validly deprive an individual of any of his constitutional rights is whether the deprivation is reasonably related to a public danger that is so "immediate, imminent, and impending" as not to admit of delay and not to permit the intervention of ordinary constitutional processes to alleviate the danger. *** Civilian Exclusion Order No. 34, banishing from a prescribed area of the Pacific Coast "all persons of Japanese ancestry, both alien and non-alien," clearly does not meet that test. Being an obvious racial discrimination, the order deprives all those within its scope of the equal protection of the laws as guaranteed by the Fifth Amendment. It further deprives these individuals of their constitutional rights to live and work where they will, to establish a home where they choose and to move about freely. In excommunicating them without benefit of hearings, this order also deprives them of all their constitutional rights to procedural due process. Yet no reasonable relation to an "immediate, imminent, and impending" public danger is evident to support this racial restriction which is one of the most sweeping and complete deprivations of constitutional rights in the history of this nation in the absence of martial law. . . .

That this forced exclusion was the result in good measure of [the] erroneous assumption of racial guilt rather than bona fide military necessity is evidenced by the Commanding General's Final Report on the evacuation from the Pacific Coast area. In it he refers to all individuals of Japanese descent as "subversive," as belonging to "an enemy race" whose "racial strains are undiluted," and as constituting "over 112,000 potential enemies . . . at large today" along the Pacific Coast. In support of this blanket condemnation of all persons of Japanese descent, however, no reliable evidence is cited to show that such individuals were generally disloyal, or had generally so conducted themselves in this area as to constitute a special menace to defense installations or war industries, or had otherwise by their behavior furnished reasonable ground for their exclusion as a group.

Justification for the exclusion is sought, instead, mainly upon questionable racial and sociological grounds not ordinarily within the realm of expert military judgment, supplemented by certain semi-military conclusions drawn from an unwarranted use of circumstantial evidence. . . .

The main reasons relied upon by those responsible for the forced evacuation, therefore, do not prove a reasonable relations between the group characteristics of Japanese Americans by people with racial and economic prejudices—the same people who have been among the foremost advocates of the evacuation. A military judgment based upon such racial and sociological considerations is not entitled to the great weight ordinarily given the judgments based upon strictly military considerations. . . .

The military necessity which is essential to the validity of the evacuation order thus resolves itself into a few intimations that certain individuals actively aided the enemy, from which it is inferred that the entire group of Japanese Americans could not be or remain loyal to the United States. . . . But to infer that examples of individual disloyalty prove group dis-

loyalty and justify discriminatory action against the entire group is to deny that under our system of law individual guilt is the sole basis for deprivation of rights. . . . To give constitutional sanction to that inference in this case, however well-intentioned may have been the military command on the Pacific Coast, is to adopt one of the cruelest of the rationales used by our enemies to destroy the dignity of the individual and to encourage and open the door to discriminatory actions against other minority groups in the passions of tomorrow.

No adequate reason is given for the failure to treat these Japanese Americans on an individual basis by holding investigations and hearings to separate the loyal from the disloyal, as was done in the case of persons of German and Italian ancestry. . . .

I dissent, therefore, from this legalization of racism. Racial discrimination in any form and in any degree has no justifiable part whatever in our democratic way of life. It is unattractive in any setting but it is utterly revolting among a free people who have embraced the principles set forth in the Constitution of the United States. All residents of this nation are kin in some way by blood or culture to a foreign land. Yet they are primarily and necessarily a part of the new and distinct civilization of the United States. They must accordingly be treated at all times as the heirs of the American experiment and as entitled to all the rights and freedoms guaranteed by the Constitution.

Mr. Justice Jackson, dissenting. . . . [I]f any fundamental assumption underlies our system, it is that guilt is personal and not inheritable. Even if all of one's antecedents had been convicted of treason, the Constitution forbids its penalties to be visited upon him, for it provides that "no attainder of treason shall work corruption of blood, or forfeiture except during the life of the person attainted." But here is an attempt to make an otherwise innocent act a crime merely because this prisoner is the son of parents as to whom he had no choice, and belongs to a race from which there is no way to resign. If Congress in peace-time legislation should enact such a criminal law, I should suppose this Court would refuse to enforce it. . . .

It would be impracticable and dangerous idealism to expect or insist that each specific military command in an area of probable operations will conform to conventional tests of constitutionality. When an area is so beset that it must be put under military control at all, the paramount consideration is that its measures be successful, rather than legal. The armed services must protect a society, not merely its Constitution. The very essence of the military job is to marshal physical force to remove every obstacle to its effectiveness, to give it every strategic advantage. Defense measures will not, and often should not, be held within the limits that bind civil authority in peace. . . .

But if we cannot confine military expedients by the Constitution, neither would I distort the Constitution to approve all that the military may deem expedient. That is what the Court appears to be doing, whether consciously or not. . . .

. . . [O]nce a judicial opinion rationalizes . . . an order [such as the Civilian Exclusion Order] to show that it conforms to the Constitution, or rather rationalizes the Constitution to show that the Constitution sanctions such an order, the Court for all time has validated the principle of racial discrimination in criminal procedure and of transplanting American citizens. The principle then lies about like a loaded weapon ready for the hand of any authority that can bring forward a plausible claim of an urgent need. Every repetition imbeds that principle more deeply

in our law and thinking and expands it to new purposes. All who observe the work of courts are familiar with what Judge Cardozo described as "the tendency of a principle to expand itself to the limit of its logic." A military commander may overstep the bounds of constitutionality, and it is an incident. But if we review and approve, that passing incident becomes the doctrine of the Constitution. There it has a generative power of its own, and all that it creates will be in its own image. Nothing better illustrates this danger than does the Court's opinion in this case. . . .

I should hold that a civil court cannot be made to enforce an order which violates constitutional limitations even if it is a reasonable exercise of military authority. The courts can exercise only the judicial power, can apply only law, and must abide by the Constitution, or they cease to be civil courts and become instruments of military policy. . . . My duties as a justice as I see them do not require me to make a military judgment as to whether General DeWitt's evacuation and detention program was a reasonable military necessity. I do not suggest that the courts should have attempted to interfere with the Army in carrying out its task. But I do not think they may be asked to execute a military expedient that has no place in law under the Constitution. I would reverse the judgment and discharge the prisoner.

United States v. United States District Court

407 U.S. 297; 92 S. Ct. 2125; 32 L. Ed. 2d 752 (1972)
Vote: 8-0

Three defendants were charged with conspiracy to destroy government property. One of them, Plamondon, was also charged with the bombing of a CIA office in Ann Arbor, Michigan. Defendants filed a pretrial motion to compel disclosure of information the government had obtained through electronic surveillance that had not been judicially approved. The government asserted that the surveillance was lawful as a reasonable exercise of the president's power to protect national security. The U.S. District Court for the Eastern District of Michigan held that

the government's surveillance violated the Fourth Amendment prohibition against unreasonable searches and seizures. The U.S. Court of Appeals for the Sixth Circuit agreed.

Mr. Justice Powell delivered the opinion of the Court.

. . . Title III of the Omnibus Crime Control and Safe Streets Act authorizes the use of electronic surveillance for classes of crimes carefully specified in 18 U.S.C. Sec. 2516. Such surveillance is subject to prior court order. Section 2518 sets forth the detailed and particularized application necessary to obtain such an order as well as carefully circumscribed conditions for its use. The Act represents a comprehensive attempt by Congress to promote more effective control of crime while protecting the privacy of individual thought and expression. Much of Title III was drawn to meet the constitutional requirements for electronic surveillance enunciated by this Court in *Berger v. New York* *** (1967) and *Katz v. United States* *** (1967).

Together with the elaborate surveillance requirements in Title III, there is the following proviso, 18 U.S.C. Sec. 2511 (3):

Nothing contained in this chapter or in section 605 of the Communications Act of 1934 shall limit the constitutional power of the President to take such measures as he deems necessary to protect the Nation against actual or potential attack or other hostile acts of a foreign power, to obtain foreign intelligence information deemed essential to the security of the United States, or to protect national security information against foreign intelligence activities. Nor shall anything contained in this chapter be deemed to limit the constitutional power of the President to take such measures as he deems necessary to protect the United States against the overthrow of the Government by force or other unlawful means, or against any other clear and present danger to the structure or existence of the Government. The contents of any wire or oral communication intercepted by authority of the President in the exercise of the foregoing powers may be received in evidence in any trial, hearing, or other proceeding only where such interception was reasonable, and shall not be otherwise used or disclosed except as is necessary to implement that power. ***

The Government relies on Sec. 2511 (3). It argues that "in excepting national security surveillances from the Act's warrant requirement Congress recognized the President's authority to conduct such surveillances without prior judicial approval." The section thus is viewed as a recognition or affirmance of a constitutional authority in the President to conduct warrantless domestic security surveillance such as that involved in this case.

We think the language of Sec. 2511 (3), as well as the legislative history of the statute, refutes this interpretation. The relevant language is that: "Nothing contained in this chapter . . . shall limit the constitu-

tional power of the President to take such measures as he deems necessary to protect . . ." against the dangers specified. At most, this is an implicit recognition that the President does have certain powers in the specified areas. Few would doubt this, as the section refers—among other things—to protection "against actual or potential attack or other hostile acts of a foreign power." But so far as the use of the President's electronic surveillance power is concerned, the language is essentially neutral.

Section 2511 (3) certainly confers no power, as the language is wholly inappropriate for such a purpose. It merely provides that the Act shall not be interpreted to limit or disturb such power as the President may have under the Constitution. In short, Congress simply left presidential powers where it found them. This view is reinforced by the general context of Title III. Section 2511 (1) broadly prohibits the use of electronic surveillance "except as otherwise specifically provided in this chapter." Subsection (2) thereof contains four specific exceptions. In each of the specified exceptions, the statutory language is as follows: "It shall not be unlawful . . . to intercept" the particular type of communication described.

The language of subsection (3), here involved, is to be contrasted with the language of the exceptions set forth in the preceding subsection. Rather than stating that warrantless presidential uses of electronic surveillance "shall not be unlawful" and thus employing the standard language of exception, subsection (3) merely disclaims any intention to "limit the constitutional power of the President." . . .

The legislative history of Sec. 2511 (3) supports this interpretation. . . .

. . . If we could accept the Government's characterization of Sec. 2511 (3) as a congressionally prescribed exception to the general requirement of a warrant, it would be necessary to consider the question of whether the surveillance in this case came within the exception and, if so, whether the statutory exception was itself constitutionally valid. But viewing Sec. 2511 (3) as a congressional disclaimer and expression of neutrality, we hold that the statute is not the measure of the executive authority asserted in this case. Rather, we must look to the constitutional powers of the President.

It is important at the outset to emphasize the limited nature of the question before the Court. This case raises no constitutional challenge to electronic surveillance as specifically authorized by Title III of the Omnibus Crime Control and Safe Streets Act of 1968. Nor is there any question or doubt as to the necessity of obtaining a warrant in the surveillance of crimes unrelated to the national security interest. *** Further, the instant case requires no judgment on the scope of the President's surveillance power with respect to the activities of foreign powers, within or without this country. The Attorney General's affidavit in this case states that the surveillances were "deemed necessary to protect the nation from attempts of domestic organizations to attack and subvert the existing structure of Government." There is no evidence of any involvement, directly or indirectly, of a foreign power. . . .

We begin the inquiry by noting that the President of the United States has the fundamental duty, under Art. II, Sec. 1, of the Constitution, "to preserve, protect, and defend the Constitution of the United States." Implicit in that duty is the power to protect our Government against those who would subvert or overthrow it by unlawful means. In the discharge of this duty, the President—through the Attorney General—may find it necessary to employ electronic surveillance to obtain intelligence information on the plans of those who plot unlawful acts against the Government. The use of such surveillance in internal security cases has been sanctioned more or less continuously by various Presidents and Attorneys General since July 1946. Herbert Brownell, Attorney General under President Eisenhower, urged the use of electronic surveillance both in internal and international security matters on the grounds that those acting against the Government "turn to the telephone to carry on their intrigue. The success of their plans frequently rests upon piecing together shreds of information received from many sources and many nests. The participants in the conspiracy are often dispersed and stationed in various strategic positions in government and industry throughout the country." ***

Though the Government and respondents debate their seriousness and magnitude, threats and acts of sabotage against the Government exist in sufficient number to justify investigative powers with respect to them. The covertness and complexity of potential unlawful conduct against the Government and the necessary dependency of many conspirators upon the telephone make electronic surveillance an effective investigatory instrument in certain circumstances. The marked acceleration in technological developments and sophistication in their use have resulted in new techniques for the planning, commission and concealment of criminal activities. It would be contrary to the public interest for Government to deny to itself the prudent and lawful employment of those very techniques which are employed against the Government and its law-abiding citizens.

It has been said that "the most basic function of any government is to provide for the security of the individual and of his property." *** And unless Government safeguards its own capacity to function and to preserve the security of its people, society itself could become so disordered that all rights and liberties would be endangered. . . .

But a recognition of these elementary truths does not make the employment by Government of electronic surveillance a welcome development—even when employed with restraint and under judicial supervision. There is, understandably, a deep-seated uneasiness and apprehension that this capability will be used to intrude upon cherished privacy of law-abiding citizens. We look to the Bill of Rights to safeguard this privacy. Though physical entry of the home is the chief evil against which the wording of the Fourth Amendment is directed, its broader spirit now shields private speech from unreasonable surveillance. . . . Our decision in *Katz* refused to lock the Fourth Amendment into instances of actual physical trespass. Rather, the Amendment governs "not only the seizure of tangible items, but extends as well to the recording of oral statements without any technical trespass under . . . local property law." *** That decision implicitly recognized that the broad and unsuspected governmental incursions into conversational privacy which electronic surveillance entails necessitate the application of Fourth Amendment safeguards.

National security cases, moreover, often reflect a convergence of First and Fourth Amendment values not present in cases of "ordinary" crime. Though the investigative duty of the executive may be stronger in such cases, so also is there greater jeopardy to constitutionally protected speech. "Historically the struggle for freedom of speech and press in England was bound up with the issue of the scope of the search and seizure power." *** History abundantly documents the tendency of Government—however benevolent and benign its motives—to view with suspicion those who most fervently dispute its policies. Fourth Amendment protections become the more necessary when the targets of official surveillance may be those suspected of unorthodoxy in their political beliefs. The danger to political dissent is acute where the Government attempts to act under so vague a concept as the power to protect "domestic security." Given the difficulty of defining the domestic security interest, the danger of abuse in acting to protect that interest becomes apparent. Senator Hart addressed this dilemma in the floor debate on Sec. 2511 (3): "As I read it—and this is my fear—we are saying that the President, on his motion, could declare—name your favorite poison—draft dodgers, Black Muslims, the Ku Klux Klan, or civil rights activists to be a clear and present danger to the structure or existence of the Government." *** The price of lawful public dissent must not be a dread of subjection to an unchecked surveillance power. Nor must the fear of unauthorized official eavesdropping deter vigorous citizen dissent and discussion of Government action in private conversation. For private dissent, no less than open public discourse, is essential to our free society.

As the Fourth Amendment is not absolute in its terms, our task is to examine and balance the basic values at stake in this case: the duty of Government to protect the domestic security, and the potential danger posed by unreasonable surveillance to individual privacy and free expression. If the legitimate need of Government to safeguard domestic security requires the use of electronic surveillance, the question is whether the needs of citizens for privacy and free expression may not be better protected by requiring a warrant before such surveillance is undertaken. We must also ask whether a warrant requirement would unduly frustrate the efforts of

Government to protect itself from acts of subversion and overthrow directed against it.

Though the Fourth Amendment speaks broadly of "unreasonable searches and seizures," the definition of "reasonableness" turns, at least in part, on the more specific commands of the warrant clause. Some have argued that "the relevant test is not whether it was reasonable to procure a search warrant, but whether the search was reasonable." *** This view, however, overlooks the second clause of the Amendment. The warrant clause of the Fourth Amendment is not dead language. Rather it has been "a valued part of our constitutional law for decades, and it has determined the result in scores and scores of cases in the courts all over this country. It is not an inconvenience to be somehow 'weighed' against the claims of police efficiency. It is, or should be, an important working part of our machinery of government, operating as a matter of course to check the 'well-intentioned but mistakenly overzealous executive officers' who are a part of any system of law enforcement." ***

Over two centuries ago, Lord Mansfield held that common law principles prohibited warrants that ordered the arrest of unnamed individuals whom the officer might conclude were guilty of seditious libel. "It is not fit," said Mansfield, "that the receiving or judging of the information ought to be left to the discretion of the officer. The magistrate ought to judge; and should give certain directions to the officer." *** Lord Mansfield's formulation touches the very heart of the Fourth Amendment directive: that where practical, a governmental search and seizure should represent both the efforts of the officer to gather evidence of wrongful acts and the judgment of the magistrate that the collected evidence is sufficient to justify invasion of a citizen's private premises or conversation. Inherent in the concept of a warrant is its issuance by a "neutral and detached magistrate." . . . The further requirement of "probable cause" instructs the magistrate that baseless searches shall not proceed.

These Fourth Amendment freedoms cannot properly be guaranteed if domestic security surveillances may be conducted solely within the discretion of the executive branch. The Fourth Amendment does not contemplate the executive officers of Government as neutral and disinterested magistrates. Their duty and responsibility is to enforce the laws, to investigate and to prosecute. . . .

But those charged with this investigative and prosecutorial duty should not be the sole judges of when to utilize constitutionally sensitive means in pursuing their tasks. The historical judgment, which the Fourth Amendment accepts, is that unreviewed executive discretion may yield too readily to pressures to obtain incriminating evidence and overlook potential invasions of privacy and protected speech. It may well be that, in the instant case, the Government's surveillance of Plamondon's conversations was a reasonable one which readily would have gained prior judicial approval. But this Court "has never sustained a search upon the sole ground that officers reasonably expected to find evidence of a particular crime and voluntarily confined their activities to the least intrusive means consistent with that end." ***

The Fourth Amendment contemplates a prior judicial judgment, not the risk that executive discretion may be reasonably exercised. This judicial role accords with our basic constitutional doctrine that individual freedoms will best be preserved through a separation of powers and division of functions among the different branches and levels of Government. . . . The independent check upon executive discretion is not satisfied, as the Government argues, by "extremely limited" post-surveillance judicial review. Indeed, post-surveillance review would never reach the surveillances which failed to result in prosecutions. Prior review by a neutral and detached magistrate is the time tested means of effectuating Fourth Amendment rights. . . .

It is true that there have been some exceptions to the warrant requirement. . . . But those exceptions are few in number and carefully delineated; in general they serve the legitimate needs of law enforcement officers to protect their own well-being and preserve evidence from destruction. Even while carving out those exceptions, the Court has reaffirmed the principle that the "police must, when-ever practicable, obtain advance judicial approval of searches and seizures through the warrant procedure." ***

The Government argues that the special circumstances applicable to domestic security surveillances necessitate a further exception to the warrant requirement. It is urged that the requirement of prior judicial review would obstruct the President in the discharge of his constitutional duty to protect domestic security. We are told further that these surveillances are directed primarily to the collecting and maintaining of intelligence with respect to subversive forces, and are not an attempt to gather evidence for specific criminal prosecutions. It is said that this type of surveillance should not be subject to traditional warrant requirements which were established to govern investigation of criminal activity, not on-going intelligence gathering.

The Government further insists that courts "as a practical matter would have neither the knowledge nor the techniques necessary to determine whether there was probable cause to believe that surveillance was necessary to protect national security." These security problems, the Government contends, involve "a large number of complex and subtle factors" beyond the competence of courts to evaluate.

As a final reason for exemption from a warrant requirement, the Government believes that disclosure to a magistrate of all or even a significant portion of the information involved in domestic security surveillances "would create serious potential dangers to the national security and to the lives of informants and agents. . . . Secrecy is the essential ingredient in intelligence gathering; requiring prior judicial authorization would create a greater danger of leaks. . . , because in addition to the judge, you have the clerk, the stenographer and some other official like a law assistant or bailiff who may be apprised of the nature of the surveillance." ***

These contentions in behalf of a complete exemption from the warrant requirement, when urged on behalf of the President and the national security in its domestic implications, merit the most careful consideration. We certainly do not reject them lightly, especially at a time of worldwide ferment and when civil disorders in this country are more prevalent than in the less turbulent periods of our history. There is, no doubt, pragmatic force to the Government's position.

But we do not think a case has been made for the requested departure from Fourth Amendment standards. The circumstances described do not justify complete exemption of domestic security surveillance from prior judicial scrutiny. Official surveillance, whether its purpose be criminal investigation or on-going intelligence gathering, risks infringement of constitutionally protected privacy of speech. Security surveillances are especially sensitive because of the inherent vagueness of the domestic security concept, the necessarily broad and continuing nature of intelligence gathering, and the temptation to utilize such surveillances to oversee political dissent. We recognize, as we have before, the constitutional basis of the President's domestic security role, but we think it must be exercised in a manner compatible with the Fourth Amendment. In this case we hold that this requires an appropriate prior warrant procedure.

We cannot accept the Government's argument that internal security matters are too subtle and complex for judicial evaluation. Courts regularly deal with the most difficult issues of our society. There is no reason to believe that federal judges will be insensitive to or uncomprehending of the issues involved in domestic security cases. Certainly courts can recognize that domestic security surveillance involves different considerations from the surveillance of ordinary crime. If the threat is too subtle or complex for our senior law enforcement officers to convey its significance to a court, one may question whether there is probable cause for surveillance.

Nor do we believe prior judicial approval will fracture the secrecy essential to official intelligence gathering. The investigation of criminal activity has long involved imparting sensitive information to judicial officers who have respected the confidentialities involved. Judges may be counted upon to be especially conscious of security requirements in national security cases. . . . Whatever security dangers clerical and secretarial personnel may pose can be minimized by proper administrative measures, possibly to the point of allowing the Government itself to provide the necessary clerical assistance.

Thus, we conclude that the Government's concerns do not justify departure in this case from the customary Fourth Amendment requirement of judicial approval prior to initiation of a search or surveillance. Although some added burden will be imposed upon the Attorney General, this inconvenience is justified in a free society to protect constitutional values. Nor do we think the Government's domestic surveillance powers will be impaired to any significant degree. A prior warrant establishes presumptive validity of the surveillance and will minimize the burden of justification in post-surveillance judicial review. By no means of least importance will be the reassurance of the public generally that indiscriminate wiretapping and bugging of law-abiding citizens cannot occur.

We emphasize, before concluding this opinion, the scope of our decision. As stated at the outset, this case involves only the domestic aspects of national security. We have not addressed, and express no opinion as to, the issues which may be involved with respect to activities of foreign powers or their agents. . . .

As the surveillance of Plamondon's conversations was unlawful, because conducted without prior judicial approval, the courts below correctly held that . . . [precedent] requires disclosure to the accused of his own impermissibly intercepted conversations. As stated in *Alderman*, "the trial court can and should, where appropriate, place a defendant and his counsel under enforceable orders against unwarranted disclosure of the materials which they may be entitled to inspect." ***

The judgment of the Court of Appeals is hereby Affirmed.

The Chief Justice concurs in the result.

Mr. Justice Rehnquist took no part in the consideration or decision of this case.

Mr. Justice Douglas, concurring. . . .

Mr. Justice White, concurring in the judgment. . . .

CHAPTER SEVEN

THE CONSTITUTION AND THE MODERN ADMINISTRATIVE STATE

... [T]he constitution has never been regarded as denying to Congress the necessary resources of flexibility and practicality, which will enable it to perform its function in laying down policies and establishing standards, while leaving to selected instrumentalities the making of subordinate rules within prescribed limits and the determination of facts to which the policy as declared by the Legislature is to apply.

Chief Justice Charles Evans Hughes, A.L.A. *Schechter Poultry Corporation v. United States* (1935)

INTRODUCTION

Even a cursory examination of American constitutional history reveals that the role of the national government has changed dramatically in the two centuries since the Constitution was adopted. In the early days of the republic, the role of the national government essentially followed Jefferson's dictum that "that government is best which governs least." For the most part, the national government left such functions as social welfare and education to state and local governments and concerned itself with the regulation of foreign trade, internal improvements such as canals and post roads, and the protection of the national security. State and local governments, in turn, tended to leave matters of social welfare and education to neighborhoods, churches, and families. Perhaps most fundamentally, individuals were regarded as responsible for their own problems as well as their own good fortune. For many years, the national government was seen neither as "big brother" nor ***parens patriae.***

In the wake of post-Civil War industrialization and the emergence of an economy dominated by giant corporations, the limited role of the national government began to change. A new ethos emerged, one in which government is primarily responsible for the solution of social problems. With the passage of the Interstate Commerce Act in 1887 and the concomitant establishment of the Interstate Commerce Commission, the relatively unobtrusive government envisaged by the Founders began to evolve in the direction of ever more complex and intrusive regulation. The era of Progressive reform and the subsequent New Deal contributed mightily to the growth of such regulation. The years elapsing since the New Deal have witnessed the institutionalization of the modern administrative state.

Whereas the classical liberals of the Enlightenment, political philosophers such as John Locke and Thomas Jefferson, espoused minimal government as consistent with the ideal of individual freedom, liberal theorists of the late nineteenth and early twentieth centuries sought to justify a broader role for government. Social theorists such as John Dewey advocated an expanded governmental role in part to realize the ideal of socioeconomic equality in an industrialized economy in which gross disparities existed between rich and poor. For modern liberal economists such as John Maynard Keynes, a greater degree of government intervention was necessary to smooth off the rough edges of the business cycle, to avoid the wild swings between periods of dramatic growth and periods of recession or even depression. According to the Keynesian perspective—dominant during the New Deal era—the very survival of capitalism depended on successful governmental management of the economy. In the decades following the New Deal, the American intellectual community, as exemplified in the work of the economist John Kenneth Galbraith, embraced the concept of "proactive" government—that is, government committed to progress through regulation, redistribution, and planning.

Today, in spite of the conservative reaction of the 1980s, the national government is regarded by most Americans as responsible for the social and economic well-being of the nation. No doubt, this expanded role of government has been reinforced by the ideas of Dewey, Keynes, and Galbraith. As a practical matter, however, the influence of pluralist politics has been even more conspicuous. One need only consider the success of numerous interest groups in shaping, perpetuating, and often enlarging government programs created (in theory) to advance the public interest. Students of American politics have long recognized that government regulators are apt to be more influenced by the interests of those who are to be regulated than by abstract notions of responsible government.

The existence of the modern administrative state poses serious questions of constitutional law—questions involving the foundational principles of limited government, the rule of law, separation of powers, federalism, and individual liberty. Chapter 5 examined, among other things, the Supreme Court's resistance to the expansion of the role of national government in the area of economic regulation, a theme that will be revisited in Chapter 10. This chapter is concerned primarily with separation of powers, the problems of legislative and judicial oversight of the federal bureaucracy, and the relationship between bureaucratic power and individual rights.

THE DELEGATION OF LEGISLATIVE POWER

The expansive role now played by the national government renders the legislative task of Congress considerably more difficult. In an increasingly complex society characterized by technological sophistication and economic interdependence, the sheer magnitude of problems demanding congressional attention and the practical difficulties of regulation obviously limit the ability of Congress to legislate comprehensively, much less effectively. Indeed, this complexity and attendant impracticability, coupled with the pluralistic politics of the legislative process, make it difficult for Congress to fashion rules the enforcement of which can be foreseen with any measure of precision. At the same time, the deliberate, tortoise-like pace of the legislative process makes it all but impossible for Congress to respond promptly to changing objective conditions, making meaningful, relevant regulations almost inconceivable. Thus, given the expansive scope of government, the nature of the legislative process, and the fact that many of the subjects of regulation are both complex and esoteric, Congress has come to rely more and more on "experts" for the development as well as the implementation of regulations. These experts are found in a host of government departments, commissions, agencies, boards, and bureaus that comprise the modern administrative state.

Through a series of broad **delegations of legislative power,** Congress has transferred to the federal bureaucracy much of the responsibility for making and enforcing the rules and regulations deemed necessary for a technological society. The Food and Drug Administration (FDA), the Nuclear Regulatory Commission (NRC), the Federal Aviation Administration (FAA), the Occupational Safety and Health Administration (OSHA), the Environmental Protection Agency (EPA), and the Securities and Exchange Commission (SEC) are just a few of the myriad government agencies to which the Congress has delegated broad authority to make public policy.

Frequently, the **enabling legislation** creating these agencies provides little more than vague generalities to guide agency rule-making. For example, in 1970, Congress gave OSHA the power to make rules that are "reasonably necessary or appropriate to provide safe and healthful employment and places of employment." The rules promulgated by OSHA as "necessary" or "appropriate" take on all the force of law.

The United States
Department of the
Treasury

A more recent example of legislative delegation is seen in the Americans with Disabilities Act (ADA) of 1990. The ADA, which built upon the existing body of federal civil rights law, mandates the elimination of discrimination against individuals with disabilities. A number of federal agencies, including the Department of Justice, the Department of Transportation, the Equal Employment Opportunity Commission (EEOC), and the Federal Communications Commission (FCC), are given extensive regulatory and enforcement powers under the act. As one of the many regulations that have been adopted in support of the statute, the Department of Justice published in the ***Federal Register*** a final rule prohibiting discrimination on the basis of disability in the provision of state and local government services. Twenty-nine pages of the *Federal Register* of July 26, 1991, are devoted to this one rule. Hundreds of pages of the *Federal Register* are devoted to regulations implementing this act alone.

It is argued that broad delegations of legislative power are necessary so that agencies can develop the programs required to deal with targeted problems. These delegations of power may be to a great extent desirable or even inevitable, but they do raise serious questions of constitutional theory.

Concern for Representative Government

While various factors have prompted Congress to delegate degrees of legislative power to the executive branch and to the "independent" agencies, the practice does not comport well with a traditional understanding of the Constitution. Specifically, two constitutional values are arguably infringed by legislative delegation. The first is the principle of representative government that lies within the grant of legislative power to Congress, whose members are chosen by the people. The constitutional grant of legislative power to an elected institution reflects the fundamental national commitment to the idea of democracy, albeit in a form limited by constitutional strictures. The delegation of legislative power to unelected bureaucrats can be viewed as antithetical to the ideal of representative government.

Concern for the Separation of Powers

Furthermore, delegation is difficult to square with the principle of separation of powers implicit in the very structure of the Constitution. Article I vests "all legislative power" in the Congress. Thus, when Congress delegates legislative power to the executive branch, it can be viewed as violating the implicit constitutional principles of representative government and separation of powers, as well as the express language of Article I. In *J. W. Hampton & Company v. United States* (1928), Chief Justice William Howard Taft recognized the constitutional problem raised by legislative delegation:

> [I]n carrying out that Constitutional division into three branches it is a breach of the national fundamental law if Congress gives up its legislative power and transfers it to the President, or to the judicial branch, or if by law attempts to vest itself of either executive or judicial power.

William Howard Taft:
Chief Justice, 1921–1930

Taft's essential point was that if the Constitution imposes meaningful limitations on government, then Congress must be very careful in transferring its own power to the other branches. On the other hand, we have already noted the radical change to a political ethos in which active, affirmative government is regarded as legitimate and even essential. Is it possible to have both an effective separation of powers and proactive government? As our system has evolved, the primary responsibility for reconciling political reality with constitutional principle has come to rest with the Supreme Court. Unfortunately, the Court has seldom been able to harmonize theory and reality in this context. Thus, it can be argued that the Court's decisions do not reflect a coherent constitutional theory justifying the modern administrative state.

Delegation in the Context of Foreign Affairs

The Supreme Court first encountered the issue of delegation of legislative power in *Brig Aurora v. United States* (1813). The case arose in connection with American efforts to remain neutral during the Napoleonic Wars. One measure designed to assure this neutrality was the Non-Intercourse Act of 1809. The act granted to the president the power to impose an embargo against either Great Britain or France, depending on the president's determination of specific facts. If the president found that either nation ceased "to violate neutral commerce" involving American ships, he was free to impose an embargo on the remaining offender. President James Madison determined that France was the first to comply and thus initiated an embargo against Great Britain. The Supreme Court sustained the act against a constitutional challenge, holding that the president's role was merely one of fact-finding, rather than lawmaking. Thus, in the Court's view, no unconstitutional delegation of power had taken place.

The Supreme Court handed down a similar ruling some eighty years later in *Field v. Clark* (1892). In this case, the Court upheld the Tariff Act of 1890, which imposed tariffs on certain imports if, in the president's judgment, the exporting country placed "reciprocally unequal and unreasonable" tariffs on American products. Here again the Court viewed the president's role as one of fact-finder, rather than lawmaker, and thus upheld the challenged act. Speaking for the majority, Justice John M. Harlan (the elder) noted that:

> The Act ... does not in any real sense invest the President with the power of legislation. ... Legislative power was exercised when Congress declared that [enforcement of the tariffs] should take effect upon a named contingency.

In 1928, however, the Court sustained "contingency" tariff legislation that not only allowed presidential discretion as to when to apply a tariff but also granted the president the power to alter the tariff rate. In *J. W. Hampton & Company v. United States,* the Court expanded the permissible scope of legislative delegations by holding that:

> If Congress shall lay down by legislative act an intelligible principle to which the person or body authorized to fix such rates is directed to conform, such legislative action is not a forbidden delegation of legislative power.

It should be noted that the challenged delegations in *Brig Aurora, Field,* and *Hampton* dealt primarily with foreign affairs. In *United States v. Curtiss-Wright Export Corporation* (1936) (discussed and reprinted in the previous chapter), the Supreme Court made it clear that delegations of legislative power in the field of foreign affairs must be assessed on different grounds than delegations involving domestic matters. Since the executive branch has been recognized as "the sole organ of the Federal government in the field of international relations," no clear standards govern delegations of power to the president in this area. In *Zemel v. Rusk* (1965), the Court elaborated on this view by saying that "Congress—in giving the Executive broad authority over matters of foreign affairs—must of necessity paint with a brush broader than that it customarily wields in domestic affairs."

Delegation in the Domestic Context

Although the Supreme Court has expressed more reservations about congressional delegation in the domestic sphere, the end result has been essentially the same: that is, to rationalize and uphold vast transfers of power from Congress to other branches and agencies of government. Implicitly acknowledging this "bottom-line" similarity, the Court has applied the "intelligible principle" standard of the *Hampton* case in assessing delegations of congressional power on the domestic side, as well as in foreign policy contexts. In fact, this parallel appeared in the Court's earliest decisions regarding delegation in the domestic sphere.

The first challenge to such a delegation of power occurred in *Wayman v. Southard* (1825). There, the Supreme Court upheld a congressional grant of power to the Court to determine its own rules of procedure. Given his desire to maximize the independence and power of the Supreme Court, it is not surprising that Chief Justice John Marshall held this delegation to be constitutional. In Marshall's view, the transfer of power was justified because: (1) the subject was of "less interest" to the Congress than the Court; and (2) the Court was merely "filling in the details" of a more general congressional provision. Of Marshall's two justifications, the latter survived to guide subsequent Court decisions in this area. This was essentially the position taken by the Court in the *Hampton* case, when the Court allowed delegations as long as executive discretion was guided by an "intelligible principle."

In two significant cases during the New Deal era, the Supreme Court demonstrated that the nondelegation doctrine could be more than a mere exhortation to Congress. In *Panama Refining Company v. Ryan* (1935) and *A.L.A. Schechter Poultry Corporation v. United States* (1935), the Court struck down provisions of the National Industrial Recovery Act (NIRA) on grounds of nondelegability. In *Panama v. Ryan,* also known as the hot oil case, the Court invalidated the NIRA's grant of power to President Roosevelt to exclude from interstate commerce oil produced in violation of state regulation. In striking down this provision, the Court noted that the Congress requires "flexibility and practicality . . . to perform its function in laying down principles and establishing standards." The Court also acknowledged that Congress often must delegate to "selected instrumentalities the making of subordinate rules within prescribed limits and the determination of facts to which the policy as declared by the legislature is to apply." Yet, while it was willing to allow limited delegations of power to the executive branch, the majority in the hot oil case viewed the NIRA as granting broad legislative power to the president, "without standard or rule, to be dealt with as he pleased." As such, it was an unacceptable delegation.

In *Schechter,* commonly known as the sick chicken case, the Court invalidated a provision of the NIRA that allowed the executive branch to promulgate "codes of fair competition" for a broad range of industries. These codes, developed in some cases in cooperation with targeted industries, were enforceable by criminal and civil penalties established by Congress. The Schechter Poultry Corporation was convicted on several counts of violating the Live Poultry Code developed by the National Recovery Administration (NRA). The development of this code was obviously based on a broad delegation of legislative power. The crucial issue was whether the delegation was accompanied by standards sufficiently clear to pass constitutional muster.

Although the preamble of the National Industrial Recovery Act had announced such general purposes as curbing unfair competition, increasing productivity, and otherwise rehabilitating industry, the grant of power to establish codes did not carry standards satisfactory to the Court. Rather, the Court asserted that the NIRA granted "virtually unfettered" discretion to the president to enact "laws for the government of trade and industry throughout the country." As such, the NIRA could not pass the nondelegation test.

The *Panama Refining Company* and *Schechter* cases stand out as the only two instances in which the Supreme Court has invalidated federal statutes on grounds that Congress impermissibly delegated its lawmaking power to the executive branch. It must be recognized that these cases were part and parcel of a larger battle between the Court and the Roosevelt administration over the New Deal (see Chapters 2 and 5). Many of the Court's critics were inclined to see the decisions in *Panama Refining Company* and *Schechter* as political attacks on the New Deal, rather than neutral applications of a legitimate constitutional principle. It is noteworthy that since the mid-1930s, the Court has not invoked the nondelegation doctrine to strike down any act of Congress, despite many sweeping delegations of power to the executive branch.

The permissiveness of the post-New Deal Supreme Court in this area was clearly manifested in *Yakus v. United States* (1944). Here, the Court upheld the Emergency Price Control Act of 1942, which established the Office of Price Administration and vested it with wide latitude to control prices and rents. The Court's decision in *Yakus* might be viewed as turning on the temporary nature of the act and the fact that the nation was at war. Subsequent decisions have made it clear, however, that *Yakus* was no fluke but rather represented a trend of judicial tolerance toward congressional delegations of power.

Perhaps the best example of the permissive approach the Court has taken toward legislative delegation is *Arizona v. California* (1963). In this case, the Court sustained an extremely vague delegation of power to the secretary of the interior under the Boulder Canyon Act of 1928. The act gave the secretary almost unlimited discretion to allocate the water of the Colorado River (which had been dammed to create reservoirs) among seven states. In making such allocations, the secretary was to follow legislative priorities indicated in the act: "first, for river regulation, improvement of navigation and flood control; second, for irrigation and domestic uses and satisfaction of present perfected rights...; and third, for [electrical] power." On the basis of these guidelines, it was difficult to determine whether the secretary was in fact acting within the "principles" established by Congress. The Court, however, gave Congress the benefit of the doubt, although not without a sharp dissent from Justice John M. Harlan (the younger). "Under the Court's construction of the Act," wrote Harlan, "Congress has made a gift to the Secretary of almost one million, five hundred thousand acre feet of water a year, to allocate virtually as he pleases...." No doubt aware of the inherent vagueness of the delegation it had sustained, the Court suggested that if the secretary of the interior acted in a fashion not consistent with congressional intent, Congress could reduce his power through subsequent legislation. Certainly this is not the approach to legislative delegations manifested in the *Hampton, Panama Refining Company,* and *Schechter* decisions.

In the 1970s, some members of the Court seemed ready to put the antidelegation doctrine to rest once and for all. For example, in *National Cable Association v. United States* (1974), Justice Thurgood Marshall's concurring opinion characterized the antidelegation rule as a remnant of a bygone era, the period before the "constitutional revolution" of 1937. According to Justice Marshall, the antidelegation rule "is surely as moribund as the substantive due process approach of the same era." Marshall's comments notwithstanding, a number of scholars have called for the revival of the nondelegation doctrine. In his influential book *The End of Liberalism* (1979), political scientist Theodore Lowi made a strong argument for resurrection of the *Schechter* rule.

In the early 1980s, certain members of the Supreme Court in fact indicated a desire to scrutinize legislative delegations more carefully. For example, in *Industrial Union Department v. American Petroleum Institute* (1980), the Court considered a challenge to an OSHA regulation that limited workers' exposure to benzene, a toxic chemical. Under law, OSHA was empowered to set exposure limits for toxic agents in the workplace so as to assure "to the extent feasible" that employees would not suffer adverse health effects. The parties to the case differed on the meaning of the phrase "to the extent feasible." The American Petroleum Institute argued that the law required OSHA to demonstrate that the benefits of the regulation outweighed its costs. A four-member plurality of the Court did not reach this issue, however, because OSHA had not made the necessary determination that benzene posed a significant health risk at the prohibited level of exposure. In a concurring opinion, Justice William Rehnquist opined that the statutory provisions before the Court offended the nondelegability doctrine. The plurality, as well as the four dissenters, avoided the delegation issue altogether.

The very next term, in *American Textile Manufacturers Institute v. Donovan* (1981), the Court sustained an OSHA "cotton dust" regulation against a challenge from the textile industry. Here, Justice Rehnquist dissented, joined by Chief Justice Warren Burger. Rehnquist reiterated his view that the OSHA Act of 1970 "unconstitutionally delegated to the Executive Branch the authority to make the 'hard policy choices' properly the task of the legislature." Rehnquist elaborated:

> In believing . . . [the challenged provision of the OSHA statute] . . . amounts to an unconstitutional delegation. . . , I do not mean to suggest that Congress, in enacting a statute, must resolve all ambiguities or must 'fill in all the blanks.' Even the neophyte student of government realizes that legislation is the art of compromise, and that an important, controversial bill is seldom enacted by Congress in the form in which it is first introduced. It is not unusual for the various factions supporting or opposing a proposal to accept some departure from the language they would prefer. . . . But that sort of compromise is a far cry from this case, where Congress simply abdicated its responsibility for the making of a fundamental and most difficult policy choice. . . .

In *Bowsher v. Synar* (1986), the Supreme Court was provided an excellent opportunity to revitalize the *Schechter* rule. The case raised the question of legislative delegation in the context of the **spending power** of Congress, clearly one of the most important legislative functions. In coping with the politically sensitive issue of the massive federal deficit, Congress adopted the Balanced Budget and Emergency Deficit Control Act of 1985, popularly known as the Gramm-Rudman-Hollings Act. This legislation required automatic cuts in federal spending in order to achieve a balanced budget. A constitutionally dubious provision of the law required such cuts to be made by the Comptroller General if Congress proved unwilling or unable to legislate such cuts within a given timetable. Arguably, this represented a delegation of Congress's spending power to an unaccountable bureaucrat. To use language from Justice Rehnquist's dissent in *American Textile Manufacturers v. Donovan*, it could be argued that Congress, in delegating spending authority to the Comptroller General, had "simply abdicated its responsibility for the making of a fundamental and most difficult policy choice. . . ."

Only a few hours after President Reagan signed Gramm-Rudman-Hollings into law, a legal challenge was filed in federal court by Oklahoma Representative Mike Synar, joined by eleven other members of Congress. Their major objection to Gramm-Rudman-Hollings was the delegation of legislative power to unelected bureaucrats. While Representative Synar ultimately won his lawsuit, the rationale adopted by the Supreme Court for invalidating the key provision of Gramm-Rudman-Hollings was quite different from that advanced by the plaintiff. Rather than holding that Congress had unconstitutionally delegated its spending power, the Court ruled 7 to 2 that since the Comptroller General was an agent of Congress, not the executive branch, Congress had encroached on the president's duty to "faithfully execute the laws." In the final opinion of his judicial career, Chief Justice Burger expressed the Court's view that

> . . . Congress has consistently viewed the Comptroller General as an officer of the Legislative Branch. Over the years, the Comptrollers General have also viewed themselves as part of the Legislative Branch. . . . [W]e see no escape from the conclusion that, because Congress had retained removal authority over the Comptroller General, he may not be entrusted with executive powers.

Thus, the Court's rationale was nearly the inverse of the argument made by Representative Synar. According to the Court, the Gramm-Rudman-Hollings provision was flawed not because it delegated legislative power to unelected officials but because it vested an agent of Congress with powers of implementation properly belonging to the executive branch. In other words, the Court managed to invalidate Gramm-Rudman-Hollings on separation of powers grounds without invoking the antidelegation doctrine. In adopting this approach, the Court was simply following the *Ashwander* rules (see Chapter 4), which counsel the justices to adopt the narrowest possible grounds in striking down legislation. Had the Court chosen the broader nondelegation rationale, the entire statutory basis of the modern administrative state might have been called into question. Obviously, some critics of bureaucratic government would like nothing better. But given the realities of modern society, it seems highly unlikely that the Supreme Court will move very far in that direction.

The Court's long-standing reluctance to invoke the nondelegation doctrine was reaffirmed in its 1989 ruling upholding Congress's creation of the U.S. Sentencing Commission and recognizing the constitutionality of detailed **sentencing guidelines** promulgated by the commission in 1987 (*Mistretta v. United States* [1989]). Eight members of the Court rejected the argument that Congress had impermissibly delegated its power to prescribe ranges of criminal sentences that federal judges were required to impose on persons convicted of crimes. The Court also rejected the argument that Congress had violated the separation of powers principle by placing the sentencing commission within the judicial branch and authorizing it to establish legally binding sentencing guidelines. In a lone dissent, Justice Antonin Scalia asserted that the separation of powers principle had been violated, concluding that the new sentencing commission amounted to a "junior varsity Congress with extensive lawmaking power."

CONGRESSIONAL CONTROL OF ADMINISTRATIVE ACTION

Although Congress has found it necessary or expedient to delegate much of its legislative authority to the executive branch, it has attempted to maintain control over executive decisions arising out of the exercise of delegated authority. It must be realized that executive agencies in many cases do not merely promulgate but also implement and enforce regulations, the traditional concept of separation of powers notwithstanding. Thus, Congress, through a variety of mechanisms, has attempted to retain control over agency discretion. These attempts include informal means as well as more formal mechanisms, such as attaching riders to agency appropriations bills, conducting oversight hearings, and reducing agency budgets. Of course, if Congress is extremely dissatisfied with the performance of a particular agency, it may rewrite the statute that created the agency in the first instance. By amending the appropriate statute(s), Congress may enlarge or contract the agency's jurisdiction, as well as the nature and scope of its **rule-making** authority.

The Legislative Veto

One of the more interesting, and certainly the most controversial, of the mechanisms by which Congress has sought to control the bureaucracy is the **legislative veto.** In existence since the early 1930s, the legislative veto is a device whereby Congress, one house of Congress, or even one congressional committee can "veto" agency decisions made pursuant to delegated authority. A legislative veto provision is written into the original act delegating legislative power to an executive agency. While such original legislation is adopted in the ordinary fashion, involving bicameral passage and **presentment** to the president, legislative veto resolutions are not subject to the formal requirements of Article I. For example, the seminal case of *Immigration and Naturalization Service v. Chadha* (1983) involved a resolution adopted by the House of Representatives reversing a deportation decision reached by the Immigration and Naturalization Service. This veto resolution was based on authority given to both houses of Congress by the Immigration and Nationality Act of 1952. As allowed under the act, the House veto resolution was neither submitted to the Senate nor presented to the president for approval. Indeed, the Supreme Court cited these reasons in striking this legislative veto in the *Chadha* case.

The Chadha Case

In *Chadha,* the Supreme Court majority chose to view the veto as a legislative act subject to the requirements of Article I. In adopting this approach, the Court not only invalidated the veto provision actually before it but rendered some two hundred similar statutory provisions presumptively unconstitutional. Thus, the *Chadha* case can be viewed as the most sweeping exercise of judicial review in the history of the Supreme Court.

Reacting to the breadth of the majority opinion, Justice Lewis Powell wrote a concurring opinion in which he parted company with the Court's rationale.

Byron White: Associate
Justice, 1962–

Like the majority, Powell found the legislative veto at issue invalid but for an entirely different reason. For him, the provision was unconstitutional not because it violated the Presentment Clause and the principle of **bicameralism** but because it authorized Congress to exercise a power that could not properly be considered "legislative" in nature. Powell viewed the exercise of the veto by the House as more judicial in character, in that the House was essentially deciding on the interests of particular individuals (such as Mr. Chadha), rather than making legislative pronouncements on policy questions. In Powell's view, judicial self-restraint dictated the narrower approach, leaving open the constitutionality of other legislative veto provisions, such as that contained in the War Powers Resolution (see Chapter 6).

In his dissenting opinion, Justice Byron White defended the legislative veto as an innovation in keeping with the notion of checks and balances. White regarded the legislative veto as an "indispensable political invention" and saw its invalidation as "regrettable."

The *Chadha* decision places the Court in an anomalous situation with respect to the modern administrative state. On one hand, the Court permits broad and vague delegations of power from Congress to the executive branch, notwithstanding obvious constitutional problems. On the other hand, it refuses to allow Congress to create a device by which it may check the exercise of the very power it delegated. How can the Court be so permissive in its interpretation of the Constitution on the delegation issue and so strict on the issue of the legislative veto? It is clear that the Court is not operating from a coherent theoretical perspective in this area of constitutional law.

While the *Chadha* decision can be faulted on several grounds, it should not be viewed as tremendously destructive of congressional oversight of the executive bureaucracy. Several mechanisms (discussed above) allow Congress to exercise a measure of control. But *Chadha* does represent a symbolic loss for the Congress and, by the same token, a symbolic victory for the executive branch and, in particular, the presidency. Indeed, one might view the *Chadha* case as representing a "hidden agenda" to rebuild a presidency "damaged" by such decisions as *United States v. Nixon* (1974) and *Train v. City of New York* (1975) (see Chapter 6). It is also interesting, and perhaps somewhat surprising, that the Court chose to announce the *Chadha* ruling at the height of anti-Court attacks in Congress aimed at the curtailment of the Court's appellate jurisdiction in certain constitutional areas.

A further indication of the limited practical effect of the *Chadha* decision is seen in the retention of the many legislative veto provisions in existing legislation and the inclusion of legislative veto provisions in numerous statutes passed since *Chadha* was decided. Some of these provisions require executive agencies to obtain approval of certain actions by congressional committees. Others authorize Congress to approve or disapprove agency decisions made pursuant to delegated authority. Thus, although presumptively invalid, the legislative veto survives, at least in the statute books.

Additional Separation of Powers Concerns

Some observers viewed the legislative veto (*Chadha*) and Gramm-Rudman-Hollings (*Bowsher*) decisions as exceptions to the Supreme Court's generally permissive view of the separation of powers requirement. They pointed to decisions of the late 1980s upholding congressional establishment of special prosecutors (see *Morrison v. Olson* [1988]) and creation of a sentencing commission (see *Mistretta v. United States* [1989]) as signifying a return to the view that the principle of separation of powers imposed no serious limitation on the authority of Congress. However, in the 1991 decision of *Metropolitan Washington Airports Authority (MWAA) v. Citizens for the Abatement of Aircraft Noise (CAAN)*, the Court made it clear that the separation of powers requirement is not to be taken lightly.

In *MWAA v. CAAN* (1991), the Court held that Congress had violated the separation of powers principle by authorizing the establishment of a board of review, consisting exclusively of members of Congress, with authority to veto decisions made by MWAA, an entity created by a compact between Virginia and Washington, D.C. The Court, in effect, saw the board of review as an agent of Congress and was not impressed by the formal requirement that board members act "in their individual capacities as representatives of airport users nationwide." Relying heavily on *Chadha* and *Bowsher,* the Court struck down an arrangement in which Congress was seeking to exercise control over an ostensibly independent regulatory entity through nonlegislative means. The *MWAA* case suggests that, contrary to the expectations of some scholars, the *Chadha* and *Bowsher* decisions were not mere anomalies. The Court continued to recognize the separation of powers principle as an important and practical limitation on the prerogatives of Congress.

JUDICIAL OVERSIGHT OF THE BUREAUCRACY

Like Congress, the federal courts play an important role in supervising the federal bureaucracy. A fundamental question arising in many cases is whether an agency has acted beyond the scope of its jurisdiction as defined by Congress. For example, in *National Association for the Advancement of Colored People v. Federal Power Commission* (1976), the Supreme Court said that the Federal Power Act and the Natural Gas Act did not endow the Federal Power Commission (FPC) with the authority to promulgate a rule requiring the electrical power industry to follow nondiscriminatory employment practices. Writing for the Court, Justice Potter Stewart said:

> The question is not whether Congress could authorize the Federal Power Commission to combat such discrimination. It clearly could. The question is simply whether or to what extent Congress did grant the Commission such authority. . . . [T]he parties point to nothing in the Acts or their legislative histories to indicate that the elimination of employment discrimination was one of the purposes that Congress had in mind when it enacted this legislation.

Naturally, if Congress wished to provide the FPC with the authority to promulgate rules against employment discrimination, it would merely have to amend the statutes that created the agency and defined its authority.

Due Process of Law

In addition to the substantive issues of agency jurisdiction and rule-making authority, there are significant procedural questions regarding administrative actions. Not only are federal regulatory agencies empowered to promulgate rules, they also have substantial powers to enforce those rules, as well as "quasi-judicial" authority to provide hearings and issue binding orders in individual cases. It is important that agency decisions follow procedural guidelines, so as to prevent arbitrary and capricious action and to safeguard the rights of parties.

Federal agency procedures are generally based on statutory requirements, most notably the Administrative Procedure Act (APA) of 1946. The APA has been called the "Magna Carta of Administrative Law." The APA deals with the two basic types of agency decision making: rule making and adjudication. The act specifies proper procedures for both types of decision making. In addition, the Supreme Court has applied the Due Process Clauses of the Fifth and Fourteenth Amendments when it has found statutory procedures inadequate to ensure fairness or to protect the fundamental rights of individuals.

Before a federal court will review any agency decision, threshold criteria such as "standing to sue," "exhaustion of remedies," and "ripeness" must be met (see Chapter 4). Assuming a federal court decides to review an administrative decision, it will generally attempt to dispose of the case on statutory grounds, for example by interpreting the Administrative Procedure Act, instead of reaching the constitutional due process issue.

In regard to agency rule making, the Supreme Court has tended to rely on the Administrative Procedure Act as an adequate framework for agency procedures. For example, in *Vermont Yankee Nuclear Power Corporation v. Natural Resources Defense Council, Inc.* (1978), the Supreme Court considered the adequacy of procedures used by the Atomic Energy Commission (now the Nuclear Regulatory Commission) for the licensure of nuclear power plants. Of particular concern was the agency's procedure in promulgating a rule governing spent nuclear fuel. The procedure in question included the scheduling of hearings prior to adoption of the rule, as required by the APA. These hearings were somewhat informal, however, and did not include full adjudicatory procedures, such as discovery and cross-examination. The Court of Appeals for the District of Columbia Circuit held that the existing procedure was inadequate under the Due Process Clause of the Fifth Amendment. The Supreme Court reversed without a dissenting vote. In his opinion for the Court, Justice Rehnquist sharply criticized the court of appeals decision, complaining that "this sort of unwarranted judicial examination of perceived procedural shortcomings of a rulemaking proceeding can do nothing but seriously interfere with that process prescribed by Congress. . . ."

During the 1970s, the Supreme Court seemed more willing to apply constitutional due process requirements in cases where agency decisions affected the economic interests of specific individuals. In such cases, the Court must make two determinations. First, it must decide whether the Due Process Clause is applicable. Administrative decisions are constrained by the Due Process Clause only if they in some meaningful way deprive an individual of "life, liberty or property." Second, assuming the Due Process Clause does apply, the Court must determine what "process" is due in order to ensure fundamental fairness.

In *Goldberg v. Kelly* (1970), the Supreme Court held that the Fourteenth Amendment Due Process Clause required a state agency to provide an evidentiary hearing before terminating a person's welfare benefits after the agency determined that the individual was no longer eligible for such benefits. However, Justice Brennan's opinion for the Court failed to clarify the nature of the individual's interest (that is, life, liberty, or property) that gave rise to due process rights. Most commentators have assumed that the welfare entitlements involved in *Goldberg v. Kelly* were viewed by the Court as property interests, hence the term "new property" is often used to describe statutory entitlements.

In *Goss v. Lopez* (1975), the Court continued along the path it paved in *Goldberg v. Kelly*. Here the Court, splitting 5 to 4, held that the ten-day suspension of a student from a public school constituted deprivation of property within the meaning of the Due Process Clause. Thus, the school was required to provide elementary procedural safeguards. The dissenting justices objected to the extension of constitutional protection to an interest they regarded as insubstantial in character.

A series of decisions in the early 1970s extended due process protections to a wide variety of claimants, including employees, automobile drivers, prisoners, and debtors. Eventually, something approaching a counterrevolution was to take place in this area of constitutional law. The first signal of this change came in 1976. In *Mathews v. Eldridge,* the Court upheld procedures under which social security disability benefits could be initially terminated without a prior evidentiary hearing. George Eldridge, who had been disabled due to "chronic anxiety and back strain," was informed by an official letter that, according to medical reports, his disability no longer existed and that benefit payments would be terminated. Although agency procedures required ample notification and an evidentiary hearing prior to final termination, the payments could be stopped initially without any hearing. Provision was also made for retroactive payments to any recipient whose disability was later determined not to have ended. Eldridge, who was concerned with the initial decision to terminate payments, relied on *Goldberg v. Kelly* in arguing that the Due Process Clause required an evidentiary hearing before any termination of benefits.

Writing for the Court in *Mathews,* Justice Lewis Powell conceded the existence of a property interest in social security benefits and thus the applicability of the Due Process Clause. But Powell said that "due process is flexible and calls for such procedural protections as the particular situation demands." In other words, the degree of procedural safeguards required by the Constitution depends on how much one stands to lose. In this case, the Court distinguished social security from welfare benefits and held that the "potential deprivation . . . is generally likely to be less" when social security payments are denied than when welfare benefits are terminated. In this way, the Court significantly narrowed the potential application of *Goldberg v. Kelly* without formally overruling it. In *Mathews,* the Court was willing to regard the existing agency procedures as adequate safeguards. To a litigant in Eldridge's position, the distinction between termination of social security and welfare benefits was purely academic. Nevertheless, from the Court's perspective, it was irrelevant that the initial termination of Eldridge's benefits resulted in the foreclosure of his mortgage and repossession of his furniture, forcing him and his family to share one bed. For better or worse, such considerations are generally not permitted to influence the Court in its development and application of constitutional principles.

The Supreme Court's recent decisions in this area are mixed, but the trend seems to be toward limiting the scope of due process protections. The doctrinal coherence that was beginning to emerge in the early 1970s has given way to an *ad hoc* approach. No single set of constitutional principles has gained dominance. As a result, the prediction of outcomes in individual cases in this area is particularly difficult.

AGENCY ACTIONS AND OTHER INDIVIDUAL RIGHTS

The vast power entrusted to the modern administrative state increases the likelihood that government actions will impinge on individual interests that are protected by the Bill of Rights. For example, FCC regulations of broadcast media have often been challenged on First Amendment grounds (see Chapter 12). In the 1930s and 1940s, the most obvious impact of enlarged governmental regulation was on property rights. But it soon became clear that no neat distinction could be drawn between these rights and other personal rights guaranteed by the Constitution. All constitutional rights may, under some circumstances, give way to compelling public interests. The difficulty, of course, lies in determining which public interests are truly compelling. (The "property issues" associated with government regulation are addressed more thoroughly in Chapter 10.)

Fourth Amendment Concerns

Many administrative practices pose threats to rights protected by the Fourth, Fifth, and Sixth Amendments. One of the more controversial examples involves the Immigration and Naturalization Service (INS), which routinely detains without hearings or the benefit of counsel persons suspected of entering this country illegally. In *Wong Wing v. United States* (1896), the Supreme Court ruled that individuals can be detained by immigration authorities without hearings as long as the purpose of the detention is not punitive. For the most part, however, the Court has refrained from reviewing federal immigration laws for compliance with substantive constitutional rights.

INS detentions of suspected illegal aliens are not the only administrative actions that threaten constitutionally protected liberties. "Administrative searches" of industrial plants are routinely conducted by such regulatory bodies as the EPA and OSHA. Traditionally, the Supreme Court has been more permissive toward administrative searches directed at business and industry than toward police searches directed at private individuals. For example, in *Frank v. Maryland* (1959) and *Ohio ex rel. Eaton v. Price* (1960), the Supreme Court found no violation of the Fourth Amendment when administrative searches were conducted without notice and without search warrants. In the 1960s and 1970s, the Court became stricter, holding that, as a general rule, warrants must be obtained to justify administrative searches (see, for example, *Camara v. Municipal Court* [1967], overruling *Frank v. Maryland* [1959]).

Following this stricter approach, in *Marshall v. Barlow's, Inc.* (1978), the Supreme Court struck down a provision of the Occupational Health and Safety Act of 1970 that allowed OSHA to conduct warrantless searches of the workplace. However, the Court was careful to point out that to obtain administrative search warrants, OSHA inspectors did not have to meet the same strict standards of probable cause that govern the issuance of warrants in criminal investigations. In *Donovan v. Dewey* (1981), the Court refused to invalidate a provision of the Federal Mine Safety and Health Act of 1977 that allowed the Department of Labor to conduct warrantless inspections of mines. The Court attempted to distinguish the case from *Barlow's,* but it seems clear that a majority of the justices preferred the more permissive approach of the pre-*Camara* period.

A more recent case that epitomizes a permissive approach to the Fourth Amendment as it relates to regulatory agency searches is *Dow Chemical Company v. United States* (1986). Here, the EPA, acting without a warrant, had employed a commercial aerial photographer to take pictures of a Dow chemical plant from an altitude of twelve hundred feet. When Dow learned of the photographic flyover, it filed suit in federal court, claiming that the EPA had violated its reasonable expectation of privacy. Splitting 5 to 4, the Supreme Court rejected Dow's claim, holding that the flyover was not a "search" within the meaning of the Fourth Amendment.

Self-Incrimination Concerns

The Self-Incrimination Clause of the Fifth Amendment is another provision of the Bill of Rights potentially endangered by administrative actions. Essentially, this clause protects the individual from being forced to divulge incriminating information. While the obvious application of the Self-Incrimination Clause is to criminal investigations, the Supreme Court has held that the protection applies in any governmental context that might ultimately lead to criminal prosecution (see *Murphy v. Waterfront Commission* [1964]). However, the Court has distinguished between verbal testimony and physical evidence, holding that the immunity against self-incrimination applies only to the former. Consequently, businesses have no real Fifth Amendment protections in the instance of compulsory production of incriminating business records. As a result of the winnowing of the Self-Incrimination Clause, businesspersons can be compelled to disclose their records to the scrutiny of government agencies. Justice Brennan consistently dissented from this view of the Fifth Amendment, arguing that business records fall within the "zone of privacy" protected by the Self-Incrimination Clause (see, for example, *Andresen v. Maryland* [1976], dissenting opinion).

Public Access to Agency Information

Other potential objections to the actions of the modern administrative state involve access to the tremendous stockpile of information maintained by various government agencies. Although the Supreme Court has never held such access to be a matter of constitutional right, Congress has created a statutory right of public access under the Freedom of Information Act and a right of individual access under the Privacy Act. While these acts do create exemptions for certain types of secret information, such as sensitive national security material, they nevertheless represent a significant attempt to open up the process of modern governance to the ordinary citizen.

Bureaucratic Support for Civil Rights and Liberties

Lest one assume that all actions of the federal bureaucracy are inimical to civil rights and liberties, it should be pointed out that, in recent decades, the federal government has created programs that foster them. For example, the Civil Rights Division of the Department of Justice is responsible for enforcing the extensive civil rights legislation adopted since the late 1950s, most notably the Civil Rights Act of 1964, the Voting Rights Act of 1965, and the Americans with Disabilities Act of 1990. Other agencies, such as the Department of Labor and the EEOC, also exercise important responsibilities in enforcing federal policies against job discrimination. Additionally, in 1974, Congress created the Legal Services Corporation to provide legal assistance to indigent persons involved in civil cases.

CONCLUSION

The German sociologist Max Weber argued that bureaucracy exists in the modern world because it is the most rational way of organizing efforts toward the achievement of collective goals. Whether or not Weber was right, bureaucracy is an inextricable component of modern government. Clearly, bureaucracy is here to stay, whether one considers the federal government, the governments of the fifty states, or the governments of the nation's major cities. However, the essence of American constitutionalism is that government derives its powers from and must operate within the limitations of the Constitution, the supreme law of the land. The existence of the mammoth federal bureaucracy and similar, if smaller, bureaucracies in all fifty states poses serious problems of constitutional theory. These problems include the delegation of legislative power and the means of legislative and judicial oversight of administrative decision making. In grappling with these issues, the Supreme Court has not developed a coherent constitutional theory. But one must recognize that no area of constitutional law is fully coherent. In the nature of things political, the Court's decisions are bound to reflect the untidy realities of politics more than the neatness of syllogisms. Yet it is in this particular realm of constitutional law that the eighteenth-century ideals of limited government and the rule of law seem to be most out of sync with the realities of twentieth-century political life. As the primary mechanism for fitting constitutional principles with political realities, the Supreme Court faces an especially formidable task in addressing questions of bureaucratic power.

FOR FURTHER READING

Barber, Sotirios A. *The Constitution and the Delegation of Congressional Power.* Chicago: University of Chicago Press, 1975.

Barry, Donald D., and Howard R. Whitcomb. *The Legal Foundations of Public Administration,* 2d ed. St. Paul: West, 1987.

Carter, Lief H., and Christine B. Harrington. *Administrative Law and Politics: Cases and Comments,* 2d ed. New York: Harper-Collins, 1991.

Davis, Kenneth C. *Discretionary Justice.* Baton Rouge: Louisiana State University Press, 1969.

Davis, Kenneth C. *Administrative Law.* St. Paul: West, 1973.

Dodd, Lawrence C., and Richard L. Schott. *Congress and the Administrative State.* New York: Wiley, 1979.

Epstein, Richard A. *Takings: Private Property and the Power of Eminent Domain.* Cambridge: Harvard University Press, 1985.

Fisher, Louis. *The Politics of Shared Power: Congress and the Executive.* Washington, D.C.: Congressional Quarterly Press, 1987.

Gellhorn, Walter, Clark Byse, and Peter L. Strauss. *Administrative Law: Cases and Comments,* 7th ed. Mineola, N.Y.: Foundation Press, 1979.

Harris, Joseph. *Congressional Control of Administration.* New York: Doubleday, 1965.

Lowi, Theodore J. *The End of Liberalism,* 2d ed. New York: Norton, 1979.

Pierce, Richard J., Jr., Sidney A. Shapiro, and Paul R. Verkuil. *Administrative Law and Process.* Mineola, N.Y.: Foundation Press, 1985.

Rohr, John A. *To Run a Constitution: The Legitimacy of the Administrative State.* Lawrence: University Press of Kansas, 1986.

Shapiro, Martin. *Who Guards the Guardians? Judicial Control of Administration.* Athens: University of Georgia Press, 1988.

Sunstein, Cass R. *After the Rights Revolution: Reconceiving the Regulatory State.* Cambridge: Harvard University Press, 1990.

Warren, Kenneth F. *Administrative Law in the American Political System.* St. Paul: West, 1982.

Weber, Max. *The Theory of Social and Economic Organization.* New York: Oxford University Press, 1947.

CASES AND READINGS

J. W. Hampton & Company v. United States

276 U.S. 394; 48 S. Ct. 348; 72 L. Ed. 624 (1928)

Vote: 9-0

Mr. Chief Justice Taft delivered the opinion of the Court.

J. W. Hampton, Jr. & Company made an importation into New York of barium dioxide which the collector of customs assessed at the dutiable rate of 6 cents per pound. This was 2 cents per pound more than that fixed by statute. *** The rate was raised by the collector by virtue of the proclamation of the President *** issued under . . . authority of . . . the Tariff Act of September 21, 1922, *** which is the so-called flexible tariff provision. Protest was made and an appeal was taken. . . . The case came . . . before the United States customs court. *** A majority held the action constitutional. Thereafter the case was appealed to the United States court of customs appeals. On the 16th day of October, 1926, the Attorney General certified that in his opinion the case was of such importance as to render expedient its review by this court. Thereafter the judgment of the United States customs court was affirmed. *** On a petition to this court for *certiorari,* . . . the writ was granted. *** . . .

The issue here is as to the constitutionality of [the Tariff Act] upon which depends the authority for the proclamation of the President and for 2 of the 6 cents per pound duty collected from [J. W. Hampton]. The contention of the taxpayers is . . . that the section is invalid in that it is a delegation to the President of the legislative power, which by Article 1, Sec. 1 of the Constitution, is vested in Congress, the power being that declared in Sec. 8 of Article 1, that the Congress shall have power to lay and collect taxes, duties, imposts, and excises. . . .

. . . It seems clear what Congress intended by [the act]. Its plan was to secure by law the imposition of customs duties on articles of imported merchandise which should equal the difference between the cost of producing in a foreign country the articles in question and laying them down for sale in the United States, and the cost of producing and selling like or similar articles in the United States, so that the duties not only secure revenue but at the same time enable domestic producers to compete on terms of equality with foreign producers in the markets of the United States. It may be that it is difficult to fix with exactness this difference, but the difference which is sought in the statute is perfectly clear and perfectly intelligible. Because of the difficulty in practically determining what that difference is, Congress seems to have doubted that the information in its possession was such as to enable it to make the adjustment accurately, and also to have apprehended that with changing conditions the difference might vary in such a way that some readjustments would be necessary to give effect to the principle on which the statute proceeds. To avoid such difficulties, Congress adopted . . . the method of describing with clearness what its policy and plan was and then authorizing a member of the executive branch to carry out its policy and plan and to find the changing difference from time to time and to make the adjustments necessary to conform the duties to the standard underlying that policy and plan. As it was a matter of great importance, it concluded to give by statute to the President . . . the function of determining the difference as it might vary. . . .

The well-known maxim *delegata potestas non potest delegari* ["that which is delegated cannot be redelegated"], applicable to the law of agency in the general and common law, is well understood and has had wide application in the construction of our Federal and state Constitutions than it has in private law. Our Federal Constitution and state Constitutions of this country divide the governmental power into three branches. The first is the legislative, the second is the executive, and the third is the judicial, and the rule is that in the actual administration of the government Congress or the legislature should exercise the legislative power, the President or the state executive, the governor, the executive power, and the courts or the judiciary the judicial power, and in carrying out that constitutional division into three branches it is a breach of the national fundamental law if Congress gives up its legislative power and transfers it to the President, or to the judicial branch, or if by law it attempts to invest itself or its members with either executive power or judicial power. This is not to say that the three branches are not coordinate parts of one government and that each in the field of its duties may not invoke the action of the two other branches in so far as the action invoked shall not be an assumption of the constitutional field of action of another branch. In determining what it may do in seeking assistance from another branch, the extent and character of that assistance must be fixed according to common sense and the inherent necessities of the governmental coordination.

The field of Congress involves all and many varieties of legislative action, and Congress had found it frequently necessary to use officers of the executive branch, within definite limits, to secure the exact effect intended by its acts of legislation, by vesting discretion in such officers to make public regulations interpreting a statute and directing the details of its execution, even to the extent of providing for penalizing a breach of such regulations. ***

Congress may feel itself unable conveniently to determine exactly when its exercise of the legislative power should become effective, because dependent on future conditions, and it may leave the determination of such time to the decision of an executive. . . .

[O]ne of the great functions conferred on Congress by the Federal Constitution is the regulation of interstate commerce and rates to be exacted by interstate carriers for the passenger and merchandise traffic. The rates to be fixed are myriad. If Congress were to be required to fix every rate, it would be impossible to exercise the power at all. Therefore, common sense requires that in the fixing of such rates, Congress may provide a Commission, as it does, called the Interstate Commerce Commission, to fix those rates, after hearing evidence and argument concerning them from interested parties, all in accord with a general rule that Congress first lays down that rates shall be just and reasonable considering the service given and not discriminatory. . . .

It is conceded by counsel that Congress may use executive officers in the application and enforcement of a policy declared in law by Congress and authorize such officers in the application of the congressional declaration to enforce it by regulation equivalent to law. But it is said that this never has been permitted to be done where Congress has exercised the power to levy taxes and fix customs duties. The authorities make no such distinction. The same principle that permits Congress to exercise its rate-making power in interstate commerce by declaring the rule which shall prevail in the legislative fixing of rates, and enables it to remit to a rate-making-body created in accordance with its provisions the fixing of such rates, justifies a similar provision for the fixing of customs duties on imported merchandise. If Congress shall lay down by legislative act an intelligible principle to which the person or body authorized to fix such rates is directed to conform, such legislative action is not a forbidden delegation of legislative power. If it is thought wise to vary the customs duties according to changing conditions of production at home and abroad, itmay authorize the Chief Executive to carry out this purpose. . . .

A.L.A. Schechter Poultry Corporation v. United States

295 U.S. 495; 55 S. Ct. 837; 79 L. Ed. 1570 (1935)

Vote: 9-0

Mr. Chief Justice Hughes delivered the opinion of the Court.

[Schechter Poultry Corporation et al.] were convicted in the District Court of the United States for the Eastern District of New York on eighteen counts of an indictment charging violations of what is known as the "Live Poultry Code," and on an additional count for conspiracy to commit such violations. . . .

The Circuit Court of Appeals sustained the conviction on the conspiracy count and on sixteen counts for violation of the code.... On the respective applications of the defendants *** ... this Court granted writs of *certiorari.* *** ...

The "Live Poultry Code" was promulgated under Sec. 3 of the National Industrial Recovery Act. That section ... authorizes the President to approve "codes of fair competition." Such a code may be approved for a trade or industry, upon application by one of more trade or industrial associations or groups, if the President finds (1) that such associations or groups "impose no inequitable restrictions on admission to membership therein and are truly representative," and (2) that such codes are not designed "to promote monopolies or to eliminate or oppress small enterprises and will not operate to discriminate against them, and will tend to effectuate the policy" *** of the act. Such codes "shall not permit monopolies or monopolistic practices." As a condition of his approval, the President may "impose such conditions (including requirements for the making of reports and the keeping of accounts) for the protection of consumers, competitors, employees and others, and in furtherance of the public interest, and may provide such exceptions to an exemptions from the provisions of such code as the President in his discretion deems necessary to effectuate the policy herein declared." Where such a code has not been approved, the President may prescribe one, either on his own motion or on complaint. Violation of any provision of a code (so approved or prescribed) "in any transaction in or affecting interstate or foreign commerce" is made a misdemeanor punishable by a fine of not more than $500 for each offense, and each day the violation continues is to be deemed a separate offense.

The "Live Poultry Code" was approved by the President on April 13, 1934....

The declared purpose is "To effect the policies of title I of the National Industrial Recovery Act." ...

The code fixes the number of hours for workdays. It provides that no employee, with certain exceptions, shall be permitted to work in excess of forty (40) hours in any one week, and that no employee, save as stated, "shall be paid in any pay period less than at the rate of fifty (50) cents per hour." ... [The code also limits child-labor practices and creates administrative procedures for the execution of the code's provisions.]

Of the eighteen counts of the indictment upon which the defendants were convicted, aside from the count for conspiracy, two counts charged violations of the minimum wage and maximum hour provisions of the code; ... ten counts, respectively, were that [Schechter, in selling] to retail dealers and butchers, had permitted "selections of individual chickens taken from particular coops and half coops."

Of the other six counts, one charged the sale to a butcher of an unfit chicken; two counts charged the making of sales without having the poultry inspected or approved in accordance with regulations or ordinances of the City of New York; two counts charged the making of false reports or the failure to make reports relating to the range of daily prices and volume and sales for certain periods; and the remaining count was for sales to slaughterers or dealers who were without licenses required by the ordinances and regulations of the City of New York.

First. Two preliminary points are stressed by the government with respect to the appropriate approach to the important questions presented. We are told that the provision of the statute authorizing the adoption of codes must be viewed in the light of the grave national crisis with which Congress was confronted. Undoubtedly, the conditions to which power is addressed are always to be considered when the exercise of power is challenged. Extraordinary conditions may call for extraordinary remedies. But the argument necessarily stops short of an attempt to justify action which lies outside the sphere of constitutional authority. Extraordinary conditions do not create or enlarge constitutional power. The Constitution establishes a national government with powers deemed to be adequate, as they have proved to be both in war and peace, but these powers of the national government are limited by the constitutional grants. Those who act under these grants are not at liberty to transcend the imposed limits because they believe that more or different power is necessary....

The further point is urged that the national crisis demanded a broad and intensive co-operative effort by those engaged in trade and industry, and that this necessary co-operation was sought to be fostered by permitting them to initiate the adoption of codes. But the statutory plan is not simply one for voluntary effort. It does not seek merely to endow voluntary trade or industrial associations or groups with privileges or immunities. It involves the coercive exercise of the law-making power. The codes of fair competition which the statute attempts to authorize are codes of laws. If valid, they place all persons within their reach under the obligation of positive law, binding equally those who assent and those who do not assent. Violations of the provisions of the codes are punishable as crimes.

Second. The question of the delegation of legislative power [:] ... the Constitution provides that "all legislative powers herein granted shall be vested in a Congress of the United States, which shall consist of a Senate and House of Representatives." *** And the Congress is authorized "to make all laws which shall be necessary and proper for carrying into execution" its general power. *** The Congress is not permitted to abdicate or to transfer to others the essential legislative functions with which it is thus vested. We have repeatedly recognized the necessity of adapting legislation to complex conditions in-volving a host of details with which the National Legislature cannot deal directly. We point out in the Panama Ref. Co. Case [*Panama Refining Company v. Ryan* (1935)] that the Constitution has never been regarded as denying to Congress the necessary resources of flexibility and practicality, which will enable it to perform its function in laying down policies and establishing standards, while leaving to selected instrumentalities the making of subordinate rules within prescribed limits and the determination of facts to which the policy as declared by the Legislature is to apply. But ... the constant recognition of the necessity and validity of such provisions, and the wide range of administrative authority which has been developed by means of them, cannot be allowed to obscure the limitations of the authority to delegate, if our constitutional system is to be maintained. ***

Accordingly, we look to the statute to see whether Congress has overstepped these limitations — whether Congress in authorizing "Codes of Fair Competition" has itself established the standards of

legal obligation, thus performing its essential legislative function, or, by the failure to enact such standards, has attempted to transfer that function to others. ...

What is meant by "fair competition" as the term is used in the act? Does it refer to a category established in the law, and is the authority to make codes limited accordingly? Or is it used as a convenient designation for whatever set of laws the formulators of a code for a particular trade or industry may propose and the President may himself prescribe, as being wise and beneficent provisions for the government of the trade or industry in order to accomplish the broad purposes of rehabilitation, correction and expansion which are stated [in the act]?

The act does not define "fair competition." "Unfair competition" as known to the common law is a limited concept. Primarily, and strictly, it relates to the palming off of one's goods as those of a rival trader. *** In recent years its scope has been extended. It has been held to apply to misappropriation as well as misrepresentation, to the selling of another's goods as one's own — to misappropriation of what equitably belongs to a competitor. *** Unfairness in competition has been predicated on acts which lie outside the ordinary course of business and are tainted by fraud, or coercion, or conduct otherwise prohibited by law. *** But it is evident that in its widest range "unfair competition," as it has been understood in the law, does not reach the objectives of the codes which are authorized by the National Industrial Recovery Act. The codes may, indeed, cover conduct which existing law condemns, but they are not limited to conduct of that sort. The government does not contend that the act contemplates such a limitation. It would be opposed both to the declared purposes of the act and to its administrative construction.

The Federal Trade Commission Act *** introduces the expression "unfair methods of competition," which were declared to be unlawful. That was an expression new in the law. Debate apparently convinced the sponsors of the legislation that the words "unfair competition," in the light of their meaning at common law, were too narrow. We have said that the substituted phrase has a broader meaning; that it does not admit of precise definition, its scope being left to judicial determination as controversies arise.

*** What are "unfair methods of competition" are thus to be determined in particular competitive conditions and of what is found to be a specific and substantial public interest. *** To make this possible Congress set up a special procedure. A commission, a quasi-judicial body, was created. Provision was made for formal complaint, for notice and hearing, for appropriate findings of fact supported by adequate evidence, and for judicial review to give assurance that the action of the Commission is taken within its statutory authority. ***

In providing for codes, the National Industrial Recovery Act dispenses with this administrative procedure and with any administrative procedure of an analogous character. But the difference between the code plan of the Recovery Act and the scheme of the Federal Trade Commission Act lies not only in procedure but in subject matter. We cannot regard the "fair competition" of the codes as antithetical to the "unfair methods of competition" of the Federal Trade Commission Act. The "fair competition" of the codes has a much broader range and a new significance. The Recovery Act provides that it shall not be construed to impair the powers of the Federal Trade Commission, but, when a code is approved, its provisions are to be the "standards of fair competition" for the trade or industry concerned, and any violation of such standards in any transaction in or affecting interstate or foreign commerce is to be deemed "an unfair method of competition" within the meaning of the Federal Trade Commission Act. ***

For a statement of the authorized objectives and content of the "codes of fair competition" we are referred repeated to the "declaration of policy" in *** the Recovery Act. Thus, the approval of a code by the President is conditioned on his finding that it "will tend to effectuate the policy of this title." *** The President is authorized to impose such conditions "for the protection of consumers, competitors, employees and others, and in furtherance of the public interest, and may provide such exceptions to and exemptions from the provisions of such code as the President in his discretion deems necessary to effectuate the policy herein declared." *** The "policy herein declared" is manifestly that set forth. . . . That declaration embraces a broad range of objectives. Among them we find the elimination of "un-

fair competitive practices." But even if this clause were to be taken to relate to practices which fall under the ban of existing law, either common law or statute, it is still only one of the authorized aims described. *** It is there declared to be "the policy of Congress"—

to remove obstructions to the free flow of interstate and foreign commerce which tend to diminish the amount thereof; and to provide for the general welfare by promoting the organization of industry for the purpose of cooperative action among trade groups, to induce and maintain united action of labor and management under adequate governmental sanctions and supervision, to eliminate unfair competitive practices, to promote the fullest possible utilization of the present productive capacity of industries, to avoid undue restriction of production (except as may be temporarily required), to increase the consumption of industrial and agricultural produces by increasing purchasing power, to reduce and rehabilitate industry and to conserve natural resources.

. . . [Under these provisions], whatever "may tend to effectuate" these general purposes may be included in the "codes of fair competition." We think the conclusion is inescapable that the authority sought to be conferred *** was not merely to deal with "unfair competitive practices" which offend against existing law, and could be the subject of judicial condemnation without further legislation, or to create administrative machinery for the application of established principles of law to particular instances of violation. Rather, the purpose is clearly disclosed to authorize new and controlling prohibitions through codes of laws which would embrace what the formulators would propose, and what the President would approve, or prescribe, as wise and beneficent measures for the government of trades and industries in order to bring about their rehabilitation, correction and development, according to the general declaration of policy. *** Codes of laws of this sort are styled "codes of fair competition." ***

The question, then, turns upon the authority which *** the Recovery Act vests in the President to approve or prescribe. . . . Congress cannot delegate legislative power to the President to exercise an unfettered discretion to make whatever laws he thinks may be needed or advisable for the rehabilitation and expansion of trade or industry. ***

Accordingly we turn to the Recovery Act to ascertain what limits have been set to the exercise of the President's discretion. First, the President, as a condition of approval, is required to find that the trade or industrial associations or groups which propose a code "impose no inequitable restrictions on admission to membership" and are "truly representative." That condition, however, relates only to the status of the initiators of the new laws and not to the permissible scope of such laws. Second, the President is required to find that the code is not "designed to promote monopolies or to eliminate or oppress small enterprises and will not operate to discriminate against them." And to this is added a proviso that the code "shall not permit monopolies or monopolistic practices." But these restrictions leave virtually untouched the field of policy envisaged *** and in what wide field of legislative possibilities the proponents of a code, refraining from monopolistic designs, may roam at will and the President may approve or disapprove their proposals as he may see fit. That is the precise effect of the further finding that the President is to make—that the code will tend to effectuate the policy of this title." While this is called a finding, it is really but a statement of an opinion as to the general effect upon the promotion of trade or industry of a scheme of laws. These are the only findings which Congress has made essential in order to put into operation a legislative code having the aims described in the "Declaration of Policy."

Nor is the breadth of the President's discretion left to the necessary implications of this limited requirement as to his findings. As already noted, the President in approving a code may impose his own conditions, adding to or taking from what is proposed, as "in his discretion" he thinks necessary "to effectuate the policy" declared by the act. Of course, he has no less liberty when he prescribes a code on his own motion or on complaint, and he is free to prescribe one if a code has not been approved. The act provides for the creation by the President of administrative agencies to assist him, but the action or reports of such agencies, or of his other assistants— their recommendations and findings in relation to the making of codes—have no sanction beyond the will of the President, who may accept, modify or reject them as he pleases. . . .

To summarize and conclude upon this point: *** the Recovery Act is without precedent. It supplies no standards for any trade, industry or activity. It does not undertake to prescribe rules of conduct to be applied to particular states of fact determined by appropriate administrative procedure. Instead of prescribing rules of conduct, it authorizes the making of codes to prescribe them. For that legislative undertaking, Sec. 3 sets up no standards, aside from the statement of the general aims of rehabilitation, correction and expansion. *** In view of the scope of that broad declaration, and of the nature of the few restrictions that are imposed, the discretion of the President in approving or prescribing codes, and thus enacting laws for the government of trade and industry throughout the country, is virtually unfettered. We think that the code-making authority thus conferred is an unconstitutional delegation of legislative power. . . .

The Court also considered Commerce Clause questions and concluded that the attempted regulation of intrastate activities exceeded the constitutional grant of power to regulate interstate commerce.

Mr. Justice Cardozo, concurring.

The delegated power of legislation which has found expression in this code is not canalized within banks that keep it from overflowing. It is unconfined and vagrant. . . .

. . . Here, in the case before us, is an attempted delegation not confined to any single act nor to any class or group of acts identified or described by reference to a standard. Here in effect is a roving commission to inquire into evils and upon discovery correct them. . . .

The code does not confine itself to the suppression of methods of competition that would be classified as unfair according to accepted business standards or accepted norms of ethics. It sets up a comprehensive body of rules to promote the welfare of the industry, if not the welfare of the nation, without reference to standards, ethical or commercial, that could be known or predicted in advance of its adoption. . . . Even if the statute itself had fixed the meaning of fair competition by way of contrast with practices that are oppressive or unfair, the code outruns the bounds of the authority conferred. What is excessive is not sporadic or superficial. It is deep-seated and pervasive. The licit and illicit sections are so combined and welded as to be incapable of severance without destructive mutilation. . . .

I am authorized to state that **Mr. Justice Stone** joins in this opinion.

Bowsher v. Synar

478 U.S. 714; 106 S. Ct. 3181; 92 L. Ed. 2d 583 (1986)
Vote: 7-2

Chief Justice Burger delivered the opinion of the Court.

The question presented by these appeals is whether the assignment by Congress to the Comptroller General of the United States of certain functions under the Balanced Budget and Emergency Deficit Control Act of 1985 violates the doctrine of separation of powers.

On December 12, 1985, the President signed into law the Balanced Budget and Emergency Deficit Control Act of 1985, *** popularly known as the "Gramm-Rudman-Hollings Act." The purpose of the Act is to eliminate the federal budget deficit. To that end, the Act sets a "maximum deficit amount" for federal spending for each of fiscal years 1986 through 1991. The size of that maximum deficit amount progressively reduces to zero in fiscal year 1991. If in any fiscal year the federal budget deficit exceeds the maximum deficit amount by more than a specified sum, the Act requires across-the-board cuts in federal spending to reach the targeted deficit level, with half of the cuts made to defense programs and the other half made to non-defense programs. The Act exempts certain priority programs from these cuts. ***

These "automatic" reductions are accomplished through a rather complicated procedure, spelled out in Sec. 251, the so-called "reporting provisions" of the Act. Each year, the Director of the Office of Management and Budget (OMB) and the Congressional Budget Office (CBO) independently estimate the amount of the federal budget deficit for the upcoming fiscal year. If that deficit exceeds the maximum target deficit amount for that fiscal year by more than

a specified amount, the Directors of OBM and CBO independently calculate, on a program-by-program basis, the budget reductions necessary to ensure that the deficit does not exceed the maximum deficit amount. The Act then requires the Directors to report jointly their deficit estimates and budget reduction calculations to the Comptroller General.

The Comptroller General, after reviewing the Directors' reports, then reports his conclusions to the President. *** The President in turn must issue a "sequestration" order mandating the spending reductions specified by the Comptroller General. *** There follows a period during which Congress may by legislation reduce spending to obviate, in whole or in part, the need for the sequestration order. If such reductions are not enacted, the sequestration order becomes effective and the spending reductions included in that order are made. . . .

Within hours of the President's signing of the Act, Congressman Synar, who had voted against the Act, filed a complaint seeking declaratory relief that the Act was unconstitutional. Eleven other Members later joined Congressman Synar's suit. A virtually identical lawsuit was also filed by the National Treasury Employees Union. The Union alleged that its members had been injured as a result of the Act's automatic spending reduction provisions, which have suspended certain cost-of-living benefit increases to the Union's members. . . .

The District Court rejected appellees' challenge that the Act violated the delegation doctrine. The court expressed no doubt that the Act delegated broad authority, but delegation of similarly broad authority has been upheld in past cases. The District

Court observed that in *Yakus v. United States* ***
(1944), this Court upheld a statute that delegated to
an unelected "Price Administrator" the power "to
promulgate regulations fixing prices of commodities." Moreover, in the District Court's view, the Act
adequately confined the exercise of administrative
discretion. The District Court concluded that "the
totality of the Act's standards, definitions, context,
and reference to past administrative practice provides an adequate 'intelligible principle' to guide
and confine administrative decision-making." ***

Although the District Court concluded that the Act
survived a delegation doctrine challenge, it held that
the role of the Comptroller General in the deficit
reduction process violated the constitutionally imposed separation of powers. The court first explained that the Comptroller General exercises executive functions under the Act. However, the
Comptroller General, while appointed by the President with the advice and consent of the Senate, is
removable not by the President but only by a joint
resolution of Congress or by impeachment. The District Court reasoned that this arrangement could not
be sustained under this Court's decisions in *Myers v.
United States* *** (1926) and *Humphrey's Executor v.
United States* *** (1935). Under the separation of
powers established by the Framers of the Constitution, the court concluded, Congress may not retain
the power of removal over an officer performing
executive functions. The congressional removal
power created a "here-and-now subservience" of the
Comptroller General to Congress. *** The District
Court therefore held that "since the powers conferred upon the Comptroller General as part of the
automatic deficit reduction process are executive
powers, which cannot constitutionally be exercised
by an officer removable by Congress, those powers
cannot be exercised and therefore the automatic deficit reduction process to which they are central cannot be implemented." ***

Appeals were taken directly to this Court. . . . We
noted probable jurisdiction and expedited consideration of the appeals. *** We affirm.

We noted recently that "[t]he Constitution sought
to divide the delegated powers of the new Federal
Government into three defined categories, Legislative, Executive, and Judicial. *** The declared pur-

pose of separating and dividing the powers of government, of course, was to "diffus[e] power the
better to secure liberty." ***

That this system of division and separation of powers produces conflicts, confusion, and discordance at
times is inherent, but it was deliberately so structured to assure full, vigorous and open debate on the
great issues affecting the people and to provide avenues for the operation of checks on the exercise of
governmental power.

The Constitution does not contemplate an active
role for Congress in the supervision of officers
charged with the execution of the laws it enacts. The
President appoints "Officers of the United States"
with the advice and Consent of the Senate. *** Once
the appointment has been made and confirmed,
however, the Constitution explicitly provides for removal of Officers of the United States by Congress
only upon impeachment by the House of Representatives and conviction by the Senate. An impeachment by the House and trial by the Senate can rest
only on "Treason, Bribery or other high Crimes and
Misdemeanors." Article II, Sec. 4. A direct congressional role in the removal of officers charged with
the execution of the laws beyond this limited one is
inconsistent with separation of powers. . . .

This Court first directly addressed this issue in
Myers v. United States *** (1925). At issue in *Myers*
was a statute providing that certain postmasters
could be removed only "by and with the advice and
consent of the Senate." The President removed one
such postmaster without Senate approval, and a lawsuit ensued. Chief Justice Taft, writing for the Court,
declared the statute unconstitutional on the ground
that for Congress to "draw to itself, or to either
branch of it, the power to remove or the right to
participate in the exercise of that power . . . would be
. . . to infringe the constitutional principle of the separation of governmental powers." ***

A decade later, in *Humphrey's Executor v. United
States* *** (1935), relied upon heavily by appellants, a
Federal Trade Commissioner who had been re-
moved by the President sought back pay. *Humphrey's
Executor* involved an issue not presented either in
the *Myers* case or in this case—i.e., the power of
Congress to limit the President's powers of removal
of a Federal Trade Commissioner. *** The relevant

statute permitted removal "by the President," but only "for inefficiency, neglect of duty, or malfeasance in office." Justice Sutherland, speaking for the Court, upheld the statute, holding that "illimitable power of removal is not possessed by the President [with respect to Federal Trade Commissioners]." *** The Court distinguished *Myers,* reaffirming its holding that congressional participation in the removal of executive officers is unconstitutional. . . .

In light of these precedents, we conclude that Congress cannot reserve for itself the power of removal of an officer charged with the execution of the laws except by impeachment. To permit the execution of the laws to be vested in an officer answerable only to Congress would, in practical terms, reserve in Congress control over the execution of the laws. As the District Court observed, "Once an officer is appointed, it is only the authority that can remove him, and not the authority that appointed him, that he must fear and, in the performance of his functions, obey." The structure of the Constitution does not permit Congress to execute the laws; it follows that Congress cannot grant to an officer under its control what it does not possess.

To permit an officer controlled by Congress to execute the laws would be, in essence, to permit a congressional veto. Congress could simply remove, or threaten to remove, an officer for executing the laws in any fashion found to be unsatisfactory to Congress. This kind of congressional control over the execution of the laws, *Chadha* makes clear, is constitutionally impermissible.

The dangers of congressional usurpation of Executive Branch functions have long been recognized. "[T]he debates of the Constitutional Convention, and the Federalist Papers, are replete with expressions of fear that the Legislative Branch of the National Government will aggrandize itself at the expense of the other two branches." *** Indeed, we also have observed only recently that "[t]he hydraulic pressure inherent within each of the separate Branches to exceed the outer limits of its power, even to accomplish desirable objectives, must be resisted." *** With these principles in mind, we turn to consideration of whether the Comptroller General is controlled by Congress.

Appellants urge that the Comptroller General performs his duties independently and is not subservient to Congress. We agree with the District Court that this contention does not bear close scrutiny.

The critical factor lies in the provisions of the statute defining the Comptroller General's Office relating to removability. Although the Comptroller General is nominated by the President from a list of three individuals recommended by the Speaker of the House of Representatives and the President pro tempore of the Senate, *** and confirmed by the Senate, he is removable only at the initiative of Congress. He may be removed not only by impeachment but also by Joint Resolution of Congress. . . .

Although the President could veto such a joint resolution, the veto could be overridden by a two-thirds vote of both Houses of Congress. Thus, the Comptroller General could be removed in the face of Presidential opposition. Like the District Court, we therefore read the removal provision as authorizing removal by Congress alone. . . .

It is clear that Congress has consistently viewed the Comptroller General as an officer of the Legislative Branch. The Reorganization Acts of 1945 and 1949, for example, both stated that the Comptroller General and the GAO are "a part of the legislative branch of the Government." *** Similarly, in the Accounting and Auditing Act of 1950, Congress required the Comptroller General to conduct audits "as an agent of the Congress." ***

Over the years, the Comptrollers General have also viewed themselves as part of the Legislative Branch. . . .

Against this background, we see no escape from the conclusion that, because Congress had retained removal authority over the Comptroller General, he may not be entrusted with executive powers. The remaining question is whether the Comptroller General has been assigned such powers in the Balanced Budget and Emergency Deficit Control Act of 1985.

The primary responsibility of the Comptroller General under the instant Act is the preparation of a "report." This report must contain detailed estimates of projected federal revenues and expenditures. The report must also specify the reductions, if any, necessary to reduce the deficit to the target for the appropriate fiscal year. The reductions must be set forth on a program-by-program basis.

In preparing the report, the Comptroller General is to have "due regard" for the estimates and reductions set forth in a joint report submitted to him by the Directory of CBO and the Director of OMB, the President's fiscal and budgetary advisor. However, the Act plainly contemplates that the Comptroller General will exercise his independent judgment and evaluation with respect to those estimates. The Act also provides that the Comptroller General's report "shall explain fully any differences between the contents of such report and the report of the Directors." *** . . .

. . . [T]he Act . . . gives the Comptroller General the ultimate authority to determine the budget cuts to be made. Indeed, the Comptroller General commands the President himself to carry out, without the slightest variation (with exceptions not relevant to the constitutional issues presented), the director of the Comptroller General as to the budget reductions:

The [Presidential] order must provide for reductions in the manner specified, *** must incorporate the provisions of the [Comptroller General's] report, and must be consistent with such report in all respects. The President may not modify or recalculate any of the estimates, determinations, specifications, bases, amounts, or percentages set forth in the report submitted under Sec. 251 (b) in determining the reductions to be specified in the order with respect to programs, projects, and activities, or with respect to budget activities, within an account. . . . ***

Congress of course initially determined the content of the Balanced Budget and Emergency Deficit Control Act; and undoubtedly the content of the Act determines the nature of the executive duty. However, as *Chadha* makes clear, once Congress makes its choice in enacting legislation, its participation ends. Congress can thereafter control the execution of its enactment only indirectly—by passing new legislation. By placing the responsibility for execution of the Balanced Budget and Emergency Deficit Control Act in the hands of an officer who is subject to removal only by itself, Congress in effect has retained control over the execution of the Act and has intruded into the executive function. The Constitution does not permit such intrusion. . . .

Because we conclude that the Comptroller General, as an officer removable by Congress, may not exercise the powers conferred upon him by the Act, we have no occasion for considering appellees' other challenges to the Act, including their argument that the assignment of powers to the Comptroller General . . . violates the delegation doctrine. ***

No one can doubt that Congress and the President are confronted with fiscal and economic problems of unprecedented magnitude, but "the fact that a given law or procedure is efficient, convenient, and useful in facilitating functions of government, standing alone, will not save it if it is contrary to the Constitution. Convenience and efficiency are not the primary objectives—or the hallmarks—of democratic government. . . ."

We conclude the District Court correctly held that the powers vested in the Comptroller General under Sec. 251 violate the command of the Constitution that the Congress play no direct role in the execution of the laws. Accordingly, the judgment and order of the District Court are affirmed. . . .

Justice Stevens, with whom *Justice Marshall* joins, concurring in the judgment.

When this Court is asked to invalidate a statutory provision that has been approved by both Houses of the Congress and signed by the President, particularly an Act of Congress that confronts a deeply vexing national problem, it should only do so for the most compelling constitutional reasons. I agree with the Court that the "Gramm-Rudman-Hollings" Act contains a constitutional infirmity so severe that the flawed provision may not stand. I disagree with Court, however, on the reasons why the Constitution prohibits the Comptroller General from exercising the powers assigned to him by . . . the Act. It is not the dormant, carefully circumscribed congressional removal power represents the primary constitutional evil. Nor do I agree with the conclusion of both the majority and the dissent that the analysis depends on a labeling of the functions assigned to the Comptroller General as "executive powers." *** Rather, I am convinced that the Comptroller General must be characterized as an agent of Congress because of his longstanding statutory responsibilities; that the powers assigned to him under the Gramm-Rudman-

Hollings Act require him to make policy that will bind the Nation; and that, when Congress, or a component or an agent of Congress, seeks to make policy that will bind the Nation, it must follow the procedures mandated by Article I of the Constitution—through passage by both Houses and presentment to the President. In short, Congress may not exercise its fundamental power to formulate national policy by delegating that power to one of its two Houses, to a legislative committee, or to an individual agent of the Congress such as the Speaker of the House of Representatives, the Sergeant at Arms of the Senate, or the Director of the Congressional Budget Office. *** That principle, I believe, is applicable to the Comptroller General....

Justice White, dissenting.

The Court, acting in the name of separation of powers, takes upon itself to strike down the Gramm-Rudman-Hollings Act, one of the most novel and far-reaching legislative responses to a national crisis since the New Deal. The basis of the Court's action is a solitary provision of another statute that was passed over sixty years ago and has lain dormant since that time. I cannot concur in the Court's action. Like the Court, I will not purport to speak to the wisdom of the policies incorporated in the legislation the Court invalidates; that is a matter for the Congress and the Executive, both of which expressed their assent to the statute barely half a year ago. I will, however, address the wisdom of the Court's willingness to interpose its distressingly formalistic view of separation of powers have rested on untenable constitutional propositions leading to regrettable results. *** Today's result is even more misguided. As I will explain, the Court's decision rests on a feature of the legislative scheme that is of minimal practical significance and that presents no substantial threat to the basic scheme of separation of powers....

The majority's ... conclusion rests on the rigid dogma that, outside of the impeachment process, any "direct congressional role in the removal of officers charged with the execution of the laws ... is inconsistent with separation of powers." *** Reliance on such an unyielding principle to strike down a statute posing no real danger of aggrandizement of congressional power is extremely misguided and in-

sensitive to our constitutional role. The wisdom of vesting "executive" powers in an officer removable by joint resolution may indeed by debatable—as may be the wisdom of the entire scheme of permitting an unelected official to revise the budget enacted by Congress—but such matters are for the most part to be worked out between the Congress and the President through the legislative process, which affords each branch ample opportunity to defend its interests. The Act vesting budget-cutting authority in the Comptroller General represents Congress' judgment that the delegation of such authority to counteract ever-mounting deficits is "necessary and proper" to the exercise of the powers granted the Federal Government by the Constitution; and the President's approval of the statute signifies his unwillingness to reject the choice made by Congress. *** Under such circumstances, the role of this Court should be limited to determining whether the Act so alters the balance of authority among the branches of government as to pose a genuine threat to the basic division between the lawmaking power and the power to execute the law. Because I see no such threat, I cannot join the Court in striking down the Act.

I dissent.

Justice Blackmun, dissenting.

The Court may be correct when it says that Congress cannot constitutionally exercise removal authority over an official vested with the budget-reduction powers that Sec. 251 of the Balanced Budget and Emergency Deficit Control Act of 1985 gives to the Comptroller General. This, however, is not because "[t]he removal powers over the Comptroller General's office dictate that he will be subservient to Congress." *** I agree with Justice White that any such claim is unrealistic. Furthermore, I think it is clear under *Humphrey's Executor v. United States* *** (1935), that "executive" powers of the kind delegated to the Comptroller General under the Deficit Control Act need not be exercised by an officer who serves at the President's pleasure; Congress certainly could prescribe the standards and procedures for removing the Comptroller General. But it seems to me that an attempt by Congress to participate directly in the removal of an executive officer—other than through the constitutionally prescribed procedure of impeachment—might well violate the principle of separation of powers by assuming for Congress part of the President's constitutional responsibility to carry out the laws.

In my view, however, that important and difficult question need not be decided in this case, because no matter how it is resolved the plaintiffs, now appellees, are not entitled to the relief they have requested. Appellees have not sought invalidation of the 1921 provision that authorizes Congress to remove the Comptroller General by joint resolution; indeed, it is far from clear they would have standing to request such a judgment. The only relief sought in this case is nullification of the automatic budget-reduction provisions of the Deficit Control Act, and

that relief should not be awarded even if the Court is correct that those provisions are constitutionally incompatible with Congress' authority to remove the Comptroller General by joint resolution. Any incompatibility, I feel, should be cured by refusing to allow congressional removal—if it ever is attempted—and not by striking down the central provisions of the Deficit Control Act. However wise or foolish it may be, that statute unquestionably ranks among the most important federal enactments of the past several decades. I cannot see the sense of invalidating legislation of this magnitude in order to preserve a cumbersome, 65-year-old removal power that has never been exercised and appears to have been all but forgotten until this litigation. . . .

Mistretta v. United States

488 U.S. 361; 109 S. Ct. 647; 102 L. Ed. 2d 714 (1989)
Vote: 8-1

Under the Sentencing Reform Act of 1984 Congress abolished the system of indeterminate criminal sentencing and parole previously applied in federal cases. Indeterminate sentencing and parole had long been criticized because of wide disparities among similarly situated defendants both in the sentences imposed by judges and in the actual time of imprisonment served prior to release on parole. One of the most controversial provisions of the Sentencing Reform Act called for the establishment of the U.S. Sentencing Commission, an independent body of seven voting members within the judicial branch. All members of the commission were to be appointed by the president, with Senate approval, and were subject to removal by the president for "neglect of duty," "malfeasance in office," or "other good cause. . . ." The statute required that at least three members of the sentencing commission be federal judges, chosen from a list of six recommended to the president by the Judicial Conference of the United States. The commission was empowered to promulgate binding sentencing guidelines that federal judges were required to follow. These guidelines prescribed ranges of determinate sentences for all types of federal offenses and

defendants, according to detailed specified factors. A federal grand jury returned a three-count indictment against John Mistretta, resulting from his alleged distribution of cocaine. Mistretta moved to have the sentencing guidelines ruled unconstitutional on the grounds that they represented an excessive delegation of authority by Congress and that they violated the principle of separation of powers. The district court denied his motion and upheld the guidelines. Mistretta then agreed to plead guilty to one count of the indictment (conspiracy to distribute) in exchange for the prosecutors' willingness to dismiss the other two counts. Accepting this negotiated guilty plea, the trial judge applied the sentencing guidelines over Mistretta's constitutional objections and sentenced him to a prison term of eighteen months. Mistretta filed a notice of appeal to the U.S. Court of Appeals for the Eighth Circuit, but both he and the government later petitioned the Supreme Court for certiorari, thus obtaining review by the High Court prior to judgment by the court of appeals. The Court's willingness to grant this expedited review underscored its recognition of the importance of constitutional questions posed by the Sentencing Reform Act.

Justice Blackmun delivered the Opinion of the Court.

... Developing proportionate penalties for hundreds of different crimes by virtually limitless array of offenders is precisely the sort of intricate, labor-intensive task for which delegation to an expert body is especially appropriate. Although Congress has delegated significant discretion to the Commission to draw judgments from its analysis of existing sentencing practice and alternative sentencing models, "Congress is not confined to that method of executing its policy which involves the least possible delegation of discretion to administrative officers." *** We have no doubt that in the hands of the Commission "the criteria which Congress has supplied are wholly adequate for carrying out the general policy and purpose" of the Act. ***

Having determined that Congress has set forth sufficient standards for the exercise of the Commission's delegated authority, we turn to Mistretta's claim that the Act violates the constitutional principle of separation of powers.

This Court consistently has given voice to, and has reaffirmed, the central judgment of the Framers of the Constitution that, within our political scheme, the separation of governmental powers into three coordinate Branches is essential to the preservation of liberty. *** Madison, in writing about the principle of separated powers, said: "No political truth is certainly of greater intrinsic value or is stamped with the authority of more enlightened patrons of liberty." ***

In applying the principle of separated powers in our jurisprudence, we have sought to give life to Madison's view of the appropriate relationship among the three coequal Branches. Accordingly, we have recognized, as Madison admonished at the founding, that while our Constitution mandates that "each of the three general departments of government [must remain] entirely free from the control or coercive influence, direct or indirect, of either of the others," *** the Framers did not require—and indeed rejected—the notion that the three Branches must be entirely separate and distinct. *** Madison, defending the Constitution against charges that it established insufficiently separate Branches, addressed the point directly. Separation of powers, he wrote, "d[oes] not mean that these [three] departments

ought to have no partial agency in, or no control over the acts of each other," but rather "that where the whole power of one department is exercised by the same hands which possess the whole power of another department, the fundamental principles of a free constitution, are subverted." *** Madison recognized that our constitutional system imposes upon the Branches a degree of overlapping responsibility, a duty of interdependence as well as independence the absence of which "would preclude the establishment of a Nation capable of governing itself effectively." ***

In adopting this flexible understanding of separation of powers, we simply have recognized Madison, "against a gradual concentration of the several powers in the same department, consists in giving to those who administer each department, the necessary constitutional means, and personal motives, to resist encroachments of the others." Accordingly, as we have noted many times, the Framers "built into the tripartite Federal Government ... a self-executing safeguard against the encroachment or aggrandizement of one branch at the expense of the other." ***

It is this concern of encroachment and aggrandizement that has animated our separation-of-powers jurisprudence and aroused our vigilance against the "hydraulic pressure inherent within each of the separate Branches to exceed the outer limits of its power." Accordingly, we have not hesitated to strike down provisions of law that either accrued to a single Branch powers more appropriately diffused among separate Branches or that undermined the authority and independence of one or another coordinate Branch. For example, just as the Framers recognized the particular danger of the Legislative Branch's accrediting to itself judicial or executive power, so too have we invalidated attempts by Congress to exercise the responsibilities of other Branches or to reassign powers vested by the Constitution in either the Judicial Branch or the Executive Branch.

In this case, the "practical consequences" of locating the Commission within the Judicial Branch pose no threat of undermining the integrity of the Judicial Branch or of expanding the powers of the Judiciary beyond constitutional bounds by uniting within the

Branch the political or quasi-legislative power of the Commission with the judicial power of the courts. . . . First, although the Commission is located in the Judicial Branch, its powers are not united with the powers of the Judiciary in a way that has meaning for separation-of-powers analysis. Whatever constitutional problems might arise if the powers of the Commission were vested in a court, the Commission is not a court, does not exercise judicial power, and is not controlled by or accountable to members of the Judicial Branch. The Commission, on which members of the judiciary may be a minority, is an independent agency in every relevant sense. In contrast to a court's exercising judicial power, the Commission is fully accountable to Congress, which can revoke or amend any or all of the guidelines as it sees fit either within the 180-day waiting period, *** or at any time. In contrast to a court, the Commission's members are subject to the President's limited powers of removal. In contrast to a court, its rulemaking is subject to the notice and comment requirements of the Administrative Procedure Act. *** While we recognize the continuing vitality of Montesquieu's admonition: " 'Were the power of judging joined with the legislative, the life and liberty of the subject would be exposed to arbitrary control,' " *** because Congress vested the power to promulgate sentencing guidelines in an independent agency, not a court, there can be no serious argument that Congress combined legislative and judicial power within the Judicial Branch.

Second, although the Commission wields rulemaking power and not the adjudicatory power exercised by individual judges when passing sentence, the placement of the Sentencing Commission in the Judicial Branch has not increased the Branch's authority. Prior to the passage of the Act, the Judicial Branch, as an aggregate, decided precisely the questions assigned to the Commission: what sentence is appropriate to what criminal conduct under what circumstances. It was the everyday business of judges, taken collectively, to evaluate and weigh the various aims of sentencing and to apply those aims to the individual cases that came before them. The Sentencing Commission does no more than this, albeit basically through the methodology of sentencing guidelines, rather than entirely individualized sen-

tencing determinations. Accordingly, in placing the Commission in the Judicial Branch, Congress cannot be said to have aggrandized the authority of that Branch or to have deprived the Executive Branch of a power it once possessed. Indeed, because the Guidelines have the effect of promoting sentencing within a narrower range than was previously applied, the power of the Judicial Branch is, if anything, somewhat diminished by the Act. And, since Congress did not unconstitutionally delegate its own authority, the Act does not unconstitutionally diminish Congress' authority. Thus, although Congress has authorized the Commission to exercise a greater degree of political judgment than has been exercised in the past by any one entity within the Judicial Branch, in the unique context of sentencing, this authorization does nothing to upset the balance of power among the Branches.

What Mistretta's argument comes down to, then, is not that the substantive responsibilities of the Commission aggrandize the Judicial Branch, but that Branch is inevitably weakened by its participation in policymaking. We do not believe, however, that the placement within the Judicial Branch of an independent agency charged with the promulgation of sentencing guidelines can possibly be construed as preventing the Judicial Branch "from accomplishing its constitutionally assigned function." *** Despite the substantive nature of its work, the Commission is not incongruous or inappropriate to the Branch. As already noted, sentencing is a field in which the Judicial Branch long has exercised substantive or political judgment. What we said in *Morrison* when upholding the power of the Special Division to appoint independent counsels applies with even greater force here: "This is not a case in which judges are given power . . . in an area in which they have no special knowledge or expertise.

Nor do the guidelines, though substantive, involve a degree of political authority inappropriate for a nonpolitical Branch. Although the guidelines are intended to have substantive effects on public behavior (as do the rules of procedure), they do not bind or regulate the primary conduct of the public or vest in the Judicial Branch the legislative responsibility for establishing minimum and maximum penalties for every crime. They do no more than fetter the discretion of sentencing judges to do what they have done for generations—impose sentences within the broad limits established by Congress. Given their limited reach, the special role of the Judicial Branch in the field of sentencing, and the fact that the guidelines are promulgated by an independent agency and not a court, it follows that as a matter of "practical consequences" the location of the Sentencing Commission within the Judicial Branch simply leaves with the Judiciary what long has belonged to it.

In sum, since substantive judgment in the field of sentencing has been and remains appropriate to the Judicial Branch, and the methodology of rulemaking has been and remains appropriate to that Branch, Congress' considered decision to combine these function in an independent Sentencing Commission and to locate that Commission with the Judicial Branch does not violate the principle of separation of powers. . . .

We conclude that in creating the Sentencing Commission—an unusual hybrid in structure and authority—Congress neither delegated excessive legislative power nor upset the constitutionally mandated balance of powers among the coordinate Branches. The Constitution's structural protections do not prohibit Congress from delegating to an expert body located within the Judicial Branch the intricate task of formulating sentencing guidelines consistent with such significant statutory direction as is present here. Nor does our system of checked and balanced authority prohibit Congress from calling upon the accumulated wisdom and experience of the Judicial Branch in creating policy on a matter uniquely within the ken of judges. Accordingly, we hold that the Act is constitutional.

The judgment of United States District Court for the Western District of Missouri is affirmed.

It is so ordered.

Justice Scalia, dissenting.

While the products of the Sentencing Commission's labors have been given the modest name "Guidelines," *** they have the force and effect of laws, prescribing the sentences criminal defendants are to receive. A judge who disregards them will be reversed. *** I dissent from today's decision because I can find no place within our constitutional system for an agency created by Congress to exercise no gov-

ernmental power other than the making of laws. . . . Today's decision follows the regrettable tendency of our recent separation-of-powers jurisprudence *** to treat the Constitution as though it were no more than a generalized prescription that the functions of the Branches should not be commingled too much—how much is too much to be determined, case-by-case, by this Court. The Constitution is not that. Rather, as its name suggests, it is a prescribed structure, a framework, for the conduct of Government. In designing that structure, the Framers themselves considered how much commingling was, in the generality of things, acceptable, and set forth their conclusions in the document. That is the meaning of the statements concerning acceptable commingling made by Madison in defense of the proposed Constitution, and now routinely used as an excuse for disregarding it. When he said, as the Court correctly quotes, that separation of power 'd[oes] not mean that these [three] departments ought to have no partial agency in, or no control over the acts of each other,' *** his point was that the commingling specifically provided for in the structure that he and his colleagues had designed—the Presidential veto over legislation, the Senate's confirmation of executive and judicial officers, the Senate's ratification of treaties, the Congress' power to impeach and remove executive and judicial officers—did not violate a proper understanding of separation of powers. He would be aghast, I think, to hear those words used as justification for ignoring that carefully designed structure so long as, in the changing view of the Supreme Court from time to time, "too much commingling" does not occur. Consideration of the degree of commingling that a particular disposition produces may be appropriate at the margins where the outline of the framework itself is not clear; but it seems to me far from a marginal question whether our constitutional structure allows for a body which is not the Congress, and yet exercises no governmental powers except the making of rules that have the effect of laws.

I think the Court errs, in other words, not so much because it mistakes the degree of commingling, but because it fails to recognize that this case is not about commingling, but about the creation of a new Branch altogether, a sort of junior-varsity Congress. It may well be that in some circumstances such a

Branch would be desirable; perhaps the agency before us here will prove to be so. But there are many desirable dispositions that do not accord with the constitutional structure we live under. And in the long run the improvisation of a constitutional structure on the basis of currently perceived utility will be disastrous.

I respectfully dissent from the Court's decision, and would reverse the judgment of the District Court.

Immigration and Naturalization Service v. Chadha

462 U.S. 919; 103 S. Ct. 2764; 77 L. Ed. 2d 317 (1983)
Vote: 7-2

Chief Justice Burger delivered the opinion of the Court.

We granted *certiorari* . . . [to address] . . . the constitutionality of the provision in 244(c)(2) of the Immigration and Nationality Act, *** authorizing one House of Congress, by resolution, to invalidate the decision of the Executive Branch, pursuant to authority delegated by Congress to the Attorney General of the United States, to allow a particular deportable alien to remain in the United States.

I

Chadha is an East Indian who was born in Kenya and holds a British passport. He was lawfully admitted to the United States in 1966 on a non-immigrant student visa. His visa expired on June 30, 1972. On October 11, 1973, the District Director of the Immigration and Naturalization Service ordered Chadha to show cause why he should not be deported for having "remained in the United States for a longer time than permitted." *** . . . [A] deportation hearing was held before an immigration judge on January 11, 1974. Chadha conceded that he was deportable for overstaying his visa and the hearing was adjourned to enable him to file an application for suspension of deportation . . . Section 244(a)(1) provides:

(a) As hereinafter prescribed in this section, the Attorney General may, in his discretion, suspend deportation and adjust the status to that of an alien lawfully admitted for permanent residence, in the case of an alien who applies to the Attorney General for suspension of deportation and—

(1) is deportable under any law of the United States except the provisions specified in paragraph (2) of this sub-

section; has been physically present in the United States for a continuous period of not less than seven years immediately preceding the date of such application, and proves that during all of such period he was and is a person of good moral character; and is a person whose deportation would, in the opinion of the Attorney General, result in extreme hardship to the alien or to his spouse, parent, or child, who is a citizen of the United States, or an alien lawfully admitted for permanent residence.

After Chadha submitted his application for suspension of deportation, the deportation hearing was resumed on February 7, 1974. On the basis of evidence adduced at the hearing, affidavits submitted with the application, and the results of a character investigation conducted by the INS, the immigration judge, on June 25, 1974, ordered that Chadha's deportation be suspended. The immigration judge found that Chadha met the requirements of 244(a)(1): he had resided continuously in the United States for over seven years, was of good moral character, and would suffer "extreme hardship" if deported.

Pursuant to 244(c)(1) of the Act, the immigration judge suspended Chadha's deportation and a report of the suspension was transmitted to Congress. Section 244(c)(1) provides:

Upon application by any alien who is found by the Attorney General to meet the requirements of subsection (a) of this section the Attorney General may in his discretion suspend deportation of such alien. If the deportation of any alien is suspended under the provisions of this subsection, a complete and detailed statement of the facts and pertinent provisions of law in the case shall be reported to the Congress with the reasons for such suspension. Such reports shall be submitted on the first day of each calendar month in which Congress is in session.

Once the Attorney General's recommendation for suspension of Chadha's deportation was conveyed to Congress, Congress had the power under 244(c)(2) of the Act, to veto the Attorney General's determination that Chadha should not be deported. Section 244(c)(2) provides:

(2) In the case of an alien specified in paragraph (1) of subsection (a) of this subsection—if during the session of the Congress at which a case is reported, or prior to the close of the session of the Congress next following the session at which a case is reported, either the Senate or the House of Representatives passes a resolution stating in substance that it does not favor the suspension of such deportation, the Attorney General shall thereupon deport such alien or authorize the alien's voluntary departure at his own expense under the order of deportation in the manner provided by law. If, within the time above specified, neither the Senate nor the House of Representatives shall pass such a resolution, the Attorney General shall cancel deportation proceedings.

The June 25, 1974, order of the immigration judge suspending Chadha's deportation remained outstanding as a valid order for a year and a half. For reasons not disclosed by the record, Congress did not exercise the veto authority reserved to it under 244(c)(2), until the first session of the 94th Congress. This was the final session in which Congress, pursuant to 244(c)(2), could act to veto the Attorney General's determination that Chadha should not be deported. The session ended on December 19, 1975. Absent Congressional action, Chadha's deportation proceedings would have been cancelled after this date and his status adjusted to that of a permanent resident alien.

On December 12, 1975, Representative Eilberg, Chairman of the Judiciary Subcommittee on Immigration, Citizenship, and International Law, introduced a resolution opposing "the granting of permanent residence in the United States to [six] aliens," including Chadha. *** The resolution was referred to the House Committee on the Judiciary. On December 16, 1975, the resolution was discharged from further consideration by the House Committee on the Judiciary and submitted to the House of Representatives for a vote. The resolution had not been printed and was not made available to other Members of the House prior to or at the time it was voted on. *** So

far as the record before us shows, the House consideration of the resolution was based on Representative Eilberg's statement from the floor that

[i]t was the feeling of the committee, after reviewing 340 cases, that the aliens contained in the resolution [Chadha and five others] did not meet these statutory requirements, particularly as it relates to hardship; and it is the opinion of the committee that their deportation should not be suspended. ***

The resolution was passed without debate or recorded vote. Since the House action was pursuant to 244(c)(2), the resolution was not treated as an Article I legislative act; it was not submitted to the Senate or presented to the President for his action.

After the House veto of the Attorney General's decision to allow Chadha to remain in the United States, the immigration judge reopened the deportation proceedings to implement the House order deporting Chadha. Chadha moved to terminate the proceedings on the ground that 244(c)(2) is unconstitutional. The immigration judge held that he has no authority to rule on the constitutional validity of 244(c)(2). On November 8, 1976, Chadha was ordered deported pursuant to the House action.

Chadha appealed the deportation order to the Board of Immigration Appeals again contending that 244(c)(2) is unconstitutional. The Board held that it had "no power to declare unconstitutional an act of Congress" and Chadha's appeal was dismissed. ***

Pursuant to 106(a) of the Act, Chadha filed a petition for review of the deportation order in the United States Court of Appeals for the Ninth Circuit. The Immigration and Naturalization Service agreed with Chadha's position before the Court of Appeals and joined him in arguing that 244(c)(2) is unconstitutional. In light of the importance of the question, the Court of Appeals invited both the Senate and the House of Representatives to file briefs *amici curiae*.

After full briefing and oral argument, the Court of Appeals held that the House was without constitutional authority to order Chadha's deportation; accordingly it directed the Attorney General "to cease and desist from taking any steps to deport this alien based upon the resolution enacted by the House of Representatives." *** The essence of its holding was that 244(c)(2) violates the constitutional doctrine of separation of powers.

We granted *certiorari* . . . and we now affirm.

Section II is not reprinted.

III

We turn now to the question whether action of one House of Congress under 244(c)(2) violates strictures of the Constitution. We begin, of course, with the presumption that the challenged statute is valid. Its wisdom is not the concern of the courts; if a challenged action does not violate the Constitution, it must be sustained. . . .

By the same token, the fact that a given law or procedure is efficient, convenient, and useful in facilitating functions of government, standing alone, will not save it if it is contrary to the Constitution. Convenience and efficiency are not the primary objectives—or the hallmarks—of democratic government and our inquiry is sharpened rather than blunted by the fact that Congressional veto provisions are appearing with increasing frequency in statutes which delegate authority to executive and independent agencies:

Since 1932, when the first veto provision was enacted into law, 295 congressional veto-type procedures have been inserted in 196 different statutes as follows: from 1932 to 1939, five statutes were affected; from 1940–49, nineteen; between 1950–59, thirty-four statutes; and from 1960–69, forty-nine. From the year 1970 through 1975, at least one hundred sixty-three such provisions were included in eighty-nine laws. ***

Justice White undertakes to make a case for the proposition that the one-House veto is a useful "political invention," and we need not challenge that assertion. We can even concede this utilitarian argument although the long-range political wisdom of this "invention" is arguable. It has been vigorously debated and it is instructive to compare the views of the protagonists. But policy arguments supporting even useful "political inventions" are subject to the demands of the Constitution which defines powers and, with respect to this subject, sets out just how those powers are to be exercised.

Explicit and unambiguous provisions of the Constitution prescribe and define the respective functions of the Congress and of the Executive in the legislative process. Since the precise terms of those familiar provisions are critical to the resolution of this case, we set them out verbatim. Art. I provides:

All legislative Powers herein granted shall be vested in a Congress of the United States, which shall consist of a Senate *and* a House of Representatives. [Art. I, Sec. 1. Emphasis added.] Every Bill which shall have passed the House of Representatives and the Senate, shall, before it becomes a Law, be presented to the President of the United States; . . .

Every Order, Resolution, or Vote to which the Concurrence of the Senate and House of Representatives may be necessary (except on a question of Adjournment) shall be presented to the President of the United States; and before the Same shall take Effect, shall be approved by him, or being disapproved by him, shall be repassed by two thirds of the Senate and House of Representatives, according to the Rules and Limitations prescribed in the Case of a Bill.

These provisions of Art. I are integral parts of the constitutional design for the separation of powers. We have recently noted that "[t]he principle of separation of powers was not simply an abstract generalization in the minds of the Framers: it was woven into the documents that they drafted in Philadelphia in the summer of 1787." *** Just as we relied on the textual provision of Art. II, Sec. 2, cl. 2, to vindicate the principle of separation of powers . . ., we find that the purposes underlying the Presentment Clauses, Art, I, Sec. 7, cls. 2, 3, and the bicameral requirement of Art. I, Sec. 1 and 7, cl. 2, guide our resolution of the important question presented in this case. The very structure of the articles delegating and separating powers under Arts. I, II, and III exemplify the concept of separation of powers and we now turn to Art. I.

The records of the Constitutional Convention reveal that the requirement that all legislation be presented to the President before becoming law was uniformly accepted by the Framers. Presentment to the President and the Presidential veto were considered so imperative that the draftsmen took special pains to assure that these requirements could not be circumvented. During the final debate on Art. I, Sec. 7, cl. 2, James Madison expressed concern that it might easily be evaded by the simple expedient of calling a proposed law a "resolution" or "vote" rather than a "bill." As a consequence, Art. I, Sec. 7, cl. 3, was added.

The decision to provide the President with a limited and qualified power to nullify proposed legislation by veto was based on the profound conviction of the Framers that the powers conferred on Congress were the powers to be most carefully circumscribed. It is beyond doubt that lawmaking was a power to be shared by both Houses and the President. . . .

The President's role in the law-making process also reflects the Framers' careful efforts to check whatever propensity a particular Congress might have to enact oppressive, improvident, or ill-considered measures.

The bicameral requirement of Art. I, Sec. 1, 7 was of scarcely less concern to the Framers than was the Presidential veto and indeed the two concepts are interdependent. By providing that no law could take effect without the concurrence of the prescribed majority of the Members of both Houses, the Framers reemphasized their belief, already remarked upon in connection with the Presentment Clauses, that legislation should not be enacted unless it has been carefully and fully considered by the Nation's elected officials. . . .

However familiar, it is useful to recall that apart from their fear that special interests could be favored at the expense of public needs, the Framers were also concerned, although not of one mind, over the apprehensions of the smaller states. Those states feared a commonality of interest among the larger states would work to their disadvantage; representatives of the larger states, on the other hand, were skeptical of a legislature that could pass laws favoring a minority of the people. It need hardly be repeated here that the Great Compromise, under which one House was viewed as representing the people and the other the states, allayed the fears of both the large and small states.

We see therefore that the Framers were acutely conscious that the bicameral requirement and the Presentment Clauses would serve essential constitutional functions. The President's participation in the legislative process was to protect the Executive Branch from Congress and to protect the whole people from improvident laws. The division of the Congress into two distinctive bodies assures that the legislative power would be exercised only after opportunity for full study and debate in separate settings. The President's unilateral veto power, in turn, was limited by the power of two thirds of both Houses of Congress to overrule a veto thereby precluding final arbitrary action in Art. I, Sec. 1, 7 represents the Framers' decision that the legislative power of the Federal government be exercised in accord with a single, finely wrought and exhaustively considered, procedure.

IV

The Constitution sought to divide the delegated powers of the new federal government into three defined categories, legislative, executive and judicial, to assure, as nearly as possible, that each Branch of government would confine itself to its assigned responsibility. The hydraulic pressure inherent within each of the separate Branches to exceed the outer limits of its power, even to accomplish desirable objectives, must be resisted.

Although not "hermetically" sealed from one another, the powers delegated to the three Branches are functionally identifiable. When any Branch acts, it is presumptively exercising the power the Constitution has delegated to it. When the Executive acts, it presumptively acts in an executive or administrative capacity as defined in Art. II. And when, as here, one House of Congress purports to act, it is presumptively acting within its assigned sphere.

Beginning with this presumption, we must nevertheless establish that the challenged action under 244(c)(2) is of the kind to which the procedural requirements of Art. I, Sec. 7 apply. Not every action taken by either House is subject to the bicameralism and presentment requirements of Art. I. Whether actions taken by either House are, in law and fact, an exercise of legislative power depends not on their form but upon "whether they contain matter which is properly to be regarded as legislative in its character and effect." ***

Examination of the action taken here by one House pursuant to 244(c)(2) reveals that it was essentially legislative in purpose and effect. In purporting to exercise power defined in Art. I, Sec. 8, cl. 4 to "establish an uniform Rule of Naturalization," the House took action that had the purpose and effect of altering the legal rights, duties and relations of persons, including the Attorney General, Executive Branch officials and Chadha, all outside the legislative branch. Section 244(c)(2) purports to authorize one House of Congress to require the Attorney General to deport an individual alien whose deportation otherwise would be cancelled under 244. The one-House veto operated in this case to overrule the Attorney General and mandate Chadha's deportation; absent the House action, Chadha would remain in the United States. Congress has acted and its action has altered Chadha's status.

The legislative character of the one-House veto in this case is confirmed by the character of the Congressional action it supplants. Neither the House of Representatives nor the Senate contends that, absent the veto provision in 244(c)(2), either of them, or both of them acting together, could effectively require the Attorney General to deport an alien once the Attorney General, in the exercise of legislatively delegated authority, had determined the alien should remain in the United States. Without the challenged provision in 244(c)(2), this could have been achieved, if at all, only by legislation requiring deportation. Similarly, a veto by one House of Congress under 244(c)(2) cannot be justified as an attempt at amending the standards set out in 244(a)(1), or as a repeal of 244 as applied to Chadha. Amendment and repeal of statutes, no less than enactment, must conform with Art. I.

The nature of the decision implemented by the one-House veto in this case further manifests its legislative character. After long experience with the clumsy, time-consuming private bill procedure, Congress made a deliberate choice to delegate to the Executive Branch, and specifically to the Attorney General, the authority to allow deportable aliens to remain in this country in certain specified circumstances. It is not disputed that this choice to delegate authority is precisely the kind of decision that can be implemented only in accordance with the procedures set out in Art. I. Disagreement with the Attorney General's decision on Chadha's deportation—that is, Congress' decision to deport Chadha—no less than Congress' original choice to delegate to the

Attorney General the authority to make that decision, involves determinations of policy that Congress can implement in only one way; bicameral passage followed by presentment to the President. Congress must abide by its delegation of authority until that delegation is legislatively altered or revoked.

Finally, we see that when the Framers intended to authorize either House of Congress to act alone and outside of its prescribed bicameral legislative role, they narrowly and precisely defined the procedure for such action. There are but four provisions in the Constitution, explicit and unambiguous, by which one House may act alone with the unreviewable force of law, not subject to the President's veto:

(a) The House of Representatives alone was given the power to initiate impeachments. Art. I, Sec. 2, cl. 6;

(b) The Senate alone was given the power to conduct trials following impeachment on charges initiated by the House and to convict following trial. Art. I, Sec. 3, cl. 5;

(c) The Senate alone was given final unreviewable power to approve or to disapprove presidential appointments. Art. II, Sec. 2, cl. 2;

(d) The Senate alone was given unreviewable power to ratify treaties negotiated by the President. Art. II, Sec. 2, cl. 2.

Clearly, when the Draftsmen sought to confer special powers on one House, independent of the other House, or of the President, they did so in explicit, unambiguous terms. Those carefully defined exceptions from presentment and bicameralism underscore the difference between the legislative functions of Congress and other unilateral but important and binding one-House acts provided for in the Constitution. These exceptions are narrow, explicit, and separately justified; none of them authorize the action challenged here. On the contrary, they provide further support for the conclusion that Congressional authority is not to be implied and for the conclusion that the veto provided for in 244(c)(2) is not authorized by the constitutional design of the powers of the Legislative Branch.

Since it is clear that the action by the House under 244(c)(2) was not within any of the express constitutional exceptions authorizing one House to act alone, and equally clear that it was an exercise of legislative power, that action was subject to the standards prescribed in Article I. The bicameral requirement, the Presentment Clauses, the President's veto, and Congress' power to override a veto were intended to erect enduring checks on each Branch and to protect the people from the improvident exercise of power by mandating certain prescribed steps. To preserve those checks, and maintain the separation of powers, the carefully defined limits on the power of each Branch must not be eroded. To accomplish what has been attempted by one House of Congress in this case requires action in conformity with the express procedures of the Constitution's prescription for legislative action: passage by a majority of both Houses and presentment to the President.

The veto authorized by 244(c)(2) doubtless has been in many respects a convenient shortcut; the "sharing" with the Executive by Congress of its authority over aliens in this manner is, on its face, an appealing compromise. In purely practical terms, it is obviously easier for action to be taken by one House without submission to the President; but it is crystal clear from the records of the Convention, contemporaneous writings and debates, that the Framers ranked other values higher than efficiency. The records of the Convention and debates in the States preceding ratification underscore the common desire to define and limit the exercise of the newly created federal powers affecting the states and the people. There is unmistakable expression of a determination that legislation by the national Congress by a step-by-step, deliberate and deliberative process.

The choices we discern as having been made in the Constitutional Convention impose burdens on governmental processes that often seem clumsy, inefficient, even unworkable, but those hard choices were consciously made by men who had lived under a form of government that permitted arbitrary governmental acts to go unchecked. There is no support in the Constitution or decisions of this Court for the proposition that the cumbersomeness and delays often encountered in complying with explicit Constitutional standards may be avoided, either by the Congress or by the President. With all the obvious flaws of delay, untidiness, and potential for abuse, we have not yet found a better way to preserve freedom than by making the exercise of power

subject to the carefully crafted restraints, spelled out in the Constitution.

V

We hold that the Congressional veto provision in 244(c)(2) is severable from the Act and that it is unconstitutional. Accordingly, the judgment of the Court of Appeals is affirmed.

Justice Powell, concurring in the judgment.

The Court's decision, based on the Presentment Clauses, Art. I, Sec. 7, cl. 2 and 3, apparently will invalidate every use of the legislative veto. The breadth of this holding gives one pause. Congress has included the veto in literally hundreds of statutes, dating back to the 1930s. Congress clearly views this procedure as essential to controlling the delegation of power to administration agencies. One reasonably may disagree with Congress' assessment of the veto's utility, but the respect due its judgment as a coordinate branch of Government cautions that our holding should be no more extensive than necessary to decide this case. In my view, the case may be decided on a narrower ground. When Congress finds that a particular person does not satisfy the statutory criteria for permanent residence in this country it has assumed a judicial function in violation of the principle of separation of powers. Accordingly, I concur only in the judgment. . . .

The Constitution does not establish three branches with precisely defined boundaries. Rather, as Justice Jackson wrote, "[w]hile the Constitution diffuses power the better to secure liberty, it also contemplates that practice will integrate the dispersed powers into a workable government. It enjoins upon its branches separateness but interdependence, autonomy but reciprocity." ***

Functionally, the doctrine may be violated in two ways. One branch may interfere impermissibly with the other's performance of its constitutionally assigned functions. Alternatively, the doctrine may be violated when one branch assumes a function that more properly is entrusted to another. This case presents the latter situation.

On its face, the House's action appears clearly adjudicatory. The House did not enact a general rule;

rather it made its own determination that six specific persons did not comply with certain statutory criteria. It thus undertook the type of decision that traditionally has been left to other branches. Even if the House did not make a *de novo* determination, but simply reviewed the Immigration and Naturalization Service's findings, it still assumed a function ordinarily entrusted to the federal courts. Where, as here, Congress has exercised a power "that cannot possibly be regarded as merely in aid of the legislative function of Congress," *** the decisions of this Court have held that Congress impermissibly assumed a function that the Constitution entrusted to another branch.

The impropriety of the House's assumption of this function is confirmed by the fact that its action raises the very danger the Framers sought to avoid — the exercise of unchecked power. In deciding whether Chadha deserves to be deported, Congress is not subject to any internal constraints that prevent it from arbitrarily depriving him of the right to remain in this country. Unlike the judiciary or an administrative agency, Congress is not bound by established substantive rules. Nor is it subject to the procedural safeguards, such as the right to counsel and a hearing before an impartial tribunal, that are present when a court or an agency adjudicates individual rights. The only effective constraint on Congress' power is political, but Congress is most accountable politically when it prescribes rules of general applicability. When it decides rights of specific persons, those rights are subject to "the tyranny of a shifting majority." ***

Chief Justice Marshall observed: "It is the peculiar province of the legislative to prescribe general rules for the government of society; the application of those rules would seem to be the duty of other departments." *** In my view, when Congress undertook to apply its rules to *Chadha*, it exceeded the scope of its constitutionally prescribed authority. I would not reach the broader question whether legislative vetoes are invalid under the Presentment Clauses.

Justice White, dissenting.

Today the Court not only invalidates 244(c)(2) of the Immigration and Nationality Act, but also sounds the death knell for nearly 200 other statutory provisions in which Congress has reserved a "legislative

veto." For this reason, the Court's decision is of surpassing importance. And it is for this reason that the Court would have been well-advised to decide the case, if possible, on the narrower grounds of separation of powers, leaving for full consideration the constitutionality of other congressional review statutes operating on such varied matters as war powers and agency rulemaking, some of which concern the independent regulatory agencies.

The prominence of the legislative veto mechanism is our contemporary political system and its importance to Congress can hardly be overstated. It has become a central means by which Congress secures the accountability of executive and independent agencies. Without the legislative veto, Congress is faced with a Hobson's choice: either to refrain from delegating the necessary authority, leaving itself with a hopeless task of writing laws with the requisite specificity to cover endless special circumstances across the entire policy landscape, or in the alternative, to abdicate its lawmaking function to the executive branch and independent agencies. To choose the former leaves major national problems unresolved; to opt for the latter risks unaccountable policymaking by those not elected to fill that role. Accordingly, over the past five decades, the legislative veto has been placed in nearly 200 statutes. The device is known in every field of governmental concern: reorganization, budgets, foreign affairs, war powers, and regulation of trade, safety, energy, the environment and the economy.

The legislative veto developed initially in response to the problems of reorganizing the sprawling government structure created in response to the Depression.

. . . [T]he legislative veto is more than "efficient, convenient, and useful." *** It is an important if not indispensable political invention that allows the President and Congress to resolve major constitutional and policy differences, assures the accountability of independent regulatory agencies, and preserves Congress' control over lawmaking. Perhaps there are other means of accommodation and accountability, but the increasing reliance of Congress upon the legislative veto suggests that the alternatives to which Congress must now turn are not entirely satisfactory.

The history of the legislative veto also makes clear that it has not been a sword with which Congress has struck out to aggrandize itself at the expense of the other branches—the concerns of Madison and Hamilton. Rather, the veto has been a means of defense, a reservation of ultimate authority necessary if Congress is to fulfill its designated role under Article I as the nation's lawmaker. While the President has often objected to particular legislative vetoes, generally those left in the hands of congressional committees, the Executive has more often agreed to legislative review as the price for a broad delegation of authority. To be sure, the President may have preferred unrestricted power, but that could be precisely why Congress thought it essential to retain a check on the exercise of delegated authority.

For all the reasons, the apparent sweep of the Court's decision today is regrettable. The Court's Article I analysis appears to invalidate all legislative vetoes irrespective of form or subject. Because the legislative veto is commonly found as a check upon rulemaking by administrative agencies and upon broad-based policy decisions of the Executive Branch, it is particularly unfortunate that the Court reaches its decision in a case involving the exercise of a veto over deportation decisions regarding particular individuals. Courts should always be wary of striking statutes as unconstitutional; to strike an entire class of statutes based on consideration of a somewhat atypical and more-readily indictable exemplar of the class is irresponsible.

If the legislative veto were as plainly unconstitutional as the Court strives to suggest, its broad ruling today would be more comprehensible. But, the constitutionality of the legislative veto is anything but clear-cut. The issue divides scholars, courts, attorneys general, and the two other branches of the National Government. If the veto devices so flagrantly disregarded the requirements of Article I as the Court today suggests, I find it incomprehensible that Congress, whose members are bound by oath to uphold the Constitution, would have placed these mechanisms in nearly 200 separate laws over a period of 50 years.

I do not suggest that all legislative vetoes are necessarily consistent with separation of powers principles. A legislative check on an inherently executive function, for example that of initiating prosecutions, poses an entirely different question. But the legislative veto device here—and in many other settings—is far from an instance of legislative tyranny over the Executive. It is a necessary check on the unavoidably expanding power of the agencies, both executive and independent, as they engage in exercising authority delegated by Congress.

I regret that I am in disagreement with my colleagues on the fundamental questions that this case presents. But even more I regret the destructive scope of the Court's holding. It reflects a profoundly different conception of the Constitution than that held by the courts which sanctioned the modern administrative state. Today's decision strikes down in one fell swoop provisions in more laws enacted by Congress than the Court has cumulatively invalidated in its history. I fear it will now be more difficult "to insure that the fundamental policy decisions in our society will be made not by an appointed official but by the body immediately responsible to the people." *** I must dissent.

Justice Rehnquist, dissenting. . . .

Metropolitan Washington Airports, Authority v. Citizens for the Abatement of Aircraft Noise

501 U.S. ___; 111 S. Ct. 2298; 115 L. Ed. 2d 236 (1991)

Vote: 6-3

Washington National and Dulles International are the only two major commercial airports owned by the U.S. government. Because of its location near the *center of the Washington, D.C., metropolitan area, National is far more convenient and heavily used than Dulles. Flight paths over densely populated ar-*

eas around these airports have caused many local residents to become concerned about aircraft safety, noise, and air pollution. In 1986, Congress passed a law transferring control of National and Dulles from the Department of Transportation to the Metropolitan Washington Airports Authority (MWAA). This entity, created by a compact between Virginia and the District of Columbia, was established to facilitate the financing of capital improvements at both airports through the sale of tax-exempt bonds. The MWAA was to be governed by an eleven-member board of directors. Fearing that the relinquishment of federal control would result in the transfer of many commercial routes from National to Dulles, Congress added provisions to the 1986 act calling for the creation of a nine-member board of review consisting of members of Congress who purportedly would serve on the board in their "individual capacities." Among the powers vested in the review board was the authority to veto decisions of the MWAA Board of Directors. In due course, the board of directors adopted a master plan providing for extensive new facilities at National. The review board decided not to veto the plan. Local residents, including Citizens for the Abatement of Aircraft Noise (CAAN), brought suit in federal court, alleging that the review board's veto power was unconstitutional. The district court ruled against CAAN, but the court of appeals reversed. The Supreme Court granted MWAA's petition for certiorari.

Justice Stevens delivered the Opinion of the Court.

. . . [T]here is no question about federal power to operate the airports. The question is whether the maintenance of federal control over the airports by means of the Board of Review, which is allegedly a federal instrumentality, is invalid, not because it invades any state power, but because Congress' continued control violated the separation of powers principle. . . . We must therefore consider whether the powers of the Board of Review may, consistent with the separation of powers, be exercised by an agent of Congress. . . .

Because National and Dulles are the property of the Federal Government and their operations directly affect interstate commerce, there is no doubt concerning the ultimate power of Congress to enact legislation defining the policies that govern those operations. Congress itself can formulate the details, or it can enact general standards and assign to the Executive Branch the responsibility for making necessary managerial decisions in conformance with those standards. The question presented is only whether the Legislature has followed a constitutionally acceptable procedure in delegating decision-making authority to the Board of Review.

The structure of our Government as conceived by the Framers of our Constitution disperses the federal power among the three branches—the Legislative, the Executive, and the Judicial—placing both substantive and procedural limitations on each. The ultimate purpose of this separation of powers is to protect the liberty and security of the governed.

Violations of the separation-of-powers principle have been uncommon because each branch has traditionally respected the prerogatives of the other two. Nevertheless, the Court has been sensitive to its responsibility to enforce the principle when necessary [Justice Stevens now quotes from the Supreme Court's decision in *Morrison v. Olson* (1988)]:

Time and again we have reaffirmed the importance in our constitutional scheme of the separation of governmental powers into the three coordinate branches. *** As we stated in *Buckley v. Valeo* *** (1976), the system of separated powers and checks and balances established in the Constitution was regarded by the Framers as 'self-executing safeguard against the encroachment or aggrandizement of one branch at the expense of the other.' *** We have not hesitated to invalidate provisions of law which violate this principle. ***

The abuses by the monarch recounted in the Declaration of Independence provide dramatic evidence of the threat to liberty posed by a too powerful executive. But, as James Madison recognized [in *The Federalist* No. 48], the representatives of the majority in a democratic society, if unconstrained, may pose a similar threat:

It will not be denied, that power is of an encroaching nature, and that it ought to be effectually restrained from passing the limits assigned to it.

The founders of our republic . . . seem never for a moment to have turned their eyes from the danger to liberty from the overgrown and all-grasping prerogative of an hereditary magistrate, supported and fortified by an hereditary branch of the legislative authority. They seem never to have recollected the danger from legislative usurpations; which by assembling all power in the same hands, must lead to the same tyranny as is threatened by executive usurpation.... [I]t is against the enterprising ambition of this department, that the people ought to indulge all their jealousy and exhaust all their precautions.

The legislative department derives a superiority in our governments from other circumstances. Its constitutional powers being at once more extensive and less susceptible of precise limits, it can with the greater facility, mask under complicated and indirect measures, the encroachments which it makes on the coordinate departments. It is not infrequently a question of real necessity in legislative bodies, whether the operation of a particular measure will, or will not extend beyond the legislative sphere. ***

To forestall the danger of encroachment "beyond the legislative sphere," the Constitutional imposes two basic and related constraints on the Congress. It may not "invest itself or its Members with either executive power or judicial power." *** And, when it exercises its legislative power, it must follow the "single, finely wrought and exhaustively considered, procedures" specified in Article I. ***

The first constraint is illustrated by the Court's holdings in *Springer v. Philippine Islands* *** (1928) and *Bowsher v. Synar* *** (1986). *Springer* involved the validity of acts of the Philippine legislature that authorized a committee of three—two legislators and one executive—to vote corporate stock owned by the Philippine Government. Because the Organic Act of the Philippine Islands incorporated the separation-of-powers principle, and because the challenged statute authorized two legislators to perform the executive function of controlling the management of the government-owned corporations, the Court held the statutes invalid. Our more recent decision in *Bowsher* involved a delegation of authority to the Comptroller General to revise the federal budget. After concluding that the Comptroller General was in effect an agent of Congress, the Court held that he could not exercise executive powers....

The second constraint is illustrated by our decision in *[Immigration and Naturalization Service v.] Chadha*. This case involved the validity of a statute that authorized either House of Congress by resolution to invalidate a decision by the Attorney General to allow a deportable alien to remain in the United States. Congress had the power to achieve that result through legislation, but the statute was nevertheless invalid because Congress cannot exercise its legislative power to enact laws without following the bicameral and presentment procedures specified in Article I. For the same reason, an attempt to characterize the budgetary action of the Comptroller General in *Bowsher* as legislative action would not have saved its constitutionally because Congress may not delegate the power to legislate to its own agents or to its own Members.

Respondents [CAAN] rely on both of these constraints in their challenge to the Board of Review. The Court of Appeals found it unnecessary to discuss the second constraint because the court was satisfied that the power exercised by the Board of Review over "key operational decisions is quintessentially executive." *** We need not agree or disagree with this characterization by the Court of Appeals to conclude that the Board of Review's power is constitutionally impermissible. If the power is executive, the Constitution does not permit an agent of Congress to exercise it. If the power is legislative, Congress must exercise it in conformity with the bicameralism and presentment requirements of Art. I, § 7. In short, when Congress "[takes] action that ha[s] the purpose and effect of altering the legal rights, duties, and relations of persons ... outside the Legislative Branch," it must take that action by the procedures authorized in the Constitution. ***

One might argue that the provision for a Board of Review is the kind of practical accommodation between the Legislature and the Executive that should be permitted in a "workable government." Admittedly, Congress imposed its will on the regional authority created by the District of Columbia and the Commonwealth of Virginia by means that are unique and that might prove to be innocuous. However, the statutory scheme challenged today provides a blueprint for extensive expansion of the legislative power beyond its constitutionally confined role. Given the scope of the federal power to dispense benefits to the States in a variety of forms and subject to a host of statutory conditions, Congress could, if this Board of Review were valid, use similar expedients to enable its Members or its agents to retain control, outside the ordinary legislative process, of the activities of state grant recipients charged with executing virtually every aspect of national policy. As

James Madison presciently observed, the legislature "can with greater facility, mask under complicated and indirect measures, the encroachments which it makes on the co-ordinate departments." Heeding his warning that legislative "power is of an encroaching nature," we conclude that the Board of Review is an impermissible encroachment.

The judgment of the Court of Appeals is affirmed.

Justice White, with whom The Chief Justice and Justice Marshall join, dissenting.

Today the Court strikes down yet another innovative and otherwise lawful governmental experiment in the name of separation of powers. To reach this result, the majority must strain to bring state enactments within the ambit of a doctrine hitherto applicable only to the Federal Government and strain again to extend the doctrine even though both Congress and the Executive argue for the constitutionality of the arrangement which the Court invalidates. These efforts are untenable because they violate the " 'cardinal principle that this Court will first ascertain whether a construction of [a] statute is fairly possible by which the [constitutional] question may be avoided.' " *** They are also untenable because the Court's separation-of-powers cases in no way compel the decision the majority reaches.

I

For the first time in its history, the Court employs separation-of-powers doctrine to invalidate a body created under state law. The majority justifies this unprecedented step on the ground that the Board of Review "exercises sufficient federal power ... to mandate separation-of-powers scrutiny." This conclusion follows, it is claimed, because the Board, as presently constituted, would not exist but for the conditions set by Congress in the Metropolitan Washington Airports Act of 1986. *** This unprecedented rationale is insufficient on at least two counts. The Court's reasoning fails first because it ignores the plain terms of every instrument relevant to this case. The Court further errs because it also misapprehends the nature of the Transfer Act as a lawful exercise of congressional authority under the Property Clause, U.S. Const., Art. IV, sec. 3, cl. 2. . . .

II

Even assuming that separation-of-powers principles apply, the Court can hold the board to be unconstitutional only by extending those principles in an unwarranted fashion. The majority contends otherwise, reasoning that the Constitution requires today's result whether the Board exercises executive or legislative power. *** Yet never before has the Court struck down a body on separation-of-powers grounds that neither Congress nor the Executive oppose. It is absurd to suggest that the Board's power represents the type of "legislative usurpation ... which, by assembling all power in the same hands ... must lead to the same tyranny" that concerned the Framers. *** More to the point, it is clear that the Board does not offend separation-of-powers principles either under our cases dealing with executive power or our decisions concerning legislative authority. . . .

III

The majority claims not to retreat from our settled rule that " '[w]hen this Court is asked to invalidate statutory provision that has been approved by both Houses of the Congress and signed by the President, . . . it should only do so for the most compelling constitutional reasons.' " *** This rule should apply with even greater force when the arrangement under challenge has also been approved by what are functionally two state legislatures and two state executives.

Since the "compelling constitutional reasons" on which we have relied in our past separation-of-powers decisions are insufficient to strike down the Board, the Court has had to inflate those reasons needlessly to defend today's decision. I cannot follow along this course. The Board violates none of the principles set forth in our cases. Still less does it provide a "blueprint for extensive expansion of the legislative power beyond its constitutionally confined role." *** This view utterly ignores the Executive's ability to protect itself through, among other things, the ample power of the veto. Should Congress ever undertake such improbable projects as transferring national parklands to the States on the condition that its agents control their oversight . . .

there is little doubt that the President would be equal to the task of safeguarding his or her interests. Least of all, finally, can it be said that the Board reflects "[t]he propensity of the legislative department to intrude upon the rights, and to absorb the powers, of the other departments," that the Framers feared. *** Accordingly, I dissent.

Vermont Yankee Nuclear Power Corporation v. Natural Resources Defense Council, Inc.

435 U.S. 519; 98 S. Ct. 1197; 55 L. Ed. 2d 460 (1978)
Vote: 7-0

In 1967, after conducting public hearings pursuant to the Administrative Procedure Act, the Atomic Energy Commission (AEC) granted a license to Vermont Yankee Nuclear Power Corporation to operate a nuclear power plant. Over the objection of the Natural Resources Defense Council (NRDC), the licensing hearing did not consider the issue of the environmental effects of reprocessing spent nuclear fuel. In 1972, after conducting another hearing, the AEC issued a rule dealing with the issue of spent nuclear fuel. NRDC filed suit, challenging the adequacy of procedures that were followed in the AEC rule-making hearing. Specifically, NRDC argued that the hearing was inadequate in that it lacked full adjudicatory procedures, such as cross-examination of witnesses and discovery of evidence. The Court of Appeals for the District of Columbia Circuit agreed, holding that the procedures of the rule-making hearing did not constitute due process of law.

Mr. Justice Rehnquist delivered the Opinion of the Court.

In 1946, Congress enacted the Administrative Procedure Act, which as we have noted elsewhere was not only "a new basic and comprehensive regulation of procedures in many agencies," *Wong Yang Sung v. McGrath* *** (1950), but was also a legislative enactment which settled "long-continued and hard-fought contentions, and enacts a formula upon which opposing social and political forces have come to rest." Section 553 of the Act, dealing with rulemaking, requires that ". . . notice of proposed rulemaking shall be published in the Federal Register. . . ," describes the contents of that notice, and goes on to require in subsection (c) that after the notice the agency "shall give interested persons an opportunity to participate in the rulemaking through submission of written data, views, or arguments with or without opportunity for oral presentation. After consideration of the relevant matter presented, the agency shall incorporate in the rules adopted a concise general statement of their basis and purpose." *** Interpreting this provision of the Act in *United States v. Allegheny-Ludlum Steel Corp.* *** (1972), and *United States v. Florida East Coast Railroad Co.* *** (1973), we held that generally speaking this section of the Act established the maximum procedural requirements which Congress was willing to have the courts impose upon agencies in conducting rule-making procedures. Agencies are free to grant additional procedural rights in the exercise of their discretion, but reviewing courts are generally not free to impose them if the agencies have not chosen to grant them. This is not to say necessarily that there are no circumstances which would ever justify a court in overturning agency action because of a failure to employ procedures beyond those required by the statute. But such circumstances, if they exist, are extremely rare. . . .

It is in the light of this background of statutory and decisional law that we granted certiorari to review two judgments of the Court of Appeals for the District of Columbia Circuit because of our concern that they had seriously misread or misapplied this statutory and decisional law cautioning reviewing courts against engrafting their own notions of proper procedures upon agencies entrusted with substantive functions of Congress. . . .

. . . [B]efore determining whether the Court of Appeals reached a permissible result, we must determine exactly what result it did reach, and in this case that is no mean feat. Vermont Yankee argues that the court invalidated the rule because of the inadequacy of the procedures employed in the proceedings. Respondent NRDC, on the other hand, labeling petitioner's view of the decision a "straw man," argues to this Court that the court merely held that the record was inadequate to enable the reviewing court to determine whether the agency had fulfilled its statutory obligation. . . .

After a thorough examination of the opinion itself, we conclude that while the matter is not entirely free from doubt, the majority of the Court of Appeals struck down the rule because of the perceived inadequacies of the procedures employed in the rulemaking proceedings. The court first determined the intervenors' primary argument to be "that the decision to preclude 'discovery or cross-examination' denied them a meaningful opportunity to participate in the proceedings as guaranteed by due process." *** . . . The court also refrained from actually ordering the agency to follow any specific procedures, but there is little doubt in our minds that the ineluctable mandate of the court's decision is that the procedures afforded during the hearings were inadequate. This conclusion is particularly buttressed by the fact that after the court examined the record, . . . and declared it insufficient, the court proceeded to discuss at some length the necessity for further procedural devices or a more "sensitive" application of those devices employed during the proceedings. ***

In prior opinions we have intimated that even in a rulemaking proceeding when an agency is making a " 'quasi-judicial' " determination by which a very small number of persons are " 'exceptionally affected, in each case upon individual grounds,' " in some circumstances additional procedures may be required in order to afford the aggrieved individuals due process. *** It might also be true, although we do not think the issue is presented in this case and accordingly do not decide it, that a totally unjustified departure from well settled agency procedures of long standing might require judicial correction.

But this much is absolutely clear. Absent constitutional constraints or extremely compelling circumstances, "the administrative agencies should be free to fashion their own rules of procedure and to pursue methods of inquiry capable of permitting them to discharge their multitudinous duties." ***

. . . NRDC argues that Sec. 553 of the Administrative Procedure Act merely establishes lower procedural bounds and that a court may routinely require more than the minimum when an agency's proposed rule addresses complex or technical factual issues or "issues of great public import." *** We have, however, previously shown that our decisions reject this view.

We also think the legislative history, even the part which it cites, does not bear out its contention. . . . Congress intended that the discretion of the agencies and not that of the courts be exercised in determining when extra procedural devices should be employed.

There are compelling reasons for construing Sec. 553 in this manner. In the first place, if courts continually review agency proceedings to determine whether the agency employed procedures which were, in the court's opinion, perfectly tailored to reach what the court perceives to be the "best" or "correct" result, judicial view would be totally unpredictable. And the agencies, operating under this vague injunction to employ the "best" procedures and facing the threat of reversal if they did not, would undoubtedly adopt full adjudicatory procedures in every instance. Not only would this totally disrupt the statutory scheme, through which Congress enacted "a formula upon which opposing social and political forces have come to rest," *** but all the inherent advantages of informal rulemaking would be totally lost.

Secondly, it is obvious that the court in this case reviewed the agency's choice of procedures on the basis of the record actually produced at the hearing, and not on the basis of the information available to the agency when it made the decision to structure the proceedings in a certain way. This sort of Monday morning quarterbacking not only encourages but almost compels the agency to conduct all rulemaking proceedings with the full panoply of procedural devices normally associated only with adjudicatory hearings.

Finally, and perhaps more importantly, this sort of review fundamentally misconceives the nature of the standard for judicial review of an agency rule. The court below uncritically assumed that additional procedures will automatically result in a more adequate record because it will give interested parties more of an opportunity to participate and contribute to the proceedings. But informal rulemaking need not be based solely on the transcript of a hearing held before an agency. Indeed, the agency need not even hold a formal hearing. *** Thus, the adequacy of the "record" in this type of proceeding is not correlated directly to the type of procedural devices employed, but rather turns on whether the agency has followed the statutory mandate of the Administrative Procedure Act or other relevant statutes. If the agency is compelled to support the rule which it ultimately adopts with the type of record produced only after a full adjudicatory hearing, it simply will have no choice but to conduct a full adjudicatory hearing prior to promulgating every rule. In sum, this sort of unwarranted judicial examination of perceived procedural shortcomings of a rulemaking proceeding can do nothing but seriously interfere with that process prescribed by Congress. . . .

Reversed and remanded.

Mr. Justice Blackmun and *Mr. Justice Powell* took no part in . . . [this decision].

Mathews v. Eldridge

424 U.S. 319; 96 S. Ct. 893; 47 L. Ed. 2d 18 (1976)
Vote: 6-2

Mr. Justice Powell delivered the opinion of the Court.

The issue in this case is whether the Due Process Clause of the Fifth Amendment requires that prior to the termination of Social Security disability benefit payments the recipient be afforded an opportunity for an evidentiary hearing.

Cash benefits are provided to workers during periods in which they are completely disabled under the disability insurance program created by the 1956 amendments to *** the Social Security Act. *** . . . Eldridge was first awarded benefits in June 1968. In March 1972, he received a questionnaire from the state agency charged with monitoring his medical condition. Eldridge completed the questionnaire, indicating that his condition had not improved and identifying the medical sources, including physicians, from whom he had received treatment recently. The state agency then obtained reports from his physician and a psychiatric consultant. After considering these reports and other information in his file the agency informed Eldridge by letter that it has made a tentative determination that his disability had ceased in May 1972. The letter included a statement of reasons for the proposed termination of benefits, and advised Eldridge that he might request reasonable time in which to obtain and submit additional information pertaining to his condition.

In his written response, Eldridge disputed one characterization of his medical condition and indicated that the agency already had enough evidence to establish his disability. The state agency then made its final determination that he had ceased to be disabled in May 1972. This determination was accepted by the Social Security Administration (SSA), which notified Eldridge in July that his benefits would terminate after that month. The notification also advised him of his right to seek reconsideration by the state agency of this initial determination within six months.

Instead of requesting reconsideration Eldridge commenced this action challenging the constitutional validity of the administrative procedures established by the Secretary of Health, Education, and Welfare for assessing whether there exists a continuing disability. He sought an immediate reinstatement of benefits pending a hearing on the issue of his disability. *** The secretary moved to dismiss on the grounds that Eldridge's benefits had been terminated in accordance with valid administrative regulations and procedures and that he had failed to exhaust available remedies. . . .

. . . [The] District Court held that prior to termination of benefits Eldridge had to be afforded an evidentiary hearing of the type required for welfare beneficiaries under *** the Social Security Act. *** [T]he Court of Appeals for the Fourth Circuit affirmed. . . . We reverse. . . .

Procedural due process imposes constraints on governmental decisions which deprive individuals of "liberty" or "property" interests within the meaning of the Due Process Clause of the Fifth or Fourteenth Amendment. The Secretary does not contend that procedural due process is inapplicable to terminations of Social Security disability benefits. He recognizes, as has been implicit in our prior decisions, *** that the interest of an individual in continued receipt of these benefits is a statutorily created "property" interest protected by the Fifth Amendment. *** Rather, the Secretary contends that the existing administration procedures . . . provide all the process that is constitutionally due before a recipient can be deprived of that interest.

This Court consistently has held that some form of hearing is required before an individual is finally deprived of a property interest. *** The "right to be heard before being condemned to suffer grievous loss of any kind, even though it may not involve the stigma and hardships of a criminal conviction, is a principle basic to our society." *** The fundamental requirement of due process is the opportunity to be heard "at a meaningful time and in a meaningful manner." *** Eldridge agrees that the review procedures available to a claimant before the initial determination of ineligibility becomes final would be adequate if disability benefits were not terminated until after the evidentiary hearing stage of the administrative process. The dispute centers upon what process is due prior to the initial termination of benefits, pending review.

In recent years this Court increasingly has had occasion to consider the extent to which due process requires an evidentiary hearing prior to the deprivation of some type of property interest even if such a hearing is provided thereafter. In only one case, *Goldberg v. Kelly,* *** has the Court held that a hearing closely approximating a judicial trial is nec-

essary. In other cases requiring some type of pretermination hearing as a matter of constitutional right the Court has spoken sparingly about the requisite procedures. . . .

These decisions underscore the truism that "[d]ue process," unlike some legal rules, is not a technical conception with a fixed content unrelated to time, place, and circumstances." *** "[D]ue process is flexible and calls for such procedural protections as the particular situation demands." *** Accordingly, resolution of the issue whether the administrative procedures provided here are constitutionally sufficient requires analysis of the governmental and private interests that are affected. *** More precisely, our prior decisions indicate that identification of the specific dictates of due process generally requires consideration of three distinct factors: first, the private interest that will be affected by the official action; second, the risk of an erroneous deprivation of such interest through the procedures used, and the probable value, if any, of additional or substitute procedural safeguards; and finally, the Government's interest, including the function involved and the fiscal and administrative burdens that the additional or substitute procedural requirement would entail. *** . . .

Despite the elaborate character of the administrative procedures provided by the Secretary, the courts below held them to be constitutionally inadequate, concluding that due process requires an evidentiary hearing prior to termination. In light of the private and governmental interests at stake here and the nature of the existing procedures, we think this was error.

Since a recipient whose benefits are terminated is awarded full retroactive relief if he ultimately prevails, his sole interest is in the uninterrupted receipt of this course of income pending final administrative decision on his claim. . . .

Only in *Goldberg* has the Court held that due process requires an evidentiary hearing prior to a temporary deprivation. It was emphasized there that welfare assistance is given to persons on the very margin of subsistence. . . . Eligibility for disability benefits, in contrast, is not based upon financial need. Indeed, it is wholly unrelated to the worker's income or support from many other sources, such as earnings of other family members, workmen's compensation awards, tort claims awards, savings, private insurance, public or private pensions, veterans' benefits, food stamps, public assistance, or the "many other important programs, both public and private, which contain provisions for disability payments affecting a substantial portion of the work force. . . ." ***

As *Goldberg* illustrates, the degree of potential deprivation that may be created by a particular decision is a factor to be considered in assessing the validity of any administrative decisionmaking process. *** The potential deprivation here is generally likely to be less than in *Goldberg,* although the degree of difference can be overstated. . . . [T]o remain eligible for benefits a recipient must be "unable to engage in substantial gainful activity." ***

As we recognized last Term, . . . "the possible length of wrongful deprivation of . . . benefits [also] is an important factor in assessing the impact of official action on the private interests." The Secretary concedes that the delay between a request for a hearing before an administrative law judge and a decision on the claim is currently between 10 and 11 months. Since a terminated recipient must first obtain a reconsideration decision as a prerequisite to invoking his right to an evidentiary hearing, the delay between the actual cut off of benefits and final decision after a hearing exceeds one year.

In view of the torpidity of this administrative review process, *** and the typically modest resources of the family unit of the physically disabled worker, the hardship imposed upon the erroneously terminated disability recipient may be significant. Still, the disabled worker's need is likely to be less than that of a welfare recipient. In addition to the possibility of access to private resources, other forms of government assistance will become available where the termination of disability benefits places a worker or his family below the subsistence level. *** In view of these potential sources of temporary income, there is less reason here than in *Goldberg* to depart from the ordinary principle, established by our decisions, that something less than an evidentiary hearing is sufficient prior to adverse administrative action.

An additional factor to be considered here is the fairness and reliability of the existing pretermination procedures, and the probable value, if any, of additional procedural safeguards. Central to the evalua-

tion of any administrative process is the nature of the relevant inquiry. *** In order to remain eligible for benefits the disabled worker must demonstrate by means of "medically acceptable clinical and laboratory diagnostic techniques" *** that he is unable "to engage in any substantial gainful activity by reason of any *medically determinable* physical or mental impairment. . . ." *** (emphasis supplied). In short, a medical assessment of the worker's physical or mental condition is required. This is a more sharply focused and easily documented decision than the typical determination of welfare entitlement. In the latter case, a wide variety of information may be deemed relevant, and issues of witness credibility and veracity often are critical to the decisionmaking process. . . .

By contrast, the decision whether to discontinue disability benefits will turn, in most cases, upon "routine, standard, and unbiased medical reports by physician specialists," *** concerning a subject whom they have personally examined. . . . To be sure, credibility and veracity may be a factor in the ultimate disability assessment in some cases. But procedural due process rules are shaped by the risk of error inherent in the truthfinding process as applied to the generality of cases, not the rare exceptions. The potential value of an evidentiary hearing, or even oral presentation to the decisionmaker, is substantially less in this context than in *Goldberg*. . . .

A further safeguard against mistake is the policy of allowing the disability recipient's representative full access to all information relied upon by the state agency. In addition, prior to the cutoff of benefits the agency informs the recipient of its tentative assessment, the reasons therefore, and provides a summary of the evidence that it considers most relevant. Opportunity is then afforded the recipient to submit additional evidence or arguments, enabling him to challenge directly the accuracy of information in his field as well as the correctness of the agency's tentative conclusions. These procedures *** enable the recipient to "mold" his argument to respond to the precise issues which the decisionmaker regards as crucial. . . .

In striking the appropriate due process balance the final factor to be assessed is the public interest. This includes the administrative burden and other societal costs that would be associated with requiring, as a matter of constitutional right, an evidentiary hearing upon demand in all cases prior to the termination of disability benefits. The most visible burden would be the incremental cost resulting from the increased number of hearings and the expense of providing benefits to ineligible recipients pending decision. No one can predict the extent of the increase, but the fact that full benefits would continue until after such hearings would assure the exhaustion in most cases of this attractive option. Nor would the theoretical right of the Secretary to recover undeserved benefits result, as a practical matter, in any substantial offset the added outlay of public funds. . . . [E]xperience with the constitutionalizing of government procedures suggests that the ultimate additional cost in terms of money and administrative burden would not be insubstantial.

Financial cost alone is not a controlling weight in determining whether due process requires a particular procedural safeguard prior to some administrative decision. But the Government's interest, and hence that of the public, in conserving scarce fiscal and administrative recourses, is a factor that must be weighed. At some point the benefit or an additional safeguard to the individual affected by the administrative action and to society, in terms of increased assurance that the action is just, may be outweighed by the cost. Significantly, the cost of protecting those whom the preliminary administrative process had identified as likely to be found undeserving may in the end come out of the pockets of the deserving since resources available for any particular program of social welfare are not unlimited. ***

But more is implicated in cases of this type than *ad hoc* weighing of fiscal and administrative burdens against the interests of a particular category of claimants. The ultimate balance involves a determination as to when, under our constitutional system, judicial-type procedures must be imposed upon administrative action to assure fairness. We reiterate the wise admonishment of Mr. Justice Frankfurter that differences in the origin and function of administrative agencies "preclude wholesale transplantation of the rules of procedure, trial, and review which have evolved from the history and experience of courts." *** The judicial model of an evidentiary hearing is neither a required, nor even the most effective, method of decisionmaking in all circumstances. The essence of due process is the requirement that "a person in jeopardy of serious loss [be given] notice of the case against him and opportunity to meet it." *** All that is necessary is that the procedures be tailored, in light of the decision to be made, to "the capacity and circumstances of those who are to be heard," *** to insure that they are given a meaningful opportunity to present their case. In assessing what process is due in this case, substantial weight must be given to the good-faith judgments of the individuals charged by Congress with the administration of social welfare programs that the procedures they have provided assure fair consideration of the entitlement claims of individuals. *** This is especially so where, as here, the prescribed procedures not only provide the claimant with an effective process for asserting his claim prior to any administrative action, but also assure a right to an evidentiary hearing, as well as to subsequent judicial review, before the denial of his claim becomes final. ***

We conclude that an evidentiary hearing is not required prior to the termination of disability benefits and that the present administrative procedures fully comport with due process.

The judgment of the Court of Appeals is reversed.

Mr. Justice Brennan, with whom **Mr. Justice Marshall** concurs, dissenting.

. . . I agree with the District Court and the Court of Appeals that, prior to termination of benefits, Eldridge must be afforded an evidentiary hearing of the type required for welfare beneficiaries. *** I would add that the Court's consideration that a discontinuance of disability benefits may cause the recipient to suffer only a limited deprivation is no argument. It is speculative. Moreover, the very legislative determination to provide disability benefits, without any prerequisite determination of need in fact, presumes a need by the recipient which is not this Court's function to denigrate. Indeed, in the present case, it is indicated that because disability benefits were terminated there was a foreclosure upon the Eldridge home and the family's furniture was repossessed, forcing Eldridge, his wife and children to sleep in one bed. *** Finally, it is also no argument that a worker, who has been placed in the untenable position of having been denied disability benefits, may still seek other forms of public assistance.

Mr. Justice Stevens took no part in the consideration or decision of this case.

Marshall v. Barlow's, Inc.

436 U.S. 307; 98 S. Ct. 1816; 56 L. Ed. 2d 305 (1978)

Vote: 5-3

Mr. Justice White delivered the opinion of the Court.

Section 8(a) of the Occupational Safety and Health Act [OSHA] of 1970 empowers agents of the Secretary of Labor (Secretary) to search the work area of any employment facility within the Act's jurisdiction. The purpose of the search is to inspect for safety hazards and violations of OSHA regulations. No search warrant or other process is expressly required under the Act.

On the morning of September 11, 1975, an OSHA inspector entered the customer service area of Barlow's, Inc., an electrical and plumbing installation business located in Pocatello, Idaho. The president and general manager, Ferrol G. "Bill" Barlow, was on hand; and the OSHA inspector, after showing his credentials, informed Mr. Barlow that he wished to conduct a search of the working areas of the business. Mr. Barlow inquired whether any complaint had been received about his company. The inspector answered no, but that Barlow's, Inc., had simply turned up on the agency's selection process. The inspector again asked to enter the nonpublic area of the business; Mr. Barlow's response was to inquire whether the inspector had a search warrant. The inspector had none. Thereupon, Mr. Barlow refused the inspector admission to the employee area of his business. He said he was relying on his rights as guaranteed by the Fourth Amendment of the United States Constitution. . . .

The Secretary urges that warrantless inspections to enforce OSHA are reasonable within the meaning of the Fourth Amendment. Among other things, he relies on 8(a) of the Act, *** which authorizes inspection of business premises without a warrant and which the Secretary urges represents a congressional construction of the Fourth Amendment that the courts should not reject. Regrettably, we are unable to agree.

The Warrant Clause of the Fourth Amendment protects commercial buildings as well as private homes. To hold otherwise would belie the origin of that Amendment, and the American colonial experience. An important forerunner of the first 10 Amendments to the United States Constitution, the Virginia Bill of Rights, specifically opposed "general warrants, whereby an officer or messenger may be commanded to search suspected places without evidence of a fact committed." The general warrant was a recurring point of contention in the Colonies immediately preceding the Revolution. The particular offensiveness it engendered was acutely felt by the merchants and businessmen whose premises and products were inspected for compliance with the several parliamentary revenue measures that most irritated the colonists. "[T]he Fourth Amendment's commands grew in large measure out of the colonists' experience with the writs of assistance . . . [that] granted sweeping power to customs officials and other agents of the king to search at large for smuggled goods." *** Against this background, it is untenable that the ban on warrantless searches was not intended to shield places of business as well as of residence.

This Court has already held that warrantless searches are generally unreasonable, and that this rule applied to commercial premises as well as homes. In *Camara v. Municipal Court* [1967], *** we held:

[E]xcept in certain carefully defined classes of cases, a search of private property without proper consent is "unreasonable unless it has been authorized by a valid search warrant."

On the same day, we also ruled:

. . . [A] search of private houses is presumptively unreasonable if conducted without a warrant. The businessman, like the occupant of a residence, has a constitutional right to go about his business free from unreasonable official entries upon his private commercial property. The businessman, too, has that right placed in jeopardy if the decision to enter and inspect for violation of regulatory laws can be made and enforced by the inspector in the field without official authority evidenced by a warrant. *See v. Seattle* *** (1967).

These same cases also held that the Fourth Amendment prohibition against unreasonable searches protects against warrantless intrusions during civil as well as criminal investigations. The reason is found in the "basic purpose of this Amendment . . . [which] is to safeguard the privacy and security of individuals against arbitrary invasions by governmental officials." *** If the government intrudes on a person's property, the privacy interest suffers whether the government's motivation is to investigate violations of criminal law or breaches of other statutory or regulatory standards. It therefore appears that unless some recognized exception to the warrant requirement applies. *See v. Seattle* would require a warrant to conduct the inspection sought in this case.

The Secretary urges that an exception from the search warrant requirement has been recognized for "pervasively regulated" industries "long subject to close supervision and inspection." *Colonnade Catering Corp. v. United States* *** (1970); *Biswell v. United States* *** (1972). These cases are indeed exceptions, but they represent responses to relatively unique circumstances. Certain industries have such a history of government oversight that no reasonable expectation of privacy, *** could exist for a proprietor over the stock of such an enterprise. Liquor (Colonnade) and firearms (Biswell) are industries of this type; when an entrepreneur embarks upon such a business, he has voluntarily chosen to subject himself to a full arsenal of governmental regulations. . . .

The clear import of our cases is that the closely regulated industry of the type involved in *Colonnade* and *Biswell* is the exception. The Secretary would make it the rule. Invoking the Walsh-Healey Act of 1936, *** the Secretary attempts to support a conclusion that all businesses involved in interstate commerce have long been subjected to close supervision of employee safety and health conditions. But the degree of federal involvement in employee working circumstances has never been of the order of specificity and pervasiveness that OSHA mandates. It is quite unconvincing to argue that the imposition of minimum wages and maximum hours on employers who contracted with the Government under the Walsh-Healey Act prepared the entirety of American interstate commerce for regulation of working conditions to the minutest detail. Nor can any but the most fictional sense of voluntary consent to later searches be found in the single fact that one conducts a business affecting interstate commerce; under current practice and law, few businesses can be conducted without having some effect on interstate commerce.

The Secretary also attempts to derive support for a *Colonnade–Biswell*-type exception by drawing analogies from the field of labor law. In *Republic Aviation Corp. v. NLRB* *** (1945), this Court upheld the rights of employees to solicit for a union during nonworking time where efficiency was not compromised. By opening up his property to employees, the employer had yielded so much of his private property rights as to allow those employees to exercise rights under the National Labor Relations Act. But this Court also held that the private property rights of an owner prevailed over the intrusion of nonemployee organizers, even in nonworking areas of the plant and during nonworking hours. ***

The critical fact in this case is that entry over Mr. Barlow's objection is being sought by a Government agent. Employees are not being prohibited from reporting OSHA violations. What they observe in their daily functions is undoubtedly beyond the employer's reasonable expectation of privacy. The Government inspector, however, is not an employee. Without a warrant he stands in no better position than a member of the public. What is observable by the public is observable, without a warrant, by the Government inspection as well. The owner of a business has not, by the necessary utilization of employees in his operation, thrown open the areas where employees alone are permitted to the warrantless scrutiny of Government agents. That an employee is free to report, and the government is free to use, any evidence of noncompliance with OSHA that the employee observes furnishes no justification for federal agents to enter a place of business from which the public is restricted and to conduct their own warrantless search.

The Secretary nevertheless stoutly argues that the enforcement scheme of the Act requires warrantless searches, and that the restrictions on search discretion contained in the Act and its regulations already protect as much privacy as a warrant would. The Secretary thereby asserts the actual reasonableness of OSHA searches, whatever the general rule against warrantless searches might be. Because "reasonableness is still the ultimate standard," *** the Secretary suggests that the Court decide whether a warrant is needed by arriving at a sensible balance between the administrative necessities of OSHA inspections and the incremental protection of privacy of business owners a warrant would afford. He suggests that only a decision exempting OSHA inspections from the Warrant Clause would give "full recognition to the competing public and private interests here at stake." ***

The Secretary submits that warrantless inspections are essential to the proper enforcement of OSHA because they afford the opportunity to inspect without prior notice and hence to preserve the advantages of surprise. While the dangerous conditions outlawed by the Act include structural defects that cannot be quickly hidden or remedied, the Act also regulates a myriad of safety details that may be amenable to speedy alteration or disguise. The risk is that during the interval between an inspector's initial request to search a plant and his procuring a warrant following the owner's refusal of permission, violations of this latter type could be corrected and thus escape the inspector's notice. To the suggestion that warrants may be issued *ex parte* and executed without delay and without prior notice, thereby preserving the element of surprise, the Secretary expresses concern for the administrative strain that would be experienced by the inspection system, and by the courts, should *ex parte* warrants issued in advance become standard practice.

We are unconvinced, however, that requiring warrants to inspect will impose serious burdens on the inspection system or the courts, will prevent inspections necessary to enforce the statute, or will make them less effective. In the first place, the great majority of businessmen can be expected in normal course to consent to inspection without warrant; the Secretary has not brought to this Court's attention any widespread pattern of refusal. . . . Nor is it immediately apparent why the advantages of surprise would be lost if, after being refused entry, procedures were available for the Secretary to seek an *ex parte*

warrant and to reappear at the premises without further notice to the establishment being inspected.

Whether the Secretary proceeds to secure a warrant or other process, with or without prior notice, his entitlement to inspect will not depend on his demonstrating probable cause to believe that conditions in violation of OSHA exist on the premises. Probable cause in the criminal law sense is not required. For purposes of an administrative search such as this, probable cause justifying the issuance of a warrant may be based not only on specific evidence of an existing violation but also on a showing that "reasonable legislative or administrative standards for conducting an . . . inspection are satisfied with respect to a particular [establishment]." *** A warrant showing that a specific business has been chosen for an OSHA search on the basis of a general administrative plan for the enforcement of the Act derived from neutral sources such as, for example, dispersion of employees in various types of industries across a given area, and the desired frequency of searches in any of the lesser divisions of the area, would protect an employer's Fourth Amendment divisions of the area, would protect an employer's Fourth Amendment rights. . . .

Finally, the Secretary urges that requiring a warrant for OSHA inspectors will mean that, as a practical matter, warrantless-search provisions in other regulatory statutes are also constitutionally infirm. The reasonableness of a warrantless search, however, will depend upon the specific enforcement needs and privacy guarantees of each statute. Some of the statutes cited apply only to a single industry, where regulations might already be so pervasive that a *Colonnade-Biswell* exception to the warrant requirement could apply. Some statutes already envision resort to federal-court enforcement when entry is refused, employing specific language in some cases and general language in others. In short, we base today's opinion on the facts and law concerned with OSHA and do not retreat from a holding appropriate to that statute because of its real or imagined effect on other, different administrative schemes.

Nor do we agree that the incremental protections afforded the employer's privacy by a warrant are so marginal that they fail to justify the administrative burdens that may be entailed. The authority to make warrantless searches devolves almost unbridled discretion upon executive and administrative officers, particularly those in the field, as to when to search and whom to search. A warrant, by contrast, would provide assurances from a neutral officer that the inspection is reasonable under the Constitution, is authorized by statute, and is pursuant to an administrative plan containing specific neutral criteria. Also, a warrant would then and there advise the owner of the scope and objects of the search, beyond which limits the inspector is not expected to proceed. These are important functions for a warrant to perform, functions which underlie the Court's prior decisions that the Warrant Clause applied to inspections for compliance with regulatory statutes. *** We conclude that the concerns expressed by the Secretary do not suffice to justify warrantless inspections under OSHA or vitiate the general constitutional requirement that for a search to be reasonable a warrant must be obtained. . . .

Mr. Justice Brennan took no part in the consideration or decision of this case.

Mr. Justice Stevens, with whom *Mr. Justice Blackmun* and *Mr. Justice Rehnquist* join, dissenting.

Congress enacted the Occupational Safety and Health Act to safeguard employees against hazards in the work areas of business subject to the act. To ensure compliance, Congress authorized the Secretary of Labor to conduct routine, nonconsensual inspections. Today the Court holds that the Fourth Amendment prohibits such inspections without a warrant. The Court also holds that the constitutionally required warrant may be issued without any showing of probable cause. I disagree with both of these holdings.

The Fourth Amendment contains two separate Clauses, each flatly prohibiting a category of governmental conduct. The first Clause states that the right to be free from unreasonable searches "shall not be violated"; the second unequivocally prohibits the issuance of warrants except "upon probable cause." In this case the ultimate question is whether the category of warrantless searches authorized by the statute is "unreasonable" within the meaning of the first Clause.

In cases involving the investigation of criminal activity, the Court has held that the reasonableness of a search generally depends upon whether it was conducted pursuant to a valid warrant. *** There is, however, also a category of searches which are reasonable within the meaning of the first Clause even though the probable-cause requirement of the Warrant Clause cannot be satisfied. *** The regulatory inspection program challenged in this case, in judgment, falls within this category.

The warrant requirement is linked "textually . . . to the probable-cause concept" in the Warrant Clause. *** The routine OSHA inspections are, by definition, not based on cause to believe there is a violation on the premises to be inspected. Hence, if the inspections were measured against the requirements of the Warrant Clause, they would be automatically and unequivocally unreasonable.

Because of the acknowledged importance and reasonableness of routine inspections in the enforcement of federal regulatory statutes such as OSHA, the Court recognizes that requiring full compliance with the Warrant Clause would invalidate all such inspection programs. Yet, rather than simply analyzing such programs under the "Reasonableness" Clause of the Fourth Amendment, the Court holds the OSHA program invalid under the Warrant Clause and then avoids a blanket prohibition on all routine, regulatory inspections by relying on the notion that the "probable cause" requirement in the Warrant Clause may be relaxed whenever the Court believes that the governmental need to conduct a category of "search" outweighs the intrusion on interests protected by the Fourth Amendment.

The Court's approach disregards the plain language of the Warrant Clause and is unfaithful to the balance struck by the Framers of the Fourth Amendment—"the one procedural safeguard in the Constitution that grew directly out of the events which immediately preceded the revolutionary struggle with England."

Since the general warrant, not the warrantless search, was the immediate evil at which the Fourth Amendment was directed, it is not surprising that the Framers placed precise limits on its issuance. The requirement that a warrant only issue on a showing of particularized probable cause was the means adopted to circumscribe the warrant power. While the subsequent course of Fourth Amendment jurisprudence in this Court emphasizes the dangers posed by warrantless searches conducted without probable cause, it is the general reasonableness standard in the first Clause, not the Warrant Clause, that the Framers adopted to limit this category of searches. It is, of course, true that the existence of a valid warrant normally satisfied the reasonableness requirement under the Fourth Amendment. But we should not dilute the requirements of the Warrant Clause in an effort to force every kind of governmental intrusion which satisfied the Fourth Amendment definition of a "search" into a judicially developed, warrant-preference scheme.

Fidelity to the original understanding of the Fourth Amendment, therefore, leads to the conclusion that the Warrant Clause has no application to routine, regulatory inspections of commercial premises. If such inspections are valid, it is because they comport with the ultimate reasonableness standard of the Fourth Amendment. If the Court were correct in its view that such inspections, if undertaken without a warrant, are unreasonable in the constitutional sense, the issuance of a "new-fangled warrant"—to use Mr. Justice Clark's characteristically expressive term—without any true showing of particularized probable cause would not be sufficient to validate them. . . .

The case before us involves an attempt to conduct a warrantless search of the working area of an electrical and plumbing contractor. The statute authorizes such an inspection during reasonable hours. The inspection is limited to those areas over which Congress has exercised its proper legislative authority. The area is also one to which employees have regular access without any suggestion that the work performed or the equipment used has any special claim to confidentiality. Congress had determined that industrial safety is an urgent federal interest requiring regulation and supervision, and further, that warrantless inspections are necessary to accomplish the safety goals of the legislation. While one may question the wisdom of pervasive governmental oversight of industrial life, I decline to question Congress' judgment that the inspection power is a necessary enforcement device in achieving the goals of a valid exercise of regulatory power.

I respectfully dissent.

Dow Chemical Company v. United States
476 U.S. 227; 106 S. Ct. 1819; 90 L. Ed. 2d 226 (1986)
Vote: 5-4

In this case, the Supreme Court reviews a court of appeals decision upholding the Environmental Protection Agency's aerial observation of a chemical plant complex. The critical question is whether the EPA action constituted a search within the meaning of the Fourth Amendment.

Chief Justice Burger delivered the opinion of the Court.

. . . Petitioner Dow Chemical Co. operates a 2,000-acre facility manufacturing chemicals at Midland, Michigan. The facility consists of numerous covered buildings, with manufacturing equipment and piping conduits located between the various buildings exposed to visual observation from the air. At all times, Dow has maintained elaborate security around the perimeter of the complex barring ground-level public views of these areas. It also investigates any low-level flights by aircraft over the facility. Dow has not undertaken, however, to conceal all manufacturing equipment within the complex from aerial views. Dow maintains that the cost of covering its exposed equipment would be prohibitive.

In early 1978, enforcement officials of EPA, with Dow's consent, made an on-site inspection of two powerplants in this complex. A subsequent EPA request for a second inspection, however, was denied, and EPA did not thereafter seek an administrative search warrant. Instead, EPA employed a commercial aerial photographer, using a standard floor-mounted, precision aerial mapping camera, to take photographs of the facility from altitudes of 12,000, 3,000, and 1,200 feet. At all times the aircraft was lawfully within navigable airspace. ***

EPA did not inform Dow of this aerial photography, but when Dow became aware of it, Dow brought suit in the District Court alleging that EPA's action violated the Fourth Amendment and was beyond EPA's statutory investigative authority. The District Court granted Dow's motion for summary judgment on the grounds that EPA had no authority to take aerial photographs and that doing so was a search violating the Fourth Amendment. EPA was permanently enjoined from taking aerial photographs of Dow's premises and from disseminating, releasing, or copying the photographs already taken. ***

The District Court accepted the parties' concession that EPA's " 'quest for evidence' " was a "search," *** and limited its analysis to whether the search was unreasonable under *Katz v. United States* *** (1967). Proceeding on the assumption that a search in Fourth Amendment terms had been conducted, the court found that Dow manifested an expectation of privacy in its exposed plant areas because it intentionally surrounded them with buildings and other enclosures. ***

The District Court held that this expectation of privacy was reasonable, as reflected in part by trade secret protections restricting Dow's commercial competitors from aerial photography of these exposed areas. *** The court emphasized that use of "the finest precision aerial camera available" permitted EPA to capture on film "a great deal more than the human eye could ever see." ***

The Court of Appeals reversed. *** It recognized that Dow indeed had a subjective expectation of privacy in certain areas from ground-level intrusions, but the court was not persuaded that Dow had a subjective expectation of being free from aerial surveillance since Dow had taken no precautions against such observation, in contrast to its elaborate ground-level precautions. *** The court rejected the argument that it was not feasible to shield any of the critical parts of the exposed plant areas from aerial surveys. The Court of Appeals, however, did not explicitly reject the District Court's factual finding as to Dow's subjective expectations.

. . . Viewing Dow's facility to be more like the "open field" in *Oliver v. United States* *** (1984), than a home or an office, [the court of appeals] held that the common-law curtilage doctrine did not apply to a large industrial complex of closed buildings connected by pipes, conduits, and other exposed manufacturing equipment. The Court of Appeals looked to "the peculiarly strong concepts of intimacy, personal autonomy and privacy associated with the home" as the basis for the curtilage protection. The court did not view the use of sophisticated photographic equipment by EPA as controlling.

The Court of Appeals then held that EPA clearly acted within its statutory powers even absent express authorization for aerial surveillance, concluding that the delegation of general investigative authority to EPA, similar to that of other law enforcement agencies, was sufficient to support the use of aerial photography.

II

The photographs at issue in this case are essentially like those commonly used in mapmaking. Any person with an airplane and an aerial camera could readily duplicate them. In common with much else, the technology of photography has changed in this century. These developments have enhanced industrial processes, and indeed all areas of life; they have also enhanced law enforcement techniques. Whether they may be employed by competitors to penetrate trade secrets is not a question presented in this case. Governments do not generally seek to appropriate trade secrets of the private sector, and the right to be free of appropriation of trade secrets is protected by law.

Dow nevertheless relies heavily on its claim that trade secret laws protect it from any aerial photography of this industrial complex by its competitors, and that this protection is relevant to our analysis of such photography under the Fourth Amendment. That such photography might be barred by state law with regard to competitors, however, is irrelevant to the questions presented here. State tort law governing unfair competition does not define the limits of the Fourth Amendment. *** The Government is seeking these photographs in order to regulate, not to compete with, Dow. If the Government were to use the photographs to compete with Dow, Dow might have a Fifth Amendment "taking" claim. Indeed, Dow alleged such a claim in its complaint, but the District Court dismissed it without prejudice. But even trade secret laws would not bar all forms of photography of this industrial complex; rather, only photography with an intent to use any trade secrets revealed by the photographs may be proscribed. Hence, there is no prohibition of photographs taken by a casual passenger on an airliner, or those taken by a company producing maps for its mapmaking purposes.

Dow claims first that EPA has no authority to use aerial photography to implement its statutory authority for "site inspection" under 114 (a) of the Clean Air Act ***; second, Dow claims EPA's use of aerial photography was a "search" of an area that, notwithstanding the large size of the plant, was within an "industrial curtilage" rather than an "open field," and that it had a reasonable expectation of privacy from such photography protected by the Fourth Amendment.

III

Congress has vested in EPA certain investigatory and enforcement authority, without spelling out precisely how this authority was to be exercised in all the myriad circumstances that might arise in monitoring matters relating to clean air and water standards. When Congress invests an agency with enforcement and investigatory authority, it is not necessary to identify explicitly each and every technique that may be used in the course of executing the statutory mission. Aerial observation authority, for example, is not usually expressly extended to police for traffic control, but it could hardly be thought necessary for a legislative body to tell police that aerial observation could be employed for traffic control of a metropolitan area, or to expressly authorize police to send messages to ground highway patrols that a particular over-the-road truck was traveling in excess of 55 miles per hour. Common sense and ordinary human experience teach that traffic violators are apprehended by observation.

Regulatory or enforcement authority generally carries with it all the modes of inquiry and investigation traditionally employed or useful to execute the authority granted. Environmental standards such as clean air and clean water cannot be enforced only in libraries and laboratories, helpful as those institutions may be.

Under 114(a)(2), the Clean Air Act provides that "upon presentation of . . . credentials," EPA has a "right of entry to, upon, or through any premises." *** Dow argues this limited grant of authority to enter does not authorize any aerial observation. In particular, Dow argues that unannounced aerial observation deprives Dow of its right to be informed that an inspection will be made or has occurred, and its right to claim confidentiality of the information contained in the places to be photographed. . . . It is not claimed that EPA has disclosed any of the photographs outside the agency.

Section 114(a), however, appears to expand, not restrict, EPA's general powers to investigate. Nor is there any suggestion in the statute that the powers conferred by this section are intended to be exclusive. There is no claim that EPA is prohibited from taking photographs from a ground-level location accessible to the general public. EPA, as a regulatory and enforcement agency, needs no explicit statutory provision to employ methods of observation commonly available to the public at large: we hold that the use of aerial observation and photography is within EPA's statutory authority.

IV

We turn now to Dow's contention that taking aerial photographs constituted a search without a warrant, thereby violating Dow's rights. Under this contention, however, Dow concedes that a simple flyover with naked-eye observation, or the taking of a photograph from a nearby hillside overlooking such a facility, would give rise to no Fourth Amendment problem. . . .

Dow plainly has a reasonable, legitimate, and objective expectation of privacy within the interior of its covered buildings, and it is equally clear that expectation is one society is prepared to observe. . . . Moreover, it could hardly be expected that Dow would erect a huge cover over a 2,000-acre tract. In contending that its entire enclosed plant complex is an "industrial curtilage," Dow argues that its exposed manufacturing facilities are analogous to the curtilage surrounding a home because it has taken every possible step to bar access from ground level.

The Court of Appeals held that whatever the limits of an "industrial curtilage" barring ground-level intrusions into Dow's private areas, the open areas exposed here were more analogous to "open fields" than to a curtilage for purposes of aerial observation. In *Oliver,* the Court described the curtilage of a dwelling as "the area to which extends the intimate activity associated with the 'sanctity of a man's home and the privacies of life.' " The intimate activities associated with family privacy and the home and its curtilage simply do not reach the outdoor areas or spaces between structures and buildings of a manufacturing plant.

Admittedly, Dow's enclosed plant complex, like the area in *Oliver,* does not fall precisely with the "open fields" doctrine. The area at issue here can perhaps be seen as falling somewhere between "open fields" and curtilage, but lacking some of the critical characteristics of both. Dow's inner manufacturing areas are elaborately secured to ensure they are not open or exposed to the public from the ground. Any actual physical entry by EPA into any enclosed area would raise significantly different questions, because "the businessman, like the occupant of a residence, has a constitutional right to go about his business free from unreasonable official entries upon his private commercial property." The narrow issue raised by Dow's claim of search and seizure, however, concerns aerial observation of a 2,000-acre outdoor manufacturing facility without physical entry.

We pointed out in *Donovan v. Dewey* *** (1981), that the Government has "greater latitude to conduct warrantless inspections of commercial property" because "the expectation of privacy that the owner of commercial property enjoys in such property differs significantly from the sanctity accorded an individual's home." We emphasized that unlike a homeowner's interest in his dwelling, the interest of the owner of commercial property is not one in being free from

any inspections." And with regard to regulatory inspections, we have held that "[w]hat is observable by the public is observable without a warrant, by the Government inspector as well."

... Here, EPA was not employing some unique sensory device that, for example, could penetrate the walls of buildings and record conversations in Dow's plants, offices, or laboratories, but rather a conventional, albeit precise, commercial camera commonly used in mapmaking. The Government asserts it has not yet enlarged the photographs to any significant degree, but Dow points out that simple magnification permits identification of objects such as wires as small as ½-inch diameter.

It may well be, as the Government concedes, that surveillance of private property by using highly sophisticated surveillance equipment not generally available to the public, such as satellite technology, might be constitutionally proscribed absent a warrant. But the photographs here are not so revealing of intimate details as to raise constitutional concerns. Although they undoubtedly give EPA more detailed information than naked-eye views, they remain limited to an outline of the facility's buildings and equipment. The mere fact that human vision is enhanced somewhat, at least to the degree here, does not give rise to constitutional problems.

An electronic device to penetrate walls or windows so as to hear and record confidential discussions of chemical formulae or other trade secrets would raise very different and far more serious questions; other protections such as trade secret laws are available to protect commercial activities from private surveillance by competitors.

We conclude that the open areas of an industrial plant complex with numerous plant structures spread over an area of 2,000 acres are not analogous to the curtilage of a dwelling for purposes of aerial complex is more comparable to an open field and as such it is open to the view and observation of persons in aircraft lawfully in the public airspace immediately above or sufficiently near the area for the reach of cameras.

We hold that the taking of aerial photographs of an industrial plant complex from navigable airspace is not a search prohibited by the Fourth Amendment. . . .

Justice Powell, with whom *Justice Brennan, Justice Marshall,* and *Justice Blackmun join,* . . . dissenting in part.

The Fourth Amendment protects private citizens from arbitrary surveillance by their Government. For nearly 20 years, this Court has adhered to a standard that ensured that Fourth Amendment rights would retain their vitality as technology expanded the Government's capacity to commit unsuspected intrusions into private areas and activities. Today, in the context of administrative aerial photography of commercial premises, the Court retreats from that standard. It holds that the photography was not a Fourth Amendment "search" because it was not accompanied by a physical trespass and because the equipment used was not the most highly sophisticated form of technology available to the Government. Under this holding, the existence of an asserted privacy interest apparently will be decided solely by reference to the manner of surveillance used to intrude on that interest. Such an inquiry will not protect Fourth Amendment rights, but rather will permit their gradual decay as technology advances. . . .

I would reverse the decision of the Court of Appeals. EPA's aerial photography penetrated into a private commercial enclave, an area in which society has recognized that privacy interests legitimately may be claimed. The photographs captured highly confidential information that Dow had taken reasonable and objective steps to preserve as private. Since the Clean Air Act does not establish a defined and regular program of warrantless inspections, see *Marshall v. Barlow's, Inc.* *** (1978), EPA should have sought a warrant from a neutral judicial officer. The Court's holding that the warrantless photography does not constitute an unreasonable search within the meaning of the Fourth Amendment is based on the absence of any physical trespass—a theory disapproved in a line of cases beginning with the decision in *Katz v. United States.* *** These cases have provided a sensitive and reasonable means of preserving interests in privacy cherished by our society. The Court's decision today cannot be reconciled with our precedents or with the purpose of the Fourth Amendment.

CHAPTER EIGHT

THE DYNAMICS OF "OUR FEDERALISM"

The states . . . retain a significant measure of sovereign authority. They do so, however, only to the extent that the Constitution has not divested them of their original powers and transferred those powers to the Federal Government . . .

Justice Harry Blackmun,
Garcia v. San Antonio Metropolitan Transit Authority (1985), majority opinion

The problems of federalism in an integrated national economy are capable of more responsible resolution than holding that the States as States retain no status apart from that which Congress chooses to let them retain.

Justice Sandra Day O'Connor, dissenting in *Garcia*

Sandra Day O'Connor:
Associate Justice, 1981–

INTRODUCTION

In a **federal system,** power is divided between a central government and a set of regional governments. A **unitary system,** by contrast, vests all authority in the central government. In the American context, **federalism** refers to the division of power between the national government on the one hand and the state and local governments on the other.

Federalism is one of the two basic structural characteristics of the American constitutional system, the other being separation of powers among branches of the national government. Over the two centuries since the republic was founded, the relationship between the national government and the states has changed dramatically. Today, there is no question of the dominance of the national government in most areas of policy-making. Yet states remain viable actors in the political system and in recent years may have become even more important. Thus, as a constitutional principle, federalism retains great importance.

"Our Federalism," as Justice Hugo L. Black described it in *Younger v. Harris* (1971), represents

> a system in which there is sensitivity to the legitimate interests of both State and National Governments, and in which the National Government, anxious though it may be to vindicate and protect federal rights and federal interests, always endeavors to do so in ways that will not unduly interfere with the legitimate activities of the States.

As an applied principle of government, federalism requires an ongoing effort by legislators, chief executives, and judges to balance many competing interests and values: among them, individual liberty and public order, local diversity and the national interest, limited government and social justice. This chapter examines the constitutional basis and evolving meaning of "Our Federalism," giving special attention to the contribution of the U.S. Supreme Court in defining the relationships and marking the boundaries between national and state functions.

DEVELOPMENT OF THE FEDERAL SYSTEM

Students will recall that prior to the ratification of the Constitution of 1787, the United States was a confederation of sovereign states. Each state was vested with the necessary powers of government, limited only by the terms of state constitutions and the traditional common law rights and immunities of individuals. States had broad taxing and spending powers, of course, but they also issued their own currency and regulated the terms of their commercial relationships with other states and foreign countries. Moreover, the states possessed **police power,** the authority to make laws to protect the public safety, health, and welfare and even to foster the morality of their citizens.

There was never any real prospect that the Constitution of 1787 would provide for a unitary system. The states existed as autonomous political entities from the time of the American Revolution and were not about to surrender to the national government rights and powers to which they had become accustomed. Moreover, there was widespread fear of concentrating too much power in the national government. The smaller states, in particular, were concerned about how their interests would be protected under the new Constitution. The solution was twofold. First, all states would enjoy equal representation in the U.S. Senate. Second, the national government would be one of definite and limited powers. In addition, the Tenth Amendment, ratified in 1791, specifically recognized the **reserved powers** of the States:

> The powers not delegated to the United States by the Constitution, nor prohibited by it to the States, are reserved to the States respectively, or to the people.

National Supremacy versus States' Rights

Although the Supremacy Clause of Article VI recognized the primacy of national authority in areas of national activity, those areas were specifically enumerated, for the most part, with the implication (made explicit in the Tenth Amendment) that the states retained autonomy in other areas. The original Constitution, however, was ambiguous on the question of where ultimate sovereign power resided. Federalist Party leaders, including Alexander Hamilton, John Marshall, and John Adams, argued eloquently that the issue must be resolved in favor of the national government.

The Democratic-Republicans, most notably James Madison and Thomas Jefferson, argued on behalf of "states' rights." In proposing the Virginia and Kentucky Resolution of 1798, Jefferson went so far as to argue that the "sovereign and independent states" had the right to nullify acts of Congress that they deemed to be unconstitutional. This was the origin of the doctrines of **nullification** and **interposition,** later employed by New England states during the War of 1812 and by South Carolina in opposition to federal tariff legislation in 1832. These doctrines were most fully developed in the writings of the South Carolina statesman and political theorist John C. Calhoun. Theories of nullification and interposition later provided a rationale for the secession of eleven Southern states in 1860 and 1861. These states' rights doctrines even figured prominently in the desegregation battles of the 1950s and '60s.

Chisholm v. Georgia

The U.S. Supreme Court rendered its first major constitutional decision in 1793. The case, *Chisholm v. Georgia,* dealt specifically with the issue of state sovereignty. An essential aspect of sovereignty in the Anglo-American tradition has been **sovereign immunity,** the doctrine that the government may be sued only with its consent. As previously noted, Article III of the Constitution granted to federal courts jurisdiction over "controversies between a state and citizens of another state." In response to criticism from the Anti-Federalists, proponents of the Constitution argued that this provision did not authorize a private individual to sue a state without its consent.

Nevertheless, shortly after the Constitution was adopted, several such suits were filed in federal court. One of these cases, *Chisholm v. Georgia,* was an original action brought in the Supreme Court by two South Carolina citizens who, as executors of the estate of a British decedent, sought to recover property confiscated by the state of Georgia during the Revolution. Georgia refused to appear in the case but filed a strong protest denying the Court's jurisdiction. In addition, a resolution was introduced in the Georgia legislature asserting that federal judicial authority to entertain such suits "would effectually destroy the retained sovereignty of the states."

By a 4-to-1 majority, the Supreme Court rejected Georgia's argument, strongly endorsing the authority of the federal judiciary in relation to the states. This decision drew an intense reaction from states' rights advocates. The result was adoption of the Eleventh Amendment in 1798, in effect barring a citizen from suing a state government in a federal court without the state's consent. Specifically, the amendment provides that

> [t]he judicial power of the United States shall not be construed to extend to any suit in law or equity, commenced or prosecuted against one of the United States by citizens of another State, or by citizens or subjects of any foreign State.

While the ratification of the Eleventh Amendment was a major victory for states' rights forces, the Amendment has not proved to be an insurmountable barrier to the federal court review of state policies (see discussion of **judicial federalism** below).

The Marshall Court Establishes National Supremacy

Although *Chisholm v. Georgia* was overruled by the Eleventh Amendment, the Supreme Court continued to embrace a nationalist point of view. This was largely due to President John Adams's appointment of John Marshall, an ardent Federalist, to be chief justice in 1801. Chief Justice Marshall provided one of the most forceful statements of national supremacy in *M'Culloch v. Maryland* (1819), in which he and his colleagues broadly interpreted the Necessary and Proper Clause as conferring on Congress the implied power to establish a national bank (see Chapter 5). The Court not only expanded congressional powers but also struck a blow against states' rights by invalidating a Maryland law imposing a tax on the Baltimore branch of the bank. Invoking the Supremacy Clause of Article VI, John Marshall declared that

> the states have no power, by taxation or otherwise, to retard, impede, burden, or in any manner control the operations of the constitutional laws enacted by Congress to carry into execution the powers vested in the general government. This is, we think, the unavoidable consequence of that supremacy which the Constitution has declared.

Marshall developed his theory of national power in large part as a constitutional rationale for limiting the broad authority reserved to the states. His Court invalidated various state commercial and financial restrictions opposed by business interests, citing infringements on federal authority. But federal power was largely dormant during the Marshall era. Marshall did not anticipate a vigorous national regulatory policy, and in fact no such policy emerged until well into the twentieth century. Thus, Marshall's nationalism went hand in hand with the growth of private enterprise. By placing restrictions on state power in the name of abstract principles of national supremacy, the Marshall Court helped clear the way for early commercial and industrial expansion.

As this economic development proceeded, basic changes took place within the political environment. Jacksonian democracy, with its emphasis on broader political participation (at least by white males), swept away most of the property qualifications for voting that had existed when the Constitution was written. With this drive toward greater political equality, economic privilege also came under attack, primarily in state legislatures. Laws were passed providing for debtor relief and more extensive regulation of business. The Court moderated its earlier negative position as it reviewed more and more legislation of this kind. This developing trend was apparent even before Marshall's death in 1835. For example, over his solitary dissent, the Court upheld an Ohio law making bankruptcy procedures available to persons who assumed debts after its passage (*Ogden v. Saunders* [1827]). A similar law, applicable to all debtors regardless of whether their obligations were incurred before or after its passage, had been declared unconstitutional by the Marshall Court a few years earlier (*Sturges v. Crowninshield*, 1819). In 1829, Marshall joined his colleagues in upholding the authority of a state to drain disease-infested marshlands as a public health measure (*Willson v. Black-Bird Creek Marsh Company* [1829]). The dam constructed for this purpose interfered with commercial navigation. Nevertheless, the Court recognized that, as a basic aspect of the state's police power, the public health objective was controlling. This decision was a limited, but significant, victory for proponents of state regulation.

The Taney Court: Renewed Emphasis on States' Rights

During the time Marshall's successor, Roger B. Taney, served as chief justice (1836 to 1864), the police powers of the states continued to expand. In addition to protecting public health and safety, the police power was also used as a justification for safeguarding the morals and general welfare of the community (see, for example, *New York v. Miln* [1837]). Moreover, the Taney Court came to recognize state power to regulate certain aspects of interstate commerce, a power that the Federalists earlier had argued was the exclusive domain of the national government (see *Cooley v. Board of Wardens* [1852], discussed below).

Slavery and the Civil War

Despite the Supreme Court's attempts to harmonize federal and state power, a conflict was brewing that would forever change the character of American federalism. The source of the conflict was the "peculiar institution" of slavery, an institution so divisive that it had threatened to derail the Constitutional Convention of 1787. During the early and middle nineteenth century, the integrity of the Union was preserved by a series of fragile congressional compromises defining the extent of slavery in the states and federal territories.

By far the most significant decision of the Taney Court was *Dred Scott v. Sandford* (1857), in which the Court sharply limited the power of the federal government to regulate slavery in the territories (see Chapter 2). Sharp regional divisions, aggravated by the Court's defense of slavery, ultimately split the nation into two armed camps. Southern states, under the banner of states' rights, asserted the right to secede from the Union and ultimately backed this assertion with the use of force. The Union, under the leadership of President Abraham Lincoln, resolved to prevent secession by any means necessary. The resulting Civil War was by far the greatest bloodbath in American history. After the loss of more than 620,000 lives and the destruction of billions of dollars worth of property, it was settled once and for all that a state could not secede from the Union. The Civil War made it clear that when state and national governments collide in exercising legal authority, the former must be subordinate to the latter.

With its decision in *Texas v. White* (1869), handed down four years after Gen. Robert E. Lee's surrender at Appomattox, the Supreme Court added its constitutional endorsement to the new order by solemnly proclaiming that a state could not withdraw from the Union without violating the basic law. Perhaps the Court contributed a measure of legal authority to the military verdict of the Civil War, but in doing so (after the fact), it merely underscored the limits of judicial power to deal with questions that profoundly divide the American people.

The Civil War Amendments

The ratification of the Thirteenth, Fourteenth, and Fifteenth Amendments in 1865, 1868, and 1870, respectively, had a significant impact on federalism. These amendments were designed primarily to protect the civil rights of the former slaves. As a means to that end, the Civil War Amendments imposed prohibitions on the state governments and authorized Congress to pass legislation in support of these prohibitions. Beginning with passage of the Civil Rights Act of 1866, Congress has used its powers under the Civil War Amendments to enact far-ranging civil rights legislation, including the Civil Rights Act of 1964 and the Voting Rights Act of 1965. Moreover, in a long series of decisions beginning in 1897, the Supreme Court held that various provisions of the Bill of Rights are enforceable against the states under the Fourteenth Amendment. The creation and extension of the doctrine of incorporation eventually resulted in increased federal judicial supervision of state and local policies (for further discussion, see Chapter 9).

The Heyday of Dual Federalism: 1890–1937

The constitutional changes wrought by the Civil War did not impede the further growth of state police power. The rapid accumulation and concentration of corporate wealth, stimulated by the upheaval and dislocation of war, drew an even more active regulatory response from state legislatures during the 1860s and 1870s. Only with the rise of organized labor in the 1880s and the appearance of the Populist party in the 1890s did a marked change in the permissive view toward state regulatory power take place. Identifying with an economic establishment that saw the specter of socialism in these movements, the Supreme Court began to use the Due Process Clause of the Fourteenth Amendment and the Commerce Clause as justifications for restricting the police power of the states.

This tendency was but one aspect of a far larger trend of constitutional interpretation through which the Court set limits on regulatory power at all levels of government. Although it placed restrictions on state police power, the Court also imposed similar curbs on the emerging national police power by invoking the Tenth Amendment and the Due Process Clause of the Fifth Amendment, the latter provision applying directly to the national government. This development contributed to the growing influence of **dual federalism** after 1890. A good example of this perspective can be seen in *Hammer v. Dagenhart* (1918), in which the Supreme Court invoked the Tenth Amendment in striking down a federal law restricting the use of child labor in factories. Writing for the Court, Justice William R. Day characterized the statute as "an invasion by the federal power" into an area reserved to the states by the Tenth Amendment.

Proponents of the dual federalism perspective not only sought a balance between state and national power, but they also contemplated a kind of constitutional "twilight zone" into which neither the states nor the national government could intrude. Dual federalism reflected the Jeffersonian view that the best government is that which governs least. From 1890 to 1937, the Supreme Court was often receptive to this view and, as a consequence, struck down a great number of laws, both federal and state, that interfered with the operations of the free market.

The Constitutional Revolution of 1937

Dual federalism remained a major factor in American constitutional development until the beginning of the "constitutional revolution of 1937" (see Chapters 2 and 5). But it was by no means the only factor at work during the half-century preceding its eventual eclipse. Accelerated industrial growth and urbanization increased the impetus toward centralized governmental authority. As noted in Chapter 5, the Court sanctioned piecemeal extension of national power under the Commerce Clause, particularly to protect conventional morality, public health, and safety. Thus, even during the period before the New Deal, the growing number of problems demanding a national response threatened to upset the balance implicit in dual federalism.

Following its 1937 confrontation with President Franklin D. Roosevelt, the Court began to sanction the exercise of national regulatory power and social welfare programs of broad scope. The Fourteenth Amendment was no longer interpreted as a restriction on state regulatory power, and the Tenth Amendment virtually disappeared as a limitation on national authority. Dual federalism eventually gave way to **cooperative federalism,** a system of shared powers that has become an essential feature of American government and politics since the late 1930s. Supreme Court decisions upholding the Social Security Act of 1935 (*Helvering v. Davis* [1937] and *Chas. C. Steward Machine Company v. Davis* [1937]) and the Fair Labor Standards Act of 1938 (*United States v. Darby* [1941]) represented this trend.

Cooperative federalism was a prominent feature of the Social Security Act. The dissenting justices in *Chas. C. Steward Machine* contended that the tax credits allowed to employers who contributed to state unemployment funds had the effect of forcing the states to participate in the social security program and that such coercion violated the Tenth Amendment. The argument did not prevail, and with the passage of time, it became apparent that cooperative arrangements between nation and state would proliferate. The traditional model of two distinct spheres of government, characteristic of dual federalism, gave way to what has been aptly described as "marble cake" federalism, due to the blending of national and state functions and responsibilities.

The Short-Lived Resurrection of the Tenth Amendment

As previously noted, the Tenth Amendment virtually disappeared as a limitation on the powers of the national government in the wake of the constitutional revolution of 1937. Yet in 1976, the Tenth Amendment was resurrected in a 5-to-4 decision by the Supreme Court. In *National League of Cities v. Usery*, the Court struck down a 1974 amendment to the Fair Labor Standards Act that extended the federal minimum wage to state and local government employees. Writing for the Court, Justice William Rehnquist opined that the Tenth Amendment prohibits Congress from infringing "traditional aspects of state sovereignty." In a stinging dissent, Justice William Brennan accused the majority of an irresponsible departure from modern principles of constitutional law. Brennan's dissent was vindicated in 1985, when a sharply divided Supreme Court overruled *National League of Cities* (*Garcia v. San Antonio Metropolitan Transit Authority* [1985]). With the *Garcia* decision, many assumed that the revitalization of the Tenth Amendment had ended. Others, however, predicted that the Court had not spoken its final word on this subject.

Since *Garcia*, the Supreme Court has further weakened and narrowed the Tenth Amendment's restrictions on national power. In *South Carolina v. Baker* (1988), in upholding a federal tax on interest from unregistered state and local bonds, the Court concluded that protections afforded by the Tenth Amendment are "structural, not substantive." Writing for the majority, Justice Brennan explained that the states "must find their protection from congressional regulation through the national political process, not through judicially defined spheres of unregulated state activity." Brennan found that "nothing in *Garcia* or the Tenth Amendment authorizes courts to second-guess the substantive basis for congressional legislation."

It is true that the Court in *Garcia* recognized the importance of the national political process in protecting the autonomy of the states. Still, the *Garcia* majority examined the question of whether the political process offered sufficient protection to state interests threatened by the minimum wage legislation at issue in that case. In *South Carolina v. Baker,* on the other hand, the Court made no such inquiry. South Carolina did not allege that it was barred from participation in the political process or that "it was singled out in a way that left it politically isolated and powerless." As the majority viewed the case, this purely procedural question was the only relevant Tenth Amendment concern. As thus interpreted, the Tenth Amendment offers no protection to the states other than their right to take part in national politics. The Supreme Court evidently assumes, rightly or wrongly, that such participation alone is a sufficient means of protecting state interests.

CHARACTERISTICS OF THE CONTEMPORARY FEDERAL SYSTEM

Taking into account both the constitutional basis and the political dimensions of American federalism, it is possible to identify the characteristics most funda-mental to this system of government. One characteristic is the continuing divi-sion of legal authority between two levels of government, national and state. Each level has an independent mechanism of government through which it enacts, interprets, and administers law. Considerable overlapping occurs, of course, but the structure of two legally distinct spheres of government, each with its own constitution, legislature, chief executive, judiciary, and administrative bureaucracy remains intact.

A second characteristic of the American federal system is that the two levels of government exercise direct authority simultaneously over persons within their jurisdictions. Dual citizenship is a fundamental part of the system, and many rights, privileges, and immunities derive from both national and state citizenship. A third characteristic is the subordination of state to national au-thority in such fields as taxation and the regulation of interstate commerce where both levels of government exercise concurrent legal power. Fourth is a growing area of shared activity in which the national government and the states jointly undertake programs in education, highway construction, public health, social security, unemployment compensation, and environmental protection, among others.

A fifth characteristic is the recognized authority of one tribunal, the U.S. Supreme Court, to mark the boundaries and allocate constitutional power be-tween the national government and the states. The fact that the federal Consti-tution is the supreme law of the land does not mean that claims of national power will always prevail over counterclaims by the states. In adjusting these competing claims, the Supreme Court performs one of its most important tra-ditional functions. Because its decisions in this area have come to be accepted with finality, subject only to reversal by constitutional amendment, the Court serves as the "umpire of the federal system."

National Preemption of State Law

In a long line of decisions, the Supreme Court has held that national law pre-empts, that is, supersedes, state law if considerations of national policy warrant it, so long as those considerations are consistent either with enumerated powers or broader national interests. (For an interesting but somewhat dated example of federal **preemption,** see *Pennsylvania v. Nelson* [1956], where the Court struck down a state law criminalizing sedition against the national government.)

As the Court made clear in the *Nelson* case, a state law may be struck down, even where there is no explicit conflict with federal law, if the Court finds that Congress has legitimately occupied the field. Questions in this area call for careful balancing of important state and national interests. Problems arise when Congress fails to make its purpose explicit—which is often the case. The Court must then draw inferences based on the presumed objectives of federal law and the supposed impact of related state action.

For example, in *Burbank v. Lockheed Air Terminal* (1973), the Supreme Court held that a local aircraft noise abatement ordinance was preempted by the federal Noise Control Act of 1972, even though the latter contained no specific preemptive language and there was no evidence that the ordinance placed a heavy burden on interstate commerce. Relying on the Supremacy Clause, Justice Douglas emphasized the potential safety hazard that could result if a "significant number of municipalities" adopted similar ordinances. The Noise Control Act established a "comprehensive scheme" of aircraft noise regulation, including a role for the Environmental Protection Agency. In the Court's opinion, it was the "pervasive nature" of this federal regulatory pattern that preempted the Burbank ordinance. The four dissenting justices cited considerations of federalism in support of their view that the ordinance should be upheld. They maintained that the "basic constitutional division of legislative competence between the states and Congress" was consistent with democratic values and that this principle should be followed. The dissenters preferred to view the ordinance as a routine exercise of the police power and thought the inquiry should be confined to the facts of the case, unaffected by speculation about the possible effect of such an ordinance if adopted by other cities.

More recently, in *California v. Federal Energy Regulatory Commission* (*FERC*) (1990), the Supreme Court held that state regulations imposing minimum flow rates on rivers used to generate hydroelectric power were preempted by the Federal Power Act. In another case involving the FERC, *Nantahala Power and Light Company v. Thornburg* (1986), the Court invoked the preemption doctrine to prohibit states from deviating from federal standards in setting intrastate rates for the sale of electrical power. Likewise, in *Mississippi Power and Light Company v. Mississippi ex rel. Moore* (1988), the Court held that FERC regulations preempted a state's authority to set rates in the area of electrical power.

The field of energy policy has tended to be one in which the Court has taken a strongly nationalistic posture. Nevertheless, in the controversial area of nuclear power, two significant preemption decisions of the 1980s were resolved in favor of the states. In *Pacific Gas and Electric Company v. State Energy Resources Conservation and Development Commission* (1983), the Supreme Court upheld a California statute imposing a moratorium on the certification of nuclear power plants, pending state approval of an effective method of nuclear waste disposal. The Court found that the state moratorium was not preempted by the Atomic Energy Act of 1954. In his majority opinion, Justice White noted that the federal Nuclear Regulatory Commission (NRC) has "exclusive jurisdiction to license the transfer, delivery receipt, acquisition, possession, and use of nuclear materials." But the NRC does not have authority over "the generation of electricity itself, or

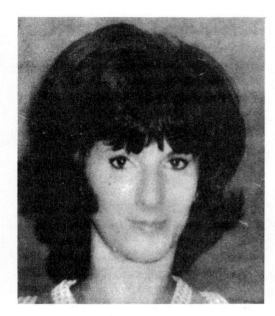

Karen Silkwood

over the economic question whether a particular plant should be built...."
Finding it "inconceivable that Congress would have left a regulatory vacuum,"
White inferred that Congress intended for the states to exercise economic judg-
ments, including assessment of nuclear waste disposal methods.

A year later, in the highly publicized Karen Silkwood case (*Silkwood v.
Kerr-McGee Corporation* [1984]), the Supreme Court upheld a state law that
permitted punitive damages in a lawsuit stemming from an incident in which a
nuclear power worker was exposed to a lethal dose of radiation. The Court
reaffirmed its earlier holding that state efforts to regulate the safety of nuclear
power were preempted by federal law but held that the punitive damages rule
at issue was primarily economic in character. The *Pacific Gas and Electric* and
Silkwood cases allow the states more regulatory leeway in a controversial field
traditionally dominated by the federal government. It is reasonable to suppose
that increased public concern over the safety of nuclear power and skepticism
about the federal government's ability to ensure nuclear safety had some impact
on the Court's willingness to accommodate increased regulatory activity at the
state level.

Judicial Federalism

Another distinctive aspect of American federalism is the relationship between
the federal and state court systems. As noted in Chapter 1, every state maintains
its own system of trial and appellate courts responsible for adjudicating issues
of state law. The decision of the highest state court with respect to matters of
state law, including interpretation of the state constitution, is final and, accordingly, unreviewable by the federal courts. Ultimately, a complete understanding

of American constitutional law must take into account the myriad state court decisions involving matters of state, as opposed to federal, constitutional interpretation.

Of course, in matters of federal constitutional law, the U.S. Supreme Court speaks with finality. This principle was firmly established by two significant decisions of the Marshall era (see *Martin v. Hunter's Lessee* [1816] and *Cohens v. Virginia* [1821], both of which are discussed in Chapter 2). In *Cohens v. Virginia,* the Supreme Court held that its constitutional jurisdiction extended to state criminal cases in which a federal question was involved. According to Chief Justice Marshall,

> The American people may certainly give to a national tribunal a supervising power over those judgments of the state courts, which may conflict with the Constitution, laws or treaties, of the United States, without converting them into federal courts, or converting the national into a state tribunal.

A notable development in the history of judicial federalism was the adoption of the Fourteenth Amendment, with its broad restrictions on state power. The Fourteenth Amendment has been interpreted to extend most of the prohibitions of the Bill of Rights to actions of state and local governments (for an extensive discussion of the "incorporation" doctrine, see Chapter 9). The application of the Bill of Rights to the states allows for increased federal judicial supervision of state courts, especially in cases dealing with the rights of the criminally accused (see Chapter 14). Nevertheless, state courts and laws are normally afforded considerable deference by federal courts in areas of the law not affected by provisions of the federal Constitution.

The federal Constitution establishes a minimum level of protection for individual rights to which states must adhere. State courts are free, however, to interpret their respective state constitutions to provide higher levels of protection to individuals within their jurisdictions. For example, the constitutions of several states (e.g. Alaska and Florida) contain provisions explicitly protecting individual privacy. State court decisions interpreting these provisions typically provide a greater degree of protection for individual privacy than is afforded by the federal courts under the implicit guarantee of privacy in the federal Constitution (see Chapter 15). According to the traditional philosophy of judicial restraint, federal courts should not overrule state court decisions recognizing broader individual rights than those afforded by the federal Constitution as long as such decisions are based on **independent state grounds.**

The Eleventh Amendment

A direct response to the Supreme Court's decision in *Chisholm v. Georgia* (discussed above), the Eleventh Amendment bars citizens of one state from suing governments of other states in federal court. Although the Eleventh Amendment does not expressly forbid suits by citizens against their own states, the Supreme Court, emphasizing the historical background out of which the amendment emerged, extended this constitutional restriction to bar such actions (*Hans v. Louisiana* [1890]). However, the immunity granted to the states by the Eleventh Amendment does not extend to local governments. For instance, a person subjected to unwarranted police brutality may sue a city government to recover monetary damages (see, for example, *Los Angeles v. Lyons* [1983]). Nor does the Eleventh Amendment bar suits against state and local officials. By way of example, in *Roe v. Wade* (1973), a woman seeking to challenge Texas's strict antiabortion statute brought suit against the Dallas County district attorney, seeking an injunction to prevent him from enforcing the law. Since one can usually bring suit against one or more state officials, the Eleventh Amendment does not pose an insurmountable barrier to an aggrieved party's effort to obtain relief against a state government by way of a federal lawsuit.

STATE POWER TO REGULATE COMMERCE

In the first two major sections of this chapter, we have surveyed the historical development and contemporary characteristics of American federalism. We turn now to a more detailed examination of the interplay between state and national power in a major area of policy-making: the regulation of commerce.

As described in Chapter 5, the power of Congress to regulate commerce "among the states" is vast but far from exclusive. The constitutional language granting this power is general and open-ended. One of the Supreme Court's most important responsibilities has been to decide how this general language relates to the exercise of state power in an endless variety of regulatory settings. No definitive rulings fixing the limits of state authority or drawing a precise line of demarcation between national and state power have emerged. The process of constitutional interpretation is heavily influenced by changes in the perceived needs and interests of society. Nowhere is this influence better illustrated than in the regulation of commerce. Cases in this area also vividly illustrate the Court's important function in policing the boundaries of our federal system.

The Commerce Clause as drafted in 1787 represented an attempt to address problems faced by a growing national economy saddled with commercial rivalries among largely independent states. But this affirmative grant of authority to Congress was not accompanied by an explicit negation of state power. Although it forbids the states to tax imports and exports (unless specifically authorized by Congress), the Constitution is silent on the nature and extent of state power to regulate commerce. We know that some of the Framers of the Constitution assumed that the commerce power was indivisible—that is, an exclusive grant of power to the national government. But experience coupled with the logical *and* political implications of federalism soon made it clear that this inflexible position was unworkable. Nevertheless, the Commerce Clause placed substantial implied limits on state power. Over the years, those limits have been defined and redefined, not only by the Supreme Court but also by Congress.

Gibbons v. Ogden

The first major decision of the Supreme Court involving state-versus-federal regulation of commerce was *Gibbons v. Ogden* (1824). The *Gibbons* case resulted from an attempt by the state of New York to create and protect a monopoly issued to a private steamboat company. A competing company, operating under a federal license, was enjoined by a New York court from operating on waters within the borders of New York state (for an extensive discussion of *Gibbons,* see Chapter 5). The Supreme Court held that: (1) the licensure of steamboats by the federal government was a valid exercise of the national power to regulate interstate commerce and (2) the attempt by New York to enforce a steamboat monopoly within its waters was a violation of the Supremacy Clause.

In terms of federalism, the thrust of *Gibbons v. Ogden* was that states could not impede the efforts of Congress to regulate commerce among the states. But the Court stopped short of holding that states had no power whatsoever to regulate interstate commerce. Suppose Congress has not acted on a matter covered by state commercial legislation. Or suppose state law merely complements existing national policy. Under such circumstances, are the states free to act, even if their actions have an impact on interstate commerce? The *Gibbons* decision left these questions unanswered.

The *Cooley* Case

It was not until 1852 that the Supreme Court made a serious effort to resolve the issue of state power to regulate interstate commerce. Before that time, the Court had upheld various state laws directly or indirectly affecting interstate commerce, ruling that they were appropriate exercises of the police power. But the concept of interstate commerce was too all-embracing and the demand for state regulatory activity too strong for the Court to avoid the issue indefinitely. Ultimately, it reached the Taney Court in *Cooley v. Board of Wardens* (1852). Justice Benjamin R. Curtis wrote the opinion of the Court, recognizing that the Commerce Clause did not automatically bar all state regulation in this field. At issue was the constitutionality of a Pennsylvania law requiring ships entering or leaving the port of Philadelphia to hire local harbor pilots. This was admittedly a regulation of both interstate and foreign commerce. Nevertheless, it was upheld because it dealt with a "subject" of commerce "imperatively demanding that diversity, which alone can meet the local necessities of navigation." Curtis reasoned that the term *commerce* covered a multitude of subjects, some requiring national uniformity in their regulation, others calling for the diversity of local control. Because the Constitution did not explicitly prohibit the states from regulating, and because Congress in 1789 had purported to authorize state regulation of pilots, he concluded that the law in question was valid. This distinction between local and national aspects of interstate commerce, although far from clear-cut, was a significant contribution to constitutional interpretation. While its application in *Cooley* was expressly limited to the facts of that case, the principle applied soon achieved the status of constitutional doctrine.

The Supreme Court's attempt to strike a balance between the values of local diversity and national uniformity has been apparent in hundreds of decisions rendered since *Cooley*. The justices have developed more sophisticated terminology than the "local-national" dichotomy used by Justice Curtis. But his perception of the complex problem of promoting commerce in a federal system remains important to this day.

Benjamin R. Curtis: Associate
Justice, 1851–1857

State Regulation of Interstate Commerce:
Divergent Perspectives

Except for the Court's general inclination to take a more critical view of economic regulation between the late 1880s and late 1930s, no consistent historical pattern has emerged in this field since the *Cooley* case. From time to time, the Court has attempted to classify state regulations with respect to their "direct" or "indirect" effect on interstate commerce or the degree to which they "burden" or "discriminate against" it. The "direct-or-indirect" test has not been in vogue since the late 1930s; but even when it was used, the Court seemed more concerned about the basic distinction between commercial regulations *per se* and police power legislation aimed at protecting the health, safety, and general welfare of the community. The Court has become less concerned than was Justice Curtis with the *subject* of commerce being regulated and more concerned with the *means* by which the regulation is implemented.

This approach has produced results in different cases that are difficult to reconcile. For instance, in *South Carolina Highway Department v. Barnwell Bros.* (1938), the Supreme Court sustained a South Carolina statute prescribing maximum weights and widths of trucks using the highways of the state. This measure imposed a substantial burden on interstate commerce, but the Court, through Justice Stone, reasoned that the countervailing safety considerations were more important. Stone pointed to the extensive control states had traditionally exerted over their public roads. He also pointed out that the highway regulation fell with equal weight on intrastate and interstate truckers—that it did not, in other words, single out businesses engaged in interstate commerce and impose added burdens on them to the advantage of intrastate economic interests. Still, the decision depended heavily on a view of state autonomy in building, maintaining, and controlling highways that was debatable even in 1938 and is open to far more serious challenge now that a nationally subsidized interstate highway system is well-established.

In sharp contrast to its decision in *Barnwell*, the Court in *Southern Pacific Railroad Company v. Arizona* (1945), invalidated a law limiting the lengths of passenger and freight trains traveling through the state to fourteen and seventy cars, respectively. The regulation imposed a substantial burden on interstate commerce, but Arizona defended it as an appropriate safety measure and pointed to the absence of conflicting federal legislation on the subject. The Supreme Court, in a sharply divided decision, declared the law unconstitutional. Harlan F. Stone, who had been elevated to chief justice in 1941, again wrote the majority opinion. He concluded that "as a safety measure" the law afforded "slight and dubious advantage, if any, over unregulated train lengths." Accordingly, the "serious burden" imposed on interstate commerce was not justified. On the other hand, before this decision was rendered, the Court had upheld a number of railroad safety measures adopted by the states, including Arkansas's "full crew" laws. These regulations fixed the minimum number of employees required to serve on trains traveling designated distances within the state. The statutes were again sustained more than twenty years after the *Southern Pacific* decision, even though they were no longer relevant to the issue of safety. As enacted in 1903 and 1907, they included the requirement of firemen on each train. By 1966, coal-burning steam engines had been replaced by diesel power, and the continued requirement of a fireman was justified, if at all, only as a means of providing local employment. Nevertheless, the Court, in an opinion by Justice Black, who had dissented in the *Southern Pacific* case, was willing to defer to state policy. Even if the laws were no longer justifiable as safety measures, Black maintained that it was up to the legislature, not the Court, to change them (*Brotherhood of Locomotive Engineers v. Chicago, Rock Island & Pacific Railroad Company* [1966]).

Cases Involving the Trucking Industry

Although the Supreme Court has continued to express deference toward state efforts to promote highway safety, it has from time to time invalidated statutes in this area when the "burden" on interstate commerce appears to outweigh the safety benefits of the regulation. Thus, in *Bibb v. Navajo Freight Lines* (1959), the Court struck down as a burden on interstate commerce an Illinois law requiring the use of contoured mudguards on trucks traversing the state's highways. A more recent example is *Kassel v. Consolidated Freightways Corporation* (1981), in which the Court struck down, as a violation of the Commerce Clause, an Iowa statute prohibiting the use of sixty-five-foot-long double-trailer trucks on its highways. The justices, however, could not agree on a rationale for their decision. A plurality of four (Powell, White, Blackmun, and Stevens) expressed the view that the Iowa statute imposed an unreasonable burden on interstate commerce, given the absence of "any significant countervailing safety interest." In a concurring opinion, Justice Brennan, joined by Justice Marshall, maintained that the Iowa legislation was protectionist in nature. He found that the primary intent underlying the statute was not to promote safety but "to discourage interstate truck traffic on Iowa's highways." Justice Rehnquist, in a dissenting opinion supported by Chief Justice Burger and Justice Stewart, took issue with Brennan's view, arguing that the statute was without doubt "a valid highway safety regulation and thus entitled to the strongest presumption of validity against Commerce Clause challenges." He maintained that Iowa's regulation of truck lengths was rational and that the safety benefits were more than slight. The "true problem" with this decision, as Rehnquist viewed it, was that the plurality and concurring opinions gave the states "no guidance whatsoever . . . as to whether their laws are valid or how to defend them."

The Nation as an Economic Unit

Any state regulation of interstate commerce aimed squarely at promoting local business interests by curtailing competition from out-of-state firms is unlikely to survive a constitutional challenge that reaches the Supreme Court. Those who drafted the Commerce Clause recognized the importance of promoting a national economy, and successive generations of Supreme Court justices have not lost sight of that objective. The 1949 decision in *H.P. Hood and Sons v. Du Mond* provides a good illustration of this point. Here, the Supreme Court invalidated a New York administrative decision denying Hood and Sons, a Massachusetts corporation, permission to increase from three to four the number of milk processing plants it operated in New York. Writing for the majority, Justice Robert Jackson viewed this limitation on Hood's source of supply as a form of economic isolationism that the state was not free to impose. It made no difference in principle that New York placed a ceiling, rather than an absolute ban, on Hood's activities within the state. "Our system, fostered by the Commerce Clause," Jackson asserted, "is that every farmer and every craftsman shall be encouraged to produce by the certainty that he will have free access to every market in the nation." Here, as in the *Southern Pacific* case, the absence of national legislation on the matter at issue was not the controlling factor. The state had acted simply to protect local interests, and that action, the Court found, was inconsistent with the negative implications of the Commerce Clause.

The Supreme Court has been equally skeptical of state regulations that pressure out-of-state businesses into moving the center of their operations to the regulating state. Even when such coercive measures are defended as legitimate health laws, the Court is not easily persuaded. In *Dean Milk Company v. Madison* (1951), for instance, the Court struck down a purported local health ordinance prohibiting the sale of milk if it came from a farm more than twenty-five miles from Madison, Wisconsin, or was bottled more than five miles away from the central square of the city. Clearly this measure discriminated against interstate commerce, something the Court was unwilling to condone, even for health purposes, if "reasonable, nondiscriminatory alternatives, adequate to conserve legitimate local interests" were available. In this instance, the Court believed such alternatives could be found.

In 1976, the Court invalidated a Mississippi regulation under which the board of health prohibited the sale of milk from another state unless Mississippi milk could be marketed there. The mandatory nature of this reciprocity was held to be an undue burden on interstate commerce and was not justified either as a health measure or as a provision promoting free trade among the states (*Great Atlantic and Pacific Tea Company v. Cottrell* [1976]).

In the 1978 case of *Philadelphia v. New Jersey,* the Supreme Court invalidated a state law prohibiting the importation of most solid and liquid waste materials from other states. Brushing aside the alleged environmental dangers posed by overuse of New Jersey's limited landfill space, the Court, through Justice Stewart, concluded that however justifiable the objectives of the law might be, the method employed to achieve them could not discriminate against articles of interstate commerce (in this instance, garbage) "unless there is some reason, apart from their origin, to treat them differently." The Court saw this attempt to bar out-of-state access to New Jersey's privately owned landfill sites, while leaving them open to in-state users, as simply another example of "parochial legislation" tending to promote state economic protectionism at the expense of national interests. The problem of preserving adequate landfill space was by no means unique to New Jersey. And yet, in the Court's view, the state was attempting through this legislation "to isolate itself from a problem common to many by erecting a barrier against the movement of interstate trade." (*Philadelphia v. New Jersey* was reaffirmed by the Supreme Court in 1992. See *Chemical Waste Management, Inc. v. Hunt,* reprinted in Appendix E.)

Regulation of Alcoholic Beverages

In 1984, the Court, by a 5-to-3 margin (Justice Brennan did not participate) invalidated a provision of the Hawaii liquor tax exempting certain locally produced alcoholic beverages (*Bacchus Imports, Ltd. v. Dias*). Writing for the majority, Justice White reasoned that although "a State may enact laws pursuant to its police powers that have the purpose and effect of encouraging domestic industry, ... [the] Commerce Clause stands as a limitation on the means by which a state can constitutionally seek to achieve that goal." He found it "irrelevant to the Commerce Clause inquiry that the motivation of the legislature was the desire to aid the makers of the locally produced beverage rather than to harm out-of-state producers." The exemption at issue violated the Commerce Clause "because it had both the purpose and effect of discriminating in favor of local products." The Court rejected a challenge to the tax exemption based on Section 2 of the Twenty-first Amendment, recognizing the power of the states to regulate the importation and sale of "intoxicating liquors" within their borders. (The Twenty-first Amendment repealed the Eighteenth Amendment, which prohibited the "manufacture, sale or transportation of intoxicating liquors" within the United States.)

In dissent, Justice Stevens, joined by Justices Rehnquist and O'Connor, maintained that the Commerce Clause argument was "squarely foreclosed by the Twenty-First Amendment." Stevens asserted that since adoption of this Amendment in 1933, the Court had "consistently reaffirmed" the view that the states may regulate commerce in intoxicating liquors "unconfined by ordinary limitations imposed ... by the Commerce Clause and other constitutional provisions."

The Supreme Court followed a line of reasoning similar to that of *Bacchus* in striking down state laws designed to keep local liquor and beer prices in line with prices charged in neighboring states. In *Healy v. Beer Institute* (1989), for example, the Court invalidated Connecticut's "beer price affirmation" statute as a violation of the Commerce Clause. This act required brewers and importers of beer to post monthly prices for each brand of beer they intended to sell in Connecticut and to affirm that these prices were no higher than prices in bordering states at the time of posting. Writing for the Court, Justice Blackmun found that this law had the effect of controlling commercial activity entirely outside Connecticut. He maintained that "the practical effect of this affirmation law, in conjunction with the many other beer pricing and affirmation laws that have been or might be enacted throughout the country, is to create just the kind of competing and interlocking local economic regulation that the Commerce Clause was meant to preclude." As in previous cases, the Court rejected the argument that because this regulation involved alcoholic beverages, it was justified under the Twenty-first Amendment. (For further discussion of this issue, see *Brown-Forman Distillers Corp. v. New York State Liquor Authority* [1986]).

State Attempts to Protect Their Natural Resources

The Supreme Court is unlikely even to permit a state to conserve its privately controlled natural resources if the conservation effort affords preferential treatment to local consumers. In a 1923 decision, for example, the Court invalidated a West Virginia law requiring local natural gas producers to give priority to the orders of in-state, as opposed to out-of-state, customers (*Pennsylvania v. West Virginia*). Of course, a state can assume ownership and direct control of its natural resources without violating the Commerce Clause. But if a state seeks to regulate privately owned businesses, even those engaged in the sale of scarce natural resources, the federal courts are almost certain to condemn the policy if it results in local favoritism.

For a long time, the Supreme Court recognized an exception to this general restriction by permitting the states to exercise broad control over interstate shipment of wild animals and fish for commercial sale. But in *Hughes v. Oklahoma* (1979), this exception was abolished. Here, the Court struck down a statute providing that minnows other than those produced in licensed hatcheries could not be sold outside Oklahoma. The law was presumably designed to protect the state's "natural" minnow population, but the Court rejected this rationale. Writing for the majority, Justice Brennan concluded that "challenges under the Commerce Clause to state regulations of wild animals should be considered according to the same general rule applied to state regulations of other natural resources." The *Hughes* decision requires courts to scrutinize state laws restricting the importation and exportation of animals and fish. It does not, however, create an insurmountable obstacle to such legislation. For example, in *Maine v. Taylor* (1986), the Supreme Court upheld a state law prohibiting the importation of live bait fish. The Court accepted Maine's argument that the restriction was necessary to protect the state's valuable fisheries from parasites and nonnative species of fish.

The "Market Participant" Exception

Despite its critical view of state economic protectionism, the Supreme Court has upheld state regulation designed to promote noneconomic objectives, even when such regulations inhibit economic competition—as long as the state is a "market participant." For example, in a sharply divided ruling, the Court upheld a Maryland law authorizing the state to pay a bounty to junk processors for the hulks of abandoned automobiles (*Hughes v. Alexandria Scrap Corporation* [1976]). To receive the bounty, a dealer had to furnish documentation of title. However, the documentation requirements were more demanding for out-of-state processors. A Virginia processor challenged the law as a violation of both the Commerce and the Equal Protection Clauses of the Fourteenth Amendment. Justice Powell, writing for the majority, conceded that the law had the practical effect of channeling economic benefits to in-state processors. Nevertheless, he concluded that "[n]othing in the purposes animating the Commerce Clause forbids a state, in the absence of congressional action, from participating in the market and exercising the right to favor its own citizens over others." In a dissenting opinion, Justice Brennan, joined by Justices White and Marshall, denied that this law differed from the kind of "economic protectionism" struck down in previous cases. He maintained that the Maryland bounty was an obvious discrimination against interstate commerce.

The "market participant" exception recognized in *Alexandria Scrap* was reaffirmed in the 1980 case of *Reeves Inc. v. Stake*. Here, the Court, by a 5-to-4 margin, upheld a South Dakota policy under which all in-state customers were supplied first with cement produced by a state-operated plant. Adhering closely to the reasoning in *Alexandria Scrap,* Justice Blackmun, writing for the majority, stated that "the Commerce Clause responds principally to state taxes and regulatory measures impeding free private trade in the national marketplace." He found "no indication of a constitutional plan to limit the ability of the states themselves to operate freely in the free market."

Three years later, in *White v. Massachusetts Council of Construction Employers, Inc.* (1983), the Court held that the Commerce Clause did not bar implementation of an executive order requiring that at least 50 percent of the workers on all city-funded construction projects be residents of Boston. In his majority opinion, Justice Rehnquist reasoned that "[i]f the city is a market participant, then the Commerce Clause establishes no barrier to conditions such as these which the city demands for its participation." The Court, however, refused to apply the "market participation" exception to an Alaska law requiring that any timber taken from state-owned land be at least partially processed before being removed from the state (*South-Central Timber Development, Inc. v. Wunnicke* [1984]).

A Constitutional Right to Engage in Interstate Commerce?

Thus far we have focused on the Commerce Clause as a source of national authority (see Chapter 5) and as a limitation on state regulatory activity. But in addition to its importance in allocating power between national and state government, the Commerce Clause has been interpreted as conferring rights on individuals. Following the Civil War, Congress passed important legislation that permitted civil suits for damages against state officials for the violation of "rights, privileges or immunities secured by the Constitution and laws" of the United States. This provision appears in Title 42, Section 1983 of the United States Code, and suits brought under its authority are commonly referred to as **Section 1983 actions.** In a 1991 decision, the Supreme Court held that the Commerce Clause grants federally protected "rights, privileges or immunities," thus authorizing Section 1983 actions for state violations of the Commerce Clause (see *Dennis v. Higgins* [1991]). Expressing the views of a seven-member majority, Justice White rejected the argument that because the Commerce Clause was designed to promote "national economic and political union," it did not confer rights within the meaning of Section 1983. White stated that "the commerce clause of its own force imposes limitations on state regulation of commerce, and is the source of a right of action . . . [by persons] injured by regulations that exceed such limitations."

At issue in *Dennis v. Higgins* was Nebraska's imposition of higher taxes and fees on out-of-state motor carriers than on those with vehicles registered in-state. An Ohio-based motor carrier, doing business in several states including Nebraska, challenged the tax and fee differential as "retaliatory" and alleged, among other things, that it deprived him of his constitutional right to engage in interstate commerce. While the Supreme Court did not determine whether his rights had in fact been violated, it held that he was entitled to pursue his Commerce Clause claim under Section 1983. Federal law (42 U.S. Code, Section 1988) provides that one who prevails in a Section 1983 action can recover attorney's fees and expenses of litigation. Emphasizing the implications of this provision for the "right" to engage in interstate commerce, Justice Anthony Kennedy, in a dissenting opinion joined by Chief Justice Rehnquist, argued that "[b]y making such fee awards available, the Court does not vindicate the purposes of Section 1983 or Section 1988, but merely shifts the balance of power away from the states and toward interstate business."

State Power to Regulate Commerce: Countervailing Considerations

The foregoing summary is far from a complete discussion of judicial interpretation of the Commerce Clause as applied to state regulatory activity. Nevertheless, this brief overview indicates the breadth of choice and the variety of alternatives open to the courts in this complex field. No single dominant theme emerges, but it appears the Supreme Court accords priority to at least two potentially conflicting considerations: (1) encouragement of the continued growth of a strong national economy and (2) promotion of state responsibility under the police power to protect the health, safety, and general welfare of the citizenry. Simultaneous commitments to national unity and local autonomy are reflected in the Court's case-by-case weighing of alternatives under the Commerce Clause.

STATE TAXING POWER

By contrast with the regulation of commerce, state power to tax was well established when the Constitution was drafted in 1787. The grant of taxing authority to Congress in Article I, Section 8, clause 1 did not withdraw or transfer this power from the states. Taxation simply became one of those concurrent powers exercised broadly by both spheres of government. Of course, the authority to tax at the local level is derived from the states. Cities, counties, and other units of local government are created and may be abolished by the states, and the scope of their taxing power is largely determined either by state constitutional provisions or by statutes—always subject, however, to federal constitutional requirements.

Routine aspects of state and local taxation do not often raise serious federal constitutional problems. The states have retained broad discretion under the federal Constitution to tap a variety of revenue sources that have widened as governmental services and costs have increased. It is only when states or their local subdivisions use taxation to block or undermine a federal constitutional principle or objective that state taxing power is likely to be limited by the Supreme Court. One such principle is the promotion of a national economy, embodied in such provisions as the Commerce Clause and the restriction on state taxation of imports and exports (see Article I, Section 10). A state tax that unfairly burdens interstate commerce to the advantage of local economic interests is vulnerable to constitutional attack. The foregoing discussion of state power to regulate commerce touched on this aspect of state taxation. Two additional problems are posed by the federal relationship, both of which have their origins in constitutional principles and reflect the gradual expansion of governmental power.

Intergovernmental Tax Immunity

First, we examine the doctrine of intergovernmental tax immunity. In *M'Culloch v. Maryland* (1819), Chief Justice Marshall asserted that Congress has not only an implied power to establish a national bank but also that a state cannot use its taxing authority to undermine that power. Marshall refused to sanction a state tax having the potential to destroy an entity constitutionally created by the national government. As he put it, characteristically "the power to tax involves the power to destroy." But in Marshall's view, this reasoning did not apply in reverse—that is, it provided no justification for imposing restrictions on *national* taxing power when that power interfered with lawful *state* objectives. But whether Marshall acknowledged it or not, the logic of his argument cut both ways.

As the doctrine of dual federalism emerged in the aftermath of the Civil War, the argument in favor of state immunity from national taxation gained support. In 1871, the Supreme Court embraced this doctrine in *Collector v. Day,* holding that the salary of a Massachusetts judge was immune from the federal income tax levied during the Civil War. The judge's salary was treated as an "instrumentality" of state government protected by the Tenth Amendment, just as the Bank of the United States had been viewed as an instrumentality of the national government protected by the Supremacy Clause. This reasoning was later applied to exempt from state as well as federal income taxes the salaries of many employees at all levels of government. Precisely why these salaries should be afforded special protection was never made clear, but the broader principle of intergovernmental tax immunity, which *Collector v. Day* established, followed logically from the assumptions underlying classical federalism.

For a number of years, the doctrine of intergovernmental tax immunity flourished in American constitutional law. The Court expanded the doctrine in the famous income tax case of 1895 by holding, among other things, that Congress could not tax income generated by state and local government securities (see *Pollock v. Farmers' Loan and Trust Company*). Although the *Pollock* decision was in large part overruled by the Sixteenth Amendment, adopted in 1913, this restriction on federal taxation remained in effect for many years. The exemption was finally challenged in 1982, when Congress imposed a tax on the interest from unregistered, long-term bonds issued by state and local governments. The state of South Carolina brought an original action in the Supreme Court attacking the constitutionality of this measure (*South Carolina v. Baker* [1988]). In upholding the tax, the Court concluded that neither the Tenth Amendment nor the doctrine of intergovernmental tax immunity prevented Congress from taxing this important source of state and local revenue. *South Carolina v. Baker* thus finally overruled the last remaining vestige of the *Pollock* decision.

Intergovernmental tax immunity had its heyday during the 1920s. In 1922, for example, the Court went so far as to strike down a state tax on income accruing to a company from oil lands it had leased from Indian tribes. Since these lands were classified as federal property, the Court concluded that the oil company, as lessee, was an instrumentality of the United States, carrying out the government's "duties to the Indians" (*Gillespie v. Oklahoma* [1922]). In a 1928 case, the states were barred from taxing royalties derived from national patents on the ground that such a tax would discourage national efforts to promote science and invention (*Long v. Rockwood*).

With growing demands for additional tax sources in response to the Great Depression, these highly restrictive decisions were overruled (*Fox Film Corporation v. Doyal* [1932]). In 1939, the Supreme Court overruled *Collector v. Day* and its progeny, thus removing the tax exemptions previously applied to the salaries of state and federal employees (*Graves v. New York ex rel. O'Keefe*). Justice Stone, who, along with Justices Oliver Wendell Holmes and Louis Brandeis, had been on the dissenting side during the heyday of reciprocal tax immunity, assumed a leading role in articulating the new approach. He rejected the rigid logic of dual federalism and recognized the practical demands imposed by two legally distinct governments, both obviously requiring more revenue to perform their expanding duties.

Neither the states nor the national government can tax essential governmental functions performed by the other. This is as true today as it was in the 1920s. The problem is determining just what constitutes an essential function of government. Presumably, Congress could not impose a tax on the publication of statutes enacted by a state legislature. Nor could a state levy a tax on the *United States Supreme Court Reports*. But once we move away from such extreme and improbable situations, the answers are not so easy. For example, although a state may not tax federal property directly, it can place a privilege tax on an individual or corporation using federal property and may base the tax on the value of such property (*United States v. City of Detroit* [1958]). States may also tax federal contractors, even if the burden of the tax is absorbed in the contract price and thus in effect passed on to the government (*Alabama v. King & Boozer* [1941]). On the other hand, the Supremacy Clause broadly protects functions of the national government from regulation through the imposition of state taxes or exercise of the state police power (*United States v. Georgia Public Service Commission* [1963]).

Basically, the Supreme Court has attempted to maximize the discretion of the taxing authority without impairing the performance of essential activities of government. Formal doctrine is less useful to the Court in making specific determinations in this field than practical assessments of political or economic reality. The gradual decline of reciprocal tax immunity since the 1930s illustrates the veracity of Justice Oliver Wendell Holmes's famous observation that the "life of the law has not been logic; it has been experience."

A modern example of the erosion of reciprocal tax immunity is provided by the 1978 decision in *Massachusetts v. United States*. Here, the Court upheld the imposition of a federal aircraft registration tax on a state-owned helicopter used exclusively for police work. It is difficult to think of a more basic governmental function than that of law enforcement, but the Court readily found the tax valid as a "user fee." Writing for the majority, Justice Brennan concluded:

> A nondiscriminatory taxing measure that operates to defray the cost of a federal program by recovering a fair approximation of each beneficiary's share of the cost is surely no more offensive to the constitutional scheme than is either a tax on the income earned by state employees or a tax on a State's sale of bottled water [see *New York v. United States* (1946)]. . . . There is no danger that such measures will not be based on benefits conferred or that they will function as regulatory devices unduly burdening essential state activities.

With respect to both federal and state taxation, the emphasis today is on enlarging, not restricting, available sources of revenue. This point is illustrated by the decision in *United States v. County of Fresno* (1977), in which the Court upheld a local property tax on U.S. Forestry Service employees whose houses were rented from the government. The tax was imposed only on those renting from owners (in this instance, the federal government) who were themselves exempt from taxation. Justice White, for the majority, found the tax to be nondiscriminatory, concluding that since it fell on individuals and not government, it was no impediment to the work of the Forestry Service.

The Imports-Exports Clause

Article I, Section 10, clause 2 of the Constitution provides: "No state shall, without the consent of the Congress, lay any imposts or duties on imports or exports, except what may be absolutely necessary for executing its inspection laws." Like the Commerce Clause, the Imports-Exports Clause was intended to promote broad national economic interests and minimize the negative influence of parochial state policies. In addition, the Imports-Exports Clause was designed to bar discrimination against both the shipment of goods into the United States from foreign countries and the shipment of American goods destined for foreign markets. Another aim of this clause was to remove the unfair advantage that seaboard states with ports of entry would otherwise have over interior states. Given the legal characteristics of "Our Federalism," however, the Imports-Exports Clause was also theoretically applicable to goods imported from or exported to other states. Despite occasional tendencies to accord it this broad interpretation, this clause has usually been confined to the movement of goods between foreign countries and the United States.

The first question the Supreme Court considered in limiting the scope of state taxing power turned on the definition of the word *import* in this clause. At what point, for state taxation purposes, does a commodity imported from a foreign country lose its distinct character as an import and thereby become subject to a state's general taxing power? Chief Justice Marshall considered this question in the 1827 case of *Brown v. Maryland*. Maryland required that importers and sellers of goods in designated forms pay a license fee of fifty dollars. The state imposed a financial penalty for failure to comply with this requirement. Four sellers of foreign merchandise challenged the Maryland law as violative of the Imports-Exports and Commerce Clauses. The Marshall Court declared the law unconstitutional on both grounds. The chief justice interpreted the Imports-Exports Clause as a broad restriction on state power. The fee at issue in this case was aimed exclusively at imports and, on the basis of his analysis, was clearly a violation of the Constitution. But Marshall went one step further and considered a question not directly at issue in this case: When does a commodity moving into a state from a foreign jurisdiction lose its distinct character as an import? He answered as follows:

> When the importer has so acted upon the thing imported, that it has become incorporated and mixed up with the mass of property within the country, it has perhaps lost its distinctive character as an import, and has become subject to the taxing power of the state; but while remaining the property of the importer, in his warehouse, in the original form or package in which it was imported, a tax upon it is too plainly a duty on imports to escape the prohibition in the Constitution.

Since the law at issue did not apply to sellers of domestic goods, it was plainly discriminatory and could have been invalidated without reference to this "original package" test. But the state attorney general, Roger B. Taney (Marshall's successor as chief justice on the Supreme Court), argued that a simple invalidation of the license fee through strict construction of the language of the Imports-Exports Clause could permanently insulate imported goods from state and local taxation. Marshall's development of the "original package" test, with its emphasis on a cutoff point beyond which the states would be free to tax, appears to have come in response to Taney's argument.

The Rise and Fall of the Original Package Doctrine

In 1872, the original package dictum was accorded formal constitutional status, providing the basis for invalidating a nondiscriminatory property tax on imported goods that, although no longer in the "stream of commerce," remained in their original packages (*Low v. Austin*). The original package doctrine had the appeal of apparent simplicity, and over time it acquired the aura accorded to many of the pronouncements of Chief Justice Marshall. But as many scholars pointed out, the doctrine was both mechanical and inconsistent with the purpose of the Imports-Exports Clause, which was simply to prevent discriminatory state taxation on goods moving from or to foreign markets.

Generally speaking, the development of American law relies heavily on **precedent.** This reliance on the authority of prior rulings is termed *stare decisis.* Although less pronounced in constitutional law than in most other legal subfields, *stare decisis* is a powerful factor in the decision-making process. Perhaps this explains the durability of the original package doctrine. However, with advances in technology and great increases in the volume of foreign trade, the doctrine became untenable. By the 1940s, legal scholars were calling for its abandonment. They urged the substitution of a simple test focusing on the question of whether a given state tax is discriminatory. Finally, in the 1976 case of *Michelin Tire Corporation v. Wages,* the Supreme Court adopted this position. It overruled *Lowe v. Austin* and upheld a nondiscriminatory Georgia tax on tires and tubes imported from France and Canada. Writing for the majority, Justice Brennan took note of the extensive criticism of the original package doctrine and of its departure from the intent of the Framers. He then concluded:

> Our independent study persuades us that a nondiscriminatory ad valorem property tax is not the type of state exaction which the Framers of the Constitution or the Court in *Brown* [*v. Maryland*] had in mind as being an "impost" or duty and the *Lowe v. Austin*'s reliance upon the *Brown* dictum to reach the contrary conclusion was misplaced.

In this way, the Court managed to nullify the original package doctrine without challenging John Marshall's initial statement of the formula, thus according deference to judicial tradition while at the same time overruling a troublesome constitutional precedent.

Other Taxation Issues

The Supreme Court has encountered other constitutional problems in determining the scope of state taxing power. These include issues of multiple taxation, the proper basis of assessment, the degree of burden that will be permitted on interstate commerce, and the procedural requirements of due process of law. This chapter, however, is concerned only with the more salient aspects of American federalism and cannot elaborate on these additional questions of state taxation. Like its national counterpart, state taxation serves regulatory as well as revenue-raising purposes. For example, certain state-imposed license fees may be upheld even though they apply to interstate as well as intrastate business activities. The question in such cases is whether the state is acting within the proper scope of its police power. The Supreme Court has not invalidated a state tax merely because of its regulatory effect. The Court has been far more concerned with whether a given tax discriminates against interstate or foreign commerce or whether it inhibits an essential function of the national government. The constitutional scope of the state taxing power is strongly influenced, even in an age of cooperative federalism, by the central objective of balancing state and national interests.

INTERSTATE RELATIONS

In addition to interaction between the national government and the states, American federalism encompasses relations *among* the states. This interstate dimension is addressed primarily by Article IV of the Constitution, with its Full Faith and Credit, Privileges and Immunities, and Rendition provisions. The Framers also provided, in Article I, Section 10, clause 3, that the states could not, without congressional consent, "enter into any agreement or compact" with other states or with foreign powers.

"Full Faith and Credit"

The Full Faith and Credit Clause requires that each state recognize and enforce the "public acts, records, and judicial proceedings of every other state" (Article IV, Section 2, clause 1). In addition to asserting this general principle, the Constitution grants Congress the power to "prescribe the manner in which such acts, records and proceedings shall be proved, and the effect thereof." To that end, Congress passed legislation in 1790 and 1804 providing for the authentication and effect of public records. As a result of this early legislation and occasional minor changes over the years, the principle of **full faith and credit** has become an integral part of our legal system.

The most difficult and important questions in this area have involved the extent to which valid final judgments by state courts are enforceable in other states. One brief illustration of the complexity characterizing this area is provided by the Supreme Court's decision in *Estin v. Estin* (1948). Here, the Court recognized a "divisible" divorce decree. Under this approach, a state must accord validity to a divorce granted by another state but is not bound by another state's decision on such related matters as alimony, child custody, and division of property.

The Privileges and Immunities Clause

The principle of full faith and credit is insufficient to promote harmonious interstate relations. Recognition of another state's "acts, records, and judicial proceedings" would be of little consequence if the states were free to favor their own citizens over those of other states. To preclude this possibility, the Framers provided in Section 2, clause 1, of Article IV that "citizens of each state shall be entitled to all privileges and immunities of citizens in the several states." This

Privileges and Immunities Clause should not be confused with a similar provision in the Fourteenth Amendment declaring: "No state shall make or enforce any law which shall abridge the privileges or immunities of citizens of the United States." Whereas the Fourteenth Amendment protects privileges and immunities of *national* citizenship only, Article IV is directed to *state* citizenship (see *The Slaughter-House Cases* [1873]). In spite of its open-ended language, this provision was until recently accorded a narrow judicial interpretation.

The first major decision interpreting Article IV's Privileges and Immunities Clause established this narrow construction but identified a number of **fundamental rights** embraced by the provision (*Corfield v. Coryell* [1823]). In this circuit court ruling, Supreme Court Justice Bushrod Washington argued that the clause protects only those privileges and immunities "which are, in their nature, fundamental; which belong of right to the citizens of all free governments." For Washington, these fundamentals included

> the right of a citizen of one state to pass through or reside in any other state . . . ; to claim the benefit of the writ of habeas corpus; to institute and maintain actions of any kind in the courts of the state; to take, hold, and dispose of property; and an exemption from higher taxes or impositions than are paid by other citizens of the state.

Justice Washington's list of fundamental rights is limited by comparison with the scope of constitutional protections today. Nevertheless, the logic underlying his position could be extended to include many rights guaranteed by other constitutional provisions. Indeed, the Privileges and Immunities Clause is closely related to such concepts as equal protection and due process, as well as to the negative implications of the Commerce Clause.

The Supreme Court did not elaborate on the "fundamental rights" formulation of *Corfield v. Coryell*. Rather, it gave greater attention to the question of whether states were granting equality of rights to citizens of other states relative to their own citizens. In any event, the Privileges and Immunities Clause has never been interpreted to preclude all differential treatment of out-of-state citizens. On occasion, the Court has allowed even discrimination involving fundamental rights if it could be shown that such discrimination could not be "reasonably . . . characterized as hostile to the rights of citizens of other states" (*Blake v. McClung* [1898]). As a result, differential state standards governing the practice of certain professions are not barred by the Privileges and Immunities Clause: Out-of-state physicians, lawyers, and other professionals may be required to prove their competency on the basis of higher standards than those applied to their in-state counterparts. Tuition rates at public colleges and universities are typically lower for in-state students. Out-of-state residents are charged more for hunting and fishing licenses than are in-state residents. Such discrepancies are generally accepted as justifiable because they advance legitimate state interests.

On this basis, the Supreme Court upheld Iowa's one-year residency requirement as a prerequisite to obtaining a divorce (*Sosna v. Iowa* [1975]). Similar durational residency requirements had been struck down as applied to welfare benefits, voting, and publicly financed health care (see, for example, *Shapiro v.*

Thompson [1969]; *Dunn v. Blumstein* [1972]). The state-imposed restrictions in those cases were justified only by budgetary and record-keeping concerns. These interests were regarded as less important than the constitutional claims of individuals burdened by the residency requirements. By contrast, Iowa could justify its residency requirement for divorce on grounds other than budgetary constraints and administrative convenience. "A decree of divorce," said Justice Rehnquist for the majority, "is not a matter in which the only interested parties are the state as a sort of 'grantor' and a plaintiff . . . in the role of 'grantee.' " He continued by observing:

> Both spouses are obviously interested in the proceedings, since it will affect their marital status and very likely their property rights. Where a married couple has minor children, a decree of divorce would usually include provisions for their custody and support. With consequences of such moment riding on a divorce decree issued by its courts, Iowa may insist that one seeking to initiate such a proceeding have the modicum of attachment to the state required here.

Thus, a state must show that its differential treatment of in-state and out-of-state residents serves some reasonable purpose.

Alaska's failure to justify such differential treatment led the court in 1978 to strike down a statute requiring employers to give preferential treatment to in-state residents (*Hicklin v. Orbeck*). Specifically, the law required "the employment of qualified Alaska residents" in preference to out-of-state residents, in connection with "all oil and gas leases, easements or right-of-way permits for oil or gas pipeline purposes . . . to which the state is a party." Alaska began to enforce this act seriously in 1975, when construction on the Trans-Alaska Pipeline was reaching its peak. As a result, Hicklin and other nonresidents who had previously worked on this project "were prevented from obtaining pipeline-related work. . . ." The Court unanimously invalidated Alaska's preferential requirement as a violation of the Privileges and Immunities Clause of Article IV. Writing for the Court, Justice Brennan concluded that this law was

> an attempt to force virtually all businesses that benefit in some way from the economic ripple effect of Alaska's decision to develop her oil and gas resources to bias their employment practices in favor of the state's residents. We believe that Alaska's ownership of the oil and gas that is the subject matter of [this legislation] simply constitutes insufficient justification for the pervasive discrimination against nonresidents that the Act mandates.

We have already noted the close relationship between the Privileges and Immunities and the Commerce Clauses. But this relationship does not mean that the two clauses are entirely equivalent in impact. Thus, a state policy that survives scrutiny under the Commerce Clause may be invalidated under Article IV, Section 2. This point is well-illustrated by the 1984 decision of *United Building and Construction Trades v. Camden*. At issue was the question of whether the Privileges and Immunities Clause was violated by a Camden, New Jersey, city ordinance requiring that a minimum of 40 percent of persons employed under city construction contracts be Camden residents. The New Jersey Supreme Court held that because the ordinance was written in terms of municipal rather than state residency, it was not subject to the Privileges and Immunities Clause. Without ruling on the constitutionality of the ordinance, the Supreme Court reversed. In his majority opinion, Justice Rehnquist concluded that the local character of the ordinance did not "somehow place it outside the scope of the Clause." The ordinance in question had state approval, but even if it had been "adopted solely by Camden, the hiring preference would still have to comport" with this constitutional provision.

Distinguishing the *Camden* decision from *White v. Massachusetts Council of Construction Employers* (1983), discussed above, Rehnquist asserted that the Commerce and the Privileges and Immunities Clauses "have different aims and set different standards for state conduct." The "market participant" rationale applied in *White* was not controlling in the *Camden* case. In supporting this conclusion, Rehnquist reasoned as follows:

> The Commerce Clause is an implied restraint upon state regulatory powers. Such powers must give way before the superior authority of Congress to legislate on (or leave unregulated) matters involving interstate commerce. When the state acts solely as a market participant, no conflict between state regulation and federal regulatory authority can arise.... The Privileges and Immunities Clause, on the other hand, imposes a direct restraint on state action in the interests of interstate harmony.... It is discrimination against out-of-state residents on matters of fundamental concern which triggers the Clause, not regulation affecting interstate commerce.

Rendition

The Full Faith and Credit Clause does not extend to criminal offenses; that is, no state need enforce the criminal laws of another state or respect those laws as a defense in a prosecution. This position has its roots in the Anglo-American concept of **due process,** which requires trial in the district where the crime was committed. Complete reliance on this tradition could have permitted any of the states to become havens of refuge for fugitives from other states. The Framers therefore included a Rendition Clause in Section 2 of Article IV:

> A person charged in any state with treason, felony, or other crime, who shall flee from justice, and be found in another state, shall on demand of the executive authority of the state from which he fled, be delivered up, to be removed to the state having jurisdiction of the crime.

Pursuant to this clause, Congress in 1793 passed legislation delineating the manner of **rendition** and obligating governors to comply with the **extradition** requirements. Those provisions, both statutory and constitutional, were presumed to cover any and all violations of a state's criminal law and required a governor to deliver a fugitive to the "requesting" state, even if the fugitive's acts would not have been criminal in the governor's state. This requirement was upheld in the 1861 case of *Kentucky v. Dennison.* Ohio Governor William Dennison had refused to comply with Kentucky's demand that he surrender a black defendant, charged in Kentucky with aiding the escape of slaves. The

Supreme Court unanimously held that although Dennison had a duty to comply with Kentucky's demand, this duty was unenforceable. This anomalous aspect of the *Dennison* case was eventually overruled by a 1987 Supreme Court decision holding that a federal judge can require a governor to perform "the ministerial duty" of delivering a fugitive upon a proper demand from another state (*Puerto Rico v. Branstad*).

Interstate Compacts

The Full Faith and Credit, Privileges and Immunities, and Rendition clauses were obviously designed to minimize friction among the states. By contrast, the Compacts Clause, although stated in negative terms, was more positive in that it paved the way for the states, with congressional consent, to enter into agreements among themselves. The relevant language of Article I, Section 10, clause 3 provides that "[n]o state shall, without the consent of Congress, . . . enter into any agreement or compact with another state, or with a foreign power . . . ." Over the years, many such agreements have been entered into with generally beneficial results. New York and New Jersey, for example, have cooperated in administering the New York Port Authority. Other states have developed agreements for the regulation of oil and gas, the management of water resources, and the like. Despite the constitutional requirement of congressional approval, the Court has sustained several interstate agreements not explicitly sanctioned by Congress.

This was the result in the 1978 case of *United States Steel Corporation v. Multistate Tax Commission*. In 1967, a multistate tax compact went into effect among seven states. By 1978, some twenty-three states had participated at various times, some remaining affiliated, others withdrawing. The purpose of this compact was to reduce the inefficiency inherent in the separate single-state administration of taxes levied on multistate businesses. The compact established a commission to carry out a number of related functions. U.S. Steel and other large corporations, believing that the commission's activities worked to their disadvantage, challenged the constitutionality of the compact, alleging that it unreasonably burdened interstate commerce. However, the Supreme Court sustained the compact in spite of the absence of explicit congressional consent.

In *Multistate Tax Commission*, the Supreme Court relied principally on the precedent of *Virginia v. Tennessee* (1893). There, the Court had sustained a compact between Virginia and Tennessee that resolved a border dispute, finding that Congress had tacitly approved the arrangement. In this early decision, Justice Stephen J. Field, speaking for the Court, added that not all compacts required even tacit approval. Approval was unnecessary if the compact did not tend to "increase the political power of the states which may encroach upon or interfere with the just supremacy of the United States." The Court applied this rationale in *Multistate Tax Commission*. Justice Powell for the majority reasoned that because the taxing authority remained in the hands of each state and because all regulations promulgated by the commission were ineffectual until state statutes authorized them, the compact did not expand state power at the expense of federal authority. Indeed, the compact gave no single state any greater power than it possessed independently. Accordingly, the compact was no greater burden on interstate commerce than were state taxes on multistate businesses previously sustained as constitutional.

Interstate compacts that are granted congressional approval function as the legal equivalent of federal treaties and statutes; that is, they are the supreme law of the land. Once approved, the terms of the compact are binding on all parties, preventing a state from unilaterally withdrawing and from using its internal domestic policy to avoid compliance with the terms of the compact. This policy is well illustrated by the case of *West Virginia ex rel. Dyer v. Sims* (1951). There, the Supreme Court overruled the West Virginia Supreme Court's holding that West Virginia's commitments under an interstate compact were invalid because they conflicted with the state constitution.

CONCLUSION

"Our Federalism" encompasses a set of complex and dynamic relationships between the states and the national government and among the states themselves. These relationships are defined and redefined through the process of judicial interpretation. In performing its role as umpire of the federal system, the Supreme Court has attempted over the years to give expression to the contending values of national unity and local diversity. Although the role of the national government has become dominant in the second half of the twentieth century, the states continue to be viable and important governmental entities. They have by no means sunk to the status of mere administrative units. In fact, there has been a significant degree of state resurgence since the early 1970s. Indeed, as a result of the "Reagan Revolution" of the 1980s, the states have had to shoulder greater policy-making and fiscal responsibilities. In the 1990s, many states are struggling to meet increased financial burdens resulting from a "new federalism" in which the national government relies increasingly on the states to manage, and fund, important but costly social programs.

This "new federalism," in some respects more accurately characterized as contentious rather than cooperative, by no means signals a return to the dual federalism of the days before the New Deal. Today, the national, state, and local governments are joint participants in programs ranging from environmental regulation to criminal law enforcement, from elementary education to "independent living" services for elderly persons. The recent and highly publicized movement to privatize some traditional governmental functions at the state and local levels has not led to a massive diminution of activity in the public sector. Despite the traditional tendency of Americans to criticize their government, the demand for public services continues to grow. The real challenge to contemporary federalism is how government at all levels can respond to these demands in an age of fiscal stress.

FOR FURTHER READING

Antieau, Chester J. *Modern Constitutional Law,* 2 vols. Rochester, N.Y.: Lawyers' Cooperative, 1969.

Anton, Thomas. *American Federalism and Public Policy.* Philadelphia: Temple University Press, 1989.

Berger, Raoul. *Federalism: The Founders' Design.* Norman: University of Oklahoma Press, 1987.

Bowman, Ann O., and Richard C. Kearney. *The Resurgence of the States.* Englewood Cliffs, N.J.: Prentice-Hall, 1986.

Calhoun, John C. *A Discourse on the Constitution and Government of the United States.* New York: Bobbs-Merrill, 1953.

Calhoun, John C. *A Disquisition on Government.* New York: Bobbs-Merrill, 1953.

Conlan, Timothy. *New Federalism: Intergovernmental Reform from Nixon to Reagan.* Washington, D.C.: Brookings Institution, 1988.

Corwin, Edward S. *Liberty against Government.* Baton Rouge: Louisiana State University Press, 1948.

Corwin, Edward S. *The Commerce Clause versus States' Rights.* Princeton: Princeton University Press, 1936.

Elazar, Daniel. *American Federalism: The View from the States,* 3d ed. New York: Harper and Row, 1984.

Frankfurter, Felix. *The Commerce Clause under Marshall, Taney and Waite.* Chapel Hill: University of North Carolina Press, 1937.

Gittell, Marilyn. *State Politics and the New Federalism.* New York: Longman, 1986.

Goldwin, Robert, ed. *A Nation of States.* New York: Rand-McNally, 1974.

Porter, Mary, and G. Allan Tarr, eds. *State Supreme Courts: Policymakers in the Federal System.* Westport, Conn.: Greenwood Press, 1982.

Pritchett, C. Herman. *Constitutional Law of the Federal System.* Englewood Cliffs, N.J.: Prentice-Hall, 1984.

Riker, William. *Federalism: Origin, Operation, Significance.* Boston: Little, Brown, 1964.

Stephens, Otis H., Jr., and Gregory J. Rathjen. *The Supreme Court and the Allocation of Constitutional Power.* San Francisco: W.H. Freeman, 1980.

CASES AND READINGS

Chisholm v. Georgia

2 Dall. (2. U.S.) 419; 1 L. Ed. 440 (1793)
Vote: 4-1

In 1777, the state of Georgia authorized two state commissioners to purchase supplies from Robert Farquhar, a merchant based in Charleston, South Carolina. Although the supplies were delivered, Farquhar never received payment. After Farquhar's death, the executor of his estate, Alexander Chisholm, brought a federal lawsuit against the state of Georgia to force payment of the claim. Relying on the ancient doctrine of sovereign immunity, Georgia responded that it could not be sued without its own consent, even by a citizen of another state proceeding in a federal tribunal. The Chisholm *case was decided by the Supreme Court on February 18, 1793. Dividing 4-to-1, the Court rejected the state's contention of immunity. In keeping with the common practice of the day, all five justices rendered opinions* seriatim. *Chief Justice John Jay and Associate Justices James Wilson, John Cushing, and John Blair wrote opinions concurring in the judgment. Justice James Iredell produced a dissenting opinion. (Although Congress in 1792 had increased the size of the Court to six justices, Justice William Paterson did not begin service on the Court until March 1793). Only Justice Wilson's concurrence and Justice Iredell's dissent are excerpted here.*

Wilson, Justice: —This is a case of uncommon magnitude. One of the parties to it is a state; certainly respectable, claiming to be sovereign. The question to be determined is whether this state, so respectable, and whose claim soars so high, is amenable to the jurisdiction of the supreme court of the United States? This question, important in itself, will depend on others, more important still; and, may, perhaps, be ultimately resolved into one, no less radical than this—"do the people of the United States form a nation?" . . .

To the Constitution of the United States the term "sovereign" is totally unknown. There is but one place where it could have been used with propriety.

But, even in that place it would not, perhaps, have comported with the delicacy of those who ordained and established that constitution. They might have announced themselves "sovereign people of the United States." But serenely conscious of the fact, they avoided the ostentatious declaration. . . .

In one sense, the term "sovereign" has for its correlative, [the term] "subject." In this sense, the term can receive no application; for it has no object in the Constitution of the United States. Under that constitution there are citizens, but no subjects. "Citizens of the United States." "Citizens of another state." "Citizens of different states." "A state or citizen thereof." The term "subject" occurs indeed, once in the instrument; but to make the contrast strongly, the epithet "foreign" is prefixed. In this sense, I presume the state of Georgia has no claim upon her own citizens: In this sense, I am certain, she can have no claim upon the citizens of another state. . . .

As a judge of this court, I know, and can decide upon the knowledge, that the citizens of Georgia, when they acted upon the large scale of the union, as part of the "People of the United States," did not surrender the supreme or sovereign power to that state; but, as to the purposes of the union, retained it to themselves. As to the purposes of the union, therefore, Georgia is not a sovereign state. . . .

Under this view, the question is naturally subdivided into two others. 1. Could the Constitution of the United States vest a jurisdiction over the State of Georgia? 2. Has that constitution vested such jurisdiction in this court? I have already remarked, that in the practice, and even in the science of politics, there has been frequently a strong current against the natural order of things; and an inconsiderate or an interested disposition to sacrifice the end to the means. This remark deserves a more particular illustration. Even in almost every nation, which has been denominated free, the state has assumed a supercilious preeminence above the people who have formed it: Hence the haughty notions of state independence, state sovereignty, and state supremacy. In despotic governments, the Government has usurped, in a similar manner, both upon the state and the people: Hence all arbitrary doctrines and pretensions concerning the supreme, absolute, and uncontrollable power of government. In each, man is degraded from the prime rank, which he ought to hold in human affairs; In the latter, the state as well as the man is degraded. Of both degradations, striking instances occur in history, in politics, and in common life. . . .

In the United States, and in the several states which compose the union, we go not so far; but still we go one step farther than we ought to go in this unnatural and inverted order of things. The states, rather than the people, for whose sakes the states exist, are frequently the objects which attract and arrest our principal attention. This, I believe, has produced much of the confusion and perplexity, which have appeared in several proceedings and several publications on state politics, and on the politics, too of the United States. Sentiments and expressions of this inaccurate kind prevail in our common, even in our convivial, language. Is a toast asked? "The United States" instead of the "People of the United States," is the toast given. This is not politically correct. The toast is meant to present to view the first great object in the union: It presents only the second; It presents only the artificial person, instead of the natural persons, who spoke it into existence. A state I cheerfully admit, is the noblest work of man: But man himself, free and honest, is, I speak as to this world, the noblest work of God. . . .

With the strictest propriety, therefore, classical and political, our national scene opens with the most magnificent object which the nation could present. "The people of the United States" are the first personages introduced. Who were those people? They were the citizens of thirteen states, each of which had a separate constitution and government, and all of which were connected together by articles of confederation. To the purposes of public strength and felicity that confederacy was totally inadequate. A requisition on the several states terminated its legislative authority; executive or judicial authority it had none. In order, therefore, to form a more perfect

union, to establish justice, to insure domestic tranquility, to provide for common defense, and to secure the blessings of liberty, those people, among whom were the people of Georgia, ordained and established the present constitution. By that constitution, legislative power is vested, executive power is vested, judicial power is vested.

The question now opens fairly to our view, could the people of those states, among whom were those of Georgia, bind those states, and Georgia, among the others, by the legislative, executive, and judicial power so vested? If the principles on which I have founded myself are just and true, this question must, unavoidably, receive an affirmative answer. If those States were the work of those people, those people, and that I may apply the case closely, the people of Georgia, in particular, could alter, as they pleased, their former work; to any given degree, they could diminish as well as enlarge it. Any or all of the former State powers they could extinguish or transfer. The inference which necessarily results is, that the constitution ordained and established by those people; and still closely to apply the case, in particular, by the people of Georgia, could vest jurisdiction or judicial power over those states, and over the state of Georgia in particular.

The next question under this head is—Has the constitution done so? Did those people mean to exercise this, their undoubted power? These questions may be resolved, either by fair and conclusive deductions, or by direct and explicit declarations. In order, ultimately, to discover, whether the people of the United States intended to bind those states by the judicial power vested by the national constitution, a previous inquiry will naturally be: Did those people intend to bind those states by the legislative power vested by that constitution? The articles of confederation, it is well known, did not operate upon individual citizens, but operated only upon states. This defect was remedied by the national constitution, which as all allow, has an operation on individual citizens. But if an opinion, which some seem to entertain, be just; the defect remedied, on one side, was balanced by a defect introduced on the other: for they seem to think, that the present constitution operates only on individual citizens, and not on states. This opinion, however, appears to be altogether unfounded. When certain laws of the states are declared to be "subject to the revision and control of the congress"; it cannot, surely be contended, that the legislature power of the national government was meant to have no operation on the several states. The fact, incontrovertibly established in one instance, proves the principle in all other instances, to which the facts will be found to apply. We may then infer, that the people of the United States intended to bind the several states, by the legislative power of the national government. . . .

Whoever considers, in a combined and comprehensive view, the general texture of the constitution, will be satisfied that the people of the United States intended to form themselves into a nation for national purposes. They instituted, for such purposes, a national government complete in all its parts, with powers legislative, executive and judiciary; and in all those powers extending over the whole nation. Is it congruous that, with regard to such purposes, any man or body of men, any person, natural or artificial, should be permitted to claim successfully an entire exemption from the jurisdiction of the national government? Would not such claims, crowned with success, be repugnant to our very existence as a nation? When so many trains of deduction, coming from different quarters, converge and unite at last in the same point, we may safely conclude, as the legitimate result of this constitution, that the State of Georgia is amenable to the jurisdiction of this court. . . .

Iredell, Justice [dissenting]: Every state in the union in every instance where its sovereignty has not been delegated to the United States, I consider to be as completely sovereign, as the United States are in respect to the powers surrendered. The United States are sovereign as to all the powers of government actually surrendered. Each state in the union is sovereign as to all the powers reserved. It must necessarily be so, because the United States have no claim to any authority but such as the states have surrendered to them. Of course the part not surrendered must remain as it did before. The powers of the general government, either of a legislative or executive nature, or which particularly concerns treaties with foreign powers, do for the most part (if not wholly) affect individuals, and not states. They

require no aid from any state authority. This is the great leading distinction between the old articles of confederation, and the present constitution. The judicial power is of a peculiar kind. It is indeed commensurate with the ordinary legislative and executive powers of the general government, and the power which concerns treaties. But it also goes further. . . .

So far as states under the constitution can be made legally liable to [the federal courts] . . . , so far to be sure they are subordinate to the authority of the United States, and their individual sovereignty is in this respect limited. But it is limited no farther than the necessary execution of such authority requires. The authority extends only to the decision of controversies in which a state is a party, and providing laws necessary for that purpose. That surely can refer only to such controversies in which a state can be a party; it can be determined, according to the principles [of law] I have supported, in no other manner than by a reference either to preexistent laws, or laws passed under the constitution and in conformity to it.

Whatever be the true construction of the constitution in this particular; whether it is to be construed as intending merely a transfer of jurisdiction from one tribunal to another, or as authorizing the legislature to provide laws for the decision of all possible controversies in which a state may be involved with an individual, without regard to any prior exception; yet it is certain that the legislature [in passing the Judiciary Act of 1789] has in fact proceeded upon the former supposition and not upon the latter. . . . [I]n instances like this before the court, this court hath a concurrent jurisdiction only; the present being one of those cases where by the judicial act this court hath original but not exclusive jurisdiction. This court, therefore, under that act, can exercise no authority in such instances but such authority as from the subject matter of it may be exercised in some other court. — There are no courts with which a concurrence can be suggested but the circuit courts, or courts of the different states. With the former it cannot be, for admitting that the constitution is not to have a restrictive operation, so as to confine all cases in which a state is a party exclusively to the supreme court (an opinion to which I am strongly inclined), yet there are no words in the definition of the powers of the circuit court which give a color to an opinion, that where a suit is brought against a state by a citizen of another state, the circuit court could exercise any jurisdiction at all. If they could, however, such a jurisdiction, by the very terms of their authority, could only be concurrent with the courts of the several States. It follows, therefore, unques-

tionably, I think, that looking at the act of Congress, which I consider is on this occasion the limit of our authority. . . , we can exercise no authority in the present instance consistently with the clear intention of the act, but such a proper state court would have been at least competent to exercise at the same time the act was passed. . . .

M'Culloch v. Maryland

4 Wheat. (17 U.S.) 316; 4 L. Ed. 579 (1819)

This case is reprinted in Chapter 5. While M'Culloch *is critically important to the issue of congressional authority—in particular, the doctrine of implied*

powers—it is equally significant with respect to basic issues of American federalism. Accordingly, students might wish to reread M'Culloch *at this point.*

Gibbons v. Ogden

9 Wheat. (22 U.S.) 1; 6 L. Ed. 23 (1824)

This case is reprinted in Chapter 5. Although Gibbons v. Ogden *is of great importance as the first Supreme Court decision recognizing broad congressional authority to regulate commerce, it is also important in*

illustrating the relationship between state and national regulatory power in this field. It may be useful to review Gibbons *before reading the remaining cases reprinted in this chapter.*

Hammer v. Dagenhart

247 U.S. 251; 38 S. Ct. 529; 62 L. Ed. 1101 (1918)
Vote: 5-4

Mr. Justice Day delivered the opinion of the Court.

A bill was filed in the United States district court for the western district of North Carolina by a father in his own behalf and as next friend of his two minor sons, one under the age of fourteen years and the other between the ages of fourteen and sixteen years, employees in a cotton mill at Charlotte, North Carolina, to enjoin the enforcement of the act of Congress intended to prevent interstate commerce in the products of child labor. ***

The district court held the act unconstitutional. . . . This appeal brings the case here. . . .

The controlling question for decision is: Is it within the authority of Congress in regulating commerce among the states to prohibit the transportation in interstate commerce of manufactured goods, the product of a factory in which, within thirty days prior to their removal therefrom, children under the age of fourteen have been employed or permitted to work, or children between the ages of fourteen and sixteen years have been employed or permitted to work, more than eight hours in any day, or more than six days in any week, or after the hour of 7 o'clock P.M. or before the hour of 6 o'clock A.M.?

The power essential to the passage of this act, the government contends, is found in the commerce clause of the Constitution, which authorizes Congress to regulate commerce with foreign nations and among the states.

. . . [The commerce] power is one to control the means by which commerce is carried on, which is directly the contrary of the assumed right to forbid commerce from moving and thus destroy it as to particular commodities. But it is insisted that adjudged cases in this court establish the doctrine that the power to regulate given to Congress incidentally includes the authority to prohibit the movement of ordinary commodities, and therefore that the subject is not open for discussion. The cases demonstrate the contrary. They rest upon the character of the particular subjects dealt with and the fact that the scope of governmental authority, state or national, possessed over them, is such that the authority to prohibit is, as to them, but the exertion of the power to regulate.

. . . [It has been held that] Congress might pass a law having the effect to keep the channels of commerce free from use in the transportation of tickets used in the promotion of lottery schemes; . . . [prohibiting] the introduction into the states by means of interstate commerce of impure food and drugs; . . . [forbidden] transportation of a woman in interstate commerce for the purpose of prostitution; . . . [prohibiting] the transportation of women in interstate commerce for the purposes of debauchery and kindred purposes; . . . [and barring] the transportation of intoxicating liquors. . . .

In each of these instances the use of interstate transportation was necessary to the accomplishment of harmful results. In other words, although the power over interstate transportation was to regulate, that could only be accomplished by prohibiting the use of the facilities of interstate commerce to effect the evil intended.

This element is wanting in the present case. The thing intended to be accomplished by this statute is the denial of the facilities of interstate commerce to those manufacturers in the states who employ chil-

dren within the prohibited ages. The act in its effect does not regulate transportation among the states, but aims to standardize the ages at which children may be employed in mining and manufacturing within the states. The goods shipped are of themselves harmless. The act permits them to be freely shipped after thirty days from the time of their removal from the factory. When offered for shipment, and before transportation begins, the labor of their production is over, and the mere fact that they were intended for interstate commerce transportation does not make their production subject to Federal control under the commerce power.

Commerce "consists of intercourse and traffic . . . and includes the transportation of persons and property, as well as the purchase, sale and exchange of commodities." The making of goods and the mining of coal are not commerce, nor does the fact that these things are to be afterwards shipped, or used in interstate commerce, make their production a part thereof. ***

Over interstate transportation, or its incidents, the regulatory power of Congress is ample, but the production of articles intended for interstate commerce is a matter of local regulation. . . . If it were otherwise, all manufacture intended for interstate shipment would be brought under Federal control to the practical exclusion of the authority of the states—a result certainly not contemplated by the framers of the Constitution when they vested in Congress the authority to regulate commerce among the states. ***

It is further contended that the authority of Congress may be exerted to control interstate commerce in the shipment of child-made goods because of the effect of the circulation of such goods in other states where the evil of this class of labor has been recognized by local legislation, and the right to thus employ child labor has been more rigorously restrained than in the state of production. In other words, that the unfair competition thus engendered may be controlled by closing the channels of interstate commerce to manufacturers in those states where the local laws do not meet what Congress deems to be the more just standard of other states.

There is no power vested in Congress to require the states to exercise their police power so as to prevent possible unfair competition. Many causes may co-operate to give one state, by reason of local laws or conditions, an economic advantage over others. The commerce clause was not intended to give to Congress a general authority to equalize such conditions....

The grant of power to Congress over the subject of interstate commerce was to enable it to regulate such commerce, and not to give it authority to control the states in their exercise of the police power over local trade and manufacture.

The grant of authority over a purely Federal matter was not intended to destroy the local power always existing and carefully reserved to the states in the 10th Amendment to the Constitution.

Police regulations relating to the internal trade and affairs of the states have been uniformly recognized as within such control....

That there should be limitations upon the right to employ children in mines and factories in the interest of their own and the public welfare, all will admit. That such employment is generally deemed to require regulation is shown by the fact that the brief of counsel states that every state in the Union has a law upon the subject, limiting the right to thus employ children. In North Carolina, the state wherein is located the factory in which the employment was had in the present case, no child under twelve years of age is permitted to work....

In interpreting the Constitution it must never be forgotten that the nation is made up of states, to which are intrusted the powers of local government. And to them and to the people the powers not expressly delegated to the national government are reserved. The power of the states to regulate their purely internal affairs by such laws as seem wise to the local authority is inherent, and has never been surrendered to the general government. *** To sustain this statute would not be, in our judgment, a recognition of the lawful exertion of congressional authority over interstate commerce, but would sanction an invasion by the Federal power of the control of a matter purely local in its character, and over which no authority has been delegated to Congress in conferring the power to regulate commerce among the states.

We have neither authority nor disposition to question the motives of Congress in enacting this legislation. The purposes intended must be attained consistently with constitutional limitations, and not by an invasion of the powers of the states. This court has no more important function than that which devolves upon it the obligation to preserve inviolate the constitutional limitations upon the exercise of authority, Federal and state, to the end that each may continue to discharge, harmoniously with the other, the duties intrusted to it by the Constitution.

... [T]he act in a twofold sense is repugnant to the Constitution. It not only transcends the authority delegated to Congress over commerce, but also exerts a power as to a purely local matter to which the Federal authority does not extend. The far-reaching result of upholding the act cannot be more plainly indicated than by pointing out that if Congress can thus regulate matters intrusted to local authority by prohibition of the movement of commodities in interstate commerce, all freedom of commerce will be at an end, and the power of the state over local matters may be eliminated, and thus our system of government be practically destroyed.

For these reasons we hold that this law exceeds the constitutional authority of Congress. It follows that the decree of the District Court must be affirmed.

Mr. Justice Holmes, dissenting.

... [I]f an act is within the powers specifically conferred upon Congress, it seems to me that it is not made any less constitutional because of the indirect effects that it may have, however obvious it may be that it will have those effects; and that we are not at liberty upon such grounds to hold it void.

The first step in my argument is to make plain what no one is likely to dispute—that the statute in question is within the power expressly given to Congress if considered only as to its immediate effects, and that if invalid it is so only upon some collateral ground. The statute confines itself to prohibiting the carriage of certain goods in interstate or foreign commerce. Congress is given power to regulate such commerce in unqualified terms. It would not be argued today that the power to regulate does not include the power to prohibit. Regulation means the prohibition of something, and when interstate commerce is the matter to be regulated I cannot doubt that the regulations may prohibit any part of such commerce that Congress sees fit to forbid....

The question, then is narrowed to whether the exercise of its otherwise constitutional power by Congress can be pronounced unconstitutional because of its possible reaction upon the conduct of the states in a matter upon which I have admitted that they are free from direct control. I should have thought that that matter had been disposed of so fully as to leave no room for doubt. I should have thought that the most conspicuous decisions of this court had made it clear that the power to regulate commerce and other constitutional powers could not be cut down or qualified by the fact that it might interfere with the carrying out of the domestic policy of any state.

Holmes reviews in a slightly different light the same set of cases supporting the prohibition of supposedly "harmful" products, discussed by Justice Day in the majority opinion, and continues:

The notion that prohibition is any less prohibition when applied to things now thought evil I do not understand. But if there is any matter upon which civilized countries have agreed,—far more unanimously than they have with regard to intoxicants, and some other matters over which this country is now emotionally aroused,—it is the evil of premature and excessive child labor. I should have thought that if we were to introduce our own moral conceptions where, in my opinion, they do not belong, this was pre-eminently a case for upholding the exercise of all its powers by the United States.

But I had thought that the propriety of the exercise of a power admitted to exist in some cases was for the consideration of Congress alone, and that this court always had disvowed the right to intrude its judgment upon questions of policy or morals. It is not for this court to pronounce when prohibition is necessary to regulation if it ever may be necessary, — to say that it is permissible as against strong drink, but not as against the product of ruined lives.

The act does not meddle with anything belonging to the states. They may regulate their internal affairs and their domestic commerce as they like. But when they seek to send their products across the state line they are no longer within their rights. If there were no Constitution and no Congress their power to cross the line would depend upon their neighbors. Under the Constitution such commerce belongs not to the states, but to Congress to regulate. It may carry out its views of public policy whatever indirect effect they may have upon the activities of the states. Instead of being encountered by a prohibitive tariff at her boundaries, the state encounters the public policy of the United States which it is for Congress to express. The public policy of the United States is shaped with a view to the benefit of the nation as a whole. . . . The national welfare as understood by Congress may require a different attitude within its sphere from that of some self-seeking state. It seems to me entirely constitutional for Congress to enforce its understanding by all the means at its command.

Mr. Justice McKenna, Mr. Justice Brandeis, and **Mr. Justice Clarke** concur in this opinion.

United States v. Darby Lumber Company
312 U.S. 100; 61 S. Ct. 451; 85 L. Ed. 609 (1941)
Vote: 9-0

Mr. Justice Stone delivered the opinion of the Court.

The two principal questions raised by the record in this case are, first, whether Congress has constitutional power to prohibit the shipment in interstate commerce of lumber manufactured by employees whose wages are less than a prescribed minimum or whose weekly hours of labor at that wage are greater than a prescribed maximum, and, second, whether it has power to prohibit the employment of work- men in the production of goods "for interstate commerce" at other than prescribed wages and hours. . . .

The Fair Labor Standards Act [FLSA] set up a comprehensive legislative scheme for preventing the shipment in interstate commerce of certain products and commodities produced in the United States under labor conditions as respects wages and hours which fail to conform to standards set up by the Act. Its purpose, as we judicially know from the declaration of policy ... is to exclude from interstate commerce goods produced for the commerce and to prevent their production for interstate commerce, under conditions detrimental to the maintenance of the minimum standards of living necessary for health and general well-being; and to prevent the use of interstate commerce as the means of competition in the distribution of goods so produced, and as the means of spreading and perpetuating such substandard labor conditions among the workers of the several states....

... [T]he statute *** prohibits certain specified acts and punishes willful violation of it by a fine of not more than $10,000 and punishes each conviction after the first by imprisonment of not more than six months or by the specified fine or both.... [The act makes it unlawful to ship in interstate commerce goods produced by employees working for less than a minimum wage of twenty-five cents per hour or for more than forty-four hours a week.]

The indictment charges that [Darby] is engaged, in the state of Georgia, in the business of acquiring raw materials, which he manufactures into finished lumber with the intent, when manufactured, to ship it in interstate commerce to customers outside the state, and that he does in fact so ship a large part of the lumber so produced. There are numerous counts charging [him] with the shipment in interstate commerce from Georgia to points outside the state of lumber in the production of which, for interstate commerce, [Darby] has employed workmen at less than the prescribed minimum wage or more than the prescribed maximum hours without payment to them of any wage for overtime....

The case comes here on assignments by the Government that the district court erred in so far as it held that Congress was without constitutional power to penalize the acts set forth in the indictment, and [Darby] seeks to sustain the decision below on the grounds that the prohibition by Congress of those Acts is unauthorized by the commerce clause....

The prohibition of shipment of the proscribed goods in interstate commerce. [The FLSA] prohibits, and the indictment charges, the shipment in interstate commerce, of goods produced for interstate commerce by employees whose wages and hours of employment do not conform to the requirements of the Act.... [T]he only question arising under the commerce clause with respect to such shipments is whether Congress has the constitutional power to prohibit them.

While manufacture is not of itself interstate commerce the shipment of manufactured goods interstate is such commerce and the prohibition of such shipment by Congress is indubitably a regulation of the commerce. The power to regulate commerce is the power "to prescribe the rule by which commerce is governed." *** It extends not only to those regulations which aid, foster and protect the commerce, but embraces those which prohibit it. *** It is conceded that the power of Congress to prohibit transportation in interstate commerce includes noxious articles, *** and articles such as intoxicating liquor or convict made goods, traffic in which is forbidden or restricted by the laws of the state of destination. ***

But it is said that the present prohibition falls within the scope of none of these categories; that while the prohibition is nominally a regulation of the commerce its motive or purpose is regulation of wages and hours of persons engaged in manufacture, the control of which has been reserved to the states and upon which Georgia and some of the states of destination have placed no restriction; that the effect of the present statute is not to exclude the prescribed articles from interstate commerce in aid of state regulation, *** but instead, under the guise of a regulation of interstate commerce, it undertakes to regulate wages and hours within the state contrary to the policy of the state which has elected to leave them unregulated.

The power of Congress over interstate commerce "is complete in itself, may be exercised to its utmost extent, and acknowledges no limitations other than are prescribed in the Constitution." *** That power can neither be enlarged nor diminished by the exercise or nonexercise of state power. *** Congress, following its own conception of public policy concerning the restrictions which may appropriately be imposed on interstate commerce, is free to exclude from the commerce articles whose use in the states for which they are destined it may conceive to be injurious to the public health, morals or welfare, even though the state has not sought to regulate their use. ***

Such regulation is not a forbidden invasion of state power merely because either its motive or its consequence is to restrict the use of articles of commerce within the states of destination and is not prohibited unless by other constitutional provisions. It is no objection to the assertion of power to regulate interstate commerce that its exercise is attended by the same incidents which attend the exercise of the police power of the states. ***

The motive and purpose of the present regulation are plainly to make effective the Congressional conception of public policy that interstate commerce should not be made the instrument of competition in the distribution of goods produced under substandard labor conditions, which competition is injurious to the commerce and to the states from and to which the commerce flows. The motive and purpose of a regulation of interstate commerce are matters for the legislative judgment upon the exercise of which the Constitution places no restriction and over which the courts are given no control. *** ... Whatever their motive and purpose, regulations of commerce which do not infringe some constitutional prohibition are within the plenary power conferred on Congress by the Commerce Clause. Subject only to that limitation, presently to be considered, we conclude that the prohibition of the shipment interstate of goods produced under the forbidden substandard labor conditions is within the constitutional authority of Congress.

In the more than a century which has elapsed since the decision of *Gibbons v. Ogden,* these principles of constitutional interpretation have been so long and repeatedly recognized by this Court as applicable to the Commerce Clause, that there would be little occasion for repeating them now were it not for the decision of this Court twenty-two years ago in *Hammer v. Dagenhart.* *** In that case it was held by a bare majority of the Court over the powerful and now classic dissent of Mr. Justice Holmes setting

forth the fundamental issues involved that Congress was without power to exclude the products of child labor from interstate commerce. The reasoning and conclusion of the Court's opinion there cannot be reconciled with the conclusion which we have reached, that the power of Congress under the Commerce Clause is plenary to exclude any article from interstate commerce subject only to the specific prohibitions of the Constitution.

Hammer v. Dagenhart has not been followed. The distinction on which the decision was rested that Congressional power to prohibit interstate commerce is limited to articles which in themselves have some harmful or deleterious property—a distinction which was novel when made and unsupported by any provision of the Constitution—has long since been abandoned. *** The thesis of the opinion that the motive of the prohibition or its effect to control in some measure the use or production within the states of the article thus excluded from the commerce can operate to deprive the regulation of its constitutional authority has long since ceased to have force. ***

The conclusion is inescapable that *Hammer v. Dagenhart* was a departure from the principles which have prevailed in the interpretation of the Commerce Clause both before and since the decision and that such vitality, as a precedent, as it then had has long since been exhausted. It should be and now is overruled.

Validity of the wage and hour requirements. ... [W]e must at the outset determine whether the particular acts charged in the courts, ... as they were construed below, constitute "production for commerce" within the meaning of the statute. As the Government seeks to apply the statute in the indictment, and as the court below construed the phrase "produced for interstate commerce," it embraces at least the case where an employer engaged, as is [Darby], in the manufacture and shipment of goods in filling orders of extrastate customers, manufactures his product with the intent or expectation that according to the normal course of his business all or some part of it will be selected for shipment to those customers.

Without attempting to define the precise limits of the phrase, we think the acts alleged in the indictment are within the sweep of the statute. The obvious purpose of the Act was not only to prevent the interstate transportation of the proscribed product, but to stop the initial step toward transportation, production with the purpose of so transporting it. Congress was not unaware that most manufacturing businesses shipping their product in interstate commerce make it in their shops without reference to its ultimate destination and then after manufacture select some of it for shipment interstate and some intrastate according to the daily demands of their business, and that it would be practically impossible, without disrupting manufacturing businesses, to restrict the prohibited kind of production to the particular pieces of lumber, cloth, furniture or the like which later move in interstate rather than intrastate commerce. *** . . .

There remains the question whether such restriction on the production of goods for commerce is a permissible exercise of the commerce power. The power of Congress over interstate commerce is not confined to the regulation of commerce among the states. It extends to those activities intrastate which so affect interstate commerce or the exercise of the power of Congress over it as to make regulation of them appropriate means to the attainment of a legitimate end, the exercise of the granted power of Congress to regulate interstate commerce. ***

While this Court has many times found state regulations of interstate commerce, when uniformity of its regulation is of national concern, to be incompatible with the Commerce Clause even though Congress has not legislated on the subject, the Court has never implied such restraint on state control over matters intrastate not deemed to be regulations of interstate commerce or its instrumentalities even though they affect the commerce. *** In the absence of Congressional legislation on the subject state laws which are not regulations of the commerce itself or its instrumentalities are not forbidden even though they affect interstate commerce. ***

But it does not follow that Congress may not by appropriate legislation regulate intrastate activities where they have a substantial effect on interstate commerce. *** . . .

In such legislation Congress has sometimes left it to the courts to determine whether the intrastate

activities have the prohibited effect on the commerce, as in the Sherman Act. It has sometimes left it to an administrative board or agency to determine whether the activities sought to be regulated or prohibited have such effect, as in the case of the Interstate Commerce Act and the National Labor Relations Act, or whether they come within the statutory definition of the prohibited Act as in the Federal Trade Commission Act. And sometimes Congress itself has said that a particular activity affects the commerce as it did in the present act, the Safety Appliance Act and the Railway Labor Act. In passing on the validity of legislation of the class last mentioned the only function of courts is to determine whether the particular activity regulated or prohibited is within the reach of the federal power. ***

Congress, having by the present Act adopted the policy of excluding from interstate commerce all goods produced for the commerce which do not conform to the specified labor standards, it may choose the means reasonably adapted to the attainment of the permitted end, even though they involve control of intrastate activities. Such legislation has often been sustained with respect to powers, other than the commerce power granted to the national government, when the means chosen, although not themselves within the granted power, were nevertheless deemed appropriate aids to the accomplishment of some purpose within an admitted power of the national government. *** A familiar like exercise of power is the regulation of intrastate transactions which are so commingled with or related to interstate commerce that all must be regulated if the interstate commerce is to be effectively controlled. *** . . .

. . . [T]he evils aimed at by the [FLSA] are the spread of substandard labor conditions through the use of the facilities of interstate commerce for competition by the goods so produced with those produced under the prescribed or better labor conditions; and the consequent dislocation of the commerce itself caused by the impairment or destruction of local businesses by competition made effective through interstate commerce. The Act is thus directed at the suppression of a method or kind of competition in interstate commerce which it has in effect condemned as "unfair," as the Clayton Act has condemned other "unfair methods of competition" made effective through interstate commerce. *** ...

The means adopted ... for the protection of interstate commerce by the suppression of the production of the condemned goods for interstate commerce is so related to the commerce and so affects it as to be within the reach of the commerce power. *** Congress, to attain its objective in the suppression of nationwide competition in interstate commerce by goods produced under substandard labor conditions, has made no distinction as to the volume or amount of shipments in the commerce or of production for commerce by any particular shipper or producer. It recognized that in present day industry, competition by a small part may affect the whole and that the total effect of the competition of many small producers may be great. *** The legislation aimed at a whole embraces all its parts. *** ...

Our conclusion is unaffected by the Tenth Amendment which provides: "The powers not delegated to the United States by the Constitution nor prohibited by it to the states are reserved to the states respectively or to the people." The amendment states but a truism that all is retained which has not been surrendered. There is nothing in the history of its adoption to suggest that it was more than declaratory of the relationship between the national and state governments as it had been established by the Constitution before the amendment or that its purpose was other than to allay fears that the new national government might seek to exercise powers not granted, and that the states might not be able to exercise fully their reserved powers. ***

From the beginning and for many years the amendment has been construed as not depriving the national government of authority to resort to all means for the exercise of a granted power which are appropriate and plainly adapted to the permitted end. *** Whatever doubts may have arisen of the soundness of that conclusion they have been put at rest by the decisions under the Sherman Act and the National Labor Relations Act....

The Act is sufficiently definite to meet constitutional demands. One who employs persons, without conforming to the prescribed wage and hour conditions, to work on goods which he ships or expects to ship across state lines, is warned that he may be subject to the criminal penalties of the Act. No more is required. *** ...

Reversed.

National League of Cities v. Usery

426 U.S. 833; 96 S. Ct. 2465; 49 L. Ed. 2d 245 (1976)
Vote: 5-4

Mr. Justice Rehnquist delivered the opinion of the Court.

Nearly 40 years ago Congress enacted the Fair Labor Standards Act, and required employers covered by the Act to pay their employees a minimum hourly wage and to pay them at one and one-half times their regular rate of pay for hours worked in excess of 40 during a work week.... This Court unanimously upheld the Act as a valid exercise of congressional authority under the commerce power in *United States v. Darby* *** ....

The original Fair Labor Standards Act passed in 1938 specifically excluded the States and their political subdivisions from its coverage. In 1974, however, Congress enacted the most recent of a series of broadening amendments to the Act. By these amendments Congress has extended the minimum wage and maximum hour provisions to almost all public employees employed by the States and by their various political subdivisions. Appellants in these cases include individual cities and States, the National League of Cities, and the National Governors' Conference; they brought an action ... which challenged the validity of the 1974 amendments. They asserted in effect when Congress sought to apply the Fair Labor Standards Act provisions virtually across the board to employees of state and municipal governments it "infringed a constitutional prohibition" running in favor of the States as States. The gist of their complaint was not that the conditions of employment of such public employees were beyond the scope of the commerce power had those employees been employed in the private sector, but that the established constitutional doctrine of intergovernmental immunity consistently recognized in a long series of our cases affirmatively prevented the exercise of this authority in the manner which Congress chose in the 1974 amendments....

[The League] in no way challenge[s] ... the breadth of authority granted Congress under the commerce power. Their contention, on the contrary, is that when Congress seeks to regulate directly the activities of States as public employers, it transgresses an affirmative limitation on the exercise of its power akin to other commerce power affirmative limitations contained in the Constitution. Congressional enactments which may be fully within the grant of legislative authority contained in the Commerce Clause may nonetheless be invalid because [they are] found to offend against the right to trial by jury contained in the Sixth Amendment *** or the Due Process Clause of the Fifth Amendment. *** [The League's] essential contention is that the 1974 amendments to the Act, while undoubtedly within the scope of the Commerce Clause, encounter a similar constitutional barrier because they are to be applied directly to the States and subdivisions of States as employers.

This Court has never doubted that there are limits upon the power of Congress to override state sovereignty, even when exercising its otherwise plenary powers to tax or to regulate commerce which are conferred by Art. I of the Constitution.... [T]he Court [has] recognized that an express declaration of this limitation is found in the Tenth Amendment:

> While the Tenth Amendment has been characterized as a "truism," stating merely that "all that is retained which has not been surrendered," *** it is not without significance. The Amendment expressly declares the constitutional policy that Congress may not exercise power in a fashion that impairs the States' integrity or their ability to function effectively in a federal system.

... [Usery] argues that the cases in which this Court has upheld sweeping exercises of authority by Congress, even though those exercises pre-empted

state regulation of the private sector, have already curtailed the sovereignty of the States quite as much as the 1974 amendments to the Fair Labor Standards Act. We do not agree. It is one thing to recognize the authority of Congress to enact laws regulating individual businesses necessarily subject to the dual sovereignty of the government of the Nation and of the State in which they reside. It is quite another to uphold a similar exercise of congressional authority directed, not to private citizens, but to the States as States. We have repeatedly recognized that there are attributes of sovereignty attaching to every state government which may not be impaired by Congress, not because Congress may lack an affirmative grant of legislative authority to reach the matter, but because the Constitution prohibits it from exercising the authority in that manner....

One undoubted attribute of state sovereignty is the States' power to determine the wages which shall be paid to those whom they employ in order to carry out their governmental functions, what hours those persons will work, and what compensation will be provided where these employees may be called upon to work overtime. The question we must resolve here, then, is whether these determinations are "functions essential to separate and independent existence," *** so that Congress may not abrogate the States' otherwise plenary authority to make them....

Quite apart from the substantial costs imposed upon the States and their political subdivisions, the Act displaces state policies regarding the manner in which they will structure delivery of those governmental services which their citizens require. The Act, speaking directly to the States *qua* States, requires that they shall pay all but an extremely limited minority of their employees the minimum wage rates currently chosen by Congress. It may well be that as a matter of economic policy it would be desirable that States, just as private employers, comply with these minimum wage requirements. But it cannot be gain-said that the federal requirement directly supplants the considered policy choices of the States' elected officials and administrators as to how they wish to structure pay scales in state employment. The State might wish to employ persons with little or no training, or those who wish to work on a casual basis, or those who for some other reason do not possess minimum employment requirements, and pay them less than the federally prescribed minimum wage. It may wish to offer part-time or summer employment to teenagers at a figure less than the minimum wage, and if unable to do so may decline to offer such employment at all. But the Act would forbid such choices by the States. The only "discretion" left to them under the Act is either to attempt to increase their revenue to meet the additional financial burden imposed upon them by paying congressionally prescribed wages to their existing complement of employees, or to reduce that complement to a number which can be paid the federal minimum wage without increasing revenue.

This dilemma presented by the minimum wage restrictions may seem not immediately different from that faced by private employers, who have long been covered by the Act and who must find ways to increase their gross income if they are to pay higher wages while maintaining current earnings. The difference, however, is that a State is not merely a factor in the "shifting economic arrangements" of the private sector of the economy, *** but is itself a coordinate element in the system established by the Framers for governing our Federal Union.

This congressionally imposed displacement of state decisions may substantially restructure traditional ways in which the local governments have arranged their affairs. Although at this point many of the actual effects under the proposed amendments remain a matter of some dispute among the parties, enough can be satisfactorily anticipated for an outline discussion of their general import. The requirement imposing premium rates upon any employment in excess of what Congress has decided is appropriate for a governmental employee's workweek, for example, appears likely to have the effect of coercing the States to structure work periods in some employment areas, such as police and fire protection, in a manner substantially different from practices which have long been commonly accepted among local governments of this Nation. . . .

Our examination of the effect of the 1974 amendments, as sought to be extended to the States and their political subdivisions, satisfies us that both the minimum wage and the maximum hour provisions will impermissibly interfere with the integral gov-

ernmental functions of these bodies. . . . If Congress may withdraw from the States the authority to make those fundamental employment decisions upon which their systems for performance of these functions must rest, we think there would be little left of the States' "separate and independent existence." *** Thus, even if appellants may have overestimated the effect which the Act will have upon their current levels and patterns of governmental activity, the dispositive factor is that Congress has attempted to exercise its Commerce Clause authority to prescribe minimum wages and maximum hours to be paid by the States in their capacities as sovereign governments. In so doing, Congress has sought to wield its power in a fashion that would impair the States' "ability to function effectively in a federal system." *** This exercise of congressional authority does not comport with the federal system of government embodied in the Constitution. We hold that insofar as the challenged amendments operate to directly displace the States' freedom to structure integral operations in areas of traditional governmental functions, they are not within the authority granted Congress by Art. I, Sec. 8, cl. 3. . . .

The judgment of the District Court is accordingly reversed and the case is remanded for further proceedings consistent with this opinion.

Mr. Justice Blackmun, concurring. . . .

Mr. Justice Brennan, with whom ***Mr. Justice White*** and ***Mr. Justice Marshall*** join, dissenting.

. . . My Brethren do not successfully obscure today's patent usurpation of the role reserved for the political process by their purported discovery in the Constitution of a restraint derived from sovereignty of the States on Congress' exercise of the commerce power. . . . [T]here is no restraint based on state sovereignty requiring or permitting judicial enforcement anywhere expressed in the Constitution; our decisions over the last century and a half have explicitly rejected the existence of any such restraint on the commerce power. . . .

My Brethren have today manufactured an abstraction without substance, founded neither in the words of the Constitution nor on precedent. An abstraction having such profoundly pernicious consequences is not made less so by characterizing the 1974 amendments as legislation directed against the "States *qua* States." *** . . .

The reliance of my Brethren upon the Tenth Amendment as "an express declaration of [a state sovereignty] limitation" *** not only suggests that they overrule governing decisions of this Court that address this question but must astound scholars of the Constitution. . . . [A]s the Tenth Amendment's significance was summarized:

The amendment states but a truism that all is retained which has not been surrendered. *There is nothing in the history of its adoption to suggest that it was more than declaratory of the relationship between the national and state governments as it had been established by the Constitution before the amendment* or that its purpose was other than to allay fears that the new national government might seek to exercise powers not granted, and that the states might not be able to exercise fully their reserved powers. . . .

From the beginning and for many years the amendment has been construed as not depriving the national government of authority to resort to all means for the exercise of a granted power which are appropriate and plainly adapted to the permitted end. *** (emphasis added). . . .

Today's repudiation of [an] unbroken line of precedents that firmly reject my Brethren's ill-conceived abstraction can only be regarded as a transparent cover for invalidating a congressional judgment with which they disagree. The only analysis even remotely resembling that adopted today is found in a line of opinions dealing with the Commerce Clause and the Tenth Amendment that ultimately provoked a constitutional crisis for the Court in the 1930's. *** We tend to forget that the Court invalidated legislation during the Great Depression, not solely under the Due Process Clause, but also and primarily under the Commerce Clause and the Tenth Amendment. It may have been the eventual abandonment of that overly restrictive construction of the commerce power that spelled defeat for the Court-packing plan, and preserved the integrity of this institution. . . . but my Brethren today are transparently trying to cut back on that recognition of the scope of the commerce power. . . .

My Brethren do more than turn aside long-standing constitutional jurisprudence that emphati-

cally rejects today's conclusion. More alarming is the startling restructuring of our federal system, and the role they create therein for the federal judiciary. This Court is simply not at liberty to erect a mirror of its own conception of a desirable governmental structure. If the 1974 amendments have any "vice," *** my Brother Stevens is surely right that it represents "merely . . . a policy issue which has been firmly resolved by the branches of government having power to decide such questions." *** It bears repeating "that effective restraints on . . . exercise [of the commerce power] must proceed from political rather than from judicial processes." ***

It is unacceptable that the judicial process should be thought superior to the political process in this area. Under the Constitution the Judiciary has no role to play beyond finding that Congress has not made an unreasonable legislative judgment respecting what is "commerce." . . .

Judicial restraint in this area merely recognizes that the political branches of our Government are structured to protect the interests of the States, as well as the Nation as a whole, and that the States are fully able to protect their own interests in the premises. Congress is constituted of representatives in both the Senate and House elected from the States. *** Decisions upon the extent of federal intervention under the Commerce Clause into the affairs of the States are in that sense decisions of the States themselves. Judicial redistribution of powers granted the National Government by the terms of the Constitution violates the fundamental tenet of our federalism that the extent of federal intervention into the States' affairs in the exercise of delegated powers shall be determined by the States' exercise of political power through their representatives in Congress. *** . . . Any realistic assessment of our federal political system, dominated as it is by representatives of the people elected from the States, yields the conclusion that it is highly unlikely that those representatives will ever be motivated to disregard totally the concerns of these States. *** . . .

We are left with a catastrophic judicial body blow at Congress' power under the Commerce Clause. Even if Congress may nevertheless accomplish its objectives—for example, by conditioning grants of federal funds upon compliance with federal minimum wage and overtime standards *** —there is an ominous portent of disruption of our constitutional structure implicit in today's mischievous decision. I dissent.

Mr. Justice Stevens, dissenting.

The Court holds that the Federal Government may not interfere with a sovereign State's inherent right to pay a substandard wage to the janitor at the state capitol. The principle on which the holding rests is difficult to perceive.

The Federal Government may, I believe, require the State to act impartially when it hires or fires the janitor, to withhold taxes from his paycheck, to observe safety regulations when he is performing his job, to forbid him from burning too much soft coal in the capitol furnace, from dumping untreated refuse in an adjacent waterway, from overloading a state-owned garbage truck, or from driving either the truck or the governor's limousine over 55 miles an hour. Even though these and many other activities of the capitol janitor are activities of the State *qua* State, I have no doubt that they are subject to federal regulation. . . .

My disagreement with the wisdom of this legislation may not, of course, affect my judgment with respect to its validity. On this issue there is no dissent from the proposition that the Federal Government's power over the labor market is adequate to embrace these employees. Since I am unable to identify a limitation on that federal power that would not also invalidate federal regulation of state activities that I consider unquestionably permissible, I am persuaded that this statute is valid. Accordingly, with respect and a great deal of sympathy for the views expressed by the Court, I dissent from its constitutional holding.

Garcia v. San Antonio Metropolitan Transit Authority

469 U.S. 528; 105 S. Ct. 1005; 83 L. Ed. 2d 1016 (1985)
Vote: 5-4

Justice Blackmun delivered the opinion of the Court.

We revisit in these cases an issue raised in *National League of Cities v. Usery*. . . . *** In that litigation, this Court, by a sharply divided vote, ruled that the Commerce Clause does not empower Congress to enforce the minimum-wage and overtime provisions of the Fair Labor Standards Act (FLSA) against the States "in areas of traditional governmental functions." *** Although *National League of Cities* supplied some examples of "traditional governmental functions," it did not offer a general explanation of how a "traditional" function is to be distinguished-from a "nontraditional" one. Since then, federal and state courts have struggled with the task, thus imposed, of identifying a traditional function for purposes of state immunity under the Commerce Clause.

In the present cases, a Federal District Court concluded that municipal ownership and operation of a mass-transit system is a traditional governmental function and thus, under *National League of Cities*, is exempt from the obligations imposed by the FLSA. Faced with the identical question, three Federal Courts of Appeals and one state appellate court have reached the opposite conclusion.

Our examination of this "function" standard applied in these and other cases over the last eight years now persuades us that the attempt to draw the boundaries of state regulatory immunity in terms of "traditional governmental function" is not only unworkable but is inconsistent with established principles of federalism and, indeed, with those very federalism principles on which *National League of Cities* purported to rest. That case, accordingly, is overruled.

The history of public transportation in San Antonio, Tex., is characteristic of the history of local mass transit in the United States generally. Passenger transportation for hire within San Antonio originally was provided on a private basis by a local transportation company. In 1913, the Texas Legislature authorized the State's municipalities to regulate vehicles providing carriage for hire. *** Two years later, San Antonio enacted an ordinance setting forth franchising, insurance, and safety requirements for passenger vehicles operated for hire. The city continued to rely on such publicly regulated private mass transit until 1959, when it purchased the privately owned San Antonio Transit Company and replaced it with a public authority known as the San Antonio Transit System (SATS). SATS operated until 1978, when the city transferred its facilities and equipment to appellee San Antonio Metropolitan Transit Authority (SAMTA), a public mass-transit authority organized on a countywide basis. *** SAMTA currently is the major provider of transportation in the San Antonio metropolitan area; between 1978 and 1980 alone, its vehicles traveled over 26 million route miles and carried over 63 million passengers.

As did other localities, San Antonio reached the point where it came to look to the Federal Government for financial assistance in maintaining its public mass transit. SATS managed to meet its operating expenses and bond obligations for the first decade of its existence without federal or local financial aid. By 1970, however, its financial position had deteriorated to the point where federal subsidies were vital for its continued operation. SATS' general manager that year testified before Congress that "if we do not receive substantial help from the Federal Government, San Antonio may . . . join the growing ranks of cities that have inferior [public] transportation or may end up with no [public] transportation at all." ***

The principal federal program to which SATS and other mass-transit systems looked for relief was the Urban Mass Transportation Act of 1964 (UMTA), *** which provides substantial federal assistance to urban mass-transit programs. *** UMTA now authorizes the Department of Transportation to fund 75 percent of the capital outlays and up to 50 percent of the operating expenses of qualifying mass-transit programs. *** SATS received its first UMTA subsidy, a $4.1 million capital grant, in December 1970. From then until February 1980, SATS and SAMTA received over $51 million in UMTA grants—more than $31 million in capital grants, over $20 million in operating assis-

tance, and a minor amount in technical assistance. During SAMTA's first two fiscal years, it received $12.5 million in UMTA operating grants, $26.8 million from sales taxes, and only $10.1 million from fares. Federal subsidies and local sales taxes currently account for about 75 percent of SAMTA's operating expenses.

The present controversy concerns the extent to which SAMTA may be subjected to the minimum-wage and overtime requirements of the FLSA. When the FLSA was enacted in 1938, its wage and overtime provisions did not apply to local mass-transit employees or, indeed, to employees of state and local governments. *** In 1961, Congress extended minimum-wage coverage to employees of any private mass-transit carrier whose annual gross revenue was not less than $1 million. *** Five years later, Congress extended FLSA coverage to state and local-government employees for the first time by withdrawing the minimum-wage and overtime exemptions from public hospitals, schools, and mass-transit carriers whose rates and services were subject to state regulation. *** At the same time, Congress eliminated the overtime exemption for all mass-transit employees other than drivers, operators, and conductors. *** The application of the FLSA to public schools and hospitals was ruled to be within Congress' power under the Commerce Clause. ***

The FLSA obligations of public mass-transit systems like SATS were expanded in 1974 when Congress provided for the progressive repeal of the surviving overtime exemption for mass-transit employees. *** Congress simultaneously brought the States and their subdivisions further within the ambit of the FLSA by extending FLSA coverage to virtually all state and local-government employees. ***

Appellees have not argued that SAMTA is immune from regulation under the FLSA on the ground that it is a local transit system engaged in intrastate commercial activity. In a practical sense, SAMTA's operations might well be characterized as "local." Nonetheless, it long has been settled that Congress' authority under the Commerce Clause extends to intrastate economic activities that affect interstate commerce. *** Were SAMTA a privately owned and operated enterprise, it could not credibly argue that Congress exceeded the bounds of its Commerce

Clause powers in prescribing minimum wages and overtime rates for SAMTA's employees. Any constitutional exemption from the requirements of the FLSA therefore must rest on SAMTA's status as a governmental entity rather than on the "local" nature of its operations.

The prerequisites for governmental immunity under *National League of Cities* were summarized by this Court in *Hodel* [v. *Virginia Surface Mining and Recl. Assn.*]. *** Under that summary, four conditions must be satisfied before a state activity may be deemed immune from a particular federal regulation under the Commerce Clause. First, it is said that the federal statute at issue must regulate "the 'States as States.' " Second, the statute must "address matters that are indisputably 'attribute[s] of state sovereignty.' " Third, state compliance with the federal obligation must "directly impair [the States'] ability 'to structure integral operations in areas of traditional governmental functions.' " Finally, the relation of state and federal interests must not be such that "the nature of the federal interest . . . justifies state submission." ***

The controversy in the present cases has focused on the third *Hodel* requirement—that the challenged federal statute trenches on "traditional governmental functions." The District Court voiced a common concern: "Despite the abundance of adjectives, identifying which particular state functions are immune remains difficult." *** Just how troublesome the task has been is revealed by the results reached in other federal cases. . . .

Thus far, this Court itself has made little headway in defining the scope of the governmental functions deemed protected under *National League of Cities*. In that case the Court set forth examples of protected and unprotected functions, *** but provided no explanation of how those examples were identified. . . .

The central theme of *National League of Cities* was that the States occupy a special position in our constitutional system and that the scope of Congress' authority under the Commerce Clause must reflect that position. Of course, the Commerce Clause by its specific language does not provide any special limitation on Congress' actions with respect to the States. *** It is equally true, however, that the text of the Constitution provides the beginning rather than the

final answer to every inquiry into questions of federalism, for "[b]ehind the words of the constitutional provisions are postulates which limit and control." *** *National League of Cities* reflected the general conviction that the Constitution precludes "the National Government [from] devour[ing] the essentials of state sovereignty." *** In order to be faithful to the underlying federal premises of the Constitution, courts must look for the "postulates which limit and control."

What has proved problematic is not the perception that the Constitution's federal structure imposes limitations on the Commerce Clause, but rather the nature and content of those limitations. One approach to defining the limits on Congress' authority to regulate the States under the Commerce Clause is to identify certain underlying elements of political sovereignty that are deemed essential to the States' "separate and independent existence." *** This approach obviously underlay the Court's use of the "traditional governmental function" concept in *National League of Cities*. It also has led to the separate requirement that the challenged federal statute "address matters that are indisputably 'attribute[s] of state sovereignty.' " *** In *National League of Cities* itself, for example, the Court concluded that decisions by a State concerning the wages and hours of its employees are an "undoubted attribute of state sovereignty." *** The opinion did not explain what aspects of such decisions made them such an "undoubted attribute," and the Court since then has remarked on the uncertain scope of the concept. *** The point of the inquiry, however, has remained to single out particular features of a State's internal governance that are deemed to be intrinsic parts of state sovereignty.

We doubt that courts ultimately can identify principled constitutional limitations on the scope of Congress' Commerce Clause powers over the States merely by relying on a priori definitions of state sovereignty. In part, this is because of the elusiveness of objective criteria for "fundamental" elements of state sovereignty, a problem we have witnessed in the search for "traditional governmental functions." There is, however, a more fundamental reason: the sovereignty of the States is limited by the Constitution itself. A variety of sovereign powers, for example, are withdrawn from the States by Article I, Sec. 10. Section 8 of the same Article works an equally sharp contraction of state sovereignty by authorizing Congress to exercise a wide range of legislative powers and (in conjunction with the Supremacy Clause of Article VI) to displace contrary state legislation. *** By providing for final review of questions of federal law in this Court, Article III curtails the sovereign power of the States' judiciaries to make authoritative determinations of law. *** Finally, the developed application, through the Fourteenth Amendment, of the greater part of the Bill of Rights to the States limits the sovereign authority that States otherwise would possess to legislate with respect to their citizens and to conduct their own affairs.

The States unquestionably do "retai[n] a significant measure of sovereign authority." *** They do so, however, only to the extent that the Constitution has not divested them of their original powers and transferred those powers to the Federal Government. . . .

. . . [T]o say that the Constitution assumes the continued role of the States is to say little about the nature of that role. Only recently, this Court recognized that the purpose of the constitutional immunity recognized in National League of Cities is not to preserve "a sacred province of state autonomy." *** With rare exceptions, like the guarantee, in Article IV, 3, of state territorial integrity, the Constitution does not carve out express elements of state sovereignty that Congress may not employ its delegated powers to displace. . . . The power of the Federal Government is a "power to be respected" as well, and the fact that the States remain sovereign as to all powers not vested in Congress or denied them by the Constitution offers no guidance about where the frontier between state and federal power lies. In short, we have no license to employ freestanding conceptions of state sovereignty when measuring congressional authority under the Commerce Clause.

When we look for the States' "residuary and inviolable sovereignty." *** in the shape of the constitutional scheme rather than in predetermined notions of sovereign power, a different measure of state sovereignty emerges. Apart from the limitation on federal authority inherent in the delegated nature of Congress' Article I powers, the principal means chosen by the Framers to ensure the role of the States in the federal system lies in the structure of the Federal Government itself. It is no novelty to observe that the composition of the Federal Government was designed in large part to protect the States from overreaching by Congress. The Framers thus gave the States a role in the selection both of the Executive and the Legislative Branches of the Federal Government. The States were vested with indirect influence over the House of Representatives and the Presidency by their control of electoral qualifications and their role in presidential elections. *** They were given more direct influence in the Senate, where each State received equal representation and each Senator was to be selected by the legislature of his State. *** The significance attached to the States' equal representation in the Senate is underscored by the prohibition of any constitutional amendment divesting a State of equal representation without the State's consent. ***

The extent to which the structure of the Federal Government itself was relied on to insulate the interests of the States is evident in the views of the Framers. James Madison explained that the Federal Government "will partake sufficiently of the spirit [of the States], to be disinclined to invade the rights of the individual States, or the prerogatives of their governments. . . ." *** In short, the Framers chose to rely on a federal system in which special restraints on federal power over the States inhered principally in the workings of the National Government itself, rather than in discrete limitations on the objects of federal authority. State sovereign interests, then, are more properly protected by procedural safeguards inherent in the structure of the federal system than by judicially created limitations on federal power. . . .

This analysis makes clear that Congress' action in affording SAMTA employees the protections of the wage and hour provisions of the FLSA contravened no affirmative limit on Congress' power under the Commerce Clause. The judgment of the District Court therefore must be reversed.

Of course, we continue to recognize that the States occupy a special and specific position in our constitutional system and that the scope of Congress' authority under the Commerce Clause must reflect that position. But the principal and basic limit on the federal commerce power is that inherent in all congressional action—the built-in restraints that our system provides through state participation in federal governmental action. The political process ensures that laws that unduly burden the States will not be promulgated. In the factual setting of these cases the internal safeguards of the political process have performed as intended.

These cases do not require us to identify or define what affirmative limits the constitutional structure might impose on federal action affecting the States under the Commerce Clause. . . . ***

Though the separate concurrence providing the fifth vote in *National League of Cities* was "not untroubled by certain possible implications" of the decision, *** the Court in that case attempted to articulate affirmative limits on the Commerce Clause power in terms of core governmental functions and fundamental attributes of state sovereignty. But the model of democratic decisionmaking the Court there identified underestimated, in our view, the solicitude of the national political process for the continued vitality of the States. Attempts by other courts since then to draw guidance from this model have proved it both impracticable and doctrinally barren. In sum, in *National League of Cities* the Court tried to repair what did not need repair.

We do not lightly overrule recent precedent. We have not hesitated, however, when it has become apparent that a prior decision has departed from a proper understanding of congressional power under the Commerce Clause. *** Due respect for the reach of congressional power within the federal system mandates that we do so now.

National League of Cities v. Usery *** is overruled. The judgment of the District Court is reversed, and these cases are remanded to that court for further proceedings consistent with this opinion.

It is so ordered.

Justice Powell, with whom ***the Chief Justice, Justice Rehnquist,*** and ***Justice O'Connor*** join, dissenting. . . .

Justice Rehnquist, dissenting. . . .

Justice O'Connor, with whom ***Justice Powell*** and ***Justice Rehnquist*** join, dissenting.

. . . In the decades since ratification of the Constitution, interstate economic activity has steadily expanded. Industrialization, coupled with advances in transportation and communications, has created a national economy in which virtually every activity occurring within the borders of a State plays a part. The expansion and integration of the national economy brought with it a coordinate expansion in the scope of national problems. This Court has been increasingly generous in its interpretation of the commerce power of Congress, primarily to assure that the National Government would be able to deal with national economic problems. Most significantly, the Court in *NLRB v. Jones & Laughlin Steel Corp.* *** rejected its previous interpretations of the commerce power which had stymied New Deal legislation. *Jones & Laughlin* and *Darby* embraced the notion that Congress can regulate intrastate activities that affect interstate commerce as surely as it can regulate interstate commerce directly. Subsequent decisions indicate that Congress, in order to regulate an activity, needs only a rational basis for a finding that the activity affects interstate commerce. *** Even if a particular individual's activity has no perceptible interstate effect, it can be reached by Congress through regulation of that class of activity in general as long as that class, considered as a whole, affects interstate commerce. ***

Incidental to this expansion of the commerce power, Congress has been given an ability it lacked prior to the emergence of an integrated national economy. Because virtually every state activity, like virtually every activity of a private individual, arguably "affects" interstate commerce, Congress can now supplant the States from the significant sphere of activities envisioned for them by the Framers. It is in this context that recent changes in the workings of Congress, such as the direct election of Senators and the expanded influence of national interest groups *** become relevant. These changes may well have lessened the weight Congress gives to the legitimate interests of States as States. As a result, there is now a real risk that Congress will gradually erase the diffusion of power between state and nation on which the Framers based their faith in the efficiency and vitality of our Republic.

It would be erroneous, however, to conclude that the Supreme Court was blind to the threat to federalism when it expanded the commerce power. The Court based the expansion on the authority of Congress, through the Necessary and Proper Clause, "to resort to all means for the exercise of a granted power which are appropriate and plainly adapted to the permitted end." *** It is through this reasoning that an intrastate activity "affecting" interstate commerce can be reached through the commerce power. . . .

It is worth recalling the cited passage in *McCulloch v. Maryland,* *** that lies at the source of the recent expansion of the commerce power. "Let the end be legitimate, let it be within the scope of the Constitution," Chief Justice Marshall said, "and all means which are appropriate, which are plainly adapted to that end, which are not prohibited, but consist with the letter and spirit of the Constitution, are constitutional." . . .

. . . the spirit of the Tenth Amendment, of course, is that the States will retain their integrity in a system in which the laws of the United States are nevertheless supreme. ***

It is not enough that the "end be legitimate"; the means to that end chosen by Congress must not contravene the spirit of the Constitution. Thus many of this Court's decisions acknowledge that the means by which national power is exercised must take into account concerns for state autonomy . . . *** The operative language of these cases varies, but the underlying principle is consistent: state autonomy is a relevant factor in assessing the means by which Congress exercises its powers.

This principle requires the Court to enforce affirmative limits on federal regulation of the States to complement the judicially crafted expansion of the interstate commerce power. *National League of Cities v. Usery* represented an attempt to define such limits. The Court today rejects *National League of Cities* and washes its hands of all efforts to protect the States. In the process, the Court opines that unwarranted federal encroachments on state authority are and will remain " 'horrible possibilities that never happen in the real world.' " *** There is ample reason to believe to the contrary.

The last two decades have seen an unprecedented growth of federal regulatory activity, as the majority

itself acknowledges. *** In 1954, one could speak of a "burden of persuasion on those favoring national intervention" in asserting that "National action has . . . always been regarded as exceptional in our polity, an intrusion to be justified by some necessity, the special rather than the ordinary case." *** Today, as federal legislation and coercive grant programs have expanded to embrace innumerable activities that were once viewed as local, the burden of persuasion has surely shifted, and the extraordinary has become ordinary. *** For example, recently the Federal Government has, with this Court's blessing, undertaken to tell the States the age at which they can retire their law enforcement officers, and the regulatory standards, procedures, and even the agenda which their utilities commissions must consider and follow. *** The political process has not protected against these encroachments on state activities, even though they directly impinge on a State's ability to make and enforce its laws. With the abandonment of *National League of Cities,* all that stands between the remaining essentials of state sovereignty and Congress is the latter's underdeveloped capacity for self-restraints.

The problems of federalism in an integrated national economy are capable of more responsible resolution than holding that the States as States retain no status apart from that which Congress chooses to let them retain. The proper resolution, I suggest, lies in weighing state autonomy as a factor in the balance when interpreting the means by which Congress can exercise its authority on the States as States. It is insufficient, in assessing the validity of congressional regulation of a State pursuant to the commerce power, to ask only whether the same regulation would be valid if enforced against a private party. That reasoning, embodied in the majority opinion, is inconsistent with the spirit of our Constitution. It remains relevant that a State is being regulated, as *National League of Cities* and every recent case have recognized. *** As far as the Constitution is concerned, a State should not be equated with any private litigant. *** Instead, the autonomy of a State is an essential component of federalism. If state autonomy is ignored in assessing the means by which Congress regulates matters affecting commerce, then federalism becomes irrelevant simply because the set of activities remaining beyond the reach of such a commerce power "may well be negligible." ***

It has been difficult for this Court to craft bright lines defining the scope of the state autonomy protected by *National League of Cities.* Such difficulty is to be expected whenever constitutional concerns as important as federalism and the effectiveness of the commerce power come into conflict. Regardless of the difficulty, it is and will remain the duty of this Court to reconcile these concerns in the final in-stance. That the Court shuns the task today by appealing to the "essence of federalism" can provide scant comfort to those who believe our federal system requires something more than a unitary, centralized government. I would not shirk the duty acknowledged by *National League of Cities* and its progeny, and I share Justice Rehnquist's belief that this Court will in time again assume its constitutional responsibility.

I respectfully dissent.

Silkwood v. Kerr-McGee Corporation
464 U.S. 238; 104 S. Ct. 615; 78 L. Ed.2d 443 (1984)
Vote: 5-4

Karen Silkwood, a laboratory analyst at Kerr-McGee's Cimarron, Oklahoma, nuclear plant, was contaminated by plutonium at the work site. On November 13, 1974, eight days after the contamination was first detected, Karen was killed in an automobile accident. Her father, Bill Silkwood, as administrator of Karen's estate, brought a diversity of citizenship action in a federal district court, seeking to recover damages for injuries resulting from the plutonium contamination. This lawsuit was based on common law tort principles embodied in Oklahoma law. The jury decided in Silkwood's favor, awarding $505,000 in compensatory damages and $10 million in punitive damages. The Court of Appeals for the Tenth Circuit reversed, holding, among other things, the punitive damages award was preempted by federal law. The Supreme Court granted Silkwood's petition for certiorari.

Justice White delivered the opinion of the Court.
. . . As we recently observed in *Pacific Gas & Electric Co. v. State Energy Resources Conservation & Development Comm'n,* *** state law can be preempted in either of two general ways. If Congress evidences an intent to occupy a given field, any state law falling within that field is pre-empted. *** Even where Congress has not entirely displaced state regulation in the field in question, state law is still pre-empted to the extent it actually conflicts with federal law, that is, when it is impossible to comply with both state and federal law, *** or where the state law stands as an obstacle to the accomplishment of the full purposes and objectives of Congress. *** Kerr-McGee contends that the award in this case is invalid under either analysis. We consider each of these contentions in turn. . . .

Kerr-McGee argues that our ruling in *Pacific Gas & Electric* is dispositive of the issue in this case. . . . Kerr-McGee submits that because the state-authorized award of punitive damages in this case punishes and deters conduct related to radiation hazards, it falls within the prohibited field. However, a review of the same legislative history which prompted our holding in *Pacific Gas & Electric,* coupled with an examination of Congress' actions with respect to other portions of the Atomic Energy Act, convinces us that the pre-empted field does not extend as far as Kerr-McGee would have it. . . .

. . . If there were nothing more, this concern over the States' inability to formulate effective standards and the foreclosure of the States from conditioning the operation of nuclear plants on compliance with state-imposed safety standards arguably would disallow resort to state-law remedies by those suffering injuries from radiation in a nuclear plant. There is, however, ample evidence that Congress had no intention of forbidding the States to provide such remedies.

Indeed, there is no indication that Congress even seriously considered precluding the use of such remedies either when it enacted the Atomic Energy Act in 1954 or when it amended it in 1959. This silence takes on added significance in light of Congress' failure to provide any federal remedy for persons injured by such conduct. It is difficult to believe that Congress would, without comment, remove all means of judicial recourse for those injured by illegal conduct. ***

More importantly, the only congressional discussion concerning the relationship between the Atomic Energy Act and state tort remedies indicates that Congress assumed that such remedies would be available. After the 1954 law was enacted, private companies contemplating entry into the nuclear industry expressed concern over potentially bankrupting state-law suits arising out of a nuclear incident. As a result, in 1957 Congress passed the Price-Anderson Act, an amendment to the Atomic Energy Act. *** That Act established an indemnification scheme under which operators of licensed nuclear facilities could be required to obtain up to $60 million in private financial protection against such suits. The Government would then provide indemnification for the next $500 million of liability, and the resulting $560 million would be the limit of liability for any one nuclear incident.

Although the Price-Anderson Act does not apply to the present situation, the discussion preceding its enactment and subsequent amendment indicates that Congress assumed that persons injured by nuclear accidents were free to utilize existing state tort law remedies.

Congress clearly began working on the Price-Anderson legislation with the assumption that in the absence of some subsequent legislative action, state tort law would apply. This was true even though Congress was fully aware of the exclusive regulatory authority over safety matters.

When it enacted the Price-Anderson Act, Congress was well aware of the need for effective national safety regulation. In fact, it intended to encourage such regulation. But, at the same time, "the right of the State courts to establish the liability of the persons involved in the normal way [was] maintained." ***

The belief that the NRC's [Nuclear Regulatory Commission] exclusive authority to set safety standards did not foreclose the use of state tort remedies was reaffirmed when the Price-Anderson Act was amended in 1966. The 1966 amendment was designed to respond to concerns about the adequacy of state-law remedies. *** It provided that in the event of an "extraordinary nuclear occurrence," licensees could be required to waive any issue of fault, any charitable or governmental immunity defense, and any statute of limitations defense of less than 10 years. *** Again, however, the importance of the legislation for present purposes is not so much in its substance, as in the assumptions on which it was based.... "Absent ... a determination [that the incident is an "extraordinary nuclear occurrence"], a claimant would have exactly the same rights that he has today under existing law—including, perhaps, benefit of a rule of strict liability if applicable State law so provides." *** Indeed, the entire discussion surrounding the 1966 amendment was premised on the assumption that state remedies were available notwithstanding the NRC's exclusive regulatory authority....

Kerr-McGee focuses on the differences between compensatory and punitive damages awards and asserts that, at most, Congress intended to allow the former. This argument, however, is misdirected because our inquiry is not whether Congress expressly allowed punitive damages awards. Punitive damages have long been a part of traditional principles of state tort law would apply with full force unless they were expressly supplanted. Thus, it is Kerr-McGee's burden to show that Congress intended to preclude such awards. *** Yet, the company is unable to point to anything in the legislative history or in the regulations that indicates that punitive damages were not to be allowed. To the contrary, the regulations issued implementing the insurance provisions of the Price-Anderson Act themselves contemplate that punitive damages might be awarded under state law.

In sum, it is clear that in enacting and amending the Price-Anderson Act, Congress assumed that state-law remedies, in whatever form they might take, were available to those injured by nuclear incidents. This was so even though it was well aware of the NRC's exclusive authority to regulate safety matters.

No doubt there is tension between the conclusion that safety regulation is the exclusive concern of the federal law and the conclusion that a State may nevertheless award damages based on its own law of liability. But as we understand what was done over the years in the legislation concerning nuclear energy, Congress intended to stand by both concepts and to tolerate whatever tension there was between them. We can do no less. It may be that the award of damages based on the state law of negligence or strict liability is regulatory in the sense that a nuclear plant will be threatened with damages liability if it does not conform to state standards, but that regulatory consequence was something that Congress was quite willing to accept.

We do not suggest that there could never be an instance in which the federal law would pre-empt the recovery of damages based on state law. But insofar as damages for radiation injuries are concerned, pre-emption should not be judged on the basis that the Federal Government has so completely occupied the field of safety that state remedies are foreclosed but on whether there is an irreconcilable conflict between the federal and state standards or whether the imposition of a state standard in a damages action would frustrate the objectives of the federal law. We perceive no such conflict or frustration in the circumstances of this case.

The United States, as amicus curiae, contends that the award of punitive damages in this case is pre-empted because it conflicts with the federal remedial scheme, noting that the NRC is authorized to impose civil penalties on licensees when federal standards have been violated. *** However, the award of punitive damages in the present case does not conflict with that scheme. Paying both federal fines and state-imposed punitive damages for the same incident would not appear to be physically impossible. Nor does exposure to punitive damages frustrate any purpose of the federal remedial scheme.

Kerr-McGee contends that the award is pre-empted because it frustrates Congress' express desire "to encourage widespread participation in the development and utilization of atomic energy for peaceful purposes." [However] Congress ... disclaimed any interest in promoting the development and utilization of atomic energy by means that fail to provide adequate remedies for those who are injured by exposure to hazardous nuclear materials.

We also reject Kerr-McGee's submission that the punitive damages award in this case conflicts with Congress' express intent to preclude dual regulation of radiation hazards. Congress did not believe that it was inconsistent to vest the NRC with exclusive regulatory authority over the safety aspects of nuclear development while at the same time allowing plaintiffs like Silkwood to recover for injuries caused by nuclear hazards. We are not authorized to second-guess that conclusion.

We conclude that the award of punitive damages in this case is not pre-empted by federal law. The judgment of the Court of Appeals with respect to punitive damages is therefore reversed, and the case is remanded to that court for proceedings consistent with this opinion.

It is so ordered.

Justice Blackmun, with whom ***Justice Marshall*** joins, dissenting.

I join Justice Powell's opinion in dissent and add comments of my own that, I believe, demonstrate (a) the incompatibility between the Court's opinion last Term in *Pacific Gas & Electric Co. v State Energy Resources Conservation & Development Comm'n* *** (1983), and its opinion in the present case, and (b) the fact that the Court is by no means compelled to reach the result it espouses today.

Justice Powell's dissent well explains the fundamental incongruity of the Court's result. The Court acknowledges that Congress pre-empted state regulation of safety aspects of nuclear operations largely out of concern that States were without the technological expertise necessary to regulate them. *** Yet the Court concludes that Congress intended to allow a jury to impose substantial penalties upon a nuclear licensee for failure to follow what the jury regards as adequate safety procedures. The Court recognizes the paradox of its disposition, but blames the irrationality on Congress. Then, with humility, the Court explains that it is duty-bound to follow the dictates of Congress. But such institutional modesty cannot transfer the blame for the tension that today's decision injects into the regulation of nuclear power. The Court, in my view, tortures its earlier decisions and, more importantly, wreaks havoc with the regulatory structure that Congress carefully created. . . .

Justice Powell, with whom the ***Chief Justice*** and ***Justice Blackmun*** join, dissenting.

The Court's decision, in effect, authorizes lay juries and judges in each of the States to make regulatory judgments as to whether a federally licensed nuclear facility is being operated safely. Such judgments then become the predicate to imposing heavy punitive damages. This authority is approved in this case even though the Nuclear Regulatory Commission (NRC) (then the Atomic Energy Commission [AEC])—the agency authorized by Congress to assure the safety of nuclear facilities—found no relevant violation of its stringent safety requirements worthy of punishment. The decision today also comes less than a year after we explicitly held that federal law has "pre-empted" all "state safety regulation" except certain limited powers "expressly ceded to the States." There is no express authorization in federal law of the authority the Court today finds in a state's common law of torts.

Punitive damages, unrelated to compensation for any injury or damage sustained by a plaintiff, are "regulatory" in nature rather than compensatory. The Court of Appeals for the Tenth Circuit so found in this case—prior even to our decision in *Pacific Gas & Electric Co.* *** It also concluded that punitive damages are "no less intrusive than direct legislative acts of the state." *** I agree with the Court of Appeals. . . .

In sum, the Court's decision will leave this area of the law in disarray. No longer can the operators of nuclear facilities rely on the regulations and oversight of the NRC. Juries unfamiliar with nuclear technology may be competent to determine and assess compensatory damages on the basis of liability without fault. They are unlikely, however, to have even the most rudimentary comprehension of what reasonably must be done to assure the safety of employees and the public. The District Court in this case, by instructing the jury that it could infer malice, fraud, or gross negligence (see ibid.), in effect authorized the jury to impose punitive damages without fault. And, to make sure that the jury understood its standardless freedom in this respect, the Court also instructed the jury that it could ignore the regulations prescribed by the AEC if in its opinion they defied "human credence" or "can be shown not to accomplish their intended purpose." ***

We hardly could have spoken more clearly in *Pacific Gas & Electric Co.* on April 20, 1983, on the issue of pre-emption. . . . This left no doubt whatever as to the sole responsibility for nuclear safety regulation under the governance of the NRC and its large staff—experts in the technology and safety controls of nuclear energy. This case makes clear the correctness of the Court's holding in *Pacific Gas & Electric Co.* Today, the Court opens a wide and inviting door to indirect regulation by juries authorized to impose damages to punish and deter on the basis of inferences even when a plant has taken the utmost precautions provided by law. Not only is this unfair, it also could discourage investment needed to further the acknowledged national need for this alternative source of energy. I would affirm the judgment of the Court of Appeals.

Cooley v. Board of Wardens
12 How. (53 U.S.) 299; 13 L. Ed. 996 (1852)
Vote: 7-2

The controversy that led to this landmark constitutional decision began when Aaron Cooley violated a Pennsylvania law by first failing to hire pilots and then refusing to pay pilotage fees on two of his ships at the port of Philadelphia. The Board of Port Wardens successfully sued him in a local trial court, and this judgment was affirmed by the Pennsylvania Supreme Court. Cooley brought his case to the U.S. Supreme Court, challenging the pilotage law on several constitutional grounds. The following excerpts from

Justice Curtis's majority opinion deal with the question of whether this law violated the Commerce Clause.

Mr. Justice Curtis delivered the opinion of the Court.

. . . That the power to regulate commerce includes the regulation of navigation, we consider settled. And when we look to the nature of the service performed by pilots, to the relations which that service and its compensations bear to navigation between the several States, and between the ports of the United States and foreign countries, we are brought to the conclusion, that the regulation of the qualifications of pilots, of the modes and times of offering and rendering their services, of the responsibilities which shall rest upon them, of the powers they shall possess, of the compensation they may demand, and of the penalties by which their rights and duties may be enforced, do constitute regulations of navigation, and consequently of commerce, within the just meaning of this clause of the Constitution.

The power to regulate navigation is the power to prescribe rules in conformity with which navigation must be carried on. It extends to the persons who conduct it, as well as to the instruments used. Accordingly, the first Congress assembled under the Constitution passed laws, requiring the masters of ships and vessels of the United States to be citizens of the United States, and established many rules for the government and regulation of officers and seamen. *** These have been from time to time added to and changed, and we are not aware that their validity has been questioned.

Now, a pilot, so far as respects the navigation of the vessel in that part of the voyage which is his pilotage ground, is the temporary master charged with the safety of the vessel and cargo, and of the lives of those on board, and intrusted with command of the crew. He is not only one of the persons engaged in navigation, but he occupies a most important and responsible place among those thus engaged. And if Congress has power to regulate the seamen who assist the pilot in the management of the vessel, a power never denied, we can perceive no valid reason why the pilot should be beyond the reach of the same power. . . .

Nor should it be lost sight of, that this subject of the regulation of pilots and pilotage has an intimate connection with, and an important relation to, the general subject of commerce with foreign nations and among the several States, over which it was one main object of the Constitution to create a national control. . . .

It becomes necessary, to consider whether this law of Pennsylvania, being a regulation of commerce, is valid.

The Act of Congress of the 7th of August, 1789, *** is as follows:

That all pilots in the bays, inlets, rivers, harbors, and ports of the United States, shall continue to be regulated in conformity with the existing laws of the States, respectively, wherein such pilots may be, or with such laws as the States may respectively hereafter enact for the purpose, until further legislative provision shall be made by Congress.

If the law of Pennsylvania, now in question, had been in existence at the date of this Act of Congress, we might hold it to have been adopted by Congress, and thus made a law of the United States, and so valid. Because this Act does, in effect, give the force of an Act of Congress, to the then existing state laws on this subject, so long as they should continue unrepealed by the State which enacted them.

But the law on which these actions are founded was not enacted till 1803. What effect, then, can be attributed to so much of the Act of 1789 as declares that pilots shall continue to be regulated in conformity "with such laws as the States may respectively hereafter enact for the purpose, until further legislative provision shall be made by Congress"?

If the States were devested of the power to legislate on this subject by the grant of the commercial power to Congress, it is plain this Act could not confer upon them power thus to legislate. If the Constitution excluded the States from making any law regulating commerce, certainly Congress cannot regrant, or in any manner reconvey to the States that power. . . . [W]e are brought directly and unavoidably to the consideration of the question, whether the grant of the commercial power to Congress, did *per se* deprive the States of all power to regulate pilots. This question has never been decided by this court, nor, in our judgment, has any case depending upon all the considerations which must govern this one, come before this court. The grant of commercial power to Congress does not contain any terms which expressly exclude the States from exercising an authority over its subject matter. If they are excluded it must be because the nature of the power, thus granted Congress, requires that a similar authority should not exist in the States. If it were conceded on the one side, that the nature of this power, like that to legislate for the District of Columbia, is absolutely and totally repugnant to the existence of similar power in the States, probably no one would deny that the grant of the power to Congress, as effectually and perfectly excludes the States from all future legislation on the subject, as if express words has been used to exclude them. And on the other hand, if it were admitted that the existence of this power in Congress, like the power of taxation, is compatible with the existence of a similar power in the states, then it would be in conformity with the contemporary exposition of the Constitution *** and with the judicial construction, given from time to time by this court, after the most deliberate consideration, to hold that the mere grant of such a power to Congress, did not imply a prohibition on the States to exercise the same power; that it is not the mere existence of such a power, but its exercise by Congress, which may be incompatible with the exercise of the same power by the States, and that the States may legislate in the absence of congressional regulations. ***

... [W]hen the nature of a power like this is spoken of, when it is said that the nature of the power requires that it should be exercised exclusively by Congress, it must be intended to refer to the subjects of that power, and to say they are of such a nature as to require exclusive legislation by Congress. Now, the power to regulate commerce, embraces a vast field, containing not only many, but exceedingly various subjects, quite unlike in their nature, some imperatively demanding a single uniform rule, operating equally on the commerce of the United States in every port; and some, like the subject now in question, as imperatively demanding that diversity, which alone can meet the local necessities of navigation.

Either absolutely to affirm, or deny, that the nature of this power requires exclusive legislation by Congress, is to lose sight of the nature of the subjects of this power, and to assert concerning all of them, what is really applicable but to a part. Whatever subjects of this power are in their nature national, or admit only of one uniform system, or plan of regu-

lation, may justly be said to be of such a nature as to require exclusive legislation by Congress. That this cannot be affirmed of laws for the regulation of pilots and pilotage is plain. The Act of 1789 contains a clear and authoritative declaration by the first Congress, that the nature of this subject is such, that until Congress should find it necessary to exert its power, it should be left to the legislation of the States; that it is local and not national; that it is likely to be the best provided for, not by one system, or plan of regulations, but by as many as the legislative discretion of the several States should deem applicable to the local peculiarities of the port within their limits. . . .

It is the opinion of a majority of the court that the mere grant to Congress of the power to regulate commerce, did not deprive the States of power to regulate pilots, and that although Congress has legislated on this subject, its legislation manifests an intention, with a single exception, not to regulate this subject, but to leave its regulation to the several States. To these precise questions, which are all we are called on to decide, this opinion must be understood to be confined. It does not extend to the question what other subjects, under the commercial power, are within the exclusive control of Congress, or may be regulated by the States in the absence of all congressional legislation; nor to the general question how far any regulation of a subject by Congress may be deemed to operate as an exclusion of all legislation by the States upon the same subject. We decide the precise questions before us, upon what we deem sound principles, applicable to this particular subject in the state in which the legislation of Congress has left it. We go no farther. . . .

We are of opinion that this state law was enacted by virtue of a power, residing in the State to legislate; that it is not in conflict with any law of Congress; that it does not interfere with any system which Congress has established by making regulations, or by intentionally leaving individuals to their own unrestricted action; that this law is therefore valid, and the judgment of the Supreme Court of Pennsylvania in each case must be affirmed.

*Messrs. **Justices McLean** and **Wayne*** dissented.

*Mr. **Justice Daniel,*** although he concurred in the judgment of the court, yet dissented from its reasoning.

Mr. Justice Daniel

I agree with the majority in their decision, that the judgments of the Supreme Court of Pennsylvania in these cases should be affirmed, though I cannot go with them in the process or argument by which their conclusion has been reached.... The true question here is, whether the power to enact pilot laws is appropriate and necessary, or rather most appropriate and necessary to the state or the federal governments. It being conceded that this power has been exercised by the States from their very dawn of existence; that it can be practically and beneficially applied by the local authorities only; it being conceded, as it must be, that the power to pass pilot laws, as such, has not been in any express terms delegated to Congress, and does not necessarily conflict with the right to establish commercial regulations, I am forced to conclude that this is an original and inherent power in the States, and not one to be merely tolerated, or held subject to the sanction of the federal government.

South Carolina Highway Department v. Barnwell

303 U.S. 177; 58 S. Ct. 510; 82 L. Ed. 734 (1938)

Vote: 7-0

Mr. Justice Stone delivered the opinion of the Court.

The Act of the General Assembly of South Carolina *** prohibits use on the state highways of motor trucks and "semi-trailer motor trucks" whose width exceeds 90 inches, and whose weight including load exceeds 20,000 pounds.... The principal question for decision is whether these prohibitions impose an unconstitutional burden upon interstate commerce.

The district court of three judges, after hearing evidence, ... enjoined the enforcement of the weight provision against interstate motor carriers on the specified highways, and also the width limitation of 90 inches, except in the case of vehicles exceeding 96 inches in width....

The trial court rested its decision that the statute unreasonably burdens interstate commerce, upon findings, not assailed here, that there is a large amount of motor truck traffic passing interstate in the southeastern part of the United States, which would normally pass over the highways of South Carolina, but which will be barred from the state by the challenged restrictions if enforced, and upon its conclusion that, when viewed in the light of their effect upon interstate commerce, these restrictions are unreasonable.

South Carolina has built its highways and owns and maintains them. It has received from the federal government, in aid of its highway improvements, money grants which have been expended upon the highways to which the injunction applies....

While the constitutional grant to Congress of power to regulate interstate commerce has been held to operate of its own force to curtail state power in some measure, it did not forestall all state action affecting interstate commerce. Ever since *Wilson v. Black Bird Creek Marsh Co.* *** it has been recognized that there are matters of local concern, the regulation of which unavoidably involves some regulation of interstate commerce but which, because of their local character and their number and diversity, may never be fully dealt with by Congress. Notwithstanding the commerce clause, such regulation in the absence of Congressional action has for the most part been left to the states by the decisions of this Court, subject to the other applicable constitutional restraints.

The commerce clause, by its own force, prohibits discrimination against interstate commerce, whatever its form or method, and the decisions of this Court have recognized that there is scope for its like operation when state legislation nominally of local concern is in point of fact aimed at interstate commerce, or by its necessary operation is a means of gaining a local benefit by throwing the attendant burdens on those without the state. ***

But the present case affords no occasion for saying that the bare possession of power by Congress to regulate the interstate traffic forces the states to conform to standards which Congress might, but has not adopted, or curtails their power to take measures to insure the safety and conservation of their highways which may be applied to like traffic moving intrastate. Few subjects of state regulation are so peculiarly of local concern as is the use of state highways. There are few matters, local regulation of which is so inseparable from a substantial effect on interstate commerce. Unlike the railroads, local highways are built, owned and maintained by the state or its municipal subdivisions. The state has a primary and immediate concern in their safe and economical administration. The present regulations, or any others of like purpose, if they are to accomplish their end, must be applied alike to interstate and intrastate traffic both moving in large volume over the highways. The fact that they affect alike shippers in interstate and intrastate commerce in large number within as well as without the state is a safeguard against their abuse.

From the beginning it has been recognized that a state can, if it sees fit, build and maintain its own highways, canals and railroads and that in the absence of Congressional action their regulation is peculiarly within its competence, even though interstate commerce is materially affected. *** Congress not acting, state regulation of intrastate carriers has been upheld regardless of its effect upon interstate commerce. *** With respect to the extent and nature of the local interests to be protected and the unavoidable effect upon interstate and intrastate commerce alike, regulations of the use of the highways are akin to local regulation of rivers, harbors, piers and docks, quarantine regulations, and game laws, which, Congress not acting, have been sustained even though they materially interfere with interstate commerce.

The nature of the authority of the state over its own highways has often been pointed out by this Court. It may not, under the guise of regulation, discriminate against interstate commerce. But "in the absence of national legislation especially covering the subject of interstate commerce, the state may rightly prescribe uniform regulations adapted to promote safety upon its highways and the conservation of their use applicable alike to vehicles moving in interstate commerce and those of its own citizens." *** This Court has often sustained the exercise of that power although it has burdened or impeded interstate commerce. It has upheld weight limitations lower than those presently imposed, applied alike to motor traffic moving interstate and intrastate. *** Restrictions favoring passenger traffic over the carriage of interstate merchandise by truck have been similarly sustained, *** as has the exaction of a reasonable fee for the use of the highways. ***

In each of these cases regulation involves a burden on interstate commerce. But so long as the state action does not discriminate, the burden is one which the Constitution permits because it is an inseparable incident of the exercise of a legislative authority, which, under the Constitution, has been left to the states.

Congress, in the exercise of its plenary power to regulate interstate commerce, may determine whether the burdens imposed on it by state regulation, otherwise permissible, are too great, and may, by legislation designed to secure uniformity or in other respect to protect the national interest in the commerce, curtail to some extent the state's regulatory power. But that is a legislative, not a judicial function, to be performed in the light of the congressional judgment of what is appropriate regulation of interstate commerce, and the extent to which, in that field, state power and local interests should be required to yield to the national authority and interest. In the absence of such legislation the judicial function, under the commerce clause . . . stops with the inquiry whether the state legislature in adopting regulations such as the present has acted within its province, and whether the means of regulation chosen are reasonably adapted to the end sought. ***

. . . [C]ourts do not sit as legislatures, either state or national. They cannot act as Congress does when, after weighing all the conflicting interests, state and national, it determines when and how much the state regulatory power shall yield to the larger interests of a national commerce. And in reviewing a state highway regulation where Congress has not acted, a court is not called upon, as are state legislatures, to determine what, in its judgment, is the most suitable restriction to be applied of those that are possible, or to choose that one which in its opinion is best adapted to all the diverse interests affected. *** When the action of a legislature is within the scope of its power, fairly debatable questions as to its reasonableness, wisdom and propriety are not for the determination of courts, but for the legislative body, on which rest the duty and responsibility of decision. *** This is equally the case when the legislative power is one which may legitimately place an incidental burden on interstate commerce. It is not any the less a legislative power committed to the states because it affects interstate commerce, and courts are not any the more entitled, because interstate commerce is affected, to substitute their own for the legislative judgment. ***

Since the adoption of one weight or width regulation, rather than another, is a legislative not a judicial choice, its constitutionality is not to be determined by weighing in the judicial scales and merits of the legislative choice and rejecting it if the weight of evidence presented in court appears to favor a different standard. *** Being a legislative judgment it is presumed to be supported by facts known to the legislature unless facts judicially known or proved preclude that possibility. Hence, in reviewing the present determination we examine the record, not to see whether the findings of the court below are supported by evidence, but ascertain upon the whole record whether it is possible to say that the legislative choice is without rational basis. *** Not only does the record fail to exclude that possibility, but it shows affirmatively that there is adequate support for the legislative judgment.

. . . The fact that many states have adopted a different standard is not persuasive. The conditions under which highways must be built in the several states, their construction and the demands made upon them, are not uniform. The road-building art, as the record shows, is far from having attained a scientific certainty and precision, and scientific precision is not the criterion for the exercise of the constitutional regulatory power of the states. *** The legislature, being free to exercise its own judgment, is not bound by that of other legislatures. It would hardly be contended that if all the states had adopted a single standard, none, in the light of its own experience and in the exercise of its judgment upon all the complex elements which enter into the problem, could change it.

The regulatory measures taken by South Carolina are within its legislative power . . . and the resulting burden on interstate commerce is not forbidden.

Reversed.

Mr. Justice Cardozo and **Mr. Justice Reed** took no part in the consideration or decision of this case.

Southern Pacific Railroad Company v. Arizona

325 U.S. 761; 65 S. Ct. 1515; 89 L. Ed. 1915 (1945)
Vote: 7-2

Mr. Chief Justice Stone delivered the opinion of the Court.

The Arizona Train Limit Law of May 16, 1912, *** makes it unlawful for any person or corporation to operate within the state a railroad train of more than fourteen passenger or seventy freight cars, and authorizes the state to recover a money penalty for each violation of the Act. The questions for decision are whether Congress has, by legislative enactment, restricted the power of the states to regulate the length of interstate trains as a safety measure and, if not, whether the statute contravenes the commerce clause of the federal Constitution.

Although the Commerce Clause conferred on the national government power to regulate commerce, its possession of the power does not exclude all state power of regulation. Ever since *Wilson v. Black Bird Creek Marsh Co.* *** it has been recognized that, in the absence of conflicting legislation by Congress, there is a residuum of power in the state to make laws governing matters of local concern which nevertheless in some measure affect interstate commerce or even, to some extent, regulate it. *** Thus the states may regulate matters which, because of their number and diversity, may never be adequately dealt with by Congress. *** When the regulation of matters of local concern is local in character and effect, and its impact on the national commerce does not seriously interfere with its operation, and the consequent incentive to deal with them nationally is slight, such regulation has been generally held to be within state authority. ***

But ever since *Gibbons v. Ogden* *** the states have not been deemed to have authority to impede substantially the free flow of commerce from state to state, or to regulate those phases of the national commerce which, because of the need of national uniformity, demand that their regulation, if any, be prescribed by a single authority. *** Whether or not this long recognized distribution of power between the national and the state governments is predicated upon the implications of the Commerce Clause itself *** or upon the presumed intention of Congress, where Congress has not spoken, *** the result is the same.

In the application of these principles some enactments may be found to be plainly within and others plainly without state power. But between these extremes lies the infinite variety of cases, in which regulation of local matters may also operate as a regulation of commerce, in which reconciliation of the conflicting claims of state and national power is to be attained only by some appraisal and accommodation of the competing demands of the state and national interests involved. ***

For a hundred years it has been accepted constitutional doctrine that the Commerce Clause, without the aid of congressional legislation, thus affords some protection from state legislation inimical to the national commerce, and that in such cases, where Congress has not acted, this Court, and not the state legislature, is under the commerce clause the final arbiter of the competing demands of state and national interests. ***

Congress has undoubted power to redefine the distribution of power over interstate commerce. It may either permit the states to regulate the commerce in a manner which would otherwise not be permissible *** or exclude state regulation even of matters of peculiarly local concern which nevertheless affect interstate commerce. ***

But in general Congress has left it to the courts to formulate the rules thus interpreting the Commerce Clause in its application, doubtless because it has appreciated the destructive consequences to the commerce of the nation if their protection were withdrawn *** and has been aware that in their application state laws will not be invalidated without the support of relevant factual material which will "afford a sure basis" for an informed judgment. *** Meanwhile, Congress has accommodated its legislation, as have the states, to these rules as an established feature of our constitutional system. There has thus been left to the states wide scope for the regulation of matters of local state concern, even though it in some measure affects the commerce, provided it does not materially restrict the free flow of commerce across state lines, or interfere with it in matters with respect to which uniformity of regulation is of predominant national concern.

Hence the matters for ultimate determination here are the nature and extent of the burden which the state regulation of interstate trains, adopted as a safety measure, imposes on interstate commerce, and whether the relative weights of the state and national interests involved are such as to make inapplicable the rule, generally observed, that the free flow of interstate commerce and its freedom from local restraints in matters requiring uniformity of regulation are interests safeguarded by the commerce clause from state interference.

While this Court is not bound by the findings of the state court, and may determine for itself the facts of a case upon which an asserted federal right depends, *** the facts found by the state trial court showing the nature of the interstate commerce involved, and the effect upon it of the train limit law, are not seriously questioned. Its findings with respect to the need for and effect of the statute as a safety measure, although challenged in some particulars which we do not regard as material to our decision, are likewise supported by evidence.

The findings show that the operation of long trains . . . is standard practice over the main lines of the railroads of the United States, and that, if the length of trains is to be regulated at all, national uniformity in the regulation adopted, such as only Congress can prescribe, is practically indispensable to the operation of an efficient and economical national railway system.... Outside of Arizona, where the length of trains is not restricted, [Southern Pacific] runs a substantial proportion of long trains. In 1939 on its comparable route for through traffic through Utah and Nevada from 66 to 85% of its freight trains were over 70 cars in length and over 43% of its passenger trains included more than fourteen passenger cars.

In Arizona, approximately 93% of the freight traffic and 95% of the passenger traffic is interstate. Because of the Train Limit Law [Southern Pacific] is required to haul over 30% more trains in Arizona than would otherwise have been necessary. The record shows a definite relationship between operating costs and the length of trains, the increase in length resulting in a reduction of operating costs per car. The additional cost of operation of trains complying with the Train Limit Law in Arizona amounts for the two railroads traversing that state to about $1,000,000 a year. The reduction in train lengths also impedes efficient operation....

The unchallenged findings leave no doubt that the Arizona Train Limit Law imposes a serious burden on the interstate commerce conducted by [Southern Pacific]. It materially impedes the movement of ... interstate trains through that state and interposes a substantial obstruction to the national policy proclaimed by Congress, to promote adequate, economical and efficient railway transportation service. *** Enforcement of the law in Arizona, while train lengths remain unregulated or are regulated by varying standards in other states, must inevitably result in an impairment of uniformity of efficient railroad operation because the railroads are subjected to regulation which is not uniform in its application. Compliance with a state statute limiting train lengths requires interstate trains of a length lawful in other states to be broken up and reconstituted as they enter each state according as it may impose varying limitations upon train lengths. The alternative is for the carrier to conform to the lowest train limit restriction of any of the states through which its trains pass, whose laws thus control the carriers' operations both within and without the regulating state.

If one state may regulate train lengths, so may all the others, and they need not prescribe the same maximum limitation. The practical effect of such regulation is to control train operations beyond the boundaries of the state exacting it because of the necessity of breaking up and reassembling long trains at the nearest terminal points before entering and after leaving the regulating state. The serious impediment to the free flow of commerce by the local regulation of train lengths and the practical necessity that such regulation, if any, must be prescribed by a single body having a nation-wide authority are apparent.

We think, as the trial court found, that the Arizona Train Limit Law, viewed as a safety measure, affords at most slight and dubious advantage, if any, over unregulated train lengths.... Its undoubted effect on the commerce is the regulation, without securing uniformity, of the length of trains operated in interstate commerce, which lack is itself a primary cause of preventing the free flow of commerce by delaying it and by substantially increasing its cost and impairing its efficiency. In these respects the case differs from those where a state, by regulatory measures affecting the commerce, has removed or reduced safety hazards without substantial interference with the interstate movement of trains. Such are measures abolishing the car stove, *** requiring locomotives to be supplied with electric headlights, *** providing for full train crews, *** and for the equipment of freight trains with cabooses. ***

The principle that, without controlling congressional action, a state may not regulate interstate commerce so as substantially to affect its flow or deprive it of needed uniformity in its regulation is not to be avoided by "simply invoking the convenient apologetics of the police power." ***

... [W]e have pointed out that when a state goes beyond safety measures which are permissible because only local in their effect upon interstate commerce and "attempts to impose particular standards as to structure, design, equipment and operation [of vessels plying interstate] which in the judgment of its authorities may be desirable but pass beyond what is plainly essential to safety and seaworthiness, the

State will encounter the principle that such requirements, if imposed at all, must be through the action of Congress which can establish a uniform rule. Whether the state in a particular matter goes too far must be left to be determined when the precise question arises."

Here we conclude that the state does go too far. Its regulation of train lengths, admittedly obstructive to interstate train operation, and having a seriously adverse effect on transportation efficiency and economy, passes beyond what is plainly essential for safety since it does not appear that it will lessen rather than increase the danger of accident. ***

South Carolina Highway Department v. Barnwell *** was concerned with the power of the state to regulate the weight and width of motor cars passing interstate over its highways, a legislative field over which the state has a far more extensive control than over interstate railroads. In that case . . . we were at pains to point out that there are few subjects of state regulation affecting interstate commerce which are so peculiarly of local concern as is the use of the state's highways. Unlike the railroads local highways are built, owned and maintained by the state or its municipal subdivisions. The state is responsible for their safe and economical administration. Regulations affecting the safety of their use must be applied alike to intrastate and interstate traffic. The fact that they affect alike shippers in interstate and intrastate commerce in great numbers, within as well as without the state, is a safeguard against regulatory abuses. Their regulation is akin to quarantine measures, game laws, and like local regulations of rivers, harbors, piers, and docks, with respect to which the state has exceptional scope for the exercise of its regulatory power, and which, Congress not acting, have been sustained even though they materially interfere with interstate commerce. ***

The contrast between the present regulation and . . . the highway safety regulation in point of the nature of the subject of regulation and the state's interest in it, illustrate and emphasize the considerations which enter into a determination of the relative weights of state and national interests where state regulating affecting interstate commerce is attempted. Here examination of all the relevant factors makes it plain that the state interest is outweighed by the interest of the nation in an adequate, economical and efficient railway transportation service, which must prevail.

Reversed.

*Mr. **Justice Rutledge*** concurs in the result.

*Mr. **Justice Black**,* dissenting.

. . . The determination of whether it is in the interest of society for the length of trains to be governmentally regulated is a matter of public policy. Someone must fix that policy—either the Congress, or the state, or the courts. A century and a half of constitutional history and government admonishes this Court to leave that choice to the elected legislative representatives of the people themselves, where it properly belongs both on democratic principles and the requirements of efficient government.

There have been many sharp divisions of this Court concerning its authority, in the absence of congressional enactment, to invalidate state laws as violating the Commerce Clause. *** That discussion need not be renewed here, because even the broadest exponents of judicial power in this field have not heretofore expressed doubt as to a state's power, absent a paramount congressional declaration, to regulate interstate trains in the interest of safety. . . .

. . . Congress could when it pleased establish a uniform rule as to the length of trains. Congress knew about the Arizona law. It is common knowledge that the Interstate Commerce Committees of the House and the Senate keep in close and intimate touch with the affairs of railroads and other national means of transportation. Every year brings forth new legislation which goes through those Committees, much of it relating to safety. The attention of the members of Congress and of the Senate has been focused on the particular problem of the length of railroad trains. We cannot assume that they were ignorant of the commonly known fact that a long train might be more dangerous in some territories and on some particular types of railroad. The history of congressional consideration of this problem leaves little if any room to doubt that the choice of Congress to leave the state free in this field was a deliberate choice, which was taken with a full knowledge of the complexities of the problems and the probable need for diverse regulations in different localities. I am therefore compelled to reach the conclusion that today's decision is the result of the belief of a majority of this Court that both the legislature of Arizona and the Congress made wrong policy decisions in permitting a law to stand which limits the length of railroad trains. . . .

When we finally get down to the gist of what the Court today actually decides, it is this: Even though more railroad employees will be injured by "slack actions" movements on long trains than on short trains, there must be no regulation of this danger in the absence of "uniform regulations." That means that no one can legislate against this danger except the Congress; and even though the Congress is perfectly content to leave the matter to the different state legislatures, this Court, on the ground of "lack of uniformity," will require it to make an express avowal of that fact before it will permit a state to guard against that admitted danger.

We are not left in doubt as to why, as against the potential peril of injuries to employees, the Court tips the scales on the side of "uniformity." For the evil it finds in a lack of uniformity is that it (1) delays interstate commerce, (2) increases its cost and (3) impairs its efficiency. All three of these boil down to the same thing, and that is that running shorter trains would increase the cost of railroad operations.

The "burden" on commerce reduces itself to mere cost because there was no finding, and no evidence to support a finding that by the expenditure of sufficient sums of money, the railroads could not enable themselves to carry goods and passengers just as quickly and efficiently with short trains as with long trains. Thus the conclusion that a requirement for long trains will "burden interstate commerce" is a mere euphemism for the statement that a requirement for long trains will increase the cost of railroad operations.

This record in its entirety leaves me with no doubt whatever that many employees have been seriously injured and killed in the past, and that many more are likely to be so in the future, because of "slack movement" in trains. . . . It may be that offsetting dangers are possible in the operation of short trains. The balancing of these probabilities, however, is not in my judgment a matter for judicial determination, but one which calls for legislative consideration. Representatives elected by the people to make their laws, rather than judges appointed to interpret those laws, can best determine the policies which govern the people. That at least is the basic principle on which our democratic society rests. I would affirm the judgment of the Supreme Court of Arizona.

Mr. Justice Douglas, dissenting. . . .

Philadelphia, City of, v. New Jersey
437 U.S. 617; 98 S. Ct. 2531; 57 L. Ed. 2d 475 (1978)
Vote: 7-2

Mr. Justice Stewart delivered the opinion of the Court.

A New Jersey law prohibits the importation of most "solid or liquid waste which originated or was collected outside the territorial limits of the State. . . ." In this case we are required to decide whether this statutory prohibition violates the Commerce Clause of the United States Constitution.

The statutory provision . . . took effect in early 1974. . . . Apart from . . . narrow exceptions, . . . New Jersey closed its borders to all waste from other States.

Immediately affected by these developments were the operators of private landfills in New Jersey, and several cities in other States that had agreements with these operators for waste disposal. They brought suit against New Jersey and its Department of Environmental Protection in state court, attacking the statute and regulations on a number of state and federal grounds. . . . [T]he trial court declared the law unconstitutional because it discriminated against interstate commerce. The New Jersey Supreme Court . . . reversed. It found that [the statute] advanced vital health and environmental objectives with no economic discrimination against, and with little burden upon, interstate commerce, and that the law was therefore permissible under the Commerce Clause of the Constitution. . . .

The state court reached this conclusion in an attempt to reconcile modern Commerce Clause concepts with several old cases of this Court holding that States can prohibit the importation of some objects because they "are not legitimate subjects of trade and commerce." *Bowman v. Chicago & Northwestern R. Co.* *** These articles include items "which, on account of their existing condition, would bring in and spread disease, pestilence, and death, such as rags or other substances infected with the germs of yellow fever or the virus of small-pox, or cattle or meat or other provisions that are diseased or decayed, or otherwise, from their condition and quality, unfit for human use or consumption." *** The state court found that . . . the state regulations banned only "those wastes which can [not] be put to effective use," and therefore those wastes were not commerce at all, unless "the mere transportation and disposal of valueless waste between states constitutes interstate commerce within the meaning of the constitutional provision." ***

We think the state court misread our cases, and thus erred in assuming that they require a two-tiered definition of commerce. In saying that innately harmful articles "are not legitimate subjects of trade and commerce," the *Bowman* Court was stating its conclusion, not the starting point of its reasoning. All objects of interstate trade merit Commerce Clause protection; none is excluded by definition at the outset. In *Bowman* . . . the Court held simply that because the articles' worth in interstate commerce was far outweighed by the dangers inhering in their very movement, States could prohibit their transportation across state lines. Hence, we reject the state court's suggestion that the banning of "valueless" out-of-state wastes . . . implicates no constitutional protection. Just as Congress has power to regulate the interstate movement of these wastes, States are not free from constitutional scrutiny when they restrict that movement. *** . . .

The opinions of the Court through the years have reflected an alertness to the evils of "economic isolation" and protectionism, while at the same time recognizing that incidental burdens on interstate commerce may be unavoidable when a State legislates to safeguard the health and safety of its people. Thus, where simple economic protectionism is effected by state legislation, a virtually *per se* rule of invalidity has been erected. *** The clearest example of such legislation is a law that overtly blocks the flow of interstate commerce at a State's borders. *** But where other legislative objectives are credibly advanced and there is no patent discrimination against interstate trade, the Court has adopted a much more flexible approach. . . . The crucial inquiry . . . must be directed to determining whether [the New Jersey statute] is basically a protectionist measure, or whether it can fairly be viewed as a law directed to legitimate local concerns, which effects upon interstate commerce that are only incidental.

. . . [Philadelphia] strenuously contend[s] that [New Jersey's law], "while outwardly cloaked 'in the currently fashionable garb of environmental protection,' . . . is actually no more than a legislative effort to suppress competition and stabilize the cost of solid waste disposal for New Jersey residents. . . ."

[New Jersey], on the other hand, [denies that its law] was motivated by financial concerns or economic protectionism. . . .

This dispute about ultimate legislative purpose need not be resolved, because its resolution would not be relevant to the constitutional issue to be decided in this case. Contrary to the evident assumption of . . . the parties, the evil of protectionism can reside in legislative means as well as legislative ends. Thus, it does not matter whether the ultimate aim of [the statute] is to reduce the waste disposal costs of New Jersey residents or to save remaining open lands from pollution, for we assume New Jersey has every right to protect its residents' pocketbooks as well as their environment. And it may be assumed as well that New Jersey may pursue those ends by slowing the flow of all waste into the State's remaining landfills, even though interstate commerce may incidentally be affected. But whatever New Jersey's ultimate purpose, it may not be accomplished by discriminating against articles of commerce coming from outside the State unless there is some reason, apart from their origin, to treat them differently. Both on its face and in its plain effect, [New Jersey's law] violates this principle of nondiscrimination.

The Court has consistently found parochial legislation of this kind to be constitutionally invalid, whether the ultimate aim of the legislation was to assure a steady supply of milk by erecting barriers to allegedly ruinous outside competition, *** or to create jobs by keeping industry within the State, *** or to preserve the State's financial resources from depletion by fencing out indigent immigrants. *** In each of these [instances], a presumably legitimate goal was sought to be achieved by the illegitimate means of isolating the State from the national economy. . . .

The New Jersey law at issue in this case falls squarely within the area that the Commerce Clause puts off-limits to state regulation. On its face, it imposes on out-of-state commercial interests the full burden of conserving the State's remaining landfill space. . . . [T]he State has overtly moved to slow or freeze the flow of commerce for protectionist reasons. . . . What is crucial is the attempt by one State to isolate itself from a problem common to many by erecting a barrier against the movement of interstate trade.

[New Jersey argues] that not all laws which facially discriminate against out-of-state commerce are forbidden protectionist regulations. In particular, they point to quarantine laws, which this Court has repeatedly upheld even though they appear to single out interstate commerce for special treatment. *** [In New Jersey's view, the statute] is analogous to such health-protective measures, since it reduces the exposure of New Jersey residents to the allegedly harmful effects of landfill sites.

It is true that certain quarantine laws have not been considered forbidden protectionist measures, even though they were directed against out-of-state commerce. *** But those quarantine laws banned the importation of articles such as diseased livestock that required destruction as soon as possible because their very movement risked contagion and other evils. Those laws thus did not discriminate against interstate commerce as such, but simply prevented traffic in noxious articles, whatever their origin.

The New Jersey statute is not such a quarantine law. There has been no claim here that the very movement of waste into or through New Jersey endangers health, or that waste must be disposed of as soon as close to its point of generation as poss- ible. The harms caused by waste are said to arise after its disposal in landfill sites, and at that point, as New Jersey concedes, there is no basis to distinguish out-of-state waste from domestic waste. If one is inherently harmful, so is the other. Yet New Jersey has banned the former while leaving its landfill sites open to the latter. The New Jersey law blocks the importation of waste in an obvious effort to saddle those outside the State with the entire burden of slowing the flow of refuse into New Jersey's remaining landfill sites. That legislative effort is clearly impermissible under the Commerce Clause of the Constitution.

Today, cities in Pennsylvania and New York find it expedient or necessary to send their waste into New Jersey for disposal, and New Jersey claims the right to close its borders to such traffic. Tomorrow, cities in New Jersey may find it expedient or necessary to send their waste into Pennsylvania or New York for disposal, and those States might then claim the right to close their borders. The Commerce Clause will protect New Jersey in the future, just as it protects her neighbors now, from efforts by one State to isolate itself in the stream of interstate commerce from a problem shared by all.

The judgment is reversed.

Mr. Justice Rehnquist, with whom **the Chief Justice** joins, dissenting.

The question presented in this case is whether New Jersey must . . . continue to receive and dispose of solid waste from neighboring States, even though these will inexorably increase . . . health problems. . . . The Court answers this question in the affirmative. New Jersey must either prohibit all landfill operations, leaving itself to cast about for a presently nonexistent solution to the serious problem of disposing of the waste generated within its own borders, or it must accept waste from every portion of the United States, thereby multiplying the health and safety problems which would result if it dealt only with such wastes generated within the State. Because past precedents establish that the Commerce Clause does not present [New Jersey] with such a Hobson's choice, I dissent. . . .

... The physical fact of life that New Jersey must somehow dispose of its own noxious items does not mean that it must serve as a depository for those of every other State.... New Jersey should be free under our past precedents to prohibit the importation of solid waste because of the health and safety problems that such waste poses to its citizens. The fact that New Jersey continues to, and indeed must continue to, dispose of its own solid waste does not mean that New Jersey may not prohibit the importation of even more solid waste into the State. I simply see no way to distinguish solid waste, on the record of this case, from germ-infected rags, diseased meat, and other noxious items....

... I do not see why a State may ban the importation of items whose movement risks contagion, but cannot ban the importation of items which, although they may be transported into the State without undue hazard, will then simply pile up in an ever increasing danger to the public's health and safety. The Commerce Clause was not drawn with a view to having the validity of state laws turn on such pointless distinctions.

... The fact that New Jersey has left its landfill sites open for domestic waste does not, of course, mean that solid waste is not innately harmful. Nor does it mean that New Jersey prohibits importation of solid waste for reasons other than the health and safety of its population. New Jersey must out of sheer necessity treat and dispose of its solid waste in some fashion.... It does not follow that New Jersey must, under the Commerce Clause, accept solid waste ... from outside its borders and thereby exacerbate its problems.

... Because I find no basis for distinguishing the laws under challenge here from our past cases upholding state laws that prohibit the importation of items that could endanger the population of the State, I dissent.

Kassel v. Consolidated Freightways Corporation

450 U.S. 662; 101 S. Ct. 1309; 67 L. Ed. 2d 580 (1981)
Vote: 6-3

Justice Powell announced the judgment of the Court and delivered an opinion, in which *Justice White, Justice Blackmun,* and *Justice Stevens* joined.

The question is whether an Iowa statute that prohibits the use of certain large trucks within the State unconstitutionally burdens interstate commerce.

Appellee Consolidated Freightways Corporation of Delaware (Consolidated) is one of the largest common carriers in the country. It offers service in 48 States under a certificate of public convenience and necessity issued by the Interstate Commerce Commission. Among other routes, Consolidated carries commodities through Iowa on Interstate 80, the principal east–west route linking New York, Chicago, and the west coast, and on Interstate 35, a major north–south route.

Consolidated mainly uses two kinds of trucks. One consists of a three-axle trailer. This unit, commonly called a single, or "semi," is 55 feet in length overall. Such trucks have long been used on the Nation's highways. Consolidated also uses a two-axle tractor pulling a single-axle trailer which, in turn, pulls a single-axle trailer. This combination, known as a double, or twin, is 65 feet long overall. Many trucking companies, including Consolidated, increasingly prefer to use doubles to ship certain kinds of commodities. Doubles have larger capacities, and the trailers can be detached and routed separately if necessary. Consolidated would like to use 65-foot doubles on many of its trips through Iowa.

The State of Iowa, however, by statute restricts the length of vehicles that may use its highways. Unlike all other States in the West and Midwest, Iowa generally prohibits the use of 65-foot doubles within its borders. Instead, most truck combinations are restricted to 55 feet in length. Doubles, mobile homes, trucks carrying vehicles such as tractors and other farm equipment, and singles hauling livestock, are permitted to be as long as 60 feet. Notwithstanding these restrictions, Iowa's statute permits cities abutting the state line by local ordinance to adopt the length limitations of the adjoining State. *** Where a city has exercised this option, otherwise oversized trucks are permitted within the city limits and in nearby commercial zones. . . .

Because of Iowa's statutory scheme, Consolidated cannot use its 65-foot doubles to move commodities through the State. Instead, the company must do one of four things: (i) use 55-foot singles; (ii) use 60-foot doubles; (iii) detach the trailers of a 65-foot double and shuttle each through the State separately; or (iv) divert 65-foot doubles around Iowa.

Dissatisfied with these options, Consolidated filed this suit in the District Court averring that Iowa's statutory scheme unconstitutionally burdens interstate commerce. Iowa defended the law as a reasonable safety measure enacted pursuant to its police power. The State asserted that 65-foot doubles are more dangerous than 55-foot singles and, in any event, that the law promotes safety and reduces road wear within the State by diverting much truck traffic to other States.

In a 14-day trial, both sides adduced evidence on safety, and on the burden on interstate commerce imposed by Iowa's law. On the question of safety, the District Court found that the "evidence clearly establishes that the twin is as safe as the semi." *** For that reason "there is no valid safety reason for barring twins for Iowa's highways because of their configuration. "The evidence convincingly, if not overwhelmingly, establishes that the 65 foot twin is as safe as, if not safer than, the 60 foot twin and the 55 foot semi. . . ."

In light of these findings, the District Court applied the standard we enunciated in *Raymond Motor Transportation, Inc. v. Rice* *** (1978), and concluded that the state law impermissibly burdened interstate commerce. . . .

. . . In *Raymond Motor Transportation, Inc. v. Rice,* the Court held that a Wisconsin statute that precluded the use of 65-foot doubles violated the Commerce Clause. This case is *Raymond* revisited. Here, as in *Raymond,* the State failed to present any persuasive evidence that 65-foot doubles are less safe

than 55-foot singles. Moreover, Iowa's law is now out of step with the laws of all other Midwestern and Western States. Iowa thus substantially burdens the interstate flow of goods by truck. In the absence of congressional action to set uniform standards, some burdens associated with state safety regulations must be tolerated. But where, as here, the State's safety interest has been found to be illusory, and its regulations impair significantly the federal interest in efficient and safe interstate transportation, the state law cannot be harmonized with the Commerce Clause.

Iowa made a more serious effort to support the safety rationale of its law than did Wisconsin in *Raymond,* but its effort was no more persuasive. As noted above, the District Court found that the "evidence clearly establishes that the twin is as safe as the semi." The record supports this finding.

The trial focused on a comparison of the performance of the two kinds of trucks in various safety categories. The evidence showed, and the District Court found, that the 65-foot double was at least the equal of the 55-foot single in the ability to brake, turn, and maneuver. The double, because of its axle placement, produces less splash and spray in wet weather. And, because of its articulation in the middle, the double is less susceptible to dangerous "off-tracking," and to wind.

None of these findings is seriously disputed by Iowa. Indeed, the State points to only three ways in which the 55-foot single is even arguably superior: singles take less time to be passed and to clear intersections; they may back up for longer distances; and they are somewhat less likely to jackknife.

The first two of these characteristics are of limited relevance on modern interstate highways. As the District Court found, the negligible difference in the time required to pass, and to cross intersections, is insignificant on 4-lane divided highways because passing does not require crossing into oncoming traffic lanes, *** and interstates have few, if any, intersections. The concern over backing capability also is insignificant because it seldom is necessary to back up on an interstate. In any event, no evidence suggest any difference in backing capability between the 60-foot doubles that Iowa permits and the 65-foot doubles that it bans. Similarly, although doubles tend to jackknife somewhat more than singles, 65-foot doubles actually are less likely to jackknife than 60-foot doubles.

Statistical studies supported the view that 65-foot doubles are at least as safe overall as 55-foot singles and 60-foot doubles. One such study, which the District Court credited, reviewed Consolidated's comparative accident experience in 1978 with its own singles and doubles. Each kind of truck was driven 56 million miles on identical routes. The singles were involved in 100 accidents resulting in 27 injuries and one fatality. The 65-foot doubles were involved in 106 accidents resulting in 17 injuries and one fatality. Iowa's expert statistician admitted that this study provided "moderately strong evidence" that singles have a higher injury rate than doubles. *** Another study, prepared by the Iowa Department of Transportation at the request of the state legislature, concluded that "[s]ixty-five foot twin trailer combinations have not been shown by experiences in other states to be less safe than 60 foot twin trailer combinations or conventional tractor-semitrailers." *** Numerous insurance company executives, and transportation officials from the Federal Government and various States, testified that 65-foot doubles were at least as safe as 55-foot singles. Iowa concedes that it can produce no study that establishes a statistically significant difference in safety between the 65-foot double and the kinds of vehicles the State permits. *** Nor, as the District Court noted, did Iowa present a single witness who testified that 65-foot doubles were more dangerous overall than the vehicles permitted under Iowa law. *** In sum, although Iowa introduced more evidence on the question of safety than did Wisconsin in *Raymond,* the record as a whole was not more favorable to the State.

Consolidated, meanwhile, demonstrated that Iowa's law substantially burdens interstate commerce. Trucking companies that wish to continue to use 65-foot doubles must route them around Iowa or detach the trailers of the doubles and ship them through separately. Alternatively, trucking companies must use the smaller 55-foot singles or 60-foot doubles permitted under Iowa law. Each of these options engenders inefficiency and added expense. The record shows that Iowa's law added about $12.6 million each year to the costs of trucking companies.

Consolidated alone incurred about $2 million per year in increased costs.

In addition to increasing the costs of the trucking companies (and, indirectly, of the service to consumers), Iowa's law may aggravate, rather than ameliorate, the problem of highway accidents. Fifty-five foot singles carry less freight than 65-foot doubles. Either more small trucks must be used to carry the same quantity of goods through Iowa, or the same number of larger trucks must drive longer distances to bypass Iowa. In either case, as the District Court noted, the restriction requires more highway miles to be driven to transport the same quantity of goods. Other things being equal, accidents are proportional to distance traveled. *** Thus, if 65-foot doubles are as safe as 55-foot singles, Iowa's law tends to increase the number of accidents, and to shift the incidence of them from Iowa to other States.

Perhaps recognizing the weakness of the evidence supporting its safety argument, and the substantial burden on commerce that its regulations create, Iowa urges the Court simply to "defer" to the safety judgment of the State. It argues that the length of trucks is generally, although perhaps imprecisely, related to safety. The task of drawing a line is one that Iowa contends should be left to its legislature.

The Court normally does accord "special deference" to state highway safety regulations. *** This traditional deference "derives in part from the assumption that where such regulations do not discriminate on this face against interstate commerce, their burden usually falls on local economic interests as well as other States' economic interests, thus insuring that a State's own political processes will serve as a check against unduly burdensome regulations." *** Less deference to the legislative judgment due, however, where the local regulation bears disproportionately on out-of-state residents and businesses. Such a disproportionate burden is apparent here. Iowa's scheme, although generally banning large doubles from the State, nevertheless has several exemptions that secure to Iowans many of the benefits of large trucks while shunting to neighboring States many of the costs associated with their use.

At the time of trial there were two particularly significant exemptions. First, singles hauling live stock or farm vehicles were permitted to be as long as 60 feet. *** As the Court of Appeals noted, this provision undoubtedly was helpful to local interests. *** Second, cities abutting other States were permitted to enact local [ordinances] adopting the larger length limitation of the neighboring State. *** This exemption offered the benefits of longer trucks to individuals and businesses in important border cities without burdening Iowa's highways with interstate through traffic. ***

The origin of the "border cities exemption" also suggests that Iowa's statute may not have been designed to ban dangerous trucks, but rather to discourage interstate truck traffic. In 1974, the legislature passed a bill that would have permitted 65-foot doubles in the State. Governor Ray vetoed the bill. He said:

I find sympathy with those who are doing business in our state and whose enterprises could gain from increased cargo carrying ability by trucks. However, with this bill, the Legislature has pursued a course that would benefit only a few Iowa-based companies while providing a great advantage for out-of-state trucking firms and competitors at the expense of our Iowa citizens. ***

After the veto, the "border cities exemption" was immediately enacted and signed by the Governor.

It is thus far from clear that Iowa was motivated primarily by a judgment that 65-foot doubles are less safe than 55-foot singles. Rather, Iowa seems to have hoped to limit the use of its highways by deflecting some through traffic. In the District Court and Court of Appeals, the State explicitly attempted to justify the law by its claimed interest in keeping trucks out of Iowa. *** The Court of Appeals correctly concluded that a State cannot constitutionally promote its own parochial interests by requiring safe vehicles to detour around it. ***

In sum, the statutory exemptions, their history, and the arguments Iowa has advanced in support of its law in this litigation, all suggest that the deference traditionally accorded a State's safety judgment is not warranted. *** The controlling factors thus are the findings of District Court, accepted by the Court of Appeals, with respect to the relative safety of the types of trucks at issue, and the substantiality of the burden on interstate commerce.

Because Iowa has imposed this burden without any significant countervailing safety interest, its statute violates the Commerce Clause. The judgment of the Court of Appeals is affirmed.

It is so ordered.

Justice Brennan, with whom ***Justice Marshall*** joins, concurring in the judgment.

Iowa's truck-length regulation challenged in this case is nearly identical to the Wisconsin regulation struck down in *Raymond Motor Transportation, Inc. v. Rice* *** as in violation of the Commerce Clause.

In my view the same Commerce Clause restrictions that dictated that holding also require invalidation of Iowa's regulation insofar as it prohibits 65-foot doubles. . . .

Justice Rehnquist, with whom ***the Chief Justice*** and ***Justice Stewart*** join, dissenting.

The result in this case suggests, to paraphrase Justice Jackson, that the only state truck-length limit "that is valid is one which this Court has not been able to get its hands on." *** Although the plurality and concurring opinions strike down Iowa's law by different routes, I believe the analysis in both opinions oversteps our "limited authority to review state legislation under the commerce clause," *** and seriously intrudes upon the fundamental right of the States to pass laws to secure the safety of their citizens. Accordingly, I dissent. . . .

. . . Iowa defends its statute as a highway safety regulation. There can be no doubt that the challenged statute is a valid highway safety regulation and thus entitled to the strongest presumption of validity against Commerce Clause challenges. As noted, all 50 States regulate the length of trucks which may use their highways. *** The American Association of State Highway and Transportation Officials (AASHTO) has consistently recommended length as well as other limits on vehicles. The Iowa Supreme Court has long viewed the provision in question as intended to promote highway safety, *** and "[t]his Court has also had occasion to point out that the sizes and weights of automobiles have an important relation to the safe and convenient use of the highways, which are matters of state control." *** There can also be no question that the particular limit chosen by Iowa— 60 feet—is rationally related to Iowa's safety objective. Most truck limits are between 55 and 65 feet, and Iowa's choice is thus well within the widely accepted range. . . .

The answering of the relevant question is not appreciably advanced by comparing trucks slightly over the length limit with those at the length limit. It is emphatically not our task to balance any incremental safety benefits from prohibiting 65-foot doubles as opposed to 60-foot doubles against the burden on inter-state commerce. Lines drawn for safety purposes will rarely pass muster if the question is whether a slight increment can be permitted without sacrificing safety. . . .

The question is rather whether it can be said that the benefits flowing to Iowa from a rational truck-length limitation are "slight or problematical." *** The particular line chosen by Iowa— 60 feet—is relevant only to the question whether the limit is a rational one. Once a court determines that it is, it considers the overall safety benefits from the regulation against burdens on interstate commerce, and not any marginal benefits from the scheme the State established as opposed to that the plaintiffs desire. ***

The difficulties with the contrary approach are patent. While it may be clear that there are substantial safety benefits from a 55-foot truck as compared to a 105-foot truck, these benefits may not be discernible in 5-foot jumps. Appellee's approach would permit what could not be accomplished in one lawsuit to be done in 10 separate suits, each challenging an additional five feet.

Any direct balancing of marginal safety benefits against burdens on commerce would make the burdens on commerce the sole significant factor, and make likely the odd result that similar state laws enacted for identical safety reasons might violate the Commerce Clause in one part of the country but not another. . . .

Both the plurality and concurring opinions attach great significance to the Governor's veto of a bill passed by the Iowa Legislature permitting 65-foot doubles. Whatever views one may have about the

significance of legislative motives, it must be emphasized that the law which the Court strikes down today was not passed to achieve the protectionist goals the plurality and the concurrence ascribe to the Governor. Iowa's 60-foot length limit was established in 1963, at a time when very few States permitted 65-foot doubles. *** Striking down legislation on the basis of asserted legislative motives is dubious enough, but the plurality and concurrence strike down the legislation involved in this case because of asserted impermissible motives for not enacting other legislation, motives which could not possibly have been present when the legislation under challenge here was considered and passed. Such action is so far as I am aware, unprecedented in this Court's history.

Furthermore, the effort in both the plurality and concurring opinions to portray the legislation involved here as protectionist is in error. Whenever a State enacts more stringent safety measures than its neighbors, in an area which affects commerce, the safety law will have the incidental effect of deflecting interstate commerce to the neighboring States. Indeed, the safety and protectionist motives cannot be separated: The whole purpose of safety regulation of vehicles is to protect the State from unsafe vehicles. If a neighboring State chooses not to protect its citizens from the danger discerned by the enacting State, that is its business, but the enacting State should not be penalized when the vehicles it considers unsafe travel through the neighboring State.

The other States with truck-length limits that exclude Consolidated's 65-foot doubles would not at all be paranoid in assuming that they might be next on Consolidated's "hit list." The true problem with today's decision is that it gives no guidance whatsoever to these States as to whether their laws are valid or how to defend them. For that matter, the decision gives no guidance to Consolidated or other trucking firms either. Perhaps, after all is said and done, the Court today neither says nor does very much at all. We know only that Iowa's law is invalid and that the jurisprudence of the "negative side" of the Commerce Clause remains hopelessly confused.

Maine v. Taylor

477 U.S. 131; 106 S. Ct. 2440; 91 L.Ed.2d 110 (1986)
Vote: 8-1

In Hughes v. Oklahoma (1974), the Supreme Court said that once a state law is shown to discriminate against interstate commerce "either on its face or in practical effect," the burden falls on the state to demonstrate both that the statute "serves a legitimate local purpose" and that this purpose could not be served as well by available nondiscriminatory means. In the instant case, the Court applies this test to a Maine law banning the importation of live bait fish. The facts are contained in Justice Blackmun's majority opinion.

Justice Blackmun delivered the opinion of the Court.

Once again, a little fish has caused a commotion. *** The fish in this case is the golden shiner, a species of minnow commonly used as live bait in sport fishing.

Appellee Robert J. Taylor (hereafter Taylor or appellee) operates a bait business in Maine. Despite a Maine statute prohibiting the importation of live baitfish, he arranged to have 158,000 live golden shiners delivered to him from outside the State. The shipment was intercepted, and a federal grand jury in the District of Maine indicted Taylor for violating and conspiring to violate the Lacey Act Amendments of 1981, *** [which make] it a federal crime "to import, export, transport, sell, receive, acquire, or purchase in interstate or foreign commerce ... any fish or wildlife taken, possessed, transported, or sold in violation of any law or regulation of any State or in violation of any foreign law."

Taylor moved to dismiss the indictment on the ground that Maine's import ban unconstitutionally burdens interstate commerce and therefore may not form the basis for a federal prosecution under the Lacey Act. Maine *** intervened to defend the validity of its statute, arguing that the ban legitimately protects the State's fisheries from parasites and nonnative species that might be included in shipments of live baitfish. The District Court found the statute constitutional and denied the motion to dismiss. *** Taylor then entered a conditional plea of guilty pursuant

to Federal Rule of Criminal Procedure 11(a)(2), reserving the right to appeal the District Court's ruling on the constitutional question. The Court of Appeals for the First Circuit reversed, agreeing with Taylor that the underlying state statute impermissibly restricts interstate trade. *** Maine appealed. . . .

The Commerce Clause of the Constitution grants Congress the power "[t]o regulate Commerce with foreign Nations, and among the several States, and with the Indian Tribes." *** "Although the Clause thus speaks in terms of powers bestowed upon Congress, the Court long has recognized that it also limits the power of the States to erect barriers against interstate trade." *** Maine's statute restricts interstate trade in the most direct manner possible, blocking all inward shipments of live baitfish at the State's border. . . .

In determining whether a State has overstepped its role in regulating interstate commerce, this Court has distinguished between state statutes that burden interstate transactions only incidentally, and those that affirmatively discriminate against such transactions. While statutes in the first group violate the Commerce Clause only if the burdens they impose on interstate trade are "clearly excessive in relation to the putative local benefits," *** statutes in the second group are subject to more demanding scrutiny. . . . The District Court and the Court of Appeals both reasoned correctly that, since Maine's import ban discriminates on its face against interstate trade, it should be subject to the strict requirements of *Hughes v Oklahoma* . . . The District Court found after an evidentiary hearing that both parts of the *Hughes* test were satisfied, but the Court of Appeals disagreed. We conclude that the Court of Appeals erred in setting aside the findings of the District Court. To explain why, we need to discuss the proceedings below in some detail.

A

The evidentiary hearing on which the District Court based its conclusions was one before a Magistrate. Three scientific experts testified for the prosecution and one for the defense. The prosecution experts testified that live baitfish imported into the State posed two significant threats to Maine's unique and fragile fisheries. First, Maine's population of wild fish—including its own indigenous golden shiners—would be placed at risk by three types of parasites prevalent in out-of-state baitfish, but not common to wild fish in Maine. *** Second, non-native species inadvertently included in shipments of live baitfish could disturb Maine's aquatic ecology to an unpredictable extent by competing with native fish for food or habitat, by preying on native species, or by disrupting the environment in more subtle ways. ***

The prosecution experts further testified that there was no satisfactory way to inspect shipments of live baitfish for parasites or commingled species. According to their testimony, the small size of baitfish and the large quantities in which they are shipped made inspection for commingled species "a physical impossibility." *** Parasite inspection posed a separate set of difficulties because the examination procedure required destruction of the fish. *** Although statistical sampling and inspection techniques had been developed for salmonids (i.e., salmon and trout), so that a shipment could be certified parasite-free based on a standardized examination of only some of the fish, no scientifically accepted procedures of this sort were available for baitfish. ***

Appellee's expert denied that any scientific justification supported Maine's total ban on the importation of baitfish. He testified that none of the three parasites discussed by the prosecution witnesses posed any significant threat to fish in the wild, and that sampling techniques had not been developed for baitfish precisely because there was no need for them. He further testified that professional baitfish farmers raise their fish in ponds that have been freshly drained to ensure that no other species is inadvertently collected.

Weighing all the testimony, the Magistrate concluded that both prongs of the *Hughes* test were satisfied, and accordingly that appellee's motion to dismiss the indictment should be denied. Appellee filed objections, but the District Court, after an independent review of the evidence, reached the same conclusions. First, the court found that Maine "clearly has a legitimate and substantial purpose in

prohibiting the importation of live bait fish," because "substantial uncertainties" surrounded the effects that baitfish parasites would have on the State's unique population of wild fish, and the consequences of introducing non-native species were similarly unpredictable. Second, the court concluded that less discriminatory means of protecting against these threats were currently unavailable, and that, in particular, testing procedures for baitfish parasites had not yet been devised. *** Even if procedures of this sort could be effective, the court found that their development probably would take a considerable amount of time. ***

Although the Court of Appeals did not expressly set aside the District Court's finding of a legitimate local purpose, it noted that several factors "cast doubt" on that finding. First, Maine was apparently the only State to bar all importation of live baitfish. *** Second, Maine accepted interstate shipments of other freshwater fish, subject to an inspection requirement. Third, "an aura of economic protectionism" surrounded statements made in 1981 by the Maine Department of Inland Fisheries and Wildlife in opposition to a proposal by appellee himself to repeal the ban. Finally, the court noted that parasites and non-native species could be transported into Maine in shipments of nonbaitfish, and that nothing prevented fish from simply swimming into the State from New Hampshire.

Despite these indications of protectionist intent, the Court of Appeals rested its invalidation of Maine's import ban on a different basis, concluding that Maine had not demonstrated that any legitimate local purpose served by the ban could not be promoted equally well without discriminating so heavily against interstate commerce. Specifically, the Court found it "difficult to reconcile" Maine's claim that it could not rely on sampling and inspection with the State's reliance on similar procedures in the case of other freshwater fish. ***

Following the reversal of appellee's conviction, Maine and the United States petitioned for rehearing on the ground that the Court of Appeals had improperly disregarded the District Court's findings of fact. The court denied the petitions, concluding that, since the unavailability of a less discriminatory alternative "was a mixed finding of law and fact," a reviewing court "was free to examine carefully the factual record and to draw its own conclusions." ***

B

Although the proffered justification for any local discrimination against interstate commerce must be subjected to "the strictest scrutiny," *** the empirical content of that scrutiny, like any other form of fact-finding, " 'is the basic responsibility of district courts, rather than appellate courts.' " *** As this Court frequently has emphasized, appellate courts are not to decide factual questions de novo, reversing any findings they would have made differently. *** The Federal Rules of Criminal Procedure contain no counterpart to Federal Rule of Civil Procedure 52(a), which expressly provides that findings of fact made by the trial judge "shall not be set aside unless clearly erroneous." But the considerations underlying Rule 52(a)—the demands of judicial efficiency, the expertise developed by trial judges, and the importance of first-hand observation—all apply with full force in the criminal context, at least with respect to factual questions having nothing to do with guilt. Accordingly, the "clearly erroneous" standard of review long has been applied to nonguilt findings of fact by district courts in criminal cases. *** We need not decide now whether all such findings should be reviewed under the "clearly erroneous" standard, because appellee concedes that the standard applies to the factual findings made by the District Court in this case. We note, however, that no broader review is authorized here simply because this is a constitutional case, or because the factual findings at issue may determine the outcome of the case. ***

No matter how one describes the abstract issue whether "alternative means could promote this local purpose as well without discriminating against interstate commerce," *** the more specific question whether scientifically accepted techniques exist for the sampling and inspection of live baitfish is one of fact, and the District Court's finding that such techniques have not been devised cannot be characterized as clearly erroneous. Indeed, the record probably could not support a contrary finding. Two prosecution witnesses testified to the lack of such procedures, and appellee's expert conceded the point, although he disagreed about the need for such

tests. That Maine has allowed the importation of other freshwater fish after inspection hardly demonstrates that the District Court clearly erred in crediting the corroborated and uncontradicted expert testimony that standardized inspection techniques had not yet been developed for baitfish. This is particularly so because the text of the permit statute suggests that it was designed specifically to regulate importation of salmonids, for which, the experts testified, testing procedures had been developed.

Before this Court, appellee does not argue that sampling and inspection procedures already exist for baitfish; he contends only that such procedures "could be easily developed." *** Perhaps this is also what the Court of Appeals meant to suggest. Unlike the proposition that the techniques already exist, the contention that they could readily be devised enjoys some support in the record. Appellee's expert testified that developing the techniques "would just require that those experts in the field . . . get together and do it." He gave no estimate of the time and expense that would be involved, however, and one of the prosecution experts testified that development of the testing procedures for salmonids had required years of heavily financed research. In light of this testimony, we cannot say that the District Court clearly erred in concluding that the development of sampling and inspection techniques for baitfish could be expected to take a significant amount of time.

More importantly, we agree with the District Court that the "abstract possibility" of developing acceptable testing procedures, particularly when there is no assurance as to their effectiveness, does not make those procedures an "[a]vailabl[e] . . . nondiscriminatory alternativ[e]" *** for purposes of the Commerce Clause. A State must make reasonable efforts to avoid restraining the free flow of commerce across its borders, but it is not required to develop new and unproven means of protection at an uncertain cost. Appellee, of course, is free to work on his own or in conjunction with other bait dealers to develop scientifically acceptable sampling and inspection procedures for golden shiners; if and when such procedures are developed, Maine no longer may be able to justify its import ban. The State need not join in those efforts, however, and it need not pretend they have already succeeded.

C

Although the Court of Appeals did not expressly overturn the District Court's finding that Maine's import ban serves a legitimate local purpose, appellee argues as an alternative ground for affirmance that this finding should be rejected. After reviewing the expert testimony presented to the Magistrate, however, we cannot say that the District Court clearly erred in finding that substantial scientific uncertainty surrounds the effect that baitfish parasites and non-native species could have on Maine's fisheries. Moreover, we agree with the District Court that Maine has a legitimate interest in guarding against imperfectly understood environmental risks, despite the possibility that they may ultimately prove to be negligible. "[T]he constitutional principles underlying the commerce clause cannot be read as requiring the State of Maine to sit idly by and wait until potentially irreversible environmental damage has occurred or until the scientific community agrees on what disease organisms are or are not dangerous before it acts to avoid such consequences." ***

Nor do we think that much doubt is cast on the legitimacy of Maine's purposes by what the Court of Appeals took to be signs of protectionist intent. Shielding in-state industries from out-of-state competition is almost never a legitimate local purpose, and state laws that amount to "simple economic protectionism" consequently have been subject to a "virtually per se rule of invalidity." *** But there is little reason in this case to believe that the legitimate justifications the State has put forward for its statute are merely a sham or a "post hoc rationalization." *** In suggesting to the contrary, the Court of Appeals relied heavily on a 3-sentence passage near the end of a 2,000-word statement submitted in 1981 by the Maine Department of Inland Fisheries and Wildlife in opposition to appellee's proposed repeal of the State's ban on the importation of live baitfish:

" '[W]e can't help asking why we should spend our money in Arkansas when it is far better spent at home? It is very clear that much more can be done here in Maine to provide our sportsmen with safe, home-grown bait. There is also the possibility that such an industry could develop a lucrative export market in neighboring states.' " ***

We fully agree with the Magistrate that "[t]hese three sentences do not convert the Maine statute into an economic protectionism measure." *** As the Magistrate pointed out, the context of the statements cited by appellee "reveals [they] are advanced not in direct support of the statute, but to counter the argument that inadequate bait supplies in Maine require acceptance of the environmental risks of imports. Instead, the Department argues, Maine's own bait supplies can be increased." *** Furthermore, the comments were made by a state administrative agency long after the statute's enactment, and thus constitute weak evidence of legislative intent in any event. ***

The other evidence of protectionism identified by the Court of Appeals is no more persuasive. The fact that Maine allows importation of salmonids, for which standardized sampling and inspection procedures are available, hardly demonstrates that Maine has no legitimate interest in prohibiting the importation of baitfish, for which such procedures have not yet been devised. Nor is this demonstrated by the fact that other States may not have enacted similar bans, especially given the testimony that Maine's fisheries are unique and unusually fragile. Finally, it is of little relevance that fish can swim directly into Maine from New Hampshire. As the Magistrate explained: "The impediments to complete success . . . cannot be a ground for preventing a state from using its best efforts to limit [an environmental] risk." ***

The Commerce Clause significantly limits the ability of States and localities to regulate or otherwise burden the flow of interstate commerce, but it does not elevate free trade above all other values. As long as a State does not needlessly obstruct interstate trade or attempt to "place itself in a position of economic isolation," *** it retains broad regulatory authority to protect the health and safety of its citizens and the integrity of its natural resources. The evidence in this case amply supports the District Court's findings that Maine's ban on the importation of live baitfish serves legitimate local purposes that could not adequately be served by available nondiscriminatory alternatives. This is not a case of arbitrary discrimination against interstate commerce; the record suggests that Maine has legitimate reasons, "apart from their origin, to treat [out-of-state baitfish] differently." *** The judgment of the Court of Appeals setting aside appellee's conviction is therefore reversed.

It is so ordered.

Justice Stevens, dissenting.

There is something fishy about this case. Maine is the only State in the Union that blatantly discriminates against out-of-state baitfish by flatly prohibiting their importation. Although golden shiners are already present and thriving in Maine (and, perhaps not coincidentally, the subject of a flourishing domestic industry), Maine excludes golden shiners grown and harvested (and, perhaps not coincidentally, sold) in other States. This kind of stark discrimination against out-of-state articles of commerce requires rigorous justification by the discriminating State. "When discrimination against commerce of the type we have found is demonstrated, the burden falls on the State to justify it both in terms of the local benefits flowing from the statute and the unavailability of nondiscriminatory alternatives adequate to preserve the local interests at stake." ***

Like the District Court, the Court concludes that uncertainty about possible ecological effects from the possible presence of parasites and nonnative species in shipments of out-of-state shiners suffices to carry the State's burden of proving a legitimate public purpose. *** The Court similarly concludes that the State has no obligation to develop feasible inspection procedures that would make a total ban unnecessary. *** It seems clear, however, that the presumption should run the other way. Since the State engages in obvious discrimination against out- of-state commerce, it should be put to its proof. Ambiguity about dangers and alternatives should actually defeat, rather than sustain, the discriminatory measure.

This is not to derogate the State's interest in ecological purity. But the invocation of environmental protection or public health has never been thought to confer some kind of special dispensation from the general principle of nondiscrimination in interstate commerce. "A different view, that the ordinance is valid simply because it professes to be a health measure, would mean that the Commerce Clause of itself imposes no restraints on state action other than those laid down by the Due Process Clause, save for the rare instance where a state artlessly discloses an avowed purpose to discriminate against interstate goods." *** If Maine wishes to rely on its interest in ecological preservation, it must show that interest, and the infeasibility of other alternatives, with far greater specificity. Otherwise, it must further that asserted interest in a manner far less offensive to the notions of comity and cooperation that underlie the Commerce Clause.

Significantly, the Court of Appeals, which is more familiar with Maine's natural resources and with its legislation than we are, was concerned by the uniqueness of Maine's ban. That court felt, as I do, that Maine's unquestionable natural splendor notwithstanding, the State has not carried its substantial burden of proving why it cannot meet its environmental concerns in the same manner as other States with the same interest in the health of their fish and ecology. ***

I respectfully dissent.

PART THREE

CIVIL RIGHTS AND LIBERTIES

CHAPTER NINE

CONSTITUTIONAL SOURCES OF CIVIL RIGHTS AND LIBERTIES

There is, of course, a sphere within which the individual may assert the supremacy of his own will, and rightfully dispute the authority of any human government, especially of any free government existing under a written constitution, to interfere with the exercise of that will. But it is equally true that in every well-ordered society charged with the duty of conserving the safety of its members, the rights of the individual in respect of his liberty may at times, under the pressure of great dangers, be subjected to such restraint, to be enforced by reasonable regulations, as the safety of the general public may demand. . . .

Justice John M. Harlan (the elder), *Jacobson v. Massachusetts* (1905)

INTRODUCTION

One of the principal objectives of the U.S. Constitution, as stated in its preamble, is "to secure the Blessings of Liberty to ourselves and our Posterity." The Framers of the Constitution thus recognized the protection of individual liberty as a fundamental goal of constitutional government.

Paraphrasing John Locke, the Declaration of Independence (1776) had declared the "unalienable" rights of man to be "life, liberty and the pursuit of happiness." Other more specific rights, including trial by jury and freedom of speech, were generally embraced by Americans, legacies of the Magna Charta (1215) and the English Bill of Rights (1689). The Framers of the Constitution sought to protect these rights by creating a system of government that would be inherently restricted in power, hence limited in its ability to transgress the rights of the individual.

The Framers were heavily influenced by the theory of **natural rights,** in which rights are seen as inherently belonging to individuals, not as created by government. According to this view, individuals have the right to do whatever they wish, within reason, unless: 1) they interfere with the rights of others or 2) government is constitutionally empowered to act to restrict the exercise of that freedom. The Framers thus conceived of the powers of government as mere islands in a vast sea of individual rights. This was especially true of the newly created national government, which was limited to the exercise of delegated powers. The original Constitution thus contained no provision guaranteeing freedom of religion, because the Constitution gave the federal government no authority to regulate religion. Yet the Framers did recognize certain rights, at least indirectly, by enumerating specific limitations on the national government and the states.

During the debate over ratification of the Constitution, a consensus emerged that the Constitution should be more explicit as to the rights of individuals. Reflecting this consensus, the First Congress in 1789 adopted the Bill of Rights, which was ratified in 1791. This prompt response by Congress and the States underscored the strong national commitment to individual freedom.

Liberty, however, is only one aspect of constitutional rights. Equally critical in a constitutional democracy is the ideal of equality. While the Framers of the original Constitution were less interested in equality than in liberty, the Constitution has come to be considerably more egalitarian over the years, both through formal amendment and through judicial interpretation. In its constitutional sense, equality means that all citizens are considered to be equal before the law, equal before the state, and equal in their possession of rights. The term **civil rights,** as distinct from **civil liberties,** is generally used to denote citizens' equality claims, as distinct from their liberty claims.

Far-Ranging Subject Matter

The subject matter of civil rights and liberties is far-ranging, touching on most contemporary social, political, and economic issues. In the 1990–1991 term alone, the Supreme Court considered a diverse set of civil rights and liberties cases, including the following controversial questions:

1) Does the First Amendment's guarantee of free speech protect the right of barroom dancers to perform totally nude? (For the answer, see *Barnes v. Glen Theatre* [1991], discussed and reprinted in Chapter 11.)
2) Does the federal government's ban on abortion counseling by birth control clinics that receive federal financial aid constitute a breach of free speech? (See *Rust v. Sullivan* [1991], discussed and reprinted in Chapter 11.)
3) May an individual who provides information to a newspaper, in exchange for a promise of anonymity, sue for damages if the newspaper breaks its promise, or are such suits barred by the First Amendment guarantee of freedom of the press? (see *Cohen v. Cowles Media Company* [1991], discussed and reprinted in Chapter 12.)
4) May police officers board buses and trains and ask passengers for permission to search their belongings without specific reason to believe that they are harboring contraband, or does the Fourth Amendment prohibit such tactics? (See *Florida v. Bostick* [1991], discussed in Chapter 14.)
5) May prosecutors introduce as evidence in a criminal case a confession made by an accused person to a fellow inmate who was also a police informant? (See *Arizona v. Fulminante* [1991], discussed in Chapter 14.)

The Supreme Court's rulings on such issues comprise a major aspect of contemporary American constitutional law and, accordingly, are the subject of Part III of this textbook.

RIGHTS RECOGNIZED IN THE ORIGINAL CONSTITUTION

As noted, the original, unamended Constitution contained few explicit protections of individual rights. This was not because the Framers did not value rights but because they thought it unnecessary to deal with them explicitly. Significantly, most of the state constitutions adopted during the American Revolution contained fairly detailed bills of rights placing limits on state and local governments. The Framers did not anticipate the growth of a pervasive national government and thus did not regard the extensive enumeration of individual rights in the federal Constitution as critical. They did, however, recognize a few important safeguards in the original Constitution.

Circumscribing the Crime of Treason

The Framers of the Constitution, having recently participated in a successful revolution, were understandably sensitive to the prospect that government could employ the crime of treason to stifle political dissent. Thus, they provided in Article III, Section 3 that "[t]reason against the United States, shall consist only in levying War against them, or in adhering to their enemies, giving them aid and comfort." To protect citizens against unwarranted prosecution for treason, the Framers further specified that "[n]o person shall be convicted of Treason unless on the Testimony of two Witnesses to the same overt Act, or on Confession in open Court."

Prohibition of Religious Tests for Public Office

Article VI of the Constitution provides, among other things, that "no religious Test shall ever be required as a Qualification to any Office or Public Trust under the United States." This clause means, in effect, that one's personal views regarding religion may not officially qualify *or* disqualify one for public service. This clause reflects the Framers' commitment to the idea that government ought to be neutral with respect to matters of religion, a view that was strongly reinforced by adoption of the Establishment Clause of the First Amendment (see below and Chapter 13).

Habeas Corpus

Article I, Section 9 of the Constitution states that "the privilege of the Writ of Habeas Corpus shall not be suspended, unless when in Cases of Invasion or Rebellion the public Safety may require it." Grounded in English common law, the writ of **habeas corpus** gives effect to the all-important right of the individual not to be held in unlawful custody. Specifically, habeas corpus enables a court to review a custodial situation and order the release of an individual who is found to have been illegally incarcerated. While the right has many applications, the most common is in the criminal context, where an individual is arrested and held in custody but denied due process of law. In adopting the habeas corpus provision of Article I, Section 9, the Framers wanted not only to recognize the right but also to limit its suspension to emergency situations. The Constitution is somewhat ambiguous as to which branch of government has the authority to suspend the writ of habeas corpus during emergencies. As noted in Chapter 6, early in the Civil War, President Lincoln authorized military commanders to suspend the writ. Congress ultimately confirmed the President's action through legislation. During the Second World War, the writ of habeas corpus was suspended in the territory of Hawaii.

The writ of habeas corpus is an important element in modern criminal procedure. As a result of legislation passed by Congress in 1867 and subsequent judicial interpretation of that legislation, one convicted of a crime in a state court and sentenced to state prison may petition a federal district court for habeas corpus relief. This permits a federal court to review the constitutional correctness of the arrest, trial, sentencing, and so on of a state prisoner (for further discussion, see Chapters 1 and 14).

Under Chief Justice Earl Warren, the Supreme Court broadened the scope of federal habeas corpus review of state criminal convictions by permitting prisoners to raise issues in federal court that they did not raise in their state appeals (see *Fay v. Noia* [1963]). The Burger Court to some degree restricted access to federal habeas corpus in the Fourth Amendment area (see *Stone v. Powell* [1976]). Nevertheless, the frequency of federal habeas corpus cases challenging state criminal convictions has prompted a movement in Congress to place further restrictions on the availability of the writ. Since Congress initially provided this jurisdiction to the federal courts by statute, Congress may modify or abolish this jurisdiction if it so desires. It is unlikely, though, that Congress would eliminate federal habeas review of state criminal cases altogether. However, during the 1990–1991 term, the Supreme Court further restricted the availability of federal habeas corpus relief to state prisoners (see, for example, *Coleman v. Thompson* [1991]; *McCleskey v. Zant* [1991]; *Ylst v. Nunnemaker* [1991]).

Ex Post Facto Laws

Article I, Section 9 of the Constitution prohibits Congress from passing **ex post facto laws.** Article I, Section 10 imposes the same prohibition on state legislatures. *Ex post facto* laws are laws passed after the occurrence of an act that alter the legal status or consequences of that act. In *Calder v. Bull* (1798), the Supreme Court held that the *ex post facto* clauses applied to criminal but not to civil laws. According to Justice Samuel Chase's opinion in that case, impermissible *ex post facto* laws are those that "create or aggravate . . . [a] crime; or increase the punishment, or change the rules of evidence, for the purpose of conviction." Retrospective laws dealing with civil matters are thus not prohibited by the *ex post facto* clauses.

In two cases decided during the late nineteenth century, *Kring v. Missouri* (1883) and *Thompson v. Utah* (1898), the Supreme Court broadened the definition of *ex post facto* laws to prohibit certain changes in criminal procedure that might prove disadvantageous to the accused. However, in *Collins v. Youngblood* (1990), the Supreme Court overruled these precedents and returned to the definition adopted in *Calder v. Bull*. For an act to be invalidated as an *ex post facto* law, two key elements must exist. First, the act must be retroactive—it must apply to events that occurred before its passage. Second, it must seriously disadvantage the accused, not merely by changes in procedure but by means that render conviction more likely or punishment more severe.

Bills of Attainder

Article I, Sections 9 and 10 also prohibit Congress and the states, respectively, from adopting **bills of attainder.** A bill of attainder is a legislative act that imposes punishment upon a person without benefit of a trial in a court of law.

Perhaps the best-known cases involving bills of attainder are the test oath cases of 1867. In *Ex parte Garland,* the Court struck down the Federal Test Act of 1865, which forbade attorneys from practicing before federal courts unless they took an oath that they had not supported the Confederacy during the Civil War. In *Cummings v. Missouri,* the Court voided a provision of the Missouri Constitution that required a similar oath of all persons who wished to be employed in variety of occupations, including the ministry. Cummings, a Catholic priest, had been fined five hundred dollars for preaching without having taken the oath. The Court found that these laws violated both the bill of attainder and *ex post facto* provisions of Article I.

Since World War II, the Supreme Court has declared only two acts of Congress invalid as bills of attainder. The first instance was *United States v. Lovett* (1946), in which the Court struck down a rider to an appropriations measure that prohibited three named federal employees from receiving compensation

FIGURE 9.1 A Reconstruction Era Loyalty Oath (signed by the great-grandfather of one of the authors of this book)

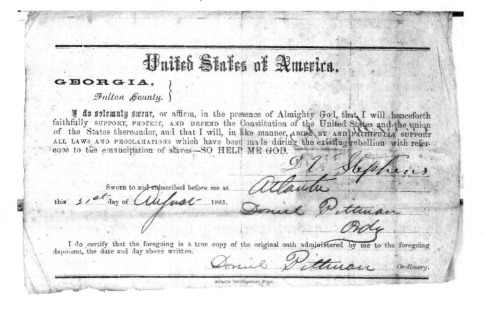

from the government. The three individuals had been branded by the House Committee on Un-American Activities as "subversives." The Court said that legislative acts "that apply either to named individuals or to easily ascertainable members of a group in such a way as to inflict punishment on them without a judicial trial are bills of attainder prohibited by the Constitution."

In *United States v. Brown* (1965), the Court invalidated a law that prohibited members of the Communist party from serving as officers in trade unions, saying that Congress had inflicted punishment on "easily ascertainable members of a group." Four justices dissented, however, citing a number of legislative prohibitions on members of the Communist party that the Court had previously upheld (see, for example, *American Communications Association v. Douds* [1950]).

The Supreme Court considered an interesting bill of attainder issue in *Nixon v. Administrator of General Services* (1977). In this case, former President Richard Nixon challenged the Presidential Recordings and Materials Preservation Act of 1974, in which Congress had placed control of Nixon's presidential papers and recordings in the hands of the General Services Administration, an agency of the federal government. Nixon argued that the law singled him out for punishment by depriving him of the traditional right of presidents to control their own presidential papers. The Court ruled 7 to 2 that the act was not a bill of attainder, concluding that Congress's purpose in passing the law was not punitive.

The Contract Clause

After the Revolutionary War, the thirteen states comprising the newly formed Union experienced a difficult period of political and economic instability. Numerous citizens, especially farmers, defaulted on their loans. Many were imprisoned under the harsh debtor laws of the period. Some state legislatures adopted laws to alleviate the plight of debtors. Cheap paper money was made legal tender; bankruptcy laws were adopted; in some states, creditors' access to the courts was restricted; some states prohibited imprisonment for debt. These policies, while commonplace today, were at that time an anathema to the wealthy. Members of the creditor class believed that serious steps had to be taken to prevent the states from abrogating debts and interfering with contracts generally.

It is fair to say that one of the motivations behind the Constitutional Convention of 1787 was the desire to secure overriding legal protection for contracts. Thus, Article I, Section 10 prohibits states from passing laws "impairing the obligation of contracts." The Contract Clause must be included among the provisions of the original Constitution that protect individual rights—in this case, the right of individuals to be free from governmental interference with their contractual relationships.

By protecting contracts, Article I, Section 10 performed an important function in the early years of American economic development. Historically, the Contract Clause was an important source of litigation in the federal courts. In modern times, it is seldom interpreted to impose significant limits on the states in the field of economic regulation. (The Contract Clause is discussed more fully in Chapter 10.)

President Thomas Jefferson

THE BILL OF RIGHTS

As previously noted, the original Constitution contained little by way of explicit protection of individual rights. In *The Federalist* No. 84, Alexander Hamilton argued that since the Constitution provided for limited government through enumerated powers, a Bill of Rights was unnecessary. In rebuttal, Anti-Federalists argued that the Necessary and Proper Clause of Article I, Section 8 could be used to justify expansive government power that might threaten individual liberties. As we have seen in Chapter 5, the Anti-Federalists were definitely on target.

The omission of a bill of rights from the original Constitution was regarded as a major defect by numerous critics and even threatened to derail ratification in some states. Thomas Jefferson, who had not participated in the Constitutional Convention due to his diplomatic duties in France, was among the most influential critics. In a letter to his close friend James Madison, Jefferson argued, "You must specify your liberties, and put them down on paper." Madison, the acknowledged father of the Constitution, thought it unwise and unnecessary to enumerate individual rights, but Jefferson's view eventually prevailed. Honoring a "gentleman's agreement" designed to secure ratification of the Constitution in several key states, the First Congress considered a proposed bill of rights drafted by Madison.

Madison's original bill of rights called for limitations on the states as well as the federal government, but this proposal was defeated by states' rights advocates in Congress. Twelve amendments to the Constitution were adopted by Congress in September 1789. Although two of these amendments were rejected by the states, the other ten were ratified in November 1791 and were added to the Constitution as the Bill of Rights.

The First Amendment

The First Amendment provides a number of crucial guarantees of freedom. The Establishment Clause prohibits Congress from making laws "respecting an establishment of religion," while the Free Exercise Clause enjoins the national government from "prohibiting the free exercise thereof." These first two clauses demonstrate the fundamental character of the Founders' devotion to freedom of religion. Today, the Religion Clauses remain both important and controversial, involving such emotional issues as prayer and the teaching of "creation science" in the public schools. (The Religion Clauses of the First Amendment are examined in Chapter 13.)

The First Amendment also protects freedom of speech and freedom of the press, often referred to jointly as freedom of expression. One can argue that freedom of expression is the most vital freedom in a democracy, in that it permits the free flow of information between the people and their government. Certainly the Framers of the Bill of Rights were aware of its fundamental importance, which is why the freedoms of speech and press were placed in the First Amendment. Finally, the First Amendment protects the "right of the people peaceably to assemble and petition the Government for a redress of grievances." Freedom of assembly remains an important right, and one that is often controversial, as when an extremist group such as the Ku Klux Klan stages a public rally. The freedom to petition government tends to be less controversial but no less

The Constitution in action: People expressing their First Amendment rights

important. Today, it is referred to as lobbying, the principal activity of interest groups. (The freedoms of speech and assembly are examined in Chapter 11; freedom of the press is dealt with in Chapter 12.)

The Second Amendment

Most Americans believe that the Constitution protects their "right to keep and bear arms." Yet the Second Amendment refers not only to the keeping and bearing of arms but also to the need for a "well regulated Militia." The Second Amendment provides:

> A well regulated Militia, being necessary to the security of a free state, the right of the people to keep and bear arms shall not be infringed.

In *United States v. Cruikshank* (1875), the Supreme Court held that the Second Amendment guaranteed states the right to maintain militias but did not guarantee to individuals the right to possess guns. Subsequently, in *United States v. Miller* (1939), the Court upheld a federal law banning the interstate transportation of certain firearms. Miller, who had been arrested for transporting a double-barreled sawed-off shotgun from Oklahoma to Arkansas, sought the protection of the Second Amendment. The Court rejected Miller's argument, asserting that "we cannot say that the Second Amendment guarantees the right to keep and bear such an instrument." In *Lewis v. United States* (1980), the Court reaffirmed the *Miller* precedent. In upholding a federal gun control act, the Court said:

> These legislative restrictions on the use of firearms are neither based on constitutionally suspect criteria, nor do they trench upon any constitutionally protected liberties. ... [T]he Second Amendment guarantees no right to keep and bear a firearm that does not have "some reasonable relationship to the preservation or efficiency of a well regulated militia."

As currently interpreted, the Second Amendment does not pose a significant constitutional barrier to the enactment or enforcement of gun control laws, whether passed by Congress, state legislatures, or local governments.

The Third Amendment

The Third Amendment prohibits military authorities from quartering troops in citizens' homes without their consent. This was a matter of serious concern to the Founders, because English troops had been forcibly billeted in colonists' homes during the Revolutionary War. Today, the Third Amendment is little more than an historical curiosity, since it has not been the subject of any significant litigation.

The Fourth Amendment

The Fourth Amendment protects citizens from unreasonable searches and seizures conducted by police and other government agents. Reflecting a serious concern of the Founders, the Fourth Amendment remains extremely important today, especially in light of the pervasiveness of crime and the national "war on drugs." In the twentieth century, the Fourth Amendment has been the source of numerous important Supreme Court decisions and has generated a tremendous and complex body of legal doctrine. For example, in *Katz v. United States* (1967), the Supreme Court under Chief Justice Warren expanded the scope of Fourth Amendment protection to include wiretapping, an important tool of modern law enforcement. The Burger and Rehnquist Courts have been decidedly more conservative in this area, facilitating police efforts to ferret out crime. (The Fourth Amendment is examined in some depth in Chapter 14.)

The Fifth Amendment

The Fifth Amendment contains a number of important provisions involving the rights of persons accused of crime. It requires the federal government to obtain an **indictment** from a **grand jury** before trying someone for a major crime. It also prohibits **double jeopardy,** that is, being tried twice for the same offense. Additionally, the Fifth Amendment protects persons against **compulsory self-incrimination,** which is what is commonly meant by the phrase "taking the Fifth." (Fifth Amendment rights of the accused are dealt with in Chapter 14.)

The Fifth Amendment also protects people against arbitrary use of **eminent domain,** the power of government to take private property for public use. The Just Compensation Clause forbids government from taking private property without paying "just compensation" to the owner (see Chapter 10). Finally, the Fifth Amendment prohibits the federal government from depriving persons of life, liberty, or property without due process of law. A virtually identical clause is found in the Fourteenth Amendment, which applies specifically to the states. The Due Process Clauses have implications both for civil and criminal cases, as well as for a variety of relationships between citizen and government. **Due process** may be the broadest and most basic protection afforded by the Constitution. (The concept of due process is more fully explicated below, as part of the discussion of the Fourteenth Amendment.)

The Sixth Amendment

The Sixth Amendment is concerned exclusively with the rights of the accused. It requires, among other things, that people accused of crimes be provided a "speedy and public trial, by an impartial jury. . . ." The right of trial by jury is one of the most cherished rights in the Anglo-American tradition, predating the Magna Charta of 1215. The Sixth Amendment also grants defendants the right to confront, or cross-examine, witnesses for the prosecution and the right to have "compulsory process" (the power of **subpoena**) to require favorable witnesses to appear in court. Significantly, considering the incredible complexity of the criminal law, the Sixth Amendment guarantees that accused persons have the "Assistance of Counsel" for their defense. The Supreme Court has regarded this right as crucial to a fair trial, holding that defendants who are unable to afford private counsel must be afforded counsel at public expense (*Gideon v. Wainwright* [1963]). (Sixth Amendment rights are examined in Chapter 14.)

Trial by jury:
A right guaranteed
by the Sixth Amendment

The Seventh Amendment

The Seventh Amendment guarantees the right to a jury trial in federal civil suits "at common law" where the amount at issue exceeds twenty dollars. Originally, it was widely assumed that the Seventh Amendment required jury trials only in traditional common law cases, for example, actions for libel, wrongful death, and trespass. But over the years, the Supreme Court expanded the scope of the Seventh Amendment to encompass civil suits seeking enforcement of statutory rights. For example, in *Curtis v. Loether* (1974), an African American woman brought suit against a number of white defendants, charging them with refusing to rent her an apartment in violation of the Fair Housing Act of 1968. The defendants requested a trial by jury, but the district court ruled that the Seventh Amendment did not apply to lawsuits seeking to enforce the rights created by the Fair Housing Act. In reversing the district court, the Supreme Court said:

> The Seventh Amendment does apply to actions enforcing statutory rights, and requires a jury trial on demand, if the statute creates legal rights and remedies, enforceable in an action for damages in the ordinary courts of law. . . . We recognize . . . the possibility that jury prejudice may deprive a victim of discrimination of the verdict to which he or she is entitled. Of course, the trial judge's power to direct a verdict, to grant judgment notwithstanding the verdict, or to grant a new trial provides substantial protection against this risk. . . .

Although it does apply to suits enforcing statutory rights, the Seventh Amendment does not apply to the adjudication of certain issues by administrative or regulatory agencies. In *Thomas v. Union Carbide* (1985), the Supreme Court said that the Seventh Amendment does not provide the right to a jury trial where Congress "has created a 'private' right that is so closely integrated into a public regulatory scheme as to be a matter appropriate for agency resolution with limited involvement by the Article III judiciary."

Under current interpretation, the Seventh Amendment does not require the traditional common law twelve-person jury in civil trials. In *Colgrove v. Battin* (1973), the Supreme Court held that a six-person jury was sufficient to try a civil case in federal court. The defendant in the case argued that the Seventh Amendment's reference to "suits at common law" required federal courts to adopt the traditional common law jury. The Supreme Court, dividing 5 to 4, disagreed. Writing for the Court, Justice William Brennan said:

> Consistently with the historical objective of the Seventh Amendment, our decisions have defined the jury right preserved in cases covered by the Amendment, as "the substance of the common-law right of trial by jury, as distinguished from mere matters of form or procedure." *** The Amendment, therefore, does not bind the federal courts to the exact procedural incidents or details of jury trial according to the common law in 1791. ***

In a lengthy dissent, Justice Thurgood Marshall stressed the need for fidelity to the traditions of the common law:

> Since some definition of "jury" must be chosen, I would ... rely on the fixed bounds of history which the Framers, by drafting the Seventh Amendment, meant to "preserve." ... It may well be that the number 12 is no more than a "historical accident" and is "wholly without significance". . . . But surely there is nothing more significant about the number six, or three or one. The line must be drawn somewhere, and the difference between drawing it in the light of history and drawing it on an *ad hoc* basis is, ultimately, the difference between interpreting a constitution and making it up as one goes along.

The controversy over the appropriate size of the jury in federal civil trials parallels the issue of jury size in criminal cases, a question examined in Chapter 14.

The Eighth Amendment

The Eighth Amendment protects persons accused of crimes from being required to post "excessive bail" to secure **pretrial release.** In *Stack v. Boyle* (1951), the Supreme Court held that bail is excessive if it is higher than is necessary to ensure a defendant's appearance for trial. But in *United States v. Salerno* (1987), a case involving the prosecution of an organized crime figure, the Court said that the Eighth Amendment does not require that defendants be released on bail, only that, if the court grants bail, it must not be "excessive."

The Eighth Amendment also forbids the imposition of "excessive fines" and the infliction of "cruel and unusual punishments" on persons convicted of crimes. Originally thought to proscribe torture, the Cruel and Unusual Punishments Clause now figures prominently in the ongoing national debate over the death penalty (see Chapter 14). Writing for the Supreme Court in *Trop v. Dulles* (1958), Chief Justice Earl Warren observed that the Cruel and Unusual Punishments Clause "must draw its meaning from the evolving standards of decency that mark the progress of a maturing society." In the *Trop* case, a soldier had lost his citizenship after being found guilty of desertion from the U.S. Army. The Supreme Court restored Trop's citizenship, noting that "[t]he civilized nations of the world are in virtual unanimity that statelessness is not to be imposed as punishment for a crime."

The Ninth Amendment

The Ninth Amendment states:

> The enumeration in the Constitution, of certain rights, shall not be construed to deny or disparage others retained by the people.

The Ninth Amendment was included in the Bill of Rights as a solution to a problem raised by James Madison; namely, that the specification of particular liberties might suggest that individuals possessed only those specified. The Ninth Amendment makes it clear that individuals retain a reservoir of rights and liberties beyond those listed in the Constitution. This reflects the dominant thinking of late-eighteenth-century America: individual rights precede and transcend the power of government; individuals possess all rights except those that have been surrendered to government for the protection of the public good.

Prior to 1965, the Ninth Amendment had little significance in constitutional law. In the words of Justice Potter Stewart,

> The Ninth Amendment, like its companion the Tenth, which this Court has held "states but a truism that all is retained which has not been surrendered," *** was framed by James Madison and adopted by the States simply to make clear that the adoption of the Bill of Rights did not alter the plan that the *Federal* government was to be a government of express and limited powers, and that all rights and powers not delegated to it were retained by the people and the individual States. *Griswold v. Connecticut* (1965) (dissenting opinion).

But in *Griswold v. Connecticut* (1965), a Supreme Court majority, in recognizing a constitutional right of privacy (discussed more fully in Chapter 15), relied in part on the Ninth Amendment. Here, the Court invalidated a Connecticut statute that made it a crime to use birth control devices. Justice Stewart, who along with Justice Hugo Black dissented in *Griswold,* expressed dismay that the Court relied on the Ninth Amendment to strike down a state statute:

> . . . [T]he idea that a federal court could ever use the Ninth Amendment to annul a law passed by the elected representatives of the people of the State of Connecticut would have caused James Madison no little wonder.

Although they have seldom relied explicitly on the Ninth Amendment, federal and state courts have over the years recognized a number of rights that Americans take for granted but which are not specifically enumerated in the Constitution. The right to marry, to determine how one's children are to be reared and educated, to choose one's occupation, to start a business, to travel freely across state lines, to sue in the courts, and to be presumed innocent of a crime until proven guilty are all examples of individual rights that have been recognized as "constitutional," despite their absence from the text of the

Constitution. Quite often these rights have been recognized under the broad Due Process Clauses of the Fifth and Fourteenth Amendments.

The Tenth Amendment

Rounding out the Bill of Rights, the Tenth Amendment provides:

> The powers not delegated to the United States by the Constitution, nor prohibited by it to the States, are reserved to the States respectively, or to the people.

Unlike other provisions of the Bill of Rights, and despite its reference to "the people," the Tenth Amendment recognizes the powers of the states vis-à-vis the federal government and does not address individual rights. Accordingly, the Tenth Amendment is largely unrelated to constitutional law in the realm of civil rights and liberties. Rather, it pertains to the area of federalism (see Chapter 8).

THE FOURTEENTH AMENDMENT

Without question, the most important amendment to the Constitution outside of the Bill of Rights is the Fourteenth Amendment. Ratified in 1868, the principal objective of the Fourteenth Amendment was to protect the civil rights and liberties of African-Americans. Although slavery had been formally abolished by the Thirteenth Amendment, ratified in 1865, questions remained about the legal status of the former slaves. One will recall that in *Dred Scott v. Sandford* (1857), the Supreme Court not only defended the institution of slavery but indicated that blacks were not citizens of the United States and possessed "no rights or privileges but such as those who held the power and the Government might choose to grant them." Section 1 of the Fourteenth Amendment made clear that *Dred Scott* was no longer the law of the land:

> All persons born or naturalized in the United States, and subject to the jurisdiction thereof, are citizens of the United States and of the State wherein they reside. No state shall make or enforce any law which shall abridge the privileges or immunities of citizens of the United States; nor shall any State deprive any person of life, liberty, or property, without due process of law; nor deny to any person within its jurisdiction the equal protection of the laws.

The federal courts have relied heavily on the Equal Protection Clause of Section 1 in advancing the civil rights of African-Americans and other minority groups. The "case of the century," *Brown v. Board of Education* (1954), in which the Supreme Court abolished racial segregation in the public schools, was based squarely on the Equal Protection Clause.

Section 5 of the Fourteenth Amendment grants to Congress the power to enforce the broad provisions of Section 1 through "appropriate legislation." Congress has relied upon Section 5 in passing civil rights legislation, such as the landmark Civil Rights Act of 1964 forbidding, among other things, racial discrimination in education and employment. (The application of the Fourteenth Amendment to issues of civil rights is examined in detail in Chapters 16 and 17.)

While the principal purpose of the Fourteenth Amendment was to protect the rights of African-Americans, it has come to be regarded as a broad shield against actions by state and local governments infringing individual rights and liberties. Of particular importance in this context is the Due Process Clause.

Due Process of Law

In its most generic sense, due process refers to the exercise of governmental power under the rule of law with due regard for the rights and interests of individuals. The concept of **procedural due process** embraces government's obligation to provide fair notice and a fair hearing to individuals before depriving them of "life, liberty or property." Thus, for example, the Supreme Court relied on the Due Process Clause of the Fourteenth Amendment in a landmark decision revolutionizing the juvenile justice system, holding that juveniles must be afforded certain procedural protections before they can be judged "delinquent" and sent to a reformatory (*In re Gault* [1967]). Similarly, the Supreme Court has invoked due process to say that police may not use methods that "shock the conscience" in attempting to gather evidence of criminal wrongdoing (*Rochin v. California* [1952]).

Historically, the concept of due process was extremely important in defending private property rights from government regulation (see Chapter 10). More recently, the courts have recognized government employment and government benefits as "property interests" subject to the requirements of due process. Thus, while there is no constitutional right to receive welfare assistance, government may not terminate a person's welfare benefits without observing certain procedural safeguards (see, for example, *Goldberg v. Kelly* [1970]).

Substantive Due Process

In addition to providing procedural protections against arbitrary and capricious government action, due process has been held to impose substantive limits on government policies as well. Under the concept of **substantive due process,** government is barred from enforcing policies that are irrational, unfair, unreasonable, or unjust, even if such policies do not run counter to other specific constitutional prohibitions.

For almost fifty years (roughly 1890 to 1937), the Supreme Court relied on substantive due process to invalidate a variety of state and federal laws regulating aspects of economic life (see Chapter 10). For example, in *Lochner v. New York* (1905), the Court struck down a state law setting maximum working hours in bakeries. The Court held that the restriction violated both the employer's and the employee's "liberty of contract," a right not specifically enumerated in the Constitution but held to be embraced within the substantive prohibitions of the Due Process Clause of the Fourteenth Amendment. While the "liberty of contract" version of substantive due process has been repudiated by the modern Supreme Court, substantive due process lives on under the rubric of the right of privacy.

The Right of Privacy

First recognized in *Griswold v. Connecticut* (1965), the right of privacy is not found in any specific provision of the Bill of Rights. Nevertheless, the Supreme Court has held that privacy is a **fundamental right** enforceable against the state governments via the Due Process Clause of the Fourteenth Amendment. As previously noted, in *Griswold*, the right of privacy was invoked to invalidate a state law prohibiting the use of birth control devices. Eight years later, in *Roe v. Wade* (1973), the right of privacy was held to be broad enough to include a woman's decision to have an abortion, touching off a constitutional debate that continues to rage. In the popular debate over *Roe*, the issue tends to be the desirability of legalized abortion. Yet the scholarly debate over *Roe v. Wade* focuses to a greater extent on the legitimacy of substantive due process as a constitutional doctrine. (The right of privacy and its application to a variety of issues, including abortion, are discussed in Chapter 15.)

The Fourteenth Amendment and "State Action"

Normally one thinks of the Fourteenth Amendment, as well as the provisions of the Bill of Rights, as placing constraints on government action. The Supreme Court has said on numerous occasions, the first being in *The Civil Rights Cases* (1883), that the prohibitions of the Fourteenth Amendment apply to **state action** but not to actions by private individuals or corporations. (This important doctrine of constitutional law is discussed at some length in Chapter 16). However, an action that is ostensibly private in character may be treated as "state action" within the purview of the Fourteenth Amendment if there is a "close nexus" between the state and the private actor. Thus, for example, the Supreme Court in 1944 invalidated the Texas Democratic party's whites-only primary election, even though the party was not, strictly speaking, an agency of the state (see *Smith v. Allwright* [1944], discussed and reprinted in Chapter 17).

Can Inaction Be "State Action"?

In modern times, the doctrine of state action has been criticized as being too restrictive. Indeed, some have argued that the Fourteenth Amendment should be interpreted to impose an affirmative duty on government to protect persons against harm in some circumstances. This argument was made in dramatic form in the 1989 case of *DeShaney v. Winnebago Social Service Department*. There, the Supreme Court, dividing 6 to 3, held that a social services agency, regardless of its prior knowledge of the danger, did not violate the Fourteenth Amendment by failing to protect a child from his abusive father. Following his parents' divorce, one-year-old Joshua DeShaney was placed in the custody of his father, who soon established legal residence in Winnebago County, Wisconsin. Two years later, county social workers began to receive reports that the father was physically abusing the child. When Joshua was four years old, his father beat him so severely as to inflict permanent brain damage, leaving the child profoundly retarded and institutionalized for life. Joshua's mother brought suit on her son's behalf, seeking monetary damages from the state, arguing that the state agency's failure to protect her son constituted an abridgment of his rights under the Fourteenth Amendment.

Writing for the majority, Chief Justice Rehnquist rejected this contention. He noted that the Court had previously recognized a state's constitutional obligation to protect the safety and well-being of those within its custody, including mentally retarded persons in state institutions. But this "affirmative duty to protect" did not arise "from the state's knowledge of the [Joshua's] predicament or from its expressions of its intent to help him." Since the state had no constitutional duty to protect Joshua from his father, its failure to do so, although calamitous, did not constitute a violation of the Due Process Clause.

In a dissenting opinion, Justice Harry Blackmun excoriated the Court for its "sterile formalism." Blackmun asserted that the "broad and stirring clauses of the Fourteenth Amendment" were "designed, at least in part, to undo the formalistic legal reasoning that infected antebellum jurisprudence. . . ." Blackmun preferred a "sympathetic reading" of the Fourteenth Amendment that recognized that "compassion need not be exiled from the province of judging."

The Incorporation of the Bill of Rights

One of the most important impacts of the Fourteenth Amendment has been the effective "nationalization" of the Bill of Rights. There is little doubt that, at the time of its ratification in 1791, the Bill of Rights was widely perceived as imposing limitations only on the powers and actions of the national government. This is suggested by the first clause of the First Amendment, which begins, "Congress shall make no law. . . ." The Court held as much in 1833 in the case of *Barron v. Baltimore,* when it refused to permit a citizen to sue a local government for violating his property rights under the Just Compensation Clause of the Fifth Amendment. Speaking for the Court, Chief Justice John Marshall said:

> We are of the opinion, that, the provision in the Fifth Amendment to the Constitution, declaring that private property shall not be taken for public use without just compensation is intended solely as a limitation on the power of the United States, and is not applicable to the legislation of the states.

The ratification of the Fourteenth Amendment in 1868 provided an opportunity for the Supreme Court to reconsider the relationship between the Bill of Rights and state and local governments. As we have seen, Section 1 of the Fourteenth Amendment imposed broad restrictions on state power, requiring the states to provide equal protection of the law to all persons, to respect the "privileges and immunities" of citizens of the United States, and, most importantly, to protect the "life, liberty, and property" of all persons. More to the point, the Fourteenth Amendment enjoined states from depriving persons of these basic rights "without due process of law." Although there is no conclusive evidence that the Framers of the Fourteenth Amendment intended for it to "incorporate" the Bill of Rights and thus make the latter applicable to actions of state and local governments, plaintiffs in federal cases began to make this argument fairly soon after the amendment was ratified.

Initially, the Supreme Court was not favorably disposed toward the **doctrine of incorporation.** In *Hurtado v. California* (1884), the Court rejected the argument that the grand jury procedure required in federal criminal cases by the Fifth Amendment was an essential feature of "due process of law" and thus required in state criminal cases by the Fourteenth Amendment. Today, the *Hurtado* decision remains "good" law; states are not required by the federal Constitution to use grand juries to bring criminal charges, although many still do.

Selective Incorporation

The fact that the *Hurtado* decision remains valid indicates that the Supreme Court has never accepted the argument that the Fourteenth Amendment incorporates the Bill of Rights *en toto*. The Court has, however, endorsed a doctrine of **selective incorporation** by which most of the provisions of the Bill of Rights have been extended to limit actions of the state and local governments. The process of selective incorporation began in 1897 in the case of *Chicago, Burlington and Quincy Railroad Company v. Chicago*. There, a conservative Court concerned about protecting private enterprise against a rising tide of government interventionism held that the Due Process Clause of the Fourteenth Amendment imposed on state and local governments the same obligation to respect private property that the Fifth Amendment imposed on the federal government. The Court said that when a state or local government takes private property under its power of eminent domain, it must provide just compensation to the owner. Thus, the Court had "incorporated" the Just Compensation Clause of the Fifth Amendment into the Due Process Clause of the Fourteenth Amendment.

The doctrine of incorporation was next applied to First Amendment freedoms, specifically the freedoms of speech and press. In *Gitlow v. New York* (1925), the Supreme Court said that

> we may and do assume that freedom of speech and of the press—which are protected by the First Amendment from abridgment by Congress—are among the fundamental personal rights and "liberties" protected by the due process clause of the Fourteenth Amendment from impairment by the states. . . .

The dictum in *Gitlow* was soon followed by decisions in which the Court relied on the doctrine of incorporation to invalidate state actions abridging the freedoms of speech and press. In *Fiske v. Kansas* (1927), the Court invalidated a state **criminal syndicalism** statute that prohibited mere advocacy of violent action, finding it to be a violation of freedom of speech. Four years later, in *Near v. Minnesota* (1931), the Court struck down a state law that permitted censorship of "malicious, scandalous and defamatory" periodicals, finding it to be a clear violation of freedom of the press. In the wake of these and related decisions, state and local policies impinging on freedom of expression became subject to challenge in the courts under the same First Amendment standards that applied to federal legislation.

In *Palko v. Connecticut* (1937), the Supreme Court refused to incorporate the Double Jeopardy Clause of the Fifth Amendment into the Due Process Clause of the Fourteenth. To merit incorporation, said Justice Benjamin N. Cardozo, a provision of the Bill of Rights must be essential to "a scheme of ordered liberty." Cardozo's majority opinion suggested that the First Amendment freedoms that had been previously incorporated represented "the matrix, the indispensable condition, of nearly every other form of freedom." The Double Jeopardy Clause, in Cardozo's view, lay on "a different plane of social and moral values."

Following *Palko v. Connecticut,* the doctrine of incorporation became the subject of an intense debate among the justices of the Supreme Court. In *Cantwell v. Connecticut* (1940), the Court incorporated the Free Exercise of Religion Clause of the First Amendment. Similarly, in *Everson v. Board of Education* (1947), the Court extended the Establishment Clause to the states under the Fourteenth Amendment (for more discussion of both cases and clauses, see Chapter 13). Yet in *Adamson v. California* (1947) and in *Rochin v. California* (1952), the Court refused to extend the Fifth Amendment privilege against compulsory self-incrimination to state criminal trials. The Court's highly selective approach to incorporation of the Bill of Rights drew the particular ire of Justices Hugo Black and William O. Douglas. In the *Adamson* case, for example, Justice Black complained that selective incorporation permitted the Court to act in a manner inconsistent with the ideal of the rule of law:

> To hold that this Court can determine what, if any, provisions of the Bill of Rights will be enforced, and if so to what degree, is to frustrate the great design of a written constitution.

In a similar vein, Justice Douglas, writing in *Rochin v. California,* argued that provisions of the Bill of Rights governing criminal procedure should be equally applicable to the state and federal courts:

> If it is a requirement of due process for a trial in the federal courthouse, it is impossible for me to say that it is not a requirement of due process for a trial in the state courthouse.

In the 1960s, the views of Justices Black and Douglas as to the applicability of the Bill of Rights to state criminal prosecutions came to be supported by a majority of justices on the Supreme Court. Indeed, one of the priorities of the Court under the leadership of Chief Justice Warren was to increase the legal protections afforded to persons accused of crimes, both in state and federal court. In a series of landmark decisions, the Warren Court incorporated nearly all of the relevant provisions of the Bill of Rights into the Due Process Clause of the Fourteenth Amendment and thus made them applicable to state criminal cases (see Table 9.1).

In one of the most significant of these decisions, *Duncan v. Louisiana* (1968), the Court made the ancient right of trial by jury applicable to defendants in state criminal cases. In a concurring opinion joined by Justice Douglas, Justice Black expressed his satisfaction with what the Court had done under the mantle of selective incorporation:

> I believe as strongly as ever that the Fourteenth Amendment was intended to make the Bill of Rights applicable to the States. I have been willing to support the selective incorporation doctrine, however, as an alternative, although perhaps less

historically supportable than complete incorporation. . . . [M]ost importantly for me, the selective incorporation process has the virtue of having already worked to make most of the Bill of Rights protections applicable to the States.

The process of selective incorporation of the Bill of Rights may have reached its terminus in 1969. In that year, in *Benton v. Maryland*, the Supreme Court overruled its earlier decision in *Palko v. Connecticut* and decided, after all, that the Double Jeopardy Clause of the Fifth Amendment warranted incorporation into the Fourteenth Amendment. The *Benton* case marks the latest and perhaps last instance of a provision of the Bill of Rights being extended to state action via the Fourteenth Amendment. As of 1992, the only provisions of the Bill of Rights that had *not* been absorbed into the Fourteenth Amendment were the Second, Third, and Seventh Amendments, the Fifth Amendment grand jury clause, and the Eighth Amendment prohibition against "excessive bail."

The principal thrust of the process of selective incorporation is that today, with few exceptions, policies of state and local government are subject to judicial

TABLE 9.1 Chronology of Incorporation of the Bill of Rights

Year	Issue and Amendment Involved	Case
1897	Just compensation (V)	*Chicago, Burlington & Quincy Railroad v. Chicago*, 166 U.S. 226
1927	Speech (I)	*Fiske v. Kansas*, 274 U.S. 380
1931	Press (I)	*Near v. Minnesota*, 283 U.S. 697
1934	Free exercise of religion (I)	*Hamilton v. Regents of the University of California*, 293 U.S. 245
1937	Assembly and petition (I)	*De Jonge v. Oregon*, 299 U.S. 353
1947	Separation of church and state (I)	*Everson v. Board of Education*, 330 U.S. 1
1948	Public trial (VI)	*In re Oliver*, 333 U.S. 257
1949	Unreasonable searches and seizures (IV)	*Wolf v. Colorado*, 338 U.S. 25
1962	Cruel and unusual punishment (VIII)	*Robinson v. California*, 370 U.S. 660
1963	Right to counsel (VI)	*Gideon v. Wainwright*, 372 U.S. 335
1964	Compulsory self-incrimination (V)	*Malloy v. Hogan*, 378 U.S. 1; *Murphy v. Waterfront Commission of New York Harbor*, 378 U.S. 52
1965	Confrontation of hostile witnesses (VI)	*Pointer v. Texas*, 380 U.S. 400
1966	Impartial jury (VI)	*Parker v. Gladden*, 385 U.S. 363
1967	Confrontation of favorable witnesses	*Washington v. Texas*, 388 U.S. 14
1967	Speedy trial (VI)	*Klopfer v. North Carolina*, 386 U.S. 371
1968	Jury trial in nonpetty criminal cases (VI)	*Duncan v. Louisiana*, 391 U.S. 145
1969	Double jeopardy (V)	*Benton v. Maryland*, 395 U.S. 784

scrutiny under the same standards that the Bill of Rights imposes on the federal government. Thus, for example, the prohibition of the First Amendment against establishment of religion applies with equal force to a school board in rural Arkansas as it does to the Congress of the United States. Likewise, the Eighth Amendment injunction against cruel and unusual punishments applies equally to high-profile federal prosecutions for treason and to sentences imposed by local courts for violations of city or county ordinances. It should be noted, however, that in a few instances, such as those governed by the Sixth Amendment right to trial by jury, the Supreme Court has been willing to give the states slightly greater latitude than the federal government in complying with Bill of Rights requirements (for further discussion, see Chapter 14).

AMENDMENTS PROTECTING VOTING RIGHTS

While the Fourteenth Amendment is the broadest, and most important, source of protection for civil rights and liberties outside of the Bill of Rights, a number of other constitutional amendments address specific civil rights issues. These Amendments (XV, XIX, XXIV, and XXVI) focus on the right to vote, which is arguably the most essential right in a democracy. The original Constitution left the matter of voting rights to the states. In 1787, voting in the United States was confined for the most part to "freeholders," that is, white male landowners above the age of twenty-one. As our society has become progressively more democratic, the Constitution has been amended to make the franchise more inclusive.

The Fifteenth Amendment

Like the Thirteenth and Fourteenth Amendments, the Fifteenth Amendment (ratified in 1870) was an outgrowth of the Civil War. Unlike the Fourteenth Amendment, however, the Fifteenth Amendment is targeted fairly narrowly, its only concern being the denial of voting rights in state and federal elections on grounds of race. As in the Thirteenth and Fourteenth Amendments, Section 5 of the Fifteenth Amendment grants Congress the power to adopt "appropriate legislation" to enforce its guarantees. In 1965, Congress employed its enforcement powers under Section 5 in adopting the landmark Voting Rights Act. Among other things, the act brought the federal government into the active supervision of electoral systems in states where racial discrimination had been pervasive. It also granted individuals the right to sue in federal court to challenge features of state and local elections deemed to be discriminatory. Without question, the Voting Rights Act of 1965 has had an enormous impact in ending racial discrimination in this area. (The issue of voting rights is examined in detail in Chapter 17.)

The Nineteenth Amendment

Like most blacks, women were originally excluded from participation in elections in this country. In 1848, a delegation of women, including the famous suffragist Elizabeth Cady Stanton, met at Seneca Falls, New York, to address the "social, civil, and religious conditions and rights of woman." The Seneca Falls

Convention adopted a resolution stating that "it is the duty of the women of this country to secure to themselves their sacred right to the elective franchise." Securing the franchise would not be easy. In 1872, Susan B. Anthony was prosecuted for attempting to vote in the presidential election. Three years later, the Supreme Court rebuffed a woman seeking to cast a ballot in a Missouri election, saying that "the Constitution of the United States does not confer the right of suffrage upon anyone" (*Minor v. Happersett* [1875]). In the last decades of the nineteenth century, a few states changed their statutes to permit female suffrage. By 1912, nine states had extended the franchise to include women. In 1918, President Woodrow Wilson took a stand in favor of women's suffrage. Following Wilson's lead, Congress adopted a constitutional amendment granting women the right to vote and submitted it to the states for ratification. In 1920, the Nineteenth Amendment was added to the Constitution:

> The right of the citizens of the United States to vote shall not be denied or abridged by the United States or by any State on account of sex.
>
> Congress shall have the power, by appropriate legislation, to enforce the provision of this article.

In one fell swoop, the size of the potential electorate was doubled! Political participation by women did not, as some critics feared, radically alter the political system or its public policy outputs.

The Twenty-fourth Amendment

Although formally granted the right to vote by the Fifteenth Amendment, many African-Americans were still effectively disenfranchised by practices such as **grandfather clauses, literacy tests, white primaries,** and poll taxes (see Chapter 17). The **poll tax** was a fee required as a condition for voting. Typically, the unpaid fees would accumulate from election to election, posing an ever-greater economic impediment to voting. Poll taxes had been common in the United States at the time the Constitution was adopted but fell into disuse by the mid-nineteenth century. They were resurrected after the ratification of the Fifteenth Amendment as a means of preventing African-Americans, most of whom were poor, from voting. In *Breedlove v. Suttles* (1937), the Supreme Court ruled that poll taxes, in and of themselves, did not violate the Fourteenth or Fifteenth Amendments. The *Breedlove* decision gave impetus to a movement to abolish the poll tax, and by 1960, poll taxes existed in only five Southern states. The Twenty-fourth Amendment, ratified in 1964, outlawed poll taxes as a requirement to vote in federal elections. A year later, the Supreme Court extended this policy when it overturned *Breedlove* and struck down poll taxes in state elections as well (*Harper v. Virginia State Board of Elections* [1966]) (see Chapter 17).

The Twenty-Sixth Amendment

During the 1960s, young people, galvanized primarily by the Vietnam War, began to assert themselves politically. Often, political participation by the young was unconventional, taking the form of demonstrations and protests. Many youth leaders argued that if eighteen-year-olds were old enough to be drafted into military service and placed in combat, they were also old enough to cast a ballot. This line of argument was not new; it had persuaded Georgia and Kentucky to lower the minimum voting age to eighteen during the Second World War.

In 1970, Congress passed a measure lowering the voting age from twenty-one to eighteen in both state and federal elections. The Supreme Court, however, declared this measure unconstitutional in *Oregon v. Mitchell* (1970). Dividing 5 to 4, the Court held that, although Congress possessed the authority to lower the voting age in *federal* elections, it could not by simple statute lower the voting age in *state* elections. This decision prompted Congress to adopt the Twenty-sixth Amendment, which was ratified by the states in record time—five weeks. Unlike women, however, young people have not taken full advantage of the extension of the franchise. People eighteen to twenty-one are considerably less likely to vote than their elders.

STANDARDS OF JUDICIAL REVIEW

We have seen that particular civil rights and liberties are protected by specific provisions of the Constitution. In addition, the Due Process Clauses of the Fifth and Fourteenth Amendments have been held to protect broad liberty and property interests.

The Rational Basis Test

In *Massachusetts Board of Retirement v. Murgia* (1976), the Supreme Court said that a law that touches on a constitutionally protected interest must, at a minimum, be "rationally related to furthering a legitimate government interest." For example, a state law that prohibits performing surgery without a license impinges on constitutionally protected interests by depriving lay persons of their right to make contracts freely and discriminating against those unable or unwilling to obtain a license. Yet the prohibition is obviously a rational means of advancing the state's legitimate interests in public health and safety. There is no doubt that, if it were challenged, the prohibition would withstand judicial review.

In applying the rational basis test, courts begin with a strong presumption that the challenged law or policy is valid. The burden of proof is on the party making the challenge to show that the law or policy is unconstitutional. To carry this burden, the party must demonstrate that there is no rational basis for the law or policy. Since this is a difficult showing to make, application of the rational basis test usually leads to a judgment sustaining the constitutionality of the challenged law or policy.

Strict Judicial Scrutiny

When a law or policy impinges on a right explicitly protected by the Constitution, such as the right to vote, it is subjected to a more searching judicial scrutiny. This approach also applies in the case of unenumerated rights that the courts have identified as fundamental, such as the right of privacy (see *Roe v. Wade* [1973]) and the right of interstate travel (see *Shapiro v. Thompson* [1969]). Strict judicial scrutiny is also warranted in cases involving forms of discrimination, such as that based on race, that have been held to be "inherently suspect" (see *Korematsu v. United States* [1944]).

Under strict scrutiny, the ordinary presumption of constitutionality is reversed, which means, in effect, that the challenged law or policy is presumed to be unconstitutional. The burden shifts to the government (local, state, or federal) to show that the law or policy furthers a **compelling government interest.** This is a heavy burden for the government to carry. Consequently, most laws subjected to strict judicial scrutiny are declared unconstitutional. However, the application of strict scrutiny is not necessarily tantamount to a declaration of unconstitutionality. For example, in *New York v. Ferber* (1982), the Supreme Court upheld a child pornography law that impinged on the First Amendment freedom of expression because, in the view of the Court, the law served a compelling interest in protecting children from the abuse typically associated with the pornography industry.

THE IMPORTANCE OF STATE CONSTITUTIONS

In trying to understand constitutional law as it relates to civil rights and liberties, one must not ignore the role of the state constitutions and courts in protecting individual rights. Under our federal system of government, the highest court of each state possesses the authority to interpret with finality its state constitution and statutes. Since every state constitution contains language protecting individual rights and liberties, many state court decisions implicate both state and federal constitutional provisions. Under the relevant language of their constitutions and statutes, state courts are free to recognize greater (but not lesser) protections of individual rights than are provided by the U.S. Constitution as interpreted by the federal courts. For example, in *In re T.W.* (1989), the Florida Supreme Court struck down as a violation of the right of privacy a statute that required parental consent in cases where minors sought abortions. The constitutionality of a similar law had been upheld on federal grounds by the U.S. Supreme Court in *Planned Parenthood v. Ashcroft* (1983). In *T.W.,* the Florida Supreme Court made it clear that it was basing its decision on an amendment to the Florida Constitution that (unlike the federal Constitution) explicitly protects the right of privacy. Similarly, in *State v. Kam* (1988), the Hawaii Supreme Court adopted an interpretation of its state constitution that affords considerably broader protection to pornography than that provided by the U.S. Constitution. These decisions, and many others like them, mean that a study of civil rights and liberties must encompass the provisions of state constitutions that parallel those of the U.S. Constitution.

CONCLUSION

This chapter has provided a broad survey of the constitutional sources of protection for civil rights and liberties. As manifestations of the ideals of liberty and equality, civil rights and liberties are regarded as indispensable features of American democracy. Yet individual rights exist in constant tension with majority rule, another essential feature of democracy. Individual rights must be balanced wisely against compelling societal interests, such as public order, national defense, and the general welfare. The task of achieving this balance rests primarily with the courts, most notably the U.S. Supreme Court. The remaining chapters of this book are devoted to an examination of the Supreme Court's jurisprudence in several key areas of civil rights and liberties.

FOR FURTHER READING

Abraham, Henry J. *Freedom and the Court: Civil Rights and Liberties in the United States,* 4th ed. New York: Oxford University Press, 1982.

Barker, Lucius J., and Twiley W. Barker, Jr. *Civil Liberties and the Constitution.* Englewood Cliffs, N.J.: Prentice-Hall, 1982.

Bonnicksen, Andrea L. *Civil Rights and Liberties.* Palo Alto, Calif.: Mayfield, 1982.

Brigham, John. *Civil Liberties and American Democracy.* Washington, D.C.: Congressional Quarterly Press, 1984.

Casper, Jonathan D. *The Politics of Civil Liberties.* New York: Harper and Row, 1972.

Dworkin, Ronald. *Taking Rights Seriously.* Cambridge: Harvard University Press, 1978.

Emerson, Thomas I., and David Haber. *Political and Civil Rights in the United States,* 2 vols. Buffalo, N.Y.: Dennis, 1958.

Morgan, Richard E. *The Law and Politics of Civil Rights and Liberties.* New York: Knopf, 1985.

Peltason, Jack W. *Corwin and Peltason's Understanding the Constitution,* 12th ed. San Diego: Harcourt Brace Jovanovich, 1991.

Perry, Michael. *The Constitution, the Courts, and Human Rights.* New Haven: Yale University Press, 1982.

Pritchett, C. Herman. *Constitutional Civil Liberties.* Englewood Cliffs, N.J.: Prentice-Hall, 1984.

Sigler, Jay A. *American Rights Policies.* Homewood, Ill.: Dorsey, 1975.

United States v. Brown

381 U.S. 437; 85 S. Ct. 1707; 14 L. Ed.2d 484 (1965)
Vote: 5-4

Under Section 504 of the Labor-Management Reporting and Disclosure Act of 1959, Congress made it a crime for a member of the Communist party to serve as an officer or employee of a labor union. Based on Congress's broad power to regulate interstate commerce, the act was justified by supporters as a means of preserving harmony in the industrial sector of the economy. Critics saw the act as an invasion of the rights of political expression and association. In American Communications Association v. Douds (1950), the Supreme Court had upheld a similar measure. By the mid-1960s, however, the disposition of the Court toward anti-Communist legislation had changed considerably.

Mr. Chief Justice Warren delivered the Opinion of the Court.

. . . Respondent has been a working longshoreman on the San Francisco docks, and an open and avowed Communist, for more than a quarter of a century. He was elected to the Executive Board of Local 10 of the International Longshoremen's and Warehousemen's Union for consecutive one-year terms in 1959, 1960, and 1961. On May 24, 1961, respondent was charged in a one-count indictment returned in the Northern District of California with "knowingly and wilfully serv[ing] as a member of an executive board of a labor organization . . . while a member of the Communist Party, in wilful violation of Section 504." It was neither charged nor proven that respondent at any time advocated or suggested illegal activity by the union, or proposed a political strike. The jury found respondent guilty and he was sentenced to six months' imprisonment. The Court of Appeals for the Ninth Circuit, sitting *en banc,* reversed and remanded with instructions to set aside the conviction and dismiss the indictment. . . .

Respondent urges . . . that the statute under which he was convicted is a bill of attainder, and therefore violates Art. I, Sec. 9, of the Constitution. We agree

that Sec. 504 is void as a bill of attainder and affirm the decision of the Court of Appeals on that basis. . . .

The Solicitor General argues that Sec. 504 is not a bill of attainder because the prohibition it imposes does not constitute "punishment." In support of this conclusion, he urges that the statute was enacted for preventive rather than retributive reasons—that its aim is not to punish Communists for what they have done in the past, but rather to keep them from positions where they will in the future be able to bring about undesirable events. He relies on *American Communications Assn. v. Douds* *** which upheld Sec. 9(h) of the National Labor Relations Act, the predecessor of the statute presently before us. . . .

This case is not necessarily controlled by *Douds.* For to prove its assertion that Sec. 9(h) was preventive rather than retributive in purpose, the Court in *Douds* focused on the fact that members of the Communist Party could escape from the class of persons specified by Congress simply by resigning from the Party:

"Here the intention is to forestall future dangerous acts; there is no one who may not, by a voluntary alteration of the loyalties which impel him to action, become eligible to sign the affidavit. We cannot conclude that this section is a bill of attainder."

Section 504, unlike Sec. 9(h), disqualifies from the holding of union office not only present members of the Communist Party, but also anyone who has within the past five years been a member of the Party. However, even if we make the assumption that the five-year provision was inserted not out of desire to visit retribution but purely out of a belief that failure to include it would lead to pro forma resignations from the Party which would not decrease the threat of political strikes, it still clearly appears that Sec. 504 inflicts "punishment" within the meaning of the Bill of Attainder clause. It would be archaic to limit the definition of "punishment" to "retribution." Punishment serves several purposes: retributive, rehabilitative deterrent—and preventive. One of the reasons society imprisons those convicted of crimes is to keep them from inflicting future harm, but that does not make imprisonment any the less punishment.

Historical considerations by no means compel restriction of the bill of attainder ban to instances of retribution. A number of English bills of attainder were enacted for preventive purposes—that is, the legislature made a judgment, undoubtedly based largely on past acts and associations (as Sec. 504 is) that a given person or group was likely to cause trouble (usually, overthrow the government) and therefore inflicted deprivations upon that person or group in order to keep it from bringing about the feared event. It is also clear that many of the early American bills attainting the Tories were passed in order to impede their effectively resisting the Revolution. . . .

We think that the Court in *Douds* misread *United States v. Lovett* [1946] when it suggested that that case could be distinguished on the ground that the sanction there imposed was levied for purely retributive reasons. In *Lovett* the Court, after reviewing the legislative history of Sec. 304 of the Urgent Deficiency Appropriation Act, concluded that the statute was the product of a congressional drive to oust from government persons whose (congressionally determined) "subversive" tendencies made their continued employment dangerous to the national welfare: "the purpose of all who sponsored Sec. 304 . . . clearly was to 'purge' the then existing and all future lists of government employees of those whom Congress deemed guilty of 'subversive activities' and therefore 'unfit' to hold a federal job." Similarly, the purpose of the statute before us is to purge the governing boards of labor unions of those whom Congress regards as guilty of subversive acts and associations and therefore unfit to fill positions which might affect interstate commerce.

The Solicitor General urges us to distinguish *Lovett* on the ground that the statute struck down there "singled out three identified individuals." It is of course true that Sec. 504 does not contain the words "Archie Brown," and that it inflicts its deprivation upon more than three people. However, the decisions of this Court, as well as the historical background of the Bill of Attainder Clause, make it crystal clear that these are distinctions without a difference.

It was not uncommon for English acts of attainder to inflict their deprivations upon relatively large groups of people, sometimes by description rather than name. Moreover, the statutes voided in *Cummings* and *Garland* were of this nature. We cannot agree that the fact that Sec. 504 inflicts its deprivation upon the membership of the Communist Party rather than upon a list of named individuals takes it out of the category of bills of attainder.

We do not hold today that Congress cannot weed dangerous persons out of the labor movement, any more than the Court held in *Lovett* that subversives must be permitted to hold sensitive government positions. Rather, we make again the point made in *Lovett:* that Congress must accomplish such results by rules of general applicability. It cannot specify the people upon whom the sanction it prescribes is to be levied. Under our Constitution, Congress possesses full legislative authority, but the task of adjudication must be left to other tribunals.

This Court is always reluctant to declare that an Act of Congress violates the Constitution, but in this case we have no alternative. . . .

Mr. Justice White, with whom **Mr. Justice Clark, Mr. Justice Harlan,** and **Mr. Justice Stewart** join, dissenting.

. . . When an enactment is challenged as an attainder, the central inquiry must be whether the disability imposed by the act is "punishment" or is "regulation" (i.e., is directed at controlling future conduct). . . . Whether a punitive purpose would be inferred has depended in past cases on a number of circumstances, including the nature of the disability, whether it was traditionally regarded as punishment, whether it is rationally connected to a permissible legislative objective, as well as the specificity of the legislature's designation of the persons to be. affected. . . .

It is not difficult to find some of the cases and statutes which the necessary implications of the Court's approach will overrule or invalidate.

American Communications Assn. v. Douds, *** which upheld the predecessor statute to Sec. 504 is obviously overruled. In that case the Court accepted the congressional findings about the Communist Party and about the propensity of Party members "to subordinate legitimate trade union objectives to obstructive strikes when dictated by Party leaders, often in support of the policies of a foreign government." Moreover, Congress was permitted to infer from a person's "political affiliations and beliefs" that such a person would be likely to instigate political strikes. Like Sec. 504, the statute there under consideration did not cover all persons who might be likely to call political strikes. Nevertheless, legislative findings that some Communists would engage in illegal activities were sufficient to sustain the exercise of legislative power. The Bill of Attainder Clause now forbids Congress to do precisely what was validated in *Douds.*

Similarly invalidated are statutes denying positions of public importance to groups of persons identified by their business affiliations, commonly known as conflict-of-interest statutes. . . .

Conflict-of-interest statutes are an accepted type of legislation. Indeed, our Constitution contains a conflict-of-interest provision in Art. I, Sec. 6, cl. 2, which prohibits any Congressman from simultaneously holding office under the authority of the United States. If the Court would save the conflict-of-interest statutes, which apparently it would, it is difficult to understand why Sec. 504 is stricken down as a bill of attainder.

Other legislative enactments relevant here are those statutes disqualifying felons from occupying certain positions. The leading case is *Hawker v. New York* *** [1889], which upheld a provision prohibiting convicted felons from practicing medicine against a claim that, as applied to one conflicted before its enactment, it was an ex post facto law. The Court noted that a legislature may establish qualifications for the practice of medicine, and character may be such a qualification. Conviction of a felony, the Court reasoned, may be evidence of character. . . .

The Court apparently agrees that the Subversive Activities Control Act was not a bill of attainder with regard to the Communist Party because, as the Court pointed out in *Communist Party v. Subversive Activities Control Board* *** [1961], the finding that the Party was a Communist-action organization was not made by the legislature but was made administratively, after a trial-type hearing and subject to judicial review. But this apparently does not settle whether the statute is a bill of attainder with respect to Party members; for under today's approach, a finding about the Party and about some of its members does not cure the vice of overinclusiveness. The Subversive Activities Control Act attaches certain disqualifications to each Party member following the administrative-judicial finding that the Party is a Communist-action organization. Among other things, each Party member is disqualified from holding union office, almost the same disqualification as is involved here. I do not see how this and the other consequences attached to Party membership in that Act could survive examination under the principles announced today.

On the other hand, if the statutes involved in *Hawker* and [related cases] are not bills of attainder, how can the Subversive Activities Control Act be an attainder with respect to members of the Communist Party? In the Communist Party case, the Board found that the "[Party's] principal leaders and a substantial number of its members are subject to and recognize the disciplinary power of the Soviet Union and its representatives. This evidences domination and control over [the Party] by the Soviet Union, and a purpose to advance the objectives of the world Communist movement." *** That finding was expressly sustained by this Court. . . . [T]hese nonlegislative findings establish a sufficient probability or likelihood with regard to Party members—a sufficient temptation to Party members who are also union officers—to permit the legislature to disqualify Party members from union office as it did in the Subversive Activities Control Act. . . .

But how does one prove that a person would be disloyal? The Communist Party's illegal purpose and its domination by a foreign power have already been adjudicated, both administratively and judicially. If this does not in itself provide a sufficient probability with respect to the individual who persists in remaining a member of the Party, or if a probability is in any event insufficient, what evidence with regard to the individual will be sufficient to disqualify him? If he must be apprehended in the act of calling one political strike or in one act of disloyalty before steps can be taken to exclude him from office, there is little or nothing left of the preventive or prophylactic function of Sec. 504. . . .

DeShaney v. Winnebago Social Services

489 U.S. 189; 109 S. Ct. 998; 103 L. Ed.2d 249 (1989)
Vote: 6-3

This case dramatizes the tension between law and justice that is inherent in a constitutional system that seeks to "establish justice" and maintain the "rule of law." At issue is whether the failure of a state agency to take action constitutes "state action" for the purposes of the Fourteenth Amendment.

Chief Justice Rehnquist delivered the opinion of the Court.

Petitioner is a boy who was beaten and permanently injured by his father, with whom he lived. The respondents are social workers and other local officials who received complaints that petitioner was being abused by his father and had reason to believe that this was the case, but nonetheless did not act to remove petitioner from his father's custody. Petitioner sued respondents claiming that their failure to act deprived him of his liberty in violation of the Due Process Clause of the Fourteenth Amendment to the United States Constitution. We hold that it did not.

I

The facts of this case are undeniably tragic. Petitioner Joshua DeShaney was born in 1979. In 1980, a Wyoming court granted his parents a divorce and awarded custody of Joshua to his father, Randy DeShaney. The father shortly thereafter moved to Neenah, a city located in Winnebago County, Wisconsin, taking the infant Joshua with him. There he entered into a second marriage, which also ended in divorce.

The Winnebago County authorities first learned that Joshua DeShaney might be a victim of child abuse in January 1982, when his father's second wife complained to the police, at the time of their divorce, that he had previously "hit the boy causing marks and [was] a prime case for child abuse." *** The Winnebago County Department of Social Services (DSS) interviewed the father, but he denied the accusations, and DSS did not pursue them further. In January 1983, Joshua was admitted to a local hospital with multiple bruises and abrasions. The examining physician suspected child abuse and notified DSS, which immediately obtained an order from a Wisconsin juvenile court placing Joshua in the temporary custody of the hospital. Three days later, the county convened an ad hoc "Child Protection Team"—consisting of a pediatrician, a psychologist, a police detective, the county's lawyer, several DSS caseworkers, and various hospital personnel—to consider Joshua's situation. At this meeting, the Team decided that there was insufficient evidence of child abuse to retain Joshua in the custody of the court. The Team did, however, decide to recommend several measures to protect Joshua, including enrolling him in a preschool program, providing his father with certain counselling services, and encouraging his father's girlfriend to move out of the home. Randy DeShaney entered into a voluntary agreement with DSS in which he promised to cooperate with them in accomplishing these goals.

Based on the recommendation of the Child Protection Team, the juvenile court dismissed the child protection case and returned Joshua to the custody of his father. A month later, emergency room personnel called the DSS caseworker handling Joshua's case to report that he had once again been treated for suspicious injuries. The caseworker concluded that there was no basis for action. For the next six months, the caseworker made monthly visits to the DeShaney home, during which she observed a number of suspicious injuries on Joshua's head; she also noticed that he had not been enrolled in school and that the girlfriend had not moved out. The caseworker dutifully recorded these incidents in her files, along with her continuing suspicions that someone in the DeShaney household was physically abusing Joshua but she did nothing more. In November 1983, the emergency room notified DSS that Joshua had been treated once again for injuries that they believed to be caused by child abuse. On the caseworker's next two visits to the DeShaney home, she was told that Joshua was too ill to see her. Still DSS took no action.

In March 1984, Randy DeShaney beat 4-year-old Joshua so severely that he fell into a life-threatening coma. Emergency brain surgery revealed a series of hemorrhages caused by traumatic injuries to the head inflicted over a long period of time. Joshua did not die, but he suffered brain damage so severe that he is expected to spend the rest of his life confined to an institution for the profoundly retarded. Randy DeShaney was subsequently tried and convicted of child abuse.

Joshua and his mother brought this action under 42 U.S.C. Sec. 1983 in the United States District Court for the Eastern District of Wisconsin against respondents Winnebago County, its Department of Social Services, and various individual employees of the Department. The complaint alleged respondents had deprived Joshua of his liberty without due process of law, in violation of his rights under the Fourteenth Amendment, by failing to intervene to protect him against a risk of violence at his father's hands of which they knew or should have known. The District Court granted summary judgment for respondents.

The Court of Appeals for the Seventh Circuit affirmed, *** holding that petitioners had not made out an actionable Sec. 1983 claim for two alternative reasons. First, the court held that the Due Process Clause of the Fourteenth Amendment does not require a state or local governmental entity to protect its citizens from "private violence, or other mishaps not attributable to the conduct of its employees." *** In so holding, they specifically rejected the position . . . that once the State learns that a particular child is in danger of abuse from third parties and actually undertakes to protect him from that danger, a "special relationship" arises between it and the child which imposes an affirmative constitutional duty to provide adequate protection. *** Second, the Court held . . . that the causal connection between respondents' conduct and Joshua's injuries was too attenuated to establish a deprivation of constitutional rights actionable under Sec 1983. *** The Court therefore found it unnecessary to reach the question whether respondents' conduct evinced that "state of mind" necessary to make out a due process claim. . . .

Because of the inconsistent approaches taken by the lower courts in determining when, if ever, the failure of a state or local governmental entity or its agents to provide an individual with adequate protective services constitutes a violation of the individual's due process rights, *** and the importance of the issue to the administration of state and local governments, we granted certiorari. *** We now affirm.

II

The Due Process Clause of the Fourteenth Amendment provides that "[n]o State shall . . . deprive any person of life, liberty, or property, without due process of law." Petitioners contend that the State deprived Joshua of his liberty interest in "free[dom] from . . . unjustified intrusions on personal security," *** by failing to provide him with adequate protection against his father's violence. The claim is one invoking the substantive rather than procedural component of the Due Process Clause; petitioners do not claim that the State denied Joshua protection without according him appropriate procedural safeguards . . . but that it was categorically obligated to protect him in these circumstances.

But nothing in the language of the Due Process Clause itself requires the State to protect the life, liberty, and property of its citizens against invasion by private actors. The Clause is phrased as a limitation on the State's power to act, not as a guarantee of certain minimal levels of safety and security. It forbids the State itself to deprive individuals of life, liberty, or property without "due process of law," but its language cannot fairly be extended to impose an affirmative obligation on the State to ensure that those interests do not come to harm through other means. Nor does history support such an expansive reading of the constitutional text. Like its counterpart in the Fifth Amendment, the Due Process Clause of the Fourteenth Amendment was intended to prevent government "from abusing [its] power, or employing it as an instrument of oppression." *** Its purpose was to protect the people from the State, not to ensure that the State protected them from each other. The Framers were content to leave the extent of governmental obligation in the latter area to the democratic political processes.

Consistent with these principles, our cases have recognized that the Due Process Clauses generally confer no affirmative right to governmental aid, even where such aid may be necessary to secure life, liberty, or property interests of which the government itself may not deprive the individual. *** If the Due Process Clause does not require the State to provide its citizens with particular protective services, it follows that the State cannot be held liable under the Clause for injuries that could have been averted had it chosen to provide them. As a general matter, then, we conclude that a State's failure to protect an individual against private violence simply does not constitute a violation of the Due Process Clause.

Petitioners contend, however, that even if the Due Process Clause imposes no affirmative obligation on the State to provide the general public with adequate protective services, such a duty may arise out of certain "special relationships" created or assumed by the State with respect to particular individuals. *** Petitioners argue that such a "special relationship" existed here because the State knew that Joshua faced a special danger of abuse at his father's hands, and specifically proclaimed, by word and by deed, its intention to protect him against that danger. *** Having actually undertaken to protect Joshua from this danger—which petitioners concede the State played no part in creating—the State acquired an affirmative "duty", enforceable through the Due Process Clause, to do so in a reasonably competent fashion. Its failure to discharge that duty, so the argument goes, was an abuse of governmental power that so "shocks the conscience," *** as to constitute a substantive due process violation. ***

We reject this argument. It is true that in certain limited circumstances the Constitution imposes upon the State affirmative duties of care and protection with respect to particular individuals. . . .

. . . While the State may have been aware of the dangers that Joshua faced in the free world, it played no part in their creation, nor did it do anything to render him any more vulnerable to them. That the State once took temporary custody of Joshua does not alter the analysis, for when it returned him to his father's custody, it placed him in no worse position than that in which he would have been had it not acted at all; the State does not become the permanent guarantor of an individual's safety by having once offered him shelter. Under these circumstances, the State had no constitutional duty to protect Joshua. . . .

Judges and lawyers, like other humans, are moved by natural sympathy in a case like this to find a way for Joshua and his mother to receive adequate compensation for the grievous harm inflicted upon them. But before yielding to that impulse, it is well to remember once again that the harm was inflicted not by the State of Wisconsin, but by Joshua's father. The most that can be said of the state functionaries in this case is that they stood by and did nothing when suspicious circumstances dictated a more active role for them. In defense of them it must also be said that had they moved too soon to take custody of the son away from the father, they would likely have been met with charges of improperly intruding into the parent-child relationship. . . .

The people of Wisconsin may well prefer a system of liability which would place upon the State and its officials the responsibility for failure to act in situations such as the present one. They may create such a system, if they do not have it already, by changing the tort law of the State in accordance with the regular law-making process. But they should not have it thrust upon them by this Court's expansion of the Due Process Clause of the Fourteenth Amendment.

Affirmed.

Justice Brennan, with whom *Justice Marshall* and *Justice Blackmun* join, dissenting. . . .

Justice Blackmun, dissenting.

Today, the Court purports to be the dispassionate oracle of the law, unmoved by "natural sympathy." But, in this pretense, the Court itself retreats into a sterile formalism which prevents it from recognizing either the facts of the case before it or the legal norms that should apply to those facts. As Justice Brennan demonstrates, the facts here involve not mere passivity, but active state intervention in the life of Joshua DeShaney—intervention that triggered a fundamental duty to aid the boy once the State learned of the severe danger to which he was exposed.

The Court fails to recognize this duty because it attempts to draw a sharp and rigid line between action and inaction. But such formalistic reasoning has no place in the interpretation of the broad and stirring clauses of the Fourteenth Amendment. Indeed, I submit that these clauses were designed, at least in part, to undo the formalistic legal reasoning that infected antebellum jurisprudence, which the late Professor Robert Cover analyzed so effectively in his significant work entitled *Justice Accused* (1975).

Like the antebellum judges who denied relief to fugitive slaves, the Court today claims that its decision, however harsh, is compelled by existing legal doctrine. On the contrary, the question presented by this case is an open one and our Fourteenth Amendment precedents may be read more broadly or narrowly depending upon how one chooses to read them. Faced with the choice, I would adopt a "sympathetic" reading, one which comports with dictates of fundamental justice and recognizes that compassion need not be exiled from the province of judging. ***

Poor Joshua! Victim of repeated attacks by an irresponsible, bullying, cowardly, and intemperate father, and abandoned by respondents who placed him in a dangerous predicament and who knew or learned what was going on, and yet did essentially nothing except, as the Court revealing observes, *** "dutifully recorded these incidents in [their] files." It is a sad commentary upon American life, and constitutional principles—so full of late patriotic fervor and proud proclamations about "liberty and justice for all," that this child, Joshua DeShaney, now is assigned to live out the remainder of his life profoundly retarded. Joshua and his mother, as petitioners here, deserve—but now are denied by this Court—the opportunity to have the facts of their case considered in the light of the constitutional protection that 42 U.S.C. Sec. 1983 is meant to provide.

Barron v. Baltimore

7 Pet. (32 U.S.) 243; 8 L. Ed. 672 (1833)
Vote: 7-0

Like the other cases reprinted in this chapter, Barron v. Baltimore *deals with the issue of whether the protections of the Bill of Rights are applicable to actions of the states and their local subdivisions. The case stemmed from an incident in which the city of Baltimore diverted the flow of certain streams, causing silt to be deposited in front of John Barron's wharf, making it unusable. Barron brought suit in state court, claiming that since the City's action amounted to a taking of private property, he was entitled to "just compensation" under the Fifth Amendment to the U.S. Constitution. The trial court agreed and awarded Barron forty-five hundred dollars. After this judgment was reversed by a state appellate court, Barron appealed to the U.S. Supreme Court on a writ of error.*

Mr. Chief Justice Marshall delivered the Opinion of the Court:

… The plaintiff in error [Barron] contends that [this case] comes within that clause in the Fifth Amendment to the Constitution which inhibits the taking of private property for public use without just compensation. He insists that this amendment, being in favor of the liberty of the citizen, ought to be so construed as to restrain the legislative power of a State, as well as that of the United States. If this proposition be untrue, the Court can take no jurisdiction of the cause.

The question thus presented is, we think, of great importance, but not of much difficulty.

The Constitution was ordained and established by the people of the United States for themselves, for their own government, and not for the government of the individual States. Each State established a constitution for itself, and in that constitution provided such limitations and restrictions on the powers of its particular government as its judgment dictated. The people of the United States framed such a government for the United States as they supposed best adapted to their situation, and best calculated to promote their interests. The powers they conferred on this government were to be exercised by itself; and the limitations on power, if expressed in general terms, are naturally, and, we think, necessarily applicable to the government created by the instrument. They are limitations of power granted in the instrument itself; not of distinct governments, framed by different persons and for different purposes.

If this proposition be correct, the Fifth Amendment must be understood as restraining the power of the general government, not as applicable to the States. In their several constitutions they have imposed such restrictions on their respective governments as their own wisdom suggested; such as they deemed most proper for themselves. It is a subject on which they judge exclusively, and with which others interfere no farther than they are supposed to have a common interest.

The counsel for the plaintiff in error insists that the Constitution was intended to secure the people of the several States against the undue exercise of power by their respective State governments; as well as against that which might be attempted by their general government. In support of this argument he relies on the inhibitions contained in the tenth section of the first article.

We think that section affords a strong if not a conclusive argument in support of the opinion already indicated by the Court.

The preceding section contains restrictions which are obviously intended for the exclusive purpose of restraining the exercise of power by the departments of the general government. Some of them use language applicable only to Congress, others are expressed in general terms. The third clause, for example, declares that "no bill of attainder or ex post facto law shall be passed." No language can be more general; yet the demonstration is complete that it applies solely to the government of the United States. In addition to the general arguments furnished by the instrument itself, some of which have been already suggested, the succeeding section, the avowed purpose of which is to restrain State legislation, contains in terms the very prohibition. It declares that "no State shall pass any bill of attainder or ex post facto law." This provision then, of the ninth section, however comprehensive its language, contains no restriction on State legislation.

The ninth section having enumerated, in the nature of a bill of rights, the limitations intended to be imposed on the powers of the general government, the tenth proceeds to enumerate those which were to operate on the State legislatures. These restrictions are brought together in the same section, and are by express words applied to the States. . . .

. . . It would be tedious to recapitulate the several limitations on the powers of the States which are contained in this section. They will be found, generally, to restrain State legislation on subjects intrusted to the government of the Union, in which the citizens of all the States are interested. In these alone were the whole people concerned. The question of their application to States is not left to construction. It is averred in positive words.

If the original Constitution, in the ninth and tenth sections of the first article, draws this plain and marked line of discrimination between the limitations it imposes on the powers of the general government and on those of the States; if in every inhibition intended to act on State power, words are employed which directly express that intent, some strong reason must be assigned for departing from this safe and judicious course in framing the amendments, before that departure can be assumed.

We search in vain for that reason.

Had the people of the several States, or any of them, required changes in their constitutions; had they required additional safeguards to liberty from the apprehended encroachments of their particular governments, the remedy was in their own hands, and would have been applied by themselves. A convention would have been assembled by the discontented State, and the required improvements would have been made by itself. The unwieldy and cumbrous machinery of procuring a recommendation from two-thirds of Congress and the assent of three-fourths of their sister States, could never have occurred to any human being as a mode of doing that which might be effected by the State itself. Had the framers of these amendments intended them to be limitations on the powers of the State governments they would have imitated the framers of the original Constitution, and have expressed that intention. Had Congress engaged in the extraordinary occupation of improving the constitutions of the several States by affording the people additional protection from the exercise of power by their own governments in matters which concerned themselves alone, they would have declared this purpose in plain and intelligible language.

But it is universally understood, it is a part of the history of the day, that the great revolution which established the Constitution of the United States was not effected without immense opposition. Serious fears were extensively entertained that those powers which the patriot statesmen who then watched over the interests of our country, deemed essential to union, and to the attainment of those invaluable objects for which union was sought, might be exercised in a manner dangerous to liberty. In almost every convention by which the Constitution was adopted, amendments to guard against the abuse of power were recommended. These amendments demanded security against the apprehended encroachments of the general government—not against those of the local governments.

In compliance with a sentiment thus generally expressed, to quiet fears thus extensively entertained, amendments were proposed by the required majority in Congress, and adopted by the States. These amendments contain no expression indicating an intention to apply them to the State governments. This Court cannot so apply them.

We are of opinion that the provision in the Fifth Amendment to the Constitution, declaring that private property shall not be taken for public use without just compensations, is intended solely as a limitation on the exercise of power by the government of the United States, and is not applicable to the legislation of the States. We are therefore of opinion that there is no repugnancy between the several acts of the General Assembly of Maryland, given in evidence by the defendants at the trial of this cause in the court of that State, and the Constitution of the United States.

This Court, therefore, has no jurisdiction of the cause, and [it] is dismissed.

Hurtado v. California

110 U.S. 516; 4 S. Ct. 111; 28 L. Ed. 232 (1884)
Vote: 7-1

Here, the Court considers whether the grand jury requirement of the Fifth Amendment is applicable to state criminal prosecutions by way of the Fourteenth Amendment. The facts are contained in Justice Matthews's majority opinion.

Mr. Justice Matthews delivered the Opinion of the Court:

The Constitution of the State of California adopted in 1879, in article I, section 8, provides as follows:

"Offenses heretofore required to be prosecuted by indictment shall be prosecuted by information after examination and commitment by a magistrate, or by indictment, with or without such examination and commitment, as may be prescribed by law. A grand jury shall be drawn and summoned at least once a year in each county."

Various provisions of the [California] Penal Code regulate proceedings before the examining and committing magistrate in cases of persons arrested and brought before them upon charges of having committed public offenses. These require, among other things, that the testimony of the witnesses shall be reduced to writing in the form of deposition; and section 872 declares that if it appears from the examination that a public offense has been committed, and there is sufficient cause to believe the defendant guilty thereof, the magistrate must indorse on the depositions an order, signed by him, to that effect, describing the general nature of the offense committed, and ordering that the defendant be held to answer thereto. Sec. 809 of the Penal Code is as follows.

"When a defendant has been examined and committed, as provided in section 872 of this Code, it shall be the duty of the district attorney, within thirty days thereafter, to file in the superior court of the county in which the offense is triable, an information charging the defendant with such offense. The information shall be in the name of the people of the State of California, and subscribed by the district attorney, and shall be in form like an indictment for the same offense."

In pursuance of the foregoing provision of the Constitution, and of the several sections of the Penal Code of California, the District Attorney of Sacramento County, on the 20th day of February, 1882, made and filed an information against the plaintiff in error, charging him with the crime of murder in the killing of one Jose Antonio Stuardo. Upon this information and without any previous investigation of the cause by any grand jury, the plaintiff in error was arraigned on the 22d day of March, 1882, and pleaded not guilty. A trial of the issue was thereafter had, and on May 7, 1882, the jury rendered its verdict, in which it found the plaintiff in error guilty of murder in the first degree.

On the 5th day of July, 1882, the Superior Court of Sacramento County, in which the plaintiff in error had been tried, rendered its judgment upon said verdict, that the said Joseph Hurtado, plaintiff in error, be punished by the infliction of death, and the day of his execution was fixed for the 20th day of July, 1882.

From this judgment an appeal was taken, and the Supreme Court of the State of California affirmed the judgment.

The proposition of law we are asked to affirm is, that an indictment or presentment by a grand jury, as known to the common law of England, is essential to that "due process of law," when applied to prosecutions for felonies, which is secured and guarantied by this provision of the Constitution of the United States, and which accordingly it is forbidden to the States respectively to dispense with in the administration of criminal law.

We are to construe this phrase in the 14th Amendment by the *usus loquendi* of the Constitution itself. The same words are contained in the 5th Amendment. That article makes specific and express provision for perpetuating the institution of the grand jury, so far as relates to prosecutions, for the most aggravated crimes under the laws of the United States. It declares that "[n]o person shall be held to answer for a capital or otherwise infamous crime, unless on a presentment or indictment of a grand jury, except in cases arising in the land or naval

forces, or in the militia when in actual service in time of war or public danger; nor shall any person be subject for the same offense to be twice put in jeopardy of life or limb; nor shall he be compelled in any criminal case to be a witness against himself." It then immediately adds: "nor be deprived of life, liberty or property, without due process of law." According to a recognized canon of interpretation, especially applicable to formal and solemn instruments of constitutional law, we are forbidden to assume, without clear reason to the contrary, that any part of this most important Amendment is superfluous. The natural and obvious inference is, that in the sense of the Constitution, "due process of law" was not meant or intended to include, *ex vi termini,* the institution and procedure of a grand jury in any case. The conclusion is equally irresistible, that when the same phrase was employed in the 14th Amendment to restrain the action of the States, it was used in the same sense and with no greater extent; and that if in the adoption of that Amendment it had been part of its purpose to perpetuate the institution of the grand jury in all the States, it would have embodied, as did the 5th Amendment, express declarations to that effect. Due process of law in the latter refers to that law of the land, which derives its authority from the legislative powers conferred upon Congress by the Constitution of the United States, exercised within the limits therein prescribed, and interpreted according to the principles of the common law. In the 14th Amendment, by parity of reason, it refers to that law of the land in each State, which derives its authority from the inherent and reserved powers of the State, exerted within the limits of those fundamental principles of liberty and justice which lie at the base of all our civil and political institutions, and the greatest security for which resides in the right of the people to make their own laws, and alter them at their pleasure.

For these reasons, finding no error therein, the judgment of the Supreme Court of California is affirmed.

Mr. Justice Harlan, dissenting.

. . . "Due process of law," within the meaning of the national Constitution, does not import one thing with reference to the powers of the States, and another with reference to the powers of the general government. If particular proceedings conducted under the authority of the general government, and involving life, are prohibited, because not constituting that due process of law required by the Fifth Amendment of the Constitution of the United States, similar proceedings, conducted under the authority of a State, must be deemed illegal as not being due process of law within the meaning of the Fourteenth Amendment. What, then, is the meaning of the words, "due process of law" in the latter amendment? . . .

According to the settled usages and modes of proceeding existing under the common and statute law of England at the settlement of this country, information in capital cases was not consistent with the "law of the land," or with "due process of law." Such was the understanding of the patriotic men who established free institutions upon this continent. Almost the identical words of Magna Charta were incorporated into most of the State Constitutions before the adoption of our national Constitution. When they declared, in substance, that no person should be deprived of life, liberty or property, except by the judgment of his peers of the law of the land, they intended to assert his right to the same guaranties that were given in the mother country by the great charter and the laws passed in furtherance of its fundamental principles. . . .

But it is said that the framers of the Constitution did not suppose that due process of law necessarily required for a capital offence the institution and procedure of a grand jury, else they would not in the same amendment prohibiting the deprivation of life, liberty, or property, without due process of law, have made specific and express provision for a grand jury where the crime is capital or otherwise infamous; therefore, it is argued, the requirement by the Fourteenth Amendment of due process of law in all proceedings involving life, liberty, and property, without specific reference to grand juries in any case whatever, was not intended as a restriction upon the power which it is claimed the States previously had, so far as the express restrictions of the national Constitution are concerned, to dispense altogether with grand juries.

This line of argument, it seems to me, would lead to results which are inconsistent with the vital prin-

ciples of republican government. If the presence in the Fifth Amendment of a specific provision for grand juries in capital cases, alongside the provision for due process of law in proceedings involving life, liberty, or property, is held to prove that "due process of law" did not, in the judgment of the framers of the Constitution, necessarily require a grand jury in capital cases, inexorable logic would require it to be, likewise, held that the right not to be put twice in jeopardy of life and limb for the same offense, nor compelled in a criminal case to testify against one's self—rights and immunities also specifically recognized in the Fifth Amendment—were not protected by that due process of law required by the settled usages and proceedings existing under the common and statute law of England at the settlement of this country. More than that, other amendments of the Constitution proposed at the same time, expressly recognize the right of persons to just compensation for private property taken for public use; their right, when accused of crime, to be informed of the nature and cause of the accusation against them, and to a speedy and public trial, by an impartial jury of the State and district wherein the crime was committed: to be confronted by the witnesses against them; and to have compulsory process for obtaining witnesses in their favor. Will it be claimed that these rights were not secured by the "law of the land" or by "due process of law," as declared and established at the foundation of our government? Are they to be excluded from the enumeration of the fundamental principles of liberty and justice, and, therefore, not embraced by "due process of law?" If the argument of my brethren be sound, those rights—although universally recognized at the establishment of our institutions as secured by that due process of law which for centuries had been the foundation of Anglo-Saxon liberty—were not deemed by our fathers as essential in the due process of law prescribed by our Constitution; because—such seems to be the argument—had they been regarded as involved in due process of law they would not have been specifically and expressly provided for, but left to the protection given by the general clause forbidding the deprivation of life, liberty, or property without due process of law. Further, the reasoning of the opinion indubitably leads to the conclusion that but for the specific provisions made in the Constitution for the security of the personal rights enumerated, the general inhibition against deprivation of life, liberty and property without due process of law would not have prevented Congress from enacting a statute in derogation of each of them. . . .

To these considerations may be added others of very great significance. When the Fourteenth Amendment was adopted, all the States of the Union, some in terms, all substantially, declared, in their constitutions, that no person shall be deprived of life, liberty, or property, otherwise than "by the judgment of his peers, or the law of the land," or "without due process of law." When that Amendment was adopted, the constitution of each State, with few exceptions, contained, and still contains, a Bill of Rights, enumerating the rights of life, liberty and property which cannot be impaired or destroyed by the legislative department. In some of them, as in those of Pennsylvania, Kentucky, Ohio, Alabama, Illinois, Arkansas, Florida, Mississippi, Missouri and North Carolina, the rights so enumerated were declared to be embraced by "the general, great and essential principles of liberty and free government"; in others, as in those of Connecticut, in 1818, and Kansas, in 1857, to be embraced by "the great and essential principles of free government." Now, it is a fact of momentous interest in this discussion, that, when the Fourteenth Amendment was submitted and adopted, the Bill of Rights and the constitutions of twenty-seven States expressly for bade criminal prosecutions, by information, for capital cases; while in the remaining ten states, they were impliedly forbidden by a general clause declaring that no person should be deprived of life otherwise than by "the judgment of his peers or the law of the land," or "without due process of law." It may be safely affirmed that, when the Amendment was adopted, a criminal prosecution, by information, for a crime involving life, was not permitted in any one of the States composing the Union. So that the court, in this case, while conceding that the requirement of due process of law protects the fundamental principles of liberty and justice, adjudges, in effect, that an immunity or right, recognized at the common law to be essential to personal security, jealously guarded by our national Constitution against violation by any tribunal or body exercising authority under the general government, and expressly or impliedly recognized, *when the Fourteenth Amendment was adopted,* in the Bill of Rights or Constitution of every State in the Union, is, yet, not a fundamental principle in governments established, as those of the States of the Union are, to secure to the citizen liberty and justice, and, therefore, is not involved in that due process of law required in proceedings conducted under the sanction of a State. My sense of duty constrains me to dissent from this interpretation of the supreme law of the land.

Mr. Justice Field did not take part in the decision of this case.

Chicago, Burlington and Quincy Railroad Company v. Chicago

166 U.S. 226; 17 S. Ct. 581; 41 L. Ed. 979 (1897)
Vote: 7-1

This case arose when the city of Chicago sought to widen Rockwell Street between West Eighteenth and West Nineteenth streets. To obtain the land necessary to widen the street, the city used its power of eminent domain, taking part of the right-of-way owned by the Chicago, Burlington and Quincy Railroad. A state trial court awarded the railroad company a mere one dollar as "just compensation" for the condemned parcels of land. The railroad took the case *to the U.S. Supreme Court on a writ of error. Although the Court ruled in favor of the city, its opinion made new law by extending the Just Compensation Clause of the Fifth Amendment to state action under the Fourteenth Amendment.*

Mr. Justice Harlan delivered the opinion of the Court.

... [A] state may not, by any of its agencies, disregard the prohibitions of the 14th Amendment. Its judicial authorities may keep within the letter of the statute prescribing forms of procedure in the courts and give the parties the fullest opportunity to be heard, and yet it might be that its final action would be inconsistent with that Amendment. In determining what is due process of law, regard must be had to substance, not to form. This court, referring to the 14th Amendment, has said: "Can a state make anything due process of law which, by its own legislation, it chooses to declare such? To affirm this is to hold that the prohibition to the states is of no avail, or has no application where the invasion of private rights is effected under the forms of state legislation." *** The same question could be propounded, and the same answer could be made, in reference to judicial proceedings inconsistent with the requirement of due process of law. If compensation for private property taken for public use is an essential element of due process of law as ordained by the 14th Amendment, then the final judgment of a state court, under the authority of which the property is in fact taken, is to be deemed the act of the state within the meaning of that Amendment.

It is proper now to inquire whether the due process of law enjoined by the 14th Amendment requires compensation to be made or adequately secured to the owner of private property taken for public use under the authority of a state.

... [A] statute declaring in terms, without more, that the full and exclusive title to a described piece of land belonging to one person should be and is hereby vested in another person, would, if effectual, deprive the former of his property without due process of law, within the meaning of the 14th Amendment. *** Such an enactment would not receive judicial sanction in any country having a written Constitution distributing the powers of government among three coordinate departments, and committing to the judiciary, expressly or by implication, authority to enforce the provisions of such Constitution. It would be treated, not as an exertion of legislative power, but as a sentence—an act of spoliation. Due protection of the rights of property has been regarded as a vital principle of republican institutions. "Next in degree to the right of personal liberty," Mr. Broom in his work on Constitutional Law says, "is that of enjoying private property without undue interference of molestation." *** The requirement that the property shall not be taken for public use without just compensation is but "an affirmance of a great doctrine established by the common law for the protection of private property. It is founded in natural equity, and is laid down as a principle of universal law. Indeed, in a free government almost all other rights would become worthless if the government possessed an uncontrollable power over the private fortune of every citizen." ***

[The remainder of Justice Harlan's lengthy opinion examines the particulars of the case at hand. He concludes as follows:]

... We have examined all the questions of law arising on the record of which this court may take cognizance, and which, in our opinion, are of sufficient importance to require notice at our hands, and finding no error, the judgment [of the state court] is affirmed.

Mr. Justice Brewer, dissenting:

I dissent from the judgment in this case. I approve that which is said in the first part of the opinion as to the potency of the 14th Amendment to restrain action by a state through either its legislative, executive or judicial departments, which deprives a party of his property rights without due compensation....

It is disappointing after reading so strong a declaration of the protecting reach of the 14th Amendment and the power and duty of this court in enforcing it as against action by a state by any of its officers or agencies, to find sustained a judgment, depriving a party—even though a railroad corporation—of valuable property without any, or, at least only nominal, compensation....

Palko v. Connecticut

302 U.S. 319; 58 S. Ct. 149; 82 L. Ed. 288 (1937)

Vote: 8-1

Mr. Justice Cardozo delivered the opinion of the Court.

A statute of Connecticut permitting appeals in criminal cases to be taken by the state is challenged by appellant as an infringement of the Fourteenth Amendment of the Constitution of the United States. Whether the challenge should be upheld is now to be determined.

Appellant was indicted in Fairfield County, Connecticut, for the crime of murder in the first degree. A jury found him guilty of murder in the second degree, and he was sentenced to confinement in the state prison for life. Thereafter the state of Connecticut, with the permission of the judge presiding at the trial, gave notice of appeal to the Supreme Court of Errors. . . . Upon such appeal, the Supreme Court of Errors reversed the judgment and ordered a new trial. *** It found that there had been error of law to the prejudice of the state. . . .

Pursuant to the mandate of the Supreme Court of Errors, defendant was brought to trial again. Before a jury was impaneled and also at later stages of the case he made the objection that the effect of the new trial was to place him twice in jeopardy for the same offense, and in so doing to violate the Fourteenth Amendment of the Constitution of the United States. Upon the overruling of the objection the trial proceeded. The jury returned a verdict of murder in the first degree, and the court sentenced the defendant to the punishment of death. The Supreme Court of Errors affirmed the judgment of conviction. *** The case is here upon appeal. ***

The execution of the sentence will not deprive appellant of his life without the process of law assured to him by the Fourteenth Amendment of the Federal Constitution.

The argument for appellant is that whatever is forbidden by the Fifth Amendment is forbidden by the Fourteenth also. The Fifth Amendment, which is not directed to the states, but solely to the federal government, creates immunity from double jeopardy. No person shall be "subject for the same offense to be twice put in jeopardy of life or limb." The Fourteenth Amendment ordains, "nor shall any state deprive any person of life, liberty, or property, without due process of law." To retry a defendant, though under one indictment and only one, subjects him, it is said, to double jeopardy in violation of the Fifth Amendment, if the prosecution is one on behalf of the United States. From this the consequence is said to follow that there is a denial of life or liberty without due process of law, if the prosecution is one on behalf of the People of a State. . . .

We do not find it profitable to mark the precise limits of the prohibition of double jeopardy in federal prosecutions. . . .

We have said that in appellant's view the Fourteenth Amendment is to be taken as embodying the prohibitions of the Fifth. His thesis is even broader. Whatever would be a violation of the original Bill of Rights (Amendments 1 to 8) if done by the federal government is now equally unlawful by force of the Fourteenth Amendment if done by a state. There is no such general rule.

The Fifth Amendment provides, among other things, that no person shall be held to answer for a capital or otherwise infamous crime unless on presentment or indictment of a grand jury. This court has held that, in prosecutions by a state, presentment or indictment by a grand jury may give way to informations at the instance of a public officer. *** The Fifth Amendment provides also that no person shall be compelled in any criminal case to be a witness against himself. This court has said that, in prosecutions by a state, the exemption will fail if the state elects to end it. *** The Sixth Amendment calls for a jury trial in criminal cases and the Seventh for a jury trial in civil cases at common law where the value in controversy shall exceed twenty dollars. This court has ruled that consistently with those amendments trial by jury may be modified by a state or abolished altogether. ***

On the other hand, the Due Process Clause of the Fourteenth Amendment may make it unlawful for a state to abridge by its statutes the freedom of speech which the First Amendment safeguards against encroachment by the Congress *** ... or the right of peaceable assembly, without which speech would be unduly trammeled or the right of one accused of crime to the benefit of counsel. *** In these and other situations immunities that are valid as against the federal government by force of the specific pledges of particular amendments have been found to be implicit in the concept of ordered liberty, and thus, through the Fourteenth Amendment, become valid as against the states.

The line of division may seem to be wavering and broken if there is a hasty catalogue of the cases on the one side and the other. Reflection and analysis will induce a different view. There emerges the perception of a rationalizing principle which gives to discrete instances a proper order and coherence. The right to trial by jury and the immunity from prosecution except as the result of an indictment may have value and importance. Even so, they are not of the very essence of a scheme of ordered liberty. To abolish them is not to violate a "principle of justice so rooted in the traditions and conscience of our people as to be ranked as fundamental." *** Few would be so narrow or provincial as to maintain that a fair and enlightened system of justice would be impossible without them. What is true of jury trials and indictments is true also, as the cases show, of the immunity from compulsory self-incrimination. *** This too might be lost, and justice still be done. Indeed, today as in the past there are students of our penal system who look upon the immunity as a mischief rather than a benefit, and who would limit its scope or destroy it altogether. No doubt there would remain the need to give protection against torture, physical or mental. *** Justice, however, would not perish if the accused were subject to a duty to respond to orderly inquiry. ...

We reach a different plane of social and moral values when we pass to the privileges and immunities that have been taken over from the earlier articles of the federal Bill of Rights and brought within the Fourteenth Amendment by a process of absorption. These in their origin were effective against the federal government alone. If the Fourteenth Amendment has absorbed them, the process of absorption

has had its source in the belief that neither liberty nor justice would exist if they were sacrificed. *** This is true, for illustration, of freedom of thought and speech. Of that freedom one may say that it is the matrix, the indispensable condition, of nearly every other form of freedom. With rare aberrations a pervasive recognition of that truth can be traced in our history, political and legal. So it has come about that the domain of liberty, withdrawn by the Fourteenth Amendment from encroachment by the states, has been enlarged by latter-day judgments to include liberty of the mind as well as liberty of action. The extension became, indeed, a logical imperative when once it was recognized, as long ago it was, that liberty is something more than exemption from physical restraint, and that even in the field of substantive rights and duties the legislative judgment, if oppressive and arbitrary, may be overridden by the courts. *** Fundamental too in the concept of due process, and so in that of liberty, is the thought that condemnation shall be rendered only after trial. *** The hearing, moreover, must be a real one, not a sham or a pretense. *** For that reason, ignorant defendants in a capital case were held to have been condemned unlawfully when in truth, though not in form, they were refused the aid of counsel. *** The decision did not turn upon the fact that the benefit of counsel would have been guaranteed to the defendants by the provisions of the Sixth Amendment if they had been prosecuted in a federal court. The decision turned upon the fact that in the particular situation laid before us in the evidence the benefit of counsel was essential to the substance of a hearing.

Our survey of the cases serves, we think, to justify the statement that the dividing line between them, if not unfaltering throughout its course, has been true for the most part to a unifying principle. On which side of the line the case made out by the appellant has appropriate location must be the next inquiry and the final one. Is that kind of double jeopardy to which the statute has subjected him a hardship so acute and shocking that our polity will not endure it? Does it violate those "fundamental principles of liberty and justice which lie at the base of all our civil and political institutions"? *** The answer surely must be "no." What the answer would have to be if the state were permitted after a trial free from error to try the accused over again or to bring another case against him, we have no occasion to consider. We deal with the statute before us and no other. The state is not attempting to wear the accused out by a multitude of cases with accumulated trials. It asks no more than this, that the case against him shall go on until there shall be a trial free from the corrosion of substantial legal error. *** This is not cruelty at all, nor even vexation in any immoderate degree. If the trial had been infected with error adverse to the accused, there might have been review at his instance, and as often as necessary to purge the vicious taint. A reciprocal privilege, subject at all times to the discretion of the presiding judge *** has now been granted to the state. There is here no seismic innovation. The edifice of justice stands, in its symmetry, to many, greater than before....

The judgment is affirmed.

Mr. Justice Butler dissents.

Adamson v. California

332 U.S. 46; 67 S. Ct. 1672; 91 L. Ed. 1903 (1947)
Vote: 5-4

In Hurtado v. California (1884), the Supreme Court held that the grand jury requirement of the Fifth Amendment was not an essential element of due process and therefore did not have to be followed in state prosecutions. In Twining v. New Jersey (1908), the Court held that the Fifth Amendment protection against compulsory self-incrimination did not have to be honored in state criminal trials. The Court revisits this question in the instant case. The student should pay close attention to the different theories of Fourteenth Amendment due process espoused in the various opinions in this case.

Mr. Justice Reed delivered the opinion of the Court.

The appellant, Adamson, a citizen of the United States, was convicted, without recommendation for mercy, by a jury in a Superior Court of the State of California of murder in the first degree. After considering the same objections to the conviction that are pressed here, the sentence of death was affirmed by the Supreme Court of the state. The provisions of California law which were challenged ... as invalid under the Fourteenth Amendment ... permit the failure of a defendant to explain or to deny evidence against him to be commented upon by court and by counsel and to be considered by court and jury. The defendant did not testify. As the trial court gave its instructions and the District Attorney argued the case in accordance with the constitutional and statutory provisions just referred to, we have for decision the question of their constitutionality.

The appellant was charged in the information with former convictions for burglary, larceny and robbery and pursuant to 1025, California Penal Code, answered that he had suffered the previous convictions. This answer barred allusion to these charges of convictions on the trial. Under California's interpretation of Sec. 1025 of the Penal Code and Sec. 2051 of the Code of Civil Procedure, however, if the defendant, after answering affirmative charges alleging prior convictions, takes the witness stand to deny or explain away other evidence that has been introduced "the commission of these crimes could have been revealed to the jury on cross-examination to impeach his testimony." This forces an accused who is a repeated offender to choose between the risk of having his prior offenses disclosed to the jury or having it draw harmful inferences from uncontradicted evidence that can only be denied or explained by the defendant.

In the first place, appellant urges that the provision of the Fifth Amendment that no person "shall be compelled in any criminal case to be a witness against himself" is a fundamental national privilege or immunity protected against state abridgment by the Fourteenth Amendment or a privilege or immunity secured, through the Fourteenth Amendment, against deprivation by state action because it is a personal right, enumerated in the federal Bill of Rights.

Secondly, appellant relies upon the due process of law clause of the Fourteenth Amendment to invalidate the provisions of the California law and as applied (a) because comment on failure to testify is permitted, (b) because appellant was forced to forego testimony in person because of danger of disclosure of his past convictions through cross-examination and (c) because the presumption of innocence was infringed by the shifting of the burden of proof to appellant in permitting comment on his failure to testify.

We shall assume, but without any intention thereby of ruling upon the issue, that permission by law to the court, counsel and jury to comment upon and consider the failure of defendant "to explain or to deny by his testimony any evidence or facts in the case against him" would infringe defendant's privilege against self-incrimination under the Fifth Amendment if this were a trial in a court of the United States under a similar law. Such an assumption does not determine appellant's rights under the Fourteenth Amendment. It is settled law that the clause of the Fifth Amendment, protecting a person against being compelled to be a witness against himself, is not made effective by the Fourteenth Amendment as a protection against state action on the ground that freedom from testimonial compulsion is a right of national citizenship, or because it is a personal privilege or immunity secured by the Federal Constitution as one of the rights of man that are listed in the Bill of Rights.

The reasoning that leads to those conclusions starts with the unquestioned premise that the Bill of Rights, when adopted, was for the protection of the individual against the federal government and its provisions were inapplicable to similar actions done by the states. *** With the adoption of the Fourteenth Amendment, it was suggested that the dual citizenship recognized by its first sentence, secured for citizens' federal protection for their elemental privileges and immunities of state citizenship. The *Slaughter-House Cases* decided, contrary to the suggestion, that these rights, as privileges and immunities of state citizenship, remained under the sole protection of the state governments. This Court, without the expression of a contrary view upon that phase of the issues before the Court, has approved this determination. The power to free defendants in state trials from self-incrimination was specifically determined to be beyond the scope of the privileges and immunities clause of the Fourteenth Amendment in *Twining v. New Jersey*. ***

We reaffirm the conclusion of the *Twining* and *Palko* Cases that protection against self-incrimination is not a privilege or immunity of national citizenship.

A right to a fair trial is a right admittedly protected by the due process clause of the Fourteenth Amendment. Therefore, appellant argues, the due process clause of the Fourteenth Amendment protects his privilege against self-incrimination. The due process clause of the Fourteenth Amendment, however, does not draw all the rights of the federal Bill of Rights under its protection. That contention was made and rejected in *Palko v. Connecticut*. *** It was rejected with citation of the cases excluding several of the rights, protected by the Bill of Rights, against infringement by the National Government. Nothing has been called to our attention that either the framers of the Fourteenth Amendment or the states that adopted it intended its due process clause to draw within its scope the earlier amendments to the Constitution. *Palko* held that such provisions of the Bill of Rights as were "implicit in the concept of ordered liberty," became secure from state interference by the clause. But it held nothing more.

For a state to require testimony from an accused is not necessarily a breach of a state's obligation to give a fair trial. Therefore, we must examine the effect of the California law applied in this trial to see whether the comment on failure to testify violates the protection against state action that the due process clause does grant to an accused. The due process clause forbids compulsion to testify by fear of hurt, torture or exhaustion. So our inquiry is directed, not at the broad question of the constitutionality of compulsory testimony from the accused under the due process clause, but to the constitutionality of the provision of the California law that permits comment upon his failure to testify. It is, of course, logically possible that while an accused might be required, under appropriate penalties, to submit himself as a witness without a violation of due process, comment by judge or jury on inferences to be drawn from his failure to testify, in jurisdictions where an accused's privilege against self-incrimination is protected, might deny due process. For example, a statute might declare that a permitted refusal to testify would compel an acceptance of the truth of the prosecution's evidence.

Generally, comment on the failure of an accused to testify is forbidden in American jurisdictions. This arises from state constitutional or statutory provisions similar in character to the federal provisions. *** California, however, is one of a few states that permit limited comment upon a defendant's failure to testify. That permission is narrow. The California law authorizes comment by court and counsel upon the "failure of the defendant to explain or to deny by his testimony any evidence or facts in the case against him." This does not involve any presumption, rebuttable or irrebuttable, either of guilt or of the truth of any fact, that is offered in evidence. It allows inferences to be drawn from proven facts. Because of this clause, the court can direct the jury's attention to whatever evidence there may be that a defendant could deny and the prosecution can argue as to inferences that may be drawn from the accused's failure to testify. California has prescribed a method for advising the jury in the search for truth. However sound may be the legislative conclusion that an accused should not be compelled in any criminal case to be a witness against himself, we see no reason why comment should not be made upon his silence. It seems quite natural that when a defendant has opportunity to deny or explain facts and determines not to do so, the prosecution should bring out the strength of the evidence by commenting upon defendant's failure to explain or deny it. The prosecution evidence may be of facts that may be beyond the knowledge of the accused. If so, his failure to testify would have little if any weight. But the facts may be such as are necessarily in the knowledge of the accused. In that case a failure to explain would point to an inability to explain.

Appellant sets out the circumstances of this case, however, to show coercion and unfairness in permitting comment. The guilty person was not seen at the place and time of the crime. There was evidence, however, that entrance to the place or room where the crime was committed might have been obtained through a small door. It was freshly broken. Evidence showed that six fingerprints on the door were petitioner's. Certain diamond rings were missing from the deceased's possession. There was evidence that appellant, sometime after the crime, asked an unidentified person whether the latter would be interested in purchasing a diamond ring. As has been stated, the information charged other crimes to appellant and he admitted them. His argument here is that he could not take the stand to deny the evidence against him because he would be subjected to a cross-examination as to former crimes to impeach his veracity and the evidence so produced might well bring about his conviction. Such cross-examination is allowable in California. Therefore, appellant contends the California statute permitting comment denies him due process.

It is true that if comment were forbidden, an accused in this situation could remain silent and avoid evidence of former crimes and comment upon his failure to testify. We are of the view, however, that a state may control such a situation in accordance with its own ideas of the most efficient administration of criminal justice. The purpose of due process is not to protect an accused against a proper conviction but against an unfair conviction. When evidence is before a jury that threatens conviction, it does not seem unfair to require him to choose between leaving the adverse evidence unexplained and subjecting himself to impeachment through disclosures of former crimes. Indeed, this is a dilemma with which any defendant may be faced. If facts, adverse to the defendant, are proven by the prosecution, there may be no way to explain them favorably to the accused except by a witness who may be vulnerable to impeachment on cross-examination. The defendant must then decide whether or not to use such a witness. The fact that the witness may also be the defendant makes the choice more difficult but a denial of due process does not emerge from the circumstances.

Mr. Justice Frankfurter, concurring.

. . . [T]he issue is not whether an infraction of one of the specific provisions of the first eight Amendments is disclosed by the record. The relevant question is whether the criminal proceedings which re sulted in conviction deprived the accused of the due process of law to which the United States Constitution entitled him. Judicial review of that guaranty of the Fourteenth Amendment inescapably imposes upon this Court an exercise of judgment upon the whole course of the proceedings in order to ascertain whether they offend those canons of decency and fairness which express the notions of justice of English-speaking peoples even toward those charged with the most heinous offenses. These standards of justice are not authoritatively formulated anywhere as though they were prescriptions in a pharmacopoeia. But neither does the application of Due Process Clause imply that judges are wholly at large. The judicial judgment in applying the Due Process Clause must move within the limits of accepted notions of justice and is not to be based upon the idiosyncracies of a merely personal judgment. The fact that judges among themselves may differ whether in a particular case a trial offends accepted notions of justice is not disproof that general rather than idiosyncratic standards are applied. An important safeguard against such merely individual judgment is an alert deference to the judgment of the State court under review.

Mr. Justice Black dissenting.

This decision reasserts a constitutional theory spelled out in *Twining v. New Jersey* *** that this Court is endowed by the Constitution with boundless power under "natural law" periodically to expand and contract constitutional standards to conform to the Court's conception of what at a particular time constitutes "civilized decency" and "fundamental liberty and justice." Invoking this *Twining* rule, the Court concludes that although comment upon testimony in a federal court would violate the Fifth Amendment, identical comment in a state court does not violate today's fashion in today's decency and fundamentals and is therefore not prohibited by the Federal Constitution as amended.

The *Twining* Case was the first, as it is the only, decision of this Court, which has squarely held that states were free, notwithstanding the Fifth and Fourteenth Amendments, to extort evidence from one

accused of crime. I agree that if *Twining* be reaffirmed, the result reached might appropriately follow. But I would not reaffirm the *Twining* decision. I think that decision and the "natural law" theory of the Constitution upon which it relies degrade the constitutional safeguards of the Bill of Rights and simultaneously appropriate for this Court a broad power which we are not authorized by the Constitution to exercise.

Whether this Court ever will, or whether it now should, in the light of past decisions, give full effect to what the Amendment was intended to accomplish is not necessarily essential to a decision here. However that may be, our prior decisions, including *Twining*, do not prevent our carrying out that purpose, at least to the extent of making applicable to the states, not a mere part, as the Court has, but the full protection of the Fifth Amendment's provision against compelling evidence from an accused to convict him of crime. And I further contend that the "natural law" formula which the Court uses to reach its conclusion in this case should be abandoned as an incongruous excrescence on our Constitution. I believe that formula to be itself a violation of our Constitution, in that it subtly conveys to courts, at the expense of legislatures, ultimate power over public policies in fields where no specific provision of the Constitution limits legislative power.

I cannot consider the Bill of Rights to be an outworn 18th Century "strait jacket" as the *Twining* opinion did. Its provisions may be thought outdated abstractions by some. And it is true that they were designed to meet ancient evils. But they are the same kind of human evils that have emerged from century to century wherever excessive power is sought by the few at the expense of the many. In my judgment the people of no nation can lose their liberty so long as a Bill of Rights like ours survives and its basic purposes are conscientiously interpreted, enforced and respected so as to afford continuous protection against old, as well as new, devices and practices which might thwart those purposes. I fear to see the consequences of the Court's practice of substituting its own concepts of decency and fundamental justice for the language of the Bill of Rights as its point of departure in interpreting and enforcing that Bill of Rights. If the choice must be between the selective process of the *Palko* decision applying some of the Bill of Rights to the States, or the *Twining* rule applying none of them, I would choose the *Palko* selective process. But rather than accept either of these choices, I would follow what I believe was the original purpose of the Fourteenth Amendment—to extend to all the people of the nation the complete protection of the Bill of Rights. To hold that this Court can determine what, if any provisions of the Bill of Rights will be enforced, and if so to what degree, is to frustrate the great design of a written Constitution.

Conceding the possibility that this Court is now wise enough to improve on the Bill of Rights by substituting natural law concepts for the Bill of Rights, I think the possibility is entirely too speculative to agree to take that course. I would therefore hold in this case that the full protection of the Fifth Amendment's proscription against compelled testimony must be afforded by California. This I would do because of reliance upon the original purpose of the Fourteenth Amendment.

Mr. Justice Douglas joins in this opinion.

Mr. Justice Murphy, with whom **Mr. Justice Rutledge** concurs, dissenting.

While in substantial agreement with the views of Mr. Justice Black, I have one reservation and one addition to make.

I agree that the specific guarantees of the Bill of Rights should be carried over intact into the first section of the Fourteenth Amendment. But I am not prepared to say that the latter is entirely and necessarily limited by the Bill of Rights. Occasions may arise where a proceeding falls so far short of conforming to fundamental standards of procedure as to warrant constitutional condemnation in terms of a lack of due process despite the absence of a specific provision in the Bill of Rights.

The point, however, need not be pursued here inasmuch as the Fifth Amendment is explicit in its provision that no person shall be compelled in any criminal case to be a witness against himself. That provision, as Mr. Justice Black demonstrates, is a constituent part of the Fourteenth Amendment.

Moreover, it is my belief that this guarantee against self-incrimination has been violated in this case. Under California law, the judge or prosecutor may comment on the failure of the defendant in a criminal trial to explain or deny any evidence or facts introduced against him. As interpreted and applied in this case, such a provision compels a defendant to be a witness against himself in one of two ways:

1. If he does not take the stand, his silence is used as the basis for drawing unfavorable inferences against him as to matters which he might reasonably be expected to explain. Thus he is compelled, through his silence, to testify against himself. And silence can be as effective in this situation as oral statements.

2. If he does take the stand, thereby opening himself to cross-examination, so as to overcome the effects of the provision in question, he is necessarily compelled to testify against himself. In that case, his testimony on cross-examination is the result of the coercive pressure of the provision rather than his own volition.

Much can be said pro and con as to the desirability of allowing comment on the failure of the accused to testify. But policy arguments are to no avail in the face of a clear constitutional command. This guarantee of freedom from self-incrimination is grounded on a deep respect for those who might prefer to remain silent before their accusers. To borrow language from *Wilson v. United States:* *** "It is not every one who can safely venture on the witness stand though entirely innocent of the charge against him. Excessive timidity, nervousness when facing others and attempting to explain transactions of a suspicious character, and offenses charged against him, will often confuse and embarrass him to such a degree as to increase rather than remove prejudices against him. It is not every one, however honest, who would, therefore, willingly be placed on the witness stand."

We are obliged to give effect to the principle of freedom from self-incrimination. That principle is as applicable where the compelled testimony is in the form of silence as where it is composed of oral statements. Accordingly, I would reverse the judgment below.

Rochin v. California

342 U.S. 165; 72 S. Ct. 205; 96 L. Ed. 183 (1952)

Vote: 8-0

Here, the Court again considers the meaning of the Due Process Clause of the Fourteenth Amendment and the relationship of the Bill of Rights to the states. Again, the specific issue is that of compulsory self-incrimination. The facts are contained in Justice Frankfurter's majority opinion.

Mr. Justice Frankfurter delivered the opinion of the Court.

Having "some information that [the petitioner] was selling narcotics," three deputy sheriffs of the County of Los Angeles, on the morning of July 1, 1949, made for the two-story dwelling house in which Rochin lived with his mother, common-law wife, brothers and sisters. Finding the outside door open, they entered and then forced open the door to Rochin's room on the second floor. Inside they found petitioner sitting partly dressed on the side of the bed, upon which his wife was lying. On a "night stand" beside the bed the deputies spied two capsules. When asked "Whose stuff is this?" Rochin seized the capsules and put them in his mouth. A struggle ensued, in the course of which the three officers "jumped upon him" and attempted to extract the capsules. The force they applied proved unavailing against Rochin's resistance. He was handcuffed and taken to a hospital. At the direction of one of the officers a doctor forced an emetic solution through a tube into Rochin's stomach against his will. This "stomach pumping" produced vomiting. In the vomited matter were found two capsules which proved to contain morphine.

Rochin was brought to trial before a California Superior Court, sitting without a jury, on the charge of possessing "a preparation of morphine" in violation of the California Health and Safety Code. *** Rochin was convicted and sentenced to sixty days' imprisonment. The chief evidence against him was the two capsules. They were admitted over petitioner's objection, although the means of obtaining them was frankly set forth in the testimony by one of the deputies, substantially as here narrated.

On appeal, the District Court of Appeal affirmed the conviction, despite the finding that the officers "were guilty of unlawfully breaking into and entering defendant's room and were guilty of unlawfully assaulting and battering defendant while in the room," and "were guilty of unlawfully assaulting, battering, torturing and falsely imprisoning the defendant at the alleged hospital." ***

This Court granted certiorari, because a serious question is raised as to the limitations which the Due Process Clause of the Fourteenth Amendment imposes on the conduct of criminal proceedings by the States. ***

In our federal system the administration of criminal justice is predominantly committed to the care of the States. The power to define crimes belongs to Congress only as an appropriate means of carrying into execution its limited grant of legislative powers. Broadly speaking, crimes in the United States are what the laws of the individual States make them, subject to the limitations of Art. 1 [sec.] 10 [cl. 1], in the original Constitution, prohibiting bills of attainder and *ex post facto* laws, and of the Thirteenth and Fourteenth Amendments.

These limitations, in the main, concern not restrictions upon the powers of the States to define crime, except in the restricted area where federal authority has preempted the field, but restrictions upon the manner in which the States may enforce their penal codes. Accordingly, in reviewing a State criminal conviction under a claim of right guaranteed by the Due Process Clause of the Fourteenth Amendment, *** "we must be deeply mindful of the responsibilities of the States for the enforcement of criminal laws, and exercise with due humility our merely negative function in subjecting convictions from state courts to the very narrow scrutiny which the Due Process Clause of the Fourteenth Amendment authorizes." Due process of law is not to be turned into a destructive dogma against the States in the administration of their systems of criminal justice.

However, this Court too has its responsibility. Regard for the requirements of the Due Process Clause "inescapably imposes upon this Court an exercise of judgment upon the whole course of the proceedings [resulting in a conviction] in order to ascertain whether they offend those canons of decency and fairness which express the notions of justice of English-speaking peoples even toward those charged with the most heinous offenses." *** These standards of justice are not authoritatively formulated anywhere as though they were specifics. Due process of law is a summarized constitutional guarantee of respect for those personal immunities which, as Mr. Justice Cardozo twice wrote for the Court, are "so rooted in the traditions and conscience of our people as to be ranked as fundamental," *** or are "implicit in the concept of ordered liberty." ***

The vague contours of the Due Process Clause do not leave judges at large. We may not draw on our merely personal and private notions and disregard the limits that bind judges in their judicial function. Even though the concept of due process of law is not final and fixed, these limits are derived from considerations that are fused in the whole nature of our judicial process. The Due Process Clause places upon this Court the duty of exercising a judgment, within the narrow confines of judicial power in reviewing State convictions, upon interests of society pushing in opposite directions.

Due process of law thus conceived is not to be derided as resort to a revival of "natural law." To believe that this judicial exercise of judgment could be avoided by freezing "due process of law" at some fixed stage of time or thought is to suggest that the most important aspect of constitutional adjudication is a function for inanimate machines and not for judges, for whom the independence safeguarded by Article 3 of the Constitution was designed and who are presumably guided by established standards of judicial behavior. Even cybernetics has not yet made that haughty claim. To practice the requisite detachment and to achieve sufficient objectivity no doubt demands of judges the habit of self-discipline and self-criticism, incertitude that one's own views are incontestable and alert tolerance toward views not shared. They are precisely the qualities society has a right to expect from those entrusted with ultimate judicial power.

Restraints on our jurisdiction are self-imposed only in the sense that there is from our decisions no immediate appeal short of impeachment or consti-

tutional amendment. But that does not make due process of law a matter of judicial caprice. The faculties of the Due Process Clause may be indefinite and vague, but the mode of their ascertainment is not self-willed. In each case "due process of law" requires an evaluation based on a disinterested inquiry pursued in the spirit of science, on a balanced order of facts exactly and fairly stated, on the detached consideration of conflicting claims. . . .

Applying these general considerations to the circumstances of the present case, we are compelled to conclude that the proceedings by which this conviction was obtained do more than offend some fastidious squeamishness or private sentimentalism about combatting crime too energetically. This is conduct that shocks the conscience. Illegally breaking into the privacy of the petitioner, the struggle to open his mouth and remove what was there, the forcible extraction of his stomach's contents—this course of proceeding by agents of government to obtain evidence is bound to offend even hardened sensibilities. They are methods too close to the rack and the screw to permit of constitutional differentiation.

It has long since ceased to be true that due process of law is heedless of the means by which otherwise relevant and credible evidence is obtained. This was not true even before the series of recent cases enforced the constitutional principle that the States may not base convictions upon confessions, however much verified, obtained by coercion. These decisions are not arbitrary exceptions to the comprehensive right of States to fashion their own rules of evidence for criminal trials. They are not sports in our constitutional law but applications of a general principle. They are only instances of the general requirement that States in their prosecutions respect certain decencies of civilized conduct. Due process of law, as a historic and generative principle, precludes defining, and thereby confining, these standards of conduct more precisely than to say that convictions cannot be brought about by methods that offend "a sense of justice." It would be a stultification of the responsibility which the course of constitutional history has cast upon this Court to hold that in order to convict a man the police cannot extract by force what is in his mind but can extract what is in his stomach.

To attempt in this case to distinguish what lawyers call "real evidence" from verbal evidence is to ignore the reasons for excluding coerced confessions. Use of involuntary verbal confessions in State criminal trials is constitutionally obnoxious not only because of their unreliability. They are inadmissible under the Due Process Clause even though statements contained in them may be independently established as true. Coerced confessions offend the community's sense of fair play and decency. So here, to sanction the brutal conduct which naturally enough was condemned by the court whose judgment is before us, would be to afford brutality the cloak of law. Nothing would be more calculated to discredit law and thereby to brutalize the temper of a society.

Mr. Justice Minton took no part in the consideration or decision of his case.

Mr. Justice Black, concurring.

Adamson v. California *** sets out reasons for my belief that state as well as federal courts and law enforcement officers must obey the Fifth Amendment's command that "No person . . . shall be compelled in any criminal case to be a witness against himself." I think a person is compelled to be a witness against himself not only when he is compelled to testify, but also when as here, incriminating evidence is forcibly taken from him by a contrivance of modern science.

In the view of a majority of the Court, however, the Fifth Amendment imposes no restraint of any kind on the states. They nevertheless hold that California's use of this evidence violated the Due Process Clause of the Fourteenth Amendment. Since they hold as I do in this case, I regret my inability to accept their interpretation without protest. But I believe that faithful adherence to the specific guarantees in the Bill of Rights insures a more permanent protection of individual liberty than that which can be afforded by the nebulous standards stated by the majority.

What the majority hold is that the Due Process Clause empowers this Court to nullify any state law if its application "shocks the conscience," offends "a sense of justice" or runs counter to the "decencies of civilized conduct." The majority emphasize that these statements do not refer to their own consciences or to their senses of justice and decency. For we are told that "we may not draw on our merely personal and private notions"; our judgment must be grounded on "considerations deeply rooted in reason, and in the compelling traditions of the legal profession." We are further admonished to measure the validity of state practices, not by our reason, or by the traditions of the legal profession, but by "the community's sense of fair play and decency"; by the "traditions and conscience of our people"; or by "those canons of decency and fairness which express the notions of justice of English-speaking peoples." These canons are made necessary, it is said, because of "interests of society pushing in opposite directions." ***

If the Due Process Clause does vest this Court with such unlimited power to invalidate laws, I am still in doubt as to why we should consider only the notions of English-speaking peoples to determine what are immutable and fundamental principles of justice. Moreover, one may well ask what avenues of investigation are open to discover "canons" of decency and fairness which express the notions of English-speaking peoples to determine what are immutable and fundamental principles of justice. Moreover, one may well ask what avenues of investigation are open to discover "canons" of conduct so universally favored that this Court should write them into the Constitution? All we are told is that the discovery must be made by an "evaluation based on a disinterested inquiry pursued in the spirit of science on a balanced order of facts." ***

Some constitutional provisions are stated in absolute and unqualified language such, for illustration, as the First Amendment stating that no law shall be passed prohibiting the free exercise of religion or abridging the freedom of speech or press. Other constitutional provisions do require courts to choose between competing policies, such as the Fourth Amendment which, by its terms, necessitates a judicial decision as to what is an "unreasonable" search or seizure. There is, however, no express constitutional language granting judicial power to invalidate *every* state law of *every* kind deemed "unreasonable" or contrary to the Court's notion of civilized decencies; yet the constitutional philosophy used by the majority has, in the past, been used to deny a state the right to fix the price of gasoline, and even the right to prevent bakers from palming off smaller for larger loaves of bread. These cases, and others, show the extent to which the evanescent standards of the majority's philosophy have been used to nullify state legislative programs passed to suppress evil economic practices. What paralyzing role this same philosophy will play in the future economic affairs of this country is impossible to predict. Of even graver concern, however, is the use of the philosophy to nullify the Bill of Rights. I long ago concluded that the accordion-like qualities of this philosophy must inevitably imperil all the individual liberty safeguards specifically enumerated in the Bill of Rights. Recent decisions of this Court sanctioning abridgment of the freedom of speech and press have strengthened this conclusion.

Mr. Justice Douglas, concurring.

The evidence obtained from this accused's stomach would be admissible in the majority of states where the question has been raised. Yet the Court now says that the rule which the majority of the states have fashioned violates the "decencies of civilized conduct." To that I cannot agree. It is a rule formulated by responsible courts with judges as sensitive as we are to the proper standards for law administration.

As an original matter it might be debatable whether the provision in the Fifth Amendment that no person "shall be compelled in any criminal case to be a witness against himself" serves the ends of justice. Not all civilized legal procedures recognize it. But the choice was made by the Framers, a choice which sets a standard for legal trials in this country.

The Framers made it a standard of due process for prosecutions by the Federal Government. If it is a requirement of due process for a trial in the federal courthouse, it is impossible for me to say it is not a requirement of due process for a trial in the state courthouse. That was the issue recently surveyed in *Adamson v. California.* *** The Court rejected the view that compelled testimony should be excluded and held in substance that the accused in a state trial can be forced to testify against himself. I disagree. Of course an accused can be compelled to be present at the trial, to stand, to sit, to turn this way or that, and to try on a cap or a coat. But I think that words taken from his lips, capsules taken from his stomach, blood taken from his veins are all inadmissible provided they are taken from him without his consent. They are inadmissible because of the command of the Fifth Amendment.

That is an unequivocal, definite and workable rule of evidence for state and federal courts. But we cannot in fairness free the state courts from that command and yet excoriate them for flouting the "decencies of civilized conduct" when they admit the evidence. That is to make the rule turn not on the Constitution but on the idiosyncrasies of the judges who sit here.

The damage of the view sponsored by the Court in this case may not be conspicuous here. But it is part of the same philosophy that produced *Betts v. Brady,* *** denying counsel to an accused in a state trial against the command of the Sixth Amendment, and *Wolf v. Colorado,* *** allowing evidence obtained as a result of a search and seizure that is illegal under the Fourth Amendment to be introduced in a state trial. It is part of the process of erosion of civil rights of the citizen in recent years.

Duncan v. Louisiana

391 U.S. 145; 88 S.Ct. 1444; 20 L.Ed.2d 491 (1968)
Vote: 7-2

This case raises the question of whether, and under what circumstances, the Due Process Clause of the Fourteenth Amendment incorporates the Sixth Amendment guarantee of trial by jury in a criminal case. The facts are set forth in Justice White's majority opinion.

Mr. Justice White delivered the opinion of the Court.

Appellant, Gary Duncan, was convicted of simple battery in the Twenty-fifth Judicial District Court of Louisiana. Under Louisiana law simple battery is a misdemeanor, punishable by a maximum of two years' imprisonment and a $300 fine. Appellant sought trial by jury, but because the Louisiana Constitution grants jury trials only in cases in which capital punishment or imprisonment at hard labor may be imposed, the trial judge denied the request. Appellant was convicted and sentenced to serve 60 days in the parish prison and pay a fine of $150. Appellant sought review in the Supreme Court of Louisiana, asserting that the denial of jury trial violated rights guaranteed to him by the United States Constitution. The Supreme Court, finding "[n]o error of law in the ruling complained of," denied appellant a writ of certiorari. . . . [A]ppellant sought review in this Court, alleging that the Sixth and Fourteenth Amendments to the United States Constitution secure the right to jury trial in state criminal prosecutions where a sentence as long as two years may be imposed. . . .

Appellant was 19 years of age when tried. While driving on Highway 23 in Plaquemines Parish on October 18, 1966, he saw two younger cousins engaged in a conversation by the side of the road with four white boys. Knowing his cousins, Negroes who had recently transferred to a formerly all-white high school, had reported the occurrence of racial incidents at the school, Duncan stopped the car, got out, and approached the six boys. At trial the white boys and white onlooker testified, as did appellant and his cousins. The testimony was in dispute on many points, but the witnesses agreed that appellant and the white boys spoke to each other, that appellant encouraged his cousins to break off the encounter and enter his car, and that appellant was about to enter the car himself for the purpose of driving away with his cousins. The whites testified that just before getting in the car appellant slapped Herman Landry, one of the white boys, on the elbow. The Negroes testified that appellant had not slapped Landry, but had merely touched him. The trial judge concluded that the State had proved beyond a reasonable doubt that Duncan had committed simple battery, and found him guilty. . . .

The Fourteenth Amendment denies the States the power to "deprive any person of life, liberty, or property, without due process of law." In resolving conflicting claims concerning the meaning of this spacious language, the Court has looked increasingly to the Bill of Rights for guidance; many of the rights guaranteed by the first eight Amendments to the Constitution have been held to be protected against state action by the Due Process Clause of the Fourteenth Amendment. That clause now protects the right to compensation for property taken by the State; the rights of speech, press, and religion covered by the First Amendment; the Fourth Amendment rights to be free from unreasonable searches and seizures and to have excluded from criminal trials any evidence illegally seized; the right guaranteed by the Fifth Amendment to be free of compelled self-incrimination; and the Sixth Amendment rights to counsel, to a speedy and public trial, to confrontation of opposing witnesses, and to compulsory process for obtaining witnesses.

The test for determining whether a right extended by the Fifth and Sixth Amendments with respect to federal criminal proceedings is also protected against state action by the Fourteenth Amendment has been phrased in a variety of ways in the opinions of this Court. The question has been asked whether a right is among those "fundamental principles of liberty and justice which lie at the base of all our civil and political institutions, " *** whether it is "basic in our system of jurisprudence," *** and whether it is "a fundamental right, essential to a fair trial." *** The claim before us is that the right to trial by jury guaranteed by the Sixth Amendment meets these tests. The position of Louisiana, on the other hand, is that the Constitution imposes upon the States no duty to give a jury trial in any criminal case, regardless of the seriousness of the crime or the size of the punishment which may be imposed. Because we believe that trial by jury in criminal cases is fundamental to the American scheme of justice, we hold that the Fourteenth Amendment guarantees a right of jury trial in all criminal cases which—were they to be tried in a federal court—would come within the Sixth Amendment's guarantee. Since we consider the appeal before us to be such a case, we hold that the Constitution was

was violated when appellant's demand for jury trial was refused.

The history of trial by jury in criminal cases has been frequently told. It is sufficient for present purposes to say that by the time our Constitution was written, jury trial in criminal cases had been in existence in England for several centuries and carried impressive credentials traced by many to *Magna Carta* [1215]. . . .

Jury trial came to America with English colonists, and received strong support from them. Royal interference with the jury trial was deeply resented. Among the resolutions adopted by the First Congress of the American Colonies (the Stamp Act Congress) on October 19, 1765 — resolutions deemed by their authors to state "the most essential rights and liberties of the colonists" — was the declaration: "That trial by jury is the inherent and invaluable right of every British subject in these colonies." The First Continental Congress, in the resolve of October 14, 1774, objected to trials before judges dependent upon the Crown alone for their salaries and to trials in England for alleged crimes committed in the colonies. . . . The Declaration of Independence stated solemn objections to the King's making "Judges dependent on his Will alone, for the tenure of their offices, and the amount and payment of their salaries," to his "depriving us in many cases, of the benefits of Trial by Jury," and to his "transporting us beyond Seas to be tried for pretended offenses." The Constitution itself, in Art. III, [Sec.] 2, commanded: "The Trial of all Crimes, except in Cases of Impeachment, shall be by Jury; and such Trial shall be held in the State where the said Crimes shall have been committed." Objections to the Constitution because of the absence of a bill of rights were met by the immediate submission and adoption of the Bill of Rights. Included was the Sixth Amendment which, among other things, provided: "In all criminal prosecutions, the accused shall enjoy the right to a speedy and public trial, by an impartial jury of the State and district wherein the crime shall have been committed."

The constitution adopted by the original States guaranteed jury trial. Also, the constitution of every State entering the Union thereafter in one form or another protected the right to jury trial in criminal cases.

Even such skeletal history is impressive support for considering the right to jury in criminal cases to be fundamental to our system of justice, an importance frequently recognized in the opinions of this Court. . . .

Jury trial continues to receive strong support. The laws of every State guarantee a right to jury trial in serious criminal cases; no State has dispensed with it; nor are there significant movements underway to do so. Indeed, the three most recent state constitutional revisions, in Maryland, Michigan, and New York, carefully preserved the right of the accused to have the judgment of a jury when tried for a serious crime.

We are aware of prior cases in this Court in which the prevailing opinion contains statements contrary to our holding today that the right to jury trial in serious criminal cases is a fundamental right and hence must be recognized by the States as part of their obligation to extend due process of law to all persons within their jurisdiction. Louisiana relies especially on *Maxwell v. Dow,* *** *Palko v. Connecticut,* *** and *Snyder v. Massachusetts.* *** None of these cases, however, dealt with a State which had purported to dispense entirely with a jury trial in serious criminal cases. *Maxwell* held that no provision of the Bill of Rights applied to the States — a position long since repudiated — and that the Due Process Clause of the Fourteenth Amendment did not prevent a State from trying a defendant for a noncapital offense with fewer than 12 men on the jury. It did not deal with a case in which no jury at all had been provided. In neither *Palko* nor *Snyder* was jury trial actually at issue, although both cases contain important dicta asserting that the right to jury trial is not essential to ordered liberty and may be dispensed with by the States regardless of the Sixth and Fourteenth Amendments. These observations, though weighty and respectable, are nevertheless dicta, unsupported by holdings in this Court that a State may refuse a defendant's demand for a jury trial when he is charged with a serious crime. Perhaps because the right to jury trial was not directly at stake, the Court's remarks about the jury in *Palko* and *Snyder* took no note of past or current developments regarding jury trials, did not consider its purposes and functions, attempted no inquiry into how well it was performing its job, and did not discuss possible distinctions between civil and criminal cases. . . . Respectfully, we reject the prior dicta regarding jury trial in criminal cases.

The guarantees of jury trial in the Federal and State Constitutions reflect a profound judgment about the way in which law should be enforced and justice administered. A right to jury trial is granted to criminal defendants in order to prevent oppression by the Government. . . .

The State of Louisiana urges that holding that the Fourteenth Amendment assures a right to jury trial will cast doubt on the integrity of every trial conducted without a jury. Plainly, this is not the import of our holding. Our conclusion is that in the American States, as in the federal judicial system, a general grant of jury trial for serious offenses is a fundamental right, essential for preventing miscarriages of justice and for assuring that fair trials are provided for all defendants. We would not assert, however, that every criminal trial—or any particular trial—held before a judge alone is unfair or that a defendant may never be as fairly treated by a judge as he would be by a jury. Thus we hold no constitutional doubts about the practices, common in both federal and state courts, of accepting waivers of jury trial and prosecuting petty crimes without extending a right to jury trial. However, the fact is that in most places more trials for serious crimes are to juries than to a court alone; a great many defendants prefer the judgment of a jury to that of a court. Even where defendants are satisfied with bench trials, the right to a jury trial very likely serves its intended purpose of making judicial or prosecutorial unfairness less likely.

Louisiana's final contention is that even if it must grant jury trials in serious criminal cases, the conviction before us is valid and constitutional because here the petitioner was tried for simple battery and was sentenced to only 60 days in the parish prison. We are not persuaded. It is doubtless true that there is a category of petty crimes or offenses which is not subject to the Sixth Amendment jury trial provision and should not be subject to the Fourteenth Amendment jury trial requirement here applied to the States. Crimes carrying possible penalties up to six months do not require a jury trial if they otherwise qualify as petty offenses. . . . The question, then, is whether a crime carrying such a penalty is an offense which Louisiana may insist on trying without a jury.

We think not. So-called petty offenses were tried without juries both in England and in the Colonies and have always been held to be exempt from the otherwise comprehensive language of the Sixth Amendment's jury trial provisions. There is no substantial evidence that the Framers intended to depart from this established common-law practice, and the possible consequences to defendants from convictions for petty offenses have been thought insufficient to outweigh the benefits to efficient law enforcement and simplified judicial administration resulting from the availability of speedy and inexpensive nonjury adjudications. These same considerations compel the same result under the Fourteenth Amendment. Of course the boundaries of the petty offense category have always been ill defined, if not ambulatory. . . .

. . . We need not, however, settle in this case the exact location of the line between petty offenses and serious crimes. It is sufficient for our purposes to hold that a crime punishable by two years in prison is, based on past and contemporary standards in this country, a serious crime and not a petty offense. Consequently appellant was entitled to a jury trial and it was error to deny it. . . .

Mr. Justice Fortas, concurring.

. . . [A]lthough I agree with the decision of the Court, I cannot agree with the implication *** that the tail must go with the hide: that when we hold, influenced by the Sixth Amendment, that "due process" requires that the States accord the right of jury trial for all but petty offenses, we automatically import all of the ancillary rules which have been or may hereafter be developed incidental to the right to jury trial in the federal courts. I see no reason whatever, for example, to assume that our decision today should require us to impose federal requirements such as unanimous verdicts or a jury of 12 upon the States. We may well conclude that these and other features of federal jury practice are by no means fundamental—that they are not essential to due process of law—and that they are not obligatory on the States.

I would make these points clear today. Neither logic nor history nor the intent of the draftsmen of the Fourteenth Amendment can possibly be said to require that the Sixth Amendment or its jury trial provision be applied to the States together with the total gloss that this Court's decisions have supplied. The draftsmen of the Fourteenth Amendment intended what they said, not more or less: that no State shall deprive any person of life, liberty, or property without due process of law. It is ultimately the duty of this Court to interpret, to ascribe specific meaning to this phrase. There is no reason whatever for us to conclude that, in so doing, we are bound slavishly to follow not only the Sixth Amendment but all of its bag and baggage, however securely or insecurely affixed they may be by law and precedent to federal proceedings. To take this course, in my judgment, would be not only unnecessary but mischievous because it would inflict a serious blow upon the principle of federalism. The Due Process Clause commands us to apply its great standard to state court proceedings to assure basic fairness. It does not command us rigidly and arbitrarily to impose the exact pattern of federal proceedings upon the 50 States. On the contrary, the Constitution's command, in my view, is that in our insistence upon state observance of due process, we should, so far as possible, allow the greatest latitude for state differences. It requires, within the limits of the lofty basic standards that it prescribes for the States as well as the Federal Government, maximum opportunity for diversity and minimal imposition of uniformity of methods and detail upon the States. Our Constitution sets up a federal union, not a monolith. . . .

Mr. Justice Black, with whom **Mr. Justice Douglas** joins, concurring.

The Court today holds that the right to trial by jury guaranteed defendants in criminal cases in federal courts by Art. III of the United States Constitution and by the Sixth Amendment is also guaranteed by the Fourteenth Amendment to defendants tried in state courts. With this holding I agree for reasons given by the Court. I also agree because of reasons given in my dissent in *Adamson v California*. . . . I am very happy to support this selective process through which our Court has since the *Adamson* case held most of the specific Bill of Rights' protections applicable to the States to the same extent they are applicable to the Federal Government. Among these are the right to trial by jury decided today, the right against compelled self-incrimination, the right to counsel, the right to compulsory process for witnesses, the right to confront witnesses, the right to a speedy and public trial, and the right to be free from unreasonable searches and seizures. . . .

. . . I believe as strongly as ever that the Fourteenth Amendment was intended to make the Bill of Rights applicable to the States. I have been willing to support the selective incorporation doctrine, however, as an alternative, although perhaps less historically supportable than complete incorporation. The selective incorporation process, if used properly, does limit the Supreme Court in the Fourteenth Amendment field to specific Bill of Rights' protections only and keeps judges from roaming at will in their own notions of what policies outside the Bill of Rights are desirable and what are not. And, most importantly for me, the selective incorporation process has the virtue of having already worked to make most of the Bill of Rights' protections applicable to the States.

Mr. Justice Harlan, whom Mr. Justice Stewart joins, dissenting.

. . . The question before us is not whether jury trial is an ancient institution, which it is; nor whether it plays a significant role in the administration of criminal justice, which it does; nor whether it will endure, which it shall. The question in this case is whether the State of Louisiana, which provides trial by jury for all felonies, is prohibited by the Constitution from trying charges of simple battery to the court alone. In my view, the answer to that question, mandated alike by our constitutional history and by the longer history of trial by jury, is clearly "no."

The States have always borne primarily responsibility for operating the machinery of criminal justice within their borders, and adapting it to their particular circumstances. In exercising this responsibility, each State is compelled to conform its procedures to the requirements of the Federal Constitution. The Due Process Clause of the Fourteenth Amendment requires that those procedures be fundamentally fair in all respects. It does not, in my view, impose or encourage nationwide uniformity for its own sake; it does not command adherence to forms that happen to be old; and it does not impose on the State the rules that may be in force in the federal courts except where such rules are also found to be essential to basic fairness.

The Court's approach to this case is an uneasy and illogical compromise among the views of various Justices on how the Due Process Clause should be interpreted. The Court does not say that those who framed the Fourteenth Amendment intended to make the Sixth Amendment applicable to the States, and the Court concedes that it finds nothing unfair about the procedure by which the present appellant was tried. Nevertheless, the Court reverses his conviction: it holds, for some reason not apparent to me, that the Due Process Clause incorporates the particular clause of the Sixth Amendment that requires trial by jury in federal criminal cases—including, as I read its opinion, the sometimes trivial accompanying baggage of judicial interpretation in federal contexts. I have raised my voice many times

before against the Court's continuing undiscriminating insistence upon fastening on the States federal notions of criminal justice, and I must do so again in this instance. With all respect, the Court's approach and its reading of history are altogether topsy-turvy. . . .

Apart from the approach taken by the absolute incorporationists, I can see only one method of analysis that has any internal logic. That is to start with the words "liberty" and "due process of law" and attempt to define them in a way that accords with American traditions and our system of government. This approach, involving a much more discriminating process of adjudication than does "incorporation," is, albeit difficult, the one that was followed throughout the 19th and most of the present century. It entails a "gradual process of judicial inclusion and exclusion," seeking, with due recognition of constitutional tolerance for state experimentation and disparity, to ascertain those "immutable principles . . . of free government which no member of the Union may disregard." . . .

CHAPTER TEN

PROPERTY RIGHTS AND ECONOMIC FREEDOM

The great and chief end . . . of Mens uniting into Commonwealths, and putting themselves under Government, is the preservation of their property.

John Locke, "Second Treatise of Government"

When . . . one devotes his property to a use in which the public has an interest, he, in effect, grants to the public an interest in that use, and must be controlled by the public for the common good, to the extent of the interest he has thus created.

Chief Justice Morrison R. Waite, Munn v. Illinois (1877)

INTRODUCTION

The twin pillars of any capitalist economy are private property and contracts. For a capitalist system to flourish, it is imperative that there be legal protection for private property and legal enforcement of contracts. Unquestionably, the protection of private property and contractual relationships was particularly important to the Framers of the Constitution.

This chapter focuses on historic Supreme Court decisions balancing individual property rights and economic freedom against the evolving **police power,** first of the states and later of the national government, to protect the health, safety, and general welfare of the community. The term "property rights" includes the ownership, acquisition, and use of private property. The term "economic freedom" more accurately indicates the cluster of rights associated with private enterprise.

Americans of the eighteenth century, including those who wrote the Constitution and Bill of Rights, generally accepted the theory of **natural rights** as expounded by such philosophers as John Locke. According to this theory, basic rights to life, liberty, and property were grounded in natural or divine law. Such rights were universal and timeless, transcending government and human law. According to Locke and most other social contract theorists of the seventeenth and eighteenth centuries, individuals living originally in a "state of nature" subordinated themselves to civil government in exchange for the protection of fundamental rights to life, liberty, and property. Government in turn was limited

The English philosopher,
John Locke. His ideas
exerted profound influence
on the American Founders

in the means by which it could interfere with the exercise of individual rights. The very existence of social order presumed some loss of personal and economic freedom. To protect individual rights and advance the public good, government might restrict liberty and might even take private property for public use. But in the latter instance, it would have to provide just compensation to the previous owner, and in limiting individual liberty, it would be required to act reasonably. In short, under this social contract theory, governmental restrictions would be balanced against the high priority afforded to individual rights.

This Lockean perspective is reflected in the Contract Clause (Article I, Section 10) of the Constitution. It is also easily recognized in the Due Process Clauses of the Fifth and Fourteenth Amendments, as well as in the Fifth Amendment provision that private property shall not be "taken for public use without just compensation." As with other general provisions of the Constitution, the Supreme Court assumed principal responsibility for interpreting such phrases as "just compensation," "due process of law," and "impairment of the obligation of contracts." The interpretation of these broad phrases defined the central theme of American constitutional lawmaking during roughly the first 150 years of Supreme Court history.

EVOLVING JUDICIAL PERSPECTIVES

The *ex post facto* provisions (Article I, Sections 9 and 10) of the original Constitution had the potential of protecting property rights against governmental encroachment. But, as noted in Chapter 9, the Supreme Court held in *Calder v. Bull* (1798) that the *ex post facto* limitation applied only to retroactive criminal statutes and not to laws affecting property rights or contractual obligations. Two of the four opinions filed in this case contain important dicta on the sources of individual rights and limitations on government. These opinions, written by Justices Samuel Chase and James Iredell, merit additional attention at this point in our discussion. Without designating any specific constitutional limitations, Justice Chase asserted that "certain vital principles in our free republican governments ... will determine and overrule an apparent and flagrant abuse of legislative power." A legislative act "contrary to the great first principles of the social compact," he continued, "cannot be considered a rightful exercise of legislative authority."

Chase's opinion in *Calder v. Bull* was grounded in natural rights theory. Although this perspective has never achieved dominance on the Supreme Court as a standard for determining the validity of governmental acts, it has occasionally influenced judicial interpretation of the nature and scope of individual rights. By contrast, Justice Iredell's opinion in *Calder* maintained that courts could not invalidate legislation "merely because it is, in their judgment, contrary to the principles of natural justice." If legislatures transgress constitutional boundaries, however, "they violate a fundamental law, which must be our guide, whenever we are called upon, as judges, to determine the validity of a legislative act." Iredell's emphasis on the written Constitution as the ultimate standard for determining the validity of legislation soon became the dominant view among the justices.

Throughout most of the nineteenth century the Supreme Court sought to balance competing public and private interests in its property-related jurisprudence. However, in the face of a rising tide of state and federal economic legislation, the Court of the late nineteenth and early twentieth centuries became more adamant in its defense of what was loosely termed laissez-faire capitalism. Although the Framers of the Constitution attached great importance to the protection of property, it is doubtful that most of them would have subscribed to the doctrines by which the Supreme Court attempted to protect economic individualism. In a series of controversial decisions between the late 1880s and the late 1930s, the Court invoked the constitutional protections of private property and economic freedom to strike down numerous laws designed to regulate economic activity. This period of "conservative activism" came to an abrupt end with the constitutional revolution of 1937, brought about by a confrontation between the Court and the elected branches over the constitutionality of Roosevelt's New Deal programs (see Chapters 2 and 5).

Modern Protection of Economic Freedom

Since 1937, the Supreme Court has largely deferred to other branches of government in the field of economic regulation. The post-New Deal Court's self-restraint in the economic area has been juxtaposed with a more liberal activism on behalf of cultural, political, or human rights largely outside the field of economic activity. The modern Court, at least until recently, has been much more concerned with matters of free expression, the rights of the accused, personal privacy, and racial and sexual equality (areas of Supreme

Court activity discussed in subsequent chapters). Of course, one must recognize that private property and private enterprise are widely shared and deeply held cultural values. Especially in the wake of the decline of communism and socialism around the world, public policy in the United States is unlikely to seriously threaten these established values. Thus, the need for judicial protection of these rights is substantially less than in the early days of the Republic, or even during the days of the Great Depression. Yet the judicial protection of private property and free enterprise played an extremely important part in the development of American constitutional law and in the institutional history of the Supreme Court.

THE CONTRACT CLAUSE

Historically, the Contract Clause of Article I, Section 10 was extremely important in the protection of economic freedom and private property. Like many important constitutional provisions, the Contract Clause was given life during the era of Chief Justice John Marshall (1801 to 1835).

Key Decisions of the Marshall Court

In *Fletcher v. Peck* (1810), the Supreme Court invalidated as a violation of the Contract Clause an act of the Georgia legislature rescinding the state's sale of land to private investors. To reach this result, it was necessary for Chief Justice Marshall, who wrote the Court's opinion, to conclude that a grant is a contract. In Marshall's view, Georgia's original grant of land carried with it an implied contractual obligation not to assert a right to reclaim the land. Once this land passed into the hands of "innocent third parties" who bought it from the original purchasers, the state could not repeal the original sale, even if it could be proved that the initial grant had been obtained by bribing members of the legislature. As Marshall and his colleagues saw it, "absolute rights" had been established under the contract: that is, they had become "vested" in the subsequent purchasers. But since the state itself was a party to the contract, how could its obligations be enforced? In Marshall's view, Georgia had a moral obligation accorded the status of law, but he was equivocal as to the ultimate source of legal authority. He concluded that Georgia was "restrained" from passing the rescinding act "either by general principles, which are common to our free institutions, or by the particular provisions of the Constitution of the United States." This ambivalence underscores the continuing influence of the "natural rights" approach adopted by Justice Chase in *Calder v. Bull*. Whereas Marshall at least recognized the appropriateness of applying constitutional provisions to protect contractual obligations, Justice William Johnson, in a concurring opinion, opted for the "natural justice" approach exclusively:

> I do not hesitate to declare that a state does not possess the power of revoking its own grants. But I do it on a general principle on the reason and nature of things, a principle which will impose laws even on the deity. . . .

The *Dartmouth College* Case

Fletcher v. Peck greatly broadened the scope and potential application of the Contract Clause. But the Court's decision nine years later in *Dartmouth College v. Woodward* (1819) had far greater influence on economic development in the nineteenth-century United States. The Court held in essence that a corporate charter was a contract, the terms of which could not be changed materially by the state without violating the Constitution. The charter in question had been issued in 1769 by the British crown for the creation of Dartmouth College. This corporate charter authorized a self-perpetuating twelve-member board of trustees to govern the college. With the American Revolution, the state of New Hampshire succeeded to the rights and obligations of the crown provided by the charter. The college soon became embroiled in state politics, leading to an attempt in 1816 to convert it from a private institution into a state university. This objective was to be accomplished by placing the college under a board of overseers appointed by the governor pursuant to state legislation. The ousted trustees sued to recover the charter, seal, and records of the college and in this way directly challenged the authority of New Hampshire to enact the legislation. Again speaking for the Court, Chief Justice Marshall determined that the charter was a valid contract and that the legislature's attempt to modify the governing structure of the college violated Article I, Section 10 of the Constitution. No specific language in the original charter required this rigid limitation on the state's power to amend it almost half a century after it was granted by King George III and at a time when none of the original parties to the contract remained on the scene. Nevertheless, Marshall found that the challenged legislation violated the spirit if not the letter of the Contract Clause. Marshall indicated that any ambiguity in the charter should be construed in favor of "the adventurers" and against the state.

Although Dartmouth College was created as a charitable educational institution, the broad principle that Marshall enunciated in this case was soon applied to profit-seeking corporations. The *Dartmouth College* decision came at a time when business corporations in such fields as insurance, canal building, and road construction were beginning to proliferate. These companies and their financial backers were tangibly aided by an interpretation of the Contract Clause that gave corporate charters firm constitutional protection.

The Marshall Court also interpreted the Contract Clause as a protection of creditor interests against some forms of state regulation. In the same year that it decided the *Dartmouth College* case, the Court, in *Sturges v. Crowninshield* (1819), struck down a New York bankruptcy law under which debtors could obtain relief from financial obligations previously incurred. Speaking through Marshall once again, the Court found that this measure amounted to an impairment of the obligation of contracts. Marshall himself went so far as to assert, eight years later, that the Contract Clause barred state bankruptcy laws that applied to debts incurred *after* their passage. But on this occasion, the legislation was upheld by a majority of his brethren, leaving Marshall to record his only dissenting opinion in a constitutional case (*Ogden v. Saunders*, 1827).

The Contribution of the Taney Court

In spite of the expanded protection of property and business interests through early interpretation of the Contract Clause, the demand for state economic regulation continued to grow. As noted in Chapter 8, the Marshall Court itself began to provide limited recognition to the state police power, and Marshall's successor, Roger B. Taney, significantly extended this recognition. The *Dartmouth College* case logically implied that corporations chartered by the state could conduct their business free of governmental regulation. This laissez-faire approach could not survive for long, even in the preindustrial United States of the early nineteenth century. Counterpressures, reflected in the rise of Jacksonian democracy, were too strong to permit the continuation of such limitations on state regulatory power.

The judicial pendulum began to swing back in the other direction with the Taney Court's 1837 decision in the case of *Charles River Bridge Company v. Warren Bridge Company*. In 1785, the Massachusetts legislature had granted a corporate charter to the Charles River Bridge Company authorizing it to build a privately owned bridge between Boston and Charlestown and to collect tolls from persons using the bridge. This highly profitable arrangement, granted for a period of seventy years, was threatened by the legislature's incorporation of the Warren Bridge Company in 1828 with authorization to build a competing bridge nearby. Within a short time, the Warren Bridge was to become free to the public as a part of the Massachusetts highway system. The Charles River Bridge Company challenged the 1828 act as a violation of the 1785 charter, which allegedly implied "that the legislature would not authorize another bridge, and especially a free one," alongside the original bridge. Rejecting this contention, Chief Justice Taney construed the language of the charter literally. He concluded that no rights were "taken from the public, or given to the corporation, beyond those which the words of the charter, by their natural and proper construction, [purported] to convey." By contrast with Marshall's approach in the *Dartmouth College* case, Taney was unwilling to restrict legislative authority on the basis of implicit contractual rights. The Court's position was effectively summed up in Taney's assertion that "[w]hile the rights of private property are sacredly guarded, we must not forget that the community also have rights, and that the happiness and well-being of every citizen depends on their faithful preservation."

Later Developments

The decline of the Contract Clause as a bulwark of vested rights began with the *Charles River Bridge* case. Some forty years later, in *Stone v. Mississippi* (1880), the Supreme Court refused to extend Contract Clause protection to a chartered lottery company subsequently prohibited from selling lottery tickets in Mississippi. By the late 1880s, the Due Process Clause of the Fourteenth Amendment had supplanted the Contract Clause as a source of constitutional restraint on state regulation of business.

The extent of the demise of the Contract Clause in the twentieth century is well illustrated by the decision in the Minnesota mortgage moratorium case

(*Home Building and Loan Association v. Blaisdell* [1934]). Here, the Court, by a 5-to-4 vote, upheld a state law, passed in 1933 in the depths of the Great Depression, authorizing the postponement of mortgage foreclosures for periods not to extend beyond May 1, 1935. Chief Justice Charles Evans Hughes, writing for the majority, emphasized the qualified nature of the Contract Clause as a limitation on state power. He concluded that "the reservation of the reasonable exercise of the protective power of the state is read into all contracts."

In summary, the Contract Clause figured prominently in the Supreme Court's protection of vested property rights during the early part of the nineteenth century. Although its influence began to be undermined by the expanding doctrine of state police power during the Taney era, the Contract Clause remained a significant weapon in defense of property interests until supplanted by the development of **substantive due process** in the late 1800s. The Supreme Court invoked the Contract Clause in invalidating state legislation in some seventy-five cases prior to 1890. But the Contract Clause has not been a major restraint on state regulatory power for more than a century. Nevertheless, it is not a dead letter and is still occasionally invoked as a constitutional limitation. For example, in 1977, the Court held that a New Jersey statute violated the Contract Clause because it impaired the state's obligation to holdees of bonds issued by the Port Authority of New York and New Jersey (*United States Trust Company v. New Jersey*). Similarly, in *Allied Structural Steel Company v. Spannaus* (1978), the Court invalidated under the Contract Clause Minnesota's attempt to regulate a company's pension fund. Writing for a five-member majority, Justice Stewart observed: "If the Contract Clause is to retain any meaning at all, . . . it must be understood to impose *some* limits on the power of a State to abridge existing contractual relationships. . ." [emphasis in the original].

THE RISE AND FALL OF ECONOMIC DUE PROCESS

State police power continued to develop through the Civil War and Reconstruction, but the protection of property rights, especially in the context of business activity, remained a prime concern of American judges, including members of the U.S. Supreme Court. Due process as a substantive limitation on governmental authority began to emerge in the 1850s, but its potential was not fully realized until some years after adoption of the Fourteenth Amendment. With the exception of the *Dred Scott* case, in which congressional regulation of slavery in the territories was held to deprive slaveowners of property without due process of law (see Chapter 2), the Fifth Amendment Due Process Clause was not invoked, prior to the Civil War, as a substantive limitation on federal authority. This is not surprising, since the national government did not play an active role in the field of economic regulation until very late in the nineteenth century.

Once Congress began to develop a national police power, especially as applied to labor-management relations, the national government encountered serious obstacles as a result of the Supreme Court's expansion of **substantive due process** rights. For example, the Court in *Adair v. United States* (1908) invalidated on Fifth Amendment due process grounds a federal act outlawing yellow-dog contracts, under which persons agreed, as a condition of employment, not to join labor unions. In the meantime, however, substantive due process had emerged as a major limitation on the exercise of the state police power.

The Origins of Substantive Due Process

It is generally agreed that substantive due process as a limitation on *state* economic regulation originated in an 1856 decision of the New York Court of Appeals (the state's highest court). In *Wynehamer v. New York,* that court held that a state criminal statute prohibiting the sale of liquor curtailed the economic liberty of a Buffalo tavern owner who had been prosecuted for violating its provisions. The Court of Appeals held that the state police power could not be used to deprive the tavern owner of his liberty to practice his livelihood, a liberty protected by the due process clause of the New York constitution.

Following adoption of the Fourteenth Amendment, lawyers representing business interests in opposition to growing state regulation began to emphasize substantive due process arguments. These arguments drew heavily on an influential legal treatise entitled *Constitutional Limitations,* written by a Michigan judge, Thomas M. Cooley. First published in 1868, the year in which the Fourteenth Amendment was ratified, Cooley's treatise went through several editions in the late 1800s and had a significant impact on the constitutional jurisprudence of the laissez-faire era.

As noted in previous chapters, substantive due process focuses on the reasonableness of legislation. By contrast with the more familiar procedural aspect, which emphasizes such elements as notice and the right to a fair hearing (in other words, *how* government should operate in relation to the individual), substantive due process stresses *what* government may or may not do.

Beginning in the late 1880s, the Supreme Court used substantive due process, as well as the Commerce Clause, the Tenth Amendment, and related constitutional provisions, to carve out an area of economic individualism that marked the limits of legislative power. State laws that, in the view of a majority of the justices, unreasonably encroached on "liberty of contract," for example, were held invalid as violations of due process of law.

Key Supreme Court Decisions, 1873 to 1963

For a number of years following the adoption of the Fourteenth Amendment, most members of the Supreme Court resisted this economic due process development. Thus, in *The Slaughter-House Cases* (1873), a narrowly divided Court upheld Louisiana's grant of a monopoly in the slaughtering business in and around New Orleans. Although officially designated as "An Act to Protect the Health of the City of New Orleans. . . ," the law was not in any meaningful sense a health measure. Its only apparent effect was to deprive more than a thousand persons of their alleged right to engage in the slaughtering trade. A number of these persons filed suit, maintaining that the state had conferred "odious and exclusive privileges upon a small number of persons at the expense of the great body of the community of New Orleans." In rejecting this contention, the Supreme Court, in an opinion by Justice Samuel F. Miller, narrowly interpreted Fourteenth Amendment

Stephen J. Field: Associate
Justice, 1863–1897

restrictions on state authority. Miller virtually read out of the Fourteenth Amendment the provision that says: "No state shall make or enforce any law which shall abridge the privileges or immunities of citizens of the United States. . . ." This language, he said, extended only to rights held by Americans as citizens of the nation, as distinguished from their rights as state citizens.

In addition to this restrictive view of the Privileges and Immunities Clause, Justice Miller also found no deprivation of rights under the Due Process and Equal Protection Clauses. He identified the central purpose of the Fourteenth Amendment as the protection of the civil rights of former slaves, although he was unwilling to say that no one else was entitled to this protection. In a strong dissenting opinion, Justice Stephen J. Field took issue with Miller's narrow interpretation of the Privileges and Immunities Clause: "The privileges and immunities designated," he maintained, "are those which of right belong to the citizens of all free governments." To this day, however, the Court has not been willing to accept the broader interpretation of the Privileges and Immunities Clause than Miller gave it in *The Slaughter-House Cases.* Such an interpretation, as a number of scholars have suggested, might have enabled the Court to develop a more plausible basis for protecting property rights than that provided by the Due Process Clause.

Of more immediate relevance in light of subsequent developments is the dissenting opinion of Justice Joseph L. Bradley. While agreeing with Field's position regarding the broad protection that should be afforded by the Privileges and Immunities Clause, Bradley went one important step further, by expressing the view that

> a law which prohibits a large class of citizens from adopting a lawful employment previously adopted, does deprive them of liberty as well as property, without due process of law. Their right of choice is a portion of their liberty; their occupation is their property.

Morrison Waite: Chief Justice,
1874–1888

"Business Affected with a Public Interest"

Four years later, the Court again sustained a broad exercise of the state police power, in this instance an act of the Illinois legislature fixing maximum storage rates charged by grain elevators and public warehouses and requiring licenses to operate these facilities. This legislation grew out of the granger movement, in which thousands of farmers sought protection against excessive freight rates charged by railroads and other businesses involved in the distribution of agricultural commodities. Chief Justice Morrison R. Waite, writing for a seven-member majority in *Munn v. Illinois* (1877), sustained the rate regulation under the English common law doctrine of "business affected with a public interest." Like common carriers, innkeepers, and other persons directly serving the public, Waite reasoned, the owners of grain elevators were equally subject to regulation under this standard. Sounding a note that aroused the anger of business leaders, Waite acknowledged that such regulatory power was subject to abuse but admonished that in such instances, "the people must resort to the polls, and not to the courts."

Dissenting in *Munn*, Justice Field contended that the regulation violated due process. He maintained that under our system of government, the legislature lacked power "to fix the price which anyone shall receive for his property of any kind." He also argued that "there is hardly any enterprise or business engaging the attention and labor of any considerable portion of the community in which the public has not an interest in the sense in which that term is used by the Court." This was a prescient observation in view of the Court's rejection, almost half a century later, of the distinction between "private" businesses and those "affected with a public interest" (*Nebbia v. New York* [1934]).

Ironically, once the concept of substantive due process came to be recognized by a court majority as a basis for invalidating economic legislation, the Court began to apply Waite's rationale negatively. For example, regulations of labor-management disputes, theater ticket scalping, and the rates charged by private employment agencies were ruled unconstitutional on the ground that the businesses involved were not "affected with a public interest" (see, e.g., *Charles Wolff Packing Company v. Court of Industrial Relations* [1923]; *Tyson v. Banton* [1927]; and *Ribnik v. McBride* [1928]).

The Court Responds to Growing Corporate Influence

Powerful corporate interests reacted sharply and decisively to the *Munn* decision. In fact, the American Bar Association was organized for the immediate purpose of leading the counterattack. In 1882, former Senator Roscoe Conkling, in an argument before the Supreme Court, unveiled his "conspiracy theory" of the Fourteenth Amendment. Conkling had participated as a member of the joint congressional committee that drafted the Fourteenth Amendment in 1866. Referring selectively to a previously undisclosed journal of committee proceedings, Conkling maintained in essence that those who drafted the amendment intended for the word "person," as used in the Equal Protection and Due Process clauses, to include corporations. Later research established that Conkling's "conspiracy theory" was of dubious validity, if not an outright fraud. But in the 1880s, the theory was eagerly received and widely supported by those who sought to justify the protection of economic rights under the Fourteenth Amendment. In 1886, the Supreme Court announced without discussion that the Equal Protection Clause did apply to corporations (*Santa Clara County v. Southern Pacific Railroad*). This conclusion extended logically to the Due Process Clause as well.

Changes in Supreme Court personnel also influenced the shift toward economic due process. Chief Justice Waite, who had written the majority opinion in the *Munn* case, died in 1888 and was succeeded by Melville W. Fuller. In 1890, David J. Brewer, a nephew of Justice Field, took the seat on the high bench vacated by Justice Stanley Matthews. These and other appointees, drawn largely from the ranks of corporation lawyers, were receptive to the limited government approach implicit in substantive due process. During this period, under the leadership of Chief Justice Fuller, the Court significantly curtailed national authority through a restrictive interpretation of the commerce and taxing powers (see Chapter 5). Theories of economic individualism, especially the "social Darwinist" views of Herbert Spencer and William Graham Sumner, were very much in vogue during the period and obviously had some impact on the justices.

The Court's changing mood was signaled clearly by Justice John Marshall Harlan (the elder) in 1887. Writing for the Court in upholding a Kansas law prohibiting the sale of certain alcoholic beverages, he warned that not all exercises of the state police power would be automatically approved: "The Courts are not bound by mere forms, nor are they to be misled by mere pretenses. They are at liberty—indeed, are under a solemn duty—to look at the substance of things" (*Mugler v. Kansas* [1887]).

Economic Due Process Comes of Age

The first major shift in the Court's position came in 1890 with the decision that a state legislature could not authorize a commission to set railroad rates with finality. Such rate making, the Court concluded, must be subject to judicial review (*Chicago, Milwaukee, & St. Paul Railway Company v. Minnesota*). In 1897, the Court invalidated Louisiana's effort to regulate out-of-state insurance companies transacting business in the state. Writing for the Court, Justice Rufus Peckham found this regulation to be an infringement of the "liberty of contract" protected by the Fourteenth Amendment Due Process Clause (*Allgeyer v. Louisiana* [1897]). ("Liberty of contract," as used by the Court in this and many subsequent due process cases, should not be confused with the Contract Clause of Article I, Section 10, discussed earlier in this chapter.)

Lochner v. New York

Justice Peckham used the same rationale eight years later in what has become the best known case of the early twentieth century: *Lochner v. New York* (1905). In *Lochner,* the Court, dividing 5 to 4, struck down a state law specifying a maximum sixty-hour work week for bakery employees. Seven years earlier, the Court had upheld, as a proper exercise of the police power, an act of the Utah legislature establishing an eight-hour work day for employees in "mines . . . smelters and all other institutions for the reduction or refining of ores or metals. . ." (*Holden v. Hardy* [1898]). The Utah statute was recognized as a reasonable health measure, but the majority in *Lochner* found no such justification for limiting working hours "in the occupation of a baker." "To the common understanding," Peckham opined, "the trade of a baker has never been regarded as an unhealthy one." However, the Court's fundamental objection to the legislation was that it was a "meddlesome interference" with business. The majority gave no consideration to the relative bargaining power of employers and employees in the baking industry. They simply regarded the law as an unjustified infringement on "the right to labor, and with the right of free contract on the part of the individual, either as employer or employee."

Justice Harlan and his celebrated colleague Oliver Wendell Holmes, Jr., filed powerful dissenting opinions in the *Lochner* case. While Harlan pursued a conventional line of analysis, Justice Holmes attacked the majority for reading laissez-faire theory into the Constitution.

> This case is decided upon an economic theory which a large part of the country does not entertain. If it were a question whether I agreed with that theory, I should desire to study it further and long before making up my mind. But I do not conceive that to be my duty, because I strongly believe that my agreement or disagreement has nothing to do with the right of a majority to embody their opinions in law. . . . The Fourteenth Amendment does not enact Mr. Herbert Spencer's *Social Statics.*

Although persuasively written, Holmes's opinion has been criticized for overstating the deference that should be accorded to the will of the popular

During the late Nineteenth and early Twentieth centuries, workers often labored for long hours at low wages under oppressive conditions

majority. As Chapter 11 will demonstrate, Holmes himself was unwilling to go this far when he believed fundamental freedoms, such as those of political expression protected by the First Amendment, were at stake (see, for example, his dissenting opinion in *Gitlow v. New York* [1925]). The majority in *Lochner* apparently viewed freedom of contract as an equally fundamental right.

Although the philosophical perspective underlying the *Lochner* ruling remained influential for a number of years, its practical effect was short-lived. In 1908, the Court upheld an Oregon act limiting the workday to ten hours for women in designated occupational fields (*Muller v. Oregon*). In this case, attorney (later Associate Justice) Louis D. Brandeis submitted a novel brief in support of the legislation, presenting extensive sociological and medical data in support of the state's contention that the limitation of working hours was directly related to the promotion of the health and welfare of women. The **Brandeis brief,** which added a new dimension to constitutional argumentation, underscored the relationship between legal principles and research in the social and biological sciences. Following the *Muller* precedent, the Court in 1917 sustained the constitutionality of a maximum-hours limitation for men as well as women employed in mills and factories (*Bunting v. Oregon*). This decision amounted to the *de facto* overruling of *Lochner,* but the Court did not specifically refer to the latter case.

The Court's willingness to sustain maximum-hours laws did not carry over into other areas of labor legislation. As previously noted, a federal anti-yellow-dog contract provision was invalidated in 1908 as a violation of the Due Process Clause of the Fifth Amendment (*Adair v. United States*). Seven years later, in *Coppage v. Kansas* (1915), the Court voided a similar state provision as a violation of the freedom of contract protected by the Fourteenth Amendment. In these cases, a Court majority blithely ignored the blatant inequality in the bargaining positions of individual nonunion employees and corporate employers. Reflecting the continuing influence of the natural rights tradition, Justice Mahlon Pitney concluded for a six-member majority:

> Since it is self-evident that, unless all things are held in common, some persons must have more property than others, it is from the nature of things impossible to uphold freedom of contract and the right of private property without at the same time recognizing as legitimate those inequalities of fortune that are the necessary result of the exercise of those rights.

In the Court's view, it was unreasonable for the legislature to interfere with the "natural order" of inequalities, no matter how great the resulting disparities between employer and employee.

Wages proved to be as invulnerable to legislative regulation as yellow-dog contracts. Thus, in 1923 a divided Court struck down a congressional measure authorizing the setting of minimum wages for women and minors employed in the District of Columbia (*Adkins v. Children's Hospital*). The stated purposes of the minimum wage were to provide women with " 'the necessary cost of living,' . . . to maintain them in good health and to protect their morals." As in *Lochner,* the government's perceived interference with liberty of contract was held to violate due process—in this instance, the Fifth Amendment's restriction on federal authority. Writing for the majority, Justice George Sutherland noted that the law was demeaning to women, especially in light of the drive toward political equality that had resulted, shortly before this decision, in ratification of the Nineteenth Amendment, which removed sex as a qualification for voting. But the real object of Sutherland's concern is unmistakably apparent from the following excerpt from his majority opinion:

> The law takes account of the necessities of only one party to the contract. It ignores the necessities of the employer by compelling him to pay not less than a certain sum, not only whether the employee is capable of earning it, but irrespective of the ability of his business to sustain the burden, generously leaving him, of course, the privilege of abandoning his business as an alternative of going on at a loss. . . .

During the 1920s, Chief Justice William Howard Taft often supported the Court's limitation of regulatory authority by way of substantive due process (see, for example, his majority opinion in *Charles Wolff Packing Company v. Court of Industrial Relations* [1923]). However, Taft dissented in the *Adkins* case. In an opinion supported by Justice Edward T. Sanford, Taft expressed his belief that because no meaningful distinction could be drawn between minimum-wage and maximum-hours legislation and since the latter had been upheld in the *Muller* and *Bunting* cases, the Washington, D.C., minimum wage should be sustained. This view was further supported, he maintained, by the fact that the law upheld in *Bunting* contained a time-and-a-half provision for overtime pay. He emphasized, moreover, that "it is not the function of this Court to hold congressional acts invalid simply because they are passed to carry out economic views which the Court believes to be unwise or unsound."

Justice Holmes wrote a separate dissenting opinion, asserting that the power of Congress to enact minimum-wage legislation seemed "absolutely free from doubt." Holmes criticized sharply the Court's development of what he called the "dogma" of liberty of contract. The word *contract,* he pointed out, is not mentioned in the Due Process Clause. Holmes viewed contract merely as "an example of doing what you want to do, embodied in the word liberty. But pretty much all law," he added, "consists in forbidding men to do some things that they want to do, and contract is no more exempt from law than other acts."

Substantive due process as a restriction on economic legislation continued to flourish through the 1920s and into the 1930s. It was an integral part of the Supreme Court's intellectual defense of business interests in general. This judicial philosophy also produced a number of rulings limiting the application of the antitrust acts as restrictions on corporate behavior while extending these restrictions to such labor practices as strikes and secondary boycotts (see, for example, *Loewe v. Lawlor* [1908]; *Duplex Printing Company v. Deering* [1921]; and *Bedford Cut Stone Company v. Journeymen Stone Cutters' Association* [1927]). The Court strongly resisted efforts during this period to restrict child labor, as well as to regulate agricultural and industrial production. Apparently economic liberties, although not officially designated as "preferred freedoms," were accorded paramount importance and often prevailed over countervailing demands for socioeconomic regulation.

Patterns of Supreme Court decision making, especially in complex areas of constitutional law, often do not follow unwavering lines of analytical precision or logical consistency. As we have noted, during the period marked by such decisions as *Lochner* and *Adkins,* the Court did not always invalidate challenged regulatory legislation. The Court still adhered (officially, at least) to the principle of the presumptive validity of legislation, and as a result, many regulatory measures were upheld during the heyday of economic due process. Nevertheless, enough state and federal measures were invalidated to retard serious efforts at economic and social reform.

The Decline of Economic Due Process

The Great Depression of the 1930s, with its crippling effect on employment, industrial production, and the economic well-being of millions of people, forced the Supreme Court to rethink its constitutional commitment to limited government in the field of economic policy. It did so in a variety of issue areas between the mid-1930s and the early 1940s. With this reappraisal came the Court's repudiation of substantive due process as a restriction on the regulation of business.

This fundamental change in the Court's posture was signaled by two key decisions in 1934. As previously indicated, in that year, the Court upheld the Minnesota Mortgage Moratorium Act, finding that its provisions did not violate the Contract Clause (*Home Building and Loan Association v. Blaisdell*). Although this decision did not turn on the meaning of due process, its implications for the Court's interpretation of "liberty of contract" under the Fifth and Fourteenth Amendments were unmistakable.

The due process issue was confronted directly in *Nebbia v. New York* (1934), in which the Court upheld by a 5-to-4 margin the power of a state to regulate the

A Depression-era
soup line

retail price of milk. Concluding that this price regulation did not violate due process, Justice Owen J. Roberts emphasized the breadth of legislative power in relation to economic matters: "It is clear that there is no closed class or category of businesses affected with a public interest." Since the *Munn* case, the Court had gradually narrowed the category of businesses thus "affected" and had established a substantial constitutional barrier against state regulation in a number of areas. In fact, during the decade or so immediately prior to the *Nebbia* decision, very few businesses other than public utilities and places of public accommodation were subject to price control with full judicial approval. Consequently, the Court's obliteration of the category of "business affected with a public interest" represented a significant turning point in constitutional development. In effect, the Court was saying in *Nebbia* that all businesses, irrespective of their supposed relationship to the public interest, are subject to regulation.

This stern repudiation of judicial activism in the field of economic liberties drew a scathing dissent from Justice James C. McReynolds, supported by Justices Willis Van Devanter, George Sutherland, and Pierce Butler. The fixing of retail prices as a means of stabilizing production was, in McReynolds's view, "not regulation, but management, control, dictation," amounting to "deprivation of the fundamental right which one has to conduct his own affairs honestly and along customary lines." He strongly suggested that the Court's decision amounted to a declaration that "rights guaranteed by the Constitution exist only so long as supposed public interest does not require their extinction." McReynolds asserted that adoption of this view "would put an end to liberty under the Constitution."

The "end to liberty" feared by Justice McReynolds was postponed in the field of economic rights for another three years. In fact, in 1936, the Court reaffirmed its controversial *Adkins* ruling by striking down a New York minimum-wage law for women (*Morehead v. New York ex rel. Tipaldo*). In this decision, the majority simply reiterated the "liberty of contract" rationale, but the decision was given added significance because it coincided with the Court's invalidation of major New Deal legislation (see, for example, *United States v. Butler* [1936]; *Carter v. Carter Coal Company* [1936], discussed and reprinted in Chapter 5). In seeking Supreme Court review of a New York Court of Appeals decision invalidating this minimum-wage statute, attorneys failed to ask specifically for reconsideration of the *Adkins* precedent. Rather, they sought to distinguish the New York minimum-wage law from the congressional act invalidated in *Adkins.* Writing for a five-member majority, Justice Butler seized on this omission and considered only the question of whether the two cases were distinguishable. He found that they were not and thus struck down the New York law.

In dissenting opinions, Chief Justice Charles Evans Hughes and Justice Harlan Fiske Stone (supported by Justices Brandeis and Benjamin Cardozo) maintained that the two laws were, in fact, distinguishable. More significantly, however, they criticized the Court for its refusal to reconsider the validity of *Adkins,* especially in light of the country's experience during the Great Depression. Justice Stone chastised his colleagues in the majority for reading their own economic views into the Constitution.

> It is not for the courts to resolve doubts whether the remedy by wage regulation is as efficacious as many believe, or is better than some other, or is better even than the blind operation of uncontrolled economic forces. The legislature must be free to choose unless government is to be rendered impotent. The Fourteenth Amendment has no more embedded in the Constitution our preference for some particular set of economic beliefs, than it has adopted, in the name of liberty, the system of theology which we may happen to approve.

Ten months later, the Supreme Court, again by a 5-to-4 vote (Justice Roberts having changed sides), dramatically overruled the *Adkins* and *Tipaldo* decisions in *West Coast Hotel Company v. Parrish* (1937). Although the votes of the justices had occurred in conference several weeks before President Franklin Roosevelt unveiled his controversial Court-packing plan on February 5, 1937, most political observers and the public in general regarded the *Parrish* decision, announced on March 29, as a clear indication that the Court had caved in to pressure from a popular presidential administration. Justice Roberts later claimed he had voted with the majority in *Tipaldo* simply because he believed that the only question presented in that case was whether the New York minimum-wage law could be distinguished from the provision struck down in *Adkins.* Whatever the true motivations of Justice Roberts, his change of position in this and several other major constitutional decisions in the spring of 1937 figured prominently in the constitutional revolution that to this day marks the single most important transition in Supreme Court history.

In *West Coast Hotel Company v. Parrish,* the Court considered the constitutionality of a Washington state minimum-wage law enacted in 1913. Chief

Justice Hughes delivered the majority opinion. He noted that in upholding the minimum wage, the Washington Supreme Court had "refused to regard the decision in the *Adkins* case as determinative." Such a ruling, Hughes declared, "demands on our part a reexamination" of the *Adkins* case. This reexamination began with the dismantling of the "freedom of contract" theory on which *Adkins* was based. Hughes pointed out that this freedom is not absolute. Moreover, "the liberty safeguarded is liberty in a social organization which requires the protection of law against the evils which menace the health, safety, morals, and welfare of the people." Thus, constitutional liberty is "necessarily subject to the restraints of due process, and regulation which is reasonable in relation to its subject and is adopted in the interests of the community is due process."

Hughes enumerated a wide array of state laws in the field of employer-employee relations previously upheld by the Supreme Court. Then, after quoting approvingly from the dissenting opinions of Chief Justice Taft and Justice Holmes in *Adkins,* he branded that decision as "a departure from the true application of the principles governing the regulation by the state of the relation of employer and employed."

In further support of the formal overruling of *Adkins* and in repudiation of the philosophy it represented, Hughes took **judicial notice** of "the unparalleled demands for relief" arising during the Great Depression and still very much in evidence at the time of this decision. Interestingly, no "Brandeis brief" had been filed in the *Parrish* case, primarily because this approach had failed in the *Tipaldo* case the previous year. Acknowledging the absence in the record of statistical data establishing the need for minimum-wage legislation, Hughes nevertheless had no doubt, based on "common knowledge," that the state of Washington had "encountered the same social problem . . . present elsewhere." The state, he concluded, was free to correct the abusive practices of "unconscionable employers" who selfishly disregard the public interest.

West Coast Hotel Company v. Parrish marked the end of an era in American constitutional law. Although the fact might not have been fully recognized at the time, substantive due process as a limitation on governmental power in the field of economic regulation was dead. Justice Sutherland, the author of the *Adkins* majority opinion, sounded a defensive, subdued note in a dissenting opinion. For him, the Constitution had a fixed meaning that did not change "with the ebb and flow of economic events." He attempted, with little success, to distinguish between the "judicial function" of constitutional interpretation and "the power of amendment under the guise of interpretation." "To miss the point of difference between the two," he said, "is to miss all that the phrase 'supreme law of the land' stands for and to convert what was intended as inescapable and enduring mandates into mere moral reflections." That was precisely what the critics of the *Lochner-Adkins-Tipaldo* approach charged that the Court had been doing. But Sutherland insisted that

> [i]f the Constitution, intelligently and reasonably construed in the light of these principles, stands in the way of desirable legislation, the blame must rest upon that instrument, and not upon the Court for enforcing it according to its terms.

Obviously, enforcing the Constitution "according to its terms" was precisely what Hughes and his colleagues in the majority believed they were doing. The terms of the Constitution in such phrases as "due process of law" are anything but clear and self-defining. And when justices of the Supreme Court speak dogmatically as though such terms are susceptible of only one interpretation, as Sutherland did in his *Parrish* dissent and as others have done in various contexts, they compromise the intellectual integrity of the Court.

Personnel changes, beginning only a few months after announcement of the *Parrish* decision, soon resulted in the replacement of all four dissenting justices in that case. The newly constituted "Roosevelt Court" continued the trend begun in *Parrish* and in other 1937 decisions upholding far-reaching economic and social legislation (see, for example, *National Labor Relations Board v. Jones & Laughlin Steel Corporation; Chas. C. Steward Machine Company v. Davis,* discussed and reprinted in Chapter 5). In 1939, the Court upheld the second Agricultural Adjustment Act (*Mulford v. Smith*), and in 1941, it sustained sweeping federal regulatory power in the areas of employer-employee relations by sustaining the Fair Labor Standards Act (*United States v. Darby,* reprinted in Chapter 8). The constitutional revolution begun by the *Parrish* case in 1937 thus applied directly not only to due process interpretation but also to other key provisions of the Constitution, including the Commerce Clause, the taxing and spending power, and the Tenth Amendment.

For more than half a century, no significant state or federal regulation of business or labor-management relations has been struck down on due process grounds. The 1963 decision in *Ferguson v. Skrupa* is representative of the modern approach in this area. Here, the Supreme Court, in an opinion by Justice Hugo Black, upheld the validity of a Kansas statute conferring a virtual monopoly on the legal profession to engage in the business of "debt adjusting." Black noted that the doctrine prevailing in the *Lochner-Coppage-Adkins* line of cases authorizing courts to invalidate laws because of a belief that the legislature acted unwisely "has long since been discarded." The Court, he continued, had "returned to the original constitutional proposition that courts do not substitute their social and economic beliefs for the judgment of legislative bodies, who are elected to pass laws." Once again, we see how the "original" meaning of the Constitution can mean diametrically opposing things to various Supreme Court justices. In any event, for Justice Black, objections to the law on grounds of social utility should be addressed to the legislature, not the courts. "Whether the legislature takes for its textbook Adam Smith, Herbert Spencer, Lord Keynes, or some other," Black concluded, "is no concern of ours." He also found no violation of the Equal Protection Clause of the Fourteenth Amendment in the legislative decision to provide lawyers a monopoly in the field of debt adjusting.

EQUAL PROTECTION AND ECONOMIC REGULATION

This discussion has not emphasized the role of the Equal Protection Clause of the Fourteenth Amendment in the area of economic regulation. It should be noted, however, that during the heyday of economic due process, the Court occasionally read similar protections into this related provision of Section 1 of the Fourteenth Amendment. For example, in *Yick Wo v. Hopkins* (1886), the Court invalidated a San Francisco ordinance requiring owners of laundries housed in wooden buildings to obtain permission from the Board of Supervisors to continue operation of their businesses. The Court found that the ordinance was being administered to the serious detriment of Chinese immigrants. While all of the affected Chinese laundry owners were denied licenses by the Board of Supervisors, nearly all non-Chinese applicants were granted licenses. Writing for the Court, Justice Stanley Matthews observed: "No reason whatever, except the will of the Supervisors, is assigned why they [the Chinese laundry owners] should not be permitted to carry on, in the accustomed manner, their harmless and useful occupation, on which they depend for a livelihood." Similarly, in 1915, the Court struck down an Arizona law requiring that a minimum of 80 percent of any company's work force had to consist of American citizens (*Truax v. Raich*). In these cases, the Court was especially concerned with the adverse impact of discriminatory legislation on the conduct of business.

Equal protection, like due process, disappeared as an important limitation on state economic regulatory power after the mid-1930s. It was used, however, in the late 1950s, to strike down a provision of an Illinois law exempting the American Express Company from the requirement that any firm selling or issuing money orders in the state obtain a license and submit to state regulation (*Morey v. Doud* [1957]). The effect of the discrimination here was not reasonably related to the underlying regulatory purpose of the statute. This ruling is an isolated exception to the modern Court's unwillingness to invalidate economic regulation on Fourteenth Amendment grounds.

PROPERTY RIGHTS AND THE "TAKINGS" ISSUE

The final provision of the Fifth Amendment states: "nor shall private property be taken for public use without just compensation." In *Barron v. Baltimore* (1833), the Supreme Court held that the Just Compensation Clause, like the other provisions of the Bill of Rights, was applicable only to the acts and policies of the national government. However, in 1897, this clause became the first provision of the Bill of Rights to be "incorporated" into the Fourteenth Amendment and thus made applicable to the states (*Chicago, Burlington, & Quincy Railroad v. Chicago*). (For further discussion of the incorporation issue and these important cases, see Chapter 9.) The salient legal questions raised by the Just Compensation Clause are: (1) What constitutes a "taking" of private property?; (2) What constitutes a "public use"?; and (3) What constitutes "just compensation"?

Although the "takings" concept has sometimes been interpreted literally to refer only to a physical appropriation of private property by the government, there are circumstances in which a regulation may be so severe as to constitute a taking. The basic problem is to determine the point at which a regulation goes beyond the legitimate scope of the police power and becomes an exercise of the power of **eminent domain.** The dominant view is that the distinction between a valid regulation and the taking of property is one of degree. Justice Holmes stated this rule in the 1922 case of *Pennsylvania Coal Company v. Mahon.* Under a duly executed deed, the coal company claimed rights to mine coal under the land on which Mahon's dwelling was located. Mahon claimed, however, that irrespective of the deed, these rights were superseded by a Pennsylvania statute preventing the mining of coal in such a way as to cause the subsidence of specified types of improved land, including that on which his house was located. The issue was whether this exercise of the state's police power amounted to a "taking" of the coal company's property without just compensation. Writing for the Court, Holmes concluded that it did, and that the company was entitled to compensation. "The general rule," he declared, "is that while property may be regulated to a certain extent, if regulation goes too far it will be recognized as a taking."

Although the general concept remains valid, the value of the *Mahon* case as a precedent has been substantially diminished by the Supreme Court's decision in *Keystone Bituminous Coal Association v. DeBenedictis* (1987). Dividing 5 to 4, the Court held that a more recent Pennsylvania law designed to prevent subsidence damage from coal mining did not on its face violate either the Takings Clause or the Contract Clause.

As the *Keystone* case suggests, the modern Court tends to give a narrow interpretation to the rights protected by the Takings Clause. Thus, in *Hawaii Housing Authority v. Midkiff* (1984), the Court ruled unanimously that the state of Hawaii had not violated the Public Use Clause by adopting a policy for the redistribution of land as a means of reducing the high concentration of ownership by a small number of individuals. After extensive hearings, the legislature had discovered in the mid-1960s that, whereas the state and federal governments owned almost 49 percent of the land in Hawaii, 47 percent of the total was in the hands of seventy-two private landowners. On the heavily populated island of Oahu, twenty-two landowners held 72.5 percent of the **fee simple** titles. The legislature concluded that such concentrated land ownership was responsible for skewing the state's real estate market in the area of home ownership, that it inflated land prices, and that it was detrimental to the public welfare.

Writing for the Supreme Court, Justice Sandra Day O'Connor found ample precedent for the exercise of such regulatory power. O'Connor acknowledged that there had to be a legitimate public purpose for taking land, even where, as here, compensation was provided. "But where the exercise of the eminent domain power is rationally related to a conceivable public purpose, the Court has never held a compensated taking to be proscribed by the Public Use Clause." O'Connor concluded that on this basis, the Hawaii land reform policy was clearly constitutional. The regulation of oligopoly and "the evils associated with it is a classic exercise of a state's police powers." The Court would inquire only as to the rationality of the act, not its wisdom or desirability as public policy. O'Connor concluded that the legislature passed this act "not to benefit a particular class of identifiable individuals, but to attack certain perceived evils of concentrated property ownership in Hawaii—a legitimate public purpose."

The Takings Issue under the Rehnquist Court

During the 1986–1987 term, the Rehnquist Court showed renewed interest in the Takings Clause as a basis for protecting property rights. In *First English*

Evangelical Lutheran Church v. County of Los Angeles (1987), the Court reviewed an ordinance that prohibited the reconstruction of privately owned buildings destroyed by a flood. The prohibition applied to a parcel of land owned by the Evangelical Lutheran Church, which filed a lawsuit seeking compensation for the loss it would sustain in not being able to continue to use its land as a camp- ground. Dividing 6 to 3, the Court found that the ordinance at issue "denied appellant all use of its property for a considerable period of years" and held that "invalidation of the ordinance without payment of fair value for the use of the property during this period of time would be a constitutionally insufficient remedy."

In another California case, the Supreme Court considered a state agency ruling that required owners of beachfront property to grant an **easement** to allow public beach access as a condition for obtaining a building permit. In *Nollan v. California Coastal Commission* (1987), the Court struck down this requirement by a 5-to-4 vote. Speaking through Justice Antonin Scalia, the Court said that the state's justification for the law was

> simply an expression of the . . . [state's] belief that the public interest will be served by a continuous strip of publicly accessible beach along the coast. The [Coastal] Commission may well be right that it is a good idea, but that does not establish that the Nollans (and other coastal residents) alone can be compelled to contribute to its realization. Rather, California is free to advance its 'comprehensive program,' if it wishes, by using its power of eminent domain. . . , but if it wants an easement across the Nollans' property, it must pay for it.

In a bitter dissent, Justice William Brennan castigated the Court's "narrow view" of the case, saying that its "reasoning is hardly suited to the complex reality of natural resource protection in the 20th century." Brennan concluded by expressing hope "that today's decision is an aberration, and that a broader vision ultimately prevails."

The decisions in *First English Evangelical Lutheran Church* and *Nollan* suggested that the Supreme Court was not as thoroughly committed to judicial restraint in the takings area as had been implied by its 1984 decision in the Hawaii land reform case. The 1987 takings decisions were warmly welcomed by advocates of renewed judicial protection for property rights. On the other hand, these decisions were severely criticized by environmentalists and others who believed in regulation of private property for the general welfare.

Several decisions handed down between 1988 and 1990 suggest that the Rehnquist Court is not committed to a wholesale rejuvenation of private property rights, however. In *Pennell v. City of San Jose* (1988), the Court rejected a challenge to a local rent control ordinance. In *Duquesne Light Co. v. Barasch* (1989), the Court upheld a state law forbidding utilities from passing along to consumers costs associated with abandoned nuclear reactors. The Court rejected a utility's claim that the restriction amounted to an uncompensated taking of property. Finally, in *Preseault v. Interstate Commerce Commission* (1990), the Court sustained an ICC ruling on the transfer of a railroad right-of-way and said that the Fifth Amendment did not demand that compensation be paid prior to or simultaneously with a government taking of private property.

Antonin Scalia: Associate
Justice, 1986–

On the other hand, the Court in 1992 indicated a willingness to scrutinize the standards that state courts apply in determining whether a regulation constitutes a "taking" under the Fifth Amendment (see *Lucas* v. *South Carolina Coastal Council*). Thus the Rehnquist Court appears inclined to seek a balance between public and private interests in this area.

PROPERTY RIGHTS AND FREE EXPRESSION

The decision in *PruneYard Shopping Center v. Robins* (1980) illustrates how property rights may overlap with the freedom of expression and how, in such instances, the modern Court is likely to strike a balance in favor of the latter. Our discussion of this case leads logically into the examination of freedom of expression in Chapter 11.

The privately owned PruneYard Shopping Center in Campbell, California, had a policy prohibiting on its premises all "expressive activity" not directly related to its commercial purposes. In accordance with this policy, the shopping center had excluded several high school students who were seeking signatures for a petition opposing a United Nations resolution against Zionism. The California Supreme Court interpreted a state constitutional provision as granting the students a right to engage in this activity on the shopping center's property. In an opinion by Justice Rehnquist, the U.S. Supreme Court rejected the shopping center owner's allegations that his federally protected property rights and freedom of speech had been violated. The Court found no violation of the constitutional guarantee against the taking of private property without just compensation. Although Rehnquist recognized that "one of the essential sticks in the bundle of property rights is the right to exclude others," he found "nothing to suggest that preventing [the shopping center] from prohibiting this activity will unreasonably impair the value or use of [the] property as a shopping center." The students were orderly and had limited their activities to the "common area" of the shopping center. PruneYard had failed to show that its "right to exclude others" was "so essential to the use or economic value of [its] property that the state-authorized limitation of it amounted to a 'taking.' " In addition, Rehnquist found that the state constitutional provision granting the right of access satisfied the test of rationality established in such cases as *Nebbia v. New York* (1934). Moreover, the state could reasonably conclude that recognizing a right of access furthered its "asserted interest in promoting more expansive rights of free speech and petition than [those] conferred by the Federal Constitution." This opinion, written by one of the most conservative justices, underscores the extent to which the modern Court defers to state policies limiting economic freedom.

CONCLUSION

For almost a century and a half, the U.S. Supreme Court extended significant constitutional protection to property rights and economic freedom. The balance between these rights and the exercise of the police power shifted to some extent from period to period. The Marshall Court, primarily through the Contract Clause, erected major safeguards for "vested rights." Coincident with the subsequent rise of Jacksonian democracy, these rights began to give way to the state police power. This trend continued from the beginning of the Taney era in the late 1830s into the 1880s. With significant personnel changes on the Court and the rising influence of corporate business interests, the Court began to interpret various provisions of the Constitution, particularly the Due Process Clauses of the Fifth and Fourteenth Amendments, as substantive limitations on economic legislation. This orientation, with its emphasis on "liberty of contract," became more pronounced around the turn of the century and, despite growing criticism from dissenting justices and legal commentators, continued as a powerful influence on constitutional interpretation until the Supreme Court's confrontation with the Great Depression and the New Deal.

Because private property and free enterprise are deeply ingrained cultural values, there is little need for heightened judicial protection of these institutions. Nevertheless, it should be recognized that American judges at all levels continue to accord great weight to the protection of private property and contractual rights. Congress, the state legislatures, and local governments are unlikely to enact measures that seriously undermine economic freedom. At the same time, substantial political support exists for economic policy measures that regulate the economy "around the margins." A strong consensus exists in support of public policy designed to foster competition, reduce inequalities, stabilize the business cycle, and protect the environment, the consumer, and the worker. Facing a political consensus, the modern Supreme Court has generally acceded to these departures from laissez-faire capitalism.

During the 1980s, conservative theorists displeased with the policies of the modern regulatory state, most notably Bernard Seigan and Richard Epstein, urged the Supreme Court to resurrect its former commitment to private property and private enterprise. As yet, there is little evidence that the Court is interested in moving very far in that direction. For now, battles over government regulation of the economy appear to be more in the province of the constitutional historian than the constitutional lawyer. Of course, given the vicissitudes of American constitutional politics, nothing in the law should be considered settled once and for all.

The Modern Concern for Noneconomic Rights

As the last vestiges of laissez-faire disappeared from the Court's majority opinions, the justices began to give significantly greater attention to the protection of cultural and political freedoms, especially as exercised by members of racial and religious minorities outside the mainstream of American life. Consistent with this reorientation, the Court also began to recognize broader constitutional safeguards for persons accused of crime.

In greater or lesser degree, the Court has continued to emphasize individual rights largely outside the economic sphere. Some observers have criticized the Court for having withdrawn so completely from the defense of property interests, but even the Court's most conservative members seem disinclined to reassert the laissez-faire-oriented judicial activism of the 1920s. Of course, the Supreme Court cannot successfully pursue a course of constitutional interpretation far removed from the prevailing national political consensus. At the same time, the Court should not be expected to relinquish its position of coequality as a branch of the national government. During the past half-century, it has found ample opportunity to shape constitutional interpretation in many areas directly affecting the lives of the American people. The remaining chapters of this book will examine the Court's performance in the most important of these areas.

FOR FURTHER READING

Abraham, Henry J. *The Judiciary,* 7th ed. Boston: Allyn and Bacon, 1987.

Ackerman, Bruce. *Private Property and the Constitution.* New Haven: Yale University Press, 1977.

Conant, Michael. *The Constitution and Capitalism.* St. Paul: West, 1974.

Corwin, Edward S. *Liberty Against Government.* Baton Rouge: Louisiana State University Press, 1948.

Dorn, James A., and Henry G. Manne, eds. *Economic Liberties and the Judiciary.* Fairfax, Va.: George Mason University Press, 1987.

Epstein, Richard A. *Takings: Private Property and the Power of Eminent Domain.* Cambridge: Harvard University Press, 1985.

Locke, John. "Second Treatise of Government." *Two Treatises of Government.* Edited by Peter Laslett. New York: Mentor Books, 1960.

Macpherson, C. B., ed. *Property: Mainstream and Critical Positions.* Toronto: University of Toronto Press, 1978.

Madison, James. "Property." *National Gazette* 1, No. 44 (29 March 1792). Reprinted in *Letters and Other Writings of James Madison,* vol 4. Philadelphia: J. B. Lippincott & Co., 1865.

Mendelson, Wallace. *Capitalism, Democracy, and the Supreme Court.* New York: Appleton-Century-Crofts, 1960.

Scalia, Antonin, and Richard A. Epstein. *Scalia v. Epstein: Two Views of Activism.* Washington, D.C.: Cato Institute, 1985.

Seigan, Bernard H. *Economic Liberties and the Constitution.* Chicago: University of Chicago Press, 1980.

Twiss, Benjamin R. *Lawyers and the Constitution.* Princeton, N.J.: Princeton University Press, 1942.

Wright, Benjamin F. *The Contract Clause of the Constitution.* Cambridge: Harvard University Press, 1938.

Ziegler, Benjamin M. *The Supreme Court and American Economic Life.* New York: Row, Peterson, 1962.

C A S E S   A N D   R E A D I N G S

Dartmouth College v. Woodward
4 Wheat. (17 U.S.) 518; 4 L. Ed 629 (1819)
Vote: 5-1

Dartmouth College was originally chartered by King George III in 1769. Under the royal charter, the trustees of the College were "forever" granted the right to govern the institution as they saw fit. However, in 1816, the New Hampshire legislature attempted to take control of the College, believing its royal charter was no longer valid. Naturally, the trustees turned to the courts for protection. Failing in the state judiciary, they appealed to the Supreme Court on a writ of error.

The opinion of the Court was delivered by [**Chief Justice Marshall**].

. . . It can require no argument to prove, that the circumstances of this case constitute a contract. An application is made to the crown for a charter to incorporate a religious and literary institution. In the application, it is stated, that large contributions have been made for the object, which will be conferred on the corporation, as soon as it shall be created. The charter is granted, and on its faith the property is conveyed. Surely, in this transaction every ingredient of a complete and legitimate contract is to be found. The points for consideration are, 1. Is this contract protected by the Constitution of the United States? 2. Is it impaired by the acts under which the defendant holds? . . .

The parties in this case differ less on general principles, less on the true construction of the Constitution in the abstract, than on the application of those principles to this case, and on the true construction of the charter of 1769. This is the point on which the cause essentially depends. If the act of incorporation be a grant of political power, if it create a civil institution, to be employed in the administration of the government, or if the funds of the college be public property, or if the state of New Hampshire, as a government, be alone interested in its transactions, the subject is one in which the legislature of the state may act according to its judgment, unrestrained by

any limitation of its power imposed by the Constitution of the United States.

But if this be a private eleemosynary institution, endowed with a capacity to take property, for objects unconnected with government, whose funds are bestowed by individuals, on the faith of the charter; if the donors have stipulated for the future disposition and management of those funds, in the manner prescribed by themselves; there may be more difficulty in the case, although neither the persons who have made these stipulations, nor those for whose benefit they were made, should be parties to the cause. Those who are no longer interested in the property, may yet retain such an interest in the preservation of their own arrangements, as to have a right to insist, that those arrangements shall be held sacred. Or, if they have themselves disappeared, it becomes a subject of serious and anxious inquiry, whether those whom they have legally empowered to represent them forever, may not assert all the rights which they possessed, while in being; whether, if they be without personal representatives, who may feel injured by a violation of the compact, the trustees be not so completely their representatives, in the eye of the law, as to stand in their place, not only as respects the government of the college, but also as respects the maintenance of the college charter. It becomes then the duty of the court, most seriously to examine this charter, and to ascertain its true character. . . .

A corporation is an artificial being, invisible, intangible, and existing only in contemplation of law. Being the mere creature of law, it possesses only those properties which the charter of its creation confers upon it, either expressly or as incidental to its very existence. These are such as are supposed best calculated to effect the object for which it was created. Among the most important are immortality, and, if the expression may be allowed, individuality; properties by which a perpetual succession of many persons are considered as the same, and may act as a single individual. . . . It is no more a state instrument than a natural person exercising the same powers would be. If, then, a natural person, employed by individuals in the education of youth, or for the government of a seminary in which youth is educated, would not become a public officer, or be considered as a member of the civil government, how is it that this artificial being, created by law for the purpose of being employed by the same individuals for the same purposes, should become a part of the civil government of the country? Is it because its existence, its capacities, its powers, are given by law? Because the government has given it the power to take and hold property in a particular form and for particular purposes, has the government a consequent right substantially to change that form, or to vary the purposes to which the property is to be applied? The principle has never been asserted or recognized, and is supported by no authority. Can it derive aid from reason?

The objects for which a corporation is created are universally such as the government wishes to promote. . . . The benefit to the public is considered as an ample compensation for the faculty it confers, and the corporation is created. If the advantages to the public constitute a full compensation for the faculty it gives, there can be no reason for exacting a further compensation, by claiming a right to exercise over this artificial being a power which changes its nature, and touches the fund for the security and application of which it was created. There can be no reason for implying a charter, given for a valuable consideration, a power which is not only not expressed, but is in direct contradiction to its express stipulations.

From the fact, then, that a charter of incorporation has been granted, nothing can be inferred which changes the character of the institution, or transfers to the government any new power over it. The character of civil institutions does not grow out of their incorporation, but out of the manner in which they are formed, and the objects for which they are created. The right to change them is not founded on their being incorporated, but on their being the instruments of government, created for its purpose. The same institutions, created for the same objects, though not incorporated, would be public institu-

tions, and, of course, be controllable by the legislature. The incorporating act neither gives nor prevents this control. Neither, in reason, can the incorporating act change the character of a private eleemosynary institution. . . .

From this review of the charter, it appears that Dartmouth College is an eleemosynary institution, incorporated for the purpose of perpetuating the application of the bounty of the donors to the specified objects of that bounty; that its trustees or governors were originally named by the founder, and invested with the power of perpetuating themselves; that they are not public officers, nor is it a civil institution, participating in the administration of government; but a charity school, or a seminary of education, incorporated for the preservation of its property, and the perpetual application of that property to the objects of its creation.

Yet a question remains to be considered of more real difficulty, on which more doubt has been entertained than on all that have been discussed. The founders of the college, at least those whose contributions were in money, have parted with the property bestowed upon it, and their representatives have no interest in that property. The donors of land are equally without interest so long as the corporation shall exist. Could they be found, they are unaffected by any alteration in its constitution, and probably regardless of its form or even of its existence. The students are fluctuating, and no individual among our youth has a vested interest in the institution which can be asserted in a court of justice. Neither the founders of the college, nor the youth for whose benefit it was founded, complain of the alteration made in its charter, or think themselves injured by it. The trustees alone complain, and the trustees have no beneficial interest to be protected. Can this be such a contract as the constitution intended to withdraw from the power of state legislation? Contracts, the parties to which have a vested beneficial interest, and those only, it has been said, are the objects about which the Constitution is solicitous, and to which its protection is extended.

The Court has bestowed on this argument the most deliberate consideration, and the result will be stated. Dr. Wheelock, acting for himself and for those who, at his solicitation, had made contributions to his school, applied for this charter, as the instrument which should enable him and them to perpetuate their beneficent intention. It was granted. An artificial, immortal being was created by the crown, capable of receiving and distributing forever, according to the will of the donors, the donations which should be made to it. On this being, the contributions which had been collected were immediately bestowed. These gifts were made, not indeed to make a profit for the donors or their posterity, but for something, in their opinion, of inestimable value; for something which they deemed a full equivalent for the money with which it was purchased. The consideration for which they stipulated, is the perpetual application of the fund to its object, in the mode prescribed by themselves. Their descendants may take no interest in the preservation of this consideration. But in this respect their descendants are not their representatives. They are represented by the corporation. The corporation is the assignee of their rights, stands in their place, and distributes their bounty, as they would themselves have distributed it had they been immortal. So with respect to the students who are to derive learning from this source. The corporation is a trustee for them also. Their potential rights, which, taken distributively, are imperceptible, amount collectively to a most important interest. These are, in the aggregate, to be exercised, asserted, and protected by the corporation. They were as completely out of the donors, at the instant of their being vested in the corporation, and as incapable of being asserted by the students, as at present. . . .

This is plainly a contract to which the donors, the trustees, and the Crown (to whose rights and obligations New Hampshire succeeds) were the original parties. It is a contract made on a valuable consideration. It is a contract on the faith of which real and personal estate has been conveyed to the corporation. It is then a contract within the letter of the Constitution, and within its spirit also, unless the fact that the property is invested by the donors in trustees, for the promotion of religion and education, for the benefit of persons who are perpetually changing, though the objects remain the same, shall create a particular exception, taking this case out of the prohibition contained in the Constitution.

It is more than possible that the preservation of rights of this description was not particularly in the view of the framers of the Constitution, when the clause under consideration was introduced into that instrument. It is probable that interferences of more frequent recurrence, to which the temptation was stronger, and of which the mischief was more extensive, constituted the great motive for imposing this restriction on the state legislatures. But although a particular and a rare case may not, in itself, be of sufficient magnitude to induce a rule, yet it must be governed by the rule, when established, unless some plain and strong reason for excluding it can be given. It is not enough to say, that this particular case was not in the mind of the Convention when the article was framed, nor of the American people when it was adopted. It is necessary to go further, and to say that, had this particular case been suggested, the language would have been so varied as to exclude it, or it would have been made a special exception. The case being within the words of the rule, must be within its operation likewise, unless there be something in the literal construction so obviously absurd or mischievous, or repugnant to the general spirit of the instrument, as to justify those who expound the Constitution in making it an exception.

On what safe and intelligible ground can this exception stand? There is no expression in the Constitution, no sentiment delivered by its contemporaneous expounders, which would justify us in making it. In the absence of all authority of this kind, is there, in the nature and reason of the case itself, that which would sustain a construction of the Constitution not warranted by its words? Are contracts of this description of a character to excite so little interest that we must exclude them from the provisions of the Constitution, as being unworthy of the attention of those who framed the instrument? Or does public policy so imperiously demand their remaining exposed to legislative alteration as to compel us, or rather permit us to say, that these words, which were introduced to give stability to contracts, and which in their plain import comprehend this contract, must yet be so construed as to exclude it? . . .

If the insignificance of the object does not require that we should exclude contracts respecting it from the protection of the Constitution, neither, as we conceive, is the policy of leaving them subject to legislative alteration so apparent, as to require a forced construction of that instrument, in order to effect it. These eleemosynary institutions do not fill the place, which would otherwise be occupied by government, but that which would otherwise remain vacant. They are complete acquisitions to literature. They are donations to education; donations, which any government must be disposed rather to encourage than to discountenance. It requires no very critical examination of the human mind, to enable us to determine, that one great inducement to these gifts is the conviction felt by the giver, that the disposition he makes of them is immutable. It is probable, that no man was, and that no man ever will be, the founder of a college, believing at the time, than an act of incorporation constitutes no security for the institution; believing, that it is immediately to be deemed a public institution, whose funds are to be governed and applied, not by the will of the donor, but by the will of the legislature. All such gifts are made in the pleasing, perhaps delusive hope, that the charity will flow forever in the channel which the givers have marked out for it. If every man finds in his own bosom strong evidence of the universality of this sentiment, there can be but little reason to imagine, that the framers of our Constitution were strangers to it, and that, feeling the necessity and policy of giving permanence and security to contracts, of withdrawing them from the influence of legislative bodies, whose fluctuating policy and repeated interferences, produced the most perplexing and injurious embarrassments, they still deemed it necessary to leave these contracts subject to those interferences. The motives for such an exception must be very powerful, to justify the construction which makes it. . . .

We next proceed to the inquiry, whether its obligation has been impaired by those acts of the legislature of New Hampshire, to which the special verdict refers? . . .

It has been already stated, that the act "to amend the charter, and enlarge and improve the corporation of Dartmouth College," increases the number of trustees to twenty-one, gives the appointment of the additional members to the executive of the state, and creates a board of overseers, to consist of twenty-five

persons, of whom twenty-one are also appointed by the executive of New Hampshire, who have power to inspect and control the most important acts of the trustees.

On the effect of this law [of 1816], two opinions cannot be entertained. Between acting directly, and acting through the agency of trustees and overseers, no essential difference is perceived. The whole power of governing the college is transferred from trustees appointed according to the will of the founder, expressed in the charter, to the executive of New Hampshire. The management and application of the funds of this eleemosynary institution, which are placed by the donors in the hands of trustees named in the charter, and empowered to perpetuate themselves, are placed by this act under the control of the government of the state. The will of the state is substituted for the will of the donors, in every essential operation of the college. This is not an immaterial change. The founders of the college contracted, not merely for the perpetual application of the funds which they gave, to the objects for which those funds were given; they contracted, also, to secure that application by the Constitution of the corporation. They contracted for a system which should, as far as human foresight can provide, retain forever the government of the literary institution they had formed, in the hands of persons approved by themselves. This system is totally changed. The charter of 1769 exists no longer. It is reorganized; and reorganized in such a manner as to convert a literary institution, moulded according to the will of its founders, and placed under the control of private literary men, into a machine entirely subservient to the will of government. This may be for the advantage of literature in general; but it is not according to the will of the donors, and is subversive of that contract on the faith of which their property was given. . . .

It results from this opinion, that the acts of the legislature of New Hampshire, which are stated in the special verdict found in this cause, are repugnant to the Constitution of the United States; and that the judgment on this special verdict ought to have been for the plaintiffs. The judgment of the State Court must therefore be reversed.

Mr. Justice Duvall dissented.

Charles River Bridge Company v. Warren Bridge Company

11 Pet. (36 U.S.) 420; 9 L. Ed. 773 (1837)
Vote 5-2

This decision was one of the Taney Court's most important contributions to American constitutional development. The case grew out of a dispute involving rival companies in the business of building and operating bridges. The constitutional issue stemmed from the fact both companies were operating under charters granted them by a state legislature. In 1785, the Massachusetts legislature incorporated the Charles River Bridge Company for forty years, for the purpose of building and operating a toll bridge over the River Charles between Boston and Cambridge. In 1792, the legislature extended the term of the charter to seventy years. In 1828, the legislature chartered another company, the Warren Bridge Company, and authorized it to build another bridge three hundred yards from the Charles River Bridge. The Charles River Bridge Company then brought suit, arguing that the legislature had implicitly granted it an exclusive right to operate a bridge in the area throughout the life of its charter. According to the Charles River Bridge Company, the grant of the charter to the Warren Bridge Company was an impairment of the obligation of contracts, forbidden by Article I, Section 10 of the Constitution. The state courts rejected this argument, and the Supreme Court took the case on a writ of error.

Mr. Chief Justice Taney delivered the opinion of the Court.

... This brings us to the act of the legislature of Massachusetts, of 1785, by which the plaintiffs were incorporated by the name of "The Proprietors of the Charles River Bridge"; and it is here, and in the law of 1792, prolonging their charter, that we must look for the extent and nature of the franchise conferred upon the plaintiffs.

Much has been said in the argument of the principles of construction by which this law is to be expounded, and what undertakings, on the part of the state, may be implied. The Court think there can be no serious difficulty on that head. It is the grant of certain franchises by the public to a private corporation, and in a matter where the public interest is concerned. The rule of construction in such cases is well settled, both in England and by the decisions of our own tribunals. ... *** In the case of the *Proprietors of the Stourbridge Canal v. Wheely* and others, the Court say[s], "The canal having been made under an act of Parliament, the rights of the plaintiffs are derived entirely from that act. This, like many other cases, is a bargain between a company of adventurers and the public, the terms of which are expressed in the statute; and the rule of construction, in all such cases, is now fully established to be this; that any ambiguity in the terms of the contract must operate against the adventurers, and in favor of the public, and the plaintiffs can claim nothing that is not clearly given them by the act." And the doctrine thus laid down is abundantly sustained by the authorities referred to in this decision. ...

... The argument in favour of the proprietors of the Charles River bridge, is ... that the power claimed by the state, if it exists, may be so used as to destroy the value of the franchise they have granted to the corporation. ... The existence of the power does not, and cannot depend upon the circumstance of its having been exercised or not.

... [T]he object and end of all government is to promote the happiness and prosperity of the community by which it is established, and it can never be assumed, that the government intended to diminish its power of accomplishing the end for which it was created. And in a country like ours, free, active, and enterprising, continually advancing in numbers and wealth, new channels of communication are daily found necessary, both for travel and trade; and are essential to the comfort, convenience and prosperity of the people. A state ought never to be presumed to surrender this power, because, like the taxing power, the whole community have an interest in preserving it undiminished. And when a corporation alleges that a state has surrendered, for seventy years, its power of improvement and public accommodation, in a great and important line of travel, along which a vast number of its citizens must daily pass, the community have a right to insist, in the language of this court above quoted, "that its abandonment ought not to be presumed in a case in which the deliberate purpose of the state to abandon it does not appear." The continued existence of a government would be of no great value, if by implications and presumptions it was disarmed of the powers necessary to accomplish the ends of its creation, and the functions it was designed to perform, transferred to the hands of privileged corporations. The rule of construction announced by the court was not confined to the taxing power; nor is it so limited in the opinion delivered. On the contrary, it was distinctly placed on the ground that the interests of the community were concerned in preserving, undiminished, the power then in question; and whenever any power of the state is said to be surrendered and diminished, whether it be the taxing power or any other affecting the public interest, the same principle applies, and the rule of construction must be the same. No one will question that the interests of the great body of the people of the state would, in this instance, be affected by the surrender of this great line of travel to a single corporation, with the right to exact toll, and exclude competition for seventy years. While the rights of private property are sacredly guarded, we must not forget that the community also have rights, and that the happiness and well-being of every citizen depends on their faithful preservation.

Adopting the rule of construction above stated as the settled one, we proceed to apply it to the charter of 1785, to the proprietors of the Charles river bridge. This act of incorporation is in the usual form, and the privileges such as are commonly given to corporations of that kind. It confers on them the ordinary faculties of a corporation, for the purpose of building the bridge; and establishes certain rates of toll, which the company are authorized to take. This is the whole grant. There is no exclusive privilege given to them over the waters of Charles River, above or below their bridge; no right to erect another bridge themselves, nor to prevent other persons from erecting one. No engagement from the state, that another shall not be erected; and no undertaking not to sanction competition, nor to make improvements that may diminish the amount of its income. Upon all these subjects, the charter is silent, and nothing is said in it about a line of travel, so

much insisted on in the argument, in which they are to have exclusive privileges. . . .

. . . In short, all the franchises and rights of property, enumerated in the charter, and there mentioned to have been granted to it, remain unimpaired. But its income is destroyed by the Warren bridge; which, being free, draws off the passengers and property which would have gone over it, and renders their franchise of no value. This is the gist of the complaint. For it is not pretended, that the erection of the Warren bridge would have done them any injury, or in any degree affected their right of property, if it had not diminished the amount of their tolls. In order, then, to entitle themselves to relief, it is necessary to show, that the legislature contracted not to do the act of which they complain; and that they impaired, or in other words, violated, that contract by the erection of the Warren bridge.

The inquiry, then, is, does the charter contain such a contract on the part of the state? Is there any such stipulation to be found in that instrument? It must be admitted on all hands, that there is none; no words that even relate to another bridge, or to the [diminution] of their tolls, or to the line of travel. If a contract on that subject can be gathered from the charter, it must be by implication; and cannot be found in the words used. Can such an agreement be implied? The rule of construction before stated is an answer to the question; in charters of this description, no rights are taken from the public, or given to corporation, beyond those which the words of the charter, by their natural and proper construction, purport to convey. There are no words which import such a contract as the plaintiffs in error contend for, and none can be implied. . . .

Indeed, the practice and usage of almost every state in the Union, old enough to have commenced the work of internal improvement, is opposed to the doctrine contended for on the part of the plaintiffs in error. Turnpike roads have been made in succession, on the same line of travel; the later ones interfering materially with the profits of the first. These corporations have, in some instances, been utterly ruined by the introduction of newer and better modes of transportation and travelling. In some cases, railroads have rendered the turnpike roads on the same line of travel so entirely useless, that the franchise of the turnpike corporation is not worth preserving. Yet in none of these cases have the corporations supposed that their privileges were invaded, or any contract violated on the part of the state. Amid the multitude of cases which have occurred, and have been daily occurring for the last forty or fifty years, this is the first instance in which such an implied contract has been contended for, and this court called upon to infer it, from an ordinary act of incorporation, containing nothing more than the usual stipulations and provisions to be found in every such law. The absence of any such controversy, when there must have been so many occasions to give rise to it, proves that neither states, nor individuals, nor corporations, ever imagined that such a contract could be implied from such charters. It shows, that the men who voted for these laws never imagined that they were forming such a contract; and if we maintain that they have made it, we must create it by a legal fiction, in opposition to the truth of the fact, and the obvious intention of the party. We cannot deal thus with the rights reserved to the states; and by legal intendments and mere technical reasoning, take away from them any portion of that power over their own internal police and improvement, which is not necessary to their well-being and prosperity.

And what would be the fruits of this doctrine of implied contracts, on the part of the states, and of property in a line of travel by a corporation if it should now be sanctioned by this court? To what results would it lead us? If it is to be found in the charter to this bridge, the same process of reasoning must discover it, in the various acts which have been passed, within the last forty years, for turnpike companies. And what is to be the extent of the privileges of exclusion on the different sides of the road? The counsel who have so ably argued this case, have not attempted to define it by any certain boundaries. How far must the new improvement be distant from the old one? How near may you approach, without invading its rights in the privileged line? If this court should establish the principles now contended for, what is to become of the numerous railroads established on the same line of travel with turnpike companies; and which have rendered the franchises of the turnpike corporations of no value? Let it once be understood, that such charters carry with them these

implied contracts, and give this unknown and undefined prosperity in a line of travelling; and you will soon find the old turnpike corporations awakening from their sleep and calling upon this court to put down the improvements which have taken their place. The millions of property which have been invested in railroads and canals, upon lines of travel which had been before occupied by turnpike corporations, will be put in jeopardy. We shall be thrown back to the improvements of the last century, and obliged to stand still, until the claims of the old turnpike corporations shall be satisfied; and they shall consent to permit these states to avail themselves of the lights of modern science, and to partake of the benefit of those improvements which are now adding to the wealth and prosperity, and the convenience and comfort, of every other part of the civilized word. Nor is this all. This court will find itself compelled to fix, by some kind of arbitrary rule, the width of this new kind of property in a line of travel; for if such a right of property exists, we have no lights to guide us in marking out its extent, unless, indeed, we resort to the old feudal grants, and to the exclusive rights of ferries, by prescription, between towns; and are prepared to decide that when a turnpike road from one town to another, had been made, no railroad or canal, between these two points, could afterwards be established. This court are not prepared to sanction principles which must lead to such results. . . .

The judgment of the supreme judicial court of the commonwealth of Massachusetts, dismissing the plaintiffs' bill, must therefore, be affirmed with costs.

Mr. Justice McLean delivered an opinion [concurring in the judgment] holding that the case should be dismissed for want of jurisdiction.

Mr. Justice Story, dissenting.

The present . . . is not the case of a royal grant, but of a legislative grant, by a public statute. The rules of the common law in relation to royal grants have, therefore, in reality, nothing to do with the case. We are to give this act of incorporation a rational and fair construction, according to the general rules which govern in all cases of the exposition of public statutes. We are to ascertain the legislative intent; and that once ascertained, it is our duty to give it a full and liberal operation. . . .

I admit, that where the terms of a grant are to impose burdens upon the public, or to create a restraint injurious to the public interests, there is sound reason for interpreting the terms, if ambiguous, in favour of the public. But at the same time, I insist, that there is not the slightest reason for saying, even in such a case, that the grant is not to be construed favourable to the grantee, so as to secure him in the enjoyment of what is actually granted. . . .

. . . Our legislatures neither have, nor affect to any royal prerogatives. There is no provision in the Constitution authorizing their grants to be construed differently from the grants of private persons, in regard to the like subject matter. The policy of the common law, which gave the crown so many exclusive privileges, and extraordinary claims, different from those of the subject, was founded in a good measure, if not altogether, upon the divine right of kings, or at least upon a sense of their exalted dignity and preeminence over all subjects, and upon the notion, that they are entitled to peculiar favour, for the protection of their kingly privileges. They were always construed according to common sense and common reason, upon their language and their intent. What reason is there, that our legislative acts should not receive a similar interpretation? Is it not at least as important in our free governments, that a citizen should have as much security for his rights and estate derived from the grants of the legislature, as he would have in England? What solid ground is there to say, that the words of a grant in the mouth of a citizen, shall mean one thing, and in the mouth of the legislature shall mean another thing? That in regard to the grant of another citizen, every word shall in case of any question of interpretation or implication be construed against him, and in regard to the grant of the government, every word shall be construed in its favour? That language shall be construed, not according to its natural import and implications from its own proper sense, and the objects of the instrument; but shall change its meaning, as it is spoken by the whole people, or by one of them? There may be very solid grounds to say, that neither grants nor charters ought to be extended beyond the fair reach of their words; and that no implications ought to be made, which are not clearly deducible from the language, and the nature and objects of the grant.

In the case of the legislative grant, there is no ground to impute surprise, imposition or mistake to the same extent as in a mere private grant of the crown. The words are the words of the legislature upon solemn deliberation, and examination, and debate. Their purport is presumed to be well known, and the public interests are watched, and guarded by all the varieties of local, personal, and professional jealousy; as well as by the untiring zeal of numbers, devoted to the public service. . . .

But it has been argued, and the argument has been pressed in every form which ingenuity could suggest, that if grants of this nature are to be construed liberally, as conferring any exclusive rights on the grantees, it will interpose an effectual barrier against all general improvements of the country. . . . For my own part, I can conceive of no surer plan to arrest all public improvements founded on private capital and enterprise, than to make the outlay of that capital uncertain, and questionable both as to security, and as to productiveness. No man will hazard his capital in any enterprise, in which, if there be a loss, it must be borne exclusively by himself; and if there be success, he has not the slightest security of enjoying the rewards of that success for a single moment. . . .

Upon the whole, my judgment is that the act of the legislature of Massachusetts granting the charter of Warren Bridge, is an act impairing the obligation of the prior contract and grant to the proprietors of Charles river bridge; and, by the Constitution of the United States, it is, therefore, utterly void. I am for reversing the decree of the state court for further proceedings. . . .

Mr. Justice Thompson concurred in this [dissenting] opinion. . . .

Home Building and Loan Association v. Blaisdell

290 U.S. 398; 54 S. Ct. 231; 78 L. Ed. 413 (1934)
Vote: 5-4

In 1933, the Minnesota legislature adopted an act designed to prevent the foreclosure of mortgages on real estate during the economic emergency produced by the Great Depression. The Mortgage Moratorium Act authorized courts to extend the redemption periods of mortgages in order to prevent foreclosures. The act was to remain in effect only during the emergency period and in no case beyond May 1, 1935.

Mr. Chief Justice Hughes delivered the opinion of the Court.

. . . The state court upheld the statute as an emergency measure. Although conceding that the obligations of the mortgage contract were impaired, the court decided that what it thus described as an impairment was, notwithstanding the contract clause of the Federal Constitution, within the police power of the state as that power was called into exercise by the public economic emergency which the legislature had found to exist. Attention is thus directed to the preamble and first section of the statute which described the existing emergency in terms that were deemed to justify the temporary relief which the statute affords. The state court, declaring that it could not say that this legislative finding was without basis, supplemented that finding by its own statement of conditions of which it took judicial notice. The court said:

In addition to the weight to be given the determination of the Legislature that an economic emergency exists which demands relief, the court must take notice of other considerations. The members of the Legislature come from every community of the state and from all the walks of life. They are familiar with conditions generally in every calling, occupation, profession, and business in the state. Not only they, but the courts must be guided by what is common knowledge. It is common knowledge that in the last few years land values have shrunk enormously. Loans made a few years ago upon the basis of the then going values cannot possibly be replaced on the basis of present values. We all know that when this law was enacted the large financial companies which had made it their business to invest in mortgages, had ceased to do so. No bank would directly or indirectly loan on real estate mortgages. Life insurance companies, large investors on such mortgages, had even declared a moratorium as to the loan provisions of their policy contracts. The President had closed banks temporarily. The Congress, in addition to many extraordinary measures looking to the relief of the economic emergency, had passed an act to supply funds whereby mortgagors may be able within a reasonable time to refinance their mortgages or redeem from sales where the redemption has not expired. With this knowledge the court cannot well hold that the Legislature had no basis in fact for the conclusion that an economic emergency existed which called for the exercise of the police power to grant relief. . . .

We approach the questions thus presented upon the assumption made below, as required by the law of the state, that the mortgage contained a valid power of sale to be exercised in case of default; that this power was validly exercised; that under the law then applicable the period of redemption from the sale was one year, and that it has been extended by the judgment of the court over the opposition of the mortgagee-purchaser; and that, during the period thus extended, and unless the order for extension is modified, the mortgagee-purchaser will be unable to obtain possession, or to obtain or convey title in fee, as he would have been able to do had the statute not been enacted. The statute does not impair the integrity of the mortgage indebtedness. The obligation for interest remains. The statute does not affect the validity of the sale of the right of a mortgagee-purchaser to title in fee, or his right to obtain a deficiency judgment, if the mortgagor fails to redeem within the prescribed period. Aside from the extension of time, the other conditions of redemption are unaltered. While the mortgagor remains in possession, he must pay the rental value as that value has been determined, upon notice and hearing, by the court. The rental value so paid is devoted to the carrying of the property by the application of the required payments to taxes, insurance, and interest on the mortgage indebtedness. While the mortgagee-purchaser is debarred from actual possession, he has, so far as rental value is concerned, the equivalent of possession during the extended period.

In determining whether the provision for this temporary and conditional relief exceeds the power of the state by reason of the clause in the Federal Constitution prohibiting impairment of the obligations of contracts, we must consider the relation of emergency to constitutional power, the historical setting of the contract clause, the development of the jurisprudence of this Court in the construction of that clause, and the principles of construction which we may consider to be established.

Emergency does not create power. Emergency does not increase granted power or remove or diminish the restrictions imposed upon power granted or reserved. The Constitution was adopted in a period of grave emergency. Its grants of power to the Federal Government and its limitations of the power of the states were determined in the light of emergency, and they are not altered by emergency. What power was thus granted and what limitations were thus imposed are questions which have always been, and always will be, the subject of close examination under our constitutional system.

While emergency does not create power, emergency may furnish the occasion for the exercise of power. "Although an emergency may not call into life a power which has never lived, nevertheless emergency may afford a reason for the exertion of a living power already enjoyed." *** The constitutional question presented in the light of an emergency is whether the power possessed embraces the particular exercise of it in response to particular conditions. Thus, the war power of the federal government is not created by the emergency of war, but it is a power to wage war successfully, and thus it permits the harnessing of the entire energies of the people in a supreme co-operative effort to preserve the nation. But even the war power does not remove constitutional limitations safeguarding essential liberties. When the provisions of the Constitution, in grant or restriction, are specific, so particularized as not to admit a state to have more than two Senators in the Congress, or permit the election of a President by a general popular vote without regard to the number of electors to which the states are respectively entitled, or permit the states to "coin money" or to "make anything but gold and silver coin a tender in payment of debts." But, where constitutional grants

and limitations of power are set forth in general clauses, which afford a broad outline, the process of construction is essential to fill in the details. That is true of the Contract Clause. . . .

In the construction of the Contract Clause, the debates in the Constitutional Convention are of little aid. But the reasons which led to the adoption of that clause, and of the other prohibitions of Section 10 of Article I, are not left in doubt, and have frequently been described with eloquent emphasis. The widespread distress following the revolutionary period, and the plight of debtors had called forth in the state an ignoble array of legislative schemes for the defeat of creditors and the invasion of contractual obligations. Legislative interferences had been so numerous and extreme that the confidence essential to prosperous trade had been undermined and the utter destruction of credit was threatened. "The sober people of America" were convinced that some "thorough reform" was needed which would "inspire a general prudence and industry, and give a regular course to the business of society." *** . . .

The inescapable problems of construction have been: What is a contract? What are the obligations of contracts? What constitutes impairment of these obligations? What residuum of power is there still in the states, in relation to the operation of contracts, to protect the vital interests of the community? Questions of this character, "of no small nicety and intricacy, have vexed the legislative halls, as well as the judicial tribunals, with an uncounted variety and frequency of litigation and speculation." ***

It is manifest . . . that there has been a growing appreciation of public needs and of the necessity of finding ground for a rational compromise between individual rights and public welfare. . . . Pressure of a constantly increasing density of population, the interrelation of the activities of our people and the complexity of our economic interests, have inevitably led to an increased use of the organization of society in order to protect the very bases of individual opportunity. Where, in earlier days, it was thought that only the concerns of individuals or of classes were involved, and that those of the state itself were touched only remotely, it has later been found that the fundamental interests of the state are directly affected; and that the question is no longer merely that of one party to a contract as against another, but of the use of reasonable means to safeguard the economic structure upon which the good of all depends.

It is no answer to say that this public need was not apprehended a century ago, or to insist that what the provision of the Constitution meant to the vision of that day it must mean to the vision of our time. If by the statement that what the Constitution meant at the time of its adoption it means to-day, in is intended to say that the great clauses of the Constitution must be confined to the interpretation which the framers, with the conditions and outlook of their time, would have placed upon them, the statement carries its own refutation. It was to guard against such a narrow conception that Chief Justice Marshall uttered the memorable warning: "We must never forget, that it is *a constitution* we are expounding"; *** "a constitution intended to endure for ages to come, and, consequently, to be adapted to the various *crises* of human affairs." *** When we are dealing with the words of the Constitution, . . . "we must realize that they have called into life a being the development of which could not have been foreseen completely by the most gifted of its begetters. . . . The case before us must be considered in the light of our whole experience and not merely in that of what was said a hundred years ago." ***

Nor is it helpful to attempt to draw a fine distinction between the intended meaning of the words of the Constitution and their intended application. When we consider the contract clause and the decisions which have expounded it in harmony with the essential reserved power of the states to protect the security of their peoples, we find no warrant for the conclusion that the clause has been warped by these decisions from its proper significance or that the founders of our government would have interpreted the clause differently had they had occasion to assume that responsibility in the conditions of the later day. The vast body of law which has been developed was unknown to the fathers, but it is believed to have preserved the essential content and the spirit of the Constitution. With a growing recognition of public needs and the relation of individual right to public security, the Court has sought to prevent the perversion of the clause through its use as

an instrument to throttle the capacity of the states to protect their fundamental interests. . . .

We are of the opinion that the Minnesota statute as here applied does not violate the Contract Clause of the Federal Constitution. Whether the legislation is wise or unwise as matter of policy is a question with which we are not concerned. . . .

Mr. Justice Sutherland, dissenting.

Few questions of greater moment than that just decided have been submitted for judicial inquiry during this generation. He simply closes his eyes to the necessary implications of the decision who fails to see in it the potentiality of future gradual but ever-advancing encroachments upon the sanctity of private and public contracts. The effect of the Minnesota legislation, though serious enough in itself, is of trivial significance compared with the far more serious and dangerous inroads upon the limitations of the Constitution which are almost certain to ensue as a consequence naturally following any step beyond the boundaries fixed by that instrument. And those of us who are thus apprehensive of the effect of this decision would, in a matter so important, be neglectful of our duty should we fail to spread upon the permanent records of the court the reasons which move us to the opposite view.

A provision of the Constitution, it is hardly necessary to say, does not admit of two distinctly opposite interpretations. It does not mean one thing at one time and an entirely different thing at another time. If the Contract Impairment Clause, when framed and adopted, meant that the terms of a contract for the payment of money could not be altered . . . by a state statute enacted for the relief of hardly pressed debtors to the end and with the effect of postponing payment or enforcement during and because of an economic or financial emergency, it is but to state the obvious to say that it means the same now. This view, at once so rational in its application to the written word, and so necessary to the stability of constitutional principles, though from time to time challenged, has never, unless recently, been put within the realm of doubt by the decisions of this Court. . . .

The provisions of the federal Constitution, undoubtedly, are pliable in the sense that in appropriate cases they have the capacity of bringing within their grasp every new condition which falls within their meaning. But their *meaning* is changeless; it is only their *application* which is extensible. *** Constitutional grants of power and restrictions upon the exercise of power are not flexible as the doctrines of the common law are flexible. These doctrines, upon the principles of the common law itself, modify or abrogate themselves whenever they are or whenever they become plainly unsuited to different or changed conditions. . . .

The whole aim of construction, as applied to a provision of the Constitution, is to discover the meaning, to ascertain and give effect to the intent, of its framers and the people who adopted it. . . . *** And if the meaning be at all doubtful, the doubt should be resolved, wherever reasonably possible to do so, in a way to forward the evident purpose with which the provision was adopted. . . .

An application of these principles to the question under review removes any doubt, if otherwise there would be any, that the Contract Impairment Clause denies to the several states the power to mitigate hard consequences resulting to debtors from financial or economic exigencies by an impairment of the obligation of contracts of indebtedness. A candid consideration of the history and circumstances which led up to and accompanied the framing and adoption of this clause will demonstrate conclusively that it was framed and adopted with the specific and studied purpose of preventing legislation designed to relieve debtors especially in time of financial distress. Indeed, it is not probable that any other purpose was definitely in the minds of those who composed the framers' convention or the ratifying state conventions which followed, although the restriction has been given a wider application upon principles clearly stated by Chief Justice Marshall in the Dartmouth College Case. *** . . .

The present exigency is nothing new. From the beginning of our existence as a nation, periods of depression, of industrial failure, of financial distress, of unpaid and unpayable indebtedness, have alternated with years of plenty. The vital lesson that expenditure beyond income begets poverty, that public or private extravagance, financed by promises to pay, either must end in complete or partial repudiation or the promises be fulfilled by self-denial and painful

effort, though constantly taught by bitter experience, seems never to be learned; and the attempt by legislative devices to shift the misfortune of debtor to the shoulders of the creditor without coming into conflict with the Contract Impairment Clause has been persistent and oft-repeated.

The defense of the Minnesota law is made upon grounds which were discountenanced by the markers of the Constitution and have many times been rejected by this court. That defense should not now succeed, because it constitutes an effort to overthrow the constitutional provision by an appeal to facts and circumstances identical with those which brought it into existence. With due regard for the process of logical thinking, it legitimately cannot be urged that conditions which produced the rule may now be invoked to destroy it.

. . . The opinion concedes that emergency does not create power, or increase granted power, or remove or diminish restrictions upon power granted or reserved. It then proceeds to say, however, that while emergency does not create power, it may furnish the occasion for the exercise of power. I can only interpret what is said on that subject as meaning that while an emergency does not diminish a restriction upon power it furnishes an occasion for diminishing it; and this, as it seems to me, is merely to say the same thing by the use of another set of words, with the effect of affirming that which has just been denied.

It is quite true that an emergency may supply the occasion for the exercise of power, depending upon the nature of the power and the intent of the Constitution with respect thereto. The emergency of war furnishes an occasion for the exercise of certain of the war powers. This the Constitution contemplates, since they cannot be exercised upon any other occasion. The existence of another kind of emergency authorizes the United States to protect each of the states of the Union against domestic violence. *** But we are here dealing not with a power granted by the federal Constitution, but with the state policy power, which exists in its own right. Hence the question is not whether an emergency furnishes the occasion for the exercise of that state power, but whether an emergency furnishes an occasion for the relaxation of the restrictions upon the power imposed by the

Contract Impairment Clause, and the difficulty is that the Contract Impairment Clause forbids state action under any circumstances, if it have the effect of impairing the obligation of contracts. That clause restricts every state power in the particular specified, no matter what may be the occasion. It does not contemplate that an emergency shall furnish an occasion for softening the restriction or making it any the less a restriction upon state action in that contingency than it is under strictly normal conditions.

The Minnesota statute either impairs the obligation of contracts or it does not. If it does not, the occasion to which it relates becomes immaterial, since then the passage of the statute is the exercise of a normal, unrestricted, state power and requires no special occasion to render it effective. If it does, the emergency no more furnishes a proper occasion for its exercise than if the emergency were nonexistent. And so, while, in form, the suggested distinction seems to put us forward in a straight line, in reality it simply carries us back in a circle, like bewildered travelers lost in a wood, to the point where we parted company with the view of the state court. . . .

I quite agree with the opinion of the Court that whether the legislation under review is wise or unwise is a matter with which we have nothing to do. Whether it is likely to work well or work ill presents a question entirely irrelevant to the issue. The only legitimate inquiry we can make is whether it is constitutional. If it is not, its virtues, if it have any, cannot save it; if it is, its faults cannot be invoked to accomplish its destruction. If the provisions of the Constitution be not upheld when they pinch as well as when they comfort, they may as well be abandoned. Being unable to reach any other conclusion than that the Minnesota statute infringes the constitutional restrictions under review, I have no choice but to say so.

I am authorized to say that **_Mr. Justice Van Devanter, Mr. Justice McReynolds_** and **_Mr. Justice Butler_** concur in this opinion.

The Slaughter-House Cases
16 Wall. (83 U.S.) 36; 21 L. Ed. 394 (1873)
Vote: 5-4

In 1869, the Louisiana legislature granted to a slaughterhouse company a monopoly for the city of New Orleans. A number of independent butchers sought injunctions against the monopoly. Unable to secure injunctions in the state courts, they turned to the Supreme Court, which granted review pursuant to a writ of error.

Mr. Justice Miller . . . delivered the opinion of the Court.

. . . The statute is denounced not only as creating a monopoly and conferring odious and exclusive privileges upon a small number of persons at the expense of the great body of the community of New Orleans, but it is asserted that it deprives a large and meritorious class of citizens—the whole of the butchers of the city—of the right to exercise their trade, the business to which they have been trained and on which they depend for the support of themselves and their families; and that the unrestricted exercise of the business of butchering is necessary to the daily subsistence of the population of the city. . . .

It is not, and cannot be successfully controverted, that it is both the right and the duty of the legislative body—the supreme power of the State or municipality—to prescribe and determine the localities where the business of slaughtering for a great city may be conducted. To do this effectively it is indispensable that all persons who slaughter animals for food shall do it in those places and nowhere else.

The statute under consideration defines these localities and forbids slaughtering in any other. It does not, as has been asserted, prevent the butcher from doing his own slaughtering. On the contrary, the Slaughter-House Company is required, under a heavy penalty, to permit any person who wishes to do so, to slaughter in their houses; and they are bound to make ample provision for the convenience of all slaughtering for the entire city. The butcher then is still permitted to slaughter, to prepare, and to sell his own meats; but he is required to slaughter at a specified place and to pay reasonable compensation for the use of the accommodations furnished him at that place.

The wisdom of the monopoly granted by the legislature may be open to question, but it is difficult to see a justification for the assertion that the butchers are deprived of the right to labor in their occupation, or the people of their daily service in preparing food, or how this statute, with the duties and guards imposed upon the company, can be said to destroy the business of the butcher, or seriously interfere with its pursuit.

The power here exercised by the legislature of Louisiana is, in its essential nature, one which has been up to the present period in the constitutional history of this country, always conceded to belong to the States, however it may now be questioned in some of its details. . . .

Unless, therefore, it can be maintained that the exclusive privilege granted by this charter to the corporation is beyond the power of the legislature of Louisiana, there can be no just exception to the validity of the statute. And in this respect we are not able to see that these privileges are especially odious or objectionable. The duty imposed as a consideration for the privilege is well defined, and its enforcement well guarded. The prices or charges to be made by the company are limited by the statute, and we are not advised that they are on the whole exorbitant or unjust.

The proposition is, therefore, reduced to these terms: Can any exclusive privileges be granted to any of its citizens, or to a corporation, by the legislature of a State? . . .

The plaintiffs in error accepting this issue, allege that the statute is a violation of the Constitution of the United States in these several particulars:

That it creates an involuntary servitude forbidden by the thirteenth article of amendment;

That it abridges the privileges and immunities of citizens of the United States;

That it denies to the plaintiffs the equal protection of the laws; and,

That it deprives them of their property without due process of law; contrary to the provisions of the first section of the fourteenth article of amendment.

This court is thus called upon for the first time to give construction to these articles.

. . . On the most casual examination of the language of [the Thirteenth, Fourteenth, and Fifteenth] amendments, no one can fail to be impressed with the one pervading purpose found in them all, lying at the foundation of each, and without which none of them would have been even suggested; we mean the freedom of the slave race, the security and firm establishment of that freedom, and the protection of the newly-made freeman and citizen from the oppressions of those who had formerly exercised unlimited dominion over him. It is true that only the Fifteenth Amendment, in terms, mentions the negro by speaking of his color and his slavery. But it is just as true that each of the other articles was addressed to the grievances of that race, and designed to remedy them as the Fifteenth.

We do not say that no one else but the negro can share in this protection. Both the language and spirit of these articles are to have their fair and just weight in any question of construction. Undoubtedly while negro slavery alone was in the mind of the congress which proposed the thirteenth article, it forbids any other kind of slavery, now or hereafter. If Mexican peonage or the Chinese cooly labor system shall develop slavery of the Mexican or Chinese race within our territory, this amendment may safely be trusted to make it void. And so if other rights are assailed by the States which properly and necessarily fall within the protection of these articles, that protection will apply, though the party interested may not be of African descent. But what we do say, and what we wish to be understood is, that in any fair and just construction of any section or phrase of these amendments, it is necessary to look to the purpose which we have said was the pervading spirit of them all, the evil which they were designed to remedy, and the process of continued addition to the Constitution, until that purpose was supposed to be accomplished, as far as constitutional law can accomplish it. . . .

The next observation is more important in view of the arguments of counsel in the present case. It is, that the distinction between citizenship of the United States and citizenship of a State is clearly recognized and established. Not only may a man be a citizen of the United States without being a citizen of a State, but an important element is necessary to convert the former into the latter. He must reside within the State to make him a citizen of it, but it is only necessary that he should be born or naturalized in the United States to be a citizen of the Union.

It is quite clear, then, that there is a citizenship of the United States, and a citizenship of a State, which are distinct from each other, and which depend upon different characteristics of circumstance in the individual.

We think this distinction and its explicit recognition in this amendment of great weight in this argument, because the next paragraph of this same section, which is the one mainly relied on by the plaintiffs in error, speaks only of privileges and immunities of citizens of the United States, and does not speak of those of citizens of the several States. The argument, however, in favor of the plaintiffs rests wholly on the assumption that the citizenship is the same, and the privileges and immunities guaranteed by the clause are the same.

The language is, "No State shall make or enforce any law which shall abridge the privileges or immunities of citizens of the United States." It is a little remarkable, if this clause was intended as a protection to the citizen of a State against the legislative power of his own State, that the [words] *citizen of the State* should be left out when it is so carefully used, and used in contradistinction to citizens of the United States, in the very sentence which precedes it. It is too clear for argument that the change in phraseology was adopted understandingly and with a purpose.

Of the privileges and immunities of the citizen of the United States, and of the privileges and immunities of the citizen of the States, and what they respectively are, we will presently consider; but we wish to state here that it is only the former which are placed by this clause under the protection of the Federal Constitution, and that the latter, whatever they may be, are not intended to have any additional protection by this paragraph of the amendment.

If, then, there is a difference between the privileges and immunities belonging to a citizen of the United States as such, and those belonging to the citizen of the State as such the latter must rest for their security and protection where they have heretofore rested; for they are not embraced by this paragraph of the amendment. . . .

Fortunately we are not without judicial construction of this clause of the Constitution, the first and the leading case on the subject is that of *Corfield v. Coryell,* *** decided by Mr. Justice Washington in the Circuit Court for the District of Pennsylvania in 1823.

"The inquiry," he says, is,

[W]hat are the privileges and immunities of citizens of the several States? We feel no hesitation in confining these expressions to those privileges and immunities which are fundamental; which belong of right to the citizens of all free governments, and which have at all times been enjoyed by citizens of the several States which compose this Union, from the time of their becoming free, independent, and sovereign. What these fundamental principles are, it would be more tedious than difficult to enumerate. They may all, however, be comprehended under the following general heads: protection by the government, with the right to acquire and possess property of every kind, to such restraints as the government may prescribe for the general good of the whole. . . .

It would be the vainest show of learning to attempt to prove by citations of authority, that up to the adoption of the recent amendments, no claim or pretense was set up that those rights depended on the Federal government for their existence or protection, beyond the very few express limitations which the Federal Constitution imposed upon the States — such, for instance, as the prohibition against *ex post facto* laws, bills of attainder, and laws impairing the obligation of contracts. But with the exception of these and a few other restrictions, the entire domain of the privileges and immunities of the citizens of the States, and without that of the Federal government. Was it the purpose of the Fourteenth Amendment, by the simple declaration that no States should make or enforce any law which abridge the privileges and immunities of citizens of the United States, to transfer the security and protection of all the civil rights which we have mentioned, from the states to the Federal government? And where it is declared that

Congress shall have the power to enforce that article, was it intended to bring within the power of Congress the entire domain of civil rights heretofore belonging exclusively to the States?

All this and more must follow, if the proposition of the plaintiffs in error be sound. For not only are these rights subject to the control of Congress whenever in its discretion any of them are supposed to be abridged by State legislation, but that body may also pass laws in advance, limiting and restricting the exercise of legislative power of the States, in their most ordinary and usual functions, as in its judgment it may think proper on all such subjects. And still further, such a construction followed by the reversal of the judgments of the Supreme Court of Louisiana in these cases, would constitute this court a perpetual censor upon all legislation of the States, on the civil rights of their own citizens, with authority to nullify such as it did not approve as consistent with those rights, as they existed at the time of the adoption of this amendment. The argument we admit is not always the most conclusive which is drawn from the consequences urged against the adoption of a particular construction of an instrument. But when, as in the case before us, these consequences are so serious, so far-reaching and pervading, so great a departure from the structure and spirit of our institutions; when the effect is to fetter and degrade the State governments by subjecting them to the control of Congress, in the exercise of powers heretofore universally conceded to them of the most ordinary and fundamental character; when in fact it radically changes the whole theory of the relations of the State and Federal governments to each other and of both of these governments to the people; the argument has a force that is irresistible, in the absence of language which expresses such a purpose too clearly to admit of doubt.

We are convinced that no such results were intended by the Congress which proposed these amendments, nor by the legislatures of the States which ratified them.

Having shown that the privileges and immunities relied on in the argument are those which belong to citizens of the States as such, and that they are left to the State governments for security and protection, and not by this article placed under the special care

of the Federal government, we may hold ourselves excused from defining the privileges and immunities of citizens of the United States which no State can abridge, until some case involving those privileges may make it necessary to do so.

But lest it be said that no such privileges and immunities are to be found if those we have been considering are excluded, we venture to suggest some which owe their existence to the Federal government, its National character, its Constitution, or its laws.

One of these is well described in the case of *Crandall* v. *Nevada*. *** It is said to be the right of the citizens of this great country, protected by implied guarantees of its Constitution, "to come to the seat of government to assert any claim he may have upon that government, to transact any business he may have with it, to seek its protection, to share its offices, to engage in administering its functions. He has the right of free access to its seaports, through which all operations of foreign commerce are conducted, to the subtreasuries, land offices, and courts of justice in the several States." And quoting from the language of Chief Justice Taney in another case, it is said "that for all the great purposes for which the Federal government was established, we are one people, with one common country, we are all citizens of the United States"; and it is, as such citizens, that their rights are supported in this court in *Crandall* v. *Nevada*. . . .

The argument has not been much pressed in these cases that the defendant's charter deprives the plaintiffs of their property without due process of law, or that it denies to them the equal protection of the law. The first of these paragraphs has been in the Constitution since the adoption of the fifth amendment, as a restraint upon the Federal power. It is also to be found in some form of expression in the constitutions of nearly all the States, as a restraint upon the power of the States. This law, then, has practically been the same as it now is during the existence of the government, except so far as the present amendment may place the restraining power over the States in this matter in the hands of the Federal government.

We are not without judicial interpretation, therefore, both State and National, of the meaning of this clause. And it is sufficient to say that under no construction of that provision that we have ever seen, or any that we deem admissible, can the restraint imposed by the state of Louisiana upon the exercise of their trade by the butchers of New Orleans be held to be a deprivation of property within the meaning of that provision.

"Nor shall any State deny to any person within its jurisdiction the equal protection of the laws."

In the light of the history of these amendments, and the pervading purpose of them, which we have already discussed, it is not difficult to give a meaning to this clause. The existence of laws in the states where the newly emancipated negroes resided, which discriminated with gross injustice and hardship against them as a class, was the evil to be remedied by this clause, and by it such laws are forbidden.

If, however, the states did not conform their laws to its requirements, then by the fifth section of the article of amendment Congress was authorized to enforce it by suitable legislation. We doubt very much whether any action of a State not directed by way of discrimination against the negroes as a class, or on account of their race, will ever be held to come within the purview of this provision. It is so clearly a provision for that race and that emergency, that a strong case would be necessary for its application to any other. But as it is a State that is to be dealt with, and not alone the validity of its laws, we may safely leave that matter until congress shall have exercised its power, or some case of State oppression, by denial of equal justice in its courts, shall have claimed a decision at our hands. We find no such case in the one before us, and do not deem it necessary to go over the argument again, as it may have relation to this particular clause of the amendment. . . .

The judgments of the Supreme Court of Louisiana in these cases are affirmed.

Mr. Justice Field, dissenting:

. . . The question presented is . . . one of the gravest importance, not merely to the parties here, but to the whole country. It is nothing less than the question whether the recent amendments to the Federal Constitution protect the citizens of the United States against the deprivation of their common rights by State legislation. In my judgment the Fourteenth Amendment does afford such protection, and was so intended by the Congress which framed and the States which adopted it.

The amendment does not attempt to confer any new privileges or immunities upon citizens, or to enumerate or define those already existing. It assumes that there are such privileges and immunities which belong of right to citizens as such, and ordains that they shall not be abridged by State legislation. If this inhibition has no reference to privileges and immunities of this character, but only refers, as held by the majority of the court in their opinion, to such privileges and immunities as were before its adoption specially designated in the Constitution or necessarily implied as belonging to citizens of the United States, it was a vain and idle enactment, which accomplished nothing, and most unnecessarily excited Congress and the people on its passage. With privileges and immunities thus designated or implied no State could ever have interfered by its laws and no new constitutional provision was required to inhibit such interference. The supremacy of the Constitution and the laws of the United States always controlled any State legislation of that character. But if the amendment refers to the natural and inalienable rights which belong to all citizens, the inhibition has a profound significance and consequence.

What, then, are the privileges and immunities which are secured against abridgment by State legislation? . . .

The terms, privileges and immunities, are not new in the Amendment; they were in the Constitution before the Amendment was adopted. They are found in the second section of the fourth article, which declares that "the citizens of each State shall be entitled to all privileges and immunities of citizens in the several States," and they have been the subject of frequent consideration in judicial decisions. In *Corfield* v. *Coryell*, Mr. Justice Washington said he had "no hesitation in confining these expressions to those privileges and immunities which were, in their nature, fundamental; which belong of right to citizens of all free governments, and which have at all times been enjoyed by the citizens of the several states which compose the Union, from the time of their becoming free, independent, and sovereign; and, in considering what those fundamental privileges were, he said that perhaps it would be more tedious than difficult to enumerate them, but that they might be "all comprehended under the following general heads: protection by the government; the enjoyment of life and liberty, with the right to acquire and possess property of every kind, and to pursue and obtain happiness and safety, subject, nevertheless, to such restraints as the government may justly prescribe for the general good of the whole." This appears to me to be a sound construction of the clause in question. The privileges and immunities designated are those which of right belong to the citizens of all free governments. Clearly among these must be placed the right to pursue a lawful employment in a lawful manner, without other restraint than such as equally affects all persons. In the discussions in Congress upon the passage of the Civil Rights Act [of 1866] repeated reference was made to this language of Mr. Justice Washington. It was cited by Senator Trumbull with the observation that it enumerated the very rights belonging to a citizen of the United States set forth in the first section of the act, and with the statement that all persons born in the United States, being declared by the act citizens of the United States, would thenceforth be entitled to the rights of citizens, and that these were the great fundamental rights set forth in the act; and that they were set forth "as appertaining to every freeman." . . .

This equality of right, with exemption from all disparaging and partial enactments, in the lawful pursuits of life, throughout the whole country, is the distinguishing privilege of citizens of the United States. To them, everywhere, all pursuits, all professions, all avocations are open without other restrictions than such as are imposed equally upon all others of the same age, sex, and condition. The State may prescribe such regulations for every pursuit and calling of life as will promote the public health, secure the good order and advance the general prosperity of society, but when once prescribed, the pursuit or calling must be free to be followed by every citizen who is within the conditions designated, and will conform to the regulations. This is the fundamental idea upon which our institutions rest, and unless adhered to in the legislation of the country our government will be a republic only in name. The Fourteenth Amendment, in my judgment, makes it essential to the validity of the legislation of every State that this equality of right should be respected. How widely this equality has been departed from, how entirely rejected and trampled upon by the act of Louisiana, I have already shown. And it is to me a matter of profound regret that is validity is recognized by a majority of this court, for by it the right of free labor, one of the most sacred and imprescriptible rights of man, is violated. . . .

I am authorized by the **Chief Justice, Mr. Justice Swayne,** and **Mr. Justice Bradley,** to state that they concur with me in this dissenting opinion.

Mr. Justice Bradley, dissenting.

. . . The right of a State to regulate the conduct of its citizens is undoubtedly a very broad and extensive one, and not to be lightly restricted. But there are certain fundamental rights which this right of regulation cannot infringe. It may prescribe the manner of their exercise, but it cannot subvert the rights themselves. . . .

The granting of monopolies, or exclusive privileges to individuals or corporations, is an invasion of the right of another to choose a lawful calling, and an infringement of personal liberty. It was so felt by the English nation as far back as the reigns of Elizabeth and James. A fierce struggle for the suppression of such monopolies, and for abolishing the prerogative of creating them, was made and was successful. . . . And ever since that struggle no English-speaking people have ever endured such an odious badge of tyranny. . . .

Can the Federal courts administer relief to citizens of the United States whose privileges and immunities have been abridged by a State? Of this I entertain no doubt. Prior to the Fourteenth Amendment this could not be done, except in a few instances, for the want of the requisite authority. . . .

Admitting, therefore, that formerly the States were not prohibited from infringing any fundamental privileges and immunities of citizens of the United States, except in a few specified cases, that cannot be said now, since the adoption of the Fourteenth Amendment. In my judgment, it was the intention of the people of this country in adopting that amendment to provide National security against violation by the States of the fundamental rights of the citizen. . . .

In my view, a law which prohibits a large class of citizens from adopting a lawful employment, or from following a lawful employment previously adopted, does deprive them of liberty as well as property, without due process of law. Their right of choice is a portion of their liberty; their occupation is their property. Such a law also deprives those citizens of the equal protection of the laws, contrary to the last clause of the section. . . .

Mr. Justice Swayne, dissenting. . . .

Munn v. Illinois

94 U.S. 113; 24 L. Ed. 77 (1877)
Vote: 7-2

Mr. Chief Justice Waite delivered the opinion of the Court.

The question to be determined in this case is whether the General Assembly of Illinois can, under the limitations upon the legislative power of the States imposed by the Constitution of the United States, fix by law the maximum of charges for the storage of grain in warehouses at Chicago and other places in the State. . . .

It is claimed that such a law is repugnant . . . [t]o that part of Amendment XIV, which ordains that no State shall "Deprive any person of life, liberty or property, without due process of law, nor deny to any person within its jurisdiction the equal protection of the laws." . . .

. . . [I]t is apparent that, down to the time of the adoption of the Fourteenth Amendment, it was not supposed that statutes regulating the use, or even the price of the use, of private property necessarily deprived an owner of his property without due process of law. Under some circumstances they may, but not under all. The Amendment does not change the law in this particular; it simply prevents the states from doing that which will operate as such a deprivation.

This brings us to inquire as to the principles upon which this power of regulation rests, in order that we may determine what is within and what without its operative effect. Looking, then, to the common law, from whence came the right which the Constitution protects, we find that when private property is "affected with a public interest, it ceases to be *juris privati* only." This was said by Lord Chief Justice Hale more than two hundred years ago, in his treatise *De Portibus Maris,* *** and has been accepted without objection as an essential element in the law of property ever since. Property does become clothed with a public interest when used in a manner to make it of public consequence, and affect the community at large. When, therefore, one devotes his property to a use in which the public has an interest, he, in effect, grants to the public an interest in that use, and must submit to be controlled by the public for the common good, to the extent of the interest he has thus created. He may withdraw his grant by discontinuing the use; but, so long as he maintains the use, he must submit to the control. . . .

. . . [W]hen private property is devoted to a public use, it is subject to public regulation. It remains only to ascertain whether the warehouses of these plaintiffs in error, and the business which is carried on there, come within the operation of this principle. . . .

. . . [T]hese plaintiffs in error . . . stand . . . in the very "gateway of commerce," and take toll from all who pass. Their business most certainly "tends to common charge, and has become a thing of public interest and use." . . . Certainly, if any business can be clothed "with a public interest, and cease to the juris privati only," this has been. It may not be made so by the operation of the constitution of Illinois or this statute, but it is by the facts.

We also are not permitted to overlook the fact that, for some reason, the people of Illinois, when they revised their constitution in 1870, saw fit to make it the duty of the General Assembly to pass laws "for the protection of producers, shippers and receivers of grain and produce," *** to require all railroad companies receiving and transporting grain in bulk or otherwise to deliver the same at any elevator to which it might be consigned, that could be reached by any track that was or could be used by such company, and that all railroad companies should permit connections to be made with their tracks, so that any public warehouse, etc., might be reached by the cars on their railroads. This indicates very clearly that during the twenty years in which this peculiar business had been assuming its present "immense proportions," something had occurred which led the whole body of the people to suppose that remedies such as are usually employed to prevent abuses by virtual monopolies might not be inappropriate here. For our purposes we must assume that, if a state of facts could exist that would justify such legislation, it actually did exist when the statute now under consideration was passed. For us the question is one of power, not of expediency. If no state of circumstances could exist to justify such a statute, then we may declare this one void, because in excess of the legislative power of the State. But if it could, we must presume it did. Of the propriety of the legislative interference within the scope of the legislative power, the Legislature is the exclusive judge.

Neither is it a matter of any moment that no precedent can be found for a statute precisely like this. It is conceded that the business is one of recent origin, that its growth has been rapid, and that it is already of great importance. And it must also be conceded that it is a business in which the whole public has a direct and positive interest. It presents, therefore, a case for the application of a long known and well established principle in social science, and this statute simply extends the law so as to meet this new development of commercial progress. There is no attempt to compel these owners to grant the public an interest in their property, but to declare their obligations, if they use it in this particular manner.

It matters not in this case that these plaintiffs in error had built their warehouses and established their business before the regulations complained of were adopted. What they did was, from the beginning, subject to the power of the body politic to require them to conform to such regulations as might be established by the proper authorities for the common good. They entered upon their busi-

ness and provided themselves with the means to carry it on subject to this condition. If they did not wish to submit themselves to such interference, they should not have clothed the public with an interest in their concerns. . . .

It is insisted, however, that the owner of property is entitled to a reasonable compensation for its use, even though it be clothed with a public interest, and that what is reasonable is a judicial and not a legislative question.

As has already been shown, the practice has been otherwise. In countries where the common law prevails, it has been customary from time immemorial for the Legislature to declare what shall be a reasonable compensation under such circumstances, or, perhaps more properly speaking, to fix a maximum beyond which any charge made would be unreasonable. Undoubtedly, in mere private contracts, relating to matters in which the public has no interest, what is reasonable must be ascertained judicially. But this is because the Legislature has no control over such a contract. So, too, in matters which do affect the public interest, and as to which legislative control may be exercised, if there are no statutory regulations upon the subject, the courts must determine what is reasonable. The controlling fact is the power to regulate at all. If that exists, the right to establish the maximum of charge, as one of the means of regulation, is implied. In fact, the common law rule, which requires the charge to be reasonable, is itself a regulation as to price. Without it the owner could make his rates at will, and compel the public to yield to his terms, or forego the use.

But a mere common law regulation of trade or business may be changed by statute. A person has no property, no vested interest, in any rule of the common law. That is only one of the forms of municipal law, and is no more sacred than any other. Rights of property which have been created by the common law cannot be taken away without due process; but the law itself, as a rule of conduct, may be changed at the will, or even at the whim, of the Legislature, unless prevented by constitutional limitations. Indeed, the great office of statutes is to remedy defects in the common law as they are developed, and to adapt it to the changes of time and circumstances. To limit the rate of charge for services rendered in a public employment, or for the use of property in which the public has an interest, is only changing a regulation which existed before. It establishes no new principle in the law, but only gives a new effect to an old one.

We know that this is a power which may be abused; but that is no argument against its existence. For protection against abuses by Legislatures the people must resort to the polls, not to the courts. . . .

Mr. Justice Field, dissenting:

I am compelled to dissent from the decision of the Court in this case, and from the reasons upon which that decision is founded. The principle upon which the opinion of the majority proceeds is, in my judgment, subversive of the rights of private property, heretofore believed to be protected by constitutional guarantees against legislative interference, and is in conflict with the authorities cited in its support. . . .

The declaration of the [Illinois] Constitution of 1870, that private buildings used for private purposes shall be deemed public institutions, does not make them so. The receipt and storage of grain in a building erected by private means for that purpose does not constitute the building a public warehouse. There is no magic in the language, though used by a constitutional convention, which can change a private business into a public one, or alter the character of the building in which the business is transacted. . . .

. . . The doctrine declared is that property "becomes clothed with a public interest when used in a manner to make it of public consequence, and affect the community at large;" and from such clothing the right of the Legislature is deduced to control the use of the property, and to determine the compensation which the owner may receive for it. When Sir Matthew Hale, and the sages of the law in his day, spoke of property as affected by a public interest, and ceasing from that cause to be juris privati solely, that is, ceasing to be held merely in private right, they referred to property dedicated by the owner to public uses, or to property the use of which was granted by the government, or in connection with which special privileges were conferred. Unless the property was thus dedicated, or some right bestowed by the government was held with the property, either by specific grant or by prescription of so long a time as to

imply a grant originally, the property was not affected by any public interest so as to be taken out of the category of property held in private right. But it is not in any such sense that the terms "clothing property with a public interest" are used in this case. From the nature of the business under consideration—the storage of grain—which, in any sense in which the words can be used, is a private business, in which the public are interested only as they are interested in the storage of other products of the soil, or in articles of manufacture, it is clear that the court intended to declare that, whenever one devotes his property to a business which is useful to the public, "affects the community at large," the Legislature can regulate the compensation which the owner may receive for its use, and for his own services in connection with it. . . .

If this be sound law, if there be no protection, either in the principles upon which our republican government is founded, or in the prohibitions of the Constitution against such invasion of private rights, all property and all business in the state are held at the mercy of a majority of its Legislature. . . .

No State "shall deprive any person of life, liberty or property without due process of law," says the Fourteenth Amendment to the Constitution. . . .

By the term "liberty," as used in the provision, something more is meant than mere freedom from physical restraint or the bounds of a prison. It means freedom to go where one may choose, and to act in such manner, not inconsistent with the equal rights of others, as his judgment may dictate for the promotion of his happiness; that is, to pursue such callings and avocations as may be most suitable to develop his capacities, and give to them their highest enjoyment.

The same liberal construction which is required for the protection of life and liberty, in all particulars in which life and liberty are of any value, should be applied to the protection of private property. If the Legislature of a State, under pretense of providing for the public good, or for any other reason, can determine against the consent of the owner, the uses to which private property shall be devoted, or the prices which the owner shall receive for its uses, it can deprive him of the property as completely as by a special Act for its confiscation or destruction. If, for instance, the owner is prohibited from using his building for the purposes for which it was designed, it is of little consequence that he is permitted to retain the title and possession; or, if he is compelled to take as compensation for its use less than the expenses to which he is subject by its ownership, he is, for all practical purposes, deprived of the property, as effectually as if the Legislature had ordered his forcible dispossession. If it be admitted that the Legislature has any control over the compensation, the extent of that compensation becomes a mere matter of legislative discretion. . . .

There is nothing in the character of the business of the defendants as warehousemen which called for the interference complained of in this case. Their buildings are not nuisances; their occupation of receiving and storing grain infringes upon no rights of others, disturbs no neighborhood, infects not the air, and in no respect prevents others from using and enjoying their property as to them may seem best. The legislation in question is nothing less than a bold assertion of absolute power by the State to control, at its discretion, the property and business of the citizen, and fix the compensation he shall receive. . . .

. . . I deny the power of any Legislature under our government to fix the price which one shall receive for his property of any kind. If the power can be exercised as to one article, it may as to all articles, and the prices of every thing, from a calico gown to a city mansion, may be the subject of legislative direction. . . .

I am of opinion that the judgment of the Supreme Court of Illinois should be reversed.

Mr. Justice Strong concurred in this dissent.

Chicago, Milwaukee & St. Paul Railway Company v. Minnesota
134 U.S. 418; 10 S. Ct. 462; 33 L. Ed. 970 (1890)
Vote: 6-3

An 1887 Minnesota law established a commission with the power to set "equal and reasonable rates of charges for the transportation of property." This case began after the commission ordered a decrease in the rate for transporting milk. The railroad company brought suit, challenging the authority of the commission, and the railroad took the case to the Supreme Court on a writ of error.

Mr. Justice Blatchford . . . delivered the opinion of the Court.

. . . The construction put upon the statute by the Supreme Court of Minnesota must be accepted by this court, for the purposes of the present case, as conclusive and not to be reexamined here as to its propriety or accuracy. The Supreme Court authoritatively declares that it is the expressed intention of the legislature of Minnesota, by the statute, that the rates recommended and published by the commission, if it proceeds in the manner pointed out by the act, are not simply advisory, nor merely *prima facie* equal and reasonable, but final and conclusive as to what are equal and reasonable charges; that the law neither contemplates nor allows any issue to be made or inquiry to be had as their equality or reasonableness in fact; that, under the statute, the rates published by the commission are the only ones that are lawful, and, therefore, in contemplation of law the only ones that are equal and reasonable; and that, in a proceeding for a mandamus under the statute, there is no fact to traverse except the violation of law in not complying with the recommendations of the commission. In other words, although the railroad company is forbidden to establish rates that are not equal and reasonable, there is no power in the courts to stay the hands of the commission, if it chooses to establish rates that are unequal and unreasonable.

This being the construction of the statute by which we are bound in considering the present case, we are of opinion that, so construed, it conflicts with the

Constitution of the United States in the particulars complained of by the railroad company. It deprives the company of its right to a judicial investigation by due process of law, under the forms and with the machinery provided by the wisdom of successive ages for the investigation judicially of the truth of a matter in controversy, and substitutes therefor, as an absolute finality, the action of a railroad commission which, in view of the powers conceded to it by the state court, cannot be regarded as clothed with judicial functions or possessing the machinery of a court of justice.

Under section 8 of the statute, which the Supreme Court of Minnesota says is the only one which relates to the matter of the fixing by the commission of general schedules of rates, and which section, it says, fully and exclusively provides for that subject, and is complete in itself, all that the commission is required to do is, on the filing with it by a railroad company of copies of its schedules of charges, to "find" that any part thereof is in any respect unequal or unreasonable, and then it is authorized and directed to compel the company to change the same and adopt such charge as the commission "shall declare to be equal and reasonable," and, to that end, it is required to inform the company in writing in what respect its charges are unequal and unreasonable. No hearing is provided for, no summons or notice to the company before the commission has found what it is to find and declared what it is to declare, no opportunity provided for the company to introduce witnesses before the commission, in fact, nothing which has the semblance of due process of law; and although, in the present case, it appears that, prior to the decision of the commission, the company appeared before it by its agent, and the commission investigated the rates charged by the company for transporting milk, yet it does not appear what the character of the investigation was or how the result was arrived at.

By the second section of the statute in question, it is provided that all charges made by a common carrier for the transportation of passengers or property shall be equal and reasonable. Under this provision, the carrier has a right to make equal and reasonable charges for such transportation. In the present case, the return alleged that the rate of charge fixed by the commission was not equal or reasonable, and the Supreme Court held that the statute deprived the company of the right to show that judicially. The question of the reasonableness of a rate of charge for transportation by a railroad company, involving as it does the element of reasonableness both as regards the company and as regards the public, is eminently a question for judicial investigation, requiring due process of law for its determination. If the company is deprived of the power of charging reasonable rates for the use of its property, and such deprivation takes place in the absence of an investigation by judicial machinery, it is deprived of the lawful use of its property, and thus, in substance and effect, of the property itself, without due process of law and in violation of the Constitution of the United States; and in so far as it is thus deprived, while other persons are permitted to receive reasonable profits upon their invested capital, the company is deprived of the equal protection of the laws. . . .

Mr. Justice Miller, concurring. . . .

Mr. Justice Bradley (with whom concurred *Mr. Justice Gray* and *Mr. Justice Lamar*) dissenting.

I cannot agree to the decision of the court in this case. It practically overrules *Munn v. Illinois* *** and the several railroad cases that were decided at the same time. The government principle of those cases was that the regulation and settlement of the fares of railroads and other public accommodations is a legislative prerogative and not a judicial one. . . .

But it is said that all charges should be reasonable, and that none but reasonable charges can be exacted; and it is urged that what is a reasonable charge is a judicial question. On the contrary, it is preeminently a legislative one, involving considerations of policy as well as of remuneration; and is usually determined by the legislature, by fixing a maximum of charges in the charter of the company, or afterwards, if its hands are not tied by contract. . . .

Thus, the legislature either fixes the charges at rates which it deems reasonable; or merely declares that they shall be reasonable; and it is only in the latter case, where what is reasonable is left open, that the courts have jurisdiction of the subject. I repeat: When the legislature declares that the charges shall be reasonable, or, which is the same thing, allows the common-law rule to that effect to prevail, and leaves the matter there; then resort may be had to the courts to inquire judicially whether the charges are reasonable. Then, and not till then, is it a judicial question. But the legislature has the right, and it is its prerogative, if it chooses to exercise it, to declare what is reasonable. . . .

It is always a delicate thing for the courts to make an issue with the legislative department of the government, and they should never do so if it is possible to avoid it. By the decision now made we declare, in effect, that the judiciary, and not the legislature, is the final arbiter in the regulation of fares and freights of railroads and the charges of other public accommodations. It is an assumption of authority on the part of the judiciary which, it seems to me, with all due deference to the judgment of my brethren, it has no right to make. . . .

I think it is perfectly clear, and well settled by the decisions of this court, that the legislature might have fixed the rates in question. If it had done so, it would have done it through the aid of committees appointed to investigate the subject, to acquire information, to cite parties, to get all the facts before them, and finally to decide and report. No one could

have said that this was not due process of law. And if the legislature itself could do this, acting by its committees, and proceeding according to the usual forms adopted by such bodies, I can see no good reason why it might not delegate the duty to a board of commissioners, charged, as the board in this case was, to regulate and fix the charges so as to be equal and reasonable. . . .

It may be that our legislatures are invested with too much power, open, as they are, to influences so dangerous to the interests of individuals, corporations and society. But such is the Constitution of our republican form of government; and we are bound to abide by it until it can be corrected in a legitimate way. If our legislatures become too arbitrary in the exercise of their powers, the people always have a remedy in their hands; they may at any time restrain them by constitutional limitations. But so long as they remain invested with the powers that ordinarily belong to the legislative branch of government, they are entitled to exercise those powers, amongst which, in my judgment, is that of the regulation of railroads and other public means of intercommunication, and the burdens and charges which those who own them are authorized to impose upon the public. . . .

Lochner v. New York

198 U.S. 45; 25 S. Ct. 539; 49 L. Ed. 937 (1905)
Vote: 5-4

Joseph Lochner, a bakery owner in Utica, N.Y., was fined $50 for violating a state law that limited employment in bakeries to ten hours a day and sixty hours a week. After his conviction was upheld by the state appellate courts, Lochner obtained review in the U.S. Supreme Court on a writ of error.

Mr. Justice Peckham delivered the opinion of the Court.

The indictment . . . charges that the plaintiff in error violated . . . the labor law of the state of New York, in that he wrongfully and unlawfully required and permitted an employee working for him to work

more than sixty hours in one week. . . . The mandate of the statute, that "no employee shall be required or permitted to work," is the substantial equivalent of an enactment that "no employee shall contract or agree to work," more than ten hours per day; and, as there is no provision for special emergencies, the statute is mandatory in all cases. It is not an act merely fixing the number of hours which shall constitute a legal day's work, but an absolute prohibition upon the employer permitting, under any circumstances, more than ten hours work to be done in his establishment. The employee may desire to earn the extra money which would arise from his working more than the prescribed time, but this statute forbids the employer from permitting the employee to earn it.

The statute necessarily interferes with the right of contract between the employer and employees, concerning the number of hours in which the latter may labor in the bakery of the employer. The general right to make a contract in relation to his business is part of the liberty of the individual protected by the 14th Amendment of the Federal Constitution. *** Under that provision no state can deprive any person of life, liberty, or property without due process of law. The right to purchase or to sell labor is part of the liberty protected by this amendment, unless there are circumstances which exclude the right. There are, however, certain powers, existing in the sovereignty of each state in the Union, somewhat vaguely termed police powers, the exact description and limitation which have not been attempted by the courts. Those powers, broadly stated, and without, at present, any attempt at a more specific limitation, relate to the safety, health, morals, and general welfare of the public. Both property and liberty are held on such reasonable conditions as may be imposed by the governing power of the state in the exercise of those powers, and with such conditions the 14th Amendment was not designed to interfere. . . .

The state, therefore, has power to prevent the individual from making certain kinds of contracts, and in regard to them the Federal Constitution offers no protection. If the contract be one which the state, in the legitimate exercise of its police power, has the right to prohibit, it is not prevented from prohibiting it by the 14th Amendment. Contracts in violation of a statute, for immoral purposes, or to do any other unlawful act, could obtain no protection from the Federal Constitution, as coming under the liberty of person or of free contract. Therefore, when the state, by its legislature, in the assumed exercise of its police powers, has passed an act which seriously limits the right to labor or the right of contract in regard to their means of livelihood between persons who are *sui juris* (both employer and employee), it becomes of great importance to determine which shall prevail, — the right of the individual to labor for such time as he may choose, or the right of the state to prevent the individual from laboring, or from entering into any contract to labor, beyond a certain time prescribed by the state.

This court has recognized the existence and upheld the exercise of the police powers of the states in many cases which might fairly be considered as border ones, and it has, in the course of its determination of questions regarding the asserted invalidity of such statutes, on the ground of their violation of the rights secured by the Federal Constitution, been guided by rules of a very liberal nature, the application of which has resulted, in numerous instances, in upholding the validity of state statutes thus assailed. Among the later cases where the state law has been upheld by this court is that of *Holden* v. *Hardy*. *** A provision in the act of the legislature of Utah was there under consideration, the act limiting the employment of workmen in all underground mines or workings, to eight hours per day, "except in cases of emergency, where life or property is in imminent danger." It also limited the hours of labor in smelting and other institutions for the reduction or refining of ores or metals to eight hours per day, except in like cases of emergency. The act was held to be a valid exercise of the police powers of the state. . . .

It must, of course, be conceded that there is a limit to the valid exercise of the police power by the state. There is no dispute concerning this general proposition. Otherwise the 14th Amendment would have no efficacy and the legislatures of the states would have unbounded power, and it would be enough to say that any piece of legislation was enacted to conserve the morals, the health, or the safety of the people; such legislation would be valid, no matter how absolutely without foundation the claim might be. The claim of the police power would be a mere pretext, — become another and delusive name for the supreme sovereignty of the state to be exercised free from constitutional restraint. This is not contended for. In every case that comes before this court, therefore, where legislation of this character is concerned, and where the protection of the Federal Constitution is sought, the question necessarily arises. Is this a fair, reasonable, and appropriate exercise of the police power of the state, or is it an unreasonable, unnecessary, and arbitrary interference with the right of the individual to his personal liberty, or to enter into those contracts in relation to labor which may seem to him appropriate or necessary for the support of himself and his family? Of course the liberty of contract relating to labor includes both parties to it. The one has as much right to purchase as the other to sell labor.

This is not a question of substituting the judgment of the court for that of the legislature. If the act be within the power of the state it is valid, although the judgment of the court might be totally opposed to the enactment of such a law. But the question would still remain: Is it within the police power of the state? And that question must be answered by the court.

The question whether this act is valid as a labor law, pure and simple, may be dismissed in a few words. There is no reasonable ground for interfering with the liberty of person or the right of free contract, by determining the hours of labor, in the occupation of a baker. There is no contention that bakers as a class are not equal in intelligence and capacity to men in other trades or manual occupations, or that they are not able to assert their rights and care for themselves without the protecting arm of the state, interfering with their independence of judgment and of action. They are in no sense wards of the state. Viewed in the light of a purely labor law, with no reference whatever to the question of health, we think that a law like the one before us involves neither the safety, the morals, nor the welfare, of the public, and that interest of the public is not in the slightest degree affected by such an act. The law must be upheld, if at all, as a law pertaining to the health of the individual engaged in the occupation of a baker. It does not affect any other portion of the public than those who are engaged in that occupation. Clean and wholesome bread does not depend upon whether the baker works but ten hours per day or only sixty hours a week. The limitation of the hours of labor does not come within the police power on that ground.

It is a question of which of two powers or rights shall prevail,—the power of the state to legislate or the right of the individual to liberty of person and freedom of contract. The mere assertion that the subject relates, though but in a remote degree, to the public health, does not necessarily render the enactment valid. The act must have a more direct relation, as a means to an end, and the end itself must be appropriate and legitimate, before an act can end,

and the end itself must be appropriate and legitimate, before an act can be held to be valid which interferes with the general right of an individual to be free in his person and in his power to contract in relation to his own labor. . . .

We think the limit of the police power has been reached and passed in this case. There is, in our judgment, no reasonable foundation for holding this to be necessary or appropriate as a health law to safeguard the public health, or the health of the individuals who are following the trade of a baker. If this statute be valid, and if, therefore, a proper case is made out in which to deny the right of an individual, *sui juris,* as employer or employee, to make contracts for the labor of the latter under the protection of the provisions of the Federal Constitution, there would seem to be no length to which legislation of this nature might not go. . . .

We think that there can be no fair doubt that the trade of a baker, in and of itself, is not an unhealthy one to that degree which would authorize the legislature to interfere with the right to labor, and with the right of free contract on the part of the individual, either as employer or employee. In looking through statistics regarding all trades and occupations, it may be true that the trade of a baker does not appear to be as healthy as some other trades, and is also vastly more healthy than still others. To the common understanding the trade of a baker has never been regarded as an unhealthy one. Very likely physicians would not recommend the exercise of that or of any other trade as a remedy for ill health. Some occupations are more healthy than others, but we think there are none which might not come under the power of the legislature to supervise and control the hours of working therein, if the mere fact that the occupation is not absolutely and perfectly healthy is to confer that right upon the legislative department of the government. . . .

It is impossible for us to shut our eyes to the fact that many of the laws of this character, while passed under what is claimed to be the police power for the purpose of protecting the public health or welfare, are, in reality, passed from other motives. We are justified in saying so when, from the character of the law and the subject upon which it legislates, it is apparent that the public health or welfare bears but the most remote relation to the law. The purpose of a statute must be determined from the natural and legal effect of the language employed; and whether it is or is not repugnant to the Constitution of the United States must be determined from the natural effect of such statutes when put into operation, and not from their proclaimed purpose. ***

It is manifest to us that the limitation of the hours of labor as provided for in this section of the statute under which the indictment was found, and the plaintiff in error convicted, has no such direct relation to, and no such substantial effect upon, the health of the employee, as to justify us in regarding the section as really a health law. It seems to us that the real object and purpose were simply to regulate the hours of labor between the master and his employees (all being men, *sui juris*), in a private business, not dangerous in any degree to morals, or in any real and substantial degree to the health of the employees. Under such circumstances the freedom of master and employee to contract with each other in relation to their employment, and in defining the same, cannot be prohibited or interfered with, without violating the Federal Constitution.

The judgment of the Court of Appeals of New York, as well as that of the Supreme Court and of the County Court of Oneida County, must be reversed and the case remanded to County Court for further proceedings not inconsistent with this opinion.

Reversed.

Mr. Justice Harlan (with whom **Mr. Justice White** and **Mr. Justice Day** concurred) dissenting:

. . . It is plain that this statute was enacted in order to protect the physical well-being of those who work in bakery and confectionery establishments. It may be that the statute had its origin, in part, in the belief that employers and employees in such establishments were not upon an equal footing, and that the necessities of the latter often compelled them to submit to such exactions as unduly taxed their strength. Be this as it may, the statute must be taken as expressing the belief of the people of New York that, as a general rule, and in the case of the average man, labor in excess of sixty hours during a week in such establishments may endanger the health of those who thus labor. Whether or not this be wise legisla-

tion it is not the province of the court to inquire. Under our system of government the courts are not concerned with the wisdom or policy of legislation. So that, in determining the question of power to interfere with liberty of contract, the court may inquire whether the means devised by the state are germane to an end which may be lawfully accomplished and have a real or substantial relation to the protection of health, as involved in the daily work of the persons, male and female, engaged in bakery and confectionery establishments. But when this inquiry is entered upon I find it impossible, in view of common experience, to say that there is here no real or substantial relation between the means employed by the state and the end sought to be accomplished by its legislation. Nor can I say that the statute has no appropriated or direct connection with that protection to health which each state owes to her citizens; or that it is not promotive of the health of the employees in question; or that the regulation prescribed by the state is utterly unreasonable and extravagant or wholly arbitrary. Still less can I say that the statute is, beyond question, a plain, palpable invasion of rights secured by the fundamental law. Therefore I submit that this court will transcend its functions if it assumes to annul the statute of New York. It must be remembered that this statute does not apply to all kinds of business. It applies only to work in bakery and confectionery establishments, in which, as all know, the air constantly breathed by workmen is not as pure and healthful as that to be found in some other establishments or out of doors. . . .

. . . [T]he state is not amenable to the judiciary, in respect of its legislative enactments, unless such enactments are plainly, palpably, beyond all question, inconsistent with the Constitution of the United States. We are not to presume that the state of New York has acted in bad faith. Nor can we assume that its legislature acted without due deliberation, or that it did not determine this question upon the fullest attainable information and for the common good. We cannot say that the state has acted without reason, nor ought we to proceed upon the theory that its action is a mere sham. Our duty, I submit, is to sustain the statute as not being in conflict with the Federal Constitution, for the reason—and such is an all-sufficient reason—it is not shown to be plainly and palpably inconsistent with that instrument. Let the state alone in the management of its purely domestic affairs, so long as it does not appear beyond all question that it has violated the Federal Constitution. This view necessarily results from the principle that the health and safety of the people of a state are primarily for the state to guard and protect.

I take leave to say that the New York statute, in the particulars here involved, cannot be held to be in conflict with the 14th Amendment, without enlarging the scope of the amendment far beyond its original purpose, and without bringing under the supervision of this court matters which have been supposed to belong exclusively to the legislative departments of the several states . . . to guard the health and safety of their citizens . . .

Mr. Justice Holmes, dissenting:

. . . This case is decided upon an economic theory which a large part of the country does not entertain. If it were a question whether I agreed with that theory, I should desire to study it further and long before making up my mind. But I do not conceive that to be my duty, because I strongly believe that my agreement or disagreement has nothing to do with the right of a majority to embody their opinions in law. It is settled by various decisions of this court that . . . state laws may regulate life in many ways which are as legislators might think as injudicious, or if you like as tyrannical, as this, and which, equally with this, interfere with the liberty to contract. Sunday laws and usury laws are ancient examples. A more modern one is the prohibition of lotteries. The liberty of the citizen to do as he likes so long as he does not interfere with the liberty of others to do the same, which has been a shibboleth for some well-known writers, is interfered with by school laws, by the post office, by every state or municipal institution which takes his money for purposes thought desirable, whether he likes it or not. The 14th Amendment does not enact Mr. Herbert Spencer's *Social Statics*. . . . But a Constitution is not intended to embody a particular economic theory, whether of paternalism and the organic relation of the citizen to the state or of laissez faire. It is made for people of fundamentally differing views, and the accident of finding certain opinions natural and familiar, or novel, and even shocking, ought not to conclude our judgment upon the question whether statutes embodying them conflict with the Constitution of the United States.

General propositions do not decide concrete cases. The decision will depend on a judgment or intuition more subtle than any articulate major premise. But I think that the proposition just stated, if it is accepted, will carry us far toward the end. Every opinion tends to become a law. I think that the word "liberty," in the 14th Amendment, is perverted when it is held to prevent the natural outcome of a dominant opinion, unless it can be said that a rational and fair man necessarily would admit that the statute proposed would infringe fundamental principles as they have been understood by the traditions of our people and our law. It does not end research to show that no such sweeping condemnation can be passed upon the statute before us. A reasonable man might think it a proper measure on the score of health. Men whom I certainly could not pronounce unreasonable would uphold it as a first installment of a general regulation of the hours of work. Whether in the latter aspect it would be open to the charge of inequality I think it unnecessary to discuss.

Adkins v. Children's Hospital

261 U.S. 525; 43 S. Ct. 394; 67 L. Ed. 785 (1923)
Vote: 5-3

In 1918, Congress created a board and empowered it to set minimum wages for women and children working in The District of Columbia. Children's Hos- *pital obtained an injunction to prevent Adkins and other board members from enforcing the minimum wage. Adkins et al. appealed to the Supreme Court.*

Mr. Justice Sutherland delivered the opinion of the Court.

... The judicial duty of passing upon the constitutionality of an act of Congress is one of great gravity and delicacy. The statute here in question has successfully borne the scrutiny of the legislative branch of the government, which, by enacting it, has affirmed its validity; and that determination must be given great weight. This Court, by an unbroken line of decisions from Chief Justice Marshall to the present day, has steadily adhered to the rule that every possible presumption is in favor of the validity of an act of Congress until overcome beyond rational doubt. But if, by clear and indubitable demonstration, a statute be opposed to the Constitution, we have no choice but to say so. The Constitution, by its own terms, is the supreme law of the land, emanating from the people, the repository of ultimate sovereignty under our form of government. A congressional statute, on the other hand, is the act of an agency of this sovereign authority, and, if it conflict with the Constitution, must fall; for that which is not supreme must yield to that which is....

The statute now under consideration is attacked upon the ground that it authorizes an unconstitutional interference with the freedom of contract included within the guarantees of the due process clause of the Fifth Amendment. That the right to contract about one's affairs is a part of the liberty of the individual protected by this clause is settled by the decisions of this Court, and is no longer open to question. *** Within this liberty are contracts of employment of labor. In making such contracts, generally speaking, the parties have an equal right to obtain from each other the best terms they can as the result of private bargaining....

There is, of course, no such thing as absolute freedom of contract. It is subject to a great variety of restraints. But freedom of contract is, nevertheless, the general rule and restraint the exception; and the exercise of legislative authority to abridge it can be justified only by the existence of exceptional circumstances. Whether these circumstances exist in the present case constitutes the question to be answered....

In the *Muller* Case the validity of an Oregon statute, forbidding the employment of any female in certain industries more than ten hours during any

one day, was upheld. The decision proceeded upon the theory that the difference between the sexes may justify a different rule respecting hours of labor in the case of women than in the case of men. It is pointed out that these consist in differences of physical structure, especially in respect of the maternal functions, and also in the fact that historically woman has always been dependent upon man, who has established his control by superior physical strength.... But the ancient inequality of the sexes, otherwise than physical as suggested in the *Muller* Case has continued "with diminishing intensity." In view of the great—not to say revolutionary—changes which have taken place since that utterance, in the contractual, political, and civil status of women, culminating in the Nineteenth Amendment, it is not unreasonable to say that these differences have now come almost, if not quite, to the vanishing point. In this aspect of the matter, while the physical differences must be recognized in appropriate cases, and legislation fixing hours or conditions of work may properly taken them into account, we cannot accept the doctrine that women of mature age, *sui juris,* require or may be subjected to restrictions upon their liberty of contract which could not lawfully be imposed in the case of men under similar circumstances. To do so would be to ignore all the implications to be drawn from the present-day trend of legislation, as well as that of common thought and usage, by which woman is accorded emancipation from the old doctrine that she must be given special protection or be subjected to special restraint in her contractual and civil relationships. In passing, it may be noted that the instant statute applies in the case of a woman employer contracting with a woman employee as it does when the former is a man.

The essential characteristics of the statute now under consideration, which differentiate it from the laws fixing hours of labor, will be made to appear as we proceed. It is sufficient now to point out that the latter ... deal with incidents of the employment having no necessary effect upon the heart of the contract; that is, the amount of wages to be paid and received. A law forbidding work to continue beyond a given number of hours leaves the parties free to contract about wages and thereby equalize whatever additional burdens may be imposed upon the employer as a result of the restrictions as to hours, by an adjustment in respect of the amount of wages. Enough has been said to show that the authority to fix hours of labor cannot be exercised except in respect of those occupations where work of long-continued duration is detrimental to health. This Court has been careful in every case where the question has been raised, to place its decision upon this limited authority of the legislature to regulate hours of labor, and to disclaim any purpose to uphold the legislation as fixing wages, thus recognizing an essential difference between the two. It seems plain that these decisions afford no real support for any form of law establishing minimum wages.

If now, in the light furnished by the foregoing exceptions to the general rule forbidding legislative interference with freedom of contract, we examine and analyze the statute in question, we shall see that it differs from them in every material respect. . . . It is simply and exclusively a price-fixing law, confined to adult women (for we are not now considering the provisions relating to minors), who are legally as capable of contracting for themselves as men. It forbids two parties having lawful capacity under penalties as to the employer to freely contract with one another in respect of the price for which one shall render service to the other in a purely private employment where both are willing, perhaps anxious, to agree, even though the consequences may be to oblige one to surrender a desirable engagement, and the other to dispense with the services of a desirable employee. . . .

The standard furnished by the statute for the guidance of the board is so vague as to be impossible of practical application with any reasonable degree of accuracy. What is sufficient to supply the necessary cost of living for a woman worker and maintain her in good health and protect her morals is obviously not a precise or unvarying sum,—not even approximately so. The amount will depend upon a variety of circumstances: The individual temperament, habits of thrift, care, ability to buy necessaries intelligently, and whether the woman lives alone or with her family. To those who practice economy, a given sum will afford comfort, while to those of contrary habit the same sum will be wholly inadequate. The cooperative economies of the family group are not taken into

account, though they constitute an important consideration in estimating the cost of living, for it is obvious that the individual expense will be less in the case of a member of a family than in the case of one living alone. The relation between earnings and morals is not capable of standardization. It cannot be shown that well-paid women safeguard their morals more carefully than those who are poorly paid. Morality rests upon other considerations than wages; and there is, certainly, no such prevalent connection between the two as to justify a broad attempt to adjust the latter with reference to the former. . . .

The law takes account of the necessities of only one party to the contract. It ignores the necessities of the employer by compelling him to pay not less than a certain sum, not only whether the employee is capable of earning it, but irrespective of the ability of his business to sustain the burden, generously leaving him, of course, the privilege of abandoning his business as an alternative for going on at a loss. Within the limits of the minimum sum, he is precluded, under penalty of fine and imprisonment, from adjusting compensation to the differing merits of his employees. It compels him to pay at least the sum fixed in any event, because the employee needs it, but requires no service of equivalent value from the employee. . . . To the extent that the sum fixed exceeds the fair value of the services rendered, it amounts to a compulsory exaction from the employer for the support of a partially indigent person, for whose condition there rests upon him no peculiar responsibility, and therefore, in effect, arbitrarily shifts to his shoulders a burden which, if it belongs to anybody, belongs to society as a whole.

The feature of this statute which, perhaps more than any other, puts upon it the stamp of invalidity is that it exacts from the employer an arbitrary payment for a purpose and upon a basis having no causal connection with his business, or the contract, or the work the employee engages to do. . . . The ethical right of every worker, man or woman, to a living wage, may be conceded. One of the declared and important purposes of trade organizations is to secure it. And with that principle and with every legitimate effort to realize it in fact, no one can quarrel; but the fallacy of the proposed method of attaining it is that it assumes that every employer is bound, at all events to furnish it. The moral requirement, implicit in every contract of employment, *viz.,* that the amount to be paid and the service to be rendered shall bear to each other some relation of just equivalence, is completely ignored. . . . Certainly the employer, by paying a fair equivalent for the service rendered, though not sufficient to support the employee, has neither caused nor contributed to her poverty. On the contrary, to the extent of what he pays, he has relieved it. In principle, there can be no difference between the case of selling labor and the case of selling goods. If one goes to the butcher, the baker, or grocer to buy food, he is morally entitled to obtain the worth of his money, but he is not entitled to more. If what he gets is worth what he pays, he is not justified in demanding more simply because he needs more; and the shopkeeper, having dealt fairly and honestly in that transaction, is not concerned in any peculiar sense with the question of his customer's necessities. . . . But a statute which prescribes payment without regard to any of these things, and solely with relation to circumstances apart from the contract of employment, the business affected by it, and the work done under it, is so clearly the product of a naked, arbitrary exercise of power, that it cannot be allowed to stand under the Constitution of the United States.

We are asked, upon the one hand, to consider the fact that several states have adopted similar statutes, and we are invited, upon the other hand, to give weight to the fact that three times as many states, presumably as well informed and as anxious to promote the health and morals of their people, have refrained from enacting such legislation. We have also been furnished with a large number of printed opinions approving the policy of the minimum wage, and our own reading has disclosed a large number to the contrary. These are all proper enough for the consideration of the lawmaking bodies, since their tendency is to establish the desirability or undesirability of the legislation; but they reflect no legitimate light upon the question of its validity, and that is what we are called upon to decide. The elucidation of that question cannot be aided by counting heads.

It is said that great benefits have resulted from the operation of such statutes, not alone in the District of Columbia, but in the several states where they have been in force. A mass of reports, opinions of special observers and students of the subject, and the like, has been brought before us in support of this statement, all of which we have found interesting but only mildly persuasive. That the earnings of women now are greater than they were formerly, and that conditions affecting women have become better in other respects, may be conceded; but convincing indications of the logical relation of these desirable changes to the law in question are significantly lacking. They may be, and quite probably are, due to other causes. . . .

Finally, it may be said that if, in the interest of the public welfare, the police power may be invoked to justify the fixing of a minimum wage, it may, when the public welfare is thought to require it, be invoked to justify a maximum wage. The power to fix high wages connotes, by like course of reasoning, the power to fix low wages. If, in the face of the guarantees of the Fifth Amendment, this form of legislation shall be legally justified, the field for the operation of the police power will have been widened to a great and dangerous degree. If, for example, in the opinion of future lawmakers, wages in the building trades shall become so high as to preclude people of ordinary means from building and owning homes, an authority which sustains the minimum wage will be invoked to support a maximum wage for building laborers and artisans, and the same argument which has been here urged to strip the employer of his constitutional liberty of contract in one direction will be utilized to strip the employee of his constitutional liberty of contract in the opposite direction. A wrong decision does not end with itself: it is a precedent, and, with the swing of sentiment, its bad influence may run from one extremity of the arc to the other.

It has been said that legislation of the kind now under review is required in the interest of social justice, for whose ends freedom of contract may lawfully be subjected to restraint. The liberty of the individual to do as he pleases, even in innocent matters, is not absolute. It must frequently yield to the common good, and the line beyond which the power of interference may not be pressed is neither definite nor unalterable, but may be made to move, within limits not well defined, with changing need and circumstance. Any attempt to fix a rigid boundary would be unwise as well as futile. But, nevertheless, there are limits to the power, and when these have been passed, it becomes the plain duty of the courts, in the proper exercise of their authority, to so declare. To sustain the individual freedom of action contemplated by the Constitution is not to strike down the common good, but to exalt it; for surely the good of society as a whole cannot be better served than by the preservation against arbitrary restraint of the liberties of its constituent members.

It follows from what has been said that the act in question passes the limit prescribed by the Constitution, and, accordingly, the decrees of the court below are affirmed.

Mr. Justice Brandeis took no part in the consideration or decision of these cases.

Mr. Chief Justice Taft, dissenting.

I regret much to differ from the Court of these cases.

The boundary of the police power, beyond which its exercise becomes an invasion of the guaranty of liberty under the Fifth and Fourteenth Amendments to the Constitution, is not easy to mark. Our Court has been laboriously engaged in pricking out a line in successive cases. We must be careful, it seems to me, to follow that line as well as we can, and not to depart from it by suggesting a distinction that is formal rather than real.

Legislatures, in limiting freedom of contract between employee and employer by a minimum wage, proceed on the assumption that employees in the class receiving least pay are not upon a full level of equality of choice with their employer, and in their necessitous circumstances are prone to accept pretty much anything that is offered. They are peculiarly subject to the overreaching of the harsh and greedy employer. The evils of the sweating system and of the long hours and low wages which are characteristic of it are well known. Now, I agree that it is a disputable question in the field of political economy how far a statutory requirement of maximum hours or minimum wages may be a useful remedy for these evils, and whether it may not make the case of the op-

pressed employee worse than it was before. But it is not the function of this Court to hold congressional acts invalid simply because they are passed to carry out economic views which the Court believes to be unwise or unsound. . . .

The right of the legislature under the Fifth and Fourteenth Amendments to limit the hours of employment on the score of the health of the employee, it seems to me, has been firmly established. As to that, one would think the line had been pricked out so that it has become a well-formulated rule. . . . In [*Bunting v. Oregon*] *** this Court sustained a law limiting the hours of labor of any person, whether man or woman, working in any mill, factory, or manufacturing establishment, to ten hours a day, with a proviso as to further hours [allowing limited overtime at one and one-half times the regular wage]. . . . The law covered the whole field of industrial employment, and certainly covered the case of persons employed in bakeries. Yet the opinion in the *Bunting* Case does not mention the Lochner Case. No one can suggest any constitutional distinction between employment in a bakery and one in any other kind of a manufacturing establishment which should make a limit of hours in the one invalid, and the same limit in the other permissible. It is impossible for me to reconcile the *Bunting* Case and the Lochner Case, and I have always supposed that the Lochner Case was thus overruled *sub silentio*. Yet the opinion of the Court herein in support of its conclusion quotes from the opinion in the Lochner Case as one which has been sometimes distinguished, but never overruled. Certainly there was no attempt to distinguish it in the Bunting Case.

However, the opinion herein does not overrule the *Bunting* Case in express terms, and therefore I assume that the conclusion in this case rests on the distinction between a minimum of wages and a maximum of hours in the limiting of liberty to contract. I regret to be at variance with the court as to the substance of this distinction. In absolute freedom of contract the one term is as important as the other, for both enter equally into the consideration given and received; a restriction as to one is not any greater in essence than the other, and is of the same kind. One is the multiplier and the other the multiplicand.

If it be said that long hours of labor have a more direct effect upon the health of the employee than the low wage, there is very respectable authority from those observers, disclosed in the record and in the literature on the subject, quoted at length in the briefs, that they are equally harmful in this regard. Congress took this view, and we cannot say it was not warranted in so doing. . . .

I am authorized to say that **Mr. Justice Sanford** concurs in this opinion.

Mr. Justice Holmes, dissenting.

The question in this case is the broad one, whether Congress can establish minimum rates of wages for women in the District of Columbia, with due provision for special circumstances, or whether we must say that Congress has no power to meddle with the matter at all. To me, notwithstanding the deference due to the prevailing judgment of the Court, the power of Congress seems absolutely free from doubt. The end—to remove conditions leading to ill health, immorality, and the deterioration of the race—no one would deny to be within the scope of constitutional legislation. The means are means that have the approval of Congress, of many states, and of those governments from which we have learned our greatest lessons. When so many intelligent persons, who have studied the matter more than any of us can, have thought that the means are effective and are worth the price, it seems to me impossible to deny that the belief reasonably may be held by reasonable men. If the law encountered no other objection than that the means bore no relation to the end, or that they cost too much, I do not suppose that anyone would venture to say that it was bad. I agree, of course, that a law answering the foregoing requirements might be invalidated by specific provisions of the Constitution. For instance, it might take private property without just compensation. But, in the present instance, the only objection that can be urged is found within the vague contours of the Fifth Amendment, prohibiting the depriving any person of liberty or property without due process of law. To that I turn.

The earlier decisions upon the same words in the Fourteenth Amendment began within our memory, and went no farther than an unpretentious assertion of the liberty to follow the ordinary callings. Later that innocuous generality was expanded into the dogma, Liberty of Contract. Contract is not specifically mentioned in the text that we have to construe. It is merely an example of doing what you want to do, embodied in the word "liberty." But pretty much all law consists in forbidding men to do some things that they want to do, and contract is no more exempt from law than other acts. Without enumerating all the restrictive laws that have been upheld, I will mention a few that seem to me to have interfered with liberty of contract quite as seriously and directly as the one before us. Usury laws prohibit contracts by which a man receives more than so much interest for the money that he lends. Statutes of frauds restrict many contracts to certain forms. Some Sunday laws prohibit practically all contracts during one-seventh of our whole life. Insurance rates may be regulated. Finally, women's hours of labor may be fixed. . . . And the principle was extended to men, with the allowance of a limited overtime, to be paid for "at the rate of time and one half of the regular wage," in *Bunting v. Oregon.* ***

I confess that I do not understand the principle on which the power to fix a minimum for the wages of women can be denied by those who admit the power to fix a maximum for their hours of work. I fully assent to the proposition that here, as elsewhere, the distinctions of the law are distinctions of degree; but I perceive no difference in the kind or degree of interference with liberty, the only matter with which we have any concern, between the one case and the other. The bargain is equally affected whichever half you regulate. *Muller v. Oregon* [1908], I take it, is as good law today as it was in 1908. It will need more than the Nineteenth Amendment to convince me that there are no differences between men and women, or that legislation cannot take those differences into account. I should not hesitate to take them into account if I thought it necessary to sustain this act. . . . But after *Bunting v. Oregon* *** I had supposed that it was not necessary, and that *Lochner v. New York* *** would be allowed a deserved repose. . . .

Nebbia v. New York

291 U.S. 502; 54 S. Ct. 505; 78 L. Ed. 940 (1934)
Vote: 5-4

The factual background of this case vividly illustrates how a trivial incident can result in a landmark constitutional decision. In 1933, the New York legislature had established a milk control board with the power to "fix minimum and maximum . . . retail prices to be charged . . . to consumers." The board set the price of milk at nine cents a quart, but Leo Nebbia, a Rochester grocer, violated this order by selling two quarts of milk and a nickel loaf of bread for eighteen cents. At his trial, Nebbia asserted that the statute and order contravened the Due Process Clause of the Fourteenth Amendment. Following his misdemeanor conviction, Nebbia renewed this contention unsuccessfully in appeals to the county court and the New York Court of Appeals. He then petitioned the U.S. Supreme Court for review.

Mr. Justice Roberts delivered the opinion of the Court.

. . . Under our form of government the use of property and the making of contracts are normally matters of private and not of public concern. The general rule is that both shall be free of governmental interference. But neither property rights nor contract rights are absolute; for government cannot exist if the citizen may at will use his property to the detriment of his fellows, or exercise his freedom of contract to work them harm. Equally fundamental with the private right is that of the public to regulate it in the common interest. . . .

The milk industry in New York has been the subject of long-standing and drastic regulations in the public interest. The legislative investigation of 1932 was persuasive of the fact that for this and other reasons unrestricted competition aggravated existing evils and the normal law of supply and demand was insufficient to correct maladjustments detrimental to the community. The inquiry disclosed destructive and demoralizing competitive conditions and unfair trade practices which resulted in retail price cutting and reduced the income of the farmer below the cost of production. We do not understand the appel-

lant to deny that in these circumstances the legislature might reasonably consider further regulation and control desirable for protection of the industry and the consuming public. That body believed conditions could be improved by preventing destructive price-cutting by stores which, due to the flood of surplus milk, were able to buy at much lower prices than the larger distributors and to sell without incurring the delivery costs of the latter. In the order of which complaint is made the Milk Control Board fixed a price of ten cents per quart for sales by a distributor to a consumer, and nine cents by a store to a consumer, thus recognizing the lower costs of the store, and endeavoring to establish a differential which would be just to both. In the light of the facts the order appears not to be unreasonable or arbitrary, or without relation to the purpose to prevent ruthless competition from destroying the wholesale price structure on which the farmer depends for his livelihood, and the community for an assured supply of milk.

But we are told that because the law essays to control prices it denies due process. Notwithstanding the admitted power to correct existing economic ills by appropriate regulation of business, even though an indirect result may be a restriction of the freedom of contract or a modification of charges for services or the price of commodities, the appellant urges that direct fixation of prices is a type of regulation absolutely forbidden. His position is that the Fourteenth Amendment requires us to hold the challenged statute void for this reason alone. The argument runs that the public control of rates or prices is *per se* unreasonable and unconstitutional, save as applied to businesses affected with a public interest; that a business so affected is one in which property is devoted to an enterprise of a sort which the public itself might appropriately undertake, or one whose owner relies on a public grant or franchise for the right to conduct the business, or in which he is bound to serve all who apply; in short, such as is commonly called a public utility; or a business in its nature a monopoly. The milk industry, it is said, possesses none of these characteristics, and, therefore, not being affected with a public interest, its charges may not be controlled by the state. Upon the soundness of this contention the appellant's case against the statute depends.

We may as well say at once that the dairy industry is not, in the accepted sense of the phrase, a public utility. We think the appellant is also right in asserting that there is in this case no suggestion of any monopoly or monopolistic practice. It goes without saying that those engaged in the business are in no way dependent upon public grants or franchises for the privilege of conducting their activities. But if, as must be conceded, the industry is subject to regulation in the public interest, what constitutional principle bars the state from correcting existing maladjustments by legislation touching prices? We think there is no such principle. The Due Process Clause makes no mention of sales or of prices any more than it speaks of business or contracts or buildings or other incidents of property. The thought seems nevertheless to have persisted that there is something peculiarly sacrosanct about the price one may charge for what he makes or sells, and that, however able to regulate other elements of manufacture or trade, with incidental effect upon price, the state is incapable of directly controlling the price itself. This view was negatived many years ago. *** . . .

It is clear that there is no closed class or category of businesses affected with a public interest, and the function of courts in the application of the Fifth and Fourteenth Amendments is to determine in each case whether circumstances vindicate the challenged regulation as a reasonable exertion of governmental authority or condemn it as arbitrary or discriminatory. *** The phrase "affected with a public interest" can, in the nature of things, mean no more than that an industry, for adequate reason, is subject to control for the public good. In several of the decisions of this court wherein the expressions "affected with a public interest," and "clothed with a public use," have been brought forward as the criteria of the validity of price control, it has been admitted that they are not susceptible of definition and form an unsatisfactory test of the constitutionality of legislation directed at business practices or prices. These decisions must

rest, finally, upon the basis that the requirements of due process were not met because the laws were found arbitrary in their operation and effect. But there can be no doubt that upon proper occasion and by appropriate measures the state may regulate a business in any of its aspects, including the prices to be charged for the products or commodities it sells.

So far as the requirement of due process is concerned, and in the absence of other constitutional restriction, a state is free to adopt whatever economic policy may reasonably be deemed to promote public welfare, and to enforce that policy by legislation adapted to its purpose. The courts are without authority either to declare such policy, or, when it is declared by the legislature, to override it. . . .

. . . The Constitution does not secure to any one liberty to conduct his business in such fashion as to inflict injury upon the public at large, or upon any substantial group of the people. Price control, like any other form of regulation, is unconstitutional only if arbitrary, discriminatory, or demonstrably irrelevant to the policy the legislature is free to adopt, and hence an unnecessary and unwarranted interference with individual liberty.

Tested by these considerations we find no basis in the Due Process Clause of the Fourteenth Amendment for condemning the provisions of the Agriculture and Markets Law here drawn into question.

The judgment is affirmed.

Mr. Justice McReynolds [joined by Justices Van Devanter, Sutherland and Butler, dissenting].

. . . Regulation to prevent recognized evils in business has long been upheld as permissible legislative action. But fixation of the price at which "A," engaged in an ordinary business, may sell, in order to enable "B," a producer, to improve his condition, has not been regarded as within legislative power. This is not regulation, but management, control, dictation—it amounts to the deprivation of the fundamental right which one has to conduct his own affairs honestly and along customary lines. The argument advanced here would support general prescription of prices for farm products, groceries, shoes, clothing, all the necessities of modern civilization, as well as labor, when some legislature finds and declares such action advisable and for the public good. This

Court has declared that a State may not by legislative fiat convert a private business into a public utility. *** And if it be now ruled that one dedicates his property to public use whenever he embarks on an enterprise which the Legislature may think it desirable to bring under control, this is but to declare that rights guaranteed by the Constitution exist only so long as supposed public interest does not require their extinction. To adopt such a view, of course, would put an end to liberty under the Constitution. . . .

West Coast Hotel Company v. Parrish

300 U.S. 379; 57 S. Ct. 578; 81 L. Ed. 703 (1937)
Vote: 5-4

In May, 1935, Elsie Parrish was discharged from her job as a chambermaid at the Cascadian Hotel (owned by the West Coast Hotel Company) in Wenatchee, Washington. She had originally been employed in the late summer of 1933 at a wage rate of twenty-two cents per hour. At the time of her dismissal, Parrish was being paid twenty-five cents an hour, still well below the $14.50 weekly minimum set by the Industrial Welfare Committee pursuant to a state minimum-wage law passed in 1913. Elsie Parrish and her husband, Ernest, promptly sued the West Coast Hotel Company for $216.19, the amount by which the minimum wage exceeded her actual earnings during the period of her employment. Although the Parrishes lost at the trial level (the judge held that the case was controlled by Adkins v. Children's Hospital*), they appealed successfully to the state supreme court. This tribunal, in spite of* Adkins, *sustained the Washington minimum-wage statute. One of the West Coast Hotel attorneys asked the judge who had written the opinion in this case how the state court could have reached such a result in light of* Adkins. *The judge said in reply, "Well, let's let the Supreme Court say it one more time." A few weeks later, the Court did just that with its ruling in* Tipaldo *striking down the New York minimum-wage statute. But the Parrishes persisted, and the Supreme Court agreed to review their case in the late fall of 1936.*

Mr. Chief Justice Hughes delivered the opinion of the Court.

This case presents the question of the constitutional validity of the minimum wage law of the state of Washington.

. . . It provides:

Sec. 1. The welfare of the State of Washington demands that women and minors be protected from conditions of labor which have a pernicious effect on their health and morals. The State of Washington, therefore, exercising herein its police and sovereign power declares that inadequate wages and unsanitary conditions of labor exert such pernicious effect.

Sec. 2. It shall be unlawful to employ women or minors in any industry or occupation within the State of Washington under conditions of labor detrimental to their health or morals; and it shall be unlawful to employ women workers in any industry within the State of Washington at wages which are not adequate for their maintenance.

Sec. 3. There is hereby created a commission to be known as the "Industrial Welfare Commission" for the State of Washington, to establish such standards of wages and conditions of labor for women and minors employed within the State of Washington, as shall be held hereunder to be reasonable and not detrimental to health and morals, and which shall be sufficient for the decent maintenance of women. . . .

The appellant conducts a hotel. The appellee Elsie Parrish was employed as a chambermaid and (with her husband) brought this suit to recover the difference between the wages paid her and the minimum wage fixed pursuant to the state law. The minimum wage was $14.50 per week of 48 hours. The appellant challenged the act as repugnant to the due process clause of the Fourteenth Amendment of the Constitution of the United States. The Supreme Court of the State, reversing the trial court, sustained the statute and directed judgment for the plaintiffs. . . .

The appellant relies upon the decision of the Court in *Adkins v. Children's Hospital* *** which held invalid the District of Columbia Minimum Wage Act, which was attacked under the Due Process Clause of the Fifth Amendment. On the argument at bar, counsel for the appellees attempted to distinguish the *Adkins* case upon the ground that the appellee was employed in a hotel and that the business of an innkeeper was affected with a public interest. That effort at distinction is obviously futile, as it appears that in one of the cases ruled by the *Adkins* opinion the employee was a woman employed as an elevator operator in a hotel. . . .

The recent case of *Morehead v. New York ex rel. Tipaldo* *** came here on *certiorari* to the New York court, which had held the New York minimum wage act for women to be invalid. A minority of this Court thought that the New York statute was distinguishable in a material feature from that involved in the *Adkins* case, and that for that and other reasons the New York statute should be sustained. But the Court of Appeals of New York had said that it found no material difference between the two statutes, and this Court held that the "meaning of the statute" as fixed by the decision of the state court "must be accepted here as if the meaning had been specifically expressed in the enactment." . . . That view led to the affirmance by this Court of the judgment in the Morehead case, as the Court considered that the only question before it was whether the *Adkins* case was distinguishable and that reconsideration of that decision had not been sought. . . .

We think that the question which was not deemed to be open in the Morehead case is open and is necessarily presented here. The Supreme Court of Washington has upheld the minimum wage statute of that State. It has decided that the statute is a reasonable exercise of the police power of the State. In reaching that conclusion the state court has invoked principles long established by this Court in the application of the Fourteenth Amendment. The state court has refused to regard the decision in the *Adkins* case as determinative and has pointed to our decisions both before and since that case as justifying its position. We are of the opinion that this ruling of the state court demands on our part a reexamination of the *Adkins* case. The importance of the question, in which many States having similar laws are concerned, the close division by which the decision in

the *Adkins* case was reached, and the economic conditions which have supervened, and in the light of which the reasonableness of the exercise of the protective power of the State must be considered, make it not only appropriate, but we think imperative, that in deciding the present case the subject should receive fresh consideration. . . .

The principle which must control our decision is not in doubt. The constitutional provision invoked is the due process clause of the Fourteenth Amendment governing the States, as the due process clause invoked in the Adkins case governed Congress. In each case the violation alleged by those attacking minimum wage regulation for women is deprivation of freedom of contract. What is this freedom? The Constitution does not speak of freedom of contract. It speaks of liberty and prohibits the deprivation of liberty without due process of law. In prohibiting that deprivation the Constitution does not recognize an absolute and uncontrollable liberty. Liberty in each of its phases has its history and connotation. But the liberty safeguarded is liberty in a social organization which requires the protection of law against the evils which menace the health, safety, morals and welfare of the people. Liberty under the Constitution is thus necessarily subject to the restraints of due process, and regulation which is reasonable in relation to its subject and is adopted in the interests of the community is due process.

This essential limitation of liberty in general governs freedom of contract in particular. More than twenty-five years ago we set forth the applicable principle in these words, after referring to the cases where the liberty guaranteed by the Fourteenth Amendment had been broadly described:

But it was recognized in the cases cited, as in many others, that freedom of contract is a qualified and not an absolute right. There is no absolute freedom to do as one wills or to contract as one chooses. The guaranty of liberty does not withdraw from legislative supervision that wide department of activity which consists of the making of contracts, or deny to government the power to provide restrictive safeguards. Liberty implies the absence of arbitrary restraint, not immunity from reasonable regulations and prohibitions imposed in the interests of the community. ***

This power under the Constitution to restrict freedom of contract has had many illustrations. That it may be exercised in the public interest with respect to contracts between employer and employee is undeniable. . . .

The point that has been strongly stressed that adult employees should be deemed competent to make their own contracts was decisively met nearly forty years ago in *Holden v. Hardy* *** where we pointed out the inequality in the footing of the parties. We said:

The legislature has also recognized the fact, which the experience of legislators in many States has corroborated, that the proprietors of these establishments and their operatives do not stand upon an equality, and that their interests are, to a certain extent, conflicting. The former naturally desire to obtain as much labor as possible from their employees, while the latter are often induced by the fear of discharge to conform to regulations which their judgment, fairly exercised, would pronounce to be detrimental to their health or strength. In other words, the proprietors lay down the rules and the laborers are practically constrained to obey them. In such cases self-interest is often an unsafe guide, and the legislature may properly interpose its authority.

And we added that the fact "that both parties are of full age and competent to contract does not necessarily deprive the state of the power to interfere where the parties do not stand upon an equality, or where the public health demands that one party to the contract shall be protected against himself." . . .

It is manifest that this established principle is peculiarly applicable in relation to the employment of women in whose protection the State has a special interest. That phase of the subject received elaborate consideration in *Muller v. Oregon* *** where the constitutional authority of the State to limit the working hours of women was sustained. We emphasized the consideration that "woman's physical structure and the performance of maternal functions place her at a disadvantage in the struggle for subsistence" and that her physical well-being "becomes an object of public interest and care in order to preserve the strength and vigor of the race." We emphasized the need of protecting women against oppression despite her possession of contractual rights. We said that "though limitations upon personal and contractual rights may be removed by legislation, there is that in her disposition and habits of life which will operate against

a full assertion of those rights. She will still be where some legislation to protect her seems necessary to secure a real equality of right." Hence she was "properly placed in a class by herself, and legislation designed for her protection may be sustained even when like legislation is not necessary for men and could not be sustained." We concluded that the limitations which the statute there in question "placed upon her contractual powers, upon her right to agree with her employer as to the time she shall labor" were "not imposed solely for her benefit, but also largely for the benefit of all." ***

. . . [T]he dissenting Justices in the *Adkins* case [argued] that the minimum wage statute [should] be sustained. The validity of the distinction made by the Court between a minimum wage and a maximum of hours in limiting liberty of contract was especially challenged. . . . That challenge persists and is without any satisfactory answer. As Chief Justice Taft observed: "In absolute freedom of contract the one term is as important as the other, for both enter equally into the consideration given and received, a restriction as to the one is not greater in essence than the other and is of the same kind. One is the multiplier and the other the multiplicand." And Mr. Justice Holmes, while recognizing that "the distinctions of the law are distinctions of degree," could "perceive no difference in the kind or degree of interference with liberty, the only matter with which we have any concern, between the one case and the other. The bargain is equally affected whichever half you regulate." . . .

The minimum wage to be paid under the Washington statute is fixed after full consideration by representatives of employers, employees and the public. It may be assumed that the minimum wage is fixed in consideration of the services that are performed in the particular occupations under normal conditions. Provision is made for special licenses at less wages in the case of women who are incapable of full service. The statement of Mr. Justice Holmes in the *Adkins* case is pertinent:

This statute does not compel anybody to pay anything. It simply forbids employment at rates below those fixed as the minimum requirement of health and right living. It is safe to assume that women will not be employed at even the lowest wages allowed unless they earn them, or unless the employer's business can sustain the burden. In short the law in its character and operation is like hundreds of so-called police laws that have been upheld.

And Chief Justice Taft forcibly pointed out the consideration which is basic in a statute of this character:

Legislatures which adopt a requirement of maximum hours or minimum wages may be presumed to believe that when sweating employers are prevented from paying unduly low wages by positive law they will continue their business, abating that part of their profits, which were wrung from the necessities of their employees, and will concede the better terms required by the law; and that while in individual cases hardship may result, the restriction will enure to the benefit of the general class of employees in whose interest the law is passed and so to that of the community at large. . . .

We think that the views thus expressed are sound and that the decision in the *Adkins* case was a departure from the true application of the principles governing the regulation by the State of the relation of employer and employed. . . .

With full recognition of the earnestness and vigor which characterize the prevailing opinion in the *Adkins* case, we find it impossible to reconcile that ruling with these well-considered declarations. What can be closer to the public interest than the health of women and their protection from unscrupulous and overreaching employers? And if the protection of women is a legitimate end of the exercise of state power, how can it be said that the requirement of the payment of a minimum wage fairly fixed in order to meet the very necessities of existence is not an admissible means to that end? The legislature of the State was clearly entitled to consider the situation of women in employment, the fact that they are in the class receiving the least pay, that their bargaining power is relatively weak, and that they are the ready victims of those who would take advantage of their necessitous circumstances. The legislature was entitled to adopt measures to reduce the evils of the "sweating system," the exploiting of workers at wages so low as to be insufficient to meet the bare cost of living, thus making their very helplessness the occasion of a most injurious competition. The legislature had the right to consider that its minimum wage requirements would be an important aid in carrying out its policy of protection. The adoption of similar requirements by many States evidences a deepseated conviction both as to the presence of the evil and as to the means adapted to check it. Legislative response to that conviction cannot be regarded as arbitrary or capricious, and that is all we have to decide. Even if the wisdom of the policy be regarded as debatable and its effects uncertain, still the legislature is entitled to its judgment.

There is an additional and compelling consideration which recent economic experience has brought into a strong light. The exploitation of a class of workers who are in an unequal position with respect to bargaining power and are thus relatively defenseless against the denial of a living wage is not only detrimental to their health and well being but casts a direct burden for their support upon the community. What these workers lose in wages the taxpayers are called upon to pay. The bare cost of living must be met. We may take judicial notice of the unparalleled demands for relief which arose during the recent period of depression and still continue to an alarming extent despite the degree of economic recovery which has been achieved. It is unnecessary to cite official statistics to establish what is of common knowledge through the length and breadth of the land. While in the instant case no factual brief has been presented, there is no reason to doubt that the state of Washington has encountered the same social problem that is present elsewhere. The community is not bound to provide what is in effect a subsidy for unconscionable employers. The community may direct its law-making power to correct the abuse which springs from their selfish disregard of the public interest. The argument that the legislation in question constitutes an arbitrary discrimination, because it does not extend to men, is unavailing. This Court has frequently held that the legislative authority, acting within its proper field, is not bound to extend its regulation to all cases which it might possibly reach. The legislature "is free to recognize degrees of harm and it may confine its restrictions to those classes of cases where the need is deemed to be clearest." *** If "the law presumably hits the evil where it is most felt, it is not to be overthrown because there are other instances to which it might have been applied." *** There is not "doctrinaire requirement" that the legislation should be couched in all embracing terms. . . .

Affirmed.

Mr. Justice Sutherland, dissenting.

Mr. Justice Van Devanter, Mr. Justice McReynolds, Mr. Justice Butler and I think the judgment of the court below should be reversed.

The principles and authorities relied upon to sustain the judgment, were considered in *Adkins v. Children's Hospital* and *Morehead v. New York ex rel. Tipaldo;* and their lack of application to cases like the one in hand was pointed out. A sufficient answer to all that is now said will be found in the opinions of the Court in those cases. Nevertheless, in the circumstances, it seems well to restate our reasons and conclusions. . . .

It is urged that the question involved should now receive fresh consideration, among other reasons, because of "the economic conditions which have supervened"; but the meaning of the Constitution does not change with the ebb and flow of economic events. We frequently are told in more general words that the Constitution must be construed in the light of the present. If by that it is meant that the Constitution is made up of living words that apply to every new condition which they include, the statement is quite true. But to say, if that be intended, that the words of the Constitution mean today what they did not mean when written—that is, that they do not apply to a situation now to which they would have applied then—is to rob that instrument of the essential element which continues it in force as the people have made it until they, and not their official agents, have made it otherwise. . . .

The judicial function is that of interpretation; it does not include the power of amendment under the guise of interpretation. To miss the point of difference between the two is to miss all that the phrase "supreme law of the land" stands for and to convert what was intended as inescapable and enduring mandates into mere moral reflections.

If the Constitution, intelligently and reasonably construed in the light of these principles, stands in the way of desirable legislation, the blame must rest upon that instrument, and not upon the Court for enforcing it according to its terms. The remedy in that situation—and the only true remedy—is to amend the Constitution. . . .

Coming, then, to a consideration of the Washington statute, it first is to be observed that it is in every substantial respect identical with the statute involved in the *Adkins* case. Such vices as existed in the latter are present in the former. And if the *Adkins* case was properly decided, as we who join in this opinion think it was, it necessarily follows that the Washington statute is invalid. . . .

Ferguson v. Skrupa

372 U.S. 726; 83 S. Ct. 1028; 10 L. Ed. 2d 93 (1963)
Vote: 9-0

Mr. Justice Black delivered the opinion of the Court.

In this case, properly here on appeal . . . , we are asked to review the judgment of a three-judge District Court enjoining, as being in violation of the Due Process Clause of the Fourteenth Amendment, a Kansas statute making it a misdemeanor for any person to engage "in the business of debt adjusting" except as an incident to "the lawful practice of law in this state." The statute defines "debt adjusting" as "the making of a contract, express, or implied with a particular debtor whereby the debtor agrees to pay a certain amount of money periodically to the person engaged in the debt adjusting business who shall for a consideration distribute the same among certain specified creditors in accordance with a plan agreed upon."

The complaint, filed by appellee Skrupa doing business as "Credit Advisor," alleged that Skrupa was engaged in the business of "debt adjusting" as defined by the statute, that his business was a "useful and desirable" one, that his business activities were not "inherently immoral or dangerous" or in any way contrary to the public welfare, and that therefore the business could not be "absolutely prohibited" by Kansas. The three-judge court heard evidence by

Skrupa tending to show the usefulness and desirability of his business and evidence by the state officials tending to show that "debt adjusting" lends itself to grave abuses against distressed debtors, particularly in the lower income brackets, and that these abuses are of such gravity that a number of States have strictly regulated "debt adjusting" or prohibited it altogether. The court found that Skrupa's business did fall within the Act's proscription and concluded, one judge dissenting, that the Act was prohibitory, not regulatory, but that even if construed in part as regulatory it was an unreasonable regulation of a "lawful business," which the court held amounted to a violation of the Due Process Clause of the Fourteenth Amendment. The court accordingly enjoined enforcement of the statute.

Under the system of government created by the Constitution, it is up to legislatures, not courts, to decide on the wisdom and utility of legislation. There was a time then the Due Process Clause was used by this Court to strike down laws which were thought unreasonable, that is, unwise or incompatible with some particular economic or social philosophy. In this manner the Due Process Clause was used, for example, to nullify laws prescribing maximum hours for work in bakeries, *Lochner v. New York,* *** outlawing "yellow dog" contracts, *Coppage v. Kansas,* *** setting minimum wages for women, *Adkins v. Children's Hospital,* *** and fixing the weight of loaves of bread, *Jay Burns Baking Co. v. Bryan.* *** This intrusion by the judiciary into the realm of legislative value judgments was strongly objected to at the time, particularly by Mr. Justice Holmes and Mr. Justice Brandeis. . . .

The doctrine that prevailed in *Lochner, Coppage, Adkins, Burns,* and like cases—that due process authorizes courts to hold laws unconstitutional when they believe the legislature has acted unwisely—has long since been discarded. We have returned to the original constitutional proposition that courts do not substitute their social and economic beliefs for the judgment of legislative bodies, who are elected to pass laws. As this Court stated in a unanimous opinion in 1941, "We are not concerned . . . with the wisdom, need, or appropriateness of the legislation." Legislative bodies have broad scope to experiment with economic problems, and this Court does not sit

to "subject the State to an intolerable supervision hostile to the basic principles of our Government and wholly beyond the protection which the general clause of the Fourteenth Amendment was intended to secure." It is now settled that States "have power to legislate against what are found to be injurious practices in their internal commercial and business affairs, so long as their laws do not run afoul of some specific federal constitutional prohibition or of some valid federal law."

. . . We conclude that the Kansas Legislature was free to decide for itself that legislation was needed to deal with the business of debt adjusting. Unquestionably, there are arguments showing that the business of debt adjusting has social utility, but such arguments are properly addressed to the legislature, not to us. We refuse to sit as a "superlegislature to weigh the wisdom of legislation," and we emphatically refuse to go back to the time when courts used the Due Process Clause "to strike down state laws, regulatory of business and industrial conditions, because they may be unwise, improvident, or out of harmony with a particular school of thought." Nor are we able or willing to draw lines by calling a law "prohibitory" or "regulatory." Whether the legislature takes for its textbook Adam Smith, Herbert Spencer, Lord Keynes, or some other is no concern of ours. The Kansas debt adjusting statute may be wise or unwise. But relief, if any be needed, lies not with us but with the body constituted to pass laws for the State of Kansas.

Nor is the statute's exception of lawyers a denial of equal protection of the laws to nonlawyers. Statutes create many classifications which do not deny equal protection; it is only "invidious discrimination" which offends the Constitution. If the State of Kansas wants to limit debt adjusting to lawyers, the Equal Protection Clause does not forbid. We also find no merit in the contention that the Fourteenth Amendment is violated by the failure of the Kansas statute's title to be as specific as appellee thinks it ought to be under the Kansas constitution.

Reversed.

Mr. Justice Harlan concurs in the judgment on the ground that this state measure bears a rational relation to a constitutionally permissible objective. ***

Hawaii Housing Authority v. Midkiff

467 U.S. 229; 104 S. Ct. 2321; 81 L. Ed. 2d 186 (1984)

Vote: 8-0

Justice O'Connor delivered the opinion of the Court.

The Fifth Amendment of the United States Constitution provides, in pertinent part, that "private property [shall not] be taken for public use, without just compensation." These cases present the question whether the Public Use Clause of that Amendment, made applicable to the States through the Fourteenth Amendment, prohibits the State of Hawaii from taking, with just compensation, title in real property from lessors and transferring it to lessees in order to reduce the concentration of ownership of fees simple in the State. We conclude that it does not.

The Hawaiian Islands were originally settled by Polynesian immigrants from the eastern Pacific. These settlers developed an economy around a feudal land tenure system in which one island high chief, the *ali'i nui,* controlled the land and assigned it for development to certain subchiefs. The subchiefs would then reassign the land to other lower ranking chiefs, who would administer the land and govern the farmers and other tenants working it. All land was held at the will of the *ali'i nui* and eventually had to be returned to his trust. There was no private ownership of land. ***

Beginning in the early 1800's, Hawaiian leaders and American settlers repeatedly attempted to divide the lands of the kingdom among the crown, the chiefs, and the common people. These efforts proved largely unsuccessful, however, and the land remained in the hands of a few. In the mid-1960's, after extensive hearings, the Hawaii Legislature discovered that, while the State and Federal Governments owned almost 49% of the State's land, another 47% was in the hands of only 72 private landowners. *** The legislature further found that 18 landholders, with tracts of 21,000 acres or more, owned more than 40% of this land and that, on Oahu, the most urbanized of the islands, 22 landowners owned 72.5% of the fee simple titles. *** The legislature concluded that concentrated land ownership was responsible for skewing the State's residential fee simple market, inflating land prices, and injuring the public tranquility and welfare.

To redress these problems, the legislature decided to compel the large landowners to break up their estates. The legislature considered requiring large landowners to sell lands which they were leasing to homeowners. However, the landowners strongly resisted this scheme, pointing out the significant federal tax liabilities they would incur. Indeed, the landowners claimed that the federal tax laws were the primary reason they previously had chosen to lease, and not sell, their lands. Therefore, to accommodate the needs of both lessors and lessees, the Hawaii Legislature enacted the Land Reform Act of 1967 (Act), *** which created a mechanism for condemning residential tracts and for transferring ownership of the condemned fees simple to existing lessees. By condemning the land in question, the Hawaii Legislature intended to make the land sales involuntary, thereby making the federal tax consequences less severe while still facilitating the redistribution of fees simple. ***

Under the Act's condemnation scheme, tenants living on single-family residential lots within developmental tracts at least five acres in size are entitled to ask the Hawaii Housing Authority (HHA) to condemn the property on which they live. *** When 25 eligible tenants, or tenants on half the lots in the tract, whichever is less, file appropriate applications, the Act authorizes HHA to hold a public hearing to determine whether acquisition by the State of all or part of the tract will "effectuate the public purposes" of the Act. *** If HHA finds that these public purposes will be served, it is authorized to designate some or all of the lots in the tract for acquisition. It then acquires, at prices set either by condemnation trial or by negotiation between lessors and lessees, the former fee owners' full "right, title, and interest" in the land. ***

After compensation has been set, HHA may sell the land titles to tenants who have applied for fee simple ownership. HHA is authorized to lend these tenants up to 90% of the purchase price, and it may condition final transfer on a right of first refusal for the first 10 years following sale. *** If HHA does not sell the lot to the tenant residing there, it may lease the lot or sell it to someone else, provided that public notice has been given. *** However, HHA may not sell to any one purchaser, or lease to any one tenant, more than one lot, and it may not operate for profit. *** In practice, funds to satisfy the condemnation awards have been supplied entirely by lessees. While the Act authorizes HHA to issue bonds and appropriate funds for acquisition, no bonds have issued and HHA has not supplied any funds for condemned lots. ***

In April 1977, HHA held a public hearing concerning the proposed acquisition of some of appellees' lands. HHA made the statutorily required finding that acquisition of appellees' lands would effectuate the public purposes of the Act. Then, in October 1978, it directed appellees to negotiate with certain lessees concerning the sale of the designated properties. Those negotiations failed, and HHA subsequently ordered appellees to submit to compulsory arbitration.

Rather than comply with the compulsory arbitration order, appellees filed suit, in February 1979, in United States District Court, asking that the Act be declared unconstitutional and that its enforcement be enjoined. The District Court temporarily restrained the State from proceeding against appellees' estates. Three months later, while declaring the compulsory arbitration and compensation formulae provisions of the Act unconstitutional, the District Court refused preliminarily to enjoin appellants from conducting the statutory designation and condemnation proceedings. Finally, in December 1979, it granted partial summary judgment to appellants, holding the remaining portion of the Act constitutional under the Public Use Clause. *** The District Court found that the Act's goals were within the bounds of the State's police powers and that the means the legislature had chosen to serve those goals were not arbitrary, capricious, or selected in bad faith.

The Court of Appeals for the Ninth Circuit reversed. *** ... [T]he Court of Appeals determined that the Hawaii Land Reform Act could not pass the requisite judicial scrutiny of the Public Use Clause. It found that the transfers contemplated by the Act were unlike those of takings previously held to constitute "public uses" by this Court. The court further

determined that the public purposes offered by the Hawaii Legislature were not deserving of judicial deference. The court concluded that the Act was simply "a naked attempt on the part of the state of Hawaii to take the private property of A and transfer it to B solely for B's private use and benefit." *** One judge dissented. ...

The majority of the Court of Appeals ... determined that the Act violates the "public use" requirement of the Fifth and Fourteenth Amendments. On this argument, however, we find ourselves in agreement with the dissenting judge in the Court of Appeals.

The starting point for our analysis of the Act's constitutionality is the Court's decision in *Berman v. Parker* [1954]. *** In *Berman,* the Court held constitutional the District of Columbia Redevelopment Act of 1945. That Act provided both for the comprehensive use of the eminent domain power to redevelop slum areas and for the possible sale or lease of the condemned lands to private interests. In discussing whether the takings authorized by that Act were for a "public use," *** the Court stated

We deal, in other words, with what traditionally has been known as the police power. An attempt to define its reach or trace its outer limits is fruitless, for each case must turn on its own facts. The definition is essentially the product of legislative determinations addressed to the purposes of government, purposes neither abstractly nor historically capable of complete definition. Subject to specific constitutional limitations, when the legislature has spoken, the public interest has been declared in terms well-nigh conclusive. In such cases the legislature, not the judiciary, is the main guardian of the public needs to be served by social legislation, whether it be Congress legislating concerning the District of Columbia ... or the States legislating concerning local affairs. ... This principle admits of no exception merely because the power of eminent domain is involved. ... ***

The Court explicitly recognized the breadth of the principle it was announcing, noting:

Once the object is within the authority of Congress, the right to realize it through the exercise of eminent domain is clear. For the power of eminent domain is merely the means to the end. ... Once the object is within the authority of Congress, the means by which it will be attained is also for Congress to determine. Here one of the means chosen is the use of private enterprise for redevelopment of the area. Appellants argue that this makes the project a taking from one businessman for the benefit of another businessman. But the means of executing the project are for Congress and Congress alone to determine, once the public purpose has been established. ***

The "public use" requirement is thus coterminous with the scope of a sovereign's police powers.

There is, of course, a role for courts to play in reviewing a legislature's judgment of what constitutes a public use, even when the eminent domain power is equated with the police power. But the Court in *Berman* made clear that it is "an extremely narrow" one. The Court in *Berman* cited with approval the Court's decision in *Old Dominion Co. v. United States* [1925], *** which held that deference to the legislature's "public use" determination is required "until it is shown to involve an impossibility." The *Berman* Court also cited to *United States ex rel. TVA v. Welch* [1946], *** which emphasized that "[a]ny departure from this judicial restraint would result in courts deciding on what is and is not a governmental function and in their invalidating legislation on the basis of their view on that question at the moment of decision, a practice which has proved impracticable in other fields." In short, the Court has made clear that it will not substitute its judgment for a legislature's judgment as to what constitutes a public use "unless the use be palpably without reasonable foundation." ***

To be sure, the Court's cases have repeatedly stated that "one person's property may not be taken for the benefit of another private person without a justifying public purpose, even though compensation be paid." *** Thus, in *Missouri Pacific R. Co. v. Nebraska* [1896], *** where the "order in question was not, and was not claimed to be, . . . a taking of private property for a public use under the right of eminent domain," *** the Court invalidated a compensated taking of property for lack of a justifying public purpose. But where the exercise of the eminent domain power is rationally related to a conceivable public purpose, the Court has never held a compensated taking to be proscribed by the Public Use Clause. ***

On this basis, we have no trouble concluding that the Hawaii Act is constitutional. The people of Hawaii have attempted, much as the settlers of the original 13 Colonies did, to reduce the perceived social and economic evils of a land oligopoly traceable to their monarchs. The land oligopoly has, according to the Hawaii Legislature, created artificial deterrents to the normal functioning of the State's residential land market and forced thousands of individual homeowners to lease, rather than buy, the land underneath their homes. Regulating oligopoly and the evils associated with it is a classic exercise of a State's police powers. *** We cannot disapprove of Hawaii's exercise of this power.

Nor can we condemn as irrational the Act's approach to correcting the land oligopoly problem. The Act presumes that when a sufficiently large number of persons declare that they are willing but unable to buy lots at fair prices the land market is malfunctioning. When such a malfunction is signaled, the Act authorizes HHA to condemn lots in the relevant tract. The Act limits the number of lots any one tenant can purchase and authorizes HHA to use public funds to ensure that the market dilution goals will be achieved. This is a comprehensive and rational approach to identifying and correcting market failure.

Of course, this Act, like any other, may not be successful in achieving its intended goals. But "whether in fact the provision will accomplish its objectives is not the question: the [constitutional requirement] is satisfied if . . . the . . . [state] Legislature rationally could have believed that the [Act] would promote its objective." *** When the legislature's purpose is legitimate and its means are not irrational, our cases make clear that empirical debates over the wisdom of takings— no less than debates over the wisdom of other kinds of socioeconomic legislation—are not to be carried out in the federal courts. Redistribution of fees simple to correct deficiencies in the market determined by the state legislature to be attributable to land oligopoly is a rational exercise of the eminent domain power. Therefore, the Hawaii statute must pass the scrutiny of the Public Use Clause. . . .

The State of Hawaii has never denied that the Constitution forbids even a compensated taking of property when executed for no reason other than to confer a private benefit on a particular private party. A purely private taking could not withstand the scrutiny of the public use requirement; it would serve no legitimate purpose of government and would thus be void. But no purely private taking is involved in this case. The Hawaii Legislature enacted its Land Reform Act not to benefit a particular class of identifiable individuals but to attack certain perceived evils of concentrated property ownership in Hawaii—a legitimate public purpose. Use of the condemnation power to achieve this purpose is not irrational. Since we assume for purposes of this appeal that the weighty demand of just compensation has been met,

the requirements of the Fifth and Fourteenth Amendments have been satisfied. Accordingly, we reverse the judgment of the Court of Appeals, and remand these cases for further proceedings in conformity with this opinion.

It is so ordered.

Justice Marshall took no part in the consideration or decision of these cases.

Nollan v. California Coastal Commission

483 U.S. 825; 107 S. Ct. 3141; 97 L. Ed. 2d 677 (1987)
Vote: 5-4

James and Marilyn Nollan leased with an option to purchase a small bungalow situated on a beachfront lot in Ventura County, California. Their option to buy was conditioned on their promise to demolish the bungalow, which had fallen into disrepair, and replace it with a new structure. In order to do so, they had to obtain a development permit from the California Coastal Commission. The commission informed the Nollans that it would grant the permit only on the condition that they grant an easement allowing for public access to the beach across their property. The Nollans filed suit in the superior court, which invalidated the easement condition and ordered that it be stricken from the permit. The California Coastal Commission appealed to the California Court of Appeals, which reversed the superior court. The Nollans appealed to the U.S. Supreme Court.

Justice Scalia delivered the Opinion of the Court.

... Had California simply required the Nollans to make an easement across their beachfront available to the public on a permanent basis in order to increase public access to the beach, rather than conditioning their permit to rebuild their house on their agreeing to do so, we have no doubt there would have been a taking. To say that the appropriation of a public easement across a landowner's premises does not constitute a taking of a property interest but

rather (as Justice Brennan contends) "a mere restriction on its use," *** is to use words in a manner that deprives them of all their ordinary meaning. Indeed, one of the principal uses of the eminent domain power is to assure that government be able to require conveyance of such interests, so long as it pays for them. *** Perhaps because the point is so obvious, we have never been confronted with a controversy that required us to rule upon it, but our cases' analysis of the effects of other governmental action lead us to the same conclusion. . . .

Given, then, that requiring uncompensated conveyance of the easement outright would violate the Fourteenth Amendment, the question becomes whether requiring it to be conveyed as a condition for issuing a land-use permit alters the outcome. We have long recognized that land use regulation does not effect a taking if it "substantially advance[s] legitimate state interests" and does not "den[y] an owner economically viable use of his land." *** Our cases have not elaborated on the standards for determining what constitutes a "legitimate state interest" or what type of connection between the regulation and the state interest satisfies the requirement that the former "substantially advance" the latter. They have made clear, however, that a broad range of governmental purposes and regulations satisfies these requirements. *** The Commission argues that among these permissible purposes are protecting the public's ability to see the beach, assisting the public in overcoming the "psychological barrier" to using the beach created by a developed shorefront, and preventing congestion on the public beaches. We assume, without deciding, that this is so—in which case the Commission unquestionably would be able to deny the Nollans their permit outright if their new house (alone, or by reason of the cumulative impact produced in conjunction with other construction) would substantially impede these purposes, unless the denial would interfere so drastically with the Nollans use of their property as to constitute a taking. ***

The Commission argues that a permit condition that serves the same legitimate police-power purpose as a refusal to issue the permit should not be found to be a taking if the refusal to issue the permit would not constitute a taking. We agree. . . . Although such a requirement, constituting a permanent grant of continuous access to the property, would have to be considered a taking if it were not attached to a development permit, the Commission's assumed power to forbid construction of the house in order to protect the public's view of the beach must surely include the power to condition construction upon some concession by the owner, even a concession of property rights, that serves the same end. If a prohibition designed to accomplish that purpose would be a legitimate exercise of the police power rather than a taking, it would be strange to conclude that providing the owner an alternative to that prohibition which accomplishes the same purpose is not.

The evident constitutional propriety disappears, however, if the condition substituted for the prohibition utterly fails to further the end advanced as the justification for the prohibition. When that essential nexus is eliminated, the situation becomes the same as if California law forbade shouting fire in a crowded theater, but granted dispensations to those willing to contribute $100 to the state treasury. While a ban on shouting fire can be a core exercise of the State's police power to protect the public safety, and can thus meet even our stringent standards for regulation of speech, adding the unrelated condition alters the purpose to one which, while it may be legitimate, is inadequate to sustain the ban. There-

fore, even though, in a sense, requiring a $100 tax contribution in order to shout fire is a lesser restriction on speech than an outright ban, it would not pass constitutional muster. Similarly here, the lack of nexus between the condition and the original purpose of the building restriction converts that purpose to something other than what it was. The purpose then becomes, quite simply, the obtaining of an easement to serve some valid governmental purpose, but without payment of compensation. Whatever may be the outer limits of "legitimate state interests" in the takings and land use context, this is not one of them. In short, unless the permit condition serves the same governmental purpose as the development ban, the building restriction is not a valid regulation of land use but "an out-and-out plan of extortion." ***

. . . It is quite impossible to understand how a requirement that people already on the public beaches be able to walk across the Nollans' property reduces any obstacles to viewing the beach created by the new house. It is also impossible to understand how it lowers any "psychological barrier" to using the public beaches, or how it helps to remedy any additional congestion on them caused by construction of the Nollans' new house. We therefore find that the Commission's imposition of the permit condition cannot be treated as an exercise of its land use power for any of these purposes. Our conclusion on this point is consistent with the approach of every other court that has considered the question, with the exception of the California state courts. ***

Justice Brennan argues that imposition of the access requirement is not irrational. In his version of the Commission's argument, the reason for the requirement is that in its absence, a person looking toward the beach from the road will see a street of residential structures including the Nollans' new home and conclude that there is no public beach nearby. If, however, that person sees people passing and repassing along the dry sand behind the Nollans' home, he will realize that there is a public beach somewhere in the vicinity. The Commission's action, however, was based on the opposite factual finding that the wall of houses completely blocked the view of the beach and that a person looking from the road would not be able to see it at all. . . .

We are left, then, with the Commission's justification for the access requirement unrelated to land use regulation:

"Finally, the Commission notes that there are several existing provisions of pass and repass lateral access benefits already given by past Faria Beach Tract applicants as a result of prior coastal permit decisions. The access required as a condition of this permit is part of a comprehensive program to provide continuous public access along Faria Beach as the lots undergo development or redevelopment." ***

That is simply an expression of the Commission's belief that the public interest will be served by a continuous strip of publicly accessible beach along the coast. The Commission may well be right that it is a good idea, but that does not establish that the Nollans (and other coastal residents) alone can be compelled to contribute to its realization. Rather, California is free to advance its "comprehensive program," if it wishes, by using its power of eminent domain for the "public purpose," see U.S. Const., Amdt. V; but if it wants an easement across the Nollans' property, it must pay for it.

Reversed.

Justice Brennan, with whom **Justice Marshall** joins, dissenting.

. . . The Court's conclusion that the permit rendition imposed on appellants is unreasonable cannot withstand analysis. First, the Court demands a degree of exactitude that is inconsistent with our standard for reviewing the rationality of a state's exercise of its police power for the welfare of its citizens. Second, even if the nature of the public access condition imposed must be identical to the precise burden on access created by appellants, this requirement is plainly satisfied. . . .

Imposition of the permit condition in this case represents the State's reasonable exercise of its police power. The Coastal Commission has drawn on its expertise to preserve the balance between private development and public access, by requiring that any project that intensifies development on the increasingly crowded California coast must be offset by gains in public access. Under the normal standard for review of the police power, this provision is eminently reasonable. Even accepting the Court's novel insistence on a precise *quid pro quo* of burdens and

benefits, there is a reasonable relationship between the public benefit and the burden created by appellants' development. The movement of development closer to the ocean creates the prospect of encroachment on public tidelands, because of fluctuation in the mean high tide line. The deed restriction ensures that disputes about the boundary between private and public property will not deter the public from exercising its right to have access to the sea.

Furthermore, consideration of the Commission's action under traditional takings analysis underscores the absence of any viable takings claim. The deed restriction permits the public only to pass and repass along a narrow strip of beach, a few feet closer to a seawall at the periphery of appellants' property. Appellants almost surely have enjoyed an increase in the value of their property even with the restriction, because they have been allowed to build a significantly larger new home with garage on their lot. . . .

. . . State agencies . . . require considerable flexibility in responding to private desires for development in a way that guarantees public access to the coast. They should be encouraged to regulate development in the context of the overall balance of competing uses of the shoreline. The Court today does precisely the opposite, overruling an eminently reasonable exercise of an expert state agency's judgment, substituting its own narrow view of how this balance should be struck. Its reasoning is hardly suited to the complex reality of natural resource protection in the 20th century. I can only hope that today's decision is an aberration, and that a broader vision ultimately prevails.

I dissent.

Justice Blackmun, dissenting.

. . . I disagree with the Court's rigid interpretation of the necessary correlation between a burden created by development and a condition imposed pursuant to the State's police power to mitigate that burden. The land-use problems this country faces require creative solutions. These are not advanced by an "eye for an eye" mentality. The close nexus between benefits and burdens that the Court now imposes on permit conditions creates an anomaly in the ordinary requirement that a State's exercise of its police power need be no more than rationally based.

In my view, the easement exacted from ap- pellants and the problems their development created are adequately related to the governmental interest in providing public access to the beach. Coastal development by its very nature makes public access to the shore generally more difficult. Appellants' structure is part of that general development and, in particular, it diminishes the public's visual access to the ocean and decreases the public's sense that it may have physical access to the beach. These losses in access can be counteracted, at least in part, by the condition on appellants' construction permitting public passage that ensures access along the beach.

Traditional takings analysis compels the conclusion that there is no taking here. The governmental action is a valid exercise of the police power, and, so far as the record reveals, has a nonexistent economic effect on the value of appellants' property. No investment-backed expectations were diminished. It is significant that the Nollans had notice of the easement before they purchased the property and that public use of the beach had been permitted for decades.

For these reasons, I respectfully dissent.

Justice Stevens, with whom **Justice Blackmun** joins, dissenting. . . .

PruneYard Shopping Center v. Robins

447 U.S. 74; 100 S. Ct. 2035; 64 L. Ed. 2d 741 (1980)
Vote: 9–0

In this case, the Court considers whether state constitutional provisions allowing individuals to exercise free speech rights on the premises of privately owned shopping centers violate the shopping center owners' rights under the Fourteenth Amendment. The facts are given in Justice Rehnquist's majority opinion.

Mr. Justice Rehnquist delivered the opinion of the Court.

We postponed jurisdiction of this appeal from the Supreme Court of California to decide the important federal constitutional questions it presented. . . .

I

Appellant PruneYard is a privately owned shopping center in the city of Campbell, Cal. It covers approximately 21 acres— 5 devoted to parking and 16 occupied by walkways, plazas, sidewalks, and buildings that contain more than 65 specialty shops, 10 restaurants, and a movie theater. The PruneYard is open to the public for the purpose of encouraging the patronizing of its commercial establishments. It has a policy not to permit any visitor or tenant to engage in any publicly expressive activity, including the circu-

lation of petitions, that is not directly related to its commercial purposes. This policy has been strictly enforced in a nondiscriminatory fashion. . . .

Appellees are high school students who sought to solicit support for their opposition to a United Nations resolution against "Zionism." On a Saturday afternoon they set up a card table in a corner of PruneYard's central courtyard. They distributed pamphlets and asked passersby to sign petitions, which were to be sent to the President and members of Congress. Their activity was peaceful and orderly and so far as the record indicates was not objected to by PruneYard's patrons.

Soon after appellees had begun soliciting signatures, a security guard informed them that they would have to leave because their activity violated PruneYard regulations. The guard suggested that they move to the public sidewalk at the PruneYard's perimeter. Appellees immediately left the premises and later filed this lawsuit. . . . They sought to enjoin appellants from denying them access to the Prune-Yard for the purpose of circulating their petitions.

The Superior Court held that appellees were not entitled under either the Federal or California Constitution to exercise their asserted rights on the shopping center property. *** It concluded that there were "adequate, effective channels of communication for [appellees] other than soliciting on the private property of the [PruneYard]." *** The California Court of Appeal affirmed.

The California Supreme Court reversed, holding that the California constitution protects "speech and petitioning, reasonably exercised, in shopping centers even when the centers are privately owned." *** It concluded that appellees are entitled to conduct their activity on PruneYard Property. In rejecting appellants' contention that such a result infringed property rights protected by the Federal Constitution, the California Supreme Court observed:

It bears repeated emphasis that we do not have under consideration the property or private rights of an individual homeowner or the proprietor of a modest retail establishment. As a result of advertising and the lure of a congenial environment, 25,000 persons are induced to congregate daily to take advantage of the numerous amenities offered by the [shopping center there]. A handful of additional orderly persons soliciting signatures and distributing handbills in connection therewith, under reasonable regulations adopted by defendant to assure that these activities do not interfere with normal business operations *** would not markedly dilute defendant's property rights. ***

. . . Before this Court, appellants contend that their constitutionally established rights under the Fourteenth Amendment to exclude appellees from adverse use of appellant's private property cannot be denied by invocation of a state constitutional provision or by judicial reconstruction of a state's laws of private property. . . .

Part II is deleted.

III

Appellants first contend that *Lloyd Corp. v. Tanner* *** (1972), prevents the State from requiring a private shopping center owner to provide access to persons exercising their state constitutional rights of free speech and petition when adequate alternative avenues of communication are available. *Lloyd* dealt with the question whether under the Federal Constitution a privately owned shopping center may prohibit the distribution of handbills on its property when the handbilling is unrelated to the shopping center's operations. *** The shopping center had adopted a strict policy against the distribution of handbills within the building complex and its malls, and it made no exceptions to this rule. *** Respondents in *Lloyd* argued that because the shopping center was open to the public, the First Amendment prevents the private owner from enforcing the handbilling restriction on shopping center premises. *** In rejecting this claim we substantially repudiated the rationale of *Food Employees v. Logan Valley Plaza* [1968], ***, which was later overruled in *Hudgens v. NLRB* [1976], *** We stated that property does not "lose its private character merely because the public is generally invited to use it for designated purposes," and that "[t]he essentially private character of a store and its privately owned abutting property does not change by virtue of being large or clustered with other stores in a modern shopping center." ***

Our reasoning in *Lloyd,* however, does not *ex proprio vigore* [of its own force] limit the authority of the State to exercise its police power or its sovereign right to adopt in its own Constitution individual liberties more expansive than those conferred by the Federal Constitution. *** In *Lloyd,* there was no state constitutional or statutory provision that had been construed to create rights to the use of private property by strangers, comparable to those found to exist by the California Supreme Court here. It is, of course, well established that a State in the exercise of its police power may adopt reasonable restrictions on private property so long as the restrictions do not amount to a taking without just compensation or contravene any other federal constitutional provision. *** *Lloyd* held that when a shopping center owner opens his private property to the public for the purpose of shopping, the First Amendment to the United States Constitution does not thereby create individual rights in expression beyond those already existing under applicable law. ***

IV

Appellants next contend that a right to exclude others underlies the Fifth Amendment guarantee against the taking of property without just compensation and the Fourteenth Amendment guarantee against the deprivation of property without due process of law.

It is true that one of the essential sticks in the bundle of property rights is the right to exclude others. *** And here there has literally been a "taking" of that right to the extent that the California Supreme Court has interpreted the State Constitution to entitle its citizens to exercise free expression and petition rights on shopping center property. But it is well established that "not every destruction or injury to property by governmental action has been held to be a 'taking' in the constitutional sense." *** Rather, the determination whether a state law unlawfully infringes a landowner's property in violation of the Taking Clause requires an examination of whether "the restriction on private property forc[es] some people alone to bear public burdens which, in all fairness and justice, should be borne by the public as a whole." *** This examination entails inquiry into such factors as the character of the governmental action, its economic impact, and its interference with reasonable investment-backed expectations. *** When "regulation goes too far it will be recognized as a taking." ***

Here the requirement that appellants permit appellees to exercise state-protected rights of free expression and petition on shopping center property clearly does not amount to an unconstitutional infringement of appellants' property rights under the Taking Clause. There is nothing to suggest that preventing appellants from prohibiting this sort of activity will unreasonably impair the value or use of their property as a shopping center. The PruneYard is a large commercial complex that covers several city blocks, contains numerous separate business establishments, and is open to the public at large. The decision of the California Supreme Court makes it clear that the PruneYard may restrict expressive activity by adopting time, place, and manner regulations that will minimize any interference with its commercial functions. Appellees were orderly, and they limited their activity to the common areas of the shopping center. In these circumstances, the fact that they may have "physically invaded" appellants' property cannot be viewed as determinative.

This case is quite different from *Kaiser Aetna v. United States* [1979]. *** *Kaiser Aetna* was a case in which the owners of a private pond had invested substantial amounts of money in dredging the pond, developing it into an exclusive marina, and building a surrounding marina community. The marina was open only to fee-paying members, and the fees were paid in part to "maintain the privacy and security of the pond." *** The Federal Government sought to compel free public use of the private marina on the ground that the marina became subject to the federal navigational servitude because the owners had dredged a channel connecting it to "navigable water."

The Government's attempt to create a public right of access to the improved pond interfered with Kaiser Aetna's "reasonable investment backed expectations." We held that it went "so far beyond ordinary regulation or improvement for navigation as to amount to a taking. . . ." *** Nor as a general proposition is the United States, as opposed to the several States, possessed of residual authority that enables it to define "property" in the first instance. A State is, of course, bound by the Just Compensation Clause of the Fifth Amendment, *** but here appellants have failed to demonstrate that the "right to exclude others" is so essential to the use or economic value of their property that the state-authorized limitation of it amounted to a "taking." . . .

V

Appellants finally contend that a private property owner has a First Amendment right not to be forced by the State to use his property as a forum for the speech of others. They state that in *Wooley v. Maynard* *** (1977), this Court concluded that a State may not constitutionally require an individual to participate in the dissemination of an ideological message by displaying it on his private property in a manner and for the express purpose that it be observed and read by the public. This rationale applies here, they argue, because the message of *Wooley* is that the State may not force an individual to display any message at all.

Wooley, however, was a case in which the government itself prescribed the message, required it to be displayed openly on appellee's personal property that was used "as part of his daily life," and refused to permit him to take any measures to cover up the motto even though the Court found that the display of the motto served no important state interest. Here, by contrast, there are a number of distinguishing factors. Most important, the shopping center by choice of its owner is not limited to the personal use of appellants. It is instead a business establishment that is open to the public to come and go as they please. The views expressed by members of the public in passing out pamphlets or seeking signatures for a petition thus will not likely be identified with those of the owner. Second, no specific message is dictated by the State to be displayed on appellants' property. There consequently is no danger of governmental discrimination for or against a particular message. Finally, as far as appears here appellants can expressly disavow any connection with the message by simply posting signs in the area where the speakers or handbillers stand. Such signs, for example, could disclaim any sponsorship of the message and could explain that the persons are communicating their own messages by virtue of state law. . . .

We conclude that neither appellants' federally recognized property rights have been infringed by the California Supreme Court's decision recognizing a right of appellees to exercise state-protected rights of expression and petition on appellants' property. The judgment of Supreme Court of California is therefore affirmed.

Mr. Justice Marshall, concurring. . . .

Mr. Justice White, concurring in part and concurring in the judgment.

. . . I agree that on the record before us there was not an unconstitutional infringement of appellants' property rights. But it bears pointing out that the Federal Constitution does not require that a shopping center permit distributions or solicitations on its property. . . . The First and Fourteenth Amendments do not prevent the property owner from excluding those who would demonstrate or communicate on his property. Insofar as the Federal Constitution is concerned, therefore, a State may decline to construe its own constitution so as to limit the property rights of the shopping center owner.

The Court also affirms the California Supreme Court's implicit holding that appellants' own free-speech rights under the First and Fourteenth Amendments were not infringed by requiring them to provide a forum for appellees to communicate with the public on shopping center property. I concur in this judgment, but I agree with Mr. Justice Powell that there are other circumstances that would present a far different First Amendment issue. May a State require the owner of a shopping center to subsidize any and all political, religious, or social-action groups by furnishing a convenient place for them to urge their views on the public and to solicit funds from likely prospects? Surely there are some limits on state authority to impose such requirements; and in this respect, I am not in entire accord with Part V of the Court's opinion.

Mr. Justice Powell with whom **Mr. Justice White** joins, concurring in part and in the judgment.

Although I join the judgment, I do not agree with all of the reasoning in Part V of the Court's opinion. I join Parts I–IV on the understanding that our decision is limited to the type of shopping center involved in this case. Significantly different questions would be presented if a State authorized strangers to picket or distribute leaflets in privately owned, free-standing stores and commercial premises. Nor does our decision today apply to all "shopping centers." This generic term may include retail establishments that vary widely in size, location, and other relevant characteristics. Even large establishments may be able to show that the number of type of persons wishing to speak on their premises would create a substantial annoyance to customers that could be eliminated only by elaborate, expensive, and possibly unenforceable time, place, and manner restrictions. As the Court observes, state power to regulate private property is limited to the adoption of reasonable restrictions that "do not amount to a taking without just compensation or contravene any other federal constitutional provision." ***

Restrictions on property use, like other state laws, are invalid if they infringe the freedom of expression and belief protected by the First and Fourteenth Amendments. In Part V of today's opinion, the Court rejects appellants' contention that "a private property owner has a First Amendment right not to be forced by the State to use his property as a forum for the speech of others." *** I agree that the owner of this shopping center has failed to establish a cognizable First Amendment claim in this case. But some of the language in the Court's opinion is unnecessarily and perhaps confusingly broad. In my view, state action that transforms privately owned property into a forum for the expression of the public's views could raise serious First Amendment questions. . . .

One easily can identify other circumstances in which a right of access to commercial property would burden the owner's First and Fourteenth Amendment right to refrain from speaking. But appellants have identified no such circumstance. Nor did appellants introduce evidence that would support a holding in their favor. . . .

On the record before us, I cannot say that customers of this vast center would be likely to assume that appellees' limited speech activity expressed the views of the PruneYard or of its owner. The shopping center occupies several city blocks. It contains more than 65 shops, 10 restaurants, and a theater. Interspersed among these establishments are common walkways and plazas designed to attract the public. *** Appellees are high school students who set up their card table in one corner of a center courtyard known as the "Grand Plaza." They showed passersby several petitions and solicited signatures. Persons solicited could not reasonably have believed that the petitions embodied the views of the shopping center merely because it owned the ground on which they stood.

Appellants have not alleged that they object to the ideas contained in the appellees' petitions. Nor do they assert that some groups who reasonably might be expected to speak at the PruneYard will express views that are so objectionable as to require a response even when listeners will not mistake their source. The record contains no evidence concerning the numbers of types of interest groups that may seek access to this shopping center, and no testimony showing that the appellants strongly disagree with any of them.

Because appellants have not shown that the limited right of access held to be afforded by the California Constitution burdened their First and Fourteenth Amendment rights in the circumstances presented, I join the judgment of the Court. I do not interpret our decision today as a blanket approval for state efforts to transform privately owned commercial property into public forums. Any such state action would raise substantial federal constitutional questions not present in this case.

CHAPTER ELEVEN

FREEDOM OF EXPRESSION, ASSEMBLY AND ASSOCIATION

[T]he guaranties of the First Amendment [are] the foundation upon which our governmental structure rests and without which it could not continue to endure as conceived and planned. . . . Freedom to speak and write about public questions is as important to the life of our government as is the heart to the human body. In fact, this privilege is the heart of our government. If that heart be weakened, the result is debilitation; if it be stilled, the result is death.

Justice Hugo Black, *Milk Wagon Drivers Union v. Meadowmoor Dairies* (1941)

INTRODUCTION

Freedoms of conscience, thought, and expression are fundamental components of American constitutional democracy. James Madison, principal author of the Bill of Rights, fully recognized the importance of these freedoms. The First Amendment, as he originally proposed it in the House of Representatives on June 8, 1789, read as follows:

> The civil rights of none shall be abridged on account of religious belief or worship, nor shall any national religion be established, nor shall the full and equal rights of conscience be in any manner, or on any pretext infringed.

> The people shall not be deprived or abridged of their right to speak, to write, or to publish their sentiments, and the freedom of the press, as one of the great bulwarks of liberty, shall be inviolable.

> The people shall not be restrained from peaceably assembling and consulting for their common good; nor from applying to the legislature by petitions, or remonstrances, for redress of their grievances.

The same principles of freedom, although less explicitly stated, are contained in the final version of the First Amendment, ratified in 1791:

> Congress shall make no law respecting an establishment of religion or prohibiting the free exercise thereof; or abridging the freedom of speech, or of the press, or the right of the people peaceably to assemble, and to petition the Government for a redress of grievances.

599

Despite the obvious importance of freedoms of thought and communication (the essence of First Amendment guarantees), the U.S. Supreme Court did not begin to give major attention to these values until after World War I. And not until the "constitutional revolution" of the late 1930s did First Amendment jurisprudence emerge as a principal field of constitutional interpretation. Since that time, First Amendment questions of increasing diversity and difficulty have continued to be among the most important concerns of the Court.

This chapter examines the Supreme Court's development of constitutional standards and guidelines broadly defining the freedoms of expression, assembly, and association. Although closely related to freedom of speech, freedom of the press, with its implications for the mass media, is addressed separately in Chapter 12.

Incorporation of Freedoms of Speech and Press

With the exception of the right of "just compensation" (discussed in Chapter 10), the expressive freedoms of speech and press were the earliest to be incorporated into the Fourteenth Amendment and thus made applicable to the states (see *Gitlow v. New York* [1925]; *Fiske v. Kansas* [1927]; *Near v. Minnesota* [1931]). The early incorporation of these freedoms was not merely an accident of history. Rather, it reflected the Supreme Court's awareness of the fundamental importance of these liberties. During debates over the original Bill of Rights, James Madison had proposed that constitutional protections in this area be provided against state encroachment. It was not until well into the twentieth century, however, that the Supreme Court converted this broad view of constitutional protection into national public policy. By the late 1940s, the Court had incorporated all First amendment guarantees into the Fourteenth Amendment, thus underscoring the fundamental importance accorded these rights. In *Palko v. Connecticut* (1937), Justice Benjamin Cardozo, writing for an eight-member majority, characterized freedom of thought and speech as "the matrix, the indispensable condition, of nearly every other form of freedom."

The "Preferred Position" of First Amendment Freedoms

During the 1940s several members of the Supreme Court suggested that the First Amendment freedoms of speech and press enjoyed a "preferred position" in relation to other constitutional guarantees. In *Murdock v. Pennsylvania* (1943), for example, Justice William O. Douglas stated for the Court that "freedom of press, freedom of speech, freedom of religion are in a preferred position." Two years later, Justice Wiley B. Rutledge, commenting on the Court's duty to choose between individual freedom and governmental power, asserted: "Choice on that border, now as always delicate, is perhaps more so where the usual presumption supporting legislation is balanced by the preferred place given in our scheme to the great, the indispensable democratic freedoms secured by the First Amendment" (*Thomas v. Collins* [1945]).

Justice Felix Frankfurter, while recognizing the fundamental nature of First Amendment freedoms, was critical of the "preferred position" terminology. As a former Harvard University law professor, he could not resist lecturing his colleagues on the finer points of constitutional law. Thus, in a concurring opinion (one of his favorite modes of communication), Frankfurter characterized the "preferred position of freedom of speech" as "a mischievous phrase, if it carries the thought, which it may safely imply, that any law touching communication is infected with presumptive invalidity" (*Kovacs v. Cooper* [1949]). In the years since Frankfurter registered his protest, the Court has not used the "preferred freedoms" language, but freedom of expression is still given a high priority.

Approaches to First Amendment Interpretation

Although the contemporary Court is not inclined, as were a majority of the justices in the 1940s, to acknowledge formally that First Amendment freedoms enjoy a preferred position under the Constitution, it is generally recognized that there is something special about the First Amendment and the values it represents. In the past half-century, First Amendment freedoms have undergone development and refinement far beyond anything that the authors of the Bill of Rights might have anticipated.

In the limited space available we can sketch only the major features of this complex development. Some forms of expression, such as political debate, are accorded very wide latitude under the First Amendment; others, such as commercial speech, are given more limited protection; and still other types of communication, including defamation and obscenity, are given little, if any. With some notable exceptions, the tendency of the Court since the late 1930s has been to expand the scope of expressive freedoms. Nevertheless, significant limits are still imposed. Few absolute guarantees are recognized, and the necessary task of line-drawing characterizes the development of First Amendment law no less than other areas of constitutional interpretation. From time to time, the Court has placed reliance on elusive standards, such as "clear and present danger," "bad tendency," and the "balancing" test. In recent years, however, the justices have been less inclined to tailor specific decisions to such verbal formulations. Although the Court has recognized the intrinsic value of free expression, it has acknowledged the validity of reasonable "time, place, and manner" restrictions on such expression. First Amendment jurisprudence is thus characterized by many gradations, nuances, and variations of emphasis.

Justices have advocated a variety of positions regarding freedom of expression, ranging from the occasional "absolutist" defense of free speech by Justice Hugo Black to the limited protection accorded by Justice John M. Harlan's "ad hoc balancing" of individual freedoms against interests of national security. As a result, no clear unified theory of First Amendment freedom in communication has emerged. Nevertheless, certain trends are clearly discernible; for example, the Court has achieved some internal consistency in articulating the values of expressive and associational freedom in the political arena. The most important early developments in this area focused on alleged threats to national security posed by "subversive" expression. We turn first to that subject.

"SUBVERSIVE" SPEECH AND INTERNAL SECURITY CONCERNS

Political dissent is ingrained in the American tradition. As is true of economic freedom, it has always been recognized as part of the core of individual liberties protected by the Constitution. But, as with any other liberty, the right of political dissent is not absolute. When those in power perceive public criticism as an effort to undermine the government, they are likely to characterize it as "subversive" or "disloyal" and to impose criminal penalties on such expression. This tendency is particularly strong during periods of actual or threatened military conflict. At such times of national stress, even judges are not inclined to draw neat distinctions between speech and conduct or between real and imagined threats to national security.

For a brief period during the administration of President John Adams, the national government sought to suppress public criticism through enforcement of the Alien and Sedition Acts, passed by Congress in 1798. Most relevant to our discussion is a provision of the Sedition Act imposing punishment for "any false, scandalous and malicious" writing against the government. A few of Thomas Jefferson's partisans were prosecuted under this statute, and it may have had a **chilling effect** on criticism of the government. Nevertheless, the provision expired on March 3, 1801, just before Jefferson and his newly victorious party took power. Jefferson pardoned those convicted under the statute, and no occasion arose for the Supreme Court to determine its constitutionality.

During the Civil War, a number of limits were imposed on freedom of expression. These included newspaper censorship and the prosecution of some of the more vociferous critics of the Lincoln administration. However, no constitutional challenges raising First Amendment issues reached the Supreme Court. The important constitutional issues relating to individual liberty on which the Court focused during this period dealt with suspension of the writ of habeas corpus.

The "Clear and Present Danger" Test

In response to criticism of the Wilson administration's decision to enter World War I, Congress passed the Espionage Act of 1917 and the Sedition Act of 1918. Two separate prosecutions initiated under the Espionage Act ultimately resulted in important First Amendment decisions by the Supreme Court in 1919. In the first of these cases, *Schenck v. United States,* Justice Oliver Wendell Holmes, Jr. articulated the famous **clear and present danger** test. In this case, a unanimous Court affirmed the conviction of Charles T. Schenck, general secretary of the Socialist party, for conspiring to print and circulate leaflets "to men who had been called and accepted for military service." The leaflets urged resistance to the draft on the ground that it violated the Thirteenth Amendment of the Constitution. Although sharply critical of the war effort, Schenck's message was confined to the advocacy of peaceful measures, such as petition for repeal of the draft. The record does not indicate that any disruption or actual draft resistance occurred as a result of Schenck's efforts; however, the Court unanimously upheld his conviction on the ground that speech intended to obstruct the war

Oliver Wendell Holmes, Jr.:
Associate Justice, 1902–
1932

effort was not entitled to constitutional protection. Writing for the Court, Justice Holmes reasoned that

> the character of every act depends upon the circumstances in which it is done. The most stringent protection of free speech would not protect a man in falsely shouting fire in a theater, and causing a panic. It does not even protect a man from an injunction against uttering words that have all the effect of force. The question in every case is whether the words used are used in such circumstances and are of such a nature as to create a clear and present danger that they will bring about the substantive evils that Congress has a right to prevent. It is a question of proximity and degree. When a nation is at war many things that might be said in time of peace are such a hindrance to its effort that their utterance will not be endured so long as men fight, and that no court could regard them as protected by any constitutional right.

The "Bad Tendency" Test

The standard that Holmes articulated in the *Schenck* case was ignored by a Court majority some eight months later in *Abrams v. United States* (1919). Here, the Court affirmed the convictions of Jacob Abrams, a self-styled "anarchist-Socialist," and several associates for distributing leaflets in New York City urging the "workers of the world" to resist, among other things, American intervention in Russia against the newly formed Bolshevik government. For Justice John H. Clarke, the Court's majority spokesman, it was enough that Abrams was advocating a general strike "in the greatest port of our land" for the purpose of "curtailing the production of ordnance and munitions necessary and essential to the prosecution of the war. . . ." In effect, Clarke was reverting to the traditional common law **bad tendency** test, according little importance to the free speech question and focusing on the possibility that Abrams's circular might in some way hinder the war effort.

In a powerful dissenting opinion, Justice Holmes, joined by Justice Louis D. Brandeis, again resorted to the clear and present danger test, but this time he used it as a basis for challenging, rather than endorsing, governmental interference with free speech:

> [T]he ultimate good desired is better reached by free trade in ideas. . . . I think that we should be eternally vigilant against attempts to check the expression of opinions that we loathe and believe to be fraught with death, unless they so immediately threaten immediate interference with the lawful and pressing purposes of the law that an immediate check is required to save the country.

Through the 1920s, a Court majority continued to adhere to the bad tendency test, while Holmes and Brandeis further developed the clear and present danger doctrine as a rationale in support of freedom of expression and association. In *Gitlow v. New York* (1925), the Court upheld a conviction under New York's Criminal Anarchy Act that prohibited advocacy of the overthrow of government "by force or violence." Prior to this decision, the Court had addressed issues of freedom of expression arising from the states strictly on the basis of the Due Process Clause of the Fourteenth Amendment, without specific reference to the First Amendment. In fact, as late as 1922 the Court observed that "the Constitution of the United States imposes upon the States no obligation to convey upon those within their jurisdiction . . . the right of free speech . . ." (*Prudential Insurance Company v. Cheek*).

In 1923, the Court invalidated on due process grounds a Nebraska law prohibiting the teaching of the German language in primary schools *(Meyer v. Nebraska)*. Similarly, in *Pierce v. Society of Sisters* (1925), the Court struck down an amendment to the Oregon constitution aimed at prohibiting parents from sending their children to private schools. In the *Meyer* and *Pierce* cases, the Court focused on the deprivation of liberty and property rights protected by the Fourteenth Amendment Due Process Clause. In the *Gitlow* case, however, Justice Edward T. Sanford, writing for the majority, stated without elaboration: "For present purposes we may and do assume that freedom of speech and of the press—which are protected by the First Amendment from abridgment by Congress—are among the fundamental personal rights and 'liberties' protected by the Due Process Clause of the Fourteenth Amendment from impairment by the states." (The Court first invalidated a state law on First Amendment freedom of speech grounds two years later in *Fiske v. Kansas* [1927].)

The incident giving rise to the *Gitlow* case was publication of the "Left Wing Manifesto," a statement of beliefs held by what the Court characterized as the most radical section of the Socialist party. In essence, the manifesto called for the destruction of established government and its replacement by a "revolutionary dictatorship of the proletariat." In affirming the conviction of Benjamin Gitlow, business manager of *The Revolutionary Age,* the Socialist Party paper that published the "Left Wing Manifesto," Justice Sanford stated the essence of the "bad tendency" test:

That a state, in the exercise of its police power, may punish those who abuse [freedom of speech and press] by utterances inimical to the public welfare, tending to corrupt public morals, incite to crime, or disturb the public peace, is not open to question. . . .

Sanford continued:

. . . The state cannot reasonably be required to measure the danger from every such utterance in the nice balance of a jeweler's scale. A single revolutionary spark may kindle a fire that, smoldering for a time, may burst into a sweeping and destructive conflagration. It cannot be said that the state is acting arbitrarily or unreasonably when, in the exercise of its judgment as to the measures necessary to protect the public peace and safety, it seeks to extinguish the spark without waiting until it has enkindled the flame or blazed into the conflagration.

Again, Justices Holmes and Brandeis dissented. They could find no clear and present danger of an effort "to overthrow the government by force on the part of the admittedly small minority who shared the defendant's views." In response to the contention that the "Left Wing Manifesto" was an incitement, Holmes asserted that:

Every idea is an incitement. It offers itself for belief and if believed it is acted on unless some other belief outweighs it or some failure of energy stifles the movement at its birth. The only difference between the expression of an opinion and an incitement in the narrower sense is the speaker's enthusiasm for the result. Eloquence may set fire to reason. But whatever may be thought of the redundant discourse before us it had no chance of starting a present conflagration. If in the long run the beliefs expressed in proletarian dictatorship are destined to be accepted by the dominant forces of the community, the only meaning of free speech is that they should be given their chance and have their way.

This ringing endorsement of the concept of a "free marketplace of ideas" contrasts sharply with Holmes's earlier deference, in the *Schenck* case, to governmental control of dissident expression. As we have seen in connection with judicial review of economic regulation (in Chapter 10), Holmes was inclined to give wide latitude to legislative discretion in matters of public policy. But his dissent in *Gitlow,* like his dissent in *Abrams v. United States,* reflected a decided shift in emphasis where First Amendment values were concerned. This change was probably influenced by Holmes's association on the Court with Justice Brandeis, a dedicated and articulate defender of civil rights and liberties, and his acquaintance with Harvard University law professor Zechariah Chafee, Jr., a widely recognized authority on the First Amendment.

Brandeis himself had occasion to discuss the "clear and present danger" formula in a concurring opinion in *Whitney v. California* (1927). In this case, the majority, speaking again through Justice Sanford, adhered to the "bad tendency" test in affirming the conviction of Charlotte Anita Whitney (a niece of Justice Stephen J. Field) for violating California's Criminal Syndicalism Act. The statute defined "criminal syndicalism" as "any doctrine or precept advocating, teaching or aiding and abetting the commission of crime, sabotage . . . or unlawful acts of force and violence or unlawful methods of terrorism as a means of accomplishing a change in industrial ownership or control, or effecting any political change." Whitney's conviction was based on her participation in the organizing convention of the Communist Labor party of California. The jury rejected her contention that at this meeting she advocated lawful, nonviolent political reform. She maintained that her conviction was a deprivation of liberty without due process of law, but she did not contend specifically that her participation in organizing the Communist Labor party constituted no clear and present danger. Sanford rejected the view that the act, as applied in this case, was

> an unreasonable or arbitrary exercise of the police power of the state, unwarrantably infringing any right of free speech, assembly or association, or that those persons are protected by the Due Process Clause who abuse such rights by joining and furthering an organization . . . menacing the peace and welfare of the state.

Because Whitney did not raise the clear and present danger issue, Brandeis and Holmes felt compelled to concur. The jury was presented with evidence of a conspiracy and under the circumstances, they concluded, its verdict should not be disturbed. Nevertheless, Brandeis took sharp issue with the majority's narrow view of the constitutional protection that should be afforded political dissent. The crux of the Brandeis-Holmes position is contained in the following excerpts:

> Those who won our independence believed that the final end of the state was to make men free to develop their faculties; and that in its government the deliberative forces should prevail over the arbitrary. They valued liberty both as an end and as a means. They believed liberty to be the secret of happiness and courage to be the secret of liberty. They believed that . . . public discussion is a political duty; and that this should be a fundamental principle of the American government. . . .
> . . . To justify suppression of free speech there must be reasonable ground to fear that serious evil will result if free speech is practiced. There must be reasonable ground to believe that the danger apprehended is imminent. There must be reasonable ground to believe that the evil to be presented is a serious one.

A Supreme Court majority first used the clear and present danger test in defense of free speech in the 1937 case of *Herndon v. Lowry*. This decision reversed a conviction for violation of a Georgia statute prohibiting "any attempt, by persuasion or otherwise," to incite insurrection. Following this decision, the Court began to apply the clear and present danger test not only to "seditious" speech but to other First Amendment issues as well.

"Clear and Probable Danger"

As a constitutional doctrine, clear and present danger reached its high point in the 1940s. Two of the strongest supporters of this prospeech test, Justices Frank Murphy and Wiley Rutledge, died in the summer of 1949. Their successors, Justices Tom Clark and Sherman Minton, were more inclined to support the government's regulation of expression, especially involving members of the Communist party. The Cold War, which had begun in the late 1940s, deepened after the United States became embroiled in the Korean conflict, and by the early 1950s, McCarthyism, with its emphasis on the alleged "communist menace" to internal security, had achieved substantial national influence.

Against this background of Cold War paranoia, the Supreme Court reviewed and affirmed the convictions of eleven leaders of the American Communist party in *Dennis v. United States* (1951). Eugene Dennis and his ten co-defendants had been convicted after a highly publicized nine-month federal trial for violation of the Internal Security Act of 1940, more commonly known as the Smith Act. The Court of Appeals for the Second Circuit upheld these convictions. In his opinion for that court, Chief Judge Learned Hand substituted a more limited defense of First Amendment freedoms than that of clear and present danger. This doctrine, popularly known as the **clear and probable danger** test, was adopted by Chief Justice Fred M. Vinson in a plurality opinion announcing the Supreme Court's judgment affirming the convictions.

The new standard that Hand articulated required courts in each case to "ask whether the gravity of the 'evil,' discounted by its improbability, justifies such invasion of free speech as is necessary to avoid the danger."

The Smith Act made it a crime "to knowingly or willfully advocate, abet, advise, or teach the duty, necessity, desirability, or propriety of overthrowing or destroying any government in the United States by force or violence. . . ." In essence, the defendants' convictions resulted from their activities in organizing and furthering the purposes of the Communist party of the United States.

Chief Justice Vinson attempted—unconvincingly, in light of later First Amendment decisions—to draw a distinction between advocacy and discussion of ideas. The former, he insisted, might be limited by Congress without interfering with the freedom of debate protected by the First Amendment. Vinson also played down the importance of verbal formulas, such as clear and present danger. He then proceeded to adopt Judge Hand's clear and probable danger alternative, a verbal formulation just as elusive as the clear and present danger test.

Two members of the *Dennis* majority, Justices Felix Frankfurter and Robert Jackson, wrote separate concurring opinions, neither of which endorsed Hand's formula or the clear and present danger test. Frankfurter maintained that the Court should defer to the legislative balancing of competing interests in the free speech area no less than in other areas of policy-making. Jackson differentiated between isolated, localized protest and what he saw as a highly organized conspiracy of international dimensions aimed at subverting the American government. He regarded the clear and present danger test as an inadequate standard for assessing a conspiracy of this magnitude. Jackson found "no constitutional right to 'gang up' on the Government."

Justice Black, who dissented along with Justice Douglas, contended that in charging the defendants with conspiracy to advocate the overthrow of government in the future, the prosecution had engaged in "a virulent form of prior censorship of speech and press." Black acknowledged that prevailing public opinion would not oppose the Court's decision but expressed the hope that "in calmer times, when present pressures, passions and fears subside, this or some later Court will restore the First Amendment liberties to the high preferred place where they belong in a free society."

Changes in public opinion and in Supreme Court personnel did in fact result in a gradual movement away from the restrictive First Amendment interpretation symbolized by the *Dennis* decision. Although, as previously indicated, the Court did not resurrect the phrase "preferred position" and did not formally overrule *Dennis,* it narrowed the scope of the Smith Act and offered greater protection to advocacy of ideas, including the forcible overthrow of government. The Court raised evidentiary standards for Smith Act prosecutions and confined its "membership clause" to "active" as distinguished from "nominal" membership in an organization advocating forcible overthrow of the government (see, for example, *Yates v. United States* [1957]; *Scales v. United States* [1961]; *Noto v. United States* [1961]; *Communist Party v. Subversive Activities Control Board* [1961]).

Ad Hoc Balancing: Weighing the Competing Interests

In the aftermath of *Dennis,* the Court moved away from the clear and present danger test and briefly relied on "ad hoc balancing" to determine the limits of First Amendment protection in the area of internal security. This weighing of "competing private and public interests," as Justice Harlan phrased it, emphasized the particular circumstances of each case (see *Barenblatt v. United States* [1959], reprinted in Chapter 5). Thus ad hoc balancing in practice amounted to a process of decision making, rather than a clear interpretive doctrine. However, it is doubtful that a standard such as clear and present danger is, on close analysis, any more definite.

By the late 1960s, the Court began to achieve greater clarity in articulating First Amendment requirements in the field of political expression. For example, by a 5-to-4 majority, the justices overturned the conviction of Robert Watts for violating a federal statute making it a crime to "knowingly and willfully . . . [threaten] to take the life or to inflict bodily harm upon the President of the United States . . ." (*Watts v. United States* [1969]). During a public rally on the grounds of the Washington Monument, Watts asserted that he would not report for his scheduled preinduction physical examination and then stated: "If they ever make me carry a rifle the first man I want to get in my sights is LBJ" (President Lyndon B. Johnson). The Court upheld the statute on its face but cautioned that a law criminalizing a form of pure speech "must be interpreted with the commands of the First Amendment clearly in mind." Threats must be distinguished from "constitutionally protected speech." The Court concluded that "the kind of political hyperbole indulged in by petitioner" was not a "threat" within the meaning of the statute.

"Imminent Lawless Action"

In *Brandenburg v. Ohio* (1969), the Court invalidated a state criminal syndicalism statute, thus explicitly overruling *Whitney v. California.* In reversing the conviction of a local Ku Klux Klan leader who had conducted a televised rally near Cincinnati, the Court held that "the constitutional guarantees of free speech and free press do not permit a State to forbid or proscribe advocacy of the use of force or of law violation except where such advocacy is directed to inciting or producing **imminent lawless action** and is likely to incite or produce such action." The Ohio statute purported to "punish mere advocacy and to forbid . . . assembly with others merely to advocate the described type of action." As such, it fell "within the condemnation of the First and Fourteenth Amendments."

The *Brandenburg* standard, with its requirement of intent to incite or produce imminent lawless action, reaffirmed and expanded the old clear and present danger test as articulated by Justices Holmes and Brandeis. The Burger Court firmly adhered to this standard in the 1970s and 1980s, as seen in *Hess v. Indiana* (1973), *Communist Party of Indiana v. Whitcomb* (1974), and *National Association for the Advancement of Colored People v. Claiborne Hardware Co.* (1982). In spite of the current Court's conservative drift, political dissent continues to receive substantial protection under the First Amendment (see, for example, *Rankin v. McPherson* [1987]; *Texas v. Johnson* [1989]).

"FIGHTING WORDS"

One of the primary responsibilities of local government is the maintenance of peace and order. At the same time, it has been recognized throughout American history that streets, parks, and similar public places are appropriate forums for the expression of ideas. The built-in tension produced by this dual commitment to order and to liberty has produced some of the most important Supreme Court decisions on fundamental free-speech questions.

It was in the context of confrontation between a street orator and a police officer that the Court drew a highly publicized line between protected and unprotected speech. In *Chaplinsky v. New Hampshire* (1942), the Court unanimously upheld a conviction under a statute providing that no person "shall address any offensive, derisive or annoying word to any other person who is lawfully in any street or other public place, nor call him by any offensive or derisive name. . . ." Walter Chaplinsky, a member of the Jehovah's Witnesses sect, was distributing religious literature at a busy intersection in Rochester, New Hampshire. Following a warning by the city marshal and the outbreak of a disturbance, a police officer "started with Chaplinsky for the police station," without informing him that he was under arrest. En route they encountered the marshal, whom Chaplinsky addressed as follows: "You are a God damned racketeer and a damned Fascist, and the whole government of Rochester are Fascists or agents of Fascists." In affirming Chaplinsky's conviction, the Supreme Court adopted the state court's construction of the statute as what "men of common intelligence would understand would be words likely to cause an average addressee to fight, . . . face-to-face words plainly likely to cause a breach of the peace by the addressee." Writing for the Court, Justice Murphy concluded:

> There are certain well defined and narrowly limited classes of speech, the prevention and punishment of which have never been thought to raise any constitutional problem. These include the lewd and obscene, the profane, the libelous, and the insulting or "fighting" words—those which by their very utterance inflict injury or tend to incite an immediate breach of the peace. It has been well observed that such utterances are no essential part of any exposition of ideas, and are of such slight social value as a step to truth that any benefit that may be derived from them is clearly outweighed by the social interest in order and morality.

This original statement of the **fighting words** exception to constitutionally protected speech was broad in scope. Speech might be punished if it inflicted injury or created a danger that the person addressed would resort to violence. The Court probably underestimated the social value of what some would regard as fighting words, and no consideration was given to the question of whether marshals or police should be expected to exercise more restraint than the average person in responding to such epithets.

In a number of subsequent cases presenting similar issues, the Court avoided or narrowed the fighting words category. For example, in *Terminiello v. Chicago* (1949), the Court specifically declined to address the fighting words concept in reversing a breach-of-the-peace conviction. The conviction of Father Arthur Terminiello resulted from an inflammatory speech he delivered to some eight hundred persons in a Chicago meeting hall. Terminiello's anti-Semitic tirade produced violent reactions from an even larger crowd that had gathered outside the auditorium. Despite police efforts to control the crowd, a number of disturbances occurred, including rock-throwing, window-breaking, and an attempt to break down the back door of the meeting hall. In instructing the jury, the trial judge defined "breach of the peace" to include speech that "stirs the public to anger, invites dispute, brings about a condition of unrest, or creates a disturbance. . . ." Justice Douglas, writing for a five-member majority, maintained that "a function of free speech under our system of government is to invite dispute." Speech may "best serve its high purpose when it induces a condition of unrest, creates dissatisfaction with conditions as they are, or even stirs people to anger." Because the ordinance proscribed speech of this very kind, it was held unconstitutional on grounds of **vagueness** and **overbreadth.** Thus, the Court did not consider the specific question of whether Terminiello's speech was constitutionally protected.

A comparison of the *Terminiello* decision with the Court's ruling two years later in *Feiner v. New York* (1951) illustrates the difficulty of drawing lines in this area. In *Feiner*, the Court upheld a disorderly conduct conviction arising from a street corner oration that produced some unrest, but no violence, in a crowd of seventy-five or eighty people—a situation far less volatile than that described in *Terminiello*. In the course of his speech, Irving Feiner, a Syracuse University student and member of the Young Progressives of America, referred to the mayor of Syracuse as a "champagne-sipping bum" and to the mayor of New York City and President Harry S. Truman as "bums." Although the precise facts were far from clear, Feiner apparently urged African-Americans in his audience to fight for equal rights. This "stirred up a little excitement" and one white onlooker threatened violence if the police did not intervene. Feiner was arrested after refusing repeated orders by the police to terminate his speech. In affirming Feiner's conviction, the Court again refused to apply the fighting words concept. Chief Justice Vinson wrote for the majority: "It is one thing to say that the police cannot be used as an instrument for the suppression of unpopular views [a point emphasized in Justice Black's dissenting opinion] and another to say that, when as here the speaker passes the bounds of argument or persuasion and undertakes incitement to riot, they are powerless to prevent a breach of the peace."

The *Feiner* decision is perhaps more accurately attributable to the Cold War climate of the early 1950s, which was reflected at the Supreme Court level in a conspicuous insensitivity to First Amendment values. In any event, the Court's civil rights demonstration cases of the 1960s had the effect of significantly limiting *Feiner* as a precedent.

Further erosion of *Feiner,* as well as a narrowing of the fighting words exception to First Amendment protection, occurred in *Cohen v. California* (1971). Here, the Court refused to classify as fighting words the message "Fuck the Draft" emblazoned on the back of a jacket worn by Paul Robert Cohen in the corridors of the Los Angeles County Courthouse. Reversing Cohen's conviction for breach of the peace, the Court, through Justice Harlan, reasoned as follows:

> While the four-letter word displayed by Cohen in relation to the draft is not uncommonly employed in a personally provocative fashion, in this instance it was clearly not "directed to the person of the hearer." *** No individual actually or likely to be present could reasonably have regarded the words on appellant's jacket as a direct personal insult. Nor do we have here an instance of the exercise of the State's police power to prevent a speaker from intentionally provoking a given group to hostile reaction.

Although the Court still gives formal recognition to the fighting words exception, it is more likely to use vagueness and overbreadth standards (discussed below) in setting aside convictions for disorderly conduct or breach of the peace. Following this approach, the Court has refused to treat as fighting words such outbursts as "you son of a bitch, I'll choke you to death," directed to a police officer (*Gooding v. Wilson* [1972]; see also *Lewis v. City of New Orleans* [1974]).

Hate Speech

During the 1980s, a number of communities adopted laws aimed at protecting African-Americans and other minority groups from so-called "hate speech." One such ordinance was enacted by the city of St. Paul, Minnesota. It provided that

> Whoever places on public or private property a symbol, object, appellation, characterization or graffiti, including, but not limited to, a burning cross or Nazi swastika, which one knows or has reasonable grounds to know arouses anger, alarm or resentment in others on the basis of race, color, creed, religion or gender commits disorderly conduct and shall be guilty of a misdemeanor.

In the widely publicized case of R.A.V. v. St. Paul (1992), the Supreme Court declared the ordinance unconstitutional. Justice Scalia summarized the rationale of the majority as follows:

> Assuming, *arguendo,* that all of the expression reached by the ordinance is proscribable under the "fighting words" doctrine, we nonetheless conclude that the ordinance is facially unconstitutional in that it prohibits otherwise permitted speech solely on the basis of the subjects the speech addresses.

R.A.V. v. City of St. Paul is reprinted in Appendix E.

SYMBOLIC SPEECH

Communication can take many forms in addition to spoken and written words. Emblems and gestures often convey opinions and ideas; as such, they are entitled to First Amendment protection. Just how much protection depends on the particular circumstances of each case and on the weighing of competing interests. The term **symbolic speech** is applied to a wide range of nonverbal communication and has received substantial attention from the post-New Deal Court. Early examples are provided by the "flag salute" cases of *Minersville School District v. Gobitis* (1940) and *West Virginia State Board of Education v. Barnette* (1943). (These cases, which also implicate freedom of religion, are discussed more fully in Chapter 13). In the first of these cases, the Court upheld a local school board directive requiring public school students to salute the American flag as part of the daily class routine. In one of the most dramatic turnabouts in its history, the Court overruled this precedent three years later in the second flag salute case. In *Barnette,* a six-member majority recognized the right of school children who were members of Jehovah's Witnesses to refrain from participation in the flag salute ritual.

Symbolic Speech in the Vietnam Era

The Vietnam War produced a number of protests that fell into the symbolic speech category. The Court held that some but not all forms of protest in this area were entitled to constitutional protection. For example, in *United States v. O'Brien* (1968), the Court rejected the First Amendment claim of a Vietnam War protester that publicly burning his draft card was a form of constitutionally protected symbolic speech. David Paul O'Brien, who had burned his Selective Service registration certificate on the steps of the South Boston Courthouse in the presence of a "sizable crowd," was convicted for violation of a federal law providing that an offense was committed by any person "who forges, alters, knowingly destroys, knowingly mutilates, or in any manner changes any such certificate. . . ."

Chief Justice Earl Warren, writing for a seven-member majority, determined that Congress had ample constitutional authority to prohibit the destruction or mutilation of draft cards. Specifically, he cited the enumerated power to "raise and support armies," as well as the implied powers to "classify and conscript manpower for military service," to "establish a system of registration for individuals liable for training and service," and to "require such individuals within reason to cooperate in the registration system. . . ." Warren stated the Court's view of the appropriate constitutional standard as follows:

> [A] government regulation is sufficiently justified if it is within the constitutional power of the Government; if it furthers an important interest; if the governmental interest is unrelated to the suppression of free expression; and if the incidental restriction on alleged First Amendment freedoms is no greater than is essential to the furtherance of that interest.

In Chief Justice Warren's view, the law under which O'Brien was convicted met all these constitutional requirements.

A less defiant form of symbolic speech in opposition to the Vietnam War was afforded First Amendment protection in *Tinker v. Des Moines Independent Community School District* (1969). High school students John Tinker and Christopher Eckhardt, along with Tinker's sister Mary Beth, wore black armbands to school to protest American involvement in the Vietnam War. Anticipating this protest, school officials had adopted a policy that students refusing to remove such armbands would be suspended until they agreed to return to school without them. The Tinkers and Eckhardt refused to remove their armbands when requested and were sent home under suspension. They then brought suit to recover nominal damages and to enjoin school officials from enforcing the regulation. A U.S. district court dismissed the complaint, concluding that in this instance, "the disciplined atmosphere of the classroom, not the plaintiffs' right to wear armbands on school premises," was "entitled to the protection of the law."

The case eventually reached the Supreme Court, where a majority of the justices took a very different view of the competing values at stake. Writing for the Court, Justice Abe Fortas rejected the district court's view that the action of school officials was "reasonable" because it was based on fear that a disturbance would result from the wearing of armbands. Fortas maintained that "in our system, undifferentiated fear or apprehension of disturbance is not enough to overcome the right to freedom of expression." He found that the wearing of armbands in this instance "was divorced from actual or potential disruptive conduct . . ." and as such was "closely akin to 'pure speech' which . . . is entitled to comprehensive protection under the First Amendment. . . ." For public school officials to justify prohibiting the "particular expression of opinion," Fortas asserted, they must be able to show that such action "was caused by something more than a mere desire to avoid the discomfort and unpleasantness that always accompany an unpopular viewpoint." The essence of the majority's position is captured in the following passage:

> In our system students may not be regarded as closed-circuit recipients of only that which the State chooses to communicate. They may not be confined to the expression of those sentiments that are officially approved. In the absence of a specific showing of constitutionally valid reasons to regulate their speech, students are entitled to freedom of expression of their views. . . .

Flag Burning

During the same year in which it decided the *Tinker* case, the Court had an opportunity to address the question of whether flag burning is entitled to constitutional protection as symbolic speech (*Street v. New York* [1969]). The Court focused on the element of verbal expression also presented in this case, however, and effectively avoided the symbolic speech issue. After learning of the assassination attempt against civil rights leader James Meredith in Mississippi, Sidney Street burned his American flag on a Brooklyn street corner. The arresting officer testified that he heard Street say to a small crowd of onlookers: "We don't need no damn flag." Street was convicted of "malicious mischief" in

Protestors burning American flags. A form of free speech?

violation of a New York state statute making it a misdemeanor to "publicly mutilate, deface, defile, or defy, trample upon or cast contempt upon, either by words or act [any flag of the United States]." Because a general verdict was rendered by the trial court, the Supreme Court, in an opinion by Justice Harlan, observed that Street might have been punished for his speech as well as for burning the flag. The Court concluded that under the circumstances, he could not be constitutionally punished for his words alone. Harlan emphasized that the Court was not ruling on the question of whether Street could be punished for flag burning, "even though the burning was an act of protest."

The Warren Court's decision left open the question of whether flag burning *per se* was a form of symbolic speech protected by the First Amendment. The Rehnquist Court, surprising many observers, answered that question in the affirmative in the highly publicized case of *Texas v. Johnson* (1989). After publicly burning the American flag outside the 1984 Republican National Convention in Dallas, Gregory Johnson was prosecuted under a Texas law prohibiting flag desecration. Johnson was convicted at trial, but his conviction was reversed by the Texas Court of Criminal Appeals, which held that Johnson's conduct was protected by the First Amendment. In an extremely controversial decision, the U.S. Supreme Court agreed, splitting 5 to 4. Perhaps most surprising to Court-watchers was the fact that two Reagan appointees, Justices Antonin Scalia and Anthony Kennedy, joined the majority. On the other hand, Justice John Paul Stevens, generally considered a liberal on civil liberties issues, was among the dissenters.

Writing for the Court in *Johnson*, Justice William Brennan observed that "[t]he expressive, overtly political nature of [Johnson's] conduct was both intentional and overwhelmingly apparent." In Brennan's view,

> Johnson was convicted for engaging in expressive conduct. The State's interest in preventing breaches of the peace does not support his conviction because Johnson's conduct did not threaten to disturb the peace. Nor does the State's interest in preserving the flag as a symbol of nationhood and national unity justify his criminal conviction for engaging in political expression.

Dissenting, Chief Justice William Rehnquist challenged the majority's conclusion that Johnson's act of flag burning was a form of political speech, saying that "flag burning is the equivalent of an inarticulate grunt or roar that . . . is most likely to be indulged in not to express any particular idea, but to antagonize others. . . ." Rehnquist stressed the "unique position" of the flag "as the symbol of our Nation, a uniqueness that justifies a governmental prohibition against flag burning. . . ." But for Justice Brennan and the majority, "[t]he way to preserve the flag's special role is not to punish those who feel differently. . . ."

In the wake of the *Johnson* decision, conservatives called for a constitutional amendment to place flag burning beyond the pale of First Amendment protection. In an attempt to address the issue by less drastic means, Congress passed the Federal Flag Protection Act of 1989, making flag burning a federal crime. In *United States v. Eichman* (1990), the Court struck down the Flag Protection Act as applied to flag burning as a means of political protest.

"Sleep Speech"?

In *Clark v. Community for Creative Non-Violence* (1984), the Court refused to extend First Amendment protection to an overnight demonstration in which participants proposed to sleep in "symbolic tents" to draw attention to the plight of the homeless. The demonstration, organized by the Community for Creative Nonviolence, was planned for Lafayette Park and the Mall in Washington, D.C. The National Park Service issued a permit allowing the erection of two symbolic tent cities but denied the request that demonstrators be allowed to sleep in the tents. The Supreme Court sustained the Park Service regulation. Writing for the majority, Justice Byron White reasoned as follows:

> That sleeping, like the symbolic tents themselves, may be expressive and part of the message delivered by the demonstration does not make the ban any less a limitation on the manner of demonstrating, for reasonable time, place, and manner regulations normally have the purpose and direct effect of limiting expression but are nevertheless valid.

In a dissenting opinion Justice Thurgood Marshall, joined by Justice Brennan, maintained that the government had not adequately explained how this regulation would advance its interest in well-kept parks in Washington, D.C., that are open to large numbers of visitors. In Marshall's view, the Court's decision, far from advancing legitimate governmental interests, advanced only "the prerogatives of a bureaucracy that over the years has shown an implacable hostility toward citizens' exercise of First Amendment rights."

OBSCENITY, INDECENCY, AND PROFANITY

Myriad state and local laws prohibit obscenity, indecent exposure, lewd and lascivious conduct, and profanity. Until fairly recently, such laws were not thought to raise constitutional problems. In 1942 (see *Chaplinsky v. New Hampshire,* discussed above), the Supreme Court said that "the lewd and obscene" and "the profane" were beyond the pale of constitutional protection. In the 1960s and '70s, the Supreme Court moved away from the *Chaplinsky* dictum and began to afford First Amendment protection to pornography, nudity, and profanity.

While the Court has consistently maintained that obscenity is not protected by the First Amendment, it has imposed a fairly strict definition of obscenity with the result that only hard-core pornography is subject to prohibition (for an in-depth discussion of obscenity, see Chapter 12). With respect to profanity, the Court's 1971 decision in *Cohen v. California* (discussed above) rejected the proposition that state and local governments, as "guardians of the public morality, may properly remove [an] offensive word from the public vocabulary." Of course, a significant factor in the *Cohen* case was that Cohen's jacket bearing the words "Fuck the Draft" made a statement on a matter of public policy. Would the current Court, clearly a more conservative body than that which decided *Cohen v. California,* permit communities to punish profanity that is unconnected to political ideas? While the prospect may seem silly, especially considering the vulgar language that is common in movies and on television, many antiprofanity ordinances are still on the books. In the 1980s, when bumper stickers reading "Shit Happens!" began to appear on automobiles around the country, some communities passed ordinances banning such displays. An interesting question to consider is whether the current Supreme Court would uphold a conviction under such an ordinance and, if so, whether that decision would necessitate overruling *Cohen v. California.*

Nude Dancing

While there is certainly no First Amendment protection for public nudity generally, nudity may acquire constitutional protection in certain contexts. As a part of a play or performance that is not legally obscene, nudity may be considered symbolic speech protected under the First Amendment. In *Doran v. Salem Inn* (1975), the Supreme Court said that "although the customary 'barroom' type of nude dancing may involve only the barest minimum of constitutional protection, . . . this form of entertainment might be entitled to First and Fourteenth Amendment protection under some circumstances."

The Court faced the nude dancing issue squarely in a widely publicized case decided late in the 1990 term: *Barnes v. Glen Theatre, Inc.* (1991). This case involved a constitutional challenge to an Indiana public indecency statute as it applied to nude dancing in bars. The Court rejected the challenge, splitting 5 to 4. Speaking for a plurality, Chief Justice Rehnquist recognized that nude dancing was "expressive conduct within the outer perimeters of the First Amendment" but held that the state's interest in fostering order and morality

Is nude dancing a form of free expression under the First Amendment?

justified the minimal burden on free expression associated with requiring dancers to wear pasties and G-strings. Justice Scalia's opinion concurring in the judgment was even more conservative in refusing to recognize any First Amendment protection for such activities. Scalia stressed society's interest in preserving traditional morality, saying that

> there is no basis for thinking that our society has shared that Thoreauvian 'you-may-do-what-you-like-as-long-as-it-does-not-injure-someone-else' beau ideal — much less for thinking that it was written into the Constitution.

Justice David Souter's decisive concurrence in *Glen Theatre* was more narrowly drawn. Like Rehnquist, Souter recognized the applicability of the First Amendment but concluded that the state's interest in eliminating "harmful secondary effects, including the crime associated with adult entertainment," justified the limited restriction on freedom of expression.

The four dissenting justices in *Glen Theatre* (White, Marshall, Blackmun, and Stevens) found the nude dancing at issue in the case to be "communicative activity" squarely within the protection of the First Amendment, saying that "nudity is itself an expressive component of the dance, not merely incidental 'conduct.'" The dissenters quoted approvingly from the Court's previous decision in *Doran v. Salem Inn,* which observed that

> while the entertainment afforded by a nude ballet at Lincoln Center to those who can pay the price may differ vastly in content (as viewed by judges) or in quality (as viewed by critics), it may not differ in substance from the dance viewed by the person who . . . wants some 'entertainment' with his beer or shot of rye.

In the wake of the Supreme Court's decision in *Glen Theatre,* cities and counties around the country where nude dancing has been permitted began to consider ordinances to restrict this activity. How far such restrictions may go remains uncertain.

RESTRICTING SPEECH BY PUBLIC EMPLOYEES AND BENEFICIARIES

Government employment, government grants and contracts, even government programs such as social security are not constitutional rights but benefits that government may eliminate altogether or deny to particular individuals, as long as it provides due process of law. May government make the enjoyment of such benefits contingent on the surrender of constitutional rights, in particular those rights guaranteed by the First Amendment?

Under the Federal Lobbying (Hatch) Act, federal civil servants are barred from actively participating in political campaigns. The Supreme Court upheld this prohibition in *United States v. Harris* (1954) and again in *United States Civil Service Commission v. National Association of Letter Carriers* (1973). Writing for the Court in the latter decision, Justice White asserted that it was essential that the political influence of federal government workers be limited in order to maintain the concept of a merit-based civil service.

The decisions upholding the Hatch Act can be read broadly to imply that government may restrict speech as a condition of employment, or they may be interpreted more narrowly, that is, limited to the special case of the federal civil service. The Supreme Court's decisions *Branti v. Finkel* (1980) and *Rankin v. McPherson* (1987) suggest the latter interpretation. In *Branti,* the Court said that the First Amendment bars the firing of public prosecutors for expressing their political sentiments. *Rankin v. McPherson* posed a similar issue but in more dramatic fashion.

Ardith McPherson, a newly hired deputy constable in Harris County, Texas, was fired after she was overheard making certain remarks about John Hinckley's attempt to assassinate President Ronald Reagan in March 1981. Upon learning of the unsuccessful assasination attempt, McPherson said, "If they go for him again, I hope they get him." When Constable Rankin learned of the remark, he summarily discharged McPherson, who was at the time a probationary employee. McPherson brought suit under 42 U.S. Code Section 1983, seeking reinstatement and monetary damages. The district court dismissed the case, holding that McPherson's remarks were not protected under the First Amendment. The court of appeals reversed, however, and the Supreme Court agreed. Writing for the majority, Justice Marshall remarked that "[v]igilance is necessary to ensure that public employers do not use authority over employees to silence discourse, not because it hampers public functions but simply because superiors disagree with the content of employees' speech."

Rankin v. McPherson was a 5-to-4 decision. Two of the members of the majority were Justices Brennan and Marshall, both of whom have since retired. Given the movement of the Supreme Court in the conservative direction as a result of recent changes in membership, it is doubtful that *Rankin* would have been similarly decided had it come to the Court four years later.

Restricting Abortion Counseling

Certainly the decision in *Rust v. Sullivan* (1991) suggests a different perspective on issues in this area. In *Rust,* the Court sustained a federal regulation barring private birth control clinics that receive federal funds from counseling their clients regarding abortion. The Department of Health and Human Services imposed this restriction in 1987 at the direction of the Reagan administration. When the Court upheld the restriction in June 1991, it was not only abortion rights activists who protested. Civil libertarians, members of the medical profession, and even some supporters of the Bush administration expressed opposition to what they perceived as an attack on free speech.

Critics of the *Rust* decision pointed out that if government could make the receipt of federal funds conditional upon the surrender of First Amendment rights, then all government benefits might be used as devices to limit constitutional rights. For example, people who live in public housing could be asked to surrender their Fourth Amendment rights or face eviction; public defenders could be limited in the defenses they provide to their indigent clients; students could have their choice of occupations dictated by conditions imposed on student loans. The most serious implication of the *Rust* ruling is that public employees, including teachers, might be prohibited from addressing controversial issues or face losing their jobs.

The NEA Funding Controversy

In the late 1980s, a controversy erupted over National Endowment for the Arts (NEA) funding of provocative works of art that offended the religious and sexual sensibilities of many people. Republican Senator Jesse Helms of North Carolina generated considerable publicity by proposing a ban on federal grants supporting "indecent" works of art. During the early stages of the 1992 presidential election campaign, President George Bush intensified the dispute by firing NEA Chairman John Frohnmeyer. Is it legitimate for the federal government to censor works of art that it subsidizes through a granting agency like the NEA? In a speech to the National Press Club on March 23, 1992, Frohnmeyer argued that "when the government does support free expression, it must do so with a level playing field—no blacklists and no ideological preconceptions." On the other hand, conservative critics of the NEA argued that the taxpayers have no obligation to support works of art that many would find offensive. As yet, the Supreme Court has not been called upon to render a decision in this matter.

FREEDOM OF ASSEMBLY

When in 1977 the American Nazi Party announced plans to march through the streets of Skokie, Illinois, a predominantly Jewish suburb of Chicago, the village council responded by passing an ordinance designed to prohibit the march. The ordinance was declared unconstitutional, but a ban on displaying the swastika was upheld by a federal appeals court under the fighting words doctrine (see *National Socialist Party v. Skokie* [1977]; *Collin v. Smith* [1978]).

The Constitution in action: Freedom of assembly in the Nation's capital

The Nazi-Skokie controversy illustrates the potential conflict between the First Amendment freedom of assembly and a community's desire to protect itself against disturbances of the public repose. While the Supreme Court has recognized legitimate community interests that may, under some conditions, justify limitations on assembly, it has tended to favor the First Amendment right of groups to assemble in the **public forum,** especially for the purpose of expressing a political message.

Civil Rights Demonstrations

Organized public protest against racial segregation in southern and border states was a critical component of the civil rights movement of the 1950s and 1960s. In *Edwards v. South Carolina* (1963), the Supreme Court reversed breach-of-the-peace convictions of 187 African-American college students who had participated in a peaceful civil rights demonstration on the grounds of the state capitol in Columbia, South Carolina. Although the capitol grounds had traditionally been the locus of political assemblies, the demonstrators were advised by the police that if they did not disperse within fifteen minutes, they would be arrested. In response, they engaged in what the city manager later described as "boisterous," "loud," and "flamboyant" conduct, consisting of "listening to a 'religious harangue' by one of their leaders, and loudly singing 'The Star Spangled Banner' and other patriotic and religious songs, while stamping their feet and clapping their hands." The subsequent convictions of these students resulted in fines of up to one hundred dollars and jail sentences of up to thirty days. The Court held that in "arresting, convicting and punishing" these students, South Carolina had infringed their "constitutionally protected rights of

free speech, free assembly, and freedom to petition for redress of their grievances." In his opinion for the majority, Justice Potter Stewart observed: "The
circumstances in this case reflect an exercise of these basic constitutional rights
in their most pristine and classic form." Distinguishing this decision from the
ruling in *Feiner v. New York* (1951), he concluded: "The Fourteenth Amendment
does not permit a state to make criminal the peaceful expression of unpopular
views."

The Supreme Court was presented with a related, but more complex, set of
issues in *Cox v. Louisiana,* (1965). A civil rights leader, Rev. B. Elton Cox, led two
thousand African-American college students in a peaceful demonstration protesting the jailing of twenty-three fellow students who had been picketing segregated lunch counters in Baton Rouge, Louisiana, in December 1961. According
to Justice Arthur Goldberg's account of the facts, Cox was given permission by
the chief of police to conduct the demonstration on the sidewalk across the
street from the courthouse and was "led to believe" that he was not acting in
violation of state law. A speech in which Cox urged the students to "sit in" at
segregated lunch counters produced some "muttering" and "grumbling" from
a crowd of one hundred to three hundred white onlookers. When the students
refused to comply with a police order to disperse, tear gas was used to break up
the demonstration. On the following day, Cox was charged with several violations of state law. He was later convicted of breach of the peace, obstructing
"public passages," and picketing near a courthouse.

Reversing the Louisiana Supreme Court's affirmance of these convictions,
the U.S. Supreme Court handed down two rulings on the same day, giving
separate treatment to the picketing conviction. In *Cox I,* the Court held that the
convictions for breach of the peace and for obstructing the sidewalk violated
Cox's First Amendment freedoms of speech and assembly. However, in *Cox II,*
the Court, while ultimately reversing the picketing conviction on due process
grounds, rejected Cox's First Amendment objections. Drawing a distinction between "speech" and "conduct"—a distinction that is at best ambiguous—Justice
Goldberg asserted for a five-member majority: "A narrowly drawn statute such as
the one under review is obviously a safeguard both necessary and appropriate
to vindicate the state's interest in assuring justice under law." Such a statute, he
continued, does not "infringe upon the constitutionally protected rights of free
speech and free assembly." He concluded: "The conduct which is the subject of
this statute—picketing and parading—is subject to regulation even though intertwined with expression and association."

A similar factual pattern was presented in the 1966 case of *Adderley v.
Florida,* but this time the Court affirmed the conviction of African-American
students who were protesting local practices of racial segregation. Like the
situation in *Cox,* the demonstrators were also denouncing the arrests of other
students, in this instance students from Florida A & M University who had
attempted to integrate movie theaters in Tallahassee. During their demonstration, Harriet Louise Adderley and other students had allegedly blocked a jail
driveway not normally used by the public. When they ignored requests to leave
this area, they were arrested and charged with violating a state law that prohibited trespass "committed with a malicious and mischievous intent."

Members of the Ku Klux Klan exercising their First Amendment rights

In justifying defendants' convictions, Justice Black, writing for a majority of five, found that nothing in the Constitution prevented Florida from "even-handed enforcement of its general trespass statute. . . ." Emphasizing the use of the driveway for vehicles providing service to the jail and playing down the symbolic significance of a civil rights protest at the place of incarceration, Black insisted: "The State, no less than a private owner of property, has power to preserve the property under its control for the use to which it is lawfully dedicated."

The *Adderley* decision may be viewed as marking the Warren Court's outer limit of tolerance for public protest. But *Adderley* is perhaps more accurately seen as a concession to public opinion. The decision was rendered at a time of great public concern over a rising tide of crime and violence in America's cities. Perhaps certain justices on the Court saw the *Adderley* case as a good opportunity to make a statement in favor of "law and order," a value that the Warren Court was seldom credited with stressing.

The civil rights and antiwar movements of the 1960s were characterized by frequent demonstrations, most of which stayed within constitutional parameters, others of which pressed the limits of constitutional tolerance for public protest. The relatively tranquil decades of the 1970s and '80s produced fewer cases involving large-scale demonstrations. The key issue for the Burger and Rehnquist Courts has been defining the concept of **public forum.**

What Constitutes a Public Forum?

The Supreme Court has recognized that the term "public forum" includes not only streets and parks but any property that government "has opened for use by the public as a place for expressive activity" (*Perry Educational Association v. Perry Local Educators' Association* [1983]). In *United States v. Grace* (1983), the

Court recognized that the sidewalks surrounding the Court's own building in Washington, D.C., qualified as a public forum and struck down the federal law forbidding use of that space for picketing or handing out leaflets.

Not every place open to the public constitutes a public forum for purposes of the First Amendment. For example, a privately owned shopping center is not considered a public forum. In *Lloyd Corporation v. Tanner* (1972), the Supreme Court observed that a privately owned shopping center does not "lose its private character merely because the public is generally invited to use it for designated purposes...." On the other hand, the Court let stand a California Supreme Court ruling that recognized shopping centers as public forums under the California Constitution (see *PruneYard Shopping Center v. Robins* [1980], discussed and reprinted in Chapter 10). The *PruneYard* decision points up the ability of state courts and state constitutions to grant civil liberties claims transcending those recognized under the federal constitution.

Is an Airport a Public Forum?

The Supreme Court has struggled with the problem of whether an airport is a public forum for the purposes of soliciting, prosyletizing and distributing literature. In *Board of Airport Commissioners v. Jews for Jesus* (1987) and *Lee v. International Society for Krishna Consciousness* (1992), the Court struck down policies that restricted such activities in public airport terminals. Although it relied in both decisions on First Amendment considerations, the Court was unable to reach agreement, however, as to whether an airport is a public forum. Given the prevalence of expressive activities in airports, it is unlikely that the Court will be unable to avoid this question forever.

TIME, PLACE, AND MANNER REGULATIONS

It is well-established that reasonable **time, place, and manner regulations** can justify the restriction of First Amendment activities in the public forum. The general rule is that such regulations must be reasonable, narrowly drawn, and neutral in content. Applying this standard, the Supreme Court struck down, as unconstitutional on its face, a local ordinance that gave unlimited discretion to the chief of police in forbidding or permitting the use of sound amplification devices, such as loudspeakers on trucks (*Saia v. New York* [1948]). A year later, in *Kovacs v. Cooper,* the Court upheld a narrowly interpreted ordinance prohibiting vehicles on the public streets from operating amplifiers or other instruments emitting "loud and raucous noises."

The requirement of content neutrality is not absolute, but government cannot depart from it without meeting a heavy burden of justification. The Court is likely to invalidate a regulation of this kind unless the government can show that it is necessary to serve a compelling interest and is narrowly drawn to achieve that purpose. The Court applied this standard in declaring unconstitutional the previously noted restriction on picketing on the sidewalks surrounding the Supreme Court building (*United States v. Grace* [1983]).

In *Boos v. Barry* (1988), the Supreme Court struck down a District of Columbia regulation that prohibited the display of signs within five hundred feet of a foreign embassy if the message displayed on the signs brought the embassy's government into "disrepute." At the same time, the Court sustained the regulation permitting police to disperse assemblies within five hundred feet of embassies. The former regulation was a restriction on the content of a political message; the latter, if applied evenhandedly, was regarded as a legitimate time, place, and manner regulation.

The Special Problem of Zoning Regulations

Time, place, and manner restrictions often take the form of local **zoning** requirements that have the effect of limiting freedom of expression. In the continuing process of First Amendment line drawing, the Supreme Court has had occasion to look closely at a number of these restrictions. In *Heffron v. International Society for Krishna Consciousness (ISKON)* (1981), a majority of five justices upheld a Minnesota "zoning" restriction limiting solicitation at the state fair, as applied to an organization wishing to distribute and sell religious literature and request donations from fair patrons. The regulation, which applied to nonprofit, charitable, and commercial enterprises alike, confined solicitation activities to booths rented on a first-come, first-served basis. ISKCON maintained that this restriction violated the First and Fourteenth Amendments by interfering with one of its sacred rituals, sankirtan, which required the faithful to distribute and sell religious literature and to solicit contributions. Writing for the majority, Justice White left no doubt that he was unimpressed by this line of argument:

> None of our cases suggest that the inclusion of peripatetic solicitation as part of a church ritual entitles church members to solicitation rights in a public forum superior to those members of other religious groups who raise money but do not purport to ritualize the process.

In the majority's view, the regulation at issue was content-neutral and nondiscriminatory in application. Moreover, it served a significant governmental interest, that of maintaining crowd control on the congested state fairgrounds. Justice Brennan, speaking for the four dissenters, saw the First Amendment issue quite differently:

> As soon as a proselytizing member of ISKCON hands out a free copy of the Bhagavad-Gita to an interested listener, or a political candidate distributes his campaign brochure to a potential voter, he becomes subject to arrest and removal from the fairgrounds. This constitutes a significant restriction on First Amendment rights.

Five years later, the Court upheld a zoning ordinance passed by the city of Renton, Washington, prohibiting the location of "adult theaters" within one thousand feet of residential, church, park, or school property (*Renton v. Playtime Theatres, Inc.* [1986]). Writing for a majority of seven, Justice Rehnquist found that the ordinance was "content-neutral," that it served a "substantial governmental interest," and that it permitted reasonable alternative "avenues of

A Recent Example of Ideological Division: The *Kokinda* Case

United States v. Kokinda (1990) provides a good illustration of ideological division on the early Rehnquist Court in the First Amendment area. Here, the Court, by a 5-to-4 margin, held that, as applied to the facts of this case, a regulation prohibiting all in-person solicitation of funds on U.S. Postal Service premises did not violate the First Amendment. The incident that led to this ruling occurred at the post office in Bowie, Maryland. A seven-foot-wide sidewalk located on Postal Service property provided the only means of access from the adjoining parking lot to the post office entrance. On August 6, 1986, Marsha Kokinda and Kevin Pearle, volunteers for the National Democratic Policy Committee, set up a table on this sidewalk for the purpose of soliciting contributions and selling organizational literature. Responding to customer complaints, the postmaster asked Kokinda and Pearle to leave the premises. When they refused to do so, they were arrested by a postal inspector. They were later tried before a federal magistrate and convicted of violating the ban on solicitation.

The Supreme Court affirmed these convictions but failed to produce a majority opinion. Writing for the plurality, Justice Sandra Day O'Connor (joined by Rehnquist, White, and Scalia) maintained that the postal sidewalk "[did] not have the characteristics of public sidewalks traditionally open to expressive activity." Since this sidewalk was thus not a public forum, the First Amendment issue should be examined under a "reasonableness" standard, rather than under the more exacting "strict scrutiny" typically applied in public forum cases. In O'Connor's view, the Postal Service could reasonably conclude that since solicitation was "inherently disruptive" of its business, a total ban on this activity was appropriate. Justice O'Connor also noted that the ban did not "discriminate on the basis of content or viewpoint."

In a concurring opinion, Justice Kennedy found it unnecessary to make a precise determination as to whether the postal sidewalk should be viewed as a public forum. He assumed that for many purposes government premises of this kind should be so regarded and that expressive activity in this setting should be given First Amendment protection. He concluded, however, that the narrowly drawn, nondiscriminatory regulation at issue served an important government interest and that it met the "traditional standards . . . applied to time, place and manner restrictions of protected expression."

Justice Brennan, in a dissenting opinion supported by Justices Marshall, Stevens, and Blackmun, asserted that the postal sidewalk was a public forum and that the regulation "[did] not qualify as a content-neutral time, place or manner restriction." That the sidewalk was open and accessible to the public was "alone sufficient to identify it as a public forum." Brennan rejected Justice O'Connor's reliance on a standard of "reasonableness," indicating his preference for a "higher level of scrutiny. . . ." He insisted, however, that even if a reasonableness standard were appropriate, the postal regulation's distinction between "solicitation and virtually all other kinds of speech" was not reasonable.

communication." He asserted that the ordinance was a "valid governmental response to the 'admittedly serious problems' created by adult theaters." The city had not used its zoning power as a "pretext for suppressing expression" but had made areas available for adult theaters and their patrons while "preserving the quality of life in the community at large." Rehnquist concluded: "This, after all, is the essence of zoning."

Again Justice Brennan filed a dissenting opinion, this time supported by Justice Marshall alone. Brennan flatly rejected the central premise of the majority opinion when he asserted that ". . . the circumstances here strongly suggest that the ordinance was designed to suppress expression, even that constitutionally protected, and thus was not to be analyzed as a content-neutral time, place and manner restriction." From Justice Brennan's criticism of the Court's analysis in this case, it is clear that the initial characterization of a law, for First Amendment purposes, is all-important. Regulations are not automatically classified as reasonable time, place, and manner restrictions simply because the legislative body enacting them uses that rationale. Ultimately, in matters touching freedom of expression, judges must determine whether a given law is to be viewed as primarily a content-neutral time, place, and manner restriction or as a deliberate attempt, under the guise of this rationale, to limit freedom of expression. The Court may apply neat verbal formulas and strive for analytical consistency, but ultimately the question comes down to one of judgment in which intuition and ideology are often decisive factors.

FREEDOM OF ASSOCIATION

Although the Constitution makes no explicit reference to freedom of association, the Supreme Court has long recognized association as a "penumbral" or "implicit" constitutional right. Different provisions of the Constitution have been identified as sources for the protection of various types of association, and some associational freedoms are given more protections than others. Intimate associations—for example, those between husband and wife or parent and child—are extensively protected by the constitutional right of privacy (see Chapter 15). On the other hand, economic associations, like property rights, are afforded more limited protection under the Due Process Clauses of the Fifth and Fourteenth Amendments. The right to associate with others for purposes of worship or devotion is obviously implied by the Free Exercise of Religion Clause of the First Amendment (see Chapter 13). Similarly, the First Amendment freedoms of speech, assembly, and petition implicitly protect the right of individuals to associate for political purposes.

Political Association

Political association, like political expression, occupies a high place in the Supreme Court's scheme of constitutional values. But, like political expression, freedom of political association is far from absolute. Thus, in *Scales v. United States* (1961), the Supreme Court was willing to place its stamp of approval on Section 2 of the Smith Act, which impinged on freedom of association by making it a crime merely to belong to the Communist party. The majority saved the constitutionality of Section 2 by interpreting it narrowly so as to apply only to "active" members of the Communist party who had a "specific intent" to bring about the violent overthrow of the United States government. Four members of the Court (Douglas, Black, Warren, and Brennan) dissented, claiming that the majority had in effect legalized guilt by association.

The constitutional controversy over communism and government efforts to rid the country of the "red menace" greatly diminished during the 1960s. On the other hand, the civil rights movement was at that time reaching its apogee. In the struggle for civil rights, the National Association for the Advancement of Colored People (NAACP) was one of the most significant political organizations. The NAACP had aroused tremendous hostility in the South and had occasionally been the target of state government attempts at intimidation and suppression. In *NAACP v. Alabama* (1958), the Supreme Court found that the state of Alabama had unconstitutionally infringed the NAACP's freedom of association by selectively enforcing a law requiring organizations based outside Alabama to register members' names and addresses with state authorities. Writing for the Court, Justice Harlan stressed the adverse effect that such disclosure would have on the NAACP's political activities:

> Petitioner [the NAACP] has made an uncontroverted showing that on past occasions revelation of the identity of its rank-and-file members has exposed these members to economic reprisal, loss of employment, threat of physical coercion, and other manifestations of public hostility. Under these circumstances, we think it apparent that compelled disclosure of . . . membership is likely to affect adversely the ability of petitioner and its members to pursue their collective effort.

In ruling in favor of the NAACP, the Supreme Court had to distinguish a precedent that cut the other way. In 1928, it had upheld a New York law under which the Ku Klux Klan was forced to disclose its membership list. In that case, *Bryant v. Zimmerman*, the Court had justified the state policy by stressing the violent and unlawful tactics of the Klan. In *NAACP v. Alabama,* the Court stressed the fact that the NAACP used lawful means in seeking its political objectives.

Freedom of Association and Discrimination

In the 1990s, there is very little controversy about the rights of minorities to organize for purposes of litigation and political action. Today, many states use their legislative powers on behalf of minority groups and women seeking integration into the economic and cultural mainstream. Public accommodations laws have been used to force civic groups and social clubs to extend membership to women and minorities. Freedom of association has often been raised as a constitutional objection to such efforts.

In *Roberts v. United States Jaycees* (1984), a unanimous Supreme Court found that Minnesota's interest in eradicating sex discrimination was sufficiently compelling to justify a decision of its human rights commission requiring local chapters of the Jaycees to admit women. Writing for the Court, Justice Brennan recognized a political dimension to the Jaycees' activities but nevertheless held that the organization's freedom of political association must give way to the superior state interest in abolishing sex discrimination. In *Rotary International v. Rotary Club of Duarte* (1987), the Court extended its decision in the *Jaycees* case to encompass the Rotary Club as well. And in 1988, the Court upheld a city ordinance requiring large all-male social clubs to admit women *(New York State Club Association v. City of New York)*. The Court's decisions dealing with "private" clubs suggest that freedom of association in that context must yield to the societal interest in eradicating racial and sexual inequality.

THE OVERBREADTH DOCTRINE

The doctrine of overbreadth is an important element in First Amendment jurisprudence, although its importance has probably declined somewhat in recent years. First articulated in *Thornhill v. Alabama* (1940), the doctrine of overbreadth proscribes a law that "does not aim specifically at evils within the allowable area of state control [but] sweeps within its ambit other activities that in ordinary circumstances constitute an exercise of freedom of speech. . . ." For example, in *Coates v. Cincinnati* (1971), the Court found an ordinance that prohibited people from congregating on the streets and "annoying" passersby to be unconstitutionally overbroad. In the Court's view, the ordinance allowed police to make arrests for constitutionally protected activity, such as legitimate political speech, as well as unprotected activity, such as fighting words. Writing for a majority of six, Justice Stewart stated:

> The First and Fourteenth Amendments do not permit a state to make criminal the exercise of the right of assembly simply because its exercise may be "annoying" to some people. If this were not the rule, the right of the people to gather in public places for social or political purposes would be continually subject to summary suspension through the good-faith enforcement of a prohibition against annoying conduct.

Justice Stewart further observed:

> The city is free to prevent people from blocking sidewalks, obstructing traffic, littering streets, committing assaults, or engaging in countless other forms of antisocial conduct. It can do so through the enactment and enforcement of ordinances directed with reasonable specificity toward the conduct to be prohibited. . . . It cannot constitutionally do so through the enactment and enforcement of an ordinance whose violation may entirely depend on whether a policeman is annoyed.

Justice Stewart's opinion in *Coates* shows the close relationship between the doctrine of overbreadth and the **void for vagueness doctrine.** A law is void for vagueness if it fails to define proscribed conduct with sufficient clarity and specificity. A fundamental principle of legality is that the individual must be able to determine which forms of conduct are permitted and which are prohibited. A criminal law that is both overbroad and vague makes this determination difficult, if not impossible.

As Justice Brennan stated in his majority opinion in *Gooding v. Wilson* (1972), the overbreadth and vagueness doctrines permit facial attacks "with no requirement that the person making the attack demonstrate that his own conduct could not be regulated by a statute drawn with the requisite narrow specificity." Such attacks resulted in numerous laws being struck down by the Supreme Court during the 1960s and early 1970s (see, for example, *Aptheker v. Secretary of State* [1964]; *Keyishian v. State Board of Regents* [1967]; *United States v. Robel* [1967]).

In the early 1970s, President Nixon's four appointees to the Supreme Court—Burger, Blackmun, Powell, and Rehnquist—expressed deep concern for the overuse of the overbreadth doctrine. Dissenting in *Gooding v. Wilson,* Justice Blackmun claimed that the doctrine "urgently need[ed] re-examination." Such reexamination did in fact occur, resulting in a modification of the doctrine. In *Broadrick v. Oklahoma* (1973), the Court held that any declaration of facial overbreadth should be the exception, rather than the rule. According to Justice White's majority opinion, "the overbreadth of a statute must not only be real, but substantial as well, judged in relation to the statute's plainly legitimate sweep."

The more conservative version of the overbreadth doctrine is less likely to result in declarations of facial overbreadth. For example, in *New York v. Ferber* (1982), the Supreme Court upheld a child pornography law against a challenge of overbreadth, saying that the law was "not substantially overbroad" and that "whatever overbreadth exists should be cured through case-by-case analysis of the situations to which its sanctions, assertedly, may not be applied." Thus, the Court's approach in *Ferber* was far removed from the dominant approach of the 1960s, in which one could successfully challenge the validity of the statute on the grounds that it might be applied at some future time to constitutionally protected activity! However, the Court has by no means discarded the overbreadth doctrine entirely (see, for example, *Board of Airport Commissioners v. Jews for Jesus* [1987]; *Houston v. Hill* [1987]).

CONCLUSION

The preceding discussion of major issues involving freedom of expression, assembly, and association, although necessarily selective, underscores several important First Amendment themes. The Supreme Court recognizes no absolutes in this area, but it does operate on the assumption that First Amendment freedoms are of fundamental importance in a democratic society. As a result, the Court generally imposes high standards in determining the constitutionality of legislation challenged on First Amendment grounds. In recent years, a majority of the justices have resisted easy generalizations and uncritical application of neat doctrinal tests in this particularly complex area of constitutional interpretation. In deciding difficult First Amendment cases, the Court attempts to accommodate legitimate governmental interests in maintaining peace, order, security, decency, and overall quality of life with an open society's vital interest in maintaining a free marketplace of ideas.

FOR FURTHER READING

Abernathy, Glenn. *The Right of Assembly and Association,* 2d ed. Columbia: University of South Carolina Press, 1981.

Berns, Walter. *The First Amendment and the Future of American Democracy.* New York: Basic Books, 1976.

Bollinger, Lee. *The Tolerant Society: Freedom of Speech and Extremist Speech in America.* New York: Oxford University Press, 1986.

Chafee, Zechariah, Jr. *Free Speech in the United States.* Cambridge: Harvard University Press, 1941.

Downs, D. A. *Nazis in Skokie: Freedom, Communication and the First Amendment.* South Bend, Ind.: Notre Dame University Press, 1985.

Emerson, Thomas I. *The System of Freedom of Expression.* New York: Random House, 1970.

Fellman, David. *The Constitutional Right of Association.* Chicago: University of Chicago Press, 1963.

Fortas, Abe. *Concerning Dissent and Civil Disobedience.* New York: New American Library, 1968.

Kalven, Harry, Jr. *A Worthy Tradition: Freedom of Speech in America.* New York: Harper and Row, 1988.

Konefsky, Samuel J. *The Legacy of Holmes and Brandeis: a Study in the Influence of Ideas.* New York: Macmillan, 1956.

Polenberg, Richard. *Fighting Faiths: The Abrams Case, the Supreme Court and Free Speech.* New York: Viking Press, 1987.

Shapiro, Martin. *Freedom of Speech: The Supreme Court and Judicial Review.* Englewood Cliffs, N.J.: Prentice-Hall, 1966.

Shiffrin, Steven H., and Jesse H. Choper. *The First Amendment.* St. Paul: West, 1991.

Smith, James M. *Freedom's Fetters: The Alien and Sedition Laws and American Civil Liberties.* Ithaca, N.Y.: Cornell University Press, 1956.

Tedford, Thomas L. *Freedom of Speech in the United States.* New York: Random House, 1985.

C A S E S   A N D   R E A D I N G S

Schenck v. United States

249 U.S. 47; 39 S. Ct. 247; 63 L. Ed. 470 (1919)
Vote: 9-0

Charles T. Schenck, general secretary of the Socialist party, was convicted of "causing and attempting to cause insubordination in the military and naval forces of the United States," as prohibited under the Espionage Act of 1917. The conviction stemmed from the Socialist party's activities in printing and distributing leaflets attacking American participation in the First World War and urging young men to oppose the military draft.

Mr. *Justice Holmes* delivered the opinion of the Court:

This is an indictment in three counts. The first charges a conspiracy to violate the Espionage Act of June 15, 1917, *** by causing and attempting to cause insubordination, etc., in the military and naval forces of the United States, and to obstruct the recruiting and enlistment service of the United States, when the United States was at war with the German Empire; to wit, that the defendant wilfully conspired to have printed and circulated to men who had been called and accepted for military service, a document set forth and alleged to be calculated to cause such insubordination and obstruction. The court alleges overt acts in pursuance of the conspiracy, ending in the distribution of the document set forth. The second count alleges a conspiracy to commit an offense against the United States; to wit, to use the mails for the transmission of matter declared to be non-mailable, *** to wit, the above-mentioned document, with an averment of the same overt acts. The third count charges an unlawful use of the mails for the transmission of same matter and otherwise as above. The defendants were found guilty on all the counts. They set up the First Amendment to the Constitution, forbidding Congress to make any law abridging the freedom of speech or of the press. . . .

According to the testimony Schenck said he was general secretary of the Socialist party and had charge of the Socialist headquarters from which the documents were sent. He identified a book found there as the minutes of the executive committee of the party. The book showed a resolution of August 13, 1917, that 15,000 leaflets should be printed . . . to be mailed to men who had passed exemption boards, and for distribution. Schenck personally attended to the printing. On August 20 the general secretary's report said, "Obtained new leaflets from the printer and started work addressing envelopes," etc.; and there was a resolve that Comrade Schenck be allowed $125 for sending leaflets through the mail. He said that he had about fifteen or sixteen thousand printed. There were files of the circular in question in the inner office. . . . Copies were proved to have been sent through the mails to drafted men. Without going into confirmatory details that were proved, no reasonable man could doubt that the defendant Schenck was largely instrumental in sending the circulars about. . . .

The document in question, upon its first printed side, recited the 1st section of the Thirteenth Amendment, said that the idea embodied in it was violated by the Conscription Act, and that a conscript is little better than a convict. In impassioned language it intimated that conscription was despotism in its worst form and a monstrous wrong against humanity, in the interest of Wall Street's chosen few. It said: "Do not submit to intimidation"; but in form at least confined itself to peaceful measures, such as a petition for the repeal of the act. The other and later printed side of the sheet was headed, "Assert Your Rights." It stated reasons for alleging that anyone violated the Constitution when he refused to recognize "your right to assert your opposition to the draft," and went on: "If you do not assert and support your rights, you are helping to deny or disparage rights which it is the solemn duty of all citizens and residents of the United States to retain." It described the arguments on the other side as coming from cunning politicians and a mercenary capitalist press, and even silent consent to the Conscription Law as helping to support an infamous conspiracy. It denied the power to send our citizens away to foreign shores to shoot up the people of other lands, and added that words could not express the condemnation such cold-blooded ruthlessness deserves, etc., etc., winding up, "You must do your share to maintain, support, and uphold the rights of the people of this country." Of course the document would not have been sent unless it had been intended to have some effect, and we do not see what effect it could be expected to have upon persons subject to the draft except to influence them to obstruct the carrying of it out. The defendants do not deny that the jury might find against them on this point.

But it is said, suppose that that was the tendency of this circular, it is protected by the First Amendment to the Constitution. Two of the strongest expressions are said to be quoted respectively from well-known public men. It well may be that the prohibition of laws abridging the freedom of speech is not confined to previous restraints, although to prevent them may have been the main purpose.... We admit that in many places and in ordinary times the defendants, in saying all that was said in the circular, would have been within their constitutional rights.

But the character of every act depends upon the circumstances in which it is done. *** The most stringent protection of free speech would not protect a man in falsely shouting fire in a theater, and causing a panic. It does not even protect a man from an injunction against uttering words that may have all the effect of force. *** The question in every case is whether the words used are used in such circumstances and are of such a nature as to create a clear and present danger that they will bring about the substantive evils that Congress has a right to prevent. It is a question of proximity and degree. When a nation is at war many things that might be said in time of peace are such a hindrance to its effort that their utterance will not be endured so long as men fight, and that no court could regard them as protected by any constitutional right. It seems to be admitted that if an actual obstruction of the recruiting service were proved, liability for words that produced that effect might be enforced. The Statute of 1917 punishes conspiracies to obstruct as well as actual obstruction. If the act (speaking, or circulating a paper), its tendency and the intent with which it is done, are the same, we perceive no ground for saying that success alone warrants making the act a crime. *** ...

Judgments affirmed.

Dennis v. United States

341 U.S. 494; 71 S. Ct. 857; 95 L. Ed. 1137 (1951)
Vote: 6-2

The Smith Act of 1940 made it a federal crime for any person "to knowingly or willfully advocate ... or teach the duty, necessity, desirability, or propriety of overthrowing or destroying any government in the United States by force or violence...." The act also made it a crime "to organize or help to organize any society, group, or assembly of persons who teach, advocate or encourage the overthrow...." Eleven high-ranking members of the American Communist party were convicted of violating the Smith Act. Their convictions were upheld by a U.S. court of appeals. The Supreme Court granted certiorari to consider whether the act, inherently or as applied, violates the First or Fifth Amendments.

Mr. Chief Justice Vinson announced the judgment of the Court and an opinion in which **Mr. Justice Reed, Mr. Justice Burton** and **Mr. Justice Minton** join.

... The obvious purpose of the statute is to protect existing Government, not from change by peaceable, lawful and constitutional means, but from change by violence, revolution and terrorism. That it is within the power of the Congress to protect the Government of the United States from armed rebellion is a proposition which requires little discussion. Whatever theoretical merit there may be to the argument that there is a "right" to rebellion against dictatorial governments is without force where the existing structure of the government provides for peaceful and orderly change. We reject any principle of governmental helplessness in the face of preparation for revolution, which principle, carried to its logical conclusion, must lead to anarchy. No one could conceive that it is not within the power of Congress to prohibit acts intended to overthrow the Government by force and violence. The question with which we are concerned here is not whether Congress has such power, but whether the means which it has employed conflict with the First and Fifth Amendments to the Constitution.

One of the bases for the contention that the means which Congress has employed are invalid takes the form of an attack on the face of the statute on the grounds that by its terms it prohibits academic discussion of the merits of Marxism-Leninism, that it stifles ideas and is contrary to all concepts of a free speech and a free press. . . .

The very language of the Smith Act negates the interpretation which petitioners would have us impose on that Act. It is directed at advocacy, not discussion. Thus, the trial judge properly charged the jury that they could not convict if they found that petitioners did "no more than pursue peaceful studies and discussions or teaching and advocacy in the realm of ideas." *** He further charged that it was not unlawful "to conduct in an American college and university a course explaining the philosophical theories set forth in the books which have been placed in evidence." *** Such a charge is in strict accord with the statutory language, and illustrates the meaning to be placed on those words. Congress did not intend to eradicate the free discussion of political theories, to destroy the traditional rights of Americans to discuss and evaluate ideas without fear of governmental sanction. Rather Congress was concerned with the very kind of activity in which the evidence showed these petitioners engaged. . . .

But although the statute is not directed at the hypothetical cases which petitioners have conjured, its application in this case has resulted in convictions

for the teaching and advocacy of the overthrow of the Government by force and violence, which, even though coupled with the intent to accomplish that overthrow, contains an element of speech. For this reason, we must pay special heed to the demands of the First Amendment marking out the boundaries of speech.

. . . [T]he basis of the First Amendment is the hypothesis that speech can rebut speech, propaganda will answer propaganda, free debate of ideas will result in the wisest governmental policies. It is for this reason that this Court has recognized the inherent value of free discourse. An analysis of the leading cases in this Court which have involved direct limitations on speech, however, will demonstrate that both the majority of the Court and the dissenters in particular cases have recognized that this is not an unlimited, unqualified right, but that the societal value of speech must, on occasion, be subordinated to other values and considerations. . . .

. . . [W]here an offense is specified by a statute in nonspeech or nonpress terms, a conviction relying upon speech or press as evidence of violation may be sustained only when the speech or publication created a "clear and present danger" of attempting or accomplishing the prohibited crime. ***

In this case we are squarely presented with the application of the "clear and present danger" test, and must decide what that phrase imports. We first note that many of the cases in which this Court has reversed convictions by use of this or similar tests have been based on the fact that the interest which the State was attempting to protect was itself too insubstantial to warrant restriction of speech. *** Overthrow of the Government by force and violence is certainly a substantial enough interest for the Government to limit speech. Indeed, this is the ultimate value of any society, for if a society cannot protect its very structure from armed internal attack, it must follow that no subordinate value can be protected. If, then, this interest may be protected, the literal problem which is presented is what has been meant by the use of the phrase "clear and present danger" of the utterances bringing about the evil within the power of Congress to punish.

Obviously, the words cannot mean that before the Government may act, it must wait until the putsch is about to be executed, the plans have been laid and the signal is awaited. If Government is aware that a group aiming at its overthrow is attempting to indoctrinate its members and to commit them to a course whereby they will strike when the leaders feel the circumstances permit, action by the Government is required. The argument that there is no need for Government to concern itself, for Government is strong, it possesses ample powers to put down a rebellion, it may defeat the revolution with ease needs no answer. For that is not the question. Certainly an attempt to overthrow the Government by force, even though doomed from the outset because of inadequate numbers or power of the revolutionists, is a sufficient evil for Congress to prevent. The damage which such attempts create both physically and politically to a nation makes it impossible to measure the validity in terms of the probability of success, or the immediacy of a successful attempt. In the instant case the trial judge charged the jury that they could not convict unless they found that petitioners intended to overthrow the Government "as speedily as circumstances would permit." *** This does not mean, and could not properly mean, that they would not strike until there was certainty of success. What was meant was that the revolutionists would strike when they thought the time was ripe. We must therefore reject the contention that success or probability of success is the criterion.

The situation with which Justice Holmes and Brandeis were concerned in *Gitlow [v. New York]* was a comparatively isolated event, bearing little relation in their minds to any substantial threat to the safety of the community. *** They were not confronted with any situation comparable to the instant one—the development of an apparatus designed and dedicated to the overthrow of the Government, in the context of world crisis after crisis.

Chief Judge Learned Hand, writing for the [U.S. court of appeals] majority below, interpreted the phrase as follows: "In each case [courts] must ask whether the gravity of the 'evil,' is discounted by its improbability, justifies such invasion of free speech as is necessary to avoid the danger." *** We adopt this statement of the rule. As articulated by Chief Judge Hand, it is as succinct and inclusive as any other we might devise at this time. It takes into consideration

those factors which we deem relevant, and relates their significance. More we cannot expect from words.

Likewise, we are in accord with the court below, which affirmed the trial court's finding that the requisite danger existed. The mere fact that from the period 1945 to 1948 petitioners' activities did not result in an attempt to overthrow the Government by force and violence is of course no answer to the fact that there was a group that was ready to make the attempt. The formation by petitioners of such a highly organized conspiracy, with rigidly disciplined members subject to call when the leaders, these petitioners, felt that the time had come for action, coupled with the inflammable nature of world conditions, similar uprisings in other countries, and the touch-and-go nature of our relations with countries with whom petitioners were in the very least ideologically attuned, convince us that their convictions were justified on this score. And this analysis disposes of the contention that a conspiracy to advocate, as distinguished from the advocacy itself, cannot be constitutionally restrained, because it comprises only the preparation. It is the existence of the conspiracy which creates the danger. *** If the ingredients of the reaction are present, we cannot bind the Government to wait until the catalyst is added.

V

We hold that [the challenged sections] of the Smith Act, do not inherently, or as construed or applied in the instant case, violate the First Amendment and other provisions of the Bill of Rights, or the First and Fifth Amendments because of indefiniteness. Petitioners intended to overthrow the Government of the United States as speedily as the circumstances would permit. Their conspiracy to organize the Communist Party and to teach and advocate the overthrow of the Government of the United States by force and violence created a "clear and present danger" of an attempt to overthrow the Government by force and violence. They were properly and constitutionally convicted for violation of the Smith Act. The judgments of conviction are Affirmed.

Mr. Justice Clark took no part in the consideration or decision of this case.

Mr. Justice Frankfurter, concurring in affirmance of the judgment. . . .

Mr. Justice Jackson, concurring.

. . . What really is under review here is a conviction of conspiracy, after a trial for conspiracy, on an indictment charging conspiracy, brought under a statute outlawing conspiracy. With due respect to my colleagues, they seem to me to discuss anything under the sun except the law of conspiracy. One of the dissenting opinions even appears to chide me for "invoking the law of conspiracy." As that is the case before us, it may be more amazing that its reversal can be proposed without even considering the law of conspiracy.

The Constitution does not make conspiracy a civil right. The Court has never before done so and I think it should not do so now. Conspiracies of labor unions, trade associations, and news agencies have been condemned, although accomplished, evidenced and carried out, like the conspiracy here, chiefly by letter-writing, meetings, speeches and organization. Indeed, this Court seems, particularly in cases where the conspiracy has economic ends, to be applying its doctrines with increasing severity. While I consider criminal conspiracy a dragnet device capable of perversion into an instrument of injustice in the hands of a partisan or complacent judiciary, it has an established place in our system of law, and no reason appears for applying it only to concerted action claimed to disturb interstate commerce and withholding it from those claimed to undermine our whole Government. . . .

Mr. Justice Black dissenting.

. . . At the outset I want to emphasize what the crime involved in this case is, and what it is not. These petitioners were not charged with an attempt to overthrow the Government. They were not charged with overt acts of any kind designed to overthrow the Government. They were not even charged with saying anything or writing anything designed to overthrow the Government. The charge was that they agreed to assemble and to talk and publish certain ideas at a later date: the indictment is that they considered to organize the Communist Party and to use speech or newspapers and other publications in the future to teach and advocate the forcible overthrow of the Government. No matter how it is worded, this is a virulent form of prior censorship of speech and press, which I believe the First Amendment forbids. I would hold Section 3 of the Smith Act authorizing this prior restraint unconstitutional on its face and as applied.

But let us assume, contrary to all constitutional ideas of fair criminal procedure, that petitioners, although not indicted for the crime of actual advocacy, may be punished for it. Even on this radical assumption, the other opinions in this case show that the only way to affirm these convictions is to repudiate directly or indirectly the established "clear and present danger" rule. This the Court does in a way which greatly restricts the protections afforded by the First Amendment. The opinions for affirmance indicate that the chief reason for jettisoning the rule is the expressed fear that advocacy of Communist doctrine endangers the safety of the Republic. Undoubtedly, a governmental policy of unfettered communication of ideas does entail dangers. To the Founders of this Nation, however, the benefits derived from free expression were worth the risk. They embodied this philosophy in the First Amendment's command that Congress "shall make no law abridging . . . the freedom of speech, or of the press. . . ." I have always believed that the First Amendment is the keystone of our Government, that the freedoms it guarantees provide the best insurance against destruction of all freedom. At least as to speech in the realm of public matters, I believe that the "clear and present danger" test does not "mark the furthermost constitutional boundaries of protected expression" but does "nor more than recognized a minimum compulsion of the Bill of Rights." ***

So long as this Court exercises the power of judicial review of legislation, I cannot agree that the First Amendment permits us to sustain laws suppressing freedom of speech and press on the basis of Congress' or our own notions of mere "reasonableness." Such a doctrine waters down the First Amendment so that it amounts to little more than an admonition to Congress. The Amendment as so construed is not likely to protect any but those "safe" or orthodox views which rarely need its protection. I must also express my objection to the holding because, as Mr.

Justice Douglas' dissent shows, it sanctions the determination of a crucial issue of fact by the judge rather than by the jury. Nor can I let this opportunity pass without expressing my objection to the severely limited grant of certiorari in this case which precluded consideration here of at least two other reasons for reversing these convictions: (1) the record shows a discriminatory selection of the jury panel which prevented trial before a representative cross-section of the community; (2) the record shows that one member of the trial jury was violently hostile to petitioners before and during the trial.

Public opinion being what it now is, few will protest the conviction of these Communist petitioners. There is hope, however, that in calmer times, when present pressures, passions and fears subside, this or some later Court will restore the First Amendment liberties to the high preferred place where they belong in a free society.

Mr. Justice Douglas, dissenting.

If this were a case where those who claimed protection under the First Amendment were teaching the techniques of sabotage, the assassination of the President, the filching of documents from public files, the planting of bombs, the art of street warfare, and the like, I would have no doubts. The freedom to speak is not absolute; the teaching of methods of terror and other seditious conduct should be beyond the pale along with obscenity and immorality. This case was argued as if those were the facts. The argument imported much seditious conduct into the record. That is easy and it has popular appeal, for the activities of Communists in plotting and scheming against the free world are common knowledge. But the fact is that no such evidence was introduced at the trial. There is a statute which makes a seditious conspiracy unlawful. Petitioners, however, were not charged with a "conspiracy to overthrow" the Government. They were charged with a conspiracy to form a party and groups and assemblies of people who teach and advocate the overthrow of our Gov-

ernment by force or violence and with a conspiracy to advocate and teach its overthrow by force and violence. It may well be that indoctrination in the techniques of terror to destroy the Government would be indictable under either statute. But the teaching which is condemned here is of a different character.

So far as the present record is concerned, what petitioners did was to organize people to teach and themselves teach the Marxist-Leninist doctrine contained chiefly in four books: *Foundations of Leninism* by Stalin (1924), *The Communist Manifesto* by Marx and Engels (1848), *State and Revolution* by Lenin (1917), *History of the Communist Party of the Soviet Union* (1939).

These books are to Soviet Communism what *Mein Kampf* was to Nazism. If they are understood, the ugliness of Communism is revealed, its deceit and cunning are exposed, the nature of its activities becomes apparent, and the chances of its success less likely. That is not, of course, the reason why petitioners chose these books for their classrooms. They are fervent Communists to whom these volumes are gospel. They preached the creed with the hope that some day it would be acted upon.

The opinion of the Court does not outlaw these texts nor condemn them to the fire, as the Communists do literature offensive to their creed. But if the books themselves are not outlawed, if they can lawfully remain on library shelves, by what reasoning does their use in a classroom become a crime? It would not be a crime under the Act to introduce these books to a class, though that would be teaching what the creed to violent overthrow of the government is. The Act, as construed, requires the element of intent—that those who teach the creed believe in it. The crime then depends not on what is taught but on who the teacher is. That is to make freedom of speech turn not on what is said, but on the intent with which it is said. Once we start down that road we enter territory dangerous to the liberties of every citizen. . . .

Brandenburg v. Ohio

395 U.S. 444; 89 S. Ct. 1827; 23 L. Ed. 2d 430 (1969)
Vote: 9-0

Per Curiam.

The appellant, a leader of a Ku Klux Klan group, was convicted under the Ohio Criminal Syndicalism statute for "advocat[ing] ... the duty, necessity, or propriety of crime, sabotage, violence, or unlawful methods of terrorism as a means of accomplishing industrial or political reform" and for "voluntarily assembl[ing] with any society, group, or assemblage of persons formed to teach or advocate the doctrines of criminal syndicalism." *** He was fined $1,000 and sentenced to one to 10 years' imprisonment. The appellant challenged the constitutionality of the criminal syndicalism statute under the First and Fourteenth Amendments to the United States Constitution, but the intermediate appellate court of Ohio affirmed his conviction without opinion. The Supreme Court of Ohio dismissed his appeal. . . . It did not file an opinion or explain its conclusions. Appeal was taken to this Court, and we noted probable jurisdiction. *** We reverse.

The record shows that a man, identified at trial as the appellant, telephoned an announcer-reporter on the staff of a Cincinnati television station and invited him to come to a Ku Klux Klan "rally" to be held at a farm in Hamilton County. With the cooperation of the organizers, the reporter and a cameraman attended the meeting and filmed the events. Portions of the films were later broadcast on the local station and on a national network.

The prosecution's case rested on the films and on testimony identifying the appellant as the person who communicated with the reporter and who spoke at the rally. The State also introduced into evidence several articles appearing in the film, including a pistol, a rifle, a shotgun, ammunition, a Bible, and a red hood worn by the speaker in the films.

One film showed 12 hooded figures, some of whom carried firearms. They were gathered around a large wooden cross, which they burned. No one was present other than the participants and the newsmen who made the film. Most of the words uttered during the scene were incomprehensible when the film was projected, but scattered phrases could be understood that were derogatory of Negroes and, in one instance, of Jews. Another scene on the same film showed the appellant, in Klan regalia, making a speech. The speech, in full, was as follows:

This is an organizers' meeting. We have had quite a few members here today which are—we have hundreds, hundreds of members throughout the State of Ohio. I can quote from a newspaper clipping from the Columbus, Ohio *Dispatch,* five weeks ago Sunday morning. The Klan has more members in the State of Ohio than does any other organization. We're not a revengent organization, but if our President, our Congress, our Supreme Court, continues to suppress the white, Caucasian race, it's possible that there might have to be some revengeance taken.

We are marching on Congress July the Fourth, four hundred thousand strong. From there we are dividing into two groups, one group to march on St. Augustine, Florida , the other group to march into Mississippi. Thank you.

The second film showed six hooded figures, one of whom, later identified as the appellant, repeated a speech very similar to that recorded on the first film. The reference to the possibility of "revengeance" was omitted, and one sentence was added: "Personally, I believe the nigger should be returned to Africa, the Jew returned to Israel." Though some of the figures in the films carried weapons, the speaker did not.

The Ohio Criminal Syndicalism Statute was enacted in 1919. From 1917 to 1920, identical or quite similar laws were adopted by 20 States and two territories. *** In 1927, this Court sustained the constitutionality of California's Criminal Syndicalism Act, the text of which is quite similar to that of the laws of Ohio. *** The Court upheld that statute on the ground that, without more, "advocating" violent means to effect political and economic change involves such danger to the security of the State that the State may outlaw it. *** But [this view] has been thoroughly discredited by later decisions. *** These later decisions have fashioned the principle that the constitutional guarantees of free speech and free press do not permit a State to forbid or proscribe advocacy of the use of force or of law violation except where such advocacy is directed to inciting or producing imminent lawless action and is likely to incite or produce such action. As we said in *Noto v. United States,* *** "the mere abstract teaching . . . of the moral propriety or even moral necessity for a resort to force and violence, is not the same as preparing a group for violent action and steeling it to such action." *** A statute which fails to draw this distinction impermissibly intrudes upon the freedoms guaranteed by the First and Fourteenth Amendments. It sweeps within its condemnation speech which our Constitution has immunized from governmental control. ***

Measured by this test, Ohio's Criminal Syndicalism Act cannot be sustained. The Act punishes persons who "advocate or teach the duty, necessity, or propriety" of violence "as a means of accomplishing industrial or political reform"; or who publish or circulate or display any book or paper containing such advocacy; or who "justify" the commission of violent acts "with intent to exemplify, spread or advocate the propriety of the doctrines of criminal syndicalism"; or who "voluntarily assemble" with a group formed "to teach or advocate the doctrines of criminal syndicalism." Neither the indictment nor the trial judge's instructions to the jury in any way refined the statute's bald definition of the crime in terms of mere advocacy not distinguished from incitement to imminent lawless action.

Accordingly, we are here confronted with a statute which, by its own words and as applied, purports to punish mere advocacy and to forbid, on pain of crim-inal punishment, assembly with others merely to advocate the described type of action. Such a statute falls within the condemnation of the First and Fourteenth Amendments. The contrary teaching of *Whitney v. California* ***cannot be supported and that decision is therefore overruled.

Reversed.

Mr. Justice Black, concurring. . . .

Mr. Justice Douglas, concurring.

. . . I see no place in the regime of the First Amendment for any "clear and present danger" test, whether strict and tight as some would make it, or freewheeling. . . .

The line between what is permissible and not subject to control and what may be made impermissible and subject to regulation is the line between ideas and overt acts.

The example usually given by those who would punish speech is the case of one who falsely shouts fire in a crowded theatre.

This is, however, a classic case where speech is brigaded with action. *** They are indeed inseparable and a prosecution can be launched for the overt acts actually caused. Apart from rare instances of that kind, speech is, I think, immune from prosecution. Certainly there is no constitutional line between advocacy of abstract ideas . . . and advocacy of political action. . . . The quality of advocacy turns on the depth of the conviction; and government has no power to invade that sanctuary of belief and conscience.

Feiner v. New York
340 U.S. 315; 71 S. Ct. 303; 95 L. Ed. 295 (1951)
Vote: 6-3

Irving Feiner was convicted of the misdemeanor of disorderly conduct by a local court in Syracuse, New York. He was sentenced to thirty days in the county jail. The conviction was affirmed by the New York Court of Appeals (the highest appellate court of that state). The Supreme Court granted certiorari to consider Feiner's claim that the conviction violated his right of free speech under the First and Fourteenth Amendments. The facts are reviewed in Chief Justice Vinson's majority opinion.

Mr. Chief Justice Vinson delivered the opinion of the Court.

On the evening of March 8, 1949, petitioner Irving Feiner was addressing an open-air meeting at the corner of South McBride and Harrison Streets in the City of Syracuse. At approximately 6:30 P.M., the police received a telephone complaint concerning the meeting, and two officers were detailed to investigate. One of these officers went to the scene immediately, the other arriving some twelve minutes later. They found a crowd of about seventy-five or eighty people, both Negro and white, filling the sidewalk and spreading out into the street. Petitioner, standing on a large wooden box on the sidewalk, was addressing the crowd through a loud-speaker system attached to an automobile. Although the purpose of his speech was to urge his listeners to attend a meeting to be held that night in the Syracuse Hotel, in its course he was making derogatory remarks concerning President Truman, the American Legion, the Mayor of Syracuse, and other local political officials.

The police officers made no effort to interfere with petitioner's speech, but were first concerned with the effect of the crowd on both pedestrian and vehicular traffic. They observed the situation from the opposite side of the street, noting that some pedestrians were forced to walk in the street to avoid the crowd. Since traffic was passing at the time, the officers attempted to get the people listening to petitioner back on the sidewalk. The crowd was restless and there was some pushing, shoving and milling around. One of the officers telephoned the police station from a nearby store, and then both policemen crossed the street and mingled with the crowd without any intention of arresting the speaker.

At this time, petitioner was speaking in a "loud, high-pitched voice." He gave the impression that he was endeavoring to arouse the Negro people against the whites, urging that they rise up in arms and fight for equal rights. The statements before such a mixed audience "stirred up a little excitement." Some of the onlookers made remarks to the police about their inability to handle the crowd and at least one threatened violence if the police did not act. There were others who appeared to be favoring petitioner's arguments. Because of the feeling that existed in the crowd both for, and against the

speaker, the officers finally "stepped in to prevent it from resulting in a fight." One of the officers approached the petitioner, not for the purpose of arresting him, but to get him to break up the crowd. He asked petitioner to get down off the box, but the latter refused to accede to his request and continued talking. The officer waited for a minute and then demanded that he cease talking. Although the officer had thus twice requested petitioner to stop over the course of several minutes, petitioner not only ignored him but continued talking. During all this time, the crowd was pressing closer around petitioner and the officer. Finally, the officer told petitioner he was under arrest and ordered him to get down from the box, reaching up to grab him. Petitioner stepped down, announcing over the microphone that "the law has arrived, and I suppose they will take over now." In all, the officer had asked petitioner to get down off the box three times over a space of four or five minutes. Petitioner had been speaking for over a half hour.

On these facts, petitioner was specifically charged with *** [disorderly conduct]. The bill of particulars, demanded by petitioner and furnished by the State, gave in detail the facts upon which the prosecution relied to support the charge of disorderly conduct. Paragraph C is particularly pertinent here: "By ignoring and refusing to heed and obey reasonable police orders issued at the time and place mentioned in the information to regulate and control said crowd and to prevent a breach or breaches of the peace and to prevent injury to pedestrians attempting to use said walk, and being forced into the highway adjacent to the place in question, and prevent injury to the public generally." ***

We are not faced here with blind condonation by a state court of arbitrary police action. Petitioner was accorded a full, fair trial. The trial judge heard testimony supporting and contradicting the judgment of the police officers that a clear danger of disorder was threatened. After weighing this contradictory evidence, the trial judge reached the conclusion that the police officers were justified in taking action to prevent a breach of the peace. The exercise of the police officers' proper discretionary power to prevent a breach of the peace was thus approved by the trial court and later by two courts on review. The courts below recognized petitioner's right to hold a street meeting at this locality, to make use of loud-speaking equipment in giving his speech, and to make derogatory remarks concerning public officials and the American Legion. They found that the officers in making the arrest were motivated solely by a proper concern for the preservation of order and protection of the general welfare, and that there was no evidence which could lend color to a claim that the acts of the police were a cover for suppression of petitioner's views and opinions. Petitioner was thus neither arrested nor convicted for the making or the content of his speech. Rather, it was the reaction which it actually engendered.

The language of *Cantwell v. Connecticut* *** is appropriate here. "The offense known as breach of the peace embraces a great variety of conduct destroying or menacing public order and tranquility. It includes not only violent acts but acts and words likely to produce violence in others. No one would have the hardihood to suggest that the principle of freedom of speech sanctions incitement to riot or that religious liberty connotes the privilege to exhort others to physical attack upon those belonging to another sect. When clear and present danger of riot, disorder, interference with traffic upon the public streets, or other immediate threat to public safety, peace, or order, appears, the power of the State to prevent or punish is obvious." *** The findings of the New York courts as to the condition of the crowd and the refusal of petitioner to obey the police requests, supported as they are by the record of this case, are persuasive that the conviction of petitioner for violation of public peace, order and authority does not exceed the bounds of proper state police action. This Court respects, as it must, the interest of the community in maintaining peace and order on its streets. *** We cannot say that the preservation of that interest here encroaches on the constitutional rights of this petitioner.

We are well aware that the ordinary murmurings and objections of a hostile audience cannot be allowed to silence a speaker, and are also mindful of the possible danger of giving overzealous police officials complete discretion to break up otherwise lawful public meetings. "A State may not unduly suppress free communication of views, religious or other, under the guise of conserving desirable conditions." ***

But we are not faced here with such a situation. It is one thing to say that the police cannot be used as an instrument for the suppression of unpopular views, and another to say that, when as here the speaker passes the bounds of argument of persuasion and undertakes incitement to riot, they are powerless to prevent a breach of the peace. Nor in this case can we condemn the considered judgment of three New York courts approving the means which the police, faced with a crisis, used in the exercise of their power and duty to preserve peace and order. The findings of the state courts as to the existing situation and the imminence of greater disorder coupled with petitioner's deliberate defiance of the police officers convince us that we should not reverse this conviction in the name of free speech.

Affirmed.

Mr. Justice Frankfurter concurs in the result.

Mr. Justice Black, dissenting.

The record before us convinces me that petitioner, a young college student, has been sentenced to the penitentiary for the unpopular views he expressed on matters of public interest while lawfully making a street-corner speech in Syracuse, New York. Today's decision, however, indicates that we must blind ourselves to this fact because the trial judge fully accepted the testimony of the prosecution witnesses on all important points. Many times in the past this Court has said that despite findings below, we will examine the evidence for ourselves to ascertain whether federally protected rights have been denied; otherwise review here would fail of its purpose in safeguarding constitutional guarantees. Even a partial abandonment of this rule marks a dark day for civil liberties in our Nation.

But still more has been lost today. Even accepting every "finding of fact" below, I think this conviction makes a mockery of the free speech guarantees of the First and Fourteenth Amendments. The end result of the affirmance here is to approve a simple and readily available technique by which cities and states can with impunity subject all speeches, political or otherwise, on streets or elsewhere, to the supervision and censorship of the local police. I will have no part or parcel in this holding which I view as a long step toward totalitarian authority. . . .

In my judgment, today's holding means that as a practical matter, minority speakers can be silenced in any city. Hereafter, despite the First and Fourteenth Amendments, the policeman's club can take heavy toll of a current administration's public critics. Criticism of public officials will be too dangerous for all but the most courageous. ***

Mr. Justice Douglas, with whom **Mr. Justice Minton** concurs, dissenting.

. . . Public assemblies and public speech occupy an important role in American life. One high function of the police is to protect these lawful gatherings so that the speakers may exercise their constitutional rights. When unpopular causes are sponsored from the public platform, there will commonly be mutterings and unrest and heckling from the crowd. When a speaker mounts a platform it is not unusual to find him resorting to exaggeration, to vilification of ideas and men, to the making of false charges. But those extravagances *** do not justify penalizing the speaker by depriving him of the platform or by punishing him for his conduct.

A speaker may not, of course, incite a riot any more than he may incite a breach of the peace by the use of "fighting words." *** But this record shows no such extremes. It shows an unsympathetic audience and the threat of one man to haul the speaker from the stage. It is against that kind of threat that speakers need police protection. If they do not receive it and instead the police throw their weight on the side of those who would break up the meetings, the police become the new censors of speech. . . .

Cohen v. California
403 U.S. 15; 91 S. Ct. 1780; 29 L. Ed. 2d 284 (1971)
Vote: 5-4

Mr. Justice Harlan delivered the opinion of the Court.

This case may seem at first blush too inconsequential to find its way into our books, but the issue it presents is of no small constitutional significance.

Appellant Paul Robert Cohen was convicted in the Los Angeles Municipal Court of violating that part of California Penal Code Sec. 415 which prohibits "maliciously and willfully disturb[ing] the peace or quiet of any neighborhood or person . . . by . . . offensive conduct. . . ." He was given 30 days' imprisonment. The facts upon which his conviction rests are detailed in the opinion of the Court of Appeal of California, Second Appellate District, as follows:

On April 26, 1968, the defendant was observed in the Los Angeles County Courthouse in the corridor outside the division 20 of the municipal court wearing a jacket bearing the words "Fuck the Draft" which were plainly visible. There were women and children present in the corridor. The defendant was arrested. The defendant testified that he wore the jacket knowing that the words were on the jacket as a means of informing the public of the depth of his feelings against the Vietnam War and the draft.

The defendant did not engage in, nor threaten to engage in, nor did anyone as the result of his conduct in fact commit or threaten to commit any act of violence. The defendant did not make any loud or unusual noise, nor was there any evidence that he uttered any sound prior to his arrest. ***

In affirming the conviction the Court of Appeal held that "offensive conduct" means "behavior which has a tendency to provoke others to acts of violence or to in turn disturb the peace," and that the State had proved this element because, on the facts of this case, "[i]t was certainly reasonably foreseeable that such conduct might cause others to rise up to commit a violent act against the person of the defendant or attempt to forcibly remove his jacket." *** . . .

I

In order to lay hands on the precise issue which this case involves, it is useful first to canvass various matters which this record does not present.

The conviction quite clearly rests upon the asserted offensiveness of the words Cohen used to convey his message to the public. The only "conduct" which the State sought to punish is the fact of communication. Thus, we deal here with a conviction resting solely upon "speech," *** not upon any separately identifiable conduct which allegedly was intended by Cohen to be perceived by others as expressive of particular views but which, on its face, does not necessarily convey any message and hence arguably could be regulated without effectively repressing Cohen's ability to express himself. *** Further, the State certainly lacks power to punish Cohen for the underlying content of the message the inscription conveyed. At least so long as there is no showing of an intent to incite disobedience to or disruption of the draft, Cohen could not, consistently with the First and Fourteenth Amendments, be punished for asserting the evident position on the inutility or immorality of the draft his jacket reflected. ***

Appellant's conviction, then, rests squarely upon his exercise of the "freedom of speech" protected from arbitrary governmental interference by the Constitution and can be justified, if at all, only as a valid regulation of the manner in which he exercised that freedom, not as a permissible prohibition on the substantive message it conveys. This does not end the inquiry, of course, for the First and Fourteenth Amendments have never been thought to give absolute protection to every individual to speak whenever or wherever he pleases, or to use any form of address in any circumstances that he chooses. In this vein, too, however, we think it important to note that several issues typically associated with such problems are not presented here. ***

In the first place, Cohen was tried under a statute applicable throughout the entire State. Any attempt to support this conviction on the ground that the statute seeks to preserve an appropriately decorous atmosphere in the courthouse where Cohen was arrested must fall in the absence of any language in the statute that would have put appellant on notice that certain kinds of otherwise permissible speech or conduct would nevertheless, under California law, not be tolerated in certain places. ***

In the second place, as it comes to us, this case cannot be said to fall within those relatively few categories of instances where prior decisions have established the power of government to deal more

comprehensively with certain forms of individual expression simply upon a showing that such a form was employed. This is not, for example, an obscenity case. Whatever else may be necessary to give rise to the States' broader power to prohibit obscene expression, such expression must be, in some significant way, erotic. *** It cannot plausibly be maintained that this vulgar allusion to the Selective Service System would conjure up such psychic stimulation in anyone likely to be confronted with Cohen's crudely defaced jacket.

This Court has also held that the States are free to ban the simple use, without a demonstration of additional justifying circumstances, of so-called "fighting words," those personally abusive epithets which, when addressed to the ordinary citizen, are, as a matter of common knowledge, inherently likely to provoke violent reaction. *** While the four-letter word displayed by Cohen in relation to the draft is not uncommonly employed in a personally provocative fashion, in this instance it was clearly not "directed to the person of the hearer." *** No individual actually or likely to be present could reasonably have regarded the words on appellant's jacket as a direct personal insult. Nor do we have here an instance of the exercise of the State's police power to prevent a speaker from intentionally provoking a given group to hostile reaction. *** There is, as noted above, no showing that anyone who saw Cohen was in fact violently aroused or that appellant intended such a result.

Finally, in arguments before this Court much has been made of the claim that Cohen's distasteful mode of expression was thrust upon unwilling or unsuspecting viewers, and that the State might therefore legitimately act as it did in order to protect the sensitive from otherwise unavoidable exposure to appellant's crude form of protest. Of course, the mere presumed presence of unwitting listeners or viewers does not serve automatically to justify curtailing all speech capable of giving offense. *** While this Court has recognized that government may properly act in many situations to prohibit intrusion into the privacy of the home of unwelcome views and ideas which cannot be totally banned from the public dialogue, *** we have at the same time consistently stressed that "we are often 'captives' outside the sanctuary of the home and subject to objectionable speech." *** The ability of government, consonant with the Constitution, to shut off discourse solely to protect others from hearing it is, in other words, dependent upon a showing that substantial privacy interests are being invaded in an essentially intolerable manner. Any broader view of this authority would effectively empower a majority to silence dissidents simply as a matter of personal predilections.

In this regard, persons confronted with Cohen's jacket were in a quite different posture than, say, those subjected to the raucous emissions of sound trucks blaring outside their residences. Those in the Los Angeles courthouse could effectively avoid further bombardment of their sensibilities simply by averting their eyes. And, while it may be that one has a more substantial claim to a recognizable privacy interest when walking through a courthouse corridor than, for example, strolling through Central Park, surely it is nothing like the interest in being free from unwanted expression in the confines of one's own home. Given the subtlety and complexity of the factors involved, if Cohen's "speech" was otherwise entitled to constitutional protection, we do not think the fact that some unwilling "listeners" in a public building may have been briefly exposed to it can serve to justify this breach of the peace conviction where, as here, there was no evidence that persons powerless to avoid appellant's conduct did in fact object to it, and where that portion of the statute upon which Cohen's conviction rests evinces no concern, either on its face or as construed by the California courts, with the special plight of the captive auditor, but, instead, indiscriminately sweeps within its prohibitions all "offensive conduct" that disturbs "any neighborhood or person." ***

II

Against this background, the issue flushed by this case stands out in bold relief. It is whether California can excise, as "offensive conduct," one particular scurrilous epithet from the public discourse, either upon the theory of the court below that its use is inherently likely to cause violent reaction or upon a more general assertion that the States, acting as guardians of public morality, may properly remove this offensive word from the public vocabulary.

The rationale of the California court is plainly untenable. At most it reflects an "undifferentiated fear or apprehension of disturbance [which] is not enough to overcome the right to freedom of expression." *** We have been shown no evidence that substantial numbers of citizens are standing ready to strike out physically at whoever may assault their sensibilities with execrations like that uttered by Cohen. There may be some persons about with such lawless and violent proclivities, but that is an insufficient base upon which to erect, consistently with constitutional values, a governmental power to force persons who wish to ventilate their dissident views into avoiding particular forms of expression. The argument amounts to little more than the self-defeating proposition that to avoid physical censorship of one who has not sought to provoke such a response by a hypothetical coterie of the violent and lawless, the State may more appropriately effectuate that censorship themselves. ***

Admittedly, it is not so obvious that the First and Fourteenth Amendments must be taken to disable the States from punishing public utterance of this unseemly expletive in order to maintain what they regard as a suitable level of discourse within the body politic. We think, however, that examination and reflection will reveal the shortcomings of a contrary viewpoint.

. . . [W]e cannot overemphasize that, in our judgment, most situations where the State has a justifiable interest in regulating speech will fall within one or more of the various established exceptions, discussed above but not applicable here, to the usual rule that governmental bodies may not prescribe the form or content of individual expression. Equally important to our conclusion is the constitutional backdrop against which our decision must be made. The constitutional right of free expression is powerful medicine in a society as diverse and populous as ours. It is designed and intended to remove governmental restraints from the arena of public discussion, putting the decision as to what views shall be voiced largely into the hands of each of us, in the hope that use of such freedom will ultimately produce a more capable citizenry and more perfect polity and in the belief that no other approach would comport with the premise of individual dignity and choice upon which our political system rests. ***

To many, the immediate consequence of this freedom may often appear to be only verbal tumult, discord, and even offensive utterance. These are, however, within established limits, in truth necessary side effects of the broader enduring values which the process of open debate permits us to achieve. That the air may at times seem filled with verbal cacophony is, in this sense, not a sign of weakness but of strength. We cannot lose sight of the fact that, in what otherwise might seem a trifling and annoying instance of individual distasteful abuse of a privilege, these fundamental societal values are truly implicated. That is why "[w]holly neutral futilities . . . come under the protection of free speech as fully as do Keats' poems or Donne's sermons," *** and why "so long as the means are peaceful, the communication need not meet standards of acceptability." ***

Against this perception of the constitutional policies involved, we discern certain more particularized considerations that peculiarly call for reversal of this conviction. First, the principle contended for by the State seems inherently boundless. How is one to distinguish this from any other offensive word? Surely the State has no right to cleanse public debate to the point where it is grammatically palatable to the most squeamish among us. Yet no readily ascertainable general principle exists for stopping short of that result were we to affirm the judgment below. For, while the particular four-letter word being litigated here is perhaps more distasteful than most others of its genre, it is nevertheless often true that one man's vulgarity is another's lyric. Indeed, we think it is largely because governmental officials cannot make principled distinctions in this area that the Constitution leaves matter of taste and style so largely to the individual.

Additionally, we cannot overlook the fact, because it is well illustrated by the episode involved here, that much linguistic expression serves a dual communicative function: it conveys not only ideas capable of relatively precise detached explication, but otherwise inexpressible emotions as well. In fact, words are often chosen as much for their emotive as their cognitive force. We cannot sanction the view that the Constitution, while solicitous of the cognitive content of individual speech, has little or no regard for that emotive function which, practically speaking, may often

be the more important element of the overall message sought to be communicated. Indeed, as Mr. Justice Frankfurter has said, "[o]ne of the prerogatives of American citizenship is the right to criticize public men and measures—and that means not only informed and responsible criticism but the freedom to speak foolishly and without moderation." ***

Finally, and in the same vein, we cannot indulge the facile assumption that one can forbid particular words without also running a substantial risk of suppressing ideas in the process. Indeed, governments might soon seize upon the censorship of particular words as a convenient guise for banning the expression of unpopular views. We have been able, as noted above, to discern little social benefit that might result from running the risk of opening the door to such grave results.

It is, in sum, our judgment that, absent a more particularized and compelling reason for its actions, the State may not, consistently with the First and Fourteenth Amendments, make the simple public display here involved of this single four-letter expletive a criminal offense. . . .

Reversed.

Mr. Justice Blackmun, with whom the **Chief Justice** and **Mr. Justice Black** join.

I dissent, and I do so for two reasons:

1. Cohen's absurd and immature antic, in my view, was mainly conduct and little speech. *** The California Court of Appeal appears so to have described it, *** and I cannot characterize it otherwise. Further, the case appears to me to be well within the sphere of *Chaplinsky v. New Hampshire,* *** where Mr. Justice Murphy, a known champion of First Amendment freedoms, wrote for a unanimous bench. As a consequence, this Court's agonizing over First Amendment values seems misplaced and unnecessary.

2. I am not at all certain that the California Court of Appeal's construction of Sec. 415 is now the authoritative California construction. The Court of Appeal filed its opinion on October 22, 1969. The Supreme Court of California declined review by a four-to-three vote on December 17. *** A month later, on January 27, 1970, the State Supreme Court in another case construed Sec. 415, evidently for the first time. *** Chief Justice Traynor, who was among

the dissenters to his court's refusal to take Cohen's case, wrote the majority opinion. He held that Sec. 415 "is not unconstitutionally vague and overbroad" and further said:

[T]hat part of Penal Code Section 415 in question here makes punishable only wilful and malicious conduct that is violent and endangers public safety and order or that creates a clear and present danger that others will engage in violence of that nature.

... [It] does not make criminal any nonviolent act unless the act incites or threatens to incite others to violence...." ***

Inasmuch as this Court does not dismiss this case, it ought to be remanded to the California Court of Appeal for reconsideration in the light of the subsequently rendered decision by the State's highest tribunal in [the case of if *In re Bushman*].

Mr. Justice White concurs in Paragraph 2 of *Mr. Justice Blackmun's* dissenting opinion.

Tinker v. Des Moines Independent Community School District

393 U.S. 503; 89 S. Ct. 733; 21 L. Ed. 2d 731 (1969)
Vote: 7-2

Mr. Justice Fortas delivered the opinion of the Court.

Petitioner John F. Tinker, 15 years old, and petitioner Christopher Eckhardt, 16 years old, attended high schools in Des Moines, Iowa. Petitioner Mary Beth Tinker, John's sister, was a 13-year-old student in junior high school.

In December 1965, a group of adults and students in Des Moines held a meeting at the Eckhardt home. The group determined to publicize their objections to the hostilities in Vietnam and their support for a truce by wearing black armbands during the holiday season and by fasting on December 16 and New Year's Eve. Petitioners and their parents had previously engaged in similar activities, and they decided to participate in the program.

The principals of the Des Moines schools became aware of the plan to wear armbands. On December 14, 1965, they met and adopted a policy that any student wearing an armband to school would be asked to remove it, and if he refused he would be suspended until he returned without the armband. Petitioners were aware of the regulation that the school authorities adopted.

On December 16, Mary Beth and Christopher wore black armbands to their schools. John Tinker wore his armband the next day. They were all sent home and suspended from school until they would come back without their armbands. They did not return to school until after the planned period for wearing armbands had expired—that is, until after New Year's Day.

This complaint was filed in the United States District Court by petitioners, through their fathers, under Sec. 1983 of Title 42 of the United States Code. It prayed for an injunction restraining the respondent school officials and the respondent members of the board of directors of the school district from disciplining the petitioners, and it sought nominal damages. After an evidentiary hearing the District Court dismissed the complaint. It upheld the constitutionality of the school authorities' action on the ground that it was reasonable in order to prevent disturbance of school discipline. *** The court referred to but expressly declined to follow the Fifth Circuit's holding in a similar case that the wearing of symbols like the armbands cannot be prohibited unless it "materially and substantially interfere[s] with the requirements of appropriate discipline in the operation of the school." ***

On appeal, the Court of Appeals for the Eighth Circuit considered the case *en banc*. The court was equally divided, and the District Court's decision was accordingly affirmed, without opinion. *** We granted *certiorari*.

I

The District Court recognized that the wearing of an armband for the purpose of expressing certain views is the type of symbolic act that is within the Free Speech Clause of the First Amendment. *** As we shall discuss, the wearing of armbands in the circumstances of this case was entirely divorced from actually or potentially disruptive conduct by those participating in it. It was closely akin to "pure speech" which, we have repeatedly held, is entitled to comprehensive protection under the First Amendment. ***

First Amendment rights, applied in light of the special characteristics of the school environment, are available to teachers and students. It can hardly be argued that either students or teachers shed their constitutional rights to freedom of speech or expression at the schoolhouse gate. This has been the unmistakable holding of this Court for almost 50 years. In *Meyer v. Nebraska* [1923] *** this Court, in opinions by Mr. Justice McReynolds, held that the Due Process Clause of the Fourteenth Amendment prevents States from forbidding the teaching of a foreign language to young students. Statutes to this effect, the Court held, unconstitutionally interfere with the liberty of teacher, student, and parent. ***

On the other hand, the Court has repeatedly emphasized the need for affirming the comprehensive authority of the States and of school officials, consistent with fundamental constitutional safeguards, to prescribe and control conduct in the schools. *** Our problem lies in the area where students in the exercise of First Amendment rights collide with the rules of the school authorities.

II

The problem posed by the present case does not relate to regulation of the length of skirts or the type of clothing, to hair style, or deportment. *** It does not concern aggressive, disruptive action or even group demonstrations. Our problem involves direct, primary First Amendment rights akin to "pure speech."

The school officials banned and sought to punish petitioners for a silent, passive expression of opinion, unaccompanied by any disorder or disturbance on the part of petitioners. There is here no evidence whatever of petitioners' interference, actual or nascent, with the schools' work or of collision with the rights of other students to be secure and to be let alone. Accordingly, this case does not concern speech or action that intrudes upon the work of the schools or the rights of other students.

Only a few of the 18,000 students in the school system wore the black armbands. Only five students were suspended for wearing them. There is no indication that the work of the schools or any class was disrupted. Outside the classrooms, a few students made hostile remarks to the children wearing armbands, but there were no threats or acts of violence on school premises.

The District Court concluded that the action of the school authorities was reasonable because it was based upon their fear or a disturbance from the wearing of the armbands. But, in our system, undifferentiated fear or apprehension of disturbance is not enough to overcome the right to freedom of expression. Any departure from absolute regimentation may cause trouble. Any variation from the majority's opinion may inspire fear. Any word spoken, in class, in the lunchroom, or on the campus, that deviates from the views of another person may start an argument or cause a disturbance. But our Constitution says we must take this risk, *** and our history says that it is this sort of hazardous freedom—this kind of openness—that is the basis of our national strength and the independence and vigor of Americans who grow up and live in this relatively permissive, often disputatious, society.

In order for the State in the person of school officials to justify prohibition of a particular expression of opinion, it must be able to show that its action was caused by something more than a mere desire to avoid the discomfort and unpleasantness that always accompany an unpopular viewpoint. Certainly where there is no finding and no showing that engaging in of the forbidden conduct would "materially and substantially interfere with the requirements of appropriate discipline in the operation of the school," the prohibition cannot be sustained. ***

In the present case, the District Court made no such finding, and our independent examination of the record fails to yield evidence that the school authorities had reason to anticipate that the wearing of the armbands would substantially interfere with the work of the school or impinge upon the rights of other students. Even an official memorandum prepared after the suspension that listed the reasons for the ban on wearing the armbands made no reference to the anticipation of such disruption.

On the contrary, the action of the school authorities appears to have been based upon an urgent wish to avoid the controversy which might result from the expression, even by the silent symbol of armbands, in opposition to this Nation's part in the conflagration in Vietnam. It is revealing, in this respect that the meeting at which the school principals decided to issue the contested regulation was called in response to a student's statement to the journalism teacher in one of the schools that he wanted to write an article on Vietnam and have it published in the school paper. (The student was dissuaded).

It is also relevant that the school authorities did not purport to prohibit the wearing of all symbols of political or controversial significance. The record shows that students in some of the schools wore buttons relating to national political campaigns, and some even wore the Iron Cross, traditionally a symbol of Nazism. The order prohibiting the wearing of armbands did not extend to these. Instead, a particular symbol—black armbands worn to exhibit opposition to this Nation's involvement in Vietnam—was singled out for prohibition. Clearly, the prohibition of expression of one particular opinion, at least without evidence that it is necessary to avoid material and substantial interference with schoolwork or discipline, is not constitutionally permissible.

In our system, state-operated schools may not be enclaves of totalitarianism. School officials do not possess absolute authority over their students. Students in school as well as out of school are "persons" under our Constitution. They are possessed of fundamental rights which the State must respect, just as they themselves must respect their obligations to the State. In our system, students may not be regarded as closed-circuit recipients of only that which the State chooses to communicate. They may not be confined to the expression of those sentiments that are officially approved. In the absence of a specific showing

of constitutionally valid reasons to regulate their speech, students are entitled to freedom of expression of their views. As Judge Gewin, speaking for the Fifth Circuit, said, school officials cannot suppress "expressions of feelings with which they do not wish to contend." ***

Under our Constitution, free speech is not a right that is given only to be so circumscribed that it exists in principle but not in fact. Freedom of expression would not truly exist if the right could be exercised only in an area that a benevolent government has provided as a safe haven for crackpots. The Constitution says that Congress (and the States) may not abridge the right to free speech. This provision means what it says. We properly read it to permit reasonable regulation of speech connected activities in carefully restricted circumstances. But we do not confine the permissible exercise of First Amendment rights to a telephone booth or the four corners of a pamphlet, or to supervised and ordained discussion in a school classroom.

If a regulation were adopted by school officials forbidding discussion of the Vietnam conflict, or the expression by any student of opposition to it anywhere on school property except as part of a prescribed classroom exercise, it would be obvious that the regulation would violate the constitutional rights of students, at least if it could not be justified by a showing that the students' activities would materially and substantially disrupt the work and discipline of the school. *** In the circumstances of the present case, the prohibition of the silent, passive "witness of the armbands," as one of the children called it, is no less offensive to the Constitution's guarantees.

As we have discussed, the record does not demonstrate any facts which might reasonably have led school authorities to forecast substantial disruption of or material interference with school activities, and no disturbances or disorders on the school premises in fact occurred. These petitioners merely went about their ordained rounds in school. Their deviation consisted only in wearing on their sleeve a band of black cloth, not more than two inches wide. They wore it to exhibit their disapproval of the Vietnam hostilities and their advocacy of a truce, to make their views known, and, by their example, to influence others to adopt them. They neither interrupted school activities nor sought to intrude in the school affairs or the lives of others. They caused discussion outside of the class rooms, but no interference with work and no disorder. In the circumstances, our Constitution does not permit officials of the State to deny their form of expression.

We express no opinion as to the form of relief which should be granted, this being a matter for the lower courts to determine. We reverse and remand for further proceedings consistent with this opinion.

Reversed and remanded.

Mr. Justice Stewart, concurring. . . .

Mr. Justice White, concurring. . . .

Mr. Justice Black, dissenting.

. . . As I read the Court's opinion it relies upon the following grounds for holding unconstitutional the judgment of the Des Moines school officials and the two courts below. First, the Court concludes that the wearing of armbands is "symbolic speech" which is "akin to 'pure speech' " and therefore protected by the First and Fourteenth Amendments. Secondly, the Court decides that the public schools are an appropriate place to exercise "symbolic speech" as long as normal school functions are not "unreasonably" disrupted. Finally, the Court arrogates to itself, rather than to the State's elected officials charged with running the schools, the decision as to which school disciplinary regulations are "reasonable."

Assuming that the Court is correct in holding that the conduct of wearing armbands for the purpose of conveying political ideas is protected by the First Amendment, *** the crucial remaining questions are whether students and teachers may use the schools at their whim as a platform for the exercise of free speech—"symbolic" or "pure"—and whether the courts will allocate to themselves the function of deciding how the pupils' school day will be spent. While I have always believed that under the First and Fourteenth Amendments neither the State nor the Federal Government has any authority to regulate or censor the content of speech, I have never believed that any person has a right to give speeches or engage in demonstrations where he pleases and when he pleases. . . .

While the record does not show that any of these armband students shouted, used profane language, or were violent in any manner, detailed testimony by some of them shows their armbands caused comments, warnings by other students, the poking of fun at them, and a warning by an older football player that other, nonprotesting students had better let them alone. There is also evidence that a teacher of mathematics had his lesson period practically "wrecked" chiefly by disputes with Mary Beth Tinker, who wore her armband for her "demonstration."

Even a casual reading of the record shows that this armband did divert students' minds from their regular lessons, and that talk, comments, etc., made John Tinker "self-conscious" in attending school with his armband. While the absence of obscene remarks or boisterous and loud disorder perhaps justifies the Court's statement that the few armband students did not actually "disrupt" the classwork, I think the record overwhelmingly shows that the armbands did exactly what the elected school officials and principals foresaw they would, that is, took the student's minds off their classwork and diverted them to thoughts about the highly emotional subject of the Vietnam war. And I repeat that if the time has come when pupils of state-supported schools, kindergartens, grammar schools, or high school, can defy and flout orders of school officials to keep their minds on their own schoolwork, it is the beginning of a new revolutionary era of permissiveness in this country fostered by the judiciary. The next logical step, it appears to me, would be to hold unconstitutional laws that bar pupils under 21 or 18 from voting, or from being elected members of the boards of education. . . .

In my view, teachers in state-controlled public schools are hired to teach there. Although Mr. Justice McReynolds may have intimated to the contrary in *Meyer v. Nebraska,* *** certainly a teacher is not paid to go into school and teach subjects the State does not hire him to teach as a part of its selected curriculum. Nor are public school students sent to the schools at public expense to broadcast political or any other views to educate and inform the public. The original idea of schools, which I do not believe is yet abandoned as worthless or out of date, was that children had not yet reached the point of experience and wisdom which enabled them to teach all of their elders. It may be that the Nation has outworn the old-fashioned slogan that "children are to be seen not heard," but one may, I hope, be permitted to harbor the thought that taxpayers send children to school on the premise that at their age they need to learn, not teach. . . .

Change has been said to be truly the law of life but sometimes the old and the tried and true are worth holding. The schools of this Nation have undoubtedly contributed to giving us tranquility and to making us a more law-abiding people. Uncontrolled and uncontrollable liberty is an enemy to domestic peace. We cannot close our eyes to the fact that some of the country's greatest problems are crimes committed by the youth, too many of school age. School discipline, like parental discipline, is an integral and important part of training our children to be good citizens—to be better citizens. Here a small number of students have crisply and summarily refused to obey a school order designed to give pupils who want to learn the opportunity to do so. One does not need to be a prophet or the son of a prophet to know that after the Court's holding today some students in Iowa schools and indeed in all schools will be ready, able, and willing to defy their teachers on practically all orders. This is the more unfortunate for the schools since groups of students all over the land are already running loose, conducting break-ins, sing-ins, lie-ins, and smash-ins. Many of these student groups, as is all too familiar to all who read the newspapers and watch the television news programs, have already engaged in rioting, property seizures, and destruction. They have picketed

schools to force students not to cross the picket lines and have too often violently attacked earnest but frightened students who wanted an education that the pickets did not want them to get. Students engaged in such activities are apparently confident that they know far more about how to operate public school systems than do their parents, teachers, and elected school officials. It is no answer to say that the particular students here have not yet reached such high points in their demands to attend classes in order to exercise their political pressures. Turned loose with lawsuits for damages and injunctions against their teachers as they are here, it is nothing but wishful thinking to imagine that young, immature students will not soon believe it is their right to control the schools rather than the right of the States that collect the taxes to hire the teachers for the benefit of the pupils. This case, therefore, wholly without constitutional reasons in my judgment, subjects all the public schools in the country to the whims and caprices of their loudest-mouthed, but maybe not their brightest, students. I, for one, am not fully persuaded that school pupils are wise enough, even with this Court's expert help from Washington, to run the 23,390 public school systems in our 50 States. I wish, therefore, wholly to disclaim any purpose on my part to hold that the Federal Constitution compels the teachers, parents, and elected school officials to surrender control of the American public school system to public school students. I dissent.

Mr. Justice Harlan, dissenting. . . .

Texas v. Johnson [note]
491 U.S. 397, 109 S. Ct. 2533, 105 L. Ed.2d 342 (1989)
Vote: 5-4

After burning an American flag as part of a public protest, Gregory Lee Johnson was convicted of desecrating a flag in violation of Texas law. The Texas Court of Criminal Appeals reversed the conviction, holding that the statute under which Johnson was

convicted was unconstitutional as applied to his particular conduct. In a widely publicized and highly controversial 5-to-4 decision, the U.S. Supreme Court upheld the Texas Court of Criminal Appeals. Perhaps the most surprising aspect of the decision was that two Reagan appointees, Justices Kennedy and Scalia, voted with Justices Brennan, Marshall, and Blackmun to create the majority. Chief Justice Rehnquist dissented, along with Justices White, O'Connor, and Stevens. An extensive excerpt from the decision is reprinted in Chapter 2.

Barnes v. Glen Theatre, Inc.

501 U.S. ____; 111 S. Ct. 2456; 115 L. Ed.2d 504 (1991)

Vote: 5-4

Two South Bend, Indiana, establishments that featured all-nude dancing brought suit in the U.S. District Court for the Northern District of Indiana seeking an injunction against enforcement of an Indiana statute prohibiting complete nudity in public places. The district court dismissed the case, concluding that "the type of dancing these plaintiffs wish to perform is not expressive activity protected by the Constitution of the United States." On appeal, the Court of Appeals for the Seventh Circuit reversed, holding that the nude dancing at issue was "expressive conduct protected by the First Amendment." The Supreme Court granted certiorari.

Chief Justice Rehnquist . . . [announced the judgment of the Court and delivered an opinion joined by Justices **O'Connor** and **Kennedy**].

. . . The Kitty Kat Lounge, Inc. (Kitty Kat) is located in the city of South Bend. It sells alcoholic beverages and presents "go-go dancing." Its proprietor desires to present "totally nude dancing," but an applicable Indiana statute regulating public nudity requires that the dancers wear "pasties" and a "G-string" when they dance. The dancers are not paid an hourly wage, but work on commission. They receive a 100 percent commission on the first $60 in drink sales during their performances. Darlene Miller, one of the respondents in the action, had worked at the Kitty Kat for about two years at the time this action was brought. Miller wishes to dance nude because she believes she would make more money doing so.

Respondent Glen Theatre, Inc. is an Indiana corporation with a place of business in South Bend. Its primary business is supplying so-called adult entertainment through written and printed materials, movie showings, and live entertainment at the

"bookstore" consists of nude and seminude performances and showings of the female body through glass panels. Customers sit in a booth and insert coins into a timing mechanism that permits them to observe the live nude and seminude dancers for a period of time. One of Glen Theatre's dancers, Gayle Ann Marie Sutro, has danced, modeled, and acted professionally for more than 15 years, and in addition to her performances at the Glen Theatre, can be seen in a pornographic movie at a nearby theater. ***

Several of our cases contain language suggesting that nude dancing of the kind involved here is expressive conduct protected by the First Amendment. In *Doran v. Salem Inn, Inc.* *** (1975), we said: "[A]lthough the customary 'barroom' type of nude dancing may involve only the barest minimum of protected expression, we recognized in *California v. LaRue* *** (1972), that this form of entertainment might be entitled to First and Fourteenth Amendment protection under some circumstances." In *Schad v. Borough of Mount Ephraim* *** (1981), we said that "[f]urthermore, as the state courts in this case recognized, nude dancing is not without its First Amendment protections from official regulation" (citations omitted). These statements support the conclusion of the Court of Appeals that nude dancing of the kind sought to be performed here is expressive conduct within the outer perimeters of the First Amendment, though we view it as only marginally so. This, of course, does not end our inquiry. We must determine the level of protection to be afforded to the expressive conduct at issue, and must determine whether the Indiana statute is an impermissible infringement of that protected activity.

Indiana, of course, has not banned nude dancing as such, but has proscribed public nudity across the board. The Supreme Court of Indiana has construed the Indiana statute to preclude nudity in what are essentially places of public accommodation such as the Glen Theatre and the Kitty Kat Lounge. In such places, respondents point out, minors are excluded and there are no non-consenting viewers. Respondents contend that while the state may license establishments such as the ones involved here, and limit the geographical area in which they do business, it may not in any way limit the performance of the dances within them without violating the First Amendment. The petitioner contends, on the other hand, that Indiana's restriction on nude dancing is a valid "time, place or manner" restriction under cases such as *Clark v. Community for Creative Non-Violence* *** (1984).

The "time, place, or manner" test was developed for evaluating restriction on expression taking place on the public property which had been dedicated as a "public forum," *** although we have on at least one occasion applied it to conduct occurring on private property. *** In *Clark* we observed that this test has been interpreted to embody much the same standards as those set forth in *United States v. O'Brien* *** (1968), and we turn, therefore, to the rule enunciated in *O'Brien*. . . .

This Court has held that when "speech" and "nonspeech" elements are combined in the same course of conduct, a sufficiently important governmental interest in regulating the nonspeech element can justify incidental limitation on First Amendment freedoms. To characterize the quality of the governmental interest which must appear, the Court has employed a variety of descriptive terms: compelling; substantial; subordinating; paramount; cogent; strong. Whatever imprecision inheres in these terms, we think it clear that a government regulation is sufficiently justified if it is within the constitutional power of the Government; if it furthers an important or substantial governmental interest; if the governmental interest is unrelated to the suppression of free expression; and if the incidental restriction on alleged First Amendment freedoms is no greater than essential to the furtherance of that interest. ***

Applying the four-part *O'Brien* test enunciated above, we find that Indiana's public indecency statute is justified despite its incidental limitations on some expressive activity. The public indecency statute is clearly within the constitutional power of the

State and furthers substantial governmental interests. It is impossible to discern, other than from the text of the statute, exactly what governmental interest the Indiana legislators had in mind when they enacted this statute, for Indiana does not record legislative history, and the state's highest court has not shed additional light on the statute's purpose. Nonetheless, the statute's purpose of protecting societal order and morality is clear from its text and history. Public indecency statutes of this sort are of ancient origin, and presently exist in at least 47 States. Public indecency, including nudity, was a criminal offense at common law, and this Court recognized the common-law roots of the offense of "gross and open indecency" in *Winters v. New York* *** (1948). Public nudity was considered an act *malum en se.* *** Public indecency statutes such as the one before us reflect moral disapproval of people appearing in the nude among strangers in public places.

This public indecency statute follows a long line of earlier Indiana statutes banning all public nudity. The history of Indiana's public indecency statute shows that it predates barroom nude dancing and was enacted as a general prohibition. At least as early as 1831, Indiana has a statute punishing "open and notorious lewdness, or . . . any grossly scandalous and public indecency." *** A gap during which no statute was in effect was filled by the Indiana Supreme Court in *Ardery v. State* *** (1977), which held that the court could sustain a conviction for exhibitions of "privates" in the presence of others. The court traced the offense to the Bible story of Adam and Eve. *** In 1881, a statute was enacted that would remain essentially unchanged for nearly a century:

Whoever, being over fourteen years of age, makes an indecent exposure of his person in a public place, or in any place where there are other persons to be offended or annoyed thereby, . . . is guilty of public indecency. . . . ***

The language quoted above remained unchanged until it was simultaneously repealed and replaced with the present statute in 1976. ***

This and other public indecency statutes were designed to protect morals and public order. The traditional police power of the States is defined as the authority to provide for the public health, safety, and morals, and we have upheld such a basis for legislation. . . .

. . . In *Bowers v. Hardwick* *** (1986), we said: The law, however, is constantly based on notion of morality, and if all laws representing essentially moral choices are to be invalidated under the Due Process Clause, the courts will be very busy indeed.

Thus, the public indecency statute furthers a substantial government interest in protecting order and morality.

This interest is unrelated to the suppression of free expression. Some may view restricting nudity on moral grounds as necessarily related to expression. We disagree. It can be argued, of course, that almost limitless types of conduct—including appearing in the nude in public—are "expressive," and in one sense of the word this is true. People who go about in the nude in public may be expressing something about themselves by so doing. But the Court rejected this expansive notion of "expressive conduct" in *O'Brien,* saying:

We cannot accept the view than an apparently limitless variety of conduct can be labelled "speech" whenever the person engaging in the conduct intends thereby to express an idea. . . .

Respondents contend that even though prohibiting nudity in public generally may not be related to suppressing expression, prohibiting the performance of nude dancing is related to expression because the state seeks to prevent its erotic message. Therefore, they reason that the application of the Indiana statute to the nude dancing in this case violates the First Amendment, because it fails the third part of the *O'Brien* test, viz: the governmental interest must be unrelated to the suppression of free expression.

But we do not think that when Indiana applies its statute to the nude dancing in these nightclubs it is proscribing nudity because of the erotic message conveyed by the dancers. Presumably numerous other erotic performances are presented at these establishments and similar clubs without any interference from the state, so long as the performers wear a scant amount of clothing. Likewise the requirement that the dancers don pasties and a G-string does not deprive the dance of whatever erotic message it con-

veys; it simply makes the message slightly less graphic. The perceived evil that Indiana seeks to address is not erotic dancing, but public nudity. The appearance of people of all shapes, sizes and ages in the nude at a beach, for example, would convey little if any erotic message, yet the state still seeks to prevent it. Public nudity is the evil the state seeks to prevent, whether or not it is combined with expressive activity.

This conclusion is buttressed by a reference to the facts of *O'Brien.* An act of Congress provided that anyone who knowingly destroyed a selective service registration certificate committed an offense. O'Brien burned his certificate on the steps of the South Boston Courthouse to influence others to adopt his anti-war beliefs. The Court upheld his conviction, reasoning that the continued availability of issued certificates served a legitimate and substantial purpose in the administration of the selective service system. O'Brien's deliberate destruction of his certificate frustrated this purpose and "for this non-communicative aspect of his conduct, and for nothing else, he was convicted." *** It was assumed that O'Brien's act in burning the certificate had a communicative element in it sufficient to bring into play the First Amendment, *** but it was for the non-communicative element that he was prosecuted. So here with the Indiana statute; while the dancing to which it was applied had a communicative element, it was not the dancing that was prohibited, but simply its being done in the nude.

The fourth part of the *O'Brien* test requires that the incidental restriction on First Amendment freedom be no greater than is essential to the furtherance of the governmental interest. As indicated in the discussion above, the governmental interest served by the text of the prohibition is societal disapproval of nudity in public places and among strangers. The statutory prohibition is not a means to some greater end, but an end in itself. It is without cavil that the public indecency statute is "narrowly tailored"; Indiana's requirement that the dancers wear at least pasties and a G-string is modest, and the bare minimum necessary to achieve the state's purpose.

The judgment of the Court of Appeals accordingly is . . . reversed.

Justice Scalia, concurring in the judgment. . . .

Justice Souter, concurring in the judgment. . . .

Justice White, with whom *Justice Marshall, Justice Blackmun,* and *Justice Stevens* join, dissenting.

. . . We are told by the Attorney General of Indiana that . . . the Indiana Supreme Court [has] held that the statute at issue here cannot and does not prohibit nudity as part of some larger form of expression meriting protection when the communication of ideas is involved. *** Petitioners also state that the evils sought to be avoided by applying the statute in this case would not obtain in the case of theatrical productions such as *Salome* or *Hair.* Neither is there any evidence that the State has attempted to apply the statute to nudity in performances such as plays, ballets or operas. "No arrests have ever been made for nudity as part of a play or ballet." ***

Thus, the Indiana statute is not a general prohibition of the type that we have upheld in prior cases. As a result, the Court's and Justice Scalia's simple references to the State's general interest in promoting societal order and morality [are] not sufficient justification for a statute which concededly reaches a significant amount of expressive activity. Instead of applying the *O'Brien* test, we are obligated to carefully examine the reasons the State has chosen to regulate this expressive conduct in a less than general statute. In other words, when the State enacts a law which draws a line between expressive conduct of the same type which is regulated and nonexpressive conduct which is not regulated, *O'Brien* places the burden on the State to justify the distinctions it has made. Closer inquiry as to the purpose of the statute is surely appropriate.

Legislators do not just randomly select certain conduct for proscription; they have reasons and those reasons illuminate the purpose of the law that is passed. Indeed, a law may have multiple purposes. The purpose of forbidding people from appearing nude in parks, beaches, hot dog stands, and like public places is to protect others from offense. But that could not possibly be the purpose of preventing nude dancing in theaters and barrooms since the viewers are exclusively consenting adults who pay money to see these dances. The purpose of the proscription in these contexts is to protect the viewers from what the State believes is the harmful message that nude dancing communicates . . .

That the performances in the Kitty Kat Lounge may not be high art, to say the least, and may not appeal to the Court, is hardly an excuse for distorting and ignoring settled doctrine. The Court's assessment of the artistic merits of nude dancing performances should not be the determining factor in deciding this case. In the words of Justice Harlan, "it is largely because governmental officials cannot make principled decisions in this area that the Constitution leaves matters of taste and style so largely to the individual." *** "[W]hile the entertainment afforded by a nude ballet at Lincoln Center to those who can pay the price may differ vastly in content (as viewed by judges) or in quality (as viewed by critics), it may not differ in substance from the dance viewed by the person who . . . wants some 'entertainment' with his beer or shot of rye." *** . . .

As I see it, our cases require us to affirm absent a compelling state interest supporting the statute. Neither the Court nor the State suggest that the statute could withstand scrutiny under that standard. . . .

Accordingly, I would affirm the judgment of the Court of Appeals, and dissent from this Court's judgment.

Rankin v. McPherson

483 U.S. 378; 107 S. Ct. 2891; 97 L. Ed.2d 315 (1987)
Vote: 5-4

In this case, a clerical employee in a county constable's office was discharged for remarking, after hearing of an attempt on the life of President Ronald   *Reagan, "If they go for him again, I hope they get him." The Supreme Court must decide whether the dismissal was a violation of the First Amendment.*

Justice Marshall delivered the opinion of the Court.

. . . On January 12, 1981, respondent Ardith McPherson was appointed a deputy in the office of the constable of Harris County, Texas. The constable is an elected official who functions as a law enforcement officer. At the time of her appointment, McPherson, a black woman, was 19 years old and had attended college for a year, studying secretarial science. Her appointment was conditional for a 90-day probationary period.

Although McPherson's title was "deputy constable," this was the case only because all employees of the constable's office, regardless of job function, were deputy constables. She was not a commissioned peace officer, did not wear a uniform, and was not authorized to make arrests or permitted to carry a gun. McPherson's duties were purely clerical. . . .

On March 30, 1981, McPherson and some fellow employees heard on an office radio that there had been an attempt to assassinate the President of the United States. Upon hearing that report, McPherson engaged a co-worker, Lawrence Jackson, who was apparently her boyfriend, in a brief conversation . . . [According to McPherson's uncontroverted testimony, she remarked,] ". . . shoot, if they go for him again, I hope they get him."

McPherson's . . . remark was overheard by another deputy constable, who, unbeknownst to McPherson, was in the room at the time. The remark was reported to Constable Rankin, who summoned McPherson. McPherson readily admitted that she had made the statement, but testified that she told Rankin, upon being asked if she made the statement, "Yes, but I didn't mean anything by it." After their discussion, Rankin fired McPherson.

McPherson brought suit in the United States District Court for the Southern District of Texas under 42 U.S.C. sec. 1983, alleging that petitioner Rankin, in discharging her, had violated her constitutional rights under color of state law. She sought reinstatement, back pay, costs and fees, and other equitable relief. . . .

[T]he District Court held . . . that the statements were not protected [under the First Amendment]. . . . [In reversing the District Court], the Court of Appeals concluded that the Government's interest did not outweigh the First Amendment interest in protecting McPherson's speech. Given the nature of McPherson's job and the fact that she was not a law enforcement officer, was not brought by virtue of her job into contact with the public, and did not have access to sensitive information, the Court of Appeals deemed her "duties . . . so utterly ministerial and her potential for undermining the office's mission so trivial" as to forbid her dismissal for expression of her political opinions. "However ill-considered Ardith McPherson's opinion was," the Court of Appeals concluded, "it did not make her unfit" for the job she held in Constable Rankin's office. ***

We . . . affirm [the judgment of the Court of Appeals]. . . .

The determination whether a public employer has properly discharged an employee for engaging in speech requires "a balance between the interests of the [employee], as a citizen, in commenting upon matters of public concern and the interest of the State, as an employer, in promoting the efficiency of the public services it performs through its employees." *** This balancing is necessary in order to accommodate the dual role of the public employer as a provider of public services and as a government entity operating under the constraints of the First Amendment. On one hand, public employers are employers, concerned with the efficient function of their operations; review of every personnel decision made by a public employer could, in the long run, hamper the performance of public functions. In the other hand, "the threat of dismissal from public employment is . . . a potent means of inhibiting speech." *** Vigilance is necessary to ensure that public employers do not use authority over employees to silence discourse, not because it hampers public functions but simply because superiors disagree with the content of employees' speech.

The threshold question in applying this balancing test is whether McPherson's speech may be "fairly characterized as constituting speech on a matter of public concern." *** "Whether an employee's speech addresses a matter of public concern must be determined by the content, form, and context of a given statement, as revealed by the whole record." *** The District Court apparently found that McPherson's speech did not address a matter of public concern. The Court of Appeals rejected this conclusion, finding that "the life and death of the President are obviously matters of public concern." ***

Considering the statement in context discloses that it plainly dealt with a matter of public concern. The statement was made in the course of a conversation addressing the policies of the President's administration. . . . While a statement that amounted to a threat to kill the President would not be protected by the First Amendment, the District Court concluded, and we agree, that McPherson's statement did not amount to a threat punishable under [the federal statute proscribing threats against public officials], or, indeed, that could properly be criminalized at all. The inappropriate or controversial character of a statement is irrelevant to the question whether it deals with a matter of public concern. . . .

Because McPherson's statement addressed a matter of public concern . . . we [must] balance McPherson's interest in making her statement against "the interest of the State, as an employer, in promoting the efficiency of the public services it performs through its employees." *** The State bears a burden of justifying the discharge on legitimate grounds. . . .

[T]he very nature of the balancing test make[s] apparent that the state interest element of the test focuses on the effective functioning of the public employer's enterprise. Interference with work, personnel relationships, or the speaker's job performance can detract from the public employer's function; avoiding such interference can be a strong state interest. From this perspective, however, petitioner fails to demonstrate a state interest that outweighs McPherson's First Amendment rights. While McPherson's statement was made at the workplace, there is no evidence that it interfered with the efficient functioning of the office. . . .

While the facts underlying Rankin's discharge of McPherson are, despite extensive proceedings in the District Court, still somewhat unclear, it is undisputed that he fired McPherson based on the content of her speech. Evidently because McPherson had made the statement, and because the constable believed that she "meant it," he decided that she was not a suitable employee to have in a law enforcement agency. But in weighing the State's interest in discharging an employee based on any claim that the content of a statement made by the employee some-

how undermines the mission of the public employer, some attention must be paid to the responsibilities of the employee within the agency. The burden of caution employees bear with respect to the words they speak will vary with the extent of authority and public accountability the employee's role entails. Where, as here, an employee serves no confidential, policymaking, or public contact role, the danger to the agency's successful function from that employee's private speech is minimal. We cannot believe that every employee in Constable Rankin's office, whether computer operator, electrician, or file clerk, is equally required, on pain of discharge, to avoid any statement susceptible of being interpreted by the Constable as an indication that the employee may be unworthy of employment in his law enforcement agency. At some point, such concerns are so removed from the effective function of the public employer that they cannot prevail over the free speech rights of the public employee.

This is such a case. McPherson's employment-related interaction with the Constable was apparently negligible. Her duties were purely clerical and were limited solely to the civil process function of the constable's office. There is no indication that she would ever be in a position to further—or indeed to have any involvement with—the minimal law enforcement activity engaged in by the constable's office. Given the function of the agency, McPherson's position in the office, and the nature of her statement, we are not persuaded that Rankin's interest in discharging her outweighed her rights under the First Amendment.

Justice Powell, concurring.

It is not easy to understand how this case has assumed constitutional dimensions and reached the Supreme Court of the United States. The fact that the case is here, however, illustrates the uniqueness of our Constitution and our system of judicial review: courts at all levels are available and receptive to claims of injustice, large and small, by each and every citizen of this country. . . .

In my view, however, the case is hardly as complex as might be expected in a dispute that now has been considered five separate times by three different federal courts. The undisputed evidence shows that McPherson made an ill-considered—but protected—comment during a private conversation, and the Constable made an instinctive, but intemperate, employment decision on the basis of this speech. I agree that on these facts, McPherson's private speech is protected by the First Amendment. I join the opinion of the Court.

Justice Scalia, with whom the **Chief Justice, Justice White,** and **Justice O'Connor** join, dissenting.

I agree with the proposition, felicitously put by Constable Rankin's counsel, that no law enforcement agency is required by the First Amendment to permit one of its employees to "ride with the cops and cheer for the robbers." *** The issue in this case is whether Constable Rankin, a law enforcement official, is prohibited by the First Amendment from preventing his employees from saying of the attempted assassination of President Reagan—on the job within hearing of other employees—"If they go for him again, I hope they get him." The Court holds that McPherson's statement was protected by the First Amendment because (1) it "addressed a matter of public concern," and (2) McPherson's interest in making the statement outweighs Rankin's interest in suppressing it. In so doing, the Court significantly and irrationally expands the definition of "public concern"; it also carves out a new and very large class of employees—i.e. those in "nonpolicy-making" positions—who, if today's decision is to be believed, can never be disciplined for statements that fall within the Court's expanded definition. Because I believe the Court's conclusions rest upon a distortion of both the record and the Court's prior decisions, I dissent. . . .

[S]peech on matters of public concern is that speech which lies "at the heart of the First Amendment's protection." *** If, but only if, an employee's speech falls within this category, a public employer seeking to abridge or punish it must show that the employee's interest is outweighed by the government's interest, "as an employer, in promoting the efficiency of the public services it performs through its employees." ***

McPherson fails this threshold requirement. The statement for which she was fired—and the only

statement the Constable heard—was, "If they go for him again, I hope they get him." ***

The District Judge rejected McPherson's argument that her statement was "mere political hyperbole," finding, to the contrary, that it was, "in context," "violent words." "This is not," he said, "the situation where one makes an idle threat to kill someone for not picking them [sic] up on time, or not picking up their [sic] clothes. It was more than that." *** He ruled against McPherson at the conclusion of the second hearing because [the district judge said,] "I don't think it is a matter of public concern to approve even more to [sic] the second attempt at assassination." ***

McPherson's statement . . . is only one step removed from statements that we have previously held entitled to no First Amendment protection even in the nonemployment context—including assassination threats against the President . . . , "fighting words," epithets or personal abuse, and advocacy of force or violence. A statement lying so near the category of completely unprotected speech cannot fairly be viewed as lying within the "heart" of the First Amendment's protection; it lies within that category of speech that can neither be characterized as speech on matters of public concern nor properly subject to criminal penalties. Once McPherson stopped explicitly criticizing the President's policies and expressed a desire that he be assassinated, she crossed the line.

The Court reaches the opposite conclusion only by distorting the concept of "public concern." It does not explain how a statement expressing approval of a serious and violent crime—assassination of the President—can possibly fall within that category. It simply rehearses the "context" of McPherson's statement, and then concludes that because of that context, and because the statement "came on the heels of a news bulletin regarding what is certainly a matter of heightened public attention; an attempt on the life of the President," the statement "plainly dealt with a matter of public concern." *** I cannot respond to this progression of reasoning except to say I do not understand it. . . .

Even if I agreed that McPherson's statement was speech on a matter of "public concern," I would still find it unprotected. It is important to be clear on what the issue is in this part of the case. . . . We are asked to determine whether, given the interests of this law enforcement office, McPherson had a right to say what she did—so that she could not only be fired for it, but could not be formally reprimanded for it, or even prevented from repeating it endlessly into the future. It boggles the mind to think that she has such a right.

Rust v. Sullivan

500 U.S.___; 111 S. Ct. 1759; 114 L. Ed.2d 233 (1991)
Vote: 5-4

In 1970, Congress passed Title X of the Public Health Service Act, which authorized federal grants to public and private organizations that provide family planning services. One of the provisions of the act barred grants to "programs where abortion is a method of family planning." For many years, this prohibition was interpreted as applying only to organizations that actually provided abortion services to their clients. In 1988, however, the Department of Health and Human Services (HHS) issued a regulation prohibiting recipients of Title X funds from counseling their clients on the subject of abortion. This so-called gag rule generated enormous political controversy and, not surprisingly, a series of lawsuits. In the instant case, Dr. Irving Rust and other doctors sued HHS Secretary Louis Sullivan, claiming that the gag rule was unlawful. Plaintiffs challenged the regulation on three grounds: (1) that it was not authorized under the terms of Title X; (2) that it violated the First Amendment rights of doctors and patients to engage in free speech about legally available medical procedures; and (3) that it infringed women's rights to choose abortion. The federal district court upheld the HHS regulation and the circuit court affirmed. For the purposes of this textbook, only those sections of the Supreme Court's decision dealing with constitutional issues have been excerpted here.

Chief Justice Rehnquist delivered the opinion of the Court.

. . . There is no question but that the statutory prohibition contained in Sec. 1008 is constitutional. In *Maher v. Roe* *** [1977], we upheld a state welfare regulation under which Medicaid recipients received payments for services related to childbirth, but not for nontherapeutic abortions. The Court rejected the claim that this unequal subsidization worked a violation of the Constitution. We held that the Government may "make a value judgment favoring childbirth over abortion, and . . . implement that judgment by the allocation of public funds." *** Here the Government is exercising the authority it possesses under *Maher* and [*Harris v.*] *McRae* *** [1980] to subsidize family planning services which will lead to conception and childbirth, and declining to "promote or encourage abortion." The Government can, without violating the Constitution, selectively fund a program to encourage certain activities it believes to be in the public interest, without at the same time funding an alternate program which seeks to deal with the problem in another way. In so doing, the Government has not discriminated on the basis of viewpoint; it has merely chosen to fund one activity to the exclusion of the other. "[A] legislature's decision not to subsidize the exercise of a fundamental right does not infringe the right." ***

To hold that the Government unconstitutionally discriminates on the basis of viewpoint when it chooses to fund a program dedicated to advance certain permissible goals, because the program in advancing those goals necessarily discourages alternate goals, would render numerous government programs constitutionally suspect. When Congress established a National Endowment for Democracy to encourage other countries to adopt democratic principles, it was not constitutionally required to fund a program to encourage competing lines of political philosophy such as Communism and Fascism. Petitioners' assertions ultimately boil down to the position that if the government chooses to subsidize one protected right, it must subsidize analogous counterpart rights. But the Court has soundly rejected that proposition. *** Within far broader limits than petitioners are willing to concede, when the government appropriates public funds to establish a program it is entitled to define the limits of that program. . . .

[T]he government is not denying a benefit to anyone, but is instead simply insisting that public funds be spent for the purposes for which they were authorized. The Secretary's regulations do not force the Title ` X grantee to give up abortion-related speech; they merely require that the grantee keep such activities separate and distinct from Title X activities. Title X expressly distinguishes between a Title X grantee and a Title X project. The grantee, which normally is a health care organization, may receive funds from a variety of sources for a variety of purposes. The grantee receives Title X funds, however, for the specific and limited purpose of establishing and operating a Title X project. The regulations govern the scope of the Title X project's activities, and leave the grantee unfettered in its other activities. The Title X grantee can continue to perform abortions, provide abortion-related services, and engage in abortion advocacy; it simply is required to conduct those activities through programs that are separate and independent from the project that receives Title X funds. . . .

By requiring that the Title X grantee engage in abortion-related activity separately from activity receiving federal funding, Congress has . . . not denied it the right to engage in abortion-related activities. Congress has merely refused to fund such activities out of the public fisc, and the Secretary has simply required a certain degree of separation from the Title X project in order to ensure the integrity of the federally funded program.

The same principles apply to petitioners' claim that the regulations abridge the free speech rights of the grantee's staff. Individuals who are voluntarily employed for a Title X project must perform their duties in accordance with the regulation's restrictions on abortion counseling and referral. . . .

We turn now to petitioners' argument that the regulations violate a woman's Fifth Amendment right to choose whether to terminate her pregnancy. We re-

cently reaffirmed the long-recognized principle that " 'the Due Process Clauses generally confer no affirmative right to governmental aid, even where such aid may be necessary to secure life, liberty, or property interests of which the government itself may not deprive the individual.' " *** The Government has no constitutional duty to subsidize an activity merely because the activity is constitutionally protected and may validly choose to fund childbirth over abortion and " 'implement that judgment by the allocation of public funds' " for medical services relating to childbirth but not to those relating to abortion. *** The Government has no affirmative duty to "commit any resources to facilitating abortions," *** and its decision to fund childbirth but not abortion "places no governmental obstacle in the path of a woman who chooses to terminate her pregnancy, but rather, by means of unequal subsidization of abortion and other medical services, encourages alternative activity deemed in the public interest." ***

That the regulations do not impermissibly burden a woman's Fifth Amendment rights is evident from the line of cases beginning with *Maher* and *McRae* and culminating in our most recent decision in *Webster*. Just as Congress' refusal to fund abortions in *McRae* left "an indigent woman with at least the same range of choice in deciding whether to obtain a medically necessary abortion as she would have had if Congress had chosen to subsidize no health care costs at all," and "Missouri's refusal to allow public employees to perform abortions in public hospitals leaves a pregnant woman with the same choices as if the State had chosen not to operate any public hospitals," *** Congress' refusal to fund abortion counseling and advocacy leaves a pregnant woman with the same choices as if the government had chosen not to fund family-planning services at all. The difficulty that a woman encounters when a Title X project does not provide abortion counseling or referral leaves her in no different position than she would have been if the government had not enacted Title X. . . .

Petitioners contend, however, that most Title X clients are effectively precluded by indigency and poverty from seeing a health care provider who will provide abortion-related services. But once again, even these Title X clients are in no worse position than if Congress had never enacted Title X. . . .

The Secretary's regulations are a permissible construction of Title X and do not violate either the First or Fifth Amendments to the Constitution. Accordingly, the judgment of the Court of Appeals is
Affirmed.

Justice Blackmun [joined by ***Justice Marshall***], dissenting.

As is discussed [below], the Regulations impose viewpoint-based restrictions upon protected speech and are aimed at a woman's decision whether to continue or terminate her pregnancy. In both respects, they implicate core constitutional values. . . .

Until today, the Court never has upheld viewpoint-based suppression of speech simply because that suppression was a condition upon the acceptance of public funds. Whatever may be the Government's power to condition the receipt of its largess upon the relinquishment of constitutional rights, it surely does not extend to a condition that suppresses the recipient's cherished freedom of speech based solely upon the content or viewpoint of that speech. *** This rule is a sound one. . . .

The Regulations are also clearly viewpoint-based. While suppressing speech favorable to abortion with one hand, the Secretary compels anti-abortion speech with the other. . . .

The advocacy Regulations at issue here, however, are not limited to lobbying but extend to all speech having the effect of encouraging, promoting, or advocating abortion as a method of family planning. Thus, in addition to their impermissible focus upon the viewpoint of regulated speech, the provisions intrude upon a wide range of communicative conduct, including the very words spoken to a woman by her physician. By manipulating the content of the doctor/patient dialogue, the Regulations upheld today force each of the petitioners "to be an instrument for fostering public adherence to an ideological point of view [he or she] finds unacceptable." ***

This type of intrusive, ideologically based regulation of speech goes far beyond the narrow lobbying limitations approved in *Regan,* and cannot be justified simply because it is a condition upon the receipt of a governmental benefit. . . .

Finally, it is of no small significance that the speech the Secretary would suppress is truthful information regarding constitutionally protected conduct of vital importance to the listener. One can imagine no legitimate governmental interest that might be served by suppressing such information. . . .

By far the most disturbing aspect of today's ruling is the effect it will have on the Fifth Amendment rights of the women who, supposedly, are beneficiaries of Title X programs. The majority rejects petitioners' Fifth Amendment claims summarily. . . .

Until today, the Court has allowed to stand only those restrictions upon reproductive freedom that, while limiting the availability of abortion, have left intact a woman's ability to decide without coercion whether she will continue her pregnancy to term. *** Today's decision abandons that principle, and with disastrous results.

Contrary to the majority's characterization, this is not a case in which individuals seek government aid in exercising their fundamental rights. The Fifth Amendment right asserted by petitioners is the right of a pregnant woman to be free from affirmative governmental interference in her decision. *Roe v. Wade* and its progeny are not so much about a medical procedure as they are about a woman's fundamental right to self-determination. Those cases serve to vindicate the idea that "liberty," if it means anything, must entail freedom from governmental domination in making the most intimate and personal of decisions. By suppressing medically pertinent information and injecting a restrictive ideological message unrelated to considerations of maternal health, the government places formidable obstacles in the path of Title X clients' freedom of choice and thereby violates their Fifth Amendment rights.

Justice Stevens, dissenting. . . .

Justice O'Connor, dissenting. . . .

Edwards v. South Carolina

372 U.S. 229; 83 S. Ct. 680; 9 L. Ed.2d 697 (1963)
Vote: 8-1

Mr. Justice Stewart delivered the opinion of the Court.

The petitioners, 187 in number, were convicted in a magistrate's court in Columbia, South Carolina, of the common-law crime of breach of the peace....

There was no substantial conflict in the trial evidence. Late in the morning of March 2, 1961, the petitioners, high school and college students of the Negro race, met at the Zion Baptist Church in Columbia. From there, at about noon, they walked in separate groups of about 15 to the South Carolina State House grounds, an area of two city blocks open to the general public. Their purpose was "to submit a protest to the citizens of South Carolina, along with the Legislative Bodies of South Carolina, our feelings and our dissatisfaction with the present condition of discriminatory actions against Negroes, in general, and to let them know that we were dissatisfied and that we would like for the laws which prohibited Negro privileges in this State to be removed."

Already on the State House grounds when the petitioners arrived were 30 or more law enforcement officers, who had advance knowledge that the petitioners were coming. Each group of petitioners entered the grounds through a driveway and parking area known in the record as the "horseshoe." As they entered, they were told by the law enforcement officials that "they had a right, as a citizen, to go through the State House grounds, as any other citizen has, as long as they were peaceful." During the next half hour or 45 minutes, the petitioners, in the same small groups, walked single file or two abreast in an orderly way through the grounds, each group carrying placards bearing such messages as "I am proud to be a Negro" and "Down with segregation."

During this time a crowd of some 200 to 300 onlookers had collected in the horseshoe area and on the adjacent sidewalks. There was no evidence to suggest that these onlookers were anything but curious, and no evidence at all of any threatening remarks, hostile gestures, or offensive language on the part of any member of the crowd. The City Manager testified that he recognized some of the onlookers, whom he did not identify, as "possible trouble makers," but his subsequent testimony made clear that nobody among the crowd actually caused or threatened any trouble. There was no obstruction of pedestrian or vehicular traffic within the State House grounds. No vehicle was prevented from entering or leaving the horseshoe area. Although vehicular traffic at a nearby street intersection was slowed down somewhat, an officer was dispatched to keep traffic moving. There were a number of bystanders on the public sidewalks adjacent to the State House grounds, but they all moved on when asked to do so, and there was no impediment of pedestrian traffic. Police protection at the scene was at all times sufficient to meet any foreseeable possibility of disorder.

In the situation and under the circumstances thus described, the police authorities advised the petitioners that they would be arrested if they did not disperse within 15 minutes. Instead of dispersing, the petitioners engaged in what the City manager described as "boisterous," "loud," and "flamboyant" conduct, which, as his later testimony made clear, consisted of listening to a "religious harangue" by one of their leaders, and loudly singing "The Star Spangled Banner" and other patriotic and religious songs, while stamping their feet and clapping their hands. After 15 minutes had passed, the police arrested the petitioners and marched them off to jail.

Upon this evidence the state trial court convicted the petitioners of breach of the peace, and imposed sentences ranging from a $10 fine or five days in jail, to a $100 fine or 30 days in jail. In affirming the judgments, the Supreme Court of South Carolina said that under the law of that State the offense of breach of the peace "is not susceptible for exact definition," but that the "general definition of the offense" is as follows:

In general terms, a breach of the peace is a violation of public order, a disturbance of the public tranquility, by any act or conduct inciting to violence ..., it includes any violation of any law enacted to preserve peace and good order. It may consist of an act of violence or an act likely to produce violence. It is not necessary that the peace be actually broken to lay the foundation for a prosecution for this offense. If what is done is unjustifiable and unlawful, tending with sufficient directness to break the peace, no more is required. Nor is actual personal violence an essential element in the offense. . . .

By "peace," as used in the law in this connection, is meant the tranquility enjoyed by citizens of a municipality or community where good order reigns among its members, which is the natural right of all person in political society. ***

. . . It has long been established that these First Amendment freedoms are protected by the Fourteenth Amendment from invasion by the States. *** The circumstances in this case reflect an exercise of these basic constitutional rights in their most pristine and classic form. The petitioners felt aggrieved by laws of South Carolina which allegedly "prohibited Negro privileges in this State." They peaceably assembled at the site of the State Government and there peaceably expressed their grievances "to the citizens of South Carolina, along with the Legislative Bodies of South Carolina." Not until they were told by police officials that they must disperse on pain of arrest did they do more. Even then, they but sang patriotic and religious songs after one of their leaders had delivered a "religious harangue." There was no violence or threat of violence on their part, or on the part of any member of the crowd watching them. Police protection was "ample."

This, therefore, was a far cry from the situation in *Feiner v. New York* [1951], *** where two policemen were faced with a crowd which was "pushing, shoving, and milling around," *** where at least one member of the crowd "threatened violence if the police did not act," *** where "the crowd was pressing closer around petitioner and the officer," *** and where "the speaker passes the bounds of argument or persuasion and undertakes incitement to riot." *** And the record is barren of any evidence of "fighting words." ***

We do not review in this case criminal convictions resulting from the even-handed application of a precise and narrowly drawn regulatory statute evincing a legislative judgment that certain specific conduct be limited or proscribed. If, for example, the petitioners had been convicted upon evidence that they had violated a law regulating traffic, or had dis-

obeyed a law reasonably limiting the periods during which the State House grounds were open to the public, this would be a different case. . . . These petitioners were convicted of an offense so generalized as to be, in the words of the South Carolina Supreme Court, "not susceptible of exact definition." And they were convicted upon evidence which showed no more than that the opinions which they were peaceably expressing were sufficiently opposed to the views of the majority of the community to attract 'a crowd and necessitate police protection. . . .

Mr. Justice Clark, dissenting.

. . . Beginning, as did the South Carolina courts, with the premise that the petitioners were entitled to assemble and voice their dissatisfaction with segregation, the enlargement of constitutional protection for the conduct here is as fallacious as would be the conclusion that free speech necessarily includes the right to broadcast from a sound truck in the public street. *** Here the petitioners were permitted without hindrance to exercise their rights of free speech and assembly. Their arrests occurred only after a situation arose in which the law-enforcement officials on the scene considered that a dangerous disturbance was imminent. The County Court found that "[t]he evidence is clear that the officers were motivated solely by a proper concern for the preservation of order and prevention of further interference with traffic upon the public streets and sidewalks." ***

. . . [I]n *Feiner v. New York* *** (1951), we upheld a conviction for breach of the peace in a situation no more dangerous than that found here. There the demonstration was conducted by only one person and the crowd was limited to approximately 80, as compared with the present lineup of some 200 demonstrators and 300 onlookers. There the petitioner was "endeavoring to arouse the Negro people against the whites, urging that they rise up in arms and fight for equal rights." *** Only one person—in a city having an entirely different historical background—was exhorting adults. Here 200 youthful Negro demonstrators were being aroused to a "fever pitch" before a crowd of some 300 people who undoubtedly were hostile. Perhaps their speech was not so animated but in this setting their actions, their placards reading "You may jail our bodies but not our souls" and their chanting of "I Shall Not Be Moved," accompanied by stamping feet and clapping hands, created a much greater danger of riot and disorder. It is my belief that anyone conversant with the almost spontaneous combustion in some Southern communities in such a situation will agree that the [city's] action may well have averted a major catastrophe.

The gravity of the danger here surely needs no further explication. The imminence of that danger has been emphasized at every stage of this proceed-ing, from the complaints charging that the demonstrations "tended directly to immediate violence" to the State Supreme Court's affirmance on the authority of *Feiner*. *** This record, then, shows no steps backward from a standard of "clear and present danger." But to say that the police may not intervene until the riot has occurred is like keeping out the doctor until the patient dies. I cannot subscribe to such a doctrine. . . .

Adderley v. Florida

385 U.S. 39; 87 S. Ct. 242; 17 L. Ed. 2d 149 (1966)
Vote: 5-4

Mr. Justice Black delivered the opinion of the Court.

Petitioners, Harriett Louise Adderley and 31 other persons, were convicted by a jury in a joint trial in the County Judge's Court of Leon County, Florida, on a charge of "trespass with a malicious and mischievous intent" upon the premises of the county jail contrary to 821.18 of the Florida statutes set out below. Petitioners, apparently all students of the Florida A. & M. University in Tallahassee, had gone from the school to the jail about a mile away, along with many other students, to "demonstrate" at the jail their protests of arrests of other protesting students the day before, and perhaps to protest more generally against state and local policies and practices of racial segregation, including segregation of the jail. The county sheriff, legal custodian of the jail and jail grounds, tried to persuade the students to leave the jail grounds. When this did not work, he notified them that they must leave, that if they did not leave he would arrest them for trespassing, and that if they resisted he would charge them with that as well. Some of the students left but others, including petitioners, remained and they were arrested. On appeal the convictions were affirmed by the Florida Circuit Court and then by the Florida District Court of Appeal. *** That being the highest state court to which they could appeal, petitioners applied to us for *certiorari* contending that, in view of petitioners' pur-pose to protest against jail and other segregation policies, their conviction denied them "rights of free speech, assembly, petition, due process of law and equal protection of the laws as guaranteed by the Fourteenth Amendment to the Constitution of the United States." On this "Question Presented" we granted *certiorari*. ***

Petitioners have insisted from the beginning of this case that it is controlled by and must be reversed because of our prior cases of *Edwards v. South Carolina* *** and *Cox v. Louisiana*. *** We cannot agree. . . .

Petitioners argue that "petty criminal statutes may not be used to violate minorities' constitutional rights." This of course is true but this abstract proposition gets us nowhere in deciding this case. . . .

Petitioners here contend that "Petitioners' convictions are based on a total lack of relevant evidence." If true, this would be a denial of due process . . . Both in the petition for *certiorari* and in the brief on the merits petitioners state that their summary of the evidence "does not conflict with the facts contained in the Circuit Court's opinion" which was in effect affirmed by the District Court of Appeal. *** That statement is correct and petitioners' summary of facts, as well as that of the Circuit Court, shows an abundance of facts to support the jury's verdict of guilty in this case.

In summary both these statements show testimony ample to prove this: Disturbed and upset by the arrest of their schoolmates the day before, a large number of Florida A. & M. students assembled on the school grounds and decided to march down to the county jail. Some apparently wanted to be put in jail too, along with the students already there. A group of around 200 marched from the school and arrived at the jail singing and clapping. They went directly to the jail-door entrance where they were met by a deputy sheriff, evidently surprised by their arrival. He asked them to move back, claiming they were blocking the entrance to the jail and fearing that they might attempt to enter the jail. They moved back part of the way, where they stood or sat, singing, clapping and dancing, on the jail driveway and on an adjacent grassy area upon the jail premises. This particular jail entrance and driveway were not normally used by the public, but by the sheriff's department for transporting prisoners to and from the courts several blocks away and by commercial concerns for servicing the jail. Even after their partial retreat, the demonstrators continued to block vehicular passage over this driveway up to the entrance of the jail. Someone called the sheriff who was at the moment apparently conferring with one of the state court judges about incidents connected with prior arrests for demonstrations. When the sheriff returned to the jail, he immediately inquired if all was safe inside the jail and was told it was. He then engaged in a conversation with two of the leaders. He told them that they were trespassing upon jail property and that he would give them 10 minutes to leave or he would arrest them. Neither of the leaders did anything to disperse the crowd, and one of them told the sheriff that they wanted to get arrested. A local minister talked with some of the demonstrators and told them not to enter the jail, because they could not arrest themselves, but just to remain where they were. After about 10 minutes, the sheriff, in a voice loud enough to be heard by all, told the demonstrators that he was the legal custodian of the jail and its premises, that they were trespassing on county property in violation of the law, that they should all leave forthwith or he would arrest them, and that if they attempted to resist arrest, he would charge them with that as a separate offense. Some of the group then left. Others, including all petitioners, did not leave. Some of them sat down. In a few minutes, realizing that the

remaining demonstrators had no intention of leaving, the sheriff ordered his deputies to surround those remaining on jail premises and placed them, 107 demonstrators, under arrest. The sheriff unequivocally testified that he did not arrest any persons other than those who were on the jail premises. Of the three petitioners testifying, two insisted that they were arrested before they had a chance to leave, had they wanted to, and one testified that she did not intend to leave. The sheriff again explicitly testified that he did not arrest any person who was attempting to leave.

Under the foregoing testimony the jury was authorized to find that the State had proven every essential element of the crime, as it was defined by the state court. That interpretation is, of course, binding on us, leaving only the question of whether conviction of the state offense, thus defined, unconstitutionally deprives petitioners of their rights to freedom of speech, press, assembly or petition. We hold it does not. The sheriff, as jail custodian, had power, as the state courts have here held, to direct that this large crowd of people get off the grounds. There is not a shred of evidence in this record that this power was exercised, or that its exercise was sanctioned by the lower courts, because the sheriff objected to what was being sung or said by the demonstrators or because he disagreed with the objectives of their protest. The record reveals that he objected only to their presence on that part of the jail grounds reserved for jail uses. There is no evidence at all that on any other occasion had similarly large groups of the public been permitted to gather on this portion of the jail grounds for any purpose. Nothing in the Constitution of the United States prevents Florida from even-handed enforcement of its general trespass statute against those refusing to obey the sheriff's order to remove themselves from what amounted to the curtilage of the jailhouse. The State, no less than a private owner of property, has power to preserve the property under its control for the use to which it is lawfully dedicated. For this reason there is no merit to the petitioners' argument that they had a constitutional right to stay on the property, over the jail custodian's objections, because this "area chosen for the peaceful civil rights demonstration was not only 'reasonable' but also particularly appropriate. . . ."

Such an argument has as its major unarticulated premise the assumption that people who want to propagandize protests or views have a constitutional right to do so whenever and however and wherever they please. That concept of constitutional law was vigorously and forthrightly rejected in . . . *Cox v. Louisiana.* *** We reject it again. The United States Constitution does not forbid a State to control the use of its own property for its own lawful nondiscriminatory purpose.

These judgments are

Affirmed.

Mr. Justice Douglas, with whom the **Chief Justice, Mr. Justice Brennan,** and **Mr. Justice Fortas** concur, dissenting.

. . . The jailhouse, like an executive mansion, a legislative chamber, a courthouse, or the statehouse itself *** is one of the seats of government, whether it be the Tower of London, the Bastille, or a small county jail. And when it houses political prisoners or those who many think are unjustly held, it is an obvious center for protest. The right to petition for the redress of grievances has an ancient history and is not limited to writing a letter or sending a telegram to a congressman; it is not confined to appearing before the local city council, or writing letters to the President or Governor or Mayor. *** Conventional methods of petitioning may be, and often have been, shut off to large groups of our citizens. Legislators may turn deaf ears; formal complaints may be routed endlessly through a bureaucratic maze; courts may let the wheels of justice grind very slowly. Those who do not control television and radio, those who cannot afford to advertise in newspapers or circulate elaborate pamphlets may have only a more limited type of access to public officials. Their methods should not be condemned as tactics of obstruction and harassment as long as the assembly and petition are peaceable, as these were.

There is no question that petitioners had as their purpose a protest against the arrest of Florida A. & M. students for trying to integrate public theatres. The sheriff's testimony indicates that he well understood the purpose of the rally. The petitioners who testified unequivocally stated that the group was protesting the arrests, and state and local policies of segrega-

tion, including segregation of the jail. This testimony was not contradicted or even questioned. The fact that no one gave a formal speech, that no elaborate handbills were distributed, and that the group was not laden with signs would seem to be immaterial. Such methods are not the *sine qua non* of petitioning for the redress of grievances. The group did sing "freedom" songs. And history shows that a song can be a powerful tool of protest. *** There was no violence; no threat of violence; no attempted jail break; no storming of a prison; no plan or plot to do anything but protest. The evidence is uncontradicted that the petitioners' conduct did not upset the jailhouse routine; things went on as they normally would. None of the group entered the jail. Indeed, they moved back from the entrance as they were instructed. There was no shoving, no pushing, no disorder or threat of riot. It is said that some of the group blocked part of the driveway leading to the jail entrance. The chief jailer, to be sure, testified that vehicles would not have been able to use the driveway. Never did the students locate themselves so as to cause interference with persons or vehicles going to or coming from the jail. Indeed, it is undisputed that the sheriff and deputy sheriff, in separate cars, were able to drive up the driveway to the parking places near the entrance and that no one obstructed their path. Further, it is undisputed that the entrance to the jail was not blocked. And whenever the students were requested to move they did so. If there was congestion, the solution was a further request to move to lawns or parking areas, not complete ejection and arrest. The claim is made that a tradesman waited inside the jail because some of the protestants were sitting around and leaning on his truck. The only evidence supporting such a conclusion is the testimony of a deputy sheriff that the tradesman "came to the door . . . and then did not leave." His remaining is just as consistent with a desire to satisfy his curiosity as it is with a restraint. Finally, the fact that some of the protestants may have felt their cause so just that they were willing to be arrested for making their protest outside the jail seems wholly irrelevant. A petition is nonetheless a petition, though its futility may make martyrdom attractive.

We do violence to the First Amendment when we permit this "petition for redress of grievances" to be turned into a trespass action. It does not help to analogize this problem to the problem of picketing. Picketing is a form of protest usually directed against private interests. I do not see how rules governing picketing in general are relevant to this express constitutional right to assemble and to petition for redress of grievances. In the first place the jailhouse grounds were not marked with "NO TRESPASSING!" signs, nor does respondent claim that the public was generally excluded from the grounds. Only the sheriff's fiat transformed lawful conduct into an unlawful trespass. To say that a private owner could have done the same if the rally had taken place on private property is to speak of a different case, as an assembly and a petition for redress of grievances run to government, not to private proprietors.

The Court forgets that prior to this day our decisions have drastically limited the application of state statutes inhibiting the right to go peacefully on public property to exercise First Amendment rights....

There may be some public places which are so clearly committed to other purposes that their use for the airing of grievances is anomalous. There may be some instances in which assemblies and petitions for redress of grievances are not consistent with other necessary purposes of public property. A noisy meeting may be out of keeping with the serenity of the statehouse or the quiet of the courthouse. No

one, for example, would suggest that the Senate gallery is the proper place for a vociferous protest rally. And in other cases it may be necessary to adjust the right to petition for redress of grievances to the other interests inhering in the uses to which the public property is normally put. *** But this is quite different from saying that all public places are off limits to people with grievances. ***

Today a trespass law is used to penalize people for exercising a constitutional right. Tomorrow a disorderly conduct statute, a breach-of-the-peace statute, a vagrancy statute will be put to the same end. It is said that the sheriff did not make the arrests because of the views which petitioners espoused. That excuse is usually given, as we know from the many cases involving arrests of minority groups for breaches of the peace, unlawful assemblies, and parading without a permit. The charge against William Penn, who preached a nonconformist doctrine in a street in London, was that he caused "a great concourse and tumult of people" in contempt of the King and "to the great disturbance of his peace." *** That was in 1670. In modern times, also such arrests are usually sought to be justified by some legitimate function of government. Yet by allowing these orderly and civilized protests against injustice to be suppressed, we only increase the forces of frustration which the conditions of second-class citizenship are generating amongst us.

National Association for the Advancement of Colored People v. Alabama

357 U.S. 449; 78 S. Ct. 1163; 2 L. Ed.2d 1488 (1958)
Vote: 9-0

In 1956, the Alabama attorney general sought to force the National Association for the Advancement of Colored People (NAACP) to turn over to the state the names of its "members" and "agents." The attorney general based his action on a statute requiring out-of-state corporations to register and report certain information. A state trial court ordered the NAACP to comply with the state's demand. When it refused to do so, the NAACP was held in contempt

and fined one hundred thousand dollars. The state supreme court refused to review the case.

Mr. Justice Harlan delivered the opinion of the Court.

... Alabama has a statute similar to those of many other States which requires a foreign corporation, except as exempted, to qualify before doing business by filing its corporate charter with the Secretary of

State and designating a place of business and an agent to receive service of process. . . . [The NAACP] has never complied with the qualification statute, from which it considered itself exempt.

In 1956 the Attorney General of Alabama brought an equity suit in the State Circuit Court, Montgomery County, to enjoin the Association from conducting further activities within, and to oust it from, the State. . . .

[T]he State moved for the production of a large number of the Association's records and papers, including bank statements, leases, deeds, and records containing the names and addresses of all Alabama "members" and "agents" of the Association. It alleged that all such documents were necessary for adequate preparation for the hearing, in view of petitioner's denial of the conduct of intrastate business within the meaning of the qualification statute. Over petitioner's objections, the court ordered the production of a substantial part of the requested records, including the membership lists. . . .

Thereafter petitioner . . . produced substantially all the data called for by the production order except its membership lists, as to which it contended that Alabama could not constitutionally compel disclosure, and moved to modify or vacate the contempt judgment, or stay its execution pending appellate review. This motion was denied. While a similar stay application, which was later denied, was pending before the Supreme Court of Alabama, the Circuit Court made a further order adjudging petitioner in continuing contempt and increasing the fine already imposed to $100,000. ***

Effective advocacy of both public and private points of view, particularly controversial ones, is undeniably enhanced by group association, as this Court has more than once recognized by remarking on the close nexus between the freedoms of speech and assembly. *** It is beyond debate that freedom to engage in association for the advancement of beliefs and ideas is an inseparable aspect of the "liberty" assured by the Due Process Clause of the Fourteenth Amendment, which embraces freedom of speech. *** Of course, it is immaterial whether the beliefs sought to be advanced by the association pertain to political, economic, religious or cultural matters, and state action which may have the effect of curtailing the freedom to associate is subject to the closest judicial scrutiny. . . .

The fact that Alabama, so far as is relevant to the validity of the contempt judgment presently under review, has taken no direct action, to restrict the right of petitioner's members to associate freely, does not end inquiry into the effect of the production order. In the domain of these indispensable liberties, whether of speech, press, or association, the decisions of this Court recognize that abridgement of such rights, even though unintended, may inevitably follow from varied forms of governmental action. . . .

It is hardly a novel perception that compelled disclosure of affiliation with groups engaged in advocacy may constitute as effective a restraint on freedom of association as the forms of governmental action in the cases above were thought likely to produce upon the particular constitutional rights there involved. This Court has recognized the vital relationship between freedom to associate and privacy in one's associations. *** Inviolability of privacy in group association may in many circumstances be indispensable to preservation of freedom of association, particularly where a group espouses dissident beliefs.

We think that the production order, in the respects here drawn in question, must be regarded as entailing the likelihood of a substantial restraint upon the exercise by petitioner's members of their right to freedom of association. Petitioner has made an uncontroverted showing that on past occasion revelation of the identity of its rank-and-file members has exposed these members to economic reprisal, loss of employment, threat of physical coercion, and other manifestations of public hostility. Under these circumstances, we think it apparent that compelled disclosure of petitioner's Alabama membership is likely to affect adversely the ability of petitioner and its members to pursue their collective effort to foster beliefs which they admittedly have the right to advocate, in that it may induce members to withdraw from the Association and dissuade others from joining it because of fear of exposure of their beliefs shown through their associations and of the consequences of this exposure.

It is not sufficient to answer, as the State does here, that whatever repressive effect compulsory disclosure of names of petitioner's members may have upon participation by Alabama citizens in petitioner's activities follows not from state action but from private community pressures. The crucial factor is the interplay of governmental and private action, for it is only after the initial exertion of state power represented by the production order that private action takes hold.

We turn to the final question whether Alabama has demonstrated an interest in obtaining the disclosures it seeks from petitioner which is sufficient to justify the deterrent effect which we have concluded these disclosures may well have on the free exercise by petitioner's members of their constitutionally protected right of association. Such a "... subordinating interest of the State must be compelling." *** ...

Whether there was "justification" in this instance turns solely on the substantiality of Alabama's interest in obtaining the memberships lists.... The exclusive purpose was to determine whether petitioner was conducting intrastate business in violation of the Alabama foreign corporation registration stature, and the membership lists were expected to help resolve this question.... Without intimating the slightest view upon the merits of these issues, we are unable to perceive that the disclosure of the names of petitioner's rank-and-file members has a substantial bearing.

As matters stand in the state court, petitioner (1) has admitted its presence and conduct of activities in Alabama since 1918; (2) has offered to comply in all respects with the state qualification statute, although preserving its contention that the statute does not apply to it; and (3) has apparently complied satisfactorily with the production order, except for the membership lists, by furnishing the Attorney General with varied business records, its charter and statement of purposes, the names of all of its directors and officers, and with the total number of its Alabama members and the amount of their dues....

We hold that the immunity from state scrutiny of membership lists which the Association claims on behalf of its members is here so related to the right of the members to pursue their lawful private interests privately and to associate freely with others in so doing as to come within the protection of the Fourteenth Amendment. And we conclude that Alabama has fallen short of showing a controlling justification for the deterrent effect on the free enjoyment of the right to associate which disclosure of membership lists is likely have. According, the judgment of civil contempt and the $100,000 fine which resulted from petitioner's refusal to comply with the production order in this respect must fall....

Roberts v. United States Jaycees

468 U.S. 609; 104 S. Ct. 3244; 82 L. Ed.2d 462 (1984)

Vote: 7-0

Justice Brennan delivered the opinion of the Court.

This case requires us to address a conflict between a State's efforts to eliminate gender-based discrimination against its citizens and the constitutional freedom of association asserted by members of a private organization. In the decision under review, the Court of Appeals for the Eighth Circuit concluded that, by requiring the United States Jaycees to admit women as full voting members, the Minnesota Human Rights Act violates the First and Fourteenth Amendment rights of the organization's members. We noted probable jurisdiction, *** and now reverse....

... An individual's freedom to speak, to worship, and to petition the government for the redress of grievances could not be vigorously protected from interference by the State unless a correlative freedom to engage in group effort toward those ends were not also guaranteed. *** According protection to collective effort on behalf of shared goals is especially important in preserving political and cultural diversity and in shielding dissident expression from suppression by the majority. *** Consequently, we have long understood as implicit in the right to engage in activities protected by the First Amendment a corresponding right to associate with others in pursuit of a wide variety of political, social, economic, educational, religious, and cultural ends. *** In view of the various protected activities in which the Jaycees engages, *** that right is plainly implicated in this case. . . .

The right to associate for expressive purposes is not, however, absolute. Infringements on that right may be justified by regulations adopted to serve compelling state interests, unrelated to the suppression of ideas, that cannot be achieved through means significantly less restrictive of associational freedoms. *** We are persuaded that Minnesota's compelling interest in eradicating discrimination against its female citizens justifies the impact that application of the statute to the Jaycees may have on the male members' associational freedoms.

On its face, the Minnesota Act does not aim at the suppression of speech, does not distinguish between prohibited and permitted activity on the basis of viewpoint, and does not license enforcement authorities to administer the statute on the basis of such constitutionally impermissible criteria. *** Nor does the Jaycees contend that the Act has been applied in this case for the purpose of hampering the organization's ability to express its views. Instead, as the Minnesota Supreme Court explained, the Act reflects the State's strong historical commitment to eliminating discrimination and assuring its citizens equal access to publicly available goods and services. *** That goal, which is unrelated to the suppression of expression, plainly serves compelling state interests of the highest order.

The Minnesota Human Rights Act at issue here is an example of public accommodations laws that were adopted by some States beginning a decade before enactment of their federal counterpart, the Civil Rights Act of 1875. . . . Indeed, when this Court invalidated that federal statute in the Civil Rights Cases, *** it emphasized the fact that state laws imposed a variety of equal access obligations on public accommodations. In response to that decision, many more States, including Minnesota, adopted statutes prohibiting racial discrimination in public accommodations. These laws provided the primary means for protecting the civil rights of historically disadvantaged groups until the Federal Government reentered the field in 1957. *** Like many other States,

Minnesota has progressively broadened the scope of its public accommodations law in the years since it was first enacted, both with respect to the number and type of covered facilities and with respect to the groups against whom discrimination is forbidden. *** In 1973, the Minnesota Legislature added discrimination on the basis of sex to the types of conduct prohibited by the statute. ***

By prohibiting gender discrimination in places of public accommodation, the Minnesota Act protects the State's citizenry from a number of serious social and personal harms. In the context of reviewing state actions under the Equal Protection Clause, this Court has frequently noted that discrimination based on archaic and overbroad assumptions about the relative needs and capacities of the sexes forces individuals to labor under stereotypical notions that often bear no relationship to their actual abilities. It thereby both deprives persons of their individual dignity and denies society the benefits of wide participation in political, economic, and cultural life. *** These concerns are strongly implicated with respect to gender discrimination in the allocation of publicly available goods and services. Thus, in upholding Title II of the Civil Rights Act of 1964, *** which forbids race discrimination in public accommodations, we emphasized that its "fundamental object . . . was to vindicate 'the deprivation of personal dignity that surely accompanies denials of equal access to public establishments.' " *** That stigmatizing injury, and the denial of equal opportunities that accompanies it, is surely felt as strongly by persons suffering discrimination on the basis of their sex as by those treated differently because of their race.

Nor is the state interest in assuring equal access limited to the provision of purely tangible goods and services. . . . Like many States and municipalities, Minnesota has adopted a functional definition of public accommodations that reaches various forms of public, quasi-commercial conduct. *** This expansive definition reflects a recognition of the changing nature of the American economy and of the importance, both to the individual and to society, of removing the barriers to economic advancement and political and social integration that have historically plagued certain disadvantaged groups, including women. *** Thus, in explaining its conclusion that the Jaycees local chapters are "place[s] of public accommodations" within the meaning of the Act, the Minnesota court noted the various commercial programs and benefits offered to members and stated that, "[l]eadership skills are 'goods,' [and] business contacts and employment promotions are 'privileges' and 'advantages.' ..." *** Assuring women equal access to such goods, privileges, and advantages clearly furthers compelling state interests.

In applying the Act to the Jaycees, the State has advanced those interests through the least restrictive means of achieving its ends. Indeed, the Jaycees have failed to demonstrate that the Act imposes any serious burdens on the male members' freedom of expressive association. *** To be sure, as the Court of Appeals noted, a "not insubstantial part" of the Jaycees' activities constitutes protected expression on political, economic, cultural, and social affairs. *** Over the years, the national and local levels of the organization have taken public positions on a number of diverse issues, *** and members of the Jaycees regularly engage in a variety of civic, charitable, lobbying, fund-raising and other activities worthy of constitutional protection under the First Amendment. *** There is, however, no basis in the record for concluding that admission of women as full voting members will impede the organization's ability to engage in these protected activities or to disseminate its preferred views. The Act requires no change in the Jaycees' creed of promoting the interests of young men, and it imposes no restrictions on the organization's ability to exclude individuals with ideologies or philosophies different from those of its existing members. *** Moreover, the Jaycees already invite women to share the group's views and philosophy and to participate in much of its training and community activities. Accordingly, any claim that admission of women as full voting members will impair a symbolic message conveyed by the very fact that women are not permitted to vote is attenuated at best. ***

While acknowledging that "the specific content of most of the resolutions adopted over the years by the Jaycees has nothing to do with sex," *** the Court of Appeals nonetheless entertained the hypothesis that women members might have a different view or agenda with respect to these matters so that, if they are allowed to vote, "some change in the Jaycees'

philosophical cast can reasonably be expected." *** It is similarly arguable that, insofar as the Jaycees is organized to promote the views of young men whatever those views happen to be, admission of women as voting members will change the message communicated by the group's speech because of the gender-based assumptions of the audience. Neither supposition, however, is supported by the record. In claiming that women might have a different attitude about such issues as the federal budget, school prayer, voting rights, and foreign relations, *** or that the organization's public positions would have a different effect if the group were not "a purely young men's association," the Jaycees relies solely on unsupported generalizations about the relative interests and perspectives of men and women. *** Although such generalizations may or may not have a statistical basis in fact with respect to particular positions adopted by the Jaycees, we have repeatedly condemned legal decisionmaking that relies uncritically on such assumptions. *** In the absence of a showing far more substantial than that attempted by the Jaycees, we decline to indulge in the sexual stereotyping that underlies appellee's contention that, by allowing women to vote, application of the Minnesota Act will change the content or impact of the organization's speech. ***

In any event, even if enforcement of the Act causes some incidental abridgement of the Jaycees' protected speech, that effect is no greater than is necessary to accomplish the State's legitimate purposes. As we have explained, acts of invidious discrimination in the distribution of publicly available goods, services, and other advantages cause unique evils that government has a compelling interest to prevent—wholly apart from the point of view such conduct may transmit. Accordingly, like violence or other types of potentially expressive activities that produce special harms distinct from their communicative impact, such practices are entitled to no constitutional protection. *** In prohibiting such practices, the Minnesota Act therefore "responds precisely to the substantive problem which legitimately concerns" the State and abridges no more speech or associational freedom than is necessary to accomplish that purpose. *** ...

The judgment of the Court of Appeals is reversed.

Justice Rehnquist concurs in the judgment.

The Chief Justice and *Justice Blackmun* took no part in the decision of this case.

Justice O'Connor, concurring in part and concurring in the judgment.

. . . On the one hand, an association engaged exclusively in protected expression enjoys First Amendment protection of both the content of its message and the choice of its members. Protection of the message itself is judged by the same standards as protection of speech by an individual. Protection of the association's right to define its membership derives from the recognition that the formation of an expressive association is the creation of a voice, and the selection of members is the definition of that voice. . . . A ban on specific group voices on public affairs violates the most basic guarantee of the First Amendment—that citizens, not the government, control the content of public discussion.

On the other hand, there is only minimal constitutional protection of the freedom of commercial association. There are, of course, some constitutional protections of commercial speech—speech intended and used to promote a commercial transaction with the speaker. But the State is free to impose any rational regulation on the commercial transaction itself. The Constitution does not guarantee a right to choose employees, customers, suppliers, or those with whom one engages in simple commercial transactions, without restraint from the State. A shopkeeper has no constitutional right to deal only with persons of one sex. . . .

Minnesota's attempt to regulate the membership of the Jaycees chapters operating in that State presents a relatively easy case for application of the expressive-commercial dichotomy. Both the Minnesota Supreme Court and the United States District Court, which expressly adopted the state court's findings, made findings of fact concerning the commercial nature of the Jaycees activities. The Court of Appeals, which disagreed with the District Court over the legal conclusions to be drawn from the facts, did not dispute any of those findings. *** "The Jaycees is not a political party, or even primarily a political pressure group, but the advocacy of political and

public causes, selected by the membership, is a not insubstantial part of what it does. . . . [A] good deal of what the [Jaycees] does indisputably comes within the right of association . . . in pursuance of the specific ends of speech, writing, belief, and assembly for redress of grievances." ***

There is no reason to question the accuracy of this characterization. Notwithstanding its protected expressive activities, the Jaycees—otherwise known as the Junior Chamber of Commerce—is, first and foremost, an organization that, at both the national and local levels, promotes and practices the art of solicitation and management. The organization claims that the training it offers its members gives them an advantage in business, and business firms do indeed sometimes pay the dues of individual memberships for their employees. Jaycees members hone their solicitation and management skills, under the direction and supervision of the organization, primarily through their active recruitment of new members. "One of the major activities of the Jaycees is the sale of memberships in the organization. It encourages continuous recruitment of members with the expressed goal of increasing membership. . . . The Jaycees itself refers to its members as customers and membership as a product it is selling. More than 80 percent of the national officers' time is dedicated to recruitment, and more than half of the available achievement awards are in part conditioned on achievement in recruitment." *** The organization encourages record-breaking performance in selling memberships: the current records are 348 for most memberships sold in a year by one person, 134 for most sold in a month, and 1,586 for most sold in a lifetime.

Recruitment and selling are commercial activities, even when conducted for training rather than for profit. The "not insubstantial" volume of protected Jaycees activity found by the Court of Appeals is simply not enough to preclude state regulation of the Jaycees' commercial activities. The State of Minnesota has a legitimate interest in ensuring nondiscriminatory access to the commercial opportunity presented by membership in the Jaycees. The members of the Jaycees may not claim constitutional immunity from Minnesota's antidiscrimination law by seeking to exercise their First Amendment rights through this commercial organization. . . .

CHAPTER TWELVE
FREEDOM OF THE PRESS: MASS MEDIA AND THE CONSTITUTION

In the First Amendment the Founding Fathers gave the free press the protection it must have to fulfill its essential role in our democracy. The press was to serve the governed, not the governors. The Government's power to censor the press was abolished so that the press would forever remain free to censure the Government.

Justice Hugo Black, concurring
in *New York Times Company v. United States* (1971)

Hugo Black: Associate Justice,
1937–1971

INTRODUCTION

Chapter 11 examined the First Amendment's explicit protection of the freedoms of speech and assembly and its implicit guarantee of freedom of association. This chapter addresses the First Amendment's express recognition of freedom of the press. Although the freedoms of speech and press are often subsumed under the broader principle of "freedom of expression," freedom of the press has its own distinctive characteristics, and its constitutional development may be distinguished analytically from that of other First Amendment protections.

While the Framers of the Bill of Rights conceived of freedom of the press in terms of the right to publish newspapers, books, pamphlets, and other writings, the concept has taken on a larger meaning with the advent of electronic media. Accordingly, this chapter examines the constitutional issues involved in the activities of the mass media. It pays special attention to rapidly changing constitutional doctrines governing broadcast media. It also analyzes two traditional limitations on press freedom—libel and obscenity—which continue to be the subjects of important litigation.

FREEDOM OF THE PRESS—A BASIC NATIONAL COMMITMENT

The constitutional commitment to freedom of the press has its roots in English common law and in colonial experience, especially during the decades immediately preceding the American Revolution. The mass media of that period, consisting of small independent newspapers and pamphlets, played a vital role in facilitating political debate as well as in disseminating information. It is worth recalling in this context that the ratification of the Constitution was vigorously debated not only in the state ratifying conventions but in the press as well. The collection of essays known as *The Federalist Papers* first appeared as a series of newspaper articles analyzing and endorsing the new Constitution. Anti-Federalists also made wide use of newspapers in expressing opposition to ratification.

The Rule against Prior Restraint

The primary contribution of the English common law to development of freedom of the press in the United States consists of the rule against **prior restraint.** In his *Commentaries on the Laws of England,* William Blackstone stated the rule in the following language: "The liberty of the press is indeed essential to the nature of a free state; but this consists in laying no previous restraints upon publications, and not in freedom from censure for criminal matter when published." This concept has been of great importance to the Supreme Court in defining freedom of the press under the First Amendment, but it has not been applied as an absolute guarantee or regarded as a complete statement of freedom of the press.

Thus, in the landmark case of *Near v. Minnesota* (1931), Chief Justice Charles Evans Hughes observed in his majority opinion:

> The criticism upon Blackstone's statement has not been because immunity from previous restraint upon publication has not been regarded as deserving of special emphasis, but chiefly because the immunity cannot be deemed to exhaust the conception of the liberty guaranteed.

In *Near v. Minnesota,* the Court struck down a state law that permitted public officials to seek an **injunction** to stop publication of any "malicious, scandalous and defamatory newspaper, magazine or other periodical." The statute was invoked to suppress publication of a small Minneapolis newspaper, the *Saturday Press,* which had strong anti-Semitic overtones and maligned local political officials, particularly the chief of police. This law provided that once a newspaper was enjoined, further publication was punishable as **contempt of court.** Hughes characterized this mode of suppression as "the essence of censorship" and declared it unconstitutional. With its decision in *Near v. Minnesota,* the Court incorporated the First Amendment freedom of the press into the Due Process Clause of the Fourteenth Amendment, thus making it fully applicable to the states.

In commenting with general approval on the rule against prior restraint, Chief Justice Hughes acknowledged that this restriction is not absolute. It would not, for example, prevent government in time of war from prohibiting publication of "the sailing dates of transports or the number and location of troops." In these and related situations, national security interests are almost certain to prevail over freedom of the press. But where is the line to be drawn? How far can the "national security" justification be extended in suppressing publication?

The Pentagon Papers Case

The Court revisited the question of prior restraint on the press in the much-heralded Pentagon papers case of 1971 (*New York Times Company v. United States*). Here, the federal government attempted to prevent the *New York Times* and the *Washington Post* from publishing excerpts from a classified study entitled "History of U.S. Decision-Making Process on Viet Nam Policy" (the Pentagon papers). By a 6-to-3 vote, the Supreme Court, in a brief *per curiam* opinion, held that the government's effort to block publication of this material amounted to an unconstitutional prior restraint. The majority was simply not convinced that such publication—several years after the events and decisions discussed in the Pentagon papers—constituted a significant threat to national security. The furor produced by this highly publicized case and the great pressure brought to bear on the Court for a speedy decision of the issue help explain why no detailed majority opinion was produced. The justices in fact wrote nine separate opinions, advancing a wide variety of rationales for and against application of the prior restraint concept. Excerpts from each of these opinions are reprinted in this chapter, and it may be useful to consider the constitutional implications of the various arguments.

The Progressive H-Bomb Case

The prior restraint issue arose again in 1979 in connection with the publication of a magazine article purporting to describe the process of making a hydrogen bomb. The federal government obtained a **preliminary injunction** against *The Progressive* blocking publication of the article pending a hearing. In the meantime, however, another magazine published a similar article, with no apparent damage to national security. As a result, the case against *The Progressive*

In June, 1971, the New York Times began a series of stories based on the Pentagon Papers

was dismissed and the injunction lifted (see *United States v. Progressive* [1979]). *The Progressive's* H-bomb article was ultimately published in November 1979. In light of the Pentagon papers and *Progressive* cases, one may conclude that, while national security may justify a departure from the rule against prior restraint, in the real world of American constitutional law, such departures tend to be rare and short-lived.

The *Hazelwood* Case

One notable exception to the protection of press freedom against prior restraint involves the publication of student-operated school newspapers. In *Hazelwood School District v. Kuhlmeier* (1988), the Supreme Court voted 5 to 3 to uphold a public school principal's decision to excise certain controversial material from the school newspaper. The principal objected to certain articles dealing with divorce and teenage pregnancy on the grounds that they were written in such a way as to permit students to identify classmates who had encountered such difficulties. The student newspaper staff hired a lawyer and challenged the principal's action in federal court. Writing for the majority, Justice Byron White concluded that "educators do not offend the First Amendment by exercising editorial control over the style and content of student speech in school-sponsored expressive activities so long as their actions are reasonably related to legitimate pedagogical concerns." Dissenting, Justice William Brennan accused the majority of eviscerating *Tinker v. Des Moines Independent Community*

School District (1969), in which the Court had accorded First Amendment protection to certain expressive activities by students in public schools (*Tinker* is discussed and reprinted in Chapter 11). According to Brennan, the majority opinion in *Hazelwood* "denudes high school students of much of the First Amendment protection that *Tinker* itself prescribed."

The controversy in *Hazelwood* centered around a student newspaper at a public high school. Would the federal courts permit officials at a state college or university to censor student-run campus newspapers? Could "legitimate pedagogical concerns" at this level ever justify such interference?

The Free Press-Fair Trial Dilemma

The courts have long recognized that media coverage of a sensational criminal case may be prejudicial to the right of the defendant to receive a fair trial by an unbiased jury (see, for example, *Sheppard v. Maxwell* [1966], discussed in Chapter 14). In exceptional circumstances, a court may depart from the prior restraint doctrine by restricting news coverage of a criminal case. Appellate courts will scrutinize such restrictions very closely, however, to ensure that they are narrowly tailored and do not unduly restrict the right of the press to inform the public about the criminal justice system.

The U.S. Supreme Court has emphasized the severe limitations against prior restraints, even in the context of a sensational criminal trial, as its decision in *Nebraska Press Association v. Stuart* (1976), indicates. In *Nebraska Press*, the Supreme Court invalidated a **gag order** issued by a state trial judge in an attempt to prevent the press from reporting certain aspects of a grisly mass murder. Writing for the Court, Chief Justice Warren E. Burger noted that "the barriers to prior restraint remain high and the presumption against its use remains intact."

LIBEL

Libel consists of injuring someone's reputation by reporting falsehoods about that person. It is not a crime, but a tort, the remedy for which is a civil suit for damages. Libelous publications have traditionally been outside the scope of First Amendment protection. However, since the mid-1960s, the Supreme Court has in effect made it easier for defendants in libel suits brought by "public persons" to avoid libel judgments. In so doing, the Court has substantially expanded First Amendment freedom in an area traditionally controlled by principles of tort law. This development reflects what Justice Brennan described as "a profound national commitment to the principle that debate on public issues should be uninhibited, robust, and wide-open" (*New York Times Company v. Sullivan* [1964]).

Actual Malice

Prior to the Supreme Court's decision in *New York Times Company v. Sullivan*, the primary defense in a libel action was proof that the published material was true. The *Sullivan* decision substituted a new rule that afforded far greater protection to published criticism of official conduct. As stated by Justice Brennan,

William Brennan: Associate Justice,
1956–1990

this standard "prohibits a public official from recovering damages for a defamatory falsehood relating to his official conduct unless he proves that the statement was made with 'actual malice'—that is, with knowledge that it was false or with reckless disregard of whether it was false or not." As long as there is an "absence of malice" on the part of the press, public officials are barred from recovering damages for the publication of false statements about them.

The *Sullivan* case emerged out of the civil rights struggle of the 1960s. L. B. Sullivan, a city commissioner in Montgomery, Alabama, brought suit against the *New York Times* for its publication of a paid advertisement in which civil rights leaders chastised Montgomery officials for police responses to civil rights demonstrations. The *Sullivan* decision broadening protection of the press against libel actions thus reflected the Warren Court's commitment to protecting free expression by minority groups facing a politically hostile environment.

Public Persons

Although *New York Times Company v. Sullivan* applied only to cases where public officials sued for libel, the principle was soon expanded to cover a broader category designated as "public figures" (see *Curtis Publishing Company v. Butts* [1967]). This category includes prominent (and not so prominent) public figures, as well as persons who thrust themselves into the glare of publicity. The theory underlying this doctrine is that public figures have sufficient access to the media to defend themselves against false charges and thus do not require the assistance of libel suits. In *Gertz v. Robert Welch, Inc.* (1974), the Supreme Court stated that "public officials and public figures usually enjoy significantly greater access to the channels of effective communication and hence have a more realistic opportunity to counteract false statements than private individuals normally enjoy." The Court went on to discuss the concept of a "public figure":

> In some instances an individual may achieve such pervasive fame or notoriety that he becomes a public figure for all purposes and in all contexts. More commonly, an individual voluntarily injects himself or is drawn into a particular public controversy and thereby becomes a public figure for a limited range of issues. In either case, such persons assume special prominence in the resolution of public questions.

The concept of "public person" has been difficult to apply, but the Supreme Court has made it clear that publicity does not necessarily make a private citizen a public figure for purposes of libel law. For example, in *Time, Inc. v. Firestone* (1976), the Court rejected an attempt by a defendant in a libel suit to characterize Dorothy Firestone, a wealthy Palm Beach socialite, as a public figure merely because she was involved in a highly publicized divorce case. Speaking for the Court, Justice William Rehnquist said that for a plaintiff in a libel suit to be considered a public figure, the alleged defamation must involve a public controversy, not merely a private dispute that has been publicized in the press. While Firestone's divorce may have generated widespread public interest, it did not involve questions of vital public concern. Moreover, Firestone had not sought public attention; it was thrust upon her by an inquiring press.

In one of its more colorful recent cases, *Hustler Magazine v. Falwell* (1988), the Supreme Court reaffirmed the *Sullivan-Gertz* rules. *Hustler* magazine published a parody of the well-known conservative evangelist Jerry Falwell that depicted Rev. Falwell having sex with his mother in an outhouse. Falwell sued for infliction of emotional distress and won a substantial judgment against *Hustler*. In a unanimous decision, the Supreme Court reversed the judgment, holding that Falwell, as a public figure, could not recover damages for infliction of emotional distress without showing that *Hustler* had published a false statement of fact with actual malice.

Invasions of Privacy

Closely related to libel is the concept of **invasion of privacy.** Many jurisdictions have laws permitting private individuals to sue the press for unwarranted invasions of their privacy. Following its decision in *New York Times Company v. Sullivan,* the Supreme Court began to restrict such lawsuits. The first major decision came in *Time, Inc. v. Hill* (1967). There, the Court set aside a judgment in an invasion of privacy suit brought against *Life Magazine. Life* had published a story about a family that had been held hostage by escaped prisoners. Unfortunately, not all of the statements made in the magazine story were true. Under New York law, family members could sue regardless of whether the story constituted libel. In setting aside the verdict for the plaintiffs, the Supreme Court said that the First Amendment "preclude[s] the application of the New York statute to redress false reports of matters of public interest in the absence of proof that the defendant published the report with knowledge of its falsity or in reckless disregard of the truth."

In a similar vein, the Supreme Court has blocked efforts to restrict the press from reporting the identities of crime victims. In *Cox Broadcasting v. Cohn* (1975), the Court reversed a judgment for the plaintiff in a case in which a television station reported the name of a rape victim. The Court emphasized the fact that the name had been contained in the indictment and was thus a part of the public record. Similarly, in *The Florida Star v. B.J.F.* (1989), the Court overturned a verdict against a newspaper that reported the name of a rape victim. The newspaper had obtained the victim's name from a police report that had been released in violation of state law and the established policy of the police department. The *Cox Broadcasting* and *Florida Star* decisions reflect a commitment to the principle that the press has the right to report information that it lawfully obtains.

A FREE PRESS AND THE "PEOPLE'S RIGHT TO KNOW"

There is little doubt that the press has a constitutional right to publish information about government activities, subject to narrow exceptions based on national security. But does it have a constitutional right of access to this information? What means can government use to keep information from the press? And what means of obtaining secret government information are constitutionally protected? These questions have yet to be fully answered, but the lines of the controversy have been drawn.

The Issue of Media Privilege

In a democracy, does the public always have a right to know what its government is doing? Some would argue that our government violates democratic principles to the extent that it maintains secret information or conducts covert activities. According to this view, the proper role of the press is to oppose any government efforts at secrecy. The press thus "represents" the public by scrutinizing and publicizing the actions of government; accordingly, the people are better informed and are better able to evaluate their leaders. An active, adversarial press is therefore vital to democracy. Of course, not everyone shares this view.

Although press freedom is often advocated in terms of democratic principles and "the people's right to know," there is evidence that the American people do not always support the claims of the press vis-à-vis their government. For example, when reporters were excluded from the Grenada invasion of December 1983, there was an uproar of righteous indignation in the media. However, an ABC News poll taken shortly after the invasion revealed that 67 percent of the public supported censorship of the news media when "national security" was at stake.

Some champions of the institutionalized press are willing to justify almost any means of obtaining secret government information. Some would even go so far as to justify the commission of certain crimes, if necessary, to obtain government information about which the "people have a right to know."

The Limits of Media Privilege

In an episode of the video seminar "The Constitution: That Delicate Balance," reporter Lyle Denniston of The (Baltimore) Sun had the following exchange (quoted in George McKenna, A Guide to the Constitution: That Delicate Balance [New York: Random House, 1984], p. 239) with Dean Benno Schmidt of the Columbia Law School:

Denniston:	Professor Schmidt, as a journalist I have only one responsibility and that is to get a story and print it.
Schmidt:	Would you steal it yourself?
Denniston:	I would.
Schmidt:	Right off [former Secretary of Defense James R.] Schlesinger's desk?
Denniston:	Exactly. And hopefully without his knowing it.
Schmidt:	Would you hold a gun to his head?
Denniston:	Mayhem might be ruled out, but I'm not even sure of that.
Schmidt:	But breaking and entering?
Denniston:	Breaking and entering is benign. . . .

Although Denniston was probably exaggerating his views for effect, some feel that the press should be immunized from prosecution for minor offenses committed during the course of an investigation. Most people would bristle at the suggestion that members of the press are endowed with a superior legal status such that they can ignore laws binding on everyone else. To many, the notion of "media privilege" is an anathema. Perhaps such views articulated by members of the elite press partially explain the downturn in public confidence in the media over the last decade.

For the most part, the Supreme Court has not taken the side of the press in the controversy over media privilege. Although it has never faced the issue squarely, dicta in a number of cases (including the Pentagon papers case) suggest that reporters are not immune from prosecution for unlawful entry or even receiving stolen information. Moreover, the Court has never recognized the right to obtain government information, as distinguished from the right to publish information already obtained. Thus, for example, in *Houchins v. KQED* (1978), the Court rejected a radio station's claim that it had a First Amendment right of access to a local jail. Writing for a plurality in *Houchins,* Chief Justice Burger observed that

> [b]eyond question, the role of the media is important; acting as the "eyes and ears" of the public, they can be a powerful and constructive force, contributing to remedial action in the conduct of public business. They have served that function since the beginning of the Republic, but like all other components of our society, media representatives are subject to limits. . . .

As a consequence of such Burger Court decisions as *Houchins,* a degree of antipathy developed between the institutional press and the Supreme Court during the 1970s. Another source of this antipathy was Chief Justice Burger's stalwart opposition to television cameras in the federal courts. Today, many state court proceedings are videotaped or even carried on live television. One wonders when, if ever, the nation will be able to see and hear oral arguments in the U.S. Supreme Court on television.

Confidential Sources

Perhaps the greatest source of antagonism between the press and the Burger Court was the 1972 decision in *Branzburg v. Hayes,* which involved the legal protection of reporters' confidential sources. The reporter's greatest asset (aside from the First Amendment) is the confidential source. The institutionalized media therefore argue strenuously that the First Amendment gives reporters an absolute privilege to maintain the confidentiality of their sources, a privilege similar to that claimed by lawyers with respect to their clients. On the other hand, prosecutors tend to argue that the public interest in finding the truth in a criminal prosecution outweighs a reporter's interest in maintaining the confidentiality of sources. While some states have **shield laws** protecting journalists in such situations, others permit reporters to be held in contempt and confined for refusing to divulge their sources.

In *Branzburg v. Hayes,* the Supreme Court confronted a situation in which a newspaper reporter subpoenaed to appear before a grand jury refused to identify certain persons he had seen using and selling illicit drugs. The reporter had observed the illegal activities during an undercover investigation of the local drug scene. Citing the First Amendment, he refused to disclose his confidential sources to the grand jury. Writing for the Supreme Court, Justice White was not amused:

> [W]e cannot seriously entertain the notion that the First Amendment protects a newsman's agreement to conceal the criminal conduct of his source, or evidence thereof, on the theory that it is better to write about crime than to do something about it.

Given the conservative orientation of the Rehnquist Court, the relationship between the Court and the press will probably remain somewhat antipathetic. The hostility was not lessened by the 1991 decision that held that the First Amendment does not immunize the press against suits for reneging on promises to maintain the confidentiality of sources. In *Cohen v. Cowles Media Company,* the Court decided a case in which a political campaign worker provided a reporter with damaging information about a rival candidate on the condition that the worker's identity be kept secret. The newspaper made an editorial decision to publish the name of the "source," who was fired by his employer as a result. The source sued the newspaper under a state **promissory estoppel** law and won two hundred thousand dollars in compensatory damages. The U.S. Supreme Court rejected the newspaper's argument that such suits were barred by the First Amendment. Writing for the Court, Justice White observed that

> [i]t is ... beyond dispute that "[t]he publisher of a newspaper has no special immunity from the application of general laws. He has no special privilege to invade the rights and liberties of others." *** Accordingly, enforcement of such general laws against the press is not subject to stricter scrutiny than would be applied to enforcement against other persons or organizations.

OBSCENITY

One of the most difficult tasks the Supreme Court has undertaken in recent decades is that of determining the First Amendment limitations on state and federal laws regulating the advertisement, distribution, and sale of obscene books, magazines, and films. Prior to the Supreme Court's entry into this field in 1957, most American courts adhered to a legal definition of obscenity derived from the 1868 English case of *Regina v. Hicklin*. The *Hicklin* test was "whether the tendency of the matter charged as obscenity is to deprave and corrupt those whose minds are open to such immoral influences, and into whose hands a publication of this sort may fall." By the mid-twentieth century, this standard was widely regarded as unduly restrictive of artistic and literary expression. The principal objection to the *Hicklin* test was that it sought to measure obscenity with reference to its supposed impact on the most vulnerable members of society.

The Prurient Interest Test

In *Roth v. United States* (1957), the Supreme Court handed down new legal guidelines for obscenity. Writing for the majority, Justice Brennan expressed the view that obscenity is "utterly without redeeming social importance" and thus entitled to no First Amendment protection. Rejecting the essence of the *Hicklin* standard, he stated the new test as "whether to the average person, applying contemporary community standards, the dominant theme of the material taken as a whole appeals to a prurient interest."

Roth v. United States, a federal case, was consolidated with the state case of *Alberts v. California,* thus making the new test applicable to every level of government in the country. But in spite of its uniform applicability and apparent simplicity, the *Roth-Alberts* test drew the Court into an interpretive quagmire from which it has not yet emerged. Virtually every term in the new obscenity test proved elusive. The Court could never reach full agreement on what constitutes an appeal to a "prurient interest." The term "redeeming social importance" also failed to generate consensus. A majority of the Court, in the years immediately following *Roth,* could not even agree on whether the term "community" referred to the nation as a whole or to individual states or localities. Although most of the justices believed that "hard-core pornography" was not entitled to First Amendment protection, they were unable to define its meaning. Justice Potter Stewart's well-known remark "I know it when I see it" (see *Jacobellis v. Ohio* [1964], concurring opinion) points up the difficulty of precise definition in this area.

In spite of the difficulty in applying the *Roth-Alberts* test, the Court during the 1960s did achieve a measure of clarity on two other aspects of the obscenity issue. In *Ginzburg v. United States* (1966), the Court held that the "pandering" of material by mailed advertisement, designed to appeal to a prurient interest, could be prosecuted under the federal obscenity statute. Ralph Ginzburg had sought, among other things, to obtain mailing privileges from local postmasters in the tiny hamlets of Blue Ball and Intercourse, Pennsylvania, for the purpose of advertising his magazine *Eros.* Even assuming the material contained in this publication was not obscene, the Court was willing to allow government to punish the "commercial exploitation of erotica solely for the sake of their prurient appeal." Three years later, in *Stanley v. Georgia* (1969), the Court held that "the First and Fourteenth Amendments prohibit making mere private possession of obscene material a crime" (for further discussion, see Chapter 15).

The *Miller* Test

Partly because of the complexity of the problem and partly as a result of the refusal of Justices Hugo Black and William O. Douglas to recognize the legitimacy of any limitations on expression in the obscenity field, the Warren Court was unable to muster a clear majority in support of all aspects of the *Roth-Alberts* test during the 1960s. The Burger Court was also sharply divided but ultimately achieved a bare majority in restating the constitutional test of obscenity. Writing for the Court in *Miller v. California* (1973), Chief Justice Burger stated that "the basic guidelines for the trier of fact" in obscenity cases are:

> (a) whether "the average person, applying contemporary community standards" would find that the work, taken as a whole, appeals to the prurient interest, . . .
> (b) whether the work depicts or describes, in a patently offensive way, sexual conduct specifically defined by the applicable state law, and (c) whether the work, taken as a whole, lacks serious literary, artistic, political, or scientific value.

The *Miller* test was somewhat more restrictive of free expression than was the original *Roth-Alberts* test as embellished and applied by the Warren Court. The Burger Court explicitly rejected the "utterly without redeeming social value" standard advanced by a minority of justices in the 1960s (see *Memoirs v. Massachusetts* [1966]). Nevertheless, the new guidelines were far from clear. The Court had indicated that the applicable "community standards" under the new test were local or at most statewide standards. But when authorities in Albany, Georgia, purportedly applying "community standards," attempted to ban the movie *Carnal Knowledge,* the Court ruled that the test had been improperly applied. Only material showing "patently offensive hard core sexual conduct" could be proscribed under the new rules (*Jenkins v. Georgia* [1974]).

In 1987, a 5-to-4 majority of the Court modified the "contemporary community standards" yardstick. Writing for the majority in *Pope v. Illinois,* Justice White declared that

> the proper inquiry is not whether an ordinary member of any given community would find serious literary, artistic, political and scientific value in allegedly obscene material, but whether a reasonable person would find such value in the material, taken as a whole.

Whether this "reasonable person" alternative represents a liberalization of the obscenity test or fosters "intolerable orthodoxy," as Justice John Paul Stevens predicted in a dissenting opinion, it is clear that First Amendment issues in the field of obscenity are far from resolved.

Child Pornography

May a state criminalize the distribution of material depicting children engaged in sexual activities, irrespective of whether the material meets the legal test of obscenity? In *New York v. Ferber* (1982), the Court answered this question in the affirmative. It held that a state has a compelling interest in protecting children from sexual abuse and found a close connection between such abuse and the use of children in the production of pornographic materials. In 1990, the Rehnquist Court went beyond the *Ferber* decision in upholding a state law prohibiting the possession and viewing of child pornography (*Osborne v. Ohio*). Justices Brennan, Marshall, and Stevens, all of whom had concurred in the *Ferber* case, dissented in *Osborne*. Justice Brennan found the law too "overly broad" and criticized the Court for departing from its earlier decision in *Stanley v. Georgia* (1969). Together, the *Ferber* and *Osborne* decisions provide a clear indication that the Supreme Court is not sympathetic to any First Amendment claim that would protect from criminal prosecution those who produce, distribute, or consume child pornography.

Pornography as an Infringement of Women's Rights?

In recent years, some feminists have been sharply critical of pornography, arguing that it debases and objectifies women. As a means of combating pornography, Andrea Dworkin, a noted feminist and lawyer, proposed that women be permitted to sue pornographers for damages under civil rights laws. In 1982, Dworkin and other feminists, in an unlikely alliance with political conservatives, succeeded in bringing about the adoption of an innovative ordinance in Indianapolis, Indiana, based on this "civil rights" approach. The ordinance defined pornography as the "sexually explicit subordination of women, graphically depicted, whether in pictures or in words. . . ." In effect, the ordinance treated pornography as an illegal form of sex discrimination or exploitation, remediable through a civil suit for damages. In subsequent federal litigation, this ordinance was declared invalid as a violation of the First Amendment (*American Booksellers Ass'n., Inc. v. Hudnut* [1984]). In her opinion in *Hudnut*, U.S. District Judge Sarah Evans Barker maintained that

> [t]he Supreme Court's finding in [*New York v.*] *Ferber* of the uncontroverted state interest in "safeguarding the physical and psychological well-being of a minor" and its resultant characterization of that interest as "compelling" . . . is an interest which inheres in children and is not . . . readily transferable to adult women as a class. Adult women generally have the capacity to protect themselves from participating in and being personally victimized by pornography, which makes the State's interest in safeguarding the physical and psychological well-being of women . . . not so compelling as to sacrifice the guarantees of the First Amendment. . . .

On appeal, the U.S. Court of Appeals for the Seventh Circuit sustained Judge Barker's ruling. The Supreme Court denied certiorari, thus leaving intact the lower court decisions striking down the ordinance. Yet the issue is far from resolved. Feminists and other critics of pornography continue to work to persuade other communities to adopt ordinances similar to the ill-fated Indianapolis law.

COMMERCIAL ADVERTISING

Prior to the mid-1970s, the Supreme Court regarded the regulation of commercial speech (a broad category including but not limited to the advertising of products and services) as simply an aspect of economic regulation, entitled to no special

First Amendment protection. In an important 1976 decision, however, the Court struck down Virginia's ban on the advertisement of prescription drug prices (*Virginia State Board of Pharmacy v. Virginia Citizens Consumer Council*). Writing for the Court, Justice Harry Blackmun stated that although reasonable time, place, and manner restrictions on commercial speech are legitimate and although the state is free to proscribe "false and misleading" advertisements, consumers have a strong First Amendment interest in the free flow of information about goods and services available in the marketplace. The Court soon extended this limited First Amendment protection to other forms of commercial speech, including attorney advertising (*Bates v. State Bar of Arizona* [1977]).

In *Central Hudson Gas and Electric Corporation v. Public Service Commission of New York* (1980), Justice Lewis Powell articulated the general rationale for First Amendment protection in this area:

> Commercial expression not only serves the economic interest of the speaker, but also assists consumers and furthers the societal interest in the fullest possible dissemination of information. In applying the First Amendment to this area, we have rejected the "highly paternalistic" view that government has complete power to suppress or regulate commercial speech.

In the same opinion, Justice Powell outlined a four-part test for evaluating regulations of commercial speech. To begin with, commercial speech must "concern lawful activity and not be misleading" if it is to be protected under the First Amendment. If this prerequisite is met, then three additional questions must be considered: (1) Is the "asserted governmental interest" in regulation substantial? (2) Does the regulation directly advance the asserted governmental interest? (3) Finally, is the regulation more extensive than is necessary to serve that purpose?

Justice Powell's analysis represented a compromise between competing approaches that stressed consumer protection on one hand and a free marketplace of ideas on the other. In 1986, a narrowly divided Supreme Court opted for the consumer-protection alternative. In *Posadas De Puerto Rico Associates v. Tourism Company,* the Court upheld a law prohibiting advertisements inviting residents of the territory of Puerto Rico to gamble legally in local casinos. In his majority opinion, Justice Rehnquist emphasized Puerto Rico's substantial interest in reducing the demand for casino gambling among its citizens and noted that the regulation at issue directly advanced this objective. He maintained that the legislature of Puerto Rico "surely could have prohibited casino gambling by the residents of Puerto Rico altogether." He concluded that this "greater power to completely ban casino gambling necessarily includes the lesser power to ban advertising of casino gambling."

In a strongly worded dissent, Justice Stevens contended that Puerto Rico had not merely banned the advertising of casino gambling. It had "blatantly" discriminated in punishing speech "depending on the publication, audience and words employed." In his view, the challenged prohibition established "a regime of prior restraint" and articulated a "hopelessly vague and unpredictable" standard. In spite of the somewhat restrictive (some would say paternalistic) ruling

The Problem of Cigarette Advertising

Federal law currently prohibits the advertising of cigarettes on television and radio. Those representing the tobacco industry have consistently maintained that this ban is unconstitutional, citing the protected status of commercial speech under the First Amendment. The Supreme Court has never ruled on this specific issue. How do you think the Court would rule in a case challenging the ban on cigarette advertising? What arguments would the government advance in support of the ban? If you were a member of the High Court, what position would you take on this question?

in *Posadas,* it is clear that a great many commercial messages today are entitled to First Amendment protection that was nonexistent two decades ago. This enlargement of freedom of expression in the commercial realm underscores the recognition that First Amendment freedoms are by no means limited to the traditional categories of political debate and social protest, important as these concerns are in a constitutional democracy.

THE SPECIAL CASE OF BROADCAST MEDIA

The Framers of the First Amendment could not have foreseen the invention of radio and television, let alone the prevalence of these electronic media in contemporary society. Nevertheless, because television and radio are used to express ideas in the public forum, most observers would agree that the electronic media deserve First Amendment protection, at least to some extent. Yet since their inception, radio and television have been regulated extensively by the federal government.

In order to operate a television or radio station, one must obtain a license from the Federal Communications Commission (FCC); to broadcast without a license from the FCC is a federal crime (as operators of "pirate" radio stations have often discovered). In granting licenses, the FCC is authorized to regulate the station's frequency, wattage, and hours of transmission. To a lesser extent, it also has the power to regulate the content of broadcasts. For example, the FCC has developed regulations to keep the airwaves free of "obscene" or "indecent" programming. Moreover, station licenses come up for renewal every three years, and the FCC is invested with tremendous discretion to determine whether a given station has been operating "in the public interest."

Clearly, government regulations that apply to the electronic media in the private sector would be unconstitutional if applied to the print media. The more permissive approach to government regulation of television and radio is predicated on the "scarcity theory," which holds that due to the limited number of available broadcast channels, the government must allocate this scarce resource in the public interest.

The FCC's Fairness Doctrine

Since its creation by Congress, the FCC has required broadcasters to devote a reasonable proportion of their air time to discussion of important public issues. Until 1987, the FCC interpreted this statutory mandate to require broadcasters engaged in editorials in which specific persons were criticized to provide notice to the persons involved and air time for rebuttal. This "fairness doctrine" was upheld by the Supreme Court in *Red Lion Broadcasting Company v. FCC* (1969). In *Red Lion,* the Court held that the FCC regulation had struck a reasonable balance between the public interest in hearing various points of view and the broadcaster's interests in free expression. Nevertheless, the fairness doctrine remained extremely controversial. It was finally repealed by the FCC in the summer of 1987.

Editorializing by Public Television and Radio Stations

Electronic media in the public sector have been subject to more restrictive government regulations on editorializing. Based on a 1967 act of Congress, the FCC prohibited public radio and television stations from engaging in editorializing altogether. However, in *FCC v. League of Women Voters* (1984), the Supreme Court declared this ban unconstitutional. Writing for a sharply divided Court, Justice Brennan concluded that the ban failed to meet a "least restrictive means test."

> [The] broad ban on all editorializing ... far exceeds what is necessary to protect against the risk of governmental interference or to prevent the public from assuming that editorials by public broadcasting stations represent the official view of government.

Restrictions of "Indecent" Programming

In a broad regulation that would almost certainly be declared unconstitutional if applied to a magazine or newspaper, the FCC has prohibited radio and television stations, whether public or private, from broadcasting "indecent" or "obscene" programs. In April 1987, the FCC made national news when it threatened to not renew the licenses of certain radio stations in New York and California. These stations were engaged in so-called "shock radio," which featured talk programs that were intentionally tasteless and given to heavy doses of profanity and frequent sexual references. Although the FCC's threats made headlines, there was little talk of litigation to challenge the agency's regulations. The Supreme Court had previously upheld restrictions on indecent broadcasting in *FCC v. Pacifica Foundation* (1978). In that case, the Court reviewed FCC regulations as applied to a radio broadcast of a monologue by comedian George Carlin that examined "seven dirty words you can't say on the radio." Attorneys for the Pacifica Foundation argued that the monologue in question did not meet the legal test of obscenity and therefore could not be banned from the radio by the FCC. Writing for the Court, Justice Stevens disagreed, observing that "when the Commission finds that a pig has entered the parlor, the exercise of its regulatory power does not depend on proof that the pig is obscene."

The growing availability of cable TV, which is not limited to a small number of channels, raises serious questions about the continued validity of the scarcity theory. However, it is unlikely that all the FCC regulations on the broadcast media will go the route of the fairness doctrine. In any event, cablecasts (as distinguished from broadcasts) are not subject to FCC content regulations. Thus, what may not be shown on CBS or one of the other broadcast networks may be shown on HBO or The Movie Channel, which are available exclusively to cable subscribers. Increasingly, there are calls for greater government regulation of so-called "premium" and "pay per view" channels, especially with regard to sexually oriented programming. The widespread diffusion of new communications technology in the 1970s and '80s has generated new constitutional questions for the 1990s.

CONCLUSION

Freedom of the press is far more than a felicitous phrase contained in the First Amendment. It represents a basic national commitment to the idea that a free press is essential to the survival of constitutional democracy. Although the American people often find fault with the mass media, most people understand and support the press in its watchdog role. For its part, the Supreme Court has buttressed the role of the media by erecting a high barrier against prior restraint and scrutinizing closely any form of press censorship. Yet, like all constitutional rights, freedom of the press is neither absolute nor unlimited. It must be balanced against the government's responsibility to protect national security, the interest of the criminal justice system in ferreting out crime, and society's interest in maintaining a modicum of public decency. Freedom of the press must also be weighed against the rights of individuals to be treated fairly and maintain a degree of personal privacy. The Supreme Court has shown that it is willing to circumscribe to some extent the First Amendment guarantee of freedom of the press in order to protect these other values.

FOR FURTHER READING

Adler, Renata. *Reckless Disregard*. New York: Vintage Books, 1986.

Clor, Harry. *Obscenity and Public Morality*. Chicago: University of Chicago Press, 1969.

Forer, Louis. *A Chilling Effect: The Mounting Threat of Libel and Invasion of Privacy Actions to the First Amendment*. New York: Norton, 1987.

Friendly, Fred W. *Minnesota Rag: The Dramatic Story of the Landmark Supreme Court Case That Gave Meaning to Freedom of the Press*. New York: Random House, 1981.

Friendly, Fred W. *The Good Guys, the Bad Guys and the First Amendment*. New York: Random House, 1976.

Labunski, Richard. *The First Amendment under Siege: The Politics of Broadcast Regulation*. Westport, Conn.: Greenwood Press, 1981.

Levy, Leonard W. *Emergence of a Free Press*. New York: Oxford University Press, 1985.

Lewis, Anthony. *Make No Law: The Sullivan Case and the First Amendment.* New York: Random House, 1991.

Lofton, John. *The Press as Guardian of the First Amendment.* Columbia: University of South Carolina Press, 1981.

McKenna, George. *A Guide to the Constitution: That Delicate Balance.* New York: Random House, 1984.

O'Brien, David. *The Public's Right to Know: The Supreme Court and the First Amendment.* New York: Praeger, 1981.

Powe, Lucas. *American Broadcasting and the First Amendment.* Berkeley: University of California Press, 1987.

Schmidt, Benno, Jr. *Freedom of the Press vs. Public Access.* New York: Praeger, 1976.

Shapiro, Martin. *The Pentagon Papers and the Courts: A Case Study in Foreign Policy Making and Freedom of the Press.* San Francisco: Chandler, 1975.

Smolla, Rodney. *Jerry Falwell v. Larry Flynt: The First Amendment on Trial.* New York: St. Martin's Press, 1988.

C A S E S   A N D   R E A D I N G S

Near v. Minnesota
283 U.S. 697; 51 S. Ct. 625; 75 L. Ed. 1357 (1931)
Vote: 5-4

Mr. Chief Justice Hughes delivered the opinion of the Court.

Chapter 285 of the Sessions Laws of Minnesota for the year 1925 provides for the abatement, as a public nuisance, of a "malicious, scandalous and defamatory newspaper, magazine or other periodical." Section one of the act is as follows:

Section 1: Any person who, as an individual, or as a member or employee of a firm, or association or organization, or as an officer, director, member or employee of a corporation, shall be engaged in the business of regularly or customarily producing, publishing or circulating, having in possession, selling or giving away, (a) an obscene, lewd and lascivious newspaper, magazine, or other periodical, or (b) a malicious, scandalous and defamatory newspaper, magazine or other periodical, is guilty of a nuisance, and all persons guilty of such nuisance may be enjoined, as hereinafter provided. . . .

In actions brought under (b) above, there shall be available the defense that the truth was published with good motives and for justifiable ends and in such actions the plaintiff shall not have the right to report [*sic*] to issues or editions of periodicals taking place more than three months before the commencement of the action.

Section two provides that whenever any such nuisance is committed or exists, the county attorney of any county where any such periodical is published or circulated, or, in case of his failure or refusal to proceed upon written request in good faith of a reputable citizen, the attorney general, or upon like failure or refusal of the latter, any citizen of the county, may maintain an action in the district court of the county in the name of the state to enjoin perpetually the persons committing or maintaining any such nuisance from further committing or maintaining it. Upon such evidence as the court shall deem sufficient, a temporary injunction may be granted. . . .

The action, by section three, is to be "governed by the practice and procedure applicable to civil actions for injunctions," and after trial the court may enter judgment permanently enjoining the defendants found guilty of violating the act from continuing the violation and, "in and by such judgment, such nuisance may be wholly abated." The court is empowered, as in other cases of contempt, to punish disobedience to a temporary or permanent injunction by fine of not more than $1,000 or by imprisonment in the county jail for not more than twelve months.

Under this statute . . . the county attorney of Hennepin county brought this action to enjoin the publication of what was described as a "malicious, scandalous and defamatory newspaper, magazine and periodical," known as "The Saturday Press," published by the defendants in the city of Minneapolis. The complaint alleged that the defendants, on September 24, 1927, and on eight subsequent dates in October and November, 1927, published and circulated editions of that periodical which were "largely devoted to malicious, scandalous and defamatory articles" concerning [various public officials and others].

Without attempting to summarize the contents of the voluminous exhibits attached to the complaint, we deem it sufficient to say that the articles charged in substance that a Jewish gangster was in control of gambling, bootlegging and racketeering in Minneapolis, and that law enforcing officers and agencies were not energetically performing their duties. Most of the charges were directed against the chief of police; he was charged with gross neglect of duty, illicit relations with gangsters, and with participation in graft. The county attorney was charged with knowing the existing conditions and with failure to take adequate measures to remedy them. The mayor was accused of inefficiency and dereliction. One member of the grand jury was stated to be in sympathy with the gangsters. A special grand jury and a special prosecutor were demanded to deal with the situation in general, and, in particular, to investigate an attempt to assassinate one Guilford, one of the original defendants, who, it appears from the articles, was shot by gangsters after the first issue of the periodical had been published. There is no question but that the articles made serious accusations against the public officers named and others in connection with the prevalence of crimes and the failure to expose and punish them.

At the beginning of the action on November 22, 1927, and upon the verified complaint, an order was made directing the defendants to show cause why a temporary injunction should not issue and meanwhile forbidding the defendants to publish, circulate or have in their possession any editions of the periodical from September 24, 1927, to November 19, 1927, inclusive, and from publishing, circulating, or having in their possession, "any future editions of said The Saturday Press" and "any publication, known by any other name whatsoever containing malicious, scandalous and defamatory matter of the kind alleged in plaintiff's complaint herein or otherwise."

The defendants demurred to the complaint upon the ground that it did not state facts sufficient to constitute a cause of action, and on this demurrer challenged the constitutionality of the statute. The district court overruled the demurrer and certified the question of constitutionality to the supreme court of the state. The supreme court sustained the statute *** and it is conceded by the appellee that the act was thus held to be valid over the objection that it violated not only the state Constitution, but also the Fourteenth Amendment of the Constitution of the United States.

Thereupon, the defendant Near, the present appellant, answered the complaint. He averred that he was the sole owner and proprietor of the publication in question. He admitted the publication of the articles in the issues described in the complaint but denied that they were malicious, scandalous or defamatory as alleged. He expressly invoked the protection of the Due Process Clause of the Fourteenth Amendment. The case then came on for trial. . . .

The district court made findings of fact, which followed the allegations of the complaint and found in general terms that the editions in question were "chiefly devoted to malicious, scandalous and defamatory articles," concerning the individuals named. The court further found that the defendants through

these publications "did engage in the business of regularly and customarily producing, publishing and circulating a malicious, scandalous and defamatory newspaper," and that "the said publication" "under said name of The Saturday Press, or any other name, constitutes a public nuisance under the laws of the state." Judgment was thereupon entered adjudging that "the newspaper, magazine and periodical known as The Saturday Press, as a public nuisance, be and is hereby abated. . . ."

The defendant Near appealed from this judgment to the supreme court of the state, again asserting his right under the Federal Constitution, and the judgment was affirmed upon the authority of the former decision. ***

From the judgment as thus affirmed, the defendant Near appeals to this Court.

This statute, for the suppression as a public nuisance of a newspaper or periodical, is unusual, if not unique, and raises questions of grave importance transcending the local interests involved in the particular action. It is no longer open to doubt that the liberty of the press and of speech is within the liberty safeguarded by the Due Process Clause of the Fourteenth Amendment from invasion by state action. It was found impossible to conclude that this essential personal liberty of the citizen was left unprotected by the general guaranty of fundamental rights of persons and property. *** Liberty of speech and of the press is not an absolute right, and the state may punish its abuse. Liberty, in each of its phases, has its history and connotation and, in the present instance, the inquiry is as to the historic conception of the liberty of the press and whether the statute under review violates the essential attributes of that liberty. . . .

If we cut through mere details of procedure, the operation and effect of the statute in substance is that public authorities may bring the owner or publisher of a newspaper or periodical before a judge upon a charge of conducting a business of publishing scandalous and defamatory matter—in particular that the matter consists of charges against public officers of official dereliction—and unless the owner or publisher is able and disposed to bring competent evidence to satisfy the judge that the charges are true and are published with good motives and for justifiable ends, his newspaper or periodical is suppressed and further publication is made punishable as a contempt. This is of the essence of censorship.

The question is whether a statute authorizing such proceedings in restraint of publication is consistent with the conception of the liberty of the press as historically conceived and guaranteed. In determining the extent of the constitutional protection, it has been generally, if not universally, considered that it is the chief purpose of the guaranty to prevent previous restraints upon publication. The struggle in England, directed against the legislative power of the licenser, resulted in renunciation of the censorship of the press. The liberty deemed to be established was thus described by Blackstone:

The liberty of the press is indeed essential to the nature of a free state; but this consists in laying no previous restraints upon publications, and not in freedom from censure for criminal matter when published. Every freeman has an undoubted right to lay what sentiments he pleases before the public; to forbid this, is to destroy the freedom of the press; but if he publishes what is improper, mischievous or illegal, he must take the consequences of his own temerity.
***

The criticism upon Blackstone's statement has not been because immunity from previous restraint upon publication has not been regarded as deserving of special emphasis, but chiefly because that immunity cannot be deemed to exhaust the conception of the liberty guaranteed by state and Federal constitutions. The point of criticism has been "that the mere exemption from previous restraints cannot be all that is secured by the constitutional provisions;" and that "the liberty of the press might be rendered a mockery and a delusion, and the phrase itself a by-word, if, while every man was at liberty to publish what he pleased, the public authorities might nevertheless punish him for harmless publications." ***

The objection has also been made that the principle as to immunity from previous restraint is stated too broadly, if every such restraint is deemed to be prohibited. That is undoubtedly true; the protection even as to previous restraint is not absolutely unlimited. But the limitation has been recognized only in exceptional cases. "When a nation is at war many things that might be said in time of peace are such a hindrance to its effort that their utterance will not be endured so long as men fight and that no court could

regard them as protected by any constitutional right." *** No one would question but that a government might prevent actual obstruction to its recruiting service or the publication of the sailing dates of transports or the number and location of troops. On similar grounds, the primary requirements of decency may be enforced against obscene publications. The security of the community life may be protected against incitements to acts of violence and the overthrow by force of orderly government. The constitutional guaranty of free speech does not "protect a man from an injunction against uttering words that may have all the effect of force. . . ."

The exceptional nature of its limitations places in a strong light the general conception that liberty of the press, historically considered and taken up by the Federal Constitution, has meant, principally, although not exclusively, immunity from previous restraints or censorship. The conception of the liberty of the press in this country has broadened with the exigencies of the colonial period and with the efforts to secure freedom from oppressive administration. That liberty was especially cherished for the immunity if afforded from previous restraint of the publication of censure of public officers and charges of official misconduct. . . .

The fact that for approximately one hundred and fifty years there has been almost an entire absence of attempts to impose previous restraints upon publications relating to the malfeasance of public officers is significant of the deep-seated conviction that such restraints would violate constitutional rights. Public officers, whose character and conduct remain open to debate and free discussion in the press, find their remedies for false accusations in actions under libel laws providing for redress and punishment, and not in proceedings to restrain the publication of newspapers and periodicals. . . .

The importance of this immunity has not lessened. While reckless assaults upon public men, and efforts to bring obloquy upon those who are endeavoring faithfully to discharge official duties, exert a baleful influence and deserve the severest condemnation in public opinion, it cannot be said that this abuse is greater, and it is believed to be less, than that which characterized the period in which our institutions took shape. Meanwhile, the administration of government has become more complex, the opportunities for malfeasance and corruption have multiplied, crime has grown to most serious proportions, and the danger of its protection by unfaithful officials and of the impairment of the fundamental security of life and property by criminal alliances and official neglect, emphasizes the primary need of a vigilant and courageous press, especially in great cities. The fact that the liberty of the press may be abused by miscreant purveyors of scandal does not make any the less necessary the immunity of the press from previous restraint in dealing with official misconduct. Subsequent punishment for such abuses as may exist is the appropriate remedy, consistent with constitutional privilege. . . .

The statute in question cannot be justified by reason of the fact that the publisher is permitted to show, before injunction issues, that the matter published is true, and is published with good motives and for justifiable ends. If such a statute, authorizing suppression and injunction on such a basis, is constitutionally valid, it would be equally permissible for the legislature to provide that at any time the publisher of any newspaper could be brought before a court, or even an administrative officer (as the constitutional protection may not be regarded as resting on mere procedural details) and required to produce proof of the truth of his publication, or of what he intended to publish, and of his motives, or stand enjoined. If this can be done, the legislature may provide machinery for determining in the complete exercise of its discretion what are justifiable ends and restrain publication accordingly. And it would be but a step to a complete system of censorship. The recognition of authority to impose previous restraint upon publication in order to protect the community against the circulation of charges of misconduct, and especially of official misconduct, necessarily would carry with it the admission of the authority of the censor against which the constitutional barrier was erected. The preliminary freedom, by virtue of the very reason for its existence, does not depend, as this court has said, on proof of truth. ***

Equally unavailing is the insistence that the statute is designed to prevent the circulation of scandal which tends to disturb the public peace and to provoke assaults and the commission of crime. Charges of reprehensible conduct, and in particular of official malfeasance, unquestionably create a public scandal, but the theory of the constitutional guaranty is that even a more serious public evil would be caused by authority to prevent publication.

For these reasons we hold the statute, so far as it authorized the proceedings in this action under clause (b) of section one, to be an infringement of the liberty of the press guaranteed by the Fourteenth Amendment. We should add that this decision rests upon the operation and effect of the statute, without regard to the question of the truth of the charges contained in the particular periodical. The fact that the public officers named in this case, and those associated with the charges of official dereliction, may be deemed to be impeccable, cannot affect the conclusion that the statute imposes an unconstitutional restraint upon publication.

Judgment reversed.

Mr. Justice Butler, dissenting:

The decision of the Court in this case declares Minnesota and every other state powerless to restrain by injunction the business of publishing and circulating among the people malicious, scandalous and defamatory periodicals that in due course of judicial procedure has been adjudged to be a public nuisance. It gives to freedom of the press a meaning and a scope not heretofore recognized and construes "liberty" in the Due Process Clause of the Fourteenth Amendment to put upon the states a Federal restriction that is without precedent. . . .

The Minnesota statute does not operate as a previous restraint on publication within the proper meaning of that phrase. It does not authorize administrative control in advance such as was formerly exercised by the licensers and censors but prescribes a remedy to be enforced by a suit in equity. In this case there was previous publication made in the course of the business of regularly producing malicious, scandalous and defamatory periodicals. The business and publications unquestionably constitute an abuse of the right of free press. The statute denounces the things done as a nuisance on the ground, as stated by the state supreme court, that they threaten morals, peace and good order. There is no question of the power of the state to denounce such transgressions.

The restraint authorized is only in respect of continuing to do what has been duly adjudged to constitute a nuisance. . . . There is nothing in the statute purporting to prohibit publications that have not been adjudged to constitute a nuisance. It is fanciful to suggest similarity between the granting or enforcement of the decree authorized by this statute to prevent further publication of malicious, scandalous and defamatory articles and the previous restraint upon the press by licensers as referred to by Blackstone and described in the history of the times to which he alludes. . . .

It is well known, as found by the state supreme court, that existing libel laws are inadequate effectively to suppress evils resulting from the kind of business and publications that are shown in this case.

The doctrine that measures such as the one before us are invalid because they operate as previous restraints to infringe freedom of press exposes the peace and good order of every community and the business and private affairs of every individual to the constant and protracted false and malicious assaults of any insolvent publisher who may have purpose and sufficient capacity to contrive and put into effect a scheme or program for oppression, blackmail or extortion.

The judgment should be affirmed.

Mr. Justice Van Devanter, Mr. Justice McReynolds, and *Mr. Justice Sutherland,* concur in this opinion.

New York Times Company v. United States (The Pentagon Papers Case)
403 U.S. 713; 91 S. Ct. 2140; 29 L. Ed.2d 822 (1971)
Vote: 6-3

Per Curiam.

We granted *certiorari* in these cases in which the United States seeks to enjoin the New York Times and the Washington Post from publishing the contents of a classified study entitled "History of U.S. Decision-Making Process on Viet Nam Policy."

"Any system of prior restraints of expression comes to this Court bearing a heavy presumption against its constitutional validity." *** The Government "thus carries a heavy burden of showing justification for the imposition of such a restraint." *** The District Court for the Southern District of New York in the *New York Times* case and the District Court for the District of Columbia and the Court of Appeals for the District of Columbia Circuit in the *Washington Post* case held that the Government had not met that burden. We agree.

The judgment of the Court of Appeals for the District of Columbia Circuit is therefore affirmed. The order of the Court of Appeals for the Second Circuit is reversed and the case is remanded with directions to enter a judgment affirming the judgment of the

District Court for the Southern District of New York. The stays entered June 25, 1971, by the Court are vacated. The judgments shall issue forthwith.

So ordered.

Mr. Justice Black, with whom *Mr. Justice Douglas* joins, concurring.

. . . I believe that every moment's continuance of the injunctions against these newspapers amounts to a flagrant, indefensible, and continuing violation of the First Amendment. . . . In my view it is unfortunate that some of my Brethren are apparently willing to hold that the publication of news may sometimes be enjoined. Such a holding would make a shambles of the First Amendment. . . .

In seeking injunctions against these newspapers and in its presentation to the Court, the Executive Branch seems to have forgotten the essential purpose and history of the First Amendment. . . .

In the First Amendment the Founding Fathers gave the free press the protection it must have to fulfill its essential role in our democracy. The press was to serve the governed, not the governors. The Government's power to censor the press was abolished so that the press would remain forever free to censure the Government. The press was protected so that it could bare the secrets of government and inform the people. Only a free and unrestrained press can effectively expose deception in government. And paramount among the responsibilities of a free press is the duty to prevent any part of the government from deceiving the people and sending them off to distant lands to die of foreign fevers and foreign shot and shell. In my view, far from deserving condemnation for their courageous reporting, the *New York Times,* the *Washington Post,* and other newspapers should be commended for serving the purpose that the Founding Fathers saw so clearly. In revealing the workings of government that led to the Vietnam war, the newspapers nobly did precisely that which the Founders hoped and trusted they would do. . . .

. . . [W]e are asked to hold that despite the First Amendment's emphatic command, the Executive Branch, the Congress, and the Judiciary can make laws enjoining publication of current news and abridging freedom of the press in the name of "national security." The Government does not even attempt to rely on any act of Congress. Instead it makes the bold and dangerously far-reaching contention that the courts should take it upon themselves to "make" a law abridging freedom of the press in the name of equity, presidential power, and national security, even when the representatives of the people in Congress have adhered to the command of the First Amendment and refused to make such a law. *** To find that the President has "inherent power" to halt the publication of news by resort to the courts would wipe out the First Amendment and destroy the fundamental liberty and security of the very people the Government hopes to make "secure." No one can read the history of the adoption of the First Amendment without being convinced beyond any doubt that it was injunctions like those sought here that Madison and his collaborators intended to outlaw in this Nation for all time.

The word "security" is a broad, vague generality whose contours should not be invoked to abrogate the fundamental law embodied in the First Amendment. The guarding of military and diplomatic secrets at the expense of informed representative government provides no real security for our Republic. The Framers of the First Amendment, fully aware of both the need to defend a new nation and the abuses of the English and colonial Governments, sought to give this new society strength and security by providing that freedom of speech, press, religion, and assembly should not be abridged. . . .

Mr. Justice Douglas, with whom **Mr. Justice Black** joins, concurring.

. . . The Government says that it has inherent powers to go into court and obtain an injunction to protect the national interest, which in this case is alleged to be national security.

Near v. Minnesota [1931] *** repudiated that expansive doctrine in no uncertain terms.

The dominant purpose of the First Amendment was to prohibit the widespread practice of governmental suppression of embarrassing information. It is common knowledge that the First Amendment was adopted against the widespread use of the common law of seditious libel to punish the dissemination of material that is embarrassing to the powers-that-be. *** The present cases will, I think, go down in history as the most dramatic illustration of that principle. A debate of large proportions goes on in the Nation over our posture in Vietnam. That debate antedated the disclosure of the contents of the present documents. The latter are highly relevant to the debate in progress.

Secrecy in government is fundamentally anti-democratic, perpetuating bureaucratic errors. Open debate and discussion of public issues are vital to our national health. On public questions there should be "uninhibited, robust, and wide-open" debate. ***

Mr. Justice Brennan, concurring.

I

I write separately in these cases only to emphasize what should be apparent: that our judgments in the present cases may not be taken to indicate the propriety, in the future, of issuing temporary stays and restraining orders to block the publication of material sought to be suppressed by the Government. So far as I can determine, never before has the United States sought to enjoin a newspaper from publishing information in its possession. The relative novelty of the question presented, the necessary haste with which decisions were reached, the magnitude of the interests asserted, and the fact that all the parties have concentrated their arguments upon the question whether permanent restraints were proper may have justified at least some of the restraints heretofore imposed in these cases. Certainly it is difficult to fault the several courts below for seeking to assure that the issues here involved were preserved for ultimate review by this Court. But even if it be assumed that some of the interim restraints were proper in the two cases before us, that assumption has no bearing upon the propriety of similar judicial action in the future. To begin with, there has now been ample time for reflection and judgment; whatever values there may be in the preservation of novel questions for appellate review may not support any restraints in the future. More important, the First Amendment stands as an absolute bar to the imposition of judicial restraints in circumstances of the kind presented by these cases.

II

The error that has pervaded these cases from the outset was the granting of any injunctive relief whatsoever, interim or otherwise. The entire thrust of the Government's claim throughout these cases has been that publication of the material sought to be enjoined "could," or "might," or "may" prejudice the national interest in various ways. But the First Amendment tolerates absolutely no prior judicial restraints of the press predicated upon surmise or conjecture that untoward consequences may result. . . .

Mr. Justice Stewart, with whom *Mr. Justice White* joins, concurring.

In the governmental structure created by our Constitution, the Executive is endowed with enormous power in the two related areas of national defense and international relations. This power, largely unchecked by the Legislative and Judicial branches, has been pressed to the very hilt since the advent of the nuclear missile age. For better or for worse, the

simple fact is that a President of the United States possesses vastly greater constitutional independence in these two vital areas of power than does, say, a prime minister of a country with a parliamentary form of government.

In the absence of the governmental checks and balances present in other areas of our national life, the only effective restraint upon executive policy and power in the areas of national defense and international affairs may lie in an enlightened citizenry—in an informal and critical public opinion which alone can here protect the values of democratic government. For this reason, it is perhaps here that a press that is alert, aware, and free most vitally serves the basic purpose of the First Amendment. For without an informed and free press there cannot be an enlightened people.

Yet it is elementary that the successful conduct of international diplomacy and the maintenance of an effective national defense require both confidentiality and secrecy. Other nations can hardly deal with this Nation in an atmosphere of mutual trust unless they can be assured that their confidences will be kept. And within our own executive departments, the development of considered and intelligent international policies would be impossible if those charged with their formulation could not communicate with each other freely, frankly, and in confidence. In the area of basic national defense the frequent need for absolute secrecy is, of course, self-evident.

I think there can be but one answer to this dilemma, if dilemma it be. The responsibility must be where the power is. If the Constitution gives the Executive a large degree of unshared power in the conduct of foreign affairs and the maintenance of our national defense, then under the Constitution the Executive must have the largely unshared duty to determine and preserve the degree of internal security necessary to exercise that power successfully. It is an awesome responsibility, requiring judgment and wisdom of a high order. I should suppose that moral, political, and practical considerations would dictate that a very first principle of that wisdom would be an insistence upon avoiding secrecy for its own sake. For when everything is classified, then nothing is classified, and the system becomes one to be disregarded by the cynical or the careless, and to be manipulated by those intent on self-protection or self-promotion. I should suppose, in short, that the hallmark of a truly effective internal security system would be the maximum possible disclosure, recognizing that secrecy can best be preserved only when credibility is truly maintained. But be that as it may, it is clear to me that it is the constitutional duty of the Executive—as a matter of sovereign prerogative and not as a matter of law as the courts know law—through the promulgation and enforcement of executive regulations, to protect the confidentiality necessary to carry out its responsibilities in the fields of international relations and national defense.

This is not to say that Congress and the courts have no role to play. Undoubtedly Congress has the power to enact specific and appropriate criminal laws to protect government property and preserve government secrets. Congress has passed such laws, and several of them are of very colorable relevance to the apparent circumstances of these cases. And if a criminal prosecution is instituted, it will be the responsibility of the courts to decide the applicability of the criminal law under which the charge is brought. Moreover, if Congress should pass a specific law authorizing civil proceedings in this field, the courts would likewise have the duty to decide the constitutionality of such a law as well as its applicability to the facts proved.

But in the cases before us we are asked neither to construe specific regulations nor to apply specific laws. We are asked, instead, to perform a function that the Constitution gave to the Executive, not the Judiciary. We are asked, quite simply, to prevent the publication by two newspapers of material that the Executive Branch insists should not, in the national interest, be published. I am convinced that the Executive is correct with respect to some of the documents involved. But I cannot say that disclosure of any of them will surely result in direct, immediate, and irreparable damage to our Nation or its people. That being so, there can under the First Amendment be but one judicial resolution of the issues before us. I join the judgments of the Court.

Mr. Justice White, with whom **Mr. Justice Stewart** joins, concurring.

I concur in today's judgments, but only because of the concededly extraordinary protection against prior restraints enjoyed by the press under our constitutional system. I do not say that in no circumstances would the First Amendment permit an injunction against publishing information about government plans or operations. Nor, after examining the materials the Government characterizes as the most sensitive and destructive, can I deny that revelation of these documents will do substantial damage to public interests. Indeed, I am confident that their disclosure will have that result. But I nevertheless agree that the United States has not satisfied the very heavy burden that it must meet to warrant an injunction against publication in these cases, as least in the absence of express and appropriately limited congressional authorization for prior restraints in circumstances such as these. . . .

Mr. Justice Marshall, concurring.

The Government contends that the only issue in these cases is whether in a suit by the United States, "the First Amendment bars a court from prohibiting a newspaper from publishing material whose disclosure would pose a 'grave and immediate danger to the security of the United States.' " With all due respect, I believe that the ultimate issue in this case is even more basic than the one posed by the Solicitor General. The issue is whether this Court or the Congress has the power to make law. . . .

It would . . . be utterly inconsistent with the concept of separation of powers for this Court to use its power of contempt to prevent behavior that Congress has specifically declined to prohibit. There would be a similar damage to the basic concept of these co-equal branches of Government if when the Executive Branch has adequate authority granted by Congress to protect "national security" it can choose instead to invoke the contempt power of a court to enjoin the threatened conduct. The Constitution provides that Congress shall make laws, the President execute laws, and courts interpret laws. It did not provide for government by injunction in which the courts and the Executive Branch can "make law" without regard to the action of Congress. It may be more convenient for the Executive Branch if it need only convince a judge to prohibit conduct rather than ask the Congress to pass a law, and it may be more convenient to enforce a contempt order than to seek a criminal conviction in a jury trial. Moreover, it may be considered politically wise to get a court to share the responsibility for arresting those who the Executive Branch has probable cause to believe are violating the law. But convenience and political considerations of the moment do not justify a basic departure from the principles of our system of government. . . .

Mr. Chief Justice Burger, dissenting.

. . . I suggest . . . these cases have been conducted in unseemly haste. Mr. Justice Harlan covers the chronology of events demonstrating the hectic pressures under which these cases have been processed and I need not restate them. The prompt setting of these cases reflects our universal abhorrence of prior restraint. But prompt judicial action does not mean unjudicial haste.

Here, moreover, the frenetic haste is due in large part to the manner in which the *Times* proceeded from the date it obtained the purloined documents. It seems reasonably clear now that the haste precluded reasonable and deliberate judicial treatment of these cases and was not warranted. The precipitate action of this Court aborting trials not yet completed is not the kind of judicial conduct that ought to attend the disposition of a great issue.

The newspapers make a derivative claim under the First Amendment; they denominate this right as the public "right to know"; by implication, the *Times* asserts a sole trusteeship of that right by virtue of its journalistic "scoop." The right is asserted as an absolute. Of course, the First Amendment right itself is not an absolute, as Justice Holmes so long ago pointed out in his aphorism concerning the right to shout "fire" in a crowded theater if there was no fire. There are other exceptions, some of which Chief Justice Hughes mentioned by way of example in *Near v. Minnesota.* There are no doubt other exceptions no one has had occasion to describe or discuss. Conceivably such exceptions may be lurking in these cases and would have been flushed had they been properly considered in the trial courts, free from unwarranted deadlines and frenetic pressures. An issue of this importance should be tried and heard in

a judicial atmosphere conducive to thoughtful, reflective deliberation, especially when haste, in terms of hours, is unwarranted in light of the long period the *Times*, by its own choice, deferred publication.

It is not disputed that the *Times* has had unauthorized possession of the documents for three to four months, during which it has had its expert analysts studying them, presumably digesting them and preparing the material for publication. During all of this time, the *Times* presumably in its capacity as trustee of the public's "right to know," had held up publication for purposes it considered proper and thus public knowledge was delayed. No doubt this was for a good reason; the analysis of 7,000 pages of complex material drawn from a vastly greater volume of material would inevitably take time and the writing of good news stories takes time. But why should the United States Government, from whom this information was illegally acquired by someone, along with all the counsel, trial judges, and appellate judges be placed under needless pressure? After these months of deferral, the alleged "right to know" has somehow and suddenly become a right that must be vindicated instanter.

Would it have been unreasonable since the newspaper could anticipate the Government's objections to release of secret material, to give the Government an opportunity to review the entire collection and determine whether agreement could be reached on publication? Stolen or not, if security was not in fact jeopardized, much of the material could no doubt have been declassified, since it spans a period ending in 1968. With such an approach—one that great newspapers have in the past practiced and stated editorially to be the duty of an honorable press—the newspapers and Government might well have narrowed the area of disagreement as to what was and was not publishable, leaving the remainder to be resolved in orderly litigation, if necessary. To me it is hardly believable that a newspaper long regarded as a great institution in American life would fail to perform one of the basic and simple duties of every citizen with respect to the discovery or possession of stolen property or secret government documents. That duty, I had thought—perhaps naively—was to report forthwith, to responsible public officers. This duty rests on taxi drivers, Justices and the *New York*

Times. The course followed by the *Times,* whether so calculated or not, removed any possibility of orderly litigation of the issues. If the action of the judges up to now has been correct, that result is sheer happenstance. . . .

Mr. Justice Harlan, with whom the **Chief Justice** and **Mr. Justice Blackmun** join, dissenting.

These cases forcefully call to mind the wise admonition of Mr. Justice Holmes. ***

"Great cases like hard cases make bad law. For great cases are called great, not by reason of their real importance in shaping the law of the future, but because of some accident of immediate overwhelming interest which appeals to the feelings and distorts the judgment. These immediate interests exercise a kind of hydraulic pressure which makes what previously was clear seem doubtful, and before which even well settled principles of law will bend." *** With all respect, I consider that the Court has been almost irresponsibly feverish in dealing with these cases."

This frenzied train of events took place in the name of the presumption against prior restraints created by the First Amendment. Due regard for the extraordinarily important and difficult questions involved in these litigations should have led the Court to shun such a precipitate timetable. . . .

Pending further hearings in each case conducted under the appropriate ground rules, I would continue the restraints on publication. I cannot believe that the doctrine prohibiting prior restraints reaches to the point of preventing courts from maintaining the status quo long enough to act responsibly in matters of such national importance as those involved here. . . .

Mr. Justice Blackmun, dissenting.

. . . The First Amendment, after all, is only one part of an entire Constitution. Article II of the great document vests in the Executive Branch primary power over the conduct of foreign affairs and places in that branch the responsibility for the Nation's safety. Each provision of the Constitution is important, and I cannot subscribe to a doctrine of unlimited absolutism for the First Amendment at the cost of downgrading other provisions. . . .

Nebraska Press Association v. Stuart
427 U.S. 539; 96 S. Ct. 2791; 49 L. Ed. 2d 683 (1976)
Vote: 9-0

This case stems from the brutal murder of six members of the Henry Kelly family in Sutherland, Nebraska, on the night of October 18, 1975. Erwin Simants, an unemployed handyman and a nearby neighbor of the Kellys, was accused of the crime. Evidence indicated that the victims died as a result of wounds inflicted with a .22-caliber rifle and that some of the victims had been sexually assaulted after the wounds had been inflicted. The grisly crime generated widespread publicity, much of which was obviously prejudicial to the accused. Three days after Simants was arrested, attorneys for the state and the defense asked the local court to issue an order restricting media coverage of the case. The court complied and issued an order prohibiting reportage of certain aspects of the case (State v.
Simants) until a trial jury could be empaneled. The Nebraska Press Association filed this civil suit challenging the constitutionality of the "gag order." After the Nebraska Supreme Court upheld the lower court's order, the Nebraska Press Association took the case to the U.S. Supreme Court on a writ of certiorari. Before the Supreme Court handed down its decision, Erwin Simants was convicted and sentenced to death. Ultimately, however, his conviction was reversed by the Nebraska Supreme Court after it was found that the local sheriff had visited the trial jurors at the motel where they were sequestered during the course of the trial. At his second murder trial, Simants was found not guilty by reason of insanity. At this time, he is still confined to a Nebraska mental hospital.

Mr. Chief Justice Burger delivered the opinion of the Court:

... The problems presented by this case are almost as old as the Republic. Neither in the Constitution nor in contemporaneous writings do we find that the conflict between these two important rights was anticipated, yet it is inconceivable that the authors of the Constitution were unaware of the potential conflicts between the right to an unbiased jury and the guarantee of freedom of the press. The unusually able lawyers who helped write the Constitution and later drafted the Bill of Rights were familiar with the historic episode in which John Adams defended British soldiers charged with homicide for firing into a crowd of Boston demonstrators; they were intimately familiar with the clash of the adversary system and the part that the passions of the populace sometimes play in influencing potential jurors. They did not address themselves directly to the situation presented by this case; their chief concern was the need for freedom of expression in the political arena and the dialogue in ideas. But they recognized that there were risks to private rights from an unfettered press. ...

The Sixth Amendment in terms guarantees "trial, by an impartial jury ..." in federal criminal prosecutions. Because "trial by jury in criminal cases is fundamental to the American scheme of justice," the Due Process Clause of the Fourteenth Amendment guarantees the same right in state criminal prosecutions. ...

In the overwhelming majority of criminal trials, pretrial publicity presents few unmanageable threats to this important right. But when the case is a "sensational" one tensions develop between the right of the accused to trial by an impartial jury and the rights guaranteed others by the First Amendment. The relevant decisions of the Court, even if not dispositive, are instructive by way of background. ...

In *Sheppard v. Maxwell* [1966] *** the Court focused sharply on the impact of pretrial publicity and a trial court's duty to protect the defendant's constitutional right to a fair trial. With only Mr. Justice Black dissenting, and he without opinion, the Court ordered a new trial for the petitioner, even though the first trial had occurred 12 years before. Beyond doubt the press had shown no responsible concern

for the constitutional guarantee of a fair trial; the community from which the jury was drawn had been inundated by publicity hostile to the defendant. But the trial judge "did not fulfill his duty to protect [the defendant] from the inherently prejudicial publicity which saturated the community and to control disruptive influences in the courtroom." *** The Court noted that "unfair and prejudicial news comment on pending trials has become increasingly prevalent. ...." Because the trial court had failed to use even minimal efforts to insulate the trial and the jurors from the "deluge of publicity" ... the Court vacated the judgment of conviction and a new trial followed, in which the accused was acquitted.

Cases such as these are relatively rare, and we have held in other cases that trials have been fair in spite of widespread publicity. ...

... [T]hese cases demonstrate that pretrial publicity—even pervasive, adverse publicity—does not inevitably lead to an unfair trial. The capacity of the jury eventually impaneled to decide the case fairly is influenced by the tone and extent of the publicity, which is in part, and often in large part, shaped by what attorneys, police, and other officials do to precipitate news coverage. The trial judge has a major responsibility. What the judge says about a case, in or out of the courtroom, is likely to appear in newspapers and broadcasts. More important, the measures a judge takes or fails to take to mitigate the effects of pretrial publicity—the measures described in *Sheppard*—may well determine whether the defendant receives a trial consistent with the requirements of due process. That this responsibility has not always been properly discharged is apparent from the decisions just reviewed.

The costs of failure to afford a fair trial are high. In the most extreme cases, ... the risk of injustice was avoided when the convictions were reversed. But a reversal means that justice has been delayed for both the defendant and the State; in some cases, because of lapse of time retrial is impossible or further prosecution is gravely handicapped. Moreover, in borderline cases in which the conviction is not reversed, there is some possibility of an injustice unredressed. The "strong measures" outlined in *Sheppard v. Maxwell* are means by which a trial judge can try to avoid exacting these costs from society or from the accused.

The state trial judge in the case before us acted responsibly, out of a legitimate concern, in an effort to protect the defendant's right to a fair trial. What we must decide is not simply whether the Nebraska courts erred in seeing the possibility of real danger to the defendant's rights, but whether in the circumstances of this case the means employed were foreclosed by another provision of the Constitution.

The First Amendment provides that "Congress shall make no law . . . abridging the freedom . . . of the press," and it is "no longer open to doubt that the liberty of the press, and of speech, is within the liberty safe-guarded by the Due Process Clause of the Fourteenth Amendment from invasion by state action." *Near v. Minnesota* [1931]. *** The Court has interpreted these guarantees to afford special protection against orders that prohibit the publication or broadcast of particular information or commentary—orders that impose a "previous" or "prior" restraint on speech. None of our decided cases on prior restraint involved restrictive orders entered to protect a defendant's right to a fair and impartial jury, but the opinions on prior restraint have a common thread relevant to this case. . . .

More recently in *New York Times Co. v. United States* [1971] *** the Government sought to enjoin the publication of excerpts from a massive, classified study of the Nation's involvement in the Vietnam conflict, going back to the end of the Second World War. The dispositive opinion of the Court simply concluded that the government had not met its heavy burden of showing justification for the prior restraint. Each of the six concurring Justices and the three dissenting Justices expressed his views separately, but "every member of the Court, tacitly or explicitly, accepted the *Near* . . . condemnation of prior restraint as presumptively unconstitutional." *** The Court's conclusion in *New York Times* suggests that the burden on the government is not reduced by the temporary nature of a restraint; in that case the Government asked for a temporary restraint solely to permit it to study and assess the impact on national security of the lengthy documents at issue.

The thread running through all these cases is that prior restraints on speech and publication are the most serious and the least tolerable infringement on First Amendment rights. . . .

. . . The extraordinary protections afforded by the First Amendment carry with them something in the nature of a fiduciary duty to exercise the protected rights responsibly—a duty widely acknowledged but not always observed by editors and publishers. It is not asking too much to suggest that those who exercise First Amendment rights in newspapers or broadcasting enterprises direct some effort to protect the rights of an accused to a fair trial by unbiased jurors.

Of course, the order at issue—like the other requested in *New York Times*—does not prohibit but only postpones publication. Some news can be delayed and most commentary can even more readily be delayed without serious injury, and there often is a self-imposed delay when responsible editors call for verification of information. But such delays are normally slight and they are self-imposed. Delays imposed by governmental authority are a different matter.

We have learned, and continue to learn, from what we view as the unhappy experiences of other nations where government has been allowed to meddle in the internal editorial affairs of newspapers. Regardless of how beneficent-sounding the purposes of controlling the press might be, we . . . remain intensely skeptical about those measures that would allow government to insinuate itself into the editorial rooms of this Nation's press. ***

. . . As a practical matter, moreover, the element of time is not unimportant if press coverage is to fulfill its traditional function of bringing news to the public promptly.

The authors of the Bill of Rights did not undertake to assign priorities as between First Amendment and Sixth Amendment rights, ranking one as superior to the other. In this case, the petitioners would have us declare the right of an accused subordinate to their right to publish in all circumstances. But if the authors of these guarantees, fully aware of the potential conflicts between them, were unwilling or unable to resolve the issue by assigning to one priority over the other, it is not for us to rewrite the Constitution by undertaking what they declined to do. It is unnecessary, after nearly two centuries, to establish a priority applicable in all circumstances. Yet it is nonetheless clear that the barriers to prior restraint remain high unless we are to abandon what the Court has said for nearly a quarter of our national existence and implied throughout all of it. The history of even wartime suspension of categorical guarantees, such as habeas corpus or the right to trial by civilian courts *** cautions against suspending explicit guarantees.

The Nebraska courts in this case enjoined the publication of certain kinds of information about the *Simants* case. There are, as we suggested earlier, marked differences in setting and purpose between the order entered here and the orders in *Near* ... and *New York Times,* but as to the underlying issue—the right of the press to be free from prior restraints on publication—those cases form the backdrop against which we must decide this case.

We turn now to the record in this case to determine whether, as Learned Hand put it, "the gravity of the 'evil,' discounted by its improbability, justifies such invasion of free speech as is necessary to avoid the danger." *** To do so, we must examine the evidence before the trial judge when the order was entered to determine (a) the nature and extent of pretrial news coverage; (b) whether other measures would be likely to mitigate the effects of unrestrained pretrial publicity; and (c) how effectively a restraining order would operate to prevent the threatened danger. The precise terms of the restraining order are also important. We must then consider whether the record supports the entry of a prior restraint on publication, one of the most extraordinary remedies known to our jurisprudence....

Our review of the pretrial record persuades us that the trial judge was justified in concluding that there would be intense and pervasive pretrial publicity concerning this case. He could also reasonably conclude, based on common human experience, that publicity might impair the defendant's right to a fair trial. He did not purport to say more, for he found only "a clear and present danger that pre-trial publicity *could* impinge upon the defendant's right to a fair trial." *** His conclusion as to the impact of such publicity on prospective jurors was of necessity speculative, dealing as he was with factors unknown and unknowable.

We find little in the record that goes to another aspect of our task, determining whether measures short of an order restraining all publication would have insured the defendant a fair trial....

We have noted earlier that pretrial publicity, even if pervasive and concentrated, cannot be regarded as leading automatically and in every kind of criminal case to an unfair trial....

... There is no finding that alternative measures would not have protected Simants' rights, and the Nebraska Supreme Court did no more than imply that such measures might not be adequate. Moreover, the record is lacking in evidence to support such a finding.

We must also assess the probable efficacy of prior restraint on publication as a workable method of protecting Simants' right to a fair trial, and we cannot ignore the reality of the problems of managing and enforcing pretrial restraining orders....

Finally, we note that the events disclosed by the record took place in a community of 850 people. It is reasonable to assume that, without any news accounts being printed or broadcast, rumors would travel swiftly by word of mouth. One can only speculate on the accuracy of such reports, given the generative propensities of rumors; they could well be more damaging than reasonably accurate news accounts. But plainly a whole community cannot be restrained from discussing a subject intimately affecting life within it.

Given these practical problems, it is far from clear that prior restraint on publication would have protected Simants' rights.

Finally, another feature of this case leads us to conclude that the restrictive order entered here is not supportable. At the outset the County Court entered a very broad restrictive order, the terms of which are not before us; it then held a preliminary hearing open to the public and the press. There was testimony concerning at least two incriminating statements made by Simants to private persons; the statement—evidently a confession—that he gave to law enforcement officials was also introduced....

To the extent that this order prohibited the reporting of evidence adduced at the open preliminary hearing, it plainly violated settled principles: "[T]here is nothing that proscribes the press from reporting events that transpire in the courtroom." *** The County Court could not know that closure of the preliminary hearing was an alternative open to it until the Nebraska Supreme Court so construed state law; but once a public hearing had been held, what transpired there could not be subject to prior restraint. . . .

The record demonstrates, as the Nebraska courts held, that there was indeed a risk that pretrial news accounts, true or false, would have some adverse impact on the attitudes of those who might be called as jurors. But on the record now before us it is not clear that further publicity, unchecked, would so distort the views of potential jurors that 12 could not be found who would, under proper instructions, fulfill their sworn duty to render a just verdict exclusively on the evidence presented in open court. We cannot say on this record that alternatives to a prior restraint on petitioners would not have sufficiently mitigated the adverse effects of pretrial publicity so as to make prior restraint unnecessary. Nor can we conclude that the restraining order actually entered would serve its intended purpose. Reasonable minds can have few doubts about the gravity of the evil pretrial publicity can work, but the probability that it would do so here was not demonstrated with the degree of certainty our cases on prior restraint require. . . .

Our analysis ends as it began, with a confrontation between prior restraint imposed to protect one vital constitutional guarantee and the explicit command of another that the freedom to speak and publish shall not be abridged. We reaffirm that the guarantees of freedom of expression are not an absolute prohibition under all circumstances, but the barriers to prior restraint remain high and the presumption against its use continues intact. We hold that, with respect to the order entered in this case prohibiting reporting or commentary on judicial proceedings held in public, the barriers have not been overcome; to the extent that this order restrained publication of such material, it is clearly invalid. To the extent that it prohibited publication based on information gained from other sources, we conclude that the heavy burden imposed as a condition to securing a prior restraint was not met and the judgment of the Nebraska Supreme Court is therefore Reversed.

Mr. Justice White, concurring. . . .

Mr. Justice Powell, concurring. . . .

Mr. Justice Brennan, with whom **Mr. Justice Stewart** and **Mr. Justice Marshall** join, concurring in the judgment.

. . . The right to a fair trial by a jury of one's peers is unquestionably one of the most precious and sacred safeguards enshrined in the Bill of Rights. I would hold, however, that resort to prior restraints on the freedom of the press is a constitutionally impermissible method for enforcing that right; judges have at their disposal a broad spectrum of devices for ensuring that fundamental fairness is accorded the accused without necessitating so drastic an incursion on the equally fundamental and salutary constitutional mandate that discussion of public affairs in a free society cannot depend on the preliminary grace of judicial censors. . . .

I unreservedly agree with Mr. Justice Black that "free speech and fair trials are two of the most cherished policies of our civilization, and it would be a trying task to choose between them." But I would reject the notion that a choice is necessary, that there is an inherent conflict and cannot be resolved without essentially abrogating one right or the other. To hold that courts cannot impose any prior restraints on the reporting of or commentary upon information revealed in open court proceedings, disclosed in public documents, or divulged by other sources with respect to the criminal justice system is not, I must emphasize, to countenance the sacrifice of precious Sixth Amendment rights on the altar of the First Amendment. For although there may in some instances be tension between uninhibited and robust reporting by the press and fair trials for criminal defendants, judges possess adequate tools short of injunctions against reporting for relieving that tension. To be sure, these alternatives may require greater sensitivity and effort on the part of judges conducting criminal trials than would the stifling of publicity through the simple expedient of issuing a restrictive order on the press; but that sensitivity and effort is required in order to ensure the full enjoyment and proper accommodation of both First and Sixth Amendment rights.

There is, beyond peradventure, a clear and substantial damage to freedom of the press whenever even a temporary restraint is imposed on reporting of material concerning the operations of the criminal justice system, an institution of such pervasive influence in our constitutional scheme. And the necessary impact of reporting even confessions can never be so direct, immediate, and irreparable that I would give credence to any notion that prior restraints may be imposed on that rationale. It may be that such incriminating material would be of such slight news value or so inflammatory in particular cases that responsible organs of the media, in an exercise of self-restraint, would choose not to publicize that material, and not make the judicial task of safeguarding precious rights of criminal defendants more difficult. Voluntary codes such as the Nebraska Bar-Press Guidelines are a commendable acknowledgment by the media that constitutional prerogatives bring enormous responsibilities, and I would encourage continuation of such voluntary cooperative efforts between the bar and the media. However, the press may be arrogant, tyrannical, abusive, and sensationalist, just as it may be incisive, probing, and informative. But at least in the context of prior restraints on publication, the decision of what, when, and how to publish is for editors, not judges. *** Every restrictive order imposed on the press in this case was accordingly an unconstitutional prior restraint on the freedom of the press, and I would therefore reverse the judgment of the Nebraska Supreme Court and remand for further proceedings not inconsistent with this opinion. . . .

Mr. Justice Stevens, concurring in the judgment. . . .

New York Times Company v. Sullivan
376 U.S. 254; 84 S. Ct. 710; 11 L. Ed. 2d 686 (1964)
Vote: 9-0

Mr. Justice Brennan delivered the opinion of the Court.

We are required in this case to determine for the first time the extent to which the constitutional protections for speech and press limit a State's power to award damages in a libel action brought by a public official against critics of his official conduct.

Respondent L. B. Sullivan is one of the three elected Commissioners of the City of Montgomery, Alabama. He testified that he was "Commissioner of Public Affairs and the duties are supervision of the Police Department, Fire Department, Department of Cemetery and Department of Scales." He brought this civil libel action against the four individual petitioners, who are Negroes and Alabama clergymen, and against petitioner the New York Times Company, a New York corporation which publishes the *New York Times,* a daily newspaper. A jury in the Circuit Court of Montgomery County awarded him damages of $500,000, the full amount claimed, against all the petitioners and the Supreme Court of Alabama affirmed. ***

Respondent's complaint alleged that he had been libeled by statements in a full-page advertisement that was carried in the *New York Times* on March 29, 1960. Entitled "Heed Their Rising Voices," the advertisement began by stating that "As the whole world knows by now, thousands of Southern Negro students are engaged in widespread non-violent demonstrations in positive affirmation of the right to live in human dignity as guaranteed by the U.S. Constitution and the Bill of Rights." It went on to charge that "in their efforts to uphold these guarantees, they are being met by an unprecedented wave of terror by those who would deny and negate that document which the whole world looks upon as setting the pattern for modern freedom. . . ." Succeeding paragraphs purported to illustrate the "wave of terror" by describing certain alleged events. The text concluded with an appeal for funds for three purposes: support of the student movement, "the struggle for the right-to-vote," and the legal defense of Dr. Martin Luther King, Jr., leader of the movement, against a perjury indictment then pending in Montgomery.

The text appeared over the names of 64 persons, many widely known for their activities in public affairs, religion, trade unions, and the performing arts. Below these names, and under a line reading "We in the south who are struggling daily for dignity and freedom warmly endorse this appeal," appeared the names of the four individual petitioners and of 16 other persons, all but two of whom were identified as clergymen in various Southern cities. The advertisement was signed at the bottom of the page by the "Committee to Defend Martin Luther King and the Struggle for Freedom in the South," and the officers of the Committee were listed.

Of the 10 paragraphs of text in the advertisement, the third and a portion of the sixth were the basis of respondent's claim of libel. They read as follows:

Third paragraph:

In Montgomery, Alabama, after students sang "My Country, 'Tis of Thee" on the State Capitol steps, their leaders were expelled from school, and truckloads of police armed with shotguns and tear-gas ringed the Alabama State College Campus. When the entire student body protested to state authorities by refusing to re-register, their dining hall was padlocked in an attempt to starve them into submission.

Sixth paragraph:

Again and again the Southern violators have answered Dr. King's peaceful protests with intimidation and violence. They have bombed his home almost killing his wife and child. They have assaulted his person. They have arrested him seven times—for "speeding," "loitering" and similar "offenses." And now they have charged him with "perjury"— a *felony* under which they could imprison him for *ten years*....

Although neither of these statements mentions respondent by name, he contended that the word "police" in the third paragraph referred to him as the Montgomery Commissioner who supervised the Police Department, so that he was being accused of "ringing" the campus with police. He further claimed that the paragraph would be read as imputing to the police, and hence to him, the padlocking of the dining hall in order to starve the students into submission. As to the sixth paragraph, he contended that since arrests are ordinarily made by the police, the statement "They have arrested [Dr. King] seven times" would be read as referring to him; he further contended that the "They" who did the arresting

would be equated with the "They" who committed the other described acts and with the "Southern violators." Thus, he argued, the paragraph would be read as accusing the Montgomery police, and hence him, of answering Dr. King's protests with "intimidation and violence," bombing his home, assaulting his person, and charging him with perjury. Respondent and six other Montgomery residents testified that they read some of all of the statements as referring to him in his capacity as Commissioner.

It is uncontroverted that some of the statements contained in the two paragraphs were not accurate descriptions of events which occurred in Montgomery. Although Negro students staged a demonstration on the State Capitol steps, they sang the National Anthem and not "My Country, 'Tis of Thee." Although nine students were expelled by the State Board of Education, this was not for leading the demonstration at the Capitol, but for demanding service at a lunch counter in the Montgomery County Courthouse on another day. Not the entire student body, but most of it, had protested the expulsion, not by refusing to register, but by boycotting classes on a single day; virtually all the students did register for the ensuing semester. The campus dining hall was not padlocked on any occasion, and the only students who may have been barred from eating there were the few who had neither signed a preregistration application nor requested temporary meal tickets. Although the police were deployed near the campus in large numbers on three occasions, they did not at any time "ring" the campus, and they were not called to the campus in connection with the demonstration on the State Capitol steps, as the third paragraph implied. Dr. King had not been arrested seven times, but only four; and although he claimed to have been assaulted some years earlier in connection with his arrest for loitering outside a courtroom, one of the officers who made the arrest denied that there was such an assault.

On the premise that the charges in the sixth paragraph could be read as referring to him, respondent was allowed to prove that he had not participated in the events described. Although Dr. King's home had in fact been bombed twice when his wife and child were there, both of these occasions antedated respondent's tenure as Commissioner, and the police were not only not implicated in the bombings, but had made every effort to apprehend those who were. Three of Dr. King's four arrests took place before respondent became Commissioner. Although Dr. King had in fact been indicted (he was subsequently acquitted) on two counts of perjury, each of which carried a possible five-year sentence, respondent had nothing to do with procuring the indictment. . . .

Because of the importance of the constitutional issues involved, we granted the separate petitions for *certiorari* of the individual petitioners and of the *Times*. *** We reverse the judgment. We hold that the rule of law applied by the Alabama courts is constitutionally deficient for failure to provide the safeguards for freedom of speech and of the press that are required by the First and Fourteenth Amendments in a libel action brought by a public official against critics of his official conduct. We further hold that under the proper safeguards the evidence presented in this case is constitutionally insufficient to support the judgment for respondent.

I

We may dispose at the outset of two grounds asserted to insulate the judgment of the Alabama courts from constitutional scrutiny. The first is the proposition relied on by the State Supreme Court—that "The Fourteenth Amendment is directed against State action and not private action." That proposition has no application to this case. Although this is a civil lawsuit between private parties, the Alabama courts have applied a state rule of law which petitioners claim to impose invalid restrictions on their constitutional freedoms of speech and press. . . .

The second contention is that the constitutional guarantees of freedom of speech and of the press are inapplicable here, at least so far as the *Times* is concerned, because the allegedly libelous statements were published as part of a paid, "commercial" advertisement. . . .

. . . That the *Times* was paid for publishing the advertisement is as immaterial in this connection as is the fact that newspapers and books are sold. *** Any other conclusion would discourage newspapers from carrying "editorial advertisements" of this type, and so might shut off an important outlet for the promulgation of information and ideas by persons who do not themselves have access to publishing facilities—who wish to exercise their freedom of speech even though they are not members of the press. *** The effect would be to shackle the First Amendment in its attempt to secure "the widest possible dissemination of information from diverse and antagonistic sources." To avoid placing such a handicap upon the freedoms of expression, we hold that if the allegedly libelous statements would otherwise be constitutionally protected from the present judgment, they do not forfeit that protection because they were published in the form of a paid advertisement.

II

Under Alabama law as applied in this case, a publication is "libelous per se" if the words "tend to injure a person . . . in his reputation" or to "bring [him] into public contempt"; the trial court stated that the standard was met if the words are such as to "injure him in his public office, or impute misconduct to him in his office, or want of official integrity, or want of fidelity to a public trust. . . ." The jury must find that the words were published "of and concerning" the plaintiff, but where the plaintiff is a public official his place in the governmental hierarchy is sufficient evidence to support a finding that his reputation has been affected by statements that reflect upon the agency of which he is in charge. Once "libel per se" has been established, the defendant has no defense as to stated facts unless he can persuade the jury that they were true in all their particulars. *** His privilege of "fair comment" for expressions of opinion depends on the truth of the facts upon which the comment is based. *** Unless he can discharge the burden of proving truth, general damages are presumed, and may be awarded without proof of pecuniary injury. A showing of actual malice is apparently a prerequisite to recovery of punitive damages, and the defendant may in any event forestall a punitive award by a retraction meeting the statutory requirements. Good motives and belief in truth do not negate an inference of malice, but are relevant only in mitigation of punitive damages if the jury chooses to accord them weight. ***

The question before us is whether this rule of liability, as applied to an action brought by a public official against critics of his official conduct, abridges the freedom of speech and of the press that is guaranteed by the First and Fourteenth Amendments.

Respondent relies heavily, as did the Alabama courts, on statements of this Court to the effect that the Constitution does not protect libelous publications. Those statements do not foreclose our inquiry here. None of the cases sustained the use of libel laws to impose sanctions upon expression critical of the official conduct of public officials.... Like insurrection, contempt, advocacy of unlawful acts, breach of the peace, obscenity, solicitation of legal business, and the various other formulae for the repression of expression that have been challenged in this Court, libel can claim no talismanic immunity from constitutional limitations. It must be measured by standards that satisfy the First Amendment....

[W]e consider this case against the background of a profound national commitment to the principle that debate on public issues should be uninhibited, robust, and wide-open, and that it may well include vehement, caustic, and sometimes unpleasantly sharp attacks on government and public officials. ***

A rule compelling the critic of official conduct to guarantee the truth of all his factual assertions—and to do so on pain of libel judgments virtually unlimited in amount—leads to a comparable "self-censorship." Allowance of the defense of truth, with the burden of proving it on the defendant, does not mean that only false speech will be deterred. Even courts accepting this defense as an adequate safeguard have recognized the difficulties of adducing legal proofs that the alleged libel was true in all its factual particulars. *** Under such a rule, would-be critics of official conduct may be deterred from voicing their criticism, even though it is believed to be true and even though it is in fact true, because of doubt whether it can be proved in court or fear of the expense of having to do so. They tend to make only statements which "steer far wider of the unlawful zone." *** The rule thus dampens the vigor and limits the variety of public debate. It is inconsistent with the First and Fourteenth Amendments.

The constitutional guarantees require, we think, a federal rule that prohibits a public official from re-covering damages for a defamatory falsehood relating to his official conduct unless he proves that the statement was made with "actual malice"—that is, with knowledge that it was false or with reckless disregard of whether it was false or not....

Such a privilege for criticism of official conduct is appropriately analogous to the protection accorded a public official when *he* is sued for libel by a private citizen.... The reason for the official privilege is said to be that the threat of damage suits would otherwise "inhibit the fearless, vigorous, and effective administration of policies of government" and "dampen the ardor of all but the most resolute, or the most irresponsible, in the unflinching discharge of their duties." *** Analogous considerations support the privilege for the citizen-critic of government. It is as much his duty to criticize as it is the official's duty to administer. *** It would give public servants an unjustified preference over the public they serve, if critics of official conduct did not have a fair equivalent of the immunity granted to the officials themselves.

We conclude that such a privilege is required by the First and Fourteenth Amendments.

III

We hold today that the Constitution delimits a State's power to award damages for libel in actions brought by public officials against critics of their official conduct. Since this is such an action, the rule requiring proof of actual malice is applicable. While Alabama law apparently requires proof of actual malice for an award of punitive damages, where general damages are concerned malice is "presumed." Such a presumption is inconsistent with the federal rule. ... Since the trial judge did not instruct the jury to differentiate between general and punitive damages, it may be that the verdict was wholly an award of one or the other. But it is impossible to know, in view of the general verdict returned. Because of this uncertainty, the judgment must be reversed and the case remanded. ***

Mr. Justice Black, with whom *Mr. Justice Douglas* joins, concurring.

... I base my vote to reverse on the belief that the First and Fourteenth Amendments not merely "delimit" a State's power to award damages to "public officials against critics of their official conduct" but completely prohibit a State from exercising such a power. The Court goes on to hold that a State can subject such critics to damages if "actual malice" can be proved against them. "Malice," even as defined by the Court, is an elusive, abstract concept, hard to prove and hard to disprove. The requirement that malice be proved provides at best an evanescent protection for the right critically to discuss public affairs and certainly does not measure up to the sturdy safeguard embodied in the First Amendment. Unlike the Court, therefore, I vote to reverse exclusively on the ground that the *Times* and the individual defendants had an absolute, unconditional constitutional right to publish in the *Times* advertisement their criticisms of the Montgomery agencies and officials. . . .

Hustler Magazine v. Falwell

485 U.S. 46; 108 S. Ct. 876; 99 L. Ed.2d 41 (1988)
Vote: 8-0

In its November 1983 issue, Hustler *magazine ran a fictional advertisement entitled "Jerry Falwell talks about his first time." The ad, which was a spoof on the popular ad campaign for Campari liqueur, portrayed Rev. Falwell as a hypocritical drunkard whose "first time" involved sex with his mother in an outhouse. At the bottom of the page, in fine print, was the disclaimer "Ad Parody—Not to Be Taken Seriously." Nevertheless, Rev. Falwell took the ad very seriously and brought a federal lawsuit suit for libel and intentional infliction of emotional distress. At trial, the jury rejected the libel claim but found for Falwell on the claim of emotional distress. The court of appeals affirmed the judgment, and* Hustler *petitioned the Supreme Court for certiorari.*

Chief Justice Rehnquist delivered the opinion of the Court.

. . . On appeal, the United States Court of Appeals for the Fourth Circuit . . . rejected petitioners' argument that the "actual malice" standard of *New York Times Co. v. Sullivan* *** (1964) must be met before respondent can recover for emotional distress. The court agreed that because respondent is concededly a public figure, petitioners are "entitled to the same level of first amendment protection in the claim for intentional infliction of emotional distress that they received in [respondent's] claim for libel." *** But this does not mean that a literal application of the actual malice rule is appropriate in the context of an emotional distress claim. In the court's view, the *New York Times* decision emphasized the constitutional importance not of the falsity of the statement or the defendant's disregard for the truth, but of the heightened level of culpability embodied in the requirement of "knowing . . . or reckless" conduct. Here, the *New York Times* standard is satisfied by the state law requirement, and the jury's finding, that the defendants have acted intentionally or recklessly. The Court of Appeals then went on to reject the contention that because the jury found that the ad parody did not describe actual facts about respondent, the ad was an opinion that is protected by the First Amendment. As the court put it, this was "irrelevant," as the issue is "whether [the ad's] publication was sufficiently outrageous to constitute intentional infliction of emotional distress." *** . . .

This case presents us with a novel question involving First Amendment limitations [on lawsuits for] the intentional infliction of emotional distress. We must decide whether a public figure may recover damages for emotional harm caused by the publication of an ad parody offensive to him, and doubtless gross and repugnant in the eyes of most. Respondent would have us find that [the public] interest in protecting public figures from emotional distress is sufficient to deny First Amendment protection to speech that is patently offensive and is intended to inflict emotional injury, even when that speech could not reasonably have been interpreted as stating actual facts about the public figure involved. This we decline to do.

At the heart of the First Amendment is the recognition of the fundamental importance of the free flow of ideas and opinions on matters of public interest and concern. "[T]he freedom to speak one's mind is not only an aspect of individual liberty—and thus a good unto itself—but also is essential to the common quest for truth and the vitality of society as a whole." *** We have therefore been particularly vigilant to ensure that individual expressions of ideas remain free from governmental imposed sanctions. The First Amendment recognizes no such thing as a "false" idea. *** Justice Holmes wrote, "[W]hen men have realized that time has upset many fighting faiths, they may come to believe even more than they believe the very foundations of their own conduct that the ultimate good desired is better reached by free trade in ideas—that the best test of truth is the power of the thought to get itself accepted in the competition of the market. . . ." ***

The sort of robust political debate encouraged by the First Amendment is bound to produce speech that is critical of those who hold public office or those public figures who are "intimately involved in the resolution of important public questions or, by reason of their fame, shape events in area of concern to society at large." *** Justice Frankfurter put it succinctly in *Baumgartner v. United States* *** (1944), when he said that "[o]ne of the prerogatives of American citizenship is the right to criticize public men and measures." Such criticism, inevitably, will not always be reasoned or moderate; public figures as well as public officials will be subject to "vehement, caustic, and sometimes unpleasantly sharp attacks." *** "[T]he candidate who vaunts his spotless record and sterling integrity cannot convincingly cry 'Foul!' when an opponent or an industrious reporter attempts to demonstrate the contrary." ***

Of course, this does not mean that any speech about a public figure is immune from sanction in the form of damages. Since *New York Times Co. v. Sullivan,* supra, we have consistently ruled that a public figure may hold a speaker liable for the damage to reputation caused by publication of a defamatory falsehood, but only if the statement was made "with knowledge that it was false or with reckless disregard of whether it was false or not." False statements of fact are particularly valueless; they interfere with the truth-seeking function of the marketplace of ideas, and they cause damage to an individual's reputation that cannot easily be repaired by counter speech, however persuasive or effective. *** But even though falsehoods have little value in and of themselves, they are "nevertheless inevitable in free debate," *** and a rule that would impose strict liability on a publisher for false factual assertions would have an undoubted "chilling" effect on speech relating to public figures that does have constitutional value. "Freedoms of expression require 'breathing space.' " *** This breathing space is provided by a constitutional rule that allows public figures to recover for libel or defamation only when they can prove both that the statement was false and that the statement was made with the requisite level of culpability.

Respondent argues, however, that a different standard should apply in this case because here the State seeks to prevent not reputational damage, but the severe emotional distress suffered by the person who is the subject of an offensive publication. *** In respondent's view, and in the view of the Court of Appeals, so long as the utterance was intended to inflict emotional distress, was outrageous, and did in fact inflict serious emotional distress, it is of no constitutional import whether the statement was a fact or an opinion, or whether it was true or false. It is the intent to cause injury that is the gravamen of the tort, and the State's interest in preventing emotional harm simply outweighs whatever interest a speaker may have in speech of this type.

Generally speaking the law does not regard the intent to inflict emotional distress as one which should receive much solicitude, and it is quite understandable that most if not all jurisdictions have chosen to make it civilly culpable where the conduct in question is sufficiently "outrageous." But in the world of debate about public affairs, many things done with motives that are less than admirable are protected by the First Amendment . . . Thus while such a bad motive may be deemed controlling for purposes of tort liability in other areas of the law, we think the First Amendment prohibits such a result in the area of public debate about public figures.

Were we to hold otherwise, there can be little doubt that political cartoonists and satirists would be subjected to damages awards without any showing that their work falsely defamed its subject. Webster's defines a caricature as "the deliberately distorted picturing or imitating of a person, literary style, etc. by exaggerating features or mannerisms for satirical effect." The appeal of the political cartoon or caricature is often based on exploration of unfortunate physical traits or politically embarrassing events—an exploration often calculated to injure the feelings of the subject of the portrayal. The art of the cartoonist is often not reasoned or evenhanded, but slashing and one-sided. One cartoonist expressed the nature of the art in these words:

"The political cartoon is a weapon of attack, of scorn and ridicule and satire; it is least effective when it tries to pat some politician on the back. It is usually as welcome as a bee sting and is always controversial in some quarters." ***

Several famous examples of this intentionally injurious speech were drawn by Thomas Nast, probably the greatest American cartoonist to date, who was associated for many years during the post-Civil War era with *Harper's Weekly.* In the pages of that publication Nast conducted a graphic vendetta against William M. "Boss" Tweed and his corrupt associates in New York City's "Tweed Ring." It has been described by one historian of the subject as "a sustained attack which in its passion and effectiveness stands alone in the history of American graphic art." *** Another writer explains that the success of the Nast cartoon was achieved "because of the emotional impact of its presentation. It continuously goes beyond the bounds of good taste and conventional manners." ***

Despite their sometimes caustic nature, from the early cartoon portraying George Washington as an ass down to the present day, graphic depictions and satirical cartoons have played a prominent role in public and political debate. Nast's castigation of the Tweed Ring, Walt McDougall's characterization of presidential candidate James G. Blaine's banquet with the millionaires at Delmonico's as "The Royal Feast of Belshazzar," and numerous other efforts have undoubtedly had an effect on the course and outcome of contemporaneous debate. Lincoln's tall, gangling posture, Teddy Roosevelt's glasses and teeth, and Franklin D. Roosevelt's jutting jaw and cigarette holder have been immortalized by political cartoons with an effect that could not have been obtained by the photographer or the portrait artist. From the viewpoint of history it is clear that our political discourse would have been considerably poorer without them.

Respondent contends, however, that the caricature in question here was so "outrageous" as to distinguish it from more traditional political cartoons. There is no doubt that the caricature of respondent and his mother published in *Hustler* is at best a distant cousin of the political cartoons described above, and a rather poor relation at that. If it were possible by laying down a principled standard to separate the one from the other, public discourse would probably suffer little or no harm. But we doubt that there is any such standard, and we are quite sure that the pejorative description "outrageous" does not supply one. "Outrageousness" in the area of political and social discourse has an inherent subjectiveness about it which would allow a jury to impose liability on the basis of the jurors' tastes or views, or perhaps on the basis of their dislike of a particular expression. An "outrageousness" standard thus runs afoul of our longstanding refusal to allow damages to be awarded because the speech in question may have an adverse emotional impact on the audience. ***

We conclude that public figures and public officials may not recover for the tort of intentional infliction of emotional distress by reason of publications such as the one here at issue without showing in addition that the publication contains a false statement of fact which was made with "actual malice," i.e., with knowledge that the statement was false or with reckless disregard as to whether or not it was true. This is not merely a "blind application" of the *New York Times* standard, *** it reflects our considered judgment that such a standard is necessary to give adequate "breathing space" to the freedoms protected by the First Amendment.

Here it is clear that respondent Falwell is a "public figure" for purposes of First Amendment law. The jury found against respondent on his libel claim when it decided that the *Hustler* ad parody could not "reasonably be understood as describing actual facts about [respondent] or actual events in which [he] participated." *** The Court of Appeals interpreted the jury's finding to be that the ad parody "was not reasonably believable," and in accordance with our custom we accept this finding. Respondent is thus relegated to his claim for damages awarded by the jury for the intentional infliction of emotional distress by "outrageous" conduct. But for reasons heretofore stated this claim cannot, consistently with the First Amendment, form a basis for the award of damages when the conduct in question is the publication of a caricature such as the ad parody involved here.

The judgment of the Court of Appeals is accordingly Reversed.

Justice Kennedy took no part in the consideration or decision of this case.

Justice White, concurring in the judgment.

As I see it, the decision in *New York Times v. Sullivan* *** has little to do with this case, for here the jury found that the ad contained no assertion of fact. But I agree with the Court that the judgment below, which penalized the publication of the parody, cannot be squared with the First Amendment. . . .

Branzburg v. Hayes
408 U.S. 665; 92 S. Ct. 2646; 33 L.Ed. 2d 626 (1972)
Vote: 5-4

Opinion of the Court by *Mr. Justice White,* announced by the *Chief Justice.*

The issue in these cases is whether requiring newsmen to appear and testify before state or federal grand juries abridges the freedom of speech and press guaranteed by the First Amendment. We hold that it does not.

The writ of *certiorari* in *Branzburg v. Hayes* *** brings before us two judgments of the Kentucky Court of Appeals, both involving petitioner Branzburg, a staff reporter for the *Courier-Journal,* a daily newspaper published in Louisville, Kentucky.

On November 15, 1969, the *Courier-Journal* carried a story under petitioner's by-line describing in detail his observations of two young residents of Jefferson County synthesizing hashish from marihuana, an activity which, they asserted, earned them about $5,000 in three weeks. The article included a photograph of a pair of hands working above a laboratory table on which was a substance identified by the caption as hashish. The article stated that petitioner had promised not to reveal the identity of the two hashish makers. Petitioner was shortly subpoenaed by the Jefferson County grand jury; he appeared, but refused to identify the individuals he had seen possessing marihuana or the persons he had seen making hashish from marihuana. A state trial court judge

ordered petitioner to answer these questions and rejected his contention that the Kentucky reporters' privilege statute, *** the First Amendment of the United States Constitution, or Sections 1, 2, and 8 of the Kentucky Constitution authorized his refusal to answer. Petitioner then sought prohibition and *mandamus* in the Kentucky Court of Appeals on the same grounds, but the Court of Appeals denied the petition. *** It held that petitioner had abandoned his First Amendment argument in a supplemental memorandum he had filed and tacitly rejected his argument based on the Kentucky Constitution. It also construed [the Kentucky statute] as affording a newsman the privilege of refusing to divulge the identity of an informant who supplied him with information, but held that the statute did not permit a reporter to refuse to testify about events he had observed personally, including the identities of those persons he had observed.

The second case involving petitioner Branzburg arose out of his later story published on January 10, 1971, which described in detail the use of drugs in Frankfort, Kentucky. The article reported that in order to provide a comprehensive survey of the "drug scene" in Frankfort, petitioner had "spent two weeks interviewing several dozen drug users in the capital city" and had seen some of them smoking marihuana. A number of conversations with and observations of several unnamed drug users were recounted. Subpoenaed to appear before a Franklin County grand jury "to testify in the matter of violation of statutes concerning use and sale of drugs," petitioner Branzburg moved to quash the summons; the motion was denied, although an order was issued protecting Branzburg from revealing "confidential associations, sources or information" but requiring that he "answer any questions which concern or pertain to any criminal act, the commission of which was actually observed by [him]." [Before he was] to appear before the grand jury, petitioner sought *mandamus* and prohibition from the Kentucky Court of Appeals, arguing that if he [had] to go before the grand jury or to answer questions regarding the identity of informants or disclose information given to him in confidence, his effectiveness as a reporter would be greatly damaged. The Court of Appeals once again denied the requested writs, reaffirming its construction of [the Kentucky statute] and rejecting petitioner's claim of a First Amendment privilege....

Petitioner sought a writ of *certiorari* to review both judgments of the Kentucky Court of Appeals, and we granted the writ. ***

... Branzburg ... claims ... that to gather news it is often necessary to agree either not to identify the source of information published or to publish only part of the facts revealed, or both; that if the reporter is nevertheless forced to reveal these confidences to a grand jury, the source so identified and other confidential sources of other reporters will be measurably deterred from furnishing publishable information, all to the detriment of the free flow of information protected by the First Amendment. Although the newsmen in these cases do not claim an absolute privilege against official interrogation in all circumstances, they assert that the reporter should not be forced either to appear or to testify before a grand jury or at trial until and unless sufficient grounds are shown for believing that the reporter possesses information relevant to a crime the grand jury is investigating, that the information the reporter has is unavailable from other sources, and that the need for the information is sufficiently compelling to override the claimed invasion of First Amendment interests occasioned by the disclosure. Principally

relied upon are prior cases emphasizing the importance of the First Amendment guarantees to individual development and to our system of representative government, decisions requiring that official action with adverse impact on First Amendment rights be justified by a public interest that is "compelling" or "paramount," and those precedents establishing the principle that justifiable government goals may not be achieved by unduly broad means having an unnecessary impact on protected rights of speech, press, or association. The heart of the claim is that the burden on news gathering resulting from compelling reporters to disclose confidential information outweighs any public interest in obtaining the information.

We do not question the significance of free speech, press, or assembly to the country's welfare. Nor is it suggested that news gathering does not qualify for First Amendment protection; without some protection for seeking out the news, freedom of the press could be eviscerated. But these cases involve no intrusions upon speech or assembly, no prior restraint or restriction on what the press may publish, and no express or implied command that the press publish what it prefers to withhold. No exaction or tax for the privilege of publishing, and no penalty, civil or criminal, related to the content of published material is at issue here. The use of confidential sources by the press is not forbidden or restricted; reporters remain free to seek news from any source by means within the law. No attempt is made to require the press to publish its sources of information or indiscriminately to disclose them on request.

The sole issue before us is the obligation of reporters to respond to grand jury subpoenas as other citizens do and to answer questions relevant to an investigation into the commission of crime. Citizens generally are not constitutionally immune from grand jury subpoenas; and neither the First Amendment nor any other constitution provision protects the average citizen from disclosing to a grand jury information that he has received in confidence. The claim is, however, that reporters are exempt from these obligations because if forced to respond to subpoenas and identify their sources or disclose other confidences, their informants will refuse or be reluctant to furnish newsworthy information in the future. This asserted burden on news gathering is said to make compelled testimony from newsmen constitutionally suspect and to require a privileged position for them.

It is clear that the First Amendment does not invalidate every incidental burdening of the press that may result from the enforcement of civil or criminal statutes of general applicability. Under prior cases, otherwise valid laws serving substantial public interests may be enforced against the press as against others, despite the possible burden that may be imposed. The Court has emphasized that "[t]he publisher of a newspaper has no special immunity from the application of general laws. He has no special privilege to invade the rights and liberties of others." *** ...

A number of States have provided newsmen a statutory privilege of varying breadth, but the majority have not done so, and none has been provided by federal statute. Until now the only testimonial privilege for unofficial witnesses that is rooted in the Federal Constitution is the Fifth Amendment privilege against compelled self-incrimination. We are asked to create another by interpreting the First Amendment to grant newsmen a testimonial privilege that other citizens do not enjoy. This we decline to do. Fair and effective law enforcement aimed at providing security for the person and property of the individual is a fundamental function of government, and the grand jury plays an important, constitutionally mandated role in this process. On the records now before us, we perceive no basis for holding that the public interest in law enforcement and in ensuring effective grand jury proceedings is insufficient to override the consequential, but uncertain, burden on news gathering that is said to result from insisting that reporters, like other citizens, respond to relevant questions put to them in the course of a valid grand jury investigation or criminal trial.

This conclusion itself involves no restraint on what newspapers may publish or on the type or quality of information reporters may seek to acquire, nor does it threaten the vast bulk of confidential relationships between reporters and their sources. Grand juries address themselves to the issues of whether crimes have been committed and who committed them. Only where news sources themselves are implicated in crime or possess information relevant to the grand jury's task need they or the reporter be concerned about grand jury subpoenas. Nothing before us indicates that a large number or percentage of *all* confidential news sources fall into either category and would in any way be deterred by our holding that the Constitution does not, as it never has, exempt the newsman from performing the citizen's normal duty of appearing and furnishing information relevant to the grand jury's task.

The preference for anonymity of those confidential informants involved in actual criminal conduct is presumably a product of their desire to escape criminal prosecution, and this preference, while understandable, is hardly deserving of constitutional protection. It would be frivolous to assert—and no one does in these cases—that the First Amendment, in the interest of securing news or otherwise, confers a license on either the reporter or his news sources to violate valid criminal laws. Although stealing documents or private wiretapping could provide newsworthy information, neither reporter nor source is immune from conviction for such conduct, whatever the impact on the flow of news. Neither is immune, on First Amendment grounds, from testifying against the other, before the grand jury or at a criminal trial. The Amendment does not reach so far as to override the interest of the public in ensuring that neither reporter nor source is invading the rights of other citizens through reprehensible conduct forbidden to all other persons. To assert the contrary proposition "is to answer it, since it involves in its very statement the contention that the freedom of the press is the freedom to do wrong with impunity and implies the right to frustrate and defeat the discharge of those which the freedom of all, including that of the press, depends. . . ."

Thus, we cannot seriously entertain the notion that the First Amendment protects a newsman's agreement to conceal the criminal conduct of his source, or evidence thereof, on the theory that it is better to write about crime than to do something about it. Insofar as any reporter in these cases undertook not to reveal or testify about the crime he witnessed, his claim of privilege under the First Amendment presents no substantial question. The crimes of news sources are no less reprehensible and threatening to the public interest when witnessed by a reporter than when they are not.

There remain those situations where a source is not engaged in criminal conduct but has information suggesting illegal conduct by others. Newsmen frequently receive information from such sources pursuant to a tacit or express agreement to withhold the source's name and suppress any information that the source wishes not published. Such informants presumably desire anonymity in order to avoid being entangled as a witness in a criminal trial or grand jury investigation. They may fear that disclosure will threaten their job security or personal safety or that it will simply result in dishonor or embarrassment.

The argument that the flow of news will be diminished by compelling reporters to aid the grand jury in a criminal investigation is not irrational, nor are the records before us silent on the matter. But we remain unclear how often and to what extent informers are actually deterred from furnishing information when newsmen are forced to testify before a grand jury. The available data indicate that some newsmen rely a great deal on confidential sources and that some informants are particularly sensitive to the threat of exposure and may be silenced if it is held by this Court that, ordinarily, newsmen must testify pursuant to subpoenas, but the evidence fails to demonstrate that there would be a significant constriction of the flow of news to the public if this Court reaffirms the prior common-law and constitutional rule regarding the testimonial obligations of newsmen. Estimates of the inhibiting effect of such subpoenas on the willingness of informants to make disclosures to newsmen are widely divergent and to a great extent speculative. It would be difficult to canvass the views of the informants themselves; surveys of reporters on this topic are chiefly opinions of predicted informant behavior and must be viewed in the light of the professional self-interest of the interviewees. Reliance by the press on confidential informants does not mean that all such sources will in fact dry up because of the later possible appearance of the newsman before a grand jury. The reporter may never be called and if he objects to testifying, the prosecution may not insist. Also, the relationship of many informants to the press is a symbiotic one which is unlikely to be greatly inhibited by the threat of subpoena: quite often, such informants are members of a minority political or cultural group that relies heavily on the media to propagate its views, publicize its aims, and magnify its exposure to the public. Moreover, grand juries characteristically conduct secret proceedings, and law enforcement officers are themselves experienced in dealing with informers, and have their own methods for protecting them without interference with the effective administration of justice. There is little before us indicating that informants whose interest in avoiding exposure is that it may threaten job security, personal safety, or peace of mind, would in fact be in a worse position, or would think they would be, if they risked placing their trust in public officials as well as reporters. We doubt if the informer who prefers anonymity but is sincerely interested in furnishing evidence of crime will always or very often be deterred by the prospect of dealing with those public authorities characteristically charged with the duty to protect the public interest as well as his.

Accepting the fact, however, that an undetermined number of informants not themselves implicated in crime will nevertheless, for whatever reason, refuse to talk to newsmen if they fear identi- fication by a reporter in an official investigation, we cannot accept the argument that the public interest in possible future news about crime from undisclosed, unverified sources must take precedence over the public interest in pursuing and prosecuting those crimes reported to the press by informants and in thus deterring the commission of such crimes in the future....

Finally, as we have earlier indicated, news gathering is not without its First Amendment protections, and grand jury investigations if instituted or conducted other than in good faith, would pose wholly different issues for resolution under the First Amendment. Official harassment of the press undertaken not for purposes of law enforcement but to disrupt a reporter's relationship with his news sources would have no justification. Grand juries are subject to judicial control and subpoenas to motions to quash. We do not expect courts will forget that grand juries must operate within the limits of the First Amendment as well as the Fifth....

Mr. Justice Powell, concurring....

Mr. Justice Douglas, dissenting.

. . . Today's decision will impede the wide-open and robust dissemination of ideas and counter-thought which a free press both fosters and protects and which is essential to the success of intelligent self-government. Forcing a reporter before a grand jury will have two retarding effects upon the ear and the pen of the press. Fear of exposure will cause dissidents to communicate less openly to trusted reporters. And, fear of accountability will cause editors and critics to with which more restrained pens. . . .

A reporter is no better than his source of information. Unless he has a privilege to withhold the identity of his source, he will be the victim of governmental intrigue or aggression. If he can be summoned to testify in secret before a grand jury, his sources will dry up and the attempted exposure, the effort to enlighten the public, will be ended. If what the Court sanctions today becomes settled law, then the reporter's main function in American society will be to pass on to the public the press releases which the various departments of government issue.

It is no answer to reply that the risk that a newsman will divulge one's secrets to the grand jury is no greater than the threat that he will in any event inform to the police. Even the most trustworthy reporter may not be able to withstand relentless badgering before a grand jury.

The record in this case is replete with weighty affidavits from responsible newsmen, telling how important is the sanctity of their sources of information. When we deny newsmen that protection, we deprive the people of the information needed to run the affairs of the Nation in an intelligent way. . . .

Today's decision is more than a clog upon news gathering. It is a signal to publishers and editors that they should exercise caution in how they use whatever information they can obtain. Without immunity they may be summoned to account for their criticism. Entrenched officers have been quick to crash their powers down upon unfriendly commentators. ***

The intrusion of government into this domain is symptomatic of the disease of this society. As the years pass the power of government becomes more and more pervasive. It is a power to suffocate both people and causes. Those in power, whatever their politics, want only to perpetuate it. Now that the fences of the law and the tradition that has protected the press are broken down, the people are the victims. The First Amendment, as I read it, was designed precisely to prevent that tragedy. . . .

Mr. Justice Stewart, with whom *Mr. Justice Brennan* and *Mr. Justice Marshall* join, dissenting.

The Court's crabbed view of the First Amendment reflects a disturbing insensitivity to the critical role of an independent press in our society. The question whether a reporter has a constitutional right to a confidential relationship with his source is of first impression here, but the principles that should guide our decision are as basic as any to be found in the Constitution. While Mr. Justice Powell's enigmatic concurring opinion gives some hope of a more flexible view in the future, the Court in these cases holds that a newsman has no First Amendment right to protect his sources when called before a grand jury. The Court thus invites state and federal authorities to undermine the historic independence of the press by attempting to annex the journalistic profession as an investigative arm of government. Not only will this decision impair performance of the press' constitutionally protected functions, but it will, I am convinced, in the long run harm rather than help the administration of justice.

I respectfully dissent.

Cohen v. Cowles Media Company

501 U.S. ___; 111 S.Ct. 2513; 115 L.Ed.2d 586 (1991)

Vote: 5-4

The issue in this case is whether the First Amendment prohibits a civil suit for damages against a newspaper that broke a promise of confidentiality given in exchange for information. Justice White's majority opinion provides a detailed discussion of the facts.

Justice White delivered the opinion of the Court.

. . . During the closing days of the 1982 Minnesota gubernatorial race, Dan Cohen, an active Republican associated with Wheelock Whitney's Independent-Republican gubernatorial campaign, approached reporters from the St. Paul *Pioneer Press Dispatch (Pioneer Press)* and the Minneapolis *Star and Tribune (Star Tribune)* and offered to provide documents relating to a candidate in the upcoming election. Cohen made clear to the reporters that he would provide the information only if he was given a promise of confidentiality. Reporters from both papers promised to keep Cohen's identity anonymous and Cohen turned over copies of two public court records concerning Marlene Johnson, the Democratic-Farmer-Labor candidate for Lieutenant Governor. The first record indicated that Johnson had been charged in 1969 with three counts of unlawful assembly, and the second that she had been convicted in 1970 of petit theft. Both newspapers interviewed Johnson for her explanation and one reporter tracked down the person who had found the records for Cohen. As it turned out, the unlawful assembly charges arose out of Johnson's participation in a protest of an alleged failure to hire minority workers on municipal construction projects and the charges were eventually dismissed. The petit theft conviction was for leaving a store without paying for $6.00 worth of sewing materials. The incident apparently occurred at a time during which Johnson was emotionally distraught, and the conviction was later vacated.

After consultation and debate, the editorial staffs of the two newspapers independently decided to publish Cohen's name as part of their stories concerning Johnson. In their stories, both papers identified Cohen as the source of the court records, indicated his connection to the Whitney campaign, and included denials by Whitney campaign officials of any role in the matter. The same day the stories appeared, Cohen was fired by his employer.

Cohen sued respondents, the publishers of the *Pioneer Press* and *Star Tribune,* in Minnesota state court, alleging fraudulent misrepresentation and breach of contract. The trial court rejected respondents' argument that the First Amendment barred Cohen's lawsuit. A jury returned a verdict in Cohen's favor, awarding him $200,000 in compensatory dam-

ages and $500,000 in punitive damages. The Minnesota Court of Appeals, in a split decision, reversed the award of punitive damages after concluding that Cohen had failed to establish a fraud claim, the only claim which would support such an award. *** However, the court upheld the finding of liability for breach of contract and the $200,000 compensatory damage award. ***

A divided Minnesota Supreme Court reversed the compensatory damages award. *** After affirming the Court of Appeals' determination that Cohen had not established a claim for fraudulent misrepresentation, the court considered his breach of contract claim and concluded that "a contract cause of action is inappropriate for these particular circumstances." *** The court then went on to address the question whether Cohen could establish a cause of action under Minnesota law on a promissory estoppel theory. Apparently, a promissory estoppel theory was never tried to the jury, nor briefed nor argued by the parties; it first arose during oral argument in the Minnesota Supreme Court when one of the justices asked a question about equitable estoppel. ***

In addressing the promissory estoppel question, the court decided that the most problematic element in establishing such a cause of action here was whether injustice could be avoided only by enforcing the promise of confidentiality made to Cohen. The court stated that "[u]nder a promissory estoppel analysis there can be no neutrality towards the First Amendment. In deciding whether it would be unjust not to enforce the promise, the court must necessarily weigh the same considerations that are weighed for whether the First Amendment has been violated. The court must balance the constitutional rights of a free press against the common law interest in protecting a promise of anonymity." *** After a brief discussion, the court concluded that "in this case enforcement of the promise of confidentiality under a promissory estoppel theory would violate defendants' First Amendment rights." ***

We granted certiorari to consider the First Amendment implications of this case. ***

The initial question we face is whether a private cause of action for promissory estoppel involves "state action" within the meaning of the Fourteenth Amendment such that the protections of the First Amendment are triggered. For if it does not, then the

First Amendment has no bearing on this case. The rationale of our decision in *New York Times Co. v. Sullivan* *** (1964) and subsequent cases compels the conclusion that there is state action here. Our cases teach that the application of state rules of law in state courts in a manner alleged to restrict First Amendment freedoms constitutes "state action" under the Fourteenth Amendment. *** In this case, the Minnesota Supreme Court held that if Cohen could recover at all it would be on the theory of promissory estoppel, a state-law doctrine which, in the absence of a contract, creates obligations never explicitly assumed by the parties. These legal obligations would be enforced through the official power of the Minnesota courts. Under our cases, that is enough to constitute "state action" for purposes of the Fourteenth Amendment.

Respondents rely on the proposition that "if a newspaper lawfully obtains truthful information about a matter of public significance then state officials may not constitutionally punish publication of the information, absent a need to further a state interest of the highest order." *** That proposition is unexceptionable, and it has been applied in various cases that have found insufficient the asserted state interests in preventing publication of truthful, lawfully obtained information. ***

This case however, is not controlled by this line of cases but rather by the equally well-established line of decisions holding that generally applicable laws do not offend the First Amendment simply because their enforcement against the press has incidental effects on its ability to gather and report the news. As the cases relied on by respondents recognize, the truthful information sought to be published must have been lawfully acquired. The press may not with impunity break and enter an office or dwelling to gather news. Neither does the First Amendment relieve a newspaper reporter of the obligation shared by all citizens to respond to a grand jury subpoena and answer questions relevant to a criminal investigation, even though the reporter might be required to reveal a confidential source. *** The press, like others interested in publishing, may not publish copyrighted material without obeying the copyright laws. *** Similarly, the media must obey the National Labor Relations Act, *** and the Fair Labor Standards Act, *** may not restrain trade in violation of the antitrust laws, *** and must pay nondiscriminatory taxes. *** It is therefore beyond dispute that "[t]he publisher of a newspaper has no special immunity from the application of general laws. He has no special privilege to invade the rights and liberties of others." *** Accordingly, enforcement of such general laws against the press is not subject to stricter scrutiny than would be applied to enforcement against other persons or organizations.

There can be little doubt that the Minnesota doctrine of promissory estoppel is a law of general applicability. It does not target or single out the press. Rather, in so far as we are advised, the doctrine is generally applicable to the daily transactions of all the citizens of Minnesota. The First Amendment does not forbid its application to the press. . . .

Respondents and *amici* argue that permitting Cohen to maintain a cause of action for promissory estoppel will inhibit truthful reporting because news organizations will have legal incentives not to disclose a confidential source's identity even when that person's identity is itself newsworthy. Justice Souter makes a similar argument. But if this is the case, it is no more than the incidental, and constitutionally insignificant, consequence of applying to the press a generally applicable law that requires those who make certain kinds of promises to keep them. Although we conclude that the First Amendment does not confer on the press a constitutional right to disregard promises that would otherwise be enforced under state law, we reject Cohen's request that in reversing the Minnesota Supreme Court's judgment we reinstate the jury verdict awarding him $200,000 in compensatory damages. *** The Minnesota Supreme Court's incorrect conclusion that the First Amendment barred Cohen's claim may well have truncated its consideration of whether a promissory estoppel claim had otherwise been established under Minnesota law and whether Cohen's jury verdict could be upheld on a promissory estoppel basis. Or perhaps the State Constitution may be construed to shield the press from a promissory estoppel cause of action such as this one. These are matters for the Minnesota Supreme Court to address and resolve in the first instance on remand. Accordingly, the judgment of the Minnesota Supreme Court is reversed, and the case is remanded for further proceedings not inconsistent with this opinion.

Justice Blackmun, with whom ***Justice Marshall*** and ***Justice Souter*** join, dissenting. . . .

Justice Souter, with whom ***Justice Marshall, Justice Blackmun*** and ***Justice O'Connor*** join, dissenting.

. . . This case does not fall within the line of authority holding the press to laws of general applicability where commercial activities and relationships, not the content of publication, are at issue. *** Even such general laws as do entail effects on the content of speech, like the one in question, may of course be found constitutional, but only, as Justice Harlan observed,

"when [such effects] have been justified by subordinating valid governmental interests, a prerequisite to constitutionality which has necessarily involved a weighing of the governmental interest involved. . . . Whenever, in such a context, these constitutional protections are asserted against the exercise of valid governmental powers a reconciliation must be effected, and that perforce requires an appropriate weighing of the respective interests involved." ***

Thus, "[t]here is nothing talismanic about neutral laws of general applicability," *** for such laws may restrict First Amendment rights just as effectively as those directed specifically at speech itself. Because I do not believe the fact of general applicability to be dispositive, I find it necessary to articulate, measure, and compare the competing interests involved in any given case to determine the legitimacy of burdening constitutional interests, and such has been the Court's recent practice in publication cases. ***

Nor can I accept the majority's position that we may dispense with balancing because the burden on publication is in a sense "self-imposed" by the newspaper's voluntary promise of confidentiality. *** This suggests both the possibility of waiver, the requirements for which have not been met here, *** as well as a conception of First Amendment rights as those of the speaker alone, with a value that may be measured without reference to the importance of the information to public discourse. But freedom of the press is ultimately founded on the value of enhancing such discourse for the sake of a citizenry better informed and thus more prudently self-governed. "[T]he First Amendment goes beyond protection of the press and the self-expression of individuals to prohibit government from limiting the stock of information from which members of the public may draw." *** In this context, " '[i]t is the right of the [public], not the right of the [media], which is paramount.' " *** For "[w]ithout the information provided by the press most of us and many of our representatives would be unable to vote intelligently or to register opinions on the administration of government generally." ***

The importance of this public interest is integral to the balance that should be struck in this case. There can be no doubt that the fact of Cohen's identity expanded the universe of information relevant to the choice faced by Minnesota voters in that State's 1982 gubernatorial election, the publication of which was thus of the sort quintessentially subject to strict First Amendment protection. *** The propriety of his leak to respondents could be taken to reflect on his character, which in turn could be taken to reflect on the character of the candidate who had retained him as an adviser. An election could turn on just such a factor; if it should, I am ready to assume that it would be to the greater public good, at least over the long run.

This is not to say that the breach of such a promise of confidentiality could never give rise to liability. One can conceive of situations in which the injured party is a private individual, whose identity is of less public concern than that of the petitioner; liability there might not be constitutionally prohibited. Nor do I mean to imply that the circumstances of acquisition are irrelevant to the balance, *** although they may go only to what balances against, and not to diminish, the First Amendment value of any particular piece of information.

Because I believe the State's interest in enforcing a newspaper's promise of confidentiality insufficient to outweigh the interest in unfettered publication of the information revealed in this case, I respectfully dissent.

Miller v. California

413 U.S. 15; 93 S. Ct. 2607; 37 L. Ed. 2d 419 (1973)
Vote: 5-4

Mr. Chief Justice Burger delivered the opinion of the Court.

This is one of a group of "obscenity-pornography" cases being reviewed by the Court in a reexamination of standards enunciated in earlier cases involving what Mr. Justice Harlan called "the intractable obscenity problem." ***

Appellant conducted a mass mailing campaign to advertise the sale of illustrated books, euphemistically called "adult" material. After a jury trial, he was convicted of violating California Penal Code [Section] 311.2 (a), a misdemeanor, by knowingly distributing obscene matter, and the Appellate Department, Superior Court of California, County of Orange, summarily affirmed the judgment without opinion. Appellant's conviction was specifically based on his conduct in causing five unsolicited advertising brochures to be sent through the mail in an envelope addressed to a restaurant in Newport Beach, California. The envelope was opened by the manager of the restaurant and his mother. They had not requested the brochures; they complained to the police.

The brochures advertise four books entitled "Intercourse," "Man-Woman," "Sex Orgies Illustrated," and "An Illustrated History of Pornography," and a film entitled "Marital Intercourse." While the brochures contain some descriptive printed material, primarily they consist of pictures and drawings very explicitly depicting men and women in groups of two or more engaging in a variety of sexual activities, with genitals often prominently displayed.

I

This case involves the application of a State's criminal obscenity statute to a situation in which sexually explicit materials have been thrust by aggressive sales action upon unwilling recipients who had in no way indicated any desire to receive such materials. This Court has recognized that the States have a legitimate interest in prohibiting dissemination or exhibition of obscene material when the mode of dissemination carries with it a significant danger of offending the sensibilities of unwilling recipients or of exposure to juveniles. *** It is in this context that we are called on to define the standards which must be used to identify obscene material that a State may regulate without infringing the First Amendment as applicable to the States through the Fourteenth Amendment. . . .

. . . In *Roth v. United States*, *** the Court sustained a conviction under a federal statute punishing the mailing of "obscene, lewd, lascivious or filthy . . ." materials. The key to that holding was the Court's rejection of the claim that obscene materials were protected by the First Amendment. Five Justices joined in the opinion stating:

All ideas having even the slightest redeeming social importance—unorthodox ideas, controversial ideas, even ideas hateful to the prevailing climate of opinion—have full protection of the [First Amendment guaranties], unless excludable because they encroach upon the limited area of more important interests. But implicit in the history of the First Amendment is the rejection of obscenity as utterly without redeeming social importance. . . .

Apart from the initial formulation in the *Roth* case, no majority of the Court has at any given time been able to agree on a standard to determine what constitutes obscene, pornographic material subject to regulation under the States' police power. *** We have seen "a variety of views among the members of the Court unmatched in any other course of constitutional adjudication." *** This is not remarkable, for in the area of freedom of speech and press the courts must always remain sensitive to any infringement on genuinely serious literary, artistic, political, or scientific expression. This is an area in which there are few eternal verities. . . .

II

This much has been categorically settled by the Court, that obscene material is unprotected by the First Amendment. *** "The First and Fourteenth

Amendments have never been treated as absolutes." *** We acknowledge, however, the inherent dangers of undertaking to regulate any form of expression. State statutes designed to regulate obscene materials must be carefully limited. *** As a result, we now confine the permissible scope of such regulation to works which depict or describe sexual conduct. That conduct must be specifically defined by the applicable state law, as written or authoritatively construed. A state office must also be limited to works which, taken as a whole, appeal to the prurient interest in sex, which portray sexual conduct in a patently offensive way, and which, taken as a whole, do not have serious literary, artistic, political, or scientific value.

The basic guidelines for the trier of fact must be: (a) whether "the average person, applying contemporary community standards" would find that the work, taken as a whole, appeals to the prurient interest, *** (b) whether the work depicts or describes, in a patently offensive way, sexual conduct specifically defined by the applicable state law, and (c) whether the work, taken as a whole, lacks serious literary, artistic, political, or scientific value. We do not adopt as a constitutional standard the *"utterly without redeeming social value"* test of *Memoirs v. Massachusetts;* *** that concept has never commanded the adherence of more than three Justices at one time. *** If a state law that regulates obscene material is thus limited, as written or construed, the First Amendment values applicable to the States through the Fourteenth Amendment are adequately protected by the ultimate power of appellate courts to conduct an independent review of constitutional claims when necessary. ***

We emphasize that it is not our function to propose regulatory schemes for the States. That must await their concrete legislative efforts. It is possible, however, to give a few plain examples of what a state statute could define for regulation under the second part (b) of the standard announced in this opinion *supra:*

(a) Patently offensive representations or descriptions of ultimate sexual acts, normal or perverted, actual or simulated.
(b) Patently offensive representations or descriptions of masturbation, excretory functions, and lewd exhibition of the genitals.

Sex and nudity may not be exploited without limit by films or pictures exhibited or sold in places of public accommodation any more than live sex and nudity can be exhibited or sold without limit in such public places. At a minimum, prurient, patently offensive depiction or description of sexual conduct must have serious literary, artistic, political, or scientific value to merit First Amendment protection. ***

Under the holdings announced today, no one will be subject to prosecution for the sale or exposure of obscene materials unless these materials depict or describe patently offensive "hard core" sexual conduct specifically defined by the regulating state law, as written or construed. We are satisfied that these specific prerequisites will provide fair notice to a dealer in such materials that his public and commercial activities may bring prosecution. *** . . .

It is certainly true that the absence, since *Roth,* of a single majority view of this Court as to proper standards for testing obscenity has placed a strain on both state and federal courts. But today, for the first time since *Roth* was decided in 1957, a majority of this Court has agreed on concrete guidelines to isolate "hard core" pornography from expression protected by the First Amendment. . . .

This may not be an easy road, free from difficulty. But no amount of "fatigue" should lead us to adopt a convenient "institutional" rationale—an absolutist, "anything goes" view of the First Amendment— because it will lighten our burdens. "Such an abnegation of judicial supervision in this field would be inconsistent with our duty to uphold the constitutional guarantees." *** Nor should be remedy "tension between state and federal courts" by arbitrarily depriving the States of a power reserved to them under the Constitution, a power which they have enjoyed and exercised continuously from before the adoption of the First Amendment to this day. *** . . .

III

Under a national Constitution, fundamental First Amendment limitations on the powers of the States do not vary from community to community, but this does not mean that there are, or should or can be, fixed, uniform national standards of precisely what appeals to the "prurient interest" or is "patently offensive." These are essentially questions of fact, and our nation is simply too big and too diverse for this Court to reasonably expect that such standards could be articulated for all 50 States in a single formulation, even assuming the prerequisite consensus exists. When triers of fact are asked to decide whether "the average person, applying contemporary community standards" would consider certain materials "prurient," it would be unrealistic to require that the answer be based on some abstract formulation. The adversary system, with lay jurors as the usual ultimate factfinders in criminal prosecution, has historically permitted triers-of-fact to draw on the standards of their community, guided always by limiting instructions on the law. To require a State to structure obscenity proceedings around evidence of a national "community standard" would be an exercise in futility. . . .

It is neither realistic nor constitutionally sound to read the First Amendment as requiring that the people of Maine or Mississippi accept public depiction of conduct found tolerable in Las Vegas, or New York City. *** People in different States vary in their tastes and attitudes, and this diversity is not to be strangled by the absolutism of imposed uniformity.

IV

The dissenting Justices sound the alarm of repression. But, in our view, to equate the free and robust exchange of ideas and political debate with commercial exploitation of obscene material demeans the grand conception of the First Amendment and its high purposes in the historic struggle for freedom. It is a "misuse of the great guarantees of free speech and free press. . . ." *** The First Amendment protects works which, taken as a whole, have serious literary, artistic, political or scientific value, regardless of whether the government or a majority of the people approve the ideas these works represent. "The protection given speech and press was fashioned to assure unfettered interchange of *ideas* for the bringing about of political and social changes desired by the people." *** But the public portrayal of hard core sexual conduct for its own sake, and for the ensuing commercial gain, is a different matter.

One can concede that the "sexual revolution" of recent years may have had useful byproducts in striking layers of prudery from a subject long irrationally kept from needed ventilation. But it does not follow that no regulation of patently offensive "hard core" materials is needed or permissible; civilized people do not allow unregulated access to heroin because it is a derivative of medicinal morphine. . . .

Mr. Justice Douglas, dissenting.

. . . Today the Court retreats from the earlier formulations of the constitutional test and undertakes to make new definitions. This effort, like the earlier ones, is earnest and well-intentioned. The difficulty is that we do not deal with constitutional terms, since "obscenity" is not mentioned in the Constitution or Bill of Rights. And the First Amendment makes no such exception from "the press" which it undertakes to protect nor, as I have said on other occasions, is an exception necessarily implied, for there was no recognized exception to the free press at the time the Bill of Rights was adopted which treated "obscene" publications differently from other types of papers, magazines, and books. So there are no constitutional guidelines for deciding what is and what is not "obscene." The Court is at large because we deal with tastes and standards of literature. What shocks me may be sustenance for my neighbor. What causes one person to boil up in rage over one pamphlet or movie may reflect only his neurosis, not shared by others. We deal here with problems of censorship which, if adopted, should be done by constitutional amendment after full debate by the people.

Obscenity cases usually generate tremendous emotional outbursts. They have no business being in the courts. If a constitutional amendment authorized censorship, the censor would probably be an administrative agency. Then criminal prosecutions could follow as, if and when publishers defied the censor and sold their literature. Under that regime a publisher would know when he was on dangerous ground. Under the present regime—whether the old standards or the new ones are used—the criminal law becomes a trap. A brand new test would put a publisher behind bars under a new law improvised by the courts after the publication. . . .

My contention is that until a civil proceeding has placed a tract beyond the pale, no criminal prosecution should be sustained. For no more vivid illustration of vague and uncertain laws could be designed than those we have fashioned. As Mr. Justice Harlan has said:

The upshot of all this divergence in viewpoint is that anyone who undertakes to examine the Court's decisions since *Roth* which have held particular material obscene or not obscene would find himself in utter bewilderment. *** ...

... The idea that the First Amendment permits government to ban publications that are "offensive" to some people puts an ominous gloss on freedom of the press. That test would make it possible to ban any paper or any journal or magazine in some benighted place. The First Amendment was designed "to invite dispute," to induce "a condition of unrest," to "create dissatisfactions with conditions as they are," and even to stir "people to anger." *** The idea that the First Amendment permits punishment for ideas that are "offensive" to the particular judge or jury sitting in judgment is astounding. No greater leveler of speech or literature has ever been designed. To give the power to the censor, as we do today, is to make a sharp and radical break with the traditions of a free society. The First Amendment was not fashioned as a vehicle for dispensing tranquilizers to the people. Its prime function was to keep debate open to "offensive" as well as to "staid" people. The tendency throughout history has been to subdue the individual and to exalt the power of government. The use of the standard "offensive" gives authority to government that cuts the very vitals out of the First Amendment. As is intimated by the Court's opinion, the materials before us may be garbage. But so is much of what is said in political campaigns, in the daily press, on TV or over the radio. By reason of the First Amendment—and solely because of it—speakers and publishers have not been threatened or subdued because their thoughts and ideas may be "offensive" to some. ...

Mr. Justice Brennan, with whom **Mr. Justice Stewart** and **Mr. Justice Marshall** join, dissenting. ...

Jenkins v. Georgia
418 U.S. 153; 94 S. Ct. 2750; 41 L. Ed.2d 642 (1974)
Vote: 9-0

Jenkins, the manager of a movie theater in Albany, Georgia, was arrested after his theater showed the film Carnal Knowledge. *After a trial in which a jury viewed the allegedly obscene film, Jenkins was convicted of "distributing obscene material" under the Georgia Penal Code. He was fined $750 and sentenced to one year probation. On appeal, the Georgia Supreme Court upheld the conviction and sentence.*

Mr. Justice Rehnquist delivered the opinion of the Court.

... There is little to be found in the record about the film "Carnal Knowledge" other than the film itself. However, appellant has supplied a variety of information and critical commentary, the authenticity of which appellee does not dispute. The film appeared on many "Ten Best" lists for 1971, the year in which it was released. Many but not all of the reviews were favorable. We believe that the following passage from a review which appeared in the *Saturday Review* is a reasonably accurate description of the film:

"[It is basically a story] of two young college men, roommates and lifelong friends forever preoccupied with their sex lives. Both are first met as virgins. [Jack] Nicholson is the more knowledgeable and attractive of the two; speaking colloquially, he is a burgeoning bastard. Art Garfunkel is his friend, the nice but troubled guy straight out of those early Feiffer cartoons, but real. He falls in love with the lovely Susan (Candice Bergen) and unknowingly shares her with his college buddy. As the 'safer' one of the two, he is selected by Susan for marriage.

"The time changes. Both men are in their thirties, pursuing successful careers in New York. Nicholson has been running through an average of a dozen women a year but has never managed to meet the right one, the one with the full bosom, the good legs, the properly rounded bottom. More than that, each and every one is a threat to his malehood and peace of mind, until at last, in a bar, he finds Ann-Margret, an aging bachelor girl with striking cleavage and, quite obviously, something of a past. 'Why don't we shack up?' she suggests. They do and a horrendous relationship ensues, complicated mainly by her paranoidal desire to marry. Meanwhile, what of Garfunkel? The sparks have gone out of his marriage, the sex has lost its savor, and Garfunkel tries once more. And later, even more foolishly, again."

The appellee [the state of Georgia] contends essentially that under *Miller* [v. *California*] the obscenity . . . of the film "Carnal Knowledge" was a question for the jury, and that the jury, having resolved the question against appellant [Jenkins], and there being some evidence to support its findings, the judgment of conviction should be affirmed. . . . *Miller* states that the questions of what appeals to the "prurient interest" and what is "patently offensive" under the obscenity test which it formulates are "essential questions of fact." *** . . . We held in *Paris Adult Theater I v. Slaton* *** (1973), decided on the same day, that expert testimony as to obscenity is not necessary when the films at issue are themselves placed in evidence. . . .

But all of this does not lead us to agree with the Supreme Court of Georgia's apparent conclusion that the jury's verdict against appellant virtually precluded all further appellate review of appellant's assertion that his exhibition of the film was protected by the First and Fourteenth Amendments. Even though questions of appeal to the "prurient interest" or of patent offensiveness are "essentially questions of fact," it would be a serious misreading of *Miller* to conclude that juries have unbridled discretion in determining what is "patently offensive." Not only did we there say that "the First Amendment values applicable to the States through the Fourteenth Amendment are adequately protected by the ultimate power of appellate courts to conduct an independent review of constitutional claims when necessary," *** but we made it plain that under that holding "no one will be subject to prosecution for the sale or exposure of obscene materials unless these materi-als depict or describe patently offensive 'hard core' sexual conduct. . . ." ***

We also took pains in *Miller* to "give a few plain examples of what a state statute could define for regulation under part (b) of the standard announced," that is, the requirement of patent offensiveness. *** These examples included "representations or descriptions of ultimate sexual acts, normal or perverted, actual or simulated," and "representations or descriptions of masturbation, excretory functions, and lewd exhibition of the genitals." *** While this did not purport to be an exhaustive catalog of what juries might find patently offensive, it was certainly intended to fix substantive constitutional limitations, deriving from the First Amendment, on the type of material subject to such a determination. It would be wholly at odds with this aspect of *Miller* to uphold an obscenity conviction based upon a defendant's depiction of a woman with a bare midriff, even though a properly charged jury unanimously agreed on a verdict of guilty.

Our own viewing of the film satisfies us that "Carnal Knowledge" could not be found under the *Miller* standards to depict sexual conduct in a patently offensive way. Nothing in the movie falls within either of the two examples given in *Miller* of material which may constitutionally be found to meet the "patently offensive" element of those standards, nor is there anything sufficiently similar to such material to justify similar treatment. While the subject matter of the picture is, in a broader sense, sex, and there are scenes in which sexual conduct including "ultimate sexual acts" is to be understood to be taking place, the camera does not focus on the bodies of the actors at such times. There is no exhibition whatever of the actors' genitals, lewd or otherwise, during these scenes. There are occasional scenes of nudity, but nudity alone is not enough to make material legally obscene under the *Miller* standards.

Appellant's showing of the film "Carnal Knowledge" is simply not the "public portrayal of hard core sexual conduct for its own sake, and for the ensuing commercial gain" which we said was punishable in *Miller*. *** We hold that the film could not, as a matter of constitutional law, be found to depict sexual conduct in a patently offensive way, and that it is therefore not outside the protection of the First and Fourteenth Amendments because it is obscene. No other basis appearing in the record upon which the judgment of conviction can be sustained, we reverse the judgment of the Supreme Court of Georgia.

Reversed.

Mr. Justice Brennan, with whom *Mr. Justice Stewart* and *Mr. Justice Marshall* join, concurring in the result.

... In order to make the review mandated by *Miller,* the Court was required to screen the film "Carnal Knowledge" and make an independent determination.... Following that review, the Court holds that "Carnal Knowledge" "could not, as a matter of constitutional law, be found to depict sexual conduct in a patently offensive way, and that it is therefore not outside the protection of the First and Fourteenth Amendments because it is obscene." ***

Thus, it is clear that as long as the *Miller* test remains in effect "one cannot say with certainty that material is obscene until at least five members of this Court, applying inevitably obscure standards, have pronounced it so." *** Because of the attendant uncertainty of such a process and its inevitable institutional stress upon the judiciary, I continue to adhere to my view that, "at least in the absence of distribution to juveniles or obtrusive exposure to unconsenting adults, the First and Fourteenth Amendments prohibit the State and Federal Governments from attempting wholly to suppress sexually oriented materials on the basis of their allegedly 'obscene' contents." *** It is clear that, tested by that constitutional standard, the Georgia obscenity statutes under which appellant Jenkins was convicted are constitutionally overbroad and therefore facially invalid. I therefore concur in the result in the Court's reversal of Jenkins' conviction.

New York v. Ferber

458 U.S. 747; 102 S. Ct. 3348; 73 L. Ed. 2d 1113 (1982)
Vote: 9-0

Justice White delivered the opinion of the Court.

At issue in this case is the constitutionality of a New York criminal statute which prohibits persons from knowingly promoting sexual performances by children under the age of 16 by distributing material which depicts such performances.

In recent years, the exploitive use of children in the production of pornography has become a serious national problem. The federal government and forty-seven States have sought to combat the problem with statutes specifically directed at the production of child pornography. At least half of such statutes do not require that the materials produced be legally obscene. Thirty-five States and the United States Congress have also passed legislation prohibiting the distribution of such materials; twenty States prohibit the distribution of material depicting children engaged in sexual conduct without requiring that the material be legally obscene.

New York is one of the twenty. In 1977, the New York legislature enacted Article 263 of its Penal Law.

Section 263.05 criminalizes as a class C felony the use of a child in a sexual performance:

A person is guilty of the use of a child in a sexual performance if knowing the character and content thereof he employs, authorizes or induces a child less than sixteen years of age to engage in a sexual performance or being a parent, legal guardian or custodian of such child, he consents to the participation by such child in a sexual performance.

A "[s]exual performance" is defined as "any performance or part thereof which includes sexual conduct by a child less than sixteen years of age," ***. "Sexual conduct" is in turn defined *** :

"Sexual conduct" means actual or simulated sexual intercourse, deviate sexual intercourse, sexual bestiality, masturbation, sado-masochistic abuse, or lewd exhibition of the genitals.

A performance is defined as "any play, motion picture, photograph or dance" or "any other visual representation exhibited before an audience." ***

At issue in this case is Sec. 263.15, defining a class D felony:

A person is guilty of promoting a sexual performance by a child when, knowing the character and content thereof, he produces, directs or promotes any performance which includes sexual conduct by a child less than sixteen years of age.

To "promote" is also defined:

"Promote" means to procure, manufacture, issue, sell, give, provide, lend, mail, deliver, transfer, transmute, publish, distribute, circulate, disseminate, present, exhibit or advertise, or to offer or agree to do the same.

A companion provision bans only the knowing dissemination of obscene material.

This case arose when Paul Ferber, the proprietor of a Manhattan bookstore specializing in sexually oriented products, sold two films to an undercover police officer. The films are devoted almost exclusively to depicting young boys masturbating. Ferber was indicted on two counts of Sec. 263.10 and two counts of Sec. 263.15, the two New York laws controlling dissemination of child pornography. After a jury trial, Ferber was acquitted of the two counts of promoting an obscene sexual performance, but found guilty of the two counts under Sec. 263.15 which did not require proof that the films were obscene. Ferber's convictions were affirmed without opinion by the Appellate Division of the New York State Supreme Court. ***

The New York Court of Appeals reversed, holding that Sec. 263.15 violated the First Amendment. *** . . . Two judges dissented. We granted the State's petition for *certiorari,* *** . . . presenting the single question:

To prevent the abuse of children who are made to engage in sexual conduct for commercial purposes, could the New York State Legislature, consistent with the First Amendment, prohibit the dissemination of material which shows children engaged in sexual conduct, regardless of whether such material is obscene?

. . . In *Miller v. California* [1973], a majority of the Court agreed that "a state offense must also be limited to works which, taken as a whole, appeal to the prurient interest in sex, which portray sexual conduct in a patently offensive way, and which, taken as a whole, do not have serious literary, artistic, political, or scientific value." *** Over the past decade,

we have adhered to the guidelines expressed in *Miller.* . . .

. . . The *Miller* standard, like its predecessors, was an accommodation between the state's interests in protecting the "sensibilities of unwilling recipients" from exposure to pornographic material and the dangers of censorship inherent unabashedly content-based laws. Like obscenity statutes, laws directed at the dissemination of child pornography run the risk of suppressing protected expression by allowing the hand of the censor to become unduly heavy. For the following reasons, however, we are persuaded that the States are entitled to greater leeway in the regulation of pornographic depictions of children.

First. It is evident beyond the need for elaboration that a state's interest in "safeguarding the physical and psychological well being of a minor" is "compelling." *** "A democratic society rests, for its continuance, upon the healthy well-rounded growth of young people into full maturity as citizens." *** Accordingly, we have sustained legislation aimed at protecting the physical and emotional well-being of youth even when the laws have operated in the sensitive area of constitutionally protected rights. In *Prince v. Massachusetts,* *** the Court held that a statute prohibiting use of a child to distribute literature on the street was valid notwithstanding the statute's effect on a First Amendment activity. In *Ginsberg v. New York,* *** we sustained a New York law protecting children from exposure to nonobscene literature. Most recently, we held that the government's interest in the "well-being of its youth" justified special treatment of indecent broadcasting received by adults as well as children. *FCC v. Pacifica Foundation.* ***

The prevention of sexual exploitation and abuse of children constitutes a government objective of surpassing importance. The legislative findings accompanying passage of the New York laws reflect this concern:

There has been a proliferation of children as subjects in sexual performances. The case of children is a sacred trust and should not be abused by those who seek to profit through a commercial network based on the exploitation of children. The public policy of the state demands the protection of children from exploitation through sexual performances.

We shall not second-guess this legislative judgment. Respondent has not intimated that we do so. Suffice it to say that virtually all of the States and the United States have passed legislation proscribing the production of or otherwise combatting "child pornography." The legislative judgment, as well as the judgment found in the relevant literature, is that the use of children as subjects of pornographic materials is harmful to the physiological, emotional, and mental health of the child. That judgment, we think, easily passes muster under the First Amendment.

Second. The distribution of photographs and films depicting sexual activity by juveniles is intrinsically related to the sexual abuse of children in at least two ways. First, the materials produced are a permanent record of the children's participation and the harm to the child is exacerbated by their circulation. Second, the distribution network for child pornography must be closed if the production of material which requires the sexual exploitation of children is to be effectively controlled. Indeed, there is no serious contention that the legislature was unjustified in believing that it is difficult, if not impossible, to halt the exploitation of children by pursuing only those who produce the photographs and movies. While the production of pornographic materials is a low-profile, clandestine industry, the need to market the resulting products requires a visible apparatus of distribution. The most expeditious if not the only practical method of law enforcement may be to dry up the market for this material by imposing severe criminal penalties on persons selling, advertising, or otherwise promoting the product. Thirty-five States and Congress have concluded that restraints on the distribution of pornographic materials are required in order to effectively combat the problem, and there is a body of literature and testimony to support these legislative conclusions. ***

Respondent does not contend that the State is unjustified in pursuing those who distribute child pornography. Rather, he argues that it is enough for the State to prohibit the distribution of materials that are legally obscene under the *Miller* test. While some States may find that this approach properly accommodates its interests, it does not follow that the First Amendment prohibits a State from going further. The *Miller* standard, like all general definitions of what may be banned as obscene, does not reflect the State's particular and more compelling interest in prosecuting those who promote the sexual exploitation of children. Thus, the question under the *Miller* test of whether a work, taken as a whole, appeals to the prurient interest of the average person bears no connection to the issue of whether a child has been physically or psychologically harmed in the production of the work. Similarly, a sexually explicit depiction need not be "patently offensive" in order to have required the sexual exploitation of a child for its production. In addition, a work which, taken on the whole, contains serious literary, artistic, political, or scientific value may nevertheless embody the hardest core of child pornography. "It is irrelevant to the child [who has been abused] whether or not the material . . . has a literary, artistic, political, or social value." *** We therefore cannot conclude that the *Miller* standard is a satisfactory solution to the child pornography problem.

Third. The advertising and selling of child pornography provides an economic motive for and is thus an integral part of the production of such materials, an activity illegal throughout the nation. "It rarely has been suggested that the constitutional freedom for speech and press extends its immunity to speech or writing used as an integral part of conduct in violation of a valid criminal statute." *** We note that were the statutes outlawing the employment of children in these films and photographs fully effective, and the constitutionality of these laws [has] been questioned, the First Amendment implications would be no greater than that presented by laws against distribution: enforceable production laws would leave no child pornography to be marketed.

Fourth. The value of permitting live performances and photographic reproductions of children engaged in lewd sexual conduct is exceedingly modest, if not *de minimis*. We consider it unlikely that visual depictions of children performing sexual acts or lewdly exhibiting their genitals would often constitute an important and necessary part of a literary performance or scientific or educational work. As the state judge in this case observed, if it were necessary for literary or artistic value, a person over the statutory age who perhaps looked younger could be utilized. Simulation outside of the prohibition of the statute could provide another alternative. Nor is there any question here of censoring a particular literary theme or portrayal of sexual activity. The First Amendment interest is limited to that of rendering the portrayal somewhat more "realistic" by utilizing or photographing children.

Fifth. Recognizing and classifying child pornography as a category of material outside the protection of the First Amendment is not incompatible with our earlier decisions. "The question whether speech is, or is not protected by the First Amendment often depends on the content of the speech." . . . *** Thus, it is not rare that a content-based classification of speech has been accepted because it may be appropriately generalized that within the confines of the given classification, the evil to be restricted so overwhelmingly outweighs the expressive interests, if any, at stake, that no process of case-by-case adjudication is required. When a definable class of material, such as that covered by Sec. 263.15, bears so heavily and pervasively on the welfare of children engaged in its production, we think the balance of competing interests is clearly struck and that it is permissible to consider these materials as without the protection of the First Amendment. . . .

It remains to address the claim that the New York statute is unconstitutionally overbroad because it would forbid the distribution of material with serious literary, scientific or educational value or material which does not threaten the harms sought to be combatted by the State. Respondent prevailed on that ground below, and it is to that issue that we now turn.

. . . While the reach of the statute is directed at the hard core of child pornography, the Court of Appeals was understandably concerned that some protected expression, ranging from medical textbooks to pictorials in *National Geographic* would fall prey to the

statute. How often, if ever, it may be necessary to employ children to engage in conduct clearly within the reach of the Sec. 263.15 in order to produce educational, medical or artistic works cannot be known with certainty. Yet we seriously doubt, and it has not been suggested, that these arguably impermissible applications of the statute amount to more than a tiny fraction of the materials within the statute's reach. Nor will we assume that the New York courts will widen the possibly invalid reach of the statute by giving an expansive construction to the proscription on "lewd exhibition[s] of the genitals." Under these circumstances, Sec. 263.15 is "not substantially overbroad and . . . whatever overbreadth may exist should be cured through case-by-case analysis of the fact situations to which its sanctions, assertedly, may not be applied." ***

Because Sec. 263.15 is not substantially overbroad, it is unnecessary to consider its application to material that does not depict sexual conduct of a type that New York may restrict consistent with the First Amendment. As applied to Paul Ferber and to others who distribute similar material, the statute does not violate the First Amendment as applied to the States through the Fourteenth. The decision of the New York Court of Appeals is reversed and the case is remanded to that court for further proceedings not inconsistent with this opinion.

So ordered.

Justice Blackmun concurs in the result.

Justice O'Connor, concurring. . . .

Justice Brennan, with whom *Justice Marshall* joins, concurring in the judgment. . . .

Justice Stevens, concurring in the judgment. . . .

American Booksellers Ass'n., Inc. v. Hudnut

771 F. 2d 323 (U.S. Ct. App., 7th Cir., 1985)
Vote: 3-0

In April 1984, the city of Indianapolis, Indiana, adopted an ordinance defining "pornography" as a practice that discriminates against women. The law

banned pornography within the city and permitted women to sue producers, distributors, and/or sellers of pornography for damages and injunctive relief.

The American Booksellers Association and numerous other plaintiffs successfully challenged the ordinance in federal district court. See American Booksellers v. Hudnut, *598 F. Supp. 1316 (1984). Mayor Hudnut of Indianapolis, the principal defendant in the case, appealed to the Seventh Circuit Court of Appeals. Judge Frank Easterbrook wrote the opinion for the unanimous circuit court.*

Easterbrook, J.:

. . . To be "obscene" under *Miller v. California* *** (1973), a "publication must, taken as a whole, appeal to the prurient interest, must contain patently offensive depictions or descriptions of specified sexual conduct, and on the whole have no serious literary, artistic, political, or scientific value." *** Offensiveness must be assessed under the standards of the community. Both offensiveness and an appeal to something other than "normal, healthy sexual desires" are essential elements of "obscenity." ***

"Pornography" under the ordinance is "the graphic sexually explicit subordination of women, whether in pictures or in words, that also includes one or more of the following:

(1) Women are presented as sexual objects who enjoy pain or humiliation; or

(2) Women are presented as sexual objects who experience sexual pleasure in being raped; or

(3) Women are presented as sexual objects tied up or cut up or mutilated or bruised or physically hurt, or as dismembered or truncated or fragmented or severed into body parts; or

(4) Women are presented as being penetrated by objects or animals; or

(5) Women are presented in scenarios of degradation, injury, abasement, torture, shown as filthy or inferior, bleeding, bruised, or hurt in a context that makes these conditions sexual; or

(6) Women are presented as sexual objects for domination, conquest, violation, exploitation, possession, or use, or through postures or positions of servility or submission or display."

The [law] provides that the "use of men, children, or transsexuals in the place of women in paragraphs (1) through (6) above shall also constitute pornography under this section." The ordinance as passed in April 1984 defined "sexually explicit" to mean actual or simulated intercourse or the uncovered exhibition of the genitals, buttocks or anus. An amendment in June 1984 deleted this provision, leaving the term undefined.

The Indianapolis ordinance does not refer to the prurient interest, to offensiveness, or to the standards of the community. It demands attention to particular depictions, not to the work judged as a whole. It is irrelevant under the ordinance whether the work has literary, artistic, political, or scientific value. The City and many *amici* point to these omissions as virtues. They maintain that pornography influences attitudes, and the statute is a way to alter the socialization of men and women rather than to vindicate community standards of offensiveness. And as one of the principal drafters of the ordinance has asserted, "if a woman is subjected, why should it matter that the work has other value?" ***

Civil rights groups and feminists have entered this case as *amici* on both sides. Those supporting the ordinance say that it will play an important role in reducing the tendency of men to view women as sexual objects, a tendency that leads to both unacceptable attitudes and discrimination in the workplace and violence away from it. Those opposing the ordinance point out that much radical feminist literature is explicit and depicts women in ways forbidden by the ordinance and that the ordinance would reopen old battles. It is unclear how Indianapolis would treat works from James Joyce's *Ulysses* to Homer's *Iliad;* both depict women as submissive objects for conquest and domination.

We do not try to balance the arguments for and against an ordinance such as this. The ordinance discriminates on the ground of the content of the speech. Speech treating women in the approved way — in sexual encounters "premised on equality" *** is lawful no matter how sexually explicit. Speech treating women in the disapproved way — as submissive in matters sexual or as enjoying humiliation — is unlawful no matter how significant the literary, artistic, or political qualities of the work taken as a whole. The state may not ordain preferred viewpoints in this way. The Constitution forbids the state to declare one perspective right and silence opponents. . . .

. . . Under the First Amendment the government must leave to the people the evaluation of ideas.

Bold or subtle, an idea is as powerful as the audience allows it to be. A belief may be pernicious—the beliefs of Nazis led to the death of millions, those of the Klan to the repression of millions. A pernicious belief may prevail. Totalitarian governments today rule much of the planet, practicing suppression of billions and spreading dogma that may enslave others. One of the things that separates our society from theirs is our absolute right to propagate opinions that the governments finds wrong or even hateful. . . .

Under the ordinance graphic sexually explicit speech is "pornography" or not depending on the perspective the author adopts. Speech that "subordinates" women and also, for example, presents women as enjoying pain, humiliation, or rape, or even presents women in "positions of servility or submission or display" is forbidden, no matter how great the literary or political value of the work taken as a whole. Speech that portrays women in positions of equality is lawful, no matter how graphic the sexual content. This is thought control. It establishes an "approved" view of women, of how they may react to sexual encounters, of how the sexes may relate to each other. Those who espouse the approved view may use sexual images; those who do not, may not.

Indianapolis justifies the ordinance on the ground that pornography affects thoughts. Men who see women depicted as subordinate are more likely to treat them so. Pornography is an aspect of dominance. It does not persuade people so much as change them. It works by socializing, by establishing the expected and the permissible. In this view pornography is not an idea; pornography is the injury.

There is much to this perspective. Beliefs are also facts. People often act in accordance with the images and patterns they find around them. People raised in a religion tend to accept the tenets of that religion, often without independent examination. People taught from birth that black people are fit only for slavery rarely rebelled against that creed; beliefs coupled with the self-interest of the masters established a social structure that inflicted great harm while enduring for centuries. Words and images act at the level of the subconscious before they persuade at the level of the conscious. Even the truth has little chance unless a statement fits within the framework of beliefs that may never have been subjected to rational study.

Therefore we accept the premises of this legislation. Depictions of subordination tend to perpetuate subordination. The subordinate status of women in turn leads to affront and lower pay at work, insult and injury at home, battery and rape on the streets. In the language of the legislature, "[p]ornography is central in creating and maintaining sex as a basis of discrimination. Pornography is a systematic practice of exploitation and subordination based on sex which differentially harms women. The bigotry and contempt it produces, with the acts of aggression it fosters, harm women's opportunities for equality and rights [of all kinds]." ***

Yet this simply demonstrates the power of pornography as speech. All of these unhappy effects depend on mental intermediation. Pornography affects how people see the world, their fellows, and social relations. If pornography is what pornography does, so is other speech. Hitler's orations affected how some Germans saw Jews. Communism is a world view, not simply a Manifesto by Marx and Engels or a set of speeches. Efforts to suppress communist speech in the United States were based on the belief that the public acceptability of such ideas would increase the likelihood of totalitarian government. Religions affect socialization in the most pervasive way. The opinion in *Wisconsin v. Yoder* *** (1972), shows how a religion can dominate an entire approach to life, governing much more than the relation between the sexes. Many people believe that the existence of television, apart from the content of specific programs, leads to intellectual laziness, to a penchant for violence, to many other ills. The Alien and Sedition Acts passed during the administration of John Adams rested on a sincerely held belief that disrespect for the government leads to social collapse and revolution—a belief with support in the history of many nations. Most governments of the world act on this empirical evidence regularly, suppressing critical speech. In the United States, however, the strength of the support for this belief is irrelevant. Seditious libel is protected speech unless the danger is not only grave but also imminent. ***

Racial bigotry, anti-Semitism, violence on television, reporters' biases—these and many more influence the culture and shape our socialization. None is directly answerable by more speech, unless that speech too finds its place in the popular culture. Yet all is protected as speech, however insidious. Any other answer leaves the government in control of all of the institutions of culture, the great censor and director of which thoughts are good for us.

Sexual responses often are unthinking responses, and the association of sexual arousal with the subordination of women therefore may have a substantial effect. But almost all cultural stimuli provoke unconscious responses. Religious ceremonies condition their participants. Teachers convey messages by selecting what not to cover; the implicit message about what is off-limits or unthinkable may be more powerful than the messages for which they present rational argument. Television scripts contain unarticulated assumptions. People may be conditioned in subtle ways. If the fact that speech plays a role in a process of conditioning were enough to permit governmental regulation, that would be the end of freedom of speech.

It is possible to interpret the claim that the pornography is the harm in a different way. Indianapolis emphasizes the injury that models in pornographic films and pictures may suffer. The record contains materials depicting sexual torture, penetration of women by red-hot irons and the like. These concerns have nothing to do with written materials subject to the statute, and physical injury can occur with or without the "subordination" of women. . . .

The more immediate point, however, is that the image of pain is not necessarily pain. In *Body Double,* a suspense film directed by Brian DePalma, a woman who has disrobed and presented in a sexually explicit display is murdered by an intruder with a drill. The drill runs through the woman's body. The film is sexually explicit and a murder occurs — yet no one believes that the actress suffered pain or died. In *Barbarella,* a character played by Jane Fonda is at times displayed in sexually explicit ways and at times shown "bleeding, bruised, [and] hurt in a context that makes these conditions sexual"—and again no one believes that Fonda was actually tortured to make the film. In *Carnal Knowledge* a woman grovels to please the sexual whims of a character played by Jack Nicholson; no one believes that

there was a real sexual submission and the Supreme Court held the film protected by the First Amendment. *** And this works both ways. The description of women's sexual domination of men in *Lysistrata* was not real dominance. Depictions may affect slavery, war, or sexual roles, but a book about slavery is not itself slavery, or a book about death by poison a murder.

Much of Indianapolis's argument rests on the belief that when speech is "unanswerable," and the metaphor that there is a "marketplace of ideas" does not apply, the First Amendment does not apply either. The metaphor is honored; Milton's *Aeropagitica* and John Stewart Mill's *On Liberty* defend freedom of speech on the ground that the truth will prevail, and many of the most important cases under the First Amendment recite this position. The Framers undoubtedly believed it. As a general matter it is true. But the Constitution does not make the dominance of truth a necessary condition of speech. To say that it does would be to confuse an outcome of free speech with a necessary condition for the application of the amendment.

A power to limit speech on the ground that truth has not yet prevailed and is not likely to prevail implies the power to declare truth. At some point the government must be able to say (as Indianapolis has said): "We know what the truth is, yet a free exchange of speech has not driven out falsity, so that we must now prohibit falsity." If the government may declare the truth, why wait for the failure of speech? Under the First Amendment, however, there is no such thing as a false idea *** so the government may not restrict speech on the ground that in a free exchange truth is not yet dominant.

At any time, some speech is ahead in the game; the more numerous speakers prevail. Supporters of minority candidates may be forever "excluded" from the political process because their candidates never win, because few people believe their positions. This does not mean that freedom of speech has failed. . . .

We come, finally, to the argument that pornography is "low value" speech, that it is enough like obscenity that Indianapolis may prohibit it. Some cases hold that speech far removed from politics and other subjects at the core of the Framers' concerns may be subjected to special regulation. *** These cases do not sustain statutes that select among viewpoints, however. In *Pacifica* the FCC sought to keep vile language off the air during certain times. The Court held that it may; but the Court would not have sustained a regulation prohibiting scatological descriptions of Republicans but not scatological descriptions of Democrats, or any other form of selection among viewpoints. . . .

At all events, "pornography" is not low value speech within the meaning of these cases. In Indianapolis it seeks to prohibit certain speech because it believes this speech influences social relations and politics on a grand scale, that it controls attitudes at home and in the legislature. This precludes a characterization of the speech as low value. True, pornography and obscenity have sex in common. But Indianapolis left out of its definition any reference to literary, artistic, political, or scientific value. The ordinance applies to graphic sexually explicit subordination in works great and small. The Court sometimes balances the value of speech against the costs of its restriction, but it does this by category of speech and not by the content of particular works. *** Indianapolis has created an approved point of view and so loses the support of these cases. . . .

Federal Communications Commission v. Pacifica Foundation
438 U.S. 726; 98 S.Ct. 3026; 57 L.Ed.2d 1073 (1978)
Vote: 5-4

*On Tuesday, October 30, 1973, at about 2 p.m., a New York radio station owned by the Pacifica Foundation broadcast a George Carlin monologue on the "seven dirty words you can't say on the radio," namely, "shit, piss, fuck, cunt, cocksucker, motherfucker, and tits." Before airing the recording, the station warned listeners of the strong content. The station received no complaints directly from listeners. Several weeks later, a man who claimed that he had heard the monologue while driving in his car with his young son filed a complaint with the Federal Communications Commission. Although it imposed no formal sanctions, the FCC indicated that the complaint would be "associated with the station's license file, and in the event that subsequent complaints are received, the Commission will then decide whether it should utilize any of the available sanctions it has been granted by Congress." *** Pacifica Foundation appealed the agency's action to the U.S. court of appeals, which reversed the FCC.*

Justice Stevens delivered the opinion of the Court . . .
. . . Obscene materials have been denied the protection of the First Amendment because their content is so offensive to contemporary moral standards. ***But the fact that society may find speech offensive is not a sufficient reason for suppressing it. Indeed, if it is the speaker's opinion that gives offense, that consequence is a reason for according it constitutional protection. For it is a central tenet of the First Amendment that the government must remain neutral in the marketplace of ideas. If there were any reason to believe that the Commission's characterization of the Carlin monologue as offensive could be traced to its political content—or even to the fact that it satirized contemporary attitudes about four-letter words—First Amendment protection might be required. But that is simply not this case. These words offend for the same reasons that obscenity offends. This place in the hierarchy of First Amendment values was aptly sketched by Justice Murphy when he said: "Such utterances are no essential part of any exposition of ideas, and are of such slight social value as a step to truth that any benefit that may be derived from them is clearly outweighed by the social interest in order and morality." ***

Although these words ordinarily lack literary, political, or scientific value, they are not entirely outside the protection of the First Amendment. Some uses of even the most offensive words are unquestionably protected. *** Indeed, we may assume, *arguendo,* that this monologue would be protected on other contexts. Nonetheless, the constitutional protection accorded to a communication containing such patently offensive sexual and excretory language need not be the same in every context. It is a characteristic of speech such as this that both its capacity to offend and its "social value," to use Justice Murphy's term, vary with the circumstances. Words that are commonplace in one setting are shocking in another. To paraphrase Justice Harlan, one man's lyric is another's vulgarity. ***

In this case it is undisputed that the content of Pacifica's broadcast was "vulgar," "offensive," and "shocking." Because content of that character is not entitled to absolute constitutional protection under all circumstances, we must consider its context in order to determine whether the Commission's action was constitutionally permissible.

We have long recognized that each medium of expression presents special First Amendment problems. And of all forms of communication, it is broadcasting that has received the most limited First Amendment protection. Thus, although other speakers cannot be licensed except under laws that carefully define and narrow official discretion, a broadcaster may be deprived of his license and his forum if the Commission decides that such an action would serve "the public interest, convenience, and necessity." *** Similarly, although the First Amendment protects newspaper publishers from being required to print the replies of those whom they criticize, *** it affords no such protection to broadcasters; on the contrary, they must give free time to the victims of their criticism. ***

The reasons for these distinctions are complex, but two have relevance to the present case. First, the broadcast media have established a uniquely pervasive presence in the lives of all Americans. Patently offensive, indecent material presented over the airwaves confronts the citizen, not only in public, but also in the privacy of the home, where the individual's right to be left alone plainly outweighs the First Amendment rights of an intruder. *** Because the broadcast audience is constantly tuning in and out, prior warnings cannot completely protect the listener or viewer from unexpected program content. To say that one may avoid further offense by turning off the radio when he hears indecent language is like saying that the remedy for an assault is to run away

after the first blow. One may hang up on an indecent phone call, but that option does not give the caller a constitutional immunity or avoid a harm that has already taken place.

Second, broadcasting is uniquely accessible to children, even those too young to read. Although Cohen's written message [see *Cohen v. California* (1971)] might have been incomprehensible to a first grader, Pacifica's broadcast could have enlarged a child's vocabulary in an instant. Other forms of offensive expression may be withheld from the young without restricting the expression at its source. Bookstores and motion picture theaters, for example, may be prohibited from making indecent material available to children. We held in *Ginsberg v. New York* *** [1968], that the government's interest in the "well-being of its young" and in supporting "parents' claim to authority in their own household" justified the regulation of otherwise protected expression. The ease with which children may obtain access to broadcast material, coupled with the concerns recognized in *Ginsberg,* amply justify special treatment of indecent broadcasting.

It is appropriate, in conclusion, to emphasize the narrowness of our holding. This case does not involve a two-way radio conversation between a cab driver and a dispatcher, or a telecast of an Elizabethan comedy. We have not decided that an occasional expletive in either setting would justify any sanction, or, indeed, that this broadcast would justify a criminal prosecution. The Commission's decision rested entirely on a nuisance rationale under which context is all-important. The concept requires consideration of a host of variables. The time of day was emphasized by the Commission. The content of the program in which the language is used will also affect the composition of the audience, and differences between radio, television, and perhaps closed-circuit transmissions, may also be relevant. As Justice Sutherland wrote, a "nuisance may be merely a right thing in the wrong place,—like a pig in the parlor instead of the barnyard." *** We simply hold that when the Commission finds that a pig has entered the parlor, the exercise of its regulatory power does not depend on proof that the pig is obscene.

The judgment of the Court of Appeals is reversed.

It is so ordered.

Justice Powell, with whom ***Justice Blackmun*** joins, concurring in part.

The issue . . . is whether the Commission may impose civil sanctions on a licensee radio station for broadcasting the monologue at two o'clock in the afternoon. The Commission's primary concern was to prevent the broadcast from reaching the ears of unsupervised children who were likely to be in the audience at that hour. In essence, the Commission sought to "channel" the monologue to hours when the fewest unsupervised children would be exposed to it. In my view, this consideration provides strong support for the Commission's holding.

The Court has recognized society's right to "adopt more stringent controls on communicative materials available to youths than on those available to adults." *** This recognition stems in large part from the fact that "a child . . . is not possessed of that full capacity for individual choice which is the presupposition of First Amendment guarantees." *** At the same time, such speech may have a deeper and more lasting negative effect on a child than on an adult. . . . The Commission properly held that the speech from which society may attempt to shield its children is not limited to that which appeals to the youthful prurient interest. The language involved in this case is as potentially degrading and harmful to children as representations of many erotic acts.

In most instances, the dissemination of this kind of speech to children may be limited without also limiting willing adults' access to it. Sellers of printed and recorded matter and exhibitors of motion pictures and live performances may be required to shut their doors to children, but such a requirement has no effect on adults' access. The difficulty is that such a physical separation of the audience cannot be accomplished in the broadcast media. . . .

In my view, the Commission was entitled to give substantial weight to this difference in reaching its decision in this case.

A second difference, not without relevance, is that broadcasting—unlike most other forms of communication—comes directly into the home, the one place where people ordinarily have the right not to be assaulted by uninvited and offensive sights and sounds. . . . The Commission also was entitled to give this factor appropriate weight in the circumstances of the instant case. This is not to say, however, that the Commission has an unrestricted license to decide what speech, protected in other media, may be banned from the airwaves in order to protect unwilling adults from momentary exposure to it in their homes. Making the sensitive judgments required in these cases is not easy. But this responsibility has been reposed initially in the Commission, and its judgment is entitled to respect. . . .

In short, I agree that on the facts of this case, the Commission's order did not violate respondent's First Amendment rights. . . .

In my view, the result in this case does not turn on whether Carlin's monologue, viewed as a whole, or the words that constitute it, have more or less "value" than a candidate's campaign speech. This is a judgment for each person to make, not one for the judges to impose upon him.

The result turns instead on the unique characteristics of the broadcast media, combined with society's right to protect its children from speech generally agreed to be inappropriate for their years, and with the interest of unwilling adults in not being assaulted by such offensive speech in their homes. Moreover, I doubt whether today's decision will prevent any adult who wishes to receive Carlin's message in Carlin's own words from doing so, and from making for himself a value judgment as to the merit of the message and words.

Justice Brennan, with whom ***Justice Marshall*** joins, dissenting.

Without question, the privacy interests of an individual in his home are substantial and deserving of significant protection. In finding these interests sufficient to justify the content regulation of protected speech, however, the Court commits two errors. First, it misconceives the nature of the privacy interest involved where an individual voluntarily chooses to admit radio communications into his home. Second, it ignores the constitutionally protected interests of both those who wish to transmit and those who desire to receive broadcasts that many—including the FCC and this Court—might find offensive. . . .

Even if an individual who voluntarily opens his home to radio communications retains privacy interests of sufficient moment to justify a ban on protected speech if those interests are "invaded in an essentially intolerable manner," *** the very fact that those interests are threatened only by a radio broadcast precludes any intolerable invasion of privacy; for unlike other intrusive modes of communication, such as sound trucks, "[t]he radio can be turned off," *** —and with a minimum of effort. . . . Whatever the minimal discomfort suffered by a listener who inadvertently tunes into a program he finds offensive during the brief interval before he can simply extend his arm and switch stations or flick the "off" button, it is surely worth the candle to preserve the broadcaster's right to send, and the right of those interested to receive, a message entitled to full First Amendment protection. . . .

The Court's balance, of necessity, fails to accord proper weight to the interests of listeners who wish to hear broadcasts the FCC deems offensive. It permits majoritarian tastes completely to preclude a protected message from entering the home of a receptive, unoffended minority. No decision of this Court supports such a result. Where the individuals constituting the offended majority may freely choose to reject the material being offered, we have never found their privacy interests of such moment to warrant the suppression of speech on privacy grounds. . . .

Most parents will undoubtedly find understandable as well as commendable the Court's sympathy with the FCC's desire to prevent offensive broadcasts from reaching the ears of unsupervised children. Unfortunately, the facial appeal of this justification for radio censorship masks its constitutional insufficiency. . . .

Because the Carlin monologue is obviously not an erotic appeal to the prurient interests of children, the Court, for the first time, allows the government to prevent minors from gaining access to materials that are not obscene, and are therefore protected, as to them. It thus ignores our recent admonition that "[s]peech that is neither obscene as to youths nor subject to some other legitimate proscription cannot be suppressed solely to protect the young from ideas or images that a legislative body thinks unsuitable for them." *** The Court's refusal to follow its own pronouncements is especially lamentable since it has the anomalous subsidiary effect, at least in the radio context at issue here,

of making completely unavailable to adults material which may not constitutionally be kept even from children. This result violates in spades the principle of *Butler v. Michigan* *** (1957). *Butler* involved a challenge to a Michigan statute that forbade the publication, sale, or distribution of printed material "tending to incite minors to violent or depraved or immoral acts, manifestly tending to the corruption of the morals of youth." Although *Roth v. United States* *** (1957) had not yet been decided, it is at least arguable that the material the statute in *Butler* was designed to suppress could have been constitutionally denied to children. Nevertheless, this Court found the statute unconstitutional. . . .

Where, as here, the government may not prevent the exposure of minors to the suppressed material, the principle of *Butler* applies *a fortiori*. . . .

[N]either . . . the intrusive nature of radio [nor] the presence of children in the listening audience . . . can . . . support the FCC's disapproval of the Carlin monologue. These two asserted justifications are further plagued by a common failing: the lack of principled limits on their use as a basis for FCC censorship. No such limits come readily to mind, and neither of the opinions constituting the Court serve to clarify the extent to which the FCC may assert the privacy and children-in-the-audience rationales as justification for expunging from the airways protected communications the Commission finds offensive. Taken to their logical extreme, these rationales would support the cleansing of public radio of any "four-letter words" whatsoever, regardless of their context. The rationales could justify the banning from radio of a myriad of literary works, novels, poems, and plays by the likes of Shakespeare, Joyce, Hemingway, Ben Jonson, Henry Fielding, Robert Burns, and Chaucer; they could support the suppression of a good deal of political speech, such as the Nixon tapes; and they could even provide the basis for imposing sanctions for the broadcast of certain portions of the Bible. . . .

To insure that the FCC's regulation of protected speech does not exceed these bounds, my Brother Powell is content to rely upon the judgment of the Commission while my Brother Stevens deems it prudent to rely on this Court's ability accurately to assess the worth of various kinds of speech. For my own part, even accepting that this case is limited to its facts, I would place the responsibility and the right to weed worthless and offensive communications from the public airways where it belongs and where, until today, it resided: in a public free to choose those communications worthy of its attention from a marketplace unsullied by the censor's hand. . . .

[T]here runs throughout the opinions of my Brothers Powell and Stevens another vein I find equally disturbing: a depressing inability to appreciate that in our land of cultural pluralism, there are many who think, act, and talk differently from the Members of this Court, and who do not share their fragile sensibilities. It is only an acute ethnocentric myopia that enables the Court to approve the censorship of communications solely because of the words they contain. . . .

Today's decision will thus have its greatest impact on broadcasters desiring to reach, and listening audiences composed of, persons who do not share the Court's view as to which words or expressions are acceptable and who, for a variety of reasons, including a conscious desire to flout majoritarian conventions, express themselves using words that may be regarded as offensive by those from different socioeconomic backgrounds. In this context, the Court's decision may be seen for what, in the broader perspective, it really is: another of the dominant culture's inevitable efforts to force those groups who do not share its mores to conform to its way of thinking, acting, and speaking.

Justice Stewart, with whom ***Justice Brennan, Justice White,*** and ***Justice Marshall*** join, dissenting.

I think that "indecent" should properly be read as meaning no more than "obscene." Since the Carlin monologue concededly was not "obscene," I believe that the Commission lacked statutory authority to ban it. Under this construction of the statute, it is unnecessary to address the difficult and important issue of the Commission's constitutional power to prohibit speech that would be constitutionally protected outside the context of electronic broadcasting. . . .

CHAPTER THIRTEEN

RELIGIOUS LIBERTY AND CHURCH-STATE RELATIONS

> We are a people whose institutions presuppose a Supreme Being.
>
> Justice William O. Douglas, *Zorach v. Clauson* (1952)

> . . . [O]ne of the mandates of the First Amendment is to promote a viable, pluralistic society and to keep government neutral, not only between sects, but also between believers and nonbelievers.
>
> Justice William O. Douglas, dissenting in *Walz v. Tax Commission* (1970)

INTRODUCTION

Religion is one of the hallmarks of American society. Americans are more likely than people in other Western democracies to hold religious beliefs, affiliate with religious denominations, and attend religious services. Another distinguishing feature of American social life is the great diversity of religious beliefs and practices that coexist peacefully. In no other society on earth can one find such a wide array of faiths: Amish, Quaker, Baptist, Jehovah's Witnesses, Seventh Day Adventist, Lutheran, Methodist, Episcopalian, Presbyterian, Roman Catholic, Eastern Orthodox, Christian Scientist, Jewish, Mormon, Islamic, and Krishna, to name but a few. Despite obvious differences in doctrine and styles of worship, all of these sects are united by their belief in a Supreme Being and their commitment to codes of proper conduct. Nevertheless, history teaches us that human beings are given to zealotry, intolerance, and even persecution in the name of God.

The Framers of the Bill of Rights were well aware of the excesses that can result when one denomination is established as the official religion, recognized and supported by government. Indeed, a thirst for freedom to worship God in one's own way, without coercion or persecution by government, was one of the avowed motivations in the formation of the American colonies. However, nine of the thirteen original American colonies set up official churches and provided them with financial support. In fact, at the time the Bill of Rights was ratified in 1791, Connecticut, Massachusetts, and New Hampshire continued to recognize the Congregational Church as the official, state-sponsored denomination. Nevertheless, opposition to officially established religion ultimately prevailed.

Thus, the First Amendment to the Constitution provides that "Congress shall make no law respecting an establishment of religion, or prohibiting the free exercise thereof. . . ."

That the protection of religious freedom was of fundamental importance to the Framers is underscored by the fact that the Religion Clauses are listed first among the safeguards contained in the Bill of Rights. These clauses not only reflect the strong desire for religious freedom held by eighteenth-century Americans, they also protect and foster the religious diversity that exists in America today.

Widespread agreement exists regarding the abstract value of the Religion Clauses of the First Amendment. Nevertheless, there is equally broad disagreement about what these clauses specifically require, permit, and forbid. Some of the Supreme Court's least popular decisions are in the realm of government involvement with religion, specifically in the area of school prayer. It should be noted, however, that these decisions are often as misunderstood as they are unpopular. This chapter attempts to clarify and explain what the Supreme Court has said in some of its many decisions interpreting the Religion Clauses of the First Amendment. Sadly, too often those who are given to strong opinions on the subject of religion are unwilling or unable to understand clearly what has been decided by the courts. While informed debate over judicial decisions is to be encouraged, criticism based on ignorance is counterproductive.

The Incorporation of the Religion Clauses

In his original draft of the Bill of Rights, James Madison proposed that state as well as federal establishments of religion be prohibited. The First Congress rejected Madison's suggestion in this respect. Thus, the First Amendment proscribed establishments of religion by the national government only. By the late 1940s, the Supreme Court had ruled, however, that the Religion Clauses of the First Amendment were of sufficient importance in a "scheme of ordered liberty" to warrant their application to the states through the Due Process Clause of the Fourteenth Amendment (for a discussion of the doctrine of incorporation, see Chapter 9). The Free Exercise Clause was definitively applied to the states in *Cantwell v. Connecticut* (1940); arguably, it had been incorporated in the 1934 case of *Hamilton v. Regents of the University of California.* The Establishment Clause was incorporated in *Everson v. Board of Education* (1947). Thus, all levels of government, from local school boards to the U.S. Congress, are now required to abide by the strictures of the Religion Clauses of the First Amendment.

WHAT IS RELIGION?

Before one can define "establishment of religion" or "the free exercise thereof," one must know what is meant by the term "religion." It comes from the Latin *religare,* which means "to tie down" or "to restrain." Since its appearance in the English language at the beginning of the thirteenth century, the term "religion" has had a distinctly theological connotation. *Webster's Third New International Dictionary of the English Language* (1986) offers seven definitions of the term.

The first is "the personal commitment to and serving of God or a god with worshipful devotion...." It goes on to define religion as "a personal awareness or conviction of the existence of a supreme being or of supernatural powers or influences controlling one's own, humanity's, or all nature's destiny...."

In the 1890 case of *Davis v. Beason,* the Supreme Court first had occasion to define religion. In a majority opinion authored by Justice Stephen J. Field, the Court stated:

> [T]he term "religion" has reference to one's view of his relations to his Creator, and to the obligations they impose of reverence for His being and character, and obedience to His will.

The Court's conception of religion in 1890 was thus strictly theistic, which no doubt mirrored popular attitudes on the subject. By the 1960s, however, American society had become much more religiously diverse, and nontheistic creeds from Asia, such as Buddhism and Taoism, were beginning to find adherents in this country.

Religion Broadly Defined

In 1965, the Supreme Court attempted to define religion in a fashion broad enough to respect the diversity of creeds that coexist in modern America. The definitional problem arose in *United States v. Seeger* (1965), a case involving four men who claimed conscientious objector status in refusing to serve in the Vietnam War. In the Universal Military Training and Service Act of 1940, Congress exempted from combat duty anyone "who, by reason of religious training and belief, is conscientiously opposed to participation in war in any form." The act defined "religious training and belief" as training or belief "in a relation to a Supreme Being involving duties superior to those arising from any human relation." Although some organized religions (such as the Quakers) do not approve of participation in war, Daniel Seeger was not a member of any such group. Nevertheless, he sought conscientious objector status on religious grounds. When specifically asked about his belief in a Supreme Being, Seeger stated that "you could call [it] a belief in the Supreme Being or God. These just do not happen to be the words that I use." Forest Peter, another man whose refusal to serve in Vietnam was before the Supreme Court in *Seeger,* claimed that after considerable meditation and reflection "on values derived from the Western religious and philosophical tradition," he determined that it would be "a violation of his moral code to take human life and that he considered this belief superior to any obligation to the state." In deciding the *Seeger* case, the Court avoided a constitutional question by interpreting the statutory definition of religion broadly. Writing for the Court, Justice Tom Clark held that

> Congress, in using the expression "Supreme Being" rather than the designation "God," was merely clarifying the meaning of religious tradition and belief so as to embrace all religions and to exclude essentially political, sociological, or philosophical views [and] the test of belief "in a relation to a Supreme Being" is whether a given belief that is sincere and meaningful occupies a place in the life of its possessor parallel to the orthodox belief in God.

Apparently the Court was persuaded that Seeger, Peter, and the others whose refusal to serve in Vietnam was before the Court, possessed such a belief and recognized them as conscientious objectors on religious grounds.

A Working Definition of Religion

Subsequent decisions in both federal and state tribunals have expanded on the definition of religion adopted by the Supreme Court in the *Seeger* case. Essentially, a creed must meet four criteria to qualify as a religion as this term is used in the First Amendment. First, as noted above, there must be a belief in God or some parallel belief that occupies a central place in the believer's life. Second, the religion must involve a moral code that transcends individual belief—it cannot be purely subjective. Third, some associational ties must be involved, that is, some community of people united by common beliefs. And fourth, there must be a demonstrable sincerity of belief. Under these criteria, even nontheistic creeds, such as Taoism or Zen Buddhism, qualify as religions. But frivolous or ridiculous beliefs, such as Stanley Oscar Brown's professed "faith" in Kozy Kitten Cat Food (see *Brown v. Pena* [1977]) fail to meet any of the above criteria. Of course, there is a long continuum between ludicrous beliefs such as Brown's and conventional religions. An interesting question to ponder is whether some of the "pop religions" in vogue since the 1960s, such as EST, Scientology, and Transcendental Meditation (TM), would qualify as religions under the above criteria. What about such well-known "cults" as the Unification Church (the "Moonies")? Are they entitled to the same constitutional protection as members of the United Church of Christ or the Assembly of God?

FREE EXERCISE OF RELIGION

What happens when religious beliefs and practices run afoul of the law? Are Rastafarians, who believe that constantly smoking marijuana is the way to develop a close relationship with God, immune from prosecution by the state of Florida? Is the Tennessee law that forbids the handling of poisonous snakes in religious services an unconstitutional infringement on the rights of those who sincerely believe that "taking up serpents" is required by the Holy Bible? To what extent does the Free Exercise Clause delimit government's authority to protect the public safety, health, welfare, and morals from religious practices that threaten these interests?

The first major pronouncement by the Supreme Court on the scope of the Free Exercise Clause, to which these questions speak, came in *Reynolds v. United States* (1879). In this landmark case, the Court upheld application of the federal antipolygamy statute to a Mormon who claimed it was his religious duty to have several wives. It is clear from the congressional debates surrounding this legislation that the law was aimed squarely at this religious minority, which had become highly controversial in nineteenth-century America.

The *Reynolds* decision was based on a sharp distinction between belief and conduct. According to Chief Justice Morrison R. Waite, "Congress was deprived of all legislative power over mere opinion, but was left free to reach actions which were in violation of social duties or subversive of good order." Although the Supreme Court has occasionally reiterated the distinction between religious belief and conduct, it has largely repudiated the position taken in *Reynolds* that religious conduct is beyond the pale of the Free Exercise Clause. After all, few if any government policies infringe religious belief *per se;* rather, they are aimed at particular kinds of actions deemed socially undesirable. In its post-New Deal expansion of civil liberties, the Court markedly increased the degree of judicial protection of religiously motivated conduct. This did not mean that religious activity ever received absolute immunity from government regulation. Rather, the Court remained willing to uphold public policies that infringed on religious practices if the government could point to an important secular justification for such infringement. Specifically, the Court came to recognize freedom of religion as a fundamental right that could be abridged only if necessary to protect a compelling governmental interest.

While the justices often disagreed over precisely which government interests should be viewed as compelling, this general standard established a strong presumption in favor of the free exercise of religion. Recent decisions of the Rehnquist Court, most notably *Employment Division v. Smith* (1990), discussed below, raise serious questions as to whether a majority of the justices continue to accept the compelling state interest test as a basis for determining whether religious freedom is entitled to constitutional protection.

Cantwell v. Connecticut (1940) was the first major decision in which the Court accorded a heightened degree of protection to religious freedom. In *Cantwell,* the Court struck down a state law that prohibited door-to-door solicitation for any religious or charitable cause without prior approval of a state agency. The law was challenged by Newton Cantwell, a member of the Jehovah's Witnesses, a sect committed to active proselytizing. Cantwell and his sons routinely went from door to door or stopped people on the street in order to communicate a message that was highly critical of the Roman Catholic church and other organized religions. Eventually they were arrested and charged with failure to obtain approval for solicitation under the state law, as well as with common law breach of the peace. The Court reversed the breach-of-the-peace conviction and invalidated the state statute:

> In the realm of religious faith, and in that of political belief, sharp differences arise. In both fields the tenets of one man may seem the rankest error to his neighbor. To persuade others to his point of view, the pleader, as we know, resorts to exaggeration, to vilification of men who have been, or are, prominent in church or state, and even to false statement. But the people of this nation have ordained in the light of history, that, in spite of the probability of excesses and abuses, these liberties are, in the long view, essential to enlightened opinion and right conduct on the part of citizens of a democracy.

In another case involving members of the Jehovah's Witnesses, the Supreme Court held that a state law requiring the payment of a tax for the privilege of solicitation could not be constitutionally applied to cases of religious solicitation (*Murdock v. Pennsylvania* [1943]). Writing for the Court, Justice William O.

Douglas observed that "a person cannot be compelled to purchase . . . a privilege freely granted by the Constitution."

In still another Jehovah's Witnesses case, *Niemotko v. Maryland* (1951), the Supreme Court held unconstitutional a city council's denial of a permit to the Jehovah's Witnesses to use the city park for a public meeting. The city council had refused to grant the permit because the Jehovah's Witnesses' answers to questions about Catholicism, military service, and other issues were "unsatisfactory." A unanimous Supreme Court regarded this denial of the public forum to an unpopular religious group as blatant censorship.

Although the Supreme Court has consistently defended the right of unpopular religious groups to meet, canvass, solicit, and proselytize in the public forum, it has generally rejected arguments that the Free Exercise Clause allows religious groups to engage in activities that are proscribed as detrimental to public health, safety, or morality. Thus in 1975, the Court refused to overturn a lower-court decision that upheld North Carolina's law prohibiting the handling of poisonous snakes in religious ceremonies (see *State ex rel. Swann v. Pack*). With few exceptions, state and federal courts have been unwilling to allow the use of psychedelic drugs by those claiming religious significance for drug-induced hallucinations (but see *People v. Woody,* Cal. Sup. Ct., 1963). *In Employment Division v. Smith* (1990), the Supreme Court rejected a claim made by members of the Native American Church that their ritualistic use of peyote constituted free exercise of religion.

Sunday Closing Laws

In a controversial set of decisions in the early 1960s called the Sunday closing cases (see, for example, *McGowan v. Maryland* [1961]), the Court upheld "blue laws" that prohibited certain businesses from operating on Sunday. In challenging the constitutionality of such laws, it was argued that they officially recognized Sunday as the Sabbath, in violation of the Establishment Clause and the Free Exercise rights of those who observed the Sabbath on Saturday. In upholding Sunday closing laws, the Supreme Court stressed the secular nature of the regulations. In the Court's view, such laws represented the community's desire for a day of rest and relaxation, independent of any religious significance. Writing for the majority in *McGowan,* Chief Justice Earl Warren noted that

> it is common knowledge that the first day of the week has come to have special significance as a rest day in this country. People of all religions and people with no religion regard Sunday as a time for family activity, for visiting friends and relatives, for late sleeping, for passive and active entertainments, for dining out, and the like.

The fact that this day of rest happened to be the day of worship for most Christians was incidental in the view of the Court. The Court's decisions in the Sunday Sunday closing cases are similar in this respect to the Court's decision in *Lynch v. Donnelly* (1984), upholding a city's sponsorship of a nativity scene during Christmas. There, the Court stressed the secular nature of the crèche as a "neutral harbinger" of the holiday season; it downplayed any religious significance relative to the birth of Christ.

In one of the Sunday closing cases, *Braunfeld v. Brown* (1961), Justice William Brennan filed a separate opinion urging that those who recognize Saturday as the Sabbath be exempted from the Sunday closing laws. In Brennan's view, the failure to exempt Sabbatarians from these laws would infringe their free exercise of religion:

> [T]he laws do not say that appellants must work on Saturday. But their effect is that appellants may not simultaneously practice their religion and their trade, without being hampered by a substantial competitive disadvantage. Their effect is that no one may at one and the same time be an Orthodox Jew and compete effectively with his Sunday observing fellow tradesmen. This clog upon the exercise of religion, this state imposed burden on Orthodox Judaism, has exactly the same economic effect as a tax levied upon the sale of religious literature.

Unemployment Benefits

Although Justice Brennan could not muster a majority to endorse this perspective on the Sunday closing laws, his position did carry the day in *Sherbert v. Verner* (1963). Adell Sherbert was a Seventh Day Adventist who was discharged from her job in a textile mill because she refused to work on Saturdays. Sherbert's application for unemployment compensation was denied because, in the state's view, she had refused "without good cause, to accept 'suitable work when offered . . . by the unemployment office or [by her] employer. . . .' " Ordinarily, dismissal from a job for just cause bars a person from collecting unemployment compensation. Here, however, the Court held that the denial of unemployment compensation significantly burdened Sherbert's free exercise rights without furthering any compelling state interest.

Sherbert v. Verner was reaffirmed by the Court's decision in *Thomas v. Review Board* (1981). In *Thomas,* the Court held that a member of Jehovah's Witnesses who quit his job after being transferred to a department that manufactured tank turrets could not be denied unemployment compensation. It is difficult to reconcile the Court's decisions in *Sherbert v. Verner* and *Thomas v. Review Board* with the Sunday closing cases. However, in light of the Court's decision in *Employment Division v. Smith* (1990), the viability of *Sherbert* and *Thomas* as precedents is open to question.

The Oregon Peyote Case

Throughout the 1980s, the Supreme Court continued to apply the rationale established in *Sherbert v. Verner* and *Thomas v. Review Board* (see, for example, *Hobbie v. Unemployment Appeals Division* [1987]). These cases stood for the proposition that, in the absence of a compelling justification, a state could not withhold unemployment compensation from an employee who resigned or was discharged due to unwillingness to depart from religious practices or beliefs that conflicted with job requirements. In 1990, however, a sharply divided Court, in *Employment Division v. Smith,* departed dramatically from this approach and imposed potentially serious limits on the scope of religious freedom protected by the First Amendment.

In *Smith,* a state's interest in prohibiting the use of illicit drugs came into conflict with well-established practices of the Native American Church, a sect outside the Judeo-Christian mainstream of American religion. Two members of this church, Alfred Smith and Galen Black, worked as drug rehabilitation counselors for a private social service agency in Oregon. Along with other church members, Smith and Black ingested peyote, a hallucinogenic drug, at a sacramental ceremony practiced by Native Americans for hundreds of years. Citing their use of peyote as "job-related misconduct," the social service agency fired Smith and Black. Recognizing no exception, even for sacramental purposes, Oregon's controlled substances statute made the possession of peyote a criminal offense. Although Smith and Black were not charged with violation of this law, its existence figured prominently in the Supreme Court's ultimate resolution of the free exercise issue in this case.

Shortly after they were fired, Smith and Black applied for unemployment compensation. The Oregon Employment Appeals Board denied their applications, accepting the employer's explanation that Smith and Black had been discharged for job-related misconduct. The former counselors successfully challenged this administrative ruling in the Oregon Court of Appeals, thus initiating a lengthy and complex judicial struggle that generated several state court decisions and two rulings by the U.S. Supreme Court. On remand from the first of these rulings, the Oregon Supreme Court held that the controlled substance law, as applied in this case, violated the Free Exercise Clause of the First Amendment and that Smith and Black were thus entitled to unemployment compensation.

Reviewing the case for a second time and finally reaching the basic constitutional issue, the U.S. Supreme Court reversed. Justice Antonin Scalia, writing for the majority, ruled that "if prohibiting the exercise of religion ... is ... merely the incidental effect of a generally applicable and otherwise valid [criminal] law, the First Amendment has not been offended." According to this reasoning, the Free Exercise Clause would be violated only if a particular religious practice were singled out for proscription. In supporting this holding, Scalia relied heavily on *Reynolds v. United States* (1879), in effect equating Oregon's drug prohibition with the federal antipolygamy statute. He maintained that the *Sherbert-Thomas* line of decisions could be distinguished since the religious practices followed by employees in those cases were not prohibited by law. Scalia also rejected the compelling state interest test on which *Sherbert, Thomas,* and similar cases were based. He contended that "[t]o make an individual's obligation to obey such a law contingent upon the law's coincidence with his religious beliefs except where the state's interest is compelling ... contradicts both constitutional tradition and common sense." The legislature, Scalia maintained, is free to make accommodations for religious practices. Such accommodations, however, are not required, no matter how "central" a particular practice might be to one's religious beliefs.

As Justice Sandra Day O'Connor's concurring opinion indicates, Scalia's rejection of the governmental interest test was the most controversial aspect of this decision. Although she supported the Court's judgment that the Free Exercise Clause had not been violated, O'Connor sharply criticized the majority opinion as a dramatic departure "from well-settled First Amendment jurispru-

Is Animal Sacrifice "Free Exercise of Religion"?

In 1987, the city of Hialeah, a Miami suburb, passed an ordinance prohibiting the sacrifice of live animals as part of religious rituals. The ordinance came in response to local concern over the sacrifical practices associated with Santeria, a blend of Roman Catholicism and West African religions brought to the Caribbean by Yoruba slaves. Santeria, which literally means "worship of the saints," involves occasional sacrifices of live animals, usually goats or chickens. According to some estimates, there are as many as 70,000 devotees of Santeria in the Miami area, and perhaps as many as one million nationwide. Ernesto Pichardo, a Santeria priest, challenged the Hiahleah law as a violation of the First Amendment. In your opinion, is Mr. Pichardo on solid constitutional ground in attacking the ordinance?

dence . . . and . . . [as] incompatible with our Nation's fundamental commitment to individual religious liberty." This part of O'Connor's opinion was supported by Justices Brennan, Marshall, and Blackmun, who dissented from the Court's decision. "The compelling interest test," O'Connor asserted, "effectuates the First Amendment's command that religious liberty is an independent liberty, that it occupies a preferred position, and that the Court will not permit encroachments upon this liberty, whether direct or indirect, unless required by clear and compelling governmental interests 'of the highest order.'"

In a separate dissenting opinion, Justice Harry Blackmun, joined by Justices Brennan and Marshall, charged the majority with "mischaracterizing" precedents and "overturning . . . settled law concerning the Religion Clauses of our Constitution." With evident sarcasm, Blackmun expressed the hope that the Court was "aware of the consequences" and that the result was not a "product of overreaction to the serious problems the country's drug crisis [had] generated." He pointed out that the Native American Church restricted and supervised the sacramental use of peyote. The state thus had no significant health or safety justification for regulating this form of drug use. Blackmun also noted that Oregon had not attempted to prosecute Smith and Black or, for that matter, any other Native Americans for the sacramental use of peyote. He concluded that "Oregon's interest in enforcing its drug laws against religious use of peyote [was] not sufficiently compelling to outweigh respondents' right to the free exercise of their religion."

Patriotic Rituals and Duties

Some religious leaders embrace "Americanism" as virtually mandated by the Almighty; others are less nationalistic. For example, the Amish and the Mennonites live largely in isolation from the mainstream of modern society, pursuing life-styles and embracing virtues reminiscent of the early nineteenth century. For the most part, they are uninterested in things political, preferring to concentrate on their families' moral and spiritual development. They are generally unwilling to serve in the armed forces, since they are opposed to war in any form. They also avoid displays of nationalism or even citizenship. To what extent does the First Amendment protect such groups from being forced to observe patriotic rituals and duties that are readily observed by most Americans?

The Flag Salute Cases

In *Minersville School District v. Gobitis* (1940), the Supreme Court upheld a local school board requirement that all public school students participate in a daily flag salute program. The requirement had been challenged by a member of the Jehovah's Witnesses whose children were being forced to salute the American flag in violation of their religious training, which held the flag salute to be the worship of a "graven image" (see Exod. 20: 4–5). In a dramatic turnabout, the *Gobitis* decision was overruled three years later in *West Virginia State Board of Education v. Barnette* (1943). In the *Gobitis* decision, Justice Felix Frankfurter had justified the compulsory flag salute as an appropriate means for the attainment of national unity, which he viewed as "the basis of national security." Writing for the Court that overruled Frankfurter's position, Justice Robert Jackson stated that "compulsory unification of opinion leads only to the unanimity of the graveyard," obviously referring to the situation in Europe in 1943. For Justice Jackson,

> [t]o believe that patriotism will not flourish if patriotic ceremonies are voluntary and spontaneous instead of a compulsory routine is to make an unflattering estimate of the appeal of our institutions to free minds.

Nothing that the Supreme Court has decided since *Barnette* indicates that government has any justification for forcing citizens to make professions of patriotism. The Court has even gone as far as to prohibit the state of New Hampshire from requiring that an automobile display a license plate inscribed with the State's motto "Live Free or Die" if such motto offends the religious sensibilities of the car's owner (see *Wooley v. Maynard* [1977]). Although the Court has not faced the question since 1931 (see *United States v. Bland*), it is interesting to speculate as to whether the current Court would require a religious pacifist who wishes to become a citizen to swear that he or she would "defend the Constitution and the laws of the United States against all enemies, foreign or domestic," which is the oath required of all naturalized citizens. The Court upheld the oath requirement in 1931. Would it do so today?

Free Exercise of Religion and Military Service

Another interesting constitutional question involves conscientious objection to military service, alluded to earlier in the discussion of the *Seeger* case. Although Congress has provided an exemption from military service for religiously motivated conscientious objectors, is such an exemption required by the Free Exercise Clause? In other words, would the Supreme Court permit religiously motivated refusal to serve in combat on constitutional grounds if there were no act of Congress providing such an exemption? On the other hand, is it not possible to argue that, in granting an exemption only to those whose refusal to serve is based on religion, Congress has run afoul of the Establishment Clause?

One of the most controversial Supreme Court decisions in the area of free exercise of religion deals with military regulations that were alleged to infringe First Amendment rights. In *Goldman v. Weinberger* (1986), the Court upheld an Air Force dress code requirement against the challenge of an Orthodox Jew who was disciplined for wearing a yarmulke while in uniform. Stressing the need for discipline and uniformity in the military, the Court rejected the challenge by a vote of 5 to 4. Writing for the sharply divided Court, Justice William Rehnquist maintained that

> when evaluating whether military needs justify a particular restriction on religiously motivated conduct, courts must give great deference to the professional judgment of military authorities concerning the relative importance of a particular military interest.

In *Goldman,* the Supreme Court thus reiterated the position taken five years before that "[j]udicial deference . . . is at its apogee when legislative action under the congressional authority to raise and support armies and make rules and regulations for their governance is challenged" (*Rostker v. Goldberg* [1981], discussed and reprinted in Chapter 16). Constitutional rights enjoyed by American citizens are to a large extent sacrificed during military service.

Freedom of Religion versus *Parens Patriae*

Our legal traditions recognize government as **parens patriae,** meaning literally "parent of the country." This term refers to the role of government as guardian of persons who are not legally competent to make their own decisions, for example, children, the severely retarded, and the mentally ill. Occasionally, the state uses this power to take custody of children who are the victims of neglect or abuse. The state's role as *parens patriae* has sometimes come into conflict with the Free Exercise Clause when parents refuse on religious grounds to allow their children to receive medical treatment. Some devoutly religious persons sincerely believe that medical science is blasphemous—that true faith is all that is necessary to promote healing. For example, in a 1983 Tennessee case that attracted wide attention, a fundamentalist preacher refused to allow a hospital to treat his young daughter for cancer. The state intervened as *parens patriae* and secured a court order requiring medical treatment (see *In the Matter of Hamilton* [1983]).

Although some state and federal court decisions have recognized the right of a competent adult to refuse medical treatment on religious and/or privacy grounds, courts are generally disinclined to uphold such Free Exercise claims where the health of children is involved. Judges generally assume that children are not sufficiently mature to make rational choices regarding medical treatment and, in some instances, must be protected against the consequences of their parents' unusual religious convictions.

In *Prince v. Massachusetts* (1944), the Supreme Court upheld a child labor law against an attack based on the Free Exercise Clause. The law prohibited boys under twelve and girls under eighteen from selling newspapers on the streets. The law was challenged by a member of the Jehovah's Witnesses whose children normally assisted her in the sale and distribution of religious literature. Dividing 8 to 1, the Court held that the state's role as *parens patriae* in protecting the safety of children overrode Prince's Free Exercise claim.

Compulsory School Attendance

In *Wisconsin v. Yoder* (1972), the Supreme Court held that a state's compulsory high school attendance law could not be constitutionally applied to members of the Old Order Amish faith, which does not permit secular education beyond the eighth grade. Writing for the Court, Chief Justice Warren E. Burger placed great stress on the fact that the education of the Amish teenager continued in the home, with emphasis on practical skills as well as religious and moral values. Based on Burger's opinion in *Yoder,* it seems unlikely that the Court would grant the Amish an exemption from compulsory primary education. Nor would it grant an exemption to members of a "religion" that strikes the Court as silly, faddish, or insincere.

SEPARATION OF CHURCH AND STATE

The Establishment Clause of the First Amendment was adopted in contradiction to the practice, prevalent not only in Europe but among the American colonies, of having official churches supported by taxation. Indeed, as previously noted, some states maintained their established churches well into the nineteenth century. Thus, the concept of "a wall of separation between church and state," as Thomas Jefferson referred to it, was an American invention whose application remained to be worked out in practice.

Competing Interpretations of the Establishment Clause

In the two centuries since the Establishment Clause went into effect, Americans both on and off the Supreme Court have disagreed sharply over the meaning of the Clause. One view is that it merely forbids the establishment of an official, state-supported religion. According to this restrictive interpretation, Congress does not run afoul of the First Amendment so long as it refrains from selecting one denomination as the official or preferred religion. However, even the literal language of the First Amendment suggests a broader prohibition than this, however. It does not say that Congress shall make no law establishing an official religion; rather, it states that "Congress shall make no law *respecting* an establishment of religion" (emphasis added). This general language indicates a broader restriction than mere prohibition of an established church. For the most part, the Supreme Court has opted for this broader interpretation.

When polled, most Americans respond approvingly to the abstract concept of separation of church and state. Yet there is no consensus on how high or how thick the "wall of separation" should be. Thus, the Supreme Court's decisions applying this concept to particular situations have been even more controversial than its decisions under the Free Exercise Clause. Many of these controversial decisions involve education, notably prayer in public schools and state aid to private religious schools.

Traditional Government Practices

Potential Establishment Clause questions are implicit in many traditional government practices. For example, consider the practice of Congress and every state legislature of paying a chaplain, usually of a particular Protestant denomination, to lead our representatives in public prayer (see *Marsh v. Chambers* [1983]). What about the inscription "In God We Trust" on American currency? Or the Supreme Court's time-honored practice of opening oral argument with the invocation "God save the United States and this honorable Court"? Or the recognition of America as "one nation under God" in the official pledge of allegiance to the flag? These and other common practices indicate the degree to which religion figures prominently in the public life of this nation. Although many Americans no doubt approve of such official endorsement and invocation of religion, what about the rights of nonbelievers? How far does the First Amendment allow the government to go in recognizing, endorsing, or accommodating religious beliefs? As the controversial Supreme Court decisions interpreting the Establishment Clause demonstrate, the answer to this question is far from clear.

The *Lemon* Test

In 1971, the Court laid down a three-pronged test for determining the constitutionality of policies challenged under the Establishment Clause (see *Lemon v. Kurtzman*). The so-called *Lemon* test synthesized various elements of the Court's Establishment Clause jurisprudence as it had evolved through the 1950s and 1960s. Although controversial from its inception, the *Lemon* test has been applied to a broad range of issues involving separation of church and state. Under the *Lemon* test, a challenged policy must meet the following criteria in order to pass muster under the Establishment Clause: (1) it must have a "secular purpose"; (2) it must not have the principal or primary effect of "inhibiting or advancing religion"; and (3) it must avoid an "excessive government entanglement with religion."

It should go without saying that the *Lemon* test does not contain hard and fast criteria for judicial decision making. Rather, like all judicial doctrines, it is subject to some degree of manipulation by those who are predisposed to a particular result. For example, how can the "purpose" of a challenged law be determined with certainty by the courts? How does one distinguish the "principal" or "primary" effects of a law from its secondary or tertiary effects? Finally, how much entanglement between religion and government is "excessive"? During the 1970s and 1980s, the Court was often criticized for inconsistency in its application of the *Lemon* test, leading some scholars to question the value of the test altogether.

Religion and Education

In *Everson v. Board of Education* (1947), the first case in which the Supreme Court applied the Establishment Clause to the states via the Fourteenth Amendment, the issue was whether a local school board could reimburse parents for expenses they incurred in transporting their children to and from Catholic schools. The payments to parents of children in parochial schools were part of a general program under which all parents of children in public schools and nonprofit private schools, regardless of religious affiliation, were entitled to reimbursement for transportation costs. However, it is worth noting that the overwhelming number of children attending nonprofit private schools in this New Jersey school district were enrolled in Catholic schools. Writing for a sharply divided Court, Justice Hugo Black justified the challenged payments on the theory that the school board was merely furthering the state's legitimate interest in getting children, "regardless of their religion, safely and expeditiously to and from accredited schools."

Justice Wiley Rutledge, joined by Justices Felix Frankfurter, Robert Jackson, and Harold Burton, dissented vigorously. Professing sympathy for the economic hardships involved in sending one's children to private, religious schools, Justice Rutledge nevertheless asserted:

> Like St. Paul's freedom, religious liberty with a great price must be bought. And for those who exercise it most fully, by insisting upon religious education for their children mixed with secular, by the terms of our Constitution the price is greater than for others.

The "child benefit" theory articulated in *Everson* has for the most part been maintained. Thus, for example, in *Board of Education v. Allen* (1968), the Supreme Court upheld a New York statute requiring local public school districts to lend textbooks on secular subjects to students in private and parochial schools. And in *Meek v. Pittenger* (1975), the Court reaffirmed this position.

"Released Time" Programs and "Equal Access" Policies

To accommodate the religious beliefs of public school students, the Court has upheld "released time" programs, which allow students to leave campus to attend religious exercises. Distinguishing a 1948 decision in which it struck down an on-campus released-time program *(McCollum v. Board of Education)*, the Court in *Zorach v. Clauson* (1952) upheld a New York policy under which public school students who received parental permission left campus to attend religious services while other students attended study hall. Writing for the Court, Justice Douglas stressed the need for governmental accommodation of religious practices:

> When the state encourages religious instruction or cooperates with religious authorities by adjusting the schedule of public events to sectarian needs, it follows the best of our traditions. For then it respects the religious nature of our people and accommodates the public service to their spiritual needs. To hold that it may not would be to find in the Constitution a requirement that the government show a callous indifference to religious groups.

As one of three dissenters in *Zorach,* Justice Jackson delivered a stinging rejoinder to the majority:

> The released time program is founded upon a use of the State's power of coercion, which, for me, determines its unconstitutionality. Stripped to its essentials, the plan has two stages, first, that the State compel each student to yield a large part of his time for secular public education and, second, that some of it be "released" to him on the condition that he devote it to sectarian religious purposes.... If public education were taking so much of the pupils' time as to injure the public or the students' welfare by encroaching on their religious opportunity, simply shortening everyone's school day would facilitate voluntary and optional attendance at Church classes. But that suggestion is rejected upon the ground that if they are made free many students will not go to the Church. Hence, they must be deprived of their freedom for this period, with Church attendance put to them as one of two possible ways of using it.

Released-time programs, although constitutionally permissible under *Zorach v. Clauson,* are not in widespread use in public schools today. More common today are policies under which religiously oriented student groups are permitted access to school facilities. In *Widmar v. Vincent* (1981), the Supreme Court said that public school facilities that have been designated an open forum may not be placed off-limits to religious groups. In *Board of Education v. Mergens* (1990), the Court upheld the Equal Access Act of 1984, in which Congress prohibited public secondary schools that receive federal funds from disallowing meetings of student groups on the basis of "religious, political, philosophical or other content of the speech at such meetings."

"Parochiaid": Government Efforts to Assist Religious Schools

In *Lemon v. Kurtzman* (1971), the Court struck down Pennsylvania and Rhode Island policies providing publicly funded salary supplements to teachers in parochial schools as fostering "excessive entanglement." Similarly, in *Committee for Public Education v. Nyguist* (1973), the Court used the three-pronged test in striking down a New York law that provided various forms of economic aid to parochial schools. Although the released-time programs approved in *Zorach* have not been recently litigated before the Supreme Court, it is highly unlikely such programs could survive a rigorous application of the *Lemon* test.

The Supreme Court reinforced its holdings in *Lemon* and *Nyguist* in two significant decisions of the mid-1980s. In *Aguilar v. Felton* (1985), the Court struck down a New York City program that used federal funds to supplement salaries of public school teachers who taught remedial courses on the premises of religious schools. Similarly, in *Grand Rapids School District v. Ball* (1985), the Court invalidated a program in which supplementary classes for students in sectarian schools were taught by public school teachers at public expense. Writing for the Court in the *Grand Rapids* case, Justice Brennan observed that

> [t]he symbolic union of church and state inherent in the provision of secular, state-provided instruction in the religious school buildings threatens to convey a message of state support for religion to students and to the general public.

Justice Byron White used the occasion to dissent not only from the Court's *Grand Rapids* holding but from the entire thrust of the Court's decisions in the area of state aid to religious schools:

> I am firmly of the belief that the Court's decisions in these cases, like its decisions in *Lemon* and *Nyguist,* are not required by the First Amendment and [are] contrary to the long-range interest of the country. . . . I am satisfied that what the States have sought to do in these cases is well within their authority and is not forbidden by the Establishment Clause.

The Continuing School Prayer Controversy

Few decisions of the modern Supreme Court have been criticized more intensely than the school prayer decisions of the early 1960s. In *Engel v. Vitale* (1962), the Court invalidated a New York Board of Regents policy that established the voluntary recitation of an official prayer by children in the public schools at the start of each school day. The brief official prayer was as follows:

> Almighty God, we acknowledge our dependence on Thee, and we beg Thy blessings upon us, our parents, our teachers and our country.

The Court divided 6 to 1 in striking down the New York Regents' prayer (Justices Frankfurter and Charles Whittaker did not participate in the decision due to health problems). Justice Black wrote the opinion for the majority:

> The Constitutional prohibition against laws respecting an establishment of religion must at least mean that in this country it is no part of the business of government to compose official prayers for any group of the American people to recite as part of a religious program carried on by government.

Justice Potter Stewart, the lone dissenter in *Engel v. Vitale,* compared the recitation of the Regents' prayer to other official recognitions of God and religion, such as the pledge of allegiance to the flag, the president's oath of office, and the invocation said prior to oral argument in the Supreme Court:

> I do not believe that this Court, or the Congress, or the President has by the actions and practices I have described established an "official religion" in violation of the Constitution. And I do not believe the State of New York has done so in this case. What each has done has been to recognize and to follow the deeply entrenched and highly cherished spiritual traditions of our Nation.

In 1963, the Court reinforced the *Engel* decision in the companion cases of *Abington School District v. Schempp* and *Murray v. Curlett* by striking down the practice of Bible reading and the recitation of the Lord's Prayer in the Pennsylvania and Maryland public schools. Again, only Justice Stewart dissented.

The reaction to the Court's school prayer decisions came fast and furious and, indeed, has still not disappeared. The Court was roundly condemned by religious leaders and conservative members of Congress and through resolutions passed by several state legislatures. Polls have consistently shown that a majority of Americans oppose the Court's ban on school prayer. On several

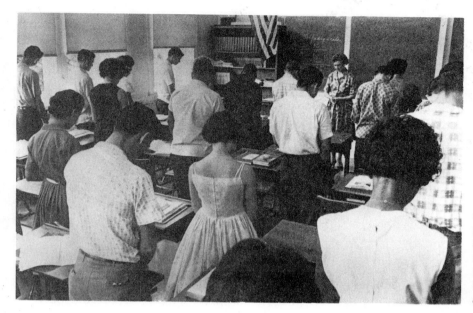

Free exercise of religion or a violation of separation of church and state? An organized prayer session in a public school classroom

occasions, constitutional amendments have been introduced in Congress aimed specifically at overturning the school prayer decisions. In November 1971, one such proposal in the House of Representatives fell only twenty-eight votes short of the two-thirds majority required for constitutional amendments. In the election of 1980, Ronald Reagan capitalized on public sentiment about school prayer by advocating the "school prayer amendment." However, once in office, President Reagan was either unwilling or unable to push this proposal through Congress.

Negative public reaction and widespread noncompliance notwithstanding, the Supreme Court has maintained, although by a shrinking majority, the position articulated in the school prayer cases. For example, in *Stone v. Graham* (1980), the Court invalidated a Kentucky law requiring that the Ten Commandments be posted in all public school classrooms. In 1985, the Court struck down an Alabama law that required public school students to observe a moment of silence "for the purpose of meditation or voluntary prayer" at the start of each school day (see *Wallace v. Jaffree*). It should be noted that in no case has the Court held that it is unconstitutional for a student to pray voluntarily in the public school classroom. What the Court has said is that it is unconstitutional for the state schools to require, endorse, or sanction prayer, either directly or indirectly. One might think that if this were better understood, some of the public hostility toward the Court's decisions would abate. On the other hand, given the nature and intensity of feelings on this issue, it is unlikely that an accurate public perception of the Court's holdings would diminish the public opprobrium. (In 1992 the Supreme Court continued to emphasize the importance of separation of church and state in the area of public education; see *Lee v. Weisman,* reprinted in Appendix E.)

The Evolution-Creationism Conflict

With the rapid expansion of public education in the early twentieth century, especially in rural areas dominated by fundamentalist Protestantism, a controversy erupted over the teaching of evolution in the public schools. The controversy achieved national prominence in 1925 when John T. Scopes, a high school biology teacher in Dayton, Tennessee, was prosecuted for teaching evolution in violation of a state law that had been passed earlier that year. Amidst a carnival-like atmosphere, the "Monkey Trial," as it was caricatured in the press, pitted famous politician and orator William Jennings Bryan against celebrated lawyer Clarence Darrow in a battle royal in the courtroom. Although Darrow outsmarted Bryan in a much-publicized debate over Biblical literalism, Scopes was nevertheless convicted of violating the state statute. The Tennessee Supreme Court reversed the conviction on technical grounds, however, preventing the U.S. Supreme Court from having to consider what was potentially the most explosive constitutional question of that decade.

In the wake of the *Scopes* trial, two states, Arkansas and Mississippi, enacted legislation similar to the Tennessee antievolution law. Yet it was not until 1965 that one of these laws was challenged in court. In that year, Susan Epperson, a high school biology teacher in Little Rock, filed a lawsuit challenging the Arkansas statute. Although the Arkansas trial court ruled in favor of Epperson and struck down the antievolution law, the state supreme court reversed and reinstated the statute. On certiorari, the U.S. Supreme Court reversed (*Epperson v. Arkansas* [1968]). Writing for the Court, Justice Abe Fortas asserted that Arkansas could not "prevent its teachers from discussing the theory of evolution because it is contrary to the belief of some that the Book of Genesis must be the exclusive source of doctrine as to the origins of man."

The *Epperson* decision put to rest the issue of whether states could prohibit the teaching of evolution in their public schools. But two decades later, the evolution-creationism conflict resurfaced in Louisiana. This time, the question was whether the state could *mandate* that creationism, or "creation science," be given equal time in the classroom along with the theory of evolution. In *Edwards v. Aguillard* (1987), the Supreme Court answered this question in the negative. Writing for a majority of seven, Justice Brennan averred that "the primary purpose" of the Louisiana Creationism Act was "to endorse a particular religious doctrine," rather than further the legitimate interests of the state in fostering different points of view in the classroom.

In the wake of such decisions as *Edwards v. Aguillard* and *Epperson v. Arkansas,* as well as the school prayer decisions discussed previously, fundamentalist Christians began to argue that, in its attempt to expunge religious teaching and symbols from the public schools, the Supreme Court had fostered a "religion" of "secular humanism." According to its detractors, secular humanism is a philosophy emphasizing the view that morality is a human invention and that moral choices are largely matters of personal values. In the view of some fundamentalists, the pervasiveness of secular humanism in public school curricula was highly corrosive to traditional values and institutions.

In 1987, a federal district court barred the use of certain widely used history, social studies, and home economics textbooks in the public schools of Mobile

County, Alabama. In essence, the district judge held that these books advanced the "religion" of secular humanism. In embracing this philosophy, the textbooks allegedly ignored or understated the historical and contemporary significance of traditional religion in American life, thus abridging the Free Exercise rights of students holding theistic beliefs. The "teaching" of secular humanism amounted to "a sweeping fundamental belief that must not be promoted by the public schools." Such promotion, the court concluded, was a violation of the Establishment Clause of the First Amendment. The Court of Appeals for the Eleventh Circuit promptly overruled this novel decision, finding that the "purpose" for using the textbooks in question was "purely secular" (see *Smith v. Board of School Commissioners of Mobile County* [1987]).

In a similar case initiated in 1986, fundamentalist parents in Hawkins County, Tennessee, sued their county school board over the reading curriculum in the local public schools, complaining of the humanist perspective embodied in the curriculum. Although plaintiffs won at trial, the judgment was overruled on appeal by the Court of Appeals for the Sixth Circuit. The Supreme Court declined to review the case (*Mozert v. Hawkins County Public Schools* [1988]), thus letting the appeals court's decision stand.

Other Public Affirmations of Religious Belief

It is natural for there to be numerous public affirmations of belief in a religious society such as ours. The Court's decision in *Abington v. Schempp* suggests, however, that government sponsorship of such affirmations is unconstitutional. Nevertheless, the Supreme Court has been unwilling to hold government-sponsored displays or affirmations of belief to the same standard of strict neutrality that underlies the school prayer decisions.

Perhaps the best example of the Court's unwillingness to extend the holding of *Abington v. Schempp* to its logical conclusion came in *Marsh v. Chambers* (1983). Here, the Court refused to invalidate Nebraska's policy of beginning legislative sessions with prayers offered by a Protestant chaplain retained at the taxpayers' expense. Writing for the Court, Chief Justice Burger made no pretense of applying the strict three-part test laid down in his own majority opinion in *Lemon v. Kurtzman*. Instead, Burger's opinion relied heavily on history and the need for accommodation of popular religious beliefs. In a caustic dissent, Justice Brennan observed that "if any group of law students were asked to apply the principles of *Lemon* to the question of legislative prayer, they would nearly unanimously find the practice to be unconstitutional."

The decision in *Marsh v. Chambers* suggested to some observers that the Supreme Court was prepared to abandon the strict tripartite *Lemon* test for determining establishment of religion. To others, *Marsh* was a mere aberration, based on the pragmatic realization that the Court would inevitably be embarrassed if it were to attempt to strike down a practice that occurs in nearly every legislature in the United States, including the U.S. Congress. This case provides a good illustration of the practical limits of judicial power.

The decision in *Lynch v. Donnelly* (1984) suggests that *Marsh* was more than a mere aberration. In *Lynch,* the Court upheld a city-sponsored nativity scene in

Warren E. Burger: Chief Justice, 1969–1986

Pawtucket, Rhode Island. Chief Justice Burger's majority opinion barely mentioned the *Lemon* test. Again Burger relied on history and the fact that the crèche had become for many a "neutral harbinger of the holiday season," rather than a symbol of Christianity.

Five years later, in the Pennsylvania case of *County of Allegheny v. American Civil Liberties Union* (1989), the Court reexamined the constitutional question posed by traditional holiday displays on public property. Here, the justices considered two separate displays: a crèche prominently situated on the grand staircase inside the county courthouse and an arrangement featuring a Christmas tree and a Hanukkah menorah placed just outside the nearby city-county building. A sign bearing the mayor's name and entitled "Salute to Liberty" was placed at the foot of the Christmas tree. Justice Blackmun, for a majority of the Court, maintained that the display of the crèche inside the courthouse, with the accompanying words "Gloria in Excelsis Deo," clearly conveyed a religious message. By authorizing the display, the county had, in Blackmun's view, indicated its endorsement of that message. Such endorsement, he concluded, was a violation of the Establishment Clause. By contrast, the Christmas tree and menorah display, in tandem with the mayor's message, was not in the Court's view "an endorsement of religious faith, but simply a recognition of cultural diversity." The overall display conveyed a predominantly secular message and thus did not violate the Establishment Clause.

The Supreme Court's decisions in *Marsh* and *Lynch* indicate that the Burger Court retreated from the "strict neutrality" approach of the Warren Court in favor of an approach that might be labeled "accommodation" or "benevolent neutrality." The *Allegheny County* decision suggested, however, that the Rehnquist Court was not prepared to abandon the strict *Lemon* test altogether. Whether the Rehnquist Court will continue to rely on *Lemon* is highly doubtful, as its 1992 decision in *Lee v. Weisman* (reprinted in Appendix E) seemed to confirm. In that case, the justices, dividing 5-4, held that the official sponsorship of prayers at a public school graduation ceremony in Rhode Island violated the Establishment Clause. In reaffirming the original school prayer decisions, the majority, speaking through Justice Kennedy, specifically refused to apply, or for that matter re-examine, the *Lemon* test.

The Problem of Tax Exemptions

Traditionally, church properties have been exempt from local property taxes and church incomes have been exempt from federal and state income taxes. Such exemptions generally are not limited to churches but extend to various private, nonprofit organizations that can be classified as charitable institutions. The existence of tax exemptions for churches and religious schools raises questions arising under both the Establishment and Free Exercise clauses of the First Amendment. On the one hand, it can be argued that a tax exemption is an indirect subsidy. Arguably, for government to exempt churches and church schools from paying taxes is to subsidize them in violation of the requirement of separation of church and state. On the other hand, one can argue that failure to exempt churches from taxation amounts to an infringement of the Free Exercise Clause, since, as Chief Justice John Marshall pointed out in *M'Culloch v. Maryland* (1819), "the power to tax involves the power to destroy."

The Supreme Court considered the constitutionality of property tax exemptions for churches in the case of *Walz v. Tax Commission* (1970). Frederick Walz brought suit against the New York City Tax Commission, arguing that the commission's grant of property tax exemptions to churches (as allowed by state law) required him to subsidize those churches indirectly. Relying heavily on the long-standing practice of religious tax exemptions and the Court's traditional deference to legislative bodies with regard to the taxing power, the Court found no constitutional violation. Writing for a majority of eight, Chief Justice Burger noted that

> [f]ew concepts are more deeply embedded in the fabric of our national life, beginning with pre-Revolutionary colonial times, than for the government to exercise ... this kind of benevolent neutrality toward churches and religious exercise generally so long as none was favored over others and none suffered interference.

Dissenting vigorously, Justice Douglas argued for strict government neutrality toward religion as distinct from the Chief Justice's "benevolent neutrality" approach:

> If believers are entitled to public financial support, so are nonbelievers. A believer and nonbeliever under the present law are treated differently because of the articles of their faith. Believers are doubtless comforted that the cause of religion is being fostered by this legislation. Yet one of the mandates of the First Amendment is to promote a viable, pluralistic society and to keep government neutral, not only between sects, but also between believers and nonbelievers.

It is interesting to compare Justice Douglas's dissent in *Walz* with his majority opinion in *Zorach v. Clauson*. In 1952, Douglas had written, apparently in earnest, about the importance of governmental accommodation of religion. In concurring opinions in the school prayer decisions of 1962 and 1963, Douglas indicated that he was reconsidering his position on the Establishment Clause generally. By 1970, his stance had shifted from accommodation to strict neutrality. Justice Douglas's forceful dissent in *Walz* to the contrary notwithstanding, it is unlikely that the Supreme Court would ever invalidate religious tax exemptions. There is simply too much public support for these long-standing policies.

To take advantage of tax exemptions for religious property, a small minority of unscrupulous individuals have established "churches" in their homes after obtaining inexpensive "doctor of divinity" degrees through the mail. For example, in the late 1970s in one small town in New York, nearly 85 percent of the residents became "ministers" and claimed tax-exempt status for their homes. This subterfuge was finally ended through state legislation that was upheld by a later court decision. The U.S. Supreme Court dismissed the appeal, thus allowing the state court decision to stand (*Hardenbaugh v. New York* [1981]).

One of the most controversial Supreme Court decisions of the early 1980s dealt with the question of whether tax-exempt status could be withdrawn from religious schools that practice race discrimination. In *Bob Jones University v. United States* (1983), the Court held that such institutions could indeed be denied their federal income tax exemptions by the Internal Revenue Service (IRS). Prior to 1975, Bob Jones University, a fundamentalist Christian college in South Carolina, had refused to admit African-Americans. After 1975, African-Americans were admitted, but interracial dating and marriage were strictly prohibited. The IRS formally revoked the school's long-standing tax exemption in 1976. Then, in 1982, the Reagan administration announced that the IRS was restoring tax-exempt status to all segregated private schools, claiming that the IRS lacked the authority to remove tax exemptions without specific authorizing legislation from Congress. The Court's 8-to-1 decision in *Bob Jones* repudiated the Reagan administration's view that the IRS lacked authority to revoke the tax-exempt status of religious schools that practice racial discrimination. With regard to the First Amendment issue, the Court held that

> [t]he governmental interest at stake here is compelling. . . . The government has a fundamental, overriding interest in eradicating racial discrimination in education. . . . That governmental interest substantially outweighs whatever burden denial of tax benefits places on petitioners' exercise of their religious beliefs.

The Court's decision in *Bob Jones* implies that tax exemptions for religious enterprises are not a matter of constitutional entitlement—they are granted through governmental benevolence and can be withdrawn for reasons of public policy.

Tuition Tax Credits

Many states have considered the idea of providing tax credits to parents of children in private and parochial schools. Indeed, in 1982, President Reagan proposed tuition tax credits of five hundred dollars per child for parents whose children attend private and parochial schools. Although the proposal did not obtain congressional approval, serious questions were raised about its constitutionality. In *Committee for Public Education v. Nyquist* (1973), the Supreme Court had struck down a state tax deduction for parents of children in parochial schools. However, the Court may be moving away from the *Nyquist* decision, at least insofar as it dealt with tax benefits. In 1983, in *Mueller v. Allen,* the Court upheld a Minnesota law that allowed parents of children in private and parochial schools to deduct as much as seven hundred dollars of school expenses from their incomes subject to state income tax. Given the conservatism of the Rehnquist Court it is unlikely that the justices will raise serious constitutional objections to tax credits that benefit parochial schools.

CONCLUSION

While the United States is a decidedly religious nation, it is also committed to secular government and religious freedom. These competing values create tensions that can never be finally resolved. Inevitably, constitutional law on the subject of religious liberty remains unsettled, reflecting the evolving views of a maturing society.

The Supreme Court of the 1990s appears to accord legitimacy to governmental efforts to accommodate traditional religious practices. In this respect, it has followed the initiatives of the Burger Court in such cases as *Widmar v. Vincent* (1981) and *Lynch v. Donnelly* (1984). The Court has been less receptive to unorthodox religious practices, especially if they are perceived to be in conflict with the imperatives of law enforcement (see, for example, *Employment Division v. Smith,* 1990). The ideological impact on the Court resulting from appointments made by Presidents Nixon, Reagan, and Bush is apparent in this area. In addition to the influence of partisan judicial appointments, we see the Court responding to a conservative trend in society's attitudes with respect to religion, crime, and deviance. The following chapter examines the changing response of the Supreme Court to constitutional questions dealing specifically with crime and punishment.

FOR FURTHER READING

Bellah, Robert, et al. *The Good Society*. New York: Knopf, 1991.

Curry, Thomas J. *The First Freedoms*. New York: Oxford University Press, 1986.

Howe, Mark DeWolfe. *The Garden and the Wilderness: Religion and Government in American Constitutional History*. Chicago: University of Chicago Press, 1985.

Irons, Peter. *The Courage of Their Convictions: Sixteen Americans Who Fought Their Way to the Supreme Court*. New York: Penguin Books, 1990. See, in particular, chapters 1, 7, 9, and 15.

Kauper, Paul. *Religion and the Constitution*. Baton Rouge: Louisiana State University Press, 1964.

Levy, Leonard. *The Establishment Clause: Religion and the First Amendment*. New York: Macmillan, 1986.

Manwaring, David. *Render Unto Caesar: The Flag Salute Controversy*. Chicago: University of Chicago Press, 1962.

Miller, William Lee. *The First Liberty: Religion and the American Republic*. New York: Knopf, 1986.

Oaks, Dallin, ed. *The Wall Between Church and State*. Chicago: University of Chicago Press, 1963.

Pfeffer, Leo. *Church, State and Freedom*. Boston: Beacon Press, 1967.

Pfeffer, Leo. *God, Caesar and the Constitution*. Boston: Beacon Press, 1975.

Sorauf, Frank. *The Wall of Separation: The Constitutional Politics of Church and State*. Princeton, N.J.: Princeton University Press, 1976.

Stokes, Anson, and Leo Pfeffer. *Church and State in the United States*. New York: Harper and Row, 1965.

Tussman, Joseph. *The Supreme Court on Church and State*. New York: Oxford University Press, 1962.

West Virginia State Board of Education v. Barnette

319 U.S. 624; 63 S. Ct. 1178; 87 L. Ed. 1628 (1943)
Vote: 6-3

In Minersville School District v. Gobitis (1940), the Supreme Court, in an 8-to-1 decision, upheld a local school board directive in Minersville, Pennsylvania, requiring public school students and teachers to participate in a flag salute ceremony conducted as a regular part of the daily classroom schedule. This requirement had been challenged by Walter Gobitis, a member of the Jehovah's Witnesses sect, whose children, Lillian and William (ages twelve and ten), were expelled from school for refusing to salute the flag. In upholding the flag salute requirement, the Court rejected Gobitis's contention that it violated First Amendment principles of religious liberty as applied to the states through the Due Process Clause of the Fourteenth Amendment.

Three years later, in a dramatic and highly publicized reversal of its position, the Supreme Court, by a 6-to-3 margin, overruled the Gobitis case by striking down a virtually identical flag salute requirement imposed by the West Virginia Board of Education. The board was acting under authority of a statute passed by the West Virginia legislature in the immediate aftermath of the Gobitis decision. This law required all schools in the state to offer classes in civics, history, and the federal and state constitutions "for the purpose of teaching, fostering, and perpetuating the ideals, principles, and spirit of Americanism, and increasing the knowledge of the organization and machinery of the Government."

Walter Barnette, and two other Jehovah's Witnesses, all of whom had children in the public schools, filed suit to enjoin the compulsory flag salute on grounds that it violated a constitutionally protected religious precept contained in the Old Testament (Exod. 20:4-5) forbidding the worship of "any graven image." Under their reading of the Scriptures, the flag salute constituted such forbidden worship.

Because this decision represents such a swift and decisive overruling of constitutional precedent, it is

interesting to compare the alignments of the justices in Gobitis *and* Barnette. *Justice Frankfurter wrote the majority opinion in the* Gobitis *case, with only Justice Stone dissenting. Justice Jackson, who along with Justice Rutledge joined the Court after that decision was announced, wrote the majority opinion in* Barnette. *Justices Black, Douglas, and Murphy, all of whom had supported Frankfurter's original majority position, switched sides and supported the majority opinion in* Barnette. *Justices Frankfurter, Reed, and Roberts dissented in the latter case.*

Mr. Justice Jackson delivered the opinion of the Court:

. . . National unity as an end which officials may foster by persuasion and example is not in question. The problem is whether under our Constitution compulsion as here employed is a permissible means for its achievement.

Struggles to coerce uniformity of sentiment in support of some end thought essential to their time and country have been waged by many good as well as by evil men. Nationalism is a relatively recent phenomenon but at other times and places the ends have been racial or territorial security, support of a dynasty or regime, and particular plans for saving souls. As first and moderate methods to attain unity have failed, those bent on its accomplishment must resort to an ever increasing severity. As governmental pressure toward unity becomes greater, so strife becomes more bitter as to whose unity it shall be. Probably no deeper division of our people could proceed from any provocation than from finding it necessary to choose what doctrine and whose program public educational officials shall compel youth to unite in embracing. Ultimate futility of such attempts to compel coherence is the lesson of every such effort from the Roman drive to stamp out Christianity as a disturber of its pagan unity, the Inquisition, as a means to religious and dynastic unity, the

Siberian exiles as a means to Russian unity, down to the fast failing efforts of our present totalitarian enemies. Those who begin coercive elimination of dissent soon find themselves exterminating dissenters. Compulsory unification of opinion achieves only the unanimity of the graveyard.

It seems trite but necessary to say that the First Amendment to our Constitution was designed to avoid these ends by avoiding these beginnings. There is no mysticism in the American concept of the State or of the nature or origin of its authority. We set up government by consent of the governed, and the Bill of Rights denies those in power any legal opportunity to coerce that consent. Authority here is to be controlled by public opinion, not public opinion by authority.

The case is made difficult not because the principles of its decision are obscure but because the flag involved is our own. Nevertheless, we apply the limitations of the Constitution with no fear that freedom to be intellectually and spiritually diverse or even contrary will disintegrate the social organization. To believe that patriotism will not flourish if patriotic ceremonies are voluntary and spontaneous instead of a compulsory routine is to make an unflattering estimate of the appeal of our institutions to free minds. We can have intellectual individualism and the rich cultural diversities that we owe to exceptional minds only at the price of occasional eccentricity and abnormal attitudes. When they are so harmless to others or to the State as those we deal with here, the price is not too great. But freedom to differ is not limited to things that do not matter much. That would be a mere shadow of freedom. The test of its substance is the right to differ as to things that touch the heart of the existing order.

If there is any fixed star in our constitutional constellation, it is that no official, high or petty, can prescribe what shall be orthodox in politics, nationalism, religion, or other matters of opinion or force citizens to confess by word or act their faith therein. If there are any circumstances which permit an exception, they do not now occur to us.

We think the action of the local authorities in compelling the flag salute and pledge transcends constitutional limitations on their power and invades the sphere of intellect and spirit which it is the purpose of the First Amendment to our Constitution to reserve from all official control.

The decision of this Court in *Minersville School Dist. v. Gobitis* and the holdings of those few *per curiam* decisions which preceded and foreshadowed it are overruled, and the judgment enjoining enforcement of the West Virginia Regulation is affirmed.

Mr. Justice Roberts and **Mr. Justice Reed** adhere to the views expressed by the Court in *Minersville School Dist. v. Gobitis,* *** and are of the opinion that the judgment below should be reversed.

Mr. Justice Black and **Mr. Justice Douglas,** concurring:

We are substantially in agreement with the opinion just read, but since we originally joined with the Court in the *Gobitis* case, it is appropriate that we make a brief statement of reasons for our change of view.

Reluctance to make the Federal Constitution a rigid bar against state regulation of conduct thought inimical to the public welfare was the controlling influence which moved us to consent to the *Gobitis* decision. Long reflection convinced us that although the principle is sound, its application in the particular case was wrong. *** We believe that the statute before us fails to accord full scope to the freedom of religion secured to the appellees by the First and Fourteenth Amendments. . . .

No well ordered society can leave to the individuals an absolute right to make final decisions, unassailable by the State, as to everything they will or will not do. The First Amendment does not go so far. Religious faiths, honestly held, do not free individuals from responsibility to conduct themselves obediently to laws which are either imperatively necessary to protect society as a whole from grave and pressingly imminent dangers or which, without any general prohibition, merely regulate time, place or manner of religious activity. Decisions as to the constitutionality of particular laws which strike at the substance of religious tenets and practices must be made by this Court. The duty is a solemn one, and in meeting it we cannot say that a failure, because of religious scruples, to assume a particular physical position and to repeat the words of a patriotic formula creates a grave danger to the nation. Such a statutory exaction is a form of test oath, and the test oath has always been abhorrent in the United States.

Words uttered under coercion are proof of loyalty to nothing but self-interest. Love of country must spring from willing hearts and free minds, inspired by a fair administration of wise laws enacted by the people's elected representatives within the bounds of express constitutional prohibitions. These laws must, to be consistent with the First Amendment, permit the widest toleration of conflicting viewpoints consistent with a society of free men.

Neither our domestic tranquility in peace nor our martial effort in war depend on compelling little children to participate in a ceremony which ends in nothing for them but a fear of spiritual condemnation. If, as we think, their fears are groundless, time and reason are the proper antidotes for their errors. The ceremonial, when enforced against conscientious objectors, more likely to defeat than to serve its high purpose, is a handy implement for disguised religious persecution. As such, it is inconsistent with our Constitution's plan and purpose.

Mr. Justice Murphy, concurring:

. . . Without wishing to disparage the purposes and intentions of those who hope to inculcate sentiments of loyalty and patriotism by requiring a declaration of allegiance as a feature of public education, or unduly belittle the benefits that may accrue therefrom, I am impelled to conclude that such a requirement is not essential to the maintenance of effective government and orderly society. To many it is deeply distasteful to join in a public chorus of affirmation of private belief. By some, including the members of this sect, it is apparently regarded as incompatible with a primary religious obligation and therefore a restriction on religious freedom. Official compulsion to affirm what is contrary to one's religious beliefs is the antithesis of freedom of worship which, it is well to recall, was achieved in this country only after what Jefferson characterized as the "severest contests in which I have ever been engaged." . . .

Mr. Justice Frankfurter, dissenting:

One who belongs to the most vilified and persecuted minority in history is not likely to be insensible to the freedoms guaranteed by our Constitution. Were my purely personal attitude relevant I should wholeheartedly associate myself with the general libertarian views in the Court's opinion, representing as they do the thought and action of a lifetime. But as judges we are neither Jew nor Gentile, neither Catholic nor agnostic. We owe equal attachment to the Constitution and are equally bound by our judicial obligations whether we derive our citizenship from the earliest or the latest immigrants to these shores. As a member of this Court I am not justified in writing my private notions of policy into the Constitution, no matter how deeply I may cherish them or how mischievous I may deem their disregard. The duty of a judge who must decide which of two claims before the Court shall prevail, that of a State to enact and enforce laws within its general competence or that of an individual to refuse obedience because of the demands of his conscience, is not that of the ordinary person. It can never be emphasized too much that one's own opinion about the wisdom or evil of a law should be excluded altogether when one is doing one's duty on the bench. The only opinion of our own even looking in that direction that is material is our opinion whether legislators could in reason have enacted such a law. In the light of all the circumstances, including the history of this question in this Court, it would require more daring than I possess to deny that reasonable legislators could have taken the action which is before us for review. Most unwillingly, therefore, I must differ from my brethren with regard to legislation like this. I cannot bring my mind to believe that the "liberty" secured by the Due Process Clause gives this Court authority to deny to the State of West Virginia the attainment of that which we all recognize as a legitimate legislative end, namely, the promotion of good citizenship, by employment of the means here chosen. . . .

Of course patriotism cannot be enforced by the flag salute. But neither can the liberal spirit be enforced by judicial invalidation of illiberal legislation. Of constant preoccupation with the constitutionality of legislation rather than with its wisdom tends to preoccupation of the American mind with a false value. The tendency of focusing attention on constitutionality is to make constitutionality synonymous with wisdom, to regard a law as all right if it is constitutional. Such an attitude is a great enemy of liberalism. Particularly in legislation affecting freedom of thought and freedom of speech much which should offend a free-spirited society is constitutional. Reliance for the most precious interests of civilization, therefore, must be found outside of their vin-

dication in courts of law. Only a persistent positive translation of the faith of a free society into the convictions and habits and actions of a community is the ultimate reliance against unabated temptations to fetter the human spirit.

Goldman v. Weinberger

475 U.S. 503; 106 S. Ct. 1310; 89 L. Ed. 2d 478 (1986)
Vote: 5-4

Justice Rehnquist delivered the opinion of the Court.

Petitioner S. Simcha Goldman contends that the Free Exercise Clause of the First Amendment to the United States Constitution permits him to wear a yarmulke while in uniform, notwithstanding an Air Force regulation mandating uniform dress for Air Force personnel. The District Court for the District of Columbia permanently enjoined the Air Force from enforcing its regulation against petitioner and from penalizing him for wearing his yarmulke. The Court of Appeals for the District of Columbia Circuit reversed on the ground that the Air Force's strong interest in discipline justified the strict enforcement of its uniform dress requirements. We granted *certiorari* because of the importance of the question, and now affirm.

Petitioner Goldman is an Orthodox Jew and ordained rabbi. In 1973, he was accepted into the Armed Forces Health Professions Scholarship Program and placed on inactive reserve status in the Air Force while he studied clinical psychology at Loyola University of Chicago. During his three years in the scholarship program, he received a monthly stipend and an allowance for tuition, books, and fees. After completing his Ph.D. in psychology, petitioner entered active service in the United States Air Force as a commissioned officer, in accordance with a requirement that participants in the scholarship program serve one year of active duty for each year of subsidized education. Petitioner was stationed at March Air Force Base in Riverside, California, and served as a clinical psychologist at the mental health clinic on the base.

Until 1981, petitioner was not prevented from wearing his yarmulke on the base. He avoided controversy by remaining close to his duty station in the health clinic and by wearing his service cap over the yarmulke when out of doors. But in April 1981, after he testified as a defense witness at a court-martial wearing his yarmulke but not his service cap, opposing counsel lodged a complaint with Colonel Joseph Gregory, the Hospital Commander, arguing that petitioner's practice of wearing his yarmulke was a violation of Air Force Regulation (AFR) 35-10. This regulation states in pertinent part that "[h]eadgear will not be worn ... [w]hile indoors except by armed security police in the performance of their duties." ***

Colonel Gregory informed petitioner that wearing a yarmulke while on duty does indeed violate AFR 35-10, and ordered him not to violate this regulation outside the hospital. Although virtually all of petitioner's time on the base was spent in the hospital, he refused. Later, after petitioner's attorney protested to the Air Force General Counsel, Colonel Gregory revised his order to prohibit petitioner from wearing the yarmulke even in the hospital. Petitioner's request to report for duty in civilian clothing pending legal resolution of the issue was denied. The next day he received a formal letter of reprimand, and was warned that failure to obey AFR 35-10 could subject him to a court-martial. Colonel Gregory also withdrew a recommendation that petitioner's application to extend the term of his active service be approved, and substituted a negative recommendation.

Petitioner then sued respondent Secretary of Defense and others, claiming that the application of AFR

35-10 to prevent him from wearing his yarmulke infringed upon his First Amendment freedom to exercise his religious beliefs....

Petitioner argues that AFR 35-10, as applied to him, prohibits religiously motivated conduct and should therefore be analyzed under the standard enunciated in *Sherbert v. Verner* *** (1963). See also *Thomas v. Review Board* *** (1981); *Wisconsin v. Yoder* *** (1972). But we have repeatedly held that "the military is, by necessity, a specialized society separate from civilian society." *** "[T]he military must insist upon a respect for duty and a discipline without counterpart in civilian life," *** in order to prepare for and perform its vital role. ***

Our review of military regulations challenged on First Amendment grounds is far more deferential than constitutional review of similar laws or regulations designed for civilian society. The military need not encourage debate or tolerate protest to the extent that such tolerance is required of the civilian state by the First Amendment; to accomplish its mission the military must foster instinctive obedience, unity, commitment, and *esprit de corps.* *** The essence of military service "is the subordination of the desires and interests of the individual...."

These aspects of military life do not, of course, render entirely nugatory in the military context the guarantees of the First Amendment. *** But "within the military community there is simply not the same [individual] autonomy as there is in the larger civilian community." *** In the context of the present case, when evaluating whether military needs justify a particular restriction on religiously motivated conduct, courts must give great deference to the professional judgment of military authorities concerning the relative importance of a particular military interest. *** Not only are courts " 'ill-equipped to determine the impact upon discipline that any particular intrusion upon military authority might have,' " *** but the military authorities have been charged by the Executive and Legislative Branches with carrying out our Nation's military policy. "Judicial deference ... is at its apogee when legislative action under the congressional authority to raise and support armies and make rules and regulations for their governance is challenged." ***

The considered professional judgment of the Air Force is that the traditional outfitting of personnel in standardized uniforms encourages the subordination of personal preferences and identities in favor of the overall group mission. Uniforms encourage a sense of hierarchical unity by tending to eliminate outward individual distinctions except for those of rank. The Air Force considers them as vital during peacetime as during war because its personnel must be ready to provide an effective defense on a moment's notice; the necessary habits of discipline and unity must be developed in advance of trouble. We have acknowledged that "[t]he inescapable demands of military discipline and obedience to orders cannot be taught on battlefields; the habit of immediate compliance with military procedures and orders must be virtually reflex with no time for debate or reflection." *** ...

Petitioner Goldman contends that the Free Exercise Clause of the First Amendment requires the Air Force to make an exception to its uniform dress requirements for religious apparel unless the accoutrements create a "clear danger" of undermining discipline and *esprit de corps.* He asserts that in general, visible but "unobtrusive" apparel will not create such a danger and must therefore be accommodated. He argues that the Air Force failed to prove that a specific exception for his practice of wearing an unobtrusive yarmulke would threaten discipline. He contends that the Air Force's assertion to the contrary is mere *ipse dixit,* with no support from actual experience or a scientific study in the record, and is contradicted by expert testimony that religious exceptions to AFR 35-10 are in fact desirable and will increase morale by making the Air Force a more humane place.

But whether or not expert witnesses may feel that religious exceptions to AFR 35-10 are desirable is quite beside the point. The desirability of dress regulations in the military is decided by the appropriate military officials, and they are under no constitutional mandate to abandon their considered professional judgment. Quite obviously, to the extent the regulations do not permit the wearing of religious apparel such as a yarmulke, a practice described by petitioner as silent devotion akin to prayer, military life may be more objectionable for petitioner and probably others. But the First Amendment does not require the military to accommodate such practices in the face of its view that they would detract from the uniformity sought by the dress regulations. The Air Force has drawn the line essentially between religious apparel which is visible and that which is not, and we hold that those portions of the regulations challenged here reasonably and evenhandedly regulate dress in the interest of the military's perceived need for uniformity. The First Amendment therefore does not prohibit them from being applied to petitioner even though their effect is to restrict the wearing of the headgear required by his religious beliefs.

The judgment of the Court of Appeals is affirmed.

Justice Stevens, with whom *Justice White* and *Justice Powell* join, concurring.

Captain Goldman presents an especially attractive case for an exception from the uniform regulations that are applicable to all other Air Force personnel. His devotion to his faith is readily apparent. The yarmulke is a familiar and accepted sight. In addition to its religious significance for the wearer, the yarmulke may evoke the deepest respect and admiration—the symbol of a distinguished tradition and an eloquent rebuke to the ugliness of anti-Semitism. Captain Goldman's military duties are performed in a setting in which a modest departure from the uniform regulation creates almost no danger of impairment of the Air Force's military mission. Moreover, on the record before us, there is reason to believe that the policy of strict enforcement against Captain Goldman had a retaliatory motive—he had worn his yarmulke while testifying on behalf of a defendant in a court-martial proceeding. Nevertheless, as the case has been argued, I believe we must test the validity of the Air Force's rule not merely as it applies to Captain Goldman but also as it applies to all service personnel who have sincere religious beliefs that may conflict with one or more military commands.

Justice Brennan is unmoved by the Government's concern "that while a yarmulke might not seem obtrusive to a Jew, neither does a turban to a Sikh, a saffron robe to a Satchidananda Ashram-Integral Yogi, nor do dreadlocks to a Rastafarian." *** He correctly points out that "turbans, saffron robes, and dreadlocks are not before us in this case," and then suggests that other cases may be fairly decided by reference to a reasonable standard based on "func-tional utility, health and safety considerations, and the goal of a polished, professional appearance." *** As the Court has explained, this approach attaches no weight to the separate interest in uniformity itself. Because professionals in the military service attach great importance to that plausible interest, it is one that we must recognize as legitimate and rational even though personal experience or admiration for the performance of the "rag-tag band of soldiers" that won us our freedom in the revolutionary war might persuade us that the Government has exaggerated the importance of that interest.

The interest in uniformity, however, has a dimension that is of still greater importance for me. It is the interest in uniform treatment for the members of all religious faiths. The very strength of Captain Goldman's claim creates the danger that a similar claim on behalf of a Sikh or a Rastafarian might readily be dismissed as "so extreme, so unusual, or so faddish an image that public confidence in his ability to perform his duties will be destroyed." *** If exceptions from dress code regulations are to be granted on the basis of a multifactored test such as that proposed by Justice Brennan, inevitably the decisionmaker's evaluation of the character and the sincerity of the requestor's faith—as well as the probable reaction of the majority to the favored treatment of a member of that faith—will play a critical part in the decision. For the difference between a turban or a dreadlock on the one hand, and a yarmulke on the other, is not merely a difference in "appearance"—it is also the difference between a Sikh or a Rastafarian, on the one hand, and an Orthodox Jew on the other. The Air Force has no business drawing distinctions between such persons when it is enforcing commands of universal application.

As the Court demonstrates, the rule that is challenged in this case is based on a neutral, completely objective standard—visibility. It was not motivated by hostility against, or any special respect for, any religious faith. An exception for yarmulkes would represent a fundamental departure from the true principle of uniformity that supports that rule. For that reason, I join the Court's opinion and its judgment.

Justice Brennan, with whom *Justice Marshall* joins, dissenting. . . .

Justice Blackmun, dissenting. . . .

Justice O'Connor, with whom *Justice Marshall* joins, dissenting.

The issue posed in this case is whether, consistent with the Free Exercise Clause of the First Amendment, the Air Force may prohibit Captain Goldman, an Orthodox Jewish psychologist, from wearing a yarmulke while he is in uniform on duty inside a military hospital.

The Court rejects Captain Goldman's claim without even the slightest attempt to weigh his asserted right to the free exercise of his religion against the interest of the Air Force in uniformity of dress within the military hospital. No test for Free Exercise claims in the military context is even articulated, much less applied. It is entirely sufficient for the court if the military perceives a need for uniformity. . . .

I believe that the Court should attempt to articulate and apply an appropriate standard for a free exercise claim in the military context, and should examine Captain Goldman's claim in light of that standard. . . .

. . . One can . . . glean at least two consistent themes from this Court's precedents. First, when the government attempts to deny a Free Exercise claim, it must show that an unusually important interest is at stake, whether that interest is denominated "compelling," "of the highest order," or "overriding." Second, the government must show that granting the requested exemption will do substantial harm to that interest, whether by showing that the means adopted is the "least restrictive" or "essential," or that the interest will not otherwise be served. These two requirements are entirely sensible in the context of the assertion of a free exercise claim. First, because the government is attempting to override an interest specifically protected by the Bill of Rights, the government must show that the opposing interest it asserts is of especial importance before there is any chance that its claim can prevail. Second, since the Bill of Rights is expressly designed to protect the individual against the aggregated and sometimes intolerant powers of the state, the government must show that the interest asserted will in fact be substantially harmed by granting the type of exemption requested by the individual.

There is no reason why these general principles should not apply in the military, as well as the civilian, context. . . . Furthermore, the test that one can glean from this court's decisions in the civilian context is sufficiently flexible to take into account the special importance of defending our Nation without abandoning completely the freedoms that make it worth defending.

The first question that the Court should face here, therefore, is whether the interest that the government asserts against the religiously based claim of the individual is of unusual importance. It is perfectly appropriate at this step of the analysis to take account of the special role of the military. The mission of our armed services is to protect our nation from those who would destroy all our freedoms. I agree that, in order to fulfill that mission, the military is entitled to take some freedoms from its members. As the Court notes, the military " 'must insist upon a respect for duty and a discipline without counterpart in civilian life.' " *** The need for military discipline and *esprit de corps* is unquestionably an especially important governmental interest.

But the mere presence of such an interest cannot end the analysis of whether a refusal by the Government to honor the free exercise of an individual's religion is constitutionally acceptable. A citizen pursuing even the most noble cause must remain within the bounds of the law. So, too, the Government may, even in pursuing its most compelling interests, be subject to specific restraints in doing so. The second question in the analysis of a Free Exercise claim under this court's precedents must also be reached here: will granting an exemption of the type requested by the individual do substantial harm to the especially important governmental interest?

I have no doubt that there are many instances in which the unique fragility of military discipline and *esprit de corps* necessitates rigidity by the Government when similar rigidity to preserve an assertedly analogous interest would not pass constitutional muster in the civilian sphere. *** Nonetheless, as Justice Brennan persuasively argues, the Government can present no sufficiently convincing proof in this case to support an assertion that granting an exemption of the type requested here would do substantial harm to military discipline and *esprit de corps*. ***

First, the Government's asserted need for absolute uniformity is contradicted by the Government's own exceptions to its rule. . . . Furthermore, the Government does not assert, and could not plausibly argue, that petitioner's decision to wear his yarmulke while indoors at the hospital presents a threat to health or safety. And finally, the District Court found as fact that in this particular case, far from creating discontent or indiscipline in the hospital where Captain Goldman worked, "[f]rom September 1977 to May 7, 1981, no objection was raised to Goldman's wearing of his yarmulke while in uniform." ***

In the rare instances where the military has not consistently or plausibly justified its asserted need for rigidity of enforcement, and where the individual seeking the exemption establishes that the assertion by the military of a threat to discipline or *esprit de corps* is in his or her case completely unfounded, I would hold that the Government's policy of uniformity must yield to the individual's assertion of the right of free exercise of religion. On the facts of this case, therefore, I would require the Government to accommodate the sincere religious belief of Captain Goldman. Napoleon may have been correct to assert that, in the military sphere, morale is to all other factors as three is to one, but contradicted assertions of necessity by the military do not on the scales of justice bear a similarly disproportionate weight to sincere religious beliefs of the individual.

I respectfully dissent.

Wisconsin v. Yoder

406 U.S. 205; 92 S. Ct. 1526; 32 L. Ed. 2d 15 (1972)
Vote: 6-1

Mr. Chief Justice Burger delivered the opinion of the Court.

On petition of the State of Wisconsin, we granted the writ of *certiorari* in this case to review a decision of the Wisconsin Supreme Court holding that respondents' convictions for violating the State's compulsory school-attendance law were invalid under the Free Exercise Clause of the First Amendment to the United States Constitution made applicable to the States by the Fourteenth Amendment. For the reasons hereafter stated we affirm the judgment of the Supreme Court of Wisconsin.

Respondents Jonas Yoder and Wallace Miller are members of the Old Order Amish religion, and respondent Adin Yutzy is a member of the Conservative Amish Mennonite Church. They and their families are residents of Green County, Wisconsin. Wisconsin's compulsory school-attendance law required them to cause their children to attend public or private school until . . . age 16 but the respondents declined to send their children, ages 14 and 15, to public school after they completed the eighth grade. The children were not enrolled in any private school, or within any recognized exception to the compulsory-attendance law, and they are conceded to be subject to the Wisconsin statute.

On complaint of the school district administrator for the public schools, respondents were charged, tried, and convicted of violating the compulsory-attendance law in Green County Court and were fined the sum of $5 each. Respondents defended on the ground that the application of the compulsory-attendance law violated their rights under the First and Fourteenth Amendments. The trial testimony showed that respondents believed, in accordance with the tenets of Old Order Amish communities generally, that their children's attendance at high school, public or private, was contrary to the Amish religion and way of life. They believed that by sending their children to high school, they would not only expose themselves to the danger of the censure of the church community, but, as found by the county court, also endanger their own salvation and that of their children. The State stipulated that respondents' religious beliefs were sincere.

In support of their position, respondents presented as expert witnesses scholars on religion and education whose testimony is uncontradicted. They expressed their opinions on the relationship of the Amish belief concerning school attendance to the more general tenets of their religion, and described the impact that compulsory high school attendance could have on the continued survival of Amish communities as they exist in the United States today. The history of the Amish sect was given in some detail, beginning with the Swiss Anabaptists of the 16th century who rejected institutionalized churches and sought to return to the early, simple, Christian life de-emphasizing material success, rejecting the competitive spirit, and seeking to insulate themselves from the modern world. As a result of their common heritage, Old Order Amish communities today are characterized by a fundamental belief that salvation requires life in a church community separate and apart from the world and worldly influence. This concept of life aloof from the world and its values is central to their faith.

A related feature of Old Order Amish communities is their devotion to a life in harmony with nature and the soil, as exemplified by the simple life of the early Christian era that continued in America during much of our early national life. Amish beliefs require members of the community to make their living by farming or closely related activities. Broadly speaking, the Old Order Amish religion pervades and determines the entire mode of life of its adherents. Their conduct is regulated in great detail by the Ordnung, or rules, of the church community. Adult baptism, which occurs in late adolescence, is the time at which Amish young people voluntarily undertake heavy obligations, not unlike the Bar Mitzvah of the Jews, to abide by the rules of the church community.

Amish objection to formal education beyond the eighth grade is firmly grounded in these central religious concepts. They object to the high school, and higher education generally, because the values they teach are in marked variance with Amish values and the Amish way of life; they view secondary school education as an impermissible exposure of their children to a "worldly" influence in conflict with their beliefs. The high school tends to emphasize intellectual and scientific accomplishments, self-distinction, competitiveness, worldly success, and social life with other students. Amish society emphasizes informal learning-through-doing; a life of "goodness," rather than a life of intellect; wisdom, rather than technical knowledge, community welfare, rather than competition; and separation from, rather than integration with, contemporary worldly society.

Formal high school education beyond the eighth grade is contrary to Amish beliefs, not only because it places Amish children in an environment hostile to Amish beliefs with increasing emphasis on competition in class work and sports and with pressure to conform to the styles, manners, and ways of the peer group, but also because it takes them away from their community, physically and emotionally, during the crucial and formative adolescent period of life. During this period, the children must acquire Amish attitudes favoring manual work and self-reliance and the specific skills needed to perform the adult role of an Amish farmer or housewife. They must learn to enjoy physical labor. Once a child has learned basic reading, writing, and elementary mathematics, these traits, skills, and attitudes admittedly fall within the category of those best learned through example and "doing" rather than in a classroom. And, at this time in life, the Amish child must also grow in his faith and his relationship to the Amish community if he is to be prepared to accept the heavy obligations imposed by adult baptism. In short, high school attendance with teachers who are not of the Amish faith— and may even be hostile to it—interposes a serious barrier to the integration of the Amish child into the Amish religious community. Dr. John Hostetler, one of the experts on Amish society, testified that the modern high school is not equipped, in curriculum or social environment, to impart the values promoted by Amish society.

The Amish do not object to elementary education through the first eight grades as a general proposition because they agree that their children must have basic skills in the "three R's" in order to read the Bible, to be good farmers and citizens, and to be able to deal with non-Amish people when necessary in the course of daily affairs. They view such a basic education as acceptable because it does not significantly expose their children to worldly values or interfere with their development in the Amish community during the crucial adolescent period. While Amish accept compulsory elementary education generally, wherever possible they have established their own elementary schools in many respects like the small local schools of the past. In the Amish belief higher learning tends to develop values they reject as influences that alienate man from God.

On the basis of such considerations, Dr. Hostetler testified that compulsory high school attendance could not only result in great psychological harm to Amish children, because of the conflicts it would produce, but would also, in his opinion, ultimately result in the destruction of the Old Order Amish church community as it exists in the United States today. The testimony of Dr. Donald A. Erickson, an expert witness on education, also showed that the Amish succeed in preparing their high school age children to be productive members of the Amish community. He described their system of learning through doing the skills directly relevant to their adult roles in the Amish community as "ideal" and perhaps superior to ordinary high school education. The evidence also showed that the Amish have an excellent record as law-abiding and generally self-sufficient members of society.

Although the trial court in its careful findings determined that the Wisconsin compulsory school-attendance law "does interfere with the freedom of the Defendants to act in accordance with their sincere religious belief" it also concluded that the requirement of high school attendance until age 16 was a "reasonable and constitutional" exercise of governmental power, and therefore denied the motion to dismiss the charges. The Wisconsin Circuit Court affirmed the convictions. The Wisconsin Supreme Court, however, sustained respondents' claim under the Free Exercise Clause of the First Amendment and reversed the convictions. A majority of the court was of the opinion that the State had failed to make an adequate showing that its interest in "establishing and maintaining an educational system overrides the defendants' right to the free exercise of their religion." ***

There is no doubt as to the power of a State, having a high responsibility for education of its citizens, to impose reasonable regulations for the control and duration of basic education. See, e.g., *Pierce v. Society of Sisters* *** (1925). Providing public schools ranks at the very apex of the function of a State. Yet even this paramount responsibility was, in *Pierce,* made to yield to the right of parents to provide an equivalent education in a privately operated system. There the Court held that Oregon's statute compelling attendance in a public school from age eight to age 16 unreasonably interfered with the interest of parents in directing the rearing of their offspring, including their education in church-operated schools. As that case suggests, the values of parental direction of the religious upbringing and education of their children in their early and formative years have a high place in our society. *** Thus, a State's interest in universal education, however highly we rank it, is not totally free from a balancing process when it impinges on fundamental rights and interests, such as those specifically protected by the Free Exercise Clause of the First Amendment, and the traditional interest of parents with respect to the religious upbringing of their children so long as they, in the words of *Pierce,* "prepare [them] for additional obligations." ***

It follows that in order for Wisconsin to compel school attendance beyond the eighth grade against a claim that such attendance interferes with the practice of a legitimate religious belief, it must appear either that the State does not deny the free exercise of religious belief by its requirement, or that there is a state interest of sufficient magnitude to override the interest claiming protection under the Free Exercise Clause. Long before there was general acknowledgment of the need for universal formal education, the Religion Clauses had specially and firmly fixed the right to free exercise of religious beliefs, and buttressing this fundamental right was an equally firm, even if less explicit, prohibition against the establishment of any religion by government. The values underlying these two provisions relating to religion have been zealously protected, sometimes even at the expense of other interests of admittedly high social importance. The invalidation of financial aid to parochial schools by government grants for a salary subsidy for teachers is but one example of the extent to which courts have gone in this regard, notwithstanding that such aid programs were legislatively determined to be in the public interest and the service of sound educational policy by States and by Congress. ***

The essence of all that has been said and written on the subject is that only those interests of the highest order and those not otherwise served can overbalance legitimate claims to the free exercise of religion. We can accept it as settled, therefore, that, however strong the State's interest in universal compulsory education, it is by no means absolute to the exclusion or subordination of all other interests. ***

We come then to the quality of the claims of the respondents concerning the alleged encroachment of Wisconsin's compulsory school-attendance statute on their rights and the rights of their children to the free exercise of the religious beliefs they and their forebears have adhered to for almost three centuries. In evaluating those claims we must be careful to determine whether the Amish religious faith and their mode of life are, as they claim, inseparable and interdependent. A way of life, however virtuous and admirable, may not be interposed as a barrier to reasonable state regulation of education if it is based on purely secular considerations; to have the protection of the Religion Clauses, the claims must be rooted in religious belief. Although a determination of what is a "religious" belief or practice entitled to constitutional protection may present a most delicate question, the very concept of ordered liberty precludes allowing every person to make his own standards on matters of conduct in which society as a whole has important interests. Thus, if the Amish asserted their claims because of their subjective evaluation and rejection of the contemporary secular values accepted by the majority, much as Thoreau rejected the social values of his time and isolated himself at Walden Pond, their claims would not rest on a religious basis. Thoreau's choice was philosophical and personal rather than religious, and such belief does not rise to the demands of the Religion Clauses.

Giving no weight to such secular considerations, however, we see that the record in this case abundantly supports the claim that the traditional way of life of the Amish is not merely a matter of personal preference, but one of deep religious conviction, shared by an organized group, and intimately related to daily living. . . .

The impact of the compulsory-attendance law on respondents' practice of the Amish religion is not only severe, but inescapable, for the Wisconsin law affirmatively compels them, under threat of criminal sanction, to perform acts undeniably at odds with fundamental tenets of their religious beliefs. *** Nor is the impact of the compulsory-attendance law confined to grave interference with important Amish religious tenets from a subjective point of view. It carries with it precisely the kind of objective danger to the free exercise of religion that the First Amendment was designed to prevent. As the record shows, compulsory school attendance to age 16 for Amish children carries with it a very real threat of undermining the Amish community and religious practice as they exist today; they must either abandon belief and be assimilated into society at large, or be forced to migrate to some other and more tolerant region.

In sum, the unchallenged testimony of acknowledged experts in education and religious history, almost 300 years of consistent practice, and strong evidence of a sustained faith pervading and regulating respondents' entire mode of life support the claim that enforcement of the State's requirement of compulsory formal education after the eighth grade would gravely endanger if not destroy the free exercise of respondents' religious beliefs.

Neither the findings of the trial court nor the Amish claims as to the nature of their faith are challenged in this Court by the State of Wisconsin. Its position is that the State's interest in universal compulsory formal secondary education to age 16 is so great that it is paramount to the undisputed claims of respondents that their mode of preparing their youth for Amish life, after the traditional elementary education, is an essential part of their religious belief and practice. Nor does the State undertake to meet the claim that the Amish mode of life and education is inseparable from and a part of the basic tenets of their religion—indeed, as much a part of their religious belief and practices as baptism, the confessional, or a sabbath may be for others.

Wisconsin concedes that under the Religion Clauses religious beliefs are absolutely free from the State's control, but it argues that "actions," even though religiously grounded, are outside the protection of the First Amendment. But our decisions have rejected the idea that religiously grounded conduct is always outside the protection of the Free Exercise

Clause. It is true that activities of individuals, even when religiously based, are often subject to regulation by the States in the exercise of their undoubted power to promote the health, safety, and general welfare, or the Federal government in the exercise of its delegated powers. *** But to agree that religiously grounded conduct must often be subject to the broad police power of the State is not to deny that there are areas of conduct protected by the Free Exercise Clause of the First Amendment and thus beyond the power of the State to control, even under regulations of general applicability. *** This case, therefore, does not become easier because respondents were convicted for their "actions" in refusing to send their children to the public high school; in this context belief and action cannot be neatly confined in logic-tight compartments. ***

Nor can this case be disposed of on the grounds that Wisconsin's requirement for school attendance to age 16 applies uniformly to all citizens of the State and does not, on its face, discriminate against religions or a particular religion, or that it is motivated by legitimate secular concerns. A regulation neutral on its face may, in its application, nonetheless offend the constitutional requirement for governmental neutrality if it unduly burdens the free exercise of religion. *** The Court must not ignore the danger that an exception from a general obligation of citizenship on religious grounds may run afoul of the Establishment Clause, but that danger cannot be allowed to prevent any exception no matter how vital it may be to the protection of values promoted by the right of free exercise. . . .

We turn, then, to the State's broader contention that its interest in its system of compulsory education is so compelling that even the established religious practices of the Amish must give way. Where fundamental claims of religious freedom are at stake, however, we cannot accept such a sweeping claim; despite its admitted validity in the generality of cases, we must searchingly examine the interests that the State seeks to promote by its requirement for compulsory education to age 16, and the impediment to those objectives that would flow from recognizing the claimed Amish exemption. ***

The State advances two primary arguments in support of its system of compulsory education. It notes, as Thomas Jefferson pointed out early in our history, that some degree of education is necessary to prepare citizens to participate effectively and intelligently in our open political system if we are to preserve freedom and independence. Further, education prepares individuals to be self-reliant and self-sufficient participants in society. We accept these propositions.

However, the evidence adduced by the Amish in this case is persuasively to the effect that an additional one or two years of formal high school for Amish children in place of their long-established program of informal vocational education would do little to serve those interests. Respondents' experts testified at trial, without challenge, that the value of all education must be assessed in terms of its capacity to prepare the child for life. It is one thing to say that compulsory education for a year or two beyond the eighth grade may be necessary when its goal is the preparation of the child for life in modern society as the majority live, but is quite another if the goal of education be viewed as the preparation of the child for life in the separated agrarian community that is the keystone of the Amish faith. ***

The State attacks respondents' position as one fostering "ignorance" from which the child must be protected by the State. No one can question the State's duty to protect children from ignorance but this argument does not square with the facts disclosed in the record. Whatever their idiosyncrasies as seen by the majority, this record strongly shows that the Amish community has been a highly successful social unit within our society, even if apart from the conventional "mainstream." Its members are productive and very law-abiding members of society; they reject public welfare in any of its usually modern forms. The Congress itself recognized their self-sufficiency by authorizing exemption of such groups as the Amish from the obligation to pay social security taxes.

It is neither fair nor correct to suggest that the Amish are opposed to education beyond the eighth grade level. What this record shows is that they are opposed to conventional formal education of the type provided by a certified high school because it comes at the child's crucial adolescent period of religious development. . . .

We must not forget that in the Middle Ages important values of the civilization of the Western World were preserved by members of religious orders who isolated themselves from all worldly influences against great obstacles. There can be no assumption that today's majority is "right" and the Amish and others like them are "wrong." A way of life that is odd or even erratic but interferes with no rights or interests of others is not to be condemned because it is different.

The State, however, supports its interest in providing an additional one or two years of compulsory high school education to Amish children because of the possibility that some such children will choose to leave the Amish community, and that if this occurs they will be ill-equipped for life. The State argues that if Amish children leave their church they should not be in the position of making their way in the world without the education available in the one or two additional years the State requires. However, on this record, that argument is highly speculative. There is no specific evidence of the loss of Amish adherents by attrition, nor is there any showing that upon leaving the Amish community Amish children, with their practical agricultural training and habits of industry and self-reliance, would become burdens on society because of educational shortcomings. Indeed, this argument of the State appears to rest primarily on the State's mistaken assumption, already noted, that the Amish do not provide any education for their children beyond the eighth grade, but allow them to grow in "ignorance." To the contrary, not only do the Amish accept the necessity for formal schooling through the eighth grade level, but continue to provide what has been characterized by the undisputed testimony of expert educators as an "ideal" vocational education for their children in the adolescent years.

There is nothing in this record to suggest that the Amish qualities of reliability, self-reliance, and dedication to work would fail to find ready markets in today's society. Absent some contrary evidence supporting the State's position, we are unwilling to assume that persons possessing such valuable vocational skills and habits are doomed to become burdens on society should they determine to leave the Amish faith, nor is there any basis in the record

to warrant a finding that an additional one or two years of formal school education beyond the eighth grade would serve to eliminate any such problem that might exist.

Insofar as the State's claim rests on the view that a brief additional period of formal education is imperative to enable the Amish to participate effectively and intelligently in our democratic process, it must fall. The Amish alternative to formal secondary school education has enabled them to function effectively in their day-to-day life under self-imposed limitations on relations with the world, and to survive and prosper in contemporary society as a separate, sharply identifiable and highly self-sufficient community for more than 200 years in this country. In itself this is strong evidence that they are capable of fulfilling the social and political responsibilities of citizenship without compelled attendance beyond the eighth grade at the price of jeopardizing their free exercise of religious belief. When Thomas Jefferson emphasized the need for education as a bulwark of a free people against tyranny, there is nothing to indicate he had in mind compulsory education through any fixed age beyond a basic education. Indeed, the Amish communities singularly parallel and reflect many of the virtues of Jefferson's ideal of the "sturdy yeoman" who would form the basis of what he considered as the ideal of a democratic society. Even their idiosyncratic separateness exemplifies the diversity we profess to admire and encourage.

The requirement for compulsory education beyond the eighth grade is a relatively recent development in our history. Less than 60 years ago, the educational requirements of almost all of the States were satisfied by completion of the elementary grades, at least where the child was regularly and lawfully employed. The independence and successful social functioning of the Amish community for a period approaching almost three centuries and more than 200 years in this country are strong evidence that there is at best a speculative gain, in terms of meeting the duties of citizenship, from an additional one or two years of compulsory formal education. Against this background it would require a more particularized showing from the State on this point to justify the severe interference with religious freedom such additional compulsory attendance would entail. . . .

Finally, the State . . . argues that a decision exempting Amish children from the State's requirement fails to recognize the substantive right of the Amish child to a secondary education, and fails to give due regard to the power of the State as *parens patriae* to extend the benefit of secondary education to children regardless of the wishes of their parents. . . .

This case, of course, is not one in which any harm to the physical or mental health of the child or to the public safety, peace, order, or welfare has been demonstrated or may be properly inferred. The record is to the contrary, and any reliance on that theory would find no support in the evidence.

Contrary to the suggestion of the dissenting opinion of Mr. Justice Douglas, our holding today in no degree depends on the assertion of the religious interest of the child as contrasted with that of the parents. It is the parents who are subject to prosecution here for failing to cause their children to attend school, and it is their right of free exercise, not that of their children, that must determine Wisconsin's power to impose criminal penalties on the parent. The dissent argues that a child who expresses a desire to attend public high school in conflict with the wishes of his parents should not be prevented from doing so. There is no reason for the Court to consider that point since it is not an issue in the case. The children are not parties to this litigation. The State has at no point tried this case on the theory that respondents were preventing their children from attending school against their expressed desires, and indeed the record is to the contrary. The State's position from the outset has been that it is empowered to apply its compulsory-attendance law to Amish parents in the same manner as to other parents—that is, without regard to the wishes of the child. That is the claim we reject today.

Our holding in no way determines the proper resolution of possible competing interests of parents, children, and the State in an appropriate state court proceeding in which the power of the State is asserted on the theory that Amish parents are preventing their minor children from attending high school despite their expressed desires to the contrary. Recognition of the claim of the State in such a proceeding would, of course, call into question traditional concepts of parental control over the religious upbringing and education of their minor children recognized in this Court's past decisions. It is clear that such an intrusion by a State into family decisions in the area of religious training would give rise to grave questions of religious freedom comparable to those raised here and those presented in *Pierce v. Society of Sisters* [1925]. *** On this record we neither reach nor decide those issues.

The State's argument proceeds without reliance on any actual conflict between the wishes of parents and children. It appears to rest on the potential that exemption of Amish parents from the requirements of the compulsory-education law might allow some parents to act contrary to the best interests of their children by foreclosing their opportunity to make an intelligent choice between the Amish way of life and that of the outside world. The same argument could, of course, be made with respect to all church schools short of college. There is nothing in the record or in the ordinary course of human experience to suggest that non-Amish parents generally consult with children of ages 14-16 if they are placed in a church school of the parents' faith.

Indeed it seems clear that if the State is empowered, as *parens patriae,* to "save" a child from himself or his Amish parents by requiring an additional two years of compulsory formal high school education, the State will in large measure influence, if not determine, the religious future of the child. [T]his case involves the fundamental interest of parents, as contrasted with that of the State, to guide the religious future and education of their children. The history and culture of Western civilization reflect a strong tradition of parental concern for the nurture and upbringing of their children. This primary role of the parents in the upbringing of their children is now established beyond debate as an enduring American tradition.

For the reasons stated we hold, with the Supreme Court of Wisconsin, that the First and Fourteenth Amendments prevent the State from compelling respondents to cause their children to attend formal high school to age 16. Our disposition of this case, however, in no way alters our recognition of the obvious fact that courts are not school boards or legislatures, and are ill-equipped to determine the "necessity" of discrete aspects of a State's program of compulsory education. This should suggest that courts must move with great circumspection in performing the sensitive and delicate task of weighing a State's legitimate social concern when faced with religious claims for exemption from generally applicable educational requirements. It cannot be overemphasized that we are not dealing with a way of life and mode of education by a group claiming to have recently discovered some "progressive" or more enlightened process for rearing children for modern life.

Aided by a history of three centuries as an identifiable religious sect and a long history as a successful and self-sufficient segment of American society, the Amish in this case have convincingly demonstrated the sincerity of their religious beliefs, the interrelationship of belief with their mode of life, the vital role that belief and daily conduct play in the continued survival of Old Order Amish communities and their religious organization, and the hazards presented by the state's enforcement of a statute generally valid as to others. Beyond this, they have carried the even more difficult burden of demonstrating the adequacy of their alternative mode of continuing informal vocational education in terms of precisely those overall interests that the State advances in support of its program of compulsory high school education. In light of this convincing showing, one that probably few other religious groups or sects could make, and weighing the minimal difference between what the State would require and what the Amish already accept, it was incumbent on the State to show with more particularity how its admittedly strong interest in compulsory education would be adversely affected by granting an exemption to the Amish. *******

Nothing we hold is intended to undermine the general applicability of the State's compulsory school-attendance statutes or to limit the power of the State to promulgate reasonable standards that, while not impairing the free exercise of religion, provide for continuing agricultural vocational education under parental and church guidance by the Old Order Amish or others similarly situated. The States have had a long history of amicable and effective relationships with church-sponsored schools,

and there is no basis for assuming that, in this related context, reasonable standards cannot be established concerning the content of the continuing vocational education of Amish children under parental guidance, provided always that state regulations are not inconsistent with what we have said in this opinion.

Affirmed.

Mr. Justice Powell and **Mr. Justice Rehnquist** took no part in the consideration or decision of this case.

Mr. Justice Stewart, with whom **Mr. Justice Brennan** joins, concurring. . . .

Mr. Justice Douglas, dissenting in part.

I agree with the Court that the religious scruples of the Amish are opposed to the education of their children beyond the grade schools, yet I disagree with the Court's conclusion that the matter is within the dispensation of parents alone. The Court's analysis assumes that the only interests at stake in the case are those of the Amish parents on the one hand, and those of the State on the other. The difficulty with this approach is that, despite the Court's claim, the parents are seeking to vindicate not only their own free exercise claims, but also those of their high-school-age children.

It is argued that the right of the Amish children to religious freedom is not presented by the facts of the case, as the issue before the Court involves only the Amish parents' religious freedom to defy a state criminal statute imposing upon them an affirmative duty to cause their children to attend high school.

First, respondents' motion to dismiss in the trial court expressly asserts, not only the religious liberty of the adults, but also that of the children, as a defense to the prosecutions. It is, of course, beyond question that the parents have standing as defendants in a criminal prosecution to assert the religious interests of their children as a defense. Although the lower courts and a majority of this Court assume an identity of interest between parent and child, it is clear that they have treated the religious interest of the child as a factor in the analysis.

Second, it is essential to reach the question to decide the case, not only because the question was squarely raised in the motion to dismiss, but also because no analysis of religious-liberty claims can take place in a vacuum. If the parents in this case are allowed a religious exemption, the inevitable effect is to impose the parents' notions of religious duty upon their children. Where the child is mature enough to express potentially conflicting desires, it would be an invasion of the child's rights to permit such an imposition without canvassing his views. As in *Prince v. Massachusetts* *** it is an imposition resulting from this very litigation. As the child has no other effective forum, it is in this litigation that his rights should be considered. And, if an Amish child desires to attend high school, and is mature enough to have that desire respected, the State may well be able to override the parents' religiously motivated objections.

Religion is an individual experience. It is not necessary, nor even appropriate, for every Amish child to express his views on the subject in a prosecution of a single adult. Crucial, however, are the views of the child whose parent is the subject of the suit. Frieda Yoder has in fact testified that her own religious views are opposed to high-school education. I therefore join the judgment of the Court as to respondent Jonas Yoder. But Frieda Yoder's views may not be those of Vernon Yutzy or Barbara Miller. I must dissent, therefore, as to respondents Adin Yutzy and Wallace Miller as their motion to dismiss also raised the question of their children's religious liberty.

This issue has never been squarely presented before today. Our opinions are full of talk about the power of the parents over the child's education. ***

And we have in the past analyzed similar conflicts between parent and State with little regard for the views of the child. *** Recent cases, however, have clearly held that the children themselves have constitutionally protectible interests....

On this important and vital matter of education, I think the children should be entitled to be heard. While the parents, absent dissent, normally speak for the entire family, the education of the child is a matter on which the child will often have decided views. He may want to be a pianist or an astronaut or an oceanographer. To do so he will have to break from the Amish tradition.

It is the future of the student, not the future of the parents, that is imperiled by today's decision. If a parent keeps his child out of school beyond the grade school, then the child will be forever barred from entry into the new and amazing world of diversity that we have today. The child may decide that that is the preferred course, or he may rebel. It is the student's judgment, not his parents', that is essential if we are to give full meaning to what we have said about the Bill of Rights and of the right of students to be masters of their own destiny. If he is harnessed to the Amish way of life by those in authority over him and if his education is truncated, his entire life may be stunted and deformed. The child, therefore, should be given an opportunity to be heard before the State gives the exemption which we honor today.

The views of the two children in question were not canvassed by the Wisconsin courts. The matter should be explicitly reserved so that new hearings can be held on remand of the case....

Employment Division v. Smith
494 U.S. 872; 110 S. Ct. 1595; 108 L. Ed.2d 876 (1990)
Vote: 6-3

Alfred Smith and Galen Black, both members of the Native American Church, were fired from their jobs as drug rehabilitation counselors on the grounds that they had used peyote during a religious ritual. They were subsequently denied unemployment benefits because they had been discharged *for "misconduct." The question before the U.S. Supreme Court is whether the refusal of the state to grant unemployment benefits in this situation constitutes an abridgement of rights under the Free Exercise Clause of the First Amendment.*

Justice Scalia delivered the opinion of the Court.

... Respondents' claim for relief rests on our decisions in *Sherbert v. Verner* *** [1963]; *Thomas v. Review Board* *** [1981]; and *Hobbie v. Unemployment Appeals Comm'n of Florida* *** [1987], in which we held that a State could not condition the availability of unemployment insurance on an individual's willingness to forego conduct required by his religion. ... [H]owever, the conduct at issue in those cases was not prohibited by law. ... [T]hat distinction [is] critical, for "if Oregon does prohibit the religious use of peyote, and if that prohibition is consistent with the Federal Constitution, there is no federal right to engage in that conduct in Oregon," and "the State is free to withhold unemployment compensation from respondents for engaging in work-related misconduct, despite its religious motivation." *** Now that the Oregon Supreme Court has confirmed that Oregon does prohibit the religious use of peyote, we proceed to consider whether that prohibition is permissible under the Free Exercise Clause. ...

The free exercise of religion means, first and foremost, the right to believe and profess whatever religious doctrine one desires. Thus, the First Amendment obviously excludes all "governmental regulation of religious beliefs as such." ***

But the "exercise of religion" often involves not only belief and profession but the performance of (or abstention from) physical acts: assembling with others for a worship service, participating in sacramental use of bread and wine, proselytizing, abstaining from certain foods or certain modes of transportation. It would be true, we think (though no case of ours has involved the point), that a state would be "prohibiting the free exercise [of religion]" *** if it sought to ban such acts or abstentions only when they are engaged in for religious reasons, or only because of the religious belief that they display. It would doubtless be unconstitutional, for example, to ban the casting of "statutes that are to be used for worship purposes," *** or to prohibit bowing down before a golden calf.

Respondents in the present case, however, seek to carry the meaning of "prohibiting the free exercise [of religion]" one large step further. They contend that their religious motivation for using peyote places them beyond the reach of a criminal law that is not specifically directed at their religious practice, and that is concededly constitutional as applied to those who use the drug for other reasons. They assert, in other words, that "prohibiting the free exercise [of religion]" includes requiring any individual to observe a generally applicable law that requires (or forbids) the performance of an act that his religious belief forbids (or requires). As a textual matter, we do not think the words must be given that meaning. It is no more necessary to regard the collection of a general tax, for example, as "prohibiting the free exercise [of religion]" by those citizens who believe support of organized government to be sinful, than it is to regard the same tax as "abridging the freedom ... of the press" of those publishing companies that must pay the tax as a condition of staying in business. It is a permissible reading of the text, in the one case as in the other, to say that if prohibiting the exercise of religion (or burdening the activity of printing) is not the object of the tax but merely the incidental effect of a generally applicable and otherwise valid provision, the First Amendment has not been offended. ...

Our decisions reveal that the latter reading is the correct one. We have never held that an individual's religious beliefs excuse him from compliance with an otherwise valid law prohibiting conduct that the State is free to regulate. ***

The only decisions in which we have held that the First Amendment bars application of a neutral, generally applicable law to religiously motivated action have involved not the Free Exercise Clause alone, but the Free Exercise Clause in conjunction with other constitutional protections, such as freedom of speech and of the press. ***

The present case does not present such a hybrid situation, but a free exercise claim unconnected with any communicative activity or parental right. Respondents urge us to hold, quite simply, that when otherwise prohibitable conduct is accompanied by religious convictions, not only the convictions but the conduct itself must be free from governmental regulation. ...

Respondents argue that even though exemption from generally applicable criminal laws need not automatically be extended to religiously motivated actors, at least the claim for a religious exemption must be evaluated under the balancing test set forth in *Sherbert v. Verner* [1963]. *** Under the *Sherbert* test, governmental actions that substantially burden a religious practice must be justified by a compelling governmental interest. . . . Applying that test we have, on three occasions, invalidated state unemployment compensation rules that conditioned the availability of benefits upon an applicant's willingness to work under conditions forbidden by his religion. *** We have never invalidated any governmental action on the basis of the *Sherbert* test except the denial of unemployment compensation. . . .

Even if we were inclined to breathe into *Sherbert* some life beyond the unemployment compensation field, we would not apply it to require exemptions from a generally applicable criminal law. . . .

We conclude today that the sounder approach, and the approach in accord with the vast majority of our precedents, is to hold the test inapplicable to such challenges. The government's ability to enforce generally applicable prohibitions of socially harmful conduct, like its ability to carry out other aspects of public policy, "cannot depend on measuring the effects of a governmental action on a religious objector's spiritual development." *** To make an individual's obligation to obey such a law contingent upon the law's coincidence with his religious beliefs, except where the State's interest is "compelling"— permitting him, by virtue of his beliefs, "to become a law unto himself," *** — contradicts both constitutional tradition and common sense.

The "compelling government interest" requirement seems benign, because it is familiar from other fields. But using it as the standard that must be met before the government may accord different treatment on the basis of race, *** is not remotely comparable to using it for the purpose asserted here. What it produces in those other fields—equality of treatment, and an unrestricted flow of contending speech—are constitutional norms; what it would produce here—a private right to ignore generally applicable laws—is a constitutional anomaly.

Nor is it possible to limit the impact of respondents' proposal by requiring a "compelling state interest" only when the conduct prohibited is "central" to the individual's religion. It is no more appropriate for judges to determine the "centrality"

of religious beliefs before applying a "compelling interest" test in the free exercise field, than it would be for them to determine the "importance" of ideas before applying the "compelling interest" test in the free speech field. What principle of law or logic can be brought to bear to contradict a believer's assertion that a particular act is "central" to his personal faith? . . .

If the "compelling interest" test is to be applied at all, then, it must be applied across the board, to all actions thought to be religiously commanded. Moreover, if "compelling interest" really means what it says (and watering it down here would subvert its rigor in the other fields where it is applied), many laws will not meet the test. Any society adopting such a system would be courting anarchy, but that danger increases in direct proportion to the society's diversity of religious beliefs, and its determination to coerce or suppress none of them. . . .

Values that are protected against government interference through enshrinement in the Bill of Rights are not thereby banished from the political process. Just as a society that believes in the negative protection accorded to the press by the First Amendment is likely to enact laws that affirmatively foster the dissemination of the printed word, so also a society that believes in the negative protection accorded to religious belief can be expected to be solicitous of that value in its legislation as well. It is therefore not surprising that a number of States have made an exception to their drug laws for sacramental peyote use. But to say that a nondiscriminatory religious-practice exemption is permitted, or even that it is desirable, is not to say that it is constitutionally required, and that the appropriate occasions for its creation can be discerned by the courts. It may fairly be said that leaving accommodation to the political process will place at a relative disadvantage those religious practices that are not widely engaged in; but that unavoidable consequence of democratic government must be preferred to a system in which each conscience is a law unto itself or in which judges weigh the social importance of all law against the centrality of all religious beliefs. . . .

Because respondent's ingestion of peyote was prohibited under Oregon law, and because that prohibition is constitutional, Oregon may, consistent with the Free Exercise Clause, deny respondents unemployment compensation when their dismissal results from use of the drug. The decision of the Oregon Supreme Court is accordingly reversed.

It is so ordered.

Justice O'Connor . . . [concurring in the judgment only].

Although I agree with the result the Court reaches in this case, I cannot join its opinion. In my view, today's holding dramatically departs from well-settled First Amendment jurisprudence, appears unnecessary to resolve the question presented, and is incompatible with our Nation's fundamental commitment to individual religious liberty. . . .

The Court today extracts from our long history of free exercise precedents the single categorical rule that "if prohibiting the exercise of religion . . . is . . . merely the incidental effect of a generally applicable and otherwise valid provision, the First Amendment has not been offended." *** Indeed, the Court holds that where the law is a generally applicable criminal prohibition, our usual free exercise jurisprudence does not even apply. To reach this sweeping result, however, the Court must not only give a strained reading of the First Amendment but must also disregard our consistent application of free exercise doctrine to cases involving generally applicable regulations that burden religious conduct. . . .

The Court today . . . interprets the Clause to permit the government to prohibit, without justification, conduct mandated by an individual's religious beliefs, so long as that prohibition is generally applicable. But a law that prohibits certain conduct—conduct that happens to be an act of worship for someone—manifestly does prohibit that person's free exercise of his religion. A person who is barred from engaging in religiously motivated conduct is barred from freely exercising his religion regardless of whether the law prohibits the conduct only when engaged in for religious reasons, only by members of that religion, or by all persons. It is difficult to deny that a law that prohibits religiously motivated conduct, even if the law is generally applicable, does not at least implicate First Amendment concerns.

The Court responds that generally applicable laws are "one large step" removed from laws aimed at specific religious practices. The First Amendment, however, does not distinguish between laws that are generally applicable and laws that target particular religious practices. Indeed, few States would be so naive as to enact a law directly prohibiting or burdening a religious practice as such. Our free exercise cases have all concerned generally applicable laws that had the effect of significantly burdening a religious practice. If the First Amendment is to have any vitality, it ought not be construed to cover only the extreme and hypothetical situation in which a State directly targets a religious practice. . . .

To say that a person's right to free exercise has been burdened, of course, does not mean that he has an absolute right to engage in the conduct. Under our established First Amendment jurisprudence, we have recognized that the freedom to act, unlike the freedom to believe, cannot be absolute. Instead, we have respected both the First Amendment's express textual mandate and the governmental interest in regulation of conduct by requiring the Government to justify any substantial burden on religiously motivated conduct by a compelling state interest and by means narrowly tailored to achieve that interest. . . .

The compelling interest test effectuates the First Amendment's command that religious liberty is an independent liberty, that it occupies a preferred position, and that the Court will not permit encroachments upon this liberty, whether direct or indirect, unless required by clear and compelling governmental interests "of the highest order." ***

In my view, however, the essence of a free exercise claim is relief from a burden imposed by government on religious practices or beliefs, whether the burden is imposed directly through laws that prohibit or compel specific religious practices, or indirectly through laws that, in effect, make abandonment of one's own religion or conformity to the religious beliefs of others the price of an equal place in the civil community. . . .

Indeed, we have never distinguished between cases in which a State conditions receipt of a benefit on conduct prohibited by religious beliefs and cases in which a State affirmatively prohibits such conduct. The *Sherbert* compelling interest test applies in both kinds of cases. . . .

Finally, the Court today suggests that the disfavoring of minority religions is an "unavoidable consequence" under our system of government and that accommodation of such religions must be left to the political process. *** In my view, however, the First Amendment was enacted precisely to protect the rights of those whose religious practices are not shared by the majority and may be viewed with hostility. The history of our free exercise doctrine amply demonstrates the harsh impact majoritarian rule has had on unpopular or emerging religious groups such as the Jehovah's Witnesses and the Amish. . . .

The Court's holding today not only misreads settled First Amendment's precedent; it appears to be unnecessary to this case. I would reach the same result applying our established free exercise jurisprudence. . . .

[T]he critical question in this case is whether exempting respondents from the State's general criminal prohibition "will unduly interfere with fulfillment of the governmental interest." *** Although the question is close, I would conclude that uniform application of Oregon's criminal prohibition is "essential to accomplish" its overriding interest in preventing the physical harm caused by the use of a Schedule I controlled substance. Oregon's criminal prohibition represents that State's judgment that the possession and use of controlled substances, even by only one person, is inherently harmful and dangerous. Because the health effects caused by the use of controlled substances exist regardless of the motivation of the user, the use of such substances, even for religious purposes, violates the very purpose of the law that prohibits them. . . .

For these reasons, I believe that granting a selective exemption in this case would seriously impair Oregon's compelling interest in prohibiting possession of peyote by its citizens. Under such circumstances, the Free Exercise Clause does not require the State to accommodate respondents' religiously motivated conduct. . . .

I would therefore adhere to our established free exercise jurisprudence and hold that the State in this case has a compelling interest in regulating peyote use by its citizens and that accommodating respondents' religiously motivated conduct "will unduly interfere with fulfillment of the governmental interest." *** Accordingly, I concur in the judgment of the Court.

Justice Blackmun, with whom **Justice Brennan** and **Justice Marshall** join, dissenting.

This Court over the years painstakingly has developed a consistent and exacting standard to test the constitutionality of a state statute that burdens the free exercise of religion. Such a statute may stand only if the law in general, and the State's refusal to allow a religious exemption in particular, are justified by a compelling interest that cannot be served by less restrictive means.

Until today, I thought this was a settled and inviolate principle of this Court's First Amendment jurisprudence. The majority, however, perfunctorily dismisses it as a "constitutional anomaly." As carefully detailed in Justice O'Connor's concurring opinion . . . the majority is able to arrive at this view only by mischaracterizing this Court's precedents. The Court discards leading free exercise cases such as *Cantwell v. Connecticut* *** (1940), and *Wisconsin v. Yoder* (1972), as "hybrid." *** The Court views traditional free exercise analysis as somehow inapplicable to criminal prohibitions (as opposed to conditions on the receipt of benefits), and to state laws of general applicability (as opposed, presumably, to laws that expressly single out religious practices). The Court cites cases in which, due to various exceptional circumstances, we found strict scrutiny inapposite, to hint that the Court is aware of the consequences, and that its result is not a product of overreaction to the serious problems the country's drug crisis has generated.

This distorted view of our precedents leads the majority to conclude that strict scrutiny of a state law burdening the free exercise of religion is a "luxury" that a well-ordered society cannot afford, and that the repression of minority religions is an "unavoidable consequence of democratic government." *** I do not believe the Founders thought their dearly bought freedom from religious persecution a "luxury," but an essential element of liberty—and they could not have thought religious intolerance "unavoidable," for they drafted the Religion Clauses precisely in order to avoid that intolerance.

For these reasons, I agree with Justice O'Connor's analysis of the applicable free exercise doctrine.... As she points out, "the critical question in this case is whether exempting respondents from the State's general criminal prohibition: 'will unduly interfere with fulfillment of the governmental interest.'" *** I do disagree, however, with her specific answer to that question.

The State's interest in enforcing its prohibition, in order to be sufficiently compelling to outweigh a free exercise claim, cannot be merely abstract or symbolic. The State cannot plausibly assert that unbending application of a criminal prohibition is essential to fulfill any compelling interest, if it does not, in fact, attempt to enforce that prohibition. In this case, the State actually has not evinced any concrete interest in enforcing its drug laws against religious users of peyote. Oregon has never sought to prosecute respondents, and does not claim that it has made significant enforcement efforts against other religious users of peyote. The State's asserted interest thus amounts only to the symbolic preservation of an unenforced prohibition....

The State proclaims an interest in protecting the health and safety of its citizens from the dangers of unlawful drugs. It offers, however, no evidence that the religious use of peyote has ever harmed anyone....

The fact that peyote is classified as a Schedule I controlled substance does not, by itself, show that any and all uses of peyote, in any circumstance, are inherently harmful and dangerous. The Federal Government, which created the classifications of unlawful drugs from which Oregon's drug laws are derived, apparently does not find peyote so dangerous as to preclude an exemption for religious use....

The carefully circumscribed ritual context in which respondents used peyote is far removed from the irresponsible and unrestricted recreational use of unlawful drugs. The Native American Church's internal restrictions on, and supervision of, its members' use of peyote substantially obviate the State's health and safety concerns....

Moreover, just as in *Yoder,* the values and interests of those seeking a religious exemption in this case are congruent, to a great degree, with those the State seeks to promote through its drug laws.... Not only does the Church's doctrine forbid nonreligious use of peyote; it also generally advocates self-reliance, familial responsibility, and abstinence from alcohol.... Far from promoting the lawless and irresponsible use of drugs, Native American Church members' spiritual code exemplifies values that Oregon's drug laws are presumably intended to foster....

Finally, although I agree with Justice O'Connor that courts should refrain from delving into questions of whether, as a matter of religious doctrine, a particular practice is "central" to the religion, I do not think this means that the courts must turn a blind eye to the severe impact of a State's restrictions on the adherents of a minority religion....

If Oregon can constitutionally prosecute them for this act of worship, they, like the Amish, may be "forced to migrate to some other and more tolerant region." *Yoder.* This potentially devastating impact must be viewed in light of the federal policy—reached in reaction to many years of religious persecution and intolerance—of protecting the religious freedom of Native Americans. ***

The American Indian Religious Freedom Act, in itself, may not create rights enforceable against government action restricting religious freedom, but this Court must scrupulously apply its free exercise analysis to the religious claims of Native Americans, however unorthodox they may be. Otherwise, both the First Amendment and the stated policy of Congress will offer to Native Americans merely an unfulfilled and hollow promise.

For these reasons, I conclude that Oregon's interest in enforcing its drug laws against religious use of peyote is not sufficiently compelling to outweigh respondents' right to the free exercise of their religion. Since the State could not constitutionally enforce its criminal prohibition against respondents, the interests underlying the State's drug laws cannot justify its denial of unemployment benefits. Absent such justification, the State's regulatory interest in denying benefits for religiously motivated "misconduct," is indistinguishable from the state interests this Court has rejected.... The State of Oregon cannot, consistently with the Free Exercise Clause, deny respondents unemployment benefits....

Everson v. Board of Education

330 U.S. 1; 67 S. Ct. 504; 91 L. Ed. 711 (1947)
Vote: 5-4

Mr. Justice Black delivered the opinion of the Court.

A New Jersey statute authorizes its local school districts to make rules and contracts for the transportation of children to and from schools. The appellee, a township board of education, acting pursuant to this statute, authorized reimbursement to parents of money expended by them for the bus transportation of their children on regular buses operated by the public transportation system. Part of this money was for the payment of transportation of some children in the community to Catholic parochial schools. These church schools give their students, in addition to secular education, regular religious instruction conforming to the religious tenets and modes of worship of the Catholic Faith. The superintendent of these schools is a Catholic priest.

The appellant, in his capacity as a district taxpayer, filed suit in a state court challenging the right of the Board to reimburse parents of parochial school students. He contended that the statute and the resolution passed pursuant to it violated both the State and the Federal Constitutions. That court held that the legislature was without power to authorize such payment under the state constitution. *** The New Jersey Court of Errors and Appeals reversed, holding that neither the statute nor the resolution passed pursuant to it was in conflict with the State constitution or the provisions of the Federal Constitution in issue. ***

Since there has been no attack on the statute on the ground that a part of its language excludes children attending private schools operated for profit from enjoying State payment for their transportation, we need not consider this exclusionary language; it has no relevancy to any constitutional question here presented. Furthermore, if the exclusion clause had been properly challenged, we do not know whether New Jersey's highest court would construe its statutes as precluding payment of the school transportation of any group of pupils, even those of a private school run for profit. Consequently, we put to one side the question as to the validity of the statute against the claim that it does not authorize payment for the transportation generally of school children in New Jersey. . . .

The New Jersey statute is challenged as a "law respecting the establishment of religion." The First Amendment, as made applicable to the states by the Fourteenth, *** commands that a state "shall make no law respecting an establishment of religion, or prohibiting the free exercise thereof. . . ." These words of the First Amendment reflected in the minds of early Americans a vivid mental picture of conditions and practices which they fervently wished to stamp out in order to preserve liberty for themselves and for their posterity. Doubtless their goal has not been entirely reached; but so far has the Nation moved toward it that the expression "law respecting the establishment of religion," probably does not so vividly remind present-day Americans of the evils, fears, and political problems that caused that expression to be written into our Bill of Rights. Whether this New Jersey law is one respecting an "establishment of religion" requires an understanding of the meaning of that language, particularly with respect to the imposition of taxes. Once again, therefore, it is not inappropriate briefly to review the background and environment of the period in which that constitutional language was fashioned and adopted.

A large proportion of the early settlers of this country came here from Europe to escape the bondage of laws which compelled them to support and attend government favored churches. The centuries immediately before and contemporaneous with the colonization of America had been filled with turmoil, civil strife, and persecutions, generated in large part by established sects determined to maintain their absolute political and religious supremacy. With the power of government supporting them, at various times and places, Catholics had persecuted Protestants, Protestants had persecuted other Protestant sects, Catholics of one shade of belief had persecuted Catholics of another shade of belief, and all of these had from time to time persecuted Jews. In efforts to force loyalty to whatever religious group happened to be on top and in league with the government of a particular time and place, men and women had been fined, cast in jail, cruelly tortured, and killed. Among the offenses for which these punishments had been inflicted were such things as speaking disrespectfully of the views of ministers of government-established churches, nonattendance at those churches, expressions of non-belief in their doctrines, and failure to pay taxes and tithes to support them.

These practices of the old world were transplanted to and began to thrive in the soil of the new America. The very charters granted by the English Crown to the individuals and companies designated to make the laws which would control the destinies of the colonials authorized these individuals and companies to erect religious establishments which all, whether believers or non-believers, would be required to support and attend. An exercise of this authority was accompanied by a repetition of many of the old-world practices and persecutions. Catholics found themselves hounded and proscribed because of their faith; Quakers who followed their conscience went to jail; Baptists were peculiarly obnoxious to certain dominant Protestant sects; men and women of varied faiths who happened to be in a minority in a particular locality were persecuted because they steadfastly persisted in worshipping God only as their own consciences dictated. And all of these dissenters were compelled to pay tithes and taxes to support government-sponsored churches whose ministers preached inflammatory sermons designed to strengthen and consolidate the established faith by generating a burning hatred against dissenters.

These practices became so commonplace as to shock the freedom-living colonials into a feeling of abhorrence. The imposition of taxes to pay ministers' salaries and to build and maintain churches and church property aroused their indignation. It was these feelings which found expression in the First Amendment. No one locality and no one group throughout the Colonies can rightly be given entire credit for having aroused the sentiment that culminated in adoption of the Bill of Rights' provisions embracing religious liberty. But Virginia, where the established church had achieved a dominant influ-

ence in political affairs and where many excesses attracted wide public attention, provided a great stimulus and able leadership for the movement. The people there, as elsewhere, reached the conviction that individual religious liberty could be achieved best under a government which was stripped of all power to tax, to support, or otherwise to assist any or all religions, or to interfere with the beliefs of any religious individual or group. . . .

The meaning and scope of the First Amendment, preventing establishment of religion or prohibiting the free exercise thereof, in the light of its history and the evils it was designed forever to suppress, have been several times elaborated by the decisions of this Court prior to the application of the First Amendment to the states by the Fourteenth. The broad meaning given the Amendment by these earlier cases has been accepted by this Court in its decisions concerning an individual's religious freedom rendered since the Fourteenth Amendment was interpreted to make the prohibitions of the First applicable to state action abridging religious freedom. There is every reason to give the same application and broad interpretation to the "establishment of religion" clause. . . .

The "establishment of religion" clause of the First Amendment means at least this: Neither a state nor the Federal Government can set up a church. Neither can pass laws which aid one religion, aid all religions, or prefer one religion over another. Neither can force nor influence a person to go to or to remain away from church against his will or force him to profess a belief or disbelief in any religion. No person can be punished for entertaining or professing religious beliefs or disbeliefs, for church attendance or nonattendance. No tax in any amount, large or small, can be levied to support any religious activities or institutions, whatever they may be called, or whatever form they may adopt to teach or practice religion. Neither a state nor the Federal Government can, openly or secretly, participate in the affairs of any religious organizations or groups and vice versa. In the words of Jefferson, the clause against establishment of religion by law was intended to erect "a wall of separation between church and State." *******

We must consider the New Jersey statute in accordance with the foregoing limitations imposed by the

First Amendment. But we must not strike that state statute down if it is within the State's constitutional power even though it approaches the verge of that power. *** New Jersey cannot consistently with the "establishment of religion" clause of the First Amendment contribute tax-raised funds to the support of an institution which teaches the tenets and faith of any church. On the other hand, other language of the amendment commands that New Jersey cannot hamper its citizens in the free exercise of their own religion. Consequently, it cannot exclude individual Catholics, Lutherans, Mohammedans, Baptists, Jews, Methodists, Non-believers, Presbyterians, or the members of any other faith, because of their faith, or lack of it, from receiving the benefits of public welfare legislation. While we do not mean to intimate that a state could not provide transportation only to children attending public schools, we must be careful in protecting the citizens of New Jersey against state-established churches, to be sure that we do not inadvertently prohibit New Jersey from extending its general state law benefits to all its citizens without regard to their religious belief.

Measured by these standards, we cannot say that the First Amendment prohibits New Jersey from spending tax-raised funds to pay the bus fares of parochial school pupils as a part of a general program under which it pays the fares of pupils attending public and other schools. It is undoubtedly true that children are helped to get to church schools. There is even a possibility that some of the children might not be sent to the church schools if the parents were compelled to pay their children's bus fares out of their own pockets when transportation to a public school would have been paid for by the State. The same possibility exists where the state requires a local transit company to provide reduced fares to school children including those attending parochial schools, or where a municipally owned transportation system undertakes to carry all school children free of charge. Moreover, state-paid policemen, detailed to protect children going to and from church schools from the very real hazards of traffic, would serve much the same purpose and accomplish much the same result as state provisions intended to guarantee free transportation of a kind which the state deems to be best for the school children's welfare.

And parents might refuse to risk their children to the serious danger of traffic accidents going to and from parochial schools, the approaches to which were not protected by policemen. Similarly, parents might be reluctant to permit their children to attend schools which the state had cut off from such general government services as ordinary police and fire protection, connections for sewage disposal, public highways and sidewalks. Of course, cutting off church schools from these services, so separate and so indisputably marked off from the religious function, would make it far more difficult for the schools to operate. But such is obviously not the purpose of the First Amendment. That Amendment requires the state to be a neutral in its relations with groups of religious believers and non-believers; it does not require the state to be their adversary. State power is no more to be used so as to handicap religions than it is to favor them.

This Court has said that parents may, in the discharge of their duty under state compulsory education laws, send their children to a religious rather than a public school if the school meets the secular educational requirements which the state has power to impose. *** It appears that these parochial schools meet New Jersey's requirements. The State contributes no money to the schools. It does not support them. Its legislation, as applied, does no more than provide a general program to help parents get their children, regardless of their religion, safely and expeditiously to and from accredited schools.

The First Amendment has erected a wall between church and state. That wall must be kept high and impregnable. We could not approve the slightest breach. New Jersey has not breached it here.

Affirmed.

Mr. Justice Jackson, dissenting.

I find myself, contrary to first impressions, unable to join in this decision. I have a sympathy, though it is not ideological, with Catholic citizens who are compelled by law to pay taxes for public schools, and also feel constrained by conscience and discipline to support other schools for their own children. Such relief to them as this case involves is not in itself a serious burden to taxpayers and I had assumed it to be as little serious in principle. Study of this case convinces me otherwise. The Court's opinion marshals every argument in favor of state aid and puts the case in its most favorable light, but much of its reasoning confirms my conclusions that there are no good grounds upon which to support the present legislation. In fact, the undertones of the opinion, advocating complete and uncompromising separation of Church from State, seem utterly discordant with its conclusion yielding support to their commingling in educational matters. The case which irresistibly comes to mind as the most fitting precedent is that of Julia who, according to Byron's reports, "whispering 'I will ne'er consent,'—consented." . . .

This policy of our Federal Constitution has never been wholly pleasing to most religious groups. They all are quick to invoke its protections; they are all irked when they feel its restraints. This Court has gone a long way, if not an unreasonable way, to hold that public business of such paramount importance as maintenance of public order, protection of the privacy of the home, and taxation may not be pursued by a state in a way that even indirectly will interfere with religious proselyting. ***

But we cannot have it both ways. Religious teaching cannot be a private affair when the state seeks to impose regulations which infringe on it indirectly, and a public affair when it comes to taxing citizens of one faith to aid another, or those of no faith to aid all. If these principles seem harsh in prohibiting aid to Catholic education, it must not be forgotten that it is the same Constitution that alone assures Catholics the right to maintain these schools at all when predominant local sentiment would forbid them. *** Nor should I think that those who have done so well without this aid would want to see this separation between Church and State broken down. If the state may aid these religious schools, it may therefore regulate them. Many groups have sought aid from tax funds only to find that it carried political controls with it. Indeed this Court has declared that "It is hardly lack of due process for the Government to regulate that which it subsidizes." ***

But in any event, the great purposes of the Constitution do not depend on the approval or convenience of those they restrain. I cannot read the history of the struggle to separate political from ecclesiastical affairs, well summarized in the opinion of Mr. Justice Rutledge in which I generally concur, without a conviction that the Court today is unconsciously giving the clock's hands a backward turn.

Mr. Justice Frankfurter joins in this opinion.

Mr. Justice Rutledge, with whom **Mr. Justice Frankfurter, Mr. Justice Jackson** and **Mr. Justice Burton** agree, dissenting.

. . . No one conscious of religious values can be unsympathetic toward the burden which our constitutional separation puts on parents who desire religious instruction mixed with secular for their children. They pay taxes for others' children's education, at the same time the added cost of instruction for their own. Nor can one happily see benefits denied to children which others receive, because in conscience they or their parents for them desire a different kind of training others do not demand.

But if those feelings should prevail, there would be an end to our historic constitutional policy and command. No more unjust or discriminatory in fact is it to deny attendants at religious schools the cost of their transportation than it is to deny them tuitions, sustenance for their teachers, or any other educational expense which others receive at public cost. . . .

Of course discrimination in the legal sense does not exist. The child attending the religious school has the same right as any other to attend the public school. But he foregoes exercising it because the same guaranty which assures this freedom forbids the public school or any agency of the state to give or aid him in securing the religious instruction he seeks.

Were he to accept the common school, he would be the first to protest the teaching there of any creed or faith not his own. And it is precisely for the reason that their atmosphere is wholly secular that children are not sent to public schools under the *Pierce* doctrine. But that is a constitutional necessity, because we have staked the very existence of our country on the faith that complete separation between the state and religion is best for the state and best for religion. ***

That policy necessarily entails hardship upon persons who forego the right to educational advantages the state can supply in order to secure others it is precluded from giving. Indeed this may hamper the parent and the child forced by conscience to that choice. But it does not make the state unneutral to withhold what the Constitution forbids it to give. On the contrary it is only by observing the prohibition rigidly that the state can maintain its neutrality and avoid partisanship in the dissensions inevitable when sect opposes sect over demands for public moneys to further religious education, teaching or training in any form or degree, directly or indirectly. Like St. Paul's freedom, religious liberty with a great price must be bought. And for those who exercise it most fully, by insisting upon religious education for their children mixed with secular, by the terms of our Constitution the price is greater than for others....

Abington School District v. Schempp

374 U.S. 203; 83 S. Ct. 1560; 10 L. Ed. 2d 844 (1963)
Vote: 8-1

Mr. Justice Clark delivered the opinion of the Court.

... The appellees Edward Lewis Schempp, his wife Sidney, and their children, Roger and Donna, are of the Unitarian faith and are members of the Unitarian Church in Germantown, Philadelphia, Pennsylvania, where they, as well as another son, Ellory, regularly attend religious services. The latter was originally a party but having graduated from the school system ... was voluntarily dismissed from the action. The other children attend the Abington Senior High School, which is a public school operated by appellant district.

On each school day at the Abington Senior High School ... opening exercises are conducted pursuant to [state law]. The exercises are broadcast into each room in the school building through an inter-communications system and are conducted under the supervision of a teacher by students attending the school's radio and television workshop. Selected students from this course gather each morning in the school's workshop studio for the exercises, which include readings by one of the students of 10 verses of the Holy Bible, broadcast to each room in the building. This is followed by the recitation of the Lord's Prayer, likewise over the intercommunications system, but also by the students in the various classrooms, who are asked to stand and join in repeating the prayer in unison. The exercises are closed with the flag salute and such pertinent announcements as are of interest to the students.

Participation in the opening exercises, as directed by the statute, is voluntary. The student reading the verses from the Bible may select the passages and read from any version he chooses, although the only copies furnished by the school are the King James version, copies of which were circulated to each teacher by the school district. During the period in which the exercises have been conducted the King James, the Douay and the Revised Standard versions of the Bible have been used, as well as the Jewish Holy Scriptures. There are no prefatory statements, no questions asked or solicited, no comments or explanations made and no interpretations given at or during the exercises. The students and parents are advised that the student may absent himself from the classroom or, should he elect to remain, not participate in the exercises....

The wholesome "neutrality" of which this Court's cases speak ... stems from a recognition of the teachings of history that powerful sects or groups might bring about a fusion of governmental and religious functions or a concert or dependency of one upon the other to the end that official support of the State or Federal Government would be placed behind the tenets of one or of all orthodoxies. This the Establishment Clause prohibits. And a further reason for neutrality is found in the Free Exercise Clause, which recognizes the value of religious training, teaching and observance and, more particularly, the right of every person to freely choose his own course with reference thereto, free of any compulsion from the state. This the Free Exercise Clause guarantees. Thus, the two clauses may overlap. . . . [T]he Establishment Clause has been directly considered by this Court eight times in the past score of years and, with only one Justice dissenting on the point, it has consistently held that the clause withdrew all legislative power respecting religious belief or the expression thereof. The test may be stated as follows: what are the purpose and the primary effect of the enactment? If either is the advancement or inhibition of religion then the enactment exceeds the scope of legislative power as circumscribed by the Constitution. That is to say that to withstand the strictures of the Establishment Clause there must be a secular legislative purpose and a primary effect that neither advances nor inhibits religion. *** The Free Exercise Clause, likewise considered many times here, withdraws from legislative power, state and federal, the exertion of any restraint on the free exercise of religion. Its purpose is to secure religious liberty in the individual by prohibiting any invasions thereof by civil authority. Hence it is necessary in a free exercise case for one to show the coercive effect of the enactment as it operates against him in the practice of his religion. The distinction between the two clauses is apparent—a violation of the Free Exercise Clause is predicated on coercion while the Establishment Clause violation need not be so attended.

Applying the Establishment Clause principles to the cases at bar we find that the States are requiring the selection and reading at the opening of the school day of verses from the Holy Bible and the recitation of the Lord's Prayer by the students in unison. These exercises are prescribed as part of the curricular activities of students who are required by law to attend school. They are held in the school buildings under the supervision and with the participation of teachers employed in those schools. . . . The trial court . . . has found that such an opening exercise is a religious ceremony and was intended by the State to be so. We agree with the trial court's finding as to the religious character of the exercises. Given that finding, the exercises and the law requiring them are in violation of the Establishment Clause. . . .

The conclusion follows that the laws require religious exercises and such exercises are being con-

ducted in direct violation of the rights of the appellees and petitioners. Nor are these required exercises mitigated by the fact that individual students may absent themselves upon parental request, for that fact furnishes no defense to a claim of unconstitutionality under the Establishment Clause. *** Further, it is no defense to urge that the religious practices here may be relatively minor encroachments on the First Amendment. The breach of neutrality that is today a trickling stream may all too soon become a raging torrent and, in the words of Madison, "it is proper to take alarm at the first experiment on our liberties." ***

It is insisted that unless these religious exercises are permitted a "religion of secularism" is established in the schools. We agree of course that the State may not establish a "religion of secularism" in the sense of affirmatively opposing or showing hostility to religion, thus "preferring those who believe in no religion over those who do believe." *** We do not agree, however, that this decision in any sense has that effect. In addition, it might well be said that one's education is not complete without a study of comparative religion or the history of religion and its relationship to the advancement of civilization. It certainly may be said that the Bible is worthy of study for its literary and historic qualities. Nothing we have said here indicates that such study of the Bible or of religion, when presented objectively as part of a secular program of education, may not be effected consistently with the First Amendment. But the exercises here do not fall into those categories. They are religious exercises, required by the State in violation of the command of the First Amendment that the Government maintain strict neutrality, neither aiding nor opposing religion.

Finally, we cannot accept that the concept of neutrality, which does not permit a State to require a religious exercise even with the consent of the majority of those affected, collides with the majority's right to free exercise of religion. While the Free Exercise Clause clearly prohibits the use of state action to deny the rights of free exercise to *anyone,* it has never meant that a majority could use the machinery of the State to practice its beliefs. . . .

The place of religion in our society is an exalted one, achieved through a long tradition of reliance on the home, the church and the inviolable citadel of the individual heart and mind. We have come to recognize through bitter experience that it is not within the power of government to invade that citadel, whether its purpose or effect be to aid or oppose, to advance or retard. In the relationship between man and religion, the State is firmly committed to a position of neutrality. Though the application of that rule requires interpretation of a delicate sort, the rule itself is clearly and concisely stated in the words of the First Amendment. Applying that rule to the facts of these cases, we affirm. . . .

Mr. Justice Douglas, concurring. . . .

Mr. Justice Goldberg, with whom *Mr. Justice Harlan* joins, concurring. . . .

Mr. Justice Stewart, dissenting.

I think the records in the two cases before us are so fundamentally deficient as to make impossible an informed or responsible determination of the constitutional issues presented. Specifically, I cannot agree that on these records we can say that the Establishment Clause has necessarily been violated. But I think there exist serious questions under both that provision and the Free Exercise Clause—insofar as each is imbedded in the Fourteenth Amendment—which require the remand of these cases for the taking of additional evidence. . . .

What our Constitution indispensably protects is the freedom of each of us, be he Jew or Agnostic, Christian or Atheist, Buddhist or Freethinker, to believe or disbelieve, to worship or not worship, to pray or keep silent, according to his own conscience, uncoerced and unrestrained by government. It is conceivable that these school boards, or even all school boards, might eventually find it impossible to administer a system of religious exercises during school hours in such a way as to meet this constitutional standard—in such a way as completely to free from any kind of official coercion those who do not affirmatively want to participate. But I think we must not assume that school boards so lack the qualities of inventiveness and good will as to make impossible the achievement of that goal.

I would remand both cases for further hearings.

Wallace v. Jaffree
472 U.S. 38; 105 S. Ct. 2479; 86 L. Ed. 2d 29 (1985)
Vote: 6-3

In 1978, the Alabama legislature passed a law that provided: "At the commencement of the first class each day in the first through the sixth grades in all public schools . . . a period of silence, not to exceed one minute in duration, shall be observed for meditation, and during any such period silence shall be maintained and no activities engaged in." In 1981, this law was amended to authorize the period of silence "for meditation or voluntary prayer." The amended version of the Alabama "moment of silence law" is before the Supreme Court in this case.

Justice Stevens delivered the opinion of the Court.
. . . [T]he narrow question for decision is whether [the challenged law], which authorizes a period of silence for "meditation or voluntary prayer," is a law respecting the establishment of religion within the meaning of the First Amendment.

Appellee Ishmael Jaffree is a resident of Mobile County, Alabama. On May 28, 1982, he filed a complaint on behalf of three of his minor children; two of them were second-grade students and the third was then in kindergarten. The complaint named members of the Mobile County School Board, various school officials, and the minor plaintiffs' three teachers as defendants. The complaint alleged that the appellees brought the action "seeking principally a declaratory judgment and an injunction restraining the Defendants and each of them from maintaining or allowing the maintenance of regular religious prayer services or other forms of religious observances in the Mobile County Public Schools in violation of the First Amendment as made applicable to states by the Fourteenth Amendment to the United States Constitution." The complaint further alleged that two of the children had been subjected to various acts of religious indoctrination "from the beginning of the school year in September, 1981"; that the defendant teachers had "on a daily basis" led their classes in saying certain prayers in unison; that the minor children were exposed to ostracism from their peer group class members if they did not participate; and that Ishmael Jaffree had repeatedly but unsuccessfully requested that the devotional services be stopped. The original complaint made no reference to any Alabama statute. . . .

Jaffree's complaint was later amended to challenge the revised "moment of silence" statute. The U.S. district court dismissed the challenge to the statute holding that "the Establishment Clause of the First Amendment to the U.S. Constitution does not prohibit the state from establishing a religion." The U.S. court of appeals reversed, finding the challenged law to be in violation of the First Amendment.

When the court has been called upon to construe the breadth of the Establishment Clause, it has examined the criteria developed over a period of many years. Thus, in *Lemon v. Kurtzman,* *** we wrote:

Every analysis in this area must begin with consideration of the cumulative criteria developed by the Court over many years. Three such tests may be gleaned from our cases. First, the statute must have a secular legislative purpose; second, its principal or primary effect must be one that neither advances nor inhibits religion, *** finally, the statute must not foster "an excessive government entanglement with religion." ***

It is the first of these three criteria that is most plainly implicated by this case. As the District Court correctly recognized, no consideration of the second or third criteria is necessary if a statute does not have a clearly secular purpose. For even though a statute that is motivated in part by a religious purpose may satisfy the first criterion, *** the First Amendment requires that a statute must be invalidated if it is entirely motivated by a purpose to advance religion.

In applying the purpose test, it is appropriate to ask "whether government's actual purpose is to endorse or disapprove of religion." In this case, the answer to that question is dispositive. For the record not only provides us with an unambiguous affirmative answer, but it also reveals that the enactment of [the amended statute] was not motivated by any clearly secular purpose—indeed, the statute had *no* secular purpose.

The sponsor of the bill that became [the challenged law], Senator Donald Holmes, inserted into the legislative record—apparently without dissent—a statement indicating that the legislation was an "effort to return voluntary prayer" to the public schools. Later Senator Holmes confirmed this purpose before the District Court. In response to the question whether he had any purpose for the legislation other than returning voluntary prayer to public schools, he stated, "No, I did not have no other purpose in mind." The State did not present evidence of *any* secular purpose. . . .

The legislative intent to return prayer to the public schools is, of course, quite different from merely protecting every student's right to engage in voluntary prayer during an appropriate moment of silence during the school day. The 1978 statute already protected that right, containing nothing that prevented any student from engaging in voluntary prayer during a silent minute of meditation. Appellants have not identified any secular purpose that was not fully served by [the original statute] before the enactment of [the amendment]. Thus, only two conclusions are consistent with the text . . . (1) the statute was enacted to convey a message of State endorsement and promotion of prayer; or (2) the statute was enacted for no purpose. No one suggests that the statute was nothing but a meaningless or irrational act.

We must, therefore, conclude that the Alabama Legislature intended to change existing law and that it was motivated by the same purpose that the Governor's Answer to the Second Amended Complaint expressly admitted; that the statement inserted in the legislative history revealed; and that Senator Holmes' testimony frankly described. The Legislature enacted [the challenged statute] for the sole purpose of expressing the State's endorsement of prayer activities for one minute at the beginning of each school day.

The addition of "or voluntary prayer" indicates that the State intended to characterize prayer as a favored practice. Such an endorsement is not consistent with the established principle that the Government must pursue a course of complete neutrality toward religion.

The importance of that principle does not permit us to treat this as an inconsequential case involving nothing more than a few words of symbolic speech on behalf of the political majority. For whenever the State itself speaks on a religious subject, one of the questions that we must ask is "whether the Government intends to convey a message of endorsement or disapproval of religion." The well-supported concurrent findings of the District Court and the Court of Appeals—that [the challenged law] was intended to convey a message of State-approval of prayer activities in the public schools—make it unnecessary, and indeed inappropriate, to evaluate the practical significance of the addition of the words "or voluntary prayer" to the statute. Keeping in mind, as we must, "both the fundamental place held by the Establishment Clause in our constitutional scheme and the myriad, subtle ways in which Establishment Clause values can be eroded," we conclude that [the challenged statute] violates the First Amendment.

The judgment of the Court of Appeals is affirmed. It is so ordered.

Justice Powell, concurring. . . .

Justice O'Connor, concurring in the judgment.

Nothing in the United States Constitution as interpreted by this Court or in the laws of the State of Alabama prohibits public school students from voluntarily praying at any time before, during, or after the school day. Alabama has facilitated voluntary silent prayers of students who are so inclined by enacting [the 1978 law] which provides a moment of silence in appellees' schools each day. The parties to these proceedings concede the validity of this enactment. At issue in these appeals is the constitutional validity of an additional and subsequent Alabama statute, *** which both the District Court and the Court of Appeals concluded was enacted solely to

officially encourage prayer during the moment of silence. I agree with the judgment of the Court that, in light of the findings of the Courts below and the history of its enactment, [the challenged law] violates the Establishment Clause of the First Amendment. In my view, there can be little doubt that the purpose and likely effect of this subsequent enactment is to endorse and sponsor voluntary prayer in the public schools. I write separately to identify the peculiar features of the Alabama law that render it invalid, and to explain why moment of silence laws in other States do not necessarily manifest the same infirmity. I also write to explain why neither history nor the Free Exercise Clause of the First Amendment validate the Alabama law struck down by the Court today. . . .

After an extensive discussion of Supreme Court decisions interpreting the religion clauses of the First Amendment, Justice O'Connor concludes:

The Court does not hold that the Establishment Clause is so hostile to religion that it precludes the States from affording schoolchildren an opportunity for voluntary silent prayer. To the contrary, the moment of silence statutes of many States should satisfy the Establishment Clause standard we have here applied. The Court holds only that Alabama has intentionally crossed the line between creating a quiet moment during which those so inclined may pray, and affirmatively endorsing the particular religious practice of prayer. This line may be a fine one, but our precedents and the principles of religious liberty require that we draw it. In my view, the judgment of the Court of Appeals must be affirmed.

Chief Justice Burger, dissenting.

Some who trouble to read the opinions in this case will find it ironic—perhaps even bizarre—that on the very day we heard arguments in this case, the Court's session opened with an invocation for Divine protection. Across the park a few hundred yards away, the House of Representatives and the Senate regularly open each session with a prayer. These legislative prayers are not just one minute in duration, but are extended, thoughtful invocations and prayers for Divine guidance. They are given, as they have been since 1789, by clergy appointed as official Chaplains and paid from the Treasury of the United States. Congress has also provided chapels in the Capitol, at public expense, where Members and others may pause for prayer, meditation—or a moment of silence.

Inevitably some wag is bound to say that the Court's holding today reflects a belief that the historic practice of the Congress and this Court is justified because members of the Judiciary and Congress are more in need of Divine guidance than are schoolchildren. Still others will say that all this controversy is "much ado about nothing," since no power on earth—including this Court and Congress— can stop any teacher from opening the school day with a moment of silence for pupils to meditate, to plan their day—or to pray if they voluntarily elect to do so. . . .

Justice White, dissenting.

. . . As I read the filed opinions, a majority of the Court would approve statutes that provided for a moment of silence but did not mention prayer. But if a student asked whether he could pray during that moment, it is difficult to believe that the teacher could not answer in the affirmative. If that is the case, I would not invalidate a statute that at the outset provided the legislative answer to the question "May I pray?" This is so even if the Alabama statute is infirm, which I do not believe it is, because of its peculiar legislative history.

I appreciate Justice Rehnquist's explication of the history of the Religion Clauses of the First Amendment. Against that history, it would be quite understandable if we undertook to reassess our cases dealing with these clauses, particularly those dealing with the Establishment Clause. Of course, I have been out of step with many of the Court's decisions dealing with this subject matter, and it is thus not surprising that I would support a basic reconsideration of our precedents.

Justice Rehnquist, dissenting.

. . . The true meaning of the Establishment Clause can only be seen in its history. *** As drafters of our Bill of Rights, the Framers inscribed the principles that control today. Any deviation from their intentions frustrates the permanence of that Charter and will only lead to the type of unprincipled decision-making that has plagued our Establishment Clause cases since *Everson.*

The Framers intended the Establishment Clause to prohibit the designation of any church as a "national" one. The Clause was also designed to stop the Federal Government from asserting a preference for one religious denomination or sect over others. Given the "incorporation" of the Establishment Clause as against the States via the Fourteenth Amendment in *Everson,* States are prohibited as well from establishing a religion or discriminating between sects. As its history abundantly shows, however, nothing in the Establishment Clause requires government to be strictly neutral between religion and irreligion, nor does that Clause prohibit Congress or the States from pursuing legitimate secular ends through nondiscriminatory sectarian means.

The Court strikes down the Alabama statute . . . because the State wished to "endorse prayer as a favored practice." *** It would come as much of a shock to those who drafted the Bill of Rights as it will to a large number of thoughtful Americans today to learn that the Constitution, as construed by the majority, prohibits the Alabama Legislature from "endorsing" prayer. George Washington himself, at the request of the very Congress which passed the Bill of Rights, proclaimed a day of "public thanksgiving and prayer, to be observed by acknowledging with grateful hearts the many and signal favors of Almighty God." History must judge whether it was the father of his country in 1789, or a majority of the Court today, which has strayed from the meaning of the Establishment Clause.

The State surely has a secular interest in regulating the manner in which public schools are conducted. Nothing in the Establishment Clause of the First Amendment, properly understood, prohibits any such generalized "endorsement" of prayer. I would therefore reverse the judgment of the Court of Appeals. . . .

Edwards v. Aguillard

482 U.S. 578; 107 S. Ct. 2573; 96 L. Ed. 2d 510 (1987)

Vote: 7-2

The teaching of evolution in the public schools has long been controversial. Indeed, some states have attempted to ban the teaching of evolution altogether. Such a prohibition was struck down in Epperson v. Arkansas (1968). More recently, states have attempted to balance the teaching of evolution with the teaching of "creation science." Whether this is a legitimate secular requirement for public school curricula or an attempt to instruct public school students in the Biblical account of creation is the issue before the Supreme Court in this case.

Justice Brennan delivered the opinion of the Court.

The question for decision is whether Louisiana's "Balanced Treatment for Creation-Science and Evolution-Science in Public School Instruction" Act (Creationism Act) *** is facially invalid as violative of the Establishment Clause of the First Amendment.

The Creationism Act forbids the teaching of the theory of evolution in public schools unless accompanied by instruction in "creation science." *** No school is required to teach evolution or creation science. If either is taught, however, the other must also be taught. *** The theories of evolution and creation science are statutorily defined as "the scientific evidences for [creation or evolution] and inferences from those scientific evidences." ***

Appellees, who include parents of children attending Louisiana public schools, Louisiana teachers, and religious leaders, challenged the constitutionality of the Act in District Court, seeking an injunction and declaratory relief. Appellants, Louisiana officials charged with implementing the Act, defended on the ground that the purpose of the Act is to protect a legitimate secular interest, namely, academic freedom. Appellees attacked the Act as facially invalid because it violated the Establishment Clause and made a motion for summary judgment. The District Court granted the motion. *** The court held that there can be no valid secular reason for prohibiting the teaching of evolution, a theory historically opposed by some religious denominations. The court further concluded that "the teaching of 'creation-science' and 'creationism,' as contemplated by the statute, involves teaching 'tailored to the principles' of a particular religious sect or group of sects." *** The District Court therefore held that the Creationism Act violated the Establishment Clause either because it prohibited the teaching of evolution or because it required the teaching of creation science with the purpose of advancing a particular religious doctrine.

The Court of Appeals affirmed. *** The court observed that the statute's avowed purpose of protecting academic freedom was inconsistent with requiring, upon risk of sanction, the teaching of creation science whenever evolution is taught. *** The court found that the Louisiana legislature's actual intent was "to discredit evolution by counterbalancing its teaching at every turn with the teaching of creationism, a religious belief." *** Because the Creationism Act was thus a law furthering a particular religious belief, the Court of Appeals held that the Act violated the Establishment Clause. A suggestion for rehearing *en banc* was denied over a dissent. *** We noted probable jurisdiction, *** and now affirm.

The Establishment Clause forbids the enactment of any law "respecting an establishment of religion." The Court has applied a three-pronged test to determine whether legislation comports with the Establishment Clause. First, the legislature must have adopted the law with a secular purpose. Second, the statute's principal or primary effect must be one that neither advances nor inhibits religion. Third, the statute must not result in an excessive entanglement of government with religion. *Lemon v. Kurtzman* *** (1971). State action violates the Establishment Clause if it fails to satisfy any of these prongs. . . .

Lemon's first prong focuses on the purpose that animated adoption of the Act. "The purpose prong of the *Lemon* test asks whether government's actual purpose is to endorse or disapprove of religion." *** A governmental intention to promote religion is clear when the State enacts a law to serve a religious purpose. This intention may be evidenced by promotion of religion in general, *** or by advancement of a particular religious belief. *** If the law was enacted for the purpose of endorsing religion, "no consideration of the second or third criteria [of *Lemon*] is necessary." *** In this case, the petitioners had identified no clear secular purpose for the Louisiana Act.

True, the Act's stated purpose is to protect academic freedom. *** This phrase might, in common parlance, be understood as referring to enhancing the freedom of teachers to teach what they will. The Court of Appeals, however, correctly concluded that the Act was not designed to further that goal. We find no merit in the State's argument that the "legislature may not [have] use[d] the terms 'academic freedom' in the correct legal sense. They might have [had] in mind, instead, a basic concept of fairness: teaching all of the evidence." *** Even if "academic freedom" is read to mean "teaching all of the evidence" with respect to the origin of human beings, the Act does not further this purpose. The goal of providing a more comprehensive science curriculum is not furthered either by outlawing the teaching of evolution or by requiring the teaching of creation science.

While the Court is normally deferential to a State's articulation of a secular purpose, it is required that the statement of such purpose be sincere and not a sham. . . .

It is clear from the legislative history that the purpose of the legislative sponsor, Senator Bill Keith, was to narrow the science curriculum. During the legislative hearings, Senator Keith stated: "My preference would be that neither [creationism nor evolution] be taught." *** Such a ban on teaching does not promote—indeed, it undermines—the provision of a comprehensive scientific education.

It is equally clear that requiring schools to teach creation science with evolution does not advance academic freedom. The Act does not grant teachers a flexibility that they did not already possess to supplant the present science curriculum with the presentation of theories, besides evolution, about the origin of life. Indeed, the Court of Appeals found that no law prohibited Louisiana public schoolteachers from teaching any scientific theory. *** As the president of the Louisiana Science Teachers Association

testified, "[a]ny scientific concept that's based on established fact can be included in our curriculum already, and no legislation allowing this is necessary." *** The Act provides Louisiana schoolteachers with no new authority. Thus the stated purpose is not furthered by it. . . .

Furthermore, the goal of basic "fairness" is hardly furthered by the Act's discriminatory preference for the teaching of creation science and against the teaching of evolution. While requiring that curriculum guides be developed for creation science, the Act says nothing of comparable guides for evolution. *** Similarly, research services are supplied for creation science but not for evolution. *** Only "creation scientists" can serve on the panel that supplies the resource services. *** The Act forbids school boards to discriminate against anyone who "chooses to be a creation-scientist" or to teach "creationism," but fails to protect those who choose to teach evolution or any other noncreation science theory, or who refuse to teach creation science. ***

If the Louisiana legislature's purpose was solely to maximize the comprehensiveness and effectiveness of science instruction, it would have encouraged the teaching of all scientific theories about the origins of humankind. But under the Act's requirements, teachers who were once free to teach any and all facets of this subject are now unable to do so. Moreover, the Act fails even to ensure that creation science will be taught, but instead requires the teaching of this theory only when the theory of evolution is taught. Thus we agree with the Court of Appeals' conclusion that the Act does not serve to protect academic freedom, but has the distinctly different purpose of discrediting "evolution by counterbalancing its teaching at every turn with the teaching of creation science. . . ." ***

Stone v. Graham [1980] invalidated the State's requirement that the Ten Commandments be posted in public classrooms. "The Ten Commandments are undeniably a sacred text in the Jewish and Christian faiths, and no legislative recitation of a supposed secular purpose can blind us to that fact." *** As a result, the contention that the law was designed to provide instruction on a "fundamental legal code" was "not sufficient to avoid conflict with the First Amendment." *** Similarly *Abington School District v.*

Schempp [1963] held unconstitutional a statute "requiring the selection and reading at the opening of the school day of verses from the Holy Bible and the recitation of the Lord's Prayer by the students in unison," despite the proffer of such secular purposes as the "promotion of moral values, the contradiction to the materialistic trends of our times, the perpetuation of our institutions and the teaching of literature." ***

As in *Stone* and *Abington,* we need not be blind in this case to the legislature's preeminent religious purpose in enacting this statute. There is a historic and contemporaneous link between the teachings of certain religious denominations and the teaching of evolution. It was this link that concerned the Court in *Epperson v. Arkansas* [1968], *** which also involved a facial challenge to a statute regulating the teaching of evolution. In that case, the Court reviewed an Arkansas statute that made it unlawful for an instructor to teach evolution or to use a textbook that referred to this scientific theory. Although the Arkansas antievolution law did not explicitly state its predominate religious purpose, the Court could not ignore that "[t]he statute was a product of the upsurge of 'fundamentalist' religious fervor" that has long viewed this particular scientific theory as contradicting the literal interpretation of the Bible. *** After reviewing the history of antievolution statutes, the Court determined that "there can be no doubt that the motivation for the [Arkansas] law was the same [as other antievolution statutes]: to suppress the teaching of a theory which, it was thought, 'denied' the divine creation of man." *** The Court found that there can be no legitimate state interest in protecting particular religions from scientific views "distasteful to them," *** and concluded "that the First Amendment does not permit the State to require that teaching and learning must be tailored to the principles or prohibitions of any religious sect or dogma." ***

These same historic and contemporaneous antagonisms between the teachings of certain religious denominations and the teaching of evolution are present in this case. The preeminent purpose of the Louisiana legislature was clearly to advance the religious viewpoint that a supernatural being created humankind. The term "creation science" was defined as embracing this particular religious doctrine by those responsible for the passage of the Creation-ism Act. Senator Keith's leading expert on creation science, Edward Boudreaux, testified at the legislative hearings that the theory of creation science included belief in the existence of a supernatural creator. *** Senator Keith also cited testimony from other experts to support the creation-science view that "a creator [was] responsible for the universe and everything in it." *** The legislative history therefore reveals that the term "creation science," as contemplated by the legislature that adopted this Act, embodies the religious belief that a supernatural creator was responsible for the creation of humankind.

Furthermore, it is not happenstance that the legislature required the teaching of a theory that coincided with this religious view. The legislative history documents that the Act's primary purpose was to change the science curriculum of public schools in order to provide persuasive advantage to a particular religious doctrine that rejects the factual basis of evolution in its entirety. The sponsor of the Creationism Act, Senator Keith, explained during the legislative hearings that his disdain for the theory of evolution resulted from the support that evolution supplied to views contrary to his own religious beliefs. According to Senator Keith, the theory of evolution was consonant with the "cardinal principle[s] of religious humanism, secular humanism, theological liberalism, aetheistism [*sic*]." *** The state senator repeatedly stated that scientific evidence supporting his religious views should be included in the public school curriculum to redress the fact that the theory of evolution incidentally coincided with what he characterized as religious beliefs antithetical to his own. The legislation therefore sought to alter the science curriculum to reflect endorsement of a religious view that is antagonistic to the theory of evolution.

In this case, the purpose of the Creationism Act was to restructure the science curriculum to conform with a particular religious viewpoint. Out of many possible science subjects taught in the public schools, the legislature chose to affect the teaching of the one scientific theory that historically has been opposed by certain religious sects. As in *Epperson,* the legislature passed the Act to give preference to those religious groups which have as one of their tenets the creation of humankind by a divine creator.

The "overriding fact" that confronted the Court in *Epperson* was "that Arkansas' law selects from the body of knowledge a particular segment which it proscribes for the sole reason that it is deemed to conflict with ... a particular interpretation of the Book of Genesis by a particular religious group." *** Similarly, the Creationism Act is designed *either* to promote the theory of creation science which embodies a particular religious tenet by requiring that creation science be taught whenever evolution is taught or to prohibit the teaching of a scientific theory disfavored by certain religious sects by forbidding the teaching of evolution when creation science is not also taught. The Establishment Clause, however, "forbids alike the preference of a religious doctrine or the prohibition of theory which is deemed antagonistic to a particular dogma." *** Because the primary purpose of the Creationism Act is to advance a particular religious belief, the Act endorses religion in violation of the First Amendment.

We do not imply that a legislature could never require that scientific critiques of prevailing scientific theories be taught. Indeed, the Court acknowledged in *Stone* that its decision forbidding the posting of the Ten Commandments did not mean that no use could ever be made of the Ten Commandments, or that the Ten Commandments played an exclusively religious role in the history of Western civilization. *** In a similar way, teaching a variety of scientific theories about the origins of humankind to schoolchildren might be validly done with the clear secular intent of enhancing the effectiveness of science instruction. But because the primary purpose of the Creationism Act is to endorse a particular religious doctrine, the Act furthers religion in violation of the Establishment Clause. . . .

Justice Powell, with whom ***Justice O'Connor*** joins, concurring. . . .

Justice White, concurring in the judgment. . . .

Justice Scalia, with whom ***the Chief Justice*** joins, dissenting.

Even if I agreed with the questionable premise that legislation can be invalidated under the Establishment Clause on the basis of its motivation alone, without regard to its effects, I would still find no justification for today's decision. The Louisiana legislators who passed the "Balanced Treatment for Creation-Science and Evolution-Science Act" (Balanced Treatment Act), *** each of whom had sworn to support the Constitution, were well aware of the potential Establishment Clause problems and considered that aspect of the legislation with great care. After seven hearings and several months of study, resulting in substantial revision of the original proposal, they approved the Act overwhelmingly and specifically articulated the secular purpose they meant it to serve. Although the record contains abundant evidence of the sincerity of that purpose (the only issue pertinent to this case), the Court today holds, essentially on the basis of "its visceral knowledge regarding what must have motivated the legislators," *** that the members of the Louisiana Legislature knowingly violated their oaths and then lied about it. I dissent. Had requirements of the Balanced Treatment Act that are not apparent on its face been clarified by an interpretation of the Louisiana Supreme Court, or by the manner of its implementation, the Act might well be found unconstitutional; but the question of its constitutionality cannot rightly be disposed of on the gallop, by impugning the motives of its supporters. . . .

Our cases interpreting and applying the purpose test have made such a maze of the Establishment Clause that even the most conscientious governmental officials can only guess what motives will be held unconstitutional. We have said essentially the following: Government may not act with the purpose of advancing religion, except when forced to do so by the Free Exercise Clause (which is now and then); or when eliminating existing governmental hostility to religion (which exists sometimes); or even when merely accommodating governmentally uninhibited religious practices, except that at some point (it is unclear where) intentional accommodation results in the fostering of religion, which is of course unconstitutional. ***

But the difficulty of knowing what vitiating purpose one is looking for is as nothing compared with the difficulty of knowing how or where to find it. For while it is possible to discern the objective "purpose" of a statute (i.e., the public good at which its provisions appear to be directed), or even the formal motivation for a statute where that is explicitly set forth (as it was, to no avail, here), discerning the subjective motivation of those enacting the statute is, to be honest, almost always an impossible task. The number of possible motivations, to begin with, is not binary, or indeed even finite. In the present case, for example, a particular legislator need not have voted for the Act either because he wanted to foster religion or because he wanted to improve education. He may have thought the bill would provide jobs for his district, or he may have wanted to make amends with a faction of his party he had alienated on another vote, or he may have been a close friend of the bill's sponsor, or he may have been repaying a favor he owed the Majority Leader, or he may have hoped the Governor would appreciate his vote and make a fundraising appearance for him, or he may have been pressured to vote for a bill he disliked by a wealthy contributor or by a flood of constituent mail, or he may have been seeking favorable publicity, or he may have been reluctant to hurt the feelings of a loyal staff member who worked on the bill, or he may have been settling an old score with a legislator who opposed the bill, or he may have been mad at his wife who opposed the bill, or he may have been intoxicated and utterly unmotivated when the vote was called, or he may have accidentally voted "yes" instead of "no," or, of course, he may have had (and very likely did have) a combination of some of the above and many other motivations. To look for the sole purpose of even a single legislator is probably to look for something that does not exist.

Putting that problem aside, however, where ought we to look for the individual legislator's purpose? We cannot of course assume that every member present (if, as is unlikely, we know who or even how many they were) agreed with the motivation expressed in a particular legislator's pre-enactment floor or committee statement. Quite obviously, "[w]hat motivates one legislator to make a speech about a statute is not necessarily what motivates scores of others to enact it." *** Can we assume, then, that they all agree with the motivation expressed in the staff-prepared committee reports they might have read—even though we are unwilling to assume that they agreed with the motivation expressed in the very statute that they voted for? Should we consider post-enactment floor statements? Or post-enactment testimony from legislators, obtained expressly for the lawsuit? Should we consider media reports on the realities of the legislative bargaining? All of these sources, of course, are eminently manipulable. Legislative histories can be contrived and sanitized, favorable media coverage orchestrated, and post-enactment recollects conveniently distorted. Perhaps most valuable of all would be more objective indications—for example, evidence regarding the individual legislators' religious affiliations. And if that, why not evidence regarding the fervor or tepidity of their beliefs?

Having achieved, through these simple means, an assessment of what individual legislators intended, we must still confront the question (yet to be addressed in any of our cases) how many of them must have the invalidating intent. If a state senate approves a bill by a vote of 26 to 25, and only one of the 26 intended solely to advance religion, is the law unconstitutional? What if 13 of the 26 had that intent? What if 3 of the 26 had the impermissible intent, but 3 of the 25 voting against the bill were motivated by religious hostility or were simply attempting to "balance" the votes of their impermissibly motivated colleagues? Or is it possible that the intent of the bill's sponsor is alone enough to invalidate it—on a theory, perhaps, that even though everyone else's intent was pure, what they produced was the fruit of a forbidden tree?

Because there are not good answers to these questions, this Court has recognized from Chief Justice Marshall *** to Chief Justice Warren *** that determining the subjective intent of the legislators is a perilous enterprise. *** It is perilous, I might note, not just for the judges who will very likely reach the wrong result, but also for the legislators who find that they must assess the validity of proposed legislation—and risk the condemnation of having voted for an unconstitutional measure—not on the basis of what the legislation contains, nor even on the basis of what they themselves intend, but on the basis of what others have in mind.

Given the many hazards involved in assessing the subjective intent of governmental decisionmakers, the first prong of *Lemon* is defensible, I think, only if the text of the Establishment Clause demands it. That is surely not the case. The Clause states that "Congress shall make no law respecting an establishment of religion." One could argue, I suppose, that any time Congress acts with the intent of advancing religion, it has enacted a "law respecting an establishment of religion"; but far from being an unavoidable reading, it is quite an unnatural one. I doubt, for example, that the Clayton Act *** could reasonably be described as a "law respecting an establishment of religion" if bizarre new historical evidence revealed that it lacked a secular purpose, even though it has no discernible nonsecular effect. It is, in short, far from an inevitable reading of the Establishment Clause that it forbids all governmental action intended to advance religion; and if not inevitable, any

reading with such untoward consequences must be wrong.

In the past we have attempted to justify our embarrassing Establishment Clause jurisprudence on the ground that it "sacrifices clarity and predictability for flexibility." *** One commentator had aptly characterized this as "a euphemism ... for ... the absence of any principled rationale." *** I think it time that we sacrifice some "flexibility" for "clarity and predictability." Abandoning *Lemon*'s purpose test—a test which exacerbates the tension between the Free Exercise and Establishment Clause, has no basis in the language or history of the amendment, and, as today's decision shows, has wonderfully flexible consequences—would be a good place to start.

Marsh v. Chambers
463 U.S. 783; 103 S. Ct. 3330; 77 L. Ed. 2d 1019 (1983)
Vote: 6-3

Chief Justice Burger delivered the opinion of the Court.

The question presented is whether the Nebraska Legislature's practice of opening each legislative day with a prayer by a chaplain paid by the State violates the Establishment Clause of the First Amendment.

The Nebraska Legislature begins each of its sessions with a prayer offered by a chaplain who is chosen biennially by the Executive Board of the Legislative Council and paid out of public funds. Robert E. Palmer, a Presbyterian minister, has served as chaplain since 1965 at a salary of $319.75 per month for each month the legislature is in session.

Ernest Chambers is a member of the Nebraska Legislature and a taxpayer of Nebraska. Claiming that the Nebraska Legislature's chaplaincy practice violates the Establishment Clause of the First Amendment, he brought this action *** seeking to enjoin enforcement of the practice. After denying a motion to dismiss on the ground of legislative immunity, the District Court held that the Establishment Clause was not breached by the prayers, but was violated by paying the chaplain from public funds. *** It therefore enjoined the legislature from using public funds

to pay the chaplain; it declined to enjoin the policy of beginning sessions with prayers. . . .

Applying the three-part test of *Lemon v. Kurtzman,* *** the [Court of Appeals] held that the chaplaincy practice violated all three elements of the test: the purpose and primary effect of selecting the same minister for 16 years and publishing his prayers was to promote a particular religious expression; use of state money for compensation and publication led to entanglement. *** Accordingly, the Court of Appeals modified the District Court's injunction and prohibited the State from engaging in any aspect of its established chaplaincy practice.

We granted *certiorari* limited to the challenge to the practice of opening sessions with prayers by a state-employed clergyman, *** and we reverse.

The opening of sessions of legislative and other deliberative public bodies with prayer is deeply embedded in the history and tradition of this country. From colonial times through the founding of the Republic and ever since, the practice of legislative prayer has coexisted with the principles of disestablishment and religious freedom. In the very courtrooms in which the United States District Judge and later three Circuit Judges heard and decided this case, the proceedings opened with an announcement that concluded, "God save the United States and this Honorable Court." The same invocation occurs at all sessions of this Court.

The tradition in many of the colonies was, of course, linked to an established church, but the Continental Congress, beginning in 1774, adopted the traditional procedure of opening its sessions with a prayer offered by a paid chaplain. *** Although prayers were not offered during the Constitutional Convention, the First Congress, as one of its early items of business, adopted the policy of selecting a chaplain to open each session with prayer. Thus on April 7, 1789, the Senate appointed a committee "to take under consideration the manner of electing Chaplains." *** An April 9, 1789, a similar committee was appointed by the House of Representatives. On April 25, 1789, the Senate elected its first chaplain, *** the House followed suit on May 1, 1789. *** A statute providing for the payment of these chaplains was enacted into law on Sept. 22, 1789. ***

On Sept. 25, 1789, three days after Congress authorized the appointment of paid chaplains, final agreement was reached on the language of the Bill of Rights. *** Clearly the men who wrote the First Amendment Religion Clauses did not view paid legislative chaplains and opening prayers as a violation of that Amendment, for the practice of opening sessions with prayer has continued without interruption ever since that early session of Congress. It has also been followed consistently in most of the states, including Nebraska, where the institution of opening legislative sessions with prayer was adopted even before the State attained statehood. ***

Standing alone, historical patterns cannot justify contemporary violations of constitutional guarantees, but there is far more here than simply historical patterns. In this context, historical evidence sheds light not only on what the draftsmen intended the Establishment Clause to mean, but also on how they thought that clause applied to the practice authorized by the First Congress—their actions reveal their intent. . . .

In *Walz v. Tax Comm'n.* [1970], *** we considered the weight to be accorded to history:

It is obviously correct that no one acquires a vested or protected right in violation of the Constitution by long use, even when that span of time covers our entire national existence and indeed predates it. Yet an unbroken practice . . . is not something to be lightly cast aside.

No more is Nebraska's practice of over a century, consistent with two centuries of national practice, to be cast aside. . . . In applying the First Amendment to the states through the Fourteenth Amendment, *** it would be incongruous to interpret that clause as imposing more stringent First Amendment limits on the States than the draftsmen imposed on the Federal Government.

This unique history leads us to accept the interpretation of the First Amendment draftsmen who saw no real threat to the Establishment Clause arising from a practice of prayer similar to that now challenged. . . .

In light of the unambiguous and unbroken history of more than 200 years, there can be no doubt that the practice of opening legislative sessions with prayer has become part of the fabric of our society. To invoke Divine guidance on a public body entrusted with making the laws is not, in these circumstances, an "establishment" of religion or a step toward establishment; it is simply a tolerable acknowledgement of beliefs widely held among the people of this country. As Justice Douglas observed, "[w]e are a religious people whose institutions presuppose a Supreme Being." ***

We turn then to the question of whether any features of the Nebraska practice violate the Establishment Clause. Beyond the bare fact that a prayer is offered, three points have been made: first, that a clergyman of only one denomination—Presbyterian—has been selected for 16 years; second, that the chaplain is paid at public expense; and third, that the prayers are in the Judeo-Christian tradition. Weighed against the historical background, these factors do not serve to invalidate Nebraska's practice.

The Court of Appeals was concerned that Palmer's long tenure has the effect of giving preference to his religious views. We, no more than Members of Congresses of this century, can perceive any suggestion that choosing a clergyman of one denomination advances the beliefs of a particular church. To the contrary, the evidence indicates that Palmer was reappointed because his performance and personal qualities were acceptable to the body appointing him. Palmer was not the only clergyman heard by the Legislature; guest chaplains have officiated at the request of various legislators and as substitutes during Palmer's absences. *** Absent proof that the chaplain's reappointment stemmed from an impermissible motive, we conclude that his long tenure does not in itself conflict with the Establishment Clause.

Nor is the compensation of the chaplain from public funds a reason to invalidate the Nebraska Legislature's chaplaincy; remuneration is grounded in historic practice initiated . . . by the same Congress that adopted the Establishment Clause of the First Amendment. . . . The content of the prayer is not of concern to judges where, as here, there is no indication that the prayer opportunity has been exploited to proselytize or advance any one, or to disparage any other, faith or belief. That being so, it is not for us to embark on a sensitive evaluation or to parse the content of a particular prayer.

We do not doubt the sincerity of those, who like respondent, believe that to have prayer in this context risks the beginning of the establishment the Founding Fathers feared. But this concern is not well founded. . . . The unbroken practice for two centuries in the National Congress, for more than a century in Nebraska and in many other states, gives abundant assurance that there is no real threat "while this Court sits." ***

The judgment of the Court of Appeals is reversed.

Justice Brennan, with whom **Justice Marshall** joins, dissenting.

. . . [D]isagreement with the Court requires that I confront the fact that some twenty years ago, in a concurring opinion in one of the cases striking down official prayer and ceremonial Bible reading in the public schools, I came very close to endorsing essentially the result reached by the Court today. Nevertheless, after much reflection, I have come to the conclusion that I was wrong then and that the Court is wrong today. I now believe that the practice of official invocational prayer, as it exists in Nebraska and most other State Legislatures, is unconstitutional. It is contrary to the doctrine as well the underlying purposes of the Establishment Clause, and it is not

saved either by its history or by any of the other considerations suggested in the Court's opinion.

I respectfully dissent.

The Court makes no pretense of subjecting Nebraska's practice of legislative prayer to any of the formal "tests" that have traditionally structured our inquiry under the Establishment Clause. That it fails to do so is, in a sense, a good thing, for it simply confirms that the Court is carving out an exception to the Establishment Clause rather than reshaping Establishment Clause doctrine to accommodate legislative prayer. For my purposes, however, I must begin by demonstrating what should be obvious: that, if the Court were to judge legislative prayer through the unsentimental eye of our settled doctrine, it would have to strike it down as a clear violation of the Establishment Clause.

The most commonly cited formulation of prevailing Establishment Clause doctrine is found in *Lemon v. Kurtzman* [1971]: ***

Every analysis in this area must begin with consideration of the cumulative criteria developed by the Court over many years. Three such tests may be gleaned from our cases. First, the statute [at issue] must have a secular legislative purpose; second, its principal or primary effect must be one that neither advances nor inhibits religion; finally, the statute must not foster "an excessive government entanglement with religion." ***

That the "purpose" of legislative prayer is preeminently religious rather than secular seems to me to be self-evident. "To invoke Divine guidance on a public body entrusted with making the laws," *** is nothing but a religious act. Moreover, whatever secular functions legislative prayer might play— formally opening the legislative session, getting the members of the body to quiet down, and imbuing them with a sense of seriousness and high purpose— could so plainly be performed in a purely nonreligious fashion that to claim a secular purpose for the prayer is an insult to the perfectly honorable individuals who instituted and continue the practice.

The "primary effect" of legislative prayer is also clearly religious. As we said in the context of officially sponsored prayers in the public schools, "prescribing a particular form of religious worship," even if the individuals involved have the choice not to participate, places "indirect coercive pressure upon religious minorities to conform to the prevailing officially approved religion...." *** More importantly, invocations in Nebraska's legislative halls explicitly link religious belief and the prestige of the State. "[T]he mere appearance of a joint exercise of legislative authority by Church and State provides a significant symbolic benefit to religion in the minds of some by reason of the power conferred." ***

Finally, there can be no doubt that the practice of legislative prayer leads to excessive "entanglement" between the State and religion. *Lemon* pointed out that "entanglement" can take two forms: First, a state statute or program might involve the state impermissibly in monitoring and overseeing religious affairs. *** In the case of legislative prayer, the process of choosing a "suitable" chaplain, whether on a permanent or rotating basis, and insuring that the chaplain limits himself to "suitable" prayers, involves precisely the sort of supervision that agencies of government should if at all possible avoid.

Second, excessive "entanglement" might arise out of "the divisive political potential" of a state statute or program.... In this case, this second aspect of entanglement is also clear. The controversy between Senator Chambers and his colleagues, which had reached the stage of difficulty and rancor long before this lawsuit was brought, has split the Nebraska Legislature precisely on issues of religion and religious conformity. *** The record in this case also reports a series of instances, involving legislators other than Senator Chambers, in which invocations by Reverend Palmer and others led to controversy along religious lines. And in general, the history of legislative prayer has been far more eventful—and divisive—than a hasty reading of the Court's opinion might indicate.

In sum, I have no doubt that, if any group of law students were asked to apply the principles of *Lemon* to the question of legislative prayer, they would nearly unanimously find the practice to be unconstitutional....

The argument is made occasionally that a strict separation of religion and state robs the nation of its spiritual identity. I believe quite the contrary. It may be true that individuals cannot be "neutral" on the question of religion. But the judgment of the Establishment Clause is that neutrality by the organs of *government* on questions of religion is both possible and imperative....

Justice Stevens, dissenting.

In a democratically elected legislature, the religious beliefs of the chaplain tend to reflect the faith of the majority of the lawmakers' constituents. Prayers may be said by a Catholic priest in the Massachusetts Legislature and by a Presbyterian minister in the Nebraska Legislature, but I would not expect to find a Jehovah's Witness or a disciple of Mary Baker Eddy or the Reverend Moon serving as the official chaplain in any state legislature. Regardless of the motivation of the majority that exercises the power to appoint the chaplain, it seems plain to me that the designation of a member of one religious faith to serve as the sole official chaplain of a state legislature for a period of 16 years constitutes the preference of one faith over another in violation of the Establishment Clause of the First Amendment.

The Court declines to "embark on a sensitive evaluation or to parse the content of a particular prayer." *** Perhaps it does so because it would be unable to explain away the clearly sectarian content of some of the prayers given by Nebraska's chaplain. Or perhaps the Court is unwilling to acknowledge that the tenure of the chaplain must inevitably be conditioned on the acceptability of that content to the silent majority.

I would affirm the judgment of the Court of Appeals.

Lynch v. Donnelly

465 U.S. 668; 104 S. Ct. 1355; 79 L. Ed. 2d 604 (1984)

Vote: 5-4

The Chief Justice delivered the opinion of the Court.

We granted *certiorari* to decide whether the Establishment Clause of the First Amendment prohibits a municipality from including a crèche, or Nativity scene, in its annual Christmas display.

I

Each year, in cooperation with the downtown retail merchants' association, the City of Pawtucket, Rhode Island, erects a Christmas display as part of its observance of the Christmas holiday season. The display is situated in a park owned by a nonprofit organization and located in the heart of the shopping district. The display is essentially like those to be found in hundreds of towns or cities across the Nation—often on public grounds—during the Christmas season. The Pawtucket display comprises many of the figures and decorations traditionally associated with Christmas, including, among other things, a Santa Claus house, reindeer pulling Santa's sleigh, candy-striped poles, a Christmas tree, carolers, cutout figures representing such characters as a clown, an elephant, and a teddy bear, hundreds of colored lights, a large banner that reads "SEASONS GREETINGS," and the crèche at issue here. All components of this display are owned by the city.

The crèche, which has been included in the display for 40 or more years, consists of the traditional figures, including the Infant Jesus, Mary and Joseph, angels, shepherds, kings, and animals, all ranging in height from 5″ to 5′. In 1973, when the present crèche was acquired, it cost the City $1,365; it now is valued at $200. The erection and dismantling of the crèche costs the City about $20 per year; nominal expenses are incurred in lighting the crèche. No money has been expended on its maintenance for the past 10 years.

Respondents, Pawtucket residents and individual members of the Rhode Island affiliate of the American Civil Liberties Union, and the affiliate itself, brought this action in the United States District Court for Rhode Island, challenging the City's inclusion of the crèche in the annual display. The District Court held that the City's inclusion of the crèche in the display violates the Establishment Clause, *** which is binding on the states through the Fourteenth Amendment. The District Court found that, by including the crèche in the Christmas display, the City has "tried to endorse and promulgate religious beliefs," *** and that "erection of the crèche has the real and substantial effect of affiliating the City with the Christian beliefs that the crèche represents." *** This "appearance of official sponsorship," it believed, "confers more than a remote and incidental benefit on Christianity." *** Last, although the court acknowledged the absence of administrative entanglement, it found that excessive entanglement has been fostered as a result of the political divisiveness of including the crèche in the celebration. *** The City was permanently enjoined from including the crèche in the display.

A divided panel of the Court of Appeals for the First Circuit affirmed. *** We granted *certiorari*, *** and we reverse.

II

A

This Court has explained that the purpose of the Establishment and Free Exercise Clauses of the First Amendment is "to prevent, as far as possible, the intrusion of either [the church or the state] into the precincts of the other." *** At the same time however, the Court has recognized that "total separation is not possible in an absolute sense. Some relationship between government and religious organizations is inevitable." *** In every Establishment Clause case, we must reconcile the inescapable tension between the objective of preventing unnecessary intrusion of either the church or the state upon the other, and the reality that, as the Court has so often noted, total separation of the two is not possible.

The Court has sometimes described the Religion Clause as erecting a "wall" between church and state. *** The concept of a "wall" of separation is a useful figure of speech probably deriving from views of Thomas Jefferson. The metaphor has served as a reminder that the Establishment Clause forbids an established church or anything approaching it. But the metaphor itself is not a wholly accurate description of the practical aspects of the relationship that in fact exists between church and state.

No significant segment of our society and no institution within it can exist in a vacuum or in total or absolute isolation from all the other parts, much less from government. "It has never been thought either possible or desirable to enforce a regime of total separation...." *** Nor does the Constitution require complete separation of church and state; it affirmatively mandates accommodation, not merely tolerance, of all religions, and forbids hostility toward any. *** Anything less would require the "callous indifference" we have said was never intended by the Establishment Clause. *** Indeed, we have observed, such hostility would bring us into "war with our national tradition as embodied in the First Amendment's guaranty of the free exercise of religion." ***

B

The Court's interpretation of the Establishment Clause has comported with what history reveals was the contemporaneous understanding of its guarantees. A significant example of the contemporaneous understanding of that Clause is found in events of the first week of the First Session of the First Congress in 1789. In the very week that Congress approved the Establishment Clause as part of the Bill of Rights for submission to the states, it enacted legislation providing for paid chaplains for the House and Senate. In *Marsh v. Chambers,* *** we noted that seventeen Members of that First Congress had been Delegates to the Constitutional Convention where freedom of speech, press and religion and antagonism toward an established church were subjects of frequent discussion. We saw no conflict with the Establishment Clause when Nebraska employed members of the clergy as official legislative Chaplains to give opening prayers at sessions of the state legislature. . . .

Our history is replete with official references to the value and invocation of Divine guidance in deliberations and pronouncements of the Founding Fathers and contemporary leaders. Beginning in the early colonial period long before Independence, a day of Thanksgiving was celebrated as a religious holiday to give thanks for the bounties of Nature as gifts from God. President Washington and his successors proclaimed Thanksgiving, with all its religious overtones, a day of national celebration and Congress made it a National Holiday more than a century ago. *** That holiday has not lost its theme of expressing thanks for Divine aid any more than has Christmas lost its religious significance.

Executive Orders and other official announcements of Presidents and the Congress have proclaimed both Christmas and Thanksgiving National Holidays in religious terms. And, by Acts of Congress, it has long been the practice that federal employees are released from duties on these National Holidays, while being paid from the same public revenues that provide the compensation of the Chaplains of the Senate and the House and the military services. Thus, it is clear that Government has long recognized—indeed it has subsidized—holidays with religious significance.

Other examples of reference to our religious heritage are found in the statutorily prescribed national motto "In God We Trust," *** which Congress and the President mandated for our currency, *** and in the language "One nation under God," as part of the Pledge of Allegiance to the American flag. That pledge is recited by thousands of public school children—and adults—every year.

Art galleries supported by public revenues display religious paintings of the 15th and 16th centuries, predominantly inspired by one religious faith. The National Gallery in Washington, maintained with Government support, for example, has long exhibited masterpieces with religious messages, notably the Last Supper, and paintings depicting the Birth of Christ, the Crucifixion, and the Resurrection, among many others with explicit Christian themes and messages. The very chamber in which oral arguments on this case were heard is decorated with a notable and permanent—not seasonal—symbol of religion: Moses with Ten Commandments. Congress has long provided chapels in the Capitol for religious worship and meditation.

There are countless other illustrations of the Government's acknowledgment of our religious heritage and governmental sponsorship of graphic manifestations of that heritage. Congress has directed the President to proclaim a National Day of Prayer each year "on which [day] the people of the United States may turn to God in prayer and meditation at churches, in groups, and as individuals." *** Our Presidents have repeatedly issued such Proclamations. Presidential Proclamations and messages have also issued to commemorate Jewish Heritage Week, *** and the Jewish High Holy Days. *** One cannot look at even this brief resume without finding that our history is pervaded by expressions of religious beliefs. . . . Equally pervasive is the evidence of accommodation of all faiths and all forms of religious expression, and hostility toward none. . . .

III

This history may help explain why the Court consistently has declined to take a rigid, absolutist view of the Establishment Clause. We have refused "to construe the Religion Clauses with a literalness that would undermine the ultimate constitutional objective *as illuminated by history*." *** In our modern, complex society, whose traditions and constitutional underpinnings rest on and encourage diversity and pluralism in all areas, an absolutist approach in applying the Establishment Clause is simplistic and has been uniformly rejected by the Court. . . .

In each case, the inquiry calls for line drawing; no fixed, *per se* rule can be framed. The Establishment Clause like the Due Process Clauses is not a precise, detailed provision in a legal code capable of ready application. The purpose of the Establishment Clause "was to state an objective, not to write a statute." *** The line between permissible relationships and those barred by the Clause can no more be straight and unwavering than due process can be defined in a single stroke or phrase or test. The Clause erects a "blurred, indistinct, and variable barrier depending on all the circumstances of a particular relationship." ***

In the line-drawing process we have often found it useful to inquire whether the challenged law or conduct has a secular purpose, whether its principal or primary effect is to advance or inhibit religion, and whether it creates an excessive entanglement of government with religion. *** But, we have repeatedly emphasized our unwillingness to be confined to any single test or criterion in this sensitive area. . . .

In this case, the focus of our inquiry must be on the crèche in the context of the Christmas season. . . . Focus exclusively on the religious component of any activity would inevitably lead to its invalidation under the Establishment Clause. . . .

The narrow question is whether there is a secular purpose for Pawtucket's display of the crèche. The display is sponsored by the City to celebrate the Holiday and to depict the origins of that Holiday. These are legitimate secular purposes. The District Court's inference, drawn from the religious nature of the crèche, that the City has no secular purpose was, on this record, clearly erroneous.

The District Court found that the primary effect of including the crèche is to confer a substantial and impermissible benefit on religion in general and on the Christian faith in particular. Comparisons of the relative benefits to religion of different forms of governmental support are elusive and difficult to make. But to conclude that the primary effect of including the crèche is to advance religion in violation of the Establishment Clause would require that we view it as more beneficial to and more an endorsement of religion, for example, than expenditure of large sums of public money for textbooks supplied throughout the country to students attending church-sponsored schools, *** expenditure of public funds for transportation of students to church-sponsored schools, *** federal grants for college buildings of church-sponsored institutions of higher education combining secular and religious education, *** noncategorical grants to church-sponsored colleges and universities, *** and tax exemptions for church properties. . . . ***

We are unable to discern a greater aid to religion deriving from inclusion of the crèche than from these benefits and endorsements previously held not violative of the Establishment Clause. . . .

Entanglement is a question of kind and degree. In this case, however, there is no reason to disturb the District Court's finding on the absence of administrative entanglement. There is no evidence of contact with church authorities concerning the content or design of the exhibit prior to or since Pawtucket's purchase of the crèche. No expenditures for maintenance of the crèche have been necessary; and since the City owns the crèche, now valued at $200, the tangible material it contributes is *de minimis*. In many respects the display requires far less ongoing, day-to-day interaction between church and state than religious paintings in public galleries. . . .

The Court of Appeals correctly observed that this Court has not held that political divisiveness alone can serve to invalidate otherwise permissible conduct. And we decline to so hold today. This case does not involve a direct subsidy to church-sponsored schools or colleges, or other religious institutions, and hence no inquiry into potential political divisiveness is even called for. *** In any event, apart from this litigation there is no evidence of political friction or divisiveness over the crèche in the 40-year history of Pawtucket's Christmas celebration. The District Court stated that the inclusion of the crèche for the 40 years has been "marked by no apparent dissension" and that the display has had a "calm history." *** Curiously, it went on to hold that the political divisiveness engendered by this lawsuit was evidence of excessive entanglement. A litigant cannot, by the very act of commencing a lawsuit, however, create the appearance of divisiveness and then exploit it as evidence of entanglement.

We are satisfied that the city has a secular purpose for including the crèche, that the city has not impermissibly advanced religion, and that including the crèche does not create excessive entanglement between religion and government.

IV

Justice Brennan describes the crèche as a "recreation of an event that lies at the heart of Christian faith." *** The crèche, like a painting, is passive; admittedly it is a reminder of the origins of Christmas. Even the traditional, purely secular displays extant at Christmas, with or without a crèche, would inevita-bly recall the religious nature of the Holiday. The display engenders a friendly community spirit of goodwill in keeping with the season. The crèche may well have special meaning to those whose faith includes the celebration of religious Masses, but none who sense the origins of the Christmas celebration would fail to be aware of its religious implications. That the display brings people into the central city, and serves commercial interests and benefits merchants and their employees, does not, as the dissent points out, determine the character of the display. That a prayer invoking Divine guidance in Congress is preceded and followed by debate and partisan conflict over taxes, budgets, national defense, and myriad mundane subjects, for example, has never been thought to demean or taint the sacredness of the invocation.

Of course the crèche is identified with one religious faith but no more so than the examples we have set out from prior cases in which we found no conflict with the Establishment Clause. *** It would be ironic, however, if the inclusion of a single symbol of a particular historic religious event, as part of a celebration acknowledged in the Western world for 20 centuries, and in this country by the people, by the Executive Branch, by the Congress, and the courts for two centuries, would so "taint" the City's exhibit as to render it violative of the Establishment Clause. To forbid the use of this one passive symbol—the crèche—at the very time people are taking note of the season with Christmas hymns and carols in public schools and other public places, and while the Congress and Legislatures open sessions with prayers by paid chaplains would be a stilted over-reaction contrary to our history and to our holdings. If the presence of the crèche in this display violates the Establishment Clause, a host of other forms of taking official note of Christmas, and of our religious heritage, are equally offensive to the Constitution.

The Court has acknowledged that the "fears and political problems" that gave rise to the Religion Clauses in the 18th century are of far less concern today. *** We are unable to perceive the Archbishop of Canterbury, the Bishop of Rome, or other powerful religious leaders behind every public acknowledgment of the religious heritage long officially recognized by the three constitutional branches of government. Any notion that these symbols pose a real danger of establishment of a state church is far-fetched indeed.

V

That this Court has been alert to the constitutionally expressed opposition to the establishment of religion is shown in numerous holdings striking down statutes or programs as violative of the Establishment Clause. *** The most recent example of this careful scrutiny is found in the case invalidating a municipal ordinance granting to a church a virtual veto power over the licensing of liquor establishments near the church. *** Taken together these cases abundantly demonstrate the Court's concern to protect the genuine objectives of the Establishment Clause. It is far too late in the day to impose a crabbed reading of the Clause on the country.

VI

We hold that, notwithstanding the religious significance of the crèche, the City of Pawtucket has not violated the Establishment Clause of the First Amendment. Accordingly, the judgment of the Court of Appeals is reversed.

It is so ordered.

Justice O'Connor, concurring. . . .

Justice Brennan, with whom ***Justice Marshall, Justice Blackmun*** and ***Justice Stevens*** join, dissenting.

. . . As we have sought to meet new problems arising under the Establishment Clause, our decisions, with few exceptions, have demanded that a challenged governmental practice satisfy the following criteria:

First the [practice] must have a secular legislative purpose; second, its principal or primary effect must be one that neither advances nor inhibits religion; finally, [it] must not foster 'an excessive government entanglement with religion.' ***

This well-defined three-part test expresses the essential concerns animating the Establishment Clause.

Thus, the test is designed to ensure that the organs of government remain strictly separate and apart from religious affairs, for "a union of government and religion tends to destroy government and degrade religion." *** And it seeks to guarantee that government maintains a position of neutrality with respect to religion and neither advances nor inhibits the promulgation and practice of religious beliefs. *** In this regard, we must be alert in our examination of any challenged practice not only for an official establishment of religion, but also for those other evils at which the Clause was aimed—"sponsorship, financial support, and active involvement of the sovereign in religious activity." ***

. . . Under our constitutional scheme, the role of safeguarding our "religious heritage" and of promoting religious beliefs is reserved as the exclusive prerogative of our nation's churches, religious institutions and spiritual leaders. Because the Framers of the Establishment Clause understood that "religion is too personal, too sacred, too holy to permit its 'unhallowed perversion' by civil [authorities]," *** the Clause demands that government play no role in this effort. The Court today brushes aside these concerns by insisting that Pawtucket has done nothing more than include a "traditional" symbol of Christmas in its celebration of this national holiday, thereby muting the religious content of the crèche. *** But the city's action should be recognized for what it is: a coercive, though perhaps small, step toward establishing the sectarian preferences of the majority at the expense of the minority, accomplished by placing public facilities and funds in support of the religious symbolism and theological tidings that the crèche conveys. As Justice Frankfurter, writing in *McGowan v. Maryland,* observed, the Establishment Clause "withdr[aws] from the sphere of legitimate legislative concern and competence a specific, but comprehensive area of human conduct: man's belief or disbelief in the verity of some transcendental idea and man's expression in action of that belief or disbelief." *** That the Constitution sets this realm of thought and feeling apart from the pressures and antagonisms of government is one of its supreme achievements. Regrettably, the Court today tarnishes that achievement.

I dissent.

Justice Blackmun, with whom **Justice Stevens** joins, dissenting.

... Not only does the Court's resolution of this controversy make light of our precedents, but also, ironically, the majority does an injustice to the crèche and the message it manifests. While certain persons, including the Mayor of Pawtucket, undertook a crusade to "keep 'Christ' in Christmas," *** the Court today has declared that presence virtually irrelevant. The majority urges that the display, "with or without a crèche," "recall[s] the religious nature of the Holiday," and "engenders a friendly community spirit of goodwill in keeping with the season." *** Before the District Court, an expert witness for the city made a similar, though perhaps more candid, point, stating that Pawtucket's display invites people "to participate in the Christmas spirit, brotherhood,

peace, and let loose with their money." *** The crèche has been relegated to the role of a neutral harbinger of the holiday season, useful for commercial purposes, but devoid of any inherent meaning and incapable of enhancing the religious tenor of a display of which it is an integral part. The city has its victory—but it is a Pyrrhic one indeed.

The import of the Court's decision is to encourage use of the crèche in a municipally sponsored display, a setting where Christians feel constrained in acknowledging its symbolic meaning and non-Christians feel alienated by its presence. Surely, this is a misuse of a sacred symbol. Because I cannot join the Court in denying either the force of our precedents or the sacred message that is at the core of the crèche, I dissent and join Justice Brennan's opinion.

Walz v. Tax Commission

397 U.S. 664; 90 S. Ct. 1409; 25 L. Ed. 2d 697 (1970)
Vote: 8-1

Mr. Chief Justice Burger delivered the opinion of the Court.

Appellant, owner of real estate in Richmond County, New York, sought an injunction in the New York courts to prevent the New York City Tax Commission from granting property tax exemptions to religious organizations for religious properties used solely for religious worship. The exemption from state taxes is authorized by Art. 16, Sec. 1, of the New York Constitution, which provides in relevant part:

Exemptions from taxation may be granted only by general laws. Exemptions may be altered or repealed except those exempting real or personal property used exclusively for religious, educational or charitable purposes as defined by law and owned by any corporation or association organized or conducted exclusively for one or more of such purposes and not operating for profit.

The essence of appellant's contention was that the New York City Tax Commission's grant of an exemption to church property indirectly requires the appellant to make a contribution to religious bodies and thereby violates provisions prohibiting estab-

lishment of religion under the First Amendment which under the Fourteenth Amendment is binding on the States.

Appellee's motion for summary judgment was granted and the Appellate Divisions of the New York Supreme Court, and the New York Court of Appeals affirmed. We noted probable jurisdiction *** and affirm.

Prior opinions of this Court have discussed the development and historical background of the First Amendment in detail. *** It would therefore serve no useful purpose to review in detail the background of the Establishment and Free Exercise Clauses of the First Amendment or to restate what the Court's opinions have reflected over the years. ...

The course of constitutional neutrality in this area cannot be an absolutely straight line; rigidity could well defeat the basic purpose of these provisions, which is to insure that no religion be sponsored or favored, none commanded, and none inhibited. The general principle deducible from the First Amendment and all that has been said by the Court is this:

that we will not tolerate either governmentally established religion or governmental interference with religion. Short of those expressly proscribed governmental acts there is room for play in the joints productive of a benevolent neutrality which will permit religious exercise to exist without sponsorship and without interference.

Each value judgment under the Religion Clauses must therefore turn on whether particular acts in question are intended to establish or interfere with religious beliefs and practices or have the effect of doing so. Adherence to the policy of neutrality that derives from an accommodation of the Establishment and Free Exercise Clauses has prevented the kind of involvement that would tip the balance toward government control of churches or governmental restraint on religious practice. Adherents of particular faiths and individual churches frequently take strong positions on public issues including ... vigorous advocacy of legal or constitutional positions. Of course, churches as much as secular bodies and private citizens have that right. No perfect or absolute separation is really possible; the very existence of the Religion Clauses is an involvement of sorts—one that seeks to mark boundaries to avoid excessive entanglement. . . .

The legislative purpose of a property tax exemption is neither the advancement nor the inhibition of religion; it is neither sponsorship nor hostility. New York, in common with the other States, has determined that certain entities that exist in a harmonious relationship to the community at large, and that foster its "moral or mental improvement," should not be inhibited in their activities by property taxation or the hazard of loss of those properties for nonpayment of taxes. It has not singled out one particular church or religious group or even churches as such; rather, it has granted exemption to all houses of religious worship within a broad class of property owned by nonprofit, quasi-public corporations which include hospitals, libraries, playgrounds, scientific, professional, historical, and patriotic groups. The State has an affirmative policy that considers these groups as beneficial and stabilizing influences in community life and finds this classification useful, desirable, and in the public interest. Qualification for tax exemption is not perpetual or immutable; some

tax-exempt groups lose that status when their activities take them outside the classification and new entities can come into being and qualify for exemption.

Governments have not always been tolerant of religious activity, and hostility toward religion has taken many shapes and forms—economic, political, and sometimes harshly oppressive. Grants of exemption historically reflect the concern of authors of constitutions and statutes as to the latent dangers inherent in the imposition of property taxes; exemption constitutes a reasonable and balanced attempt to guard against those dangers. The limits of permissible state accommodation to religion are by no means coextensive with the noninterference mandated by the Free Exercise Clause. To equate the two would be to deny a national heritage with roots in the Revolution itself. *** We cannot read New York's statute as attempting to establish religion; it is simply sparing the exercise of religion from the burden of property taxation levied on private profit institutions. . . .

Granting tax exemptions to churches necessarily operates to afford an indirect economic benefit and also gives rise to some, but yet a lesser, involvement than taxing them. In analyzing either alternative the questions are whether the involvement is excessive, and whether it is a continuing one calling for official and continuing surveillance leading to an impermissible degree of entanglement. Obviously a direct money subsidy would be a relationship pregnant with involvement and, as with most governmental grant programs, could encompass sustained and detailed administrative relationships for enforcement of statutory or administrative standards, but that is not this case. The hazards of churches supporting government are hardly less in their potential than the hazards of government supporting churches, each relationship carries some involvement rather than the desired insulation and separation. We cannot ignore the instances in history when church support of government led to the kind of involvement we seek to avoid.

The grant of a tax exemption is not sponsorship since the government does not transfer part of its revenue to churches but simply abstains from demanding that the church support the state. No one has ever suggested that tax exemption has converted libraries, art galleries, or hospitals into arms of the state or put employees "on the public payroll." There is no genuine nexus between tax exemption and establishment of religion. As Mr. Justice Holmes commented in a related context "a page of history is worth a volume of logic." *** The exemption creates only a minimal and remote involvement between church and state and far less than taxation of churches. It restricts the fiscal relationship between church and state, and tends to complement and reinforce the desired separation insulating each from the other.

Separation in this context cannot mean absence of all contact; the complexities of modern life inevitably produce some contact and the fire and police protection received by houses of religious worship are no more than incidental benefits accorded all persons or institutions within a State's boundaries, along with many other exempt organizations. The appellant has not established even an arguable quantitative correlation between the payment of an *ad valorem* property tax and the receipt of these municipal benefits.

All of the 50 States provide for tax exemption of places of worship, most of them doing so by constitutional guarantees. For so long as federal income taxes have had any potential impact on churches—over 75 years—religious organizations have been expressly exempt from the tax. Such treatment is an "aid" to churches no more and no less in principle than the real estate tax exemption granted by States. Few concepts are more deeply embedded in the fabric of our national life, beginning with pre-Revolutionary colonial times, than for the government to exercise at the very least this kind of benevolent neutrality toward churches and religious exercise generally so long as none was favored over others and none suffered interference. . . .

It is obviously correct that no one acquires a vested or protected right in violation of the Constitution by long use, even when that span of time covers our entire national existence and indeed predates it. Yet an unbroken practice of according the exemption to churches, openly and by affirmative state action, not covertly or by state inaction, is not something to be lightly cast aside. Nearly 50 years ago Mr. Justice Holmes stated:

"If a thing has been practiced for two hundred years by common consent, it will need a strong case for the Fourteenth Amendment to affect it. . . ." ***

Nothing in this national attitude toward religious tolerance and two centuries of uninterrupted freedom from taxation has given the remotest sign of leading to an established church or religion and on the contrary it has operated affirmatively to help guarantee the free exercise of all forms of religious belief. Thus, it is hardly useful to suggest that tax exemption is but the "foot in the door" or the "nose of the camel in the tent" leading to an established church. If tax exemption can be seen as this first step toward "establishment" of religion, as Mr. Justice Douglas fears, the second step has been long in coming. . . .

The argument that making "fine distinctions" between what is and what is not absolute under the Constitution is to render us a government of men, not laws, gives too little weight to the fact that it is an essential part of adjudication to draw distinctions, including fine ones, in the process of interpreting the Constitution. We must frequently decide, for example, what are "reasonable" searches and seizures under the Fourth Amendment. Determining what acts of government tend to establish or interfere with religion falls well within what courts have long been called upon to do in sensitive areas.

It is interesting to note that while the precise question we now decide has not been directly before the Court previously, the broad question was discussed by the Court in relation to real estate taxes assessed nearly a century ago on land owned by and adjacent to a church in Washington, D.C. At that time Congress granted real estate tax exemptions to buildings devoted to art, to institutions of public charity, libraries, cemeteries, and "church buildings, and grounds actually occupied by such buildings." In denying tax exemption as to land owned by but not used for the church, but rather to produce income, the Court concluded:

In the exercise of this [taxing] power, Congress, like any State legislature unrestricted by constitutional provisions, may at its discretion wholly exempt certain classes of property from taxation, or may tax them at a lower rate than other property. ***

It appears that at least up to 1885 this Court, reflecting more than a century of our history and uninterrupted practice, accepted without discussion the proposition that federal or state grants of tax exemption to churches were not a violation of the

Religion Clauses of the First Amendment. As to the New York statute, we now confirm that view.
Affirmed.

Mr. Justice Brennan, concurring. . . .

. . . *Mr. Justice Harlan* [concurring] . . . .

Mr. Justice Douglas, dissenting.

Petitioner is the owner of real property in New York and is a Christian. But he is not a member of any of the religious organizations, "rejecting them as hostile." The New York statute exempts from taxation real property "owned by a corporation or association organized exclusively for . . . religious . . . purposes" and used "exclusively for carrying out" such purposes. Yet nonbelievers who own realty are taxed at the usual rate. The question in the case therefore is whether believers—organized in church groups— can be made exempt from real estate taxes, merely because they are believers, while nonbelievers, whether organized or not, must pay the real estate taxes. . . .

Churches perform some functions that a State would constitutionally be empowered to perform. I refer to nonsectarian social welfare operations such as the care of orphaned children and the destitute and people who are sick. A tax exemption to agencies performing those functions would therefore be as constitutionally proper as the grant of direct subsidies to them. Under the First Amendment a State may not, however, provide worship if private groups fail to do so. As Mr. Justice Jackson said:

[A State] may socialize utilities and economic enterprises and make taxpayers' business out of what conventionally had been private business. It may make public business of individual welfare, health, education, entertainment or security. But it cannot make public business of religious worship or instruction, or of attendance at religious institutions of any character. . . . That is a difference which the Constitution sets up between religion and almost every other subject matter of legislation, a difference which goes to the very root of religious freedom and which the Court is overlooking today. ***

That is a major difference between churches, on the one hand and the rest of the nonprofit organizations on the other. Government could provide or finance operas, hospitals, historical societies, and all the rest because they represent social welfare programs within the reach of the police power. In contrast, government may not provide or finance worship because of the Establishment Clause any more than it may single out "atheistic" or "agnostic" centers or groups and create or finance them.

The Brookings Institution, writing in 1933, before the application of the Establishment Clause of the First Amendment to the States, said about tax exemptions of religious groups:

Tax exemption, no matter what its form, is essentially a government grant or subsidy. Such grants would seem to be justified only if the purpose for which they are made is one for which the legislative body *would be equally willing to make* a direct appropriation from public funds equal to the amount of the exemption. This test would not be met except in the case where the exemption is granted to encourage certain activities of private interests, which, if not thus performed, would have to be assumed by the government at an expenditure at least as great as the value of the exemption.

Since 1947, when the Establishment Clause was made applicable to the States, that report would have to state that the exemption would be justified only where "the legislative body *could make*" an appropriation for the cause.

On the record of this case, the church *qua* nonprofit, charitable organization is intertwined with the church *qua* church. A church may use the same facilities, resources, and personnel in carrying out both its secular and its sectarian activities. The two are unitary and on the present record have not been separated one from the other. The state has a public policy of encouraging private public welfare organizations, which it desires to encourage through tax exemption. Why may it not do so and include churches *qua* welfare organizations on a nondiscriminatory basis? That avoids, it is argued, a discrimination against churches and in a real sense maintains neutrality toward religion which the First Amendment was designed to foster. Welfare services, whether performed by churches or by nonreligious groups, may well serve the public welfare.

Whether a particular church seeking an exemption for its welfare work could constitutionally pass muster would depend on the special facts. The assumption is that the church is a purely private institution, promoting a sectarian cause. The creed, teaching, and beliefs of one may be undesirable or even repulsive to others. Its sectarian faith sets it apart from all others and makes it difficult to equate its constituency with the general public. The extent that its facilities are open to all may only indicate the nature of its proselytism. Yet though a church covers up its religious symbols in welfare work, its welfare activities may merely be a phase of sectarian activity. I have said enough to indicate the nature of this tax exemption problem.

Direct financial aid to churches or tax exemptions to the church *qua* church is not, in my view, even arguably permitted. Sectarian causes are certainly not antipublic and many would rate their own church or perhaps all churches as the highest form of welfare. The difficulty is that sectarian causes must remain in the private domain not subject to public control or subsidy. That seems to me to be the requirement of the Establishment Clause. . . .

The exemptions provided here insofar as welfare projects are concerned may have the ring of neutrality. But subsidies either through direct grant or tax exemption for sectarian causes, whether carried on by church *qua* church or by church *qua* welfare agency, must be treated differently, lest we in time allow the church *qua* church to be on the public payroll, which, I fear, is imminent. . . .

If believers are entitled to public financial support, so are nonbelievers. A believer and nonbeliever under the present law are treated differently because of the articles of their faith. Believers are doubtless comforted that the cause of religion is being fostered by this legislation. Yet one of the mandates of the First Amendment is to promote a viable, pluralistic society and to keep government neutral, not only between sects, but also between believers and nonbelievers. The present involvement of government in religion may seem *de minimis*. But it is, I fear, a long step down the Establishment path. Perhaps I have been misinformed. But as I have read the Constitution and its philosophy, I gathered that independence was the price of liberty.

I conclude that this tax exemption is unconstitutional.

CHAPTER FOURTEEN

THE CONSTITUTION AND CRIMINAL JUSTICE

We could, of course, facilitate the process of administering justice to those who violate criminal laws by ignoring . . . the entire Bill of Rights—but it is the very purpose of the Bill of Rights to identify values that may not be sacrificed to expediency. In a just society those who govern, as well as those who are governed, must obey the law.

Justice John P. Stevens, dissenting in *United States v. Leon* (1984)

INTRODUCTION

Protecting citizens against crime is one of the fundamental obligations of any government. In the United States, of course, government must perform the function of crime control while respecting the constitutional rights of individuals. Balancing the public interest in crime control against the values of individual liberty and privacy is, without question, the most common problem facing trial and appellate courts today. Many of the nation's courts, especially in major metropolitan areas, are flooded with criminal cases, many of which raise vexing questions of constitutional law. This chapter examines the development of constitutional standards in this extremely important area of the law.

Relevant Constitutional Provisions

The most obvious source of constitutional protection for persons suspected, accused or convicted of crimes is the Bill of Rights. Numerous provisions of the Bill of Rights bear directly on the administration of criminal justice in the United States (see Table 14.1). Several restrictions in the original Constitution, together with guarantees in the Fourth, Fifth, Sixth, and Eighth Amendments, were designed to prevent government from subjecting individuals to arbitrary arrest, prosecution, and punishment. Both the national government and the states are prohibited from enacting **ex post facto laws** and **bills of attainder** (Article I, Sections 9 and 10). By contrast, the **habeas corpus** guarantee (Article I, Section 9) applies only to the national government, leaving the preservation of this right in state jurisdictions up to the states themselves. Most provisions of the Bill of Rights, including those pertaining to criminal justice, have been incorporated

815

into the Due Process Clause of the Fourteenth Amendment, thereby making them applicable to the states as well as the national government. (For a discussion of *ex post facto* laws, bills of attainder, habeas corpus, and "selective incorporation" of the Bill of Rights, see Chapter 9).

SEARCH AND SEIZURE

The Fourth Amendment recognizes a right of personal privacy entitling the American people to protection against arbitrary intrusions by law enforcement officers. The Framers of the Bill of Rights were acutely sensitive to the need to insulate people from unlimited governmental powers of search and seizure. One of the chief complaints of the American colonists was the power of police and customs officials to conduct "general" searches under the dreaded Writs of Assistance authorized by Parliament in 1662. In 1761, James Otis reviled the Writs of Assistance as "the worst instrument of arbitrary power, the most destructive of English liberty and the fundamental principles of law, that was ever found in an English law book" (quoted in *Boyd v. United States* [1886]).

When the First Congress considered the Bill of Rights, most state constitutions already contained limitations on government powers in this area. Thus, there was little objection in Congress to the search and seizure amendment contained in James Madison's proposal for a Bill of Rights. After minor changes in language, the Fourth Amendment was adopted:

> The right of the people to be secure in their persons, houses, papers and effects, against unreasonable searches and seizures, shall not be violated, and no warrants shall issue, but upon probable cause, supported by Oath or Affirmation, and particularly describing the place to be searched, and the persons or things to be seized.

TABLE 14.1 Key Provisions of the Bill of Rights Affecting Criminal Justice

Amendment	Provision
IV	Prohibits unreasonable searches and seizures
V	Requires grand jury in serious criminal cases
	Prohibits double jeopardy
	Protects against compulsory self-incrimination
	Requires due process of law in criminal cases
VI	Grants defendant a speedy and public trial
	Guarantees an impartial jury
	Requires that defendants be notified of charges
	Permits defendants to confront hostile witnesses
	Allows defendants to compel testimony of favorable witnesses
	Provides right to counsel in criminal cases
VIII	Prohibits excessive bail
	Proscribes excessive fines
	Bars infliction of "cruel and unusual punishments"

Like many of the broad provisions of the Constitution, the Fourth Amendment raises as many questions as it answers. It is clear that government cannot subject people to unreasonable searches and seizures, but what is meant by "unreasonable"? What exactly is a search? What is the precise meaning of "probable cause"? In our legal system, these are questions for the Supreme Court to answer. Unfortunately for the student, the police on the street, the criminal suspect, and the ordinary, law-abiding citizen, these answers can be very complicated and confusing.

"Reasonable Expectations of Privacy"

One of the most difficult problems in applying the eighteenth-century language of the Fourth Amendment to modern conditions is determining the scope of the privacy to be protected. Obviously, the Amendment prohibits unreasonable searches of one's dwelling. But what about the search of an individual's automobile, motorhome, or boat? What about one's telephone conversations, fax transmissions, or electronic mail? Are such communications protected by the Fourth Amendment?

In *Olmstead v. United States* (1928), the Supreme court took a very strict view of the scope of the Fourth Amendment. Roy Olmstead, a suspected bootlegger, was charged with conspiracy to violate the National Prohibition Act. The government's evidence consisted of transcripts of Olmstead's telephone conversations obtained through a wiretap placed outside his property. The agents had obtained no warrant authorizing the wiretap. Although there was no search or seizure of his person or physical property, Olmstead maintained that the Fourth Amendment had been violated. The term "effects," as used in the Fourth Amendment, could have been interpreted to include telephone conversations, but the Court opted for a narrower construction. Writing for the majority, Chief Justice William Howard Taft stated:

> The reasonable view is that one who installs in his house a telephone instrument with connecting wires intends to project his voice to those quite outside, and that the wires beyond his house, and messages passing over them, are not within the protection of the Fourth Amendment.

Justice Louis Brandeis, along with three of his colleagues, dissented. In one of his most forward-looking opinions, he asserted the need to keep the Constitution relevant to changing technological conditions:

> The progress of science in furnishing the government with means of espionage is not likely to stop with wiretapping. Ways may some day be developed by which the government, without removing papers from secret drawers, can reproduce them in court, and by which it will be enabled to expose to a jury the most intimate occurrences of the home. . . . Can it be that the Constitution affords no protection against such invasions of individual security?

In 1928, the telephone was in fairly wide use; today, it is virtually omnipresent. Perhaps it was this reality that motivated the Supreme Court in 1967 to overturn *Olmstead* in the landmark decision of *Katz v. United States.* Here, the

Court reversed a conviction in which government agents, acting without a warrant, attached a "bug," or listening device, to the outside of a public telephone booth from which Charles Katz, a suspected bookie, often placed calls. Writing for the Court, Justice Potter Stewart stated that "the Fourth Amendment protects people—not places."

Adhering to Justice John M. Harlan's concurrence in *Katz,* the Supreme Court has since held that the Fourth Amendment extends to any place or any thing in which an individual has a **reasonable expectation of privacy.** The Court has demonstrated a willingness to consider hotel rooms, garages, offices, automobiles, sealed letters, suitcases, and other closed containers as protected by the Fourth Amendment. On the other hand, the Court has held that there is no Fourth Amendment protection for abandoned or discarded property or for "open fields" (see *Oliver v. United States* [1984]).

Probable Cause

The fundamental requirement imposed on government by the Fourth Amendment is that searches and seizures must be based on **probable cause.** Probable cause is a term of art, without precise meaning. The Supreme Court has observed that "probable cause is fluid concept—turning on the assessment of probabilities in particular factual contexts—not readily, or even usefully, reduced to a neat set of legal rules" (*Illinois v. Gates* [1983]). As interpreted by the Court, probable cause means in effect that for a search to be valid, a police officer must have good reason to believe that it will produce evidence of crime. According to the Court's decision in *Brinegar v. United States* (1949), officers have probable cause when

> the facts and circumstances within their knowledge, and of which they had reasonably trustworthy information, [are] sufficient in themselves to warrant a man of reasonable caution in the belief that an offense has been or is being committed.

The Warrant Requirement

To help ensure that probable cause does exist before police undertake to search private premises, the Fourth Amendment imposes a warrant requirement. A **search warrant** is simply an order issued by a judge or magistrate that authorizes a search. To obtain a search warrant, a law enforcement officer must take an oath or sign an **affidavit** attesting to certain facts that, if true, constitute probable cause to support the issuance of a warrant.

In *Coolidge v. New Hampshire* (1971), the Supreme Court invalidated a warrant that was issued by the state's attorney general, rather than a judicial officer. Thus, the Court places great importance on the role of the "neutral and detached magistrate" in maintaining the integrity of the Fourth Amendment. This amendment also requires that search warrants describe with particularity "the place to be searched, and the persons or things to be seized." This provision reflects the Framers' distaste for the general warrants used in colonial America. In *Stanford v. Texas* (1965), the Supreme Court reaffirmed this long-standing distaste for "dragnet" searches when it invalidated a five-hour search of a Communist party headquarters resulting in the seizure of some five thousand items, including books by Justice Hugo Black and Pope John XXIII.

Confidential and Anonymous Informants

One of the most controversial questions concerning the issuance of search warrants involves the use of confidential or anonymous informants. Police often use tips provided by confidential informants to obtain search warrants that lead to the discovery of incriminating evidence. In *Aguilar v. Texas* (1963), police obtained a warrant simply by swearing that they "had received reliable information from a credible person" that illegal drugs would be found at a certain location. The Supreme Court ultimately invalidated the warrant, holding that an affidavit must inform the magistrate of

> the underlying circumstances from which the informant concluded that the narcotics were where he claimed they were, and some of the underlying circumstances from which the officer concluded that the informant, whose identity need not be disclosed, . . . was "credible" or his information "reliable."

Five years later, the Court reaffirmed this two-pronged test in the case of *Spinelli v. United States* (1969). The so-called *Aguilar–Spinelli* test made it more difficult for police to obtain warrants based on tips from confidential informants. Accordingly, on this issue, as on several others, the Warren Court was much criticized for "handcuffing the police." In 1983, a more conservative Supreme Court under Chief Justice Warren E. Burger abandoned the rigorous *Aguilar-Spinelli* test in favor of a **totality of circumstances** approach that makes it easier for police to get search warrants. In *Illinois v. Gates,* Justice William Rehnquist asserted that the *Aguilar-Spinelli* test could not "avoid seriously impeding the task of law enforcement" because "anonymous tips seldom could survive a rigorous application of either of the *Spinelli* prongs." Dissenting, Justice William Brennan argued that

> the Court [gave] virtually no consideration to the value of insuring that findings of probable cause are based on information that a magistrate can reasonably say has been obtained in a reliable way by an honest or credible person. I . . . fear that the Court's rejection of *Aguilar* and *Spinelli* . . . "may foretell an evisceration of the probable cause standard."

In recent years, the Supreme Court has moved beyond *Gates* and manifested an even greater level of permissiveness toward police reliance on anonymous tips (see, for example, *Alabama v. White* [1990]). Critics of these decisions argue that the Court's interest in facilitating law enforcement is eclipsing its traditional concern for the privacy of citizens subjected to police searches.

Warrantless Searches

Although the Fourth Amendment clearly indicates a preference for search warrants, the Supreme Court has held that, under **exigent circumstances,** a warrantless search may nevertheless be "reasonable." One example of a legitimate warrantless search is that which is incidental to a lawful arrest. In *Chimel v. California* (1969), Justice Stewart's majority opinion stated:

> When an arrest is made, it is reasonable for the arresting officer to search the person arrested in order to remove any weapons that the latter might seek to use in order to resist arrest or effect his escape.... In addition, it is entirely reasonable for the arresting officer to search for and seize any evidence on the arrestee's person in order to prevent its concealment or destruction.

An obvious example of a legitimate warrantless search is one based on the consent of the individual whose privacy is to be invaded. It is an elementary principle of law that individuals may waive their constitutional rights; Fourth Amendment protections are no exception. In *Schneckloth v. Bustamonte* (1973), the Supreme Court upheld a search based on consent even though the police failed to advise the individual that he was not obligated to consent to the police request. Nevertheless, the burden of proof rests on the prosecution to show that no coercion was used to obtain consent. To determine whether consent was given voluntarily, and knowingly, the Court looks to the totality of circumstances surrounding the search. In *Florida v. Bostick,* a highly publicized 1991 decision, the Court upheld the controversial police practice of boarding interstate buses in big-city terminals, approaching persons matching a **drug courier profile,** and asking them for permission to search their belongings.

Other accepted justifications for warrantless searches include **plain view** (see *Coolidge v. New Hampshire* [1971]), **hot pursuit** (see *Warden v. Hayden* [1967]), **evanescent evidence** (see *Schmerber v. California* [1966]), and **emergency searches** (see *Michigan v. Tyler* [1978]). In each of these examples, compelling exigencies make the warrant requirement itself unreasonable, at least in the view of the nation's highest court.

Automobile Searches

One of the most interesting, and most problematic, exceptions to the warrant requirement is the automobile search. In *Carroll v. United States* (1925), the Supreme Court upheld the warrantless search of an automobile believed to be carrying illegal liquor. The Court stressed, however, that probable cause was essential to justify a warrantless automobile search. Indiscriminately stopping and searching passing motorists in an effort to discover evidence of crime could never be constitutionally justified.

The case of *Arkansas v. Sanders* (1979) presented the Court with an interesting question. Can warrantless searches of automobiles extend to all the contents of said vehicles, or do police still need a warrant to search luggage taken from the trunk? In *Sanders,* the Court disallowed the search of the luggage, suggesting to some observers that the automobile exception was "in trouble." However, in *United States v. Ross* (1982), the Supreme Court demonstrated otherwise. In a 6-to-3 decision, the Court upheld a warrantless search of a paper bag and a leather pouch found in the locked trunk of a stopped automobile, a search that produced thirty-two hundred dollars in cash and a sizable quantity of heroin. Writing for the Court, Justice John Paul Stevens clarified the legitimate scope of a warrantless automobile search as that "no greater than a magistrate could have authorized by issuing a warrant based on the probable cause that justified the search." Dissenting vehemently, Justice Thurgood Marshall assailed the majority position as "flatly inconsistent ... with established Fourth Amendment principles...." In 1991, the Court went one step further and formally overruled *Arkansas v. Sanders* (see *California v. Acevedo*), removing any lingering doubts about judicial distinctions between searches of automobiles and closed containers found therein.

"Stop and Frisk"

One of the most controversial forms of police search is the so-called **stop and frisk.** This type of limited search occurs when police confront suspicious persons in an effort to prevent a crime from taking place. The seminal case in this area is *Terry v. Ohio* (1968). Here, an experienced plainclothes officer observed three men acting suspiciously. The officer concluded that they were preparing to rob a nearby store and approached them. He identified himself as a police officer and asked for their names. Unsatisfied with their mumbled responses, he then subjected one of the trio to a "pat-down" search, which produced a gun for which the individual had no permit. In this instance, the police officer had no warrant; indeed, he did not have probable cause in its traditional sense. The Court nevertheless allowed the pat-down search on the basis of **reasonable suspicion.** The Court attempted, however, to limit the scope of the stop and frisk:

> The sole justification of the search ... is the protection of the police officer and others nearby, and it therefore must be confined in scope to an intrusion reasonably designed to discover guns, knives, clubs or other hidden instruments for the assault of the police officer.

Of course, if police discover contraband or other evidence of crime in the process of performing the pat-down for weapons, such evidence is admissible under a theory analogous to the plain view doctrine.

Investigatory Detention

The type of police encounter upheld in *Terry v. Ohio* and numerous subsequent court decisions has come to be known as **investigatory detention** or the "*Terry* stop." Police may stop and question suspicious persons, pat them down for weapons, and even subject them to nonintrusive search procedures, such as the use of metal detectors and drug-sniffing dogs. While a suspect is being detained, a computer search can be performed to determine if the suspect is wanted for crimes in other jurisdictions. If so, then he or she may be arrested and a search conducted incident to that arrest.

Investigatory detention has become extremely important in the highly publicized "war on drugs," as police officers have been given the power to detain, question, and investigate suspected drug couriers. In *United States v. Sokolow*

(1989), the Supreme Court upheld a search and seizure that stemmed from a *Terry* stop conducted at an international airport. The defendant in the case aroused the suspicions of federal Drug Enforcement Administration (DEA) agents by conforming to a controversial "drug courier profile" developed by the DEA.

United States v. Sokolow is consistent with a host of judicial decisions affording law enforcement officers wide latitude to investigate and detain suspected drug smugglers at international airports. In one widely publicized case, such a suspect was held for sixteen hours while airport security officers obtained a court order permitting a rectal examination of the suspect. During the exam, officers retrieved a plastic balloon filled with cocaine and placed the suspect under arrest. Over the next few days, the suspect passed eighty-eight similar balloons! The Supreme Court upheld the long detention, even though security personnel lacked probable cause to make the initial stop. As in *Terry v. Ohio*, the Court found that there was reasonable suspicion to justify the original detention (*United States v. Montoya de Hernandez* [1985]).

Detention of an Automobile Based on an Anonymous Tip

The Supreme Court has become increasingly permissive as to what constitutes "reasonable suspicion" for purposes of investigatory detention. For example, in *Alabama v. White* (1990), the Court upheld a *Terry* stop of an automobile based solely on an anonymous tip that described a certain car that would be at a specific location. Police went to the location, located the vehicle, and detained the driver, Vanessa White. The encounter led ultimately to the discovery of marijuana and cocaine in the automobile. Writing for the Court, Justice Byron White noted that "[a]lthough it is a close case, we conclude that under the totality of the circumstances, the anonymous tip, as corroborated, exhibited sufficient indicia of reliability to justify the investigatory stop of respondent's car." In a dissenting opinion joined by Justices Brennan and Marshall, Justice Stevens wrote:

> Anybody with enough knowledge about a given person to make her the target of a prank, or to harbor a grudge against her, will certainly be able to formulate a tip about her like the one predicting Vanessa White's excursion. In addition, under the Court's holding, every citizen is subject to being seized and questioned by any officer who is prepared to testify that the warrantless stop was based on an anonymous tip predicting whatever conduct the officer had just observed.

The Court's willingness to permit the stop and detention in *Alabama v. White* stands in sharp contrast to the Warren Court's carefully drawn stop and frisk policy delineated in *Terry v. Ohio*.

Drug Testing

No treatment of permissible search and seizure would be complete without at least some discussion of the emerging constitutional problem of drug testing. Does the Fourth Amendment permit government agencies to administer drug

John Paul Stevens:
Associate Justice, 1975–

tests to their employees? In *National Treasury Employees Union v. Von Raab* (1989), the Supreme Court upheld a drug testing program adopted by the U.S. Customs Service. The program was limited, however, to personnel seeking positions as customs inspectors, who have a large role to play in the interdiction of illegal drugs. Persons who failed the drug tests were denied positions but were not subjected to criminal investigation. On the same day that it decided *Von Raab,* the Court handed down a ruling in *Skinner v. Railway Labor Executives Association.* Here, the Court upheld federal regulations that required drug and alcohol testing of railroad employees involved in serious train accidents. It remains to be seen whether the Rehnquist Court will approve broader and more consequential drug-testing measures without imposing a probable cause or reasonable suspicion requirement. But the seriousness of the drug epidemic and society's warlike response to it is likely to create considerable pressure for the courts to accommodate such policies.

ARREST

An **arrest** entails the deprivation of one's liberty by a law enforcement officer or other person with legal authority. Normally, an arrest occurs when one suspected of having committed a crime is taken into custody by a police officer. Since an arrest is, in effect, a "seizure," it must conform to the probable cause and warrant requirements of the Fourth Amendment. In *Ker v. California* (1963), the Supreme Court held that the legality of arrests by state and local officers should be determined by the same standards applicable to federal law enforcement officials.

Use of Force by Police in Making Arrests

Since suspects often resist arrest, police on occasion must use force to take a person into custody. The courts have generally recognized that the Fourth Amendment permits police to use only such force as is "reasonable" and "necessary" in effectuating an arrest. In *Tennessee v. Garner* (1985), the Supreme Court held that police officers may use *deadly* force only when necessary to apprehend a fleeing felon and only when "the officer has probable cause to believe that the suspect poses a significant threat of death or physical injury to the officer or others." While most police officers take care to exercise force responsibly, police have committed acts of brutality in numerous instances. In such cases, police officers are subject not only to internal departmental sanctions but also to civil suit and even criminal prosecution under applicable state and federal statutes.

The Rodney King Episode

The issue of police brutality took on tremendous political significance in early May 1992, when a riot erupted in Los Angeles after a jury acquitted several Los Angeles police officers of charges stemming from the beating of African-American motorist Rodney King, which was videotaped by an onlooker and televised nationally. The national outrage in response to the acquittal led the Justice Department to bring charges against the officers under federal civil rights laws.

The Arrest Warrant

Arrests are often made pursuant to warrants based on preliminary investigations. An **arrest warrant,** like a search warrant, is issued by a judge or magistrate upon a showing of probable cause. Under some circumstances, however, warrantless arrests are permissible. The most common of these is where police observe someone committing a crime or have direct knowledge of criminal activity. Whether or not it is made pursuant to a warrant, an arrest must be based on probable cause.

The Probable Cause Hearing

As the warrant requirement of the Fourth Amendment implies, the legality of detention after arrest also depends on the existence of probable cause. It follows logically that a person arrested *without* a warrant must be brought *promptly* before a judicial officer for a probable cause determination. This principle had in fact emerged in English common law by the late seventeenth century, long before ratification of the Fourth Amendment in 1791. It was not until 1975 that the Supreme Court, in *Gerstein v. Pugh,* explicitly recognized the **probable cause hearing** as a Fourth Amendment requirement in cases of warrantless arrest. This decision, however, did not specify the maximum time that a person could be held in custody prior to a probable cause determination. In *County of Riverside v. McLaughlin* (1991), the Rehnquist Court adopted a permissive interpretation of the probable cause hearing requirement. In this controversial

5-to-4 decision, the majority, speaking through Justice Sandra Day O'Connor, held that an individual could be detained for as long as forty-eight hours prior to a probable cause hearing without necessarily violating the Fourth Amendment.

In the *McLaughlin* case, the Court balanced Fourth Amendment rights against state interests in administrative convenience and local autonomy. In a sharply worded dissent, Justice Antonin Scalia, generally favorable to law enforcement claims, criticized the majority for going far beyond the Court's prevailing concern that criminals not go unpunished. He argued that the Court had improperly applied the *Gerstein* precedent, repudiating one of the "core applications" of the Fourth Amendment "so that the presumptively innocent may be left in jail." By definition, the failure to find probable cause points to the innocence of the arrestee. According to the many critics of the *McLaughlin* decision, the majority lost sight of this consideration in its apparent zeal to accommodate the practical demands of law enforcement.

THE FOURTH AMENDMENT EXCLUSIONARY RULE

In addition to the difficult questions involving police methods of obtaining incriminating evidence is the controversial issue of how violations of the Fourth Amendment are to be remedied and deterred. As far back as 1886, in *Boyd v. United States,* the Supreme Court suggested that evidence obtained in violation of the Fourth Amendment should be excluded from trial. In *Weeks v. United States,* (1914) the Court made this dictum a formal requirement of criminal procedure in federal courts. Justice William R. Day's opinion for the Court suggested that exclusion of tainted evidence was implicit in the requirements of the Fourth Amendment:

> If letters and private documents can thus be [illegally] seized and held and used in evidence against a citizen accused of an offense, the protection of the 4th Amendment ... is of no value ... and might as well be stricken from the Constitution.

It was not until *Mapp v. Ohio* (1961) that the Court extended the **exclusionary rule,** as it is called, to state criminal prosecutions by way of the Fourteenth Amendment. The *Mapp* decision was certainly one of the Warren Court's major contributions to the law of criminal procedure, and accordingly, it remains a very controversial holding. Those who believe the exclusionary rule is merely a judicially created rule of evidence have criticized the Supreme Court for extending its supervisory power to the state courts. On the other hand, if the exclusionary rule is implicit in the Fourth Amendment and if the Fourth Amendment is made applicable to the states through the Fourteenth Amendment, then it follows that the exclusionary rule must be respected in state criminal prosecutions.

The Supreme Court under Chief Justice Burger substantially curtailed the application of the exclusionary rule. In *United States v. Calandra* (1974), the Burger Court made its philosophy quite clear:

> [T]he rule is a judicially created remedy designed to safeguard Fourth Amendment Rights generally through its deterrent effect, rather than a personal constitutional right of the party aggrieved.

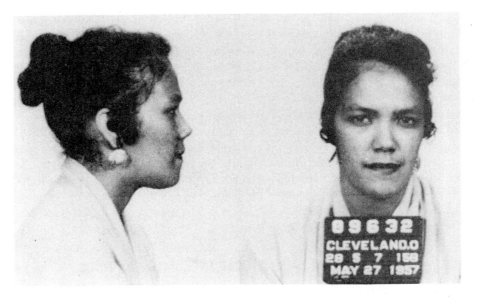

Dollree Mapp

The Court's current approach to cases involving the exclusionary rule is to weigh the perceived costs of its application against the potential benefits of deterring police misconduct. Using this approach, the Court has refused to extend the exclusionary rule to grand jury proceedings (*United States v. Calandra* [1974]) and to federal civil proceedings where evidence was obtained unlawfully by state agents (*United States v. Janis* [1976]). A majority on the current Supreme Court evidently agree with Chief Justice Burger's assessment (dissenting in *Bivens v. Six Unknown Named Federal Narcotics Agents* [1971]) of the social costs of suppressing otherwise valid evidence:

> Some clear demonstration of the benefits and effectiveness of the exclusionary rule is required to justify it in view of the high price it extracts from society—the release of countless guilty criminals.... But there is no empirical evidence to support the claim that the rule actually deters illegal conduct of law enforcement officials.

The Good-Faith Exception

Without question, the most important Burger Court decisions on the exclusionary rule were the companion cases of *United States v. Leon* and *Massachusetts v. Sheppard* (1984). In these cases, the Court adopted a limited **good-faith exception** to the exclusionary rule where officers seize evidence in good faith, relying on search warrants later held to be defective. In *Leon,* police officers obtained a search warrant acting on a tip from a confidential informant of unproven reliability. A subsequent search of a residence turned up a substantial amount of illegal drugs. At an evidentiary hearing prior to trial, a judge ruled that the warrant had been wrongly issued, that there was insufficient information to constitute probable cause. The Supreme Court ultimately held that the evidence could nevertheless be admitted against the defendants, because to exclude such evidence would have no deterrent effect on police misconduct. The error was made by the magistrate who issued the warrant, not by the police who were deemed to be acting in good faith. In like manner, in *Massachusetts v. Sheppard,* the Court held that use of the wrong warrant form as authorization for a search in a murder investigation did not render the seized evidence inadmissible. Dissenting in the *Leon* case, Justice Brennan exploded:

> The Court seeks to justify this result on the ground that the "costs" of adhering to the exclusionary rule ... exceed the "benefits." But ... it is clear that we have not been treated to an honest assessment of the merits of the exclusionary rule but have instead been drawn into a curious world where the "costs" of excluding illegally obtained evidence loom to exaggerated heights and where the "benefits" of such exclusion are made to disappear with a mere wave of the hand.

It is clear that the intense intra-Court conflict in *Leon* and *Sheppard* stems from basic differences of opinion as to the constitutional foundations of the exclusionary rule. If one agrees with Justice Brennan that suppression of illegally obtained evidence is a personal right under the Fourth Amendment, then clearly the exclusionary rule cannot be sacrificed on the altar of cost-benefit analysis. On the other hand, if the rule is nothing more than a judicially created rule of evidence or procedure designed to deter future police misconduct, then the Court is free to apply or dispense with the rule depending on its perceived utility.

The controversy over the exclusionary rule is far from over. It remains to be seen whether the Rehnquist Court will extend the good-faith exception to warrantless searches involving unintended violations of constitutionally protected privacy. A step in that direction was taken in *Illinois v. Krull* (1987), where the Rehnquist Court extended the good-faith exception to warrantless searches authorized under a statute that was later declared unconstitutional. The statute that permitted the police to perform searches without warrants was analogized to the magistrate's erroneous issuance of a search warrant in the *Leon* case. Among the provisions in President George Bush's "crime package" proposed to Congress as recently as January 1992 was a measure calling for a good-faith exception for warrantless searches by federal agents.

Civil Suits to Enforce the Fourth Amendment

During the 1985 term, the Court handed down a decision that revived a long-disputed alternative to the exclusionary rule. In *Malley v. Briggs* (1986), the Court allowed civil suits under 42 U.S. Code Section 1983 against police officers who "knowingly violate the law" or act in a fashion that "no reasonably competent officer" would consider to be legal in conducting arrests, searches, and seizures. In the *Malley* case, a Rhode Island state trooper obtained a warrant for the arrest of a prominent couple who were charged with "conspiring to possess marijuana." The warrant was based on a suggestion overheard by police wire-tappers that the couple had hosted a marijuana party some three months earlier. The couple was taken into custody, but no physical evidence of any crime was discovered. Consequently, the grand jury refused to hand down an indictment. Not satisfied with this after-the-fact vindication, the couple filed a civil suit for damages against the police officer. The federal district court dismissed the case, holding that a police officer could not be held liable for actions based on a warrant issued by a magistrate. Ultimately, however, the Supreme Court disagreed, underscoring its previous recognition of civil suits as means of enforcing Fourth Amendment rights.

The civil remedy was advanced as an alternative to the exclusionary rule by Justice Felix Frankfurter in the 1949 case of *Wolf v. Colorado.* In a strongly worded dissenting opinion in *Wolf,* Justice Frank Murphy cast grave doubt on the viability of the civil remedy as a realistic alternative. The Warren Court, as reflected in its decisions on the exclusionary rule, apparently agreed with Murphy's assessment. But the civil liability approach was resurrected by Chief Justice Burger in his dissent in the *Bivens* case. Finally, in *Malley,* a majority of the Court found occasion to apply the civil remedy in the context of an outrageous Fourth Amendment violation.

POLICE INTERROGATION AND CONFESSIONS OF GUILT

Another of the Warren Court's controversial contributions to the criminal process was its enlargement of protection for criminal suspects subjected to police interrogation. Clearly, police must have the authority to question suspects in order to solve crimes. But the Supreme Court held as far back as 1897 (*Bram v. United States*) that a coerced confession violates the Self-Incrimination Clause of the Fifth Amendment. Of course, the Self-Incrimination Clause was not incorporated into the Fourteenth Amendment until well into the 1960s. Prior to incorporation, the Court's scrutiny of police interrogation in the states was limited to a broad due process inquiry that examined the "totality of circumstances" in each case with one eye on the fairness of the defendant's trial and the other on methods of police interrogation.

The traditional test used by the Court was whether a challenged confession could reasonably be deemed to have been voluntary. Subjective voluntariness, however, is extremely difficult to discern, even through direct observation, let alone through appellate hindsight years later. Consequently, the Supreme Court's decisions in this area were often unclear and inconsistent. For example, in the 1944 case of *Ashcraft v. Tennessee,* the Court overturned a murder conviction on grounds that the defendant's alleged confession was coerced because it had been preceded by a thirty-six-hour period of continuous police interrogation. Writing for a six-member majority, Justice Black made no attempt to weigh the effect of this long and intense period of questioning on the suspect. Black simply concluded that thirty-six hours of questioning was "inherently coercive" and that use of the confession violated the Due Process Clause of the Fourteenth Amendment. Justice Robert H. Jackson dissented sharply, pointing out that coerciveness could not be measured simply by reference to the clock. Just over a month later, in *Lyons v. Oklahoma* (1944), the Court, dividing 5 to 4, held to be "voluntary" a confession repeated some twelve hours after the suspect, during incommunicado detention in the dead of night, had been forced to hold in his lap a pan containing the charred bones of his alleged murder victims.

By the 1960s, many believed that another approach to the law governing police interrogation was necessary. The Court's decision in *Malloy v. Hogan* (1964) to incorporate the Self-Incrimination Clause paved the way for a stricter attitude toward interrogation by state law enforcement personnel. A sharp break with the "voluntariness" approach came in 1964 when the Supreme Court decided *Escobedo v. Illinois*. Here, the Court held that once a police interrogation

> has begun to focus on a particular suspect, the suspect has been taken into custody, the police carry out a process of interrogations that lends itself to incriminating statements, the suspect has requested and been denied an opportunity to consult with his lawyer, and the police have not effectively warned him of his absolute constitutional right to remain silent . . . no statement elicited by the police during the interrogation may be used against him during the criminal trial.

In effect, *Escobedo* adopted an exclusionary rule similar to that of *Mapp v. Ohio* but applied to enforce Fifth and Sixth Amendment rights. Two years later, in *Miranda v. Arizona* (1966), the Court elaborated on the need for constitutional safeguards to protect citizens from "inherently coercive" police interrogation.

> It is obvious that such an interrogation environment is created for no purpose other than to subjugate the individual to the will of his examiner. This atmosphere carries its own badge of intimidation. To be sure this is not physical intimidation, but is equally destructive to human dignity. The current practice of incommunicado interrogation is at odds with one of our Nation's most cherished principles— that the individual may not be compelled to incriminate himself.

The Miranda Warnings

To safeguard the immunity against self-incrimination, the Court developed the well-known **Miranda warnings**. Unless police inform suspects of their rights to remain silent and have an attorney present during questioning and unless police obtain voluntary waivers of these rights, suspects' confessions and other statements are inadmissible at trial. When the *Miranda* decision came down in 1966, the Court was harshly criticized, especially by the law enforcement community, for "coddling criminals" and "hamstringing the police." However, the practice of "Mirandizing" suspects soon became standard operating procedure in law enforcement. Today, many in law enforcement support the *Miranda* decision as a means of professionalizing police conduct and, perhaps more importantly, protecting legitimate confessions from later challenges. As long as the police provide suspects with the warning and avoid coercion, anything said by the suspect can be used against him or her in a court of law. Whereas, prior to *Miranda*, there was something of a presumption against the admissibility of a confession, today the presumption is clearly in favor of admitting confessions as evidence, as long as the requirements of *Miranda* have been observed by the police.

Although the Supreme Court has reaffirmed the *Miranda* decision, it has substantially narrowed the scope of its requirements. For example, in *Harris v.*

New York (1971), the Court ruled that confessions excluded from trial under *Miranda* could nevertheless be used to impeach the credibility of a defendant who takes the stand to testify in his or her own behalf. Writing for the Court, Chief Justice Burger pointed out that

> [e]very criminal defendant is privileged to testify in his own defense, or to refuse to do so. But that privilege cannot be construed to include the right to commit perjury.

The "Public Safety Exception" to *Miranda*

In 1984, the Supreme Court created the public safety exception to the requirement that *Miranda* warnings be given before any questioning of the suspect takes place. In *New York v. Quarles,* the Court examined an interesting factual situation. Two New York City police officers were approached by a woman who claimed she had just been raped and that her assailant had gone into a nearby grocery store. The police were informed that the assailant was carrying a gun. The officers proceeded to the store and immediately spotted Benjamin Quarles, who matched the description given by the victim. Upon seeing the police, Quarles turned and ran. One of the police officers drew his service revolver and ordered Quarles to freeze. Quarles complied with the officer's request. The officer frisked Quarles and discovered an empty shoulder holster. Before reading Quarles the *Miranda* warnings, the officer asked where the gun was. Quarles nodded in the direction of some empty boxes and said, "The gun is over there." He was then placed under arrest and given the *Miranda* warnings. Later, Quarles moved to have his statement suppressed from evidence since it was made prior to the *Miranda* warnings. He also moved for suppression of the gun under the **fruit of the poisonous tree** doctrine (see *Wong Sun v. United States* [1963]). The Supreme Court allowed both pieces of evidence to be used against Quarles, notwithstanding the delay in the *Miranda* warnings. Obviously, the Court felt that the officers were justified in locating a discarded weapon prior to Mirandizing Quarles. In so holding, the Court created the **public safety exception.**

> We conclude that the need for answers to questions in a situation posing a threat to the public safety outweighs the need for the prophylactic rule protecting the . . . privilege against self-incrimination.

The Inevitable Discovery Exception

Another exception to the *Miranda* exclusionary rule is based on inevitable discovery of physical evidence that is challenged as the "fruit of the poisonous tree." In a macabre case decided in 1984 (*Nix v. Williams*), the Court allowed evidence to be admitted even though it was obtained through the statement of a suspect who had indicated his desire to remain silent until he could meet with his attorney. After one of the police officers involved made a speech emphasizing the need for a "Christian burial" for the victim, the suspect led police to the body of a young girl he had kidnapped and murdered. In allowing the body to be used as evidence, the Court reasoned that the body was not the "fruit of a poisonous tree" since a search underway in the area would eventually have located the body anyway. Hence, the Court created an **inevitable discovery exception** to the exclusionary rule.

Police Deception

The Court has refused to expand the scope of custodial interrogation beyond an actual arrest or significant "deprivation of freedom." In *Oregon v. Mathiason* (1977), the Court allowed the use of a confession obtained by police during voluntary interrogation of a suspect who was not at the time under arrest. An interesting fact in the *Mathiason* case is that the police officer who obtained the confession lied to the suspect about his fingerprints being found at the scene of the crime. Only after this deception did Mathiason confess. Nevertheless, he was not under formal arrest at the time and had even come to the station house unescorted to talk to police. In the Court's view, this was a "noncustodial" situation; hence, *Miranda* did not apply.

In another controversial decision involving police deception, *Moran v. Burbine* (1986), the Court further delimited the scope of the *Miranda* rule. Police arrested Burbine for burglary and later obtained information that linked him to an unsolved murder. Burbine's sister, unaware of the possible murder charge, retained an attorney to represent her brother. The attorney telephoned the police, who assured her that Burbine was not to be questioned until the next day but failed to tell her of a possible murder charge against her client. Despite their assurances to the contrary, the police then interrogated Burbine, failing to tell him that an attorney had been obtained for him and had attempted to contact him. Burbine waived his rights to counsel and to remain silent and eventually confessed to the killing. The Supreme Court found no constitutional violation, holding that Burbine had knowingly, intelligently, and voluntarily waived his rights.

In one of the most significant recent decisions in this area, *Arizona v. Fulminante* (1991), the Supreme Court disallowed the use of a confession that was obtained by a prisoner who was also a confidential Federal Bureau of Investigation (FBI) informant. Oreste Fulminante, who was suspected of murdering his eleven-year-old step-daughter Jeneane, was incarcerated in federal prison on an unrelated charge. He was befriended by Anthony Sarivola, a former police officer serving time for extortion. Sarivola led Fulminante to believe that he had organized-crime connections and could protect Fulminante from other prisoners who had heard that Fulminante was suspected of killing his step-daughter. Sarivola insisted, however, that Fulminante tell him what really happened to his step-daughter. Fulminante then confided in Sarivola that he had indeed taken his step-daughter on his motorcycle into the desert where, in the words of Justice White, "he choked her, sexually assaulted her, and made her beg for her life, before shooting her twice in the head." Sarivola gave this information to the FBI, which, in turn, passed it along to Arizona authorities. After being released from prison, Fulminante was indicted for the murder of his step-daughter. Denying his motion to suppress, the Arizona trial court allowed the confession to be introduced and subsequently found Fulminante guilty of first-degree murder. In reviewing this conviction, the Supreme Court found that

Fulminante's confession had been coerced. However, the most significant aspect of the Court's decision was its holding that a coerced confession is subject to **harmless error** analysis. Prior to this holding, a defendant was automatically entitled to reversal of his or her conviction if a coerced confession had been introduced into evidence at trial. Under the *Fulminante* decision, an appellate court is permitted to affirm a conviction if it determines that the defendant would have been convicted on other evidence even in the absence of the coerced confession. It should be noted that the Supreme Court found that the use of Fulminante's confession was not harmless error and therefore reversed his conviction. Irrespective of this result, the *Fulminante* decision has been criticized as a further erosion of the constitutional protection against coerced confessions.

THE RIGHT TO COUNSEL

Historically, the Sixth Amendment right to counsel in "all criminal prosecutions" meant no more than that the government could not prevent a person accused of a crime from hiring a lawyer if he or she could afford to do so. The Supreme Court moved significantly away from this traditional view in the celebrated Scottsboro case. Here, the Court reversed the convictions of a group of young African-American men who had been sentenced to death in an Alabama court for allegedly raping two white women. During the rushed investigation and trial, conducted in an atmosphere of extreme racial animosity, the defendants were

Some of the defendants who challenged their convictions in *Powell v. Alabama*

Clarence Earl Gideon

not represented by counsel in any meaningful sense. In *Powell v. Alabama* (1932), the Supreme Court found that the defendants had been denied due process of law in violation of the Fourteenth Amendment. Justice George Sutherland's majority opinion placed great importance on the failure of the trial judge to ensure effective representation and adequate time to prepare a defense.

The *Gideon* Decision

Under Chief Justice Earl Warren, the Supreme Court placed enormous stress on the need for professional representation of persons suspected or accused of crimes. In its *Escobedo* and *Miranda* decisions, for example, the Warren Court was obviously concerned about the absence of defense counsel during custodial police interrogation. In *Gideon v. Wainwright* (1963), the Court overruled precedent and held that the Sixth Amendment right to counsel as applied to the states via the Due Process Clause of the Fourteenth Amendment requires states to provide counsel to defendants who cannot afford to hire attorneys on their own. The *Gideon* Court recognized that

> in our adversary system of criminal justice, any person haled into court, who is too poor to hire a lawyer, cannot be assured a fair trial unless counsel is provided for him. This seems to us to be an obvious truth.

In a related case decided the same day as *Gideon* (*Douglas v. California* [1963]), the Court held that a state must provide counsel to an indigent defendant who has a right under state law to appeal a conviction to a higher court. (However, in *Pennsylvania v. Finley* [1987], the Court made clear what had been only implicit in *Douglas v. California,* namely that "the right to appointed counsel extends to the first appeal . . . and no further.")

Because *Gideon* was made retroactive, it had a tremendous impact on the criminal justice system. For example, in Florida, where the *Gideon* case originated, the state was required to retry hundreds of convicted felons who had not been represented by counsel at their first trials. In many cases, the key witnesses were no longer available, and the state was forced to drop its charges. In the wake of *Gideon,* many states decided it would be more economical in the long run to set up permanent offices to handle indigent defense rather than to have judges appoint counsel ad hoc. Most states now have public defenders to make good on the state's responsibility under the Due Process Clause of the Fourteenth Amendment. Although many state judges, legislators, governors, and law enforcement officers resented the Court's "meddling" in their affairs, the *Gideon* decision has come, like so many other Supreme Court rulings, to be accepted and even praised by state officials.

For the most part, the Burger Court maintained this commitment to providing counsel to indigent defendants. In *Argersinger v. Hamlin* (1972), the Court extended the *Gideon* ruling to cover misdemeanor trials (*Gideon* applied only to felonies):

> We hold ... that absent a knowing and intelligent waiver, no person may be imprisoned for any offense, whether classified as petty, misdemeanor or felony, unless he was represented by counsel at his trial.

The *Argersinger* decision was ambiguous, however, on the issue of whether misdemeanor defendants were entitled to counsel if they faced *possible* jail terms or only if their convictions *actually resulted* in incarceration. In *Scott v. Illinois* (1979), the Supreme Court clarified the situation, holding that counsel had to be provided to indigent misdemeanants only if conviction would actually result in imprisonment. Writing for the Court, Justice Rehnquist thus opted for a narrow interpretation of *Argersinger,* arguing that "any extension would create confusion and impose unpredictable, but necessarily substantial costs on fifty quite diverse states."

Effectiveness of Appointed Counsel

One of the most elusive contemporary issues in the right to counsel area is that of effective representation. As the Court recognized in *Powell v. Alabama* (1932), the right to counsel is useless unless one is competently represented. Until recently, most federal courts followed the "mockery of justice" test in determining the competency of appointed counsel. The question was whether the attorney was so ineffective as to constitute "a farce or mockery of justice" (see for example, *Edwards v. United States* [1958]). This permissive standard was rapidly adopted by most of the state supreme courts. However, the federal circuit courts adopted different standards of varying strictness. In 1984, the Supreme Court finally standardized the test that courts must follow to comply with the Sixth Amendment. In *Strickland v. Washington,* the Court held that an indigent appellant must show (1) that his or her trial lawyer was less than reasonably effective and (2) that there is a reasonable probability that the outcome of the trial would have been different had counsel been more effective. Obviously, this is a difficult test to meet, allowing for reversal only in cases of egregious incompetence.

Self-Representation

Although decisions such as *Powell v. Alabama* and *Gideon v. Wainwright* stressed the importance of counsel in ensuring a fair trial, the Supreme Court has made it quite clear that a defendant has a constitutional right to refuse counsel, as long as the waiver is made "knowingly and intelligently." In *Faretta v. California* (1975), the Court decided a case in which Faretta, accused of grand theft, requested permission from the trial court to represent himself, arguing that the public defender's office was too busy to provide him with effective representation. The trial judge refused the request and appointed an assistant public defender to represent him. Faretta's conviction was ultimately vacated by the Supreme Court by a 6-to-3 vote. The majority asserted that

> [t]he language and spirit of the Sixth Amendment contemplate that counsel, like the other defense tools guaranteed by the Amendment, shall be an aid to a willing defendant—not an organ of the state interposed between an unwilling defendant and his right to defend himself personally.

Although the *Faretta* decision did not produce a rash of *pro se* defenses (those in which the defendant conducts his or her own defense), occasionally a defendant will "go it alone" in the courtroom. To such defendants, many lawyers would say that "anybody who chooses to represent himself has a fool for a client." An interesting question to ponder is whether one who chose to represent him- or herself at trial and was convicted could ever secure reversal on appeal by claiming that his or her lawyer was incompetent!

BAIL AND PRETRIAL DETENTION

Since persons accused of crime are presumed innocent until proven guilty, it is customary for defendants to be released from custody prior to **arraignment** and trial. Ordinarily, courts require defendants to post **bail** (a sum of money), which is forfeited if the defendant flees to escape prosecution. The Eighth Amendment prohibits "excessive bail." The Supreme Court has recognized that the purpose of bail is not to inflict punishment but to ensure that a defendant appears in court. In *Stack v. Boyle* (1951), the Court said that "[b]ail set at a figure higher than an amount reasonably calculated to fulfill this purpose is 'excessive' under the Eighth Amendment." However, the Court has never held that the Excessive Bail Clause is incorporated by the Fourteenth Amendment, leaving the issue of excessive bail in state criminal prosecutions to state constitutions, legislatures, and courts.

It has been a long-standing practice for courts to deny bail to defendants who are deemed especially dangerous or pose an unusual likelihood of fleeing to avoid prosecution. This raises the question of whether the Eighth Amendment implies a right to pretrial release. In *United States v. Salerno* (1987), the Supreme Court answered this question in the negative. Here, the Court upheld the Bail Reform Act of 1984, which permits pretrial detention in federal cases where a court determines that the release of a defendant would pose a serious threat to public safety. Writing for the Court, Chief Justice Rehnquist agreed that "a primary function of bail is to safeguard the courts' role in adjudicating the guilt or innocence of defendants" but rejected "the proposition that the Eighth Amendment categorically prohibits the government from pursuing other admittedly compelling interests through the regulation of pretrial release." In a vehement dissenting opinion, Justice Marshall observed that

> Throughout the world today there are men, women and children interned indefinitely, awaiting trials which may never come or which may be a mockery of the word, because their governments believe them to be "dangerous." Our Constitution . . . can shelter us forever from the evils of such unchecked power. . . . But it cannot protect us if we lack the courage, and the self-restraint, to protect ourselves. Today a majority of the Court applies itself to an ominous exercise in demolition. Theirs is truly a decision which will go forth without authority, and come back without respect.

The Court's decision in *Salerno,* while applying formally only to federal criminal cases, suggests the validity of state laws denying bail to persons accused of violent felonies, especially where such persons have a record of violent crimes. It is doubtful that the Supreme Court would approve a policy of long-term pretrial detention for defendants accused of nonviolent crimes.

PLEA BARGAINING

Most books dealing with the rights of the accused focus on problems associated with the criminal trial, such as jury selection, jury verdicts, the "public trial" controversy, and so on. It must be recognized, however, that only a small proportion of criminal cases ever gets to trial. In a typical jurisdiction, only about 5 percent of felony arrests result in trials. Many cases are dropped by the prosecution after key evidence has been suppressed on Fourth, Fifth, or Sixth Amendment grounds. Other cases must be dropped because key witnesses cannot be located or made to testify. But the main reason that criminal cases do not often result in trials is the existence of **plea bargaining**. Plea bargaining results in an agreement by the accused to plead guilty in exchange for some concession from the prosecution. This concession might be a reduction in the severity or number of the charges brought, or it might simply be a promise by the prosecutor not to seek the maximum sentence allowed by law.

Conventional wisdom holds that plea bargaining occurs because of the scarce resources allocated to the processing of criminal cases. The criminal trial can be a protracted process. There simply are not enough prosecutors, public defenders, and judges to try all the criminal cases coming into the system. Nor does the public or its elected representatives seem inclined to provide the necessary resources. Even if such resources were miraculously furnished, there is reason to believe plea bargaining would still occur. The evidence indicates that plea bargaining occurs in those jurisdictions where scarce resources are really not a problem. In addition, an incentive to plea bargain may be built into the very nature of the criminal justice process. We know that organizations generally try to minimize uncertainties associated with their activities. The defense counsel group is probably no different. Lawyers especially dislike the uncertainty inherent in a trial governed by due process. The legal technicalities associated with proving guilt and the unpredictability of juries make the criminal trial a very uncertain enterprise. Many prosecutors and defense lawyers would rather settle on a plea bargain that is certain than to go into the courtroom and take their chances on losing the case. This suggests that plea bargaining is here to stay.

Plea bargaining has been and will continue to be an object of criticism. Some are offended by what they perceive to be insufficient penalties meted out to criminals through plea bargains. Others are concerned that our historic commitment to due process of law is being sacrificed on the altar of expediency.

The Supreme Court has addressed the issue of plea bargaining in several cases dating from the late 1960s (see for example, *Jackson v. United States* [1968]; *Boykin v. Alabama* [1969]; *Brady v. United States* [1970]; and *Santobello v. New York* [1971]). Basically, the Court has manifested concern over plea bargaining but nevertheless has recognized its practicality, if not its inevitability. However, the Court has stated emphatically that a trial judge must ascertain that the defendant has made a "knowing and intelligent" waiver of the right to a trial before accepting the defendant's plea of guilty. As the Court noted in *Boykin v. Alabama*,

> a plea of guilty is more than an admission of conduct, it is a conviction. Ignorance, incomprehension, coercion, terror, inducements, subtle or blatant threats might be a cover-up of unconstitutionality.

One of the more difficult cases decided by the Court in the area of plea bargaining was *Bordenkircher v. Hayes* (1978). Paul Hayes was indicted by a Kentucky grand jury for writing a bad check. It was not his first offense. The prosecutor informed Hayes that if he did not plead guilty, he (the prosecutor) would return to the grand jury to seek a tougher indictment based on the state's habitual offender statute. The defendant refused to "cop a plea," and the prosecutor carried out his threat. The grand jury handed down the more serious indictment. Hayes was tried, convicted, and sentenced to life imprisonment. Was this threat by the prosecutor constitutionally permissible? Dividing 5 to 4, the Supreme Court ruled that it was, since Hayes was "properly chargeable" under the recidivist statute from the start. Dissenting, Justice Harry Blackmun refused to approve what he perceived as "prosecutorial vindictiveness." In Blackmun's view, Hayes was being punished for the exercise of constitutional rights. The sharp division in *Bordenkircher* underscores the fact that reasonable people, including those trained in the law, can disagree on what offends the "fundamental fairness" required by due process.

TRIAL BY JURY

In spite of the pervasiveness of plea bargaining, the jury trial still plays a prominent role not only in American political mythology but also in the day-to-day operation of the criminal justice process. Trial by jury is recognized as a federal constitutional right in criminal and civil cases. Reference to jury trial appears once in the original Constitution and twice in the Bill of Rights. Article III provides: "The trial of all Crimes, except in Cases of Impeachment, shall be by

Jury. . . ." The Seventh Amendment requires that "the right of trial by jury shall be preserved" in civil suits. Most pertinent to our concerns is the Sixth Amendment, which states: "In all criminal prosecutions, the accused shall enjoy the right to a speedy and public trial by an impartial jury. . . ." Of course, prior to the incorporation of this provision into the Fourteenth Amendment in 1968 (see *Duncan v. Louisiana*), "all criminal prosecutions" meant all *federal* criminal prosecutions.

The Problem of Pretrial Publicity

Even before the Sixth Amendment right to trial by jury was incorporated into the Fourteenth Amendment, the Supreme Court had occasion to reverse jury verdicts in state criminal cases where the fairness of the trial was prejudiced by excessive publicity. In so doing, the Court used the "fair trial" doctrine under the Fourteenth Amendment, rather than the Sixth Amendment jury trial provision. *Sheppard v. Maxwell* (1966) is an excellent case in point. There, the Court reversed a murder conviction reached in a trial conducted against a backdrop of sensationalistic publicity. The circumstances surrounding the *Sheppard* case are almost comical in retrospect. Local officials allowed Dr. Sam Sheppard's murder trial to degenerate into a circus. As Justice Black noted in his opinion for the Court,

> [t]he fact is that bedlam reigned at the courthouse during the trial and newsmen took over practically the entire courtroom, hounding most of the participants in the trial, especially Sheppard.

The jurors in the *Sheppard* case were constantly exposed to the intense media coverage of the case right up until the time that they began their deliberations. Under these circumstances, the guilty verdict was virtually a foregone conclusion. Concluding that fundamental fairness had been denied, the Supreme Court reversed Sheppard's conviction.

Sheppard v. Maxwell leads one to wonder just what steps can be legitimately taken to insulate a trial jury from prejudicial publicity in a sensational case. One possibility is to take extreme care in the jury selection process, possibly by increasing the number of **peremptory challenges** available to the defense and the prosecution (such challenges, while limited in number, do not ordinarily require an explanation by counsel or a ruling by the trial judge). Another common step is to sequester the jury during the course of the trial. Another frequent measure is to postpone the trial until the publicity dies down. A less common approach is to change the venue of the trial to a locale less affected by the pretrial publicity. Although there is no question about the propriety of these measures, considerable doubt remains as to their efficacy.

Some judges have attempted more drastic means of protecting the defendant's right to a fair trial. One of these is to impose gag orders on the press, prohibiting the reportage of certain facts or incidents related to a sensational crime. In *Nebraska Press Association v. Stuart* (1976), the Supreme Court invalidated a **gag order** imposed by a trial judge to safeguard the rights of a man accused of a brutal mass murder. The Court viewed the order as a prior restraint in violation of the First Amendment's protection of the freedom of the press. The

Nebraska Press case vividly illustrates the head-on conflict of two cherished constitutional principles: freedom of the press and the right to a fair trial. Although the Court was unanimous in striking down the gag order, Chief Justice Burger's majority opinion left open the possibility that such orders might be permissible under extreme circumstances (for further discussion, see Chapter 12).

Another more drastic means of protecting the defendant's right to a fair trial is closure of pretrial proceedings. In *Gannet v. DePasquale* (1979), the Court allowed the closure of a pretrial hearing to determine the admissibility of evidence with the consent of both the prosecution and the defense. Writing for a divided Court, Justice Stewart stated that the right to a "public trial" guaranteed by the Sixth Amendment is personal to the defendant, not a general right of public access. Stewart went on to say that any First Amendment right of access by the press was outweighed by the right of the accused to receive a fair trial. In 1980, the Court appeared to alter its position somewhat. In *Richmond Newspapers v. Virginia,* the Court voted 7 to 1 to disallow the closure of a criminal trial. Although there was no majority opinion, the justices seemed to have agreed that the First Amendment prohibits trial closure. The very next year, in *Chandler v. Florida* (1981), the Court allowed television coverage of criminal trials, suggesting that *Richmond Newspapers* was no anomaly. The Court's decision in *Waller v. Georgia* (1984) also suggests a strong commitment to the value of a public trial. In *Waller,* the Court refused to allow closure of a pretrial suppression hearing that had been granted by the trial court over the objection of the accused. Although the Court in *Waller* suggested that extreme circumstances might allow the closure of a pretrial proceeding despite the objection of the defendant, the Court adopted a test that makes it very difficult to justify closure.

Jury Size

Historically, trial juries in the United States were composed of twelve persons, all of whom had to agree in order to convict a defendant. Although this is still the case in most states, some jurisdictions allow for six-person juries in noncapital cases. And four states (Oregon, Louisiana, Oklahoma, and Texas) no longer require juries to be unanimous to convict defendants, at least in some noncapital cases. In *Williams v. Florida* (1970), the Supreme Court approved Florida's use of six-person juries in noncapital cases. Justice White's opinion for the Court discussed the relationship between jury size and the Sixth Amendment:

> [T]he fact that the jury at common law was composed of precisely twelve is a historical accident, unnecessary to effect the purposes of the jury system and wholly without significance. . . . To read the Sixth Amendment as forever codifying a feature so incidental to the real purpose of the Amendment is to ascribe a blind formalism to the Framers. . . .

Serious questions exist about the factual assertions made by the Court in the *Williams* case. Is it true, as the Court asserted, that "neither currently available evidence nor theory suggests that the twelve-member jury is necessarily more advantageous to the defendant . . ."? Some experts on jury behavior have concluded otherwise. However, in *Ballew v. Georgia* (1978), the Court drew the line on jury size when it refused to permit the use of five-person juries. The Court cited studies to show that "the purpose and functioning of the jury . . . is seriously impaired . . . by a reduction in size to below six members." Thus, state legislatures are free to specify the number of persons to serve on juries in noncapital cases as long as they observe the constitutional minimum of six.

The Unanimity Principle

In *Johnson v. Louisiana* (1972) and its companion case *Apodaca v. Oregon* (1972), the Supreme Court surprised many observers by allowing state criminal trials to depart from the historic unanimity rule. In *Johnson,* the state of Louisiana passed a law allowing for convictions by nine votes on twelve-person juries in noncapital cases. Writing for a sharply divided Court, Justice White tried to reconcile nonunanimity with the "reasonable doubt" standard required by due process:

> Of course, the State's proof could be regarded as more certain if it had convinced all 12 jurors instead of only nine; it would have been even more compelling if it had . . . convinced 24 or 36 jurors. But the fact remains that nine jurors—a substantial majority of the jury—were convinced by the evidence. In our view disagreement of three jurors does not alone establish reasonable doubt.

One can argue, as Justice Marshall did in his dissent, that the refusal of three presumably reasonable jurors to sanction a guilty verdict might in and of itself indicate a reasonable doubt as to the guilt of the accused:

> The juror whose dissenting voice is unheard may be a spokesman, but simply for himself—and that, in my view, is enough. The doubts of a single juror are in my view evidence that the government has failed to carry its burden of proving guilt beyond a reasonable doubt.

The Court's decisions in *Williams v. Florida* and *Johnson v. Louisiana* left many observers wondering whether the Court would permit nonunanimous verdicts by six-member juries. In *Burch v. Louisiana* (1979), the Court allayed the fears of those who thought it was going too far to facilitate criminal convictions. Justice Rehnquist wrote the opinion for a unanimous Court:

> We agree . . . that the question presented is a "close" one. Nevertheless, we believe that conviction by a nonunanimous six-member jury in a state criminal trial for a nonpetty offense deprives an individual of his constitutional right to trial by jury.

Exclusion of Minorities from Juries

Another problem that has beset the courts with respect to trial juries is the exclusion of women, African-Americans, and other minority groups from juries, especially where defendants are members of such groups. Although the Court has quite clearly stated that there is no constitutional right of a defendant to have on the jury individuals of his or her gender or ethnic identity, it has also held that the systematic exclusion of such groups is unconstitutional under the Fourteenth

Amendment (see *Swain v. Alabama* [1965]). The Court has recognized that a jury should, at least ideally, represent a cross-section of the community in order to be completely fair and just to the accused.

One of the more difficult issues in jury selection is the use of the peremptory challenge to eliminate prospective jurors on the grounds of race. In *Batson v. Kentucky* (1986), the Supreme Court held that a prosecutor's use of peremptory challenges to exclude African-Americans from a jury trying an African-American defendant constituted a basis for reversal on appeal. Consequently, today in the trial of an African-American defendant, the exclusion of a single African-American juror can be the basis for the trial court to deny the use of a peremptory challenge, if the judge is persuaded that the challenge is racially motivated. In 1991, the *Batson* rule was broadened so that a defendant need not be of the same race as the excluded juror to successfully challenge that juror's exclusion (*Powers v. Ohio*). In the same year, the Supreme Court extended the *Batson* rule to encompass civil trials as well (*Edmondson v. Leesville Concrete Company*). In 1992, the Court went one important step further by prohibiting racially-motivated peremptory by defendants in criminal cases (see *Georgia v. McCollum*).

THE PROTECTION AGAINST DOUBLE JEOPARDY

The Fifth Amendment provides that no person "shall . . . be subject for the same offense to be twice put in jeopardy of life or limb." This protection against double jeopardy has deep roots in the soil of the common law. To allow the government to continue to prosecute a defendant on the same charge, using the same evidence that had previously resulted in acquittal, would seem to violate "fundamental canons of decency and fairness." Yet, in *Palko v. Connecticut* (1937), the Supreme Court held otherwise in refusing to incorporate the Double Jeopardy Clause into the Fourteenth Amendment. This holding has been overruled (see *Benton v. Maryland* [1969]), and the Double Jeopardy Clause has taken its place among those protections deemed "essential to a scheme of ordered liberty." However, the question of what exactly constitutes double jeopardy remains open. Essentially, the clause prevents the government from attempting to convict the accused of an illegal act after it has once failed to do so. A number of exceptions to this general rule exist.

Given our system of federalism, it is possible for one set of actions to lead to separate criminal prosecutions in the state and federal courts. According to the Supreme Court's decision in *Bartkus v. Illinois* (1959), the "dual sovereignty" of the state and federal governments permits separate prosecutions for the same act. However, statutes in nearly every state prohibit successive prosecutions, thus rendering this issue largely academic.

Another legitimate deviation from the double jeopardy principle occurs in the case of a mistrial granted on the request of the defense. Judges often declare a **mistrial** if there is some extraordinary event, such as the death of a juror or attorney; some prejudicial error that cannot be corrected; or a "hung jury" (that is, a jury unable to reach a verdict). The declaration of a mistrial, at least on the motion of the defendant, has the effect of "wiping the slate clean," of declaring that no trial took place. Thus, the state's renewal of its prosecution of the accused does not violate the Double Jeopardy Clause.

CRUEL AND UNUSUAL PUNISHMENTS

The Framers of the Bill of Rights were well aware of the sordid history of torture that characterized criminal punishment in pre-Revolutionary Europe. In *O'Neil v. Vermont* (1892), the Supreme Court said that the Eighth Amendment prohibition of "cruel and unusual punishments" was directed to "punishments which inflict torture, such as the rack, the thumb-screw, the iron boot, the stretching of limbs and the like, which are attended with acute pain and suffering." Yet the Court recognized that the Eighth Amendment also proscribed "punishments which by their excessive length or severity are greatly disproportionate to the offense charged."

Torture is no longer a significant legal issue in this country. Indeed, corporal punishment has been abolished as a penalty for criminal acts. Yet the question of proportionality of punishments and crimes remains a viable problem for contemporary courts of law. In *Robinson v. California* (1962), the Supreme Court held that state courts were bound by the Cruel and Unusual Punishments Clause. Since then, there have been numerous challenges to state sentencing statutes but none more controversial than those involving the death penalty.

The Death Penalty

Although already in decline, the death penalty was in widespread use when the Constitution was adopted—not only for murder but also for an array of lesser offenses. The Due Process Clauses of the Fifth and Fourteenth Amendments explicitly recognize, although they do not necessarily endorse, the death penalty: "no person shall be deprived of *life,* liberty or property without due process of law" (emphasis added). In *Trop v. Dulles* (1958), however, Chief Justice Warren indicated that the Cruel and Unusual Punishments Clause "must draw its meaning from the evolving standards of decency that mark the progress of a maturing society." By the 1960s, it was clear that public support for the death penalty had diminished substantially. By 1966, public opinion polls were finding that a majority of Americans opposed capital punishment. Reflecting this change in societal attitudes, only two persons were executed in the United States between 1967 and the Supreme Court's decision in *Furman v. Georgia* (1972), which struck down the Georgia death penalty law.

With the *Furman* case, five justices voted to strike down Georgia's death penalty. There was, however, only a brief *per curiam* opinion announcing the judgment of the Court. For the majority's rationale, one had to look at five separate concurring opinions. Two of the five justices—Brennan and Marshall—held that the death penalty itself was cruel and unusual punishment, given the "evolving standards of decency." Throughout their subsequent tenure on the Court, Brennan and Marshall steadfastly maintained the position that the death penalty is inherently unconstitutional (Justice Brennan retired in 1990; Justice Marshall followed suit in 1991).

The death penalty: Just desserts or "cruel and unusual punishment"?

If "evolving standards of decency" have anything to do with public opinion, then the Brennan-Marshall position on the death penalty is difficult to defend. Since the late 1960s, probably as a result of the increasing salience of the crime problem, the level of support for the death penalty has risen steadily, to 69 percent in 1977. It is thus difficult to make the evolving-standards argument unless one is talking about one's own standards! However, it is generally considered unacceptable for judges to impose their personal standards of morality on public policy under the aegis of the Constitution. Thus, Justice Marshall, dissenting in *Gregg v. Georgia* (1976), took the position that "the American people, fully informed as to the purposes of the death penalty and its liabilities, would in my view reject it as morally unacceptable." Justice Marshall's statement was regarded by many critics as arrogant, but it should be admitted that we simply do not know whether Marshall's assertion was correct. His hypothesis is possibly testable through empirical or experimental research; unfortunately, such research has yet to reach fruition.

Of the five justices who voted to invalidate the death penalty in the *Furman* case, Justice Stewart's opinion seems to have been the most influential. For Stewart, the problem with the death penalty was not the punishment itself but the manner in which it was being administered. Trial juries were being left with virtually unfettered discretion in deciding when to impose capital punishment. The result, according to Stewart, was that the death penalty was "wantonly and . . . freakishly imposed." Although Stewart explicitly linked his objection to the Cruel and Unusual Punishment Clause, it seems as though he was making a "due process" argument: the death penalty was invalid because it was being administered in an arbitrary and capricious fashion.

In the wake of the *Furman* decision, some thirty-five state legislatures rewrote their death penalty laws. Georgia's revamped death penalty statute was before the Supreme Court in the *Gregg* case of 1976. The revised Georgia law requires a bifurcated trial for capital crimes: In the first stage, guilt is determined in the usual manner; the second stage deals with the appropriate sentence. For the jury to impose the death penalty, it has to find at least one of several statutorily prescribed **aggravating factors.** Automatic appeal to the state supreme court is also provided. The appellate review must consider not only the procedural regularity of the trial but also whether the evidence supports the finding of the aggravating factor and whether the death sentence is disproportionate to the penalty imposed in similar cases.

The Court had little difficulty upholding the new Georgia statute, with only Justices Brennan and Marshall dissenting. Justice Stewart's opinion announcing the judgment stated:

> The new Georgia sentencing procedures . . . focus the jury's attention on the particularized nature of the crime and the particularized characteristics of the individual defendant. . . . In this way the jury's discretion is channeled. No longer can a jury wantonly and freakishly impose the death sentence, it is always circumscribed by the legislative guidelines.

Thus, after a hiatus of four years, the death penalty was reinstated. Although Justice Stewart's opinion in *Gregg* makes much of the procedural safeguards required by the Georgia law, one suspects that the marked increase in public support for the death penalty that occurred during the four years after *Furman* had something to do with the Court's decision to uphold Georgia's revised law. In this, as in other areas, the Court seldom strays far from a clear national consensus. Fortunately for the Court, the restraint demonstrated by several of the justices in *Furman* (by deciding the case on fairly narrow grounds) facilitated the reinstatement of the death penalty in *Gregg* four years later without the necessity of overruling a recent precedent.

Although the Court now recognizes the death penalty, it has refused to allow states to execute criminals convicted of lesser crimes than first-degree murder. In *Coker v. Georgia* (1977), the Court invalidated an attempt to execute a man convicted of rape. Writing for a plurality, Justice White characterized the death sentence for rape as "disproportionate" and "excessive."

Recent Supreme Court decisions indicate an increasingly permissive stance toward imposition of capital punishment. For the most part, the Court has been unsympathetic to challenges to the legal sufficiency of procedures used to impose the death penalty. For example, in *Pulley v. Harris* (1984), the Court rejected the argument that trial judges must engage in **comparative proportionality review** (one of the features of the revised Georgia law upheld in *Gregg*) before imposing the death penalty. In another significant case, *Lockhart v. McCree* (1986), the Court facilitated the use of capital punishment by ruling that potential jurors could be excluded before trial if their opposition to the death penalty was so intense that it would impair their ability to perform as impartial jurors. In *McCleskey v. Kemp* (1987), the Court upheld the death sentence imposed on Warren McCleskey, an African-American defendant who relied on a thorough statistical study in contending that capital punishment in Georgia was infected by pervasive racial discrimination. And in *Walton v. Arizona* (1990), the Court upheld a state law permitting the trial judge, rather than the jury, to determine the existence of aggravating and **mitigating circumstances.** In this case, the Court also concluded that Arizona's characterization of "heinous, cruel or depraved" conduct as an aggravating factor was sufficiently specific to meet the requirements of the Eighth Amendment.

One departure from the more conservative trend in death penalty decisions came in the summer of 1986. In *Ford v. Wainwright*, the Supreme Court held that the Eighth Amendment prohibits the execution of a prisoner who is insane. Invoking the "evolving standards of decency" test, the Court asserted that "the intuition that such an execution . . . offends humanity is shared across this Nation." However, in *Penry v. Lynaugh* (1989), the Court held that mild mental retardation, in and of itself, is not a sufficient basis to bar the imposition of the death penalty. Moreover, while the Court recognizes the youth of the defendant as a mitigating factor, it has upheld imposition of the death penalty on juveniles who were sixteen or seventeen at the time they committed their crimes.

In the late 1980s, growing concern for the rights of crime victims led some states to enact laws permitting the introduction of **victim impact statements** at the penalty phase of capital trials. Such statements related to personal characteristics of murder victims and to the impact of their murders on family members. In *Booth v. Maryland* (1987) and *South Carolina v. Gathers* (1989), the Supreme Court declared that the introduction of such "victim-impact evidence" violated the Eighth Amendment. In a dramatic reversal of this position, a more conservative Court in 1991 held that "the Eighth Amendment erects no *per se* bar" to "the admission of victim impact evidence and prosecutorial argument on that subject . . ." (*Payne v. Tennessee*). While victims' rights advocates praised this decision, civil libertarians and defense attorneys objected sharply to what they perceived as an invitation to infuse excessive emotion into the criminal process. In one of the last opinions he wrote before retiring, Justice Marshall, dissenting, delivered a broadside against the Rehnquist Court's disregard of precedent:

> In dispatching *Booth* and *Gathers* to their graves, today's majority ominously suggests that an even more extensive upheaval of this Court's precedents may be in store. . . . The majority today sends a clear signal that scores of established constitutional liberties are now ripe for reconsideration. . . .

Although *Furman v. Georgia* has never been formally overruled, the current Court seems to be moving away from the concerns expressed in that decision. On the other hand, the death penalty is a volatile issue in American society, and the pendulum of public opinion might someday swing in the other direction. As with other constitutional questions shaped by societal values, the issue of capital punishment invites periodic reexamination by the Court.

Mandatory Life Imprisonment

Can imprisonment alone constitute cruel and unusual punishment? The answer to this general question depends on the circumstances of individual cases and the makeup of the Supreme Court at any given time. For example, in *Rummel v. Estelle* (1980), the Court upheld a mandatory life sentence imposed on a man who had committed three nonviolent felonies. In three separate cases over a period of years, Rummel had been convicted of the fraudulent use of a credit card, forging a check, and obtaining money under false pretenses. Under Texas law, he was adjudged a habitual offender and sentenced to life in prison. In a similar case three years later, the Court struck down a South Dakota statute that authorized life imprisonment for habitual felons (see *Solem v. Helm* [1983]). Bcause the South Dakota law did not provide for release on parole, the Court distinguished this case from *Rummel v. Estelle*. In 1991, the Supreme Court, in *Harmelin v. Michigan,* upheld a life sentence without possibility of parole imposed on an individual for possessing 772 grams of cocaine. Michigan law required the automatic imposition of this sentence on anyone convicted of possessing 650 grams or more of any mixture containing cocaine. In all three of the aforementioned cases, the Court divided 5 to 4, indicating the absence of consensus in this area.

Prisoners' Rights

Because they have been convicted of serious crimes, the inmates in our nation's crowded prison system have lost many of the rights we take for granted. They have forfeited their right to live in civil society, to move about freely, to associate with whom they choose, and to make decisions about everyday matters such as eating, sleeping, recreation, and work. Many have forfeited their right to vote or to hold public office. But they have not been stripped of all constitutional rights and protections. Just which of the many constitutional rights are retained by those confined to prison is still unclear. Judicial restraint dictates that such questions be left open until raised in specific controversies; the Court has yet to decide more than a handful of cases in this area.

Prior to the 1960s, courts appeared indifferent to the rights of prisoners. The main reason for this is that so few cases were ever filed; for the most part, prisoners were denied access to counsel and the courts. As a result of favorable Supreme Court decisions of the 1950s and early '60s, however, prisoners began to obtain access to the federal judiciary, using petitions for writs of habeas corpus. Then, in the 1970s, their cases began to reach the level of the Supreme Court. Today, several pronouncements from the High Court guide lower-court judges, legislators, and prison officials in dealing with the legal aspects of prison confinement (see, for example, *Cruz v. Beto* [1972]; *Procunier v. Martinez* [1974]; *Baxter v. Palmigiano* [1976]).

In *Hutto v. Finney* (1978), the Supreme Court upheld a federal court order imposing a thirty-day limit on the use of punitive isolation by a state prison. The case, which began in 1969 under the name *Holt v. Sarver,* involved an Eighth Amendment challenge to the conditions of confinement in the Arkansas prison system, particularly the notorious Cummins Farm. The challenged conditions included corporal punishment and torture; abysmal sanitation, diet, and health care; and an overall atmosphere of violence. The conditions that prevailed at Cummins Farm were not altogether atypical of conditions in maximum security state prisons at the time the litigation began. Today, as a result of increased judicial oversight, such conditions are rare exceptions.

In 1992, the Supreme Court demonstrated continuing solicitude toward prisoners subjected to inhumane treatment. In *Hudson v. McMillian,* the Court held that a prisoner who is beaten maliciously by guards may bring a civil suit to recover damages under a claim of cruel and unusual punishment, even if the injuries sustained are not serious. In one of his first dissenting opinions on the High Court, Justice Clarence Thomas (joined by Justice Scalia) expressed the view that nonserious injury to a prisoner does not rise to the level of cruel and unusual punishment.

Many people, especially prison officials, regard judicial oversight of prisons with disdain. Few observers beyond prisoners themselves and a few groups representing their interests are prepared to lavish praise on the federal courts for their involvement in this area. As a group, prisoners have very little political power and even less public support. Nevertheless, some argue that one of the most important functions of the judiciary is to protect "discrete and insular minorities" who have no effective means of representing themselves in the political process. Certainly prisoners are such a minority. And although they may well deserve harsh punishment, they are nevertheless persons and, as such, are entitled to the applicable protections of the Constitution.

APPEAL AND POSTCONVICTION RELIEF

The federal Constitution makes no mention of a defendant's right to appeal from a criminal conviction, although one could argue that such a right is implicit in the concept of procedural due process. In *McKane v. Durston* (1894), the Supreme Court held that there is no such constitutional right. Given the expansiveness of modern notions of due process, it is likely that the Supreme Court would reconsider *McKane v. Durston* but for the fact that Congress and all fifty state legislatures have created statutory rights of appeal. Indeed, a federal defendant's right of appeal is of fairly ancient vintage, having first been granted by the Judiciary Act of 1789.

The so-called **appeal by right** granted by federal and state statutes applies to defendants who are convicted over their pleas of "not guilty." The only situation in which a defendant who pleads guilty retains the right of appeal is where such a provision is made pursuant to a plea bargain. The prosecution is never permitted to appeal from the acquittal of the defendant but may appeal certain pretrial rulings resulting in the dismissal of the case.

The appeal by right is an important means whereby defendants assert constitutional rights alleged to have been violated in their apprehension or the investigation, prosecution or trial of their case. The appeal by right thus permits appellate courts to perform the important function of **error correction.** Of course, not all errors constitute the basis for reversal on appeal. Only those errors deemed prejudicial to the accused necessitate reversal; other mistakes are referred to as harmless errors (see *Chapman v. California* [1967]).

In 1991, the Supreme Court made news when it decided that, under certain circumstances, the use of an involuntary confession as evidence at trial constitutes a harmless error (see *Arizona v. Fulminante,* discussed above). Previously, the use of an illegally obtained confession was considered a sufficient basis for reversal of a conviction, regardless of the strength of the other evidence against the accused.

Beyond the right to one appeal, defendants may petition higher courts to review their convictions, but such review is granted at the discretion of the higher court. In the U.S. Supreme Court and most state supreme courts, discretionary review involves the issuance of a writ of certiorari. In essence, the writ of certiorari is issued to the lower court, directing it to provide the record in a given case so that the higher court may conduct its review. The use of this type of discretionary review is usually limited to new and important issues of law, especially where the lower appellate courts are in conflict.

Federal Habeas Corpus Review of State Criminal Cases

A state prisoner who has exhausted his or her appeals in the state courts may petition a federal district court for a writ of habeas corpus. The power of federal courts to issue habeas corpus in state cases can be traced to an act of Congress adopted just after the Civil War (see *Ex parte McCardle* [1869], discussed and reprinted in Chapter 3). Rarely used prior to the 1950s, in the modern era, this aspect of federal jurisdiction has played an important role in the development of constitutional law as it relates to the criminal process. In *Brown v. Allen* (1953), the Supreme Court held that state prisoners could readjudicate issues on federal habeas review that had already been addressed in state proceedings. Then in *Fay v. Noia* (1963), the Warren Court further expanded federal habeas corpus by deciding that state prisoners could raise issues in their federal habeas corpus petitions that they failed to raise in state appeals. Moreover, unless it was found that they deliberately abused the writ, there was no limit on the number of habeas corpus petitions that state prisoners could file in federal district courts (see *Sanders v. United States* [1963]).

The Warren Court's decision to expand federal habeas corpus helped fuel the "criminal justice revolution" of the 1960s. Federal district courts could look at and correct the state courts' failures to implement the pronouncements of the High Court in such key areas as search and seizure, confessions, double jeopardy, and the right to counsel. Accordingly, one of the strategies of the Burger and Rehnquist Courts' "counterrevolution" in the criminal process area has been to restrict federal habeas review of state criminal convictions.

The Appellate Odyssey of Robert Alton Harris

In a protracted series of appeals spanning some fourteen years, federal and state courts wrangled with a variety of legal issues surrounding the death sentence imposed on Robert Alton Harris, who was convicted of murdering two teenage boys in San Diego, California, in 1978. In trying to escape the death sentence, Harris filed nine petitions for habeas corpus in California state courts and four federal habeas corpus petitions. Harris's appellate odyssey provides a case study in the complex appeals process that often occurs in death penalty cases.

March 6, 1979	Harris is convicted and sentenced to die in California's gas chamber.
February 11, 1981	On appeal, the California Supreme Court upholds Harris's conviction and death sentence.
October 5, 1981	The U.S. Supreme Court denies Harris's petition for certiorari.
November, 1981	Harris files three habeas corpus petitions in California state courts; all are denied.
March 5, 1982	Harris files the first of several habeas corpus petitions in U.S. District Court for the Southern District of California.
March 12, 1982	The federal district court denies Harris's first habeas corpus petition.
August 13, 1982	Harris files a second federal habeas corpus petition in the federal district court.
October, 1984	After fine points have been resolved by the U.S. Supreme Court and the Ninth Circuit Court of Appeals, the district court denies Harris's second petition for habeas corpus.
July 8, 1988	The Ninth Circuit Court of Appeals affirms the district court's denial of habeas corpus relief.
September 28, 1989	The appeals court denies Harris's petition for *en banc* rehearing.
January 5, 1990	Harris files a fourth state habeas petition in the California court.
January 16, 1990	The U.S. Supreme Court declines Harris's petition for review of the district court's denial of federal habeas corpus.
February 5, 1990	A state judge in San Diego schedules Harris's execution for April 3.
March 16, 1990	The California Supreme Court rejects Harris's fourth state habeas corpus petition.
March 26, 1990	Harris files a third federal habeas corpus petition.
March 29, 1990	The federal district court denies the third habeas corpus petition.
March 30, 1990	A judge on the Ninth Circuit Court of Appeals issues a stay of execution.
April 2, 1990	The U.S. Supreme Court rejects California's request to vacate the stay of execution.
August 29, 1990	The Ninth Circuit Court of Appeals rejects claims raised in Harris's third federal habeas corpus petition.
November 30, 1990	Harris petitions the federal district court for a new hearing on the third habeas corpus petition.
March 22, 1991	The Ninth Circuit Court of Appeals orders the district court to consider the request for rehearing.
May 15, 1991	The federal district court denies the petition for rehearing.

August 21, 1991	The appeals court upholds the district court's denial of the petition for rehearing.
November 8, 1991	The appeals court denies the petition for an *en banc* rehearing on its decision upholding the district court's denial of rehearing.
March 2, 1992	The U.S. Supreme Court rejects Harris's petition for review of the lower-court rulings on his third federal habeas corpus petition.
March 13, 1992	A state court in San Diego sets April 21 as Harris's execution date.
April 16, 1992	Harris files his ninth habeas corpus petition in California courts.
April 17, 1992	The California Supreme Court rejects Harris's ninth state habeas corpus petition.
April 18, 1992	Harris files a fourth habeas corpus petition in the U.S. District Court for Southern California; it is summarily denied.
April 18, 1992	A judge on the U.S. District Court for the Northern District of California issues an order prohibiting the state of California from executing anyone by means of the gas chamber.
April 19, 1992	The Ninth Circuit Court of Appeals vacates the district court order prohibiting the use of the gas chamber.

In the early morning hours of April 21, 1992, four separate stays of execution were issued by different judges on the Ninth Circuit Court of Appeals. Each of these stays was immediately vacated by the U.S. Supreme Court. The fourth of these stays came at 3:51 A.M. Pacific time, after Harris had been strapped into the chair in the gas chamber. At 5:45, the Supreme Court issued an order prohibiting lower federal courts from issuing any additional stays of execution. The vote on the high court was 7 to 2, with Justices Blackmun and Stevens dissenting. This final action by the Supreme Court cleared the way for Harris's execution, which began at 6:10 A.M. Harris's final words to the prison warden were "You can be a king or a street sweeper, but everybody dances with the Grim Reaper." Harris was pronounced dead at 6:21 A.M.

Source: Katherine Bishop, "The Legal Journey of a Death Sentence," *New York Times*, 22 April 1992, p. C-23.

The first significant limitation on federal habeas corpus came in *Stone v. Powell* (1976). There, the Burger Court decided that state prisoners could not use federal habeas corpus petitions to raise Fourth Amendment issues where they had been provided "a full and fair opportunity" to litigate those issues in the state courts. Subsequently, in *Engle v. Isaac* (1982), the Court refused to allow a state prisoner to use federal habeas corpus to challenge a questionable jury instruction to which he failed to object during trial. Other decisions of the Burger Court chipped away at the Warren Court's expansive interpretations of federal habeas corpus relief (see, for example, *Kuhlmann v. Wilson* [1986]; *Straight v. Wainwright* [1986]).

The Rehnquist Court continued the trend toward limiting access to federal habeas corpus. In 1991, the Court barred Warren McCleskey, still on death row in Georgia, from filing a second federal habeas corpus petition, holding that he had "abused the writ" (see *McCleskey v. Zant*). In the *McCleskey* case, the Court held that a state need not prove that a petitioner deliberately abandoned a constitutional claim in his or her first habeas corpus petition for the petitioner to be barred from raising the claim in a subsequent petition. The Court thus moved away from the "deliberate abandonment" standard the Warren Court had articulated in *Sanders v. United States* (1963). In another bitter dissent, Justice Marshall blasted the Court for departing from precedent, saying that "whatever 'abuse of the writ' today's decision is designed to avert pales in comparison with the majority's own abuse of the norms that inform the proper judicial function."

It should be noted that the Supreme Court's decision in *McCleskey v. Zant* came at a time when Congress was debating further restrictions on federal habeas corpus. Clearly, both the Court and Congress were responding to a widespread perception that state prisoners were being afforded excessive opportunities to challenge their convictions. While one can argue that federal habeas corpus has been subject to abuse by state prisoners, most serious commentators would agree that eliminating this aspect of federal jurisdiction altogether would remove some of the pressure that has led to an increased awareness of and appreciation for defendants' rights in the state courts. Indeed, in the *McCleskey* case, the Rehnquist Court expressed a commitment to the "continued efficacy" of federal habeas corpus to prevent miscarriages of justice in the state courts. In its 1991 term, the Rehnquist Court continued its curtailment of federal habeas corpus. In *Keeney v. Tamayo-Reyes* (1992), the Court overturned *Townsend v. Sain* (1963), in which the Warren Court had held that state prisoners had the right to seek federal habeas corpus relief unless they had deliberately by-passed the state courts.

JUVENILE JUSTICE

At the time of the founding of the United States, children were treated essentially as adults for the purposes of criminal justice. It was not uncommon for teenagers to be hanged, flogged, or placed in the public pillory as punishment for their crimes. Toward the end of the nineteenth century, public outcry against such treatment led to the establishment of a separate justice system for juveniles. Reformatories and specialized courts were created to deal with young offenders not as hardened criminals but as misguided youth in need of special care. This special treatment was legally justified by the *parens patriae* concept: that the state is responsible for caring for those incapable of caring for themselves. The newly created juvenile courts were usually separate from the regular tribunals; often the judges or referees that presided over these courts did not have formal legal training. There was little procedural regularity or even opportunity for the juvenile offender to confront his or her accusers.

The abuses that came to be associated with juvenile courts were addressed by the Supreme Court in the landmark case *In re Gault* (1967). Along with *Mapp v. Ohio, Gideon v. Wainwright,* and *Miranda v. Arizona, Gault* is considered to be one of the "four horsemen" of the Warren Court's revolution in the criminal justice area. In *Gault,* the Court essentially made the juvenile courts adhere to standards of due process, applying most of the basic procedural safeguards enjoyed by adults accused of crimes. Moreover, *Gault* held that juvenile courts must respect the right of counsel, the freedom from compulsory self-incrimination, and the right to confront (cross-examine) hostile witnesses.

For the most part, the Supreme Court has reaffirmed the *Gault* decision (see, for example, *Breed v. Jones* [1975]). In *McKeiver v. Pennsylvania* (1971), however, the Court refused to extend the right to trial by jury to juvenile pro-ceedings. Writing for a plurality, Justice Blackmun concluded that juries are not indispensable "to fair and equitable juvenile proceedings." Thirteen years later, in *Schall v. Martin* (1984), the Court upheld a pretrial detention program for juveniles that might well have been found violative of due process had it applied to adults. Writing for the Court, Justice Rehnquist stressed that "the Constitution does not mandate elimination of all differences in the treatment of juveniles." At this point, it appears likely that the Supreme Court will maintain the requirements imposed in *Gault* and a few subsequent cases. But further expansion of juvenile due process seems unlikely.

Capital Punishment of Juveniles

One of the most difficult issues facing the courts in the area of juvenile justice is whether, and under what circumstances, persons below the age of legal majority (but who are tried as adults in regular criminal courts) should face the death penalty when convicted of capital crimes. In *Eddings v. Oklahoma* (1982), the Supreme Court voted 5 to 4 to vacate the death sentence of a sixteen-year-old boy. In 1988, the Court divided 6 to 3 in ruling that the Constitution forbids execution of juveniles who are fifteen or younger at the time they committed their capital crimes (*Thompson v. Oklahoma*). One year later, in *Stanford v. Kentucky* (1989), the Court split 5 to 4 in deciding that juveniles sixteen and older at the time of their crimes may be sentenced to death. According to Justice O'Connor's controlling opinion in *Stanford,* "it is sufficiently clear that no na-tional consensus forbids the imposition of capital punishment on 16 or 17-year-old capital murderers." Thus, for the time being, the line appears to be drawn at sixteen years; juveniles who were, at the time of their crimes, sixteen or older may be subject to the death penalty without offending the current Court's in-terpretation of the Eighth Amendment. This line, of course, is subject to alter-ation as the membership of the Court and national opinion change.

CONCLUSION

This chapter has summarized the development of constitutional standards in the field of criminal justice. Here, as in much of its First Amendment jurisprudence, the Supreme Court has attempted to balance legitimate interests of public safety and public order with equally legitimate interests in individual liberty and privacy. In seeking to protect the constitutional rights of persons suspected, accused, or convicted of crimes, the Court has often challenged established law enforcement methods. This tendency began in the 1930s and was most pronounced in the areas of search and seizure, police interrogation, and the right to counsel. Sharp criticism resulted from Supreme Court efforts to "police the police" and to upgrade standards of criminal procedure in the courts. Such criticism was particularly strong toward the end of the Warren era in the late 1960s.

Reflecting strong currents of change in public opinion, as well as the impact of the Nixon, Reagan, and Bush appointments, the Supreme Court since the 1970s has been decidedly more sympathetic to law enforcement than was the Warren Court. In refusing to extend or in some cases overturning Warren Court precedents, the Burger and Rehnquist Courts opened themselves to the charge of insensitivity to the rights of individuals. This criticism has been particularly strident with respect to decisions in the area of search and seizure.

The reason the Framers of the Bill of Rights imposed constraints on law enforcement was not that the Framers were opposed to law and order. Rather, they were deeply distrustful of power; they feared what well-meaning but overzealous officials might do if not constrained by the rule of law. Certainly there was ample historical evidence to support their fears. Consequently, they gave us a Bill of Rights that makes it more difficult for government to investigate, prosecute, and punish crime.

But what we as a society lose in our ability to control crime, we gain in increased liberty and privacy. It is hard to have it both ways, but, of course, most of us would like to! The great challenge to courts, especially the Supreme Court, is to strike a delicate balance between society's need for crime control and our equally strong desires for individual privacy and freedom.

FOR FURTHER READING

Abraham, Henry J. *Freedom and the Court: Civil Rights and Liberties in the United States,* 4th ed. New York: Oxford University Press, 1982.

Amsterdam, Anthony. *Perspectives on the Fourth Amendment.* St. Paul: Minnesota Law Review Foundation, 1974.

Baker, Liva. *Miranda: Crime, Law and Politics.* New York: Atheneum Press, 1983.

Bedau, Hugo Adam, ed. *The Death Penalty in America,* 3d ed. New York: Oxford University Press, 1982.

Berns, Walter. *For Capital Punishment.* New York: Basic Books, 1979.

Black, Charles, Jr. *Capital Punishment: The Inevitability of Caprice and Mistake.* New York: Norton, 1974.

Carter, Lief H. *The Limits of Order.* Lexington: Lexington Books, 1974.

Dershowitz, Alan M. *The Best Defense.* New York: Random House, 1982.

Eisenstein, James, Roy B. Fleming, and Peter F. Nardulli. *The Contours of Justice: Communities and Their Courts.* Boston: Little, Brown, 1988.

Heumann, Milton. *Plea Bargaining: The Experiences of Prosecutors, Judges and Defense Attorneys.* Chicago: University of Chicago Press, 1978.

Israel, Jerold H., Yale Kamisar, and Wayne R. LaFave. *Criminal Procedure and the Constitution.* St. Paul: West, 1988.

Jacob, Herbert. *Law and Politics in the United States.* Boston: Little, Brown, 1986.

Kalven, Harry, and Hans Zeisel. *The American Jury.* Chicago: University of Chicago Press, 1966.

Kamisar, Yale. *Police Interrogation and Confessions: Essays in Law and Policy.* Ann Arbor: University of Michigan Press, 1980.

Landynski, Jacob W. *Search and Seizure and the Supreme Court.* Baltimore: Johns Hopkins University Press, 1978.

Levy, Leonard W. *Against the Law: The Nixon Court and Criminal Justice.* New York: Harper and Row, 1974.

Lewis, Anthony. *Gideon's Trumpet.* New York: Vintage, 1964.

Miller, Leonard G. *Double Jeopardy and the Federal System.* Chicago: University of Chicago Press, 1968.

Neubauer, David W. *America's Courts and the Criminal Justice System,* 3d ed. Pacific Grove, Calif.: Brooks/Cole, 1988.

Packer, Herbert L. *The Limits of the Criminal Sanction.* Stanford, Calif.: Stanford University Press, 1968.

Scheb, John M., and John M. Scheb, II. *Criminal Law and Procedure.* St. Paul: West, 1989.

Scheingold, Stuart A. *The Politics of Law and Order: Street Crime and Public Policy.* New York: Longman, 1984.

Schlesinger, Stephen. *Exclusionary Injustice.* New York: Dekker, 1977.

Sigler, Jay. *Double Jeopardy: The Development of a Legal and Social Policy.* Ithaca, N.Y.: Cornell University Press, 1969.

Stephens, Otis H., Jr. *The Supreme Court and Confessions of Guilt.* Knoxville: University of Tennessee Press, 1973.

Way, H. Frank. *Criminal Justice and the American Constitution.* Belmont, Calif.: Duxbury Press, 1980.

White, Welsh. *The Death Penalty in the Eighties.* Ann Arbor: University of Michigan Press, 1988.

Whitebread, Charles H., and Christopher Slobogin. *Criminal Procedure: An Analysis of Cases and Concepts,* 3rd ed. Westbury, N.Y.: Foundation Press, 1993.

CASES AND READINGS

Olmstead v. United States

277 U.S. 438; 48 S. Ct. 564; 72 L. Ed. 944 (1928)
Vote: 5-4

Mr. Chief Justice Taft delivered the opinion of the Court.

These cases are here by *certiorari* from the Circuit Court of Appeals for the Ninth Circuit. They were granted with the distinct limitation that the hearing should be confined to the single question whether the use of evidence of private telephone conversations between the defendants and others, intercepted by means of wire tapping, amounted to a violation of the 4th and 5th Amendments.

The petitioners were convicted in the District Court for the Western District of Washington of a conspiracy to violate the National Prohibition Act by unlawfully possessing, transporting and importing intoxicating liquors and maintaining nuisances, and by selling intoxicating liquors. Seventy-two others in addition to the petitioners were indicted. Some were not apprehended, some were acquitted, and others pleaded guilty.

The evidence in the records discloses a conspiracy of amazing magnitude to import, possess and sell liquor unlawfully. It involved the employment of not less than fifty persons, of two seagoing vessels for the transportation of liquor to British Columbia, of smaller vessels for coastwise transportation to the state of Washington, the purchase and use of a ranch beyond the suburban limits of Seattle, with a large underground cache for storage and a number of smaller caches in that city, the maintenance of a central office manned with operators, the employment of executives, salesmen, deliverymen, dispatchers, scouts, bookkeepers, collectors and an attorney. In a bad month sales amounted to $176,000; the aggregate for a year must have exceeded two millions of dollars.

Olmstead was the leading conspirator and the general manager of the business. He made a contribution of $10,000 to the capital; eleven others contributed $1,000 each. The profits were divided one-half to Olmstead and the remainder to the other

eleven. Of the several offices in Seattle the chief one was in a large office building. In this there were three telephones on three different lines. There were telephones in an office of the manager in his own home, at the homes of his associates, and at other places in the city. Communication was had frequently with Vancouver, British Columbia. Times were fixed for the deliveries of the "stuff," to places along Puget Sound near Seattle, and from there the liquor was removed and deposited in the caches already referred to. One of the chief men was always on duty at the main office to receive orders by the telephones and to direct their filing by a corps of men stationed in another room—the "bull pen." The call numbers of the telephones were given to those known to be likely customers. At times the sales amounted to 200 cases of liquor per day.

The information which led to the discovery of the conspiracy and its nature and extent was largely obtained by intercepting messages on the telephones of the conspirators by four Federal prohibition officers. Small wires were inserted along the ordinary telephone wires from the residences of four of the petitioners and those leading from the chief office. The insertions were made without trespass upon any property of the defendants. They were made in the basement of the large office building. The taps from house lines were made in the streets near the houses.

The gathering of evidence continued for many months. Conversations of the conspirators, of which refreshing stenographic notes were currently made, were testified to by the government witnesses. They revealed the large business transactions of the partners and their subordinates. Men at the wires heard the orders given for liquor by customers, and the acceptances; they became auditors of the conversations between the partners. All this disclosed the conspiracy charged in the indictment. Many of the intercepted conversations were not merely reports but parts of the criminal acts. The evidence also disclosed the difficulties to which the conspirators were subjected, the reported news of the capture of vessels, the arrest of their men and the seizure of cases of liquor in garages and other places. It showed the dealing by Olmstead, the chief conspirator, with members of the Seattle police, the messages to them which secured the release of arrested members of the conspiracy, and also direct promises to officers of payments as soon as opportunity offered.

The 4th Amendment provides: "The right of the people to be secure in their persons, houses, papers, and effects, against unreasonable searches and seizures, shall not be violated, and no warrants shall issue, but upon probable cause, supported by oath or affirmation, and particularly describing the place to be searched, and the persons or things to be seized." And the 5th: "No person . . . shall be compelled, in any criminal case, to be a witness against himself." . . .

There is no room in the present case for applying the 5th Amendment unless the 4th Amendment was first violated. There was no evidence of compulsion to induce the defendants to talk over their many telephones. They were continually and voluntarily transacting business without knowledge of the interception. Our consideration must be confined to the 4th Amendment. . . .

The well-known historical purpose of the 4th Amendment, directed against general warrants and writs of assistance, was to prevent the use of governmental force to search a man's house, his person, his papers, and his effects, and to prevent their seizure against his will. . . .

The Amendment itself shows that the search is to be of material things—the person, the house, his papers or his effects. The description of the warrant necessary to make the proceeding lawful is that it must specify the place to be searched and the person or *things* to be seized. . . .

. . . The 4th Amendment may have proper application to a sealed letter in the mail because of the constitutional provision for the Post Office Department and the relations between the government and those who pay to secure protection of their sealed letters. . . . It is plainly within the words of the Amendment to say that the unlawful rifling by a government agent of a sealed letter is a search and seizure of the sender's papers or effects. The letter is a paper, an effect, and in the custody of a government that forbids carriage except under its protection.

The United States takes no such care of telegraph or telephone messages as of mailed sealed letters. The Amendment does not forbid what was done here. There was no searching. There was no seizure. The evidence was secured by the use of the sense of hearing and that only. There was no entry of the house or offices of the defendants.

By the invention of the telephone fifty years ago, and its application for the purpose of extending communications, one can talk with another at a far distant place.

The language of the Amendment can not be extended and expanded to include telephone wires reaching to the whole world from the defendant's house or office. The intervening wires are not part of his house or office, any more than are the highways along which they are stretched.

This court, in *Carroll v. United States* [1925],*** declared:

The 4th Amendment is to be construed in the light of what was deemed an unreasonable search and seizure when it was adopted and in a manner which will conserve public interests as well as the interests and rights of individual citizens. . . .

Congress may, of course, protect the secrecy of telephone messages by making them, when intercepted, inadmissible in evidence in Federal criminal trials, by direct legislation, and thus depart from the common law of evidence. But the courts may not adopt such a policy by attributing an enlarged and unusual meaning to the 4th Amendment. The reasonable view is that one who installs in his house a telephone instrument with connecting wires intends to project his voice to those quite outside, and that the wires beyond his house and messages while passing over them are not within the protection of the 4th Amendment. Here those who intercepted the projected voices were not in the house of either party to the conversation. . . .

We think, therefore, that the wire tapping here disclosed did not amount to a search or seizure within the meaning of the 4th Amendment. . . .

The judgments of the Circuit Court of Appeals are affirmed....

Mr. Justice Holmes: [dissenting]. ...

Mr. Justice Brandeis, dissenting:

... The government makes no attempt to defend the methods employed by its officers. Indeed, it concedes that if wire-tapping can be deemed a search and seizure within the 4th Amendment, such wire-tapping as was practiced in the case at bar was an unreasonable search and seizure, and that the evidence thus obtained was inadmissible. But it relies on the language of the Amendment; and it claims that the protection given thereby cannot properly be held to include a telephone conversation.

"We must never forget," said Mr. Chief Justice Marshall in *M'Culloch v. Maryland,* *** "that it is a Constitution we are expounding." Since then, this court has repeatedly sustained the exercise of power by Congress, under various clauses of that instrument, over objects of which the Fathers could not have dreamed....

"... [T]ime works changes, brings into existence new conditions and purposes." Subtler and more far-reaching means of invading privacy have become available to the government. Discovery and invention have made it possible for the government, by means far more effective than stretching upon the rack, to obtain disclosures in court of what is whispered in the closet.

Moreover, "in the applications of a constitution, our contemplation cannot be only of what has been, but of what may be." The progress of science in furnishing the government with means of espionage is not likely to stop with wire-tapping. Ways may some day be developed by which the government, without removing papers from secret drawers, can reproduce them in court, and by which it will be enabled to expose to a jury the most intimate occurrences of the home. Advances in the psychic and related sciences may bring means of exploring unexpressed beliefs, thoughts and emotions.... Can it be that the Constitution affords no protection against such invasions of individual security? ...

Time and again, this court, in giving effect to the principle underlying the 4th Amendment, has refused to place an unduly literal construction upon it....

The protection guaranteed by the Amendments is much broader in scope. The makers of our Constitution undertook to secure conditions favorable to the pursuit of happiness. They recognized the significance of man's spiritual nature, of his feelings and of his intellect. They knew that only a part of the pain, pleasure and satisfactions of life are to be found in material things. They sought to protect Americans in their beliefs, their thoughts, their emotions and their sensations. They conferred, as against the government, the right to be let alone—the most comprehensive of rights and the right most valued by civilized men. To protect that right, every unjustifiable intrusion by the government upon the privacy of the individual, whatever the means employed, must be deemed a violation of the 4th Amendment. And the use, as evidence in a criminal proceeding, of facts ascertained by such intrusion must be deemed a violation of the 5th.

Applying to the 4th and 5th Amendments the established rule of construction, the defendants' objections to the evidence obtained by a wiretapping must, in my opinion, be sustained. It is, of course, immaterial where the physical connection with the telephone wires leading into the defendants' premises was made. And it is also immaterial that the intrusion was in aid of law enforcement. Experience should teach us to be most on our guard to protect liberty when the government's purposes are beneficent. Men born to freedom are naturally alert to repel invasion of their liberty by evil-minded rulers. The greatest dangers to liberty lurk in insidious encroachment by men of zeal, well-meaning, but without understanding....

Decency, security, and liberty alike demand that government officials shall be subjected to the same rules of conduct that are commands to the citizen. In a government of laws, existence of the government will be imperilled if it fails to observe the law scrupulously. Our government is the potent, the omnipresent, teacher. For good or for ill, it teaches the whole people by its example. Crime is contagious. If the government becomes a law-breaker, it breeds contempt for law; it invites every man to become a law unto himself; it invites anarchy. To declare that in the administration of the criminal law the end justifies the means—to declare that the government may commit crimes in order to secure the conviction of a private criminal—would bring terrible retribution. Against that pernicious doctrine this court should resolutely set its face.

Mr. Justice Butler, dissenting:

. . . This court has always construed the Constitution in the light of the principles upon which it was founded. The direct operation or literal meaning of the words used do not measure the purpose or scope of its provisions. Under the principles established and applied by this court, the 4th Amendment safeguards against all evils that are like and equivalent to those embraced within the ordinary meaning of its words. That construction is consonant with sound reason and in full accord with the course of decisions since *M'Culloch v. Maryland.* . . .

When the facts in these cases are truly estimated, a fair application of that principle decides the constitutional question in favor of the petitioners. With great deference, I think should be given a new trial.

Mr. Justice Stone, dissenting. . . .

Katz v. United States
389 U.S. 347; 88 S. Ct. 507; 19 L. Ed. 2d 576 (1967)
Vote: 7-1

Mr. Justice Stewart delivered the opinion of the Court.

The petitioner was convicted in the District Court for the Southern District of California under an eight-count indictment charging him with transmitting wagering information by telephone from Los Angeles to Miami and Boston in violation of a federal statute. At trial the Government was permitted, over the petitioner's objection, to introduce evidence of the petitioner's end of telephone conversations, overheard by FBI agents who had attached an electronic listening and recording device to the outside of the public telephone booth from which he had placed his calls. In affirming his conviction, the Court of Appeals rejected the contention that the recordings had been obtained in violation of the Fourth Amendment, because "[t]here was no physical entrance into the area occupied by [the petitioner]." We granted *certiorari* in order to consider the constitutional questions thus presented.

The petitioner has phrased those questions as follows:

A. Whether a public telephone booth is a constitutionally protected area so that evidence obtained by attaching an electronic listening recording device to the top of such a booth is obtained in violation of the right to privacy of the user of the booth.

B. Whether physical penetration of a constitutionally protected area is necessary before a search and seizure can be said to be violative of the Fourth Amendment to the United States Constitution.

We decline to adopt this formulation of the issues. In the first place the correct solution of Fourth Amendment problems is not necessarily promoted by incantation of the phrase "constitutionally protected area." Secondly, the Fourth Amendment cannot be translated into a general constitutional "right to privacy." That Amendment protects individual privacy against certain kinds of governmental intrusion, but its protections go further, and often have nothing to do with privacy at all. Other provisions of the Constitution protect personal privacy from other forms of governmental invasion. But the protection of a person's general right to privacy—his right to be let alone by other people—is, like the protection of his property and of his very life, left largely to the law of the individual States.

Because of the misleading way the issues have been formulated, the parties have attached great significance to the characterization of the telephone booth from which the petitioner placed his calls. The petitioner has strenuously argued that the booth was a "constitutionally protected area." The Government has maintained with equal vigor that it was not. But this effort to decide whether or not a given "area," viewed in the abstract, is "constitutionally protected" deflects attention from the problem presented by this case. For the Fourth Amendment protects people, not places. What a person knowingly exposes to the public, even in his own home or office, is not a subject of Fourth Amendment protection. But what he seeks to preserve as private, even in an area accessible to the public, may be constitutionally protected.

The Government stresses the fact that the telephone booth from which the petitioner made his calls was constructed partly of glass, so that he was as visible after he entered it as he would have been if he had remained outside. But what he sought to exclude when he entered the booth was not the intruding eye—it was the uninvited ear. He did not shed his right to do so simply because he made his calls from a place where he might be seen. No less than an individual in a business office, in a friend's apartment, or in a taxicab, a person in a telephone booth may rely upon the protection of the Fourth Amendment. One who occupies it, shuts the door behind him, and pays the toll that permits him to place a call is surely entitled to assume that the words he utters into the mouthpiece will not be broadcast to the world. To read the Constitution more narrowly is to ignore the vital role that the public telephone has come to play in private communication.

The Government contends, however, that the activities of its agents in this case should not be tested by Fourth Amendment requirements, for the surveillance technique they employed involved no physical penetration of the telephone booth from which the petitioner placed his calls. It is true that the absence of such penetration was at one time thought to foreclose further Fourth Amendment inquiry, *** for that Amendment was thought to limit only searches and seizures of tangible property. But "[t]he premise that property interests control the right of the Government to search and seize has been discredited." Thus, although a closely divided Court supposed in Olmstead that surveillance without any trespass and without the seizure of any material object fell outside the ambit of the Constitution, we have since departed from the narrow view on which that decision rested. Indeed, we have expressly held that the

Fourth Amendment governs not only the seizure of tangible items, but extends as well to the recording of oral statements overheard without any "technical trespass under ... local property law." Once this much is acknowledged, and once it is recognized that the Fourth Amendment protects people—and not simply "areas"—against unreasonable searches and seizures it becomes clear that the reach of the Amendment cannot turn upon the presence or absence of a physical intrusion into any given enclosure.

We conclude that the underpinnings of ... [*Olmstead v. United States*] ... have been so eroded by our subsequent decisions that the "trespass" doctrine there enunciated can no longer be regarded as controlling. The Government's activities in electronically listening to and recording the petitioner's words violated the privacy upon which he justifiably relied while using the telephone booth and thus constituted a "search and seizure" within the meaning of the Fourth Amendment. The fact that the electronic device employed to achieve that end did not happen to penetrate the wall of the booth can have no constitutional significance.

The question remaining for decision, then, is whether the search and seizure conducted in this case complied with constitutional standards. In that regard, the Government's position is that its agents acted in an entirely defensible manner. They did not begin their electronic surveillance until investigation of the petitioner's activities had established a strong probability that he was using the telephone in question to transmit gambling information to persons in other States, in violation of federal law. Moreover, the surveillance was limited, both in scope and in duration, to the specific purpose of establishing the contents of the petitioner's unlawful telephone communications. The agents confined their surveillance to the brief periods during which he used the telephone booth, and they took great care to overhear only the conversations of the petitioner himself.

Accepting this account of the Government's actions as accurate, it is clear that this surveillance was so narrowly circumscribed that a duly authorized magistrate, properly notified of the need for such investigation, specifically informed of the basis on which it was to proceed, and clearly apprised of the precise intrusion it would entail, could constitutionally have authorized, with appropriate safeguards, the very limited search and seizure that the Government asserts in fact took place.

The Government urges that, because its agents ... did no more here than they might properly have done with prior judicial sanction, we should retroactively validate their conduct. That we cannot do. It is apparent that the agents in this case acted with restraint. Yet the inescapable fact is that this restraint was imposed by the agents themselves, not by a judicial officer. They were not required, before commencing the search, to present their estimate of probable cause for detached scrutiny by a neutral magistrate. They were not compelled, during the conduct of the search itself, to observe precise limits established in advance by a specific court order. Nor were they directed, after the search had been completed, to notify the authorizing magistrate in detail of all that had been seized. In the absence of such safeguards, this Court has never sustained a search upon the sole ground that officers reasonably expected to find evidence of a particular crime and voluntarily confined their activities to the least intrusive means consistent with that end. Searches conducted without warrants have been held unlawful "notwithstanding facts unquestionably showing probable cause," for the Constitution requires "that the deliberate, impartial judgment of a judicial officer ... be interposed between the citizen and the police...." "Over and again this Court has emphasized that the mandate of the [Fourth] Amendment requires adherence to judicial processes," and that searches conducted outside the judicial process, without prior approval by judge or magistrate, are *per se* unreasonable under the Fourth Amendment—subject only to a few specifically established and well-delineated exceptions.

It is difficult to imagine how any of those exceptions could ever apply to the sort of search and seizure involved in this case. Even electronic surveillance substantially contemporaneous with an individual's arrest could hardly be deemed an "incident" of that arrest. Nor could the use of electronic surveillance without prior authorization be justified on grounds of "hot pursuit." And, of course, the very nature of electronic surveillance precludes its use pursuant to the suspect's consent.

The Government does not question these basic principles. Rather, it urges the creation of a new exception to cover this case. It argues that surveillance of a telephone booth should be exempted from the usual requirement of advance authorization by a magistrate upon a showing of probable cause. We cannot agree. Omission of such authorization

bypasses the safeguards provided by an objective predetermination of probable cause, and substitutes instead the far less reliable procedure of an after-the-event justification for the ... search, too likely to be subtly influenced by the familiar shortcomings of hindsight judgment. ***

And bypassing a neutral predetermination of the scope of a search leaves individuals secure from Fourth Amendment violations "only in the discretion of the police." ***

These considerations do not vanish when the search in question is transferred from the setting of a home, an office, or a hotel room to that of a telephone booth. Wherever a man may be, he is entitled to know that he will remain free from unreasonable searches and seizures. The government agents here ignored "the procedure of antecedent justification ... that is central to the Fourth Amendment," *** a procedure that we hold to be a constitutional precondition of the kind of electronic surveillance involved in this case. Because the surveillance here failed to meet that condition, and because it led to the petitioner's conviction, the judgment must be reversed.

Mr. Justice Marshall took no part in the consideration or decision of this case.

Mr. Justice Douglas, with whom **Mr. Justice Brennan** joins, concurring....

Mr. Justice Harlan, concurring.

I join the opinion of the Court, which I read to hold only (a) that an enclosed telephone booth is an area where, like a home, a person has a constitutionally protected reasonable expectation of privacy; (b) that electronic as well as physical intrusion into a place that is in this sense private may constitute a violation of the Fourth Amendment; and (c) that the invasion of a constitutionally protected area by federal authorities is, as the Court has long held, presumptively unreasonable in the absence of a search warrant.

As the Court's opinion states, "the Fourth Amendment protects people, not places." The question, however, is what protection it affords to those people. Generally, as here, the answer to that question requires reference to a "place." My understanding of the rule that has emerged from prior decisions is that there is a twofold requirement, first that a person have exhibited an actual (subjective) expectation of privacy and, second, that the expectation be one that society is prepared to recognize as "reasonable." Thus a man's home is, for most purposes, a place where he expects privacy, but objects, activities, or statements that he exposes to the "plain view" of outsiders are not "protected" because no intention to keep them to himself has been exhibited. On the other hand, conversations in the open would not be protected against being overheard, for the expectation of privacy under the circumstances would be unreasonable.

The critical fact in this case is that "[o]ne who occupies it [a telephone booth], shuts the door behind him, and pays the toll that permits him to place a call is surely entitled to assume" that his conversation is not being intercepted. The point is not that the booth is "accessible to the public" at other times, but that it is a temporarily private place whose momentary occupants' expectations of freedom from intrusion are recognized as reasonable. . . .

Mr. Justice White, concurring. . . .

Mr. Justice Black, dissenting.

My basic objection is twofold: (1) I do not believe that the words of the Amendment will bear the meaning given them by today's decision, and (2) I do not believe that it is the proper role of this Court to rewrite the Amendment in order "to bring it into harmony with the times" and thus reach a result that many people believe to be desirable.

While I realize that an argument based on the meaning of words lacks the scope, and no doubt the appeal, of broad policy discussions and philosophical discourses on such nebulous subjects as privacy, for me the language of the Amendment is the crucial

place to look in construing a written document such as our Constitution. The Fourth Amendment says that

The right of the people to be secure in their persons, houses, papers, and effects, against unreasonable searches and seizures, shall not be violated, and no Warrants shall issue, but upon probable cause, supported by Oath or affirmation, and particularly describing the place to be searched, and the persons or things to be seized.

The first clause protects "persons, houses, papers, and effects, against unreasonable searches and seizures. . . ." These words connote the idea of tangible things with size, form, and weight, things capable of being searched, seized, or both. The second clause of the Amendment still further established its Framers' purpose to limit its protection to tangible things by providing that no warrants shall issue but those "particularly describing the place to be searched, and the persons or things to be seized." A conversation overheard by eavesdropping, whether by plain snooping or wire-tapping, is not tangible and, under the normally accepted meanings of the words, can neither be searched nor seized. In addition the language of the second clause indicates that the Amendment refers not only to something tangible so it can be seized but to something already in existence so it can be described. Yet the Court's interpretation would have the Amendment apply to overhearing future conversations which by their very nature are nonexistent until they take place. How can one "describe" a future conversation, and, if one cannot, how can a magistrate issue a warrant to eavesdrop one in the future? It is argued that information showing what is expected to be said is sufficient to limit the boundaries of what later can be admitted into evidence; but does such general information really meet the specific language of the Amendment which says "particularly describing"? Rather than using language in a completely artificial way, I must conclude that the Fourth Amendment simply does not apply to eavesdropping.

Tapping telephone wires, of course, was an unknown possibility at the time the Fourth Amendment was adopted. But eavesdropping (and wiretapping is nothing more than eavesdropping by telephone) was, "an ancient practice which at common law was condemned as a nuisance. In those days the eavesdropper listened by naked ear under the eaves of houses or their windows, or beyond their walls seeking out private discourse." *** There can be no doubt that the Framers were aware of this practice, and if they had desired to outlaw or restrict the use of evidence obtained by eavesdropping, I believe that they would have used the appropriate language to do so in the Fourth Amendment. They certainly would not have left such a task to the ingenuity of language-stretching judges. No one, it seems to me, can read the debates on the Bill of Rights without reaching the conclusion that its Framers and critics well knew the meaning of the words they used, what they would be understood to mean by others, their scope and their limitations. Under these circumstances it strikes me as a charge against their scholarship, their common sense and their candor to give to the Fourth Amendment's language the eavesdropping meaning the Court imputes to it today.

I do not deny that common sense requires and that this Court often has said that the Bill of Rights' safeguards should be given a liberal construction. This principle, however, does not justify construing the search and seizure amendment as applying to eavesdropping or the "seizure" of conversations. The

Fourth Amendment was aimed directly at the abhorred practice of breaking in, ransacking and searching homes and other buildings and seizing people's personal belongings without warrants issued by magistrates. The Amendment deserves, and this Court has given it, a liberal construction in order to protect against warrantless searches of buildings and seizures of tangible personal effects. But until today this Court has refused to say that eavesdropping comes within the ambit of Fourth Amendment restrictions.

Since I see no way in which the words of the Fourth Amendment can be construed to apply to eavesdropping, that closes the matter for me. In interpreting the Bill of Rights, I willingly go as far as a liberal construction of the language takes me, but I simply cannot in good conscience give a meaning to words which they have never before been thought to have and which they certainly do not have in common ordinary usage. I will not distort the words of the Amendment in order to "keep the Constitution up to date" or "to bring it into harmony with the time." It was never meant that this Court have such power, which in effect would make us a continuously functioning constitutional convention.

Illinois v. Gates

462 U.S. 213; 103 S. Ct. 2317; 76 L. Ed. 2d 527 (1983)
Vote: 6-3

Justice Rehnquist delivered the opinion of the Court.

Respondents Lance and Susan Gates were indicted for violation of state drug laws after police officers, executing a search warrant, discovered marijuana and other contraband in the automobile and home. Prior to trial the Gateses moved to suppress evidence seized during the search. The Illinois Supreme Court affirmed the decisions of lower state courts granting the motion. It held that the affidavit submitted in support of the State's application for a warrant to search the Gateses' property was inadequate under this Court's decisions in *Aguilar v. Texas* *** (1964) and *Spinelli v. United States* *** (1969). . . .

We now turn to the question presented in the State's original petition for *certiorari,* which requires us to decide whether respondents' rights under the Fourth and Fourteenth Amendments were violated by the search of their car and house. A chronological statement of events usefully introduces the issues at stake. Bloomingdale, Ill., is a suburb of Chicago located in DuPage County. On May 3, 1978, the Bloomingdale Police Department received by mail an anonymous handwritten letter which read as follows:

This letter is to inform you that you have a couple in your town who strictly make their living on selling drugs. They are Sue and Lance Gates, they live on Greenway, off Bloomingdale Rd. in the condominiums. Most of their buys are done in Florida. Sue his wife drives their car to Florida, where she leaves it to be loaded up with drugs, then Lance flys down and drives it back. Sue flys back after she drops the car off in Florida. May 3 she is driving down there again and Lance will be flying down in a few days to drive it back. At the time Lance drives the car back he has the trunk loaded with over $100,000.00 in drugs. Presently, they have over $100,000.00 worth of drugs in their basement. They brag about the fact they never have to work, and make their entire living on pushers.

I guarantee if you watch them carefully you will make a big catch. They are friends with some big drug dealers, who visit their house often.

The letter was referred by the Chief of Police of the Bloomingdale Police Department to Detective Mader, who decided to pursue the tip. Mader learned, from the office of the Illinois Secretary of State, that an Illinois driver's license had been issued to one Lance Gates, residing at a stated address in Bloomingdale. He contacted a confidential informant, whose examination of certain financial records revealed a more recent address for the Gates, and he also learned from a police officer assigned to O'Hare Airport that "L. Gates" had made a reservation on Eastern Airlines flight 245 to West Palm Beach, Fla., scheduled to depart from Chicago on May 5 at 4:15 P.M.

Mader then made arrangements with an agent of the Drug Enforcement Administration for surveillance of the May 5 Eastern Airlines flight. The agent later reported to Mader that Gates had boarded the flight, and that federal agents in Florida had observed him arrive in West Palm Beach and take a taxi to the nearby Holiday Inn. They also reported that Gates went to a room registered to one Susan Gates and that, at 7:00 A.M. the next morning, Gates and an unidentified woman left the motel in a Mercury bearing Illinois license plates and drove northbound on an interstate frequently used by travelers to the Chicago area. In addition, the DEA [Drug Enforcement Administration] agent informed Mader that the license plate number on the Mercury was registered to a Hornet station wagon owned by Gates.

Mader signed an affidavit setting forth the foregoing facts, and submitted it to a judge of the Circuit Court of DuPage County, together with a copy of the anonymous letter. The judge of that court thereupon issued a search warrant for the Gateses' residence and for their automobile. The judge, in deciding to

issue the warrant, could have determined that the *modus operandi* of the Gateses had been substantially corroborated.

At 5:15 A.M. on March 7th, only 36 hours after he had flown out of Chicago, Lance Gates, and his wife, returned to their home in Bloomingdale, driving the car in which they had left West Palm Beach some 22 hours earlier. The Bloomingdale police were awaiting them, searched the trunk of the Mercury, and uncovered approximately 350 pounds of marijuana. A search of the Gateses' home revealed marijuana, weapons, and other contraband. The Illinois Circuit Court ordered suppression of all these items, on the ground that the affidavit submitted to the Circuit Judge failed to support the necessary determination of probable cause to believe that the Gateses' automobile and home contained the contraband in question. This decision was affirmed in turn by the Illinois Appellate Court and by a divided vote of the Supreme Court of Illinois. ***

The Illinois Supreme Court concluded—and we are inclined to agree—that, standing alone, the anonymous letter sent to the Bloomingdale Police Department would not provide the basis for a magistrate's determination that there was probable cause to believe contraband would be found in the Gateses' car and home. The letter provides virtually nothing from which one might conclude that its author is either honest or his information reliable; likewise, the letter gives absolutely no indication of the basis for the writer's predictions regarding the Gateses' criminal activities. Something more was required, then, before a magistrate could conclude that there was probable cause to believe that contraband would be found in the Gateses' home and car. ***

The Illinois Supreme Court also properly recognized that Detective Mader's affidavit might be capable of supplementing the anonymous letter with information sufficient to permit a determination of probable cause. *** In holding that the affidavit in fact did not contain sufficient additional information to sustain a determination of probable cause, the Illinois court applied a "two-pronged test," derived from our decision in *Spinelli v. United States.* *** The Illinois Supreme Court, like some others, apparently understood *Spinelli* as requiring that the anonymous letter satisfy each of two independent requirements before it could be relied on. According to this view, the letter, as supplemented by Mader's affidavit, first had to adequately reveal the "basis of knowledge" of the letter writer—the particular means by which he came by the information given in his report. Second, it had to provide facts sufficiently establishing either the "veracity" of the affiant's informant, or, alternatively, the "reliability" of the informant's report in this particular case.

The Illinois court, alluding to an elaborate set of legal rules that have developed among various lower courts to enforce the "two-pronged test," found that the test had not been satisfied. First, the "veracity" prong was not satisfied because, "there was simply no basis [for] ... conclud[ing] that the anonymous person [who wrote the letter to the Bloomingdale Police Department] was credible." The court indicated that corroboration by police of details contained in the letter might never satisfy the "veracity" prong, and in any event, could not do so if, as in the present case, only "innocent" details are corroborated. *** In addition, the letter gave no indication of the basis of its writer's knowledge of the Gateses' activities. The Illinois court understood *Spinelli* as permitting the detail contained in a tip to be used to infer that the informant had a reliable basis for his statements, but it thought that the anonymous letter failed to provide sufficient detail to permit such an inference. Thus, it concluded that no showing of probable cause had been made.

We agree with the Illinois Supreme Court that an informant's "veracity," "reliability" and "basis of knowledge" are all highly relevant in determining the value of his report. We do not agree, however, that these elements should be understood as entirely separate and independent requirements to be rigidly exacted in every case, which the opinion of the Supreme Court of Illinois would imply. Rather, as detailed below, they should be understood simply as closely intertwined issues that may usefully illuminate the commonsense, practical question whether there is "probable cause" to believe that contraband or evidence is located in a particular place.

This totality-of-the-circumstances approach is far more consistent with our prior treatment of probable cause than is any rigid demand that specific "tests" be satisfied by every informant's tip. Perhaps

the central teaching of our decisions bearing on the probable cause standard is that it is a "practical, nontechnical conception." *** "In dealing with probable cause, ... as the very name implies, we deal with probabilities. These are not technical, they are the factual and practical considerations of everyday life on which reasonable and prudent men, not legal technicians, act." ***

[P]robable cause is a fluid concept—turning on the assessment of probabilities in particular factual contexts—not readily, or even usefully, reduced to a neat set of legal rules. Informants' tips doubtless come in many shapes and sizes from many different types of persons. "Informants' tips, like all other clues and evidence coming to a policeman on the scene, may vary greatly in their value and reliability." Rigid legal rules are ill-suited to an area of such diversity. "One simple rule will not cover every situation." ***

Moreover, the "two-pronged test" directs analysis into two largely independent channels—the informant's "veracity" or "reliability" and his "basis of knowledge." There are persuasive arguments against according these two elements such independent status. Instead, they are better understood as relevant considerations in the totality-of-the-circumstances analysis that traditionally has guided probable cause determinations: a deficiency in one may be compensated for, in determining the overall reliability of a tip, by a strong showing as to the other, or by some other indicia of reliability. ***

If, for example, a particular informant is known for the unusual reliability of his predictions of certain types of criminal activities in a locality, his failure, in a particular case, to thoroughly set forth the basis of his knowledge surely should not serve as an absolute bar to a finding of probable cause based on his tip. *** Likewise, if an unquestionably honest citizen comes forward with a report of criminal activity—which if fabricated would subject him to criminal liability—we have found rigorous scrutiny of the basis of his knowledge unnecessary.... Conversely, even if we entertain some doubt as to an informant's motives, his explicit and detailed description of alleged wrongdoing, along with a statement that the event was observed firsthand, entitles his tip to greater weight than might otherwise be the case.

Unlike a totality-of-the-circumstances analysis, which permits a balanced assessment of the relative weights of all the various indicia of reliability (and unreliability) attending an informant's tip, the "two-pronged test" has encouraged an excessively technical dissection of informants' tips, with undue attention being focused on isolated issues that cannot sensibly be divorced from the other facts presented to the magistrate.

As early as *Locke v. United States* *** (1813), Chief Justice Marshall observed, in a closely related context, that "the term 'probable cause,' according to its usual acceptation, means less than evidence which would justify condemnation. . . . It imports a seizure made under circumstances which warrant suspicion." More recently, we said that "the quanta . . . of proof" appropriate in ordinary judicial proceedings are inapplicable to the decision to issue a warrant. *** Finely tuned standards such as proof beyond a reasonable doubt or by a preponderance of the evidence, useful in formal trials, have no place in the magistrate's decision. While an effort to fix some general, numerically precise degree of certainty corresponding to "probable cause" may not be helpful, it is clear that "only the probability, and not a *prima facie* showing, of criminal activity is the standard of probable cause." ***

We also have recognized that affidavits "are normally drafted by nonlawyers in the midst and haste of a criminal investigation. Technical requirements of elaborate specificity once exacted under common law pleading have no proper place in this area." *** Likewise, search and arrest warrants long have been issued by persons who were neither lawyers or judges, and who certainly do not remain abreast of each judicial refinement of the nature of "probable cause." *** The rigorous inquiry into the *Spinelli* prongs and the complex superstructure of evidentiary and analytical rules that some have seen implicit in our *Spinelli* decision, cannot be reconciled with the fact that many warrants are—quite properly, *** issued on the basis of nontechnical common-sense judgments of laymen applying a standard less demanding than those used in more formal legal proceedings. . . .

Similarly, we have repeatedly said that after-the-fact scrutiny by courts of the sufficiency of an affidavit should not take the form of *de novo* review. A magistrate's determination of probable cause should be paid great deference by reviewing courts." ***

If the affidavits submitted by police officers are subjected to the type of scrutiny some courts have deemed appropriate, police might well resort to warrantless searches, with the hope of relying on consent or some other exception to the warrant clause that might develop at the time of the search. In addition, the possession of a warrant by officers conducting an arrest or search greatly reduces the perception of unlawful or intrusive police conduct, by assuring "the individual whose property is searched or seized of the lawful authority of the executing officer, his need to search, and the limits of his power to search." *** Reflecting this preference for the warrant process, the traditional standard for review of an issuing magistrate's probable cause determination has been that so long as the magistrate has a "substantial basis for . . . conclud[ing]" that a search would uncover evidence of wrongdoing, the Fourth Amendment requires no more. *** We think reaffirmation of this standard better serves the purpose of encouraging recourse to the warrant procedure and is more consistent with our traditional deference to the probable cause determinations of magistrates than is the "two-pronged test."

Finally, the direction taken by decisions following *Spinelli* poorly serves "[t]he most basic function of any government": "to provide for the security of the individual and of his property." *** The strictures that inevitably accompany the "two-pronged test" cannot avoid seriously impeding the task of law enforcement. *** . . . Ordinary citizens, like ordinary witnesses, generally do not provide extensive recitations of the basis of their everyday observations. Likewise, as the Illinois Supreme Court observed in this case, the veracity of persons supplying anonymous tips is by hypothesis largely unknown and unknowable. As a result, anonymous tips seldom could survive a rigorous application of either of the *Spinelli* prongs. Yet, such tips, particularly when supplemented by independent police investigation, frequently contribute to the solution of otherwise "perfect crimes." While a conscientious assessment of the basis for crediting such tips is required by the Fourth Amendment, a standard that leaves virtually no place for anonymous citizen informants is not.

For all these reasons, we conclude that it is wiser to abandon the "two-pronged test" established by our decisions in *Aguilar* and *Spinelli*. In its place we reaffirm the totality of the circumstances analysis that traditionally has informed probable cause determinations. *** We are convinced that this flexible, easily applied standard will better achieve the accommodation of public and private interests that the Fourth Amendment requires than does the approach that has developed from *Aguilar* and *Spinelli*. . . .

Justice White, concurring in the judgment. . . .

Justice Brennan, with whom **Justice Marshall** joins, dissenting.

. . . In recognition of the judiciary's role as the only effective guardian of Fourth Amendment rights, this Court has developed over the last half century a set of coherent rules governing a magistrate's consideration of a warrant application and the showings that are necessary to support a finding of probable cause. We start with the proposition that a neutral and detached magistrate, and not the police, should determine whether there is probable cause to support the issuance of a warrant. . . .

In order to emphasize the magistrate's role as an independent arbiter of probable cause and to insure that searches and seizures are not effected on less than probable cause, the Court has insisted that police officers provide magistrates with the underlying facts and circumstances that support the officer's conclusions. . . .

To suggest that anonymous informants' tips are subject to the tests established by *Aguilar* and *Spinelli* is not to suggest that they can never provide a basis for a finding of probable cause. It is conceivable that police corroboration of the details of the tip might establish the reliability of the informant under *Aguilar's* veracity prong, as refined in *Spinelli*, and that the details in the tip might be sufficient to qualify under the "self-verifying detail" test established by *Spinelli* as a means of satisfying *Aguilar's* basis of knowledge prong. The *Aguilar* and *Spinelli* tests must be applied to anonymous informants' tips, however, if we are to continue to insure that findings of probable cause, and attendant intrusions, are based on information provided by an honest or cred-

ible person who has acquired the information in a reliable way. . . .

In light of the important purposes served by *Aguilar* and *Spinelli*, I would not reject the standards they establish. If anything, I simply would make more clear that *Spinelli*, properly understood, does not depart in any fundamental way from the test established by *Aguilar*. For reasons I shall next state, I do not find persuasive the Court's justifications for rejecting the test established by *Aguilar* and refined by *Spinelli*. . . .

. . . [O]ne can concede that probable cause is a "practical, nontechnical" concept without betraying the values that *Aguilar* and *Spinelli* reflect. *** *Aguilar* and *Spinelli* require the police to provide magistrates with certain crucial information. They also provide structure for magistrates' probable cause inquiries. In so doing, *Aguilar* and *Spinelli* preserve the role of magistrates as independent arbiters of probable cause determinations, and advance the substantive value of precluding findings of probable cause, and attendant intrusions, based on anything less than information from an honest or credible person who has acquired his information in a reliable way. Neither the standards nor their effects are inconsistent with a "practical, nontechnical" conception of probable cause. Once a magistrate has determined that he has information before him that he can reasonably say has been obtained in a reliable way by a credible person, he has ample room to use his common sense and to apply a practical, nontechnical conception of probable cause. . . .

The Court also insists that the *Aguilar-Spinelli* standards must be abandoned because they are inconsistent with the fact that non-lawyers frequently serve as magistrates. *** To the contrary, the standards help to structure probable cause inquiries and, properly interpreted, may actually help a non-lawyer magistrate in making a probable cause determination. Moreover, the *Aguilar* and *Spinelli* tests are not inconsistent with deference to magistrates' determinations of probable cause. . . .

At the heart of the Court's decision to abandon *Aguilar* and *Spinelli* appears to be its belief that "the direction taken by decisions following *Spinelli* poorly serves 'the most basic function of any government: to provide for the security of the individual and of his property.' " *** This conclusion rests on the judgment that *Aguilar* and *Spinelli* "seriously imped[e] the task of law enforcement," *** and render anonymous tips valueless in police work. *** Surely, the Court overstates its case. *** But of particular concern to all Americans must be that the Court gives virtually no consideration to the value of insuring that findings of probable cause are based on information that a magistrate can reasonably say has been obtained in a reliable way by an honest or credible person. I share Justice White's fear that the court's rejection of *Aguilar* and *Spinelli* and its adoption of a new totality of the circumstances test, "may foretell an evisceration of the probable cause standard. . . ." ***

The Court's complete failure to provide any persuasive reason for rejecting *Aguilar* and *Spinelli* doubtlessly reflects impatience with what it perceives to be "overly technical" rules governing searches and seizures under the Fourth Amendment. Words such as "practical," "nontechnical," and "commonsense," as used in the Court's opinion, are but code words for an overly permissive attitude toward police practices in derogation of the rights secured by the Fourth Amendment. Everyone shares the Court's concern over the horror of drug trafficking, but under our Constitution only measures consistent with the Fourth Amendment may be employed by government to cure this evil. We must be ever mindful of Justice Stewart's admonition in *Coolidge v. New Hampshire,* *** (1971), that "[i]n times of unrest, whether caused by crime or racial conflict or fear of internal subversion, this basic law and the values that it represents may appear unrealistic or 'extravagant' to some. But the values were those of the authors of our fundamental constitutional concepts." ***

Rights secured by the Fourth Amendment are particularly difficult to protect because their "advocates are usually criminals." But the rules "we fashion [are] for the innocent and guilty alike." *** . . . [T]oday's decision threatens to "obliterate one of the most fundamental distinctions between our form of government, where officers are under the law, and the police-state where they are the law." ***

Justice Stevens, with whom ***Justice Brennan*** joins, dissenting.

The fact that Lance and Sue Gates made a 22-hour nonstop drive from West Palm Beach, Florida, to Bloomingdale, Illinois, only a few hours after Lance had flown to Florida provided persuasive evidence that they were engaged in illicit activity. The fact, however, was not known to the magistrate when he issued the warrant to search the home.

What the magistrate did know at the time was that the anonymous informant had not been completely accurate in his or her predictions. The informant had indicated that "Sue drives their car to Florida where she leaves it to be loaded up with drugs. . . . She flies back after she drops the car off in Florida." *** Yet Detective Mader's affidavit reported that she "left the West Palm Beach area driving the Mercury northbound." ***

The discrepancy between the informant's predictions and the facts known to Detective Mader is significant for three reasons. First, it cast doubt on the informant's hypothesis that the Gateses already had "over $100,000 worth of drugs in their basement." *** The informant had predicted an itinerary that always kept one spouse in Bloomingdale, suggesting that the Gateses did not want to leave their home unguarded because something valuable was hidden within. That inference obviously could not be drawn when it was known that the pair was actually together over a thousand miles from home.

Second, the discrepancy made the Gateses' conduct seem substantially less unusual than the informant had predicted it would be. It would have been odd if, as predicted, Sue had driven down to Florida on Wednesday, left the car, and flown right back to Illinois. But the mere facts that Sue was in West Palm Beach with the car, that she was joined by her husband at the Holiday Inn on Friday, and that the couple drove north together the next morning are neither unusual nor probative of criminal activity.

Third, the fact that the anonymous letter contained a material mistake undermines the reasonableness of relying on it as a basis for making a forcible entry into a private home.

Of course, the activities in this case did not stop when the magistrate issued the warrant. The Gateses drove all night to Bloomingdale, the officers searched the car and found 400 pounds of marijuana, and then they searched the house. However, none of these subsequent events may be considered in evaluating the warrant, and the search of the house was legal only if the warrant was valid. *** I cannot accept the Court's casual conclusion that, before the Gateses arrived in Bloomingdale, there was probable cause to justify a valid entry and search of a private home. No one knows who the informant in this case was, or

what motivated him or her to write the note. Given that the note's predictions were faulty in one significant respect, and were corroborated by nothing except ordinary innocent activity, I must surmise that the Court's evaluation of the warrant's validity has been colored by subsequent events. . . .

Chimel v. California

395 U.S. 752; 89 S. Ct. 2034; 23 L. Ed. 2d 685 (1969)
Vote: 7-2

Mr. *Justice Stewart* delivered the opinion of the Court.

This case raises basic questions concerning the permissible scope under the Fourth Amendment of a search incident to a lawful arrest.

The relevant facts are essentially undisputed. Late in the afternoon of September 13, 1965, three police officers arrived at the Santa Ana, California, home of the petitioner with a warrant authorizing his arrest for the burglary of a coin shop. The officers knocked on the door, identified themselves to the petitioner's wife, and asked if they might come inside. She ushered them into the house, where they waited 10 or 15 minutes until the petitioner returned home from work. When the petitioner entered the house, one of the officers handed him the arrest warrant and asked for permission to "look around." The petitioner objected, but was advised that "on the basis of the lawful arrest," the officers would nonetheless conduct a search. No search warrant had been issued.

Accompanied by the petitioner's wife, the officers then looked through the entire three-bedroom house, including the attic, the garage, and a small workshop. In some rooms the search was relatively cursory. In the master bedroom and sewing room, however, the officers directed the petitioner's wife to open drawers and "to physically move contents of the drawers from side to side so that [they] might view any items that would have come from [the] burglary." After completing the search, they seized numerous items—primarily coins, but also several

medals, tokens, and a few other objects. The entire search took between 45 minutes and an hour.

At the petitioner's subsequent state trial on two charges of burglary, the items taken from his house were admitted into evidence against him, over his objection that they had been unconstitutionally seized. He was convicted, and the judgments of conviction were affirmed by both the California Court of Appeal, *** and the California Supreme Court. *** Both courts accepted the petitioner's contention that the arrest warrant was invalid because the supporting affidavit was set out in conclusory terms, but held that since the arresting officers had procured the warrant "in good faith," and since in any event they had had sufficient information to constitute probable cause for the petitioner's arrest, that arrest had been lawful. From this conclusion the appellate courts went on to hold that the search of the petitioner's home had been justified, despite the absence of a search warrant, on the ground that it had been incident to a valid arrest. We granted *certiorari* in order to consider the petitioner's substantial constitutional claims. ***

Without deciding the question, we proceed on the hypothesis that the California courts were correct in holding that the arrest of the petitioner was valid under the Constitution. This brings us directly to the question whether the warrantless search of the petitioner's entire house can be constitutionally justified as incident to that arrest. The decisions of this Court bearing upon that question have been far from consistent, as even the most cursory review makes evident. . . .

In 1950 . . . came *United States v. Rabinowitz,* ******* the decision upon which California primarily relies in the case now before us. In *Rabinowitz,* federal authorities had been informed that the defendant was dealing in stamps bearing forged overprints. On the basis of that information they secured a warrant for his arrest, which they executed at his one-room business office. At the time of the arrest, the officers "searched the desk, safe, and file cabinets in the office for about an hour and a half," ******* and seized 573 stamps with forged overprints. The stamps were admitted into evidence at the defendant's trial, and this Court affirmed his conviction, rejecting the contention that the warrantless search had been unlawful. The Court held that the search in its entirety fell within the principle giving law enforcement authorities "[t]he right 'to search the place where the arrest is made in order to find and seize things connected with the crime. . . .' " ******* The test, said the Court, "is not whether it is reasonable to procure a search warrant, but whether the search was reasonable."

Rabinowitz has come to stand for the proposition, *inter alia,* that a warrantless search "incident to a lawful arrest" may generally extend to the area that is considered to be in the "possession" or under the "control" of the person arrested. And it was on the basis of that proposition that the California courts upheld the search of the petitioner's entire house in this case. That doctrine, however, at least in the broad sense in which it was applied by the California courts in this case, can withstand neither historical nor rational analysis.

Even limited to its own facts, the *Rabinowitz* decision was, as we have seen, hardly founded on an unimpeachable line of authority. . . .

Nor is the rationale by which the State seeks here to sustain the search of the petitioner's house supported by a reasoned view of the background and purpose of the Fourth Amendment. Mr. Justice Frankfurter wisely pointed out in his *Rabinowitz* dissent that the Amendment's proscription of "unreasonable searches and seizures" must be read in light of "the history that gave rise to the words"—a history of "abuses so deeply felt by the Colonies as to be one of the potent causes of the Revolution. . . ." ******* The Amendment was in large part a reaction to the general warrants and warrantless searches that had so alienated the colonists and had helped speed the movement for independence. In the scheme of the Amendment, therefore, the requirement that "no Warrants shall issue, but upon probable cause," plays a crucial part. . . .

A similar analysis underlies the "search incident to arrest" principle, and marks its proper extent. When an arrest is made, it is reasonable for the arresting officer to search the person arrested in order to remove any weapons that the latter might seek to use in order to resist arrest or effect his escape. Otherwise, the officer's safety might well be endangered, and the arrest itself frustrated. In addition, it is entirely reasonable for the arresting officer to search for and seize any evidence on the arrestee's person in order to prevent its concealment or destruction. And the area into which an arrestee might reach in order to grab a weapon or evidentiary items must, of course, be governed by a like rule. A gun on a table or in a drawer in front of one who is arrested can be as dangerous to the arresting officer as one concealed in the clothing of the person arrested. There is ample justification, therefore, for a search of the arrestee's person and the area "within his immediate control"—construing that phrase to mean the area from within which he might gain possession of a weapon or destructible evidence.

There is no comparable justification, however, for routinely searching any room other than that in which an arrest occurs—or, for that matter, for searching through all the desk drawers or other closed or concealed areas in that room itself. Such searches, in the absence of well-recognized exceptions, may be made only under the authority of a search warrant. . . .

It is argued in the present case that it is "reasonable" to search a man's house when he is arrested in it. But that argument is founded on little more than a subjective view regarding the acceptability of certain sorts of police conduct, and not on considerations relevant to Fourth Amendment interests. Under such an unconfined analysis, Fourth Amendment protection in this area would approach the evaporation point. It is not easy to explain why, for instance, it is less subjectively "reasonable" to search a man's house when he is arrested on his front lawn—or just down the street—than it is when he happens to be in the house at the time of arrest. . . .

The petitioner correctly points out that one result of decisions such as *Rabinowitz* and *Harris* is to give law enforcement officials the opportunity to engage in searches not justified by probable cause, by the simple expedient of arranging to arrest suspects at home rather than elsewhere. We do not suggest that the petitioner is necessarily correct in his assertion that such a strategy was utilized here, but the fact remains that had he been arrested earlier in the day, at his place of employment rather than at home, no search of his house could have been made without a search warrant. In any event, even apart from the possibility of such police tactics, the general point so forcefully made by Judge Learned Hand in *United States v. Kirschenblatt,* *** remains:

After arresting a man in his house, to rummage at will among his papers in search of whatever will convict him, appears to us to be indistinguishable from what might be done under a general warrant; indeed, the warrant would give more protection, for presumably it must be issued by a magistrate. True, by hypothesis the power would not exist, if the supposed offender were not found on the premises; but it is small consolation to know that one's papers are safe only so long as one is not at home. ***

Rabinowitz and *Harris* have been the subject of critical commentary for many years, and have been relied upon less and less in our own decisions. It is time, for the reasons we have stated, to hold that on their own facts, and insofar as the principles they stand for are inconsistent with those that we have endorsed today, they are no longer to be followed.

Application of sound Fourth Amendment principles to the facts of this case produces a clear result.

The search here went far beyond the petitioner's person and the area from within which he might have obtained either a weapon or something that could have been used as evidence against him. There was no constitutional justification, in the absence of a search warrant, for extending the search beyond that area. The scope of the search was, therefore, "unreasonable" under the Fourth and Fourteenth Amendments, and the petitioner's conviction cannot stand.

Mr. Justice Harlan, concurring. . . .

Mr. Justice White, with whom *Mr. Justice Black* joins, dissenting.

Few areas of the law have been as subject to shifting constitutional standards over the last 50 years as that of the search "incident to an arrest." There has been a remarkable instability in this whole area, which has seen at least four major shifts in emphasis. Today's opinion makes an untimely fifth. In my view, the Court should not abandon the old rule. . . .

An arrested man, by definition conscious of the police interest in him, and provided almost immediately with a lawyer and a judge, is in an excellent position to dispute the reasonableness of his arrest and contemporaneous search in a full adversary proceeding. I would uphold the constitutionality of this search contemporaneous with an arrest since there were probable cause both for the search and for the arrest, exigent circumstance involving the removal or destruction of evidence, and a satisfactory opportunity to dispute the issues of probable cause shortly thereafter. In this case, the search was reasonable.

United States v. Ross
456 U.S. 798; 102 S. Ct. 2157; 72 L. Ed. 2d 572 (1982)
Vote: 6-3

Justice Stevens delivered the opinion of the Court.
In *Carroll v. United States* [1925], *** the Court held that a warrantless search of an automobile stopped by police officers who had probable cause to believe

the vehicle contained contraband was not unreasonable within the meaning of the Fourth Amendment. The Court in *Carroll* did not explicitly address the scope of the search that is permissible. In this case, we consider the extent to which police officers—who have legitimately stopped an automobile and who have probable cause to believe that contraband is concealed somewhere within it—may conduct a probing search of compartments and containers within the vehicle whose contents are not in plain view. We hold that they may conduct a search of the vehicle that is as thorough as a magistrate could authorize in a warrant "particularly describing the place to be searched."

In the evening of November 27, 1978, an informant who had previously proved to be reliable telephoned Detective Marcum of the District of Columbia Police Department and told him that an individual known as "Bandit" was selling narcotics kept in the trunk of a car parked at 439 Ridge Street. The informant stated that he had just observed "Bandit" complete a sale and that "Bandit" had told him that additional narcotics were in the trunk. The informant gave Marcum a detailed description of "Bandit" and stated that the car was a "purplish maroon" Chevrolet Malibu with District of Columbia license plates.

Accompanied by Detective Cassidy and Sergeant Gonzales, Marcum immediately drove to the area and found a maroon Malibu parked in front of 439 Ridge Street. A license check disclosed that the car was registered to Albert Ross; a computer check on Ross revealed that he fit the informant's description and used the alias "Bandit." In two passes through the neighborhood the officers did not observe anyone matching the informant's description. To avoid alerting persons on the street, they left the area.

The officers returned five minutes later and observed the maroon Malibu turning off Ridge Street onto Fourth Street. They pulled alongside the Malibu, noticed that the driver matched the informant's description, and stopped the car. Marcum and Cassidy told the driver—later identified as Albert Ross, the respondent in this action—to get out of the vehicle. While they searched Ross, Sergeant Gonzales discovered a bullet on the car's front seat. He searched the interior of the car and found a pistol in the glove compartment. Ross then was arrested and handcuffed. Detective Cassidy took Ross' keys and opened the trunk, where he found a closed brown paper bag. He opened the bag and discovered a

number of glassine bags containing a white powder. Cassidy replaced the bag, closed the trunk, and drove the car to headquarters.

At the police station Cassidy thoroughly searched the car. In addition to the "lunch-type" brown paper bag, Cassidy found in the trunk a zippered red leather pouch. He unzipped the pouch and discovered $3,200 in cash. The police laboratory later determined that the powder in the paper bag was heroin. No warrant was obtained.

Ross was charged with possession of heroin with intent to distribute. *** Prior to trial, he moved to suppress the heroin found in the paper bag and the currency found in the leather pouch. After an evidentiary hearing, the District Court denied the motion to suppress. The heroin and currency were introduced in evidence at trial and Ross was convicted.

A three-judge panel of the Court of Appeals reversed the conviction. It held that the police had probable cause to stop and search Ross' car and that, *** the officers lawfully could search the automobile—including its trunk—without a warrant. The court considered separately, however, the warrantless search of the two containers found in the trunk. On the basis of *Arkansas v. Sanders* *** the court concluded that the constitutionality of a warrantless search of a container found in an automobile depends on whether the owner possesses a reasonable expectation of privacy in its contents. Applying that test, the court held that the warrantless search of the paper bag was valid but the search of the leather pouch was not. The court remanded for a new trial at which the items taken from the paper bag, but not those from the leather pouch, could be admitted.

The entire Court of Appeals then voted to rehear the case *en banc*. A majority of the court rejected the panel's conclusion that a distinction of constitutional significance existed between the two containers found in respondent's trunk; it held that the police should not have opened either container without first obtaining a warrant.

The *en banc* Court of Appeals considered, and rejected, the argument that it was reasonable for the police to open both the paper bag and the leather pouch because they were entitled to conduct a warrantless search of the entire vehicle in which the two containers were found. The majority concluded that this argument was foreclosed by *Sanders*.

Three dissenting judges interpreted *Sanders* differently. Other courts also have read the *Sanders* opinion in different ways. Moreover, disagreement concerning the proper interpretation of *Sanders* was at least partially responsible for the fact that *Robbins v. California* *** was decided last Term without a Court opinion.

There is, however, no dispute among judges about the importance of striving for clarification in this area of the law. For countless vehicles are stopped on highways and public streets every day, and our cases demonstrate that it is not uncommon for police officers to have probable cause to believe that contraband may be found in a stopped vehicle. In every such case a conflict is presented between the individual's constitutionally protected interest in privacy and the public interest in effective law enforcement. No single rule of law can resolve every conflict, but our conviction that clarification is feasible led us to grant the Government's petition for *certiorari* in this case and to invite the parties to address the question whether the decision in *Robbins* should be reconsidered.

... [T]he exception to the warrant requirement established in *Carroll*—the scope of which we consider in this case—applied only to searches of vehicles that are supported by probable cause. In this class of cases, a search is not unreasonable if based on facts that would justify the issuance of a warrant, even though a warrant has not actually been obtained.

The rationale justifying a warrantless search of an automobile that is believed to be transporting contraband arguably applies with equal force to any movable container that is believed to be carrying an illicit substance. . . .

... A lawful search of fixed premises generally extends to the entire area in which the object of the search may be found and is not limited by the possibility that separate acts of entry or opening may be required to complete the search. Thus, a warrant that authorizes an officer to search a home for illegal weapons also provides authority to open closets, chests, drawers, and containers in which the weapon might be found. A warrant to open a footlocker to search for marihuana would also authorize the opening of packages found inside. A warrant to search a vehicle would support a search of every part of the vehicle that might contain the object of the search. When a legitimate search is under way, and when its purpose and its limits have been precisely defined, nice distinctions between closets, drawers, and containers, in the case of a home, or between glove compartments, upholstered seats, trunks, and wrapped packages, in the case of a vehicle, must give way to the interest in the prompt and efficient completion of the task at hand.

This rule applies equally to all containers, as indeed we believe it must. One point on which the Court was in virtually unanimous agreement in *Robbins* was that a constitutional distinction between "worthy" and "unworthy" containers would be improper. Even though such a distinction perhaps could evolve in a series of cases in which paper bags, locked trunks, lunch buckets, and orange crates were placed on one side of the line or the other, the central purpose of the Fourth Amendment forecloses such a distinction. . . .

The scope of a warrantless search of an automobile thus is not defined by the nature of the container in which the contraband is secreted. Rather, it is defined by the object of the search and the places in which there is probable cause to believe that it may be found. Just as probable cause to believe that a stolen lawnmower may be found in a garage will not support a warrant to search an upstairs bedroom, probable cause to believe that undocumented aliens are being transported in a van will not justify a warrantless search of a suitcase. Probable cause to believe that a container placed in the trunk of a taxi contains contraband or evidence does not justify a search of the entire cab.

Our decision today is inconsistent with the disposition in *Robbins v. California* and with the portion of the opinion in *Arkansas v. Sanders* on which the plurality in *Robbins* relied. Nevertheless, the doctrine of *stare decisis* does not preclude this action. Although we have rejected some of the reasoning in *Sanders*, we adhere to our holding in that case; although we reject the precise holding in *Robbins*, there was no Court opinion supporting a single rationale for its judgment, and the reasoning we adopt today was not presented by the parties in that case. Moreover, it is clear that no legitimate reliance interest can be frustrated by our decision today. Of greatest importance, we are convinced that the rule we apply in this case is faithful to the interpretation of the Fourth Amendment that the Court has followed with substantial consistency throughout our history.

. . . The exception recognized in *Carroll* is unquestionably one that is "specifically established and well delineated." *** We hold that the scope of the warrantless search authorized by that exception is no broader and no narrower than a magistrate could legitimately authorize by warrant. If probable cause justifies the search of a lawfully stopped vehicle, it justifies the search of every part of the vehicle and its contents that may conceal the object of the search.

The judgment of the Court of Appeals is reversed. The case is remanded for further proceedings consistent with this opinion.

It is so ordered.

Justice Blackmun, concurring. . . .

Justice Powell, concurring. . . .

Justice White, dissenting. . . .

Justice Marshall, with whom **Justice Brennan** joins, dissenting.

The majority today not only repeals all realistic limits on warrantless automobile searches, it repeals the Fourth Amendment warrant requirement itself. By equating a police officer's estimation of probable cause with a magistrate's, the Court utterly disregards the value of a neutral and detached magistrate.

According to the majority, whenever police have probable cause to believe that contraband may be found within an automobile that they have stopped on the highway, they may search not only the automobile but also any container found inside it, without obtaining a warrant. The scope of the search, we are told, is as broad as a magistrate could authorize in a warrant to search the automobile. The majority makes little attempt to justify this rule in terms of recognized Fourth Amendment values. The Court

simply ignores the critical function that a magistrate serves. And although the Court purports to rely on the mobility of an automobile and the impracticability of obtaining a warrant, it never explains why these concerns permit the warrantless search of a *container,* which can easily be seized and immobilized while police are obtaining a warrant.

The new rule adopted by the Court today is completely incompatible with established Fourth Amendment principles, and takes a first step toward an unprecedented "probable cause" exception to the warrant requirement. In my view, under accepted standards, the warrantless search of the containers in this case clearly violates the Fourth Amendment. . . .

The majority's rule is flatly inconsistent with these established Fourth Amendment principles concerning the scope of the automobile exception and the importance of the warrant requirement. Historically, the automobile exception has been limited to those situations where its application is compelled by the justifications described above. Today, the majority makes no attempt to base its decision on these justifications. This failure is not surprising, since the traditional rationales for the automobile exception plainly do not support extending it to the search of a container found inside a vehicle.

The practical mobility problem—deciding what to do with both the car and the occupants if an immediate search is not conducted—is simply not present in the case of movable containers, which can easily be seized and brought to the magistrate. The lesser expectation of privacy rationale also has little force. A container, as opposed to the car itself, does not reflect diminished privacy interests. Moreover, the practical corollary that this Court has recognized— that depriving occupants of the use of a car may be a greater intrusion than an immediate search—is of doubtful relevance here, since the owner of a container will rarely suffer significant inconvenience by being deprived of its use while a warrant is being obtained.

Ultimately the majority, unable to rely on the justifications underlying the automobile exception, simply creates a new "probable cause" exception to the warrant requirement for automobiles. We have soundly rejected attempts to create such an exception in the past, and we should do so again today.

The only convincing explanation I discern for the majority's broad rule is expediency: it assists police in conducting automobile searches, ensuring that the private containers into which criminal suspects often place goods will no longer be a Fourth Amendment shield.

This case will have profound implications for the privacy of citizens traveling in automobiles, as the Court well understands. "For countless vehicles are stopped on highways and public streets every day and our cases demonstrate that it is not uncommon for police officers to have probable cause to believe that contraband may be found in a stopped vehicle." *** A closed paper bag, a toolbox, a knapsack, a suitcase, and an attache case can alike be searched without the protection of the judgment of a neutral magistrate, based only on the rarely disturbed decision of a police officer that he has probable cause to search for contraband in the vehicle. The Court derives satisfaction from the fact that its rule does not exalt the rights of the wealthy over the rights of the poor. A rule so broad that all citizens lose vital Fourth Amendment protection is no cause for celebration.

I dissent.

Terry v. Ohio

392 U.S. 1; 88 S. Ct. 1868; 20 L. Ed. 2d 889 (1968)
Vote: 8-1

Mr. Chief Justice Warren delivered the opinion of the Court.

This case presents serious questions concerning the role of the Fourth Amendment in the confrontation on the street between the citizen and the policeman investigating suspicious circumstances.

Petitioner Terry was convicted of carrying a concealed weapon and sentenced to the statutorily prescribed term of one to three years in the penitentiary. Following the denial of a pretrial motion to suppress, the prosecution introduced in evidence two revolvers and a number of bullets seized from Terry and a codefendant, Richard Chilton, by Cleveland Police Detective Martin McFadden. At the hearing on the motion to suppress this evidence, Officer McFadden testified that while he was patrolling in plain clothes in downtown Cleveland at approximately 2:30 in the afternoon his attention was attracted by two men, Chilton and Terry, standing on the corner of Huron Road and Euclid Avenue. He had never seen the two men before, and he was unable to say precisely what first drew his eye to them. However, he testified that he had been a policeman for 39 years and a detective for 35 and that he had been assigned to patrol this vicinity of downtown Cleveland for shoplifters and pickpockets for 30 years. He explained that he had developed routine habits of observation over the years and that he would "stand and watch people or walk and watch people at many intervals of the day." He added: "Now, in this case when I looked over they didn't look right to me at the time."

His interest aroused, Officer McFadden took up a post of observation in the entrance to a store 300 to 400 feet away from the two men. "I get more purpose to watch them when I seen their movements," he testified. He saw one of the men leave the other one and walk southwest on Huron Road, past some stores. The man paused for a moment and looked in a store window, then walked on a short distance, turned around and walked back toward the corner, pausing once again to look in the same store window. He rejoined his companion at the corner, and the two conferred briefly. Then the second man went through the same series of motions, strolling down Huron Road, looking in the same window, walking on a short distance, turning back, peering in the store window again, and returning to confer with the first man at the corner. The two men repeated this ritual alternately between five and six times apiece—in all roughly a dozen trips. At one point, while the two were standing together on the corner, a third man approached them and engaged them briefly in conversation. This man then left the two other and walked west on Euclid Avenue. Chilton and Terry resumed their measured pacing, peering, and conferring. After this had gone on for 10 to 12 minutes, the two men walked off together, heading west on Euclid Avenue, following the path taken earlier by the third man.

By this time Officer McFadden had become thoroughly suspicious. He testified that after observing this elaborately casual and oft-repeated reconnaissance of the store window on Huron Road, he suspected the two men of "casing a job, a stick-up," and that he considered it his duty as a police officer to investigate further. He added that he feared "they may have a gun." Thus, Officer McFadden followed Chilton and Terry and saw them stop in front of Zucker's store to talk to the same man who had conferred with them earlier on the street corner. Deciding that the situation was ripe for direct action, Officer McFadden approached the three men, identified himself as a police officer and asked for their names. At this point his knowledge was confined to what he had observed. He was not acquainted with any of the three men by name or by sight, and he had received no information concerning them from any other source. When the men "mumbled something" in response to his inquiries, Officer McFadden grabbed petitioner Terry, spun him around so that they were facing the other two, with Terry between McFadden and the other, and patted down the outside of his clothing. In the left breast pocket of Terry's overcoat Officer McFadden felt a pistol. He reached inside the overcoat pocket, but was unable to remove the gun. At this point, keeping Terry between himself and the other, the officer ordered all three men to enter Zucker's store. As they went in, he removed Terry's overcoat completely, removed a .38-caliber revolver from the pocket and ordered all three men to face the wall with their hands raised. Officer McFadden proceeded to pat down the outer clothing of Chilton and the third man, Katz. He discovered another revolver in the outer pocket of Chilton's overcoat, but no weapons were found on Katz. The officer testified that he only patted the men down to see whether they had weapons, and that he did not put his hands beneath the outer garments of either Terry or Chilton until he felt their guns. So far as appears from the record, he never placed his hands beneath Katz' outer garments. Officer McFadden seized Chilton's gun, asked the proprietor of the store to call a police wagon, and took all three men to the station, where Chilton and Terry were formally charged with carrying concealed weapons.

On the motion to suppress the guns the prosecution took the position that they had been seized following a search incident to a lawful arrest. The trial court rejected this theory, stating that it "would be stretching the facts beyond reasonable comprehension" to find that Officer McFadden had probable cause to arrest the men before he patted them down for weapons. However, the court denied the defendants' motion on the ground that Officer McFadden, on the basis of his experience, "had reasonable cause to believe ... that the defendants were conducting themselves suspiciously, and some interrogation should be made of their action." Purely for his own protection, the court held, the officer had the right to pat down the outer clothing of these men, who he had reasonable cause to believe might be armed. The court distinguished between a investigatory "stop" and an arrest, and between a "frisk" of the outer clothing for weapons and a full-blown search for evidence of crime. The frisk, it held, was essential to the proper performance of the officer's investigatory duties, for without it, "the answer to the police officer may be a bullet, and a loaded pistol discovered during the frisk is admissible."

After the court denied their motion to suppress, Chilton and Terry waived jury trial and pleaded not guilty. The court adjudged them guilty, and the Court of Appeals for the Eighth Judicial District, Cuyahoga County, affirmed. *** The Supreme Court of Ohio dismissed their appeal on the ground that no "substantial constitutional question" was involved. We granted *certiorari*, *** to determine whether the admission of the revolvers in evidence violated petitioner's rights under the Fourth Amendment, made applicable to the States by the Fourteenth. *** We affirm the conviction.

... Unquestionably petitioner was entitled to the protection of the Fourth Amendment as he walked down the street in Cleveland. *** The question is whether in all the circumstances of this on-the-street encounter, his right to personal security was violated by an unreasonable search and seizure. ...

Our first task is to establish at what point in this encounter the Fourth Amendment becomes relevant. That is, we must decide whether and when Officer McFadden "seized" Terry and whether and when he conducted a "search." There is some suggestion in the use of such terms as "stop" and "frisk" that such police conduct is outside the purview of the Fourth Amendment because neither action rises to the level of a "search" or "seizure" within the meaning of the Constitution. We emphatically reject this notion. It is quite plain that the Fourth Amendment governs "seizures" of the person which do not eventuate in a trip to the station house and prosecution for crime—"arrest" in traditional terminology. It must be recognized that whenever a police officer accosts an individual and restrains his freedom to walk away, he has "seized" that person. And it is nothing less than sheer torture of the English language to suggest that a careful exploration of the outer surfaces of a person's clothing all over his or her body in an attempt to find weapons is not a "search." Moreover, it is simply fantastic to urge that such a procedure performed in public by a policeman while the citizen stands helpless, perhaps facing a wall with his hands raised, is a "petty indignity." It is a serious intrusion upon the sanctity of the person, which may inflict great indignity and arouse strong resentment, and it is not to be undertaken lightly.

The danger in the logic which proceeds upon distinctions between a "stop" and an "arrest," or "seizure" of the person, and between a "frisk" and a "search" is twofold. It seeks to isolate from constitutional scrutiny the initial stages of the contact between the policeman and the citizen. And by suggesting a rigid all-or-nothing model of justification and regulation under the Amendment, it obscures the utility of limitations upon the scope, as well as the initiation, of police action as a means of constitutional regulation. This Court has held in the past that a search which is reasonable at its inception may violate the Fourth Amendment by virtue of its intolerable intensity and scope. *** The scope of the search must be "strictly tied to and justified by" the circumstances which rendered its initiation permissible. ***

The distinctions of classical "stop-and-frisk" theory thus serve to divert attention from the central inquiry under the Fourth Amendment—the reasonableness in all the circumstances of the particular governmental invasion of a citizen's personal security. "Search" and "seizure" are not talismans. We therefore reject the notions that the Fourth Amendment does not come into play at all as a limitation upon police conduct if the officers stop short of something called a "technical arrest" or a "full-blown search."

In this case there can be no question, then, that Officer McFadden "seized" petitioner and subjected him to a "search" when he took hold of him and patted down the outer surfaces of his clothing. We must decide whether at that point it was reasonable for Officer McFadden to have interfered with petitioner's personal security as he did. And in determining whether the seizure and search were "unreasonable" our inquiry is a dual one—whether the officer's action was justified at its inception, and whether it was reasonably related in scope to the circumstances which justified the interference in the first place.

If this case involved police conduct subject to the Warrant Clause of the Fourth Amendment, we would have to ascertain whether "probable cause" existed to justify the search and seizure which took place. However, that is not the case. We do not retreat from our holdings that the police must, whenever practicable, obtain advance judicial approval of searches and seizures through the warrant procedure, *** or that in most instances failure to comply with the warrant requirement can only be excused by exigent circumstances. *** But we deal here with an entire rubric of police conduct—necessarily swift action predicated upon the on-the-spot observations of the officer on the beat—which historically has not been, and as a practical matter could not be, subjected to the warrant procedure. Instead, the conduct involved in this case must be tested by the Fourth Amendment's general proscription against unreasonable searches and seizures.

Nonetheless, the notions which underlie both the warrant procedure and the requirement of probable cause remain fully relevant in this context. In order to assess the reasonableness of Officer McFadden's conduct as a general proposition, it is necessary "first to focus upon the governmental interest which allegedly justifies official intrusion upon the constitutionally protected interests of the private citizen," for there is "no ready test for determining reasonableness other than by balancing the need to search [or seize] against the invasion which the search [or seizure] entails." *** And in justifying the particular intrusions the police officer must be able to point to specific and articulable facts which, taken together with rational inferences from those facts, reasonably warrant that intrusion. . . .

Applying these principles to this case, we consider first the nature and extent of the governmental interests involved. One general interest is of course that of effective crime prevention and detection; it is this interest which underlies the recognition that a police officer may in appropriate circumstances and in an appropriate manner approach a person for purposes of investigating possible criminal behavior even though there is no probable cause to make an arrest. . . .

The crux of this case, however, is not the propriety of Officer McFadden's taking steps to investigate petitioner's suspicious behavior, but rather, whether there was justification for McFadden's invasion of Terry's personal security by searching him for weapons in the course of that investigation. We are now concerned with more than the governmental interest in investigating crime; in addition, there is the more immediate interest of the police officer in taking steps to assure himself that the person with whom he is dealing is not armed with a weapon that could unexpectedly and fatally be used against him. Certainly it would be unreasonable to require that police officers take unnecessary risks in the performance of their duties. . . .

In view of these facts, we cannot blind ourselves to the need for law enforcement officers to protect themselves and other prospective victims of violence in situations where they may lack probable cause for an arrest. When an officer is justified in believing that the individual whose suspicious behavior he is investigating at close range is armed and presently dangerous to the officer or to others, it would appear to be clearly unreasonable to deny the officer the power to take necessary measures to determine whether the person is in fact carrying a weapon and to neutralize the threat of physical harm.

We must consider, however, the nature and quality of the intrusion on individual rights which must be accepted if police officers are to be conceded the right to search for weapons in situations where probable cause to arrest for crime is lacking. Even a limited search of the outer clothing for weapons constitutes a severe, though brief, intrusion upon cherished personal security, and it must surely bean annoying, frightening, and perhaps humiliating experience. . . .

We conclude that the revolver seized from Terry was properly admitted in evidence against him. At the time he seized petitioner and searched him for weapons, Officer McFadden had reasonable grounds to believe that petitioner was armed and dangerous, and it was necessary for the protection of himself and others to take swift measures to discover the true facts and neutralize the threat of harm if it materialized. The policeman carefully restricted his search to what was appropriate to the discovery of the particular items which he sought. Each case of this sort will, of course, have to be decided on its own facts. We merely hold today that where a police officer observes unusual conduct which leads him reasonably to conclude in light of his experience that criminal activity may be afoot and that the persons with whom he is dealing may be armed and presently dangerous, where in the course of investigating this behavior he identifies himself as a policeman and makes reasonable inquiries, and where nothing in the initial stages of the encounter serves to dispel his reasonable fear for his own or others' safety, he is entitled for the protection of himself and others in the area to conduct a carefully limited search of the outer clothing of such persons in an attempt to discover weapons which might be used to assault him. Such a search is a reasonable search under the Fourth Amendment, and any weapons seized may properly be introduced in evidence against the person from whom they were taken.

Affirmed.

Mr. Justice Black concurs in the judgment and the opinion except where the opinion quotes from and relies upon this Court's opinion in *Katz v. United States* and the concurring opinion in *Warden v. Hayden.*

Mr. Justice Harlan, concurring. . . .

Mr. Justice White, concurring. . . .

Mr. Justice Douglas, dissenting.

I agree that petitioner was "seized" within the meaning of the Fourth Amendment. I also agree that frisking petitioner and his companions for guns was a "search." But it is a mystery how that "search" and that "seizure" can be constitutional by Fourth Amendment standards, unless there was "probable cause" to believe that (1) a crime had been committed or (2) a crime was in the process of being committed or (3) a crime was about to be committed.

The opinion of the Court disclaims the existence of "probable cause." If loitering were in issue and that was the offense charged, there would be "probable cause" shown. But the crime here is carrying concealed weapons; and there is no basis for concluding that the officer had "probable cause" for believing that that crime was being committed. Had a warrant been sought, a magistrate would, therefore, have been unauthorized to issue one, for he can act only if there is a showing of "probable cause." We hold today that the police have greater authority to make a "seizure" and conduct a "search" than a judge has to authorize such action.

We have said precisely the opposite over and over again.

In other words, police officers up to today have been permitted to effect arrests or searches without warrants only when the facts within their personal knowledge would satisfy the constitutional standard of probable cause. At the time of their "seizure" without a warrant they must possess facts concerning the person arrested that would have satisfied a magistrate that "probable cause" was indeed present. The term "probable cause" rings a bell of certainty that is not sounded by phrases such as "reasonable suspicion. . . ."

The infringement on personal liberty of any "seizure" of a person can only be "reasonable" under the Fourth Amendment if we require the police to possess "probable cause" before they seize him. Only that line draws a meaningful distinction between an officer's mere inkling and the presence of facts within the officer's personal knowledge which would convince a reasonable man that the person seized has committed, is committing, or is about to commit a particular crime. . . .

United States v. Sokolow

490 U.S. 1; 109 S. Ct. 1581; 104 L. Ed.2d 1 (1989)
Vote: 7-2

At issue here is the Drug Enforcement Administration's use of a "drug courier profile" as means of identifying suspected drug smugglers. Does the fact that a passenger arriving at an international airport fits a profile of characteristics associated with drug smugglers constitute "reasonable suspicion" to allow an investigatory detention? The relevant facts are provided in the Court's opinion.

Chief Justice Rehnquist delivered the opinion of the Court.

. . . This case involves a typical attempt to smuggle drugs through one of the Nation's airports. On a Sunday in July 1984, respondent went to the United Airlines ticket counter at Honolulu Airport, where he purchased two round-trip tickets for a flight to Miami

leaving later that day. The tickets were purchased in the names of "Andrew Kray" and "Janet Norian," and had open return dates. Respondent paid $2,100 for the tickets from a large roll of $20 bills, which appeared to contain a total of $4,000. He also gave the ticket agent his home telephone number. The ticket agent noticed that respondent seemed nervous; he was about 25 years old; he was dressed in a black jumpsuit and wore gold jewelry; and he was accompanied by a woman, who turned out to be Janet Norian. Neither respondent nor his companion checked any of their four pieces of luggage.

After the couple left for their flight, the ticket agent informed Officer John McCarthy of the Honolulu Police Department of respondent's cash purchase of tickets to Miami. Officer McCarthy determined that the telephone number respondent gave to the ticket agent was subscribed to a "Karl Herman," who resided at 348-A Royal Hawaiian Avenue in Honolulu. Unbeknownst to McCarthy (and later to the DEA agents), respondent was Herman's roommate. The ticket agent identified respondent's voice on the answering machine at Herman's number. Officer McCarthy was unable to find any listing under the name "Andrew Kray" in Hawaii. McCarthy subsequently learned that return reservations from Miami to Honolulu had been made in the names of Kray and Norian, with their arrival scheduled for July 25, three days after respondent and his companion had left. He also learned that Kray and Norian were scheduled to make stopovers in Denver and Los Angeles.

On July 25, during the stopover in Los Angeles, DEA agents identified respondent. He "appeared to be very nervous and was looking all around the waiting area." *** Later that day, at 6:30 P.M., respondent and Norian arrived in Honolulu. As before, they had not checked their luggage. Respondent was still wearing a black jumpsuit and gold jewelry. The couple proceeded directly to the street and tried to hail a cab, where Agent Richard Kempshall and three other DEA agents approached them. Kempshall displayed his credentials, grabbed respondent by the arm and moved him back onto the sidewalk. Kempshall asked respondent for his airline ticket and identification; respondent said that he had neither. He told the agents that his name was "Sokolow," but that he was traveling under his mother's maiden name, "Kray."

Respondent and Norian were escorted to the DEA office at the airport. There, the couple's luggage was examined by "Donker," a narcotics detector dog, which alerted to respondent's brown shoulder bag. The agents arrested respondent. He was advised of his constitutional rights and declined to make any statements. The agents obtained a warrant to search the shoulder bag. They found no illicit drugs, but the bag did contain several suspicious documents indicating respondent's involvement in drug trafficking. The agents had Donker reexamine the remaining luggage, and this time the dog alerted to a medium-sized Louis Vuitton bag. By now, it was 9:30 P.M., too late for the agents to obtain a second warrant. They allowed respondent to leave for the night, but kept his luggage. The next morning, after a second dog confirmed Donker's alert, the agents obtained a warrant and found 1,063 grams of cocaine inside the bag.

Respondent was indicted for possession with the intent to distribute cocaine in violation of 21 U.S.C. Sec. 841(a) (1). The United States District Court for Hawaii denied his motion to suppress the cocaine and other evidence seized from his luggage, finding that the DEA agents had a reasonable suspicion that he was involved in drug trafficking when they stopped him at the airport. Respondent then entered a conditional plea of guilty to the offense charged.

The United States Court of Appeals for the Ninth Circuit reversed respondent's conviction by a divided vote, holding that the DEA agents did not have a reasonable suspicion to justify the stop. ***

We granted *certiorari* to review the decision of the Court of Appeals, *** because of its serious implication for the enforcement of the federal narcotics laws. We now reverse.

The Court of Appeals held that the DEA agents seized respondent when they grabbed by the arm and moved him back onto the sidewalk. *** The Government does not challenge that conclusion, and we assume—without deciding—that a stop occurred here. Our decision, then, turns on whether the agents had a reasonable suspicion that respondent was engaged in wrongdoing when they encountered him on the sidewalk. In *Terry v. Ohio* *** (1968), we held that the police can stop and briefly detain a person for investigative purposes if the officer has a reasonable suspicion supported by articulable facts that criminal activity "may be afoot," even if the officer lacks probable cause.

The officer, of course, must be able to articulate something more than an "inchoate and unparticularized suspicion or 'hunch.' " The Fourth Amendment requires "some minimal level of objective justification" for making the stop. *** That level of suspicion is considerably less than proof of wrongdoing by a preponderance of the evidence. We have held that probable cause means "a fair probability that contraband or evidence of a crime will be found," *** and the level of suspicion required for a *Terry* stop is obviously less demanding than that for probable cause. ***

The concept of reasonable suspicion, like probable cause, is not "readily, or even usefully, reduced to a neat set of legal rules." *** We think the Court of Appeals' effort to refine and elaborate the requirements of "reasonable suspicion" in this case create unnecessary difficulty in dealing with one of the relatively simple concepts embodied in the Fourth Amendment. In evaluating the validity of a stop such as this, we must consider "the totality of the circumstances—the whole picture." ***

The rule enunciated by the Court of Appeals, in which evidence available to an officer is divided into evidence of "ongoing criminal behavior" on the one hand, and "probabilistic" evidence, on the other, is not in keeping with the quoted statements from our decisions. It also seems to us to draw a sharp line between types of evidence, the probative value of which varies only in degree. The Court of Appeals classified evidence of traveling under an alias, or evidence that the suspect took an evasive or erratic path through an airport, as meeting the test for showing "ongoing criminal activity." But certainly instances are conceivable in which traveling under an alias would not reflect ongoing criminal activity: for example, a person who wished to travel to a hospital or clinic for an operation and wished to conceal that fact. One taking an evasive path through an airport might be seeking to avoid a confrontation with an angry acquaintance or with a creditor. This is not to say that each of these types of evidence is not highly probative, but they do not have the sort of iron-clad significance attributed to them by the Court of Appeals.

On the other hand, the factors in this case that the Court of Appeals treated as merely "probabilistic" also have probative significance. Paying $2,100 in cash for two airplane tickets is out of the ordinary, and it is even more out of the ordinary to pay that sum from a roll of $20 bills containing nearly twice that amount of cash. Most business travelers, we feel confident, purchase airline tickets by credit card or check so as to have a record for tax or business purposes, and few vacationers carry with them thousands of dollars in $20 bills. We also think the agents had a reasonable ground to believe that respondent was traveling under an alias; the evidence was by no means conclusive, but it was sufficient to warrant

consideration. While a trip from Honolulu to Miami, standing alone, is not a cause for any sort of suspicion, here there was more: surely few residents of Honolulu travel from that city for 20 hours to spend 48 hours in Miami during the month of July.

Any one of these factors is not by itself proof of any illegal conduct and is quite consistent with innocent travel. But we think taken together they amount to reasonable suspicion. *** We do not agree with respondent that our analysis is somehow changed by the agents' belief that his behavior was consistent with one of the DEA's "drug courier profiles." A court sitting to determine the existence of reasonable suspicion must require the agent to articulate the factors leading to that conclusion, but the fact that these factors may be set forth in a "profile" does not somehow detract from their evidentiary significance as seen by a trained agent.

Respondent also contends that the agents were obligated to use the least intrusive means available to verify or dispel their suspicions that he was smuggling narcotics. In respondent's view, the agents should have simply approached and spoken with him, rather than forcibly detaining him. . . . The reasonableness of the officer's decision to stop a suspect does not turn on the availability of less intrusive investigatory techniques. Such a rule would unduly hamper the police's ability to make swift on-the-spot decisions . . . and it would require courts to "indulge in 'unrealistic second-guessing.'" *** We hold that the agents had a reasonable basis to suspect that respondent was transporting illegal drugs on these facts. The judgment of the Court of Appeals is therefore reversed and the case remanded for further proceedings consistent with our decision. . . .

Justice Marshall, with whom **Justice Brennan** joins, dissenting.

Because the strongest advocates of Fourth Amendment rights are frequently criminals, it is easy to forget that our interpretations of such rights apply to the innocent and the guilty alike. *** In the present case, the chain of events set in motion when respondent Andrew Sokolow was stopped by Drug Enforcement Administration (DEA) agents at Honolulu International Airport led to the discovery of cocaine and, ultimately, to Sokolow's conviction for drug trafficking. But in sustaining this conviction on the ground that the agents reasonably suspected Sokolow of ongoing criminal activity, the Court diminishes the rights of *all* citizens "to be secure in their persons," *** as they traverse the Nation's airports. Finding this result constitutionally impermissible, I dissent.

The Fourth Amendment cabins government's authority to intrude on personal privacy and security by requiring that searches and seizures usually be supported by a showing of probable cause. The reasonable-suspicion standard is a derivation of the probable cause command, applicable only to those brief detentions which fall short of being full-scale searches and seizures and which are necessitated by law-enforcement exigencies such as the need to stop ongoing crimes, to prevent imminent crimes, and to protect law-enforcement officers in highly charged situations. *** By requiring reasonable suspicion as a prerequisite to such seizures, the Fourth Amendment protects innocent persons from being subjected to "overbearing or harassing" police conduct carried out solely on the basis of imprecise stereotypes of what criminals look like, or on the basis of irrelevant personal characteristics such as race. ***

To deter such egregious police behavior, we have held that a suspicion is not reasonable unless officers have based it on "specific and articulable facts." *** It is not enough to suspect that an individual has committed crimes in the past, harbors unconsummated criminal designs, or has the propensity to commit crimes. On the contrary; before detaining an individual, law enforcement officers must reasonably suspect that he is engaged in, or poised to commit, a criminal act *at that moment.* *** The rationale for permitting brief, warrantless seizures is, after all, that it is impractical to demand strict compliance with the Fourth Amendment's ordinary probable-cause requirement in the face of ongoing or imminent criminal activity demanding "swift action predicated upon the on-the-spot observations of the officer on the beat." *** Observations raising suspicions of past criminality demand no such immediate action, but instead should appropriately trigger routine police investigation, which may ultimately generate sufficient information to blossom into probable cause.

Evaluated against this standard, the facts about Andrew Sokolow known to the DEA agents at the time they stopped him fall short of reasonably indicating that he was engaged at the time in criminal activity. It is highly significant that the DEA agents stopped Sokolow because he matched one of the DEA's "profiles" of a paradigmatic drug courier. In my view, a law enforcement officer's mechanistic application of a formula of personal and behavioral traits in deciding whom to detain can only dull the officer's ability and determination to make sensitive and fact-specific inferences "in light of his experience," *** particularly in ambiguous or border-line cases. Reflexive reliance on a profile of a drug courier characteristics runs a far greater risk than does ordinary, case-by-case police work, of subjecting innocent individuals to unwarranted police harassment and detention. This risk is enhanced by the profile's "chameleon-like way of adapting to any particular set of observations." *** In asserting that it is not "somehow" relevant that the agents who stopped Sokolow did so in reliance on a prefabricated profile of criminal characteristics, *** the majority thus ducks serious issues relating to a questionable law enforcement practice, to address the validity of which we granted certiorari in this case. . . .

The facts known to the DEA agents at the time they detained the traveler in this case are scarcely . . . suggestive of ongoing criminal activity. . . . Sokolow gave no indications of evasive activity. On the contrary, the sole behavioral detail about Sokolow noted by the DEA agents was that he was nervous. With news accounts proliferating of plane crashes, near-collisions and air terrorism, there are manifold and good reasons for being agitated while awaiting flight, reasons that have nothing to do with one's involvement in a criminal endeavor.

The remaining circumstantial facts known about Sokolow, considered either singly or together, are scarcely indicative of criminal activity. . . . [T]he fact that Sokolow took a brief trip to a resort city for which he brought only carry-on luggage also "describe[s] a very large category of presumably innocent travelers." That Sokolow embarked from Miami, "a source city for illicit drugs," is no more suggestive of illegality; thousands of innocent persons travel from "source cities" every day and, judging from the

DEA's testimony in past cases, nearly every major city in the country may be characterized as a source or distribution city. That Sokolow had his phone listed in another person's name also does not support the majority's assertion that the DEA agents reasonably believed Sokolow was using an alias; it is commonplace to have one's phone registered in the name of a roommate, which, it later turned out, was precisely what Sokolow had done. That Sokolow was dressed in a black jumpsuit and wore gold jewelry also provides no grounds for suspecting wrongdoing, the majority's repeated and unexplained allusions to Sokolow's style of dress notwithstanding. *** For law enforcement officers to base a search, even in part, on a pop guess that persons dressed in a particular fashion are likely to commit crimes not only stretches the concept of reasonable suspicion beyond recognition, but also is inimical to the self-expression which the choice of wardrobe may provide.

Finally, that Sokolow paid for his tickets in cash indicates no imminent or ongoing criminal activity. The majority "feel[s] confident" that "[m]ost business travelers . . . purchase airline tickets by credit card or check." *** Why the majority confines its focus only to "business travelers" I do not know, but I would not so lightly infer ongoing crime from the use of legal tender. Making major cash purchases, while surely less common today, may simply reflect the traveler's aversion to, or inability to obtain, plastic money. Conceivably, a person who spends large amounts of cash may be trying to launder his proceeds from *past* criminal enterprises by converting them into goods and services. But, as I have noted, investigating completed episodes of crime goes beyond the appropriately limited purview of brief, *Terry*-style seizure. Moreover, it is unreasonable to suggest that, had Sokolow left the airport, he would have been gone forever and thus immune from subsequent investigation. *** Sokolow, after all, had given the airline his phone number, and the DEA, having ascertained that it was indeed Sokolow's voice on the answering machine at that number, could have learned from that information where Sokolow resided.

The fact is that, unlike the taking of patently evasive action, *** the use of an alias, *** the casing of a store, *** the provision of a reliable report from an informant that wrongdoing is imminent, *** nothing about the characteristics shown by airport traveler Sokolow reasonably suggests that criminal activity is afoot. The majority's hasty conclusion to the contrary serves only to indicate its willingness, when drug crimes or anti-drug policies are at issue, to give short shrift to constitutional rights. *** In requiring that seizures be based on at least some evidence of criminal conduct, the Court of Appeals was faithful to the Fourth Amendment principle that law enforcement officers must reasonably suspect a person of criminal activity before they can detain him. Because today's decision, though limited to its facts, *** ignores this important constitutional command, I dissent.

Weeks v. United States

232 U.S. 383; 34 S. Ct. 341; 58 L. Ed. 652 (1914)
Vote: 9-0

Mr. Justice Day delivered the opinion of the Court:

An indictment was returned against the plaintiff in error, defendant below, and herein so designated, in the District Court of the United States for the Western District of Missouri, containing nine counts. The seventh count, upon which a conviction was had, charged the use of the mails for the purpose of transporting certain coupons or tickets representing chances or shares in a lottery . . . in violation of the Criminal Code. Sentence of fine and imprisonment was imposed. This writ of error is to review that judgment.

The defendant was arrested by a police officer, so far as the record shows, without warrant, at the Union Station in Kansas City, Missouri, where he was employed by an express company. Other police officers had gone to the house of the defendant, and being told by a neighbor where the key was kept, found it and entered the house. They searched the defendant's room and took possession of various papers and articles found there, which were afterwards turned over to the United States marshal. Later in the same day police officers returned with the marshal, who thought he might find additional evidence, and, being admitted by someone in the house, probably a boarder, in response to a rap, the marshal searched the defendant's room and carried away certain letters and envelopes found in the drawer of a chiffonier. Neither the marshal nor the police officers had a search warrant.

The defendant filed in the cause before time for trial ... [a] ... Petition to Return Private Papers, Books, and Other Property.

Upon consideration of the petition the court entered an order directing the return of such property as was not pertinent to the charge against the defendant, but denied the petition as to pertinent matter, reserving the right to pass upon the pertinency at a later time. In obedience to the order the district attorney returned part of the property taken, and retained the remainder, concluding a list of the latter with the statement that, "all of which last above described property is to be used in evidence in the trial of the above-entitled cause, and pertains to the alleged sale of lottery tickets of the company above named."

After the jury had been sworn and before any evidence had been given, the defendant again urged his petition for the return of his property, which was denied by the court. Upon the introduction of such papers during the trial, the defendant objected on the ground that the papers had been obtained without a search warrant, and by breaking into his home, in violation of the 4th and 5th Amendments to the Constitution of the United States, which objection was overruled by the court. Among the papers retained and put in evidence were a number of lottery tickets and statements with reference to the lottery, taken at the first visit of the police to the defendant's room, and a number of letters written to the defendant in respect to the lottery, taken by the marshal upon his search of defendant's room.

The defendant assigns error, among other things, in the court's refusal to grant his petition for the return of his property, and in permitting the papers to be used at the trial.

It is thus apparent that the question presented involves the determination of the duty of the court with reference to the motion made by the defendant for the return to certain letters, as well as other papers, taken from his room by the United States marshal, who, without authority of process, if any such could have been illegally issued, visited the room of the defendant for the declared purpose of obtaining additional testimony to support the charge against the accused, and, having gained admission to the house, took from the drawer of a chiffonier there found certain letters written to the defendant, tending to show his guilt. These letters were placed in the control of the district attorney, and were subsequently produced by him and offered in evidence against the accused at the trial. The defendant contends that such appropriation of his private correspondence was in violation of rights secured to him by the 4th and 5th Amendments to the Constitution of the United States. We shall deal with the 4th Amendment. . . .

The history of this Amendment is given with particularity in the opinion of Mr. Justice Bradley, speaking for the court in *Boyd v. United States* [1884]. *** As was there shown, it took its origin in the determination of the framers of the Amendments to the Federal Constitution to provide for that instrument a Bill of Rights, securing to the American people, among other things, those safeguards which had grown up in England to protect the people from unreasonable searches and seizures, such as were permitted under the general warrants issued under authority of the government, by which there had been invasions of the home and privacy of the citizens, and the seizure of their private papers in support of charges, real or imaginary, made against them. Such practices had also received sanction under warrants and seizures under the so-called writs of assistance, issued in the American colonies. Resistance to these practices had established the principle which was enacted into the fundamental law in the 4th Amendment, that a man's house was his castle, and not to be invaded by any general authority to search and seize his goods and papers.

The effect of the 4th Amendment is to put the courts of the United States and Federal officials, in the exercise of their power and authority, under limitations and restraints as to the exercise of such power and authority, and to forever secure the people, their persons, houses, papers, and effects, against all unreasonable searches and seizures under the guise of law. This protection reaches all alike, whether accused of crime or not, and the duty of giving to it force and effect is obligatory upon all intrusted under our Federal system with the enforcement of the laws. The tendency of those who execute the criminal laws of the country to obtain conviction by means of unlawful seizures and enforced confessions, the latter often obtained after subjecting accused persons to unwarranted practices destructive of rights secured by the Federal Constitution, should find no sanction in the judgments of the courts, which are charged at all times with the support of the Constitution, and to which people of all conditions have a right to appeal for the maintenance of such fundamental rights.

What, then, is the present case? Before answering that inquiry specifically, it may be well by a process of exclusion to state what it is not. It is not an assertion of the right on the part of the government, always recognized under English and American law, to search the person of the accused when legally arrested, to discover and seize the fruits or evidences of crime. Nor is it the case of testimony offered at a trial where the court is asked to stop and consider the illegal means by which proofs, otherwise competent, were obtained,—of which we shall have occasion to treat later in this opinion. Nor is it the case of burglar's tools or other proofs of guilt found upon his arrest within the control of the accused.

The case in the aspect in which we are dealing with it involves the right of the court in a criminal prosecution to retain for the purposes of evidence the letters and correspondence of the accused, seized in his house in his absence and without his authority, by a United States marshal holding no warrant for his arrest and none for the search of his premises. If letters and private documents can thus be seized and held and used in evidence against a citizen accused of an offense, the protection of the 4th Amendment, declaring his right to be secure against such searches and seizures, is of no value, and, so far as those thus placed are concerned, might as well be stricken from the Constitution. The efforts of the courts and their officials to bring the guilty to punishment, praise-worthy as they are, are not to be aided by the sacrifice of those great principles established by years of endeavor and suffering which have resulted in their embodiment in the fundamental law of the land. The United States marshal could only have invaded the house of the accused when armed with a warrant issued as required by the Constitution, upon sworn information, and describing with reasonable particularity the thing for which the search was to be made. Instead, he acted without sanction of law, doubtless prompted by the desire to bring further proof to the aid of the government, and under color of his office undertook to make a seizure of private papers in direct violation of the constitutional prohibition against such action. Under such circumstances, without sworn information and particular description, not even an order of court would have justified such procedure; much less was it within the authority of the United States marshal to thus invade the house and privacy of the accused.

We therefore reach the conclusion that the letters in question were taken from the house of the accused by an official of the United States, acting under color of his office, in direct violation of the constitutional rights of the defendant; that having made a seasonable application for their return, which was heard and passed upon by the court, there was involved in the order refusing the application of denial of the constitutional rights of the accused, and that the court should have restored these letters to the accused. In holding them and permitting their use upon the trial, we think prejudicial error was committed. . . .

It results that the judgment of the court below must be reversed, and the case remanded for further proceedings in accordance with this opinion.

Reversed.

Mapp v. Ohio

367 U.S. 643; 81 S. Ct. 1684; 6 L. Ed. 2d 1081 (1961)

Vote: 6-3

Mr. Justice Clark delivered the opinion of the Court.

Appellant stands convicted of knowingly having had in her possession and under her control certain lewd and lascivious books, pictures, and photographs in violation of *** Ohio's Revised Code. . . . [T]he Supreme Court of Ohio found that her conviction was valid though "based primarily upon the introduction in evidence of lewd and lascivious books and pictures unlawfully seized during an unlawful search of defendant's home. . . ."

On May 23, 1957, three Cleveland police officers arrived at appellant's residence in that city pursuant to information that "a person [was] hiding out in the home, who was wanted for questioning in connection with a recent bombing, and that there was a large amount of policy [gambling] paraphernalia being hidden in the home." Miss Mapp and her daughter by a former marriage lived on the top floor of the two-family dwelling. Upon their arrival at that house, the officers knocked on the door and demanded entrance but appellant, after telephoning her attorney, refused to admit them without a search warrant. They advised their headquarters of the situation and undertook a surveillance of the house.

The officers again sought entrance some three hours later when four or more additional officers arrived on the scene. When Miss Mapp did not come to the door immediately at least one of the several doors to the house was forcibly opened and the policemen gained admittance. Meanwhile Miss Mapp's attorney arrived, but the officers, having secured their own entry, and continuing in their defiance of the law, would permit him neither to see Miss Mapp nor to enter the house. It appears that Miss Mapp was halfway down the stairs from the upper floor to the front door when the officers, in this high-handed manner, broke into the hall. She demanded to see the search warrant. A paper, claimed to be a warrant, was held up by one of the officers. She grabbed the "warrant" and placed it in her bosom. A struggle ensued in which the officers recovered the piece of paper and as a result of which they handcuffed appellant because she had been "belligerent" in resisting their official rescue of the "warrant" from her person. Running roughshod over appellant, a policeman "grabbed" her, "twisted [her] hand," and she "yelled [and] pleaded with him" because "it was hurting." Appellant, in handcuffs, was then forcibly taken upstairs to her bedroom where the officers searched a dresser, a chest of drawers, a closet and some suitcases. They also looked into a photo album and through personal papers belonging to the appellant. The search spread to the rest of the second floor including the child's bedroom, the living room, the kitchen and a dinette. The basement of the building and a trunk found therein were also searched. The obscene materials for possession of which she was ultimately convicted were discovered in the course of that widespread search.

At the trial no search warrant was produced by the prosecution, nor was the failure to produce one explained or accounted for. At best, "There is, in the record, considerable doubt as to whether there ever was any warrant for the search of defendant's home." *** The Ohio Supreme Court believed a "reasonable argument" could be made that the conviction should be reversed "because the 'methods' employed to obtain the [evidence] . . . were such as to 'offend "a sense of justice," ' ' " but the court found determinative the fact that the evidence had not been taken "from defendant's person by the use of brutal or offensive force. . . ."***

The State says that even if the search were made without authority, or otherwise unreasonably, it is not prevented from using the unconstitutionally seized evidence at trial, citing *Wolf v. Colorado* [1949], in which this Court did indeed hold "that in a prosecution in a State court for a State crime the Fourteenth Amendment does not forbid the admission of evidence obtained by an unreasonable search and seizure." *** On this appeal, of which we have noted probable jurisdiction, *** it is urged once again that we review that holding. . . .

[I]n the year 1914, in the *Weeks* Case, this Court "for the first time" held that, "in a federal prosecution the Fourth Amendment barred the use of evidence secured through an illegal search and seizure." *** This Court has ever since required of federal law officers a strict adherence to that command which this Court has held to be a clear, specific, and constitutionally required—even if judicially implied—deterrent safeguard without insistence upon which the Fourth Amendment would have been reduced to "a form of words." *** It meant, quite simply, that "conviction by means of unlawful seizures and enforced confessions . . . should find no sanction in the judgments of the courts. . . ." ***

There are in the cases of this Court some passing references to the *Weeks* rule as being one of evidence. But the plain and unequivocal language of *Weeks*—and its later paraphrase in *Wolf*—to the effect that the *Weeks* rule is of constitutional origin, remains entirely undisturbed. In *Byars v. United States*** (1927), a unanimous Court declared that "the doctrine [cannot] . . . be tolerated under our constitutional system, that evidences of crime discovered by a federal officer in making a search without lawful warrant may be used against the victim of the unlawful search where a timely challenge has been interposed." . . .

In 1949, 35 years after *Weeks* was announced, this Court, in *Wolf v. Colorado* for the first time discussed the effect of the Fourth Amendment upon the States through the operation of the Due Process Clause of the Fourteenth Amendment. It said: "[W]e have no hesitation in saying that were a State affirmatively to sanction such police incursion into privacy it would run counter to the guaranty of the Fourteenth Amendment." *** Nevertheless, after declaring that the "security of one's privacy against arbitrary intrusion by the police" is "implicit in 'the concept of ordered liberty' and as such enforceable against the States through the Due Process Clause," and announcing that it "stoutly adhere[d]" to the *Weeks* decision, the Court decided that the *Weeks* exclusionary rule would not then be imposed upon the States as "an essential ingredient of the right." *** The Court's reasons for not considering essential to the right to privacy, as a curb imposed upon the States by the Due Process Clause, that which decades

before had been posited as part and parcel of the Fourth Amendment's limitation upon federal encroachment of individual privacy, were bottomed on factual considerations.

While they are not basically relevant to a decision that the exclusionary rule is an essential ingredient of the Fourth Amendment as the right it embodies is vouchsafed against the States by the Due Process Clause, we will consider the current validity of the factual grounds upon which *Wolf* was based.

The Court in *Wolf* first stated that "[t]he contrariety of views of the States" on the adoption of the exclusionary rule of *Weeks* was "particularly impressive"; . . . and, in this connection that it could not "brush aside the experience of States which deem the incidence of such conduct by the police too slight to call for a deterrent remedy . . . by overriding the [States'] relevant rules of evidence." *** While in 1949, prior to the *Wolf* Case, almost two-thirds of the States were opposed to the use of the exclusionary rule, now, despite the *Wolf* Case, more than half of those since passing upon it, by their own legislative or judicial decision, have wholly or partly adopted or adhered to the *Weeks* rule. . . . Significantly, among those now following the rule is California, which, according to its highest court, was "compelled to reach that conclusion because other remedies have completely failed to secure compliance with the constitutional provisions. . . ." . . . The experience of California that such other remedies have been worthless and futile is buttressed by the experience of other States. The obvious futility of relegating the Fourth Amendment to the protection of other remedies has, moreover, been recognized by this Court since *Wolf*.***

Likewise, time has set its face against what *Wolf* called the "weighty testimony" of *People v. Defore* *** (1926). There Justice (then Judge) Cardozo, rejecting adoption of the *Weeks* exclusionary rule in New York, had said that "[t]he Federal rule as it stands is either too strict or too lax." *** However, the force of that reasoning has been largely vitiated by later decisions of this Court. These include the recent discarding of the "silver platter" doctrine which allowed federal judicial use of evidence seized in violation of the Constitution by state agents; *** the relaxation of the formerly strict requirements as to standing to challenge the use of evidence, thus seized, so that now the procedure of exclusion, "ultimately referable to constitutional safeguards," is available to anyone even "legitimately on [the] premises" unlawfully searched; *** and, finally, the formulation of a method to prevent state use of evidence unconstitutionally seized by federal agents. *** Because there can be no fixed formula, we are admittedly met with "recurring questions of the reasonableness of searches," but less is not to be expected when dealing with a Constitution, and, at any rate, "[r]easonableness is in the first instance for the [trial court] . . . to determine."***

It, therefore, plainly appears that the factual considerations supporting the failure of the *Wolf* Court to include the *Weeks* exclusionary rule when it recognized the enforceability of the right to privacy against the States in 1949, while not basically relevant to the constitutional consideration, could not, in any analysis, now be deemed controlling. . . .

Since the Fourth Amendment's right of privacy has been declared enforceable against the States through the Due Process Clause of the Fourteenth, it is enforceable against them by the same sanction of exclusion as is used against the Federal Government. Were it otherwise, then just as without the *Weeks* rule the assurance against unreasonable federal searches and seizures would be "a form of words," valueless and undeserving of mention in a perpetual charter of inestimable human liberties, so too, without that rule the freedom from state invasions of privacy would be so ephemeral and so neatly severed from its conceptual nexus with the freedom from all brutish means of coercing evidence as not to merit this Court's high regard as a freedom "implicit in the concept of ordered liberty." At the time that the Court held in *Wolf* that the Amendment was applicable to the States through the Due Process Clause, the cases of this Court, as we have seen, had steadfastly held that as to federal officers the Fourth Amendment included the exclusion of the evidence seized in violation of its provisions. Even *Wolf* "stoutly adhered" to that proposition. The right to privacy, when conceded operatively enforceable against the States, was not susceptible of destruction by avulsion of the sanction upon which its protection and enjoyment had always been deemed dependent under the *Boyd, Weeks* and

Silverthorne cases. Therefore, in extending the substantive protections of due process to all constitutionally unreasonable searches—state or federal—it was logically and constitutionally necessary that the exclusion doctrine—an essential part of the right to privacy—be also insisted upon as an essential ingredient of the right newly recognized by the *Wolf* case. In short, the admission of the new constitutional right by *Wolf* could not consistently tolerate denial of its most important constitutional privilege, namely, the exclusion of the evidence which an accused had been forced to give by reason of the unlawful seizure. To hold otherwise is to grant the right but in reality to withhold its privilege and enjoyment. Only last year the Court itself recognized that the purpose of the exclusionary rule "is to deter—to compel respect for the constitutional guaranty in the only effectively available way—by removing the incentive to disregard it." . . .

Moreover, our holding that the exclusionary rule is an essential part of both the Fourth and Fourteenth Amendments is not only the logical dictate of prior cases, but it also makes very good sense. There is no war between the Constitution and common sense. Presently, a federal prosecutor may make no use of evidence illegally seized, but a State's attorney across the street may, although he supposedly is operating under the enforceable prohibitions of the same Amendment. Thus the State, by admitting evidence unlawfully seized, serves to encourage disobedience to the Federal Constitution which it is bound to uphold. Moreover, . . . "[t]he very essence of a healthy federalism depends upon the avoidance of needless conflict between state and federal courts." . . .

Federal–state cooperation in the solution of crime under constitutional standards will be promoted, if only by recognition of their now mutual obligation to respect the same fundamental criteria in their approaches. "However much in a particular case insistence upon such rules may appear as a technicality that inures to the benefit of a guilty person, the history of the criminal law proves that tolerance of shortcut methods in law enforcement impairs its enduring effectiveness." *** Denying shortcuts to only one of two cooperating law enforcement agencies tends naturally to breed legitimate suspicion of "working arrangements" whose results are equally tainted.***

There are those who say, as did Justice (then Judge) Cardozo, that under our constitutional exclusionary doctrine "[t]he criminal is to go free because the constable has blundered." *** In some cases this will undoubtedly be the result. But, . . . "there is another consideration—the imperative of judicial integrity." *** The criminal goes free, if he must, but it is the law that sets him free. Nothing can destroy a government more quickly than its failure to observe its own laws, or worse, its disregard of the charter of its own existence. As Mr. Justice Brandeis, dissenting, said in *Olmstead v. United States:* "Our Government is the potent, the omnipresent teacher. For good or for ill, it teaches the whole people by its example. . . . If the Government becomes a lawbreaker, it breeds contempt for law; it invites every man to become a law unto himself; it invites anarchy." *** Nor can it lightly be assumed that, as a practical matter, adoption of the exclusionary rule fetters law enforcement. Only last year this Court expressly considered that contention and found that "pragmatic evidence of a sort" to the contrary was not wanting. . . .

The ignoble shortcut to conviction left open to the State tends to destroy the entire system of constitutional restraints on which the liberties of the people rest. Having once recognized that the right to privacy embodied in the Fourth Amendment is enforceable against the States, and that the right to be secure against rude invasions of privacy by state officers is, therefore, constitutional in origin, we can no longer permit that right to remain an empty promise. Because it is enforceable in the same manner and to like effect as other basic rights secured by the Due Process Clause, we can no longer permit it to be revocable at the whim of any police officer who, in the name of law enforcement itself, chooses to suspend its enjoyment. Our decision, founded on reason and truth, gives to the individual no more than that which the Constitution guarantees him, to the police officer no less than that to which honest law enforcement is entitled, and, to the courts, that judicial integrity so necessary in the true administration of justice.

The judgment of the Supreme Court of Ohio is reversed and the case remanded for further proceedings not inconsistent with this opinion.

Reversed and remanded.

Mr. Justice Black, concurring.

I am still not persuaded that the Fourth Amendment, standing alone, would be enough to bar the introduction into evidence against an accused of papers and effects seized from him in violation of its commands. For the Fourth Amendment does not itself contain any provision expressly precluding the use of such evidence, and I am extremely doubtful that such a provision could properly be inferred from nothing more than the basic command against unreasonable searches and seizures. Reflection on the problem, however, in the light of cases coming before the Court since *Wolf,* has led me to conclude that when the Fourth Amendment's ban against unreasonable searches and seizures is considered together with the Fifth Amendment's ban against compelled self-incrimination, a constitutional basis emerges which not only justifies but actually requires the exclusionary rule. . . .

Mr. Justice Douglas, concurring. . . .

Mr. Justice Harlan, whom **Mr. Justice Frankfurter** and **Mr. Justice Whittaker** join, dissenting.

In overruling the *Wolf* case the Court, in my opinion, has forgotten the sense of judicial restraint which, with due regard for *stare decisis,* is one element that should enter into deciding whether a past decision of this Court should be overruled. Apart from that I also believe that the *Wolf* rule represents sounder Constitutional doctrine than the new rule which now replaces it.

From the Court's statement of the case one would gather that the central, if not controlling, issue on this appeal is whether illegally state-seized evidence is Constitutionally admissible in a state prosecution, an issue which would of course face us with the need for re-examining *Wolf.* However, such is not the situation. For, although that question was indeed raised here and below among appellant's subordinate points, the new and pivotal issue brought to the Court by this appeal is whether section 2905.34 of the Ohio Revised Code making criminal the mere knowing possession or control of obscene material, and under which appellant has been convicted, is consistent with the rights of free thought and expression assured against state action by the Fourteenth

Amendment. That was the principal issue which was decided by the Ohio Supreme Court, which was tendered by appellant's Jurisdictional Statement, and which was briefed and argued in this Court.

In this posture of things, I think it fair to say that five members of this Court have simply "reached out" to overrule *Wolf.* With all respect for the views of the majority, and recognizing that *stare decisis* carries different weight in Constitutional adjudication than it does in nonconstitutional decision, I can perceive no justification for regarding this case as an appropriate occasion for re-examining *Wolf.* . . .

I would not impose upon the States this federal exclusionary remedy. The reasons given by the majority for now suddenly turning its back on *Wolf* seem to me notably unconvincing.

First, it is said that "the factual grounds upon which *Wolf* was based" have since changed, in that more States now follow the *Weeks* exclusionary rule than was so at the time *Wolf* was decided. While that is true, a recent survey indicates that at present one-half of the States still adhere to the common-law non-exclusionary rule, and one, Maryland, retains the rule as to felonies. . . . But in any case surely all this is beside the point, as the majority itself indeed seems to recognize. Our concern here, as it was in *Wolf,* is not with the desirability of that rule but only with the question whether the States are constitutionally free to follow it or not as they may themselves determine, and the relevance of the disparity of views among the States on this point lies simply in the fact that the judgment involved is a debatable one. Moreover, the very fact on which the majority relies, instead of lending support to what is now being done, points away from the need of replacing voluntary state action with federal compulsion.

The preservation of a proper balance between state and federal responsibility in the administration of criminal justice demands patience on the part of those who might like to see things move faster among the States in this respect. . . .

Memorandum of *Mr. Justice Stewart.*

Agreeing fully with Part I of Mr. Justice Harlan's dissenting opinion, I express no view as to the merits of the constitutional issue which the Court today decides. I would, however, reverse the judgment in this case, because I am persuaded that the provision . . . upon which the petitioner's conviction was based is, in the words of Mr. Justice Harlan, not "consistent with the rights of free thought and expression assured against state action by the Fourteenth Amendment."

United States v. Leon

468 U.S. 897; 104 S. Ct. 3405; 82 L. Ed. 2d 677 (1984)

Vote: 6-3

*Justice **White*** delivered the opinion of the Court.

This case presents the question whether the Fourth Amendment exclusionary rule should be modified so as not to bar the use in the prosecution's case-in-chief of evidence obtained by officers acting in reasonable reliance on a search warrant issued by a detached and neutral magistrate but ultimately found to be unsupported by probable cause. To resolve this question, we must consider once again the tension between the sometimes competing goals of, on the one hand, deterring official misconduct and removing inducements to unreasonable invasions of privacy and, on the other, establishing procedures under which criminal defendants are "acquitted or convicted on the basis of all the evidence which exposes the truth."***

In August 1981, a confidential informant of unproven reliability informed an officer of the Burbank Police Department that two persons known to him as 'Armando' and 'Patsy' were selling large quantities of cocaine and methaqualone from their residence at 620 Price Drive in Burbank, Cal. The informant also indicated that he had witnessed a sale of methaqualone by "Patsy" at the residence approximately five months earlier and had observed at that time a shoebox containing a large amount of cash that belonged to "Patsy." He further declared that "Armando" and "Patsy" generally kept only small quantities of drugs at their residence and stored the remainder at another location in Burbank.

On the basis of this information, the Burbank police initiated an extensive investigation focusing first on the Price Drive residence and later on two other residences as well. Cars parked at the Price Drive residence were determined to belong to respondents Armando Sanchez, who had previously been arrested for possession of marihuana, and Patsy Stewart, who had no criminal record. During the course of the investigation, officers observed an automobile belonging to respondent Ricardo Del Castillo, who had previously been arrested for possession of 50 pounds of marihuana, arrive at the Price residence. The driver of that car entered the house, exited shortly thereafter carrying a small paper sack, and drove away. A check of Del Castillo's probation records led the officers to respondent Alberto Leon, whose telephone number Del Castillo had listed as his employer's. Leon had been arrested in 1980 on drug charges, and a companion had informed the police at that time that Leon was heavily involved in the importation of drugs into this country. Before the current investigation began, the Burbank officers had learned that an informant had told a Glendale police officer that Leon stored a large quantity of methaqualone at his residence in Glendale. During the course of this investigation, the Burbank officers learned that Leon was living at 716 South Sunset Canyon in Burbank.

Subsequently, the officers observed several persons, at least one of whom had prior drug involvement, arriving at the Price Drive residence and leaving with small packages; observed a variety of other material activity at the two residences as well as at a condominium at 7902 Via Magdalena; and witnessed a variety of relevant activity involving respondents' automobiles. The officers also observed respondents Sanchez and Stewart board separate flights for Miami. The pair later returned to Los Angeles together, consented to a search of their luggage that revealed only a small amount of marihuana, and left the airport. Based on these and other observations summarized in the affidavit, Officer Cyril Rombach of the Burbank Police Department, an experienced and well-trained narcotics investigator, prepared an application for a warrant to search 620 Price Drive, 716 South Sunset Canyon, 7902 Via Magdalena, and automobiles registered to each of the respondents for an extensive list of items believed to be related to respondent's drug-trafficking activities. Officer Rombach's extensive application was reviewed by several Deputy District Attorneys.

A facially valid search warrant was issued in September 1981 by a State Superior Court Judge. The ensuing searches produced large quantities of drugs at the Via Magdalena and Sunset Canyon addresses and a small quantity at the Price Drive residence. Other evidence was discovered at each of the residences and in Stewart's and Del Castillo's automobiles. . . .

The respondents then filed motions to suppress the evidence seized pursuant to the warrant. The District Court . . . concluded that the affidavit was insufficient to establish probable cause, but did not suppress all of the evidence as to all of the respondents because none of the respondents had standing to challenge all of the searches. In response to a request from the Government, the court made clear that Officer Rombach had acted in good faith, but it rejected the Government's suggestion that the Fourth Amendment exclusionary rule should not apply where evidence is seized in reasonable, good-faith reliance on a search warrant. . . .

The Fourth Amendment contains no provision expressly precluding the use of evidence obtained in violation of its commands, and an examination of its origin and purposes makes clear that the use of fruits of a past unlawful search or seizure "work[s] no new Fourth Amendment wrong." *** The wrong condemned by the Amendment is "fully accomplished" by the unlawful search or seizure itself, *** and the exclusionary rule is neither intended nor able to "cure the invasion of the defendant's rights which he has already suffered." *** The rule thus operates as "a judicially created remedy designed to safeguard Fourth Amendment rights generally through its deterrent effect, rather than a personal constitutional right of the person aggrieved."***

Whether the exclusionary sanction is appropriately imposed in a particular case, our decisions make clear, is "an issue separate from the question whether the Fourth Amendment rights of the party seeking to invoke the rule were violated by police conduct." *** Only the former question is currently before us, and it must be resolved by weighing the costs and benefits of preventing the use in the prosecution's case-in-chief of inherently trustworthy tangible evidence obtained in reliance on a search warrant issued by a detached and neutral magistrate that ultimately is found to be defective.

The substantial social costs exacted by the exclusionary rule for the vindication of Fourth Amendment rights have long been a source of concern. "Our cases have consistently recognized that unbending application of the exclusionary sanction to enforce ideals of government rectitude would impede unacceptably the truth-finding functions of judge and jury." *** An objectionable collateral consequence of this interference with the criminal justice system's truth-finding function is that some guilty defendants may go free or receive reduced sentences as a result of favorable plea bargains. Particularly when law enforcement officers have acted in objective good faith or their transgressions have been minor, the magnitude of the benefit conferred on such guilty defendants offends basic concepts of the criminal justice system. *** Indiscriminate application of the exclusionary rule, therefore, may well "generat[e] disrespect for the law and the administration of justice." *** Accordingly, "[a]s with any remedial device, the application of the rule has been restricted to those areas where its remedial objectives are thought most efficaciously served." ***

... The Court has, to be sure, not seriously questioned, "in the absence of a more efficacious sanction, the continued application of the rule to suppress evidence from the [prosecution's] case where a Fourth Amendment violation has been substantial and deliberate...." *** Nevertheless, the balancing approach that has evolved in various contexts—including criminal trial—"forcefully suggest[s] that the exclusionary rule be more generally modified to permit the introduction of evidence obtained in the reasonable good-faith belief that a search or a seizure was in accord with the Fourth Amendment." ...

As cases considering the use of unlawfully obtained evidence in criminal trials themselves make clear, it does not follow from the emphasis on the exclusionary rule's deterrent value that "anything which deters illegal searches is thereby commanded by the Fourth Amendment." *** In determining whether persons aggrieved solely by the introduction of damaging evidence unlawfully obtained from their co-conspirators or co-defendants could seek suppression, for example, we found that the additional benefits of such an extension of the exclusionary rule would not outweigh its costs. *** Standing to invoke the rule has thus been limited to cases in which the prosecution seeks to use the fruits of an illegal search or seizure against the victim of police misconduct....

Because a search warrant "provides the detached scrutiny of a neutral magistrate, which is a more reliable safeguard against improper searches than the hurried judgment of a law enforcement officer 'engaged in the often competitive enterprise of ferreting out crime,' " *** we have expressed a strong preference for warrants and declared that "in a doubtful or marginal case a search under a warrant may be sustainable where without one it would fall." *** Reasonable minds frequently may differ on the question whether a particular affidavit establishes probable cause, and we have thus concluded that the preference for warrants is most appropriately effectuated by according "great deference" to a magistrate's determination. ***

Deference to the magistrate, however, is not boundless. It is clear, first, that the deference accorded to a magistrate's finding of probable cause does not preclude inquiry into the knowing or reckless falsity of the affidavit on which that determination was based. *** Second, the courts must also insist that the magistrate purport to "perform his 'neutral and detached' function and not serve merely as a rubber stamp for the police." ...

Third, reviewing courts will not defer to a warrant based on an affidavit that does not "provide the magistrate with a substantial basis for determining the existence of probable cause." ... Even if the warrant application was supported by more than a "bare bones" affidavit, a reviewing court may properly conclude that, notwithstanding the deference that magistrates deserve, the warrant was invalid because the magistrate's probable-cause determination reflected an improper analysis of the totality of the circumstances, *** or because the form of the warrant was improper in some respect.

Only in the first of these three situations, however, has the Court set forth a rationale for suppressing evidence obtained pursuant to a search warrant; in the other areas, it has simply excluded such evidence without considering whether Fourth Amendment interests will be advanced. To the extent that proponents of exclusion rely on its behavioral effects on judges and magistrates in these areas, their reliance is misplaced. First, the exclusionary rule is designed to deter police misconduct rather than to punish the errors of judges and magistrates. Second, there exists no evidence suggesting that judges and magistrates are inclined to ignore or subvert the Fourth Amendment or that lawlessness among those actors requires application of the extreme sanction of exclusion.

Third, and most important, we discern no basis, and are offered none, for believing that exclusion of evidence seized pursuant to a warrant will have a significant deterrent effect on the issuing judge or magistrate.... Judges and magistrates are not adjuncts to the law enforcement team; as neutral judicial officers, they have no stake in the outcome of particular criminal prosecutions. The threat of exclusion thus cannot be expected significantly to deter them. Imposition of the exclusionary sanction is not necessary meaningfully to inform judicial officers of their errors, and we cannot conclude that admitting evidence obtained pursuant to a warrant while at the same time declaring that the warrant was somehow defective will in any way reduce judicial officers' professional incentives to comply with the Fourth Amendment, encourage them to repeat their mistakes, or lead to the granting of all colorable warrant requests.

If exclusion of evidence obtained pursuant to a subsequently invalidated warrant is to have any deterrent effect, therefore, it must alter the behavior of individual law enforcement officers or the policies of their departments....

We have frequently questioned whether the exclusionary rule can have any deterrent effect when the offending officers acted in the objectively reasonable belief that their conduct did not violate the Fourth Amendment. "No empirical researcher, proponent or opponent of the rule, has yet been able to establish with any assurance whether the rule has a deterrent effect...." *** But even assuming that the rule effectively deters some police misconduct and provides incentives for the law enforcement profession as a whole to conduct itself in accord with the Fourth Amendment, it cannot be expected, and should not be applied, to deter objectively reasonable law enforcement activity....

We conclude that the marginal or nonexistent benefits produced by suppressing evidence obtained in objectively reasonable reliance on a subsequently invalidated search warrant cannot justify the substantial costs of exclusion....

When the principles we have enunciated today are applied to the facts of this case, it is apparent that the judgment of the Court of Appeals cannot stand. The Court of Appeals applied the prevailing legal standards to Officer Rombach's warrant application and concluded that the application could not support the magistrate's probable-cause determination. In so doing, the court clearly informed the magistrate that he had erred in issuing the challenged warrant. This aspect of the court's judgment is not under attack in this proceeding.

Having determined that the warrant should not have issued, the Court of Appeals understandably declined to adopt a modification of the Fourth Amendment exclusionary rule that this court had not previously sanctioned. Although the modification finds strong support in our previous cases, the Court of Appeals' commendable self-restraint is not to be criticized. We have now re-examined the purposes of the exclusionary rule and the propriety of its application in cases where officers have relied on a subsequently invalidated search warrant. Our conclusion is that the rule's purposes will only rarely be served by applying it in such circumstances....

Accordingly, the judgment of the Court of Appeals is reversed.

Justice Blackmun, concurring. . . .

Justice Brennan, with whom ***Justice Marshal*** joins, dissenting.

Ten years ago in *United States v. Calandra,* *** (1974), I expressed the fear that the Court's decision "may signal that a majority of my colleagues have positioned themselves to reopen the door [to evidence secured by official lawlessness] still further and abandon altogether the exclusionary rule in search-and-seizure cases." *** Since then, in case after case, I have witnessed the Court's gradual but determined strangulation of the rule. It now appears that the Court's victory over the Fourth Amendment is complete. That today's decision represents the *piece de résistance* of the Court's past efforts cannot be doubted, for today the Court sanctions the use in the prosecution's case-in-chief of illegally obtained evidence against the individual whose rights have been violated—a result that had previously been thought to be foreclosed.

The Court seeks to justify this result on the ground that the "costs" of adhering to the exclusionary rule in cases like those before us exceed the "benefits." But the language of deterrence and of cost/benefit analysis, if used indiscriminately, can have a narcotic effect. It creates an illusion of technical precision and ineluctability. It suggests that not only constitutional principle but also empirical data supports the majority's result. When the Court's analysis is examined carefully, however, it is clear that we have not been treated to an honest assessment of the merits of the exclusionary rule, but have instead been drawn into a curious world where the "costs" of excluding illegally obtained evidence loom to exaggerated heights and where the "benefits" of such exclusion are made to disappear with a mere wave of the hand.

The majority ignores the fundamental constitutional importance of what is at stake here. While the machinery of law enforcement and indeed the nature of crime itself have changed dramatically since the Fourth Amendment became part of the Nation's fundamental law in 1791, what the Framers understood then remains true today—that the task of combating crime and convicting the guilty will in every era seem of such critical and pressing concern that we may be lured by the temptations of expediency into forsaking our commitment to protecting individual liberty and privacy. It was for that very reason that the Framers of the Bill of Rights insisted that law enforcement efforts be permanently and unambiguously restricted in order to preserve personal freedoms. In the constitutional scheme they ordained,

the sometimes unpopular task of ensuring that the government's enforcement efforts remain within the strict boundaries fixed by the Fourth Amendment was entrusted to the courts. . . . If those independent tribunals lose their resolve, however, as the Court has done today, and give way to the seductive call of expediency, the vital guarantees of the Fourth Amendment are reduced to nothing more than a "form of words."***

A proper understanding of the broad purposes sought to be served by the Fourth Amendment demonstrates that the principles embodied in the exclusionary rule rest upon a far firmer constitutional foundation than the shifting sands of the Court's deterrence rationale. But even if I were to accept the Court's chosen method of analyzing the question posed by these cases, I would still conclude that the Court's decision cannot be justified. . . .

At bottom, the Court's decision turns on the proposition that the exclusionary rule is merely a "'judicially created remedy designed to safeguard Fourth Amendment rights generally through its deterrent effect, rather than a personal constitutional right.'" *** The germ of that idea is found in *Wolf v. Colorado,* *** and although I had thought that such a narrow conception of the rule had been forever put to rest by our decision in *Mapp v. Ohio,* *** it has been revived by the present Court and reaches full flower with today's decision. The essence of this view, as expressed initially in the *Calandra* opinion and as reiterated today, is that the sole "purpose of the Fourth Amendment is to prevent unreasonable governmental intrusions into the privacy of one's person, house, papers, or effects. The wrong condemned is the unjustified governmental invasion of these areas of an individual's life. That wrong . . . is *fully accomplished* by the original search without probable cause." *** This reading of the Amendment implies that its proscriptions are directed solely at those government agents, who may actually invade an individual's constitutionally protected privacy. The courts are not subject to any direct constitutional duty to exclude illegally obtained evidence, because the question of the admissibility of such evidence is not addressed by the Amendment. This view of the scope of the Amendment relegates the judiciary to the periphery. Because the only constitutionally cognizable injury has already been "fully accomplished" by the police by the time a case comes before the courts, the Constitution is not itself violated if the judge decides to admit the tainted evidence. Indeed, the most the judge *can* do is wring his hands and hope that perhaps by excluding such evidence he can deter future transgressions by the police.

Such a reading appears plausible, because, as critics of the exclusionary rule never tire of repeating, the Fourth Amendment makes no express provision of the exclusion of evidence secured in violation of its commands. A short answer to this claim, of course, is that many of the Constitution's most vital imperatives are stated in general terms and the task of giving meaning to these precepts is therefore left to subsequent judicial decisionmaking in the context of concrete cases. The nature of our Constitution, as Chief Justice Marshall long ago explained, "requires that only its great outlines should be marked, its important objects designated, and the minor ingredients which compose those objects be deduced from the nature of the objects themselves."***

A more direct answer may be supplied by recognizing that the Amendment, like other provisions of the Bill of Rights, restrains the power of the government as a whole; it does not specify only a particular agency and exempt all others. The judiciary is responsible, no less than the executive, for ensuring that constitutional rights are respected....

... It is difficult to give any meaning at all to the limitations imposed by the Amendment if they are read to proscribe only certain conduct by the police but to allow other agents of the same government to take advantage of evidence secured by the police in violation of its requirements. The Amendment therefore must be read to condemn not only the initial unconstitutional invasion of privacy—which is done, after all, for the purpose of securing evidence—but also the subsequent use of any evidence so obtained.

The Court evades this principle by drawing an artificial line between the constitutional rights and responsibilities that are engaged by actions of the police and those that are engaged when a defendant appears before the courts. According to the Court, the substantive protections of the Fourth Amendment are wholly exhausted at the moment when police unlawfully invade an individual's privacy and thus no substantive force remains to those protections at the time of trial when the government seeks to use evidence obtained by the police.

I submit that such a crabbed reading of the Fourth Amendment casts aside the teaching of those Justices who first formulated the exclusionary rule, and rests ultimately on an impoverished understanding of judicial responsibility in our constitutional scheme. For my part, "[t]he right of the people to be secure in their persons, houses, papers and effects, against unreasonable searches and seizures" comprises a personal right to exclude all evidence secured by means of unreasonable searches and seizures. The right to be free from the initial invasion of privacy and the right of exclusion are coordinate components of the central embracing right to be free from unreasonable searches and seizures....

Justice Stevens, dissenting....

Miranda v. Arizona
384 U.S. 436; 86 S. Ct. 1602; 16 L. Ed. 2d 694 (1966)
Vote: 5-4

Mr. Chief Justice Warren delivered the opinion of the Court.

The cases before us raise questions which go to the roots of our concepts of American criminal jurisprudence: the restraints society must observe consistent with the Federal Constitution in prosecuting individuals for crime. More specifically, we deal with the admissibility of statements obtained from an individual who is subjected to custodial police interrogation and the necessity for procedures which assure that the individual is accorded his privilege under the Fifth Amendment to the Constitution not to be compelled to incriminate himself.

We dealt with certain phases of this problem recently in *Escobedo v. Illinois* *** (1964).

We start here, as we did in *Escobedo,* with the premise that our holding is not an innovation in our jurisprudence, but is an application of principles long recognized and applied in other settings. We have undertaken a thorough re-examination of the *Escobedo* decision and the principles it announced, and we reaffirm it. That case was but an explication of basic rights that are enshrined in our Constitution — that "No person . . . shall be compelled in any criminal case to be a witness against himself," and that "the accused shall . . . have the Assistance of Counsel" — rights which were put in jeopardy in that case through official overbearing. These precious rights were fixed in our Constitution only after centuries of persecution and struggle. And in the words of Chief Justice Marshall, they were secured "for ages to come, and . . . designed to approach immortality as nearly as human institutions can approach it."***

Our holding will be spelled out with some specificity in the pages which follow but briefly stated it is this: the prosecution may not use statements, whether exculpatory or inculpatory, stemming from custodial interrogation of the defendant unless it demonstrates the use of procedural safeguards effective to secure the privilege against self-incrimination. By custodial interrogation, we mean questioning initiated by law enforcement officers after a person has been taken into custody or otherwise deprived of his freedom of action in any significant way. As for the procedural safeguards to be employed, unless other fully effective means are devised to inform accused persons of their right of silence and to assure a continuous opportunity to exercise it, the following measures are required. Prior to any questioning, the person must be warned that he has a right to remain silent, that any statement he does make may be used as evidence against him, and that he has a right to the presence of an attorney, either retained or appointed. The defendant may waive effectuation of these rights, provided the waiver is made voluntarily, knowingly and intelligently. If, however, he indicates

in any manner and at any stage of the process that he wishes to consult with an attorney before speaking there can be no questioning. Likewise, if the individual is alone and indicates in any manner that he does not wish to be interrogated, the police may not question him. The mere fact that he may have answered some questions or volunteered some statements on his own does not deprive him of the right to refrain from answering any further inquiries until he has consulted with an attorney and thereafter consents to be questioned.

The constitutional issue we decide . . . is the admissibility of statements obtained from a defendant questioned while in custody or otherwise deprived of his freedom of action in any significant way. In each, the defendant was questioned by police officers, detectives, or a prosecuting attorney in a room in which he was cut off from the outside world. In none of these cases was the defendant given a full and effective warning of his rights at the outset of the interrogation process. In all the cases, the questioning elicited oral admissions, and in three of them, signed statements as well which were admitted at their trials. They all thus share salient features — *incommunicado* interrogation of individuals in a police-dominated atmosphere, resulting in self-incriminating statements without full warnings of constitutional rights.

An understanding of the nature and setting of this in-custody interrogation is essential to our decisions today. The difficulty in depicting what transpires at such interrogations stems from the fact that in this country they have largely taken place *incommunicado.* From extensive factual studies undertaken in the early 1930's, including the famous Wickersham Report to Congress by a Presidential Commission, it is clear that police violence and the "third degree" flourished at that time. In a series of cases decided by this Court long after these studies, the police resorted to physical brutality — beating, hanging, whipping — and to sustained and protracted questioning *incommunicado* in order to extort confessions. The Commission on Civil Rights in 1961 found much evidence to indicate that "some policemen still resort to physical force to obtain confessions." The use of physical brutality and violence is not, unfortunately, relegated to the past or to any part of the country. Only recently in Kings County, New York, the police brutally beat, kicked and placed lighted cigarette butts on the back of a potential witness under interrogation for the purpose of securing a statement incriminating a third party.***

The examples given above are undoubtedly the exception now, but they are sufficiently widespread to be the object of concern. Unless a proper limitation upon custodial interrogation is achieved—such as these decisions will advance—there can be no assurance that practices of this nature will be eradicated in the foreseeable future.

Again we stress that the modern practice of in-custody interrogation is psychologically rather than physically oriented. Interrogation still takes place in privacy. Privacy results in secrecy and this in turn results in a gap in our knowledge as to what in fact goes on in the interrogation rooms. A valuable source of information about present police practices, however, may be found in various police manuals and texts which document procedures employed with success in the past, and which recommended various other effective tactics. These texts are used by law enforcement agencies themselves as guides. It should be noted that these texts professedly present the most enlightened and effective means presently used to obtain statements through custodial interrogation. By considering these texts and other data, it is possible to describe procedures observed and noted around the country.

Even without employing brutality, the "third degree" or the specific strategems described above, the very fact of custodial interrogation exacts a heavy toll on individual liberty and trades on the weakness of individuals.

In the cases before us today, given this background, we concern ourselves primarily with this interrogation atmosphere and the evils it can bring.

In these cases, we might not find the defendants' statements to have been involuntary in traditional terms. Our concern for adequate safeguards to protect precious Fifth Amendment rights is, of course, not lessened in the slightest. In each of the cases, the defendant was thrust into an unfamiliar atmosphere and run through menacing police interrogation procedures. The potentiality for compulsion is forcefully apparent, for example, in *Miranda,* where the indigent Mexican defendant was a seriously disturbed individual with pronounced sexual fantasies. . . .

It is obvious that such an interrogation environment is created for no purpose other than to subjugate the individual to the will of his examiner. This atmosphere carries its own badge of intimidation. . . . The current practice of *incommunicado* interrogation is at odds with one of our Nation's most cherished principles—that the individual may not be compelled to incriminate himself. Unless adequate protective devices are employed to dispel the compulsion inherent in custodial surroundings, no statement obtained from the defendant can truly be the product of his free choice.

From the foregoing, we can readily perceive an intimate connection between the privilege against self-incrimination and police custodial questioning. It is fitting to turn to history and precedent underlying the Self-Incrimination Clause to determine its applicability in this situation.

We sometimes forget how long it has taken to establish the privilege against self-incrimination, the sources from which it came and the fervor with which it was defended. Its roots go back into ancient times.

As a "noble principle often transcends its origins," the privilege has come rightfully to be recognized in part as an individual's substantive right, a "right to a private enclave where he may lead a private life. That right is the hallmark of our democracy." *** We have recently noted that the privilege against self-incrimination—the essential mainstay of our adversary system—is founded on a complex of values. . . . All these policies point to one overriding thought: the constitutional foundation underlying the privilege is the respect a government—state or federal—must accord to the dignity and integrity of its citizens.

We are satisfied that all the principles embodied in the privilege apply to informal compulsion exerted by law-enforcement officers during in-custody questioning. An individual swept from familiar surroundings into police custody, surrounded by antagonistic forces, and subjected to the techniques of persuasion described above cannot be otherwise than under compulsion to speak. As a practical matter, the compulsion to speak in the isolated setting of the police station may well be greater than in courts or other official investigations, where there are often impartial observers to guard against intimidation or trickery.

The presence of counsel, in all the cases before us today, would be the adequate protective device necessary to make the process of police interrogation conform to the dictates of the privilege. His presence would insure that statements made in the government-established atmosphere are not the product of compulsion.

It is impossible for us to foresee the potential alternatives for protecting the privilege which might be devised by Congress or the States in the exercise of their creative rulemaking capacities. Therefore we cannot say that the Constitution necessarily requires adherence to any particular solution for the inherent compulsions of the interrogation process as it is presently conducted. Our decision in no way creates a constitutional straitjacket which will handicap sound efforts at reform, nor is it intended to have this effect. We encourage Congress and the States to continue their laudable search for increasingly effective ways of protecting the rights of the individual while promoting efficient enforcement of our criminal laws.

A recurrent argument made in these cases is that society's need for interrogation outweighs the privilege. This argument is not unfamiliar to this Court. See, e.g., *Chambers v. Florida.****

In announcing these principles, we are not unmindful of the burdens which law enforcement officials must bear, often under trying circumstances. We also fully recognize the obligation of all citizens to aid in enforcing the criminal laws. This Court, while protecting individual rights, has always given ample latitude to law enforcement agencies in the legitimate exercise of their duties. The limit we have placed on the interrogation process should not constitute an undue interference with a proper system of law enforcement. As we have noted, our decision does not in any way preclude police from carrying out their traditional investigatory functions. Although confessions may play an important role in some convictions, the cases before us present graphic-examples of the overstatement of the "need" for confessions.

Therefore, in accordance with the foregoing, the judgment of the Supreme Court of Arizona . . . [is] reversed. . . .

Mr. Justice Harlan, whom *Mr. Justice Stewart* and *Mr. Justice White* join, dissenting. . . .

Mr. Justice White, with whom *Mr. Justice Harlan* and *Mr. Justice Stewart* join, dissenting.

. . . The obvious underpinning of the Court's decision is a deep-seated distrust of all confessions. As the Court declares that the accused may not be interrogated without counsel present, absent a waiver of the right to counsel, and as the Court all but admonishes the lawyer to advise the accused to remain silent, the result adds up to a judicial judgment that evidence from the accused should not be used against him in any way, whether compelled or not. This is the not so subtle overtone of the opinion—that it is inherently wrong for the police to gather evidence from the accused himself. And this is precisely the nub of this dissent. I see nothing wrong or immoral, and certainly nothing unconstitutional, in the police's asking a suspect whom they have reasonable cause to arrest whether or not he killed his wife or in confronting him with the evidence on which the arrest was based, at least where he has been plainly advised that he may remain completely silent. . . .

This is not to say that the value of respect for the inviolability of the accused's individual personality should be accorded no weight or that all confessions should be indiscriminately admitted. This Court has long read the Constitution to proscribe compelled confessions, a salutary rule from which there should be no retreat. But I see no sound basis, factual or otherwise, and the Court gives none, for concluding that the present rule against the receipt of coerced confessions is inadequate for the task of sorting out inadmissible evidence and must be replaced by the *per se* rule which is now imposed. Even if the new concept can be said to have advantages of some sort over the present law, they are far outweighed by its likely undesirable impact on other very relevant and important interests.

The most basic function of any government is to provide for the security of the individual and of his property. These ends of society are served by the criminal laws which for the most part are aimed at the prevention of crime. Without the reasonably effective performance of the task of preventing private violence and retaliation, it is idle to talk about human dignity and civilized values.

The rule announced today will measurably weaken the ability of the criminal law to perform these tasks. It is a deliberate calculus to prevent interrogations, to reduce the incidence of confessions and pleas of guilty and to increase the number of trials.

There is, in my view, every reason to believe that a good many criminal defendants who otherwise would have been convicted on what this Court has previously thought to be the most satisfactory kind of evidence will now, under this new version of the Fifth Amendment, either not be tried at all or will be acquitted if the State's evidence, minus the confession, is put to test of litigation.

I have no desire whatsoever to share the responsibility for any such impact on the present criminal process.

In some unknown number of cases the Court's rule will return a killer, a rapist or other criminal to the streets and to the environment which produced him, to repeat his crime whenever it pleases him. As a consequence, there will not be a gain, but a loss, in human dignity. The real concern is not the unfortunate consequences of this new decision on the criminal law as an abstract, disembodied series of authoritative proscriptions, but the impact on those who rely on the public authority for protection and who without it can only engage in violent self-help with guns, knives and the help of their neighbors similarly inclined. There is, of course, a saving factor: the next victims are uncertain, unnamed and unrepresented in this case.

Nor can this decision do other than have a corrosive effect on the criminal law as an effective device to prevent crime. A major component in its effectiveness in this regard is its swift and sure enforcement. The easier it is to get away with rape and murder, the less the deterrent effect on those who are inclined to attempt it. This is still good common sense. If it were not, we should posthaste liquidate the whole law enforcement establishment as a useless, misguided effort to control human conduct.

And what about the accused who has confessed or would confess in response to simple, noncoercive questioning and whose guilt could not otherwise be proved? Is it so clear that release is the best thing for him in every case? Has it so unquestionably been

resolved that in each and every case it would be better for him not to confess and to return to his environment with no attempt whatsoever to help him? I think not. It may well be that in many cases it will be no less than a callous disregard for his own welfare as well as for the interests of his next victim.

Much of the trouble with the Court's new rule is that it will operate indiscriminately in all criminal cases, regardless of the severity of the crime or the circumstances involved. It applies to every defendant, whether the professional criminal or one committing a crime of momentary passion who is not part and parcel of organized crime. It will slow down the investigation and the apprehension of confederates in those cases where time is of the essence, such as kidnapping, those involving the national security, and some of those involving organized crime. In the latter context the lawyer who arrives may also be the lawyer for the defendant's colleagues and can be relied upon to insure that no breach of the organization's security takes place even though the accused may feel that the best thing he can do is to cooperate.

At the same time, the Court's *per se* approach may not be justified on the ground that it provides a "bright line" permitting the authorities to judge in advance whether interrogation may safely be pursued without jeopardizing the admissibility of any information obtained as a consequence. Nor can it be claimed that judicial time and effort, assuming that is a relevant consideration, will be conserved because of the ease of application of the new rule. Today's decision leaves open such questions as whether the accused was in custody, whether his statements were spontaneous or the product of interrogation, whether the accused has effectively waived his rights, and whether nontestimonial evidence introduced at trial is the fruit of statements made during a prohibited interrogation, all of which are certain to prove productive of uncertainty during investigation and litigation during prosecution. For all these reasons, if further restrictions on police interrogation are desirable at this time, a more flexible approach makes much more sense than the Court's constitutional strait jacket which forecloses more discriminating treatment by legislative or rule-making pronouncements. . . .

Mr. Justice Clark, dissenting. . . .

Nix v. Williams

467 U.S. 431; 104 S. Ct. 2501; 81 L. Ed. 2d 377 (1984)
Vote: 7-2

Chief Justice Burger delivered the opinion of the Court.

We granted *certiorari* to consider whether, at respondent Williams' second murder trial in state court, evidence pertaining to the discovery and condition of the victim's body was properly admitted on the ground that it would ultimately or inevitably have been discovered even if no violation of any constitutional or statutory provision had taken place.

On December 24, 1968, 10-year-old Pamela Powers disappeared from a YMCA building in Des Moines, Iowa, where she had accompanied her parents to watch an athletic contest. Shortly after she disappeared, Williams was seen leaving the YMCA carrying a large bundle wrapped in a blanket; a 14-year-old boy who had helped Williams open his car door reported that he had seen "two legs in it and they were skinny and white."

Williams' car was found the next day 160 miles east of Des Moines in Davenport, Iowa. Later several items of clothing belonging to the child, some of Williams' clothing, and an army blanket like the one used to wrap the bundle that Williams carried out of the YMCA were found at a rest stop on Interstate 80 near Grinnell, between Des Moines and Davenport. A warrant was issued for Williams' arrest.

Police surmised that Williams had left Pamela Powers or her body somewhere between Des Moines and the Grinnell rest stop where some of the young girl's clothing had been found. On December 26, the Iowa Bureau of Criminal Investigation initiated a large-scale search. Two hundred volunteers divided into teams began the search 21 miles east of Grinnell, covering an area several miles to the north and south of Interstate 80. They moved westward from Poweshiek County, in which Grinnell was located, into Jasper County. Searchers were instructed to check all roads, abandoned farm buildings, ditches, culverts, and any other place in which the body of a small child could be hidden.

Meanwhile, Williams surrendered to local police in Davenport.... Williams contacted a Des Moines attorney who arranged for an attorney in Davenport to meet Williams at Davenport police station. Des Moines police informed counsel they would pick Williams up in Davenport and return him to Des Moines without questioning him. Two Des Moines detectives then drove to Davenport, took Williams into custody, and proceeded to drive him back to Des Moines.

During the return trip, one of the policemen, Detective Leaming, began a conversation with Williams, saying:

I want to give you something to think about while we're traveling down the road.... They are predicting several inches of snow for tonight, and I feel that you yourself are the only person that knows where this little girl's body is ... and if you get a snow on top of it you yourself may be unable to find it. And since we will be going right past the area [where the body is] on the way to Des Moines, I feel that we could stop and locate the body, that the parents of this little girl should be entitled to a Christian burial for the little girl who was snatched away from them on Christmas [E]ve and murdered.... [A]fter a snow storm [we may not be] able to find it at all.

Leaming told Williams he knew the body was in the area of Mitchellville—a town they would be passing on the way to Des Moines. He concluded the conversation by saying, "I do not want you to answer me.... Just think about it...."

Later, as the police car approached Grinnell, Williams asked Leaming whether the police had found the young girl's shoes. After Leaming replied that he was unsure, Williams directed the police to a point near a service station where he said he had left the shoes; they were not found. As they continued the drive to Des Moines, Williams asked whether the blanket had been found and then directed the officers to a rest area in Grinnell where he said he had disposed of the blanket; they did not find the blanket. At this point Leaming and his party were joined by the officers in charge of the search. As they approached Mitchellville, Williams, without any further conversation, agreed to direct the officers to the child's body.

The officers directing the search had called off the search at 3 P.M., when they left the Grinnell Police Department to join Leaming at the rest area. At that time, one search team near the Jasper County-Polk County line was only two and one-half miles from where Williams soon guided Leaming and his party to the body. The child's body was found next to a culvert in a ditch beside a gravel road in Polk County, about two miles south of Interstate 80, and essentially within the area to be searched.

In February 1969 Williams was indicted for first-degree murder. Before trial in the Iowa court, his counsel moved to suppress evidence of the body and all related evidence including the condition of the body as shown by the autopsy. The ground for the motion was that such evidence was the "fruit" or product of Williams' statements made during the automobile ride from Davenport to Des Moines and prompted by Leaming's statements. The motion to suppress was denied.

The jury found Williams guilty of first-degree murder; the judgment of conviction was affirmed by the Iowa Supreme Court. *** Williams then sought release on *habeas corpus* in the United States District Court. . . . That court concluded that the evidence in question had been wrongly admitted at Williams' trial; *** a divided panel of the Court of Appeals for the Eighth Circuit agreed. ***

We granted *certiorari*, *** and a divided Court affirmed, holding that Detective Leaming had obtained incriminating statements from Williams by what was viewed as interrogation in violation of his right to counsel. *Brewer v. Williams* *** (1977). This Court's opinion noted, however, that although Williams' incriminating statements could not be introduced into evidence at a second trial, evidence of the body's location and condition "might well be admissible on the theory that the body would have been discovered in any event, even had incriminating statements not been elicited from Williams." ***

At Williams' second trial in 1977 in the Iowa court, the prosecution did not offer Williams' statements into evidence, nor did it seek to show that Williams had directed the police to the child's body. However, evidence of the condition of her body as it was found, articles and photographs of her clothing, and the results of postmortem medical and chemical tests on the body were admitted. The trial court concluded that the State had proved by a preponderance of the evidence that, if the search had not been sus-

pended and Williams has not led the police to the victim, her body would have been discovered "*within a short time*" in essentially the same condition as it was actually found. The trial court also ruled that if the police had not located the body, "the search would clearly have been taken up again where it left off, given the extreme circumstances of this case and the body would [have] been found in *short order*." ***

In finding that the body would have been discovered in essentially the same condition as it was actually found, the court noted that freezing temperatures had prevailed and tissue deterioration would have been suspended. *** The challenged evidence was admitted and the jury again found Williams guilty of first-degree murder; he was sentenced to life in prison.

On appeal, the Supreme Court of Iowa again affirmed. . . .

In 1980 Williams renewed his attack on the state-court conviction by seeking a writ of *habeas corpus* in the United States District Court for the Southern District of Iowa. The District Court conducted its own independent review of the evidence and concluded, as had the state courts, that the body would inevitably have been found by the searchers in essentially the same condition it was in when Williams led police to its discovery. The District Court denied Williams' petition. ***

The Court of Appeals for the Eighth Circuit reversed. . . .

We granted the State's petition for *certiorari*, *** and we reverse. . . .

Williams contends that evidence of the body's location and condition is "fruit of the poisonous tree," i.e., the "fruit" or product of Detective Leaming's plea to help the child's parents give her "a Christian burial," which this Court had already held equated to interrogation. He contends that admitting the challenged evidence violated the Sixth Amendment whether it would have been inevitably discovered or not. Williams also contends that, if the inevitable discovery doctrine is constitutionally permissible, it must include a threshold showing of police good faith.

The doctrine requiring courts to suppress evidence as the tainted "fruit" of unlawful governmental conduct had its genesis in *Silverthorne Lumber Co. v. United States* *** (1920); there, the Court held that the exclusionary rule applies not only to the illegally obtained evidence itself, but also to other incriminating evidence derived from the primary evidence. The holding of *Silverthorne* was carefully limited, however, for the Court emphasized that such information does not automatically become "sacred and inaccessible." . . .

Wong Sun v. United States, *** (1963), extended the exclusionary rule to evidence that was the indirect product or "fruit" of unlawful police conduct, but there again the Court emphasized that evidence that has been illegally obtained need not always be suppressed. . . . The Court thus pointedly negated the kind of good-faith requirement advanced by the Court of Appeals in reversing the District Court.

Although *Silverthorne* and *Wong Sun* involved violations of the Fourth Amendment, the "fruit of the poisonous tree" doctrine has not been limited to cases in which there has been a Fourth Amendment violation. The Court has applied the doctrine where the violations were of the Sixth Amendment, *** as well as of the Fifth Amendment.

The core rationale consistently advanced by this Court for extending the exclusionary rule to evidence that is the fruit of unlawful police conduct has been that this admittedly drastic and socially costly course is needed to deter police from violations of constitutional and statutory protections. This Court has accepted the argument that the way to ensure protection is to exclude evidence seized as a result of such violations notwithstanding the high social cost of letting persons obviously guilty go unpunished for their crimes. On this rationale, the prosecution is not to be put in a better position than it would have been in if no illegality had transpired.

By contrast, the derivative evidence analysis ensures that the prosecution is not put in a worse position simply because of some earlier police error or misconduct. The independent source doctrine allows admission of evidence that has been discovered by means wholly independent of any constitutional violation. That doctrine, although closely related to the inevitable discovery doctrine, does not apply here; Williams' statements to Leaming indeed led police to the child's body, but that is not the whole story. The independent source doctrine teaches us that the interest of society in deterring unlawful police conduct and the public interest in having juries receive all probative evidence of a crime are properly balanced by putting the police in the same, not a worse, position than they would have been in if no police error or misconduct had occurred. *** When the challenged evidence has an independent source, exclusion of such evidence would put the police in a worse position than they would have been in absent any or violation. There is a functional similarity between these two doctrines in that exclusion of evidence that would inevitably have been discovered would also put the government in a worse position, because the police would have obtained that evidence if no misconduct had taken place. Thus, while the independent source exception would not justify admission of evidence in this case, its rationale is wholly consistent with and justifies our adoption of the ultimate or inevitable discovery exception to the Exclusionary Rule.

It is clear that the cases implementing the exclusionary rule "began with the premise that the challenged evidence is in some sense the product of illegal governmental activity." *** Of course, this does not end the inquiry. If the prosecution can establish by a preponderance of the evidence that the information ultimately or inevitably would have been discovered by lawful means—here the volunteers' search—then the deterrence rationale has so little basis that the evidence should be received. Anything less would reject logic, experience, and common sense. . . .

Exclusion of physical evidence that would inevitably have been discovered adds nothing to either the integrity or fairness of a criminal trial. The Sixth Amendment right to counsel protects against unfairness by preserving the adversary process in which the reliability of proffered evidence may be tested in cross-examination. *** Here, however, Detective Leaming's conduct did nothing to impugn the reliability of the evidence in question—the body of the child and its condition as it was found, articles of clothing found on the body, and the autopsy. No one would seriously contend that the presence of counsel in the police car when Leaming appealed to Williams' decent human instincts would have had any bearing on the reliability of the body as evidence. Suppression, in these circumstances, would do nothing whatever to promote the integrity of the trial process, but would inflict a wholly unacceptable burden on the administration of criminal justice.

Nor would suppression ensure fairness on the theory that it tends to safeguard the adversary system of justice. To assure the fairness of trial proceedings, this Court has held that assistance of counsel must be available at pretrial confrontation where "the subsequent trial [cannot] cure a[n otherwise] one-sided confrontation between prosecuting authorities and the uncounseled defendant." *** Fairness can be assured by placing the State and the accused in the same positions they would have been in had the impermissible conduct not taken place. However, if the government can prove that the evidence would have been obtained inevitably and, therefore, would have been admitted regardless of any overreaching by the police, there is no rational basis to keep that evidence from the jury in order to ensure the fairness of the trial proceedings. In that situation, the State has gained no advantage at trial and the defendant has suffered no prejudice. Indeed, suppression of that evidence would operate to undermine the adversary system by putting the State in a worse position than it would have occupied without any police misconduct. Williams' argument that inevitable discovery constitutes impermissible balancing of values is without merit. . . .

The Court of Appeals did not find it necessary to consider whether the record fairly supported the finding that the volunteer search party would ultimately or inevitably have discovered the victim's body. However, three courts independently reviewing the evidence have found that the body of the child inevitably would have been found by the searchers. Williams challenges these findings, asserting that the record contains only the "*post hoc* rationalization" that the search efforts would have proceeded two and one-half miles into Polk County where Williams had led police to the body. . . .

On [the] record it is clear that the search parties were approaching the actual location of the body, and we are satisfied, along with three courts earlier, that the volunteer search teams would have resumed the search had Williams not earlier led the police to the body and the body inevitably would have been found. . . .

The judgment of the Court of Appeals is reversed, and the case is remanded for further proceedings consistent with this opinion.

It is so ordered.

Justice White, concurring. . . .

Justice Stevens, concurring in the judgment. . . .

Justice Brennan, with whom **Justice Marshall** joins, dissenting.

. . . To the extent that today's decision adopts this "inevitable discovery" exception to the exclusionary rule, it simply acknowledges a doctrine that is akin to the "independent source" exception first recognized by the Court in *Silverthorne Lumber Co. v. United States.* *** In particular, the Court concludes that unconstitutionally obtained evidence may be admitted at trial if it inevitably would have been discovered in the same condition by an independent line of investigation that was already being pursued when the constitutional violation occurred. As has every federal Court of Appeals previously addressing this issue, . . . I agree that in these circumstances the "inevitable discovery" exception to the exclusionary rule is consistent with the requirements of the Constitution.

In its zealous efforts to emasculate the exclusionary rule, however, the Court loses sight of the crucial difference between the "inevitable discovery" doctrine and the "independent source" exception from which it is derived. When properly applied, the "independent source" exception allows the prosecution to use evidence only if it was, in fact, obtained by fully lawful means. It therefore does no violence to the constitutional protections that the exclusionary rule is meant to enforce. The "inevitable discovery" exception is likewise compatible with the Constitution, though it differs in one key respect from its next of kin: specifically, the evidence sought to be introduced at trial has not actually been obtained from an independent source, but rather would have been discovered as a matter of course if independent investigations were allowed to proceed.

In my view, this distinction should require that the government satisfy a heightened burden of proof before it is allowed to use such evidence. The inevitable discovery exception necessarily implicates a hypothetical finding that differs in kind from the factual findings that precedes application of the independent source rule. To ensure that this hypothetical finding is narrowly confined to circumstances that are functionally equivalent to an independent source, and to protect fully the fundamental rights served by the exclusionary rule, I would require

clear and convincing evidence before concluding that the government had met its burden of proof on this issue. *** Increasing the burden of proof serves to impress the factfinder with the importance of the decision and thereby reduces the risk that illegally obtained evidence will be admitted. *** Because the lower courts did not impose such a requirement, I would remand this case for application of this heightened burden of proof by the lower courts in the first instance. I am therefore unable to join either the Court's opinion or its judgment.

New York v. Quarles
467 U.S. 649; 104 S. Ct. 2626; 81 L. Ed.2d 550 (1984)
Vote: 5-3-1

Justice Rehnquist delivered the opinion of the Court.

Respondent Benjamin Quarles was charged in the New York trial court with criminal possession of a weapon. The trial court suppressed the gun in question, and a statement made by respondent, because the statement was obtained by police before they read respondent his "Miranda rights." That ruling was affirmed on appeal through the New York Court of Appeals. We granted *certiorari,* *** and we now reverse. We conclude that under the circumstances involved in this case, overriding considerations of public safety justify the officer's failure to provide Miranda warnings before he asked questions devoted to locating the abandoned weapon.

On September 11, 1980, at approximately 12:30 A.M., Officer Frank Kraft and Officer Sal Scarring were on road patrol in Queens, New York, when a young woman approached their car. She told them that she had just been raped by a black male, approximately six feet tall, who was wearing a black jacket with the name "Big Ben" printed in yellow letters on the back. She told the officers that the man had just entered an A & P supermarket located nearby and that the man was carrying a gun.

The officers drove the woman to the supermarket, and Officer Kraft entered the store while Officer Scarring radioed for assistance. Officer Kraft quickly

spotted respondent, who matched the description given by the woman, approaching a checkout counter. Apparently upon seeing the officer, respondent turned and ran toward the rear of the store, and Officer Kraft pursued him with a drawn gun. When respondent turned the corner at the end of an aisle, Officer Kraft lost sight of him for several seconds, and upon regaining sight of respondent, ordered him to stop and put his hands over his head.

Although more than three other officers had arrived on the scene by that time, Officer Kraft was the first to reach respondent. He frisked him and discovered that he was wearing a shoulder holster which was then empty. After handcuffing him, Officer Kraft asked him where the gun was. Respondent nodded in the direction of some empty cartons and responded, "the gun is over there." Officer Kraft thereafter retrieved a loaded .38 caliber revolver from one of the cartons, formally placed respondent under arrest, and read him his Miranda rights from a printed card. Respondent indicated that he would be willing to answer questions without an attorney present. Officer Kraft then asked respondent if he owned the gun and where he had purchased it. Respondent answered that he did own it and that he had purchased it in Miami, Florida.

In the subsequent prosecution of respondent for criminal possession of a weapon, the judge excluded the statement, "the gun is over there," and the gun because the officer had not given respondent the warnings required by our decision in *Miranda v. Arizona,* *** before asking him where the gun was located. The judge excluded the other statements about respondent's ownership of the gun and the place of purchase, as evidence tainted by the prior *Miranda* violation. The Appellate Division of the Supreme Court of New York affirmed without opinion.

The Court of Appeals ... concluded that respondent was in "custody" within the meaning of *Miranda* during all questioning and rejected the state's argument that the exigencies of the situation justified Officer Kraft's failure to read respondent his Miranda rights until after he had located the gun. The court declined to recognize an exigency exception to the usual requirements of *Miranda* because it found no indication from Officer Kraft's testimony at the suppression hearing that his subjective motivation in asking the question was to protect his own safety or the safety of the public. *** For the reasons which follow, we believe that this case presents a situation where concern for public safety must be paramount to adherence to the literal language of the prophylactic rules enunciated in *Miranda.* ...

In this case we have before us no claim that respondent's statements were actually compelled by police conduct which overcame his will to resist. *** Thus the only issue before us is whether Officer Kraft was justified in failing to make available to respondent the procedural safeguards associated with the privilege against compulsory self-incrimination since *Miranda.*

The New York Court of Appeals was undoubtedly correct in deciding that the facts of this case come within the ambit of the *Miranda* decision as we have subsequently interpreted it. We agree that respondent was in police custody because we have noted that "the ultimate inquiry is simply whether there is a 'formal arrest or restraint on freedom of movement' of the degree associated with a formal arrest." *** Here Quarles was surrounded by at least four police officers and was handcuffed when the questioning at issue took place. As the New York Court of Appeals observed, there was nothing to suggest that any of the officers were any longer concerned for their safety. The New York Court of Appeals' majority

declined to express an opinion as to whether there might be an exception to the *Miranda* rule if the police had been acting to protect the public, because the lower courts in New York had made no factual determination that the police had acted with that motive. ***

We hold that on these facts there is a "public safety" exception to the requirement that Miranda warnings be given before a suspect's answers may be admitted into evidence, and the availability of that exception does not depend upon the motivation of the individual officers involved. In a kaleidoscopic situation such as the one confronting these officers, where spontaneity rather than adherence to a police manual is necessarily the order of the day, the application of the exception which we recognize today should not be made to depend on *post hoc* findings at a suppression hearing concerning the subjective motivation of the arresting officer. Undoubtedly most police officers, if placed in Officer Kraft's position, would act out of a host of different, instinctive, and largely unverifiable motives—their own safety, the safety of others, and perhaps as well the desire to obtain incriminating evidence from the suspect.

Whatever the motivation of individual officers in such a situation, we do not believe that the doctrinal underpinnings of *Miranda* required that it be applied in all its rigor to a situation in which police officers ask questions reasonably prompted by a concern for the public safety. The *Miranda* decision was based in large part on this Court's view that the warnings which it required police to give to suspects in custody would reduce the likelihood that the suspects would fall victim to constitutionally impermissible practices of police interrogation in the presumptively coercive environment of the station house. *** The dissenters warned that the requirement of Miranda warnings would have the effect of decreasing the number of suspects who respond to police questioning. *** The *Miranda* majority, however, apparently felt that whatever the cost to society in terms of fewer convictions of guilty suspects, that cost would simply have to be borne in the interest of enlarged protection for the Fifth Amendment privilege.

The police in this case, in the very act of apprehending a suspect, were confronted with the immediate necessity of ascertaining the whereabouts of a gun which they had every reason to believe the suspect had just removed from his empty holster and discarded in the supermarket. So long as the gun was concealed somewhere in the supermarket, with its actual whereabouts unknown, it obviously posed more than one danger to the public safety: an accomplice might make use of it, a customer or employee might later come upon it.

In such a situation, if the police are required to recite the familiar Miranda warnings before asking the whereabouts of the gun, suspects in Quarles' position might well be deterred from responding. Procedural safeguards which deter a suspect from responding were deemed acceptable in *Miranda* in order to protect the Fifth Amendment privilege; when the primary social cost of those added protections is the possibility of fewer convictions, the *Miranda* majority was willing to bear that cost. Here, had Miranda warnings deterred Quarles from responding to Officer Kraft's question about the whereabouts of the gun, the cost would have been something more than merely the failure to obtain evidence useful in convicting Quarles but to insure that further danger to the public did not result from the concealment of the gun in a public area.

We conclude that the need for answers to questions in a situation posing a threat to the public safety outweighs the need for the prophylactic rule protecting the Fifth Amendment's privilege against self-incrimination. We decline to place officers such as Officer Kraft in the untenable position of having to consider, often in a matter of seconds, whether it best serves society for them to ask the necessary questions without the Miranda warnings and render whatever probative evidence they uncover inadmissible, or for them to give the warnings in order to preserve the admissibility of evidence they might uncover but possibly damage or destroy their ability to obtain that evidence and neutralize the volatile situation confronting them.

In recognizing a narrow exception to the *Miranda* rule in this case, we acknowledge that to some degree we lessen the desirable clarity of that rule. At least in part in order to preserve its clarity, we have over the years refused to sanction attempts to expand our *Miranda* holding. ***But as we have pointed out, we believe that the exception which we recognize today lessens the necessity of that on-the-scene balancing process. The exception will not be difficult for police officers to apply because in each case it will be circumscribed by the exigency which justifies it. We think police officers can and will distinguish almost instinctively between questions necessary to secure their own safety or the safety of the public and questions designed solely to elicit testimonial evidence from a suspect.

The facts of this case clearly demonstrate that distinction and an officer's ability to recognize it. Officer Kraft asked only the question necessary to locate the missing gun before advising respondent of his rights. It was only after securing the loaded revolver and giving the warnings that he continued with investigatory questions about the ownership and place of purchase of the gun. The exception which we recognize today, far from complicating the thought processes and the on-the-scene judgments of police officers, will simply free them to follow their legitimate instincts when confronting situations presenting a danger to the public safety.

We hold that the Court of Appeals in this case erred in excluding the statement, "the gun is over there," and the gun because of the officer's failure to read respondent his Miranda rights before attempting to locate the weapon. Accordingly we hold that it also erred in excluding the subsequent statements as illegal fruits of a *Miranda* violation. We therefore reverse and remand for further proceedings not inconsistent with this opinion.

It is so ordered.

Justice O'Connor, concurring in part in the judgment and dissenting in part.

... Were the Court writing from a clean slate, I could agree with its holding. But *Miranda* is now the law and, in my view, the Court has not provided sufficient justification for departing from it or for blurring its now clear strictures. Accordingly, I would require suppression of the initial statement taken from respondent in this case. On the other hand, nothing in *Miranda* or the privilege itself requires exclusion of nontestimonial evidence derived from informal custodial interrogation, and I therefore agree with the Court that admission of the gun in evidence is proper....

Justice Marshall, with whom *Justice Brennan* and *Justice Stevens* join, dissenting.

The police in this case arrested a man suspected of possessing a firearm in violation of New York law. Once the suspect was in custody and found to be unarmed, the arresting officer initiated an interrogation. Without being advised of his right not to respond, the suspect incriminated himself by locating the gun. The majority concludes that the State may rely on this incriminating statement to convict the suspect of possessing a weapon. I disagree. The arresting officers had no legitimate reason to interrogate the suspect without advising him of his rights to remain silent and to obtain assistance of counsel. By finding on these facts justification for unconsented interrogation, the majority abandons the clear guidelines enunciated in *Miranda v. Arizona* *** and condemns the American judiciary to a new era of *post hoc* inquiry into the propriety of custodial interrogations. More significantly and in direct conflict with this Court's long-standing interpretation of the Fifth Amendment, the majority has endorsed the introduction of coerced self-incriminating statements in criminal prosecutions. I dissent. . . .

The majority's entire analysis rests on the factual assumption that the public was at risk during Quarles' interrogation. This assumption is completely in conflict with the facts as found by New York's highest court. Before the interrogation began, Quarles had been "reduced to a condition of physical powerlessness." *** Contrary to the majority's speculations, *** Quarles was not believed to have, nor did he in fact have, an accomplice to come to his rescue. When the questioning began, the arresting officers were sufficiently confident of their safety to put away their guns. As Officer Kraft acknowledged at the suppression hearing, "the situation was under control." *** Based on Officer Kraft's testimony, the New York Court of Appeals found: "Nothing suggests that any of the officers was by that time concerned for his own physical safety." *** The Court of Appeals also determined that there was no evidence that the interrogation was prompted by the arresting officers' concern for the public's safety. *** . . .

The majority's treatment of the legal issues presented in this case is no less troubling than its abuse of the facts. Before today's opinion, the Court had

twice concluded that, under *Miranda v. Arizona,* police officers conducting custodial interrogations must advise suspects of their rights before any questions concerning the whereabouts of incriminating weapons can be asked. *** Now the majority departs from these cases and rules that police may withhold Miranda warnings whenever custodial interrogations concern matters of public safety.

The majority contends that the law, as it currently stands, places police officers in a dilemma whenever they interrogate a suspect who appears to know of some threat to the public's safety. If the police interrogate the suspect without advising him of his rights, the suspect may reveal information that the authorities can use to defuse the threat, but the suspect's statements will be inadmissible at trial. If, on the other hand, the police advise the suspect of his rights, the suspect may be deterred from responding to the police's questions, and the risk to the public may continue unabated. According to the majority, the police must now choose between establishing the suspect's guilt and safeguarding the public from danger.

The majority proposes to eliminate this dilemma by creating an exception to *Miranda v. Arizona* for custodial interrogations concerning matters of public safety. *** Under the majority exception, police would be permitted to interrogate suspects about such matters before the suspects have been advised of their constitutional rights. Without being "deterred" by the knowledge that they have a constitutional right not to respond, these suspects will be likely to answer the questions. Should the answers also be incriminating, the State would be free to introduce them as evidence in a criminal prosecution. Through this "narrow exception to the *Miranda* rule," *** the majority proposes to protect the safety without jeopardizing the prosecution of criminal defendants. I find in this reasoning an unwise and unprincipled departure from our Fifth Amendment precedents.

Before today's opinion, the procedures established in *Miranda v. Arizona* had "the virtue of informing police and prosecutors with specificity as to what they may do in conducting custodial interrogation, and of informing courts under what circumstances statements obtained during such interrogations are not admissible." *** In a chimerical quest for public safety, the majority has abandoned the rule that brought eighteen years of doctrinal tranquillity to the field of custodial interrogations. As the majority candidly concedes, a public-safety exception destroys forever the clarity of *Miranda* for both law enforcement officers and members of the judiciary. The Court's candor cannot mask what a serious loss the administration of justice has incurred.

This case is illustrative of the chaos the "public-safety" exception will unleash. The circumstances of Quarles' arrest have never been in dispute. After the benefit of briefing and oral argument, the New York Court of Appeals concluded that there was "no evidence in the record before us that there were exigent circumstances posing a risk to the public safety." Upon reviewing the same facts and hearing the same arguments, a majority of this Court has come to precisely the opposite conclusion: "So long as the gun was concealed somewhere in the supermarket, with its actual whereabouts unknown, it obviously posed more than one danger to the public safety...." ***

If after plenary review two appellate courts so fundamentally differ over the threat to public safety presented by the simple and uncontested facts of this case, one must seriously question how law enforcement officers will respond to the majority's new rule in the confusion and haste of the real world.... Not only will police officers have to decide whether the objective facts of an arrest justify an unconsented custodial interrogation; they will also have to remember to interrupt the interrogation and read the suspect his Miranda warnings once the focus of the inquiry shifts from protecting the public's safety to ascertaining the suspect's guilt. Disagreements of the scope of the "public-safety" exception and mistakes in its application are inevitable....

Though unfortunate, the difficulty of administering the "public-safety" exception is not the most profound flaw in the majority's decision. The majority has lost sight of the fact that *Miranda v. Arizona* and our earlier custodial-interrogation cases all implemented a constitutional privilege against self-incrimination. The rules established in these cases were designed to protect criminal defendants against prosecutions based on coerced self-incriminating statements. The majority today turns its back on these constitutional considerations, and invites the government to prosecute through the use of what necessarily are coerced statements....

Powell v. Alabama (The Scottsboro Case)
287 U.S. 45; 53 S. Ct. 55; 77 L. Ed. 158 (1932)
Vote: 7-2

Mr. Justice Sutherland delivered the opinion of the Court.

The petitioners, hereinafter referred to as defendants, are negroes charged with the crime of rape, committed upon the person of two white girls. The crime is said to have been committed on March 25, 1931. The indictment was returned in a state court of first instance on March 31 and the record recites that on the same day the defendants were arraigned and entered pleas of not guilty. There is a further recital to the effect that upon the arraignment they were represented by counsel. But no counsel had been employed, and aside from a statement made by the trial judge several days later during a colloquy immediately preceding the trial, the record does not disclose when, or under what circumstances, an appointment of counsel was made, or who was appointed. During the colloquy referred to, the trial judge, in response to a question, said that he had appointed all the members of the bar for the purpose of arraigning the defendants and then of course anticipated that the members of the bar would continue to help the defendants if no counsel appeared. Upon the argument here both sides accepted that as a correct statement of the facts concerning the matter.

... Each of the three trials was completed within a single day. Under the Alabama statute the punishment for rape is to be fixed by the jury, and in its discretion may be from ten years' imprisonment to death. The juries found defendants guilty and imposed the death penalty upon all. The trial court overruled motions for new trials and sentenced the defendants in accordance with the verdicts. The judgments were affirmed by the state supreme court. Chief Justice Anderson thought the defendants had not been accorded a fair trial and strongly dissented. ***

In this court the judgments are assailed upon the grounds that the defendants, and each of them, were denied due process of law and the equal protection of the laws, in contravention of the Fourteenth Amendment, specifically as follows: (1) they were not given a fair, impartial and deliberate trial; (2) they were denied the right to counsel, with the accustomed incidents of consultation and opportunity of preparation for trial; and (3) they were tried before juries from which qualified members of their own race were systematically excluded. . . .

The only one of the assignments which we shall consider is the second, in respect of the denial of counsel; and it becomes unnecessary to discuss the facts of the case or the circumstances surrounding the prosecution except in so far as they reflect light upon that question.

The record shows that on the day when the offense is said to have been committed, these defendants, together with a number of other negroes, were upon a freight train on its way through Alabama. On the same train were seven white boys and two white girls. A fight took place between the negroes and the white boys, in the course of which the white boys, with the exception of one named Gilley, were thrown off the train. A message was sent ahead, reporting the fight and asking that every negro be gotten off the train. The participants in the fight, and the two girls, were in an open gondola car. The two girls testified that each of them was assaulted by six different negroes in turn, and they identified the seven defendants as having been among the number. None of the white boys was called to testify, with the exception of Gilley, who was called in rebuttal.

Before the train reached Scottsboro, Alabama, a sheriff's posse seized the defendants and two other negroes. Both girls and the negroes then were taken to Scottsboro, the county seat. Word of their coming

and of the alleged assault had preceded them, and they were met at Scottsboro by a large crowd. It does not sufficiently appear that the defendants were seriously threatened with, or that they were actually in danger of, mob violence; but it does appear that the attitude of the community was one of great hostility. The sheriff thought it necessary to call for the militia to assist in safeguarding the prisoners. Chief Justice Anderson pointed out in his opinion that every step taken from the arrest and arraignment to the sentence was accompanied by the military. Soldiers took the defendants to Gadsden for safekeeping, brought them back to Scottsboro for arraignment, returned them to Gadsden for safekeeping while awaiting trial, escorted them to Scottsboro for trial a few days later, and guarded the courthouse and grounds at every stage of the proceedings. It is perfectly apparent that the proceedings, from beginning to end, took place in an atmosphere of tense, hostile and excited public sentiment. During the entire time, the defendants were closely confined or were under military guard. The record does not disclose their ages, except that one of them was nineteen; but the record clearly indicates that most, if not all, of them were youthful, and they are constantly referred to as "the boys." They were ignorant and illiterate. All of them were residents of other states, where alone members of their families or friends resided.

However guilty defendants, upon due inquiry might prove to have been, they were, until convicted, presumed to be innocent. It was the duty of the court having their cases in charge to see that they were denied no necessary incident of a fair trial. With any error of the state court involving alleged contravention of the state statutes or constitution we, of course, have nothing to do. The sole inquiry which we are permitted to make is whether the federal Constitution was contravened *** and as to that, we confine ourselves, as already suggested, to the inquiry whether the defendants were in substance denied the right to counsel, and if so, whether such denial infringes the Due Process Clause of the Fourteenth Amendment.

First. The record shows that immediately upon the return of the indictment defendants were arraigned and pleaded not guilty. Apparently they were not asked whether they had, or were able to employ, counsel, or wished to have counsel appointed; or whether they had friends or relatives who might assist in that regard if communicated with. . . .

It is hardly necessary to say that the right to counsel being conceded, a defendant should be afforded a fair opportunity to secure counsel of his own choice. Not only was that not done here, but such designation of counsel as was attempted was either so indefinite or so close upon the trial as to amount to a denial of effective and substantial aid in that regard. This will be amply demonstrated by a brief review of the record.

April 6, six days after indictment, the trial began. When the first case was called, the court inquired whether the parties were ready for trial. The state's attorney replied that he was ready to proceed. No one answered for the defendants or appeared to represent or defend them. Mr. Roddy, a Tennessee lawyer, not a member of the local bar, addressed the court, saying that he had not been employed, but that people who were interested had spoken to him about the case. He was asked by the court whether he intended to appear for the defendants, and answered that he would like to appear along with counsel that the court might appoint. The record then proceeds:

The Court: If you appear for these defendants, then I will not appoint counsel; if local counsel are willing to appear and assist you under the circumstances all right, but I will not appoint them.
Mr. Roddy: Your Honor has appointed counsel, is that correct?
The Court: I appointed all the members of the bar for the purpose of arraigning the defendants and then of course I anticipated them to continue to help them if no counsel appears.
Mr. Roddy: Then I don't appear then as counsel but I do want to stay in and not be ruled out in this case.
The Court: Of course I would not do that—
Mr. Roddy: I just appear here through the courtesy of Your Honor.
The Court: Of course I give you that right; . . .

. . . [T]his action of the trial judge in respect of appointment of counsel was little more than an expansive gesture, imposing no substantial or definite obligation upon any one . . . during perhaps the most critical period of the proceedings against these de-

fendants, that is to say, from the time of their arraignment until the beginning of their trial, when consultation, thorough-going investigation and preparation were vitally important, the defendants did not have the aid of counsel in any real sense, although they were as much entitled to such aid during that period as at the trial itself. ***

Nor do we think the situation was helped by what occurred on the morning of the trial. At that time, as appears from the colloquy printed above, Mr. Roddy stated to the court that he did not appear as counsel, but that he would like to appear along with counsel that the court might appoint; that he had not been given an opportunity to prepare the case; that he was not familiar with the procedure in Alabama, but merely came down as a friend of the people who were interested; that he thought the boys would be better off if he should step entirely out of the case. Mr. Moody, a member of the local bar, expressed a willingness to help Mr. Roddy in anything he would do under the circumstances. To this the court responded, "All right, all the lawyers that will; of course I would not require a lawyer to appear if—." And Mr. Moody continued, "I am willing to do that for him as a member of the bar; I will go ahead and help do anything I can do." With this dubious understanding, the trials immediately proceeded. The defendants, young, ignorant, illiterate, surrounded by hostile sentiment, haled back and forth under guard of soldiers, charged with an atrocious crime regarded with especial horror in the community where they were to be tried, were thus put in peril of their lives within a few moments after counsel for the first time charged with any degree of responsibility began to represent them.

It is not enough to assume that counsel thus precipitated into the case thought there was no defense, and exercised their best judgment in proceeding to trial without preparation. Neither they nor the court could say what a prompt and thorough-going investigation might disclose as to the facts. No attempt was made to investigate. No opportunity to do so was given. Defendants were immediately hurried to trial. Chief Justice Anderson, after disclaiming any intention to criticize harshly counsel who attempted to represent defendants at the trials, said: " . . . The record indicates that the appearance was rather *pro forma* than zealous and active. . . ." Under the circumstances disclosed, we hold that defendants were not accorded the right of counsel in any substantial sense. To decide otherwise, would simply be to ignore actualities. . . .

The prompt disposition of criminal cases is to be commended and encouraged. But in reaching that result a defendant, charged with a serious crime, must not be stripped of his right to have sufficient time to advise with counsel and prepare his defense. To do that is not to proceed promptly in the calm spirit of regulated justice but to go forward with the haste of the mob. . . .

Second. The Constitution of Alabama provides that in all criminal prosecutions the accused shall enjoy the right to have the assistance of counsel; and a state statute requires the court in a capital case, where the defendant is unable to employ counsel, to appoint counsel for him. The state supreme court held that these provisions had not been infringed. . . . The question, however, which it is our duty, and within our power, to decide, is whether the denial of the assistance of counsel contravenes the Due Process Clause of the Fourteenth Amendment to the federal Constitution.

If recognition of the right of a defendant charged with a felony to have the aid of counsel depended upon the existence of a similar right at common law as it existed in England when our Constitution was adopted, there would be great difficulty in maintaining it as necessary to due process. Originally, in England, a person charged with treason or felony was denied the aid of counsel, except in respect of legal questions which the accused himself might suggest. At same time parties in civil cases and persons accused of misdemeanors were entitled to the full assistance of counsel. After the revolution of 1688, the rule was abolished as to treason, but was otherwise steadily adhered to until 1836, when by act of Parliament the full right was granted in respect of felonies generally. ***

An affirmation of the right to the aid of counsel in petty offenses, and its denial in the case of crimes of the gravest character, where such aid is most needed, is so outrageous and so obviously a perversion of all sense of proportion that the rule was constantly, vigorously and sometimes passionately assailed by English statesmen and lawyers. As early as 1758, Blackstone, although recognizing that the rule was settled at common law, denounced it as not in keeping with the rest of the humane treatment of prisoners by the English law. "For upon what face of reason," he says, "can that assistance be denied to save the life of a man, which yet is allowed him in prosecutions for every petty trespass?" *** One of the grounds upon which Lord Coke defended the rule was that in felonies the court itself was counsel for the prisoner. *** But how can a judge, whose functions are purely judicial, effectively discharge the obligations of counsel for the accused? He can and should see to it that in the proceedings before the court the accused shall be dealt with justly and fairly. He cannot investigate the facts, advise and direct the defense, or participate in those necessary conferences between counsel and accused which sometimes partake of the inviolable character of the confessional. . . .

In light of the facts outlined in the forepart of this opinion—the ignorance and illiteracy of the defendants, their youth, the circumstances of public hostility, the imprisonment and the close surveillance of the defendants by the military forces, the fact that their friends and families were all in other states and communication with them necessarily difficult, and above all that they stood in deadly peril of their lives—we think the failure of the trial court to give them reasonable time and opportunity to secure counsel was a clear denial of due process.

But passing that, and assuming their inability, even if opportunity had been given, to employ counsel, as the trial court evidently did assume, we are of opinion that, under the circumstances just stated, the necessity of counsel was so vital and imperative that the failure of the trial court to make an effective appointment of counsel was likewise a denial of due process within the meaning of the Fourteenth Amendment. Whether this would be so in other criminal prosecutions, or under other circumstances, we need not determine. All that it is necessary now to decide, as we do decide, is that in a capital case, where the defendant is unable to employ counsel, and is incapable adequately of making his own defense because of ignorance, feeble-mindedness, illiteracy, or the like, it is the duty of the court, whether requested or not, to assign counsel for him as a necessary requisite of due process of law; and that duty is not discharged by an assignment at such a time or under such circumstances as to preclude the giving of effective aid in the preparation and trial of the case. To hold otherwise would be to ignore the fundamental postulate, already adverted to, "that there are certain immutable principles of justice which inhere in the very idea of free government which no member of the Union may disregard." *** In a case such as this, whatever may be the rule in other cases, the right to have counsel appointed, when necessary, is a logical corollary from the constitutional right to be heard by counsel. . . .

The judgments must be reversed and the causes remanded for further proceedings not inconsistent with this opinion.

Judgments reversed.

Mr. Justice Butler, dissenting.

If correct, the ruling that the failure of the trial court to give petitioners time and opportunity to secure counsel was denial of due process is enough, and with this the opinion should end. But the Court goes on to declare that "the failure of the trial court to make an effective appointment of counsel was likewise a denial of due process within the meaning of the Fourteenth Amendment." This is an extension of federal authority into a field hitherto occupied exclusively by the several States. Nothing before the Court calls for a consideration of the point. It was not suggested below and petitioners do not ask for its decision here. The Court, without being called upon to consider it, adjudges without a hearing an important constitutional question concerning criminal procedure in state courts.

It is a wise rule firmly established by a long course of decisions here that constitutional questions—even when properly raised and argued—are to be decided only when necessary for a determination of the rights of the parties in controversy before it. . . .

The record wholly fails to reveal that petitioners have been deprived of any right guaranteed by the Federal Constitution, and I am of opinion that the judgment should be affirmed.

Mr. Justice McReynolds concurs in this opinion.

Gideon v. Wainwright
372 U.S. 335; 83 S. Ct. 792; 9 L. Ed. 2d 799 (1963)
Vote: 9-0

Mr. Justice Black delivered the opinion of the Court.

Petitioner was charged in a Florida state court with having broken and entered a poolroom with intent to commit a misdemeanor. This offense is a felony under Florida law. Appearing in court without funds and without a lawyer, petitioner asked the court to appoint counsel for him, whereupon the following colloquy took place:

The Court: Mr. Gideon, I am sorry, but I cannot appoint Counsel to represent you in this case. Under the laws of the State of Florida, the only time the Court can appoint Counsel to represent a Defendant is when that person is charged with a capital offense. I am sorry, but I will have to deny your request to appoint Counsel to defend you in this case. The Defendant: The United States Supreme Court says I am entitled to be represented by Counsel.

Put to trial before a jury, Gideon conducted his defense about as well as could be expected from a layman. He made an opening statement to the jury, cross-examined the State's witnesses, presented witnessed in his own defense, declined to testify himself, and made a short argument "emphasizing his innocence to the charge contained in the Information filed in this case." The jury returned a verdict of guilty, the petitioner was sentenced to serve five years in the state prison. Later, petitioner filed in the Florida Supreme Court this *habeas corpus* petition attacking his conviction and sentence on the ground that the trial court's refusal to appoint counsel for him denied him rights "guaranteed by the Constitution and the Bill of Rights by the United States Government." Treating the petition for *habeas corpus* as properly before it, the State Supreme Court, "upon consideration thereof" but without an opinion, denied all relief. Since 1942, when *Betts v. Brady,* *** was decided by a divided Court, the problem of a defendant's federal constitutional right to counsel in a state court has been a continuing source of controversy and litigation in both state and federal courts. To give this problem another review here, we granted *certiorari.* Since Gideon was proceeding *in forma pauperis,* we appointed counsel to represent him and requested both sides to discuss in their briefs and oral arguments the following: "Should this Court's holding in *Betts v. Brady* be reconsidered?"

Since the facts and circumstances of the two cases are so nearly indistinguishable, we think the *Betts v. Brady* holding if left standing would require us to reject Gideon's claim that the Constitution guarantees him the assistance of counsel. Upon full reconsideration we conclude that *Betts v. Brady* should be overruled.

The facts upon which Betts claimed that he had been unconstitutionally denied the right to have counsel appointed to assist him are strikingly like the facts upon which Gideon here bases his federal constitutional claim.

The Sixth Amendment provides, "In all criminal prosecutions, the accused shall enjoy the right . . . to have the Assistance of Counsel for his defense." We have construed this to mean that in federal courts counsel must be provided for defendants unable to employ counsel unless the right is competently and intelligently waived. Betts argued that this right is extended to indigent defendants in state courts by the Fourteenth Amendment. In response the Court stated that, while the Sixth Amendment laid down "no rule for the conduct of the states, the question recurs whether the constraint laid by Amendment upon the national courts expresses a rule so fundamental and essential to a fair trial, and so, to due process of law, that it is made obligatory upon the States by the Fourteenth Amendment." In order to decide whether the Sixth Amendment's guarantee of counsel is of this fundamental nature, the Court in *Betts* set out and considered "[r]elevant data on the subject . . . afforded by constitutional and statutory provisions subsisting in the colonies and the States prior to the inclusion of the Bill of Rights in the

national Constitution, and in the constitutional, legislative, and judicial history of the States to the present date." *** On the basis of this historical data the Court concluded that "appointment of counsel is not a fundamental right, essential to a fair trial." *** It was for this reason the *Betts* Court refused to accept the contention that the Sixth Amendment's guarantee of counsel for indigent federal defendants was extended to or, in the words of that Court, "made obligatory upon the States by the Fourteenth Amendment." *** Plainly, had the Court concluded that appointment of counsel for an indigent criminal defendant was "a fundamental right, essential to a fair trial," *** it would have held that the Fourteenth Amendment requires appointment of counsel in a state court, just as the Sixth Amendment requires in a federal court.

We think the Court in *Betts* had ample precedent for acknowledging that those guarantees of the Bill of Rights which are fundamental safeguards of liberty immune from federal abridgment are equally protected against state invasion by the Due Process Clause of the Fourteenth Amendment. This same principle was recognized, explained, and applied in *Powell v. Alabama,* *** a case upholding the right of counsel, where the Court held that despite sweeping language to the contrary in *Hurtado v. California,* *** the Fourteenth Amendment "embraced" those " 'fundamental principles of liberty and justice which lie at the base of all our civil and political institutions,' " even though they had been "specifically dealt with in another part of the federal Constitution." *** In many cases other than *Powell* and *Betts,* this Court has looked to the fundamental nature of original Bill of Rights guarantees to decide whether the Fourteenth Amendment makes them obligatory on the States.

In light of these and many other prior decisions of this Court, it is not surprising that the *Betts* Court, when faced with the contention that "one charged with crime, who is unable to obtain counsel, must be furnished counsel by the State," *** conceded that "[e]xpressions in the opinions of this court lend color to the argument. . . ." *** The fact is that in deciding as it did—that "appointment of counsel is not a fundamental right, essential to a fair trial" *** —the Court in *Betts v. Brady* made an abrupt break with its own well-considered precedents. In returning to these old precedents, sounder we believe than the new, we but restore constitutional principles established to achieve a fair system of justice. Not only these precedents but also reason and reflection require us to recognize that in our adversary system of criminal justice, any person haled into court, who is too poor to hire a lawyer, cannot be assured a fair trial unless counsel is provided for him. This seems to us to be an obvious truth. Governments, both state and federal, quite properly spend vast sums of money to establish machinery to try defendants accused of crime. Lawyers to prosecute are everywhere deemed essential to protect the public's interest in an orderly society. Similarly, there are few defendants charged with crime, few indeed, who fail to hire the best lawyers they can get to prepare and present their defenses. That government hires lawyers to prosecute and defendants who have the money hire lawyers to defend are the strongest indications of the widespread belief that lawyers in criminal courts are necessities, not luxuries. The right of one charged with crime to counsel may not be deemed fundamental and essential to fair trials in some countries, but it is in ours. From the very beginning, our state and national constitutions and laws have laid great emphasis on procedural and substantive safeguards designed to assure fair trials before impartial tribunals in which every defendant stands equal before the law. This noble ideal cannot be realized if the poor man charged with crime has to face his accusers without a lawyer to assist him.

The Court in *Betts v. Brady* departed from the sound wisdom upon which the Court's holding in *Powell v. Alabama* rested. Florida, supported by two other States, has asked that *Betts v. Brady* be left intact. Twenty-two States, as friends of the Court, argue that *Betts* was "an anachronism when handed down" *** and that it should now be overruled. We agree.

The judgment is reversed and the cause is remanded to the Supreme Court of Florida for further action not inconsistent with this opinion.

Mr. Justice Douglas, concurring. . . .

Mr. Justice Clark, concurring in the result. . . .

Mr. Justice Harlan, concurring.

. . . In agreeing with the Court that the right to counsel in a case such as this should now be expressly recognized as a fundamental right embraced in the Fourteenth Amendment, I wish to make a further observation. When we hold a right or immunity, valid against the Federal Government, to be "implicit in the concept of ordered liberty" and thus valid against the States, I do not read our past decisions to suggest that by so holding, we automatically carry over an entire body of federal law and apply it in full sweep to the States. Any such concept would disregard the frequently wide disparity between the legitimate interest of the States and of the Federal Government, the divergent problems that they face, and the significantly different consequences of their actions. In what is done today I do not understand the Court to depart from the principles laid down in *Palko v. Connecticut,* *** or to embrace the concept that the Fourteenth Amendment "incorporates" the Sixth Amendment as such.

On these premises I join in the judgment of the Court.

Bordenkircher v. Hayes

434 U.S. 357; 98 S. Ct. 663; 54 L. Ed.2d 604 (1978)

Vote: 5-4

Mr. Justice Stewart delivered the opinion of the Court.

The question in this case is whether the Due Process Clause of the Fourteenth Amendment is violated when a state prosecutor carries out a threat made during plea negotiations to reindict the accused on more serious charges if he does not plead guilty to the offense with which he was originally charged.

I

The respondent, Paul Lewis Hayes, was indicted by a Fayette County, Ky., grand jury on a charge of uttering a forged instrument in the amount of $88.30, an offense then punishable by a term of two to 10 years in prison. *** After arraignment, Hayes, his retained counsel, and the Commonwealth's attorney met in the presence of the clerk of the court to discuss a possible plea agreement. During these conferences the prosecutor offered to recommend a sentence of five years in prison if Hayes would plead guilty to the indictment. He also said that if Hayes did not plead guilty and "save the court the inconvenience of a trial," he would return to the grand jury to seek an indictment under the Kentucky Habitual Criminal Act, *** which would subject Hayes to a mandatory sentence of life imprisonment by reason of his two prior felony convictions. Hayes chose not to plead guilty, and the prosecutor did obtain an indictment charging him under the Habitual Criminal Act. It is not disputed that the recidivist charge was fully justified by the evidence, that the prosecutor was in possession of this evidence at the time of the original indictment, and that Hayes' refusal to plead guilty to the original charge was what led to his indictment under the habitual criminal statute.

A jury found Hayes guilty on the principal charge of uttering a forged instrument and, in a separate proceeding, further found that he had twice before been convicted of felonies. As required by the habitual offender statute, he was sentenced to a life term in the penitentiary. The Kentucky Court of Appeals rejected Hayes' constitutional objectives to the enhanced sentence, holding in an unpublished opinion that imprisonment for life with the possibility of parole was constitutionally permissible in light of the previous felonies of which Hayes had been convicted, and that the prosecutor's decision to indict him as an habitual offender was a legitimate use of available leverage in the plea bargaining process.

On Hayes' petition for a federal writ of *habeas corpus,* the United States District Court for the Eastern District of Kentucky agreed that there had been no constitutional violation in the sentence or the indictment procedure, and denied the writ. The Court of Appeals for the Sixth Circuit reversed the District Court's judgement. *** While recognizing "that plea bargaining now plays an important role in our criminal justice system," *** the appellate court thought that the prosecutor's conduct during the bargaining negotiations had violated the principles ... which "protect[ed] defendants from the vindictive exercise of a prosecutor's discretion." *** We granted *certiorari* to consider a constitutional question of importance in the administration of criminal justice.

II

It may be helpful to clarify at the outset the nature of the issue in this case. While the prosecutor did not actually obtain the recidivist indictment until after the plea conferences had ended, his intention to do so was clearly put forth at the outset of the plea negotiations. Hayes was thus fully informed of the true terms of the offer when he made his decision to plead not guilty. This is not a situation, therefore, where the prosecutor without notice brought an additional and more serious charge after plea negotiations relating only to the original indictment had ended with the defendant's insistence on pleading not guilty. As a practical matter, in short, this case would be no different if the grand jury had indicted Hayes as a recidivist from the outset, and the prosecutor had offered to drop that charge as part of the plea bargain.

III

We have recently had occasion to observe that "whatever might be the situation in an ideal world, the fact is that the guilty plea and the often concomitant plea bargain are important components of this country's criminal justice system. Properly administered, they can benefit all concerned." *** The open acknowledgment of this previously clandestine practice had led this Court to recognize the importance of counsel during plea negotiations, *** the need for a public record indicating that a plea was knowingly and voluntarily made, *** and the requirement that a prosecutor's plea bargaining promise must be kept. ***

To punish a person because he has done what the law plainly allows him to do is a due process violation of the most basic sort, ... and for an agent of the State to pursue a course of action whose objective is to penalize a person's reliance on his legal rights is "patently unconstitutional. . . ." *** But in the "give-and-take" of plea bargaining, there is no such element of punishment or retaliation so long as the accused is free to accept or reject the prosecution's offer.

Plea bargaining flows from "the mutuality of advantage" to defendants and prosecutors, each with his own reasons for wanting to avoid trial. *** Defendants advised by competent counsel and protected by other procedural safeguards are presumptively capable of intelligent choice in response to prosecutorial persuasion, and unlikely to be driven to false self-condemnation. *** Indeed, acceptance of the basic legitimacy of plea bargaining necessarily implies rejection of any notion that a guilty plea is involuntary in a constitutional sense simply because it is the end result of the bargaining process. By hypothesis, the plea may have been induced by promises of a recommendation of a lenient sentence or a reduction of charges, and thus by fear of the possibility of a greater penalty upon conviction after a trial. ***

While confronting a defendant with the risk of more severe punishment clearly may have a "discouraging effect on the defendant's assertion of his trial rights, the imposition of these difficult choices [is] an inevitable"—and permissible—"attribute of any legitimate system which tolerates and encourages the negotiation of pleas. . . ." *** It follows that, by tolerating and encouraging the negotiation of pleas, this Court has necessarily accepted as constitutionally legitimate the simple reality that the prosecutor's interest at the bargaining table is to persuade the defendant to forego his right to plead not guilty.

It is not disputed here that Hayes was properly chargeable under the recidivist statute, since he had in fact been convicted of two previous felonies. In our system, so long as the prosecutor has probable cause to believe that the accused committed an offense defined by statute, the decision whether or not to prosecute, and what charge to file or bring before a grand jury, generally rests entirely in his discretion. Within the limits set by the legislature's constitutionally valid definition of chargeable offenses, "the conscious exercise of some selectivity in enforcement is not in itself a federal constitutional violation" so long

as "the selection was [not] deliberately based upon an unjustifiable standard such as race, religion, or other arbitrary classification. . . ." *** To hold that the prosecutor's desire to induct a guilty plea is an "unjustifiable standard," which, like race or religion, may play no part in his charging decision, would contradict the very premises that underlie the concept of plea bargaining itself. Moreover, a rigid constitutional rule that would prohibit a prosecutor from acting forthrightly in his dealings with the defense could only invite unhealthy subterfuge that would drive the practice of plea bargaining back into the shadows from which it has so recently emerged. ***

There is no doubt that the breadth of discretion that our country's legal system vests in prosecuting attorneys carries with it the potential for both individual and institutional abuse. And broad though that discretion may be there are undoubtedly constitutional limits upon its exercise. We hold only that the course of conduct engaged in by the prosecutor in this case, which no more than openly presented the defendant with the unpleasant alternatives of foregoing trial or facing charges on which he was plainly subject to prosecution, did not violate the Due Process Clause of the Fourteenth Amendment.

Accordingly, the judgment of the Court of Appeals is reversed.

Mr. Justice Blackmun, with whom **Mr. Justice Brennan** and **Mr. Justice Marshall** join, dissenting.

. . . Prosecutorial vindictiveness, it seems to me, in the present narrow context, is the fact against which the Due Process Clause ought to protect. I perceive little difference between vindictiveness after what the Court describes *** as the exercise of a "legal right to attack his original conviction," and vindictiveness in the " 'give-and-take negotiation common in plea bargaining.' " *** Prosecutorial vindictiveness in any context is still prosecutorial vindictiveness. The Due Process Clause should protect an accused against it, however it asserts itself. The Court of Appeals rightly so held, and I would affirm the judgment.

It might be argued that it really makes little difference how this case, now that it is here, is decided. The Court's holding gives plea bargaining full sway despite vindictiveness. A contrary result, however, merely would prompt the aggressive prosecutor to bring the greater charge initially in every case, and only thereafter to bargain. The consequences to the accused would still be adverse, for then he would bargain against a greater charge, face the likelihood of increased bail, and run the risk that the court would be less inclined to accept a bargained plea. Nonetheless, it is far preferable to hold the prosecution to the charge it was originally content to bring and to justify in the eyes of its public.

Mr. Justice Powell, dissenting.

Although I agree with much of the Court's opinion, I am not satisfied that the result in this case is just or that the conduct of the plea bargaining met the requirements of due process. . . .

There may be situations in which a prosecutor would be fully justified in seeking a fresh indictment for a more serious offense. The most plausible justification might be that it would have been reasonable and in the public interest initially to have charged the defendant with the greater offense. In most cases a court could not know why the harsher indictment was sought, and an inquiry into the prosecutor's motive would neither be indicated nor likely to be fruitful. In those cases, I would agree with the majority that the situation would not differ materially from one in which the higher charge was brought at the outset. ***

But this is not such a case. Here, any inquiry into the prosecutor's purpose is made unnecessary by his candid acknowledgment that he threatened to procure and in fact procured the habitual criminal indictment because of respondent's insistence on exercising his constitutional rights. . . .

The plea-bargaining process, as recognized by this Court, is essential to the functioning of the criminal-justice system. It normally affords genuine benefits to defendants as well as to society. And if the system is to work effectively, prosecutors must be accorded the widest discretion, within constitutional limits, in conducting bargaining. . . . This is especially true when a defendant is represented by counsel and presumably is fully advised of his rights. Only in the most exceptional case should a court conclude that the scales of the bargaining are so unevenly balanced as to arouse suspicion. In this case, the prosecutor's actions denied respondent due process because their admitted purpose was to discourage and then to penalize with unique severity his exercise of constitutional rights. Implementation of a strategy calculated solely to deter the exercise of constitutional rights is not a constitutionally permissible exercise of discretion. I would affirm the opinion of the Court of Appeals on the facts of this case.

Batson v. Kentucky

476 U.S. 79; 106 S. Ct. 1712; 90 L. Ed.2d 69 (1986)
Vote: 7–2

Justice Powell delivered the opinion of the Court.

This case requires us to reexamine that portion of *Swain v. Alabama* *** (1965), concerning the evidentiary burden placed on a criminal defendant who claims that he has been denied equal protection through the State's use of peremptory challenges to exclude members of his race from the petit jury.

Petitioner, a black man, was indicted in Kentucky on charges of second-degree burglary and receipt of stolen goods. On the first day of trial in Jefferson Circuit Court, the judge conducted voir dire examination of the venire, excused certain jurors for cause, and permitted the parties to exercise peremptory challenges. The prosecutor used his peremptory challenges to strike all four black persons on the venire, and a jury composed only of white persons was selected. Defense counsel moved to discharge the jury before it was sworn on the ground that the prosecutor's removal of the black veniremen violated petitioner's rights under the Sixth and Fourteenth Amendments to a jury drawn from a cross-section of the community, and under the Fourteenth Amendment to equal protection of the laws. Counsel requested a hearing on his motion. Without expressly ruling on the request for a hearing, the trial judge observed that the parties were entitled to use their peremptory challenges to "strike anybody they want to." The judge then denied petitioner's motion, reasoning that the cross-section requirement applies only to selection of the venire and not to selection of the petit jury itself.

The jury convicted petitioner on both counts. ***

The Supreme Court of Kentucky affirmed. *** We granted certiorari *** and now reverse.

In *Swain v. Alabama*, this Court recognized that a "State's purposeful or deliberate denial to Negroes on account of race of participation as jurors in the administration of justice violates the Equal Protection Clause." *** This principle has been "consistently and repeatedly" reaffirmed, *** in numerous decisions of this Court both preceding and following Swain. We reaffirm the principle today.

More than a century ago, the Court decided that the State denies a black defendant equal protection of the laws when it puts him on trial before a jury from which members of his race have been purposefully excluded. *Strauder v. West Virginia,* ***(1880). That decision laid the foundation for the Court's unceasing efforts to eradicate racial discrimination in the procedures used to select the venire from which individual jurors are drawn. In *Strauder,* the Court explained that the central concern of the recently ratified Fourteenth Amendment was to put an end to governmental discrimination on account of race. *** Exclusion of black citizens from service as jurors constitutes a primary example of the evil the Fourteenth Amendment was designed to cure.

In holding that racial discrimination in jury selection offends the Equal Protection Clause, the Court in *Strauder* recognized, however, that a defendant has no right to a "petit jury composed in whole or in part of persons of his own race." *** "The number of our races and nationalities stands in the way of evolution of such a conception" of the demand of equal protection. *** But the defendant does have the right to be tried by a jury whose members are selected pursuant to nondiscriminatory criteria. *** The Equal Protection Clause guarantees the defendant that the State will not exclude members of his race from the jury venire on account of race, *** or on the false assumption that members of his race as a group are not qualified to serve as jurors. ***

Purposeful racial discrimination in selection of the venire violates a defendant's right to equal protection because it denies him the protection that a trial by jury is intended to secure. "The very idea of a jury is a body *** composed of the peers or equals of the person whose rights it is selected or summoned to determine; that is, of his neighbors, fellows, associates, persons having the same legal status in society as that which he holds." *** The petit jury has occupied a central position in our system of justice by safeguarding a person accused of crime against the arbitrary exercise of power by prosecutor or judge. *** Those on the venire must be "indifferently chosen" to secure the defendant's right under the Fourteenth Amendment to "protection of life and liberty against race or color prejudice." ***

Racial discrimination in selection of jurors harms not only the accused whose life or liberty they are summoned to try. Competence to serve as a juror ultimately depends on an assessment of individual qualifications and ability impartially to consider evidence presented at a trial. *** A person's race simply "is unrelated to his fitness as a juror." *** As long ago as *Strauder,* therefore, the Court recognized that by denying a person participation in jury service on account of his race, the State unconstitutionally discriminated against the excluded juror. ***

The harm from discriminatory jury selection extends beyond that inflicted on the defendant and the excluded juror to touch the entire community. Selection procedures that purposefully exclude black persons from juries undermine public confidence in the fairness of our system of justice. *** Discrimination within the judicial system is most pernicious because it is "a stimulant to that race prejudice which is an impediment to securing to [black citizens] that equal justice which the law aims to secure to all others." ***

In *Strauder,* the Court invalidated a state statute that provided that only white men could serve as jurors. *** We can be confident that no state now has such a law. The Constitution requires, however, that we look beyond the face of the statute defining juror qualifications and also consider challenged selection practices to afford "protection against action of the State through its administrative officers in effecting the prohibited discrimination." *** Thus, the Court has found a denial of equal protection where the procedures implementing a neutral statute operated to exclude persons from the venire on racial grounds, and has made clear that the Constitution prohibits all forms of purposeful racial discrimination in selection of jurors. While decisions of this Court have been concerned largely with discrimination during selection of the venire, the principles announced there also forbid discrimination on account of race in selection of the petit jury. Since the Fourteenth Amendment protects an accused throughout the proceedings bringing him to justice, *** the State may not draw up its jury lists pursuant to neutral procedures but then resort to discrimination at "other stages in the selection process." ***

Accordingly, the component of the jury selection process at issue, here, the State's privilege to strike individual jurors through peremptory challenges, is subject to the commands of the Equal Protection Clause. Although a prosecutor ordinarily is entitled to exercise permitted peremptory challenges "for any reason at all, as long as that reason is related to his view concerning the outcome" of the case to be tried, *** the Equal Protection Clause forbids the prosecutor to challenge potential jurors solely on account of their race or on the assumption that black jurors as a group will be unable impartially to consider the State's case against a black defendant.

The principles announced in *Strauder* never have been questioned in any subsequent decision of this Court. Rather, the Court has been called upon repeatedly to review the application of those principles to particular facts. A recurring question in these cases, as in any case alleging a violation of the Equal Protection Clause, was whether the defendant had met his burden of proving purposeful discrimination on the part of the State. *** That question also was at the heart of the portion of *Swain v. Alabama* we reexamine today.

Swain required the Court to decide, among other issues, whether a black defendant was denied equal protection by the State's exercise of peremptory challenges to exclude members of his race from the petit jury. *** The record in Swain showed that the prosecutor had used the State's peremptory challenges to strike the six black persons included on the petit jury venire. *** While rejecting the defendant's claim for failure to prove purposeful discrimination, the Court nonetheless indicated that the Equal Protection Clause placed some limits on the State's exercise of peremptory challenges. ***

The Court sought to accommodate the prosecutor's historical privilege of peremptory challenge free of judicial control, *** and the constitutional prohibition on exclusion of persons from jury service on account of race. *** While the Constitution does not confer a right to peremptory challenges, *** those challenges traditionally have been viewed as one means of assuring the selection of a qualified and unbiased jury. *** To preserve the peremptory nature of the prosecutor's challenge, the Court in *Swain* declined to scrutinize his actions in a particular case by relying on a presumption that he properly exercised the State's challenges. ***

The Court went on to observe, however, that a state may not exercise its challenges in contravention of the Equal Protection Clause. It was impermissible for a prosecutor to use his challenges to exclude blacks from the jury "for reasons wholly unrelated to the outcome of the particular case on trial" or to deny to blacks "the same right and opportunity to participate in the administration of justice enjoyed by the white population." *** Accordingly, a black defendant could make out a prima facie case of purposeful discrimination on proof that the peremptory challenge system was "being perverted" in that manner. For example, an inference of purposeful discrimination would be raised on evidence that a prosecutor, "in case after case, whatever the circumstances, whatever the crime and whoever the defendant or the victim may be, is responsible for the removal of Negroes who have been selected as qualified jurors by the jury commissioners and who have survived challenges for cause, with the result that no Negroes ever serve on petit juries." *** Evidence offered by the defendant in *Swain* did not meet that standard. While the defendant showed that prosecutors in the jurisdiction had exercised their strikes to exclude blacks from the jury, he offered no proof of the circumstances under which prosecutors were responsible for striking black jurors beyond the facts of his own case. ***

A number of lower courts following the teaching of *Swain* reasoned that proof of repeated striking of blacks over a number of cases was necessary to establish a violation of the Equal Protection Clause. Since this interpretation of *Swain* has placed on defendants a crippling burden of proof, prosecutors' peremptory challenges are now largely immune from constitutional scrutiny. For reasons that follow, we reject this evidentiary formulation as inconsistent with standards that have been developed since *Swain* for assessing a prima facie case under the Equal Protection Clause. ***

As in any equal protection case, the "burden is, of course," on the defendant who alleges discriminatory selection of the venire "to prove the existence of purposeful discrimination." *** In deciding if the defendant has carried his burden of persuasion, a court must undertake "a sensitive inquiry into such circumstantial and direct evidence of intent as may be available." *** Circumstantial evidence of invidious intent may include proof of disproportionate impact. *** We have observed that under some circumstances proof of discriminatory impact "may for all practical purposes demonstrate unconstitutionality because in various circumstances the discrimination is very difficult to explain on nonracial grounds." *** For example, "total or seriously disproportionate exclusion of Negroes from jury venires is itself such an 'unequal application of the law *** as to show intentional discrimination.' " ***

Moreover, since *Swain*, we have recognized that a black defendant alleging that members of his race have been impermissibly excluded from the venire may make out a prima facie case of purposeful discrimination by showing that the totality of the relevant facts gives rise to an inference of discriminatory purpose. *** Once the defendant makes the requisite showing, the burden shifts to the State to explain adequately the racial exclusion. *** The State cannot meet this burden on mere general assertions that its officials did not discriminate or that they properly performed their official duties. *** Rather, the State must demonstrate that "permissible racially neutral selection criteria and procedures have produced the monochromatic result." ***

The showing necessary to establish a prima facie case of purposeful discrimination in selection of the venire may be discerned in this Court's decisions. *** The defendant initially must show that he is a member of a racial group capable of being singled out for differential treatment. *** In combination with the evidence, a defendant may then make a prima facie case by proving that in the particular jurisdiction members of his race have not been summoned for jury service over an extended period of time. *** Proof of systematic exclusion from the venire raises an inference of purposeful discrimination because the "result bespeaks discrimination." ***

Since the ultimate issue is whether the State has discriminated in selecting the defendant's venire, however, the defendant may establish a prima facie case "in other ways than by evidence of long-continued unexplained absence" of members of his race "from many panels." *** In cases involving the venire, this Court has found a prima facie case on proof that members of the defendant's race were substantially underrepresented on the venire from which his jury was drawn, and that the venire was selected under a practice providing "the opportunity for discrimination." *** This combination of factors raises the necessary inference of purposeful discrimination because the Court has declined to attribute to chance the absence of black citizens on a particular jury array where the selection mechanism is subject to abuse. When circumstances suggest the need, the trial court must undertake a "factual inquiry" that "takes into account all possible explanatory factors" in the particular case. ***

Thus, since the decision in *Swain*, this Court has recognized that a defendant may make a prima facie showing of purposeful racial discrimination in selection of the venire by relying solely on the facts concerning its selection *in his case*. These decisions are in accordance with the proposition *** that "a consistent pattern of official racial discrimination" is not "a necessary predicate to a violation of the Equal Protection Clause. A single invidiously discriminatory governmental act" is not "immunized by the absence of such discrimination in the making of the comparable decisions." *** For evidentiary requirements to dictate that "several must suffer discrimination" before one could object, *** would be inconsistent with the promise of equal protection to all.

The standards for assessing a prima facie case in the context of discriminatory selection of the venire have been fully articulated since *Swain*. *** These principles support our conclusion that a defendant may establish a prima facie case of purposeful discrimination in selection of the petit jury solely on evidence concerning the prosecutor's exercise of peremptory challenges at the defendant's trial. To establish such a case, the defendant first must show that he is a member of a cognizable racial group, *** and that the prosecutor has exercised peremptory challenges to remove from the venire members of the defendant's race. Second, the defendant is entitled to rely on the fact, as to which there can be no dispute, that peremptory challenges constitute a jury selection practice that permits "those to discriminate who are of a mind to discriminate." *** Finally, the defendant must show that these facts and any other relevant circumstances raise an inference that the prosecutor used that practice to exclude the veniremen from the petit jury on account of their race. This combination of factors in the empanelling of the petit jury, as in the selection of the venire, raises the necessary inference of purposeful discrimination.

In deciding whether the defendant has made the requisite showing, the trial court should consider all relevant circumstances. For example, a "pattern" of strikes against black jurors included in the particular venire might give rise to an inference of discrimination. Similarly, the prosecutor's questions and statements during voir dire examination and in exercising his challenges may support or refute an inference of discriminatory purpose. These examples are merely illustrative. We have confidence that trial judges, experienced in supervising voir dire, will be able to decide if the circumstances concerning the prosecutor's use of peremptory challenges creates a prima facie case of discrimination against black jurors.

Once the defendant makes a prima facie showing, the burden shifts to the State to come forward with a neutral explanation for challenging black jurors. Though this requirement imposes a limitation in some cases on the full peremptory character of the historic challenge, we emphasize that the prosecutor's explanation need not rise to the level justifying exercise of a challenge for cause. But the prosecutor may not rebut the defendant's prima facie case of discrimination by stating merely that he challenged jurors of the defendant's race on the assumption—or his intuitive judgment—that they would be partial to the defendant because of their shared race. *** Just as the Equal Protection Clause forbids the States to exclude black persons from the venire on the assumption that blacks as a group are unqualified to serve as jurors, *** so it forbids the States to strike black veniremen on the assumption that they will be biased in a particular case simply because the defendant is black. The core guarantee of equal protection, ensuring citizens that their State will not discriminate on account of race, would be meaningless were we to approve the exclusion of jurors on the basis of such assumptions, which arise solely from the jurors' race. Nor may the prosecutor rebut the defendant's case merely by denying that he had a discriminatory motive or "affirming his good faith in individual selections." *** If these general assertions were accepted as rebutting a defendant's prima facie case, the Equal Protection Clause "would be but a vain and illusory requirement." *** The prosecutor therefore must articulate a neutral explanation related to the particular case to be tried. The trial court then will have the duty to determine if the defendant has established purposeful discrimination.

The State contends that our holding will eviscerate the fair trial values served by the peremptory challenge. Conceding that the Constitution does not guarantee a right to peremptory challenges and that *Swain* did state that their use ultimately is subject to the strictures of equal protection, the State argues that the privilege of unfettered exercise of the challenge is of vital importance to the criminal justice system.

While we recognize, of course, that the peremptory challenge occupies an important position in our trial procedures, we do not agree that our decision today will undermine the contribution the challenge generally makes to the administration of justice. The reality of practice, amply reflected in many state and federal court opinions, shows that the challenge may be, and unfortunately at times has been, used to discriminate against black jurors. By requiring trial courts to be sensitive to the racially discriminatory use of peremptory challenges, our decision enforces the mandate of equal protection and furthers the ends of justice. In view of the heterogeneous population of our nation, public respect for our criminal justice system and the rule of law will be strengthened if we ensure that no citizen is disqualified from jury service because of his race.

Nor are we persuaded by the State's suggestion that our holding will create serious administrative difficulties. In those states applying a version of the evidentiary standard we recognize today, courts have not experienced serious administrative burdens, and the peremptory challenge system has survived. We decline, however, to formulate particular procedures to be followed upon a defendant's timely objection to a prosecutor's challenges.

In this case, petitioner made a timely objection to the prosecutor's removal of all black persons on the venire. Because the trial court flatly rejected the objection without requiring the prosecutor to give an explanation for his action, we remand this case for further proceedings. If the trial court decides that the facts establish, prima facie, purposeful discrimination and the prosecutor does not come forward with a neutral explanation for his action, our precedents require that petitioner's conviction be reversed. ***

It is so ordered.

Justice White, concurring. ***

Justice Marshall, concurring. ***

Justice Stevens, with whom ***Justice Brennan*** joins, concurring. . . .

Justice Rebnquist, with whom ***The Chief Justice*** joins, dissenting.

*** I cannot subscribe to the Court's unprecedented use of the Equal Protection Clause to restrict the historic scope of the peremptory challenge, which has been described as "a necessary part of trial by jury." *** In my view, there is simply nothing "unequal" about the State using its peremptory challenges to strike blacks from the jury in cases involving black defendants, so long as such challenges are also used to exclude whites in cases involving white defendants, Hispanics in cases involving Hispanic

defendants, Asians in cases involving Asian defendants, and so on. This case-specific use of peremptory challenges by the State does not single out blacks, or members of any other race for that matter, for discriminatory treatment. Such use of peremptories is at best based upon seat-of-the-pants instincts, which are undoubtedly crudely stereotypical and may in many cases be hopelessly mistaken. But as long as they are applied across the board to jurors of all races and nationalities, I do not see—and the Court most certainly has not explained—how their use violates the Equal Protection Clause.

Nor does such use of peremptory challenges by the State infringe upon any other constitutional interests. The Court does not suggest that exclusion of blacks from the jury through the State's use of peremptory challenges results in a violation of either the fair cross-section or impartiality component of the Sixth Amendment. *** And because the case-specific use of peremptory challenges by the State does not deny blacks the right to serve as jurors in cases involving non-black defendants, it harms neither the excluded jurors nor the remainder of the community.

The use of group affiliations, such as age, race, or occupation, as a "proxy" for potential juror partiality, based on the assumption or belief that members of one group are more likely to favor defendants who belong to the same group, has long been accepted as a legitimate basis for the State's exercise of peremptory challenges. *** Indeed, given the need for reasonable limitations on the time devoted to voir dire, the use of such "proxies" by both the State and the defendant may be extremely useful in eliminating from the jury persons who might be biased in one way or another. The Court today holds that the State may not use its peremptory challenges to strike black prospective jurors on this basis without violating the Constitution. But I do not believe there is anything in the Equal Protection Clause, or any other Constitutional provision, that justifies such a departure. *** Petitioner in the instant case failed to make a sufficient showing to overcome the presumption announced in *Swain* that the State's use of peremptory challenges was related to the context of the case. I would therefore affirm the judgment of the court below.

Johnson v. Louisiana

406 U.S. 356; 92 S. Ct. 1620; 32 L. Ed. 2d 152 (1972)

Vote: 5-4

*Mr. Justice **White*** delivered the opinion of the Court.

Under the Louisiana Constitution and Code of Criminal Procedure, criminal cases in which the punishment is necessarily at hard labor are tried to a jury of 12 and the vote of nine jurors is sufficient to return either a guilty or not guilty verdict. The principal question in this case is whether these provisions allowing less-than-unanimous verdicts in certain cases are valid under the Due Process and Equal Protection Clauses of the Fourteenth Amendment.

Appellant Johnson was arrested at his home on January 20, 1968. There was no arrest warrant, but the victim of an armed robbery had identified Johnson from photographs as having committed the crime. He was then identified at a lineup, at which he had counsel, by the victim of still another robbery. The latter crime is involved in this case. Johnson pleaded not guilty, was tried on May 14, 1968, by a 12-man jury and was convicted by a nine-to-three verdict. His due process and equal protection challenges to the Louisiana constitutional and statutory provisions were rejected by the Louisiana courts, and he appealed here. We noted probable jurisdiction. Conceding that under *Duncan v. Louisiana,* the Sixth Amendment is not applicable to his case, appellant presses his equal protection and due process claims, together with a Fourth Amendment claim also rejected by the Louisiana Supreme Court. We affirm.

Appellant argues that in order to give substance to the reasonable doubt standard, which the State, by virtue of the Due Process Clause of the Fourteenth Amendment, must satisfy in criminal cases, that clause must be construed to require a unanimous-jury verdict in all criminal cases. In so contending, appellant does not challenge the instructions in this case. Concededly, the jurors were told to convict only if convinced of guilt beyond a reasonable doubt. Nor is there any claim that, if the verdict in this case had been unanimous, the evidence would have been insufficient to support it. Appellant focuses instead on the fact that less than all jurors

voted to convict and argues that, because three voted to acquit, the reasonable-doubt standard has not been satisfied and his conviction is therefore infirm.

We note at the outset that this Court has never held jury unanimity to be a requisite of due process of law. Indeed, the Court has more than once expressly said that "[i]n criminal cases due process of law is not denied by a state law . . . which dispenses with the necessity of a jury of twelve, or unanimity in the verdict." *** These statements, moreover, co-existed with cases indicating that proof of guilt beyond a reasonable doubt is implicit in constitutions recognizing "the fundamental principles that are deemed essential for the protection of life and liberty." ***

. . . It is our view that the fact of three dissenting votes to acquit raises no question of constitutional substance about either the integrity or the accuracy of the majority verdict of guilt. Appellant's contrary argument breaks down into two parts, each of which we shall consider separately: first, that nine individual jurors will be unable to vote conscientiously in favor of guilt beyond a reasonable doubt when three of their colleagues are arguing for acquittal, and second, that guilt cannot be said to have been proved beyond a reasonable doubt when one or more of a jury's members at the conclusion of deliberation still possess such a doubt. Neither argument is persuasive.

In considering the first branch of appellant's argument, we can find no basis for holding that the nine jurors who voted for his conviction failed to follow their instructions concerning the need for proof beyond such a doubt or that the vote of any one of the nine failed to reflect an honest belief that guilt had been so proved. We have no grounds for believing that majority jurors, aware of their responsibility and power over the liberty of the defendant, would simply refuse to listen to arguments presented to them in favor of acquittal, terminate discussion, and render a verdict. On the contrary it is far more likely that a juror presenting reasoned argument in favor of acquittal would either have his arguments answered or would carry enough other jurors with him to prevent conviction. A majority will cease discussion and outvote a minority only after reasoned discussion has ceased to have persuasive effect or to serve any other purpose—when a minority, that is, continues to insist upon acquittal without having persuasive reasons in support of its position. At that juncture there is no basis for denigrating the vote of so large a majority of the jury or for refusing to accept their decision as being, at least in their minds, beyond a reasonable doubt. Indeed, at this point, a "dissenting juror should consider whether his doubt was a reasonable one . . .[when it made] no impression upon the minds of so many men, equally honest, equally intelligent with himself." *** Appellant offers no evidence that majority jurors simply ignore the reasonable doubts of their colleagues or otherwise act irresponsibly in casting their votes in favor of conviction, and before we alter our own long-standing perceptions about jury behavior and overturn a considered legislative judgment that unanimity is not essential to reasoned jury verdicts, we must have some basis for doing so other than unsupported assumptions.

We conclude, therefore, that, as to the nine jurors who voted to convict, the State satisfied its burden of proving guilt beyond any reasonable doubt. The remaining question under the Due Process Clause is whether the vote of three jurors for acquittal can be said to impeach the verdict of the other nine and to demonstrate that guilt was not in fact proved beyond such doubt. We hold that it cannot.

Of course, the State's proof could be regarded as more certain if it had convinced all 12 jurors instead of only nine; it would have been even more compelling if it had been required to convince and had, in fact, convinced 24 or 36 jurors. But the fact remains that nine jurors—a substantial majority of the jury—were convinced by the evidence. In our view disagreement of three jurors does not alone establish reasonable doubt, particularly when such a heavy majority of the jury, after having considered the dissenters' views, remains convinced of guilt. That rational men disagree is not in itself equivalent to a failure of proof by the State, nor does it indicate infidelity to the reasonable-doubt standard. Jury verdicts finding guilt beyond a reasonable doubt are regularly sustained even though the evidence was such that the jury would have been justified in

having a reasonable doubt, even though the trial judge might not have reached the same conclusion as the jury, and even though appellate judges are closely divided on the issue whether there was sufficient evidence to support a conviction. That want of jury unanimity is not to be equated with the existence of a reasonable doubt emerges even more clearly from the fact, that, when a jury in a federal court, which operates under the unanimity rule and is instructed to acquit a defendant if it has a reasonable doubt about his guilt, cannot agree unanimously upon a verdict, the defendant is not acquitted, but is merely given a new trial. If the doubt of a minority of jurors indicates the existence of a reasonable doubt, it would appear that a defendant should receive a directed verdict of acquittal rather than a retrial. We conclude, therefore, that verdicts rendered by nine out of 12 jurors are not automatically invalidated by the disagreement of the dissenting three.

Appellant also attacks as violative of the Equal Protection Clause the provisions of Louisiana law requiring unanimous verdicts in capital and five-man jury cases, but permitting less-than-unanimous verdicts in cases such as his. We conclude, however, that the Louisiana statutory scheme serves a rational purpose and is not subject to constitutional challenge.

In order to "facilitate, expedite, and reduce expense in the administration of criminal justice," *** Louisiana has permitted less serious crimes to be tried by five jurors with unanimous verdicts, more serious crimes have required the assent of nine of 12 jurors, and for the most serious crimes a unanimous verdict of 12 jurors is stipulated. In appellant's case, nine jurors rather than five or 12 were required for a verdict. We discern nothing invidious in this classification. We have held that the States are free under the Federal Constitution to try defendants with juries of less than 12 men. Three jurors here voted to acquit, but from what we have earlier said, this does not demonstrate that appellant was convicted on a lower standard of proof. To obtain a conviction in any of the categories under Louisiana law, the State must prove guilt beyond reasonable doubt, but the number of jurors who must be so convinced increases with the seriousness of the crime and the severity of the punishment that may be imposed. We perceive nothing unconstitutional or invidiously discriminatory, however, in a State's insisting that its burden of proof be carried with more jurors where more serious crimes or more severe punishments are at issue.

Appellant nevertheless insists that dispensing with unanimity in his case disadvantaged him as compared with those who commit less serious or capital crimes. With respect to the latter, he is correct; the State does make conviction more difficult by requiring the assent of all 12 jurors. Appellant might well have been ultimately acquitted had he committed a capital offense. But as we have indicated, this does not constitute a denial of equal protection of the law; the State may treat capital offenders differently without violating the constitutional rights of those charged with lesser crimes. As to the crimes triable by a five-man jury, if appellant's position is that it is easier to convince nine of 12 jurors than to convince all of five, he is simply challenging the judgment of the Louisiana Legislature. That body obviously intended to vary the difficulty of proving guilt with the gravity of the offense and the severity of the punishment. We remain unconvinced by anything appellant has presented that this legislative judgment was defective in any constitutional sense.

The judgment of the Supreme Court of Louisiana is therefore Affirmed.

Mr. Justice Blackmun, concurring. . . .

Mr. Justice Powell, concurring. . . .

Mr. Justice Douglas, with whom *Mr. Justice Brennan* and *Mr. Justice Marshall* concur, dissenting.

. . . The result of today's decision is anomalous: though unanimous jury decisions are not required in state trials, they are constitutionally required in federal prosecutions. How can that be possible when both decisions stem from the Sixth Amendment?

Rule 31 (a) of the Federal Rules of Criminal Procedure states, "The verdict shall be unanimous." That Rule was made by this Court with the concurrence of Congress. . . . After today a unanimous verdict will be required in a federal prosecution but not in a state prosecution. Yet the source of the right in each case is the Sixth Amendment. I fail to see how with reason we can maintain those inconsistent dual positions. . . .

Mr. Justice Brennan, with whom *Mr. Justice Marshall* joins, dissenting. . . .

Mr. Justice Stewart, with whom *Mr. Justice Brennan* and *Mr. Justice Marshall* join, dissenting. . . .

Mr. Justice Marshall, with whom *Mr. Justice Brennan* joins, dissenting.

Today the Court cuts the heart out of two of the most important and inseparable safeguards the Bill of Rights offers a criminal defendant: the right to submit his case to a jury, and the right to proof beyond a reasonable doubt. Together, these safeguards occupy a fundamental place in our constitutional scheme, protecting the individual defendant from the awesome power of the State. After today, the skeleton of these safeguards remains, but the Court strips them of life and of meaning. I cannot refrain from adding my protest to that of my Brothers Douglas, Brennan, and Stewart, whom I join.

My dissenting Brothers have pointed to the danger, under a less-than-unanimous rule, of excluding from the process members of minority groups, whose participation we have elsewhere recognized as a constitutional requirement. It should be emphasized, however, that the fencing-out problem goes beyond the problem of identifiable minority groups. The juror whose dissenting voice is unheard may be a spokesman, not for any minority viewpoint, but simply for himself—and that, in my view, is enough. The doubts of a single juror are in my view evidence that the government has failed to carry its burden of proving guilt beyond a reasonable doubt. I dissent.

Furman v. Georgia

408 U.S. 238; 92 S. Ct. 2726; 33 L. Ed. 2d 346 (1972)
Vote: 5-4

Per Curiam.

. . . The Court holds that the imposition and carrying out of the death penalty in these cases constitutes cruel and unusual punishment in violation of the Eighth and Fourteenth Amendments. The judgment in each case is therefore reversed insofar as it leaves undisturbed the death sentence imposed, and the cases are remanded for further proceedings.

Mr. Justice Douglas, Mr. Justice Brennan, Mr. Justice Stewart, Mr. Justice White, and **Mr. Justice Marshall** have filed separate opinions in support of the judgments. The **Chief Justice, Mr. Justice Blackmun, Mr. Justice Powell,** and **Mr. Justice Rehnquist** have filed separate dissenting opinions.

Mr. Justice Douglas concurring.

In these three cases [including *Branch v. Texas* and *Jackson v. Georgia*] the death penalty was imposed, one of them for murder, and two for rape. In each the determination of whether the penalty should be death or a lighter punishment was left by the State to the discretion of the judge or of the jury. In each of the three cases the trial was to a jury. They are here on petitions for *certiorari* which we granted limited to the question whether the imposition and execution of the death penalty constitutes "cruel and unusual punishment" within the meaning of the Eighth Amendment as applied to the States by the Fourteenth. I vote to vacate each judgment, believing that the exaction of the death penalty does violate the Eighth and Fourteenth Amendments. . . .

The words "cruel and unusual" certainly include penalties that are barbaric. But the words, at least when read in light of the English proscription against selective and irregular use of penalties, suggest that it is "cruel and unusual" to apply the death penalty—or any other penalty selectively to minorities whose numbers are few, who are outcasts of society, and who are unpopular, but whom society is willing to see suffer though it would not countenance general application of the same penalty across the board. . . .

Jackson, a black, convicted of the rape of a white woman, was 21 years old. A court-appointed psychiatrist said that Jackson was of average education and average intelligence, that he was not an imbecile, or schizophrenic, or psychotic, that his traits were the product of environmental influences, and that he was competent to stand trial. Jackson had entered the house after the husband left for work. He held scissors against the neck of the wife, demanding money. She could find none and a struggle ensued for the scissors, a battle which she lost; and she was then raped, Jackson keeping the scissors pressed against her neck. While there did not appear to be any long-term traumatic impact on the victim, she was bruised and abraded in the struggle but was not hospitalized. Jackson was a convict who had escaped from a work gang in the area, a result of a three-year sentence for auto theft. He was at large for three days and during that time had committed several other offenses—burglary, auto theft, and assault and battery.

Furman, a black, killed a householder while seeking to enter the home at night. Furman shot the deceased through a closed door. He was 26 years old and had finished the sixth grade in school. Pending trial he was committed to the Georgia Central State Hospital for a psychiatric examination on his plea of insanity tendered by a court-appointed counsel. The superintendent reported that a unanimous staff diagnostic conference on the same date had concluded "that this patient should retain his present diagnosis of Mental Deficiency, Mild to Moderate, with psychotic episodes associated with Convulsive Disorder." The physicians agreed that "at present the patient is not psychotic, but he is not capable of cooperating with his counsel in the preparation of his defense," and the staff believed "that he is in need of further psychiatric hospitalization and treatment."

Later the superintendent reported that the staff diagnosis was Mental Deficiency, Mild to Moderate, with Psychotic Episodes associated with Convulsive

Disorder. He concluded, however, that Furman was "not psychotic at present, knows right from wrong and is able to cooperate with his counsel in preparing his defense."

Branch, a black, entered the rural home of a 65-year-old widow, a white, while she slept and raped her, holding his arm against her throat. Thereupon he demanded money and for 30 minutes or more the widow searched for money, finding little. As he left, Jackson said if the widow told anyone what happened, he would return to kill her. The record is barren of any medical or psychiatric evidence showing injury to her as a result of Branch's attack.

He had previously been convicted of felony theft and found to be a borderline mentally deficient and well below the average IQ of Texas prison inmates. He had the equivalent of five and a half years of grade school education. He had a "dull intelligence" and was in the lowest fourth percentile of his class.

We cannot say from facts disclosed in these records that these defendants were sentenced to death because they were black. Yet our task is not restricted to an effort to divine what motives impelled these death penalties. Rather, we deal with a system of law and of justice that leaves to the uncontrolled discretion of judges or juries the determination whether defendants committing these crimes should die or be imprisoned. Under these laws no standards govern the selection of the penalty. People live or die, dependent on the whim of one man or of 12. . . .

In a Nation committed to equal protection of the laws there is no permissible "caste" aspect of law enforcement. Yet we know that the discretion of judges and juries in imposing the death penalty enables the penalty to be selectively applied, feeding prejudices against the accused if he is poor and despised, lacking political clout, or if he is a member of a suspect or unpopular minority, and saving those who by social position may be in a more protected position. In ancient Hindu law a Brahman was exempt from capital punishment, and in those days, "[g]enerally, in the law books, punishment increased in severity as social status diminished." We have, I fear, taken in practice the same position, partially as a result of making the death penalty discretionary and partially as a result of the ability of the rich to purchase the services of the most respected and most resourceful legal talent in the Nation.

The high service rendered by the "cruel and unusual" punishment clause of the Eighth Amendment is to require legislatures to write penal laws that are evenhanded, nonselective, and nonarbitrary, and to require judges to see to it that general laws are not applied sparsely, selectively, and spottily to unpopular groups.

A law that stated that anyone making more than $50,000 would be exempt from the death penalty would plainly fall, as would a law that in terms said that blacks, those who never went beyond the fifth grade in school, those who made less than $3,000 a year, or those who were unpopular or unstable should be the only people executed. A law which in the overall view reaches that result in practice has no more sanctity than a law which in terms provides the same.

Thus, these discretionary statutes are unconstitutional in their operation. They are pregnant with discrimination and discrimination is an ingredient not compatible with the idea of equal protection of the laws that is implicit in the ban on "cruel and unusual" punishments. . . .

Mr. Justice Brennan, concurring.

. . . Ours would indeed be a simple task were we required merely to measure a challenged punishment against those that history has long condemned. That narrow and unwarranted view of the Clause, however, was left behind with the 19th century. Our task today is more complex. We know "that the words of the [Clause] are not precise and that their scope is not static." We know, therefore, that the Clause "must draw its meaning from the evolving standards of decency that mark the progress of a maturing society." *** That knowledge, of course, is but the beginning of the inquiry.

. . . [T]he question is whether [a] penalty subjects the individual to a fate forbidden by the principle of civilized treatment guaranteed by the [Clause]." It was also said that a challenged punishment must be examined "in light of the basic prohibition against inhuman treatment" embodied in the Clause. ***

. . . "The basic concept underlying the [Clause] is nothing less than the dignity of man. While the State has the power to punish, the [Clause] stands to assure that this power be exercised within the limits of civilized standards." *** At bottom, then, the Cruel and Unusual Punishment Clause prohibits the infliction of uncivilized and inhuman punishments. The State, even as it punishes, must treat its members with respect for their intrinsic worth as human beings. A punishment is "cruel and unusual," therefore, if it does not comport with human dignity.

This formulation, of course, does not of itself yield principles for assessing the constitutional validity of particular punishments. Nevertheless, even though "[t]his Court has had little occasion to give precise content to the [Clause]," there are principles recognized in our cases and inherent in the clause sufficient to permit a judicial determination whether a challenged punishment comports with human dignity. . . .

In sum, the punishment of death is inconsistent with all four principles: Death is an unusually severe and degrading punishment; there is a strong probability that it is inflicted arbitrarily; its rejection by contemporary society is virtually total; and there is no reason to believe that it serves any penal purpose more effectively than the less severe punishment of imprisonment. The function of these principles is to enable a court to determine whether a punishment comports with human dignity. Death, quite simply, does not. . . .

Mr. Justice Stewart, concurring.

The penalty of death differs from all other forms of criminal punishment, not in degree but in kind. It is unique in its total irrevocability. It is unique in its rejection of rehabilitation of the convict as a basic purpose of criminal justice. And it is unique, finally in its absolute renunciation of all that is embodied in our concept of humanity.

For these and other reasons, at least two of my Brothers have concluded that the infliction of the death penalty is constitutionally impermissible in all circumstances under the Eighth and Fourteenth Amendments. Their case is a strong one. But I find it unnecessary to reach the ultimate question they would decide. ***

Legislatures—state and federal—have sometimes specified that the penalty of death shall be the mandatory punishment for every person convicted of engaging in certain designated criminal conduct.

If we were reviewing death sentences imposed under these or similar laws, we would be faced with the need to decide whether capital punishment is unconstitutional for all crimes and under all circumstances. We would need to decide whether a legislature—state or federal—could constitutionally determine that certain criminal conduct is so atrocious that society's interest in deterrence and retribution wholly outweighs any considerations of reform or rehabilitation of the perpetrator, and that, despite the inconclusive empirical evidence, only the automatic penalty of death will provide maximum deterrence.

On that score I would say only that I cannot agree that retribution is a constitutionally impermissible ingredient in the imposition of punishment. The instinct for retribution is part of the nature of man, and channeling that instinct in the administration of criminal justice serves as important purpose in promoting the stability of a society governed by law. When people begin to believe that organized society is unwilling or unable to impose upon criminal offenders the punishment they "deserve," then there are sown the seeds of anarchy—of self-help, vigilante justice and lynch law.

The constitutionality of capital punishment in the abstract is not, however, before us in these cases. For the Georgia and Texas Legislatures have not provided that the death penalty shall be imposed upon all those who are found guilty of forcible rape. And the Georgia Legislature has not ordained that death shall be the automatic punishment for murder. . . .

Instead, the death sentences now before us are the product of a legal system that brings them, I believe, within the very core of the Eighth Amendment's guarantee against cruel and unusual punishments, a guarantee applicable against the States through the Fourteenth Amendment. *** In the first place, it is clear that these sentences are "cruel" in the sense that they excessively go beyond, not in degree but in kind, the punishments that the state legislatures have determined to be necessary. *** In the second place, it is equally clear that these sentences are "unusual" in the sense that the penalty of death is infrequently imposed for murder, and that its imposition for rape is extraordinarily rare. But I do not rest my conclusion upon these two propositions alone.

These death sentences are cruel and unusual in the same way that being struck by lightning is cruel and unusual. For, of all the people convicted of rapes and murders in 1967 and 1968, many just as reprehensible as these, the petitioners are among a capriciously selected random handful upon whom the sentence of death has in fact been imposed. My concurring Brothers have demonstrated that, if any basis can be discerned for the selection of these few to be sentenced to die, it is the constitutionally impermissible basis of race. *** But racial discrimination has not been proved, and I put it to one side. I simply conclude that the Eighth and Fourteenth Amendments cannot tolerate the infliction of a sentence of death under legal systems that permit this unique penalty to be so wantonly and so freakishly imposed. . . .

Mr. Justice White, concurring.

The facial constitutionality of statutes requiring the imposition of the death penalty for first-degree murder, for more narrowly defined categories of murder, or for rape would present quite different issues under the Eighth Amendment than are posed by the cases before us. In joining the Court's judgments, therefore, I do not at all intimate that the death penalty is unconstitutional *per se* or that there is no system of capital punishment that would comport with the Eighth Amendment. That question, ably argued by several of my Brethren, is not presented by these cases and need not be decided.

The narrow question to which I address myself concerns the constitutionality of capital punishment statutes under which (1) the legislature authorizes the imposition of the death penalty for murder or rape; (2) the legislature does not itself mandate the penalty in any particular class or kind of case (that is, legislative will is not frustrated if the penalty is never imposed), but delegates to judges or juries the decisions as to those cases, if any, in which the penalty will be utilized; and (3) judges and juries have ordered the death penalty with such infrequency that the odds are now very much against imposition and execution of the penalty with respect to any convicted murderer or rapist. It is in this

context that we must consider whether the execution of these petitioners would violate the Eighth Amendment. . . .

. . . Like my Brethren, I must arrive at judgment; and I can do no more than state a conclusion based on 10 years of almost daily exposure to the facts and circumstances of hundreds and hundreds of federal and state criminal cases involving crimes for which death is the authorized penalty. That conclusion, as I have said, is that the death penalty is exacted with great infrequency even for the most atrocious crimes and that there is no meaningful basis for distinguishing the few cases in which it is imposed from the many cases in which it is not. The short of it is that the policy of vesting sentencing authority primarily in juries—a decision largely motivated by the desire to mitigate the harshness of the law and to bring community judgment to bear on the sentence as well as guilt or innocence—has so effectively achieved its aims that capital punishment within the confines of the statutes now before us has for all practical purposes run its course. . . .

. . . I add only that past and present legislative judgment with respect to the death penalty loses much of its force when viewed in light of the recurring practice of delegating sentencing authority to the jury and the fact that a jury, in its own discretion and without violating its trust or any statutory policy, may refuse to impose the death penalty no matter what the circumstances of the crime. Legislative "policy" is thus necessarily defined not by what is legislatively authorized but by what juries and judges do in exercising the discretion so regularly conferred upon them. In my judgment what was done in these cases violated the Eighth Amendment. . . .

Mr. Justice Marshall, concurring.

The criminal acts with which we are confronted are ugly, vicious, reprehensible acts. Their sheer brutality cannot and should not be minimized. But, we are not called upon to condone the penalized conduct; we are asked only to examine the penalty imposed on each of the petitioners and to determine whether or not it violates the Eighth Amendment. The question then is not whether we condone rape or murder, for surely we do not; it is whether capital punishment is "a punishment no longer consistent with our own self-respect" and therefore, violative of the Eighth Amendment. . . .

Perhaps the most important principle in analyzing "cruel and unusual" punishment questions is one that is reiterated again and again in the prior opinions of the Court: i.e., the cruel and unusual language "must draw its meaning from the evolving standards of decency that mark the progress of a maturing society." Thus, a penalty that was permissible at one time in our Nation's history is not necessarily permissible today.

Faced with an open question, we must establish our standards for decision. The decisions discussed in the previous section imply that a punishment may be deemed cruel and unusual for any one of four distinct reasons.

First, there are certain punishments that inherently involve so much physical pain and suffering that civilized people cannot tolerate them—e.g., use of the rack, the thumbscrew, or other modes of torture. *** Regardless of public sentiment with respect to imposition of one of these punishments in a particular case or at any one moment in history, the Constitution prohibits it. These are punishments that have been barred since the adoption of the Bill of Rights.

Second, there are punishments that are unusual, signifying that they were previously unknown as penalties for a given offense. *** If these punishments are intended to serve a humane purpose, they may be constitutionally permissible. . . .

Third, a penalty may be cruel and unusual because it is excessive and serves no valid legislative purpose. The decisions previously discussed are replete with assertions that one of the primary functions of the cruel and unusual punishments clause is to prevent excessive or unnecessary penalties; *** these punishments are unconstitutional even though popular sentiment may favor them. . . .

Fourth, where a punishment is not excessive and serves a valid legislative purpose, it still may be invalid if popular sentiment abhors it. . . .

It is immediately obvious, then, that since capital punishment is not a recent phenomenon, if it violates the Constitution, it does so because it is excessive or unnecessary, or because it is abhorrent to currently existing moral values. . . .

In order to assess whether or not death is an excessive or unnecessary penalty, it is necessary to consider the reasons why a legislature might select it as punishment for one or more offenses, and examine whether less severe penalties would satisfy the legitimate legislative wants as well as capital punishment. If they would, then the death penalty is unnecessary cruelty, and, therefore, unconstitutional. . . .

There are six purposes conceivably served by capital punishment: retribution, deterrence, prevention of repetitive criminal acts, encouragement of guilty pleas and confessions, eugenics, and economy. [*Justice Marshall finds none of these purposes persuasive.*]

In addition, even if capital punishment is not excessive, it nonetheless violates the Eighth Amendment because it is morally unacceptable to the people of the United States at this time in their history.

In judging whether or not a given penalty is morally acceptable, most courts have said that the punishment is valid unless "it shocks the conscience and sense of justice of the people." . . .

While a public opinion poll obviously is of some assistance in indicating public acceptance or rejection of a specific penalty, its utility cannot be very great. This is because whether or not a punishment is cruel and unusual depends, not on whether its mere mention "shocks the conscience and sense of justice of the people," but on whether people who were fully informed as to the purposes of the penalty and its liabilities would find the penalty shocking, unjust, and unacceptable.

In other words, the question with which we must deal is not whether a substantial proportion of American citizens would today, if polled, opine that capital punishment is barbarously cruel, but whether they would find it to be so in the light of all information presently available. . . .

This information would almost surely convince the average citizen that the penalty was unwise, but a problem arises as to whether it would convince him that the penalty was morally reprehensible. This problem arises from the fact that the public's desire for retribution, even though this is a goal that the legislature cannot constitutionally pursue as its sole justification for capital punishment, might influence the citizenry's view of the morality of capital punishment. The solution to the problem lies in the fact that no one has ever seriously advanced retribution as a legitimate goal of our society. Defenses of capital punishment are always mounted on deterrent or other similar theories. This should not be surprising. It is the people of this country who have urged in the past that prisons rehabilitate as well as isolate offenders, and it is the people who have injected a sense of purpose into our penology. I cannot believe that at this stage in our history, the American people would ever knowingly support purposeless vengeance. Thus, I believe that the great mass of citizens would conclude on the basis of the material already considered that the death penalty is immoral therefore unconstitutional. . . .

In striking down capital punishment, this Court does not malign our system of government. On the contrary, it pays homage to it. Only in a free society could right triumph in difficult times, and could civilization record its magnificent advancement. In recognizing the humanity of our fellow beings, we pay ourselves the highest tribute. We achieve "a major milestone in the long road up from barbarism" and join the approximately 70 other jurisdictions in the world which celebrate their regard for civilization and humanity by shunning capital punishment. . . .

Mr. Chief Justice Burger, with whom **Mr. Justice Blackmun,** and **Mr. Justice Rehnquist,** join, dissenting.

At the outset it is important to note that only two members of the Court, Mr. Justice Brennan and Mr. Justice Marshall, have concluded that the Eighth Amendment prohibits capital punishment for all crimes and under all circumstances. Mr. Justice Douglas has also determined that the death penalty contravenes the Eighth Amendment, although I do not read his opinion as necessarily requiring final abolition of the penalty. . . .

Mr. Justice Stewart and Mr. Justice White have concluded that petitioners' death sentences must be set aside because prevailing sentencing practices do not comply with the Eighth Amendment. . . .

If we were possessed of legislative power, I would either join with Mr. Justice Brennan and Mr. Justice Marshall or, at the very least, restrict the use of capital punishment to a small category of the most heinous crimes. Our constitutional inquiry, however, must be divorced from personal feelings as to the morality and efficacy of the death penalty, and be confined to the meaning and applicability of the uncertain language of the Eighth Amendment. There is no novelty in being called upon to interpret a constitutional provision that is less than self-defining, but, of all our fundamental guarantees, the ban on "cruel and unusual punishments" is one of the most difficult to translate into judicially manageable terms. The widely divergent views of the Amendment expressed in today's opinions reveals the haze that surrounds this constitutional command. Yet it is essential to our role as a court that we not seize upon the enigmatic character of the guarantee as an invitation to enact our personal predilections into law.

Although the Eighth Amendment literally reads as prohibiting only those punishments that are both "cruel" and "unusual," history compels the conclusion that the Constitution prohibits all punishments of extreme and barbarous cruelty, regardless of how frequently or infrequently imposed. . . .

But where, as here, we consider a punishment well known to history, and clearly authorized by legislative enactment, it disregards the history of the Eighth Amendment and all the judicial comment that has followed to rely on the term "unusual" as affecting the outcome of these cases. Instead, I view these cases as turning on the single question whether capital punishment is "cruel" in the constitutional sense. The term "unusual" cannot be read as limiting the ban on "cruel" punishments or as somehow expanding the meaning of the term "cruel." For this reason I am unpersuaded by the facile argument that since capital punishment has always been cruel in the everyday sense of the word, and has become unusual due to decreased use, it is, therefore, now "cruel and unusual." . . .

Since there is no majority of the Court on the ultimate issue presented in these cases, the future of capital punishment in this country has been left in an uncertain limbo. Rather than providing a final and unambiguous answer on the basic constitutional question, the collective impact of the majority's ruling is to demand an undetermined measure of change from the various state legislatures and the Congress. While I cannot endorse the process of decisionmaking that has yielded today's result and the restraints that that result imposes on legislative action, I am not altogether displeased that legislative bodies have been given the opportunity, and indeed unavoidable responsibility, to make a thorough re-evaluation of the entire subject of capital punishment. If today's opinions demonstrate nothing else, they starkly show that this is an area where legislatures can act far more effectively than courts. . . .

The highest judicial duty is to recognize the limits on judicial power and to permit the democratic processes to deal with matters falling outside of those limits. The "hydraulic pressure[s]" that Holmes spoke of as being generated by cases of great import have propelled the Court to go beyond the limits of judicial power, while fortunately leaving some room for legislative judgment.

Mr. Justice Blackmun, dissenting.

I join the respective opinions of The Chief Justice, Mr. Justice Powell, and Mr. Justice Rehnquist, and add only the following, somewhat personal, comments.

. . . Cases such as these provide for me an excruciating agony of the spirit. I yield to no one in the depth of my distaste, antipathy, and, indeed, abhorrence, for the death penalty, with all its aspects of physical distress and fear and of moral judgment exercised by finite minds. That distaste is buttressed by a belief that capital punishment serves no useful purpose that can be demonstrated. For me, it violates childhood's training and life's experiences, and is not compatible with the philosophical convictions I have been able to develop. It is antagonistic to any sense of "reverence for life." Were I legislator, I would vote against the death penalty for the policy reasons argued by counsel for the respective petitioners and expressed and adopted in the several opinions filed by the Justices who vote to reverse these convictions.

Although personally I may rejoice at the Court's result, I find it difficult to accept or to justify as a matter of history, of law, or of constitutional pronouncement. I fear the Court has overstepped. It has sought and has achieved an end.

Mr. Justice Powell, with whom **the Chief Justice, Mr. Justice Blackmun,** and **Mr. Justice Rehnquist** join, dissenting.

The Court granted *certiorari* in these cases to consider whether the death penalty is any longer a permissible form of punishment. *** It is the judgment of five Justices that the death penalty, as customarily prescribed and implemented in this country today, offends the constitutional prohibition against cruel and unusual punishments. The reasons for that judgment are stated in five separate opinions, expressing as many separate rationales. In my view, none of these opinions provides a constitutionally adequate foundation for the Court's decision. . . .

Perhaps enough has been said to demonstrate the unswerving position that this Court has taken in opinions spanning the last hundred years. On virtually every occasion that any opinion has touched on the question of the constitutionality of the death penalty, it has been asserted affirmatively, or tacitly assumed, that the Constitution does not prohibit the penalty. No Justice of the Court, until today, has dissented from this consistent reading of the Constitution. The petitioners in these cases now before the Court cannot fairly avoid the weight of this substantial body of precedent merely by asserting that there is no prior decision precisely in point. *Stare decisis,* if it is a doctrine founded on principle, surely applies where there exists a long line of cases endorsing or necessarily assuming the validity of a particular matter of constitutional interpretation. . . .

I know of no case in which greater gravity and delicacy have attached to the duty that this Court is called on to perform whenever legislation—state or federal—is challenged on constitutional grounds. It seems to me that the sweeping judicial action undertaken today reflects a basic lack of faith and confidence in the democratic process. Many may regret, as I do, the failure of some legislative bodies to address the capital punishment issue with greater frankness or effectiveness. Many might decry their failure either to abolish the penalty entirely or selectively, or to establish standards for its enforcement. But impatience with the slowness, and even the unresponsiveness; of legislatures is no justification for judicial intrusion upon their historic powers. . . .

Mr. Justice Rehnquist, with whom ***the Chief Justice, Mr. Justice Blackmun,*** and ***Mr. Justice Powell*** join, dissenting.

. . . Whatever its precise rationale, today's holding necessarily brings into sharp relief the fundamental question of the role of judicial review in a democratic society. How can government by the elected representatives of the people co-exist with the power of the federal judiciary, whose members are constitutionally insulated from responsiveness to the popular will, to declare invalid laws duly enacted by the popular branches of government?

Sovereignty resides ultimately in the people as a whole and, by adopting through their States a written Constitution for the Nation and subsequently adding amendments to that instrument, they have both granted certain powers to the National Government, and denied other powers to the National and the State Governments. Courts are exercising no more than the judicial function conferred upon them by Art. III of the Constitution when they assess, in a case before them, whether or not a particular legislative enactment is within the authority granted by the Constitution to the enacting body, and whether it runs afoul of some limitation placed by the Constitution on the authority of that body. For the theory is that the people themselves have spoken in the Constitution, and therefore its commands are superior to the commands of the legislature, which is merely an agent of the people.

The Founding Fathers thus wisely sought to have the best of both worlds, the undeniable benefits of both democratic self-government and individual rights protected against possible excesses of that form of government.

The courts in cases properly before them have been entrusted under the Constitution with the last word, short of constitutional amendment, as to whether a law passed by the legislature conforms to the Constitution. But just because courts in general, and this Court in particular, do have the last word, the admonition of Mr. Justice Stone dissenting in *United States v. Butler* must be constantly borne in mind:

[W]hile unconstitutional exercise of power by the executive and legislative branches of the government is subject to judicial restraint, the only check upon our own exercise of power is our own sense of self-restraint. ***

Rigorous attentions to the limits of this Court's authority is likewise enjoined because of the natural desire that beguiles judges along with other human beings into imposing their own views of goodness, truth, and justice upon others. Judges differ only in that they have power, if not the authority, to enforce their desires. This is doubtless why nearly two centuries of judicial precedent from this Court counsel the sparing use of that power. The most expansive reading of the leading constitutional cases does not remotely suggest that this Court has been granted a roving commission, either by the Founding Fathers or by the Framers of the Fourteenth Amendment, to strike down laws that are based upon notions of policy or morality suddenly found unacceptable by a majority of this Court. . . .

While overreaching by the Legislative and Executive Branches may result in the sacrifice of individual protections that the Constitution was designed to secure against action of the State, judicial overreaching may result in sacrifice of the equally important right of the people to govern themselves. The Due Process and Equal Protection Clauses of the Fourteenth Amendment were "never intended to destroy the States' power to govern themselves." ***

The very nature of judicial review, as pointed out by Justice Stone in his dissent in the *Butler* case, makes the courts the least subject to Madisonian check in the event that they shall, for the best of motives, expand judicial authority beyond the limits contemplated by the Framers. It is for this reason that judicial self-restraint is surely an implied, if not an expressed, condition of the grant of authority of judicial review. The Court's holding in these cases has been reached, I believe, in complete disregard of that implied condition.

Gregg v. Georgia

428 U.S. 153; 96 S. Ct. 2909; 49 L. Ed. 2d 859 (1976)

Vote: 7-2

Troy Gregg was convicted of murder and armed robbery and sentenced to death by a Georgia court. The evidence established that Gregg had robbed and killed two men who had picked him up hitchhiking. Under Georgia's death penalty statute, revised in the wake of Furman v. Georgia, *Gregg's trial was conducted in two separate stages, the first to determine guilt and the second to determine the sentence. The constitutionality of the revised Georgia statute is before the Supreme Court in this case.*

Judgment of the Court, and opinion of **Mr. Justice Stewart, Mr. Justice Powell** and **Mr. Justice Stevens,** announced by **Mr. Justice Stewart.**

The issue in this case is whether the imposition of the sentence of death for the crime of murder under the law of Georgia violates the Eighth and Fourteenth Amendments. . . .

Before considering the issues presented it is necessary to understand the Georgia statutory scheme for the imposition of the death penalty. The Georgia statute, as amended after our decision in *Furman v. Georgia,* *** retains the death penalty for six categories of crime: murder, kidnapping for ransom or where the victim is harmed, armed robbery, rape, treason, and aircraft hijacking. *** The capital defendant's guilt or innocence is determined in the traditional manner, either by a trial judge or a jury, in the first stage of a bifurcated trial.

If trial is by jury, the trial judge is required to charge lesser included offenses when they are supported by any view of the evidence. *** After a verdict, finding, or plea of guilty to a capital crime, a presentence hearing is conducted before whoever made the determination of guilt. The sentencing procedures are essentially the same in both bench and jury trials. At the hearing:

[T]he judge [or jury] shall hear additional evidence in extenuation, mitigation, and aggravation of punishment, in-cluding the record of any prior criminal convictions and pleas of guilty or pleas of *nolo contendere* of the defendant, or the absence of any prior conviction and pleas:. Provided, however, that only such evidence in ag-

gravation as the State has made known to the defendant prior to his trial shall be admissible. The judge [or jury] shall also hear argument by the defendant or his counsel and the prosecuting attorney . . . regarding the punishment to be imposed. ***

The defendant is accorded substantial latitude as to the types of evidence that he may introduce. *** Evidence considered during the guilt stage may be considered during the sentencing stage without being resubmitted. ***

In the assessment of the appropriate sentence to be imposed the judge is also required to consider or to include in his instructions to the jury "any mitigating circumstances or aggravating circumstances otherwise authorized by law and any of [ten] statutory aggravating circumstances which may be supported by the evidence. . . ." *** The scope of the nonstatutory aggravating or mitigating circumstances is not delineated in the statute. Before a convicted defendant may be sentenced to death, however, except in cases of treason or aircraft hijacking, the jury, or the trial judge in cases tried without a jury, must find beyond a reasonable doubt one of the 10 aggravating circumstances specified in the statute. If the verdict is death the jury or judge must specify the aggravating circumstance(s) found. *** In jury cases, the trial judge is bound by the jury's recommended sentence. ***

In addition to the conventional appellate process available in all criminal cases, provision is made for special expedited direct review by the Supreme Court of Georgia of the appropriateness of imposing the sentence of death in the particular case. The court is directed to consider "the punishment as well as any errors enumerated by way of appeal," and to determine:

(1) Whether the sentence of death was imposed under the influence of passion, prejudice, or any other arbitrary factor, and

(2) Whether, in cases other than treason or aircraft hijacking, the evidence supports the jury's or judge's finding of a statutory aggravating circumstance. . . .

(3) Whether the sentence of death is excessive or disproportionate to the penalty imposed in similar cases, considering both the crime and defendant. ***

If the court affirms a death sentence, it is required to include in its decision reference to similar cases that it has taken into consideration. ***

A transcript and complete record of the trial, as well as a separate report by the trial judge, are transmitted to the court for its use in reviewing the sentence. *** The report is in the form of a 6½-page questionnaire, designed to elicit information about the defendant, the crime, and the circumstances of the trial. It requires the trial judge to characterize the trial in several ways designed to test for arbitrariness and disproportionality of sentence. Included in the report are responses to detailed questions concerning the quality of the defendant's representation, whether race played a role in the trial, and, whether, in the trial court's judgment, there was any doubt about the defendant's guilt or the appropriateness of the sentence. A copy of the report is served upon defense counsel. Under its special review authority, the court may either affirm the death sentence or remand the case for resentencing. In cases in which the death sentence is affirmed there remains the possibility of executive clemency. . . .

The Court on a number of occasions has both assumed and asserted the constitutionality of capital punishment. In several cases that assumption provided a necessary foundation for the decision, as the Court was asked to decide whether a particular method of carrying out a capital sentence would be allowed to stand under the Eighth Amendment. But until *Furman v. Georgia,* *** the Court never confronted squarely the fundamental claim that the punishment of death always, regardless of the enormity of the offense or the procedure followed in imposing the sentence, is cruel and unusual punishment in violation of the Constitution. Although this issue was presented and addressed in *Furman,* it was not resolved by the Court. Four Justices would have held that capital punishment is not unconstitutional *per se;* two Justices would have reached the opposite conclusion; and three Justices, while agreeing that the statutes then before the Court were invalid as applied, left open the question whether such punishment may ever be imposed. We now hold that the punishment of death does not invariably violate the Constitution. . . .

Four years ago, the petitioners in *Furman* and its companion cases predicated their argument primarily upon the asserted proposition that standards of decency had evolved to the point where capital punishment no longer could be tolerated. The petitioners in those cases said, in effect, that the evolutionary process had come to an end, and that standards of decency required that the Eighth Amendment be construed finally as prohibiting capital punishment for any crime regardless of its depravity and impact on society. This view was accepted by two Justices. Three other Justices were unwilling to go so far; focusing on the procedures by which convicted defendants were selected for the death penalty rather than on the actual punishment inflicted they joined in the conclusion that the statutes before the Court were constitutionally invalid.

The petitioners in the capital cases before the Court today renew the "standards of decency" argument, but developments during the four years since *Furman* have undercut substantially the assumptions upon which their argument rested. Despite the continuing debate, dating back to the 19th century, over the morality and utility of capital punishment, it is now evident that a large proportion of American society continues to regard it as an appropriate and necessary criminal sanction.

The most marked indication of society's endorsement of the death penalty for murder is the legislative response to *Furman.* The legislatures of at least 35 States have enacted new statutes that provide for the death penalty for at least some crimes that result in the death of another person. And the Congress of the United States, in 1974, enacted a statute providing the death penalty for aircraft piracy that results in death. These recently adopted statutes have attempted to address the concerns expressed by the Court in *Furman* primarily (i) by specifying the factors to be weighed and the procedures to be followed in deciding when to impose a capital sentence, or (ii) by making the death penalty mandatory for specified crimes. But all of the post-*Furman* statutes make clear that capital punishment itself has not been rejected by the elected representatives of the people.

In the only statewide referendum occurring since *Furman* and brought to our attention, the people of California adopted a constitutional amendment that authorized capital punishment, in effect negating a prior ruling by the Supreme Court of California *** that the death penalty violated the California Constitution.

The jury also is a significant and reliable objective index of contemporary values because it is so directly involved. *** The Court has said that "one of the most important functions any jury can perform in making ... a selection [between life imprisonment and death for a defendant convicted in a capital case] is to maintain a link between contemporary community values and the penal system." *** It may be true that evolving standards have influenced juries in recent decades to be more discriminating in imposing the sentence of death. But the relative infrequency of jury verdicts imposing the death sentence does not indicate rejection of capital punishment *per se.* Rather, the reluctance of juries in many cases to impose the sentence may well reflect the humane feeling that this most irrevocable of sanctions should be reserved for a small number of extreme cases. *** Indeed, the actions of juries in many States since *Furman* is fully compatible with the legislative judgments, reflected in the new statutes, as to the continued utility and necessity of capital punishment in appropriate cases. At the close of 1974 at least 254 persons had been sentenced to death since *Furman,* and by the end of March 1976, more than 460 persons were subject to death sentences.

As we have seen, however, the Eighth Amendment demands more than that a challenged punishment be acceptable to contemporary society. The Court also must ask whether it comports with the basic concept of human dignity at the core of the Amendment. *** Although we cannot "invalidate a category of penalties because we deem less severe penalties adequate to serve the ends of penology," *** the sanction imposed cannot be so totally without penological justification that it results in the gratuitous infliction of suffering. ***

The death penalty is said to serve two principal social purposes: retribution and deterrence of capital crimes by prospective offenders.

In part, capital punishment is an expression of society's moral outrage at particularly offensive conduct. This function may be unappealing to many, but it is essential in an ordered society that asks its citizens to rely on legal processes rather than self-help

to vindicate their wrongs. "Retribution is no longer the dominant objective of the criminal law," *** but neither is it a forbidden objective nor one inconsistent with our respect for the dignity of men. *** Indeed, the decision that capital punishment may be the appropriate sanction in extreme cases is an expression of the community's belief that certain crimes are themselves so grievous an affront to humanity that the only adequate response may be the penalty of death.

Statistical attempts to evaluate the worth of the death penalty as a deterrent to crimes by potential offenders have occasioned a great deal of debate. The results simply have been inconclusive....

Although some of the studies suggest that the death penalty may not function as a significantly greater deterrent than lesser penalties, there is no convincing empirical evidence either supporting or refuting this view. We may nevertheless assume safely that there are murderers, such as those who act in passion, for whom the threat of death has little or no deterrent effect. But for many others, the death penalty undoubtedly is a significant deterrent. There are carefully contemplated murders, such as murder for hire, where the possible penalty of death may well enter into the cold calculus that precedes the decision to act. And there are some categories of murder, such as murder by a life prisoner, where other sanctions may not be adequate.

The value of capital punishment as a deterrent of crime is a complex factual issue the resolution of which properly rests with the legislatures, which can evaluate the results of statistical studies in terms of their own local conditions and with a flexibility of approach that is not available to the courts. *** Indeed, many of the post-*Furman* statutes reflect just such a responsible effort to define those crimes and those criminals for which capital punishment is most probably an effective deterrent.

In sum, we cannot say that the judgment of the Georgia legislature that capital punishment may be necessary in some cases is clearly wrong. Considerations of federalism, as well as respect for the ability of a legislature to evaluate, in terms of its particular state the moral consensus concerning the death penalty and its social utility as a sanction, require us to conclude, in the absence of more convincing evidence, that the infliction of death as a punishment for murder is not without justification and thus is not unconstitutionally severe.

Finally, we must consider whether the punishment of death is disproportionate in relation to the crime for which it is imposed. There is no question that death as a punishment is unique in its severity and irrevocability. *** When a defendant's life is at stake, the Court has been particularly sensitive to insure that every safeguard is observed. *** But we are concerned here only with the imposition of capital punishment for the crime of murder, and when a life has been taken deliberately by the offender, we cannot say that the punishment is invariably disproportionate to the crime. It is an extreme sanction, suitable to the most extreme of crimes.

We hold that the death penalty is not a form of punishment that may never be imposed, regardless of the circumstances of the offense, regardless of the character of the offender, and regardless of the procedure followed in reaching the decision to impose it. . . .

. . . We now turn to consideration of the constitutionality of Georgia's capital-sentencing procedures. In the wake of *Furman,* Georgia amended its capital punishment statute, but chose not to narrow the scope of its murder provisions. Thus, now as before *Furman,* in Georgia "[a] person commits murder when he unlawfully and with malice aforethought, either express or implied, causes the death of another human being." *** All persons convicted of murder "shall be punished by death or by imprisonment for life." ***

Georgia did act, however, to narrow the class of murderers subject to capital punishment by specifying 10 statutory aggravating circumstances, one of which must be found by the jury to exist beyond a reasonable doubt before a death sentence can ever be imposed. In addition, the jury is authorized to consider any other appropriate aggravating or mitigating circumstances. *** The jury is not required to find any mitigating circumstance in order to make a recommendation of mercy that is binding on the trial court, *** but it must find a statutory aggravating circumstance before recommending a sentence of death.

These procedures require the jury to consider the circumstances of the crime and the criminal before

it recommends sentence. No longer can a Georgia jury do as Furman's jury did: reach a finding of the defendant's guilt and then, without guidance or direction, decide whether he should live or die. Instead, the jury's attention is directed to the specific circumstances of the crime: Was it committed in the course of another capital felony? Was it committed for money? Was it committed upon a peace officer or judicial officer? Was it committed in a particularly heinous way or in a manner that endangered the lives of many persons? In addition, the jury's attention is focused on the characteristics of the person who committed the crime: Does he have a record of prior convictions for capital offenses? Are there any special facts about this defendant that mitigate against imposing capital punishment (e.g., his youth, the extent of his cooperation with the police, his emotional state at the time of the crime). As a result, while some jury discretion still exists, "the discretion to be exercised is controlled by clear and objective standards so as to produce non-discriminatory application." ***

As an important additional safeguard against arbitrariness and caprice, the Georgia statutory scheme provides for automatic appeal of all death sentences to the State's Supreme Court. That court is required by statute to review each sentence of death and determine whether it was imposed under the influence of passion or prejudice, whether the evidence supports the jury's finding of a statutory aggravating circumstance, and whether the sentence is disproportionate compared to those sentences imposed in similar cases. ***

In short, Georgia's new sentencing procedures require as a prerequisite to the imposition of the death penalty, specific jury findings as to the circumstances of the crime or the character of the defendant. Moreover to guard further against a situation comparable to that presented in *Furman,* the Supreme Court of Georgia compares each death sentence with the sentences imposed on similarly situated defendants to ensure that the sentence of death in a particular case is not disproportionate. On their face these procedures seem to satisfy the concerns of *Furman.* No longer should there be "no meaningful basis for distinguishing the few cases in which [the death penalty] is imposed from the many cases in which it is not." ***

The basic concern of *Furman* centered on those defendants who were being condemned to death capriciously and arbitrarily. Under the procedures before the Court in that case, sentencing authorities were not directed to give attention to the nature or circumstances of the crime committed or to the character or record of the defendant. Left unguided, juries imposed the death sentence in a way that could only be called freakish. The new Georgia sentencing procedures, by contrast, focus the jury's attention on the particularized nature of the crime and the particularized characteristics of the individual defendant. While the jury is permitted to consider any aggravating or mitigating circumstances, it must find and identify at least one statutory aggravating fact before it may impose a penalty of death. In this way the jury's discretion is channeled. No longer can a jury wantonly and freakishly impose the death sentence; it is always circumscribed by the legislative guidelines. In addition, the review function of the Supreme Court of Georgia affords additional assurance that the concerns that prompted our decision in *Furman* are not present to any significant degree in the Georgia procedure applied here.

Mr. Justice White, with whom **The Chief Justice** and **Mr. Justice Rehnquist** join, concurring in the judgment. . . .

Mr. Justice Blackmun, concurring in the judgment. . . .

Mr. Justice Brennan, dissenting. . . .

Mr. Justice Marshall, dissenting.

In *Furman v. Georgia* *** I set forth at some length my views on the basic issue presented to the court in these cases. The death penalty, I concluded, is a cruel and unusual punishment prohibited by the Eighth and Fourteenth Amendments. That continues to be my view.

In *Furman* I concluded that the death penalty is constitutionally invalid for two reasons. First, the death penalty is excessive. *** And second, the American people, fully informed as to the purposes of the death penalty and its liabilities, would in my view reject it as morally unacceptable. ***

Since the decision in *Furman,* the legislatures of 35 States have enacted new statutes authorizing the imposition of the death sentence for certain crimes, and Congress has enacted a law providing the death penalty for air piracy resulting in death. *** I would be less than candid if I did not acknowledge that these developments have a significant bearing on a realistic assessment of the moral acceptability of the death penalty to the American people. But if the constitutionality of the death penalty turns, as I have urged, on the opinion of an informed citizenry, then even the enactment of new death statutes cannot be viewed as conclusive. A recent study, conducted after the enactment of the post-*Furman* statutes, has confirmed that the American people know little about the death penalty, and that the opinions of an informed public would differ significantly from those of a public unaware of the consequences and effects of the death penalty.

Even assuming, however, that the post-*Furman* enactment of statutes authorizing the death penalty renders the prediction of the views of an informed citizenry an uncertain basis for a constitutional decision, the enactment of those statutes has no bearing whatsoever on the conclusion that the death penalty is unconstitutional because it is excessive. An excessive penalty is invalid under the Cruel and Unusual Punishments Clause "even though popular sentiment may favor" it. *** The inquiry here, then, is simply whether the death penalty is necessary to accomplish the legitimate legislative purposes in punishment, or whether a less severe penalty—life imprisonment—would do as well. ***

The two purposes that sustain the death penalty as nonexcessive in the Court's view are general deterrence and retribution. In *Furman,* I canvassed the relevant data on the deterrent effect of capital punishment. *** The available evidence, I concluded in *Furman,* was convincing that "capital punishment is not necessary as a deterrent to crime in our society." ***

. . . The other principal purpose said to be served by the death penalty is retribution. The notion that retribution can serve as a moral justification for the sanction of death finds credence in the opinion of My Brothers Stewart, Powell, and Stevens, and . . . White. . . . It is this notion that I find to be the most disturbing aspect of today's unfortunate decisions.

The concept of retribution is a multifaceted one, and any discussion of its role in the criminal law must be undertaken with caution. On one level, it can be said that the notion of retribution or reprobation is the basis of our insistence that only those who have broken the law be punished, and in this sense the notion is quite obviously central to a just system of criminal sanctions. But our recognition that retribution plays a crucial role in determining who may be punished by no means requires approval of retribution as a general justification for punishment. It is the question whether retribution can provide a moral justification for punishment—in particular, capital punishment—that we must consider.

. . . The mere fact that the community demands the murderer's life in return for the evil he has done cannot sustain the death penalty, for as the plurality reminds us, "the Eighth Amendment demands more than that a challenged punishment be acceptable to contemporary society." *** To be sustained under the Eighth Amendment, the death penalty must "[comport] with the basis concept of human dignity at the core of the Amendment" *** . . . . Under these standards, the taking of life "because the wrongdoer deserves it" surely must fall, for such a punishment has as its very basis the total denial of the wrongdoer's dignity and worth.

The death penalty, unnecessary to promote the goal of deterrence or to further any legitimate notion of retribution, is an excessive penalty forbidden by the Eighth and Fourteenth Amendments. I respectfully dissent from the Court's judgment upholding the sentences of death imposed upon the petitioners in these cases.

McCleskey v. Kemp
481 U.S. 279; 107 S. Ct. 1756; 95 L. Ed. 2d 262 (1987)
Vote: 5-4

In this case, the Court considers one of the long-standing objections to capital punishment—that it is racially discriminatory. The case is interesting in that the challenge to Georgia's death penalty is based almost entirely on a study performed by social scientists.

Justice Powell delivered the opinion of the Court.

This case presents the question whether a complex statistical study that indicates a risk that racial considerations enter into capital sentencing determinations proves that petitioners McCleskey's capital sentence is unconstitutional under the Eighth or Fourteenth Amendment.

McCleskey, a black man, was convicted of two counts of armed robbery and one count of murder in the Superior Court of Fulton County, Georgia, on October 12, 1978. McCleskey's convictions arose out of the robbery of a furniture store and the killing of a white police officer during the course of the robbery. The evidence at trial indicated that McCleskey and three accomplices planned and carried out the robbery. All four were armed. McCleskey entered the front of the store while the other three entered the rear. McCleskey secured the front of the store by rounding up the customers and forcing them to lie face down on the floor. The other three rounded up the employees in the rear and tied them up with tape. The manager was forced at gunpoint to turn over the store receipts, his watch, and $6.00. During the course of the robbery, a police officer, answering a silent alarm, entered the store through the front door. As he was walking down the center aisle of the store, two shots were fired. Both struck the officer. One hit him in the face and killed him.

Several weeks later, McCleskey was arrested in connection with an unrelated offense. He confessed that he had participated in the furniture store robbery, but denied that he had shot the police officer. At trial, the State introduced evidence that at least one of the bullets that struck the officer was fired from a .38 caliber Rossi revolver. This description matched the description of the gun that McCleskey had carried during the robbery. The State also introduced the testimony of two witnesses who had heard McCleskey admit to the shooting.

The jury convicted McCleskey of murder. At the penalty hearing, the jury heard arguments as to the appropriate sentence. Under Georgia law, the jury could not consider imposing the death penalty unless it found beyond a reasonable doubt that the murder was accompanied by one of the statutory aggravating circumstances. *** The jury in this case found two aggravating circumstances to exist beyond a reasonable doubt: the murder was committed during the course of an armed robbery, *** and the murder was committed upon a peace officer engaged in the performance of his duties. *** In making its decision whether to impose the death sentence, the jury considered the mitigating and aggravating circumstances of McCleskey's conduct. McCleskey offered no mitigating evidence. The jury recommended that he be sentenced to death on the murder charge and to consecutive life sentences on the armed robbery charges. The court followed the jury's recommendation and sentenced McCleskey to death. . . .

McCleskey . . . filed a petition for a writ of *habeas corpus* in the federal District Court for the Northern District of Georgia. His petition raised 18 claims, one of which was that the Georgia capital sentencing process is administered in a racially discriminatory manner in violation of the Eighth and Fourteenth Amendments to the United States Constitution. In support of his claim, McCleskey proffered a statistical study performed by Professors David C. Baldus, George Woodworth, and Charles Pulanski (the Baldus study) that purports to show a disparity in the imposition of the death sentence in Georgia based on the race of the murder victim and, to a lesser extent, the race of the defendant. The Baldus study is actually two sophisticated statistical studies that examine over 2,000 murder cases that occurred in Georgia during the 1970s. The raw numbers collected by Professor Baldus indicate that defendants charged with killing white persons received the death penalty in 11% of the cases, but defendants charged with killing blacks received the death penalty in only 1% of the cases. The raw numbers also indicate a reverse racial disparity according to the race of the defendant: 4% of the black defendants received the death penalty, as opposed to 7% of the white defendants.

Baldus also divided the cases according to the combination of the race of the defendant and the race of the victim. He found that the death penalty was assessed in 22% of the cases involving black defendants and white victims; 8% of the cases involving white defendants and white victims; 1% of the cases involving black defendants and black victims; and 3% of the cases involving white defendants and black victims. Similarly, Baldus found that prosecutors sought the death penalty in 70% of the cases involving black defendants and white victims; 32% of the cases involving white defendants and white victims; 15% of the cases involving black defendants and black victims; and 19% of the cases involving white defendants and black victims.

Baldus subjected his data to an extensive analysis, taking account of 230 variables that could have explained the disparities on nonracial grounds. One of his models concludes that, even after taking account of 39 nonracial variables, defendants charged with killing white victims were 4.3 times as likely to receive a death sentence as defendants charged with killing blacks. According to this model, black defendants were 1.1 times as likely to receive a death sentence as other defendants. Thus, the Baldus study indicates that black defendants, such as McCleskey, who kill white victims have the greatest likelihood of receiving the death penalty.

McCleskey's first claim is that the Georgia capital punishment statute violates the Equal Protection Clause of the Fourteenth Amendment. He argues that race has infected the administration of Georgia's statute in two ways: persons who murder whites are more likely to be sentenced to death than persons who murder blacks, and black murderers are more likely to be sentenced to death than white murderers.

As a black defendant who killed a white victim, McCleskey claims that the Baldus study demonstrates that he was discriminated against because of his race and because of the race of his victim. In its broadest form, McCleskey's claim of discrimination extends to every actor in the Georgia capital sentencing process from the prosecutor who sought the death penalty and the jury that imposed the sentence, to the State itself that enacted the capital punishment statute and allows it to remain in effect despite its allegedly discriminatory application. We agree with the Court of

Appeals, and every other court that has considered such a challenge, that this claim must fail.

Our analysis begins with the basic principle that a defendant who alleges an equal protection violation has the burden of proving "the existence of purposeful discrimination." *** A corollary to this principle is that a criminal defendant must prove that the purposeful discrimination "had a discriminatory effect" on him. *** Thus, to prevail under the Equal Protection Clause, McCleskey must prove that the decisionmakers in his case acted with discriminatory purpose. He offers no evidence specific to his own case that would support an inference that racial considerations played a part in his sentence. Instead, he relies solely on the Baldus study. McCleskey argues that the Baldus study compels an inference that his sentence rests on purposeful discrimination. McCleskey's claim that these statistics are sufficient proof of discrimination, without regard to the facts of a particular case, would extend to all capital cases in Georgia, at least where the victim was white and the defendant is black. . . .

McCleskey also suggests that the Baldus study proves that the State as a whole has acted with a discriminatory purpose. He appears to argue that the State has violated the Equal Protection Clause by adopting the capital punishment statute and allowing it to remain in force despite its allegedly discriminatory application. But " '[d]iscriminatory purpose' . . . implies more than intent as volition or intent as awareness of consequences. It implies that the decisionmaker, in this case a state legislature, selected or reaffirmed a particular course of action at least in part 'because of,' not merely 'in spite of,' its adverse effects upon an identifiable group." *** For this claim to prevail, McCleskey would have to prove that the Georgia Legislature enacted or maintained the death penalty statute because of an anticipated racially discriminatory effect. In *Gregg v. Georgia* *** (1976), this Court found that the Georgia capital sentencing system could operate in a fair and neutral manner. There was no evidence then, and there is none now, that the Georgia Legislature enacted the capital punishment statute to further a racially discriminatory purpose.

Nor has McCleskey demonstrated that the legislature maintains the capital punishment statute be-cause of the racially disproportionate impact suggested by the Baldus study. As legislatures necessarily have wide discretion in the choice of criminal laws and penalties, and as there were legitimate reasons for the Georgia Legislature to adopt and maintain capital punishment, *** we will not infer a discriminatory purpose on the part of the State of Georgia. Accordingly, we reject McCleskey's equal protection claims.

McCleskey also argues that the Baldus study demonstrates that the Georgia capital sentencing system violates the Eighth Amendment. . . .

. . . [O]ur decisions since *Furman* have identified a constitutionally permissible range of discretion in imposing the death penalty. First, there is a required threshold below which the death penalty cannot be imposed. In this context, the State must establish rational criteria that narrow the decisionmaker's judgment as to whether the circumstances of a particular defendant's case meet the threshold. Moreover, a societal consensus that the death penalty is disproportionate to a particular offense prevents a State from imposing the death penalty for that offense. Second, States cannot limit the sentencer's consideration of any relevant circumstance that could cause it to decline to impose the penalty. In this respect, the State cannot channel the sentencer's discretion, but must allow it to consider any relevant information offered by the defendant.

In light of our precedents under the Eighth Amendment, McCleskey cannot argue successfully that his sentence is "disproportionate to the crime in the traditional sense." *** He does not deny that he committed a murder in the course of a planned robbery, a crime for which this Court has determined that the death penalty constitutionally may be imposed. *** His disproportionality claim "is of a different sort." *** McCleskey argues that the sentence in his case is disproportionate to the sentences in other murder cases.

On the one hand, he cannot base a constitutional claim on an argument that his case differs from other cases in which defendants did receive the death penalty. On automatic appeal, the Georgia Supreme Court found that McCleskey's death sentence was not disproportionate to other death sentences imposed in the State. *** The court supported this conclusion with an appendix containing citations to 13 cases involving generally similar murders. *** Moreover, where the statutory procedures adequately channel the sentencer's discretion, such proportionality review is not constitutionally required. *** . . .

Two additional concerns inform our decision in this case. First, McCleskey's claim, taken to its logical conclusion, throws into serious question the principles that underlie our entire criminal justice system. The Eighth Amendment is not limited in application to capital punishment, but applies to all penalties. *** Thus, if we accepted McCleskey's claim that racial bias has impermissibly tainted the capital sentencing decision, we could soon be faced with similar claims as to other types of penalty. Moreover, the claim that his sentence rests on the irrelevant factor of race easily could be extended to apply to claims based on unexplained discrepancies that correlate to membership in other minority groups, and even to gender. Similarly, since McCleskey's claim relates to the race of his victim, other claims could apply with equally logical force to statistical disparities that correlate with the race or sex of other actors in the criminal justice system, such as defense attorneys or judges. Also, there is no logical reason that such a claim need be limited to racial or sexual bias. If arbitrary and capricious punishment is the touchstone under the Eighth Amendment, such a claim could—at least in theory—be based upon any arbitrary variable, such as the defendant's facial characteristics, or the physical attractiveness of the defendant or the victim, that some statistical study indicates may be influential in jury decisionmaking. As these examples illustrate, there is no limiting principle to the type of challenge brought by McCleskey. The Constitution does not require that a State eliminate any demonstrable disparity that correlates with a potentially irrelevant factor in order to operate a criminal justice system that includes capital punishment. . . .

Second, McCleskey's arguments are best presented to the legislative bodies. It is not the responsibility—or indeed even the right—of this Court to determine the appropriate punishment for particular crimes. It is the legislatures, the elected representatives of the people, that are "constituted to respond to the will and consequently the moral val-

ues of the people." *** Legislatures also are better qualified to weigh and "evaluate the results of statistical studies in terms of their own local conditions and with a flexibility of approach that is not available to the courts." *** Capital punishment is now the law in more than two-thirds of our States. It is the ultimate duty of courts to determine on a case-by-case basis whether these laws are applied consistently with the Constitution. Despite McCleskey's wideranging arguments that basically challenge the validity of capital punishment in our multiracial society, the only question before us is whether in his case, *** the law of Georgia was properly applied. We agree with the District Court and the Court of Appeals for the Eleventh Circuit that this was carefully and correctly done in this case.

Accordingly, we affirm the judgment of the Court of Appeals for the Eleventh Circuit.

Justice Brennan, with whom **_Justice Marshall_** joins, and with whom **_Justice Blackmun_** and **_Justice Stevens_** join [in part], dissenting.

Adhering to my view that the death penalty is in all circumstances cruel and unusual punishment forbidden by the Eighth and Fourteenth Amendments, I would vacate the decision below insofar as it left undisturbed the death sentence imposed in this case. The Court observes that "[t]he _Gregg_-type statute imposes unprecedented safeguards in the special context of capital punishment," which "ensure a degree of care in the imposition of the death penalty that can be described only as unique." Notwithstanding these efforts, murder defendants in Georgia with white victims are more than four times as likely to receive the death sentence as are defendants with black victims. Nothing could convey more powerfully the intractable reality of the death penalty: "that the effort to eliminate arbitrariness in the infliction of that ultimate sanction is so plainly doomed to failure that it—and the death penalty—must be abandoned altogether."

Even if I did not hold this position, however, I would reverse the Court of Appeals, for petitioner McCleskey has clearly demonstrated that his death sentence was imposed in violation of the Eighth and Fourteenth Amendments. . . . I write separately to emphasize how conclusively McCleskey has also demonstrated precisely the type of risk of irrationality in sentencing that we have consistently condemned in our Eighth Amendment jurisprudence. . . .

Justice Blackmun, with whom ***Justice Marshall*** and ***Justice Stevens*** join and with whom ***Justice Brennan*** joins [in part], dissenting.

The Court today sanctions the execution of a man despite his presentation of evidence that establishes a constitutionally intolerable level of racially based discrimination leading to the imposition of his death sentence. I am disappointed with the Court's action not only because of its denial of constitutional guarantees to petitioner McCleskey individually, but also because of its departure from what seems to me to be well-developed constitutional jurisprudence. . . .

Justice Stevens, with whom ***Justice Blackmun*** joins, dissenting.

There "is a qualitative difference between death and any other permissible form of punishment" and hence, " 'a corresponding difference in the need for reliability in the determination that death is the appropriate punishment in a specific case.' " *** Even when considerations far less repugnant than racial discrimination are involved, we have recognized the "vital importance to the defendant and to the community that any decision to impose the death sentence be, and appear to be, based on reason rather than caprice or emotion." *** [A]lthough not every imperfection in the deliberative process is sufficient, even in a capital case, to set aside a state-court judgment, the severity of the sentence mandates careful scrutiny in the review of any colorable claim of error."

In this case it is claimed—and the claim is supported by elaborate studies which the Court properly assumes to be valid—that the jury's sentencing process was likely distorted by racial prejudice. The studies demonstrate a strong probability that McCleskey's sentencing jury, which expressed "the community's outrage—its sense that an individual has lost his moral entitlement to live," *** —was influenced by the fact that McCleskey is black and his victim was white, and that this same outrage would not have been generated if he had killed a member of his own race. This sort of disparity is constitutionally intolerable. It flagrantly violates the Court's prior "insistence that capital punishment be imposed fairly, and with reasonable consistency, or not at all." ***

The Court's decision appears to be based on a fear that the acceptance of McCleskey's claim would sound the death knell for capital punishment in Georgia. If society were indeed forced to choose between a racially discriminatory death penalty (one that provides heightened protection against murder "for whites only") and no death penalty at all, the choice mandated by the Constitution would be plain. *** But the Court's fear is unfounded. One of the lessons of the Baldus study is that there exist certain categories of extremely serious crimes for which prosecutors consistently seek, and juries consistently impose, the death penalty without regard to the race of the victim or the race of the offender. If Georgia were to narrow the class of death-eligible defendants to those categories, the danger of arbitrary and discriminatory imposition of the death penalty would be significantly decreased, if not eradicated. . . .

Hutto v. Finney

437 U.S. 678; 98 S. Ct. 2565; 57 L. Ed. 2d 522 (1978)
Vote: 6-2-1

Mr. Justice Stevens delivered the opinion of the Court.

After finding that conditions in the Arkansas penal system constitute cruel and unusual punishment, the District Court entered a series of detailed remedial orders. On appeal to the United States Court

of Appeals for the Eighth Circuit, petitioners challenged . . . an order placing a maximum limit of 30 days on confinement in punitive isolation. . . . The Court of Appeals affirmed. . . . We granted *certiorari* *** and now affirm.

This litigation began in 1969; it is a sequel to two earlier cases holding that conditions in the Arkansas prison system violated the Eighth and Fourteenth Amendments. Only a brief summary of the facts is necessary to explain the basis for the remedial order.

The routine conditions that the ordinary Arkansas convict had to endure were characterized by the District Court as "a dark and evil world completely alien to the free world." *** That characterization was amply supported by the evidence.[1]

The inmates slept together in large, 100-man barracks and some convicts, known as "creepers," would slip from their beds to crawl along the floor, stalking their sleeping enemies. In one 18-month period, there were 17 stabbings, all but one occurring in the barracks. Homosexual rape was so common and uncontrolled that some potential victims dared not sleep; instead they would leave their beds and spend the night clinging to the bars nearest the guards' station. The punishments for misconduct not serious enough to result in punitive isolation were cruel,[2] unusual,[3] and unpredictable.[4] It is the discipline known as "punitive isolation" that is most relevant for present purposes.

Confinement in punitive isolation was for an indeterminate period of time. An average of four, and sometimes as many as 10 or 11, prisoners were crowded into windowless 8' × 10' cells containing no furniture other than a source of water and a toilet that could only be flushed from outside the cell. At night the prisoners were given mattresses to spread on the floor. Although some prisoners suffered from infectious diseases such as hepatitis and venereal disease, mattresses were removed and jumbled together each morning, then returned to the cells at random in the evening. Prisoners in isolation received fewer than 1,000 calories a day; their meals consisted primarily of 4-inch squares of "grue," a substance created by mashing meat, potatoes, oleo, syrup, vegetables, eggs, and seasoning into a paste and baking the mixture in a pan.

After finding the conditions of confinement unconstitutional, the District Court did not immediately impose a detailed remedy of its own. Instead, it directed the Department of Correction to "make a substantial start" on improving conditions and to file reports on its progress. *** When the Department's progress proved unsatisfactory, a second hearing was held. The District Court found some improvements, but concluded that prison conditions remained unconstitutional. *** Again the court offered prison administrators an opportunity to devise a plan of their own for remedying the constitutional violations, but this time the court issued guidelines, identifying four areas of change that would cure the worst evils: improving conditions in the isolation cells, increasing inmate safety, eliminating the barracks sleeping arrangements, and putting an end to the trusty system.

*** The Department was ordered to move as rapidly as funds became available. ***

After this order was affirmed on appeal, *** more hearings were held in 1972 and 1973 to review the

---

[1] The administrators of Arkansas' prison system evidently tried to operate their prisons at a profit. Cummins Farm, the institution at the center of this litigation, required its 1,000 inmates to work in the fields 10 hours a day, six days a week, using mule-drawn tools and tending crops by hand. The inmates were sometimes required to run to and from the fields, with a guard in an automobile or on horseback driving them on. They worked in all sorts of weather, so long as the temperature was above freezing, sometimes in unsuitable light clothing or without shoes.

[2] Inmates were lashed with a wooden-handled leather strap five feet long and four inches wide. Although it was not official policy to do so, some inmates were apparently whipped for minor offenses until their skin was bloody and bruised.

[3] The "Tucker telephone," a hand-cranked device, was used to administer electrical shocks to various sensitive parts of an inmate's body.

[4] Most of the guards were simply inmates who had been issued guns. Although it had 1,000 prisoners, Cummins employed only eight guards who were not themselves convicts. Only two nonconvict guards kept watch over the 1,000 men at night. While the "trusties" maintained an appearance of order, they took a high toll from the other prisoners. Inmates could obtain access to medical treatment only if they bribed the trusty in charge of sick call. As the District Court found, it was "within the power of a trusty guard to murder another inmate with practical impunity," because trusties with weapons were authorized to use deadly force against escapees. "Accidental shootings" also occurred; and one trusty fired his shotgun into a crowded barracks because the inmates would not turn off their TV. Another trusty beat an inmate so badly the victim required partial dentures.

Department's progress. Finding substantial improvements, the court concluded that continuing supervision was no longer necessary. The court held, however, that its prior decrees would remain in effect and noted that sanctions, as well as an award of costs and attorney's fees, would be imposed if violations occurred. ***

The Court of Appeals reversed the District Court's decision to withdraw its supervisory jurisdiction, *** and the District Court held a fourth set of hearings. *** It found that, in some respects, conditions had seriously deteriorated since 1973, when the court had withdrawn its supervisory jurisdiction. Cummins Farm, which the court had condemned as overcrowded in 1970 because it housed 1,000 inmates, now had a population of about 1,500. *** The situation in the punitive isolation cells was particularly disturbing. The court concluded that either it had misjudged conditions in these cells in 1973 or conditions had become much worse since then. *** There were still twice as many prisoners as beds in some cells. And because inmates in punitive isolation are often violently antisocial, overcrowding led to persecution of the weaker prisoners. The "grue" diet was still in use, and practically all inmates were losing weight on it. The cells had been vandalized to a "very substantial" extent *** Because of their inadequate numbers, guards assigned to the punitive isolation cells frequently resorted to physical violence, using nightsticks and Mace in their efforts to maintain order. Prisoners were sometimes left in isolation for months, their release depending on "their attitudes as appraised by prison personnel."

The court concluded that the constitutional violations identified earlier had not been cured. It entered an order that placed limits on the number of men that could be confined in one cell, required that each have a bunk, discontinued the "grue" diet, and set 30 days as the maximum isolation sentence. The District Court gave detailed consideration to the matter of fees and expenses, made an express finding that petitioners had acted in bad faith, and awarded counsel "a fee of $20,000.00 to be paid out of [the] Department of Correction funds." *** The Court of Appeals affirmed and assessed an additional $2,500 to cover fees and expenses on appeal. ***

... The Eighth Amendment's ban on inflicting cruel and unusual punishments, made applicable to the States by the Fourteenth Amendment, "proscribes more than physically barbarous punishments." *** It prohibits penalties that are grossly disproportionate to the offense, *** as well as those that transgress today's "broad and idealistic concepts of dignity, civilized standards, humanity, and decency." *** Confinement in a prison or in an isolation cell is a form of punishment subject to scrutiny under Eighth Amendment standards. Petitioners do not challenge this proposition; nor do they disagree with the District Court's original conclusion that Arkansas prisons, including its punitive isolation cells, constituted cruel and unusual punishment. Rather, petitioners single out that portion of the District Court's most recent order that forbids the Department to sentence inmates to more than 30 days in punitive isolation. Petitioners assume that the District Court held that indeterminate sentences to punitive isolation always constitute cruel and unusual punishments. This assumption misreads the District Court's holding.

Read in its entirety, the District Court's opinion makes it abundantly clear that the length of isolation sentences was not considered in a vacuum. In the court's words, punitive isolation "is not necessarily unconstitutional, but it may be, depending on the duration of the confinement and the conditions thereof." *** It is perfectly obvious that every decision to remove a particular inmate from general prison population for an indeterminate period could not be characterized as cruel and unusual. If new conditions of confinement are not materially different from those affecting other prisoners, a transfer for the duration of a prisoner's sentence might be completely unobjectionable and well within the authority of the prison administrator. *** It is equally plain, however, that the length of confinement cannot be ignored in deciding whether the confinement meets constitutional standards. A filthy, overcrowded cell and a diet of "grue" might be tolerated for a few days and intolerably cruel for weeks or months.

The question before the trial court was whether past constitutional violations had been remedied. The court was entitled to consider the severity of those violations in assessing the constitutionality of conditions in the isolation cells. The court took note of the inmates' diet, the continued overcrowding, the rampant violence, the vandalized cells, and the "lack of professionalism and good judgment on the part of maximum security personnel." *** The length of time each inmate spent in isolation was simply one consideration among many. We find no error in the court's conclusion that, taken as a whole, conditions in the isolation cells continued to violate the prohibition against cruel and unusual punishment. . . .

The judgment of the Court of Appeals is accordingly affirmed.

Mr. Justice Powell, with whom the ***Chief Justice*** joins, concurring in part and dissenting in part. . . .

Mr. Justice Rehnquist, dissenting.

. . . No person of ordinary feeling could fail to be moved by the Court's recitation of the conditions formerly prevailing in the Arkansas prison system.

Yet I fear the Court has allowed itself to be moved beyond the well-established bounds limiting the exercise of remedial authority by the federal district courts. . . .

The District Court's order limiting the maximum period of punitive isolation to 30 days in no way related to any condition found offensive to the Constitution. It is, when stripped of descriptive verbiage, a prophylactic rule, doubtless well designed to assure a more humane prison system in Arkansas, but not complying with [the limitations on district court remedies]. . . .

Certainly the provision is not remedial in the sense that it "restore[s] the victims of discriminatory conduct to the position they would have occupied in the absence of such conduct." *** The sole effect of the provision is to grant future offenders against prison discipline greater benefits than the Constitution requires; it does nothing to remedy the plight of past victims of conditions which may well have been unconstitutional. . . .

In Re Gault

387 U.S. 1; 87 S. Ct. 1428; 18 L. Ed. 2d 527 (1967)
Vote: 7-1-1

Mr. Justice Fortas delivered the opinion of the Court.

. . . On Monday, June 8, 1965, at about 10 A.M., Gerald Francis Gault and a friend, Ronald Lewis, were taken into custody by the Sheriff of Gila County. Gerald was then still subject to a six months' probation order which had been entered on February 25, 1964, as a result of his having been in the company of another boy who had stolen a wallet from a lady's purse. The police action on June 8 was taken as the result of a verbal complaint by a neighbor of the boys, Mrs. Cook, about a telephone call made to her in which the caller or callers made lewd or indecent remarks. It will suffice for purposes of this opinion to say that the remarks or questions put to her were of the irritatingly offensive, adolescent, sex variety.

At the time Gerald was picked up, his mother and father were both at work. No notice that Gerald was

being taken into custody was left at the home. No other steps were taken to advise them that their son had, in effect, been arrested. Gerald was taken to the Children's Detention Home. When his mother arrived home at about 6 o'clock, Gerald was not there. Gerald's older brother was sent to look for him at the trailer home of the Lewis family. He apparently learned then that Gerald was in custody. He so informed his mother. The two of them went to the Detention Home. The deputy probation officer, Flagg, who was also superintendent of the Detention Home, told Mrs. Gault "why Jerry was there" and said that a hearing would be held in Juvenile Court at 3 o'clock the following day, June 9.

Officer Flagg filed a petition with the court on the hearing day, June 9, 1964. It was not served on the Gaults. Indeed, none of them saw this petition until the *habeas corpus* hearing on August 17, 1964. The petition was entirely formal. It made no reference to any factual basis for the judicial action which it initiated. It recited only that "said minor is under the age of eighteen years, and is in need of the protection of this Honorable court; [and that] said minor is a delinquent minor." It prayed for a hearing and an order regarding "the care and custody of said minor." Officer Flagg executed a formal affidavit in support of the petition.

On June 9, Gerald, his mother, his older brother, and Probation Officers Flagg and Henderson appeared before the Juvenile Judge in chambers. Gerald's father was not there. He was at work out of the city. Mrs. Cook, the complainant, was not there. No one was sworn at this hearing. No transcript or recording was made. No memorandum or record of the substance of the proceedings was prepared. Our information about the proceedings and the subsequent hearing on June 15, derives entirely from the testimony of the Juvenile Court Judge, Mr. and Mrs. Gault and Officer Flagg at the *habeas corpus* proceeding conducted two months later. From this, it appears that at the June 9 hearing Gerald was questioned by the judge about the telephone call. There was conflict as to what he said. His mother recalled that Gerald said he only dialed Mrs. Cook's number and handed the telephone to his friend, Ronald. Officer Flagg recalled that Gerald had admitted making the lewd remarks. Judge McGhee testified that Gerald "admitted making one of these [lewd] statements." At the conclusion of the hearing, the judge said he would "think about it." Gerald was taken back to the Detention Home. He was not sent to his own home with his parents. On June 11 or 12, after having been detained since June 8, Gerald was released and driven home. There is no explanation in the record as to why he was kept in the Detention Home or why he was released. At 5 P.M. on the day of Gerald's release, Mrs. Gault received a note signed by Officer Flagg. It was on plain paper, not letterhead. Its entire text was as follows:

Mrs. Gault:

Judge McGhee has set Monday, June 15, 1964 at 11:00 A.M. as the date and time for further Hearings on Gerald's delinquency.

/s/Flagg

At the appointed time on Monday, June 15, Gerald, his father and mother, Ronald Lewis and his father, and Officers Flagg and Henderson were present before Judge McGhee. Witnesses at the *habeas corpus* proceeding differed in their recollections of Gerald's testimony at the June 15 hearing. Mr. and Mrs. Gault recalled that Gerald again testified that he had only dialed the number and that the other boy had made the remarks. Officer Flagg agreed that at this hearing Gerald did not admit making the lewd remarks. But Judge McGhee recalled that "there was some admission again of some of the lewd statements. He—he didn't admit any of the more serious lewd statements." Again, the complainant, Mrs. Cook, was not present. Mrs. Gault asked that Mrs. Cook be present "so she could see which boy that done the talking, the dirty talking over the phone." The Juvenile Judge said "she didn't have to be present at that hearing." The judge did not speak to Mrs. Cook or communicate with her at any time. Probation Officer Flagg had talked to her once—over the telephone on June 9.

At this June 15 hearing a "referral report" made by the probation officers was filed with the court, although not disclosed to Gerald or his parents. This listed the charge as "Lewd Phone Calls." At the conclusion of the hearing, the judge committed Gerald as a juvenile delinquent to the State Industrial School "for the period of his minority [that is, until 21] unless sooner discharged by due process of law." . . .

No appeal is permitted by Arizona law in juvenile cases. On August 3, 1964, a petition for a writ of *habeas corpus* was filed with the Supreme Court of Arizona and referred by it to the Superior Court for hearing.

At the *habeas corpus* hearing on August 17, Judge McGhee was vigorously cross-examined as to the basis for his actions. He testified that he had taken into account the fact that Gerald was on probation. He was asked "under what section of . . . the code you found the boy delinquent."

His answer is set forth in the margin. In substance, he concluded that Gerald came within ARS 8-201-6(a), which specifies that a "delinquent child" includes one "who has violated a law of the state or an ordinance or regulation of a political subdivision thereof." The law which Gerald was found to have violated . . . provides that a person who "in the presence of hearing of any woman or child . . . uses vulgar, abusive or obscene language, is guilty of a misdemeanor. . . ." The penalty specified in the Criminal Code, which would apply to an adult, is $5 to $50, or imprisonment for not more than two months. The judge also testified that he acted under ARS 8-201-6(d) which includes in the definition of a "delinquent child" one who, as the judge phrased it, is "habitually involved in immoral matters."

Asked about this basis for his conclusion that Gerald was "habitually involved in immoral matters," the judge testified, somewhat vaguely, that two years earlier, on July 2, 1962, a "referral" was made concerning Gerald, "where the boy had stolen a baseball glove from another boy and lied to the Police Department about it." The judge said there was "no hearing," and "no accusation" relating to this incident, "because of lack of material foundation." But it seems to have remained in his mind as a relevant factor. The judge also testified that Gerald had admitted making other nuisance phone calls in the past which, as the judge recalled the boy's testimony, were "silly calls, or funny calls, or something like that."

The Superior Court dismissed the writ, and appellants sought review in the Arizona Supreme Court. . . .

The Supreme Court handed down an elaborate and wide-ranging opinion affirming dismissal of the writ and stated the court's conclusions as to the issues raised by appellants and other aspects of the juvenile process. In their jurisdictional statement and brief in this Court, appellants do not urge upon us all of the points passed upon by the Supreme Court of Arizona. They urge that we hold the Juvenile Code of Arizona invalid on its face or as applied in this case because, contrary to the Due Process Clause of the Fourteenth Amendment, the juvenile is taken from the custody of his parents and committed to a state institution pursuant to proceedings in which the Juvenile Court has virtually unlimited discretion, and in which the following basic rights are denied:

1. Notice of the charges;
2. Right to counsel;
3. Right to confrontation and cross-examination;
4. Privilege against self-incrimination;
5. Right to a transcript of the proceedings; and
6. Right to appellate review.

. . . From the inception of the juvenile court system, wide differences have been tolerated—indeed insisted upon—between the procedural rights accorded to adults and those of juveniles. In practically all jurisdictions, there are rights granted to adults which are withheld from juveniles. In addition to the specific problems involved in the present case, for example, it has been held that the juvenile is not entitled to bail, to indictment by grand jury, to a public trial or to trial by jury. It is frequent practice that rules governing the arrest and interrogation of adults by the police are not observed in the case of juveniles. . . .

It is claimed that juveniles obtain benefits from the special procedures applicable to them which more than offset the disadvantages of denial of the substance of normal due process. As we shall discuss, the observance of due process standards, intelligently and not ruthlessly administered, will not compel the States to abandon or displace any of the substantive benefits of the juvenile process. But it is important, we think, that the claimed benefits of the juvenile process should be candidly appraised. Neither sentiment or folklore should cause us to shut our eyes, for example, to such startling findings as that reported in an exceptionally reliable study of repeaters or recidivism conducted by the Stanford Research Institute for the President's Commission on Crime in the District of Columbia. This Commission's Report states:

In fiscal 1966 approximately 66 percent of the 16- and 17-year-old juveniles referred to the court by the Youth Aid Division had been before the court previously. 1965, 56 percent of those in the Receiving Home were repeaters. The SRI study revealed that 61 percent of the sample Juvenile Court referrals in 1965 had been previously referred at least once and that 42 percent had been referred at least twice before. ***

Certainly, these figures and the high crime rates among juveniles to which we have referred, could not lead us to conclude that the absence of constitutional protections reduces crime, or that the juvenile system, functioning free of constitutional inhibitions as it has largely done, is effective to reduce crime or rehabilitate offenders. We do not mean by this to denigrate the juvenile court process or to suggest that there are no aspects of the juvenile system relating to offenders which are valuable. But the features of the juvenile system which its proponents have asserted are of unique benefit will not be impaired by constitutional domestication. For example, the commendable principles relating to the processing and treatment of juveniles separately from adults are in no way involved or affected by the procedural issues under discussion. Further, we are told that one of the important benefits of the special juvenile court procedures is that they avoid classifying the juvenile as a "criminal." The juvenile offender is now classed as a "delinquent." There is, of course, no reason why this should not continue. It is disconcerting, however, that this term has come to involve only slightly less stigma than the term "criminal" applied to adults. It is also emphasized that in practically all jurisdictions, statutes provide that an adjudication of the child as a delinquent shall not operate as a civil disability or disqualify him for civil service appointment. There is no reason why the application of due process requirements should interfere with such provisions. . . .

Further, it is urged that the juvenile benefits from informal proceedings in the court. The early conception of the Juvenile Court proceeding was one in which a fatherly judge touched the heart and conscience of the erring youth by talking over his problems, by paternal advice and admonition, and in which, in extreme situations, benevolent and wise institutions of the State provided guidance and help "to save him from a downward career." Then, as now, goodwill and compassion were admirably prevalent. But recent studies have, with surprising unanimity, entered sharp dissent as to the validity of this gentle conception. They suggest that the appearance as well as the actuality of fairness, impartiality and orderliness—in short, the essentials of due process—may be a more impressive and more therapeutic attitude so far as the juvenile is concerned. . . .

Ultimately, however, we confront the reality of that portion of the Juvenile Court process with which we deal in this case. A boy is charged with misconduct. The boy is committed to an institution where he may be restrained of liberty for years. It is of no constitutional consequence—and of limited practical meaning—that the institution to which he is committed is called an Industrial School. The fact of the matter is that, however euphemistic the title, a "receiving home" or an "industrial school" for juveniles is an institution of confinement in which the child is incarcerated for a greater or lesser time. His world becomes "a building with whitewashed walls, regimented routine and institutional hours. . . ." Instead of mother and father and sisters and brothers and friends and classmates, his world is peopled by guards, custodians, state employees, and "delinquents" confined with him for anything from waywardness to rape and homicide.

In view of this, it would be extraordinary if our Constitution did not require the procedural regularity and the exercise of care implied in the phrase "due process." Under our Constitution, the condition of being a boy does not justify a kangaroo court. The traditional ideas of Juvenile Court procedure, indeed, contemplated that time would be available and care would be used to establish precisely what the juvenile did and why he did it—was it a prank of adolescence or a brutal act threatening serious consequences to himself or society unless corrected? Under traditional notions, one would assume that in a case like that of Gerald Gault, where the juvenile appears to have a home, a working mother and father, and an older brother, the Juvenile Judge would have made a careful inquiry and judgment as to the possibility that the boy could be disciplined and dealt with at home, despite his previous transgressions. Indeed, so far as appears in the record before us . . . the points to which the judge directed his attention were little different from those that would be involved in determining any charge of violation of a penal statute. The essential difference between Gerald's case and a normal criminal case is that safeguards available to adults were discarded in Gerald's case. The summary procedure as well as the long commitment was possible because Gerald was 15 years of age instead of over 18. . . .

Appellants allege that the Arizona Juvenile Code is unconstitutional or alternatively that the proceedings before the Juvenile Court were constitutionally defective because of failure to provide adequate notice of the hearings. . . .

. . . Notice, to comply with due process requirements, must be given sufficiently in advance of scheduled court proceedings so that reasonable opportunity to prepare will be afforded, and it must "set forth the alleged misconduct with particularity." It is obvious that no purpose of shielding the child from the public stigma of knowledge of his having been taken into custody and scheduled for hearing is served by the procedure approved by the court below. The "initial hearing" in the present case was a hearing on the merits. Notice at that time is not timely; and even if there were a conceivable purpose served by the deferral proposed by the court below, it would have to yield to the requirements that the child and his parents or guardian be notified, in writing, of the specific charge or factual allegations to be considered at the hearing, and that such written notice be given at the earliest practicable time, and in any event sufficiently in advance of the hearing to permit preparation. . . .

Appellants charge that the Juvenile Court proceedings were fatally defective because the court did not advise Gerald or his parents of their right to counsel, and proceeded with the hearing, the adjudication of delinquency and the order of commitment in the absence of counsel for the child and his parents or an express waiver of the right thereto. . . . A proceeding where the issue is whether the child will be found to be "delinquent" and subjected to the loss of his liberty for years is comparable in seriousness to a felony prosecution. The juvenile needs the assistance of counsel to cope with problems of law, to make skilled inquiry into the facts, to insist upon regularity of the proceedings, and to ascertain whether he has a defense and to prepare and submit it. The child "requires the guiding hand of counsel at every step in the proceedings against him." . . .

We conclude that the Due Process Clause of the Fourteenth Amendment requires that in respect of proceedings to determine delinquency which may result in commitment to an institution in which the juvenile's freedom is curtailed, the child and his parents must be notified of the child's right to be represented by counsel retained by them, or if they are unable to afford counsel, that counsel will be appointed to represent the child. . . .

Appellants urge that the writ of *habeas corpus* should have been granted because of the denial of the rights of confrontation and cross-examination in

the Juvenile Court hearings, and because the privilege against self-incrimination was not observed. . . .

The privilege against self-incrimination is, of course, related to the question of the safeguards necessary to assure that admissions or confessions are reasonably trustworthy, that they are not the mere fruits of fear or coercion, but are reliable expressions of the truth. The roots of the privilege are, however, far deeper. They tap the basic stream of religious and political principle because the privilege reflects the limits of the individual's attornment to the state and—in a philosophical sense—insists upon the equality of the individual and the state. In other words, the privilege has a broader and deeper thrust than the rule which prevents the use of confessions which are the product of coercion because coercion is thought to carry with it the danger of unreliability. One of its purposes is to prevent the state, whether by force or by psychological domination, from overcoming the mind and will of the person under investigation and depriving him of the freedom to decide whether to assist the state in securing his conviction.

It would indeed be surprising if the privilege against self-incrimination were available to hardened criminals but not to children. The language of the Fifth Amendment, applicable to the States by operation of the Fourteenth Amendment, is unequivocal and without exception. And the scope of the privilege is comprehensive. . . .

Against the application to juveniles of the right to silence, it is argued that juvenile proceedings are "civil" and not "criminal," and therefore the privilege should not apply. It is true that the statement of the privilege in the Fifth Amendment, which is applicable to the States by reason of the Fourteenth Amendment, is that no person "shall be compelled in any criminal case to be a witness against himself." However, it is also clear that the availability of the privilege does not turn upon the type of proceeding in which its protection is invoked, but upon the nature of the statement or admission and the exposure which it invites. The privilege may, for example, be claimed in a civil or administrative proceeding, if the statement is or may be inculpatory.

It would be entirely unrealistic to carve out of the Fifth Amendment all statements by juveniles on the grounds that these cannot lead to "criminal" involvement. In the first place, juvenile proceedings to determine "delinquency," which may lead to commitment to a state institution, must be regarded as "criminal" for purposes of the privilege against self-incrimination. To hold otherwise would be to disregard substance because of the feeble enticement of the "civil" label-of-convenience which has been attached to juvenile proceedings. Indeed, in over half of the States, there is no even assurance that the juvenile will be kept in separate institutions, apart from adult "criminals." In those States juveniles may be placed in or transferred to adult penal institutions after having been found "delinquent" by a juvenile court. For this purpose, at least, commitment is a deprivation of liberty. It is incarceration against one's will, whether it is called "criminal" or "civil." And our Constitution guarantees that no person shall be "compelled" to be a witness against himself when he is threatened with deprivation of his liberty—a command which this Court has broadly applied and generously implemented in accordance with the teaching of the history of the privilege and its great office in mankind's battle for freedom. . . .

We conclude that the constitutional privilege against self-incrimination is applicable in the case of juveniles as it is with respect to adults. We appreciate that special problems may arise with respect to waiver of the privilege by or on behalf of children, and that there may well be some differences in technique—but not in principle—depending upon the age of the child and the presence and competence of parents. The participation of counsel will, of course, assist the police, Juvenile Courts and appellate tribunals in administering the privilege. If counsel was not present for some permissible reason when an admission was obtained, the greatest care must be taken to assure that the admission was voluntary, in the sense not only that it was not coerced or suggested, but also that it was not the product of ignorance of rights or of adolescent fantasy, fright or despair. . . .

Absent a valid confession adequate to support the determination of the Juvenile Court, confrontation and sworn testimony by witnesses available for cross-examination were not essential for a finding of "delinquency. . . ."

. . . We now hold that, absent a valid confession, a determination of delinquency and an order of commitment to a state institution cannot be sustained in the absence of sworn testimony subjected to the opportunity for cross-examination in accordance with our law and constitutional requirements.

Appellants urge that the Arizona statute is unconstitutional under the Due Process Clause because, as construed by its Supreme Court, "there is no right of appeal from a juvenile court order. . . ." The court held that there is no right to a transcript because there is no right to appeal and because the proceedings are confidential and any record must be destroyed after a prescribed period of time. Whether a transcript or other recording is made, it held, is a matter for the discretion of the juvenile court. . . .

As the present case illustrates, the consequences of failure to provide an appeal, to record the proceedings, or to make findings or state the grounds for the juvenile court's conclusion may be to throw a burden upon the machinery for *habeas corpus,* to saddle the reviewing process with the burden of attempting to reconstruct a record, and to impose upon the Juvenile Judge the unseemly duty of testifying under cross-examination as to the events that transpired in the hearings before him.

For the reasons stated, the judgment of the Supreme Court of Arizona is reversed and the cause remanded for further proceedings not inconsistent with this opinion.

It is so ordered.

Mr. Justice Black concurring. . . .

Mr. Justice White, concurring. . . .

Mr. Justice Harlan, concurring in part and dissenting in part. . . .

Mr. Justice Stewart, dissenting.

The Court today uses an obscure Arizona case as a vehicle to impose upon thousands of juvenile courts throughout the Nation restrictions that the Constitution made applicable to adversary criminal trials. I believe the Court's decision is wholly unsound as a matter of constitutional law, and sadly unwise as a matter of judicial policy.

Juvenile proceedings are not criminal trials. They are not civil trials. They are simply not adversary proceedings. Whether treating with a delinquent child, a neglected child, a defective child, or a dependent child, a juvenile proceeding's whole purpose and mission is the very opposite of the mission and purpose of a prosecution in a criminal court. The object of the one is correction of a condition. The object of the other is conviction and punishment for a criminal act.

In the last 70 years many dedicated men and women have devoted their professional lives to the enlightened task of bringing us out of the dark world of Charles Dickens in meeting our responsibilities to the child in our society. The result has been the creation in this century of a system of juvenile and family courts in each of the 50 States. There can be no denying that in many areas the performance of these agencies has fallen disappointingly short of the hopes and dreams of the courageous pioneers who first conceived them. For a variety of reasons, the reality has sometimes not even approached the ideal, and much remains to be accomplished in the administration of public juvenile and family agencies—in personnel, in planning, in financing, perhaps in the formulation of wholly new approaches.

I possess neither the specialized experience nor the expert knowledge to predict with any certainty where may lie the brightest hope for progress in dealing with the serious problems of juvenile delinquency. But I am certain that the answer does not lie in the Court's opinion in this case, which serves to convert a juvenile proceeding into a criminal prosecution. . . .

CHAPTER FIFTEEN

PERSONAL AUTONOMY AND THE CONSTITUTIONAL RIGHT OF PRIVACY

. . . [T]here is a sphere of action in which society, as distinguished from the individual, has, if any, only an indirect interest; comprehending all that portion of a person's life and conduct which affects only himself, or if it also affects others, only with their free, voluntary and undeceived consent and participation.

John Stuart Mill, *On Liberty* (1859)

INTRODUCTION

The constitutional right of privacy protects the individual from unwarranted government interference in intimate personal relationships or activities. As it has taken shape since the mid-1960s, the right of privacy includes the freedom of the individual to make fundamental choices involving sex, reproduction, family life, and other intimate personal relationships. Of the various constitutional rights addressed in this book, the right of privacy remains the most intensely disputed. The controversy stems in part from the absence of any specific reference to privacy in the Constitution. Some scholars and judges still adhere to Justice Hugo Black's view that a "right of privacy" cannot reasonably be inferred from the language of the original Constitution or any of its amendments. However, it is clear that this is a minority position in the 1990s. Among recent Supreme Court nominees, only Judge Robert Bork has categorically denied the existence of a right of privacy. For most Americans, the debate over privacy has less to do with competing theories of constitutional interpretation than with the profound implications of the privacy principle for divisive social and moral questions, such as abortion, gay rights, and euthanasia.

In *Roe v. Wade* (1973), the Supreme Court held that the right of privacy "is broad enough to encompass a woman's decision whether or not to terminate her pregnancy." As the ongoing protest against legal abortion makes clear, abortion is hardly an ordinary issue of public policy. Nor was *Roe v. Wade* a run-of-the-mill Supreme Court decision. Unlike most constitutional decisions, *Roe* aroused deep philosophical conflict and even deeper political and emotional turmoil. *Roe v. Wade* drew the Supreme Court into a firestorm of political controversy that continues unabated after two decades. This controversy has dominated public discussion of the Court, often eclipsing other important issues and likewise influencing the debate surrounding the Supreme Court nominations of David Souter and Clarence Thomas.

While abortion is the focal point of the debate over the right of privacy, the viability of the right of privacy is not based solely on the continued vitality of *Roe v. Wade*. Even if *Roe* were to be overturned, the right of privacy would still exist as an independent constitutional right, albeit somewhat circumscribed. The right of privacy is now well-established in both federal and state constitutional law and has application to numerous questions of public policy beyond abortion. This chapter examines some of the more salient ones.

Philosophical Foundations of the Right of Privacy

When the Supreme Court invoked the right of privacy to effectively legalize abortion within stated limits, it was giving expression to a sense of moral individualism deeply rooted in American culture. However, countervailing notions of traditional morality are also deeply ingrained in American society, as the relentless and widespread attacks on *Roe v. Wade* demonstrate. In no other area of constitutional law are individualism and traditional morality so sharply antagonistic as in the area of privacy rights.

The moral individualism underlying the constitutional right of privacy was conceived in the political liberalism of the Age of Enlightenment. This classical liberalism gained ascendancy in the nineteenth century. Today, it is most closely approximated by the philosophy of libertarianism, which holds that individual freedom is the highest good and that law should be interpreted to maximize the scope of liberty.

During and after the 1960s, the libertarian perspective became increasingly widespread among Americans, especially younger people. In the late 1960s and throughout the '70s, a large number of people began to question the authority of government to regulate the private lives of individuals in the name of traditional morality. In the libertarian view, the legitimate role of government is protection of individuals from one another, not from their own vices. Thus, libertarians often object to laws regulating sexual conduct, living arrangements, and the private use of drugs—even to laws mandating that motorcycle riders wear helmets. Perhaps the ultimate libertarian position is opposition to the criminal law against suicide. In the libertarian view, the individual has the right to make basic decisions regarding his or her own life—or death.

The countervailing position, which might be dubbed "classical conservatism," holds that individuals must often be protected against their own vices. Classical conservatives not only defend traditional morality but the embodiment of that morality in the law. On the contemporary Supreme Court, Justice Antonin Scalia has endorsed the classical conservative view of law and morality. In *Barnes v. Glen Theatre, Inc.* (1991) (the "nude dancing" decision discussed and reprinted in Chapter 11), Scalia wrote that

> Our society prohibits, and all human societies have prohibited, certain activities not because they harm others but because they are considered . . . immoral. In

American society, such prohibitions have included, for example, sadomasochism, cockfighting, bestiality, suicide, drug use, prostitution and sodomy. While there might be a great diversity of views on whether various of these prohibitions should exist, . . . there is no doubt that absent specific constitutional protection for the conduct involved, the Constitution does not prohibit them simply because they regulate "morality."

The debate over the constitutional right of privacy is ultimately a debate between two sharply divergent views of the law. In the libertarian view, the law exists to protect individuals from one another. In this view, morality is not in and of itself a legitimate basis for law. The classical conservative view, on the other hand, sees law and morality as inseparable and holds that the maintenance of societal morality is one of the essential functions of the legal system.

CONSTITUTIONAL FOUNDATIONS OF THE RIGHT OF PRIVACY

While libertarianism has roots in the liberalism of the Enlightenment, it is doubtful that any of the Framers of the Constitution were libertarians in the modern sense of the term. Certainly the Framers believed in individual freedom, but most did not conceive of freedom as including the right to flout traditional principles of conduct embodied in the common law. Yet the right of privacy, in essence the constitutionalization of libertarianism, has been "found" by the Supreme Court to emanate from various provisions of the Bill of Rights (see *Griswold v. Connecticut* [1965]).

Several provisions of the Bill of Rights were adopted to protect individuals from unreasonable invasions of privacy. The Third Amendment explicitly protects the privacy of the home in peacetime from soldiers seeking quarters. The Fourth Amendment protects individuals from unreasonable searches and seizures where they have a "reasonable expectation of privacy" (*Katz v. United States* [1967], Harlan, J., concurring). The Fifth Amendment prohibits compulsory self-incrimination, thus protecting the privacy of an accused individual's thoughts. The First Amendment ensures freedom of conscience in both political and religious matters, again recognizing the autonomy of the individual. Finally, the First Amendment's implicit guarantee of freedom of association protects one's right to choose one's friends, one's spouse, one's business partners. In *Griswold v. Connecticut* (1965), the Supreme Court interpreted these protections as embodying a right to be free of those government intrusions into the realm of intimate personal decisions.

Proponents of a constitutional right of privacy often cite the Ninth Amendment, which guarantees rights "retained by the people" even though they are not enumerated in the Constitution. Indeed, historically, the courts have recognized a variety of unenumerated constitutional rights. The right to marry, to choose one's spouse, to select an occupation, to travel freely within the country, and to enter into contracts are all examples of long-standing rights retained by the people although they are not explicitly provided for in the Constitution. They have achieved constitutional status by virtue of the fact that they are elements of the "liberty" protected by the Due Process Clauses of the Fifth and Fourteenth Amendments.

Dissenting in *Olmstead v. United States* (1928), Justice Louis Brandeis wrote:

> The makers of our Constitution undertook to secure conditions favorable to the pursuit of happiness. They recognized the significance of man's spiritual nature, of his feelings and his intellect. They knew that only a part of his pain, pleasure, and satisfactions of life are to be found in material things. They sought to protect Americans in their beliefs, their thoughts, their emotions and their sensations. They conferred, as against the Government, the right to be let alone—the most comprehensive of rights and the right most valued by civilized men.

These words were written by way of dissent in a case dealing with the scope of the Fourth Amendment's protection against wiretapping (see Chapter 14). Yet they may be interpreted as foreshadowing the modern right of privacy, which is, in essence, the "right to be let alone."

Substantive Due Process

To understand the emergence of the constitutional right of privacy, one must return to the era of economic due process (see Chapter 10). In a landmark decision in 1905, the Supreme Court interpreted the Due Process Clause of the Fourteenth Amendment broadly to impose a restriction on the power of state legislatures to engage in economic regulation. In *Lochner v. New York*, the Court held that the "liberty of contract" protected by the Fourteenth Amendment had been infringed when the state of New York adopted a law restricting the working hours of bakery employees. While *Lochner* and related decisions were concerned exclusively with the protection of individual property rights (see Chapter 10), they paved the way for the creation of the right of privacy by giving a substantive (as distinct from a strictly procedural) interpretation to the Due Process Clause of the Fourteenth Amendment. Under the "substantive due process" formula, courts can "discover" in the Fourteenth Amendment rights that are "fundamental" or "implicit in a scheme of ordered liberty." Again, the Ninth Amendment's recognition of rights "retained by the people" provides additional justification for the substantive interpretation of the Fourteenth Amendment.

In the first two decades of the twentieth century, substantive due process was by and large confined to the protection of economic liberties from government regulation. Just two months before the Court handed down its controversial decision in *Lochner,* it refused to find in the Due Process Clause a prohibition against compulsory vaccination laws (*Jacobson v. Massachusetts* [1905]). Nevertheless, Justice John M. Harlan's majority opinion did recognize that

> [t]here is, of course, a sphere within which the individual may assert the supremacy of his own will and rightfully dispute the authority of any human government, especially of any free government existing under a written constitution, to interfere with the exercise of that will.

For Justice Harlan and most of his brethren, the state's interest in promoting the public health through compulsory vaccination was superior to the individual "exercise of will." Nevertheless, in *Jacobson,* the Court suggested that the Four-teenth Amendment might protect certain noneconomic aspects of individual autonomy.

The expansion of substantive due process to include noneconomic rights took a quantum leap in 1923. In that year, the Court recognized that citizens have the right to study foreign languages in private schools, state statutes to the contrary notwithstanding (*Meyer v. Nebraska*). Two years later, the Court em-phasized the right to a private education by striking down an Oregon law that required parents to send their children to public schools (*Pierce v. Society of Sisters* [1925]).

PROCREATION AND BIRTH CONTROL

The slowly emerging right of privacy experienced a temporary setback in *Buck v. Bell* (1927). There, the Court refused to find in the Fourteenth Amend-ment an immunity against compulsory sterilization for mentally retarded per-sons. Carrie Buck, a young woman crassly characterized by the Court as "feeble minded," was committed to a state institution, where her mother was also con-fined. Pursuant to state law, the director of the institution sought to have Carrie Buck sterilized after she had given birth to a mentally retarded child. Carrie Buck's attorneys immediately challenged the constitutionality of the statute, but the Supreme Court, in an 8-to-1 decision, upheld the sterilization law. Writing for the Court, Justice Oliver Wendell Holmes, Jr. declared that the principle announced in *Jacobson v. Massachusetts* was "broad enough to cover cutting the Fallopian tubes." In one of his more memorable (and most gratuitous) lines, Holmes went on to write that "[t]hree generations of imbeciles are enough."

Although *Buck v. Bell* has never been formally overruled, it is unlikely that it would command a majority today. In 1942, the Court struck down a state law providing for the compulsory sterilization of criminals (*Skinner v. Oklahoma*). Although the decision was based on the Equal Protection Clause of the Four-teenth Amendment, rather than on substantive due process, *Skinner* in effect recognized a constitutional right of procreation. The Court characterized the right to procreate as "one of the basic civil rights of man." The Court's decisions in *Meyer v. Nebraska, Pierce v. Society of Sisters,* and *Skinner v. Oklahoma* paved the way for the landmark 1965 decision in *Griswold v. Connecticut* recognizing an independent constitutional right of privacy.

The Connecticut Birth Control Controversy

The *Griswold* case involved a challenge to an 1879 Connecticut law that made the sale and possession of birth control devices a misdemeanor. The law also forbade anyone from assisting, abetting, or counseling another in the use of birth control devices. In 1961, the Supreme Court voted 5 to 4 to dismiss a challenge to the Connecticut law (see *Poe v. Ullman,* reprinted in Chapter 4). The challenge stemmed not from a criminal prosecution but from a lawsuit brought by a married couple and their physician who complained of state interference in the doctor-patient relationship. Writing for a four-member plurality, Justice Felix Frankfurter said that there was no real "case or controversy" and that the issue was unripe for judicial review. Frankfurter alluded to a "tacit agreement" whereby the birth control law would no longer be enforced. In a forceful dissent, Justice William O. Douglas pointed out that an earlier criminal prosecution had effectively prevented birth control clinics from operating in the state. Douglas not only asserted that the case was properly before the Court but characterized the statute as "an invasion of the privacy implicit in a free society." Douglas's sharp dissent in *Poe v. Ullman* anticipated the Court's decision in *Griswold* four years later.

Estelle Griswold was the director of Planned Parenthood in Connecticut. Just three days after Planned Parenthood opened a clinic in New Haven, Griswold was arrested. Reportedly, she had given detectives a tour of the clinic, pointing out contraceptives that the clinic was dispensing. After a short trial, Griswold was convicted and fined one hundred dollars. As expected, the Connecticut courts upheld her conviction, rejecting the contention that the state law was unconstitutional. Also as expected, Griswold's attorneys filed a petition for certiorari in the U.S. Supreme Court. When the Court agreed to take the case, it was clear that the justices were going to rule on the constitutionality of the Connecticut law.

Griswold's attorneys argued that the birth control law infringed a right of privacy implicit in the Bill of Rights, as embodied in the concept of personal liberty protected by the Fourteenth Amendment. Moreover, they maintained that the Connecticut statute lacked a reasonable relationship to a legitimate legislative purpose. The state of Connecticut responded by emphasizing its broad police powers, arguing that the birth control law was a rational means of promoting the welfare of Connecticut's people. Interestingly, however, Connecticut's brief failed to state the particular legislative purpose behind the birth control law. Rather, the brief was designed chiefly to persuade the justices that they should not second-guess the wisdom or desirability of social legislation.

On June 7, 1965, the Supreme Court announced its decision striking down the Connecticut birth control law. The vote was 7 to 2. Justice Douglas was given the task of writing the majority opinion. After a disclaimer that "we do not sit as a super-legislature to determine the wisdom, need and propriety of laws...," Douglas proceeded to explain why, in his view, the Connecticut law ran afoul of the Constitution. As an advocate of "total incorporation" (see Chapter 9), Justice Douglas sought to identify an implicit right of privacy in the Bill of Rights, rather than in the vague notions of "liberty" that the Court had in the past attached to the Due Process Clause of the Fourteenth Amendment. In what has become frequently quoted language, Douglas asserted that

> specific guarantees in the Bill of Rights have penumbras, formed by emanations from those guarantees that help give them life and substance. Various guarantees create zones of privacy....

Justice Douglas reasoned that the explicit language of the Bill of Rights, specifically the First, Third, Fourth, Fifth, and Ninth Amendments, when considered along with their "emanations" and "penumbras" as defined by previous decisions of the Court, add up to a general, independent right of privacy. In

Douglas's view, this general right was infringed by the state of Connecticut when it outlawed birth control. In the sharpest language of the majority opinion, Douglas wrote:

> Would we allow the police to search the sacred precincts of marital bedrooms for telltale signs of the use of contraceptives? The very idea is repulsive to the notions of privacy surrounding the marriage relationship.

While the prospect of the police searching one's bedroom for evidence of contraception is no doubt repulsive to many, the question is whether the law allowing such a search is constitutional. Obviously, Justices John Harlan and Byron White, who voted to strike down the Connecticut law, were not altogether persuaded by Justice Douglas's discovery of a general right of privacy in the Bill of Rights. In their separate opinions concurring in the judgment, Harlan and White maintained that the Connecticut law infringed the "liberty" protected by the Fourteenth Amendment, a liberty that, in their view, transcends the particular protections of the Bill of Rights. In taking this course, Justices Harlan and White were not embarking on uncharted jurisprudential waters; they were merely using the substantive due process approach that had been employed in *Meyer v. Nebraska, Pierce v. Society of Sisters,* and the numerous cases in which the Court had used "liberty of contract" to invalidate economic legislation.

Dissenting sharply, Justice Black criticized what he perceived as a blatant attempt to amend the Constitution through loose interpretation:

> I realize that many good and able men have eloquently spoken . . . about the duty of this Court to keep the Constitution in tune with the times. The idea is that the Constitution must be changed from time to time and that this Court is charged with a duty to make those changes. For myself, I must with all deference reject that philosophy. The Constitution makers knew the need for change and provided for it. Amendments . . . can be submitted to the people . . . for ratification. That method of change was good enough for our Fathers, and being somewhat old-fashioned I must add that it is good enough for me.

Justice Black never hesitated to urge invalidation of a legislative act if he believed it ran afoul of a specific provision of the Constitution. Consequently, he and Douglas often found themselves voting together in civil liberties cases, thus earning the label "judicial activists." But, as one who preferred to adhere strictly to the text of the Constitution, Black refused in *Griswold* to go along with what he regarded as a discredited approach to constitutional interpretation:

> I cannot rely on the Due Process Clause or the Ninth Amendment or any mysterious and uncertain natural law concept as a reason for striking down this state law. . . . I had thought that we had laid that formula, as a means of striking down state legislation, to rest once and for all. . . .

The debate over modes of constitutional interpretation is certainly a legitimate one. Cogent jurisprudential arguments can be made for and against the Court's decision in *Griswold.* However, it must be recognized that the Court's decision was not based on a radical departure from traditional jurisprudence, as a few extreme critics have claimed. Rather, there is ample precedent for the broad interpretation of the Constitution in general (for example, *Marbury v. Madison*), and the substantive due process formula in particular, in the rich history of the Court's constitutional decision making.

Although *Griswold* was sharply criticized by commentators who shared Justice Black's view of constitutional interpretation and by a few staunch social conservatives, the Court's decision was not subjected to the kind of public outcry occasioned by the desegregation decisions of the 1950s or the school prayer decisions of the early 1960s. Obviously, the average person is not particularly concerned with the legal aspects of a Supreme Court decision; he or she is much more likely to focus on the Court's substantive policy output. As a matter of public policy, *Griswold* was quite well-received.

A Gallup Poll conducted in 1965 found that 81 percent of the American public agreed with the statement that "birth control information should be available to anyone who wants it." There can be little doubt that changing societal attitudes about sex, procreation, and contraception had more to do with the Court's decision in *Griswold* than did "emanations" from the Bill of Rights!

Beyond the Marital Bedroom

In the *Griswold* case, the Court was careful to invalidate the Connecticut law only insofar as it invaded marital privacy, thus leaving open the question of whether states could prohibit the use of birth control devices by unmarried persons. In *Eisenstadt v. Baird* (1972), the Court faced a challenge to a Massachusetts law that prohibited unmarried persons from obtaining and using contraceptives. William Baird, a former medical student, was arrested after he delivered a lecture on birth control at Boston University during which he provided some contraceptive foam to a female student. In reversing his conviction and striking down the Massachusetts law, the Court established the right of privacy as an individual right, not a right enjoyed solely by married couples. As Justice William Brennan's opinion for the Court stated,

> [t]he marital couple is not an independent entity with a mind and heart of its own, but an association of two individuals each with separate intellectual and emotional makeup. If the right of privacy means anything, it is the right of the individual, married or single, to be free from unwarranted governmental intrusion into matters so fundamentally affecting a person as the decision whether or not to beget a child.

Having thus articulated an independent right of privacy protecting individual decisions in the area of sex and procreation, *Eisenstadt v. Baird* paved the way for the most controversial decision the Supreme Court was to make during the Chief Justiceship of Warren Burger: *Roe v. Wade.*

THE ABORTION CONTROVERSY

Norma McCorvey, also known as Jane Roe, was a twenty-five-year-old unmarried Texas woman who was faced with an unwanted pregnancy resulting from an alleged gang rape that she later admitted never occurred. After her doctor

Norma McCorvey,
a.k.a. "Jane Roe"

informed her that abortion was illegal in Texas, she went to see an attorney. That
attorney, Linda Coffee, introduced McCorvey to Sarah Weddington, a young
woman just out of law school, who ultimately argued the case before the Supreme Court. Weddington expressed her view that the Constitution allows a
woman to control her own body, including the decision to terminate an unwanted pregnancy. Shortly thereafter, Coffee and Weddington filed suit in federal
district court against Dallas District Attorney Henry Wade, seeking to enjoin him
from enforcing what was claimed to be an unconstitutional law. The suit was
filed as a class action, that is, not only on behalf of Jane Roe but on behalf of all
women "similarly situated." The district court declared the Texas law unconstitutional but refused to issue the injunction, invoking the doctrine of abstention
(see Chapter 4). As permitted in cases of this kind, Jane Roe appealed directly to
the Supreme Court.

The Supreme Court Decides *Roe v. Wade*

On January 22, 1973, the Supreme Court handed down a 7-to-2 decision striking
down the Texas law. Justice Harry A. Blackmun wrote the majority opinion. After
determining that the case was properly before the Court, Blackmun reviewed
prior decisions on the right of privacy. In what is perhaps the best known
statement from his opinion in *Roe,* Blackmun concluded that right of privacy "is
broad enough to encompass a woman's decision whether or not to terminate
her pregnancy." Yet Blackmun's analysis did not end with this pronouncement,
because the right of privacy, like all constitutional rights, may be limited if there
is a sufficiently strong justification by the state. Specifically, because the Court

dubbed the right of privacy "fundamental," the state of Texas had to demonstrate a "compelling interest" to justify regulating or prohibiting abortion. The Court recognized a compelling interest in protecting maternal health that justifies "reasonable" state regulations of abortions performed after the first trimester of pregnancy. However, the state of Texas sought not only to regulate but also to proscribe abortion altogether and claimed a compelling state interest in protecting unborn human life. The Court recognized this interest as legitimate but held that it does not become compelling until that point in pregnancy when the fetus becomes "viable," that is, capable of "meaningful life outside the mother's womb." Beyond the point of viability, according to the Court, the state may prohibit abortion, except in cases where it is necessary to preserve the life or health of the mother.

The Court summarily rejected the argument that a fetus is a "person" as that term is used in the Constitution and thus possessed of a right to life, holding that the term "has application only postnatally." If a fetus is regarded as a person from the point of conception, then any abortion is certainly homicide. If that were the case, then states could not allow abortions even in cases of rape or where the pregnancy endangers the life of the mother (as the Texas law challenged in *Roe* allowed). Nor would intrauterine devices or "morning after" pills, both of which prevent implantation after conception, be permissible. Like abortion, these forms of birth control, which are regarded by most as morally acceptable, would be tantamount to murder. Clearly, the Court was not inclined to make such a pronouncement. Nor was it prepared to assert that the woman's right to obtain an abortion is absolute: "that she is entitled to terminate at whatever time, in whatever way and for whatever reason she alone chooses. . . ." The Court tried to steer a middle course, to accommodate what it regarded as legitimate interests on both sides of the issue.

Roe v. Wade was the product of sharp conflict, bargaining, and compromise within the Supreme Court. Although the Court's decision attempted to strike a reasonable balance between the state's interest in protecting unborn life and a woman's interest in controlling her own body, the abortion decision was not viewed by the "prolife" forces as an acceptable compromise. The hostile reaction to *Roe v. Wade* was immediate and intense. Justices of the Supreme Court, especially Harry Blackmun, received hate mail and even death threats. The 1980s saw frequent public demonstrations, harassment of women entering abortion clinics, and even the occasional bombing of such facilities. Militant confrontation between prolife and prochoice forces continues in the 1990s.

Since the *Roe* decision came down in 1973, public opinion has remained sharply divided on the abortion question. This sharp division was reflected in the U.S. Senate, which, in 1983, defeated by one vote a proposed constitutional amendment that would have provided that "[t]he right to an abortion is not secured by this Constitution." While it is difficult to say with certainty which side of the issue is favored by public opinion, it was clear until recently, that the antiabortion forces manifest greater intensity in their opposition to abortion than the prochoice forces do in their support. In politics, intensity may count for as much as numbers. In constitutional law, neither is supposed to matter; but there is considerable evidence that both do!

Regulation of Abortion in the Wake of *Roe v. Wade*

In the wake of *Roe v. Wade,* many state and local governments enacted regulations governing the performance of abortions. As previously noted, the Court in *Roe* allowed for "reasonable" regulation of abortions to effectuate the state's legitimate interest in protecting maternal health. However, many state statutes and local ordinances affecting abortion were not intended to promote maternal health at all but to deter women from obtaining abortions.

In *Planned Parenthood of Central Missouri v. Danforth* (1976), the Court struck down a Missouri law that required minors to obtain the consent of their husbands or parents before obtaining an abortion. Three years later, in *Bellotti v. Baird* (1979), the Court struck down a similar law passed by the state of Massachusetts. This law required an unmarried pregnant minor to obtain parental consent for an abortion or, if parental consent was not given, to obtain authorization from a judge who was to determine whether the abortion was in the minor's best interest. Taken together, the decisions in *Bellotti* and *Danforth* emphasized the personal nature of the abortion decision. Other parties, whether one's spouse, parents, or the state, cannot be given a veto over the exercise of one's constitutional rights.

In 1983, the Court appeared to back away from the strong position taken in *Bellotti* and *Danforth.* In *Planned Parenthood v. Ashcroft,* the Court upheld a Missouri law that required parental consent for "unemancipated" minors but apparently only because the law provided a mechanism whereby exceptionally mature minors could obtain abortions by seeking judicial intervention.

The same day *Ashcroft* came down, the Court announced its decision in *Akron v. Akron Center for Reproductive Health* (1983). In this case, the Court struck down a city ordinance that, in addition to requiring parental consent for minors' abortions, required: (a) that all abortions be performed in hospitals; (b) a twenty-four-hour waiting period before abortions could be performed; (c) that physicians make certain specified statements to the woman seeking abortion to ensure that her decision is truly an informed one; and (d) that all fetal remains be disposed of in a manner that is both humane and sanitary. The Court found that these requirements imposed significant burdens on a woman's exercise of her constitutional rights without substantially furthering the state's legitimate interests. The "humane and sanitary" disposal requirement was invalidated as "impermissibly vague" in obliquely suggesting an intention on the part of the city to "mandate some sort of 'decent burial' of the embryo at the earliest stages of formation."

Restrictions on Public Funding of Abortions

One of the more successful legislative assaults on abortion involves the exemption of abortions not deemed to be medically necessary from medical welfare programs. As a matter of public policy, this exemption is highly questionable. For one thing, it creates a double standard for rich and poor. Moreover, it seems likely to increase the numbers of future dependents on food stamps, Aid to Families with Dependent Children, and Medicaid. However, as the Supreme

The Constitution in action: A "pro-life" demonstration

Court has frequently observed, the wisdom of a particular public policy and the constitutionality thereof are separate questions. In *Maher v. Roe* (1977), the Court voted 6 to 3 to uphold a Connecticut welfare regulation that denied Medicaid benefits to indigent women seeking to have abortions, unless their attending physicians certified their abortions as "medically necessary." The Court's decision was based on the "new due process-equal protection" analysis developed by the Court over the last two decades (see Chapter 16). In a nutshell, the Court held that the denial of Medicaid benefits to poor women seeking elective abortions neither discriminated against a "suspect class" of persons nor unduly burdened the exercise of fundamental rights. Therefore, the Court judged the Connecticut regulation to be permissible under both the Equal Protection and Due Process Clauses of the Fourteenth Amendment.

Three years later, in *Harris v. McRae* (1980), the Court upheld a provision of federal law, commonly known as the Hyde Amendment, forbidding the use of federal funds to support nontherapeutic abortions. Writing for a sharply divided Court, Justice Potter Stewart concluded that

> [i]t simply does not follow that a woman's freedom of choice carries with it a constitutional entitlement to the financial resources to avail herself of the full range of protected choices. . . . Although government may not place obstacles in the path of a woman's exercise of her freedom of choice, it need not remove those not of its own creation. Indigency falls in the latter category.

The Hyde Amendment restricted federal funding of abortions, leaving states to decide whether to impose similar restrictions on the use of state funds. As noted, the U.S. Supreme Court upheld Connecticut's restriction on abortion funding in *Maher v. Roe* (1977). Yet several state supreme courts have invalidated similar restrictions under their state constitutions (see, for example, *Committee to Defend Reproductive Rights v. Myers* [Cal. S.Ct. 1981]; *Moe v. Secretary of Administration* [Mass. S.Jud.Ct. 1981]; *Right to Choose v. Byrne* [N.J. S.Ct. 1982]).

Eroding Support for *Roe v. Wade* on the Supreme Court

By the early 1980s, the bloc of justices supportive of *Roe v. Wade* had begun to erode. In the *Akron Center* decision of 1983, the Court had explicitly reaffirmed *Roe* but by one less vote than the *Roe* majority of 1973. While Potter Stewart had voted with the majority in *Roe,* his successor on the Court, Sandra Day O'Connor, dissented in the *Akron* case. In one of her most significant early opinions, Justice O'Connor expressed considerable dissatisfaction with the "trimester framework" adopted by the Court in *Roe v. Wade.* O'Connor's *Akron* dissent went well beyond a critique of the particular formulation adopted by the Court in *Roe,* however. Her opinion suggested that a state has a sufficiently compelling interest in protecting potential life to allow it to ban abortion at any stage of pregnancy. O'Connor's apparent dissent from the *Roe* decision did not necessarily indicate that she opposed legalized abortion. It did indicate that O'Connor believed that the state legislature (not a court of law) is the proper forum for resolving the abortion issue. Again, quoting from her dissent in *Akron v. Akron Center,* "[i]t is . . . difficult to believe that this Court, without the resources available to those bodies entrusted with making legislative choices, believes itself competent to make these inquiries. . . ."

Substantial support exists, even among those who favor some form of legalized abortion, for the position adopted by Justice O'Connor. Some would argue that the question of abortion is simply not one that courts should decide. These critics would call for judicial restraint, for deference to the legislative judgment. While many state legislators have criticized the Supreme Court for usurping the role of the legislature in deciding *Roe v. Wade,* others have expressed relief that the judiciary has "taken the heat" on the abortion issue. Few legislators relish the prospect of voting on the abortion question. On both sides of the issue are powerful interest groups, and a middle ground on abortion is difficult to locate, much less defend.

The Supreme Court reaffirmed *Roe v. Wade* again in *Thornburgh v. American College of Obstetricians and Gynecologists* (1986). However, in *Thornburgh*, the vote in favor of a constitutional right to abortion was 5 to 4, because Chief Justice Burger switched sides and joined the dissenters. Although Burger retired after the 1985 term, his departure did not strengthen the position of *Roe v. Wade*. President Ronald Reagan elevated Associate Justice William Rehnquist to the position of chief justice and appointed Antonin Scalia, a conservative, to fill the vacancy.

In 1987, it appeared that the opponents of legalized abortion were only one vote away from overturning *Roe v. Wade*. In that year, Justice Lewis Powell, a member of the *Roe* majority, retired from the Court. It looked as if the Court would be divided 4 to 4 on the abortion issue, possibly making the next appointee to the Court the swing vote on whether to overrule *Roe v. Wade*. To a great extent, this fact explains the furor surrounding President Reagan's nomination of conservative federal judge Robert Bork to fill the vacancy left by Justice Powell. A well-known critic of *Roe* and of the right of privacy generally, Bork entered a firestorm of political controversy when he appeared before the Senate Judiciary Committee. The Senate, controlled by the Democrats, ultimately rejected Bork, in no small measure due to his stand on the right of privacy. Eventually, the Senate confirmed Reagan's nomination of another federal judge, Anthony Kennedy. In his confirmation hearing, Kennedy was asked repeatedly about his views on abortion. He replied, "If I had a . . . fixed view . . . I might be obliged to disclose that to you. I don't have such a view." The nation would have to wait two years for Kennedy to register his opinion in the abortion debate.

The Webster Decision

Without question, the most significant abortion case of the 1980s was *Webster v. Reproductive Health Services* (1989). Many thought the *Webster* case would be the one in which the Supreme Court would overturn *Roe v. Wade*. Those who favored such an outcome were disappointed by the decision. Yet those who supported legalized abortion found cause for alarm in what they perceived as a significant departure from the philosophy of *Roe*.

The *Webster* case involved a challenge to a Missouri statute containing a number of restrictions on abortions. Most worrisome from the prochoice perspective was the statement in the preamble of the law that "the life of each human being begins at conception." In its various provisions, the law forbade state employees from performing, assisting in, or counseling women to have abortions. It also prohibited the use of any state facilities for these purposes. Finally, it required all doctors who would perform abortions to conduct viability tests on fetuses at or beyond twenty weeks' gestation.

The Supreme Court, splitting 5 to 4, sustained the constitutionality of the Missouri statute. Yet in deciding the issues in *Webster*, the Supreme Court could not agree on a majority opinion. A plurality (Chief Justice Rehnquist and Associate Justices White, Kennedy, and O'Connor) expressed the view that the legislation could be sustained without overruling *Roe v. Wade*. In her separate concurrence, Justice O'Connor stressed the "fundamental rule of judicial restraint," which dictates that courts not decide major issues unless absolutely necessary. Only Justice Scalia, in a separate concurrence, called for the explicit overruling of *Roe* and chided his colleagues in the majority for not facing the issue squarely: "Of the four courses we might have chosen today—to reaffirm *Roe,* to overrule it explicitly, to overrule it *sub silentio,* or to avoid the question— the last is the least responsible." Justice Blackmun, the author of the Court's opinion in *Roe v. Wade,* accused the plurality of undermining *Roe:*

> With feigned restraint, the plurality announces that its analysis leaves *Roe* "undis-
> turbed," albeit "modif[ied] and narrow[ed]." *** But this disclaimer is totally mean-
> ingless. The plurality opinion is filled with winks, and nods, and knowing glances
> to those who would do away with *Roe* explicitly, but turns a stone face to anyone
> in search of what the plurality conceives as the scope of a woman's right under the
> Due Process Clause to terminate a pregnancy free from the coercive and brooding
> influence of the State.

Rust v. Sullivan: Restricting Information about Abortion

Supporters of legalized abortion were dealt another setback during the spring of 1991. In *Rust v. Sullivan,* the Supreme Court upheld a federal regulation that barred birth control clinics that received federal funds from providing information about abortion services to their clients. The regulation had been imposed in 1987 by the Department of Health and Human Services (HHS) at the direction of the Reagan administration, which opposed legalized abortion. The Supreme Court found the regulation to be a legitimate condition imposed on the receipt of financial assistance from the government. In the Court's view, the regulation was neither an invasion of privacy rights nor of freedom of speech, as plaintiffs in the lawsuit alleged. Congress, with broad public support, passed a measure designed to overturn the HHS regulation. However, this act was vetoed by President George Bush, and Congress was unable to muster the two-thirds vote necessary to override the veto.

The Last Gasp of *Roe v. Wade?*

In *Rust v. Sullivan,* as in the *Webster* decision two years earlier, the Court did not face squarely the question of whether *Roe v. Wade* should be maintained as the law of the land. Yet these decisions did send a strong signal that the Court was prepared to tolerate greater restrictions on legalized abortion. On January 21, 1992, on the eve of the nineteenth anniversary of its landmark decision in *Roe v. Wade,* the Supreme Court announced that it would hear a case challenging a Pennsylvania law that contained a series of restrictions on abortion (*Planned Parenthood v. Casey* [1992]). Among other things, the law required spousal notification, parental consent in cases of minors, and a twenty-four-hour waiting period before an abortion could be performed. Identical requirements had been declared invalid by the Supreme Court in previous decisions, but the Third Circuit Court of Appeals in Philadelphia upheld most of the provisions of the Pennsylvania statute. The appellate court based its ruling largely on the Supreme Court's 1989 *Webster* decision, which it interpreted as a significant retreat from the "strict scrutiny" to which abortion regulations had been subjected.

On April 22, 1992, the Supreme Court heard oral arguments in *Planned Parenthood v. Casey.* Ernest Preate, Jr., attorney general of Pennsylvania, defended the constitutionality of the statute, contending, among other things, that "*Roe* did not establish an absolute right to abortion on demand, but rather a limited right subject to reasonable State regulations. . . ." Attacking the statute, Kathryn Kolbert, counsel for the American Civil Liberties Union, characterized Pennsylvania's regulations not only as unreasonable but as "cruel and oppressive." U.S. Solicitor General Kenneth W. Starr, speaking on behalf of the Bush administration, urged the Court to abandon the "compelling state interest" test and adopt a more lenient "rational basis test" for determining the constitutionality of statutes in this area. When asked by Justice White whether the adoption of such a test would lead to a conclusion that the Pennsylvania law should be upheld, Starr replied, "Exactly."

The Supreme Court handed down its much anticipated decision in *Planned Parenthood v. Casey* on June 29, 1992, the last day of the Court's 1991 term (the decision is reprinted in Appendix E). To the surprise of many observers, the Court reaffirmed by a 5-to-4 vote the essential holding in *Roe v. Wade* that the constitutional right of privacy is broad enough to include a woman's decision to terminate her pregnancy. The Court was highly fragmented, however, producing five opinions. Two justices, Blackmun and Stevens, took the position that *Roe v. Wade* should be reaffirmed and that all of the challenged provisions of the Pennsylvania statute should be declared invalid. Four justices, Rehnquist, Scalia, White, and Thomas, took the view that *Roe* should be overruled and all of the Pennsylvania restrictions upheld. Adopting an extremely unusual method of presentation underscoring the gravity of the case, Justices O'Connor, Kennedy, and Souter jointly authored the controlling opinion of the Court. This lengthy joint opinion thoroughly reexamined *Roe v. Wade,* its underlying rationale and formulation, and the line of cases it spawned. While joining Justices Blackmun and Stevens in explicitly reaffirming *Roe,* the joint opinion abandoned the trimester framework and declared a new "undue burden" test for judging regulations of abortion. Applying this test, the joint opinion upheld the parental consent, waiting period, and record-keeping and reporting provisions but invalidated the spousal notification requirement.

The *Casey* decision was greeted with dismay and derision from both prolife and prochoice groups. Prochoice groups expressed alarm that the Court was willing to overturn recent precedent (*Akron v. Akron Center for Reproductive Health* [1983]; *Thornburgh v. American College of Obstetricians and Gynecologists* [1986]) and uphold Pennsylvania's restrictions on abortion. Prolife advocates were disappointed that two Reagan appointees (Kennedy and O'Connor) and one Bush appointee (Souter) voted to reaffirm *Roe v. Wade.*

Although *Planned Parenthood v. Casey* reaffirmed the essential holding of *Roe v. Wade,* it is likely that the Court will revisit this issue in the near future.

In their separate opinions in *Casey,* Chief Justice Rehnquist and Justice Scalia, supported by Justices White and Thomas, made it clear that four members of the Court are fully prepared to overrule *Roe v. Wade.* And Justice Blackmun, who was eighty-three at the time of the *Casey* decision, gave notice that he could not remain on the Court indefinitely. On the other hand, the election of Bill Clinton to the presidency in 1992 appeared to reverse the momentum for overruling *Roe.*

Even if the Court were to overrule *Roe v. Wade,* this would by no means result in the immediate recriminalization of abortion. If *Roe* is overruled, states will be free, just as they were prior to 1973, to determine their own policies with respect to abortion. Undoubtedly, some states would move to ban abortion altogether, while others would opt for continued broad availability of abortions. To those who see abortion as a "fundamental right," as well to those who see it as a fundamental wrong, the patchwork of state policies that would follow on overturning of *Roe* would be unacceptable. Many Americans, not comfortable with either extreme, believe that state legislatures ought to be permitted to experiment with various policies in an effort to achieve a workable compromise on this, the toughest social and moral issue of our time.

The principle of **judicial federalism** has tremendous significance for the abortion issue. Even in the absence of *Roe v. Wade,* state courts would be free to determine whether restrictions on abortion violate relevant provisions of their state constitutions. It is quite conceivable that some state supreme courts would take this position. For example, Florida is one of four states whose constitutions contain explicit recognition of the right of privacy (the others are Alaska, California, and Montana). The Florida Supreme Court has said that "[s]ince the people of this state exercised their prerogative and enacted an

The Constitution in action: A "pro-choice" demonstration

amendment to the Florida Constitution which expressly and succinctly provides for a strong right of privacy. . . , it can only be concluded that the right is much broader in scope than that of the federal constitution" (*Winfield v. Division of Pari-Mutuel Wagering* [Fla. S.Ct. 1985]). That court has also indicated quite clearly that a woman's right to choose abortion is protected by the privacy amendment to the state constitution (see *In re T.W.* [Fla. S.Ct. 1989]). Thus, even if the Supreme Court were to overturn *Roe v. Wade,* it would not *ipso facto* return the abortion issue to the exclusive domain of the state legislatures.

The abortion issue is *the* constitutional question of our time. But it is far more complex than most observers of American law and politics realize, going well beyond the domain of the U.S. Supreme Court and the fate of *Roe v. Wade.* It will be many years before this question is finally resolved.

THE RIGHT OF PRIVACY AND LIVING ARRANGEMENTS

While Supreme Court decisions in the area of reproductive freedom receive most of the public attention, the Court's decisions applying the constitutional right of privacy are by no means confined to contraception and abortion. The right of privacy has also been applied in reviewing city ordinances governing residential occupancy. In *Belle Terre v. Boraas* (1974), the Supreme Court upheld a village ordinance that limited residential land use to one-family dwellings. A couple who had leased a house to six unrelated college students challenged the law on the ground that it "trenche[d] on the newcomers' rights of privacy." The Court, adopting the traditional "rational basis test," found the ordinance to be a valid exercise of the police power. Justice Thurgood Marshall dissented, maintaining that fundamental rights of privacy and association were infringed and that the village failed to demonstrate a compelling justification for this infringement.

In *Moore v. City of East Cleveland* (1977), the Court struck down an ordinance that limited the occupancy of residences to members of single families. However, the East Cleveland ordinance defined "family" in such a way as to prohibit a grandmother from cohabiting with her two grandsons. Distinguishing the ordinance from the one upheld in *Belle Terre,* which primarily affected unrelated individuals, the Court stressed the "freedom of choice in matters of marriage and family life."

> Our decisions teach that the Constitution protects the sanctity of the family precisely because the institution of the family is deeply rooted in our history and tradition. [Ours] is by no means a tradition limited to respect for [the] nuclear family. The tradition of uncles, aunts, cousins, and especially grandparents sharing a household along with parents and children has roots equally venerable and equally deserving of constitutional recognition.

In a rather caustic concurrence, Justice Brennan noted that "in today's America, the nuclear family is the pattern so often found in much of white suburbia" but that "the Constitution cannot tolerate the imposition by government upon the rest of us of white suburbia's preference in patterns of family living."

PRIVACY AND GAY RIGHTS

In *Eisenstadt v. Baird* (1972), the Supreme Court tacitly acknowledged the right of an unmarried adult to engage in heterosexual activity. If this right is based on the premise that one may decide what to do with his or her own body without interference by the state, how can laws that prohibit private, consensual homosexual conduct be justified? What is the compelling interest on the part of the state that could be advanced to justify such prohibitions? The question has been raised in federal court. In *Doe v. Commonwealth's Attorney* (1976), the Supreme Court summarily affirmed a federal district court decision that upheld Virginia's antisodomy law. The district court, dividing 2 to 1, cited Justice Harlan's dissent in the 1961 case of *Poe v. Ullman,* which, although supportive of sexual privacy within marriage, suggested that homosexual conduct could be prosecuted even if practiced privately. The Supreme Court, in refusing to hear the appeal in *Doe v. Commonwealth's Attorney,* in effect endorsed Justice Harlan's position.

In *Bowers v. Hardwick* (1986), the Supreme Court reached the merits of a case challenging the application of Georgia's sodomy law to homosexual activity. Michael Hardwick, an admitted homosexual, was charged with committing sodomy with a consenting male adult in the privacy of his home. Although the state prosecutor decided not to take the case to the grand jury, Hardwick brought suit in federal court, seeking a declaration that the statute was unconstitutional. The district court dismissed the case, but the appeals court reversed, remanding the suit for trial. The Supreme Court granted the state's petition for certiorari and reversed the court of appeals.

In arguing his case before the Supreme Court, Hardwick relied on *Griswold v. Connecticut* and *Roe v. Wade,* as well as on the Court's 1969 decision in *Stanley v. Georgia.* In *Stanley,* the Court held that the First Amendment prohibits

A "gay rights" march in San Francisco

a state from punishing a person merely for the private possession of obscene materials. Although ostensibly a First Amendment case, the *Stanley* decision suggested that the home was a sanctuary from prosecution for acts that might well be criminal outside the home.

Dividing 5 to 4 in *Hardwick,* the Court upheld the Georgia law, refusing to recognize "a fundamental right to engage in homosexual sodomy." Writing for the Court, Justice White stressed the traditional legal and moral prohibitions against sodomy. Responding to the libertarian argument that the state has no right to legislate solely on the basis of morality, White wrote that "law . . . is constantly based on notions of morality, and if all laws representing essentially moral choices are to be invalidated. . . , the Courts will be very busy indeed."

Dissenting, Justice Blackmun disputed the Court's characterization of the issue. For Blackmun and three of his colleagues, the case was not about a "fundamental right to engage in homosexual sodomy" but the more general right of an adult, homosexual or heterosexual, to engage in consensual sexual acts with another adult. Striking a libertarian chord, Justice John Paul Stevens wrote that "the fact that the governing majority in a State has traditionally viewed a practice as immoral is not a sufficient reason for upholding a law prohibiting the practice. . . ."

Whether the Supreme Court would uphold a sodomy law as applied to heterosexual activity remains to be seen. If the Supreme Court were to strike down sodomy laws as applied to married couples, there would probably be little criticism of the Court. If, however, the Court were to invalidate sodomy laws as applied to unmarried persons, whether heterosexual or homosexual, then questions might be raised regarding the constitutionality of laws against prostitution, incest, and polygamy. In *Hardwick,* Justice White averred that the Court was "reluctant to start down that road."

Interestingly, retired Supreme Court Justice Lewis Powell, one of the members of the *Hardwick* majority, has expressed reservations about his vote in that case. In talking to a group of law students at New York University in October 1990, Justice Powell said, "I think I probably made a mistake in that one." In a subsequent interview, Powell said that the case was a "close call" and that his decision to support the majority was based in part on the fact that the sodomy law had been largely unenforced. Powell minimized the importance of the case, referring to it as "frivolous" and suggesting that it had been filed "just to see what the court would do . . ." (*Washington Post,* 26 October 1990, p. A-3).

OTHER "VICTIMLESS CRIMES"

Controversy has long surrounded the so-called victimless crimes of gambling, use of "recreational" drugs, prostitution, and so forth. Libertarians argue that the state has no business criminalizing conduct where no individual claims to have been injured. Individuals charged with such offenses have some times invoked the right of privacy by way of defense.

The Private Use of "Recreational" Drugs

In a widely publicized decision in 1975, *Ravin v. State,* the Alaska Supreme Court held that the right of privacy under both the federal and Alaska constitutions was broad enough to encompass the right to possess marijuana for personal use. In its opinion, the court noted the strong libertarian orientation of Alaskans. To date, the Alaska Supreme Court decision has not been emulated by the federal courts or by the courts of other states. Of course, even if the U.S. Supreme Court were to rule that the right of privacy under the Constitution did not protect the private use of marijuana, the Alaska decision would still be valid on independent state constitutional grounds. The Alaska Supreme Court is the authoritative interpreter of the Alaska Constitution. Interestingly, the Alaska Constitution contains an explicit right of privacy, unlike the U.S. Constitution and the constitutions of most states. Of course, this explicit right of privacy did not prevent Alaska voters in 1990 from approving a constitutional amendment in effect overruling *Ravin v. State.* Like the U.S. Supreme Court, a state supreme court is the final authority on matters of constitutional interpretation unless and until the constitution is amended. In 1990, amidst the widespread public concern over the problem of drug abuse, Alaskans decided through a referendum that their state constitution should not condone even the private use of illicit drugs.

Helmet and Seat Belt Laws

Another application of the right of privacy is in the area of safety laws, as exemplified by laws requiring motorcyclists to wear protective helmets and drivers to wear seat belts. Again, the libertarian thesis would be that the government has no right to protect the individual from him- or herself. In *State v. Albertson* (1970), the Idaho Supreme Court rejected a privacy-based challenge to that state's motorcycle helmet law, citing an important public safety interest. In all likelihood, most state courts would find sufficient public safety interests to uphold helmet laws, as well as mandatory seat belt laws.

REFUSAL OF MEDICAL TREATMENT AND THE "RIGHT TO DIE"

Since the mid-1970s, the right of privacy has been successfully asserted as a basis for refusing medical treatment. For example, in *Superintendent of Belchertown State School v. Saikewicz* (Mass. 1977), the Massachusetts Supreme Judicial Court permitted the guardian of an elderly, retarded man to assert his ward's right of privacy and refuse chemotherapy treatment for the elderly man's leukemia. Under the right of privacy, courts have also authorized the discontinuation of artificial means of life support, even if it results in the immediate death of the patient. For example, in the case of *Guardianship of Andrew Barry* (1984), a Florida appellate court allowed the removal of a respirator that was maintaining the life of a comatose infant. Andrew Barry was one of twins, the other of whom died at birth. Andrew had a serious brain defect that kept him comatose and unable to breathe without mechanical assistance. After it became clear that

Andrew would never achieve a "sapient existence" and would spend his life on the ventilator, his parents asked the hospital to remove the machine. Not surprisingly, the hospital refused to do so without a court order.

The Karen Quinlan Case

In both *Saikewicz* and *Barry*, courts relied on the doctrine of "substituted judgment" whereby legal guardians are permitted to exercise the rights of persons under their authority. The best known case involving the doctrine of substituted judgment in relation to the so-called right to die is *In re Quinlan* (N.J. 1976). Karen Quinlan was a healthy young woman who became permanently comatose after she ingested large quantities of drugs and alcohol. In this condition, she was unable to maintain normal breathing without a ventilator. After it became clear that Karen Quinlan would not regain consciousness, her parents asked her physicians to remove the respirator. The physicians refused, no doubt concerned about possible criminal prosecution or civil liability. The Quinlans went to court and obtained an order allowing removal of the life-support machine. According to the New Jersey Supreme Court, the right of privacy was "broad enough to encompass [Karen Quinlan's] decision to decline medical treatment under certain circumstances, in much the same way as it is broad enough to encompass a woman's decision to terminate pregnancy...." Of course, Karen Quinlan, lying comatose in the hospital, was unable to communicate her intentions to exercise this aspect of the right of privacy. According to the Court's opinion, the "only practical way to prevent destruction of [Karen Quinlan's] right is to permit the guardian and family ... to render their best judgment as to whether she would exercise [the right to decline treatment] in these circumstances."

After Karen Quinlan was taken off the breathing machine, she lived for nine years in a coma, taking food and water through a nasogastric tube. Her parents never asked that this feeding be discontinued, but therein lies another troubling question. Does the right of privacy empower a terminally ill patient to refuse food and water provided through a nasogastric tube? In *Bouvia v. Superior Court* (Cal. 1986), the California Supreme Court answered this question in the affirmative in a case involving a young woman who, although competent, was suffering the terrible effects of an advanced degenerative illness.

A Right to Commit Suicide?

Court decisions such as *Quinlan* and *Bouvia* have led to a national debate over the right to die. In what circumstances and by what means does a person have a right to bring about his or her own demise? Critics of the right to die argue that it is a "slippery slope" leading inexorably to the legal recognition of "mercy killing" and suicide. If the right of privacy allows an individual to make "fundamental life choices" and to decide what happens to his or her body, then how can laws that forbid suicide (or aiding and abetting suicide) be constitutional? In 1991, the public debate over the right to die took an eerie turn when Dr. Jack Kevorkian was prosecuted after assisting several people to commit suicide.

Kevorkian, an advocate of euthanasia, had developed a "suicide machine" by which individuals could self-administer lethal injections of drugs and thereby achieve painless death. The case of Dr. Kevorkian and his suicide machine raises troubling questions, one that the courts will be grappling with in the years to come.

The Nancy Cruzan Case

The U.S. Supreme Court's only significant decision to date involving the right to die is the 1990 case of *Cruzan v. Missouri Health Department*. When the case reached the Supreme Court, Nancy Cruzan had for six years been confined to a hospital bed in a state of unconsciousness. Her condition was the result of extreme brain damage that occurred in an automobile accident. When it became apparent that Cruzan's condition was irreversible, her parents asked the hospital to remove the nasogastric tube that was keeping her alive. The hospital refused absent a court order. The trial court issued the order, but the Missouri Supreme Court reversed, citing the state's "policy strongly favoring the preservation of life." The Missouri Supreme Court said that since Nancy Cruzan was unable to communicate, there would have to be clear and convincing evidence of her desire to have the feeding tube removed. Dividing 5 to 4, the U.S. Supreme Court upheld the Missouri Supreme Court's decision. Writing for the Court, Chief Justice Rehnquist held that, although Nancy Cruzan had a right to terminate life-prolonging treatment, it was reasonable for the state to impose the clear and convincing evidence standard as a means of guarding against potential abuse of the "substituted judgment" doctrine.

Dr. Jack Kevorkian and his "suicide machine"

Critics of the right to die, many of whom also oppose legalized abortion, hailed the *Cruzan* decision as a victory for the prolife movement. It remains to be seen, however, whether the *Cruzan* decision represents a turnaround in the development of the right to die or merely the fine-tuning of a right that is now well-established in American jurisprudence. It is likely that state, rather than federal, courts will continue to take the lead in developing this important new area of the law.

THE PROTECTION OF PRIVATE INFORMATION

In a society that relies so heavily on computerized data bases capable of storing vast amounts of information about individuals, it was inevitable that the Supreme Court would be asked to determine the degree to which the right of privacy insulates a person from having to disclose personal information to government agencies. The question arose in regard to a New York law that established a compulsory official record of prescriptions for drugs for which there is a substantial illegal market. In an effort to control the abuse and illegal sale of certain substances, the law required the recording of the names and addresses of individuals for whom prescriptions were written, as well as the pharmacies designated to fill such prescriptions. The law did, however, contain safeguards designed to preserve the confidentiality of these records. The purpose here was to protect the privacy and reputations of those whose medical prescriptions contained substances associated with drug abuse. In *Whalen v. Roe* (1977), the Supreme Court unanimously upheld the law, finding no invasion of protected privacy. Justice Stevens's opinion for the Court acknowledged "the threat to privacy implicit in the accumulation of vast amounts of personal information . . ." but held that the New York law provided a "proper concern with, and protection of, the individual's interest in privacy." No doubt other such laws where the government's concern for individual privacy is less pronounced will eventually reach the Court.

Drug Testing

The recent proliferation of mandatory and random drug testing in the workplace has raised serious constitutional issues. May government, as a condition of employment, military service, or licensure, require an individual to submit to urinalysis? While the concept of privacy is obviously relevant here, it is likely that the Supreme Court will address such issues in the general context of Fourth Amendment prohibitions against unreasonable searches and seizures and the Fifth Amendment immunity against compulsory self-incrimination (see, for example, *National Treasury Employees Union v. Von Raab* [1989]; *Skinner v. Railway Labor Executives* [1989]).

CONCLUSION

The modern Supreme Court has fashioned a general, independent constitutional right of privacy by drawing on the Fourteenth Amendment and on various provisions of the Bill of Rights. While the legal logic underlying the right of privacy is debatable, the right is now firmly established in American constitutional law. The right of privacy has been recognized by the courts of most states, and several state constitutions now even contain explicit protections of the right of privacy.

It is unclear whether, and how far, the courts will further extend the right of privacy. In 1965, when the Supreme Court decided *Griswold v. Connecticut,* public sentiment had become decidedly more liberal in the area of sex and reproduction. The 1973 abortion decision did not meet with the same extent of popular approbation, and the opposition to abortion has been much more intense than the opposition to the use of devices that prevent conception. The so-called right to die, if it is limited to the withholding of extraordinary means of life prolongation, seems to be socially acceptable. But there would be considerable opposition to the legalization of active euthanasia or suicide. At this point, prevailing social norms do not condone homosexual conduct or the private use of "recreational" drugs. For courts to assert constitutional protections for such activities would be a bold move indeed, leading inevitably to political retaliation. One certainly would not expect the U.S. Supreme Court, which has become steadily more conservative in recent years, to adopt such libertarian positions in the near future. The evolution of the right of privacy thus illustrates the "give and take" of American constitutional law. It also dramatizes the fact that constitutional rights do not exist in a social, political, or moral vacuum.

FOR FURTHER READING

Barnett, Randy, ed. *The Rights Retained by the People: The History and Meaning of the Ninth Amendment.* Fairfax, Va.: George Mason University Press, 1989.

Breckenridge, Adam Carlyle. *The Right to Privacy.* Lincoln: University of Nebraska Press, 1970.

Hayden, Trudy, and Jack Novik. *Your Rights to Privacy.* New York: Avon Books, 1980.

Johnson, Charles A., and Bradley C. Canon. *Judicial Policies: Implementation and Impact.* Washington, D.C.: Congressional Quarterly Press, 1984.

Luker, Kristin. *Abortion and the Politics of Motherhood.* Berkeley: University of California Press, 1980.

Mayer, Michael. *Rights of Privacy.* New York: Law-Arts, 1972.

McClellan, Grant S., ed. *The Right to Privacy.* New York: H. W. Wilson, 1976.

Mill, John Stuart. *On Liberty.* New York: Appleton-Century-Crofts, 1947.

Miller, Arthur R. *The Assault on Privacy.* Ann Arbor: University of Michigan Press, 1971.

O'Brien, David M. *Privacy, Law and Public Policy.* New York: Praeger, 1979.

Pennock, J. Roland, and John W. Chapman, eds. *Privacy.* New York: Atherton, 1970.

Rubin, Eva R. *Abortion, Politics and the Courts:* Roe v. Wade *and Its Aftermath.* New York: Greenwood Press, 1987.

Shattuck, John H. F. *Rights of Privacy.* Skokie, Ill.: National Textbook Company, 1977.

Steiner, Gilbert Y., ed. *The Abortion Dispute and the American System.* Washington, D.C.: Brookings Institution, 1983.

Tribe, Laurence. *Abortion: The Clash of Absolutes.* New York: Norton, 1990.

Westin, Alan F. *Privacy and Freedom.* New York: Atheneum, 1970.

Woodward, Bob, and Armstrong, Scott. *The Brethren: Inside the Supreme Court.* New York: Simon and Schuster, 1979.

CASES AND READINGS

Jacobson v. Massachusetts

197 U.S. 11; 25 S. Ct. 358; 49 L. Ed. 643 (1905)
Vote: 7-2

Acting under authority of state law, the board of health of Cambridge, Massachusetts, adopted a regulation requiring that, with certain exceptions, inhabitants of the city be vaccinated against smallpox. State law imposed a five-dollar fine for violation of the vaccination requirement. Henning Jacobson, a resident of Cambridge, refused to comply with the regulation. As a result, charges were filed against him; he was convicted, and the fine was imposed. Jacobson appealed his conviction, contending that the compulsory vaccination law and implementing regulation violated his rights under the Fourteenth Amendment. The state, in response, argued that the statute was a legitimate exercise of its police power. The Massachusetts Supreme Judicial Court sustained the constitutionality of the law, and Jacobson obtained review by the U.S. Supreme Court.

Mr. Justice Harlan delivered the opinion of the Court:

This case involves the validity, under the Constitution of the United States, of certain provisions in the statutes of Massachusetts relating to vaccination. . . .

We pass without extended discussion the suggestion that the particular section of the statute of Massachusetts now in question *** is in derogation of rights secured by the preamble of the Constitution of the United States. Although that preamble indicates the general purposes for which the people ordained and established the Constitution, it has never been regarded as the source of any substantive power conferred on the government of the United States, or on any of its departments. Such powers embraced only those expressly granted in the body of the Constitution, and such as may be implied from those so granted. Although, therefore, one of the declared objects of the Constitution was to secure the blessings of liberty to all under the sovereign jurisdiction and authority of the United States, no power can be exerted to that end by the United States, unless, apart

from the preamble, it be found in some express delegation of power, or in some power to be properly implied therefrom.

We also pass without discussion the suggestion that the above section of the statute is opposed to the spirit of the Constitution. Undoubtedly, as observed by Chief Justice Marshall, speaking for the court in *Sturges v. Crowninshield,* *** "the spirit of an instrument, especially of a constitution, is to be respected not less than its letter; yet the spirit is to be collected chiefly from its words." We have no need in this case to go beyond the plain, obvious meaning of the words in those provisions of the Constitution which, it is contended, must control our decision. . . .

Is the statute . . . inconsistent with the liberty which the Constitution of the United States secures to every person against deprivation by the state?

The authority of the state to enact this statute is to be referred to what is commonly called the police power—a power which the state did not surrender when becoming a member of the Union under the Constitution. Although this court has refrained from any attempt to define the limits of that power, yet it has "health laws of every description;" indeed, all laws that relate to matters completely within its territory and which do not by their necessary operation affect the people of other states. According to settled principles, the police power of a state must be held to embrace, at least, such reasonable regulations established directly by legislative enactment as will protect the public health and the public safety. ***

We come, then, to inquire whether any right given or secured by the Constitution is invaded by the statute as interpreted by the state court. The defendant insists that his liberty is invaded when the state subjects him to fine or imprisonment for neglecting or refusing to submit to vaccination; that a compulsory vaccination law is unreasonable, arbitrary, and oppressive, and, therefore, hostile to the inherent right of every freeman to care for his own body and health in such a way as to him seems best; and that the execution of such a law against one who objects to vaccination, no matter for what reason, is nothing short of an assault upon his person. But the liberty secured by the Constitution of the United States to every person within its jurisdiction does not import an absolute right in each person to be, at all times and in all circumstances, wholly freed from restraint. There are manifold restraints to which every person is necessarily subject for the common good. On any other basis organized society could not exist with safety to its members. Society based on the rule that each one is a law unto himself would soon be confronted with disorder and anarchy. Real liberty for all could not exist under the operation of a principle which recognizes the right of each individual person to use his own, whether in respect of his person or his property, regardless of the injury that may be done to others. . . .

Applying these principles to the present case, it is to be observed that the legislature of Massachusetts required the inhabitants of a city or town to be vaccinated only when, in the opinion of the board of health, that was necessary for the public health or the public safety. The authority to determine for all what ought to be done in such an emergency must have been lodged somewhere or in some body; and surely it was appropriate for the legislature to refer that question, in the first instance, to a board of health composed of persons residing in the locality affected, and appointed, presumably, because of their fitness to determine such questions. To invest such a body with authority over such matters was not an unusual, nor an unreasonable or arbitrary, requirement. Upon the principle of self-defense, of paramount necessity, a community has the right to protect itself against an epidemic of disease which threatens the safety of its members. . . .

There is, of course, a sphere within which the individual may assert the supremacy of his own will, and rightfully dispute the authority of any human government, especially of any free government existing under a written constitution, to interfere with the exercise of that will. But it is equally true that in every well-ordered society charged with the duty of conserving the safety of its members the rights of the individual in respect of his liberty may at times,

under the pressure of great dangers, be subjected to such restraint, to be enforced by reasonable regulations, as the safety of the general public may demand. . . .

Whatever may be thought of the expediency of this statute, it cannot be affirmed to be, beyond question, in palpable conflict with the Constitution. Nor, in view of the methods employed to stamp out the disease of smallpox, can anyone confidently assert that the means prescribed by the state to that end has no real or substantial relation to the protection of the public health and the public safety. Such an assertion would not be consistent with the experience of this and other countries whose authorities have dealt with the disease of smallpox. And the principle of vaccination as a means to prevent the spread of smallpox has been enforced in many states by statutes making the vaccination of children a condition of their right to enter or remain in public school. ***

We are not prepared to hold that a minority, residing or remaining in any city or town where smallpox is prevalent, and enjoying the general protection afforded by an organized local government, may thus defy the will of its constituted authorities, acting in good faith for all, under the legislative sanction of the state. If such be the privilege of a minority, then a like privilege would belong to each individual of the community, and the spectacle would be presented of the welfare and safety of an entire population being subordinated to the notions of a single individual who chooses to remain a part of that population. We are unwilling to hold it to be an element in the liberty secured by the Constitution of the United States that one person, or a minority of persons, residing in any community and enjoying the benefits of its local government, should have the power thus to dominate the majority when supported in their action by the authority of the state. While this court should guard with firmness every right appertaining to life, liberty, or property as secured to the individual by the supreme law of the land, it is of the last importance that it should not invade the domain of local authority except when it is plainly necessary to do so in order to enforce that law. The safety and the health of the people of Massachusetts are, in the first instance, for that commonwealth to guard and protect. They are matters that d not ordinarily concern the national government. So far as they can be reached by any government, they depend, primarily, upon such action as the state, in its wisdom, may take; and we do not perceive that this legislation has invaded any right secured by the Federal Constitution. . . .

We now decide only that the statute covers the present case, and that nothing clearly appears that would justify this Court in holding it to be unconstitutional and inoperative in its application to the plaintiff in error.

The judgment of the court below must be affirmed. It is so ordered.

Mr. Justice Brewer and *Mr. Justice Peckham* dissent.

Meyer v. Nebraska

262 U.S. 390; 43 S. Ct. 625; 67 L. Ed. 1042 (1923)

Vote: 7-2

Mr. Justice McReynolds delivered the opinion of the Court.

Plaintiff in error was tried and convicted in the District Court for Hamilton County, Nebraska, under an information which charged that on May 25, 1920, while an instructor in Zion Parochial School, he unlawfully taught the subject of reading in the German language to Raymond Parpart, a child of ten years, who had not attained and successfully passed the eighth grade. The information is based upon "An act relating to the teaching of foreign languages in the States of Nebraska," approved April 9, 1919. . . .

The following excerpts from the opinion [of the Supreme Court of Nebraska] sufficiently indicate the reasons advanced to support [its] conclusion.

The salutary purpose of the statute is clear. The legislature had seen the baneful effects of permitting foreigners, who had taken residence in this country, to rear and educate their children in the language of their native land. The result of that condition was found to be inimical to our own safety. To allow the children of foreigners, who had emigrated here, to be taught from early childhood the language of the country of their parents was to rear them with that language as their mother tongue. It was to educate them so that they must always think in that language, and, as a consequence, naturally inculcate in them the ideas and sentiments foreign to the best interests of this country. The statute, therefore, was intended not only to require that the education of all children be conducted in the English language, but that, until they had grown into that language and until it had become a part of them, they should not in the schools be taught any other language.

The obvious purpose of this statute was that the English language should become the mother tongue of all children reared in this state. The enactment of such a statute comes reasonably within the police power of the state. ***

While this Court has not attempted to define with exactness the liberty [guaranteed by the Fourteenth Amendment], the term has received much consideration and some of the included things have been definitely stated. Without doubt, it denotes not merely freedom from bodily restraint but also the right of the individual to contract, to engage in any of the common occupations of life, to acquire useful knowledge, to marry, establish a home and bring up children, to worship God according to the dictates of his own conscience, and generally to enjoy those privileges long recognized at common law as essential to the orderly pursuit of happiness by free men. . . . The established doctrine is that this liberty may not be interfered with, under the guise of protecting the public interest, by legislative action which is arbitrary or without reasonable relation to some purpose within the competency of the State to effect. Determination by the legislature of what constitutes proper exercise of police power is not final or conclusive but is subject to supervision by the courts. . . .

Corresponding to the right of control, it is the natural duty of the parent to give his children education suitable to their station in life; and nearly all the States, including Nebraska, enforce this obligation by compulsory laws.

Practically, education of the young is only possible in schools conducted by especially qualified persons who devote themselves thereto. The calling always has been regarded as useful and honorable, essential, indeed, to the public welfare. Mere knowledge of the German language cannot reasonably be regarded as harmful. Heretofore it has been commonly looked upon as helpful and desirable. Plaintiff in error taught this language in school as part of his occupation. His right thus to teach and the right of parents to engage him so to instruct their children, we think, are within the liberty of the Amendment.

The challenged statute forbids the teaching in school of any subject except in English; also the teaching of any other language until the pupil has attained and successfully passed the eighth grade, which is not usually accomplished before the age of twelve. The Supreme Court of the State has held that "the so-called ancient or dead languages" are not "within the spirit or the purpose of the act." . . . Latin, Greek, Hebrew are not proscribed; but German, French, Spanish, Italian and every other alien speech are within the ban. Evidently the legislature has attempted materially to interfere with the calling of modern language teachers, with the opportunities of pupils to acquire knowledge, and with the power of parents to control the education of their own. . . .

Mr. Justice Holmes [with whom *Justice Sutherland* concurred], dissenting.

We all agree, I take it, that it is desirable that all the citizens of the United States should speak a common tongue, and therefore that the end aimed at by the statute is a lawful and proper one. The only question is whether the means adopted deprive teachers of the liberty secured to them by the Fourteenth Amendment. It is with hesitation and unwillingness that I differ from my brethren with regard to a law like this but I cannot bring my mind to believe that in some circumstances, and circumstances existing it is said in Nebraska, the statute might not be regarded as a reasonable or even necessary method of reaching the desired result. The part of the act with which we are concerned deals with the teaching of young children. Youth is the time when familiarity with a language is established and if there are sections in the State where a child would hear only Polish or French or German spoken at home I am not prepared to say that it is unreasonable to provide that in his early years he shall hear and speak only English at school. But if it is reasonable it is not an undue restriction of the liberty either of teacher or scholar. No one would doubt that a teacher might be forbidden to teach many things, and the only criterion of his liberty under the Constitution that I can think of it "whether, considering the end in view, the statute passes the bounds of reason and assumes the character of a merely arbitrary fiat." . . . I think I appreciate the objection to the law but it appears to me to present a question upon which men reasonably might differ and therefore I am unable to say that the Constitution of the United States prevents the experiment being tried. . . .

Buck v. Bell

274 U.S. 200; 47 S. Ct. 584; 71 L. Ed. 1000 (1927)
Vote: 8-1

Mr. Justice Holmes delivered the opinion of the Court.

This is a writ of error to review a judgment of the Supreme Court of Appeals of the State of Virginia, affirming a judgment of the Circuit Court of Amherst County, by which the defendant in error [Dr. J. H. Bell], the superintendent of the State Colony for Epileptics and Feeble Minded, was ordered to perform the operation of salpingectomy upon Carrie Buck, the plaintiff in error, for the purpose of making her sterile. *** The case comes here upon the contention that the statute authorizing the judgment is void under the Fourteenth Amendment as denying to the plaintiff in error due process of law and the equal protection of the laws.

Carrie Buck is a feeble minded white woman who was committed to the State Colony above mentioned in due form. She is the daughter of a feeble minded mother in the same institution, and the mother of an illegitimate feeble minded child. She was eighteen years old at the time of the trial of her case in the Circuit Court, in the latter part of 1924. An Act of Virginia, approved March 20, 1924, recites that the health of the patient and the welfare of society may be promoted in certain cases by the sterilization of mental defectives, under careful safeguard. . . .

The attack is not upon the procedure but upon the substantive law. . . . In view of the general declarations of the legislature and the specific findings of the Court, obviously we cannot say as matter of law that the grounds do not exist, and if they exist they justify the result. . . . It is better for all the world, if instead of waiting to execute degenerate offspring for crime, or to let them starve for their imbecility, society can prevent those who are manifestly unfit from continuing their kind. The principle that sus-

tains compulsory vaccination is broad enough to cover cutting the Fallopian tubes. Three generations of imbeciles are enough.

But, it is said, however it might be if this reasoning were applied generally, it fails when it is confined to the small number who are in the institutions named and is not applied to the multitudes outside. It is the usual last resort of constitutional arguments to point out shortcomings of this sort. But the answer is that the law does all that is needed when it does all that it can, indicates a policy, applies it to all within the lines, and seeks to bring within the lines all similarly situated so far and so fast as its means allow. Of course so far as the operations enable those who otherwise must be kept confined to be returned to the world, and thus open the asylum to others, the equality aimed at will be more nearly reached.

Judgment affirmed.

Mr. Justice Butler dissents.

Poe v. Ullman

367 U.S. 497; 81 S. Ct. 1752; 6 L. Ed.2d 989 (1961)

In this case, the Supreme Court considers the constitutionality of state laws forbidding the use of artificial means of birth control. The Court dismisses the case as unripe for judicial review (the Court's opinion is reprinted in Chapter 3). However, Justice Harlan's dissenting opinion is noteworthy for its conceptualization of the constitutional right of privacy.

Mr. Justice Harlan, dissenting.

I consider that this Connecticut legislation, as construed to apply to these appellants, violates the Fourteenth Amendment. I believe that a statute making it a criminal offense for married couples to use contraceptives is an intolerable and unjustifiable invasion of privacy and in the conduct of the most intimate concerns of an individual's personal life. I reach this conclusion, even though I find it difficult and unnecessary at this juncture to accept appellants' other argument that the judgment of policy behind

the statute, so applied, is so arbitrary and unreasonable as to render the enactment invalid for that reason alone. Since both the contentions draw their basis from no explicit language of the Constitution, and have yet to find expression in any decision of this Court, I feel it desirable at the outset to state the framework of Constitutional principles in which I think the issue must be judged.

In reviewing state legislation, whether considered to be in the exercise of the State's police powers, or in provision for the health, safety, morals or welfare of its people, it is clear that what is concerned are "the powers of government inherent in every sovereignty." *** Only to the extent that the Constitution so requires may this Court interfere with the exercise of this plenary power of government. *** But precisely because it is the Constitution alone which warrants judicial interference in sovereign operations of the State, the basis of judgment as to the Constitutionality of state action must be a rational one, approaching the text which is the only commission for our power not in a literalistic way, as if we had a tax statute before us, but as the basic charter of our society, setting out in spare but meaningful terms the principles of government. But as inescapable as is the rational process in Constitutional adjudication in general, nowhere is it more so than in giving meaning to the prohibitions of the Fourteenth Amendment and, where the Federal Government is involved, the Fifth Amendment, against the deprivation of life, liberty or property without due process of law.

It is but a truism to say that this provision of both Amendments is not self-explanatory. As to the Fourteenth, which is involved here, the history of the Amendment also sheds little light on the meaning of the provision. *** It is important to note, however, that two views of the Amendment have not been accepted by this Court as delineating its scope. One view, which was ably and insistently argued in response to what were felt to be abuses by this Court of its reviewing power, sought to limit the provision to a guarantee of procedural fairness. *** The other view which has been rejected would have it that the Fourteenth Amendment, whether by way of the Privileges and Immunities Clause or the Due Process Clause, applied against the States only and precisely those restraints which had prior to the Amendment been applicable merely to federal action. However, "due process" in the consistent view of this Court has ever been a broader concept than the first view and more flexible than the second.

Were due process merely a procedural safeguard it would fail to reach those situations where the deprivation of life, liberty or property was accomplished by legislation which by operating in the future could, given even the fairest possible procedure in application to individuals, nevertheless destroy the enjoyment of all three. ***

However it is not the particular enumeration of rights in the first eight Amendments which spells out the reach of Fourteenth Amendment due process, but rather, as was suggested in another context long before the adoption of that Amendment, those concepts which are considered to embrace those rights "which are fundamental, which belong to the citizens of all free governments," *** for "the purposes [of securing] which men enter into society." *** Again and again this Court has resisted the notion that the Fourteenth Amendment is no more than a shorthand reference to what is explicitly set out elsewhere in the Bill of Rights. *** Indeed the fact that an identical provision limiting federal action is found among the first eight Amendments, applying to the Federal Government, suggests that due process is a discrete concept which subsists as an independent guaranty of liberty and procedural fairness, more general and inclusive than the specific prohibitions. ***

Due process has not been reduced to any formula; its content cannot be determined by reference to any code. The best that can be said is that through the course of this Court's decisions it has represented the balance which our Nation, built upon postulates of respect for the liberty of the individual has struck between that liberty and the demands of organized society. If the supplying of content to this Constitutional concept has of necessity been a rational process, it certainly has not been one where judges have felt free to roam where unguided speculation might take them. The balance of which I speak is the balance struck by this country, having regard to what history teaches are the traditions from which it developed as well as the traditions from which it broke. That tradition is a living thing. A decision of this Court which radically departs from it could not long survive, while a decision which builds on what has survived is likely to be sound. No formula could serve as a substitute, in this area, for judgment and restraint.

It is this outlook which has led the Court continuingly to perceive distinctions in the imperative character of Constitutional provisions, since that character must be discerned from a particular provision's larger context. And inasmuch as this context is not one of words, but of history and purposes, the full scope of the liberty guaranteed by the Due Process Clause cannot be found in or limited by the precise terms of the specific guarantees elsewhere provided in the Constitution. This "liberty" is not a series of isolated points pricked out in terms of the taking of property; the freedom of speech, press, and religion; the right to keep and bear arms; the freedom from unreasonable searches and seizures; and so on. It is a rational continuum which, broadly speaking, includes a freedom from all substantial arbitrary impositions and purposeless restraints *** and which also recognizes, what a reasonable and sensitive judgment must, that certain interests require particularly careful scrutiny of the state needs asserted to justify their abridgment.

Each new claim to Constitutional protection must be considered against a background of Constitutional purposes, as they have been rationally perceived and historically developed. Though we exercise limited and sharply restrained judgment, yet there is no "mechanical yardstick," no "mechanical answer." The decision of an apparently novel claim must depend on grounds which follow closely on well-accepted principles and criteria. The new decision must take "its place in relation to what went before and further [cut] a channel for what is to come." ***

On these premises I turn to the particular Constitutional claim in this case.

Appellants contend that the Connecticut statute deprives them, as it unquestionably does, of a substantial measure of liberty in carrying on the most intimate of all personal relationships, and that it does so arbitrarily and without any rational, justifying purpose. The State, on the other hand, asserts that it is acting to protect the moral welfare of its citizenry, both directly, in that it considers the practice of contraception immoral in itself, and instrumentally, in that the availability of contraceptive materials tends to minimize "the disastrous consequence of dissolute action," that is fornication and adultery.

It is argued by appellants that the judgment, implicit in this statute—that the use of contraceptives by married couples is immoral—is an irrational one, that in effect it subjects them in a very important matter to the arbitrary whim of the legislature, and that it does so for no good purpose. Where, as here, we are dealing with what must be considered "a basic liberty," *** [t]here are limits to the extent to which the presumption of constitutionality can be pressed," *** and at the mere assertion that the action of the State finds justification in the controversial realm of morals cannot justify alone any and every restriction it imposes. ***

Yet the very inclusion of the category of morality among state concerns indicates that society is not limited in its objects only to the physical well-being of the community, but has traditionally concerned itself with the moral soundness of its people as well. Indeed to attempt a line between public behavior and that which is purely consensual or solitary would be to withdraw from community concern a range of subjects with which every society in civilized times has found it necessary to deal. The laws regarding marriage which provide both when the sexual powers may be used and the legal and societal context in which children are born and brought up, as well as laws forbidding adultery, fornication and homosexual practices which express the negative of the proposition, confining sexuality to lawful marriage, form a pattern so deeply pressed into the substance of our social life that any Constitutional doctrine in this area must build upon that basis. ***

It is in this area of sexual morality, which contains many proscriptions of consensual behavior having little or no direct impact on others, that the State of Connecticut has expressed its moral judgment that all use of contraceptives is improper. Appellants cite an impressive list of authorities who, from a great variety of points of view, commend the considered use of contraceptives by married couples. What they do not emphasize is that not too long ago the current of opinion was very probably quite the opposite and that even today the issue is not free of controversy. Certainly, Connecticut's judgment is no more demonstrably correct or incorrect than are the varieties of judgment, expressed in law, on marriage and divorce, on adult consensual homosexuality, abortion, and sterilization, or euthanasia and suicide. If we had a case before us which required us to decide simply, and in abstraction, whether the moral judgment implicit in the application of the present statute to married couples was a sound one, the very controversial nature of these questions would, I think, require us to hesitate long before concluding that the Constitution precluded Connecticut from choosing as it has among these various views. ***

But, as might be expected, we are not presented simply with this moral judgment to be passed on as an abstract proposition. The secular state is not an examiner of consciences: it must operate in the realm of behavior, of overt actions, and where it does so operate, not only the underlying, moral purpose of its operations, but also the choice of means becomes relevant to any Constitutional judgment on what is done. The moral presupposition on which appellants ask us to pass judgment could form the basis of a variety of legal rules and administrative choices, each presenting a different issue for adjudication. For example, one practical expression of the moral view propounded here might be the rule that a marriage in which only contraceptive relations had taken place had never been consummated and could be annulled. *** Again, the use of contraceptives might be made a ground for divorce, or perhaps tax benefits and subsidies could be provided for large families. Other examples also readily suggest themselves.

Precisely what is involved here is this: the State is asserting the right to enforce its moral judgment by intruding upon the most intimate details of the marital relation with the full power of the criminal law. Potentially, this could allow the deployment of all the incidental machinery of the criminal law, arrests, searches and seizures; inevitably it must mean at the very least the lodging of criminal charges, a public trial, and testimony as to the *corpus delicti*. Nor could any imaginable elaboration of presumptions, testimonial privileges, or other safeguards, alleviate the necessity for testimony as to the mode and manner of the married couples' sexual relations, or at least the opportunity for the accused to make denial of the charges. In sum, the statute allows the State to enquire into, prove and punish married people for the private use of their marital intimacy.

This, then, is the precise character of the enactment whose Constitutional measure we must take. The statute must pass a more rigorous Constitutional test than that of going merely to the plausibility of its underlying rationale. *** This enactment involves what, by common understanding throughout the English-speaking world, must be granted to be a most fundamental aspect of "liberty," the privacy of the home in its most basic sense, and it is this which requires that the statute be subjected to "strict scrutiny." ***

That aspect of liberty which embraces the concept of the privacy of the home receives explicit Constitutional protection at two places only. These are the Third Amendment, relating to the quartering of soldiers, and the Fourth Amendment, prohibiting unreasonable searches and seizures. While these Amendments reach only the Federal Government, this Court has held in the strongest terms, and today again confirms, that the concept of "privacy" embodied in the Fourth Amendment is part of the "ordered liberty" assured against state action by the 14th Amendment. ***

It is clear, of course, that this Connecticut statute does not invade the privacy of the home in the usual sense, since the invasion involved here may, and doubtless usually would, be accomplished without any physical intrusion whatever into the home. What the statute undertakes to do, however, is to create a crime which is grossly offensive to this privacy, while the Constitution refers only to methods of ferreting out substantive wrongs, and the procedure it requires presupposes that substantive offenses may be committed and sought out in the privacy of the home. But such an analysis forecloses any claim to Constitutional protection against this form of deprivation of privacy, only if due process in this respect is limited to what is explicitly provided in the Constitution, divorced from the rational purposes, historical roots, and subsequent developments of the relevant provisions. . . .

I think the sweep of the Court's decisions, under both the Fourth and Fourteenth Amendments, amply shows that the Constitution protects the privacy of the home against all unreasonable intrusion of whatever character. "[These] principles *** affect the very essence of constitutional liberty and security. They reach farther than [a] concrete form of the case *** before the court, with its adventitious circumstances; they apply to all invasions on the part of the government and its employees of the sanctity of a man's home and the privacies of life." *** "The security of one's privacy against arbitrary intrusion by the police—which is at the core of the Fourth Amendment—is basic to a free society." ***

It would surely be an extreme instance of sacrificing substance to form were it to be held that the Constitutional principle of privacy against arbitrary official intrusion comprehends only physical invasions by the police. To be sure, the times presented the Framers with two particular threats to that principle, the general warrant, *** and the quartering of soldiers in private homes. But though "[l]egislation, both statutory and constitutional, is enacted, *** from an experience of evils *** its general language should not, therefore, be necessarily confined to the form that evil had theretofore taken. *** [A] principle, to be vital, must be capable of wider application than the mischief which gave it birth." ***

Although the form of intrusion here—the enactment of a substantive offense—does not, in my opinion, preclude the making of a claim based on the right of privacy embraced in the "liberty" of the Due Process Clause, it must be acknowledged that there is another sense in which it could be argued that this intrusion on privacy differs from what the Fourth Amendment, and the similar concept of the Fourteenth, were intended to protect; here we have not an intrusion into the home so much as on the life which characteristically has its place in the home. But to my mind such a distinction is so insubstantial as to be captious: if the physical curtilage of the home is protected, it is surely as a result of solicitude to protect the privacies of the life within. Certainly the safeguarding of the home does not follow merely from the sanctity of property rights. The home derives its pre-eminence as the seat of family life. And the integrity of that life is something so fundamental that it has been found to draw to its protection the principles of more than one explicitly granted Constitutional right. . . .

Of this whole "private realm of family life" it is difficult to image what is more private or more intimate than a husband and wife's marital relations. We would indeed be straining at a gnat and swallowing a camel were we to show concern for the niceties of property law involved in our recent decision, under the Fourth Amendment, *** and yet fail at least to see any substantial claim here.

Of course, just as the requirement of a warrant is not inflexible in carrying out searches and seizures, *** so there are countervailing considerations at this more fundamental aspect of the right involved. "[T]he family *** is not beyond regulation," *** and it would be an absurdity to suggest either that offenses may not be committed in the bosom of the family or that the home can be made a sanctuary for crime. The right of privacy most manifestly is not an absolute.

Thus, I would not suggest that adultery, homosexuality, fornication and incest are immune from criminal enquiry, however privately practiced. So much has been explicitly recognized in acknowledging the State's rightful concern for its people's moral welfare. *** But not to discriminate between what is involved in this case and either the traditional offenses against good morals or crimes which, though they may be committed anywhere, happen to have been committed or concealed in the home, would entirely misconceive the argument that is being made.

Adultery, homosexuality and the like are sexual intimacies which the State forbids altogether, but the intimacy of husband and wife is necessarily an essential and accepted feature of the institution of marriage, an institution which the State not only must allow, but which always and in every age it has fostered and protected. It is one thing when the State exerts its power either to forbid extra-marital sexuality altogether, or to say who may marry, but it is quite another when, having acknowledged a marriage and the intimacies inherent in it, it undertakes to regulate by means of the criminal law the details of that intimacy.

In sum, even though the State has determined that the use of contraceptives is an iniquitous as any act of extra-marital sexual immorality, the intrusion of the whole machinery of the criminal law into the very heart of marital privacy, requiring husband and wife to render account before a criminal tribunal of their uses of that intimacy, is surely a very different thing indeed from punishing those who establish intimacies which the law has always forbidden and which can have no claim to social protection.

In my view the appellants have presented a very pressing claim for Constitutional protection. Such difficulty as the claim presents lies only in evaluating it against the State's countervailing contention that it be allowed to enforce, by whatever means it deems appropriate, its judgment of the immorality of the practice this law condemns. In resolving this conflict a number of factors compel me to conclude that the decision here must most emphatically be for the appellants. Since, as it appears to me, the statute marks an abridgment of important fundamental liberties protected by the Fourteenth Amendment, it will not do to urge in justification of that abridgement simply that the statute is rationally related to the effectuation of a proper state purpose. A closer scrutiny and stronger justification than that are required. *****

Though the State has argued the Constitutional permissibility of the moral judgment underlying this statute, neither its brief, not its argument, nor anything in any of the opinions of its highest court in these or other cases even remotely suggests a justification for the obnoxiously intrusive means it has chosen to effectuate that policy. To me the very circumstance that Connecticut has not chosen to press the enforcement of this statute against individual users, while it nevertheless persists in asserting its right to do so at any time—in effect a right to hold this statute as an imminent threat to the privacy of the households of the State—conduces to the inference either that it does not consider the policy of the statute a very important one, or that it does not regard the means it has chosen for its effectuation as appropriate or necessary.

But conclusive, in my view, is the utter novelty of this enactment. Although the Federal Government and many States have at one time or other had on their books statutes forbidding or regulating the distribution of contraceptives, none, so far as I can find, has made the use of contraceptives a crime. Indeed, a diligent search has revealed that no nation, including several which quite evidently share Connecticut's moral policy, has seen fit to effectuate that policy by the means presented here.

Though undoubtedly the States are and should be left free to reflect a wide variety of policies and should be allowed broad scope in experimenting with various means of promoting those policies, I must agree with Mr. Justice Jackson that "[t]here are limits to the extent to which a legislatively represented majority may conduct ***** experiments at the expense of the dignity and personality" of the individual. ***** In this instance these limits are, in my view, reached and passed. . . .

Griswold v. Connecticut
381 U.S. 479; 85 S. Ct. 1678; 14 L. Ed. 2d 510 (1965)
Vote: 7-2

Mr. Justice Douglas delivered the opinion of the Court.

Appellant Griswold is Executive Director of the Planned Parenthood League of Connecticut. Appellant Buxton is a licensed physician and a professor at the Yale Medical School who served as Medical Director for the League at its Center in New Haven—a center open and operating from November 1 to November 10, 1961, when appellants were arrested.

They gave information, instruction and medical advice to *married persons* as to the means of preventing conception. They examined the wife and prescribed the best contraceptive device or material for her use. Fees were usually charged, although some couples were serviced free.

The statutes whose constitutionality is involved in this appeal [provide]:

Any person who uses any drug, medicinal article or instrument for the purpose of preventing conception shall be fined not less than fifty dollars or imprisoned not less than

sixty days nor more than one year or be both fined and imprisoned.

Any person who assists, abets, counsels, causes, hires or commands another to commit any offense may be prosecuted and punished as if he were the principal offender.

The appellants were found guilty as accessories and fined $100 each, against the claim that the accessory statute as so applied violated the Fourteenth Amendment. The Appellate Division of the Circuit Court affirmed. The Supreme Court of Errors affirmed that judgment. . . . *****

We think that appellants have standing to raise the constitutional rights of the married people with whom they had a professional relationship. . . . Certainly the accessory should have standing to assert that the offense which he is charged with assisting is not, or cannot constitutionally be, a crime. . . .

Coming to the merits, we are met with a wide range of questions that implicate the Due Process Clause of the Fourteenth Amendment. Overtones of some arguments suggest that *Lochner v. New York,* *** should be our guide. But we decline that invitation.... We do not sit as a super-legislature to determine the wisdom, need, and propriety of laws that touch economic problems, business affairs, or social conditions. This law, however, operates directly on an intimate relation of husband and wife and their physician's role in one aspect of that relation.

The association of people is not mentioned in the Constitution nor in the Bill of Rights. The right to educate a child in a school of the parents' choice—whether public or private or parochial—is also not mentioned. Nor is the right to study any particular subject or any foreign language. Yet the First Amendment has been construed to include certain of those rights.

By *Pierce v. Society of Sisters,* the right to educate one's children as one chooses is made applicable to the States by the force of the First and Fourteenth Amendments. By *Meyer v. Nebraska,* the same dignity is given the right to study the German language in a private school. In other words, the State may not, consistently with the spirit of the First Amendment, contract the spectrum of available knowledge. The right of freedom of speech and press includes not only the right to utter or to print, but the right to distribute, the right to receive, the right to read *** and freedom of inquiry, freedom of thought, and freedom to teach *** indeed the freedom of the entire university community. *** Without those peripheral rights the specific rights would be less secure. And so we reaffirm the principle of the *Pierce* and the *Meyer* cases.

In *NAACP v. Alabama,* *** we protected the "freedom to associate and privacy in one's associations," noting that freedom of association was a peripheral First Amendment right. Disclosure of membership lists of a constitutionally valid association, we held, was invalid "as entailing the likelihood of a substantial restraint upon the exercise by petitioner's members of their right to freedom of association." In other words, the First Amendment has a penumbra where privacy is protected from governmental intrusion. In like context, we have protected forms of "association" that are not political in the customary sense but pertain to the social, legal, and economic benefit of the members....

[Previous] ... cases suggest that specific guarantees in the Bill of Rights have penumbras, formed by emanations from those guarantees that help give them life and substance. Various guarantees create zones of privacy. The right of association contained in the penumbra of the First Amendment is one, as we have seen. The Third Amendment in its prohibition against the quartering of soldiers "in any house" in time of peace without the consent of the owner is another facet of that privacy. The Fourth Amendment explicitly affirms the "right of the people to be secure in their persons, houses, papers, and effects, against unreasonable searches and seizures." The Fifth Amendment in its Self-Incrimination Clause enables the citizen to create a zone of privacy which government may not force him to surrender to his detriment. The Ninth Amendment provides: "The enumeration in the Constitution, of certain rights, shall not be construed to deny or disparage others retained by the people."

The Fourth and Fifth Amendments were described in *Boyd v. United States* *** as protection against all governmental invasions "of the sanctity of a man's home and the privacies of life." We recently referred in *Mapp v. Ohio* *** to the Fourth Amendment as creating a "right to privacy, no less important than any other right carefully and particularly reserved to the people." ***

We have had many controversies over these penumbral rights of "privacy and repose." *** These cases bear witness that the right of privacy which presses for recognition here is a legitimate one.

The present case, then, concerns a relationship lying within the zone of privacy created by several fundamental constitutional guarantees. And it concerns a law which, in forbidding the *use* of contraceptives rather than regulating their manufacture or sale, seeks to achieve its goals by means having a maximum destructive impact upon that relationship. Such a law cannot stand in light of the familiar principle, so often applied by this Court, that a "governmental purpose to control or prevent activities constitutionally subject to state regulation may not be achieved by means which sweep unnecessarily broadly and thereby invade the area of protected freedoms." *** Would we allow the police to search the sacred precincts of marital bedrooms for telltale signs of the use of contraceptives? The very idea is repulsive to the notions of privacy surrounding the marriage relationship. . . .

Mr. Justice Goldberg, whom **the Chief Justice** and **Mr. Justice Brennan** join, concurring.

I agree with the Court that Connecticut's birth-control law unconstitutionally intrudes upon the right of marital privacy, and I join in its opinion and judgment. Although I have not accepted the view that "due process" as used in the Fourteenth Amendments incorporates all of the first eight Amendments, . . . I do agree that the concept of liberty protects those personal rights that are fundamental, and is not confined to the specific terms of the Bill of Rights. My conclusion that the concept of liberty is not so restricted and that it embraces the right of marital privacy though that right is not mentioned explicitly in the Constitution is supported both by numerous decisions of this Court, referred to in the Court's opinion, and by the language and history of the Ninth Amendment. *** In reaching the conclusion that the right of marital privacy is protected, as being within the protected penumbra of specific guarantees of the Bill of Rights, the Court refers to the Ninth Amendment, *** I add these words to emphasize the relevance of that Amendment to the Court's holding. . . .

The Ninth Amendment reads, "The enumeration in the Constitution, of certain rights, shall not be construed to deny or disparage others retained by the people." The Amendment is almost entirely the work of James Madison. It was introduced in Congress by him and passed the House and Senate with little or no debate and virtually no change in language. It was proffered to quiet expressed fears that a bill of specifically enumerated rights could not be sufficiently broad to cover all essential rights and that the specific mention of certain rights would be interpreted as a denial that others were protected. . . .

. . . The Ninth Amendment to the Constitution may be regarded by some as a recent discovery and may be forgotten by others, but since 1791 it has been a basic part of the Constitution which we are sworn to uphold. To hold that a right so basic and fundamental and so deep-rooted in our society as the right of privacy in marriage may be infringed because that right is not guaranteed in so many words by the first eight amendments to the Constitution is to ignore the Ninth Amendment and to give it no effect whatsoever. Moreover, a judicial construction that this fundamental right is not protected by the Constitution because it is not mentioned in explicit terms by one of the first eight amendments or elsewhere in the Constitution would violate the Ninth Amendment. . . .

A dissenting opinion suggests that my interpretation of the Ninth Amendment somehow "broaden[s] the powers of this Court." *** With all due respect, I believe that it misses the import of what I am saying. I do not take the position of my Brother Black in his dissent in *Adamson v. California* *** that the entire Bill of Rights is incorporated in the Fourteenth Amendment, and I do not mean to imply that the Ninth Amendment is applied against the States by the Fourteenth. Nor do I mean to state that the Ninth Amendment constitutes an independent source of rights protected from infringement by either the States or the Federal Government. Rather, the Ninth Amendment shows a belief of the Constitution's authors that fundamental rights exist that are not expressly enumerated in the first eight amendments and an intent that the list of rights included there not be deemed exhaustive. As any student of this Court's opinions knows, this Court has held, often unanimously, that the Fifth and Fourteenth Amendments protect certain fundamental personal liberties from abridgment by the Federal Government or the States. *** The Ninth Amendment simply shows the intent of the Constitution's authors that other fundamental personal rights should not be denied such protection or disparaged in any other way simply because they are not specifically listed in the first eight constitutional amendments. I do not see how this broadens the authority of the Court; rather it serves to support what this Court has been doing in protecting fundamental rights.

Nor am I turning somersaults with history in arguing that the Ninth Amendment is relevant in a case dealing with a *State's* infringement of a fundamental right. While the Ninth Amendment—and indeed the entire Bill of Rights—originally concerned restrictions upon *federal* power, the subsequently enacted Fourteenth Amendment prohibits the States as well from abridging fundamental personal liberties. And, the Ninth Amendment, in indicating that not all such liberties are specifically mentioned in the first eight amendments, is surely relevant in showing the existence of other fundamental personal rights, now protected from state, as well as federal, infringement. In sum, the Ninth Amendment simply lends strong support to the view that the "liberty" protected by the Fifth and Fourteenth Amendments from infringement by the Federal Government or the States is not restricted to rights specifically mentioned in the first eight amendments. ***

In determining which rights are fundamental, judges are not left at large to decide cases in light of their personal and private notions. Rather, they must look to the "traditions and [collective] conscience of our people" to determine whether a principle is "so rooted [there] . . . as to be ranked as fundamental." *** The inquiry is whether a right involved "is of such a character that it cannot be denied without violating those 'fundamental principles of liberty and justice which lie at the base of all our civil and political institutions'. . . ." . . .

The entire fabric of the Constitution and the purposes that clearly underlie its specific guarantees demonstrate that the rights to marital privacy and to marry and raise a family are of similar order and magnitude as the fundamental rights specifically protected.

Although the Constitution does not speak in so many words of the right of privacy in marriage, I cannot believe that it offers these fundamental rights no protection. The fact that no particular provision of the Constitution explicitly forbids the State from disrupting the traditional relation of the family—a relation as old and as fundamental as our entire civilization—surely does not show that the Government was meant to have the power to do so. Rather, as the Ninth Amendment expressly recognizes, there are fundamental personal rights such as this one, which are protected from abridgment by the Government though not specifically mentioned in the Constitution. . . .

The logic of the dissents would sanction federal or state legislation that seems to me even more plainly unconstitutional than the statute before us. Surely the Government, absent a showing of a compelling subordinating state interest, could not decree that all husbands and wives must be sterilized after two children have been born to them. Yet by their reasoning such an invasion of marital privacy would not be subject to constitutional challenge because, while it might be "silly," no provision of the Constitution specifically prevents the Government from curtailing the marital right to bear children and raise a family. While it may shock some of my Brethren that the Court today holds that the Constitution protects the right of marital privacy, in my view it is far more shocking to believe that the personal liberty guaranteed by the Constitution does not include protection against such totalitarian limitation of family size, which is at complete variance with our constitutional concepts. Yet, if upon a showing of a slender basis of rationality, a law outlawing voluntary birth control by married persons is valid, then, by the same reasoning, a law requiring compulsory birth control also would seem to be valid. In my view, however, both types of law would unjustifiably intrude upon rights of marital privacy which are constitutionally protected.

In a long series of cases this Court has held that where fundamental personal liberties are involved, they may not be abridged by the States simply on a showing that a regulatory statute has some rational relationship to the effectuation of a proper state purpose. . . .

Although the Connecticut birth-control law obviously encroaches upon a fundamental personal liberty, the State does not show that the law serves any "subordinating [state] interest which is compelling" or that it is "necessary . . . to the accomplishment of a permissible state policy." The State, at most, argues that there is some rational relation between this statute and what is admittedly a legitimate subject of state concern—the discouraging of extra-marital relations. It says that preventing the use of birth-control devices by married persons helps prevent the indulgence by some in such extra-marital relations. The rationality of this justification is dubious, particularly in light of the admitted widespread availability to all persons in the State of Connecticut, unmarried as well as married, of birth-control devices for the prevention of disease, as distinguished from the prevention of conception. *** But, in any event, it is clear that the state interest in safeguarding marital fidelity can be served by a more discriminately tailored statute, which does not, like the present one, sweep unnecessarily broadly, reaching far beyond the evil sought to be dealt with and intruding upon the privacy of all married couples. . . .

Finally, it should be said of the Court's holding today that it in no way interferes with a State's proper regulation of sexual promiscuity or misconduct. . . .

Adultery, homosexuality and the like are sexual intimacies which the State forbids . . . but the intimacy of husband and wife is necessarily an essential and accepted feature of the institution of marriage, an institution which the State not only must allow, but which always and in every age it has fostered and protected. It is one thing when the State exerts its power either to forbid extra-marital sexuality . . . or to say who may marry, but it is quite another when, having acknowledged a marriage and the intimacies inherent in it, it undertakes to regulate by means of the criminal law the details of that intimacy. *******

In sum, I believe that the right of privacy in the marital relation is fundamental and basic—a personal right "retained by the people" within the meaning of the Ninth Amendment. Connecticut cannot constitutionally abridge this fundamental right, which is protected by the Fourteenth Amendment from infringement by the States. I agree with the Court that petitioners' convictions must therefore be reversed.

Mr. Justice Harlan, concurring in the judgment.

I fully agree with the judgment of reversal, but find myself unable to join the Court's opinion. The reason is that it seems to me to evince an approach to this case very much like that taken by my Brothers Black and Stewart in dissent, namely: the Due Process Clause of the Fourteenth Amendment does not touch this Connecticut statute unless the enactment is found to violate some right assured by the letter or penumbra of the Bill of Rights.

In other words, what I find implicit in the Court's opinion is that the "incorporation" doctrine may be used to *restrict* the reach of Fourteenth Amendment Due Process. For me this is just as unacceptable constitutional doctrine as is the use of the "incorporation" approach to *impose* upon the States all the requirements of the Bill of Rights as found in the provisions of the first eight amendments and in the decisions of this court interpreting them. *******

In my view, the proper constitutional inquiry in this case is whether this Connecticut statute infringes the Due Process Clause of the Fourteenth Amendment because the enactment violates basic values "implicit in the concept of ordered liberty." ******* For reasons stated at length in my dissenting opinion in *Poe v. Ullman,* I believe that it does. While the relevant inquiry may be aided by resort to one or more of the provisions of the Bill of Rights, it is not dependent on them or any of their radiations. The Due Process Clause of the Fourteenth Amendment stands, in my opinion, on its own bottom. . . .

While I could not more heartily agree that judicial "self restraint" is an indispensable ingredient of sound constitutional adjudication, I do submit that the formula suggested for achieving it is more hollow than real. "Specific" provisions of the Constitution, no less than "due process," lend themselves as readily to "personal" interpretations by judges whose constitutional outlook is simply to keep the Constitution in supposed "tune with the times." . . .

Judicial self-restraint will not, I suggest, be brought about in the "due process" area by the historically unfounded incorporation formula long advanced by my Brother Black, and now in part espoused by my Brother Stewart. It will be achieved in this area, as in other constitutional areas, only by continual insistence upon respect for the teachings of history, solid recognition of the basic values that underlie our society, and wise appreciation of the great roles that the doctrines of federalism and separation of powers have played in establishing and preserving American freedoms. ******* Adherence to these principles will not, of course, obviate all constitutional differences of opinion among judges, nor should it. Their continued recognition will, however, go farther toward keeping most judges from roaming at large in the constitutional field than will the interpolation into the Constitution of an artificial and largely illusory restriction on the content of the Due Process Clause.

Mr. Justice White, concurring in the judgment.

In my view this Connecticut law as applied to married couples deprives them of "liberty" without due process of law, as that concept is used in the Fourteenth Amendment. I therefore concur in the judgment of the Court reversing these convictions under the Connecticut aiding and abetting statute. . . .

Mr. Justice Black, with whom **Mr. Justice Stewart** joins, dissenting.

I agree with my Brother Stewart's dissenting opinion. And like him I do not to any extent whatever base my view that this Connecticut law is constitutional on a belief that the law is wise or that its policy is a good one. In order that there may be no room at all to doubt why I vote as I do, I feel constrained to add that the law is every bit as offensive to me as it is to my Brethren of the majority and my Brothers Harlan, White and Goldberg who, reciting reasons why it is offensive to them, hold it unconstitutional. There is no single one of the graphic and eloquent strictures and criticisms fired at the policy of this Connecticut law either by the Court's opinion or by those of my concurring brethren to which I cannot subscribe—except their conclusion that the evil qualities they see in the law make it unconstitutional.

. . . I get nowhere in this case by talk about a constitutional "right of privacy" as an emanation from one or more constitutional provisions. I like my privacy as well as the next one, but I am nevertheless compelled to admit that government has a right to invade it unless prohibited by some specific constitutional provision. For these reasons I cannot agree with the Court's judgment and the reasons it gives for holding this Connecticut law unconstitutional. . . .

I realize that many good and able men have eloquently spoken and written, sometimes in rhapsodical strains, about the duty of this Court to keep the Constitution in tune with the times. The idea is that the Constitution must be changed from time to time and that this Court is charged with a duty to make those changes. For myself, I must with all deference reject that philosophy. The Constitution makers knew the need for change and provided for it. Amendments suggested by the people's elected representatives can be submitted to the people or their selected agents for ratification. That method of change was good enough for our Fathers, and being somewhat old-fashioned I must add it is good enough for me. And so, I cannot rely on the Due Process Clause or the Ninth Amendment or any mysterious and uncertain natural law concept as a reason

for striking down this state law. The Due Process Clause with an "arbitrary and capricious" or "shocking to the conscience" formula was liberally used by this Court to strike down economic legislation in the early decades of this century, threatening, many people thought, the tranquility and stability of the Nation. *** That formula, based on subjective considerations of "natural justice," is no less dangerous when used to enforce this Court's views about personal rights than those about economic rights. I had thought that we had laid that formula, as a means for striking down state legislation, to rest once and for all. . . .

Mr. Justice Stewart, whom **Mr. Justice Black** joins, dissenting.

Since 1879 Connecticut has had on its books a law which forbids the use of contraceptives by anyone. I think this is an uncommonly silly law. As a practical matter, the law is obviously unenforceable, except in the oblique context of the present case. As a philosophical matter, I believe the use of contraceptives in the relationship of marriage should be left to personal and private choice, based upon the individual's moral, ethical, and religious beliefs. As a matter of social policy, I think professional counsel about methods of birth control should be available to all, so that each individual's choice can be meaningfully made. But we are not asked in this case to say whether we think this law is unwise, or even asinine. We are asked to hold that it violates the United States Constitution. And that I cannot do.

In the course of its opinion the Court refers to no less than six Amendments to the Constitution: the First, the Third, the Fourth, the Fifth, the Ninth, and the Fourteenth. But the Court does not say which of these Amendments, if any, it thinks is infringed by this Connecticut law.

We *are* told that the Due Process Clause of the Fourteenth Amendment is not, as such, the "guide" in this case. With that much I agree. There is no claim that this law, duly enacted by the Connecticut Legislature, is unconstitutionally vague. There is no claim that the appellants were denied any of the elements of procedural due process at their trial, so as to make their convictions constitutionally invalid. And, as the Court says, the day has long passed since the Due

Process Clause was regarded as a proper instrument for determining "the wisdom, need, and propriety" of state laws. *** My Brothers Harlan and White to the contrary, "[w]e have returned to the original constitutional proposition that courts do not substitute their social and economic beliefs for the judgment of legislative bodies, who are elected to pass laws." ***

As to the First, Third, Fourth, and Fifth Amendments, I can find nothing in any of them to invalidate this Connecticut law, even assuming that all those Amendments are fully applicable against the States. It has not even been argued that this is a law "respecting an establishment of religion, or prohibiting the free exercise thereof." And surely, unless the solemn process of constitutional adjudication is to descend to the level of a play on words, there is not involved here any abridgment of "the freedom of speech, or of the press; or the right of the people peaceably to assemble, and to petition the Government for a redress of grievances." No soldier has been quartered in any house. There has been no search, and no seizure. Nobody has been compelled to be a witness against himself.

The Court also quotes the Ninth Amendment, and my Brother Goldberg's concurring opinion relies heavily upon it. But to say that the Ninth Amendment has anything to do with this case is to turn somersaults with history. The Ninth Amendment, like its companion the Tenth, which this Court held "states but a truism that all is retained which has not been surrendered," *** was framed by James Madison and adopted by the States simply to make clear that the adoption of the Bill of Rights did not alter the plan that the *Federal* Government was to be a government of express and limited powers, and that all rights and powers not delegated to it were retained by the people and the individual States. Until today no member of this Court has ever suggested that the Ninth Amendment meant anything else, and the idea that a federal court could ever use the Ninth Amendment to annul a law passed by the elected representatives of the people of the State of Connecticut would have caused James Madison no little wonder.

What provision of the Constitution, then, does make this state law invalid? The Court says it is the right of privacy "created by several fundamental constitutional guarantees." With all deference, I can find no such general right of privacy in the Bill of Rights, in any other part of the Constitution, or in any case ever before decided by this Court.

At the oral argument in this case we were told that the Connecticut law does not "conform to current community standards." But it is not the function of this Court to decide cases on the basis of community standards. We are here to decide cases "agreeably to the Constitution and laws of the United States." It is the essence of judicial duty to subordinate our own personal views, our own ideas of what legislation is wise and what is not. If, as I should surely hope, the law before us does not reflect the standards of the people of Connecticut, the people of Connecticut can freely exercise their true Ninth and Tenth Amendment rights to persuade their elected representative to repeal it. That is the constitutional way to take this law off the books.

Roe v. Wade

410 U.S. 113; 93 S. Ct. 705; 35 L. Ed. 2d 147 (1973)

Vote: 7-2

Mr. Justice Blackmun delivered the opinion of the Court.

. . . The Texas statutes that concern us here . . . make it a crime to "procure an abortion," as therein defined, or to attempt one, except with respect to "an abortion procured or attempted by medical advice for the purpose of saving the life of the mother." Similar statutes are in existence in a majority of the States.

Texas first enacted a criminal abortion statute in 1854. *** This was soon modified into language that has remained substantially unchanged to the present time. ***

Jane Roe, a single woman who was residing in Dallas County, Texas, instituted this federal action in March 1970 against the District Attorney of the county. She sought a declaratory judgment that the Texas criminal abortion statutes were unconstitutional on their face, and an injunction restraining the defendant from enforcing the statutes.

Roe alleged that she was unmarried and pregnant; that she wished to terminate her pregnancy by an abortion "performed by a competent, licensed physician, under safe, clinical conditions"; that she was unable to get a "legal" abortion in Texas because her life did not appear to be threatened by the continuation of her pregnancy; and that she could not afford to travel to another jurisdiction in order to secure a legal abortion under safe conditions. She claimed that the Texas statutes were unconstitutionally vague and that they abridged her right of personal privacy, protected by the First, Fourth, Fifth, Ninth, and Fourteenth Amendments. By an amendment to her complaint Roe purported to sue "on behalf of herself and all other women" similarly situated. . . .

The principal thrust of appellant's attack on the Texas statutes is that they improperly invade a right, said to be possessed by the pregnant woman, to choose to terminate her pregnancy. Appellant would discover this right in the concept of personal "liberty" embodied in the Fourteenth Amendment's Due Process Clause; or in personal, marital, familial, and sexual privacy said to be protected by the Bill of Rights or its penumbras, *** or among those rights reserved to the people by the Ninth Amendment. *** Before addressing this claim, we feel it desirable briefly to survey, in several aspects, the history of abortion, for such insight as that history may afford us, and then to examine the state purposes and interests behind the criminal abortion laws. . . .

Three reasons have been advanced to explain historically the enactment of criminal abortion laws in the 19th century and to justify their continued existence.

It has been argued occasionally that these laws were the product of a Victorian social concern to discourage illicit sexual conduct. Texas, however, does not advance this justification in the present case, and it appears that no court or commentator has taken the argument seriously. . . .

A second reason is concerned with abortion as a medical procedure. When most criminal abortion laws were first enacted, the procedure was a hazardous one for the woman. This was particularly true prior to the development of antisepsis. Antiseptic techniques, of course, were based on discoveries by Lister, Pasteur, and others first announced in 1867, but were not generally accepted and employed until about the turn of the century. Abortion mortality was high. Even after 1900, and perhaps until as late as the development of antibiotics in the 1940s, standard modern techniques such as dilation and curettage were not nearly so safe as they are today. Thus, it has been argued that a State's real concern in enacting a criminal abortion law was to protect the pregnant woman, that is, to restrain her from submitting to a procedure that placed her life in serious jeopardy.

Modern medical techniques have altered this situation. Mortality rates for women undergoing early abortions, where the procedure is legal, appear to be as low as or lower than the rates for normal childbirth. Consequently, any interest of the State in protecting the woman from an inherently hazardous procedure, except when it would be equally dangerous for her to forgo it, has largely disappeared. Of course, important state interests in the area of health and medical standards do remain. . . .

The third reason is the State's interest—some phrase it in terms of duty—in protecting prenatal life. Some of the argument for this justification rests on the theory that a new human life is present from the moment of conception. The State's interest and general obligation to protect life then extends, it is argued, to prenatal life. Only when the life of the pregnant mother herself is at stake, balanced against the life she carries within her, should the interest of the embryo or fetus not prevail. Logically, of course, a legitimate state interest in this area need not stand or fall on acceptance of the belief that life begins at conception or at some other point prior to live birth. In assessing the State's interest, recognition may be given to the less rigid claim that as long as at least *potential* life is involved, the State may assert interests beyond the protection of the pregnant woman alone. . . .

The Constitution does not explicitly mention any right of privacy. In a line of decisions, *** the Court has recognized that a right of personal privacy or a guarantee of certain areas or zones of privacy, does exist under the Constitution. . . .

This right of privacy, whether it be founded in the Fourteenth Amendment's concept of personal liberty and restrictions upon state action, as we feel it is, or, as the District Court determined, in the Ninth Amendment's reservation of rights to the people, is broad enough to encompass a woman's decision whether or not to terminate her pregnancy. The detriment that the State would impose upon the pregnant woman by denying this choice altogether is apparent. Specific and direct harm medically diagnosable even in early pregnancy may be involved. Maternity, or additional offspring, may force upon the woman a distressful life and future. Psychological harm may be imminent. Mental and physical health may be taxed by child care. There is also the distress, for all concerned, associated with the unwanted child, and there is the problem of bringing a child into a family already unable, psychologically and otherwise, to care for it. In other cases, as in this one, the additional difficulties and continuing stigma of unwed motherhood may be involved. All these are factors the woman and her responsible physician necessarily will consider in consultation.

On the basis of elements such as these, appellant and some *amici* argue that the woman's right is absolute and that she is entitled to terminate her pregnancy at whatever time, in whatever way, and for whatever reason she alone chooses. With this we do not agree. Appellant's arguments that Texas either has no valid interest at all in regulating the abortion decision, or no interest strong enough to support any limitation upon the woman's sole determination, is unpersuasive. The Court's decisions recognizing a right of privacy also acknowledge that some state regulation in areas protected by the right is appropriate. As noted above, a State may properly assert important interests in safeguarding health, in maintaining medical standards, and in protecting potential life. At some point in pregnancy, these respective interests become sufficiently compelling to sustain regulation of the factors that govern the abortion decision. The privacy right involved, therefore, cannot be said to be absolute. . . .

We, therefore, conclude that the right of personal privacy includes the abortion decision, but that this right is not unqualified and must be considered against important state interests in regulation.

We note that those federal and state courts that have recently considered abortion law challenges have reached the same conclusion. A majority, in addition to the District Court in the present case, have held state laws unconstitutional, at least in part, because of vagueness or because of overbreadth and abridgment of rights. ***

Although the results are divided, most of these courts have agreed that the right of privacy, however based, is broad enough to cover the abortion decision; that the right, nonetheless, is not absolute and is subject to some limitations; and that at some point the state interests as to protection of health, medical standards, and prenatal life, become dominant. We agree with this approach.

Where certain "fundamental rights" are involved, the Court has held that regulation limiting these rights may be justified only by a "compelling state interest," *** and that legislative enactments must be narrowly drawn to express only the legitimate state interests at stake. ***

The District Court held that the appellee failed to meet his burden of demonstrating that the Texas statute's infringement upon Roe's rights was necessary to support a compelling state interest, and that, although the appellee presented "several compelling justifications for state presence in the area of abortions," the statutes outstripped these justifications and swept "far beyond any areas of compelling state interest." Appellant and appellee both contest that holding. Appellant, as has been indicated, claims an absolute right that bars any state imposition of criminal penalties in the area. Appellee argues that the State's determination to recognize and protect prenatal life from and after conception constitutes a compelling state interest. As noted above, we do not agree fully with either formulation.

The appellee and certain *amici* argue that the fetus is a "person" within the language and meaning of the Fourteenth Amendment. In support of this, they outline at length and in detail the well-known facts of fetal development. If this suggestion of personhood is established, the appellant's case, of course, collapses, for the fetus' right to life is then guaranteed specifically by the Amendment. The appellant conceded as much on reargument. On the other hand, the appellee conceded on reargument that no case could be cited that holds that a fetus is a person within the meaning of the Fourteenth Amendment.

The Constitution does not define "person" in so many words. Section 1 of the Fourteenth Amendment contains three references to "person." The first, in defining "citizens," speaks of "persons born or naturalized in the United States." The word also appears both in the Due Process Clause and in the Equal Protection Clause. "Person" is used in other places in the Constitution: in the listing of qualifications for Representatives and Senators, Art. I, Sec. 2, cl. 2, and 3, cl. 3; in the Apportionment Clause, Art. I, Sec. 2, cl. 3; in the Migration and Importation provision, Art. I, Sec. 9, cl. 1; in the Emolument Clause, Art. I, Sec. 9, cl. 8; in the Electors provisions, Art. II, Sec. 1, cl. 2, and the superseded cl. 3; in the provision outlining qualifications for the office of President, Art. II, Sec. 1, cl. 5; in the Extradition provisions, Art. IV, Sec. 2, cl. 2, and the superseded Fugitive Slave Clause 3; and in the Fifth, Twelfth, and Twenty-second Amendments, as well as in Sec. 2 and Sec. 3 of the Fourteenth Amendment. But in nearly all these instances, the use of the word is such that it has application only postnatally. None indicates, with any assurance, that it has any possible prenatal application.[1]

All this, together with our observation, that throughout the major portion of the 19th century prevailing legal abortion practices were far freer than they are today, persuades us that the word "person," as used in the Fourteenth Amendment, does not include the unborn.

This conclusion, however, does not of itself fully answer the contentions raised by Texas, and we pass on to other considerations.

---

[1]When Texas urges that a fetus is entitled to Fourteenth Amendment protection as a person, it faces a dilemma. Neither in Texas nor in any other State are all abortions prohibited. Despite broad proscription, an exception always exists. The exception contained in Art. 1196, for an abortion procured or attempted by medical advice for the purpose of saving the life of the mother, is typical. But if the fetus is a person who is not to be deprived of life without due process of law, and if the mother's condition is the sole determinant, does not the Texas exception appear to be out of line with the Amendment's command?

The pregnant woman cannot be isolated in her privacy. She carries an embryo and, later, a fetus, if one accepts the medical definitions of the developing young in the human uterus. The situation there is inherently different from marital intimacy, or bedroom possession of obscene material, or marriage, or procreation, or education. . . . As we have intimated above, it is reasonable and appropriate for a State to decide that at some point in time another interest, that of health of the mother or that of potential human life, becomes significantly involved. The woman's privacy is no longer sole and any right of privacy she possesses must be measured accordingly.

Texas urges that, apart from the Fourteenth Amendment, life begins at conception and is present throughout pregnancy, and that, therefore, the State has a compelling interest in protecting that life from and after conception. We need not resolve the difficult question of when life begins. When those trained in the respective disciplines of medicine, philosophy, and theology are unable to arrive at any consensus, the judiciary, at this point in the development of man's knowledge, is not in a position to speculate as to the answer.

It should be sufficient to note briefly the wide divergence of thinking on this most sensitive and difficult question. There has always been strong support for the view that life does not begin until live birth. This was the belief of the Stoics. It appears to be the predominant, though not the unanimous, attitude of the Jewish faith. It may be taken to represent also the position of a large segment of the Protestant community, insofar as that can be ascertained; organized groups that have taken a formal position on the abortion issue have generally regarded abortion as a matter for the conscience of the individual and her family. As we have noted, the common law found greater significance in quickening. Physicians and their scientific colleagues have regarded that event with less interest and have tended to focus either upon conception, upon live birth, or upon the interim point at which the fetus becomes "viable," that is, potentially able to live outside the mother's womb, albeit with artificial aid. Viability is usually placed at about seven months (28 weeks) but may occur earlier, even at 24 weeks. The Aristotelian theory of "mediate animation," that held sway throughout the Middle Ages and the Renaissance in Europe, continued to be official Roman Catholic dogma until the 19th century, despite opposition to this "ensoulment" theory from those in the Church who would recognize the existence of life from the moment of conception. The latter is now, of course, the official belief of the Catholic Church. As one of the briefs *amicus* discloses, this is a view strongly held by many non-Catholics as well, and by many physicians. Substantial problems for precise definition of this view are posed, however, by new embryological data that purport to indicate that conception is a "process" over time, rather than an event, and by new medical techniques such as menstrual extraction, the "morning-after" pill, implantation of embryos, artificial insemination, even artificial wombs.

In areas other than criminal abortion, the law has been reluctant to endorse any theory that life, as we recognize it, begins before live birth or to accord legal rights to the unborn except in narrowly defined situations and except when the rights are contingent upon live birth. For example, the traditional rule of tort law denied recovery for prenatal injuries even though the child was born alive. That rule has been changed in almost every jurisdiction. In most States, recovery is said to be permitted only if the fetus was viable, or at least quick, when the injuries were sustained, though few courts have squarely so held. In a recent development, generally opposed by the commentators, some States permit the parents of a stillborn child to maintain an action for wrongful death because of prenatal injuries. Such an action, however, would appear to be one to vindicate the parents' interest and is thus consistent with the view that the fetus, at most, represents only the potentiality of life. Similarly, unborn children have been recognized as acquiring rights or interests by way of inheritance or other devolution of property, and have been represented by guardians *ad litem*. Perfection of the interests involved, again, has generally been contingent upon live birth. In short, the unborn have never been recognized in the law as persons in the whole sense.

In view of all this, we do not agree that, by adopting one theory of life, Texas may override the rights of the pregnant woman that are at stake. We repeat, however, that the State does have an important and legitimate interest in preserving and protecting the health of the pregnant woman, whether she be a resident of the State or a nonresident who seeks medical consultation and treatment there, and that it has still another important and legitimate interest in protecting the potentiality of human life. These interests are separate and distinct. Each grows in substantiality as the woman approaches term and, at a point during pregnancy, each becomes "compelling."

With respect to the State's important and legitimate interest in the health of the mother, the "compelling" point, in the light of present medical knowledge, is at approximately the end of the first trimester. This is so because of the now-established medical fact that until the end of the first trimester mortality in abortion may be less than mortality in normal childbirth. It follows that, from and after this point, a State may regulate the abortion procedure to the extent that the regulation reasonably relates to the preservation and protection of maternal health. Examples of permissible state regulation in this area are requirements as to the qualifications of the person who is to perform the abortion; as to the licensure of that person; as to the facility in which the procedure is to be performed, that is, whether it must be a hospital or may be a clinic or some other place of less-than-hospital status; as to the licensing of the facility; and the like.

This means, on the other hand, that for the period of pregnancy prior to this "compelling" point, the attending physician, in consultation with his patient, is free to determine, without regulation by the State, that, in his medical judgment, the patient's pregnancy should be terminated. If that decision is reached, the judgment may be effectuated by an abortion free of interference by the State.

With respect to the State's important and legitimate interest in potential life, the "compelling" point is at viability. This is so because the fetus then presumably has the capability of meaningful life outside the mother's womb. State regulation protective of fetal life after viability thus has both logical and biological justifications. If the State is interested in protecting fetal life after viability, it may go so far as to proscribe abortion during that period, except when it is necessary to preserve the life or health of the mother.

Measured against these standards, the Texas Penal Code, in restricting legal abortions to those "procured or attempted by medical advice for the purpose of saving the life of the mother," sweeps too broadly. The statute makes no distinction between abortions performed early in pregnancy and those performed later, and it limits to a single reason, "saving" the mother's life, the legal justification for the procedure. The statute, therefore, cannot survive the constitutional attack made upon it here.

To summarize and to repeat:

1. A state criminal abortion statute of the current Texas type, that excepts from criminality only a *life-saving* procedure on behalf of the mother, without regard to pregnancy stage and without recognition of the other interests involved, is violative of the Due Process Clause of the Fourteenth Amendment.

   (a) For the stage prior to approximately the end of the first trimester, the abortion decision and its effectuation must be left to the medical judgment of the pregnant woman's attending physician.

   (b) For the stage subsequent to approximately the end of the first trimester, the State, in promoting its interest in the health of the mother, may, if it chooses, regulate the abortion procedure in ways that are reasonably related to maternal health.

   (c) For the stage subsequent to viability, the State in promoting its interest in the potentiality of human life may, if it chooses, regulate, and even proscribe, abortion except where it is necessary, in appropriate medical judgment, for the preservation of the life or health of the mother.

This holding, we feel, is consistent with the relative weights of the respective interests involved, with the lessons and examples of medical and legal history, with the lenity of the common law, and with the demands of the profound problems of the present day. The decision leaves the State free to place increasing restrictions on abortion as the period of pregnancy lengthens, so long as those restrictions are tailored to the recognized state interests. The decision vindicates the right of the physician to administer medical treatment according to his professional judgment up to the points where important state interests provide compelling justifications for intervention. Up to those points, the abortion decision in all its aspects is inherently, and primarily, a medical decision, and basic responsibility for it must rest with the physician. If an individual practitioner abuses the privilege of exercising proper medical judgment, the usual remedies, judicial and intraprofessional, are available. . . .

Mr. Chief Justice Burger, concurring.

I agree that, under the Fourteenth Amendment to the Constitution, the abortion statutes of Georgia and Texas impermissibly limit the performance of abortions necessary to protect the health of pregnant women, using the term health in its broadest medical context. *** I am somewhat troubled that the Court has taken notice of various scientific and medical data in reaching its conclusion; however, I do not believe that the Court has exceeded the scope of judicial notice accepted in other contexts. . . .

I do not read the Court's holdings today as having the sweeping consequences attributed to them by dissenting Justices; the dissenting views discount the reality that the vast majority of physicians observe the standards of their profession, and act only on the basis of carefully deliberated medical judgments relating to life and health. Plainly, the Court today rejects any claim that the Constitution requires abortion on demand.

Mr. Justice Douglas, concurring. . . .

Mr. Justice Stewart, concurring. . . .

Mr. Justice White, with whom Mr. Justice Rehnquist joins, dissenting.

At the heart of the controversy in these cases are those recurring pregnancies that pose no danger whatsoever to the life or health of the mother but are, nevertheless, unwanted for any one or more of a variety of reasons — convenience, family planning, economics, dislike of children, the embarrassment of illegitimacy, etc. The common claim before us is that for any one of such reasons, or for no reason at all, and without asserting or claiming any threat to life or health, any woman is entitled to an abortion at her request if she is able to find a medical advisor willing to undertake the procedure.

The Court for the most part sustains this position: During the period prior to the time the fetus becomes viable, the Constitution of the United States values the convenience, whim, or caprice of the putative mother more than the life or potential life of the fetus; the Constitution, therefore, guarantees the right to an abortion as against any state law or policy seeking to protect the fetus from an abortion not prompted by more compelling reasons of the mother.

With all due respect, I dissent. I find nothing in the language or history of the Constitution to support the Court's judgment. The Court simply fashions and announces a new constitutional right for pregnant mothers and, with scarcely any reason or authority for its action, invests that right with sufficient substance to override most existing state abortion statutes. The upshot is that the people and the legislatures of the 50 States are constitutionally disentitled to weigh the relative importance of the continued existence and development of the fetus, on the one hand, against a spectrum of possible impacts on the mother, on the other hand. As an exercise of raw judicial power, the Court perhaps has authority to do what it does today; but in my view its judgment is an improvident and extravagant exercise of the power of judicial review that the Constitution extends to this Court. . . .

Mr. Justice Rehnquist, dissenting.

. . . The Due Process Clause of the Fourteenth Amendment undoubtedly does place a limit, albeit a broad one, on legislative power to enact laws such as this. If the Texas statute were to prohibit an abortion even where the mother's life is in jeopardy, I have little doubt that such a statute would lack a rational relation to a valid state objective. . . . But the Court's sweeping invalidation of any restrictions on abortion during the first trimester is impossible to justify under that standards, and the conscious weighing of competing factors that the Court's opinion appar-

ently substitutes for the established test is far more appropriate to a legislative judgment than to a judicial one.

The Court eschews the history of the Fourteenth Amendment in its reliance on the "compelling state interest" test. But the Court adds a new wrinkle to this test by transposing it from the legal considerations associated with the Equal Protection Clause of the Fourteenth Amendment to this case arising under the Due Process Clause of the Fourteenth Amendment. Unless I misapprehend the consequences of this transplanting of the "compelling state interest test," the Court's opinion will accomplish the seemingly impossible feat of leaving this area of the law more confused than it found it.

. . . While the Court's opinion quotes from the dissent of Mr. Justice Holmes in *Lochner v. New York,* the result it reaches is more closely attuned to the majority opinion of Mr. Justice Peckham in that case. As in *Lochner* and similar cases applying substantive due process standards to economic and social welfare legislation, the adoption of the compelling state interest standard will inevitably require this Court to examine the legislative policies and pass on the wisdom of these policies in the very process of deciding whether a particular state interest put forward may or may not be "compelling." The decision here to break pregnancy into three distinct terms and to outline the permissible restrictions the State may impose in each one, for example, partakes more of judicial legislation than it does of a determination of the intent of the drafters of the Fourteenth Amendment.

The fact that a majority of the States reflecting, after all, the majority sentiment in those States, have had restrictions on abortions for at least a century is a strong indication, it seems to me, that the asserted right to an abortion is not "so rooted in the traditions and conscience of our people as to be ranked as fundamental. . . ." Even today, when society's views on abortion are changing, the very existence of the debate is evidence that the "right" to an abortion is not so universally accepted as the appellants would have us believe. . . .

Maher v. Roe

432 U.S. 464; 97 S. Ct. 2376; 53 L. Ed. 2d 484 (1977)
Vote: 6-3

Mr. Justice Powell delivered the opinion of the Court.

A regulation of the Connecticut Welfare Department limits state medicaid benefits for first trimester abortions to those that are "medically necessary," a term defined to include psychiatric necessity. *** Connecticut enforces this limitation through a system of prior authorization from its Department of Social Services. In order to obtain authorization for a first trimester abortion, the hospital or clinic where the abortion is to be performed must submit, among other things, a certificate from the patient's attending physician stating that the abortion is medically necessary.

This attack on the validity of the Connecticut regulation was brought against Appellant Maher, the Commissioner of Social Services, by Appellees Poe and Roe, two indigent women who were unable to obtain a physician's certificate of medical necessity. In a complaint filed in the United States District Court for the District of Connecticut, they challenged the regulation both as inconsistent with the requirements of Title XIX of the Social Security Act, *** and as violative of their constitutional rights, including the Fourteenth Amendment's guarantees of due process and equal protection. Connecticut originally defended its regulation on the theory that Title XIX of the Social Security Act prohibited the funding of abortions that were not medically necessary. After certifying a class of women unable to obtain medicaid assistance for abortions because of the regulation, the District Court held that the Social Security Act not only allowed state funding of nontherapeutic abortions but also required it. *** On appeal, the Court of Appeals for the Second Circuit read the Social Security Act to allow, but not to require, state funding of such abortions. *** Upon remand for consideration of the constitutional issues raised in the complaint, a three-judge District Court was convened. That court invalidated the Connecticut regulation. ***

Although it found no independent constitutional right to a state-financed abortion, the District Court held that the Equal Protection Clause forbids the exclusion of nontherapeutic abortions from a state welfare program that generally subsidizes the medical expenses incident to pregnancy and childbirth. The court found implicit in *Roe v. Wade* *** (1973), and *Doe v. Bolton,* *** the view that "abortion and childbirth, when stripped of the sensitive moral arguments surrounding the abortion controversy, are simply two alternative medical methods of dealing with pregnancy...." *** ... [T]he court held that the Connecticut program "weights the choice of the pregnant mother against choosing to exercise her constitutionally protected right" to a nontherapeutic abortion and "thus infringes upon a fundamental interest." *** The court found no state interest to justify this infringement. The State's fiscal interest was held to be "wholly chimerical because abortion is the least expensive medical response to a pregnancy." *** And any moral objection to abortion was deemed constitutionally irrelevant:

The state may not justify its refusal to pay for one type of expense arising from pregnancy on the basis that it morally opposes such an expenditure of money. To sanction such a justification would be to permit discrimination against those seeking to exercise a constitutional right on the basis that the state simply does not approve of the exercise of that right. ***

The District Court enjoined the State from requiring the certificate of medical necessity for Medicaid-funded abortions. The court also struck down the related requirements of prior written request by the pregnant woman and prior authorization by the Department of Social Services, holding that the State could not impose any requirements on Medicaid payments for abortions that are not "equally applicable to Medicaid payments for childbirth, if such conditions or requirements tend to discourage a woman from choosing an abortion or to delay the occurrence of an abortion that she has asked her physician to perform." *** We noted probable jurisdiction to consider the constitutionality of the Connecticut regulation. ***

The Constitution imposes no obligation on the States to pay the pregnancy-related medical expenses of indigent women, or indeed to pay any of the medical expenses of indigent women, or indeed to pay any of the medical expenses of indigents. But when a State decides to alleviate some of the hardships of poverty by providing medical care, the manner in which it dispenses benefits is subject to constitutional limitations. Appellees' claim is that Connecticut must accord equal treatment to both abortion and childbirth, and may not evidence a policy preference by funding only the medical expenses incident to childbirth. This challenge to the classifications established by the Connecticut regulation presents a question arising under the Equal Protection Clause of the Fourteenth Amendment. The basic framework of analysis of such a claim is well settled.

We must decide, first, whether [state legislation] operated to the disadvantage of some suspect class or impinges upon a fundamental right explicitly or implicitly protected by the Constitution, thereby requiring strict judicial scrutiny.... If not, the [legislative] scheme must still be examined to determine whether it rationally furthers some legitimate, articulated state purpose and therefore does not constitute an invidious discrimination....

... Applying this analysis here, we think the District Court erred in holding that the Connecticut regulation violated the Equal Protection Clause of the Fourteenth Amendment.

This case involves no discrimination against a suspect class. An indigent woman desiring an abortion does not come within the limited category of disadvantaged classes so recognized by our cases. Nor does the fact that the impact of the regulation falls upon those who cannot pay lead to a different conclusion. In a sense, every denial of welfare to an indigent creates a wealth classification as compared to nonindigents who are able to pay for the desired goods or services. But this Court has never held that financial need alone identifies a suspect class for purposes of equal protection analysis. *** Accordingly, the central question in this case is whether the regulation "impinges upon a fundamental right explicitly or implicitly protected by the Constitution." *** The District Court read our decisions in *Roe v. Wade*, *** and the subsequent cases applying it, as establishing a fundamental right to abortion and

therefore concluded that nothing less than a compelling state interest would justify Connecticut's different treatment of abortion and childbirth. We think the District Court misconceived the nature and scope of the fundamental right recognized in *Roe*.

At issue in *Roe* was the constitutionality of a Texas law making it a crime to procure or attempt to procure an abortion, except on medical advice for the purpose of saving the life of the mother. Drawing on a group of disparate cases restricting governmental intrusion, physical coercion, and criminal prohibition of certain activities, we concluded that the Fourteenth Amendment's concept of personal liberty affords constitutional protection against state interference with certain aspects of an individual's personal "privacy," including a woman's decision to terminate her pregnancy. ***

The Texas statute imposed severe criminal sanctions on the physicians and other medical personnel who performed abortions, thus drastically limiting the availability and safety of the desired service. As Mr. Justice Stewart observed, "it is difficult to imagine a more complete abridgment of a constitutional freedom...." *** We held that only a compelling state interest would justify such a sweeping restriction on a constitutionally protected interest, and we found no such state interest during the first trimester. Even when judged against this demanding standard, however, the State's dual interests in the health of the pregnant woman and the potential life of the fetus were deemed sufficient to justify substantial regulation of abortions in the second and third trimesters. "These interests are separate and distinct. Each grows in substantiality as the woman approaches term and, at a point during pregnancy, each becomes 'compelling.' " *** In the second trimester, the State's interest in the health of the pregnant woman justifies state regulation reasonably related to that concern. *** At viability, usually in the third trimester, the State's interest in the potential life of the fetus justifies prohibition with criminal penalties, except where the life or health of the mother is threatened. ***

The Texas law in *Roe* was a stark example of impermissible interference with the pregnant woman's decision to terminate her pregnancy. In subsequent cases, we have invalidated other types of restrictions, different in form but similar in effect, on the woman's freedom of choice. Thus, in *Planned Parenthood of Missouri v. Danforth,* *** we held that Missouri's requirement of spousal consent was unconstitutional because it "granted [the husband] the right to prevent unilaterally, and for whatever reason, the effectuation of his wife's and her physician's decision to terminate her pregnancy." Missouri had interposed an "absolute obstacle to a woman's decision that *Roe* held to be constitutionally protected from such interference. . . ."

These cases recognize a constitutionally protected interest "in making certain kinds of important decisions" free from governmental compulsion. *** . . .[T]he right in *Roe v. Wade* can be understood only by considering both the woman's interest and the nature of the State's interference with it. *Roe* did not declare an unqualified "constitutional right to an abortion," as the District Court seemed to think. Rather, the right protects the woman from unduly burdensome interference with her freedom to decide whether to terminate her pregnancy. It implies no limitation on the authority of a State to make a value judgment favoring childbirth over abortion, and to implement that judgment by the allocation of public funds.

The Connecticut regulation before us is different in kind from the laws invalidated in our previous abortion decisions. The Connecticut regulation places no obstacles—absolute or otherwise—in the pregnant woman's path to an abortion. An indigent woman who desires an abortion suffers no disadvantage as a consequence of Connecticut's decision to fund childbirth; she continues as before to be dependent on private sources for the service she desires. The State may have made childbirth a more attractive alternative, thereby influencing the woman's decision, but it has imposed no restriction on access to abortions that was not already there. The indigency that may make it difficult—and in some cases, perhaps, impossible—for some women to have abortions is neither created nor in any way affected by the Connecticut regulation. We conclude that the Connecticut regulation does not impinge upon the fundamental right recognized in *Roe*.

Our conclusion signals no retreat from *Roe* or the cases applying it. There is a basic difference between direct state interference with a protected activity and

state encouragement of an alternative activity consonant with legislative policy. Constitutional concerns are greatest when the State attempts to impose its will by force of law; the State's power to encourage actions deemed to be in the public interest is necessarily far broader.

This distinction is implicit in two cases cited in *Roe* in support of the pregnant woman's right under the Fourteenth Amendment. *Meyer v. Nebraska,* *** involved a Nebraska law making it criminal to teach foreign languages to children who had not passed the eighth grade. Nebraska's imposition of a criminal sanction on the providers of desired services makes *Meyer* closely analogous to *Roe*. In sustaining the constitutional challenge brought by a teacher convicted under the law, the Court held that the teacher's "right thus to teach and the right of parents to engage him so to instruct their children" were "within the liberty of the Amendment." In *Pierce v. Society of Sisters,* *** the Court relied on Meyer to invalidate an Oregon criminal law requiring the parent or guardian of a child to send him to public school, thus precluding the choice of a private school. Reasoning that the Fourteenth Amendment's concept of liberty "excludes any general power of the State to standardize its children by forcing them to accept instruction from public teachers only," the Court held that the law "unreasonably interfere[d] with the liberty of parents and guardians to direct the upbringing and education of children under their control." ***

Both cases invalidate substantial restrictions on constitutionally protected liberty interests: in *Meyer,* the parent's right to have his child taught a particular foreign language; in *Pierce,* the parent's right to choose private rather than public school education. But neither case denied to a State the policy choice of encouraging the preferred course of action. Indeed, in *Meyer* the Court was careful to state that the power of the State "to prescribe a curriculum" that included English and excluded German in its free public schools "is not questioned." *** Similarly, *Pierce* casts no shadow over a State's power to favor public education by funding it—a policy choice pursued in some States for more than a century. . . . Yet, were we to accept appellees' argument, an indigent parent could challenge the state policy of favoring public rather than private schools, or of preferring instruction in English rather than German, on grounds identical in principle to those advanced here. We think it abundantly clear that a State is not required to show a compelling interest for its policy choice to favor normal childbirth any more than a State must so justify its election to fund public but not private education.

The question remains whether Connecticut's regulation can be sustained under the less demanding test of rationality that applies in the absence of a suspect classification or the impingement of a fundamental right. This test requires that the distinction drawn between childbirth and nontherapeutic abortion by the regulation be "rationally related" to a "constitutionally permissible" purpose. *** We hold that the Connecticut funding scheme satisfies this standard. . . .

We certainly are not unsympathetic to the plight of an indigent woman who desires an abortion, but "the Constitution does not provide judicial remedies for every social and economic ill." *** Our cases uniformly have accorded the States a wider latitude in choosing among competing demands for limited public funds. In *Dandrige v. Williams*, *** despite recognition that laws and regulations allocating welfare funds involve "the most basic economic needs of impoverished human beings," we held that classifications survive equal protection challenge when a "reasonable basis" for the classification is shown. As the preceding discussion makes clear, the state interest in encouraging normal childbirth exceeds this minimal level.

The decision whether to expend state funds for nontherapeutic abortion is fraught with judgments of policy and value over which opinions are sharply divided. Our conclusion that the Connecticut regulation is constitutional is not based on a weighing of its wisdom or social desirability, for this Court does not strike down state laws "because they may be unwise, improvident, or out of harmony with a particular school of thought." *** Indeed, when an issue involves policy choices as sensitive as those implicated by public funding of nontherapeutic abortions, the appropriate forum for their resolution in a democracy is the legislature. We should not forget that "legislatures are ultimate guardians of the liberties

and welfare of the people in quite as great a degree as the courts." ***

In conclusion, we emphasize that our decision today does not proscribe government funding of nontherapeutic abortions. It is open to Congress to require provision of Medicaid benefits for such abortions as a condition of state participation in the Medicaid program. Also, . . . Connecticut is free—through normal democratic processes—to decide that such benefits should be provided. We hold only that the Constitution does not require a judicially imposed resolution of these difficult issues.

The District Court also invalidated Connecticut's requirements of prior written request by the pregnant woman and prior authorization by the Department of Social Services. Our analysis above rejects the basic premise that prompted invalidation of these procedural requirements. It is not unreasonable for a State to insist upon a prior showing of medical necessity to insure that its money is being spent only for authorized purposes. The simple answer to the argument that similar requirements are not imposed for other medical procedures is that such procedures do not involve the termination of a potential human life. In *Planned Parenthood of Central Missouri v. Danforth*, *** we held that the woman's written consent to an abortion was not an impermissible burden under *Roe*. We think that decision is controlling on the similar issue here.

The judgment of the District Court is reversed, and the case is remanded for further proceedings consistent with this opinion.

Mr. Chief Justice Burger, concurring. . . .

Mr. Justice Brennan, with whom ***Mr. Justice Marshall*** and ***Mr. Justice Blackmun*** join, dissenting.

The District Court held:

When Connecticut refuses to fund elective abortions while funding therapeutic abortions and prenatal and postnatal case, it weights the choice of the pregnant mother against choosing to exercise her constitutionally protected right to an elective abortion. . . . Her choice is affected not simply by the absence of payment for the abortion, but by the availability of public funds for childbirth if she chooses not to have the abortion. When the state thus infringes upon a fundamental interest, it must assert a compelling state interest. ***

This Court reverses on the ground that "the District Court misconceived the nature and scope of the fundamental right recognized in *Roe* ***" and therefore that Connecticut was not required to meet the "compelling interest" test to justify its discrimination against elective abortion but only "the less demanding test of rationality that applies in the absence of . . . the infringement of a fundamental right." *** This holding, the Court insists, "places no obstacles— absolute or otherwise—in the pregnant woman's path to an abortion"; she is still at liberty to finance the abortion from "private sources." *** True, "the State may [by funding childbirth] have made childbirth a more attractive alternative, thereby influencing the woman's decision, but it has imposed no restriction on access to abortions that was not already there." True, also indigency "may make it more difficult—and in some cases, perhaps impossible— for some women to have abortions," but that regrettable consequence "is neither created nor in any way affected by the Connecticut regulation." ***

But a distressing insensitivity to the plight of impoverished pregnant women is inherent in the Court's analysis. The stark reality for too many, not just "some," indigent pregnant women is that indigency makes access to competent licensed physicians not merely "difficult" but "impossible." As a practical matter, many indigent women will feel they have no choice but to carry their pregnancies to term because the State will pay for the associated medical services, even though they would have chosen to have abortions if the State had also provided funds for that procedure, or indeed if the State had provided funds for neither procedure. This disparity in funding by the State clearly operates to coerce indigent pregnant women to bear children they would not otherwise choose to have, and just as clearly, this coercion can only operate upon the poor, who are uniquely the victims of this form of financial pressure. . . .

None can take seriously the Court's assurance that its "conclusion signals no retreat from *Roe* [*v. Wade*] or the cases applying it. . . ." Indeed, it cannot be gainsaid that today's decision seriously erodes the principles that *Roe* and *Doe* announced to guide the determination of what constitutes an unconstitutional infringement of the fundamental right of pregnant women to be free to decide whether to have an abortion.

The Court's premise is that only an equal protection claim is presented here. Claims of interference with enjoyment of fundamental rights have, however, occupied a rather protean position in our constitutional jurisprudence. Whether or not the Court's analysis may reasonably proceed under the Equal Protection Clause, the Court plainly errs in ignoring, as it does, the unanswerable argument of appellee, and holding of the District Court, that the regulation unconstitutionally impinges upon her claim of privacy derived from the Due Process Clause. . . .

Until today, I had not thought the nature of the fundamental right established in *Roe* was open to question, let alone susceptible to the interpretation advanced by the Court. The fact that the Connecticut scheme may not operate as an absolute bar preventing all indigent women from having abortions is not critical. What is critical is that the State has inhibited their fundamental right to make that choice free from state interference. . . .

Although Connecticut does not argue it as justification, the Court concludes that the State's interest "in protecting the potential life of the fetus" suffices. *** Since only the first trimester of pregnancy is involved in this case, that justification is totally foreclosed if the Court is not overruling the holding of *Roe v. Wade* that "[w]ith respect to the State's important and legitimate interest in potential life, the 'compelling point is at viability,'" occurring at about the end of the second trimester. *** The [State] also argues a further justification not relied upon by the Court, namely, that it needs "to control the amount of its limited public funds which will be allocated to its public welfare budget." *** The District Court correctly held, however, that the asserted interest was "wholly chimerical" because the "state's assertion that it saves money when it declines to pay the cost of a welfare mother's abortion is simply contrary to indisputed facts." ***

Finally, the reasons that render the Connecticut regulation unconstitutional also render invalid in my view the requirement of a prior written certification by the woman's attending physician that the abortion is "medically necessary," and the requirement that the hospital submit a Request for Authorization of professional Services including a "statement indicating the medical need for the abortion." *** For the same reasons, I would also strike down the requirement for prior authorization of payment by the Connecticut Department of Social Services.

Mr. Justice Marshall dissenting. . . .

Mr. Justice Blackmun, joined by *Mr. Justice Brennan* and *Mr. Justice Marshall,* dissenting. . . .

Bellotti v. Baird

443 U.S. 622; 99 S. Ct. 3035; 61 L. Ed.2d 797 (1979)
Vote: 8-1

In this case, the Supreme Court considers a challenge to a Massachusetts law restricting the access of minors to abortions.

Mr. Justice Powell announced the judgment of the Court and delivered an opinion in which *The Chief Justice, Mr. Justice Stewart,* and *Mr. Justice Rehnquist* joined.

. . . On August 2, 1974, the Legislature of the Commonwealth of Massachusetts passed, over the Governor's veto, an Act pertaining to abortions performed within the State. *** According to its title, the statute was intended to regulate abortions "within present constitutional limits." Shortly before the Act was to go into effect, the class action from which these appeals arise was commenced in the District Court to enjoin, as unconstitutional, the provision of the Act now codified as Mass. Gen. Laws Ann., ch. 112, Sec. 12S (West Supp. 1979).

Section 12S provides in part:

"If the mother is less than eighteen years of age and has not married, the consent of both the mother and her parents [to an abortion to be performed on the mother] is required. If one or both of the mother's parents refuse such consent, consent may be obtained by order of a judge of the superior court for good cause shown, after such hearing as he deems necessary. Such a hearing will not require the appointment of a guardian for the mother. If one of the parents has died or has deserted his or her family, consent by the remaining parent is sufficient. If both parents have died or have deserted their family, consent of the mother's guardian or other person having duties similar to a guardian, or any person who had assumed the care and custody of the mother is sufficient. The commissioner of public health shall prescribe a written form for such consent.

Such form shall be signed by the proper person or persons and given to the physician performing the abortion who shall maintain it in his permanent files."

Physicians performing abortions in the absence of the consent required by Sec. 12S are subject to injunctions and criminal penalties. ***

. . . Unquestionably, there are many competing theories about the most effective way for parents to fulfill their central role in assisting their children on the way to responsible adulthood. While we do not pretend any special wisdom on this subject, we cannot ignore that central to many of these theories, and deeply rooted in our Nation's history and tradition, is the belief that the parental role implies a substantial measure of authority over one's children. Indeed, "constitutional interpretation has consistently recognized that the parents' claim to authority in their own household to direct the rearing of their children is basic in the structure of our society." ***

Properly understood, then, the tradition of parental authority is not inconsistent with our tradition of individual liberty; rather, the former is one of the basic presuppositions of the latter. Legal restrictions on minors, especially those supportive of the parental role, may be important to the child's chances for the full growth and maturity that make eventual participation in a free society meaningful and rewarding. Under the Constitution, the State can "properly conclude that parents and others, teachers for example, who have [the] primary responsibility for children's well-being are entitled to the support of laws designed to aid discharge of that responsibility." ***

With these principles in mind, we consider the specific constitutional questions presented by these appeals. . . . Massachusetts has attempted to reconcile the constitutional right of a woman, in consultation with her physician, to choose to terminate her pregnancy as established by *Roe v. Wade* *** with the special interest of the State in encouraging an unmarried pregnant minor to seek the advice of her parents in making the important decision whether or not to bear a child. . . .

The pregnant minor's options are much different from those facing a minor in other situations, such as deciding whether to marry. A minor not permitted to marry before the age of majority is required simply to postpone her decision. She and her intended spouse may preserve the opportunity for later marriage should they continue to desire it. A pregnant adolescent, however, cannot preserve for long the possibility of aborting, which effectively expires in a matter of weeks from the onset of pregnancy.

Moreover, the potentially severe detriment facing a pregnant woman *** is not mitigated by her minority. Indeed, considering her probable education, employment skills, financial resources, and emotional maturity, unwanted motherhood may be exceptionally burdensome for a minor. In addition, the fact of having a child brings with it adult legal responsibility, for parenthood, like attainment of the age of majority, is one of the traditional criteria for the termination of the legal disabilities of minority. In sum, there are few situations in which denying a minor the right to make an important decision will have consequences so grave and indelible.

Yet, an abortion may not be the best choice for the minor. The circumstances in which this issue arises will vary widely. In a given case, alternatives to abortion, such as marriage to the father of the child, arranging for its adoption, or assuming the responsibilities of motherhood with the assured support of family, may be feasible and relevant to the minor's best interests. Nonetheless, the abortion decision is one that simply cannot be postponed, or it will be made by default with far-reaching consequences.

For these reasons *** "the State may not impose a blanket provision . . . requiring the consent of a parent or person *in loco parentis* as a condition for abortion of an unmarried minor during the first 12 weeks of her pregnancy." Although *** such deference to parents may be permissible with respect to

other choices facing a minor, the unique nature and consequences of the abortion decision make it inappropriate "to give a third party an absolute, and possibly arbitrary, veto over the decision of the physician and his patient to terminate the patient's pregnancy, regardless of the reason for withholding the consent." *** We therefore conclude that if the State decides to require a pregnant minor to obtain one or both parents' consent to an abortion, it also must provide an alternative procedure whereby authorization for the abortion can be obtained.

A pregnant minor is entitled in such a proceeding to show either: (1) that she is mature enough and well enough informed to make her abortion decision, in consultation with her physician, independently of her parents' wishes, or (2) that even if she is not able to make this decision independently, the desired abortion would be in her best interests. The proceeding in which this showing is made must assure that a resolution of the issue, and any appeals that may follow, will be completed with anonymity and sufficient expedition to provide an effective opportunity for an abortion to be obtained. In sum, the procedure must ensure that the provision requiring parental consent does not in fact amount to the "absolute, and possibly arbitrary, veto" that was found impermissible in [*Planned Parenthood of Central Missouri v.*] *Danforth* *** [1976].

It is against these requirements that [Sec.] 12S must be tested. We observe initially that as authoritatively construed by the highest court of the State, the statute satisfies some of the concerns that require special treatment of a minor's abortion decision. It provides that if parental consent is refused, authorization may be "obtained by order of a judge of the superior court for good cause shown, after such hearing as he deems necessary." A superior court judge . . . "must disregard all parental objections, and other considerations, which are not based exclusively on what would serve the minor's best interests." ***

Despite these safeguards, . . . [the challenged provision] falls short of constitutional standards in certain respects. We now consider these. Among the questions certified to the [Massachusetts] Supreme Judicial Court was whether Sec. 12S permits any minors—mature or immature—to obtain judicial consent to an abortion without any parental consultation whatsoever. *** The state court answered that, in general, it does not. "[T]he consent required by [Sec. 12S must] be obtained for every nonemergency abortion where the mother is less than eighteen years of age and unmarried." *** The text of Sec. 12S itself states an exception to this rule, making consent unnecessary from any parent who has "died or has deserted his or her family." The Supreme Judicial Court construed the statute as containing an additional exception: Consent need not be obtained "where no parent (or statutory substitute) is available." *** The court also ruled that an available parent must be given notice of any judicial proceedings brought by a minor to obtain consent for an abortion. ***

We think that, construed in this manner, Sec. 12S would impose an undue burden upon the exercise by minors of the right to seek an abortion. As the District Court recognized, "there are parents who would obstruct, and perhaps altogether prevent, the minor's right to go to court." *** There is no reason to believe that this would be so in the majority of cases where consent is withheld. But many parents hold strong views on the subject of abortion, and young pregnant minors, especially those living at home, are particularly vulnerable to their parents' efforts to obstruct both an abortion and their access to court. It would be unrealistic, therefore, to assume that the mere existence of a legal right to seek relief in superior court provides an effective avenue of relief for some of those who need it the most.

We conclude, therefore, that under state regulation such as that undertaken by Massachusetts, every minor must have the opportunity—if she so desires—to go directly to a court without first consulting or notifying her parents. If she satisfies the court that she is mature and well enough informed to make intelligently the abortion decision on her own, the court must authorize her to act without parental consultation or consent. If she fails to satisfy the court that she is competent to make this decision independently, she must be permitted to show that an abortion nevertheless would be in her best interests. If the court is persuaded that it is, the court must authorize the abortion. If, however, the court is not persuaded by the minor that she is mature or that the

abortion would be in her best interests, it may decline to sanction the operation.

There is, however, an important state interest in encouraging a family rather than a judicial resolution of a minor's abortion decision. Also, as we have observed above, parents naturally take an interest in the welfare of their children—an interest that is particularly strong where a normal family relationship exists and where the child is living with one or both parents. These factors properly may be taken into account by a court called upon to determine whether an abortion in fact is in a minor's best interests. If, all things considered, the court determines that an abortion is in the minor's best interests, she is entitled to court authorization without any parental involvement. On the other hand, the court may deny the abortion request of an immature minor in the absence of parental consultation if it concludes that her best interests would be served thereby, or the court may in such a case defer decision until there is parental consultation in which the court may participate. But this is the full extent to which parental involvement may be required. For the reasons stated above, the constitutional right to seek an abortion may not be unduly burdened by state-imposed conditions upon initial access to court.

Sec. 12S requires that both parents consent to a minor's abortion. The District Court found it to be "custom" to perform other medical and surgical procedures on minors with the consent of only one parent, and it concluded that "nothing about abortions . . . requires the minor's interest to be treated differently." ***

We are not persuaded that, as a general rule, the requirement of obtaining both parents' consent unconstitutionally burdens a minor's right to seek an abortion. The abortion decision has implications far broader than those associated with most other kinds of medical treatment. At least when the parents are together and the pregnant minor is living at home, both the father and mother have an interest—one normally supportive—in helping to determine the course that is in the best interests of a daughter. Consent and involvement by parents in important decisions by minors long have been recognized as protective of their immaturity. In the case of the abortion decision, for reasons we have stated, the focus of the parents' inquiry should be the best interests of their daughter. As every pregnant minor is entitled in the first instance to go directly to the court for a judicial determination without prior parental notice, consultation, or consent, the general rule with respect to parental consent does not unduly burden the constitutional right. Moreover, where the pregnant minor goes to her parents and consent is denied, she still must have recourse to a prompt judicial determination of her maturity or best interests.

Another of the questions certified by the District Court to the Supreme Judicial Court was the following: "If the superior court finds that the minor is capable [of making], and has, in fact, made and adhered to, an informed and reasonable decision to have an abortion, may the court refuse its consent based on a finding that a parent's, or its own, contrary decision is a better one?" *** To this the state court answered:

"[W]e do not view the judge's role as limited to a determination that the minor is capable of making, and has made, an informed and reasonable decision to have an abortion. Certainly the judge must make a determination of those circumstances, but, if the statutory role of the judge to determine the best interests of the minor is to be carried out, he must make a finding on the basis of all relevant views presented to him. We suspect that the judge will give great weight to the minor's determination, if informed and reasonable, but in circumstances where he determines that the best interests of the minor will not be served by an abortion, the judge's determination should prevail, assuming that his conclusion is supported by the evidence and adequate findings of fact." ***

The Supreme Judicial Court's statement reflects the general rule that a State may require a minor to wait until the age of majority before being permitted to exercise legal rights independently. *** But we are concerned here with the exercise of a constitutional right of unique character. *** As stated above, if the minor satisfies a court that she has attained sufficient maturity to make a fully informed decision, she then is entitled to make her abortion decision independently. We therefore agree with the District Court that Sec. 12S cannot constitutionally permit judicial disregard of the abortion decision of a minor who has been determined to be mature and fully

competent to assess the implications of the choice she has made.

Although it satisfies constitutional standards in large part, Sec. 12S falls short of them in two respects: First, it permits judicial authorization for an abortion to be withheld from a minor who is found by the superior court to be mature and fully competent to make this decision independently. Second, it requires parental consultation or notification in every instance, without affording the pregnant minor an opportunity to receive an independent judicial determination that she is mature enough to consent or that an abortion would be in her best interests. Accordingly, we affirm the judgment of the District Court insofar as it invalidates this statute and enjoins its enforcement.

Affirmed.

Mr. Justice Rehnquist, concurring. . . .

Mr. Justice Stevens, with whom ***Mr. Justice Brennan, Mr. Justice Marshall,*** and ***Mr. Justice Blackmun,*** join, concurring in the judgment.

. . . The Massachusetts statute is, on its face, simple and straightforward. It provides that every woman under 18 who has not married must secure the consent of both her parents before receiving an abortion. "If one or both of the mother's parents refuse such consent, consent may be obtained by order of a judge of the superior court for good cause shown." ***

Whatever confusion or uncertainty might have existed as to how this statute was to operate *** has been eliminated by the authoritative construction of its provisions by the Massachusetts Supreme Judicial Court. *** The statute was construed to require that every minor who wishes an abortion must first seek the consent of both parents, unless a parent is not available or unless the need for the abortion constitutes " 'an emergency requiring immediate action.' " *** Both parents, so long as they are available, must also receive notice of judicial proceedings brought under the statute by the minor. In those proceedings, the task of the judge is to determine whether the best interests of the minor will be served by an abortion. The decision is his to make, even if he finds "that the minor is capable of making, and has made, an informed and reasonable decision to have an abortion." *** Thus, no minor in Massachusetts, no matter how mature and capable of informed decisionmaking, may receive an abortion without the consent of either both her parents or a superior court judge. In every instance, the minor's decision to secure an abortion is subject to an absolute third-party veto.

In *Planned Parenthood of Central Missouri v. Danforth* *** this Court invalidated statutory provisions requiring the consent of the husband of a married woman and of one parent of a pregnant minor to an abortion. As to the spousal consent, the Court concluded that "we cannot hold that the State has the constitutional authority to give the spouse unilaterally the ability to prohibit the wife from terminating her pregnancy, when the State itself lacks that right." *** And as to the parental consent, the Court held that "[j]ust as with the requirement of consent from the spouse, so here, the State does not have the constitutional authority to give a third party an absolute, and possibly arbitrary, veto over the decision of the physician and his patient to terminate the patient's pregnancy, regardless of the reason for withholding the consent." *** These holdings, I think, equally apply to the Massachusetts [law that] requires the consent of both of the woman's parents. It does, of course, provide an alternative in the form of a suit initiated by the woman in superior court. But in that proceeding, the judge is afforded an absolute veto over the minor's decisions, based on his judgment of her best interests. In Massachusetts, then, as in Missouri, the State has imposed an "absolute limitation on the minor's right to obtain an abortion," *** applicable to every pregnant minor in the State who has not married.

The provision of an absolute veto to a judge—or, potentially, to an appointed administrator—is to me particularly troubling. The constitutional right to make the abortion decision affords protection to both of the privacy interests recognized in this Court's cases: "One is the individual interest in avoiding disclosure of personal matters, and another is the interest in independence in making certain kinds of important decisions." *** It is inherent in the right to make the abortion decision that the right may be exercised without public scrutiny and in defiance of the contrary opinion of the sovereign or other third parties. In Massachusetts, however, every minor who cannot secure the consent of both her parents—which under *Danforth* cannot be an absolute prerequisite to an abortion—is required to secure the consent of the sovereign. As a practical matter, I would suppose that the need to commence judicial proceedings in order to obtain a legal abortion would impose a burden at least as great as, and probably greater than, that imposed on the minor child by the need to obtain the consent of a parent. Moreover, once this burden is met, the only standard provided for the judge's decision is the best interest of the minor. That standard provides little real guidance to the judge, and his decision must necessarily reflect personal and societal values and mores whose enforcement upon the minor—particularly when contrary to her own informed and reasonable decision—is fundamentally at odds with privacy interests underlying the constitutional protection afforded to her decision.

In short, it seems to me that this case is governed by *Danforth;* to the extent this statute differs from that in *Danforth,* it is potentially even more restrictive of the constitutional right to decide whether or not to terminate a pregnancy. Because the statute has been once authoritatively construed by the Massachusetts Supreme Judicial Court, and because it is clear that the statute as written and construed is not constitutional, I agree with Mr. Justice Powell that the District Court's judgment should be affirmed. Because his opinion goes further, however, and addresses the constitutionality of an abortion statute that Massachusetts has not enacted, I decline to join his opinion.

Mr. Justice White, dissenting.

I was in dissent in *Planned Parenthood of Central Missouri v. Danforth* *** on the issue of the validity of requiring the consent of a parent when an unmarried woman under 18 years of age seeks an abortion. I continue to have the views I expressed there and also agree with much of what Mr. Justice Stevens said in dissent in that case *** I would not, therefore, strike down this Massachusetts law.

But even if a parental consent requirement of the kind involved in *Danforth* must be deemed invalid, that does not condemn the Massachusetts law, which, when the parents object, authorizes a judge to permit an abortion if he concludes that an abortion is in the best interests of the child. Going beyond *Danforth,* the Court now holds it unconstitutional for a State to require that in all cases parents receive notice that their daughter seeks an abortion and, if they object to the abortion, an opportunity to participate in a hearing that will determine whether it is in the "best interests" of the child to undergo the surgery. Until now, I would have thought inconceivable a holding that the United States Constitution forbids even notice to parents when their minor child who seeks surgery objects to such notice and is able to convince a judge that the parents should be denied participation in the decision.

With all due respect, I dissent.

Akron v. Akron Center for Reproductive Health
462 U.S. 416; 103 S.Ct. 2481; 76 L. Ed. 2d 687 (1983)
Vote: 6-3

Justice Powell delivered the opinion of the Court.

In this litigation we must decide the constitutionality of several provisions of an ordinance enacted by the city of Akron, Ohio, to regulate the performance of abortions.

[This case comes] to us a decade after we held in *Roe v. Wade* *** that the right of privacy, grounded in the concept of personal liberty guaranteed by the Constitution, encompasses a woman's right to decide whether to terminate her pregnancy. Legislative responses to the Court's decision have required us on several occasions, and again today, to define the limits of a State's authority to regulate the performance of abortions. And arguments continue to be made . . . that we erred in interpreting the Constitution. Nonetheless, the doctrine of *stare decisis,* while perhaps never entirely persuasive on a constitutional question, is a doctrine that demands respect in a society governed by the rule of law. We respect it today, and reaffirm *Roe v. Wade.*

In February 1978 the city council of Akron enacted Ordinance No. 160–1978, entitled "Regulation of Abortions." The ordinance sets forth 17 provisions that regulate the performance of abortions, five of which are at issue in this case:

(i) Section 1870.03 requires that all abortions performed after the first trimester of pregnancy be performed in a hospital.

(ii) Section 1870.05 sets forth requirements for notification of and consent by parents before abortions may be performed on unmarried minors.

(iii) Section 1870.06 requires that the attending physician make certain specified statements to the patient "to insure that the consent for an abortion is truly informed consent."

(iv) Section 1870.07 requires a 24-hour waiting period between the time the woman signs a consent form and the time the abortion is performed.

(v) Section 1870.16 requires that fetal remains be "disposed of in a humane and sanitary manner."

A violation of any section of the ordinance is punishable as a criminal misdemeanor. If any provision is invalidated, it is to be severed from the remainder of the ordinance. The ordinance became effective on May 1, 1978.

On April 19, 1978, a lawsuit challenging virtually all of the ordinance's provisions was filed in the District Court of the Northern District of Ohio. The plaintiffs, respondents and cross-petitioners in this Court were three corporations that operate abortion clinics in Akron and a physician who has performed abortions at one of the clinics. The defendants, petitioners and cross-respondents here were the city of Akron and three city officials. . . .

In August 1979, after hearing evidence, the District Court ruled on the merits. It found that plaintiffs lacked standing to challenge seven provisions of the ordinance, none of which is before this Court. The District Court invalidated four provisions, including 1870.05 (parental notice and consent), 1870.06(B) (requiring disclosure of facts concerning the woman's pregnancy, fetal development, the complications of abortion, and agencies available to assist the woman) and 1870.16 (disposal of fetal remains). The court upheld the constitutionality of the remainder of the ordinance, including 1870.03 (hospitalization for abortions after the first trimester), 1870.60(C) (requiring disclosure of the particular risks of the woman's pregnancy and the abortion technique to be employed), and 1870.07 (24-hour waiting period).

All parties appealed some portion of the District Court's judgment. The Court of Appeals for the Sixth Circuit affirmed in part and reversed in part. . . .

Three separate petitions for *certiorari* were filed. In light of the importance of the issue presented, and in particular the conflicting decisions as to whether a State may require that all second-trimester abortions be performed in a hospital, we granted both Akron's and the plaintiffs' petitions. *** . . . We now reverse the judgment of the Court of Appeals upholding Akron's hospitalization requirement, but affirm the remainder of the decision invalidating the provisions on parental consent, informed consent, waiting period, and disposal of fetus remains.

In *Roe v. Wade,* the Court held that the "right to privacy, . . . founded in the Fourteenth Amendment's concept of personal liberty and restrictions upon state action, . . . is broad enough to encompass a woman's decision whether or not to terminate her pregnancy." *** Although the Constitution does not specifically identify this right, the history of this Court's constitutional adjudication leaves no doubt that "the full scope of the liberty guaranteed by the Due Process Clause cannot be found in or limited by the precise terms of the specific guarantees elsewhere provided in the Constitution." *** Central among these protected liberties is an individual's "freedom of personal choice in matters of marriage and family life." *** The decision in *Roe* was based firmly on this long-recognized and essential element of personal liberty.

The Court also has recognized, because abortion is a medical procedure, that the full vindication of the woman's fundamental right necessarily requires that her physician be given "the room he needs to make his best medical judgment." *** The physician's exercise of this medical judgment encompasses both assisting the woman in the decision-making process and implementing her decision should she choose abortion. ***

At the same time, the Court in *Roe* acknowledged that the woman's fundamental right "is not unqualified and must be considered against important state interests in abortion." *** But restrictive state regulation of the right to choose abortion, as with other fundamental rights subject to searching judicial examination, must be supported by a compelling state interest. *** We have recognized two such interests that may justify state regulation of abortions.

First, a State has an "important and legitimate interest in protecting the potentiality of human life." *** Although the interest exists "throughout the course of the woman's pregnancy," *** it becomes compelling only at viability, the point at which the fetus "has the capability of meaningful life outside the mother's womb." *** At viability this interest in protecting the potential life of the unborn child is so important that the State may proscribe abortions altogether, "except when it is necessary to preserve the life or health of the mother." ***

Second, because a State has legitimate concern with the health of women who undergo abortions, "a State may properly assert important interests in safeguarding health [and] in maintaining medical standards." *** We held in *Roe,* however, that this health interest does not become compelling until "approximately the end of the first trimester" of pregnancy. Until that time, a pregnant woman must be permitted, in consultation with her physician, to decide to have an abortion and to effectuate that decision "free of interference by the State." ***

This does not mean that a State never may enact a regulation touching on the first weeks of pregnancy. Certain regulations that have no significant impact on the woman's exercise of her right may be permissible where justified by important state health objectives. In [*Planned Parenthood of Central Missouri v. Danforth* (1976)], we unanimously upheld two Missouri statutory provisions, applicable to the first trimester, requiring the woman to provide her informed written consent to the abortion and the physician to keep certain records, even though comparable requirements were not imposed on most other medical procedures. The decisive factor was that the State met its burden of demonstrating that these regulations furthered important health-related State concerns. But even these minor regulations on the abortion procedure during the first trimester may not interfere with physician-patient consultation or with the woman's choice between abortion and childbirth.

From approximately the end of the first trimester of pregnancy, the State "may regulate the abortion procedure to the extent that the regulation reasonably relates to the preservation and protection of maternal health. *** The State's discretion to regulate on this basis does not, however, permit it to adopt abortion regulations that depart from accepted medical practice." *** We have rejected a State's attempt to ban a particular second-trimester abortion procedure, where the ban would have increased the costs and limited the availability of abortions without promoting important health benefits. If a State requires licensing or undertakes to regulate the performance of abortions during this period, the health standards adopted must be "legitimately related to the objective the State seeks to accomplish." ***

Section 1870.03 of the Akron ordinance requires that any abortion performed "upon a pregnant woman subsequent to the end of the first trimester of her pregnancy" must be "performed in a hospital." A "hospital" is "a general hospital or special hospital devoted to gynecology or obstetrics which is accredited by the Joint Commission on Accreditation of Hospitals or by the American Osteopathic Association." Accreditation by these organizations requires compliance with comprehensive standards governing a wide variety of health and surgical services. The ordinance thus prevents the performance of abortions in outpatient facilities that are not part of an acute-care, full-service hospital.

In the District Court plaintiffs sought to demonstrate that this hospitalization requirement has a serious detrimental impact on a woman's ability to obtain a second-trimester abortion in Akron and that it is not reasonably related to the State's interest in the health of the pregnant woman. The District Court did not reject this argument, but rather found the evidence "not . . . so convincing that it is willing to discard the Supreme Court's formulation in *Roe*" of a line between impermissible first-trimester regulation and permissible second-trimester regulation. We believe that the courts below misinterpreted this Court's prior decisions, and we now hold that 1870.03 is unconstitutional.

In *Roe v. Wade* the Court held that after the end of the first trimester of pregnancy the State's interest becomes compelling, and it may "regulate the abortion procedure to the extent that the regulation reasonably relates to the preservation and protection of maternal health." *** We noted, for example, that States could establish requirements relating "to the facility in which the procedure is to be performed, that is, whether it must be in a hospital or may be a clinic or some other place less-than-hospital status." *** In the companion case of *Doe v. Bolton* the Court invalidated a Georgia requirement that all abortions be performed in a hospital licensed by the State Board of Health and accredited by the Joint Commission on Accreditation of Hospitals. We recognized the State's legitimate health interests in establishing, for second-trimester abortions, "standards for licensing all facilities where abortions may be performed." *** We found, however, that "the State must show more than [was shown in *Doe*] in order to prove that only the full resources of a licensed hospital, rather than those of some other appropriately licensed institution, satisfy these health interests." ***

We reaffirm today that a State's interest in health regulation becomes compelling at approximately the end of the first trimester. The existence of a compelling state interest in health, however, is only the beginning of the inquiry. The State's regulation may be upheld only if it is reasonably designed to further that state interest. *** And the Court in *Roe* did not hold that it always is reasonable for a State to adopt an abortion regulation that applies to the entire second trimester. A State necessarily must have latitude in adopting regulations of general applicability in this sensitive area. But if it appears that during a substantial portion of the second trimester the State's regulation "depart[s] from accepted medical practice." *** the regulation may not be upheld simply because it may be reasonable for the remaining portion of the trimester. Rather, the State is obligated to make a reasonable effort to limit the effect of its regulations to the period of the trimester during which its health interest will be furthered.

There can be no doubt that 1870.03's second-trimester hospitalization requirement places a significant obstacle in the path of women seeking an abortion. A primary burden created by the requirement is additional cost to the woman. . . .

Akron does not contend that 1870.03 imposes only an insignificant burden on women's access to abortion, but rather defends it as a reasonable health regulation. This position had strong support at the time of *Roe v. Wade,* as hospitalization for second-trimester abortions was recommended by the American Public Health Association (APHA), and the American College of Obstetricians and Gynecologists (ACOG). *** Since then, however, the safety of second-trimester abortions has increased dramatically. The principal reason is that the D&E [dilation and evacuation] procedure is now widely and successfully used for second-trimester abortions. The Court of Appeals found that there was "an abundance of evidence that D&E is the safest method of performing post-first trimester abortions today." *** The availability of the D&E procedure during the interval between approximately 12 and 16 weeks of pregnancy, a period during which other second-trimester abortion techniques generally cannot be used, has meant that women desiring an early second-trimester abortion no longer are forced to incur the health risks of waiting until at least the sixteenth week of pregnancy.

For our purposes, an even more significant factor is that experience indicates that D&E may be performed safely on an outpatient basis in appropriate nonhospital facilities. The evidence is strong enough to have convinced the APHA to abandon its prior recommendation of hospitalization for all second-trimester abortions. . . . Similarly, the ACOG no longer suggests that all second-trimester abortions be performed in a hospital. It recommends that abortions performed in a physician's office or out-patient clinic be limited to 14 weeks of pregnancy, but it indicates that abortions may be performed safely in "a hospital-based or in a free-standing ambulatory surgical facility, or in an out-patient clinic meeting the criteria required for a free-standing surgical facility, until 18 weeks of pregnancy." ***

These developments, and the professional commentary supporting them, constitute impressive evidence that—at least during the early weeks of the second trimester—D&E abortions may be performed as safely in an outpatient clinic as in a full-service

hospital. We conclude, therefore, that "present medical knowledge," convincingly undercuts Akron's justification for requiring that *all* second-trimester abortions be performed in a hospital.

Akron nonetheless urges that "[t]he fact that some mid-trimester abortions may be done in a minimally equipped clinic does not invalidate the regulations." *** It is true that a state abortion regulation is not unconstitutional simply because it does not correspond perfectly in all cases to the asserted state interest. But the lines drawn in a state regulation must be reasonable, and this cannot be said of 1870.03. By preventing the performance of abortions in an appropriate nonhospital setting, Akron has imposed a heavy, and unnecessary, burden on women's access to a relatively inexpensive, otherwise accessible, and safe abortion procedure . . . *** and therefore unreasonably infringes upon a woman's constitutional right to obtain an abortion.

We turn next to the provision prohibiting a physician from performing an abortion on a minor pregnant woman under the age of 15 unless he obtains "the informed written consent of one of her parents or her legal guardian" or unless the minor obtains "an order from a court having jurisdiction over her that the abortion be performed or induced." The District Court invalidated this provision because "[i]t does not establish a procedure by which a minor can avoid a parental veto of her abortion decision by demonstrating that her decision is, in fact, informed. Rather, it requires, in all cases, both the minor's informed consent and either parental consent or a court order." The Court of Appeals affirmed on the same basis.

The relevant legal standards are not in dispute. The Court has held that "the State may not impose a blanket provision . . . requiring the consent of a parent or person *in loco parentis* as a condition for abortion of an unmarried minor." *** . . . [I]t is clear that Akron may not make a blanket determination that *all* minors under the age of 15 are too immature to make this decision or that an abortion never may be in the minor's best interests without parental approval. . . .

The Akron ordinance provides that no abortion shall be performed except "with the informed written consent of the pregnant woman, . . . given freely and without coercion." Furthermore, "in order to insure that the consent for an abortion is truly informed consent," the woman must be "orally informed by her attending physician" of the status of her pregnancy, the development of her fetus, the date of possible viability, the physical and emotional complications that may result from an abortion, and the availability of agencies to provide her with assistance and information with respect to birth control, adoption, and childbirth. 1870.06(B). In addition, the attending physician must inform her "of the particular risks associated with her own pregnancy and the abortion technique to be employed . . . [and] other information which in his own medical judgment is relevant to her decision as to whether to have an abortion or carry her pregnancy to term." ***

The District Court found that 1870.06(B) was unconstitutional, but that 1870.06(C) was related to a valid state interest in maternal health. The Court of Appeals concluded that both provisions were unconstitutional. *** We affirm. . . .

The Akron ordinance prohibits a physician from performing an abortion until 24 hours after the pregnant woman signs a consent form. The District Court upheld this provision on the ground that it furthered Akron's interest in ensuring "that a woman's abortion decision is made after careful consideration of all the facts applicable to her particular situation." *** The Court of Appeals reversed, finding that the inflexible waiting period had "no medical basis," and that careful consideration of the abortion decision by the woman "is beyond the state's power to require." *** We affirm the Court of Appeals' judgment.

The District Court found that the mandatory 24-hour waiting period increases the cost of obtaining an abortion by requiring the woman to make two separate trips to the abortion facility. Plaintiffs also contend that because of scheduling difficulties the effective delay may be longer than 24 hours, and that such a delay in some cases could increase the risk of an abortion. Akron denies that any significant health risk is created by a 24-hour waiting period, and argues that a brief period of delay—with the opportunity for reflection on the counseling received—often will be beneficial to the pregnant woman.

We find that Akron has failed to demonstrate that any legitimate state interest is furthered by an arbitrary and inflexible waiting period. There is no evidence suggesting that the abortion procedure will be performed more safely. Nor are we convinced that the State's legitimate concern that the woman's decision be informed is reasonably served by requiring a 24-hour delay as a matter of course. The decision whether to proceed with an abortion is one as to which it is important to "affor[d] the physician adequate discretion in the exercise of his medical judgment." *** In accordance with the ethical standards of the profession, a physician will advise the patient to defer the abortion when he thinks this will be beneficial to her. But if a woman, after appropriate counseling, is prepared to give her written informedconsent and proceed with the abortion, a State may not demand that she delay the effectuation of that decision.

Section 1870.16 of the Akron ordinance requires physicians performing abortions to "insure that the remains of the unborn child are disposed of in a humane and sanitary manner." The Court of Appeals found that the word "humane" was impermissibly vague as a definition of conduct subject to criminal prosecution. The court invalidated the entire provision, declining to sever the word "humane" in order to uphold the requirement that disposal be "sanitary." We affirm this judgment.

Akron contends that the purpose of 1870.16 is simply "'preclude the mindless dumping of aborted fetuses on garbage piles.'" *** It is far from clear, however, that this provision has such a limited intent. The phrase "humane and sanitary" does, as the Court of Appeals noted, suggest a possible intent to "mandate some sort of 'decent burial' of an embryo at the earliest stages of formation." *** This level of uncertainty is fatal where criminal liability is imposed. Because 1870.16 fails to give a physician "fair notice that his contemplated conduct is forbidden," *** we agree that it violates the Due Process Clause.

We affirm the judgment of the Court of Appeals invalidating those sections of Akron's "Regulations of Abortions" ordinance that deal with parental consent, informed consent, a 24-hour waiting period, and the disposal of fetal remains. The remaining portion of the judgment, sustaining Akron's requirement that all second-trimester abortions be performed in a hospital, is reversed.

It is so ordered.

Justice O'Connor, with whom *Justice White* and *Justice Rehnquist* join, dissenting.

The trimester or "three-stage" approach adopted by the Court in *Roe,* and, in a modified form, employed by the Court to analyze the state regulations in these cases, cannot be supported as a legitimate or useful framework for accommodating the woman's right and the State's interests. The decision of the Court today graphically illustrates why the trimester approach is a completely unworkable method of accommodating the conflicting personal rights and compelling state interests that are involved in the abortion context.

As the Court indicates today, the State's compelling interest in maternal health changes as medical technology changes, and any health regulation must not "depart from accepted medical practice." *** In applying this standard, the Court holds that "the safety of second-trimester abortions has increased dramatically" *** since 1973, when Roe was decided. Although a regulation such as one requiring that all second-trimester abortions be performed in hospitals "had strong support" in 1973 "as a reasonable health regulation," *** this regulation can no longer stand because, according to the Court's diligent research into medical and scientific literature, the dilation and evacuation procedure (D&E), used in 1973 only for first-trimester abortions, "is now widely and successfully used for second trimester abortions." *** Further, the medical literature relied on by the Court indicates that the D&E procedure may be performed in an appropriate non-hospital setting for "at least . . . the early weeks of the second trimester. . . ." *** The Court then chooses the period of 16 weeks of gestation as that point at which D&E procedures may be performed safely in a non-hospital setting, and thereby invalidates the Akron hospitalization regulation.

It is not difficult to see that despite the Court's purported adherence to the trimester approach adopted in *Roe,* the lines drawn in that decision have now been "blurred" because of what the Court accepts as technological advancement in the safety of abortion procedure. The State may no longer rely on a "bright line" that separates permissible from impermissible regulation, and it is no longer free to consider the second trimester as a unit and weigh the risks posed by all abortion procedures throughout that trimester. Rather, the State must continuously and conscientiously study contemporary medical and scientific literature in order to determine whether the effect of a particular regulation is to "depart from accepted medical practice" insofar as particular procedures and particular periods within the trimester are concerned. Assuming that legislative bodies are able to engage in this exacting task, it is difficult to believe that our Constitution *requires* that they do it as a prelude to protecting the health of their citizens. It is even more difficult to believe that this Court, without the resources available to those bodies entrusted with making legislative choices, believes itself competent to make these inquiries and to revise these standards every time the American College of Obstetricians and Gynecologists (ACOG) or similar group revises its views about what is and what is not appropriate medical procedure in this area. Indeed, the ACOG standards on which the Court relies were changed in 1982 after trial in the present cases. Before ACOG changed its standards in 1982, it recommended that all mid-trimester abortions be performed in a hospital. As today's decision indicates, medical technology is changing, and this change will necessitate our continued functioning as the nation's "ex officio medical board with powers to approve or disapprove medical and operative practices and standards throughout the United States." *** . . .

Just as improvements in medical technology inevitably will move forward the point at which the State may regulate for reasons of maternal health, different technological improvements will move *backward* the point of viability at which the State may proscribe abortions except when necessary to preserve the life and health of the mother.

In 1973, viability before 28 weeks was considered unusual. The standard on which the Court relied in *Roe* for its understanding of viability, stated that "[a]ttainment of a [fetal] weight of 1,000 g [or a fetal age of approximately 28 weeks gestation] is . . . widely used as the criterion of viability." *** However, recent studies have demonstrated increasingly earlier fetal viability. It is certainly reasonable to believe that fetal viability in the first trimester of pregnancy may be possible in the not too distant future. Indeed, the

Court has explicitly acknowledged that *Roe* left the point of viability "flexible for anticipated advancements in medical skill." *** "[W]e recognized in *Roe* that viability was a matter of medical judgment, skill, and technical ability, and we preserved the flexibility of the term." ***

The *Roe* framework, then, is clearly on a collision course with itself. As the medical risks of various abortion procedures decrease, the point at which the State may regulate for reasons of maternal health is moved further forward to actual childbirth. As medical science becomes better able to provide for the separate existence of the fetus, the point of viability is moved further back toward conception. Moreover, it is clear that the trimester approach violates the fundamental aspiration of judicial decision making through the application of neutral principles "sufficiently absolute to give them roots throughout the community and continuity over significant periods of time. . . ." *** The *Roe* framework is inherently tied to the state of medical technology that exists whenever particular litigation ensues. Although legislatures are better suited to make the necessary factual judgments in this area, the Court's framework forces legislatures, as a matter of constitutional law, to speculate about what constitutes "accepted medical practice" at any given time. Without the necessary expertise or ability, courts must then pretend to act as science review boards and examine those legislative judgments.

The Court adheres to the *Roe* framework because the doctrine of *stare decisis* "demands respect in society governed by the rule of law." *** Although respect for *stare decisis* cannot be challenged, "this Court's considered practice [is] not to apply *stare decisis* as rigidly in constitutional as in nonconstitutional cases." *** Although we must be mindful of the "desirability of continuity of decision in constitutional questions, . . . when convinced of former error, this Court has never felt constrained to follow precedent. In constitutional questions, where correction depends on amendment and not upon legislative action this Court throughout its history has freely exercised its power to reexamine the basis of its constitutional decisions." ***

Even assuming that there is a fundamental right to terminate pregnancy in some situations, there is no justification in law or logic for the trimester framework adopted in Roe and employed by the Court today on the basis of *stare decisis*. For the reasons stated above, that framework is clearly an unworkable means of balancing the fundamental right and the compelling state interests that are indisputably implicated.

The Court in *Roe* correctly realized that the State has important interests "in the areas of health and medical standards" and that "[t]he State has a legitimate interest in seeing to it that abortion, like any other medical procedure, is performed under circumstances that insure maximum safety for the patient." *** The Court also recognized that the State has "another important and legitimate interest in protecting the potentiality of human life." *** I agree completely that the State has these interests, but in my view, the point at which these interests become compelling does not depend on the trimester of pregnancy. Rather, these interests are present *throughout* pregnancy.

This Court has never failed to recognize that "a State may properly assert important interests in safeguarding health [and] in maintaining medical standards." *** It cannot be doubted that as long as a state statute is within "the bounds of reason and [does not] assum[e] the character of a merely arbitrary fiat . . . [then] [t]he State . . . must decide upon measures that are needful for the protection of its people. . . ." *** "There is nothing in the United States Constitution which limits the State's power to require that medical procedures be done safely. . . ." *** "The mode and procedure of medical diagnostic procedures is not the business of judges." *** Under the *Roe* framework, however, the state interest in maternal health cannot become compelling until the onset of the second trimester of pregnancy because "until the end of the first trimester mortality in abortion may be less than mortality in normal childbirth." *** Before the second trimester, the decision to perform an abortion "must be left to the medical judgment of the pregnant woman's attending physician." ***

The fallacy inherent in the *Roe* framework is apparent: just because the State has a compelling interest in ensuring maternal safety once an abortion may be more dangerous than childbirth, it simply does not follow that the State has no interest before that point that justifies state regulation to ensure that first-trimester abortions are performed as safely as possible.

The state interest in potential human life is likewise extant throughout pregnancy. In *Roe,* the Court held that although the State had an important and legitimate interest in protecting potential life, that interest could not become compelling until the point at which the fetus was viable. The difficulty with this analysis is clear: *potential* life is no less potential in the first weeks of pregnancy than it is at viability or afterward. At any stage in pregnancy, there is the *potential* for human life. Although the Court refused to "resolve the difficult question of when life begins," *** the Court chose the point of viability—when the fetus is *capable* of life independent of its mother—to permit the complete proscription of abortion. The choice of viability as the point at which the state interest in *potential* life becomes compelling is no less arbitrary than choosing any point before viability or any point afterward. Accordingly, I believe that the State's interest in protecting potential human life exists throughout the pregnancy.

Although the State possesses compelling interests in the protection of potential human life and in maternal health throughout pregnancy, not every regulation that the State imposes must be measured against the State's compelling interests and examined with strict scrutiny. This Court has acknowledged that "the right in *Roe v. Wade* can be understood only by considering both the woman's interest and the nature of the State's interference with it. *Roe* did not declare an unqualified 'constitutional right to an abortion.' . . . Rather, the right protects the woman from unduly burdensome interference with her freedom to decide whether to terminate her pregnancy." *** The Court and its individual Justices have repeatedly utilized the "unduly burdensome" standard in abortion cases. . . .

In determining whether the State imposes an "undue burden," we must keep in mind that when we are concerned with extremely sensitive issues, such as the one involved here, "the appropriate forum for their resolution in a democracy is the legislature. . . ." ***

Webster v. Reproductive Health Services
492 U.S. 490; 109 S. Ct. 3040; 106 L. Ed.2d 410 (1989)
Vote: 5-4

In 1986, Missouri enacted a statute declaring that "the life of each human being begins at conception" and that "unborn children have protectable interests in life, health and well-being." Specifically, the law prohibited public employees in the state from performing or assisting in abortions except as necessary to save the life of the mother. It barred the use of public facilities for the performance of proscribed abortions and prohibited the expenditure of any public funds for "encouraging or counseling" women to have such abortions. Additionally, all physicians were required to perform "viability tests" on fetuses during or after the twentieth week of gestation. A number of health care professionals, some employed by the state at public facilities, others by private, nonprofit corporations providing abortion

services, brought suit in federal district court to challenge the statute. The district court declared the law unconstitutional and enjoined its enforcement. The Court of Appeals for the Eighth Circuit affirmed.

Chief Justice Rehnquist, with whom **Justice White** and **Justice Kennedy** join, announced the judgment of the court. . . .

This appeal concerns the constitutionality of a Missouri statute regulating the performance of abortions. The United States Court of Appeals for the Eighth Circuit struck down several provisions of the statute on the ground that they violated this Court's decision in *Roe v. Wade* *** (1973), and cases following it. We noted probable jurisdiction, and now reverse. . . .

Decision of this case requires us to address four sections of the Missouri Act: (a) the preamble; (b) the prohibition on the use of public facilities or employees to perform abortions; (c) the prohibition on public funding of abortion counseling; and (d) the requirement that physicians conduct viability tests prior to performing abortions. We address these seriatim.

[A] The Act's preamble . . . sets forth "findings" by the Missouri legislature that "[t]he life of each human being begins at conception," and that "[u]nborn children have protectable interests in life, health, and well-being." *** The Act then mandates that state laws be interpreted to provide unborn children with "all the rights, privileges, and immunities available to other persons, citizens, and residents of this state," subject to the Constitution and this Court's precedents.

The State contends that the preamble itself is precatory and imposes no substantive restrictions on abortions, and that appellees therefore do not have standing to challenge it. Appellees, on the other hand, insist that the preamble is an operative part of the Act intended to guide the interpretation of other provisions of the Act. They maintain, for example, that the preamble's definition of life may prevent physicians in public hospitals from dispensing certain forms of contraceptives, such as the intrauterine device. . . .

In our view, the Court of Appeals misconceived the meaning of the *Akron* [*v. Akron Center for Reproductive Health* (1983)] dictum, which was only that a State could not "justify" an abortion regulation otherwise invalid under *Roe v. Wade* on the ground that it embodied the State's view about when life begins. Certainly the preamble does not by its terms regulate abortion or any other aspect of appellees' medical practice. The Court has emphasized that *Roe v. Wade* "implies no limitation on the authority of a State to make a value judgment favoring childbirth over abortion." *** The preamble can be read simply to express that sort of value judgment.

We think the extent to which the preamble's language might be used to interpret other state statutes or regulations is something that only the courts of Missouri can definitively decide. . . . We therefore need not pass on the constitutionality of the Act's preamble.

[B] Section 188.210 provides that "[i]t shall be unlawful for any public employee within the scope of his employment to perform or assist an abortion, not necessary to save the life of the mother," while Sec. 188.215 makes it "unlawful for any public facility to be used for the purpose of performing or assisting an abortion not necessary to save the life of the mother." The Court of Appeals held that these provisions contravened this Court's abortion decisions. We take the contrary view.

As we said earlier this Term in *DeShaney v. Winnegago County Dept. of Social Services* *** (1989), "our cases have recognized that the Due Process Clauses generally confer no affirmative right to governmental aid, even where such aid may be necessary to secure life, liberty, or property interests of which the government itself may not deprive the individual." In *Maher v. Roe,* *** the Court upheld a Connecticut welfare regulation under which Medicaid recipients received payments for medical services related to childbirth, but not for nontherapeutic abortions. Relying on *Maher,* the Court in *Poelker v. Doe* *** (1977), held that the city of St. Louis committed "no constitutional violation . . . in electing, as a policy choice, to provide publicly financed hospital services for childbirth without providing corresponding services for nontherapeutic abortions."

More recently, in *Harris v. McRae* *** (1980), the Court upheld "the most restrictive version of the Hyde Amendment," which withheld from States federal funds under the Medicaid program to reimburse the costs of abortions, " 'except where the life of the mother would be endangered if the fetus were carried to term.' " As in *Maher* and *Poelker,* the Court required only a showing that Congress' authorization of "reimbursement for medically necessary services generally, but not for certain medically necessary abortions," was rationally related to the legitimate governmental goal of encouraging childbirth. . . .

Just as Congress' refusal to fund abortions in *McRae* left "an indigent woman with at least the same range of choice in deciding whether to obtain a medically necessary abortion as she would have had if Congress had chosen to subsidize no health care costs at all," Missouri's refusal to allow public employees to perform abortions in public hospitals leaves a pregnant woman with the same choices as if the State had chosen not to operate any public hospitals at all. The challenged provisions only restrict a woman's ability to obtain an abortion to the extent that she chooses to use a physician affiliated with a public hospital. This circumstance is more easily remedied, and thus considerably less burdensome, than indigency, which "may make it difficult—and in some cases, perhaps impossible—for some women to have abortions" without public funding. *** Having held that the State's refusal to fund abortions does not violate *Roe v. Wade,* it strains logic to reach a contrary result for the use of public facilities and employees. If the State may "make a value judgment favoring childbirth over abortion and . . . implement that judgment by the allocation of public funds," *** surely it may do so through the allocation of other public resources, such as hospitals and medical staff. . . .

Maher, Poelker, and *McRae* all support the view that the State need not commit any resources to facilitating abortions, even if it can turn a profit by doing so. In *Poelker,* the suit was filed by an indigent who could not afford to pay for an abortion, but the ban on the performance of nontherapeutic abortions in city-owned hospitals applied whether or not the pregnant woman could pay. The Court emphasized that the Mayor's decision to prohibit abortions in city hospitals was "subject to public debate and approval or disapproval at the polls," and that "the Constitution does not forbid a State or city, pursuant to democratic processes, from expressing a preference for normal childbirth as St. Louis has done." *** Thus we uphold the Act's restrictions on the use of public employees and facilities for the performance or assistance of nontherapeutic abortions. . . .

[D] Section 188.029 of the Missouri Act provides:

"Before a physician performs an abortion on a woman he has reason to believe is carrying an unborn child of twenty or more weeks gestational age, the physician shall first determine if the unborn child is viable by using and exercising that degree of care, skill and proficiency commonly exercised by the ordinarily skillful, careful, and prudent physician engaged in similar practice under the same or similar conditions. In making this determination of viability, the physician shall perform or cause to be performed such medical examinations and tests as are necessary to make a finding of the gestational age, weight, and lung maturity of the unborn child and shall enter such findings and determination of viability in the medical record of the mother."

As with the preamble, the parties disagree over the meaning of this statutory provision. The State emphasizes the language of the first sentence, which speaks in terms of the physician's determination of viability being made by the standards of ordinary skill in the medical profession. Appellees stress the language of the second sentence, which prescribes such "tests as are necessary" to make a finding of gestational age, fetal weight, and lung maturity. . . .

We think the viability-testing provision makes sense only if the second sentence is read to require only those tests that are useful to making subsidiary findings as to viability. If we construe this provision to require a physician to perform those tests needed to make the three specified findings in all circumstances, including when the physician's reasonable professional judgment indicates that the tests would be irrelevant to determining viability or even dangerous to the mother and the fetus, the second sentence of Sec. 188.029 would conflict with the first sentence's requirement that a physician apply his reasonable professional skill and judgment. It would also be incongruous to read this provision, especially the word "necessary," to require the performance of tests irrelevant to the expressed statutory purpose of determining viability. . . .

The viability-testing provision of the Missouri Act is concerned with promoting the State's interest in potential human life rather than in maternal health. Section 188.029 creates what is essentially a presumption of viability at 20 weeks, which the physician must rebut with tests indicating that the fetus is not viable prior to performing an abortion. It also directs the physician's determination as to viability by specifying consideration, if feasible, of gestational age, fetal weight, and lung capacity. The District Court found that "the medical evidence is uncontradicted that a 20-week fetus is not viable," and that "23 ½ weeks to 24 weeks gestation is the earliest point in pregnancy where a reasonable possibility of viability exists." *** But it also found that there may be a 4-week error in estimating gestational age, which supports testing at 20 weeks.

In *Roe v. Wade,* the Court recognized that the State has "important and legitimate" interests in protecting maternal health and in the potentiality of human life. During the second trimester, the State "may, if it chooses, regulate the abortion procedure in ways that are reasonably related to maternal health." After viability, when the State's interest in potential human life was held to be compelling, the State "may, if it chooses, regulate, and even proscribe, abortion except where it is necessary, in appropriate medical judgment, for the preservation of the life or health of the mother." ***

We think that the doubt cast upon the Missouri statute by [*Roe* and subsequent decisions] is not so much a flaw in the statute as it is a reflection of the fact that the rigid trimester analysis of the course of a pregnancy enunciated in *Roe* has resulted in subsequent cases ... making constitutional law in this area a virtual Procrustean bed. Statutes specifying elements of informed consent to be provided abortion patients, for example, were invalidated if they were thought to "structur[e] ... the dialogue between the woman and her physician. *** As the dissenters in *Thornburgh* pointed out, such a statute would have been sustained under any traditional standard of judicial review, *** or for any other surgical procedure except abortion. ***

Stare decisis is a cornerstone of our legal system, but it has less power in constitutional cases, where, save for constitutional amendments, this Court is the only body able to make needed changes. *** We have not refrained from reconsideration of a prior construction of the Constitution that has proved "unsound in principle and unworkable in practice." ***

In the first place, the rigid *Roe* framework is hardly consistent with the notion of a Constitution cast in general terms, as ours is, and usually speaking in general principles, as ours does. The key elements of the *Roe* framework—trimesters and viability—are not found in the text of the Constitution or in any place else one would expect to find a constitutional principle. Since the bounds of the inquiry are essentially indeterminate, the result has been a web of legal rules that have become increasingly intricate, resembling a code of regulations rather than a body of constitutional doctrine. As Justice White has put it, the trimester framework has left this Court to serve as the country's "ex officio" medical board with powers to approve or disapprove medical and operative practices and standards throughout the United States." ***

In the second place, we do not see why the State's interest in protecting potential human life should come into existence only at the point of viability, and that there should therefore be a rigid line allowing state regulation after viability but prohibiting it before viability. The dissenters in *Thornburgh*, writing in the context of the *Roe* trimester analysis, would have recognized this fact by positing against the "fundamental right" recognized in *Roe* the State's "compelling interest" in protecting potential human life throughout pregnancy. "[T]he State's interest, if compelling after viability, is equally compelling before viability." ***

The tests that Sec. 188.029 requires the physician to perform are designed to determine viability. The State here has chosen viability as the point at which its interest in potential human life must be safeguarded. *** It is true that the tests in question increase the expense of abortion, and regulate the discretion of the physician in determining the viability of the fetus. Since the tests will undoubtedly show in many cases that the fetus is not viable, the tests will have been performed for what were in fact second-trimester abortions. But we are satisfied that the requirement of these tests permissibly furthers the State's interest in protecting potential human life, and we therefore believe Sec. 188.029 to be constitutional.

The dissent takes us to task for our failure to join in a "great issues" debate as to whether the Constitution includes an "unenumerated" general right to privacy as recognized in cases such as *Griswold v. Connecticut* *** and *Roe*. But *Griswold v. Connecticut*, unlike *Roe*, did not purport to adopt a whole framework, complete with detailed rules and distinctions, to govern the cases in which the asserted liberty interest would apply. As such, it was far different from the opinion, if not the holding, of *Roe v. Wade*, which sought to establish a constitutional framework for judging state regulation of abortion during the entire term of pregnancy. That framework sought to deal with areas of medical practice traditionally subject to state regulation, and it sought to balance once and for all by reference only to the calendar the claims of the State to protect the fetus as a form of human life against the claims of a woman to decide for herself whether or not to abort a fetus she was carrying. The experience of the Court in applying Roe v. Wade in later cases suggests to us that there is wisdom in not unnecessarily attempting to elaborate the abstract differences between a "fundamental *right" to abortion, as the Court described it in Akron,* a "limited fundamental constitutional right," which Justice Blackmun's dissent today treats *Roe* as having established, or a liberty interest protected by the Due Process Clause, which we believe it to be. The Missouri testing requirement here is reasonably designed to ensure that abortions are not performed where the fetus is viable—an end which all concede is legitimate—and that is sufficient to sustain its constitutionality....

Both appellants and the United States as *amicus curiae* have urged that we overrule our decision in *Roe v. Wade.* The facts of the present case, however, differ from those at issue in *Roe.* Here, Missouri has determined that viability is the point at which its interest in potential human life must be safeguarded. In *Roe,* on the other hand, the Texas statute criminalized the performance of all abortions, except when the mother's life was at stake. This case therefore affords us no occasion to revisit the holding of *Roe,* which was that the Texas statute unconstitutionally infringed the right to an abortion derived from the Due Process Clause, and we leave it undisturbed. To the extent indicated in our opinion, we would modify and narrow *Roe* and succeeding cases.

Because none of the challenged provisions of the Missouri Act properly before us conflict[s] with the Constitution, the judgment of the Court of Appeals is Reversed.

Justice O'Connor, ... concurring in part.

... Nothing in the record before us or the opinions below indicates that subsections 1(1) and 1(2) of the preamble to Missouri's abortion regulation statute will affect a woman's decision to have an abortion. Justice Stevens suggests that the preamble may also "interfere with contraceptive choices," because certain contraceptive devices act on a female ovum after it has been fertilized by a male sperm. *** The Missouri Act defines "conception" as "the fertilization of the ovum of a female by a sperm of a male," ... and invests "unborn children" with "protectable interests in life, health, and well-being,"

from "the moment of conception." *** Justice Stevens asserts that any possible interference with a woman's right to use such postfertilization contraceptive devices would be unconstitutional under *Griswold v. Connecticut* and our subsequent contraception cases. Similarly, certain *amici* suggest that the Missouri Act's preamble may prohibit the developing technology of in vitro fertilization, a technique used to aid couples otherwise unable to bear children in which a number of ova are removed from the woman and fertilized by male sperm....

It may be correct that the use of postfertilization contraceptive devices is constitutionally protected by *Griswold* and its progeny but, as with a woman's abortion decision, nothing in the record or the opinions below indicates that the preamble will affect a woman's decision to practice contraception.... Neither is there any indication of the possibility that the preamble might be applied to prohibit the performance of *in vitro* fertilization. I agree with the Court, therefore, that all of these intimations of unconstitutionality are simply too hypothetical to support the use of declaratory judgment procedures and injunctive remedies in this case.

Similarly, it seems to me to follow directly from our previous decisions concerning state or federal funding of abortions, that appellees' facial challenge to the constitutionality of Missouri's ban on the utilization of public facilities and the participation of public employees in the performance of abortions not necessary to save the life of the mother cannot succeed. Given Missouri's definition of "public facility" as "any public institution, public facility, public equipment, or any physical asset owned, leased, or controlled by this state or any agency or political subdivisions thereof," *** there may be conceivable applications of the ban on the use of public facilities that would be unconstitutional. Appellees and *amici* suggest that the State could try to enforce the ban against private hospitals using public water and sewage lines, or against private hospitals leasing state-owned equipment or state land. Whether some or all of these or other applications of Sec. 188.215 would be constitutional need not be decided here. *Maher, Poelker,* and *McRae* stand for the proposition that some quite straightforward applications of the Missouri ban on the use of public facilities for performing abortions would be constitutional and that is enough to defeat appellees' assertion that the ban is facially unconstitutional. . . .

Justice Scalia, . . . concurring in part.

. . . I share Justice Blackmun's view that [the plurality opinion] would effectively overrule *Roe v. Wade*. *** I think that should be done, but would do it more explicitly. Since today we contrive to avoid doing it, and indeed to avoid almost any decision of national import, I need not set forth my reasons, some of which have been well recited in dissents of my colleagues in other cases. . . .

The outcome of today's case will doubtless be heralded as a triumph of judicial statesmanship. It is not that, unless it is statesmanlike needlessly to prolong this Court's self-awarded sovereignty over a field where it has little proper business since the answers to most of the cruel questions posed are political and not juridical—a sovereignty which therefore quite properly, but to the great damage of the Court, makes it the object of the sort of organized public pressure that political institutions in a democracy ought to receive. . . .

Justice Blackmun, with whom **Justice Brennan** and **Justice Marshall** join, . . . dissenting in part.

Today, *Roe v. Wade,* and the fundamental constitutional right of women to decide whether to terminate a pregnancy, survive but are not secure. Although the Court extricates itself from this case without making a single, even incremental, change in the law of abortion, the plurality and Justice Scalia would overrule *Roe* (the first silently, the other explicitly) and would return to the States virtually unfettered authority to control the quintessentially intimate, personal, and life-directing decision whether to carry a fetus to term. Although today, no less than yesterday, the Constitution and the decisions of this Court prohibit a State from enacting laws that inhibit women from the meaningful exercise of that right, a plurality of this Court implicitly invites every state legislature to enact more and more restrictive abortion regulations in order to provoke more and more test cases, in the hope that sometime down the line the Court will return the law of procreative freedom to the severe limitations that generally prevailed in this country before January 22, 1973. Never in my memory has a plurality announced a judgment of this Court that so foments disregard for the law and for our standing decisions.

Nor in my memory has a plurality gone about its business in such a deceptive fashion. At every level of its review, from its effort to read the real meaning out of the Missouri statute, to its intended evisceration of precedents and its deafening silence about the protections that it would jettison, the plurality obscures the portent of its analysis. With reigned restraint, the plurality announces that its analysis leaves *Roe* "undisturbed," albeit "modif[ied] and narrow[ed]." But this disclaimer is totally meaningless. The plurality opinion is filled with winks, and nods, and knowing glances to those who would do away with *Roe* explicitly, but turns a stone face to anyone in search of what the plurality conceives as the scope of a woman's right under the Due Process Clause to terminate a pregnancy free from the coercive and brooding influence of the State. The simple truth is that *Roe* would not survive the plurality's analysis, and that the plurality provides no substitute for *Roe*'s protective umbrella.

I fear for the future. I fear for the liberty and equality of the millions of women who have lived and come of age in the 16 years since *Roe* was decided. I fear for the integrity of, and public esteem for, this Court.

I dissent. . . .

Justice Stevens, . . . dissenting in part. . . .

Moore v. City of East Cleveland

431 U.S. 494; 97 S. Ct. 1932; 52 L. Ed. 2d 531 (1977)
Vote: 5-4

Mr. Justice Powell announced the judgment of the Court, and delivered an opinion in which *Mr. Justice Brennan, Mr. Justice Marshall,* and *Mr. Justice Blackmun* joined.

East Cleveland's housing ordinance, like many throughout the country, limits occupancy of a dwelling unit to members of a single family. But the ordinance contains an unusual and complicated definitional section that recognizes as a "family" only a few categories of related individuals. Because her family, living together in her home, fits none of those categories, appellant stands convicted of a criminal offense. The question in this case is whether the ordinance violates the Due Process Clause of the Fourteenth Amendment.

Appellant, Mrs. Inez Moore, lives in her East Cleveland home together with her son, Dale Moore, Sr., and her two grandsons, Dale, Jr., and John Moore, Jr. The two boys are first cousins rather than brothers; we are told that John came to live with his grandmother and with the elder and younger Dale Moores after his mother's death.

In early 1973, Mrs. Moore received a notice of violation from the city, stating that John was an "illegal occupant" and directing her to comply with the ordinance. When she failed to remove him from her home, the city filed a criminal charge. Mrs. Moore moved to dismiss, claiming that the ordinance was constitutionally invalid on its face. Her motion was overruled, and upon conviction she was sentenced to five days in jail and a $25 fine. The Ohio Court of Appeals affirmed after giving full consideration to her constitutional claims, and the Ohio Supreme Court denied review. We noted probable jurisdiction of her appeal.

The city argues that our decision in *Village of Belle Terre v. Boraas,* *** (1974), requires us to sustain the ordinance attacked here. Belle Terre, like East Cleveland, imposed limits on the types of groups that could occupy a single dwelling unit. Applying the constitutional standard announced in this Court's leading land-use case, *Euclid v. Ambler Realty Co.* ***

(1926), we sustained the Belle Terre ordinance on the ground that it bore a rational relationship to permissible state objectives.

But one overriding factor sets this case apart from *Belle Terre*. The ordinance there affected only unrelated individuals. It expressly allowed all who were related by "blood, adoption, or marriage" to live together, and in sustaining the ordinance we were careful to note that it promoted "family needs" and "family values." East Cleveland, in contrast, has chosen to regulate the occupancy of its housing by slicing deeply into the family itself. This is no mere incidental result of the ordinance. On its face it selects certain categories of relatives who may live together and declares that others may not. In particular, it makes a crime of a grandmother's choice to live with her grandson in circumstances like those presented here.

When a city undertakes such intrusive regulation of the family, neither *Belle Terre* nor *Euclid* governs; the usual judicial deference to the legislature is inappropriate. "This Court has long recognized that freedom of personal choice in matters of marriage and family life is one of the liberties protected by the Due Process Clause of the Fourteenth Amendment." *** A host of cases, tracing their lineage to *Meyer v. Nebraska* *** (1923), and *Pierce v. Society of Sisters* *** (1925), have consistently acknowledged a "private realm of family life which the state cannot enter." *** ... When the government intrudes on choices concerning family living arrangements, this Court must examine carefully the importance of the governmental interests advanced and the extent to which they are served by the challenged regulation. ***

When thus examined, this ordinance cannot survive. The city seeks to justify it as a means of preventing overcrowding, minimizing traffic and parking congestion, and avoiding an undue financial burden on East Cleveland's school system. Although these are legitimate goals, the ordinance before us serves them marginally, at best. For example, the ordinance permits any family consisting only of husband, wife, and unmarried children to live together, even if the family contains a half dozen licensed drivers, each with his or her own car. At the same time it forbids an adult brother and sister to share a household, even if both faithfully use public transportation. The ordinance would permit a grandmother to live with a single dependent son and children, even if his school-age children number a dozen, yet it forces Mrs. Moore to find another dwelling for her grandson John, simply because of the presence of his uncle and cousin in the same household. We need not labor the point. [The ordinance] has but a tenous relation to alleviation of the conditions mentioned by the city.

The city would distinguish the cases based on *Meyer* and *Pierce*. It points out that none of them "gives grandmothers any fundamental rights with respect to grandsons," *** and suggests that any constitutional right to live together as a family extends only to the nuclear family—essentially a couple and its dependent children.

To be sure, these cases did not expressly consider the family relationship presented here. They were immediately concerned with freedom of choice with respect to childbearing, *** or with the rights of parents to the custody and companionship of their own children, *** or with traditional parental authority in matters of child rearing and education. *** But unless we close our eyes to the basic reasons why certain rights associated with the family have been accorded shelter under the Fourteenth Amendment's Due Process Clause, we cannot avoid applying the force and rationale of these precedents to the family choice involved in this case.

Understanding those reasons requires careful attention to this Court's function under the Due Process Clause. Mr. Justice Harlan described it eloquently:

Due process has not been reduced to any formula; its contents cannot be determined by reference to any code. The best that can be said is that through the course of this Court's decisions it has represented the balance which our Nation, built upon postulates of respect for the liberty of the individual, has struck between that liberty and the demands of organized society. If the supplying of content to this Constitutional concept has of necessity been a rational process, it certainly has not been one where judges have felt free to roam where unguided speculation might take them. The balance of which I speak is the balance struck by

this country, having regard to what history teaches are the traditions from which it developed as well as the traditions from which it broke. That tradition is a living thing. A decision of this Court which radically departs from it could not long survive, while a decision which builds on what has survived is likely to be sound. No formula could serve as a substitute, in this area, for judgment and restraint.

. . . [T]he full scope of the liberty guaranteed by the Due Process Clause cannot be found in or limited by the precise terms of the specific guarantees elsewhere provided in the Constitution. This "liberty" is not a series of isolated points pricked out in terms of the taking of property; the freedom of speech, press, and religion; the right to keep and bear arms; the freedom from unreasonable searches and seizures; and so on. It is a rational continuum which, broadly speaking, includes a freedom from all substantial arbitrary impositions and purposeless restraints, . . . and which also recognizes, what a reasonable and sensitive judgment must, that certain interests require particularly careful scrutiny of the state needs asserted to justify their abridgment. ***

Substantive due process has at times been a treacherous field for this court. There are risks when the judicial branch gives enhanced protection to certain substantive liberties without the guidance of the more specific provisions of the Bill of Rights. As the history of the *Lochner* era demonstrates, there is reason for concern lest the only limits to such judicial intervention become the predilections of those who happen at the time to be Members of this Court. That history counsels caution and restraint. But it does not counsel abandonment, nor does it require what the city urges here: cutting off any protection of family rights at the first convenient, if arbitrary boundary— the boundary of the nuclear family.

Appropriate limits on substantive due process come not from drawing arbitrary lines but rather from careful "respect for the teachings of history [and] solid recognition of the basic values that underlie our society." *** Our decisions establish that the Constitution protects the sanctity of the family precisely because the institution of the family is deeply rooted in this Nation's history and tradition. It is through the family that we inculcate and pass down many of our most cherished values, moral and cultural.

Ours is by no means a tradition limited to respect for the bonds uniting the members of the nuclear family. The tradition of uncles, aunts, cousins, and especially grandparents sharing a household along with parents and children has roots equally venerable and equally deserving of constitutional recognition. Over the years millions of our citizens have grown up in just such an environment, and most, surely, have profited from it. Even if conditions of modern society have brought about a decline in extended family households, they have not erased the accumulated wisdom of civilization, gained over the centuries and honored throughout our history, that supports a larger conception of the family. Out of choice, necessity, or a sense of family responsibility, it has been common for close relatives to draw together and participate in the duties and the satisfactions of a common home. Decisions concerning child rearing . . . long have been shared with grandparents or other relatives who occupy the same household—indeed who may take on major responsibility for the rearing of the children. Especially in times of adversity, such as the death of a spouse or economic need, the broader family has tended to come together for mutual sustenance and to maintain or rebuild a secure home life. This is apparently what happened here.

Whether or not such a household is established because of personal tragedy, the choice of relatives in this degree of kinship to live together may not lightly be denied by the state. *Pierce* struck down an Oregon law requiring all children to attend the State's public schools, holding that the Constitution "excludes any general power of the State to standardize its children by forcing them to accept instruction from public teachers only." *** By the same token the Constitution prevents East Cleveland from standardizing its children—and its adults—by forcing all to live in certain narrowly defined family patterns.

Reversed.

Mr. Justice Brennan, with whom **Mr. Justice Marshall** joins, concurring. . . .

Mr. Justice Stevens, concurring in the judgment.

In my judgment the critical question presented by this case is whether East Cleveland's housing ordinance is a permissible restriction on appellant's right to use her own property as she sees fit. . . .

Long before the original States adopted the Constitution, the common law protected an owner's right to decide how best to use his own property. This basic right has always been limited by the law of nuisance which proscribes uses that impair the enjoyment of other property in the vicinity. But the question whether an individual owner's use could be further limited by a municipality's comprehensive zoning plan was not finally decided until this century.

The holding in *Euclid* v. *Ambler Realty Co.* *** that a city could use its police power, not just to abate a specific use of property which proved offensive, but also to create and implement a comprehensive plan for the use of land in the community, vastly diminished the rights of individual property owners. It did not, however, totally extinguish those rights. On the contrary, that case expressly recognized that the broad zoning power must be exercised within constitutional limits. . . .

There appears to be no precedent for an ordinance which excludes any of an owner's relatives from the group of persons who may occupy his residence on a permanent basis. Nor does there appear to be any justification for such a restriction on an owner's use of his property. The city has failed totally to explain the need for a rule which would allow a homeowner to have two grandchildren live with her if they are brothers, but not if they are cousins. Since this ordinance has not been shown to have any "substantial relation to the public health, safety, morals or general welfare" of the city of East Cleveland, and since it cuts so deeply into a fundamental right normally associated with the ownership of residential property—that of an owner to decide who may reside on his or her property—it must fall under the limited standard of review of zoning decisions which this Court preserved in *Euclid* . . . . Under that standard, East Cleveland's unprecedented ordinance constitutes a taking of property without due process and without just compensation.

For these reasons, I concur in the Court's judgment.

Mr. Chief Justice Burger, dissenting.

It is unnecessary for me to reach the difficult constitutional issue this case presents. Appellant's deliberate refusal to use a plainly adequate administrative remedy provided by the city should foreclose her from pressing in this Court any constitutional objections to the city's zoning ordinance. Considerations of federalism and comity, as well as the finite capacity of federal courts, support this position. In courts, as in hospitals, two bodies cannot occupy the same space at the same time; when any case comes here which could have been disposed of long ago at the local level, it takes the place of some other case, which, having no alternative remedy, might well have been given.

The single-family zoning ordinances of the city of East Cleveland define the term "family" to include only the head of the household and his or her most intimate relatives, principally the spouse and unmarried and dependent children. Excluded from the definition of "family," and hence from cohabitation, are various persons related by blood or adoption to the head of the household. The obvious purpose of the city is the traditional one of preserving certain areas as family residential communities.

The city has established a Board of Building Code Appeals to consider variances from this facially stringent single-family limit when necessary to alleviate "practical difficulties and unnecessary hardships" and "to secure the general welfare and [do] substantial justice. . . ." *** The Board has power to grant variances to "[a]ny person adversely affected by a decision of any City official made in the enforcement of any [zoning] ordinance," so long as appeal is made to the Board within 10 days of notice of the decision appealed from. ***

After appellant's receipt of the notice of violation, her lawyers made no effort to apply to the Board for a variance to exempt her from the restrictions of the ordinance, even though her situation appears on its face to present precisely the kind of "practical difficulties and unnecessary hardships" the variance procedure was intended to accommodate. Appellant's counsel does not claim appellant was unaware of the right to go to the Board and seek a variance, or that any attempt was made to secure relief by an application to the Board. Indeed, appellant's counsel makes no claim that the failure to seek a variance was due to anything other than a deliberate decision to forgo the administrative process in favor of a judicial forum. . . .

Mr. Justice Stewart, with whom **Mr. Justice Rehnquist** joins, dissenting.

In *Village of Belle Terre v. Boraas,* *** the Court considered a New York village ordinance that restricted land use within the village to single-family dwellings. That ordinance defined "family" to include all persons related by blood, adoption, or marriage who lived and cooked together as a single-housekeeping unit; it forbade occupancy by any group of three or more persons who were not so related. We held that the ordinance was a valid effort by the village government to promote the general community welfare, and that it did not violate the Fourteenth Amendment nor infringe any other rights or freedoms protected by the Constitution.

The present case brings before us a similar ordinance of East Cleveland, Ohio, one that also limits the occupancy of any dwelling unit to a single family, but that defines "family" to include only certain combinations of blood relatives. The question presented, as I view it, is whether the decision in *Belle Terre* is controlling, or whether the Constitution compels a different result because East Cleveland's definition of "family" is more restrictive than that before us in the *Belle Terre* case. . . .

In my view, the appellant's claim that the ordinance in question invades constitutionally protected rights of association and privacy is in large part answered by the *Belle Terre* decision. The argument was made there that a municipality could not zone its land exclusively for single-family occupancy because to do so would interfere with protected rights of privacy or association. We rejected this contention, and held that the ordinance at issue "involve[d] no 'fundamental' right guaranteed by the Constitution, such as . . . the right of association, . . . or any rights of privacy."

The *Belle Terre* decision thus disposes of the appellant's contentions to the extent that they focus not on her blood relationships with her sons and grandsons but on more general notions about the "privacy of the home." Her suggestions that every person has a constitutional right permanently to share his residence with whomever he pleases, and that such choices are "beyond the province of legitimate governmental intrusion," amounts to the same argument that was made and found unpersuasive in *Belle Terre*.

To be sure, the ordinance involved in *Belle Terre* did not prevent blood relatives from occupying the same dwelling, and the Court's decision in that case does not, therefore, foreclose the appellant's arguments based specifically on the ties of kinship present in this case. Nonetheless, I would hold, for the reasons that follow, that the existence of those ties does not elevate either the appellant's claim of associational freedom or her claim of privacy to a level invoking constitutional protection.

To suggest that the biological fact of common ancestry necessarily gives related persons constitutional rights of association superior to those of unrelated persons is to misunderstand the nature of the associational freedoms that the Constitution has been understood to protect. Freedom of association has been constitutionally recognized because it is often indispensable to effectuation of explicit First Amendment guarantees. *** But the scope of the associational right, until now, at least, has been limited to the constitutional need that created it; obviously not every "association" is for First Amendment purposes or serves to promote the ideological freedom that the First Amendment was designed to protect.

The "association" in this case is not for any purpose relating to the promotion of speech, assembly, the press, or religion. And wherever the outer boundaries of constitutional protection of freedom of association may eventually turn out to be, they surely do not extend to those who assert no interest other than the gratification, convenience, and economy of sharing the same residence.

The appellant is considerably closer to the constitutional mark in asserting that the East Cleveland ordinance intrudes upon "the private realm of family life which the state cannot enter." *** Several decisions of the Court have identified specific aspects of what might broadly be termed "private family life" that are constitutionally protected against state interference. ***

Although the appellant's desire to share a single-dwelling unit also involves "private family life" in a sense, that desire can hardly be equated with any of the interests protected in the cases just cited. The ordinance about which the appellant complains did not impede her choice to have or not to have children, and it did not dictate to her how her own children were to be nurtured and reared. The ordinance clearly does not prevent parents from living together or living with their unemancipated offspring.

But even though the Court's previous cases are not directly in point, the appellant contends that the importance of the "extended family" in American society requires us to hold that her decision to share her residence with her grandsons may not be interfered with by the State. This decision, like the decisions involved in bearing and raising children, is said to be an aspect of "family life" also entitled to substantive protection under the Constitution. Without pausing to inquire how far under this argument an "extended family" might extend, I cannot agree. When the Court has found that the Fourteenth Amendment placed a substantive limitation on a State's power to regulate, it has been in those rare cases in which the personal interests at issue have been deemed " 'implicit in the concept of ordered liberty.' " *** The interest that the appellant may have in permanently sharing a single kitchen and a suite of contiguous rooms with some of her relatives simply does not rise to that level. To equate this interest with the fundamental decisions to marry and to bear and raise children is to extend the limited substantive contours of the Due Process Clause beyond recognition. . . .

Mr. Justice White, dissenting. . . .

Dronenburg v. Zech

741 F. 2d 1388 (1984)
Vote: 3-0

In this case, the U.S. Court of Appeals for the District of Columbia considers a challenge to a U.S. Navy regulation requiring mandatory discharge for homosexual conduct. James Dronenburg, a twenty-seven-year-old petty officer, was found to have engaged in such activity on a repeated basis. He admitted the allegations but argued that his constitutional right of privacy protected him against discharge under the Navy regulation. The opinion is authored by Judge Robert H. Bork, who would later be nominated (unsuccessfully) to serve on the Supreme Court.

Bork, Circuit Judge:

... Appellant advances two constitutional arguments, a right of privacy and a right to equal protection of the laws. Resolution of the second argument is to some extent dependent upon that of the first. Whether the appellant's asserted constitutional right to privacy is based upon fundamental human rights, substantive due process, the ninth amendment or emanations from the Bill of Rights, if no such right exists, then appellant's right to equal protection is not infringed unless the Navy's policy is not rationally related to a permissible end. *** We think neither right has been violated by the Navy.

According to appellant, *Griswold v. Connecticut* *** (1965), and the cases that came after it ... have "developed a right of privacy of constitutional dimension ..." Appellant finds in these cases a thread of principle: that the government should not interfere with an individual's freedom to control intimate personal decisions regarding his or her own body" except by the least restrictive means available and in the presence of a compelling state interest. *** Given this principle, he urges, private consensual homosexual activity must be held to fall within the zone of constitutionally protected privacy. ***

Whatever thread of principle may be discerned in the right-of-privacy cases, we do not think it is the one discerned by appellant. Certainly the Supreme Court has never defined the right so broadly as to encompass homosexual conduct.... More to the point, the Court in *Doe v. Commonwealth's Attorney for Richmond* *** (1976), summarily affirmed a district court judgment, upholding a Virginia statute making it a criminal offense to engage in private consensual homosexual conduct. The district court in *Doe* had found that the right to privacy did not extend to private homosexual conduct because the latter bears no relation to marriage, procreation, or family life. *** The Supreme Court's summary disposition of a case constitutes a vote on the merits; as such, it is binding on lower federal courts. *** ...

But even should we agree that *Doe v. Commonwealth's Attorney* is somewhat ambiguous precedent, we would not extend the right of privacy created by the Supreme Court to cover appellant's conduct here. An examination of the cases cited by appellant shows that they contain little guidance for lower courts.... [Judge Bork proceeds to review the Supreme Court's decisions dealing with the right of privacy, including *Griswold v. Connecticut* (1965), *Loving v. Virginia* (1967), *Eisenstadt v. Baird* (1972), *Roe v. Wade* (1973) and *Carey v. Population Services International* (1977).]

... These cases, and the suggestion that we apply them to protect homosexual conduct in the Navy, pose a peculiar jurisprudential problem. When the Supreme Court decides cases under a specific provision or amendment to the Constitution it explicates the meaning and suggests the contours of a value already stated in the document or implied by the Constitution's structure and history. The lower court judge finds in the Supreme Court's reasoning about those legal materials, as well as in the materials themselves, guidance for applying the provision or amendment to a new situation. But when the court creates new rights, ... lower courts have none of these materials available and can look only to what the Supreme Court has stated to be the principle involved.

In this group of cases, ... we do not find any principle articulated even approaching in breadth that which appellant seeks to have us adopt. The Court has listed as illustrative of the right of privacy such matters as activities relating to marriage, procreation, contraception, family relationships, and child rearing and education. It need hardly be said that none of these covers a right to homosexual conduct.

The question then becomes whether there is a more general principle that explains these cases and is capable of extrapolation to new claims not previously decided by the Supreme Court. It is true that the principle appellant advances would explain all of these cases, but then so would many other, less sweeping principles. The most the Court has said on that topic is that only rights that are "fundamental" or "implicit in the concept of ordered liberty" are included in the right of privacy. These formulations are not particularly helpful to us, however, because they are less prescriptions of a mode of reasoning than they are conclusions about particular rights enunciated. We would find it impossible to conclude that a right to homosexual conduct is "fundamental" or "implicit in the concept of ordered liberty" unless any and all private sexual behavior falls within those categories, a conclusion we are unwilling to draw.

In dealing with a topic like this, in which we are asked to protect from regulation a form of behavior never before protected, and indeed traditionally condemned, we do well to bear in mind ... "[t]hat the Court has ample precedent for the creation of new constitutional rights should not lead it to repeat the process at will." ... If it is any degree doubtful that the Supreme Court should freely create new constitutional rights, we think it certain that lower courts should not do so. We have no guidance from the Constitution or, as we have shown with respect to the case at hand, from articulated Supreme Court principle. If courts of appeals should, in such circumstances, begin to create new rights freely, the volume of decisions would mean that many would evade Supreme Court review, a great body of judge-made law would grow up, and we would have "preempt(ed) for (ourselves) another part of the governance of the country without express constitutional authority." *** If the revolution in sexual mores that appellant proclaims is in fact ever to arrive, we think

it must arrive through the moral choices of the people and the elected representatives, not through the usage of this court. ...

We conclude, therefore, that we can find no constitutional right to engage in homosexual conduct and that, as judges, we have no warrant to create one. We need ask, therefore, only whether the Navy's policy is rationally related to a permissible end. ... We have said that legislation may implement morality. So viewed, this regulation bears a rational relationship to a permissible end. It may be argued, however, that a naval regulation, unlike the act of a legislature, must be rationally related not to morality for its own sake but to some further end which the Navy is entitled to pursue because of the Navy's assigned function. We need not decide that question because, if such a connection is required, this regulation is plainly a rational means of advancing a legitimate, indeed a crucial, interest common to all our armed forces. To ask the question is to answer it. The effects of homosexual conduct within a naval or military unit are almost certain to be harmful to morale and discipline. The Navy is not required to produce social science data or the results of controlled experiments to prove what common sense and common experience demonstrate. This very case illustrates dangers of the sort the Navy is entitled to consider. ... Episodes of this sort are certain to be deleterious to morale and discipline, to call into question the even-handedness of superiors' dealings with lower ranks, to make personal dealings uncomfortable where the relationship is sexually ambiguous, to generate dislike and disapproval among many who find homosexuality morally offensive, and, it must be said, given the powers of military superiors over their inferiors, to enhance the possibility of homosexual seduction. The Navy's policy requiring discharge of those who engage in homosexual conduct serves legitimate state interests. ... We believe that the policy requiring discharge for homosexual conduct is a rational means of achieving these legitimate interests. *** The unique needs of the military, "a specialized society separate from civilian society," *** justify the Navy's determination that homosexual conduct impairs its capacity to carry out its mission.

Affirmed.

Bowers v. Hardwick

478 U.S. 186; 106 S. Ct. 2841; 92 L. Ed. 2d 140 (1986)
Vote: 5-4

Justice White delivered the opinion of the Court.

In August 1982, respondent was charged with violating the Georgia statute criminalizing sodomy by committing that act with another adult male in the bedroom of respondent's home. After a preliminary hearing, the District Attorney decided not to present the matter to grand jury unless further evidence developed.

Respondent then brought suit in the Federal District Court, challenging the constitutionality of the statute insofar as it criminalized consensual sodomy. He asserted that he was a practicing homosexual, that the Georgia sodomy statute, as administered by the defendants, placed him in imminent danger of arrest, and that the statute for several reasons violates the Federal Constitution. The District Court granted the defendants' motion to dismiss [relying on *Doe v. Commonwealth's Attorney* (1976)]. . . .

A divided panel of the Court of Appeals for the Eleventh Circuit reversed. *** . . . Relying on our decisions in *Griswold v. Connecticut,* *** *Eisenstadt v. Baird,* *** *Stanley v. Georgia,* *** and *Roe v. Wade,* *** the court went on to hold that the Georgia statute violated respondent's fundamental rights because his homosexual activity is a private and intimate association that is beyond the reach of the state regulation by reason of the Ninth Amendment and the Due Process Clause of the Fourteenth Amendment. The case was remanded for trial, at which, to prevail, the State would have to prove that the statute is supported by a compelling interest and is the most narrowly drawn means of achieving that end.

Because other Courts of Appeals have arrived at judgments contrary to that of the Eleventh Circuit in this case, we granted the State's petition for *certiorari.* . . .

This case does not require a judgment on whether laws against sodomy between consenting adults in general, or between homosexuals in particular, are wise or desirable. It raises no question about the right or propriety of state legislative decisions to repeal their laws that criminalize homosexual sodomy, or of state court decisions invalidating those laws on state constitutional grounds. The issue presented is whether the Federal Constitution confers a fundamental right upon homosexuals to engage in sodomy and hence invalidates the laws of the many States that still make such conduct illegal and have done so for a very long time. The case also calls for some judgment about the limits of the Court's role in carrying out its constitutional mandate.

We first register our disagreement with the Court of Appeals and with respondent that the Court's prior cases have construed the Constitution to confer a right of privacy that contends to homosexual sodomy and for all intents and purposes have decided this case. . . .

Accepting the decisions in these cases and the above description of them, we think it evident that none of the rights announced in those cases bears any resemblance to the claimed constitutional right of homosexuals to engage in acts of sodomy, that is asserted in this case. No connection between family, marriage, or procreation on the one hand and homosexual activity on the other has been demonstrated, either by the Court of Appeals or by respondent. Moreover, any claim that these cases nevertheless stand for the proposition that any kind of private sexual conduct between consenting adults is constitutionally insulated from state proscription is unsupportable. Indeed, the Court's opinion in *Carey [v. Population Services]* twice asserted that the privacy right, which the *Griswold* line of cases found to be one of the protections provided by the Due Process Clause, did not reach so far. ***

Precedent aside, however, respondent would have us announce, as the Court of Appeals did, a fundamental right to engage in homosexual sodomy. This we are quite unwilling to do. It is true that despite the language of the Due Process Clauses of the Fifth and Fourteenth Amendments, which appears to focus only on the processes by which life, liberty, or property is taken, the cases are legion in which Clauses have been interpreted to have substantive content, subsuming rights that to a great extent are immune from federal or state regulation or proscription. Among such cases are those recognizing rights that have little or no textual support in the constitutional language. . . .

Striving to assure itself and the public that announcing rights not readily identifiable in the constitution's text involves much more than the imposition of the Justices' own choice of values on the States and the Federal Government, the Court has sought to identify the nature of the rights qualifying for heightened judicial protection. In *Palko v. Connecticut* *** (1937), it was said that this category includes those fundamental liberties that are "implicit in the concept of the record liberty," such that "neither liberty nor justice would exist if [they] were sacrificed." A different description of fundamental liberties appeared in *Moore v. East Cleveland* *** where they are characterized [by Justice Powell] as those liberties that are "deeply rooted in this Nation's history and tradition."

It is obvious to us that neither of these formulations would extend a fundamental right to homosexuals to engage in acts of consensual sodomy. Proscriptions against that conduct have ancient roots. *** Sodomy was a criminal offense at common law and was forbidden by the laws of the original thirteen States when they ratified the Bill of Rights. In 1868, when the Fourteenth Amendment was ratified, all but 5 of the 37 States in the Union had criminal sodomy laws. In fact, until 1961, all States outlawed sodomy, and today, 24 States and the District of Columbia continue to provide criminal penalties for sodomy performed in private and between consenting adults. *** Against this background, to claim that a right to engage in such conduct is "deeply rooted in this Nation's history and tradition" or "implicit in the concept of ordered liberty" is, at best, facetious. . . .

Nor are we inclined to take a more expansive view of our authority to discover new fundamental rights imbedded in the Due Process Clause. The Court is most vulnerable and comes nearest to illegitimacy when it deals with judge-made constitutional law having little or no cognizable roots in the language or design of the Constitution. That this is so was painfully demonstrated by the face-off between the Executive and the Court in the 1930's, which resulted in the repudiation of much of the substantive gloss

that the Court had placed on the Due Process Clause of the Fifth and Fourteenth Amendments. There should be therefore, great resistance to expand the substantive reach of those Clauses, particularly if it requires redefining the category of rights deemed to be fundamental. Otherwise, the Judiciary necessarily takes to itself further authority to govern the country without express constitutional authority. The claimed right pressed on us today falls far short of overcoming this resistance.

Respondent, however, asserts that the result should be different where the homosexual conduct occurs in the privacy of the home. He relies on *Stanley v. Georgia* *** (1969), where the Court held that the First Amendment prevents conviction for possessing and reading obscene material in the privacy of his home: "If the First Amendment means anything, it means that a State has no business telling a man, sitting alone in his house, what books he may read or what films he may watch." ***

Stanley did protect conduct that would not have been protected outside the home, and it partially prevented the enforcement of state obscenity laws; but the decision was firmly grounded in the First Amendment. The right pressed upon us here has no similar support in the text of the Constitution, and it does not qualify for recognition under the prevailing principles for construing the Fourteenth Amendment. Its limits are also difficult to discern. Plainly enough, otherwise illegal conduct is not always immunized whenever it occurs in the home. Victimless crimes, such as the possession and use of illegal drugs, do not escape the law where they are committed at home. *Stanley* itself recognized that its holding offered no protection for the possession in the home of drugs, firearms, or stolen goods. *** And if respondent's submission is limited to the voluntary sexual conduct between consenting adults, it would be difficult, except by fiat, to limit the claimed right to homosexual conduct while leaving exposed to prosecution adultery, incest, and other sexual crimes even though they are committed in the home. We are unwilling to start down that road.

Even if the conduct at issue here is not a fundamental right, respondent asserts that there must be a rational basis for the law and that there is none in this case other than the presumed belief of a majority of the electorate in Georgia that homosexual sodomy is immoral and unacceptable. This is said to be an inadequate rationale to support the law. The law, however, is constantly based on notions of morality, and if all laws representing essentially moral choices are to be invalidated under the Due Process Clause, the courts will be very busy indeed. Even respondent makes no such claim, but insists that majority sentiments about the morality of homosexuality should be declared inadequate. We do not agree, and are unpersuaded that the sodomy laws of some 25 States should be invalidated on this basis. . . .

Accordingly, the judgment of the Court of Appeals is reversed.

Chief Justice Burger, concurring.

I join the Court's opinion, but I write separately to underscore my view that in constitutional terms there is no such thing as a fundamental right to commit homosexual sodomy.

As the Court notes, *** the proscriptions against sodomy have very "ancient roots." Decisions of individuals relating to homosexual conduct have been subject to state intervention throughout the history of Western Civilization. Condemnation of those practices is firmly rooted in Judeo-Christian moral and ethical standards. Homosexual sodomy was a capital crime under Roman law. *** During the English Reformation when powers of the ecclesiastical courts were transferred to the King's Courts, the first English statute criminalizing sodomy was passed. *** Blackstone described "the infamous crime against nature" as an offense of "deeper malignity" than rape, an heinous act "the very mention of which is a disgrace to human nature," and "a crime not fit to be named." *** The common law of England, including its prohibition of sodomy, became the received law of Georgia and the other Colonies. In 1816 the Georgia Legislature passed the statute at issue here, and that statute has been continuously in force in one form or another since that time. To hold that the act of homosexual sodomy is somehow protected as a fundamental right would be to cast aside millennia of moral teaching.

This is essentially not a question of personal "preferences" but rather that of the legislative authority of the State. I find nothing in the Constitution depriving a State of the power to enact the statute challenged here.

Justice Powell, concurring. . . .

Justice Blackmun, with whom **Justice Brennan, Justice Marshall,** and **Justice Stevens** join, dissenting.

This case is no more about "a fundamental right to engage in homosexual sodomy," as the Court purports to declare, *** than *Stanley v. Georgia* *** (1969) was about a fundamental right to watch obscene movies, or *Katz v. United States* *** (1967) was about a fundamental right to place interstate bets from a telephone booth. Rather, this case is about "the most comprehensive of rights and the right most valued by civilized men," namely, "the right to be let alone." ***

The statute at issue denies individuals the right to decide for themselves whether to engage in particular forms of private, consensual sexual activity. The Court concludes that [it] is valid essentially because "the laws of . . . many States . . . still make such conduct illegal and have done so for a very long time." *** But the fact that the moral judgments expressed by statutes like [such] may be "natural and familiar . . . ought not to conclude our judgment upon the question whether statutes embodying them conflict with the Constitution of the United States." ***

Like Justice Holmes, I believe that "[i]t is revolting to have no better reason for a rule of law than that so it was laid down in the time of Henry IV. It is still more revolting if the grounds upon which it was laid down have vanished long since, and the rule simply persists from blind imitation of the past." *** I believe we must analyze respondent's claim in the light of the values that underlie the constitutional right to privacy. If that right means anything, it means that, before Georgia can prosecute its citizens for making choices about the most intimate aspects of their lives, it must do more than assert that the choice they have made is an " 'abominable crime not fit to be named among Christians.' " ***

In its haste to reverse the Court of Appeals and hold that the Constitution does not "confe[r] a fundamental right upon homosexuals to engage in sodomy," the Court relegates the actual statute being challenged to a footnote and ignores the procedural posture of the case before it. A fair reading of the statute and of the complaint clearly reveals that the majority has distorted the question this case presents.

First, the Court's almost obsessive focus on homosexual activity is particularly hard to justify in light of the broad language Georgia has used. Unlike the Court, the Georgia Legislature has not proceeded on the assumption that homosexuals are so different from other citizens that their lives may be controlled in a way that would not be tolerated if it limited the choices of those other citizens. *** Rather, Georgia has provided that "[a] person commits the offense of sodomy when he performs or submits to any sexual act involving the sex organs of one person and the mouth or anus of another." *** The sex or status of the persons who engage in the act is irrelevant as a matter of state law. In fact, to the extent I can discern a legislative purpose for Georgia's 1968 enactment ... that purpose seems to have been to broaden the coverage of the law to reach heterosexual as well as homosexual activity. I therefore see no basis for the Court's decision to treat this case as an "as applied" challenge to Sec. 16-6-2, *** or for Georgia's attempt, both in its brief and at oral argument, to defend Sec. 16-6-2 solely on the grounds that it prohibits homosexual activity. Michael Hardwick's standing may rest in significant part on Georgia's apparent willingness to enforce against homosexuals a law it seems not to have any desire to enforce against heterosexuals. *** But his claim that Sec. 16-6-2 involves an unconstitutional intrusion into his privacy and his right of intimate association does not depend ... on his sexual orientation.

Until 1968, Georgia defined sodomy as "the carnal knowledge and connection against the order of nature, by man with man, or in the same unnatural manner with woman." *** In *Thompson v. Aldredge* *** (1939), the Georgia Supreme Court held that [the law] did not prohibit lesbian activity. And in *Riley v. Garrett* *** (1963), the Georgia Supreme Court held that [the law] did not prohibit heterosexual cunnilingus. Georgia passed the act-specific statute currently in force "perhaps in response to the restrictive court decisions such as *Riley.*" ***

Second, I disagree with the Court's refusal to consider whether [the sodomy law] runs afoul of the Eighth or Ninth Amendments or the Equal Protection Clause of the Fourteenth Amendment. *** Respondent's complaint expressly invoked the Ninth Amendment, *** and he relied heavily before this Court on *Griswold v. Connecticut* *** (1965), which identifies that Amendment as one of the specific constitutional provisions giving "life and substance" to our understanding of privacy. *** More importantly, the procedural posture of the case requires that we affirm the Court of Appeals' judgment if there is any ground on which respondent may be entitled to relief. ...

Despite historical views of homosexuality, it is no longer viewed by mental health professionals as a "disease" or disorder. *** But, obviously, neither is it simply a matter of deliberate personal election. Homosexual orientation may well form part of the very fiber of an individual's personality. Consequently, ... the Eighth Amendment may pose a constitutional barrier to sending an individual to prison for acting on that attraction regardless of the circumstances. An individual's ability to make constitutionally protected "decisions concerning sexual relations," *** is rendered empty indeed if he or she is given no real choice but a life without any physical intimacy.

With respect to the Equal Protection Clause's applicability to [the challenged law], I note that Georgia's exclusive stress before this Court on its interest in prosecuting homosexual activity despite the gender-neutral terms of the statute may arise serious questions of discriminatory enforcement, questions that cannot be disposed of before the Court on a motion to dismiss. *** The legislature having decided that the sex of the participants is irrelevant to the legality of the acts, I do not see why the State can defend [the law] on the ground that individuals singled out for prosecution are of the same sex as their partners. Thus, under the circumstances of this case, a claim under the Equal Protection Clause may well be available without having to reach the more controversial question whether homosexuals are a suspect class. ***

"Our cases long have recognized that the Constitution embodies a promise that a certain private sphere of individual liberty will be kept largely beyond the reach of government." *** In construing the right to privacy, the Court has proceeded along two somewhat distinct, albeit complementary lines. First, it has recognized a privacy interest with reference to certain decisions that are properly for the individual to make. . . .

The Court concludes today that none of our prior cases dealing with various decisions that individuals are entitled to make free of governmental interference "bears any resemblance to the claimed constitutional right of homosexuals to engage in acts of sodomy that is asserted in this case." *** While it is true that these cases may be characterized by their connection to protection of the family, *** the Court's conclusion that they extend no further than this boundary ignores the warning in *Moore v. East Cleveland*, *** against "clos[ing] our eyes to the basic reasons why certain rights associated with the family have been accorded shelter under the Fourteenth Amendment's Due Process Clause." We protect those rights not because they contribute, in some direct and material way, to the general public welfare, but because they form so central a part of an individual's life. "[T]he concept of privacy embodies the 'moral fact that a person belongs to himself and not others nor to society as a whole.' " ***

In a variety of circumstances we have recognized that a necessary corollary of giving individuals freedom to choose how to conduct their lives is acceptance of the fact that different individuals will make different choices. For example, in holding that the clearly important state interest in public education should give way to a competing claim by the Amish to the effect that extended formal schooling threatened their way of life, the Court declared: "There can be no assumption that today's majority is 'right' and the Amish and others like them are 'wrong.' A way of life that is odd or even erratic but interferes with no rights or interests of others is not to be condemned because it is different." *** The Court claims that its decision today merely refuses to recognize a fundamental right to engage in homosexual sodomy; what the Court really has refused to recognize is the fundamental interest all individuals have in controlling the nature of their intimate associations with others.

The behavior for which Hardwick faces prosecution occurred in his own home, a place to which the Fourth Amendment attaches special significance. The Court's treatment of this aspect of the case is symptomatic of its overall refusal to consider the broad principles that have informed our treatment of privacy in specific cases. Just as the right to privacy is more than the mere aggregation of a number of entitlements to engage in specific behavior, so too, protecting the physical integrity of the home is more than merely a means of protecting specific activities that often take place there. Even when our understanding of the contours of the right to privacy depends on "reference to a 'place,' " *** the essence of a Fourth Amendment violation is 'not the breaking of [a person's] doors, and the rummaging of his drawers,' but rather is "the invasion of his indefeasible right of personal security, personal liberty and private property.' " ***

The Court's interpretation of the pivotal case of *Stanley v. Georgia* *** is entirely unconvincing. *Stanley* held that Georgia's undoubted power to punish the public distribution of constitutionally unprotected, obscene material did not permit the State to punish the private possession of such material. According to the majority here, *Stanley* relied entirely on the First Amendment, and thus, it is claimed, sheds no light on cases not involving printed materials. *** But that is not what *Stanley* said. Rather, the *Stanley* Court anchored its holding in the Fourth Amendment's special protection for the individual in his home. . . .

Indeed, the right of an individual to conduct intimate relationships in the intimacy of his or her own home seems to me to be the heart of the Constitution's protection of privacy. . . .

Justice Stevens, with whom **Justice Brennan** and **Justice Marshall** join, dissenting. . . .

Cruzan v. Director, Missouri Health Department

497 U.S. 261; 110 S. Ct. 2841; 111 L. Ed.2d 224 (1990)
Vote: 5-4

State courts have decided numerous cases involving the termination of medical treatments sustaining the life of terminally ill or injured patients. The case of Nancy Cruzan was the first case of this kind to reach the U.S. Supreme Court. The pertinent facts are provided in the Court's opinion.

Chief Justice Rehnquist delivered the opinion of the Court.

Petitioner Nancy Beth Cruzan was rendered incompetent as a result of severe injuries sustained during an automobile accident. Co-petitioners Lester and Joyce Cruzan, Nancy's parents and co-guardians, sought a court order directing the withdrawal of their daughter's artificial feeding and hydration equipment after it became apparent that she had virtually no chance of recovering her cognitive faculties. The Supreme Court of Missouri held that because there was no clear and convincing evidence of Nancy's desire to have life-sustaining treatment withdrawn under such circumstances, her parents lacked authority to effectuate such a request. We granted certiorari, *** and now affirm.

On the night of January 11, 1983, Nancy Cruzan lost control of her car as she traveled down Elm Road in Jasper County, Missouri. The vehicle overturned, and Cruzan was discovered lying face down in a ditch without detectable respiratory or cardiac function. Paramedics were able to restore her breathing and heartbeat at the accident site, and she was transported to a hospital in an unconscious state. An attending neurosurgeon diagnosed her as having sustained probable cerebral contusions compounded by significant anoxia (lack of oxygen). The Missouri trial court in this case found that permanent brain damage generally results after 6 minutes in an anoxic state; it was estimated that Cruzan was deprived of oxygen from 12 to 14 minutes. She remained in a coma for approximately three weeks and then progressed to an unconscious state in which she was able to orally ingest some nutrition. In order to ease feeding and further the recovery,

surgeons implanted a gastrostomy feeding and hydration tube in Cruzan with the consent of her then husband. Subsequent rehabilitative efforts proved unavailing. She now lies in a Missouri state hospital in what is commonly referred to as a persistent vegetative state: generally, a condition in which a person exhibits motor reflexes but evinces no indications of significant cognitive function. The State of Missouri is bearing the cost of her care.

After it had become apparent that Nancy Cruzan had virtually no chance of regaining her mental faculties her parents asked hospital employees to terminate the artificial nutrition and hydration procedures. All agree that such a removal would cause her death. The employees refused to honor the request without court approval. The parents then sought and received authorization from the state trial court for termination. The court found that a person in Nancy's condition had a fundamental right under the State and Federal Constitutions to refuse or direct the withdrawal of "death prolonging procedures." *** The Court also found that Nancy's "expressed thoughts at age twenty-five in somewhat serious conversation with a housemate friend that if sick or injured she would not wish to continue her life unless she could live at least halfway normally suggests that given her present condition she would not wish to continue on with her nutrition and hydration." ***

The Supreme Court of Missouri reversed by a divided vote. The court recognized a right to refuse treatment embodied in the common-law doctrine of informed consent, but expressed skepticism about the application of that doctrine in the circumstances of this case. *** The court also declined to read a broad right of privacy into the State Constitution which would "support the right of a person to refuse medical treatment in every circumstance," and expressed doubt as to whether such a right existed under the United States Constitution. *** It then decided that the Missouri Living Will statute, *** embodied a state policy strongly favoring the preservation of life. *** The court found that Cruzan's statements to her roommate regarding her desire to live or die under certain conditions were "unreliable for the purpose of determining her intent," *** "and thus insufficient to support the co-guardians' claim to exercise substituted judgment on Nancy's behalf." *** It rejected the argument that Cruzan's parents were entitled to order the termination of her medical treatment, concluding that "no person can assume that choice for an incompetent in the absence of the formalities required under Missouri's Living Will statutes or the clear and convincing, inherently reliable evidence absent here." *** The court also expressed its view that "[b]road policy questions bearing on life and death are more properly addressed by representative assemblies" than judicial bodies. ***

We granted certiorari to consider the question of whether Cruzan has a right under the United States Constitution which would require the hospital to withdraw life-sustaining treatment from her under these circumstances. . . .

In the [*In re*] Quinlan [N.J. 1976] case, young Karen Quinlan suffered severe brain damage as the result of anoxia, and entered a persistent vegetative state. Karen's father sought judicial approval to disconnect his daughter's respirator. The New Jersey Supreme Court granted the relief, holding that Karen had a right of privacy grounded in the Federal Constitution to terminate treatment. *** Recognizing that this right was not absolute, however, the court balanced it against asserted state interests. Noting that the State's interest "weakens and the individual's right to privacy grows as the degree of bodily invasion increases and the prognosis dims," the court concluded that the state interests had to give way in that case. *** The court also concluded that the "only practical way" to prevent the loss of Karen's privacy right due to her incompetence was to allow her guardian and family to decide "whether she would exercise it in these circumstances." ***

After *Quinlan*, however, most courts have based a right to refuse treatment either solely on the common law right to informed consent or on both the common law right and a constitutional privacy right.

The Fourteenth Amendment provides that no State shall "deprive any person of life, liberty, or property, without due process of law." The principle that a competent person has a constitutionally protected liberty interest in refusing unwanted medical treatment may be inferred from our prior decisions. In *Jacobson v Massachusetts* *** (1905), for instance, the Court balanced an individual's liberty interest in declining an unwanted smallpox vaccine against the State's interest in preventing disease. Decisions prior to the incorporation of the Fourth Amendment into the Fourteenth Amendment analyzed searches and seizures involving the body under the Due Process Clause and were thought to implicate substantial liberty interests.

[In *Washington v. Harper* (1990)], . . . in the course of holding that a State's procedures for administering antipsychotic medication to prisoners were sufficient to satisfy due process concerns, we recognized that prisoners possess "a significant liberty interest in avoiding the unwanted administration of antipsychotic drugs under the Due Process Clause of the Fourteenth Amendment." ***

But determining that a person has a "liberty interest" under the Due Process Clause does not end the inquiry; "whether respondent's constitutional rights have been violated must be determined by balancing his liberty interests against the relevant state interests." ***

Petitioners insist that under the general holdings of our cases, the forced administration of life-sustaining medical treatment, and even of artificially delivered food and water essential to life, would implicate a competent person's liberty interest. Although we think the logic of the cases discussed above would embrace such a liberty interest, the dramatic consequences involved in refusal of such treatment would inform the inquiry as to whether the deprivation of that interest is constitutionally permissible. But for purposes of this case, we assume that the United States Constitution would grant a competent person a constitutionally protected right to refuse lifesaving hydration and nutrition.

Petitioners go on to assert that an incompetent person should possess the same right in this respect as is possessed by a competent person. . . . The difficulty with petitioners' claim is that in a sense it begs the question: an incompetent person is not able to make an informed and voluntary choice to exercise a hypothetical right to refuse treatment or any other right. Such a "right" must be exercised for her, if at all, by some sort of surrogate. Here, Missouri has in effect recognized that under certain circumstances a surrogate may act for the patient in electing to have hydration and nutrition withdrawn in such a way as to cause death, but it has established a procedural safeguard to assure that the action of the surrogate conforms as best it may to the wishes expressed by the patient while competent. Missouri requires that evidence of the incompetent's wishes as to the withdrawal of treatment be proved by clear and convincing evidence. The question, then, is whether the United States Constitution forbids the establishment of this procedural requirement by the State. We hold that it does not.

Whether or not Missouri's clear and convincing evidence requirement comports with the United States Constitution depends in part on what interests the State may properly seek to protect in this situation. Missouri relies on its interest in the protection and preservation of human life, and there can be no gainsaying this interest. As a general matter, the States—indeed, all civilized nations—demonstrate their commitment to life by treating homicide as serious crime. Moreover, the majority of States in this country have laws imposing criminal penalties on one who assists another to commit suicide. We do not think a State is required to remain neutral in the face of an informed and voluntary decision by a physically-able adult to starve to death.

But in the context presented here, a State has more particular interests at stake. The choice between life and death is a deeply personal decision of obvious and overwhelming finality. We believe Missouri may legitimately seek to safeguard the personal element of this choice through the imposition of heightened evidentiary requirements. It cannot be disputed that the Due Process Clause protects an interest in life as well as an interest in refusing life-sustaining medical treatment. Not all incompetent patients will have loved ones available to serve as surrogate decisionmakers. And even where family members are present, "[t]here will, of course, be some unfortunate situations in which family members will not act to protect a patient." *** A State is entitled to guard against potential abuses in such situations. Similarly, a State is entitled to consider

that a judicial proceeding to make a determination regarding an incompetent's wishes may very well not be an adversarial one, with the added guarantee of accurate fact-finding that the adversary process brings with it. *** Finally, we think a State may properly decline to make judgments about the "quality" of life that a particular individual may enjoy, and simply assert an unqualified interest in the preservation of human life to be weighed against the constitutionally protected interests of the individual.

In our view, Missouri has permissibly sought to advance these interests though the adoption of a "clear and convincing" standard of proof to govern such proceedings. "The function of a standard of proof, as that concept is embodied in the Due Process Clause and in the realm of factfinding, is to 'instruct the factfinder concerning the degree of confidence our society thinks he should have in the correctness of factual conclusions for a particular type of adjudication.'" *** Further, this level of proof, "or an even higher one, has traditionally been imposed in cases involving allegations of civil fraud, and in a variety of other kinds of civil cases involving such issues as . . . lost wills, oral contracts to make bequests, and the like." ***

We think it self-evident that the interests at stake in the instant proceedings are more substantial, both on an individual and societal level, than those involved in a run-of-the-mind civil dispute. But not only does the standard of proof reflect the importance of a particular adjudication, it also serves as "a societal judgment about how the risk or error should be distributed between the litigants." *** The more stringent the burden of proof a party must bear, the more that party bears the risk of an erroneous decision. We believe that Missouri may permissibly place an increased risk of an erroneous decision on those seeking to terminate an incompetent individual's life-sustaining treatment. An erroneous decision not to terminate results in a maintenance of the status quo; the possibility of subsequent developments such as advancements in medical science, the discovery of new evidence regarding the patient's intent, changes in the law, or simply the unexpected death of the patient despite the administration of life-sustaining treatment, at least create the potential that a wrong decision will eventually be corrected or its impact mitigated. An erroneous decision to withdraw life-sustaining treatment, however, is not susceptible of correction. . . . The same must surely be said of the decision to discontinue hydration and nutrition of a patient such as Nancy Cruzan, which all agree will result in her death.

It is also worth noting that most, if not all, States simply forbid oral testimony entirely in determining the wishes of parties in transactions which, while important, simply do not have the consequences that a decision to terminate a person's life does. At common law and by statute in most States, the parole evidence rule prevents the variations of the terms of a written contract by oral testimony. The statute of frauds makes unenforceable oral contracts to leave property by will, and statutes regulating the making of wills universally require that those instruments be in writing. *** There is no doubt that statutes requiring wills to be in writing, and statutes of frauds which require that a contract to make a will be in writing, on occasion frustrate the effectuation of the intent of a particular decedent, just as Missouri's requirement of proof in this case may have frustrated the effectuation of the not-fully-expressed desires of Nancy Cruzan. But the Constitution does not require general rules to work faultlessly; no general rule can.

In sum, we conclude that a State may apply a clear and convincing evidence standard in proceedings where a guardian seeks to discontinue nutrition and hydration of a person diagnosed to be in a persistent vegetative state. We note that many courts which have adopted some sort of substituted judgment procedure in situations like this, whether they limit consideration of evidence to the prior expressed wishes of the incompetent individual, or whether they allow more general proof of what the individual's decision would have been, require a clear and convincing standard of proof for such evidence. ***

The Supreme Court of Missouri held that in this case the testimony adduced at trial did not amount to clear and convincing proof of the patient's desire to have hydration and nutrition withdrawn. In so doing, it reversed a decision of the Missouri trial court which had found that the evidence "suggest[ed]" Nancy Cruzan would not have desired to continue such measures, App to Pet for Cert A98, but which had not adopted the standard of "clear and convinc-

ing evidence" enunciated by the Supreme Court. The testimony adduced at trial consisted primarily of Nancy Cruzan's statements made to a housemate about a year before her accident that she would not want to live should she face life as "vegetable," and other observations to the same effect. The observations did not deal in terms with withdrawal of medical treatment or of hydration and nutrition. We cannot say that the Supreme Court of Missouri committed constitutional error in reaching the conclusion that it did.

Petitioners alternatively contend that Missouri must accept the "substituted judgment" of close family members even in the absence of substantial proof that their views reflect the views of the patient. . . . No doubt is engendered by anything in this record but that Nancy Cruzan's mother and father are loving and caring parents. If the State were required by the United States Constitution to repose a right of "substituted judgment" with anyone, the Cruzans would surely qualify. But we do not think the Due Process Clause requires the State to repose judgment on these matters with anyone but the patient herself. Close family members may have a strong feeling—a feeling not at all ignoble or unworthy, but not entirely disinterested, either—that they do not wish to witness the continuation of the life of a loved one which they regard as hopeless, meaningless, and even degrading. But there is no automatic assurance that the view of close family members will necessarily be the same as the patient's would have been had she been confronted with the prospect of her situation while competent. All of the reasons previously discussed for allowing Missouri to require clear and convincing evidence of the patient's wishes lead us to conclude that the State may choose to defer only to those wishes, rather than confide the decision to close family members.

The judgment of the Supreme Court of Missouri is affirmed.

Justice Scalia, concurring.

The various opinions in this case portray quite clearly the difficult, indeed agonizing, questions that are presented by the constantly increasing power of science to keep the human body alive for longer than any reasonable person would want to inhabit it.

The States have begun to grapple with these problems through legislation. I am concerned, from the tenor of today's opinions, that we are poised to confuse that enterprise as successfully as we have confused the enterprise of legislating concerning abortion—requiring it to be conducted against a background of federal constitutional imperatives that are unknown because they are being newly crafted from Term to Term. That would be a great misfortune.

While I agree with the Court's analysis today, and therefore join in its opinion, I would have preferred that we announce, clearly and promptly, that the federal courts have no business in this field; that American law has always accorded the State the power to prevent, by force if necessary, suicide—including suicide by refusing to take appropriate measures necessary to preserve one's life; that the point at which life becomes "worthless," and the point at which the means necessary to preserve it become "extraordinary" or "inappropriate," are neither set forth in the Constitution nor known to the nine Justices of this Court any better than they are known to nine people picked at random from the Kansas City telephone directory; and hence, that even when it is demonstrated by clear and convincing evidence that a patient no longer wishes certain measures to be taken to preserve her life, it is up to the citizens of Missouri to decide, through their elected representatives, whether that wish will be honored. It is quite impossible (because the Constitution says nothing about the matter) that those citizens will decide upon a line less lawful than the one we would choose; and it is unlikely (because we know no more about "life-and-death" than they do) that they will decide upon a line less reasonable. . . .

Justice Brennan, with whom **_Justice Marshall_** and **_Justice Blackmun_** join, dissenting.

. . . Nancy Cruzan has dwelt in [a] twilight zone for six years. She is oblivious to her surroundings and will remain so. *** Her body twitches only reflexively, without consciousness. *** The areas of her brain that once thought, felt, and experienced sensations have degenerated badly and are continuing to do so. The cavities remaining are filling with cerebrospinal fluid. The " 'cerebral cortical atrophy is

irreversible, permanent, progressive and ongoing.' " *** "Nancy will never interact meaningfully with her environment again. She will remain in a persistent vegetative state until her death." *** Because she cannot swallow, her nutrition and hydration are delivered through a tube surgically implanted in her stomach.

A grown woman at the time of the accident, Nancy had previously expressed her wish to forgo continuing medical care under circumstances such as these. Her family and her friends are convinced that this is what she would want. A guardian _ad litem_ appointed by the trial court is also convinced that this is what Nancy would want. Yet the Missouri Supreme Court, alone among state courts deciding such a question, has determined that an irreversibly vegetative patient will remain a passive prisoner of medical technology—for Nancy, perhaps for the next 30 years. ***

Today the Court, while tentatively accepting that there is some degree of constitutionally protected liberty interest in avoiding unwanted medical treatment such as artificial nutrition and hydration, affirms the decision of the Missouri Supreme Court. The majority opinion, as I read it, would affirm that decision on the ground that a State may require "clear and convincing" evidence of Nancy Cruzan's prior decision to forgo life-sustaining treatment under circumstances such as hers in order to ensure that her actual wishes are honored. *** Because I believe that Nancy Cruzan has a fundamental right to be free of unwanted artificial nutrition and hydration, which right is not outweighed by any interests of the State, and because I find that the improperly biased procedural obstacles imposed by the Missouri Supreme Court impermissibly burden that right, I respectfully dissent. Nancy Cruzan is entitled to choose to die with dignity. . . .

Justice Stevens, dissenting.

Our Constitution is born of the proposition that all legitimate governments must secure the equal right of every person to "Life, Liberty, and the pursuit of Happiness." In the ordinary case we quite naturally assume that these three ends are compatible, mutually enhancing, and perhaps even coincident.

The Court would make an exception here. It permits the State's abstract, undifferentiated interest in the preservation of life to overwhelm the best interests of Nancy Beth Cruzan, interests which would, according to an undisputed finding, be served by allowing her guardians to exercise her constitutional right to discontinue medical treatment. Ironically, the Court reaches this conclusion despite endorsing three significant propositions which should save it from any such dilemma. First, a competent individual's decision to refuse life-sustaining medical procedures is an aspect of liberty protected by the Due Process Clause of the Fourteenth Amendment. *** Second, upon a proper evidentiary showing, a qualified guardian may make that decision on behalf of an incompetent ward. Third, in answering the important question presented by this tragic case, it is wise "not to attempt by any general statement, to cover every possible phase of the subject." *** Together, these considerations suggest that Nancy Cruzan's liberty to be free from medical treatment must be understood in light of the facts and circumstances particular to her.

I would so hold: in my view, the Constitution requires the State to care for Nancy Cruzan's life in a way that gives appropriate respect to her own best interests. . . .

In this case, as is no doubt true in many others, the predicament confronted by the healthy members of the Cruzan family merely adds emphasis to the best interests finding made by the trial judge. Each of us has an interest in the kind of memories that will survive after death. To that end, individual decisions are often motivated by their impact on others. A member of the kind of family identified in the trial court's findings in this case would likely have not only a normal interest in minimizing the burden that her own illness imposes on others, but also an interest in having their memories of her filled predominantly with thoughts about her past vitality rather than her current condition. The meaning and completion of her life should be controlled by persons who have her best interests at heart—not by a state legislature concerned only with the "preservation of human life."

The Cruzan family's continuing concern provides a concrete reminder that Nancy Cruzan's interests did not disappear with her vitality or her consciousness. However commendable may be the State's interest in human life, it cannot pursue that interest by appropriating Nancy Cruzan's life as a symbol for its own purposes. Lives do not exist in abstraction from persons, and to pretend otherwise is not to honor but to desecrate the State's responsibility for protecting life. A State that seeks to demonstrate its commitment to life may do so by aiding those who are actively struggling for life and health. In this endeavor, unfortunately, no State can lack for opportunities: there can be no need to make an example of tragic cases like that of Nancy Cruzan.

I respectfully dissent.

CHAPTER SIXTEEN

EQUAL PROTECTION AND THE ANTIDISCRIMINATION PRINCIPLE

Our constitution is color-blind, and neither knows nor tolerates classes among citizens. In respect of civil rights all are equal before the law. The humblest is the peer of the most powerful. The law regards man as man, and takes no account of his color when his civil rights as guaranteed by the supreme law of the land are involved.

Justice John M. Harlan (the elder), dissenting in *Plessy v. Ferguson* (1896)

John M. Harlan (the elder):
Associate Justice, 1877–1911

INTRODUCTION

One of the philosophical foundations of American democracy is the idea that all individuals are equal before the law. This ideal is expressed both in the Declaration of Independence and in the Equal Protection Clause of the Fourteenth Amendment, which provides that no state shall "deny to any person within its jurisdiction the equal protection of the laws." The Equal Protection Clause prohibits states from denying any person or class of persons the same protection and rights that the law extends to other "similarly situated" persons or classes of persons.

Like other rights guaranteed by the post-Civil War Amendments, the Equal Protection Clause was motivated in large part by a desire to protect the civil rights of African-Americans recently freed from slavery. However, the text of the Clause makes no mention of race; rather, it refers to any person within the jurisdiction of a state. Although the Supreme Court attempted initially to limit the scope of the Equal Protection Clause to discrimination claims brought by African Americans (see *The Slaughter-House Cases* [1873]; *Strauder v. West Virginia* [1880]), the Clause has been developed into a broad prohibition against unreasonable governmental discrimination directed at any identifiable group.

In the late nineteenth century, the Supreme Court declared that the word *person* in the Equal Protection Clause included corporations (see *Santa Clara County v. Southern Pacific Railroad Company* [1886]). Occasionally, the Clause was employed as a basis for invalidating discriminatory business regulation (see *Yick Wo v. Hopkins* [1886]). In the modern era, the Equal Protection Clause has been invoked successfully to challenge discrimination against racial and ethnic minorities, as well as discrimination against women, the poor, illegitimate children, the mentally retarded, and even illegal aliens. Under the so-called New Equal Protection, the Supreme Court has used the Equal Protection Clause to scrutinize closely any state law or practice that discriminates among groups in their enjoyment of "fundamental rights." Without question, the scope of the Equal Protection Clause has been expanded far beyond the expectations of its authors. Along with the Due Process Clause of the Fourteenth Amendment, the Equal Protection Clause has become the principal basis for challenging the constitutionality of a broad range of state laws, actions, and policies.

The "Equal Protection Component" of the Fifth Amendment

Since the Fourteenth Amendment applies only to the states and since the Bill of Rights contains no explicit equal protection provision, does it follow that the national government is under no constitutional obligation to provide equal protection of the laws? The Supreme Court has answered this question emphatically in the negative, "finding" an "equal protection component" in the Due Process Clause of the Fifth Amendment. The Court has concluded that the values underlying the equal protection guarantee are embraced within the broad definition of due process of law (see *Bolling v. Sharpe* [1954]). Since the Fourteenth Amendment contains a Due Process Clause virtually identical to that found in the Fifth Amendment, one might conclude that the Equal Protection Clause of the Fourteenth Amendment is superfluous. While this may be true in a formal, logical sense, the Equal Protection Clause was the historic basis for judicial scrutiny of governmental policies challenged as discriminatory. In the absence of the Equal Protection Clause, such scrutiny would have been more difficult to justify.

LEVELS OF JUDICIAL SCRUTINY IN EQUAL PROTECTION CASES

Although the adoption and early development of the Equal Protection Clause must be understood in the context of the historic struggle for racial equality in this country, courts have over the years entertained a variety of equal protection claims going well beyond issues of racial discrimination. The Supreme Court has developed a set of standards for judging the constitutionality of policies that are challenged on equal protection grounds.

The Rational Basis Test

State and federal laws are replete with discriminations, or classifications, of various kinds. Yet very few of these classifications are considered constitutionally offensive. For example, a state law that requires a person to possess a license to practice psychiatry discriminates against those persons who are unable to meet the qualifications necessary to obtain a license. Yet few would question the reasonableness of such discrimination. Similarly, when the state limits the driving privilege to persons sixteen and older, it is engaging in age discrimination. But, again, few would challenge the reasonableness of such discrimination.

The traditional test employed by courts in judging challenged legislative classifications is the **rational basis test** (first articulated by the Supreme Court in *Gulf, Colorado & Santa Fe Railway Company v. Ellis* [1897]). Under this deferential approach, the burden is on the party challenging the statute to show that: (1) the purpose of the challenged discrimination is an illegitimate state objective and (2) the means employed by the state are not rationally related to the achievement of its objective. Thus, for example, the state law requiring psychiatrists to be licensed reflects a legitimate state interest in protecting the public health and safety and is rationally related to that end. The rational basis test remains the primary test for determining the constitutionality of classifications that impinge on economic interests.

As noted in previous chapters, during the "age of conservative activism" (1890 to 1937), the Supreme Court emphasized the protection of private property against government regulation and redistribution. Although the Equal Protection Clause played a limited role in this protection, the Court relied more heavily on the Due Process Clauses of the Fifth and Fourteenth Amendments. In the wake of the constitutional revolution of 1937, the locus of Supreme Court activism moved away from the protection of economic individualism. Instead, the post-New Deal Court focused its attention on civil rights and liberties, especially the rights of traditionally disadvantaged minorities. In a famous footnote to his opinion in *United States v. Carolene Products Company* (1938), Justice Harlan Fiske Stone stated that

> prejudice against discrete and insular minorities may be a special condition, which tends seriously to curtail the operation of those political processes ordinarily to be relied upon to protect minorities and . . . may call for a more searching judicial scrutiny.

The Court's desire to protect "discrete and insular minorities" who lack political clout in Congress and/or the state legislatures resulted in numerous controversial decisions concerning the rights of the accused, prisoners, aliens (legal and illegal), persons with disabilities and unorthodox religious sects. The Equal Protection Clause figured prominently in this process. In expanding the scope of the Equal Protection Clause, the Court developed a style of analysis that to a great extent superseded the traditional rational basis test.

The Suspect Classification Doctrine

Korematsu v. United States (1944) provided the first real indication that the Court was embarking on a new approach to the Equal Protection Clause. In *Korematsu,* the Court upheld the constitutionality of the "relocation" of Japanese Americans living on the West Coast during the Second World War (for further discussion, see Chapter 6). In his majority opinion, Justice Hugo Black stated that

> all legal restrictions which curtail the civil rights of a single group are immediately suspect. That is not to say that all such restrictions are unconstitutional. It is to say that courts must subject them to the most rigid scrutiny. Pressing public necessity may sometimes justify the existence of such restrictions; racial antagonism never can.

It is now widely recognized that no compelling justification supported the relocation order. However, the majority in *Korematsu* apparently did not have full access to information, later made public, clearly indicating that the relocation order stemmed more from racial prejudice than from military necessity. Although on its face the *Korematsu* decision was hardly a victory for civil rights, it marked the inception of the **suspect classification doctrine,** which holds that certain kinds of discrimination are inherently suspect and therefore must be subjected to **strict judicial scrutiny.** Included among those laws that are inherently suspect are those that classify persons based on race, religion, or ethnicity, as well as those that impinge on fundamental rights.

Operationally speaking, strict judicial scrutiny means that the ordinary **presumption of constitutionality** is reversed; the government carries the **burden of proof** that its challenged policy is constitutional. To carry that burden, government must show that its policy is necessary to the achievement of a **compelling interest.** Although these tests are far from precise, the compelling interest test is generally understood to be far more stringent than the traditional rational basis test. Using the suspect classification doctrine, the Court has invalidated, explicitly or implicitly, virtually all public policies that overtly discriminate among persons on the basis of their race (see, for example, *Loving v. Virginia* [1967]). In the Court's view, it is virtually impossible for government to have a compelling interest that would require or justify racial or ethnic discrimination.

Judging the Disparate Impact of Facially Neutral Policies

The suspect classification doctrine applies only to policies that overtly discriminate on the basis of race, religion, or ethnicity. What standard should be applied to judge policies that are neutral on their face but have disparate impacts on people of different races? In *Washington v. Davis* (1976), the Supreme Court considered a challenge to the practice of requiring applicants to the District of Columbia police department to pass a verbal skills test that was used widely in the federal civil service. African-American applicants were approximately four times as likely to fail this test as were white applicants. The Court rejected the argument that the testing requirement should be subjected to strict scrutiny under the suspect classification doctrine. Writing for the Court, Justice Byron White said:

> A rule that a statute designed to serve neutral ends is nevertheless invalid, absent compelling justification, if in practice it benefits or burdens one race more than another would be far-reaching and would raise serious questions about, and perhaps invalidate, a whole range of tax, welfare, public service, regulatory and licensing statutes. . . .

Under *Washington v. Davis* and similar decisions, a policy that is racially neutral on its face but has a disparate racial impact will be upheld unless plaintiffs can show that it was adopted to serve a racially discriminatory purpose.

Heightened Scrutiny

To complicate matters further, the Supreme Court has developed still another level of equal protection review, falling somewhere between the rational basis test and the suspect classification doctrine. This approach, often described as **heightened scrutiny,** has been applied most prominently, but not exclusively, to sex discrimination claims. (Heightened scrutiny is discussed more fully below under the topic of sex discrimination.) Thus, there are currently three tiers of review for judging equal protection claims. Shortly before his retirement in 1991, Justice Thurgood Marshall suggested that the Court adopt a "sliding scale" that would embrace a "spectrum of standards" of review. Others on the Court have been put off by what they regard as needless doctrinal complexity. Justice John Paul Stevens, for example, has argued for a return to the rational basis standard, which he believes to be adequate to invalidate all invidious forms of discrimination. Others on the Court, most notably Chief Justice William Rehnquist, are dissatisfied with the modern Court's special solicitude for the claims of "discrete and insular minorities." Given the conservative character of the contemporary Supreme Court, we can anticipate significant doctrinal changes in the Court's equal protection jurisprudence.

THE STRUGGLE FOR RACIAL EQUALITY

While the Equal Protection Clause is now recognized as a broad shield against arbitrary governmental action, little doubt exists that the Fourteenth Amendment was adopted primarily to combat state-sponsored racial discrimination. Specifically, the Fourteenth Amendment was designed to provide constitutional authority for newly enacted federal civil rights legislation aimed at ending discrimination against African-Americans. Section Five of the Fourteenth Amendment gives Congress the power to enforce, "by appropriate legislation," the abstract promises of the Equal Protection Clause and other provisions of the Amendment.

Early Interpretations of the Equal Protection Clause

Shortly before the Fourteenth Amendment was ratified, Congress passed the Civil Rights Act of 1866, which, among other things, protected the right of African-Americans to inherit, own, and convey property. In the wake of the Civil War, many of the Southern states had adopted "Black Codes," which denied such basic economic rights to former slaves. Under the new Civil Rights Act, violation of these rights was made a federal offense where it could be shown that the violator was acting "under color of state law." Apparently having some reservations about the constitutionality of this law, Congress rushed to adopt the Fourteenth Amendment, believing that the Equal Protection Clause of Section 1 together with the enforcement provision of Section 5 would provide an adequate constitutional basis for far-ranging civil rights legislation.

The Civil Rights Cases of 1883

While the modern Supreme Court recognizes broad congressional power under the Fourteenth Amendment, the Supreme Court's early view of congressional authority in the field of civil rights was much more restrictive. In adopting the Civil Rights Act of 1875, Congress made a serious attempt to eradicate racial discrimination in "places of public accommodation," including hotels, taverns, restaurants, theaters, and "public conveyances." In the *Civil Rights Cases* (1883), the Supreme Court struck down the key provisions of this act, ruling that the Fourteenth Amendment limited congressional action to the prohibition of official, state-sponsored discrimination as distinct from discrimination practiced by privately owned places of public accommodation. The Supreme Court's decision in *The Civil Rights Cases* may have been motivated by a desire to promote reconciliation between North and South and between the federal and state governments. Unfortunately, any such reconciliation was achieved at the expense of African-Americans.

Adoption of Jim Crow Laws

Not only did the Court's decision in the *Civil Rights Cases* preserve widespread practices of racial discrimination in restaurants, hotels, and the like, it was also regarded as a green light for the passage of legislation mandating strict racial segregation. The so-called Jim Crow laws adopted in the aftermath of the *Civil Rights Cases* required segregation in virtually every area of public life. They required blacks and whites to attend separate schools, to use separate parks, to ride in separate railroad cars, and even to be buried in separate cemeteries. Perhaps the most ludicrous of the many Jim Crow laws required white and black witnesses in court to take their oaths on separate Bibles!

Federal Civil Rights Statutes Passed during Reconstruction

During the Reconstruction Era, Congress passed four major civil rights acts. Some provisions of these statutes remain important components of contemporary civil rights law.

THE CIVIL RIGHTS ACT OF 1866.
This act provided that citizens of all races have the same rights to make and enforce contracts, to sue and give evidence in the courts, and to own, purchase, sell, rent, and inherit real and personal property. For modern counterparts, see 42 U.S. Code Sections 1981 and 1982.

THE CIVIL RIGHTS ACT OF 1870.
Also known as the Ku Klux Klan Act, this statute made it a federal crime to conspire to "injure, oppress, threaten or intimidate any citizen in the free exercise of any right or privilege secured to him by the Constitution or laws of the United States." For modern counterpart, see 18 U.S. Code Section 241. The statute also criminalized any act under color of state law that subjects persons to deprivations of constitutional rights. See 18 U.S. Code Section 242.

THE CIVIL RIGHTS ACT OF 1871.
This statute made individuals acting under color of state law personally liable for acts violating the constitutional rights of others. Civil actions under this statute are commonly referred to as "Section 1983 actions" because the act is codified at 42 U.S. Code Section 1983. The 1871 act also permitted civil suits against those conspiring to violate civil rights of others (codified at 42 U.S. Code Section 1985).

THE CIVIL RIGHTS ACT OF 1875.
This statute forbade denial of equal rights and privileges by places of public accommodation. It was declared invalid as applied to privately owned public accommodations in *The Civil Rights Cases* (1883). Access to public accommodations was ultimately achieved under Title II of the Civil Rights Act of 1964.

The "Separate but Equal" Doctrine

In *Plessy v. Ferguson* (1896), the Supreme Court upheld racial segregation in the context of public transportation. The Court's ruling provided a rationale for government-mandated segregation on a broad scale. At issue in *Plessy* was an 1890 Louisiana law requiring passenger trains operating within the state to provide "equal but separate" accommodations for the "white and colored races." Homer Plessy, who was considered "colored" under Louisiana law because one of his great grandparents was black, was ordered to leave a railroad car reserved for whites. Plessy, who intended to challenge the constitutionality of the law, refused to vacate his seat and was arrested. Dividing 7 to 1 (Justice David Brewer not participating), the Court sustained the Louisiana statute. Writing for the majority, Justice Henry Billings Brown asserted that

> in the nature of things, [the Fourteenth Amendment] could not have been intended to abolish distinctions based upon color, or to enforce social, as distinguished from political, equality, or a commingling of the two races upon terms unsatisfactory to either.

The "colored entrance" to a movie theater during the era of segregation

In one of the most widely quoted opinions in American constitutional law, Justice John M. Harlan (the elder) dissented vehemently. For Justice Harlan, ironically a former Kentucky slave owner, the "arbitrary separation of citizens on the basis of race" was tantamount to imposing a "badge of servitude" on the Negro race. He asserted that "our Constitution is color-blind, and neither knows nor tolerates classes among citizens."

The "separate but equal" doctrine approved in *Plessy* remained the authoritative interpretation of the Equal Protection Clause for fifty-eight years. Ultimately, of course, it was repudiated by the Supreme Court in *Brown v. Board of Education of Topeka* (1954). The **state action** doctrine announced in *The Civil Rights Cases* remains authoritative to this day, and not until the 1960s was Congress willing or able to prohibit discrimination in places of public accommodation. When Congress did finally act in passing the Civil Rights Act of 1964, it had to rely primarily on its broad powers under the Commerce Clause, rather than on Section 5 of the Fourteenth Amendment (see Chapter 5).

Thurgood Marshall on *Plessy v. Ferguson*

Prior to his appointment to the Supreme Court, Justice Thurgood Marshall served as counsel for the National Association for the Advancement of Colored People (NAACP). In his brief to the Supreme Court in *Brown v. Board of Education* (1954), Marshall wrote:

While the majority opinion [in *Plessy*] sought to rationalize its holding on the basis that separation of races was conducive to public peace and order, Justice Harlan knew all too well that the seeds of continuing racial animosities had been planted. . . . It is the dissenting opinion of Justice Harlan, rather than the majority opinion in *Plessy v. Ferguson,* that is in keeping with the scope and meaning of the Fourteenth Amendment. . . .

The net effect of *The Civil Rights Cases* and *Plessy v. Ferguson* was to defer the dream of legal and political equality for African-Americans for nearly a century after ratification of the Fourteenth Amendment. During this period, racial discrimination was simply a way of life for many Americans, both black and white. In the 1990s, although considerable progress toward racial equality has been achieved, racial discrimination and hatred have by no means disappeared from American society.

The Decline of *De Jure* Racial Segregation

The Court's decision in *Plessy v. Ferguson* rested on two obvious fictions: (1) that racial segregation conveyed no negative statement about the status of African-Americans and (2) that separate accommodations and facilities for blacks were in fact equal to those reserved for whites. Blacks, and no doubt most whites, knew better. As time went by, it became increasingly obvious to the Supreme Court that the separate but equal doctrine was a mere rationalization for relegating African-Americans to second-class citizenship.

In a series of cases decided between 1938 and 1950, the Supreme Court chipped away at the separate but equal doctrine, as applied to higher education, without repudiating the doctrine altogether. In *Missouri ex rel. Gaines v. Canada* (1938), the Court mandated the admission of a qualified African-American resident of Missouri to the state university law school. The Court held that a state could not escape its obligation by making provisions for its African-American students to attend out-of-state law schools. The Supreme Court reaffirmed its holding in *Gaines* a decade later in *Sipuel v. Oklahoma Board of Regents* (1948). Two years later, in *McLaurin v. Oklahoma State Regents* (1950), the Court disallowed an attempt by the University of Oklahoma to segregate a black graduate student from his white colleagues after he was admitted pursuant to a court order. In class, the student, McLaurin, was required to sit in a row of desks restricted to blacks. In the cafeteria, he was required to eat alone at a particular table. He was restricted to a designated table in the library. He was even prohibited from visiting his professors during their regular office hours in order to

Thurgood Marshall: Associate
Justice, 1967–1991

minimize his interactions with white students. In the Court's view, this isolation
significantly detracted from McLaurin's educational experience and thus could
not be justified under the separate but equal doctrine.

In *Sweatt v. Painter* (1950), the Court considered an attempt by the state of
Texas to provide a separate law school for African-Americans. The Court found
that the newly created law school at the Texas College for Negroes was substantially inferior, in terms of both measurable and intangible factors, to the white-
only law school at the University of Texas.

Desegregation

By the early 1950s, it was clear that the Supreme Court would no longer tolerate
the provision of demonstrably inferior services or facilities to African-Americans
under the aegis of the separate but equal doctrine. But considerable uncertainty
remained, both within and outside the Court, as to whether the justices would,
or should, abandon the *Plessy* doctrine altogether. The NAACP mounted a major
challenge to segregated public schools, instituting lawsuits in four states and the
District of Columbia. These cases were first argued before the Supreme Court in
1952, but because of the political magnitude of the issue presented, the Court
directed that the cases be reargued in 1953. Before the second round of oral
argument, Chief Justice Fred M. Vinson died and was replaced by Earl Warren.

The *Brown* Decision

Finally, on May 17, 1954, the uncertainty regarding segregated public schools
came to an end when the Court handed down its landmark decision in
Brown v. Board of Education. In one of the most important decisions in its

Clarence Thomas on *Brown v. Board of Education*

Prior to his appointment to the Supreme Court in 1991, Clarence Thomas wrote in the *Howard Law Journal* (1987):

The great flaw in *Brown* is that it did not rely on Justice Harlan's dissent in *Plessy*, which understood well that the fundamental issue of guidance by the Founders' constitutional principles lay at the heart of the segregation issue. . . . Justice Harlan's *Plessy* opinion is a good example of thinking in the spirit of the Founding. His arguments can be fully appreciated only in light of the Founders' intentions. Largely as a result of the dubious reasoning of the post-*Plessy* Court, and a national indifference to the rights of all Americans, Justice Harlan's argument that the Constitution is "colorblind" did not rally supporters.

history, the Court unanimously struck down racial segregation in the public schools of Kansas, South Carolina, Delaware, and Virginia. Speaking for the Court in *Brown,* Chief Justice Warren declared that "in the field of public education, the doctrine of 'separate but equal' has no place. Separate educational facilities are inherently unequal." Thus, in a concise and forceful opinion, the Warren Court abandoned a long-standing constitutional precedent and precipitated a revolution in public education.

In a companion case to *Brown, Bolling v. Sharpe,* the Court held that the operation of segregated schools by the District of Columbia violated the Due Process Clause of the Fifth Amendment. Here, as noted at the beginning of this chapter, the Court recognized an "equal protection component" in the Fifth Amendment due process requirement, indicating that uniform antidiscrimination mandates were to be applied to the federal government as well as the states.

Implementation of *Brown*

The *Brown* decision of 1954 left open the question of how and when desegregation would have to be achieved. In a follow-up decision in 1955 (referred to as *Brown* II), the Court blunted the revolutionary potential of the original decision by adopting a formula calling for implementation of desegregation with "all deliberate speed." Recognizing that compliance would be more difficult to achieve in the South than in other sections of the country, the Court left it up to federal district judges to apply this formula, taking into account the particular circumstances characterizing race relations within their respective jurisdictions. This approach ensured great diversity in the implementation of *Brown* I and invited the use of delaying tactics by state and local officials. Despite its concern for the difficulties public officials would face in bringing about desegregation, the Court was reviled in many quarters for "meddling" in state and local affairs. Some of the Court's harsher critics went so far as to call for the impeachment of Chief Justice Warren.

Some of the more extreme critics of school desegregation called for militant noncompliance with the Court's directive. John Kasper, a well-known white

Clarence Thomas:
Associate Justice, 1991–

supremacist and self-styled protégé of the fascist poet Ezra Pound, went around the country preaching the use of violence and intimidation to prevent black students from entering formerly all-white public schools. In the late summer of 1956, Kasper went to Clinton, Tennessee, where he succeeded in fomenting violent resistance to court-ordered integration of Clinton High School. In late August, Kasper was ordered by federal judge Robert Taylor "to cease hindering, obstructing, or in any wise interfering" with court-ordered integration. Kasper persisted in his efforts, and Clinton experienced a turbulent fall replete with riots, beatings, death threats directed at various school officials, and harassment of African-American students. After the National Guard was called in to restore order, Kasper was arrested and convicted for violating the federal court injunction. Ultimately, peace returned to Clinton, and desegregation proceeded apace.

The Little Rock Crisis

In one of the best known and most dramatic efforts to resist the Supreme Court's desegregation decisions, Arkansas Governor Orval Faubus called out the National Guard in 1957 to prevent nine African-American students from entering Little Rock Central High School. The Guard was soon withdrawn, but an angry mob of whites continued to harass the black students. President Dwight D. Eisenhower, who had expressed serious reservations about the *Brown* decision, nevertheless intervened with federal troops to quell the violence and enforce the court-ordered integration. In *Cooper v. Aaron* (1958), the Court delivered a sharp rebuke to Arkansas officials who had attempted to frustrate the Court's mandate (see Chapter 3). Would the Court's language in *Cooper v. Aaron* have been so strong in the absence of Eisenhower's intervention in Little Rock?

A scene from the Little Rock School desegregation crisis, September 1957

The Court Repudiates "All Deliberate Speed"

In efforts less dramatic than what transpired in Little Rock, state and local governments intent on avoiding desegregation adopted a strategy of "legislate and litigate" that delayed universal compliance with *Brown* for well over two decades. But in *Alexander v. Holmes County* (1969), after many years of delay, the Supreme Court finally abandoned the permissive "all deliberate speed" policy and ordered desegregation "at once."

The Busing Controversy

As previously noted, the Supreme Court's *Brown* II decision left the implementation of school desegregation largely to the discretion of federal district judges. Of the various measures that these judges employed in dismantling "dual" school systems, forced busing was by far the most controversial. In *Swann v. Charlotte-Mecklenburg Board of Education* (1971), the Supreme Court unanimously approved the use of court-ordered busing to achieve the goal of desegregation. In 1973, the Court turned its attention to school desegregation outside the South. In *Keyes v. Denver School District*, the Court, with only Justice Rehnquist dissenting, found *de jure* discrimination where a series of administrative decisions in the 1960s had helped to maintain racially segregated public schools in the city of Denver. Thus, in *Keyes*, as in *Swann*, the Supreme Court upheld a busing plan imposed by a federal district court.

As court-ordered busing became more pervasive, it erupted into a major political issue. In the 1972 presidential campaign, candidate George Wallace exploited the busing issue quite successfully, goading incumbent Richard Nixon into taking a stronger antibusing posture than he had previously maintained. Perhaps as a reaction to widespread criticism of *Swann* and *Keyes*, as well as antibusing rumblings in Congress, the Supreme Court backed away from busing in the case of *Milliken v. Bradley* (1974). *Milliken* involved a challenge to a court-ordered desegregation plan for greater Detroit that involved busing students across school district lines within the metropolitan area. Although *Milliken* by no means overturned *Swann* and *Keyes*, a 5-to-4 majority of the justices held that court-ordered busing of students across school district lines is permissible only if all affected districts had been guilty of past discriminatory practices. By thus limiting interdistrict busing plans, the Supreme Court placed substantial limits on this approach to school desegregation in metropolitan areas.

To the proponents of racial busing, the decision in *Milliken* was an unfortunate retreat from the Court's long-standing commitment to integration. For others, *Milliken* was a welcome concession to public opinion, which was generally negative toward busing. Clearly, the effect of the *Milliken* decision was to defuse much of the harsh criticism that had previously been directed at the Court over the busing issue. Nevertheless, interdistrict busing schemes continued to be ordered by federal judges where interdistrict violations were uncovered. In the unfortunate case of Boston, interdistrict busing in 1974 produced intense hostility and violence.

The use of busing to achieve desegregation continues to this day, although it is not as pervasive as it was in the early seventies. Indeed, African-American intellectuals and educators no longer uniformly support busing. Some reject what they regard as a racist implication that black children cannot improve themselves without exposure to white children. Clearly, the political and intellectual impetus behind racial busing has diminished dramatically. Consequently, busing is no longer a salient political issue. The Supreme Court continues to hear cases in this area, but the major thrust of current litigation is toward the termination, rather than the continued implementation, of busing and related desegregation plans. In a significant 1991 decision, *Board of Education v. Dowell,* the Court granted federal district courts clear authority to terminate desegregation orders provided that two conditions are met: (1) the local school board in question has complied in good faith with the desegregation decree and (2) all vestiges of prior discrimination have been effectively removed. The *Dowell* decision left many questions unanswered, but the Court made it clear that judicial supervision of school desegregation is, after all, temporary in nature.

In 1992, the Supreme Court amplified its decision in *Dowell* in permitting a federal district court that for many years had supervised desegregation of the DeKalb County, Georgia, schools to relinquish supervision over certain aspects of school administration (see *Freeman v. Pitts* reprinted in Appendix E). The Court held that district judges have discretion to relinquish supervision of school systems where racial imbalances stemming from *de jure* segregation have disappeared, even if schools remain "racially identifiable" due to demographic factors. Under the approach taken in *Dowell* and *Freeman*, local school districts that show good-faith efforts to comply with court-mandated desegregation plans will eventually regain full control of their school systems.

Affirmative Action

The furor over court-ordered busing that occurred during the 1970s has now largely subsided. As is usually the case in American politics, a new controversy has developed to take its place. The controversy involves **affirmative action:** the compensatory preferential treatment of members of traditionally disfavored minority groups. The affirmative action concept is manifested in three major areas of distributive policy: employment, government contracts, and higher education. Affirmative action emerged through executive orders handed down during the Kennedy, Johnson, and Nixon administrations of the 1960s and early '70s. Initially, it was limited to the requirement that federal government contractors make increased efforts to recruit minority employees. Thereafter, state higher education programs were subjected to affirmative action guidelines as a condition of accepting federal subsidies. Soon federal and state courts were adopting "race-conscious remedies" (for example, racial busing) in resolving desegregation lawsuits. Eventually, what began as little more than a public exhortation became a series of goals, quotas, and timetables designed to integrate African-Americans, Hispanics, Native Americans, and other traditionally disfavored minorities into the economic and educational mainstream.

Although the ultimate objective of affirmative action was, and is, universally applauded, the means of achieving it—quotas, formulas, and ratios based on immutable racial characteristics—are distasteful to many and appear downright unjust to others. To many critics, affirmative action represents an unfortunate degeneration of the noble ideal of equality of opportunity into "statistical parity." For some legal critics, affirmative action is a violation of the color-blind Constitution idealized by Justice Harlan's dissent in *Plessy v. Ferguson.* Still others, some of them members of nonpreferred ethnic minorities object to affirmative action not on principle but because they have not been given preferred status. Yet, the many defenders of affirmative action characterize it as the only practicable means of realizing the American dream for those who have been traditionally locked out.

Competing Models of Justice

Affirmative action is problematic legally because it involves two competing models of racial justice. One theory views race discrimination and its appropriate remedies in terms of identifiable *groups.* Under this theory, all individuals properly belonging to a traditionally disfavored minority are entitled to partake of a remedy. The competing individualistic theory holds that remedies are to be provided only to those *individuals* who can show that they have been the targets of invidious discrimination. The conflict can also be viewed as one between contemporary politics and traditional principles of law. In the contemporary pluralistic political process, we are accustomed to thinking in terms of group interests. However, our system of law rests on a foundation of individualism and does not easily accommodate the concept of "group rights."

Naturally, people on all sides of the affirmative action controversy looked to the Supreme Court for a settlement of the issue. The Supreme Court initially avoided the constitutionality of affirmative action when it decided *DeFunis v. Odegaard* (1974), holding that the question presented in this case was moot.

The *Bakke* and *Fullilove* Cases

Eventually, however, the Supreme Court did hand down a ruling on affirmative action, but *Regents of the University of California v. Bakke* (1978) could hardly be regarded as a definitive resolution of the issue. Alan Bakke, a thirty-seven-year-old white male engineer, brought suit to challenge the affirmative action policy of the medical school at the University of California at Davis (Cal-Davis). Bakke had been denied admission to the medical school, although his objective indicators (that is, Medical College Admission Test score and grade point average) were better than those of several of the sixteen minority students admitted under a "set aside" policy. The California Supreme Court found this to be a violation of equal protection and ordered Bakke to be admitted to the medical school. Seeking a more authoritative resolution of the issue, the university appealed. Bakke ultimately won the appeal, completed his medical school program, and is now a practicing anesthesiologist.

In one of the least comprehensible sets of opinions issued by the U.S. Supreme Court since *Chisholm v. Georgia* (1793), the Court voted 5 to 4 to invalidate the Cal-Davis quota system and admit Alan Bakke to medical school. However, also by a 5-to-4 margin, the Court endorsed affirmative action in the abstract, by recognizing race as a legitimate criterion of admission to medical school. According to Justice Lewis Powell's controlling opinion in *Bakke,* the state has a compelling interest in achieving diversity in its medical school, and this interest justifies the use of race as one of several criteria of admission. However, the use of a rigid quota system

> tells applicants who are not Negro, Asian or Chicano that they are totally excluded from a specific percentage of the seats in an entering class. No matter how strong their qualifications, quantitative and extracurricular, including their own potential for contribution to educational diversity, they are never afforded the chance to compete with applicants from the preferred groups for the special admissions seats.

For Justice Powell, this was the fatal flaw in the Cal-Davis affirmative action plan. Powell's brethren were less equivocal. Four members of the Court—Burger, Stewart, Rehnquist, and Stevens—would have declared the entire policy to be in violation of the Civil Rights Act, which, in their judgment, requires government to observe a standard of color-blindness. On the other hand, Justices Brennan, Marshall, White, and Blackmun found no statutory or constitutional violation in the minority "set aside" policy. According to Justice William Brennan, "[g]overnment may take race into account when it acts not to demean or insult any racial group, but to remedy disadvantages cast on minorities by past racial prejudice. . . ."

An equally equivocal endorsement of affirmative action was provided by the Supreme Court in *Fullilove v. Klutznick* (1980). In *Fullilove,* the Court upheld a federal public works program that provided a 10 percent "set-aside" of federal funds for "minority business enterprises." Since this case involved an act of Congress, rather than state action, the set-aside policy was challenged as a violation of the equal protection component of the Fifth Amendment Due Process Clause. The Supreme Court upheld the minority set-aside by a vote of 6 to 3. Unfortunately, as in *Bakke,* the Court was unable to produce a majority opinion. Chief Justice Warren Burger's plurality opinion stressed Congress' broad powers under Section 5 of the Fourteenth Amendment but stopped far short of providing a wholesale endorsement of affirmative action. In a concurring opinion Justice Brennan echoed the strong proaffirmative action position he had taken in *Bakke:*

> [The] principles outlawing the irrelevant or pernicious use of race [are] inapposite to racial classifications that provide benefits to minorities for the purpose of remedying the present effects of past racial discrimination. Such classifications may disadvantage some whites, but whites as a class lack the "traditional indicia of suspectness: the class is not saddled with such disabilities, or subjected to such a history of purposeful unequal treatment, or relegated to such a position of political powerlessness as to command extraordinary protection from the majoritarian political process."

Justice Stewart, joined by Justice Rehnquist, cited Justice Harlan's *Plessy* dissent as a barrier to any sort of race preferences, while Justice Stevens's dissenting opinion focused on Congress's failure to demonstrate that remedial preferences were being bestowed on a truly disadvantaged class. The Court's failure to produce majority opinions in *Bakke* and *Fullilove* compounded the uncertainties surrounding the myriad affirmative action policies in effect by the early 1980s.

The Supreme Court has continued to grapple with the affirmative action issue, most notably through a series of decisions interpreting federal civil rights statutes. The Court often has been supportive of affirmative action programs (see, for example, *Steelworkers v. Weber* [1979]; *Sheet Metal Workers v. Equal Employment Opportunity Commission* [1986]; *Firefighters v. Cleveland* [1986]; *Johnson v. Transportation Agency of Santa Clara* [1987]). Despite its general acceptance of affirmative action as a remedial device, the Court has, however, placed limits on the scope of affirmative action policies, for example by refusing to allow affirmative action objectives to override seniority in determining layoffs (see *Memphis Firefighters v. Stotts* [1984]). The Court has also held that, if their interests are adversely affected, white employees may challenge the legality of affirmative action plans that are established under **consent decrees,** even if they were not parties to the original litigation (*Martin v. Wilks* [1989]).

The *Croson* Case

The most significant Rehnquist Court decision on affirmative action thus far is *City of Richmond v. J. A. Croson Company* (1989). In 1983, the Richmond City Council passed an ordinance requiring that construction companies awarded city contracts in turn award at least 30 percent of their subcontracts to minority-owned business enterprises. A plumbing contractor, the J. A. Croson Company, sued the city in federal court, arguing that the set-aside was unconstitutional. The federal district court upheld the ordinance, relying heavily on the Supreme Court's earlier decision in *Fullilove v. Klutznick*. The Court of Appeals reversed, however, and the city of Richmond asked the Supreme Court to review the case.

The personnel on the High Court had changed significantly since *Fullilove*, of course. Justice Stewart had been replaced by Justice Sandra Day O'Connor in 1981. Justice Antonin Scalia had joined the Court after Chief Justice Burger retired, and Justice Rehnquist became chief justice in 1986. Justice Anthony Kennedy joined the Court in 1988 after the retirement of Justice Powell. These personnel changes produced a shift in the ideological character of the Court, moving it substantially to the right. It was no surprise, therefore, that the Court, voting 6 to 3, struck down the Richmond set-aside plan. Writing for the Court, Justice O'Connor noted that "[t]he Richmond Plan denies certain citizens the opportunity to compete for a fixed percentage of public contracts based solely upon their race." After reviewing the relevant history and facts, Justice O'Connor concluded that

> the city has failed to demonstrate a compelling interest in apportioning public contracting opportunities on the basis of race. To accept Richmond's claim that past societal discrimination alone can serve as the basis for rigid racial preferences would be to open the door to competing claims for "remedial relief" for every disadvantaged group. The dream of a Nation of equal citizens in a society where race is irrelevant to personal opportunity and achievement would be lost in a mosaic of shifting preferences based on inherently unmeasurable claims of past wrongs. . . .

In a bitter dissent, Justice Marshall (joined by Justices Brennan and Blackmun) characterized the decision as a "deliberate and giant step backward" and "a full-scale retreat from the Court's long-standing solicitude to race-conscious remedial efforts. . . ." Marshall predicted that the decision would "inevitably discourage or prevent governmental entities, particularly States and localities, from acting to rectify the scourge of past discrimination."

In her *Croson* opinion, Justice O'Connor attempted to distinguish the Richmond set-aside plan from the congressional program that the Court had approved in *Fullilove v. Klutznick*. O'Connor emphasized the broad powers of Congress under Section 5 of the Fourteenth Amendment, indicating that municipalities lack equally broad powers. Many critics of the *Croson* decision found this distinction unpersuasive. Students reading *Croson* and *Fullilove* should consider whether the two cases can in fact be distinguished from one another.

It is interesting to speculate as to how the Supreme Court would have decided *Fullilove* if that case had come to the Court in 1989, instead of 1980. As the Court became even more conservative with the departures of Justices Marshall and Brennan and the arrival of Justices Souter and Thomas, it appeared possible that the *Croson* case was the beginning of a process of dismantling affirmative action policies.

The Ongoing Problem of Racial Discrimination

Students will readily recall the enormous violence and destruction that ravaged areas of Los Angeles in early May 1992. The catalyst for the riot was the acquittal of several city police officers accused of brutality in the beating of African-American motorist Rodney King, who had been stopped by police for an automobile violation. The acquittal and subsequent riot sent shock waves through the American political and legal systems. People of all races questioned whether, nearly forty years after *Brown v. Board of Education,* the nation had made significant progress toward the constitutional ideal of racial justice. In the early 1990s, the terrible problems of America's inner cities, the disportionate "representation" of African-Americans in the Nation's prisons, and the persistence of racial animosity ensure that race will continue to be a serious political and legal problem for many years to come. For the Supreme Court in particular, the issue of racial equality remains a difficult challenge.

SEX DISCRIMINATION

Women are hardly a "discrete and insular minority." In fact, they comprise a majority of the adult population. Nevertheless, women have been historically subjected to considerable legal discrimination. Some of this discrimination was ostensibly benign, reflecting the paternalism of a patriarchal society. Not only were women once thought unfit to vote or hold public office, they were also regarded as in need of special protection from a cruel world. Thus, some gender-based classifications actually benefited females and burdened males. For example, a number of states and the federal government for a time maintained minimum-wage requirements for women but not for men. Most graphically, women have traditionally been exempted from compulsory military service.

Until very recently, the Supreme Court refused to recognize even the most blatant forms of sex discrimination as constitutionally offensive. In *Bradwell v. State* (1873), the Court upheld an Illinois law that prohibited women from practicing law. Similarly, in *Minor v. Happersett* (1875), the Court held that women had no constitutional right to vote. Even as late as 1948, the Court upheld a Michigan law that prohibited women from serving as bartenders (see *Goesaert v. Cleary*). These decisions reflected broader societal attitudes that relegated women, much like African-Americans, to a position of social inferiority and second-class citizenship.

The Second World War did much to change the social status of women. Women in great numbers left the home and entered the industrial workplace, often assuming jobs many thought they were incapable of handling. By the 1970s, women had begun to compete with men for managerial and professional positions. Although women are still on average paid less than men, even for equal work, society has come to accept women in the workplace. Society is also learning to accept women in political roles: in Congress, in state legislatures, as mayors, governors, presidential candidates, and as justices of the Supreme Court. Naturally, the changing role of women is accompanied by demands for legal equality.

During the 1970s, women's rights became a major constitutional issue

Congressional Responses to Demands for Sexual Equality

Congress responded to growing demands for legal equality between the sexes by passing the Equal Pay Act of 1963, the 1972 Amendments to Title VII of the Civil Rights Act of 1964, and Title IX of the Federal Education Act of 1972. The first and second of these statutes were aimed at eliminating sex discrimination in the workplace. The third authorized the withholding of federal funds from educational institutions that engaged in sex discrimination. These statutes have been an important source of civil rights for women and have given rise to a number of significant Supreme Court decisions. For example, in *Meritor Savings Bank, FSB v. Vinson* (1986), the Court held that Title VII of the Civil Rights Act of 1964 bars sexual harassment on the job.

The Equal Rights Amendment

In 1972, Congress attempted to broaden legal protection of women's rights by adopting a constitutional amendment that read as follows:

Section 1. Equality of rights under the law shall not be denied or abridged by the United States or by any State on account of sex.

Section 2. The Congress shall have the power to enforce, by appropriate legislation, the provisions of this article.

Section 3. This amendment shall take effect two years after the date of ratification.

Like all constitutional amendments, the Equal Rights Amendment (ERA) had to be ratified by at least three-fourths of the states to become part of the Constitution. Initially, the ERA met with much enthusiasm and little controversy in the state legislatures. By 1976, it had been ratified by thirty-five of the necessary thirty-eight states. However, in the late 1970s, opposition to the ERA crystallized in those states that had yet to ratify. Although Congress extended the period for ratification until 1982, the Amendment ultimately failed to win approval by the requisite number of states.

Judicial Scrutiny of Gender-Based Discrimination

The demise of the Equal Rights Amendment left constitutional interpretation in the field of sex discrimination largely in the domain of the Fourteenth Amendment. In the early 1970s, it appeared that the Supreme Court was going to add sex to the list of "suspect classifications" under the Fourteenth Amendment. In *Reed v. Reed* (1971), the Court struck down a provision of the Idaho Probate Code that required probate judges to prefer males to females in appointing administrators of estates. Writing for the majority in *Reed,* Chief Justice Burger noted that "to give a mandatory preference to members of either sex over members of the other . . . is to make the very kind of arbitrary legislative choice forbidden by the Equal Protection Clause."

In *Frontiero v. Richardson* (1973), the Supreme Court divided 8 to 1 (Justice Rehnquist dissenting) in upholding Lt. Sharron Frontiero's claim that the Air Force violated the equal protection component of the Fifth Amendment in requiring women, but not men, to demonstrate that their spouses were in fact dependents for the purpose of receiving medical and dental benefits. While the Court was receptive to the equal protection claim, it was unable to achieve majority support for the proposition that sex is a suspect classification. Expressing the views of four members of the Court, Justice Brennan's plurality opinion was unequivocal in declaring gender-based discrimination to be inherently suspect and thus presumptively unconstitutional:

> . . . [S]ince sex, like race and national origin, is an immutable characteristic determined solely by the accident of birth, the imposition of special disabilities upon the members of a particular sex because of their sex would seem to violate "the basic concept of our system that legal burdens should bear some relationship to individual responsibility. . . ."

The remaining four members of the majority were not prepared to go so far. In an opinion concurring in the judgment only, Justice Powell wrote that "[i]t is unnecessary for the Court in this case to characterize sex as a suspect classification, with all of the far-reaching implications of such a holding."

"Heightened Scrutiny"

As yet, the Court has not officially recognized sex discrimination as inherently suspect, but it has nevertheless invalidated a number of gender-based policies under a "heightened scrutiny" or "intermediate scrutiny" approach. For example, in *Weinberger v. Wiesenfeld* (1975), the Court unanimously voided a provision of the Social Security Act that authorized survivors' benefits for the widows of deceased workers but withheld them for men in the same situation. Similarly, in *Califano v. Goldfarb* (1977), a sharply divided Court struck down another social security requirement that widowers, but not widows, had to demonstrate their financial dependence on their deceased spouses as a condition for obtaining survivors' benefits.

In *Craig v. Boren* (1976), the Court articulated a test for judging gender-based policies under the intermediate standard of review. According to this test, a gender-based policy must be substantially related to an important government objective. Presumably, this test is stricter than the rational basis test but less strict than the compelling state interest test.

In *Craig v. Boren*, the Court struck down an Oklahoma law that forbade the sale of "3.2 beer" to females under the age of eighteen and males under twenty-one. Oklahoma attempted to justify the statute as a means of promoting its interest in traffic safety, citing data that were purported to show that men in the eighteen-to-twenty-one age bracket were more likely to be arrested for drunk driving than were women in the same age bracket. Unpersuaded by the statistical evidence, the Court held that the state had failed to demonstrate a substantial relationship between its sexually discriminatory policy and its admittedly important interest in traffic safety. In a sharp dissent, Justice Rehnquist challenged the new intermediate standard of equal protection review. In Rehnquist's view, the terms "important objective" and "substantial relation" were so ". . . elastic as to invite subjective judicial preferences or prejudices." Despite this criticism, the Court has maintained the intermediate standard of review for gender-based policies.

In *Orr v. Orr* (1979), the Court considered the question of differential alimony requirements for men and women. The Alabama law in question required divorced men, under certain circumstances, to make alimony payments to their ex-wives but exempted women in the same circumstances from paying alimony to their ex-husbands. Somewhat disingenuously, the state argued that its gender-based alimony policy was designed to compensate women for economic discrimination produced by the institution of marriage. The Court accepted the state's asserted interest as both legitimate and important but rejected the argument that its alimony policy was substantially related to the achievement of this objective. Writing for the Court, Justice Brennan asserted that

> Alabama's alleged compensatory purpose may be effectuated without placing burdens solely on husbands. Progress toward fulfillment of such a purpose would not be hampered, and it would cost the state nothing more, if it were to treat men and women equally by making alimony burdens independent of sex. . . . Thus, "[t]he [wives] who benefit from the disparate treatment are those who were . . . nondependent on their husbands. . . ." They are precisely those who are not "needy

spouses" and who are the "least likely to have been victims of discrimination" by the institution of marriage.

The preceding sample of cases is not meant to suggest that the Supreme Court's sex-discrimination decisions have uniformly cut in one direction. On the contrary, the flexible approach to sex discrimination employed by the Court has resulted in a number of decisions upholding challenged gender-based policies. For example, in *Kahn v. Shevin* (1974), the Court let stand a Florida statute that gave property tax exemptions to widows but not widowers. According to Justice William O. Douglas's majority opinion, the distinction was

> reasonably designed to further the state policy of cushioning the financial impact of spousal loss upon the sex for which that loss imposes a disproportionately heavy burden. . . . The financial difficulties confronting the lone woman in Florida or any other state exceed those facing the man.

The same year, in *Geduldig v. Aiello* (1974), the Court upheld a state health insurance policy that excluded pregnancy from the list of disabilities for which a state employee could be compensated. In approving the policy, the Court concluded that it did not discriminate

> against any definable group or class in terms of the aggregate risk protection derived by the group or class from the program. There is no risk from which men are protected and women are not. Likewise, there is no risk from which women are protected and men are not.

Not surprisingly, a number of observers took issue with the Court's assumption that a state's refusal to extend its disability policy to include pregnancy was gender-neutral.

One of the most controversial issues in the area of sex discrimination is the role that women should play in military service. Opponents of the Equal Rights Amendment argued that adoption of the Amendment would result in women being drafted into combat, a prospect that many people still find unacceptable. In *Rostker v. Goldberg* (1981), the Supreme Court considered the constitutionality of the male-only draft registration law. Emphasizing its traditional deference to Congress in the area of military affairs, the Court upheld the challenged policy by a vote of 6 to 3. Writing for the majority, Justice Rehnquist asserted that exclusion of women from the draft "was not an 'accidental by-product of a traditional way of thinking about women.' " According to Justice Rehnquist, men and women "are simply not similarly situated for purposes of a draft or registration for a draft." No doubt many women and men would challenge Rehnquist's assumption, especially in light of the expanded role women played in the war against Iraq in early 1991.

It is difficult to say with any precision what principles have guided the Court's treatment of sex discrimination cases under the intermediate scrutiny approach. Perhaps each decision rests on each justice's intuitive sense of whether the challenged discrimination is "benign" or "invidious." As Justice Oliver Wendell Holmes, Jr. pointed out in his dissent in *Lochner v. New York* (1905), judicial decisions often "depend on a judgment or intuition more subtle than any articulate major premise." What Holmes was suggesting was that judicial decision making is preeminently political behavior: that any exercise in legal methodology is subordinate to the assertion of judicial values. While this position can be overstated, one cannot examine the history of American constitutional decision making and deny the essential validity of Holmes's observation.

Sex Discrimination by Educational Institutions

In perhaps the most significant of its sex discrimination decisions, the Burger Court voted 5 to 4 to require the Mississippi University for Women (MUW) to admit a male student to its nursing school (*Mississippi University for Women v. Hogan* [1982]). Joe Hogan was a registered nurse working in Columbus, the city where MUW is located. Lacking a bachelor's degree, he applied for admission to the MUW nursing program and was denied solely on account of sex, although the school did inform him that he could register on a noncredit basis. Rather than quit his job to enroll in another state institution, Hogan filed suit. The state of Mississippi argued that operating a school solely for women compensated for sex discrimination in the past. Additionally, the state argued that the presence of men would detract from the performance of female students. Writing for the Supreme Court, Justice O'Connor gave both of the state's arguments short shrift. Justice O'Connor rejected the "compensation" argument as contrived since the state had made no showing that women had historically lacked opportunities in the field of nursing. O'Connor then pointed out that the state's argument that male students would adversely affect the performance of females was undermined by the university's willingness to accept male students as auditors. In O'Connor's view, the principal effect of the female-only nursing program was to "perpetuate the stereotyped view of nursing as an exclusively women's job."

In a strongly worded dissent, Justice Powell asserted that the Court's decision adversely affected the opportunities of women by forbidding the "States from providing women with an opportunity to choose the type of university they prefer." Powell further suggested that the Court's decision

> bows deeply to conformity. Left without honor . . . is an element of diversity that has characterized much of American education and enriched much of American life.

The *Hogan* decision addressed the question of whether state-operated professional schools could limit enrollment to one sex. It did not address the broader question of whether publicly operated or supported educational institutions generally may constitutionally impose such restrictions. While this general constitutional question has not yet been addressed, a number of suits have been brought against colleges that limit enrollment to one sex. In one highly publicized case, a federal district judge ruled that the male-only admissions policy at Virginia Military Institute did not violate the Equal Protection Clause (see *United States v. Virginia* [W.D. Va., 1991]). One can expect active litigation in this area over the next few years. It is likely that the Supreme Court will, sooner or later, address this difficult issue.

An emerging issue of special concern to college students is whether universities can maintain sexually segregated athletic programs. Is the separate but equal doctrine appropriate when considering collegiate athletics? Suppose a female student wants to play football at a state university. Since the university does not have a women's football program, does the Equal Protection Clause require the university to let the woman try out for the men's team? While some may feel that such issues trivialize the Constitution, these matters tend to be far from trivial in the minds of plaintiffs.

OTHER FORMS OF DISCRIMINATION

As of 1992, the only suspect classifications that have been identified by the Supreme Court are those based on race, national origin, and religious affiliation. As previously noted, gender-based classifications, which are the subject of much current controversy, have not been added to the inventory of suspect classifications. Rather, sex discrimination, along with several other types of discrimination, occupies a middle tier in what has become a complex, multitiered approach to judging challenged classifications.

Illegitimacy

Although laws discriminating against persons based on illegitimacy have not been declared to be inherently suspect, blatant instances of this type of discrimination have been invalidated. For example, in *Weber v. Aetna Casualty and Surety Company* (1972), the Supreme Court struck down a Louisiana law barring illegitimate offspring from collecting death benefits under workers' compensation. And in *Jimenez v. Weinberger* (1974), the Court invalidated a federal provision that denied welfare benefits to the illegitimate dependent children of disabled persons. However, in a case reminiscent of the landmark sex discrimination case *Reed v. Reed,* the Court upheld a law subordinating illegitimate offspring to other relatives in determining intestate succession (*Labine v. Vincent* [1971]). And in *Lalli v. Lalli* (1978), the Court upheld a law allowing illegitimate children to inherit from their intestate fathers only if paternity had been judicially determined during the lifetime of the deceased.

More recently, in *Michael H. v. Gerald D.* (1989), the Court upheld a California statute that created a legal presumption that a child born to a married woman living with her husband is the product of that marriage, thus making it more difficult for natural fathers of children who are the product of extramarital affairs to establish paternity. While clear principles are difficult to discern in this area, the Court has not hesitated to invalidate laws it perceives to be based solely on prejudice against illegitimate children. At the same time, however, it has recognized the primacy of the nuclear family and the social undesirability of producing children outside of wedlock.

Persons with Disabilities

Although disabled persons can be viewed as constituting a "discrete and insular minority," policies and practices that discriminate against the disabled have not been recognized as "inherently suspect" under the Fourteenth Amendment. Nor has the Supreme Court yet held that the Constitution imposes an obligation on government to equalize physical access for the handicapped to government buildings or other physical facilities. Arguably, a government's failure to provide a wheelchair ramp at a place where votes are cast could be viewed as an unreasonable burden on the exercise of a "fundamental right." Congress has attempted to increase access to the polls for handicapped persons through passage of the Voting Accessibility Act of 1984. For the most part it has been the Congress, not the Supreme Court, that has taken the lead in recognizing the rights of handicapped persons. With the passage of Title V of the Rehabilitation Act of 1973, the Education for all Handicapped Children Act of 1975, and especially the Americans with Disabilities Act of 1990, Congress has attempted to remove barriers confronting persons with disabilities in such areas as employment, education, and public transportation. However, some commentators have criticized the Supreme Court for narrowly interpreting legislation in this field, thus constraining the rights of disabled persons.

On the other hand, the Supreme Court has not been completely insensitive to the rights of handicapped individuals. For example, in *Cleburne v. Cleburne Living Center* (1985), the Court struck down a zoning law that had been applied to prohibit a home for the mentally retarded from operating in a residential neighborhood. Justice White's majority opinion not only rejected the argument that retardation is a suspect classification but also rejected the lower court's characterization of retardation as "quasi-suspect." Opting for the traditional standard of review, Justice White nevertheless found no rational basis for the city's decision. The *Cleburne* case demonstrates that the rational basis standard is not necessarily synonymous with judicial deference.

Residency and Alienage

The Fifth and Fourteenth Amendments do not protect citizens alone from arbitrary or unjust government actions. Rather, the Amendments use the broader term "persons." The Supreme Court has stressed the text of the Fourteenth Amendment in striking down a number of state laws that differentiate between residents and nonresidents or between citizens and aliens. For example, in *Shapiro v. Thompson* (1969), the Supreme Court struck down a series of laws that imposed one-year waiting periods on new state residents seeking welfare benefits. Then, in *Sugarman v. Dougall* (1973), the Court struck down a New York law that denied civil service jobs to aliens. In 1976, the Court extended this ruling to invalidate similar federal civil service restrictions *(Hampton v. Mow Sun Wong).*

In a controversial 1982 decision, the Supreme Court went so far as to invalidate discrimination against the children of illegal aliens. In *Plyler v. Doe,* the Court voted 5 to 4 to strike down a Texas law that denied free public education to the children of illegal immigrants. Using "heightened scrutiny," Justice Brennan found no "substantial interest" of the state to justify the denial of educational benefits to the children of illegal aliens. Dissenting sharply, Chief Justice Burger complained that "if ever a court was guilty of an unabashedly result-oriented approach, this case is a prime example." The Court's decisions in

Shapiro v. Thompson and *Plyler v. Doe* involved not merely the distinction between residents and nonresidents or between legal residents and illegal aliens, they implicated the underlying issue of poverty.

Wealth, Poverty, and Equal Protection

Discrimination based on wealth has never been held to be inherently suspect, although some justices on the Supreme Court have indicated a desire to do so. However, the Court has often invalidated forms of economic discrimination that prevent individuals from exercising their constitutional rights. Wealth-based discriminations that burden fundamental rights have been subjected to strict judicial scrutiny; those that do not involve fundamental rights have been judged by the traditional rational basis test. For example, in the case of *Shapiro v. Thompson*, described above, the Court found that the state residency requirement infringed the fundamental right of interstate travel. Similarly, in *Harper v. Virginia State Board of Elections* (1966), the Supreme Court invalidated a state's poll tax as a denial of equal protection. Certainly the imposition of a tax on voting can be seen as a burden on the exercise of a fundamental right (see Chapter 17).

In *Gideon v. Wainwright* (1963), the Court, relying on the Sixth Amendment right to counsel, required states to appoint counsel for indigent defendants accused of felonies. On the same day, in *Douglas v. California*, the Court required states to provide counsel to indigent defendants seeking appellate review in state courts. These wealth-discrimination rulings of the Warren Court were closely related to the maintenance of procedural due process in the context of criminal prosecutions.

To what extent does the Equal Protection Clause require the equalization of services or benefits provided by state and local governments? May a city's provision of public goods, such as roads, sewage systems, parks, and recreational facilities, vary according to neighborhood property tax revenues? The answer depends on whether such discriminations involve fundamental rights or "interests." But which interests are "fundamental"? Is education a fundamental right?

The Controversy over Public School Funding

In *San Antonio v. Rodriguez* (1973), the Court considered a challenge to the Texas system of financing public schools primarily through local property taxes. The Texas system, which is similar to that employed in most states, resulted in dramatically different amounts of money being spent among the state's school districts. In reviewing the Texas system of school funding, a sharply divided Court employed the traditional rational basis test, refusing to recognize wealth as a suspect classification. Using this approach, the Court found no constitutional violation. According to Justice Powell's majority opinion, the school finance system

> allegedly discriminates against a large, diverse, and amorphous class, unified only by the common factor of residence in districts which happen to have less taxable wealth than other districts. The system of alleged discrimination and the class it defines have none of the traditional indicia of suspectness; the class is not saddled

with such disabilities, or subjected to such history of purposeful unequal treatment, or relegated to such a position of political powerlessness as to command extraordinary protection from the majoritarian political process.

Justice Marshall protested vehemently in *Rodriguez,* arguing that education was a "fundamental interest" and that "poverty" was indeed a "suspect classification." According to Justice Marshall,

> [the] Court has never suggested that because some "adequate" level of benefits is provided to all, discrimination in the provision of services is therefore constitutionally excusable. The Equal Protection Clause is not addressed to the minimal sufficiency but to the unjustifiable inequalities of state action.

The Supreme Court's interpretation of the Fourteenth Amendment in *Rodriguez* in no way prevents state courts from adopting a contrary view of the relevant provisions of their state constitutions. Indeed, the California Supreme Court did so in *Serrano v. Priest* (1971). Since then, more than twenty state supreme courts have followed suit in holding that disparities in funding among school districts violate state constitutional requirements of equal protection. This trend nicely illustrates the principle of **judicial federalism,** under which state courts are free to interpret their state laws in a way that provides additional rights beyond those secured by federal law. At a time in which the U.S. Supreme Court is dominated by conservatives, advocates of civil rights and liberties may find state tribunals receptive to claims that would be rejected by the federal courts.

Restriction of Abortion Funding for Indigent Women

Another controversial issue reaching the Burger Court under the aegis of the New Equal Protection was the dispute over legislative efforts to cut off government funds to support abortions. In *Maher v. Roe* (1977), the Court upheld the constitutionality of a Connecticut policy withholding Medicaid payments for nonessential abortions. Writing for a majority of six justices, Justice Powell opined that

> [a]n indigent woman desiring an abortion does not come within the limited category of disadvantaged classes so recognized by our cases. Nor does the fact that the impact of the regulation falls upon those who cannot pay lead to a different conclusion. In a sense, every denial of welfare to an indigent creates a wealth classification as compared to nonindigents who are able to pay for the desired goods or services. But this Court has never held that financial need alone identifies a suspect class for purposes of Equal Protection analysis.

Subsequently, in *Harris v. McRae* (1980), the Court upheld the so-called Hyde Amendment, a federal law that severely limited the use of federal funds to support abortions for indigent women. Writing for the sharply divided bench, Justice Stewart observed that

> [t]he Hyde Amendment, like the Connecticut welfare regulation at issue in *Maher,* places no governmental obstacle in the path of a woman who chooses to terminate her pregnancy, but rather, by means of unequal subsidization of abortion and other medical services, encourages alternative activity deemed in the public in-

terest. The present case does differ factually from *Maher* insofar as that case involved a failure to fund nontherapeutic abortions, whereas the Hyde Amendment withholds funding of certain medically necessary abortions.

Nevertheless, Justice Stewart concluded that

> [h]ere as in *Maher,* the principal impact of the Hyde Amendment falls on the indigent. But that fact does not itself render the funding restriction constitutionally invalid, for this Court has held repeatedly that poverty, standing alone, is not a suspect classification. . . .

Dissenting, Justice Marshall chastised the majority for its insensitivity to the plight of the poor, saying that "[t]here is another world 'out there,' the existence of which the Court . . . either chooses to ignore or refuses to recognize." In Marshall's view, "it is only by blinding itself to that other world" that the Court could uphold the Hyde Amendment. (This issue is also addressed in Chapter 15.)

Possible Interpretations of Economic Equal Protection

Although most commentators have associated an expansion of the Equal Protection Clause to protect economic interests with liberal, redistributive policy objectives, such a broadening of equal protection might well turn out to be a double-edged sword. If a more conservative Supreme Court were to make "wealth," as distinct from "poverty," a suspect classification, then government presumably would have to show a compelling interest to justify progressive taxation, subsidies, and a host of redistributive policies. Just as the Due Process Clause was once used to frustrate progressivism, populism, and the New Deal, so the Equal Protection Clause could conceivably be employed by a more conservative Supreme Court to attack the welfare state.

As we have pointed out repeatedly in this book, constitutional language, such as "due process" and "equal protection," is sufficiently broad to embrace various potential applications. Indeed, socialists could "find" in the Equal Protection Clause a requirement that government equalize material conditions in society. Similarly, the Takings Clause of the Fifth Amendment could be cited to provide a constitutional justification for the nationalization of private industries. This is not to say that the Constitution has no plain or obvious meanings, which it surely does. It is only to say that certain language in the Constitution, such as the Equal Protection Clause, is written broadly enough to allow for various, even opposing, interpretations. The constitutional values that are actualized through decision making depend greatly on the political ideologies of the justices who happen to be on the Court and on the broader political culture within which the Court functions.

Discrimination on the Basis of Sexual Orientation

While some states and cities have enacted laws protecting homosexuals against discrimination in housing, employment, and the like, there is no such protection under federal civil rights laws. Moreover, the federal courts have had little to say about "gay rights" in terms of the equal protection requirements of the Constitution.

One question of gay rights that came to the fore during the 1980s was the military's policy of discharging persons who admitted to being homosexual. In *Watkins v. U.S. Army* (1988), the U.S. Court of Appeals for the Ninth Circuit court invalidated this policy. Writing for the court, Judge Norris concluded that "the Army's regulations violate the constitutional guarantee of equal protection of the laws because they discriminate against persons of homosexual orientation, a suspect class, and because the regulations are not necessary to promote a legitimate compelling governmental interest." On *en banc* rehearing the Court of Appeals affirmed the judgment but did so on nonconstitutional grounds, finding it "unnecessary to reach the constitutional issues. . . ." The Supreme Court denied certiorari, thus leaving open the constitutional question as to whether the military's ban on homosexuals violates constitutional equal protection standards. Shortly after his election to the presidency in November 1992, Bill Clinton announced that he intended to issue an executive order abolishing the military's ban on homosexuals. Once implemented, this order would obviate constitutional litigation of this issue.

The Supreme Court has not, thus far, determined whether discrimination against homosexuals violates the equal protection requirement. However, this issue was raised in *San Francisco Arts and Athletics, Inc. v. United States Olympic Committee* (1987). In that case, the United States Olympic Committee (USOC) obtained an injunction barring San Francisco Arts and Athletics (SFAA), from holding a series of athletic events designated as the "Gay Olympics." SFAA alleged that this action on the part of USOC amounted to unconstitutional discrimination in view of the fact that USOC had permitted other organizations to conduct events such as the "Junior Olympics" and the "Special Olympics." The Supreme Court avoided the question of discrimination by holding that USOC was not a "governmental actor" and was thus not subject to constitutional equal protection requirements. While recognizing a close connection between Congress and the USOC, the Court nevertheless refused to view Congress as a "joint participant" in the decisions of the Olympic Committee.

Although the Supreme Court has thus far managed to avoid the substantive constitutional questions involving gay rights, it is likely that pressure will continue to build for the Court to address these issues.

THE ONGOING PROBLEM OF PRIVATE DISCRIMINATION

As we have seen in such cases as SFAA v. USOC, the equal protection requirements of the Fifth and Fourteenth Amendments prohibit only government or persons acting under the authority of government from engaging in certain proscribed forms of discrimination. However, these constitutional safeguards do not apply directly to private, that is, nongovernmental, discrimination. Private discrimination may be remediable, however, through the application of federal, state, and even local civil rights laws.

The repudiation of the separate but equal doctrine in *Brown* and subsequent decisions led to the virtual disappearance of *de jure* racial segregation, that is, segregation required or created by law or public policy. Yet, *de facto* segregation in housing, employment and education nevertheless still exists to a great extent, as a function of both social norms and economic disparities. Segregation that is purely *de facto* is beyond the purview of the Equal Protection Clause *per se*. Many forms of *de facto* segregation, however, may be within the remedial power of both state and federal statutes. For example, under the Fair Housing Act of 1968, Congress prohibited racial discrimination in the rental or sale of homes where the transaction is handled by a licensed agent. The questions surrounding such attempts at eradicating *de facto* discrimination are by no means closed.

As previously noted, the Supreme Court in 1883 drew a sharp distinction between racial discrimination that is purely private in character and that which is supported by state action. Without formally overruling the *Civil Rights Cases,* the Court has blurred this distinction as applied to racial discrimination. Nevertheless, the Court has shown no inclination to abandon the state action doctrine. For example, in the case of a racially restrictive private club's refusal to serve the African-American guest of a white member, the Court determined that the mere grant of a liquor license did not convert the club's discriminatory policy into state action under the Fourteenth Amendment (*Moose Lodge v. Irvis* [1972]). A decade earlier, in *Burton v. Wilmington Parking Authority* (1961), the Court had found state action when a state agency leased property to a restaurant that refused to serve African-Americans. Legalistically, whether there is state

Blacks attempt to order lunch at a "whites only" lunch counter

action in support of discrimination depends on whether there is a "close nexus" between the functions of the state and the private discrimination. More realistically, it probably depends on whether circumstances foster a perception that the state approves of the discrimination at issue.

Restrictive Covenants

A classic form of private discrimination was the "restrictive covenant" whereby a group of homeowners agreed not to sell or rent their homes to African-Americans, Jews, and other disfavored minorities. Under the decision in the *Civil Rights Cases*, this purely private form of racial discrimination was deemed to be beyond the purview of the Equal Protection Clause. However, in *Shelley v. Kraemer* (1948), the Supreme Court held such covenants to be unenforceable in state courts, because any such enforcement would amount to state action in contravention of the Fourteenth Amendment. Arguably, for a state court to enforce such an agreement would foster a public perception that the state approves of racially restrictive covenants. On the other hand, it would be a mistake to conclude that the mere judicial enforcement of every private agreement necessarily constitutes state action for purposes of the Fourteenth Amendment. In fact, ordinary contracts and other private transactions are generally not brought within the limitations of the Fourteenth Amendment merely because they are enforced in court. *Shelley v. Kraemer* seems to stand for the proposition that questions of private racial discrimination constitute a unique category.

Although restrictive covenants are no longer judicially enforceable, racial restrictions are still written into many deeds, a fact that aroused considerable public attention during the 1986 Senate confirmation hearings on the elevation of William Rehnquist to be chief justice. In the course of these hearings, it was revealed that the deed to a piece of property owned by Rehnquist himself contained a restrictive covenant.

Finally, it should be noted that although the decision in the *Civil Rights Cases* has not been overruled, Congress has employed its broad powers, chiefly under the Commerce Clause (Article I, Section 8) to prohibit racial discrimination by places of public accommodation whose operations affect interstate commerce (see Chapter 5). In *Heart of Atlanta Motel v. United States* (1964), the Supreme Court upheld Title II of the 1964 Civil Rights Act, thus allowing Congress to accomplish under its commerce power what the Court in 1883 prevented it from doing under the Fourteenth Amendment.

State Powers to Prohibit Private Discrimination

Historically, the state governments were anything but leaders in the struggle for civil rights. Yet today, many states have civil rights or "human rights" statutes. An emerging constitutional issue is the extent to which states can act affirmatively to foster integration. Can a state adopt legislation that outlaws racial discrimination in the places of public accommodation perceived as not currently subject to federal civil rights laws? Can the states require "quasi-public" organizations, such as the Rotary Club, the Kiwanis, or the Jaycees, to admit women? What about private social clubs? Can the states require racially or religiously exclusive country clubs to admit those their membership policies currently exclude? Here, we have a classic confrontation between the state's legitimate interest in eradicating invidious discrimination and the freedom of association protected by the First and Fourteenth Amendments. In the landmark decision *Roberts v. United States Jaycees* (1984) (reprinted in Chapter 11), the Court upheld a Minnesota human rights law requiring a civic organization to accept women as full members, despite the organization's reliance on the First Amendment. For Justice Brennan, the state's interest in eradicating discrimination was more compelling than the Jaycees' claim to free association. However, Justice O'Connor was careful to point out that the Jaycees behaved more like a commercial enterprise than a political organization or a private club. Justice O'Connor's concurrence left open the question of whether "less public" entities are subject to state intervention.

The principle articulated in the *Jaycees* decision has been followed consistently by the Supreme Court. For example, in 1987, the Court unanimously extended this principle to encompass the Rotary Club as well *(Rotary International v. Rotary Club of Duarte)*. Likewise, in 1988, a unanimous Court relied on *Roberts v. Jaycees* in upholding a New York City ordinance that required certain all-male social clubs to admit women *(New York Club Association v. City of New York)*. Whether the Supreme Court continues to expand the powers of state and local governments to combat private discrimination depends significantly on the views of future appointees to the Court.

CONCLUSION

In a brief introductory essay, it is impossible to discuss all the important issues of equal protection, both actual and potential. After more than two decades of the New Equal Protection, it is clear that any government policy that differentiates among identifiable groups poses a potential equal protection problem. For example, as longevity of the American population increases and more people stay on the job beyond the traditional age of retirement, discrimination against the elderly is becoming a more prominent equal protection issue. Another issue on the horizon is whether laws forbidding single-sex marriage unreasonably discriminate against homosexuals.

In spite of recent changes in the ideological makeup of the Supreme Court, there exists an elaborate framework of statutes and judicial decisions reflecting a strong national commitment to the antidiscrimination principle. Some observers may view recent limitations on affirmative action programs and disengagement of the federal courts from supervision of public school desegregation as departures from this commitment. The antidiscrimination principle, however, is far broader than specific remedial measures adopted to address immediate problems. The fundamental commitment to this principle is likely to outlast ephemeral changes in the political landscape.

Politically, one of the most important applications of the Equal Protection Clause has been to the historic problem of legislative malapportionment. This problem, along with other issues related to the themes of representation and political participation, is examined in Chapter 17.

FOR FURTHER READING

Abraham, Henry J. *Freedom and the Court,* 5th ed. New York: Oxford University Press, 1988.

Baer, Judith. *Equality Under the Constitution: Reclaiming the Fourteenth Amendment.* Ithaca, N.Y.: Cornell University Press, 1983.

Berger, Raoul. *Government by Judiciary: The Transformation of the Fourteenth Amendment.* Cambridge: Harvard University Press, 1977.

Bonnicksen, Andrea. *Civil Rights and Liberties.* Palo Alto, Calif.: Mayfield, 1982.

Brigham, John. *Civil Liberties and American Democracy.* Washington, D.C.: Congressional Quarterly Press, 1984.

Finch, Minnie. *The NAACP: Its Fight for Justice.* Metuchen, N.J.: Scarecrow Press, 1981.

Franklin, John Hope. *From Slavery to Freedom: A History of Negro Americans.* New York: Knopf, 1980.

Ginsberg, Ruth. *Constitutional Aspects of Sex-Based Discrimination.* St. Paul: West, 1974.

Glazer, Nathan. *Affirmative Discrimination: Ethnic Inequality and Public Policy.* New York: Basic Books, 1975.

Graham, Hugh Davis. *The Civil Rights Era: Origins and Development of a National Policy.* New York: Oxford University Press, 1990.

Kluger, Richard. *Simple Justice.* New York: Vintage Books, 1975.

Morgan, Richard E. *The Law and Politics of Civil Rights and Liberties.* New York: Knopf, 1985.

O'Connor, Karen. *Women's Organizations' Use of the Courts.* Lexington, Mass.: Lexington Books, 1980.

Orfield, Gary. *Must We Bus?* Washington, D.C.: Brookings Institute, 1978.

Peltason, Jack W. *58 Lonely Men: Southern Federal Judges and School Desegregation.* Urbana: University of Illinois Press, 1961.

Pritchett, C. Herman. *Constitutional Civil Liberties.* Englewood Cliffs, N.J.: Prentice-Hall, 1984.

Rhode, Deborah. *Justice and Gender.* Cambridge: Harvard University Press, 1989.

Rossum, Ralph. *Reverse Discrimination: The Constitutional Debate.* New York: Dekker, 1980.

Sandoz, Ellis. *Conceived in Liberty: American Individual Rights Today.* North Scituate, Mass.: Duxbury Press, 1978.

Scheingold, Stuart. *The Politics of Rights.* New Haven: Yale University Press, 1974.

Schwartz, Bernard, ed. *The Fourteenth Amendment.* New York: New York University Press, 1970.

Sindler, Allan P. *Bakke, DeFunis and Minority Admissions.* New York: Longman, 1978.

Thomas, William R. *The Burger Court and Civil Liberties,* rev. ed. Brunswick, Ohio: Kings Court Communications, 1979.

Wasby, Stephen L., Anthony A. D'Amato, and Rosemary Metrailer. *Desegregation from* Brown *to* Alexander: *An Exploration of Supreme Court Strategies.* Carbondale: Southern Illinois University Press, 1977.

Wilkinson, J. Harvie III. *From* Brown *to* Bakke: *The Supreme Court and School Integration: 1954–1978.* New York: Oxford University Press, 1981.

Wolters, Raymond. *The Burden of* Brown: *Thirty Years of School Desegregation.* Knoxville: University of Tennessee Press, 1984.

Woodward, C. Vann. *The Strange Career of Jim Crow.* New York: Oxford University Press, 1968.

Yarbrough, Tinsley, ed. *The Reagan Administration and Human Rights.* New York: Praeger, 1985.

CASES AND READINGS

The Civil Rights Cases
109 U.S. 3; 3 S. Ct. 18; 27 L. Ed. 835 (1883)
Vote: 8-1

Mr. Justice Bradley delivered the opinion of the Court:

These cases are all founded on the . . . "Civil Rights Act," passed March 1, 1875. . . . Two of the cases . . . are indictments for denying to persons of color the accommodations and privileges of an inn or hotel; two of them, . . . for denying to individuals the privileges and accommodations of a theater. . . . The case of Robinson and wife against the Memphis & Charleston Railroad Company was an action . . . to recover the penalty of $500 given by the second section of the act; and the gravamen was the refusal by the conductor of the railroad company to allow the wife to ride in the ladies' car, [because] she was a person of African descent.

The sections of the law referred to provide as follows:

Sec. 1. That all persons within . . . United States shall be entitled to the full and equal enjoyment of the accommodations, advantages, facilities, and privileges of inns, public conveyances on land or water, theaters, and other places of public amusement; subject only to the conditions and limitations established by law, and applicable alike to citizens of every race and color, regardless of any previous condition of servitude.

Sec. 2. That any person who shall violate the foregoing section . . . shall, for every such offense, forfeit and pay the sum of $500 to the person aggrieved [and] be deemed guilty of a misdemeanor, and upon conviction thereof shall be fined not less than $500 nor more than $1,000, or shall be imprisoned not less than 30 days nor more than one year. . . .

The first section of the Fourteenth Amendment . . . declares that "no state shall make or enforce any law which shall abridge the privileges or immunities of citizens of the United States; nor shall any state deprive any person of life, liberty, or property without due process of law; nor deny to any person within its jurisdiction, the equal protection of the laws." It is state action of a particular character that is prohibited. Individual invasion of individual rights is not the subject-matter of the amendment. . . . It nullifies and makes void all state legislation, and state action of every kind, which impairs the privileges and immunities of citizens of the United States, or which injures them in life, liberty, or property without due process of law, or which denies to any of them the equal protection of the laws. [T]he last section of the amendment invests Congress with power to enforce it by appropriate legislation. To enforce what? To enforce the prohibition. To adopt appropriate legislation for correcting the effects of such prohibited state law and state acts, and thus to render them effectually null, void, and innocuous. . . . It does not invest Congress with power to legislate upon subjects which are within the domain of state legislation. . . . It does not authorize Congress to create a code of municipal law for the regulation of private rights; but to provide modes of redress against the operation of state laws, and the action of state officers, executive or judicial, when these are subversive of the fundamental rights specified in the amendment. . . .

An inspection of the law shows that it makes no reference whatever to any supposed or apprehended violation of the Fourteenth Amendment on the part of the states. . . . It proceeds *ex directo* to declare that certain acts committed by individuals shall be deemed offenses, and shall be prosecuted and punished by proceedings in the courts of the United States. It does not profess to be corrective of any constitutional wrong committed by the states. . . . [I]t steps into the domain of local jurisprudence, and lays down rules for the conduct of individuals in society towards each other . . . without referring in any manner to any supposed action of the state or its authorities.

If this legislation is appropriate for enforcing the prohibitions of the amendment, it is difficult to see where it is to stop. Why may not Congress, with equal show of authority, enact a code of laws for the enforcement and vindication of all rights of life, liberty, and property? If it is supposable that the states may deprive persons of life, liberty and property without due process of law (and the amendment itself does suppose this), why should not Congress proceed at once to prescribe due process of law for the protection of every one of these fundamental rights, in every possible case, as well as to prescribe equal privileges in inns, public conveyances, and theaters. The truth is that the implication of a power to legislate in this manner is based upon the assumption that if the states are forbidden to legislate or act in a particular way on a particular subject, and power is conferred upon Congress to enforce the prohibition, this gives Congress power to legislate generally upon that subject, and not merely power to provide modes of redress against such state legislation or action. The assumption is certainly unsound. It is repugnant to the Tenth Amendment. . . .

. . . [C]ivil rights, such as are guarantied by the Constitution against state aggression, cannot be impaired by the wrongful acts of individuals, unsupported by state authority in the shape of laws, customs, or judicial or executive proceedings. The wrongful act of an individual, unsupported by any such authority, is simply a private wrong, or a crime of that individual. . . . An individual cannot deprive a man of his right to vote, to hold property, to buy and to sell, to sue in the courts, or to be a witness or a juror; he may, by force or fraud, interfere with the enjoyment of the right in a particular case; . . . but unless protected in these wrongful acts by some shield of state law or state authority, he cannot destroy or injure the right; he will only render himself amenable to satisfaction or punishment; and amenable therefor to the laws of the state where the wrongful acts are committed. Hence, in all those cases where the Constitution seeks to protect the rights of the citizen against discriminative and unjust laws of the state by prohibiting such laws, it is not individual offenses, but abrogation and denial of rights, which it denounces, and for which it clothes the Congress with power to provide a remedy. This abrogation and denial of rights, for which the states alone were or could be responsible, was the great seminal and fundamental wrong which was intended to be remedied. . . .

Of course, these remarks do not apply to those cases in which Congress is clothed with direct and plenary powers of legislation over the whole subject, accompanied with an express or implied denial of such power to the states, as in the regulation of commerce with foreign nations, among the several states, and with the Indian tribes, the coining of money, the establishment of post-offices and post-roads, the declaring of war, etc. In these cases Congress has power to pass laws for regulating the subjects specified, in every detail, and the conduct and transactions of individuals in respect thereof. . . .

But the power of Congress to adopt direct and primary, as distinguished from corrective, legislation on the subject in hand, is sought, in the second place, from the Thirteenth Amendment, which . . . declares "that neither slavery, nor involuntary servitude, except as a punishment for crime, whereof the party shall have been duly convicted, shall exist within the United States, or any place subject to their jurisdiction;" and it gives Congress power to enforce the amendment by appropriate legislation. . . .

. . . [I]t is assumed that the power vested in Congress to enforce the article by appropriate legislation, clothes Congress with power to pass all laws necessary and proper for abolishing all badges and incidents of slavery in the United States; and upon this assumption it is claimed that this is sufficient authority for declaring by law that all persons shall have equal accommodations and privileges in all inns, public conveyances, and places of public amusement; the argument being that the denial of such equal accommodations and privileges is in itself a subjection to a species of servitude within the meaning of the amendment. . . .

. . . [T]he civil rights bill of 1866, passed in view of the Thirteenth Amendment, before the Fourteenth was adopted, understood to wipe out these burdens and disabilities, the necessary incidents of slavery, constituting its substance and visible form; and to secure to all citizens of every race and color, and without regard to previous servitude, those fundamental rights which are the essence of civil freedom, namely, the same right to make and enforce contracts, to sue, be parties, give evidence, and to inherit, purchase, lease, sell, and convey property, as is enjoyed by white citizens. Whether this legislation was fully authorized by the Thirteenth Amendment alone, without the support which it afterwards received from the Fourteenth Amendment, after the adoption of which it was re-enacted with some additions, it is not necessary to inquire. It is referred to for the purpose of showing that at that time (in 1866) Congress did not assume, under the authority given by the Thirteenth Amendment, to adjust what may be called the social rights of men and races in the community; but only to declare and vindicate those fundamental rights which appertain to the essence of citizenship, and the enjoyment or deprivation of which constitutes the essential distinction between freedom and slavery.

. . . Many wrongs may be obnoxious to the prohibitions of the Fourteenth Amendment which are not, in any just sense, incidents or elements of slavery. Such, for example, would be the taking of private property without due process of law; or allowing persons who have committed certain crimes (horse-stealing, for example) to be seized and hung by the *posse comitatus* without regular trial; or denying to any person, or class of persons, the right to pursue any peaceful avocations allowed to others. What is called class legislation would belong to this category, and would be obnoxious to the prohibitions of the Fourteenth Amendment, but would not necessarily be so to the Thirteenth, when not involving the idea of any subjection of one man to another. . . . Can the act of a mere individual, the owner of the inn, the public conveyance, or place of amusement, refusing the accommodation, be justly regarded as imposing any badge of slavery or servitude upon the applicant, or only as inflicting an ordinary civil injury. . . ? [S]uch an act of refusal has nothing to do with slavery or involuntary servitude, . . . if it is violative of any right of the party, his redress is to be sought under the laws of the state; or, if those laws are adverse to his rights and do not protect him, his remedy will be found in the corrective legislation which Congress has adopted, or may adopt, for counter-acting the effect of state laws, or state action, prohibited by the Fourteenth Amendment. It would be running the slavery argument into the ground to make it apply to every act of discrimination which a person may see fit to make as to the guests he will entertain, or as to the people he will take into his coach or cab or car, or admit to his concert or theater, or deal with in other matters of intercourse or business. Innkeepers and public carriers, by the laws of all the states, so far as we are aware, are bound, to the extent of their facilities, to furnish proper accommodation to all unobjectionable persons who in good faith apply for them. If the laws themselves make any unjust discrimination, amenable to the prohibitions of the Fourteenth Amendment, Congress has full power to afford a remedy under that amendment and in accordance with it.

. . . There were thousands of free colored people in this country before the abolition of slavery, enjoying all the essential rights of life, liberty, and property the same as white citizens; yet no one, at that time, thought that it was any invasion of their personal status as freemen because they were not admitted to all the privileges enjoyed by white citizens, or because they were subjected to discriminations in the enjoyment of accommodations in inns, public conveyances, and places of amusement. Mere discriminations on account of race or color were not regarded as badges of slavery. . . .

On the whole, we are of the opinion that no countenance of authority for the passage of the law in question can be found in either the Thirteenth or Fourteenth Amendment of the Constitution; and no other ground of authority for its passage being suggested, it must necessarily be declared void. . . .

Mr. Justice Harlan, dissenting.

The opinion in these cases proceeds, as it seems to me, upon grounds entirely too narrow and artificial. The substance and spirit of the recent amendments of the Constitution have been sacrificed by a subtle and ingenious verbal criticism. . . .

The Thirteenth Amendment, my brethren concede, did something more than to prohibit slavery as an institution, resting upon distinctions of race, and upheld by positive law. They admit that it established and decreed universal civil freedom throughout the United States. But did the freedom thus established involve nothing more . . . than to forbid one man from owning another as property? . . . I do not contend that the Thirteenth Amendment invests Congress with authority, by legislation, to regulate the entire body of the civil rights which citizens enjoy, or may enjoy, in the several states. But I do hold that since slavery . . . was the moving or principal cause of the adoption of that amendment, and since that institution rested wholly upon the inferiority, as a race, of those held in bondage, their freedom necessarily involved immunity from, and protection against, all discrimination against them, because of their race, in respect of such civil rights as belong to freemen of other races. Congress, therefore, under its express power to enforce that amendment, by appropriate legislation, may enact laws to protect that people against the deprivation, on account of their race, of any civil rights enjoyed by other freemen in the same state; and such legislation may be of a direct and primary character, operating upon states, their officers and agents, and also upon, at least, such individuals and corporations as exercise public functions and wield power and authority under the State. . . .

I am of the opinion that . . . discrimination practised by corporations and individuals in the exercise of their public or quasi-public functions is a badge of servitude, the imposition of which Congress may prevent under its power through appropriate legislation, to enforce the Thirteenth Amendment. . . .

It remains now to consider these cases with reference to the power Congress has possessed since the adoption of the Fourteenth Amendment. . . .

The first clause of the first section—"all persons born or naturalized in the United States, and subject to the jurisdiction thereof, are citizens of the United States, and of the state wherein they reside"—is of a distinctly affirmative character. In its application to the colored race, previously liberated, it created and granted, as well citizenship of the United States, as citizenship of the state in which they respectively resided. . . . Further, they were brought, by this supreme act of the nation, within the direct operation of the provision of the Constitution which declares that "the citizens of each state shall be entitled to all privileges and immunities of citizens in the several states." ***

The citizenship thus acquired by that race, in virtue of an affirmative grant by the nation, may be protected, not alone by the judicial branch of the government, but by congressional legislation of a primary direct character; this, because the power of Congress is not restricted to the enforcement of prohibitions upon state laws or state action. It is, in terms distinct and positive, to enforce "the provisions of this article" of amendment; not simply those

of a prohibitive character, but the provisions,—all of the provisions,—affirmative and prohibitive, of the amendment. . . .

But what was secured to colored citizens of the United States—as between them and their respective states—by the grant to them of state citizenship? With what rights, privileges, or immunities did this grant from the nation invest them? There is one, if there be no others—exemption from race discrimination in respect of any civil right belonging to citizens of the white race in the same state. . . . It is fundamental in American citizenship that, in respect of such rights, there shall be no discrimination by the state, or its officers, or by individuals, or corporations exercising public functions or authority, against any citizen because of his race or previous condition of servitude.

. . . [T]o hold that the amendment remits that right to the states for their protection, primarily, and stays the hands of the nation, until it is assailed by state laws or state proceedings, is to adjudge that the amendment, so far from enlarging the powers of Congress,—as we have heretofore said it did,—not only curtails them, but reverses the policy which the general government has pursued from its very organization. Such an interpretation of the amendment is a denial to Congress of the power, by appropriate legislation, to enforce one of its provisions. In view of the circumstances under which the recent amendments were incorporated into the Constitution, and especially in view of the peculiar character of the new rights they created and secured, it ought not to be presumed that the general government has abdicated its authority, by national legislation, direct and primary in its character, to guard and protect privileges and immunities secured by that instrument. . . . It was perfectly well known that the great danger to the equal enjoyment by citizens of their rights, as citizens, was to be apprehended, not altogether from unfriendly state legislation, but from the hostile action of corporations and individuals in the states. And it is to be presumed that it was intended, by [the Fourteenth Amendment] to clothe Congress with power and authority to meet that danger. . . .

It is said that any interpretation of the Fourteenth Amendment different from that adopted by the court, would authorize Congress to enact a municipal code for all the states, covering every matter affecting the life, liberty, and property of the citizens of the several states. Not so. Prior to the adoption of that amendment the constitutions of the several states, without, perhaps, an exception, secured all persons against deprivation of life, liberty, or property, other-wise than by due process of law, and, in some form, recognized the right of all persons to the equal protection of the laws. These rights, therefore, existed before that amendment was proposed or adopted. . . .

Plessy v. Ferguson

163 U.S. 537; 16 S. Ct. 1138; 41 L. Ed. 256 (1896)
Vote: 7-1

A Louisiana law passed in 1890 required all passenger trains in the state to have "equal but separate accommodations for the white, and colored races." Homer Plessy, claiming that he "was seven-eighths Caucasian and one-eighth African blood; that the mixture of colored blood was not discernible in him; and that he was entitled to every right . . . of the white race," was arrested after refusing to vacate a seat in a car that was reserved for white passengers. Plessy's attack on the statute's constitutionality was unsuccessful in the Louisiana courts. He appealed.

Mr. Justice Brown . . . delivered the opinion of the Court.

. . . That [the statute] does not conflict with the Thirteenth Amendment, which abolished slavery and involuntary servitude, except as a punishment for crime, is too clear for argument. Slavery implies involuntary servitude,—a state of bondage; the ownership of mankind as a chattel, or, at least, the control of the labor and services of one man for the benefit of another, and the absence of a legal right to the disposal of his own person, property, and services. This amendment . . . was regarded by the statesmen of that day as insufficient to protect the colored race from certain laws which had been enacted in the Southern states, imposing upon the colored race onerous disabilities and burdens, and curtailing their rights in the pursuit of life, liberty, and property to such an extent that their freedom was of little value; and . . . the Fourteenth Amendment was devised to meet this exigency. . . .

The object of the amendment was undoubtedly to enforce the absolute equality of the two races before the law, but, in the nature of things, it could not have been intended to abolish distinctions based upon color, or to enforce social, as distinguished from political, equality, or a commingling of the two races upon terms unsatisfactory to either. Laws permitting, and even requiring, their separation, in places where they are liable to be brought into contact . . . have been generally, if not universally, recognized as within the competency of the state legislatures in the exercise of their police power. The most common instance of this is connected with the establishment of separate schools for white and colored children, which have been [upheld] even by courts of states where the political rights of the colored race have been longest and most earnestly enforced.

One of the earliest of these cases is that of *Roberts v. City of Boston,* *** (1849). "The great principle," said Chief Justice Shaw, "advanced by the learned and eloquent advocate for the plaintiff (Mr. Charles Sumner), is that, by the constitution and laws of Massachusetts, all persons, without distinction of age or sex, birth, or color, origin or condition, are equal before the law. . . . But, when this great principle comes to be applied to the actual and various conditions of persons in society, it will not warrant the assertion that men and women are legally clothed with the same civil and political powers, and that children and adults are legally to have the same functions and be subject to the same treatment; but only that the rights of all, as they are settled and regulated by law, are equally entitled to the paternal consideration and protection of the law for their maintenance and security." Similar laws have been enacted by Congress under its general power of legislation over the District of Columbia, as well as by the legislatures of many of the states, and have been generally, if not uniformly, sustained by the courts. ***

Laws forbidding the intermarriage of the two races may be said in a technical sense to interfere with the freedom of contract, and yet have been universally recognized as within the police power of the state. ***

The distinction between laws interfering with the political equality of the negro and those requiring the separation of the two races in schools, theaters, and railway carriages has been frequently drawn by this court.

[It is suggested] that the same argument that will justify the state legislature in requiring railways to provide separate accommodations for the two races will also authorize them to require separate cars to be provided for people whose hair is of a certain color, or who are aliens, or who belong to certain nationalities, or to enact laws requiring colored people to walk upon one side of the street, and white people upon the other, or requiring white men's houses to be painted white, and colored men's black, or their vehicles or business signs to be of different colors, upon the theory that one side of the street is as good as the other, or that a house or vehicle of one color is as good as one of another color. The reply to all this is that every exercise of the police power must be reasonable, and extend only to such laws as are enacted in good faith for the promotion of the public good, and not for the annoyance or oppression of a particular class. ***

So far, then, as a conflict with the Fourteenth Amendment is concerned, the case reduces itself to the question whether the statute of Louisiana is a reasonable regulation, and with respect to this there must necessarily be a large discretion on the part of the legislature. In determining the question of reasonableness, it is at liberty to act with reference to the established usages, customs, and traditions of the people, and with a view to the promotion of their comfort, and the preservation of the public peace and good order. Gauged by this standard, we cannot say [that this law] is unreasonable, or more obnoxious to the Fourteenth Amendment than the acts of Congress requiring separate schools for colored children in the District of Columbia, the constitutionality of which does not seem to have been questioned, or the corresponding acts of state legislatures.

We consider the underlying fallacy of the plaintiff's argument to consist in the assumption that the enforced separation of the two races stamps the colored race with a badge of inferiority. If this be so, it is not by reason of anything found in the act, but solely because the colored race chooses to put that construction upon it. The argument necessarily assumes that if, as has been more than once the case, and is not unlikely to be so again, the colored race should become the dominant power in the state legislature, and should enact a law in precisely similar terms, it would thereby relegate the white race to an inferior position. We imagine that the white race, at least, would not acquiesce in this assumption. The argument also assumes that social prejudices may be overcome by legislation, and that equal rights cannot be secured to the negro except by an enforced commingling of the two races. We cannot accept this proposition. If the two races are to meet upon terms of social equality, it must be the result of natural affinities, a mutual appreciation of each other's merits, and a voluntary consent of individuals. . . . Legislation is powerless to eradicate racial instincts, or to abolish distinctions based upon physical differences, and the attempt to do so can only result in accentuating the difficulties of the present situation. If the civil and political rights of both races be equal, one cannot be inferior to the other civilly or politically. If one race be inferior to the other socially, the Constitution of the United States cannot put them upon the same plane. . . .

Affirmed.

Mr. Justice Brewer did not . . . participate in the decision of this case.

Mr. Justice Harlan dissenting.

. . . In respect of civil rights, common to all citizens, the Constitution of the United States does not, I think, permit any public authority to know the race of those entitled to be protected in the enjoyment of such rights. Every true man has pride of race, and under appropriate circumstances, when the rights of others, his equals before the law, are not to be affected, it is his privilege to express such pride and to take such action based upon it as to him seems proper. But I deny that any legislative body or judicial tribunal may have regard to the race of citizens when the civil rights of those citizens are involved. Indeed, such legislation as that here in question is inconsistent not only with that equality of rights which pertains to citizenship, national and state, but with the personal liberty enjoyed by every one within the United States.

The Thirteenth Amendment does not permit the withholding or the deprivation of any right necessarily inhering in freedom. It not only struck down the institution of slavery as previously existing in the United States, but it prevents the imposition of any burdens or disabilities that constitute badges of slavery or servitude.... It was followed by the Fourteenth [and Fifteenth] amendment[s], which added greatly to the dignity and glory of American citizenship, and to the security of personal liberty....

It was said in argument that the statute of Louisiana does not discriminate against either race, but prescribes a rule applicable alike to white and colored citizens. But this argument does not meet the difficulty. Everyone knows that the statute in question had its origin in the purpose, not so much to exclude white persons from railroad cars occupied by blacks, as to exclude colored people from coaches occupied by or assigned to white persons.... No one would be so wanting in candor as to assert the contrary. The fundamental objection, therefore, to the statute, is that it interferes with the personal freedom of citizens. "Personal liberty," it has been well said, "consists in the power of locomotion, of changing situation, or removing one's person to whatsoever places one's own inclination may direct, without imprisonment or restraint, unless by due course of law." *** If a white man and a black man choose to occupy the same public conveyance on a public highway, it is their right to do so; and no government, proceeding alone on grounds of race, can prevent it without infringing the personal liberty of each.

... If a state can prescribe, as a rule of civil conduct, that whites and blacks shall not travel as passengers in the same railroad coach, why ... may it not require sheriffs to assign whites to one side of a court room, and blacks to the other? And why may it not also prohibit the commingling of the two races in the galleries of legislative halls or in public assemblages convened for the consideration of the politi-

cal questions of the day? [W]hy may not the state require the separation in railroad coaches of native and naturalized citizens of the United States, or of Protestants and Roman Catholics? ...

The white race deems itself to be the dominant race in this country. And so it is, in prestige, in achievements, in education, in wealth, and in power. So, I doubt not, it will continue to be for all time, if it remains true to its great heritage, and holds fast to the principles of constitutional liberty. But in view of the Constitution, in the eye of the law, there is in this country no superior, dominant, ruling class of citizens. There is no caste here. Our Constitution is color-blind, and neither knows nor tolerates classes among citizens. ...

In my opinion, the judgment this day rendered will, in time, prove to be quite as pernicious as the decision made by this tribunal in the Dred Scott Case *** that the descendants of Africans who were imported into this country, and sold as slaves, were not included nor intended to be included under the word "citizens" in the Constitution; ... that, at the time of the adoption of the Constitution, they were "considered as a subordinate and inferior class of beings, who had been subjugated by the dominant race, and, whether emancipated or not, yet remained subject to their authority, and had not rights or privileges but such as those who held the power and the government might choose to grant them." *** The recent amendments of the Constitution, it was supposed, has eradicated these principles from our institutions. But it seems that we have yet, in some of the states, a dominant race,—a superior class of citizens,—which assumes to regulate the enjoyment of civil rights, common to all citizens, upon the basis of race. The present decision ... will encourage the belief that it is possible by means of state enactments, to defeat the beneficent purposes which the people of the United States had in view when they adopted the recent amendments of the Constitution.... What can more certainly arouse race hate, what more certainly create and perpetuate a feeling of distrust between these races, than state enactments which, in fact, proceed on the ground that colored citizens are so inferior and degraded that they cannot be allowed to sit in public coaches occupied by white citizens? ... This question is not met by the suggestion that social equality cannot exist between the white and black races in this country . . . for social equality no more exists between two races when traveling in a passenger coach or a public highway than when members of the same races sit by each other in a street car or in the jury box, or stand or sit with each other in a political assembly. . . .

If evils will result from the comminglings of the two races upon public highways established for the benefit of all, they will be infinitely less than those that will surely come from state legislation regulating the enjoyment of civil rights upon the basis of race. We boast of the freedom enjoyed by our people above all other peoples. But it is difficult to reconcile that boast with a state of the law which, practically, puts the brand of servitude and degradation upon a large class of our fellow citizens,—our equals before the law. The thin disguise of "equal" accommodations for passengers in railroad coaches will not mislead any one, nor atone for the wrong this day done. . . .

I do not deem it necessary to review the decisions of state courts to which reference was made in argument. Some, and the most important, of them, are wholly inapplicable, because rendered prior to the adoption of the last amendments of the Constitution. . . . Others were made at a time when public opinion, in many localities, was dominated by the institution of slavery; when it would not have been safe to do justice to the black man; and when, so far as the rights of blacks were concerned, race prejudice was, practically, the supreme law of the land. Those decisions cannot be guides in the era introduced by the recent amendments of the supreme law, which established universal civil freedom. . . .

Shelley v. Kraemer
334 U.S. 1; 68 S. Ct. 836; 92 L. Ed. 1161 (1948)
Vote: 6-0

Mr. Chief Justice Vinson delivered the opinion of the Court:

These cases present for our consideration questions relating to the validity of court enforcement of private agreements, generally described as restrictive covenants, which have as their purpose the exclusion of persons of designated race or color from the ownership or occupancy of real property. Basic constitutional issues of obvious importance have been raised.

The first of these cases comes to this Court on *certiorari* to the Supreme Court of Missouri. On February 16, 1911, thirty out of a total of thirty-nine owners of property fronting both sides of Labadie Avenue between Taylor Avenue and Cora Avenue in the city of St. Louis, signed an agreement, which was subsequently recorded, providing in part:

. . . The said property is hereby restricted to the use and occupancy for the term of Fifty (50) years from this date, so that it shall be a condition all the time and whether recited and referred to as [*sic*] not in subsequent conveyances and shall attach to the land, as a condition precedent to the sale of the same, that hereafter no part of said property or any portion thereof shall be, for said term of Fifty years, occupied by any person not of the Caucasian race, it being intended hereby to restrict the use of said property for said period of time against the occupancy as owners or tenants of any portion of said property for resident or other purpose by people of the Negro or Mongolian Race. . . .

On August 11, 1945, pursuant to a contract of sale, petitioners Shelley, who are Negroes, for valuable consideration received from one Fitzgerald a warranty deed to the parcel in question. The trial court found that petitioners had no actual knowledge of the restrictive agreement at the time of the purchase.

On October 9, 1945, respondents, as owners of other property subject to the terms of the restrictive convenant, brought suit in the Circuit Court of the city of St. Louis praying that petitioners Shelley be restrained from taking possession of the property and that judgment be entered divesting title out of petitioners Shelley and revesting title in the immediate grantor or in such other person as the court should direct. The trial court denied the requested relief on the ground that the restrictive agreement, upon which respondents based their action, had never become final and complete because it was the intention of the parties to that agreement that it was not to become effective until signed by all property owners in the district, and signatures of all the owners had never been obtained.

The Supreme Court of Missouri sitting *en banc* reversed and directed the trial court to grant the relief for which respondents had prayed. That court held the agreement effective and concluded that enforcement of its provisions violated no rights guaranteed to petitioners by the Federal Constitution. At the time the court rendered its decision, petitioners were occupying the property in question. . . .

Petitioners have placed primary reliance on their contentions, first raised in the state courts, that judicial enforcement of the restrictive agreements in these cases has violated rights guaranteed to petitioners by the Fourteenth Amendment of the Federal Constitution and Acts of Congress passed pursuant to that Amendment. Specifically, petitioners urge that they have been denied the equal protection of the laws, deprived of property without due process of law, and have been denied privileges and immunities of citizens of the United States. We pass to a consideration of those issues.

I

Whether the equal protection clause of the Fourteenth Amendment inhibits judicial enforcement by state courts of restrictive covenants based on race or color is a question which this Court has not heretofore been called upon to consider. . . .

It is well, at the outset, to scrutinize the terms of the restrictive agreements involved in these cases. In the Missouri case, the covenant declares that no part of the affected property shall be "occupied by any person not of the Caucasian race, it being intended hereby to restrict the use of said property . . . against the occupancy as owners or tenants of any portion of said property for resident or other purpose by people of the Negro or Mongolian Race." Not only does the restriction seek to proscribe use and occupancy of the affected properties by members of the ex-

cluded class, but as construed by the Missouri courts, the agreement requires that title of any person who uses his property in violation of the restriction shall be divested. . . .

It cannot be doubted that among the civil rights intended to be protected from discriminatory state action by the Fourteenth Amendment are the rights to acquire, enjoy, own and dispose of property. Equality in the enjoyment of property rights was regarded by the framers of that Amendment as an essential pre-condition to the realization of other basic civil rights and liberties which the Amendment was intended to guarantee. Thus . . . the Civil Rights Act of 1866 which was enacted by Congress while the Fourteenth Amendment was also under consideration provides:

"All citizens of the United States shall have the same right, in every State and Territory, as is enjoyed by white citizens thereof to inherit, purchase, lease, sell, hold, and convey real and personal property." This Court has given specific recognition to the same principle. ***

It is likewise clear that restrictions on the right of occupancy of the sort sought to be created by the private agreements in these cases could not be squared with the requirements of the Fourteenth Amendment if imposed by state statute or local ordinance. . . .

But the present cases, unlike those just discussed, do not involve action by state legislatures or city councils. Here the particular patterns of discrimination and the areas in which the restrictions are to operate, are determined, in the first instance, by the terms of agreements among private individuals. Participation of the State consists in the enforcement of the restrictions so defined. The crucial issue with which we are here confronted is whether this distinction removes these cases from the operation of the prohibitory provisions of the Fourteenth Amendment.

Since the decision of this Court in *The Civil Rights Cases,* *** the principle has become firmly embedded in our constitutional law that the action inhibited by the first section of the Fourteenth Amendment is only such action as may fairly be said to be that of the States. That Amendment erects no shield against merely private conduct, however discriminatory or wrongful.

We conclude, therefore, that the restrictive agreements standing alone cannot be regarded as violative of any rights guaranteed to petitioners by the Fourteenth Amendment. So long as the purposes of those agreements are effectuated by voluntary adherence to their terms, it would appear clear that there has been no action by the State and the provisions of the Amendment have not been violated. ***

But here there was more. These are cases in which the purposes of the agreements were secured only by judicial enforcement by state courts of the restrictive terms of the agreements. The respondents urge that judicial enforcement of private agreements does not amount to state action; or, in any event, the participation of the States is so attenuated in character as not to amount to state action within the meaning of the Fourteenth Amendment. Finally, it is suggested, even if the States in these cases may be deemed to have acted in the constitutional sense, their action did not deprive petitioners of rights guaranteed by the Fourteenth Amendment. We move to a consideration of these matters.

II

That the action of state courts and of judicial officers in their official capacities is to be regarded as action of the State within the meaning of the Fourteenth Amendment, is a proposition which has long been established by decisions of this Court. That principle was given expression in the earliest cases involving the construction of the terms of the Fourteenth Amendment. . . .

The short of the matter is that from the time of the adoption of the Fourteenth Amendment until the present, it has been the consistent ruling of this Court that the action of the States to which the Amendment has reference, includes action of state courts and state judicial officials. Although, in construing the terms of the Fourteenth Amendment, differences have from time to time been expressed as to whether particular types of state action may be said to offend the Amendment's prohibitory provisions, it has never been suggested that state court action is immunized from the operation of those provisions simply because the act is that of the judicial branch of the state government.

III

Against this background of judicial construction, extending over a period of some three-quarters of a century, we are called upon to consider whether enforcement by state courts of the restrictive agreements in these cases may be deemed to be the acts of those States; and, if so, whether that action has denied these petitioners the equal protection of the laws which the Amendment was intended to insure.

We have no doubt that there has been state action in these cases in the full and complete sense of the phrase. The undisputed facts disclose that petitioners were willing purchasers of properties upon which they desired to establish homes. The owners of the properties were willing sellers; and contracts of sale were accordingly consummated. It is clear that but for the active intervention of the state courts, supported by the full panoply of state power, petitioners would have been free to occupy the properties in question without restraint.

These are not cases, as has been suggested, in which the States have merely abstained from action, leaving private individuals free to impose such discriminations as they see fit. Rather, these are cases in which the States have made available to such individuals the full coercive power of government to deny to petitioners, on the grounds of race or color, the enjoyment of property rights in premises which petitioners are willing and financially able to acquire and which the grantors are willing to sell. The difference between judicial enforcement and nonenforcement of the restrictive covenants is the difference to petitioners between being denied rights of property available to other members of the community and being accorded full enjoyment of those rights on an equal footing. . . .

We hold that in granting judicial enforcement of the restrictive agreements in these cases, the States have denied petitioners the equal protection of the laws and that, therefore, the action of the state courts cannot stand. We have noted that freedom from discrimination by the States in the enjoyment of property rights was among the basic objectives sought to be effectuated by the framers of the Fourteenth Amendment. That such discrimination has occurred in these cases is clear. Because of the race or color of these petitioners they have been denied rights of ownership or occupancy enjoyed as a matter of course by other citizens of different race or color. . . .

Respondents urge, however, that since the state courts stand ready to enforce restrictive covenants excluding white persons from ownership or occupancy of property covered by such agreements, enforcement of covenants excluding colored persons may not be deemed a denial of equal protection of the laws to the colored persons who are thereby affected. This contention does not bear scrutiny. The parties have directed our attention to no case in which a court, state or federal, has been called upon to enforce a covenant excluding members of the white majority from ownership or occupancy of real property on grounds of race or color. But there are more fundamental considerations. The rights created by the first section of the Fourteenth Amendment are, by its terms, guaranteed to the individual. The rights established are personal rights. It is, therefore, no answer to these petitioners to say that the courts may also be induced to deny white persons rights of ownership and occupancy on grounds of race or color. Equal protection of the laws is not achieved through indiscriminate imposition of inequalities. . . .

The historical context in which the Fourteenth Amendment became a part of the Constitution should not be forgotten. Whatever else the Framers sought to achieve, it is clear that the matter of primary concern was the establishment of equality in the enjoyment of basic civil and political rights and the preservation of those rights from discriminatory action on the part of the States based on considerations of race or color. Seventy-five years ago this Court announced that the provisions of the Amendment are to be construed with this fundamental purpose in mind. Upon full consideration, we have concluded that in these cases the States have acted to deny petitioners the equal protection of the laws guaranteed by the Fourteenth Amendment. Having so decided, we find it unnecessary to consider whether petitioners have also been deprived of property without due process of law or denied privileges and immunities of citizens of the United States. . . .

Reversed.

Justices Reed, Jackson, and **Rutledge** took no part in the consideration or decision of these cases.

Sweatt v. Painter

339 U.S. 629; 70 S. Ct. 848; 94 L. Ed. 1114 (1950)
Vote: 9-0

Mr. Chief Justice Vinson delivered the opinion of the Court:

This case and *McLaurin v. Oklahoma State Regents* *** present different aspects of this general question: To what extent does the Equal Protection Clause of the Fourteenth Amendment limit the power of a state to distinguish between students of different races in professional and graduate education in a state university? Broader issues have been urged for our consideration, but we adhere to the principle of deciding constitutional questions only in the context of the particular case before the Court. We have frequently reiterated that this Court will decide constitutional questions only when

necessary to the disposition of the case at hand, and that such decisions will be drawn as narrowly as possible. *** Because of this traditional reluctance to extend constitutional interpretations to situations or facts which are not before the Court, much of the excellent research and detailed argument presented in these cases is unnecessary to their disposition.

In the instant case, petitioner filed an application for admission to the University of Texas Law School for the February 1946 term. His application was rejected solely because he is a Negro. Petitioner thereupon brought this suit for *mandamus* against the appropriate school officials, respondents here, to compel his admission. At that time, there was no law school in Texas which admitted Negroes.

The state trial court recognized that the action of the State in denying petitioner the opportunity to gain a legal education while granting it to others deprived him of the equal protection of the laws guaranteed by the Fourteenth Amendment. The court did not grant the relief requested, however, but continued the case for six months to allow the State to supply substantially equal facilities. At the expiration of the six months, in December 1946 the court denied the writ on the showing that the authorized university officials had adopted an order calling for the opening of a law school for Negroes the following February. While petitioner's appeal was pending, such a school was made available, but petitioner refused to register therein. The Texas Court of Civil Appeals set aside the trial court's judgment and ordered the case "remanded generally to the trial court for further proceedings without prejudice to the rights of any party to this suit."

On remand, a hearing was held on the issue of the equality of the educational facilities at the newly established school as compared with the University of Texas Law School. Finding that the new school offered petitioner "privileges, advantages, and opportunities for the study of law substantially equivalent to those offered by the State to white students at the University of Texas," the trial court denied *mandamus*. The Court of Civil Appeals affirmed. *** Petitioner's application for a writ of error was denied by the Texas Supreme Court. We granted *certiorari* *** because of the manifest importance of the constitutional issues involved.

The University of Texas Law School, from which petitioner was excluded, was staffed by a faculty of sixteen full-time and three part-time professors, some of whom are nationally recognized authorities in their field. Its student body numbered 850. The library contained over 65,000 volumes. Among the other facilities available to the students were a law review, moot court facilities, scholarship funds, and Order of the Coif affiliation. The school's alumni occupy the most distinguished positions in the private practice of the law and in the public life of the State. It may properly be considered one of the nation's ranking law schools.

The law school for Negroes which was to have opened in February, 1947, would have had no independent faculty or library. The teaching was to be carried on by four members of the University of Texas Law School faculty, who were to maintain their offices at the University of Texas while teaching at both institutions. Few of the 10,000 volumes ordered for the library had arrived; nor was there any full-time librarian. The school lacked accreditation.

Since the trial of this case, respondents report the opening of a law school at the Texas State University for Negroes. It is apparently on the road to full accreditation. It has a faculty of five full-time professors; a student body of 23; a library of some 16,500 volumes serviced by a full-time staff; a practice court and legal aid association; and one alumnus who has become a member of the Texas Bar.

Whether the University of Texas Law School is compared with the original or the new law school for Negroes, we cannot find substantial equality in the educational opportunities offered white and Negro law students by the State. In terms of number the faculty, variety of courses and opportunity for specialization, size of the student body, scope of the library, availability of law review and similar activities, the University of Texas Law School is superior. What is more important, the University of Texas Law School possesses to a far greater degree those qualities which are incapable of objective measurement but which make for greatness in a law school. Such qualities, to name but a few, include reputation of the faculty, experience of the administration, position and influence of the alumni, standing in the community, traditions and prestige. It is difficult to believe that one who had a free choice between these law schools would consider the question close.

Moreover, although the law is a highly learned profession, we are well aware that it is an intensely practical one. The law school, the proving ground for legal learning and practice, cannot be effective in isolation from the individuals and institutions with which the law interacts. Few students and no one who has practiced law would choose to study in an academic vacuum, removed from the interplay of ideas and the exchange of views with which the law is concerned. The law school to which Texas is willing to admit petitioner excludes from its student body members of the racial groups which number 85% of the population of the State and include most of the lawyers, witnesses, jurors, judges and other officials with whom petitioner will inevitably be dealing when he becomes a member of the Texas Bar. With such a substantial and significant segment of society excluded, we cannot conclude that the education offered petitioner is substantially equal to that which he would receive if admitted to the University of Texas Law School.

It may be argued that excluding petitioner from that school is no different from excluding white students from the new law school. This contention overlooks realities. It is unlikely that a member of a group so decisively in the majority, attending a school with rich traditions and prestige which only a history of consistently maintained excellence could command, would claim that the opportunities afforded him for legal education were unequal to those held open to petitioner. That such a claim, if made, would be dishonored by the State, is no answer. "Equal protection of the laws is not achieved through indiscriminate imposition of inequalities." ***

It is fundamental that these cases concern rights which are personal and present. This court has stated unanimously that "The State must provide [legal education] for [petitioner] in conformity with the Equal Protection Clause of the Fourteenth Amendment and provide it as soon as it does for applicants of any other group." *** That case "did not present the issue whether a state might not satisfy the Equal Protection

Clause of the Fourteenth Amendment by establishing a separate law school for Negroes." *** In *Missouri ex rel. Gaines v. Canada,* *** the Court, speaking through Chief Justice Hughes, declared that "petitioner's right was a personal one. It was as an individual that he was entitled to the equal protection of the laws, and the State was bound to furnish him within its borders facilities for legal education substantially equal to those which the State there afforded for persons of the white race, whether or not other negroes sought the same opportunity." These are the only cases in this Court which present the issue of the constitutional validity of race distinctions in state-supported graduate and professional education.

In accordance with these cases, petitioner may claim his full constitutional right: legal education equivalent to that afforded by the State to students of other races. Such education is not available to him in a separate law school as offered by the State. We cannot, therefore, agree with respondents that the doctrine of *Plessy v. Ferguson* *** requires affirmance of the judgment below. Nor need we reach petitioner's contention that *Plessy v. Ferguson* should be re-examined in the light of contemporary knowledge respecting the purposes of the Fourteenth Amendment and the effects of racial segregation.

We hold that the Equal Protection Clause of the Fourteenth Amendment requires that petitioner be admitted to the University of Texas Law School. The judgment is reversed and the cause is remanded for proceedings not inconsistent with this opinion.

Reversed.

Brown v. Board of Education of Topeka I

347 U.S. 483; 74 S. Ct. 686; 98 L. Ed. 873 (1954)
Vote: 9-0

Mr. Chief Justice Warren delivered the opinion of the Court:

These cases come to us from the States of Kansas, South Carolina, Virginia, and Delaware. They are premised on different facts and different local conditions, but a common legal question justifies their consideration in this consolidated opinion.

In each of the cases, minors of the Negro race, through their legal representatives, seek the aid of the courts in obtaining admission to the public schools of their community on a nonsegregated basis. In each instance, they had been denied admission to schools attended by white children under laws requiring or permitting segregation according to race. This segregation was alleged to deprive the plaintiffs of the equal protection of the laws under the Fourteenth Amendment. In each of the cases other than the Delaware case, a three-judge federal district court denied relief to the plaintiffs on the so-called "separate but equal" doctrine announced by this Court in *Plessy v. Ferguson.* *** Under that doctrine, equality of treatment is accorded when the races are provided substantially equal facilities, even though these facilities be separate. In the Delaware case, the Supreme Court of Delaware adhered to that doctrine, but ordered that the plaintiffs be admitted to the white schools because of their superiority to the Negro schools. . . .

Because of the obvious importance of the question presented, the Court took jurisdiction. Argument was heard in the 1952 Term, and reargument was heard this Term on certain questions propounded by the Court.

Reargument was largely devoted to the circumstances surrounding the adoption of the Fourteenth Amendment in 1868. It covered exhaustively consideration of the Amendment in Congress, ratification by the states, then existing practices in racial segregation, and the views of proponents and opponents of the Amendment. This discussion and our own investigation convince us that, although these sources cast some light, it is not enough to resolve the problem with which we are faced. At best, they are inconclusive. The most avid proponents of the post-War Amendments undoubtedly intended them to remove all legal distinctions among "all persons born or naturalized in the United States." Their opponents, just as certainly, were antagonistic to both the letter and the spirit of the Amendments and wished them to have the most limited effect. What others in Congress and the state legislatures had in mind cannot be determined with any degree of certainty.

An additional reason for the inconclusive nature of the Amendment's history, with respect to segregated schools, is the status of public education at that time. In the South, the movement toward free common schools, supported by general taxation, had not yet taken hold. Education of white children was largely in the hands of private groups. Education of Negroes was almost nonexistent, and practically all of the race were illiterate. In fact, any education of Negroes was

forbidden by law in some states. Today, in contrast, many Negroes have achieved outstanding success in the arts and sciences as well as in the business and professional world. It is true that public education had already advanced further in the North, but the effect of the Amendment on Northern States was generally ignored in the congressional debates. Even in the North, the conditions of public education did not approximate those existing today. The curriculum was rudimentary; ungraded schools were common in rural areas; the school term was but three months a year in many states; and compulsory school attendance was virtually unknown. As a consequence, it is not surprising that there should be so little in the history of the Fourteenth Amendment relating to its intended effect on public education.

In the first cases in this Court construing the Fourteenth Amendment, decided shortly after its adoption, the Court interpreted it as proscribing all state-imposed discriminations against the Negro race. The doctrine of "separate but equal" did not make its appearance in this Court until 1896 in the case of *Plessy v. Ferguson,* *** involving not education but transportation. American courts have since labored with the doctrine for over half a century. In this Court, there have been six cases involving the "separate but equal" doctrine in the field of public education. In *Cumming v. County Board of Education,* *** and *Gong Lum v. Rice,* *** the validity of the doctrine itself was not challenged. In more recent cases, all on the graduate school level, inequality was found in that specific benefits enjoyed by white students were denied to Negro students of the same educational qualifications. *** In none of these cases was it necessary to reexamine the doctrine to grant relief to the Negro plaintiff. And in *Sweatt v. Painter,* *** the Court expressly reserved decision on the question whether *Plessy v. Ferguson* should be held inapplicable to public education.

In the instant cases, that question is directly presented. Here, unlike *Sweatt v. Painter,* there are findings below that the Negro and white schools involved have been equalized, or are being equalized, with respect to buildings, curricula, qualifications and salaries of teachers, and other "tangible" factors. Our decision, therefore, cannot turn on merely a comparison of these tangible factors in the Negro and white schools involved in each of the cases. We must look instead to the effect of segregation itself on public education.

In approaching this problem, we cannot turn the clock back to 1868 when the Amendment was adopted, or even to 1896 when *Plessy v. Ferguson* was written. We must consider public education in the light of its full development and its present place in American life throughout the Nation. Only in this way can it be determined if segregation in public schools deprives these plaintiffs of the equal protection of the laws.

Today, education is perhaps the most important function of state and local governments. Compulsory school attendance laws and the great expenditures for education both demonstrate our recognition of the importance of education to our democratic society. It is required in the performance of our most basic public responsibilities, even service in the armed forces. It is the very foundation of good citizenship. Today it is a principal instrument in awakening the child to cultural values, in preparing him for later professional training, and in helping him to adjust normally to his environment. In these days, it is doubtful that any child may reasonably be expected to succeed in life if he is denied the opportunity of an education. Such an opportunity, where the state has undertaken to provide it, is a right which must be made available to all on equal terms.

We come then to the question presented: Does segregation of children in public schools solely on the basis of race, even though the physical facilities and other "tangible" factors may be equal, deprive the children of the minority group of equal educational opportunities? We believe that it does.

In *Sweatt v. Painter,* in finding that a segregated law school for Negroes could not provide them equal educational opportunities, this Court relied in large part on "those qualities which are incapable of objective measurement but which make for greatness in a law school." In *McLaurin v. Oklahoma State Regents,* *** the Court, in requiring that a Negro admitted to a white graduate school be treated like all other students, again resorted to intangible considerations: ". . . his ability to study, to engage in discussions and exchange views with other students, and, in general, to learn his profession." Such considerations apply with added force to children in grade and high schools. To separate them from others of similar age and qualifications solely because of their race generates a feeling of inferiority as to their status in the community that may affect their hearts and minds in a way unlikely ever to be undone. The effect of this separation on their educational opportunities was well stated by a finding in the Kansas case by a court which nevertheless felt compelled to rule against the Negro plaintiffs:

Segregation of white and colored children in public schools has a detrimental effect upon the colored children. The impact is greater when it has the sanction of the law; for the policy of separating the races is usually interpreted as denoting the inferiority of the Negro group. A sense of inferiority affects the motivation of a child to learn. Segregation with the sanction of law, therefore, has a tendency to retard the educational and mental development of Negro children and to deprive them of some of the benefits they would receive in a racially integrated school system.

Whatever may have been the extent of psychological knowledge at the time of *Plessy v. Ferguson,* this finding is amply supported by modern authority. Any language in *Plessy v. Ferguson* contrary to this finding is rejected.

We conclude that in the field of public education the doctrine of "separate but equal" has no place. Separate educational facilities are inherently unequal. Therefore, we hold that the plaintiffs and others similarly situated for whom the actions have been brought are, by reason of the segregation complained of, deprived of the equal protection of the laws guaranteed by the Fourteenth Amendment. This disposition makes unnecessary any discussion whether such segregation also violates the Due Process Clause of the Fourteenth Amendment.

Because these are class actions, because of the wide applicability of this decision, and because of the great variety of local conditions, the formulation of decrees in these cases presents problems of considerable complexity. On reargument, the consideration of appropriate relief was necessarily subordinated to the primary question—the constitutionality of segregation in public education. We have now announced that such segregation is a denial of the equal protection of the laws. In order that we may have the full assistance of the parties in formulating decrees, the cases will be restored to the docket, and the parties are requested to present further argument. . . .

It is so ordered.

Brown v. Board of Education of Topeka II

349 U.S. 294; 75 S. Ct. 753; 99 L. Ed. 1083 (1955)

Mr. Chief Justice Warren delivered the opinion of the Court.

These cases were decided on May 17, 1954. The opinions of that date, declaring the fundamental principle that racial discrimination in public education is unconstitutional, are incorporated herein by reference. All provisions of federal, state, or local law requiring or permitting such discrimination must yield to this principle. There remains for consideration the manner in which relief is to be accorded.

Because these cases arose under different local conditions and their disposition will involve a variety of local problems, we requested further argument on the question of relief. In view of the nationwide importance of the decision, we invited the Attorney General of the United States and the Attorneys General of all states requiring or permitting racial discrimination in public education to present their views on that question. The parties, the United States, and the States of Florida, North Carolina, Arkansas, Oklahoma, Maryland, and Texas filed briefs and participated in the oral argument.

These presentations were informative and helpful to the Court in its consideration of the complexities arising from the transition to a system of public education freed of racial discrimination. The presentations also demonstrated that substantial steps to eliminate racial discrimination in public schools have already been taken, not only in some of the communities in which these cases arose, but in some of the states appearing as *amici curiae,* and in other states as well. Substantial progress has been made in the District of Columbia and in the communities in Kansas and Delaware involved in this litigation. The defendants in the cases coming to us from South Carolina and Virginia are awaiting the decision of this Court concerning relief.

Full implementation of these constitutional principles may require solution of varied local school problems. School authorities have the primary responsibility for elucidating, assessing, and solving these problems; courts will have to consider whether the action of school authorities constitutes good faith implementation of the governing constitutional principles. Because of their proximity to local conditions and the possible need for further hearings, the courts which originally heard these cases can best perform this judicial appraisal. Accordingly, we believe it appropriate to remand the cases to those courts.

In fashioning and effectuating the decrees, the courts will be guided by equitable principles. Traditionally, equity has been characterized by a practical flexibility in shaping its remedies and by a facility for adjusting and reconciling public and private needs. These cases call for the exercise of these traditional attributes of equity power. At stake is the personal interest of the plaintiffs in admission to public schools as soon as practicable on a nondiscriminatory basis. To effectuate this interest may call for elimination of a variety of obstacles in making the transition to school systems operated in accordance with the constitutional principles set forth in our May 17, 1954, decision. Courts of equity may properly take into account the public interest in the elimination of such obstacles in a systematic and effective manner. But it should go without saying that the vitality of these constitutional principles cannot be allowed to yield simply because of disagreement with them.

While giving weight to these public and private considerations, the courts will require that the defendants make a prompt and reasonable start toward full compliance with our May 17, 1954, ruling. Once such a start has been made, the courts may find that additional time is necessary to carry out the ruling in an effective manner. The burden rests upon the defendants to establish that such time is necessary in the public interest and is consistent with good faith compliance at the earliest practicable date. To that end, the courts may consider problems related to administration, arising from the physical condition of the school plant, the school transportation system, personnel, revision of school districts and attendance areas into compact units to achieve a system of determining admission to the public schools on a nonracial basis, and revision of local laws and regulations which may be necessary in solving the foregoing problems. They will also consider the adequacy of any plans the defendants may propose to meet these problems and to effectuate a transition to a racially nondiscriminatory school system. During this period of transition, the courts will retain jurisdiction of these cases.

The judgments below, except that in the Delaware case, are accordingly reversed and remanded to the District courts to take such proceedings and enter such orders and decrees consistent with this opinion as are necessary and proper to admit to public schools on a racially nondiscriminatory basis with all deliberate speed the parties to these cases. The judgment in the Delaware case—ordering the immediate admission of the plaintiffs to schools previously attended only by white children—is affirmed on the basis of the principles stated in our May 17, 1954, opinion, but the case is remanded to the Supreme Court of Delaware for such further proceedings as that court may deem necessary in light of this opinion.

It is so ordered.

Loving v. Virginia
388 U.S. 1; 87 S. Ct. 1817; 18 L. Ed. 2d 1010 (1967)
Vote: 9-0

Mr. Chief Justice Warren delivered the opinion of the Court.

This case presents a constitutional question never addressed by this Court: whether a statutory scheme adopted by the State of Virginia to prevent marriages between persons solely on the basis of racial classifications violates the . . . Fourteenth Amendment. For reasons which seem to us to reflect the central meaning of those constitutional commands, we conclude that these statutes cannot stand consistently with the Fourteenth Amendment.

In June 1958, two residents of Virginia, Mildred Jeter, a Negro woman, and Richard Loving, a white man, were married in the District of Columbia pursuant to its laws. Shortly after their marriage, the Lovings returned to Virginia and established their marital abode in Caroline County. At the October Term, 1958, of the Circuit Court of Caroline County, a grand jury issued an indictment charging the Lovings and violating Virginia's ban on interracial marriages. On January 6, 1959, the Lovings pleaded guilty to the charge and were sentenced to one year in jail; however the trial judge suspended the sentence for a period of 25 years on the condition that the Lovings leave the State and not return to Virginia together for 25 years, stating that:

Almighty God created the races white, black, yellow, malay, and red, and he placed them on separate continents. And but for the interference with his arrangements there would be no cause for such marriages. The fact that he separated the races shows that he did not intend for the races to mix.

After their convictions the Lovings took up residence in the District of Columbia. On November 6, 1963, they filed a motion in the state trial court to vacate the judgment and set aside the sentence on the ground that the statutes which they had violated were repugnant to the Fourteenth Amendment. The motion not having been decided by October 28, 1964, the Lovings instituted a class action in the United States District Court for the Eastern District of Virginia requesting that a three-judge court be convened to declare the Virginia antimiscegenation statutes unconstitutional and to enjoin state officials from enforcing their convictions. On January 22, 1965, the state trial judge denied the motion to vacate the sentences, and the Lovings perfected an appeal to the Supreme Court of Appeals of Virginia. On February 11, 1965, the three-judge District Court continued the case to allow the Lovings to present their constitutional claims to the highest state court.

The [Virginia] Supreme Court of Appeals upheld the constitutionality of the antimiscegenation statutes and, after modifying the sentence, affirmed the convictions. The Lovings appealed this decision, and we noted probable jurisdiction on December 12, 1966.

The two statutes under which appellants were convicted and sentenced are part of a comprehensive statutory scheme aimed at prohibiting and punishing interracial marriages. The Lovings were convicted of violating Sec. 20-58 of the Virginia Code:

Leaving State to Evade Law. If any white person and colored person shall go out of this State, for the purpose of being married, and with the intention of returning, and be married out of it, and afterwards return to and reside in it, cohabiting as man and wife, they shall be punished as provided in Section 20-59, and the marriage shall be governed by the same law as if it had been solemnized in this State. The fact of their cohabitation here as man and wife shall be evidence of their marriage.

Section 20-59, which defines the penalty for miscegenation, provides:

Punishment for Marriage. If any white person intermarry with a colored person, or any colored person intermarry with a white person, he shall be guilty of a felony and shall be punished by confinement in the penitentiary for not less than one nor more than five years.

Other central provisions in the Virginia statutory scheme are Section 20-57, which automatically voids all marriages between "a white person and a colored person" without any judicial proceeding, and Sections 20-54 and 1-14 which, respectively, define "white persons" and "colored persons and Indians" for purposes of the statutory prohibitions. The Lovings have never disputed in course of this litigation that Mrs. Loving is a "colored person" or that Mr. Loving is a "white person" within the meanings given those terms by the Virginia statutes.

Virginia is now one of 16 States which prohibit and punish marriages on the basis of racial classifications. Penalties for miscegenation arose as an incident to slavery and have been common in Virginia since the colonial period. The present statutory scheme dates from the adoption of the Racial Integrity Act of 1924, passed during the period of extreme nativism which followed the end of the First World War. The central features of this Act, and current Virginia law, are the absolute prohibition of a "white person" marrying other than another "white person," a prohibition against issuing marriage licenses until the issuing official is satisfied that the applicants' statements as to their race are correct, certificates of "racial composition" to be kept by both local and state registrars, and the carrying forward of earlier prohibitions against racial intermarriage.

I

In upholding the constitutionality of these provisions in the decision below, the Supreme Court of Appeals of Virginia referred to its 1955 decision in *Naim v. Naim,* *** as stating the reasons supporting the validity of these laws. In *Naim,* the state court concluded that the State's legitimate purposes were "to preserve the racial integrity of its citizens," and to prevent "the corruption of blood," "a mongrel breed of citizens," and "the obliteration of racial pride," obviously an endorsement of the doctrine of White Supremacy. The court also reasoned that marriage has traditionally been subject to state regulation without federal intervention, and, consequently, the regulation of marriage should be left to exclusive state control by the Tenth Amendment.

While the state court is no doubt correct in asserting that marriage is a social relation subject to the State's police power, *** the State does not contend in its argument before this Court that its powers to regulate marriage are unlimited notwithstanding the commands of the Fourteenth Amendment. Nor could it do so in light of *Meyer v. State of Nebraska* *** (1923) and *Skinner v. State of Oklahoma* *** (1942). Instead, the State argues that the meaning of the Equal Protection Clause, as illuminated by the statements of the Framers, is only that state penal laws containing an interracial element as part of the definition of the offense must apply equally to whites and Negroes in the sense that members of each race are punished to the same degree. Thus, the State contends that, because its miscegenation statutes punish equally both the white and the Negro participants in an interracial marriage, these statutes, despite their reliance on racial classifications do not constitute an invidious discrimination based upon race. The second argument advanced by the State assumes the validity of its equal application theory. The argument is that, if the Equal Protection Clause does not outlaw miscegenation statutes because of their reliance on racial classifications, the question of constitutionality would thus become whether there was any rational basis for a State to treat interracial marriages differently from other marriages. On this question, the State argues, the scientific evidence is substantially in doubt and, consequently, this Court should defer to the wisdom of the state legislature in adopting its policy of discouraging interracial marriages.

Because we reject the notion that the mere "equal application" of a statute containing racial classification is enough to remove the classifications from the Fourteenth Amendment's proscription of all invidious racial discriminations, we do not accept the State's contention that these statutes should be upheld if there is any possible basis for concluding that they serve a rational purpose. The mere fact of equal application does not mean that our analysis of this statute should follow the approach we have taken in case involving no racial discrimination where the Equal Protection Clause has been arrayed against a statute discriminating between the kinds of advertising which may be displayed on trucks in New York City, *** or an exemption in Ohio's *ad valorem* tax for merchandise owned by a non-resident in a storage warehouse. *** In these cases, involving distinctions not drawn according to race, the Court has merely asked whether there is any rational foundation for the discriminations, and has deferred to the wisdom of the state legislatures. In the case at bar, however, we deal with statutes containing racial classifications, and the fact of equal application does not immunize the statute from the very heavy burden of justification which the Fourteenth Amendment has traditionally required of state statutes drawn according to race.

The State argues that statements in the Thirty-ninth Congress about the time of the passage of the Fourteenth Amendment indicate that the Framers did not intend the Amendment to make unconstitutional state miscegenation laws. Many of the statements alluded to by the State concern the debates over the Freemen's Bureau Bill, which President Johnson vetoed, and the Civil Rights Act of 1966, enacted over his veto. While these statements have some relevance to the intention of Congress in submitting the Fourteenth Amendment, it must be understood that they pertained to the passage of specific statutes and not to the broader, organic purpose of a constitutional amendment. As for the various statements directly concerning the Fourteenth Amendment, we have said in connection with a related problem, that although these historical sources "cast some light" they are not sufficient to resolve the problem; "[a]t

best, they are inconclusive. The most avid proponents of the post-War Amendments undoubtedly intended them to remove all legal distinctions among 'all persons born or naturalized in the United States.' Their opponents, just as certainly, were antagonistic to both the letter and the spirit of the Amendments and wished them to have the most limited effect." *** We have rejected the proposition that the debates in the Thirty-ninth Congress or in the state legislatures which ratified the Fourteenth Amendment supported the theory advanced by the State, that the requirement of equal protection of the laws is satisfied by penal laws defining offenses based on racial classifications so long as white and Negro participants in the offense were similarly punished. ***

The State finds support for its "equal application" theory in the decision of the Court in *Pace v. Alabama* *** (1882). In that case, the Court upheld a conviction under an Alabama statute forbidding adultery or fornication between a white person and a Negro which imposed a greater penalty than that of a statute proscribing similar conduct by members of the same race. The Court reasoned that the statute could not be said to discriminate against Negroes because the punishment for each participant in the offense was the same. However, as recently as the 1964 Term, in rejecting the reasoning of that case, we stated "*Pace* represents a limited view of the Equal Protection Clause which has not withstood analysis in the subsequent decisions of this Court." *** As we there demonstrated, the Equal Protection Clause requires the consideration of whether the classifications drawn by any statute constitute an arbitrary and invidious discrimination. The clear and central purpose of the Fourteenth Amendment was to eliminate all official state sources of invidious racial discrimination in the States. ***

There can be no question but that Virginia's miscegenation statutes rest solely upon distinctions drawn according to race. The statutes proscribe generally accepted conduct if engaged in by members of different races. Over the years, this Court has consistently repudiated "[d]istinctions between citizens solely because of their ancestry" as being "odious to a free people whose institutions are founded upon the doctrine of equality." *** At the very least, the Equal Protection Clause demands that racial classifications, especially suspect in criminal statutes, be subjected to the "most rigid scrutiny," *** and, if they are ever to be upheld, they must be shown to be necessary to the accomplishment of some permissible state objective, independent of the racial discrimination which it was the object of the Fourteenth Amendment to eliminate. Indeed, two members of this Court have already stated that they "cannot conceive of a valid legislative purpose . . . which makes the color of a person's skin the test of whether his conduct is a criminal offense." ***

There is patently no legitimate overriding purpose independent of invidious racial discrimination which justifies this classification. The fact that Virginia only prohibits interracial marriages involving white persons demonstrates that the racial classifications must stand on their own justification, as measures designed to maintain White Supremacy. We have consistently denied the constitutionality of measures which restrict the rights of citizens on account of race. There can be no doubt that restricting the freedom to marry solely because of racial classification violates the central meaning of the Equal Protection Clause. . . .

These convictions must be reversed. It is so ordered.

Mr. Justice Stewart, concurring.

I have previously expressed the belief that "it is simply not possible for a state law to be valid under our Constitution which makes the criminality of an act depend upon the race of the actor." *** Because I adhere to that belief, I concur in the judgment of the Court.

Swann v. Charlotte-Mecklenburg Board of Education

402 U.S. 1; 91 S. Ct. 1267; 28 L. Ed. 2d 554 (1971)
Vote: 9-0

In Charlotte-Mecklenburg, North Carolina, the nation's forty-third largest school district, the board of education devised a desegregation plan in order to comply with the Supreme Court's ruling in the Brown *case. The U.S. district court, however, rejected the board's plan as not producing sufficient racial integration at the elementary level. Instead, the district court accepted a plan prepared by an outside expert that called for, among other things, racial quotas, altering attendance zones, and busing of students. In this case, the Supreme Court considers the permissibility of such measures.*

Mr. Chief Justice Burger delivered the opinion of the Court, saying in part:

. . . The central issue in this case is that of student assignment, and there are essentially four problem areas: (1) to what extent racial balance or racial quotas may be used as an implement in a remedial order to correct a previously segregated system; (2) whether every all-Negro and all-white school must be eliminated as an indispensable part of a remedial process of desegregation; (3) what are the limits, if any, on the rearrangement of school districts and attendance zones, as a remedial measure; and (4) what are the limits, if any, on the use of transportation facilities to correct state-enforced racial school segregation.

(1) Racial Balance or Racial Quotas.

The constant theme and thrust of every holding from *Brown* I (1954) to date is that state-enforced separation of races in public schools is discrimination that violates the Equal Protection clause. The remedy commanded was to dismantle dual school systems.

We are concerned in these cases with the elimination of the discrimination inherent in the dual school systems, not with myriad factors of human existence which can cause discrimination in a multitude of ways on racial, religious, or ethnic grounds. The target of the cases from *Brown* I to the present was the dual school system. The elimination of racial discrimination in public schools is a large task and one that should not be retarded by efforts to achieve broader purposes lying beyond the jurisdiction of school authorities. One vehicle can carry only a limited amount of baggage. . . .

Our objective in dealing with the issues presented by these cases is to see that school authorities exclude no pupil or a racial minority from any school, directly or indirectly, on account of race; it does not and cannot embrace all the problems of racial prejudice, even when those problems contribute to disproportionate racial concentrations in some schools.

In this case it is urged that the District Court has imposed a racial balance requirement of 71%-29% on individual schools. . . . If we were to read the holding of the District Court to require, as a matter of substantive constitutional right, any particular degree of racial balance or mixing, that approach would be disapproved and we would be obliged to reverse. The constitutional command to desegregate schools does not mean that every school in every community must always reflect the racial composition of the school system as a whole. . . .

. . . The use made of mathematical ratios was no more than a starting point in the process of shaping a remedy, rather than an inflexible requirement. From that starting point the District Court proceeded to frame a decree that was within its discretionary powers, an equitable remedy for the particular circumstances. As we said in *Green* [v. *County School Board*] a school authority's remedial plan or a district court's remedial decree is to be judged by its effectiveness. Awareness of the racial composition of the whole school system is likely to be a useful starting point in shaping a remedy to correct past constitutional violations. In sum, the very limited use made of mathematical ratios was within the equitable remedial discretion of the District Court.

(2) One-Race Schools.

The record in this case reveals the familiar phenomenon that in metropolitan areas minority groups are often found concentrated in one part of the city. In some circumstances certain schools may remain all or largely of one race until new schools can be provided or neighborhood patterns change. Schools all or predominately of one race in a district of mixed population will require close scrutiny to determine that school assignments are not part of state-enforced segregation.

In light of the above, it should be clear that the existence of some small number of one-race, or virtually one-race, schools within a district is not in and of itself the mark of a system which still practices segregation by a law. . . . Where the school authority's proposed plan for conversion from a dual to a unitary system contemplates the continued existence of some schools that are all or predominately of one race, they have the burden of showing that such school assignments are genuinely nondiscriminatory. The court should scrutinize such schools, and the burden upon the school authorities will be to satisfy the court that their racial composition is not the result of present or past discriminatory action on their part.

An optional minority-to-minority transfer provision has long been recognized as a useful part of every desegregation plan. Provision for optional transfer of those in the majority racial group of a particular school to other schools where they will be in the minority is an indispensable remedy for those students willing to transfer to other schools in order to lessen the impact on them of the state-imposed stigma of segregation. In order to be effective, such a transfer arrangement must grant the transferring student free transportation and space must be made available in the school to which he desires to move. *** The court orders in this and the companion *Davis* case now provide such an option.

(3) Remedial Altering of Attendance Zones.

The maps submitted in these cases graphically demonstrate that one of the principal tools employed by school planners and by courts to break up the dual school system has been a frank—and sometimes drastic—gerrymandering of school districts and attendance zones. An additional step was pairing, "clustering," or "grouping" of schools with attendance assignments made deliberately to accomplish the transfer of Negro students out of formerly segregated Negro schools and transfer of white students to formerly all-Negro schools. More often than not, these zones are neither compact nor contiguous; indeed they may be on opposite ends of the city. As in interim corrective measure, this cannot be said to be beyond the broad remedial powers of a court.

Absent a constitutional violation there would be no basis for judicially ordering assignment of students on a racial basis. All things being equal, with no history of discrimination, it might well be desirable to assign pupils to schools nearest their homes. But all things are not equal in a system that has been deliberately constructed and maintained to enforce racial segregation. . . .

No fixed or even substantially fixed guidelines can be established as to how far a court can go, but it must be recognized that there are limits. The objective is to dismantle the dual school system. "Racially neutral" assignment plans proposed by school authorities to a district court may be inadequate; such plans may fail to counteract the continuing effects of past school segregation resulting from discriminatory location of school sites or distortion of school size in order to achieve or maintain an artificial racial separation. When school authorities present a district court with a "loaded game board," affirmative action in the form of remedial altering of attendance zones is proper to achieve truly nondiscriminatory assignments. In short, an assignment plan is not acceptable simply because it appears to be neutral. . . .

We hold that the pairing and grouping of noncontiguous school zones is a permissible tool and such action is to be considered in light of the objectives sought. . . .

(4) Transportation of Students.

The scope of permissible transportation of students as an implement of a remedial decree has never been defined by this Court and by the very nature of the problem it cannot be defined with precision. . . .

The importance of bus transportation as a normal and accepted tool of educational policy is readily discernible in this and the companion case. The Charlotte school authorities did not purport to assign students on the basis of geographically drawn zones until 1965 and then they allowed almost unlimited transfer privileges. The District Court's conclusion that assignment of children to the school nearest their home serving their grade would not produce an effective dismantling of the dual system is supported by the record.

Thus the remedial techniques used in the District Court's order were within that court's power to provide equitable relief; implementation of the decree is well within the capacity of the school authority.

The decree provided that the buses used to implement the plan would operate on direct routes. Students would be picked up at schools near their homes and transported to the schools they were to attend. The trips for elementary school pupils average about seven miles and the District Court found that they would take "not over 35 minutes at the most." This system compares favorably with the transportation plan previously operated in Charlotte under which each day 23,600 students on all grade levels were transported an average of 15 miles one way for an average trip requiring over an hour. In these circumstances, we find no basis for holding that the local school authorities may not be required to employ bus transportation as one tool of school desegregation. Desegregation plans cannot be limited to the walk-in school. . . .

. . . At some point, these school authorities and others like them should have achieved full compliance with this Court's decision in *Brown* I. The systems will then be "unitary" in the sense required by our decisions in *Green [v. County School Board]* and *Alexander [v. Holmes County Board of Education]*.

It does not follow that the communities served by such systems will remain demographically stable, for in a growing, mobile society, few will do so. Neither school authorities nor district courts are constitutionally required to make year-by-year adjustments of the racial composition of student bodies once the affirmative duty to desegregate has been accomplished and racial discrimination through official action is eliminated from the system. This does not mean that federal courts are without power to deal with future problems; but in the absence of a showing that either the school authorities or some other agency of the State has deliberately attempted to fix or alter demographic patterns to affect the racial composition of the schools, further intervention by a district court should not be necessary. . . .

It is so ordered.

Milliken v. Bradley

418 U.S. 717; 94 S. Ct. 3112; 41 L. Ed. 2d 1069 (1974)

Vote: 5-4

Ronald and Richard Bradley, along with several other Detroit public school students and the National Association for the Advancement of Colored People (NAACP), brought a class action against Michigan Governor William Milliken and other state and city officials alleging racial segregation in the past and present operation of the Detroit school system, resulting primarily from the drawing of school district and attendance zone boundaries. This challenge was sustained by the U.S. District Court for the Eastern District of Michigan, which ordered the Detroit School Board to formulate desegregation plans for the city school system and ordered state officials to submit desegregation plans encompassing the three-county metropolitan area, despite the fact that the eighty-five outlying school districts in these counties were not parties to the action and there was no claim that they had committed constitutional violations. Outlying school districts were later allowed to intervene in the lawsuit but were not permitted to assert any claim or defense on issues previously adjudicated or to reopen any issue previously decided. They were allowed merely to advise the court as to the propriety of a metropolitan plan and to submit any objections, modifications, or alternatives to such a plan. The district court then ruled that it was proper to consider metropolitan plans, that Detroit-only plans submitted by the board and others were inadequate to accomplish desegregation, and that therefore it would seek a solution beyond the limits of the Detroit School District. It concluded that "(s)chool district lines are simply matters of political convenience and may not be used to deny constitutional rights." Without having evidence that the suburban school districts had committed acts of de jure segregation, the district court appointed a panel to submit a plan for the Detroit schools that would encompass an entire designated desegregation area consisting of fifty-three of the eighty-five suburban school districts plus Detroit and ordered the Detroit School Board to acquire at least 295 school buses to provide transportation under an interim plan to be developed for the 1972–73 school year.

The U.S. Court of Appeals for the Sixth Circuit affirmed as to the findings of de jure segregation in the Detroit school district and the propriety and necessity of the metropolitan desegregation plan, concluding that the state was responsible for the segregation in Detroit and had authority to control local school districts. However, the Court remanded the case for more extensive participation by the affected suburban districts. It also vacated the district court's order as to acquisition of school buses, subject to that court's right to consider reimposing the order at an appropriate time. Governor Milliken and other state officials sought Supreme Court review on certiorari.

Mr. Chief Justice Burger delivered the opinion of the Court.

We granted *certiorari* in these consolidated cases to determine whether a federal court may impose a multidistrict, areawide remedy to a single district *de jure* segregation problem absent any finding that the other included school districts have failed to operate unitary school systems within their districts, absent any claim or finding that the boundary lines of any affected school district were established with the purpose of fostering racial segregation in public schools, absent any finding that the included districts committed acts which effected segregation within the other districts, and absent a meaningful opportunity for the included neighboring school districts to present evidence or be heard on the propriety of a multidistrict remedy or on the question of constitutional violations by those neighboring districts. . . .

Viewing the record as a whole, it seems clear that the District Court and the Court of Appeals shifted the primary focus from a Detroit remedy to the metropolitan area only because of their conclusion that total desegregation of Detroit would not produce the racial balance which they perceived as desirable. Both courts proceeded on an assumption that the Detroit schools could not be truly desegregated—in their view of what constituted desegregation—unless the racial composition of the student body of each school substantially reflected the racial composition of the population of the metropolitan areas as a whole. The metropolitan area was then defined as Detroit plus 53 of the outlying school districts. . . .

The record before us, voluminous as it is, contains evidence of *de jure* segregated conditions only in the Detroit schools; indeed, that was the theory on which the litigation was initially based and on which the District Court took evidence. *** With no showing of significant violation by the 53 outlying school districts and no evidence of any interdistrict violation or effect, the court went beyond the original theory of the case as framed by the pleadings and mandated a metropolitan area remedy. To approve the remedy ordered by the court would impose on the outlying districts, not shown to have committed any constitutional violation, a wholly impermissible remedy based on a standard not hinted at in *Brown* I and II or any holding of this Court.

In dissent Mr. Justice White and Mr. Justice Marshall undertake to demonstrate that agencies having statewide authority participated in maintaining the dual school system found to exist in Detroit. They are apparently of the view that once such participation is shown, the District Court should have a relatively free hand to reconstruct school districts outside of Detroit in fashioning relief. Our assumption . . . that state agencies did participate in the maintenance of the Detroit system, should make it clear that it is not on this point that we part company. The difference between us arises instead from established doctrine laid down by our cases. *Brown, Green, Swann,* . . . [etc.] . . . each addressed the issue of constitutional wrong in terms of an established geographic and administrative school system populated by both Negro and White children. In such a context, terms such as "unitary" and "dual" systems, and "racially identifiable schools," have meaning, and the necessary federal authority to remedy the constitutional wrong is firmly established. But the remedy is necessarily designed, as all remedies are, to restore the victims of discriminatory conduct to the position they would have occupied in the absence of such conduct. Disparate treatment of White and Negro students occurred within the Detroit school system, and not elsewhere, and on this record the remedy must be limited to that system. ***

The constitutional right of the Negro respondents residing in Detroit is to attend a unitary school system in that district. Unless petitioners drew the district lines in a discriminatory fashion, or arranged for White students residing in the Detroit district to attend schools in Oakland and Macomb Counties, they were under no constitutional duty to make provisions for Negro students to do so. The view of the dissenters, that the existence of a dual system in Detroit can be made the basis for a decree requiring cross-district transportation of pupils cannot be supported on the grounds that it represents merely the devising of a suitably flexible remedy for the violation of rights already established by our prior decisions. It can be supported only by drastic expansion of the constitutional right itself, an expansion without any support in either constitutional principle or precedent. . . .

. . . Accepting . . . the correctness of . . . [the lower courts'] finding of State responsibility for the segregated conditions within the city of Detroit, it does not follow that an interdistrict remedy is constitutionally justified or required. With a single exception, . . . there has been no showing that either the State or any of the 85 outlying districts engaged in activity that had a cross-district effect. The boundaries of the Detroit School District, which are coterminous with the boundaries of the city of Detroit, were established over a century ago by neutral legislation when the city was incorporated; there is no evidence in the record, nor is there any suggestion by the respondents, that either the original boundaries of the Detroit School District, or any other school district in Michigan, were established for the purpose of creating, maintaining or perpetuating segregation of races. There is no claim and there is no evidence hinting that petitioners and their predecessors, or the 40-odd other school districts in the tri-county area—but outside the District Court's "desegregation area"—have ever maintained or operated anything but unitary school systems. Unitary school systems have been required for more than a century by the Michigan Constitution as implemented by state law. Where the schools of only one district have been affected, there is no constitutional power in the courts to decree relief balancing the racial composition of that district's schools with those of the surrounding districts. . . .

We conclude that the relief ordered by the District Court and affirmed by the Court of Appeals was based upon an erroneous standard and was unsupported by . . . evidence that acts of the outlying districts affected the discrimination found to exist in the schools of Detroit. Accordingly, the judgment of the Court of Appeals is vacated and the case is remanded for further proceedings consistent with this opinion leading to prompt formulation of a decree directed to eliminating the segregation found to exist in Detroit city schools, a remedy which has been delayed since 1970.

Reversed and remanded.

Mr. Justice Stewart, concurring. . . .

Mr. Justice Douglas dissenting. . . .

Mr. Justice White, with whom *Mr. Justice Douglas, Mr. Justice Brennan,* and *Mr. Justice Marshall* join, dissenting.

. . . Regretfully, and for several reasons, I can join neither the Court's judgment nor its opinion. The core of my disagreement is that deliberate acts of segregation and their consequences will go unremedied, not because a remedy would be infeasible or unreasonable in terms of the usual criteria governing school desegregation cases, but because an effective remedy would cause what the Court considers to be undue administrative inconvenience to the State. The result is that the State of Michigan, the entity at which the Fourteenth Amendment is directed, has successfully insulated itself from its duty to provide effective desegregation remedies by vesting sufficient power over its public schools in its local school districts. If this is the case in Michigan, it will be the case in most States. . . .

I am surprised that the Court, sitting at this distance from the State of Michigan, claims better insight than the Court of Appeals and the District Court as to whether an interdistrict remedy for equal protection violations practiced by the State of Michigan would involve undue difficulties for the State in the management of its public schools. In the area of what constitutes an acceptable desegregation plan, "we must of necessity rely to a large extent, as this Court has for more than 16 years, on the informed judg-

ment of the district courts in the first instance and on courts of appeals." *** Obviously, whatever difficulties there might be, they are surmountable; for the Court itself concedes that had there been sufficient evidence of an interdistrict violation, the District Court could have fashioned a single remedy for the districts implicated rather than different remedy for each district in which the violation had occurred or had an impact.

I am even more mystified how the Court can ignore the legal reality that the constitutional violations, even if occurring locally, were committed by governmental entities for which the State is responsible and that it is the State that must respond to the command of the Fourteenth Amendment. An interdistrict remedy for the infringements that occurred in this case is well within the confines and powers of the State, which is the governmental entity ultimately responsible for desegregation of its schools. . . .

Finally, I remain wholly unpersuaded by the Court's assertion that "the remedy is necessarily designed, as all remedies are, to restore the victims of discriminatory conduct to the position they would have occupied in the absence of such conduct." *** In the first place, under this premise the court's judgment is itself infirm; for had the Detroit school system not followed an official policy of segregation throughout the 1950's and 1960's, Negroes and whites would have been going to school together. There would have been no, or at least not as many, recognizable Negro schools and no, or at least not as many, white schools, but "just schools," and neither Negroes nor whites would have suffered from the effects of segregated education, with all its shortcomings. Surely the Court's remedy will not restore to the Negro community, stigmatized as it was by the dual school system, what it would have enjoyed over all or most of this period if the remedy is confined to present-day Detroit; for the maximum remedy available with that area will leave many of the schools almost totally black, and the system itself will be predominantly black and will become increasingly so. Moreover, when a State has engaged in acts of official segregation over a lengthy period of time, as in the case before us, it is unrealistic to suppose that the children who were victims of the State's unconstitutional conduct could now be provided the benefits of which they were wrongfully deprived. Nor can the benefits which accrue to school systems in which school children have not been officially segregated, and to the communities supporting such school systems, be fully and immediately restored after a substantial period of unlawful segregation. The education of children of different races in a desegregated environment has unhappily been lost along with the social, economic, and political advantages which accompany a desegregated school system as compared with an unconstitutionally segregated system. It is for these reasons that the Court has consistently followed the course of requiring the effects of past official segregation to be eliminated "root and branch" by imposing, in the present, the duty to provide a remedy which will achieve "the greatest possible degree of actual desegregation, taking into account the practicalities of the situation." It is also for these reasons that once a constitutional violation has been found, the District Judge obligated to provide such a remedy "will thus necessarily be concerned with the eliminating of one-race schools." These concerns were properly taken into account by the District Judge in this case. Confining the remedy to the boundaries of the Detroit district is quite unrelated either to the goal of achieving maximum desegregation or to those intensely practical considerations, such as the extent and expense of transportation, that have imposed limits on remedies in cases such as this. The Court's remedy, in the end, is essentially arbitrary and will leave serious violations of the Constitution substantially unremedied. . . .

Mr. Justice Marshall, with whom **Mr. Justice Douglas, Mr. Justice Brennan,** and **Mr. Justice White** join, dissenting.

. . . Nowhere in the court's opinion does the majority confront, let alone respond to, the District Court's conclusion that a remedy limited to the city of Detroit would not effectively desegregate the Detroit city schools. . . .

. . . The rippling effects on residential patterns caused by purposeful acts of segregation do not automatically subside at the school district border. With rare exceptions, these effects naturally spread through all the residential neighborhoods within a metropolitan area. . . .

The State must also bear part of the blame for the white flight to the suburbs which would be forthcoming from a Detroit-only decree and would render such a remedy ineffective. Having created a system where whites and Negroes were intentionally kept apart so that they could not become accustomed to learning together, the State is responsible for the fact that many whites will react to the dismantling of that segregated system by attempting to flee to the suburbs. Indeed, by limiting the District Court to a Detroit-only remedy and allowing that flight to the suburbs to succeed, the Court today allows the State to profit from its own wrong and to perpetuate for years to come the separation of the races it achieved in the past by purposeful state action. . . .

One final set of problems remains to be considered. We recognized in *Brown* II, and have reemphasized ever since, that in fashioning relief in desegregation cases, "the courts will be guided by equitable principles. Traditionally equity has been characterized by a practical flexibility in shaping its remedies and by a facility for adjusting and reconciling public and private needs." ***

Though not resting its holding on this point, the majority suggests that various equitable considerations militate against inter-district relief. The Court refers to, for example, financing and administrative problems, the logistical problems attending large scale transportation of students, and the prospect of the District Court's becoming a "*de facto* 'legislative authority'" and "'school superintendent' for the entire area." *** The entangling web of problems woven by the Court, however, appears on further consideration to be constructed of the flimsiest of threads. . . .

Some disruption, of course, is the inevitable product of any desegregation decree, whether it operates within one district or on an interdistrict basis. . . .

Desegregation is not and was never expected to be an easy task. Racial attitudes ingrained in our Nation's childhood and adolescence are not quickly thrown aside in its middle years. But just as the inconvenience of some cannot be allowed to stand in the way of the rights of others, so public opposition, no matter how strident, cannot be permitted to divert this Court from the enforcement of the constitutional principles at issue in this case. Today's holding, I fear, is more a reflection of a perceived public mood that we have gone far enough in enforcing the Constitution's guarantee of equal justice than it is the product of neutral principles of law. In the short run, it may seem to be the easier course to allow our great metropolitan areas to be divided up each into two cities—one white, the other black—but it is a course, I predict, our people will ultimately regret. I dissent.

Fullilove v. Klutznick

448 U.S. 448; 100 S. Ct. 2758; 65 L. Ed. 2d 902 (1980)
Vote: 6-3

Mr. Chief Justice Burger announced the judgment of the Court and delivered an opinion in which *Mr. Justice White* and *Mr. Justice Powell* joined.

In May 1977, Congress enacted the Public Works Employment Act of 1977, *** which amended the Local Public Works Capital Development and Investment Act of 1976. *** The 1977 amendments authorized an additional $4 billion appropriation for federal grants to be made . . . to state and local governmental entities for use in local public works projects. . . . Section 103(f)(2) of the 1977 Act, referred to as the "minority business enterprise" or "MBE" provision, requires that:

[N]o grant shall be made under this Act for any local public works project unless the applicant gives satisfactory assurance to the Secretary that at least 10 per centum of the amount of each grant shall be expended for minority business enterprises. For purposes of this paragraph, the term "minority business enterprise" means a business at least 50 per centum of which is owned by minority group members. . . . For the purposes of the preceding sentence minority group members are citizens of the United States who are Negroes, Spanish speaking, Orientals, Indians, Eskimos, and Aleuts. . . .

The 1976 Act was intended as a short-term measure to alleviate the problem of national unemployment and to stimulate the national economy by assisting state and local governments to build needed public facilities. . . . The 1977 Act . . . retained the underlying objective to direct funds into areas of high unemployment. The 1977 Act also added new restrictions on applicants seeking to qualify for federal grants; among these was the MBE provision. . . .

. . . A program that employs racial or ethnic criteria, even in a remedial context, calls for close exam-

ination; yet we are bound to approach our task with appropriate deference to the Congress, a co-equal branch. . . .

The clear objective of the MBE provision is disclosed by our . . . review of its legislative and administrative background. The program was designed to ensure that, to the extent federal funds were granted under the Public Works Employment Act of 1977, grantees who elect to participate would not employ procurement practices that Congress had decided might result in perpetuation of the effects of prior discrimination which had impaired or foreclosed access by minority businesses to public contracting opportunities. The MBE program does not mandate the allocation of federal funds according to inflexible percentages solely based on race or ethnicity.

In enacting the MBE provision, it is clear that Congress employed an amalgam of its specifically delegated powers. The Public Works Employment Act of 1977, by its very nature, is primarily an exercise of the Spending Power. . . .

. . . The legislative history of the MBE provision shows that there was a rational basis for Congress to conclude that the subcontracting practices of prime contractors could perpetuate the prevailing impaired access by minority businesses to public contracting opportunities, and that this inequity has an effect on interstate commerce. Thus Congress could take necessary and proper action to remedy the situation. . . .

In certain contexts, there are limitations on the reach of the Commerce Power to regulate the actions of state and local governments. *** To avoid such complications, we look to Section 5 of the Fourteenth Amendment for the power to regulate the procurement practices of state and local grantees of federal funds. *** A review of our cases persuades us that the objectives of the MBE program are within the power of Congress under Section 5 "to enforce, by appropriate legislation," the equal protection guarantees of the Fourteenth Amendment....

With respect to the MBE provision, Congress had abundant evidence from which it could conclude that minority businesses have been denied effective participation in public contracting opportunities by procurement practices that perpetuated the effects of prior discrimination.... Although much of this history related to the experience of minority businesses in the area of federal procurement, there was direct evidence before the Congress that this pattern of disadvantage and discrimination existed with respect to state and local construction contracting as well. In relation to the MBE provision, Congress acted within its competence to determine that the problem was national in scope....

We now turn to the question whether, as a *means* to accomplish these plainly constitutional objectives, Congress may use racial and ethnic criteria, in this limited way, as a condition attached to a federal grant. We are mindful that "[i]n no matter should we pay more deference to the opinion of Congress than in its choice of instrumentalities to perform a function that is within its power." *** However, Congress may employ racial or ethnic classifications in exercising its spending or other legislative powers only if those classifications do not violate the equal protection component of the Due Process Clause of the Fifth Amendment. We recognize the need for careful judicial evaluation to assure that any congressional program that employs racial or ethnic criteria to accomplish the objective of remedying the present effects of past discrimination is narrowly tailored to the achievement of that goal....

Our review of the regulations and guidelines governing administration of the MBE provision reveals that Congress enacted the program as a strictly remedial measure; moreover, it is a remedy that functions prospectively, in the manner of an injunctive decree....

As a threshold matter, we reject the contention that in the remedial context the Congress must act in a wholly "colorblind" fashion. In *Swann v. Charlotte-Mecklenburg Board of Education*, *** we rejected this argument in considering a court-formulated school desegregation remedy on the basis that examination of the racial composition of student bodies was an unavoidable starting point and that racially based attendance assignments were permissible so long as no absolute racial balance of each school was required....

Here we deal...not with the limited remedial powers of a federal court...but with the broad remedial powers of Congress. It is fundamental that in no organ of government, state or federal, does there repose a more comprehensive remedial power than in the Congress, expressly charged by the Constitution with competence and authority to enforce equal protection guarantees. Congress not only may induce voluntary action to assure compliance with existing federal statutory or constitutional antidiscrimination provisions, but also, where Congress has authority to declare certain conduct unlawful, it may, as here, authorize and induce state action to avoid such conduct. ***

A more specific challenge to the MBE program is the charge that it impermissibly deprives nonminority businesses of access to at least some portion of the government contracting opportunities generated by the Act. It must be conceded that by its objective of remedying the historical impairment of access, the MBE provision can have the effect of awarding some contracts to MBE's which otherwise might be awarded to other businesses, who may themselves be innocent of any prior discriminatory actions. Failure of nonminority firms to receive certain contracts is, of course, an incidental consequence of the program, not part of its objective....

It is not a constitutional defect in this program that it may disappoint the expectations of nonminority firms. Where effectuating a limited and properly tailored remedy to cure the effects of prior discrimination, such "a sharing of the burden" by innocent parties is not impermissible. *** The actual "burden" shouldered by nonminority firms is relatively light in this connection when we consider the scope of this public works program as compared with overall construction contracting opportunities. Moreover, although we may assume that the complaining parties are innocent of any discriminatory conduct, it was within congressional power to act on the assumption that in the past some nonminority businesses may have reaped competitive benefit over the years from the virtual exclusion of minority firms from these contracting opportunities. . . .

. . . The history of governmental tolerance of practices using racial or ethnic criteria for the purpose or with the effect of imposing an invidious discrimination must alert us to the deleterious effects of even benign racial or ethnic classifications when they stray from narrow remedial justifications. Even in the context of a facial challenge such as is presented in this case, the MBE provision cannot pass muster unless, with due account for its administrative program, it provides a reasonable assurance that application of racial or ethnic criteria will be limited to accomplishing the remedial objectives of Congress and that misapplications of the program will be promptly and adequately remedied administratively. . . .

The administrative program contains measures to effectuate the congressional objective of assuring legitimate participation by disadvantaged MBE's. Administrative definition has tightened some less definite aspects of the statutory identification of the minority groups encompassed by the program. There is administrative scrutiny to identify and eliminate from participation in the program MBE's who are not "*bona-fide*" within the regulations and guidelines; for example, spurious minority-front entities can be exposed. A significant aspect of this surveillance is the complaint procedure available for reporting "unjust participation by an enterprise or individuals in the MBE program." *** And even as to specific contract awards, waiver is available to avoid dealing with an MBE who is attempting to exploit the remedial aspects of the program by charging an unreasonable price, i.e., a price not attributable to the present effects of past discrimination. *** We must assume that Congress intended close scrutiny of false claims and prompt action on them. . . .

Any preference based on racial or ethnic criteria must necessarily receive a most searching examination to make sure that it does not conflict with constitutional guarantees. This case is one which requires, and which has received, that kind of examination. . . . The MBE provision of the Public Works Employment Act of 1977 does not violate the Constitution.

Mr. Justice Powell, concurring.

Although I would place greater emphasis than the Chief Justice on the need to articulate judicial standards of review in conventional terms, I view his opinion announcing the judgment as substantially in accord with my own views. Accordingly, I join that opinion and write separately to apply the analysis set forth by my opinion in *University of California v. Bakke.* *** . . .

A race-conscious remedy should not be approved without consideration of an additional crucial factor—the effect of the set-aside upon innocent third parties. *** In this case, the petitioners contend with some force that they have been asked to bear the burden of the set-aside even though they are innocent of wrongdoing. I do not believe, however, that their burden is so great that the set-aside must be disapproved. As noted above, Congress knew that minority contractors were receiving only 1% of federal contracts at the time the set-aside was enacted. The [1977 Act] appropriated $4 billion for public work projects, of which it could be expected that approximately $400 million would go to minority contractors. The Court of Appeals calculated that the set-aside would reserve about .25% of all the funds expended yearly on construction work in the United States for approximately 4% of the Nation's contractors who are members of a minority group. *** The set-aside would have no effect on the ability of the remaining 96% of contractors to compete for 99.75% of construction funds. In my view, the effect of the set-aside is limited and so widely dispersed that its use is consistent with fundamental fairness.

Consideration of these factors persuades me that the set-aside is a reasonably necessary means of furthering the compelling governmental interest in redressing the discrimination that affects minority contractors. Any marginal unfairness to innocent nonminority contractors is not sufficiently significant—or sufficiently identifiable—to outweigh the governmental interest served . . . When Congress acts to remedy identified discrimination, it may exercise discretion in choosing a remedy that is reasonably necessary to accomplish its purpose. Whatever the exact breadth of that discretion, I believe that it encompasses the selection of the set-aside in this case. . . .

Mr. Justice Marshall, with whom **Mr. Justice Brennan** and **Mr. Justice Blackmun** join, concurring in the judgment.

My resolution of the constitutional issue in this case is governed by the separate opinion I coauthored in *University of California Regents v. Bakke.* ***

In *Bakke,* I joined my Brothers Brennan, White, and Blackmun in articulating the view that "racial classifications are not *per se* invalid under the [Equal Protection Clause of] the Fourteenth Amendment." *** We acknowledged that "a government practice or statute which . . . contains 'suspect classifications' is to be subjected to 'strict scrutiny' and can be justified only if it furthers a compelling government purpose and, even then, only if no less restrictive alternative is available." *** Thus, we reiterated the traditional view that racial classifications are prohibited if they are irrelevant. *** In addition, we firmly adhered to "the cardinal principle that racial classifications that stigmatize—because they are drawn on the presumption that one race is inferior to another or because they put the weight of government behind racial hatred and separatism—are invalid without more." ***

We recognized, however, that these principles outlawing the irrelevant or pernicious use of race were inapposite to racial classifications that provide benefits to minorities for the purpose of remedying the present effects of past racial discrimination. Such classifications may disadvantage some whites, but whites as a class lack the " 'traditional indicia of suspectness: the class is not saddled with such disabilities, or subjected to such a history of purposeful unequal treatment, or relegated to such a position of political powerlessness as to command extraordinary protection from the majoritarian political process.' " *** Because the consideration of race is relevant to remedying the continuing effects of past racial discrimination, and because governmental programs employing racial classifications for remedial purposes can be crafted to avoid stigmatization, we concluded that such programs should not be subjected to conventional "strict scrutiny"—scrutiny that is strict in theory, but fatal in fact. ***

Nor did we determine that such programs should be analyzed under the minimally rigorous rational-basis standard of review. *** We recognized that race has often been used to stigmatize politically powerless segments of society, and that efforts to ameliorate the effects of past discrimination could be based on paternalistic stereotyping, not on a careful consideration of modern social conditions. In addition, we acknowledged that governmental classification on the immutable characteristic of race runs counter to the deep national belief that state-sanctioned benefits and burdens should bear some relationship to individual merit and responsibility. ***

We concluded, therefore, that because a racial classification ostensibly designed for remedial purposes is susceptible to misuse, it may be justified only by showing "an important and articulated purpose for its use." *** "In addition any statute must be stricken that stigmatizes any group or that singles out those least well represented in the political process to bear the brunt of a benign program." *** In our view, then, the proper inquiry is whether racial classifications designed to further remedial purposes serve important governmental objectives and are substantially related to achievement of those objectives. ***

Judged under this standard, the 10% minority set-aside provision at issue in this case is plainly constitutional. Indeed, the question is not even a close one. . . .

Mr. Justice Stewart, with whom **Mr. Justice Rehnquist** joins, dissenting.

"Our Constitution is color-blind, and neither knows nor tolerates classes among citizens. . . . The law regards man as man, and takes no account of his surroundings or of his color . . ." Those words were written by a Member of this Court 84 years ago. *Plessy v. Ferguson* *** (Harlan, J., dissenting). His colleagues disagreed with him, and held that a statute that required the separation of people on the basis of their race was constitutionally valid because it was a "reasonable" exercise of legislative power and had been "enacted in good faith for the promotion [of] the public good. . . ." *** Today, the Court upholds a statute that accords a preference to citizens who are "Negroes, Spanish-speaking, Orientals, Indians, Eskimos, and Aleuts," for much the same reasons. I think today's decision is wrong for the same reason that *Plessy v. Ferguson* was wrong, and I respectfully dissent.

The equal protection standard of the Constitution has one clear and central meaning—it absolutely prohibits invidious discrimination by government. That standard must be met by every State under the Equal Protection Clause of the Fourteenth Amendment. *** And that standard must be met by the United States itself under the Due Process Clause of the Fifth Amendment. Under our Constitution, any official action that treats a person differently on account of his race or ethnic origin is inherently suspect and presumptively invalid. *** Under our Constitution, the government may never act to the detriment of a person solely because of that person's race.... In short, racial discrimination is by definition invidious discrimination.

The rule cannot be any different when the persons injured by a racially biased law are not members of a racial minority. The guarantee of equal protection is "universal in [its] application, to all persons ... without regard to any differences of race, of color, or of nationality." *** The command of the equal protection guarantee is simple but unequivocal: In the words of the Fourteenth Amendment, "No State shall ... deny to *any* person ... the equal protection of the laws." Nothing in this language singles out some "persons" for more "equal" treatment than others. Rather, as the Court made clear in *Shelley v. Kraemer,* *** the benefits afforded by the Equal Protection Clause "are, by its terms, guaranteed to the individual. [They] are personal rights." From the perspective of a person detrimentally affected by a racially discriminatory law, the arbitrariness and unfairness is entirely the same, whatever his skin color and whatever the law's purpose, be it purportedly "for the promotion of the public good" or otherwise....

The Court's attempt to characterize the [1977 Act] as a proper remedial measure to counteract the effects of past or present racial discrimination is remarkably unconvincing. The Legislative Branch of government is not a court of equity. It has neither the dispassionate objectivity nor the flexibility that are needed to mold a race-conscious remedy around the single objective of eliminating the effects of past or present discrimination....

... Certainly, nothing in the Constitution gives Congress any greater authority to impose detriments on the basis of race than is afforded the Judicial Branch. And a judicial decree that imposes burdens on the basis of race can be upheld only where its sole purpose is to eradicate the actual effects of illegal race discrimination. *** ...

The Fourteenth Amendment was adopted to ensure that every person must be treated equally by each State regardless of the color of his skin.... Today, the Court derails this achievement and places its imprimatur on the creation once again by government of privileges based on birth.

The Court, moreover, takes this drastic step without, in my opinion, seriously considering the ramifications of its decision. Laws that operate on the basis of race require definitions of race. Because of the Court's decision today, our statute books will once again have to contain laws that reflect the odious practice of delineating the qualities that make one person a Negro and make another white. Moreover, racial discrimination, even "good faith" racial discrimination, is inevitably a two-edged sword. "[P]referential programs may only reinforce common stereotypes holding that certain groups are unable to achieve success without special protection based on a factor having no relationship to individual worth." *** Most importantly, by making race a relevant criterion once again in its own affairs, the Government implicitly teaches the public that the apportionment of rewards and penalties can legitimately be made according to race—rather than according to merit or ability—and that people can, and perhaps should, view themselves and others in terms of their racial characteristics. Notions of "racial entitlement" will be fostered, and private discrimination will necessarily be encouraged. ***

There are those who think that we need a new Constitution, and their views may someday prevail. But under the Constitution we have, one practice in which government may never engage is the practice of racism—not even "temporarily" and not even as an "experiment." ...

Mr. Justice Stevens, dissenting.

The 10% set-aside contained in the Public Works Employment Act of 1977 *** creates monopoly privileges in a $4,000,000,000 market for a class of investors defined solely by racial characteristics. The direct beneficiaries of these monopoly privileges are the relatively small number of persons within the racial classification who represent the entrepreneurial subclass—those who have, or can borrow, working capital. . . .

The legislative history of the Act discloses that there is a group of legislators in Congress identified as the "Black Caucus" and that members of that group argued that if the Federal Government was going to provide $4,000,000,000 of new public contract business, their constituents were entitled to "a piece of the action." . . .

. . . [A]n absolute preference that is unrelated to a minority firm's ability to perform a contract inevitably will engender resentment on the part of competitors excluded from the market for a purely racial reason and skepticism on the part of customers and suppliers aware of the statutory classification. . . . [A] statute of this kind inevitably is perceived by many as resting on an assumption that those who are granted this special preference are less qualified in some respect that is identified purely by their race. Be-

cause that perception—especially when fostered by the Congress of the United States—can only exacerbate rather than reduce racial prejudice, it will delay the time when race will become a truly irrelevant, or at least insignificant, factor. . . .

. . . [R]ather than take the substantive position expressed in Mr. Justice Stewart's dissenting opinion, I would hold this statute unconstitutional on a narrower ground. It cannot fairly be characterized as a "narrowly tailored" racial classification because it simply raises too many serious questions that Congress failed to answer or even to address in a responsible way. . . .

. . . It is up to Congress to demonstrate that its unique statutory preference is justified by a relevant characteristic that is shared by the members of the preferred class. In my opinion, because it has failed to make that demonstration, it has also failed to discharge its duty to govern impartially embodied in the Fifth Amendment to the United States Constitution.

I respectfully dissent.

City of Richmond v. J.A. Croson Company

488 U.S. 469; 109 S. Ct. 706; 102 L. Ed.2d 854 (1989)
Vote: 6-3

The J.A. Croson Company, a plumbing contractor based in Ohio, brought suit against the city of Richmond, Virginia, challenging an ordinance enacted by the city council. The ordinance called for nonminority contractors (such as Croson) that were awarded contracts by the city to in turn award at least 30 percent of the dollar value of their subcontracts to "minority business enterprises." The city council sought to justify this set-aside requirement by the fact that, although the city was 50 percent African-American, minority-owned firms were receiving less than 1 percent of the city's construction contracts. A federal district judge ruled that the program was constitutional, relying heavily on the Supreme Court's decision in Fullilove v. Klutznick *(1980). The court of appeals reversed, however, and the city of Richmond sought and obtained review by the Supreme Court.*

Justice O'Connor delivered the opinion of the Court [joined *en toto* by *Justice Stevens* and, for the most part, by *Chief Justice Rehnquist, Justice White* and *Justice Kennedy*] . . .

I. [omitted]

II. [omitted]

III.

A. The Richmond Plan denies certain citizens the opportunity to compete for a fixed percentage of public contracts based solely upon their race. To whatever racial group these citizens belong, their "personal rights" to be treated with equal dignity and respect are implicated by a rigid rule erecting race as the sole criterion in an aspect of public decisionmaking.

Absent searching judicial inquiry into the justification for such race-based measure, there is simply no way of determining what classifications are "benign" or "remedial" and what classifications are in fact motivated by illegitimate notions of racial inferiority or simple racial politics. Indeed, the purpose of strict scrutiny is to "smoke out" illegitimate uses of race by assuring that the legislative body is pursuing a goal important enough to warrant use of a highly suspect tool. The test also ensures that the means chosen "fit" this compelling goal so closely that there is little or no possibility that the motive for the classification was illegitimate racial prejudice or stereotype.

Classifications based on race carry a danger of stigmatic harm. Unless they are strictly reserved for remedial settings, they may in fact promote notions of racial inferiority and lead to a politics of racial hostility. *** We thus reaffirm the view . . . that the standard of review under the Equal Protection Clause is not dependent on the race of those burdened or benefitted by a particular classification. . . .

Under the standard proposed by Justice Marshall's dissent, "[r]ace-conscious classifications designed to further remedial goals" are forthwith subject to a relaxed standard of review. How the dissent arrives at the legal conclusion that a racial classification is "designed to further remedial goals," without first engaging in an examination of the factual basis for its enactment and the nexus between its scope and that factual basis we are not told. However, once the "remedial" conclusion is reached, the dissent's standard is singularly deferential, and bears little resemblance to the close examination of legislative purpose we have engaged in when reviewing classifications based either on race or gender. . . . The dissent's watered-down version of equal protection review effectively assures that race will always be relevant in American life, and that the "ultimate goal" of "eliminat[ing] entirely from governmental decisionmaking such irrelevant factors as a human being's race" *** will never be achieved.

Even were we to accept a reading of the guarantee of equal protection under which the level of scrutiny varies according to the ability of different groups to defend their interests in the representative process, heightened scrutiny would still be appropriate in the circumstances of this case. One of the central arguments for applying a less exacting standard to "benign" racial classifications is that such measures essentially involve a choice made by dominant racial groups to disadvantage themselves. If one aspect of the judiciary's role under the Equal Protection Clause is to protect "discrete and insular minorities" from majoritarian prejudice or indifference, *** some maintain that these concerns are not implicated when the "white majority" places burdens upon itself. ***

In this case, blacks comprise approximately 50% of the population of the city of Richmond. Five of the nine seats on the City Council are held by blacks. The concern that a political majority will more easily act to the disadvantage of a minority based on unwarranted assumptions or incomplete facts would seem to militate for, not against, the application of heightened judicial scrutiny in this case.

B. The District Court found the city council's "findings sufficient to ensure that, in adopting the Plan, it was remedying the present effects of past discrimination in the construction industry." Like the "role model" theory employed in *Wygant,* a generalized assertion that there has been past discrimination in an entire industry provides no guidance for a legislative body to determine the precise scope of the injury it seeks to remedy. It "has no logical stopping point." *** "Relief" for such an ill-defined wrong could extend until the percentage of public contracts awarded to MBEs [minority business enterprises] in Richmond mirrored the percentage of minorities in the population as a whole.

Appellant argues that it is attempting to remedy various forms of past discrimination that are alleged to be responsible for the small number of minority businesses in the local contracting industry. Among these the city cites the exclusion of blacks from skilled construction trade unions and training programs. This past discrimination has prevented them "from following the traditional path from laborer to entrepreneur." The city also lists a host of nonracial factors which would seem to face a member of any racial group attempting to establish a new business enterprise, such as deficiencies in working capital, inability to meet bonding requirements, unfamiliarity with bidding procedures, and disability caused by an inadequate track record.

While there is no doubt that the sorry history of both private and public discrimination in this country has contributed to a lack of opportunities for black entrepreneurs, this observation, standing alone, cannot justify a rigid racial quota in the awarding of public contracts in Richmond, Virginia. Like the claim that discrimination in primary and secondary schooling justifies a rigid racial preference in medical school admissions, an amorphous claim that there has been past discrimination in a particular industry cannot justify the use of an unyielding racial quota.

It is sheer speculation how many minority firms there would be in Richmond absent past societal discrimination, just as it was sheer speculation how many minority medical students would have been admitted to the medical school at Davis absent past discrimination in educational opportunities. Defining these sorts of injuries as "identified discrimination" would give local governments license to create a patchwork of racial preferences based on statistical generalizations about any particular field of endeavor.

These defects are readily apparent in this case. The 30% quota cannot in any realistic sense be tied to any injury suffered by anyone. The District Court relied upon five predicate "facts" in reaching its conclusion that there was an adequate basis for the 30% quota: (1) the ordinance declares itself to be remedial; (2) several proponents of the measure stated their views that there had been past discrimination in the construction industry; (3) minority businesses received .67% of prime contracts from the city while minorities constituted 50% of the city's population; (4) there were very few minority contractors in local and state contractors' associations; and (5) in 1977, Congress made a determination that the effects of past discrimination had stifled minority participation in the construction industry nationally.

None of these "findings," singly or together, provide[s] the city of Richmond with a "strong basis in evidence for its conclusion that remedial action was necessary." *** There is nothing approaching a *prima facie* case of a constitutional or statutory violation by anyone in the Richmond construction industry.

The District Court accorded great weight to the fact that the city council designated the Plan as "remedial." But the mere recitation of a "benign" or legitimate purpose for a racial classification, is entitled to little or no weight. . . .

The District Court also relied on the highly conclusionary statement of a proponent of the Plan that there was racial discrimination in the construction industry "in this area, and the State, and around the nation." It also noted that the city manager had related his view that racial discrimination still plagued the construction industry in his home city of Pittsburgh. . . . These statements are of little probative value in establishing identified discrimination in the Richmond construction industry. The fact-finding process of legislative bodies is generally entitled to a presumption of regularity and deferential review by the judiciary. But when a legislative body chooses to employ a suspect classification, it cannot rest upon a generalized assertion as to the classification's relevance to its goals. . . .

Reliance on the disparity between the number of prime contracts awarded to minority firms and the minority population of the city of Richmond is similarly misplaced. . . .

In the employment context, we have recognized that for certain entry level positions or positions requiring minimal training, statistical comparisons of the racial composition of an employer's workforce to the racial composition of the relevant population may be probative of a pattern of discrimination. . . . But where special qualifications are necessary, the relevant statistical pool for purposes of demonstrating discriminatory exclusion must be the number of minorities qualified to undertake the particular task. . . .

In this case, the city does not even know how many MBE's in the relevant market are qualified to undertake prime or subcontracting work in public construction projects. . . . Nor does the city know what percentage of total city construction dollars minority firms now receive as subcontractors on prime contracts let by the city.

To a large extent, the set-aside of subcontracting dollars seems to rest on the unsupported assumption that white prime contractors simply will not hire minority firms. . . . Without any information on minority participation in subcontracting, it is quite simply impossible to evaluate overall minority representation in the city's construction expenditures.

The city and the District Court also relied on evidence that MBE membership in local contractors' associations was extremely low. Again, standing alone this evidence is not probative of any discrimination in the local construction industry. There are numerous explanations for this dearth of minority participation, including past societal discrimination in education and economic opportunities as well as both black and white career and entrepreneurial choices. Blacks may be disproportionately attracted to industries other than construction. . . . The mere fact that black membership in these trade organizations is low, standing alone, cannot establish a *prima facie* case of discrimination.

Finally, the city and the District Court relied on Congress' finding in connection with the set-aside approved in Fullilove that there had been nationwide discrimination in the construction industry. The probative value of these findings for demonstrating the existence of discrimination in Richmond is extremely limited. By its inclusion of a waiver procedure in the national program addressed in *Fullilove,* Congress explicitly recognized that the scope of the problem would vary from market area to market area. . . .

Moreover, as noted above, Congress was exercising its powers under Sec. 5 of the Fourteenth Amendment in making a finding that past discrimination would cause federal funds to be distributed in a manner which reinforced prior patterns of discrimination. While the States and their subdivision may take remedial action when they possess evidence that their own spending practices are exacerbating a pattern of prior discrimination, they must identify that discrimination, public or private, with some specificity before they may use race-conscious relief. Congress has made national findings that there has been societal discrimination in a host of fields. If all a state or local government need do is find a congressional report on the subject to enact a set-aside program, the constraints of the Equal Protection Clause will, in effect, have been rendered a nullity. . . .

In sum, none of the evidence presented by the city points to any identified discrimination in the Richmond construction industry. We, therefore, hold that the city has failed to demonstrate a compelling interest in apportioning public contracting opportunities on the basis of race. To accept Richmond's claim

that past societal discrimination alone can serve as the basis for rigid racial preferences would be to open the door to competing claims for "remedial relief" for every disadvantaged group. The dream of a Nation of equal citizens in a society where race is irrelevant to personal opportunity and achievement would be lost in a mosaic of shifting preferences based on inherently unmeasurable claims of past wrongs. . . .

The foregoing analysis applies only to the inclusion of blacks within the Richmond set-aside program. There is absolutely no evidence of past discrimination against Spanish-speaking, Oriental, Indian, Eskimo, or Aleut persons in any aspect of the Richmond construction industry. The District Court took judicial notice of the fact that the vast majority of "minority" persons in Richmond were black. It may well be that Richmond has never had an Aleut or Eskimo citizen. The random inclusion of racial groups that, as a practical matter, may never have suffered from discrimination in the construction industry in Richmond, suggests that perhaps the city's purpose was not in fact to remedy past discrimination.

If a 30% set-aside was "narrowly tailored" to compensate black contractors for past discrimination, one may legitimately ask why they are forced to share this "remedial relief" with an Aleut citizen who moves to Richmond tomorrow? The gross overinclusiveness of Richmond's racial preference strongly impugns the city's claim of remedial motivation. . . .

IV

As noted by the court below, it is almost impossible to assess whether the Richmond Plan is narrowly tailored to remedy prior discrimination since it is not linked to identified discrimination in any way. We limit ourselves to two observations in this regard.

First, there does not appear to have been any consideration of the use of race-neutral means to increase minority business participation in city contracting. . . . Many of the barriers to minority participation in the construction industry relied upon by the city to justify a racial classification appear to be race-neutral. If MBEs disproportionately lack capital or cannot meet bonding requirements, a race-neutral program of city financing for small firms would, *a fortiori,* lead to greater minority participation. The principal opinion in *Fullilove* found that Congress had carefully examined and rejected race-neutral alternatives before enacting the MBE set-aside.

Second, the 30% quota cannot be said to be narrowly tailored to any goal, except perhaps outright racial balancing. It rests upon the "completely unrealistic" assumption that minorities will choose a particular trade in lockstep proportion to their representation in the local population. . . .

Since the city must already consider bids and waivers on a case-by-case basis, it is difficult to see the need for a rigid numerical quota. As noted above, the congressional scheme upheld in *Fullilove* allowed for a waiver of the set-aside provision where an MBE's higher price was not attributable to the effects of past discrimination. Based upon proper findings, such programs are less problematic from an equal protection standpoint because they treat all candidates individually, rather than making the color of an applicant's skin the sole relevant consideration. Unlike the program upheld in *Fullilove,* the Richmond Plan's waiver system focuses solely on the availability of MBEs; there is no inquiry into whether or not the particular MBE seeking a racial preference has suffered from the effects of past discrimination by the city or prime contractors.

Given the existence of an individualized procedure, the city's only interest in maintaining a quota system rather than investigating the need for remedial action in particular cases would seem to be simple administrative convenience. But the interest in avoiding the bureaucratic effort necessary to tailor remedial relief to those who truly have suffered the effects of prior discrimination cannot justify a rigid line drawn on the basis of a suspect classification. . . . Under Richmond's scheme, a successful black, Hispanic, or Oriental entrepreneur from anywhere in the country enjoys an absolute preference over other citizens based solely on their race. We think it obvious that such a program is not narrowly tailored to remedy the effects of prior discrimination.

V

Nothing we say today precludes a state or local entity from taking action to rectify the effects of identified discrimination within its jurisdiction. If the city of Richmond had evidence before it that nonminority contractors were systematically excluding minority businesses from subcontracting opportunities it could take action to end the discriminatory exclusion. Where there is a significant statistical disparity between the number of qualified minority contractors willing and able to perform a particular service and the number of such contractors actually engaged by the locality or the locality's prime contractors, an inference of discriminatory exclusion could arise. Under such circumstances, the city could act to dismantle the closed business system by taking appropriate measures against those who discriminate on the basis of race or other illegitimate criteria. In the extreme case, some form of narrowly tailored racial preference might be necessary to break down patterns of deliberate exclusion. . . .

Proper findings in this regard are necessary to define both the scope of the injury and the extent of the remedy necessary to cure its effects. Such findings also serve to assure all citizens that the deviation from the norm of equal treatment of all racial and ethnic groups is a temporary matter, a measure taken in the service of the goal of equality itself. Absent such findings, there is a danger that a racial classification is merely the product of unthinking stereotypes or a form of racial politics. "[I]f there is no duty to attempt either to measure the recovery by the wrong or to distribute that recovery within the injured class in an evenhanded way, our history will adequately support a legislative preference for almost any ethnic, religious, or racial group with the political strength to negotiate 'a piece of the action' for its members." *** Because the city of Richmond has failed to identify the need for remedial action in the awarding of its public construction contracts, its treatment of its citizens on a racial basis violates the dictates of the Equal Protection Clause. According, the judgment of the Court of Appeals for the Fourth Circuit is Affirmed.

Justice Stevens, concurring in part.

. . . I . . . do not agree with the premise that seems to underlie today's decision, that a governmental decision that rests on a racial classification is never permissible except as a remedy for a past wrong. I do, however, agree with the Court's explanation of why the Richmond ordinance cannot be justified as a remedy for past discrimination, and therefore join Parts I, III-B, and IV of its opinion.

Justice Kennedy, concurring in part.

I join all but Part II of Justice O'Connor's opinion and give this further explanation.... The moral imperative of racial neutrality is the driving force of the Equal Protection Clause. Justice Scalia's opinion underscores that proposition, quite properly in my view. The rule suggested in his opinion, which would strike down all preferences which are not necessary remedies to victims of unlawful discrimination, would serve important structural goals, as it would eliminate the necessity for courts to pass upon each racial preference that is enacted. Structural protections may be necessities if moral imperatives are to be obeyed. His opinion would make it crystal clear to the political branches, at least those of the States, that legislation must be based on criteria other than race.

Nevertheless, given that a rule of automatic invalidity for racial preferences in almost every case would be a significant break with our precedent that requires a case-by-case test, I am not convinced we need adopt it at this point. On the assumption that it will vindicate the principle of race neutrality found in the Equal Protection Clause, I accept the less absolute rule contained in Justice O'Connor's opinion, a rule based on the proposition that any racial preference must face the most rigorous scrutiny by the courts. My reasons for doing so are as follows. First, I am confident that, in application, the strict scrutiny standard will operate in a manner generally consistent with the imperative of race neutrality, because it forbids the use even of narrowly drawn racial classifications except as a last resort. Second, the rule against race-conscious remedies is already less than an absolute one, for that relief may be the only adequate remedy after a judicial determination that a State or its instrumentality has violated the Equal Protection Clause. I note, in this connection, that evidence which would support a judicial finding of intentional discrimination may suffice also to justify remedial legislative action, for it diminishes the constitutional responsibilities of the political branches

to say they must wait to act until ordered to do so by a court. Third, the strict scrutiny rule is consistent with our precedents, as Justice O'Connor's opinion demonstrates.

Justice Scalia, concurring.

I agree with much of the Court's opinion, and, in particular, with its conclusion that strict scrutiny must be applied to all governmental classification by race, whether or not its asserted purpose is "remedial" or "benign." I do not agree, however, with the Court's dicta suggesting that, despite the Fourteenth Amendment, state and local governments may in some circumstances discriminate on the basis of race in order (in a broad sense) "to ameliorate the effects of past discrimination." The benign purpose of compensating for social disadvantages, whether they have been acquired by reason of prior discrimination or otherwise, can no more be pursued by the illegitimate means of racial discrimination than can other assertedly benign purposes we have repeatedly rejected. *** The difficulty of overcoming the effects of past discrimination is as nothing compared with the difficulty of eradicating from our society the source of those effects, which is the tendency—fatal to a nation such as ours—to classify and judge men and women on the basis of their country of origin or the color of their skin....

Justice Marshall, with whom Justice Brennan and Justice Blackmun join, dissenting.

[T]oday's decision marks a deliberate and giant step backward in this Court's affirmative action jurisprudence. Cynical of one municipality's attempt to redress the effects of past racial discrimination in a particular industry, the majority launches a grapeshot attack on race-conscious remedies in general. The majority's unnecessary pronouncements will inevitably discourage or prevent governmental entities, particularly States and localities, from acting to rectify the scourge of past discrimination. This is the harsh reality of the majority's decision, but it is not the Constitution's command....

My view has long been that race-conscious classifications designed to further remedial goals "must serve important governmental objectives and must be substantially related to achievement of those objectives" in order to withstand constitutional scrutiny. . . . Analyzed in terms of this two-prong standard, Richmond's set-aside, like the federal program on which it was modeled, is "plainly constitutional". . . .

Turning first to the governmental interest inquiry, Richmond has two powerful interests in setting aside a portion of public contracting funds for minority-owned enterprises. The first is the city's interest in eradicating the effects of past racial discrimination. It is far too late in the day to doubt that remedying such discrimination is a compelling, let alone an important, interest. . . .

Richmond has a second compelling interest in setting aside, where possible, a portion of its contracting dollars. That interest is the prospective one of preventing the city's own spending decisions from reinforcing and perpetuating the exclusionary effects of past discrimination.

When government channels all its contracting funds to a white-dominated community of established contractors whose racial homogeneity is the product of private discrimination, it does more than place its imprimatur on the practices which forged and which continue to define that community. It also provides a measurable boost to those economic entities that have thrived within it, while denying important economic benefits to those entities which, but for prior discrimination, might well be better qualified to receive valuable government contracts. In my view, the interest in ensuring that the government does not reflect and reinforce prior private discrimination in dispensing public contracts is every bit as strong as the interest in eliminating private discrimination—an interest this Court has repeatedly deemed compelling.

The remaining question with respect to the "governmental interest" prong of equal protection analysis is whether Richmond has proffered satisfactory proof of past racial discrimination to support its twin interests in remediation and in governmental nonperpetuation. Although the Members of this Court have differed on the appropriate standard of review for race-conscious remedial measure, we have always regarded this factual inquiry as a practical one. Thus, the Court has eschewed rigid tests which require the provision of particular species of evidence, statistical or otherwise. At the same time we have required that

government adduce evidence that, taken as a whole, is sufficient to support its claimed interest and to dispel the natural concern that it acted out of mere "paternalistic stereotyping, not on a careful consideration of modern social conditions." ***

Richmond's reliance on localized, industry-specific findings is a far cry from the reliance on generalized "societal discrimination" which the majority decries as a basis for remedial action. But characterizing the plight of Richmond's minority contractors as mere "societal discrimination" is not the only respect in which the majority's critiques shows an unwillingness to come to grips with why construction-contracting in Richmond is essentially a whites-only enterprise. The majority also takes the disingenuous approach of disaggregating Richmond's local evidence, attacking it piecemeal, and thereby concluding that no single piece of evidence adduced by the city, "standing alone," suffices to prove past discrimination. But items of evidence do not, of course, "stan[d] alone" or exist in alien juxtaposition; they necessarily work together, reinforcing or contradicting each other.

In any event, the majority's criticisms of individual items of Richmond's evidence rest on flimsy foundations. The majority states, for example, that reliance on the disparity between the share of city contracts awarded to minority firms (.67%) and the minority population of Richmond (approximately 50%) is "misplaced" . . . first, considering how minuscule the share of Richmond public construction contracting dollars received by minority-owned businesses is, it is hardly unreasonable to conclude that this case involves a "gross statistical disparit[y]." There are roughly equal numbers of minorities and nonminorities in Richmond—yet minority-owned businesses receive one-seventy-fifth the public contracting funds that other businesses receive. . . .

Second, and more fundamentally, where the issue is not present discrimination but rather whether past discrimination has resulted in the continuing exclusion of minorities from an historically tightknit industry, a contrast between population and work force is entirely appropriate to help gauge the degree of the exclusion. . . . This contrast is especially illuminating in cases like this, where a main avenue of introduction into the work force—here, membership in the trade associations whose members presumably train apprentices and help them procure subcontracting assignments—is itself grossly dominated by nonminorities. The majority's assertion that the city "does not even know how many MBE's in the relevant market are qualified," is thus entirely beside the point. . . . The city's requirement that prime public contractors set aside 30% of their subcontracting assignments for minority-owned enterprises, subject to the ordinance's provision for waivers where minority-owned enterprises are unavailable or unwilling to participate, is designed precisely to ease minority contractors into the industry.

Had the majority paused for a moment on the facts of the Richmond experience, it would have discovered that the city's leadership is deeply familiar with what racial discrimination is. The members of the Richmond City Council have spent long years witnessing. . .the deliberate diminution of black residents' voting rights, resistance to school desegregation, and publicly sanctioned housing discrimination. Numerous of federal courts chronicle this disgraceful recent history. . . .

When the legislatures and leaders of cities with histories of pervasive discrimination testify that past discrimination has infected one of their industries, armchair cynicism like that exercised by the majority has no place. . . . Disbelief is particularly inappropriate here in light of the fact that appellee Croson, which had the burden of proving unconstitutionality at trial, *** has at no point come forward with any direct evidence that the City Council's motives were anything other than sincere.

Finally, I vehemently disagree with the majority's dismissal of the congressional and Executive Branch findings noted in *Fullilove* as having "extremely limited" probative value in this case. The majority concedes that Congress established nothing less than a "presumption" that minority contracting firms have been disadvantaged by prior discrimination. The majority, inexplicable, would forbid Richmond to "share" in this information, and permit only Congress to take note of these ample findings. In thus requiring that Richmond's local evidence be severed from the context in which it was prepared, the majority would require cities seeking to eradicate the effects of past discrimination within their borders to

reinvent the evidentiary wheel and engage in unnecessarily duplicative, costly, and time-consuming fact-finding.

No principle of federalism or of federal power, however, forbids a state or local government from drawing upon a nationally relevant historical record prepared by the Federal Government. . . . Of course, Richmond could have built an even more compendious record of past discrimination, one including additional stark statistics and additional individual accounts of past discrimination. But nothing in the Fourteenth Amendment imposes such onerous documentary obligations upon States and localities once the reality of past discrimination is apparent.

In my judgment, Richmond's set-aside plan also comports with the second prong of the equal protection inquiry, for it is substantially related to the interests it seeks to serve in remedying past discrimination and in ensuring that municipal contract procurement does not perpetuate that discrimination. The most striking aspect of the city's ordinance is the similarity it bears to the "appropriately limited" federal set-aside provision upheld in *Fullilove*. Like the federal provision, Richmond's is limited to five years in duration, and was not renewed when it came up for reconsideration in 1988. Like the federal provision, Richmond's contains a waiver provision freeing from its subcontracting requirements those nonminority firms that demonstrate that they cannot comply with its provisions. Like the federal provision, Richmond's has a minimal impact on innocent third parties. While the measure affects 30% of public contracting dollars, that translates to only 3% of overall Richmond area contracting. . . .

Finally, like the federal provision, Richmond's does not interfere with any vested right of a contractor to a particular contract; instead it operates entirely prospectively. . . .

As for Richmond's 30% target, the majority states that this figure "cannot be said to be narrowly tailored to any goal, except perhaps outright racial balancing." The majority ignores two important facts. First, the set-aside measure affects only 3% of overall city contracting; thus, any imprecision in tailoring has far less impact than the majority suggests. But more important, the majority ignores the fact that Richmond's 30% figure was patterned directly on the

Fullilove precedent. Congress' 10% figure fell "roughly halfway between the present percentage of minority contractors and the percentage of minority group members in the Nation." *** The Richmond City Council's 30% figure similarly falls roughly halfway between the present percentage of Richmond-based minority contractors (almost zero) and the percentage of minorities in Richmond (50%). In faulting Richmond for not presenting a different explanation for its choice of a set-aside figure, the majority honors *Fullilove* only in the breach. . . .

Today, for the first time, a majority of this Court has adopted strict scrutiny as its standard of Equal Protection Clause review of race-conscious remedial measures. This is an unwelcome development. A profound difference separates governmental actions that themselves are racist, and governmental actions that seek to remedy the effects of prior racism or to prevent neutral governmental activity from perpetuating the effects of such racism. . . .

I am also troubled by the majority's assertion that, even if it did not believe generally in strict scrutiny of race-based remedial measures, "the circumstances of this case" require this Court to look upon the Richmond City Council's measure with the strictest scrutiny. The sole such circumstance which the majority cites, however, is the fact that blacks in Richmond are a "dominant racial grou[p]" in the city. In support of this characterization of dominance, the majority observes that "blacks comprise approximately 50% of the population of the city of Richmond" and that "[f]ive of the nine seats on the City Council are held by blacks."

While I agree that the numerical and political supremacy of a given racial group is a factor bearing upon the level of scrutiny to be applied, this Court has never held that numerical inferiority, standing alone, makes a racial group "suspect" and thus entitled to strict scrutiny review. Rather, we have identified other "traditional indicia of suspectness": whether a group has been "saddled with such disabilities, or subjected to such a history of purposeful unequal treatment, or relegated to such a position of political powerlessness as to command extraordinary protection from the majoritarian political process." *** . . .

The majority today sounds a full-scale retreat from the Court's long-standing solicitude to race-conscious remedial efforts "directed toward deliverance of the century-old promise of equality of economic opportunity." *** The new and restrictive tests it applies scuttle one city's effort to surmount its discriminatory past, and imperil those of dozens more localities. I, however, profoundly disagree with the cramped vision of the Equal Protection Clause which the majority offers today and with its application of that vision to Richmond, Virginia's laudable set-aside plan. The battle against pernicious racial discrimination or its effects is nowhere near won. I must dissent.

Justice Blackmun, with whom **Justice Brennan** joins, dissenting.

I never thought that I would live to see the day when the city of Richmond, Virginia, the cradle of the Old Confederacy, sought on its own, within a narrow confine, to lessen the stark impact of persistent discrimination. But Richmond, to its great credit, acted. Yet, this Court, the supposed bastion of equality, strikes down Richmond's efforts as though discrimination had never existed or was not demonstrated in this particular litigation. Justice Marshall convincingly discloses the fallacy and the shallowness of that approach. History is irrefutable, even though one might sympathize with those who—though possibly innocent in themselves—benefit from the wrongs of past decades.

So the Court today regresses. I am confident, however, that, given time, it one day again will do its best to fulfill the great promises of the Constitution's Preamble and of the guarantees embodied in the Bill of Rights—a fulfillment that would make this Nation very special.

Frontiero v. Richardson

411 U.S. 677; 93 S. Ct. 1764; 36 L. Ed.2d 583 (1973)

Vote: 8-1

Mr. Justice Brennan announced the judgment of the Court and an opinion in which **Mr. Justice Douglas, Mr. Justice White,** and **Mr. Justice Marshall** join.

The question before us concerns the right of a female member of the uniformed services to claim her spouse as a "dependent" for the purposes of obtaining increased quarters allowances and medical and dental benefits . . . on an equal footing with male members. Under [the statutes at issue], a serviceman may claim his wife as a "dependent" without regard to whether she is in fact dependent upon him for any part of her support. A servicewoman, on the other hand, may not claim her husband as a "dependent" under these programs unless he is in fact dependent upon her for over one-half of his support. *** Thus, the question for decision is whether this difference in treatment constitutes an unconstitutional discrimination against servicewomen in violation of the [equal protection component] of the Fifth Amendment. A three-judge District Court for the Middle District of Alabama, one judge dissenting, rejected this contention and sustained the constitutionality of the provisions of the statutes making this distinction. *** We noted probable jurisdiction. *** We reverse.

I

In an effort to attract career personnel through reenlistment, Congress established . . . a scheme for the provision of fringe benefits to members of the uniformed services on a competitive basis with business and industry. . . . [A] member of the uniformed services with dependents is entitled to an increased "basic allowance for quarters" and . . . a member's dependents are provided comprehensive medical and dental care.

Appellant Sharron Frontiero, a lieutenant in the United States Air Force, sought increased quarters allowance, and housing and medical benefits for her husband, appellant Joseph Frontiero, on the ground

that he was her "dependent." Although such benefits would automatically have been granted with respect to the wife of a male member of the uniformed services, appellant's application was denied because she failed to demonstrate that her husband was dependent on her for more than one-half of his support. Appellants then commenced this suit, contending that, by making this distinction, the statutes unreasonably discriminate on the basis of sex in violation of the Due Process Clause of the Fifth Amendment. In essence, appellants asserted that the discriminatory impact of the statutes is two-fold: first, as a procedural matter, a female member is required to demonstrate her spouse's dependency, while no such burden is imposed upon male members; and second, as a substantive matter, a male member who does not provide more than one-half of his wife's support receives benefits, while a similarly situated female member is denied such benefits. Appellants therefore sought a permanent injunction against the continued enforcement of these statutes and an order directing the appellees to provide Lieutenant Frontiero with the same housing and medical benefits that a similarly situated male member would receive.

Although the legislative history of these statutes sheds virtually no light on the purposes underlying the differential treatment accorded male and female members, a majority of the three-judge District Court surmised that Congress might reasonably have concluded that, since the husband in our society is generally the "breadwinner" in the family—and the wife typically the "dependent" partner—"it would be more economical to require married female members claiming husbands to prove actual dependency than to extend the presumption of dependency to such members." *** Indeed, given the fact that approximately 99% of all members of the uniformed services are male, the District Court speculated that such differential treatment might conceivably lead to a "considerable saving of administrative expense and manpower." ***

II

At the outset, appellants contend that classifications based upon sex, like classifications based upon race, alienage, and national origin, are inherently suspect and must therefore be subjected to close judicial scrutiny. We agree and, indeed, find at least implicit support for such an approach in our unanimous decision only last Term in *Reed v. Reed.* ***

In *Reed,* the Court considered the constitutionality of an Idaho statute providing that, when two individuals are otherwise equally entitled to appointment as administrator of an estate, the male applicant must be preferred to the female. Appellant, the mother of the deceased, and appellee, the father, filed competing petitions for appointment as administrator of their son's estate. Since the parties, as parents of the deceased, were members of the same entitlement class, the statutory preference was invoked and the father's petition was therefore granted. Appellant claimed that this statute, by giving a mandatory preference to males over females without regard to their individual qualifications, violated the Equal Protection Clause of the Fourteenth Amendment.

The Court noted that the Idaho statute "provides that different treatment be accorded to the applicants on the basis of their sex; it thus establishes a classification subject to scrutiny under the Equal Protection Clause." *** Under "traditional" equal protection analysis, a legislative classification must be sustained unless it is "patently arbitrary" and bears no rational relationship to a legitimate governmental interest. ***

In an effort to meet this standard, appellee contended that the statutory scheme was a reasonable measure designed to reduce the workload on probate courts by eliminating one class of contests. Moreover, appellee argued that the mandatory preference for male applicants was in itself reasonable since "men [are] as a rule more conversant with business affairs than . . . women." Indeed, appellee maintained that "it is a matter of common knowledge, that women still are not engaged in politics, the professions, business or industry to the extent that men are." And the Idaho Supreme Court, in upholding the constitutionality of this statute, suggested that the Idaho Legislature might reasonably have "concluded that in general men are better qualified to act as an administrator than are women."

Despite these contentions, however, the Court held the statutory preference for male applicants unconstitutional. In reaching this result, the Court implicitly rejected appellee's apparently rational explanation of the statutory scheme, and concluded that, by ignoring the individual qualifications of particular applicants, the challenged statute provided "dissimilar treatment for men and women who are . . . similarly situated." *** The Court therefore held that, even though the State's interest in achieving administrative efficiency "is not without some legitimacy," "[t]o give a mandatory preference to members of either sex over members of the other, merely to accomplish the elimination of hearings on the merits, is to make the very kind of arbitrary legislative choice forbidden by the [Constitution]. . . ."*** This departure from "traditional" rational basis analysis with respect to sex-based classifications is clearly justified.

There can be no doubt that our Nation has had a long and unfortunate history of sex discrimination. Traditionally, such discrimination was rationalized by an attitude of "romantic paternalism" which, in practical effect, put women not on a pedestal, but in a cage. Indeed, this paternalistic attitude became so firmly rooted in our national consciousness that, exactly 100 years ago, a distinguished member of this Court was about to proclaim:

"Man is, or should be, woman's protector and defender. The natural and proper timidity and delicacy which belongs to the female sex evidently unfits it for many of the occupations of civil life. The constitution of the family organizations, which is founded in the divine ordinance, as well as in the nature of things, indicates the domestic sphere as that which properly belongs to the domain and functions of womanhood. The harmony, not to say identity, of interests and views which belong, or should belong, to the family institution is repugnant to the ideas of a woman adopting distinct and independent career from that of her husband. . . . . . . The paramount destiny and mission of woman are to fulfill the noble and benign offices of wife and mother. This is the law of the Creator." ***

As a result of notions such as these, our statute books gradually became laden with gross, stereotypical distinctions between the sexes and, indeed, throughout much of the 19th century the position of women in our society was, in many respects, comparable to that of blacks under the pre-Civil War slave codes. Neither slaves nor women could hold office, serve on juries, or bring suit in their own names, and married women traditionally were denied the legal capacity to hold or convey property or to serve as legal guardians of their own children. *** And although blacks were guaranteed the right to vote in 1870, women were denied even that right—which is itself "preservative of other basic civil and political rights"—until adoption of the Nineteenth Amendment half a century later.

It is true, of course, that the position of women in America has improved markedly in recent decades. Nevertheless, it can hardly be doubted that, in part because of the high visibility of the sex characteristic, women still face pervasive, although at times more subtle, discrimination in our educational institutions, on the job market and, perhaps most conspicuously, in the political arena. ***

Moreover, since sex, like race and national origin, is an immutable characteristic determined solely by the accident of birth, the imposition of special disabilities upon the members of a particular sex because of their sex would seem to violate "the basic concept of our system that legal burdens should bear some relationship to individual responsibility...." *** And what differentiates sex from such nonsuspect statutes as intelligence or physical disability, and aligns it with the recognized suspect criteria, is that the sex characteristic frequently bears no relation to ability to perform or contribute to society. As a result, statutory distinctions between the sexes often have the effect of invidiously relegating the entire class of females to inferior legal status without regard to the actual capabilities of its individual members.

We might also note that, over the past decade, Congress has itself manifested an increasing sensitivity to sex-based classifications. In Title VII of the Civil Rights Act of 1964, for example, Congress expressly declared that no employer, labor union, or other organization subject to the provisions of the Act shall discriminate against any individual on the basis of "race, color, religion, sex, or national origin." Similarly, the Equal Pay Act of 1963 provides that no employer covered by the Act "shall discriminate ... between employees on the basis of sex." And Section 1 of the Equal Rights Amendment, passed by Congress on March 22, 1972, and submitted to the legislatures

of the States for ratification, declares that "[e]quality of rights under the law shall not be denied or abridged by the United States or by any State on account of sex." Thus, Congress has itself concluded that classifications based upon sex are inherently invidious, and this conclusion of a coequal branch of government is not without significance to the question presently under consideration. ***

With these considerations in mind, we can only conclude that classifications based upon sex, like classifications based upon race, alienage, or national origin, are inherently suspect, and must therefore be subjected to strict judicial scrutiny. Applying the analysis mandated by that stricter standard of review, it is clear that the statutory scheme now before us is constitutionally invalid.

III

The sole basis of the classification established in the challenged statutes is the sex of the individuals involved. Thus ... a female member of the uniformed services seeking to obtain housing and medical benefits for her spouse must prove his dependency in fact, whereas no such burden is imposed upon male members. In addition, the statutes operate so as to deny benefits to a female member, such as appellant Sharron Frontiero, who provides less than one-half of her spouse's support, while at the same time granting such benefits to a male member who likewise provides less than one-half of his spouse's support. Thus to this extent at least, it may fairly be said that these statutes command "dissimilar treatment for men and women who are ... similarly situated." ***

Moreover, the Government concedes that the differential treatment accorded men and women under these statutes serves no purpose other than mere "administrative convenience." In essence, the Government maintains that, as an empirical matter, wives in our society frequently are dependent upon their husbands, while husbands rarely are dependent upon their wives. Thus, the Government argues that Congress might reasonably have concluded that it would be both cheaper and easier simply conclusively to presume that wives of male members are financially dependent upon their husbands, while burdening female members with the task of establishing dependency in fact.

The Government offers no concrete evidence, however, tending to support its view that such differential treatment in fact saves the Government any money. In order to satisfy the demands of strict judicial scrutiny, the Government must demonstrate, for example, that it is actually cheaper to grant increased benefits with respect to all male members, than it is to determine which male members are in fact entitled to such benefits and to grant increased benefits only to those members whose wives actually meet the dependency requirement. Here, however, there is substantial evidence that, if put to the test, many of the wives of male members would fail to qualify for benefits. And in light of the fact that the dependency determination with respect to the husbands of female members is presently made solely on the basis of affidavits, rather than through the more costly hearing process, the Government's explanation of the statutory scheme is, to say the least, questionable.

In any case, our prior decisions make clear that, although efficacious administration of governmental programs is not without some importance, "the Constitution recognizes higher values than speed and efficiency." *** And when we enter the realm of "strict judicial scrutiny," there can be no doubt that "administrative convenience" is not a shibboleth, the mere recitation of which dictates constitutionality. *** On the contrary, any statutory scheme which draws a sharp line between the sexes, solely for the purpose of achieving administrative convenience, necessarily commands "dissimilar treatment for men and women who are . . . similarly situated," and therefore involves the "very kind of arbitrary legislative choice forbidden by the [Constitution]. . . ." *** We therefore conclude that, by according differential treatment to male and female members of the uniformed services for the sole purpose of achieving administrative convenience, the challenged statutes violate the Due Process Clause of the Fifth Amendment insofar as they require a female member to prove the dependency of her husband.

Reversed.

Mr. Justice Stewart concurs in the judgment, agreeing that the statutes before us work an invidious discrimination in violation of the Constitution. ***

Mr. Justice Rehnquist dissents. . . .

Mr. Justice Powell, with whom **The Chief Justice** and **Mr. Justice Blackmun** join, concurring in the judgment.

I agree that the challenge statutes constitute an unconstitutional discrimination against service women in violation of the Due Process Clause of the Fifth Amendment, but I cannot join the opinion of Mr. Justice Brennan, which would hold that all classifications based upon sex, "like classifications based upon race, alienage, and national origin," are "inherently suspect and must therefore be subjected to close judicial scrutiny." *** It is unnecessary for the Court in this case to characterize sex as a suspect classification, with all of the far-reaching implications of such a holding. *** In my view, we can and should decide this case on the authority of *Reed* and reserve for the future any expansion of its rationale.

There is another, and I find compelling, reason for deferring a general categorizing of sex classifications as invoking the strictest test of judicial scrutiny. The Equal Rights Amendment, which if adopted will resolve the substance of this precise question, has been approved by the Congress and submitted for ratification by the States. If this Amendment is duly adopted, it will represent the will of the people accomplished in the manner prescribed by the Constitution. By acting prematurely and unnecessarily, as I view it, the Court has assumed a decisional responsibility at the very time when state legislatures, functioning within the traditional democratic process, are debating the proposed Amendment. It seems to me that this reaching out to pre-empt by judicial action a major political decision which is currently in process of resolution does not reflect appropriate respect for duly prescribed legislative processes.

There are times when this Court, under our system, cannot avoid a constitutional decision on issues which normally should be resolved by the elected representatives of the people. But democratic institutions are weakened, and confidence in the restraint of the Court is impaired, when we appear unnecessarily to decide sensitive issues of broad social and political importance at the very time they are under consideration within the prescribed constitutional processes.

Rostker v. Goldberg

453 U.S. 57; 101 S. Ct. 2646; 69 L. Ed.2d 478 (1981)

Vote: 6-3

Justice Rehnquist delivered the opinion of the Court.

The question presented is whether the Military Selective Service Act [MSSA] *** violates the Fifth Amendment to the United States Constitution in authorizing the President to require the registration of males and not females.

Congress is given the power under the Constitution "To raise and support Armies," "To provide and maintain a Navy," and "To make Rules for the Government and Regulation of the land and naval Forces." *** Pursuant to this grant of authority, Congress has enacted the Military Selective Service Act. *** Section 3 of the Act *** empowers the President, by proclamation, to require the registration of "every male citizen" and male resident aliens between the ages of 18 and 26.... The MSSA registration provision serves no other purpose beyond providing a pool for subsequent induction.

Registration for the draft...was discontinued in 1975.... In early 1980, President Carter determined that it was necessary to reactivate the draft registration process. The immediate impetus for this decision was the Soviet armed invasion of Afghanistan.... The Selective Service System had been inactive, however, and funds were needed before reactivating registration. The President therefore recommended that funds be transferred from the Department of Defense to the separate Selective Service System.... He also recommended that Congress take action to amend the MSSA to permit the registration and conscription of women as well as men....

Congress agreed that it was necessary to reactivate the registration process, and allocated funds for that purpose in a Joint Resolution which passed the House on April 22 and the Senate on June 12.... The Resolution did not allocate all the funds originally requested by the President, but only those necessary to register males. *** Although Congress considered the question at great length, *** it declined to amend the MSSA to permit the registration of women.

On July 2, 1980, the President, by Proclamation, ordered the registration of specified groups of young men pursuant to the authority conferred by the Act. Registration was to commence on July 21, 1980....

On Friday, July 18, 1980, three days before registration was to commence, the District Court issued an opinion finding that the Act violated the Due Process Clause of the Fifth Amendment and permanently enjoined the Government from requiring registration under the Act....

Whenever called upon to judge the constitutionality of an Act of Congress—"the gravest and most delicate duty that this Court is called upon to perform," *** the Court accords "great weight to the decisions of Congress." *** The Congress is a coequal branch of government whose Members take the same oath we do to uphold the Constitution of the United States. As Justice Frankfurter noted in *Joint Anti-Fascist Refugee Committee v. McGrath* *** (1951) (concurring opinion), we must have "due regard to the fact that this Court is not exercising a primary judgment but is sitting in judgment upon those who also have taken the oath to observe the Constitution and who have the responsibility for carrying on government." The customary deference accorded the judgments of Congress is certainly appropriate when, as here, Congress specifically considered the question of the Act's constitutionality. ***

This is not, however, merely a case involving the customary deference accorded congressional decisions. The case arises in the context of Congress' authority over national defense and military affairs, and perhaps in no other area has the Court accorded Congress greater deference. In rejecting the registration of women, Congress explicitly relied upon its constitutional powers.... The "specific findings" section of the Report of the Senate Armed Services Committee, later adopted by both Houses of Congress, began by stating:

Article I, section 8 of the Constitution commits exclusively to the Congress the powers to raise and support armies, provide and maintain a Navy, and make rules for Government and regulation of the land and naval forces, and pursuant to these powers it lies within the discretion of the

Congress to determine the occasions for expansion of our Armed Forces, and the means best suited to such expansion should it prove necessary. ***

. . . This Court has consistently recognized Congress' "broad constitutional power" to raise and regulate armies and navies. ***

Not only is the scope of Congress' constitutional power in this area broad, but the lack of competence on the part of the courts is marked. . . .

This case is quite different from several of the gender-based discrimination cases we have considered [in an omitted portion of this opinion] in that, despite appellees' assertions, Congress did not act "unthinkingly" or "reflexively and not for any considered reason." *** The question of registering women for the draft not only received considerable national attention and was the subject of wide-ranging public debate, but also was extensively considered by Congress in hearings, floor debate, and in committee. Hearings held by both Houses of Congress in response to the President's request for authorization to register women adduced extensive testimony and evidence concerning the issue. . . . These hearings built on other hearings held the previous year addressed to the same question.

. . . While proposals to register women were being rejected in the course of transferring funds to register males, Committees in both Houses which had conducted hearings on the issue were also rejecting the registration of women. . . .

The foregoing clearly establishes that the decision to exempt women from registration was not the " 'accidental by-product of a traditional way of thinking about females.' "

. . . Congress determined that any future draft, which would be facilitated by the registration scheme, would be characterized by a need for combat troops. The Senate Report explained, in a specific finding later adopted by both Houses, that "[i]f mobilization were to be ordered in a wartime scenario, the primary manpower need would be for combat replacements." *** The purpose of registration, therefore, was to prepare for a draft of combat troops.

Women as a group, however, unlike men as a group, are not eligible for combat. The restrictions on the participation of women in combat in the Navy and Air Force are statutory. . . . The Army and Marine Corps preclude the use of women in combat as a matter of established policy. *** Congress specifically recognized and endorsed the exclusion of women from combat in exempting women from registration. In the words of the Senate Report:

The principle that women should not intentionally and routinely engage in combat is fundamental, and enjoys wide support among our people. It is universally supported by military leaders who have testified before the Committee. . . . Current law and policy exclude women from being assigned to combat in our military forces, and the Committee reaffirms this policy. ***

. . . The existence of the combat restrictions clearly indicates the basis for Congress' decision to exempt women from registration. The purpose of registration was to prepare for a draft of combat troops. Since women are excluded from combat, Congress concluded that they would not be needed in the event of a draft, and therefore decided not to register them. . . .

. . . The reason women are exempt from registration is not because military needs can be met by drafting men. This is not a case of Congress arbitrarily choosing to burden one of two similarly situated groups, such as would be the case with an all-black or all-white, or an all-Catholic or all-Lutheran, or an all-Republican or all-Democratic registration. Men and women, because of the combat restrictions on women, are simply not similarly situated for purposes of a draft or registration for a draft.

Congress' decision to authorize the registration of only men, therefore, does not violate the Due Process Clause. The exemption of women from registration is not only sufficiently but also closely related to Congress' purpose in authorizing registration. . . . The fact that Congress and the Executive have decided that women should not serve in combat fully justifies Congress in not authorizing their registration, since the purpose of registration is to develop a pool of potential combat troops. . . . The Constitution requires that Congress treat similarly situated persons similarly, not that it engage in gestures of superficial equality. . . .

In sum, Congress carefully evaluated the testimony that 80,000 women conscripts could be usefully employed in the event of a draft and rejected it in the permissible exercise of its constitutional responsibility. . . .

In light of the foregoing, we conclude that Congress acted well within its constitutional authority when it authorized the registration of men, and not women, under the Military Selective Service Act. The decision of the District Court holding otherwise is accordingly
Reversed.

Justice White, with whom ***Justice Brennan*** joins, dissenting. . . .

Justice Marshall, with whom ***Justice Brennan*** joins, dissenting.

The Court today places its imprimatur on one of the most potent remaining public expressions of "ancient canards about the proper role of women." *** It upholds a statute that requires males but not females to register for the draft, and which thereby categorically excludes women from a fundamental civic obligation. Because I believe the Court's decision is inconsistent with the Constitution's guarantee of equal protection of the laws, I dissent.

. . . By now it should be clear that statutes like the MSSA, which discriminate on the basis of gender, must be examined under the "heightened" scrutiny mandated by *Craig v. Boren*. *** Under this test, a gender-based classification cannot withstand constitutional challenge unless the classification is substantially related to the achievement of an important governmental objective. *** This test applies whether the classification discriminates against males or females. *** The party defending the challenged classification carries the burden of demonstrating both the importance of the governmental objective it serves and the substantial relationship between the discriminatory means and the asserted end. *** Consequently before we can sustain the MSSA, the Government must demonstrate that the gender-based classification it employs bears "a close and substantial relationship to [the achievement of] important governmental objectives." *** . . .

. . . The relevant inquiry under the *Craig v. Boren* test is not whether a gender-neutral classification would substantially advance important governmental interests. Rather, the question is whether the gender-based classification is itself substantially related to the achievement of the asserted governmental inter-

ests. Thus, the Government's task in this case is to demonstrate that excluding women from registration substantially furthers the goal of preparing for a draft of combat troops. Or to put it another way, the Government must show that registering women would substantially impede its efforts to prepare for such a draft. Under our precedents, the Government cannot meet this burden without showing that a gender-neutral statute would be a less effective means of attaining this end. . . . In this case, the Government makes no claim that preparing for a draft of combat troops cannot be accomplished just as effectively by registering both men and women but drafting only men if only men turn out to be needed. Nor can the Government argue that this alternative entails the additional cost and administrative inconvenience of registering women. This Court has repeatedly stated that the administrative convenience of employing a gender classification is not an adequate constitutional justification under the *Craig v. Boren* test. . . .

The fact that registering women in no way obstructs the governmental interest in preparing for a draft of combat troops points up a second flaw in the Court's analysis. The Court essentially reduces the question of the constitutionality of male-only registration to the validity of a hypothetical program for conscripting only men. The Court posits a draft in which all conscripts are either assigned to those specific combat posts presently closed to women or must be available for rotation into such positions. . . .

. . . But even addressing the Court's reasoning on its own terms, its analysis is flawed because the entire argument rests on a premise that is demonstrably false. As noted, the majority simply assumes that registration prepares for a draft in which every draftee must be available for assignment to combat. But the majority's draft scenario finds no support in either the testimony before Congress, or more importantly, in the findings of the Senate report. Indeed, the scenario appears to exist only in the Court's imagination, for even the Government represents only that "in the event of mobilization, approximately two-thirds of the demand on the induction system would be for combat skills." . . . For my part, rather than join the Court in imagining hypothetical drafts, I prefer to examine the findings in the Senate Report and the testimony presented to Congress. . . .

... In some 106 instances since this Court was established it has determined that congressional action exceeded the bounds of the Constitution. I believe the same is true of this statute. In an attempt to avoid its constitutional obligation, the Court today "pushes back the limits of the Constitution" to accommodate an Act of Congress.

I would affirm the judgment of the District Court.

Mississippi University for Women v. Hogan
458 U.S. 718; 102 S. Ct. 3331; 73 L. Ed.2d 1090 (1982)
Vote: 5-4

Justice O'Connor delivered the opinion of the Court:

This case presents the narrow issue of whether a state statute that excludes males from enrolling in a state-supported professional nursing school violates the Equal Protection Clause of the Fourteenth Amendment.

I

The facts are not in dispute. In 1884, the Mississippi legislature created the Mississippi Industrial Institute and College for the Education of White Girls of the State of Mississippi, now the oldest state-supported all-female college in the United States. *** The school, known today as Mississippi University for Women (MUW), has from its inception limited its enrollment to women.

In 1971, MUW established a School of Nursing, initially offering a two-year associate degree. Three years later, the school instituted a four-year baccalaureate program in nursing and today also offers a graduate program. The School of Nursing has its own faculty and administers its own criteria for admission.

Respondent, Joe Hogan, is a registered nurse but does not hold a baccalaureate degree in nursing. Since 1974, he has worked as a nursing supervisor in a medical center in Columbus, the city in which MUW is located. In 1979, Hogan applied for admission to the MUW School of Nursing's baccalaureate program. Although he was otherwise qualified, he was denied admission solely because of his sex. School officials informed him that he could audit the courses in which he was interested, but could not enroll for credit. ...

II

We begin our analysis aided by several firmly established principles. Because the challenged policy expressly discriminates among applicants on the basis of gender, it is subject to scrutiny under the Equal Protection Clause. *** That this statute discriminates against males rather than against females does not exempt it from scrutiny or reduce the standard of review. *** Our decisions also establish that the party seeking to uphold a statute that classifies individuals on the basis of their gender must carry the burden of showing an "exceedingly persuasive justification" for the classification. *** The burden is met only by showing at least that the classification serves "important governmental objectives and that the discrimination means employed" are "substantially related to the achievement of those objectives." ***

Although the test for determining the validity of a gender-based classification is straightforward, it must be applied free of fixed notions concerning the roles and abilities of males and females. Care must be taken in ascertaining whether the statutory objective itself reflects archaic and stereotypic notions. Thus, if the statutory objective is to exclude or "protect" members of one gender because they are presumed to suffer from an inherent handicap or to be innately inferior, the objective itself is illegitimate. ***

If the State's objective is legitimate and important, we next determine whether the requisite direct, substantial relationship between objective and means is present. The purpose of requiring that close relationship is to assure that the validity of a classification is determined through reasoned analysis rather than through the mechanical application of traditional, often inaccurate, assumptions about the proper roles of men and women. The need for the requirement is amply revealed by reference to the broad range of statutes already invalidated by this Court, statutes that relied upon the simplistic, outdated assumption that gender could be used as a "proxy for other, more germane bases of classification," *** to establish a link between objective and classification.

Applying this framework, we now analyze the arguments advanced by the State to justify its refusal to allow males to enroll for credit in MUW's School of Nursing.

III

A

The State's primary justification for maintaining the single-sex admissions policy of MUW's School of Nursing is that it compensates for discrimination against women and, therefore, constitutes educational affirmative action. As applied to the School of Nursing, we find the State's argument unpersuasive....

It is readily apparent that a State can evoke a compensatory purpose to justify an otherwise discriminatory classification only if members of the gender benefited by the classification actually suffer a disadvantage related to the classification....

... Mississippi has made no showing that women lacked opportunities to obtain training in the field of nursing or to attain positions of leadership in that field when the MUW School of Nursing opened its doors or that women currently are deprived of such opportunities. In fact, in 1970, the year before the School of Nursing's first class enrolled, women earned 94 percent of the nursing baccalaureate degrees conferred in Mississippi and 98.6 percent of the degrees earned nationwide. *** That year was not an aberration; one decade earlier, women had earned all the nursing degrees conferred in Mississippi and 98.9 percent of the degrees earned nationwide. ***

Rather than compensate for discriminatory barriers faced by women, MUW's policy of excluding males from admission to the School of Nursing tends to perpetuate the stereotyped view of nursing as an exclusively woman's job. By assuring that Mississippi allots more openings in its state-supported nursing schools to women than it does to men, MUW's admissions policy lends credibility to the old view that women, not men, should become nurses, and makes the assumption that nursing is a field for women a self-fulfilling prophecy. ***

The policy is invalid also because it fails the second part of the equal protection test, for the State has made no showing that the gender-based classification is substantially and directly related to its proposed compensatory objective. To the contrary, MUW's policy of permitting men to attend classes as auditors fatally undermines its claim that women, at least those in the School of Nursing, are adversely affected by the presence of men.

... The uncontroverted record reveals that admitting men to nursing classes does not affect teaching style, that the presence of men in the classroom would not affect the performance of the female nursing students, and that men in coeducational nursing schools do not dominate the classroom. In sum, the record in this case is flatly inconsistent with the claim that excluding men from the School of Nursing is necessary to reach any of MUW's educational goals.

Thus, considering both the asserted interest and the relationship between the interest and the methods used by the State, we conclude that the State has fallen far short of establishing the "exceedingly persuasive justification" needed to sustain the gender-based classification. Accordingly, we hold that MUW's policy of denying males the right to enroll for credit in its School of Nursing violates the Equal Protection Clause of the Fourteenth Amendment.

B

In an additional attempt to justify its exclusion of men from MUW's School of Nursing, the State contends that MUW is the direct beneficiary "of specific congressional legislation which, on its face, permits the institution to exist as it has in the past." The argument is based upon the language of 901(a) in Title IX of the Education Amendments of 1972. *** Although 901(a) prohibits gender discrimination in education programs that receive federal financial assistance, subsection 5 exempts the admissions policies of undergraduate institutions "that traditionally and continually from [their] establishment [have] a policy of admitting only students of one sex" from the general prohibition. Arguing that Congress enacted

Title IX in furtherance of its power to enforce the Fourteenth Amendment, a power granted by Sec. 5 of that Amendment, the State would have us conclude that 901(a)(5), is but "a congressional limitation upon the broad prohibitions of the Equal Protection Clause of the Fourteenth Amendment." ***

The argument requires little comment. Initially, it is far from clear that Congress intended . . . to exempt MUW from any constitutional obligation. Rather, Congress apparently intended, at most, to exempt MUW from the requirements of Title IX.

Even if Congress envisioned a constitutional exemption, the State's argument would fail. Section 5 of the Fourteenth Amendment gives Congress broad power indeed to enforce the command of the Amendment and "to secure to all persons the enjoyment of perfect equality of civil rights and the equal protection of the laws against State denial or invasion. . . ." Congress' power under Sec. 5 grants Congress no power to restrict, abrogate, or dilute these guarantees. Although we give deference to congressional decisions and classifications, neither Congress nor a State can validate a law that denies the rights guaranteed by the Fourteenth Amendment. . . .

Chief Justice Burger, dissenting.

I agree generally with Justice Powell's dissenting opinion. I write separately, however, to emphasize that the Court's holding today is limited to the context of a professional nursing school. *** Since the Court's opinion relies heavily on its finding that women have traditionally dominated the nursing profession, *** it suggests that a State might well be justified in maintaining, for example, the option of an all-women's business school or liberal arts program.

Justice Blackmun, dissenting. . . .

Justice Powell, with whom **Justice Rehnquist** joins, dissenting.

. . . The Court's opinion bows deeply to conformity. Left without honor—indeed, held unconstitutional—is an element of diversity that has characterized much of American education and enriched much of American life. The Court in effect holds today that no State now may provide even a single institution of higher learning open only to women

students. It gives no heed to the efforts of the State of Mississippi to provide abundant opportunities for young men and young women to attend coeducational institutions, and none to the preferences of the more than 40,000 young women who over the years have evidenced their approval of an all-women's college by choosing Mississippi University for Women (MUW) over seven coeducational universities within the State. The Court decides today that the Equal Protection Clause makes it unlawful for the State to provide women with a traditionally popular and respected choice of educational environment. It does so in a case instituted by one man, who represents no class, and whose primary concern is personal convenience.

. . . [Hogan's] constitutional complaint is based upon a single asserted harm: that he must travel to attend the state-supported nursing schools that concededly are available to him. The Court characterizes this injury as one of "inconvenience." This description is fair and accurate, though somewhat embarrassed by the fact that there is, of course, no constitutional right to attend a state-supported university in one's home town. . . .

I

Coeducation, historically, is a novel educational theory. From grade school through high school, college, and graduate and professional training, much of the nation's population during much of our history has been educated in sexually segregated classrooms. At the college level, for instance, until recently some of the most prestigious colleges and universities—including most of the Ivy League—had long histories of single-sex education. As Harvard, Yale, and Princeton remained all-male colleges well into the second half of this century, the "Seven Sister" institutions established a parallel standard of excellence for women's colleges. Of the Seven Sisters, Mount Holyoke opened as a female seminary in 1837 and was chartered as a college in 1888. Vassar was founded in 1865, Smith and Wellesley in 1875, Radcliffe in 1879, Bryn Mawr in 1885, and Barnard in 1889. Mount Holyoke, Smith, and Wellesley recently have made considered decisions to remain essentially single-sex institutions. ***

The sexual segregation of students has been a reflection of, rather than an imposition upon, the preference of those subject to the policy. It cannot be disputed, for example, that the highly qualified women attending the leading women's colleges could have earned admission to virtually any college of their choice. Women attending such colleges have chosen to be there, usually expressing a preference for the special benefits of a single-sex institutions. Similar decisions were made by the colleges that elected to remain open to women only.

The arguable benefits of single-sex colleges also continue to be recognized by students of higher education. The Carnegie Commission on Higher Education has reported that it "favor[s] the continuation of colleges for women. They provide an element of diversity . . . and [an environment in which women] generally . . . speak up more in their classes, . . . hold more positions of leadership on campus, . . . and have more role models and mentors among women teachers and administrators." ***

Despite the continuing expressions that single-sex institutions may offer singular advantages to their students, there is no doubt that coeducational institutions are far more numerous. But their numerical predominance does not establish—in any sense properly cognizable by a court—that individuals' preferences for single-sex education are misguided or illegitimate, or that a State may not provide its citizens with a choice.

II

The issue in this case is whether a State transgresses the Constitution when—within the context of a public system that offers a diverse range of campuses, curricula, and educational alternatives—it seeks to accommodate the legitimate personal preferences of those desiring the advantages of an all-women's college. In my view, the court errs seriously by assuming—without argument or discussion—that the equal protection standard generally applicable to sex discrimination is appropriate here. That standard was designed to free women from "archaic and overbroad generalizations." *** In no previous case have we applied it to invalidate state efforts to expand women's choices. Nor are there prior sex discrimination decisions by this Court in which a male plaintiff, as in this case, had the choice of an equal benefit. . . .

By applying heightened equal protection analysis to this case, the Court frustrates the liberating spirit of the Equal Protection Clause. It forbids the States from providing women with an opportunity to choose the type of university they prefer. And yet it is these women whom the Court regards as the victims of an illegal, stereotyped perception of the role of women in our society. The Court reasons this way in a case in which no woman has complained, and the only complainant is a man who advances no claims on behalf of anyone else. His claim, it should be recalled, is not that he is being denied a substantive educational opportunity, or even the right to attend an all-male or a coeducational college. *** It is only that the colleges open to him are located at inconvenient distances.

III

The Court views this case as presenting a serious equal protection claim of sex discrimination. I do not and I would sustain Mississippi's right to continue MUW on a rational basis analysis. But I need not apply this "lowest tier" of scrutiny. I can accept for present purposes the standard applied by the Court: that there is a gender-based distinction that must serve an important governmental objective by means that are substantially related to its achievement. The record in this case reflects that MUW has a historic position in the State's educational system dating back to 1884. More than 2,000 women presently evidence their preference for MUW by having enrolled there. The choice is one that discriminates invidiously against no one. And the State's purpose in preserving that choice is legitimate and substantial. Generations of our finest minds, both among educators and students, have believed that single-sex college-level institutions afford distinctive benefits. There are many persons, of course, who have different views. But simply because there are these differences is no reason— certainly none of constitutional dimension—to conclude that no substantial state interest is served when such a choice is made available.

In arguing to the contrary, the Court suggests that the MUW is so operated as to "perpetuate the stereotyped view of nursing as an exclusively women's job." *** But as the Court itself acknowledges, *** MUW's School of Nursing was not created until 1971—about 90 years after the single-sex campus itself was founded. This hardly supports a link between nursing as a woman's profession and MUW's single-sex admission policy. Indeed, MUW's School of Nursing was established at the coeducational University of Mississippi at Jackson. The School of Nursing makes up only one part—a relatively small part—of a diverse modern university campus and curriculum. The other departments on the MUW campus offer a typical range of degrees and a typical range of subjects. There is no indication that women suffer fewer opportunities at other Mississippi state campuses because of MUW's admission policy.

In sum, the practice of voluntarily chosen single-sex education is an honored tradition in our country, even if it now rarely exists in state colleges and universities. Mississippi's accommodation of such student choices is legitimate because it is completely consensual and is important because it permits students to decide for themselves the type of college education they think will benefit them most. Finally, Mississippi's policy is substantially related to its long-respected objective.

IV

A distinctive feature of America's tradition has been respect for diversity. This has been characteristic of the peoples from numerous lands who have built our country. It is the essence of our democratic system. At stake in this case as I see it is the preservation of a small aspect of this diversity. But that aspect is by no means insignificant, given our heritage of available choice between single-sex and coeducational institutions of higher learning. The Court answers that there is discrimination—not just that which may be tolerable, as for example between those candidates for admission able to contribute most to an educational institution and those able to contribute less—but discrimination of constitutional dimension. But, having found "discrimination," the Court finds it difficult to identify the victims. It hardly can claim that women are discriminated against. A constitutional case is held to exist solely because one man found it inconvenient to travel to any of the other institutions made available to him by the State of Mississippi. In essence he insists that he has a right to attend a college in his home community. This simply is not a sex discrimination case. The Equal Protection Clause was never intended to be applied to this kind of case.

Plyler v. Doe

457 U.S. 202; 102 S. Ct. 2382; 72 L. Ed.2d 786 (1982)
Vote: 5-4

Justice Brennan delivered the opinion of the Court.

The question presented by these cases is whether, consistent with the Equal Protection Clause of the Fourteenth Amendment, Texas may deny to undocumented school age children the free public education that it provides to children who are citizens of the United States or legally admitted aliens.

Since the late 19th century, the United States has restricted immigration into this country. Unsanctioned entry into the United States is a crime, *** and those who have entered unlawfully are subject to deportation.... *** But despite the existence of these

legal restrictions, a substantial number of persons have succeeded in unlawfully entering the United States, and now live within various States including the State of Texas.

In May 1975, the Texas Legislature revised its education laws to withhold from local school districts any state funds for the education of children who were not "legally admitted" into the United States. The 1975 revision also authorized local school districts to deny enrollment in their public schools to children not "legally admitted" to the country. ***

This is a class action, filed in the United States District Court for the Eastern District of Texas in

September 1977, on behalf of certain school age children of Mexican origin residing in Smith County, Tex., who could not establish that they had been legally admitted into the United States. The action complained of the exclusion of plaintiff children from the public schools of the Tyler Independent School District. The Superintendent and members of the Board of Trustees of the School District were named as defendants; the State of Texas intervened as a party-defendant. . . .

The District Court held that illegal aliens were entitled to the protection of the Equal Protection Clause of the Fourteenth Amendment, and that [the Texas law] violated that Clause. . . .

. . . With respect to equal protection, however, the Court of Appeals affirmed in all essential respects the analysis of the District Court, *** concluding that [the Texas law] was "constitutionally infirm regardless of whether it was tested using the mere rational basis standard or some more stringent test . . ." ***

The Fourteenth Amendment provides that "[n]o State shall . . . deprive any person of life, liberty, or property, without due process of law; nor deny to any person within its jurisdiction the equal protection of the laws." Appellants argue at the outset that undocumented aliens, because of their immigration status, are not "persons within the jurisdiction" of the State of Texas, and that they therefore have no right to the equal protection of Texas law. We reject this argument. Whatever his status under the immigration laws, an alien is surely a "person" in any ordinary sense of that term. Aliens, even aliens whose presence in this country is unlawful, have long been recognized as "persons" guaranteed due process of law by the Fifth and Fourteenth Amendments. ***

Appellants seek to distinguish our prior cases, emphasizing that the Equal Protection Clause directs a State to afford its protection to persons within its jurisdiction while the Due Process Clauses of the Fifth and Fourteenth Amendments contain no such assertedly limiting phrase. In appellants' view, persons who have entered the United States illegally are not "within the jurisdiction" of a State even if they are present within a State's boundaries and subject to its laws. Neither our cases nor the logic of the Fourteenth Amendment supports that constricting construction of the phrase "within its jurisdiction." We

have never suggested that the class of persons who might avail themselves of the equal protection guarantee is less than coextensive with that entitled to due process. To the contrary, we have recognized that both provisions were fashioned to protect an identical class of persons, and to reach every exercise of state authority. . . .

Our conclusion that the illegal aliens who are plaintiffs in these cases may claim the benefit of the Fourteenth Amendment's guarantee of equal protection only begins the inquiry. The more difficult question is whether the Equal Protection Clause has been violated by the refusal of the State of Texas to reimburse local school boards for the education of children who cannot demonstrate that their presence within the United States is lawful, or by the imposition by those school boards of the burden of tuition on those children. It is to this question that we now turn.

The Equal Protection Clause directs that "all persons similarly circumstanced shall be treated alike." *** But so too, "[t]he Constitution does not require things which are different in fact or opinion to be treated in law as though they were the same." *** The initial discretion to determine what is "different" and what is "the same" resides in the legislatures of the States. A legislature must have substantial latitude to establish classifications that roughly approximate the nature of the problem perceived, that accommodate competing concerns both public and private, and that account for limitations on the practical ability of the State to remedy every ill. In applying the Equal Protection Clause to most forms of state action, we thus seek only the assurance that the classification at issue bears some fair relationship to a legitimate public purpose.

But we would not be faithful to our obligations under the Fourteenth Amendment if we applied so deferential a standard to every classification. The Equal Protection Clause was intended as a restriction on state legislative action inconsistent with elemental constitutional premises. Thus we have treated as presumptively invidious those classifications that disadvantage a "suspect class," or that impinge upon the exercise of a "fundamental right." With respect to such classifications, it is appropriate to enforce the mandate of equal protection by requiring the State to demonstrate that its classification has been precisely tailored to serve a compelling governmental interest. In addition, we have recognized that certain forms of legislative classification, while not facially invidious, nonetheless give rise to recurring constitutional difficulties; in these limited circumstances we have sought the assurance that the classification reflects a reasoned judgment consistent with the ideal of equal protection by inquiring whether it may fairly be viewed as furthering a substantial interest of the State. We turn to a consideration of the standard appropriate for the evaluation of [the Texas law].

Sheer incapability or lax enforcement of the laws barring entry into this country, coupled with the failure to establish an effective bar to employment of undocumented aliens, has resulted in the creation of a substantial "shadow population" of illegal migrants—numbering in the millions—within our borders. This situation raises the specter of a permanent caste of undocumented resident aliens, encouraged by some to remain here as a source of cheap labor, but nevertheless denied the benefits that our society makes available to citizens and lawful residents. The existence of such an underclass presents most difficult problems for a Nation that prides itself on adherence to principles of equality under law.

The children who are plaintiffs in these cases are special members of this underclass. Persuasive arguments support the view that a State may withhold its beneficence from those whose very presence within the United States is the product of their own unlawful conduct. These arguments do not apply with the same force to classifications imposing disabilities on the minor children of such illegal entrants. At the least, those who elect to enter our territory by stealth and in violation of our law should be prepared to bear the consequences, including, but not limited to, deportation. But the children of those illegal entrants are not comparably situated. Their "parents have the ability to conform their conduct to societal norms," and presumably the ability to remove themselves from the state's jurisdiction; but the children who are plaintiffs in these cases "can affect neither their parents' conduct nor their own status." *** Even if the State found it expedient to control the conduct of adults by acting against their children, legislation directing the onus of a parent's misconduct against his

children does not comport with fundamental conceptions of justice. . . .

Of course, undocumented status is not irrelevant to any proper legislative goal. Nor is undocumented status an absolutely immutable characteristic since it is the product of conscious, indeed unlawful, action. But [the Texas law] is directed against children, and imposes its discriminatory burden on the basis of a legal characteristic over which children can have little control. It is thus difficult to conceive of a rational justification for penalizing these children for their presence within the United States. Yet that appears to be precisely the effect of [the Texas law].

Public education is not a "right" granted to individuals by the Constitution. *** But neither is it merely some governmental "benefit" indistinguishable from other forms of social welfare legislation. Both the importance of education in maintaining our basic institutions, and the lasting impact of its deprivation on the life of the child, mark the distinction. The "American people have always regarded education and [the] acquisition of knowledge as matters of supreme importance." *** In addition to the pivotal role of education in sustaining our political and cultural heritage, denial of education to some isolated group of children poses an affront to one of the goals of the Equal Protection Clause: the abolition of governmental barriers presenting unreasonable obstacles to advancement on the basis of individual merit. Paradoxically, by depriving the children of any disfavored group of an education, we foreclose the means by which that group might raise the level of esteem in which it is held by the majority. But more directly, "education prepares individuals to be self-reliant and self-sufficient participants in society." *** Illiteracy is an enduring disability. The inability to read and write will handicap the individual deprived of a basic education each and every day of his life. The inestimable toll of that deprivation on the social, economic, intellectual, and psychological well-being of the individual, and the obstacle it poses to individual achievement, make it most difficult to reconcile the cost of the principle of a status-based denial of basic education with the framework of equality embodied in the Equal Protection Clause. . . .

. . . Undocumented aliens cannot be treated as a suspect class because their presence in this country in violation of federal law is not a "constitutional irrelevancy." Nor is education a fundamental right; a State need not justify by compelling necessity every variation in the manner in which education is provided to its population. *** But more is involved in these cases than the abstract question whether [the Texas law] discriminates against a suspect class, or whether education is a fundamental right. [The Texas law] imposes a lifetime hardship on a discrete class of children not accountable for their disabling status. The stigma of illiteracy will mark them for the rest of their lives. By denying these children a basic education, we deny them the ability to live within the structure of our civic institutions, and foreclose any realistic possibility that they will contribute in even the smallest way to the progress of our Nation. In determining the rationality of [the Texas law] we may appropriately take into account its costs to the Nation and to the innocent children who are its victims. In light of these countervailing costs, the discrimination contained in [the Texas law] can hardly be considered rational unless it furthers some substantial goal of the State.

It is the State's principal argument, and apparently the view of the dissenting Justices, that the undocumented status of these children *vel non* establishes a sufficient rational basis for denying them benefits that a State might choose to afford other residents. The State notes that while other aliens are admitted "on an equality of legal privileges with all citizens under nondiscriminatory laws," *** the asserted right of these children to an education can claim no implicit congressional imprimatur. Indeed, in the State's view, Congress' apparent disapproval of the presence of these children within the United States, and the evasion of the federal regulatory program that is the mark of undocumented status, provides authority for its decision to impose upon them special disabilities. Faced with an equal protection challenge respecting the treatment of aliens, we agree that the courts must be attentive to congressional policy; the exercise of congressional power might well affect the State's prerogatives to afford differential treatment to a particular class of aliens. But we are unable to find in the congressional immigration scheme any statement of policy that might weigh significantly in arriving at an equal protection bal-

ance concerning the State's authority to deprive these children of an education. . . .

Appellants argue that the classification at issue furthers an interest in the "preservation of the state's limited resources for the education of its lawful residents." *** Of course, a concern for the preservation of resources standing alone can hardly justify the classification used in allocating those resources. *** The State must do more than justify its classification with a concise expression of an intention to discriminate. *** Apart from the asserted state prerogative to act against undocumented children solely on the basis of their undocumented status—an asserted prerogative that carries only minimal force in the circumstances of these cases—we discern three colorable state interests that might support [the Texas law].

First, appellants appear to suggest that the State may seek to protect itself from an influx of illegal immigrants. While a State might have an interest in mitigating the potentially harsh economic effects of sudden shifts in population, [the Texas law] hardly offers an effective method of dealing with an urgent demographic or economic problem. There is no evidence in the record suggesting that illegal entrants impose any significant burden on the State's economy. To the contrary, the available evidence suggests that illegal aliens underutilize public services, while contributing their labor to the local economy and tax money to the state fisc. *** The dominant incentive for illegal entry into the State of Texas is the availability of employment; few if any illegal immigrants come to this country, or presumably to the State of Texas, in order to avail themselves of a free education. Thus, even making the doubtful assumption that the net impact of illegal aliens on the economy of the State is negative, we think it clear that "[c]harging tuition to undocumented children constitutes a ludicrously ineffectual attempt to stem the tide of illegal immigration," at least when compared with the alternative of prohibiting the employment of illegal aliens. ***

Second, while it is apparent that a State may "not . . . reduce expenditures for education by barring [some arbitrarily chosen class of] children from its schools," *** appellants suggest that undocumented children are appropriately singled out for exclusion because of the special burdens they impose on the State's ability to provide high quality public education. But the record in no way supports the claim that exclusion of undocumented children is likely to improve the overall quality of education in the State. . . .

Finally, appellants suggest that undocumented children are appropriately singled out because their unlawful presence within the United States renders them less likely than other children to remain within the boundaries of the state, and to put their education to productive social or political use within the State. Even assuming that such an interest is legitimate, it is an interest that is most difficult to quantify. The State has no assurance that any child, citizen or not, will employ the education provided by the State within the confines of the State's borders. In any event, the record is clear that many of the undocumented children disabled by this classification will remain in this country indefinitely, and that some will become lawful residents or citizens of the United States. It is difficult to understand precisely what the State hopes to achieve by promoting the creation and perpetuation of a subclass of illiterates within our boundaries, surely adding to the problems and costs of unemployment, welfare, and crime. It is thus clear that whatever savings might be achieved by denying these children an education, they are wholly insubstantial in light of the costs involved to these children, the State, and the Nation.

If the State is to deny a discrete group of innocent children the free public education that it offers to other children residing within its borders, that denial must be justified by a showing that it furthers some substantial state interest. No such showing was made here. . . .

Justice Marshall, concurring. . . .

Justice Blackmun, concurring. . . .

Justice Powell, concurring. . . .

Chief Justice Burger, with whom *Justice White, Justice Rehnquist,* and *Justice O'Connor* join, dissenting.

Were it our business to set the Nation's social policy, I would agree without hesitation that it is senseless for an enlightened society to deprive any children—including illegal aliens—of an elementary education. I fully agree that it would be folly—and wrong—to tolerate creation of a segment of society made up of illiterate persons, many having a limited or no command of our language. However, the Constitution does not constitute us as "Platonic Guardians" nor does it vest in this Court the authority to strike down laws because they do not meet our standards of desirable social policy, "wisdom," or "common sense." *** We trespass on the assigned function of the political branches under our structure of limited and separated powers when we assume a policy-making role as the Court does today.

The Court makes no attempt to disguise that it is acting to make up for Congress' lack of "effective leadership" in dealing with the serious national problems caused by the influx of uncountable millions of illegal aliens across our borders. *** The failure of enforcement of the immigration laws over more than a decade and the inherent difficulty and expense of sealing our vast borders have combined to create a grave socioeconomic dilemma. It is a dilemma that has not yet even been fully assessed, let alone addressed. However, it is not the function of the judiciary to provide "effective leadership" simply because the political branches of government fail to do so. . . .

In a sense, the Court's opinion rests on such a unique confluence of theories and rationales that it will likely stand for little beyond the results in these particular cases. Yet the extent to which the Court departs from principled constitutional adjudication is nonetheless disturbing.

. . . The Equal Protection Clause does not mandate identical treatment of different categories of persons. ***

The dispositive issue in these cases, simply put, is whether, for purposes of allocating its finite resources, a state has a legitimate reason to differentiate between persons who are lawfully within the state and those who are unlawfully there. The distinction the State of Texas has drawn—based not only upon its own legitimate interests but on classifications established by the Federal Government in its immigration laws and policies—is not unconstitutional. . . .

... [T]he Equal Protection Clause does not preclude legislators from classifying among persons on the basis of factors and characteristics over which individuals may be said to lack "control." Indeed, in some circumstances persons generally, and children in particular, may have little control over or responsibility for such things as their ill health, need for public assistance, or place of residence. Yet a state legislature is not barred from considering, for example, relevant differences between the mentally healthy and the mentally ill, or between the residents of different counties, simply because these may be factors unrelated to individual choice or to any "wrongdoing." The Equal Protection Clause protects against arbitrary and irrational classifications, and against invidious discrimination stemming from prejudice and hostility; it is not an all-encompassing "equalizer" designed to eradicate every distinction for which persons are not "responsible."

... This Court has recognized that in allocating governmental benefits to a given class of aliens, one "may take into account the character of the relationship between the alien and this country." *** When that "relationship" is a federally prohibited one, there can, of course, be no presumption that a state has a constitutional duty to include illegal aliens among the recipients of its governmental benefits. ...

Once it is conceded—as the Court does—that illegal aliens are not a suspect class, and that education is not a fundamental right, our inquiry should focus on and be limited to whether the legislative classification at issue bears a rational relationship to a legitimate state purpose. *** ...

Without laboring what will undoubtedly seem obvious to many, it simply is not "irrational" for a state to conclude that it does not have the same responsibility to provide benefits for persons whose very presence in the state and this country is illegal as it does to provide for persons lawfully present. By definition, illegal aliens have no right whatever to be here, and the state may reasonably, and constitutionally, elect not to provide them with governmental services at the expense of those who are lawfully in the state. The Court has failed to offer even a plausible explanation why illegality of residence in this country is not a factor that may legitimately bear upon the *bona fides* of state residence and entitlement to the benefits of lawful residence.

It is significant that the Federal Government has seen fit to exclude illegal aliens from numerous social welfare programs, such as the food stamp program, *** the old-age assistance, aid to families with dependent children, aid to the blind, aid to the permanently and totally disabled, and supplemental security income programs, *** the Medicare hospital insurance benefits program, *** and the Medicaid hospital insurance benefits for the aged and disabled program ***. Although these exclusions do not conclusively demonstrate the constitutionality of the State's use of the same classification for comparable purposes, at the very least they tend to support the rationality of excluding illegal alien residents of a State from such programs so as to preserve the State's finite revenues for the benefit of lawful residents. *** ...

Congress, "vested by the Constitution with the responsibility of protecting our borders and legislating with respect to aliens," bears primary responsibility for addressing the problems occasioned by the millions of illegal aliens flooding across our southern border. Similarly, it is for Congress, and not this Court, to assess the "social costs borne by our Nation when select groups are denied the means to absorb the values and skills upon which our social order rests." *** While the "specter of a permanent caste" of illegal Mexican residents of the United States is indeed a disturbing one, *** it is but one segment of a larger problem, which is for the political branches to solve. I find it difficult to believe that Congress would long tolerate such a self-destructive result—that it would fail to deport these illegal alien families or to provide for the education of their children. Yet instead of allowing the political processes to run their course—albeit with some delay—the Court seeks to do Congress' job for it, compensating for congressional inaction. It is not unreasonable to think that this encourages the political branches to pass their problems to the judiciary.

The solution to this seemingly intractable problem is to defer to the political processes, unpalatable as that may be to some.

City of Cleburne, Texas v. Cleburne Living Center

473 U.S. 432; 105 S. Ct. 3249; 87 L. Ed.2d 313 (1985)
Vote: 9-0

Justice White delivered the opinion of the Court.

A Texas city denied a special use permit for the operation of a group home for the mentally retarded, acting pursuant to a municipal zoning ordinance requiring permits for such homes. The Court of Appeals for the Fifth Circuit held that mental retardation is a "quasi-suspect" classification and that the ordinance violated the Equal Protection Clause because it did not substantially further an important governmental purpose. We hold that a lesser standard of scrutiny is appropriate, but conclude that under that standard the ordinance is invalid as applied in this case.

In July, 1980, respondent Jan Hannah purchased a building at 201 Featherston Street in the city of Cleburne, Texas, with the intention of leasing it to Cleburne Living Centers, Inc. (CLC), for the operation of a group home for the mentally retarded. It was anticipated that the home would house 13 retarded men and women, who would be under the constant supervision of CLC staff members. . . .

The city informed CLC that a special use permit would be required for the operation of a group home at the site, and CLC accordingly submitted a permit application. In response to a subsequent inquiry from CLC, the city explained that under the zoning regulations applicable to the site, a special use permit, renewable annually, was required for the construction of "[h]ospitals for the insane or feeble-minded, or alcoholic [*sic*] or drug addicts, or penal or correctional institutions." The city had determined that the proposed group home should be classified as a "hospital for the feeble-minded." After holding a public hearing on CLC's application, the city council voted three to one to deny a special use permit.

CLC then filed suit in Federal District Court against the city and a number of its officials, alleging, *inter alia,* that the zoning ordinance was invalid on its face and as applied because it discriminated against the mentally retarded in violation of the equal protection rights of CLC and its potential residents. . . .

The Equal Protection Clause of the Fourteenth Amendment commands that no State shall "deny to any person within its jurisdiction the equal protection of the laws," which is essentially a direction that all persons similarly situated should be treated alike. *** Section 5 of the Amendment empowers Congress to enforce this mandate, but absent controlling congressional direction, the courts have themselves devised standards for determining the validity of state legislation or other official action that is challenged as denying equal protection. The general rule is that legislation is presumed to be valid and will be sustained if the classification drawn by the statute is rationally related to a legitimate state interest. . . . *** When social or economic legislation is at issue, the Equal Protection Clause allows the states wide latitude, *** and the Constitution presumes that even improvident decisions will eventually be rectified by the democratic processes.

The general rule gives way, however, when a statute classifies by race, alienage or national origin. These factors are so seldom relevant to the achievement of any legitimate state interest that laws grounded in such considerations are deemed to reflect prejudice and antipathy—a view that those in the burdened class are not as worthy or deserving as others. For these reasons and because such discrimination is unlikely to be soon rectified by legislative means, these laws are subject to strict scrutiny and will be sustained only if they are suitably tailored to serve a compelling state interest. *** Similar oversight by the courts is due when state laws impinge on personal rights protected by the Constitution. ***

Legislative classifications based on gender also call for a heightened standard of review. That factor generally provides no sensible ground for different treatment. Rather than resting on meaningful considerations, statutes distributing benefits and burdens between the sexes in different ways very likely reflect outmoded notions of the relative capabilities of men and women. A gender classification fails unless it is substantially related to a sufficiently important governmental interest. *** Because illegitimacy is beyond the individual's control and bears "no relation to the individual's ability to participate in and contribute to society," *** official discriminations resting on that characteristic are also subject to somewhat heightened review. Those restrictions "will survive equal protection scrutiny to the extent they are substantially related to a legitimate state interest." ***

We have declined, however, to extend heightened review to differential treatment based on age:

While the treatment of the aged in this Nation has not been wholly free of discrimination, such persons, unlike, say, those who have been discriminated against on the basis of race or national origin, have not experienced a "history of purposeful unequal treatment" or been subjected to unique disabilities on the basis of stereotyped characteristics not truly indicative of their abilities. ***

... Where individuals in the group affected by a law have distinguishing characteristics relevant to interests the state has the authority to implement, the courts have been very reluctant, as they should be in our federal system and with respect for the separation of powers, to closely scrutinize legislative choices as to whether, how and to what extent whose interests should be pursued. In such cases, the Equal Protection Clause requires only a rational means to serve a legitimate end.

Against this background, we conclude for several reasons that the Court of Appeals erred in holding mental retardation a quasi-suspect classification calling for a more exacting standard of judicial review than is normally accorded economic and social legislation. First, it is undeniable, and it is not argued otherwise here, that those who are mentally retarded have a reduced ability to cope with and function in the everyday world. Nor are they all cut from the same pattern: as the testimony in this record indicates, they range from those whose disability is not immediately evident to those who must be constantly cared for. They are thus different, immutably so, in relevant respects, and the states' interest in dealing with and providing for them is plainly a legitimate one. How this large and diversified group is to be treated under the law is a difficult and often a technical matter, very much a task for legislators guided by qualified professionals and not by the perhaps ill-informed opinions of the judiciary. Heightened scrutiny inevitably involves substantive judgments about legislative decisions, and we doubt that the predicate for such judicial oversight is present where the classification deals with mental retardation.

Second, the distinctive legislative response, both national and state, to the plight of those who are mentally retarded demonstrates not only that they have unique problems, but also that the lawmakers have been addressing their difficulties in a manner that belies a continuing antipathy or prejudice and a corresponding need for more intrusive oversight by the judiciary. Thus, the federal government has not only outlawed discrimination against the mentally retarded in federally funded programs, *** but it has also provided the retarded with the right to receive "appropriate treatment, services, and habilitation" in a setting that is "least restrictive of [their] personal liberty." *** In addition, the government has conditioned federal education funds on a State's assurance that retarded children will enjoy an education that, "to the maximum extent appropriate," is integrated with that of non-mentally retarded children. *** The government has also facilitated the hiring of the mentally retarded into the federal civil service by exempting them from the requirement of competitive examination. *** The State of Texas has similarly enacted legislation that acknowledges the special status of the mentally retarded by conferring certain rights upon them, such as "the right to live in the least restrictive setting appropriate to [their] individual needs and abilities," including "the right to live ... in a group home."

Such legislation thus singling out the retarded for special treatment reflects the real and undeniable differences between the retarded and others. That a civilized and decent society expects and approves such legislation indicates that governmental consideration of those differences in the vast majority of situations is not only legitimate but desirable. It may be, as CLC contends, that legislation designed to benefit, rather than disadvantage, the retarded would generally withstand examination under a test of heightened scrutiny. *** The relevant inquiry, however, is whether heightened scrutiny is constitutionally mandated in the first instance. Even assuming that many of these laws could be shown to be substantially related to an important governmental purpose, merely requiring the legislature to justify its efforts in these terms may lead it to refrain from acting at all. Much recent legislation intended to benefit the retarded also assumes the need for measures that might be perceived to disadvantage them. The Education of the Handicapped Act, for example, requires an "appropriate" education, not one that is equal in all respects to the education of non-retarded children; clearly, admission to a class that exceeded the abilities of a retarded child would not be appropriate. Similarly, the Developmental Disabilities Assistance Act and the Texas act give the retarded the right to live only in the "least restrictive setting" appropriate to their abilities, implicitly assuming the need for at least some restrictions that would not be imposed on others. Especially given the wide variation in the abilities and needs of the retarded themselves, governmental bodies must have a certain amount of flexibility and freedom from judicial oversight in shaping and limiting their remedial efforts.

Third, the legislative response, which could hardly have occurred and survived without public support, negates any claim that the mentally retarded arepolitically powerless in the sense that they have no ability to attract the attention of the lawmakers. Any minority can be said to be powerless to assert direct control over the legislature, but if that were a criterion for higher level scrutiny by the courts, much economic and social legislation would now be suspect.

Fourth, if the large and amorphous class of the mentally retarded were deemed quasi-suspect for the reasons given by the Court of Appeals, it would be difficult to find a principled way to distinguish a variety of other groups who have perhaps immutable disabilities setting them off from others, who cannot themselves mandate the desired legislative responses, and who can claim some degree of prejudice from at least part of the public at large. One need mention in this respect only the aging, the disabled, the mentally ill, and the infirm. We are reluctant set out on that course, and we decline to do so.

Doubtless, there have been and there will continue to be instances of discrimination against the retarded that are in fact invidious, and that are

properly subject to judicial correction under constitutional norms. But the appropriate method of reaching such instances is not to create a new quasi-suspect classification to more searching evaluation. Rather, we should look to the likelihood that governmental action premised on a particular classification is valid as a general matter, not merely to the specifics of the case before us. Because mental retardation is a characteristic that the government may legitimately take into account in a wide range of decisions, and because both state and federal governments have recently committed themselves to assisting the retarded, we will not presume that any given legislative action, even one that disadvantages retarded individuals, is rooted in considerations that the Constitution will not tolerate.

Our refusal to recognize the retarded as a quasi-suspect class does not leave them entirely unprotected from invidious discrimination. To withstand equal protection review, legislation that distinguishes between the mentally retarded and others must be rationally related to a legitimate governmental purpose. This standard, we believe, affords government the latitude necessary both to pursue policies designed to assist the retarded in realizing their full potential, and to freely and efficiently engage in activities that burden the retarded in what is essentially an incidental manner. The State may not rely on a classification whose relationship to an asserted goal is so attenuated as to render the distinction arbitrary or irrational. *** Furthermore, some objectives—such as "a bare . . . desire to harm a politically unpopular group," *** —are not legitimate state interests. *** Beyond that, the mentally retarded, like others, have and retain their substantive constitutional rights in addition to the right to be treated equally by the law.

We turn to the issue of the validity of the zoning ordinance insofar as it requires a special use permit for homes for the mentally retarded. We inquire first whether requiring a special use permit for the Featherston home in the circumstances here deprives respondents of the equal protection of the laws. If it does, there will be no occasion to decide whether the special use permit provision is facially invalid where the mentally retarded are involved, or to put it another way, whether the city may never insist on a special use permit for a home for the mentally retarded in an R-3 zone. This is the preferred course of adjudication since it enables courts to avoid making unnecessarily broad constitutional judgments. ***

The constitutional issue is clearly posed. The City does not require a special use permit in an R-3 zone for apartment houses, multiple dwellings, boarding and lodging houses, fraternity or sorority houses, dormitories, apartment hotels, hospitals, sanitariums, nursing homes for convalescents or the aged (other than for the insane or feeble-minded or alcoholics or drug addicts), private clubs or fraternal orders, and other specified uses. It does, however, insist on a special permit for the Featherston home, and it does so, as the District Court found, because it would be a facility for the mentally retarded. May the city require the permit for this facility when other care and multiple dwelling facilities are freely permitted?

It is true . . . that the mentally retarded as a group are indeed different from others not sharing their misfortune, and in this respect they may be different from those who would occupy other facilities that would be permitted in an R-3 zone without a special permit. But this difference is largely irrelevant unless the Featherston home and those who would occupy it would threaten legitimate interests of the city in a way that other permitted uses such as boarding houses and hospitals would not. Because in our view the record does not reveal any rational basis for believing that the Featherston home would pose any special threat to the city's legitimate interests, we affirm the judgment below insofar as it holds the ordinance invalid as applied in this case. . . .

The short of it is that requiring the permit in this case appears to us to rest on an irrational prejudice against the mentally retarded, including those who would occupy the Featherston facility and who would live under the closely supervised and highly regulated conditions expressly provided for by state and federal law.

The judgment of the Court of Appeals is affirmed insofar as it invalidates the zoning ordinance as applied to the Featherston home. The judgment is otherwise vacated.

It is so ordered.

Justice Stevens, with whom *The Chief Justice* joins, concurring.

The Court of Appeals disposed of this case as if a critical question to be decided were which of three clearly defined standards of equal protection review should be applied to a legislative classification discriminating against the mentally retarded. In fact, our cases have not delineated three—or even one or two—such well defined standards. Rather, our cases reflect a continuum of judgmental responses to differing classifications which have been explained in opinions by terms ranging from "strict scrutiny" at one extreme to "rational basis" at the other. I have never been persuaded that these so called "standards" adequately explain the decisional process. Cases involving classifications based on alienage, illegal residency, illegitimacy, gender, age, or—as in this case—mental retardation, do not fit well into sharply defined classifications.

"I am inclined to believe that what has become known as the [tiered] analysis of equal protection claims does not describe a completely logical method of deciding cases, but rather is a method the Court has employed to explain decisions that actually apply a single standard in a reasonably consistent fashion." *** In my own approach to these cases, I have always asked myself whether I could find a "rational basis" for the classification at issue. The term "rational," of course, includes a requirement that an impartial lawmaker could logically believe that the classification would serve a legitimate public purpose that transcends the harm to the members of the disadvantaged class. Thus, the word "rational"—for me at least—includes elements of legitimacy and neutrality that must always characterize the performance of the sovereign's duty to govern impartially.

The rational basis test, properly understood, adequately explains why a law that deprives a person of the right to vote because his skin has a different pigmentation than that of other voters violates the Equal Protection Clause. It would be utterly irrational to limit the franchise on the basis of height or weight; it is equally invalid to limit it on the basis of skin color. None of these attributes has any bearing at all on the citizen's willingness or ability to exercise that civil right. We do not need to apply a special standard, or to apply "strict scrutiny," or even "heightened scrutiny," to decide such cases.

In every equal protection case, we have to ask certain basic questions. What class is harmed by the legislation, and has it been subjected to a "tradition of disfavor" by our laws? What is the public purpose that is being served by the law? What is the characteristic of the disadvantaged class that justifies the disparate treatment? In most cases the answer to these questions will tell us whether the statute has a "rational basis." The answers will result in the virtually automatic invalidation of racial classifications and in the validation of most economic classifications, but they will provide differing results in cases involving classifications based on alienage, gender, or illegitimacy. But that is not because we apply an "intermediate standard of review" in these cases; rather it is because the characteristics of these groups are sometimes relevant and sometimes irrelevant to a valid public purpose, or, more specifically, to the purpose that the challenged laws purportedly intended to serve.

Every law that places the mentally retarded in a special class is not presumptively irrational. The differences between mentally retarded persons and those with greater mental capacity are obviously relevant to certain legislative decisions. An impartial lawmaker—indeed, even a member of a class of persons defined as mentally retarded—could rationally vote in favor of a law providing funds for special education and special treatment for the mentally retarded. A mentally retarded person could also recognize that he is a member of a class that might need special supervision in some situations, both to protect himself and to protect others. Restrictions on his right to drive cars or to operate hazardous equipment might well seem rational even though they deprived him of employment opportunities and the kind of freedom of travel enjoyed by other citizens. . . .

The discrimination against the mentally retarded that is at issue in this case is the city's decision to require an annual special use permit before property in an apartment house district may be used as a group home for persons who are mildly retarded. The record convinces me that this permit was required because of the irrational fears of neighboring property owners, rather than for the protection of the mentally retarded persons who would reside in respondent's home. . . .

San Antonio Independent School District v. Rodriguez

411 U.S. 1; 93 S. Ct. 1278; 36 L. Ed.2d 16 (1973)
Vote: 5-4

When this litigation began, the school system in San Antonio, Texas, was financed by a combination of state funds and local property tax revenues. In 1971, the state markedly increased the amount of state aid to poorer school districts. Nevertheless, substantial disparities in spending still existed across districts, attributable to disparities in property tax revenues. This case raises the question of whether such spending disparities violate the Equal Protection Clause of the Fourteenth Amendment.

Mr. Justice Powell delivered the opinion of the Court.

Despite . . . recent increases [in state aid], substantial interdistrict disparities in school expenditures found by the District Court to prevail in San Antonio and in varying degrees throughout the State still exist. And it was these disparities, largely attributable to differences in the amounts of money collected through local property taxation, that led the District Court to conclude that Texas's dual system of public school finance violated the Equal Protection Clause. The District Court held that the Texas system discriminates on the basis of wealth in the manner in which education is provided for its people. Finding that wealth is a "suspect" classification and that education is a "fundamental" interest, the District Court held that the Texas system could be sustained only if the State could show that it was premised upon some compelling state interest. On this issue the court concluded that "[n]ot only are defendants unable to demonstrate compelling state interests . . . they fail even to establish a reasonable basis for these classifications." ***

. . . We must decide, first, whether the Texas system of financing public education operates to the disadvantage of some suspect class or impinges upon a fundamental right explicitly or implicitly protected by the Constitution, thereby requiring strict judicial scrutiny. If so, the judgment of the District Court should be affirmed. If not, the Texas scheme must still be examined to determine whether it rationally furthers some legitimate, articulated state purpose and therefore does not constitute an invidious discrimination in violation of the Equal Protection Clause of the Fourteenth Amendment. . . .

The wealth discrimination discovered by the District Court in this case, and by several other courts that have recently struck down school financial laws in other States, is quite unlike any of the forms of wealth discrimination heretofore reviewed by this Court. Rather than focusing on the unique features of the alleged discrimination, the courts in these cases have virtually assumed their findings of a suspect classification through a simplistic process of analysis: since, under the traditional systems of financing public schools, some poorer people receive less expensive educations than other more affluent people, these systems discriminate on the basis of wealth. This approach largely ignores the hard threshold questions, including whether it makes a difference for purposes of consideration under the Constitution that the class of disadvantaged "poor" cannot be identified or defined in customary equal protection terms, and whether the relative—rather than absolute—nature of the asserted deprivation is of significant consequence. Before a State's laws and the justifications for the classifications they create are subjected to strict judicial scrutiny, we think these threshold considerations must be analyzed more closely than they were in the court below.

The case comes to us with no definitive description of the classifying facts or delineation of the disfavored class. Examination of the District Court's opinion and of appellees' complaint, briefs, and contentions at oral argument suggests, however, at least three ways in which the discrimination claimed here might be described. The Texas system of school

finance might be regarded as discriminating (1) against "poor" persons whose incomes fall below some identifiable level of poverty or who might be characterized as functionally "indigent," or (2) against those who are relatively poorer than others, or (3) against all those who, irrespective of their personal incomes, happen to reside in relatively poorer school districts. Our task must be to ascertain whether, in fact, the Texas system has been shown to discriminate on any of these possible bases and, if so, whether the resulting classification may be regarded as suspect. . . .

. . . Even a cursory examination . . . demonstrates that neither of the two distinguishing characteristics of wealth classifications can be found here. First, in support of their charge that the system discriminates against the "poor," appellees have made no effort to demonstrate that it operates to the peculiar disadvantage of any class fairly definable as indigent, or as composed of persons whose incomes are beneath any designated poverty level. Indeed, there is no reason to believe that the poorest families are not necessarily clustered in the poorest property districts. A recent and exhaustive study of school districts in Connecticut concluded that "[i]t is clearly incorrect . . . to contend that the 'poor' live in 'poor' districts. . . . Thus, the major factual assumption . . . —that the educational finance system discriminates against the 'poor'—is simply false in Connecticut." *** Defining "poor" families as those below the Bureau of the Census "poverty level," the Connecticut study found, not surprisingly, that the poor were clustered around commercial and industrial areas— those same areas that provide the most attractive sources of property tax income for school districts. Whether a similar pattern would be discovered in Texas is not known, but there is no basis on the record in this case for assuming that the poorest people—defined by reference to any level of absolute impecunity—are concentrated in the poorest districts.

[N]either appellees nor the District Court addressed the fact that . . . lack of personal resources has not occasioned an absolute deprivation of the desired benefit. The argument here is not that the children in districts having relatively low assessable property values are receiving no public education; rather, it is that they are receiving a poorer quality education than that available to children in districts having more assessable wealth. Apart from the unsettled and disputed question whether the quality of education may be determined by the amount of money expended for it, a sufficient answer to appellees' argument is that at least where wealth is involved the Equal Protection Clause does not require absolute equality of precisely equal advantages. . . . The State repeatedly asserted in its briefs in this Court that . . . it now assures "every child in every school district an adequate education." No proof was offered at trial persuasively discrediting or refuting the State's assertion.

For these two reasons—the absence of any evidence that the financing system discriminates against any definable category of "poor" people or that it results in the absolute deprivation of education—the disadvantaged class is not susceptible to identification in traditional terms. . . .

The Court here considers and repudiates the argument that there is a correlation between family income in a district and the amount spent by government on education.

This brings us, then, to the third way in which the classification scheme might be defined—district wealth discrimination. Since the only correlation indicated by the evidence is between district property wealth and expenditures, it may be argued that discrimination might be found without regard to the individual income characteristics of district residents. Assuming a perfect correlation between district property wealth and expenditures from top to bottom, the disadvantaged class might be viewed as encompassing every child in every district except the district that has the most assessable wealth and spends the most on education. . . .

However described, it is clear that appellees ask this Court to extend its most exacting scrutiny to review a system that allegedly discriminates against a large, diverse, and amorphous class, unified only by the common factor of residence in districts that happen to have less taxable wealth than other districts. The system of alleged discrimination and the class it defines have none of the traditional indicia of suspectness: the class is not saddled with such disabilities, or subjected to such history of purposeful unequal treatment, or relegated to such a position of political powerlessness as to command extraordinary protection from the majoritarian political process.

We thus conclude that the Texas system does not operate to the peculiar disadvantage of any suspect class. But in recognition of the fact that this Court has never heretofore held that wealth discrimination alone provides an adequate basis for invoking strict scrutiny, appellees have not relied solely on this contention. They also assert that the State's system impermissibly interferes with the exercise of a "fundamental" right and that accordingly the prior decisions of this Court require the application of the strict standard of judicial review. It is this question—whether education is a fundamental right, in the sense that it is among the rights and liberties protected by the Constitution—which has so consumed the attention of courts and commentators in recent years. . . .

Education, of course, is not among the rights afforded explicit protection under our Federal Constitution. Nor do we find any basis for saying it is implicitly so protected. It is appellees' contention, however, that education . . . is itself a fundamental personal right because it is essential to the effective exercise of First Amendment freedoms and to intelligent utilization of the right to vote. . . .

We need not dispute any of these propositions. The Court has long afforded zealous protection against unjustifiable governmental interference with the individual's rights to speak and to vote. Yet we have never presumed to possess either the ability or the authority to guarantee to the citizenry the most effective speech or the most informed electoral choice. . . .

Even if it were conceded that some identifiable quantum of education is a constitutionally protected prerequisite to the meaningful exercise of either right, we have no indication that the present levels of education expenditure in Texas provide an education that falls short. . . .

. . . In one further respect we find this a particularly inappropriate case in which to subject state action to strict judicial scrutiny. The present case, in another basic sense, is significantly different from any of the cases in which the Court has applied strict scrutiny to state or federal legislation touching upon constitutionally protected rights. Each of our prior cases involved legislation which "deprived," "infringed," or "interfered" with the free exercise of some such fundamental personal right or liberty.... A critical distinction between those cases and the one now before us lies in what Texas is endeavoring to do with respect to education. Every step leading to the establishment of the system Texas utilizes today—including the decisions permitting localities to tax and expand locally, and creating and continuously expanding state aid—was implemented in an effort to extend public education and to improve its quality. Of course, every reform that benefits some more than others may be criticized for what it fails to accomplish. But we think it plain that, in substance, the thrust of the Texas system is affirmative and reformatory and, therefore, should be scrutinized under judicial principles sensitive to the nature of the State's efforts and to the rights reserved to the States under the Constitution....

We need not rest our decision, however, solely on the inappropriateness of the strict scrutiny test. A century of Supreme Court adjudication under the Equal Protection Clause affirmatively supports the application of the traditional standard of review, which requires only that the State's system be shown to bear some rational relationship to legitimate state purposes. This case represents far more than a challenge to the manner in which Texas provides for the education of its children. We have here nothing less than a direct attack on the way in which Texas has chosen to raise and disburse state and local tax revenues....

Justice Powell here defends the correctness of the more lenient standards of judicial review in the field of taxation.

... The Texas system of school finance ... permits and encourages a large measure of participation in and control of each district's schools at the local level. In an era that has witnessed a consistent trend toward centralization of the functions of government, local sharing of responsibility for public education has survived....

The persistence of attachment to government at the lowest level where education is concerned re-

flects the depth of commitment of its supporters. In part, local control means ... the freedom to devote more money to the education of one's children. Equally important, however, is the opportunity it offers for participation in the decision-making process that determines how those local tax dollars will be spent. Each locality is free to tailor local programs to local needs. Pluralism also affords some opportunity for experimentation, innovation, and a healthy competition for educational excellence....

... Appellees suggest that local control could be preserved and promoted under other financing systems that resulted in more equality in educational expenditures. While it is no doubt true that reliance on local property taxation for school revenues provides less freedom of choice with respect to expenditures for some districts than for others, the existence of "some inequality" in the manner in which the State's rationale is achieved is not alone a sufficient basis for striking down the entire system.... Only where state action impinges on the exercise of fundamental constitutional rights or liberties must it be found to have chosen the least restrictive alternative.... It is also well to remember that even those districts that have reduced ability to make free decisions with respect to how much they spend on education still retain under the present system a large measure of authority as to how available funds will be allocated. They further enjoy the power to make numerous other decisions with respect to the operation of the schools. The people of Texas may be justified in believing that other systems of school finance, which place more of the financial responsibility in the hands of the State, will result in a comparable lessening of desired local autonomy. That is, they may believe that along with increased control of the purse strings at the state level will go increased control over local policies....

... One also must remember that the system here challenged is not peculiar to Texas or to any other State. In its essential characteristics the Texas plan for financing public education reflects what many educators for a half century have thought was an enlightened approach to a problem for which there is no perfect solution. We are unwilling to assume for ourselves a level of wisdom superior to that of legislators, scholars, and educational authorities in

49 States, especially where the alternatives proposed are only recently conceived and nowhere yet tested. The constitutional standard under the Equal Protection Clause is whether the challenged state action rationally furthers a legitimate state purpose or interest.... We hold that the Texas plan abundantly satisfies this standard.

Mr. Justice Stewart, concurring....

Mr. Justice Brennan, dissenting.

... Here, there can be no doubt that education is inextricably linked to the right to participate in the electoral process and to the rights of free speech and association guaranteed by the First Amendment. This being so, any classification affecting education must be subjected to strict judicial scrutiny, and since even the State concedes that the statutory scheme now before us cannot pass constitutional muster under this stricter standard of review, I can only conclude that the Texas school financing scheme is constitutionally invalid....

Mr. Justice White, with whom *Mr. Justice Douglas* and *Mr. Justice Brennan* join, dissenting.

The Texas public schools are financed through a combination of state funding, local property tax revenue, and some federal funds. Concededly, the system yields wide disparity in per-pupil revenue among the various districts. In a typical year, for example, the Alamo Heights district had total revenues of $594 per pupil, while the Edgewood district had only $356 per student. The majority and the State concede, as they must, the existence of major disparities in spendable funds. But the State contends that the disparities do not invidiously discriminate against children and families in districts such as Edgewood, because the Texas scheme is designed "to provide an adequate education for all, with local autonomy to go beyond that as individual school districts desire and are able.... It leaves to the people of each district the choice whether to go beyond the minimum and, if so, by how much...."

The difficulty with the Texas system ... is that it provides a meaningful option to Alamo Heights and like school districts but almost none to Edgewood and those other districts with a low per-pupil real estate tax base. In these latter districts, no matter how desirous parents are of supporting their schools with greater revenues, it is impossible to do so through the use of the real estate property tax. In these districts the Texas system utterly fails to extend a realistic choice to parents, because the property tax, which is the only revenue-raising mechanism extended to school districts, is practically and legally unavailable....

In order to equal the highest yield in any other Bexar County district, Alamo Heights would be required to tax at the rate of $.68 per $100 of assessed valuation. Edgewood would be required to tax at the prohibitive rate of $5.76 per $100. But state law places a $1.50 per $100 ceiling on the maintenance tax rate, a limit that would surely be reached long before Edgewood attained an equal yield. Edgewood is thus precluded in law, as well as in fact, from achieving a yield even close to that of some other districts.

The Equal Protection Clause permits discriminations between classes but requires that the classification bear some rational relationship to a permissible object sought to be attained by the statute. It is not enough that the Texas system before us seeks to achieve the valid, rational purpose of maximizing local initiative; the means chosen by the State must also be rationally related to the end sought to be achieved....

... Requiring the State to establish only that unequal treatment is in furtherance of a permissible goal, without also requiring the State to show that the means chosen to effectuate that goal are rationally related to its achievement, makes equal protection analysis no more than an empty gesture. In my view, the parents and children in Edgewood, and in like districts, suffer from an invidious discrimination violative of the Equal Protection Clause....

There is no difficulty in identifying the class that is subject to the alleged discrimination and that is entitled to the benefits of the Equal Protection Clause. I need go no farther than the parents and children in the Edgewood district, who are plaintiffs here and who assert that they are entitled to the same choice as Alamo Heights to augment local expenditures for schools but are denied that choice by state law. This group constitutes a class sufficiently definite to invoke the protection of the Constitution. They are as entitled to the protection of the Equal Protection Clause as were the voters in allegedly unrepresented counties in the reapportionment cases. . . .

Mr. Justice Marshall, with whom **Mr. Justice Douglas** concurs, dissenting.

. . . We sit . . . not to resolve disputes over educational theory but to enforce our Constitution. It is an inescapable fact that if one district has more funds available per pupil than another district, the former will have greater choice in educational planning than will the latter. In this regard, I believe the question of discrimination in educational quality must be deemed to be an objective one that looks to what the State provides its children, not to what the children are able to do with what they receive. That a child is forced to attend an underfunded school with poorer physical facilities, less experienced teachers, larger classes, and a narrower range of courses than a school with substantially more funds—and thus with greater choice in educational planning—may nevertheless excel is to the credit of the child, not the State. . . . *** Indeed, who can ever measure for such a child the opportunities lost and the talents wasted for want of a broader, more enriched education? Discrimination in the opportunity to learn that is afforded a child must be our standard. . . .

. . . I must once more voice my disagreement with the Court's rigidified approach to equal protection analysis. . . . The court apparently seeks to establish today that equal protection cases fall into one of two neat categories which dictate the appropriate standard of review—strict scrutiny or mere rationality. But this Court's decisions in the field of equal protection defy such easy categorization. A principled reading of what this Court has done reveals that it has applied a spectrum of standards in reviewing discrimination allegedly violative of the Equal Protection Clause. This spectrum clearly comprehends variations in the degree of care with which the Court will scrutinize particular classifications, depending, I believe, on the constitutional and societal impor-

tance of the interest adversely affected and the recognized invidiousness of the basis upon which the particular classification is drawn. . . .

. . . [It] seems to me inescapably clear that this Court has consistently adjusted the care with which it will review state discrimination in light of the constitutional significance of the interests affected and the invidiousness of the particular classification. In the context of economic interests, we find that discriminatory state action is almost always sustained, for such interests are generally far removed from constitutional guarantees. Moreover, "[t]he extremes to which the Court has gone in dreaming up rational bases for state regulation in that area may in many instances be ascribed to a healthy revulsion from the Court's earlier excesses in using the Constitution to protect interests that have more than enough power to protect themselves in the legislative halls." *** But the situation differs markedly when discrimination against important individual interests with constitutional implications and against particularly disadvantaged or powerless classes is involved. The majority suggests, however, that a variable standard of review would give this Court the appearance of a "super-legislature." Such an approach seems to me a part of the guarantees of our Constitution and of the historic experiences with oppression of and discrimination against discrete, powerless minorities which underlie that document. In truth, the Court itself will be open to the criticism raised by the majority so long as it continues on its present course of effectively selecting in private which cases will be afforded special consideration without acknowledging the true basis of its action. . . .

The nature of our inquiry into the justifications for state discrimination is essentially the same in all equal protection cases: We must consider the substantiality of the state interests sought to be served, and we must scrutinize the reasonableness of the means by which the State has sought to advance its interests. . . . Differences in the application of this test are, in my view, a function of the constitutional importance of the interests at stake and the invidiousness of the particular classification. In terms of the asserted state interests, the Court has indicated that it will require, for instance, a "compelling," *** or a

"substantial" or "important," *** state interest to justify discrimination affecting individual interests of
constitutional significance. Whatever the differences,
if any, in these descriptions of the character of the
state interest necessary to sustain such discrimination, basic to each is, I believe, a concern with the
legitimacy and the reality of the asserted state interests. Thus, when interests of constitutional importance are at stake, the Court does not stand ready to
credit the State's classification with any conceivable
legitimate purpose, but demands a clear showing
that there are legitimate state interests which the
classification was in fact intended to serve. Beyond
the question of the adequacy of the State's purpose
for the classification, the Court traditionally has become increasingly sensitive to the means by which a
State chooses to act as its action affects more directly
interests of constitutional significance. . . . Thus, by
now, "less restrictive alternatives" analysis is firmly
established in equal protection jurisprudence. *** . . .
Here both the nature of the interest and the classification dictate close judicial scrutiny of the purposes
which Texas seeks to serve with its present educational financing scheme and of the means it has selected to serve that purpose. . . .

CHAPTER SEVENTEEN

REPRESENTATION AND VOTING RIGHTS

Undoubtedly, the right of suffrage is a fundamental matter in a free and democratic society. Especially since the right to exercise the franchise in a free and unimpaired manner is preservative of other basic civil and political rights, any alleged infringement of the right of citizens to vote must be carefully and meticulously scrutinized.

Chief Justice Earl Warren, *Reynolds v. Sims* (1964)

INTRODUCTION

The right to vote is essential to **representative democracy,** that form of government in which policy decisions are made by representatives chosen in periodic competitive elections based on the principle of **universal suffrage.** Democratic theory thus rests on a premise of political equality. While individuals may be inherently unequal with respect to their talents and virtues, democratic theory holds that they are nevertheless equal in their essential worth and dignity as human beings. They are therefore equal before the law and equal before the state. Each has an equal right to participate in politics, to make his or her interests, preferences, and values known to the government. In the United States, such participation takes many forms, among which voting is considered to be the most fundamental. Democratic theory requires that all citizens, at least all law-abiding adults, retain a legal right to vote in free and fair elections. As the Supreme Court recognized in *Yick Wo v. Hopkins* (1886), voting is "a fundamental political right, because [it is] preservative of other rights."

While the United States today is clearly a democratic country, the term "democracy" was an anathema to many of the Framers of the Constitution. They accepted the notion of **popular sovereignty** in the abstract, but they certainly did not believe that every question of policy was to be subjected to majority rule. Many of the delegates to the Constitutional Convention shared Alexander Hamilton's view that democracy was little more than legitimized mob rule, an ever-present danger to personal security, liberty, and property. The Framers thus sought to establish a *constitutional republic,* where public policy would be made by elected representatives within limits delineated in the Constitution. As we have noted in previous chapters, the Constitution was adopted to place certain values above the political fray, in order to protect individual rights from the tyranny of transient majorities. With its several elitist elements and many limitations on majority rule, the Framers' Constitution can be seen as rather undemocratic. But two centuries of history have witnessed the democratization of the Constitution. What was conceived as a constitutional *republic* has become a constitutional *democracy*.

The Democratization of America

It should be remembered that property qualifications for voting still existed in 1787 and that the franchise was granted originally only to white males. With the advent of Jacksonian democracy in the 1830s, property qualifications rapidly diminished and were virtually nonexistent by the time of the Civil War. The Fifteenth Amendment, adopted in 1870, theoretically extended the franchise to African-Americans, although another century of struggle was necessary to realize the promise of the Amendment. The Nineteenth Amendment, ratified in 1920, removed sex as a qualification for voting. In addition to women's suffrage, another accomplishment of the progressive movement was passage of the Seventeenth Amendment in 1913, providing for the direct election of U.S. senators. The Twenty-fourth Amendment, ratified in 1964, abolished poll taxes as prerequisites for voting in federal elections. Finally, the minimum voting age was lowered to eighteen with the adoption of the Twenty-sixth Amendment in 1971. Thus, through two centuries of political change highlighted by historic amendments, the U.S. Constitution has evolved substantially in the direction of democracy.

Despite theories of the "ruling class" and the "power elite" that portray a concentration of power in a few hands, most observers would agree that political influence is more widely dispersed in the United States than in most other countries. Through mass media, political parties, interest group activity, and public demonstrations, the American people have numerous opportunities to make their demands and preferences known to their political leaders. And, of course, many of these leaders are accountable to the public through regular, competitive elections. The American people elect an astonishing array of public officials from the president all the way down to local school board members. Unfortunately, however, election practices, and even the laws governing elections, have not always reflected a serious commitment to the ideal of political equality.

Policing the Democratic Process

What happens when the majority decides to strip the minority of certain rights, even to exclude it from political participation? In a political system based solely on majority rule, there would be no remedy for the minority group. The problem is far from hypothetical. History resounds with instances of majorities oppressing minorities. Even in the United States, the "people's representatives" have passed laws isolating minority groups, diluting their right to vote, and even excluding them from the political process altogether. Such sordid conduct underscores the need for limitations on legislative power, especially in the area of voting rights. Those constitutional amendments safeguarding the right to vote and to organize politically are essential to a minority group's ability to protect itself from a hostile majority. Equally important, however, is the role that courts have played in ensuring that minorities are not locked out of the political process. Indeed, one of the paradoxes of American democracy is that the U.S. Supreme Court, a fundamentally elitist institution, has played a major part in the progressive democratization of the country. Through its exercise of judicial review, the Court, especially during the first half of the twentieth century, struck down a number of laws restricting the right to vote. More recently, it has upheld and thus reinforced the constitutional legitimacy of statutes, such as the Voting Rights Act of 1965, designed to safeguard and expand the franchise.

Justice Harlan Fiske Stone's famous footnote in *United States v. Carolene Products* (1938) recognized potential problems resulting from efforts to limit political participation, including "restrictions upon the right to vote," "restraints upon the dissemination of information," "interferences with political organizations," and "prohibition[s] of peaceable assembly." Stone asserted that "prejudice against discrete and insular minorities may be a special condition, which tends seriously to curtail the operation of those political processes ordinarily to be relied upon to protect minorities. . . ." Accordingly, claims brought by groups that have been locked out of the political process call for a "more searching judicial inquiry."

RACIAL DISCRIMINATION IN VOTING RIGHTS

As previously noted, the ratification of the Fifteenth Amendment in 1870 did not result in the immediate enfranchisement of most African-Americans. In some areas, public officials blatantly refused to honor the mandates of the Fifteenth Amendment. In other areas, groups such as the Ku Klux Klan resorted to terrorism to prevent African-Americans from exercising their newly won right to vote. The Supreme Court initially aided such resistance by limiting congressional power to enforce the Fifteenth Amendment. In *United States v. Reese* (1876), the Court struck down the Enforcement Act of 1870, by which Congress attempted to protect the right of blacks to vote in state elections. By 1884, however, the Court changed course and recognized Congress's power to enforce the Fifteenth Amendment (see *Ex parte Yarbrough*). By this time, however, Congress was not particularly concerned with the rights of African-Americans. Nevertheless, once it became clear that the Court would permit the federal government to secure blacks' voting rights, states bent on maintaining African-Americans in a position of second-class citizenship resorted to disingenuous methods designed to exclude them from the political process.

"Grandfather Clauses"

Perhaps the most blatant official means of preventing black Americans from exercising their newly granted constitutional right to vote was the **grandfather clause.** First enacted by Mississippi in 1890, this device soon spread throughout

Southern and border states. Oklahoma's version, adopted as an amendment to the state constitution in 1910, was typical in that it required literacy tests for all voters whose ancestors had not been entitled to vote prior to 1866. The overall effect of grandfather clauses was to subject almost all potential black voters to literacy tests arbitrarily administered by white officials, while exempting numerous illiterate whites from this requirement.

Largely in response to invidious discrimination of this kind, the National Association for the Advancement of Colored People (NAACP) was formed in the early twentieth century. The first of many legal victories won by the NAACP came in 1915 when the Supreme Court struck down the Oklahoma grandfather clause (*Guinn v. United States*). Undaunted, the Oklahoma legislature in 1916 adopted a new law aimed at keeping African-Americans from the polls. This statute granted permanent voting registration to all persons who had voted in 1914, when the grandfather clause was still in effect. All other persons were required to register to vote during a twelve-day period or be permanently disqualified from voting. Not surprisingly, the Supreme Court ultimately invalidated this subterfuge as well (see *Lane v. Wilson* [1939]).

The White Primary

After the demise of the grandfather clause, Southern states resorted to the equally infamous **white primary.** This device was an extremely effective means of keeping African-Americans from exercising their right to vote in any meaningful sense. Until the 1960s, the "solid South" maintained a virtual one-party political system. Thus, in all but a few areas, nomination by the Democratic party was tantamount to election. In fact, Republicans seldom bothered to run in the general elections. In order to keep African-Americans out of the political process, the Democratic party in many states adopted a rule excluding them from party membership. Concomitantly, state legislatures closed the primaries to everyone except party members. The Supreme Court had previously ruled that political parties were private organizations, not part of the government election apparatus (see *Newberry v. United States* [1921]). Consequently, through the white primary device, blacks were effectively disenfranchised but, arguably, not by official state action.

In a series of cases from the late 1920s through the early 1950s, the Supreme Court grappled with the white primary issue. In two early decisions, it effectively barred formal state endorsement of the white primary (see *Nixon v. Herndon* [1927]; *Nixon v. Condon* [1932]). However, in *Grovey v. Townsend* (1935), the Supreme Court upheld a Texas white primary based not on legislative enactment but exclusively on a resolution adopted by the state Democratic Party. The Court's decision in *Grovey* thus reinforced the prevailing legal view that political parties were merely private organizations beyond the purview of the Equal Protection Clause. In *United States v. Classic* (1941), however, the Court moved away from this highly artificial view of party primaries. The *Classic* case involved the question of whether the federal government could regulate party primaries in order to prevent election fraud. In upholding this exercise of congressional power, the Court overruled *Newberry* and undercut the logic of *Grovey v.*

Townsend. In *Smith v. Allwright* (1944), the Court struck down the white primary as violative of the Fifteenth Amendment, thus overruling the *Grovey* decision. Writing for the Court, Justice Stanley Reed expressed a pragmatic view of the concept of state action:

> This grant to the people of the opportunity for choice is not to be nullified by a State through casting its electoral process in a form which permits a private organization to practice racial discrimination in the election. Constitutional rights would be of little value if they could be thus indirectly denied.

In an attempt to circumvent the Supreme Court's ruling in *Smith v. Allwright,* Texas Democrats established the "Jaybird Democratic Association," from which African-Americans were excluded. The Jaybirds held "preprimary" elections in which candidates for the Democratic primaries were selected. This none-too-subtle attempt at further evasion of constitutional requirements was invalidated by the Supreme Court (*Terry v. Adams* [1953]). In *Terry,* the Court observed that under the preprimary scheme, both the primary and the general election were little more than "perfunctory ratifiers" of the Jaybirds' choices for elected officials.

Literacy Tests

The eradication of grandfather clauses and white primaries was insufficient to integrate African-Americans into the political process, as die-hard racism manifested itself in alternative exclusionary tactics. For example, many states relied on **literacy tests** that, despite superficial neutrality, were administered in a highly discriminatory manner. Quite frequently, white people were not required to take the tests, even if their literacy was questionable. However, since the Constitution had left the determination of voting qualifications to the states and since these tests were on their face racially neutral, the Supreme Court refused to strike them down. In *Lassiter v. Northampton County Board of Education* (1959), the Court explicitly upheld the use of literacy tests. Writing for the Court, Justice William O. Douglas reasoned that "in our society where newspapers, periodicals, books and other printed matter canvass and debate campaign issues, a State might conclude that only those who are literate should exercise the franchise." Ultimately, literacy tests as devices of racial discrimination were done away with, not by the Supreme Court but by Congress through the landmark Voting Rights Act of 1965.

Poll Taxes

Another less common but equally effective means of keeping African-Americans from voting was the **poll tax.** At the time the Constitution was adopted, poll taxes were widely used as a legitimate means of raising revenue. During the 1780s, however, poll taxes did not significantly hamper voting because only white property owners were entitled to vote anyway! By the mid-nineteenth century, poll taxes had virtually disappeared. Around 1900, a number of states resurrected the poll tax for the obvious purpose of preventing African-Americans from voting. The tax generally amounted to two dollars per election—quite sufficient to deter most blacks, as well as poor whites, from exercising the franchise. On its face, however, the poll tax was racially neutral, and the Supreme Court initially refused to strike it down (see *Breedlove v. Suttles* [1937]). Eventually, however, the poll tax was thoroughly repudiated. In 1963, the poll tax was abolished in federal elections through adoption of the Twenty-fourth Amendment. Three years later, in *Harper v. Virginia Board of Elections* (1966), the Supreme Court held that poll taxes in state elections violated the Fourteenth Amendment. Writing for the Court, Justice Douglas emphasized the arbitrariness of the tax:

> To introduce wealth, or payment of a fee as a measure of a voter's qualifications is to introduce a capricious or irrelevant factor. . . . Wealth, like race, creed, or color, is not germane to one's ability to participate intelligently in the electoral process.

Racial Gerrymandering

Perhaps the most outrageous attempt to disenfranchise African-American voters occurred in Tuskegee, Alabama, in 1957. At the city's behest, the all-white Alabama legislature dramatically altered the boundaries of Tuskegee from a square to a twenty-eight-sided figure. The purpose of the **gerrymander** was obvious in that all but five of the city's four hundred black voters were placed outside the city limits, while no white voters were displaced. A number of the "former residents" of Tuskegee brought suit in federal court, seeking a declaratory judgment that the redistricting measure was unconstitutional and an injunction to prohibit its enforcement. The U.S. District Court for the Middle District of Alabama dismissed the case for lack of jurisdiction, stating that it had "no control over, no supervision over, and no power to change any boundaries of a municipal corporation fixed by a duly convened legislative body. . . ." The Court of Appeals for the Fifth Circuit agreed. But the Supreme Court reversed the lower courts and reinstated the complaint, saying that the "petitioners are entitled to prove their allegations at trial." Speaking for a unanimous bench, Justice Felix Frankfurter stated that if the plaintiffs' allegations were proven, it would be "difficult to appreciate what stands in the way of adjudging [the redistricting measure] invalid . . ." (*Gomillion v. Lightfoot* [1960]). Indeed, plaintiffs prevailed at trial, and the gerrymander was invalidated.

The Voting Rights Act of 1965

A 1961 report of the U.S. Commission on Civil Rights documented the pervasiveness of voting discrimination in the South. According to the report, less than 10 percent of eligible African-Americans were registered to vote in at least 129 counties in ten Southern states. In counties where blacks comprised a majority of the population, the average level of black registration was only 3 percent. As the civil rights movement of the early 1960s galvanized the nation's conscience, the demand for federal action grew. The federal government responded with the Civil Rights Act of 1964 and the Voting Rights Act of 1965, both of which were pushed through Congress under the skillful leadership of President Lyndon B. Johnson.

Earl Warren:
Chief Justice, 1953–1969

The Voting Rights Act employed a rough index of discrimination to apply the scrutiny of the federal government to those states that had historically been most recalcitrant in refusing to allow African-Americans to vote: Alabama, Georgia, Louisiana, Mississippi, South Carolina, and Virginia. Specifically, the act waived accumulated poll taxes and abolished literacy tests and similar devices in those areas to which the statute applied. The act also required the aforementioned states to obtain "preclearance" from the U.S. Department of Justice before making changes in their electoral systems. Not surprisingly, this historic and far-reaching act was challenged on the ground that Congress had exceeded its power to enforce the Fifteenth Amendment. The Supreme Court, although recognizing the Voting Rights Act as "inventive," upheld the law (see *South Carolina v. Katzenbach* [1966]). Writing for a nearly unanimous Court (only Justice Hugo Black partially dissented), Chief Justice Earl Warren expressed characteristic optimism about the Voting Rights Act:

> Hopefully, millions of non-white Americans will now be able to participate for the first time on an equal basis in the government under which they live. We may finally look forward to the day when truly "the right of citizens of the United States to vote shall not be denied or abridged by the United States or by any State on account of race, color or previous condition of servitude."

Despite its strong endorsement by the Warren Court and subsequent extension by Congress, the Voting Rights Act remains controversial. Of particular concern to many are the strict "preclearance" requirements of Section 5, under which designated states must submit proposed changes in election laws to the Justice Department for approval. Equally controversial is Section 2, which allows plaintiffs in any jurisdiction to challenge electoral schemes that impermissibly dilute the voting strength of minority groups. These provisions led many conservatives to oppose renewal of the Voting Rights Act in 1982. The Reagan administration, more conservative than its Democratic and Republican predecessors in the field of civil rights, initially opposed the extension of the act without major changes in these controversial provisions. However, bipartisan support in Congress for extending the act forced the administration to back down. The act was renewed and strengthened in 1982.

While some civil rights activists argue that the Voting Rights Act has not been enforced vigorously enough, one must recognize the very real impact that it has had on minority political participation. Enforcement of the Voting Rights Act has resulted in substantially higher levels of voter registration among African-Americans, particularly in the Deep South. Accordingly, many politicians who formerly made overt appeals to white supremacy tempered their racist rhetoric in order to draw support from new black voters. Perhaps the best example of this metamorphosis was Alabama Governor George Wallace who, in the face of the civil rights movement of the 1960s, maintained a strong segregationist stance. In the late 1970s and early 1980s, Wallace dropped the racist rhetoric in order to appeal to newly enfranchised African-Americans who might be tempted to vote Republican. Another excellent example of this political realism is seen in the long career of Republican Senator Strom Thurmond of South Carolina. In 1948, when he was the Democratic governor of the state, Thurmond ran for president on the strongly segregationist Dixiecrat ticket. With the enfranchisement of African-Americans, however, Thurmond began actively soliciting (and often receiving) their support in his U.S. Senate races.

At-Large Elections

As African-Americans began to register and vote in greater numbers, black politicians made substantial gains, especially at the local level. Seeking to thwart the growing influence of black voters, a number of white-dominated cities and counties adopted basic structural changes in their systems of representation. Since the overt racial gerrymander had been declared unconstitutional in *Gomillion v. Lightfoot* (1960), these communities converted to **at-large elections** in which local candidates ran for office on a citywide or countywide basis. This election method was by no means novel in the United States, but its use as a deliberate means of limiting the political clout of African-American voters raised new constitutional issues. At-large systems of voting were often coupled with the annexation of predominantly white suburban areas, thereby further diluting black voting power. Since the 1970s, many of these at-large and annexation schemes have been challenged in court as unlawful attempts to undermine the voting strength of minority groups.

The Supreme Court Rules on At-Large Elections

In 1980, the Supreme Court handed down a ruling on the constitutionality of at-large elections (*Mobile v. Bolden*). Since 1911, the city of Mobile, Alabama, had used at-large elections to choose its three-member city commission. At the time the lawsuit was filed, more than 35 percent of the residents of Mobile were

African-American. Despite several attempts, however, no African-American had ever been elected to the city commission. Plaintiffs argued that the at-large system was unconstitutional because it had the effect of unfairly diluting the voting strength of racial minorities. The U.S. District Court for the Southern District of Alabama agreed, as did the Fifth Circuit Court of Appeals. The Supreme Court reversed, holding that there must be a showing of a discriminatory intent on the part of public officials in order to warrant a finding that the Constitution has been violated. Dissenting vehemently, Justice Thurgood Marshall asserted that "Such judicial deference to official decision making has no place under the Fifteenth Amendment." Marshall went on to accuse the Court of being "an accessory to the perpetuation of racial discrimination."

In spite of, or perhaps in response to Justice Marshall's accusatory rhetoric in *Mobile v. Bolden,* the Supreme Court in 1982 demonstrated that the "intentional discrimination" standard can in fact be met. In *Rogers v. Lodge,* the Court, voting 6 to 3, struck down an at-large election scheme in Burke County, Georgia, on the basis of the standard handed down in the *Mobile* case. In this case, the Court reasserted a commitment to the Fifteenth Amendment that some critics found lacking in *Mobile v. Bolden.*

The "Effects" Test under the 1982 Voting Rights Act Amendments

In its 1982 extension of the Voting Rights Act, Congress amended Section 2 to allow plaintiffs to prevail in voting dilution cases on the basis of an "effects" test, rather than on the "intent" standard of *Mobile v. Bolden.* In other words, Congress accomplished through statute what the Supreme Court refused to do under the Fifteenth Amendment. Thus, *Mobile v. Bolden* is essentially irrelevant to a group of minority plaintiffs seeking to challenge an election scheme. It matters not to plaintiffs whether they prevail under a provision of the federal Constitution or under Section 2 of the Voting Rights Act. Here is an important lesson for students of the American legal system: civil rights law is by no means the exclusive province of courts and constitutions. Legislatures may act to enhance civil rights through their power to adopt ordinary legislation. This point was driven home forcefully during the fall of 1991 when Congress passed and President George Bush signed a major civil rights act that, among other things, rejected Supreme Court interpretations narrowly applying earlier statutory prohibitions against discrimination (for additional discussion, see Chapter 16).

The Problem of Proportionate Representation

The voting dilution cases raise the serious question of proportionate representation (not to be confused with *proportional* representation existing under some parliamentary systems). A scheme of proportionate representation would require citizens to be represented by individuals possessing specific racial, sexual, religious, occupational, or other characteristics in proportion to their occurrence in the population. Thus, under a scheme of racial proportionate representation, African-Americans in Mobile (see *Mobile v. Bolden,* discussed above) would be "entitled" to one seat on the city commission. Indeed, ostensibly because of its opposition to racially proportionate representation, the Reagan Administration consistently opposed the effects standard in voting rights litigation, whether brought under the Fourteenth Amendment or Section 2 of the Voting Rights Act.

The Supreme Court has said repeatedly that the Constitution does not require or permit proportionate representation. Few would disagree with the Court on this point of theory. The problem is of a more practical nature. Suppose a federal district judge finds that a city's system of at-large elections was established for the single purpose of diluting the voting strength of African-Americans. Clearly, the court may order the city to set up a system of single-member districts, but how should those districts be drawn? Should the court impose a scheme that virtually assures proportionate representation of African-Americans on the city council? Would such a "race-conscious remedy" be constitutionally acceptable? While this question is being litigated in the federal judiciary, the Supreme Court has yet to face the question squarely. In fact, what usually happens in voting rights cases is that both the plaintiff and the defendant submit remedial plans and the court attempts to fashion an equitable compromise. The final remedy that emerges will almost certainly enhance the electoral prospects for African-American candidates but may not ensure proportionate representation.

Challenges to Judicial Election Systems

When Congress extended the Voting Rights Act in 1982, it changed the statutory language in a way that eventually proved to be highly significant. Instead of applying only to elections of "legislators," the act now refers to "representatives." This suggests the applicability of Voting Rights Act challenges to nonlegislative elections, but which elections? In a controversial 6-to-3 decision, the Supreme Court held in 1991 that plaintiffs may challenge judicial election systems under Section 2 of the Voting Rights Act. In *Chisom v. Roemer,* the Court decided that the statutory term "representatives" includes elected judges. The *Chisom* case is one of myriad examples of important civil rights policies being determined through statutory, as opposed to constitutional, interpretation. Students of constitutional law must realize that much of the important law of civil rights stems not from judicial interpretation of the Fourteenth and Fifteenth Amendments but from the broad-gauged statutes passed under Congress's power to enforce the guarantees of those Amendments.

Chisom v. Roemer involved a challenge to Louisiana's system for electing judges to the state supreme court. Under that system, five of the seven state supreme court judges were elected from single-member districts; the remaining two jurists were elected at-large from a sixth district that included predominantly black Orleans Parish and several other parishes where African-Americans were in the minority. Plaintiffs in the case argued that this scheme had the effect of diluting the voting strength of blacks in New Orleans. Had Orleans Parish been set up as a separate single-member district, an African-American candidate would have had a greater chance of being elected to the state supreme court. Under the existing system, no black had ever been elected to Louisiana's highest tribunal, despite a number of attempts. After a bench trial, the U.S. district court concluded that there had been no violation of the Voting Rights Act under the standard set forth in the landmark case of *Thornburgh v. Gingles* (1986). On appeal, the Fifth Circuit Court of Appeals concluded that the Voting Rights Act did not apply to judicial elections, holding that the district court should have dismissed the complaint altogether. On certiorari, the Supreme Court reversed, declaring that "[w]hen each of several members of a court must be a resident of a different district, and must be elected by the voters of that district, it seems both reasonable and realistic to characterize the winners as representatives of that district." The Supreme Court expressed no opinion on the merits of the plaintiffs' case. It merely remanded the case to the Fifth Circuit Court of Appeals for further consideration.

In a related case, the Supreme Court decided that Section 2 of the Voting Rights Act applies also to the election of state trial judges. In *Houston Lawyers' Association v. Attorney General of Texas* (1991), the Court said that "[i]f a State decides to elect its trial judges, . . . those elections must be conducted in compliance with the Voting Rights Act." Since at least half the states still use elections to select some or all of their judges, the Court's decisions in *Chisom v. Roemer* and *Houston Lawyers' Association* have plowed a fertile field for litigation. It remains to be seen whether plaintiffs will be successful in mounting challenges to judicial elections. However, one can be sure that the Supreme Court will be revisiting this new area of voting rights law.

THE REAPPORTIONMENT DECISIONS

Questions of inequality with respect to voting rights are by no means limited to the issue of racial discrimination. For many years, one of the most intractable and pervasive forms of inequality was that of legislative **malapportionment.**

Representation in the U.S. House of Representatives, in all fifty state legislatures, and in most local governments is apportioned on the basis of population. Representatives in state legislatures and in the U.S. House are elected from single-member districts. Malapportionment exists to the extent that the number of voters comprising such districts is unequal. Malapportionment can come about in two ways. It has generally occurred as a function of natural population shifts due to urbanization and interstate migration. It has also come about through gerrymandering, where district lines are intentionally drawn to create inequalities for political purposes.

Historically, malapportionment of the state legislatures and the U.S. House favored rural over urban interests. In many states, it was not uncommon for urban districts to be ten times as populous as rural districts, thus diluting the value of urban votes by a factor of ten. A particularly egregious example of malapportionment was provided by Georgia's "county unit system" (declared unconstitutional by the Supreme Court in *Gray v. Sanders* [1963]). Under that scheme, Fulton County (comprising much of metropolitan Atlanta) with a population of more than half a million was entitled to three seats in the state House of Representatives. Echols County in rural south Georgia, with a 1960 population of only 1,876, was entitled to one representative. Thus, the discrepancy in representation was more than a hundred to one in favor of Echols County!

Even though apportionment discrepancies throughout the United States were great and growing, it was unrealistic to expect elected officials (many of whom benefited from the status quo) to address the problem. Yet most Americans seemed to assume that this problem, like so many others, had a legal solution. Accordingly, voters from grossly underrepresented urban areas turned for relief to the federal courts, citing, among other things, the Equal Protection Clause of the Fourteenth Amendment. In *Colegrove v. Green* (1946), the Supreme Court invoked the political questions doctrine to foreclose judicial relief, at least from the federal bench. Writing for a plurality of the Court, Justice Frankfurter warned of the dangers of entering the "political thicket" of malapportionment:

> It is hostile to a democratic system to involve the judiciary in the politics of the people. . . . The remedy for unfairness in districting is to secure state legislatures that will apportion properly, or to invoke the ample powers of Congress.

The Reapportionment Revolution

Between 1946 and 1962, groups representing urban interests tried, without much success, to secure reapportionment through the state legislatures and through the ballot box. Beginning in 1962, however, the Supreme Court produced a series of decisions on reapportionment that would permanently alter the American political landscape and draw the Court into a firestorm of criticism.

In *Baker v. Carr* (1962), the Supreme Court opened the doors of the federal courthouse to plaintiffs pressing reapportionment claims. The Court reversed its previous position and declared malapportionment to be justiciable (see Chapter 4). Shortly thereafter, the Court declared malapportionment in its various contexts unconstitutional (see Table 17.1). Reapportionment, wrote Chief Justice Warren in *Reynolds v. Sims* (1964), would have to follow the principle of "one person, one vote." In *Reynolds,* the Court held that "the Equal

TABLE 17.1 Major Supreme Court Decisions Extending Reapportionment

Case	Year	Target of Reapportionment
Gray v. Sanders	1963	Georgia "county unit" system of apportioning state legislature
Wesberry v. Sanders	1964	Congressional districts
Reynolds v. Sims	1964	All state legislatures
Lucas v. Colorado 44th General Assembly	1964	State legislative apportionment based on constitutional provisions
Avery v. Midland County	1968	Local governing bodies
Hadley v. Junior College District	1970	School boards

Protection Clause requires that a State make an honest and good faith effort to construct districts, in both houses of its legislature, as nearly of equal population as is practicable."

Not surprisingly, many observers soon began to wonder just how strict the Court would be in requiring population equality among legislative districts. In *Reynolds,* Chief Justice Warren had observed that

> it is a practical impossibility to arrange legislative districts so that each one has an identical number of residents, or citizens, or voters. Mathematical exactness is hardly a workable constitutional requirement. . . .

In 1969, the Court provided an indication of just how strict it intended to be when it struck down an apportionment scheme for congressional districts in Missouri. The plan invalidated by the Court in *Kirkpatrick v. Preisler* involved a 6 percent population deviation between the smallest and the largest districts and only a 1.8 percent average deviation from the ideal district population. Many praised the Court for its rigorous application of the one person, one vote principle. Others decried the Court's meddling in the technicalities of legislative apportionment. Regardless of the position one takes on this issue, the importance of the Court's reapportionment decisions can hardly be overstated. Indeed, on a number of occasions, Chief Justice Warren himself pointed without hesitation to the reapportionment decisions as his principal contribution to constitutional law.

Reapportionment under the Burger Court

For the most part, the Supreme Court under Chief Justice Warren Burger maintained the Warren Court's strong commitment to the one person, one vote principle. The counterrevolution many critics feared from a more conservative Court did not materialize, at least not in the realm of apportionment cases. The Burger Court, however, did allow state legislatures more leeway in determining state legislative boundaries than in drawing congressional district lines. The Court made it clear that, in scrutinizing state districts, it was willing to entertain "legitimate considerations incident to the effectuation of a rational state policy." Thus, in *Brown v. Thomson* (1983), the Court upheld an apportionment scheme for the Wyoming legislature based on county lines, even though the scheme had a population deviation of nearly 90 percent between the largest and the smallest districts. On the very same day, in *Karcher v. Daggett,* the Court invalidated a New Jersey scheme for congressional districts where the maximum deviation was less than 1 percent! The majority agreed with the federal district court that the plan was "not a good-faith effort to achieve population equality using the best available census data."

The 1990 Census and Congressional Reapportionment

While state legislatures are responsible for drawing the boundaries of congressional districts, the Constitution empowers Congress to determine the number of representatives that each state shall have. Every ten years, after completion of the census, Congress reallocates congressional seats among the states. Article I, Section 2 of the Constitution imposes three restrictions on the exercise of Congress's discretion in this area: (1) every state is guaranteed at least one congressional seat; (2) district lines may not cross state borders; and (3) no district shall include less than thirty thousand persons.

In 1941, Congress enacted a law specifying that "the method of equal proportions" would be used to ascertain the number of congressional seats to which each state would be entitled. Applying this method to the results of the 1990 census, Congress determined that Montana would lose one of its two congressional seats. After reapportionment, the average population of congressional districts was 572,466, while Montana's population was 803,655. Montana's single district was thus 231,189 persons larger than the average district. Had Montana retained two districts, each would have been 170,638 persons smaller than the average district. Since the loss of a congressional seat means the decline of influence in Congress and the Electoral College, Montana promptly filed suit to challenge the allocation. Relying on *Wesberry v. Sanders* (1964) and *Kirkpatrick v. Preisler* (1969), the state argued that the greater discrepancy between actual and ideal district size by its loss of a seat violated the principle of one person, one vote. A three-judge district court issued a summary judgment upholding Montana's claim and declaring the 1941 statute unconstitutional. On direct appeal, the Supreme Court unanimously reversed (*Department of Commerce v. Montana* [1992] reprinted in Appendix E). Writing for the Court, Justice John Paul Stevens concluded that Congress had ample power to adopt the method of least proportions or any other reasonable method as long as it is applied consistently after each census. The *Montana* decision suggests that the contemporary Supreme Court is willing to accord far more latitude to Congress than to state legislatures in the field of reapportionment.

Assessing the Reapportionment Decisions

The Supreme Court's reapportionment decisions have been sharply criticized by conservative scholars and by some politicians. In the mid-1960s, a widely publicized effort to overrule the reapportionment decisions through constitutional amendment was spearheaded by Senate Minority Leader Everett Dirksen (R-Illinois). Despite auspicious beginnings, the Dirksen Amendment proved to be a flash in the pan. It soon became clear that the American people fundamentally approved of the reapportionment decisions, irrespective of the strident attacks by many elected officials. A Gallup Poll conducted shortly after *Reynolds v. Sims* was decided found that 47 percent approved of the decision, 30 percent disapproved, and 23 percent expressed no opinion. Apparently the one person, one vote principle appealed to the American people's sense of fair play.

While many observers believe that the Supreme Court's school prayer and desegregation decisions were somewhat damaging to its prestige and credibility, the reapportionment decisions seem to have had the opposite effect. Thus, while the continuing debate over the proper role of the Court is important, the Court's legitimacy does not depend so much on fastidious adherence to legal principles, procedures, and traditions as it does on public support for the substance of the

Court's decisions. One of the great ironies of American democracy (and perhaps its greatest strength) is that the judicial elite must from time to time interfere with the people's elected representatives for the purpose of maintaining the norm of political equality.

For some jurisprudential thinkers, such as John Hart Ely, the primary utility of and justification for judicial review is to maintain the integrity of the democratic process. Certainly the reapportionment decisions make sense from this perspective. It is noteworthy that the reapportionment decisions, although much reviled by incumbent politicians, were met with a far greater degree of compliance than, for example, the school prayer decisions. The strong public support for reapportionment *as a policy* was undoubtedly a critical factor promoting legislative compliance. The clarity of the Supreme Court's one person, one vote mandate likewise facilitated implementation of reapportionment. Finally, the easy observability of noncompliance probably had a substantial effect on legislative willingness to abide by the Court's decisions.

POLITICAL PARTIES AND ELECTORAL FAIRNESS

Although the Framers of the Constitution neither desired nor anticipated the development of political parties, by 1800 a two-party system had taken root in the young republic. While particular political parties have come and gone since then, the two-party system remains an established feature of the political order. Most political scientists regard the two-party system as a source of desirable political stability.

The merits of the two-party system aside, there is surely a constitutional right for disaffected voters to form new parties or support independent candidates who challenge the established order. Despite ideological disagreements, the two established parties tend to collaborate in suppressing competition by rival third parties and independent candidates. State legislatures frequently adopt laws making it difficult, if not impossible, for third parties to get candidates on the ballot. Unrealistic filing deadlines and petition requirements are often employed to frustrate the electoral ambitions of third-party and independent candidates.

In 1980, independent presidential candidate John Anderson filed suit in federal court to challenge Ohio's March filing deadline for the November general elections. In *Anderson v. Celebrezze* (1983), Anderson received a favorable ruling from the Supreme Court, which declared the Ohio regulation to be excessively burdensome on the efforts of independent candidates. Anderson's belated legal victory, however, did not altogether eliminate problems that third-party and independent candidates encounter when attempting to get their names on the ballot, as both David Duke and Ross Perot discovered during their 1992 presidential campaigns.

Partisan Gerrymandering

Historically, one of the weapons of interparty competition has been the gerrymander, the intentional drawing of district lines for political purposes. Although legislative apportionment must proceed on the principle of one person, one vote and must not be based on race discrimination, there remains the prospect that the party in power in the state legislature will redraw district lines so as to minimize the likelihood that the opposing party will gain seats in the next election. The process of reapportionment, which occurs after each decennial census, thus provides an opportunity for the party holding the majority of seats in the legislature to further strengthen its position. Until recently, this **partisan gerrymandering** was thought to be constitutionally unassailable.

In a significant 1986 decisions, however, the Supreme Court upheld the justiciability of cases challenging partisan gerrymandering. In *Davis v. Bandemer* (1986), the Court ruled that Indiana Democrats could challenge a 1981 reapportionment plan adopted by the Republican-controlled state legislature. A plurality of four justices maintained, however, that to prevail in such cases, plaintiffs would have to make "a threshold showing of discriminatory vote dilution. . . ." In a concurring opinion reminiscent of Justice Frankfurter's plea for judicial restraint in *Colegrove v. Green,* Justice Sandra Day O'Connor lamented the Court's "far-reaching step into the 'political thicket' " and predicted dire consequences. According to Justice O'Connor, a former state legislator,

> [t]o turn these matters over to the federal judiciary is to inject the courts into the most heated partisan issues. It is predictable that the courts will respond by moving away from the nebulous standard a plurality of the Court fashions today and toward some form of proportional representation.

The consequences of federal court involvement in partisan gerrymandering will certainly be closely examined by lawyers, scholars, and politicians. Whether *Davis v. Bandemer* represents a permanent entry into the field remains to be seen.

CONCLUSION

The fundamental question of whether courts of law ought to have the power to invalidate legislative and executive acts has long since been put to rest. Yet there remains substantial controversy over the appropriate role of courts in applying the tenets of the Constitution to challenged legislation. Many are troubled by substantive due process decisions in which the Supreme Court has invalidated legislative policies on the basis of arguably dubious principles, such as liberty of contract and the right of privacy, nowhere mentioned in the Constitution. While the appropriate role of the Supreme Court in addressing substantive issues of policy is debatable, there is little disagreement about the legitimacy of the Court's role in maintaining the integrity of the democratic process.

Applying a standard of **strict scrutiny,** the Supreme Court since *Baker v. Carr* (1962) and *Reynolds v. Sims* (1964) has had a significant impact in the area of representation and voting rights. The Court's major decisions in the area reflect three fundamental principles: first, suffrage must be universally available; second, all votes must count equally; and, third, elections must offer the voter a diversity of candidates and parties. Although politicians may resent the Court's "meddling" with the political process, the principles underlying the Court's decisions are essential to the realization of constitutional democracy.

Attempts by legislative majorities to close the channels of political participation to disfavored groups of citizens, whether they be city dwellers, ethnic minorities, or rival political parties, are antithetical to the ideals underlying our system of representative government. Guarding the ideal of political equality is thus without question one of the most important obligations of the Supreme Court. Like its concern for separation of powers, checks and balances, and freedom of expression, the Court's protection of voting rights is critical to the preservation of constitutional democracy in the United States.

FOR FURTHER READING

Baker, Gordon E. *The Reapportionment Revolution.* New York: Random House, 1966.

Ball, Howard. *The Warren Court's Conceptions of Democracy: An Evaluation of the Supreme Court's Apportionment Cases.* Rutherford, N.J.: Fairleigh Dickinson University Press, 1971.

Berger, Raoul. *Government by Judiciary: The Transformation of the Fourteenth Amendment.* Cambridge: Harvard University Press, 1977.

Bullock, Charles S., and Kathryn S. Butler. "Voting Rights." In Tinsley E. Yarbrough, ed., *The Reagan Administration and Human Rights.* New York: Praeger, 1985.

Cortner, Richard C. *The Reapportionment Cases.* Knoxville: University of Tennessee Press, 1970.

Dixon, Robert G., Jr. *Democratic Representation: Reapportionment in Law and Politics.* New York: Oxford University Press, 1968.

Ely, John Hart. *Democracy and Distrust.* Cambridge: Harvard University Press, 1980.

Hamilton, Howard D., ed. *Legislative Reapportionment: Key to Power.* New York: Harper and Row, 1964.

Hanson, Royce. *The Political Thicket: Reapportionment and Constitutional Democracy.* Englewood Cliffs, N.J.: Prentice-Hall, 1966.

Mendelson, Wallace. *Discrimination.* Englewood Cliffs, N.J.: Prentice-Hall, 1962.

Polsby, Nelson W., ed. *Reapportionment in the 1970s.* Berkeley: University of California Press, 1971.

Rodell, Fred. "It Is the Earl Warren Court." *New York Times Magazine,* 13 March 1966.

Taper, Bernard. *Gomillion v. Lightfoot: Apartheid in Alabama.* New York: McGraw-Hill, 1967.

United States Commission on Civil Rights. *1961 Report.* Washington, D.C.: U.S. Government Printing Office, 1961.

Smith v. Allwright

321 U.S. 649; 64 S. Ct. 757; 88 L. Ed. 987 (1944)
Vote: 8-1

In 1927, the Texas legislature passed a law that au-thorized political parties to set qualifications for party membership. Pursuant to this law, the state Democratic party, at its convention in May 1932, adopted the following resolution: "Be it resolved that all white citizens of the State of Texas who are qual-ified to vote under the Constitution and laws of the State shall be eligible to membership in the Demo-cratic Party and, as such, entitled to participate in its deliberations." Lonnie Smith, a black resident of Texas, sued S. E. Allwright, an election judge, for re-fusing to allow him to vote in a Democratic primary at which candidates for state and national office were to be nominated. Through the efforts of the National Association for the Advancement of Col-ored People, this case ultimately reached the U.S. Su-preme Court. Thurgood Marshall, as counsel for the NAACP, participated in the argument of the case on behalf of Smith.

Mr. Justice Reed delivered the opinion of the Court.

. . . The Democratic party of Texas is held by the Supreme Court of that State to be a "voluntary asso-ciation," *** protected by [the] constitution of Texas, from interference by the State except that:

"In the interest of fair methods and a fair expres-sion by their members of their preferences in the selection of their nominees, the State may regulate such elections by proper laws." ***

That court stated further:

Since the right to organize and maintain a political party is one guaranteed by the Bill of Rights of this State, it neces-sarily follows that every privilege essential or reasonably appropriate to the exercise of that right is likewise guaranteed,—including, of course, the privilege of deter-mining the policies of the party and its membership. With-out the privilege of determining the policy of a political association and its membership, the right to organize such an association would be a mere mockery. We think these

rights,—that is, the right to determine the membership of a political party and to determine its policies, of necessity are to be exercised by the state convention of such party, and cannot, under any circumstances, be conferred upon a state or governmental agency. *** . . .

Texas is free to conduct her elections and limit her electorate as she may deem wise, save only as her action may be affected by the prohibitions of the United States Constitution or in conflict with powers delegated to and exercised by the National Govern-ment. The Fourteenth Amendment forbids a State from making or enforcing any law which abridges the privileges or immunities of citizens of the United States and the Fifteenth Amendment specifically in-terdicts any denial or abridgement by a State of the right of citizens to vote on account of color. Respon-dents appeared in the District Court and the Circuit Court of Appeals and defended on the ground that the Democratic party of Texas is a voluntary organi-zation with members banded together for the pur-pose of selecting individuals of the group represent-ing the common political beliefs as candidates in the general election. As such a voluntary organization, it was claimed, the Democratic party is free to select its own membership and limit to whites participation in the party primary. Such action, the answer asserted, does not violate the Fourteenth, Fifteenth or Seven-teenth Amendments as officers of government can-not be chosen at primaries and the Amendments are applicable only to general elections where govern-mental officers are actually elected. . . .

Since *Grovey v. Townsend* and prior to the present suit, no case from Texas involving primary elections has been before this Court. We did decide, however, *United States v. Classic.* *** We there held that Section 4 of Article I of the Constitution autho-rized Congress to regulate primary as well as gen-eral elections, "where the primary is by law made an integral part of the election machinery." *** Consequently, in the *Classic* case, we upheld the applicability to frauds in a Louisiana primary of Sections 19 and 20 of the Criminal Code. . . . *Classic* bears upon *Grovey v. Townsend* not because exclusion of Negroes from primaries is any more or less state action by reason of the unitary character of the electoral process but because the recognition of the place of the primary in the electoral scheme makes clear that state delegation to a party of the power to fix the qualifications of primary elections is delegation of a state function that may make the party's action the action of the State. When *Grovey v. Townsend* was written, the Court looked upon the denial of a vote in a primary as a mere refusal by a party of party membership. *** As the Louisiana statutes for holding primaries are similar to those of Texas, our ruling in *Classic* as to the unitary character of the electoral process calls for a reexamination as to whether or not the exclusion of Negroes from a Texas party primary was state action. . . .

It may now be taken as a postulate that the right to vote in such a primary for the nomination of candidates without discrimination by the State, like the right to vote in a general election, is a right secured by the Constitution. *** By the terms of the Fifteenth Amendment that right may not be abridged by any State on account of race. Under our Constitution the great privilege of the ballot may not be denied a man by the State because of his color.

We are thus brought to an examination of the qualifications for Democratic primary electors in Texas, to determine whether state action or private action has excluded Negroes from participation. Despite Texas' decision that the exclusion is produced by private or party action *** federal courts must for themselves appraise the facts leading to that conclusion. It is only by the performance of this obligation that a final and uniform interpretation can be given to the Constitution, the "supreme Law of the Land." ***

Primary elections are conducted by the party under state statutory authority. The county executive committee selects precinct election officials and the county, district or state executive committees, respectively, canvass the returns. These party committees or the state convention certify the party's candidates to the appropriate officers for inclusion on the official ballot for the general election. No name which has not been so certified may appear upon the ballot for the general election as a candidate of a political party. No other name may be printed on the ballot which has not been placed in nomination by qualified voters who must take oath that they did not participate in a primary for the selection of a candidate for the office for which the nomination is made.

The state courts are given exclusive original jurisdiction of contested elections and of *mandamus* proceedings to compel party officers to perform their statutory duties.

We think that this statutory system for the selection of party nominees for inclusion on the general election ballot makes the party which is required to follow these legislative directions an agency of the State in so far as it determines the participants in a primary election. The party takes its character as a state agency from the duties imposed upon it by state statutes; the duties do not become matters of private law because they are performed by a political party. The plan of the Texas primary follow substantially that of Louisiana, with the exception that in Louisiana the State pays the cost of the primary while Texas assesses the cost against candidates. In numerous instances, the Texas statutes fix or limit the fees to be charged. Whether paid directly by the State or through state requirements, it is state action which compels. When primaries become a part of the machinery for choosing officials, state and national, as they have here, the same tests to determine the character of discrimination or abridgement should be applied to the primary as are applied to the general election. If the State requires a certain electoral procedure, prescribes a general election ballot made up of party nominees so chosen and limits the choice of the electorate in general elections for state offices, practically speaking, to those whose names appear on such a ballot, it endorses, adopts and enforces the discrimination against Negroes, practiced by a party entrusted by Texas law with the determination of the qualifications of participants in the primary. This is state action within the meaning of the Fifteenth Amendment. ***

The United States is a constitutional democracy. Its organic law grants to all citizens a right to participate in the choice of elected officials without restriction by any State because of race. This grant to the people of the opportunity for choice is not to be nullified by a State through casting its electoral process in a form which permits a private organization to practice racial discrimination in the election. Constitutional rights would be of little value if they could be thus indirectly denied. ***

... In reaching this conclusion we are not unmindful of the desirability of continuity of decision in constitutional questions. However, when convinced of former error, this Court has never felt constrained to follow precedent. In constitutional questions, where correction depends upon amendment and not upon legislative action this Court throughout its history has freely exercised its power to reexamine the basis of its constitutional decisions. This has long been accepted practice, and this practice has continued to this day. This is particularly true when the decision believed erroneous is the application of a constitutional principle rather than an interpretation of the Constitution to extract the principle itself. Here we are applying, contrary to the recent decision in *Grovey v. Townsend,* the well-established principle of the Fifteenth Amendment, forbidding the abridgement by a State of a citizen's right to vote. *Grovey v. Townsend* is overruled.

Judgment reversed.

Mr. Justice Frankfurter concurs in the result.

Mr. Justice Roberts:

... I have expressed my views with respect to the present policy of the court freely to disregard and to overrule considered decisions and the rules of law announced in them. This tendency, it seems to me, indicates an intolerance for what those who have composed this court in the past have conscientiously and deliberately concluded, and involves an assumption that knowledge and wisdom reside in us which was denied to our predecessors. I shall not repeat what I there said for I consider it fully applicable to the instant decision, which but points the moral anew. ...

The reason for my concern is that the instant decision, overruling that announced about nine years ago, tends to bring adjudications of this tribunal into the same class as a restricted railroad ticket, good for this day and train only. I have no assurance, in view of current decisions, that the opinion announced today may not shortly be repudiated and overruled by justices who deem they have new light on the subject. In the present term the court has overruled three cases.

In the present case, *** the court below relied, as it was bound to, upon our previous decision. As that court points out, the statutes of Texas have not been altered since *Grovey v. Townsend* was decided. The same resolution is involved as was drawn in question in *Grovey v. Townsend.* Not a fact differentiates that case from this except the names of the parties.

It is suggested that *Grovey v. Townsend* was overruled *sub silentio* in *United States v. Classic.* *** If so, the situation is even worse than that exhibited by the outright repudiation of an earlier decision, for it is the fact that, in the *Classic* case, *Grovey v. Townsend* was distinguished in brief and argument by the Government without suggestion that it was wrongly decided, and was relied on by the appellee, not as a controlling decision, but by way of analogy. The case is not mentioned in either of the opinions in the *Classic* case. Again and again it is said in the opinion of the court in that case that the voter who was denied the right to vote was a fully qualified voter. In other words, there was no question of his being a person entitled under state law to vote in the primary. The offense charged was the fraudulent denial of his conceded right by an election officer because of his race. Here the question is altogether different. It is whether, in a Democratic primary, he who tendered his vote was a member of the Democratic party. ...

It is regrettable that in an era marked by doubt and confusion, an era whose greater need is steadfastness of thought and purpose, this court, which has been looked to as exhibiting consistency in adjudication, and a steadiness which would hold the balance even in the face of temporary ebbs and flows of opinion, should now itself become the breeder of fresh doubt and confusion in the public mind as to the stability of our institutions.

Gomillion v. Lightfoot

364 U.S. 339; 81 S. Ct. 125; 5 L. Ed. 2d 110 (1960)
Vote: 9-0

Mr. Justice Frankfurter delivered the opinion of the Court.

This litigation challenges the validity, under the United States Constitution, of Local Act No. 140, passed by the Legislature of Alabama in 1957, redefining the boundaries of the City of Tuskegee. Petitioners, Negro citizens of Alabama who were, at the time of this redistricting measure, residents of the City of Tuskegee, brought an action in the United States District Court for the Middle District of Alabama for a declaratory judgment that Act 140 is unconstitutional, and for an injunction to restrain the Mayor and officers of Tuskegee and the officials of Macon County, Alabama, from enforcing the Act against them and other Negroes similarly situated. Petitioners' claim is that enforcement of the statute, which alters the shape of Tuskegee from a square to an uncouth twenty-eight–sided figure, will constitute a discrimination against them in violation of the Due Process and Equal Protection Clauses of the Fourteenth Amendment to the Constitution and will deny them the right to vote in defiance of the Fifteenth Amendment.

The respondents moved for dismissal of the action for failure to state a claim upon which relief could be granted and for lack of jurisdiction of the District Court. The court granted the motion, stating, "This court has no control over, no supervision over, and no power to change any boundaries of municipal corporations fixed by a duly convened and elected legislative body, acting for the people for the State of Alabama." *** On appeal, the Court of Appeals for the Fifth Circuit affirmed the judgment, one judge dissenting. *** We brought the case here since serious questions were raised concerning the power of a State over its municipalities in relation to the Fourteenth and Fifteenth Amendments. *** . . . The essential inevitable effect of this redefinition of Tuskegee's boundaries is to remove from the city all save only four or five of its 400 Negro voters while not removing a single white voter or resident. The result of the Act is to deprive the Negro petitioners discrimi-

natorily of the benefits of residence in Tuskegee, including, *inter alia*, the right to vote in municipal elections.

These allegations, if proven, would abundantly establish that Act 140 was not an ordinary geographic redistricting measure even within familiar abuses of gerrymandering. If these allegations upon a trial remained uncontradicted or unqualified, the conclusion would be irresistible, tantamount for all practical purposes to a mathematical demonstration, that the legislation is solely concerned with segregating white and colored voters by fencing Negro citizens out of town so as to deprive them of their preexisting municipal vote.

It is difficult to appreciate what stands in the way of adjudging a statute having this inevitable effect invalid in light of the principles by which this Court must judge, and uniformly has judged, statutes that, howsoever speciously defined, obviously discriminate against colored citizens. "The [Fifteenth] Amendment nullified sophisticated as well as simpleminded modes of discrimination." ***

The complaint amply alleges a claim of racial discrimination. Against this claim the respondents have never suggested, either in their brief or in oral argument, any countervailing municipal function which Act 140 is designed to serve. The respondents invoke generalities expressing the State's unrestricted power—unlimited, that is, by the United States Constitution—to establish, destroy, or reorganize by contraction or expansion its political subdivisions, to wit, cities, counties, and other local units. We freely recognize the breadth and importance of this aspect of the State's political power. To exalt this power into an absolute is to misconceive the reach and rule of this Court's decisions. . . .

. . . The Court has never acknowledged that the States have power to do as they will with municipal corporations regardless of consequences. Legislative control of municipalities, no less than other state power, lies within the scope of relevant limitations imposed by the United States Constitution. . . .

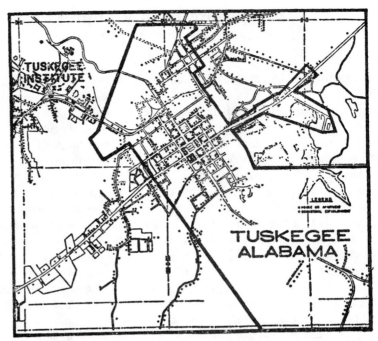

FIGURE 17.1 Tuskegee, Alabama, Before and After Act 140

The entire area of the square comprised the city prior to Act 140. The irregular black-bordered figure within the square represents the post-enactment city.

Appendix to Opinion of the Court

. . . Such power, extensive though it is, is met and overcome by the Fifteenth Amendment to the Constitution of the United States, which forbids a State from passing any law which deprives a citizen of his vote because of his race. The opposite conclusion, urged upon us by respondents, would sanction the achievement by a State of any impairment of voting rights whatever so long as it was cloaked in the garb of the realignment of political subdivisions. "It is inconceivable that guaranties embedded in the Constitution of the United States may thus be manipulated out of existence." ***

When a State exercises power wholly within the domain of state interest, it is insulated from federal judicial review. But such insulation is not carried over when state power is used as an instrument for circumventing a federally protected right. This principle has had many applications. It has long been recognized in cases which have prohibited a State from exploiting a power acknowledged to be abso-lute in an isolated context to justify the imposition of an "unconstitutional condition." What the Court has said in those cases is equally applicable here, viz., that "Act generally lawful may become unlawful when done to accomplish an unlawful end, *** and a constitutional power cannot be used by way of condition to attain an unconstitutional result." The petitioners are entitled to prove their allegations at trial.

For these reasons, the principal conclusions of the District Court and the Court of Appeals are clearly erroneous and the decision below must be

Reversed.

Mr. Justice Douglas, [concurring]. . . .

Mr. Justice Whittaker, concurring.

I concur in the Court's judgment, but not in the whole of its opinion. It seems to me that the decision should be rested not on the Fifteenth Amendment, but rather on the equal Protection Clause of the

Fourteenth Amendment to the Constitution. I am doubtful that the averments of the complaint, taken for present purposes to be true, show a purpose by Act No. 140 to abridge petitioners' "right . . . to vote," in the Fifteenth Amendment sense. It seems to me that the "right . . . to vote" that is guaranteed by the Fifteenth Amendment is but the same right to vote as is enjoyed by all others within the same election precinct, ward or other political division. And, inasmuch as no one has the right to vote in a political division, or in a local election concerning only an area in which he does not reside, it would seem to follow that one's right to vote in Division A is not abridged by a re-

districting that places his residence in Division B if he there enjoys the same voting privileges as all others in that Division, even though the redistricting was done by the State for the purposes of placing a racial group of citizens in Division B rather than A.

But it does seem clear to me that accomplishment of a State's purpose—to use the Court's phrase—of "fencing Negro citizens out of" Division A and into Division B is an unlawful segregation of races of citizens, in violation of the Equal Protection Clause of the Fourteenth Amendment, *** and, as stated, I would think the decision should be rested on that ground. . . .

South Carolina v. Katzenbach

383 U.S. 301; 86 S. Ct. 803; 15 L. Ed. 2d 769 (1966)
Vote: 8-1

The Voting Rights Act of 1965 is one of the most significant pieces of civil rights legislation ever adopted by the Congress. Essentially, it brings the power of the federal government to bear on traditional practices designed to keep minorities from participating in the electoral process. More specifically, the act utilizes a triggering formula to target those areas in which voting discrimination is most egregious. In such areas, the act abolishes literacy tests, waives poll taxes that have accumulated, and forbids the state from implementing new voting requirements until they have been found by the federal courts or the U.S. attorney general to be nondiscriminatory. Additionally, the act allows for federal examiners to be appointed to supervise the conduct of elections. Finally, the act authorizes civil and criminal penalties for those who interfere with the rights guaranteed by the act. In this case, the state of South Carolina challenged the constitutionality of various provisions of the Voting Rights Act.

Mr. Chief Justice Warren delivered the opinion of the Court.

. . . The Voting Rights Act of 1965 reflects Congress' firm intention to rid the country of racial discrimination in voting. The heart of the Act is a complex scheme of stringent remedies aimed at areas where voting discrimination has been most flagrant. . . .

At the outset, we emphasize that only some of the many portions of the Act are properly before us. . . .

The Court then undertakes a detailed review of the challenged provisions: the coverage or "triggering" formula; the suspension of certain "tests or devices," including property requirements and literacy tests; the review of new voting requirements by the attorney general or the federal courts; and the appointment of federal examiners to supervise elections.

These provisions of the Voting Rights Act of 1965 are challenged on the fundamental ground that they exceed the powers of Congress and encroach on an area reserved to the States by the Constitution. . . . Has Congress exercised its powers in an appropriate manner with relation to the states?

The ground rules for resolving this question are clear. The language and purpose of the Fifteenth Amendment, the prior decisions construing its several provisions, and the general doctrines of constitutional interpretation, all point to one fundamental principle. As against the reserved powers of the States, Congress may use any rational means to effectuate the constitutional prohibition of racial discrimination in voting. . . .

Section 1 of the Fifteenth Amendment declares that "[t]he right of citizens of the United States to vote shall not be denied or abridged on account of race, color or previous condition of servitude." This declaration has always been treated as self-executing and has repeatedly been construed, without further legislative specification, to invalidate state voting qualifications or procedures which are discriminatory on their face or in practice. . . . [Here the Court cites numerous cases to illustrate its point.] The gist of the matter is that the Fifteenth Amendment supersedes contrary exertions of state power. "When a State exercises power wholly within the domain of state interest, it is insulated from federal judicial review. But such insulation is not carried over when state power is used as an instrument for circumventing a federally protected right." ***

South Carolina contends that the cases cited above [omitted] are precedents only for the authority of the judiciary to strike down state statutes and procedures—that to allow an exercise of this authority by Congress would be to rob the courts of their rightful constitutional role. On the contrary, Section 2 of the Fifteenth Amendment expressly declares that "Congress shall have the power to enforce this article by appropriate legislation." By adding this authorization, the Framers indicated that Congress was to be chiefly responsible for implementing the rights created in Section 1. . . .

Congress has repeatedly exercised these powers in the past, and its enactments have repeatedly been upheld. *** On the rare occasions where the Court has found an unconstitutional exercise of these powers, in its opinion Congress had attacked evils not comprehended by the Fifteenth Amendment. ***

The basic test to be applied in a case involving Section 2 of the Fifteenth Amendment is the same in all cases concerning the express powers of Congress with relation to the reserved powers of the States. Chief Justice Marshall laid down the classic formulation, 50 years before the Fifteenth Amendment was ratified.

Let the end be legitimate, let it be within the scope of the constitutional, and all means which are appropriate, which are plainly adapted to that end, which are not prohibited, but consist with the letter and spirit of the Constitution, are constitutional. ***

We therefore reject South Carolina's argument that Congress may appropriately do no more than to forbid violations of the Fifteenth Amendment in general terms. . . .

Congress exercised its authority . . . in an inventive manner when it adopted the Voting Rights Act of 1965. First: the measure prescribes remedies for voting discrimination which go into effect without any need for prior adjudication. This was clearly a legitimate response to the problem, for which there is ample precedent under other constitutional provisions. *** Congress had found that case-by-case litigation was inadequate to combat widespread and persistent discrimination in voting, because of the inordinate amount of time and energy required to overcome the obstructionist tactics invariably encountered in these lawsuits. After enduring nearly a century of systematic resistance to the Fifteenth Amendment, Congress might well shift the advantage of time and inertia from the perpetrators of the evil to its victims. . . .

Second: The Act intentionally confines these remedies to a small number of states and political subdivisions which in most instances were familiar to Congress by name. This, too, was a permissible method of dealing with the problem. Congress had learned that substantial voting discrimination presently occurs in certain sections of the country, and it knew no way of accurately forecasting whether the evil might spread elsewhere in the future. In acceptable legislative fashion, Congress chose to limit its attention to the geographic areas where immediate action seemed necessary. *** The doctrine of the equality of States, invoked by South Carolina, does not bar this approach, for that doctrine applies only to the terms upon which States are admitted to the Union, and not to the remedies for local evils which have subsequently appeared. ***

COVERAGE FORMULA

We now consider the related question of whether the specific States and political subdivisions . . . were an appropriate target for the new remedies. . . .

To be specific, the new remedies of the Act are imposed on three States—Alabama, Louisiana, and Mississippi—in which federal courts have repeatedly found substantial voting discrimination. Section 4(b) of the Act also embraces two other States—Georgia and South Carolina—plus large portions of a third State—North Carolina—for which there was more fragmentary evidence of recent voting discrimination mainly adduced by the Justice Department and the Civil Rights Commission. All these areas were appropriately subjected to the new remedies. . . .

The area listed above, for which there was evidence of actual voting discrimination, share two characteristics incorporated by Congress into the coverage formula: the use of tests and devices for voter registration, and a voting rate in the 1964 presidential election at least 12 points below the national average. Tests and devices are relevant to voting discrimination because of their long history as a tool for perpetrating the evil; a low voting rate is pertinent for the obvious reason that widespread disenfranchisement must inevitably affect the number of actual voters. Accordingly, the coverage formula is rational in both practice and theory. It was therefore permissible to impose the new remedies on the few remaining States and their political subdivisions covered by the formula. . . .

SUSPENSION OF TESTS

We now arrive at consideration of the specific remedies prescribed by the Act for areas included within the coverage formula. South Carolina assails the temporary suspension of existing voting qualifications. . . . The record shows that in most of the States covered by the Act, including South Carolina, various tests and devices have been instituted with the purpose of disenfranchising Negroes, have been framed in such a way to facilitate this aim, and have been administered in a discriminatory fashion for many years. Under these circumstances, the Fifteenth Amendment has clearly been violated. ***

The Act suspends literacy tests and similar devices for a period of five years from the last occurrence of substantial voting discrimination. This was a legitimate response to the problem, for which there is ample precedent in Fifteenth Amendment cases. *** Underlying the response was the feeling that States and political subdivisions which had been allowing white illiterates to vote for years could not sincerely

complain about "dilution" of their electorates through the registration of Negro illiterates. Congress knew that continuance of the tests and devices in use at the present time, no matter how fairly administered in the future, would freeze the effect of past discrimination in favor of unqualified white registrants. Congress permissably rejected the alternative of requiring a complete re-registration of all voters, believing that this would be too harsh on whites who had enjoyed the franchise for their entire adult lives.

REVIEW OF NEW RULES

The Act suspends voting regulations pending scrutiny by federal authorities to determine whether their use would violate the Fifteenth Amendment. This may have been an uncommon exercise of Congressional power, as South Carolina contends, but the Court has recognized that exceptional conditions can justify legislative measures not otherwise appropriate. *** Under the compulsion of these unique circumstances, Congress responded in a permissibly decisive manner. . . .

FEDERAL EXAMINERS

The Act authorizes the appointment of federal examiners to list qualified applicants who are thereafter entitled to vote, subject to an expeditious challenge procedure. This was clearly an appropriate response to the problem, closely related to remedies authorized in prior cases. *** In many of the political subdivisions covered by . . . the Act, voting officials have persistently employed a variety of procedural tactics to deny Negroes the franchise, often in direct defiance or evasion of federal court decrees. Congress realized that merely to suspend voting rules which have been misused or are subject to misuse might leave this localized evil undisturbed. . . .

After enduring nearly a century of widespread resistance to the Fifteenth Amendment, Congress has marshalled an array of potent weapons against the evil, with authority by the Attorney General to employ them effectively. Many of the areas affected by this development have indicated their willingness to abide by any restraints legitimately imposed upon them. We here hold that the portions of the Voting Rights

Act properly before us are a valid means for carrying out the commands of the Fifteenth Amendment. Hopefully, millions of non-white Americans will now be able to participate for the first time on an equal basis in the government under which they live. . . .

The bill of complaint is dismissed.

Justice Black, concurring [in part] and dissenting [in part]. . . .

Mobile v. Bolden

446 U.S. 55; 100 S. Ct. 1490; 64 L. Ed.2d 47 (1980)
Vote: 6-3

In this case, the Supreme Court considers a challenge to at-large local elections based on the Voting Rights Act of 1965 and the Fifteenth Amendment.

Mr. Justice Stewart announced the judgment of the court and delivered an opinion, in which ***The Chief Justice, Mr. Justice Powell,*** and ***Mr. Justice Rehnquist*** joined.

The City of Mobile, Ala., has since 1911 been governed by a City Commission consisting of three members elected by the voters of the city at large. The question in this case is whether this at-large system of municipal elections violates the rights of Mobile's Negro voters in contravention of federal statutory or constitutional law.

The appellees brought this suit in the Federal District Court for the Southern District of Alabama as a class action on behalf of all Negro citizens of Mobile. Named as defendants were the city and its three incumbent Commissioners, who are the appellants before this Court. The complaint alleged that the practice of electing the City Commissioners at large unfairly diluted the voting strength of Negroes in violation of [Section] 2 of the Voting Rights Act of 1965, of the Fourteenth Amendment, and of the Fifteenth Amendment. Following a bench trial, the District Court found that the constitutional rights of the appellees had been violated, entered a judgment in their favor, and ordered that the City Commission be disestablished and replaced by a municipal government consisting of a Mayor and a City Council with members elected from single-member districts. *** The Court of Appeals affirmed the judgment in its entirety. ***

In Alabama, the form of municipal government a city may adopt is governed by state law. Until 1911, cities not covered by specific legislation were limited to governing themselves through a mayor and city council. In that year, the Alabama Legislature authorized every large municipality to adopt a commission form of government. Mobile established its City Commission in the same year, and has maintained that basic system of municipal government ever since.

Three Commissioners jointly exercise all legislative, executive, and administrative power in the municipality. They are required after election to designate one of their number as Mayor, a largely ceremonial office, but no formal provision is made for allocating specific executive or administrative duties among the three. As required by the state law enacted in 1911, each candidate for the Mobile City Commission runs for election in the city at large for a term of four years in one of three numbered posts, and may be elected only by a majority of the total vote. This is the same basic electoral system that is followed by literally thousands of municipalities and other local governmental units throughout the Nation.

Although required by general principles of judicial administration to do so, *** neither the District Court nor the Court of Appeals addressed the complaint's statutory claim—that the Mobile electoral system violates [Section] 2 of the Voting Rights Act of 1965. Even a cursory examination of that claim, however, clearly discloses that it adds nothing to the appellees' complaint.

Section 2 of the Voting Rights Act provides:

"No voting qualification or prerequisite to voting, or standard, practice, or procedure shall be imposed or applied by any State or political subdivision to deny or abridge the right of any citizen of the United States to vote on account of race or color." ***

Assuming, for present purposes, that there exists a private right of action to enforce this statutory provision, it is apparent that the language of [Section] 2 no more than elaborates upon that of the Fifteenth Amendment, and the sparse legislative history of [Section] 2 makes clear that it was intended to have an effect no different from that of the Fifteenth Amendment itself.

Section 2 was an uncontroversial provision in proposed legislation whose other provisions engendered protracted dispute. The House Report on the bill simply recited that [Section] 2 "grants . . . a right to be free from enactment or enforcement of voting qualifications . . . or practices which deny or abridge the right to vote on account of race or color." *** The view that this section simply restated the prohibitions already contained in the Fifteenth Amendment was expressed without contradiction during the Senate hearings. Senator Dirksen indicated at one point that all States, whether or not covered by the pre-clearance provisions of [Section] 5 of theproposed legislation, were prohibited from dis-criminating against Negro voters by [Section] 2, which he termed "almost a rephrasing of the 15th [A]mendment." Attorney General Katzenbach agreed. ***

In view of the section's language and its sparse but clear legislative history, it is evident that this statutory provision adds nothing to the appellees' Fifteenth Amendment claim. We turn, therefore, to a consideration of the validity of the judgment of the Court of Appeals with respect to the Fifteenth Amendment.

The Court's early decision under the Fifteenth Amendment established that it imposes but one limitation on the powers of the States. It forbids them to discriminate against Negroes in matters having to do with voting. *** The Amendment's command and effect are wholly negative. "The Fifteenth Amendment does not confer the right of suffrage upon any one," but has "invested the citizens of the United States with a new constitutional right which is within the protecting power of Congress. That right is exemption from discrimination in the exercise of the elective franchise on account of race, color, or previous condition of servitude." ***

Our decisions, moreover, have made clear that action by a State that is racially neutral on its face violates the Fifteenth Amendment only if motivated by a discriminatory purpose. ***

The Court's more recent decisions confirm the principle that racially discriminatory motivation is a necessary ingredient of a Fifteenth Amendment violation. ***

While other of the Court's Fifteenth Amendment decisions have dealt with different issues, none has questioned the necessity of showing purposeful discrimination in order to show a Fifteenth Amendment violation. The cases of *Smith v. Allwright* *** [1944] and *Terry v. Adams* *** [1953] for example, dealt with the question whether a State was so involved with racially discriminatory voting practices as to invoke the Amendment's protection. . . .

The answer to the appellees' argument is that, as the District Court expressly found, their freedom to vote has not been denied or abridged by anyone. The Fifteenth Amendment does not entail the right to have Negro candidates elected, and neither *Smith v. Allwright* nor *Terry v. Adams* contains any implication to the contrary. That Amendment prohibits only purposefully discriminatory denial or abridgment by government of the freedom to vote "on account of race, color, or previous condition of servitude." Having found that Negroes in Mobile "register and vote without hindrance," *** the District Court and Court of Appeals were in error in believing that the appellants invaded the protection of that Amendment in the present case.

The Court of Appeals also agreed with the District Court that Mobile's at-large electoral system violates the Equal Protection Clause of the Fourteenth Amendment. There remains for consideration, therefore, the validity of its judgment on that score.

The claim that at-large electoral schemes unconstitutionally deny to some persons the equal protection of the laws has been advanced in numerous cases before this Court. That contention has been raised most often with regard to multimember constituencies within a state legislative apportionment system. The constitutional objection to multimember districts is not and cannot be that, as such, they depart from apportionment on a population basis in violation of *Reynolds v. Sims* [1964] and its progeny.

Rather the focus in such cases has been on the lack of representation multimember districts afford various elements of the voting population in a system of representative legislative democracy. "Criticism [of multimember districts] is rooted in their winner-take-all aspects, their tendency to submerge minorities. . . , a general preference for legislatures reflecting community interests as closely as possible and disenchantment with political parties and elections as devices to settle policy differences between contending interests." ***

Despite repeated constitutional attacks upon multimember legislative districts, the Court has consistently held that they are not unconstitutional *per se*. *** We have recognized, however, that such legislative apportionments could violate the Fourteenth Amendment if their purpose were invidiously to minimize or cancel out the voting potential of racial or ethnic minorities. *** To prove such a purpose it is not enough to show that the group allegedly discriminated against has not elected representatives in proportion to its numbers. ***

The judgment is reversed, and the case is remanded to the Court of Appeals for further proceedings.

It is so ordered.

Mr. Justice Blackmun, concurring in the result.

Assuming that proof of intent is a prerequisite to appellees' prevailing on their constitutional claim of vote dilution, I am inclined to agree with Mr. Justice White that, in this case, "the findings of the District Court amply support an inference of purposeful discrimination." *** I concur in the Court's judgment of reversal, however, because I believe that the relief afforded appellees by the District Court was not commensurate with the sound exercise of judicial discretion.

It seems to me that the city of Mobile, and its citizenry, have a substantial interest in maintaining the commission form of government that has been in effect there for nearly 70 years. The District Court recognized that its remedial order, changing the form of the city's government to a mayor-council system, "raised serious constitutional issues." *** Nonetheless, the court was "unable to see how the impermissibly unconstitutional dilution can be effectively corrected by any other approach." *** . . .

Contrary to the District Court, I do not believe that, in order to remedy the unconstitutional vote dilution it found, it was necessary to convert Mobile's city government to a mayor-council system. In my view, the District Court should have at least considered alternative remedial orders that would have maintained some of the basic elements of the commission system Mobile long ago had selected. . . .

Mr. Justice Stevens, concurring in the judgment. . . .

Mr. Justice Brennan, dissenting.

I dissent because I agree with Mr. Justice Marshall that proof of discriminatory impact is sufficient in these cases. I also dissent because, even accepting the plurality's premise that discriminatory purpose must be shown, I agree with Mr. Justice Marshall and Mr. Justice White that the appellees have clearly met that burden.

Mr. Justice White, dissenting.

In *White v. Regester* *** (1973), this Court unanimously held the use of multimember districts for the election of state legislators in two counties in Texas violated the Equal Protection Clause of the Fourteenth Amendment because, based on a careful assessment of the totality of the circumstances, they were found to exclude Negroes and Mexican-Americans from effective participation in the political processes in the counties. Without questioning the vitality of *White v. Regester* and our other decisions dealing with challenges to multimember districts by racial or ethnic groups, the Court today inexplicably rejects a similar holding based on meticulous factual findings and scrupulous application of the principles of these cases by both the District Court and the Court of Appeals. The Court's decision is flatly inconsistent with *White v. Regester* and it cannot be understood to flow from our recognition in *Washington v. Davis* *** (1976), that the Equal Protection Clause forbids only purposeful discrimination. Both the District Court and the Court of Appeals properly found that an invidious discriminatory purpose could be inferred from the totality of facts in this case. The Court's cryptic rejection of their conclusions ignores the principles that an invidious discriminatory purpose can be inferred from objective factors of the kind relied on in *White v. Regester* and that the trial courts are in a special position to make such intensely local appraisals. . . .

Because I believe that the findings of the District Court amply support an inference of purposeful discrimination in violation of the Fourteenth and Fifteenth Amendments, I respectfully dissent.

Mr. Justice Marshall, dissenting.

. . . The plurality concludes that our prior decisions establish the principle that proof of discriminatory intent is a necessary element of a Fifteenth Amendment claim. In contrast, I continue to adhere to my conclusion . . . that "[t]he Court's decisions relating to the relevance of purpose-and/or-effect analysis in testing the constitutionality of legislative enactments are somewhat less than a seamless web." . . . [A]t various times the Court's decisions have seemed to adopt three inconsistent approaches: (1) that purpose alone is the test for unconstitutionality; (2) that effect alone is the test; and (3) that purpose or effect, either alone or in combination, is sufficient to show unconstitutionality. *** In my view, our Fifteenth Amendment jurisprudence on the necessity of proof of discriminatory purpose is no less unsettled than was our approach to the importance of such proof in Fourteenth Amendment racial discrimination cases prior to *Washington v. Davis* *** (1976). What is called for in the present cases is a fresh consideration—similar to our inquiry in *Washington v. Davis* with regard to Fourteenth Amendment discrimination claims—of whether proof of discriminatory purpose is necessary to establish a claim under the Fifteenth Amendment. . . .

. . . [I]t is beyond dispute that a standard based solely upon the motives of official decisionmakers creates significant problems of proof for plaintiffs and forces the inquiring court to undertake an unguided, tortuous look into the minds of officials in the hope of guessing why certain policies were adopted and others rejected. . . . An approach based on motivation creates the risk that officials will be able to adopt policies that are the products of discriminatory intent so long as they

sufficiently mask their motives through the use of subtlety and illusion. . . .

I continue to believe, then, that under the Fifteenth Amendment an "[e]valuation of the purpose of a legislative enactment is just too ambiguous a task to be the sole tool of constitutional analysis. . . . [A] demonstration of effect ordinarily should suffice. If, of course, purpose may conclusively be shown, it too should be sufficient to demonstrate a statute's unconstitutionality." *** The plurality's refusal in this case even to consider this approach bespeaks an indifference to the plight of minorities who, through no fault of their own, have suffered diminution of the right preservative of all other rights.

The American approach to government is premised on the theory that, when citizens have the unfettered right to vote, public officials will make decisions by the democratic accommodation of competing beliefs, not by deference to the mandates of the powerful. The American approach to civil rights is premised on the complementary theory that the unfettered right to vote is preservative of all other rights. The theoretical foundations for these approaches are shattered where, as in the present cases, the right to vote is granted in form, but denied in substance.

It is time to realize that manipulating doctrines and drawing improper distinctions under the Fourteenth and Fifteenth Amendments, as well as under Congress' remedial legislation enforcing those Amendments, make this Court an accessory to the perpetuation of racial discrimination. The plurality's requirement of proof of intentional discrimination, so inappropriate in today's cases, may represent an attempt to bury the legitimate concerns of the minority beneath the soil of a doctrine almost as impermeable as it is spacious. If so, the superficial tranquility created by such measures can be but short-lived. If this Court refuses to honor our long-recognized principle that the Constitution "nullifies sophisticated as well as simple-minded modes of discrimination," *** it cannot expect the victims of discrimination to respect political channels of seeking redress. I dissent.

Rogers v. Lodge

458 U.S. 613; 102 S. Ct. 3272; 73 L. Ed. 2d 1012 (1982)
Vote: 6-3

Justice White delivered the opinion of the Court.

The issue in this case is whether the at-large system of elections in Burke County, Ga., violates the Fourteenth Amendment rights of Burke County's black citizens.

I

Burke County is a large, predominately rural county located in eastern Georgia. Eight hundred and thirty-one square miles in area, it is approximately two-thirds the size of the State of Rhode Island. According to the 1980 census, Burke County had a total population of 19,349, of whom 10,385, or 53.6%, were black. The average age of blacks living there is lower than the average age of whites and therefore whites constitute a slight majority of the voting age population. As of 1978, 6,373 persons were registered to vote in Burke County, of whom 38% were black.

The Burke County Board of Commissioners governs the county. It was created in 1911, *** and consists of five members elected at large to concurrent 4-year terms by all qualified voters in the county. The county has never been divided into districts, either for the purpose of imposing a residency requirement on candidates or for the purpose of requiring candidates to be elected by voters residing in a district. In order to be nominated or elected, a candidate must receive a majority of the votes cast in the primary or general election, and a runoff must be held if no candidate receives a majority in the first primary or general election. *** Each candidate must run for a specific seat on the Board, and a voter may vote only once for any candidate. No Negro has been elected to the Burke County Board of Commissioners.

Appellees, eight black citizens of Burke County, filed this suit in 1976 in the United States District Court for the Southern District of Georgia. The suit was brought on behalf of all black citizens in Burke County. The class was certified in 1977. The complaint alleged that the county's system of at-large elections violates appellees' First, Thirteenth, Fourteenth and Fifteenth Amendment rights ... by diluting the voting power of black citizens. Following a bench trial at which both sides introduced extensive evidence, the court issued an order on September 29, 1978, stating that appellees were entitled to prevail and ordering that Burke County be divided into five districts for purposes of electing County Commissioners....

The Court of Appeals affirmed. *** It stated that while the proceedings in the District Court took place prior to the decision in *Mobile v. Bolden,* *** the District Court correctly anticipated *Mobile* and required appellees to prove that the at-large voting system was maintained for a discriminatory purpose. *** The Court of Appeals also held that the District Court's findings were not clearly erroneous, and that its conclusion that the at-large system was maintained for invidious purpose was "virtually mandated by the overwhelming proof." *** We noted probable jurisdiction, and now affirm. ***

II

At-large voting schemes and multimember districts tend to minimize the voting strength of minority groups by permitting the political majority to elect all representatives of the district. A distinct minority, whether it be a racial, ethnic, economic, or political group, may be unable to elect any representatives if the political unit is divided into single-member districts. The minority's voting power in a multimember district is particularly diluted when bloc voting occurs and ballots are cast along strict majority–minority lines. While multimember districts have been challenged for "their winner-take-all aspects, their tendency to submerge minorities and to overrepresent the winning party," *** this Court has repeatedly held that they are not unconstitutional *per se.* *** The Court has recognized, however, that multimember districts violate the Fourteenth Amendment if "conceived or operated as purposeful devices to further racial discrimination" by minimizing, canceling out or diluting the voting strength of racial elements in the voting population. *** Cases charging that multimember districts unconstitutionally dilute the voting strength of racial minorities are thus subject to the standard of proof generally applicable to Equal Protection Clause cases. *** In order for the Equal Protection Clause to be violated, "the invidious quality of a law claimed to be racially discriminatory must ultimately be traced to a racially discriminatory purpose."

Arlington Heights [v. *Metropolitan Housing Development Corp.*] *** and *Washington v. Davis* *** both rejected the notion that a law is invalid under the Equal Protection Clause simply because it may affect a greater proportion of one race than another. However, both cases recognized that discriminatory intent need not be proved by direct evidence. "Necessarily, an invidious discriminatory purpose may often be inferred from the totality of the relevant facts, including the fact, if it is true, that the law bears more heavily on one race than another." *** Thus determining the existence of a discriminatory purpose "demands a sensitive inquiry into such circumstantial and direct evidence of intent as may be available." ***

In *Mobile v. Bolden,* the Court was called upon to apply these principles to the at-large election system in Mobile, Ala. Mobile is governed by three commissioners who exercise all legislative, executive, and administrative power in the municipality. *** Each candidate for the City Commission runs for one of three numbered posts in an at-large election and can only be elected by a majority vote. *** Plaintiffs brought a class action on behalf of all Negro citizens of Mobile alleging that the at-large scheme diluted their voting strength in violation of several statutory and constitutional provisions. The District Court concluded that the at-large system "violates the constitutional rights of the plaintiffs by improperly restricting their access to the political process," *** and ordered that the commission form of government be replaced by a mayor and a nine-member City Council elected from single-member districts. *** The Court of Appeals affirmed. *** This Court reversed.

Justice Stewart, writing for himself and three other Justices, noted that to prevail in their contention that the at-large voting system violates the Equal Protection Clause of the Fourteenth Amendment, plaintiffs had to prove the system was " 'conceived or operated as [a] purposeful devic[e] to further racial ...

discrimination.' " *** Such a requirement "is simply one aspect of the basic principle that only if there is purposeful discrimination can there be a violation of the Equal Protection Clause of the Fourteenth Amendment." ***

The plurality went on to conclude that the District Court had failed to comply with this standard. The District Court had analyzed plaintiffs' claims in light of the standard which had been set forth in *Zimmer v. McKeithen.* *** *Zimmer* set out a list of factors ... that a court should consider in assessing the constitutionality of at-large and multimember district voting schemes. Under *Zimmer,* voting dilution is established "upon proof of the existence of an aggregate of these factors." ***

The plurality in *Mobile* was of the view that *Zimmer* was "decided upon the misunderstanding that it is not necessary to show a discriminatory purpose in order to prove a violation of the Equal Protection Clause—that proof of a discriminatory effect is sufficient." *** The plurality observed that while "the presence of the indicia relied on in *Zimmer* may afford some evidence or a discriminatory purpose," the mere existence of those criteria is not a substitute for a finding of discriminatory purpose. *** The District Court's standard in *Mobile* was likewise flawed. Finally, the plurality concluded that the evidence on which the lower courts had relied was "insufficient to prove an unconstitutionally discriminatory purpose in the present case." *** Justice Stevens rejected the intentional discrimination standard but concluded that the proof failed to satisfy the legal standard that in his view was the applicable rule. He therefore concurred in the judgment of reversal. ...

Because the District Court in the present case employed the evidentiary factors outlined in *Zimmer,* it is urged that its judgment is infirm for the same reasons that led to the reversal in *Mobile.* We do not agree. First, and fundamentally, we are unconvinced that the District Court in this case applied the wrong legal standard.

The District Court ... demonstrated its understanding by observing that a determination of discriminatory intent is "a requisite to a finding of unconstitutional vote dilution" under the Fourteenth Amendments. *** Furthermore, while recognizing that the evidentiary factors identified in *Zimmer* were to be considered, the District Court was aware that it was "not limited in its determination only to the *Zimmer* factors" but could consider other relevant factors as well. *** The District Court then proceeded to deal with what it considered to be the relevant proof and concluded that the at-large scheme of electing commissioners," although racially neutral when adopted, is being maintained for invidious purposes." *** That system "while neutral in origin . . . has been subverted to invidious purposes." ***

III

. . . The District court found that blacks have always made up a substantial majority of the population in Burke County, *** but that they are a distinct minority of the registered voters. *** There was also overwhelming evidence of bloc voting along racial lines. Hence, although there had been black candidates, no black had ever been elected to the Burke County Commission. These facts bear heavily on the issue of purposeful discrimination. Voting along racial lines allows those elected to ignore black interests without fear of political consequences, and without bloc voting the minority candidates would not lose elections solely because of their race. Because it is sensible to expect that at least some blacks would have been elected in Burke County, the fact that none have ever been elected is important evidence of purposeful exclusion. ***

Under our cases, however, such facts are insufficient in themselves to prove purposeful discrimination absent other evidence such as proof that blacks have less opportunity to participate in the political processes and to elect candidates of their choice. *** Both the District Court and the Court of Appeals thought the supporting proof in this case was sufficient to support an inference of intentional discrimination. . . .

The District Court began by determining the impact of past discrimination on the ability of blacks to participate effectively in the political process. Past discrimination was found to contribute to low black voter registration because prior to the Voting Rights Act of 1965, blacks had been denied access to the political process by means such as literacy tests, poll

taxes, and white primaries. The result was that "Black suffrage in Burke County was virtually non-existent." *** Black voter registration in Burke County has increased following the Voting Rights Act to the point that some 38% of blacks eligible to vote are registered to do so. *** On that basis the District Court inferred that "past discrimination has had an adverse effect on black voter registration which lingers to this date." *** Past discrimination against blacks in education also had the same effect. Not only did Burke County schools discriminate against blacks as recently as 1969, but also some schools still remain essentially segregated and blacks as a group have completed less formal education than whites. ***

The District Court found further evidence of exclusion from the political process. Past discrimination had prevented blacks from effectively participating in Democratic Party affairs and in primary elections. Until this lawsuit was filed, there had never been a black member of the County Executive Committee of the Democratic Party. There were also property ownership requirements that made it difficult for blacks to serve as chief registrar in the county. There had been discrimination in the selection of grand jurors, the hiring of county employees, and in the appointments to boards and committees which oversee the county government. *** The District Court thus concluded that historical discrimination had restricted the present opportunity of blacks effectively to participate in the political process. Evidence of historical discrimination is relevant to drawing an inference of purposeful discrimination, particularly in cases such as this one where the evidence shows that discriminatory practices were commonly utilized, that they were abandoned when enjoined by courts or made illegal by civil rights legislation, and that they were replaced by laws and practices which, though neutral on their face, serve to maintain the status quo.

Extensive evidence was cited by the District Court to support its finding that elected officials of Burke County have been unresponsive and insensitive to the needs of the black community, which increases the likelihood that the political process was not equally open to blacks. This evidence ranged from the effects of past discrimination which still haunt the county courthouse to the infrequent appointment of blacks to county boards and committees; the overtly discriminatory pattern of paving county roads; the reluctance of the county to remedy black complaints, which forced blacks to take legal action to obtain school and grand jury desegregation; and the role played by the County Commissioners in the incorporation of an all-white private school to which they donated public funds for the purchase of band uniforms. ***

The District Court also considered the depressed socio-economic status of Burke County blacks. It found that proportionately more blacks than whites have incomes below the poverty level. *** Nearly 53% of all black families living in Burke County had incomes equal to or less than three-fourths of a poverty-level income. *** Not only have blacks completed less formal education than whites, but also the education they have received "was qualitatively inferior to a marked degree." *** Blacks tend to receive less pay than whites, even for similar work, and they tend to be employed in menial jobs more often than whites. *** Seventy-three percent of houses occupied by blacks lacked all or some plumbing facilities; only 16% of white-occupied houses suffered the same deficiency. *** The District Court concluded that the depressed socioeconomic status of blacks results in part from "the lingering effects of past discrimination. ***

Although finding that the state policy behind the at-large electoral system in Burke County was "neutral in origin," the District Court concluded that the policy "has been subverted to invidious purposes." *** As a practical matter, maintenance of the state statute providing for at-large elections in Burke County is determined by Burke County's state representatives, for the legislature defers to their wishes on matters of purely local application. The court found that Burke County's state representatives "have retained a system which has minimized the ability of Burke County Blacks to participate in the political system." ***

The trial court considered, in addition, several factors which this Court has indicated enhance the tendency of multimember districts to minimize the voting strength of racial minorities. *** It found that the sheer geographic size of the county, which is nearly two-thirds the size of Rhode Island, "has made it more difficult for blacks to get to polling places or to campaign for office." The court concluded, as a matter of law, that the size of the county tends to impair the access of blacks to the political process. The majority vote requirement was found "to submerge the will of the minority" and thus "deny the minority's access to the system." *** The court also found the requirements that candidates run for specific seats, enhances appellees' lack of access because it prevents a cohesive political group from concentrating on a single candidate. Because Burke County has no residency requirement, "[a]ll candidates could reside in Waynesboro, or in '[lily]-white' neighborhoods. To that extent, the denial of access becomes enhanced." ***

None of the District Court's findings underlying its ultimate finding of intentional discrimination appears to us to be clearly erroneous; and as we have said, we decline to overturn the essential finding of the District Court, agreed to by the Court of Appeals, that the at-large system in Burke County has been maintained for the purpose of denying blacks equal access to the political processes in the county. As in *White v. Regester,* *** the District Court's findings were "sufficient to sustain [its] judgment . . . and, on this record, we have no reason to disturb them."

We also find no reason to overturn the relief ordered by the District Court. Neither the District Court nor the Court of Appeals discerned any special circumstances that would militate against utilizing single-member districts. Where "a constitutional violation has been found, the remedy is tailored to cure the 'condition that offends the Constitution.' " *** ...

The judgment of the Court of Appeals is affirmed.

Justice Powell, with whom *Justice Rehnquist* joins, dissenting.

I

Mobile v. Bolden *** establishes that an at-large voting system must be upheld against constitutional attack unless maintained for a discriminatory purpose. In *Mobile* we reversed a finding of unconstitutional vote dilution because the lower courts had relied on factors insufficient as a matter of law to establish discriminatory intent. *** The District Court and Court of Appeals in this case based their findings of unconstitutional discrimination on the same factors held insufficient in *Mobile*. Yet the Court now finds their conclusion unexceptionable. The *Mobile* plurality also affirmed that the concept of "intent" was no mere fiction, and held that the District Court had erred in "its failure to identify the state officials whose intent it considered relevant." *** Although the courts below did not answer that question in this case, the Court today affirms their decision.

Whatever the wisdom of *Mobile,* the Court's opinion cannot be reconciled persuasively with that case. There are some variances in the largely sociological evidence presented in the two cases. But *Mobile* held that this kind of evidence was not enough. Such evidence, we found in *Mobile,* did not merely fall short, but "fell far short[,] of showing that [an at-large electoral scheme was] 'conceived or operated [as a] purposeful devic[e] to further racial . . . discrimination.' " *** Because I believe that *Mobile* controls this case, I dissent.

II

The Court's decision today relies heavily on the capacity of the federal district courts—essentially free from any standards propounded by this Court—to determine whether at-large voting systems are "being maintained for the invidious purpose of diluting the voting strength of the black population." Federal courts thus are invited to engage in deeply subjective inquiries into the motivations of local officials in structuring local governments. Inquiries of this kind not only can be "unseemly" . . . ; they intrude the federal courts—with only the vaguest constitutional direction—into an area of intensely local and political concern. . . .

Justice Stevens, dissenting.

Our legacy of racial discrimination has left its scars on Burke County, Georgia. The record in this case amply supports the conclusion that the governing officials of Burke County have repeatedly denied black citizens rights guaranteed by the Fourteenth and Fifteenth Amendments to the Federal Constitution. No one could legitimately question the validity of remedial measures, whether legislative or judicial, designed to prohibit discriminatory conduct by pub-

lic officials and to guarantee that black citizens are effectively afforded the rights to register and to vote. Public roads may not be paved only in areas in which white citizens live; black citizens may not be denied employment opportunities in country government; segregated schools may not be maintained.

Nor, in my opinion, could there be any doubt about the constitutionality of an amendment to the Voting Rights Act that would require Burke County and other covered jurisdictions to abandon specific kinds of at-large voting schemes that perpetuate the effects of past discrimination. . . .

The Court's decision today, however, is not based on either its own conception of sound policy or any statutory command. The decision rests entirely on the Court's interpretation of the requirements of the Federal Constitution. Despite my sympathetic appraisal of the Court's laudable goals, I am unable to agree with its approach to the constitutional issue that is presented. In my opinion, this case raises questions that encompass more than the immediate plight of disadvantaged black citizens. I believe the Court errs by holding the structure of the local governmental unit unconstitutional without identifying an acceptable, judicially manageable standard for adjudicating cases of this kind. . . .

Ever since I joined the Court, I have been concerned about the Court's emphasis on subjective intent as a criterion for constitutional adjudication. Although that criterion is often regarded as a restraint on the exercise of judicial power, it may in fact provide judges with a tool for exercising power that otherwise would be confined to the legislature. My principal concern with the subjective-intent standard, however, is unrelated to the quantum of power it confers upon the judiciary. It is based on the quality of that power. For in the long run constitutional adjudication that is premised on a case-by-case appraisal of the subjective intent of local decisionmakers cannot possibly satisfy the requirement of impartial administration of the law that is embodied in the Equal Protection Clause of the Fourteenth Amendment.

The facts of this case illustrate the ephemeral character of a constitutional standard that focuses on subjective intent. When the suit was filed in 1976, approximately 58 percent of the population of Burke

County was black and approximately 42 percent was white. Because black citizens had been denied access to the political process—through means that have since been outlawed by the Voting Rights Act of 1965—and because there had been insufficient time to enable the registration of black voters to overcome the history of past injustice, the majority of registered voters in the county were white. The at-large electoral system therefore served, as a result of the presence of bloc voting, to maintain white control of the local government. Whether it would have continued to do so would have depended on a mix of at least three different factors—the continuing increase in voter registration among blacks, the continuing exodus of black residents from the county,

and the extent to which racial block voting continued to dominate local politics.

If those elected officials in control of the political machinery had formed the judgment that these factors created a likelihood that a bloc of black voters was about to achieve sufficient strength to elect an entirely new administration, they might have decided to abandon the at-large system and substitute five single-member districts with the boundary lines drawn to provide a white majority in three districts and a black majority in only two. Under the Court's intent standard, such a change presumably would violate the Fourteenth Amendment. It is ironic that the remedy ordered by the District fits that pattern precisely. . . .

Reynolds v. Sims

377 U.S. 533; 84 S. Ct. 1362; 12 L. Ed. 2d 506 (1964)
Vote: 8-1

Prior to this lawsuit, the apportionment scheme for the Alabama legislature created a 35-member senate elected from districts whose population varied from 15,417 to 634,864 and a house of representatives with 106 members elected from districts whose populations varied from 6,731 to 104,767. Registered voters from two urban counties brought this lawsuit challenging the constitutionality of the existing apportionment. The U.S. district court ruled for the plaintiffs and ordered a temporary reapportionment plan. On appeal, the Supreme Court affirmed the lower court's decision.

Mr. Chief Justice Warren delivered the opinion of the Court.

. . . A predominant consideration in determining whether a State's legislative apportionment scheme constitutes an invidious discrimination violative of rights asserted under the Equal Protection Clause is that the rights allegedly impaired are individual and personal in nature. . . . [T]he judicial focus must be concentrated upon ascertaining whether there has been any discrimination against certain of the State's citizens which constitutes an impermissible impair-

ment of their constitutionally protected right to vote. . . . Undoubtedly, the right of suffrage is a fundamental matter in a free and democratic society. Especially since the right to exercise the franchise in a free and unimpaired manner is preservative of other basic civil and political rights, any alleged infringement of the right of citizens to vote must be carefully and meticulously scrutinized. . . .

Legislators represent people, not trees or acres. Legislators are elected by voters, not farms or cities or economic interests. As long as ours is a representative form of government, and our legislatures are those instruments of government elected directly by and directly representative of the people, the right to elect legislators in a free and unimpaired fashion is a bedrock of our political system. It could hardly be gainsaid that a constitutional claim had been asserted by an allegation that certain otherwise qualified voters had been entirely prohibited from voting for members of their state legislature. And, if a State should provide that the votes of citizens in one part of the State should be given two times, or five times, or 10 times the weight of votes of citizens in another part of the State, it could hardly be contended that the right to vote of those residing in the disfavored area had not been effectively diluted. It would appear extraordinary to suggest that a State could be constitutionally permitted to enact a law providing that certain of the State's voters could vote two, five, or 10 times for their legislative representatives, while voters living elsewhere could vote only once. And it is inconceivable that a state law to the effect that, in counting votes for legislators, the votes of citizens in one part of the State would be multiplied by two, five, or 10, while the votes of persons in another area would be counted only at face value, could be constitutionally sustainable. Of course, the effect of state legislative districting schemes which give the same number of representatives to unequal numbers of constituents is identical. Overweighting and overvaluation of the votes of those living here has the certain effect of dilution and under valuation of the votes of those living there. The resulting discrimination against those individual voters living in disfavored areas is easily demonstrable mathematically. Their right to vote is simply not the same right to vote as that of those living in a favored part of the State. Two, five, or 10 of them must vote before the effect of their voting is equivalent to that of their favored neighbor. Weighting the votes of citizens differently, by any method or means, merely because of where they happen to reside, hardly seems justifiable. . . .

State legislatures are, historically, the fountainhead of representative government in this country. . . . Most citizens can achieve [full and effective] participation only as qualified voters through the election of legislators to represent them. Full and effective participation by all citizens in state government requires, therefore, that each citizen have an equally effective voice in the election of members of his state legislature. Modern and viable state government needs, and the Constitution demands, no less.

Logically, in a society ostensibly grounded on representative government, it would seem reasonable that a majority of the people of a State could elect a majority of that State's legislators. To conclude differently, and to sanction minority control of state legislature bodies, would appear to deny majority rights in a way that far surpasses any possible denial of minority rights that might otherwise be thought to result. Since legislatures are responsible for enacting laws by which all citizens are to be governed, they should be bodies which are collectively responsive to the popular will. And the concept of equal protection has been traditionally viewed as requiring the uniform treatment of persons standing in the same relation to the governmental action questioned or challenged. With respect to the allocation of legislative representation, all voters, as citizens of a State, stand in the same relation regardless of where they live. Any suggested criteria for the differentiation of citizens are insufficient to justify any discrimination, as to the weight of their votes, unless relevant to the permissible purposes of legislative apportionment. Since the achieving of fair and effective representation for all citizens is concededly the basic aim of legislative apportionment, we conclude that the Equal Protection Clause guarantees the opportunity for equal participation by all voters in the election of state legislators. Diluting the weight of votes because of place of residence impairs basic constitutional rights under the Fourteenth Amendment just as much as invidious discriminations based upon factors such as race *** or economic status. *** Our constitutional system amply provides for the protection of minorities by means other than giving them majority control of state legislatures. And the democratic ideals of equality and majority rule, which have served this Nation so well in the past, are hardly of any less significance for the present and the future.

We are told that the matter of apportioning representation in a state legislature is a complex and many-faceted one. We are advised that States can rationally consider factors other than population in apportioning legislative representation. We are admonished not to restrict the power of the States to impose differing views as to political philosophy on their citizens. We are cautioned about the dangers of entering into political thickets and mathematical quagmires. Our answer is this: a denial of constitutionally protected rights demands judicial protection; our oath and our office require no less of us.

To the extent that a citizen's right to vote is debased, he is that much less a citizen. The fact that an individual lives here or there is not a legitimate reason for overweighting or diluting the efficacy of his vote. The complexions of societies and civilizations change, often with amazing rapidity. A nation once primarily rural in character becomes predominantly urban. Representation schemes once fair and equitable become archaic and outdated. But the basic principle of representative government remains, and must remain, unchanged—the weight of a citizen's vote cannot be made to depend on where he lives. Population is, of necessity, the starting point for consideration and the controlling criterion for judgment in legislative apportionment controversies. A citizen, a qualified voter, is no more nor no less so because he lives in the city or on the farm. This is the clear and strong command of our Constitution's Equal Protection Clause. This is an essential part of the concept of a government of laws and not men. This is at the heart of Lincoln's vision of "government of the people, by the people, [and] for the people." The Equal Protection Clause demands no less than substantially equal state legislative representation for all citizens, of all places as well as of all races. . . .

By holding that as a federal constitutional requisite both houses of a state legislature must be apportioned on a population basis, we mean that the Equal Protection Clause requires that a State make an honest and good faith effort to construct districts, in both houses of its legislature, as nearly of equal population as is practicable. We realize that it is a practical impossibility to arrange legislative districts so that each one has an identical number of residents, or citizens, or voters. Mathematical exactness or precision is hardly a workable constitutional requirement. . . .

. . . So long as the divergences from a strict population standard are based on legitimate considerations incident to the effectuation of a rational state policy, some deviations from the equal-population principle are constitutionally permissible with respect to the apportionment of seats in either or both of the two houses of a bicameral state legislature. But neither history alone, nor economic or other sorts of group interests, are permissible factors in attempting to justify disparities from population-based representation. Citizens, not history or economic interests, cast votes. Considerations of area alone provide an insufficient justification for deviations from the equal-population principle. Again, people, not land or trees or pastures, vote. Modern developments and

improvements in transportation and communications make rather hollow, in the mid-1960's, most claims that deviations from population-based representation can validly be based solely on geographical considerations. Arguments for allowing such deviations in order to insure effective representation for sparsely insettled areas and to prevent legislative districts from becoming so large that the availability of access of citizens to their representatives is impaired are today, for the most part, unconvincing.

A consideration that appears to be of more substance in justifying some deviations from population-based representation in state legislatures is that of insuring some voice to political subdivisions, as political subdivisions. . . . In many States much of the legislature's activity involves the enactment of so-called local legislation, directed only to the concerns of particular political subdivisions. And a State may legitimately desire to construct districts along political subdivision lines to deter the possibilities of gerrymandering. But if, even as a result of a clearly rational state policy of according some legislative representation to political subdivisions, population is submerged as the controlling consideration in the apportionment of seats in the particular legislative body, then the right of all of the State's citizens to cast an effective and adequately weighted vote would be unconstitutionally impaired. . . .

Mr. Justice Clark, concurring. . . .

Mr. Justice Stewart, concurring. . . .

Mr. Justice Harlan, dissenting:

. . . The Court's constitutional discussion . . . is remarkable . . . for its failure to address itself at all to the Fourteenth Amendment as a whole or to the legislative history of the Amendment pertinent to the matter at hand. Stripped of aphorisms, the Court's argument boils down to the assertion that appellee's right to vote has been invidiously "debased" or "diluted" by systems of apportionment which entitle them to vote for fewer legislators than other voters, an assertion which is tied to the Equal Protection Clause only by the constitutionally frail tautology that "equal" means "equal."

Had the Court paused to probe more deeply into the matter, it would have found that the Equal Protection Clause was never intended to inhibit the States in choosing any democratic method they pleased for the apportionment of their legislatures....

The history of the adoption of the Fourteenth Amendment provides conclusive evidence that neither those who proposed nor those who ratified the Amendment believed that the Equal Protection Clause limited the power of the States to apportion their legislatures as they saw fit. Moreover, the history demonstrates that the intention to leave this power undisturbed was deliberate and was widely believed to be essential to the adoption of the Amendment....

Although the Court—necessarily, as I believe—provides only generalities in elaboration of its main thesis, its opinion nevertheless fully demonstrates how far removed these problems are from fields of judicial competence. Recognizing that "indiscriminate districting" is an invitation to "partisan gerrymandering," *** the Court nevertheless excludes virtually every basis for the formation of electoral districts other than "indiscriminate districting." In one or another of today's opinions, the Court declares it unconstitutional for a State to give effective consideration to any of the following in establishing legislative districts:

1. history;
2. "economic or other sorts of group interests";
3. area;
4. geographical considerations;
5. a desire "to insure effective representation for sparsely settled areas";
6. "availability of access of citizens to their representatives";
7. theories of bicameralism (except those approved by the Court);
8. occupation;
9. "an attempt to balance urban and rural power";
10. the preference of a majority of voters in the State.

So far as presently appears, the only factor which a State may consider, apart from numbers, is political subdivisions. But even "a clearly rational state policy" recognizing this factor is unconstitutional if "population is submerged as the controlling consideration...."

I know of no principle of logic or practical or theoretical politics, still less any constitutional principle, which establishes all or any of these exclusions. Certain it is that the Court's opinion does not establish them. So far as the Court says anything at all on this score, it says only that "legislators represent people, not trees or acres," ... that "citizens, not history or economic interests, cast votes," ... that "people, not land or trees or pastures, vote." ... All this may be conceded. But it is surely equally obvious, and, in the context of elections, more meaningful to note that people are not ciphers and that legislators can represent their electors only by speaking for their interests—economic, social, political—many of which do reflect the place where the electors live. The Court does not establish, or indeed even attempt to make a case for the proposition that conflicting interests within a State can only be adjusted by disregarding them when voters are grouped for purposes of representation....

Karcher v. Daggett

462 U.S. 725; 103 S. Ct. 2653; 77 L. Ed. 2d 133 (1983)
Vote: 5-4

Justice Brennan delivered the opinion of the Court.

The question presented by this appeal is whether an apportionment plan for congressional districts satisfies Article I, Section 2, of the Constitution without need for further justification if the population of the largest district is less than one percent greater than the population of the smallest district. A three-judge District Court declared New Jersey's 1982 reapportionment plan unconstitutional on the authority of *Kirkpatrick v. Preisler* *** (1969) and *White v. Weiser* (1973), *** because the population deviations among districts, although small, were not the result of a good-faith effort to achieve population equality. We affirm.

I

After the results of the 1980 decennial census had been tabulated, the Clerk of the United States House of Representatives notified the governor of New Jersey that the number of Representatives to which the State was entitled had decreased from 15 to 14. Accordingly, the New Jersey Legislature was required to reapportion the State's congressional districts. The State's 199th Legislature passed two reapportionment bills. One was vetoed by the Governor, and the second, although signed into law, occasioned significant dissatisfaction among those who felt it diluted minority voting strength in the city of Newark. *** In response, the 200th Legislature returned to the problem of apportioning congressional districts when it convened in January 1982, and it swiftly passed a bill (S-711) introduced by Senator Feldman, President *pro tem* of the State Senate, which created the apportionment plan at issue in this case. The bill was signed by the Governor on January 19, 1982. . . .

Like every plan considered by the legislature, the Feldman Plan contained 14 districts, with an average population per district (as determined by the 1980 census) of 526,059. Each district did not have the same population. On the average, each district differed from the "ideal" figure by 0.1384%, or about 726 people. The largest district, the Fourth District, which includes Trenton, had a population of 527,472, and the smallest, the Sixth District, embracing most of Middlesex County, a population of 523,798. The difference between them was 3,674 people, or 0.6984% of the average district. The populations of the other districts also varied. The Ninth District, including most of Bergen County, in the northeastern corner of the State, had a population of 527,349, while the population of the Third District, along the Atlantic shore, was only 524,825. ***

The legislature had before it other plans with appreciably smaller population deviations between the largest and smallest districts. The one receiving the most attention in the District Court was designed by

Dr. Ernest Reock, a political science professor at Rutgers University and Director of the Bureau of Government Research. A version of the Reock Plan introduced in the 200th Legislature by Assemblyman Hardwick had a maximum population difference of 2,375, or 0.4514% of the average figure. ***

Almost immediately after the Feldman Plan became law, a group of individuals with varying interests, including all incumbent Republican Members of Congress from New Jersey, sought a declaration that the apportionment plan violated Article I, Section 2, of the Constitution and an injunction against proceeding with the primary election for United States Representatives under the plan. . . .

Shortly thereafter, the District Court issued an opinion and order declaring the Feldman Plan unconstitutional. Denying the motions for summary judgment and resolving the case on the record as a whole, the District Court held that the population variances in the Feldman Plan were not "unavoidable despite a good-faith effort to achieve absolute equality." *** The court rejected appellants' argument that a deviation lower than the statistical imprecision of the decennial census was "the functional equivalent of mathematical equality." *** It also held that appellants had failed to show that the population variances were justified by the legislature's purported goals of preserving minority voting strength and anticipating shifts in population. Ibid. The District Court enjoined appellants from conducting primary or general elections under the Feldman Plan, but that order was stayed pending appeal to this Court. . . .

II

Article I, Section 2, establishes a "high standard of justice and common sense" for the apportionment of congressional districts: "equal representation for equal numbers of people." *** Precise mathematical equality, however, may be impossible to achieve in an imperfect world; therefore the "equal representation" standard is enforced only to the extent of requiring that districts be apportioned to achieve population equality "as nearly as is practicable." *** As we explained further in *Kirkpatrick v. Preisler*:

[T]he "as nearly as practicable" standard requires that the State make a good-faith effort to achieve precise mathematical equality. *** Unless population variances among congressional districts are shown to have resulted despite such effort, the State must justify each variance, no matter how small. ***

Article I, Section 2, therefore, "permits only the limited population variances which are unavoidable despite a good-faith effort to achieve absolute equality, or for which justification is shown." ***

Thus two basic questions shape litigation over population deviations in state legislation apportioning congressional districts. First, the court must consider whether the population differences among districts could have been reduced or eliminated altogether by a good-faith effort to draw districts of equal population. Parties challenging apportionment legislation must bear the burden of proof on this issue, and if they fail to show that the differences could have been avoided the apportionment scheme must be upheld. If, however, the plaintiffs can establish that the population differences were not the result of a good-faith effort to achieve equality, the State must bear the burden of proving that each significant variance between districts was necessary to achieve some legitimate goal. ***

III

Appellants' principal argument in this case is addressed to the first question described above. They contend that the Feldman Plan should be regarded *per se* as the product of a good-faith effort to achieve population equality because the maximum population deviation among districts is smaller than the predictable undercount in available census data.

A

Kirkpatrick squarely rejected a nearly identical argument. "The whole thrust of the 'as nearly as practicable' approach is inconsistent with adoption of fixed numerical standards which excuse population variances without regard to the circumstances of each particular case." *** Adopting any standard other than population equality, using the best census data available, *** would subtly erode the Constitution's ideal of equal representation. If state legisla-

tors knew that a certain *de minimis* level of population differences was acceptable, they would doubtless strive to achieve that level rather than equality. ***

Furthermore, choosing a different standard would import a high degree of arbitrariness into the process of reviewing apportionment plans. *** In this case, appellants argue that a maximum deviation of approximately 0.7% should be considered *de minimis*. If we accept that argument, how are we to regard deviations of 0.8%, 0.9%, 1%, or 1.1%?

Any standard, including absolute equality, involves a certain artificiality. As appellants point out, even the census data are not perfect, and the well-known restlessness of the American people means that population counts for particular localities are outdated long before they are completed. Yet problems with the data at hand apply equally to any population-based standard we could choose. As between two standards—equality or something less than equality—only the former reflects the aspirations of Article I, Section 2.

To accept the legitimacy of unjustified, though small population deviations in this case would mean to reject the basic premise of *Kirkpatrick* and *Wesberry* [v. *Sanders*]. We decline appellants' invitation to go that far. The unusual rigor of their standard has been noted several times. Because of that rigor, we have required that absolute population equality be the paramount objective of apportionment only in the case of congressional districts, for which the command of Article I, Section 2 as regards the National Legislature outweighs the local interests that a State may deem relevant in apportioning districts for representatives to state and local legislatures.... The principle of population equality for congressional districts has not proved unjust or socially or economically harmful in experience. *** If anything, this standard should cause less difficulty now for state legislatures than it did when we adopted it in *Wesberry*. The rapid advances in computer technology and education during the last two decades make it relatively simple to draw contiguous districts of equal population and at the same time to further whatever secondary goals the State has. Finally, to abandon unnecessarily a clear and oft-confirmed constitutional interpretation would impair our authority in other cases, *** would implicitly open the door to a plethora of requests that we reexamine other rules that some may consider burdensome, and would prejudice those who have relied upon the rule of law in seeking an equipopulous congressional apportionment in New Jersey. *** We thus reaffirm that there are no *de minimis* population variations, which could practically be avoided, but which nonetheless meet the standard of Article I, Section 2, without justification.

The sole difference between appellants' theory and the argument we rejected in *Kirkpatrick* is that appellants have proposed a *de minimis* line that gives the illusion of rationality and predictability: the "inevitable statistical imprecision of the census." They argue: "Where, as here, the deviation from ideal district size is less than the known imprecision of the census figures, that variation is the functional equivalent of zero." *** There are two problems with this approach. First, appellants concentrate on the extent to which the census systematically undercounts actual population—a figure which is not known precisely and which, even if it were known, would not be relevant to this case. Second, the mere existence of statistical imprecisions does not make small deviations among districts the functional equivalent of equality. . . .

The census may systematically undercount population, and the rate of undercounting may vary from place to place. Those facts, however, do not render meaningless the differences in population between congressional districts, as determined by uncorrected census counts. To the contrary, the census data provide the only reliable—albeit less than perfect—indication of the districts' "real"relative population levels. Even if one cannot say with certainty that one district is larger than another merely because it has a higher census count, one can say with certainty that the district with a larger census count is more likely to be larger than the other district than it is to be smaller or the same size. That certainty is sufficient for decision-making. *** Furthermore, because the census count represents the "best population data available," *** it is the only basis for good-faith attempts to achieve population equality. Attempts to explain population deviations

on the basis of flaws in census data must be supported with a precision not achieved here. ***

Section B is omitted.

C

Given that the census-based population deviations in the Feldman Plan reflect real differences among the districts, it is clear that they could have been avoided or significantly reduced with a good-faith effort to achieve population equality. For that reason alone, it would be inappropriate to accept the Feldman Plan as "functionally equivalent" to a plan with districts of equal population.

The District Court found that several other plans introduced in the 200th Legislature had smaller maximum deviations than the Feldman Plan. *** Appellants object that the alternative plans considered by the District Court were not comparable to the Feldman Plan because their political characters differed profoundly. *** We have never denied that apportionment is a political process, or that state legislatures could pursue legitimate secondary objectives as long as those objectives were consistent with a good-faith effort to achieve population equality at the same time. Nevertheless, the claim that political considerations require population differences among congressional districts belongs more properly to the second level of judicial inquiry in these cases, *** in which the State bears the burden of justifying the differences with particularity.

In any event, it was unnecessary for the District Court to rest its finding on the existence of alternative plans with radically different political effects. As in *Kirkpatrick,* "resort to the simple device of transferring entire political subdivisions of known population between contiguous districts would have produced districts much closer to numerical equality." *** Starting with the Feldman Plan itself and the census data available to the legislature at the time it was enacted, *** one can reduce the maximum population deviation of the plan merely by shifting a handful of municipalities from one district to another. ***

Thus the District Court did not err in finding that the plaintiffs had met their burden of showing that the Feldman Plan did not come as nearly as practicable to population equality.

IV

By itself, the foregoing discussion does not establish that the Feldman Plan is unconstitutional. Rather, appellees' success in proving that the Feldman Plan was not the product of a good-faith effort to achieve population equality means only that the burden shifted to the State to prove that the population deviations in its plan were necessary to achieve some legitimate state objective. *White v. Weiser* demonstrates that we are willing to defer to state legislative policies, so long as they are consistent with constitutional norms, even if they require small differences in the population of congressional districts. *** Any number of consistently applied legislative policies might justify some variance, including, for instance, making districts compact, respecting municipal boundaries, preserving the cores of prior districts, and avoiding contests between incumbent Representatives. As long as the criteria are nondiscriminatory, *** these are all legitimate objectives that on a proper showing could justify minor population deviations. ***

The State must, however, show with some specificity that a particular objective required the specific deviations in its plan, rather than simply relying on general assertions. The showing required to justify population deviations is flexible, depending on the size of the deviations, the importance of the State's interests, the consistency with which the plan as a whole reflects those interests, and the availability of alternatives that might substantially vindicate those interests yet approximate population equality more closely. By necessity, whether deviations are justified requires case-by-case attention to these factors....

V

The District Court properly applied the two-part test of *Kirkpatrick v. Preisler* to New Jersey's 1982 apportionment of districts for the United States House of Representatives. It correctly held that the population deviations in the plan were not functionally equal as a matter of law, and it found that the plan was not a good-faith effort to achieve population equality using the best available census data. It also correctly rejected appellants' attempt to justify the population deviations as not supported by the

evidence. The judgment of the District Court, therefore, is affirmed.

Justice Stevens, concurring....

Justice White, with whom ***the Chief Justice, Justice Powell,*** and ***Justice Rehnquist*** join, dissenting.

... "[T]he achieving of fair and effective representation for all citizens is concededly the basis aim of legislative apportionment." *** One must suspend credulity to believe that the Court's draconian response to a trifling 0.6984% maximum deviation promotes "fair and effective representation" for the people of New Jersey....

There can be little question but that the variances in the New Jersey plan are "statistically insignificant." Although the Government strives to make the decennial census as accurate as humanly possible, the Census Bureau has never intimated that the results are a perfect count of the American population. The Bureau itself estimates the inexactitude in the taking of the 1970 census at 2.3%, a figure which is considerably larger than the 0.6984% maximum variance in the New Jersey plan, and which dwarfs the 0.2470% difference between the maximum deviations of the selected plan and the leading alternative plan.... Because the amount of undercounting differs from district to district, there is no point for a court of law to act under an unproved assumption that such tiny differences between redistricting plans reflect actual differences in population....

Even if the 0.6984% deviation here is not encompassed within the scope of the statistical imprecision of the census, it is minuscule when compared with the variations among the districts inherent in translating census numbers into citizens' votes. First, the census "is more of an event than a process." *** "It measures population at only a single instant in time. District populations are constantly changing, often at different rates in either direction, up or down." As the Court admits, "the well-known restlessness of the American people means that population counts for particular localities are outdated long before they are completed." *** Second, far larger differences among districts are introduced because a substantial percentage of the total population is too young to register or is disqualified by alienage. Third, census figures cannot account for the proportion of all those otherwise eligible individuals who fail to register. The differences in the number of eligible voters per district for these reasons overwhelm the minimal variations attributable to the districting plan itself.

Accepting that the census, and the districting plans which are based upon it, cannot be perfect represents no backsliding in our commitment to assuring fair and equal representation in the election of Congress. I agree with the views of Judge Gibbons, who dissented in the District Court, that *Kirkpatrick* should not be read as a "prohibition against toleration of *de minimis* population variances. which have no statistically relevant effect on relative representation." A plus–minus deviation of 0.6984% surely falls within this category.

If today's decision simply produced an unjustified standard with little practical import, it would be bad enough. Unfortunately, I fear that the Court's insistence that "there are no *de minimis* population variations, which could practically be avoided, but which nonetheless meet the standard of Article I, Section 2, without justification," *** invites further litigation of virtually every congressional redistricting plan in the Nation. At least 12 States which have completed redistricting on the basis of the 1980 census have adopted plans with a higher deviation than that presented here, and 4 others have deviations quite similar to New Jersey's. Of course, under the

Court's rationale, even Rhode Island's plan—whose two districts have a deviation of 0.02% or about 95 people—would be subject to constitutional attack.

In all such cases, state legislatures will be hard pressed to justify their preference for the selected plan. A good-faith effort to achieve population equality is not enough if the population variances are not "unavoidable." The court must consider whether the population differences could have been further "reduced or eliminated altogether." *** With the assistance of computers, there will generally be a plan with an even more minimal deviation from the mathematical ideal. Then, "the State must bear the burden of proving that each significant variance between districts was necessary to achieve some legitimate goal." *** As this case illustrates, literally any variance between districts will be considered "significant." . . .

Yet no one can seriously contend that such an inflexible insistence upon mathematical exactness will serve to promote "fair and effective representation." The more likely result of today's extension of *Kirkpatrick* is to move closer to fulfilling Justice Fortas' prophecy that "a legislature might have to ignore the boundaries of common sense, running the congressional district line down the middle of the corridor of an apartment house or even dividing the residents of a single-family house between two districts." *** Such sterile and mechanistic application only brings the principle of "one man, one vote" into disrepute. . . .

Justice Powell, dissenting. . . .

Brown v. Thomson
462 U.S. 835; 103 S. Ct. 2690; 77 L. Ed. 2d 214 (1983)
Vote: 5-4

Justice Powell delivered the opinion of the Court.

The issue is whether the State of Wyoming violated the Equal Protection Clause by allocating one of the 64 seats in its House of Representatives to a county the population of which is considerably lower than the average population per state representative.

I

Since Wyoming became a State in 1890, its legislature has consisted of a Senate and a House of Representatives. The State's Constitution provides that each of the State's counties "shall constitute a senatorial and representative district" and that "[e]ach county shall have at least one senator and one representative." The senators and representatives are required to be "apportioned among the said counties as nearly as may be according to the number of their inhabitants." *** The State has had 23 counties since 1922.... [T]he apportionment of the Wyoming House has been challenged three times in the past 20 years....

The present case is a challenge to Wyoming's 1981 statute reapportioning its House of Representatives in accordance with the requirements of Article 3, Section 3 of the state Constitution. The 1980 census placed Wyoming's population at 469,557. The statute provided for 64 representatives, meaning that the ideal apportionment would be 7,337 persons per representative. Each county was given one representative, including the six counties the population of which fell below 7,337. The deviations from population equality were similar to those in prior decades, with an average deviation of 16% and maximum deviation of 89%.

The issue in this case concerns only Niobrara County, the State's least populous county. Its population of 2,924 is less than half of the ideal district of 7,337. Accordingly, the general statutory formula would have dictated that its population for purposes of representation be rounded down to zero. This would have deprived Niobrara County of its own representative for the first time since it became a county in 1913. The state legislature found, however, that "the opportunity for oppression of the people of this state or any of them is greater if any county is deprived a representative in the legislature than if each is guaranteed at least one (1) representative." It therefore followed the state Constitution's requirement and expressly provided that a county would receive a representative even if the statutory for formula rounded the county's population to zero. Niobrara County thus was given one seat in a 64-seat House. The legislature also provided that if this representation for Niobrara County were held unconstitutional, it would be combined with neighboring county in a single representative district. The House then would consist of 63 representatives.

Appellants, members of the state League of Women Voters and residents of seven counties in which the population per representative is greater than the state average, filed this lawsuit in the District Court for the District of Wyoming. They alleged that "[b]y granting Niobrara County a representative to which it is not statutorily entitled, the voting privileges of Plaintiffs and other citizens and electors of Wyoming similarly situated have been improperly and illegally diluted in violation of the 14th Amendment...." *** They sought declaratory and injunctive relief that would prevent the State from giving a separate representative to Niobrara County, thus implementing the alternative plan calling for 63 representatives.

The three-judge District Court upheld the constitutionality of the statute. *** The court noted that the narrow issue presented was the alleged discriminatory effect of a single county's representative, and concluded, citing expert testimony, that "the 'dilution' of the plaintiffs' votes is *de minimis* when Niobrara County has its own representative." *** The court also found that Wyoming's policy of granting a representative to each county was rational and, indeed, particularly well suited to the special needs of Wyoming.

We noted probable jurisdiction *** and now affirm.

II

A

In *Reynolds v. Sims* *** the Court held that "the Equal Protection Clause requires that the seats in both house of a bicameral state legislature must be apportioned on a population basis." This holding requires only "that a State make an honest and good faith effort to construct districts ... as nearly of equal population as is practicable," for "it is a practical impossibility to arrange legislative districts so that each one has an identical number of residents, or citizens or voters." ***

We have recognized that some deviations from population equality may be necessary to permit the States to pursue other legitimate objectives such as "maintain[ing] the integrity of various political subdivisions" and "provid[ing] for compact districts of contiguous territory." *** ... "An unrealistic overemphasis on raw population figures, a mere nose count in the districts, may submerge these other considerations and itself furnish a ready tool for ignoring factors that in day-to-day operation are important to an acceptable representation and apportionment arrangement." ***

In view of these considerations, we have held that "minor deviations from mathematical equality among state legislative districts are insufficient to make out a *prima facie* case of invidious discrimination under the Fourteenth Amendment so as to require justification by the State." *** Our decisions have established, as a general matter, that an apportionment plan with a maximum population deviation under 10% falls within this category of minor deviations. A plan with larger disparities in population, however, creates a *prima facie* case of discrimination and therefore must be justified by the State. The ultimate inquiry, therefore, is whether the legislature's plan "may reasonably be said to advance [a] rational state policy" and, if so, "whether the population disparities among the districts that have resulted from the pursuit of this plan exceed constitutional limits." ***

imate state policy. This does not mean that population deviations of any magnitude necessarily are acceptable. Even a neutral and consistently applied criterion such as use of counties as representative districts can frustrate *Reynolds*'s mandate of fair and effective representation if the population disparities are excessively high. "[A] State's policy urged in justification of disparity in district population, however rational, cannot constitutionally be permitted to emasculate the goal of substantial equality." *** It remains true, however, as the Court in *Reynolds* noted, that consideration must be given "to the character as well as the degree of deviations from a strict population basis." *** The consistency of application and the neutrality of effect of the nonpopulation criteria must be considered along with the size of the population disparities in determining whether a state legislative apportionment plan contravenes the Equal Protection Clause.

B

In this case there is no question that Niobrara County's deviation from population equality— 60% below the mean—is more than minor. There also can be no question that Wyoming's constitutional policy— followed since statehood—of using counties as representative districts and ensuring that each county has one representative is supported by substantial and legitimate state concerns. *** ... The State's policy of preserving county boundaries is based on the state Constitution, has been followed for decades, and has been applied consistently throughout the State. As the District Court found, this policy has particular force given the peculiar size and population of the State and the nature of its governmental structure. *** In addition, population equality is the sole other criterion used, and the State's apportionment formula ensures that population deviations are no greater than necessary to preserve counties as representative districts. *** Finally, there is no evidence of "a built-in bias tending to favor particular political interests or geographic areas." ***

In short, this case presents an unusually strong example of an apportionment plan the population variations of which are entirely the result of the consistent and nondiscriminatory application of a legit-

C

Here we are not required to decide whether Wyoming's nondiscriminatory adherence to county boundaries justified the population deviations that exist throughout Wyoming's representative districts. Appellants deliberately have limited their challenge to the alleged dilution of their voting power resulting from the one representative given to Niobrara County. The issue therefore is not whether a 16% average deviation and an 89% maximum deviation, considering the state apportionment plan as a whole, are constitutionally permissible. Rather, the issue is whether Wyoming's policy of preserving county boundaries justifies the additional deviations from population equality resulting from the provision of representation to Niobrara County.

It scarcely can be denied that in terms of actual effect on appellants' voting power, it matters little whether the 63-member or 64-member House is used. The District Court noted, for example, that the seven counties in which appellants reside will elect 28 representatives under either plan. The only difference, therefore, is whether they elect 43.75% of the legislature (28 of 64 members) or 44.44% of the legislature (28 of 63 members). *** The District Court aptly described this difference as *"de minimis."* ***

We do not suggest that a State is free to create and allocate an additional representative seat in any way it chooses simply because that additional seat will have little or no effect on the remainder of the State's voters. The allocation of representative to a particular political subdivision still may violate the Equal Protection Clause if it greatly exceed the population variations existing in the rest of the State and if the State provides no legitimate justifications for the creation of that seat. Here, however, considerable population variations will remain even if Niobrara County's representative is eliminated. Under the 63-member plan, the average deviation per representative would be 13% and the maximum deviation would be 66%. *** These statistics make clear that the grant of a representative to Niobrara County is not a significant cause of the population deviations that exist in Wyoming.

Moreover, we believe that the differences between the two plans are justified on the basis of Wyoming's longstanding and legitimate policy of preserving county boundaries. *** Particularly where there is no "taint of arbitrariness or discrimination," substantial deference is to be accorded the political decisions of the people of a State acting through their elected representatives. Here it is noteworthy that by enacting the 64-member plan the State ensured that its policy of preserving county boundaries applied nondiscriminatorily. The effect of the 63-member plan would be to deprive the voters of Niobrara County of their own representative, even though the remainder of the House of Representatives would be constituted so as to facilitate representation of the interests of each county. *** In these circumstances, we are not persuaded that Wyoming has violated the Fourteenth Amendment by permitting Niobrara County to have its own representative.

The judgment of the District Court is affirmed.

Justice O'Connor, with whom **Justice Stevens** joins, concurring.

By its decisions today in this case and in *Karcher v. Daggett,* *** the Court upholds, in the former, the allocation of one representative to a county in a state legislative plan with an 89% maximum deviation from population equality and strikes down, in the latter, a congressional reapportionment plan for the State of New Jersey where the maximum deviation is 0.6984%. As a member of the majority in both cases, I feel compelled to explain the reasons for my joinder in these apparently divergent decisions.

In my view, the "one-person, one-vote" principle is the guiding ideal in evaluating both congressional and legislative redistricting schemes. In both situations, however, ensuring equal representation is not simply a matter of numbers. There must be flexibility in assessing the size of the deviation against the importance, consistency, and neutrality of the state policies alleged to require the population disparities.

Both opinions recognize this need for flexibility in examining the asserted state policies. In *Karcher,* New Jersey has not demonstrated that the population variances in congressional districts were necessary to preserve minority voting strength—the only justification offered by the State. *** Here, by contrast, there can be no doubt that the population deviation resulting from the provision of one representative to Niobrara County is the product of the consistent and nondiscriminatory application of Wyoming's longstanding policy of preserving county boundaries.

In addition, as the Court emphasizes, in this case we are not required to decide whether, and do not suggest that, "Wyoming's nondiscriminatory adherence to county boundaries justifies the population deviations that exist throughout Wyoming's representative districts." *** Thus, the relevant percentage in this case is not the 89% maximum deviation when the State of Wyoming is viewed as a whole, but the additional deviation from equality produced by the allocation of one representative to Niobrara County. ***

In this regard, I would emphasize a point acknowledged by the majority. *** Although the maximum deviation figure is not the controlling element in an apportionment challenge, even the consistent and nondiscriminatory application of a legitimate state policy cannot justify substantial population deviations throughout the State where the effect would be to eviscerate the one-person, one-vote principle. In short, there is clearly some outer limit to the magnitude of the deviation that is constitutionally permissible even in the face of the strongest justifications.

In the past, this Court has recognized that a state legislative apportionment scheme with a maximum population deviation exceeding 10% creates a *prima facie* case of discrimination. *** Moreover, *** we suggested that a 16.4% maximum deviation "may well approach tolerable limits." I have the gravest doubts that a statewide legislative plan with an 89% maximum deviation could survive constitutional scrutiny despite the presence of the State's strong interest in reserving county boundaries. I join the Court's opinion on the understanding that nothing in it suggests that this Court would uphold such a scheme.

Mr. Justice Brennan, with whom *Justice White, Justice Marshall,* and *Justice Blackmun* join, dissenting.

The Court today upholds a reapportionment scheme for a state legislature featuring an 89% maximum deviation and a 16% average deviation from population equality. I cannot agree.

I

Although I disagree with today's holding, it is worth stressing how extraordinarily narrow it is, and how empty of likely precedential value. The Court goes out of its way to make clear that because appellants have chosen to attack only one small feature of Wyoming's reapportionment scheme, the Court weighs only the marginal unequalizing effect of that one feature, and not the overall constitutionality of the entire scheme. *** Hence, although in my view the Court reaches the wrong result in the case at hand, it is unlikely that any future plaintiffs challenging a state reapportionment scheme as unconstitutional will be so unwise as to limit their challenge to the scheme's single most objectionable feature. Whether this will be a good thing for the speed and cost of constitutional litigation remains to be seen. But at least plaintiffs henceforth will know better than to exercise moderation or restraint in mounting constitutional attacks on state apportionment statutes, lest they forfeit their small claim by omitting to assert a big one.

II

A

The Equal Protection Clause of the Fourteenth Amendment requires that a State, in apportioning its legislature, "make an honest and good faith effort to construct districts . . . as nearly of equal population as is practicable." *** Under certain conditions the Constitution permits small deviations from absolute equality in state legislative districts, but we have carefully circumscribed the range of permissible deviations as to both degree and kind. What is required is "a faithful adherence to a plan of population-based representation, with such minor deviations only as may occur in recognizing certain factors that are free from any taint of arbitrariness or discrimination." "[T]he overriding objective must be substantial equality of population among the various districts, so that the vote of any citizen is approximately equal in weight to that of any other citizen in the State." ***

Our cases since *Reynolds* have clarified the structure of constitutional inquiry into state legislative apportionments, setting up what amounts to a four-step test. First, a plaintiff must show that the deviations at issue are sufficiently large to make out a *prima facie* case of discrimination. We have come to establish a rough threshold of 10% maximum deviation from equality (adding together the deviations from average district size of the most underrepresented and most overrepresented districts); below that level, deviations will ordinarily be considered *de minimis*. *** Second, a court must consider the quality of the reasons advanced by the State to explain the deviations. Acceptable reasons must be "legitimate considerations incident to the effectuation of a rational state policy," *** and must be "free from any taint of arbitrariness or discrimination. . . ." *** Third, the State must show that "the state policy urged . . . to justify the divergences . . . is, indeed, furthered by the plan. . . ." *** This necessarily requires a showing that any deviations from equality are not significantly greater than is necessary to serve the State's asserted policy; if another plan could serve that policy substantially as well while providing smaller deviations from equality, it can hardly be said that the larger deviations advance the policy. *** Fourth, even if the State succeeds in showing that the deviations in its plan are justified by their furtherance of a rational state policy, the court must nevertheless consider whether they are small enough to be constitutionally tolerable. "For a State's policy urged in justification of disparity in district population, however rational, cannot constitutionally be permitted to emasculate the goal of substantial population equality." ***

B

It takes little effort to show that Wyoming's 1981 House of Representatives apportionment is manifestly unconstitutional under the test established by our cases, whether one considers the instance of Niobrara County alone or in combination with the large deviations present in the rest of the scheme. . . .

Davis v. Bandemer

478 U.S. 109; 106 S. Ct. 2797; 92 L. Ed. 2d 85 (1986)
Vote: 7-2

Justice White announced the judgment of the Court. . . .

In this case, we review a judgment from a three-judge District Court, which sustained an equal protection challenge to Indiana's 1981 state apportionment on the basis that the law unconstitutionally diluted the votes of Indiana Democrats. *** Although we find such political gerrymandering to be justiciable, we conclude that the District Court applied an insufficiently demanding standard in finding unconstitutional vote dilution. Consequently, we reverse.

The Indiana Legislature, also known as the "General Assembly," consists of a House of Representatives and a Senate. There are 100 members of the House of Representatives, and 50 members of the Senate. The members of the House serve 2-year terms, with elections held for all seats every 2 years. The members of the Senate serve 4-year terms, and Senate elections are staggered so that half of the seats are up for election every two years. The members of both Houses are elected from legislative districts; but, while all Senate members are elected from single-member districts, House members are elected from a mixture of single-member and multi-member districts. The division of the State into districts is accomplished by legislative enactment, which is signed by the Governor into law. Reapportionment is required every 10 years and is based on the federal decennial census. There is no prohibition against more frequent reapportionments.

In early 1981, the General Assembly initiated the process of reapportioning the State's legislative districts pursuant to the 1980 census. At this time, there were Republican majorities in both the House and the Senate, and the Governor was Republican. Bills were introduced in both Houses, and a reapportionment plan was duly passed and approved by the Governor. This plan provided 50 single-member districts for the Senate; for the House, it provided 7 triple-member, 9 double-member, and 61 single-member districts. In the Senate plan, the population deviation between districts was 1.15%; in the House plan, the deviation was 1.05%. The multi-member districts generally included the more metropolitan areas of the State, although not every metropolitan area was in a multi-member district. Marion County, which includes Indianapolis, was combined with portions of its neighboring counties to form five triple-member districts. Fort Wayne was divided into two parts, and each part was combined with portions of the surrounding county or counties to make two double-member districts. On the other hand, South Bend was divided and put partly into a double-member district and partly into a single-member district (each part combined with part of the surrounding county or counties). Although county and city lines were not consistently followed, township lines generally were. The two plans, the Senate and the House, were not nested; that is, each Senate district was not divided exactly into two House districts. There appears to have been little relation between the lines drawn in the two plans.

In early 1982, this suit was filed by several Indiana Democrats (here the appellees) against various state officials (here the appellants), alleging that the 1981 reapportionment plans constituted a political gerrymander intended to disadvantage Democrats. Specifically, they contended that the particular district lines that were drawn and the mix of single- and multi-member districts were intended to and did violate their right, as Democrats, to equal protection under the Fourteenth Amendment. A three-judge District Court was convened to hear these claims.

In November 1982, before the case went to trial, elections were held under the new districting plan. All of the House seats and half of the Senate seats were up for election. Over all the House races statewide, Democratic candidates received 51.9% of the vote. Only 43 Democrats, however, were elected to the House. Over all the Senate races statewide, Democratic candidates received 53.1% of the vote. Thirteen (of 25) Democrats were elected. In Marion and Allen Counties, both divided into multi-member House districts, Democratic candidates drew 46.6% of the vote, but only 3 of the 21 House seats were filled by Democrats.

On December 13, 1984, a divided District Court issued a decision declaring the reapportionment to be unconstitutional, enjoining the appellants from holding elections pursuant to the 1981 redistricting, ordering the General Assembly to prepare a new plan, and retaining jurisdiction over the case. ***

The defendants appealed, seeking review of the District Court's rulings that the case was justiciable and that, if justiciable, an equal protection violation had occurred. We noted probable jurisdiction. ***

We address first the question whether this case presents a justiciable controversy or a nonjusticiable political question. Although the District Court never explicitly stated that the case was justiciable, its holding clearly rests on such a finding. The appellees urge that this Court has in the past acknowledged and acted upon the justiciability of purely political gerrymandering claims. The appellants contend that we have affirmed on the merits decisions of lower courts finding such claims to be nonjusticiable.

Since *Baker v. Carr* *** we have consistently adjudicated equal protection claims in the legislative districting context regarding inequalities in population between districts. In the course of these cases, we have developed and enforced the "one person, one vote" principle. ***

Our past decisions also make clear that even where there is no population deviation among the districts, racial gerrymandering presents a justiciable equal protection claim. In the multi-member district context, we have reviewed, and on occasion rejected, districting plans that unconstitutionally diminished the effectiveness of the votes of racial minorities. *** We have also adjudicated claims that the configuration of single-member districts violated equal protection with respect to racial and ethnic minorities, although we have never struck down an apportionment plan because of such a claim.

In the multi-member district cases, we have also repeatedly stated that districting that would "operate to minimize or cancel out the voting strength of racial or political elements of the voting population" would raise a constitutional question. *** Finally, in *Gaffney v. Cummings,* *** we upheld against an equal protection political gerrymandering challenge a state legislative single-member redistricting scheme that was formulated in a bipartisan effort to try to provide political representation on a level approximately proportional to the strength of political parties in the State. In that case, we adjudicated the type of purely political equal protection claim that is brought here, although we did not, as a threshold matter, expressly hold such a claim to be justiciable. Regardless of this lack of a specific holding, our consideration of the merits of the claim in *Gaffney* in the face of a discussion of justiciability in appellant's brief, combined with our repeated reference in other opinions to the constitutional deficiencies of plans that dilute the vote of political groups, at the least supports an inference that these cases are justiciable.

In the years since *Baker v. Carr,* both before and after *Gaffney,* however, we have also affirmed a number of decisions in which the lower courts rejected the justiciability of purely political gerrymandering claims. In *WMCA, Inc. v. Lomenzo,* *** the most frequently cited of these cases, we affirmed the decision of a three-judge District Court upholding a temporary apportionment plan for the State of New York. The District Court had determined that political gerrymandering equal protection challenges to this plan were nonjusticiable. *** Justice Harlan, in his opinion concurring in the Court's summary affirmance, expressed his understanding that the affirmance was based on the Court's approval of the lower court's finding of nonjusticiability. *** Although these summary affirmances arguably support an inference that these claims are not justiciable, there are other cases in which federal or state courts adjudicated political gerrymandering claims and we summarily affirmed or dismissed for want of a substantial federal question. ***

These sets of cases may look in different directions, but to the extent that our summary affirmances indicate the nonjusticiability of political gerrymander cases, we are not bound by those decisions. As we have observed before, "[i]t is not at all unusual for the Court to find it appropriate to give full consideration to a question that has been the subject of previous summary action." *** The issue that the appellants would have us find to be precluded by these summary dispositions is an important one, and it deserves further consideration.

The outlines of the political question doctrine were described and to a large extent defined in *Baker v. Carr.* . . .

It is true that the type of claim that was presented in *Baker v. Carr* was subsequently resolved in this Court by the formulation of the "one person, one vote" rule. *** The mere fact, however, that we may not now similarly perceive a likely arithmetic presumption in the instant context does not compel a conclusion that the claims presented here are nonjusticiable. The one person, one vote principle had not yet been developed when *Baker* was decided. At that time, the Court did not rely on the potential for such a rule in finding justiciability. Instead, as the language quoted above clearly indicates, the Court contemplated simply that legislative line-drawing in the districting context would be susceptible of adjudication under the applicable constitutional criteria.

Furthermore, in formulating the one-person, one-vote formula, the Court characterized the question posed by election districts of disparate size as an issue of fair representation. In such cases, it is not that anyone is deprived of a vote or that any person's vote is not counted. Rather, it is that one electoral district elects a single representative and another district of the same size elects two or more—the elector's vote in the former district having less weight in the sense that he may vote for and his district be represented by only one legislator, while his neighbor in the adjoining district votes for and is represented by two or more. . . .

Since the achieving of fair and effective representation for all citizens is concededly the basic aim of legislative apportionment, we conclude that the Equal Protection Clause guarantees the opportunity for equal participation by all voters in the election of State legislators. Diluting the weight of votes because of place of residence impairs basic constitutional rights under the Fourteenth Amendment just as much as invidious discriminations based upon factors such as race. . . . ***

Reynolds [*v. Sims*] surely indicates the justiciability of claims going to the adequacy of representation in state legislatures.

The issue here is of course different. . . . Not only does everyone have the right to vote and to have his vote counted, but each elector may vote for and be represented by the same number of lawmakers. Rather, the claim is that each political group in a State should have the same chance to elect representatives of its choice as any other political group. Nevertheless, the issue is one of representation, and we decline to hold that such claims are never justiciable. . . .

Having determined that the political gerrymandering claim in this case is justiciable, we turn to the question whether the District Court erred in holding that appellees had alleged and proved a violation of the Equal Protection Clause. . . . [The Court finds that the District Court erred in this respect.]

In sum, we hold that political gerrymandering cases are properly justiciable under the Equal Protection Clause. We also conclude, however, that a threshold showing of discriminatory vote dilution is required for a *prima facie* case of an equal protection violation. In this case, the findings made by the District Court of an adverse effect on the appellees do not surmount the threshold requirement. Consequently, the judgment of the District Court is reversed.

Chief Justice Burger, concurring in the judgment. . . .

Justice O'Connor, with whom *the Chief Justice* and *Justice Rehnquist* join, concurring in the judgment.

Today the Court holds that claims of political gerrymandering lodged by members of one of the political parties that make up our two-party system are justiciable under the equal Protection Clause of the Fourteenth Amendment. Nothing in our precedents compels us to take this step, and there is every reason not to do so. I would hold that the partisan gerrymandering claims of major political parties raise a nonjusticiable political question that the judiciary should leave to the legislative branch as the Framers of the Constitution unquestionably intended. Accordingly, I would reverse the District Court's judgment on the grounds that appellees' claim is nonjusticiable.

There can be little doubt that the emergence of a strong and stable two-party system in this country has contributed enormously to sound and effective government. The preservation and health of our political institutions, state and federal, depends to no small extent on the continued vitality of our two-party system, which permits both stability and measured change. The opportunity to control the drawing of electoral boundaries through the legislative process of apportionment is a critical and traditional part of politics in the United States, and one that plays no small role in fostering active participation in the political parties at every level. Thus, the legislative business of apportionment is fundamentally a political affair, and challenges to the manner in which an apportionment has been carried out—by the very parties that are responsible for this process—present a political question in the truest sense of the term.

To turn these matters over to the federal judiciary is to inject the courts into the most heated partisan issues. It is predictable that the courts will respond by moving away from the nebulous standard a plurality of the Court fashions today and toward some form of rough proportional representation for all political groups. The consequences of this shift will be as immense as they are unfortunate. I do not believe, and the Court offers not a shred of evidence to suggest, that the Framers of the Constitution intended the judicial power to encompass the making of such fundamental choices about how this Nation is to be governed. Nor do I believe that the proportional representation towards which the Court's expansion of equal protection doctrine will lead is consistent with our history, our traditions, or our political institutions.

The Court pays little heed to these considerations, which should inform any sensible jurisprudence of Article III and of the Equal Protection Clause. . . .

In cases such as this one, which may profoundly affect the governance of this Nation, it is not enough to cite precedent: we should examine it for possible limits, and if they are lacking, for possible flaws. . . .

If members of the major political parties are protected by the Equal Protection Clause from dilution of their voting strength, then members of every identifiable group that possesses distinctive interests and tends to vote on the basis of those interests should be able to bring similar claims. Federal courts will have no alternative but to attempt to recreate the complex process of legislative apportionment in the context of adversary litigation in order to reconcile the competing claims of political, religious, ethnic, racial, occupational, and socioeconomic groups. Even if there were some way of limiting such claims to organized political parties, the fact remains that the losing party or the losing group of legislators in every reapportionment will now be invited to fight the battle anew in federal court. Apportionment is so important to legislators and political parties that the burden of proof the plurality places on political gerrymandering plaintiffs is unlikely to deter the routine lodging of such complaints. Notwithstanding the plurality's threshold requirement of discriminatory effects, the Court's holding that political gerrymandering claims are justiciable has open the door to pervasive and unwarranted judicial superintendance of the legislative task of apportionment. There is simply no clear stopping point to prevent the gradual evolution of a requirement of roughly proportional representation for every cohesive political group.

In my view, this enterprise is flawed from its inception. The Equal Protection Clause does not supply judicially manageable standards for resolving purely political gerrymandering claims, and no group right to an equal share of political power was ever intended by the Framers of the Fourteenth Amendment. The Court rests its case on precedent, but the cases on which the Court relies do not require that we take this next and most far-reaching step into the "political thicket." ***

Justice Powell, with whom ***Justice Stevens*** joins, concurring in part . . . and dissenting.

This case presents the question whether a state legislature violates the Equal Protection Clause by adopting a redistricting plan designed solely to preserve the power of the dominant political party, when the plan follows the doctrine of "one person, one vote" but ignores all other neutral factors relevant to the fairness of redistricting.

In answering this question, the plurality expresses the view, with which I agree, that a partisan political gerrymander violates the Equal Protection Clause only on proof of "both intentional discrimination against an identifiable political group and an actual discriminatory effect on that group." *** The plurality acknowledges that the record in this case supports a finding that the challenged redistricting plan was adopted for the purpose of discriminating against Democratic voters. *** The plurality argues however, that appellees failed to establish that their voting strength was diluted statewide despite uncontradicted proof that certain key districts were grotesquely gerrymandered to enhance the election prospects of Republican candidates. This argument appears to rest solely on the ground that the legislature accomplished its gerrymander consistent with "one person, one vote," in the sense that the legislature designed voting districts of approximately equal population and erected no direct barriers to Democratic voters' exercise of the franchise. Since the essence of a gerrymandering claim is that the members of a political party as a group have been denied their right to "fair and effective representation," *** I believe that the claim cannot be tested solely by reference to "one person, one vote." Rather, a number of other relevant neutral factors must be considered. Because the plurality ignores such factors and fails to enunciate standards by which to determine whether a legislature has enacted an unconstitutional gerrymander, I dissent. . . .

In conclusion, I want to make clear the limits of the standard that I believe the Equal Protection Clause imposes on legislators engaged in redistricting. Traditionally, the determination of electoral districts within a State has been a matter left to the legislative branch of the state government. Apart from the doctrine of separation of powers and the federal system prescribed by the Constitution, federal judges are ill-equipped generally to review legislative decisions respecting redistricting. As the plurality opinion makes clear, however, our precedents hold that a colorable claim of discriminatory gerrymandering presents a justiciable controversy under the Equal Protection Clause. Federal courts in exercising their duty to adjudicate such claims should impose a heavy burden of proof on those who allege that a redistricting plan violates the Constitution. In light of *Baker v. Carr, Reynolds v. Sims,* and their progeny, including such comparatively recent decisions as *Gaffney v. Cummings,* this case presents a paradigm example of unconstitutional discrimination against the members of a political party that happened to be out of power. The well-grounded findings of the District Court to this effect have not been, and I believe cannot be, held clearly erroneous.

Accordingly, I would affirm the judgment of the District Court.

THE CONSTITUTION OF THE UNITED STATES OF AMERICA

We the People of the United States, in Order to form a more perfect Union, establish Justice, insure domestic Tranquility, provide for the common defence, promote the general Welfare, and secure the Blessings of Liberty to ourselves and our Posterity, do ordain and establish this Constitution for the United States of America.

ARTICLE I

Section 1. All legislative Powers herein granted shall be vested in a Congress of the United States, which shall consist of a Senate and House of Representatives.

Section 2. The House of Representatives shall be composed of Members chosen every second Year by the People of the several States, and the Electors in each State shall have the Qualifications requisite for Electors of the most numerous Branch of the State Legislature.

No Person shall be a Representative who shall not have attained to the age of twenty five Years, and been seven Years a Citizen of the United States, and who shall not, when elected, be an Inhabitant of that State in which he shall be chosen.

Representatives and direct Taxes shall be apportioned among the several States which may be included within this Union, according to their respective Numbers, which shall be determined by adding to the whole Number of free Persons, including those bound to Service for a term of Years, and excluding Indians not taxed, three fifths of all other Persons. The actual Enumeration shall be made within three Years after the first Meeting of the Congress of the United States, and within every subsequent Term of ten Years, in such Manner as they shall by Law direct. The number of Representatives shall not exceed one for every thirty Thousand, but each State shall have at Least one Representative; and until such enumeration shall be made, the State of New Hampshire shall be entitled to chuse three, Massachusetts eight, Rhode Island and Providence Plantations one, Connecticut five, New York six, New Jersey four, Pennsylvania eight, Delaware one, Maryland six, Virginia ten, North Carolina five, South Carolina five, and Georgia three.

When vacancies happen in the Representation from any State, the Executive Authority thereof shall issue Writs of Election to fill such Vacancies.

The House of Representatives shall chuse their Speaker and other Officers; and shall have the sole Power of Impeachment.

Section 3. The Senate of the United States shall be composed of two Senators from each State, chosen by the Legislature thereof, for six Years; and each Senator shall have one Vote.

Immediately after they shall be assembled in Consequence of the first Election, they shall be divided as equally as may be into three Classes. The Seats of the Senators of the first Class shall be vacated at the Expiration of the second Year, of the second Class at the Expiration of the fourth Year, and of the third Class at the Expiration of the sixth Year, so that one third may be chosen every second Year; and if Vacancies happen by Resignation, or otherwise, during the Recess of the Legislature of any State, the Executive thereof may make temporary Appointments until the next Meeting of the Legislature, which shall then fill such Vacancies.

No Person shall be a Senator who shall not have attained to the Age of thirty Years, and been nine Years a Citizen of the United States, and who shall not, when elected, be an Inhabitant of that State for which he shall be chosen.

The Vice President of the United States shall be President of the Senate, but shall have no Vote, unless they be equally divided.

The Senate shall chuse their other Officers, and also a President pro tempore, in the Absence of the Vice President, or when he shall exercise the Office of President of the United States.

The Senate shall have the sole Power to try all Impeachments. When sitting for that Purpose, they shall be on Oath or Affirmation. When the President of the United States is tried the Chief Justice shall preside: And no Person shall be convicted without the Concurrence of two thirds of the Members present.

Judgment in Cases of Impeachment shall not extend further than to removal from Office, and disqualification to hold and enjoy any Office of honor, Trust or Profit under the United States: but the Party convicted shall nevertheless be liable and subject to Indictment, Trial, Judgment and Punishment, according to Law.

Section 4. The Times, Places and Manner of holding Elections for Senators and Representatives, shall be prescribed in each State by the Legislature thereof; but the Congress may at any time by Law make or alter such Regulations, except as to the Places of chusing Senators.

The Congress shall assemble at least once in every Year, and such Meeting shall be on the first Monday in December, unless they shall by Law appoint a different Day.

Section 5. Each House shall be the Judge of the Elections, Returns and Qualifications of its own Members, and a Majority of each shall constitute a Quorum to do Business; but a smaller Number may adjourn from day to day, and may be authorized to compel the Attendance of absent Members, in such Manner, and under such Penalties as each House may provide.

Each House may determine the Rules of its Proceedings, punish its Members for disorderly Behaviour, and, with the Concurrence of two thirds, expel a Member.

Each House shall keep a Journal of its Proceedings, and from time to time publish the same, excepting such Parts as may in their Judgment require Secrecy; and the Yeas and Nays of the Members of either House on any question shall, at the Desire of one fifth of those Present, be entered on the Journal.

Neither House, during the Session of Congress, shall, without the Consent of the other, adjourn for more than three days, nor to any other Place than that in which the two Houses shall be setting.

Section 6. The Senators and Representatives shall receive a Compensation for their Services, to be ascertained by Law, and paid out of the Treasury of the United States. They shall in all Cases, except Treason, Felony and Breach of the Peace, be privileged from Arrest during their Attendance at the Session of their respective Houses, and in going to and returning from the same; and for any Speech or Debate in either House, they shall not be questioned in any other Place.

No Senator or Representative shall, during the Time for which he was elected, be appointed to any civil Office under the Authority of the United States, which shall have been created, or the Emoluments whereof shall have been encreased during such time; and no Person holding any Office under the United States, shall be a Member of either House during his Continuance in Office.

Section 7. All Bills for raising Revenue shall originate in the House of Representatives; but the Senate may propose or concur with amendments as on other Bills.

Every Bill which shall have passed the House of Representatives and the Senate, shall, before it become a Law, be presented to the President of the United States; If he approve he shall sign it, but if not he shall return it, with his Objections to that House in which it shall have originated, who shall enter the Objections at large on their Journal, and proceed to reconsider it. If after such Reconsideration two thirds of that House shall agree to pass the Bill, it shall be sent, together with the Objections, to the other House, by which it shall likewise be reconsidered, and if approved by two thirds of that House, it shall become a Law. But in all such Cases the Votes of both Houses shall be determined by Yeas and Nays, and the Names of the Persons voting for and against the Bill shall be entered on the Journal of each House respectively. If any Bill shall not be returned by the President within ten Days (Sunday excepted) after it shall have been presented to him, the Same shall be a Law, in like Manner as if he had signed it, unless the Congress by their Adjournment prevent its Return, in which Case it shall not be a Law.

Every Order, Resolution, or Vote to which the Concurrence of the Senate and House of Representatives may be necessary (except on a question of Adjournment) shall be presented to the President of the United States; and before the Same shall take Effect, shall be approved by him, or being disapproved by him, shall be repassed by two thirds of the Senate and House of Representatives, according to the Rules and Limitations prescribed in the Case of a Bill.

Section 8. The Congress shall have Power To lay and collect Taxes, Duties, Imposts and Excises, to pay the Debts and provide for the common Defence and general Welfare of the United States; but all Duties, Imposts and Excises shall be uniform throughout the United States;

To borrow Money on the credit of the United States;

To regulate Commerce with foreign Nations, and among the several States, and with the Indian Tribes;

To establish an uniform Rule of Naturalization, and uniform Laws on the subject of Bankruptcies throughout the United States;

To coin Money, regulate the Value thereof, and of foreign Coin, and fix the Standard of Weights and Measures;

To provide for the Punishment of counterfeiting the Securities and current Coin of the United States;

To establish Post Offices and post Roads;

To promote the Progress of Science and useful Arts, by securing for limited Times to Authors and Inventors the exclusive Right to their respective Writings and Discoveries;

To constitute Tribunals inferior to the supreme Court;

To define and punish Piracies and Felonies committed on the high Seas, and Offenses against the Law of Nations;

To declare War, grant Letters of Marque and Reprisal, and make Rules concerning Captures on Land and Water;

To raise and support Armies, but no Appropriation of Money to that Use shall be for a longer Term than two Years;

To provide and maintain a Navy;

To make Rules for the Government and Regulation of the land and naval Forces;

To provide for calling forth the Militia to execute the Laws of the Union, suppress Insurrections and repel Invasions;

To provide for organizing, arming, and disciplining, the Militia, and for governing such Part of them as may be employed in the Service of the United States, reserving to the States respectively, the Appointment of the Officers, and the Authority of training the Militia according to the discipline prescribed by Congress;

To exercise exclusive Legislation in all Cases whatsoever, over such District (not exceeding ten Miles square) as may, by Cession of particular States, and the Acceptance of Congress, become the Seat of the Government of the United States, and to exercise like Authority over all Places purchased by the Consent of the Legislature of the State in which the Same shall be, for the Erection of Forts, Magazines, Arsenals, dock-Yards, and other needful Buildings;—And

To make all laws which shall be necessary and proper for carrying into Execution the foregoing Powers, and all other Powers vested by this Constitution in the Government of the United States, or in any Department or Officer thereof.

Section 9. The Migration or Importation of such Persons as any of the States now existing shall think proper to admit, shall not be prohibited by the Congress prior to the Year one thousand eight hundred and eight, but a Tax or duty may be imposed on such Importation, not exceeding ten dollars for each Person.

The Privilege of the Writ of Habeas Corpus shall not be suspended, unless when in Cases of Rebellion or Invasion the public Safety may require it.

No Bill of Attainder or ex post facto Law shall be passed.

No Capitation, or other direct, Tax shall be laid, unless in Proportion to the Census or Enumeration herein before directed to be taken.

No Tax or Duty shall be laid on Articles exported from any State.

No Preference shall be given by any Regulation of Commerce or Revenue to the Ports of one State over those of another; nor shall Vessels bound to, or from, one State, be obliged to enter, clear or pay Duties in another.

No Money shall be drawn from the Treasury, but in Consequence of Appropriations made by Law; and a regular Statement and Account of the Receipts and Expenditures of all public Money shall be published from time to time.

No Title of Nobility shall be granted by the United States: And no Person holding any Office of Profit or Trust under them, shall, without the Consent of the Congress, accept of any present, Emolument, Office, or Title, of any kind whatever, from any King, Prince or foreign State.

Section 10. No State shall enter into any Treaty, Alliance, or Confederation; grant Letters of Marque and Reprisal; coin Money; emit Bills of Credit; make any Thing but gold and silver Coin a Tender in Payment of Debts; pass any Bill of Attainder, ex post facto Law, or Law impairing the Obligation of Contracts, or grant any Title of Nobility.

No State shall, without the Consent of the Congress, lay any Imposts or Duties on Imports or Exports, except what may be absolutely necessary for executing its inspection Laws: and the net Produce of all Duties and Imposts, laid by any State on Imports or Exports, shall be for the Use of the Treasury of the United States; and all such Laws shall be subject to the Revision and Controul of the Congress.

No State shall, without the Consent of Congress, lay any Duty of Tonnage, keep Troops, or Ships of War in time of Peace, enter into any Agreement or Compact with another State, or with a foreign Power, or engage in War, unless actually invaded, or in such imminent Danger as will not admit of delay.

ARTICLE II

Section 1. The executive Power shall be vested in a President of the United States of America. He shall hold his Office during the Term of four Years, and, together with the Vice President, chosen for the same Term, be elected, as follows:

Each State shall appoint, in such Manner as the Legislature thereof may direct, a Number of Electors, equal to the whole Number of Senators and Representatives to which the State may be entitled in the Congress: but no Senator or Representative, or Person holding an Office of Trust or Profit under the United States, shall be appointed an Elector.

The Electors shall meet in their respective States, and vote by Ballot for two Persons, of whom one at least shall not be an Inhabitant of the same State with themselves. And they shall make a List of all the Persons voted for, and of the Number of Votes for each; which List they shall sign and certify, and transmit sealed to the Seat of the Government of the United States, directed to the President of the Senate. The President of the Senate shall, in the presence of the Senate and House of Representatives, open all the Certificates, and the Votes shall then be counted. The Person having the greatest Number of Votes shall be the President, if such Number be a Majority of the whole Number of Electors appointed; and if there be more than one who have such Majority, and have an equal Number of Votes, then the House of Representatives shall immediately chuse by Ballot one of them for President; and if no Person have a Majority, then from the five highest on the List the said House shall in like Manner chuse the President. But in chusing the President, the Votes shall be taken by States, the Representation from each State having one Vote; a quorum for this Purpose shall consist of a Member or Members from two thirds of the States, and a Majority of all the States shall be necessary to a Choice. In every Case, after the Choice of the President, the Person having the greatest Number of Votes of the Electors shall be the Vice President. But if

there should remain two or more who have equal Votes, the Senate shall chuse from them by Ballot the Vice President.

The Congress may determine the Time of chusing the Electors, and the Day on which they shall give their Votes; which Day shall be the same throughout the United States.

No Person except a natural born Citizen, or a Citizen of the United States, at the time of the Adoption of this Constitution, shall be eligible to the Office of President; neither shall any Person be eligible to that Office who shall not have attained to the Age of thirty five Years, and been fourteen Years a Resident within the United States.

In Case of the Removal of the President from Office, or of his Death, Resignation, or Inability to discharge the Powers and Duties of the said Office, the Same shall devolve on the Vice President, and the Congress may by Law provide for the Case of Removal, Death, Resignation or Inability, both of the President and Vice President, declaring what Officer shall then act as President, and such Officer shall act accordingly, until the Disability be removed, or a President shall be elected.

The President shall, at stated Times, receive for his Services, a Compensation, which shall neither be increased nor diminished during the Period for which he shall have been elected, and he shall not receive within that Period any other Emolument from the United States, or any of them.

Before he enter on the Execution of his Office, he shall take the following Oath or Affirmation:—"I do solemnly swear (or affirm) that I will faithfully execute the Office of President of the United States, and will to the best of my Ability, preserve, protect and defend the Constitution of the United States."

Section 2. The President shall be Commander in Chief of the Army and Navy of the United States, and of the Militia of the several States, when called into the actual Service of the United States; he may require the Opinion, in writing, of the principal Officer in each of the executive Departments, upon any Subject relating to the Duties of their respective Offices, and he shall have Power to grant Reprieves and Pardons for Offenses against the United States, except in Cases of Impeachment.

He shall have Power, by and with the Advice and Consent of the Senate, to make Treaties, provided two thirds of the Senators present concur; and he shall nominate, and by and with the Advice and Consent of the Senate, shall appoint Ambassadors, other public Ministers and Consuls, Judges of the supreme Court, and all other Officers of the United States, whose Appointments are not herein otherwise provided for, and which shall be established by Law: but the Congress may by Law vest the Appointment of such inferior Officers, as they think proper, in the President alone, in the Courts of Law, or in the Heads of Departments.

The President shall have Power to fill up all Vacancies that may happen during the Recess of the Senate, by granting Commissions which shall expire at the End of their next Session.

Section 3. He shall from time to time give to the Congress Information of the State of the Union, and recommend to their Consideration such Measures as he shall judge necessary and expedient; he may, on extraordinary Occasions, convene both Houses, or either of them, and in Case of Disagreement between them, with Respect to the Time of Adjournment, he may adjourn them to such Time as he shall think proper; he shall receive Ambassadors and other public Ministers; he shall take Care that the Laws be faithfully executed, and shall Commission all the Officers of the United States.

Section 4. The President, Vice President and all Civil Officers of the United States, shall be removed from Office on Impeachment for, and Conviction of, Treason, Bribery, or other high Crimes and Misdemeanors.

ARTICLE III

Section 1. The judicial Power of the United States, shall be vested in one supreme Court, and in such inferior Courts as the Congress may from time to time ordain and establish. The Judges, both of the supreme and inferior Courts, shall hold their Offices during good Behaviour, and shall, at stated Times, receive for their Services, a Compensation, which shall not be diminished during their Continuance in Office.

Section 2. The judicial Power shall extend to all Cases, in Law and Equity, arising under this Constitution, the Laws of the United States, and Treaties made, or which shall be made, under their Authority;—to all Cases affecting Ambassadors, other public Ministers and Consuls;—to all Cases of admiralty and maritime Jurisdiction;—to Controversies to which the United States shall be a Party;—to Controversies between two or more States;—between a State and Citizens of another State;—between Citizens of different States;—between Citizens of the same State claiming Lands under Grants of different States, and between a State, or the Citizens thereof, and foreign States, Citizens or Subjects.

In all Cases affecting Ambassadors, other public Ministers and Consuls, and those in which a State shall be Party, the supreme Court shall have original Jurisdiction. In all the other Cases before mentioned, the supreme Court shall have appellate Jurisdiction, both as to Law and Fact, with such Exceptions, and under such Regulations as the Congress shall make.

The Trial of all Crimes, except in Cases of Impeachment, shall be by Jury; and such Trial shall be held in the State where the said Crimes shall have been committed; but when not committed within any State, the Trial shall be at such Place or Places as the Congress may by Law have directed.

Section 3. Treason against the United States, shall consist only in levying War against them, or in adhering to their Enemies, giving them Aid and Comfort. No Person shall be convicted of Treason unless on the Testimony of two Witnesses to the same overt Act, or on Confession in open Court.

The Congress shall have Power to declare the Punishment of Treason, but no Attainder of Treason shall work Corruption of Blood, or Forfeiture except during the Life of the Person attainted.

ARTICLE IV

Section 1. Full Faith and Credit shall be given in each State to the public Acts, Records, and judicial Proceedings of every other State. And the Congress may by general Laws prescribe the Manner in which such Acts, Records and Proceedings shall be proved, and the Effect thereof.

Section 2. The Citizens of each State shall be entitled to all Privileges and Immunities of Citizens in the several States.

A Person charged in any State with Treason, Felony, or other Crime, who shall flee from Justice, and be found in another State, shall on Demand of the executive Authority of the State from which he fled, be delivered up, to be removed to the State having Jurisdiction of the Crime.

No Person held to Service of Labour in one State, under the Laws thereof, escaping into another, shall, in Consequence of any Law or Regulation therein, be discharged from such Service or Labour, but shall be delivered up on Claim of the Party to whom such Service or Labour may be due.

Section 3. New States may be admitted by the Congress into this Union; but no new State shall be formed or erected within the Jurisdiction of any other State; nor any State be formed by the Junction of two or more States, or Parts of States, without the Consent of the Legislatures of the States concerned as well as of the Congress.

The Congress shall have Power to dispose of and make all needful Rules and Regulations respecting the Territory or other Property belonging to the United States; and nothing in this Constitution shall be so construed as to Prejudice any Claims of the United States, or of any particular State.

Section 4. The United States shall guarantee to every State in this Union a Republican Form of Government, and shall protect each of them against Invasion; and on Application of the Legislature, or of the Executive (when the Legislature cannot be convened) against domestic Violence.

ARTICLE V

The Congress, whenever two thirds of both Houses shall deem it necessary, shall propose Amendments to this Constitution, or, on the Application of the Legislatures of two thirds of the several States, shall call a Convention for proposing Amendments, which, in either Case, shall be valid to all Intents and Purposes, as Part of this Constitution, when ratified by the Legislatures of three fourths of the several States, or by Conventions in three fourths thereof, as the one or the other Mode of Ratification may be proposed by the Congress; Provided that no Amendment which may be made prior to the Year One thousand eight hundred and eight shall in any Manner affect the first and fourth Clauses in the Ninth Section of the first Article; and that no State, without its Consent, shall be deprived of its equal Suffrage in the Senate.

ARTICLE VI

All Debts contracted and Engagements entered into, before the Adoption of this Constitution, shall be as valid against the United States under this Constitution, as under the Confederation.

This Constitution, and the Laws of the United States which shall be made in Pursuance thereof; and all Treaties made, or which shall be made, under the Authority of the United States, shall be the supreme Law of the Land; and the Judges in every State shall be bound thereby, any Thing in the Constitution or Laws of any State to the Contrary notwithstanding.

The Senators and Representatives before mentioned, and the Members of the several State Legislatures, and all executive and judicial Officers, both of the United States and of the several States, shall be bound by Oath or Affirmation, to support this Constitution; but no religious Test shall ever be required as a Qualification to any Office or Public Trust under the United States.

ARTICLE VII

The Ratification of the Conventions of nine States, shall be sufficient for the Establishment of this Constitution between the States so ratifying the Same.

Articles in Addition to, and Amendment of, the Constitution of the United States of America, Proposed by Congress, and Ratified by the Several States, Pursuant to the Fifth Article of the Original Constitution

AMENDMENT I [1791]

Congress shall make no law respecting an establishment of religion, or prohibiting the free exercise thereof; or abridging the freedom of speech, or of the press; or the right of the people peaceably to assemble, and to petition the Government for a redress of grievances.

AMENDMENT II [1791]

A well regulated Militia, being necessary to the security of a free state, the right of the people to keep and bear Arms, shall not be infringed.

AMENDMENT III [1791]

No Soldier shall, in time of peace be quartered in any house, without the consent of the Owner, nor in time of war, but in a manner to be prescribed by law.

AMENDMENT IV [1791]

The right of the people to be secure in their persons, houses, papers, and effects, against unreasonable searches and seizures, shall not be violated, and no Warrants shall issue, but upon probable cause, supported by Oath or affirmation, and particularly describing the place to be searched, and the persons or things to be seized.

AMENDMENT V [1791]

No person shall be held to answer for a capital, or otherwise infamous crime, unless on a presentment or indictment of a Grand Jury, except in cases arising in the land or naval forces, or in the Militia, when in actual service in time of War or public danger; nor shall any person be subject for the same offence to be twice put in jeopardy of life or limb; nor shall be compelled in any criminal case to be a witness against himself, nor be deprived of life, liberty, or property, without due process of law; nor shall private property be taken for public use, without just compensation.

AMENDMENT VI [1791]

In all criminal prosecutions, the accused shall enjoy the right to a speedy and public trial, by an impartial jury of the State and district wherein the crime shall have been committed, which district shall have been previously ascertained by law, and to be informed of the nature and cause of the accusation; to be confronted with the witnesses against him; to have compulsory process for obtaining witnesses in his favor, and to have the Assistance of Counsel for his defence.

AMENDMENT VII [1791]

In Suits at common law, where the value in controversy shall exceed twenty dollars, the right of trial by jury shall be preserved, and no fact tried by a jury, shall be otherwise re-examined in any Court of the United States, than according to the rules of the common law.

AMENDMENT VIII [1791]

Excessive bail shall not be required, nor excessive fines imposed, nor cruel and unusual punishments inflicted.

AMENDMENT IX [1791]

The enumeration in the Constitution, of certain rights, shall not be construed to deny or disparage others retained by the people.

AMENDMENT X [1791]

The powers not delegated to the United States by the Constitution, nor prohibited by it to the States, are reserved to the States respectively, or to the people.

AMENDMENT XI [1798]

The Judicial power of the United States shall not be construed to extend to any suit in law or equity, commenced or prosecuted against one of the United States by Citizens of another State, or by Citizens or Subjects of any Foreign State.

AMENDMENT XII [1804]

The Electors shall meet in their respective states and vote by ballot for President and Vice-President, one of whom, at least, shall not be an inhabitant of the same state with themselves; they shall name in their ballots the person voted for as President, and in distinct ballots the person voted for as Vice-President, and they shall make distinct lists of all persons voted for as President, and of all persons voted for as Vice-President, and of the number of votes for each, which lists they shall sign and certify, and transmit sealed to the seat of the government of the United States, directed to the President of the Senate;—The President of the Senate shall, in the presence of the Senate and House of Representatives, open all the certificates and the votes shall then be counted;—The person having the greatest number of votes for President, shall be the President, if such number be a majority of the whole number of Electors appointed; and if no person have such majority, then from the persons having the highest numbers not exceeding three on the list of those voted for as President, the House of Representatives shall choose immediately, by ballot, the President. But in choosing the President, the votes shall be taken by states, the representation from each state having one vote; a quorum for this purpose shall consist of a member or members from two-thirds of the states, and a majority of all the states shall be necessary to a choice. And if the House of Representatives shall not choose a President whenever the right of choice shall devolve upon them, before the fourth day of March next following, then the Vice-President shall act as President, as in the case of the death or other constitutional disability of the President—The person having the greatest number of votes as Vice-President, shall be the Vice-President, if such number be a majority of the whole number of Electors appointed, and if no person have a majority, then from the two highest numbers on the list, the Senate shall choose the Vice-President; a quorum for the purpose shall consist of two-thirds of the whole number of Senators, and a majority of the whole number shall be necessary to a choice. But no person constitutionally ineligible to the office of President shall be eligible to that of Vice-President of the United States.

AMENDMENT XIII [1865]

Section 1. Neither slavery nor involuntary servitude, except as a punishment for crime whereof the party shall have been duly convicted, shall exist within the United States, or any place subject to their jurisdiction.

Section 2. Congress shall have power to enforce this article by appropriate legislation.

AMENDMENT XIV [1868]

Section 1. All persons born or naturalized in the United States and subject to the jurisdiction thereof, are citizens of the United States and of the State wherein they reside. No State shall make or enforce any law which shall abridge the privileges or immunities of citizens of the United States; nor shall any State deprive any person of life, liberty, or property, without due process of law; nor deny to any person within its jurisdiction the equal protection of the laws.

Section 2. Representatives shall be apportioned among the several States according to their respective numbers, counting the whole number of persons in each State, excluding Indians not taxed. But when the right to vote at any election for the choice of electors for President and Vice President of the United States, Representatives in Congress, the Executive and Judicial officers of a State, or the members of the Legislature thereof, is denied to any of the male inhabitants of such State, being twenty-one years of age, and citizens of the United States, or in any way abridged, except for participation in rebellion, or other crime, the basis of representation therein shall be reduced in the proportion which the number of such male citizens shall bear to the whole number of male citizens twenty-one years of age in such State.

Section 3. No person shall be a Senator or Representative in Congress, or elector of President and Vice President, or hold any office, civil or military, under the United States, or under any State, who, having previously taken an oath, as a member of Congress, or as an officer of the United States, or as a member of any State legislature, or as an executive or judicial officer of any State, to support the Constitution of the United States, shall have engaged in insurrection or rebellion against the same, or given aid or comfort to the enemies thereof. But Congress may by a vote of two-thirds of each House, remove such disability.

Section 4. The validity of the public debt of the United States, authorized by law, including debts incurred for payment of pensions and bounties for services in suppressing insurrection or rebellion, shall not be questioned. But neither the United States nor any State shall assume or pay any debt or obligation incurred in aid of insurrection or rebellion against the United States, or any claim for the loss or emancipation of any slave; but all such debts, obligations and claims shall be held illegal and void.

Section 5. The Congress shall have power to enforce, by appropriate legislation, the provisions of this article.

AMENDMENT XV [1870]

Section 1. The right of citizens of the United States to vote shall not be denied or abridged by the United States or by any State on account of race, color, or previous condition of servitude.

Section 2. The Congress shall have power to enforce this article by appropriate legislation.

AMENDMENT XVI [1913]

The Congress shall have power to lay and collect taxes on incomes, from whatever source derived, without apportionment among the several States, and without regard to any census or enumeration.

AMENDMENT XVII [1913]

The Senate of the United States shall be composed of two Senators from each State, elected by the people thereof, for six years; and each Senator shall have one vote. The electors in each State shall have the qualifications requisite for electors of the most numerous branch of the State legislatures.

When vacancies happen in the representation of any State in the Senate, the executive authority of such State shall issue writs of election to fill such vacancies: *Provided,* That the legislature of any State may empower the executive thereof to make temporary appointments until the people fill the vacancies by election as the legislature may direct.

This amendment shall not be so construed as to affect the election or term of any Senator chosen before it becomes valid as part of the Constitution.

AMENDMENT XVIII [1919]

Section 1. After one year from the ratification of this article the manufacture, sale, or transportation of intoxicating liquors within, the importation thereof into, or the exportation thereof from the United States and all territory subject to the jurisdiction thereof for beverage purposes is hereby prohibited.

Section 2. The Congress and the several States shall have concurrent power to enforce this article by appropriate legislation.

Section 3. This article shall be inoperative unless it shall have been ratified as an amendment to the

Constitution by the legislatures of the several States, as provided in the Constitution, within seven years from the date of the submission hereof to the States by the Congress.

AMENDMENT XIX [1920]

The right of citizens of the United States to vote shall not be denied or abridged by the United States or by any State on account of sex.

Congress shall have power to enforce this article by appropriate legislation.

AMENDMENT XX [1933]

Section 1. The terms of the President and Vice President shall end at noon on the 20th day of January, and the terms of Senators and Representatives at noon on the 3d day of January, of the years in which such terms would have ended if this article had not been ratified; and the terms of their successors shall then begin.

Section 2. The Congress shall assemble at least once in every year, and such meeting shall begin at noon on the 3d day of January, unless they shall by law appoint a different day.

Section 3. If, at the time fixed for the beginning of the term of the President, the President elect shall have died, the Vice President elect shall become President. If a President shall not have been chosen before the time fixed for the beginning of his term, or if the President elect shall have failed to qualify, then the Vice President elect shall act as President until a President shall have qualified; and the Congress may by law provide for the case wherein neither a President elect nor a Vice President elect shall have qualified, declaring who shall then act as President, or the manner in which one who is to act shall be selected, and such person shall act accordingly until a President or Vice President shall have qualified.

Section 4. The Congress may by law provide for the case of the death of any of the persons from whom the House of Representatives may choose a President whenever the right of choice shall have devolved upon them, and for the case of the death of any of the persons from whom the Senate may choose a Vice President whenever the right of choice shall have devolved upon them.

Section 5. Sections 1 and 2 shall take effect on the 15th day of October following the ratification of this article.

Section 6. This article shall be inoperative unless it shall have been ratified as an amendment to the Constitution by the legislatures of three-fourths of the States within seven years from the date of its submission.

AMENDMENT XXI [1933]

Section 1. The eighteenth article of amendment to the Constitution of the United States is hereby repealed.

Section 2. The transportation or importation into any State, Territory or possession of the United States for delivery or use therein of intoxicating liquors, in violation of the laws thereof, is hereby prohibited.

Section 3. This article shall be inoperative unless it shall have been ratified as an amendment to the Constitution by conventions in the several States, as provided in the Constitution, within seven years from the date of the submission hereof to the States by the Congress.

AMENDMENT XXII [1951]

Section 1. No person shall be elected to the office of the President more than twice, and no person who has held the office of President, or acted as President, for more than two years of a term to which some other person was elected President shall be elected to the office of the President more than once. But this Article shall not apply to any person holding the office of President when this Article was proposed by the Congress, and shall not prevent any person who may be holding the office of President, or acting as President, during the term within which this Article becomes operative from holding the office of President or acting as President during the remainder of such term.

Section 2. This Article shall be inoperative unless it shall have been ratified as an amendment to the Constitution by the legislatures of three-fourths of the several States within seven years from the date of its submission to the States by the Congress.

AMENDMENT XXIII [1961]

Section 1. The District constituting the seat of Government of the United States shall appoint in such manner as the Congress may direct:

A number of electors of President and Vice President equal to the whole number of Senators and Representatives in Congress to which the District would be entitled if it were a State, but in no event more than the least populous State; they shall be in addition to those appointed by the States, but they shall be considered, for the purposes of the election of President and Vice President, to be electors appointed by a State; and they shall meet in the District and perform such duties as provided by the twelfth article of amendment.

Section 2. The Congress shall have power to enforce this article by appropriate legislation.

AMENDMENT XXIV [1964]

Section 1. The right of citizens of the United States to vote in any primary or other election for President or Vice President, for electors for President or Vice President, or for Senator or Representative in Congress, shall not be denied or abridged by the United States or any State by reason of failure to pay any poll tax or other tax.

Section 2. The Congress shall have power to enforce this article by appropriate legislation.

AMENDMENT XXV [1967]

Section 1. In case of the removal of the President from office or of his death or resignation, the Vice President shall become President.

Section 2. Whenever there is a vacancy in the office of the Vice President, the President shall nominate a Vice President who shall take office upon confirmation by a majority vote of both Houses of Congress.

Section 3. Whenever the President transmits to the President pro tempore of the Senate and the Speaker of the House of Representatives has written declaration that he is unable to discharge the powers and duties of his office, and until he transmits to them a written declaration to the contrary, such powers and duties shall be discharged by the Vice President as Acting President.

Section 4. Whenever the Vice President and a majority of either the principal officers of the executive departments or of such other body as Congress may by law provide, transmit to the President pro tempore of the Senate and the Speaker of the House of Represen-

tatives their written declaration that the President is unable to discharge the powers and duties of his office, the Vice President shall immediately assume the powers and duties of the office as Acting President.

Thereafter, when the President transmits to the President pro tempore of the Senate and the Speaker of the House of Representatives his written declaration that no inability exists, he shall resume the powers and duties of his office unless the Vice President and a majority of either the principal officers of the executive department or of such other body as Congress may by law provide, transmit within four days to the President pro tempore of the Senate and the Speaker of the House of Representatives their written declaration that the President is unable to discharge the powers and duties of his office. Thereupon Congress shall decide the issue, assembling within forty-eight hours for that purpose if not in session. If the Congress, within twenty-one days after receipt of the latter written declaration, or, if Congress is not in session, within twenty-one days after Congress is required to assemble, determines by two-thirds vote of both Houses that the President is unable to discharge the powers and duties of his office, the Vice President shall continue to discharge the same as Acting President; otherwise, the President shall resume the powers and duties of his office.

AMENDMENT XXVI [1971]

Section 1. The right of citizens of the United States, who are eighteen years of age or older, to vote shall not be denied or abridged by the United States or by any State on account of age.

Section 2. The Congress shall have power to enforce this article by appropriate legislation.

AMENDMENT XXVII [Proposed 1789; Ratified 1992]

No law, varying the compensation for the services of Senators and Representatives, shall take effect until an election of Representatives have intervened.

A P P E N D I X B

CHRONOLOGY OF JUSTICES OF THE UNITED STATES SUPREME COURT

Years of Court as Constituted	Chief Justice	Associate Justices								
1789	*Jay*	Rutledge, J.	Cushing	Wilson	Blair					
1790–91	*Jay*	Rutledge, J.	Cushing	Wilson	Blair	Iredell				
1792	*Jay*	Johnson, T.	Cushing	Wilson	Blair	Iredell				
1793–94	*Jay*	Paterson	Cushing	Wilson	Blair	Iredell				
1795	*Rutledge, J.*	Paterson	Cushing	Wilson	Blair	Iredell				
1796–97	*Ellsworth*	Paterson	Cushing	Wilson	Chase, S.	Iredell				
1798–99	*Ellsworth*	Paterson	Cushing	Washington	Chase, S.	Iredell				
1800	*Ellsworth*	Paterson	Cushing	Washington	Chase, S.	Moore				
1801–03	*Marshall, J.*	Paterson	Cushing	Washington	Chase, S.	Moore				
1804–05	*Marshall, J.*	Paterson	Cushing	Washington	Chase, S.	Johnson, W.				
1806	*Marshall, J.*	Livingston	Cushing	Washington	Chase, S.	Johnson, W.				
1807–10	*Marshall, J.*	Livingston	Cushing	Washington	Chase, S.	Johnson, W.	Todd			
1811–12	*Marshall, J.*	Livingston	Story	Washington	Duvall	Johnson, W.	Todd			
1813–25	*Marshall, J.*	Thompson	Story	Washington	Duvall	Johnson, W.	Todd			
1826–28	*Marshall, J.*	Thompson	Story	Washington	Duvall	Johnson, W.	Trimble			
1829	*Marshall, J.*	Thompson	Story	Washington	Duvall	Johnson, W.	McLean			
1830–34	*Marshall, J.*	Thompson	Story	Baldwin	Duvall	Johnson, W.	McLean			
1835	*Marshall, J.*	Thompson	Story	Baldwin	Duvall	Wayne	McLean			
1836	*Taney*	Thompson	Story	Baldwin	Barbour	Wayne	McLean			
1837–40	*Taney*	Thompson	Story	Baldwin	Barbour	Wayne	McLean	Catron	McKinley	
1841–44	*Taney*	Thompson	Story	Baldwin	Daniel	Wayne	McLean	Catron	McKinley	
1845	*Taney*	Nelson	Woodbury	(vacant)	Daniel	Wayne	McLean	Catron	McKinley	
1846–50	*Taney*	Nelson	Woodbury	Grier	Daniel	Wayne	McLean	Catron	McKinley	
1851–52	*Taney*	Nelson	Curtis	Grier	Daniel	Wayne	McLean	Catron	McKinley	
1853–57	*Taney*	Nelson	Curtis	Grier	Daniel	Wayne	McLean	Catron	Campbell	
1858–60	*Taney*	Nelson	Clifford	Grier	Daniel	Wayne	McLean	Catron	Campbell	
1861	*Taney*	Nelson	Clifford	Grier	(vacant)	Wayne	McLean	Catron	Campbell	
1862	*Taney*	Nelson	Clifford	Grier	Miller	Wayne	Swayne	Catron	Davis	
1863	*Taney*	Nelson	Clifford	Grier	Miller	Wayne	Swayne	Catron	Davis	Field
1864–65	*Chase, S. P.*	Nelson	Clifford	Grier	Miller	Wayne	Swayne	Catron	Davis	Field
1866–67	*Chase, S. P.*	Nelson	Clifford	Grier	Miller	Wayne	Swayne	(ended)*	Davis	Field
1868–69	*Chase, S. P.*	Nelson	Clifford	Grier	Miller	(vacant)	Swayne		Davis	Field

*Congress ended the use of a ten-person Court in this year.

Years of Court as Constituted	Chief Justice	Associate Justices							
1870–71	*Chase, S. P.*	Nelson	Clifford	Strong	Miller	Bradley	Swayne	Davis	Field
1872–73	*Chase, S. P.*	Hunt	Clifford	Strong	Miller	Bradley	Swayne	Davis	Field
1874–76	*Waite*	Hunt	Clifford	Strong	Miller	Bradley	Swayne	Davis	Field
1877–79	*Waite*	Hunt	Clifford	Strong	Miller	Bradley	Swayne	Harlan	Field
1880	*Waite*	Hunt	Clifford	Woods	Miller	Bradley	Swayne	Harlan	Field
1881	*Waite*	Hunt	Gray	Woods	Miller	Bradley	Matthews	Harlan	Field
1882–87	*Waite*	Blatchford	Gray	Woods	Miller	Bradley	Matthews	Harlan	Field
1888	*Fuller*	Blatchford	Gray	Lamar, L.	Miller	Bradley	Matthews	Harlan	Field
1889	*Fuller*	Blatchford	Gray	Lamar, L.	Miller	Bradley	Brewer	Harlan	Field
1890–91	*Fuller*	Blatchford	Gray	Lamar, L.	Brown	Bradley	Brewer	Harlan	Field
1892	*Fuller*	Blatchford	Gray	Lamar, L.	Brown	Shiras	Brewer	Harlan	Field
1893	*Fuller*	Blatchford	Gray	Jackson, H.	Brown	Shiras	Brewer	Harlan	Field
1894	*Fuller*	White	Gray	Jackson, H.	Brown	Shiras	Brewer	Harlan	Field
1895–97	*Fuller*	White	Gray	Peckham	Brown	Shiras	Brewer	Harlan	Field
1898–1901	*Fuller*	White	Gray	Peckham	Brown	Shiras	Brewer	Harlan	McKenna
1902	*Fuller*	White	Holmes	Peckham	Brown	Shiras	Brewer	Harlan	McKenna
1903–05	*Fuller*	White	Holmes	Peckham	Brown	Day	Brewer	Harlan	McKenna
1906–08	*Fuller*	White	Holmes	Peckham	Moody	Day	Brewer	Harlan	McKenna
1909	*Fuller*	White	Holmes	Lurton	Moody	Day	Brewer	Harlan	McKenna
1910–11	*White, E.*	Van Devanter	Holmes	Lurton	Lamar, J.	Day	Hughes	Harlan	McKenna
1912–13	*White, E.*	Van Devanter	Holmes	Lurton	Lamar, J.	Day	Hughes	Pitney	McKenna
1914–15	*White, E.*	Van Devanter	Holmes	McReynolds	Lamar, J.	Day	Hughes	Pitney	McKenna
1916–20	*White, E.*	Van Devanter	Holmes	McReynolds	Brandeis	Day	Clarke	Pitney	McKenna
1921	*Taft*	Van Devanter	Holmes	McReynolds	Brandeis	Day	Clarke	Pitney	McKenna
1922	*Taft*	Van Devanter	Holmes	McReynolds	Brandeis	Butler	Sutherland	Pitney	McKenna
1923–24	*Taft*	Van Devanter	Holmes	McReynolds	Brandeis	Butler	Sutherland	Sanford	McKenna
1925–29	*Taft*	Van Devanter	Holmes	McReynolds	Brandeis	Butler	Sutherland	Sanford	Stone
1930–31	*Hughes*	Van Devanter	Holmes	McReynolds	Brandeis	Butler	Sutherland	Roberts	Stone
1932–36	*Hughes*	Van Devanter	Cardozo	McReynolds	Brandeis	Butler	Sutherland	Roberts	Stone
1937	*Hughes*	Black	Cardozo	McReynolds	Brandeis	Butler	Sutherland	Roberts	Stone
1938	*Hughes*	Black	Cardozo	McReynolds	Brandeis	Butler	Reed	Roberts	Stone
1939	*Hughes*	Black	Frankfurter	McReynolds	Douglas	Butler	Reed	Roberts	Stone
1940	*Hughes*	Black	Frankfurter	McReynolds	Douglas	Murphy	Reed	Roberts	Stone
1941–42	*Stone*	Black	Frankfurter	Byrnes	Douglas	Murphy	Reed	Roberts	Jackson, R.
1943–44	*Stone*	Black	Frankfurter	Rutledge, W.	Douglas	Murphy	Reed	Roberts	Jackson, R.
1945	*Stone*	Black	Frankfurter	Rutledge, W.	Douglas	Murphy	Reed	Burton	Jackson, R.
1946–48	*Vinson*	Black	Frankfurter	Rutledge, W.	Douglas	Murphy	Reed	Burton	Jackson, R.
1949–52	*Vinson*	Black	Frankfurter	Minton	Douglas	Clark	Reed	Burton	Jackson, R.
1953–54	*Warren*	Black	Frankfurter	Minton	Douglas	Clark	Reed	Burton	Jackson, R.
1955	*Warren*	Black	Frankfurter	Minton	Douglas	Clark	Reed	Burton	Harlan
1956	*Warren*	Black	Frankfurter	Brennan	Douglas	Clark	Reed	Burton	Harlan
1957	*Warren*	Black	Frankfurter	Brennan	Douglas	Clark	Whittaker	Burton	Harlan
1958–61	*Warren*	Black	Frankfurter	Brennan	Douglas	Clark	Whittaker	Stewart	Harlan
1962–65	*Warren*	Black	Goldberg	Brennan	Douglas	Clark	White, B.	Stewart	Harlan
1965–67	*Warren*	Black	Fortas	Brennan	Douglas	Clark	White, B.	Stewart	Harlan
1967–69	*Warren*	Black	Fortas	Brennan	Douglas	Marshall, T.	White, B.	Stewart	Harlan
1969	*Burger*	Black	Fortas	Brennan	Douglas	Marshall, T.	White, B.	Stewart	Harlan
1969–70	*Burger*	Black	(vacant)	Brennan	Douglas	Marshall, T.	White, B.	Stewart	Harlan
1970–71	*Burger*	Black	Blackmun	Brennan	Douglas	Marshall, T.	White, B.	Stewart	Harlan
1972–75	*Burger*	Powell	Blackmun	Brennan	Douglas	Marshall, T.	White, B.	Stewart	Rehnquist

Years of Court as Constituted	Chief Justice	Associate Justices							
1975–81	*Burger*	Powell	Blackmun	Brennan	Stevens	Marshall, T.	White, B.	Stewart	Rehnquist
1981–86	*Burger*	Powell	Blackmun	Brennan	Stevens	Marshall, T.	White, B.	O'Connor	Rehnquist
1986–87	*Rehnquist*	Powell	Blackmun	Brennan	Stevens	Marshall, T.	White, B.	O'Connor	Scalia
1987–90	*Rehnquist*	Kennedy	Blackmun	Brennan	Stevens	Marshall, T.	White, B.	O'Connor	Scalia
1990–91	*Rehnquist*	Kennedy	Blackmun	Souter	Stevens	Marshall, T.	White, B	O'Connor	Scalia
1991–	*Rehnquist*	Kennedy	Blackmun	Souter	Stevens	Thomas	White, B.	O'Connor	Scalia

SUPREME COURT JUSTICES
By Appointing President, State Appointed from, and Political Party

Justice	State Appointed from	Political Party
Washington		
John Jay (1745–1829)*	N.Y.	Federalist
John Rutledge (1739–1800)	S.C.	Federalist
William Cushing (1732–1810)	Mass.	Federalist
James Wilson (1724–1798)	Pa.	Federalist
John Blair (1732–1800)	Va.	Federalist
James Iredell (1751–1799)	N.C.	Federalist
Thomas Johnson (1732–1819)	Md.	Federalist
William Paterson (1745–1806)	N.J.	Federalist
Samuel Chase (1741–1811)	Md.	Federalist
Oliver Ellsworth (1745–1807)	Conn.	Federalist
Adams, J.		
Bushrod Washington (1762–1829)	Va.	Federalist
Alfred Moore (1755–1810)	N.C.	Federalist
John Marshall (1755–1835)	Va.	Federalist
Jefferson		
William Johnson (1771–1834)	S.C.	Democratic–Republican
Henry Livingston (1757–1823)	N.Y.	Democratic–Republican
Thomas Todd (1765–1826)	Va.	Democratic–Republican
Madison		
Gabriel Duvall (1752–1844)	Md.	Democratic–Republican
Joseph Story (1779–1845)	Mass.	Democratic–Republican
Monroe		
Smith Thompson (1768–1843)	N.Y.	Democratic–Republican
Adams, J. Q.		
Robert Trimble (1776–1828)	Ky.	Democratic–Republican

*Dates in parentheses indicate birth and death dates.

Justice	State Appointed from	Political Party
Jackson		
John McLean (1785–1861)	Ohio	Democrat (later Rep.)
Henry Baldwin (1780–1844)	Penn.	Democrat
James M. Wayne (1790–1867)	Ga.	Democrat
Roger B. Taney (1777–1864)	Va.	Democrat
Philip P. Barbour (1783–1841)	Va.	Democrat
Van Buren		
John Catron (1778–1865)	Tenn.	Democrat
John McKinley (1780–1852)	Ala.	Democrat
Peter V. Daniel (1784–1860)	Va.	Democrat
Tyler		
Samuel Nelson (1792–1873)	N.Y.	Democrat
Polk		
Levi Woodbury (1789–1851)	N.H.	Democrat
Robert C. Grier (1794–1870)	Pa.	Democrat
Fillmore		
Benjamin R. Curtis (1809–1874)	Mass.	Whig
Pierce		
John A. Campbell (1811–1889)	Ala.	Democrat
Buchanan		
Nathan Clifford (1803–1881)	Maine	Democrat
Lincoln		
Noah H. Swayne (1804–1884)	Ohio	Republican
Samuel F. Miller (1816–1890)	Iowa	Republican
David Davis (1815–1886)	Ill.	Republican (later Dem.)
Stephen J. Field (1816–1899)	Calif.	Democrat
Salmon P. Chase (1808–1873)	Ohio	Republican
Grant		
William Strong (1808–1895)	Pa.	Republican
Joseph P. Bradley (1813–1892)	N.J.	Republican
Ward Hunt (1810–1886)	N.Y.	Republican
Morrison Waite (1816–1888)	Ohio	Republican
Hayes		
John M. Harlan (1833–1911)	Ky.	Republican
William B. Woods (1824–1887)	Ga.	Republican
Garfield		
Stanley Matthews (1824–1889)	Ohio	Republican
Arthur		
Horace Gray (1828–1902)	Mass.	Republican
Samuel Blatchford (1820–1893)	N.Y.	Republican

Justice	State Appointed from	Political Party
Cleveland		
Lucius Q. C. Lamar (1825–1893)	Miss.	Democrat
Melville W. Fuller (1833–1910)	Ill.	Democrat
Harrison		
David J. Brewer (1837–1910)	Kans.	Republican
Henry B. Brown (1836–1913)	Mich.	Republican
George Shiras, Jr. (1832–1924)	Pa.	Republican
Howell E. Jackson (1832–1895)	Tenn.	Democrat
Cleveland		
Edward D. White (1845–1921)	La.	Democrat
Rufus W. Peckham (1838–1909)	N.Y.	Democrat
McKinley		
Joseph McKenna (1843–1926)	Calif.	Republican
Roosevelt, T.		
Oliver W. Holmes (1841–1935)	Mass.	Republican
William R. Day (1849–1923)	Ohio	Republican
William H. Moody (1853–1917)	Mass.	Republican
Taft		
Horace H. Lurton (1844–1914)	Tenn.	Democrat
Charles E. Hughes (1862–1948)	N.Y.	Republican
Willis Van Devanter (1859–1941)	Wyo.	Republican
Joseph R. Lamar (1857–1916)	Ga.	Democrat
Mahlon Pitney (1858–1924)	N.J.	Republican
Wilson		
James C. McReynolds (1862–1946)	Tenn.	Democrat
Louis D. Brandeis (1856–1941)	Mass.	Independent
John H. Clarke (1857–1945)	Ohio	Democrat
Harding		
William H. Taft (1857–1930)	Conn.	Republican
George Sutherland (1862–1942)	Utah	Republican
Pierce Butler (1866–1939)	Minn.	Democrat
Edward T. Sanford (1865–1930)	Tenn.	Republican
Coolidge		
Harlan F. Stone (1872–1946)	N.Y.	Republican
Hoover		
Owen J. Roberts (1875–1955)	Pa.	Republican
Benjamin N. Cardozo (1870–1938)	N.Y.	Democrat
Roosevelt, F. D.		
Hugo L. Black (1886–1971)	Ala.	Democrat
Stanley F. Reed (1884–1980)	Ky.	Democrat

Justice	State Appointed from	Political Party
Felix Frankfurter (1882–1965)	Mass.	Independent
William O. Douglas (1898–1980)	Conn.	Democrat
Frank Murphy (1890–1949)	Mich.	Democrat
James F. Byrnes (1879–1972)	S.C.	Democrat
Robert H. Jackson (1892–1954)	N.Y.	Democrat
Wiley B. Rutledge (1894–1949)	Iowa	Democrat
Truman		
Harold H. Burton (1888–1964)	Ohio	Republican
Fred M. Vinson (1890–1953)	Ky.	Democrat
Tom C. Clark (1899–1977)	Texas	Democrat
Sherman Minton (1890–1965)	Ind.	Democrat
Eisenhower		
Earl Warren (1891–1974)	Calif.	Republican
John M. Harlan (1899–1971)	N.Y.	Republican
William J. Brennan (b.1906)	N.J.	Democrat
Charles E. Whittaker (1901–1973)	Mo.	Republican
Potter Stewart (1915–1986)	Ohio	Republican
Kennedy		
Byron R. White (b.1917)	Colo.	Democrat
Arthur J. Goldberg (b.1908)	Ill.	Democrat
Johnson		
Abe Fortas (1910–1982)	Tenn.	Democrat
Thurgood Marshall (b.1908)	N.Y.	Democrat
Nixon		
Warren E. Burger (b.1907)	Minn.	Republican
Harry R. Blackmun (b.1908)	Minn.	Republican
Lewis F. Powell, Jr. (b.1907)	Va.	Democrat
William H. Rehnquist (b.1924)	Ariz.	Republican
Ford		
John Paul Stevens (b.1920)	Ill.	Republican
Reagan		
Sandra Day O'Connor (b.1930)	Ariz.	Republican
Antonin Scalia (b.1936)	N.J.	Republican
Anthony M. Kennedy (b.1936)	Calif.	Republican
Bush		
David Souter (b.1939)	N.H.	Republican
Clarence Thomas (b.1948)	Va.	Republican

APPENDIX D

GLOSSARY OF LEGAL TERMS

abate To do away with or lessen the impact of, as in abatement of a nuisance.

abstention The doctrine under which the U.S. Supreme Court and other federal courts do not decide on, or interfere with, state cases even when empowered to do so. This doctrine is typically invoked when a case can be decided on the basis of state law.

accessory One who aids in the commission of a crime.

accusatorial system A system of criminal justice in which the prosecution bears the burden of proving the defendant's guilt.

acquittal A judicial finding that a defendant is not guilty of a crime with which he or she has been charged.

actual malice The deliberate intention to cause harm or injury.

ad hoc "For this." For a special purpose.

ad hoc balancing An effort by a court to balance competing interests in the context of the unique facts of a given case. In constitutional law, this term is used most frequently in connection with the adjudication of First Amendment issues.

adjudication The process of judging wherein a court determines the issues and pronounces judgment in a case.

ad litem For the lawsuit; pending the lawsuit, as in "guardian *ad litem.*"

administrative law The body of law dealing with the structure, authority, policies, and procedures of administrative and regulatory agencies.

ad valorem "According to the value." Referring to a tax or duty guaranteed according to the assessed value of the matter taxed.

adversary proceeding A legal action involving parties with adverse or opposing interests. A basic aspect of the American legal system, the adversary proceeding provides the framework within which most constitutional cases are decided. For an exception to this generalization, see *ex parte.*

advisory opinion A judicial opinion, not involving adverse parties in a "case or controversy," that is given at the request of the legislature or the executive. It has been a long-standing policy of the U.S. Supreme Court not to render advisory opinions.

affiant One who makes an affidavit.

affidavit A person's voluntary sworn declaration attesting to a set of facts.

affirm To uphold, confirm, or ratify the decision of a lower court.

affirmative action A program under which women and/or persons of particular minority groups are granted special consideration in employment, government contracts, and/or admission to programs of higher education.

a fortiori With greater force of reason.

aggravating factor   A fact attending the commission of a crime that makes the crime more reprehensible and thus justifies increased punishment.

allegation   A charge, claim, or complaint.

amici   "Friends," usually in reference to "friends of the Court." See *amicus curiae.*

amicus curiae   "Friend of the court." An individual or organization allowed to take part in a judicial proceeding, not as one of the adversaries, but as a party interested in the outcome. Usually an *amicus curiae* files a brief in support of one side or the other but occasionally takes a more active part in the argument of the case.

amnesty   A blanket pardon issued to a large group of lawbreakers.

appeal   A distinct stage in a continuing judicial proceeding in which the losing party requests a higher court to review the record and decision of a lower court.

appeal by right   An appeal brought to a higher court as a matter of right under federal or state law.

appellant   The losing party in a judicial action who appeals to a higher court.

appellate courts   Higher courts that review the decisions of lower courts.

appellate jurisdiction   The legal authority of a court of law to hear an appeal from or otherwise review a decision by a lower court.

appellee   The party against whom a case is appealed to a higher court.

apportionment   The allocation of representatives among a set of legislative districts.

arguendo   For the sake of argument.

arraignment   The process of bringing an accused person before a trial court for the purpose of entering a plea to criminal charges.

arrest   To take someone into custody or otherwise deprive that person of his or her freedom of movement.

arrest warrant   A court order authorizing police to take a specified individual into custody.

Articles of Confederation   The constitution under which the United States was governed between 1781 and 1789.

assign   To transfer or grant a legal right.

assignee   One to whom a legal right is transferred.

at bar   Before the court, as in "the case at bar."

at-large election   An election in which a number of officials are chosen to represent the district, as opposed to an arrangement under which each of the officials represents one smaller district or ward.

bad tendency test   A restrictive interpretation of the First Amendment under which government may prohibit expression having a tendency to cause people to break the law.

bail   The conditional release from custody of a person charged with a crime pending adjudication of the case.

bench trial   A trial before a judge rather than a jury.

bicameralism   The characteristic of having two houses or chambers. The U.S. Congress is a bicameral body in that it has a Senate and a House of Representatives.

bifurcated trial   A capital trial with separate phases for determining guilt and punishment.

bill of attainder   A legislative act imposing punishment on a party without the benefit of a judicial proceeding.

Bill of Rights   The first ten amendments to the U.S. Constitution, ratified in 1791, concerned primarily with individual rights and liberties.

bloc   A group of decision makers in a collegial body who usually vote the same way. In judicial politics, the term refers to groups of judges or justices on appellate courts who usually vote together.

bona fide   "In good faith." Acting without the attempt to defraud or deceive.

brief   In judicial decision making, a document submitted by counsel setting forth legal arguments germane to a particular case; in the study of constitutional law, a summary of a given case, reviewing the essential facts, issues, holding and reasoning of the court.

burden of proof   The requirement of introducing evidence to prove an allegation.

bureaucracy   Any large, complex, hierarchical organization staffed by appointed officials.

Cabinet   The collective term for the heads of the executive departments of the federal government, such as the secretary of state, the attorney general, and the secretary of defense.

capital offense   A crime punishable by death.

case   A legal dispute between adverse parties to be resolved by a court of law.

case law   Law made by courts through specific decisions, as distinguished from statutes and other sources of law.

case or controversy requirement   Article III of the U.S. Constitution extends the federal judicial power to actual cases or controversies, not to hypothetical or abstract questions of law.

case reporter   A series of books reprinting the decisions of a given court or set of courts. For example, the decisions of the U.S. Courts of Appeals are reported in the *Federal Reporter*, published by West Publishing Company.

cause   A synonym for **case.** See also **show cause, probable cause.**

censorship   Broadly defined, any restriction imposed by the government on speech, publication, or other form of expression.

certification   A procedure under which a lower court requests a decision by a higher court on specified questions in a case, pending a final decision by the lower court.

certiorari   "To be informed." A petition similar to an appeal, but it may be granted or refused at the discretion of the appellate court.

certiorari, **writ of**   An order from a higher court to a lower court directing that the record of a particular case be sent up for review. See also **certiorari.**

challenge for cause   An objection to a prospective juror on some specified ground.

checks and balances   Refers to constitutional powers granted each branch of government to prevent one branch from dominating the others.

civil action   A judicial proceeding, outside the criminal law, by which a party seeks to enforce rights or to obtain redress for wrongs.

civil case   See **civil action.**

civil liberties   The freedoms protected by the Constitution and statutes, for example, freedom of speech, religion, and assembly.

civil rights   Legal protection against invidious discrimination in citizens' exercise of the rights of life, liberty, and property. The right to equality before the law and equal treatment by government.

civil service   The system under which government employees are selected and retained based on merit, rather than political patronage.

class action   A lawsuit brought by one or more parties on behalf of themselves and others similarly situated.

clear and present danger doctrine   The doctrine that the First Amendment protects expression up to the point that it poses a clear and present danger of bringing about some substantive evil that government has a right to prevent.

clear and probable danger test   A somewhat more restrictive First Amendment test than clear and present danger. The test is "whether the gravity of the 'evil,' discounted by its improbability, justifies such invasion of speech as is necessary to avoid the danger."

clemency   A grant of mercy by an executive official pardoning a criminal or commuting his or her sentence.

code   A systematic collection of laws.

collateral attack   The attempt to defeat the outcome of a judicial proceeding by challenging it in another court.

collateral estoppel   Being barred from making a claim in one judicial proceeding that has been adjudicated in another, earlier proceeding.

comity   Courtesy, respect, civility. A matter of good will and tradition, rather than of right. Particularly important in a federal system where one jurisdiction is bound to respect the judgments of another.

commander in chief   Refers to the president's authority to command the armed forces of the country.

common law   A body of law that develops primarily through judicial decisions, rather than legislative enactments. The common law is not a fixed system but an ever-changing body of rules and principles articulated by judges and applied to changing needs and circumstances. See also **English common law.**

comparative proportionality review   A judicial examination to determine whether the sentence imposed in a given criminal case is proportionate to sentences imposed in similar cases.

compelling interest   An interest or justification of the highest order.

compulsory process   The requirement that witnesses appear and testify in court or before a legislative committee. See also **subpoena.**

compulsory self-incrimination   The requirement that an individual give testimony leading to his or her own criminal conviction. Forbidden by the U.S. Constitution, Amendment V.

concurrent jurisdiction   Jurisdiction that is shared by different courts of law.

concurrent powers   Powers exercised jointly by the state and federal governments.

concurrent resolution   An act expressing the will of both houses of the legislature but lacking a mechanism through which to enforce that will on parties outside the legislature.

concurring opinion   An opinion by a judge or justice agreeing with the decision of the court. A concurring opinion may or may not agree with the rationale adopted by the court in reaching its decision (See **opinion of the Court**).

conference   As applied to the appellate courts, a private meeting of judges to decide a case or to determine whether to grant review in a case.

confidential informant   An informant known to the police but whose identity is held in confidence.

consent   Voluntarily yielding to the will or desire of another person.

consent decree   A court-enforced agreement reached by mutual consent of parties in a civil case or administrative proceeding.

conspiracy   The crime of two or more persons planning to commit a specific criminal act.

constitutional case   A judicial proceeding involving an issue of constitutional law.

constitutional law   The fundamental and supreme law of the land defining the structure and powers of government and the rights of individuals vis-à-vis government.

contempt   An action that embarrasses, hinders, obstructs, or is calculated to lessen the dignity of a judicial or legislative body.

continuance   The postponement of a trial or hearing.

contraband   Any property that is inherently illegal to produce or possess.

cooperative federalism   A modern approach to American federalism in which powers and functions are shared among national, state, and local authorities.

corporal punishment   Punishment that inflicts pain or injury on a person's body.

court martial   A military court.

court of general jurisdiction   A trial court with broad authority to hear and decide a wide range of civil and criminal cases.

court of limited jurisdiction   A trial court with narrow authority to hear and decide cases, typically misdemeanors and/or small claims.

court system   A set of trial and appellate courts established to resolve legal disputes in a particular jurisdiction.

criminal action   A judicial proceeding initiated by government against a person charged with the commission of a crime.

criminal case   A judicial proceeding in which a person is accused of a crime.

criminal conspiracy   See **conspiracy.**

criminal law   The law defining crimes and punishments.

criminal syndicalism   The former crime of advocating political or economic change to be accomplished through revolution, sabotage, terrorism, or other violent means.

damages   A sum of money awarded in a civil suit as compensation for loss or injury or, in the case of punitive damages, as a penalty for wrongful conduct.

death-qualified jury A trial jury composed of persons who do not entertain scruples against imposing the death penalty.

decision on the merits A judicial decision that reaches the subject matter of a case.

declaratory judgment A judicial ruling conclusively declaring the rights, duties, or status of the parties but imposing no additional order, restriction, or requirement on them.

de facto In fact; as a matter of fact.

defamation A tort involving the injury to one's reputation by the malicious or reckless dissemination of a falsehood.

defendant A person charged with a crime or against whom a civil action is brought.

de jure In law; as a matter of law.

delegation of legislative power A legislative act authorizing an administrative or regulatory agency to promulgate rules and regulations having the force of law.

de minimis Minimal, trifling, trivial.

demurrer An action of a defendant admitting to a set of alleged facts but nevertheless challenging the legal sufficiency of a complaint or criminal charge.

de novo Anew; for a second time.

deposition The oral testimony of a witness taken out of court and committed to writing.

deterrence The prevention of criminal activity by punishing criminals so that others will refrain from committing similar crimes.

dicta See **obiter dicta.**

dismissal A judicial order terminating a case, putting it out of court.

dissent An appellate judge's formal vote against the judgment of the court in a given case.

dissenting opinion An opinion by a judge or justice setting forth reasons for disagreeing with a particular decision of the court.

distributive articles Articles I, II, and III of the U.S. Constitution, delineating the powers and functions of the legislative, executive, and judicial branches, respectively, of the national government.

diversity jurisdiction The authority of a federal court to entertain a civil suit in which the parties are citizens of different states and the amount in controversy exceeds fifty thousand dollars.

diversity of citizenship action A federal civil suit in which the parties are citizens of different states and the amount in controversy exceeds fifty thousand dollars.

docket The list of cases pending before a court of law.

doctrine A legal principle or rule developed through judicial decisions.

domicile A person's permanent and established home.

double jeopardy The condition of being prosecuted a second time for the same offense.

drug courier profile A controversial law enforcement practice of identifying possible drug smugglers by relying on a set of characteristics and patterns of behavior believed to typify persons who smuggle drugs.

dual federalism A concept of federalism in which the national and state governments exercise authority within separate, self-contained areas of public policy and public administration.

due process of law Legal protection against arbitrary, capricious, or unreasonable government action depriving persons of life, liberty, or property.

duty A person's legal obligation, either to another person or to the community. If one person has a right to something, another person has a duty to avoid interfering with that right.

easement A right of use over the property of another. This term frequently refers to a right-of-way across privately owned land.

Electoral College The body of electors chosen by the voters of each state and the District of Columbia for the purpose of formally electing the president and vice-president of the United States. The number of electors (538) is equivalent to the total number of representatives and senators to which each state is entitled, plus three electors from the District of Columbia.

emergency search A warrantless search performed during an emergency, such as a fire or potential explosion.

eminent domain The power of government, or of individuals and corporations authorized to perform public functions, to take private property for public use.

enabling legislation As applied to public law, a statute authorizing the creation of a government program or agency and defining the functions and powers thereof.

en banc "In the bench." Refers to a hearing or decision by the entire membership of a court, rather than a panel thereof.

English common law A system of legal rules and principles recognized and developed by English judges prior to the colonization of America and accepted as a basic aspect of the American legal system.

enumerated powers Powers specified in the text of the federal and state constitutions.

equity Historically, a system of rules, remedies, customs, and principles developed in England to supplement the harsh common law by emphasizing the concept of fairness. In addition, because the common law served only to recompense after injury, equity was devised to prevent injuries that could not be repaired or recompensed after the fact. While American judges continue to distinguish between law and equity, these systems of rights and remedies are, for the most part, administered by the same courts.

error correction Refers to the function of appellate courts in correcting more or less routine errors committed by lower courts.

error, writ of An order issued by an appellate court for the purpose of correcting an error revealed in the record of a lower-court proceeding.

establishment of religion Official government support of religion or religious institutions. Prohibited by the First Amendment. See also **separation of church and state.**

et al. "And others."

evanescent evidence Evidence that will likely disappear if not immediately seized.

evidentiary hearing A hearing on the admissibility of evidence into a civil or criminal trial.

exclusionary rule A rule barring the use of illegally obtained evidence in a criminal prosecution.

executive agreement An agreement between the United States and one or more foreign countries entered into by the president without ratification by the Senate.

executive order An order by a president or governor directing some particular action to be taken.

executive privilege The right of the president to withhold certain information from Congress or a court of law.

exhaustion of remedies The requirement that a party seeking review by a court first exhaust all legal options for resolution of the issue by nonjudicial authorities or lower courts.

exigent circumstances Situations that demand unusual or immediate action.

ex officio By virtue of the office.

ex parte "On or from one side only." An application to a court made by one party without giving notice to the adverse party. In American constitutional law this term often appears in connection with a habeas corpus proceeding.

ex post facto law A law criminalizing or punishing conduct that was innocent at the time it occurred.

ex proprio vigore By its own force.

ex rel. "On the relation or information of." Usually designating the name of a person on whose behalf the government is bringing legal action against another party.

extradition The surrender of a person by one state or country at the request of another for trial or punishment on criminal charges, either before or after conviction.

ex vi termini By definition; from the very meaning of the term or expression used.

facial attack A legal attack on the constitutionality of a law as it is written, as opposed to how it is applied in practice.

facial neutrality   A law that on its face does not discriminate between or among classes of persons.

facial validity   A law that is valid on its face. Such a law may nevertheless be invalid as applied in a given case.

federal courts   The courts operated by the U.S. government.

federalism   The constitutional division of authority and responsibility between the national government and the states.

federal question   An issue arising under the U.S. Constitution or a federal statute, executive order, regulation, or treaty.

federal question jurisdiction   The authority of federal courts to decide issues of national law.

Federal Register   The publication containing all regulations proposed and promulgated by federal agencies.

fee simple   Ownership of real property; the highest interest in real estate the law will permit.

felony   A serious crime for which a person may be incarcerated for more than one year.

felony murder   A homicide committed during the commission of another felony, such as armed robbery.

fighting words   Utterances inherently likely to provoke violence from the average person to whom they are addressed.

free exercise of religion   The constitutional right to be free from government coercion or restraint with respect to religious beliefs and practices. Guaranteed by the First Amendment.

fruit of the poisonous tree doctrine   The doctrine that evidence derived from illegally obtained and thus inadmissible evidence is tainted and therefore likewise inadmissible.

full faith and credit   The constitutional requirement (Article IV, Section 1) that states recognize and give effect to the records and legal proceedings of other states.

full opinion decision   An appellate judicial decision rendered with one or more written opinions expressing the views of the judges in the case.

fundamental error   In a judicial proceeding, an error of such gravity as to require the outcome of the proceeding to be reversed by a higher court.

fundamental rights   Those rights, whether or not explicitly stated in the Constitution, deemed to be basic and essential to a person's liberty and dignity.

gag order   An order by a judge prohibiting certain parties from speaking publicly or privately about a particular case.

gerrymandering   The intentional manipulation of legislative districts for political purposes.

good faith exception   The doctrine holding that if police officers acting in reasonable good faith obtain a warrant that is later declared invalid, the fruits of a search based on the warrant are exempted from the Fourth Amendment exclusionary rule.

grandfather clause   In its modern, general sense, any legal provision protecting someone from losing a right or benefit as a result of a change in policy. In its historic sense, a legal provision limiting the right to vote to persons whose ancestors held the right to vote prior to passage of the Fifteenth Amendment in 1870.

grand jury   A group of twelve to twenty-three citizens convened to hear evidence in criminal cases to determine whether indictment is warranted.

habeas corpus, writ of   A judicial order issued to an official holding someone in custody, requiring the official to bring the prisoner to court for the purpose of allowing the court to determine whether that person is being held legally.

habitual offender statute   A law that imposes an additional punishment on a criminal who has been convicted of previous felonies.

harmless error   A procedural or substantive error that does not affect the outcome of a judicial proceeding.

hearing   A public proceeding in a court of law, legislature, or administrative body for the purpose of ascertaining facts and deciding matters of law or policy.

heightened scrutiny   The requirement that government justify a challenged policy by showing that it is substantially necessary to the achievement of an important objective.

high crimes and misdemeanors   Offenses for which an official of the federal government may be impeached and removed from office by Congress.

holding   The specific legal principle drawn from a judicial decision.

hot pursuit   The right of police to cross jurisdictional lines to apprehend a fleeing suspect; also refers to Fourth Amendment doctrine allowing police to make warrantless searches and seizures where police pursue a fleeing suspect into a protected area.

hypothetical question   A question based on an invented or assumed set of facts.

imminent lawless action   The First Amendment doctrine under which advocacy of lawlessness is protected up to that point where lawless action is imminent.

immunity   Exemption from civil suit or criminal prosecution.

impeachment   A legislative act bringing a charge against a public official that, if proven, will result in the official's removal from office; in criminal procedure, impugning the credibility of a witness by introducing contradictory evidence or proving his or her bad character.

implied powers, doctrine of   A basic doctrine of American constitutional law derived from the Necessary and Proper Clause of Article I, Section 8. Under this doctrine, Congress is not limited to exercising those powers specifically enumerated in Article I but rather may exercise powers reasonably related to the fulfillment of its broad constitutional powers and responsibilities.

impoundment   Action by a president in refusing to allow expenditures approved by Congress.

in camera   "In a chamber." In private. Refers to a judicial proceeding or conference from which the public is excluded.

incite   To provoke or set in motion.

inciting a riot   The crime of instigating or provoking a riot.

incorporation, doctrine of   The doctrine under which most provisions of the Bill of Rights have been extended to limit state action by way of the Due Process Clause of the Fourteenth Amendment. Specific protections of the Bill of Rights are said to be incorporated within the Fourteenth Amendment's broad restrictions on the states.

independent state grounds   The doctrine that an individual's claim to a right or benefit not supported by federal law will nevertheless be recognized by a federal court if a state court has found that the claimed right or benefit rests on a valid provision of state law.

indictment   A formal criminal charge handed down by a grand jury.

indigency   Poverty; inability to afford legal representation.

in forma pauperis   "In the manner of a pauper."

information   A legal document filed by a prosecutor bringing criminal charges against a named party.

infra   Below.

inherent power   The power existing in an agency, institution, or individual by definition of the office.

inherently suspect   A law, policy, or classification that is, from a constitutional standpoint, questionable on its face.

injunction   A judicial order requiring a person to do, or to refrain from doing, a designated thing.

in loco parentis   "In the place of the parent(s)."

in personam   Refers to legal actions brought against a person, as distinct from actions against property (see **in rem**).

in propria persona   "In one's proper person." Referring to the proper person to bring a legal action or make a motion before a court of law.

in re   "In the matter of."

in rem   Refers to legal actions brought against things rather than persons.

inter alia   "Among other things."

intermediate appellate courts   Appellate courts positioned below the supreme or highest appellate court. Their primary function is to decide routine appeals not deserving review by the Supreme Court.

intermediate scrutiny See **heightened scrutiny.**

interposition The archaic doctrine holding that when the federal government attempts to act unlawfully on an object within the domain of the state governments, a state may interpose itself between the federal government and the object of the federal government's action.

interpretivism The theory of constitutional interpretation holding that judges should confine themselves to the plain meaning of the text, the intentions of the Framers, and/or the historical meaning of the document.

interrogatories Written questions put to a witness prior to trial of a civil or criminal case.

interstate commerce Commercial activity between or among states.

interstate compacts Agreements between or among state governments, somewhat analogous to treaties.

invalidate To deprive of legal force or efficacy.

invasion of privacy A tort involving the unreasonable or unwarranted intrusion on the privacy of an individual.

investigatory detention The brief detention and questioning of a person based on reasonable suspicion that criminal activity is afoot.

invidious Arousing animosity, envy, or resentment.

ipse dixit "He himself said it." An assertion resting on the authority of an individual.

ipso facto "By the mere fact."

irreparable injury An injury for which the award of money may not be adequate compensation and that may require the issuance of an injunction to fulfill the requirements of justice.

item veto The power of the chief executive to veto one or more parts of a bill without rejecting the bill in its entirety.

joint resolution An act expressing the will of both houses of Congress in attempting to impose duties or limitations on parties outside the Congress. Joint resolutions must be presented to the president for signature or veto.

judgment A judicial determination of the rights and claims of the parties in a lawsuit. In a criminal case, the court's formal declaration to the accused regarding the legal consequences of a determination of guilt.

judicial activism Defined variously, but the underlying philosophy is that judges should exercise power vigorously. See also **judicial restraint.**

judicial federalism The constitutional relationship between federal and state courts of law.

judicial notice The doctrine under which courts may accept as fact matters of common knowledge without requiring that such facts be subjected to formal proof.

judicial restraint Defined variously, but the underlying philosophy is that judges should exercise power cautiously and show deference to precedent to the decisions of other branches of government. See also **judicial activism.**

judicial review Generally, the review of any issue by a court of law. In American constitutional law, judicial review refers to the authority of a court to invalidate acts of government on constitutional grounds.

jurisdiction "To speak the law." The geographical area within which, the subject matter with respect to which, and the persons over whom a court can properly exercise its power.

juris privati "The private law," including such areas as torts, contracts, and property.

jurist One who is skilled or well-versed in the law.

just compensation The constitutional requirement that a party whose property is taken by government under the power of eminent domain be justly compensated for the loss.

justiciability The quality of appropriateness for judicial decision. A justiciable dispute is one that can be effectively decided by a court of law.

juvenile One who is below the age of legal majority.

laissez-faire   The theory holding that a capitalist economy functions best when government refrains from interfering with the marketplace.

law clerk   A judge's staff attorney.

legislative veto   A statutory provision under which a legislative body is permitted to overrule a decision of an executive agency.

liability   A broad legal term connoting debt, responsibility, or obligation. The condition of being bound to pay a debt, obligation, or judgment. This responsibility can be either civil or criminal.

libel   The tort of defamation through published material. See **defamation.**

libertarianism   A philosophy that stresses individual freedom as the highest good.

liberty of contract   The freedom to enter into contracts without undue interference from government.

limiting doctrines   Doctrines by which courts may refuse to render a decision on the merits in a case. See **abstention, exhaustion of remedies, political questions doctrine, mootness, standing.**

line-item veto   See **item veto.**

literacy test   A test of reading and/or writing skills, often given as a prerequisite to employment. At one time, literacy tests were required by many states as preconditions for voting in elections.

litigant   A party to, or participant in, a legal action.

magistrate   A judicial officer authorized to handle minor matters, such as misdemeanors.

Magna Charta   The "Great Charter" signed by King John in 1215 guaranteeing the legal rights of English subjects. Generally considered the foundation of Anglo-American constitutionalism.

majority opinion   An opinion joined by a majority of judges or justices on a collegial court.

malfeasance   Misconduct that adversely affects the performance of official duties.

mandamus, writ of   "We command." A judicial order commanding a public official or an organization to perform a specified duty.

memorandum decision   A judicial decision rendered without a supporting opinion of the court.

mens rea   Guilty mind, criminal intent.

militia   Historically, a military force composed of all able-bodied citizens, in service only during time of war, rebellion, or emergency.

miscarriage of justice   A decision of a court that is inconsistent with the substantial rights of a party to the case.

misdemeanor   A minor crime usually punishable by a fine or confinement for less than one year.

mistrial   A trial that is terminated due to misconduct, procedural error, or a "hung jury" (one that is unable to reach a verdict).

mitigating circumstances   Facts that tend to diminish the degree of seriousness of a crime.

mootness   Refers to a question that does not involve rights currently at issue in, or pertinent to, the outcome of a case.

motion   An application to a court to obtain a particular ruling or order.

narrowness doctrine   The doctrine that judicial decisions should be framed in the narrowest possible terms or based on the narrowest possible grounds.

natural law   Principles of human conduct believed to be ordained by God or nature, existing prior to and superseding human law.

natural rights   Rights believed to be inherent in human beings, the existence of which is not dependent on their recognition by government. In classical liberalism, natural rights are "life, liberty and property." As recognized by the Declaration of Independence, they are "life, liberty and the pursuit of happiness."

"new equal protection"   A modern interpretation of the Equal Protection Clause of the Fourteenth Amendment under which policies that impinge on fundamental rights or discriminate on the basis of suspect classifications are presumed invalid by the courts.

nolo contendere   "I do not contend it." A plea to a criminal charge whereby the defendant does not admit guilt but does not contest the validity of the charge.

noninterpretivism   A term referring to a variety of theories of constitutional interpretation the common property of which is the rejection of interpretivism. See **interpretivism.**

nullification   The act of rendering something invalid; the process by which something may be invalidated. Historically, a doctrine under which states claimed the right to nullify actions of the national government.

obiter dicta   "Something said in passing." Incidental statements in a judicial opinion that are not binding and are unnecessary to support the decision.

obscenity   Sexually oriented material that is patently offensive, appeals to a prurient interest in sex, and lacks serious scientific, artistic, or literary content.

obstruction of justice   The crime of impeding or preventing law enforcement or the administration of justice.

opinion   A written statement accompanying a judicial decision, authored by one or more judges, supporting or dissenting from that decision.

opinion of the court   An opinion announcing both the decision of the court and its supporting rationale. The opinion can either be a majority opinion or a unanimous opinion.

oral argument   A hearing before an appellate court in which counsel for the parties appear for the purpose of making statements and answering questions from the bench.

original intent, doctrine of   The doctrine holding that the Constitution should be interpreted and applied according to the intentions of its Framers, insofar as those intentions can be determined.

original jurisdiction   The authority to hear a case for the first time, usually to conduct a trial or hearing.

overbreadth doctrine   The First Amendment doctrine that holds that a law is invalid if it can be applied to punish people for engaging in constitutionally protected expression.

overrule   To supersede or overturn. In constitutional law, this term usually refers to the superseding of a previous judicial decision by a later decision. A decision may be overruled by the court

that originally rendered it or by a higher court in the same judicial system. In trial procedure, the term refers to a judge's denial of an objection made by counsel.

pardon   An act of executive clemency by which a convicted criminal is absolved of his or her guilt.

parens patriae   "Father of the country." A doctrine embracing the power of a government to take care of dependent children and legally incompetent persons or in some cases to function as general guardian of its people.

parole   The conditional early release from prison.

partisan gerrymandering   The intentional manipulation of legislative district lines in order to provide one political party a competitive advantage over another.

party   A person taking part in a legal transaction. This term includes plaintiffs and defendants in lawsuits but has a far broader legal connotation. In politics, an organization established for the principal purpose of recruiting and nominating candidates for public office.

patently offensive   Plainly or obviously offensive, disgusting.

penal   Containing or imposing a penalty.

penumbra   An implied right or power emanating from an enumerated right or power.

per curiam   "By the court." Refers to an opinion attributed to a court collectively, usually not identified with the name of any particular member of the court.

peremptory challenge   The right of counsel to challenge the suitability of a prospective juror without having to state the reason for regarding that person as unsuitable.

per se   In itself; inherently; taken alone.

petit jury   A trial jury in a civil or criminal case.

petition   A written request, usually addressed to a court, asking for a specified action. Sometimes the term indicates written requests in an *ex parte* proceeding, where there is no adverse party. In some jurisdictions, the term refers to the first pleading in a lawsuit.

petitioner   The party presenting a legal request to a court. In U.S. Supreme Court cases, this term usually refers to the party seeking review by way of a writ of certiorari.

plaintiff   The party initiating legal action; the complaining party.

plain view   The doctrine under which police who are lawfully in a given area may make a warrantless seizure of plainly visible contraband or other evidence of crime.

plea bargain   A judicially approved agreement reached between the prosecution and the defendant in a criminal case whereby the latter agrees to plead guilty in exchange for some concession by the former.

plenary   Full, complete. Often used with reference to the nature and extent of governmental powers enumerated in the federal Constitution.

pluralism   A social or political system in which diverse groups compete for status or power; the theory that the role of government is to serve as broker among competing interest groups.

plurality opinion   An opinion that states the judgment of the Court but that does not have the endorsement of a majority of justices.

pocket veto   The power of a chief executive to effectively veto legislation by not acting on a bill passed within ten days prior to adjournment of a legislative session.

police power   The government's authority to make and enforce laws designed to protect the public health, safety, morality, and general welfare. In American constitutional law, this term was originally applied to state power but has come to refer to broad governmental authority at all levels.

political question   Refers to a question that a court believes to be appropriate for decision by the legislative or the executive branch of government and thus improper for judicial decision making.

poll tax   A tax that must be paid before a person is permitted to vote in an election.

popular sovereignty   The idea that political authority is vested ultimately not in the rulers but in the people they rule.

precedent   A judicial decision on a point of law giving direction to or authority for later cases presenting the same legal problem, although involving different parties.

preemption   In constitutional law, the doctrine under which a field of public policy, previously open to action by the states, is brought by the U.S. Congress within the primary or exclusive control of the national government.

preferred freedoms doctrine   The doctrine that certain freedoms, in particular those protected by the First Amendment, occupy a preferred position in relation to other freedoms.

preliminary hearing   In a criminal case, a hearing held to determine the sufficiency of evidence to warrant a trial of the accused.

preliminary injunction   An injunction issued pending a trial on the merits of the case.

presentment   The requirement that legislation be sent to the chief executive for signature or veto; also, a synonym for **indictment.**

presumption of validity   The doctrine of constitutional law holding that laws are presumed to be constitutional with the burden of proof resting on the plaintiff to demonstrate otherwise.

pretrial detention   The holding of a defendant in custody prior to trial.

pretrial motion   Any of a variety of motions made by counsel prior to the inception of a trial.

pretrial release   The release of a defendant pending trial.

prima facie   At first glance; on the face of it. Referring to a point that will be considered true if uncontested or unrefuted.

prior restraint   An official act preventing publication of a particular work.

privilege   In general, an activity in which a person may engage without interference. The term is often used interchangeably with "right" in American constitutional law, as with reference to the Privileges and Immunities Clauses of Article IV and the Fourteenth Amendment of the U.S. Constitution.

probable cause Knowledge of specific facts providing reasonable grounds for believing that criminal activity is afoot.

probation The process under which one convicted of a crime is given a suspended sentence but placed under the supervision of the state.

procedural due process To ensure fundamental fairness, certain procedures that must be followed when government attempts to deprive a person of life, liberty, or property.

profanity Vulgar, coarse, or filthy language.

pro forma Merely for the sake of form.

prohibition, writ of An appellate court order preventing a lower court from exercising its jurisdiction in a particular case.

promissory estoppel The doctrine of contract law under which a promise that induces action on the part of the promisee may be legally enforceable.

proper forum The correct court or other institution in which to press a particular claim.

proportional representation An electoral system in which the percentage of votes received by a given political party entitles that party to the same percentage of seats in the legislature.

proportionate representation The idea that certain groups should be represented by ensuring that the legislature is composed according to the proportion of such groups in society.

proscribe To forbid, prohibit.

prurient interest An excessive or unnatural interest in sex.

public forum An area open to the public reserved for or suited to expressive activities protected by the First Amendment.

public law A general classification of law consisting of constitutional law, administrative law, criminal law, international law, and statutes dealing with the powers and responsibilities of government.

qua As; in the character or capacity of.

quash To annul, set aside, overthrow, suppress. The term is used with reference to action by a court.

rational basis test The test of the validity of a statute inquiring whether it is rationally related to a legitimate government objective.

reapportionment The redrawing of legislative district lines so as to remedy malapportionment.

reasonable doubt The doubt that a reasonable person could have with respect to the veracity of a given proposition after hearing the evidence.

reasonable expectation of privacy A person's reasonable expectation that his or her activities in a certain place are private; society's expectations with regard to whether activities in certain places are private.

reasonable suspicion A reasonable person's belief that criminal activity may be afoot.

recusal A decision of a judge to withdraw from a case, usually due to bias or personal interest in the outcome.

recuse To disqualify oneself from hearing a court case.

referendum An election in which voters decide a question of public policy.

regulation A legally binding rule or order prescribed by a controlling authority. The term is generally used with respect to the rules promulgated by administrative and regulatory agencies.

remand To send back, as from a higher court to a lower court for the latter to take specified action in a case or to follow proceedings designated by the higher court.

remedy The means through which a legal right is enforced or an injury is redressed.

rendition The act of one state in surrendering a fugitive to another state.

repeal A legislative act removing an existing law from the books.

reserved powers Powers reserved to the states or the people under the Tenth Amendment.

res judicata "A thing decided." A thing or matter decided by a judgment, connoting the firmness and finality of the judgment as it affects the parties to the lawsuit. *Res judicata* has the general effect of bringing litigation on a contested point to an end.

res nova   "New thing." A new issue or case.

resolution   A legislative act expressing the will of one or both houses of the legislature. Unlike a statute, a resolution has no enforcement clause. See also, **concurrent resolution; joint resolution.**

respondent   The party against whom a civil suit is filed or against whom an appeal is taken to a higher court.

restitution   The requirement that one party compensate another for an injury inflicted.

restrictive covenant   An agreement among property holders restricting the use of property or prohibiting the rental or sale of it to certain parties.

retribution   Something demanded in payment for a debt; in criminal law, the demand that a criminal pay his or her debt to society.

retroactive   Changing the legal status or character of past events or transactions.

reverse   To annul or set aside, as when an appellate court reverses the decision of a lower court.

review   An examination by an appellate court of a lower court's decision.

rider   An attachment of a small provision to a contract, document, or bill.

right   Anything to which a person has a just and valid claim.

ripeness   Readiness for review by a court of law. An issue is "ripe for review" in the Supreme Court when a case presents adverse parties who have exhausted all other avenues of appeal.

rule making   The power of a court or agency to promulgate rules; the process through which rules are promulgated.

Rule of Four   The requirement that at least four justices of the Supreme Court agree before the Court will grant certiorari in a given case.

rule of law   The idea that legitimate authority is based on principles of law, not on the desires of individual rulers.

rules of procedure   Rules promulgated by courts governing civil, criminal, and appellate procedure.

saving construction, doctrine of   The doctrine that, given two plausible interpretations of a statute, a court will adopt the interpretation that prevents the statute from being declared unconstitutional.

search warrant   A court order authorizing a search of a specified area for a specified purpose.

Section 1983 action   A federal lawsuit brought under 42 U.S. Code Section 1983 to redress violations of civil and/or constitutional rights.

sedition   The crime of inciting insurrection or attempting to overthrow the government.

selective incorporation   Doctrine under which selected provisions comprising most of the Bill of Rights are deemed applicable to the states by way of the Fourteenth Amendment.

sentencing guidelines   Rules governing the imposition of criminal sentences in comparable cases under which judges are directed to impose sentences within specified ranges.

separate but equal doctrine   A now defunct doctrine that permitted racial segregation as long as equal facilities or accommodations were provided.

separation of powers   The distribution of legislative, executive, and judicial functions among separate branches of government.

seriatim   Serially, individually.

severability, doctrine of   The doctrine under which courts will declare invalid only the offending provision of a statute and allow the other provisions to remain in effect.

severability clause   A clause found in a statute indicating that if any particular provision of the law is invalidated, the other provisions remain in effect.

show cause   A court order requiring a party to appear and present a legal justification for a particular act.

sine qua non   "Without which not." A necessary or indispensable condition or prerequisite.

slander   Defamation of character through the spoken word. See **defamation.**

small claims   Minor civil suits.

social contract   The theory that government is the product of agreement among rational individuals to subordinate themselves to collective authority in exchange for security of life, liberty, and property.

Social Darwinism   The theory that society improves through unrestricted competition and the "survival of the fittest."

sodomy   Oral or anal sex between persons, or sex between a person and an animal (the latter is often referred to as bestiality).

solicitation   The crime of offering someone money or other thing of value in order to persuade that person to commit a crime; an active effort on the part of an attorney or other professional to obtain business.

sovereign immunity   A common law doctrine under which the sovereign may be sued only with its consent.

special prosecutor   A prosecutor appointed specifically to investigate a particular episode and, if criminal activity is found, to prosecute those involved.

specific intent   The mental purpose to accomplish a certain prohibited act.

specific performance   A court-imposed requirement that a party perform obligations incurred under a contract.

standing   The legal requirement that a party must have sustained or be likely to sustain a direct, substantial injury or have a substantial stake in the outcome of a decision in order to bring suit to redress the injury or challenge the decision.

stare decisis   "To stand by decided matters." The principle that past decisions should stand as precedents for future decisions. This principle, which stands for the proposition that precedents are binding on later decisions, is said to be followed less rigorously in constitutional law than in other branches of the law.

state action, doctrine of   The doctrine that limits constitutional prohibitions to official government or government-sponsored action, as opposed to action that is merely private in character.

states' rights   The constitutional rights and powers reserved to state governments under the Tenth Amendment. Historically, the philosophy that states should be accorded broad latitude within the American federal system.

statute   A written law enacted by a legislature.

statutory construction   The official interpretation of a statute rendered by a court of law.

stay   To postpone, hold off, or stop the execution of a judgment.

stop and frisk   An investigatory detention in which a suspect is subjected to a "pat-down" search for weapons.

strict judicial scrutiny   The judicial review of a challenged policy in which a court presumes the policy to be invalid and requires the government to show a compelling interest to justify the policy.

strict necessity, doctrine of   The doctrine that a court should consider a constitutional question only when strictly necessary to resolve the case at bar.

sua sponte   "Of its own will." Voluntarily, without coercion or suggestion.

subpoena   "Under penalty." A judicial order requiring a person to appear in court in connection with a designated proceeding.

subpoena duces tecum   "Under penalty you shall bring with you." A judicial order requiring a party to bring certain described records, papers, books, or documents to court.

substantive due process   The doctrine that legislation must be fair, reasonable, and just in its content.

sui juris   Under law.

summary judgment   A decision rendered without extended argument where no material legal question is presented in a case.

supra   Above.

suspect classification doctrine   The doctrine that laws classifying people according to race, ethnicity, and religion are inherently suspect and subjected to strict judicial scrutiny.

sustain   To grant, uphold, or support.

symbolic speech   An activity that expresses a point of view or message symbolically, rather than through pure speech.

third party   A person not directly connected with a legal proceeding but potentially affected by its outcome.

time, place, and manner regulations   Reasonable government regulations as to the time, place, and manner of expressive activities protected by the Constitution.

tort   A wrongful act resulting in injury to a person or his or her property that falls outside the realm of criminal law. Remediable through a civil suit for damages.

totality of circumstances   The entire collection of relevant facts in a particular case.

treaty   A legally binding agreement between one or more countries. In the United States, treaties are negotiated by the president but must be ratified by the Senate.

trespass   An unlawful interference with another person's property.

trial   A judicial proceeding for the purpose of determining issues of fact or law that divide parties to a case.

trial courts   Courts whose primary function is the conduct of civil and/or criminal trials.

two-party system   A political system, such as that of the United States, organized around two major competing political parties.

Uniform Code of Military Justice   The set of statutes adopted by Congress defining crimes and punishments to be enforced by military authorities.

unitary system   A political system in which all power is vested in one central government.

universal suffrage   The requirement that all citizens (at least all competent adults not guilty of serious crimes) be eligible to vote in elections.

use immunity   A grant of immunity forbidding prosecutors from using certain immunized testimony as evidence in criminal prosecutions.

vacate   To set aside or annul, as when an appellate court vacates the judgment of a lower court.

vagrancy   The crime of going about without visible means of support.

venire   The set of persons summoned for jury duty. The actual jury is selected from the venire. See ***voir dire***.

venue   The geographical area in which a given court has authority to hear and decide cases.

veto   The power of a chief executive to block adoption of a law by refusing to sign the legislation.

void-for-vagueness   The doctrine under which laws that are excessively vague are held to violate due process in that they fail to provide adequate notice as to what conduct is permissible and what conduct is proscribed.

voir dire   The process of questioning potential jurors to determine their suitability to serve in a particular case.

waiver   The intentional and voluntary relinquishment of a right, or conduct from which such a relinquishment may be inferred.

warrant   A court order authorizing a search, seizure, or arrest.

white primary   Historically, a primary election in which participation was limited to whites.

writ   An order issued by a court of law requiring or prohibiting the performance of some specific action.

writ of certiorari   See **certiorari, writ of.**

writ of error   See **error, writ of.**

writ of habeas corpus   See **habeas corpus, writ of.**

writ of mandamus   See **mandamus, writ of.**

writ of prohibition   See **prohibition, writ of.**

writs of assistance   Ancient writs issuing from the Court of Exchequer in England granting sheriffs broad powers of search and seizure for the purpose of assisting in the collection of debts owed to the Crown.

wrongful death   A death that is attributable to the willful conduct or negligence of another party.

zoning   Laws regulating the use of land.

APPENDIX E

SUMMARY OF THE SUPREME COURT'S 1991 TERM

The Supreme Court concluded its 1991 term on Monday, June 29, 1992, ending on a sensational note with the long-awaited decision in *Planned Parenthood v. Casey,* the Pennsylvania abortion law case. Although the Court handed down the fewest full-opinion decisions in more than two decades, its 108 plenary decisions addressed a number of important constitutional questions.

Generally speaking, the Court's decisions were less conservative politically, and less disruptive of precedent, than many observers had expected. Only Justices Rehnquist, Scalia, and Thomas voted in a consistently conservative fashion. Justices Blackmun and Stevens generally voted in a liberal direction, while Justices O'Connor, Kennedy, Souter, and White occupied the middle of the Court's ideological spectrum.

The Court's performance in the 1991 term provides further confirmation that, although presidents can and do shape the direction of the Court, the Court remains an independent institution. The justices evidently attach paramount importance to the value of institutional integrity. This is particularly important in the abortion and school prayer decisions discussed and excerpted below.

This appendix is divided into two parts. First, it presents a general overview of important decisions handed down during the term, organized according to the chapter framework of this book. Second, it provides lengthy excerpts from six of the most significant of these decisions.

OVERVIEW OF THE 1991 TERM

Chapter 5: Congress and the Development of National Power.

New York v. United States. The Court invalidated part of a federal statute, the "take title" provision of the Low-

Level Radioactive Waste Policy Amendments Act of 1985, finding it to be an infringement of state sovereignty in violation of the Tenth Amendment. In reaching this result, however, the Court avoided overruling *Garcia v. San Antonio Metropolitan Transit Authority* (1985).

Chapter 8: The Dynamics of "Our Federalism"

Chemical Waste Management, Inc. v. Hunt. The Court invalidated an Alabama law that imposed a tax on waste products originating outside the state and shipped into Alabama for disposal. The Court, relying on its decision in *Philadelphia v. New Jersey* (1978), found that the tax impedes the free flow of interstate commerce by discriminating against materials originating outside the state.

Fort Gratiot Sanitary Landfill, Inc. v. Michigan Department of Natural Resources. The Court struck down a law requiring landfill operators to obtain a special permit from the county in which they were located before accepting trash generated outside the county.

Chapter 11: Freedom of Expression, Assembly, and Association

Dawson v. Delaware. The Court considered the constitutionality of introducing testimony at the sentencing phase of a capital trial indicating that, while in prison, the defendant had been a member of the Aryan Brotherhood, a racist gang. The Court disallowed this evidence on First Amendment grounds, pointing out that the defendant's gang membership was protected as freedom of association and was irrelevant to the issue before the trial court.

Forsyth County v. Nationalist Movement. The Court struck down a local ordinance imposing a fee of up to one thousand dollars for a permit to hold a public demonstration. Under the ordinance, the amount of the fee varied according to the level of trouble expected by local officials.

International Society for Krishna Consciousness v. Lee. The Court upheld a ban on the solicitation of funds in a publicly owned airport. However, the Court invalidated a prohibition on the distribution of literature within the airport.

R.A.V. v. St. Paul. The Court struck down a St. Paul, Minnesota, ordinance that made it a crime to engage in speech or conduct likely to arouse anger or alarm on the basis of race, color, creed, religion, or gender. In striking the law, the Court barred the prosecution of a white teenager who had burned a cross on the lawn of a black family.

Chapter 12: Freedom of the Press: Mass Media and the Constitution

Simon and Schuster v. New York State Crime Victim's Board. The Court struck down New York's "Son of Sam" statute under which a criminal's profits from books or movies would be placed in a fund to assist crime victims. The Court said that the state could not confiscate profits from expressive activities while leaving untouched profits from other types of activities.

Chapter 13: Religious Liberty and Church-State Relations

Lee v. Weisman. The Court reaffirmed its three decade-long ban on prayer in the public schools. The Court held unconstitutional a practice of inviting a member of the clergy to deliver a nonsectarian prayer at a public school graduation ceremony.

Chapter 14: The Constitution and Criminal Justice

Georgia v. McCollum. The Court, extending its 1986 ruling in *Batson v. Kentucky,* held that the Equal Protection Clause of the 14th Amendment forbids the defense in a criminal case from exercising purposeful racial discrimination in the use of peremptory challenges to prospective jurors.

Foucha v. Louisiana. The Court held that an inmate incarcerated after being found not guilty by reason of insanity must be released from custody when and if he or she is restored to sanity.

Jacobson v. United States. The Court reversed the federal pornography conviction of a Nebraska man on the ground that he was entrapped. The Court found that the government had induced the defendant to order child pornography through the mail when he was not predisposed to do so.

Keeney v. Tamayo-Reyes. The Court overturned the Warren Court decision in *Townsend v. Sain* (1963), which held that state prisoners had the right to seek federal habeas corpus relief unless they had deliberately bypassed the state courts.

Hudson v. McMillian. The Court held that a prisoner who was beaten maliciously by guards may bring a civil suit for damages under a claim of cruel and unusual punishment, even if the injuries sustained were not serious.

Wright v. West. The Court refused to adopt the Bush administration's recommendation that federal judges be required to accept the findings of state courts in habeas corpus cases involving state prisoners.

Chapter 15: Personal Autonomy and the Constitutional Right of Privacy

Planned Parenthood v. Casey. The Court reaffirmed *Roe v. Wade* (1973), the landmark decision recognizing a constitutional right to abortion. However, the Court also upheld several regulations on abortion imposed by the state of Pennsylvania and indicated that, henceforth, abortion regulations would be subjected to a more lenient standard of judicial review.

Chapter 16: Equal Protection and the Antidiscrimination Principle

United States v. Fordice. The Court held that the state of Mississippi had not proven that it had effectively dismantled its dual system of higher education for whites and blacks. Although the Court recognized the value of traditionally black state colleges, many observers believed that this ruling would have the practical effect of making it impossible for these educational institutions to survive.

Freeman v. Pitts. The Court held that certain facets of the administration of a school district can be released from the supervision of a federal court even though other facets remain subject to supervision due to the lingering effects of segregation. One practical result of this decision was to set aside a busing order imposed by a federal appeals court on DeKalb County, Georgia.

Chapter 17: Representation and Voting Rights

Burson v. Freeman. The Court upheld Tennessee's law prohibiting campaigning within one hundred feet of polling places on election day.

U.S. Department of Commerce v. Montana. The Court upheld the method by which U.S. House districts are reallocated among the states following each decennial census. After the 1990 census, the state of Montana had lost one of its two seats in the House.

EXCERPTS FROM MAJOR DECISIONS
Chemical Waste Management, Inc. v. Hunt
504 U.S.; 112 S. Ct. 2009; 119 L. Ed.2d 121 (1992)
Vote: 8-1

The state of Alabama imposed a disposal fee on hazardous wastes imported into the state for disposal. The fee did not apply to similar wastes produced in-state. Chemical Waste Management, Inc. filed suit in state court to challenge the constitutionality of the fee, arguing, among other things, that it violated the Commerce Clause of the federal Constitution. The Supreme Court granted certiorari to review the Alabama Supreme Court's decision upholding the disposal fee.

Justice White delivered the opinion of the Court.

. . . Chemical Waste Management, Inc., a Delaware corporation with its principal place of business in Oak Brook, Illinois, owns and operates one of the Nation's oldest commercial hazardous waste land disposal facilities, located in Emelle, Alabama. Opened in 1977 and acquired by petitioner in 1978, the Emelle facility is a hazardous waste treatment, storage, and disposal facility operating pursuant to permits issued by the Environmental Protection Agency (EPA) under the Resource Conservation and Recovery Act of 1976 (RCRA), *** and the Toxic Substances Control Act, *** and by the State of Alabama under [the] Alabama Code. . . . Alabama is 1 of only 16 States that have commercial hazardous waste landfills, and the Emelle facility is the largest of the 21 landfills of this kind located in these 16 States. ***

The parties do not dispute that the wastes and substances being landfilled at the Emelle facility "include substances that are inherently dangerous to human health and safety and to the environment. Such waste consists of ignitable, corrosive, toxic and reactive wastes which contain poisonous and cancer causing chemicals and which can cause birth defects, genetic damage, blindness, crippling and death." *** Increasing amounts of out-of-state hazardous wastes are shipped to the Emelle facility for permanent storage each year. From 1985 through 1989, the tonnage of hazardous waste received per year has more than doubled, increasing from 341,000 tons in 1985 to

788,000 tons by 1989. Of this, up to 90% of the tonnage permanently buried each year is shipped in from other States.

Against this backdrop Alabama enacted Act No. 90-326 (the Act). *** Among other provisions, the Act includes a "cap" that generally limits the amount of hazardous wastes or substances that may be disposed of in any 1-year period, and the amount of hazardous waste disposed of during the first year under the Act's new fees becomes the permanent ceiling in subsequent years. *** The cap applies to commercial facilities that dispose of over 100,000 tons of hazardous wastes or substances per year, but only the Emelle facility, as the only commercial facility operating within Alabama, meets this description. The Act also imposes a "base fee" of $25.60 per ton on all hazardous wastes and substances disposed of at commercial facilities, to be paid by the operator of the facility. *** Finally, the Act imposes the "additional fee" at issue here, which states in full:

"For waste and substances which are generated outside of Alabama and disposed of at a commercial site for the disposal of hazardous waste or hazardous substances in Alabama, an additional fee shall be levied at the rate of $72.00 per ton." ***

Petitioner filed suit in state court requesting declaratory relief against the respondents and seeking to enjoin enforcement of the Act. In addition to state law claims, petitioner contended that the Act violated the Commerce, Due Process, and Equal Protection Clauses of the United States Constitution, and was preempted by various federal statutes. The Trial Court declared the base fee and the cap provisions of the Act to be valid and constitutional; but, finding the only basis for the additional fee to be the origin of the wastes, the Trial Court declared it to be in violation of the Commerce Clause. *** Both sides appealed. The Alabama Supreme Court affirmed the rulings concerning the base fee and cap provisions but reversed the decision regarding the additional fee. . . .

Chemical Waste Management, Inc., petitioned for writ of certiorari, challenging all aspects of the Act. Because of the importance of the federal question and the likelihood that it had been decided in a way conflicting with applicable decisions of this Court, *** we granted certiorari limited to petitioner's Commerce Clause challenge to the additional fee. *** We now reverse.

II

No State may attempt to isolate itself from a problem common to the several States by raising barriers to the free flow of interstate trade. Today, in *Fort Gratiot Sanitary Landfill, Inc. v. Michigan Dept. of Natural Resources,* *** we have also considered a Commerce Clause challenge to a Michigan law prohibiting private landfill operators from accepting solid waste originating outside the county in which their facilities operate. In striking down that law, we adhered to our decision in *Philadelphia v. New Jersey* *** (1978), where we found New Jersey's prohibition of solid waste from outside that State to amount to economic protectionism barred by the Commerce Clause. . . .

The Act's additional fee facially discriminates against hazardous waste generated in States other than Alabama, and the Act overall has plainly discouraged the full operation of petitioner's Emelle facility. Such burdensome taxes imposed on interstate commerce alone are generally forbidden: "[A] State may not tax a transaction or incident more heavily when it crosses states lines than when it occurs entirely within the State." ***

The State, however, argues that the additional fee imposed on out-of-state hazardous waste serves legitimate local purposes related to its citizens' health and safety. Because the additional fee discriminates both on its face and in practical effect, the burden falls on the State "to justify it both in terms of the local benefits flowing from the statute and the unavailability of nondiscriminatory alternatives adequate to preserve the local interests at stake." *** "At a minimum such facial discrimination invokes the strictest scrutiny of any purported legitimate local purpose and of the absence of nondiscriminatory alternatives." ***

The State's argument here does not significantly differ from the Alabama Supreme Court's conclusions on the legitimate local purposes of the additional fee imposed, which were:

"The Additional Fee serves these legitimate local purposes that cannot be adequately served by reasonable nondiscriminatory alternatives: (1) protection of the health and safety of the citizens of Alabama from toxic substances; (2) conservation of the environment and the state's natural resources; (3) provision for compensatory revenue for the costs and burdens that out-of-state waste generators impose by dumping their hazardous waste in Alabama; (4) reduction of the overall flow of wastes traveling on the state's highways, which flow creates a great risk to the health and safety of the state's citizens." ***

These may all be legitimate local interests, and petitioner has not attacked them. But only rhetoric, and not explanation, emerges as to why Alabama targets *only* interstate hazardous waste to meet these goals. As found by the Trial Court, "[a]lthough the Legislature imposed an additional fee of $72.00 per ton on waste generated outside Alabama, there is absolutely no evidence before this Court that waste generated outside Alabama is more dangerous than waste generated in Alabama. The Court finds under the facts of this case that the only basis for the additional fee is the origin of the waste." *** In the face of such findings, invalidity under the Commerce Clause necessarily follows, for "whatever [Alabama's] ultimate purpose, it may not be accomplished by discriminating against articles of commerce coming from outside the State unless there is some reason, apart from their origin, to treat them differently." *** The burden is on the State to show that "the discrimination is demonstrably justified by a valid factor unrelated to economic protectionism," *** and it has not carried this burden. ***

Ultimately, the State's concern focuses on the volume of the waste entering the Emelle facility. Less discriminatory alternatives, however, are available to alleviate this concern, not the least of which are a generally applicable per-ton additional fee on all hazardous waste disposed of within Alabama, *** or a per-mile tax on *all* vehicles transporting hazardous waste across Alabama roads, *** or an evenhanded cap on the total tonnage landfilled at Emelle, *** which would curtail volume from all sources. To the extent Alabama's concern touches environmental conservation and the health and safety of its citizens, such concern does not vary with the point of origin of the waste, and it remains within the State's power to monitor and regulate more closely the transportation and disposal of *all* hazardous waste within its borders. Even with the possible future financial and environmental risks to be borne by Alabama, such risks likewise do not vary with the waste's State of origin in a way allowing foreign, but not local, waste to be burdened. In sum, we find the additional fee to be "an obvious effort to saddle those outside the State" with most of the burden of slowing the flow of waste into the Emelle facility. *** "That legislative effort is clearly impermissible under the Commerce Clause of the Constitution." ***

Our decisions regarding quarantine laws do not counsel a different conclusion. The Act's additional fee may not legitimately be deemed a quarantine law because Alabama permits both the generation and landfilling of hazardous waste within its borders and the importation of still more hazardous waste subject to payment of the additional fee. In any event, while it is true that certain quarantine laws have not been considered forbidden protectionist measures, even though directed against out-of-state commerce, those laws "did not discriminate against interstate commerce as such, but simply prevented traffic in noxious articles, whatever their origin." ***

The law struck down in *Philadelphia v. New Jersey* left local waste untouched, although no basis existed by which to distinguish interstate waste. But "[i]f one is inherently harmful, so is the other. Yet New Jersey has banned the former while leaving its landfill sites open to the latter." *** Here, the additional fee applies only to interstate hazardous waste, but at all points from its entrance into Alabama until it is landfilled at the Emelle facility, every concern related to quarantine applies perforce to local hazardous waste, which pays no additional fee. For this reason, the additional fee does not survive the appropriate scrutiny applicable to discriminations against interstate commerce.

Maine v. Taylor *** (1986) provides no additional justification. Maine there demonstrated that the out-of-state baitfish were subject to parasites foreign to in-state baitfish. This difference posed a threat to the State's natural resources, and absent a less discriminatory means of protecting the environment—and none was available—the importation of baitfish could properly be banned. *** To the contrary, the record establishes that the hazardous waste at issue in this case is the same regardless of its point of origin. . . . Because no unique threat is posed, and because adequate means other than overt discrimination meet Alabama's concerns, *Maine v. Taylor* provides the State no respite.

III

The decision of the Alabama Supreme Court is reversed, and the cause remanded for proceedings not inconsistent with this opinion, including consideration of the appropriate relief to petitioner. ***

Chief Justice Rehnquist, dissenting.

I have already had occasion to set out my view that States need not ban all waste disposal as a precondition to protecting themselves from hazardous or noxious materials brought across the State's borders. *** In a case also decided today, I express my further view that States may take actions legitimately directed at the preservation of the State's natural resources, even if those actions incidentally work to disadvantage some out-of-state waste generators. *** I dissent today, largely for the reasons I have set out in those two cases. Several additional comments that pertain specifically to this case, though, are in order.

Taxes are a recognized and effective means for discouraging the consumption of scarce commodities—in this case the safe environment that attends appropriate disposal of hazardous wastes. *** I therefore see nothing unconstitutional in Alabama's use of a tax to discourage the export of this commodity to other States, when the commodity is a public good that Alabama has helped to produce. *** Nor do I see any significance in the fact that Alabama has chosen to adopt a differential tax rather than an outright ban. Nothing in the Commerce Clause requires Alabama to adopt an "all or nothing" regulatory approach to noxious materials coming from without the State. ***

In short, the Court continues to err by its failure to recognize that waste—in this case admittedly *hazardous* waste—presents risks to the public health and environment that a State may legitimately wish to avoid, and that the State may pursue such an objective by means less Draconian than an outright ban. Under force of this Court's precedent, though, it increasingly appears that the only avenue by which a State may avoid the importation of hazardous wastes is to ban such waste disposal altogether, regardless of the waste's source of origin. I see little logic in creating, and nothing in the Commerce Clause that requires us to create, such perverse regulatory incentives. The Court errs in substantial measure because it refuses to acknowledge that a safe and attractive environment is the commodity really at issue in cases such as this. *** The result is that the Court today gets it exactly backward when it suggests that Alabama is attempting to "isolate itself from a problem common to the several States." *** To the contrary, it is the 34 States that have no hazardous waste facility whatsoever, not to mention the remaining 15 States with facilities all smaller than Emelle, that have isolated themselves.

There is some solace to be taken in the Court's conclusion that Alabama may impose a substantial fee on the disposal of all hazardous waste, or a per-mile fee on all vehicles transporting such waste, or a cap on total disposals at the Emelle facility. None of these approaches provide[s] Alabama the ability to tailor its regulations in a way that the State will be solving only that portion of the problem that it has created. *** But they do at least give Alabama some mechanisms for requiring waste-generating States to compensate Alabama for the risks the Court declares Alabama must run.

Of course, the costs of any of the proposals that the Court today approves will be less than fairly apportioned. For example, should Alabama adopt a flat transportation or disposal tax, Alabama citizens will be forced to pay a disposal tax equal to that faced by dumpers from outside the State. As the Court acknowledges, such taxes are a permissible effort to recoup compensation for the risks imposed on the State. Yet Alabama's general tax revenues presumably already support the State's various inspection and regulatory efforts designed to ensure the Emelle facility's safe operation. Thus, Alabamians will be made to pay twice, once through general taxation and a second time through a specific disposal fee. Permitting differential taxation would, in part, do no more than recognize that, having been made to bear all the risks from such hazardous waste sites, Alabama should not in addition be made to pay *more* than others in supporting activities that will help to minimize the risk.

Other mechanisms also appear open to Alabama to achieve results similar to those that are seemingly foreclosed today. There seems to be nothing, for example, that would prevent Alabama from providing subsidies or other tax breaks to domestic industries that generate hazardous wastes. Or Alabama may, under the market participant doctrine, open its own facility catering only to Alabama customers. *** But certainly we have lost our way when we require States to perform such gymnastics, when such performances will in turn produce little difference in ultimate effects. In sum, the only sure by-product of today's decision is additional litigation. Assuming that those States that are currently the targets for large volumes of hazardous waste do not simply ban hazardous waste sites altogether, they will undoubtedly continue to search for a way to limit their risk from sites in operation. And each new arrangement will generate a new legal challenge, one that will work to the principal advantage only of those States that refuse to contribute to a solution.

For the foregoing reasons, I respectfully dissent.

R.A.V. v. City of St. Paul

505 U.S. ___; 112 S. Ct. 2538; 120 L. Ed.2d 305 (1992)
Vote: 9-0

In this case, the Court confronts the highly volatile issue of "hate speech." Specifically, the Court strikes down a St. Paul, Minnesota, ordinance providing:

"Whoever places on public or private property a symbol, object, appellation, characterization or graffiti, including, but not limited to, a burning cross or

Nazi swastika, which one knows or has reasonable grounds to know arouses anger, alarm or resentment in others on the basis of race, color, creed, religion or gender commits disorderly conduct and shall be guilty of a misdemeanor." While the Court is unanimous in its conclusion that the ordinance violated the First Amendment, it is anything but unanimous with respect to doctrinal considerations.

Justice Scalia delivered the opinion of the Court.

In the predawn hours of June 21, 1990, petitioner and several other teen-agers allegedly assembled a crudely made cross by taping together broken chair legs. They then allegedly burned the cross inside the fenced yard of a black family that lived across the street from the house where petitioner was staying. Although this conduct could have been punished under any of a number of laws, one of the two provisions under which respondent, City of St. Paul, chose to charge petitioner (then a juvenile) was the St. Paul Bias-Motivated Crime Ordinance [quoted above] . . . .

Petitioner moved to dismiss this count on the ground that the St. Paul ordinance was substantially overbroad and impermissible content-based and therefore facially invalid under the First Amendment. The trial court granted this motion, but the Minnesota Supreme Court reversed. That court rejected petitioner's overbreadth claim because, as construed in prior Minnesota cases, the modifying phrase "arouses anger, alarm or resentment in others" limited the reach of the ordinance to conduct that amounts to "fighting words," i.e. "conduct that itself inflicts injury or tends to incite immediate violence," *** and therefore the ordinance reached only expression "that the First Amendment does not protect."

The court also concluded that the ordinance was not impermissible content-based because, in its view, "the ordinance is a narrowly tailored means toward accomplishing the compelling governmental interest in protecting the community against bias-motivated threats to public safety and order." ***

In construing the St. Paul ordinance, we are bound by the construction given to it by the Minnesota court. Accordingly, we accept the Minnesota Supreme Court's authoritative statement that the ordinance reaches only those expressions that constitute "fighting words" . . . .

We find it unnecessary to consider this issue. Assuming, *arguendo,* that all of the expression reached by the ordinance is proscribable under the "fighting words" doctrine, we nonetheless conclude that the ordinance is facially unconstitutional in that it prohibits otherwise permitted speech solely on the basis of the subjects the speech addresses.

The First Amendment generally prevents government from proscribing speech, or even expressive conduct, because of disapproval of the ideas expressed. Content-based regulations are presumptively invalid. From 1791 to the present, however, our society, like other free but civilized societies, has permitted restrictions upon the content of speech in a few limited areas, which are "of such slight social value as a step to truth that any benefit that may be derived from them is clearly outweighed by the social interest in order and morality." ***

We have sometimes said that these categories of expression are "not within the area of constitutionally protected speech," or that the "protection of the First Amendment does not extend" to them. Such statements must be taken in context, however, and are no more literally true than is the occasionally repeated shorthand characterizing obscenity "as not being speech at all." What they mean is that these areas of speech can, consistently with the First Amendment, be regulated because of their constitutionally proscribable content (obscenity, defamation, etc.) not that they are categories of speech entirely invisible to the Constitution, so that they may be made the vehicles for content discrimination unrelated to their distinctively proscribable content. Thus, the government may proscribe libel; but it may not make the further content discrimination of proscribing only libel critical of the government. . . .

Our cases surely do not establish the proposition that the First Amendment imposes no obstacle whatsoever to regulation of particular instances of such proscribable expression, so that the government "may regulate (them) freely." That would mean that a city council could enact an ordinance prohibiting only those legally obscene works that contain criticism of the city government or, indeed, that do not include endorsement of the city government.

Fighting words are thus analogous to a noisy sound truck: Each is, as Justice Frankfurter recognized, a "mode of speech," [in that] *** both can be used to convey an idea; but neither has, in and of itself, a claim upon the First Amendment. As with the sound truck, however, so also with fighting words: The government may not regulate use based on hostility or favoritism towards the underlying message expressed.

Applying these principles to the St. Paul ordinance, we conclude that, even as narrowly construed by the Minnesota Supreme Court, the ordinance is facially unconstitutional. Although the phrase in the ordinance, "aroused anger, alarm or resentment in others," has been limited by the Minnesota Supreme Court's construction to reach only those symbols or displays that amount to "fighting words," the remaining, unmodified terms make clear that the ordinance applies only to "fighting words" that insult, or provoke violence, "on the basis of race, color, creed, religion or gender."

Displays containing abusive invective, no matter how vicious or severe, are permissible unless they are addressed to one of the specified disfavored topics. Those who wish to use "fighting words" in connection with other ideas to express hostility, for example, on the basis of political affiliation, union membership, or homosexuality are not covered. The First Amendment does not permit St. Paul to impose special prohibitions on those speakers who express views on disfavored subjects.

In its practical operation, moreover, the ordinance goes even beyond mere content discrimination, to actual viewpoint discrimination. Displays containing some words, odious racial epithets, for example, would be prohibited to proponents of all views. But "fighting words" that do not themselves invoke race, color, creed, religion, or gender aspersions upon a person's mother, for example, would seemingly be usable *ad libitum* in the placards of those arguing in favor of racial, color, etc. tolerance and equality, but could not be used by that speaker's opponents. One could hold up a sign saying, for example, that all "anti-Catholic bigots" are misbegotten; but not that all "papists" are, for that would insult and provoke violence "on the basis of religion." St. Paul has no such authority to license one side of a debate to fight freestyle, while requiring the other to follow Marquis of Queensbury Rules.

St. Paul has not singled out an especially offensive mode of expression. It has not, for example, selected for prohibition only those fighting words that communicate ideas in a threatening (as opposed to a merely obnoxious) manner. Rather, it has proscribed fighting words of whatever manner that communicate messages of racial, gender, or religious intolerance. Selectivity of this sort creates the possibility that the city is seeking to handicap the expression of particular ideas.

The dispositive question in this case, therefore, is whether content discrimination is reasonably necessary to achieve St. Paul's compelling interests; it plainly is not. An ordinance not limited to the favored topics, for example, would have precisely the same beneficial effect. In fact the only interest distinctively served by the content limitation is that of displaying the City Council's special hostility towards the particular biases thus singled out. That is precisely what the First Amendment forbids. The politicians of St. Paul are entitled to express that hostility but not through the means of imposing unique limitations upon speakers who (however benightedly) disagree.

Let there be no mistake about our belief that burning a cross in someone's front yard is reprehensible. But St. Paul has sufficient means at its disposal to prevent such behavior without adding the First Amendment to the fire.

Justice White, concurring in the judgment.

I agree with the majority that the judgment of the Minnesota Supreme Court should be reversed. However, our agreement ends there.

This case could easily be decided within the contours of established First Amendment law by holding, as petitioner argues, that the St. Paul ordinance is fatally overbroad because it criminalizes not only unprotected expression but expression protected by the First Amendment.

But in the present case, the majority casts aside long-established First Amendment doctrine without the benefit of briefing and adopts an untried theory.

This Court's decisions have plainly stated that expression falling within certain limited categories so lacks the values the First Amendment was designed to protect that the Constitution affords no protection to that expression.

Nevertheless, the majority holds that the First Amendment protects those narrow categories of expression long held to be undeserving of First Amendment protection, at least to the extent that lawmakers may not regulate some fighting words more strictly than others because of their content. The Court announces that such content-based distinctions violate the First Amendment because "the government may not regulate use based on hostility or favoritism towards the underlying message expressed." Should the government want to criminalize certain fighting words, the Court now requires it to criminalize all fighting words.

To borrow a phrase, "Such a simplistic, all-or-nothing approach to First Amendment protection is at odds with common sense and with our jurisprudence as well." It is inconsistent to hold that the government may proscribe an entire category of speech because the content of that speech is evil, but that the government may not treat a subset of that category differently without violating the First Amendment; the content of the subset is by definition worthless and undeserving of constitutional protection.

The majority's observation that fighting words are "quite expressive indeed," is no answer. Fighting words are not a means of exchanging views, rallying supporters, or registering a protest; they are directed against individuals to provoke violence or to inflict injury. Therefore, a ban on all fighting words or on a subset of the fighting words category would restrict only the social evil of hate speech, without creating the danger of driving viewpoints from the marketplace. ·

Any contribution of this holding to First Amendment jurisprudence is surely a negative one, since it necessarily signals that expressions of violence, such as the message of intimidation and racial hatred conveyed by burning a cross on someone's lawn, are of sufficient value to outweigh the social interest in order and morality that has traditionally placed such fighting words outside the First Amendment. Indeed, by characterizing fighting words as a form of "debate," the majority legitimates hate speech as a form of public discussion.

Furthermore, the Court obscures the line between speech that could be regulated freely on the basis of content (i.e., the narrow categories of expression falling outside the First Amendment) and that which could be regulated on the basis of content only upon a showing of a compelling state interest (i.e., all remaining expression). By placing fighting words, which the Court has long held to be valueless, on at least equal constitutional footing with political discourse and other forms of speech that we have deemed to have the greatest social value, the majority devalues the latter category.

Under the majority's view, a narrowly drawn, content-based ordinance could never pass constitutional muster if the object of that legislation could be accomplished by banning a wider category of speech. This appears to be a general renunciation of strict scrutiny review, a fundamental tool of First Amendment analysis.

Justice Blackmun, concurring in the judgment.

I regret what the Court has done in this case. The majority opinion signals one of two possibilities: it will serve as precedent for future cases, or it will not. Either result is disheartening.

In the first instance, by deciding that a state cannot regulate speech that causes great harm unless it also regulates speech that does not (setting law and logic on their heads), the Court seems to abandon the categorical approach, and inevitably to relax the level of scrutiny applicable to content-based laws. As Justice White points out, this weakens the traditional protections of speech.

In the second instance is the possibility that this case will not significantly alter First Amendment jurisprudence, but, instead will be regarded as an aberration, a case where the Court manipulated doctrine to strike down an ordinance whose premise it opposed, namely, that racial threats and verbal assaults are of greater harm than other fighting words. I fear that the Court has been distracted from its proper mission by the temptation to decide the issue over "politically correct speech" and "cultural diversity," neither of which is presented here. If this is the meaning of today's opinion, it is perhaps even more regrettable.

I see no First Amendment values that are compromised by a law that prohibits hoodlums from driving minorities out of their homes by burning crosses on their lawns, but I see great harm in preventing the people of St. Paul from specifically punishing the race-based fighting words that so prejudice their community.

I concur in the judgment, however, because I agree with Justice White that this particular ordinance reaches beyond fighting words to speech protected by the First Amendment.

Justice Stevens [joined in part by Justices White, Blackmun, and O'Connor], concurring in the judgment.

Conduct that creates special risks or causes special harms may be prohibited by special rules. Lighting a fire near an ammunition dump or a gasoline storage tank is especially dangerous; such behavior may be punished more severely than burning trash in a vacant lot. Threatening someone because of her race or religious beliefs may cause particularly severe trauma or touch off a riot, and threatening a high public official may cause substantial social disruption; such threats may be punished more severely than threats against someone based on, say, his support of a particular athletic team. There are legitimate, reasonable, and neutral justifications for such special rules.

This case involves the constitutionality of one such ordinance. Because the regulated conduct has some communicative content, a message of racial, religious or gender hostility, the ordinance raises two quite different First Amendment questions. Is the ordinance "overbroad" because it prohibits too much speech? If not, is it "underbroad" because it does not prohibit enough speech?

As an initial matter, the Court's revision of the categorical approach seems to me something of an adventure in a doctrinal wonderland, for the concept of "obscene antigovernment" speech is fantastical. The category of the obscene is very narrow; to be obscene, expression must be found by the trier of fact to "appeal (1) to the prurient interest, . . . depic(t) or describ(e), in a patently offensive way, sexual conduct, (and) taken as a whole, lac(k) serious literary, artistic, political or scientific value." *** "Obscene antigovernment" speech, then, is a contradiction in terms: If expression is antigovernment, it does not "lac(k) serious . . . political . . . value" and cannot be obscene.

Our First Amendment decisions have created a rough hierarchy in the constitutional protection of speech. Core political speech occupies the highest, most protected position; commercial speech and non-obscene, sexually explicit speech are regarded as a sort of second-class expression; obscenity and fighting words receive the least protection of all. Assuming that the Court is correct that this last class of speech is not wholly "unprotected," it certainly does not follow that fighting words and obscenity receive the same sort of protection afforded core political speech. Yet in ruling that proscribable speech cannot be regulated based on subject matter, the Court does just that. Perversely, this gives fighting words greater protection than is afforded commercial speech. . . .

In sum, the central premise of the Court's ruling that "(c)ontent-based regulations are presumptively invalid" has simplistic appeal, but lacks support in our First Amendment jurisprudence. To make matters worse, the Court today extends this overstated claim to reach categories of hitherto unprotected speech and, in doing so, wreaks havoc in an area of settled law. Finally, although the Court recognizes exceptions to its new principle, those exceptions undermine its very conclusion that the St. Paul ordinance is unconstitutional. Stated directly, the majority's position cannot withstand scrutiny.

Lee v. Weisman
505 U.S. ____; 112 S. Ct. 2649; 120 L. Ed. 2d 467 (1992)
Vote: 5-4

In this case, the Supreme Court considers whether a prayer offered by a member of the clergy at a public school graduation ceremony violates the First Amendment prohibition against establishment of religion.

Justice Kennedy delivered the opinion of the Court.

School principals in the public school system of the city of Providence, Rhode Island, are permitted to invite members of the clergy to offer invocation and benediction prayers as part of the formal graduation ceremonies for middle schools and high schools. The question before us is whether including clerical members who offer prayers as part of the official school graduation ceremony is consistent with the religion clauses of the First Amendment....

Deborah Weisman graduated from Nathan Bishop Middle School, a public school in Providence, at a formal ceremony in June 1989.... For many years it has been the policy of the Providence School Committee and the Superintendent of Schools to permit principals to invite members of the clergy to give invocations and benedictions at middle school and high school graduations.... Acting for himself and his daughter, Deborah's father, Daniel Weisman, objected to any prayers at Deborah's middle school graduation, but to no avail. The school principal, petitioner Robert E. Lee, invited a rabbi to deliver prayers at the graduation exercises for Deborah's class. Rabbi Leslie Gutterman, of the Temple Beth El in Providence, accepted.

It has been the custom of Providence school officials to provide invited clergy with a pamphlet entitled "Guidelines for Civic Occasions," prepared by the National Conference of Christians and Jews.... The principal gave Rabbi Gutterman the pamphlet before the graduation and advised him the invocation and benediction should be nonsectarian.

Rabbi Gutterman's prayers were as follows:

Invocation:

God of the Free, Hope of the Brave, for the legacy of America where diversity is celebrated and the rights of minorities are protected, we thank You. May these young men and women grow up to enrich it.

For the liberty of America, we thank You. May these new graduates grow up to guard it.

For the political process of America in which all its citizens may participate, for its court system where all may seek justice we thank You. May those we honor this morning always turn to it in trust.

For the destiny of America we thank You. May the graduates of Nathan Bishop Middle School so live that they might help to share it.

May our aspirations for our country and for these young people, who are our hope for the future, be richly fulfilled. Amen.

Benediction:

O God, we are grateful to You for having endowed us with the capacity for learning which we have celebrated on this joyous commencement. Happy families give thanks for seeing their children achieve an important milestone.

Send Your blessings upon the teachers and administrators who helped prepare them. The graduates now need strength and guidance for the future, help them to understand that we are not complete with academic knowledge alone. We must each strive to fulfill what You require of us all: To do justly, to love mercy, to walk humbly.

We give thanks to You, Lord, for keeping us alive, sustaining us and allowing us to reach this special, happy occasion. Amen.

The school board ... argued that these short prayers and others like them at graduation exercises are of profound meaning to many students and parents throughout this country who consider that due respect and acknowledgement for divine guidance and for the deepest spiritual aspirations of our people ought to be expressed at an event as important in life as a graduation. We assume this to be so in addressing the difficult case now before us, for the significance of the prayers lies also at the heart of Daniel and Deborah Weisman's case....

Deborah and her family attended the graduation, where the prayers were recited. In July 1989, Daniel Weisman filed an amended complaint seeking a permanent injunction barring petitioners, various officials of the Providence public schools, from inviting the clergy to deliver invocations and benedictions at future graduations....

The District Court held that petitioners' practice of including invocation and benedictions in public school graduations violated the establishment clause of the First Amendment, and it enjoined petitioners from continuing the practice. The court applied the three-part establishment clause test set forth in *Lemon v. Kurtzman* *** (1971). Under that test as described in our past cases, to satisfy the establishment clause a governmental practice must (1) reflect a clearly secular purpose; (2) have a primary effect that neither advances nor inhibits religion; and (3) avoid excessive government entanglement with religion. The District Court held that petitioners' actions violated the second part of the test, and so did not address either the first or the third. *** The court determined that the practice of including invocations and benedictions, even so-called nonsectarian ones, in public school graduations creates an identification of governmental power with religious practice, endorses religion, and violates the establishment clause. ***

On appeal, the United States Court of Appeals for the First Circuit affirmed. *** . . .

The principle that government may accommodate the free exercise of religion does not supersede the fundamental limitations imposed by the establishment clause. It is beyond dispute that, at a minimum, the Constitution guarantees that government may not coerce anyone to support or participate in religion or its exercise, or otherwise act in a way which "establishes a (state) religion or religious faith, or tends to do so." *** The State's involvement in the school prayers challenged today violates these central principles.

That involvement is as troubling as it is undenied. A school official, the principal, decided that an invocation and a benediction should be given; this is a choice attributable to the State, and from a constitutional perspective it is as if a state statute decreed that the prayers must occur. The principal chose the religious participant, here a rabbi, and that choice is also attributable to the State. . . .

The State's role did not end with the decision to include a prayer and with the choice of clergyman. Principal Lee provided Rabbi Gutterman with a copy of the "Guidelines for Civic Occasions," and advised him that his prayers should be nonsectarian. Through these means the principal directed and controlled the content of the prayer. . . .

The First Amendment's religion clauses mean that religious beliefs and religious expression are too precious to be either proscribed or prescribed by the State. The design of the Constitution is that preservation and transmission of religious beliefs and worship is a responsibility and a choice committed to the private sphere, which itself is promised freedom to pursue that mission. . . .

These concerns have particular application in the case of school officials, whose effort to monitor prayer will be perceived by the students as inducing a participation they might otherwise reject. . . .

The lessons of the First Amendment are as urgent in the modern world as in the 18th century when it was written. One timeless lesson is that if citizens are subjected to state-sponsored religious exercises, the State disavows its own duty to guard and respect that sphere of inviolable conscience and belief which is the mark of a free people. To compromise that principle today would be to deny our own tradition and forfeit our standing to urge others to secure the protections of that tradition for themselves. . . .

Finding no violation under these circumstances would place objectors in the dilemma of participating, with all that implies, or protesting. We do not address whether that choice is acceptable if the affected citizens are mature adults, but we think the State may not, consistent with the establishment clause, place primary and secondary school children in this position. Research in psychology supports the common assumption that adolescents are often susceptible to pressure from their peers towards conformity, and that the influence is strongest in matters of social convention. . . .

There was a stipulation in the District Court that attendance at graduation and promotional ceremonies is voluntary. Petitioners and the United States, as *amicus,* made this a center point of the case, arguing that the option of not attending the graduation excuses any inducement or coercion in the ceremony itself. The argument lacks all persuasion. . . . Everyone knows that in our society and in our culture high school graduation is one of life's most significant occasions. . . .

The importance of the event is the point the school district and the United States rely upon to argue that a formal prayer ought to be permitted, but it becomes one of the principal reasons why their argument must fail. Their contention, one of considerable force were it not for the constitutional constraints applied to state action, is that the prayers are an essential part of these ceremonies because for many persons an occasion of this significance lacks meaning if there is no recognition, however brief, that human achievements cannot be understood apart from their spiritual essence. We think the Government's position that this interest suffices to force students to choose between compliance or forfeiture demonstrates fundamental inconsistency in its argumentation. It fails to acknowledge that what for many of Deborah's classmates and their parents was a spiritual imperative was for Daniel and Deborah Weisman religious conformance compelled by the State. While in some societies the wishes of the majority might prevail, the establishment clause of the First Amendment is addressed to this contingency and rejects the balance urged upon us. The Constitution forbids the State to exact religious conformity from a student as the price of attending her own high school graduation....

Justice Blackmun, joined by *Justice Stevens* and *Justice O'Connor,* concurring....

...[I]t is not enough that the government restrain from compelling religious practices: it must not engage in them either. The Court repeatedly has recognized that a violation of the establishment clause is not predicated on coercion....

The mixing of government and religion can be a threat to free government, even if no one is forced to participate. When the government puts its imprimatur on a particular religion, it conveys a message of exclusion to all those who do not adhere to the favored beliefs....

Justice Souter, joined by *Justice Stevens* and *Justice O'Connor,* concurring.

That government must remain neutral in matters of religion does not foreclose it from ever taking religion into account. The State may "accommodate" the free exercise of religion by relieving people from generally applicable rules that interfere with their religious callings. Contrary to the views of some, such accommodation does not necessarily signify an official endorsement of religious observance over disbelief....

Whatever else may define the scope of accommodation permissible under the establishment clause, one requirement is clear: accommodation must lift a discernible burden on the free exercise of religion....

Religious students cannot complain that omitting prayers from their graduation ceremony would, in any realistic sense, "burden" their spiritual callings. To be sure, many of them invest this rite of passage with spiritual significance, but they may express their religious feelings about it before and after the ceremony. They may even organize a privately sponsored baccalaureate if they desire the company of like-minded students. Because they accordingly have no need for the machinery of the State to affirm their beliefs, the government's sponsorship of prayer at the graduation ceremony is most reasonably understood as an official endorsement of religion and, in this instance, of theistic religion....

Justice Scalia, joined by *Chief Justice Rehnquist, Justice White* and *Justice Thomas,* dissenting.

In holding that the establishment clause prohibits invocations and benedictions at public-school graduation ceremonies, the Court, with nary a mention that it is doing so, lays waste a tradition that is as old as public-school graduation ceremonies themselves, and that is a component of an even more long-standing American tradition of nonsectarian prayer to God at public celebrations generally.... Today's opinion shows more forcefully than volumes of argumentation why our Nation's protection, that fortress which is our Constitution, cannot possibly rest upon the changeable philosophical predilections of the Justices of this Court, but must have deep foundations in the historic practices of our people.

In addition to this general tradition of prayer at public ceremonies, there exists a more specific tradition of invocations and benedictions at public-school graduation exercises....

The Court declares that students' "attendance and participation in the (invocation and benediction) are in a fair and real sense obligatory." *** But what exactly is this "fair and real sense"? According to the Court, students at graduation who want "to avoid the fact or appearance of participation" in the invocation and benediction are psychologically obligated by "public pressure, as well are peer pressure,... to stand as a group or, at least, maintain respectful silence" during those prayers. *** This assertion, the very linchpin of the Court's opinion, is almost as intriguing for what it does not say as for what it says. It does not say, for example, that students are psychologically coerced to bow their heads, place their hands in a Dürer-like prayer position, pay attention to the prayers, utter "Amen," or in fact pray....

I also find it odd that the Court concludes that high school graduates may not be subjected to this supposed psychological coercion, yet refrains from addressing whether "mature adults" may. I had thought that the reason graduation from high school is regarded as so significant an event is that it is generally associated with transition from adolescence to young adulthood. Many graduating seniors, of course, are old enough to vote. Why, then, does the Court treat them as though they were first-graders? Will we soon have a jurisprudence that distinguishes mature and immature adults?

The deeper flaw in the Court's opinion does not lie in its wrong answer to the question whether there was state-induced "peer pressure" coercion; it lies, rather, in the Court's making violation of the establishment clause hinge on such a precious question. The coercion that was a hallmark of historical establishments of religion was coercion of religious orthodoxy and of financial support by force of law and threat of penalty. Typically, attendance at the state church was required; only clergy of the official church could lawfully perform sacraments, and dissenters, if tolerated, faced an array of civil disabilities.... But there is simply no support for the proposition that the officially sponsored nondenominational invocation and benediction read by Rabbi Gutterman with no one legally coerced to recite them violated the Constitution of the United States. To the contrary, they are so characteristically American they could have come from the pen of George Washington or Abraham Lincoln himself.

The narrow context of the present case involves a community's celebration of one of the milestones in its younger citizens' lives, and it is a bold step for this Court to seek to banish from that occasion, and from thousands of similar celebrations throughout this land, the expression of gratitude to God that a majority of the community wishes to make....

Planned Parenthood v. Casey

505 U.S. ____; 112 S. Ct. 2791; 120 L. Ed.2d 674 (1992)

Vote: (see comment below)

The Court waited until the last day of the 1991 term to hand down its most anticipated decision, Planned Parenthood v. Casey. *In this case, Planned Parenthood of Southeastern Pennsylvania brought suit against Pennsylvania Governor Robert Casey to challenge the constitutionality of a series of provisions of the Pennsylvania Abortion Control Act of 1982 as amended in 1988 and 1989. As delineated in the Court's decision, "[t]he Act requires that a woman seeking an abortion give her informed consent prior to the abortion procedure, and specifies that she be provided with certain information at least 24 hours before the abortion is performed.... For a minor to obtain an abortion, the Act requires the informed consent of one of her parents, but provides for a judicial bypass option if minor does not wish or cannot obtain a parent's consent.... Another provision of the Act requires that, unless certain exceptions*

apply, a married woman seeking an abortion must sign a statement indicating that she has notified her husband of her intended abortion.... The Act exempts compliance with these three requirements in the event of a 'medical emergency....' In addition..., the Act imposes certain reporting requirements on facilities that provide abortion services." After a trial, the federal district court declared all of these provisions unconstitutional. The Court of Appeals for the Third Circuit reversed in part, upholding all of the requirements with the exception of the spousal notification provision. A fragmented Supreme Court upheld all of the statutory provisions with the exception of the spousal notification requirement. The Court produced five opinions. Two justices, Blackmun and Stevens, took the position (in separate opinions concurring in part and dissenting in part) that Roe v. Wade *should be reaffirmed and that all of the statutory provisions should be declared invalid. Four justices, Rehnquist, Scalia, White, and Thomas, took the view that* Roe *should be overruled and that all of the Pennsylvania restrictions should be upheld. The controlling opinion, co-authored by Justices O'Connor, Kennedy, and Souter, joined Justices Blackmun and Stevens in explicitly reaffirming* Roe v. Wade. *However, the "joint opinion" abandoned the* Roe *trimester framework and declared a new "unduly burdensome" test for judging regulations of abortion. Applying this test, the joint opinion upheld the parental consent and informed consent provisions but invalidated the spousal notification requirement. Thus, the vote on the Court was 5 to 4 to reaffirm* Roe v. Wade *and invalidate the spousal notification requirement and 7 to 2 to uphold the other statutory provisions.*

Justice O'Connor, Justice Kennedy, and **Justice Souter** . . . delivered the opinion of the Court. . . .

I

Liberty finds no refuge in a jurisprudence of doubt. Yet 19 years after our holding that the Constitution protects a woman's right to terminate her pregnancy in its early stages, *Roe v. Wade* *** (1973), that definition of liberty is still questioned. Joining the respondents as *amicus curiae,* the United States, as it has done in five other cases in the last decade, again asks us to overrule *Roe.* *** . . .

. . . [A]t oral arguments in this Court, the attorney for the parties challenging the statute took the position that none of the enactments can be upheld without overruling *Roe v. Wade.* *** We disagree with that analysis; but we acknowledge that our decisions after *Roe* cast doubt upon the meaning and reach of its holding. . . . State and Federal courts as well as legislatures throughout the union must have guidance as they seek to address this subject in conformance with the Constitution. Given these premises, we find it imperative to review once more the principles that define the rights of the woman and the legitimate authority of the state respecting the termination of pregnancies by abortion procedures.

After considering the fundamental constitutional questions resolved by *Roe,* principles of institutional integrity, and the rule of *stare decisis,* we are led to conclude this: the essential holding of *Roe v. Wade* should be retained and once again reaffirmed.

It must be stated at the outset and with clarity that *Roe's* essential holding, the holding we reaffirm, has three parts. First is a recognition of the right of the woman to choose to have an abortion before viability and to obtain it without undue interference from the State. Before viability, the state's interests are not strong enough to support a prohibition of abortion or the imposition of a substantial obstacle to the woman's effective right to elect the procedure. Second is a confirmation of the state's power to restrict abortions after fetal viability, if the law contains exceptions for pregnancies which endanger a woman's life or health. And third is the principle that the state has legitimate interests from the outset of the pregnancy in protecting the health of the woman and the life of the fetus that may become a child. These principles do not contradict one another; and we adhere to each.

II

. . . Men and women of good conscience can disagree, and we suppose some always shall disagree, about the profound moral and spiritual implications of terminating a pregnancy, even in its earliest stage. Some of us as individuals find abortion offensive to our most basic principles of morality, but that cannot control our decision. Our obligation is to define the liberty of all, not to mandate our own moral code. The underlying constitutional issue is whether the state can resolve these philosophic questions in such a definitive way that a woman lacks all choice in the matter, except perhaps in those rare circumstances in which the pregnancy is itself a danger to her own life or health, or is the result of rape or incest.

It is conventional constitutional doctrine that where reasonable people disagree the Government can adopt one position or the other. *** That theorem, however, assumes a state of affairs in which the choice does not intrude upon a protected liberty. Thus, while some people might disagree about whether or not the flag should be saluted, or disagree about the proposition that it may not be defiled, we have ruled that a state may not compel or enforce one view or the other. ***

... Our cases recognize "the right of the individual, married or single, to be free from unwarranted governmental intrusion into matters so fundamentally affecting a person as the decision whether to bear or beget a child." *** Our precedents "have respected the private realm of family life which the state cannot enter." *** These matters, involving the most intimate and personal choices a person may make in a lifetime, choices central to personal dignity and autonomy, are central to the liberty protected by the Fourteenth Amendment. At the heart of liberty is the right to define one's own concept of existence, of meaning, of the universe, and of the mystery of human life. Beliefs about these matters could not define the attributes of personhood were they formed under compulsion of the State.

These considerations begin our analysis of the woman's interest in terminating her pregnancy but cannot end it, for this reason: though the abortion decision may originate within the zone of conscience and belief, it is more than a philosophic exercise. Abortion is a unique act. It is an act fraught with consequences for others: for the woman who must live with the implications of her decision; for the persons who perform and assist in the procedure; for the spouse, family, and society which must confront the knowledge that these procedures exist, procedures some deem nothing short of an act of violence against innocent human life; and, depending on one's beliefs, for the life or potential life that is aborted. Though abortion is conduct, it does not follow that the State is entitled to proscribe it in all instances. That is because the liberty of the woman is at stake in a sense unique to the human condition and so unique to the law. . . .

III

... [W]hen this Court reexamines a prior holding, its judgment is customarily informed by a series of prudential and pragmatic considerations designed to test the consistency of overruling a prior decision with the ideal of the rule of law, and to gauge the respective costs of reaffirming and overruling a prior case. Thus, for example, we may ask whether the rule has proved to be intolerable simply in defying practical workability, *** whether the rule is subject to a kind of reliance that would lend a special hardship to the consequences of overruling and add inequity to the cost of repudiation, *** whether related principles of law have so far developed as to have left the old rule no more than a remnant of abandoned doctrine, *** or whether facts have so changed or come to be seen so differently, as to have robbed the old rule of significant application or justification. *** . . .

Although *Roe* has engendered opposition, it has in no sense proven "unworkable," *** representing as it does a simple limitation beyond which a state law is unenforceable. While *Roe* has, of course, required judicial assessment of state laws affecting the exercise of the choice guaranteed against government infringement, and although the need for such review will remain as a consequence of today's decision, the required determinations fall within judicial competence.

... [F]or two decades of economic and social developments, people have organized intimate relationships and made choices that define their views of themselves and their places in society, in reliance on the availability of abortion in the event that contraception should fail. The ability of women to participate equally in the economic and social life of the nation has been facilitated by their ability to control their reproductive lives. *** The Constitution serves human values, and while the effect of reliance on *Roe* cannot be exactly measured, neither can the certain cost of overruling *Roe* for people who have ordered their thinking and living around that case be dismissed.

No evolution of legal principle has left *Roe*'s doctrinal footings weaker than they were in 1973. No development of constitutional law since the case was decided has implicitly or explicitly left *Roe* behind as a mere survivor of obsolete constitutional thinking. . . .

We have seen how time has overtaken some of *Roe*'s factual assumptions: advances in maternal health care allow for abortions safe to the mother later in pregnancy than was true in 1973, *** and advances in neonatal care have advanced viability to a point somewhat earlier. *** But these facts go only to the scheme of time limits on the realization of competing interests, and the divergences from the factual premises of 1973 have no bearing on the validity of *Roe*'s central holding, that viability marks the earliest point at which the state's interest in fetal life is constitutionally adequate to justify a legislative ban on nontherapeutic abortions.

The soundness or unsoundness of that constitutional judgment in no sense turns on whether viability occurs at approximately 28 weeks, as was usual at the time of *Roe,* at 23 to 24 weeks, as it sometimes does today, or at some moment even slightly earlier in pregnancy, as it may if fetal respiratory capacity can somehow be enhanced in the future. Whenever it may occur, the attainment of viability may continue to serve as the critical fact, just as it has done since *Roe* was decided; which is to say that no change in *Roe*'s factual underpinning has left its central holding obsolete, and none supports an argument for overruling it.

The sum of the precedential inquiry to this point shows *Roe*'s underpinnings unweakened in any way affecting its central holding. While it has engendered disapproval, it has not been unworkable. An entire generation has come of age free to assume *Roe*'s concept of liberty in defining the capacity of women to act in society, and to make reproductive decisions; no erosion of principle going to liberty or personal autonomy has left *Roe*'s central holding a doctrinal remnant; *Roe* portends no developments at odds with other precedent for the analysis of personal liberty; and no changes of fact have rendered viability more or less appropriate as the point at which the balance of interests tips. Within the bounds of normal *stare decisis* analysis, then, and subject to the considerations on which it customarily turns, the stronger argument is for affirming *Roe*'s central holding, with whatever degree of personal reluctance any of us may have, not for overruling it. . . .

The Court's duty in the present case is clear. In 1973, it confronted the already-divisive issue of governmental power to limit personal choice to undergo abortion, for which it provided a new resolution based on the due process guaranteed by the Fourteenth Amendment. Whether or not a new social consensus is developing on that issue, its divisiveness is no less today than in 1973, and pressure to overrule the decision, like pressure to retain it, has grown only more intense. A decision to overrule *Roe*'s essential holding under the existing circumstances would address error, if error there was, at the cost of both profound and unnecessary damage to the Court's legitimacy, and to the Nation's commitment to the rule of law. It is therefore imperative to adhere to the essence of *Roe*'s original decision, and we do so today.

IV

From what we have said so far it follows that it is a constitutional liberty of the woman to have some freedom to terminate her pregnancy. We conclude that the basic decision in *Roe* was based on a constitutional analysis which we cannot now repudiate. The woman's liberty is not so unlimited, however, that from the outset the State cannot show its concern for the life of the unborn, and at a later point in fetal development the state's interest in life has sufficient force so that the right of the woman to terminate the pregnancy can be restricted. . . .

Yet it must be remembered that *Roe v. Wade* speaks with clarity in establishing not only the woman's liberty but also the state's "important and legitimate interest in potential life." *** That portion of the decision in *Roe* has been given too little acknowledgement and implementation by the Court in its subsequent cases. Those cases decided that any regulation touching upon the abortion decision must survive strict scrutiny, to be sustained only if drawn in narrow terms to further a compelling state interest. *** Not all of the cases decided under that formulation can be reconciled with the holding in *Roe* itself that the state has legitimate interests in the health of the woman and in protecting the potential life within her. In resolving this tension, we choose to rely upon *Roe,* as against the later cases.

. . . Regulations which do no more than create structural mechanisms by which the state, or the parent or guardian of a minor, may express profound respect for the life of the unborn are permitted, if they are not a substantial obstacle to the woman's exercise of the right to choose. *** Unless it has that effect on her right of choice, a state measure designed to persuade her to choose childbirth over abortion will be upheld if reasonably related to that goal. Regulations designed to foster the health of a woman seeking an abortion are valid if they do not constitute an undue burden.

Even when jurists reason from shared premises, some disagreement is inevitable. *** That is to be expected in the application of any legal standard which must accommodate life's complexity. We do not expect it to be otherwise with respect to the undue burden standard. We give this summary:

(a) To protect the central right recognized by *Roe v. Wade* while at the same time accommodating the state's profound interest in potential life, we will employ the undue burden analysis. . . . An undue burden exists, and therefore a provision of law is invalid, if its purpose or effect is to place a substantial obstacle in the path of a woman seeking an abortion before the fetus attains viability.

(b) We reject the rigid trimester framework of *Roe v. Wade*. To promote the state's profound interest in potential life, throughout pregnancy the state may take measures to ensure that the woman's choice is informed, and measures designed to advance this interest will not be invalidated as long as their purpose is to persuade the woman to choose childbirth over abortion. The measures must not be an undue burden on the right.

(c) As with any medical procedure, the state may enact regulations to further the health or safety of a woman seeking an abortion. Unnecessary health regulations that have the purpose or effect of presenting a substantial obstacle seeking an abortion impose an undue burden on the right.

(d) Our adoption of the undue burden analysis does not disturb the central holding of *Roe v. Wade,* and we reaffirm that holding. Regardless of whether exceptions are made for particular circumstances, a State may not prohibit any woman from making the ultimate decision to terminate her pregnancy before viability.

(e) We also reaffirm *Roe*'s holding that "subsequent to viability, the State in promoting its interest in the potentiality of human life may, if it chooses, regulate, and even proscribe, abortion except where it is necessary, in appropriate medical judgment, for the preservation of the life or health of the mother." ***

V

The Court of Appeals applied what it believed to be the undue burden standard and upheld each of the provisions [of the Pennsylvania law] except for the husband notification requirement. We agree generally with this conclusion, but refine the undue burden analysis in accordance with the principles articulated above. We now consider the separate statutory sections at issue.

A

Because it is central to the operation of other requirements, we begin with the statute's definition of medical emergency. Under the statute, a medical emergency is "[t]hat condition which, on the basis of the physician's good faith clinical judgment, so complicates the medical condition of a pregnant woman as to necessitate the immediate abortion of her pregnancy to avert her death or for which a delay will create serious risk of substantial and irreversible impairment of a major bodily function." ***

. . . [T]he Court of Appeals . . . stated: "we read the medical emergency exception as intended by the Pennsylvania legislature to assure that compliance with its abortion regulations would not in any way pose a significant threat to the life or health of a woman." *** Normally, . . . we defer to the construction of a state statute given it by the lower federal courts. Indeed, we have said that we will defer to lower court interpretations of state law unless they amount to "plain" error. . . . We adhere to that course today, and conclude that, as construed by the Court of Appeals, the medical emergency definition imposes no undue burden on a woman's abortion right.

B

We next consider the informed consent requirement. *** Except in a medical emergency, the statute requires that at least 24 hours before performing an abortion a physician inform the woman of the nature of the procedure, the health risks of the abortion and of childbirth, and the "probable gestational age of the unborn child." *** The physician or a qualified nonphysician must inform the woman of the availability of printed materials published by the State describing the fetus and providing information about medical assistance for childbirth, information about child support from the father, and a list of agencies which provide adoption and other services as alternatives to abortion. An abortion may not be performed unless the woman certifies in writing that she has been informed of the availability of these printed materials and has been provided them if she chooses to view them.

Our prior decisions establish that as with any medical procedure, the State may require a woman to give her written informed consent to an abortion. *** In this respect, the statute is unexceptional. Petitioners challenge the statute's definition of informed consent because it includes the provision of specific information by the doctor and the mandatory 24-hour waiting period. The conclusions reached by a majority of the Justices in the separate opinions filed today and the undue burden standard adopted in this opinion require us to overrule in part some of the Court's past decisions, decisions driven by the trimester framework's prohibition of all pre-viability regulations designed to further the State's interest in fetal life.

In *Akron [v. Akron Center for Reproductive Health]* *** (1983), we invalidated an ordinance which required that a woman seeking an abortion be provided by her physician with specific information "designed to influence the woman's informed choice between abortion or childbirth." *** As we later described the *Akron* holding in *Thornburgh v. American College of Obstetricians and Gynecologists,* *** there were two purported flaws in the Akron ordinance: the information was designed to dissuade the woman from having an abortion and the ordinance imposed "a rigid requirement that a specific body of information be given in all cases, irrespective of the particular needs of the patient. . . ." ***

To the extent *Akron* and *Thornburgh* find a constitutional violation when the government requires, as it does here, the giving of truthful, nonmisleading information about the nature of the procedure, the attendant health risks and those of childbirth, and the "probable gestational age" of the fetus, those cases go too far, are inconsistent with *Roe*'s acknowledgement of an important interest in potential life, and are overruled. This is clear even on the very terms of *Akron* and *Thornburgh*. Those decisions, along with *[Planned Parenthood of Central Missouri v.] Danforth* [1976], recognize a substantial government interest justifying a requirement that a woman be

apprised of the health risks of abortion and childbirth. *** It cannot be questioned that psychological well-being is a facet of health. Nor can it be doubted that most women considering an abortion would deem the impact on the fetus relevant, if not dispositive, to the decision. In attempting to ensure that a woman apprehend the full consequences of her decision, the State furthers the legitimate purpose of reducing the risk that a woman may elect an abortion, only to discover later, with devastating psychological consequences, that her decision was not fully informed. If the information the State requires to be made available to the woman is truth and not misleading, the requirement may be permissible.

We also see no reason why the State may not require doctors to inform a woman seeking an abortion of the availability of materials relating to the consequences to the fetus, even when those consequences have no direct relation to her health. An example illustrates the point. We would think it constitutional for the State to require that in order for there to be informed consent to a kidney transplant operation the recipient must be supplied with information about risks to the donor as well as risk to himself or herself. A requirement that the physician make available information similar to that mandated by the statute here was described in *Thornburgh* as "an outright attempt to wedge the Commonwealth's message discouraging abortion into the privacy of the informed-consent dialogue between the woman and her physician." *** We conclude, however, that informed choice need not be defined in such narrow terms that all considerations of the effect on the fetus are made irrelevant. As we have made clear, we depart from the holdings of *Akron* and *Thornburgh* to the extent that we permit a State to further its legitimate goal of protecting the life of the unborn by enacting legislation aimed at ensuring a decision that is mature and informed, even when in so doing the State expresses a preference for childbirth over abortion. In short, requiring that a woman be informed of the availability of information relating to fetal development and the assistance available should she decide to carry the pregnancy to full term is a reasonable measure to insure an informed choice, one which might cause the woman to choose childbirth over abortion. This requirement cannot be considered a substantial obstacle to obtaining an abortion, and, it follows, there is no undue burden.

Our prior cases also suggest that the "straitjacket," *** of particular information which must be given in each case interferes with a constitutional right of privacy between a pregnant woman and her physician.... Whatever constitutional status the doctor-patient relation may have as a general matter, in the present context it is derivative of the woman's position. The doctor-patient relation does not underlie or override the two more general rights under which the abortion right is justified: the right to make family decisions and the right to physical autonomy. On its own, the doctor-patient relation here is entitled to the same solicitude it receives in other contexts. Thus, a requirement that a doctor give a woman certain information as part of obtaining her consent to an abortion is, for constitutional purposes, no different from a requirement that a doctor give certain specific information about any medical procedure....

The Pennsylvania statute also requires us to reconsider the holding in *Akron* that the State may not require that a physician, as opposed to a qualified assistant, provide information relevant to a woman's informed consent. *** Since there is no evidence on this record that requiring a doctor to give the information as provided by the statute would amount in practical terms to a substantial obstacle to a woman seeking an abortion, we conclude that it is not an undue burden. Our cases reflect the fact that the Constitution gives the States broad latitude to decide that particular functions may be performed only by licensed professionals, even if an objective assessment might suggest that those same tasks could be performed by others. *** Thus, we uphold the provision as a reasonable means to insure that the woman's consent is informed.

Our analysis of Pennsylvania's 24-hour waiting period between the provision of the information deemed necessary to informed consent and the performance of an abortion under the undue burden standard requires us to reconsider the premise behind the decision in *Akron* in invalidating a parallel requirement.... In *Akron* we said: "Nor are we convinced that the State's legitimate concern that the woman's decision be informed is reasonably served

by requiring a 24-hour delay as a matter of course." *** We consider that conclusion to be wrong. The idea that important decisions will be more informed and deliberate if they follow some period of reflection does not strike us as unreasonable, particularly where the statute directs that important information become part of the background of the decision. The statute, as construed by the Court of Appeals, permits avoidance of the waiting period in the event of a medical emergency and the record evidence shows that in the vast majority of cases, a 24-hour delay does not create any appreciable health risk. In theory, at least, the waiting period is a reasonable measure to implement the State's interest in protecting the life of the unborn, a measure that does not amount to an undue burden....

[O]n the record before us, and in the context of this facial challenge, we are not convinced that the 24-hour waiting period constitutes an undue burden.

We are left with the argument that the various aspects of the informed consent required are unconstitutional because they place barriers in the way of abortion on demand. Even the broadest reading of *Roe,* however, has not suggested that there is a constitutional right to abortion on demand. *** Rather, the right protected by *Roe* is a right to decide to terminate a pregnancy free of undue interference by the State. Because the informed consent requirement facilitates the wise exercise of that right it cannot be classified as an interference with the right *Roe* protects. The informed consent requirement is not an undue burden on that right.

C

... Pennsylvania's abortion law provides, except in cases of medical emergency, that no physician shall perform an abortion on a married woman without receiving a signed statement from the woman that she has notified her spouse that she is about to undergo an abortion. The woman has the option of providing an alternative signed statement certifying that her husband is not the man who impregnated her; that her husband could not be located; that the pregnancy is the result of spousal sexual assault which she has reported; or that the woman believes that notifying her husband will cause him or someone else to inflict bodily injury upon her. A physician who performs an abortion on a married woman without receiving the appropriate signed statement will have his or her license revoked, and is liable to the husband for damages. . . .

. . . In well-functioning marriages, spouses discuss important intimate decisions such as whether to bear a child. But there are millions of women in this country who are the victims of regular physical and psychological abuse at the hands of their husbands. Should these women become pregnant, they may have very good reasons for not wishing to inform their husbands of their decision to obtain an abortion. Many may have justifiable fears of physical abuse, but may be no less fearful of the consequences of reporting prior abuse to the Commonwealth of Pennsylvania. Many may have a reasonable fear that notifying their husbands will provoke further instances of child abuse; these women are not exempt from [the] notification requirement. Many may fear devastating forms of psychological abuse from their husbands, including verbal harassment, threats of future violence, the destruction of possessions, physical confinement to the home, the withdrawal of financial support, or the disclosure of the abortion to family and friends. These methods of psychological abuse may act as even more of a deterrent to notification than the possibility of physical violence, but women who are the victims of the abuse are not exempt from [the] notification requirement. And many women who are pregnant as a result of sexual assaults by their husbands will be unable to avail themselves of the exception for spousal sexual assault *** because the exception requires that the woman have notified law enforcement authorities within 90 days of the assault, and her husband will be notified of her report once an investigation begins. *** If anything in this field is certain, it is that victims of spousal sexual assault are extremely reluctant to report the abuse to the government; hence, a great many spousal rape victims will not be exempt from the notification requirement. . . .

The spousal notification requirement is thus likely to prevent a significant number of women from obtaining an abortion. It does not merely make abortions a little more difficult or expensive to obtain; for many women, it will impose a substantial obstacle. We must not blind ourselves to the fact that the significant number of women who fear for their safety and the safety of their children are likely to be deterred from procuring an abortion as surely as if the Commonwealth had outlawed abortion in all cases. . . .

. . . It is an undue burden, and therefore invalid.

This conclusion is in no way inconsistent with our decisions upholding parental notification or consent requirements. *** Those enactments, and our judgment that they are constitutional, are based on the quite reasonable assumption that minors will benefit from consultation with their parents and that children will often not realize that their parents have their best interests at heart. We cannot adopt a parallel assumption about adult women. . . .

D

We next consider the parental consent provision. Except in a medical emergency, an unemancipated young woman under 18 may not obtain an abortion unless she and one of her parents (or guardian) provides informed consent as defined above. If neither a parent nor a guardian provides consent, a court may authorize the performance of an abortion upon a determination that the young woman is mature and capable of giving informed consent and has in fact given her informed consent, or that an abortion would be in her best interests.

We have been over most of this ground before. Our cases establish, and we reaffirm today, that a State may require a minor seeking an abortion to obtain the consent of a parent or guardian, provided that there is an adequate judicial bypass procedure. *** Under these precedents, in our view, the one-parent consent requirement and judicial bypass procedure are constitutional. . . .

E

Under the recordkeeping and reporting requirements of the statute, every facility which performs abortions is required to file a report stating its name and address as well as the name and address of any related entity, such as controlling or subsidiary organization. In the case of state-funded institutions, the information becomes public.

For each abortion performed, a report must be filed identifying: the physician (and the second physician where required); the facility; the referring physician or agency; the woman's age; the number of prior pregnancies and prior abortions she has had; gestational age; the type of abortion procedure; the date of the abortion; whether there were any pre-existing medical conditions which would complicate pregnancy; medical complications with the abortion; where applicable, the basis for the determination that the abortion was medically necessary; the weight of the aborted fetus; and whether the woman was married, and if so, whether notice was provided or the basis for the failure to give notice. Every abortion facility must also file quarterly reports showing the number of abortions performed broken down by trimester. *** In all events, the identity of each woman who has had an abortion remains confidential.

In *Danforth,* *** we held that recordkeeping and reporting provisions "that are reasonably directed to the preservation of maternal health and that properly respect a patient's confidentiality and privacy are permissible." We think that under this standard all the provisions at issue here except that relating to spousal notice are constitutional. Although they do not relate to the State's interest in informing the woman's choice, they do relate to health. The collection of information with respect to actual patients is a vital element of medical research, and so it cannot be said that the requirements serve no purpose other than to make abortions more difficult. Nor do we find that the requirements impose a substantial obstacle to a woman's choice. At most they might increase the cost of some abortions by a slight amount. While at some point increased cost could become a substantial obstacle, there is no such showing on the record before us.

Subsection (12) of the reporting provision requires the reporting of, among other things, a married woman's "reason for failure to provide notice" to her husband. *** This provision in effect requires women, as a condition of obtaining an abortion, to provide the Commonwealth with the precise information we have already recognized that many women have pressing reasons not to reveal. Like the spousal notice requirement itself, this provision places an undue burden on a woman's choice, and must be invalidated for that reason.

VI

Our Constitution is a covenant running from the first generation of Americans to us and then to future generations. It is a coherent succession. Each generation must learn anew that the Constitution's written terms embody ideas and aspirations that must survive more ages than one. We accept our responsibility not to retreat from interpreting the full meaning of the covenant in light of all our precedents. We invoke it once again to define the freedom guaranteed by the Constitution's own promise, the promise of liberty. . . .

Justice Stevens, concurring in part and dissenting in part.

. . . The Court is unquestionably correct in concluding that the doctrine of *stare decisis* has controlling significance in a case of this kind, notwithstanding an individual justice's concerns about the merits. The central holding of *Roe v. Wade,* *** has been a "part of our law" for almost two decades. It was a natural sequel to the protection of individual liberty established in *Griswold v. Connecticut.* *** The societal costs of overruling *Roe* at this late date would be enormous. *Roe* is an integral part of a correct understanding of both the concept of liberty and the basic equality of men and women. . . .

In my opinion, the principles established in [the] long line of cases [since *Roe v. Wade*] . . . should govern our decision today. Under these principles, [the informed consent provisions] of the Pennsylvania statute are unconstitutional. Those sections require a physician or counselor to provide the woman with a range of materials clearly designed to persuade her to choose not to undergo the abortion. . . .

The 24-hour waiting period raises even more serious concerns. . . . Part of the constitutional liberty to choose is the equal dignity to which each of us is entitled. A woman who decides to terminate her pregnancy is entitled to the same respect as a woman who decides to carry the fetus to term. The mandatory waiting period denies women that equal respect. . . .

Justice Blackmun, concurring in part and dissenting in part.

Three years ago, in *Webster v. Reproductive Health Serv.,* *** four members of this Court appeared poised to "cas(t) into darkness the hopes and visions of every woman in this country" who had come to believe that the Constitution guaranteed her the right to reproductive choice. *** All that remained between the promise of *Roe* and the darkness of the plurality was a single, flickering flame. Decisions since *Webster* gave little reason to hope that this flame would cast much light. But now, just when so many expected the darkness to fall, the flame has grown bright.

I do not underestimate the significance of today's joint opinion. Yet I remain steadfast in my belief that the right to reproductive choice is entitled to the full protection afforded by the Court before *Webster.* And I fear for the darkness as four Justices anxiously await the single vote necessary to extinguish the light. . . .

Make no mistake, the joint opinion of Justices O'Connor, Kennedy, and Souter is an act of personal courage and constitutional principle. In contrast to previous decisions in which Justices O'Connor and Kennedy postponed reconsideration of *Roe v. Wade,* *** the authors of the joint opinion today join Justice Stevens and me in concluding that "the essential holding of *Roe* should be retained and once again reaffirmed." *** In brief, five members of this Court today recognize that "the Constitution protects a woman's right to terminate her pregnancy in its early stages." ***

A fervent view of individual liberty and the force of *stare decisis* have led the Court to this conclusion. . . .

In one sense, the Court's approach is worlds apart from that of the Chief Justice and Justice Scalia. And yet, in another sense, the distance between the two approaches is short—the distance is but a single vote. I am 83 years old. I cannot remain on this Court forever, and when I do step down, the confirmation process for my successor well may focus on the issue before us today. That, I regret, may be exactly where the choice between the two worlds will be made.

Chief Justice Rehnquist, with whom **Justice White, Justice Scalia,** and **Justice Thomas** join, concurring in part and dissenting in part.

The joint opinion, following its newly-minted variation on *stare decisis,* retains the outer shell of *Roe v. Wade,* but beats a wholesale retreat from the substance of that case. We believe that *Roe* was wrongly decided, and that it can and should be overruled consistently with our traditional approach to *stare decisis* in constitutional cases. We would adopt the approach of the plurality in *Webster v. Reproductive Health Services* *** and uphold the challenged provisions of the Pennsylvania statute in their entirety. . . .

The joint opinion of Justices O'Connor, Kennedy, and Souter cannot bring itself to say that *Roe* was correct as an original matter, but the authors are of the view that "the immediate question is not the soundness of *Roe*'s resolution of the issue, but the precedential force that must be accorded to its holding." ***

Instead of claiming that *Roe* was correct as a matter of original constitutional interpretation, the opinion therefore contains an elaborate discussion of *stare decisis.* . . .

In our view, authentic principles of *stare decisis* do not require that any portion of the reasoning in *Roe* be kept intact. "*Stare decisis* is not . . . a universal, inexorable command," *** especially in cases involving the interpretation of the Federal Constitution. Erroneous decisions in such constitutional cases are uniquely durable, because correction through legislation action, save for constitutional amendment, is impossible. It is therefore our duty to reconsider constitutional interpretations that "depart(t) from a proper understanding" of the Constitution. . . .

The Judicial Branch derives its legitimacy, not from following public opinion, but from deciding by its best lights whether legislative enactments of the popular branches of Government comport with the Constitution. The doctrine of *stare decisis* is an adjunct of this duty, and should be no more subject to the vagaries of public opinion than is the basic judicial task. . . .

The decision in *Roe* has engendered large demonstrations, including repeated marches on this Court and on Congress, both in opposition to and in support of that opinion. A decision either way on *Roe* can therefore be perceived as favoring one group or the other. But this perceived dilemma arises only if one assumes, as the joint opinion does, that the Court should make its decisions with a view toward speculative public perceptions. . . .

The sum of the joint opinion's labors in the name of *stare decisis* and "legitimacy" is this: *Roe v. Wade* stands as a sort of judicial Potemkin Village, which may be pointed out to passers by as a monument to the importance of adhering to precedent. But behind the facade, an entirely new method of analysis, without any roots in constitutional law, is imported to decide the constitutionality of state laws regulating abortion. Neither *stare decisis* nor "legitimacy" are truly served by such an effort. . . .

Justice Scalia, with whom the **Chief Justice, Justice White,** and **Justice Thomas** join, concurring in part and dissenting in part.

My views on this matter are unchanged . . . The states may, if they wish, permit abortion-on-demand, but the Constitution does not require them to do so.

The permissibility of abortion, and the limitations upon it, are to be resolved like most important questions in our democracy: by citizens trying to persuade one another and then voting. As the Court acknowledges, "where reasonable people disagree the government can adopt one position or the other." ***

The Court is correct in adding the qualification that this "assumes a state of affairs in which the choice does not intrude upon a protected liberty," *** but the crucial part of that qualification is the penultimate word. A State's choice between two positions on which reasonable people can disagree is constitutional even when (as is often the case) it intrudes upon a "liberty" in the absolute sense.

Laws against bigamy, for example—which entire societies of reasonable people disagree with—intrude upon men and women's liberty to marry and live with one another. But bigamy happens not to be a liberty specially "protected" by the Constitution.

That is, quite simply, the issue in this case: not whether the power of a woman to abort her unborn child is a "liberty" in the absolute sense; or even whether it is a liberty of great importance to many women. Of course it is both. The issue is whether it is a liberty protected by the Constitution of the United States. I am sure it is not.

I reach that conclusion not because of anything so exalted as my views concerning the "concept of existence, of meaning, of the universe, and of the mystery of life." *** Rather, I reach it for the same reason that bigamy is not constitutionally protected—because of two simple facts: (1) the Constitution says absolutely nothing about it, and (2) the longstanding traditions of American society have permitted it to be legally proscribed. . . .

The Court's description of the place of *Roe* in the social history of the United States is unrecognizable. Not only did *Roe* not, as the Court suggests, resolve the deeply divisive issue of abortion; it did more than anything else to nourish it, by elevating it to the national level where it is infinitely more difficult to resolve.

National politics were not plagued by abortion protests, national abortion lobbying, or abortion marches on Congress, before *Roe v. Wade* was decided. Profound disagreement existed among our citizens over the issue—as it does over other issues, such as the death penalty—but that disagreement was being worked out at the state level. As with many other issues, the division of sentiment within each State was not as closely balanced as it was among the population of the Nation as a whole, meaning not only that more people would be satisfied with the results of state-by-state resolution, but also that those results would be more stable. Pre-*Roe,* moreover, political compromise was possible.

Roe's mandate for abortion-on-demand destroyed the compromises of the past, rendered compromises impossible for the future, and required the entire issue to be resolved, uniformly, at the national level. At the same time, *Roe* created a vast new class of abortion consumers and abortion proponents by eliminating the moral opprobrium that had attached to the act ("If the Constitution guarantees abortion, how can it be bad?"—not an accurate line of thought, but a natural one).

Many favor all of those developments, and it is not for me to say that they are wrong. But to portray *Roe* as the statesmanlike "settlement" of a divisive issue, a jurisprudential Peace of Westphalia that is worth preserving, is nothing less than Orwellian. . . .

Freeman v. Pitts

503 U.S. ___; 112 S. Ct. 1430; 118 L. Ed. 2d 108 (1992)
Vote: 8-0

In Green v. County School Board (1968), the Supreme Court held that schools that were previously segregated by law must immediately produce workable desegregation plans. The Court required that such plans eliminate racial discrimination in six areas: student assignments, faculty, staff, transportation, extracurricular activities, and physical facilities. In the wake of Green, African-American school children and their parents promptly filed a class action in federal court for the desegregation of the DeKalb County, Georgia, school system, which, like most school systems in the South, had previously been segregated by state law. The school system, in collaboration with the federal government, soon devised a comprehensive desegregation plan that was approved by the district court in a consent order issued in June 1969. Over the next seventeen years, the district court, while retaining supervisory jurisdiction, undertook only infrequent and limited intervention in the affairs of the school system. During this period, the proportion of blacks enrolled in the DeKalb County schools rose from 5.6 to 47 percent of the total, while a shift in residential patterns led to a concentration of whites in the northern half of the county and blacks in the southern half. In 1986, school officials filed a motion for final dismissal of the case, arguing that the goal of establishing a unitary system had been achieved. The district court found that the school system had "traveled the road to unitary status almost to its end" but that vestiges of the dual system of segregation remained in several areas; namely, teacher and principal assignments, resource allocation, and quality of education. Only in these areas would the school system be required to address continuing problems. The U.S. Court of Appeals for the Eleventh Circuit reversed in part and remanded the case to the district court. The court of appeals held that the district court had erred in considering the aforementioned Green factors as separate categories and said that a district court may relinquish its supervision only after a school district had satisfied all the Green factors for a number of

years. By a unanimous vote (with Justice Clarence Thomas not participating in the decision), the Supreme Court reversed and remanded the case to the court of appeals. The Court's decision is summed up in the final portion of Justice Kennedy's majority opinion, which represents the views of five of the justices (Kennedy, Rehnquist, White, Scalia, and Souter). In an opinion concurring in the judgment only, Justice Blackmun (joined by Justices O'Connor and Stevens) expresses a quite different position as to why the case should be remanded to the court of appeals. This decision thus demonstrates that consensus on the legal disposition of a case does not necessarily indicate agreement on the substantive issues involved.

Justice Kennedy delivered the opinion of the Court.

. . . We reach now the question whether the Court of Appeals erred in prohibiting the District Court from returning to DCSS [the DeKalb County School System] . . . partial control over some of its affairs. We decide that the Court of Appeals did err in holding that, as a matter of law, the District Court had no discretion to permit DCSS to regain control over student assignment, transportation, physical facilities, and extracurricular activities, while retaining court supervision over the areas of faculty and administrative assignments and the quality of education, where full compliance had not been demonstrated. . . .

That there was racial imbalance in student attendance zones was not tantamount to a showing that the school district was in noncompliance with the decree or with its duties under the law. Racial balance is not to be achieved for its own sake. It is to be pursued when racial imbalance has been caused by a constitutional violation. Once the racial imbalance due to the *de jure* violation has been remedied, the school district is under no duty to remedy imbalance that is caused by demographic factors. *** If the unlawful *de jure* policy of a school system has been the cause of the racial imbalance in student attendance, that condition must be remedied. The school district bears the burden of showing that any current imbalance is not traceable, in a proximate way, to the prior violation.

The findings of the District Court that the population changes which occurred in DeKalb County were not caused by the policies of the school district, but rather by independent factors, are consistent with the mobility that is a distinct characteristic of our society. In one year (from 1987 to 1988) over 40 million Americans, or 17.6 percent of the total population, moved households. *** Over a third of those people moved to a different county, and over six million migrated between States. *** In such a society it is inevitable that the demographic makeup of school districts, based as they are on political subdivisions such as counties and municipalities, may undergo rapid change.

The effect of changing residential patterns on the racial composition of schools though not always fortunate is somewhat predictable. Studies show a high correlation between residential reaggregation and school segregation. *** The District Court in this case heard evidence tending to show that racially stable neighborhoods are not likely to emerge because whites prefer a racial mix of 80% white and 20% black, while blacks prefer a 50%-50% mix.

Where resegregation is a product not of state action but of private choices, it does not have constitutional implications. It is beyond the authority and beyond the practical ability of the federal courts to try to counteract these kinds of continuous and massive demographic shifts. To attempt such results would require ongoing and never-ending supervision by the courts of school districts simply because they were once *de jure* segregated. Residential housing choices, and their attendant effects on the racial composition of schools, present an ever-changing pattern, one difficult to address through judicial remedies.

In one sense of the term, vestiges of past segregation by state decree do remain in our society and in our schools. Past wrongs to the black race, wrongs committed by the State and in its name, are a stubborn fact of history. And stubborn facts of history linger and persist. But though we cannot escape our history, neither must we overstate its consequences

in fixing legal responsibilities. The vestiges of segregation that are the concern of the law in a school case may be subtle and intangible but nonetheless they must be so real that they have a causal link to the *de jure* violation being remedied. It is simply not always the case that demographic forces causing population change bear any real and substantial relation to a *de jure* violation. And the law need not proceed on that premise.

As the *de jure* violation becomes more remote in time and these demographic changes intervene, it becomes less likely that a current racial imbalance in a school district is a vestige of the prior *de jure* system. The causal link between current conditions and the prior violation is even more attenuated if the school district has demonstrated its good faith. In light of its finding that the demographic changes in DeKalb County are unrelated to the prior violation, the District Court was correct to entertain the suggestion that DCSS had no duty to achieve systemwide racial balance in the student population. It was appropriate for the District Court to examine the reasons for the racial imbalance before ordering an impractical, and no doubt massive, expenditure of funds to achieve racial balance after 17 years of efforts to implement the comprehensive plan in a district where there were fundamental changes in demographics, changes not attributable to the former *de jure* regime or any later actions by school officials. The District Court's determination to order instead the expenditure of scarce resources in areas such as the quality of education, where full compliance had not yet been achieved, underscores the uses of discretion in framing equitable remedies.

To say, as did the Court of Appeals, that a school district must meet all six *Green* factors before the trial court can declare the system unitary and relinquish its control over school attendance zones, and to hold further that racial balancing by all necessary means is required in the interim, is simply to vindicate a legal phrase. The law is not so formalistic. A proper rule must be based on the necessity to find a feasible remedy that insures systemwide compliance with the court decree and that is directed to curing the effects of the specific violation.

We next consider whether retention of judicial control over student attendance is necessary or practicable to achieve compliance in other facets of the school system. Racial balancing in elementary and secondary school student assignments may be a legitimate remedial device to correct other fundamental inequities that were themselves caused by the constitutional violation. We have long recognized that the *Green* factors may be related or interdependent. Two or more *Green* factors may be intertwined and synergistic in their relation, so that a constitutional violation in one area cannot be eliminated unless the judicial remedy addresses other matters as well. We have observed, for example, that student segregation and faculty segregation are often related problems. *** As a consequence, a continuing violation in one area may need to be addressed by remedies in another. ***

There was no showing that racial balancing was an appropriate mechanism to cure other deficiencies in this case. It is true that the school district was not in compliance with respect to faculty assignments, but the record does not show that student reassignments would be a feasible or practicable way to remedy this defect. To the contrary, the District Court suggests that DCSS could solve the faculty assignment problem by reassigning a few teachers per school. The District Court, not having our analysis before it, did not have the opportunity to make specific findings and conclusions on this aspect of the case, however. Further proceedings are appropriate for this purpose.

The requirement that the school district show its good-faith commitment to the entirety of a desegregation plan so that parents, students and the public have assurance against further injuries or stigma also should be a subject for more specific findings. We stated in *Dowell* that the good-faith compliance of the district with the court order over a reasonable period of time is a factor to be considered in deciding whether or not jurisdiction could be relinquished. *** A history of good-faith compliance is evidence that any current racial imbalance is not the product of a new *de jure* violation, and enables the district court to accept the school board's representation that it has accepted the principle of racial equality and will not suffer intentional discrimination in the future. ***

When a school district has not demonstrated good faith under a comprehensive plan to remedy on-going violations, we have without hesitation approved comprehensive and continued district court supervision. ***

... [T]he District Court in this case stated that throughout the period of judicial supervision it has been impressed by the successes DCSS has achieved and its dedication to providing a quality education for all students, and that DCSS "has travelled the often long road to unitary status almost to its end." With respect to those areas where compliance had not been achieved, the District Court did not find that DCSS had acted in bad faith or engaged in further acts of discrimination since the desegregation plan went into effect. This, though, may not be the equivalent of a finding that the school district has an affirmative commitment to comply in good faith with the entirety of a desegregation plan, and further proceedings are appropriate for this purpose as well.

The judgment is reversed and the case is remanded to the Court of Appeals. It should determine what issues are open for its further consideration in light of the previous briefs and arguments of the parties and in light of the principles set forth in this opinion. Thereupon it should order further proceedings as necessary or order an appropriate remand to the District Court....

Justice Thomas took no part in the consideration or decision of this case.

Justice Scalia, concurring.

The District Court in the present case found that the imbalances in student assignment were attributable to private demographic shifts rather than governmental action. Without disturbing this finding, and without finding that revision of student assignments was necessary to remedy some other unlawful government action, the Court of Appeals ordered DeKalb County to institute massive busing and other programs to achieve integration. The Court convincingly demonstrates that this cannot be reconciled with our cases, and I join its opinion.

Our decision will be of great assistance to the citizens of DeKalb County, who for the first time since 1969 will be able to run their own public schools, at least so far as student assignments are concerned. It will have little effect, however, upon the many other school districts throughout the country that are still being supervised by federal judges, since it turns upon the extraordinarily rare circumstance of a finding that no portion of the current racial imbalance is a remnant of prior *de jure* discrimination. While it is perfectly appropriate for the Court to decide this case on that narrow basis, we must resolve—if not today, then soon—what is to be done in the vast majority of other districts, where, though our cases continue to profess that judicial oversight of school operations is a temporary expedient, democratic processes remain suspended, with no prospect of restoration, 38 years after *Brown v. Board of Education*. *** ...

Justice Souter, concurring.

I join the Court's opinion holding that where there are vestiges of a dual system in some of a judicially supervised school system's aspects, or *Green*-type factors, a district court will retain jurisdiction over the system, but need not maintain constant supervision or control over factors as to which compliance has been achieved. I write separately only to explain my understanding of the enquiry required by a district court applying the principle we set out today.

We recognize that although demographic changes influencing the composition of a school's student population may well have no causal link to prior *de jure* segregation, judicial control of student assignments may still be necessary to remedy persisting vestiges of the unconstitutional dual system, such as remaining imbalance in faculty assignments. *** This is, however, only one of several possible causal relationships between or among unconstitutional acts of school segregation and various *Green*-type factors. I think it is worth mentioning at least two others: the dual school system itself as a cause of the demographic shifts with which the district court is faced when considering a partial relinquishment of supervision, and a *Green*-type factor other than student assignments as a possible cause of imbalanced student assignment patterns in the future.

The first would occur when demographic change toward segregated residential patterns is itself caused by past school segregation and the patterns of thinking that segregation creates. Such demographic change is not an independent, supervening cause of racial imbalance in the student body, and we have said before that when demographic change is not independent of efforts to segregate, the causal relationship may be considered in fashioning a school desegregation remedy. *** Racial imbalance in student assignments caused by demographic change is not insulated from federal judicial oversight where the demographic change is itself caused in this way, and before deciding to relinquish supervision and control over student assignments, a district court should make findings on the presence or absence of this relationship.

The second and related causal relationship would occur after the district court has relinquished supervision over a remedied aspect of the school system, when future imbalance in that remedied *Green*-type factor (here, student assignments) would be caused by remaining vestiges of the dual system. Even after attaining compliance as to student composition, other factors such as racial composition of the faculty, quality of the physical plant, or per-pupil expenditures may leave schools racially identifiable. In this very case, for example, there is a correlation in particular schools of overrepresentation of black principals and administrators, lower per pupil expenditures, and high percentages of black students. Moreover, the schools in the predominately black southern section of the school district are the only ones that use "portable classrooms," i.e., trailers. *** If such other factors leave a school identifiable as "black," as soon as the district court stops supervising student assignments, nearby white parents may move in the direction of racially identifiable "white" schools, or may simply move their children into these schools. In such a case, the vestige of discrimination in one factor will act as an incubator for resegregation in others. Before a district court ends its supervision of student assignments, then, it should make a finding that there is no immediate threat of unremedied *Green*-type factors causing population or student enrollment changes that in turn may imbalance student composition in this way. And, because the district court retains jurisdiction over the case, it should of course reassert control over student assignments if it finds that this does happen.

Justice Blackmun, with whom ***Justice Stevens*** and ***Justice O'Connor*** join, concurring in the judgment.

It is almost 38 years since this Court decided *Brown v. Board of Education* *** (1954). In those 38 years the students in DeKalb County, Georgia never have attended a desegregated school system even for one day. The majority of black students never have attended a school that was not disproportionately black. Ignoring this glaring dual character of the De-Kalb County School System (DCSS), part "white" and part "black," the District Court relinquished control over student assignments, finding that the school district had achieved "unitary status" in that aspect of the system. No doubt frustrated by the continued existence of duality, the Court of Appeals ordered the school district to take extraordinary measures to correct all manifestations of this racial imbalance. Both decisions, in my view, were in error, and I therefore concur in the Court's decision to vacate the judgment and remand the case. . . .

I also am in agreement with what I consider to be the holdings of the Court. I agree that in some circumstances the District Court need not interfere with a particular portion of the school system, even while, in my view, it must retain jurisdiction over the entire system until all vestiges of state-imposed segregation have been eliminated. *** I also agree that whether the District Court must order DCSS to balance student assignments depends on whether the current imbalance is traceable to unlawful state policy and on whether such an order is necessary to fashion an effective remedy. . . .

The District Court apparently has concluded that DCSS should be relieved of its responsibility to desegregate because such responsibility would be burdensome. To be sure, changes in demographic patterns aggravated the vestiges of segregation and made it more difficult for DCSS to desegregate. But an integrated school system is no less desirable because it is difficult to achieve, and it is no less a constitutional imperative because that imperative has gone unmet for 38 years.

Although respondents challenged the District Court's causation conclusions in the Court of Appeals, that court did not reach the issue. Accordingly, in addition to the issues the Court suggests be considered in further proceedings, I would remand for the Court of Appeals to review . . . the District Court's finding that DCSS has met its burden of proving the racially identifiable schools are in no way the result of past segregative action.

U.S. Department of Commerce v. Montana
503 U.S. ____; 112 S. Ct. 1415; 118 L. Ed.2d 87 (1992)
Vote: 9-0

After losing one of its two congressional seats as a result of demographic changes revealed by the 1990 census, the state of Montana brought suit to challenge the method by which Congress allocates representatives among the states.

Justice Stevens delivered the opinion of the Court.

Article I, sec. 2, of the Constitution requires apportionment of Representatives among the several States "according to their respective Numbers." An Act of Congress passed in 1941 provides that after each decennial census "the method known as the method of equal proportions" shall be used to determine the number of Representatives to which each State is entitled. In this case a three-judge District Court held that statute unconstitutional because it found that the method of equal proportions resulted in an unjustified deviation from the ideal of equal representation. The Government's appeal from that holding requires us to consider the standard that governs the apportionment of Representatives among the several States. In view of the importance of this issue and its significance in this year's congressional and Presidential elections, we noted probable jurisdiction and ordered expedited briefing and argument. *** We now reverse.

I

The 1990 census revealed that the population of certain States, particularly California, Florida, and Texas, had increased more rapidly than the national average. The application of the method of equal proportions to the 1990 census caused 8 States to gain a total of 19 additional seats in the House of Representatives and 13 States to lose an equal number. Montana was one of those States. Its loss of one seat cut its delegation in half and precipitated this litigation.

According to the 1990 census, the population of the 50 States that elect the numbers of the House of Representatives is 249,022,783. The average size of the 435 congressional districts is 572,466. Montana's population of 803,655 forms a single congressional district that is 231,189 persons larger than the ideal congressional district. If it had retained its two districts, each would have been 170,638 persons smaller than the ideal district. In terms of absolute difference, each of the two districts would have been closer to ideal size than the single congressional district.

The State of Montana, its Governor, Attorney General, and Secretary of State, and the State's two Senators and Representatives (hereinafter collectively referred to as Montana) filed suit against appropriate federal defendants (the Government) in the United States District Court for the District of Montana, asserting that Montana was entitled to retain its two seats. They alleged that the existing apportionment method violates Article I, sec. 2, of the Constitution because it "does not achieve the greatest possible equality in the number of individuals per representative" and also violates Article I, sec. 2, and Article I, sec. 7, because reapportionment is effected "through application of a mathematical formula by the Department of Commerce and the automatic transmittal of the results to the states" rather than by legislation on which Members of Congress vote in the normal manner. A three-judge District Court ... granted Montana's motion for summary judgment on the first claim.

The majority of the three-judge District Court decided that the principle of equal representation for equal numbers of people that was applied to intrastate districting in *Wesberry v. Sanders* *** (1964),

should also be applied to the apportionment of seats among the States. Under that standard the only population variances that are acceptable are those that "are unavoidable despite a good faith effort to achieve absolute equality, or for which justification is shown." *** The District Court held that the variance between the population of Montana's single district and the ideal district could not be justified under that standard. The majority refused to accord deference to the congressional decision to adopt the method of equal proportions in 1941 because that decision was made without the benefit of this Court's later jurisprudence adopting the "one-person, one-vote" rule. Accordingly, the District Court entered a judgment declaring the statute void and enjoining the Government from effecting any reapportionment of the House of Representatives pursuant to the method of equal proportions. . . .

II

The general admonition in Article I, sec. 2, that Representatives shall be apportioned among the several States "according to their respective Numbers" is constrained by three requirements. The number of Representatives shall not exceed one for every 30,000 persons; each State shall have at least one Representative; and district boundaries may not cross state lines. Although the text of Article I determined the original apportionment that the Framers had agreed upon, it did not explain how that specific allocation had been made.

When Congress first confronted the task of apportionment after the census of 1790 (and after Vermont and Kentucky had been admitted to the Union), it considered using the constitutional minimum of 30,000 persons as the size of each district. Dividing that number into the total population of 3,615,920 indicated that the House of Representatives should contain 120 members. When that number was divided into the population of individual States, each quotient was a whole number with a fractional remainder. Thus, the use of the 30,000 divisor for Connecticut's population of 236,841 indicated that it should have 7.89 Representatives, while Rhode Island, with a population of 68,446, should have 2.28 Representatives. Because each State must be represented by a whole number of legislators, it was necessary either to disregard fractional remainders entirely or to treat some or all of them as equal to a whole Representative.

In the first apportionment bill passed by Congress, an additional Representative was assigned to the nine States whose quotas had the highest fractional remainders. Thus, Connecticut's quota of 7.89 gave it 8 and Rhode Island's smaller remainder was disregarded, giving it only 2. Although that method was supported by Alexander Hamilton, Thomas Jefferson persuaded President Washington to veto the bill, in part because its allocation of eight Representatives to Connecticut exceeded the constitutional limit of one for every 30,000 persons.

In response to that veto, Congress adopted a proposal sponsored by Thomas Jefferson that disregarded fractional remainders entirely (thus giving Connecticut only 7 Representatives). To overcome the basis for the veto, the size of the House was reduced from 120 to 105 members, giving each Representative an approximate constituency of 33,000 instead of 30,000 persons. Although both the total number of Representatives and the size of their districts increased, Jefferson's method of disregarding fractional remainders was used after each of the next four censuses. Today mathematicians sometimes refer to that method as the "method of greatest divisors," and suggest that it tends to favor large States over smaller States.

In 1832, Congress considered, but did not adopt, a proposal sponsored by John Quincy Adams that was the exact opposite of the Jefferson method. Instead of disregarding fractional remainders, Adams would have treated every fraction as a unit. Thus, using the former example as a hypothetical, both Connecticut and Rhode Island would have received one more Representative under the Adams method than they actually received under the Jefferson method. The Adams method is sometimes described as the "method of smallest divisors" and is said to favor the smaller States. It has never been endorsed by Congress.

In 1842, Congress abandoned the Jefferson method in favor of an approach supported by Senator Daniel Webster. The Webster method took account of fractional remainders that were greater than one-half by allocating "one additional representative for each State having a fraction greater than one moiety." Thus, if that method had been used in 1790, Connecticut's quota of 7.89 would have entitled it to 8 Representatives, whereas Rhode Island, with a quota of 2.28, would have received only 2. The Webster method is also described as the "method of major fractions."

In 1850, Congress enacted legislation sponsored by Representative Vinton endorsing the approach that had been sponsored by Alexander Hamilton after the first census. Although this method was used during the balance of the 19th century, it occasionally seemed to produce paradoxical results. Congress rejected it in 1911, reverting to the Webster method. In that year Congress also passed legislation that ultimately fixed the number of Representatives at 435.

After the 1920 census Congress failed to pass a reapportionment Act, but debates over the proper method of apportionment ultimately led to a request to the National Academy of Sciences to appoint a committee of experts to review the subject. That committee, composed of respected mathematicians, recommended the adoption of the "method of equal proportions." Congress used that method in its apportionment after the 1930 census, and formally adopted it in the 1941 statute at issue in this case.

The report of the National Academy of Sciences committee noted that Congress had properly rejected the Hamilton/Vinton method, and concluded that the use of only five methods could lead to a workable solution of the fractional remainder problem. In the opinion of the committee members, given the fact that it is impossible for all States to have districts of the same size, the best method was the one that minimized the discrepancy between the size of the districts in any pair of States. Under their test of fairness, a method is satisfactory if, for any pair of States, the transfer of one Representative would not decrease the discrepancy between those States' districts. The choice of a method depended on how one decided to measure the discrepancy between district sizes. Each of the five methods could be described as the "best" in the sense of minimizing the discrepancy between districts, depending on the discrepancy measure selected. The method of the harmonic mean, for example, yielded the fairest apportionment if the discrepancy was measured by the absolute difference between the number of persons per Representative. The method of major fractions was the best method if the discrepancy was measured by the absolute difference between the number of Representatives per person (also known as each person's "share" of a Representative). The method of equal proportions produced the fairest apportionment if the discrepancy was measured by the "relative difference" in either the size of the district or the share of a Representative.

The report concluded by endorsing the method of equal proportions. The committee apparently preferred this method for two reasons. First, the method of equal proportions minimized the relative difference both between the size of congressional districts and between the number of Representatives per person. Second, in comparison with the other four methods considered, this method occupied an intermediate position in terms of favoring small States over large States; it favored small States more than major fractions and greatest divisors, but not as much as smallest divisors or the harmonic mean.

If either the method of smallest divisors or the method of the harmonic mean, also known as the "Dean Method," had been used after the 1990 census, Montana would have received a second seat. Under the method of equal proportions, which was actually used, five other States had stronger claims to an additional seat because Montana's claim to a second seat was the 441st on the equal proportions "priority list." Montana would not have received a second seat under either the method of major fractions or greatest divisors. . . .

III

The Government argues that Congress' selection of any of the alternative apportionment methods involved in this litigation is not subject to judicial review. Relying principally on *Baker v. Carr* *** (1962), the Government contends that the choice among these methods presents a "political question" not amenable to judicial resolution. . . .

The case before us today is "political" in the same sense that *Baker v. Carr* was a "political case." *** It

raises an issue of great importance to the political branches. The issue has motivated partisan and sectional debate during important portions of our history. Nevertheless, the reasons that supported the justiciability of challenges to state legislative districts, as in *Baker v. Carr,* as well as state districting decisions relating to the election of Members of Congress *** apply with equal force to the issues presented by this litigation. The controversy between Montana and the Government turns on the proper interpretation of the relevant constitutional provisions. As our previous rejection of the political question doctrine in this context should make clear, the interpretation of the apportionment provisions of the Constitution is well within the competence of the Judiciary. *** The political question doctrine presents no bar to our reaching the merits of this dispute and deciding whether the District Court correctly construed the constitutional provisions at issue.

Our previous apportionment cases concerned States' decisions creating legislative districts; today we review the actions of Congress. Respect for a coordinate branch of Government raises special concerns not present in our prior cases, but those concerns relate to the merits of the controversy rather than to our power to resolve it. As the issue is properly raised in a case otherwise unquestionably within our jurisdiction, we must determine whether Congress exercised its apportionment authority within the limits dictated by the Constitution. *** Without the need for another exploration of the *Baker* factors, it suffices to say that, as in *Baker* itself and the apportionment cases that followed, the political question doctrine does not place this kind of constitutional interpretation outside the proper domain of the Judiciary.

IV

In *Wesberry v. Sanders* [1964] *** the Court considered the claim of voters in Fulton County, Georgia, that the disparity between the size of their congressional district (823,680) and the average size of the ten districts in Georgia (394,312) deprived them of the right "to have their votes for Congressmen given the same weight as the votes of other Georgians."

This Court upheld the claim, concluding that Article I, sec. 2, had established a "high standard of justice and common sense" for the apportionment of congressional districts: "equal representation for equal numbers of people." The constitutional command that Representatives be chosen "by the People of the several States" meant that "as nearly as is practicable one man's vote in a congressional election is to be worth as much as another's." Writing for the Court, Justice Black explained:

"It would defeat the principle solemnly embodied in the Great Compromise—equal representation in the House for equal numbers of people—for us to hold that, within the States, legislatures may draw the lines of congressional districts in such a way as to give some voters a greater voice in choosing a Congressman than others. The House of Representatives, a Convention agreed, was to represent the people as individuals, and on a basis of complete equality for each voter." ***

In subsequent cases, the Court interpreted that standard as imposing a burden on the States to "make a good faith effort to achieve precise mathematical equality." ***

Our cases applying the *Wesberry* standard have all involved disparities in the size of voting districts within the same State. In this case, however, Montana contends, and a majority of the District Court agreed, that the *Wesberry* standard also applies to apportionment decisions made by Congress and that it was violated because of an unjustified variance between the population of Montana's single district and the ideal district size.

Montana's evidence demonstrated that if Congress had used the method of the harmonic mean (sometimes referred to as the "Dean method) instead of the method of equal proportions (sometimes called the "Hill method") to apportion the districts, 48 of the States would have received the same number of Representatives, while Washington would have received one less—eight instead of nine—and Montana would have received one more. Under an apportionment undertaken according to the Hill method, the absolute difference between the population of Montana's single district (803,655) and the ideal (572,466) is 231,189; the difference between the average Washington district (543,105) and the ideal is 29,361. Hence, the sum of the differences

between the average and the ideal district size in the two States is 260,550. Under the Dean method, Montana would have two districts with an average population of 401,838, representing a deviation from the ideal of 170,638; Washington would then have eight districts averaging 610,993, which is a deviation of 38,527 from the ideal district size. The sum of the deviations from the ideal in the two States would thus be 209,165 under the Dean method (equal proportions). More generally, Montana emphasizes that the Dean method is the best method for minimizing the absolute deviations from ideal district size.

There is some force to the argument that the same historical insights that informed our construction of Article I, sec. 2 in the context of intrastate districting should apply here as well. As we interpreted the constitutional command that Representatives be chosen "by the People of the several States" to require the States to pursue equality in representation, we might well find that the requirement that Representatives be apportioned among the several States "according to their respective Numbers" would also embody the same principle of equality. Yet it is by no means clear that the facts here establish a violation of the *Wesberry* standard. In cases involving variances within a State, changes in the absolute differences from the ideal produce parallel changes in the relative differences. Within a State, there is no theoretical incompatibility entailed in minimizing both the absolute and the relative differences. In this case, in contrast, the reduction in the absolute difference between the size of Montana's district and the size of the ideal district has the effect of increasing the variance in the relative difference between the ideal and the size of the districts in both Montana and Washington. Moreover, whereas reductions in the variances among districts within a given State bring all of the affected districts closer to the ideal, in this case a change that would bring Montana closer to the ideal pushes the Washington districts away from that ideal.

What is the better measure of inequality—absolute difference in district size, absolute difference in share of a Representative, relative difference in district size or share? Neither mathematical analysis nor constitutional interpretation provides a conclusive answer. In none of these alternative measures of inequality do we find a substantive principle of commanding constitutional significance. The polestar of equal representation does not provide sufficient guidance to allow us to discern a single constitutionally permissible course.

A State's compliance with *Wesberry*'s "high standard of justice and common sense" begins with a good faith effort to produce complete equality for each voter. As our cases involving variances of only a fraction of one percent demonstrate, that goal is realistic and appropriate for State districting decisions. *** In this case, however, whether Montana has one district or two, its variance from the ideal will exceed 40 percent.

The constitutional guarantee of a minimum of one Representative for each State inexorably compels a significant departure from the ideal. In Alaska, Vermont, and Wyoming, where the statewide districts are less populous than the ideal district, every vote is more valuable than the national average. Moreover, the need to allocate a fixed number of indivisible Representatives among 50 States of varying populations makes it virtually impossible to have the same size district in any pair of States, let alone in all 50. Accordingly, although "common sense" supports a test requiring "a good faith effort to achieve precise mathematical equality" within each State, *** the constraints imposed by Article I, sec. 2, itself make that goal illusory for the Nation as a whole.

This commonsense understanding of a characteristic of our Federal Government must have been obvious to the masters of compromise who framed our Constitution. The spirit of compromise that provided two Senators for every State and Representatives of the People "according to their respective Numbers" in the House must also have motivated the original allocation of Representatives specified in Article I, sec. 2, itself. Today, as then, some compromise between the interests of larger and smaller States must be made to achieve a fair apportionment for the entire country.

The constitutional framework that generated the need for compromise in the apportionment process must also delegate to Congress a measure of discre-

tion that is broader than that accorded to the States in the much easier task of determining district sizes within State borders. Article I, sec. 8, cl. 18, expressly authorizes Congress to enact legislation that "shall be necessary and proper" to carry out its delegated responsibilities. Its apparently good faith choice of a method of apportionment of Representatives among the several States "according to their respective Numbers" commands far more deference than a state districting decision that is capable of being reviewed under a relatively rigid mathematical standard.

The District Court suggested that the automatic character of the application of the method of equal proportions, was inconsistent with Congress' responsibility to make a fresh legislative decision after each census. We find no merit in this suggestion. Indeed, if a set formula is otherwise constitutional, it seems to us that the use of a procedure that is administered efficiently and that avoids partisan controversy supports the legitimacy of congressional action, rather than undermining it. To the extent that the potentially divisive and complex issues associated with apportionment can be narrowed by the adoption of both procedural and substantive rules that are consistently applied year after year, the public is well served, provided, of course, that any such rule remains open to challenge or change at any time. We see no constitutional obstacle preventing Congress from adopting such a sensible procedure.

The decision to adopt the method of equal proportions was made by Congress after decades of experience, experimentation, and debate about the substance of the constitutional requirement. Independent scholars supported both the basic decision to adopt a regular procedure to be followed after each census, and the particular decision to use the method of equal proportions. For a half century the results of that method have been accepted by the States and the Nation. That history supports our conclusion that Congress had ample power to enact the statutory procedure in 1941 and to apply the method of equal proportions after the 1990 census.

The judgment of the District Court is reversed.

TABLE OF CASES

Principal cases are in bold type. Non-principal cases are in roman type.
References are to Pages.

Abington Township v. Schempp, 374 U.S. 203, 83 S.Ct. 1560, 10 L.Ed.2d 844 (1963), 92, 754, 757, 788

Abrams v. United States, 250 U.S. 616, 40 S.Ct. 17, 63 L.Ed. 1173 (1919), 603, 605

Adair v. United States, 208 U.S. 161, 28 S.Ct. 277, 52 L.Ed. 436 (1908), 527, 533

Adamson v. California, 332 U.S. 46, 67 S.Ct. 1672, 91 L.Ed. 1903 (1947), 483, 505

Adderley v. Florida, 385 U.S. 39, 87 S.Ct. 242, 17 L.Ed.2d 149 (1966), 621, 622, 662

Adkins v. Children's Hospital, 261 U.S. 525, 43 S.Ct. 394, 67 L.Ed. 785 (1923), 53, 534, 535, 537, 538, 539, 573

Aguilar v. Felton, 473 U.S. 402, 105 S.Ct. 3232, 87 L.Ed.2d 290 (1985), 753

Aguilar v. Texas, 375 U.S. 812, 84 S.Ct. 86, 11 L.Ed. 2d 48 (1963), 819

Akron v. Akron Center for Reproductive Health, Inc., 462 U.S. 416, 103 S.Ct. 2481, 76 L.Ed.2d 687 (1983), 963, 965, 968, 1010

Alabama v. King & Boozer, 314 U.S. 1, 62 S.Ct. 43, 86 L.Ed. 3 (1941), 408

Alabama v. White, 496 U.S. 325, 110 S.Ct. 2412, 110 L.Ed.2d 301 (1990), 819, 822

A.L.A. Schechter Poultry Corporation v. United States, 295 U.S. 495, 55 S.Ct. 837, 79 L.Ed. 1570 (1935), 53, 93, 182, 273, 329, 330, 331, 343

Alberts v. California, 354 U.S. 476, 77 S.Ct. 1304 (1957), 683, 684

Albertson, State v., 93 Idaho 640, 470 P.2d 300 (Idaho 1970), 973

Alexander v. Holmes County, 396 U.S. 19, 90 S.Ct. 29, 24 L.Ed.2d 19 (1969), 1055

Allegheny, County of v. American Civil Liberties Union, 492 U.S. 573, 109 S.Ct. 3086, 106 L.Ed.2d 472 (1989), 758

Allgeyer v. Louisiana, 165 U.S. 578, 17 S.Ct. 427, 41 L.Ed. 832 (1897), 532

Allied Structural Steel Co. v. Spannaus, 438 U.S. 234, 98 S.Ct. 2716, 57 L.Ed.2d 727 (1978), 527

American Booksellers Ass'n, Inc. v. Hudnut, 771 F.2d 323 (7th Cir.1985), 728

American Booksellers Ass'n, Inc. v. Hudnut, 598 F.Supp. 1316 (D.C.Ind.1984), 685

American Communications Ass'n v. Douds, 339 U.S. 382, 70 S.Ct. 674, 94 L.Ed. 925 (1950), 470

American Textile Mfrs. Institute, Inc. v. Donovan, 452 U.S. 490, 101 S.Ct. 2478, 69 L.Ed.2d 185 (1981), 331

Anderson v. Celebrezze, 460 U.S. 780, 103 S.Ct. 1564, 75 L.Ed.2d 547 (1983), 1161

Andresen v. Maryland, 427 U.S. 463, 96 S.Ct. 2737, 49 L.Ed.2d 627 (1976), 340

Andrew Barry, Guardianship of, 445 So.2d 365 (Fla. App. 2 Dist.1984), 973, 974

Apodaca v. Oregon, 406 U.S. 404, 92 S.Ct. 1628, 32 L.Ed.2d 184 (1972), 840

Aptheker v. Secretary of State, 378 U.S. 500, 84 S.Ct. 1659, 12 L.Ed.2d 992 (1964), 629

Argersinger v. Hamlin, 407 U.S. 25, 92 S.Ct. 2006, 32 L.Ed.2d 530 (1972), 834

Arizona v. California, 373 U.S. 546, 83 S.Ct. 1468, 10 L.Ed.2d 542 (1963), 330

Arizona v. Fulminante, ___ U.S. ___, 111 S.Ct. 1246, 113 L.Ed.2d 302 (1991), 466, 831, 832, 848

Arkansas v. Sanders, 442 U.S. 753, 99 S.Ct. 2586, 61 L.Ed.2d 235 (1979), 820, 821

Ashcraft v. Tennessee, 322 U.S. 143, 64 S.Ct. 921, 88 L.Ed. 1192 (1944), 828

Ashwander v. Tennessee Valley Authority, 297 U.S. 288, 56 S.Ct. 466, 80 L.Ed. 688 (1936), 128, 129, 130, **161**, 332

Bacchus Imports, Ltd. v. Dias, 468 U.S. 263, 104 S.Ct. 3049, 82 L.Ed.2d 200 (1984), 402, 403

Bailey v. Drexel Furniture Co., 259 U.S. 20, 42 S.Ct. 449, 66 L.Ed. 817 (1922), 190

Baker v. Carr, 369 U.S. 186, 82 S.Ct. 691, 7 L.Ed. 2d 663 (1962), 55, 127, 128, **151**, 1158, 1162

Ballew v. Georgia, 435 U.S. 223, 98 S.Ct. 1029, 55 L.Ed.2d 234 (1978), 839

Barenblatt v. United States, 360 U.S. 109, 79 S.Ct. 1081, 3 L.Ed.2d 1115 (1959), 89, 175, 176, **212**, 608

Barnes v. Glen Theatre, Inc., ___ U.S. ___, 111 S.Ct. 2456, 115 L.Ed.2d 504 (1991), 466, 616, 617, 618, **650**, 954

Barnes v. Kline, 759 F.2d 21, 245 U.S.App.D.C. 1 (D.C.Cir.1984), 264

Barron v. Baltimore, 32 U.S. 243, 8 L.Ed. 672 (1833), 481, 496, 540

Barrow, People v., 133 Ill.2d 226, 139 Ill.Dec. 728, 549 N.E.2d 240 (Ill.1989), 29

Bartkus v. Illinois, 359 U.S. 121, 79 S.Ct. 676, 3 L.Ed.2d 684 (1959), 841

Bates v. State Bar of Arizona, 433 U.S. 350, 97 S.Ct. 2691, 53 L.Ed.2d 810 (1977), 686

Batson v. Kentucky, 476 U.S. 79, 106 S.Ct. 1712, 90 L.Ed.2d 69 (1986), 841, **916**, App. E-2

Battaglia v. General Motors Corporation, 169 F.2d 254 (2nd Cir.1948), 87

Baxter v. Palmigiano, 425 U.S. 308, 96 S.Ct. 1551, 47 L.Ed.2d 810 (1976), 847

Bedford Cut Stone Co. v. Journeyman Stone Cutters' Ass'n, 274 U.S. 37, 47 S.Ct. 522, 71 L.Ed. 916 (1927), 535

Belle Terre v. Boraas, 416 U.S. 1, 94 S.Ct. 1536, 39 L.Ed.2d 797 (1974), 970

Bellotti v. Baird, 443 U.S. 622, 99 S.Ct. 3035, 61 L.Ed.2d 797 (1979), 963, **1005**

Belmont, United States v., 301 U.S. 324, 57 S.Ct. 758, 81 L.Ed. 1134 (1937), 276

Benton v. Maryland, 395 U.S. 784, 89 S.Ct. 2056, 23 L.Ed.2d 707 (1969), 484, 841

Bibb v. Navajo Freight Lines, Inc., 359 U.S. 520, 79 S.Ct. 962, 3 L.Ed.2d 1003 (1959), 400

Bivens v. Six Unknown Named Federal Narcotics Agents, 403 U.S. 388, 91 S.Ct. 1999, 29 L.Ed.2d 619 (1971), 826, 828

Blake v. McClung, 172 U.S. 239, 19 S.Ct. 165, 43 L.Ed. 432 (1898), 412

Bland, United States v., 283 U.S. 636, 51 S.Ct. 569, 75 L.Ed. 1319 (1931), 748

Board of Airport Com'rs v. Jews for Jesus, Inc., 482 U.S. 569, 107 S.Ct. 2568, 96 L.Ed.2d 500 (1987), 623, 629

Board of Education v. Allen, 389 U.S. 1031, 88 S.Ct. 767, 19 L.Ed.2d 819 (1968), 752

Board of Educ. v. Dowell, 498 U.S. 237, 111 S.Ct. 630, 112 L.Ed.2d 715 (1991), 1056

Board of Educ. v. Mergens, 496 U.S. 226, 110 S.Ct. 2356, 110 L.Ed.2d 191 (1990), 753

Bob Jones University v. United States, 461 U.S. 574, 103 S.Ct. 2017, 76 L.Ed.2d 157 (1983), 760

Bolling v. Sharpe, 347 U.S. 497, 74 S.Ct. 693, 98 L.Ed. 884, 53 O.O. 331 (1954), 1044, 1053

Boos v. Barry, 485 U.S. 312, 108 S.Ct. 1157, 99 L.Ed.2d 333 (1988), 624

Booth v. Maryland, 482 U.S. 496, 107 S.Ct. 2529, 96 L.Ed.2d 440 (1987), 845

Bordenkircher v. Hayes, 434 U.S. 357, 98 S.Ct. 663, 54 L.Ed.2d 604 (1978), 837, **913**

Bouvia v. Superior Court, 179 Cal.App.3d 1127, 225 Cal.Rptr. 297 (Cal.App. 2 Dist.1986), 974

Bowers v. Hardwick, 478 U.S. 186, 106 S.Ct. 2841, 92 L.Ed.2d 140 (1986), 971, 972, **1030**

Bowsher v. Synar, 478 U.S. 714, 106 S.Ct. 3181, 92 L.Ed.2d 583 (1986), 130, 331, 335, 348

Boyd v. United States, 116 U.S. 616, 6 S.Ct. 524, 29 L.Ed. 746 (1886), 816, 825

Boykin v. Alabama, 395 U.S. 238, 89 S.Ct. 1709, 23 L.Ed.2d 274 (1969), 837

Bradley v. United States, 410 U.S. 605, 93 S.Ct. 1151, 35 L.Ed.2d 528 (1973), 133

Bradwell v. Illinois, 83 U.S. 130, 21 L.Ed. 442 (1872), 1061

Brady v. United States, 397 U.S. 742, 90 S.Ct. 1463, 25 L.Ed.2d 747 (1970), 837

Bram v. United States, 168 U.S. 532, 18 S.Ct. 183, 42 L.Ed. 568 (1897), 828

Branch v. Texas, 408 U.S. 238, 92 S.Ct. 2726, 33 L.Ed.2d 346 (1972), 925

Brandenburg v. Ohio, 395 U.S. 444, 89 S.Ct. 1827, 23 L.Ed.2d 430, 48 O.O.2d 320 (1969), 133, 608, 609, 637

Branti v. Finkel, 445 U.S. 507, 100 S.Ct. 1287, 63 L.Ed.2d 574 (1980), 618

Branzburg v. Hayes, 408 U.S. 665, 92 S.Ct. 2646, 33 L.Ed.2d 626 (1972), 682, 712

Braunfeld v. Brown, 366 U.S. 599, 81 S.Ct. 1144, 6 L.Ed.2d 563, 17 O.O.2d 241 (1961), 745

Breed v. Jones, 421 U.S. 519, 95 S.Ct. 1779, 44 L.Ed.2d 346 (1975), 852

Breedlove v. Suttles, 302 U.S. 277, 58 S.Ct. 205, 82 L.Ed. 252 (1937), 486, 1152

Brewer v. Williams, 430 U.S. 387, 97 S.Ct. 1232, 51 L.Ed.2d 424 (1977), 27

Brewster, United States v., 408 U.S. 501, 92 S.Ct. 2531, 33 L.Ed.2d 507 (1972), 168

Brinegar v. United States, 338 U.S. 160, 69 S.Ct. 1302, 93 L.Ed. 1879 (1949), 818

Broadrick v. Oklahoma, 413 U.S. 601, 93 S.Ct. 2908, 37 L.Ed.2d 830 (1973), 118, 629

Brotherhood of Locomotive Engineers v. Chicago, Rock Island & Pacific Railroad Co., 382 U.S. 423, 86 S.Ct. 594, 15 L.Ed.2d 501 (1966), 400

Brown v. Allen, 344 U.S. 443, 73 S.Ct. 397, 97 L.Ed. 469 (1953), 848

Brown v. Board of Education (Brown II), 349 U.S. 294, 75 S.Ct. 753, 99 L.Ed. 1083, 57 O.O. 253 (1955), 1053, 1055, **1092**

Brown v. Board of Education (Brown I), 347 U.S. 483, 74 S.Ct. 686, 98 L.Ed. 873, 53 O.O. 326 (1954), 33, 55, 90, 131, 478, 1050, 1051, 1052, 1053, 1054, 1055, 1061, 1072, **1089**

Brown v. Maryland, 25 U.S. 419, 6 L.Ed. 678 (1827), 409

Brown v. Pena, 441 F.Supp. 1382 (D.C.Fla.1977), 742

Brown v. Thomson, 462 U.S. 835, 103 S.Ct. 2690, 77 L.Ed.2d 214 (1983), 1159, **1189**

Brown, United States v., 381 U.S. 437, 85 S.Ct. 1707, 14 L.Ed.2d 484 (1965), 470, **490**

Brown–Forman Distillers Corp. v. New York State Liquor Authority, 476 U.S. 573, 106 S.Ct. 2080, 90 L.Ed.2d 552 (1986), 403

Bryant v. Zimmerman, 278 U.S. 63, 49 S.Ct. 61, 73 L.Ed. 184 (1928), 627

Buck v. Bell, 274 U.S. 200, 47 S.Ct. 584, 71 L.Ed. 1000 (1927), 957, **981**

Buckley v. Valeo, 424 U.S. 1, 96 S.Ct. 612, 46 L.Ed. 2d 659 (1976), 193, 266

Bunting v. Oregon, 243 U.S. 426, 37 S.Ct. 435, 61 L.Ed. 830 (1917), 533, 534

Burbank v. Lockheed Air Terminal Inc., 411 U.S. 624, 93 S.Ct. 1854, 36 L.Ed.2d 547 (1973), 187, 394

Burch v. Louisiana, 441 U.S. 130, 99 S.Ct. 1623, 60 L.Ed.2d 96 (1979), 840

Burnet v. Coronado Oil & Gas Co., 285 U.S. 393, 52 S.Ct. 443, 76 L.Ed. 815 (1932), 131

Burson v. Freeman, ___ U.S. ___, 112 S.Ct. 1846, 119 L.Ed.2d 5 (1992), App. E-2

Burton v. Wilmington Parking Authority, 365 U.S. 715, 81 S.Ct. 856, 6 L.Ed.2d 45 (1961), 1073

Butler, United States v., 297 U.S. 1, 56 S.Ct. 312, 80 L.Ed. 477 (1936), 190, 191, 192, 193, **241, 537**

Calandra, United States v., 414 U.S. 338, 94 S.Ct. 613, 38 L.Ed.2d 561, 66 O.O.2d 320 (1974), 825, 826

Calder v. Bull, 3 U.S. 386, 1 L.Ed. 648 (1798), 468, 522, 523, 524

Califano v. Goldfarb, 430 U.S. 199, 97 S.Ct. 1021, 51 L.Ed.2d 270 (1977), 1064

California v. Acevedo, ___ U.S. ___, 111 S.Ct. 1982, 114 L.Ed.2d 619 (1991), 821

California v. Federal Energy Regulatory Commission (FERC), 495 U.S. 490, 110 S.Ct. 2024, 109 L.Ed. 2d 474 (1990), 394

Camara v. Municipal Court, 387 U.S. 523, 87 S.Ct. 1727, 18 L.Ed.2d 930 (1967), 339

Cantwell v. Connecticut, 310 U.S. 296, 60 S.Ct. 900, 84 L.Ed. 1213 (1940), 483, 740, 743

Carey v. Population Services Intern., 431 U.S. 678, 97 S.Ct. 2010, 52 L.Ed.2d 675 (1977), 1028

Carolene Products Co., United States v., 304 U.S. 144, 58 S.Ct. 778, 82 L.Ed. 1234 (1938), 132, 1045, 1149

Carolene Products Co., United States v., 104 F.2d 969 (7th Cir.1939), 55

Carroll v. United States, 60 Ct.Cl. 1032 (Ct.Cl.1925), 820

Carter v. Carter Coal Co., 298 U.S. 238, 56 S.Ct. 855, 80 L.Ed. 1160 (1936), 182, **226, 537**

Central Hudson Gas & Elec. Corp. v. Public Service Com'n of New York, 447 U.S. 557, 100 S.Ct. 2343, 65 L.Ed.2d 341 (1980), 686

Champion v. Ames, 188 U.S. 321, 23 S.Ct. 321, 47 L.Ed. 492 (1903), 181

Champlin Refining Co. v. Corporation Commission of Oklahoma, 286 U.S. 210, 52 S.Ct. 559, 76 L.Ed. 1062 (1932), 132

Chandler v. Florida, 449 U.S. 560, 101 S.Ct. 802, 66 L.Ed.2d 740 (1981), 839

Chaplinsky v. New Hampshire, 315 U.S. 568, 62 S.Ct. 766, 86 L.Ed. 1031 (1942), 609, 616

Chapman v. California, 386 U.S. 18, 87 S.Ct. 824, 17 L.Ed.2d 705 (1967), 848

Charles River Bridge v. Warren Bridge, 36 U.S. 420, 9 L.Ed. 773 (1837), 526, 550

Chas. C. Steward Machine Co. v. Davis, 301 U.S. 548, 57 S.Ct. 883, 81 L.Ed. 1279 (1937), 192, 246, 391, 392, 539

Chemical Waste Management, Inc. v. Hunt, ___ U.S. ___, 112 S.Ct. 2009, 119 L.Ed.2d 121 (1992), 402, App. E-1, **App. E-3**

Chicago, Burlington and Quincy Railroad Co. v. Chicago, 166 U.S. 226, 17 S.Ct. 581, 41 L.Ed. 979 (1897), 482, **501**, 540

Chicago, Milwaukee and St. Paul Railway Co. v. Minnesota, 134 U.S. 418, 10 S.Ct. 462, 33 L.Ed. 970 (1890), 50, 532, **567**

Chimel v. California, 395 U.S. 752, 89 S.Ct. 2034, 23 L.Ed.2d 685 (1969), 820, **868**

Chisholm v. Georgia, 2 U.S. 419, 1 L.Ed. 440 (1793), 90, 387, 388, **396**, **418**, 1058

Chisom v. Roemer, ___ U.S. ___, 111 S.Ct. 775, 112 L.Ed.2d 838 (1991), 1156, 1157

City of (see name of city)

Civil Rights Cases, The, 109 U.S. 3, 3 S.Ct. 18, 27 L.Ed. 835 (1883), 480, 1048, 1049, 1050, 1051, 1073, 1074, **1077**

Clark v. Community for Creative Non–Violence, 468 U.S. 288, 104 S.Ct. 3065, 82 L.Ed.2d 221 (1984), 615

Classic, United States v., 313 U.S. 299, 61 S.Ct. 1031, 85 L.Ed. 1368 (1941), 1150

Cleburne v. Cleburne Living Center, Inc., 473 U.S. 432, 105 S.Ct. 3249, 87 L.Ed.2d 313 (1985), 1068, **1134**

Coates v. Cincinnati, 402 U.S. 611, 91 S.Ct. 1686, 29 L.Ed.2d 214, 58 O.O.2d 481 (1971), 628

Cohen v. California, 403 U.S. 15, 91 S.Ct. 1780, 29 L.Ed.2d 284 (1971), 133, 611, 616, 641

Cohen v. Cowles Media Co., ___ U.S. ___, 111 S.Ct. 2513, 115 L.Ed.2d 586 (1991), 466, 682, **716**

Cohens v. Virginia, 19 U.S. 264, 5 L.Ed. 257 (1821), 48, 396

Coker v. Georgia, 433 U.S. 584, 97 S.Ct. 2861, 53 L.Ed.2d 982 (1977), 844

Colegrove v. Green, 328 U.S. 549, 66 S.Ct. 1198, 90 L.Ed. 1432 (1946), 127, 1158, 1162

Coleman v. Thompson, ___ U.S. ___, 111 S.Ct. 2546, 115 L.Ed.2d 640 (1991), 468

Colgrove v. Battin, 413 U.S. 149, 93 S.Ct. 2448, 37 L.Ed.2d 522 (1973), 476

Collector v. Day, 78 U.S. 113, 20 L.Ed. 122 (1870), 406, 407

Collin v. Smith, 578 F.2d 1197 (7th Cir.1978), 619

Collins v. Youngblood, 497 U.S. 37, 110 S.Ct. 2715, 111 L.Ed.2d 30 (1990), 468

Committee for Public Ed. v. Nyquist, 413 U.S. 756, 93 S.Ct. 2955, 37 L.Ed.2d 948 (1973), 753, 761

Committee to Defend Reproductive Rights v. Myers, 172 Cal.Rptr. 866, 625 P.2d 779 (Cal.1981), 965

Communist Party v. Subversive Activities Control Bd., 351 U.S. 115, 76 S.Ct. 663, 100 L.Ed. 1003 (1956), 129

Communist Party v. Subversive Activities Control Bd., 367 U.S. 1, 81 S.Ct. 1357, 6 L.Ed.2d 625 (1961), 608

Communist Party of Indiana v. Whitcomb, 414 U.S. 441, 94 S.Ct. 656, 38 L.Ed.2d 635 (1974), 609

Cooley v. Board of Wardens, 53 U.S. 299, 13 L.Ed. 996 (1851), 389, 398, 399, **441**

Coolidge v. New Hampshire, 403 U.S. 443, 91 S.Ct. 2022, 29 L.Ed.2d 564 (1971), 818, 820

Cooper v. Aaron, 358 U.S. 1, 78 S.Ct. 1401, 3 L.Ed. 2d 5, 3 L.Ed.2d 19 (1958), 96, **112**, 1054

Coppage v. Kansas, 236 U.S. 1, 35 S.Ct. 240, 59 L.Ed. 441 (1915), 533, 539

Corfield v. Coryell, 6 Fed.Cas. 546 (C.C.Pa.1823), 412

County of (see name of county)

Cox v. Louisiana, 379 U.S. 559, 85 S.Ct. 476, 13 L.Ed.2d 487 (1965), 621

Cox Broadcasting Corp. v. Cohn, 420 U.S. 469, 95 S.Ct. 1029, 43 L.Ed.2d 328 (1975), 680

Craig v. Boren, 429 U.S. 190, 97 S.Ct. 451, 50 L.Ed. 2d 397 (1976), 1064

Crockett v. Reagan, 558 F.Supp. 893 (D.C.D.C. 1982), 127, **158**, 279

Cruikshank, United States v., 92 U.S. 542, 23 L.Ed. 588 (1875), 473

Cruz v. Beto, 405 U.S. 319, 92 S.Ct. 1079, 31 L.Ed. 2d 263 (1972), 847

Cruzan v. Missouri Health Dept., 497 U.S. 261, 110 S.Ct. 2841, 111 L.Ed.2d 224 (1990), 975, 976, **1035**

Cummings v. Missouri, 71 U.S. 277, 18 L.Ed. 356 (1866), 469

Curtis v. Loether, 415 U.S. 189, 94 S.Ct. 1005, 39 L.Ed.2d 260 (1974), 475

Curtis Publishing Co. v. Butts, 388 U.S. 130, 87 S.Ct. 1975, 18 L.Ed.2d 1094 (1967), 678

Curtiss–Wright Export Corporation, United States v., 299 U.S. 304, 57 S.Ct. 216, 81 L.Ed. 255 (1936), 173, 273, 274, **298, 328**

Dames & Moore v. Regan, 453 U.S. 654, 101 S.Ct. 2972, 69 L.Ed.2d 918 (1981), 276

Daniel v. Paul, 395 U.S. 298, 89 S.Ct. 1697, 23 L.Ed.2d 318 (1969), 186

Darby, United States v., 312 U.S. 100, 61 S.Ct. 451, 85 L.Ed. 609 (1941), 183, 184, 185, 392, 424, 425, 539

Dartmouth College v. Woodward, 17 U.S. 518, 4 L.Ed. 629 (1819), 525, 526, **546**

Davis v. Bandemer, 478 U.S. 109, 106 S.Ct. 2797, 92 L.Ed.2d 85 (1986), 1162, **1194**

Davis v. Beason, 133 U.S. 333, 10 S.Ct. 299, 33 L.Ed. 637 (1890), 741

Davis, Helvering v., 301 U.S. 619, 301 U.S. 672, 57 S.Ct. 904, 81 L.Ed. 1307 (1937), 192, 391

Dawson v. Delaware, ___ U.S. ___, 112 S.Ct. 1093, 117 L.Ed.2d 309 (1992), App. E-1

Dean Milk Co. v. Madison, 340 U.S. 349, 71 S.Ct. 295, 95 L.Ed. 329 (1951), 401

Debs, In re, 158 U.S. 564, 15 S.Ct. 900, 39 L.Ed. 1092 (1895), 262

DeFunis v. Odegaard, 416 U.S. 312, 94 S.Ct. 1704, 40 L.Ed.2d 164 (1974), 124, 125, **143, 1058**

Dennis v. Higgins, 498 U.S. 439, 111 S.Ct. 865, 112 L.Ed.2d 969 (1991), 405

Dennis v. United States, 341 U.S. 494, 71 S.Ct. 857, 95 L.Ed. 1137 (1951), 607, 608, **632**

Department of Commerce v. Montana, ___ U.S. ___, 112 S.Ct. 1415, 118 L.Ed.2d 87 (1992), 1160, App. E-2, **App. E-29**

DeShaney v. Winnebago Social Services Department, 489 U.S. 189, 109 S.Ct. 998, 103 L.Ed.2d 249 (1989), 480, **493**

Detroit, City of, United States v., 355 U.S. 466, 78 S.Ct. 474, 2 L.Ed.2d 424 (1958), 408

Doe v. Bolton, 410 U.S. 179, 93 S.Ct. 739, 35 L.Ed. 2d 201 (1973), 1012

Doe v. Commonwealth's Attorney, 425 U.S. 985, 96 S.Ct. 2192, 48 L.Ed.2d 810 (1976), 971, 1030

Donovan v. Dewey, 452 U.S. 594, 101 S.Ct. 2534, 69 L.Ed.2d 262 (1981), 339

Doran v. Salem Inn, Inc., 422 U.S. 922, 95 S.Ct. 2561, 45 L.Ed.2d 648 (1975), 616, 617

Doremus, United States v., 249 U.S. 86, 39 S.Ct. 214, 63 L.Ed. 493 (1919), 190

Douglas v. California, 372 U.S. 353, 83 S.Ct. 814, 9 L.Ed.2d 811 (1963), 833, 1069

Dow Chemical Co. v. United States, 476 U.S. 227, 106 S.Ct. 1819, 90 L.Ed.2d 226 (1986), 339, **378**

Dr. Bonham's Case, 8 Coke Reports 107 (1610), 43

Dred Scott v. Sandford, 60 U.S. 393, 15 L.Ed. 691 (1856), 48, 49, 50, 52, 53, 69, 91, 135, 390, 478, 527

Dronenburg v. Zech, 741 F.2d 1388, 239 U.S.App. D.C. 229 (D.C.Cir.1984), **1028**

Duke Power Co. v. Carolina Environmental Study Group, Inc., 438 U.S. 59, 98 S.Ct. 2620, 57 L.Ed. 2d 595 (1978), 123

Duncan v. Louisiana, 391 U.S. 145, 88 S.Ct. 1444, 20 L.Ed.2d 491, 45 O.O.2d 198 (1968), 483, **513,** 838

Dunn v. Blumstein, 405 U.S. 330, 92 S.Ct. 995, 31 L.Ed.2d 274 (1972), 413

Duplex Printing Press Co. v. Deering, 254 U.S. 443, 41 S.Ct. 172, 65 L.Ed. 349 (1921), 535

Duquesne Light Co. v. Barasch, 488 U.S. 299, 109 S.Ct. 609, 102 L.Ed.2d 646 (1989), 542

Eakin v. Raub, 12 Sergeant & Rawle 330 (1825), 47, 63

Eastland v. United States Servicemen's Fund, 421 U.S. 491, 95 S.Ct. 1813, 44 L.Ed.2d 324 (1975), 176

E. C. Knight Co., United States v., 156 U.S. 1, 15 S.Ct. 249, 39 L.Ed. 325 (1895), 52, 53, 180, 183, **221**

Eddings v. Oklahoma, 455 U.S. 104, 102 S.Ct. 869, 71 L.Ed.2d 1 (1982), 852

Edmonson v. Leesville Concrete Co., Inc., ___ U.S. ___, 111 S.Ct. 2077, 114 L.Ed.2d 660 (1991), 841

Edwards v. Aguillard, 482 U.S. 578, 107 S.Ct. 2573, 96 L.Ed.2d 510 (1987), 756, 794

Edwards v. South Carolina, 372 U.S. 229, 83 S.Ct. 680, 9 L.Ed.2d 697 (1963), 620, **660**

Edwards v. United States, 358 U.S. 847, 79 S.Ct. 74, 3 L.Ed.2d 82 (1958), 834

Eichman, United States v., 496 U.S. 310, 110 S.Ct. 2404, 110 L.Ed.2d 287 (1990), 92, 615

Eisenstadt v. Baird, 405 U.S. 438, 92 S.Ct. 1029, 31 L.Ed.2d 349 (1972), 960, 971, 1028

Employment Div. v. Smith, 494 U.S. 872, 110 S.Ct. 1595, 108 L.Ed.2d 876 (1990), 743, 744, 745, 746, 761, 778

Engel v. Vitale, 370 U.S. 421, 82 S.Ct. 1261, 8 L.Ed. 2d 601, 20 O.O.2d 328 (1962), 754

Engle v. Isaac, 456 U.S. 107, 102 S.Ct. 1558, 71 L.Ed.2d 783 (1982), 850

Epperson v. Arkansas, 393 U.S. 97, 89 S.Ct. 266, 21 L.Ed.2d 228 (1968), 756

Escobedo v. Illinois, 378 U.S. 478, 84 S.Ct. 1758, 12 L.Ed.2d 977, 32 O.O.2d 31 (1964), 829, 833

Estin v. Estin, 334 U.S. 541, 68 S.Ct. 1213, 92 L.Ed. 1561 (1948), 411

Everson v. Board of Education, 330 U.S. 1, 67 S.Ct. 504, 91 L.Ed. 711 (1947), 483, 740, 752, 784

Ex parte (see name of party)

Faretta v. California, 422 U.S. 806, 95 S.Ct. 2525, 45 L.Ed.2d 562 (1975), 835

Fay v. Noia, 372 U.S. 391, 83 S.Ct. 822, 9 L.Ed.2d 837, 24 O.O.2d 12 (1963), 468, 848

Federal Communications Commission v. League of Women Voters, 468 U.S. 364, 104 S.Ct. 3106, 82 L.Ed.2d 278 (1984), 688

Federal Communications Commission v. Pacifica Foundation, 438 U.S. 726, 98 S.Ct. 3026, 57 L.Ed.2d 1073 (1978), 688, 732

Federal Energy Regulatory Com'n v. Mississippi, 456 U.S. 742, 102 S.Ct. 2126, 72 L.Ed.2d 532 (1982), 186

Feiner v. New York, 340 U.S. 315, 71 S.Ct. 303, 95 L.Ed. 295 (1951), 610, 611, 621, 638

Ferguson v. Skrupa, 372 U.S. 726, 83 S.Ct. 1028, 10 L.Ed.2d 93 (1963), 54, 134, 539, 585

Field v. Clark, 143 U.S. 649, 12 S.Ct. 495, 36 L.Ed. 294 (1892), 328

Firefighters v. Cleveland, 478 U.S. 501, 106 S.Ct. 3063, 92 L.Ed.2d 405 (1986), 1059

First English Evangelical Lutheran Church v. County of Los Angeles, 482 U.S. 304, 107 S.Ct. 2378, 96 L.Ed.2d 250 (1987), 541, 542

Fisher, United States v., 6 U.S. 358, 2 L.Ed. 304 (1805), 171

Fiske v. Kansas, 274 U.S. 380, 47 S.Ct. 655, 71 L.Ed. 1108 (1927), 482, 600, 604

Flast v. Cohen, 392 U.S. 83, 88 S.Ct. 1942, 20 L.Ed. 2d 947 (1968), 121, 122

Fletcher v. Peck, 10 U.S. 87, 3 L.Ed. 162 (1810), 47, 524, 525

Flint v. Stone Tracy Co., 220 U.S. 107, 31 S.Ct. 342, 55 L.Ed. 389 (1911), 52

Florida v. Bostick, ___ U.S. ___, 111 S.Ct. 2382, 115 L.Ed.2d 389 (1991), 466, 820

Florida v. Meyers, 456 U.S. 380, 104 S.Ct. 1852, 80 L.Ed.2d 381 (1984), 31

Ford v. Wainwright, 477 U.S. 399, 106 S.Ct. 2595, 91 L.Ed.2d 335 (1986), 845

Fordice, United States v., ___ U.S. ___, 112 S.Ct. 2727, 120 L.Ed.2d 575 (1992), App. E-2

Forsyth County v. Nationalist Movement, ___ U.S. ___, 112 S.Ct. 2395, 120 L.Ed.2d 101 (1992), App. E-1

Fort Gratiot Sanitary Landfill, Inc. v. Michigan Dept. of Natural Resources, ___ U.S. ___, 112 S.Ct. 2019, 119 L.Ed.2d 139 (1992), App. E-1

Foucha v. Louisiana, ___ U.S. ___, 112 S.Ct. 1780, 118 L.Ed.2d 437 (1992), App. E-2

Fox Film Corporation v. Doyal, 286 U.S. 123, 52 S.Ct. 546, 76 L.Ed. 1010 (1932), 407

Frank v. Maryland, 359 U.S. 360, 79 S.Ct. 804, 3 L.Ed.2d 877 (1959), 339

Freeman v. Pitts, ___ U.S. ___, 112 S.Ct. 1430, 118 L.Ed.2d 108 (1992), 1056, App. E-2, App. E-25

Fresno, County of, United States v., 429 U.S. 452, 97 S.Ct. 699, 50 L.Ed.2d 683 (1977), 408

Frontiero v. Richardson, 411 U.S. 677, 93 S.Ct. 1764, 36 L.Ed.2d 583 (1973), 1063, 1117

Frothingham v. Mellon, 288 F. 252 (C.A.D.C.1923), 121

Fullilove v. Klutznick, 448 U.S. 448, 100 S.Ct. 2758, 65 L.Ed.2d 902 (1980), 193, 1058, 1059, 1060, 1103

Furman v. Georgia, 408 U.S. 238, 92 S.Ct. 2726, 33 L.Ed.2d 346 (1972), 134, 268, 842, 844, 846, 925

Gambino, United States v., 566 F.2d 414 (1978), 187

Gannett Co., Inc. v. DePasquale, 443 U.S. 368, 99 S.Ct. 2898, 61 L.Ed.2d 608 (1979), 839

Garber v. United States, 73 F.R.D. 364 (D.C.D.C. 1976), 194

Garcia v. San Antonio Metropolitan Transit Authority, 469 U.S. 528, 105 S.Ct. 1005, 83 L.Ed.2d 1016 (1985), 184, 185, 392, 432, App. E-1

Garland, Ex parte, 71 U.S. 333, 18 L.Ed. 366 (1866), 268, 469

Gault, In re, 387 U.S. 1, 87 S.Ct. 1428, 18 L.Ed.2d 527, 40 O.O.2d 378 (1967), 479, 851, 852, 945

Geduldig v. Aiello, 417 U.S. 484, 94 S.Ct. 2485, 41 L.Ed.2d 256 (1974), 1065

General Motors Corp. v. United States, 215 Ct.Cl. 1086 (Ct.Cl.1977), 194

Georgia v. McCollum, ___ U.S. ___, 112 S.Ct. 2348, 120 L.Ed.2d 33 (1992), 841, App. E-2

Georgia Public Service Commission, United States v., 371 U.S. 285, 83 S.Ct. 397, 9 L.Ed.2d 317 (1963), 408

Gerstein v. Pugh, 420 U.S. 103, 95 S.Ct. 854, 43 L.Ed.2d 54 (1975), 824, 825

Gertz v. Robert Welch, Inc., 418 U.S. 323, 94 S.Ct. 2997, 41 L.Ed.2d 789 (1974), 678, 679

Gibbons v. Ogden, 22 U.S. 1, 6 L.Ed. 23 (1824), 47, 177, 178, 180, 181, **216,** 397, 398, 421

Gideon v. Wainwright, 372 U.S. 335, 83 S.Ct. 792, 9 L.Ed.2d 799, 23 O.O.2d 258 (1963), 474, 833, 834, 835, 851, **911,** 1069

Gillespie v. Oklahoma, 257 U.S. 501, 42 S.Ct. 171, 66 L.Ed. 338 (1922), 407

Ginzburg v. United States, 383 U.S. 463, 86 S.Ct. 942, 16 L.Ed.2d 31 (1966), 683

Gitlow v. New York, 268 U.S. 652, 45 S.Ct. 625, 69 L.Ed. 1138 (1925), 482, 533, 600, 604, 605

Glidden Co. v. Zdanok, 370 U.S. 530, 82 S.Ct. 1459, 8 L.Ed.2d 671 (1962), 89

Goesaert v. Cleary, 335 U.S. 464, 69 S.Ct. 198, 93 L.Ed. 163 (1948), 1061

Goldberg v. Kelly, 397 U.S. 254, 90 S.Ct. 1011, 25 L.Ed.2d 287 (1970), 337, 338, 479

Goldman v. Weinberger, 475 U.S. 503, 106 S.Ct. 1310, 89 L.Ed.2d 478 (1986), 749, 766

Goldwater v. Carter, 481 F.Supp. 949 (D.C.D.C. 1979), 127

Gomillion v. Lightfoot, 364 U.S. 339, 81 S.Ct. 125, 5 L.Ed.2d 110 (1960), 1152, 1154, **1167**

Gooding v. Wilson, 405 U.S. 518, 92 S.Ct. 1103, 31 L.Ed.2d 408 (1972), 611, 628, 629

Goss v. Lopez, 419 U.S. 565, 95 S.Ct. 729, 42 L.Ed. 2d 725 (1975), 337

Grace, United States v., 461 U.S. 171, 103 S.Ct. 1702, 75 L.Ed.2d 736 (1983), 622, 623

Grand Rapids School District v. Ball, 473 U.S. 373, 105 S.Ct. 3216, 87 L.Ed.2d 267 (1985), 753, 754

Graves v. New York ex rel. O'Keefe, 306 U.S. 466, 59 S.Ct. 595, 83 L.Ed. 927 (1939), 407

Gray v. Sanders, 372 U.S. 368, 83 S.Ct. 801, 9 L.Ed. 2d 821 (1963), 1157

Great Atlantic & Pac. Tea Co., Inc. v. Cottrell, 424 U.S. 366, 96 S.Ct. 923, 47 L.Ed.2d 55 (1976), 402

Gregg v. Georgia, 428 U.S. 153, 96 S.Ct. 2909, 49 L.Ed.2d 859 (1976), 843, 844, 845, **933**

Griswold v. Connecticut, 381 U.S. 479, 85 S.Ct. 1678, 14 L.Ed.2d 510 (1965), 126, 134, 477, 480, 955, 957, 958, 959, 960, 971, 977, **987,** 1028

Grosso v. United States, 390 U.S. 62, 88 S.Ct. 709, 19 L.Ed.2d 906, 43 O.O.2d 226 (1968), 194

Grove City College v. Bell, 465 U.S. 555, 104 S.Ct. 1211, 79 L.Ed.2d 516 (1984), 89, 90

Grovey v. Townsend, 295 U.S. 45, 55 S.Ct. 622, 79 L.Ed. 1292 (1935), 1150, 1151

Guardianship of (see name of party)

Guinn v. United States, 238 U.S. 347, 35 S.Ct. 926, 59 L.Ed. 1340 (1915), 1150

Gulf, Colorado & Santa Fe Railway Co. v. Ellis, 165 U.S. 150, 17 S.Ct. 255, 41 L.Ed. 666 (1897), 1045

Haig v. Agee, 453 U.S. 280, 101 S.Ct. 2766, 69 L.Ed.2d 640 (1981), 273, 274

Hamilton, Matter of, 657 S.W.2d 425 (Tenn.App. 1983), 749

Hamilton v. Regents of the University of Calif., 293 U.S. 245, 55 S.Ct. 197, 79 L.Ed. 343 (1934), 740

Hammer v. Dagenhart, 247 U.S. 251, 38 S.Ct. 529, 62 L.Ed. 1101 (1918), 53, 180, 184, 190, 391, 421

Hampton v. Mow Sun Wong, 426 U.S. 88, 96 S.Ct. 1895, 48 L.Ed.2d 495 (1976), 1068

Hans v. Louisiana, 134 U.S. 1, 10 S.Ct. 504, 33 L.Ed. 842 (1890), 396

Hardenbaugh v. New York, 454 U.S. 958, 102 S.Ct. 496, 70 L.Ed.2d 374 (1981), 760

Harmelin v. Michigan, ___ U.S. ___, 111 S.Ct. 2680, 115 L.Ed.2d 836 (1991), 846

Harper v. Virginia State Bd. of Elections, 383 U.S. 663, 86 S.Ct. 1079, 16 L.Ed.2d 169 (1966), 486, 1069, 1152

Harris v. McRae, 448 U.S. 297, 100 S.Ct. 2671, 65 L.Ed.2d 784 (1980), 965, 1070

Harris v. New York, 401 U.S. 222, 91 S.Ct. 643, 28 L.Ed.2d 1 (1971), 829

Harris, United States v., 216 F.2d 690 (5th Cir. 1954), 618

Hawaii Housing Authority v. Midkiff, 467 U.S. 229, 104 S.Ct. 2321, 81 L.Ed.2d 186 (1984), 541, 587

Hazelwood School Dist. v. Kuhlmeier, 484 U.S. 260, 108 S.Ct. 562, 98 L.Ed.2d 592 (1988), 676, 677

Healy v. Beer Institute, Inc., 491 U.S. 324, 109 S.Ct. 2491, 105 L.Ed.2d 275 (1989), 403

Heart of Atlanta Motel, Inc. v. United States, 379 U.S. 241, 85 S.Ct. 348, 13 L.Ed.2d 258 (1964), 237

Heart of Atlanta Motel, Inc. v. United States, ___ U.S. ___, 85 S.Ct. 1, 13 L.Ed.2d 12 (1964), 185, 1074

Heffron v. International Soc. for Krishna Consciousness, Inc. (ISKON), 452 U.S. 640, 101 S.Ct. 2559, 69 L.Ed.2d 298 (1981), 624

Helvering v. ___(see opposing party)

Herndon v. Lowry, 301 U.S. 242, 57 S.Ct. 732, 81 L.Ed. 1066 (1937), 606

Hess v. Indiana, 414 U.S. 105, 94 S.Ct. 326, 38 L.Ed.2d 303 (1973), 609

Hicklin v. Orbeck, 437 U.S. 518, 98 S.Ct. 2482, 57 L.Ed.2d 397 (1978), 413

Hicklin, Regina v., L.R. 3 Q.B. 360 (1868), 683

Hipolite Egg Co. v. United States, 220 U.S. 45, 31 S.Ct. 364, 55 L.Ed. 364 (1911), 181

Hirabayashi v. United States, 320 U.S. 81, 63 S.Ct. 1375, 87 L.Ed. 1774 (1943), 282

Hobbie v. Unemployment Appeals Com'n, 480 U.S. 136, 107 S.Ct. 1046, 94 L.Ed.2d 190 (1987), 745

Hodel v. Virginia Surface Mining and Reclamation Ass'n, Inc., 452 U.S. 264, 101 S.Ct. 2352, 69 L.Ed.2d 1 (1981), 186

Hoke v. United States, 227 U.S. 308, 33 S.Ct. 281, 57 L.Ed. 523 (1913), 169, 181

Holden v. Hardy, 169 U.S. 366, 18 S.Ct. 383, 42 L.Ed. 780 (1898), 532

Holt v. Sarver, 300 F.Supp. 825 (D.C.Ark.1969), 847

Home Building & Loan Ass'n v. Blaisdell, 290 U.S. 398, 54 S.Ct. 231, 78 L.Ed. 413 (1934), 527, 535, 554

Hopfmann v. Connolly, 471 U.S. 459, 105 S.Ct. 2106, 85 L.Ed.2d 469 (1985), 31

Houchins v. KQED, Inc., 438 U.S. 1, 98 S.Ct. 2588, 57 L.Ed.2d 553 (1978), 681

Houston v. Hill, 482 U.S. 451, 107 S.Ct. 2502, 96 L.Ed.2d 398 (1987), 629

Houston, East & West Texas Railway Co. v. United States, 234 U.S. 342, 34 S.Ct. 833, 58 L.Ed. 1341 (1914), 181

Houston Lawyers' Ass'n v. Attorney General of Texas, ___ U.S. ___, 111 S.Ct. 2376, 115 L.Ed.2d 379 (1991), 1157

H. P. Hood & Sons v. Du Mond, 336 U.S. 525, 69 S.Ct. 657, 93 L.Ed. 865 (1949), 401

Hudson v. McMillian, ___ U.S. ___, 112 S.Ct. 995, 117 L.Ed.2d 156 (1992), 847, App. E-2

Hughes v. Alexandria Scrap Corp., 426 U.S. 794, 96 S.Ct. 2488, 49 L.Ed.2d 220 (1976), 404

Hughes v. Oklahoma, 441 U.S. 322, 99 S.Ct. 1727, 60 L.Ed.2d 250 (1979), 403

Humphrey's Executor v. United States, 295 U.S. 602, 55 S.Ct. 869, 79 L.Ed. 1611 (1935), 267

Hurd v. Hodge, 334 U.S. 24, 68 S.Ct. 847, 92 L.Ed. 1187 (1948), 129

Hurtado v. California, 110 U.S. 516, 4 S.Ct. 111, 28 L.Ed. 232 (1884), 482, 498

Hustler Magazine v. Falwell, 485 U.S. 46, 108 S.Ct. 876, 99 L.Ed.2d 41 (1988), 679, 709

Hutchinson v. Proxmire, 443 U.S. 111, 99 S.Ct. 2675, 61 L.Ed.2d 411 (1979), 168

Hutto v. Finney, 437 U.S. 678, 98 S.Ct. 2565, 57 L.Ed.2d 522 (1978), 847, 942

Hylton v. United States, 3 U.S. 171, 1 L.Ed. 556 (1796), 44

Illinois v. Gates, 462 U.S. 213, 103 S.Ct. 2317, 76 L.Ed.2d 527 (1983), 131, 818, 819, **862**

Illinois v. Krull, 480 U.S. 340, 107 S.Ct. 1160, 94 L.Ed.2d 364 (1987), 827

Illinois v. Rodriguez, 497 U.S. 177, 110 S.Ct. 2793, 111 L.Ed.2d 148 (1990), 29

Immigration and Naturalization Service v. Chadha, 462 U.S. 919, 103 S.Ct. 2764, 77 L.Ed. 2d 317 (1983), 10, 132, 167, 264, 272, 279, 333, 334, 335, 357

Industrial Union Dept. v. American Petroleum Institute, 448 U.S. 607, 100 S.Ct. 2844, 65 L.Ed.2d 1010 (1980), 331

In re (see name of party)

International Soc. for Krishna Consciousness, Inc. v. Lee, ___ U.S. ___, 112 S.Ct. 2701, 120 L.Ed.2d 541 (1992), App. E-2

Jackson v. Georgia, 408 U.S. 238, 92 S.Ct. 2726, 33 L.Ed.2d 346 (1972), 925

Jackson v. United States, 393 U.S. 899, 89 S.Ct. 75, 21 L.Ed.2d 192 (1968), 837

Jacobellis v. Ohio, 378 U.S. 184, 84 S.Ct. 1676, 12 L.Ed.2d 793, 28 O.O.2d 101 (1964), 683

Jacobson v. Massachusetts, 197 U.S. 11, 25 S.Ct. 358, 49 L.Ed. 643 (1905), 956, 957, 978

Jacobson v. United States, ___ U.S. ___, 112 S.Ct. 1535, 118 L.Ed.2d 174 (1992), App. E-2

Jaffree v. Board of School Com'rs of Mobile County, 459 U.S. 1314, 103 S.Ct. 842, 74 L.Ed.2d 924 (1983), 96

Janis, United States v., 428 U.S. 433, 96 S.Ct. 3021, 49 L.Ed.2d 1046 (1976), 826

Jenkins v. Georgia, 418 U.S. 153, 94 S.Ct. 2750, 41 L.Ed.2d 642 (1974), 684, 723

Jimenez v. Weinberger, 417 U.S. 628, 94 S.Ct. 2496, 41 L.Ed.2d 363 (1974), 1067

Johnson v. Louisiana, 406 U.S. 356, 92 S.Ct. 1620, 32 L.Ed.2d 152 (1972), 840, **922**

Johnson v. Transportation Agency of Santa Clara, 480 U.S. 616, 107 S.Ct. 1442, 94 L.Ed.2d 615 (1987), 1059

Johnson, United States v., 383 U.S. 169, 86 S.Ct. 749, 15 L.Ed.2d 681 (1966), 168

Jones v. Alfred H. Mayer Co., 392 U.S. 409, 88 S.Ct. 2186, 20 L.Ed.2d 1189, 47 O.O.2d 43 (1968), 195

Jones University, Bob v. United States, 461 U.S. 574, 103 S.Ct. 2017, 76 L.Ed.2d 157 (1983), 760

J. W. Hampton, Jr., & Co. v. United States, 276 U.S. 394, 48 S.Ct. 348, 72 L.Ed. 624 (1928), 326, 328, 329, 330, **342**

Kahn v. Shevin, 416 U.S. 351, 94 S.Ct. 1734, 40 L.Ed.2d 189 (1974), 1065

Kahriger, United States v., 345 U.S. 22, 73 S.Ct. 510, 97 L.Ed. 754 (1953), 188, 194

Kam, State v., 69 Haw. 483, 748 P.2d 372 (Hawaii 1988), 488

Karcher v. Daggett, 462 U.S. 725, 103 S.Ct. 2653, 77 L.Ed.2d 133 (1983), 1159, **1184**

Kassel v. Consolidated Freightways Corp., 450 U.S. 662, 101 S.Ct. 1309, 67 L.Ed.2d 580 (1981), 400, **453**

Katz v. United States, 389 U.S. 347, 88 S.Ct. 507, 19 L.Ed.2d 576 (1967), 27, 474, 817, 818, **858,** 955

Katzenbach v. McClung, 379 U.S. 294, 85 S.Ct. 377, 13 L.Ed.2d 290 (1964), **240**

Katzenbach v. McClung, ___ U.S. ___, 85 S.Ct. 6, 13 L.Ed.2d 15 (1964), 185

Katzenbach v. Morgan, 384 U.S. 641, 86 S.Ct. 1717, 16 L.Ed.2d 828 (1966), 196, 197

Keeney v. Tamayo–Reyes, ___ U.S. ___, 112 S.Ct. 1715, 118 L.Ed.2d 318 (1992), 851, App. E-2

Kentucky v. Dennison, 65 U.S. 66, 16 L.Ed. 717 (1860), 414, 415

Ker v. California, 374 U.S. 23, 83 S.Ct. 1623, 10 L.Ed.2d 726, 24 O.O.2d 201 (1963), 823

Keyes v. Denver School Dist., 413 U.S. 189, 93 S.Ct. 2686, 37 L.Ed.2d 548 (1973), 1055, 1056

Keyishian v. State Board of Regents, 385 U.S. 589, 87 S.Ct. 675, 17 L.Ed.2d 629 (1967), 629

Keystone Bituminous Coal Ass'n v. DeBenedictis, 480 U.S. 470, 107 S.Ct. 1232, 94 L.Ed.2d 472 (1987), 541

Kilbourn v. Thompson, 103 U.S. 168, 26 L.Ed. 377 (1880), 173, 174, 175

Kirkpatrick v. Preisler, 394 U.S. 526, 89 S.Ct. 1225, 22 L.Ed.2d 519 (1969), 1159, 1160

Kissinger v. Halperin, 452 U.S. 713, 101 S.Ct. 3132, 69 L.Ed.2d 367 (1981), 271

Knowlton v. Moore, 178 U.S. 41, 20 S.Ct. 747, 44 L.Ed. 969 (1900), 52

Kokinda, United States v., 497 U.S. 720, 110 S.Ct. 3115, 111 L.Ed.2d 571 (1990), 625

Korematsu v. United States, 323 U.S. 214, 65 S.Ct. 193, 89 L.Ed. 194 (1944), 132, 262, 282, **311,** 488, 1046

Kovacs v. Cooper, 336 U.S. 77, 69 S.Ct. 448, 93 L.Ed. 513 (1949), 601, 623

Kring v. Missouri, 107 U.S. 221, 2 S.Ct. 443, 27 L.Ed. 506 (1883), 468

Kuhlmann v. Wilson, 477 U.S. 436, 106 S.Ct. 2616, 91 L.Ed.2d 364 (1986), 850

Labine v. Vincent, 401 U.S. 532, 91 S.Ct. 1017, 28 L.Ed.2d 288 (1971), 1067

Lalli v. Lalli, 439 U.S. 259, 99 S.Ct. 518, 58 L.Ed.2d 503 (1978), 1067

Lane v. Wilson, 307 U.S. 268, 59 S.Ct. 872, 83 L.Ed. 1281 (1939), 1150

Lassiter v. Northampton County Bd. of Elections, 360 U.S. 45, 79 S.Ct. 985, 3 L.Ed.2d 1072 (1959), 196, 1151

Lauf v. E.G. Shinner & Co., 303 U.S. 323, 58 S.Ct. 578, 82 L.Ed. 872 (1938), 87

Lee v. International Soc. for Krishna Consciousness, Inc., ___ U.S. ___, 112 S.Ct. 2709, 120 L.Ed.2d 669 (1992), 623

Lee v. Weisman, ___ U.S. ___, 112 S.Ct. 2649, 120 L.Ed.2d 467 (1992), 755, 759, App. E-2, **App. E-10**

Lemon v. Kurtzman, 403 U.S. 602, 91 S.Ct. 2105, 29 L.Ed.2d 745 (1971), 751, 753, 757, 758, 759

Leon, United States v., 468 U.S. 897, 104 S.Ct. 3405, 82 L.Ed.2d 677 (1984), 826, 827, **889**

Lewis v. City of New Orleans, 415 U.S. 130, 94 S.Ct. 970, 39 L.Ed.2d 214 (1974), 611

Lewis v. United States, 445 U.S. 55, 100 S.Ct. 915, 63 L.Ed.2d 198 (1980), 473

Lloyd Corp. v. Tanner, 407 U.S. 551, 92 S.Ct. 2219, 33 L.Ed.2d 131 (1972), 623

Lochner v. New York, 198 U.S. 45, 25 S.Ct. 539, 49 L.Ed. 937 (1905), 53, 54, 134, 135, 479, 532, 533, 534, 535, 538, 539, 569, 956, 1065

Lockhart v. McCree, 476 U.S. 162, 106 S.Ct. 1758, 90 L.Ed.2d 137 (1986), 845

Loewe v. Lawlor, 208 U.S. 274, 28 S.Ct. 301, 52 L.Ed. 488 (1908), 535

Long v. Rockwood, 277 U.S. 142, 48 S.Ct. 463, 72 L.Ed. 824 (1928), 407

Los Angeles v. Lyons, 461 U.S. 95, 103 S.Ct. 1660, 75 L.Ed.2d 675 (1983), 397

Lovett, United States v., 328 U.S. 303, 66 S.Ct. 1073, 90 L.Ed. 1252 (1946), 469

Loving v. Virginia, 388 U.S. 1, 87 S.Ct. 1817, 18 L.Ed.2d 1010 (1967), 1093

Loving v. Virginia, 386 U.S. 952, 87 S.Ct. 1017, 18 L.Ed.2d 101 (1967), 1028, 1046

Low v. Austin, 80 U.S. 29, 20 L.Ed. 517 (1871), 410

Lucas v. South Carolina Coastal Council, ___ U.S. ___, 112 S.Ct. 2886, 120 L.Ed.2d 798 (1992), 543

Luther v. Borden, 48 U.S. 1, 12 L.Ed. 581 (1849), 127, 149

Lynch v. Donnelly, 465 U.S. 668, 104 S.Ct. 1355, 79 L.Ed.2d 604 (1984), 744, 757, 758, 761, 803

Lyons v. Oklahoma, 322 U.S. 596, 64 S.Ct. 1208, 88 L.Ed. 1481 (1944), 828

Maher v. Roe, 432 U.S. 464, 97 S.Ct. 2376, 53 L.Ed.2d 484 (1977), 964, 965, 1000, 1070

Maine v. Taylor, 477 U.S. 131, 106 S.Ct. 2440, 91 L.Ed.2d 110 (1986), 403, 458

Malley v. Briggs, 475 U.S. 335, 106 S.Ct. 1092, 89 L.Ed.2d 271 (1986), 827, 828

Malloy v. Hogan, 378 U.S. 1, 84 S.Ct. 1489, 12 L.Ed.2d 653 (1964), 829

Mapp v. Ohio, 367 U.S. 643, 81 S.Ct. 1684, 6 L.Ed. 2d 1081, 16 O.O.2d 384 (1961), 825, 829, 851, 885

Marbury v. Madison, 5 U.S. 137, 2 L.Ed. 60 (1803), 9, 22, 35, 44, 45, 46, 47, 48, 58, 60, 88, 90, 171, 172, 177, 960

Marchetti v. United States, 390 U.S. 39, 88 S.Ct. 697, 19 L.Ed.2d 889, 43 O.O.2d 215 (1968), 194

Marsh v. Chambers, 463 U.S. 783, 103 S.Ct. 3330, 77 L.Ed.2d 1019 (1983), 751, 757, 758, 799

Marshall v. Barlow's, Inc., 436 U.S. 307, 98 S.Ct. 1816, 56 L.Ed.2d 305 (1978), 339, 374

Martin v. Hunter's Lessee, 14 U.S. 304, 4 L.Ed. 97 (1816), 48, 396

Martin v. Wilks, 490 U.S. 755, 109 S.Ct. 2180, 104 L.Ed.2d 835 (1989), 1059

Maryland v. Wirtz, 392 U.S. 183, 88 S.Ct. 2017, 20 L.Ed.2d 1020 (1968), 184, 185

Massachusetts v. Laird, 400 U.S. 886, 91 S.Ct. 128, 27 L.Ed.2d 140 (1970), 127, 135, 155, 278

Massachusetts v. Sheppard, 468 U.S. 981, 104 S.Ct. 3424, 82 L.Ed.2d 737 (1984), 826, 827

Massachusetts v. United States, 435 U.S. 444, 98 S.Ct. 1153, 55 L.Ed.2d 403 (1978), 408

Massachusetts Bd. of Retirement v. Murgia, 427 U.S. 307, 96 S.Ct. 2562, 49 L.Ed.2d 520 (1976), 487

Mathews v. Eldridge, 424 U.S. 319, 96 S.Ct. 893, 47 L.Ed.2d 18 (1976), 337, 338, 370

Matter of (see name of party)

Mayor, Aldermen and Commonalty of City of New York v. Miln, 36 U.S. 102, 9 L.Ed. 648 (1837), 389

McCardle, Ex parte, 74 U.S. 506, 19 L.Ed. 264 (1868), 88, 89, 103

McCardle, Ex parte, 73 U.S. 318, 18 L.Ed. 816 (1867), 28, 848

McCleskey v. Kemp, 481 U.S. 279, 107 S.Ct. 1756, 95 L.Ed.2d 262 (1987), 845, 938

McCleskey v. Zant, ___ U.S. ___, 111 S.Ct. 1454, 113 L.Ed.2d 517 (1991), 468, 851

McCollum v. Board of Education, 333 U.S. 203, 68 S.Ct. 461, 92 L.Ed. 649 (1948), 752

McCray v. United States, 195 U.S. 27, 24 S.Ct. 769, 49 L.Ed. 78 (1904), 189, 190

McGowan v. Maryland, 366 U.S. 420, 81 S.Ct. 1101, 6 L.Ed.2d 393, 17 O.O.2d 151 (1961), 744

McGrain v. Daugherty, 273 U.S. 135, 47 S.Ct. 319, 71 L.Ed. 580 (1927), 174, 203

McKane v. Durston, 153 U.S. 684, 14 S.Ct. 913, 38 L.Ed. 867 (1894), 847

McKeiver v. Pennsylvania, 403 U.S. 528, 91 S.Ct. 1976, 29 L.Ed.2d 647 (1971), 852

McLaurin v. Oklahoma State Regents, 339 U.S. 637, 70 S.Ct. 851, 94 L.Ed. 1149 (1950), 1051

M'Culloch v. Maryland, 17 U.S. 316, 4 L.Ed. 579 (1819), 10, 47, 171, 172, 176, 177, 195, 196, 199, 388, 406, 421, 759

Meek v. Pittenger, 421 U.S. 349, 95 S.Ct. 1753, 44 L.Ed.2d 217 (1975), 752

Memoirs v. Massachusetts, 383 U.S. 413, 86 S.Ct. 975, 16 L.Ed.2d 1 (1966), 684

Memphis Firefighters v. Stotts, 467 U.S. 561, 104 S.Ct. 2576, 81 L.Ed.2d 483 (1984), 1059

Meritor Sav. Bank, FSB v. Vinson, 477 U.S. 57, 106 S.Ct. 2399, 91 L.Ed.2d 49 (1986), 1062

Merryman, Ex parte, 17 Fed.Cas. 144 (C.C.Md. 1861), 280

Metropolitan Washington Airports Authority (MWAA) v. Citizens for Abatement of Aircraft Noise, Inc. (CAAN), ___ U.S. ___, 111 S.Ct. 2298, 115 L.Ed.2d 236 (1991), 335, 364

Meyer v. Nebraska, 262 U.S. 390, 43 S.Ct. 625, 67 L.Ed. 1042 (1923), 604, 957, 959, 980

Michael H. v. Gerald D., 491 U.S. 110, 109 S.Ct. 2333, 105 L.Ed.2d 91 (1989), 1067

Michelin Tire Corp. v. Wages, 423 U.S. 276, 96 S.Ct. 535, 46 L.Ed.2d 495 (1976), 410

Michigan v. Tyler, 436 U.S. 499, 98 S.Ct. 1942, 56 L.Ed.2d 486 (1978), 820

Midwest Oil Co., United States v., 236 U.S. 459, 35 S.Ct. 309, 59 L.Ed. 673 (1915), 262

Miller v. California, 413 U.S. 15, 93 S.Ct. 2607, 37 L.Ed.2d 419 (1973), 684, 720

Miller, United States v., 307 U.S. 174, 59 S.Ct. 816, 83 L.Ed. 1206 (1939), 473

Milligan, Ex parte, 71 U.S. 2, 18 L.Ed. 281 (1866), 280, 281, 308

Milliken v. Bradley, 418 U.S. 717, 94 S.Ct. 3112, 41 L.Ed.2d 1069 (1974), 1056, 1099

Minersville School Dist. v. Gobitis, 310 U.S. 586, 60 S.Ct. 1010, 84 L.Ed. 1375 (1940), 612, 748

Minor v. Happersett, 88 U.S. 162, 22 L.Ed. 627 (1874), 486, 1061

Miranda v. Arizona, 384 U.S. 436, 86 S.Ct. 1602, 16 L.Ed.2d 694 (1966), 829, 830, 831, 833, 851, 894

Mississippi Power & Light Co. v. Mississippi ex rel. Moore, 487 U.S. 354, 108 S.Ct. 2428, 101 L.Ed. 2d 322 (1988), 394

Mississippi University for Women v. Hogan, 458 U.S. 718, 102 S.Ct. 3331, 73 L.Ed.2d 1090 (1982), 1066, 1124

Missouri ex rel. Gaines, v. Canada, 305 U.S. 337, 59 S.Ct. 232, 83 L.Ed. 208 (1938), 1051

Missouri v. Holland, 252 U.S. 416, 40 S.Ct. 382, 64 L.Ed. 641 (1920), 275

Mistretta v. United States, 488 U.S. 361, 109 S.Ct. 647, 102 L.Ed.2d 714 (1989), 332, 335, 353

Mobile v. Bolden, 446 U.S. 55, 100 S.Ct. 1490, 64 L.Ed.2d 47 (1980), 1154, 1155, 1172

Moe v. Secretary of Administration, 382 Mass. 629, 417 N.E.2d 387 (Mass.1981), 965

Monroe v. Pape, 365 U.S. 167, 81 S.Ct. 473, 5 L.Ed. 2d 492 (1961), 26

Montoya de Hernandez, United States v., 473 U.S. 531, 105 S.Ct. 3304, 87 L.Ed.2d 381 (1985), 822

Moore v. City of East Cleveland, 431 U.S. 494, 97 S.Ct. 1932, 52 L.Ed.2d 531 (1977), 970, 1023

Moose Lodge v. Irvis, 407 U.S. 163, 92 S.Ct. 1965, 32 L.Ed.2d 627 (1972), 1073

Moran v. Burbine, 475 U.S. 412, 106 S.Ct. 1135, 89 L.Ed.2d 410 (1986), 831

Morehead v. New York ex rel. Tipaldo, 298 U.S. 587, 56 S.Ct. 918, 80 L.Ed. 1347 (1936), 537, 538

Morey v. Doud, 354 U.S. 457, 77 S.Ct. 1344, 1 L.Ed.2d 1485 (1957), 540

Morrison v. Olson, 487 U.S. 654, 108 S.Ct. 2597, 101 L.Ed.2d 569 (1988), 266, 335

Mozert v. Hawkins County Public Schools, 484 U.S. 1066, 108 S.Ct. 1029, 98 L.Ed.2d 993 (1988), 757

Mueller v. Allen, 463 U.S. 388, 103 S.Ct. 3062, 77 L.Ed.2d 721 (1983), 761

Mugler v. Kansas, 123 U.S. 623, 8 S.Ct. 273, 31 L.Ed. 205 (1887), 531

Mulford v. Smith, 307 U.S. 38, 59 S.Ct. 648, 83 L.Ed. 1092 (1939), 192, 539

Muller v. Oregon, 208 U.S. 412, 28 S.Ct. 324, 52 L.Ed. 551 (1908), 533, 534

Munn v. Illinois, 94 U.S. 113, 24 L.Ed. 77 (1876), 530, 531, 536, 564

Murdock v. Pennsylvania, 319 U.S. 105, 63 S.Ct. 870, 87 L.Ed. 1292 (1943), 600, 743

Murphy v. Waterfront Commission, 378 U.S. 52, 84 S.Ct. 1594, 12 L.Ed.2d 678 (1964), 340

Murray v. Curlett, 374 U.S. 203, 83 S.Ct. 1560 (1963), 754

Muskrat v. United States, 219 U.S. 346, 31 S.Ct. 250, 55 L.Ed. 246 (1911), 119

Myers v. United States, 272 U.S. 52, 47 S.Ct. 21, 71 L.Ed. 160 (1926), 266, 267

Nantahala Power and Light Co. v. Thornburg, 476 U.S. 953, 106 S.Ct. 2349, 90 L.Ed.2d 943 (1986), 394

National Ass'n for Advancement of Colored People v. Alabama, 357 U.S. 449, 78 S.Ct. 1163, 2 L.Ed.2d 1488 (1958), 627, 665

National Association for the Advancement of Colored People v. Claiborne Hardware Co., 458 U.S. 886, 102 S.Ct. 3409, 73 L.Ed.2d 1215 (1982), 609

National Association for the Advancement of Colored People v. Federal Power Com'n, 425 U.S. 662, 96 S.Ct. 1806, 48 L.Ed.2d 284 (1976), 336

National Cable Television Ass'n, Inc. v. United States, 415 U.S. 352, 94 S.Ct. 1155, 39 L.Ed.2d 370 (1974), 330

National Labor Relations Board v. Jones & Laughlin Steel Corp., 301 U.S. 1, 57 S.Ct. 615, 81 L.Ed. 893 (1937), 54, 95, 129, 183, **228,** 539

National League of Cities v. Usery, 426 U.S. 833, 96 S.Ct. 2465, 49 L.Ed.2d 245 (1976), 183, 184, 185, 392, **428**

National Socialist Party v. Skokie, 434 U.S. 1327, 98 S.Ct. 14, 54 L.Ed.2d 38 (1977), 619

National Treasury Employees Union v. Von Raab, 489 U.S. 656, 109 S.Ct. 1384, 103 L.Ed.2d 685 (1989), 823, 976

Natural Gas Pipeline Co. v. Slattery, 302 U.S. 300, 58 S.Ct. 199, 82 L.Ed. 276 (1937), 126

Neagle, In re, 39 F. 833 (C.C.Cal.1889), 261, 262

Near v. Minnesota, 283 U.S. 697, 51 S.Ct. 625, 75 L.Ed. 1357 (1931), 482, 600, 674, 675, **691**

Nebbia v. New York, 291 U.S. 502, 54 S.Ct. 505, 78 L.Ed. 940 (1934), 530, 535, 536, 544, **579**

Nebraska Press Ass'n v. Stuart, 427 U.S. 539, 96 S.Ct. 2791, 49 L.Ed.2d 683 (1976), 677, **700,** 838, 839

Newberry v. United States, 256 U.S. 232, 41 S.Ct. 469, 65 L.Ed. 913 (1921), 1150

New York v. Ferber, 458 U.S. 747, 102 S.Ct. 3348, 73 L.Ed.2d 1113 (1982), 488, 629, 684, 685, 725

New York v. Quarles, 467 U.S. 649, 104 S.Ct. 2626, 81 L.Ed.2d 550 (1984), 830, **903**

New York v. United States, 620 F.Supp. 374 (D.C. N.Y.1985), App. E-1

New York State Club Ass'n, Inc. v. City of New York, 487 U.S. 1, 108 S.Ct. 2225, 101 L.Ed.2d 1 (1988), 628, 1075

New York, State of v. United States, 326 U.S. 572, 66 S.Ct. 310, 90 L.Ed. 326 (1946), 408

New York Times Co. v. Sullivan, 376 U.S. 254, 84 S.Ct. 710, 11 L.Ed.2d 686 (1964), 677, 678, 679, 705

New York Times Co. v. United States (The Pentagon Papers Case), 403 U.S. 713, 91 S.Ct. 2140, 29 L.Ed.2d 822 (1971), 34, 35, 262, 675, **695**

Niemotko v. Maryland, 340 U.S. 268, 71 S.Ct. 328, 95 L.Ed. 280 (1951), 744

Nix v. Williams, 467 U.S. 431, 104 S.Ct. 2501, 81 L.Ed.2d 377 (1984), 27, 830, **899**

Nixon v. Administrator of General Services, 433 U.S. 425, 97 S.Ct. 2777, 53 L.Ed.2d 867 (1977), 470

Nixon v. Condon, 286 U.S. 73, 52 S.Ct. 484, 76 L.Ed. 984 (1932), 1150

Nixon v. Fitzgerald, 457 U.S. 731, 102 S.Ct. 2690, 73 L.Ed.2d 349 (1982), 271

Nixon v. Herndon, 273 U.S. 536, 47 S.Ct. 446, 71 L.Ed. 759 (1927), 1150

Nixon, United States v., 418 U.S. 904, 94 S.Ct. 3193, 41 L.Ed.2d 1152 (1974), 10, 30

Nixon, United States v., 418 U.S. 683, 94 S.Ct. 3090, 41 L.Ed.2d 1039 (1974), 72, 258, 261, 270, 335

Nollan v. California Coastal Com'n, 483 U.S. 825, 107 S.Ct. 3141, 97 L.Ed.2d 677 (1987), 542, 590

Noto v. United States, 367 U.S. 290, 81 S.Ct. 1517, 6 L.Ed.2d 836 (1961), 608

O'Brien v. Brown, 409 U.S. 1, 92 S.Ct. 2718, 34 L.Ed.2d 1 (1972), 29

O'Brien, United States v., 391 U.S. 367, 88 S.Ct. 1673, 20 L.Ed.2d 672 (1968), 612

Ogden v. Saunders, 25 U.S. 212, 6 L.Ed. 606 (1827), 389, 525

Ohio ex rel. Eaton v. Price, 364 U.S. 263, 80 S.Ct. 1463, 4 L.Ed.2d 1708, 13 O.O.2d 55 (1960), 339

Okanogan Indians v. United States, 279 U.S. 655, 49 S.Ct. 463, 73 L.Ed. 894 (1929), 264

Oklahoma Natural Gas Co. v. Russell, 261 U.S. 290, 43 S.Ct. 353, 67 L.Ed. 659 (1923), 126

Oliver v. United States, 466 U.S. 170, 104 S.Ct. 1735, 80 L.Ed.2d 214 (1984), 818

Olmstead v. United States, 277 U.S. 438, 48 S.Ct. 564, 72 L.Ed. 944 (1928), 817, **855,** 859, 956

O'Neil v. Vermont, 144 U.S. 323, 12 S.Ct. 693, 36 L.Ed. 450 (1892), 842

Oregon v. Mathiason, 429 U.S. 492, 97 S.Ct. 711, 50 L.Ed.2d 714 (1977), 831

Oregon v. Mitchell, 400 U.S. 112, 91 S.Ct. 260, 27 L.Ed.2d 272 (1970), 92, 487

Orr v. Orr, 440 U.S. 268, 99 S.Ct. 1102, 59 L.Ed.2d 306 (1979), 1064

Osborne v. Ohio, 495 U.S. 103, 110 S.Ct. 1691, 109 L.Ed.2d 98 (1990), 685

Pacific Gas & Elec. Co. v. State Energy Resources Conservation & Development Com'n, 461 U.S. 190, 103 S.Ct. 1713, 75 L.Ed.2d 752 (1983), 394, 395

Pack, State ex rel. Swann v., 527 S.W.2d 99 (Tenn. 1975), 744

Palko v. Connecticut, 302 U.S. 319, 58 S.Ct. 149, 82 L.Ed. 288 (1937), 482, 483, 484, 503, 600, 841

Panama Refining Co. v. Ryan, 293 U.S. 388, 55 S.Ct. 241, 79 L.Ed. 446 (1935), 329, 330

Parker v. Dugger, 876 F.2d 1470 (11th Cir.1989), 29

Paul v. Davis, 424 U.S. 693, 96 S.Ct. 1155, 47 L.Ed. 2d 405 (1976), 135

Payne v. Tennessee, ___ U.S. ___, 111 S.Ct. 2597, 115 L.Ed.2d 720 (1991), 845

Pennell v. City of San Jose, 485 U.S. 1, 108 S.Ct. 849, 99 L.Ed.2d 1 (1988), 542

Pennsylvania v. Finley, 481 U.S. 551, 107 S.Ct. 1990, 95 L.Ed.2d 539 (1987), 833

Pennsylvania v. Nelson, 350 U.S. 497, 76 S.Ct. 477, 100 L.Ed. 640 (1956), 89, 393, 394

Pennsylvania v. West Virginia, 262 U.S. 553, 43 S.Ct. 658, 67 L.Ed. 1117 (1923), 403

Pennsylvania Coal Co. v. Mahon, 260 U.S. 393, 43 S.Ct. 158, 67 L.Ed. 322 (1922), 540, 541

Penry v. Lynaugh, 492 U.S. 302, 109 S.Ct. 2934, 106 L.Ed.2d 256 (1989), 845

People v. ___(see opposing party)

Perez v. United States, 1971 WL 485 (C.D.Cal. 1971), 187

Perry Educ. Ass'n v. Perry Local Educators' Ass'n, 460 U.S. 37, 103 S.Ct. 948, 74 L.Ed.2d 794 (1983), 622

Philadelphia v. New Jersey, 437 U.S. 617, 98 S.Ct. 2531, 57 L.Ed.2d 475 (1978), 402, 450, App. E-1

Pierce v. Society of Sisters, 268 U.S. 510, 45 S.Ct. 571, 69 L.Ed. 1070 (1925), 604, 957, 959

Pink, United States v., 315 U.S. 203, 62 S.Ct. 552, 86 L.Ed. 796 (1942), 276

Planned Parenthood v. Ashcroft, 462 U.S. 476, 103 S.Ct. 2517, 76 L.Ed.2d 733 (1983), 488, 963

Planned Parenthood v. Casey, ___ U.S. ___, 112 S.Ct. 2791, 120 L.Ed.2d 674 (1992), 967, 968, 969, App. E-1, App. E-2, App. E-14

Planned Parenthood v. Danforth, 428 U.S. 52, 96 S.Ct. 2831, 49 L.Ed.2d 788 (1976), 963, 1011

Plessy v. Ferguson, 163 U.S. 537, 16 S.Ct. 1138, 41 L.Ed. 256 (1896), 36, 120, 131, 1049, 1050, 1051, 1052, 1057, 1059, 1081

Plyler v. Doe, 457 U.S. 202, 102 S.Ct. 2382, 72 L.Ed.2d 786 (1982), 1068, 1069, 1128

Poe v. Ullman, 367 U.S. 497, 81 S.Ct. 1752, 6 L.Ed.2d 989 (1961), 126, 137, 957, 958, 971, 982

Pollock v. Farmers' Loan & Trust Co., 157 U.S. 429, 15 S.Ct. 673, 39 L.Ed. 759 (1895), 51, 52, 91, 170, 407

Pope v. Illinois, 481 U.S. 497, 107 S.Ct. 1918, 95 L.Ed.2d 439 (1987), 684

Posadas De Puerto Rico Associates v. Tourism Co., 478 U.S. 328, 106 S.Ct. 2968, 92 L.Ed.2d 266 (1986), 686, 687

Powell v. McCormack, 395 U.S. 486, 89 S.Ct. 1944, 23 L.Ed.2d 491 (1969), 168, 259

Powell v. Alabama (The Scottsboro Case), 287 U.S. 45, 53 S.Ct. 55, 77 L.Ed. 158 (1932), 832, 833, 834, 835, 907

Powers v. Ohio, ___ U.S. ___, 111 S.Ct. 1364, 113 L.Ed.2d 411 (1991), 841

Preseault v. Interstate Commerce Commission, 494 U.S. 1, 110 S.Ct. 914, 108 L.Ed.2d 1 (1990), 186, 542

Prince v. Massachusetts, 321 U.S. 158, 64 S.Ct. 438, 88 L.Ed. 645 (1944), 750

Prize Cases, The, 67 U.S. 635, 17 L.Ed. 459 (1862), 277, 278, 301

Procunier v. Martinez, 416 U.S. 396, 94 S.Ct. 1800, 40 L.Ed.2d 224, 71 O.O.2d 139 (1974), 847

Progressive, Inc., United States v., 467 F.Supp. 990 (D.C.Wis.1979), 676

Prudential Ins. Co. v. Cheek, 259 U.S. 530, 42 S.Ct. 516, 66 L.Ed. 1044 (1922), 604

PruneYard Shopping Center v. Robins, 447 U.S. 74, 100 S.Ct. 2035, 64 L.Ed.2d 741 (1980), 543, 593, 623

Puerto Rico v. Branstad, 483 U.S. 219, 107 S.Ct. 2802, 97 L.Ed.2d 187 (1987), 415

Pulley v. Harris, 465 U.S. 37, 104 S.Ct. 871, 79 L.Ed.2d 29 (1984), 845

Quinlan, In re, 70 N.J. 10, 355 A.2d 647 (N.J.1976), 974

Rankin v. McPherson, 483 U.S. 378, 107 S.Ct. 2891, 97 L.Ed.2d 315 (1987), 609, 618, 653

R.A.V. v. St. Paul, ___ U.S. ___, 112 S.Ct. 2538, 120 L.Ed.2d 305 (1992), 611, App. E-2, App. E-6

Ravin v. State, 537 P.2d 494 (Alaska 1975), 973

Red Lion Broadcasting Co. v. F. C. C., 395 U.S. 367, 89 S.Ct. 1794, 23 L.Ed.2d 371 (1969), 688

Reed v. Reed, 404 U.S. 71, 92 S.Ct. 251, 30 L.Ed.2d 225 (1971), 1063, 1067

Reese, United States v., 92 U.S. 214, 23 L.Ed. 563 (1875), 1149

Reeves, Inc. v. Stake, 447 U.S. 429, 100 S.Ct. 2271, 65 L.Ed.2d 244 (1980), 404

Regan v. Wald, 468 U.S. 222, 104 S.Ct. 3026, 82 L.Ed.2d 171 (1984), 273, 274

Regina v. ___ (see opposing party)

Renton v. Playtime Theatres, Inc., 475 U.S. 41, 106 S.Ct. 925, 89 L.Ed.2d 29 (1986), 624

Reynolds v. Sims, 377 U.S. 533, 84 S.Ct. 1362, 12 L.Ed.2d 506 (1964), 92, 1158, 1159, 1160, 1162, 1181

Reynolds v. United States, 98 U.S. 145, 25 L.Ed. 244 (1878), 742, 743, 746

Ribnik v. McBride, 277 U.S. 350, 48 S.Ct. 545, 72 L.Ed. 913 (1928), 531

Richardson, United States v., 498 F.2d 9 (8th Cir. 1974), 121, 122, 123

Richmond, City of v. J.A. Croson Co., 488 U.S. 469, 109 S.Ct. 706, 102 L.Ed.2d 854 (1989), 1059, 1060, 1108

Richmond Newspapers, Inc. v. Virginia, 448 U.S. 555, 100 S.Ct. 2814, 65 L.Ed.2d 973 (1980), 839

Right to Choose v. Byrne, 91 N.J. 287, 450 A.2d 925 (N.J.1982), 965

Riverside, County of v. McLaughlin, ___ U.S. ___, 111 S.Ct. 1661, 114 L.Ed.2d 49 (1991), 824, 825

Robel, United States v., 389 U.S. 258, 88 S.Ct. 419, 19 L.Ed.2d 508 (1967), 629

Roberts v. United States Jaycees, 468 U.S. 609, 104 S.Ct. 3244, 82 L.Ed.2d 462 (1984), 627, 667, 1075

Robinson v. California, 370 U.S. 660, 82 S.Ct. 1417, 8 L.Ed.2d 758 (1962), 842

Rochin v. California, 342 U.S. 165, 72 S.Ct. 205, 96 L.Ed. 183 (1952), 479, 483, 510

Roe v. Wade, 410 U.S. 113, 93 S.Ct. 705, 35 L.Ed. 2d 147 (1973), 26, 33, 55, 92, 124, 125, 131, 397, 480, 488, 953, 954, 960, 961, 962, 963, 965, 966, 967, 968, 969, 970, 971, 993, 1020, 1028, App. E-2

Rogers v. Lodge, 458 U.S. 613, 102 S.Ct. 3272, 73 L.Ed.2d 1012 (1982), 1155, 1176

Ross, United States v., 456 U.S. 798, 102 S.Ct. 2157, 72 L.Ed.2d 572 (1982), 820, 870

Rostker v. Goldberg, 453 U.S. 57, 101 S.Ct. 2646, 69 L.Ed.2d 478 (1981), 749, 1065, 1121

Rotary Intern. v. Rotary Club of Duarte, 481 U.S. 537, 107 S.Ct. 1940, 95 L.Ed.2d 474 (1987), 627, 1075

Roth v. United States, 354 U.S. 476, 77 S.Ct. 1304, 1 L.Ed.2d 1498, 14 O.O.2d 331 (1957), 683, 684

Rummel v. Estelle, 445 U.S. 263, 100 S.Ct. 1133, 63 L.Ed.2d 382 (1980), 846

Rust v. Sullivan, ___ U.S. ___, 111 S.Ct. 1759, 114 L.Ed.2d 233 (1991), 466, 619, 657, 967

Saia v. New York, 334 U.S. 558, 68 S.Ct. 1148, 92 L.Ed. 1574 (1948), 623

Salerno, United States v., 481 U.S. 739, 107 S.Ct. 2095, 95 L.Ed.2d 697 (1987), 476, 835, 836

San Antonio v. Rodriguez, 411 U.S. 1, 93 S.Ct. 1278, 36 L.Ed.2d 16 (1973), 1069, 1070, 1138

Sanders v. United States, 375 U.S. 844, 84 S.Ct. 95, 11 L.Ed.2d 71 (1963), 848, 851

San Francisco Arts & Athletics, Inc. v. United States Olympic Committee, 483 U.S. 522, 107 S.Ct. 2971, 97 L.Ed.2d 427 (1987), 1072

Santa Clara County v. Southern Pacific Railroad Co., 118 U.S. 394, 6 S.Ct. 1132, 30 L.Ed. 118 (1886), 531, 1044

Santobello v. New York, 404 U.S. 257, 92 S.Ct. 495, 30 L.Ed.2d 427 (1971), 837

Scales v. United States, 367 U.S. 203, 81 S.Ct. 1469, 6 L.Ed.2d 782 (1961), 608, 626

Schall v. Martin, 467 U.S. 253, 104 S.Ct. 2403, 81 L.Ed.2d 207 (1984), 852

Schenck v. United States, 249 U.S. 47, 39 S.Ct. 247, 63 L.Ed. 470 (1919), 602, 603, 605, 631

Schick v. Reed, 419 U.S. 256, 95 S.Ct. 379, 42 L.Ed.2d 430 (1974), 268, 293

Schmerber v. California, 384 U.S. 757, 86 S.Ct. 1826, 16 L.Ed.2d 908 (1966), 820

Schneckloth v. Bustamonte, 412 U.S. 218, 93 S.Ct. 2041, 36 L.Ed.2d 854 (1973), 820

Scopes v. State, 152 Tenn. 424, 278 S.W. 57 (Tenn. 1925), 756

Scott v. Illinois, 440 U.S. 367, 99 S.Ct. 1158, 59 L.Ed.2d 383 (1979), 834

Seeger, United States v., 380 U.S. 163, 85 S.Ct. 850, 13 L.Ed.2d 733 (1965), 741, 742, 748

Serrano v. Priest, 96 Cal.Rptr. 601, 487 P.2d 1241 (Cal.1971), 1070

Shapiro v. Thompson, 394 U.S. 618, 89 S.Ct. 1322, 22 L.Ed.2d 600 (1969), 412, 488, 1068, 1069

Sheet Metal Workers v. Equal Employment Opportunity Commission, 478 U.S. 421, 106 S.Ct. 3019, 92 L.Ed.2d 344 (1986), 1059

Shelley v. Kraemer, 334 U.S. 1, 68 S.Ct. 836, 92 L.Ed. 1161 (1948), 129, 1074, 1084

Sheppard v. Maxwell, 384 U.S. 333, 86 S.Ct. 1507, 16 L.Ed.2d 600, 35 O.O.2d 431 (1966), 677, 838

Sherbert v. Verner, 374 U.S. 398, 83 S.Ct. 1790, 10 L.Ed.2d 965 (1963), 745, 746

Sierra Club v. Morton, 405 U.S. 727, 92 S.Ct. 1361, 31 L.Ed.2d 636 (1972), 122

Silkwood v. Kerr–McGee Corp., 464 U.S. 238, 104 S.Ct. 615, 78 L.Ed.2d 443 (1984), 395, 438

Simon & Schuster, Inc. v. New York State Crime Victims Bd., ___ U.S. ___, 112 S.Ct. 501, 116 L.Ed.2d 476 (1991), App. E-2

Singleton v. Wulff, 428 U.S. 106, 96 S.Ct. 2868, 49 L.Ed.2d 826 (1976), 121

Sipuel v. Oklahoma Board of Regents, 199 Okl. 586, 190 P.2d 437 (Okl.1948), 1051

Skinner v. Oklahoma, 316 U.S. 535, 62 S.Ct. 1110, 86 L.Ed. 1655 (1942), 957

Skinner v. Railway Labor Executives' Ass'n, 489 U.S. 602, 109 S.Ct. 1402, 103 L.Ed.2d 639 (1989), 823, 976

Slaughter–House Cases, The, 83 U.S. 36, 21 L.Ed. 394 (1872), 412, 528, 529, **558,** 1044

Smith v. Allwright, 321 U.S. 649, 64 S.Ct. 757, 88 L.Ed. 987 (1944), 480, 1151, **1164**

Smith v. Board of School Com'rs of Mobile County, 827 F.2d 684 (11th Cir.1987), 757

Sokolow, United States v., 490 U.S. 1, 109 S.Ct. 1581, 104 L.Ed.2d 1 (1989), 821, 822, **878**

Solem v. Helm, 463 U.S. 277, 103 S.Ct. 3001, 77 L.Ed.2d 637 (1983), 846

Sonzinsky v. United States, 300 U.S. 506, 57 S.Ct. 554, 81 L.Ed. 772 (1937), 190

Sosna v. Iowa, 419 U.S. 393, 95 S.Ct. 553, 42 L.Ed. 2d 532 (1975), 412

South Carolina v. Baker, 485 U.S. 505, 108 S.Ct. 1355, 99 L.Ed.2d 592 (1988), 392, 407

South Carolina v. Gathers, 490 U.S. 805, 109 S.Ct. 2207, 104 L.Ed.2d 876 (1989), 845

South Carolina v. Katzenbach, 383 U.S. 301, 86 S.Ct. 803, 15 L.Ed.2d 769 (1966), 195, 196, 1153, 1169

South Carolina State Highway Dept. v. Barnwell Bros., 303 U.S. 177, 58 S.Ct. 510, 82 L.Ed. 734 (1938), 399, 400, 444

South–Central Timber Development, Inc. v. Wunnicke, 467 U.S. 82, 104 S.Ct. 2237, 81 L.Ed.2d 71 (1984), 404

South Dakota v. Dole, 483 U.S. 203, 107 S.Ct. 2793, 97 L.Ed.2d 171 (1987), 193, 249

Southern Pac. Co. v. Arizona, 325 U.S. 761, 65 S.Ct. 1515, 89 L.Ed. 1915 (1945), 446

Southern Pacific Company v. Arizona, ___ U.S. ___, 65 S.Ct. 863 (1945), 400, 401

Spinelli v. United States, 393 U.S. 410, 89 S.Ct. 584, 21 L.Ed.2d 637 (1969), 819

Springer v. United States, 102 U.S. 586, 26 L.Ed. 253 (1880), 51, 52

Stack v. Boyle, 342 U.S. 1, 72 S.Ct. 1, 96 L.Ed. 3 (1951), 476, 835

Stafford v. Wallace, 258 U.S. 495, 42 S.Ct. 397, 66 L.Ed. 735 (1922), 182

Stanford v. Kentucky, 492 U.S. 361, 109 S.Ct. 2969, 106 L.Ed.2d 306 (1989), 852

Stanford v. Texas, 380 U.S. 926, 85 S.Ct. 879, 13 L.Ed.2d 813 (1965), 818

Stanley v. Georgia, 394 U.S. 557, 89 S.Ct. 1243, 22 L.Ed.2d 542 (1969), 130, 683, 685, 971, 972

State v. ___(see opposing party)

State ex rel. v. ___(see opposing party and relator)

State of (see name of state)

Steelworkers v. Weber, 443 U.S. 193, 99 S.Ct. 2721, 61 L.Ed.2d 480 (1979), 1059

Stone v. Graham, 449 U.S. 39, 101 S.Ct. 192, 66 L.Ed.2d 199 (1980), 755

Stone v. Mississippi, 101 U.S. 814, 25 L.Ed. 1079 (1879), 526

Stone v. Powell, 428 U.S. 465, 96 S.Ct. 3037, 49 L.Ed.2d 1067 (1976), 468, 850

Straight v. Wainwright, 475 U.S. 1099, 106 S.Ct. 1502, 89 L.Ed.2d 903 (1986), 850

Strauder v. West Virginia, 100 U.S. 303, 25 L.Ed. 664 (1879), 1044

Street v. New York, 394 U.S. 576, 89 S.Ct. 1354, 22 L.Ed.2d 572 (1969), 613

Strickland v. Washington, 466 U.S. 668, 104 S.Ct. 2052, 80 L.Ed.2d 674 (1984), 834

Students Challenging Regulatory Agency Procedures (SCRAP), United States v., 412 U.S. 669, 93 S.Ct. 2405, 37 L.Ed.2d 254 (1973), 122

Sturges v. Crowninshield, 17 U.S. 122, 4 L.Ed. 529 (1819), 389, 525

Sugarman v. Dougall, 413 U.S. 634, 93 S.Ct. 2842, 37 L.Ed.2d 853 (1973), 1068

Superintendent of Belchertown State School v. Saikewicz, 373 Mass. 728, 370 N.E.2d 417 (Mass. 1977), 973, 974

Swain v. Alabama., 382 U.S. 944, 86 S.Ct. 399, 15 L.Ed.2d 353 (1965), 841

Swann v. Charlotte–Mecklenburg Bd. of Ed., 402 U.S. 1, 91 S.Ct. 1267, 28 L.Ed.2d 554 (1971), 1055, 1056, 1096

Swann, State ex rel. v. Pack, 527 S.W.2d 99 (Tenn. 1975), 744

Sweatt v. Painter, 339 U.S. 629, 70 S.Ct. 848, 94 L.Ed. 1114 (1950), 1052, 1087

Swift & Co. v. United States, 196 U.S. 375, 25 S.Ct. 276, 49 L.Ed. 518 (1905), 182

Tennessee v. Garner, 471 U.S. 1, 105 S.Ct. 1694, 85 L.Ed.2d 1 (1985), 824

Terminiello v. Chicago, 337 U.S. 1, 69 S.Ct. 894, 93 L.Ed. 1131 (1949), 610

Terry v. Adams, 345 U.S. 461, 73 S.Ct. 809, 97 L.Ed. 1152 (1953), 1151

Terry v. Ohio, 392 U.S. 1, 88 S.Ct. 1868, 20 L.Ed. 2d 889, 44 O.O.2d 383 (1968), 821, 822, 874

Texas v. Johnson, 491 U.S. 397, 109 S.Ct. 2533, 105 L.Ed.2d 342 (1989), 26, 56, 77, 92, 609, 614, 615, 649

Texas v. White, 74 U.S. 700, 19 L.Ed. 227 (1868), 390

The Aurora v. United States, 11 U.S. 382, 3 L.Ed. 378 (1813), 327, 328

The Florida Star v. B.J.F., 491 U.S. 524, 109 S.Ct. 2603, 105 L.Ed.2d 443 (1989), 680

Thomas v. Collins, 323 U.S. 516, 65 S.Ct. 315, 89 L.Ed. 430 (1945), 600

Thomas v. Review Bd., 450 U.S. 707, 101 S.Ct. 1425, 67 L.Ed.2d 624 (1981), 745, 746

Thomas v. Union Carbide, 473 U.S. 568, 105 S.Ct. 3325, 87 L.Ed.2d 409 (1985), 475

Thompson v. Oklahoma, 487 U.S. 815, 108 S.Ct. 2687, 101 L.Ed.2d 702 (1988), 852

Thompson v. Utah, 170 U.S. 343, 18 S.Ct. 620, 42 L.Ed. 1061 (1898), 468

Thornburg v. Gingles, 478 U.S. 30, 106 S.Ct. 2752, 92 L.Ed.2d 25 (1986), 1157

Thornburgh v. American College of Obstetricians and Gynecologists, 476 U.S. 747, 106 S.Ct. 2169, 90 L.Ed.2d 779 (1986), 966, 968

Thornhill v. Alabama, 310 U.S. 88, 60 S.Ct. 736, 84 L.Ed. 1093 (1940), 628

Time, Inc. v. Firestone, 424 U.S. 448, 96 S.Ct. 958, 47 L.Ed.2d 154 (1976), 679

Time, Inc. v. Hill, 385 U.S. 374, 87 S.Ct. 534, 17 L.Ed.2d 456 (1967), 679

Tinker v. Des Moines Independent Community School Dist., 393 U.S. 503, 89 S.Ct. 733, 21 L.Ed. 2d 731, 49 O.O.2d 222 (1969), 26, 120, 613, 645, 676, 677

Townsend v. Sain, 372 U.S. 293, 83 S.Ct. 745, 9 L.Ed.2d 770 (1963), 851, App. E-2

Train v. City of New York, 420 U.S. 35, 95 S.Ct. 839, 43 L.Ed.2d 1 (1975), 272, 335

Trevett v. Weeden (1786) (unreported), 43

Trop v. Dulles, 356 U.S. 86, 78 S.Ct. 590, 2 L.Ed.2d 630 (1958), 476, 842

Truax v. Raich, 239 U.S. 33, 36 S.Ct. 7, 60 L.Ed. 131 (1915), 540

T.W., In re, 551 So.2d 1186 (Fla.1989), 488, 970

Tyson v. Banton, 273 U.S. 418, 47 S.Ct. 426, 71 L.Ed. 718 (1927), 531

United Bldg. and Const. Trades v. Camden, 465 U.S. 208, 104 S.Ct. 1020, 79 L.Ed.2d 249 (1984), 413, 414

United Public Workers v. Mitchell, 330 U.S. 75, 67 S.Ct. 556, 91 L.Ed. 754 (1947), 125

United States v. _____ (see opposing party)

United States Civil Service Commission v. National Ass'n of Letter Carriers, AFL–CIO, 413 U.S. 548, 93 S.Ct. 2880, 37 L.Ed.2d 796 (1973), 618

United States Dist. Court, United States v., 407 U.S. 297, 92 S.Ct. 2125, 32 L.Ed.2d 752 (1972), 282, 315

United States Steel Corp. v. Multistate Tax Commission, 434 U.S. 452, 98 S.Ct. 799, 54 L.Ed.2d 682 (1978), 415

United States Trust Co. v. New Jersey, 431 U.S. 1, 97 S.Ct. 1505, 52 L.Ed.2d 92 (1977), 527

University of California Board of Regents v. Bakke, 438 U.S. 265, 98 S.Ct. 2733, 57 L.Ed.2d 750 (1978), 124, 1058, 1059

Uphaus v. Wyman, 360 U.S. 72, 79 S.Ct. 1040, 3 L.Ed.2d 1090 (1959), 89

Valley Forge Christian College v. Americans United for Separation of Church and State, Inc., 454 U.S. 464, 102 S.Ct. 752, 70 L.Ed.2d 700 (1982), 122, 140

Veazie Bank v. Fenno, 75 U.S. 533, 19 L.Ed. 482 (1869), 189

Vermont Yankee Nuclear Power Corp. v. Natural Resources Defense Council, Inc., 435 U.S. 519, 98 S.Ct. 1197, 55 L.Ed.2d 460 (1978), 337, 368

Virginia v. Tennessee, 148 U.S. 503, 13 S.Ct. 728, 37 L.Ed. 537 (1893), 415

Virginia, United States v., 766 F.Supp. 1407 (W.D. Va.1991), 1066

Virginia State Bd. of Pharmacy v. Virginia Citizens Consumer Council, Inc., 425 U.S. 748, 96 S.Ct. 1817, 48 L.Ed.2d 346 (1976), 686

Wabash, St. Louis & Pacific Railway Co. v. Illinois, 118 U.S. 557, 7 S.Ct. 4, 30 L.Ed. 244 (1886), 179

Wallace v. Jaffree, 472 U.S. 38, 105 S.Ct. 2479, 86 L.Ed.2d 29 (1985), 790

Wallace v. Jaffree, 469 U.S. 1102, 105 S.Ct. 771, 83 L.Ed.2d 768 (1985), 755

Waller v. Georgia, 467 U.S. 39, 104 S.Ct. 2210, 81 L.Ed.2d 31 (1984), 839

Walton v. Arizona, 497 U.S. 639, 110 S.Ct. 3047, 111 L.Ed.2d 511 (1990), 845

Walz v. Tax Commission, 397 U.S. 664, 90 S.Ct. 1409, 25 L.Ed.2d 697 (1970), 759, 760, **808**

Warden v. Hayden, 387 U.S. 294, 87 S.Ct. 1642, 18 L.Ed.2d 782 (1967), 820

Warth v. Seldin, 422 U.S. 490, 95 S.Ct. 2197, 45 L.Ed.2d 343 (1975), 123

Washington v. Davis, 426 U.S. 229, 96 S.Ct. 2040, 48 L.Ed.2d 597 (1976), 1047

Washington v. Harper, 494 U.S. 210, 110 S.Ct. 1028, 108 L.Ed.2d 178 (1990), 1036

Watkins v. United States, 354 U.S. 178, 77 S.Ct. 1173, 1 L.Ed.2d 1273 (1957), 89, 130, 175, **206**

Watkins v. United States Army, 847 F.2d 1329 (9th Cir.1988), 1072

Watts v. United States, 394 U.S. 705, 89 S.Ct. 1399, 22 L.Ed.2d 664 (1969), 608

Wayman v. Southard, 23 U.S. 1, 6 L.Ed. 253 (1825), 328

Weber v. Aetna Cas. & Sur. Co., 406 U.S. 164, 92 S.Ct. 1400, 31 L.Ed.2d 768 (1972), 1067

Webster v. Reproductive Health Services, 492 U.S. 490, 109 S.Ct. 3040, 106 L.Ed.2d 410 (1989), 966, 967, 968, **1017**

Weeks v. United States, 232 U.S. 383, 34 S.Ct. 341, 58 L.Ed. 652 (1914), 825, **882**

Weinberger v. Wiesenfeld, 420 U.S. 636, 95 S.Ct. 1225, 43 L.Ed.2d 514 (1975), 1064

Wesberry v. Sanders, 376 U.S. 1, 84 S.Ct. 526, 11 L.Ed.2d 481 (1964), 167, 1160

West Coast Hotel Co. v. Parrish, 300 U.S. 379, 57 S.Ct. 578, 81 L.Ed. 703 (1937), 537, 538, 539, **581**

West Virginia ex rel. Dyer v. Sims, 341 U.S. 22, 71 S.Ct. 557, 95 L.Ed. 713, 44 O.O. 364 (1951), 416

West Virginia State Board of Education v. Barnette, 319 U.S. 624, 63 S.Ct. 1178, 87 L.Ed. 1628 (1943), 612, 748, 763

Whalen v. Roe, 429 U.S. 589, 97 S.Ct. 869, 51 L.Ed. 2d 64 (1977), 976

White v. Massachusetts Council of Const. Employers, Inc., 460 U.S. 204, 103 S.Ct. 1042, 75 L.Ed.2d 1 (1983), 404, 414

Whitney v. California, 274 U.S. 357, 47 S.Ct. 641, 71 L.Ed. 1095 (1927), 605, 608

Wickard v. Filburn, 317 U.S. 111, 63 S.Ct. 82, 87 L.Ed. 122 (1942), 183, **233**

Widmar v. Vincent, 454 U.S. 263, 102 S.Ct. 269, 70 L.Ed.2d 440 (1981), 753, 761

Wiener v. United States, 357 U.S. 349, 78 S.Ct. 1275, 2 L.Ed.2d 1377 (1958), 267, **296**

Wilkinson v. United States, 365 U.S. 399, 81 S.Ct. 567, 5 L.Ed.2d 633 (1961), 176

Williams v. Florida, 399 U.S. 78, 90 S.Ct. 1893, 26 L.Ed.2d 446, 53 O.O.2d 55 (1970), 839, 840

Willson v. Black–Bird Creek Marsh Co., 27 U.S. 245, 7 L.Ed. 412 (1829), 389

Winfield v. Division of Pari–Mutuel Wagering, 477 So.2d 544 (Fla.1985), 970

Wisconsin v. Yoder, 406 U.S. 205, 92 S.Ct. 1526, 32 L.Ed.2d 15 (1972), 750, 770

Wolf v. Colorado, 338 U.S. 25, 69 S.Ct. 1359, 93 L.Ed. 1782 (1949), 828

Wolff Packing Co. v. Court of Industrial Relations, 262 U.S. 522, 43 S.Ct. 630, 67 L.Ed. 1103 (1923), 531, 534

Wong Sun v. United States, 371 U.S. 471, 83 S.Ct. 407, 9 L.Ed.2d 441 (1963), 830

Wong Wing v. United States, 163 U.S. 228, 16 S.Ct. 977, 41 L.Ed. 140 (1896), 339

Woody, People v., 35 Cal.Rptr. 708 (Cal.App.1963), 744

Wooley v. Maynard, 430 U.S. 705, 97 S.Ct. 1428, 51 L.Ed.2d 752 (1977), 748

Worcester v. Georgia, 31 U.S. 515, 8 L.Ed. 483 (1832), 97

Wright v. West, ___ U.S. ___, 112 S.Ct. 2482, 120 L.Ed.2d 225 (1992), App. E-2

Wynehamer v. New York, 13 N.Y. 378 (1856), 528

Yakus v. United States, 321 U.S. 414, 64 S.Ct. 660, 88 L.Ed. 834 (1944), 87, 330

Yarbrough, Ex parte, 110 U.S. 651, 4 S.Ct. 152, 28 L.Ed. 274 (1884), 1149

Yates v. United States, 354 U.S. 298, 77 S.Ct. 1064, 1 L.Ed.2d 1356 (1957), 608

Yick Wo v. Hopkins, 118 U.S. 356, 6 S.Ct. 1064, 30 L.Ed. 220 (1886), 540, 1044, 1147

Ylst v. Nunnemaker, ___ U.S. ___, 111 S.Ct. 2590, 115 L.Ed.2d 706 (1991), 468

Younger v. Harris, 401 U.S. 37, 91 S.Ct. 746, 27 L.Ed.2d 669 (1971), 126, 146, 386

Youngstown Sheet & Tube Co. v. Sawyer, 343 U.S. 579, 72 S.Ct. 863, 96 L.Ed. 1153 (1952), 261, 262, **286**

Zemel v. Rusk, 381 U.S. 1, 85 S.Ct. 1271, 14 L.Ed. 2d 179 (1965), 328

Zorach v. Clauson, 343 U.S. 306, 72 S.Ct. 679, 96 L.Ed. 954 (1952), 752, 753, 760

INDEX

Abortion
  conflict over, 131, 480, 960–63
    eroding support on the Supreme Court, 965–70
    restrictions on public funding of, 963–65,
      1070–71
  and the Eleventh Amendment, 397
  and mootness, 124–25
  proposed amendment allowing, 92
  restriction of counseling on, 619
  restriction of information about, 967
Abstention doctrine, 126–27
Accused. *See* Criminal justice
  rights of, and civil rights and liberties, 474
Act to Improve the Administration of Justice (1988),
  21
Actual malice, in libel cases, 677–78
Adams, John
  and enforcement of Alien and Sedition Acts, 602
  as Federalist, 387
  midnight appointments of, 44, 388
Adderley, Harriet Louise, 621
Administrative action
  congressional control of
    legislative veto, 333–35
    separation of powers concerns, 335
Administrative Procedure Act (1946), 336–37
Advertising
  commercial, 685–87
  problem of cigarette, 687
Advisory opinions, 119
Affidavit in search and seizure, 818–19
Affirm, 33
Affirmative action, 1057–60
Agency actions, 338
  bureaucratic support for civil rights and liberties,
    340

  Fourth Amendment concerns, 339
  public access to agency information, 340
  self-incrimination concerns, 339–40
Aggravating factors, and the death penalty, 844
Agricultural Adjustment Act, 190, 191, 192, 539
Airport, as public forum, 623
Alcoholic beverages, state regulation of, 402–3
Alienage, and discrimination, 1068–69
Alien and Sedition Acts, enforcement of the, 602
Americans with Disabilities Act (1990), 326, 340, 1068
Amicus curiae brief, 32
Amish beliefs
  and compulsory school attendance, 750
  and patriotic rituals and duties of, 747–48
Amnesties, 268–69
Anderson, John, 1161
Animals
  sacrifice of, as free exercise of religion, 747
  and use of poisonous snakes in religious ceremony,
    744
Anonymous informants, 819
Anonymous tip, detention of an automobile based on
  an, 822
Anthony, Susan B., 486
Antidelegation rule, 330
Anti-Federalists, 674
Anti-yellow-dog contract provision, invalidation of,
  533
Appeal and postconviction relief, 847–48
  federal habeas corpus review of state criminal
    cases, 848, 850–51
Appeal by right, 21, 28, 847–48
Appellate jurisdiction, 14, 20
Appointment power
  as check on the judiciary, 93–95
  of president, 265–67

Arms, right to bear, and civil rights and liberties, 473
Arraignment, 835
Arrest, 823
    probable cause hearing on, 824–25
    police force in making, 824
    warrant for, 824
Articles of Confederation, 2–3
    lack of judicial system in, 16
Assembly, freedom of, 472, 619–20
    and civil rights demonstrations, 620–22
    and determination of public forum, 622–23
Association, 626
    and discrimination, 627–28
    political, 626–27
At-large elections, 1154–56
Atomic Energy Act (1954), 394–95
Automobile searches, 820–21

Bad tendency test, and subversive speech, 603–6
Bail and pretrial detention, 835–36
Bail Reform Act (1984), 835
Balanced Budget and Emergency Deficit Control Act
    (1985), 130, 331–32
Barbary pirates, 277
Barker, Sarah Evans, 685
Barnes, Michael, 264
Beard, Charles A., 4
Benevolent neutrality approach, 759
Bicameralism, 166–67, 334
Bill of Rights, 7, 90, 471. *See also*
    specific amendments in
    criminal justice protections in, 815–16
    incorporation of, 481–85
    privacy rights in, 955–56
    ratification of, 466
Bills of Attainder, 469–70, 815
Birth control, and privacy rights, 957–60
Black, Galen, 746
Black, Hugo
    on bicameralism, 167
    on civil rights demonstrations, 622
    on clear and probable danger, 607
    on distinguishing the unconstitutional, 134
    on economic activity, 54
    on economic due process, 539
    on education, 752
    on executive power, 262
    on federalism, 386
    on fighting words, 610
    on First Amendment, 599, 601
    on incorporation of Bill of Rights, 483–84
    on individual rights, 194
    on interstate commerce, 400
    on Ninth Amendment, 477
    on obscenity, 684
    on Pentagon Papers case, 34, 277
    on pretrial publicity, 838
    on privacy, 953, 959–60
    retirement of, 93
    and ripeness doctrine, 125–26
    on school prayer, 754
    on suspect classification doctrine, 1046
    on voting rights, 1153
Black Codes, 1048
Blackmun, Harry A.
    on abortion, 961, 962, 967, 968, 969
    on affirmative action, 1058, 1060
    on commercial advertising, 686
    on federalism, 385
    on gay rights, 972
    ideology of, 37, 55
    on interstate commerce, 400
    on juvenile justice, 852
    on market participant exception, 404
    on mootness, 125
    nomination of, 93, 629
    on Pentagon case, 34
    on plea bargaining, 837
    on regulation of alcoholic beverages, 403
    on religious freedom, 747, 758
    on state action, 481
    on Tenth Amendment, 185
Blackstone, William, 674
Blocs, 37
Boland Amendments, 274
Bork, Robert H., 22, 56, 131, 270, 953, 966
Boulder Canyon Act (1928), 330
Bradley, Joseph L., 529
Brandeis, Louis D.
    on clear and present danger test, 604
    on economic due process, 533, 537
    on imminent lawless action, 609
    on intergovernmental tax immunity, 407
    and judicial review, 128
    on political association, 626
    on privacy, 817, 956
    and *stare decisis,* 131
    on zoning regulation, 626
Brandeis brief, 533
Brennan, William
    on affirmative action, 1058–59, 1060
    on automobile detention, 822

on child pornography, 745
on compelling interest test, 747
on death penalty, 842, 844
on due process, 337
on flag burning, 615
on freedom of press, 676–78
on gender-based discrimination, 1064–65
on good-fault exception, 827
ideology of, 37
on informants, 819
on intergovernmental tax immunity, 408
on interstate commerce, 400–1
on market participant exception, 404
on original package doctrine, 410
on overbreadth doctrine, 628–29
on parochiaid, 753
on Pentagon case, 34
on political association, 626
on political questions doctrine, 128
on privacy, 960, 970
on private discrimination, 1075
on privileges and immunities clause, 413
on protection of natural resources, 403
on prurient interests test, 683
on regulation of alcoholic beverages, 402
on residency, 1068
on restricting speech of public employees, 618
retirement of, 22, 56
on Seventh Amendment, 476
on sleep speech, 615
on Sunday closing laws, 745
on takings issue, 542
on Tenth Amendment, 185, 186, 392
on voting rights, 196, 197
on zoning regulations, 624
Bricker, John, 275
Bricker Amendment, 275–76, 276
Brief
  method of preparing, 36
  submission of, 32
Broadcast media, 687
  editorializing by public television and radio
    stations, 688
  and FCC's fairness doctrine, 688
  restrictions of "indecent" programming,
    688–89
Brown, Henry Billings, 1049
Brown, John, 173
Bryan, William Jennings, 756
Budget and Impoundment Act, 272
Burden of proof, 1046

Bureaucratic support for civil rights and liberties, 340
Burger, Warren E.
  on abortion, 966
  on affirmative action, 1058, 1059, 1060
  on appointment power, 93
  on bicameralism, 167
  on compulsory school attendance, 750
  on death penalty, 134
  on delegation of power, 331
  on Fourth Amendment, 474, 825, 826, 828
  on gender-based discrimination, 1063
  on habeas corpus, 468
  on imminent lawless action, 609
  on interstate commerce, 401
  on media privilege, 681
  on Miranda warnings, 830
  nomination of, 55, 629
  on Pentagon Papers, 34
  on presidential authority, 274
  on prurient interest test, 684
  on reapportionment, 1159
  on religious freedom, 757, 758, 759
  on residency, 1068
  on spending power of Congress, 193
  on Tenth Amendment, 185
  on totality of circumstances approach, 819
Burr, Aaron, trial of, 269
Burton, Harold, 752
Bush, George
  and abortion issue, 92, 967
  and civil rights, 1155
  court nominations of, 22–23
  on economic due process, 537
  on item veto, 265
  and Persian Gulf War, 256, 279–80
Butler, Pierce, 536

Calhoun, John C., 387
Campbell, John, 49
Cantwell, Newton, 743
Capital punishment, 842–46
  of juveniles, 852
Cardozo, Benjamin N., 192, 482, 537, 600
Carlin, George, 688
Carsell, G. Harold, 93
Carter, Jimmy
  foreign policy of, 127, 275
  and granting of amnesty to draft evaders, 268–69
  influence of, on judiciary, 23
Case reporters, 35

Catron, John, 49
Certification, 28
Chafee, Zechariah, Jr., 605
Chaplinsky, Walter, 609
Charitable causes, door-to-door solicitation for, 743
Chase, Samuel, 25, 169, 189, 468, 523, 524
Checks and balances, 4, 6
Child benefit theory, 752
Child pornography, 684–85
Chilling effect, 602
Chisholm, Alexander, 90
Choate, Joseph H., 52
Church, separation of state and, 750–57
Cigarette advertising, problem of, 687
Citizenship, dual, 393
Civil cases, 15
Civil Rights Act (1866), 26, 390, 1049
Civil Rights Act (1870), 1049
Civil Rights Act (1871), 1049
Civil Rights Act (1875), 1048, 1049
Civil Rights Act (1964), 96, 186, 340, 390, 1062, 1152
Civil Rights Amendments. *See also* Fifteenth
  Amendment; Fourteenth Amendment; Thirteenth
  Amendment
  congressional enforcement of, 194–97
Civil rights and liberties, 2
  in Bill of Rights, 471
    Eighth Amendment, 476–77
    Fifth Amendment, 474
    First Amendment, 472–73
    Fourth Amendment, 473–74
    Ninth Amendment, 477–78
    Second Amendment, 473
    Seventh Amendment, 475–76
    Sixth Amendment, 474
    Tenth Amendment, 478
    Third Amendment, 473
  bureaucratic support for, 340
  and Commerce Clause, 185–86
  Fourteenth Amendment on, 478–79
    due process, 479–80
    and incorporation of Bill of Rights, 481–85
    and state action, 480–81
  and importance of state constitution, 488
  and judicial review, 487
    rational basis test, 487
    and strict judicial scrutiny, 487–88
  obscenity, indecency, and profanity, 616
    nude dancing, 616–18
  rights recognized in original constitution, 467
    bills of attainder, 469–70

circumscribing crime of treason, 467
  contract clause, 470
  ex post facto laws, 468–69
  habeas corpus, 467–68
  prohibition of religious tests for public office, 467
subject matter of, 466
and voting rights, 485
  Fifteenth Amendment on, 485
  Sixteenth Amendment on, 485–86
  Twenty-Fourth Amendment on, 486
  Twenty-Sixth Amendment on, 486–87
Civil rights demonstrations, and freedom of assembly,
  620–22
Civil Rights Restoration Act (1988), 89–90
Civil service employees, 265
Civil suits, 25–26
  presidential immunity from, 270–71
Civil War, 8, 389–90
Civil War Amendments, 7–8, 91, 390. *See also*
  Fifteenth Amendment; Fourteenth Amendment;
  Thirteenth Amendment
Civil War cases, 280–81
Clark, Tom, 606–7, 741
Clarke, John H., 603–4
Class actions, 15
Classical conservatism, 954–55
Clean Air Act, 186
Clear and present danger test, 602–3
Clear and probable danger test, 606–8
Clinton, Bill, 969
Coffee, Linda, 961
Cohen, Paul Robert, 611
Commander in chief, president as, 259
Commerce
  congressional exercise of, 179
  state power to regulate, 397–405
    countervailing considerations, 405–6
  Supreme Court restriction of, 180–82
Commerce Clause, 397
  and civil rights, 185–86
  early interpretation of, 176–79
  and federal criminal law, 187
  modern interpretation of the, 182–87
Commercial advertising, 685–87
Comparative proportionality review, and the death
  penalty, 845
Compelling government interest, 488
Compelling interest, 282, 1046
Competing interests, ad-hoc balancing in weighing,
  608
Compulsory process, 174

Compulsory school attendance, and religious freedom, 750
Compulsory self-incrimination, 474
Concurrent jurisdiction, 20
Concurring in the judgment, 33
Concurring opinion, 33
Conference and decision, 32–33
Confidential and anonymous informants, 819
Confidential sources, protection of, 682
Congress. *See* U.S. Congress
Congressional committees, rights of individuals called before, 174–76
Conkling, Roscoe, 531
Conscientious objectors, 741–42, 748–49
Consent, and warrantless searches, 820
Consent decrees, 1059
Conservative activism, period of, 50–54
Constitution, U.S. *See also specific amendments; clauses*
adoption and ratification of the, 2–7
amending, 7–10
amendments to, of overruling court decision, 89–92
as conservative document, 5–6
flexibility in, 8–10
judicial interpretation of the, 9–10
and modern government, 10
Constitutional cases, 15
Constitutional Convention, 3–6
Constitutional democracy, 8
Constitutional interpretation
interpretivism, 56–57
natural law, 57
noninterpretivism, 57
ongoing dialogue in, 57
Constitutional law
components of, 2
definition of, 2
reasons for studying, 2
Constitutional law cases, genesis of, 25–28
Constitutional revolution of 1937, 54
Consumer Credit Protection Act, 187
Contempt of court, 95, 675
Contract Clause
and civil rights and liberties, 470
contributions of Taney court, 526
and key decisions of Marshall court, 524–25
later developments, 526–27
Contract doctrine, freedom of, 53
Cooley, Thomas M., 528
Cooperative federalism, 391–92

Counsel
effectiveness of appointed, 834
right to, 832–35
Court of Military Appeals, 19
Courts
federal systems, 16–17
specialized federal tribunals, 19
U.S. Courts of Appeals, 18–19
U.S. District Courts, 17–18
U.S. Supreme Court, 19–22
overview of American, 14
state systems, 15
Courts-martial, 19
Courts of general jurisdiction, 15
Courts of limited jurisdiction, 15
Court system, 14
Cox, Archibald, 269–70
Cox, B. Elton, 621
Creationism-evolution conflict, 756–57
Crime victims, press reporting of identities of, 680
Criminal cases, 15
Criminal justice
appeal and postconviction relief, 847–48
federal habeas corpus review of state criminal cases, 848
arrest, 823
probable cause hearing, 824–25
use of force by police in making arrests, 824
warrant, 824
bail and pretrial detention, 835–36
cruel and unusual punishments, 842
death penalty, 842–46
mandatory life imprisonment, 846
prisoners' rights, 846–47
Fourth Amendment exclusionary rule, 825–26
civil suits, 827–28
good-faith exception, 826–27
importance of habeas corpus in, 468
jury trials, 837–38
exclusion of minorities from juries, 840–41
jury size, 839–40
problem of pretrial publicity, 838–39
unanimity principle, 840
juvenile justice, 851–52
plea bargaining, 836–37
police interrogation and confessions of guilt, 828–29
Miranda warnings, 829–31
police deception, 831–32
protection against double jeopardy, 841–42
relevant constitutional provisions, 815–16
right to counsel, 832

effectiveness of appointed counsel, 834
self-representation, 835
search and seizure, 816–17
automobile searches, 820–21
confidential and anonymous informants, 819
drug testing, 822–23
investigatory detention, 821–22
probable cause, 818
reasonable expectations of privacy, 817–18
stop and frisk, 821
warrantless searches, 819–20
warrant requirement, 818–19
Criminal prosecutions, 26–27
Criminal syndicalism, 133, 482
Cruel and unusual punishments, 842
death penalty, 842–46
mandatory life imprisonment, 846
prisoners' rights, 846–47
Cruzan, Nancy, 975–76
Cults, and religious freedom, 742
Curtis, Benjamin R., 49, 398, 399

Damages, 26
Daniel, Peter, 49
Darrow, Clarence, 756
Day, William R., 391, 825
Death penalty, 842–46
for juveniles, 852
Decision on the merits, 28
Declaration of Independence, 465
Declaratory judgments, 26, 87
De facto segregation, 1072–73
Defendant, 15, 25
DeFunis, Marco, 124
De jure segregation, 1072
decline of, 1051–52
Democracy, representative, 1147
Demurrer, 26, 49
Denial of certiorari, 31
Dennis, Eugene, 607
Dennison, William, 414–15
Desegregation, 1052–56. See also Racial discrimination
DeShaney, Joshua, 480–81
Devanter, Willis Van, 536
Dewey, John, 324
DeWitt, J. L., 281
Dies, Martin, 175
Direct-or-indirect test for interstate commerce, 399
Dirksen, Everett, 92, 1160

Disability, of president, 257–58
Disabled persons, discrimination of, 1067–68
Discrimination. See also Racial discrimination; Sex discrimination
on the basis of sexual orientation, 1071–72
of disabled persons, 1067–68
and freedom of association, 627–28
and illegitimacy, 1067
ongoing problem of private, 1072–75
and poverty, 1069–71
and residency and alienage, 1068–1069
Disparate impact, judging of facially neutral policies, 1046–47
Dissenting opinion, 33
Distributive articles, 165
Diversity jurisdiction, 119
Diversity of citizenship cases, 17
Domestic context, delegation of legislative powers in, 328–32
Door-to-door solicitation for religious or charitable causes, 743
Double jeopardy, 474
and the Fifth Amendment, 482–83, 484
protection against, 841–42
Douglas, William O.
and appellate jurisdiction, 89
on birth control, 958–59
and clear and present danger test, 607
and First Amendment freedom, 600, 610
and impeachment charges, 169
on literacy tests, 1151
on obscenity, 684
and Pentagon Papers case, 34
and political association, 626
on poll taxes, 1152
and religious freedom, 739, 743–44, 752, 760
and ripeness doctrine, 125–26
and selective incorporation, 483–84
on sex discrimination, 1065
on standing, 123
and taxpayer suits, 122
Drug courier profile, 820
Drugs
private use of recreational, 130, 973
religious use of, 744, 746, 747
and use of investigatory detention, 821–22
Drug testing
and privacy rights, 976
and religious freedom, 746
and search and seizure, 822–23
Dual citizenship, 393

Dual federalism, 390–91, 406
Due Process Clause, 49–50, 189
  in Fifth Amendment, 474
  in Fourteenth Amendment, 391
Due process of law, 336–38, 474
  economic, 527–39
  procedural, 479
  right of privacy, 480
  substantive, 479–80
Duke, David, 1161
Dworkin, Andrea, 685

Easement, granting of, 542
Eckhardt, Christopher, 613
Economic due process, 527–28
  decline of, 535–39
  key Supreme Court decisions on, 528–39
  and origins of substantive due process, 528
Economic equal protection, possible interpretations
  of, 1071
Economic freedom
  inclusions in, 521
  modern protection of, 523–24
Economic regulation, and equal protection, 539–40
Economic unit, nation as an, 401–5
Editorializing by public television and radio stations,
  688
Education
  and affirmative action, 1058–60
  and busing controversy, 1055–56
  desegregation in, 1052–56
  and religious freedom, 752
    equal access policies, 753
    and evolution-creationism conflict, 756–57
    parochiaid, 753–54
    released-time programs, 752–53
    and school prayer controversy, 92, 96, 754–55
  and sex discrimination, 1066–67
Education Amendments (1972), 89
Education for all Handicapped Children Act (1975),
  1068
Effects test, under Voting Rights Act Amendments,
  1155
Eighteenth Amendment, 402
Eighth Amendment, 476–77
Eisenhower, Dwight D.
  court nominations of, 93
  and executive privilege, 267
  and school desegregation, 1054
  use of impoundment by, 272

Eldridge, George, 337–38
Elections. *See also* Voting rights
  challenges to judicial systems, 1156–57
  fairness in, and partisan gerrymandering, 1161–62
  at-large, 1154–56
Electoral college, 6, 170, 257
Eleventh Amendment, 90–91, 396–97, 388
Ely, John Hart, 1161
Emergency Powers Act (1977), 276
Emergency Price Control Act, 87
Emergency searches, 820
Eminent domain, 474, 540
Enabling legislation, 325
En banc, 19
Enforcement Act (1870), 1149
English Bill of Rights, 465
English common law courts, 43
Enumerated powers, of president, 168, 255, 259–60
Environmental interests, standing to assert, 122–23
Environmental protection, and Commerce Clause,
  186–87
Environmental Protection Act, 186
Environmental Protection Agency (EPA), 325
Epperson, Susan, 756
Equal Access Act (1984), 753
Equal access policies, and religious freedom, 753
Equal Pay Act (1963), 1972 amendments to Title VII of
  the, 1062
Equal protection
  for disabled persons, 1067–68
  and discrimination on the basis of sexual
    orientation, 1071–72
  and economic regulation, 539–40
  and illegitimacy, 1067
  levels of judicial scrutiny, 1045
    heightened scrutiny, 1047
    rational basis test, 1045–46
    suspect classification doctrine, 1046–47
  ongoing problem of private discrimination,
    1072–74
    restrictive covenants, 1074
    state powers to prohibit, 1074–75
  and residency and alienage, 1068–69
  sex discrimination, 1061
    congressional responses to demands for sexual
      equality, 1062
    by educational institutions, 1066–67
    equal rights amendment, 1062–63
    heightened scrutiny, 1064–66
    judicial scrutiny of gender-based discrimination,
      1063–66

struggle for racial equality, 1047–48
    early interpretations of the Equal Protection
        Clause, 1048–51
    wealth, poverty, and equal protection, 1069–71
Equal Protection Clause
    early interpretations of, 1048–51
    of the Fourteenth Amendment, 196
Equal Rights Amendment, 1062–63
Error correction, 20, 848
Espionage Act (1917), 602
    Establishment Clause, competing interpretations of,
        and separation of church and state, 750–51
Ethics in Government Act (1978), 266
Evanescent evidence, 820
Evolution-creationism conflict, 756–57
Exclusionary rule, 825–26
    good-faith exception to, 131, 826–27
Executive agreements, power of president in, 276–77
Executive orders, 15
Executive privilege, 269
Exhaustion of remedies, 126
Exigent circumstances, and warrantless searches,
    819–20
Ex post facto laws, 468–69, 815
    and property rights, 522–23
Expression, freedom of, 472–73. *See also* Speech
    and property rights, 543–44
Extradition, 414

Fair Housing Act (1968), 96, 195, 1073
Fair Labor Standards Act (1938), 184, 392, 539
Fairness doctrine, 688
Falwell, Jerry, 679
Faubus, Orval, 96, 1054
Federal Aviation Administration (FAA), 325
Federal Communications Commission (FCC), 687
    Fairness doctrine of, 688
Federal courts, 15, 16–17
    jurisdiction of lower, 86–88
Federal criminal law, and Commerce Clause, 187
Federal Election Campaign Act (1972), 266
Federal Flag Protection Act (1989), 615
Federalism, 6
    cooperative, 391–92
    definition of, 386
    dual, 390–91, 406
    judicial, 388, 395–97, 969–70, 1076
Federalist Papers, 7, 24, 97, 99–102, 255, 471
Federal Lobbying (Hatch) Act, 618
Federal Mine Safety and Health Act (1977), and
    Fourth Amendment concerns, 339

Federal Power Act, 336, 394
Federal Power Commission (FPC), 336
Federal question jurisdiction, 118–19
Federal Register, 326
Federal system
    characteristics of the contemporary, 393
        judicial federalism, 395–97
        national preemption of state law, 393–95
    definition of, 386
    development of, 386–93
Fee simple titles, 541
Feiner, Irving, 609
Felonies, 15
Field, Stephen J., 415, 529, 530, 531, 605, 741
Fifteenth Amendment, 7, 91, 170, 195, 390, 485, 1148,
    1149, 1153, 1155
Fifth Amendment, 174, 194, 474
    Double Jeopardy Clause of the, 482–83
    and due process, 49, 336–38
    equal protection component, 1044–45
    and privacy rights, 955
    and self-incrimination concerns, 339–40
Fighting words exception, to constitutionally
    protected speech, 609–11
Firestone, Dorothy, 679
First Amendment
    and fighting words exception, 609–11
    interpretation of, 601
    original wording of, 599
    overbreadth doctrine, 628–29
    preferred position of, 600–1
    and privacy rights, 955
    subversive speech and internal security concerns,
        602
        ad hoc balancing: weighing the competing
            interests, 608
        bad tendency test, 603–6
        clear and present danger test, 602–3
        clear and probable danger test, 606–8
        imminent lawless action, 608–9
    time, place, and manner regulations, 623–24
    zoning regulations, 624–26
Fitzgerald, A. Ernest, 271
Flag-burning
    issue of, 26–27, 56, 92
    and symbolic speech, 613–15
Flag salute cases, 748
Food and Drug Administration (FDA), 325
Force, use of, by police, in making arrests, 824
Ford, Gerald
    and impeachment of Douglas, 169
    and pardoning of Nixon, 268

Foreign affairs, delegation of legislative power in context of, 327–28
Foreign Intelligence Surveillance Act (1978), 282
Foreign policy
  and political questions doctrine, 127
  power of president to make, 272–77
Fortas, Abe
  on evolution-creationism, 756–57
  resignation of, 93, 169
  on symbolic speech, 613
Fourteenth Amendment, 7, 8, 91, 170, 390, 478–79
  and due process, 336–38, 391, 479
    procedural due process, 479
    right of privacy, 480
    substantive due process, 479–80
  Equal Protection Clause of, 196
  incorporation of freedom of speech and press, 600
  incorporation of the Bill of Rights, 481–85
  ratification of, 481
  and state action, 480–81
Fourth Amendment, 26, 194, 473–74
  exclusionary rule, 825–26
    civil suits, 827–28
    good-faith exception, 826–27
  good faith exception to, 131
  and individual rights, 339
Frankfurter, Felix, 13
  on birth control, 958
  and clear and probable danger test, 607
  on First Amendment freedoms, 600–1
  and the flag salute, 748
  and legislative reapportionment, 127
  on partisan gerrymandering, 1162
  on racial gerrymandering, 1152
  and religious education, 752
  on taxation, 188
Freedom of Information Act, 340
Free Exercise Clause, 472, 740
Free expression. See Speech
Fruit of the poisonous tree doctrine, 830
Fuller, Melville, 180, 183, 531
Full faith and Credit Clause, 411
Full opinion decisions, 28
Fulton, Robert, 177
Fundamental rights, 412
  privacy as, 480

Gag order, and freedom of press, 677, 838–39
Galbraith, John Kenneth, 324
Gay rights. See also Homosexuality
  and privacy, 971–72

Gender-based discrimination. See Sexual discrimination
General Welfare Clause, 191
Gerrymandering
  partisan, 1161–62
  racial, 1152
Gibson, John B., 47
Gideon, Clarence Earl, 833–34
Ginsberg, Douglas, 22
Goldberg, Arthur, 621
Good-faith exception to the exclusionary rule, 131, 826–27
Government interest test, 746
Gramm-Rudman-Hollings Act (1985), 130, 331–32
Grandfather clauses, 486, 1149–50
Grand jury, indictment from, 474
Great Depression, 8
Grenada, 279
Grier, Robert C., 277
Guilt, confessions of, 828–29
Gulf of Tonkin Resolution of 1964, 278
Gun control. See Arms
Habeas corpus, 27, 169, 467–68, 815
  in review of state criminal cases, 848, 850–51

Habeas Corpus Act (1867), 86–87
Halperin, Morton, 271
Hamilton, Alexander, 256
  and constitutional convention, 3
  on democracy, 1147
  as Federalist, 7, 24–25, 90, 99–102, 387, 471
  on General Welfare Clause, 191
  and implied powers, 171
  on presidential powers, 259–60
Handicapped, discrimination of, 1067–68
Harlan, John Marshall
  on ad hoc balancing, 601, 608
  on affirmative action, 1057, 1059
  on birth control, 959
  on civil rights, 465
  on commerce, 180
  and corporate influence, 531, 532–33
  and delegation of legislative power, 328
  on equal protection, 1043
  on fighting words exception, 611
  on flag burning, 614
  on individual rights, 194
  on Pentagon Papers case, 34
  on political association, 627
  on privacy rights, 818
  retirement of, 93

on separate but equal doctrine, 1050
on substantive due process, 956–57
on voting rights, 197
Harmless error analysis, 832
Harris, Robert Alton, 849–50
Harrison, William Henry, death of, 257–58
Hatch Act, 125
Hate speech, 611
Haynsworth, Clement, 93
Hearing, probable cause, 824–25
Heightened scrutiny, 1047
in educational institutions, 1066–67
in sex discrimination, 1064–66
Helmet laws, 973
Helms, Jesse, 619
Henry, Patrick, 6
Hill, Anita, 23
Holmes, Oliver Wendell
on bad tendency test, 604, 605
on birth control, 957
on clear and present danger test, 602–3, 609
on commerce, 180, 182
on corporate influence, 532–33
on economic regulation, 54
on heightened scrutiny, 1065–66
on intergovernmental tax immunity, 407, 408
on judicial restraint, 53
on minimum wage, 534–35
on taking issue, 540–41
on unconstitutionality, 134
Homosexuality
and discrimination on the basis of sexual
orientation, 1071–72
and gay rights, 971–72
Hoover, Herbert, 53, 267
Hopkinson, Joseph, 171
Hot pursuit, 820
House Un-American Activities Committee (HUAC), 175
Hughes, Charles Evans, 95, 323
on commerce, 181
on court packing, 94
on economic due process, 537, 538
letter to Senator Burton K. Wheeler, March 21,
1937, 107–9
photographic memory of, 32
on prior restraint, 674–75
on statutory construction, 129–30
on substantive due process, 527
Humphrey, William, 267
Hussein, Saddam, 279
Hyde Amendment, 965

Illegitimacy, and discrimination, 1067
Immigration and Nationality Act (1952), 132–33, 333
Imminent lawless action, and subversive speech,
608–9
Immunity, 174
Impeachment
against Andrew Jackson, 168, 258–59
against Richard Nixon, 258, 259, 284–86
against Samuel Chase, 25
against William Douglas, 169
difficulty of, 93
Implied powers, 10, 170–71
Imports-Exports Clause, 408–10
Impoundment, presidential power of, 271–72
Income tax, Supreme Court rulings on, 51–52
Incorporation
doctrine of, 390, 482–85
of freedoms of speech and press, 600
of the Religion Clauses, 740
Independent state grounds, 396
Indictment, 26
by a grand jury, 474
Individual rights
and agency actions, 338
bureaucratic support for civil rights and liberties,
340
before congressional committees, 174–76
Fourth Amendment concerns, 339
public access to agency information, 340
self-incrimination concerns, 339–40
versus presidential powers, 280–81
as restraints on the taxing and spending powers,
194
Inevitable discovery exception, to the exclusionary
rule, 830–31
Informants
anonymous, 819
confidential, 819
In forma pauperis, 28
Inherently suspect, 282
Inherent powers, of president, 259–60
Injunction, 26, 87
in freedom of press cases, 675–76
Intergovernmental tax immunity, 406–8
intermediate appellate courts, 15
Internal politics, influence of, on Supreme Court
decision, 37
Internal security concerns, and subversive speech,
602–9
Interposition, 387
Interpretivism, 56–57

Interstate commerce. *See also* Commerce Clause
  as constitutional right, 404–5
  direct versus indirect effects on, 182
  regulation of, 176–87
  state regulation of
    divergent perspectives, 399–400
    and the trucking industry, 400–1
Interstate Commerce Act (1887), 323
Interstate Commerce Commission, 323
Interstate compacts, 415–16
Interstate relations, 411
  Full Faith and Credit Clause, 411
  interstate compacts, 415–16
  Privileges and Immunities Clause, 411–14
  rendition, 414–15
Investigate, power of Congress to, 172–74
Investigatory detention, 821–22
Iran-Contra affair, 255, 274
Iran hostage crisis, 255
Iredell, James, 523
Item veto, 265

Jackson, Andrew, veto of Bank of the United States,
  66–69
Jackson, Howell, 52
Jackson, Jesse, 197
Jackson, Robert H.
  on clear and probable danger, 607
  on Commerce Clause, 183
  and equal access, 753
  and flag salute cases, 748
  on judicial power, 85, 86
  and police interrogation, 828
  and religious freedom, 752
  on stewardship theory, 262
Jaffree, Ishmael, 96
Japanese-Americans, relocation of, 281–82
Jaworski, Leon, 269
Jay, John, 7, 20, 119
Jay Treaty, 269
Jefferson, Thomas
  on Bill of Rights, 7, 471
  and executive privilege, 269
  on federal judiciary, 25
  and impoundment, 271
  and judicial review, 44, 45, 173–74
  on minimal government, 323, 324
  on states rights, 387
  on subversive speech, 602
  war powers under, 277

Jehovah's Witnesses, 750
  and flag saluting, 748
  and religious freedom, 743–44, 745
Jim Crow laws, adoption of, 1048
Johnson, Andrew, 88
  impeachment charges against, 168, 258–59
Johnson, Gregory, 614–15
Johnson, Lyndon B., 608
  use of impoundment by, 272
  and Vietnam War, 278
  and voting rights, 1152
Johnson, William, 178, 524
Jones, Walter, 171
Judge
  appointment and removal of federal, 22–25, 92–95
  impeachment of, 25
  tenure of federal, 24–25
Judges Bill. *See* Judiciary Act (1925)
Judicial activism, 37, 50
Judicial dependency on Congress, 86–92
Judicial election systems, challenges to, 1156–57
Judicial federalism, 388, 395–97
  and equal protection, 1076
  and significance for the abortion issue, 969–70
Judicial interpretation, of the U.S. Constitution, 9–10
Judicial notice, 186, 538
Judicial oversight and due process of law, 336–38
Judicial power
  appointment and removal of federal judges, 22–25,
    92–95
  decisions on the merits, 128
    distinguishing the unconstitutional from the
      merely
    objectionable, 133–34
    doctrine of saving construction, 129–30
    doctrine of strict necessity, 128–29
    narrowness doctrine, 130–31
    presumption of constitutionality, 131–32
    severability doctrine, 132–33
    stare decisis, 131
    "unconstitutional as applied...," 133
  enforcement of court decisions, 95–97
  external constraints on, 86
  judicial dependency on Congress, 86–92
  threshold requirements, 118
    case or controversy requirement, 119–20
    doctrine of abstention, 126
    exhaustion of remedies, 126
    jurisdiction, 118–19
    mootness, 124–25
    political questions doctrine, 127–28

ripeness doctrine, 125–26
standing to sue, 120–24
Judicial restraint, 37, 53
definition of, 118
Judicial review, 22, 43
as American invention, 43
association of, with U.S. Supreme Court, 43–44
definition of, 43
development of, 47–56
establishment of, 44–47
standards, 487
rational basis test, 487
strict judicial scrutiny, 487–88
Judicial scrutiny
levels of, in equal protection cases
heightened scrutiny, 1047
rational basis test, 1045–46
suspect classification doctrine, 1046–47
Judiciary
appointment power as check on, 93–95
presidential influence on, 23–24
Judiciary Act (1789), 16–17, 17, 19, 46, 48, 86, 87
Judiciary Act (1801), 44, 45
Judiciary Act (1891), 18
Judiciary Act (1925), 21
Juries
exclusion of minorities from, 840–41
size of, 839–40
Jurisdiction, 14
appellate, 14, 20
concurrent, 20
diversity, 119
federal question, 118–19
of lower federal courts, 86–88
original, 14, 20, 45, 86
Jury trial, 837–38
exclusion of minorities from juries, 840–41
jury size, 839–40
problem of pretrial publicity, 838–39
rights to, and civil rights and liberties, 475–76
unanimity principle, 840
Just Compensation Clause, 474, 482
Juvenile justice, 851–52
Juveniles, capital punishment of, 852

Kasper, John, 1053–54
Katz, Charles, 818
Kennedy, Anthony
on abortion, 966, 968
confirmation of, 22
as conservative, 37
on flag burning, 614
on interstate commerce, 405
nomination of, 1060
Kennedy, John F.
assassination of, 258
foreign policy under, 275
Kevorkian, Jack, 974–75
Keynes, John Maynard, 324, 539
Kilbourn, Hallet, 173–74
King, Rodney, 824, 1061
Kissinger, Henry, 271
Ku Klux Klan, 1149

Law clerks, 30
Learned Hand, 607
Lee, Richard Henry, 6
Legal Services Corporation, 340
Legislative power. *See also* Congress
delegation of, 324–26
concern for representative government, 326
concern for the separation of powers, 326–27
in the context of foreign affairs, 327–28
in the domestic context, 328–32
Legislative veto, 333–35
Libel, 677
actual malice, 677–78
definition of, 677
invasion of privacy, 679–80
and public persons, 678–79
Libya, 279
Life imprisonment, mandatory, 846
Limiting doctrines, 118
Lincoln, Abraham, 169, 390
war powers under, 277–78
Literacy, and voting rights, 196, 1151
Literacy tests, 486, 1151
Litvinov Agreements, 276
Living arrangements, and right of privacy, 970
Livingston, Robert, 177
Locke, John, 4, 324, 465, 521
Lowi, Theodore, 330

Madison, James
and Bill of Rights, 599, 600, 740
and calling of constitutional convention, 3, 4, 6
as Federalist, 1, 7, 90, 97, 165, 255, 259–60, 471
and foreign policy, 327
on General Welfare Clause, 191

on Ninth Amendment, 477
as secretary of state, 44
on states rights, 387
Magna Charta, 465
Majority opinion, 33
Malapportionment, 1157
Malice, actual, in libel cases, 677–78
Mandatory life imprisonment, 846
Marbury, William, 44–45, 46
Marital privacy, 960
Market participant exception, to state regulation of interstate commerce, 404
Marshall, John
as Chief Justice, 33, 329
on Commerce Clause, 177–78, 180, 182
on Contract Clause, 524–25
and development of original package test, 409, 410
on implied powers, 171, 172
and incorporation of Bill of Rights, 481
on intergovernmental tax immunity, 406
and judicial review, 9, 44–48
on national supremacy, 387, 388–89
and sovereign immunity, 90
on tax exemptions, 759
on voting rights, 195
Marshall, Thurgood, 1052
on abortion funding, 1071
on affirmative action, 1058, 1060
on anonymous tip, 822
on antidelegation rule, 330
on at-large elections, 1155
on child pornography, 685
on death penalty, 842, 843, 844, 845
on flag burning, 56
ideology of, 37
on interstate commerce, 400–1
on Pentagon Papers, 34
on pretrial detention, 836
on privacy, 970
on public school funding, 1070
on religious freedom, 747
on restrictions of speech of public employees, 618
retirement of, 23
on separate but equal doctrine, 1051
on Seventh Amendment, 476
on sleep speech, 615
on Tenth Amendment, 185
on unanimity principle, 840
Martin, Luther, 171
Matthews, Stanley, 531, 540
Maximum-hours laws, court sustaining of, 533

McCardle, William H., 88
McCarthyism, 607
McCleskey, Warren, 851
McCorvey, Norma, 960–61
McLean, John, 49
McPherson, Ardith, 618
McReynolds, James C., 536, 537
M'Culloch, James W., 171
Media privilege. *See also* Press
issue of, 680–81
limits of, 681
Medical treatment, refusal of, and privacy rights, 973–76
Meeker, Leonard, 278
Meese, Edwin, 56
Memorandum decisions, 28
Mennonites, beliefs of, 747–48
Meredith, James, 613
Merryman, John, 280
Military affairs, and political questions doctrine, 127
Military service
and free exercise of religion, 741–42, 748–49
role of women in, 1065
Miller, Samuel F., 174, 528–29
Minimum-wage legislation, 534–35
constitutionality of, 536–38
Minnesota Mortgage Moratorium Act, 535
Minorities, exclusion of, from juries, 840–41
Minton, Sherman, 606–7
Miranda warnings, 829–31
Misdemeanors, 15
Missouri Compromise, 91
Mistrial, 841–42
Mitchell, John, 271
Mitigating circumstances, and the death penalty, 845
Mootness, 124–25
Moral individualism, 954
Morgan, Christine, 196
Morgan, John P., 196
Morrison, Justice, 521
Murphy, Frank, 606, 609, 828
Myers, Frank, 266

Narrowness doctrine, 130–31
Nation, as an economic unit, 401–5
National Association for the Advancement of Colored People (NAACP), 1150
National Endowment for the Arts funding controversy, 619
National Environmental Policy Act (1969), 122–23

National Industrial Recovery Act (1933), 93–94, 182, 329

National Labor Relations Act (1935), 183

National Prohibition Act, 817

National Recovery Administration, Supreme Court on, 53

National security, peacetime threats to, 282

National supremacy
role of Marshall Court in establishing, 388–89
versus states rights, 387–88

Native American Church, and use of peyote, 744, 746, 747

Nativity scenes, public display of, 744

Natural Gas Act, 336

Natural law, 55

Natural resources, state attempts to protect their, 403

Natural rights, 55, 465, 521, 523

Necessary and Proper Clause, 9–10, 171, 172

Nelson, Samuel, 49

Neutral policies, judging disparate impact of facially, 1046–47

New Deal, constitutional battle over, 53–54

Nineteenth Amendment, 170, 485–86, 1148

Ninth Amendment, 477–78
and privacy rights, 955–56

Nixon, Richard M.
court appointments of, 55
and foreign policy, 275
impeachment charges against, 258, 259, 284–86
and impoundment, 272
judicial appointments of, 93
and national security threats, 282
pardoning of, 268
and Pentagon Papers case, 262–63
presidential papers of, 470
resignation of, 168
and school busing, 1055
and Vietnam War, 278
and War Powers Resolution, 278–79
and Watergate tapes controversy, 269–70

Noise Control Act (1972), 187, 394

Non-Intercourse Act (1809), 327

Norris-LaGuardia Act (1932), 87

North, Oliver, 172, 175, 274

Nuclear Regulatory Commission (NRC), 325, 394–95

Nude dancing, and obscenity, 616–18

Nullification, 387

O'Brien, David Paul, 612

Obscenity, 682–83

child pornography, 684–85
Miller test of, 684
pornography as an infringement of women's rights, 685
prurient interest test of, 683

Occupational Health and Safety Act (1970), 186, 331
and Fourth Amendment concerns, 339

Occupational Safety and Health Administration (OSHA), 325, 331

O'Connor, Sandra Day
on abortion, 965–98
on capital punishment of juveniles, 852
on federalism, 385
on government interest test, 746–97
ideology of, 37
nomination of, 23, 1060
and partisan gerrymandering, 1162
on probable cause hearing, 825
on sexual discrimination, 1066
on spending power of Congress, 193
on takings issues, 541
on Tenth Amendment, 185

Office of Economic Opportunity (OEO), 272

Ogden, Aaron, 177

Olmstead, Roy, 817

Opinion of the Court, 33

Oral argument, 32

Orders, 15

Ordinances, 15

Organized Crime Control Act (1970), 187

Original intent, 9, 56

Original jurisdiction, 14, 20, 45

Original package doctrine, rise and fall of, 410

Original package test, 409

Otis, James, 816

Overbreadth doctrine, 609
and First Amendment, 628–29

Oversight, 173

Packers and Stockyard Act (1921), 182

Panama Canal Treaty, 275

Pardons, president power of granting, 268–69

Parens Patriae, 323
freedom of religion versus, 749–50
and juvenile justice, 851

Parochiaid, 753–54

Partisan gerrymandering, 1161–62

Patriotic rituals and duties, and religious freedom, 747–49

Peckham, Rufus, 532

Pentagon papers case, 262–63, 277, 675

People's right to know, 680–82

Per curiam opinion, 31, 34

Peremptory challenges, 838

Perot, Ross, 1161

Persian Gulf War, role of Bush in, 279–80

Persian Gulf War Resolution, 307–8

Peter, Forest, 741

Petition, right to, 472

Petitioner, 28

Peyote, use of, in Native American Church, 744, 746, 747

Pierce, Franklin, war powers under, 277

and unemployment benefits, 745–47

Pinckney, William, 171

Pitney, Mahlon, 534

Plaintiff, 15, 25

Plain view, 820

Plea bargaining, 836–37

Plurality opinion, 34

Pocket veto, 264–65

Police deception, 831–32

Police interrogation, 828–29

Miranda warnings, 829–31

police deception in, 831–32

Police power, 521

Congressional exercise of, 169

and national basis test, 970

state exercise of, 179, 521

Political Activities Act (1939), 125

Political association, and freedom of association, 626–27

Political environment, influence of, on Supreme Court decision, 37

Political parties, and partisan gerrymandering, 1161–62

Political questions doctrine, 127–28

Polk, James K., war powers under, 277

Poll taxes, 170, 486, 1151–52

Popular sovereignty, 1147

Pornography

child, 684–85

as infringement of women's rights, 685

Post-civil war era, Supreme Court in, 50

Postconviction relief. *See* Appeal and postconviction relief

Poverty, and discrimination, 1069–71

Powell, Lewis, 117

on abortion, 966

on affirmative action, 1058

on commercial advertising, 686

on Due Process Clause, 338

on gay rights, 972

on gender-based discrimination, 1063

on immunity from civil suits, 271

on interstate commerce, 400

on legislative veto, 333–34

on market participation exception, 404

nomination of, 55, 93

on overbreadth doctrine, 629

on public school funding, 1069–70

on residency, 1068–69

retirement of, 22, 56

on sex discrimination, 1066

on standing, 123

on Tenth Amendment, 185

Preate, Ernest, Jr., 968

Precedent, 131

Preemption, national, of state law, 393–95

Preliminary injunction, in freedom of press cases, 675–76

Presidency

appointment powers of, 265–67

disability of, 257–58

and the electoral college, 257

enumerated powers of, 259–60

executive privilege of, 269–70

expansion of powers, 255–56

foreign policy powers, 272–77

immunity from civil suits, 270–71

impeachment and removal from office, 258–59

impoundment powers of, 271–72

versus individual rights, 280–81

influence on the judiciary, 23–24

inherent powers of, 259–60

pardon granting powers, 268–69

removal powers of, 265–67

stewardship theory of, 260–63

structural aspects of American, 256–59

succession of, 257–58

term of office, 257

veto powers of, 263–65

war powers of, 277–82

Presidential Recordings and Materials Preservation Act (1974), 470

Press. *See also* Media privilege

broadcast media, 687

editorializing by public television and radio stations, 688

FCC's fairness doctrine, 688

restrictions of "indecent" programming, 688–89

commercial advertising, 685–87

freedom of, 472–73, 673, 674

free press-fair trial dilemma, 677
incorporation of freedoms of, 600
libel, 677
    actual malice, 677–78
    invasions of privacy, 679–80
    and public persons, 678–79
obscenity, 682–83
    child pornography, 684–85
    Miller test, 684
    pornography as infringement of women's rights, 685
    prurient interest test, 683
and the "people's right to know," 680
    confidential sources, 682
    issue of media privilege, 680–81
and problem of pretrial publicity, 838–39
rule against prior restraint, 674–75
    Hazelwood case, 676–77
    Pentagon Papers case, 675
    Progressive H-Bomb case, 675–76
Presumption of constitutionality, 131–32, 1046
Pretrial motion, 26
Pretrial publicity, problem of, 838–39
Pretrial release, 476
Price-Anderson Act, 123
Prior restraint, rule against, 674–75
Prisoners' rights, 846–47
Privacy
    abortion controversy, 480, 960–63
        eroding support on the Supreme Court, 965–70
        restrictions on public funding of, 963–65
    constitutional foundations of the right of, 955–56
        substantive due process, 956–57
    constitutional right of, 953–54
    and gay rights, 971–72
    invasion of, and libel, 679–80
    and living arrangements, 970
    philosophical foundations of the right, 954–55
    procreation and birth control, 957
        beyond the marital bedroom, 960
        Connecticut birth control controversy, 957–60
    protection of private information, 976
        drug testing, 976
    reasonable expectations of, 817–18
    refusal of medical treatment and the right to die, 973–76
    right to, 480
    and victimless crimes, 972
        helmet and seat belt laws, 973
        private use of recreational drugs, 973

Privacy Act, 340
Private discrimination, 1072–74
    restrictive covenants in, 1074
    state powers to prohibit, 1074–75
Private information, protection of, 976
Privileges and Immunities Clause, 411–14
Probable cause, 282
    hearing for, 824–25
    and search and seizure, 818
Procedural due process, 479
Procreation
    beyond the marital bedroom, 960
    and privacy rights, 957–60
Promissory estoppel, and protection of confidential sources, 682
Property rights, 521–22
    Contract Clause, 524
        contribution of the Taney Court, 526
        key decisions of the Marshall Court, 524–25
        later developments, 526–27
    economic due process, 527–28
        key Supreme Court decisions, 528–39
        origins of substantive due process, 528
    equal protection and economic regulation, 539–40
    evolving judicial perspectives, 522–24
    and free expression, 543–44
    inclusions in, 521
    and the "takings" issue, 540–44
Property taxes, exemption of religious property from, 759–61
Proportionate representation, problem of, 1155–56
Prurient interest test of obscenity, 683
Public access to agency information, 340
Public employees and beneficiaries
    restricting speech by, 618
        in abortion counseling, 619
        and NEA funding controversy, 619
Public forum, determination of, 622–23
Public office, prohibition of religious tests for, 467
Public person, concept of, and libel, 678–79
Public safety exception, 830
Public school funding, controversy over, 1069–70
Publius, 7
Punishment
    cruel and unusual, 842–47
    death penalty, 842–46, 852

Quarles, Benjamin, 830
Quinlan, Karen, 974

Racial discrimination
  at-large elections, 1154–56
    challenges to judicial election systems,
      1156–57
  ongoing problem of, 1061
  in voting rights, 1149
    grandfather clauses, 486, 1149–50
    literacy tests, 1151
    poll taxes, 170, 486, 1151–52
    racial gerrymandering, 1152
    Voting Rights Act (1965), 1152–54
    white primary, 1150–51
Racial equality
  struggle for, 1047–48
    affirmative action, 1057–60
    decline of *de jure* racial segregation, 1051–52
    desegregation, 1052–56
    early interpretations of Equal Protection Clause,
      1048–51
    ongoing problem of discrimination in, 1061
Racial gerrymandering, 1152
Racketeer Influenced and Corrupt Organizations
  (RICO), 187
Randolph, Edmund, 16
Rankin, Constable, 618
Rational basis test, 487
  in equal protection cases, 1045–46
  and privacy rights, 970
Reagan, Ronald
  court appointments of, 23–24
  and Gramm-Rudman-Hollings Act, 332
  on item veto, 265
  nominations of, 22
  and the pocket veto, 264
  popularity of, 256
  and renewal of Voting Rights Act, 1154
  on school prayer, 755
  on term of office, 257
  on tuition tax credit, 760–61
  and war powers resolution, 279
Reapportionment, 127–28, 1157–58
  assessing, 1160–61
  effect of 1990 census on, 1159–60
  reapportionment revolution, 1158–59
  under the Burger Court, 1159
Reasonable suspicion, 821
Reconstruction Act (1867), 88
Recused, 45
Reed, Stanley, 1151
Rehabilitation Act (1973), 1068

Rehnquist, William, 24
  on abortion, 969
  on affirmative action, 1058, 1059, 1060
  on bail, 835–36
  on commercial advertising, 686
  on confidential and anonymous informants, 819
  on conscientious objections, 749
  on *de jure* discrimination, 1055
  on delegation of legislative powers, 331
  on due process, 337
  on elevation to Chief Justice, 23, 55, 966
  on flag burning, 615
  on foreign relations, 274
  on Fourth Amendment, 474
  on good-faith exception, 827
  on heightened scrutiny, 1064, 1065
  ideology of, 37
  on inaction as state action, 481
  on interstate commerce, 401, 405
  on juvenile justice, 852
  on market participant exception, 404
  nomination of, 93
  on nude dancing, 616, 617
  on overbreadth doctrine, 629
  on presidential immunity from civil suits, 271
  on Privileges and Immunities Clause, 413, 414
  on probable cause hearing, 824–25
  on property rights and freedom of speech, 543–44
  on public affirmations of religious beliefs, 758–59
  on public persons, 679
  on regulation of alcoholic beverages, 402
  on restrictive covenants, 1074
  on right to counsel, 834
  on standing, 122
  takings issue under, 541–43
  on Tenth Amendment, 184, 185, 392
  on unanimity principle, 840
  on zoning regulation, 624–25
Released time programs, and religious freedom, 752–53
Religion Clauses
  of the First Amendment, 472
  incorporation of, 740
Religious belief, public affirmations of, 757–59
Religious freedom, 739–40
  and animal sacrifice, 747
  and compulsory school attendance, 750
  defining religion, 740–42
  and door-to-door solicitation, 743
  and drug use, 744, 746, 747
  and education, 752

evolution-creationism conflict, 756–57
  "Parochiaid," 753–54
  "released time" programs and "equal access"
    policies, 752–53
  school prayer controversy, 92, 96, 754–55
  and tuition tax credits, 760–61
incorporation of the Religion Clauses, 740
and military service, 741–42, 748–49
versus *Parens Patriae,* 949–50
separation of church and state, 750
and patriotic rituals and duties, 747–49
  competing interpretations of the Establishment
    Clause, 750–51
and Sunday closing laws, 744–75
and tax exemptions, 759–61
and unemployment benefits, 745–47
Religious tests, prohibition of, for public office, 467
Remedy, 26
Removal, president powers of, 265–67
Rendition, 414–15
Reporters, and protection of confidential sources, 682
Representative democracy, 1147
Representative government, concern for legislative
  power in, 326
Reserved powers, 387
Residency, and discrimination, 1068–69
Residential occupancy, and right of privacy, 970
Restrictive covenants in private discrimination, 1074
Reverse, 33
Richardson, Elliot, 269
Right to die, and privacy rights, 973–76
Ripeness doctrine, 125–26
Roane, Spencer, 48, 171–72
Roberts, Owen J.
  on congressional spending powers, 191, 192
  and economic due process, 536, 537
Roche, John P., 4
Rockelshaus, William, 269–70
Roosevelt, Franklin D.
  court-packing plan of, 54, 93–95, 109–12, 182, 537
  "Fireside Chat," March 9, 1937, 104–7
  foreign policy under, 273, 275, 276
  on national regulatory power, 391
  New Deal of, 190, 539
  and relocation of Japanese Americans, 281–82
  removal powers of, 267
  Senate Judiciary Committee Report on Court-
    spending by, 271–72
  and term of office restrictions, 257
Roosevelt, Theodore, 260

Rule of four, 31
Rule of law, 6
Rules of procedure, 28–29
Rutledge, Wiley, 87–88, 600, 606, 752

St. Clair, Arthur, 269
SALT I treaty, 275
Sandford, John, 49
Sanford, Edward T., 534, 604–5
Santeria, 747
"Saturday Night Massacre," 269–70
Saving construction, doctrine of, 129–30
Sawyer, Charles, 262
Scalia, Antonin
  on abortion, 967, 969
  on flag burning, 614
  on hate speech, 611
  ideology of, 37, 1060
  on nude dancing, 617
  on prisoner's rights, 847
  on privacy, 954
  on probable cause hearing, 825
  on property rights and free expression, 543–44
  on religious freedom, 746
  on separation of powers, 332
  on takings issue, 542
Schenck, Charles T., 602
School prayer, 92, 96, 754–55
Scopes, John T., 756
Search and seizure, 816–17
  automobile searches, 820–21
  confidential and anonymous informants, 819
  drug testing, 822–23
  investigatory detention, 821–22
  probable cause, 818
  reasonable expectations of privacy, 817–18
  stop and frisk, 821
  warrantless searches, 819–20
  warrant requirement, 818–19
Search warrant, 282
  in search and seizure, 818–19
Seat belt laws, 973
Second Amendment, 473
Section 1983 actions, 405
Securities and Exchange Commission (SEC), 325
Sedition Act (1918), 602
Seeger, Daniel, 741
Segregation. *See also* Racial discrimination
  de facto, 1072–73
  de jure, 1051–52, 1072

Selective incorporation, 482–85
Self-Incrimination Clause of the Fifth Amendment,
828–29
Self-representation, 835
Senate Judiciary committee report, on Roosevelt's
court-packing plan, 109–12
Seneca Falls Convention, 485–86
Sentencing guidelines, 332–33
Sentiments, 49
Separate but equal doctrine, 1049–51
Separation of powers, 4, 6
concern for legislative power in, 326–27
and Congressional control of administrative actions,
335
and nondelegation doctrine, 332
Separation of state, and church, 750–57
Seventeenth Amendment, 1148
Seventh Amendment, 475–76
Seventh Day Adventists, and religious freedom, 745
Severability doctrine, 132–33
Sex discrimination, 1061
congressional responses to demands for sexual
equality, 1062
and equal rights amendment, 1062–63
judicial scrutiny of, 1063–66
Sexual harassment, as issue in Thomas nomination, 23
Sexual orientation, discrimination on the basis of,
1071–72
Shays, Daniel, 3
Shays' rebellion, 3
Sherbert, Adell, 745
Sherman Antitrust Act (1890), 52
Shield laws, 682
Shock radio, 688
Silkwood, Karen, 395
Sixteenth Amendment, 91–92, 170, 189, 407
Sixth Amendment, 474
Slavery, 389–90
Sleep speech, and symbolic speech, 615
Small claims, 15
Smith, Adam, 539
Smith, Alfred, 746
Smith Act, 608, 626
Snakes, use of poisonous, in religious ceremony, 744
Social contract theorists, 4
Social Security Act (1935), 391–92
Souter, David
on abortion, 968
ideology of, 37, 1060
nomination, 22–23, 37, 954

on nude dancing, 617
on privacy rights, 954
Sovereign immunity, 25, 90, 387–88
Specialized federal tribunals, 19
Special prosecutors, appointment of, 266
Speech
distinction between protected and unprotected,
609–11
and fighting words exception to protected, 609–11
freedom of, 472–73
hate, 611
incorporation of freedoms of, 600
and obscenity, 616–18
and property rights, 543–44
restriction of, by public employees and
beneficiaries, 618–19
subversive, 602
ad hoc balancing, 608
bad tendency test, 603–6
clear and present danger test, 602–3
clear and probable danger test, 606–8
and imminent lawless action, 608–9
symbolic, 612
flag burning, 613–15
sleep speech, 615
in the Vietnam era, 612–13
Speech or Debate Clause, 168
Spencer, Herbert, 539
Spending power of Congress, 190–92, 331–32
individual rights as restraints on, 194
modern approach to, 192–93
Stalin, Joseph, 276
Standing, opposing philosophies of, 123
Standing to sue, 120–24
Stanton, Elizabeth Cady, 485
Stare decisis, 131
Starr, Kenneth W., 968
State
importance of constitutions, in civil rights and
liberties, 488
national preemption of laws of, 393–95
powers of
to prohibit private discrimination, 1074–75
to regulate commerce, 397–405
taxing, 406–11
State action doctrine, 1050
and Fourteenth Amendment, 480–81
States' rights, 10
versus national supremacy, 387–88
renewed emphasis on, under Taney, 389

States' rights advocates, 48
Statutory construction, 129–30
Stevens, John Paul, 823
  on abortion, 968
  on affirmative action, 1058
  on broadcast media, 688–89
  on child pornography, 685
  on commercial advertising, 686
  on congressional reapportionment, 1160
  on criminal justice, 815
  on detention of automobile based on anonymous
    tip, 822
  on flag burning, 614
  ideology of, 37
  on interstate commerce, 400
  on prurient interest test, 684
  on regulation of alcoholic beverages, 402
  on summary decisions, 31
  on Tenth Amendment, 185
Stewardship theory of presidential power, 260–63
Stewart, Potter
  on abortion, 965, 1070–71
  on affirmative action, 1058, 1059
  on civil rights demonstrations, 621
  on Commerce Clause, 187
  on interstate commerce, 401
  on judicial oversight of bureaucracy, 336
  on Ninth Amendment, 477
  on overbreadth doctrine, 628
  on Pentagon Papers, 34
  on pretrial publicity, 839
  on prurient interest test, 683
  replacement of, 1060
  on school prayer, 754
  on unconstitutionality, 134
Stone, Harlan Fiske, 55
  on economic due process, 537
  on intergovernmental tax immunity, 407
  on interstate commerce, 400
  on New Deal, 192
  on political participation, 1149
  on presumption of constitutionality, 132
  on Tenth Amendment, 183–84, 185
Stop and frisk, 821
Story, Joseph, 48, 191
Stream of Commerce doctrine, 181–82
Street, Sidney, 613
Strict judicial scrutiny, 487–88, 1046
Strict necessity, doctrine of, 128–29
Submission of briefs, 32
Subpoena, 95, 174, 474

Subpoena duces tecum, 174
Substantive due process, 49–50, 479
  and Contract Clause, 527
  and economic due process, 527–28
  origins of, 528
  and right to privacy, 480, 956–57
Substituted judgment doctrine, 975
Subversive speech, and internal security concerns,
  602–9
Succession, of president, 257–58
Sugar Trust, Supreme Court rulings on, 52
Suicide, right to, and privacy rights, 974–75
Summary decisions, 31
Sunday closing laws, 744–75
Supreme Court. *See* U.S. Supreme Court
Supreme Court Reporter, 35
Suspect classification doctrine in equal protection
  cases, 1046–47
Sutherland, George, 273, 534, 536, 538–39
Symbolic speech
  flag burning, 613–15
  sleep speech, 615
  in the Vietnam era, 612–13
Synar, Mike, 130, 332

Taft, William Howard
  and appointment and reserved powers, 266–67
  as chief justice, 182, 266–67, 326
  and child labor, 190
  and economic due process, 538
  on privacy, 817
  and separation of powers, 326
  and stewardship theory of presidential power, 260
  and stream of commerce doctrine, 182
  and substantive due process, 534
  Supreme Court rulings on, 51–52
Taft-Hartley Act, 262
Takings issue
  and property rights, 540–44
  under the Rehnquist Court, 541–43
Taney, Roger B.
  as Chief Justice, 49, 280, 389
  on Contract Clause, 526
  on Import-Export Clause, 409
  on individual rights versus presidential powers,
    280
  on political question doctrine, 127
  on slavery, 49
  on states' rights, 389
Tariff Act (1890), 328

Taxation
    exemptions, and religious freedom, 759–61
    federal, as a means of regulation, 189–90
    individual rights as restraints on, 194
    as source of congressional power, 188–89
    of states, 406–11
Tax Court, 19
Taxpayer suits, and standing to sue, 121–22
Taylor, Robert, 1054
Tenth Amendment, 169, 179, 189, 392–93, 478
    decline of, 183–85
Term of office, for president, 257
Third Amendment, 473
    and privacy rights, 955
Thirteenth Amendment, 7, 91, 169, 170, 195, 390
Thomas, Clarence, 1054
    on abortion, 969
    on affirmative action, 1060
    ideology of, 37
    nomination of, 23, 954
    on prisoners' rights, 847
    on school desegregation, 1053
Thompson, John G., 174
Threshold issues, 118
Thurmond, Strom, 1154
Tinker, John, 613
Title IX of the Federal Education Act (1972), 1062
Tort claims, 19
Totality of circumstances, 819
Train, Russell, 272
Treason, circumscribing crime of, 467
Treaties, power of presidents in, 275–76
Trial, dilemma over fair, and press coverage, 677
Trial courts, 14
Trucking industry, interstate commerce cases
    involving, 400–1
Truman, Harry S, 263, 267, 610
    foreign policy under, 275
    and labor relations, 262
    use of impoundment by, 272
Tuition tax credits, 760–61
Twelfth Amendment, passage of, 257
Twenty-Fifth Amendment, 258
Twenty-First Amendment, 402
Twenty-Fourth Amendment, 170, 486, 1148
Twenty-Second Amendment, 257
Twenty-Sixth Amendment, 92, 170, 486–87, 1148
Twenty-Third Amendment, 170
Two-party system, 257
Tyler, John, 127
    succession of, 257–58

Unanimity principle, 840
Unemployment benefits, and free exercise of religion,
    745–47
Uniform Code of Military Justice, 19
Unitary system, definition of, 386
U.S. Claims Court, 19
U.S. Court of International Trade, 19
U.S. Courts of Appeals, 18–19
U.S. District Courts, 17–18
United States Reports, 35
U.S. Supreme Court, 19, 28
    assignment and preparation of opinions, 34–35
    caseload, 30
    case selection, 30–31
    Congressional control in, 28–29
    decisions invalidating acts of Congress, 51
    enforcement of decisions, 95–97
    factors that influence decisions of, 35–38
    New Deal legislation invalidated by, 54
    number of justices, 28
    opinion day, 35
    political role of, 14
    priorities of the modern, 55–56
    publication of decisions of, 35
    recognition of Congress's power to investigate, 173
    restriction of jurisdiction, 88–89
    summary decisions, 31
        conference and decision, 32–33
        oral argument, 32
        submission of briefs, 32
        Supreme Court opinions, 33–34
    taking case to, 28
    term, 29–30
United States Supreme Court Reports, Lawyers'
Edition, 35
U.S. Claims Court, 19
U.S. Congress
    constitutional sources of power, 168–69
        doctrine of implied powers, 170–72
        enumerated powers, 169–70
        enforcement of civil rights amendments,
            194–197
    control of administrative action, 333
        legislative veto, 333–35
        separation of powers concerns, 335
    judicial dependency on, 86–92
    power to investigate, 172–74
        rights of individuals called before Congressional
            committees, 174–76
    reapportionment, 127–28, 1157–61
    regulation of interstate commerce, 176

congressional exercise of commerce power, 179
early interpretation of Commerce Clause, 176–79
modern interpretation of Commerce Clause,
182–87
Supreme Court restriction of commerce power,
180–82
spending power of, 190–92, 331–32
individual rights as restraints on, 194
modern approach to, 192–93
structural aspects of, 166
bicameralism, 166–67
congressional terms, 167
immunities of members of, 168
qualifications of members, 168
taxation as source of power, 188–89
federal taxation as means of regulation, 189–90
individual rights as restraints on, 194
U.S. Court of International Trade, 19
U.S. Courts of Appeals, 18–19
U.S. District Courts, 17–18
U.S. Supreme Court, 19
Universal Military Training and Service Act (1940), 741
Universal suffrage, 1147
Use immunity, 175

Vagueness, void for, 609, 628
Veto
item, 265
legislative, 333–35
pocket, 264–65
power of president in, 63–65
Victim impact statements, and the death penalty, 845
Victimless crimes, 972
helmet laws, 973
seat belt laws, 973
use of recreational drugs, 973
Vietnam War, 255
president power in, 278
and symbolic speech in, 612–13
Vinson, Fred M.
on clear and probable danger, 607
death of, 1052
and fighting words concept, 610
Void for vagueness doctrine, 609, 628
Voting Accessibility Act (1984), 1068
Voting rights, 1147–49
at-large elections, 1154–56
challenges to judicial election systems, 1156–57
Fifteenth Amendment on, 7, 91, 170, 195, 390, 485,
1148, 1149, 1153, 1155

Nineteenth Amendment on, 170, 485–86, 1148
racial discrimination in, 1149
challenges to judicial election systems, 1156–57
grandfather clauses, 486, 1149–50
literacy tests, 1151
poll taxes, 170, 486, 1151–52
racial gerrymandering, 1152
white primary, 1150–51
Twenty-Fourth Amendment on, 170, 486, 1148
Twenty-Sixth Amendment on, 92, 170, 486–87, 1148
Voting Rights Act (1965), 96, 195–97, 390, 485,
1152–54
enforcement of, 340
impact of, 485
and literacy, 196, 1151
Voting Rights Act (1982), 1154
effects test under, 1155

Wade, Henry, 26, 961
Wages
legislative regulation of, 534
minimum, 534–38
Wage Stabilization Board, 262
Wagner Act (1935), 129
Waite, Morrison R., 530, 742–43
Wallace, George, 1055, 1154
War powers of president, 277–82
War Powers Act, 279
War Powers Resolution (1973), 278–79, 304–7
Warrant
arrest, 824
search, 818–19
Warrantless searches, 819–20
of automobiles, 820–21
Warren, Earl, 1153
and civil rights and liberties, 55, 195
on criminal rights, 194, 483
on cruel and unusual punishment, 476
on habeas corpus review, 468
ideology of, 93
on legislative reapportionment, 128, 1158–59
nomination of, 93
on political association, 626
and reapportionment, 1159–1160
resignation of, 93
and school desegregation, 33, 1052, 1053
strict neutrality approach of, 758
on Sunday closing laws, 744
support for impeachment of, 25
on symbolic speech, 612

on voting rights, 1147
on wiretapping, 474
Washington, Bushrod, 412
Washington, George
    at Constitutional Convention, 256
    election of, 5
    and executive privilege, 269
    influence on judiciary, 23
    and international law, 119
Watergate scandal, 255
Watergate tapes controversy, 269–70
Watkins, John, 175
Watts, Robert, 608
Wayne, James, 49
Wealth, and discrimination, 1069–71
Webster, Daniel, 171
Weddington, Sarah, 961
Wheeler, Burton K., 94
    Charles Evans letter to (March 21, 1937), 107–9
White, Byron, 334
    on abortion, 969
    on affirmative action, 1058
    on birth controls, 959
    on confidential sources, 682
    on death penalty, 844
    on disabled persons, 1068
    on gay rights, 972
    ideology of, 37
    on immunity from civil suits, 271
    on interstate commerce, 400
    on jury size, 839
    on market participant exception, 404
    on nuclear energy, 394
    on overbreadth doctrine, 629
    on parochiaid, 754
    on Pentagon Papers, 34

    on police deception, 831
    on press freedoms, 676
    on prurient interest test, 684
    on restricting speech by public employees, 618
    on Section 1983 actions, 405
    on sleep speech, 615
    on Tenth Amendment, 185
    on unanimity principle, 840
    on zoning regulations, 624
White, Edward D., 189
White, Vanessa, 822
White primary, 486, 1150–51
Whitney, Charlotte Anita, 605–6
Whittaker, Charles, 754
Wilder, Douglas, 197
Wilson, James, 5
Wilson, Woodrow, 258, 266, 486
Wiretapping, 474
Wirt, William, 171
Women. *See also* Abortion; Sex discrimination
    pornography as infringement of rights of, 685
    restriction of abortion funding for indigent,
        1070–71
    voting rights for, 170, 485–86, 1148
Writ(s), 19
    of assistance, 816
    of certiorari, 21, 28
        denial of, 31
    of error, 20
    of mandamus, 45

Yellow dog contracts, and legislative regulation, 534

Zoning regulations, and freedom of assembly, 624–26